A CONCISE GAZETTEER OF THE WORLD

WITH DETAILED
DESCRIPTION OF
LAND, PEOPLE AND
NATURAL RESOURCES

R. BROOKES

GIAN PUBLISHING HOUSE

4348/4C, Madan Mohan Street, Ansari Road
New Delhi-110002

GIAN PUBLISHING HOUSE
4348, Madan Mohan Street,
4 C, Ansari Road, Daryaganj,
New Delhi-110002

First Reprint, 1989

ISBN 81-212-0254-X

PRINTED IN INDIA

Published by Mrs. Gayatri Garg at Goyal Offset Printers,
308/6E, Shahzada Bagh, Daya Basti, Delhi

INTRODUCTION.

Geography treats of the figure, magnitude, position, and motion of the earth, and of the situation, extent, divisions, subdivisions, and boundaries of the different places upon its surface; to which is usually subjoined an abstract of the religion, history, character, government, manners, commerce, and population of every kingdom. This science is, however, in many respects so closely connected with Astronomy, that it will be proper to give a general outline of the latter as well as the former.

THE UNIVERSE.

The term *universe* comprehends the whole frame of Nature, to the utmost extent of Creation. How magnificent and exalted, then, are the ideas presented to the human mind by its contemplation! In the formation and preservation of this stupendous structure, the wonders of Omnipotence are illustriously displayed; and the more accurate and extensive our knowledge of the universe, the more elevated will be our conceptions of the Supreme Being.

THE SOLAR SYSTEM.

The *solar system* is that portion of the universe which comprehends the sun, planets, satellites, and comets. The sun is the centre of this system, and there are eleven planets which revolve around him, each in its orbit. The names of these, according to their distance from the Sun, are Mercury, Venus, the Earth, Mars, Ceres,* Pallas,* Vesta,* Juno,* Jupiter, Saturn, and the Georgium Sidus. The first two, moving within the orbit of the Earth, are denominated inferior planets; the others move without that orbit, and are therefore denominated superior planets. The Earth, Jupiter, Saturn, and the Georgian, are attended by secondary planets, called *satellites*, or *moons*, which revolve about them as centres, and are regulated in their motions by the same laws which regulate the motions of the planets in their orbits round the sun. The Earth is attended by *one* Moon, revolving at the distance of 240,000 miles, Jupiter, *four*; Saturn, *seven*; and the Georgian, *six*. Saturn, also, besides his moons, is encircled by two concentric *rings*, at a considerable distance from his body, which, like satellites or moons, revolve round about him in his planes.

The planets have likewise a motion of rotation each round its own axis; at least observation renders it certain that Venus, the Earth, Jupiter, and Saturn have such a motion; and it is natural, from analogy, to infer that the rest have a similar motion.

The planets are opaque spherical bodies, and, having no light of their own, shine by borrowed light from the sun, which is both the centre of their motions and the source of their light and heat. They complete their revolutions in a greater or less time in proportion to their distances from the sun, there being a constant and very curious relation between their distances from him and their periodical times. †

* *Ceres* was discovered by M. Piazzi, astronomer royal at Palermo, on the 1st of January, 1801: to the naked eye it is not visible, nor will glasses of a very high magnifying power show it with a distinctly defined diameter. *Pallas*, which is still smaller, was discovered in 1802, by Dr. Olbers, at Hamburgh. *Juno* was discovered by M. Harding, in 1804; and *Vesta* by Dr. Olbers, in 1807.

† It was first discovered by Kepler, a Prussian astronomer, that the squares of the periodic times of the planets are proportional to the cubes of their mean distances from the sun.

The following Table shows the distances of the planets from the sun; with their magnitudes and periods, according to the latest observations.

NAMES.	Mean distances from the Sun.	Periodic Revolutions round the Sun.	Times of rotation on their axis.	Diameters in English miles.
	Miles.	*d. h. m.*	*d. h. m.*	
Sun	. . . . . .	. . . .	25 15 16	883,217
Mercury . . .	37,000,000	87 23 15	unknown.	3,222
Venus	68,000,000	224 16 49	23 22	[illegible],687
The Earth . .	95,000,000	365 6 9	23 56	7,964
Moon	95,000,000	365 6 9	29 12 44	2,160
Mars	144,000,000	686 23 30	24 39	4,189
Ceres	260,000,000	1,681 0 0	unknown.	160
Pallas	265,000,000	1,682 0 0	unknown.	110
Vesta	282,000,000	1,848 0 0	uncertain.	unknown.
Juno	290,000,000	2,007 12 0	uncertain.	unknown.
Jupiter . . .	490,000,000	4,332 8 51	9 56	87,000
Saturn	900,000,000	10,759 14 36	10 16	79,042
Georgian Planet	1800,000,000	30,686 18 0	unknown.	35,109

The *fixed stars* are distinguished from the planets by being more luminous, and by exhibiting that appearance termed the twinkling of the stars. They shine by their own native light, and are therefore, by analogy, and with the highest probability, supposed to be so many *suns*, each illuminating a considerable number of *planets* or *worlds*, which circulate round it. Indeed, it is unreasonable to think that these vast bodies of light and fire should be placed at such immense distances in the infinity of space, for no other purpose than to give a feeble light to the earth and the other planets in our solar system. Their distance from our earth is so inconceivably great, that, were the nearest of them to be removed out of its present situation 200 millions of miles in any direction, its change of place would not be in the smallest degree perceived by any observer on the earth, although aided by the best instruments; hence it appears that a luminous spherical body, 200 millions of miles in diameter, if viewed at the distance of the nearest fixed star, would appear as a mere lucid point, without any sensible diameter.

Besides the planets, there are other bodies belonging to our solar system, called *comets*, which also revolve round the sun as a centre, but the orbits of which do not approach so near to circles as those of the planets; for they are very long ellipses, having the sun in one of their foci. Hence it happens, that, during one part of its revolution, a comet goes off to an immense distance from the sun, and therefore cannot be seen from our earth; and during another part it comes much nearer to him, and may then become visible for a short time. The comets differ also considerably in other respects from the planets; for the paths of the latter in the heavens are all found within the *zodiac*, which is a tract extending to a small distance on each side of the ecliptic, or the path which the sun appears to describe round the heavens; whereas the path of the former is found sometimes in one quarter of the heavens and sometimes in another. The planets likewise move all in one direction about the sun, viz. from west to east, but the comets appear to move in all directions. They are also much more numerous than the planets, calculations having been made upon the orbits of upwards of eighty of them, by astronomers.

FIGURE AND MAGNITUDE OF THE EARTH.

The earth which we inhabit seems comparatively a small point in the universe, the sun being above two millions of times larger than the earth; and there is reason to suppose that similar is the fact with respect to all the stars.

It is one of the fundamental principles in *geography*, that the earth is of a round form; for, from the scientific measurements that have been made in various countries, it is proved that its form is that of a sphere, slightly flattened at the poles, from the effect of its diurnal motion. The difference of the equatorial and polar diameters is now ascertained to be 26 miles, and the four hundred and seventy-eighth thousandth part of a mile; or in the proportion of 298 to 299. This deviation from a true sphere is almost inappreciable in any representation of the earth's surface; for in a globe of 16 inches in diameter, it would vary only in the proportion of one-twentieth part of an inch—a quantity too small to be regarded; but in the actual measurement of any considerable portion of the earth's surface, this variation becomes more manifest from the inequality of the curve described by the polar circumference, while the degrees of latitude, which are always geographically divided into 60 miles, or minutes, the *measured length of a degree, increases with the latitude*, as the following table, resulting from the actual measurements, made with every refinement which science can command, by commissioners of various nations, men of the first eminence, will show.

COUNTRY.	Lat. of the middle of the Arc.	Length of a degree in feet.	Ditto in British statute miles.
	deg. m. s.		*m. f. yds.*
Sweden	66 . 20 . 10	365,782	69 . 2 . 47
Russia	58 . 17 . 37	365,368	69 . 1 . 129
England	52 . 35 . 45	364,971	69 . 0 . 217
France	46 . 52 . 2	364,872	69 . 0 . 184
Ditto	44 . 51 . 2	364,535	69 . 0 . 75
Rome	42 . 59 . 0	364,262	68 . 7 . 200
North America, United States	39 . 12 . 0	363,786	68 . 7 . 42
Cape of Good Hope	33 . 18 . 30	363,713	68 . 7 . 17
India	16 . 8 . 22	363,044	68 . 6 . 14
Ditto	12 . 32 . 21	363,013	68 . 6 . 4
Peru	1 . 31 . 0	362,808	68 . 5 . 156

In representation of the earth, its *surface* may also be considered as being smooth: its inequalities have been compared to those on the rind of an orange; but even this is an exaggeration. The loftiest mountain is known not to exceed five miles in perpendicular height, and this is only 1-1600th part of the earth's diameter; consequently, it must be represented, on a globe of 16 inches in diameter, by an elevation of 1-100th part of an inch, or the thickness of common drawing-paper; but as the general elevation of the land is very much below this, or even one-fourth of it, it must be within the thickness of the thinnest writing-paper. The ocean, supposing its depth to be equal to the height of the land, would not appear more on a similar globe than the wash of colour left by a brush in tinting a drawing.

The greater or equatorial diameter is	41,847,426 feet, or	7925·648 miles.
The lesser, or polar diameter	41,707,620 „	7899·170 „
Difference of diameters, or polar compression	139,806 „	26·478 „
Equatorial circumference		24,899·000 „

MOTIONS OF THE EARTH.

The earth turns uniformly round, once in twenty-four hours, in a direction from west to east, upon an axis, which is an imaginary line passing through its centre: this is called its *diurnal motion.* It is likewise carried in the same direction round the sun, in an orbit nearly circular, and completes its revolutions in a year: this is called its *annual motion.* As some of the divisions of our globe, of great importance in geography, depend upon these motions, we will now consider them more particularly.

By the diurnal motion of the earth, all places on its surface are carried uniformly round its axis from west to east, in the course of the natural day. This *real* motion causes the sun and the other heavenly bodies to have an *apparent* motion in the contrary direction, from east to west. Hence it is that we have the continual succession of day and night; for as the sun can only illuminate by his rays one half of a spherical body, one half of our earth must be in darkness while the other enjoys the light; it is therefore day at any place when, by the diurnal rotation, that place is turned towards the sun, and night at the same place when turned away from the sun.

The two points on the surface of the earth, which are the extremities of its axis, are called the *north* and *south poles.* A circle described upon the surface of the earth, equally distant from its two poles, is called the *equator;* this circle divides the surface of the earth into two equal parts, called the Northern and Southern Hemispheres.

As by a real motion of the earth about its axis there is produced an apparent motion of all the heavenly bodies, so, in like manner, by the real annual motion of the earth round the sun, there is produced an apparent annual motion of the sun round the earth; and thus the sun appears to make a complete revolution round the heavens once in a year. The circle which the sun appears to describe, in the course of the year, through the heavens, is called the ECLIPTIC. Astronomers have conceived this circle to be divided into twelve equal parts, called *signs*, and have given them the following names; *Aries*, *Taurus*, *Gemini*, *Cancer*, *Leo*, *Virgo*, *Libra*, *Scorpio*, *Sagittarius*, *Capricorn*, *Aquarius*, and *Pisces.* The ecliptic passes through the middle of the zodiac, and hence these signs are also called the *signs of the zodiac.*

INEQUALITY OF THE DAYS AND NIGHTS, AND CHANGES OF THE SEASONS.

Were the sun and the earth perfectly at rest with respect to each other, it is evident that one half of the earth would be continually in light, and the other in darkness, as the sun can only illuminate one half of its surface at a time. Suppose the earth to revolve about its axis, yet the position of the axis, with respect to the sun, will very much affect the distribution of light and darkness to the various places on its surface. For example, were the earth's axis to point directly towards the sun, or to coincide with a line joining the centres of the earth and the sun, still one of our hemispheres would be continually in the light, and the other in darkness. Again, suppose the earth to revolve uniformly about an axis perpendicular to a line joining the centres of the earth and sun, then all places upon the surface would be in light and darkness alternately, and an equal interval of time in each, or the days and nights would be each twelve hours long throughout the globe.

If either half of the earth's axis, for example the northern, were to make an acute angle with a line joining the centres of the earth and sun, and of consequence the southern half an obtuse angle, it would follow that the north pole, and a certain tract round it, would remain always in the light, or would have continual day, notwithstanding the earth's rotation. Even such places, in the northern hemisphere, as were turned by the diurnal rotation away from the sun, would pass sooner through the dark hemisphere of the earth than that exposed to the light, and would thus have their nights shorter than their days; at the equator the days and nights would be equal; but, in the southern hemisphere, the phenomena would be the very reverse of those which took place in the northern hemisphere, and the south pole and its neighbourhood would be in darkness. It is evident, also, that in this case the sun would be on the north side of the equator, and vertical to a certain circle parallel to it, which would be nearer to, or farther from it, according as the acute angle formed by the northern half of the earth's axis, and a line joining the centres of sun and earth, was greater or less. Now, the two last suppositions respecting the situation of the axis are such as really take place in nature; for, while the earth moves in its orbit round the sun, its axis remains continually parallel to itself, or points always in the same direction, making an angle with a perpendicular to its orbit of 23½ degrees; and as, by the earth's motion, the line joining its centre with that of the sun is continually changing its direction, it is evident that the angle contained by that line and the axis must be continually varying in magnitude, and of course the position of the poles of the earth with respect to the sun (which, as we have seen, depends entirely on that angle), must be always changing.

About the 20th of March, when the sun, as seen from the earth, enters the constellation Aries, the line joining the centres is perpendicular to the earth's axis; therefore, both poles are situated alike with respect to the sun, which is now over the equator, and the days and nights are equal throughout the world. At this time of the year, which is called the *vernal equinox*, spring commences to the inhabitants of the northern hemisphere, and autumn to those of the southern. During the time that the sun is passing through Aries, Taurus, Gemini, and till he enters Cancer, which happens about the 20th of June, and is the time of the *summer solstice*, the angle contained by the north half of the earth's axis and the line which joins the centres of the sun and earth is always diminishing, by reason of that line changing its position while the axis moves parallel to itself. Hence it happens that the north pole is turning more and more towards the sun, and the phenomena take place which we have already described as peculiar to this situation of the axis. About the 20th of June the angle is at the least, and presently begins to increase, as well as the pole to turn away from the sun, which now passes through Cancer, Leo, and Virgo, and enters Libra on the 20th of September, when the axis has a position similar to that which it had on the 20th of March, and the days and nights are again equal; this is called the autumnal equinox. The sun now appears to cross the equator, and the south pole, which during the last six months was in the dark, begins to turn towards the sun, when precisely the same phenomena are exhibited to the southern hemisphere that we have already described in the case of the northern. The *winter solstice* is about the 20th of December, when the sun enters Capricorn. Thus, by a combination of the annual and diurnal motions of the earth, with the parallelism of its axis, and its obliquity to the plane of the earth's orbit, the various seasons are produced, and the same quantity of light and darkness, upon the whole, is distributed in the course of the year to all the regions of the globe.

THE CIRCLES DESCRIBED ON THE SURFACE OF THE EARTH.

The poles of the earth are two points on its surface diametrically opposite to each other. They are the extremities of the axis of the earth's diurnal revolution. The one is called the *north* and the other the *south pole*.

The *equator* is an imaginary circle on the surface of the earth, equally distant from both poles. It divides the earth's surface into two equal parts, called the *northern* and *southern hemispheres*.

The *meridian* of any place on the earth is an imaginary circle passing through that place and the two poles. This circle with respect to that place divides the earth's surface into two equal portions, called the *eastern* and *western hemispheres*.

All places, directly north and south to each other, have the same meridian; but those places which lie in any other direction from each other have different meridians. The meridians of all places on the globe are perpendicular to the equator.

The *latitude* of a place is its distance from the equator, reckoned in degrees and minutes, on an arc of its meridian, and is north or south according as that place lies in the northern or southern hemisphere; for example, the latitude of Edinburgh is 55 degrees 58 minutes N.; that of the Cape of Good Hope is about 34 degrees S. &c. No place can have a greater latitude than 90 degrees.

Parallels of latitude are circles on the earth's surface parallel to the equator. All places directly east and west from each other are equally distant from the equator, and are said to lie in the same parallel of latitude. Such places as lie in any other direction from each other are in different parallels of latitude.

The *longitude* of a place is the degrees and minutes in an arc of the equator, intercepted between its meridian and the meridian of some other given place, from which the longitude is reckoned. The geographers of different countries generally reckon the longitude eastward and westward from the meridians passing through the capitals of these countries. Thus, in Britain, we reckon the longitude eastward and westward from the meridian of London : the longitude of Edinburgh, for example, is three degrees west; that of Petersburgh about thirty degrees east. No place can have its longitude greater than 180 degrees. The degrees of longitude are not like those of latitude, but diminish in proportion as the meridians incline, or their distance contracts in approaching the pole. Hence, in 60 degrees of latitude, a degree of longitude is but half the quantity of a degree on the equator ; and so of the rest.

The *horizon* of a place is that apparent circle which bounds the view of a spectator at that place. When the celestial bodies come above the eastern part of the horizon they are said to *rise*, and when they descend below the western part, they are said to *set.*

DIVISION OF THE EARTH INTO ZONES.

A *zone* is a broad space upon the earth, included between two parallels of latitude. There are five zones, which take their names from the degrees of heat and cold to which they are exposed, by the poles of the earth being turned alternately to and from the sun.

The *torrid zone* is that portion of the earth over which the sun is perpendicular at one time or other in the course of the year. This zone is about 47 degrees in breadth, extending to about 23½ degrees on each side of the equator. The parallel of latitude by which it is limited in the northern hemisphere is called the *tropic of cancer*, because the sun is directly over this parallel when he enters the sign of that name ; and, for a similar reason, the limiting parallel in the southern hemisphere is called the *tropic of capricorn.*

The *frigid zones* are those regions about the poles where the sun does not rise for some days at one time of the year, and does not set for some days at another time of the year. The zones extend round the poles to the distance of about 23½ degrees. That in the northern hemisphere is called the *north frigid zone*, and is bounded by a parallel of latitude called the *arctic polar circle ;* the other, in the southern hemisphere, is called the *south frigid zone*, and the parallel of latitude which bounds it the *antarctic polar circle.*

The two *temperate zones* are the spaces between the torrid and frigid zones.

The *superficies* of the several zones are as follow :—

	square miles.
The torrid zone	16,500,375
The two temperate zones	103,114,775
The two frigid zones	79,328,600
	198,943,750

NATURAL DIVISIONS OF THE EARTH.

The surface of the earth is naturally divided into land and water.

Land is divided into continents, islands, peninsulas, isthmuses, mountains, capes, hills, and cliffs.

Water is divided into oceans, seas, channels, gulfs, straits, lakes, rivers, and rivulets.

A *continent* is a large tract of land comprehending many contiguous kingdoms, states, &c., without any entire separation of its parts by water. The world is usually divided into two great continents, the Old and the New. The old continent comprehends Europe, Asia, and Africa ; and the new, North and South America.

An *island* is a tract of land entirely surrrounded by water, as Britain, Ireland, Sicily, &c.

A *peninsula* is a tract of land joined to a continent only by a narrow neck, being everywhere else encompassed by water, as the Morea in Greece, Jutland, the Crimea, &c.

An *isthmus* is the neck which joins a peninsula to the adjacent land, and forms the passage between them, as the Isthmus of Suez, the Isthmus of Darien, &c.

A *mountain* is a part of the land greatly elevated above the adjacent country.

A *cape* or *promontory* is a portion of land stretching out into the sea, as the North Cape, the Cape of Good Hope, &c.

A *cliff* is a steep shore, hill, or mountain.

The *ocean* is that vast collection of salt water, which covers the greater part of the globe. It is divided by geographers into three parts. 1. The *Atlantic* or *European Ocean*, lying between part of Europe, Africa, and America. 2. The *Indian Ocean*, lying between Africa, the East Indian Islands, and New Holland. 3. The *Pacific Ocean*, or *Great South Sea*, which lies between the Philippine Islands, China, Japan, and New Holland on the W., and the coast of America on the E. The same Ocean takes different names from the countries upon which it borders, as the British Ocean, the German Ocean, &c.

A *sea* is a branch of the ocean flowing between some parts of the continent, or separating an island from the continent, as the Mediterranean Sea, the Euxine Sea, the Baltic Sea, &c.

A *channel* is a narrow sea confined between an island and a continent, or between two islands, as the English Channel, and St. George's Channel.

A *gulf* or *bay* is a part of the ocean or sea contained between two shores, and surrounded by land every where, except at its entrance, where it communicates with the ocean, seas, or other bays, as the Gulf of Venice, the Gulf of Mexico, &c.

A *strait* is a narrow passage by which there is a communication between a gulf and its neighbouring seas, or between one part of the ocean and another, as the Straits of Gibraltar, the Straits of Babelmandel, &c.

A *lake* is a collection of water surrounded on all sides by land, as Lake Ladoga, the Lake Geneva, Loch Tay, Loch Lomond, &c.

A *river* is a current of fresh water, formed by the confluence of several rivulets, and flowing in a channel from its source to the sea.

A *rivulet* or *brook* is a small stream arising from a spring, and is the commencement of a river.

THE TIDES.

It is found by experience to be a general law of nature, that all the particles of matter which compose the universe, however remote they may be from one another, have a continual tendency to approach each other. This tendency is called *universal gravitation*, and is stronger or weaker according as the particles are situated nearer to, or farther from, each other, its intensity being always inversely proportional to the square of their distance. The planets are retained in their orbits, and move round the sun as a centre, in consequence of their tendency towards the sun being combined with a motion impressed on them, in the direction of a straight line touching their orbits. The same principle of universal gravitation likewise connects the earth and moon, and causes the moon to revolve in an orbit, of which the earth is the centre, while, on the other hand, the moon, by the force of attraction which she exerts upon the earth, produces those alternate elevations and depressions of the waters of the ocean, called *tides*.

It is in consequence of the law of universal gravitation that all the particles of matter which compose the earth are heavy, or gravitate towards its centre; but, as they must also gravitate towards the moon, it is evident that the waters of the ocean directly under the moon, being nearer to her than the central parts of the earth, will be more attracted towards her than those parts, and therefore will have their gravity towards the centre somewhat diminished. Again, the central parts being nearer the moon than the waters on the opposite side of the earth, must be more attracted by her than the waters, by which means the waters of the ocean on the opposite side of the earth will also have the gravity towards the centre somewhat diminished.

As for those parts of the ocean which are 90 degrees from the point directly under the moon, since they are nearly at the same distance from her as the central parts of the earth, they will be attracted with nearly the same force; but because they are attracted in lines directed to the moon's centre, the effect produced upon the whole is a small increase of their gravity towards the centre of the earth. Since, therefore, by the unequal action of the moon upon the waters, their gravity is in some places increased, and in others diminished, and their equilibrium thus disturbed, it is evident, from the nature of fluids, that the ocean will arrange itself so as to restore the equilibrium, and will assume a spherical or egg-like form, having its longest diameter directed towards the moon. Hence, as the earth turns round its axis, from the moon to the moon again, in 24 hours 48 minutes, the elevated parts of the ocean, which always keep nearly under her and opposite to her, will shift and move round the earth in the same time; and as it is high water, or flood, at any place when the elevated parts of the watery spheroid pass that place, so it will be low water, or ebb, when the depressed parts of the spheroid pass that place; thus there will be two tides of flood, and two of ebb, succeeding each other within that time, or at intervals of 6 hours and 12 minutes.

We have hitherto considered only the action of the moon in producing the tides, but it is evident that, for the same reasons, the inequality of the sun's action on different parts of the earth must produce a similar effect; so that there are in reality two tides every natural day, from the action of the sun, as there are in the lunar day, from that of the moon; however, by reason of the sun's immense distance from the earth, its effect in producing the tides is considerably less than that of the moon.

At the time of the new moon, or when the moon is in conjunction with the sun, and at the time of full moon, or when the moon is in direct opposition to the sun, it is evident that their effects in raising the waters will be conjoined; hence, twice in the course of every month the tides are greater than usual; these are called *spring tides.*

When the moon is entering her second and last quarter, she is then 90 degrees distant from the sun, and, when they are in this position, their effects in raising the tides are opposed to one another, by which means the one raises the water where the other depresses it, and thus the tides are twice every month lower than usual: these are called *neap tides.*

The time of high water is not precisely when the moon comes to the meridian, but generally an hour or two after; for, by the motion of the earth on its axis, the most elevated part of the water is carried beyond the point directly under the moon, in the direction of the diurnal rotation, so that the water continues to rise after it has passed directly under the moon, though her action begins there to decrease. The greatest spring tides also do not happen till the second or third day after the new or full moon; and a similar observation is to be made with respect to the neap tides. To these observations may be added the following:—1. The elevation of the waters towards the moon a little exceeds the opposite one. 2. The action of the sun and moon is greater the nearer those bodies are to the earth. 3. The greatest tides happen a little before the vernal and a little after the autumnal equinox. 4. All these phenomena obtain in the open sea, where the ocean is extensive enough to be subject to these motions; but the particular situation of places, as to shores, capes, straits, &c., disturb the motion of the waters, and occasion a deviation in some measure from the general rules.

Small inland seas, such as the Baltic and the Mediterranean, are but little subject to the tides, because the action of the sun and moon is nearly the same over the whole extent of such seas. In very high latitudes, also, the tides are very inconsiderable; for the sun and moon, acting in the neighbourhood of the equator, and always raising the water towards the middle of the torrid zone, the regions adjoining to the poles must consequently be deprived of these waters, and the sea must, within the frigid zones, be low relatively to other parts.

THE WINDS.

The currents of the atmosphere, which constitute *winds*, are produced by various parts, but of these the heat of the sun seems to be the most general and powerful; and an *east wind*, which blows continually round the globe, is produced by the rarefaction of the air by means of the solar heat within the tropical regions, and even to a considerable distance beyond them.

The following observations on this subject have been made by skilful seamen, and by the celebrated Dr. Halley:—

Within the limits of 60 degrees, viz. from 30 degrees of N. latitude to 30 degrees of S. latitude, there is a constant east wind throughout the year, blowing on the Atlantic and Pacific Oceans. This is called the *trade wind.*

The trade winds near the northern limits blow between the north and east; and near their southern limits they blow between the south and east.

These general motions of the wind are distributed on the continent and near the coasts.

In some parts of the Indian Ocean there are periodical winds, which are called *monsoons*, that is, such as blow one half of the year one way, and the other half the contrary way.

In the Atlantic Ocean, near the coast of Africa, at about 100 leagues from the shore, between the latitudes of 28 degrees and 10 degrees N., seamen constantly meet with a fresh gale of wind blowing from the north-east.

Those bound to the Caribbee Islands, across the Atlantic Ocean, find, as they approach the American side, that the said N. E. wind becomes easterly, or seldom blows more than a point from the east, either to the northward or southward. These trade winds, on the American side, extend to 30, 31, or even 32 degrees of N. latitude, which is about 4 degrees farther than they extend on the African side. To the southward of the equator, the trade winds extend three or four degrees farther towards the coast of Brazil, on the American side, than they do near the Cape of Good Hope, on the African side.

Between the latitude of 4 degrees N. and 4 degrees S., the wind always blows between the south and east; on the African side the winds are nearest the south, and on the American side nearest the east.

The winds are somewhat changed by the seasons of the year; for, when the sun is far northward, the Brazil S. E. gets to the south, and the N. E. wind to the east; and, when the sun is far south, the S. E. become east, and the N. E. winds on this side the equator veer more to the north.

Along the coast of Guinea, from Sierra Leone to the island of St. Thomas, (under the equator,) which is about 50 leagues, the southerly and S. W. winds blow perpetually; for the S. E. trade wind having passed the equator, and approaching the Guinea coast within 80 or 100 leagues, inclines towards the shore, and becomes S., then S. E., and by degrees, as it comes nearer the land, it veers about to S., S. S. W., and, in with the land, it is S. W., and sometimes W. S. W. This tract is troubled with frequent calms and violent and sudden gusts of winds, called *tornadoes*, blowing from all points of the horizon.

Between the fourth and tenth degrees of N. latitude, and between the longitudes of Cape Verd and the farthest east of the Cape Verd Isles, there is a tract of sea which seems to be condemned to perpetual calms, attended with terrible thunder and lightnings, and such frequent rains that it is called *the rains*.

Between the southern latitudes of 10 degrees and 30 degrees in the Indian Ocean, the general trade wind, about the S. E. by S., is found to blow all the year in the same manner as in the like latitudes in the Ethiopic Ocean; and, during the six months from May to December, these winds reach to within two degrees of the equator; but during the other six months, from November to June, a N. W. wind blows in the tract lying between 3 degrees and 10 degrees of S. latitude, in the meridian of the north end of Madagascar, and between 2 degrees and 12 degrees of S. latitude near the longitude of Sumatra and Java.

In the tract between Sumatra and the African coast, and from 3 degrees S. latitude quite northward to the Asiatic coasts, including the Arabian Sea and the Gulf of Bengal, the monsoons blow from September to April on the N. E.; and from March to October on the S. W. In the former half year the winds are more steady and gentle, and the weather clearer than in the latter, and the wind is more strong and steady in the Arabian Sea than in the Bay of Bengal.

Between the island of Madagascar and the coast of Africa, and thence northward as far as the equator, there is a tract wherein, from April to October, there is a constant fresh S. S. W. wind, which to the northward changes into a W. S. W. wind, blowing at that time in the Arabian Sea.

To the eastward of Sumatra and Malacca, on the north of the equator, and along the coasts of Cambodia and China, quite through the Philippines, as far as Japan, the monsoons blow northerly and southerly; the northern setting in about October or November, and the southern about May. These winds are not quite so certain as those in the Arabian seas.

Between Sumatra and Java to the west, and New Guinea to the east, the same northerly and southerly winds are observed, but the first half year monsoon inclines to the N. W., and the latter to the S. E. These winds begin a month or six weeks after those in the Chinese seas set in, and are quite as variable.

These contrary winds do not shift from one point to its opposite all at once; in some places the time of the change is attended with calms, in others by variable winds; and it often happens on the coasts of Coromandel and China, towards the end of the monsoons, that there are most violent storms, greatly resembling the hurricanes in the West Indies, wherein the wind is so very strong that hardly any thing can resist its force.

REPRESENTATIONS OF THE EARTH'S SURFACE.

The earth, as before described, is divided by the equator into two equal hemispheres, of which the north and south poles are the respective centres. As in all circles, the equator is divided into 360 degrees of 60 minutes geographic miles, which, on the equator, are about equal to 68 2-3rds British miles. Through these divisions the meridians of longitude are imagined to pass and cross the poles, and are, of course, at right angles to the equator. These meridians are also divided into 360 degrees, or by the equator and the poles into four quadrants of 90 degrees each, and these are called degrees of latitude, counting from 0 degree on the equator to 90 degrees at the poles. These consist of 60 geographic miles, but, from the ellipticity of the earth, they are not of equal length, but increase toward the poles (see Table on page v.). This variation is generally disregarded in maps and representations of the earth. The parallels of latitude intersect the meridians at right angles, and are parallel to the equator. As they approach the pole, it will be evident that they approach each other, and consequently that the degrees of longitude decrease in length in proportion, till, at 60 degrees of latitude, it is but one half the length of the equatorial degree, and at the pole it is nothing.

The only correct representation of the earth's surface can be made on a body of a similar form, or a globe, but as they are very inconvenient, or inapplicable to most purposes, maps are constructed on a flat surface, which are far more useful and preferable to a globe, but they *distort*, in a greater or less degree, the true figures of the countries they represent. They may be divided into three classes: *maps*, or representations of the *land*, showing its rivers, mountains, towns, &c.; *charts*, or representations of the *sea*, for nautical purposes, showing the depths of water, sandbanks, rocks, &c.; and *plans*, which represent *minutely* a small portion of a country, as a town or district, showing its roads, buildings, &c. A map illustrates *geography*, a chart belongs to *hydrography*, and a plan shows the *topography* of a place.

The *projection* of a map is a representation of the meridians and parallels on a plane surface, and may be generally considered as being constructed on two methods—globular projection and Mercator's projection. Maps are on globular, and charts always on Mercator's projection, while in plans, from the small portion represented, it is usually disregarded. Globular projection may be thus described. A circle of the intended diameter of the hemisphere is divided by a horizontal line passing through its centre, and representing the equator; through the centre, and at right angles to the equator, is drawn another line, which will represent a meridian; where this line cuts the circle, at the top and bottom, will be the north and south poles, and the circle, which will represent one-half the globe, is thus divided into four equal quadrants. The equator is divided into 180 parts or degrees, and the centre meridian into 180 degrees also; which will represent the degrees of latitude, reckoning from the equator N. and S. The circumference is divided into 360 degrees, or 90 degrees in each quadrant, corresponding with the centre meridian. Curved lines are now drawn through each of the subdivisions of the central meridian to those in the circumference on each side of it, and through those on the equator to the north and south poles. The whole hemisphere, or circle, will now be covered with a network of lines, each supposed to be a degree, or 60 geographic miles apart, and on these lines the configurations of the earth's surface is represented, and the distances and area are to be calculated by them; but they are unequal; the degrees of latitude, that is, the parallels, diverge from the centre, which is supposed to be 180 degrees long, to the circumference, which is also supposed to be of two portions of 180 degrees each, and consequently a degree of the circumference is much longer than on the centre, and does not bear the same proportion to the degree of longitude; so that in all large portions of the earth, it must be represented more or less distorted on a flat surface. A map of a country, as Spain, Italy, England, is represented on a portion of such a projection, and the degrees of latitude and longitude are numbered on the margin, the top being usually considered as the north, and the right hand the east, unless otherwise expressed.

Mercator's projection was invented by Gerhard Mercator, a Flemish geographer, in 1566; but the true principles on which it is constructed were first explained by Edward Wright, an Englishman, in 1599. It is used for charts, and possesses several advantages over all other projections, though it differs essentially from the *true* figure of the earth; by it the bearings and distances between places may be ascertained with much greater facility.

In this projection the figure of the earth is supposed to be developed on a cylinder, instead of a sphere. Mercator conceived a transparent cylinder of infinite length, in which an elastic globe of the same diameter is placed, and on which the meridians and parallels are drawn. By expanding this globe it will fill the cylinder, and it is evident that while the equatorial degrees remain the same, by being confined by the cylinder, the meridians, as they approach the pole, instead of converging or decreasing as before, become parallel and equal, and the degrees of latitude are increased exactly in the same proportion or ratio as the expansion of those of longitude; and therefore the great difference between this and other projections is, that the degrees of longitude are invariable, and represented by parallel straight lines, and the degrees of latitude are made to bear the same proportion to the longitude, or increasing toward the poles, while the true figure is that in which the longitude decreases, and the latitude invariable.

All straight lines on the earth's surface will be represented by straight lines on this projection, and all bearings are truly represented, though the relative size of the countries represented is increased in proportion to the latitude; so that the polar regions will be on a much larger scale than those on the equator, though not otherwise distorted. There are other modes of projecting representations of the earth on a plane surface, but the above are the most generally used.

POPULATION OF THE WORLD

ACCORDING TO VARIOUS LATE AUTHORITIES.

STATES OF EUROPE.

STATES.	Title.	Form of Government.	Religion.	Reigning Sovereign.	Area in Sq. Miles	Population.
Andorra	Limited Republic	2 Courts & Council	Catholic	. .	190	15,300
Belgium	Kingdom	Limited Monarchy	Catholic	Leopold I.	12,569	4,230,000
Cracow	Republic	Senate & Chamber	Catholic	. .	490	124,300
Denmark	Kingdom	Absolute Monarchy	Lutheran	Christian VIII.	59,762	2,097,400
Ecclesiastical States	Popedom	Abs. Sovereignty	Catholic	Gregory XVI.	17,048	2,590,000
France	Kingdom	Limited Monarchy	Catholic	Louis Philippe	202,125	33,600,000
Confederation of Germany in their political order:						
Austria	Empire	Absolute Monarchy	Catholic	Ferdinand	255,226	34,100,000
Prussia	Kingdom	Absolute Monarchy	Evangel.	Fred. W. IV.	106,302	13,800,000
Bavaria	Kingdom	Limited Monarchy	Catholic	Louis	28,435	4,300,000
Saxony	Kingdom	Limited Monarchy	Protestant	Frederic	5,705	1,680,000
Hanover	Kingdom	Limited Monarchy	Protestant	Ernest August.	14,600	1,679,000
Wirtemberg	Kingdom	Limited Monarchy	Lutheran	William	7,568	1,610,000
Baden	Grand Duchy	Limit. Sovereignty	Evangel.	Ch. Leopold Fr.	[illegible]	1,240,000
Hesse Cassel	Electorate	Limit. Sovereignty	Reformed	William II.	4,386	699,000
Hesse Darmstadt	Grand Duchy	Limit. Sovereignty	Lutheran	Louis II.	3,198	765,000
Holstein and Lunenberg	Duchy	Limited Monarchy	Lutheran	Christian	3,685	394,000
Saxe Weimar	Grand Duchy	Limited Monarchy	Lutheran	Ch. Frederick	1,403	243,000
Saxe Gotha	Duchy	Limited Monarchy	Lutheran	Ernest	582	83,000
Saxe Meiningen	Duchy	Limited Monarchy	Lutheran	} Bernard {	720	40,000
Saxe Hildburghausen	Duchy	Limited Monarchy	Lutheran		225	71,500
Saxe Coburg	Duchy	Limited Monarchy	Lutheran	Ernest	969	139,440
Mecklenburg Schwerin	Grand Duchy	Limited Monarchy	Lutheran	Paul Frederick	4,701	472,000
Mecklenburg Strelitz	Grand Duchy	Limited Monarchy	Lutheran	George V	1,094	85,300
Brunswick	Duchy	Limit. Sovereignty	Lutheran	William	1,525	250,000
Nassau	Duchy	Limit. Sovereignty	Evangel.	William	1,736	372,700
Anhalt Dessau	Duchy	Abso. Sovereignty	Evangel.	Leopold	337	57,600
Anhalt Bernburg	Duchy	Abso. Sovereignty	Evangel.	Alexis	336	45,500
Anhalt Kothen	Duchy	Abso. Sovereignty	Reformed	Henry	310	36,400
Schwarzburg	Principality	Limited Monarchy	Lutheran	Gunther II.	756	118,500
Holstein Oldenburg	Grand Duchy	Abso. Sovereignty	Lutheran	Augustus	2,470	260,000
Hohenzollern Hechingen	Principality	Limit. Sovereignty	Catholic	Fred. William	136	21,000
Hohenzollern Sigmaringen	Principality	Limit. Sovereignty	Catholic	Charles	383	42,800
Lichtenstein	Principality	Limited Monarchy	Catholic	John Joseph	52	5,800
Waldeck	Principality	Limit. Sovereignty	Evangel.	George	455	56,000
Reuss	Principalities	Limit. Sovereignty	Lutheran	Henry LXII.	588	83,400
Lippe Detmold	Principality	Limit. Sovereignty	Reformed	Leopold	432	79,000
Lippe Schauenburg	Principality	Limit. Sovereignty	Reformed	Geo. William	205	26,000
Hesse Homburg	Landgraviate	Abso. Sovereignty	Reformed	Phil. Augustus	154	24,000
Frankfort-on-the-Maine	Free City	Republic	Lutheran	. .	91	56,000
Lubeck	Free City	Republic	Lutheran	. .	142	46,500
Bremen	Free City	Republic	Calvinist	. .	67	57,800
Hamburg	Free City	Republic	Lutheran	. .	149	153,000
Great Britain and Ireland	Kingdom	Limited Monarchy	Protestant	Victoria	116,700	27,000,000
Greece	Kingdom	Limited Monarchy	Greek Ch.	Otho	10,206	810,000
Holland (with Luxembourg)	Kingdom	Limited Monarchy	Reformed	William II.	13,890	2,820,000
Ionian Islands	Republic	Under British Pro.	Greek Ch.	. .	998	242,000
Lucca	Duchy	Limit. Sovereignty	Catholic	Charles Louis	410	145,000
Modena and Massa	Duchy	Abso. Sovereignty	Catholic	Francis IV.	2,073	390,000
Monaco	Principality	Abso. Sovereignty	Catholic	. .	50	6,700
Parma	Duchy	Abso. Sovereignty	Catholic	Maria Louisa	2,184	440,000
Portugal	Kingdom	Limited Monarchy	Catholic	Maria II.	34,500	3,400,000
Russia	Empire	Absolute Monarchy	Greek Ch.	Nicholas I.	2,041,809	51,100,000
San Marino	Republic	Senate and Council	Catholic	. .	21	7,500
Sardinia	Kingdom	Absolute Monarchy	Catholic	Charles Albert	28,830	4,500,000
Sicilies, Two	Kingdom	Limited Monarchy	Catholic	Ferdinand II.	41,521	7,650,000
Spain	Kingdom	Limited Monarchy	Catholic	Isabella II.	176,480	11,963,000
Sweden and Norway	Kingdom	Limited Monarchy	Lutheran	Charles XIV.	284,530	4,1[illegible]0,000
Switzerland	Republic	Confederation	Various	. .	17,208	2,116,000
Turkey	Empire	Absolute Monarchy	Mahom.	Abdul Medjid	183,140	12,000,000
Tuscany	Grand Duchy	Abso. Sovereignty	Catholic	Leopold II.	8,302	1,330,000

Total area, 3,704,710 square miles. Total population, 235,265,140.

ASIA.

Area about 17,805,146 square miles. Population variously stated at **390 millions, 480 millions, and** 608 millions.

States, &c.	Title.	Capital.	Religion.	Reigning Sovereign.	Population.
Anam	Empire	Hué	Buddhism	Ming Ming	5,194,000
Afghanistan	Kingdom	Cabul	Mahom	Shoo-ja	10,000,000
Arabia	. . . .	Mecca	Mahom.	Yahya	7,500,000
Beloochistan	Kingdom	Kelat	Mahom.	Mehrab (k. 1839)	2,700,000
Birmah	Empire	Ava	Buddhism	Ser-a-wa	3,500,000
China	Empire	Pe-king	Confucian.	Tao-kwang	252,866,000
Japan	Empire	Jedo	Sinto	The Kubo	30,000,000
Lahore, or Seiks	Province	Lahore	Seik	Shere Singh	8,000,000
Malacca	. . . .	. . . .	. . . .	. . . .	600,000
Nepaul	Kingdom	Katmandu	Bramin.	Radzhindra Bikramsah	2,500,000
Persia	Empire	Tehran	Mahom.	Mohammed	11,240,000
Russia	Empire	Petersburgh	Greek Ch.	Nicholas I.	12,407,190
Siam	Empire	Bankok	Buddhism	Kroma-mon-tshit	5,000,000
Sindia	Empire	Hyderabad	Mahom.	Dzankodzi-rao	4,000,000
Turkestan	Indep. Tartary	. . . .	. . . .	. . . . . .	6,978,000
Turkey	Empire	Constantinople	Mahom.	Abdul Medjid	11,064,000

Islands—Independent population, 20,824,000. British Possessions, 112,822,132. Of other European Powers, 9,660,267. Total population, 608,516,019.

AFRICA.

Area about 11,647,428 square miles. Population estimated by different authors as 60 millions, 99 millions, 102 millions, or 100 millions.

Abyssinia	4,500,000	Nubia	1,900,000
Ashantee	3,000,000	Senegambia	10,000,000
Barca	300,000	Sennaar	1,500,000
Bournou	2,000,000	Soudan, the Sahara, &c.	20,000,000
Dar Fur	200,000	Jellatah tribes	2,000,000
Egypt	2,000,000	Tripoli	1,500,000
Guinea	7,000,000	Tunis	3,000,000
Morocco	8,500,000	Interior and Eastern Africa	29,000,000

Possessions of European Powers, 1,236,674. Total population, 101,498,411.

NORTH AMERICA.

Area about eight million square miles.

State.	Title.	Capital.	Presidents, &c.	Population.
British Provinces	. . .	Quebec	... ...	... ...
United States	Republic	Washington	John Tyler	17,068,666
Mexico	Republic	Mexico	Anasto. Bustamente	7,687,000
Guatimala	Republic	S. Salvador	... ...	2,000,000
Yucatan	Republic	Merida	Migl. Barbachano	479,400
Hayti	Republic	C. Haytien	J. P. Boyer	933,000
Texas	Republic	Austin	Samuel Houston	150,000

SOUTH AMERICA.

Area about seven million square miles. Population about fourteen millions.

State.	Title.	Capital.	Presidents, &c.	Population.
Argentine Republic	Republic	Buenos Ayres	Don J. M. de Rosas	2,000,000
Peru	Republic	Lima	General Gamarra	1,700,000
New Granada	Republic	Bogota	Jose. J. de Marquez	1,687,000
Bolivia	Republic	Chuquisaca	General Santa Cruz	1,500,000
Chili	Republic	Santiago	Joaquim Prieto	1,500,000
Venezuela	Republic	Caraccas	General Paez	900,000
Ecuador	Republic	Quito	V. Rocafuerte	600,000
Panama	Republic	Panama	Thomas Herrara	....
Paraguay	Republic	Assumption	....	300,000
Uruguay	Republic	Monte Video	Fructuoso Rivera	150,000
Brazil	Empire	Rio Janeiro	Pedro II. (Emperor.)	5,130,418

OCEANICA, or OCEANIA.

Area between three and four million square miles.—Population extremely uncertain, estimated by different authors at two, or at twenty millions.

POPULATION AND EXTENT OF THE GLOBE.

	According to Balbi.			Weimar Almanac, 1840.		
	Population.	Eng. Sq. Mls.	Pop. to Sq. Mile.	Population.	Eng. Sq. Mls.	Pop. to Sq. Mile.
Europe . .	227,700,000	3,700,000	61·5	233,240,043	3,807,195	61·2
Asia . .	390,000,000	16,045,000	24·3	608,516,019	17,805,146	34·2
Africa . .	60,000,000	11,254,000	5·	101,498,411	11,647,428	8·6
America . .	39,000,000	14,730,000	2·3	48,077,150	13,542,400	3·5
Oceanica . .	20,300,000	4,105,000	4·96	1,838,194	3,347,840	0·4
Total ...	737,000,000	49,834,000	14·8	993,108,537	50,150,009	19·8

POPULATION OF ENGLAND.

COUNTIES.	1801.	Increase per Cent.	1811.	Increase per Cent.	1821.	Increase per Cent.	1831.	Increase per Cent.	1841.
Bedford . . .	63,393	11	70,213	19	83,716	14	95,483	13·	107,937
Berks . . .	109,215	8	118,277	11	131,977	10	145,389	10·2	160,226
Buckingham . .	107,444	9	117,650	14	134,068	9	146,529	6·4	155,989
Cambridge . .	89,346	13	101,109	20	121,909	18	143,955	14·2	164,509
Chester . . .	191,751	18	227,[illegible]31	19	270,098	24	334,391	18·5	395,300
Cornwall . .	188,269	15	216,667	19	257,447	17	300,938	13·4	341,269
Cumberland . .	117,230	14	133,744	17	156,124	10	169,681	4·8	177,912
Derby . . .	161,142	15	185,487	15	213,333	11	237,170	14·7	272,202
Devon . . .	343,001	12	383,308	15	439,040	13	494,478	7·8	533,731
Dorset . . .	115,319	8	124,693	16	144,499	10	159,252	9·7	174,743
Durham . . .	160,361	11	177,625	17	207,673	22	253,910	27·7	324,277
Essex . . .	226,437	11	252,473	15	289,424	10	317,507	8·6	344,995
Gloucester . .	250,809	12	285,514	18	335,843	15	387,019	11·4	431,307
Hereford . .	89,191	5	94,073	10	103,243	7	111,211	2·9	114,438
Hertford . .	97,577	14	111,654	16	129,714	10	143,341	9·6	157,237
Huntingdon . .	37,568	12	42,208	15	48,771	9	53,192	10·3	58,699
Kent . . .	307,624	21	373,095	14	426,016	12	479,155	14·4	548,161
Lancaster . .	672,731	23	828,309	27	1,052,859	27	1,336,854	24·7	1,667,064
Leicester . .	130,081	16	150,419	16	174,571	13	197,003	9·5	215,855
Lincoln . . .	208,557	14	237,891	19	283,058	12	317,465	14·2	362,717
Middlesex . .	818,129	17	953,276	20	1,144,531	19	1,358,330	16·	1,576,616
Monmouth . .	45,582	36	62,127	15	71,833	36	98,130	36·9	134,349
Norfolk . . .	273,371	7	291,999	18	344,368	13	390,054	5·7	412,621
Northampton .	131,757	7	141,353	15	162,483	10	179,336	10·9	199,061
Northumberland .	157,101	9	172,161	15	198,965	12	222,912	12·2	250,268
Nottingham . .	140,350	16	162,900	15	186,873	20	225,327	10·8	249,773
Oxford . . .	109,620	9	119,191	15	136,971	11	152,156	6·1	161,573
Rutland . . .	16,356	...	16,380	13	18,487	5	19,385	10·	21,340
Salop . . .	167,639	16	194,298	6	206,153	8	222,938	7·2	239,014
Somerset . .	273,750	12	303,180	17	355,314	13	404,200	7·8	436,002
Southampton (Hants)	219,656	12	245,080	15·5	283,298	11	314,280	12·9	354,940
Stafford . . .	239,153	21	2[illegible]5,153	17	345,895	19	410,512	24·2	510,206
Suffolk . . .	210,431	11	234,211	15	270,542	9	296,317	6·3	315,129
Surrey . . .	269,043	20	323,851	23	398,658	22	486,334	19·7	582,613
Sussex . . .	159,311	19	190,083	22	233,019	17	272,340	10·	299,770
Warwick . .	208,190	10	228,735	20	274,392	23	336,610	19·4	402,121
Westmoreland .	41,617	10	45,922	12	51,359	7	55,041	2·5	56,469
Wilts . . .	185,107	5	193,828	15	222,157	8	240,156	8·2	260,007
Worcester . .	139,333	15	160,546	15	184,424	15	211,365	10·4	233,484
York (East Riding)	110,992	16	134,437	14	154,010	10	168,891	14·6	193,676
City of York and Ainstey .	24,393	12	27,304	12	30,451	17	35,362	8·3	38,322
York (North Riding)	158,225	7	169,391	11	187,452	2	190,756	7·2	204,662
York (West Riding)	565,282	16	655,042	22	801,274	22	976,350	18·2	1,154,924
ENGLAND .	8,331,434	14·5	9,538,827	17·5	11,261,437	16	13,091,005	14·5	14,995,508

POPULATION OF WALES.

COUNTIES.	1801.	Increase per Cent.	1811.	Increase per Cent.	1821.	Increase per Cent.	1831.	Increase per Cent.	1841.
Anglesea	33,806	10	37,045	21	45,063	7	48,325	5 3	50,890
Brecon	31,633	19	37,735	16	43,603	10	47,763	11·5	53,295
Cardigan	42,956	17	50,260	15	57,784	10	64,780	5·5	68,380
Carmarthen	67,317	15	77,217	17	90,239	12	100,740	6.	106,482
Carnarvon	41,521	19	49,336	17	57,958	15	66,448	22·	81,068
Denbigh	60,352	6	64,240	19	76,511	8	83,629	6·7	89,291
Flint	39,622	17	46,518	15	53,784	11	60,012	10·8	66,547
Glamorgan	71,525	18	85,067	19	101,737	24	126,612	37·	173,462
Merioneth	27,506	4	30,924	11	34,382	3	35,315	11·1	39,238
Montgomery	47,978	8	51,931	15	59,899	9	66,482	4·1	69,220
Pembroke	56,280	7	60,615	22	74,009	9	81,425	7·9	88,262
Radnor	19,050	9	20,900	7	22,459	9	24,651	2·1	25,186
WALES	541,546	13	611,788	17	717,438	12	806,182	13·	911,321

POPULATION OF SCOTLAND.

COUNTIES.	1801.	Increase per Cent.	1811.	Increase per Cent.	1821.	Increase per Cent.	1831.	Increase per Cent.	Decrease per Cent.	1841.
Aberdeen	123,082	10	135,075	15	155,387	14	177,657	8·2	......	192,283
Argyll	71,859	19	85,585	14	97,316	4	100,973	......	3·9	97,140
Ayr	84,306	23	103,954	22	127,299	14	145,055	13·4	......	164,522
Banff	35,807	2	36,668	19	43,561	12	48,604	3·	......	50,076
Berwick	30,621	1	30,779	8	33,385	2	34,048	1·1	......	34,427
Bute	11,791	2	12,033	15	13,797	3	14,151	10·9	......	15,695
Caithness	22,609	4	23,419	29	30,238	14	34,529	4·8	......	36,197
Clackmannan	10,858	11	12,010	10	13,263	11	14,729	29·7	......	19,116
Dumbarton	20,710	17	24,189	13	27,317	22	33,211	33·3	......	44,295
Dumfries	54,597	15	62,960	13	70,878	4	73,770	......	1·3	72,825
Edinburgh	122,954	21	148,607	29	191,514	15	219,345	2·8	......	225,623
Elgin (Moray)	26,705	5	28,108	11	31,162	10	34,231	2·2	......	34,994
Fife	93,743	8	101,272	13	114,556	12	128,839	8·9	......	140,310
Forfar	99,127	8	107,264	6	113,430	23	139,606	22·	......	170,380
Haddington	29,986	4	31,164	13	35,127	3	36,145	......	1·	35,781
Inverness	74,292	5	78,336	15	90,157	5	94,797	3·	......	97,615
Kincardine	26,349	4	27,439	6	29,118	8	31,431	5·1	......	33,052
Kinross	6,725	8	7,245	7	7,762	17	9,072	......	3·5	8,763
Kirkcudbright	29,211	15	33,684	15	38,903	4	40,590	1·2	......	41,099
Lanark	146,699	31	191,752	27	244,387	30	316,819	34·8	......	427,113
Linlithgow	17,844	9	19,451	17	22,685	3	23,291	15·2	......	26,848
Nairn	8,257	...	8,251	9	9,006	4	9,354	6.	......	9,923
Orkney and Shetland	46,824	...	46,153	15	53,124	10	58,239	3·	......	60,007
Peebles	8,735	14	9,935	1	10,046	5	10,578	......	·5	10,520
Perth	126,366	7	135,093	3	139,050	3	142,894	......	3·4	138,151
Renfrew	78,056	19	92,596	21	112,175	19	133,443	15·9	......	54,755
Ross and Cromarty	55,343	10	60,853	13	68,828	9	74,820	4·3	......	78,058
Roxburgh	33,682	11	37,230	10	40,892	7	43,663	5·4	......	46,062
Selkirk	5,070	16	5,889	13	6,637	2	6,833	16·9	......	7,989
Stirling	50,825	14	58,174	12	65,376	11	72,621	13·1	......	82,179
Sutherland	23,117	2	23,629	...	23,840	7	25,518	......	3·4	24,666
Wigtown	22,918	17	26,891	23	33,240	9	36,258	21·5	......	44,068
Barracks	. . .	...	....	...	....	...	....	......	......	4,425
SCOTLAND	1,599,068	14	1,805,688	16	2,093,456	13	2,365,114	11·1	.....	2,628,957

POPULATION OF THE ISLANDS IN THE BRITISH SEAS.

ISLANDS.	1821.	Increase per Cent.	1831.	Increase per Cent.	1841.
Jersey . . .	28,600	27.9	36,582	30	47,556
Guernsey, Alderney, Sark, Herm, and Jethou . .	20,827	25.4	26,128	9·2	21,538
Man . . .	40,081	2.2	41,000	17	47,985
Total . .	89,508	15.8	103,710	19·6	124,079

SUMMARY.

GREAT BRITAIN AND ISLANDS IN THE BRITISH SEAS.

	1801.	Increase per Cent.	1811.	Increase per Cent.	1821.	Increase per Cent.	1831.	Increase per Cent.	1841.
ENGLAND . .	8,331,434	14·5	9,538,827	17·5	11,261,437	16	13,091,005	14·5	14,995,508
WALES . .	541,546	13	611,788	17	717,438	12	806,182	13	911,321
Persons ascertained to have been travelling by Railways and Canals during the night of June 6, 1841 .	. .	. .	. .	. .	. . .	. .	. .	. .	4,896
England and Wales	8,872,980	14	10,150,615	17	11,978,875	16	13,897,187	14·5	15,911,725
SCOTLAND . .	1,599,068	14	1,813,688	16	2,093,456	13	2,365,114	11·1	2,628,957
Islands in the British Seas . . .	. .	. .	. .	. .	89,508	15·8	103,710	19·6	124,079
GREAT BRITAIN	10,472,048	14·2	11,964,303	17·6	14,161,839	15·5	16,366,011	14	18,664,761

POPULATION OF THE UNITED STATES.

	1800.	1810.	1820.	1830.	1840.	SLAVES. 1840.
MAINE				399,462	501,793	
Portland (City)					15,218	
Bangor (City)					8,627	
Thomaston					6,227	
Bath					5,141	
NEW HAMPSHIRE			244,161	269,533	284,574	
Concord					4,897	
Portsmouth					7,887	
Dover					6,458	
VERMONT			235,764	280,679	291,948	
Montpelier					3,725	
Bennington					3,429	
Woodstock					3,315	
Middlebury					3,162	
Burlington					4,271	
MASSACHUSETS			523,287	610,014	737,699	
Boston					93,383	
Lowell					20,796	
Salem					15,082	
New Bedford					12,087	
Charlestown					11,484	
Springfield					10,985	
Nantucket					9,012	
Cambridge					8,409	
Taunton					7,645	
Worcester					7,497	
Newbury Port					7,161	
Plymouth					5,281	
RHODE ISLAND			83,059	97,212	108,830	
Providence				16,832	23,171	
Newport				8,010	8,333	
Smithfield					9,534	
Warwick					6,726	
Cumberland					5,225	
New Providence					4,207	
Scituate					4,090	
CONNECTICUT			275,248	297,711	301,015	
Hartford (City)				9,789	12,793	
New Haven (City)				10,678	14,390	
Norwich (City)				4,179	7,239	
Middletown (City)				6,892	7,210	
New London (City)				4,356	5,528	
Bridgeport (City)					4,570	
Wethersfield					3,824	
Fairfield				4,226	3,654	
NEW YORK			1,372,812	1,093,508	2,428,921	
Northern District			944,262	1,366,467	1,683,068	
Southern District			428,550	537,041	745,853	
Albany (City)					33,721	
New York (City)					312,710	
Brooklyn (City)					36,233	
Rochester (City)					20,191	
Troy (City)					19,334	
Buffalo (City)					18,213	
Utica (City)					12,782	
Salina					11,013	
Fishkill					10,437	
Watervliet					10,141	
Poughkeepsie					10,006	
Lockport					9,125	
Newburg					8,933	
Mount Pleasant					7,307	
Seneca					7,073	
Schenectady					6,784	
Hudson (City)					5,672	
Onondaga					5,658	
Canandaigua					5,652	
Saratoga Springs					3,384	
NEW JERSEY		245,562	277,575	320,779	373,306	674
Trenton				3,925	4,035	
Newark				10,953	17,290	
New Brunswick				7,831	8,693	
Paterson				7,331	7,596	
Elizabeth Town					4,184	

POPULATION OF THE UNITED STATES.—*Continued*

	1800.	1810.	1820.	1830.	1840.	SLAVES. 1840.
PENNSYLVANIA	. .	. .	1,049,458	1,367,672	1,724,033	. .
Eastern District	. .	. .	727,977	775,577	908,744	. .
Harrisburg	1,472	2,289	2,990	4,311	5,980	. .
Philadelphia	70,287	96,287	119,325	167,325	228,691	. .
Lancaster	4,292	5,404	6,663	7,704	8,417	. .
Reading	2,385	3,463	4,352	5,859	8,410	. .
Easton	1,045	1,657	2,370	3,529	4,865	. .
York	2,503	2,847	3,545	4,216	4,779	. .
Carlisle	2,032	2,491	2,908	3,708	4,351	. .
Western District	. .	. .	321,481	592,095	815,289	. .
Pittsburg	1,565	4,768	7,248	12,542	21,115	. .
Alleghany	. .	. .	. .	2,081	10,089	. .
Erie	81	394	635	1,329	3,412	. .
DELAWARE	. .	72,694	72,749	76,739	78,085	2,605
Dover	. .	. .	. .	. .	3,790	. .
Wilmington	. .	. .	. .	. .	8,367	. .
Newcastle	. .	. .	. .	. .	2,737	. .
MARYLAND	. .	. .	. .	446,913	469,232	89,495
Annapolis	. .	. .	2,260	2,623	2,792	. .
Baltimore	23,791	46,556	62,738	80,625	102,313	. .
Frederick	. .	. .	3,037	4,427	5,182	. .
Hagerstown	. .	. .	2,690	3,371	7,197	. .
VIRGINIA	. .	. .	. .	1,211,271	1,239,797	448,987
Eastern District	. .	. .	. .	832,979	806,942	. .
Western District	. .	. .	. .	378,293	432,855	. .
Richmond	5,737	9,785	12,067	16,960	20,153	. .
Petersburg	2,521	5,663	6,690	8,322	11,136	. .
Norfolk	6,926	9,193	8,478	9,816	10,920	. .
Wheeling	. .	. .	. .	2,200	7,885	. .
Lynchburg	. .	. .	. .	4,626	6,395	. .
Fredericksburgh	. .	. .	. .	3,307	3,974	. .
Winchester	. .	. .	2,870	3,400	3,454	. .
NORTH CAROLINA	. .	. .	. .	738,470	753,419	245,817
Raleigh	669	. .	2,674	. .	2,244	. .
Wilmington	1,689	. .	2,633	. .	4,744	. .
Fayetteville	1,656	. .	3,532	. .	4,285	. .
Newbern	2,467	. .	3,663	. .	3,690	. .
SOUTH CAROLINA	. .	. .	. .	581,185	594,398	327,038
Charleston	18,712	24,711	24,780	30,289	29,261	. .
Columbia	. .	. .	. .	3,310	4,340	. .
GEORGIA	. .	. .	. .	516,823	691,932	280,944
Savannah	. .	. .	. .	7,776	11,214	. .
Augusta	. .	. .	. .	4,000	6,403	. .
Macon	. .	. .	. .	. .	3,927	. .
Columbus	. .	. .	. .	1,152	3,114	. .
ALABAMA	. .	. .	. .	309,527	590,756	253,532
Northern District	. .	. .	. .	120,215	185,776	. .
Southern District	. .	. .	. .	189,312	404,980	. .
MISSISSIPPI	. .	. .	. .	. .	375,651	195,211
Northern District	. .	. .	. .	. .	146,820	. .
Southern District	. .	. .	. .	. .	228,831	. .
Natchez	. .	. .	2,184	. .	4,800	. .
Vicksburgh	. .	. .	. .	. .	3,104	. .
LOUISIANA	. .	. .	. .	215,739	352,411	168,452
Eastern District	. .	. .	. .	155,399	249,641	. .
Western District	. .	. .	. .	60,340	102,770	. .
New Orleans	. .	. .	. .	46,310	102,193	. .
ARKANSAS	. .	. .	. .	30,388	97,574	19,935
TENNESSEE	. .	. .	. .	681,904	829,210	183,059
Eastern District	. .	. .	. .	196,301	224,259	. .
Middle District	. .	. .	. .	374,749	411,710	. .
Western District	. .	. .	. .	110,854	193,241	. .
Nashville	. .	. .	. .	5,565	6,929	. .
OHIO	. .	. .	. .	937,679	1,519,467	. .
Columbus	. .	. .	. .	2,437	6,048	. .
Cincinnati	. .	. .	. .	24,831	46,338	. .
Cleveland	. .	. .	. .	1,076	6,071	. .
Dayton	. .	. .	. .	2,965	6,067	. .
Steubenville	. .	. .	. .	2,937	5,203	. .
Zanesville	. .	. .	. .	3,094	4,766	. .
Chillicothe	. .	. .	. .	2,846	3,977	. .
Lancaster	. .	. .	. .	1,530	3,272	. .
Canton	. .	. .	. .	1,257	3,299	. .
Newark	. .	. .	. .	999	2,705	. .

POPULATION OF THE UNITED STATES.—*Continued.*

	1800.	1810.	1820.	1830.	1840.	SLAVES. 1840.
KENTUCKY	. .	. .	. .	. .	779,828	182,258
Frankfort	. .	1,099	1,679	1,680	1,917	. .
Louisville	. .	1,357	4,012	10,352	21,210	. .
Lexington	. .	4,226	5,279	6,104	6,997	. .
Maysville	. .	335	1,130	2,040	2,741	. .
MICHIGAN	. .	4,528	9,048	32,538	212,276	. .
Detroit	. .	. .	. .	. .	9,102	. .
Ypsilanti	. .	. .	. .	. .	2,419	. .
Pontiac	. .	. .	. .	. .	1,904	. .
Marshall	. .	. .	. .	. .	1,763	. .
Monroe	. .	. .	. .	. .	1,703	. .
INDIANA	. .	. .	. .	. .	685,866	. .
Indianapolis	. .	. .	. .	. .	2,692	. .
Madison	. .	. .	. .	. .	3,798	. .
New Albany	. .	. .	. .	. .	4,226	. .
Richmond	. .	. .	. .	. .	2,670	. .
ILLINOIS	. .	. .	. .	. .	476,183	. .
Springfield	. .	. .	. .	. .	2,579	. .
Chicago	. .	. .	. .	. .	4,470	. .
Alton	. .	. .	. .	. .	2,340	. .
Quincy	. .	. .	. .	. .	2,319	. .
Galina	. .	. .	. .	. .	1,843	. .
Peoria	. .	. .	. .	. .	1,467	. .
MISSOURI	. .	. .	. .	140,455	383,702	58,240
FLORIDA TERRITORY	. .	. .	. .	. .	54,477	25,717
Tallahassee	. .	. .	. .	. .	1,616	. .
St. Augustine	. .	. .	. .	. .	2,459	. .
Key West	. .	. .	. .	. .	688	. .
WISCONSIN TERRITORY	. .	. .	. .	. .	30,945	. .
Milwaukie	. .	. .	. .	. .	1,712	. .
IOWA TERRITORY	. .	. .	. .	. .	43,111	. .
DISTRICT OF COLUMBIA	. .	. .	33,039	39,859	30,657	4,694
Washington	3,210	8,208	13,247	18,827	23,364	. .
Alexandria	4,196	7,227	8,218	8,263	8,459	. .
Georgetown	. .	4,948	7,360	8,441	7,312	. .

Total population of the United States . . . 17,068,666

POPULATION OF THE PRINCIPAL CITIES OF THE UNITED STATES.

	1790.	1800.	1810.	1820.	1830.	1840.
New York	33,131	60,489	96,373	123,706	203,007	312,710
Philadelphia	42,520	70,287	96,664	108,116	167,118	228,891
Baltimore	13,503	26,614	46,555	62,738	80,625	102,313
New Orleans	. .	. .	17,242	27,176	46,310	102,193
Boston	18,038	24,927	32,250	43,298	61,392	93,383
Cincinnati	. .	750	2,540	9,644	24,831	46,338
Brooklyn	. .	3,298	4,402	7,175	12,042	36,233
Albany	3,498	5,349	9,356	12,630	24,238	33,721
Charleston	16,359	18,712	24,711	24,480	30,289	29,261
Washington	. .	3,210	8,208	13,247	18,827	23,364
Providence	. .	7,614	10,071	11,767	16,832	23,171
Louisville	. .	. .	1,357	4,012	10,352	21,210
Pittsburg	. .	1,565	4,768	7,248	12,542	21,115
Lowell	. .	. .	. .	. .	6,474	20,796
Rochester	. .	. .	. .	1,502	9,269	20,191
Richmond	. .	5,537	9,735	12,046	16,060	20,153
Troy	. .	. .	3,885	5,264	11,401	19,334
Buffalo	. .	. .	1,508	2,095	8,653	18,213
Newark	. .	. .	. .	6,507	10,953	17,290
St. Louis	. .	. .	. .	4,598	5,852	16,469
Portland	. .	3,677	7,169	8,581	12,601	15,218
Salem	7,921	9,457	12,613	12,731	13,886	15,082

POPULATION OF THE COLONY OF NEW SOUTH WALES,

ACCORDING TO THE CENSUS OF MARCH 2, 1841.

Free Males	61,324	
Free Females	40,425	
Total Free		101,749
Bond Males	23,844	
Bond Females	3,133	
Total Bond		26,977
Employed in Colonial Vessels		2,130
Total population		130,856

MALES.

Born in the Colony, 14,189 Arrived Free, 30,745 Other Free persons, 15,760

FEMALES.

Born in the Colony, 14,630 Arrived Free, 22,158 Other Free persons, 3,637

BOND MALES.		BOND FEMALES.	
Tickets of leave	5,843	Tickets of leave	316
Government employ	6,658	Government service	979
Assigned	11,343	Assigned	1,838

RELIGION.

Church of England	73,727	Roman Catholics	35,690
Church of Scotland	13,153	Jews	856
Wesleyan Methodists	3,236	Mahomedans and Pagans	207
Other Protestant Dissenters	1,857		

NUMBER OF HOUSES.

Stone, or brick, 6,375 Wood, 10,401 Total, 16,776

COUNTIES.

Argyle	3,397	Hunter	999
Bathurst	2,465	King	598
Bligh	46	Macquarie	2,409
Brisbane	1,560	Murray	2,111
Camden	6,286	Northumberland	9,975
Cook	2,892	Philip	453
Cumberland	58,108	Roxburgh	1,520
Durham	6,238	St. Vincent	1,762
Georgiana	749	Wellington	510
Gloucester	1,424		

COMMISSIONERS' DISTRICTS BEYOND THE BOUNDARIES.

Wellington	935	Peel's River	1,591
Bligh	672	New England	1,115
Lachlan	1,245	Clarence River	416
Monaroo	1,833	M'Leay River	584
Murrumbidgee	1,539		

MORETON BAY (Penal Settlement) . . 200

POPULATION OF THE COLONY OF NEW SOUTH WALES,—*Continued.*

NORFOLK ISLAND, (Penal Settlement.)

Free Males	254	Bond Males	1,288
Free Females	102	Bond Females	3
	356		1,291

Total 1,647

PORT PHILIP DISTRICT.

Free Males	7,756	Bond Males	518
Free Females	3,458	Bond Females	6
	11,214		524

Total of Port Philip . . . 11,738

POPULATION OF TASMANIA, OR VAN DIEMEN'S LAND.—Sept. 27, 1841.

Free Males	19,298	
Free Females	13,517	
Total Free		32,815
Bond Males	15,115	
Bond Females	2,275	
Total Bond		17,390
Employed in Government Vessels	64	
Total Population	50,269	

FREE MALES.		FREE FEMALES.	
Born in the Colony	5,836	Born in the Colony	5,915
Arrived Free	6,676	Arrived Free	5,922
Other Free persons	6,786	Other Free persons	1,680

BOND MALES.		BOND FEMALES.	
Holding Tickets of leave	3,140	Holding Tickets of leave	379
In Government employ	7,133	In Government employ	765
In private assignment	4,142	In private assignment	1,131

RELIGION.

Church of England	32,656	Roman Catholics	3,931
Church of Scotland	3,619	Jews	259
Wesleyan Methodists	1,944	Mahommedans and Pagans	60
Other Protestant Dissenters	1,650		

NUMBER OF HOUSES.

Stone, or brick, 3,459 Wood, 3,489 Total, 6,948

POLICE DISTRICTS.

Hobart	14,602	Oatlands	1,393	Westbury	1,218
Launceston	7,332	Brighton	2,129	Waterloo Point	817
New Norfolk	1,759	Campbell Town	1,832	Spring Bay	422
Norfolk Plains	2,627	Morven	1,924	Avoca	677
Richmond	4,158	George Town	544	Hamilton	1,029
Bothwell	958	Southport	252	Circular Head	330

Convicts employed on Public Works, 5,030. Convicts at Port Arthur, 1,099.

THE

LONDON GAZETTEER;

OR,

GEOGRAPHICAL DICTIONARY.

AA, a term applied anciently to a collection of waters, derived from the Latin *aqua*, and still the name of several European rivers; the following are the principal, viz.—in Russia, runs through the Duchy of Courland into the bay of Riga; in Saxony, falling into Lake Blanken; in Switzerland, falling into Lake Lucerne, into Lake Walstadten, and into the Aar river; in Westphalia, falling into the Wehr, into the Vecht, and into the Ems; in Holland, falling into the Vecht, at Swartsluys, into the Oldyssel; in Overyssel, falling into Lake Giter; in Brabant, falling into the Dommel; in Pas de Calais, France, falling into the sea at Gravelines, &c.

AACH, the name of a river in Switzerland, and of two others in Suabia, and also of a town in Suabia, about 30 miles N. of Constance.

AAHAUS, the chief town of a small district of the same name, in the government of Munster, one of the Prussian states, in the province of Westphalia.

AALBORG, one of the four bishoprics of the peninsular province of Jutland, being the most northerly part, and about 120 square miles in extent, containing about 90,000 inhabitants. The chief town of the same name is situate on the south coast of the Gulf of Lymfiord, in N. lat. 56. 50. E. long. 9. 46. Next to Copenhagen it is the most considerable town in Denmark. It has an exchange for merchants; the episcopal palace, two churches, two poor-houses, an hospital, convent, and cathedral school-house, are all respectable edifices; and it has a considerable trade in corn, herrings, fire-arms, saddles, gloves, &c. It was taken by the Swedes, in 1643 and 1658.

AAR, AARE, or AR, a large river in Switzerland, which rises in a lake, near Mount Saalberg, in the S. of the Canton of Bern, and, running N. W. through the whole extent of the lake of Brienz and Thun to Bern, takes a circuitous course to Soleure; whence it flows E. to Arburg, and N. E. to Brugg; below which, being joined by the Reuss and Limmat, it falls into the Rhine opposite Waldschut: also the name of two other rivers, one rising in the Grand Duchy of the Lower Rhine, falling into the Rhine; the other rising in Nassau, falling into the Lahn.

AARAU, chief town of Aargau canton, Switzerland, seated on the Aar; has a brisk trade, and manufactures of linen and cutlery, and is the place of general assembly for the Protestant cantons.

AARGAU, or ARGOVIA, a canton of Switzerland, bounded on the N. by the Rhine. It was made an independent canton in 1798; and in 1803 received further accessions of territory, and from one of the smallest became one of the largest cantons. Area, 650 square miles. Pop. 135,000. It has considerable manufactures, and is tolerably fruitful.

AARHAUS, the second of the four bishoprics of Jutland: it is a very fruitful district, on the E. side of the peninsula, extending for about 60 miles along the shore of the Cattegat; bounded on the W. by the bishopric of Viborg, intersected by numerous streams, abounding with fish, and is richly adorned with forests. It contains the residences of a great portion of the nobility of Denmark. The chief town of the same name is situate on the coast, in 56. 10. N. lat. 10. 13. E. long. The town is divided into two unequal parts, by water conveyed from a lake about 15 miles in the interior. It is large and populous; and has six gates, two principal churches, two market-places, a university, a free-school, and a well-endowed hospital, and has a considerable trade in grain, timber, &c.

AARON'S ISLAND. *See* ST. MALO.

AARONSBURG, a town of Northumberland co. in Pennsylvania, North America, 5 miles below Sunbury.

AASZY, a river of Syria, the ancient Orontes. It rises in Mount Lebanon, and, passing Antakia (Antioch), falls into the Mediterranean at Souvadia.

ABABDE, a tribe of Bedouin Arabs, in Nubia, on the Red Sea.

ABACH, or WELTENBURG, a market town in Lower Bavaria, seated on the Danube, 7 miles from Ratisbon. It is defended by a citadel, and is remarkable for Roman antiquities, as well as for its mineral waters, which are celebrated for curing various diseases. Long. 11. 56. E. lat. 48. 53. N.

ABADEH, or SHEIK ABADE, a village of Egypt, on the left bank of the Nile, 80 miles S. of Cairo. Immense architectural ruins testify its having been the site of a great and populous city.

ABADEH, a considerable town at the mouth of the Tigris, province of Fars, Persia.

ABAKANSK, a town situate on a branch of the river Yenesei, in the province of Kolhyvane, government of Tobolsk, Asiatic Russia. It was founded in 1707, and rebuilt in 1725, and since fortified: some ancient tombs, with fine inscriptions, bespeak it to have been a place of importance prior to the conquest of Siberia by Russia. N. lat. 54. E. long. 91. 14.

ABALAK, a town in the vicinity of Siberia, celebrated for an image of the Virgin, which is visited by many pilgrims, and carried in procession annually to Tobolsk.

ABANCAY, a province of Peru, S. America; the chief town thereof, of the same name, is situate about 60 miles N. W. of Cusco. There is also a river of the same name, flowing through the province, and another town in Cuenca, province of Quito.

ABANO, a considerable town of Italy, in the vicinity of Padua, distinguished for its hot sulphureous baths.

ABASCIA, or ABGAH, a country of Asiatic Russia, lying between the Caspian and Black Seas. The inhabitants are estimated at about 150,000, subsisting chiefly by hunting and plunder, and speaking a language peculiar to themselves.

ABA-UJVAR, a palatinate of Upper Hungary, about 700 square miles in extent, divided into 102 parishes. Pop. about 120,000.

ABB, a town in Yamen, Arabia.

ABBERBURY, or ALBERBURY, a large parish divided into 5 townships, in Shropshire, and 4 others in Montgomeryshire. The village of Alberbury is 7 miles W. of Shrewsbury. It was formerly the site of an alien priory and castle.

ABBEVILLE, a considerable town of France, in the department of Somme, and late province of Picardy, seated in a pleasant valley, where the river Somme divides into several branches, and separates the town into two parts. It is pretty well peopled; has a woollen manufactory, besides manufactories of sail-cloth. It lies 15 miles E. from the British Channel, 20 N. W. from Amiens, 60 S. of Calais, and 80 N. W. of Paris. Long. 1. 5. E. lat. 50. 7. N.

ABBEVILLE, a county of S. Carolina, about 700 square miles in extent. The lands are agreeably diversified with hill and dale, well watered, and productive. Pop. 23,167. The chief town, of the same name, is situate on Savannah river, 118 miles W. by N. of Columbia.

ABBEY BOYLE, a town in Ireland, on the river Boyle, 107 miles from Dublin: near the town are the picturesque ruins of the abbey.

•ABBEYFEALE, a parish in Connello, Upper Barony, county of Limerick, Ireland. It had formerly a monastery, and in the vicinity are the ruins of Purt Castle.

ABBEY-GREEN, a village in the parish of Lesmahagow, county of Lanark; 6 miles S. W. of the town of Lanark. It had formerly an abbey, and also a priory.

ABBEY-HOLME, a quarter of the parish of Holm Cultram, co. of Cumberland, pleasantly situate on the river Waver, 27 miles N. of Penrith.

ABBEYLEIX, a parish in Cullinagh Barony, Queen's co., Ireland. The town is sometimes called Clonkyne; 62 miles S. W. of Dublin.

ABBEY-MAHON, a parish in Ireland, county of Cork; 7½ miles S. of Bandon Bridge.

ABBEY-SIDE, a parish in Ireland, county of Waterford.

ABBOTS-ANN, ABBOTS-LEIGH, or ABBERLEY, ABBOTS-MORTON, ABBOTS-WOOD, co. of Worcester; ABBOTS, or PAGET'S BROMLEY, ABBOTS, or APEWOOD-CASTLE, Stafford; ABBOTSBURY, ABBOTS-STOKE, Dorset; ABBOTS, or ABBASCOMBE, ABBOTS-ISLE, ABBOTS-LEIGH, Somerset; ABBOTS-HAM, ABBOTS-KERSWELL, Devon; ABBOTSIDE, High and Low, N. R. of York; ABBOTS-LANGLEY, Herts; ABBOTS-LEIGH, Huntingdon; ABBOTSTON, Gloucester; ABBOTSTON, Wilts; ABBOTS-ANN, ABBOTSWORTH, Hants.

Towns and villages, in the several counties affixed in England. The prefix, *Abbey*, denotes their having formerly been monastic abodes, but none of them now deserve any particular notice, except Abbotsbury, in Dorset, for the former magnificence of its abbey; and Abbots-Langley, as having given birth to Nicholas Brakespeare, who attained to pontifical dignity, as Pope Adrian IV.

ABB'S HEAD, ST., a promontory, forming the southern extremity of the Frith of Forth, lying in the parish of Coldingham, and the county of Berwick, Scotland, about 10 miles N. of Berwick, and the same distance S. from Dunbar. W. long. 2. 8. lat. 55. 55. N.

ABDA, a small but fertile prov. of Morocco.

ABENRADE, or APENRADE, a town of Denmark, in Sleswick, now very flourishing, being double the extent it was formerly, and built in a better taste. It is seated on a spacious open bay in the Little Belt, surrounded on three sides by high mountains, which render the harbour safe. Pop. 2800. Long. 9. 26. E. lat. 55. 3. N.

ABENSPERG, or ABENSBERG, a town in the circle of Regen, Bavaria, seated on the Abens, near the Danube, 15 miles S. W. of Ratisbon.

ABER, a village in Caernarvonshire, N. Wales, 6 miles E. from Bangor, on the direct road from London to Holyhead. The word *Aber* signifies the fall of a lesser water into a greater, and usually refers to a place situate at the mouth of a river.

Aberarch, par. Caernarvon, Wales, 2 miles from Pwllhelli.

Aberavon, tn. Glamorgan, Wales, 18 miles N. W. from Cowbridge. In the neighbourhood are extensive iron, copper, and tin works. It is included in the Swansea dist. for sending 1 member to parliament.

Aberbrothock, or Arbroath, an ancient royal burgh and sea-port, situate at the estuary of the r. Brothock, partly in a par. of the same name, and partly in that of St. Vigeans, in the co. of Forfar, Scotland, 56 miles N. N. E. of Edinburgh, in 56. 34. N. lat. and 2. 35. W. long. William I., surnamed the Lion, king of Scotland, founded a magnificent abbey at Arbroath, in 1178, and conferred upon it very extensive immunities. Some vestiges of the building still remain to attest its former grandeur. A harbour was formed in 1194, to the eastward of the present one; the importance of the town declined with the devastation of the abbey, during the ruthless period of the reformation. The commerce of the town revived about the year 1738, when the linen manufacture was introduced, which progressively extended up to the commencement of the war in 1793, when it was vastly promoted by the increased demand for sail-cloth. 4000 to 5000 tons of shipping belong to the town, part of which is employed in the importation of flax, deals, &c. from the Baltic. A new town-hall has been more recently erected, and the town at large has undergone considerable improvement. The harbour, at spring tides, will only admit vessels of about 200 tons burthen, but being exceedingly well sheltered and commodious, and easily made, it affords security to vessels of easy draught of water. Arbroath is, however, a manufacturing rather than a commercial town. The Bell-rock lighthouse, one of the principal buildings of this kind in Britain, is off this town. It has 3 fairs annually, 31st of Jan., 3rd Wed. of June, and 18th of July.

Aberconway, or Conway, a sea-port tn. and par., Wales, co. Caernarvon, at the mouth of the Conway r., 14 miles N. by W. of Bangor. It is surrounded by walls strengthened by towers, which are still in good preservation, being one of the most complete ancient fortifications in the kingdom. The remains of its castle, built in the reign of Edward I., 1284, stand on a rocky promontory, and consist of 8 round towers, outworks, &c. The town itself is poor and inconsiderable. The new line of road passes through this town, and crosses the Conway by a suspension bridge of 300 feet span. The harbour is obstructed by shoals. Market on Friday.

Abercorn, a vil. and par. in the co. of Linlithgow, Scotland, on the S. bank of the Frith of Forth, 12 miles W. by N. of Edinburgh. A monastery existed here in the 7th century; and the castle of Abercorn was a place of great strength in the family of the Douglasses. It was dismantled in 1445, and no trace of either monastery or castle now remains. Abercorn still gives the British title of Marquis, and the Scottish title of Earl, to a branch of the family of Hamilton. The Roman wall is said to have begun in this parish.

Abercorn, a town of Georgia, N. America, 13 miles N. W. of Savannah.

Aberdare, town, Glamorgan, Wales, 4 miles W. from Merthyr Tydvil, included in the Cardiff dist. for sending 1 member to parliament.

Aberdeen, a county of Scotland, bounded on the N. W. by Banffshire, and the r. Deveron; on the N. and N. E. by the German Ocean; on the S. by the co. Kincardine, Forfar, and Perth; and on the W. by Elgin and Inverness-shire. It is divided into 8 districts; the S. part is wild, rugged, and mountainous, some of the hills rising to the height of 4000 ft. above the level of the sea, covered, in some parts, with extensive natural forests; the N. part is bleak and barren; but the midland parts of the co. are more fertile, and, since the period of 1786, have undergone improvements equal to any part of Scotland. Its rivers are the Dee, Don, Ythan, Bogie, Urie, Ugie, Cruden, and the Deveron; all of which abound, more or less, with salmon, and on the Ythan some valuable pearls have been found. Its mineral productions are various, but none of much note, except the granite, the exportation of which constantly employs several hundred tons of shipping. It sends 1 member to parliament.

Aberdeen, the principal city in the north of Scotland, situated on the coast of the German Ocean, at the efflux of the rivers Dee and Don, 127 miles N. E. from Edinburgh. It has an observatory; in long. 2. 29. W. lat. 57. 9. N. Under the denomination of Aberdeen are comprehended two towns, distinguished by the *Old* and *New*, which, however, are almost united by their respective suburbs.

Aberdeen, Old, formerly Aberdon, in the parish of Old Machar, or St. Machar, is pleasantly situated on an eminence near the mouth of the river Don, about a mile north of the New Town. It is of great antiquity, and was of some importance so long ago as 893, when, according to tradition, king Gregory the Great conferred on it some peculiar privileges; but no authentic records are extant prior to 1154. By charter, the free burgesses of the town are vested with the power of choosing their own magistracy, who are a provost, 3 bailies, a treasurer, and council, with the deacons of 6 incorporated trades. The town consists chiefly of one long street. There is a neat town-house—a new building—and a trades hospital for decayed freemen and their widows, and an hospital for 12 poor men, founded by Bishop William Dunbar, in 1532. But the chief ornament of Old Aberdeen is the large and stately fabric of King's College, founded by Bishop Elphinstone, in 1494, situated on the S. side of the town It is built round a square, with cloisters on the south side. The structure contains a chapel, library, museum, common hall, and lecture-rooms, with a long range of modern houses, for the accommodation of the professors and students. The library and museum are well furnished. The old town, being formerly the seat of a bishop, had a most magnificent cathedral, first founded in 1154, but the present edifice was begun by Bishop Kinnimonth, in 1357, and was 80 years in building; it was dedicated to St. Machar, but, like many others, it fell a sacrifice to the religious frenzy of the reformers. Two very antique spires, and one aisle, which is used as a church, is all that is now left. In this cathedral there was a fine library, which was also destroyed. Over the Don, at Old Aberdeen, there is a noble Gothic bridge, built by Bishop Cheyne, in 1281, of one arch, 67 feet span, and 34½ high from the surface of the river. On both sides it rests on a solid ledge of rock.

Aberdeen, New, is the capital of the shire of Aberdeen. For extent, trade, and beauty, it far exceeds any town in the north of Scotland. It is built on a gentle eminence, rising from a small bay, formed by the river Dee, over which there is an elegant bridge of 7 arches, rebuilt in 1724, the first having been built by Bishop Dunbar, in 1532. The streets are numerous, spacious, and well paved; the houses are built of granite (from adjoining quarries), generally four stories high, remarkably neat and elegant, having, almost universally, gardens in their rear. The whole town is about two miles in circumference. The municipal government is vested in a provost, 4 bailies, a dean of guild, treasurer, a town-clerk, a town council, and 7 deacons of incorporated trades. The town is a royal burgh, and, uniting with Aberbrothock, Brechin, Inverbervie, and Montrose, sends a member to parliament. New Aberdeen is graced with an elegant college, founded by George Keith, the Earl Marischal of Scotland, in 1593. Its other public buildings are the town-hall, market-house, the house of the Aberdeen Banking Company, a cross, an octagon building of curious workmanship, a dispensary, infirmary, and lunatic asylum, a poor-house, bridewell, gaol, and extensive barracks. An elegant street from the S. is continued over an arch of cut granite, 132 ft. span, 29 in height, and 40 wide between the parapets. Aberdeen had formerly several religious houses; besides the university, there is a respectable grammar-school and several almshouses, and upwards of 20 places for religious worship. The harbour was formerly dangerous, but has been rendered safe and commodious, by a pier of 1200 ft. in length, and the construction of wet docks. Aberdeen was formerly celebrated for the manufacture of knit stockings, and woollen fabrics generally. The linen and cotton manufactures are now carried on to a great extent. There is a valuable salmon fishery in the Dee; a considerable number of vessels are built at Aberdeen, and about 40,000 tons belong to it. It has several public breweries, rope works, iron founderies, &c., and three fairs annually, on the 31st Jan., 3rd Wed. in June, and 13th of July: a canal 19 miles in length to Inverary, contributes not a little to the advantage of both places. The whale and other fisheries employ much shipping, so that upon the whole between 300 and 400 vessels, collectively of the burden of 40,000 tons, belong to this port.

Aberdour, a parish in the N. of Aberdeenshire, on the S. coast of Murray Frith. Also another parish and village 2 miles W. of Burnt Island, in the county of Fife, Scotland.

Aberffraw, a village pleasantly situate near the coast of Caernarvon bay, on the isle of Anglesea, 9 miles S. by W. of Llangefni, on the direct road from Bangor to Holyhead; it had formerly a palace, at which 11 Princes of Wales are said to have resided. It has 4 fairs annually, 7th March, Wed. after Trinity, 23rd Oct., and 11th Dec.

Abergavenny, a town of Monmouthshire, situate at the confluence of the river Gavenny with the Usk; over the latter is a fine bridge of 15 arches, 12 miles W. of Monmouth; there are some considerable iron works in the vicinity, and it also participates in the flannel manufacture. It has a considerable market on Tues., and 3 fairs annually, on May 1st, Tues. after Trinity, and Sep. 25th.

Abergeley, tn., Denbighshire, Wales, pleasantly situate on the coast of the Irish Sea, on the direct road from Chester to Holyhead, 7 miles W. of St. Asaph, and 218 from London; it is much frequented in the summer season for bathing, has a market on Saturday, and 3 fairs annually.

Abergwilly, a village near Caermarthen, S, Wales, situate at the confluence of the river Guilly with the Towy. It contains the only episcopal palace belonging to the see of St. David's.

Abernethy, a town in Perthshire, Scotland, seated near the junction of the Erne with the Tay, 7 miles from Perth. It is said to have been the seat of the Pictish kings, as well as the see of an archbishop. In the town churchyard is a round tower 74 feet high and 48 in circumference, the only one besides that of Brechin in Scotland. It participates in the manufactures of Perth, and has 3 fairs annually. Also the name of another parish, from 150 to 180 square miles in extent, partly in Elgin and partly in Inverness-shire, abounding with natural forests of fir, which form an extensive traffic.

Aberystwith, a town of S. Wales, in Cardiganshire, seated on the Ystwith near its confluence with the Rhydol, where they fall into the bay of Cardigan; over the Rhydol is a handsome stone bridge. It lies 207 miles W. N. W. from London, and 39 N. E. from Cardigan. It was formerly fortified with a castle, and defended with walls; but both are now in ruins. It is, however, a flourishing town, having a great trade in lead, a considerable fishery of herrings, cod, and whitings, and a good weekly market on Monday; about 8000 tons of shipping belong to this town. In the bathing season, it is much frequented as a fashionable watering-place. Long. 3. 58. W., lat. 52. 25. N. It is contributory, in the Cardigan dist. in sending 1 member to parliament.

Abex, a country of Africa, on the Red Sea, which bounds it on the east; on the west it is bounded by Abyssinia and Nubia, on the north by Egypt, and on the south by the coast of Ajan. The chief towns are Arkeko, or Ercoco, and Sua-quam; which last is the capital, and the seat of a governor. It is subject to the Turks; and is very sandy and barren, being destitute of water. The heat is excessive, and the air unhealthy to Europeans. In the mountains are forests of ebony trees; abounding with wild beasts. It is 500 miles in length, and 100 in breadth. The inhabitants are Mahometans.

Abiad, Bahr el, or White river, Africa. Now generally acknowledged as the true head of the Nile. Its source is still unknown, but it flows in a N. E. direction from the interior of the continent, and joins the other principal branch, the *Bahr el Azrek*, or Blue river, at Halfaiah, forming the peninsula of Sennaar; the combined streams are then known by the name of the Nile.

Abingdon, a mkt. and borough tn. in Berkshire, England, and, with the exception of Reading, the chief tn. in the co. It is situate on the S. bank of the river Thames, 6 miles S. of Oxford, and 56 W. from London. It is a place of great antiquity, and has frequently been the abode of royalty. The market-place is spacious, in the centre of which is a respectable edifice, a spacious hall, supported by lofty pillars, in which the summer assizes for the co. are held, the space beneath serving for a market-place. The market for grain and malt on Mon. and Fri. is very great, and it has a considerable manufacture of coarse linen, sacking, &c. It is divided into two parishes, each having a church, and sends 1 member to parliament.

Abington, a post town, and capital of Washington county, Virginia, situated near the east side of the north branch of Holstein river. Here is a jail, and a court-house, where the district and county-courts are held. It is 322 miles W. S. W. of Richmond, and 587 from Philadelphia. Also the name of a township, in the state of Maryland, and another in Massachusets, N. America; and of a village, 12 miles N. of Philadelphia.

Abo, a sea-port, and chief town of what was formerly Swedish Finland, but which was wrested from that power by Russia, in 1808. The port and town of Abo are finely located in N. lat. 60. 27. W. long. 22. 18, at the southern extremity of the Promontory of Finland, on the E. shore of the Gulf of Bothnia, where it forms its junction with the Gulf of Finland. Under the Swedish government Abo was the see of a bishop, suffragan of Upsal, and had a university, founded by Queen Christina, in 1640, endowed with the same privileges as that of Upsal; and also a school, founded by Gustavus Adolphus, for 300 scholars. It was the seat of the conference where the treaty of peace was concluded between Russia and Sweden, in 1743. The town has flourished considerably, since its transfer to Russia; its chief trade is in timber, deals, and grain. Pop. about 12,000.

Abomey, a populous town, the capital of the kingdom of Dahomey, on the Gold Coast of Africa. N. lat. 7. 35. E. long. 2. 55. Pop. about 25,000.

Aboukir, a town of Egypt, in N. lat. 31. 18. E. long. 30. 38, about 6 leagues E. of Alexandria. A British army of 12,000 men, commanded by Sir Ralph Abercrombie, landed here in 1801. The bay, formed on the W. by a neck of land on which the town is situate, and on the E. by another neck of land which bounds the Rosetta branch of the Nile, is very spacious, and will for ever be memorable in history, as the scene of one of the most splendid and decisive naval battles on record, in which 9 French ships of the line were taken, and 2 others destroyed, by Lord Nelson, on the 1st August, 1798.

Aboyne, par. Aberdeen, Scotland, 5 miles W. of Kincardine.

Abrantes, a town of Portugal, in Estremadura, seated on the Tagus, 45 miles E. by N. of Lisbon, and belonging to a marquis of that title. It is situated on high ground, surrounded with gardens and olive-trees, and contains about 35,000 inhabitants, and has 4 convents, an hospital, and an alms-house.

Abrolhos, dangerous shoals on the coast of Brazil. S. lat. 17. 58. W. long. 38. 26.

Abruzzo, one of the four great provinces of Naples, bounded on the E. by the Gulf of Venice, on the N. and W. by Ancona, Umbria, and the Campagna di Roma, and on the S. by the Terra di Lavora and Molise. It is divided into two parts by the river Pescara, called Ulteriore and Citeriore. The former has Aquila, and the latter Sulmona, for its capital. It is fertile in corn, rice, fruits, saffron, vines, and olives. Pop. 590,000.

Abs, a town in France, in the department of Ardeche, formerly the chief town of Vivares, and a bishop's see, now in a very ruinous state.

Abutige, a town in Upper Egypt, on the site of the ancient Abotis, near the Nile, where great quantities of poppies grow, of which the natives make the best opium in the Levant. Long. 33. 0. E. lat. 26. 30. N.

Abyo or Abuyo, one of the Philippine islands, in the East Indies, between Mindanao and Luzon. Long. 122. 15. E. lat. 10. 0. N.

Abyssinia, a kingdom on the E. side of Africa, extending in length from about the 9th to the 17th deg. of N. lat. and its southern base, from about the 35th to the 43rd deg. of E. long. and at the N. from about the 35th to the 38th of do. forming an area of about 140,000 sq. miles, bounded on the N. by Sennaar, on the E. by the Arabian Gulf, or Red Sea, and on the S. and W. by very undefined limits, and countries very little known. A range of rugged mountains of considerable altitude, extending along the whole line of coast of the Red Sea, shut in Abyssinia, and nearly exclude it from all advantages of maritime intercourse. Some fine and fruitful plains pervade the southern part of the territory, but the prevailing characteristic of Abyssinia is mountainous and wild, and its inhabitants are as rude and ferocious as their country is wild and rugged. Its climate is various, but on the whole fine; it is exceedingly rich in vegetable productions, both of utility and beauty. The elephant, rhinoceros, buffaloes, leopards of various species, zebra, and especially the hyæna, abound; the latter is particularly ferocious and destructive; there are no tigers, and the lion is not common; there are various other wild animals, as well as the domestic ones common to Europe; the horses are strong and handsome, and there is a species of oxen with horns 4 ft. in length, and 20 inches in circumference at the root; the hippopotami and crocodile are common to the swamps and rivers which flow into the Nile. Amongst the numerous feathered tribes common to the country is the golden and black eagle, and some owls of extraordinary size and beauty; bees abound to such a degree, that honey, in the southern parts of the country, forms the staple article of production, and standard of value in exchange for all other commodities, and constitutes the principal article of food; locusts commit great devastation, and there is a species of fly extremely annoying, and even destructive to the cattle in the rainy season. The whole of the external traffic of Abyssinia is carried on at Massowah, a small island on the coast of the Red Sea, in N. lat. 15. 34. E. long. 39. 37, where elephants' teeth, rhinoceros' horns, gold-dust, honey, wax, and slaves are exchanged for spices, iron, led, copper, tin, and manufactured goods generally. The country is formed into three great divisions. 1st. Tigre, N. of which the towns are Adowa, Antalo, Dixan, and Axum; 2nd. Amhara, W. of the Tacazze river, of which Gondar and Empras are the chief towns, and the former the capital of the whole kingdom; 3rd. Shoa Efat, S. of which Ankober and Tegulet are the chief towns. The Abyssinians profess to be Christians, and some of their churches are spacious edifices, but their religious ceremonies are made up of the crude formalities of the Jewish worship, and of the Greek Christians. Their language is a dialect of the Arabic, and is called the Amharic. It contains a population of about 7,600,000.

Acadie, co. Canada, dist. of Montreal. There are manufactures of cloth, flannel, and linen. Pop. 11,470.

Acapulco, a town of Mexico, on the shores of the Pacific Ocean, in lat. 16. 55. N. and 100. 54. W. long. During the domination of Spanish rule in South America, Acapulco was the principal trading town of all New Spain; one, and sometimes two ships, annually, of several 100 tons burthen, used to arrive from the Philippine Islands, laden with all the choicest productions of Asia, to be exchanged for the gold and silver of Mexico; but this intercourse ceased with the wars which followed the French revolution in 1792, since which period to the present time, the commerce of all S. America has been exposed to numerous vicissitudes, and Acapulco has sunk into the utmost insignificance. Its harbour is one of the finest in the world, being formed into a basin by the small island of Roqueta, and defended by a fort on the N. W. The town contains only about 4000 inhabitants, and is exceedingly unhealthy, the temperature prevailing as high as 96, and hardly ever below 86, of Fahrenheit.

Acasabastlan, a river of Mexico, in the province of Vera Paz, which runs into the Gulf of Dulce. There is also a village of the same name, in the province of Chiapa.

Acayucan, an Indian settlement on the co. of the Gulf of Mexico.

Accomack, a co. of Virginia, U. S. of America, forming the N. part of a promontory, bounded on the W. by Chesapeake Bay, and on the E. by the Atlantic Ocean, extending from the S. E. corner of the state of Maryland. Pop. 17,096. Accomack Town, 207. E. by N. of Drummond, is the chief town.

Accrington, New, township, Lancashire, England. Here are extensive cotton thread manufactories, and a colliery.

Acheen, a kingdom, forming the N. W. part of the island of Sumatra, the head of Point Pedro, the most northerly part being in 5. 42. N. lat. and 95. 35. E. long. and extending about 50 miles E. by S. During the early period of the intercourse of Europe with Asia, by the Cape of Good Hope, Acheen was a powerful state, and carried on an extensive trade with the Malay and Coromandel coasts, and other parts of Asia; and on the Portuguese successively attempting to form a settlement upon the island of Sumatra, in the early part of the 16th century, they were completely expelled by the Acheenese; and, although considerably declined in power and importance, the Acheenese are still an active, and, when compared with other Asiatics, an efficient and industrious people. The chief town of the same name is situate on a river about 2 miles from the bay formed by King's Point, in N. lat. 5. 33. and 95. 17. E. long. and Point Pedro above mentioned.

Achill, an island, forming part of the county of Mayo, on the western coast of Ireland, in 54. 7. N. lat. 10. 31. W. long.

Achmim, or Ekhmim, a town of Egypt, the residence of an emir, or prince of the country. It has manufactures of coarse cottons, and stands on a small eminence, on the right bank of the Nile, 200 miles S. of Cairo. Of its ancient splendour but little now remains, but it is still one of the handsomest towns in Upper Egypt. Long. 31. 56. E. lat. 26. 40. N.

Achonry, a populous parish in Leney barony, co. of Sligo, Ireland.

Achen, a town of Lower Saxony, in the duchy of Magdeburg, with a citadel, on the Elbe, 5 miles N. W. of Dessau.

Aci Reale, a town in Sicily, at the foot of Mount Etna. It is clean and healthy, and is principally built of lava. Pop. about 14,000.

Ackworth, township, Yorkshire, 3½ miles S. S. W. of Pontefract. Here is a benevolent school of the Quakers, founded in 1777.

Acklam, a village 12 miles from York, where the body of the Emperor Severus, who died at York, was burnt to ashes, agreeably to the custom of the Romans.

Acoma, or St. Estevan de Acoma, a town of New Mexico, seated on a hill, with a good castle. The town is ascended by a flight of steps cut out of the rock. It was formerly the capital of that province. Long. 104. 15. W. lat. 35. 0. N.

ACONCAGUA, one of the provinces of Chili, intersected by the 32nd degree of S. lat. and 70th of W. long. It is inconsiderable both in extent and population. There is a town of the same name, and also a river running through the province and that of Quillota, into the sea.

ACQUA, a town in Tuscany, noted for its warm baths, 15 miles E. of Leghorn.

ACQUI, a town of Italy, in the Duchy of Montferrat, on the river Bormia; it has considerable manufactures of silk. Pop. about 7000.

ACRA or ACCARA, a territory of Guinea, on the Gold Coast, where some European states have forts, and each fort its village. Lat. 5. 25. N. 0. 10. W. long.

ACRE, or ST. JEAN D'ACRE, a seaport of Syria, in Palestine, and a bishop's see. It was originally named Accho, and afterwards Ptolemais. It was called by its present name by the knights of St. John of Jerusalem. It is small and well fortified, and appears handsome on approaching it, but the streets are narrow. The houses are built of stone, and have terrace roofs. The town is unhealthy, in consequence of the neighbouring marshes, and stands on a plain at the N. point of a bay, which extends in a semicircle of nine miles, to the point of Mount Carmel, near the mouth of the Kardanah, or ancient Belus. In the time of the crusades it underwent several sieges; and nothing is now to be seen of this ancient city, but the remains of monuments erected by the Christians, and some ruins of a church dedicated to St. Andrew. The palace of the grand master of the order of St. John of Jerusalem, is the residence of the chief of Acre. Here are three mosques, four churches, and a synagogue. The chief articles of commerce are corn and cotton. In 1759, great damage was done by an earthquake; and the year following, 5000 persons, near one third of the inhabitants, died by the plague. In 1799, aided by the British, under Sir Sidney Smith, it withstood a severe siege by the French under Buonaparte, who retreated after failing in the twelfth assault. It was again taken in 1840 by the British, for the Ottoman Porte. It is 27 miles S. of Tyre, and 80 miles N. N. W. of Jerusalem. N. lat. 30. 0. E. long. 35. 10. Pop. about 10,000.

ACRON, a district of the Fantee territory, on the Gold Coast of Africa, about 50 miles E.N.E. of Cape Coast Castle.

ACTON, the name of six villages, and a prefix to ten others, in different parts of England, signifying places originally situate among oaks; *ac* being the Saxon word for oak.

ACTOPAN, the capital of a district of the same name in the Intendencia de Mexico, about 70 miles N. N. E. of the city of Mexico.

ADALIA, or SATALIA, a sea-port town in Asia Minor, at the head of the gulf of that name, and the largest city on this coast. It is beautifully seated round a small harbour, and is built on the declivity of a hill, rising like the seats of an amphitheatre. Pop. about 8000. It was the ancient Attalia.

ADAMS, the name of three counties in different states of N. America, named after the second president of the federal union. 1st. In Pennsylvania; pop. 23,044; chief town, Getysburg. 2nd. In Mississippi; pop. 19,434; chief town, Natchez. 3rd. In Ohio; pop. 13,183; chief town, West Union; also the name of several townships in various parts of United States.

ADAM'S BRIDGE, a ledge of sand-banks, connecting Ceylon with the Coromandel coast.

ADAM'S PEAK, a remarkable mountain, the highest in Ceylon; 38 miles E. by S. from Colombo—an object of great veneration.

ADANA, a town of Asiatic Turkey, in Karamania, and a bishop's see, with a strong castle. It has a trade in corn, wine, and fruits; and is seated on a river of the same name, 12 miles from the Mediterranean, in N. lat. 36. 48. E. long. 85. 8. Pop. 5000.

ADARE, a town in the county of Limerick, Ireland. Here are the ruins of two friaries.

ADDA, a river of Switzerland, which rises in the Grisons, passes through the lake Como, the Valteline, and the N. part of the Milanese, and falls into the Po 5 miles above Cremona.

ADDERBURY, a parish in Oxfordsh. England.

ADDINGHAM, a parish in the W. R. Yorkshire, England. Population chiefly employed in cotton and worsted manufactures.

ADDISON, a county in the state of Vermont, N. America, bounded on the W., for about 25 miles in extent, by lake Champlain. Pop. 23,583. Chief town, Middlebury.

ADDLE, a parish in the W. R. Yorkshire, England, 5½ miles N. of Leeds.

ADEL, a kingdom of Africa, called also ZEILA, from a rich trading town of that name, situated near its coast by the Red Sea. It seldom rains here; but the country is well watered by rivers, and abounds with wheat, millet, frankincense, and pepper. The inhabitants are Mahometans. It was formerly a part of Abyssinia.

ADELAIDE, a city of S. Australia, the capital of the colony, on the E. side of the Gulf of St. Vincent, about 7 miles from the port. It is seated in a pleasant plain, but the site is remarkably ill-chosen; and, though it at present contains a population of 7 or 8000, it is probable that it will not arrive at any stability or eminence. Lat. 35. 57. S. long. 38. 43. E.

ADELFORS, a town of Sweden, in Smaland, noted for its gold mines, about 70 miles N. W. of Calmar.

ADEN, a sea-port of Arabia, and capital of a small state of the same name, once the most opulent city of Arabia.

ADIGE, a river of Lombardy, which rises S. of the lake of Glace, and, passing by Tyrol, Brixen, Trent, and Verona, falls into the Gulf of Venice, a little N. of the mouth of the Po.

ADMIRALTY-ISLANDS, a cluster of islands in the S. Pacific Ocean, to the N. W. of New Ireland. They were discovered in 1767, and are between twenty and thirty in number; some of them appear of considerable extent; and the W. end of the principal island is in 2. 6. S. lat. and 146. 57. E. long.

ADOUR, a river of France, which rises in the

department of Upper Pyrenees, nows by Tarbes and Dax, and enters the Bay of Biscay below Bayonne. The Duke of Wellington effected a passage across this river, with the allied English and Spanish army, in the middle of February, 1814, after considerable difficulty, in the presence of the French army, commanded by Marshal Soult.

Adowa, the capital and residence of the sovereign of Abyssinia, and the place through which the commerce of the inland parts of Abyssinia is maintained with Massowah, in the Red Sea.

Adpar, a town in Cardigan, Wales; in the Cardigan district for returning one member to parliament.

Adra, a seaport of Spain, in Granada, 47 miles S. E. of Granada. Long. 3. 7. W. lat. 36. 45. N.

Adramiti, a town of Asiatic Turkey, in Natolia, on the E. coast of a gulf, of its name, 70 miles N. by W. of Smyrna. Long. 27. 0. E. lat. 39. 35. N.

Adria, a town of Italy, in Polesino di Rovigo, which gives name to the Adriatic Sea, and was formerly of great note, but has been much reduced by frequent inundations. It is seated on the Tartaro, 25 miles S. S. W. of Venice.

Adrianople, or Edreneh, a city of European Turkey, in Romania, the see of a Greek archbishop, and formerly the European seat of the Turkish dominion. It is 8 miles in circumference, situate in a plain, on the river Marissa, which here receives two tributary streams. Several of the mosques are very splendid, and many of the houses neat, but the streets are narrow and devious. The seraglio is separated from the city by the river Arda, and commands an extensive view of the country, which is fertile, and famous for excellent vines. The commerce of the city, by the river, is considerable, and celebrated for its beautiful red dye. The Turks took this city from the Greeks, in 1362. It is 135 miles N. W. of Constantinople. Long. 22. 30. E. lat. 41. N.

Adriatic Sea. *See* Venice, Gulf of.

Adventure Bay, at the S. E. end of Van Diemen's land, so called from the ship in which Captain Furneaux sailed. Long. 147. 30. E. lat. 43. 23. S.

Ætna, or Etna, a celebrated burning mountain of Sicily, now called by the natives *Monte Gibello.* It is situated in the eastern part of the island, in long. 15. 0. E. lat. 38. 0. N. Pindar, who lived 435 years before Christ, calls it the *Pillar of Heaven,* on account of its great height, which is 10,874 feet, and its circumference at the base 70 miles. It affords an epitome of all the differences of climate. The summit is a league in circumference, and within, formed like a vast amphitheatre, from whence flames, ashes, and smoke issue in divers places. Eruptions of this mountain are mentioned by Diodorus Siculus, as happening 1693 years before Christ; and Thucydides speaks of three eruptions, which happened in 734, 477, and 425, B.C. From this period till 1447, there were about 18 different eruptions, the most destructive of which were in 1169 and 1329; there have been other eruptions since, which have done immense damage, particularly those in 1669, 1755, 1780, and 1787. In 1809, eruptions took place in twelve different parts of the mountain, and covered the adjacent lands with lava to the depth of 40 feet; and another eruption occurred in 1822.

Affane, a parish in the county of Waterford, Ireland. Sir Walter Raleigh first introduced cherries from the Canary Islands to this place.

Afghanistan, a country of Asia, stretching from the mountains of Tartary to the Arabian sea, and from the Indus to the confines of Persia. The inhabitants of this wide domain have no written character, and speak a language peculiar to themselves. They are a robust, hardy race of men, and, being generally addicted to a state of predatory warfare, their manners partake of a barbarous insolence. They avow a fixed contempt for the occupations of civil life, and are esteemed the most negligent of religious observances of all the Mahometans. They are of the sect of the Soonees, whilst their neighbours the Persians are Sheeahs—two sects of the Mahometan religion fiercely opposed to each other. Their common dress consists of a shirt, which falls over the upper part of long and narrow trousers; a woollen vest, fitted closely to the body, and reaching to the mid-leg; and a high turned-up cap of broad cloth or cotton, usually of one colour, and of a conic form, with two small parallel slits in the upper edge of its facing. The principal cities of Afghanistan are Candahar and Cabul, the former of which was the capital; but the late and present sultans have kept their court at Cabul. About the year 1720, an army of Afghans invaded Persia, took Ispahan, and made the sultan Husseyn prisoner. They kept possession of Ispahan and the southern provinces for ten years, when they were defeated in several battles, and driven out of the country by Nadir Kuli, commonly known in Europe by the name of Kouli Khan. After Nadir had deposed his sovereign, Shah Thamas, he laid siege to and took Candahar; but afterward received a considerable body of Afghans into his army, who became his favourite foreign troops. On his assassination, in 1747, the general of the Afghan troops, though furiously attacked by the whole Persian army, effected a safe retreat into his own country, where he caused himself to be acknowledged sovereign of the Afghan kingdom, over which he ruled till 1773. In 1761 he defeated the Mahrattas at Paniput, in one of the most sanguinary battles known in India. He was succeeded by his son, who reigned till 1792. On his death it was divided between his two sons, and a civil war broke out; and, after various depositions, Shah-Soojah, one of the brothers, attained the throne; who was again deposed by Dost Mahommed Khan. In 1797 the kingdom was threatened by Runjeet Singh, sovereign of the Punjab, but was prevented by the British, who subsequently deposed Dost Mohammed, in favour of the rightful heir, Shah-Soojah; but the country is far from being in a settled state.

Africa, one of the four great divisions of the world, forming a peninsula to Asia, to which it is connected by a neck of land at the N. E. extremity, about 60 miles across, called the Isthmus of Suez. In its extreme length it extends from Cape Negro, in lat. 37. 21. N. to False Cape, in lat. 34. 25. S., being about 4300 miles; and in its extreme breath from Cape Verd, in 17. 34. W., to Cape Guardafui, in 51, 32. E. long. being about 4100 miles. The whole superficies is about 13,450,000 square miles. The population is very variously estimated—between 70,000,000 and 160,000,000; but the absence of sufficient data will not allow of any thing conclusive on this head. N. Africa is subdivided into a great number of kingdoms, states, and territories; the most prominent of which are Galla, Abyssinia, Sennaar, and Nubia on the E. bordering on the Red Sea; Egypt, at the N. E. extremity; Libya, Fezzan, and Barbary (comprising Tripoli, Tunis, Algiers, and Fez) on the N. bordering on the Mediterranean; and Morocco at the N. W. extremity, bounded by the Atlantic Ocean. A large extent of coast S. of Morocco, is called Azanago, and S. of the river Senegal, in lat. 16. N. to Sierra Leone, in lat. 8. 30, the coast is occupied by several negro tribes, the limits of whose territories are very imperfectly defined. Inland, S. of the Great Desert are the kingdoms of Timbuctoo, Houssa, Cassina, and Wangara; and E. of the desert are Ashber, Bornou, Beghermé, Bergoo, Darfur, &c. With the exception of the deserts and the more mountainous districts, this part of Africa is well watered, and exceedingly fertile. The most celebrated river is the Nile, which, rising from various sources on the N. side of the great chain of mountains, and flowing through Abyssinia, Sennaar, Nubia, and Egypt, falls into the Mediterranean Sea, by several channels, between the lat. of 30. 16. and 31. 50. E. The river Niger has long furnished a subject of considerable interest to the learned. It is now ascertained that it takes its rise in the mountains of Kong, on the western side of the continent, whence proceeding in an easterly direction to Timbuctoo, and thence southerly to the Bight of Benin. Numerous streams and lakes intersect all the interior part of the country situate between the desert of Sahara, and the chain of mountains which divide the continent into two parts. Several rivers fall into the Atlantic Ocean S. of the Great Desert; the first of these is the Senegal, the entrance of which from the sea is in lat. 15. 53. N. 2nd. The Gambia, in lat. 13. 8. N.; and further S. the Pongos, Rio Grande, Nunez, and Sierra Leone, in lat. 8. 30. N.

Independently of the great chain of mountains which divides Africa into two parts, a ridge of considerable altitude extends along the whole extent of the shores of the Red Sea; and the states of Barbary are bounded on the S. by another chain called the Atlas, which at the greatest elevation rises to the height of 13,000 feet above the level of the sea.

The complexion, habits, manners, and condition of the people of Africa will be explained and illustrated when treating of its respective divisions. The physical condition of Europeans has hitherto proved exceedingly ill adapted to the climate of Africa, consequently our knowledge of the details of boundaries, population, production, and intercourse are necessarily imperfect; but, as far as our knowledge does extend, nature appears in Africa to have displayed a bold and lavish hand, alike in the animal, the feathered, and the vegetable creation; most of the domestic animals and feathered tribes common to Europe are found in various parts of N. Africa; in addition to which, in all the fertile plains, the buffalo abounds; and the forests and mountains are occupied by the rhinoceros, hyæna, leopard, panther, tiger, and lion, whilst the majestic and sagacious elephants roam in large herds, feasting on the odoriferous and luxuriant vegetation, which periodical rains and a diurnal sun constantly occasion an exhaustless soil to produce. There is also another animal, the camel, which it would be ungracious not to notice. In all the N. parts of N. Africa this gentle, unwearying, heavy-burthen and privation-sustaining animal abounds, and serves to enable the inhabitants of all the states bordering on the Atlantic Ocean and Mediterranean Sea to maintain an intercourse across the deserts (impassable by any other means) with the countries S. thereof. At the head of the feathered tribe is the ostrich, the feathers of which constitute a valuable branch of the external commerce of Africa. Winged insects are multitudinous. Bees are so numerous that honey constitutes one of the chief articles of food in all the states and territories previously enumerated, and wax an extensive article of export. Hives of locusts at times darken the atmosphere for many miles, by their number and density, and occasionally commit great ravages on the vegetation of the cultivated parts. Alligators abound in all the rivers flowing into the Atlantic Ocean; and in the marshes and streams in the interior, and on the E. side, which fall into the Nile, hippopotami and crocodiles are numerous, as are also reptiles and serpents of every description. In the vegetable kingdom, the baobab, the mangrove, the shea, lotus-tree, and palm, claim the first notice. The kingdom of Flora has been but little explored, but Nature appears to have been lavish in bestowing upon Africa a profuse share of the majesty, variety, and beauty, of every class of creation, whilst, on the other hand, innumerable obstacles have hitherto interposed to prevent their enjoyment, and the human portion of creation in Africa are of the rudest and most unsocial class of any in the known world. Trafficking in each other (slavery) appears to have prevailed amongst all the tribes and communities of Africa, from the earliest period of its being populated, but its unsocializing and debasing influence has been greatly aggravated, during the last two centuries, by the mean, avaricious, and mistaken policy of those European states who have established and maintained an intercourse with them. The religious ceremonies of the inhab. of Africa are an admixture of Paganism, Judaism, Christianity, and Mahomedism, each predominating in different parts; which will be more particularly exemplified when treating of the respective divisions.

The coast of Guinea, on which several of the European states have forts and settlements, is occupied by several powerful tribes of negroes, with whom the Europeans carry on a very extensive traffic, with the manufactured productions of Europe in general, in exchange for gold dust, ivory, skins, bees' wax, palm oil, barwood, &c. S. of the coast of Guinea, for about 15 degrees of lat., the coast is also occupied with several Negro tribes, who live in constant collision with each other, and from amongst whom about 100,000 annually at the period of 1820—1828, were transported as slaves by the ships of France, Portugal, and Spain, for working the plantations of those states in S. America and the W. Indies. The remaining portion of the W. coast, as well as all the interior, and the E. coast of this part of Africa, is very little known; but, as far as knowledge has been obtained, the inhab. appear more rude and unsocial than even those of N. Africa. In addition to all the wild animals common to the N. part, the beautiful and stately, though somewhat disproportioned quadruped the cameleopard, as well as the zebra, is common towards the S. extremity of this part of Africa; the feathered and vegetable part of nature are much the same as in N. Africa. The principal river of the S. is the Congo, which falls into the Atlantic Ocean in lat. 6. 30. S. It is supposed by some that the Congo is the channel by which the waters in the interior of N. Africa discharge themselves into the sea; if so, there must be a break in the mountains somewhere between the 18th to the 22d deg. of E. long. Capt. Tuckey, by order of the British government, in the year 1817, attempted to explore the country bordering on the Congo, but, after sailing about 200 miles up the river, felt obliged to desist from the undertaking. Several other rivers of inferior note fall into the Atlantic Ocean, as well as into the Indian Ocean. A very rude and unsocial people, the Hottentots, occupy the more S. extremity of the continent extending to the Cape of Good Hope; who will be more particularly adverted to when treating of that settlement. Numerous islands flank the several coasts of both N. and S. Africa, the chief of which are the Azores, in lat. 39. 40. to 37. N.; the Madeiras, in lat. 32. 38. N.; the Canaries, in 29. 25. to 27. 48. N.; Cape Verds, in 17. to 14. 48. N.; a cluster at the entrance to the Rio Grande, in lat. about 11. N.; Isles de Los, in lat. about 9. 22. N.; Fernando, Princes, and St. Thomas's, in 3. 28. to 0. 27. N.; and Annabona, in 1. 33. S. The islands of Ascension and St. Helena, though situated 300 leagues from the coast, are also considered as a part of Africa; and on the E. side, in the Indian Ocean, is the large island of Madagascar, extending from 25. 40. to 12. 2. S. lat., and the Comoro group, lying between the N. end of Madagascar and the mainland, Socotra, to the E. of Cape Guardafui, completing the list, unless the Isles of France and Bourbon, situate about 10 deg. to the E. of Madagascar, be included.

AGADEER, a seaport of Morocco, on the Atlantic, 152 miles S. W. from Morocco.

AGAHLY, a province in the centre of N. Africa. The chief town, of the same name, is situate in about 20. N. lat. and 13. E. long.

AGALLELA or GALLELA, an island of Africa, near Madagascar. Long. 24. 8. E. lat. 10. 12. N.

AGAMENTICUS, a mountain of the district of Maine, about 8 miles from York Harbour. Long. 70. 30. W. lat. 43. 16. N.

AGDE, a town of France, in the department of Herault, on the river Herault, not far from its mouth in the Gulf of Lyon, where there is a fort to defend the entrance. It is 17 miles N. E. of Narbonne. Long. 3. 28. E. lat. 43. 19. N.

AGEN, a city of France, capital of the department of Lot and Garonne, and a bishop's see. Prunes form here a considerable object of commerce; and it has manufactures of camlets, serges, and canvas. It is seated in a fertile country, on the banks of the Garonne, 80 miles E. S. E. of Bordeaux. Long. 0. 36. E. lat. 44. 12. N.

AGGA, AGGONA, or ACONAH, a town and district on the coast of Guinea, in which is a very high hill, called the Devil's Mount. The English have a fort here. Long. 0. 5. E. lat. 6. 0. N.

AGGERHUUS, a fortress of Norway, in the government of the same name, which is full of mountains. *See* CHRISTIANIA.

AGHA. There are several townships or parishes in Ireland, the names of which commence with Agha; as, AGHABOE, par. Queen's co., an ancient place, and was once a bishop's see; AGHABOG, par. co. Monaghan; AGHACRUE, par. co. Cork, &c.

AGHOGHILL, town, county of Antrim.

AGHRAMULLIN, a parish in the co. Monaghan, Ireland.

AGHRIM, properly AUGHRIM. *See* AUGH.

AGIMERE, or AJMEER, a town of Hindostan, capital of a province of the same name. It stands at the foot of a high mountain, on the top of which is a fortress of great strength. It was at Ajmeer that Sir Wm. Rowe, as English ambassador, was introduced to the Great Mogul in 1716: it is 150 miles W. by S. of Agra. Long. 75. 20. E. lat. 26. 35. N.

AGINCOURT, a village of France, in the department of Pas de Calais, famous in history for the battle fought here in 1405, wherein Henry V. of England, with an army of 10,000 men, defeated the French army of 60,000, leaving nearly 10,000 dead on the field. It is 7 miles N. of Hesdin.

AGLISH, the name of several parishes in Ireland, viz., in the co. of Kilkenny; in Kerry; in Cork; in Waterford; which do not require specific notice.

AGMAT, a town of Morocco, on the river of the same name, and on the W. side of one of the mountains of Atlas, 16 miles S. of Morocco.

AGMONDESHAM. *See* AMERSHAM.

AGNANO, a circular lake in the kingdom of Naples, 7 miles from Puzzoli. It is about half a mile in diameter, surrounded by mountains. On its margin is the famous Grotto del Cane, where many dogs have been tortured and suffocated, to show the effect of a vapour which rises a foot above the bottom of the cave, and is destructive to animal life.

Agnes, St., par. Cornwall, England. In its neighbourhood are some of the richest mines in the county.

Agnes, St., one of the Scilly islands, off the Land's End, Cornwall: there is a light-house upon it. Lat. 42. 54. N. 6. 19. W. long.

Agon, Agou, or Agoen, an island of Sweden, in the Gulf of Bothnia, with a good harbour. Long. 18. 10. E. lat. 61. 20. N.

Agosta, an island in the Adriatic Sea, near the coast of Dalmatia, 18 miles in circumference, and 18. S. W. of the island of Gurzola. Long. 17. 0. E. lat. 42. 55. N.

Agosta, a town of Sicily, in Val di Noto, with an excellent harbour on the E. coast, 18 miles N. of Syracuse. Long. 15. 10. E. lat. 37. 20. N.

Agra, a city of Hindostan Proper, capital of a province of the same name, with a strong fort. It was once the most splendid of all the Indian cities, and now exhibits the most magnificent ruins. About the year 1566, the emperor Acbar made it his capital, and gave his name to it; since which time it is often named Acbarabad. In the 17th century, the great Mogul frequently resided here; his palace was prodigiously large; the palaces of the omrahs and others are very numerous; and there were above 60 caravanseras, 800 baths, 700 mosques, and two magnificent mausoleums. It has since rapidly declined. In the war with the Mahrattas, in 1803, it was taken by the British. It stands on the right bank of the Jumna, a branch of the Ganges, 100 miles S. by E. of Delhi. Long. 78. 30. E. lat. 27. 16. N.

Agram, or Zagrab, a strong town of Croatia, capital of the county of Zagrab, and a bishop's see; seated on the Save, 27 miles N. E. of Carlstadt. Long. 16. 18. E. lat. 45. 48. N.

Agria, a town of Upper Hungary, and a bishop's see, with a citadel. It was besieged by the Turks, in 1552, with 70,000 men; they lost 8000 men in one day, and were obliged to raise the siege, though the garrison consisted only of 2000 Hungarians, assisted by the women, who performed wonders on this occasion. It is seated on the Agra, 47 miles N. E. of Buda. Long. 20. 10. E. lat. 48. 10. N.

Agrigan, or Island of Xavier, one of the Ladrone islands, 43 miles in compass, and has several volcanic mountains. Long. 146. 0. E. lat. 19. 40. N.

Aguas Callientes, a city in the province of Guadalaxara, Mexico: it is situate about 250 miles N. N. W. of the city of Mexico, on the direct route to Santa Fe, and is noted for its warm springs.

Aguillas, or l'Agulhas Cape, the most southern point of Africa, 13 leagues E. S. E. of the Cape of Good Hope. Long. 20. 18. E. lat. 34. 55. S.

Ahanta, a district on the Gold Coast, Africa, Axim, the chief town, is on the coast, in 4. 57. N. lat. 2. 55. W. long. Dixcove and Secondee are other stations on the coast, through which considerable traffic is carried on with the inland parts.

Ahascragh, a town in the county of Galway, Ireland.

Ahmedabad. *See* Amedabad.

Ahmednagur. *See* Amednagur.

Ahmedpore, a town in the province of Orissa, Hindostan, 34 miles S. from Cuttack.

Ahoghill, a populous parish in the county of Antrim, Ireland. There is a town of the same name.

Aich, or Aichach, a town of Bavaria, with a castle, seated on the Par, 18 miles S. of Neuberg.

Aichstadt, a town of Franconia in Bavaria. In the church is a piece of curious workmanship, called the Sun of the Holy Sacrament, which is of massy gold, enriched with diamonds, pearls, rubies, and other precious stones. It is seated on the Altmuhl, 40 miles S. by E. of Nuremberg. Long. 11. 10. E. lat. 48. 50. N.

Aidal, the principal seaport of Nubia, seated on a mountain, on the coast of the Red Sea. It has a trade in ebony and aromatic plants. Long. 35. 57. E. lat. 22. 20. N.

Aigen, a town of Austria, on the confines of Bohemia, 24 miles N. W. of Steyre.

Aigle, a town of Switzerland, in the canton of Band. All the houses, even the meanest, are built of white marble, found in the neighbourhood. It is seated near the Rhone, 6 miles from its entrance into the lake of Geneva.

Aigle, a town of France, in the department of Orne, 47 miles S. W. of Rouen.

Aignan, St., a town of France, in the department of Loire and Cher, on the river Cher, 24 miles S. by E. of Blois.

Ailah, a town of Arabia Petrea, at the head of an inlet of the Red Sea, 108 miles E. S. E. of Suez. Long. 34. 10. E. lat. 29. 10. N.

Ailly, a town of France, in the department of Somme, 9 miles S. S. E. of Amiens.

Ailsa, an insulated rock, in the Frith of Clyde, off the coast of Ayrshire, Scotland. It consists of a stupendous assemblage of precipitous cliffs, 940 ft. high. The ruins of a chapel, and of a castle, are still seen. It gives the title of Baron to the family of Kennedy, Earls of Cassillis, in Scotland.

Aimtab. *See* Antab.

Ain, a department of France, which takes its name from the river; bounded on the N. E. and S. by the departments of Jura, Mont Blanc, and Isere, and on the W. by those of the Rhone and the Loire, and Saon and Loire. Bourg is the capital.

Airdrie, a town in the parish of New Monkland, co. of Lanark, Scotland, included in the Falkirk dist. which sends 1 member to parliament. It has an iron foundry, and a considerable trade in the distillation of malt spirits. It is ten miles E. of Glasgow, on the direct road to Edinburgh.

Aire, a town of France, in the department of Landes, seated on the side of a mountain, on the river Adour, 65 miles S. of Bordeaux. Long. 0. 10. E. lat. 43. 42. N.

Aire, a town of France, in the department of Pas de Calais. It communicates with St. Omer, by a canal, 22 miles S. of Dunkirk. Long. 2. 24. E. lat. 30. 42. N.

Aire, a river in Yorkshire, which issues from a lake on Mallam Moor, near Settle, flows by Skipton, Keighley, Leeds, and Snaith, and enters the Ouse, below Howden.

Aisne, a department of France, including the territories of Soissonnois and Vermandois. It takes its name from a river which runs by Soissons, and enters the Oise, above Compeigne. It was overrun by the allied armies in 1814, and was the scene of several sanguinary and bloody battles fought between the allies and French, in the months of February and March, of the same year. Laon is the capital.

Aix, an ancient city of France, capital of the department of the Mouths of the Rhone, and an archbishop's see. It was founded by C. S. Calvinus, a Roman General, 120 B. C., and was formerly the capital of Provence, when it had a parliament. It is seated in a plain, where there are hot baths near the river Arc, accidentally discovered in 1704; but several medals and other antiques, dug up at that time, confirm the baths being known to the Romans. It is 75 miles E. of Montpelier. Long. 5. 27. E. lat. 43. 32. N.

Aix, a town of Savoy, on the lake Bourget. Here are mineral waters, much frequented. It is 12 miles N. by E. of Chamberry.

Aix, a small island of France, between the isle of Oleron and the Continent. It is 12 miles N. W. of Rochfort. Long. 1. 10. W. lat. 46. 5. N.

Aix-la-Chapelle, a city of France, capital of the department of Roer, and a bishop's see; lately an imperial city of Germany, in the duchy of Juliers. Charlemagne was so delighted with the beauty of the place, that he chose it for his residence; he is interred in the church of Notre Dame, where they keep his sword and belt. Its famous mineral waters draw a great number of persons every year; and near it are mines of iron, calamine, sulphur, and coal. In 1668 and 1748, it was distinguished by two celebrated treaties of peace. It was taken by the French in 1792, retaken by the Austrians in 1793, and again taken by the French in 1794; the allies entered it in 1814, and it was subsequently the seat of a congress of the sovereigns of the great powers of Europe, to adjust the indemnities to be paid by France, for the aggressions of the emperor Napoleon. It is seated in a bottom, surrounded by mountains, 22 miles N. E. of Liege. Long. 5. 58. E. lat. 50. 48. N.

Aizenay, a town of France, 29 miles S. of Nantes.

Ajaccio, a seaport of Corsica, capital of the department of Liamone, and a bishop's see. This is the birth-place of Napoleon Buonaparte. It stands on the west side of the island, on a point of land that juts into the gulf, 160 miles S. E. of Toulon. Long. 8. 43. E. lat 41. 56. N.

Ajan, or Ajen, a country on the eastern coast of Africa, extending from Magadoxa to Cape Guardafui, 1500 leagues. It is divided into several states or kingdoms; the principal of which are Adel and Magadoxa. The south coast of Ajan is sandy and barren, but to the N. it is more fertile. The kings of Ajan are frequently at war with the emperor of Abyssinia, and sell the prisoners which they take. Ivory, gold, and horses of excellent breed, are the articles of trade. It is the Azania of Ptolemy.

Ajazzo, Aias, or Ajasso, a seaport of Asiatic Turkey, in Syria, seated on the Mediterranean, on the site of the ancient Issus, where Alexander fought his second battle with Darius. It is 30 miles S. of Antioch, and 40 W. of Aleppo. Long. 36. 10. E. lat. 36. 0. N.

Akerman. *See* Bielgorod.

Ak-hissar, a town of Asiatic Turkey, in Natolia, the ancient Thyatira, built in a fine plain, above 17 miles over, which produces corn and cotton. It is seated on the river Hermus, 45 miles S. E. of Pergamo. Long. 28. 30. E. lat. 38. 48. N.

Akshehr, a town in Karamania, on the confines of Natolia, in Asia Minor, about 250 miles E. of Smyrna, to which place it sends considerable supplies of wool, fine carpets, wax, gum tragacanth, and galls.

Alabama, part of the Mississippi territory, admitted as a state into the confederacy of the United States of America on the 14th Dec. 1819. It is bounded on the N. by Tennessee, W. by Mississippi, S. by the Gulf of Mexico and W. Florida, and E. by Georgia. It is about 275 miles in mean length, and 185 in mean breadth, giving a superficies of 32,560,000 English statute acres. It is divided into 33 counties; Cahawba, 915 miles S. W. of Washington, is the seat of government. The total population of the state is 590,756, of whom 253,532 are slaves. The culture of cotton, which is progressively extending, is their chief occupation. The river Tombecbee runs parallel with the boundary line on the western or Mississippi side of the state, and, near to its entrance into the sea, is joined by the Alabama, which flows from the east. The towns of Mobile on the western, and Blakeley on the eastern banks of these rivers, at their confluence by several channels with the sea, are the ports for the exportation of all the surplus produce of the state. Two tribes of Indians, the Creeks and Cherokees, occupy the N. E. part of the state, bordering upon Tennessee and Georgia.

Aladulia, a maritime province of Asiatic Turkey, bounded on the S. by the N. E. extremity of the Levant Sea. The chief town is Adana.

Alais, a town of France, in the department of Gard. It has a citadel, and is seated near the river Gard, at the foot of the Cevennes, 28 miles N. W. of Nisones. Long. 2. 54. E. lat. 44. 8. N.

Alaman, a town of Switzerland, in the canton of Bern, 9 miles N. E. of Nion.

Aland, a cluster of islands in the Baltic, at the entrance of the Gulf of Bothnia. The principal island, from which the rest take their names, is 40 miles long, and near 16 broad;

and is 95 miles N. E. of Stockholm. Pop. about 12,000. Long. 20. 28. E. lat. 60. 10. N. They were ceded, with Finland, by Sweden to Russia, in the treaty of 1809.

ALARCON, a town of Spain, in New Castile. It is seated on the Xucar, 50 miles S. of Cuenca.

ALATAMAHA, a river of the United States, also called St. George's river. It rises in the Allegany mountains, and, taking a S. E. direction through Georgia, enters the Atlantic 60 miles S. W. of the river Savanna. *See* DARIEN.

ALATYR, a town of Russia, on the river Suru, 40 miles E. of Kasan.

ALANTA, a river of European Turkey, which rises in the mountains that separate Moldavia from Transylvania, flows through Wallachia, and enters the Danube, near Nicopolis.

ALAYA, a town of Asia Minor, on a lofty promontory resembling Gibraltar, surrounded by very ancient Cyclopean walls. It is a miserably constructed town.

ALBA, a town of Piedmont, in Montferrat, and an ancient bishopric. It contains three parochial and three other churches, besides the cathedral and seven convents. It is seated on the Tanaro, 20 miles S. E. of Turin.

ALBANIA, a maritime province of European Turkey, 240 miles long, and 60 broad; bounded on the N. by Dalmatia and Bosnia, E. by Macedonia and Janna, S. by Livadia, and W. by the Adriatic and Ionian Seas. It produces excellent wine. It was formerly an independent kingdom. Durazzo is the capital.

ALBANO, a town of Italy, on a lake of the same name, in Campagna di Roma. The environs produce the best wine in all this country. It is 15 miles S. S. E. of Rome.

ALBANO, a town of Naples, in Basilicata, on the river Basiento, 15 miles E. by S. of Potenza.

ALBANOPOLIS, a town of European Turkey, formerly the capital of Albania, but now a poor place, seated on the Drino, 43 miles E. of Alessio.

ALBANS, ST., a borough town in Hertfordshire, distinguished in every period of English history. It was once the metropolis of Britain, and, on the invasion of the country by the Romans, became one of their most important stations; they gave it the name of Verulam, and, by the privileges conferred upon it, so attached the native inhabitants to their interest, as to excite the vengeance of queen Boadicea, who massacred 70,000 of them, after which she was completely defeated by Suetonius Paulinus, the then Roman governor of Britain. St. Albans again became tranquil, and flourished till the Diocletian persecution, about the commencement of the fourth century, when it became distinguished for the martyrdom of its saint, whose name the town at present bears. After this period, St. Albans declined, till in the ninth century, Offa, king of the Mercians, in expiation for his unprovoked murder of St. Ethelbert, king of the East Angles, whom he had invited to his court to be his son-in-law, erected and endowed a most magnificent abbey and monastery, for Benedictine monks. After this period St. Albans experienced various alterations of fortune, till the final dissolution of its monastery, in the reign of Henry VIII., which led to the demolition of this magnificent establishment, of which the gateway now only remains, now used as the borough prison. The abbey church was rescued from impending destruction by the inhabitants, who purchased it of the succeeding monarch, Edward VI., for 400*l.*, when it was made parochial; but was exposed to the plunder and fanaticism of Cromwell, during the period of his predominance. It has since been repaired at various times, and recently by subscription of gentlemen of the county, and many vestiges of its former grandeur still remain; it is one of the largest ecclesiastical edifices in Europe. There are three other churches, in one of which (St. Michael) is a monument to the memory of the illustrious Francis Bacon. St. Albans is governed by a mayor, twelve aldermen, and returns two members to parliament. Its market, on Saturdays, is considerable in grain, &c., and especially for straw plait. The town is situate on the banks of the little river Ver, on which there are two mills for throwing silk. It is 21 miles N. of London.

ALBANY, a county of the State of New York, bounded on the E. by Hudson's river, N. by the Mohawk river, N. W. by Schenectady county, W. by Schoharie county, and S. by Greene county. It is divided into nine townships, and its pop. 68,593, of whom 413 were slaves; the chief place of the county is a city of the same name, situate on the W. bank of the Hudson river, 160 miles N. of New York, 170 W. of Boston, and 230 S. of Montreal. It is the seat of the legislative government of New York, and, next to the city of New York, is the most important place in the state. A canal, 353 miles in extent, unites the waters of the Hudson river at Albany with the great chain of lakes westward of Lake Erie, at Buffalo, in Niagara county, and another canal, 62 miles in extent, unites the Hudson from the same point with Lake Champlain, at Whitehall, in Washington county.

ALBANY, a district of the Cape of Good Hope. Chief towns, Enon, Graham's, Bathurst, &c.

ALBANY, a river of Upper Canada, which flows E. through several small lakes into James's Bay. There is a fort of the same name at its mouth. Long. 82. W. lat. 52. 14. N.

ALBARAZIN, a town of Spain in Arragon, and a bishop's see. Its wool is the best in Arragon. It is seated on the Guadalaviar, 100 miles E. of Madrid.

ALBACETE, a town of Spain, in Murcia, with manufactures in iron and steel; seated in a fertile country on the post road from Madrid, (dis. 40 leag.) to Carthagena, dis. 33½ leag.

ALBECK, a town and castle of Suabia, on the river Alb, 5 miles N. by E. of Ulm.

ALBEMARLE, or AUMALE, a town of France, in the department of Lower Seine, with a manufacture of serges and other stuffs, 20 miles S. W of Dieppe, and 32 N. N. W. of Rouen.

Albemarle, a central county of the state of Virginia, N. America. Pop. 22,924 Charlottesville is the chief town.

Albemarle Sound, an inlet of the Atlantic Ocean, in N. Carolina, 60 miles long, and from 8 to 12 broad. It is 30 miles N. of Pamtico Sound; and is united with Chesapeake Bay at Norfolk, by a canal cut through the Dismal Swamp.

Albenga, a strong seaport on the coast of Genoa, surrounded by olive-trees, 37 miles S. W. of Genoa. Long. 8. 7. E. lat. 44. 6. N.

Albion, a name sometimes applied to Britain, and probably given to it by Julius Cæsar, from the white cliffs on the S. E. shôre. (Lat. *albus.)* Scotland has been called *Albany;* but that is more probably derived from the Celtic *alb, alp*, high, from its mountainous character; the Gaels calling themselves Albannich.

Albion, New, a name given by Sir Francis Drake, who explored the coast in 1578, to a country on the W. coast of N. America, extending from 35 to 48 of N. lat.; but the northern part is now comprehended in the Missouri territory, and the southern in New California.

Albona, a town of Italy, in Istria, near the Gulf of Carnero, 16 miles E. by S. of Rovigno.

Albourne, a town in Wiltshire, England; 7 miles N. E. from Marlborough. Market on Tuesday.

Albret, a town of France in the department of Gironde, 37 miles S. of Bordeaux.

Albufeira, a town on the S. coast of Algarves, Portugal; pop. about 2000. Also a town of Valencia, on the sea-coast, Spain.

Albuquerque, a town of Spain, in Estremadura, with a strong castle. It has a considerable trade in wool and cloth, and is 18 miles N. N. W. of Badajoz. Also a town on the Rio del Norte, a few miles S. of Santa Fe, Mexico. There is also a village of the same name in the province of Puebla, Mexico.

Alby, or Albi, an ancient city of France, in the department of Tarn, seated on the river of that name. It is the chief city of the Albigeois, and was formerly the see of an archbishop. The cathedral was dedicated to St. Cecilia, and before the revolution was ornamented with a valuable silver shrine, of exquisite workmanmanship, of the Mosaic kind, and contained the relics of St. Clair, the first bishop of this city. The chapel of this saint is a magnificent building, adorned with paintings. Alby has manufactures of both linens and woollens, and four gates, which open into beautiful and fruitful plains.

Alcala de Henarez, a beautiful and extensive city of Spain, in New Castile, seated upon the river Henarez. The university, which had gone to decay, was re-established in 1494, by Cardinal Francis Ximenes; at whose charge, and under whose direction, the first polyglot Bible was printed in this town. Without the walls is a spring, the water of which is so pure and well tasted, that it is enclosed for the king of Spain's own use, from whence it is carried to Madrid. It is 11 miles S. W. of Guadalaxara, and 15 N. E. of Madrid.

Alcala la Real, a city of Spain, with a fine abbey, situate on the summit of the Sierra de Granade, on the high road from Madrid to Granade, from which it is distant 18 miles, and 190 from Madrid.

Alcala de Guadayra, a town of Spain, distant 6 miles from Seville, on the road to Madrid.

Alcama, a town of Sicily, in Val di Mazaro, 25 miles S. W. of Palermo.

Alcaniz, a town of Arragon, in Spain. It was formerly the capital of the kingdom of the Moors. It has a remarkable fountain, which throws up water through forty-two pipes. It is seated on the river Bergantes, 12 miles from Caspe.

Alcantara, a fortified town of Spain, in Estremadura, and the chief place of the knights of that name. It has a celebrated stone bridge over the Tajo, or Tagus, built in the time of Trajan. It was taken by the Earl of Galway, in 1706, but retaken the same year. It is situate on the high post road from Badajoz to Ciudad Rodrigo.

Alcantara, or Alcantarilla, a town of Spain, in Andalusia, near the river Guadalquiver. Here is a bridge, built by the Romans, to pass the marshes formed by the river. It is 14 miles S. of Seville.

Alcantara, a town of Portugal, near Lisbon, having a royal palace. There is also a town of the same name in Brazil, in the province of Maranham.

Alcaraz, a town of Spain, in New Castile, with a strong castle, and a remarkable ancient aqueduct. It is situate near the source of the Guadalquiver, 80 miles E. by S. of Calatrava. Long. 2. 20. W. lat. 38. 28. N.

Alcaraz, or Alcarraz, a town of Arragon, Spain, 2 leagues from Lerida, on the road to Madrid.

Alcazar de Sal, a town of Portugal, in Estremadura. Fine white salt is made here. It is seated on the Cadoan, 15 miles from the sea, and 35. S. E. of Lisbon. Long. 9. 5. W. lat. 38. 18. N.

Alcazar Quiber, a town of the kingdom of Fez, near which Sebastian, king of Portugal, lost his life in a battle with the Moors, in 1578. It is seated on the Lucos, 36 miles S. of Tangier.

Alcazar Seguer, a town of the kingdom of Fez, on the Strait of Gibraltar. It was taken by Alphonso, king of Portugal, in 1468, but soon after abandoned. It is 14 miles E. of Tangier.

Alcester, or Alncester, tn., Warwickshire. Many Roman coins, bricks, &c., have been found near it, and the Icknield street passes through the town. It is situate at the confluence of the Alne with the Arrow, 14 miles W. S. W. of Warwick. Market on Tuesday.

Alcmaer, or Alkmaer, a city of North Holland. It is a handsome city, and one of the cleanest in Holland. The streets and houses are extremely neat and regular, and the public buildings very beautiful. The Spaniards, under Frederick of Toledo, besieged it, after they had taken Haarlem, in 1578; but were forced to raise the siege, after lying before it three months. It opened its gates to the British troops in 1799, after the second battle near Bergen; and here the treaty for the evacuation of Holland by the invaders was afterwards concluded. It is recorded, in the register of this city, that, in the year 1639, 120 tulips, with the off-sets, sold for 90,000 florins; and, in particular, that one of them, called the *Viceroy*, sold for 4203 guilders! The States at last put a stop to this extravagant and ruinous passion for flowers. The town has a good trade in butter and cheese, which is esteemed the best in Holland. It is about 4 miles from the sea, 15 from Haerlem, and 20 N. from Amsterdam.

ALCOBACA, tn. Portugal, prov. Estremadura. Here is a celebrated abbey, the general place of sepulture of the sovereigns of Portugal.

ALCOUTIN, a town of Portugal, in Algarves, with a strong castle, seated on an island in the Guadiana, opposite to San Lucar, 16 miles from the entrance of the Guadiana into the Gulf of Cadiz, 22 miles N. N. E. of Tavira.

ALCUDIA, a town of Majorca, situate on the N. E. coast, between two large harbours. Long. 3. 0. E. lat. 39. 50. N.

ALDAN, a river of Siberia, joining the Lena, on which the finest sables are found.

ALDBOROUGH, or ALDEBURGH, seaport, Suffolk, England. The town was formerly much larger, but the sea has taken away whole streets. Markets on Wednesday and Saturday.

ALDBOROUGH, tn. W. R. Yorkshire, England, now disfranchised by parliament. Here are many remains of Roman works. It is 15 miles N. E. of York.

ALDENBURG, a town of Westphalia, 20 miles E. S. E. of Dusseldorf.

ALDERBURY, a town in Wiltshire, on a hill near the Avon, 3 miles from Salisbury. It has a manufacture of fustians. By a fire in 1777, 200 houses were destroyed.

ALDERHOLM, an island in Sweden, formed by the three arms of the river Gefle, in the Gulf of Bothnia. It has a considerable trade in planks and deals. It is 80 miles N. of Stockholm.

ALDERNEY, an island in the English channel, 8 miles in circumference, separated from France by a strait called the Race of Alderney, which is a dangerous passage, on account of the rocks under water. It is fertile in corn and pasture, and is celebrated for a breed of small cattle, which yield an abundance of very rich milk. There is a town of the same name. Long. 2. 12. W. lat. 49. 45. N.

ALDSTONE. *See* ALSTON-MOOR.

ALEGRE, a town of France, in the department of Upper Loire, 15 miles S.E. of Brioude.

ALENCON, town of France, cap. of depart. of Orne. It has a considerable trade. 58 miles S. by E. from Caen.

ALENTEJO, the largest, in its superficies, of the 6 provinces of Portugal, bounded on the north by the Tagus, and south by the ancient kingdom of Algarves. Its superficial extent is 883 Fr. leagues, and the population 380,480. Evora is the capital.

ALEPPO, the capital of Syria, and, next to Constantinople and Cairo, the most considerable city in the Turkish empire. It stands on eight hills, in the middle of a fruitful plain, and is of an oval figure. The castle is on the highest hill, in the centre of the city; and the houses are better than in other places in Turkey. As usual in the East, they consist of a large court, with a dead wall to the street, an arcade running round it, paved with marble, and a marble fountain in the middle. The streets are narrow, but well paved with large square stones, and kept very clean. Here are many stately mosques and caravanseras, fountains and reservoirs of water, and vineyards and gardens. The water in the wells is brackish, but good water is brought from some springs about 5 miles off, by an aqueduct, said to have been built by the empress Helena. The Christians have their houses and churches in the suburbs, and carry on a considerable trade in silks, camlets, and leather. Large caravans frequently arrive from Bagdad and Bassorah, charged with the products of Persia and India. Several European nations have factories here, and the merchants live in greater splendour and safety than in any other city in the Turkish empire. Coaches are not used here, but persons of quality ride on horseback, with a number of servants before them, according to their rank. Aleppo and its suburbs are 7 miles in compass; an old wall, and a broad ditch, now in many places turned into gardens, surround the city, which was estimated by Dr. Russell to contain 230,000 inhabitants, of whom 30,000 were Christians, and 5000 Jews; but, at present, according to Mr. Eton, it does not contain more than 50,000, which depopulation, occasioned chiefly by the plague, has taken place since 1770; whole streets being uninhabited and bazaars abandoned. All the inhabitants of both sexes smoke tobacco to great excess; even the very servants have almost constantly a pipe in their mouths. Eighteen miles S. E. of Aleppo is a large plain, bounded by low rocky hills, called the Valley of Salt: this is overflowed in winter, and in April, the water being soon evaporated by the sun, leaves a cake of salt, in some places half an inch thick, which is sufficient to supply all this part of the country. Aleppo is seated on a rivulet, 70 miles S. E. of Alexandretta, or Scanderoon, and 150 N. of Damascus. Long. 37. 16. E. lat. 35. 40. N. It suffered greatly by a succession of earthquakes in 1822.

ALESSANDRIA, a city of Piedmont, 48 miles S. W. of Milan. Pop. about 36,000. The town contains a cathedral, 14 churches, 17 convents, and numerous handsome buildings.

ALESSANO, a town of Naples, near the extremity of the Promontory of the Terra d'Otranto, 15 miles S. W. of Otranto.

ALESSIO, a town of European Turkey, in Dalmatia, and a bishop's see, seated on the Drino, near its entrance into the Adriatic Sea,

20 miles S. of Scutari. Long. 19. 30. E. lat. 41. 53. N.

ALET, a town of France, in the department of Aude, lately an episcopal see. It is noted for its baths, and stands near the Pyrenees, on the river Aude, 15 miles S. by W. of Carcassone.

ALEUTIAN ISLANDS. *See* ARCHIPELAGO, NORTHERN.

ALEXANDER, a county of the state of Illinois, at its southern extremity, bounded on the E. by the Ohio river to the point where it unites with the Mississippi, which bounds the county on the W. Pop. 3313. Unity is the chief town.

ALEXANDRETTA, or SCANDEROON, a town of Syria, on the Mediterranean Sea, and the port of Aleppo. It is now a poor place, the tombs being more numerous than the houses. It is 60 miles N. W. of Aleppo. Long. 36. 15. E. lat. 36. 35. N.

ALEXANDRIA, a celebrated city of Egypt, now much decayed, though there are still some remains of its ancient splendour, particularly an obelisk full of hieroglyphics, called Cleopatra's Needle; and Pompey's Pillar, which is one entire piece of granite, 70 ft. high, and 25 in circumference. The ancient Pharos, so famous in antiquity, that it was numbered among the seven wonders of the world, is now a castle called Pharillon, and still used to direct vessels into the harbour. From the harbour is a canal to the west branch of the Nile, at Rhamanie. This city was built by Alexander the Great, and now consists chiefly of one long street, facing the harbour, the rest being a heap of ruins; part of the walls are standing, with great square towers, 200 paces distant; and the gates are of Thebaic and granite marble. It was formerly a place of great trade, all the treasures of the East Indies being deposited there, before the discovery of the route by the Cape of Good Hope. It is subject to the grand seignor, who, however, has but a limited authority. Alexandria was taken by the French, under Buonaparte, in 1798, and taken from them by the English in 1801. It surrendered to the English in 1807, but was soon after evacuated. It is seated on the Mediterranean, 125 miles N. W. of Cairo. Long. 30. 16. E. lat. 31. 11. N.

ALEXANDRIA, a co. of the district of Columbia, U. S. of America. Pop 9965, including 1374 slaves.

ALEXANDRIA, a city and port of entry in the foregoing county, situate on the W. bank of the Potomac, 7 miles S. of the city of Washington. Very considerable quantities of flour are shipped from Alexandria to the northern ports of the United States, and, occasionally, to Europe and other parts of the world. In other respects its commerce is inconsiderable. Pop. 8459. There are several townships named Alexandria in the United States of America, but none that deserve any particular notice.

ALFAYATES, a town of Portugal, in Beira, defended by a wall and castle. It is 150 miles N. E. of Lisbon. Long. 5. 48. W. lat. 40. 9. N.

ALFEIZERAO, a town of Portugal, on the seaside, 75 miles N. N. E. of Lisbon. Long. 9. 15. W. lat. 39. 30. N.

ALFELD, a town of Lower Saxony, 15 miles S. S. W. of Hildesheim.

ALFORD, tn. Lincolnshire, with a market on Tuesday; 6 miles from the sea, 25 N. of Boston.

ALFORD, a parish of Scotland, in Aberdeenshire. This parish is rendered memorable by a battle fought in it, wherein the marquis of Montrose defeated General Baillie and a party of the Covenanters, on the 2nd July, 1645; and there was lately discovered in one of the mosses a man in armour on horseback, supposed to have been drowned in attempting to escape.

ALFRETON, a town in Derbyshire, with a market on Monday and Friday. Here are manufactures of stockings and brown earthenware, and two iron-works. It is seated on a hill, 13 miles N. of Derby, and 142 N. N. W. of London.

ALGAIOLA, a small fortified seaport, on the N. W. coast of Corsica, at the mouth of the Arengo, 28 miles W. by S. of Bastia.

ALGARVA, or ALGARVES, a province of Portugal. Its superficies is 232 sq. leagues, and contained 127,600 inhabitants. It forms the S. extremity of Portugal. Lagos, Faro, and Tavira, all on the S. coast, are the chief towns. It is fertile in figs, oranges, almonds, dates, olives, and excellent wine.

ALGESIRAS, a fortified town of Andalusia, Spain, situate on the coast W. of the Bay of Gibraltar.

ALGEZIRAS, or DIARBEK, a province of Asiatic Turkey, between the Tigris and Euphrates. It is mountainous, but fertile. Chief towns, Jezireh, Diarbekir, and Karkissia.

ALGIERIA, a country of Barbary, comprising the ancient Numidia, and part of Mauritania. It is 600 miles from E. to W., and 170 in breadth; bounded on the E. by Tunis, N. by the Mediterranean, S. by Mount Atlas, and W. by Morocco. Mineral springs and waters are met with in many places, and several of the chains of mountains contain lead and copper. In the interior of the country commence the dreary deserts. The principal rivers are the Shellif, Mazafran, Malva, and Zaine. The land toward the N. is fertile in corn, and the valleys are full of fruit. The melons have an exquisite taste, some of which are ripe in summer, and others in winter. The stems of the vines are very large, and the bunches of grapes are a foot and a half long. This country is divided into the provinces of Mascari, Titeri, and Constantina, and the territory of the city of Algier. Previously to the late successes of the French, the whole was in the hands of the Turks, and was governed by a sovereign called the dey, who, however, could do nothing of consequence without the council of the Janisaries. The Arabs, who live in tents, are a distinct people, governed by their own laws and magistrates. The beys or viceroys of the provinces had each an army under his command; and the late dey of Algiers had several thousand Moors, both horse and foot, in his service. The religion of the Algerines is Mahomedism, and their language a dialect of the Arabic. They have likewise a jargon, composed of Italian, French, and Spanish, called Lingua Franca, which is understood by the common people and merchants.

Algier, a strong city, capital of the whole country of Algier. It is buit on the side of a mountain, in the form of an amphitheatre, next the harbour; and the houses appearing one above another, of a resplendent whiteness, make a fine appearance from the sea. The tops of the houses are flat, covered with earth, and form a sort of gardens. The streets are narrow, and serve to keep off the extreme heat of the sun. There are five gates, but no public places or squares of considerable extent. The larger mosques are ten, but, except the one begun to be built about the year 1790, which is beautiful, there is nothing remarkable in their architecture; and the dey's palace is far from being spacious and extensive. The harbour is small, shallow, and insecure, and its entrance is incommoded with numerous rocks. The mole of the harbour is 500 paces in length, extending from the continent to a small island, where there is a castle and a large battery of guns. The country about Algier is adorned with gardens and fine villas, watered by fountains and rivulets; and thither the inhabitants resort in the hot season. The Turkish soldiers usually stationed here have exercised the greatest tyranny—often going to the farm-houses in the country, living at free quarters for twenty days together, and making use of every thing on which they could lay their hands. The chief subsistence of the inhabitants has constantly been derived from their piracies, on account of which they have frequently provoked the resentment of the most powerful states in Christendom. The emperor Charles V. lost a fine fleet and army in an expedition against Algiers in 1541. The English burnt their vessels in the harbour in 1635 and 1670; and it was bombarded by the French in 1688. In 1775, the Spaniards attacked it by sea and land, but were repulsed with great loss. In 1783 and 1784 they renewed their attacks by sea to destroy the city and galleys; but were forced to retire without effecting either its capture or destruction. In 1816, a British squadron, under the command of Lord Exmouth, bombarded the town and fleet in the harbour, with such destructive effect, as induced the dey immediately to release the Christian slaves then in his territory, and subscribe to all the terms of submission and restraint from future depredation, which the victors thought proper to dictate. This however, did not prevent them from resuming their piratical practices; and in 1830 the French undertook an expedition against them, of which the naval force reached the coasts of Algiers on the 13th of June, and on the morning of the 14th all the troops had disembarked. Their preparations had been magnificent, and their success was complete. On the 5th of July they took possession of the city, which, with its territory, is still in their hands. On hearing of the recent revolution in France, the late dey of Algiers is said to have exclaimed —" God is great! God is great! Charles X. deposed me, and now he is deposed: God is great!" The external commerce of Algier is principally with Gibraltar, whence they draw considerable supplies of European manufactures, spices, and India piece goods, in exchange for cattle, fruits, &c., for the supply of the town and garrison.

Algoa Bay, South Africa. It was selected as the landing-place for emigrants to this quarter; but the settlement is a considerable distance from the shore; about 500 miles from Cape Town.

Alhama, a town of Spain, in Granada, celebrated for its warm baths. It is surrounded by craggy mountains, and is seated on the Frio, 25 miles S. W. of Granada.

Alicant, a sea-port of Spain, in Valencia, famous for its excellent wine and fruits. It has also a great trade in barilla, and the English, Dutch, French, and Italians, have consuls here. The castle, on a high rock, was formerly reckoned impregnable, but was taken by the English in 1706. It was likewise taken by the French and Spaniards, after a siege of almost two years, when part of the rock was blown up. It is seated on the Mediterranean, on a bay of the same name, 64 French leagues S. E. of Maderia, 23 S. of Valencia, and 21 N. of Carthagena. Long. 0. 29. W. lat. 38. 20. N.

Alicata, a sea-port of Sicily, in Val di Mazara, with a fortress on a small cape at the mouth of the Salso, 22 miles S. E. of Girgenti. Long. 14. 7. E. lat. 37. 14. N.

Alicudi, the most western of the Lipari islands, in the Mediterranean, 10 miles W. of Felicuda. Long. 14. 32. E. lat. 38. 33. N.

Alifi, a town of Naples, at the foot of the Apennines, 25 miles N. W. of Benevento.

Allahabad, an interior province of Hindostan, 160 miles long, and 120 broad; bounded on the N. by Oude, E. by Bahar, S. by Orissa and Berar, and W. by Malwa and Agra. The Nerbudda, which rises on the S. E. border of the province, flows from E. to W. near its side; and the Ganges crosses it from W. to E. near its north side.

Allahabad, a city of Hindostan, capital of the above province, with a magnificent citadel. It was founded in 1583 by the emperor Acbar, who intended it as a place for arms; but its fortifications will hardly resist the battering of a field-piece. It is seated at the confluence of the Jumna with the Ganges, 470 miles W. N. W. of Calcutta. Long. 82. 0. E. lat. 25. 45. N. It was finally ceded, together with the province, to the English East India Company, in 1801.

Allah Shehr, or City of God, the ancient Philadelphia; it is now occupied by about 300 families, principally Greeks. It is situate in the province of Natolia, Asiatic Turkey, about 80 miles due E. of Smyrna.

Allegany, or Apalachian, Mountains, a long range of mountains in North America, between the Atlantic, the Mississippi, and the lakes; extending parallel with the sea-coast, 900 miles in length, and from 60 to 200 in breadth. The different ridges which compose this immense range have different names in the different states. Advancing from the S. the first ridge, commencing in Georgia, and extending through North Carolina, Virginia, and Pennsylvania, is the Blue ridge, or South Mountain, from 130 to 200 miles from the sea, and about 4000 ft. high from its base. Between this and the North Mountain spreads a large fertile vale. Next lies the *Allegany*, which is the principal ridge, and has been descriptively called the *back-bone* of the United States. Beyond this is the long ridge, called the Laurel Mountains, in a spur of which, in lat. 36, is a spring of water, 50 ft. deep, very cold, and as blue as indigo. From these several ridges proceed innumerable nameless branches or spurs. The Kittatiny, or Blue Mountains, run through the northern parts of New Jersey and Pennsylvania. These mountains are sometimes called the *Apalachian*, from a river, whose original source proceeds from this ridge, called the Apalachicola. They are not confusedly scattered and broken, but stretch along in uniform ridges, scarcely half a mile high. In several places they diverge, and some of them terminate in high perpendicular bluffs; others, towards the south, gradually subside into a level country, giving rise to the rivers which run southerly into the Gulf of Mexico.

ALLEGHANY, a river of the United States, which rises in the S. W. corner of the state of New York, in lat. 42. It is navigable, for keel-boats of 10 tons burthen, to Hamilton, 260 miles above Pittsburg, where it joins the Monongahela, and then assumes the name of Ohio. *See* OHIO.

ALLEGHANY, the name of three counties in the United States of North America; viz. 1st. in New York, pop. 40,975, of which Angelica, 272 W. by S. of Albany, is the capital; 2nd, in Pennsylvania, pop. 81,235, of which Pittsburg, 200 miles W. of Harrisburg, is the capital; and 3rd, in Maryland, pop. 15,690, of which Cumberland, 173 miles W. N. W. of Annapolis, is the chief town; also the name of several townships in Pennsylvania.

ALLEN, a county of Kentucky, U. S. of North America, pop. 7329. Scotsville, 160 miles S. W. by S. of Frankfort, is the chief town; also the name of a newly formed county in the state of Ohio.

ALLENBURG, a town of Prussia, on the river Alle, 25 miles E. S. E. of Konigsberg.

ALLENDALE, a parish and mining district at the foot of Fuller Hill in the county of Northumberland.

ALLENDORF, a town of Germany, famous for its salt-water, and three bridges over the Werra. It is 15 miles E. of Cassel; also the name of several other small towns in Germany.

ALLEN, LOUGH, a lake of Ireland, co. Leitrim, in which the Shannon has its chief source. A railway has been made to Lough Gill, about 10 miles distant.

ALLERTON, the name of a village in Lancashire, England; another in Somerset; and of 6 others in Yorkshire.

ALLERTON, NORTH. *See* NORTH ALLERTON.

ALLIER, a department of France. It is so called from a river, which flows by Moulins, and enters the Loire, below Nevers. Pop. 254,558.

ALLOA, a sea-port, Clackmannanshire, Scotland, near the mouth of the river into the Firth of Forth. Here is a custom-house, and an excellent dry dock, and its harbour is the resort of all the coal-vessels in the neighbourhood. It has a glass-house, two distilleries, and two breweries, the produce of which is in great repute. Near the town is a tower of 90 ft. in height, with walls 11 ft. in thickness. It is 30 miles W. N. W. of Edinburgh.

ALMADA, a town of Portugal, seated on a point of land on the south bank of the Tagus, nearly opposite Lisbon.

ALMADEN DE LAZOGUE, a town of Spain, in Mancha, famous for its rich mines of mercury and vermilion, 45 miles S. W. of Ciudad Real.

ALMADEN DE LA PLATA, a town of Spain, in Andalusia, on the river Colar, 34 miles N. by E. of Seville.

ALMANZA, a town of Spain, in Murcia, remarkable for the victory gained by the French and Spaniards over the allies, in 1707, when most of the English were killed or taken, having been abandoned by the Portuguese horse at the first charge. It is situate in a fertile plain, on the frontiers of Valencia, 35 miles S. W. of Xativa, and 62 N. of Murcia. Long. 1. 10. W. lat. 38. 48. N.

ALMEIDA, a fortified town of Portugal, in Beira. It was taken by the French, after a short siege, in 1810, who afterwards demolished the fortifications. It is situate on the river Coa, and near the borders of Spain, 18 miles N. E. of Guarda.

ALMERIA, a seaport of Spain, in Granada, and a bishop's see, seated at the mouth of the Almeria, 62 miles S. E. of Granada. Long. 2. 31. W. lat. 36. 51. N.

ALMISSA, a town of Dalmatia, famous for its wines. It stands at the foot of a high rock, and at the mouth of the Cetina, 12 miles E. of Spalatro.

ALMODOVAR, a town of Portugal, province of Alentejo. Pop. about 2000.

ALMODOVAR DEL CAMPO, a town of Spain, New Castile, a handsome town, at the foot of the Sierra Morena, 18 miles S. S. W. of Ciudad Real.

ALMONDBURY, a village W. R. Yorkshire, seated on the Calder, 2 miles S. S. E. of Huddersfield. It was the Campodonum of the Romans, afterward a seat of the Saxon kings, and had once a castle and a cathedral.

ALMUNETAR, a town of Spain, in Granada, seated on the Mediterranean, with a good harbour, defended by a strong castle, 30 miles S. S. E. of Alhama. Long. 3. 45. W. lat. 36. 40. N.

ALNWICK, a considerable town in Northumberland, on the road to Scotland; a place peculiarly fatal to some of the ancient Scottish monarchs. Here Malcolm III., making an inroad in Northumberland, was killed, with Edward his son and his army defeated, by Robert

Mowbray, earl of this county, in 1093; and here too his great grandson, William I., invading England with an army of 80,000 men, was encountered, his army routed, and himself made prisoner, in 1174. The town appears to have been formerly fortified, from the vestiges of a wall still to be seen in several parts, and three gates, which remain almost entire. Alnwick is a well built town; and is ornamented by a stately old Gothic castle, the seat of the Duke of Northumberland. It is seated on the Alne, 310 miles N. by W. from London, 33 N. of Newcastle, and 26 S. of Berwick.

ALPNACH, a town of Switzerland, in Underwalden, seated on an arm of the lake of the Four Cantons, 6 miles S. of Lucern.

ALPS, (from the *Celtic Alb*, or *Alp*, high) a chain of mountains in Europe, which begins at the Gulf of Genoa, to the E. of Nice, passes into Switzerland, crosses that country and Tyrol, separates Germany from Italy, and terminates at the N. part of the Gulf of Venice. This grand chain is sometimes divided into two or more ridges, ranging one by another, with only narrow valleys between; and the different portions have distinct appellations, as the Maritime, Pennine, Lepontine, Helvetian, Rhetian, Julian, &c. They are composed of stupendous rocky masses, two, four, and even six being piled upon each other; Mont Blanc, the chief, being 15,735 feet in height, and visible at a distance of 140 miles. There are few passes over them, and those of difficult access. Switzerland has the central part of these mountains, and the valleys between them. The famous Hannibal attempted to cross the Alps on the side of Piedmont, in the winter season, when he invaded Italy, and lost most of his elephants among them. They were passed successfully by a numerous French army under the command of Napoleon Buonaparte, in 1800.

ALPS, UPPER, a department of France, including part of the late province of Dauphiny. It is so called from its vicinity to the mountains of that name. The capital is Embrun.

ALPS, LOWER, a department of France, including part of the late province of Provence. The capital is Digne.

ALPS, MARITIME, a late department of France, including the county of Nice. The capital is Nice.

ALPUXARES, high mountains in Spain, in Granada, near the Mediterranean. They are inhabited by the Moriscos, who carefully cultivate the ground, which produces excellent wines and fruits.

ALRESFORD, a town in Hampshire, with a market on Thurs. and a manufacture of linseys. To the S. W. of the town is a piece of water, covering about 200 acres, which forms a head to the river Itchin. It is 18 miles N. E. of Southampton, and 57 W. S. W. of London.

ALSACE, a late province of France, now divided into the Upper and Lower Rhine, which see.

ALSEN, a fertile island of Denmark, in the Little Belt, between Sleswick and Funen, 100 miles W. of Copenhagen. Pop. 16 000. The chief town is Sonderborg.

ALSFELD, a town of Germany, with a castle, 12 miles E. of Marburg.

ALSHEDA, a town of Sweden, in Smaland, near which a gold mine was discovered in 1738.

ALSIERA, a town of Naples, in the Molise, on the river Tiserno, 33 miles N. E. of Molise.

ALSLEBEN, a town of Upper Saxony, 9 miles S. S. W. of Bernburg.

ALSTADT, a town of Upper Saxony, in Thuringia, with a castle, on the rivulet Rane, 8 miles W. of Querfurt.

ALSTADT, a town of Moravia, in the circle of Olmutz, near the source of the Morau, 35 miles N. N. W. of Olmutz.

ALSTON-MOOR, or ALDSTONE, a town in Cumberland, with a market on Saturday. Here is an iron-foundry, and a shot-manufacture; and in its vicinity are numerous lead-mines. It is seated on the side of a hill, on the S. branch of the Tyne, 20 miles E. by S. of Carlisle, and 271 N. by W. of London.

ALTAI MOUNTAINS, a range of mountains, intersecting Asia from S. to N., commencing W. of the Indus, in W. long. about 68, and diverging northward by several ridges towards East Cape, in E. long. 170.

ALTAMURA, a town of Naples, at the foot of the Apennines, 10 miles N. E. of Gravina. Pop. about 16,000.

ALTENAN, a town of Lower Saxony, in the territory of Brunswick, 8 miles S. of Goslar.

ALTENBERG, a town of Upper Saxony, in Misnia, celebrated for its tin mine, 20 miles S. of Dresden.

ALTENBURG, a town of Upper Saxony in Thuringia, with a castle on a rock. It is seated on the Pleisse, 20 miles S. of Leipsic.

ALTENBURG, a town of Lower Hungary, on the river Leitha, at its entrance into the Danube. Here are two churches and a college· and its ancient castle is now principally used for a corn magazine. It is 17 miles S. S. E. of Presburg.

ALTENKIRCHEN, a town of Germany, in the Westerwald; chief of the county of Sayn, with a castle, 15 miles N. N. E. of Coblentz.

ALTEESON, a town of Piedmont, between the rivers Doire and Stura, 3 miles N. of Turin.

ALTKIRCH, a town of France, in the department of Upper Rhine, on an eminence, near the source of the river Ill, 25 miles S. of Colmar.

ALTON, a town in Hampshire, with a market on Saturday. It has manufactures of worsted stuffs and round the town are plantations of hops. It is seated on the Wey, 28 miles E. N. E. of Southampton, and 47 W. S. W. of London.

ALTONA, a city and sea-port of Lower Saxony, in Holstein, seated on the Elbe, contiguous to Hamburgh. The Danes built it in this situation, that it might rival Hamburgh in commerce. It was burnt by the Swedes in 1712, but has been beautifully rebuilt, and is estimated to contain 30,000 inhabitants. Long. 9. 58. E. lat. 53. 34. N.

ALTORF, a town of Franconia, in the territory of Nuremberg, with a university, 16 miles S. E. of Nuremberg.

ALTORF, or ALTDORF, a town of Switzerland, capital of the canton of Uri. Here are two stone pillars, 130 paces from each other, at which distance Tell is said to have shot the apple from his son's head. This deliverer of his country lived at Burgli, near this place, and his cottage is changed into a chapel, where mass is solemnly said. Altorf stands on the lake of Lucern, near the influx of the river Russ, 20 miles S. E. of Lucern.

ALTRINGHAM, tn., Cheshire, market on Tuesday. Here are several manufactures of worsted and cotton; and much fruit and vegetables are sent hence to Manchester. It is seated near the Duke of Bridgewater's Canal, 30 miles N. E. of Chester, and 180 N. W. of London.

ALTUNKUPRI, a town of Asiatic Turkey, the capital of Kurdistan, and the residence of a pacha. It is situate on the river Altun, which flows into the Tigris, 50 miles S. E. of Mosul. Long. 44. 30. E. lat. 35. 45. N.

ALVA DE TORMES, a town of Spain, in Leon, with a castle, once the residence of the celebrated Duke of Alva, seated on the Tormes, 16 miles S. E. of Salamanca.

ALVARADO, a river of Mexico, in the province of Vera Cruz, which rises 40 miles above the town of Cordova, and flows N. E. till it enters the Gulf of Mexico, at a town of the same name, 40 miles S. E. of Vera Cruz.

ALVASTON, a village in Gloucestershire, 8 miles N. by E. of Bristol. On the top of a hill, near the Severn, is a round camp, called Oldbury, where several antiquities have been dug up.

ALZIRA, or ALCIRA, a populous town of Spain, which has a great trade in silk. It is surrounded by the Zucar, 17 miles S. of Valencia.

AMADAN, or HAMADAN, a town of Persia, in Irac Ajemi. Here are many Jews, who allege that the tombs of Mordecai and Esther are in the place which serves them for a synagogue. Amadan is a very ancient city; on its site, or near it, the ancient Ecbatana is supposed to have stood. It is said to have been destroyed by Nebuchadnezzar, and rebuilt by Darius, who brought hither all his riches. It is situate to the N. of the upper road from Bagdad to Ispahan, about 15 miles from Kenghey. It has considerable manufactures of leather, and contains about 40,000 inhabitants.

AMADIA, a town of Asiatic Turkey, in Kurdistan, governed by a bey, seated on a high mountain, 40 miles S. E. of Gezira. Long. 41. 35. E. lat. 37. 20. N.

AMAK, or AMAGER, an island of Denmark, on which part of Copenhagen, called Christianshafen, is built. It is eight miles long and four broad, and separated from Zealand by a narrow channel, over which are two bridges that communicate with Copenhagen. It is laid out in gardens and pastures, and supplies Copenhagen with milk, butter, and vegetables.

AMAL, a town of Sweden, in Gothland, with a good harbour on the lake Wenner. It has a great trade in timber, deals, and tar; and is 175 miles S. W. of Upsal.

AMALFI, a sea-port of Naples, in Principato Citeriore, and an archbishop's see. Flavio Gioia, who is said to have invented the mariner's compass, was a native of this town. It is seated on the N. W. side of the Gulf of Salerno, 13 miles S. W. of Salerno. Long. 14. 45. E. lat. 40. 28. N.

AMAND, ST., a town of France, in the department of Cher, near the river Cher, 21 miles S. of Bourges.

AMAND, ST., a town of France, in the department of Nord, with an abbey; seated on the Scarp, 7 miles N. of Valenciennes.

AMANTEA, a sea-port of Naples, near the bay of Eufemia, 20 miles S. W. of Cosenza.

AMAPALLA, a sea-port of Guatimala, in Nicaragua, seated on an island on the W. side of the entrance of the Gulf of Fonseca. Long. 88. 30. W. lat. 13. 10. N.

AMARAPURA. *See* UMMERAPOORA.

AMASIA, or AMASIEH, a town of Asiatic Turkey, in Natolia, the birth-place of Strabo, the geographer. It is the capital of a province which produces excellent wines and fruits. It was devastated by an earthquake, in 1794. It is seated on the Casalmack, which falls into the Black Sea, 36 miles N. of Tocat. Long. 36. 0. E. lat. 40. 31. N.

AMAZON, or MARANON, a river of South America, and the greatest in the world. Its source is in Peru, not far from the Pacific Ocean, and, running E., it enters the Atlantic Ocean, directly under the equinoctial line. Its course is 3300 miles, its mouth is 150 miles broad, and, 1500 miles from its mouth, it is 30 fathoms deep. It receives, in its progress, near 200 rivers, many of which have a course of 1500 miles, and some of them not inferior to the Danube or the Nile In the rainy season it overflows its banks, and fertilizes the adjacent country.

AMBA-GESHEN, a rock in Abyssinia, of a most prodigious steepness, in the form of a castle built of freestone, and almost impregnable. The Ethiopic princes were formerly banished hither by their fathers, the emperors, that they might not attempt any thing against the state; and that their residence might be as noted for its height as their birth.

AMBERG, a fortified town of Bavaria, with a strong castle. The magnificent church of St. Martin contains many beautiful paintings and curiosities; and the mint is esteemed one of the finest buildings of the kind in Germany. In 1743, it was taken by the Austrians, and in 1796, by the French. It is seated on the river Ills, or Wills, on the confines of the principality of Sultzbach, 40 miles E. of Nuremberg. Long. 11. 48. E. lat. 49. 27. N.

AMBERT, a town of France, in the department of Puy de Dome. There are numerous paper makers in its vicinity, and it has a trade in coarse laces, camlets, ferrets, &c. It is seated in a beautiful valley, on the river Dore, 21 miles E. of Issoire.

AMBLESIDE, town of Westmoreland, standing on the site of a Roman city, called *Dictus*, with a market on Wednesday. Here is a manufacture of woollen cloth. It is seated on the Rotha, near the head of Windermere-water, 13 miles N. W. of Kendal, and 276 N. N. W. of London.

AMBLETEUSE, a seaport of France, in the department of Pas de Calais, defended by a battery. At this port Cæsar embarked his cavalry when he passed over into England; and here James II. landed on his departure from England, in 1688. It is seated on the English channel, 8 miles N. of Boulogne. Long. 1. 36. E. lat. 50. 49. N.

AMBOISE, a town of France, in the department of the Indre and Loire. The town is mean and ill-built; but has been rendered famous in history, by the conspiracy of the Huguenots, in 1560, which opened the fatal religious wars in France. Here Louis XI. instituted the order of St. Michael; it was also the birth-place of the poet Jesuit Commine, and where Charles VIII. died. It is seated at the confluence of the Massee with the Loire, 12 miles E. by N. of Tours, and 118 S. by W. of Paris.

AMBOYNA, an island of the Moluccas, in the Indian Ocean. It is 56 miles in length from N. to S. and divided on the W. side by a large bay, into two parts; the largest of which is called Hitou, and the other Leytimor. The face of this island is beautiful; woody mountains and verdant plains being interspersed with hamlets, and enriched by cultivation. The chief products are cloves, nutmegs, sugar, coffee, and many delicious fruits, but more especially cloves. The principal animals are deer and wild hogs. The English and Dutch had factories here at the beginning of the 17th century; but the Dutch expelled the English, and tortured and put to death many of them. The natives wear large whiskers, and their dress is only a slight piece of stuff wrapped round their middle. The men buy their wives of their parents, and, if they prove barren, the marriage is void. They are generally Mahometans; but there are some Christians among them. This island was taken by the English in 1796, and restored by the treaty of Amiens in 1802; recaptured in 1810, and again restored to the Dutch by the treaty at Paris in 1814, and confirmed in 1824. The chief town is of the same name, neatly built, and stands near the S. W. extremity. Fort Victoria is in long. 128. 15. E. lat. 3. 40. S.

AMBROSE, St., an island on the coast of Chili, 15 miles W. from St. Felix Island. The crew of Captain Roberts, in 1792, killed and cured here 13,000 seal skins, in seven weeks. Long. 80. 55. W. lat. 26. 13. S.

AMBRYM, one of the New Hebrides, in the Pacific Ocean, 50 miles in circumference. Long. 168. 12. E. lat. 16. 10. N.

AMEDABAD, or AHMEDABAD, a city of Hindostan; the capital of Guzerat. The walls are 6 miles in circumference, and contain twelve gates; but now not a quarter of the area is inhabited. The mosque and tomb of the founder, Tatay Ahmed, are built of stone and marble, the last of exquisite workmanship. It was taken by General Goddard, in 1780, from the Poonah Mahrattas, to whom it was restored in 1783. It is seated in a level country, on a navigable river that enters the Gulf of Cambay, 320 miles N. of Bombay. Long. 72. 27. E. lat. 23. 13. N.

AMEDNAGUR, a city and fort of Hindoostan, once the capital of the soubah of its name, which is now better known by that of Dowlatabad. This city was the residence of the emperor Aurungzebe, during his conquest of the Deccan and the Carnatic. In 1803 it was taken by the British army, under General Wellesley, (now Duke of Wellington.) It is 73 miles N. E. of Poonah. Long. 75. 0. E. lat. 19. 10. N.

AMEENABAD, a town of Hindostan, in Lahore, 35 miles N. by W. of Lahore.

AMELIA, an island on the coast of East Florida, 13 miles long and 2 broad; extending about 2 miles from the continent, between the rivers St. Mary and Nassau. It is very fertile, and has a town with an excellent harbour, at its north end. Long. 82. 0. W. lat. 30. 45. N.

AMELIA, a town of Italy, seated on a mountain between the Tiber and Nira, 20 miles S. W. of Spoleto, and 45 N. of Rome.

AMELIA, an inland county of Virginia. Pop. 10,320. The court-house of the county is 58 miles W. S. W. of Richmond.

AMERICA, in its most comprehensive sense and present acceptation, may be considered as comprising half of the terrestrial globe, or the whole of the western hemisphere. It has been usual to speak of America as constituting one of the four quarters, or four grand divisions of the globe; but it is equally matter for surprise as well as for regret, that the western hemisphere should so long have remained subject to a misnomer so obvious, and a designation so inappropriate and indefinite. Recent researches in Danish literature have brought to light the fact, that America was visited long before its re-discovery by Columbus. It is proved that the Northmen first discovered this continent in the year 986, and visited it for more than two centuries afterwards. Greenland was colonized by Erik Raude, an Icelander, about the commencement of the 10th century; and one of these colonists, Leif, visited the continent of North America, and named the districts of Helluland, Markland, and Vinland, the last being the present territory of the United States; many other particulars and descriptions are still preserved. During the ignorance of the middle ages, these discoveries were totally forgotten, and not revived till the present century by the antiquaries of Copenhagen. The western hemisphere again became known to Europe in the year 1493 of the Christian era, when Christopher Columbus, a native of Genoa, who, from a long and close application to the study of geography and navigation, had obtained a knowledge of the figure of the earth, much superior to the general notions of the age in which he lived, in order that the terraqueous globe might be properly balanced, and the lands and seas proportioned to each other, was led to conceive that another continent existed. Having fully satisfied himself of the truth of this system, he became impatient to reduce it to practice, and accordingly laid his scheme before the senate of Genoa, making his native country the first offer of his services. They, however, rejected his proposal as the dream of a chimerical projector. It met with the same fate at the courts of Portugal, Spain, and England, and some of the other European powers of less note; but, still undiscouraged, he applied again to the court of Spain, who were at length induced to fit out a squadron of three small vessels, of which Columbus was made admiral; and with these he set out on his voyage of discovery, in 1492, in which voyage he discovered several of the Bahama islands, with those of Cuba and Hispaniola, and returned to Spain in the following year. In a second voyage he discovered many more of the West India islands; and in a third he attained the great object of his ambition, by discovering the southern division of the continent, near the mouth of the Oroonoko. Amongst the crowd of new adventurers who now followed from all parts of Europe, was one Americus Vespucius, a Florentine, who, with much art, and some degree of elegance, drew up an amusing history of his voyage, in which he insinuated that he first discovered what is commonly called the continent of the New World. This being published, and read with admiration, the country at large was, from him, called *America*, though it is now well understood that Columbus was the first discoverer. The celebrity of Columbus and Americus Vespucius soon resounded throughout all Europe, inspiring numbers of adventurers to witness the fruits of their discoveries. Among the rest, Giovanni Gabota (anglicised Cabot) a Venetian, and his three sons, under the auspices of Henry VII. of England, sailed from Bristol, in 1497, and traced the coast of Labrador as far as the 57th deg. of N. lat. On a second voyage, in the following year, in a ship furnished by the king, accompanied by four small barques provisioned by the merchants of Bristol, under the direction of Giovanni's second son, Sebastian, (who had been born in Bristol, hence the claim of the northern division of the western hemisphere having been discovered by an Englishman,) they discovered the island of Newfoundland in N. lat. about 47, and coasted southward as far as Florida. Cabot made a third voyage to Newfoundland in 1502. In 1519, a body of Spaniards, under the command of Cortez, landed at Vera Cruz, and discovered the populous district of Mexico. In 1524, the French sent an expedition, which traversed the coast from the lat. of 28. to 50. N. France, Spain, and England each sent successive expeditions to North America, and made attempts to establish settlements; but so unsuccessfully, that it is believed, that at the commencement of the 17th century, not a single European remained north of Mexico. In 1608, renewed efforts were made by England; since when, the extent, features, population, and productions of the whole of the western hemisphere have progressively been developed to Europe. America, or the western hemisphere, is sub divided by nature into two grand divisions, *north* and *south*; very distinct in character and feature, connected with each other by a straggling extent of territory, stretching from about the 8th to the 15th deg. of N. lat.

The northern division extends from the polar regions to the 15th deg. of N. lat., the more northern part, as far as lat. 50., extending from about the 56th to the 130th deg. of W. long., and at lat. 65. as far W. as 168 of long. From the 50th to the 30th deg. of lat. the country assumes a very compact form, extending at the N. from about the 62nd to the 124th deg. of long., gradually converging southerly, and at lat. 30 extending only from about the 81st to the 115th deg. of long. at about the 30th deg. of N. lat. The great Gulf of Mexico bounds the land from about the 80th to the 97th deg. of long., the land converging into a promontory of about 10 deg. at the N., extending S. to the chain which unites the northern with the grand southern division, gradually converging in long. to about 1 deg. only, in N. lat. 15, and in W. long. 95. The population of North America is estimated at 50,000,000, but it is somewhat uncertain. The area is about 8,000,000 sq. miles. The extreme length of the grand northern division, in a straight, unbroken line, from the mouth of the Coppermine River, which runs S. to N. into the Icy Sea, in lat. 70, to Acapulco, in lat. 17, is about 3200 miles, and the extreme breadth, from the mouth of the Penobscot river, which falls into the Atlantic Ocean in N. lat. 44. 24. W. long. 68. 45, to the mouth of Columbia river, which falls into the North Pacific Ocean in N. lat. 46. W. long. 124, the distance is about 2500. The northern part of this grand division of the western hemisphere is indented by Hudson's Bay, which extends from the line of the Arctic circle, to the 51st deg. of N. lat., and, in its extreme breadth, from the 78th to the 95th deg. of W. long. It is also intersected by a chain of fresh water lakes of vast extent. Athapescow, and the Slave Lake, (the latter of great extent,) discharge their waters into the Icy Sea; Winnipeg, and several of lesser extent and note, discharge their waters into Hudson's Bay; whilst Superior, Michigan, Huron, Erie, Ontario, and Champlain, between the latitudes of 42 and 48. N. discharge their waters by the great river St. Lawrence into the Gulf of St. Lawrence, in the lat. of 50. N. and W. long. about 65, the western extremity of Lake Superior being in long. about 92. Innumerable streams of water intersect the country in all directions, which, by unions, form themselves into noble rivers, several of which run into Hudson's Bay, whilst those S. of the great chain of lakes and the St. Lawrence, run a course from N. to S. or S. E. falling into the Atlantic Ocean. Taking them in order from N. to S. the most prominent are, St. John's, the Penobscot, Kenebeck, Androscoggin, Piscataqua, Merrimac, Connecticut, the Hudson or North River, Delaware, Susquehannah, Potomac, Rappahanock, James river, Roanoke, Santee, and Savannah. All these rivers have their source E. of a chain of mountains, called the Allegany, running parallel with the Atlantic coast, from about the 34th to the 43rd deg. of N. lat., and 2 to 300 miles from the ocean. South of the 34th deg. of lat. the Appalochicola, Alabama, Tombechbee, and some other rivers of less note, run a course due S. falling into the Gulf of Mexico. West of the Allegany mountains, innumerable other streams have their source, forming another collection of noble rivers, the most important of which are the Ohio and Tennessee, running from E. to W., the Missouri, Kanzas, and Arkansas, and the Red River, running from W. to E., all of which fall into one grand channel, called the Mississippi, which has its source about the 47th deg. of N. lat., running a course nearly due S., falling into the Gulf of Mexico in lat. 29. 5. N. and 89. 8. W. long. The Rio del Norte, or Rio Bravo, another noble river, has its source westward of the Arkansas and Red Rivers, in N. lat. about 42, and falls into the Gulf of Mexico in N. lat. 26. W. long. 97. 25. On the western coast, the Columbia and Colorado are the only rivers of importance, and they are not considerable; the first falls into the Pacific Ocean in N. lat. about 45, and the other into the Gulf of California in N. lat. about 32. A ridge of mountains runs parallel with the western coast, the whole extent of the N. division, from the point of the promontory S. in lat. 15, to the lat. of 70. N., bearing W. from the 95th to the 122nd or 123rd of long., and about 10 deg. from the western coast or shore of the Pacific Ocean; this ridge, which seems to be a continuation of the Andes of the southern division, from the 15th to about the 40th deg. of N. lat., is called the Cordilleras, and, more northerly, the Rocky Mountains; the greatest altitude is in N. lat. about 19, where the Popocatepest issues forth volcanic eruptions at a height of 17,720 ft. above the level of the sea. Another range of mountains runs parallel with the eastern or Atlantic coast, from about the 35th to the 45th deg. of N. lat., diverging into several distinct and parallel ridges, designated the Blue, Tuscarora, and Allegany mountains, and the Laurel and Chesnut ridges; and collectively they are called the Allegany; the greatest altitude does not exceed 4000 ft. above the level of the sea.

On the discovery of this vast territory, at the periods previously stated, it was found, to the N. of the 30th deg. of lat., to be thinly populated with inhabitants, and, except the Esquimaux at the more northern part, possessing one common character, and speaking one common language, though somewhat varied in dialect. In person, tall and well-proportioned; complexion coppery, with long, straight, and somewhat coarse, black hair; localized into various tribes or communities, none of whom were found to have made any, or very little, progress in the arts which contribute to the comfort of life; spears and arrows being their only instruments of attack and subsistence, whilst skins, mats, and the coarsest cloth of reeds, grass, or hemp, constituted their chief clothing and protection from the inclemency of the weather. They were, nevertheless, found possessing many manly qualities and social virtues, until corrupted and debased by the vicious refinements of their invaders, before whom they have progressively receded as from a pestilence; and from the effects of whisky and rum, exchanged for the furs which they collected for the traders; and still more, by the dreadful destruction from the small-pox, also introduced by Europeans, whole tribes are becoming extinct, and the names alone, of many powerful and numerous nations, exist now as historical remembrances. Of their origin no trace or vestige, either traditional or historical, has as yet been discovered; but from many similarities in manners, customs, religious ceremonies, and peculiarities of language, of the ancient Peruvians and Mexicans, and some of the modern tribes, which may be almost identified with those of the Malays, Indo-Chinese, and Mongolians, and which are found certainly to extend, more or less, throughout the whole of the Polynesian islands, render the hypothesis good, that the population has been derived in an *easterly* direction from the older countries and people of Asiatic origin.

Northerly, from the 30th deg. of lat., this division of the western hemisphere contains no very remarkable natural features, either of aspect or productions, animal, mineral, or vegetable, beyond the rivers and mountains already described, except the falls of Niagara, and the natural bridge in Virginia, which will be found detailed under those heads, and a few animals, especially the beaver, peculiar to the latitudes of 45 to 48, in this hemisphere. In the plains between the Allegany and Rocky Mountains, fossil bones of animals have been found, far exceeding in dimensions those of any known animal at present existing, or that have ever been found in any part of the eastern hemisphere; neither the elephant, lion, tiger, leopard, panther, nor hyæna, have been found in the northern division, but in the more northern part, bears, wolves, foxes, and a variety of smaller animals abound; the feathered and vegetable kingdoms are various and abundant, but exhibit nothing remarkable. In the rivers S. of the 35th deg. of N. lat. the alligator is common. The promontory S. of the 30th deg. of N. lat. exhibits more sublimity of aspect, variety and richness of production; which will be found more particularly elucidated under the head of Mexico.

The northern division of the western hemisphere is at present divided into three great parts; viz. 1st N., under the dominion of Great Britain, which part extends N. from the Icy Sea and polar regions, to about the 48th deg. of N. lat., subdivided into seven provinces or territories: viz. Nova Scotia, New Brunswick, Canada Lower and Upper, Labrador, New South Wales, and the N. W. territory, 2nd, the central part, from the boundary of the British territories on the N., to the Gulf of Mexico S. and W. from the Atlantic Ocean to about the

100th deg. of W. long., and from the 42nd to the 49th deg. of N. lat. extending W. to the Pacific Ocean, under the rule of the federal government of the *U. S. of America;* and, 3rd, the part extending from the United States territory N., to the isthmus which unites the northern with the grand southern division. This part for three centuries continued under the dominion of Spain; but, from the period of 1820 or 1821, it may be considered as forming a separate and independent territory, which will be found more fully exemplified under the head of Mexico; whilst the 1st and 2nd parts will be found more fully treated under the heads of British and U. S. of America.

South Division.—The southern division of the western hemisphere is subtended from the *chain* which connects it with the northern division, and extends through 68 deg. of lat. from Cape la Vela in 12. 12. N. to Cape Horn in 55. 58. S., being about 4100 miles, and, under the lat. of 5. S., extends through 45 deg. of long., from Cape St. Roque in 35. 40, to Cape Blanco in 81. 10. W. It contains an area of about 7,000,000 sq. miles, and a population of 13,000,000. This division of the western hemisphere, as previously stated, was first discovered by Columbus (on his third voyage from Spain,) on the 1st of August, 1498; but it was not till the year 1531 that any inroad was made, or knowledge obtained, of its extent and productions; in which year three low and unprincipled adventurers, Pizarro, Almagro, and the priest Lucques, landed on the *chain* of the Isthmus of Panama, and proceeding S. they discovered the rich and then populous districts of Quito and Peru. In the year 1500, the Portuguese admiral, Alvarez de Cabral, commanding a squadron of 13 sail, with 1200 men on board, destined for the East Indies by the Cape of Good Hope, having been carried by westerly winds beyond the intended longitude, accidentally discovered, on the 24th of April, the southern division of the western hemisphere, about 4 deg. S. of the equator, and, on the following day, landed and took possession of the country, since called the Brazils, in the name of the then potentate of Portugal; and, although near half a century elapsed before any effectual efforts were made by the Portuguese to form a permanent settlement, the whole of the southern division of the western hemisphere (with the exception of a comparatively trifling extent of territory between the 3rd and 7th deg. of N. lat., settled by the Dutch, and the southern extremity, continuing in possession of the natives,) fell under the dominion of Spain and Portugal, the Spanish portion being divided into five departments: viz. New Granada, Venezuela, Peru, Buenos Ayres, and Chili, each subdivided into several provinces: the whole of the Portuguese portion continuing under one general government, the Brazils subdivided into several captaincies, which will be found detailed under the head Brazils. Since the period of 1825, the domination and rule of both Spain and Portugal has entirely ceased over every part of the great southern division of the western hemisphere, new and distinct governments having established themselves, giving rise to new boundaries and subdivisions of territory; which will be found detailed under the several heads of Columbia, Peru, United Provinces of La Plata, or South America, Chili, and the Brazils, and the remaining portion under the heads of Amazonia, Guiana, and Patagonia.

The natural features of this division of the western hemisphere are in the highest degree grand and imposing; extensive fertile plains, yielding variety and abundance of every thing calculated for the comfort of man, whilst the mountains display the majesty of creation, yielding abundance of malleable and indestructible metals, and innumerable streams, forming themselves into noble rivers, yielding their proportion of supply, and affording facility of conveyance, eminently contributing to promote the sociality, enjoyment, and happiness of society. The range of mountains called the Andes, adverted to in the elucidation of the northern division, as extending from the chain to the Icy Sea, extends from the utmost extremity of this division south, to the chain which unites it with the north, running parallel with the shores of the Pacific Ocean, at the distance of 100 to 200 miles from the sea, and occasionally diverging into parallel ridges, the main ridge maintaining an average altitude of 12,000 to 15,000 ft. above the level of the sea, nearly the whole extent of the continent. In 1802, the Prussian travellers, Messrs. Humboldt and Bonpland, ascended the peak of the Andes called Chimborazo, in the province of Quito, to the height of 19,400 ft., its extreme altitude being 21,440. The peak of Cotopaxi, 40 miles S. E. of the ancient city of Quito, is volcanic, and frequently emits, with terrific violence, from its summit, 18,898 ft. above the level of the sea. Various mountain ridges intersect the more eastern parts of the continent, all running from south to north, similar in diversity and altitude to the Allegany of the northern division. The rivers run in every direction: taking them from north to south, the first demanding notice is the Magdalena; 2nd, Oroonoko; 3rd, the Japura, Tunguragua, Ucayale, Madeira, and Tapajos, branches which form the Amazons; 4th, the Araguay; 5th, the Parnaiba, or Marahnam; 6th, the Francisco; and, 7th, the Uruguay, Parana, Paraguay, Pilcomayo, Vermejo, and Salado branches, which form the Rio de la Plata, all of which will be found detailed under their respective heads. The inhabitants of this division of the western hemisphere, on the first inroads of the Spaniards, at the commencement of the 16th century, appeared to be of the same stock, and possessing the same common character of feature and colour, as those of the north, but, on the western side, much further advanced in the arts of social life and enervation; but of their origin no credible account, either of history or tradition, could be obtained. Instead of an Adam, formed of the dust of the earth, and an Eve, formed of Adam's rib, the

Peruvians had a Manca-Capac, who came from an island on a great lake south, to instruct their men in agriculture and other useful employments, and a Mama-Oello, to instruct the women in spinning and weaving. Of the precise era, however, of their appearance, their chronology was too imperfect to define; they enumerated 14 reigns of incas or sovereigns since their time, which would carry the epoch back to about the end of the 12th, or beginning of the 13th century. In the face of evidence so imperfect, it would be absurd to hazard even a conjecture, much more an assertion, upon the subject of the first peopling of the south. It may, however, be fairly inferred that the north division, subsequent to the last great periodical immersion of the northern hemisphere, was first peopled by emigrants from the south, rather than from any part of the eastern hemisphere. This seems probable, as well from the similarity of general feature and character, as from the regular gradation of the athletic power and energy which seemed to prevail amongst them from south to north. The most healthy and robust of the race would doubtless be most likely to advance onward.

The other part of the animal creation is not so powerful as in the eastern hemisphere. The elephant is nowhere found, either in the north or south. The jaguar and cougar species of the tiger, and the puma, a species of the lion, are common over every part of the southern division of the western hemisphere, as well as the panther, leopard, and ounce; the lama and vicuna are peculiar to this part of the world; the lama is not very dissimilar to the camel, but inferior in utility, and the vicuna still more so; the wool or hair, however, promises to become a useful article for manufacturing purposes. Every species of deer and furred animals are common ; whose skins form great articles of traffic.

Birds are various in species, and numerous, the condor of the Andes is considered superior in majesty to the ostrich of the deserts of Africa; in the plains is another large bird of a species between the ostrich and cassoury of New Holland; there are eagles of various kinds, and an endless variety of smaller birds of exquisitely beautiful plumage. It is considered, however, that in physiognomy and tone, the birds of the western hemisphere are inferior to those of the eastern. The winged tribe and insects are various and infinite, some surpassing in beauty, and others in noxiousness; but, next to the volcanic eruptions and natural convulsions of the earth, the greatest terror of the southern division of the western hemisphere is the reptiles, which exceed in variety, number, and voracity, those of any other part of the world. Of the inhabitants of the waters, the electric eel and ink-fish are peculiar to the eastern coast of the equatorial latitudes of this hemisphere; in addition to which, nearly all the species common to other seas and rivers are also abundant. Indestructible metals and gems are more abundant in this division of the western hemisphere, than in any other part of the world; and those infatuation-exciting metals, gold and silver, seem to abound to such a degree as is likely soon to satiate the mania, and even predilection for their possession. Copper, in several parts, is also abundant. The vegetable productions also exceed in variety, beauty, and utility, those of Asia, or any other part of the globe, whether considered in reference to sustenance, or to luxury, taste, and adornment in art. The climate, though noxious in certain confined and local situations, is on the whole delightful; in short, nothing is wanting but judicious and well-directed means, on the part of man, to render the whole southern division of the western hemisphere the abode of enjoyment and happiness. There are several islands on different parts of the coast of the western hemisphere: taking them in order, beginning with the eastern coast from the north, they stand as follows: viz. Mansfield, at the entrance of Hudson's Bay; Anticosti at the mouth, and St. John's, or Prince Edward's, in Newfoundland, and Cape Breton, at the entrance of the Gulf of St. Lawrence; the Bermudas, lat. 32; Bahamas, Carribee, or West India, comprising Cuba, Hispaniola, or St. Domingo, Jamaica, and numerous others; Trinidad, at the mouth of the Oroonoko; Falkland's, in lat. 52. S.; South Georgia, in 54. S. and 36. W. long; Staten Island, and Terra del Fuego, at the extreme south point of the continent; Chiloe, Juan Fernandez, the Galapagos, Queen Charlotte's, and the Fox Islands, off the western coast, all of which, as well as Guatimala, the provinces of Yucatan, Honduras, Nicaragua, Mosquitia, Veragua, Panama, and Terra Firma, which compose the chain which unites the two grand divisions, will be fonnd detailed under their respective heads.

AMERPORE, a town of Nepaul, 10 miles W. of Moowanpoor.

AMERKOTE, a fort of Hindostan, in the extensive sandy desert between the Indus and the Puddar. This place is celebrated as the retreat of the emperor Humaioon, during his troubles; and here was born his son, the illustrious Akbar. It is 160 miles E. N. E. of Tatta.

AMERSFORT, a town of Holland, in the state of Utrecht. A considerable quantity of tobacco is grown in the neighbourhood. It has a trade in beer, and goods from Germany are shipped here for Amsterdam. It is seated in a fertile country, on the river Ems, 10 miles E. N. E. of Utrecht.

AMERSHAM, or AGMONDESHAM, a town in Buckinghamshire; market on Tuesday. It has a considerable manufacture of black lace. The town-hall is the handsomest in the county. 26 miles N. W. of London.

AMESBURY, or AMBRESBURY, a town in Wiltshire; market on Friday. It is seated on the lower Avon, at the place where a number of Britons were treacherously murdered, and near that famous monument of antiquity, Stonehenge. Here are the ruins of a venerable abbey. This place gave birth to the celebrated Joseph Addison. It is 6 miles N. of Salisbury, and 77 W. of London.

AMHARA, a district of Abyssinia, between the Dender and Tacazze branches of the Nile.

AMHERST, a small inland county of Virginia, on the north bank of James's River. The courthouse of the county is 130 miles W. of Richmand. Pop. 12,576. Also the name of the chief town of Hilsborough county, New Hampshire, and of another town in Massachusets, and another in Cumberland county, Nova Scotia.

AMHERST, a settlement belonging to the British on the W. coast of Siam, at the entrance of Martaban Bay.

AMHERSTBURG, a town and fort of Upper Canada, on the east side of the river Detroit, at its entrance into Lake Erie. Long. 82. 56. W. lat. 42. 36. N.

AMIENS, a large and populous town of France, in the department of Somme. It is a place of great antiquity; being mentioned by Cæsar (by whom it is called Samaro-Briva) as a town that had made a vigorous resistance against the Romans, and where he convened a general assembly of the Gauls. The town is encompassed with a wall and other fortifications; and the ramparts are planted with trees, which form a delightful walk. The city has five gates. At the gate of Noyon there is a suburb, remarkable for the abbey of St. Achen. The cathedral is one of the largest and most magnificent churches in France. Three branches of the river Somme pass through this city, and afterwards unite. Amiens was taken by the Spaniards in 1597, but retaken by Henry IV., who built a citadel in it. A treaty of peace was concluded here, March 27, 1802, between Spain, Holland, France, and England. It has manufactures of linen and woollen cloth, which employ, in the city and adjacent country, 30,000 people. It is 20 miles S. E. of Abbeville, and 75 N. of Paris.

AMLWCH, a town of Wales, on the N. coast of Anglesey, with a harbour for small vessels. It is 15 miles N. W. of Beaumaris, and 266 N. W. of London. In 1768, when the Parys copper mine was opened, it did not contain above six houses. This mine yields a prodigious quantity of ore, the purest of which is exported to Swansea to be smelted.

AMMAN, a town of Syria, anciently the capital of the Ammonites, called Rabbah Ammon, and by the Greeks Philadelphia, and now the principal place of a district. It is 30 miles S. W. of Bosra, and 52 N. of Jerusalem.

AMOL, a town of Usbeck Tartary, in Bucharia, and a place of considerable trade. It is seated on the Amu, which falls into the sea of Aral, 60 miles W. of Bucharia. Long. 60. 40. E. lat. 39. 20. N.

AMOL, a town of Persia, in Mazanderan, with the remains of an ancient fortress and palace. It has manufactures of cotton, and in the neighbourhood are iron-mines and cannon-foundries. It stands in a plain at the foot of Mount Taurus, and on the borders of the Caspian Sea, 30 miles N. W. of Ferabad. Long. 52. 38. E. lat. 37. 30. A.

AMORGO, an island of the Archipelago, fertile in wine, oil, and corn. The best cultivated parts belong to a monastery. It is 30 miles in circumference, and 67 N. of Candia. Long. 26. 15. E. lat. 36. 20. N.

AMOUR, or AMUR, a river of Chinese Tartary. *See* SAGHALIEN.

AMOY, an island on the S. E. coast of China, 15 miles in circumference. The English had a factory here, but abandoned it on account of the impositions of the inhabitants. Its port, on the west side, is capable of receiving 1000 ships. Long. 118. 45. E. lat. 24. 20. N.

AMPLEPUIS, a town of France, in the department of Rhone, celebrated for its wines. It is 16 miles W. of Villefranche, and 26 N. W. of Lyons.

AMPTHILL, a town in Bedfordshire. Market on Thursday. It was the residence of Catherine, queen of Henry VIII., during the time that her unjust divorce was in agitation. It is situate between two hills, 8 miles S. of Bedford, and 45 N. W. of London.

AMPURIAS, a sea-port of Spain, in Catalonia, at the mouth of the Fluvia, 70 miles N. E. of Barcelona. Long. 3. 0. E. lat. 42. 9. N.

AMRAS, a castle or palace of Germany in Tyrol, at the foot of a mountain, 2 miles S. E. of Inspruck.

AMSTERDAM, the principal city of Holland Proper, situate on the south bank of an inlet of the Zuyder Zee. It was formerly an insignificant fishing town; became a place of some importance towards the close of the 14th century; in 1482 it was first fortified; and towards the close of the 16th, and commencement of the 17th centuries, increased greatly in population and consequence, and after the decline of Venice and Genoa as emporiums of commerce, when the intercourse with Asia by the Cape of Good Hope had become established, Amsterdam became one of the most considerable commercial cities in Europe. Although its external intercourse was greatly impeded during the French revolutionary war, subsequent to 1795, and greatly rivalled by Rotterdam and Antwerp since the peace of 1814, and somewhat decreased in population, Amsterdam still ranks amongst the largest and most respectable commercial cities in Europe. Few places have their public buildings so fine, numerous, and well kept. Here are many handsome churches, colleges, and hospitals for all religions and countries. The exchange is one of the principal ornaments of the city, and the harbour is one of the finest in Europe. The foundation of this town is laid upon piles, driven into a morass, and under the stadthouse alone are 13,659. The streets are broad and well paved, and most of them have canals, with rows of trees on each side; but there are no spacious public places, or squares. It surrendered to the king of Prussia, in Oct. 1787, when that prince invaded Holland, in favour of the stadtholder; and it received the French troops in Jan. 1795 without any resistance. The French, however were expelled in November. 1813, by the inhabitants, and the ancient government restored. The river Amstell divides the town into two parts, the Old, or Eastern, and the New, or Western. It is 70 miles N. W. of Cleves, and

80 N. by E. of Antwerp. Long. 4. 52. E. lat. 52. 22. N.

AMSTERDAM and ST. PAUL, two islands in the Indian Ocean, lying in the same longitude, at 40 miles distance. Their names are reversed by navigators, but most of them call the northern one St. Paul, and the southern Amsterdam. The former is high land, and upward of 4 miles long, and 2 miles broad. It has evident marks of volcanic eruption in every part, and is almost wholly covered with a deep fertile soil, but is destitute of trees. On the east side is a great crater, into which the sea has made a narrow and shallow entrance; its shelving sides are 700 feet in perpendicular height, in which, and in the causeway dividing it from the sea, are several hot springs of fresh water. Amsterdam, or the southern island, presents no very high land, or any rise in a conic form. It is covered with shrubs and low trees, but has no convenient landing-place. Long. 77. 48. E. lat. 37. 51. S.

AMSTERDAM, NEW, one of the Friendly Islands. *See* TONGATABOO.

AMU GIHON, AMI, or OXUS, a river of Independent Tartary, formed by numerous streams which issue from the mountains of Belur, on the confines of India and Persia, and, flowing W. by N. through Bucharia, enters the S. extremity of the lake Aral after a course of 1200 miles, part of which is through a desert.

AMWELL, a village in Hertfordshire, a mile S. of Ware, famous for originally giving rise to the New River, which supplies a great part of London with water.

ANACOPIA, the capital of the nation of the Abkahs, on the river Makai, near its entrance into the Black Sea. Long. 40. 30. E. lat. 43.20. N.

ANADIR, a r. of Siberia, which has its source out of a lake in the province of Tchukotski, and runs into Notchen Bay, near Behring's Straits.

ANA CAPRI. *See* CAPRI.

ANADOLI. *See* NATOLIA.

ANAH, a town of Asiatic Turkey, in Diarbeck, in a country producing abundance of corn and fruit. It stands on a river that flows into the Euphrates, 80 miles W. N. W. of Bagdad, and 240 S. S. E. of Diarbekir. Long. 42. 28. E. lat. 34. 6. N.

ANANTPOUR, a town of Hindostan, in Mysore, 100 miles N. E. of Chittledroog, and 120 N. of Bangalore.

ANAPA, a town in Circassia, on the Black Sea. It is now much reduced.

ANAQUITO, a district in the province of Quito, and kingdom of Peru, where Almagro and Pizarro (joint discoverers of Peru) engaged each other in battle, in 1546.

ANATTOM, an island, the most southern of the New Hebrides, in the Pacific Ocean. Long. 170. 9. E. lat. 20. 10. N.

ANBAR, a town of Asiatic Turkey, in Irac Arabi, seated on the Euphrates, 50 m. W. of Bagdad.

ANCARANI, a town of Italy, 5 miles N. of Ascoli, and 82 N. E. of Rome.

ANCASTER, a village in Lincolnshire, 15 miles S. of Lincoln. It gives the title of duke to the family of Bertie.

ANCENIS, a town of France, in the department of Lower Loire, seated on the Loire, 20 miles E. of Nantes.

ANCLAM, a fortified town of Hither Pomerania, on the river Peene, 20 miles S. E. of Gripswald.

ANCOBER, a territory of Guinea, on the Gold Coast, to the W. of Axim. It has a river of the same name flowing through it; and at its mouth is a town with a good harbour. Long. 1. 10. W. lat. 4. 50. N.

ANCONA, MARQUISATE OF, a maritime province of the states of the church, Italy, bounded on the E. by the Adriatic, and on the W. by the Appennines; it is very fruitful in corn, fruits, and silk.

ANCONA, a city and seaport of Italy, in the above province, and a bishop's see, with a citadel on a hill. The cathedral stands upon another hill, and the houses extend down the side of the eminence towards the Gulf of Venice. Clement XII. built a mole, to render the harbour safe; it is erected on the ruins of the ancient mole, raised by Trajan, and is above 2000 ft. in length. Near this stands the beautiful triumphal arch of Trajan. Here likewise Clement XII. erected a lazaretto, which advances a little way into the sea, in the form of a pentagon. Great numbers of Jews are settled in this city, where they have a synagogue; and they have the principal share of its commerce. Ancona was taken in 1796 by the French, who surrendered it to the Austrians in 1799. It is 116 miles N. by E. of Rome. Long. 13. 29. E. lat. 43. 38. N. Pop. about 20,000.

ANCOVE, a district of Madagascar, in the centre of the island. Pop. about 25,000. The soil is barren, and but little agriculture is carried on; but the slave trade was the principal employment. Ancove, or Tannane Arivou, the chief town of the district, is in lat. 20. 20. S. long. 46. 18. E.

ANCYRA, the capital of Galatia, near the river Halys, said to have been built by Midas, king of Phrygia, and so named from an anchor found there. *See* ANGOURA.

ANDAHUILAS, the chief town of a district of the same name, in the intendency of Guamanga, Peru, about 100 miles W. of Cusco.

ANDALUSIA, a province of Spain, which in its largest sense comprises the kingdoms of Granada, Seville, Cordova, Jaen, and the colony of Sierra Morena; bounded on the N. by Estremadura and La Mancha, E. by Murcia, S. by the Mediterranean, and W. by the Atlantic and Portugal. The Guadalquiver runs through its whole length; and it is the most fertile and trading country in Spain. Its aggregate superficies is 2281 French leagues, and pop. about 1,900,000. The French overran this province in 1810, but evacuated it in consequence of the battle of Salamanca, in 1812. The capital is Seville.

ANDALUSIA, NEW. *See* PARIA.

ANDAMAN ISLANDS, several islands on the E. side of the Bay of Bengal. The largest, called Great Andaman, is 120 miles long and 16 broad, indented by deep bays affording good harbours, and intersected by vast creeks, one of which passes quite through the island, and at high water is navigable for small vessels. The forests afford some precious trees, as ebony, and the nicobar bread-fruit ; and the edible bird's nests abound here. The only quadrupeds seem to be wild hogs, monkeys, and rats. The inhabitants are in a state of barbarism, and live chiefly on fish, fruits, and herbs ; they perfectly resemble negroes, and their canoes are of the rudest kind. In 1793, the English made a settlement on the N. end of Great Andaman, the largest island, which is called Port Cornwallis, and has a commodious harbour, to shelter ships during the N. E. monsoon. Long. 93. 0. E. lat. 13. 30. N.

ANDAYE, a fortified town of France, in the department of Lower Pyrenees, famous for its brandy. It is situate near the mouth of the Bidassoa, almost opposite Fontarabia, in Spain, 18 miles S. W. of Bayonne.

ANDELFINGEN, a town in Switzerland, canton of Zurich, on the Thur river, over which is a covered bridge.

ANDELY, a town of France, in the department of Eure, divided by a paved road into Great and Little Andely, a mile from each other. Great Andely is on the rivulet Gamons, and Little Andely on the Seine. The cloths manufactured here are in high esteem. It is 17 miles N. E. of Evreux, and 20 S. E. of Rouen.

ANDERAB, a town of Turkestan, in Usbek Tartary, or Himalaya. In its vicinity are rich quarries of lapis lazuli. It is seated on a branch of the Gihon Amu, and near a pass through the mountains of Hindoo-koosh, into the kingdom of Caubul, 240 miles E. S. E. of Balk. Long. 68. 58. E. lat. 36. 10. N.

ANDERO, ST. *See* SANTANDER.

ANDERNACH, a town in the grand duchy of the Lower Rhine, now forming part of the Prussian territory. Great quantities of timber are collected here, which are formed into vast rafts, and floated hence to Dordrecht, in Holland. It is seated on the Rhine, 20 miles N. W. of Coblentz.

ANDES, a chain of mountains running through the whole extent of both the S. and N. divisions of the western hemisphere, from the utmost extremity of the southern division, in S. lat. 54. to about the lat. of 18. S.; they continue, in an unbroken line, to run parallel with the shore of the Pacific Ocean, at a distance of 100 to 200 miles, with here and there parallel ridges further east, and at an altitude of 12,000 to 15,000 feet above the level of the sea; from about the 18th to the 15th degree of S. lat. the chain is somewhat broken, but further N. they assume a more grand and imposing form, diverging into parallel ridges, and rising near the equator to an altitude of 21,464 feet, and in several places issue forth volcanic eruptions with terrific violence. N. of the equator they diverge into four parallel and distinct ridges, running to the shores of the Caribbean Sea, and the outermost ridge skirting the coast of that sea to the Atlantic. Through the *chain* which unites the two grand divisions of America, or the western hemisphere, the mountains are considerably broken ; but at about the 15th degree of N. lat., through the territory of Mexico, they again assume their wonted grandeur, rising to a height of 17,720 feet, and again pouring forth volcanic matter, and proceed in an unbroken line at a somewhat greater distance from the sea than through the S. division, by the name of the Rocky Mountains, to the Icy Sea. in the 70th deg. N. lat. From the 40th deg. of lat. S. to the 30th N. the Andes abound with gold, silver, copper, and other metallic substances. For more minute details see AMERICA, and the several countries through which the Andes run.

ANDERSON, a co. of the state of Tennessee, pop. 5658. Clinton is the chief town, 150 miles E. by N. of Murfreesborough.

ANDLAU, a town of France, in the department of Lower Rhine, with a castle, situate on a mountain, 18 miles S. S. W. of Strasburg.

ANDOVER, borough, Hampshire, returning two members to parliament; market on Saturday; a manufacture of shalloons, and a considerable trade in malt. It is situate near the river Ande, 14 miles W. by N. of Winchester, and 63 W. by S. of London.

ANDOVER, a town of Massachusets, in Essex county. Here is an excellent academy called Philip's Academy; also manufactures of paper and gunpowder. It is situate on the Shawsheen, 20 miles W. S. W. of Newbury Port, and 22 N. N. W. of Boston. Also the name of several other towns in the U. S. of America.

ANDRAGIRY, or INDRAGIRI, the capital of a kingdom on the E. coast of the island of Sumatra. The chief produce is pepper. It is seated on a river commodious for trade, 200 miles N. by W. of Bencoolen. Long. 102. 0. E. lat. 0. 58. S.

ANDRARUM, a town of Sweden, in Gothland, with the greatest alum-work in the kingdom. It is ten miles S. of Christianstadt.

ANDREASBERG, a town of Lower Saxony, in the duchy of Brunswick, with good silver mines, 28 miles N. E. of Gottingen.

ANDREW, ST., a town of Germany, in Carinthia, and a bishop's see ; seated on the river Lavant, 20 miles E. N. E. of Clagenfurt.

ANDREW, ST., a seaport town of New Brunswick, at the entrance of Passamaquoddy River.

ANDREW, ST., a city of Scotland, in Fifeshire, once the metropolis of the Pictish kingdom, and the see of an archbishop, and still the seat of the oldest Scotch university. The university was founded by Bishop Wardlaw, in 1411, and consists of two colleges. The cathedral, the chapel of St. Regulus, the church of St. Salvador, and the priory, have been noble structures. The castle was the scene of the cruelty and punishment of Cardinal Beton : the window is still shown from which he beheld the martyrdom of George Wishart, who was burnt on the spot beneath; and in this castle he himself was assassinated in 1546. It is a place of little trade, and the harbour is in bad condition. It is seated at the bottom of a bay, on the level top of a small hill, 30 miles N. N. E. of Edinburgh. Long. 2. 50. W. lat. 56. 18. N.

ANDRO, an island in the Archipelago, 24 miles long and 8 broad. It is one of the ancient Cyclades. It has fertile plains, which are well watered; and it wants only a good harbour. The inhabitants are of the Greek church, and have a bishop and several monasteries. The principal riches of this island consist in silks, and the fields produce oranges, citrons, mulberries, pomegranates, and figs. The capital is of the same name; and about two miles from it are to be seen the ruins of a strong wall, with the fragments of many columns, chapiters, bases, broken statues, and several inscriptions, some of which mention the senate and people of Andros, and the priests of Bacchus; from which it is probable that this was the site of the ancient city. Long. 25. 2. E. lat. 38. 0. N.

ANDROS ISLES, a group of islands separated by intricate channels, forming part of the Bahamas in the W. Indies. They are low and thinly populated.

ANDROSCOGGIN, a river rising from Umbagog Lake, on the W. side of the state of Maine, runs into New Hampshire, and re-enters Maine, falling into the Kennebeck, about 18 miles above its confluence with the sea.

ANDUSE, a town of France, dep. Gard; manufactures, hats, stockings, and woollen fabrics. Pop. 5000.

ANDUXAR, or ANDUJAR, a town of Spain, in Andalusia, with a castle and some beautiful churches and convents. The environs abound in wheat, wine, oil, honey, and fruit. It is seated on the Guadalquiver, and on the great post road from Madrid, distant 51½ leagues, by way of Cordova to Seville and Cadiz.

ANEGADA, the most northern of the English Virgin Islands. Long. 64. 7. W. lat. 18. 40. N. It is low, and exceedingly dangerous to ships coming from the E.

ANEMUR, or ANAMOUR, CAPE, the southern extremity of Caramania, opposite the Isle of Cyprus; on the promontory are the ruins of the ancient city Anemuriam. N. lat. 36. 2. E. long. 32. 52. N.

ANGARA, prov. of Peru, capital Guancabelica. Great quantities of cattle are reared in this district; also wheat and other grains, and the sugar-cane, are cultivated.

ANGELICA, the chief tn. of Allegany county, state of New York, 285 miles W. of Albany. Pop. in 1820, 1510.

ANGELO, ST., a town of Italy, 14 miles S. W. of Urbino.

ANGELO, ST., a town of Naples, 6 miles N. N. W. of Conza.

ANGELOS, a city of Mexico. *See* PUEBLA DE LOS ANGELOS.

ANGERBURG, a town of Prussia, with a castle, seated on the N. side of a lake, to which it gives name, 70 miles S. E. of Konigsberg. Long 22. 15. E. lat. 54. 8. N.

ANGERMANIA, or ANGERMANLAND, a province of Sweden, in Nordland, 150 miles long, and from 25 to 80 broad, the widest part being to the E. on the Gulf of Bothnia. It is mountainous and woody, and in it are considerable iron-works. The chief town is Hernosand.

ANGERMUNDE, a town of Brandenburg, in the Ucker Mark, on the lake Munde, 48 miles N. N. E. of Berlin.

ANGERS, a large city of France, in the department of Maine and Loire, situated near the confluence of the Sarte, the Loire, and the Maine, which divides the city into two equal parts, between which there is a communication by two large bridges. Angers contains 36,000 inhabitants. The castle is situated in the centre of the city, on a rock overhanging the river. The cathedral is a venerable and elegant structure: the principal gate is surrounded with three steeples. Here lies interred with her ancestors the renowned Margaret, daughter of René, King of Sicily, and Queen of Henry VI. of England, who expired after many intrepid but ineffectual efforts to replace her husband on the throne, in 1482, at the castle of Dampierre. The university of Angers was founded in 1398, and the academy of belles lettres in 1685. It has a considerable manufacture of handkerchiefs and canvas; and the produce of the slate quarries, at the extremity of the suburb of Bressigny, forms likewise an important article of commerce. The walls with which king John of England surrounded it in 1214, remain nearly entire, and are of very great circumference. It is 50 miles E. N. E. of Nantes, and 175 S. W. of Paris. Long. 0. 33. W. lat. 47. 28. N.

ANGLEN, or ANGELEN, a small country of Denmark, in the duchy of Sleswick. Many authors suppose that from the people of this country the English originated; being called in to assist the Britons against the invaders from Norway, they in process of time became masters of the country, and gave it the name of England.

ANGLESEY, an island and co. at the N. W. extremity of Wales. It is separated from Carnarvonshire by a long and narrow channel called Menai, over which is a noble suspension bridge, consisting of one principal opening of 560 ft. and seven stone arches. The roadway is elevated 100 ft. above high water. The length of the suspended part is 579 ft. 5 in. That part of the island which borders this strait is finely wooded, recalling to the mind its ancient state, when it was the celebrated seat of the Druids, whose terrific religious rites were performed in the gloom of the thickest woods. Rude mounds and heaps of stone, said to be druidical remains, are still to be seen; but a little way within, the whole appears a naked tract, without trees or hedges, watered by numerous rills, fertile in grass and corn, and abounding in cattle. This island produces vast quantities of copper and sulphur, and in the N. W. part is a quarry of green marble intermixed with asbestos. It returns one member to parliament. Beaumaris and Holyhead are the chief towns; the latter of which is the principal resort of travellers to the Irish capital.

ANGOLA, the whole extent of territory on the western coast of S. Africa, from near the equator to the 13th or 14th deg. of S. lat., comprehending Loango, Congo, Angola Proper, and

Benguela, is commonly called Angola; but Angola Proper, or the kingdom of Angola, lies S. of the Congo, between the lat. of 7. to 9. S. All this part of the coast of S. Africa is well watered, and exceedingly capable of yielding abundance, not only of subsisting, but of luxuriant productions; but it is divided into numerous petty states and sovereignties, the chiefs of which live in constant collision with each other; since the restriction of the traffic in slaves to the S. of the equator, rapine and cruelty have reigned with uncontrolled sway over the whole of this fine and extensive district; and since the period of 1815, 1816, more than 100,000 of the natives have been annually transported as slaves, by the French, Spaniards, and Portuguese, to Martinique, Guadaloupe, Cuba, and the Brazils. St. Paulo de Loango, in lat. about 8. 30. S., is the principal place on the coast of Angola Proper, at which the Brazilians more particularly carry on their operations of slave-traffic. Abstracted from the unsocializing and debasing influence which the slave-traffic is so strongly calculated to excite and promote, the inhabitants of this part of S. Africa are much addicted to habits of idleness, idolatry, and polygamy.

ANGORA, or ANGOURI, the ancient Ancyra, a city of Asiatic Turkey, in Natolia, and a Greek archbishop's see, remarkable for its remains of antiquity; such as inscriptions, pillars, ruins of temples, &c. The castle has a triple enclosure, and the walls are of white marble and stone, resembling porphyry. The inhabitants are estimated at 100,000. Here are bred the finest goats in the world; the hair, being almost like silk, is worked into fine stuffs. It stands in a lofty situation, 212 miles S. E. of Constantinople. Long. 32. 50. E. lat. 40. 4. N.

ANGORA, or ANGARA, a river of Siberia, issuing from Lake Baikal. It joins the Tungouska, after passing Irkutsk.

ANGOULEME, a town of France, capital of the department of Charente, and the see of a bishop. It is seated on a mountain surrounded by rocks. The river Charente runs at the foot of it; and there are some paper manufactures in its environs. It is 50 miles W. S. W. of Limoges. Long. 0. 9. E. lat. 45. 39. N.

ANGOUMAIS, a late prov. of France, bounded on the N. by Poitou, E. by Limosin and Marche, S. by Perricord, and W. by Saintonge. It is now distributed among the departments of Charente, Dordogne, and Deux Sevres.

ANGRA, the capital of Terceira, one of the Azores. It is a bishop's see, and the residence of the governor of the Azores. The town is well built, and populous; and here are royal magazines for all sorts of naval stores, a cathedral, five churches, and several monastic houses. It stands on a bay, between two mountains, on the S. side of the island. Long. 27. 12. W. lat. 38. 39. N.

ANGROGNA, a commune of Piedmont, on a river of the same name, 7 miles W. of Pignerol.

ANGUILLA, or SNAKE ISLAND, the most northerly of the English Leeward islands in the West Indies. It is 30 miles long and 3 broad, winding somewhat in the manner of a snake, and is 60 miles N. W. of St. Christopher. Long. 62. 35. W. lat. 18. 15. N. One of the Bahama islands is also called Anguilla.

ANGUSSHIRE, or FORFARSHIRE, a maritime county on the N. E. coast of Scotland; bounded on the S. by the Frith of Tay, W. by the county of Perth, and N. by Kincardineshire. The chief towns are Dundee, Arbroath, Forfar, Montrose, and Brechin. It is prettily diversified with hill, dale, and water. In the vicinity of Forfar are several lakes, or lochs, as they are here termed. It sends one member to parliament.

ANHALT, a principality of Germany, in Upper Saxony, 42 miles long and 10 broad; bounded on the S. by Mansfield, W. by Halberstadt, E. by the duchy of Saxony, and N. by Magdeburg. It abounds in corn, and is watered by the Salde and Mulda. Its ancient castle is gone to decay. Zerbst is the capital.

ANHOLT, an island of Denmark, in the Categat, surrounded by sand-banks so dangerous to seamen, that on it is a light-house. The English took possession of it in 1810, and made it a place of rendezvous for the North Sea squadron. Long. 11. 35. E. lat. 56. 38. N.

ANIANE, a town of France, in the department of Herault, 13 miles W. N. W. of Montpelier. It has an extensive manufacture of mineral alkali.

ANJENGA, a town of Hindostan, in Travancore, which has a trade in pepper and calicoes. It stands at the mouth of a river, 46 miles W. N. W. of Travancore. Long. 76. 40. E. lat. 8. 40. N.

ANIMALY, a town of Hindostan, in the province of Coimbetore, with a fort. It has a trade in drugs, honey, and wax, collected in the hills to the south, and is seated on the Alima, 21 miles S. of Coimbetore.

ANIWA, BAY and CAPE, at the S. extremity of the peninsula of Saghalien, on the E. coast of Asia. The Japanese have a settlement here. Lat. 46. 41. N. long. 142. 32. E.

ANJOU, a late province of France, bounded on the N. by Maine, W. by Bretagne, S. by Poitou, and E. by Touraine. It formerly belonged to the sovereigns of England. It now forms the department of Mayenne, Loire, &c.

ANKOBER, a tn. of Abyssinia, capital of Shoa and Efat provinces, 300 miles S. E. of Gondar.

ANN, ST., a town of New Brunswick, situate on the river St. John, nearly opposite to Frederic-town, and 80 miles above the city of St. John. Also the name of the chief town of the province of Parana, in Paraguay, and of a lake in Upper Canada, to the N. of Lake Superior.

ANN-ARUNDEL, a county of Maryland, on the western shore of Chesapeake Bay. Pop. 29,532. Annapolis, 40 miles E. by N. of Washington, is the chief town, and seat of the legislative government of the state of Maryland.

ANN, CAPE, a point of land which forms the N. side of Massachusets Bay. A lighthouse on the point is in N. lat. 42. 40. W. long. 70. 38.

ANN, FORT, a town in Washington county,

state of New York, between the North River and Lake Champlain. Pop. 3559.

Anna, a town of Asiatic Turkey, prov. of Bagdad, pleasantly seated on the left bank of the Euphrates: the vicinity is fertile in grain and cotton. It was plundered and burnt by the Wahabees in 1827, since which the population has been about 3000.

Annaberg, St., a town of Upper Saxony, in Misnia, noted for silver mines and the manufacture of lace, 17 miles S. of Chemnitz.

Annagh, an island on the W. coast of Ireland, 5 miles in circumference, between the isle of Achil and the coast of the county of Mayo. Long. 9. 39. W. lat. 53. 58. N. Also the name of three parishes in different parts of Ireland; 1st. in the co. of Kerry, pop. 2089; 2nd. in Cavan, pop. 10,488; 3rd. in Mayo, pop. 5749.

Annagh is also a prefix to several other parishes in Ireland, such as Annagh-*clone*, *down*, *duff*, &c.

Annamaboe, one of the principal commercial places on the Gold Coast of North Africa, during the slave-trade; in N. lat. 5. 9. W. long. 1. 41.

Annamooka, one of the Friendly Islands, discovered by Tasman, in 1643, and visited by Captain Cook in 1774 and 1777. It is well cultivated in many places, consisting of plantations of yams and plantains, enclosed with neat fences of reed. The bread-fruit and cocoa-nut trees are interspersed with little order, but chiefly near the habitations of the natives; and the other parts of the island, especially towards the sea, are covered with trees and bushes. It is situate about 187. E. long. 20. S. lat.

Annan, a borough of Scotland, in Dumfriesshire, seated on the river Annan, three miles from its mouth, which forms a good harbour for vessels of 250 tons burden. Here was a fine castle, built by one of the Bruces, the ruins of which still remain. Much corn is exported hence; and there is a manufacture for carding and spinning. It is 16 miles E. S. E. of Dumfries, and 80 S. of Edinburgh. Long. 3. 8. W. lat. 55. 2. N.

Annapolis, the capital of Ann-Arundel county, and seat of the legislative government of the state of Maryland. The state-house, a noble building, stands in the centre of the city, from which point the streets diverge in every direction. Here also is St. John's College, which, with Washington College at Chester, constitute one university, named the University of Maryland. Annapolis is situate on the E. side of Chesapeake Bay, at the mouth of the Severn, 40 miles E. by N. of Washington, and 35 S. of Baltimore. Long. 76. 43. W. lat. 39. 0. N.

Annapolis, a seaport of Nova Scotia, on the E. side of the Bay of Fundy. It has one of the finest harbours in the world; but the entrance is through a difficult strait, called the Gut of Annapolis. The town stands on the S. side of the harbour, at the mouth of a river of its name, 86 miles W. by N. of Halifax. Long. 64. 55. W. lat. 44. 50. N.

Annecy, a town of Savoy, seated on a lake of its name, whence issues the canal of Thioux, which runs through the town, and then enters the river Sier. It was lately the see of a bishop, who also assumed the title of bishop and prince of Geneva. Annecy is the largest town in Savoy next to Chambery, and is 16 miles S. of Geneva. Long. 6. 5. E. lat. 45. 53. N.

Annobon, an island near the coast of Guinea, so called because it was discovered by the Portuguese on New Year's-day. It is well stocked with cattle, and abounds with palm-trees and fruit. Long. 5. 10. E. lat. 1. 50. S.

Annonay, a town of France, in the department of Ardeche, with manufacture of very fine paper; seated at the confluence of the Cances and Deumes, 12 miles S. W. of Vienne.

Annover, village, New Castile, Spain, on the Tagus, with manufactures of saltpetre, 16 miles E. N. E. of Toledo.

Anson, a county of N. Carolina, bordering on S. Carolina, and bounded on the N. E. by the Yadkin River. Pop. 15,077. Wadesborough, 142 miles S. W. by W. of Raleigh, is the chief town.

Anson's, Lord, Isle, in the Pacific Ocean, Lat. 5. 0. S. long. 154. 34. E. The shores are bold, and covered with cocoa-nut plantations.

Anspach, or Anolzbach, a principality of Germany, in the S. part of the circle of Franconia. It has iron mines, and several medicinal springs; and the soil produces considerable quantities of corn, and feeds great numbers of cattle.

Anspach, a city and capital of the above principality, with a castle, a palace, and an excellent academy. It has many handsome buildings; and the principal manufacture is lace. It is seated on the Retzat, 24 miles W. S. W. of Nuremberg. Long. 10. 28. E. lat. 49. 18. N.

Anstruther, East and West, two boroughs of Scotland, on the S. E. coast of Fifeshire. They adjoin each other; and East Anstruther, which is much the largest, is little more than a fishing village, 9 miles S. S. E. of St. Andrew. They contribute in sending one member to parliament.

Antab, or Aintab, a town at the N. E. extremity of Syria, situate on two hills, and the valley that lies between them is watered by the Sejour. It is three miles in circumference, with a strong old castle on a rock, and had formerly a considerable manufacture of printed calicoes. Many modals of the Syrian kings have been found here, and some also of the kings of Cappadocia. It is 50 miles E. of Alexandretta, and 60 N. by E. of Aleppo. Long. 37. 35. E. lat. 36. 35. N.

Antalow, a town in Abyssinia, prov. Tigré, 25 leagues S. S. E. of Axum. It is a considerable place seated on the side of a mountain.

Antarctic Regions, around the S. Pole. The probability of a southern continent seems to be revived from the recent discoveries in this part of the world. It was believed to exist till the voyage of Cook in 1774, when he reached the lat. of 71. 10. S., and his further progress was impeded by vast mountains and fields of ice, but without any discovery of land, and the belief of this continent was then abandoned. In Feb. 1831, land was discovered by Captain Biscoe, in lat. 66. 0. and long. 45. 0. E., which he named Enderby's Land; and afterwards, in Feb. 1832, he discovered Adelaide Island, in lat. 67. 1. S. and long. 71. 48. W. lying off Graham's, or Gherritz Land, to the southward of the South Shetland group; in 1838, land adjoining to Graham's Land was discovered by Captain D'Urville, and named Land of Louis Philippe. In 1839, Sabrina Land was discovered, in lat. 65. 0. S. long. 117. 0. E., and the Balleny Islands, in 66. 0. S. lat. and 164. 0. E. long.; they are volcanic. In 1840 (Jan. 18), Captain D'Urville discovered the Land of Adelie, between lat. 66. and 67. S. long. 140. 0. E. In 1841, Captains Ross and Crosier discovered the Land of Victoria, in long. 168. E., along which they sailed as high as lat. 78½., the nearest approach to the S. pole which has yet been made. In lat. 77. 50. is Mount Erebus, an active volcano 12,000 ft. high; and to the S. of which a chain of lofty mountains extend. Their progress to the eastward was impeded by vast fields and cliffs of ice. These explorations render it probable that there is a continued line of coast for a great distance in the Antarctic Ocean; but which is very difficult of access, from the vast accumulation of ice.

ANTEQUERA, a town of Spain, in Granada, divided into the Upper and the Lower. The Upper is seated on a hill, and has a castle: the Lower stands in a fertile plain, and is watered by many brooks. Here are large quantities of natural salt quarries, of excellent stone, and a spring famous for the cure of the gravel. It is 26 miles N. N. W. of Malaga. Long. 4. 30. W. lat. 37. 1. N.

ANTEQUERA, a tn. of Mexico. *See* GUAXACA.

ANTHONY, ST., FALLS OF, on the Mississippi River, in N. lat. 45. W. long. 93., being more than 2000 miles above the entrance of the river into the Gulf of Mexico. There is a fort in the Missouri territory, on the point of land formed by the St. Peter's River, which river falls into the Mississippi just below the falls of St. Anthony.

ANTIBES, a tn. of France, in the department of Var, with a strong castle, and harbour for small vessels. Its territory produces excellent fruit; and it is seated on the Mediterranean, 11 miles S. S. W. of Nice. Long. 7. 7. E. lat. 43. 35. N.

ANTICOSTI, an island at the mouth of the river St. Lawrence, 90 miles long and 20 broad. It is full of rocks, covered with wood, and has no harbour; but excellent cod is found on the shores.

ANTIGUA, one of the English Leeward Islands, in the West Indies, about 20 miles in length and breadth, and 60 E. by S. of St. Christopher. It is destitute of water, and the inhabitants are obliged to save the rain-water in cisterns. The chief produce is sugar, of which it annually produces about 10,000 hogsheads. It was taken by the French in 1782, but restored in 1783. The capital is St. John.

ANTILLES, the name which the French give to the Caribbee, or West India islands, which see.

ANTIOCH, or ANTAKIA, town of Syria, of which it was formerly the capital. This ancient city, in which the disciples of Christ were first called Christians, and yet the see of a Greek patriarch, is now almost come to nothing; but the magnificent ruins of it still remain. It is seated on the river Orontes, now called Aaszi, 15 miles from the Mediterranean, and 50 N.W. of Aleppo. Long. 36. 40. E. lat. 36. 10. N.

ANTIOCHETTA, a town of Asiatic Turkey, in Caramania, and a bishop's see, seated on the shore of the Levant, opposite Cyprus, 88 miles S. of Konieh. Long. 32. 26. E. lat. 36. 30. N.

ANTIOGO, ST., an island on the S. W. coast of Sardinia, 14 miles long and 3 broad. In 1793 it was taken by the French, but evacuated soon after.

ANTIOQUIA, or ST. FE DE ANTIOQUIA, a town in the new department of Cauca, Columbia. It is seated on the banks of the river Cauca, about 200 miles N. N. W. of St. Fe de Bogota.

ANTIPAROS (the ancient OLEAROS), an island of the Archipelago, 2 miles W. of Paros. It is only a rock, 16 miles in circuit; yet in some parts is well cultivated, and produces as much barley as serves a small village. It has a remarkable grotto, about 80 yards high and 100 broad, which contains a vast variety of figures, of a white transparent crystalline substance, resembling vegetables, marble pillars, and a superb marble pyramid. Long. 25. 44. E. lat. 37. 8. N.

ANTI-PAXO, one of the Ionian Islands on the W. coast of Greece, south of Paxo.

ANTISANA, a peak of the Andes, in the department of Quito, which is volcanic, 19,150 ft. above the level of the sea. There is a village of the same name, a few leagues E. of the city of Quito, at a height of 13,500 ft., being the highest inhabited place on the globe.

ANTI-TAURUS, a considerable chain of mountains in Asia Minor. It joins the Taurus Mountains in Karamania.

ANTIVARI, a town in European Turkey, 24 miles W. of Scutari. Here is a castle, built on a steep rock.

ANTOINE, ST., a town of France, in the department of Isere, 5 miles N.E. of St. Marcellan.

ANTONIO, ST., the most northern of the Cape Verde islands, 15 miles from St. Vincent. It is full of high mountains, whence proceed streams of excellent water, which render the land fruitful. The principal town is seated among the mountains. Long. 25. 0. W. lat. 17. 0. N.

ANTONIO DE CAPO, ST., a town of Brazil, in the province of Pernambuco, situate near Cape St. Augustine, 30 miles S. S. W. of Olinda.

There are near 100 other towns and streams in different parts of South America and Mexico, dedicated to the tutelar saint of the Portuguese and Spaniards, *Anthony*, or *San Antonio*, who does not appear to have done much for them, as they are mostly insignificant.

ANTRIM, a maritime county on the N.E. coast

of Ireland. It has two great natural curiosities; Lough Neagh, a large lake, the area of which exceeds 100,000 acres, the waters being of a petrifying quality; and the Giant's Causeway, consisting of lofty pillars of basaltes, all of angular shapes, from three sides to eight, and extending three miles along the north shore. The linen manufacture is carried on very extensively in this county, and since about 1823 the cotton manufacture has been making considerable progress. The principal towns are Belfast, Lisburne, and Carrickfergus, each of which (in addition to the two for the county) returns one member to the parliament of the United Kingdom. Carrickfergus is the assize town. For extent of superficies, population, &c., *see Gorton's Topographical Dictionary.*

ANTRIM, a city and parish of the above county, about 19 miles N. W. of Belfast. The town is situate on the bank of a small stream, which runs through Lough Neagh, at a short distance on the N. E.

ANTWERP, a celebrated city of Brabant, and, after the decline of Venice and Genoa, it became one of the most considerable commercial depôts of Europe. It is situate on the east bank of the Scheldt, in N. lat. 51. 13. and 4. 24. E. long. The era of its greatest importance was about the commencement of the 17th century, when its population amounted to about 200,000, but the devastating policy of Austria and Spain involved it in the bigoted and ruthless contentions of that period; further, by the extent of the commercial transactions, which its localities tended to make the centre, it greatly rivalled the transactions of Rotterdam and Amsterdam, and as such excited the grovelling jealousy of the Hollanders; the navigation of the Scheldt was therefore obstructed in 1648, by the treaty of Westphalia between Spain and Holland, and Antwerp in consequence progressively declined in population and importance, until the period of the French revolution. When the French overran this part of Europe in 1794, they proclaimed the free navigation of the Scheldt, and after the renewal of the war subsequent to the peace, or rather the respite of Amiens in 1802, Antwerp claimed the especial notice of Napoleon, who constructed a basin to hold about 20 sail of the line, and a noble quay, along the east bank of the river, and made it his principal naval arsenal for the northern part of his empire. It was not, however, till subsequent to the general peace of Europe in 1814, when the Neitherlands were ceded to Holland, and Antwerp declared a free port for the *transit* of merchandise, that it began to resume its former wanted activity and importance. Since that period, Brussels, and a vast extent of country westward of the Rhine, draw their supplies of foreign produce from Antwerp, which is, in consequence, progressively, though slowly, increasing in population and interest. It has, however, but few articles of export, either within itself, or of transit. The principal architectural ornament of Antwerp is the cathedral, the tower of which is surmounted, at a height of 400 ft., with a lantern of open lattice-work of exquisitely beautiful workmanship; the interior is ill-proportioned and void of effect, and its decorations of art have been overrated. There are four other churches and one or two monastic establishments deserving attention. The exchange, so long celebrated, is very commodious, forming nearly a square of great amplitude, with an interior piazza; but as an architectural edifice it is unworthy of notice. The fortifications on the land side are very complete; and, since 1816, extensive fortifications have been constructed opposite to the town on the west side of the Scheldt, calculated to afford protection in the event of any attempt at assault by water. The citadel was retained for the king of Holland by Gen. Chassé, on the separation of Belgium from Holland, but was taken by the French, as the allies of Belgium. Pop. about 65,000. 22 miles N. of Brussels, and 65 S. of Amsterdam.

ANZERMA, a town of New Granada, in the province of Popayan, where there are mines of gold. It is seated on the river Cauca, 140 miles N. N. E. of Popayan. Long. 75. 25. W. lat. 4. 58. N.

ANZI, a town of Naples, 13 miles S. E. of Potenza. Pop. 3090.

ANZIKO, a kingdom of Guinea, lying E. of Gabon and N. of Congou, but is little known. The king is styled the Micoco, whence the country is sometimes so called. The capital is Monsol.

AOSTA, or AOUST, duchy of, a province of Piedmont, bounded on the W. and N. by the Alps, or rather on the N. by the Valais, for the mountains run from N. to S. into Aoust, which may be considered altogether as a mountainous district. Pop. about 65,000. The principal city of the same name, which is a bishop's see, is situate about the centre of the province, between two streams of the Baltea River, which falls into the Po, and on the great high road from the pass of St. Bernard to Turin. It contains several monuments of the Romans. Pop. about 5500.

APALACHIAN. *See* ALLEGANY MOUNTAINS.

APALACHICOLA, a river of North America, formed by the junction of the Chatahouche and Flint, at an old Indian fort of the same name on the south confines of Georgia, and thence flows between West and East Florida into Apalaches Bay, in the Gulf of Mexico, E. of Cape Blaize.

APANORMIA, a town of the island of Santorin, seated on the N. W. coast, 7 miles N.N.W. of Scauro, at the entrance of the Grecian Archipelago.

APEE, one of the New Hebrides, near Malicollo, in the Pacific Ocean. Long. 168. 27. E. lat. 16. 46. S.

APENRADE. *See* ABENRADE.

APHIOM, or AFIUM-KARA-HISSAR, a town of Asiatic Turkey, in Natolia, built round a high rock, on the top of which is a fortress. It is three miles in circumference, and has a considerable trade. The chief manufacture is carpets; and the country around produces much opium, called aphiom by the Turks. It stands on the Mindra, 150 miles E. of Smyrna. Long. 31. 10. E. lat. 38. 35. N.

APOLDA, a tn. of Upper Saxony in Thuringia, 8 miles N. of Jena, and 40 S. W. of Leipsic.

APPENNINES, a chain of mountains, in Europe, which begins near Oneglia, on the Gulf of Genoa, passes round that gulf at no great distance from the sea, then proceeds E. to the centre of Italy, and afterward divides that country in a mediate S. E. direction to the extremities of the kingdom of Naples. Hence proceed all the rivers which water Italy. The Appennines are at first a branch of the Alps, but, in general, they may rather be regarded as hills than as mountains.

APPENZEL, a canton in the N. E. part of Switzerland, bordering on Tyrol. It is divided into twelve communities; six, called the interior, are Roman Catholics, about 16,000 in number, subsisting chiefly by agriculture; and six, exterior, bordering on the canton of St. Gallen, are Protestants, about 40,000 in number, a great portion of which are employed by the manufacturers of the city of St. Gallen.

APPENZEL, the chief town of the above canton, is situate on the bank of the river Sitter on the interior side, and containing about 3000 inhab.

APPIN, a town in Scotland, Argyleshire. The parish is of great extent.

APPLEBY, the county-town of Westmoreland. Market on Saturday. It was a Roman station, and has been twice destroyed by the Scots, and it now consists of only one broad street of mean houses. At the upper end, or S. part, is the castle, and at the lower end is the church. The town is almost encircled by the Eden. It is 20 miles N. N. E. of Kendal, and 270 N. N. W. of London.

APPLECROSS, a parish extending for about 20 miles along the western coast of Ross-shire, Scotland. The population subsists mainly by the herring fishery. There is a town of the same name, in which the population are principally concentrated.

APPLEDORE, a vill. in the parish of Northam, Devonshire, situate at the mouth of the Towridge, in Barnstaple Bay, 3 miles N. by E. of Bideford. Here the Danes landed, under Hubba, in the time of Alfred. It is now resorted to for bathing.

APPOLLONIA, a district extending about 100 miles on the S. W. coast of North Africa. Cape Appollonia is in 5 N. lat. and 3. 57. W. long.

APPOLOBAMBA, a town in La Paz, one of the united provinces of Paraguay, on the border of Peru.

APSHERON, or ABSHARON, a cape in the Caspian Sea, into which it projects from Baku, and contains a prodigious quantity of naphtha.

APT, a town in France, in the department of Mouths of the Rhone. It has a trade in prunes, coarse serges, and wax chandlery; and contains many fine Roman antiquities. It is seated on the Calaron, 20 miles N. of Aix.

APURE, a river of Columbia, rising from various sources on the E. side of the eastern range of the Andes, falling into the Oroonoko.

APURIMAC, a river of Peru, which rises 10 miles N. of Arequipa, and flows N. about 430 miles; receiving the Paucartambo, and Vilcomayo from the E., and the Jauja or Mantaro from the W. It then takes the name of Ucayale, and, continuing its course 470 miles further, enters the river Amazon, in long. 72. 46. W.

AQUI, a town of Piedmont, in the duchy of Montferrat, with a citadel, and baths of mineral water; seated on the north bank of the Bormida, 15 miles S. of Alexandria.

AQUILA, a fine large city of the kingdom of Naples, anciently called Avia, and Avella, the capital of Abruzzo, seated on a hill, E. of the Appennines, on the banks of the river Alterno, or Pescara, near its source. It has an ancient castle, and is a bishop's see. An earthquake was so violent here, in February, 1703, that 24,000 people perished, and great numbers were wounded. It is situate 35 miles W. from the Adriatic, and 92 E. of Rome. Long. 14. 20. E. lat. 42. 50. N.

AQUILEIA, an ancient and large city of the Carni, or Veneti, in Italy, seated near the coast at the head of the Gulf of Venice. A Roman colony was settled in it, between the first and second Macedonian wars, to be a bulwark against the Huns and Goths. In 425, it was beseiged by Attila, with an innumerable host of barbarians. Three months were consumed without effect in the siege; till the want of provisions, and the clamour of his army, compelled Attila to issue his orders, that the troops should strike their tents the next morning, and begin their retreat. But as he rode round the wall, pensive, angry, and disappointed, he observed a stork preparing to leave her nest in one of the towers, and to fly, with her infant family, towards the country; this he interpreted as an omen that those towers were devoted to impending ruin and solitude. The siege was renewed and prosecuted with fresh vigour; a large breach was made in the part of the wall from whence the stork had taken her fight; the Huns mounted to the assault with irresistible fury; and the succeeding generation could scarcely discover the ruins of Aquileia.

AQUINO, a tn. of Naples, in Terra di Lavoro, ruined by the emperor Conrade. It is the birthplace of Juvenal, and seated near the Carigliano, on the great high road from Rome to Naples, 20 miles S. by E. of Sora.

ARABAT, a town and fort of the Crimea, and province of Taurida, on the borders of the Sea of Asoph, 20 miles N. by E. of Caffa.

ARABIA, a country of Asia, extending from the 12th to the 32nd deg. of N. lat. and from the 33rd to the 58th of W. long., being about 1480 miles in length, and 1200 in breadth; bounded on the W. by the Red Sea, and the Isthmus of Suez, N. E. by the Euphrates, which divides it from Diarbekar; E. by the Gulfs of Persia and Ormuz; and S. by the Indian Ocean. It is divided into three parts—Arabia Petrea, Deserta, and Felix, so named by Europeans, from their supposed qualities of soil and climate. Arabia Petrea, much the smallest of the three, lies to the S. of Syria along the E. coast of the Red Sea. The north part is mountainous, and in general stony, sandy, and barren; but some parts yield sufficient nourishment for cattle, whose milk, and camels' flesh, is the chief food of its few in-inhabitants. Arabia Deserta lies S. of Syria, and E. of Arabia Petrea and the Red Sea. It is for the most part desert, being intersected by barren mountains, and many of the plains are nothing but great sands and heaths; but there are some plains and valleys that feed great flocks of sheep and goats; there are also great numbers of ostriches, and a fine breed of camels in several places, and the horses are the noblest of the species. Arabia Felix, so called on account of its fertility with regard to the rest, lies to the S. of Arabia Deserta, between the Red Sea and the Indian Ocean. It is by far the most considerable part; and, though the centre is occupied by very dry deserts, there are many rich provinces on the coasts, producing a variety of fruits, honey, wax, cinnamon, cassia, manna, spikenard, frankincense, myrrh, and coffee, of which latter great quantities are exported from Mocha. The Arabs are of a middle stature, and brown complexion, and have always a grave and melancholy air. They derive their subsistence from their flocks, from hunting, and from what they acquire by plunder of the caravans which pass from Aleppo to Bassora, and from Bassora to Mecca. They acknowledge no sovereign, but the emirs of their tribes, who are their natural princes, and to whom they pay obedience. They have also scheiks, or chiefs, of an advanced age, whom they often consult, and whose advice they follow. The dress of the Arabs consists of a white robe, bound round with a broad leather girdle, fastened by a strong buckle, or large clasp. Their drawers are made of linen, and descend to the lower part of the leg. They wear a kind of red cap on the head; and sometimes they wear slippers, after the manner of the Turks, but are generally in half boots, that they may be ready to get on horseback. Winter and summer they wear a large cloak, striped black and white, made of the hair of goats or some other animal. Their emirs dress in the same manner, except that their cloaks are for the most part all black. The Arabs in the deserts live in tents, and remove from place to place, partly for the sake of pasture, and partly to lie in wait for the caravans. The famous Mahomet was a native of this country; and his followers, soon after his death, conquered a great part of Asia, Africa, and Europe, establishing their religion wherever they came. The interior of this vast territory is very little known, but it seems nearly destitute of water, as but very few rivers are found around its coasts for near 2500 miles. Medina, Mecca, and Mocha, all on the coast of the Red Sea, are the chief towns.

Arabian Gulf. *See* Red Sea.

Aracan, Reccan, or Arracan, a maritime and fertile country of Asia, on the E. coast of the Bay of Bengal, bounded on the E. by Birmah. The rainy season continues from April to October, and the rest of the year is called summer. The inhabitants are idolaters. The women are tolerably fair, but the longest ears are reckoned the most beautiful, and in these they wear many rings. They are a dastardly race of people, and have only courage to attack defenceless merchants and boatmen. There are such numbers of elephants, buffaloes, and tigers, that but few places are inhabited, on account of the ravages made by these animals. The chief productions of commerce are salt, elephants' teeth, bees' wax, and rice; but its trade was never very considerable. Aracan was long an independent nation, governed by a king; but it was subdued by the Birmans in 1783; and was taken from them by the British in 1825.

Aracan, the capital of the country of the same name, with an extensive fort. It is situate at the head of an inlet of the sea, which forms one of the finest and most capacious harbours for shipping in the world. The river Aracan runs through the city, and waters the streets by means of several arms or canals, into which it is divided. It was taken by the Birmans in 1783. It is 260 miles S. S. E. of Islamabad, and 230 W. S. W. of Ava. Long. 93. 10. E. lat. 20. 38. N.

Arad, an interior county of Upper Hungary. Population about 155,000. There are two towns of the same name; the Old, which is the capital of the county, on the N., and the New town on the S. side of the Marosch river. The old town is a great mart for cattle, and is about 24 miles N. N. E. of Tamewer.

Arafat, or Gebel Orphat, a mountain of Arabia, about 1500 feet in height, 15 miles S. S. E. of Mecca. Its name implies the mountain of knowledge, and as such is an object of adoration with the devotees of Mahomet; in 1807, upward of 80,000 pilgrims, including 45,000 mounted Wahabees, were assembled about it.

Araguaya, a noble river of South America, which rises in the lat. of about 19. S. near to the Parana, which runs from N. to S., whilst the Araguaya runs through the heart of Brazil from S. to N., to the lat. of about 7. S., where it is joined by the Tocantins, and about 5 deg. further it diverges into two branches, one falling into the Amazon, and the other forming a separate channel into the Atlantic, called Para, in lat of 0. 20. S. and 48. 20. W. long.

Aral, a lake of Independent Tartary, 120 miles E. of the Caspian Sea. It is 200 miles in length, and in some places 70 in breadth, intersected by the lines of 45. N. lat. and 60. W. long. The water is salt, and there are many small saline lakes in the vicinity, but it has no visible communication with the sea.

Aramon, a town of France, department of Gard, on the Rhone; it has several manufactures.

Aranjuez, a town of Spain, in New Castile, with broad streets intersecting each other at right angles. The great square is surrounded by porticoes, and has a fountain that supplies the town with water. Here are three churches, and a theatre for bull-fights; but the glory of Aranjuez is the royal palace and gardens, situate on an island formed by the Tagus, the

Xarama, and a canal. This palace justly ranks among the finest and most agreeable residences in Europe; it was in it, the supreme junta of government of the kingdom, on the declaration in favour of Ferdinand VII., were installed, and held their first meeting, September 25th, 1808. Aranjuez is seated on the Tajo, 20 miles S. of Madrid.

ARARAT, a mountain of Armenia, situated near the chain of Taurus, in lat. 39. 42. N. and long. 44. 30. E. It is an insulated mountain whose summit forms two distinct cones, the highest of which is 17,260 feet above the level of the sea, the other about 4000 feet lower. The principal summit is a circular plain about 200 feet in diameter, and encrusted with perpetual ice. The ascent is so difficult that it was not accomplished till 1829, after the third attempt, by Dr. Parrot. Tradition asserts that the ark rested on the summit after the flood; and the Armenians believe that the remains exist to this day.

ARASSI, a maritime town of the territory of Genoa, 5 miles S. W. of Albenga.

ARAU, a town of Switzerland, capital of the department of Lower Argo, canton of Berne, with manufactures of cotton, printed linen, and cutlery. A treaty between the Protestant and Catholic cantons was concluded here in 1712. It is seated on the river Aar, 27 miles W. of Zurich.

ARAUCA, a district extending from the 42nd to the 37th deg. of S. lat., on the shore of the Pacific Ocean; bounded on the E. by the Andes, and is considered as belonging to Chili, but it is inhabited almost exclusively by natives, who have not only successfully resisted every attempt of the Spaniards to become masters of the country, but frequently made incursions into their territory. The district contains both gold and silver, is watered by several streams, is very fertile, and the climate is delightful. The Spaniards constructed a fort about 40 miles S. of Concepcion, (named after the district,) as a defence against the incursions of the Araucans.

ARAXES, or ARAS, a river of Asia, which rises in Georgia, flows S. E. across Armenia, and joins the Kur, near its entrance into the Caspian Sea. It is a very rapid river, and is supposed to be the Gihon mentioned by Moses.

ARBE, an island 30 miles in circumference, on the coast of Dalmatia, from which it is 5 miles distant. The soil is rich, but the inhabitants are indolent. It has a town of the same name. Long. 14. 55. E. lat. 45. 5. N.

ARBERG, a town of Switzerland, in the canton of Berne, on an island formed by two branches of the Aar. It is 10 miles W. by N. of Berne.

ARBEL, a town of Asiatic Turkey, in Curdistan, ancient Erbila, near which Alexander defeated Darius. Here are the remains of an ancient castle; and in the vicinity are naphtha pits. It is seated in an extensive plain, 36 miles N. of Altunkupri, and 50 E. of Mosul.

ARBOIS, a town of France, in the department of Jura, famous for its white wines. It is 22 miles S. W. of Besançon.

ARBOGA, a town of Sweden, Westmanland, seated on the Ulvison, by which river, and a canal, it has a communication with the lakes Hielmar and Maeler. It is 25 miles E. N. E. of Orebro.

ARBON, a town of Switzerland, situate on a point of land jetting into the lake of Constance, 12 miles S. E. of Constance.

ARBROATH. *See* ABERBROTHOCK.

ARBURG, a town of Switzerland, in the canton of Berne, with a citadel on a rock, seated on the Aar, opposite Olten, 12 miles E. of Soleure.

ARCADIA, a town of European Turkey, on the W. coast of the Morea, near the gulf of its name, 22 miles N. of Navarin. Long. 21. 42. E. lat. 37. 24. N.

ARCHANGEL, a large province of Russia, bounded on the N. by the Arctic Ocean. It is divided into eight circles, viz.: Archangel, Chencourisk, Cholmegar, Kem, Kola, Meson, Onega, and Senega. It is a very dreary district, especially the eastern part; it supplies some fir timber and deals, and contains many wild animals, which are slaughtered for their fat; and tallow and bristles form great articles of export.

ARCHANGEL, or ST. MICHAEL, the chief town of the above province, is situate on the E. bank of the Dwina River, a short distance above its entrance into a bay of the White Sea, in N. lat. 64. 34. E. long. 38. 59. It was for many years the principal seaport of Russia, and was first resorted to by the English in 1553; and, although greatly declined in importance since the building of St. Petersburg, it still exports considerable quantities of tallow, deals, and some bristles; but as it is only attained by the dreary coast of Norway, and the North Cape, in lat. 71. 10., it is accessible only a few months in the year, say July, August, and September, during which short period it is resorted to by 60 or 70 sail of vessels annually, principally English. It was nearly destroyed by fire in 1793, but has since been rebuilt with neatness, principally of wood, the severity of the winter being counteracted by stoves. Pop. about 7000, who have about a dozen churches, one Lutheran, one Calvinist, and the others Greek. Archangel is about 400 miles N. E. of St. Petersburg.

ARCHIPELAGO, is a term applied to a cluster or group of islands; hence the Grecian, Eastern, Northern, &c. &c.; but the most celebrated group is the Grecian at the head of the Mediterranean Sea, having Romania on the N., Natolia on the E., the island of Candia on the S., Macedonia, Livadia, and the Morea on the W. It is partly in Europe, and partly in Asia, containing the islands of Rhodes, Negropont, Lemnos, Tenedos, Scyros, Mitylene, Scio, Samos, Patmos, Paros, Antiparos, Cerigo, Santorini, Andros, Tina, Naxia, Milo, Delos, Argentiera, and many others.

ARCHIPELAGO, NORTHERN, a part of the Pacific Ocean, having the peninsula of Kamschatka on the W., and the coast of America on the E. It includes a number of islands, among which are four principal groups. The first, called Sasignan, contains five islands; the second, called Khoa, includes eight islands; and both these groups together are styled the Aleutian Islands. The third group is called the Andreoffski Ostrova, and comprises 16 islands. The fourth group is the Lissie Ostrova, or the Fox Islands, 16 in number. They all belong to Russia, and are valuable chiefly for the skins of animals found there, particularly the sea-otter. *See* Fox Islands.

Arcis-sur-Aube, a town of France, in the department of Aube, seated on the river Aube. 15 miles N. of Troyes.

Arco, a town and castle of Germany, in Tyrol, taken by the French in 1703, and abandoned soon after. It stands on the Sarca, near the head of the lake Garda, and 15 miles W. S. W. of Trent.

Arcos, a town of Spain, in Andalusia, seated on a craggy rock, on the river Guadaleto, 28 miles N. E. of Cadiz. It is the residence of the vicar general of the metropolitan church of Seville. There are several other towns of the same name in Spain and Portugal.

Arcot, a city of Hindostan, capital of the Carnatic, which became subject to the English East India Company in 1801. The citadel is large, and esteemed a place of some strength; but the nabob often resides at Madras. In the vicinity are several celebrated temples, visited by numerous pilgrims. Arcot has a manufacture of coarse cotton cloth. It is seated on the S. bank of the Paliar, 66 miles W. by S. of Madras, and 180 E. by N. of Seringapatam. Long. 79. 24. E. lat. 12. 51. N.

Arctic Highlands, a country on the N. E. of Baffin's Bay, discovered by Captain John Ross, in 1818. Inhabited by Esquimaux, who supposed themselves the only inhabitants of the world.

Ardagh, the name of a barony in the county of Longford, Ireland, containing the parishes and the towns of Longford and Edgworthstown; and which, united with Kilmore, gives name to a bishopric; but there is neither cathedral nor episcopal residence in Ardagh. There are many other parishes in different parts of Ireland, beginning with *Ard.*

Ardebil, a town of Persia, in Azerbijan, the residence and burial-place of many kings, particularly of Sheik Sessi, the founder of the Persian sect. Pilgrims resort to this place from all parts of Persia; and caravans are frequently passing to and from Constantinople and Smyrna. It is 35 miles E. S. E. of Tauris. Long. 47. 10. E. lat. 38. 20. N.

Ardeche, a department of France, including the late territory of Vivarez. It takes its name from a river, which flows into the Rhone, at the south extremity of the department. Privas is the capital. Pop. about 285,000.

Ardee, a town of Ireland, in the county of Louth. Here is a large mount, apparently artificial: some suppose it to have been a burial-place of the Irish kings; others that it was a place where the people assembled to deliberate on public affairs. It is 14 miles N. W. of Drogheda.

Ardennes, a department of France, containing part of the late province of Champagne. It is so named from a famous forest, lying on the river Meuse. The principal town is Sedan. Pop. 266,985.

Ardfert, a town of Ireland, in the county of Kerry, and a bishop's see united with Aghadoe to Limerick. It was formerly the capital of the county, but is now a poor place, with extensive ruins. It is seated on a river, which runs into Tralee Bay, seven miles N. N. W. of Tralee.

Ardglass, a seaport town of Ireland, county Down; the nearest part of Ireland to the Isle of Man, and may be considered the best watering place in the north of Ireland.

Ardnaree, a town of Ireland, county Sligo, on the river Moy. There are valuable salmon fisheries in the neighbourhood.

Ardmore, a town of Ireland, in the county of Waterford, on a cape and bay of its name, 10 miles S. S. W. of Dungarvon.

Ardra, a small kingdom of Guinea, on the Slave coast, at the bottom of the Gulf of St. Thomas. The country is fertile in maize, palm wine, plants, and fruits, which last all the year; and produces a great deal of salt. It has a town of the same name. Long. 3. 5. E. lat. 6. 0. N.

Ardres, a town of France, in the department of Pas de Calais. On an open plain between the town and Guisnes was the celebrated interview between Francis I. of France, and Henry VIII. of England, in 1520. It is 10 miles S. S. E. of Calais.

Ardvert, a seaport town of France, department of Lower Charente. Pop. 3000. Chief trade in fresh and cured fish.

Areca, an island in the Gulf of Persia, three miles S. W. of Ormus. The Dutch attempted to establish a factory, and built a fort here, but were expelled by the Persians.

Arekea, a seaport of Abyssinia.

Aremberg, a duchy of Germany, near Cologne.

Arensborg, the capital of a county of the same name, in the duchy of Westphalia. It is seated on a hill, by the river Roer, 22 miles S. S. E. of Ham, and 63 N. E. of Cologne. Long. 8. 10. E. lat. 51. 23. N.

Arensburg, a seaport of Russia, in the government of Riga, capital of the isle of Osel, and a bishop's see. Long. 25. 40. E. lat. 58. 15. N.

Arensharde, a district in Denmark, in the duchy of Sleswick, containing the greatest part of the famous rampart built by king Gotric, in the beginning of the 9th century, as a defence against the irruptions of the Saxons. It extends across the country, about 9 miles in length.

Arequipa, an episcopal town of Peru, founded by Pizarro, in 1539. Near it is a volcano. It has been four times laid in ruins by earthquakes. It stands in a fertile country, a few miles S. of a small lake, which is the source of the Apurimac branch of the Amazon River; 240 miles S. of Cusco, and 460 S. E. of Lima. Long. 72. 30. W. lat. 16. 40. S.

Arezzo, a town of Tuscany, in the Florentino. Guy Aretin, a Benedictine monk, inventor of the musical notes, ut, re, &c. was born here; also the celebrated Francis Petrarch, and Mecænas. It stands on a hill, at the conflux of the Chianno and Arno, 15 miles W. of Citta di Castello.

Argau. *See* Aargau.

Argences, a town of France, in the department of Calvados, on the river Menace, 10 miles E. of Caen.

Argentan, a town of France, in the department of Orne, which has a considerable trade in lace. It is seated on an eminence, in the middle of a fertile plain, on the banks of the Orne, 12 miles N. W. of Seez, and 110 W. of Paris.

Argenteuil, a town of France, on the river Seine, 5 miles N. W. of Paris. It has a fine vineyard, and in the environs are quarries of the plaster of Paris.

Argentiera, a barren island of the Archipelago, so called from the silver mines in it. There is but one village, and it has no water but what is kept in cisterns. Long. 23. 10. E. lat. 36. 50. N.

Argentiere, a town of France, department Ardeche. Pop. 10,000. Some exhausted lead mines are here, but silk is now the principal manufacture.

Argenton, a town of France, in the department of Indre, divided into two parts by the river Creuse. It is 37 miles S. W. of Bourges.

Argos, a seaport of European Turkey, in the Morea, 25 miles S. of Corinth. Long. 23. 5. E. lat. 37. 30. N.

Argostoli, a town of the island of Cefalonia, with a fortress, and the best harbour in the island. It is 8 miles W. S. W. of Cefalonia.

Argueil, a town of France, in the department of Lower Seine, 18 miles N. E. of Rouen.

Arguin, an island and fort on the coast of Zahara, 30 miles S. E. of Cape Blanco. It was taken by the Dutch from the Portuguese, in 1637; afterwards the French took it from the Dutch. Long. 17. 5. W. lat. 20. 30. N.

Argun, a river of Asia. *See* Saghalien.

Argunskoi, a town of Siberia, on the frontiers of Chinese Tartary. There are mines of silver and lead near it, and a pearl fishery in the river Argun, on the W. bank of which the town is situate. It is 70 miles S. E. of Nertchinsk. Long. 118. E. lat. 52. 30. N.

Argyleshire, a county of Scotland, bounded on the N. by Inverness-shire, E. by the counties of Perth and Dumbarton, and S. and W. by the Atlantic Ocean, by which it is broken into islands and peninsulas. It is 110 miles long from the Mull of Cantyre to its N. E. extremity; its breadth is very unequal—about 40 miles where greatest. To the N. W. is a peninsula, nearly detached from the rest of the county; it contains the districts of Ardnamurchan, Morven, Sunart, and Ardgowar. The peninsulas of Cantyre and Cowal are likewise very large. The chief islands attached to this county are Mull, Islay, Jura, Tirey, and Col. The soil of Argyleshire, in the high grounds, though little fitted for cultivation, affords excellent pasture. Some parts are covered with heath, and others exhibit rugged and bare rocks. The sides of the hills and lakes are interspersed with woods; and there are rich mines of copper, iron, and lead, which have become peculiarly valuable since the opening of the Crinan canal. The chief town is Inverary.

Ariano, a town of Naples. Pop. 10,000.

Arica, a seaport at the S. extremity of Peru. It is but badly fortified, and has been much injured by earthquakes. Here the treasure brought from Potosi is shipped; and there are many farms employed in the cultivation of Guinea pepper, in which it has a great trade. It is 550 miles S. E. of Lima. Long. 70. 25. W. lat. 18. 27. S.

Arienzo, a town of Naples, in Terra di Lavoro, 14 miles N. E. of Naples.

Arindal, a town of Norway, in the government of Bergen, noted for the productive iron mines in its vicinity. It is seated near the sea, 10 miles N. N. E. of Christiansand.

Arisch, or El Arisch, a town and fort of Egypt, on a gulf of the Mediterranean, to which it gives name. The French became masters of it in 1798; but it was retaken by the Turks and English at the end of the year. In 1800, the Turks and French signed a convention here, by which the troops of the latter were to evacuate Egypt; but the English admiral refused to ratify the capitulation. Arisch stands on the confines of Arabia and Palestine, 36 miles S. W. of Gaza, and 120 N. E. of Suez, in N. lat. 31. 8. E. long. 34. 3.

Arispe, the chief town of the extensive district of Sonora, Mexico. Arispe is situate at the foot of the Cordilleras, near the source of the Hia, or Yaqui River, in the lat. of about 31. N. and 109. W. long.

Arkansas, a territory of the U. S. of North America, formed in March 1809, by the S. extremity of the Missouri territory. The Arkansas lies between the latitudes of 33. and 36. 50. N. and 90. to 100. of W. long., being being about 500 m. in mean length from E. to W., and 242 in mean breadth from N. to S.—equal to about 121,000 square m., or 77,440,000 statute acres. It is bounded on the S. by the Red River, and on the W. conventionally by the line of the 100th deg. of W. long. which separates it on those two sides from the unsettled parts of Mexico; on the N. by the Missouri territory and state; and on the east by the Mississippi River. It was originally divided into seven counties, and in 1820 contained a population of only 14,273, of whom 1617 were slaves. The present population is 97,574, including 19,935 slaves. The Arkansas River, which has its source in about the 40th deg. of N. lat., near that of the Rio del Norte, enters the territory between the long. of 97. and 98., and after being joined by the four forks of the

Canadian, about the centre of the territory, falls into the Mississippi, in lat. 34. N.; the White and Big Black River, composed of about a dozen branches, rising in the state of Missouri, falls into the state of Mississippi about 20 miles above the Arkansas. Buffaloes, deer, elks, bears, wolves, panthers, &c., are very numerous in this territory, and S. of the Arkansas River is a race of fleet wild horses, which are hunted and caught in a way similar to those of Paraguay. About 10,000 of the Osage, Pawnee, and Cherokee tribes of Indians still occupy different parts of the territory. South of the Arkansas River, and about 100 miles W. from its mouth, and near the source of the Washita, which falls into the Red River, is a hot spring, the waters of which are peculiarly efficacious in chronic diseases, and paralytic affections; and, although in the bosom of a wilderness, it has frequently 200 or 300 visitors at a time, and is held so sacred by the Indians, that whatever differences may exist among them, they subside when here, and the spot is consecrated to peace. The banks of the numerous rivers are composed of a rich alluvial soil, which at no distant day are doubtless destined to become fields of activity and abundance. There is a town called Arkansas on the N. bank of the river, about 65 miles above its mouth; but the capital and seat of government of the territory is Arkopolis, situate on the S. bank of the river, 180 miles above Arkansas.

Arkeeko, a town of Abyssinia, situated on the shore of the Red Sea; it is built of clay and grass, with a few houses of stone.

Arklow, a barony containing 13 parishes, and the towns of Arklow, and part of Wicklow, in the county of Wicklow, Ireland. The town of Arklow is situate on the shore of St. George's Channel, about 13 m. S. of Wicklow.

Arles, an ancient city of France, in the department of Mouths of the Rhone, lately an archiepiscopal see. It was the chief city of ancient Gaul during the reign of Constantine, and Boson made it the capital of the kingdom of Burgundy. The country around produces good wine, vermilion, manna, oil, and fruits. There are a great number of antiquities, of which the amphitheatre and obelisk are the most remarkable. It is seated on the Rhone, 20 miles S. E. of Nismes. Long. 5. 37. E. lat. 43. 40. N.

Armagh, an interior county in the N. E. part of Ireland, 32 miles long, and 19 broad; bounded on the E. by Down, W. by Tyrone and Monaghan, N. by Lough Neagh, and S. by Louth. It contains 20 parishes, and sends three members to parliament, two for the county, and one for the city of Armagh. The soil is reckoned the richest in Ireland; but a tract called the Fewes is hilly and barren, and there are also some considerable bogs. Some good marble is found in this county; and the linen manufacture flourishes in all its branches. It has no river of consequence but the Blackwater, which separates it from Tyrone. The chief lakes are Carlough and Lough Clay.

Armagh, a populous parish and city of Ireland, the capital of the county of its name, and the see of an archbishop, who is primate of all Ireland. It has one of the best linen markets in Ulster, and many bleaching grounds in its vicinity. It is seated on the river Kalin, 45 miles S. E. of Londonderry, and 62 N. by W. of Dublin. Long. 7. 6. W. lat. 54. 20. N.

Armagnac, a late province of France, in Guienne, 55 miles long and 40 broad. It is fertile in corn and wine, and has a trade in brandy and wool. This province, with Gascony, now forms the department of Gers.

Armenia, a country of Asiatic Turkey, bordering on the S. E. extremity of the Black Sea, and extending eastward into Persia; it lies between the 38th and 45th deg. of E. long., and under the 39th and 40th of N. lat. The Euphrates, which has its source at the S. E. extremity of the country, runs parallel with its S. boundary; it is watered by several other rivers falling into the Black Sea, and the Karsi, which rises in the centre of the country, runs eastward, falls into the Caspian. It is a mountainous country (Ararat rising to the height of 17,260 ft.) and abounds in minerals, whilst the valleys yield abundance of corn and fruit. The inhab. are much addicted to commerce, and have a high reputation for probity; they are the chief merchants for the eastern commerce of Turkey, as the Greeks are for the western. The Armenians form a distinct sect of Christians, under a patriarch and an archbishop. Erzerum, or Arz Roum, in N lat. 40. and 40. 50. E. long. is the capital. Of the civil, judicial, or military institutions, or extent of population of Armenia, but very little is known to Europeans; the Persians claim authority over the eastern parts, and the Kurds interfere from the south.

Armentiers, a town of France, in the department of Nord, seated on the Lis, 8 miles W. N. W. of Lisle.

Armiers, a town of France, in the department of Nord, seated on the Sambre, 20 miles S. of Mons

Armyro, a town of European Turkey, in Thessaly, on the Gulf of Velo, 30 miles S. E. of Larissa. Long. 23. 22. E. lat. 39. 30. N.

Armstrong, an interior and remote county in the western part of Pennsylvania. Pop. 28,365. Kittaning, 214 miles W. by N. of Harrisburg, is the chief town. The Alleghany river enters the county at the N. W. extremity, runs in an angle to the centre, and leaves it at the S. W. extremity. Kittaning is situate on the east bank, near the centre of the county.

Armuyden, a town of Holland, in the island of Walcheren, now inconsiderable, the sea having stopped up the harbour. The salt-works are its chief resource. It is 3 miles E. of Middleburg.

Arnay le Duc, a town of France, in the department of Cote d'Or, seated in a valley near the river Arroux, 25 miles N. W. of Baune.

Arneburg, a town of Brandenburg, in the Old Mark, with a ruined castle, on a hill on the river Elbe, 3 miles from Werben.

Arnedo, a seaport of Peru, with a good harbour in the Pacific Ocean, 25 miles N. of Callao. Long. 76. 53. W. lat. 11. 40. S.

ARNHEIM, a strong town of Holland, in Gelderland, capital of the quarter or county of its name. It was formerly the residence of the dukes of Gelderland, and is seated on the Rhine, 8 miles N. of Nimeguen. Long. 5. 54. E. lat. 52. 2. N.

ARNHEIM Bay, on the N. W. side of the great Gulf of Carpentaria.

ARNO, a celebrated river of Tuscany, which rises in the Appennines, and, passing by Florence and Pisa, enters the Gulf of Genoa a little below the latter town.

ARNSHEIM, the name of two towns in the palatinate of the Lower Rhine, one near Worms, and the other about 10 miles east of New Baumberg.

ARNSTADT, a town of Upper Saxony, in the principality of Gotha, with a castle, a palace, and three churches; seated on the Gera, 11 miles S. of Erfurt.

ARNSTEIN, a town of Franconia, in the principality of Wurtzburg, with a castle, seated on the Weren, 9 miles S. W. of Schweinfurt, and about the same distance E. from Carlstadt.

AROLSEN, a town of Germany, in the electorate of Hesse, county of Waldech, near the river Aar, 29 miles S. S. E. of Paderborn.

ARONA, a town of Italy, in the Milanese, with a ruined castle, on the lake Maggiore, 30 miles N. W. of Milan.

ARPINO, a town of Naples, in Terra di Lavoro, 8 miles N. of Aquino.

ARQUA, a town of Italy, in the Paduan, remarkable for the tomb of Petrarch. It is 10 miles S. of Padua.

ARQUATA, a town of the territory of Genoa, seated on the Scrivia, 25 miles N. of Genoa.

ARQUES, a town of France, in the department of Lower Seine, with an ancient castle. Here Henry IV. gained a complete victory over the Duke of Mayenne, general of the league, in 1589. It stands on a river of its name, 4 miles S. E. of Dieppe.

ARRAGON, a province of the kingdom of Spain. Arragon was formerly an independent kingdom, and comprehended Arragon Proper, Catalonia, Valencia, and the Balearic Isles of Majorca, Minorca, Ivica, Cabrera, and Formentera. The kingdom of Arragon Proper is an interior district, extending S. from New Castile, in the lat. of 40. N. in a N. E. direction to the Pyrenees, bounded on the N. W. by Old Castile and Navarre; and on the E. by the N. end of Valencia, and Catalonia; its superficies is about 1230 sq. French leagues, and its population about 660,000. The river Ebro enters the territory from the N. W., and runs through the middle of it in a S. E. direction. Saragossa, seated on the banks of the Ebro, is the chief and only place of importance in the whole territory, nor is it remarkable for any natural productions; whilst the domination of the priestcraft, which pervades all Spain, operates as a barrier to all social enterprise and improvement.

ARRAH, a town of Hindostan, in Bahar 33 miles W. by S. of Patna.

ARRAN, an island of Scotland, in the Frith of Clyde, to the S. of the Isle of Bute. It is of an oval form, 20 miles long and 12 broad, and constitutes the greatest part of the county of Bute. Ridges of rugged mountains extend across the island, and Goatfell is near 3000 ft. in height. The southern parts present low and cultivated grounds. The climate is heathful, and invalids resort hither to drink the whey of goat's milk. Robert Bruce took refuge in this island, during the time of his greatest distress. Among the rocks are found iron-ore, spar, and a great variety of beautiful pebbles. On the coast are many wonderful caverns, which often afford shelter to smugglers. It is divided into two parishes, Kilbride and Kilmorey. Total pop. 6541. The principal place is Lamlash.

ARRAS, a fortified city of France, capital of the department of Pas de Calais, and an episcopal see, and one of the most ancient towns of France; it was the seat of the Atrebates in the time of Cæsar. It is divided into two towns; one named the city, which is the most ancient; and the other the town, which is modern. The great square is full of fine buildings, surrounded with piazzas. It was the birth-place of Robespierre, and is seated on the Scarpe, 22 miles W. N. W. of Cambray. Long. 2. 46. E. lat. 50. 17. N. Pop. about 19,000.

ARRIEGE, a department of France, containing the late provinces of Couserans and Foix. It is so named from a river, which rises in the Pyrenees, and, passing by Foix and Pamiers, enters the Garonne near Toulouse. Gold dust is found among its sands. Foix is the capital. Pop. about 225,000.

ARROE, or AAROE, and ÆROE, two islands of Denmark, the first about the middle of the Little Belt, and the other at its entrance into the Baltic. There are a cluster of Islands also called Arroe, just within the Red Sea, opposite to Mocha.

ARROUCHES, a town of Portugal, province of Alentejo, 95 miles E. from Lisbon.

ARROO, five islands in the Indian Ocean, to the S. and W. of New Guinea, extending from 5. 30. to 7. 0. S. lat. with narrow channels between them. The chief product is sago. During the dry or western monsoon, numerous flocks of the birds of paradise, from New Guinea, reside in these islands, where great numbers are killed, dried, and exported to Banda. The Arroo isles are considered as belonging to the Dutch.

ARSAMAS, a town of Russia, situate near the source of the Techa, a branch of the Oka river, in the province of Nishnei, or Lower Novogorod. It is about 100 miles E. of Moscow, and has a variety of manufactures. Pop. about 6000.

ARSOUF, a town of the coast of Syria, in Palestine, with a fortress, 10 miles N. of Jaffa.

ARTA, a sea-port of European Turkey, in Albania, and a Greek archbishop's see. It has a considerable trade in tobacco and skins, and is seated on the Arta, 70 miles N. N. W. of Lepanto. Long. 21. 30. E. lat. 39. 28. N.

Arta, Gulf of, on the W. coast of Greece; and which is the boundary of the kingdom, as the Gulf of Volo is on the E. coast.

Artaki, a town of Asiatic Turkey, in Natolia, on the S. coast of the Sea of Marmora, 76 miles S. W. of Constantinople. Long. 27. 40. E. lat. 39. 30. N.

Artakui, a town of European Turkey, in Romania, 48 miles N. W. of Gallipoli.

Artern, a town of Upper Saxony, in the county of Mansfield, circle of Thuringia, on the river Unstrutt, 29 miles N. N. E. of Erfurt.

Artois, a late province of France, bounded on the N. and E. by Flanders, and S. and W. by Hainault, Cambresis, and Picardy. It is now included in the department of Pas de Calais.

Aruba, an island 15 miles in circumference, in the West Indies; one of the Leeward Islands, and belonging to Holland. Long. 70. 5. W. lat. 12. 10. N.

Arundel, a borough in Sussex, returning one member. Market on Wed. and Sat. It is seated on the side of a hill, on the river Arun, about 5 miles from the sea, and has a venerable Gothic church, formerly collegiate. Its castle, the ancient seat of the dukes of Norfolk, stands on the hill, and is of great extent; a vast sum was expended upon it by Charles, the 12th duke. The possession of this castle confers an earldom on the proprietor. The river is navigable for barges, and great quantities of timber are sent hence for the dock-yards. It is 11 miles E. of Chichester, and 56 S. S. W. of London.

Arva, a county at the northern extremity of Lower Hungary, intersected by the Carpathian mountains; it contains a pop. of about 75,000, subsisting chiefly by agriculture, more particularly flax for domestic manufacture, and some for trade. There is a town which gives name to the county, situate on a stream which falls into the Wag river.

Arve, a rapid river of Savoy, which rises in Faucigny, and, watering Salenche, Cluse, and Bonneville, joins the Rhone below Geneva.

Arwangen, a town and castle of Switzerland, in the canton of Berne, on the river Aar, 12 miles E. of Soleure.

Arzew, a sea-port town of Algier, about 15 miles W. of Oran. It appears to be the ancient Arsenaria, there being many relics of antiquity in the neighbourhood.

Arzignano, a town of Italy, in the kingdom of Lombardy, 11 miles W. S. W. of Vicenza. Pop. 3305.

Arzilla, a sea-port in the kingdom of Fez, about 30 miles S. of Cape Spartel, and 50 S. S. W. of Tangier. It was formerly a Roman colony, and a place of considerable importance, but at present does not contain more than 1000 inhabitants.

Arzingan, a town of Armenia, on the W. bank of a branch of the Euphrates, 45 miles S. W. of Arz Roum.

Asab, or Assab, a town of Abyssinia, in Dancali, on a bay in the Straits of Babelmandel, 36 miles S. E. of Bailur.

Asangaro, a town and district of Peru, W of the Andes, N. of the lake Chuiento. It is very thinly peopled.

Asaph, St., a city of Wales, and a bishop's see, in Flintshire, on the river Elway, where it unites with the Clwyd. It is a poor place, of note only for its cathedral, but has a market on Saturday. It is 25 miles W. of Chester, and 208 N. W. of London, on the line of road to Holyhead.

Asben, an interior country of North Africa, of which Agadas is the capital: it is bounded on the E. by Bornou, and N. and W. by the deserts of Zaara and Tuarick.

Ascalon, or Askelon, a town on the coast of Palestine, distinguished in Jewish history as one of the chief cities of the Philistines. It is now an insignificant place; about 30 miles S. W. of Jerusalem, and 10 N. of Gaza.

Ascension, a barren island, in the Atlantic Ocean, 600 miles N. W. of St. Helena. It has a safe harbour, at which the East India ships often touch, to procure turtles, which are here plentiful and large. Long. 13. 50. W. lat. 7. 57. S.

Asch, or Ausch, a town of Bohemia, in the circle of Leutmeritz, situate on the banks of a small river which falls into the Elbe, about 20 miles above the town of Leutmeritz.

Aschach, a considerable town of Upper Austria, in the quarter of Hausruck, on the S. bank of the Danube.

Aschaffenburg, a town of Germany, lately in the territory of Mentz, but now the capital of a principality of the same name, in the circle of the Lower Rhine, insulated in that of Franconia. Here is a place in which George II. of England took up his quarters the night before the battle of Dettingen, in 1748. It was taken by the French in 1796 and 1800. It is situate near the conflux of the Aschaff with the Maine, on the E. side of the latter river, 20 miles E. S. E. of Frankfort, and 40 W. N. W. of Wurtzburgh. Long. 9. 5. E. lat. 50. 0. N.

Aschersleben, a considerable town on the W. bank of the Saal, in the principality of Anhault, circle of Upper Saxony. Pop. 8730.

Ascoli, a town of Italy, in the marquisate of Ancona, with two citadels; seated on a mountain, by the River Tronto, 80 miles N. E. of Rome. Long. 13. 29. E. lat. 42. 44. N.

Ascoli di Satriano, a town of Naples, in Capitanata, seated on a mountain, 70 miles E. of Naples. Long. 15. 50. E. lat. 41. 8. N.

Ascorca, a town in the island of Majorca, with a church containing a celebrated image of the Virgin, much resorted to by pilgrims.

Ashantee, an interior territory of North Africa, extending from the meridional line to the 5th or 6th degree of W. long.; bounded by the Gold Coast. The Ashantees have for a long period been the most powerful of all the negro tribes of Western Africa, not only in their contests with their neighbours, but they have frequently defied the scientific and destructive means of European warfare. During the period of the uncontrolled sway of the slave trade, previous to the commencement of the present century, the Ashantees, though little known upon the coast, were the main instruments in the interior, by which that debasing traffic was carried on, being constantly at war with their neighbours, for the obtaining of prisoners to send to the coast as slaves; and it was the Ashantees who gave rise to the famous, or rather infamous, Assiente contract of the Spaniards. Since the restriction of the slave trade to the S. of the equator, the Ashantees, though still full of thirst for war, have directed more of their attention to commerce. It was in 1806 that they first appeared formidable on the coast against the Annamboes; and in 1823 they completely defeated the whole British force of the coast, which took the field against them; the governor, who commanded in person, being slain in the conflict, and the wreck of the army compelled to take refuge in the forts.

ASHBORNE, a town of Derbyshire. Market on Saturday. It is famous for cheese, and seated between the rivers Dove and Compton, 10 miles N. E. of Uttoxeter, and 139 N. N.W. of London.

ASHBURTON, a borough in Devonshire, with a market on Tuesday for wool and yarn, and on Saturday for provisions. It is one of the four stannary towns, and has a considerable manufacture of serges. It is seated among hills (remarkable for tin and copper) near the river Dart, 14 miles S. W. of Exeter, and 192 W. by S. of London. It returns one member to parliament.

ASHBY DE LA ZOUCH, a tn. in Leicestershire. Market on Saturday. It had a castle with a very high tower, some ruins of which are standing. Here are manufactures of stockings, hats, and ribbons, and a considerable trade in malt. Ashby is 13 miles S. of Derby, and 115 N. N. W. of London. A vein of coal, of a very superior quality, was opened in the vicinity about the year 1816, and a mineral water in the same neighbourhood, since about the same period, has been much resorted to.

ASHDOD. *See* AZOTUS.

ASHEREFF, or ESHREFF, a town of Persia, situate on a small rivulet which falls into the Caspian Sea at its south end.

ASHFORD, a town in Kent, governed by a mayor. Market on Tuesday. The church is large, and was formerly collegiate. It is seated on the Ash, near its confluence with the Stour, 14 miles S. W. of Canterbury, and 55 S. E. of London.

ASHMUNEIN, a town of Egypt, built on the ruins of a city, supposed to be the ancient Hermopolis, on the left bank of the Nile, 140 miles S. S. W. of Cairo. Long. 31. 7. E. lat. 28. 10. N.

ASHNAGUR, a town of Hindostan, in the province of Cabul, seated on the Kameh, 80 miles N. of Attock, and 110 S. E. of Cabul.

ASHOVER, a parish of Derbyshire, England, 6 miles S. of Chesterfield, and 157 from London.

ASHTABULA, a county at the N. E. extremity of the state of Ohio, bordering on Lake Erie. Pop. 23,724. Jefferson, 234 miles N. E. of Columbus, is the chief town.

ASHTON IN MAKERFIELD, a township of Lancashire, England, 3 miles N. of Newton, and 196 from London.

ASHTON-UNDER-LYNE, a borough and populous parish of Lancashire; the town is seated on a high bank which rises from the river Tame, 6 miles E. of Manchester. The parish is divided into four districts, forming together one of the most important seats of the cotton manufacture, containing upwards of sixty large establishments for spinning and machine-weaving, four iron and brass foundries, as many machine manufactories, and about thirty establishments for the manufacture of hats. It has also extensive collieries in its vicinity, and it is intersected by the Manchester, and the Huddersfield and Peak Forest canals; and returns one member to parliament.

ASIA, one of the three grand divisons of the eastern hemisphere: its boundaries are so exceedingly irregular as to render it difficult to convey an accurate idea of its position, limits, and extent, except by a map; it lies, however, wholly north of the equator. Point Romaine, the most southerly point of the Malaya promontory, being in lat. 1. 23. 30. N., bounded on the N. by the Arctic Ocean, or, as a medial line, by the 70th deg. of N. lat.; from west to east it extends in its extreme limits from the Dardanelles in 26. to Behring's Straits in 190. E.; but exclusive of the promontories of Natolia, Hindostan, Malay, Kamstchatka, and the islands under the equator, Asia may be considered as lying between the 15th and 70th deg. of N. lat. and the 40th and 130th of E. long., and containing an area of 20,432,205 square miles; and the population is estimated at 480,000,000. Asia is separated from Europe on the W. by the Oural or Ural mountains, extending from the line of the Arctic circle in the long. of 63. E., bearing west to the long. of 54. in the lat. of 63., from which point they again bear to the east to the long. of 59. in the lat of 55., from which point, while the Oural mountains run in a parallel line with the 59th of long. the Asiatic boundary becomes partly conventional, bearing west to the sea of Asoph; from which, the Black Sea, the Sea of Marmora, the Dardanelles, and Levant, form the western boundary to the Isthmus of Suez, which separates it from Africa; the Arabian Gulf, or Red Sea, then forms the remainder of its western boundary, and the Arabian Sea, Indian Ocean, and China Sea, bound it on the south, and the North Pacific Ocean on the E., and the Arctic Ocean, as previously stated, forms its northern boundary; this vast extent of territory is divided into eleven great parts; viz., Siberia, Chinese Tartary, China, Thibet, Western or Independent Tartary, the Birman empire, Hindostan, Persia, Arabia, Asiatic Turkey, and Japan, the latter being exclusively insular. Several noble rivers flow in various directions; the Obi, the Yenesei, and Lena, fall into the Arctic Ocean; the Amoor or Saghalien, into the Sea of Ochotsk, in the North Pacific; the Yellow and Great Rivers intersect China from west to east, falling into the Bay of Nankin, and the Ganges, Indus, and Euphrates flowing from north to south; but it is worthy of remark, that neither in Asia or Europe, or in either of the two grand divisions of the western hemisphere, are there any rivers of importance that flow from east to west, whilst in Africa there are none that flow from west to east.

Although the rivers of Asia do not vie in magnificence with those of the western hemisphere, Asia far exceeds it in the magnificence of its mountains. The Himalaya range, which separate Hindostan from Tartary in the lat. of 29. N., rises to the prodigious height of 27,677 ft. above the level of the sea; the Ural, or Oural ridge extends in a uniform and unbroken chain, from the line of the Arctic circle to the sea of Aral, and, although not rising in altitude more than about 4500 ft., they are emphatically denominated by the Russians, the back, and by the Tartars, the girdle of the world; the Altaian chain intersects the entire territory in a N. E. direction, from the Arabian Sea to the East Cape in Behring's Straits, and in the lat. of 49. N. rises to the height of 12,800 ft., and Mounts Caucasus, Taurus, Ararat, &c. &c. spread over the western part of Asia, rising to the height of 8 to 10,000 ft. The Caspian, Baikal, and Sea of Aral, are the only inland waters that merit notice in this place; and, when compared with those of the north division of the western hemisphere, they are very insignificant. The islands of the eastern ocean are so numerous, and so diffusely scattered, as to render it difficult to decide which properly belong to Asia, and which do not; those, however, which admit of no dispute may be enumerated as follow, beginning at the north; viz. Saghalien, Jesso, the Japanese, Formosa, Hainan, the Philippines, Borneo, the Celebes, Java, Sumatra, Ceylon, the Maldive, and Laccadives; the Ladrone, New Carolinas, Pellew, New Guinea, Solomon's, New Hebrides, New Caledonia, Sandwich, Society, Friendly, New Zealand, and Van Diemen's Land will most probably hereafter become more particularly identified with Australasia; they will, however, all be treated of under their respective heads.

Asia was the parent of nations, and the scene of most of those remarkable transactions which are recorded in sacred history. After the deluge, Noah is said to have settled near the borders of the Euphrates, and to have peopled the whole continent; the posterity of Shem occupying the central regions, Japhet the northern, and Ham the southern. Javan and his descendants, Ashkenaz, Dodanim, Tarshish, Elishah, Togermah, and Riphath, are supposed to have been the ancient inhabitants of Asia Minor. The Canaanites and Amalekites were the people of Syria and Arabia Petræa. Modern writers have referred the present natives of Asia to those different stocks of Hebrews, Indians, and Tartars, the propriety of which will appear from their make, features, and languages. There are, however, some large tribes which cannot be referred to any of these classes. Mr. Pinkerton observes that the population of Asia is allowed by all authors to be wholly primitive, with the exception of the Tshuktshis, (whom the Russian historians supposed to have passed from the opposite coast of America,) the colonies that have migrated from Russia to the northern parts, as far as the sea of Kamtschatka, the well-known European settlements, and a few others. Asia certainly contains an amazing original population, and presents an ample field for the study of man in all the stages of his progress from barbarism to civilization. The western parts of Asia appear to have been occupied by numerous petty sovereignties, whose very names are now extinct. At a somewhat later period, the Babylonian empire extended over the greater part of Western Asia; the Persians next reigned paramount on that side, 328 years before the Christian era; Alexander of Macedon extended his arms as far as the Ganges, but his exploits in Asia may be considered as incursions rather than conquests.

The ascendancy of the Persians in its turn yielded to the still greater ascendant influence and power of the Tartars from the north, who also in the 12th century subdued China in the East; and indeed such was the extent of their power, that at one period nearly the whole of Asia, as well as a great part of Europe, fell under their dominion.

The Mogul empire succeeded the Tartar, whilst the greater part of Eastern Tartary became united to China, which for several centuries has remained comparatively undisturbed; but at the present time, a company of English traders, under the denomination of "The United Company of Merchants of England trading to the East Indies," may be regarded as the ascendant power, and as reigning paramount over all Asia. The Russians, however, occupy the whole of the north of Asia, from the Arctic Sea to the 50th degree of N. latitude; and it will probably be their turn next to rule the south as well as the north.

The productions of Asia, animal, mineral, vegetable, as well as birds, insects, reptiles, and fishes, are as majestic, valuable, and useful, as they are various and infinite. The elephant in Asia, like the camel in Africa, is made the instrument of burthen, and in war and pageantry ranks highest in importance; the lion and tiger of Asia are the noblest of their species, and as distinguished for the beauty of their symmetry as for their agility, strength, and ferocity. The inferior classes of the animal creation will be more particularly adverted to under the heads of the several divisions of Asia. Although apparently not so rich in precious minerals as the southern division of the western hemisphere, Asia indicates abundance of gold, and some silver, and its gems are deservedly held in the highest estimation. Of the inferior metals, if they abound, a subduing species of policy precludes their preparation for utility, and Asia draws considerable supplies of iron, copper, tin, and lead from Europe.

Rice for food, and cotton for clothing, are the main productions of the soil over all the south parts of Asia and China, and in the latter country, a decoction of the well known tea-shrub constitutes the principal drink of that populous empire, whilst the vegetable tallow-tree supplies many of their domestic wants.

Mahomedism is established in the central and western parts, while Paganism, and the most degrading and cruel superstitions, prevail in all the other regions of Asia. Christianity is scarcely known throughout this part of the globe, except in Siberia and in Greece, where the profession of it has been perpetuated amidst cruelty and oppression; nor have any adequate exertions been made by Europeans for its introduction, the small tract of India brought under cultivation by our missionaries being only as a single oasis in a vast and dreary desert.

The governments of Asia appear in all ages to have been arbitrary and despotic in the extreme; much addicted to parade and pageantry, and that to a degree of which Europe has exhibited no parallel. The government of China, although in name and form a complete despotism, appears however to be administered not only with temperance, but with a paternal solicitude for the welfare of the great body of the people, who may yet at the same time be ranked amongst the most abject of the human race. The ascendancy of the English at the close of the 18th and commencement of the 19th century, is unquestionably the most important era in the history of Asia; and, although much that is objectionable and reprehensible prevails, in some respects it indicates brighter and better prospects to Asia than it has ever before experienced.

Asia Minor comprehends that part of western Asia under the dominion of the Turks, bordering N. on the Black Sea, and S. on the Levant, including the provinces of Natolia, Caramania, and Roum, which see.

Asiago, a considerable town of Italy, in Vicentino, 20 miles north of Vicenza.

Asinara, an island in the Mediterranean, on the N. W. coast of Sardinia, 17 miles N. by W. of Sassari. It is 28 miles in compass, and is fertile and populous.

Askeaton, a town and parish of Ireland, in the county of Limerick, noted for its castle, and for one of the most perfect abbeys in the country, built by one of the earls of Desmond. It is seated on the Deel, near its confluence with the Shannon, 20 miles W. S. W. of Limerick.

Askrig, a town in N. R. Yorkshire; market on Thursday; seated near the Ure, 18 miles W. S. W. of Richmond, and 246 N. of London.

Asna. *See* Esne.

Asnieras, a town of France, in the department of Upper Vienne, 10 miles N. W. of Bellac.

Asola, a town of Italy, in Bresciano, 20 miles S. E. of Brescia.

Asolo, a town of Italy, in Trevisano, with a spacious citadel on a hill. It is surrounded by walls, and situated near the Musone, 17 miles N. W. of Treviso.

Asoph, or Azof, a sea, anciently the Palus Mæotis, lying N. of the Black Sea, with which it communicates by the Strait of Caffa, the ancient Cimmerian Bosphorus. The sea, which is sometimes called the Sea of Zabak, extends 240 miles from S. W. to N. E., between the latitude of 42. to 47. N. and 34. to 39 of W. long.

Asoph, a district of the Russian empire, in the province of Catharineslaf, including a large tract of territory to the E. and W. of the town of Asoph. It was ceded by the Turks in 1774, and after that period, several new towns were built by Catherine II.; one of which, Catharineslaf, is now the captital.

Asoph, a town of Russia, lately the capital of a district of the same name, seated on the east bank of the Don, near it entrance into the sea of Asoph. It has been several times taken by the Turks and Russians. It is not of the importance it was in the reign of Peter the Great; the river being now so choked with sand as scarcely to admit the smallest vessel. Long. 38. 32. E. lat. 46. 58. N.

Asperen, a town of Holland, famous for a long siege which it held out against the Geldrians, in 1517. It is seated on the Linghe, 13 miles S. of Utrecht, and 22 E. of Rotterdam.

Aspern, a town of Austria, on the north bank of the eastern branch of the Danube, a little below Vienna, distinguished for a great battle fought between the French and Austrians in 1809, during which the town was totally destroyed, but has been since rebuilt.

Assam, an interior country of Asia, bounded on the W. by Bengal and Bootan, N. by Thibet, and S. E. and S. by Meckley. It is divided into two provinces, Upper and Lower. Among the products are many kinds of valuable fruits, with silk, musk, pepper, cocoa-nuts, sugar, and ginger. The open parts are marked with population and tillage; the woods abound with elephants. The mountains are inhabited by a savage tribe called Nancs, who go naked, and eat dogs, cats, mice, locusts, and any thing they can find. The other inhabitants of Assam are base and unprincipled, have no fixed religion, nor any rule but their inclination. They eat all flesh except human, and even animals that die a natural death, and are dreadfully addicted to the use of opium. They are enterprising, savage, vindictive, and fond of war. They have neither horses, asses, nor camels; but they are sometimes brought there from other countries. Asses they are fond of, but are so much afraid of a horse, that one trooper would put a hundred of them to flight. The invention of gunpowder is ascribed to the Assamese. It was known in China and Hindostan in very remote antiquity; and in the code of Gentoo laws there is a prohibition of the use of fire-arms; but what these fire-arms were is not distinctly known. The tea-plant has lately been discovered growing wild in this country, and, in the present state of the commerce with China, may prove of much importance. Mr. Bruce has found it growing in extensive tracts all along the river, from Jaipore, the capital of Lower Assam, to above Jorehaut, the capital of the Upper Province. It is found in the natural jungle, which covers a large portion of the country, and under the shade of which the tea-tree flourishes spontaneously, and as thick as they can grow

They have probably been introduced by the emigrants, from the neighbouring province of Munkum.

ASSANCALE, or HASANKALA, a town of Turkish Armenia, which has hot baths much frequented. It is seated on the Ares, 22 miles E. of Erzerum.

ASSARPOUR, a town of Hindostan, in the country of Cutch, at the most eastern mouth of the Indus, 38 miles W. of Boogebooge.

ASSEERGUR, a strong hill fort of Hindostan, in Candeish. In the war with the Mahrattas, in 1803, it surrendered to the British. It is 20 miles N. E. of Burhanpour.

ASSEN, a town of Holland in Overyssel, 12 miles S. of Groningen, and 51 N. N. W. of Coevordon.

ASSENEDE, a town of Belgium, a province of East Flanders; 13 miles N. N. E. of Ghent.

ASSENHEIM, a town of Germany, in the circle of Upper Rhine, at the conflux of the Wetter with the Nidda, 11 miles N. E. of Frankfort.

ASSENS, a seaport of Denmark, in the island of Funen. It is the common passage from the duchy of Sleswick to Copenhagen, and is 17 miles S. W. of Odensee. Long. 10. 2. E. lat. 55. 17. N.

ASSINIBOINS, or ASSENEBOYNE, a river of North America, falling into the S. W. end of Lake Winnipeg; the North West Fur Trading Company have a house on the S. bank of the river, about 15 miles above its entrance into the lake.

ASSISI, a town of Italy, in the duchy of Spoleto, with a magnificent church, 22 miles N. W. of Spoleto.

ASSOMPTION, a township and village of Lower Canada, situate on the bank of a river of the same name, which falls into the St. Lawrence a little below Montreal.

ASSOS, a seaport of Asiatic Turkey, in Natolia, on a bay of the Archipelago, 12 miles S. E. of Troas. Long. 26. 36. E. lat. 39. 32. N.

ASSUMPTION, an episcopal city, capital of a province of Paraguay. It stands in a fertile country, on the E. bank of the river Paraguay, a little above the confluence of the Pilcomayo. Long. 57. 40. W. lat. 22. 47. S. Also the name of one of the Ladrone islands, in N. lat. 19. 45. and 45. 35. E. long. and of a parish in the state of Louisiana, on the W. bank of the Mississippi, intersected by the line of 30 N. lat. Pop. about 3576, of whom 1149 were slaves.

ASSYE, a small town in Hindostan, province of Berar, 38 miles N. E. of Aurungabad. A remarkable victory was gained here by General Wellesley, on September 23, 1803.

ASTABAT, a town of Persian Armenia, 3 miles from the river Aras, and 32 S. E. of Naksivan.

ASTARA, a town of Persia, in Ghilan, on a river of the same name, near its entrance into the S. W. end of the Caspian Sea. Long. 50. 40. E. lat. 38. 30. N.

ASTERABAD, or ESTERABAD, a town of Persia, capital of a province of its name, at the S. E. part of the Caspian Sea. It stands at the mouth of a river, which forms a bay convenient for trade, 110 miles E. of Ferabad. Long. 54. 58. E. lat. 37. 16. N.

ASTI, a city of Piedmont, capital of the department of Tanaro, with a citadel. Beside the cathedral, it contains upwards of thirty other churches. It is seated on the Tanaro, 24 miles E. of Turin. Pop. 21,225.

ASTORGA, an episcopal town of Spain, in Leon, well fortified by art and nature. It is seated in a plain, on the river Tueria, 25 miles S. W. of Leon, and about midway on the high road from Corunna to Madrid.

ASTORIA, a commercial establishment on the Colombia River, on the W. coast of North America. It was founded in 1811, for the fur trade, by J. J. Astor, a private citizen of the United States, but was ceded to the English North West Company.

ASTRABAD, a tongue of land on the N. E. coast of the Crimea, extending into the Sea of Asoph.

ASTRABAD, capital of a province of the same name, on the S. E. of the Caspian Sea. It has a considerable commerce with Russia, &c.

ASTRACAN, a city of the Caucasus, and the principal city of Asiatic Russia, capital of a province of the same name, and an archbishop's see. It is situate on an island formed by two branches of the Volga River, near its entrance into the N. end of the Caspian Sea, in the lat. of 46., and has a good harbour. It is surrounded by walls, and on the W. has a triangular fortress. Here are 25 Russian churches, and two convents; the Armenians, Lutherans, and Papists, have their places of worship; and the Hindoos of Moultan have been permitted to erect a temple. The houses are in general of wood; and the inhabitants are estimated at 45,938. It seldom rains here, but the river Volga overflows, like the Nile, and when the water is run off, vegetation is very rapid. Here are several large vineyards, from which some wine is made for home consumption; also manufactures of gunpowder and nitre, and on the side of the Caspian Sea are long marshes which produce a great quantity of salt. The Volga, either of itself, or by its numerous branches, intersects half of the interior provinces of European Russia, and affords to Astracan a facility of communication by water, of inestimable advantage. It communicates with Moscow by the Kashma branch, and with St. Petersburg from Twer, partly by canal, and partly by intermediate waters. The mouths of the river abound with *beluga*, a species of sturgeon, from the sound of which is made the finest isinglass, which forms a very extensive branch of the commerce of Astracan, which is also the centre of all the commerce of Russia with Persia and the East, in which Russians, Persians, Armenians, Greeks, Tartars, Jews, Hindoos, French, and English, all participate. It was taken from the Mongol Tartars about the middle of the 15th century, and is about 770 miles S. E. of Moscow, and 1050 S. S. E. of St. Petersburg.

ASTURIAS, a maritime province of the N. W of Spain, extending for about 120 miles along the shore of the Bay of Biscay. It is divided into two parts, Asturias d'Oviedo and Asturias de Santillana, so named from the chief towns. This province is full of mountains and forests; its wine and horses are excellent, and it has mines of gold, lapis lazuli, and vermilion. The eldest son of the King of Spain is styled prince of the Asturias. It was formerly a principality of the kingdom of Leon, and is bounded on the S. by the province of Leon; on the W. by Gallicia; and on the E. by Biscay and Old Castile: it extends inland from the Bay of Biscay about 45 miles, and contains a superficies of 308 square leagues, and a population of 364,238. St. Andero, at the eastern extremity of the province, in lat. 43. 28. N. and 3. 40. W. long., and distant by way of Segovia 87, and by Aranda 71½ leagues N. from Madrid, is the principal town on the coast, and Oviedo, 75½ leagues N. W. from Madrid, is the chief town inland.

Atacama, a seaport and province of Peru. The province has a great desert of the same name, which separates Peru from Chili. The town is remarkable for the fish called tollo, with which it carries on a great trade with the inland provinces. It is 210 miles S. by E. of Arica. Long. 69. 30. W. lat. 21. 20. S.

Atchinsk, a considerable town in the government of Tobolsk, on the frontiers of Colyvan. It is situate on a branch of the Obe River, in the lat. of 56. 20. N. and 89. 30. E. long.

Atena, a town of Naples, in Principato Citeriore, near the river Negro, 22 miles N. of Policastro.

Ath, a fortified town of the Netherlands, in Hainault. It has been often taken, and is seated on the Dender, 12 miles N. W. of Mons, on the road from Brussels to Tournay. Pop. 7800.

Athabasca, Lake, British territories of North America, 200 miles long, 15 broad. Lat. 59. 0. N. long. 108. 0. W. Its chief outlet joins the Slave River.

Athaboli, a town of European Turkey, in Romania, on the coast of the Black Sea, 70 miles N. E. of Adrianople.

Athboy, a parish and town in the county of Meath, Ireland. The town is 30 miles N. of Dublin, and has three annual fairs.

Athelney, an island in Somersetshire, at the confluence of the Thone and Parret, a few miles below Taunton, memorable for having afforded shelter to King Alfred. Here he collected some of his retainers, on which account he called it Æthelingay, or the Isle of Nobles, and hence he made frequent sallies upon the Danes.

Athenrey, a populous parish and town in the county of Galway, Ireland.

Athens, a once celebrated city, situate on a promontory at the southern extremity of eastern Europe; supposed to have been founded by Cecrops, 1556 years antecedent to the Christian era, or about the period of the height of Egyptian glory in the age of Moses; it became the seat of kingly authority under Codrus, about the period of the reign of David in Palestine; and, in about 1000 years subsequent to its foundation, it had attained the summit of its glory, when it became the chief city of the Grecian republic, which successfully contended against the powerful arms of the Persian monarchy, and excelled in all the arts of poetry, painting, sculpture, and architecture; the two last the Athenians may be said to have perfected, for all that succeeding ages have done has been to copy, mix, and transform. Eighty-six years antecedent to the Christian era, when refinement among the Athenians had sunk into licentiousness, and patriotism into selfish ambition and individual aggrandisement, Athens fell a prey to the furious arm of Sylla, who sacked it of some of its choicest treasures; from this period it may be considered as having passed the meridian of its glory. In the 50th year of the Christian era, it was visited by the apostle Paul, whose speech to the multitude from the celebrated temple on Mars' Hill, as recorded in the 18th chap. of the Acts of the Apostles, verse 22nd, will best testify the social and moral condition of its inhabitants at that period. It subsequently became a prey to internal commotions, as well as to external enemies, and, after experiencing various alterations of fortune, it became tributary to the Turks, on their establishing their dominion in Europe. It has since become, once more, the capital of Attica and of Greece, and the projected improvements in its vicinity will render it a handsome town. It contains about 12,000 inhabitants, the greater portion of whom are Greeks; who, having the advantage of a delightful climate, live in comparative ease. Numerous vestiges of architectural grandeur still remain to attest the supremacy of the Athenians in that noble and useful art. In 1808 Lord Elgin, then ambassador from England at Constantinople, ransacked the Parthenon of the choicest vestiges of its friezes, &c., which now adorn the national Museum in London. Athens stands in a spacious plain: the hill of Mars, on the summit of which stood the temple dedicated to the idol of that name, was, during the zenith of its greatness, in the centre of the city, but now at some distance from the present town, which is bounded on one side by Mount Hymettus, deservedly celebrated for the honey which it produces. On the sea side it has three ports; the Phalereus, Munychia, and Piræus, now Port Leoné, about 5 miles distant from the town, and through which it carries on some little external traffic in honey, wax, oil, olives, silk, &c. in exchange for the manufactures of western Europe generally; it is in lat. 37. 58. N. and 23. 46. W. long.

Athens is also the name of a county in the S. E. end of the state of Ohio, a nook bordering on the Ohio river. Pop. 6338. The chief town of the same name is finely located in the centre of the country, on a tongue of land formed by the detour of the river Hockhocking, which intersects the county from the N. W. to the S. E. corner, where it falls into the Ohio. The town is 71 miles S. E. of Columbus.

Athens is the name of another town in Greene county, state of New York, on the W. bank of the Hudson River, nearly opposite the city of Hudson. Pop. 9109. There are several other townships named Athens, in different parts of the United States.

Atherston, a tn. in Warwickshire; market on Tuesday. Manufactures of hats, ribbons, and shalloons. It is seated near the Anker, on the high road from London to Holyhead, by Chester, 13 miles N. of Coventry, and 103 N. W. of London.

Athlete, or Castel Pelegrino, a town in Palestine, on a small peninsula jutting into the Mediterranean, surrounded with extensive ruins.

Athlone, a borough of Ireland, partly in the county of West Meath, and partly in Roscommon. It stands on both sides of the Shannon, over which is a long bridge, that is the grand pass between the provinces of Leinster and Connaught. It is 60 miles W. of Dublin. This town was unsuccessfully besieged by William, prince of Orange, after the battle of the Boyne, in 1690; but was taken by storm the following year, after the battle of Aughrim, by General Ginkle, one of the Orange followers, who was created Baron of Aughrim and Earl of Athlone for the exploit. It is now one of the most extensive military stations in all Ireland; and sends one member to parliament.

Athos, or Monte Santo, a high mountain of Greece in Macedonia, on a peninsula at the entrance of the Gulf of Contessa. It has been celebrated in all ages for its singular locality, and the majesty of its appearance, and became an object of such great attraction to the Greeks, as to draw devotees from all parts of eastern Europe, who have interspersed it with numerous churches, monasteries, and hermitages; hence it has acquired the name of Monte Santo, or the Holy Mountain. The monks amount to about 6000, who subsist chiefly by preying on the numerous devotees whom their affected sanctity and craft continually draw around them; they, however, cultivate the olive and the vine to some extent, and there are four establishments of education for Greek ecclesiastics; there is a fortified town called Kareis, about half way up the mountain, at which a Turkish aga resides. It is about 70 miles E. of Salonica, and in lat. 40. 7. N. and 24. 15. E. long.

Athy, a town of Ireland, in the county of Kildare, at which the assizes are held alternately with Naas. It is seated on the river Barrow, 12 miles S. of Kildare, and communicates with Dublin daily by passage-boats, by the line of the Grand Canal. The remains of an old castle now serve for a county jail, and there are ruins of two monasteries in the vicinity.

Atlantic, or Atlantic Ocean, takes its name from Mount Atlas in Africa, and lies between the west continents of Africa and Europe, and the east continent of America. Its least breadth, from Guinea in Africa, to Brazil in South America, is 2300 miles. On one side of the equator, it is called the North Atlantic Ocean, and on the other the South Atlantic Ocean. It is remarkable for its currents, the principal of which, the Gulf Stream, is occasioned by the constant trade winds, which drive the waters, in a westerly direction, through the passages of the West India islands into the Gulf of Mexico; whence it flows, with great velocity, by the coast of Florida, making a curvilinear sweep of almost the whole breadth of the ocean. The surface of the Atlantic is estimated to be from 19 to 22 feet higher than the Pacific at the Isthmus of Panama.

Atlas, a chain of high mountains in Africa, separating Barbary from Biledulgerid, and extending E. from the coast of the Atlantic to the border of Egypt, upwards of 2000 miles; their greatest altitude is about 13,000 ft. above the level of the sea. Silver, copper, iron, lead, and antimony, are found in different parts of these mountains. Another chain, called the Little Atlas, extends from the Strait of Gibraltar to Bona in the state of Algiers. These mountains have different names, according to the various countries they pass through, and the plains and valleys by which they are intersected. They are inhabited almost in every place, except where the extreme cold will not permit.

Atlisco, a tn. of Mexico, in Tlascala, seated in an extensive plain of its name, 20 miles W. S. W. of Puebla de los Angelos.

Atol, the name of each separate group of the Maldive Islands, in the Indian Ocean.

Atooi, or Tauai, one of the Sandwich islands, in the North Pacific Ocean. It is 30 miles long, and contains a great portion of gently rising land. On the S. W. is a good road and anchoring place, called Wymoa. Long. 159. 40. W. lat. 21. 57. N. Pop. about 55,000.

Atoyaque, a town of Mexico, S. of the river Zacatula, and a few miles inland from the Pacific Ocean, in lat. 18. N.

Atrato, a river of Columbia, which rises between the first and second ridge of the Andes, and runs from S. to N. about 250 miles, into the Gulf of Darien, in lat. 8. N. and W. long. 77. 6.

Atri, a town of Naples, in Abruzzo Ulteriore, on a craggy mountain. It was the birth-place of the emperor Adrian. It is about four miles from the shore of the Adriatic, and 10 S. E. of Teramo. Long. 14. 2. E. lat. 42. 40. N.

Attica, an ancient state of Greece, of which Athens was the chief city. It is now called Livadia, which see.

Attleborough, a town in Norfolk; market on Tuesday; 14 miles N. E. of Thetford. It was formerly a city and chief town of the county.

Attock, or Attock Benares, a city and fortress of Hindostan, in the province of Lahore. It stands on the E. bank of the Indus, near the confluence of the Cabul, and on the site of the Taxila of Alexander, where he crossed that river, and advanced onwards to the Ganges, in the year 328 antecedent to the Christian era. Attock is about 700 miles above the entrance of the Indus into the Arabian Sea, and about midway between Cabul and Lahore, or 180 to 200 miles from each, in lat. 33. 6. N. and 71. 15. E. long. The present fortress was built by the Emperor Acbar, in 1581.

Attoor, a strong town of Hindostan, in the Carnatic, 60 miles N. of Tritchinopoly, and 80 W. S. W. of Pondicherry

AUB, a town of Germany, in the principality of Wurtzburg, on the river Gollach, 10 miles S. E. of Wurtzburg.

AUBAGNE, a town of France, department of Bouches du Rhone. Pop. 6620.

AUBE, an interior department in the N. E. of France, containing part of the late province of Champagne. It takes its name from a river, which, passing by Bar-sur-Aube and Arcis, joins the Seine, above Nugent. Troyes is the capital. Pop. about 240,000.

AUBENAS, a town of France, in the department of Ardeche, with manufactures of woollen cloths, red cotton, and silk; seated on the Ardeche, at the foot of the Cevennes, 15 miles S. of Viviers.

AUBENTON, a town of France, in the department of Somme, situated on the Aine, 10 miles S. of Virvins.

AUBETERRE, a town of France, on the frontiers of Charente and Dordogne, seated on the Drome, 22 miles S. of Angouleme. Long. 0. 12. E. lat. 45. 17. N.

AUBIERES, a town of France, in the department of Puy de Dome, 3 miles S. E. of Clermont.

AUBIGNE, or AUBIGNY, a small town of France, in the department of Cher, seated in a fine plain, 24 miles N. of Bourges, surrounded with strong walls, wide ditches, and high counterscarps. The castle is within the town, and is very handsome.

AUBIN, ST., a town of the island of Jersey with a fort standing on a bay of the same name, opening to the south. *See* ST. HELIER.

AUBONNE, a town of Switzerland, in the Pays de Vaud, on a river of its name, which falls into the Lake of Geneva, 10 miles W. of Lausanne.

AUBURN, the chief town of the county of Cayuga, the N. end of which borders on Lake Ontario, state of New York. Auburn is a thriving town; it was incorporated out of the township of Aurelius. Pop. 5626. It is 9 miles E. of the town of Cayuga, and 170 W. by N. of Albany.

AUBUSSON, a town of France, in the department of Creuse, with a manufacture of tapestry; seated on the river Creuse, 37 miles N. E. of Limoges.

AUCAGURAL, the capital of the kingdom of Adel, seated on an eminence near the river Hawash. Long. 44. 25. E. lat. 8. 56. N.

AUCH, a city of France, capital of the department of Gers; lately an archiepiscopal see, and the capital of Gascony. The cathedral is one of the finest in France. Here are manufactures of velvet, serges, crapes, hats, and leather. It is seated by the summit and side of a hill, on the river Gers, 37 miles W. of Toulouse. Long. 0. 37. E. lat. 43. 39. N.

AUCKLAND, BISHOPS, a town of Durham, at which the bishop has a palace. Market on Thursday. It has a beautiful castle, and a chapel, whose architecture is very curious. Here are manufactures of cotton and muslin. It is seated by the side of a hill, on the river Wear, 8 miles S. by W. of Durham, and 249 N. N. W. of London.

AUCKLAND, the intended capital of New Zealand; it is seated on the Waitemata harbour, in lat. 36. 41. S. long. 174. 45. E.

AUCKLAND ISLES, Pacific Ocean, S. of New Zealand; discovered by Capt. Bristow in 1806. Lat. 50. 38½. S. long. 165. 52. E.

AUDE, a maritime department of France, at the S. E. extremity, containing part of the late province of Languedoc. It receives its name from a river which rises in the Pyrenees, and, flowing by Quillan, Limeux, and Carcassone, enters the Mediterranean near Narbonne, and which, by the Royal Canal and Garonne, is united with the Atlantic Ocean. Carcassone is the capital.

AUDIERNE, a town of France, in the department of Finisterre, seated in the Bay of Biscay, 18 miles W. of Quimper.

AUDLEM, a town of Cheshire, England, 6 miles S. from Nantwich, 162 from London.

AUERBACH, a town on the E. side of the Vogtland, in the S. W. corner of the circle of Upper Saxony.

AUERSTADT, a village of Thuringia, circle of Upper Saxony, W. of the Saal River, celebrated for a battle between Napoleon and the Prussians, on the 14th October, 1806.

AUGGUR, tn. Hindostan, province Malwa, on an elevated plain, 40 miles from Oujein.

AUGILA, a territory of North Africa, lying to the S. of Barca, between Fezzan and Egypt. It abounds in dates; and many of the inhabitants engage in the caravan trade. The capital is of the same name, 220 miles W. of Siwah, and 510 E. by N. of Mourzouk. Long. 23. 40. E. lat. 29. 33. N.

AUGSBURG, a city of Suabia, lately imperial, and a bishop's see, but now the capital of a principality subject to Bavaria. It is a large fortified place, has a variety of manufactures, and is one of the principal trading towns, and for the negotiation of bills of exchange, in the interior of Germany. The cathedral, townhouse, and other public buildings, are magnificent. In the bishop's palace, the Lutherans presented their confession of faith to the emperor Charles V., in 1550, hence called the Confession of Augsburg. It was taken by the French in 1703, and again in 1796. It is seated between the Werdach and Lech, 30 miles N. W. of Munich. Long. 10. 55. E. lat. 48. 17. N.

AUGUSTA, a county in the centre of the state of Virginia, lying between two parallel ridges of the Allegany Mountains. Pop. 19,628. Staunton, in the centre of the county, 126 miles N. W. by W. from Richmond, is the chief town. Also the name of a township in Oneida county, state of New York, 112 miles W. by N. of Albany. Pop. 2175.

AUGUSTA, a town of the state of Georgia, in Richmond county, lately the capital of the state. It has the advantage of a central situation between the upper and lower countries; and seated in a fine plain, on the S. W. bank of the Savanna River, 52 miles N. N. E. of Louisville, and 127 N. N. W. of Savanna. Pop. 6403. Long. 81. 45. W. lat. 33. 20. N.

Augusta, a city of Sicily, near the ancient Syracuse. The inhabitants still collect the celebrated honey of Hybla, from which much profit is derived.

Augustin, St., the chief tn. of East Florida, situate at the foot of a hill, on the E. coast, which is too shallow to be approached by vessels that draw more than 12 feet of water. It is defended by a strong castle. Long. 81. 50. W. lat. 29. 56. N.

Augustin, St., a cape on the coast of Brazil, 300 miles N. E. of the Bay of All Saints. Long. 35. 40. W. lat. 8. 30. S. Also the name of a river, bay, and port, on the coast of Labrador, in the Straits of Belleisle; and of a river and bay, at the S. W. end of the island of Madagascar; and of several other rivers, points, and bays, in different parts of the world.

Augustow, a town of Poland, in Polachia, seated on the Narieu, 44 miles N. of Bielisk.

Augustus, Fort, a fortress of Scotland, in Inverness-shire, at the influx of the Oich into the S. extremity of Loch Ness, 34 miles S.S.W. of Inverness.

Augustburg. *See* Schellenberg.

Aulendorf, a town of Suabia, situate on the river Schus, 8 miles N. of Ravensburg.

Aulnay, two towns of France, adjoining each other, in the department of Calvados, 14 miles S. W. of Caen. Pop. about 3500. Also the name of another town in the department of the Lower Charente.

Aumale. *See* Albemarle.

Aumont, a town of France, in the department of Lozere, 15 miles N. W. of Mende.

Aumore, a town of Hindostan, in Bengal, 30 miles S. of Rajemal, and 46 N. N. W. of Moorshedabad.

Aunis, lately a small territory of France, in the S.W. part of Poitou, and now forming part of the department of Lower Charente.

Aurach, a fortified town of Suabia, seated at the foot of a mountain, on the rivulet Ermst, 15 miles E. of Tubingen.

Auras, a town of Silesia, on the river Oder, 12 miles N. W. of Breslau.

Auray, a town of France, in the department of Morbihan, on a river of its name, near its entrance into the Gulf of Morbihan, in the Bay of Biscay, 8 miles W. of Vannes.

Aurelius. *See* Auburn.

Aurich, the capital of East Friesland, in the kingdom of Hanover, seated in a plain surrounded by forests, 13 miles N. E. of Emden.

Aurillac, a town of France, in the department of Cantal. Quantities of lace and velvet are manufactured here. It is seated on the Jordanne, 30 miles S. W. of St. Flour. Pop. 10,500.

Auriol, a town of France, in the department of the Mouths of the Rhone, 12 miles S. E. of Axis, and 12 N. N. E. of Marseilles.

Aurora, an island, one of the New Hebrides in the Pacific Ocean. It is 36 miles long and 6 broad, affords plenty of wood and water, and has a small bay on the N. W. coast. Long. 168. 18. E. lat. 15. 8. S. Also the name of a town in Cayuga county, on the E. bank of Cayuga Lake, state of New York, 183 miles W. of Albany; and of another town in Erie county, near the E. end of Lake Erie, in the same state, containing 2909 inhabitants; 298 miles W. of Albany.

Aurungabad, a considerable city of Hindostan, capital of Dowlatabad. It owes the greatest part of its magnificence to the great Aurungzebe, who made it his place of residence and gave it the present name. It stands in a fertile plain, almost surrounded by mountains, 110 miles S. by W. of Burhanpour, and 250 E. S. E. of Surat. Long. 76. 2. E. lat. 19. 45. N.

Aurungabunder, a town of Hindostan, in the province of Tatta, on a branch of the Indus, to which it gives name; 40 miles S. by W. of Tatta.

Ausa, formerly **Alsa**, a river of Carniola, which running southward by Aquileia, after a short course falls into the Adriatic. On the banks of this river, Constantine, the son of Constantine the Great, fighting against Constans, was slain.

Auspitz, a town of Moravia, 20 miles S. S. E. of Brun.

Aussig, a town of Bohemia, seated on the Elbe, 11 miles N. N. W. of Leutmeritz.

Austell, St., a town of Cornwall, in the centre of an extensive mining district. Market on Friday. In the environs is also got fine clay, which is sent to Liverpool, Bristol, and Staffordshire, for the potteries. It is seated near the English Channel, 13 miles E. N. E. of Truro, and 245 W. S. W. of London.

Austerlitz, or **Slawkow**, a tn. of Moravia. Near this place a great and decisive victory was obtained by the French, commanded by Buonaparte, over the Austrians and Russians, on the 2nd December, 1805, which led to the treaty of Presburg. It is 12 miles E. of Brun, and 30 S. S. W. of Olmutz. Also the name of a town in Columbia county, state of New York, W. of the Hudson River, and on the border of Massachusets; 28 miles S. E. of Albany.

Australasia, a name conventionally applied to the extensive territory of Australia, and the several groups of islands, including New Zealand, S. of the equator, in the Pacific Ocean. *See* New Holland.

Australia, the largest island in the world, having an extent nearly equal to Europe, being 2400 miles from E. to W., and 1200 in breadth. Western Australia is from the long. 129. 0. E. westward; South Australia lies between long. 132. 0. and 141. 0. E.; and Eastern Australia, or New South Wales, comprises the E. portion of the continent. The British settlements are on the E. coast, of which Sydney is the capital, (*see* Wales, New South;) on the S. coast, at Port Philip, Melbourne is the capital; in St. Vincent Gulf, of which Adelaide is the capital; on the W. coast at Swan River, of which Perth is the principal town; and on the N. in Coburg peninsula, at the town of Victoria. (*See* Port Essington.)

It is probable that this great territory was

first discovered by the Portuguese, in the early part of the 16th century; they saw the N. coast after exploring the shores of New Guinea. The first exploration of its shores was on the W. coast, by a Dutch navigator, Dirk Harto, in 1616. It was again visited by the Dutch in 1619 and 1620, when the coast about Swan River was discovered. The S. coast was discovered also by the Dutch in 1627, and the N. shores by them in 1623 and 1644; this part was ordered by the States General, in 1655, to be called New Holland—a name now changed for Australia, the South Land. The whole of the E. coast was discovered in 1770, by Capt. Cook, and called by him New South Wales, and was first colonized in 1788.

Of the interior nothing is known, or can scarcely be conjectured; the S. E. angle has been peopled by the British, but the part known does not comprehend more than one-eighth of the whole. What is known in that quarter consists of a tolerably fertile district, near the coasts, for 1000 or 1500 miles inland, but beyond that the country is of low elevation and a dead level, without a hill to break the N. W. horizon; the rivers flow through this arid tract, but have no tributaries, and are nearly dried up in summer.

It was formerly thought that the great outlet of the waters was on the N. W. coast, but recent researches prove the contrary. No river of magnitude has been discovered in that quarter, except the Victoria, in long. 130., which has been traced for about 120 miles in a S. E direction; and in this country of anomalies, every theory which has been advanced has wanted confirmation, or has been subverted by the facts discovered.

AUSTRALIA, NORTH. *See* ESSINGTON, PORT.

AUSTRALIA, SOUTH, a new province erected into a free colony, on Aug. 15, 1834, having the meridians of 132. 0. and 141. 0. E. for its E. and W. boundaries, and the parallel of 26. 0. S. on the N.; and the Gulfs of St. Vincent and Spencer on the S., and contains nearly 200,000,000 acres. The northern part of the province is unfit for the occupation of man. It was penetrated by Mr. Eyre, who left Adelaide on June 18th, 1840, who found, that the whole of the country to the N. and E. of the head of Spencer's Gulf was of low elevation, with the exception of some ridges running in a N. and E. direction; and beyond which, and forming a crescent, lies Lake Torrens, a collection of salt water, which he in vain endeavoured to reach. This salt lake is, perhaps, a collection of surface water, which may extend over a vast extent of the low and desert country, which apparently forms the interior of the continent; and from the failure of his expedition, in discovering any useful river, or inland sea, as had been expected, much of the ardour for penetrating the interior has dissipated.

The southern part is a level country, and from the total deficiency of mountains, with the exception of the Mount Lofty range of 1000 or 1500, and the peak, which is 3000 feet high, there is no river of consequence. The Murray, which falls into Lake Alexandrina, passes through a country totally unfit for colonization, and does not receive a single tributary within the colony. The soil is moderately fertile, and well adapted for sheep grazing; but the country labours under the effects of drought, so peculiar to Australia in general. The climate is delicious, and exceedingly salubrious; during the summer, in Jan., Feb., and March, the thermometer is as high sometimes as 96. or 100.; but during the other parts of the year it is temperate. Adelaide is the capital.

AUSTRALIA, WESTERN, a British settlement formed in 1829, in consequence of the official announcement of the French to colonize it, which led to its formation by England. The territory of Western Australia is divided from the rest of the continent by the meridian of 129. 0. E. The colony is at the S. W. angle of the continent, and is divided into 26 counties. The country consists, generally, of a coast belt of sandy inferior land, with richer tracts near the rivers, bounded on the coast by a range of primitive mountains, between 3 and 4000 feet high, extending more than 500 miles in a N. and S. direction. Beyond these the country is generally level, and the soil superior to the coast, but not in a very high degree productive, and affords excellent sheep pasture. It is not heavily timbered, and is tolerably well watered. The principal rivers are the Swan, flowing from the N. E.; the Canning, which unites with it, and forms a large basin in lat. 32., at the head of which is the town of Perth, and at the mouth is Freemantle. The other towns are Albany, in King George's Sound, on the S. coast; and Augusta, in Flinder's Bay. North of the present colony, is the district of Victoria, in which coal has been discovered, and several large rivers, among which are the Hutt, Greenough, and Arrowsmith. At the mouth of the Hutt, in lat. 28. 54. S., is the settlement of Australind.

AUSTRIA, EMPIRE, CIRCLE, and ARCHDUCHY OF, in Europe. The Austrian empire comprehends the ancient kingdoms of Bohemia, Moravia, and Hungary, the Italian States of the Tyrol, and the ancient republic of Venice, Dalmatia, the duchies of Mantua and Milanese, parts of the circle of Bavaria, of Switzerland, and of Poland, (the particulars of which, with their several subdivisions, will be found under their respective heads,) and the circle which includes the archduchy. This fine empire lies between the 45th and the 51st deg. of N. lat. and the 9th and 27th of E. long., and contains a superficies of about 300,000 square miles, and 28,000,000 of inhabitants. In an aggregate sense, the Austrian empire may be considered an interior and agricultural, rather than a maritime and commercial country; the only part that borders upon the sea being the Italian States on the S., which may be considered tributary rather than integral parts of the empire, and as such are held by too precarious a tenure, and under circumstances too prescribed to excite a spirit of commercial enterprise. That noble river, the Danube, runs from W. to E.

through the heart of the empire, and by its numerous branches, intersects almost every part, affording great internal facility of communication and advantages; but the peculiar locality of its communication with the Black Sea, within the Dardanelles, precludes it from affording any very great external advantages. The Elbe rises in Bohemia; but its course is too circuitous, and too much liable to political impediments, to afford any advantages to Austria, to be relied on; all the useful branches of manufacture, however, in. wool, flax, silk, and leather, and most of the useful arts which contribute to the comfort and sociality of society, are carried on over every part of the empire, from materials drawn from its own internal resources. Several mountain districts supply abundance of every species of metallic and semi-metallic substances; the forests supply abundance of timber, and the plains such abundance of cattle and sheep, as to afford several million lbs. weight of wool to be annually exported, after supplying their own internal demands. The Italian States furnish silks, olives, and oil; and Hungary the choicest wines: and, indeed, the Austrian empire may be considered as containing within itself all the means of substantial subsistence and of comfort, and much of luxury; and lthough Austria is not destitute of genius, enterprise, and efficiency in the higher departments of art, a bigoted and idolatrous species of religious faith, and self-sufficiency of political ascendancy, tend to subdue rather than excite the mental faculties, and preclude all great exertion of social enterprise. The government is absolute in form, and the formularies of the church of Rome are the established religion of the empire; the first is, however, at present, administered, if not with mildness, not sanguinary, and the religion is rendered tolerant. The ruling passion of the government is military parade, to maintain which a revenue of 100 millions of florins, or 12 millions of English money, are abstracted annually from the productive classes of the empire.

The Circle of Austria is bounded on the E. by Hungary, N. by Moravia and Bohemia, W. by Bavaria, Suabia, and Switzerland, and S. by the Austrian and Italian States, and the Gulf of Venice, and contains a superficies of about 50,000 square miles, and 4,500,000 inhabitants. It is divided into the Voralberg, and the counties of Bregen and Tyrol, the bishopric of Trent, the duchies of Stiria, Carinthia, and Carniola, each subdivided into upper and lower, Friuli, and Istria, the bishoprics of Salzburg and Passau insulated in the circle of Bavaria, and two small territories of the Teutonic knights, insulated in the circle of Suabia and Franconia, all of which will be found more amply elucidated under their respective heads.

The Archduchy of Austria is bounded on the N. by Bohemia and Moravia, E. by Hungary, S. by Upper Austria, and W. by Bavaria; it forms the N. E. part of the circle, and is divided into West, Upper, East, and Lower. Upper Austria is again subdivided into the Inn Quarter, Mihel Quarter, Quarter of Hausruck, and Black and Traun Quarters; and Lower Austria N. of the Danube is subdivided into the circles west above and east below the Manhartsberg, and S. of the Danube, into the circles above and below the forest of Vienna. Upper Austria contains about 5100 square miles, 100 cities and towns, numerous villages, and 630,000 inhabitants; and Lower Austria about 73,000 square miles, 280 cities and towns, numerous villages, and 1,100,000 inhabitants. The archduchy of Austria constitutes what conventionally is considered the hereditary dominions of the house of Hapsburg, the reigning and ruling family; and the city of Vienna, situate on the S. bank of the Danube, in the circle below the forest of Vienna, in Lower Austria, is the seat of government of the whole Austrian empire. Except Vienna, which will be more fully elucidated under its proper head, there are no other cities or towns in the archduchy of Austria, that merit any particular notice; it may be considered an agricultural, and a somewhat fruitful district, and its peasantry are considered to be the happiest and best conditioned of any in Europe. To form, however, a just view, and to draw a just conclusion of their condition, and indeed of the condition of any people, it is necessary to weigh well the circumstances under which they are born, and by which they are surrounded. The peasants of Austria have been born under the influence of the star of *passive obedience*, which for years past has been preached to them with mildness and persuasion, rather than violence, and, as such, has made them a quiet and contented people; and, as far as contentment constitutes happiness, the peasantry of the archduchy of Austria may, perhaps, justly be considered as the happiest and best conditioned in Europe: but after all, in the legitimate sense of the term happiness, it is a condition alike repugnant to common sense and derogatory to the character of man. The character of the government, courtiers, and privileged classes of the archduchy of Austria, although tending somewhat to self-importance, is on the whole courteous, affable, and condescending: and whilst the peasantry of the archduchy may be considered the most contented, the court may be considered the least licentious of any in Europe.

AUTUN, a city of France, and an episcopal see, in the department of Saone and Loire. It contains many vestiges of Roman magnificence, particularly the temples of Janus and Cybele. Here are manufactures of tapestry, carpets, coverlets, and delft ware. The cathedral of St. Lazarus, the college, and the seminary, are worthy of notice. Autun is seated on the Arroux, at the foot of three mountains, 45 miles E. by S. of Nevers, and 162 S. E. of Paris.

AUVERGNE, a late province of France, 100 miles long, and 75 broad; bounded on the N. by the Bourbonnois, E. by Forez and Velay, S. by Rouergue and the Cevennes and W. by

Limosin, Querci, and La Marche. It now forms the two departments of Cantal and Puy de Dome.

AUVILLARD, a town of France, in the department of Lot and Garonne, situate on the river Garonne, 13 miles S. E. of Agen.

AUXERRE, a city of France, capital of the department of Yonne, and lately an episcopal see. It contains many fountains and squares, and the episcopal palace is deemed one of the most beautiful in France. It is seated on the side of a hill, on the river Yonne, 75 miles W. N. W. of Dijon, and 90 S. S. E. of Paris. Pop. 12,044.

AUXON, a town of France, in the department of Aube, 13 miles S. of Troyes.

AUXONNE, a town of France, in the department of Cote d'Or, with a castle, an arsenal, a foundry for cannon, and a school for the artillery. It is seated on the Saone, 17 miles E. of Dijon. Pop. about 5300.

AUZEN, or TIGRE, a town of Abyssinia, capital of the province of Tigre, and a place of considerable commerce. It is seated on a river that flows into the Tacazze, 170 miles N. E. of Gondar. Long. 39. 33. E. lat. 14. 4. N.

AVA, a country of Asia, now generally called BIRMAH, which see.

AVA, a large city, formerly the metropolis of the Birman empire. It is divided into an upper and lower city, both of which are fortified; the lower is the most extensive, about four miles in circumference, protected by a lofty wall, now mouldering into decay. The materials of the houses, consisting chiefly of wood, were removed about the year 1783, to the new city; and its numerous temples, on which the Birmans never lay sacrilegious hands, are dilapidated by time. Clumps of bamboos, a few plantain trees, and tall thorns, occupy most of the area of this lately flourishing capital. It is situate on the S. side of the Erabatty, 4 miles S. W. of Ummerapoora, the present capital, in N. lat. 22. E. long. 96. 5.

AVALON, a town of France, in the department of Yonne, which has a great trade in grain, wine, and cattle, and a manufacture of cloth. It is seated on the Cousin, 24 miles S. S. E. of Auxerre. Pop. about 4300.

AVALLON, a town of France, on the E. side of the department of Yonne, about 20 miles S. by E. of Auxerre.

AVATSCHA, or AWATSHA, a large bay, forming a very commodious harbour for ships of the largest burthen, near the S. E. extremity of the coast of Kamtschatka. The town of St. Peter and St. Paul, on the N. side of the bay, is in lat. 53. 1. N. and 15. 8. E. long. Saratounka is another town on the S. side.

AVEIRO, a town of Portugal, in Beira, with a good harbour for vessels of a moderate size. The chief trade is in salt, of which great quantities are made in its vicinity. It stands on a small gulf, at the mouth of the Vouga, 33 miles S. of Oporto. Long. 8. 40. W. lat. 40. 40. N.

AVEIRON, an interior department of the S. of France, including the late province of Rouergue. It is named from a river, which rises near Severac le Chateau, and, flowing by Rodez and Villefranche, joins the Garonne below Montauban. The Lot intersects the northern, and the Tarn the southern part of the department; it is divided into five arrondissements, Villefranche, Milhau, St. Afrique, Espalion, and Rhodez; the last is the capital of the department, which contains a population of about 320,000.

AVELLA, a town of Naples, in Terra di Lavoro, celebrated for its honey and apples; 15 miles N. E. of Naples.

AVELLINO, a town of Naples, in Principato Ulteriore. It was almost ruined by an earthquake in 1694, and again in 1805. Near it is the celebrated convent of Monte Virgine, on a wild mountain, which formerly had a sumptuous temple of Cybele. Avellino is famous for the dye of cloth, also for nuts and macaroni. It is 25 miles E. of Naples. Pop. about 9000.

AVENAY, a town of France, in the department of Marne, on the river Marne, 15 miles W. N. W. of Chalons-sur-Marne.

AVENCHE, a town of Switzerland, in the canton of Berne, formerly the capital of Helvetia, but now greatly decayed, grain and tobacco being grown on the site of part of the ancient city. It stands at the S. end of the lake Merat, 15 miles W. of Berne.

AVERBACH, a town of Upper Saxony, in Vogtland, near which is a rock famous for pale topazes. It is 14 miles S. of Zwickau.

AVERNO, a lake of Naples, in Terra di Lavoro, 600 yards in diameter, near Puzzoli. Virgil and others have said the water was so bad, that birds dropped dead when flying over it, and hence they call it the Lake of Hell; but it now has no such poisonous quality, for birds swim upon it. A little to the W. of the lake is a cave, where some pretend they went formerly to consult the Cumæan sybil. There are also some old walls, which some suppose to be the ruins of a temple of Apollo, and others of Pluto.

AVERSA, a town of Naples, in Terra di Lavoro. In 1805 it suffered greatly by an earthquake. It is seated in a fine plain 10 miles N. E. of Naples.

AVERYSBOROUGH, a town of North Carolina, situate on Cape Fear river, 25 miles N. of Fayetteville, and 30 S. W. of Raleigh.

AVES, or THE ISLANDS OF BIRDS, so called from the great numbers of birds that frequent them, though they have not a tree. They are 70 miles E. of Curacoa, and 100 N. of the coast of Colombia, in N. lat. 15. 50. W. long. 63. 43.

AVESNES, a frontier town of France, in the S. of the department of Nord, seated on the high road from Mons to Paris.

AVESTADT, a town of Sweden, in Westmania, noted for its copper-works, and a mint for copper money, 35 miles N. N. W. of Westeros.

Avezzano, a town of Naples, in Abruzzo Ulteriore, 18 miles S. of Aquila.

Aviano, a town of Italy, in Friuli, 13 miles W. of Udina.

Avigliano, a fortified town of Piedmont, on a hill, near the Cottian Alps, 10 miles W. of Turin.

Avignon, a city of the S. of France, capital of the department of Vaucluse, and a bishop's see. It was formerly dependent on the pope, and an archbishop's see, but became annexed to France in 1791. It has a university, several handsome churches, and a synagogue, and numerous manufacturing establishments. It is seated in the heart of a very fruitful district, (in which the olive, vine, and fruits of all kinds are very abundant,) on the E. bank of the Rhone, near the confluence of the Durance, about 20 miles N. E. of Nismes. Pop. about 23,500.

Avila, a town of Spain, in Old Castile, and a bishop's see, with a university, and a manufacture of fine cloth. It is seated on the Adaga, in a large plain, surrounded by mountains covered with fruit-trees and vineyards; 56 miles N. W. of Madrid. It was formerly one of the most considerable cities of Spain, but does not now contain more than 4000 inhabitants.

Aviles, a town of Spain, in Asturias, near the Bay of Biscay, 16 miles N. of Oviedo.

Avis, a town of Portugal, in Alentejo, seated on an eminence, with a castle, near the river Avis. Hence the military order of the knights of Avis have their name. It is 25 miles N. W. of Estremos.

Aviso, a town of Naples, in Terra di Lavoro, 6 miles E. of Sora.

Avlona. *See* Valona.

Avon, a river of England, celebrated for its association with the name of Shakspere. It rises from several springs in Naseby Field, Northamptonshire. It runs W. and joins the Severn at Tewkesbury, whilst the Nez, which rises within a quarter of a mile of it, flows E. and falls into the German Ocean. It is navigable from Stratford, the birth-place of Shakspere, 40 miles from Tewkesbury, and has numerous corn and paper mills on its banks. There is also another river of the same name in England, which rises in the N. of Wiltshire, runs past Malmesbury and Chippenham to Bath, falling into the Bristol Channel; this, in contradistinction to the other, is called the *Lower Avon*.

Avon, another river which rises near Bedwin, in Wiltshire, running past Salisbury, and skirting the edge of the New Forest, falling into Christchurch Bay, in the English Channel.

Avranches, a town of France, in the S. of the maritime department of La Manche. It is situate on an eminence, about 2 miles from the sea, in a fine agricultural district. It was formerly a bishop's see, to which Henry II. of England went to obtain absolution from the pope's nuncio, for the murder of Thomas à Becket in 1172. Although much declined in importance, the cathedral, episcopal palace, and castle, give it some consequence; and it contains about 6000 inhabitants; 10 miles E. of St. Malo.

Aw, Loch, a lake of Scotland, in Argyleshire, 30 miles long, and in some parts above 2 broad. It contains four little islands, tufted with trees, on one of which are the ruins of an ancient castle; and, on a peninsula of the lake are the noble ruins of Kilchurn Castle. At the N. extremity rises the mountain of Cruachan, elevated 3390 feet above the surface of the lake; and near its top is the spring which forms this beautiful expanse of water. The river Aw, the outlet of this lake, runs into Loch Etive, at the village of Bonaw.

Awatska. *See* Avatscha.

Aweri, or Overo, a kingdom of Africa, dependent on Benin, with a town of the same name, on the river Formosa. Long. 5. 10. E. lat. 6. 10. N.

Awen, a town of Suabia, on the river Cochin, 20 miles W. S. W. of Oeting.

Axbridge, a town in Somersetshire; market on Thursday; seated on the river Ax, under the Mendip hills; 10 miles N. W. of Wells, and 130 W. of London.

Axel, a town of the Netherlands, in Flanders, seated in a morass; 10 miles N. of Ghent.

Axim, a territory of Guinea, on the Gold Coast, with a river of the same name flowing through it, and a town on the E. side, at its entrance into the ocean. The Dutch have a fort and a factory here, called St. Anthony. Long. 1. 3. W. lat. 4. 42. N.

Axminster, a town in Devonshire, on the river Ax; market on Saturday. King Athelstan established a minster here to the memory of the princes slain in his army, when he defeated the Danes in this neighbourhood. Here is a manufacture of leather gloves, &c., and a famous one of carpets. It is 27 miles E. by N. of Exeter, and 147 W. of London.

Axum, a town, anciently the capital of Abyssinia. Its ruins are very extensive, among which are many obelisks of granite, with sculptures, but no hieroglyphics. It is 70 miles N. W. of Auzen. Long. 38. 45. E. lat. 14. 10. N.

Ayamonte, a seaport of Spain, in Andalusia, with a castle on a rock, at the mouth of the river Guadiana, opposite Castro-Marino, 80 miles N. W. of Cadiz. Long. 7. 15. W. lat. 37. 12. N.

Aylesbury, a borough in Buckinghamshire, market on Saturday, and returns two members to parliament. The spring assizes are held here. It is the centre of the business of the fertile vale of Aylesbury. Many people here derive their support from a peculiar manner of rearing early ducks for the London market; and the making of lace is carried on to a great extent. It is 17 miles S. E. of Buckingham, and 38 N. W. of London.

Aylesham, a town in Norfolk; market on Thursday; 12 miles N. of Norwich, and 118 N. E. of London. There is a spa about a mile from the town, very efficacious in chronic disorders. It is seated on the S. bank of the river Bure, which is navigable to Yarmouth.

AYR, a county, parish, royal burgh, and river of Scotland. The county extends for about 55 miles along the S. W. coast, and is about 20 in mean breadth. It is one of the most productive counties in Scotland, and exports considerable quantities of grain to Liverpool; and the N. part of the county participates largely in the cotton manufacture. It also abounds in coal and iron, and has some veins of copper and antimony; and some kelp is made on the coast, from sea weed, which is also extensively used as manure. It is watered by several small lakes and streams; the Garnock rises in the N. extremity of the county, and runs S. to Irvine; the Irvine and Ayr rise on the W. border, and flow E. to the sea; the Don runs from S. to N. towards Ayr; and the Girvan and Stinchar rise S. of Ayr, and run parallel with the coast into the sea, toward the S. end of the county. It has been proposed to intersect the N. part of the county with a canal from Adrossan to the Clyde at Glasgow, but, after having been completed for about 12 miles from the Clyde, the work has been suspended. Agates, porphyry, jasper, and calcareous petrifactions, are found in various parts of the county; whilst lime and freestone abound; and on the river Ayr is obtained the whetstone, so useful in sharpening of agricultural cutlery. For divisions, extent of superficies, rent, and population, see *Appendix*. The principal towns beside Ayr, are Kilmarnock, Kilwinning, and Irvine, N.; St. Quivox, Mauchline, Muirkirk, in the centre; Maybole, Kirkmichael, Dailey, Girvan, and Ballantrae, S.

The Royal Burgh of Ayr is situate in the parish, and at the mouth of the river of the same name, on the sea coast, the light-house being in lat 54. 35. N. and 4. 26. W. long. It is a place of considerable antiquity, having been a royal burgh as far back as 1202; its commercial importance declined with the rise of Glasgow, but has revived somewhat since the commencement of the present century. Its export of coal is very great. About 6000 tons of shipping belong to the place, a portion of which is employed in the timber trade to British America. Its buildings do not merit any particular notice. The Ayr river, as well as the Don, affords a considerable supply of salmon.

AZAMOR, a town of Morocco, on the river Morbeys, near the sea; 80 miles N. of Morocco.

AZAREDO, a seaport of Brazil, in the Bay of Spirito Santo, celebrated for sugar. Long. 40. 10. W. lat. 20. 18. S.

AZERBIJAN, a province of Persia, in the N. W. angle of the kingdom. Pop. 2,000,000. The Guebres, or Fire-worshippers, have here their principal temples, which are numerous. Tabriz is the capital.

AZOF. *See* ASOPH.

AZORES, or WESTERN ISLANDS, a group of islands in the Atlantic, between 25. and 30. W. long. and 37. and 40. N. lat., 900 miles W. of Portugal. They are nine in number, viz. St. Maria, St. Michael, Terceira, St. George, Graciosa, Fayal, Pico, Flores, and Corvo. They were first discovered in 1439, by John Vanderberg, a merchant of Bruges, who was driven here by stress of weather. On his arrival at Lisbon, he boasted of his discovery; on which the Portuguese set sail, and took possession of them, which they have retained ever since. They have all a clear sky and salubrious air; are extremely fertile in corn, wine, and various fruits; and breed great numbers of cattle. It is said they are quite free of venomous animals; but they are subject to earthquakes and volcanic eruptions. They are seen at a great distance, one of them having a very high mountain, called the Pico, or Peak of the Azores. The governor-general resides at Angra, in Terceira; but St. Michael is the largest island. In the year 1819, they exported to Great Britain 51,706 boxes of oranges, and in 1824–5 a still greater quantity.

AZOTUS, ASHDOD, or SHDOOD, one of the five cities of the Philistines, and a celebrated seaport of the Mediterranean. The town is now called by the Arabs *Hasaneyun*. It is but thinly inhabited, though the situation is very pleasant. The town is about a mile and a half in circumference, and has in it a mosque, a public bath, a market-place, and two inns. Here is an old structure, with fine marble pillars, which the inhabitants say was the house that Samson pulled down; and to the S. E. just out of the town, is the water where Philip baptized the Ethiopian eunuch. There are several ancient buildings, with capitals and pillars standing. It is situated about 14 or 15 miles S. of Ekron, between that and Ascalon.

AZREK, BAHR EL, or BLUE RIVER, one of the principal tributaries of the Nile. It rises in the Lake Dembea in Abyssinia, and joins the White River at Halfaiah, in Sennaar, which together form the Nile.

B.

BAALBEC. *See* BALBEC.

BABA, a town of Turkey in Asia, prov. Andoli. Pop. 4000. Also a town of South America, repub. Colombia, in the Gulf of Guayaquil.

BABA, or BABADAG, a town of European Turkey, in Bulgaria, celebrated for its knives and sword blades. It stands on a gulf of its name, in the Black Sea, 90 miles N. E. of Silistria. Long 28. 38. E. lat. 44. 40. N.

BABELMANDEL, or BAB-EL-MANDEB, a strait between the coast of Abyssinia and Arabia, uniting the Red Sea with the Indian Ocean. In it is a small island and a mountain of the same name. Long. 43. 28. E. lat. 12. 35. N.

Babenhausen, a town of Suabia, in Germany, 5 miles N. of Tubingen.

Babic, or Bababeg, a town of Persia, on the confines of the Desert of Kerman, situate at about an equal distance from the cities of Kerman, Shwaz, and Zed.

Babuyanes, a cluster of six or seven small islands in the North Pacific Ocean, 10 leagues N. of the Isle of Luconia. The chief produce is wax, ebony, bananas, cocoas, and plantains.

Babylon, the capital of the ancient kingdom of Babylonia or Chaldea. Semiramis is said by some, and Belus by others, to have founded this city. But by whomsoever it was founded, Nebuchadnezzar embellished it, and made it one of the wonders of the world. The most famous works in and about it were the walls of the city, the temple of Belus, Nebuchadnezzar's palace, the hanging gardens, the banks of the river, the artificial lake, and the canals. The walls were 87 feet thick, 350 feet high, and 60 miles in circumference, forming an exact square, having 100 gates of solid brass, 25 on each side, with a street running from each in a straight line to the opposite gate; so that there were in all 50 great streets, each 15 miles long. The site is near the present town of Helleh or Hillah, which see. Alexander of Macedon died here April 21, B. C. 323.

Baca, or Baza, a town of Spain, in Granada, 15 N. E. of Guadix. Pop. about 15,000.

Bach, or Batha, a town of Hungary, formerly the see of a bishop, seated near the Danube, 30 miles E. N. E. of Funfkirchen, and 85. S of Buda.

Bacharach, a town of Germany, in the palatinate of the Rhine. It is famous for its wine, and stands at the foot of a mountain, near the Rhine, 24 miles S. by E. of Coblentz. The Counts palatine had formerly a castle here, and levied toll on the produce and merchandise passing up and down the Rhine, which, from the extent of the exaction, was denominated the golden toll. It at present forms part of the Prussian territory.

Bacheserai, a town of Russia, in the province of Taurida. It was lately the residence of the Tartar clans of the Crimea, and the palace is a curious species of painted Chinese structure. Near this place, on a high rock, is an old fort called the Jews' Citadel, so named as having been from time immemorial inhabited by about 200 families of Jews. Bacheserai is seated in a deep valley, on the rivulet Katza, 18 miles S. S. W. of Simferopol.

Bachian, an island, the largest and most southern of the proper Moluccas. It is 70 miles in circumference. The Dutch first formed a settlement here in 1610. Zabonga is the chief town. Long. 127. 0. E. lat. 0. 25. S.

Bachu, or Baku, a city of Shirvan, in Persia, situate on the shore of a fine haven on the W. side of the Caspian Sea. It was taken possession of by Russia at the commencement of the last century; ceded back to Persia in 1735, and repossessed by Russia since 1801. The country round abounds in petroleum, and, in places, constantly emits flame, but without producing any very sensible degree of heat. It was probably this district that gave rise to the sect of the Parsees, Guebres, or Fire Worshippers, by whom it was formerly much resorted to. Baku is now an inconsiderable place; it is in 40. 5. N. lat. and 50. 10. E. long.

Back River, or Thleeweechodezeth, a river of North America, discovered by Captain Sir George Back. It rises in Sussex Lake, near the Great Slave Lake, and flows to the sea, S. of the land of Boothia Felix.

Badajoz, a town in Spain, capital of Estremadura, and a bishop's see. It is famous for a bridge built by the Romans over the Guadiana. On this bridge the Portuguese were defeated by Don John of Asturias, in 1661. Badajoz was taken by the French in 1809, and retaken by the allied army, under Lord Wellington, by storm, on the 6th of April, 1812. It is a frontier town towards Portugal, and well fortified. It is 14 miles E. of Elvas, and 175 S. by W. of Madrid. Long. 6. 40. W. lat. 38. 45. N.

Badakshan, or Budakshan, a city of Usbec Tartary, or Great Bokhara, capital of the province of Kilan. Gold, silver, and rubies are found in its vicinity; and caravans pass by this city to Cabul and China. It is seated on the main branch of the Gihon, about 100 miles from its source, at the foot of the Belur mountains, 120 miles E. of Balk. Long. 68. 50. N. lat. 37. 10. E.

Badelona, a town of Spain, in Catalonia, seated on the Mediterranean, 10 miles N. E. of Barcelona.

Baden, or Baaden, formerly a margraviate, in the circle of Suabia, stretching along the E. bank of the Rhine. It was divided into Upper and Lower, or Baden-Baden and Baden-Durlach, from the names of the chief towns of the two divisions. Under Napoleon Buonaparte's formation of the Rhenish confederacy in 1806, Baden was constituted a grand duchy in 1809; it was divided into the ten following circles, viz. the Lake, Danube, Weisen, Treisam, Kinzig, Murg, Pfuiz and Enz, Neckar, Odenwald, and Main and Tauber, being names of so many rivers intersecting the territory, and the seat of government, established at Carlsruhe, about two miles from Durlach. The whole territory contains about 5600 square miles, and a population of about 925,000, from the productive portion of whom a revenue of about 600,000*l.* annually is collected for military and state purposes. That portion of the territory bordering on the Rhine, including the old margraviate, is exceedingly fruitful, and contains about 180,000 inhabitants. The forests yield abundance of materials for building and fuel.

Baden, the capital of Upper Baden, with a castle on the top of a hill, where the prince often resides. It is remarkable for its hot baths, and is seated between the Murg and the Rhine, 40 miles W. of Stuttgard, and 20 S. of Carlsruhe. Long. 8. 22. E. lat. 48. 48. N.

BADEN, a town in Switzerland, in Argau, capital of the county of the same name. Near it are some warm baths, mentioned by the ancients under the names of Aquæ and Thermæ Helveticæ. In 1714, a treaty was concluded here between Germany and Spain. It is seated on the Limmat, 10 miles N. W. of Zurich. Long. 8. 24. E. lat. 47. 26. N.

BADEN, a town of Austria, famous for its numerous hot baths; seated on the Suechat, 15 miles S. S. W. of Vienna. Also of a village in the Valais, Switzerland, with a hot bath of a sufficient degree of heat to boil an egg.

BADENWEILER, a town of the grand duchy of Baden, in the circle of Weisen, much frequented for its hot baths, seated near the Rhine, 5 miles S. S. W. of Sulzburg.

BADRINATH, a town in Kumaoon, North Hindostan, elevated 10,000 feet, and celebrated for its temple, visited by 50,000 pilgrims annually.

BAEZA, or BAÇA, a town in Spain, in Andalusia, seated near the source of the Guadalquiver. It was once the residence of a Moorish king, and was since a bishop's see, and seat of a university, but is now deemed of little importance, although its population is still considerable. It lies four leagues E. of the great post road from Madrid to Cadiz by Cordova, and about 10 N. of Jaen.

BAFFO, a seaport town at the W. end of the Isle of Cyprus, with a fort, near the ancient Paphos, of which considerable ruins remain, particularly some broken columns, which probably belonged to the temple of Venus. Long. 32. 30. E. lat. 34. 50. N.

BAFFIN'S BAY, dividing Greenland from the eastern shores of North America—the largest gulf that has yet been explored; it was discovered by William Baffin, in 1616, but his testimony was disbelieved, till 1818, when Captain Parry circumnavigated it, and established his veracity. In 1819, Parry entered Lancaster Sound, and discovered the range of islands now known by his name; and several expeditions have followed in this direction, to ascertain the N. W. passage to the Pacific, but which has not hitherto been accomplished. The N. extremity of the Bay, or Ross Bay, is in lat. 77. 45. N. The centre of it is occupied by impenetrable ice, leaving in the summer a channel round the shores, which abounded with whales and sea calves, but which have now in a great measure deserted them.

BAFRA, a town of Turkey, in Asia, on the Kizil Ermak, 3 miles from the Black Sea.

BAGDAD, a celebrated city of Asiatic Turkey, the capital of a pachalic of the same name, or, as it is now more commonly called, Irak Arabi; which see. Bagdad is finely seated on the E. bank of the noble river Tigris, and, previous to the route to India by the Cape of Good Hope, it was the centre of a very extensive commerce. It was the capital of the Saracen empire, till taken by the Turks in the 13th century; since which it has often been an object of contention between the Turks and Persians, until it was taken the last time by the Turks in 1631. It still continues to be a place of considerable resort, for all the commodities of Natolia, Syria, Persia, and India; but has lost much of its ancient splendour, and is not so opulent as when in the possession of the Persians. The tomb of the Jewish prophet Ezekiel is still shown here. It has several manufactories of silk, cotton, wool, and leather, and has a cannon foundry. The city is surrounded by a wall about five miles in circumference, and contains some commodious houses, but its general character is mean and dirty. Its markets are abundantly supplied with all kinds of provisions; but the great heat of its climate renders it uncomfortable in the summer season. It is about 50 miles N. of the site of the ancient Babylon, 250 N. of Bassora, and 8 deg. due E. of Damascus. Lat. 33. 20. N. and 44. 46. E. long. Pop. estimated at from 60,000 to 90,000, three-fourths of whom are Turks; the remainder are Jews, Persians, and of various nations.

BAGLANA, a country of the Deccan of Hindostan, bounded on the N. by Guzerat, E. by Candeish and Dowlatabad, S. by Visiapour, and W. by the ocean. It is exceedingly mountainous, but fertile in many places.

BAGNALUCA, or BANJALUKA, a town of European Turkey, in the N. W. corner of Bosnia, on the border of Croatia, 55 miles N. W. of Serai.

BAGNARA, a seaport of Naples, in Calabria Ulteriore. Here are several high waterfalls; and among the rocks are the ruins of the former town, in which 3017 persons perished by an earthquake in 1783. It is situate near the strait of Messina, 15 miles N. N. E. of Reggio. Long. 16. 8. E. lat. 38. 15. N. Pop. about 5000.

BAGNAREA, a town of Italy, in the patrimony of St. Peter, 5 miles S. of Orvieto.

BAGNERES, a town of France, in the department of Upper Pyrenees, famous for its baths and mineral waters; seated on the river Adour, 10 miles S. of Tarbes.

BAGNOLES, a town of France, in the department of Gard, near the river Cese, 8 miles S. of Pont St. Esprit. It has manufactures of silk.

BAGSHOT, a village in Surrey, 12 miles N. by E. of Farnham. It is surrounded by an extensive heath, bordered on the W. by Windsor park. Since 1800 a considerable portion has been enclosed and brought under cultivation.

BAHAMAS, or LUCAYOS ISLANDS, a group of islands, forming part of the British West Indies, extending from the long. of 79. W. in the lat. of 28. in a S. E. direction, to the long. of 70. in the lat. of 21. N. The northern part lies contiguous to the coast of Florida, and the southern contiguous to the N. end of St. Domingo. The greater portion are mere rocks and uninhabited; the following, with their lat. and long., are the principal islands: —

	Lat.	Long.
Bahama	26 43	79 0
Abaco	26 19	77 0
Andreas	25 20	78 10
New Providence	25 0	77 37
Eleuthera	24 37	76 22
Exuma	23 33	75 51
Cat Island	24 37	75 50
Long Island	23 0	75 10
Crooked ditto	22 49	74 19
Mariguana	22 31	73 10
Great Caycos	21 34	71 27
Grand Turk	21 32	71 4
Inagua	21 0	73 0
Square Handkerchief	20 53	70 55

Of these, Cat Island first deserves notice, as being the first land of the western hemisphere discovered by Columbus on the 12th of October, 1492, by whom it was called Guanahani. New Providence is the best cultivated, producing a little sugar, coffee, and cotton, and exporting large quantities of pines to the United States of America. Exuma and Turk Islands have exported 30,000 tons of salt annually, but the chief occupation of the inhabitants is the turtle fishery. The passage between the northernmost island and the coast of Florida is called the Bahama channel, and another passage between Long and Crooked islands is called the windward passage, and forms the route of the ships bound from Jamaica to Europe; the Jamaica packet touches at Crooked Island homeward bound, as the point of departure. Population probably amounts to about 17,000.

Bahar, an interior province of Hindostan, W. of Bengal; bounded on the N. by Nepaul, W. by Oude and Allahabad, and S. by Bezar and Orissa. It is intersected by the Ganges from W. to E., which receives several tributary streams in its course through the province, the most considerable of which are, the Coosey, from the N., and the Soane from the S. It is an exceedingly fertile district; its rice is the finest of all Hindostan; sugar, silk, indigo, cotton, and saltpetre are produced in great abundance. Patna, on the S. bank of the Ganges, is the chief town. The town of Bahar, formerly the capital, is about 35 miles S. E. of Patna. The whole province is subject to the English.

Bahia, one of the twelve capitanias of Brazil, lying S. of Pernambuco, and extending from the 11th to nearly the 16th deg. of S. lat. and W. from the Atlantic Ocean in the long. of 40., to a ridge of mountains in 44., which bound it on the W. Bahia contains a surface of 54,649 square miles, and is the most extensively cultivated district of all Brazil; sugar, coffee, cotton, and tobacco are all produced in great abundance, and the culture is progressively extending. The forests abound in a variety of wood, and are so dense as to be almost impenetrable. Pop. 560,000. The chief town of the same name, or, as it is sometimes called, St. Salvador, is situate in lat. 13. 0. S. and 38. 29. W. long. on the E. bank of a noble bay, called the Bay of All Saints, which runs up from S. to N. about 40 miles, being about 8 miles wide at its mouth. Next to Rio Janeiro, Bahia is the most important town of the Brazils, and in point of commerce is the greatest. The houses are in general well built, mostly of stone, and it has several churches and convents of considerable magnitude. Pop. about 100,000.

Bahlingen, a town of Wurtemburg, situate near the source of the Teyah, a branch of the Neckar River, about 20 miles S. W. of Hohengollern.

Bahr el Abiad. *See* Abiad.

Bahr el Azrek. *See* Azrek.

Bahraitch, a town of Hindostan, in the province of Oude, 62 miles N. N. W. of Fyzabad, and 65 N. E. of Lucknow. Long. 81. 56. E. lat. 27. 30. N.

Bahrenburg, a town of Westphalia, in the county of Hoya, on the river Suhlingen, 20 miles W. of Nieuburg.

Bahrein, a town of Arabia, situate on an island 30 miles long, in the Gulf of Persia. It gives name not only to the island on which it is built, but also to a cluster of them, celebrated for the pearl fishery; and likewise to a province extending along the W. coast of the gulf. The town is fortified, and belonged once to the Portuguese, but now belongs to Busheer. It stands on the W. side of the island, 70 miles N. E. of Lahsa. Long. 49. 5. E. lat. 26. 20. N.

Baia, a town of Naples, in Terra di Lavoro, formerly famous for its hot baths and elegant palaces, of which some ruins remain. It is seated on the Bay of Naples, 12 miles W. of Naples.

Baja, a town of Lower Hungary, on the E. bank of the Danube, 85 miles N. W. of Esseg.

Baias, or Payas, a town of Syria, at the N. E. corner of the Gulf of Alexandretto, or Iskenderoon, supposed to have been the ancient Issus, celebrated for the victory of Alexander over Darius.

Baibourdi, an inland town of Armenia, 40 miles N. of Arz Roum.

Baikal, a lake of Siberia, in the province of Irkutsk, 350 miles in length, but its greatest breadth, not above 40, between the lat. of 52. and 55. N. and 104. to 109. E. long. The water is fresh, and the Russians speak of it with reverence, calling it the Holy Sea. There are many seals in it of a blackish colour, and abundance of fish; also several islands; and that of Olchon, the largest, has sulphureous springs, and naphtha sometimes floats on its surface. It receives the Selinga from the S., and its outlet is the Angara, which flows N. into the Yenisei.

Bailleul, a town of France, in the department of Nord, 9 miles S. W. of Ypres. It is a manufacturing town. Pop. about 9000. There are several other towns of the same name, in different parts of France.

Bailur, a seaport of Abyssinia, and chief town in the country of Dancali. It stands on a spacious bay of the Red Sea, 340 miles E. by N. of Gondar. Long. 42. 40. E. lat. 13. 3. N.

Bain, a town of France, in the department of Ille and Vilaine, 16 miles S. of Rennes.

Bairdstown, the chief tn. of Nelson county, Kentucky, 47 miles S. W. of Frankfort.

Bairout, or **Beyrut**, anciently Berytus, a seaport of Syria, in Palestine, and the chief town of the Druses. The port is nearly choked with sand and ruins; but many cottons and silks are exported hence for Cairo. It stands on the N. side of a broad promontory, 50 miles W. N. W. of Damascus. Long. 36. 10. E. lat. 33. 45. N. Pop. about 7500.

Baireuth, a town of Bavaria, seated in a pleasant valley, and regularly built. Pop. 14,000. *See* **Bayreuth**.

Bakewell, an extensive parish and town, in the Peak of Derbyshire, with a market on Friday. Here is a large cotton-mill; and near it, at the village of Ashford, are marble works, where the black and grey marbles found in the vicinity are sawn and polished. It is seated on the Wye, 27 miles N. N. W. of Derby, and 153 of London.

Bakow, or **Bakou**, a tn. of European Turkey, in Moldavia, on the river Bistritza, 60 miles S. W. of Jassy.

Bakshishiserai, a town of Russia, 60 miles N. of Caffa in the Crimea. It is an irregularly built place. Pop. 6000.

Baku, or **Bachu**, a town of Persia, in the province of Schirvan, the most commodious haven of the Caspian Sea, on the W. coast of which it is situate. The vicinity produces much rock salt, sulphur, and naphtha, and it is famous for saffron. Baku is a fortress, surrounded by high brick walls, 300 miles S. of Astracan. Long. 49. 15. E. lat. 40. 2. N.

Bala, a corporate tn. of Wales, in Merionethshire, with a market on Saturday. It is seated on the Lake of Bala, or Pemblemere, which is 3 miles long and 1 broad, and abounds with a fish called guinard, resembling a salmon in shape, and tasting like a trout. The river Dee issues from this lake. It has the remains of three Roman camps, which seem to have been used as exploratory stations, before the Ordovices were totally subdued. The inhabitants carry on a considerable trade in knit woollen stockings. It is 40 miles S. E. of Caernarvon, and 195 N. W. of London.

Balacheo, a tn. of European Russia, situate on a branch of the Don, 90 miles W. of Saratov.

Balachna, a town of Russia, situate near the Volga, 40 miles W. N. W. of Niznei Novogorod.

Balaguer, a fortified town of Spain, in Catalonia, on the river Segra, at the foot of a craggy rock, 75 miles W. N. W. of Barcelona. Long. 0. 40. E. lat. 41. 43. N.

Balaganskoi, a town in the province of Irkoutsk, Siberia, about 30 miles N. of the city of Irkoutsk.

Balaghaut, a district in central India, presidency of Madras, ceded to the British in 1800. Capital, Ahmednagur.

Balaklawa, a seaport at the S. W. end of the Crimea. It is much frequented.

Balambangan, a small but very fruitful island, off the N. end of Borneo, in lat. 7. 16. N. and 116. 58. W. long.

Balambuan. *See* **Palambuan**.

Balapura, Chica, a town of Hindostan, in Mysore, noted for the manufacture of sugar-candy and clayed sugar, 15 miles N. E. of Doda Balapura.

Balapura, Doda, a town of Hindostan, in Mysore, surrounded by a mud-wall and hedge, and has a strong mud fort, with a palace. Here are manufactures of cloth and sugar It is 22 miles N. by W. of Bangalore, and 57 S. E. of Sera.

Balaruc, a town of France, in the department of Herault, famous for its baths. It is 12 miles from Montpelier.

Balasore, a seaport of Hindostan, in Orissa, and a place of considerable trade; situate on the Gongahar, 20 miles from its mouth in the Bay of Bengal, and 124 S. W. of Calcutta. Long. 86. 46. E. lat. 21. 26. N.

Balaton, a lake in the S. part of Lower Hungary, 40 miles in length, and 1 to 4 broad. The N. end is about 5 miles from Stuht-Weisenburg, and 36 more from the Danube.

Balbastro, an episcopal town in Spain, in Arragon, on the river Vero, near its conflux with the Cinca, 45 miles E. N. E. of Saragossa. Pop. 7000.

Balbec, or **Baalbec**, the ancient Heliopolis, a town of Syria, at the foot of Mount Libanus, near the N. E. extremity of the fertile valley of Bocat. On the E. side are magnificent ruins, particularly those of the temple dedicated to the sun. The town was nearly destroyed by an earthquake in 1759, and is now a poor place, 37 miles N. N. W. of Damascus.

Balbriggan, a town in Ireland, county of Dublin. It has a small harbour, and the inhabitants are engaged in fishery, and the manufacture of silk and cotton.

Baldock, a town in Hertfordshire, with a market on Thursday; seated among the hills, 9 miles W. S. W. of Royston, and 37 N. N. W. of London. It was originally built by the knights templars, in the 12th century, on the site of the Roman way, called the Ikeneild-street.

Balearic Isles, five islands in the Mediterranean, forming part of the province of Arragon; they are named Majorca, Minorca, Ivica, Formentera, and Cabrera, which see.

Balfrush, a town of Persia, in Mazanderan, on the S. shore of the Caspian Sea, 12 miles W. of Ferabad.

Balga, a town of Prussia, on the Frisch Haff, 24 miles S. W. of Konigsberg.

Bali, or **Bally**, an island, 75 miles long, and 45 broad, at the E. end of the isle of Java, from which it is separated by a channel called the Strait of Bali. It is populous, abounds in rice and fruits, and furnishes slaves, cotton yarn, and pickled pork. Long. 11. 50. E. lat. 8. 30. S.

Balize, a river which divides the provinces of Yucatan and Guatimala, falling into the Bay of Honduras in lat. 14. 50. N. 91. 15. W. long. There is a town of the same name near the mouth of the river, which forms the principal settlement of the English for supplying mahogany and logwood, to the extent of 20,000 tons annually. Pop. about 18,000.

BALKAN, or EMINEH DAGH, a chain of mountains in European Turkey, forming the N. boundary of Roumelia and Bulgaria, and terminates at the Black Sea.

BALKH, a southern province of Independent Tartary, bordering on Persia, now subject to Cabul. The principal city of the same name is situate on the Dewash, a branch of the Oxus or Amu river, and is a place of great antiquity, once the capital of Persia, and the residence of Cyrus. It is still a place of considerable importance and intercourse between the inhabitants of the countries bordering on the eastern shores of the Caspian Sea and the sea of Aral and Bokhara on one side, and of Hindostan on the other. The khan's castle is a magnificent structure, built of marble, dug out of the neighbouring mountains. It is about 220 miles S. E. of Bokhara, and 260 N. W. of Attock Benares on the Indus, in 36. 28. N. lat. and 65. 20. W. long. Pop. about 7000.

BALLANTRAE, a town of Scotland, in Ayrshire, near the mouth of the Stinchar, 24 miles S. S. W. of Ayre.

BALLENSTADT, a town of Germany, in the duchy of Anhalt. It is gloomy and ill-built. Pop. 2000.

BALLIBAY, a town of Ireland, in the county of Monaghan, 76 miles from Dublin.

BALLIEBOROUGH, a parish and town in the county of Cavan, Ireland.

BALLIMONEY, a town of Ireland, county of Antrim, 150 miles from Dublin. Linen markets are held here.

BALLINA, a town in the county of Mayo, Ireland, 7 miles S. of Killala, and 120 W. by N. of Dublin. It was occupied by the French in 1798.

BALLINAKILL, a town of Ireland, Queen's county, 66 miles from Dublin.

BALLINASLOE, a town chiefly in the parish of Kilcloony, county of Galway, but extends into the parish of Creagh, in the county of Roscommon, Ireland. It is distinguished for its great annual sheep fair the first week in Oct., when about 100,000 sheep and 10,000 head of horned cattle are brought to market. It is 12 miles W. of Athlone, and 72 W. of Dublin. It is sometimes called Dunloe.

BALLINGARRY, a parish and town in the county of Limerick, Ireland.

BALLINROBE, a town of Ireland, county of Mayo, 147 miles from Dublin. A permanent military station.

BALLON, a town of France, 9 miles from Rochelle. Pop. 2500.

BALLSTON, a town of Saratoga county, state of New York, 23 miles N. W. of Albany. Pop. 2047.

BALLSTON SPA, a mineral spring in the adjoining township of Milton, 3 miles N. of the town of Ballston. It is a celebrated resort of valetudinarians and of fashion in North America.

BALLY, in Irish, signifies *town*; there are upwards of 150 parishes, towns, and villages in Ireland beginning with *Bally*.

BALLYCASTLE, a town of Ireland, county Antrim, 180 miles from Dublin. There is coal in the vicinity.

BALLYJAMESDUFF, a town of Ireland, county Cavan, 57 miles from Dublin.

BALLYMAHON, a town of Ireland, county Longford, 68 miles from Dublin, seated on the river Inny.

BALLYMENA, a town of Ireland, county Antrim, 132 miles from Dublin, with a good market for butter and linens.

BALLYRAGGET, a town of Ireland, county Kilkenny, 76 miles from Dublin.

BALLYSHANNON, a town of Ireland, county Donegal, on the side of a hill, on the river Erne, 127 miles from Dublin.

BALMERINO, a town of Scotland, in Fifeshire, which has a trade in corn and salmon. The ruins of its once magnificent abbey, founded in 1229, are much admired. It is seated on the Frith of Tay, opposite Dundee; 10 miles N. W. of St. Andrews.

BALTIC, an inland sea, in the N. W. of Europe, between the coasts of Sweden, Russia, Courland, Prussia, Germany, and Denmark, extending from the 54th to the 60th degree of N. lat., the Gulf of Bothnia running up to the lat. of 66. and lying between the 16th and 22nd degree of W. long., the Gulf of Livonia extending 2 degrees further W., and that of Finland as far as 30. Its surface is estimated at 120,000 square miles; it contains a great number of islands, the principal of which are Aland, Dago, Oesel, Gothland, Oeland, Bornholm, Rugen, and Laland; and the islands of Zealand and Funen separate it from the Cattegat, by which it communicates with the ocean. There are three navigable channels into the Baltic from the sea called the Cattegat, which communicates with the German Ocean: 1st. which is the most northerly and most frequented, is called the Sound, between the coast of Sweden N. and the coast of the Isle of Zealand S. This passage is about 4 miles across, and is navigated by 8000 to 9000 sail of vessels annually, which pay a trifling tax to the Danish government, for the maintenance of the light-houses on the coasts of the several channels. The middle channel, between the S. side of the Isle of Zealand and the Isles of Funen and Laland, is called the Great Belt; and the most southerly, between the Isles of Funen and Laland, and the coast of Jutland, the Little Belt; but the navigation of both is circuitous and intricate compared with the Sound, and they are only availed of under very particular circumstances. There is little or no tide within the Baltic, and, as such, the channels and harbours are generally frozen up three to four months in the winter. Amber is found on the coast of Prussia.

BALTIMORE, a county of the state of Maryland. Pop. 134,379. The chief town, of the same name, is finely located, at the head of an inlet called Petapsco River, on the W. side of Chesapeake Bay, in lat. 39. 22. N. and long. 76. 55. W. A stream called Jones's Falls divides the city into two parts, the town and Fell's Point, connected by bridges. Baltimore is the centre of an extensive commerce, and has risen into importance more rapidly than any other place in the Union. In 1765 the spot was a dreary swamp, and in 1820 contained a population of 62,629, about 12,000 of whom were blacks, possessing 68,674 tons of shipping. Present pop. 102,313. The houses are in general well built, principally of brick; it has upwards of 30 religious edifices, but none that merit any particular notice. The harbour is entered by a narrow strait, exceedingly well defended by a fort. During the war of 1813-14, the English made an unsuccessful attempt to possess Baltimore.

Baltinglass, a town and parish of Ireland, in the county of Wicklow. It has some manufactures of linen and woollen, and is seated on the Slaney, 29 miles S. W. of Dublin.

Baloochistan. *See* **Beloochistan.**

Bamba, a town of the kingdom of Congo, in a rich province of the same name. It carries on a traffic in slaves, and is seated on the Loze, 160 miles S. W. of St. Salvador. Long. 13. 45. E. lat. 7. 2. S.

Bambara, a kingdom of Negroland, which lies to the S. W. of that of Tombuctoo. The cultivation of corn is here carried on to a great extent; and the inhabitants are hospitable to strangers. Sego is the capital. It is intersected from W. to E. by a river, the supposed Niger, navigable for canoes the whole extent of the country.

Bamberg, the territory of, formerly an imperial bishopric, but made over to Bavaria in the Buonapartean territorial arrangements in 1803, and is now called the circle of the Maine. It is intersected by the lines of 50. N. lat. and the 11th of E. long. containing a surface of about 1430 square miles, several towns and villages, and a population of 210,000. The chief town, of the same name, is situate in the centre of the territory, on the E. bank of the Rednitz river, a little above its conflux with the Maine. It is the seat of a university, and the cathedral and episcopal palace are stately edifices.

Bamberg, a town of Bohemia, at the foot of a mountain, 30 miles S. of Glatz.

Bamborough, a village in Northumberland, on the sea coast, 14 miles N. of Alnwick. It was once a borough, and gave name to a tract called Bamboroughshire. It has a castle, on a rock, inaccessible on all sides, except the south, said to have been built by King Ida, about 560.

Bambouk, a kingdom of Africa, between the rivers Faleme and Senegal. It is said to be very populous, and on the borders of the rivers fertile, but in other parts sandy and barren. The most remarkable animals are a species of white apes, which they will not allow to be sent out of the country, white foxes, and the giraffe, or cameleopard, an animal of extraordinary swiftness. There are mines of gold, silver, tin, lead, and iron. The capital is of the same name. Long. 9. 30. W. lat. 13. 30. N.

Bamian, a city of Cabul, in Affghanistan. Here are a great number of apartments and recesses cut out of a mountain, some of which, from their ornamental work and extraordinary dimensions, are supposed to have been temples. It is seated near a river of the same name, 170 miles S. S. E. of Balk, and 100 W. of Cabul. Long. 66. 10. E. lat. 34. 30. N.

Bammakoo, a town of Central Africa, on the Niger. Long. 3. 48. W. lat. 12. 47. N.

Bamoa, or **Bhanmo**, a town on the north borders of the kingdom of Birmah, with a fort, seated on the Irrawaddy, 170 miles N. N. E. of Ummerapoora.

Bampton, a town in Oxfordshire, with a market on Wednesday. The remains of its ancient castle yet exist; and it has a trade in leather gloves, jackets, and breeches. It is seated near the Thames, 12 miles W. of Oxford, and 71 W. by N. of London.

Bampton, a town in Devonshire, with a market on Saturday, a chalybeate spring, and a manufacture of serges. It is seated in a bottom, surrounded by hills, 20 miles N. N. E. of Exeter, and 163 W. by S. of London.

Banagher, a borough of Ireland, in King's County, seated on the Shannon, 15 miles S. of Athlone.

Banawara, a town of Hindostan, in Mysore, with a fine mud fort, and the ruins of an extensive palace. Much tobacco is cultivated in the vicinity. It is 68 miles N. W. of Seringapatam.

Banbridge, a town in Ireland, county Down, 76 miles from Dublin; manufactures linen.

Banbury, a borough in Oxfordshire, governed by a mayor; with a market on Thursday. It is noted for its cakes and ale, and is seated on the Charwell, 71 miles N. N. W. of London, and on the line of the Oxford Canal. It has a manufacture of silk plush, and returns one member to parliament.

Banca, an island on the S. E. coast of Sumatra, celebrated for its productive tin mines. It has a town and strait of the same name. It was possessed by the English during the war of 1812-13, but ceded back to the Dutch in 1814.

Bancali, a seaport on an island off the E. coast of Sumatra, in the Straits of Malacca; where the Dutch have a settlement. It is 130 miles S. of Malacca. Long. 101. 7. E. lat. 1. 15. N.

Bancallary, the chief town of the island of Madura. It is the residence of the sultan, and populous.

Bancapour, a frontier town of Mysore, in lat. 14. 58. N., belonging to the Mahrattas.

Banrock, a town of the kingdom of Siam, with a fort; seated near the mouth of the Meinan, 49 miles S. of Siam. Long. 101. 48. E. lat. 13. 44. N.

Bancout, or **Fort Victoria**, a town and fortress of Hindostan, on the coast of the Concan, with a good harbour, and a trade in salt. It was taken by the British in 1755; and is 66 miles S. of Bombay. Long. 72. 48. E. lat. 18. 5. N.

Banda, a town of North Hindostan, province of Allahabad, a prosperous town, the seat of an excellent cotton manufacture.

Banda, the chief of the Banda, or Nutmeg Islands in the Indian Ocean. The group comprises this isle, called also Lantor, and six or seven others. The nutmeg, covered with mace, grows principally on these islands; and they have been subject to the Dutch ever since 1609, when they expelled both the English and natives. They are all very small, the largest being only 20 miles in circumference, and are subject to earthquakes. Banda was taken by the English in 1796, and restored in 1802, retaken in 1810, and restored again at the peace in 1814. Lat. 4. 40. S. long. 129. 30. E.

Banda-Oriental. *See* Uruguay.

Bandon, or **Bandon-bridge**, a borough of Ireland, in the county of Cork. It is commonly a military station, and has manufactures of cotton, camlets, ticking, &c. It is situate on a river of the same name, 13 miles S. W. of Cork. It returns one member to parliament.

Bandora, a town of Hindostan, on tne S. side of the island of Salsette, which is separated from that of Bombay by a narrow channel. It is 6 miles N. of Bombay.

Bancas, a tn. of Syria, 20 miles S. of Latakia.

Banff, a county of Scotland, bounded on the N. by the ocean, S. E. by Aberdeenshire, and W. by Murrayshire. Its greatest length is 50 miles, and its extent along the coast 22, but the main breadth is not more than 16. The S. part is very mountainous, but the northern district is level and fertile. The principal rivers are the Deveron and Spey, which form a part of its E. and W. boundaries, and yield abundance of fine salmon. The Avon rises from a small lake at the S. extremity of the county, falling into the Spey, where that river divides the county from Murrayshire. The principal towns are Gamry, Cullen, Fochabers, Keith, Aberdour, and Kirkmichael. Some minerals are found in the county, and great quantities of hones and whetstones. It returns one member to parliament.

Banff, the chief town of the preceding county, is situate at its N. W. extremity, on the E. bank of the Deveron, over which is a hand some bridge of seven arches. It has some manufactures of linen and cotton, but it is more a place of fashionable resort than either a manufacturing or commercial town. The town hall was built in 1798, and is a handsome edifice. It is a royal burgh, governed by a provost, four baillies, and 12 councillors; 45 miles N. of Aberdeen, and 167 of Edinburgh, and returns one member to parliament.

Bangalore, a city of Hindostan, in Mysore. It had a strong fort, built by Hyder, deemed the bulwark of Mysore, toward Arcot: it was taken by the English in 1791, and restored the next year to Tippoo, who destroyed it; but since reverted to the English. The palace is composed of mud, yet not without some degree of magnificence; and there are two extensive gardens made by the two sultans. The chief manufactures are silk and cotton cloths, muslins, leather, and oil. It is 74 miles N. E. of Seringapatam. Long. 77. 37. E. lat. 13. 0. N.

Bang-kok, or **Bankok**, a town of Asia, in Siam, on the river Menam-kong. The houses are mostly of wood, and on piles. An abundance of teak timber for ship-building is found in the neighbourhood. Pop. 40,000.

Bangor, a city of Wales, in Caernarvonshire, with a market on Wednesday. It is situate on the E. shore of the Menai Strait, on the high road from London to Holyhead. It was once so considerable, that it was called Bangor the Great, and defended by a castle. The principal buildings are the cathedral and the bishop's palace. The see is of very great antiquity. The church was dedicated to St. Daniel, who was bishop about the year 516. It is 36 miles W. of St. Asaph, and 251 N. W. of London. It contributes in sending one member to parliament.

Bangor, a town and populous parish in Ireland, in the county of Down, seated on the S. shore of the Bay of Carrickfergus, opposite the town of that name; 90 miles N. by E. of Dublin, and about 10 E. of Belfast.

Bangor, a town in the United States, state of Maine, with considerable trade, and a theological seminary. Pop. 8,627.

Banjaluka. *See* Bagnaluka.

Banjer, or **Bender**, a considerable river in the island of Borneo, which flows almost due S. from the centre of the country to the harbour of Banjermassing; and at its mouth the Dutch have their principal factory.

Banjermassing, or **Bendermassing**, a kingdom in the S. part of the island of Borneo, the capital of which is Metapura. The country produces great quantities of pepper; also gold, iron, diamonds, canes, birds'-nests, wax, and dragon's-blood. It has a town of the same name, with a good harbour, at the mouth of the river Banjer. Long. 114. 30. E. lat. 3. 15. S.

Banks Peninsula, on the E. side of New Zealand, in the Pacific Ocean; about 100 miles in circumference. Long. 184. 0. E. lat. 34. 30. S.

Banks Island, an island in the Pacific Ocean, near the W. coast of North America, about 60 miles long and 5 broad. Long. 130. 0. W. lat. 53. 30. N.

Bann, a river of Ireland, which issues from the Mourne mountains, in the county of Down, flows N. W. into Armagh, through Lough Neagh, and thence forms the boundary between Londonderry and Antrim, entering the sea four miles below Coleraine.

Bannalec, a town in the S. E. part of the department of Finisterre, France, 15 miles E. of Quimper.

Bannbridge, a town of Ireland, in the county of Down, on the river Bann, 14 miles N. by E. of Newry, on the road to Belfast.

Bannockburn, a village of Scotland, in the parish of St. Ninians, on the river Bannock, two miles S. of Stirling. It is noted for a battle between Edward II. and Robert Bruce, in 1314, in which the former was defeated. Here also James III., in 1487, was defeated by his subjects, wounded, and soon after murdered by a priest, taking his confession.

Bantam, a town on the N. W. coast of Java, capital of a kingdom of the same name, with two forts. It is divided into two parts by a river. The English and Danes had factories here till 1682, when they were expelled by the Dutch. The chief produce of the country is pepper, of which vast quantities were formerly exported by the Dutch, who deposed the kings of the ancient race, and monopolized the entire traffic of the country. Bantam, once populous and flourishing, is now a poor place, its harbour being so choked up that it is inaccessible to vessels of burden; its commerce is transferred to Batavia. Long. 105. 26. E. lat. 6. 20. S. Pop. of the province, 230,000.

Bantry, a capacious bay, at the S. W. extremity of Ireland, on the coast of Cork, capable of containing all the shipping of Europe; but somewhat exposed to the swells of the Atlantic Ocean. A French fleet endeavoured to land succours of arms in this bay to the adherents of James II. in 1689, and they made another unsuccessful attempt to effect a landing with a formidable force in 1796. It is 26 miles long, 3 broad, and 40 fathoms deep in the middle. There is a town named *Bantry*, at the head of the bay on the E. side, the spacious harbour of which is defended from the swells of the ocean by the island of Whiddy. It is 46 miles W. by S. of Cork, and 163 from Dublin.

Banyuwangy, a town in Java, East Indies; a Dutch military station for suppressing piracies. Here is the volcano Goonong Marapi. Pop. of the territory, 8800.

Bapaume, a town of France, in the department of Pas de Calais, 12 miles S. E. of Arras. Pop. 3150. There is a river of the same name, falling into the Seine, which drives about 20 paper-mills.

Bar, a town of Podolia, in Russian Poland, on a river that flows E. into the Bug. In 1768, a catholic confederation was held here, to protect the religion of the country from the encroachment of dissenters. It is 48 miles E.N.E. of Kaminieck, and 55 N. W. of Braclaw. Long. 27. 40. E. lat. 49. 14. N.

Bar, a town of Hindostan, in Bahar, near the Ganges, 34 miles E. S. E. of Patna.

Bar, or **Barrois**, a late duchy of France, lying on both sides of the Meuse, between Lorraine and Champagne. It now forms the department of Meuse.

Baracoa, a town on the N.E. coast of Cuba, with a good harbour for small vessels, 90 miles E. N. E. of St. Jago de Cuba. Long. 74. 42. W. lat. 20. 30. N.

Baranco de Malambo, or **Raranguilla**, a town of Colombia, in the province of Magdalena, and a bishop's see, with a good harbour, at the mouth of the Magdalena, 70 miles N.E. of Carthagena. Long. 74. 50. W. lat. 11. 20. N.

Barant, or **Baranwahr**, a town of Lower Hungary, capital of the county of Barany, taken from the Turks in 1684. It is seated in an island, formed by the river Crasso, 14 miles N. of Esseg, and 120 S. of Buda. Long. 19. 16. E. lat. 45. 42. N.

Barbacoa, a town of Colombia, in Cauca, on the river Tolembi. 110 miles S. W. of Popayan.

Barbacoa, a town of Colombia, in Venezuela, on the E. side of the lake Maracaybo, 130 miles S. by W. of Venezuela.

Barbadoes, the most easterly of the Windward Islands, in the West Indies, 25 miles long and 15 broad; subject to Great Britain. The soil is beautifully undulated, and yields most of the productions common to the climate; but the chief object of culture is the sugar-cane, the produce of which is about 15,000 tons of sugar annually, which, with some ginger and arrow-root, form its main exports. The island suffered greatly by a storm, on the 10th of October, 1780, when upwards of 4000 persons perished by its violence; and, at the commencement of the 19th century, was considerably on the decline, the soil indicating symptoms of exhaustion, until the year 1813, when a very singular phenomenon occurred, which contributed essentially to its resuscitation: a vast dense cloud of matter from the eastward, composed of volcanic eruption, fell, and covered nearly the whole surface of the island, which tended greatly to its fertility. Barbadoes was constituted an ecclesiastical see over the whole of the Caribbee Islands in 1824. It is also the chief seat of the commissariat for the same, which occasions the internal commerce of the island to be considerable. It was first settled by the English in 1624: after the restoration of Charles II., a duty of 4½ per cent. was exacted upon all produce exported, under the pretext of maintaining and keeping in repair the forts of the island, and for other protection. The duty has continued 150 years, and in 1820 amounted to 18,637*l.*, but wholly converted into *pensions*, and the expenses of the island defrayed out of the taxes levied in England. It is divided into five districts and eleven parishes. Bridgetown, the chief town, is in lat. 13. 5. N. and 59. 43. W. long. Charles's, James's, and Speight's towns, are the other towns of the island. Pop. 81,939.

Barbantane, a town of France, department Bouches du Rhone, 6 miles from Avignon. Pop. 2300. Excellent wine is made here.

Barbara, St., a town on the W. coast of North America, capital of a jurisdiction of its name. It stands in a rugged, barren country, but has a good roadstead. Long. 119. 17. W. lat. 34. 54. N.

Barbareen, a village of Ceylon, on the W. coast, 35 miles S. of Colombo. It has a harbour for ship-boats, and a considerable manufacture of cordage and cables from the cocoa-tree.

Barbary, or the **Barbary States**, comprise the whole northern coast of North Africa, bordering on the Mediterranean Sea, from the Atlantic Ocean to Egypt; bounded, or rather intersected on the S. by the Atlas chain of mountains, and bounded by the deserts of Sahara, Tuarick, and Libya, extending in length from the long of 10. W. to 25. E., and varying in breadth from 300 to 600 or 700 miles, between the lat. of 29. and 37. N., divided into the six following sovereignties, or states; viz. first, beginning with the west; Morocco, bor dering wholly on the Atlantic Ocean, Fez, forming the north-west corner of the African continent, and Algier, Tunis, Tripoli, and Barca, all bordering on the Mediterranean. This extensive territory was known to the ancients by the names of Mauritania, Numidia, Africa Proper, and Libya, and at one period contended with Rome for the empire of the world; and although at the present day its inhabitants are amongst the most unsocial and illiterate of the communities of civilization, they were at one period as distinguished for their attainments in art, as in arms. The whole country abounds in local beauties, and possesses all the advantages of soil and climate which man need desire; the soil yields great crops of maize and corn, and all the choice fruits, such as lemons, oranges, the vine, olives, figs, almonds, and dates, are in great profusion; the mountains are rich in mineral substances, and all the domestic animals common to Europe abound over the whole country, and the horses are much esteemed for their fleetness and beauty. The lion, panther, and hyæna, and other ferocious animals, are numerous in the mountains, and frequently make inroads into the plains. Reptiles are also very numerous, and the boa constrictor, the head, and most ferocious of that species of animated nature, is common on the borders of the deserts. The external commerce of the country is limited, but will be more particularly adverted to when treating of the respective divisions. Mahometanism, in its utmost degree of personal indulgence and wantonness of power, prevails alike in all the states, and restrains all rational and social advancement.

Barberino, a town of Tuscany, at the foot of the Appennines, on the river Sieva, 12 miles N. of Florence.

Barbezieux, a town of France, in the department of Charente, with a mineral spring, and a manufacture of linen cloth. It is 45 miles N. E. of Bordeaux. Pop. 2750.

Barbuda, one of the Leeward Islands, in the West Indies, 20 miles long and 10 broad. It has a good road for shipping, but the inhabitants (about 1500) are chiefly employed in raising corn and breeding cattle, for the use of the neighbouring islands. It is 35 miles N. of Antigua. Long. 61. 50. W. lat. 17. 50. N.

Barby, a town in the Prussian principality of Anhalt, circle of Upper Saxony, capital of a county of its name, with an ancient castle, and an academical college, founded by the United Brethren in 1754. It is seated on the Elbe, 15 miles S. E. of Magdeburg. Long. 12. 4. E. lat. 52. 2. N.

Barca, one of the six Barbary states, the ancient Cyrenaica, on the south coast of the Mediterranean, between Tripoli and Egypt. The south part is a barren desert, inhabited by wandering Arabs. The north part along the coast is fertile and well peopled. It belonged to the Turks, and is governed by a sangiac, dependent on the bashaw, who resides at Tripoli. Derna is the capital.

Barcellos, a town of Portugal, province of Entre Douro e Minho, famous for its fans. Pop. 3900.

Barcelona, a city of Spain, capital of Catalonia, and a bishop's see, with a good harbour on the Mediterranean. It is of an oblong form, defended by a strong fort, called Montjuich, which stands on a rocky mountain, a mile west of the town. It has double walls on the north and east, and the sea on the south, with a mole for the security of ships. It is divided into the New and Old town, by a wall and a ditch; and the sea having retired considerably from the portgates, a whole quarter of the town now stands on the sands that were once the bottom of the harbour. It has a fine university, an inquisition, a cathedral with two lofty towers, a palace for the viceroy, a large exchange, an extensive cannon foundry, an arsenal containing arms for several thousand men, and docks for the building of galleys. It has various manufactures, but is more particularly distinguished for those of fire-arms of all kinds, swords, cutlery, and soap; and there are several very extensive distilleries of brandy: its commerce is general. In 1705 it was taken by the Earl of Peterborough, after a siege of three weeks. In 1706, Philip V. invested it with a numerous army, but was obliged to raise the siege. In 1714 it was taken by the French and Spaniards, and a citadel built to keep it in awe. The French took this city by treachery in 1808. In 1823, it held out to the last in favour of the constitutionalists, and did not yield until all hope or expectation of successful resistance was obviously useless. It is 250 miles E. by N. of Madrid. Long. 2. 12. E. lat. 41. 23. N. Pop. of the city about 100,000, and the new town or suburb of Barcelonetta 10,000 to 12,000 more.

Barcelona is also the name of a populous seaport town, situate at the mouth of the little river Neveri in the new province of Oronoko, Columbia, about 50 miles W. of Cumana. It is a mean dirty place; the inhabitants about 14,000, under the proscribed system of Old Spain, where the chief medium of the smuggling is carried on between Trinidad and the interior parts of the country.

Barcelonette, a town of France, situate among the Alpine mountains, in the department of the Lower Alps, about 10 miles S. of Embrun.

Barcelore, or Barcura, a town of Hindostan, on the coast of Canara, which gives name to a district, but has been long in ruins. It is 40 miles N. N. W. of Mangalore.

Barcelos, a very ancient town of Portugal, in Entre Douro e Minho, near the river Cavado, 10 miles W. S. W. of Braga, supposed to have been founded by Hamilcar, 250 B. C.

Bard, and Bardin, two towns in the prov. of Kerman, Persia. Bardin is on the route from Ormus to Lake Gezel, and Bard about 10 miles E. of Bardin.

Bardewick, a town of Lower Saxony, in the duchy of Lunenburg, on the river Ilmenau, 17 miles S. E. of Hamburg.

Bardi, a town of Italy, in the Parmesan,

with a magnificent castle, 30 miles S. W. of Parma.

Bardt, or Barth, a town of Swedish Pomerania, with a castle and harbour, near the Baltic, 15 miles W. by N. of Stralsund. Long. 12. 50. E. lat. 54. 25. N.

Bareberg, a town of Sweden, capital of Skaraborg, on Lake Wener.

Bareges, a town of France, in the department of Upper Pyrenees, much frequented on account of its mineral baths. It is seated in a valley of the same name, 24 miles S. of Tarbes.

Bareily, a town of Hindostan, district of the same name, province of Delhi. It is tolerably built, and has several fine mosques; a fort also has been erected S. of the town. The manufactures are swords, &c. Pop. 65,790, one-third of which are Mohammedans, the remainder Hindoos. The district is level, fertile, and well watered; the Ganges flows on its W. boundary.

Barenton, a town of France, in the department of Manche, 20 miles E. S. E. of Avranches.

Barfleur, a town of France, in the department of Manche. It was from this port that William the Norman embarked on his expedition to England in the 11th century. Barfleur was destroyed by the English in 1346, and the harbour filled up. The cape of that name is 12 miles E. of Cherburg, and near it part of the navy of France was destroyed by the English in 1692. It is 175 miles N. W. of Paris. Long. 1. 10. W. lat. 49. 40. N.

Barga, a considerable town of Italy, about 10 miles N. of Lucca. Pop. about 9000.

Barge, or Barges, a town of Piedmont, 7 miles S. of Pinerola.

Barguzinsk, or Barghouzin, a town of Siberia, in the government of Irkutsk, on the E. side of the lake Baikal, at the influx of the Barguzin, 170 miles N. N. E. of Selenginsk. Long. 109. 30. E. lat. 53. 20. N.

Bari, or Terra di Bari, a maritime province of Naples, on the shore of the Adriatic, bounded on the S. E. by Otranto, S. W. by Basilicata, and N. W. by Capitanata. The soil is fertile, but there are many serpents and tarantulas. *See* Trani.

Bari, a seaport of Naples, capital of Terra di Bari, and an archbishop's see. It is seated on the shore of the Adriatic, has a good harbour, and is well fortified. The trade principally consists in olives and almonds. It is 26 miles E. by S. of Trani. Long. E. 17. 0. lat. 41. 15. N. Pop. 18,937.

Barjols, a town of France, in the department of Var, 19 miles S. S. W. of Riez.

Barking, a town in Essex, with a market on Saturday. It was celebrated for a magnificent nunnery, of which a gateway and part of the walls are still visible. It is chiefly inhabited by fishermen, and seated on the river Roding, near the Thames; 7 miles E. of London.

Barletta, a seaport of Naples, in Bari. It has a large stone pier, and a trade in corn, almonds, and salt. It is seated on the shore of the Adriatic, 25 miles W. S. W. of Bari. Long. 16. 32. E. lat. 41. 19. N.

Barmouth, a small seaport of Wales, in the parish of Corwen, Merionethshire, with a market on Tuesday and Friday, for fish and poultry. It has a good trade in flannels and hose, and is much frequented in the bathing season. It stands on a bay of the same name, 12 miles S. of Harlech, and 222 N. W. of London. Long. 3. 58. W. lat. 52. 44. N.

Barnaoul, a considerable town in the province of Kolyvan, Asiatic Russia, situate at the mouth of a river of the same name, falling into the Obe, about 200 miles S. of the city of Kolyvan. It is the seat of the supreme court of all the mines in the Altaian mountains. Pop. about 5000.

Barnard Castle. *See* Bernard Castle.

Barnet, a town in Hertfordshire, with a market on Monday. Near this place was fought, in 1471, the decisive battle between the houses of York and Lancaster; and at the meeting of the St. Albans and Hatfield roads is a column with an inscription to commemorate this event. Barnet is 11 miles N. by W. of London.

Barnevelt's Islands, two small islands a little north of Cape Horn, and to the south of Terra del Fuego. Long. 66. 58. W. lat. 55. 49. S.

Barneveldt, or Barnweld, an interior town of Guelderland, Holland, situate about an equal distance from Arnheim and Amersfort. Pop. about 5000.

Barnsley, a town of West Yorkshire, with a market on Wednesday. Here are considerable manufactures of coarse linen, and in the vicinity are many bleaching-grounds, a glass manufacture, and several coal mines. It has a canal to the Calder, and another to the Don, and is seated near the Dearne, 19 miles S. of Leeds, and 172 N. by W. of London.

Barnstable, a county formed of a promontory to the state of Massachusets, North America, divided into 14 townships, and containing a population of 32,548. The chief town of the same name is situate on the N. side of the county, on the shore of a spacious bay, formed by a curve of the land extending to Cape Cod. It is 62 miles S. E. of Boston. Pop. 4301.

Barnstaple, a seaport and borough in Devonshire, governed by a mayor, with a market on Friday. It had formerly a castle, but none of the works remain except the mount. Here are manufactures of tammies, shalloons, baize, &c.; and a variety of articles are exported. It is seated on the river Taw, 12 miles E. of Barnstaple Bay, in the Bristol Channel, 35 miles N. N. W. of Exeter, and 192 W. by S. of London. Long. 4. 5. W. lat. 51. 8. N. It sends two members to parliament.

Barnwell, a county or district on the S. side of the state of South Carolina, bounded on the S. by the Savannah, and N. by the Edisto River. Pop. 21,471, of whom 10,503 are slaves, who are chiefly occupied in the culture and cleaning of cotton. The chief town, of the same name, is situate in the centre of the district, 116 miles S. by W. of Columbia.

BAROACH, a town and fortress of Hindostan, Gujerat, with considerable manufactures of cotton, seated on the N. bank of the Nerbudda, near its entrance into the Gulf of Cambay, 40 miles N. by E. of Surat. Long. 72. 55. E. lat. 21. 45. N. Pop. 32,700.

BARODA, a town of Hindostan, province of Gujerat; a large and wealthy place, and capital of a district of the same name.

BARQUISIMETO, an ancient inland town of the province of Venezuela, Columbia. It is situate in a fertile plain, about 20 miles from the E. shore of the Bay of Maracaybo, and 120 W. by S. of the city of Caraccas.

BARRA, or BARRAY, one of the Hebrides of Scotland, to the S. of South Uist. It is 12 miles long and 4 broad, and has a mountainous appearance, but the soil in many parts is fertile. Great quantities of cod and ling are caught on the coast; and shell-fish, especially cockles, are found in great abundance. On the N. E. side is a good harbour. Long. 7. 27. W. lat. 57. 2. N.

BARRA, a town of Naples, in the vicinity of the city of Naples. Pop. about 5000.

BARRA, a fertile and populous district, N. of the Gambia, in North Africa, bordering on the Atlantic Ocean.

BARRA INDING, or BARRANDING, situate on the W. bank of a small river which falls into the Gambia, near its conflux with the Atlantic Ocean; it is the capital town of the territory of Barra, and is a place of considerable traffic. There is another town of the same name, about 100 miles up the river, on the N. bank, between the rivers Kolar and Bandiboo.

BARRACONDA, a considerable town in the interior of North Africa, about 400 miles up the Gambia, where there are some falls which impede the navigation of that river.

BARRACKPOOR, a military cantonment, Hindostan, presidency of Bengal, exceedingly healthy and agreeable. The governor-general has his palace in the vicinity; 15 miles from Calcutta.

BARRAGON, a small town about 12 miles below Buenos Ayres, situate on the shore of a bay to which it gives name.

BARRADY, a river of Syria, pachalic of Damascus, and on which the city stands; it falls into the Bahr-el-Mardj.

BARRAUX, a fortress of France, in the Alpine department of Isere, at the entrance of the valley of Gresivauden, and on the river Isere; 6 miles S. of Chamberry.

BARRE, a town of Massachusets, in Worcester county, noted for its butter and cheese; 24 miles N. W. of Worcester.

BARREN, an inland county in the S. central part of the state of Kentucky. Pop. 17,288. Glasgow, the chief town, is 134 miles S.W. by S. of Frankfort. Two rivers, one called the Little, and the other the Big Barren, have their source within the county, running in different directions, but both falling into the Green River.

BARROW, a river of Ireland, which rises in the N. part of Queen's County, and flows S. by Athy, Carlow, and New Ross, into Waterford harbour.

BARROW STRAIT, an inlet of Baffin's Bay, in continuation of Lancaster Sound, and which leads to the Parry Islands, &c. discovered in 1819. Prince Regent's Inlet flows into this strait.

BAR LE DUC, or BAR-SUR-ORNAIN, a town of France, capital of the department of Meuse, with a castle. Its wine is as delicate as champagne, and it has several manufactories. It is seated on the side of a hill, by the rivulet Ornain; 30 miles W. of Toul, and 138 E. of Paris. Pop. 12,520.

BAR-SUR-AUBE, a town of France, in the department of Aube, famous for its wines; seated at the foot of a mountain; 18 miles S. W. of Joinville. Pop. 3600.

BAR-SUR-SEINE, a town of France, in the department of Aube, on the river Seine, at the foot of a mountain; 20 miles S.W. of Bar-sur-Aube. Pop. 2300.

BARS, an interior county in the N. part of Lower Hungary; a town of the same name, formerly fortified, was once the capital. Kremoni, in the centre of a mining district, is now the chief town.

BARSAC, a town of France, on the W. bank of the Garonne, about 20 miles S. E. of Bordeaux. It gives name to a favourite wine.

BARTFELDT, a town in the county of Saros, N. part of Upper Hungary, situate among the Carpathian mountains. It had a printing press in the 16th century. It has manufactures of linen, and contains about 4000 inhabitants.

BARTEN, and BARTENSTEIN, two interior towns of the kingdom of Prussia Proper, 30 to 40 miles E. of Konigsberg.

BARTHE, LA, a town of France, department of Hauts Pyrenees, on the river Nestes; 12 miles from Tarbes. Pop. 3834.

BARTHOLOMEW, a river of North America, which rises in the Arkansas territory, and falls into the Washita, in the state of Louisiana, a little below the town of Washington.

BARTHOLOMEW, a small island, in the Pacific Ocean, one of the New Hebrides. Long. 167. 18. E. lat. 15. 42. S.

BARTHOLOMEW, ST., one of the Caribbee islands, in the West Indies, 24 miles in circumference, and 25 N. of St. Christopher. The French ceded it to the Swedes in 1785; and it was taken by the British in 1801, but restored to Sweden in 1814. The chief exports are drugs and lignum vitæ; and it has a good harbour. Long. 63. 40. W. lat. 17. 46. N.

BARTON, a town in Lincolnshire, with a market on Monday. It has two large churches, and was formerly a considerable place, surrounded by a rampart and fosse, the remains of which are yet visible. Four miles E. S. E. are the noble ruins of Thornton Abbey. Barton is seated on the Humber, over which is a ferry into Yorkshire; 34 miles N. of Lincoln, and 167 of London.

BARTON is also the name of a populous township in the parish of Eccles, situate on the banks of the Irwell, 7 miles E. of Manchester. There are also 30 other towns or villages called Barton in different parts of England.

BARUTH, a town of Lusatia, on the frontiers of Brandenburg; 26 miles S. by E. of Potsdam.

BARVAS, a town and parish on the N. W. coast of the isle of Lewis. The town is situate on the shore of a fine bay.

BAS, a small island off the N. coast of the department of Finisterre, France, in N. lat. 48. 46. W. long. 4. 2.

BASARDCHIK, a town of European Turkey, in Romania. It has a great trade, and is seated on the river Meritz. Long. 24. 40. E. lat. 42. 19. N.

BASCHKIRS, a tribe of Russia. They amount to about 1,000,000, and lead a pastoral life, their principal riches consisting in their horses and cattle. They differ but little from the Tartars, but their origin is not known. Formerly they led a nomadic life, but have now settled along the Ural and Volga.

BASEL, BASLE, or BALE, a canton of Switzerland, 24 miles long and 21 broad; bounded on the N. by Brisgau, E. by the Forest towns, S. by the canton of Soleure, and W. by the bishopric of Basel and France. It contains about 38,000 inhabitants, and is of the reformed religion.

BASEL, a bishopric in the N. W. part of Switzerland; bounded on the E. by the canton of Basel, S. by that of Soleure, and W. and N. by France. The bishop was a prince of the German empire. In 1798 the French seized on this territory, annexed it to France, and made it a new department, called Mont Terrible.

BASEL, the capital of the canton of the same name, and the largest town in Switzerland, is situate at the N. extremity of the canton, on the frontiers of France on the W., and the duchy of Baden on the E. It is surrounded by thick walls, flanked by towers and bastions, and is divided into two parts by the Rhine, which communicate by a handsome bridge. The largest part is on the side of Switzerland, and the least on that of Germany. The larger has five gates, six suburbs, numerous streets and fountains, and is partly seated on a hill; the other stands on a plain, and has but two gates, with several streets and fountains. The principal church is an elegant Gothic building, but disfigured by rose-coloured paint spread over the whole edifice. Under a marble tomb in it is interred the great Erasmus, who died here in 1536. The town-house, and fine paintings in fresco, are much admired. The university, founded in 1459, has a fine library, and a rich cabinet of medals. The clocks here are always an hour too fast, because the town-clock went so on a day appointed to murder the magistrates, by which the conspiracy was disconcerted. Basel has several manufactures, particularly of papers, ribbons, and cottons; and it carries on an extensive trade. Three treaties of peace were concluded here in one year (1795) with the French republic; namely, by Prussia, Spain, and Hesse Cassel. The allies passed through this city, when they invaded France, in December, 1813. Basel is capable of containing 100,000 inhabitants; but the number is scarcely more than 14,000. It is 174 miles N. by E. of Geneva, and 250 E. by S. of Paris. Long. 7. 30. E. lat. 47. 35. N.

BASHEE, an island in the China Sea, the most eastern of a cluster called, from this the Bashee Islands, lying to the S. of Formosa. The productions are plantains, bananas, pine-apples, sugar-canes, potatoes, yams, and cotton. The quadrupeds are goats and hogs. Bashee is of a circular form, six miles in diameter, and has a town of the same name. Long. 121. 50. E. lat. 20. 30. N.

BASILICATA, a maritime province, in the S. of Naples, bounded on the N. by Capitanata and Bari, E. by the Gulf of Taranta, S. by Calabria Citeriore, and W. by Principato Citeriore and Ulteriore. It has some mountains continually covered with snow, but is fertile in corn, wine, oil, cotton, honey, and saffron. Acerenza is the capital.

BASILIPOTAMO, a river of European Turkey. in the Morea, which flows into the Gulf of Colocythia. It was called Eurotas by the ancients.

BASINGSTOKE, a corporate town in Hampshire, with a market on Wednesday. It has a great trade in corn and malt, a manufacture of druggets and shalloons, and a navigable canal to the river Wey, near its entrance into the Thames; and, being situate at the junction of several great roads, from all parts of the W. of England, it is a place of considerable bustle. It is 18 miles N. N. E. of Winchester, and 45 W. by S. of London.

The village of *Old Basing*, which is a township in the parish of Basingstoke, situate about two miles to the E., is distinguished for the determined stand which it made against the forces of Cromwell, by whom it was ultimately taken, when he put nearly the whole garrison to the sword, and rased the fortress, which was the residence of the Marquis of Winchester, to the ground.

BASQUES, a late territory of France, which included Lower Navarre, Labourd, and Soule, and now forms, with Bearn, the department of Lower Pyrenees. The inhabitants still retain the ancient Iberian dialect.

BASS, an insulated rock near the coast of Scotland, at the entrance of the Frith of Forth, between the towns of North Berwick and Dunbar. On the S. side it is almost conic, on the other it overhangs the sea in a tremendous manner. It is inaccessible on all sides, except the S. W., and there it is with difficulty a man can climb up by the help of a rope or ladder. In May and June it is quite covered with the nests, eggs, and young birds of the gannets and solan geese. The rock is one mile in circumference, and has a rabbit warren, and pasture for a few sheep. A ruinous castle, once the state prison of Scotland, stands at the edge of the precipice. The garrison, in 1694, surrendered to King William, and the fortifications were demolished.

BASS'S STRAIT, a channel about 40 leagues wide, which separates Van Diemen's Land from the S. extremity of New Holland. It contains a chain of small islands that run N. and S. This strait was discovered, in 1798, by Surgeon Bass, in an open whale boat, and passed through by him and Lieutenant Flinders, in the Norfolk, in 1799.

BASSANO, a town in the N. of Italy, in Vincentino, on the E. bank of the river Brenta, in a country productive of excellent wine and oil. The French defeated the Austrians at this place in 1796. It is 18 miles N. of Vicenza.

BASSEE, or LA BASSE, a town of France, in the department of Nord, formerly of great strength, but dismantled by Louis XIV. It is seated on the Deule, 18 miles S. W. of Lisle.

BASSEEN, a tn. of Hindostan, in the country of Baglana. It was taken by the English in 1780, but restored to the Mahrattas in 1783. It stands on the sea-coast, opposite the N. W. point of the island of Salsette, 20 miles N. of Bombay. Long. 72. 40. E. lat. 19. 20. N.

BASSENTHWAITE-WATER, a lake in Cumberland, 3 miles N. W. of Keswick. It is 4 miles long, bounded on one side by high hills, wooded in many places to their bases; on the other, by the fields and the skirts of Skiddaw. The river Derwent flows through its whole length. There is a village named Bassenthwaite on the E. bank of the lake, containing 549 inhabitants.

BASSETERRE, the capital of St. Christopher; built by the French, when this part of the island was in their possession, before it was ceded to the English, in 1713. It is situate on the S. E. end of the island, and is defended by three forts. Long. 63. 13. W. lat. 17. 10. N.

BASSETERRE, the capital of Guadaloupe, on the S. W. part of the island, defended by a citadel and other fortifications. Long. 61. 59. W. lat. 15. 59. N.

BASSIEN, or PERSAIM, a city of Pegu, capital of the province of Bassien. It is a trading place, situate on a river of the same name, which is the W. branch of the Irrawaddy, 110 miles S. W. of Pegu. Long. 94. 53. E. lat. 16. 22. N.

BASSORAH, or BASRA, a city and sea-port of Asiatic Turkey, in Irac Arabi. It stands on the W. bank of the Euphrates, or Shat-ul Arab; navigable for ships of 500 tons burthen up to the town, about 65 miles above the entrance of the river into the Gulf of Persia. Bassorah appears to have been founded about the middle of the seventh century, and progressively advanced into importance until it became the most considerable trading town of all western Asia; and, previous to the route to India by the Cape of Good Hope, it was the medium through which a great portion of the commerce of Asia passed to Venice and Genoa, and from thence over western Europe. It was taken possession of by the Turks, in 1688, since which period it has continued to decline, having been alternately exposed to the irruptions of the Persians, Arabs, and Turks; and, since the commencement of the nineteenth century, when the tide of commerce began to set from the W. to the E., Smyrna has become what Bassorah was for so many centuries—the emporium of the greater portion of the commerce of that part of the world. Bassorah, however, still continues to be a place of considerable traffic, which is participated in, more or less, by most of the trading nations both of Europe and Asia. The city is surrounded by a wall of clay, said to be 6 miles in circumference, mounted with a great number of cannon; the streets are bad and narrow, and the houses, constructed of bricks, have a mean aspect. It is nominally under the dominion of Turkey, but governed by an Arab chieftain, with little deference to the Ottoman authority. The great desert of Arabia runs up nearly to the town; the immediate vicinity, however, is very fertile. A wall of several miles in extent has been constructed on the side of the desert, as a check on the predatory incursions of the Arabs, who frequently commit depredations under the very walls of the town. The population is estimated at about 60,000, among whom are a considerable number of Jews, Armenians, and Arabs, and natives of the more eastern parts of Asia. It is about 210 miles S. W. of Ispahan, in lat. 30. 30. N. and 47. 45. E. long.

BASTIA, a sea-port of European Turkey, in Albania, opposite the island of Corfu, at the mouth of the Calamu. Long. 20. 20. E. lat. 39. 40. N.

BASTIA, a city on the N. E. coast of the island of Corsica, with a good harbour and a strong castle. It was taken by the English in 1794. It is 80 miles S. S. W. of Leghorn. Long. 9. 20. E. lat. 42. 38. N. Pop. about 11,500. It was considered the capital of the island, but Ajaccio is now usually called so.

BASTOGNE, a city of the Netherlands, in Luxemburg, near the forest of Ardennes. It was fortified by the French, in 1688, and commonly known among them by the name of Paris in Ardennes. It is 23 miles N. N. W. of Luxemburg.

BASWAPATANNA, a town of Hindostan, in Mysore, with a fort and a celebrated mosque; 60 miles E. by N. of Nagura.

BATABANO, a town on the S. coast of Cuba; situate on the N. side of a large bay, opposite Pinos Island, 55 miles S. S. W. of Havannah. Long. 82. 0. W. lat. 22. 20. N.

BATACOLE, tn. of Hindostan, on the coast of Canara. The country produces a great quantity of pepper. It is 10 miles N. of Barcelore.

BATACOLO, a small fortress on the E. side of Ceylon, built by the Dutch. It is of great importance, on account of the extreme fertility of the adjacent country, which, during a war, or times of scarcity in the district of Trincomalee, can supply the garrisons there with all kinds of provisions. It surrendered to the English in 1796; it is situate at the head of a deep bay, 54 miles S. S. E. of Trincomalee.

BATALHA, a tn. of Portugal, in Estremadura, celebrated for its rich monastery, founded, in 1386, by John I., who is interred here, with his queen Philippa. It is 8 miles S. S. W. of Leirida.

BATAVIA, the ancient name of an island in

Holland; whence the Dutch are sometimes called Batavians.

Batavia, a city and sea-port on the N.E. part of the island of Java, capital of all the Dutch settlements in the East Indies, finely situate on the bosom of a spacious bay. The fort is built of coral rock, brought from some of the adjoining islands, and has a fortification of brick. A part of the town wall is built of dense lava, from the mountains in the centre of Java. No stone, of any kind, is to be found for many miles beyond this city; but marble and granite are brought here from China. The harbour is excellent, and there are canals in the principal streets, planted on each side with trees, after the manner of the towns in Holland. The inhabitants are composed of natives from nearly all the countries and islands of Asia and the Indian Ocean, as well as of most of the chief trading parts of Europe and America, amongst whom the number of Chinese is considerable.

The city was first founded in 1619, and rose rapidly into importance, and during the eighteenth century it was deemed the finest European settlement in all Asia; and although considered unhealthy, from the influence of the heat of the climate on the mud and stagnant waters of the canals and streams by which it is intersected, it was vainly denominated by the Dutch, the "Queen of the East." The houses of two streets, forming the European part of the town, are handsome and commodious, and vie, if they do not excel in capaciousness and convenience, those of the best towns in Holland; but the parts occupied by the Javanese, Chinese, and other natives of the East, like most of the Asiatic towns, are crowded, mean, and dirty. Batavia was very sensibly affected by the war of 1793, and became almost deserted, until its capture, with the whole of the island of Java, by the English, in 1811, when it became again the centre of an extensive commerce. It was ceded back to the Dutch on the peace of 1814, who, having relaxed somewhat from their former system of proscription and monopoly in their commercial regulations, Batavia continues a flourishing and important place. The stadthouse is the principal edifice deserving of notice. The natives of the several nations and countries who compose the population, which amounts to about 50,000, have each their churches, mosques, and temples, but there are none that merit any particular notice. The nature of its commerce will be more fully elucidated under the head of Java. The observatory is in lat. 6. 9. S. and 106. 52. E. long.

Batavia, the chief town of Genesee county, in the state of New York, 258 miles W. of Albany, on the direct road to Buffalo, at the E. end of Lake Erie. Pop. 4219. There is an Indian village in the township, called *Tonnewanta.*

Bath, a city of England, in the E. corner of the county of Somerset, on the confines of Gloucester and Wilts; it is bounded on the N. by a range of hills, up the declivity of which buildings have been constructed in varied ornamental and tasteful styles of architecture, terraces, crescents, &c. of a beautiful white stone, dug on the spot. The origin of this city, which derived its celebrity from its hot springs, is involved in uncertainty and fable. The ancient Britons, by whom it was called *Yr ennaint-twymin,* dated the discovery of the waters as far back as the time of Bladud, 870 years antecedent to the Christian era; be this as it may, their properties and virtues immediately attracted the enlightened attention of the Romans, on their arrival in that part of the country, 44 years, B.C., by whom they were denominated *Aquæ Solis,* Waters of the Sun, and *Fontes Calidæ,* the Fountains of Heat, and who manifested their appreciation of the waters by the erection of extensive baths, constructed with all possible regard to taste, luxury, and utility, and a temple dedicated to Minerva; and at the period of their finally withdrawing from the country, about the middle of the fifth century, the city extended upwards of two miles in length, surrounded by a wall, regularly fortified. The waters were equally appreciated by the Saxons, by whom the city was called *Caer Badon;* but it obtained no additional distinction, until the commencement of the eighteenth century, about which period it became the resort alike of all the afflicted, the idle, the gay, and the dissipated, whose means enabled them to reach it. The general influx of visitors excited a spirit of exertion and enterprise among the inhabitants, to afford accommodations suitable to the rank and taste of the most affluent classes; and, for more than half a century, popularity and improvement in all that contributed to the adornment, as well as the comfort and convenience of the city, to those who visited it for the benefit of health, or for indulgence in gaiety, pleasure, or dissipation, kept pace with each other, until it became justly celebrated as the most beautiful and agreeable abode in the British dominions. There are six public baths, and a magnificent hospital for the reception of those who come to partake of the waters, who would otherwise be excluded the benefit by the inadequacy of their means.

Bath, in conjunction with Wells, is an ecclesiastical see, and the cathedral, or abbey church, was first founded by king Osric, in 676. The present building, begun in 1465 and finished in 1606, is a beautiful specimen of Gothic architecture. There are eight other churches of the establishment, and several dissenting places of worship: a guildhall and theatre are among the other public buildings which adorn the city. The city is governed by a mayor, ten aldermen, and twenty-four common councilmen, from amongst whom are appointed a chamberlain, two bailiffs, and two constables annually. It returns two members to parliament, formerly elected by the corporation.

The waters of Bath are peculiarly efficacious in cases of gout, paralytic, and bilious affections, and various other diseases, for which they are taken internally, as well as availed of in vapour, shower, and immersion, varying in heat from 93 to 117 degrees of Fahrenheit; and, until some revolution of nature shall dry up their source, or direct their subterranean current to other openings, Bath will doubtless retain a due share of appreciation; although, notwithstanding the peculiar charm of its natural local beauties, and artificial attractions, so volatile, tasteless, and capricious is fashion, that Brighton, Cheltenham, Leamington, and other places, are dividing, and each contending for the palm of popularity. Its markets are abundantly supplied with corn, flesh, fish, vegetables, fruits, &c. on Wednesdays and Saturdays. It is 13 miles S. by E. of Bristol, 19 E. by N. of Wells, and 106 W. of London.

BATH is also the name of several towns and villages in North America, which, like the *Badens* of continental Europe, derive their name from hot or medicinal waters.

BATH, an interior county of the state of Virginia, intersected by two ridges (running parallel with each other) of the Allegany mountains, between which, and 183 miles W.N.W. of Richmond, are the hot springs which give name to the county. There is another spring a few miles north, called the Warm Spring; the north and south forks of the Jackson River run through the plain between the two ridges of mountains and the Cow Pasture River, east of the eastern ridge, all of which fall into James River, at the south end of the county. There is another hot spring in Berkeley county, Virginia, between the foot of the bluff of the Cacapon ridge of the Allegany Mountains and the Potomac River; about 40 miles N. by W. of the city of Washington. Pop. 4,300.

BATH, a town on the east bank of Hudson River, state of New York, immediately opposite Albany.

BATH, the chief town of Steuben county, state of New York, situate on the east bank of the main branch of the Tuga River; 283 miles W. by S. of Albany.

BATH, a well-built and respectable town in the state of Maine, North America, situate on the west bank of the Kennebec River (which supplies abundance of fine salmon and other fish,) a little below the junction of the Androscoggin, and a few miles above its conflux with the ocean. The river forms a capacious harbour for ships of any burthen, and ship-building constitutes the chief occupation of the inhabitants; the ships being principally employed on freight, between the southern states and Europe. Pop. 5,141. It is 39 miles N. E. of Portland.

BATHA. *See* BACH.

BATHGATE, a town of Scotland, in Linlithgowshire, 19 miles W. by S. of Edinburgh, on the high road to Glasgow. Population principally employed in weaving.

BATHOR, an interior town of Upper Hungary, in the county of Szabolts, about 30 miles N.W. of Debretzin.

BATHURST, an English settlement on the W. coast of North Africa, at the entrance of the river Gambia.

BATHURST, a settlement in N. S. Wales, consisting of a government house, military barracks, and commissariat stores. It has recently been laid out for a town. 114 miles from Sydney.

BATINDA, the chief town of a fertile district of the same name, on the N. W. confines of Delhi, bordering on the desert of Moultan.

BATOA, a small island in the Indian Ocean, near the west side of Sumatra, on the equinoctial line, in long. 98. 0. E.

BATOPILAS, a considerable town of the Andes, or Cordilleras of Mexico, in the intendency of Durango.

BATOUMI, a town at the mouth of a river of the same name, falling into the Black Sea, and forming the N. E. boundary of Armenia.

BATROUN, a town on the coast of Syria, pachalic of Tripoli; one of the best ports in the Maronite country. It exports silk, cotton, and potash; 11 miles S. of Tripoli.

BATTA, two towns on the west bank of the Danube, in Lower Hungary; one a few miles S. of Buda, and the other a few miles E. of Funfkirchen.

BATTALLAH, a town of Hindostan, about 60 miles E. by S. of Lahore, in the province of that name.

BATTAS, a country in the Island of Sumatra. The inhabitants are ruled by a number of rajahs; but they obey, or rather have a blind adoration for the king of Menongkaboo. They are more industrious than the Malays, and are exceedingly superstitious. Pop. estimated at 1,500,000.

BATTECOLA, a town on the Malabar coast, about 100 miles N. of Mangalore.

BATTENBURG, a town of Holland, in Guelderland, with a castle on the north bank of the Meuse; 10 miles S. W. of Nimeguen.

BATTENBURGH, a town and castle of Germany, in Upper Hesse, seated on the Eder; 14 miles N. of Marburg.

BATTERSEA, a village in Surrey, on the north bank of the Thames, 4 miles W. S. W. of London. Here was the seat of the St. Johns, where the famous Lord Bolingbroke was born, and died. On the site of it now stands a distillery, and a horizontal air-mill for grinding malt. Here is a timber bridge over the river to Chelsea. Population chiefly occupied in gardening and supplying the London markets with vegetables.

BATTLE, a town in Sussex, with a market on Thursday. Near this place, William, duke of Normandy, defeated Harold, king of England, in 1066, and in memory of this victory, he founded here an abbey, which, from its remains, appears to have been magnificent. This town is famous for a manufacture of gunpowder. It is 24 miles E. of Lewes, 6 N. of Hastings, and 56 S. E. of London.

BAUBELTHOUAP, an island of the Pacific Ocean, and the largest of the Pelew group. It is 24 miles long, and is well timbered, and produces yams, cocoa-nuts, and the usual tropical fruits. Lat. of E. end, 7. 41. N. long. 134. 55. E.

BAUCHERVILLE, a beautiful located village, on the W. bank of the river St. Lawrence; about 10 miles W. of Montreal.

BAUD, a town of France, department of Morbihan. Pop. 4600; 15 miles from Pontioi.

BAUG, a town of Hindostan, province of Malwa, standing in a pleasant valley on the road between Malwa and Gujerat, and containing about 2000 inhabitants. Iron ore is found in the vicinity, and is smelted in the town.

BAUGE, a town of France, department of Maine et Loire, on the river Coesnon, over which is a fine new bridge; 27 miles from Angers. Pop. 3134.

BAULEAH, a town of Hindostan, in Bengal, on the left bank of the Ganges. It is one of the principal stations for collecting of silk; 22 miles N. E. of Moorshedabad.

BAUMAN'S ISLANDS, three islands in the Pacific Ocean, discovered by Bauman, a Dutchman, who accompanied Roggewein, in 1722. They are covered with fruit trees, and divers sorts of vegetables. The inhabitants are numerous, and armed with bows and arrows; but of a gentle and humane disposition, and friendly to strangers. The largest island is about 22 miles in circumference. Long. 170. 0. W. lat. 14. 0. S.

BAUME LES NONES, or BAUME LES DAMES, a town of France, in the department of Doubs. It has a nunnery, from which it received its appellation, and is seated on the Doubs; 15 miles N. E. of Besancon.

BAUSK, or BAUTKA, a town of Courland, on the frontiers of Poland, with a castle on a rock. It is seated on the Musza; 15 miles S. E. of Mittau.

BAUTZEN, or BUDISSEN, the capital of Upper Lusatia, with a citadel on a rock, called Ortenburg. The trade, arising from various manufactures, is considerable. It is famous for a great battle having been fought here on May 20, 1813, between the allied army under the emperor of Russia and the king of Prussia, and the French army commanded by Napoleon Buonaparte, in which the former were defeated. It stands on the river Spree; 30 miles E. by N. of Dresden. Long. 14. 30. E. lat. 51. 10. N.

BAUX, a town of France, in the department of Mouths of the Rhone, seated on a rock, at the top of which is a castle; 10 miles E. by N. of Arles.

BAVARIA, PALATINATE, DUCHY, ELECTORATE, CIRCLE, and KINGDOM OF. The former *circle of Bavaria* lies between the 47th and 50th deg. of N. lat. and the 11th and 14th of E. long.; is bounded on the N.E. by Bohemia, S.E. and S. by Austria and the Tyrol, S.W. by Suabia, and N.W. by Franconia; and comprises the palatinate and principalities of Sulzbach and Neuberg, in the N.; the duchy, which constituted the greater portion of the circle, divided into Lower and Upper, the county of Werdenfels in the S.W.; the bishopric of Passau on the E.; the provostship of Berchtolsgaden, insulated in the archbishopric of Saltzburg, which formed the S.E. part of the circle, forming together an area of about 16,500 square miles, and containing a population of 1,300,000.

The Duchy of Bavaria, which formed about two-thirds of the circle, was part of the ancient Noricum, peopled from ancient Gaul, from which they were driven about 590 years B.C. It was constituted a duchy in the early part of the 10th century of the Christian era, under which title it continued uninterrupted until the reign of the emperor Ferdinand of Germany, who raised Bavaria into an *electorate* of the Germanic confederacy; but Maximilian Emanuel, grandson of the first elector, forfeited his possessions, by violating his allegiance, in entering into alliance with France against the emperor. He was, however, reinstated in his possessions in 1714, and the succeeding elector, Charles, introduced numerous salutary regulations into the social institutions of the state, under which it rose in prosperity and reputation, and continued to make advances in social improvement, and to retain its influence in the Germanic diet, until Napoleon Buonaparte interposed his power and influence, at the commencement of the 19th century, when the elector was again induced to withdraw from the Germanic confederacy, under the pledge of being vested with regal authority, and guaranteed in an accession of territory at the expense of Austria; hence the

Kingdom of Bavaria, which was acknowledged by the emperor of Austria at the peace of Presburg in 1805: the accessions of territory obtained with the regal title lay on the side of Franconia, Suabia, and the Tyrol. The disaster experienced by Napoleon at Moscow, in the winter of 1812, 1813, induced the new king to conclude a secret treaty with the confederate powers against his former patron, on condition of being guaranteed in the integrity of his newly-acquired dominions; and at the congress of Vienna, in 1818, the boundaries of the Bavarian kingdom were finally adjusted, when the territory was divided into the eight following circles, with the chief towns of each annexed as follows, viz.—

1.	The Rhine	W.	Spires
2.	Lower Maine	N.	Wurzburgh
3.	Upper ditto	N.	Bayreuth
4.	Rezat	N.W.	Anspach
5.	Upper Danube	S.W.	Augsburg
6.	Iser	S.	Munich
7.	Lower Danube	E.	Passau
8.	Regen	N.E.	Ratisbon

Of these divisions the first lies on both sides of the Rhine, at the northern extremity of the territory of the Grand Duke of Baden, and is detached from the other seven. Nos. 2, 3, and 4, formed part of the circle of Franconia, and No. 5 of Suabia; the last three previously forming the grand duchy and the palatinate, the archbishopric of Saltzburg having been ceded to Austria. The whole of this territory comprises about 32,000 square miles, and a population of about 3,600,000. The frontier parts of the kingdom of Bavaria are in general rugged and mountainous, but the inland parts are fertile in corn and pasture; all the various branches of manufacture of flax, wool, some silk, leather, and working of metals, are followed more or less as domestic occupations over most parts of the country. Having but little surplus produce of any kind for external traffic, Bavaria may be regarded as possessing within itself all the means of domestic and social comfort. It is exceedingly well watered; the Danube, which rises on the border of the Black Forest in Suabia, runs from W. to E.

through the heart of the country, passes Dilligen, Donawerth, Neuberg, Ingolstadt, and Ratisbon, to Passau, where it enters the archduchy of Austria. The Inn, Iser, Lech, and Iller, run from S. to N. into the Danube, and the Maine runs from E. to W., past Schweinfurth and Wurtzburg into the Rhine. Four-fifths of the inhabitants are Roman Catholics, and the remainder Protestants: the latter, however, not only enjoy the unrestrained exercise of their worship, but are eligible to civil offices and military appointments. Like all the other Germanic states, military pretension and parade is the ruling passion of the government, and from 40,000 to 50,000 men are held under military discipline; to sustain which, and other expenses of the state, taxes, equal to about 2,500,000*l.* English money are levied annually on the produce of the labour of the people. Munich is the capital of the whole kingdom, and the seat of government, which is unlimited, and vested in the king, the title to which is hereditary. The power has, however, been exercised with discretion, prudence, and mildness, although not with all the wisdom and efficiency to be desired. Education has of late years been widely diffused through the Bavarian states; academies, lyceums, and universities have been multiplied; productions of foreign literature have been imported; and the effects are already apparent in the improved condition of society and the gradual advance of moral and physical renovation. Bavaria may now be considered as holding the first rank among the secondary class of European states.

BAVAY, a town of France, in the department of Nord. It was taken by the Austrians in 1792, but recovered the same year. It is 6 miles N. E. of Quesnoy, and 12 S.W. of Mons.

BAWTRY, a town in West Yorkshire, with a market on Saturday. It has a trade in lead, millstones, and grindstones, and is seated on the river Idle; 9 miles S. by E. of Doncaster, and 153 N. of London.

BAYA. *See* BAJA.

BAYA, a seaport of Guinea, on the Gold Coast; 60 miles E. S. E. of Acra. Long. 1. 59. E. lat. 5. 45. N.

BAY OF ISLANDS, in the N. Island of New Zealand, and contains the missionary settlement at Paheha.

BAYAGUANA, an inland town of the Island of St. Domingo, about 35 miles N. E. of the city of St. Domingo.

BAYAMO, a town in the E. part of Cuba, on the river Estero, which forms a bay on the coast, 20 miles below the town; 80 miles W. S. W. of St. Jago. Long. 77. 20. W. lat. 20. 45. N.

BAYAZIA, or BAIAZIA, a large town of Asiatic Turkey, in the S. E. corner of Armenia, near the source of the Euphrates, on the confines of Persia. It is surrounded by a wall, and contains two mosques, and several other edifices of great architectural beauty, and about 30,000 inhabitants.

BAYERSDORF, a town of the Bavarian circle of the Upper Maine, with a seat of justice and a large synagogue; seated on the Rednitz; 4 miles N. of Erlang.

BAYEUX, a town of France, in the department of Calvados, and a bishop's see. The cathedral is very noble, and contains an exhibition, on tapestry, of the Conquest of England by William the Norman; and there are 17 other churches. The chief trade is in leather. It is seated on the river Aure; 4 miles from the English Channel, and 140 W. by N. of Paris. Long. 0. 42. W. lat. 49. 17. N. Pop. about 10,500.

BAYON, a town of France, in the department of Meurthe, on the river Moselle; 12 miles S. of Nancy.

BAYONA, a town of Spain, in Gallicia, on a small gulf of the Atlantic, with a convenient harbour; 12 miles W. by N. of Tuy.

BAYONNE, a city and seaport of France, in the department of Lower Pyrenees, and a bishop's see. The Nive and Adour unite their streams in the middle of the city, and proceed to the sea, at the distance of a mile. The first, which is deeper and more rapid than the Adour, divides the town into two unequal parts, the smallest of which is called the Bourg-neuf, or New Town: they have a communication by three timber bridges. A bank of sand, at the mouth of the Adour, renders the entrance of the harbour difficult. The citadel is the strongest in France, and the cathedral is remarkable for the height of the nave and the delicacy of the pillars which support it. The military weapon, the bayonet, bears the name of this city, in which it was invented. The chocolate of Bayonne is famous; and it also exports wines, woollen cloths, silks, cottons, &c. The chief trade arises out of its relation with Spain; and it is a kind of emporium for the merchandise of that country. The court of France was held here for some time in 1808, when the king of Spain and his son, the prince of the Asturias, were invited here to settle their differences before Buonaparte; the result of which was, that they were made to sign a treaty, resigning the crown of Spain into his hands. Bayonne was besieged by the English in 1814, during which the French made a sally, and attacked the English with success, but were at length driven back. The loss of the British in this affair was considerable, and their commander wounded and taken prisoner. It is 25 miles S. W. of Dax, and 518 S. by W. of Paris. Long. 1. 29. W. lat. 43. 29. N.

BAYPOUR, a town of Hindostan, in the prov. of Malabar, on a river capable of receiving vessels of 400 tons. It is 15 miles S. by E. of Calicut.

BAYREUTH, a city of Franconia, capital of a principality of the same name, with a palace, a fine castle, and a famous college. Near it, forming a kind of suburb, is the town of Georgen, which has a large castle, a manufacture of excellent brown and white porcelain, and a house of correction, in which the marble of the country is polished by means of a machine. In 1783 the archives of the principality were brought to Bayreuth from Plassenburg;

(*see* Culmbach;) and in 1791, the margravate of Bayreuth, with that of Anspach, was abdicated by the reigning prince, in favour of the king of Prussia; but both were annexed and guaranteed by Buonaparte, and afterwards confirmed by the congress at Vienna, to the kingdom of Bavaria, (which see;) and Bayreuth is now the capital of the circle of Upper Maine. It is 32 miles E. of Bamberg. Long. 11. 44. E. lat. 49. 55. N.

Baza, a town of Spain, in Granada, seated on the Guadalantin, 21 miles E. N. E. of Guadix.

Bazas, a town of France, in the department of Gironde, and lately an episcopal see. It is seated on a rock, 5 miles from the river Garonne, and 42 S. E. of Bordeaux. Long. 0. 2. W. lat. 44. 22. N.

Beachy Head, the highest promontory on the south coast of England, between Hastings and Seaford. Long. 0. 15. E. lat. 50. 44. N.

Beaconsfield, a town in Buckinghamshire, with a market on Thursday. The poet Waller lived here, and is interred in the churchyard. It is seated on a hill; 23 miles W. N. W. of London.

Beaminster, a town in Dorsetshire, with a market on Thursday, and manufactures of canvas, iron, and copper. This place suffered greatly by fire in 1781. It is 15 miles W. N.W. of Dorchester, and 132 W. by S. of London.

Bear Island, an island in Bantry Bay, on which are fortifications which constitute a strong defence to the head of the bay. The island is about 12 miles from the town of Bantry.

Bear Lake, Great, an extensive lake in North America, on the Arctic Circle, which empties itself into the Mackenzie River. The Indians who inhabit its shores are hospitable and inoffensive. It has formed the starting-point of several Arctic land expeditions. Franklin, in 1820, proceeded to the Coppermine River; and in 1837–1840, Messrs. Dease and Simpson have ventured here in their expeditions W. and E. on the northern coast of the continent.

Bearn, a late province of France, 40 miles long and 30 broad; bounded on the E. by Bigorre, S. by Spanish Navarre, W. by Soule and a part of Lower Navarre, and N. by Gascony and Armagnac. The plains are fertile, especially in pastures, and the hills are loaded with vines. It now forms, with Basques, the department of the Lower Pyrenees.

Beat, St., a town of France, in the department of Upper Garonne; the houses are built of marble, there being no other stone in the neighbourhood. It is seated on the Garonne; 12 miles S. S. E. of St. Bertrand.

Beaucaire, a town of France, in the department of Gard, on the Rhone, about 20 miles from the sea, where the river forms a spacious harbour, and has a communication by a bridge of boats with Tarascon on the opposite bank of the river. Much trade is carried on here, and an annual fair held for six days, in the month of July, was formerly the most famous in Europe, but is now of little importance. It is 11 miles E. of Nismes.

Beauce, a late province of France, between the Isle of France, Blasois, and Orleanois. It is so fertile in wheat that it is called the granary of Paris. It now forms the department of Eure and Loire.

Beaufort, a maritime district, forming the south-east corner of the state of South Carolina; bounded on the south-west by the Savannah River. It is a low swampy district, but very productive in rice and cotton. Pop. 35,794, of whom 29,682 are slaves, and 462 free blacks. In addition to the Savannah on the south, it is bounded on the north by the Bigslake-hatchie River, and the Coosawhatchie intersects the district from north-west to south-east, dividing into two branches about the centre of the district, and forming an island, called Port Royal Island, on which is a town named *Beaufort*, formerly the capital of the district, but the courts are now held at the town of Coosawhatchie; about 20 miles N. W. of Beaufort, and 193 S. of Columbia, the capital of the state.

Beaufort, a town of South Africa, Graff Reynet district, on the Great Leeuwin River. Lat. 32. 36. S. long. 23. 1. E.

Beaufort is also the name of a county in North Carolina, divided into two parts by the Pamtico River, at its entrance into Pamtico Sound; it is a swampy and dreary district, with a population of 12,225, of whom 4472 are slaves. Washington, 130 miles E. by S. of Raleigh, is the chief town.

Beaufort, a seaport of North Carolina, chief town of Carteret county. It is situate on the N. E. side of Core Sound, 55 miles S. S. E. of Newbern. Long. 76. 50. W. lat. 34. 38. N.

Beaufort, a town of France, in the department of Mayenne and Loire, with a castle; 15 miles E. of Angers. Pop. 6000.

Beaufort, a town of Savoy, on the river Oron, a branch of the Ysere, 12 miles N. E. of Moutier. Pop. about 3000.

Beaugency, a town of France, in the department of Loire, famous for its wines; seated on the river Loire; 6 miles W. of Orleans.

Beaujeu, a town of France, in the department of Rhone, with an ancient castle, seated on the Ardiere, at the foot of a mountain; 13 miles N. N. W. of Villefranche. Pop. 1600.

Beaujolois, a late province of France, 30 miles long and 24 broad. It lies north of the Lyonois, and both of them now form the department of Rhone.

Beauley, a river of Scotland, in Inverness-shire, formed by the union of the rivulets Farrah, Cannich, and Glass, on the borders of Ross-shire. It takes a north-east course, and, after forming the falls of Kilmorack, and other cascades, flows to the town of Beauley, where it enters the head of Murray Frith. It produces a considerable supply of salmon for the London market.

Beauley, a town of Scotland, in the parish of Kilmorack, in Inverness-shire, at the mouth of the river Beauley; 12 miles W. of Inverness.

Beaulieu, a village in Hampshire, on a river of its name; six miles S. S. W. of Southampton. It has a manufacture of coarse sacking; and on the opposite side of the river are the remains of its famous abbey, founded by King John.

Beaumarches, a town of France, in the department of Gers; 13 miles W. of Mirande.

Beaumaris, a borough of Wales, capital of Anglesea; a market on Wednesday and Saturday; governed by a mayor, a recorder, 24 burgesses, and other officers, who return one member to parliament. It stands on the Strait of Menai, was fortified with a castle by Edward I., and has a good harbour. It is 59 miles W. by N. of Chester, and 251 N. W. of London. Long. 4. 15. W. lat. 53. 15. N.

Beaumont, a town of Belgium, on the frontiers of the department du Nord, France, about eight miles E. of Maubeuge. There are eight other towns in different parts of France called Beaumont, but none that merit any particular notice, unless one in the department of Vaucluse, the residence of Mirabeau.

Beaune, a town of France, in the department of Cote d'Or, remarkable for its excellent wine. It is 25 miles S. S. W. of Dijon.

Beaurivage, a river of Lower Canada, S. of the St. Lawrence; it falls into the Chaudiere, about four miles above the entrance of that river into the St. Lawrence.

Beauvais, a town of France, capital of the department of Oise, and lately an episcopal see. The cathedral is admired for its fine architecture; and the church of St. Stephen is remarkable for its curious windows. It was besieged in 1463, by the Duke of Burgundy, at the head of 80,000 men, when the women, under the conduct of Jean de Hachette, obliged the duke to raise the siege. The inhabitants carry on a good trade in beautiful tapestry. It is seated on the Thesin, 42 miles N. of Paris. Pop. about 30,000.

Beaver, a county at the W. extremity of the state of Pennsylvania, bordering on Ohio; it is intersected by the Ohio River, and contains a population of 29,368.

Beaver, or **Beaverton**, the chief town of the county, is situate at the junction of the Beaver River with the Ohio, near the centre of the county; 240 miles W. by N. of Harrisburg.

Beaver Islands, a cluster of islands at the N. extremity of Lake Michigan.

Beaver Creek, in the township of Brookfield, Madison county, state of New York.

Beaver Dam, in Southampton township, Long Island, and in Roxbury township, Delaware county, and in Bern township, Albany county, and *Beaver-kill*, in Hurly township, Ulster county, all in the State of New York.

Beauvoir, a town of France, in the department of Vendee, on the Bay of Biscay, 32 miles N. N. W. of Sables d'Olonne.

Beban el Malook, a village of Egypt, on the W. bank of the Nile, remarkable for its numberless tombs, containing mummies, excavated in the banks of the river.

Beblingen, a town of the kingdom of Wurtemburg, with a castle on a hill; 10 miles N. W. of Stuttgard.

Bec, a town of France, in the department of Lower Seine, with a noble Benedictine abbey; 18 miles S. W. of Rouen.

Becancour, a river of Lower Canada, which falls into the St. Lawrence, from the south, opposite the town of Three Rivers.

Beccles, a corporate town in Suffolk, with a market on Saturday. It has a noble church, with a lofty steeple, and a grammar school, endowed with 10 scholarships for Emanuel College, Cambridge. It is seated on the Waveney; 12 miles S. W. of Yarmouth, and 109 N. E. of London.

Bechin, a town of Bohemia, capital of a circle of the same name, in which are several medicinal springs and mines of salt. It has an ancient fortified castle, and stands on the river Lausnitz; 57 miles S. by W. of Prague. Long. 14. 28. E. lat. 49. 18. N.

Beckum, a town of Westphalia, in the principality of Munster, at the source of the Verse; 20 miles S. E. of Munster.

Bedale, a town in North Yorkshire, with a market on Tuesday; the surrounding district is distinguished for its breed of horses, and of other cattle. 10 miles S. E. of Richmond, and 222 N. N. W. of London.

Bedarieux, a town of France, in the department of Herault, with a manufacture of druggets and other woollen stuffs; seated on the Orbre; 16 miles N. of Bezieres. Population 3350.

Beddington, a village in Surrey, two miles W. of Croydon. Here is Beddington-park, one of the many said to have been the residence of Queen Elizabeth. The church is a Gothic pile, with stalls in the aisles, like a cathedral.

Beder, a town of France, in the department of Ille and Vilaine; 10 miles W. N. W. of Rennes.

Beder, a fortified town of Hindostan, in Dowlatabad, situate on the S. bank of the Manzorah River; once the capital of a considerable kingdom, and still celebrated for the number and magnificence of its pagodas. It is 80 miles N. W. of Hydrabad. Long. 78. 2. E. lat. 17. 48. N.

Bedford, an inland county of England. At the time Britain was invaded by the Romans, Cassibelaunus, the chief of the inhabitants of this part of the country, was appointed to the command of all the forces of Britain, against Cæsar; and, under the heptarchy of the Saxons, it formed part of the kingdom of Mercia; and the county town is supposed to have been the burial-place of King Offa. It was afterwards the scene of many contests between the Britons, Saxons, and Danes, and at later periods became involved in the collisions between King John and the barons; and, in 1642, it took the side of the people against the kingly authority of Charles I. The river Ouse intersects it by a very winding course from W to E.; and the Ivel, with several tributary streams, waters the S. part. The face of the country is varied with small hills and valleys; and on the S. is a range of chalky hills, which, rising to a considerable elevation, and projecting irregularly over the valleys, give the landscape a bold and remarkable appearance. From the S. E. corner to the middle of the county runs a line of good meadow-land; and the N. and E. portions have a deep soil, which is well cultivated, and produces large crops of corn. The mineral productions are limestone, coarse marble, and imperfect coal; and fuller's earth is obtained in considerable quantities. Mineral springs are found in different parts of the county, but they have not acquired much celebrity. The manufactures are chiefly confined to the making of lace, and preparing straw-plait for bonnets, baskets, toys, &c. The remains of both Saxon and Gothic architecture are to be seen in several of the churches, as also a few specimens of stained glass in their windows. Roman antiquities have also been frequently discovered in the county; and it is intersected by three Roman roads. It sends two members to parliament.

Bedford, the chief town of the preceding county, is situate about the centre of the county, on a spacious plain, N. of the Chiltern hills, which run across the S. part. The river Ouse, over which there is a beautiful stone bridge of five arches, divides the town into two parts. It has five churches, a county hospital and lunatic asylum, a well endowed public school, and about 50 alms-houses, liberally endowed by a Sir William Harpur, knight, a former inhabitant of the town. It is a borough town, governed by a mayor, recorder, aldermen, two chamberlains, and 13 common council, and returns two members to parliament, formerly sent by the suffrage of the male inhabitants at large. It is the seat of assize, and of election for the county; holds markets on Tuesdays and Saturdays. 27 miles E. by N. of Buckingham, and 50 N. by W. of London.

Bedford Level, a tract of fenny land, about 300,000 acres, in the counties of Norfolk, Suffolk, Cambridge, Huntingdon, Northampton, and Lincoln. After various attempts to drain these fens, in the reign of Henry VI. and Charles I., William, earl of Bedford, in 1649, undertook and completed it; and, in the reign of Charles II., a corporation was established for the government of this great level. In these fens are several decoys, in which innumerable quantities of wild fowl are taken during the season.

Bedford, an interior county in the S. of Virginia, bounded on the W. by the Blue ridge of the Allegany Mountains, on the N. by James River, and on the S. by Staunton, a branch of the Roanoke. Pop. 20,203. Liberty, the chief town, in the centre of the county, is 162 miles W. by S. of Richmond.

Bedford is also the name of a county in the state of Tennessee. Pop. 20,546, and of which Shellbyville, 35 miles S. of Murfreesborough, is the chief town.

Bedford, another county in the S. part of Pennsylvania, bordering on Maryland, lying between the Tuscarora and the main ridge of the Allegany Mountains. Pop. 29,335. The chief town, of the same name, in the centre of the county, is 105 miles W. of Harrisburg.

Bedford, a town on the frontier of Connecticut, in Westchester county, E. of Hudson River, in the state of New York; 125 miles S by E. of Albany, and about 35 N. by E. o New York. Pop. 2822.

Bedford is also the name of a village in the township of Brooklyn, in Long Island, opposite New York Harbour; and of a seaport town in Bristol county, state of Massachusets; it owns considerable shipping employed in the South Sea whale fisheries. It is about 60 miles due S. of Boston.

Bednore, a district of Hindostan, forming the N. W. corner of the Mysore, intersected by the Ghaut Mountains. The chief town of the district, and which was formerly the capital of Canara, is situate E. of the mountains, and is supposed once to have been a magnificent and important place; but, having been repeatedly subjected to the assaults of the Mahrattas, the British, and Tippoo Saib, it is much reduced. It is seated on a branch of the Toombudra River; 185 miles N. W. of Seringapatam.

Bedouins, tribes of wandering Arabs, who live in tents, and are dispersed all over Arabia, Egypt, and the N. of Africa, governed by their own chiefs, in the same manner as the patriarchs lived and governed anciently; the principal employment of both, the grazing of cattle. They profess the Mohammedan faith.

Bedwin, Great, a village in Wiltshire, five miles S. W. of Hungerford, and 70 W. of London.

Bedworth, a town in the county of Warwick, England, seated on the great coal strata, which is here extensively worked. A number of persons are also employed in the ribbon manufacture; 5 miles N. of Coventry.

Beemah, a river of Hindostan, which rises in the mountains to the N. of Poonah, and flows S. E upwards of 300 miles, till it joins the Kistna, near Edghir.

Beeralston, a town in Cornwall, England; 3 miles N. of Saltash, and 212 from London.

Beering's Bay, a bay formerly called Admiralty Bay, in N. lat. 59. 18. on the W. coast of North America.

Beering's Island, an island in the Pacific Ocean, about 90 miles long and 30 wide, 30 leagues E. of the coast of Kamtschatka. Long. 166. 30. E. lat. 55. 30. N.

Beering's Strait, the narrow sea between the W. coast of North America and the E. coast of Asia. It is 13 leagues wide in the narrowest part, between the Capes Prince of Wales and Tchukotskoi, in lat. 65. 45. N. 168. 17. W. long.

Beeroo, a country of Negroland, between

Zahara on the N. and Bambara on the S. Walet is the capital.

Bees, St., a village in Cumberland, near the sea; 5 miles S. of Whitehaven. Here is a noted free-school; also the remains of a priory, the nave of its church being now used as the parish church. Two miles to the N. W. is a lofty promontory, called St. Bees' Head, on which is a lighthouse.

Beesko, a town in Brandenburg, in Middlemark, with a cloth manufacture; seated on the Spree; 40 miles S. E. of Berlin.

Befort, or Belfort, a fortified town of France, in the department of Upper Rhine, with manufactures of excellent iron. It stands at the foot of a mountain; 34 miles S. W. of Colmar. Pop. about 5000.

Begemder, a province of Abyssinia, 200 miles long, and 50 broad. It is the central and most important province of Abyssinia, and from which are derived the principal supplies in time of war.

Begherme, an interior country, in the centre of North Africa, S. of Bornou. The capital, of the same name, is situate in the lat. of 17. N. and 22. 50. E. long. A salt lake, in the centre of the territory, supplies a great extent of country with that indispensable article.

Behaban, a town of Persia, province of Fars; 160 miles S. by W. of Ispahan. Pop. 11,000.

Behabur, a town of Hindostan, in Lahore; 75 miles W. by N. of Lahore, on the road to Cashmere.

Behker, or Bhakor, a town of Hindostan, capital of a country of the same name. It stands on an island formed by the Indus; 160 miles S. by W. of Moultan. Long. 70. 2. E. lat. 27. 30. N.

Behrings. *See* Beerings.

Beilstein, the name of several towns in different parts of Germany: 1st, in the Duchy of Wurtemberg, at which is a mineral bath, about 20 miles N. by E. of Stuttgard; 2nd, in the Prussian states of the Grand Duchy of the Lower Rhine, on the E. bank of the Moselle, about 5 miles N. of Zell and 22 S. W. of Coblentz; 3rd, a little to the W. of Leon, on the Maine.

Beinheim, a town of France, in the department of Lower Rhine, seated on the Sur, near its confluence with the Rhine; 22 miles N. N. E. of Strasburg.

Beira, a province of Portugal, bordering on the Atlantic Ocean, extending from the mouth of the Mondego River, S. in lat. 40. to the Douro, which forms its northern boundary, in lat. 41. 11. N. It is bounded on the E. by the Spanish province of Salamanca, and S. by the Portuguese province of Estremadura, and contains an area of 823 square leagues, and a population of 922,500. The province is interspersed with mountains, from which rise several streams, some falling into the Tagus, and others into the Douro, in addition to the Mondego, which intersects nearly the whole province from E. to W., and is, on the whole, a fine and fruitful district. The capital is Coimbra, and the other chief towns are Lamego, Viseu, Pinhel, Almeida, Guarda, and Castel Branco.

Beirout. *See* Bairout.

Beit el Faki, a town of Arabia, in Yemen, famous as being a great mart for coffee. It is 24 miles E. S. E. of Hodeida, and about 70 N. by E. of Mocha.

Beith, a parish and town of Scotland; the parish is partly in Ayr and partly in Renfrewshire. The town, in which the greater portion of the population is concentrated, and employed in the cotton manufacture, is in Ayrshire, about 10 miles S. by W. of Paisley.

Beja, a town of Portugal, in Alentejo, supposed to have been the Pax Julia of the Romans; seated on an eminence in an extensive plain, near a lake of its name; 72 miles S. E. of Lisbon. Long. 7. 40. W. lat. 37. 58. N. Pop. about 6000.

Bejapour. *See* Visiapour.

Bekesh, a tn. in a county of the same name, in Upper Hungary, situate in a fork of the Korasch River, a few miles E. of Tur.

Bela, a large town of Upper Hungary, situate among the Carpathian Mountains, on the frontiers of Poland.

Bel-Alcasar, or Balcazar, a town of Cordovia, Spain, situate on the E. bank of the Goga River, 35 miles N. N. W. of Cordovia.

Belabre, or Balabre, a town of France, in the department of Indre; 25 miles S. W. of Chateauroux.

Belaspoor, a town of Hindostan, on the river Sutlej. It is a well built town, and prinpally of stone. Pop. 3500.

Belbeis, a considerable town of Egypt; 35 miles N. E. of Cairo, and 45 N. W. of Suez.

Belcastro, a town of Naples, in Calabria Ulteriore, seated on a mountain, 8 miles from the Gulf of Squillace, and 12 S. W. of St. Severino.

Belchite, a town of Spain, in Arragon, on the river Almonazir; 20 miles S. of Saragossa.

Belcz, or Belz, a town of Gallicia; about 25 miles N. by E. of Lemberg.

Belem, a village of Portugal, in Estremadura, on the N. side of the Tajo, 4 miles below Lisbon. Here is a royal monastery, where the kings and queens of Portugal are interred; a strong fort, which defends the entrance to the city; and to the N. a noble modern aqueduct.

Belestat, a town of France, in the department of Aude; 27 miles S. W. of Carcassone.

Belfast, a town in the county of Antrim, Ireland, situate at the head of a spacious bay, about 15 miles in length, which forms a safe and commodious harbour. Vessels drawing more than 8 or 9 feet of water, load and unload by lighters about 7 miles below the town. Belfast is a regular, well-built town; the principal street runs in a straight line from the head of the bay, and is very handsome. It is the entrepot for a great portion of the linens manufactured in the N. of Ireland, for the storing of which there is a spacious edifice called the Linen Hall, on the plan of the cloth halls in Leeds. It has a theatre and an exchange, over which is an assembly-room, two handsome churches, and several meeting-houses; and, in 1808, a public school on an extensive scale was founded; there are also very extensive barracks on the N. side of the town; the river Lagan, over which there is a bridge of twenty-one arches, falls into the bay on the S. E. side, and communicates with Lough Neagh by a canal. The markets are exceedingly well supplied with all kinds of provisions; and large quantities of linens, in small parcels, are brought in for sale by the country people, for whose accommodation there is a separate market. In addition to large quantities of linens, butter, salt provisions, and grain, shipped to Great Britain, partly in exchange for manufactures, Belfast carries on a direct trade to the West Indies, Spain, America, and the Baltic; builds and owns a considerable extent of shipping, and has several manufactures of leather, chemicals, glass, cotton, &c. The Belfast canal connects the town with Lough Neagh, and passes several marble quarries. It is 102 miles N. of Dublin. It returns two members to parliament.

Belfast, a town beautifully located on the shore of a fine bay, on the S. side of the Penobscot river, in the state of Maine, North America; it owns some shipping, and carries on a trade in timber. Pop. about 1400; about 251 miles N. E. of Boston.

Belford, a town of Northumberland, on the line of the high road from London to Edinburgh; 49 miles N. by W. of Newcastle, and 15 S. by E. of Berwick. It has a market on Thursdays.

Belgard, a town of Prussian Pomerania, immediately contiguous to Corbin, and about 15 miles S. by E. of Colberg.

Belgaum, a town of Hindostan, province of Bejapoor. Pop. 5000. It is strongly fortified, and has an abundant supply of water. It has been adopted as a cantonment for troops; 115 miles from Bejapoor.

Belgern, a town of Saxony proper, with a good trade in beer; seated on the Elbe; 8 miles S. E. of Torgau.

Belgium, a kingdom of Europe, bounded on the N. by Holland, W. by the North Sea, S. by France, E. by the Duchy of Luxembourg and of the Rhine, containing an area of 14,459 square miles, and pop. 4,000,000. The principal rivers are the Scheldt, (l'Escaut,) Meuse, (Maas,) and the Our, but it abounds in minor streams, and is entirely without lakes, in which it varies much from Holland. The southern part rises into hills of moderate elevation, but the N. W. is a part of the level of the Netherlands. It is a country of exceeding fertility and beauty. The plains in the N. are composed of luxuriant meadows, or polders, covered with cattle, while the more undulating S. is clothed with wood, and affords a pattern of agricultural skill. There are coal-pits near Namur and Mons, and Liege is famous for its hardware and its iron-works. Here is one of the largest engineering establishments in the world. There is now established a system of

dom, and which all centre at Mechlin as a starting-point. They commence at Ostend, and are connected with the Rhine, and will probably, ere long, be united to the Parisian lines.

The capital is Brussels, (Bruxelle,) but the principal commercial town is Antwerp, (Anvers.) It is divided into nine provinces, viz. Antwerp, Brabant, E. and W. Flanders, Liege, Limburg, Namur, and Luxembourg. The language of the better classes is French, which is also spoken in the southern province; but in the N. W. the Flemish is principally spoken.

The history of Belgium is identical with that of the Netherlands, till 1830, when the Belgians revolted, and, in 1831, chose Prince Leopold, of Saxe Coburg, for their sovereign, under the name of Leopold I. He is assisted in the executive by a chamber of representatives and a senate.

Belgrade, a celebrated town and fortress of European Turkey, capital of Servia, and a Greek bishop's see, seated at the confluence of the Saave with the Danube, immediately contiguous to the Sclavonian fortress of Semlin. It was first possessed by the Turks in 1522, retaken by the confederated German powers in 1688, but again taken by the Turks in 1690. It was taken by Prince Eugene in 1717, and kept till 1739, when it was ceded to the Turks. It was again taken in 1789, and restored at the peace of Reichenbach in 1790; and in 1806 it surrendered to an insurgent force of Servians, in opposition to the wanton authority of the janissaries. In addition to its eminence as a fortress, it is one of the most considerable trading towns in Western Turkey. It is about 440 miles N. W. of Constantinople, and 160 S. S. E. of Pest.

Belgrade, a town of European Turkey, in Romania, on the strait of Constantinople, 20 miles N. of that city. It was the residence of Lady M. W. Montague; and is now comparatively deserted.

Belgrado, a town of Italy, in Friuli, seated near the Tojamenta; 81 miles S. by W. of Udina.

Belida, or Bleeda, a town of Algiers, in the province of Titeria, at the foot of a ridge of mountains; 15 miles S. E. of Algiers.

Belitz, a tn. of Brandenburg, in the Middle Mark, with a manufacture of cloth; seated on a river of the same name; 27 miles S.W. of Berlin.

Bellac, a town of France, in the department of Upper Vienne, seated on the Vincon; 20 miles N. of Limoges. Pop. about 4000.

Bellaire, a town of Maryland, capital of Harford county; 22 miles N. E. of Baltimore, and 86 W. S.W. of Philadelphia.

Bellegarde, a fortress of France, in the department of Eastern Pyrenees, and an important place, on account of its being a passage to the Pyrenees. It was taken by the Spaniards in 1793, but retaken the next year. It is 15 miles S. of Perpignan.

Bellegarde, a tn. of France, in the depart

ment of Saone and Loire, on the river Saone; 15 miles N. E. of Chalons.

Belleisle, an island of France, 15 miles from the coast of Bretagne. It is 10 miles long and three broad, diversified with craggy mountains, salt-works, and fertile plains. The principal place is Palais, a fortified town, with a citadel. It was taken by the English in 1761, and restored in 1762. It now forms part of the department of Morbihan, and contains a population of about 5800. Long. 3. 5. W. lat. 47. 17. N.

Belleisle, an island at the N. E. end of a channel, between New Britain and Newfoundland, called the Strait of Belleisle. The island is 20 miles in circuit, and has a small harbour on the N. W. side. Long. 55. 25. W. lat. 51. 58. N.

Bellesme, a town of France, in the department of Orne, with an ancient castle; 24 miles E. S. E. of Alencon, and 80 S. W. of Paris.

Belley, a town of France, in the department of Ain, and lately a bishop's see; seated near the Rhone; 40 miles S. E. of Bourg. Long. 5. 44. E. lat. 45. 47. N. Pop. about 3800.

Belheim, a town in the Bavarian circle of the Rhine, lying between Laudan and Phillipsburg, on the W. side of the river.

Bellin, a town of Brandenburg, in the New Mark, E. of the Oder Canal, about 18 miles N. N.W. of Kustin.

Bellingham, a tn. in Northumberland, with a market on Tuesday; seated on the N. branch of the Tyne; 15 miles N. N. W. of Hexham, and 300 of London.

Bellinzona, a town of Switzerland, capital of the canton of Tessin. It is seated on the Tesino, 5 miles above its entrance into the lake Maggiore, and 22 W. S.W. of Chiavenna. Long. 8. 55. E. lat. 46. 8. N.

Bell Rock, or Inch Cape, a ledge of partly sunken rocks, off the E. coast of Scotland, between the Friths of Forth and Tay, formerly very dangerous in foggy weather, and by night, but somewhat obviated since 1811, by the erection of a light-house upon the most prominent point, in lat. 56. 26. N. and long. 2. 23. W.

Bellunese, a district of Italy, lying between Friuli, Cadorino, Feltrino, and Tyrol. It has large woods, and iron mines; and is fertile in corn, wine, and fruit. Belluno is the only place of note.

Belluno, a town of Italy, capital of the Bellunoso, and a bishop's see, seated among the Alps, on the river Piave; 15 miles N. E. of Feltri. Long. 12. 9. E. lat. 43. 13. N. Pop. about 7500.

Belmont, a county on the E. side of the state of Ohio, bordering on the Ohio River, which separates it from Virginia. The population in 1810 was 11,097, and in 1840, 30,901. St. Clairsville, the chief town, is 123 miles E. of Columbus.

Belmont, the name of two inconsiderable towns in France, one in the department of Loire, and the other in Aveiron.

Belover, a town in the N. E. part of Croatia, near the frontiers of Sclavonia.

Beloochistan, a country of Asia, lying between Persia and the Indus, the boundaries of which are very imperfectly defined. The inhabitants, consisting wholly of pastoral tribes, extend their territory wherever pasture and fertility invite, and the power of their arms prove sufficient to defend them against interruption; in fact, instead of Beloochistan being designated a country, it would be more proper to consider it as the eastern part of Persia, inhabited by numerous predatory and lawless tribes, possessing peculiar Mahometan tenets, from which the name of Belooches has been derived, and which will be more fully elucidated under the head of Persia. Kelat is the capital.

Belluza, a town of Hindostan, in Mysore, with a citadel, both of them strongly fortified with a mud wall and a ditch. In the vicinity is much fine rice ground, and a great number of sheep are bred. It is 38 miles N. of Seringapatam.

Belper, a town in Derbyshire, with a market on Saturday. Here are several large cotton-mills, a bleaching-mill, and an iron-forge, and about a dozen large establishments for the manufacture of nails. It is seated on the Derwent, eight miles N. of Derby, and 134 N. N. W. of London.

Belpre, a town of the state of Ohio, on the N.W. bank of the Ohio, opposite the mouth of the Little Kanhaway; 14 miles S.W. of Marietta, and 46 N.E. of Galliopolis.

Belpuig, a town of Spain, in Catalonia, with a famous convent; 18 miles E. N. E. of Lerida.

Belt, Great, a strait of Denmark, between the islands of Zealand and Funen, which forms a communication between the Cattegat and the Baltic. Owing to its more circuitous course it is not so much frequented as the Sound. (*See* Baltic.) In 1658 the whole strait was frozen so hard, that Charles Gustavus, king of Sweden, marched over it with a design to take Copenhagen.

Belt, Little, a strait, W. of the Great Belt, between Funen and North Jutland. It is one of the passages from the Cattegat to the Baltic, though not three miles in breadth, and very crooked.

Belturbet, a tn. in the N. part of the county of Cavan, Ireland; it is in the parish of Annagh. Previous to the union it returned a member to the Irish parliament. Nine miles N. N.W. of Cavan, and 61 of Dublin.

Belvedere, a town of European Turkey, capital of a fertile province of the same name, in the Morea. The raisins called Belvederes come from this place. It is 17 miles N. E. of Chirenza. Long. 21. 45. E. lat. 38. 0. N.

Belvedere is the name of several small towns in different parts of Italy.

Belvez, a town of France, in the department of Dordogne; 27 miles S.S. E. of Perigueux. Pop. about 3000.

Belum, a town of Hanover, near the mouth of the Oste; 24 miles N. W. of Stade. Considerable quantities of flax are grown in its vicinity.

Belur, a town of Usbec Tartary, capital of a

province of the same name, which is a hilly country, bounded on the N. and E. by the Belur Tagler, or Dark Mountains, anciently the Imaus. The capital is 200 miles E. of Budakshan. Long. 74. 10. E. lat. 36. 35. N.

Belzig, a town of Saxony Proper, with a castle, seated on the Walse; 25 miles N. N. W. of Wittenburg.

Bemba, a province of Congo, Africa. The inhabitants are idolatrous, and clothe in the unprepared skins of animals.

Ben, a name prefixed to most of the mountains in Scotland; the following are among the most considerable, with the counties in which situate, and their altitude above the level of the sea:—

		Feet.
Ben Ardlanich	Perth	3500
Beauchonzie	——	2922
Beinglo	——	3725
Abourd	Aberdeen	3940
Avon	———	2920
Choachan	Ross	3000
Cloch	Clackmannan	2420
Ivas	Perth	4000
Nevis	Inverness	4370
Lomond	Stirling	3240

Bena, or Bene, a fortified town of Piedmont, in the N. W. part of the province of Mondovi; 28 miles S. by E. of Turin. Pop. about 5000.

Benares, an exceedingly fertile district of Hindostan, in the N.E. part of the province of Allahabad, between those of Bahar and Oude. It contains the circars of Benares, Jionpour, Chunar, and Gazypour; and was ceded to the English in 1775. It is very productive in rice, sugar, silk, cotton, and indigo.

Benares, the chief town of the district, is one of the finest and most populous towns of all Hindostan. It is beautifully located on the N. bank of the Ganges, and celebrated as the ancient seat of Brahminical learning. Several Hindoo temples embellish the high banks of the river; and many other public and private buildings are magnificent. The streets are narrow, the houses high, and some of them five stories each, inhabited by different families, but the more wealthy Gentoos live in detached houses, with an open court, surrounded by a wall. Nearly in the centre of the city is a considerable Mahometan mosque, built by the emperor Aurungzebe, who destroyed a magnificent Hindoo temple to make room for it. There is also a very superb temple, built by the rajah Cheytsing, who was driven from Benares for exciting an insurrection against the British in 1781, and who was finally deposed in 1783. There are ruins of several Hindoo temples in the vicinity, destroyed by the intolerance of Mahometans. In addition to the consequence derived from the vast congregation of persons, occasioned by the priestcraft of Benares, it is the centre of a very extensive traffic for all the productions and manufactures of the east, and is distinguished for its trade in diamonds, and works in gold and jewellery. It is the seat of a British jurisdiction, and is about 130 miles W. by S. of Patna, and 460 W. by N. of Calcutta. Pop. about 600,000.

Benatek, a town in the circle of Bunzlau, Bohemia, situate on the west bank of the Iser River; about 30 miles N. E. of Prague. Tycho Brahè died here in 1601.

Benavari, a town of Spain, in Arragon; 17 miles N. of Lerida.

Benavente, a town of Spain, in Leon, on the river Esla; 35 miles S. S. W. of Leon.

Benavente, a town of Portugal in Alentejo, on the river Soro, near its confluence with the Tajo; 30 miles E. N. E. of Lisbon.

Benbecula, an island of Scotland, one of the Hebrides, between North and South Uist, from the last of which it is separated by a narrow channel, nearly dry at low water. It is of a circular form, including the inlets of the sea 9 miles in diameter. The soil is sandy and unproductive, but much kelp is made from the sea-weed thrown on the coast.

Bencoolen, a settlement of the English East India Company, on the south-west side of the island of Sumatra. The settlement was first formed in 1690, after the valiant Dutch drove all the English from Batavia. The unhealthiness of the spot first chosen destroyed, in 1692, nearly the whole of the European population: a new site was chosen, and the fort called Fort Marlborough has proved more congenial to the physical constitutions of Europeans; but it is still considered the most disagreeable place in all the British dominions of the east. The town is inhabited by natives from all parts of Asia. The chief occupation of the people of the country is the culture of the pepper plant, the extent of the produce of which is very great, and constitutes its exclusive means of external commerce. Fort Marlborough is in lat. 3. 48. S. and 102. 28. E. long.

Bencoonat, a town at the south-west extremity of the island of Sumatra; about 120 miles S. E. of Bencoolen.

Bencowse, a town of Algier, in the province of Constantine, 25 miles S. S. E. of Seteef.

Bendala, a town of Bornou, North Africa; about 200 miles E. of the capital.

Bender, or Teken, a fortified town of European Turkey, capital of Bessarabia. Here Charles XII. of Sweden resided, after his defeat at Pultowa in 1709. Previous to 1770, when the Russians took Bender by storm, and totally destroyed the town, and afterwards abandoned it, it contained about 30,000 inhabitants. In 1789, it was taken again by the Russians almost without a struggle, but restored to the Turks in the following year; again taken by the Russians, to whom, with the whole of Bessarabia and all that part of Moldavia east of the Pruth, it was confirmed by treaty in 1812. It is seated on the west bank of the Dniester, about 100 miles E. by S. of Jassy, and 410 N. of Constantinople. Present pop. about 10,000.

Bender Major, Begh, and Risher, three towns on the north-east shore of the Persian gulf.

Bendorf, a town on the east bank of the Rhine; about 5 miles N. of Coblentz.

Beneadi, a large town of Upper Egypt,

on the west side of the Nile, in lat. about 27. 30. N.

BENE. *See* BENA.

BENEDETTO, ST., a town of Italy, in the Mantuan, near the river Po; 15 miles S. S. E. of Mantua; distinguished, before the revolution, for one of the richest and finest convents in all Italy. There is also another town of the same name in Piedmont, 12 miles E. of Bena.

BENEDICT, a town of Maryland, in Charles county, situate on the Patuxent; 16 miles W. of Port Tobacco.

BENEDICT, ST., a market town of Hungary, on the west bank of the Gran; about 5 miles W. of Pukanz.

BENESCHAU, a town in the south-west part of Silesia, on the frontier of the principality of Troppau. Also the name of four small towns in Bohemia.

BENEVENTE, a town of France in the department of Creuse; 10 miles N. N. W. of Borganeuf.

BENEVENTO, a city of Naples, and an archbishop's see; capital of Principato Ulteriore, and of a small duchy of its name, lately belonging to the pope. Benevento has suffered greatly by earthquakes, particularly in 1688, when the archbishop was dug out of the ruins alive. Except Rome, no city of Italy can boast of so many ruins of ancient sculpture as are to be found in this place. It is seated near the confluence of the Sabato and Caloro; 35 miles N. E. of Naples. Long. 14. 47. E. lat. 41. 8. N. Pop. 20,350.

BENFELDEN, a town of France, in the department of Lower Rhine, on the river Ill; 12 miles S. S. W. of Strasburg.

BENGAL, a maritime province, forming the N. E. extremity of the great promontory of Hindostan, lying between the lat. of 22. and 26. 30. N. and the 86th and 92nd degree of E. long. It is bounded on the N. E. and N. by Meckley, Assam, and Bootan, countries at present but little known; N. W. by Bahar; S. by Orissa; and S. E. by the ocean, or Bay of Bengal, and contains an area of upwards of 100,000 square miles. The river Ganges intersects the province from N.W. to S.E., dividing into numerous channels before it falls into the sea, between the 88th and 91st degree of long. The Burrampooter enters the province from Assam, at the N. E. extremity, and unites with the most northern, which is the main branch of the Ganges, at its confluence with the sea, whilst the Dummooda waters the S. side of the province, falling into the Hoogly, or southern branch of the Ganges, below Calcutta: these rivers, with their numerous tributary streams, afford a facility of communication by water to almost every town in the province, and by their periodical overflowings add fertility to the luxuriant and exhaustless soil. Bengal is altogether a level country, formed of a continuity of vast plains, bounded only by the horizon, yielding, with but little aid of culture, all the plants and fruits peculiar to a tropical climate. Rice, cotton, silk, and saltpetre, are its indigenous and staple productions, and sugar and indigo have been recently cultivated with great success, and to a vast extent. Tobacco, hemp, and flax, are also produced for internal consumption; but, being inferior in quality to the like productions of America and Europe, they are not exported. Gums and medicinal plants are various and abundant. Of animals, the elephant and tiger hold the first rank; the former are highly appreciated for their docility, and utility for burthen, pageantry, and war; and command a value exceeding the value of the horse in Europe, according to their age and condition, in proportion as they exceed the horse in strength and power. Buffaloes and horned cattle are numerous, and horses of various kinds are common. Birds and domestic poultry of all kinds are very abundant. Previous to the commencement of the 13th century, Bengal was inhabited by an unmixed and feeble race of Hindoos, who at that period yielded their authority to a horde of Mahometan marauders from the confines of Persia and Tartary, who established their seat of empire at Delhi, and to whom Bengal continued tributary for about 140 years, when it regained, and retained its independence for nearly two centuries, when it was invaded by Shere Shah, and afterwards by the emperor Akbar, who again rendered it tributary to Delhi, to which it continued subject until the year 1756, when the whole province became subject to the authority of the English East India Company, who for half a century previously had established settlements on the banks of the Ganges, and progressively extended their influence. They have since divided it into three districts for civil and judicial purposes: viz. Calcutta, Dacca, and Moorshedabad, and formed six great military stations; of which Calcutta is the chief, as well as the seat of government of the whole British empire in Asia. The total population is about 3,000,000, of whom about nine-tenths are native Hindoos, and the remainder a mixed race of Mahometans, descendants of the early conquerors by intermarriages with the natives, and a few Europeans. Manufactures of cotton, or silk, are carried on in almost every town of the province, and in the principal cities the works in gold and jewellery are very extensive. The nature and present extent of the commerce of Bengal will be more fully elucidated under the head of CALCUTTA, and the nature and extent of revenual exactions under the head of HINDOSTAN, which see.

BENGAZI, a town of North Africa, on the shore of the Mediterranean, and has a good harbour in the state of Barca, in the beylik of Tripoli. Pop. 50,000.

BENGUELA, a maritime district on the W. coast of South Africa, lying S. of the Congo river, between the lat. 10. 30. and 16. S. There are two towns or settlements of the Portuguese on the coast, called Benguela, Old and New, the former in the lat. of 10. 50., and the other in about 12. 30. S., from whence the Portuguese and Brazilian ships obtain a considerable portion of their slaves. *See* ANGOLA.

BENI, a large river of South America, rising

near the S. extremity of La Paz, running N. parallel with, and within the most easterly ridge of the Andes, and forming the E. branch of the Ucayale, which falls into the Amazon after running from S. to N. through the whole interior of Peru. The Jesuits founded some settlements on the banks of the Beni, of which St. Francisco, Trinidad, and Reyez, in the lat. of 12. to 14. S., are the chief.

BENICARLO, a town of Valencia, Spain, a few miles N. of Peniscola. It is celebrated for its wines, of which considerable quantities are exported.

BENIGNO, ST., a populous village of Piedmont, situate on the high road to the Alps, about 10 miles N. of Turin. Pop. about 4500.

BENIHASSEN, a maritime province of Fez, bordering on the Atlantic, of which New Salee or Rabat in lat. 34. 5. N. is the principal outport.

BENIN, a country of North Africa, towards the E. extremity of Upper Guinea, lying principally N. and W. of the river Formosa, the entrance to which is in lat. 5. 33. N. and 4. 35. E. long. It is bounded on the W. by Dahomey; on the E. by Waree; and N. by undefined boundaries and countries but little known. Benin exhibits many beautiful landscapes; but the air is noxious near the coast, on account of the gross vapours from the marshes. Oranges and lemons grow on the sides of the roads, and the cotton and pepper plants are indigenous to the soil, but both are very imperfectly cultivated. Among the animals are elephants in great number, tigers, leopards, stags, wild boars, civet and mountain cats, horses, hares, and hairy sheep; a vast number of serpents and other reptiles; and the principal birds are paroquets, pigeons, partridges, storks, and ostriches. The dress of the natives is neat. The rich wear white calico or cotton petticoats, but the upper part of the body is commonly naked. The women use great art in dressing their hair, which they reduce into a variety of forms. The people are skilful in making various sorts of dyes; and they manufacture some cotton into cloths. Polygamy is allowed, and the number of wives is limited by the state of their circumstances only. Though jealous of each other, they offer their wives to Europeans. Their religion is paganism, the king himself being *fetiche*, and, as such, the chief object of adoration in his dominions. The chief town, called also *Benin*, is one of the most populous of all Western Africa, containing about 15,000 inhabitants. It is situate inland about 40 miles from Gatto, a town situate at the head of a large inlet of the Formosa river. The road from Gatto to Benin is over a level country, in some places swampy and thickly wooded, and the country around the town of Benin is also thickly wooded. Like all other African towns, Benin is very unequally laid out. The houses are all built of clay, and covered with reeds, straw, or leaves. The royal palace is of vast extent, but neither elegant nor commodious. All male slaves here are foreigners; for the inhabitants cannot be sold for slaves, only they bear the name of the king's slaves. Since the restriction of the slave-trade to the S. of the equator, Benin, in common with the whole extent of the western coast of Africa, from the river Gambia, in lat. 13. N. to Malemba, in lat. 5. S., has shown itself capable of affording all the means requisite for the formation of an intercourse, as social and reciprocal as the slave-traffic was debasing, partial, and vicious. The commerce of Great Britain with this part of Africa is inconsiderable.

BENIN-DAZY, ST., a town of France, department of Nievre, having several iron-mines in its vicinity. Pop. 1600.

BENISUEF, or BENISOUEF, a town of Egypt, with manufactures of carpets, and woollen and linen stuffs, seated on the Nile, 60 miles S. of Cairo. The town has a splendid appearance, from the numerous mosques.

BENKENSTEIN, or BENNECKENSTEIN, a town of the Prussian states, in the duchy of Saxony, 11 miles S. W. of Halberstadt.

BENNINGEN, a village of Wirtemburg, on the Neckar, where the remains of a Roman town were discovered in 1597.

BENNINGTON, a county forming the S. W. part of the state of Vermont, bordering on the state of Bew York. Pop. 16,872.

BENNINGTON, the chief town of the preceding county. Though the largest and oldest town in the state, the judicial courts are commonly held at Rutland and Windsor alternately. In or near this town, Colonel Stark gained two battles, on Aug. 16th, 1777, which contributed to the subsequent surrender of General Burgoyne's army. Bennington is situate at the foot of the Green Mountains, near the S. W. corner of the state; 30 miles E. by N. of Albany, and 129 S. S. W. of Montpelier. Pop. 3429.

BENSBERG, a town of the duchy of Berg, Westphalia; 7 miles E. of Mulheim, on the Rhine.

BENSHEIM, a town of Germany, 25 miles N. N. W. of Heidelberg, and 10 N. E. of Worms. Pop. about 3100.

BENSINGTON, commonly called BENSON, a town in Oxfordshire, on the high road from London to Oxford. It was formerly the abode of royalty, and has an hospital called God's House.

BENTHEIM, formerly a county of the circle of Westphalia, but now forming part of the kingdom of Hanover. It is about 18 miles in breadth and 45 in length, bordering on the United Provinces of Holland, intersected from S. to N. by the Vecht. Pop. about 25,000. There is a town of the same name, inconsiderable. The chief towns are Neinhus, Northorn, and Schuttorf.

BENTIVOGLIO, a town of Italy, in Bolognese, 10 miles N. E. of Bologna.

BENZHAUSEN, a populous village, with several iron-forges, in the mining district of Smalcalden, county of Henneberg, circle of Franconia.

BERAR, an interior province of the Deccan of

Hindostan, bounded on the N. by Malwa and Allahabad, E. by Orissa, S. by Golconda, and W. by Dowlatabad and Candeish. The principal part of it is nominally subject to a rajah, under the surveillance of the English East India Company, the other to the Nizam of the Deccan. The rajah's country extends 550 miles from E. to W., and, in some places, 200 from N. to S. Its capital is Nagpour. Little is known respecting the interior; but that about Nagpour is fertile and well cultivated. The general appearance of the country, particularly between Nagpour and Orissa, is that of a forest, thinly set with villages and towns.

Berat, or Arnauth Belgrade, the ancient Eordea, a large interior town of Albania; about 40 miles N. E. of Valona. Pop. about 12,000.

Beraun-Podbrad, an interior circle of Bohemia, lying between 49. 25. and 50. of N. lat., and 13. 45. and 14. 30. of E. long. It is intersected from S. to N. by the Moldau river, which falls into the Elbe, about 20 miles N. of Prague. *Beraun*, the chief town, is situate near the northern frontier of the circle, on the S. bank of a river of the same name, which rises near the frontiers of Bavaria, and falls into the Moldau a few miles S. of Prague. It has manufactures of fire-arms and earthenware. 15 miles W. S. W. of Prague.

Berbera, the projecting coast of Eastern Africa, extending from the Straits of Babelmandel to Cape Guardafui. At a town of the same name upon the coast, in lat. 10. 25. N. and 45. 8. E. long. a large annual fair is held, at which the manufactured productions of Persia and India are exchanged for gum, frankincense, myrrh, and various other commodities. This seems to be a point of the African coast from whence a more advantageous intercourse might be established with the interior than any other, either on the western or eastern coasts.

Berbice, a river of South America, the entrance to which is in lat. 6. 29. N. and 57. 11. W. long. Plantations formed by the Dutch extend on both sides of the river for about 150 miles along the coast. The colony surrendered to the English in 1790; given up at the peace of Amiens; retaken on the renewal of the war, and confirmed to England at the peace of 1814. Cotton and coffee are now largely cultivated on its banks.

Berchtolsgaden, provostship of, encircled by the archbishopric of Saltzburg, formerly part of the circle of Bavaria, but now of the Austrian empire. The chief town of the same name is situate at the N. E. part of the district, about 14 miles S. of Saltzburg. It has a handsome church. Pop. about 3000, who are much employed in the manufacture of wooden toys, large quantities of which are exported to England; the district produces great quantities of salt.

Berdickzow, a town of Russia, in Europe, government of Volhynia. Pop. 10,000, chiefly Jews. Here is a celebrated image of the Virgin, preserved in a Carmelite friary.

Berdoa, a town of Persia, in Erivan, seated in a fertile plain; 16 miles E. S. E. of Gangea.

Berdoa. *See* Burgu.

Bere Regis, a town in Dorsetshire, with a market on Wednesday. On Woodbury-hill, half a mile to the N. E., is a circular Roman camp, enclosed within three trenches. The town is seated on the Bere, near its confluence with the Piddle; 12 miles E. by N. of Dorchester, and 112 S. W. of London.

Beregh, a frontier county of Upper Hungary, bounded on the S. by the river Theiss, and N. by the Carpathian mountains. Pop. about 46,000.

Beregh, and Bereghszaz, two of the principal towns, are situate in the S. W. part of the preceding county.

Bereilly, a city of Hindostan, capital of Rohilla, which was conquered by the nabob of Oude, in 1774. It is 120 miles N. N. W. of Lucknow. Long. 79. 40. E. lat. 28. 30. N.

Berelos, a lake of Egypt, between Damietta and Rosetta, of an oval form. 32 miles long, and 10 broad in the middle.

Berenice, an ancient port of Said, or Upper Egypt, the ruins of which still remain. The harbour is safe and commodious.

Beretsk, a town at the S. E. frontier of Transylvania, near the pass of Oitosch.

Berezina, a river of Lithuania, which has its source near a village of the same name, in lat. 54. 50. N., and, after receiving several tributary streams, and running S. through the palatinate of Minsk, parallel with the Dnieper, through nearly three degrees of lat., falls into that river a little above Rzeczyca. It is memorable for the disasters which its passage occasioned to the French army on its retreat from Moscow in 1812. There is a small river of the same name falling into the Vistula, a few miles S. E. of Thorn.

Berezinskoi, a town of Siberia, on the Irtisch river; about 40 miles S. E. of Tobolsk.

Berezov, a considerable town of Siberia, situate near the confluence of the Soswa river, with the W. branch of the Obe; in lat. 64.

Berg, a duchy of Westphalia, lying along the river Rhine, to the S. of the duchy of Cleve, about 60 miles in length, and from 10 to 22 in breadth. It is full of woods and mountains, but fertile upon the banks of the Rhine, and in the valleys; and has mines of lead, iron, and coal. Dusseldorf is the capital. It now forms a part of the Prussian provinces of the Lower Rhine. Pop. about 295,000.

Berg is also the name of several towns in different parts of Germany.

Berga, a town of Spain, in Catalonia, seated on the Lobrogat; 18 miles E. N. E. of Solsona.

Berga is also the name of two towns in Saxony, one in Switzerland, and another in Norway.

Bergamasco, a province of Italy, bounded by Brescia, the Valteline, and the Milanese. Toward the N. it is mountainous and rocky, and has mines of iron; some of the valleys produce much wine and oil; and in the vicinity of the capital, Bergamo, it is very fertile. It formed part of the kingdom of Italy, under Buonaparte, but was transferred to Austria at the congress of Vienna, subsequently to the peace of 1815. Pop. about 365,000.

BERGAMO, an ancient city of Italy, and a bishop's see, capital of Bergamasco, with a citadel. It is famous for its sewing-silk; and its fair, on St. Bartholomew's day, is resorted to by merchants from distant parts. It stands on a hill, between the rivers Bremba and Serio; 30 miles N. E. of Milan; it contains several fine edifices, and is distinguished as a birth-place of several eminent artists and literati. Pop. about 30,000.

BERGAMO, a city of Natolia. *See* PERGAMI.

BERGEDORF, a town on the N. bank of the Elbe; about 10 miles E. of Hamburg.

BERGEN, a city and seaport of Norway, capital of a government of the same name, and a bishop's see, with a castle. It forms a semicircle round a small gulf of the sea, and is the most populous town in Norway, containing 20,844 inhabitants. On the land side it is defended by mountains, and on the other by several fortifications. All the churches, and many of the houses, are of stone, but most of the latter are constructed of wood. The castle and cathedral are remarkable edifices. It carries on a great trade in skins, fir-wood, deals, tar, and dried fish; it is 170 miles W. by N. of Christiana. Long. 5. 20. E. lat. 60. 24. N.

BERGEN, a town of North Holland, noted for two bloody battles in 1799, between the English and Russian forces opposed by the Dutch and French, which terminated in favour of the former. It is situate among woods; 4 miles N. N. E. of Alcmaar.

BERGEN, the chief town of the island of RUGEN, which see.

BERGEN, a considerable town of New Jersey. The inhabitants are mostly descendants from the Dutch settlers. It is surrounded by water, except on the north, and separated by the river Hudson from the city of New York, 3 miles distant. The county contains a population of 13,223. The courts are held at Hackensack, 74 miles N. E. of Trenton.

BERGEN-OP-ZOOM, a town of Dutch Brabant, capital of a marquisate of the same name. It is a handsome place, and its fortress is one of the strongest in the Netherlands, seated partly on a hill, and partly on the river Zoom, which communicates with the Scheldt by a canal. It has several times been besieged to no purpose; but was taken by the French, in 1747, and in 1794. In 1814, the English attempted to carry this place by storm; but, after forcing a passage into the town, their retreat was cut off, when they were nearly all killed or made prisoners. It is 15 miles N. of Antwerp, and 22 S. W. of Breda. Long. 4. 22. E. lat. 51. 30. N.

BERGERAC, a town of France, in the department of Dordogne, seated on the north bank of the river Dordogne; 24 miles S. by W. of Perigueux, and 48 E. of Bordeaux. Pop. 8600.

BERGOO, an interior district of North Africa, lying to the east of Bergherme; *Wara* is the chief town.

BERG-REICHENSTEIN, and BERGSTADT, two towns in the circle of Prachin Bohemia, situate in a mining district, on the frontiers of Bavaria.

BERGUES, a fortified town of France, in the department of Nord, on the river Colme, at the foot of a mountain; 5 miles S. of Dunkirk.

BERGZABERN, a town of Bavaria, circle of the Rhine, seated on the Erlbach; 6 miles S. S. W. of Landau, and 34 S. E. of Deux Ponts.

BERKHAMPSTEAD, a town in Hertfordshire, with a market on Saturday. Roman coins have been often dug up here; and on the north side are the remains of a castle, the residence of the kings of Mercia. In 697 a parliament was held here, and Ina's laws published. Here William the Conqueror swore to his nobility, to maintain the laws made by his predecessors. Henry II. kept his court in this town, and granted to it many privileges; and James I., whose children were nursed here, made it a corporation; but this government was dropped in the civil wars. The church is a handsome Gothic structure. It is seated on the west branch of the river Gade, on the Grand Junction Canal, and near the Birmingham railway; 26 miles N. W. of London.

BERKELEY, a town in Gloucestershire, governed by a mayor, with a market on Wednesday. It has a trade in timber, coals, malt, and cheese, which is benefited by means of a canal from Gloucestershire. Here is an ancient castle on a rising ground, in which Edward II. was murdered. Berkeley has the honour of giving birth to the justly celebrated Dr. Edward Jenner, the discoverer of vaccine inoculation. It is seated on the Little Avon, near its confluence with the Severn; 15 miles S.W. of Gloucester, and 114 W. of London.

BERKELEY, a frontier county of Virginia, bounded on the north by the Potomac River, which separates it from Pennsylvania. Pop. in 1820, 11,211, being about 350 less than in 1810, and in 1840, 10,972. Martinsburg, 192 miles N. by W. of Richmond, is the chief town.

BERKS, or BERKSHIRE, an inland and very irregular shaped county of England: its length is 48 miles, its breadth 29, and its circumference nearly 208 miles. The river Thames, by a very circuitous course, divides it on the north and east from the counties of Oxford and Bucks, and it is bounded on the west by Wiltshire, and south by Hampshire. Reading, 39 miles west of London, is the chief town; but the assizes for the county are held alternately at Abingdon. At the east end of the county, on the south bank of the Thames, is the castle and extensive domain of Windsor, a residence of the kings of England, and one of the most stately and magnificent abodes in Europe, or the world. The other principal towns are Maidenhead, Newbury, and Hungerford. The county has but few manufactures; some sacking is made in the vicinity of Abingdon, and some ribbons and silk plush in the vicinity of Reading; but its supply of colonial, foreign, and manufactured productions is obtained by means of a surplus of grain, flour, malt, wool, some cattle and sheep, and a considerable quantity of oak timber. In this county are also Frogmore, Cumberland Lodge, Cranbourn Lodge, and other residences of the royal family, with numerous seats belonging to the nobility and gentry. It returns three members to parliament.

BERKS, an interior county of Pennsylvania, bounded on the north-west by the Blue Ridge of the Allegany Mountains, and intersected from the north-west to south-east by the Schulkyl River. Pop. 64,569. Reading, 52 miles E. by N. of Harrisburg, is the chief town.

BERKSHIRE, a county forming the whole western boundary of the state of Massachusets, bordering on the state of New York. Pop. 41,745. Lenox, the chief town, in the centre of the county, is 129 miles due west of Boston.

BERLAMONT, a town of France, in the department of Nord; 6 miles E. S. E. of Quesnoy.

BERLEBURG, a town of Germany, in the Electorate of Hesse, with a castle, seated on the Berlebach, near its confluence with the Eder; 20 miles N. W. of Marburg, and 70 S. E. of Cassel.

BERLIN, a city of Germany, capital of the Electorate of Brandenburg, and of the whole Prussian dominions; one of the largest, best built, and best governed of any in Germany. It is defended partly by walls, partly by palisades, and has sixteen gates. The streets are straight, wide, and long; and its large squares, magnificent palaces, churches, and other buildings, are scarcely to be equalled. The magnificent avenue of lime trees, "Unter dem linden," is 2082 feet long, and 170 broad. It is 12 miles in circumference; but within this inclosure are numerous gardens; and many beautiful houses are let in stories to mechanics. The population is 236,830. The royal palace contains a fine library, a rich cabinet of curiosities and medals, and the supreme colleges of government. Near the palace stands the magnificent cathedral. Here are also several academies and hospitals, an astronomical observatory, a superb arsenal, and a royal cloth manufacture. Berlin has a flourishing trade, occasioned by its numerous manufactures of silk, wool, cotton, camel's hair, linen, Prussian blue, cutlery, and porcelain; and by its enamelled, inlaid, and embroidered works. It is seated on the river Spree, from which there is a canal to the Oder on the east, and another to the Elbe on the west; but it has a communication by water, both with the Baltic Sea and the German Ocean. This city was taken, in 1760, by an army of Russians, Austrians, and Saxons, who were obliged to evacuate it in a few days. In 1806, ten days after the battle of Jena, the French entered this city, and Buonaparte held a court in the palace. It is 100 miles N. of Dresden, and 185 N. W. of Breslau. Long. 13. 22. E. lat. 52. 31. N.

BERLIN, a town in Renssalaer county, state of New York, on the E. bank of the Hudson River; 15 miles E. of Albany. Pop. 1794. It is also the name of several other towns in different parts of the United States.

BERMEO, or BORMEO, a town of Spain, in Biscay, on the Bay of Biscay, near the Cape of Machicaco; 15 miles E. of Bilboa.

BERMUDA HUNDRED, or CITY POINT, a port of Virginia, in Chesterfield county. The exports from this place are collected at Richmond, 20 miles above it, and to which it is the out-port. City Point, from which it is named, is on the S. bank of James River, four miles S. S. W. of the town. Long. 77. 31. W. lat. 37. 16. N.

BERMUDAS, or SOMERS ISLANDS, four islands in the Atlantic Ocean; 500 miles E. of Carolina, and surrounded by rocks. They were discovered by Juan Bermudas, a Spaniard, in 1527; but not inhabited till 1609, when Sir George Somers was cast away upon them; and they have belonged to Britain ever since. They abound in cedar wood, with which a number of small vessels are built. Some sugar and coffee is cultivated for exportation. They are much subject to hurricanes and tornadoes. Pop. 11,000. The principal island is called St. George, and the town, of the same name, is in lat. 32. 22. N. and 64. 33. W. long.

BERN, or BERNE, the largest of the cantons of Switzerland, being 150 miles long and 75 broad. It is the most fertile country in Switzerland, and divided into two principal parts, called the German and Roman, but the last is most commonly called the Pays de Vaud. It is intersected from S. to N. by the river Aar; on the S. E. part are the lakes of Thun and Brienz, and on the N. W. it extends to Lake Neufchatel, and to that of Geneva. The religion is Calvinism. Pop. about 338,000.

BERNE, a town of Switzerland, capital of the canton of Berne. Here is a celebrated academy and a rich library. It is a strong place, in a peninsula formed by the river Aar; it is estimated to contain 18,000 inhabitants. The houses are built of freestone, and pretty uniform, particularly in the principal street, and there are piazzas on each side, with a walk raised four feet above the level of the street, very commodious in wet weather. The streets are traversed by a canal, and the public buildings are magnificent. In the arsenal are preserved the figure and armour of the celebrated William Tell, in the act of taking aim at the apple on his son's head. Berne was taken in 1798 by the French. It is 70 miles N. E. of Geneva. Long. 7. 29. E. lat. 46. 57. N.

BERNARD, GRAND ST., a mountain on the Pennine Alps, on the frontiers of Piedmont; 15 miles N. N. W. of Aosta. On the summit, at a height of 11,000 feet, is a large convent, where the monks entertain all travellers gratis, for three days. It was by this passage Buonaparte conducted his army into Italy in 1800. Little St. Bernard, to the S. W., is 7194 ft. in height.

BERNARD CASTLE, or BARNARD CASTLE, a town in the county of Durham, with a market on Wednesday, and manufactures of stockings and camlets. It takes its name from a castle built by Bernard Baliol, king of Scotland, who founded an hospital here. It is seated on the river Tees; 24 miles S. W. of Durham, and 246 N. N. W. of London.

BERNAW, a fortified town of Brandenburg, in the Middle Mark. The principal commerce is in beer, of which large quantities are brewed.

It is seated on the Pancho; 15 miles N. N. E. of Berlin.

Bernay, a town of France, in the department of Eure, seated on the Carantonne; 20 miles S. W. of Rouen. Pop. 6500.

Bernburg, a town of Upper Saxony, in the principality of Anhalt, seated on the Saale; 22 miles S. W. of Magdeburg. Pop. about 2500.

Berncastle, a town of Germany, remarkable for good wine; seated on the Moselle; 18 miles N. E. of Treves.

Berngries, or Beilngries, a town of Franconia, in the principality of Aichstadt, on the Altmuhl; 17 miles N. E. of Aichstadt, and 28 W. of Ratisbon.

Bernstadt, a town of Silesia, in the principality of Oels, with a castle, seated on the Weida; 20 miles E. of Breslau. Pop. 2350.

Berre, a town of France, in the department of Mouths of the Rhone, formerly one of the strongest towns of Provence. 18 miles from Aix.

Berrima, an assize town of N. S. Wales, with a court-house and gaol on the Wingeecarribee river. 83 miles from Sydney.

Berry, a late province of France, bounded on the N. by the Orleanois and Blaisois, E. by the Nivernois and Bourbonnois, S. by the Bourbonnois and Marche, and W. by Touraine and Poitou. It produces corn, fruit, hemp, and flax; and excellent wine in some places. It now forms the two departments of Cher and Indre.

Bersello, a town of Italy, in the Modenese, with a castle, seated on the Po, at the influx of the Linza; 10 miles N. N. E. of Parma.

Bertie, a county of North Carolina, bounded on the S. by the Roanoke River, and E. by Albemarle Sound. Pop. 12,175, of whom 6728 are slaves. Windsor, the chief town, is 194 miles E. by N. of Raleigh.

Bertinero, a town of Italy, in Romagna, with a citadel, seated on a hill; 15 miles S. of Ravenna.

Bertrand, St., a town of France, in the department of Upper Garonne. It was lately an episcopal see: it is 45 miles S. of Auch. Long. 0. 48. E. lat. 42. 56. N.

Bervie, or Inverbervie, a borough of Scotland, in Kincardineshire, at the mouth of the Bervie, which forms a harbour for small vessels; 12 miles N. E. of Montrose.

Berwick-upon-Tweed, a borough on the borders of England and Scotland, with a market on Saturday. It is a county of itself, governed by a mayor; and was once a strong fortress of great importance, when England and Scotland were hostile nations, to each of which it alternately belonged, or was considered as a district separate from both countries. It now belongs to the bishopric of Durham, and the English judges hold the assizes here. It is still fortified, and has good barracks for the garrison, but its castle is now in ruins. It supplies the London markets with considerable quantities of salmon, pickled pork, and grain, and has some manufactures. It returns two members to parliament: it is seated on the N. side of the Tweed, near the sea; 54 miles S. E. of Edinburgh, and 337 N. by W. of London. Long. 2. 0. W. lat. 55. 46. N.

Berwickshire, a maritime, and the S. E. border county of Scotland. Coldstream, Greenlaw, Dunse, and Lauder, are the principal towns. It is an agricultural county, and has but few manufactures. It is of considerable notoriety in the history of the border wars.

Berwick, North, a borough of Scotland, in Haddingtonshire, on the Frith of Forth; 9 miles N. of Haddington, and 22 E. N. E. of Edinburgh.

Berwick, a town of the state of Maine, in York county; 7 miles N. W. of York, and 86 N. of Boston.

Berwick, a town of Pennsylvania, in York, county, at the head of Conewago Creek; 13 miles W. by S. of York, and 45 E. S. E. of Shippensburg; also the name of a town in Columbia county, and of another in Northumberland county, both in Pennsylvania.

Besalu, a town of Spain, in Catalonia, seated near the Fluvia; 44 miles N. N. W. of Gerona.

Besançon, a fortified city of France, and an archiepiscopal see; capital of the department of Doubs. It has a citadel, on a high rock, the base of which touches two sides of the Doubs, which here forms a peninsula; also a university, an academy of sciences, a literary military society, and a public library in the abbey of St. Vincent. The triumphal arch of Aurelian, and other Roman antiquities, are still to be seen. It is 52 miles E. of Dijon, and 228 S. E. of Paris. It has several manufactures. Pop. 28,795.

Besigheim, a town of Suabia, in the kingdom of Wirtemburg, with two old castles, at the confluence of the Neckar and Ens; 25 miles N. by W. of Stuttgard. Pop. about 2000.

Bessarabia, or Budzac, a territory of European Turkey, on the N. W. coast of the Black Sea, between the mouths of the Danube and the Dniester. On the banks of the last river the Tartar inhabitants rove from place to place. Their common food is the flesh of oxen and horses, cheese, and mares' milk. Bender is the capital. Pop. 315,000.

Bessay, a town of France, in the department of Allier; 8 miles S. of Moulins.

Besse, a town of France, in the department of Puy de Dome; 18 miles S. of Clermont.

Bessenay, a town of France, in the department of Rhone; 12 miles W. of Lyons.

Bestricia, a town of Transylvania, with gold mines in its neighbourhood. It is 85 miles N. W. of Hermanstadt. Long. 28. 45. E. lat. 47. 30. N.

Betanzos, a town of Spain, in Gallicia, seated on the Mandeo, at its entrance into a bay of the Atlantic; 20 miles S. of Ferrol. Long. 8. 6. W. lat. 43. 20. N.

Betelfaugi, or Beit-el-fakih, a town of Arabia Felix, famous for the vast quantity of coffee bought and sold in it. It is 25 miles E. of the Red Sea. Long. 57. 20. E. lat. 15. 40. N.

Bethabra, a town of North Carolina, in Stoke's County, noted for being the first settlement of the Moravians in those parts, begun in 1753. It is 6 miles N. of Salem.

Bethania, or Bethany, a village at the foot of Mount Olivet, on the E. side; about 4 miles to the E. of Jerusalem. A grotto is shown as the sepulchre of Lazarus, and a cell where Mary Magdalen did penance.

Bethlehem, or Beit-Lehem, a town of Syria, in Palestine, famous for the birth of Christ. It was once a flourishing town, but now an inconsiderable place. Here is a church erected by the famous Helena, in the form of a cross; also a chapel, called the Chapel of the Nativity, where they pretend to show the manger in which Christ was laid; another called the Chapel of Joseph; and a third of the Holy Innocents. Bethlehem is much visited by pilgrims: it is seated on a ridge of hills, 6 miles S. E. of Jerusalem.

Bethlehem, a town of Pennsylvania, in Northampton county, situate on the Lehigh, a branch of the Delaware. The town being partly on an eminence, and partly on the lower banks of the Manakes (a fine creek), has a pleasant and healthy situation. It is the principal settlement in America of the Moravians, who were fixed here by Count Zinzendorf, in 1741. The German language is more in use than the English. It is 53 miles N. N. W. of Philadelphia. Long. 75. 8. W. lat. 40. 37. N.; also the name of a township in Albany county, state of New York; pop. 5114; and of another town in Orange county, and of several others in different parts of the United States.

Bethnal-Green, one of the out-parishes on the N. E. side of London, in which there were about 10,000 looms employed in the broad silk manufacture.

Bethune, a fortified town of France, in the department of Pas de Calais, with a castle. It was taken by the allies, in 1710, and restored by the treaty of Utrecht. It is seated on a rock by the river Brette; 120 miles N. of Paris.

Betley, a town in Staffordshire, with a market on Tuesday; 18 miles N. N. W. of Stafford, and 157 of London.

Bethis, a town of European Turkey, formerly the capital of Kurdistan. It is now the residence of a bey, who is neither subject to the Turks nor Persians, and has a numerous army of horsemen and infantry. It stands on the Khabur, between two mountains; 150 miles N. N. W. of Altunkupri. Long. 43. 20. E. lat. 37. 20. N.

Bettenhausen, a populous village of the county of Henneberg, Saxony; 6 miles W. of Meinungen. It has considerable manufactures of linen.

Bettiah, a town of Hindostan, in Bahar; 85 miles N. N. W. of Patna.

Betzko, a considerable town of Lower Hungary, situate on the E. bank of the Waag River, a few miles S. of Trentschin.

Betuve, an island of Holland, in Guelderland, 40 miles long and 10 broad, formed by the bifurcation of the Rhine above Nimeguen, and by the union of its streams, under different appellations, near Worcum. It was the ancient Batavia, and formerly gave the name of Bataveeren, or Batavians, to the inhabitants of the Dutch Netherlands. In this island the ancestors of the present race first settled, when they emigrated from Germany. The principal place is Nimeguen.

Beuthen, a town in Silesia, capital of a lordship of the same name. It stands near a branch of the Oder, on the frontiers of Poland; 45 miles E. N. E. of Ratisbon. Long. 18. 53. E. lat. 50. 21. N.

Beuthen, a town of Silesia, in the principality of Carolath, on the River Oder; 13 miles N. W. of Glogau.

Bevecum, a town of the Netherlands, in Brabant; 10 miles S. of Louvain.

Beveland, North, and South, two islands of Holland, in Zealand, between the E. and W. branches of the Scheldt. They were occupied by the English at the period of their disastrous expedition to Walcheren, in 1809.

Bevergern, a town of Westphalia, in the principality of Munster, on the river Ems; 5 miles N. W. of Tecklenburg.

Beveren, a populous town of the Netherlands; 5 miles N. N. E. of Oudenarde.

Beverley, a borough in East Yorkshire, governed by a mayor; with a market on Wednesday and Saturday. It has two churches, besides the minster; and a large market-place, adorned with a beautiful cross. The chief trade is in malt, oatmeal, and tanned leather. It is famous for being the retirement of John de Beverley, archbishop of York, who lived here four years, built a monastery, and died in 1211; in honour of whom several kings, particularly Athelstan, who chose him guardian saint, endowed the place with many privileges and immunities. It is seated near the river Hull; 28 miles E. by S. of York, and 183 N. of London. It returns two members to parliament.

Beverley, a seaport of Massachusets, in Essex county, separated from Salem by a handsome bridge. A cotton manufacture has been established here. It is 15 miles N. E. of Boston. Pop. about 4500.

Beverungen, a town of Westphalia, in the principality of Paderborn, at the confluence of the Bever and Weser; 24 miles S. E. of Paderborn.

Beverwyck, a town of North Holland, on the Wyckermeer, which communicates with the Wye; 7 miles N. of Haarlem, and 11. S. by W. of Alkmaer.

Bewdley, a borough in Worcestershire, with a market on Saturday. It has a good trade in malt, leather, salt, and iron ware; and a free-school founded by James I. It is seated on the Severn; 14 miles N. of Worcester, and 129 N. W. of London. It returns one member to parliament.

Bewzeville, a town of France, department of Eure, Normandy. Pop. 2500. 12 miles from Pont Audemer.

Bex, a town of Switzerland, in the canton of Bern, noted for its salt rocks; 43 miles S. W. of Bern.

Beyhar, a town of Hindostan, presidency of Bengal, capital of the Cooch Beyhar district; 30 miles N. of Runghpoor. The temples were destroyed in 1661 by the Mohammedans.

BEZIERS, a city of France, in the department of Herault; lately an episcopal see. The remains of a circus, and some inscriptions, bespeak its ancient grandeur. It is seated near the Royal Canal, on a hill, at the foot of which flows the Orbre, a few miles from the sea; 85 miles E. by S. of Toulouse, and 30 S. W. of Montpelier. Long. 3. 12. E. lat. 43. 20. N. Pop. 12,500.

BHANMO. *See* BAMOA.

BHATGONG, a considerable town of Nepaul, about 8 miles E. by S. of the capital, Catmandoo; it is the principal residence of the chief Brahmin of Nepaul. Pop. about 7000.

BHOOJ, a town of Hindostan, province of Cutch. It has a handsome appearance, from its white buildings and temples. It is badly fortified. Pop. 20,000.

BHOPAUL, a district and town of Hindostan, in the province of Malwa, on the Nurbuddah river. The valleys are fertile. The town is surrounded by a wall.

BHOREGHAUT, "the great pass," through the W. mountains of Hindostan, opening a carriage communication with the Deccan.

BHURTPORE, a town and fortress of Hindostan, in the province of Agra. The British took it by storm, in 1805. It is 38 miles W. of Agra.

BIAFRA, a country of Guinea, to the S. E. of Benin, of which little is known; but it is said to have a capital of the same name, on the River Camerones, which enters the Atlantic in long. 11. 30. E. lat. 3. 28. N.

BIALA, a town of Gallicia, on the frontiers of Silesia, opposite to Bilitz; it participates in the linen manufacture of the district. Pop. about 2300. It is the name of three other small towns in different parts of Germany.

BIALYSTOCK, a considerable town of Russian Poland; seated on the Biala, a branch of the Vistula River; 15 miles E. of Wilna.

BIANA, a town of Hindostan, province of Agra; a decayed town, though still of importance; 50 miles S. W. from Agra.

BIAR, a town of Spain, in Valencia. Its principal riches consist in honey. It is 6 miles from Villena.

BIBB, a county of the newly-formed state of Alabama, North America. Pop. 3676; Centreville, 112 miles N. by E. of Cahwaroba, is the seat of judicature for the county.

BIBERACH, a town of Suabia, with a manufacture of fustians, seated in a fertile valley, on the Reuss; 20 miles S. S. W. of Ulm. Pop. about 4500. It belongs to Wurtemburg.

BIBRA, a town of Upper Saxony, in Thuringia, much frequented on account of its mineral spring. It is 9 miles S. of Querfurt.

BICESTER, a town in Oxfordshire, with a market on Friday; 11 miles N. N. E. of Oxford, and 54 W. by N. of London, on the mail coach road to Leamington and Warwick.

BICKANEER, a town of Hindostan, capital of a circar, in the country of Agimere. It is 42 miles W. of Nagore. Long. 74. 0. E. lat. 27. 12. N.

BIDACHE, a town of France, in the department of Lower Pyrenees, with a castle, seated on the Bidouse; 12 miles E. of Bayonne. Pop. about 2000.

BIDASSOA, a river of Spain, which rises in the Pyrenees, and enters the Bay of Biscay, at Fontarabia. This river was a long time a subject of dispute between France and Spain, but it is now common between the two nations; the duties paid by those who pass from Spain to France belonging to the latter, and by those who pass the contrary way to the former.

BIDBURG, a town of the Netherlands, in the duchy of Luxemburg; 30 miles N. N. E. of Luxemburg.

BIDEFORD, a seaport of England, in Devonshire, governed by a mayor, with a market on Tuesday. It has a trade in coal, culm, timber, and oak bark, also in the herring and Newfoundland fisheries. It is seated on both sides of the Torridge, over which is an ancient Gothic bridge of 24 arches; 16 miles S. by W. of Ilfracomb, and 201 W. of London.

BIDDEFORD, a seaport of the district of Maine, in York county. The county courts are sometimes held here. It is situate on the sea coast, at the mouth of the Saco; 14 miles S. S. W. of Portland. Long. 70. 35. W. lat. 43. 26. N.

BIDDENORE. *See* NAGARA.

BIDZIGUR, or BIDJEEGHUR, a town of Hindostan, in Allahabad, with a fort on a steep and lofty rock; 50 miles S. of Benares.

BIEDENKOPF, a town of the grand duchy of Hesse, situate on the N. bank of the Lahn, near its source; 15 miles N. W. of Marburg.

BIEEZ, a town of Poland, in Cracovia, remarkable for its mines of vitriol; seated on the Weseloke; 50 miles S. E. of Cracow.

BIEL, or BIENNE, a town of Switzerland, capital of a small territory, lately subject to the bishop of Basil. It stands near a lake of the same name, on the river Suss; 17 miles N. W. of Bern.

BIELA, a town of Piedmont, and capital of a province of the same name, bounded on the W. by Aoust. The town is situate near the river Cerva; 24 miles W. of Vercelli. Pop. about 8300.

BIELA, a town of European Russia, in the government of Novogorod; a place of commerce in corn, cattle, and candles. Pop. 3000.

BIELAW, a populous town of Silesia, with considerable manufactures of linen and cotton; 15 miles E. of Buntzlaw. Pop. about 7000.

BIELFELD, a town of Westphalia, in the county of Ravensberg. The linen made and bleached here is much esteemed. It is 18 miles N. of Lipstadt. Pop. about 5500.

BIELGOROD, a town of Russia, in the government of Kursk, and an archbishop's see; 80 miles S. S. W. of Kursk. Pop. about 10,000.

BIELGOROD, or AKERMAN, a strong town of European Turkey, in Bessarabia, on the coast of the Black Sea, at the mouth of the Dniester: 70 miles S. S. E. of Bender. Long. 31. 15. E. lat. 46. 8. N.

Bieloi, a town of Russia, in the government of Smolensk; 60 miles N. E. of Smolensk.

Bielozersk, a town of Russia, in the government of Novogorod, on the S. side of the lake Bielo; 210 miles N. E. of Novogorod, and about the same distance E. of St. Petersburg. Pop. about 3000.

Bielsk, a town of Prussian Poland, capital of Podiakia, seated on the Biala, one of the sources of the Vistula; 130 miles E. N. E. of Warsaw. Long. 23. 39. E. lat. 52. 40. N.

Biervliet, a town of the Netherlands, in Flanders, situate on the West Scheldt, and on a small island of its name; 20 miles N. N. W. of Ghent.

Biggar, a town of Scotland, in Lanarkshire, with the ruins of a collegiate church; 10 miles S. E. of Carnwarth.

Biggleswade, a town in Bedfordshire, with a market on Wednesday; seated on the Ivel; 10 miles E. S. E. of Bedford, and 45 N. N. W. of London.

Bigorre, a late province of France, bounded on the N. by Armagnac, E. by Comminges, W. by Bearn, and S. by the Pyrenees. *See* Pyrenees, Upper.

Bighorn, a river of the Missouri territory, North America, rising from the Rocky Mountains in the lat. of about 41. N.; runs N. into the Yellow Stone, which falls into the Missouri, in the lat. of 48. N. It is represented as flowing through a fertile, but at present an uninhabited country.

Big Sandy, a river which divides the state of Virginia from that of Kentucky, falling into the Ohio, opposite Burlington, in Lawrence county, state of Ohio.

Biguba, a kingdom on the W. coast of Africa, watered by the Rio Grande. The capital is of the same name, seated on the N. bank of the river, about 100 miles from its mouth. Long. 13. 50. W. lat. 11. 12. N.

Bihar, a county of Upper Hungary, bordering on Transylvania. It is intersected by the Korosh river. Groswarden is the capital. The E. part is mountainous, and inhabited by Wallachians. Pop. about 223,000, chiefly Hungarians.

Bihatz, a town of Croatia, on the frontiers of Bosnia, seated on an isle formed by the river Unna; 65 miles S. E. of Carlstadt. Long. 16. 32. E. lat. 44. 51. N.

Bilboa, a city and seaport of Spain, capital of Biscay. The upper part is built mostly of wood, and has narrow streets, which terminate in a great square; the lower part is of freestone and brick, with fine broad streets. The houses are rather high, and fully inhabited. The principal exports are wool, oil, chesnuts, sword-blades, and other manufactures in iron and steel. It is seated in a fertile country, on the banks of the Durango river, which forms a good harbour near the Bay of Biscay; 50 miles W. of St. Sebastian, and 72¼ leagues N. of Madrid, by way of Aranda, and 88 by way of Valladolid and Segovia. Long. 2. 44. W. lat. 43. 14. N.

Bildeston, a town in Suffolk, seated on the river Breton; 12 miles S. E. of Bury and 63 N. E. of London. It has two fairs annually. Pop. 836.

Biledulgerid, (*Beled-el-dgerid*, the country of dates,) a country of Barbary, bounded on the N. by Tunis and Algier, E. by Tripoli, S. by Guergula, and W. by Tuggurt. The air is hot and unhealthy. The country is mountainous and sandy, producing little sustenance except dates, which are exchanged with the neighbouring countries for wheat. The inhabitants are deemed lewd, treacherous, thievish, and cruel. They are a mixture of ancient Africans and wild Arabs; the former living in towns, and the latter in tents.

Bilitz, a town of Silesia, with a castle, and considerable manufacture of cloth; situate on the Biala, on the verge of Poland; 18 miles E. N. E. of Teschen. Pop. about 3400.

Billericay, a town in Essex, with a market on Tuesday; seated on a hill; 9 miles S. W. of Chelmsford, and 23 E. of London.

Billiton, an island in the East Indies, on the N. of the sea of Java, abounding in iron ore. It was ceded to the British in 1812. Long. 108. 0. E. lat. 3. 0. S.

Billom, a town of France, in the department of Puy de Dome, seated on an eminence; 15 miles E. S. E. of Clermont. Population 5200.

Bilmah, a vast burning desert of Africa, between Fezzan and Bournou; which caravans are ten days passing. The town, of the same name, is near the salt-lakes of Domboo.

Bilsah, a town of Hindostan, in Malwa, capital of a circar, noted for producing excellent tobacco. It is situate near the source of the Betwa river; 120 miles E. of Ougein.

Bilsen, a town of the Netherlands, in the territory of Liege. Near it is Munster Bilsen, a celebrated temporal foundation and abbey for noble ladies. It is situate on the Demer; 15 miles N. N. W. of Liege. Pop. about 2000.

Bilstein, a town of Germany, in the duchy of Westphalia, situate on a mountain; 24 miles S. S. E. of Arensburg.

Bilston, a large village of Staffordshire, two miles S. E. of Wolverhampton. It has a navigable canal, communicating with the Staffordshire and Worcestershire canals, and several great rivers. Near it are large mines of coal, iron-stone, &c.; also furnaces, forges, and slitting-mills; and manufactures of japanned and enamelled goods.

Bimini, one of the Bahama islands, near the channel of Bahama; 8 miles long, and nearly as broad. It has a good harbour. Long. 79. 30. W. lat. 25. 0. N.

Bimlepatam, a town of Hindostan, on the coast of the Circars; 12 miles N. of Vizagapatam.

Binaros, or Vinaros, a town of Spain, in Valencia, seated near the Mediterranean, at the mouth of a river, which forms a small harbour; 7 miles N. by E. of Peniscola, and 23 S. of Tortosa.

Binch, a fortified town of the Netherlands,

in Hainault, in the river Haye; 9 miles E. of Mons. Pop. 4500.

BINGEN, a town of Germany, seated at the confluence of the Nahe with the Rhine; 15 miles W. by S. of Mentz. Pop. 2700.

BINGENHEIM, a town of Germany, in the circle of Upper Rhine; 16 miles N. N. E. of Frankfort.

BINGHAM, a town of Nottinghamshire, in the vale of Belvoir, with a market on Thursday; 9 miles E. of Nottingham, and 124 N. by W. of London.

BINGLEY, a town in West Yorkshire, with a market on Tuesday; seated on the Aire; 14 miles S. E. of Skipton, and 202 N. N. W. of London.

BIOBIO, the largest river of Chili, which rises in the Andes, runs through veins of gold, and fields of sarsaparilla, and, passing the city of Concepcion, enters the Pacific Ocean, in lat. 36. 56. S. It is the boundary between Chili and the country of the Araucan Indians.

BIORNEBURG, a town of Russian Finland, near the mouth of the Kune, in the Gulf of Bothnia; 75 miles N. of Abo. Long. 22. 5. E. lat. 61. 42. N.

BIR, EL-BIR, BEER, or BIREDGIK, a town of Asiatic Turkey, in Diarbeck, with a castle. It stands on the E. bank of the Euphrates, near a high mountain, in a fruitful country; 60 miles N. E. of Aleppo. This is the point which is proposed for the steam navigation of the Euphrates to commence, the merchandise being conveyed overland from the Gulf of Iskenderoon, to which this is the nearest part of the river.

BIRBOOM, a town of Hindostan, in Bengal; 66 miles W. S. W. of Moorshedabad, and 115 N. N. W. of Calcutta.

BIRD ISLANDS, in the Caribbean Sea, E. of Curacoa.

BIRKENFIELD, a town of Germany, in the county of Sponheim, in the circle of Upper Rhine; seated near the source of the river Nahe; 25 miles E. S. E. of Treves. It is distinguished for its cattle fairs.

BIRMAH, an extensive empire in Asia, to the E. of the Bay of Bengal; containing the kingdoms of Birmah, Cassay, Arracan, and Pegu, and all the W. coast of Siam, to the promontory of Malay, extending from the 10th to the 24th deg. of N. lat. The *kingdom* of Birmah, frequently called Ava, from the name of its ancient capital, has Pegu on the S., and occupies both sides of the river Irrawaddy, or Errabatty, to the frontiers of Assam on the N.; on the W. it has Arracan and Cassay, and on the E. China and Upper Siam. This kingdom was conquered in 1752, by the king of Pegu, who carried the Birman monarch prisoner to Pegu, and caused him to be murdered there in 1754; but Alompra, a Birman of low distinction, who was continued by the conqueror as chief at Monchaban, a small place to the N. of Ava, revolted against the Peguese, got possession of Ava in 1755, and, after continued battles, with various success, became the conqueror of Pegu, in 1757. This deliverer of his country continued in a state of warfare to his death, in 1760; and his successors have since added the other countries, which now form the *Birman Empire.* The climate of Birmah is very salubrious; the seasons being regular, and the extremes of heat and cold seldom experienced. The soil is remarkably fertile, producing rice, sugar-canes, tobacco, indigo, cotton, and all the tropical fruits, in perfection; and on the banks of the Irrawaddy, which runs S. through the whole country, is produced pure amber, and the finest teak timber in the world. The kingdom of Birmah abounds in minerals; it has mines of gold, silver, rubies, and sapphires; and affords amethysts, garnets, chrysolites, jasper, loadstone, and marble. The general disposition of the Birmans is strikingly contrasted with that of the natives of Hindostan, though separated only by a narrow ridge of mountains, in several places admitting of an easy intercourse. The Birmans are a lively, inquisitive race, active, irascible, and impatient; but the character of their Bengal neighbours is known to be the reverse. The passion of jealousy, which prompts most eastern nations to immure their women, and surround them with guards, seems to have little influence on the minds of the Birmans; for their wives and daughters have as free intercourse with the other sex as the rules of European society admit. The Birmans are extremely fond both of poetry and music. Their religion is, in fact, that of the Hindoos, though they are not votaries of Brama, but sectaries of Boodh. Their system of jurisprudence is distinguished above any other Hindoo commentary, for perspicuity and good sense. The emperor of Birmah is a despotic monarch, and, like the sovereigns of China, acknowledges no equal. The prevailing characteristic of the Birman court is pride. There are no hereditary dignities or employments in the government, for all honours and offices, on the demise of the possessor, revert to the crown. A white elephant is here paid almost divine honours, and has a palace, and allowed rank next to the king, and above the queen. The capital of the kingdom, and metropolis of the empire, is Ummerapoora, in lat. 22. N. and 96. E. long., and the principal seaport is *Rangoon.* Hostilities commenced between the Birmese and Anglo-Indians, in 1824, and at the close of 1825 continued with equivocal results to both parties. Rangoon, the maritime capital, surrendered to the English on the 1st of Feb. 1825.

BIRMINGHAM, a large, inland, populous, and important town of England, in Warwickshire, bordering on the counties of Worcester and Stafford. It is a place of great antiquity, and has long been celebrated for its works in every kind of metal, and the manufacture of hardware, fire-arms, cutlery, japanned wares, and trinkets. The era of its pre-eminence, however, is comparatively recent: its commencement may be dated subsequent to the war of 1776—1783; since when it has more than doubled in extent and population. The Staffordshire border abounds in iron and coal of the finest quality, which contributes essentially to the excellence and facility of most of its manufactures. The town is considered peculiarly healthy, the chief part being built along the ridge of a hill, having a dry, sandy soil. The streets are regular, and the buildings spacious. The church of St. Philip, built in 1711, is a stately and fine edifice, and since 1800 two other churches have been built, both equally handsome. It has several sectarian meeting-houses, a well-endowed public school, a handsome theatre, and an extensive suite of baths. The perspective of the town, especially on the E. side, is very imposing; and, independent of its innate importance, being nearly in the centre of the kingdom, it is a place of vast intercourse. It has a canal basin at its highest level, from whence cuts diverge in every direction, and by which the manufactures of the district are conveyed to all the ports of the kingdom, for distribution over every part of the habitable globe. Its principal improvement is the magnificent railway between this town and London, one of the greatest and most important works ever executed, and which communicates, by means of the Grand Junction Railway, with Liverpool, Derby, York, Sheffield, &c., the North Midland, and the Midland Counties Railways, forming a chain of communication with all parts of England; which may be considered as a national pride. The surrounding country is very fertile, and its market on Thursdays is in consequence exceedingly well supplied with all the essentials of subsistence. Birmingham, notwithstanding its size and importance, had no representatives in parliament, until the passing of the Reform Bill: it now returns two members. It is governed by two bailiffs and two constables; and there are several resident magistrates, who are chosen annually from the most respectable part of the community. In 1643, Birmingham was besieged and taken by Prince Rupert, and ordered to be burnt to the ground, but, owing to some propitious circumstances, the conflagration did very little damage. In 1665, or 1666, the town suffered severely from the plague. It began shortly after this period to be considerably enlarged, though in 1700 it consisted of only 30 streets; whereas there are now upwards of 300. Within 2 miles of the town are the Soho Works, celebrated as the engineering establishment of Boulton and Watt. It is 109 miles N. N. W. of London, by way of Coventry or Warwick, from each of which it is distant 18 miles; and 116 by way of Oxford, from which it is distant 58 miles.

Birnam, a hill of Scotland, in Perthshire, celebrated by Shakspere, in his Macbeth, 1580 feet above the level of the sea. It was anciently a forest and part of the royal domain of Scotland.

Birr, a parish and town of Ireland, in King's County, near the borders of Tipperary. The town is sometimes called Parson's Town: it is 34 miles N. E. of Limerick, and 34 N. N. W. of Kilkenny.

Birviesca, a town of Spain, in Old Castile; 13 miles N. of Burgos.

Birza, a town of Poland, in Samogitia; 42 miles S. E. of Mittau.

Bisaccia, a town of Naples, in Principato Ulteriore; 15 miles N. E. of Conza.

Biscara, a town of Algier, in the province of Constantina, and the chief place of the district of Zaab. It is an ancient town; 120 miles S. S. W. of Constantina. Long. 5. 12. W. lat. 33. 35. N.

Biscay, a maritime province on the N. coast of Spain, extending from the Bidassoa, which divides Spain from France, in the long of 1. 40. W. to Santona, in 3. 18. W. lying on the shore of the Bay of Biscay, nearly in a straight line, in the lat. of 43. 20. N. extending inland, in nearly a pyramidal form, to Logrono, in Old Castile; its area being 248 square leagues, and a pop. of 311,000. It is bounded on the W. by Asturias and Old Castile, and E. by Navarre. The river Ebro, which runs S. into the Mediterranean, rises nearly in the centre of the province, and afterwards forms part of its western boundary. It is divided into three parts, viz. Alava, S., chief town, Vittoria; Guipuscoa, E., chief town, St. Sebastian, the most populous part; Biscay Proper, on the W., chief town, Bilboa. The country is in some parts mountainous, but well covered with wood, and yielding abundance of iron and lead. The plains and valleys are well cultivated, yielding ample supplies of all that is essential to the comfort of the inhabitants. The Biscayans are a brave, choleric people, possessing a character and speaking a language distinct from that of every other part of Spain; and through all the mutations to which Spain has been exposed, during a period of 2000 years, by the irruptions of Romans, Carthaginians, Moors, &c., Biscay has retained its ancient Cantabrian laws and independence, and at the present time forms an independent republic under the protection of Spain, rather than an integral part of the kingdom. It admits a corregidor and commissary appointed by the crown, but permits no taxes to be levied without the sanction of the province, and yields none to the crown but as gratuitous donations, and sanctions no title of the king but that of lord. The language is a dialect of the Celtic.

Biscay, Bay of, a large bay of the Atlantic Ocean, washing the N. coast of Spain, from Cape Ortegal, and the W. coast of France. During a prevalence of westerly winds, the swell of the Atlantic Ocean sets into this bay, and renders the reach of the British Channel, to vessels from the S. and S. W., exceedingly difficult, and, if the gales are powerful, quite unattainable until they subside; there being, however, plenty of sea-room, it is a position of tediousness and labour, rather than of danger.

Biscay, New, a name given by the Spaniards to a part of the W. coast of Mexico; now incorporated with the intendancy of Sonora, Durango, and Guadalaxara, (all of which see.)

Bischofstein, a town of Prussia Proper

about 50 miles S. of Konigsberg, and 5 S. E. of Heilsburg.

BISCHOFSHEIM, a town of the duchy of Wurtzburg, seated on the Tauber; 20 miles S. S. W. of Wurtzburg. Another, seated on the Rhom; 44 miles N. by E. of Wurtzburg.

BISCHOFSLACK, a town of Upper Carniola, with a good trade in linen and worsted; 17 miles W. by N. of Laybach.

BISCHOFSWERDA, a town of Upper Saxony, in Misnia, seated on the Weiseritz; 18 miles E. of Dresden.

BISCHOFSWERDER, a town of Prussia, in the province of Oberland, on the river Oss; 28 miles N. E. of Culm.

BISCHOFZELL, a town of Switzerland, in Thurgau, with a castle; seated at the confluence of the Sitter and Thur; 12 miles S. of Constance.

BISCHWELLER, a town of France, province of Alsace. Pop. 4400; who manufacture leather, cloth, &c.; 10 miles from Strasburg.

BISEGLIA, a town of Naples, in Terra di Bari, on a hill, near the shore of the Adriatic; 6 miles E. of Trani. Pop. 10,600.

BISERTA, BIZERTA, or BINZERT, a seaport of the kingdom of Tunis, in a country abounding with corn, fruit, oil, cotton, and other valuable productions. It stands on a canal, which communicates with a gulf of the Mediterranean; 37 miles N. W. of Tunis. Long. 9. 59. E. lat. 37. 20. N.

BISENTZ, a town of Moravia, near the frontier of Hungary; 15 miles S. W. of Hradisch. Pop. about 2600.

BISHOPS-AUCKLAND, Stortford, Waltham, and Wearmouth. *See* AUCKLAND, &c.

BISHOPS-CASTLE, a town in Shropshire, with a market on Friday, much frequented by the Welsh. It is seated near the river Clun; 8 miles S. E. of Montgomery, and 159 W. N. W. of London.

There are about thirty-six other towns and villages with *Bishop*, or *Bishops* prefixed to their names, in different parts of England.

BISIGNANO, a town of Naples, in Calabria Citeriore, with a castle; seated on a hill, near the river Boccono; 16 miles N. of Cosenza.

BISLEY, a town in Gloucestershire; 3 miles S. E. of Stroud. It has a large church, standing on an eminence. Population much employed in the woollen manufacture.

BISNAGUR, or BIJNAGUR, tn. of Hindostan, in the country of Sanore. It was the capital of the ancient kingdom of Narsinga, and formerly a large city. It is seated on the S. bank of the Toombudra; 28 miles S. S. E. of Sanore, and 105 N. by W. of Chitteldroog. Long. 76. 0. E. lat. 15. 20. N.

BISNEE, a town of Bootan, capital of a district on the borders of Bengal and Assam. It is 50 miles E. N. E. of Rangamutty, and 130 S. E. of Tassasudon. Long. 90. 45. E. lat. 26. 27. N.

BISSAGOS, or BEJUGAS, a cluster of islands and shoals on the W. coast of Africa. The largest, called Bissao, is 80 miles in circuit, inhabited by Portuguese and Negroes, and well cultivated. Its N. end is opposite the mouth of the Rio Grande. Long. 15. 10. W. lat. 10 58. N.

BISSUNPOUR, a town of Hindostan, capital of a circar in Bengal; 74 miles N. W. of Calcutta.

BISTRICZ, a populous town in the N. E. part of Transylvania, on the river Bistricz; 142 miles N. E. of Coloswar. Also the name of another town in the circle of Prerau, Moravia.

BITCHE, a fortified town of France, in the department of Moselle, with a castle on a rock. It is seated at the foot of a mountain, near the river Schwelb; 30 miles N. by W. of Strasburg. Pop. 2300.

BITETTO, a town of Naples, in Terra di Bari; 11 miles S. S. W. of Bari.

BITONTO, a town of Naples, in Terra di Bari; 10 miles W. S. W. of Bari. Pop. 14,000.

BITTERFELD, a tn. of the kingdom of Saxony, seated on the Mulda; 14 miles S. of Dessau.

BLACKBURN, an extensive parish and borough in the centre of the county of Lancaster, England, intersected by the Leeds and Liverpool canal. Parts of the parish are bleak and dreary, but it is partly situate on the great coal strata, which supplies abundance of fuel. The town of Blackburn is seated in a valley, on both sides of a stream called the Derwent, over which there are four bridges, and it is skirted by the Leeds and Liverpool Canal. Next to Manchester, it is one of the principal focuses of the cotton manufacture, there being about a dozen large establishments for spinning, forty considerable employers in the manufacture of calicoes, twenty large establishments for printing ditto, with all the attendant occupations of bleaching, dyeing, iron-founding, and machine and reed-making. It has three public breweries. Markets on Wednesdays and Saturdays. It has a free grammar-school, with an endowment of about 150*l.* per annum, and also a female charity school, with nearly a similar endowment; four churches, two of them handsome, and several meeting-houses; 12 miles E. by S. of Preston, and 23 N. W. of Manchester. It sends two members to parliament.

BLACK FOREST, a mountainous and woody district of Germany, part of the ancient Hyrcinian Forest, extending N. from the frontiers of Switzerland, for about 100 miles parallel with the N. course of the Rhine. It is in some places rich in iron and other metals; and its wood is very valuable, as well for fuel, as for building, both of houses and vessels for navigating the Rhine.

BLACKHEATH, an elevated and spacious plain, the ascent to which is 5 miles E. of London Bridge. It is partly in the parish of Greenwich, and the upper part of the park of the hospital of Greenwich is part of the plain. It is intersected by the great high road from London to Dover, and is celebrated in several periods of English history. The Danes encamped upon it in 1012. In 1390, the celebrated Wat Tyler assembled 100,000 men against the government, to avenge an insult offered to his daughter by a petty tax-gatherer at Dartford. In 1450, Jack Cade assembled his forces on the same spot; and in 1497 it was the scene of a contest between Henry VII. and Lord Audley. It is surrounded by detached, and ranges of handsome buildings, residences of some of the more opulent classes connected with the transactions of London. It commands some fine prospects, and in the summer season, especially, is a beautiful and interesting spot. In the side of the ascent from London is a cavern consisting of seven large rooms, which communicate by arched avenues; the sides and roofs of rocks of chalk; and it has a well of clear water, 27 feet deep.

Blackness-Castle, a fort of Scotland, in Linlithgowshire, built on a kind of peninsula on the Frith of Forth; 9 miles N. E. of Linlithgow. It consists of four bastions, and is one of the forts which, by the Articles of Union, are to be kept in repair.

Blackpool, a village in Lancashire, 3 miles W. of Poulton; much resorted to for sea-bathing.

Black River, the name of several rivers in different parts of the world. 1st. In the county of Mayo, Ireland, falling into Lake Mask. 2nd. In the S. W. part of the island of Jamaica, falling into the Caribbean Sea. 3rd. In Upper Canada, falling into Black Bay, Lake Superior. 4th. In Orleans county, Vermont, falling into Lake Memphramagog. 5th. In Windsor county, ditto, falling into the Connecticut. 6th. In Virginia, falling into the Nottoway, on the frontiers of North Carolina. 7th. Intersecting Darlington district, South Carolina, falling into the great Pedee. 8th. Falling into Lake Michigan, towards the S. E. end; and several others, but all inconsiderable.

Black-Rock, a town of the United States of North America, state of New York; a harbour on Lake Erie.

Black Sea. *See* Euxine.

Blackwall, an appendage of the metropolis of the British empire, situate in a nook at the S. E. extremity of the county of Middlesex. It is bounded on the E. by the river Lea, which divides it from the county of Essex, at its junction with the Thames, which from Blackwall towards London Bridge makes a very considerable detour, the distance by the course of the river being about 10 miles; which led to the construction of a tide canal, nearly a mile in length, across the isthmus, but which is now disused; and also to the construction of basins or docks for the reception of all the ships arriving from the West and East Indies. The West India dock establishment is the most magnificent and complete work of the kind in the world; it consists of two outer basins from the river at Blackwall, which lead to the grand receiving basin, an oblong square, 1200 yards in length. It was first opened in 1802. Between the West India docks and the river Lea are two spacious basins for the reception of all the ships from China and the East Indies, with store-houses for the ships' stores, saltpetre, and some of the more bulky productions; but all the more valuable articles are stored in warehouses in different parts of the E. side of London. There is also the largest private ship-building yard in the world, where eight or ten ships, averaging 1000 tons each, are occasionally on the stocks, or repairing, at one time. Blackwall commands a very extensive view down the river, which draws a constant succession of visitors to witness the unrivalled passing scene of vessels from and to all parts of the world, which almost every flood and ebb of the tide presents. It is connected with the heart of London by means of a railway, with stationary engines.

Blackwater, a river of Ireland, which flows through the counties of Cork and Waterford into Youghal Bay.

Blackwater, a river in Essex, which flows into Blackwater Bay, near the mouth of the Thames. It is also the name of four or five rivers in the United States of America, but all inconsiderable.

Bladen, a county in the S. part of North Carolina, bordering on the maritime county of Brunswick. It is intersected by Cape Fear River. Pop. 8022, of whom 3413 are people of colour. Elizabeth Town, 98 miles S. of Raleigh, is the chief town.

Bladenoch, a river of Scotland, which rises in the hills in the N. part of Wigtonshire, and, after a winding course of 24 miles, enters Wigton Bay. Several islands are formed in its bed, which are famous for the resort of eagles.

Bladensburg, a town of Maryland, in George county, on the E. side of the Potomac, 9 miles from its mouth, at Washington, and 38 S. W. of Baltimore. The American army sustained a defeat by the British at this place, on the 24th of August, 1814, in attempting to arrest the progress of the British towards Washington, which they afterwards entered, and burnt most of the public buildings.

Blain, a town of France, in the department of Lower Loire; 22 miles N. N. W. of Nantes.

Blair Athol, a town of Scotland, in Perthshire, with a castle, the seat of the Duke of Athol; 36 miles N. N. W. of Perth.

Blair Gowrie, a town of Scotland, in Perthshire, with a manor-house, built in the form of a castle; 22 miles N. N. E. of Perth. Population partly employed in the cotton manufacture.

Blasois, a late province of France, bounded on the N. by Beauce, E. by Orleanois, S. by Berry, and W. by Touraine. It now forms the department of Loire and Cher.

Blaison, a town of France, in the department of Mayenne and Loire; 8 miles S. E. of Angers.

Blamont, a town of France, in the department of Meurthe, seated on the Vezouze; 12 miles E. of Luneville.

Blanc. *See* Mont Blanc.

Blanc-en-berry, a town of France, in the department of Indre, with a castle, seated on the Creuse; 35 miles E. of Poitiers. Pop. 3850.

Blanco, a cape of Patagonia; 130 miles N. E. of Port St. Julien. Long. 65. 56. W. lat. 47. 20. S.

Blanco, a cape of Peru; 120 miles S. W. of Guiaquil. Long. 81. 10. W. lat. 4. 24. S.

Blanco, a cape on the W. coast of Africa; 180 miles N. of the river Senegal. Long. 17. 10. W. lat. 20. 55. N. It is the name of many other capes or promontories in different parts of the world.

Blandford, a corporate town in Dorsetshire, with a market on Saturday. In 1731, almost all the town was burnt down; but it was soon rebuilt, and a neat town-hall of Portland stone, on columns, in which is a pump, was erected in remembrance of that dire disaster, and provision against the like. It has a considerable manufacture of thread and shirt-buttons, and is seated on the river Stour, near the Downs; 18 miles N. E. of Dorchester, and 103 W. by S. of London.

Blandford, a town of Massachusets, in Hampshire county; 25 miles S. W. of Northampton, and 116 W. by S. of Boston.

Blandford, a town of Virginia, in Prince George county. It has a large trade in tobacco, and is situate on the E. branch of the Appamattox; 4 miles N. E. of Petersburg. Blandford is also the name of several other towns in different parts of the United States of America.

Blanes, a town of Spain, in Catalonia, near the mouth of the Tordera; 20 miles S. of Gironne.

Blankenberg, a town and fort of the Netherlands, in Flanders, situate on the German Ocean; 8 miles N. E. of Ostend.

Blankenberg, a town of Westphalia, at the S. end of the duchy of Berg, on the river Sieg; 12 miles E. of Bonn.

Blankenburg, a town of Lower Saxony, capital of a principality of the same name, in the Hartz district, containing about 140 square miles. The castle stands on a craggy mountain, and is one of the finest buildings of the kind in Germany. It was the residence of Louis XVIII. during a part of his exile. The town contains about 3000 inhabitants, and is 9 miles S. of Halberstadt.

Blankenburg, a town in the principality of Schwartzenburg, circle of Thuringia; 5 miles N. W. of Saalfield.

Blankenesse, a town of Holstein on the N. bank of the Elbe; 9 miles W. by N. of Hamburg. Pop. about 2000.

Blankenhayn, a town of Saxony; 10 miles S. W. of Jena. Pop. about 1850.

Blarney, a parish and town in the county of Cork, Ireland. The town is situate about 4 miles N. W. of Cork, on a branch of the river Lee, which works a paper-mill: the cotton manufacture was attempted to be introduced about 1820. Here is a castle, on the top of which is the famous Blarney Stone.

Blas, San, a sea-port town of Mexico, on an island at the mouth of the Rio Grande, or Santiago river, which falls into the Pacific Ocean in lat. 21. 30. N. and 104. 46. W. long.

Blaubeuren, a town of Suabia, in the kingdom of Wirtemburg, with a castle on a hill. Great quantities of fustian and linen cloth are made here. It is seated at the confluence of the Ach with the Blau; 11 miles W. of Ulm.

Blaye, a sea-port of France, in the department of Gironde, on the E. bank of the river of that name; 17 miles below Bordeaux. It has a good citadel, and a fort on an island in the Gironde, or Garonne, which is here 3800 yards wide. Its trade consists in the wines of the adjacent country. Its harbour is much frequented, being the out-port to Bordeaux, as Gravesend is to London; and ships bound to Bordeaux having guns on board, leave them at Blaye. Pop. about 5000.

Blekingen, a province of Sweden, in Gothland, on the coast of the Baltic. It is 90 miles long, and 21 broad; and, though mountainous, is one of the most agreeable countries in the kingdom. The principal trade is in potash, pitch, tar, tallow, hides, and timber. The chief town is Carlscrona.

Blenheim, a village of Suabia, now in the Bavarian circle of the Upper Danube, seated on the Danube; 3 miles N. of Hochstat. It is memorable for the signal victory over the French and Bavarians, gained August 2nd, 1704, by the Duke of Marlborough. The Austrians were defeated by the French near this place in 1800.

Blenheim, a hamlet in the parish of Woodstock, Oxfordshire, in which is the noble mansion and demesne conferred by the nation on the first Duke of Marlborough, for his victories.

Blere, a town of France, in the department of Indre and Loire, on the river Cher; 18 miles E. by S. of Tours. Pop. 2600.

Blessington, a parish and town in the county of Wicklow, Ireland. The parish contains quarries of granite, which are very extensively worked. The town is 14 miles W. by S. of Dublin, on the border of Kildare.

Bletchingly, a village of Surrey, seated on a hill; 4 miles E. of Ryegate, and 21 S. of London.

Block Island, an island of the state of Rhode Island, North America, lying 21 miles S. S. W. of Newport, and in Newport county. It is 7 miles in length, and 4 in its extreme breadth, and famous for cattle, sheep, butter, and cheese. The S. part of it is in lat. 41. 8. N.; inhabited by about 700 persons, a considerable portion of whom subsist by the fishery.

Blockzyl, a town of Holland, in Overyssel, with a fort; seated at the mouth of the Aa, on the Zuyder Zee, where there is a good harbour; 8 miles N. W. of Steenwick. Long. 5. 39. E. lat. 52. 44. N

Blois, a city of France, capital of the department of Loire and Cher, and lately an episcopal see. The cathedral is a large structure, seated on an eminence at one extremity of the city; and on another eminence at the other end is a magnificent castle. In this castle Louis XII. was born; and here, in 1588, Henry III. caused the Duke of Guise, and his brother the Cardinal, to be assassinated. Here are some fine fountains, supplied by an aqueduct, supposed to have been erected by the Romans. The principal commerce is in wine and brandy; and the chief manufactures are serges and ticken. It is seated on the Loire, over which is a handsome bridge; 37 miles E. N. E. of Tours, and 100 S. S. W. of Paris. Pop. about 13,000.

Bloniez, a town of Poland, in Masovia; 20 miles W. of Warsaw.

Blore, a village in Staffordshire; 10 miles N. of Uttoxeter. Its heath is famous for a battle between the houses of York and Lancaster, in which Nevil, Earl of Salisbury, for York, with 500 men only, defeated Lord Audley with 10,000. The latter was killed, and on the spot is erected a stone cross to his memory.

Blue Mountains, several mountains so called in different parts of the world; viz. 1st. Intersecting the island of Jamaica from E. to W.; North Peak is 8180 feet above the level of the sea. 2nd. The most easterly ridge of the Allegany, in the state of Pennsylvania, extending in a S.W. direction, from the Delaware to S. of the Susquehannah river; altitude 3000 to 4000 feet. 3rd. A more southern branch of the same ridge, extending in the same direction from the N. of the Potomac river, through the state of Virginia into North Carolina; Otter Peak is 3103 feet high, and is the highest point in all Virginia: the passage of the Potomac river through this ridge is peculiarly grand. 4th. An extensive range in New South Wales, dividing the districts on the coast, from Bathurst Plains. 5th. Intersecting the island of Java in various directions.

Blyth, a large parish and town at the N.W. extremity of the county of Nottingham, bordering on Yorkshire. The town is 5 miles N. of Worksop; it has a market on Thursday.

Blyth, a town of Northumberland, England, situate at the mouth of a river of the same name, which falls into the German Ocean; 14 miles N. N. E. of Newcastle. It has a convenient quay, from which a considerable quantity of coal is shipped. There are two other rivers of the same name in England: viz. one in the county of Suffolk, falling into the sea at Southwold, and another in the county of Warwick, falling into the Tame, below Coleshill.

Boad, a town of Hindostan, in Orissa, on the river Mahanuddy; 65 miles S. S. E. of Sumbulpour, and 115 W. of Cuttack.

Bobbio, a town of Italy, in the Milanese, on the river Trebia; 25 miles S. E. of Pavia. Pop. 3500.

Bobenhausen, a town of Germany, in Hesse Darmstadt, with a castle; seated on the Gersbrentz; 49 miles S. E. of Frankfort on the Maine.

Bober, a river of Germany, which rises in Silesia, on the borders of Bohemia, flows N. by Lowenburg, Buntzlau, and Sagan, and joins the Oder below Crossen.

Bobersberg, a town of Brandenburg, in the New Mark, and duchy of Crossen; seated on the side of a hill, by the river Bober; 5 miles S. of Crossen.

Bobingen, a town of Bavaria; 9 miles S. of Augsburg. Pop. about 1500.

Bobrawa, a town in the circle of Brunn, Moravia; 4 miles S. W. of Bistitz.

Bobretz, a town in the county of Liptau, Upper Hungary, among the Carpathian Mountains. Pop. about 1700.

Bobrysk, a town in the palatinate of Minsk, Lithuania; situate E. of the Bobrigia river, just above its confluence with the Berezina.

Boca, signifying mouth, is a term which has been prefixed by the Spaniards, to the names of several straits or sea-passages in different parts of South America; the most celebrated is the north strait, between the island of Trinidad and the coast of Cumana, called the *Boca del Drago*, or Dragon's Mouth.

Boca Tigris, a strait in Canton river, China.

Bochetta, a chain of mountains in the territory of Genoa, over which is the road into Lombardy. On the highest mountain is a strong pass that will hardly admit three men to go abreast; and this is, properly, the Bochetta. It is the key of Genoa, and was forced by the French in 1796, and by the Austrians in 1800.

Bochnia, a town of Poland, in the palatinate of Cracow, with large salt mines; 20 miles E. S. E. of Cracow. Pop. about 3300.

Bocholt, a town of Westphalia, in the principality of Munster, on the river Aa; 40 miles W. of Munster.

Bockenheim, a town of Lower Saxony, in the principality of Hildesheim, on the river Nette; 13 miles S. S. E. of Hildesheim.

Bocking, a large village in Essex, adjoining to Braintree. Its church is spacious; and here is a great manufacture of baize.

Bockum, a town of Westphalia, in the county of Mark; 26 miles S. E. of Wesel.

Boden See. *See* Constance, Lake of.

Bodmin, a borough in Cornwall, governed by a mayor, with a market on Saturday. The summer assizes are held here. It has some manufactures of serge, and a trade in wool and yarn. The church is the largest in the county; and the remains of an episcopal palace and a priory are still to be seen. It is 32 miles N. E. of Falmouth, and 235 W. by S. of London. It returns two members to parliament.

Bodrogh, a river of Upper Hungary, rising among the Carpathian mountains, and falling into the Theiss at Tokay.

Bodrun, a town of Asiatic Turkey, in Natolia, on the north side of the Gulf of Scalanova; 18 miles S. of Smyrna. Another, on the site of the ancient Halicarnassus, on the north side of the Gulf of Stanchio; 45 miles W. by S. of Melassa.

Bog, or Bug, a river which rises on the south border of Volhynia, in Poland, flows through Podolia and Budzac Tartary, and enters the Black Sea, between Oczackow and the river Dnieper.

Boglio, or Beuil, a town of Savoy, situate on the Tinea; 21 miles N. N. W. of Nice.

Boglion, a town of Austrian Istria; about 30 miles S. S. E. of Trieste.

Boglipour, a town of Hindostan, capital of a circar in Bengal; seated on the Ganges; 112 miles N. E. of Moorshedabad.

Bognor, a village in Sussex; 7 miles S. of Chichester. It is an improving place, and much frequented in summer for sea-bathing.

Bogodouk, or Bogoduchow, a large inland town of European Russia, in the province of Kharkov. It has considerable manufactures of leather. Pop. about 7000.

Bogota, a river of Columbia, which falls into the Pacific Ocean, in the lat. of 1. N.

Bogoroditsk, a handsome town, containing about 5000 inhabitants; in the province of Toula, Russia.

Bogota, St. Fe de, a large town of South America. During the rule of the Spaniards in that part of the world, it was the capital of the viceroyalty of New Granada, and was then more commonly called St. Fee. Since the organization and establishment of the republic of Columbia, it has been more commonly called Bogota, and made the chief town of the province of Cundinamarco, and seat of the whole republican government of Columbia. It is situate on a spacious and fertile plain, on the most easterly ridge of the Andes, in the lat. of 4. 36. N. and 73. 30. of W. long., at an elevation of upwards of 8000 feet above the level of the sea, which, notwithstanding its contiguity to the equator, renders its climate comparatively temperate and agreeable. It is intersected by a small river called the Bogota (hence its recent appellation), which falls into the Magdalena, W. of the ridge of mountains on which the town is situate. The town is tolerably well laid out, having four squares, containing some handsome buildings; and although its remoteness from the sea, and destitution of water communication, will militate against its becoming a place of the first magnitude, should it continue to be the seat of government it will doubtless considerably increase both in extent and population, which at presents amounts to about 40,000. It is about 450 miles N. E. of Quito. About 15 miles S. W. of the town, at a place called Tequendama, the river Bogota falls down a precipice with great fury, and is an object of considerable attraction to the strangers who visit Bogota.

Bogwanpoor, a town of Bahar, Hindostan; a few miles S. E. of Benares.

Bohemia, a kingdom and very compact territory in the centre of Europe; supposed to have derived its name from a tribe of Celts called the Boii, and was originally more extensive, including Lusatia and Silesia on the N. E. and Moravia on the S. E. Previous to 1547 it was an independent kingdom, having an elective form of government, the popularity of which excited the jealousy of the emperor of Germany, Ferdinand I., who obtained at that period the consent of the Germanic diet, to declare it an hereditary appendage of the dominion of Austria. This union was severely contested on the part of the Bohemians, for about seventy years; but since 1690 they have implicitly yielded to the Austrian yoke. Bohemia, in its present extent, is in the form of a diamond, and lies between the lat. of 48. 35. and 51. 5. N. and 12. 20. to 16. 30. of W. long. Its southern point borders on Upper Austria, and it is bounded by Bavaria on the S. W., Saxony on the N. W., Lusatia and Silesia on the N. E., and Moravia on the S. E. Its extreme length and breadth will be about 180 by 190 miles, but each of the four sides of its quadrilateral figure will not average more than about 125, and as such give a superficial extent of 15,625 square miles.

Since 1751, it has been divided into the twelve following circles, named after twelve of the principal towns, (exclusive of Prague, the metropolis of the whole territory, which has a separate jurisdiction:) viz.

Leutmeritz	N.	Saatz ... N. W. including the small territory of Egen.	
Bunzlau ...	N.		
Konigingratz	N. E.		
Chrudim ...	E.	Rakownitz	Interior.
Tchaslau ...	S. E.	Kaurzim	Interior.
Bechin ..	S.	Beraund-Podrad	Interior.
Prachin	S.	Pilsen ... N. W.	

Bohemia is considered the most elevated part of Europe, no rivers running into it. The Spree, the Neisse, and the Bober, running north through Lusatia and Silesia, have their source on the frontiers of the circles of Bunzlau and Konigingratz, and the Elbe has its source in the latter circle, near the frontier of Silesia, running south into the circle of Chrudim, and then takes a north-west course, bounding the circle of Buntzlau on the south, intersecting Leutmeritz towards Dresden, in Saxony. The Moldau rises near the frontier of Austria, at the south extremity of the circle of Bechin, and runs nearly due north past Prague, into the Elbe at Milnik, in Buntzlau. Several streams have their sources in the circle of Pilsen, which unite near the town of that name, and there form the Beraun, which runs into the Moldau a little below Prague. The Egen intersects the circle of Saatz from south-west to north-east, falling into the Elbe a little below the town of Leutmeritz. These rivers, with their several tributary streams, contribute alike to the diversity and fertility of the country. There are also several small lakes in the south part of the circle of Bechin. The frontiers on all sides, except on that of Moravia, are mountainous and woody, whilst the whole of the interior possesses a soil of great capability; but as a species of feudal tyranny pervades the whole territory, it naturally precludes all excitement to social exertion, and its productions are consequently confined to a bare means of subsistence. It grows a considerable quantity of flax, which, as well as their wool, is manufactured into linens and cloths, for domestic use, and some on the side of Lusatia and Silesia for exportation. Almost every kind of mineral is found in one part of the country or the other; and, having but little external intercourse, every branch of manufacture is carried on as domestic occupations for internal supply. It has several mineral springs, but is deficient in the essential article of salt, part of the supply being obtained from external sources.

On the subjugation of Bohemia by Austria, he ancient form of government was retained, but it was merely the form: an absolute and despotic dictation nullified whatever was calculated to justify or vindicate the rights of man, and the conduct of blind passive obedience may now be considered as firmly established in Bohemia, as in any part of Europe, or the world. The established religion of Bohemia is the Roman Catholic, and, before the year 1781, the Protestants were not permitted the free exercise of their worship: at present all religious creeds are tolerated. Out of a population of about 3,000,000, the dissentients from Catholicism do not exceed 100,000, about half of whom are Jews. In time of peace, about 50,000 men are maintained in arms, to support whom, and other state pretensions, exactions, equal to about 2,000,000*l.*, English money, are imposed on the productive labours of the people. The original language of Bohemia seems to have been Sclavonic, a dialect of which is still common in the country; but the German or high Dutch is spoken with considerable purity.

BOHMERWALD, a dense mountain forest, forming the S.W. boundary of Bohemia. The term implies *Bohemian Forest, Baum* in German signifying wood; *Bohm* is probably a corruption of that term in Bohemia, and may have given name to the country, signifying a woody country, and the two following places as situated in woods.

BOHMISCH AICHE, a town of Bohemia, in the circle of Bunzlau; 20 miles N. of Jung Bunzlau.

BOHMISCH BROD, a town of Bohemia, in the circle of Kaurzim; 14 miles E. S. E. of Prague.

BOHOL, one of the Philippine islands, to the N. of Mindanao. Long. 124. 5. E. lat. 10. 0. N.

BOHOL, or BOOL, a town at the mouth of a river of the same name, falling into the Sooloo Sea, on the N. coast of the Isle of Celebes.

BOHUS, or BAHUS, a small district of West Gothland, Sweden, bordering on the Cattegat, N. of Gottenburg. Stromstadt, on the coast in lat. 58. 56. N. and 11. 15. E. long., is the principal town.

BOJADOR, a cape on the W. coast of Africa, doubled by the Portuguese in 1433. Long. 14. 27. W. lat. 26. 12. N.

BOIANO, a town of Naples, in the Molise, at the foot of the Appennines, on the E., near the river Tilerno. In 1803 it suffered greatly by an earthquake, and most of the inhabitants were destroyed. It is 45 miles N. N. E. of Naples.

BOIS LE DUC, a fortified city of Dutch Brabant, capital of a district of the same name, which contains also the towns of Helmont and Eyndhoven. It has a castle named Papenbriel, and a little to the S. are two forts, called Isabella and St. Anthony. It was taken by the French in 1794. It is situate among morasses, on the river Dommel, where it receives the Aa; 22 miles E. by N. of Breda, and 45 S. S. E. of Amsterdam. Pop. about 13,000

BOISCOMMUN a town of France, in the department of Loiret; 25 miles N. E. of Orleans.

BOITZENBURG, a town of Lower Saxony, in Mecklenburg, at the confluence of the Boitze with the Elbe; 30 miles S. W. of Schwerin.

BOITZENBURG, a town of Brandenburg, in the Upper Mark; 10 miles W. of Prenslow.

BOKHARA, a city of Bokhara. It disputes, with Samarcand, the title of capital, and stands on a rising ground, surrounded by a slender wall of earth, and a dry ditch, on the S. side of the river Sodg. The houses are low, and mostly built of mud; but the caravanseras and mosques, which are numerous, are all of brick. The bazaars, or market-places, have been stately buildings, but the greatest part of them are now in ruins. Here is also a stately building for the education of the priests. Great numbers of Jews and Arabians frequent this place; and the trade with Russia and Persia is considerable. In 1220, Bokhara was taken by Jenghis Khan, with a numerous army, who burnt the city, and demolished the castle; but after the city had remained in ruins some years, he at length ordered it to be rebuilt. It is 138 miles W. by S. of Samarcand. Long. 62. 56. E. lat. 39. 4. N.

BOKHARA, or BUCHARIA, a country of Asia, bounded on the N. by Turkestan, E. by Cashgur, S. by Hindostan and Persia, and W. by Khorasan and Kharesm. It is fertile in corn and fruit, and the best cultivated of any part of Tartary. The inhabitants, chiefly Usbec Tartars, are in general tawny, with black hair, but some are white and well made. They are cleanly in their food, which often consists of minced meat, and tea is the general drink. They are not warlike, but use the bow, lance, and sabre. The original inhabitants are a Persian colony, and still use the Persian language. They live in cities, and carry on commerce with Russia and Persia. The government is despotic; religion Mohammedan.

BOKHARIA, Little. *See* CASHGUR.

BOLABOLA, one of the Society Islands, in the Pacific Ocean; 4 leagues N. W. of Otaha. Long. 151. 52. W. lat. 16. 32. S.

BOLCHERESK, a town of Kamtschatka, on the river Bolchoireka, 22 miles from its mouth, in the sea of Okotsk. Long. 156. 37. E. lat. 52. 54. N.

BOLINGBROKE, a town in Lincolnshire, with a market on Tuesday. It was the birthplace of Henry IV. 29 miles E. of Lincoln, and 133 N. by E. of London.

BOLIVIA, or UPPER PERU, a new republic of South America, bounded on the E. by Brazil, S. by La Plata, or the Argentine republic, W. by the Pacific and Chili, and N. W. by Peru. In 1778, when the Peruvian viceroyalty was divided, the districts of La Paz, Potosi-Charcas, and Santa Cruz, were added to the viceroyalty of Buenos Ayres. These now form the republic ot Bolivia. Peru was the last of the Spanish colonies that succeeded in throwing off the yoke, which was accomplished by the brilliant victory of Aracucho, on Dec. 9th, 1824. Since that time there have been many changes in these two republics, which renders all knowledge of their present state uncertain. It is divided into six departments, and contains 310,000 square miles, and 1,200,000 inhabitants. *See* Peru.

Bolkenhayn, a town of Silesia, in the principality of Schweidnitz, a few miles W. of the town of Schweidnitz; the inhabitants are chiefly employed in the linen manufacture.

Bolkowitz, or Polkwitz, a town of Silesia; 12 miles S. of Glogau.

Bologna, a city of Italy, capital of the Bolognese, and an archbishop's see. It is about 5 miles in circumference, and contains 80,000 inhabitants. It has long been distinguished as a school of science; the university being one of the most ancient and celebrated in Europe. An academy of arts and sciences was founded in 1712, and contributed greatly to that fame which the city has acquired. As a school of painting, it is immortalized by the number of masters it has produced. There are here 169 churches, and these, as well as the numerous mansions of the nobles, are most munificently furnished with their best productions. Nor have the exertions of art been confined to the sphere of painting; the city exhibits some of the finest monuments of architecture, such as the palace of Capraria, the marble fountain in the Place-del-Gigante, and in fact almost every building of any note. The academy of arts and sciences is a building of great magnificence, and the public theatre is one of the largest and most beautiful in Italy. The church of St. Petronius is the largest in Bologna, but is more remarkable for its pavement, where Cassino drew his meridian line, 180 feet long. The trade of Bologna is very considerable, being situated in a fertile country, and having an easy conveyance of its produce by a canal to the Po. The exuberance of the adjacent country enables the inhabitants to furnish all Europe with the greatest delicacies in confectionary, distilled waters, essences, &c.; oil, wine, flax, hemp, and silk, also furnish abundant sources of trade and employment. The Reno, which passes by the city, turns no less than 400 mills for silk-works. It is situated at the foot of the Appennines; 22 miles S. E. of Modena, and 175 N. W. of Rome. Long. 11. 21. E. lat. 44. 30. N. It was taken possession of by the French in 1796, but restored to the states of Rome at the general peace.

Bolognese, a province of Italy, bounded on the N. by the Ferrarese, W. by Modena, S. by Tuscany, and E. by Romagna. It is watered by many small rivers, and produces all sorts of grain and fruit, particularly rich muscadine grapes. Some miles before the entrance into Bologna, the country seems one continued garden. The vineyards are not divided by hedges, but by rows of elms and mulberry-trees; the vines hanging in festoons from one tree to another. There are also mines of alum and iron. Bologna is the capital. There are about 300 other towns, containing a population of about 210,000.

Bolsena, a town of Italy, in the patrimony of St. Peter, on the lake of its name; 18 miles N. N. W. of Viterbo.

Bolsover, a town in Derbyshire, with a market on Friday. It has a spacious castle on the brow of a hill; and is noted for the manufacture of tobacco pipes. It is 6 miles E. of Chesterfield, and 145 N. N. W. of London.

Bolswaert, a town of Holland, in Friesland, near the Zuyder Zee; 10 miles N. of Sloten. Near this town, which is about 2 miles in extent, was formerly an abbey of the Cistertians, where the Munster Anabaptists took refuge in 1534, and where William, count of Holland, was buried in the 14th century.

Bolton-le-Moors, a large and populous borough in Lancashire, consisting of two townships, Great and Little Bolton. It is so called from its situation amidst several extensive moors, and also to distinguish it from another town in the N. part of the county, called *Bolton-le-Sands*. It is 11 miles N. W. of Manchester, on the mail-coach road to Preston and Glasgow, and, next to Manchester, is one of the most considerable stations of the cotton manufacture, the branches more particularly pursued being those of muslins, dimities, and counterpanes. The canal to Manchester, from which there is a branch to Bury, has added materially to the prosperity of the place; and the railway to Leigh, by affording facilities for an additional supply of coal, has reduced the price of that indispensable fuel. Besides the parish church, here are two other episcopal churches of recent erection, a Roman Catholic chapel, and about sixteen meeting-houses for dissenters, with various schools and charitable institutions. A town hall, for the transaction of public business, has been lately erected. Market on Mondays, well supplied with provisions. Under the Reform Bill, it sends two members to parliament. The Earl of Derby was executed here, in 1651, for proclaiming Charles II.

There are 12 other towns and villages named Bolton, besides Bolton on the Sands, in different parts of England; viz. three in Cumberland, one each in Northumberland and Westmoreland, seven in Yorkshire, and several in different parts of the United States of North America; but none that merit any particular notice.

Bomal, a town of the Netherlands, in Luxemburg, on the river Ourt; 20 miles S. of Liege.

Bombay, (*Bom-bahia*, good bay, Portuguese,) an island, city, and presidency on the W. coast of the Deccan of Hindostan. It came to the English by the marriage of Charles II. with Catherine of Portugal, and was made over to the East India Company in 1688, when it was made the seat of government of all their possessions on that side of Hindostan, which was previously at Surat, and it is now one of the three presidencies by which their oriental territories are governed. It contains a strong and capacious fortress, a city, dockyard, and marine arsenal. Here the finest merchant ships are built, all of teak supplied from the neighbouring countries, which is more durable than the best English oak; and in 1810, the Minden, 74 gun ship, was launched, having been built entirely under the superintendence of a Parsee. The ground is in general barren, and good water scarce; but it has abundance of cocoa-nuts, and its markets are well supplied with every delicacy. The population of the territory of Bombay is estimated at 225,000, three-fourths of whom are Hindoos, the remainder Mahometans, Armenians, and Jews, and about 8000 Parsees, or Fire Worshippers. The city of Bombay, next to Calcutta, may be considered the most commercial place in all Hindostan; its interchange with China is very great, the export of cotton sometimes amounting to 350,000 bales per annum. It is much resorted to by traders from Persia, Arabia, Abyssinia, Armenia, and all parts of western Asia, as well as from most of the islands of the Indian Ocean, and all the eastern parts of Asia; and the commercial transactions are conducted with more integrity than is usual in Asiatic cities. It is about 180 miles S. of Surat, and 1300 W. by S. of Calcutta. The light-house, which is a very prominent object, and visible for 20 miles out at sea, is in lat. 18. 53. N. and 72. 53. E. long.

BOMENE, a seaport of Holland, in Zealand, on the N. shore of the island of Schowen; 3 miles E. of Browershaven.

BOMMEL, a town of South Holland, in the isle of Overflakke; 7 miles W. of Williamstadt.

BOMMEL, a strong town of Holland, in Guelderland, in the island of Bommelwert, on the river Waal; 21 miles S. by E. of Utrecht, and 7 N. of Bois-le-Duc. Pop. about 3000.

BOMMELWERT, an island of Holland, formed by the junctions of the Waal and Maese. It lies in the province of Guelderland, except a small district in the west end, which belongs to South Holland. It is fifteen miles in length, from Lowestein to Fort St. Andrew, and is not more than four miles in the broadest part. It was taken by the French in 1672, and again in 1794.

BONA, a seaport of Algier, in the province of Constantina. Near it are the ruins of the ancient Hippo Regius. It has a trade in corn, oil, wax, and wool: it is 270 miles E. of Algier. Long. 7. 45. E. lat. 36. 52. N.

BONAIR, or BUEN AYRE, a fertile island in the Caribbean Sea, to the E. of Curacoa. It is 60 miles in circuit, and has a good harbour and road on the S. W. side. Long. 68. 18. W. lat. 12. 10. N.

BONAVISTA, one of the Cape Verd islands, so called from its beautiful appearance to the first discoverers, in 1450; but it is now become barren, through the extreme idleness of the inhabitants. Long. 22. 47. W. lat. 16. 6. N.

BONAVISTA, a cape on the E. side of the island of Newfoundland. Long. 52. 32. W. lat. 48. 15. N.

BOND, an interior county of the state of Illinois. It is intersected by the Kaskaskia river. Pop 2931. Independence, 10 miles S. by W. of Vandalia, is the chief town.

BONDORF, a town of Suabia, in the Black Forest, capital of a county which joins the Brisgau. It is 7 miles S. by W. of Furstenburg, now included in the territory of the duchy of Baden.

BONDOU, an interior country of North Africa, lying between the rivers Senegal and Gambia, inhabited by the Foulah race of negroes, who are industrious and social in their habits, and Mahometans in religion.

BONESS, or BORROWSTONESS, a town of Scotland, in Linlithgowshire, with a safe and commodious harbour on the Frith of Forth. It has a considerable trade in ship-building and coal, and extensive manufactures of salt and stoneware. It is 5 miles N. of Linlithgow.

BONI, or BONY, a spacious bay between the two southern promontories of the Isle of Celebes. It has numerous shoals and rocks, and is commonly called Bugges Bay by Europeans. Near the upper end of the bay, on the shore of the western promontory, is the town of Boni, which is the capital of a kingdom of the same name, but little known. The inhabitants are partly Mahometans. It is in the lat. of 3. S. and 120. 30. of E. long.

BONIFACIO, a fortified seaport of Corsica, with a good harbour and a coral fishery. It stands on a small peninsula, at the S. extremity of the island; 37 miles S. of Ajaccio. Long. 9. 20. E. lat. 41. 25. N. Pop. about 3000.

BONN, a city of Germany, in the territory of Cologne. It has a flourishing university, four parish churches, and several religious foundations. It was taken by the Duke of Marlborough, in 1703, and by the French in 1794. It is seated on the Rhine; 14 miles S. by E. of Cologne. Pop. 10,556.

BONNAT, a town of France, in the department of La Creuse. Pop. about 2000.

BONNETABLE, a town of France, in the department of Sarte; 15 miles N. E. of Mons. Pop. 4500.

BONNEVAL, a town of France, in the department of Eure and Loire; seated on the Loire; 8 miles N. of Châteaudun.

BONNEVILLE, a town of Savoy, capital of Faucigny, seated on the river Arve, at the foot of a mountain called the Mole; 20 miles S. E. of Geneva.

BONNY, a kingdom of Guinea, North Africa, lying between Waree and Calabar. The inhabitants are less social than their neighbours, and live in constant collision with those of Calabar.

BONTHAIN, a seaport at the S. extremity of the western promontory of the island of Celebes, seated on the shore of a large bay, where ships may lie in security during both the monsoons. The town has a palisadoed fort, and stands on the S. side of a small but deep river. Long. 120. 32. E. lat. 5. 31. S.

BOODROOM, a town of Asia Minor, situate on a gulf of the name, in the Gulf of Kos, probably the ancient Halicarnassus. The harbour, now decayed, is used by the Turkish navy, and the abundant ruins in its vicinity certify its former importance. Lat. 37. 5. N. long. 27. 10. E.

BOOL. *See* BOHOL.

Boom, a town of Brabant, on the N. bank of the river Nethes; 10 miles S. of Antwerp. Pop. about 3500

Boone, a frontier country of the state of Kentucky, nearly encircled by the Ohio River, which divides the N. end from the states of Ohio and Indiana, opposite to where the Miami river falls into the Ohio. Pop. 10,034. Burlington, 90 miles N. by E. of Frankfort, is the chief town.

Boondee, a city and district of Hindostan, province of Ajmeer. It is a remarkable and interesting city, from its pagodas, fountains, and Hindoo temples; it is divided into Old and New Boondee, and stands near a lake.

Boonsborough, a town of the United States, in Madison county, seated on Red River, which runs into the Kentucky; 33 miles E. S. E. of Lexington.

Boorhanpoor, a city of Hindostan, province of Candeesh, formerly the capital of a large and well-built city, mostly of brick, and paved with stone. It is famous for its delicious grapes.

Boosnah, a town of Hindostan, in Bengal; 98 miles N. E. of Calcutta.

Bootan, or **Bhotan**, a mountainous country of Hindostan Proper, lying between the province of Bengal and Thibet. It is a feudatory province of Thibet, and abounds in mountains covered with verdure, and rich with abundant forest trees; there is scarcely a mountain whose base is not washed by some torrent, and many of the loftiest bear populous villages, amid orchards and plantations, on their summits and on their sides. The southernmost ridge of the Bootan mountains rises near a mile and a half above the plains of Bengal, in a horizontal distance of only 15 miles; and from the summit the astonished traveller looks on the plains below as on an extensive ocean. The Booteas are much fairer and more robust than their neighbours the Bengalees, with broader faces and higher cheek-bones; their hair is invariably black, and cut short; their eyes small and black, with long pointed corners; and their skins remarkably smooth. The houses are built on props, though the country is hilly, and ascended by a ladder: the lower part, closed on all sides, serves for holding stores, and accommodating hogs, cows, and other animals. The capital is Tassasudon.

Boothia Felix, a district in the Arctic regions, discovered by Captain John Ross, in 1829. It lies to the W. of the Gulf of Boothia, a continuation of Prince Regent's Inlet, but the S. shore is unexplored. It is remarkable as containing the northern magnetic pole, in lat. 70. 0. 4. N. long. 96. 45. W.

Bootle, a village in Lancashire, contiguous to Liverpool, which it supplies with fine fresh water, from abundant and never-failing springs, near the sea-shore.

Bopal. *See* **Bhopaul**.

Bopfingen, a town of Suabia, on the river Eger; 19 miles N.W. of Donawert.

Boppart, a town of Germany, seated at the foot of a mountain, near the Rhine; 8 miles S. of Coblentz.

Borahs, a town of West Gothland, Sweden; about 10 miles E. of Gottenburg.

Borba, a town of Alentejo, Portugal, lying between Estremoz and Villa-Vicosa.

Borcholz, a town on the W. side of the bishopric of Paderborn, Westphalia, now part of the Prussian States.

Bord, or **Boit**, a town of France, in the department of Correze. It was the birth-place of Marmontel.

Bordentown, a town of New Jersey, in Burlington county, on the W. side of the Delaware; 6 miles below Trenton, and 23 N. E. of Philadelphia.

Borg, a town of Denmark, the chief place in the island of Femern, with a fort, on Femern Sound. Long. 11. 17. E. lat. 54. 27. N.

Borgentryck, or **Bergentrych**, a town on the S.W. side of the bishopric of Paderborn, Westphalia.

Borghetto, a town on the E. bank of the Adige, at the southern extremity of the bishopric of Trent. Also the name of a village in the vicinity of Mantua, where a severe battle was fought between the French and Austrians, in 1796.

Borgholm, a fortified town on the W. side of the isle of Oland, in the Baltic, part of the province of East Gothland.

Borg, **Barg**, or **Bergholzhausen**, a town in the county of Ravensburg, Westphalia.

Borgne, a large lake or inlet of the sea, between the states of Mississippi and Louisiana, communicating with the Gulf of Mexico, and inland with Lake Pontchartrain.

Borgo, a seaport town of Russian Finland, lying between Helsingfurt and Lovisa. In lat. 60. 21. N. and 25. 45. E. long.

Borgo, **Rusz**, **Prunt**, and **Pass**, three towns contiguous to each other, near the source of the Bistritz river, on the eastern frontier of Transylvania, bordering on the Bukowine. They have salt-springs and some manufactures of earthenware. The population is considerable, principally Wallachians.

Borgo, **St. Donnini**, a town in the duchy of Parma, so called from the martyrdom of Donnini, who was beheaded here in 304. It is a bishop's see, and is situate about midway on the road from Placentia to Parma.

Borgo di St. Sepolcro, a town of Tuscany, in the Florentino, with a fort, seated near the source of the Tiber; 12 miles N. E. of Arezzo. In 1789, about 1000 of the inhabitants were destroyed by an earthquake.

Borgoforte, a town of Italy, in the Mantuan, on the river Po, at the influx of the Oglia, 10 miles S. of Mantua; and nine others, all inconsiderable.

Borgo, or **Burgo D'Osma**, a town of Spain, surrounded with walls, and containing about 200 families; 33 miles W. of Soria, and 40 S. E. of Burgos.

Burgo di St. Angelo, a fortress of the island of Malta, a little to the E. of Valetta.

Borja, or **Bergosa**, a town of Spain, in Arragon, in a fruitful spot, near Mount Cayo, at the foot of the Pyrenees; 42 miles W. N. W. of Saragossa.

BORJA, a town of Columbia, situate on the head waters of the river Amazon, 300 miles E. by N. of Paita, and 90 W. by N. of Jean. Long. 76. 36. W. lat. 4. 15. S.

BORJA, a town in the province of Buenos Ayres, near the frontier of Brazil. It was founded by the Jesuits.

BORISOGLEBSK, a town of Russia, situate on the banks of the Verona, near the S. end of the province of Tamboy, about 300 miles S. E. of Moscow. It is also the name of a town in the province of Jaroslav, on the W. bank of the Volga, a few miles N. of the city of Jaroslav. Pop. of each about 3000.

BORISSOW, a town of Russian Poland, on the banks of the Berezina; about 35 miles E. of Minsk.

BORKELO, a strong town of Holland, in the county of Zutphen, remarkable for having been the subject of two wars: one in 1665, against the Bishop of Munster, and the other with France, in 1672. It is seated on the river Borkel, 15 miles E. N. E. of Zutphen.

BORKEN, a town of Westphalia, in the principality of Munster, with a collegiate church; seated on the Aa; 38 miles W. of Munster.

BORKUM, an island of the kingdom of Hanover, lying between the E. and W. channels of the Ems river. It is partly inundated at high water. It has a town of the same name, the inhabitants subsisting chiefly by fishing.

BORMIO, a town of Switzerland, capital of a county of its name, on the confines of Tyrol. About a mile from the town are medicinal baths. It is seated at the foot of the mountains, on the river Fredolso, near its confluence with the Adda; 40 miles S. E. of Coire. Long. 10. 20. E. lat. 46. 17. N.

BORMIO, or BORMIDA, a large river of Piedmont, which rises in the territory of Finale, runs N., intersecting the duchy of Montferrat, falling into the Tanaro, a little below Alessandria.

BORNA, a town of Upper Saxony, in the circle of Leipsic, with a manufacture of stuffs; seated near the river Pleysse; 13 miles S. E. of Leipsic, on the road to Altenburg.

BORNEO, an island of Asia, in the Indian Ocean, discovered by the Portuguese in 1521; lying between the lat. of 4. 10. S. and 7. N., and 109. 15. to 119. 25. W. long., being in its extreme length 775 miles, and 650 in extreme breadth; a surface greater than that of any island in the world, except New Holland, being about 360,000 square miles, or nearly five times larger than Great Britain. Although under the equator, the air is not so excessively hot as might be expected, being frequently refreshed with showers and cool breezes, the thermometer varying from 82. to 94. of Fahrenheit. In the monsoon, from April to September, the wind is westerly, and the rains are constant and heavy, attended with violent storms of thunder and lightning. The rainy season continues for eight months, and during that time all the flat country, from ten to twenty miles from the coast, is overflowed, and the air rendered very unhealthy. For this reason the inhabitants build their houses on floats, which they make fast to trees. They have but one floor, with partitions made with canes; and the roofs are covered with palmetto-leaves, the eaves of which reach within four or five feet of the bottom. Some of their houses are built upon pillars, a sufficient height from the surface not to be deluged. The countries on the coast are inhabited by a mixture of Malays, Javanese, and Macassars. The aborigines of the island, however, live in the interior, and are called Biadjoos, Biayos, or Dijakkese, &c., who are represented as the most uncouth and unsocial of the human race. Indeed, it seems to be here where Nature has united the chain of animated creation, and placed the orang-outang, as the connecting link between the articulating, modulating, and assigning, and the instinctive; or, in other words, between the biped and the quadruped race of animals. On one side of the orang-outang, which seems to be a native of the soil of Borneo, are apes, monkeys, bears, goats, deer, horses, buffaloes and other horned cattle, tigers, and the elephant; whilst on the other side is a class of beings with apparently no other claim to the character of man but that of the power of articulation; and yet, amidst this unsocial and unappreciating race of beings, Nature seems to have bestowed, in lavish profusion, all her most delectable gifts; with iron, tin, and various other metals, for purposes of utility, gold, diamonds, and various other precious gems for ornament abound. It is here that the salangane, a species of swallow, constructs its edible nest, which is exchanged, to gratify the luxurious palates of the Chinese, at a rate double its weight of silver. In the vegetable kingdom, in addition to rice and maize for substantial subsistence, the sensations of taste and smell are here to be gratified in the highest possible degree. Cassia, cinnamon, frankincense, and myrrh, are indigenous productions of the country. The *laurus camphoratus* yields an endless abundance of its fragrant and inflammable substance; whilst agaric, musk, aloes, and various other substances and plants, are dispersed over the country in endless profusion, to aid the domestic and social economy of man, and to serve as alteratives in case of accident or disease. On the other hand, the pernicious and poisonous class of plants and reptiles are also common; and the natives appear equally adept at applying them in revenge against their enemies, as in the application of alteratives to avoid their consequences. Thus, whilst the soil of Borneo appears susceptible, by social arrangements and due cultivation, to subsist, in a high degree of comfort and enjoyment, a fourth of the whole population of the globe, the total number of inhabitants are supposed not to exceed 3,000,000, divided into numerous petty sovereignties. With the exception, however, of the coast, very little is known as to the extent and condition of the population. The English East India Company formed some settlements upon the coast, towards the close of the 17th century; but, in 1706, the Dutch, in the heyday of their valour, drove the English entirely from the country, and for more than a century were the only European nation that maintained any direct intercourse with the island; and their grovelling policy has ever been to preclude the world from all knowledge of the position, people, condition, and resources of the countries with which they trade, as far as it is possible for them to do so. During the war, subsequently to the peace of Amiens, in 1802, when in their turn the Dutch were driven from all their positions in Asia, the English again established themselves on the coast of Borneo, and were making progress in the arts of cultivation and social economy, when, by treaty, in 1816, the Dutch were reinstated in their possessions, and Borneo again exposed to their exclusive line of policy. As far as our knowledge of the country does extend, whilst the coast on all sides is low and swampy, the interior seems much intersected by mountains; a river, called the Banjar, has its source in the centre of the country, about two degrees north of the equator, runs south into the sea of Java; and there are two or three rivers running from E. to W. falling into the sea on the west side; but the north and east coasts appear deficient in the essential of rivers for internal communication by water. There are, however, several fine harbours and roadsteads round the coast; the principal is Bandermassing, at the mouth of the Banjar; Sambar, at the south-west point; Sambas, on the west coast; Borneo, at the north-west; and Passir, at the south-east.

Borneo, the principal city and capital of a kingdom of the same name, at the north part of the above island, is situate up a river, about 10 miles from the sea, in the lat. of 4. 55. N. and 114. 15. E. long. Like most, or all the other towns on the coast, the houses are built on piles driven into the swamps, inundated at high water; and the trading transactions, which are here very considerable with the Chinese, and other eastern nations, are carried on in boats and wherries.

Bornheim, a town in the electorate of Cologne; about 15 miles W. by N. of Bonn. Pop. about 1100. Also a town of the Netherlands; about 1[illegible]iles N. E. of Dendermonde.

Bornholm, an island of Denmark, just within the Baltic; of an oval form; about 22 miles in circumference, and nearly surrounded by rocks. The soil is stony, but fertile, with excellent pasture; and there are mines of coal, and quarries of marble. It lies 10 miles S. E. of the southern extremity of Sweden. The chief town is Roune, on the west side; the north end is in lat. 55. 18. N. and 14. 49. E. long.

Bornos, a town of the province of Seville; about 15 miles N. E. of Cadiz. Pop. about 3000.

Bornou, an extensive empire in the interior of North Africa, having Howssa on the west, and Nubia on the east. It consists of a number of oases, or fertile spots, interspersed with arid wastes. The climate is said to be characterized by excessive, though not by uniform heat. Two seasons, one commencing soon after the middle of April, the other at the same period in October, divide the year. The first is introduced by violent winds from the south-east and south, with intense heat, a deluge of sultry rain, and such tempests of thunder and lightning as destroy multitudes of the cattle, and many of the people. At the commencement of the second season, the ardent heat subsides; the air becomes soft and mild, and the weather perfectly serene. Maize, rice, the horse-bean, cotton, hemp, and indigo, are cultivated; and there are figs, grapes, apricots, pomegranates, lemons, limes, and melons. The most valuable tree is called redeynah, in form and height like an olive, the leaf resembling that of a lemon, and bearing a nut, the kernel and shell of which are in great estimation, the first as a fruit, the last on account of the oil it produces. Horses, asses, mules, dogs, horned cattle, goats, sheep, and camels (the flesh of which is much esteemed), are the common animals. Bees are so numerous, that the wax is often thrown away as an article of no value. The game consists of partridges, wild ducks, and ostriches, the flesh of which is prized above every other. The other animals are the lion, leopard, civet cat, wolf, fox, elephant, buffalo, antelope, and cameleopardalis; and there are many snakes, scorpions, centipedes, and toads. The complexion of the natives is black; but they are not of the Negro cast. The dress of the greater part consists of shirts of blue cotton, manufactured in the country, of a red cap, brought from Tripoli, and a white muslin turban, from Cairo. Nose-rings of gold are worn by the principal people. But the only covering of the poorer sort is a kind of girdle for the waist. In their manners the people are courteous and humane; they are passionately fond of play; the lower classes, of draughts, and the higher excel in chess. More than thirty different languages are said to be spoken in Bornou and its dependencies; and the reigning religion is the Mahometan. The monarchy is elective. The sultan is said to have five hundred ladies in his seraglio, and that his stud contains likewise five hundred horses. His dominions extend beyond the desert into the fertile country of Negroland, of which he possesses a large portion. He has a vast army, which consists almost entirely of horse: the sabre, pike, and bow, are their weapons of offence, and a shield of hides is their armour.

Bornou, the capital of the empire of the same name, with a palace like a citadel. The whole city is surrounded by a high wall, encompassed with a ditch; but the other towns of the kingdom are open. The principal trade is in gold-dust, slaves, horses, ostriches' feathers, salt, and civet. It is seated on the Yeu; 750 miles E. N. E. of the mouth of the Niger. Long. 14. 5. E. lat 19. 45. N.

Boro Budor, the chief temple of the Javanese; situate about 60 miles from Samarang, nearly in the centre of the island. It is dedicated to Boohd, and contains several hundred snbordinate idols.

Borodino, a village of Russia, near the river Moskwa; about 90 miles W. of Moscow. It will long be memorable in the annals of Russia, for the desperate conflict between the French and Russian armies, during the march of the former towards Moscow, on the 7th of September, 1812, when about 30,000 men on each side were either killed or wounded.

BOROUGHBRIDGE, a town in West Yorkshire. Market on Saturday. It is 18 miles N. W. of York, and 206 N. by W. of London.

BOROVITCHI, a town of Russia, on the S. E. side of the province of Novogorod; bordering on Twer; seated on the S. bank of the Msta river; about 170 miles S. E. of St. Petersburgh. Pop. 2600.

BOROWISK, or BOROVSK, another town of Russia; about 60 miles S. W. of Moscow.

BORRIANO, or BORRIAL, a town of Spain, in Valencia, near the mouth of the Minjares; 21 miles N. of Valencia. Pop. about 4000.

BORRIS, in Ossory, a villlage in the parish of Aghaboe, Queen's County, Ireland; 63 miles W. by S. of Maryborough.

BORROS, a parish in Queen's County, Ireland, which includes the town of Maryborough, by which name the parish is sometimes called. *See* MARYBOROUGH.

BORROMEI ISLES, four beautiful isles, in the S. part of Lake Maggiore, N. Italy. On Isola Bella there is a fine palace and gardens.

BORROWDALE, a village in Cumberland; 6 miles S. of Keswick. It stands at the end of a narrow and crooked valley, and is famous for mines of wadd, or black-lead, a substance almost peculiar to England, and the vicinity of Malaga, Spain.

BORROWSTONESS. *See* BONESS.

BORROD, a county in the N. part of Upper Hungary, bounded on the E. by the Shajo branch of the Sheif river. It is one of the most fertile districts of the country. Pop. about 95,000. Mishkoltz is the capital.

BOSA, a seaport on the W. coast of Sardinia, and a bishop's see, with a castle, on a river of the same name; 17 miles S. S. E. of Argeri. Long. 8. 50. E. lat. 40. 29. N.

BOSCAWEN ISLAND, an island in the Pacific Ocean; about 10 miles in circumference. Long. 175. 10. W. lat. 15. 50. S.

BOSCO, or BOSCHI, a town of Italy, in the Milanese, seated on the Orbe; 5 miles E. of Alexandria.

BOSCOBEL, a village in Shropshire, 9 miles S. E. of Newport, where Charles II. was concealed in an oak, after the battle of Worcester.

BOSHUANA, or BECHUANA, an extensive tract of country in the interior of South Africa, extending through about 5. deg. of lat. from 25. to 20. S., inhabited by numerous tribes of people, of whom at present very little is known. They seem, physically considered, to be of the same stock as the Caffres, but somewhat more advanced in social economy, which seems to improve northwards. Hence it may be inferred, that civilization and improvement in Africa gradually extended itself from the north. The chief town, as far as the country is at present known, is Latakoo, represented to have contained about 15,000 inhabitants, reduced to 7 or 8000 during the 2nd decinary of the present century, by the continued intestine broils of the different tribes. They cultivate various kinds of grain, and look upon fish, as an article of food, with horror. As far as pretension to worship prevails, the people are idolaters; but they seem indifferent to worship of any kind: polygamy is general; the elder men have usually one young wife, and another who is past child-bearing. Mahomedism appears not to have reached them. Their dress is principally of skins, which they tan into leather; and, in the more northern parts, they appear to have made some progress in the smelting and working of iron. *See* CAFFRARIA.

BOSNA SERAI, the capital of Bosnia. It has a considerable trade with Dalmatia, and manufactures of swords and cutlery. It is of considerable extent, and interspersed with gardens; 125 miles S. W. of Belgrade. Pop. 60,400.

BOSNIA, a compact and naturally fertile district of European Turkey, lying between the lat. of 43. 18. and 45. 10. N., and the 17th and 20th of W. long. It is bounded on the W. by the Austrian province of Croatia; N. by the Saave river, which falls into the Danube, and divides it from Sclavonia; on the E. by the Turkish province of Servia; and S. by the N. end of Albania and Dalmatia. It has some mountain districts, and is intersected by several rivers, running from the N. into the Saave; and the Narenta, which rises in the S. part of the province, runs S. through Dalmatia, into the Adriatic at Narisi, a few miles N. of Ragusa. Its area may be stated at about 15,000 square miles; yet the population is supposed not to ceed 80,000. As a frontier district, it is principally occupied by Turkish soldiery, who are sanctioned in subsisting themselves upon the products of the occupiers of the soil; and, as the soldiery of the province amount to 40 or 50,000, they of course tend to subdue all excitement to agricultural exertion; and thus, although the vine and the olive would yield fruit in abundance, one of the finest districts in Europe is kept a wilderness, by an undisciplined, lawless, and ruthless horde of soldiery. The principal towns are Bosnia Serai, the the capital; Banjaluka, Sworniek, Traunik, (the seat of the pacha,) and Prisrendi. As far as any external commercial intercourse is maintained with Bosnia, it is principally through Dalmatia from Ragusa. The greater part of the province formerly belonged to Hungary. The inhabitants are principally Sclavonians, speaking the Sclavonic with great purity, and professing the formulary of the Greek church.

BOSPHORUS, the narrow strait, 20 miles in length, and from 1 to 1½ broad, which unites the Black Sea with the Sea of Marmora. It is sometimes called the Strait of Constantinople. It is of exceeding beauty, and the shores are lined with splendid kiosks and houses of the Constantinopolitans, for almost its whole length.

BOSSINY, or TREVENNA, a vill. in Cornwall, seated near the Bristol Channel; 17 miles N. W. of Launceston, and 233 W. by S. of London.

Bost, a strong town of Persia, capital of Segistan, or Seistan. It is seated on the Heermund, and on the route of the caravans from Ispahan to Caubul; about 170 miles W. S. W. of Candahar. Long. 64. 15. E. lat. 32. 30. N.

Bostan, a town of Asiatic Turkey, in the N. part of the province of Aladeul, situate near the eastern confines of Caramania, and near the source of a river which falls into the Levant at Adanah.

Boston, a borough and seaport tn. of Lincolnshire, England. When the idle, the crafty, and the vicious, sought subsistence and refuge, and the oppressed and indigent relief, from monastic institutions, Boston ranked among the most important towns in the country, having had not less than ten fraternal establishments; all of which were annulled, and the inmates dispersed, under the general demolition of those institutions by Henry VIII. After this reverse, when England exchanged her agricultural productions and raw materials, for the haberdashery and other manufactures of Germany and Holland, Boston became one of the principal markets in the kingdom for wool, which used to be exported in large quantities to Holland and the Hanse Towns; but, on the exportation of wool being totally prohibited, Boston was doomed to a further reverse, and gradually declined until towards the close of the last century. It has, since the commencement of the present century, gradually been rising in population and importance. The town is situate on both the banks of the river Witham, over which is a handsome bridge, of one arch, of cast iron, eighty-six feet in span, a few miles above the entrance of the river into the sea called Boston Wash, with which river, and by canals, it communicates with a considerable portion of the interior of the country; and, in addition to its very considerable trade in grain for the London market, it carries on a direct trade with the Baltic for deals, hemp, tar, &c. The parish church, founded by St. Botolph, in 1309, is a very stately edifice, being 300 feet in length, supported by Corinthian pillars, lighted by pointed windows, and its steeple ascended by steps, corresponding in number with the months, weeks, and days in the year. The steeple or tower is 286 feet in height, surmounted with a lantern, which serves as a beacon for many miles out at sea, and the country being very level inland, it forms a beautiful and interesting object in the perspective, many miles distant. The town is governed by a mayor, recorder, twelve aldermen, and eighteen common councilmen, with subordinate officers, who are vested with the admiralty jurisdiction of the adjoining coasts. The corporation, since 1800, have erected a commodious fish market, which is abundantly suppled, and large quantities are conveyed into the interior counties of Nottingham and Leicester. The markets for grain, &c., are on Wednesdays and Saturdays; and it has four fairs annually. It has two endowed schools; and returns two members to parliament. It is 36 miles S. E. of Lincoln, and 116 N. of London.

Boston Deeps, is the sea channel of the inlet called the Wash, leading from the German Ocean by the Lincolnshire coast, up to the port of Boston. The opposite side. which washes the coast of Norfolk, is called Lynn Deeps. The bottom of the Wash is a large shoal, partly dry at low water; and even the Deeps are the reverse of what their name implies, not admitting, at the most vessels of more than 200 tons burthen. It is proposed to recover a large portion of this bay from the sea, by means of an embankment.

Boston, the chief town of New England, North America, N. of New York, and the seat of the legislative government of the state of Massachusets. The town is beautifully located on a peninsula of an irregular form, about 5 miles in circumference, united on the S. side with the main land by an isthmus nearly a mile in length, and about the eighth of a mile broad; situate at the head of a spacious bay, and surrounded inland, at a distance of 5 to 7 miles, with a range of hills running in a semicircular direction, beautifully diversified with foliage, and forming altogether a very prepossessing scene. The bay is about 10 miles in length, formed by Alderton Point S., and Nahant Point N. Between these points, nearest to Alderton, is a cluster of small islands, on the most southern of which is a lighthouse, in the lat. of 42. 22. N. and 70. 53. W. long., being 10 miles E. of the town. On this island is the signal station for announcing to the town the number and description of vessels approaching from sea; and between it and Alderton Point is the principal ship channel into the bay, which contains about eighty small islands, mostly uninhabited, but several of them affording pasture for cattle and sheep. On one of them, within about 4 miles of the town, is a fort and garrison, peculiarly well adapted to protect the town from any external attack, and for the maintenance of all maritime regulations, the ship channel being within pistol-shot of the N. side of the island. Having passed this island, a vessel is considered within the harbour, which has been known to have been frozen so as to enable persons to travel on foot from the town to the fort; but this is of rare occurrence, and the harbour may be considered accessible at all seasons of the year, and as affording secure accommodation for 1000 sail of vessels of the largest capacity. There is sufficient depth of water for ships of 500 to 600 tons burthen, proceeding quite up to the town, and discharging their cargoes directly upon the quays. A tongue of land projects into the harbour from the main part of the town, on which is a spring of fine fresh water, which supplies all the shipping of the port, under local and judicious regulations. The ground is of sufficient width to afford convenient quay room and passage between it and a range of warehouses originally constructed of wood, but since 1800 substantially rebuilt four stories high, of brick. This is called Long Wharf, and is the principal focus of the coasting vessels. It leads from the harbour in a direct line up the principal street of the town, called State-street, in which are all the insurance offices and banking establishments, in and about which the principal merchants and traders assemble daily. At the upper end of this street is the old state-house, and contiguous is the court-house, record, and post-offices. Since 1806 vast improvements have taken place S. of Long Wharf; several extensive ranges of warehouses have been built, including a new custom-house, public sale-room, and observatory. The house in which the legislature of the state hold their sittings is on the W. side of the town; it is a spacious edifice of brick, and, having an elevated site, and being surmounted with a dome, is a very prominent object. The private residences on this side of the town are spacious and handsome, and exceeded by none in all America. In the market-place, N. of State-street, is a ponderous edifice supported by pillars, called Faneuil Hall, in which the town meetings are held. It has a theatre, several literary and benevolent institutions, and about thirty places for religious worship; and, independent of the neck, it is connected with the main land by four bridges; the first is on the N. side of the town, leading to Charlestown, a populous and important place; and, although not within the civil jurisdiction of Boston, commercially it may be regarded as an integral part, the two being as closely identified as Southwark and London. This bridge is upwards of 1500 feet in length; the second, on the W. side of the town, is about two-thirds of a mile in length, leading to Cambridge, distant about 4 miles, at which is the principal university in all America; the third is on the S. side of the town; and the last constructed is between those of Charlestown and Cambridge. These bridges are all of wood, but are well constructed, and the last two are as substantial and elegant as the materials of which they are constructed admit. They are all private or joint-stock properties, and encumbered with tolls. Boston is distinguished as the birth-place of Benjamin Franklin, and as the place which engendered the revolution that led to the independence of the United States. At an early period after the confederacy was acknowledged, the Bostonians embarked in the fur trade of the N. W. coast, which, by exchanging the skins in China for teas and silks, proved a source of vast wealth, and thereby laid the foundation of a general commerce, more extensive and important than in any other town of the union, except New York. Boston has several distilleries of rum from molasses, which is imported in large quantities from the Havannah and other West India islands, in exchange for flour, rice, lumber, and fish. It has a manufacture of window-glass, several roperies, and various manufactures of articles of primary necessity; and in the vicinity there are extensive tanneries and paper-mills. It is at present deficient in water communication inland; the harbour has been united with the Merrimack river by a canal, but the traffic has hitherto been inconsiderable. The local jurisdiction of the town is vested in seven select men, twelve overseers, and about fifty subordinate officers, elected annually. The population is 93,333, and if to this be added the population of Charlestown, and the population contiguous to Cambridge Bridge, and of Roxbury, continuous to the isthmus, all of which, in a social point of view, may be considered as having one common interest, and forming an undivided community, it will give a total population of 122,365. It is about 300 miles S. S. E. of Montreal, 210 N. E. of New York, and 436 N. E. by E. of Washington.

Bosworth, Market, a town in Leicestershire, with a market on Wednesday. In its vicinity, in 1468, was fought the famous battle between Richard III. and the Earl of Richmond, afterwards Henry VII., in which the former lost his crown and life. It is seated on a hill; 13 miles W. of Leicester, and 106 N. N. W. of London.

Bosworth, Husband, another town in Leicestershire; 14 miles S. of Leicester.

Boszra, a town of Syria, where Mahomet is said to have received much information from a Nestorian monk, towards founding his religious doctrines. It is 100 miles S. of Damascus.

Botany Bay, a bay of New South Wales, discovered by Cook in 1770, and so called from the great quantity of plants found on the shore. The promontories which form its entrance are named Cape Banks and Point Solander. The N. shore is 5¾ miles S. of Sydney, and was the first place colonized by Britain in 1788; the settlement was afterwards removed to Port Jackson. Here is a tower, and a memorial of Captain Cook's first landing, and also a column surmounted by a globe, to the memory of the unfortunate La Perouse. *See* New South Wales. Long. 151. 21. E. lat. 34. 0. S.

Botany Island, a small island in the Pacific Ocean, to the S. E. of New Caledonia. Long. 167. 17. E. lat. 22. 27. S.

Botesdale, a town in Suffolk, with a market on Thursday; seated in a valley; 15 miles N. E. of Bury, and 86 of London.

Botetourt, an interior county of Virginia, lying between the two most easterly ridges of the Allegany Mountains. The Roanoke and James Rivers have both their sources within this county; and it is bounded on the N. by the valley over which is the natural bridge, 90 feet in length, and 200 feet above the surface of the water. (*See* Cedar Creek.) Pop. 11,679. Fincastle, 194 miles W. of Richmond, is the chief town.

Bothnia, Gulf of, a large gulf of the Baltic, forming its northern continuity, extending in a N. by E. direction, from the Isle of Aland, in the lat. of 60., to Tornea, in the lat of 66. N., and having an average breadth of about 3 degrees of long., between 17. and 25. E. It is bounded on the W. by Sweden, and E. by Finland. It is completely frozen over in winter, and affords a convenient communication between Russia and the coasts of Sweden.

Bothnia, East, the northern Province of

Finland, extending from Finland Proper, in the lat. of 62. N., to the line of the arctic circle, which divides it from Lapland; lying on the E. shore of the Gulf of Bothnia, between 21. and 30. of E. longitude, bounded on the E. by the Russian province of Olonetz; containing an area of about 28,000 square miles, but having only about 70,000 inhabitants. It is generally low and marshy, intersected by lakes and small rivers abounding with fish—some salmon. The climate is generally unfavourable to vegetation. It has, however, some herds of small horned cattle, and bears and other furred animals are common; and it exports some fir timber, deals, tar, and pitch. It is divided into 28 parishes, under the ecclesiastical jurisdiction of the see of Abo, which favours the tenets of Luther. The inhabitants, with some little exception of Swedish, speak the Finnish language. The chief towns are Kazana, on the E. side, and Uleaborg, Brahestad, Carleby, Jacobstadt, Wasa, and Christianstadt, all on the shore of the Gulf of Bothnia. This province, with Finland, was ceded by Sweden to Russia in 1809.

BOTHNIA, WEST, a province of Sweden, lying between the W. shore of the Gulf of Bothnia and Lapland, extending S. from Angermanland, in the lat. of 63. 50. to that of 67. N. and 19. to 25. E. long. Its area is about half that of East Bothnia, and the population does not exceed 50,000. It differs but little in character from the eastern province; it abounds somewhat more in furred animals, which serve alike for subsistence and traffic. It is intersected by numerous streams, all running from W. to E. into the gulf. The four principal, rising from the mountains which divide Lapland from Norland, give name to as many districts and towns: viz. Tornea, at the head of the gulf, Lulea, Pitea, and Umea, at the S. extremity of the province, all upon the coast of the gulf. It contains some veins of copper and iron; but its chief exports are timber, deals, and tar. It is under the ecclesiastical jurisdiction of the see of Hernosand.

BOTHWELL, a town of Scotland, in the county of Lanark, situate on the E. bank of the Clyde, between Hamilton and Glasgow. It is distinguished for the battle fought in its vicinity in 1679, between the covenanters and the royal forces commanded by the Duke of Monmouth, when the former were completely defeated.

BOTTESFORD, a village in Leicestershire, on the confines of Nottinghamshire and Lincolnshire; 7 miles W. by N. of Grantham. Near it, on a lofty eminence, is Belvoir Castle, the ancient seat of the dukes of Rutland. In the church are several handsome monuments of that noble family; and many Roman antiquities have been found in the neighbourhood.

BOTWAR, a town in the N. part of the duchy of Wirtemburg, on a river of its name; 15 miles S. S. E. of Heilbron. Pop. about 2000.

BOTZEN, a large town in the interior of the Tyrol, beautifully located near the junction of the Eich and Eisach branches of the Adige river. It has some manufactures of silks, and has four fairs annually, numerously attended. The surrounding country produces excellent wine. It was taken by the French in March, 1797, but retaken by the Austrians immediately after. An Austrian commandant resides here. It is about 18 miles N. of Trent. Pop. about 8000.

BOTZEMBURGH, a town of Brandenburgh, in the Ucker Mark; 9 miles S. W. of Prentzlau, and about 50 N. of Berlin. It has a manufacture of silk.

BOUCHAIN, a fortified town of France, in the department of Nord, divided into two parts by the Scheldt. It was taken by the allies in 1711, under the Duke of Marlborough, but retaken the year following; and was invested by the Austrians in 1793, but soon relieved. It is 9 miles W. of Valenciennes.

BOUCHART, a town of France, in the department of Indre and Loire, situate on an island in the river Vienne; 15 miles S. S. W. of Tours.

BOUCHEMAIN, a town of France, in the department of Mayenne and Loire; 4 miles S. of Angers.

BOUCLANS, a town of France, in the department of Doubs; 8 miles E. of Besançon.

BOUDRY, a town of Switzerland, in the county of Neufchatel; 4 miles S. W. of Neufchatel. It was the birthplace of Marat.

BOUGAINVILLE'S STRAIT, in the South Pacific Ocean, between an island of the same name and the N. end of Solomon's Island, in the lat. of 7. S. and 156. E. long.

BOUILLON, a town of the Netherlands, in Luxemburg, with a castle, on an almost inaccessible rock. The French took it in 1676, when Louis XIV. gave it to the Duke of Bouillon. In 1794, this town was taken by storm, by General Beaulieu, after defeating a considerable body of French republicans, and given up to pillage. It is seated near the river Semoy, on the frontier of France; 6 miles N. N. E. of Sedan, and 46 W. by N. of Luxemburg.

BOUILLY, a town of France, in the department of Aube; 7 miles S. of Treves.

BOULAY, a town of France, in the department of Moselle; 13 miles N. of Metz.

BOULOGNE, a seaport of France, in the department of Pas de Calais. It is divided into two towns, the Upper and the Lower; the former is strongly fortified; but the latter is merely surrounded with walls. The port has for a long time been so shallow that no ships of burden could enter it; but, owing to some recent improvements, it is represented to hold ten feet at low water; and a large basin has lately been constructed to contain seventeen feet. The harbour is protected by a mole, to which very strong fortifications have been added. Under Buonaparte, Boulogne was made a royal port, and no merchant vessel, privateers, nor even prizes were admitted, unless loaded with ordnance or military stores, being the principal depôt of the armaments which he intended for the invasion of Britain. Since the peace in 1815 it has been much resorted to by the English, a great number of whom permanently reside here, which, with the influx of visitors from England, contribute essentially to the interest of the town and neighbourhood. Buonaparte commenced the erection of a tower, apparently intended to be carried to a great height, on which the French have recently erected his statue. It is 16 miles S. W. of Calais, in lat. 50. 46. N. and 1. 37. E. long. There is also another town of the same name in France, in the department of Upper Garonne, having several tanneries. It is 12 miles N. by W. of St. Gaudins.

Bounarbashi, a village in Asia Minor, province of Anadoli, near the Dardanelles, the undoubted site of ancient Troy. The plain of the Troad may still be traced, although some alterations have taken place in the various streams, &c.; but the main features remain to this day, and afford a proof of the veracity of the Homeric poem.

Bourbon, an island in the Indian Ocean, 50 miles long and 35 broad, lying 400 miles E. of Madagascar. It has not a safe harbour, but there are some roads for shipping. On the S. E. is a volcano. It is a fertile island; producing, in particular, the finest cotton, and excellent coffee. The French settled here in 1672. It surrendered to the English, after the capture of the Isle of France, on the 3rd of December, 1810. But Bourbon was restored at the general peace, in 1815; since when, the culture of sugar, coffee, and cotton, has been pursued with great avidity, by the aid of slaves obtained from Madagascar. It also produces a variety of woods, resins, gums, and flints. Wild goats and hogs abound in the mountains and woods. The cattle in the plains are numerous; and the coasts supply abundance of fish. On the whole, this island affords, not only all the means of subsistence, but of enjoyment, in a very high degree. Pop. about 150,000. St. Denis is the chief town, in lat. 20. 52. N. and 55. 30. E. long., about 100 miles S. of the Isle of France; which see.

Bourbon, an interior county in the N. W. part of the state of Kentucky. Pop. 14,478. Paris, situate in a fork of the S. branch of the Lickeny river, 40 miles E. of Frankfort, is the chief town.

Bourbon Lancy, a town of France, on the W. side of the department of Saone and Loire, celebrated for its hot mineral waters, and a large marble pavement, called the Great Bath, which is a work of the Romans. It is 28 miles S. W. of Autun. Pop. 2800.

Bourbon l'Archambaud, a town of France, in the department of Allier, celebrated for its hot baths, and for giving name to the family of the kings of France. It is situate near the river Allier; 15 miles W. of Moulins. Pop. 2600.

Bourbonne les Bains, a town of France, in the department of Upper Marne, famous for its hot baths; 18 miles E. N. E. of Langres. Pop. 3200.

Bourbonnois, a late province of France, bounded on the N. by Nivernois and Berry, W. by Berry and Marche, S. by Auvergne, and E. by Burgundy and Forez. It abounds in corn, fruit, pasture, wood, game, and wine. It now forms the department of Allier.

Bourbourg, a town of France, in the department of Nord, seated near the river Aa, and on a canal that communicates with Calais and Dunkirk; 10 miles S. W. of Dunkirk. Pop. 4100.

Bourdeaux, or Bordeaux, an ancient, large, and fine town of France, in the department of Gironde. It is built in the form of a crescent, on the W. bank of the river Garonne. The town has twelve gates; and the public edifices are noble, and the streets regular and handsome. The castle, called the Trumpet, is situated at the entrance of the quay, and the river runs round its walls. Most of the great streets lead to the quay. The quays are four miles in length, and the river, over which has been erected a magnificent bridge, is considerably broader than the Thames at London Bridge. On the opposite side, a range of hills, covered with woods, vineyards, churches, and villas, extend beyond the view. Almost in the centre of the town, a fine equestrian statue, in bronze, was erected to Louis XV. in 1743. The beauty of the Garonne, and the fertility of the adjoining country, were probably the causes which induced the Romans to lay the foundation of this city. The ruins of a very large amphitheatre yet remain, constructed under the Emperor Gallienus. During the irruptions of the barbarous nations, and particularly in those which the Normans repeatedly made, Bordeaux was ravaged, burnt, and almost entirely destroyed. But when Henry II. of England united it to his dominions, by his marriage with Eleanor of Aquitaine, he made it a principal object of his policy to rebuild and restore it to its ancient lustre. Edward, the Black Prince, brought his royal captive, John, king of France, to this city, after the battle of Poictiers, in 1356; and held his court and residence here during eleven years. His exalted character, his uninterrupted series of good fortune, his victories, and his munificence, drew strangers to Bordeaux from every part of Europe. Here his son, Richard II., was born. Bordeaux contains upwards of 100,000 inhabitants, and is one of the first cities in France for magnitude and beauty; and is justly esteemed as one of the most agreeable abodes in Europe. The cathedral, and the churches belonging to the late religious orders, the Dominicans and Chartreux, are much admired. According to the present religious establishment of France, Bordeaux is the seat of an archbishop. The town has a university, and an academy of arts and sciences; and a considerable export trade, particularly in fruit, wine, and brandy. In March, 1812, Bordeaux was entered by the English, after the battle of Orphes, but evacuated on the restoration of the Bourbons. It was the birthplace of Ausonius. It lies 87 miles S. of Rochelle, and 325 S. W. of Paris. Long. 0. 34. W. lat. 44. 50. N. There is a village of the same name, department of Drome, 18 miles N. of Nyons. It was the birthplace of Casaubon, and contains 1200 inhabitants.

BOURG-EN-BRASSE, the capital of the department of Ain. Near it is the magnificent church and monastery of the Augustins, which contains the mausoleum of Margaret of Austria, and of Charles V. The principal commerce is in corn, horses, cattle, and white leather. It stands in a marshy but fertile country, on the river Ressousse; 36 miles N. E. of Lyons, and 233 S. S. E. of Paris. It was the birthplace of Lalande. Pop. about 7300.

BOURG-SUR-MER, in the department of Gironde, with a tide-harbour on the Dordogne, near the point of land formed by the junction of that river with the Garonne, on its north side. It has a great trade in wine, and is 15 miles N. by E. of Bordeaux. Pop. 2700.

BOURG ACHARD, and THEROUDE, department of Eure; ST. ANDEOL, of Ardeche; ARGENTAL, of the Rhone; D'AULT, of Somme; DEOLS, of Indre; LASTIC, of Isere; D'OISANS, of ditto; DE PEAGE, of the Drone; LA REINE, of the Seine, &c., are all inconsiderable.

BOURGANEUF, a town of France, in the department of Creuse. Here is a lofty tower, faced with stones cut diamond-wise, erected by Zisim, brother of Bajazet II., emperor of the Turks, when he was obliged to exile himself, after the loss of a decisive battle. Bourganeuf is seated on the Taurion; 20 miles N. E. of Limoges. Pop. about 2000.

BOURGAS, a town in Turkey in Europe, pach. Roumelia, on the N. shore of a gulf of the same name, on the Black Sea; 130 miles N. W. of Constantinople.

BOURGES, a city of France, capital of the department of Cher, and an archiepiscopal see, with a university, founded by Louis XI., the Nero of France, who was born here. In extent, it is one of the greatest cities in France. The principal manufactures are cloth, woollen stuffs, and stockings; but the trade is inconsiderable. It is seated at the conflux of the Auron and Yevre; 25 miles N. W. of Nevers, and 125 S. of Paris. Pop. 18,200.

BOURGET, a town of Savoy, on a lake of the same name, near the Rhone; 6 miles N. of Chambery.

BOURGNEUF, a seaport of France, in the department of Lower Loire. The chief trade is in salt, made from the adjacent salt-marshes. It stands on a bay to which it gives name; 20 miles S. W. of Nantes. It has an oyster fishery on the coast. Pop. about 2000. Long. 1. 51. W. lat. 47. 3. N.

BOURGOIN, a town of France, in the department of Isere. Some hemp is grown in the vicinity, and it has some manufactures in chintz. Pop. about 3600.

BOURGUEIL, a town of France, in the department of Indre and Loire; 22 miles W. of Tours. It has a Benedictine abbey and castle. Pop. about 2800.

BOURLOS, a large lake, or bay, lying between Rosetta and Damietta branches of the Nile. On the East Cape is a town called *Bourlos*, in the lat. of 31. 36. N. and 31. 27. E. long.

BOURMONT, a town of France, in the department of Upper Marne, on a steep mountain; 20 miles E. by N. of Chaumont.

BOURN, a town in Lincolnshire, with a market on Saturday. It has a navigable canal to Boston, and is seated at the source of a rivulet that runs to Spalding; 35 miles S. of Lincoln, and 97 N. of London.

BOURO, one of the Molucca islands, in the Banda Sea, between Celebes and Ceram; about 90 miles long and 30 broad. Some mountains in it are extremely high, and the sea on one side is uncommonly deep. It is represented as being exceedingly fertile, yielding abundance of rice. One of its peculiar vegetable productions is the *melaleuca catigolia*, from the leaves of which the cajeputa oil is extracted, which forms one of the principal articles of traffic. The nutmeg, clove, cocoa, banana, and ebony trees, as well as the orange, lemon, citron, &c., are also common to the island. The natives, who live mostly in the interior, are represented to be as rude and unsocial as those of Borneo, to whom they bear a close affinity in feature, manner, and character. Wild boars, goats, and hog deer, range in the woods, which are also much infested with reptiles, and some of an enormous size. There is a town of the same name, on the shore of a commodious bay, called Cajeli, on the N. E. part of the island, in lat. 3. 25. S. and 127. E. long., where the Dutch have a fort; whose policy precludes alike all social improvement among the natives, whilst it constitutes a barrier to the attainment of all knowledge of the details of their numbers, economy, and resources. Some Mahometans, and natives of other islands, who live in subservience to the Dutch., inhabit the towns upon the coast. Pop. 60,000.

BOURTHES, a town of France, in the department of Pas de Calais; 12 miles S. E. of Boulogne.

BOUSSAC, a town of France, in the department of Creuse, with a castle on a rock; 25 miles N. E. of Gueret.

BOUTON, an island of the Indian Ocean, lying off the S. E. promontory of the island of Celebes; about 180 miles in length from N. to S., and 25 in breadth. It is in part mountainous and woody, but in other parts exceedingly fertile. The natives appear to be of Malayan origin, professing the Mahometan faith. It is governed by a sultan, who lives in considerable state, and whose authority extends over some small islands contiguous. Forts are constructed on several inaccessible heights, in different parts of the island. It is said to produce cotton of a very superior quality, which the natives manufacture into cloth. The N. point of the island is in lat. 4. 21. S. and 123. 5. E. long. The Dutch attempted to establish themselves upon this island; but their perfidy led to a general massacre, and they have not since renewed the attempt. There is a town of the same name at the N. W. extremity of the island, at which the sultan usually resides. There is also another island (a small one) called *Bouton*, off the Malay coast, in lat. 6. 25. N. and 99. 15. E. long.

BOUTONNE, a river of France, rising in the department of *Deux Sevres*, becomes navigable at St. Jean D'Angely, and falls into the Charente, about 10 miles above Rochefort. There is a town of the same name, on the N. bank of the river; about 18 miles W. of St. Jean D'Angely.

BOUVIGNES, a small fortified town of the Netherlands, on the W. bank of the Meuse; about 14 miles S. of Namur.

BOUZDOGAN, a town in the S.W. part of Natolia; about 18 miles N.W. of Melasso.

BOUZOK, a town of Asiatic Turkey, near the N.E. confines of Caramania, and near the source of a branch of the Kisil Irmak river, which falls into the Black Sea.

BOUZONVILLE, a town of France, in the department of Moselle, on the river Nied; 27 miles N. E. of Metz.

BOVA, a town of Naples, in Calabria Ultra, at the southern extremity of the promontory of Italy. The inhabitants are supposed to be descendants of Albanians, great numbers of whom are scattered over the adjacent country. Pop. of Bova about 2300.

BOVELLES, a town of France, in the department of Somme; 6 miles W. S. W. of Amiens.

BOVENDEN, or BAWARDEN, a town in the principality of Callenberg; about 3 miles N. of Gottingen.

BOVENSE, or BORGENSE, a town on the N. coast of the island of Funen, from whence there is a ferry over to Klakring, in Jutland.

BOVES, a populous town in Piedmont; a few miles S. of Coni.

BOVIGNES, a town of the Netherlands, in Namur, on the river Meuse; 10 miles S. of Namur.

BOVINO, a town of Naples, in Capitanata, seated at the foot of the Appennines; 15 miles N. E. of Benevento.

BOW, or STRATFORD-LE-BOW, one of the out-parishes of London, on the E. side. The church is 4 miles from the Royal Exchange. Bow is situate at the S. E. extremity of the county of Middlesex, separated from Essex by the river Lea. (*See* BLACKWALL.) The church is very ancient; and an old stone bridge over the river is supposed to have been the first erected in England, and the curve or bow of the arch to have given name to the town. Over this bridge is the great outlet from London, to the three eastern counties of England, viz. Essex, Suffolk, and Norfolk.

BOW, one of the Society Isles at the S. E. extremity of the cluster, in lat. 18. 23. S. and 141. 10. W. long. It was discovered by Captain Cook, on his first voyage; but, with 130 fathom of line, no bottom could be found for anchorage. It seemed barren; but from appearance of smoke, it was conjectured either to be inhabited or volcanic.

BOWES, a town at the N.W. extremity of the county of York, situate at the foot of the mountains on the frontier of Westmoreland, on one of the Roman military ways, now the high road from London to Carlisle. Its antiquity is further manifest, from a stone in the church, which, at the commencement of the last century, was used as a communion-table, on which is an adulatory inscription to the Emperor Adrian. It holds a market on Fridays; 53 miles S. by E. of Carlisle; and 250 N. by W. of London.

BOWMORE, a town of the isle of Islay, on the coast of Argyleshire, on the E. coast of Loch Indal.

BOWNES, a village in Westmoreland, on the E. side of Windermere-water; 9 miles W. by N. of Kendal. It is a great mart for fish and charcoal, and the chief place for trading, and pleasure-boats used in navigating the lake.

BOWNESS, a village in Cumberland, at the W. end of the Picts' Wall, on Solway Frith; 13 miles W. by N. of Carlisle. It was a Roman station, called Blatum Bulgium; and from hence Antoninus began his Itinerary.

BOXBERG, a town of Germany, in the grand duchy of Baden, with an ancient castle on an eminence; seated on the Tauber; 13 miles W. of Mergentheim.

BOXTEL, a town of the Netherlands, in Brabant, seated on the river Commel, and furnished with sluices. Here the British and Dutch troops, under the Duke of York, were defeated by the French in 1704. It is 8 miles S. of Bois le Duc. Pop. 2650.

BOYLE, a populous parish and town of Ireland, in the county of Roscommon, on the frontier of Sligo. Here are the ruins of an abbey, near the lake Key, and manufactures of linen and yarn. It has extensive barracks; seated on the river Boyle; 23 miles N. of Roscommon, and 86 N.W. of Dublin.

BOYNE, a river of Ireland, which rises in the N. part of the county of Kildare, crosses the county of Meath, past Trim and Navan, and enters the Irish Channel below Drogheda. In this river and on its banks James II. was defeated by William III. in 1690.

BOZOLO, a fortified town of Italy, in the Mantuan; seated on the Oglio; 15 miles S. W. of Mantua.

BRA, a large town of Piedmont, in the province of Alba, situate near the junction of the Stura with the Tanaro river; 10 miles S. E. of Carmagnola. Pop. about 10,000. Cherasco, with a further population of about 11,000, is situate on the opposite bank of the river.

BRAAN, a river of Scotland, in Perthshire, which descends from the hills E. of Loch Tay, and flows into the Tay above Dunkeld. Upon this river is a grand scene, at a place called the Rumbling-bridge. Under an arch, thrown over a narrow chasm, between two projecting rocks, the river is precipitated in a fall of near 50 feet.

BRABANT, a territory in the N. W. part of Europe, lying between the lat. of 50. 30. and 51. 35. N. and 4. and 5. 10. E. long., divided between Belgium and Holland.

BRABANT, NORTH, a province and kingdom of Holland; 90 miles long and 45 miles broad, and contains a population of 305,000. It was made a duchy in the 7th century, and was considered as the first state of the kingdom of the Netherlands. This portion of the duchy was seized by the republic of Holland, in the 17th century, when it acquired the name of Dutch Brabant, and in 1810 was annexed to the French empire, but was restored to the Dutch. Principal towns are Bois le Duc, Bergen-op-Zoom, and Breda.

Brabant, South, a province of Belgium; 63 miles in length, 36 miles broad, and contains a population of 450,700. It is beautiful and fertile. It was separated from Holland by the Belgian insurrection in 1830, and is now the principal province of the kingdom. Brussels is the capital.

Bracadale, a town and parish on the W. coast of the isle of Skye, one of the Hebrides, or Western Islands of Scotland.

Bracciano, a town of Italy, in the patrimony of St. Peter; celebrated for manufactures of paper, the ruins of Veig, and some warm baths in its vicinity. It is situated on a lake of the same name; 12 miles N.W. of Rome.

Bracciglano, a town of Naples, in Principato Citeriore; 7 miles N.N. W. of Salerno.

Bracken, a frontier county on the N. E. side of Kentucky, bounded by the Ohio River. Pop. 5280. Augusta, on the Ohio, 90 miles N. E. of Frankfort, is the chief town.

Brackenheim, a town of the duchy of Wirtemberg; about 6 miles W. of the Neckar at Lauffen, and 18 N. of Stuttgard. Pop. about 1500. It has a well endowed hospital.

Brackenidge, or Breckenridge, another frontier county of Kentucky, towards the N. E., bounded also by the Ohio river. Pop. 7845. Hardenberg, in the centre of the county, 110 miles W. S. W. of Frankfort, is the chief town.

Brackley, a town of Northamptonshire; market on Wednesday. It contains two churches, and had formerly a college, now a free school. It is seated on the Ouse; 18 miles S. S. W. of Northampton, and 63 N.W. of London.

Braclaw, a strong town in the S. of Russian Poland, capital of the palatinate of its name, in Podolia. It stands on the river Bog; 85 miles E. of Kaminiek.

Bradfield, a town in Essex, seated on the river Blackwater; 16 miles N. of Chelmsford, and 44 N. N. E. of London.

Bradfield is also the name of a township in the parish of Ecclesfield; 6 miles N. of Sheffield, in the manufactures of which it is extensively occupied. It is also the name of seven other towns and villages in different parts of England; all inconsiderable.

Bradford, a town in Wiltshire, with a market on Monday. It is the centre of the greatest fabric of superfine cloths in England. It stands on the side of a rocky hill, on the Lower Avon; 10 miles N. by W. of Warminster, and 100 W. of London.

Bradford, a large and populous parish and borough in the West Riding of Yorkshire. It returns one member to parliament. In the town are about forty large dealers in wool, about thirty large establishments for the spinning of ditto, and sixty employers for the weaving of ditto into various kinds of stuffs. It has five or six extensive iron foundries, as many machine manufactories, and several employers both in the manufacture of hats and combs; the cotton manufacture has also established itself here, which is thus one of the principal manufacturing towns in the kingdom. The town is situate at the foot of the ridge of mountains which divides the West Riding of Yorkshire from Lancashire, on the banks of a small river, falling into the Aire on the south side. It has also the advantage of a collateral cut to the Leeds and Liverpool Canal; and consequently a facility of communication by water with all parts of the kingdom. The surrounding country abounds in iron ore, coal, flag-stones, and slates. The parish church is a stately Gothic edifice: a new church, built by subscription, was opened in 1815. It has several other religious places of worship, a free grammar school, and a market-hall for the exhibition of the worsted stuffs brought for sale. Market on Thursday. It is 10 miles W. of Leeds, and 9 N. E. of Halifax.

Bradford, derived from two Saxon words, implying *broad ford*, is the name of six other towns and villages in different parts of England, situate on the banks of streams that formerly used to be forded.

Bradford, a north frontier county of Pennsylvania, bordering on Tioga and Broome counties, state of New York. It is intersected by the E. branch of the Susquehannah river, which receives numerous collateral branches flowing from all directions within the county. Pop. 32,769. Meansville, or Towanda, 189 miles N. by E. of Harrisburg, is the chief town.

Bradford, a town of Massachusets, in Essex county, where some vessels are built, and shoes made for exportation. It is situate on the Merimack, opposite Haverhill; 10 miles W. of Newbury Port. It is also the name of several other towns in different parts of the United States.

Bradley, derived from two Saxon words, *broad ley*, the latter signifying meadow or pasture land, is the name of about twenty towns and villages in different parts of England; all inconsiderable.

Braga, a city of Portugal, capital of Entre Douro-e-Minho, and the see of an archbishop, primate of Portugal. It contains four churches, besides the cathedral, and eight convents. There are some ruins of an amphitheatre, and an aqueduct. It is seated in a fertile country, on the Cavado; about 25 miles N. by E. of Oporto, and 180 miles N. of Lisbon.

Braganza, a city of Portugal, in Trazos Montes, capital of a duchy of the same name. It is divided into the Old and the New Town: the former is on an eminence, surrounded by double walls, now in ruins; and the latter is on a plain, at the foot of a mountain, defended by a fort. It seated on the Fervanza; 32 miles N. N. W. of Miranda, and 88 N. E. of Oporto. The duchy was constituted in 1442, and the possessor of the title was raised to the throne of Portugal in 1640, and has continued in succession to the present time. Pop. 2700.

BRAHESTAD, one of the five principal towns of the Russian province of East Bothnia, situate on the E. coast of the Gulf of Bothnia; about 30 miles S. S. W. of Uleaborg; in lat. 64. 40. N. and 24. 30. E. long.

BRAHMAPOOTRA. *See* BURAMPOOTER.

BRAILA, BRAHILOW, or IBRAILA, a fortified town of European Turkey, situate on the N. bank of the Danube, at the E. extremity of the province of Wallachia, a few miles S. of Galatz, and about 320 N. by W. of Constantinople. Pop. 30,000.

BRAILOW, or BRAHYLOW, a town of Poland, in Podolia, on the river Bog; 30 miles N. W. of Braclaw.

BRAIN LE COMTE, a town of the Netherlands, in Hainault; 15 miles S. S. W. of Brussels. Pop. about 3000.

BRAINTREE, a town of Essex, with a market on Wednesday. It has a considerable manufacture of baize, and is joined on the N. by the extensive village of Bocking. It is seated on the river Blackwater; 11 miles N. by E. of Chelmsford, and 40 N. E. of London.

BRAINTREE, a town of Massachusets, in Norfolk county, seated on a bay; 8 miles S. by E. of Boston. It was the birthplace of John Adams, second, and father of the sixth president, of the United States.

BRAKEL, a town of Westphalia, in the principality of Paderborn, on the rivulet Brught; 16 miles E. of Paderborn.

BRALIO, a mountain of the Alps, in the country of the Grisons, which separates the valley of Munster from the county of Bormio. It is supposed to be the same which Tacitus mentions under the name of Juga Rhætica.

BRAMANT, a town of Savoy, on the river Arc; 20 miles E. S. E. of St. Jean de Maurienne.

BRAMBER, a village in Sussex. It is seated on the Adur, immediately contiguous to Steyning; 51 miles S. by W. of London.

BRAMPTON, a town in Cumberland, with a market on Tuesday. On the top of a high hill is a fortified trench, called the Moat. It is seated on the river Irthing; 9 miles E. N. E. of Carlisle, and 311 N. N. W. of London.

BRAMPTON is the name of twelve other towns and villages; and *Bram*, derived from a Saxon word implying a bushy country, precedes the termination of the names of upwards of twenty other towns and villages in different parts of England; all inconsiderable.

BRAMSTEDT, a town of Lower Saxony, in Holstein, near which is a medicinal spring. It is seated on the Bram; 21 miles N. of Hamburg.

BRANAW, or BRAUNAU, a town of Bohemia, on the confines of Silesia, with a manufacture of coloured cloth; 11 miles N. W. of Glatz.

BRANCALEONE, a town of Naples, in Calabria Ulteriore; 9 miles S. E. of Bova, at the S. extremity of the promontory of Italy.

BRANCASTER, a village in Norfolk; 4 miles W. by N. of Burnham. It was the ancient Branodunum, a considerable Roman city, and has now a great trade in malt.

BRANDEIS, a town of Bohemia, in the circle of Kaurzim, on the S. bank of the river Elbe; 10 miles N. E. of Prague.

BRANDENBURG, ELECTORAL MARQUISATE OF, an interior and irregularly shaped territory of Europe, in the circle of Upper Saxony; lying between the lats. of 51. 45. and 54. N.; and 11. and 16. of E. long. It is separated from the Baltic, on the north, by Mecklenburg and Pomerania; bounded on the east by Prussian Poland, and on the south by the duchy of Saxony and principality of Anhalt; and on the west by Magdeburg. Its area may be estimated at about 12,000 square miles. From the tenth to the fifteenth century this territory passed under various governments subject to Poland, when, in 1417, it was vested in perpetuity, by the emperor Sigismund, with consent of the Germanic confederacy, to Frederic VI. of Nuremberg, and his descendants; a succeeding margrave having been acknowledged sovereign of the then duchy of Prussia, which in 1701 was converted into a kingdom. The seat of government was transferred from Konigsberg, in Prussia, to Berlin in Brandenburg, which has thereby become the chief part of the Prussian dominions. It is divided into the five following parts: viz. the Old Mark, W.; Prignitz, N. W.; Middle Mark, S.; Ucker Mark, N.; and the New Mark, on the E. It is in part a sandy and sterile district; but, having the advantage of several navigable rivers, and by the aid of culture, it is rendered tolerably productive in all that is necessary for subsistence and comfort. The revocation of the edict of Nantes, which, in 1685, drove thousands of the most industrious and intelligent of the manufacturing population of France from their homes, led to a number of them settling in this part of Europe, where they introduced their respective occupations in the manufacture of silk and worsted stuffs, which now contributes essentially to the reciprocal benefit of the various classes of the country. The principal rivers are, 1st, the Oder, which enters the New Mark from the S., runs N. past Frankfort, Kustrin, and Schwedt, through Pomerania, into the Baltic; 2nd, the Netze, enters the New Mark from the E., and falls into the Oder at Kustrin; 3rd, the Spree, enters the Middle Mark from the S., runs W. by N., falling into the Havel W. of Berlin; 4th, the Havel rises near the S. confines of the Ucker Mark, runs S. to Potsdam, when it makes a circuitous course W., to the town of Brandenburg, then N. to Havelberg, where it falls into the Elbe; 5th, the Elbe, from the S. E., divides the Old Mark from the Prignitz; the Havel is also united with the Elbe by a canal across the principality of Magdeburg, from Brandenburg, past Gentin; and with the Oder by another canal from Liebenwalde, past Neustadt, to Oderberg; the Spree is also united with the Oder by a canal from the S. E. extremity of the Middle Mark, to the point where the Oder enters the New Mark from Lusatia. The population of this part of the Prussian dominions amounts to about 1,250,000, who contribute a money tax equal to about 1,000,000*l*.

sterling per annum. The inhabitants are mostly dissenters from the church of Rome, indulging in the peculiar tenets of Luther, who promulgated his doctrines at Wittemberg; and some of Calvin; but the state makes no distinction; religious profession, be it what it may, being no obstacle to civil service. The following is a statement of the principal towns in each of the five divisions: viz.—

1. *Prignitz*, Wittemberg, Putlitz, Perleberg.
2. *Old Mark*, Werben, Osterberg, Kalbe.
3. *Middle ditto*, Brandenburg, Potsdam, Berlin.
4. *Ucker ditto*, Prenzlo, Boytzenburg, Angermunde.
5. *New ditto*, Falkenburg, Arenswald, Kustrin.

BRANDENBURG, the city which gives name to the preceding territory, is divided into two parts, Old and New; the former on the N. bank of the river Havel, and the latter on the S. It is a place of considerable antiquity, supposed to have been first founded by the Sclavonians, and fortified in the early part of the tenth century, as a barrier against the incursions of the Huns. It has various manufactures. Pop. about 13,000. It is about 30 miles S. of Havelsberg, and about the same distance W. of Berlin. There are two other towns named Brandenburg; one in Mecklenburg-Strelitz, surrounded by walls. The streets are wide and straight; the church of St. Mary is a large structure, and the town-house is worthy of notice. It is situate on the Toliensee; 72 miles N. of Berlin: and the other in East Prussia, with an ancient castle, at the S. end of the Frische Haff; 13 miles S. W. of Konigsberg.

BRANDON, a town in Suffolk, with a market on Friday. It stands on the Little Ouse, over which is a bridge, and a ferry a mile below, for conveying goods to and from the isle of Ely. It has a great trade in corn, malt, coal, timber, &c.; and in the vicinity are extensive rabbit warrens. It is 15 miles N. by W. of Bury, and 78 N. N. E. of London.

BRANDYWINE, a river of Chester county, in the S. E. part of Pennsylvania, which falls into the Delaware, a little below Wilmington. It is distinguished in American history for a defeat sustained by the revolutionary army, on the 11th of September, 1777.

BRASIL. *See* BRAZIL.

BRASLAW, or BRESLAU, a city of Lithuania, in the palatinate of Wilna, on the N. side of a lake which co nunicates with the Dwina; 76 miles N. N. E. of Wilna.

BRASSA, or BRESSAY, one of the Shetland islands. Between this and the principal island, called Mainland, is the noted Brassa Sound, where 1000 sail of vessels may at once find commodious mooring.

BRASSAW, or CRONSTADT, a strong town in the S. E. part of Transylvania, on the river Burezel; 50 miles E. by N. of Hermanstadt.

BRASS TOWN, a town of Tennessee, situate near the source of the Hiwasse, about 100 miles S. of Knoxville. Two miles S. of this town is the Enchanted Mountain, much famed for the curiosities found on its rocks, which consist of impressions resembling the tracks of turkeys, bears, horses, and human beings, as perfect as they could be made on snow or sand.

BRATTLEBOROUGH, a town of Vermont, in Winham county, situate on the Connecticut; 28 miles E. of Bennington, and 70 N. N. W. of Boston.

BRAUBACH, a town of Germany, in the Westerwald, with a castle; seated on the Rhine; 8 miles S. of Coblentz.

BRAUNAU, a fortified town of Bavaria, formerly the residence of the elector. In 1742 it was taken by the Austrians; and, in 1779, by the peace of Teschen, the town and its district were ceded to Austria. In 1805 it was captured by the French and Bavarians. It is seated on the E. bank of the river Inn, on the frontier of Upper Austria; 28 miles S. W. of Passau, to which country it now belongs.

BRAUNAU, a town on the eastern frontier of the circle of Koningsgratz, bordering on Silesia. It is a manufacturing town, and has a rich Benedictine abbey.

BRAUNFELS, capital of the county of Solms. Here is a magnificent palace, the seat of the prince of Solms-Braunfels; and near it is the decayed castle of Solms. It is seated near the Lahn; 10 miles W. by S. of Wetzlar. Long. 8. 23. E. lat. 50. 30. N.

BRAUNSBURG, a town of West Prussia, in Ermeland. It has an academy for catholics, established in 1783; and is seated on the Passarge, near its entrance into the Frische Haff. It exports great quantities of linen yarn to England; 18 miles N. E. of Elbing. Long. 19. 58. E. lat. 54. 30. N.

BRAUNSTON, a village in Northamptonshire; 4 miles N. W. of Daventry, and 73 from London; on the confines of Warwickshire. Here commences the Grand Junction Canal, under a tunnel three-fourths of a mile in length, to the Thames, which, with the Oxford and Coventry canals, renders it the centrical place of inland navigation.

BRAVA, a republic on the southern extremity of the kingdom of Magadoxa, and the only one in Africa. It was founded by seven Arabian brethren, who fled hither from the tyranny of Lacah, a petty monarch of Arabia. Finding a most delightful situation between two rivers, near their confluence into the Indian Ocean, they built the city of Brava, which is now large and populous, and the greatest mart on all the coast. Its merchants are rich, carrying on an extensive trade in gold, silver, elephants' teeth, ambergris, silk, cotton, and other stuffs. The republic is under the protection of the king of Portugal, for which they pay a tribute of about 20*l.* annually. The city of Brava lies in long. 43. 25. E. lat. 1. 20. N.

BRAVA, one of the Cape Verd Islands; 12 miles W. S. W. of Fuego, and inhabited by the Portuguese. The land is high and mountainous, but fertile; and horses, beeves, asses, and hogs are numerous. It has three harbours, but Porto Ferreo, on the S. side, is the best for large ships. Long. 24. 39. W. lat. 14. 52. N.

Bray, a town of Ireland, in the county of Wicklow, seated on the river Bray, near St. George's Channel; 13 miles S. of Dublin.

Bray, a village in Berkshire; 1 mile S. of Maidenhead. It is famous in song for its vicar, who was twice a papist and twice a protestant, in four successive reigns; and, when taxed with being a turncoat, said, "he always kept to his principle, to live and die vicar of Bray."

Brazil, a vast territory of South America, lying between the lats. of 4. N. and 35. S., and 35. and 72. of W. long.: but, being triangular in form, converging into a point southerly, its area will not exceed 2,000,000 of square miles, though estimated by some writers as exceeding 3,000,000. The first discovery of Brazil has been claimed for a Martin Behmen, who is said to have visited it in 1487; but the credit of making it known to Europeans is assigned to the Portuguese admiral Pedro Alvades Cabral, who sailed from Lisbon on the 9th of March, 1500, with a squadron of thirteen sail, destined for the East Indies; when, stretching more than usual to the westward, to avoid the storms that prevail off the Cape of Good Hope, he accidentally discovered this fine territory, in the lat. of 16. S., on the 24th of April; and, having communicated with the natives, who manifested a social disposition, anchored his squadron in the Bay of Porto Seguro, and, on the following day, landed and planted the cross, and took possession of the territory in the name of Emanuel, the then king of Portugal. For nearly fifty years, however, it was but little appreciated; there being no indications of gold, silver, or gems, upon the coast: it was merely availed of as a place for transportation for criminals, the ships conveying them carrying back nothing but the red wood so important in dyeing: and its capabilities would probably have remained much longer undisclosed, but for the banishment of the Jews from Portugal in 1549; who, by the assistance of their friends in other parts of the world, introduced the sugar-cane from Madeira, which flourished to such a degree as soon to render it an object of great importance; and although its profuse treasures of gold, silver, and gems remained undisclosed, enough had been discovered, and the celebrity of the colony became sufficiently general, by the close of the century, to excite the jealousy and cupidity alike of the French, Spaniards, and Dutch; and in 1624 the Dutch dispatched a squadron, under the command of Admiral Willikens, who succeeded in taking possession of St. Salvador, or Bahia, the then principal settlement, and proclaimed the possession of the whole territory; and, after having published a manifesto, allowing *liberty of conscience* to all who were disposed to subscribe an oath of fidelity to the Dutch republic, and plundered the town, he returned to Holland. The Spaniards next sent a formidable squadron, who completely dislodged the Dutch; but, in 1630, the Dutch again returned to the charge with a force of not less than forty-six armed ships, and, after seven or eight years of continued warfare, succeeded in extending their influence over more than half the country; but their oppressive and exclusive policy became so obnoxious to the settlers as to render their tenure exceedingly precarious; so that, after various collisions and alternations of success between Dutch, Spaniards, and Portuguese, towards the close of the seventeenth century, the Dutch, by treaty, ceded all their interest to the Portuguese; and the influence of the Spaniards having been previously subverted, at the commencement of the 18th century the whole territory came into the possession of the Portuguese, with whom it remained for more than a century, silently advancing in cultivation and importance, though, comparatively speaking, but little known to the world, until the events of the twenty years' war, growing out of the French revolution in 1793, led, in 1807, to the emigration of the Portuguese court from Lisbon, under the protection of a British squadron, to seek shelter at Rio Janeiro.

From this period, the barriers which had previously confined the intercourse of the Brazils to Portugal, were at once annihilated, and its features, condition, character, and resources, laid fairly open to the view and intercourse of the world. Since then, cultivation has been vastly extended, and its supply of productions doubled, trebled, and, in some cases, quadrupled. For purposes of civil and military jurisdiction, it has been divided into the 13 following districts, viz., 1st. Guiana, comprising the whole extent of country N. of the main branch of the Amazon river, bounded on the N. by the New Colombian territory and French Guiana. 2nd. Para, which comprises a vast tract extending from the frontier of Peru, the whole breadth of the country parallel with Para, S. of the main branch of the Amazon, to the Atlantic Ocean; and the following nine border on the Atlantic coast, beginning at the N., viz.

3. Maranham.	8. Rio Janeiro.
4. Seara.	9. St. Paul.
5. Pernambuco.	10. St. Catharine.
6. Bahia.	11. Rio Grande.
7. Minas Geraes.	

12. Goyaz, interior; and, 13, Matto Grosso, on the frontier of the United Provinces of Buenos Ayres. The extent and production of each of these districts will be more fully elucidated under their respective heads. Independent of the noble river Amazon, which has one of its sources near the shore of the Pacific Ocean, and, by numerous collateral branches, opens a communication with the whole interior of Peru, and dividing the before-mentioned provinces of Guiana and Para, the Madeira, Tapajoz, Xingu, Araguay, and the Tocantins, all flowing from the S. into the Amazon, intersect all the interior and northern part of Brazil; whilst the Paraguay and Parana, with innumerable branches, intersect all the southern part, running S. into the great river La Plata. In addition to these,

the Pinare, Barbadoes, Parnaiba, St. Francisco, and numerous others of minor note, intersect all the maritime provinces, falling into the Atlantic Ocean.

A chain of mountains intersect the maritime provinces from S. to N., from Rio Grande to the St. Francisco River, which separates the province of Bahia from Pernambuco. The ground rises gradually from the coast to the summit of this ridge, which varies in altitude from 3000 to 5000 feet above the level of the sea. Westward of this ridge, the ground gradually slopes till it again ascends to form another mountain ridge of somewhat greater altitude than the preceding, dividing Goyaz from the maritime provinces, and running E. of, and parallel with, the Tocantins to its entrance into the Para mouth of the Amazons. From this chain a collateral ridge branches off, intersecting the province of Seara, in a direction from S. to N., to near the shore of the Atlantic Ocean.

Over so vast a tract of land, it cannot be imagined that the climate will be found at all equal, or the seasons uniform. The northern provinces are subject to heavy rains, variable winds, tornadoes, storms, and the utmost fury of the elements; while the southerly regions are favoured with all the comforts which a fine fertile soil and temperate climate can afford. In some of the provinces the heat of the climate favours the generation of a variety of poisonous insects and reptiles; some of which, as the *liboya*, or roebuck snake, are said to extend to the length of thirty feet, and to be two or three yards in circumference. The rattlesnake, and other reptiles of the same kind, grow likewise to an enormous size; and the serpent called *ibabaloka* is affirmed to be seven yards long, and half a yard in circumference, possessed too of a poison instantaneously fatal to the human race. Here also are scorpions, ant-bears, tigers, the jaguar, porcupines, janonveras, and an animal called *tapirassou*, which is the production of a bull and an ass, having a great resemblance to both. No part of the world affords a greater number of beautiful birds, or greater variety of the most exquisite fruits; the chief indigenous vegetable production, which gave name to the country and title of prince to the heir presumptive of the sovereignty of Portugal, is the *lignum Brasilianum*, or Brazil wood, so justly celebrated for its colouring properties. Forests of trees, as stately in size as endless in variety, intermixed with brambles and creeping plants, flowering in every variety and tinge of colour, emitting the most delicious odours, and for hundreds of square miles in extent so dense as to be quite impenetrable, except to the native Indians, are spread over the greater part of the country from the sea-coast to the Araguay river, which separates Goyaz from Matto Grosso, which is, as its name partly implies, a sandy and arid district. In the cultivated parts, the *palma Christi*, orange, lemon, citron, and various other trees and plants, flourish in the utmost luxuriance; and among the inducted plants, the sugar-cane, coffee tree, and cotton plant, are yielding an increasing supply of their respective products, of the very choicest quality; but the productions for which Brazil has hitherto been the most celebrated, are its gems, gold, and silver. The gems are as various as beautiful; and, although diamonds have been appreciated from the earliest periods of social refinement, the largest and most appreciated ever known, was found in the Brazils, weighing, in its rough state, 1680 carats, or 14 oz. troy, which, according to the imaginary and conventional rule of valuation—2*l.* for the first carat—would be equal in value to 5,644,800*l.* The quantity of gold and silver during a series of years, averaged in money about 5,000,000*l.* English per annum. On the gold and silver, the government levied a tax of one-fifth of the produce, but restricted the searching for diamonds, and cutting of the lignum Brasilianum, to its own agents, subjecting the violators of the law to the severest penalties. Rich as Brazil is, in a comparative sense, in gems and metals, they have obviously retarded, rather than advanced, the genuine prosperity of the country, having tended to divert the inhabitants from the more rational and socializing pursuit of agriculture. Since 1806, however, cultivation has been pursued with greater avidity, and, its superior advantages once established, it will probably increase in estimation, whilst the infatuating pursuits in search of diamonds and gold will subside. The revolutionary spirit, so widely spread over all Spanish America during the first and second decinaries of the present century, extended itself into Brazil. Pernambuco, in 1817, revolted against the government; and the whole country manifesting rather an equivocal disposition towards the ruling family, the court of Rio Janeiro, in 1821, emigrated back to Lisbon, leaving Don Pedro, the eldest son of the king, as viceroy, who no sooner felt himself separated from paternal allegiance, than he began to turn his thoughts to his individual aggrandisement, and strove to cherish, rather than subdue, the revolutionary spirit which had previously been excited; and on the 11th of Sept., all allegiance to Portugal was formerly denounced, and Don Pedro proclaimed emperor of Brazil. His reign, however, comparatively speaking, proved but of short duration. After maintaining for some time a profitless and inglorious contest with Buenos Ayres, in regard to the *Banda Oriental*, disquietude and suspicion surrounded him in his imperial abode, and on the 7th of April, 1831, he abdicated in favour of his son, Don Pedro II., a child of five years of age; and Don Pedro I., with all the rest of his family, embarked for Europe on board a British ship of war.

Notwithstanding these political contentions, the country is progressively increasing its productions, more especially in coffee, the growth of which, in 1831, amounted to 80,000,000 of pounds, whilst its imports from Great Britain alone exceeded 2,500,000*l.* sterling.

Of the extent of the population accounts are much at variance. The induction of slaves from the coast of Africa, since the excitements to agriculture commenced, has been very great, and must have added at least 50,000 annually to the population of the coast, unless the mortality has been proportionably great with the induction. The aggregate population probably amounts to near a million, four-fifths of whom are slaves and people of colour. The natives who inhabit the inland parts are copper-coloured, strong, lively, and gay, and subject to few diseases. They are divided into a great number of tribes, each of which have their peculiar customs, which they scrupulously observe; and among some of which it is said cannibalism prevails. The number of tribes is probably between 200 and 300, but their extent is generally unknown. *See* LISBON, PORTUGAL, RIO JANEIRO.

BRAZZA, an island in the Adriatic, near the coast of Dalmatia; 30 miles long, and 10 broad. The soil is stony, but it produces much excellent wine; and this article, with fire-wood and sheep, form the chief trade. It has a town of the same name, several villages, and an aggregate population of about 15,000. Long. 17. 35. E. lat. 43. 50. N.

BREAGE, a populous village on the shore of Mount's Bay, Cornwall, with ten mines in its vicinity; 4 miles W. of Helstone, and 10 E. by S. of Penzance.

BRECHIN, a borough of Scotland, in Forfar, anciently a bishop's see, and the county town. The cathedral is partly ruinous, but one of its aisles serves for the parish church. Adjoining to this is a curious antique round tower, which tapers from the bottom, and is very slender in proportion to its height. Here is a manufacture of linen and cotton, and a considerable tannery. It is seated on the South Esk; 8 miles W. of Montrose, and 12 E. N. E. of Forfar.

BRECKERFELD, a town of Westphalia, in the county of the Mark; about 30 miles N. N. E. of Cologne. Pop. 1100.

BRECON, or BRECKNOCKSHIRE, a border county of South Wales, bounded on the E. by the counties of Hereford and Monmouth, N. by Radnor, W. by Carmarthen and Cardiganshire, and S. by Glamorgan. It is a mountainous district, yielding iron, coal, and limestone in great abundance, and some copper and lead; and at Lanelly, on the border of Glamorganshire, the smelting of iron is carried on to some extent. It has some fertile valleys, and is watered by the rivers Wye and Uske, and other streams, and has the advantage of a canal for barges of 25 tons burthen, from the centre of the county to the Bristol Channel, at Newport. It has few or no manufactures; but, in addition to its iron, it produces a surplus of grain, cattle, and butter, and some wool, out of which a considerable rent and other taxes are discharged, and a supply of manufactured, colonial, and foreign productions obtained. The four principal towns are Brecon, Builth, Crickhowel, and Hay. This county contains the Vann, or Brecknock beacon, reckoned the loftiest mountain in South Wales. It sends one member to parliament.

BRECKNOCK, or BRECON, a borough and chief town of the preceding county, with a market on Wednesday and Friday. It is an ancient place, as appears by the Roman coins that are often dug up; and its once magnificent castle is now an insignificant ruin. It contains three churches, one of which is collegiate; and in that part of the town called the Watton is a fine arsenal. To the east of the town is a considerable lake, well stored with fish, whence runs a rivulet into the Wye. It is seated at the confluence of the Hondey with the Uske, which falls into the Bristol Channel, and with which it communicates by a canal to Newport, near the mouth of the Uske; 34 miles N. W. of Monmouth, and 171 W. by N. of London. It sends one member to parliament.

BREDA, a fortified town of Dutch Brabant, surrounded on all sides by water and morasses. The great church is a noble structure, with a lofty spire, 362 feet in height. In 1625 the Spaniards, after a memorable siege of ten months, reduced this city; but, in 1637, the Prince of Orange retook it. In 1793 it surrendered to the French, after a siege of only three days, but was retaken soon after. It is seated on the river Merk; 25 miles N. N. E. of Antwerp, and 60 S. of Amsterdam. Pop. 14,000.

BREDON, a considerable village in Leicestershire; 5 miles N. N. E. of Ashby-de-la-Zouch; seated at the base of a high limestone rock, on the summit of which the church stands, and commands very extensive views.

BREDSTEDT, a town of Denmark, in the duchy of Sleswick; 21 miles W. N. W. of Sleswick. Pop. about 1500.

BREEDS HILL, an eminence, on the N. side of Charlestown, in Massachusets, immediately contiguous to Boston; celebrated for the stand made by the Americans against the British troops, at the commencement of hostilities with the mother country. This action, usually called the battle of Bunker's Hill, (another hill near it,) happened on the 17th of June, 1775.

BREGENTZ, or BERGENS, a town of Germany, in Tyrol, with a castle on an eminence; seated at the mouth of a river of its name, on the E. end of the lake of Constance; 6 miles S. E. of Lindau. Pop. about 3500.

BREGLIO, a town of the continental part of Sardinia; 19 miles N. E. of Nice.

BREHAR, the most mountainous of the Scilly islands; 30 miles W. of the Land's End. Long. 6. 47. W. lat. 50. 2. N.

BREHNA, a town of the duchy of Saxony; 8 miles N. E. of Hallo.

BREITENBACH, a town of Central Germany, in the kingdom of Saxony; 15 miles S. of Erfurt. Manufactures, sulphur, alum, and china. Pop. 2500.

BRELADE, ST., a parish of the island of Jersey, English Channel. The church is near the coast of Brelades Bay, and romantically situated. Pop. 2069.

BREME, a town of Italy, in the Milanese, near the confluence of the Sessia with the Po, on the frontiers of Montferrat; 28 miles W. of Pavia.

Bremen, a duchy and maritime district of Germany, in the circle of Lower Saxony, lying between the Weser and the Elbe; the former of which separates it from Oldenberg, and the other from Holstein. The country is fertile and populous, but in winter is subject to inundations. It formerly belonged to the Swedes, but was sold to the Elector of Hanover, in 1719. Stade, on the S. bank of the Elbe, is the seat of regency. It is about 2100 square miles in extent; contains a population of about 170,000; and now forms part of the kingdom of Hanover.

Bremen, a free city, and capital of the duchy of the same name. The Weser divides it into the Old and New Town, both of which are fortified: the former is the largest, and in it stands the cathedral. It has a harbour, nine miles below the town, and carries on a considerable trade, but which was formerly much more extensive. In 1757 it was taken by the French, who were driven out in 1758, by the Hanoverians. It is 22 miles E. of Oldenburg, and 54 S. W. of Hamburg. Pop. about 37,000. Long. 8. 40. E. lat. 53. 5. N.

Bremenvord, a town in the duchy of Bremen, defended by a castle. The chancery of the duchy is kept here. It stands near the Oste; 32 miles N. by E. of Bremen.

Bremgarten, a town of Switzerland, in the free lower bailiwicks, between the cantons of Zurich and Bern. The inhabitants deal chiefly in paper; and it is seated on the Reuss; 10 miles W. of Zurich.

Breno, a town of Italy, in Bresciano, seated on the Oglio; 36 miles N. of Brescia. Pop. about 2000.

Brenta, a river which rises in the principality of Trent, passes by Bassano and Padua, and enters the Gulf of Venice, a little S. of Venice.

Brentford, an appendage to London; 7 miles from Hyde Park Corner, on the great western road. It is seated on the N. bank of the Thames, where the Grand Junction Canal originally communicated with the river. It has some very extensive flour mills, distilleries, soap works, pan, tile, and coarse pottery works, extensive nursery grounds, and various other occupations dependent on the metropolis. It is a very old town, as may be inferred from its name being derived from the Saxon, implying a ford over the little river Brent, which here falls into the Thames, and in earlier times it was distinguished as having a market on Tuesday; whilst now, from the continual intercourse with London, it has every day the appearance of holding a great fair. At the W. end of the town is a magnificent edifice, called Sion House, formerly a monastery, now belonging to the dukedom of Northumberland. The election of the two members of parliament for the metropolitan county of Middlesex was held here; and during a contest, the whole line of road from London to, and Brentford itself, presented a scene of gaiety, animation, and spirit, that must be seen to be understood.

Bresciano, a province in the N. of Italy, lying between the lat. of 45. 10. and 46. 20. N. and 10. and 10. 45. of E. long., bounded on the S. by Mantua and the Cremonese, W. by Bergamasco, N. by the country of the Grisons, and E. by the principality of Trent, the Veronese, and Mantua. The Oglio has its source in the N. extremity of this province; runs S. for about 30 miles, when it forms the lake of Jeso, and afterwards the boundary between Bergamasco and the Cremonese. The Chiese intersects the E. side, falling into the Oglio at the S. E. extremity of the province; the Smela and several other streams intersect the centre and southern part of province, all falling into the Oglio, and Lake Garda divides it from the Veronese on the E. Its superficies may be stated at about 3000 square miles, and population at 306,000. It has some dreary spots; but on the whole it may be considered a fertile district, producing corn, wine, and oil, in abundance. The vine, olive, and mulberry, all luxuriate in its soil; and the lakes and rivers supply abundance of fish. It exports some silk; but its manufactures do not much, if at all, exceed the demand and consumption of the province. Besides Brescia, the capital, the other principal towns are Breno, Chiari, Orci, Novi, and Salo. It was formerly a part of the republic of Venice; but is now under the dominion of Austria.

Brescia, an ecclesiastical city, and capital of the preceding province, situate in a spacious and fertile plain, between the rivers Mela and Navilo, on the high road from Bergamo to Mantua. It is well fortified, and has a good citadel, on an eminence. It has twelve churches, and thirty convents. The cathedral and the palace are adorned with beautiful paintings, and in the former is shown the standard of Constantine. Here are several flourishing manufactures, and its fire-arms are particularly celebrated. This city has been taken and retaken several times, by the Austrians and French. Pop. 32,000. A stream, called the Garza, runs through the city, afterwards falling into the Mela. It is about 50 miles N. of Parma, 40 N. W. of Mantua, and 30 S. E. of Bergamo.

Bresello, a town of Italy, in the Modenese, on the river Po; 27 miles N. W. of Modena.

Breslau, an ecclesiastical city and capital of a principality of the same name, and of all Silesia; seated on the banks of the Oder, just below the junction of the little river Ohlau, which runs through several of the streets, and forms two islands. It has a Lutheran and twenty-six Catholic churches, and is surrounded by walls, strengthened by ramparts and other works. It has a great trade in linen, leather, Hungarian wines, &c., and contains 82,789 inhabitants. The public squares are spacious, the streets tolerably wide, and the houses lofty. The royal palace was obtained by the Jesuits, where they founded a university, in 1702, at which there are generally about 400 students. The two principal churches belong to the Protestants; near one of which is a college. This city became subject to the King of Prussia in

1741. It was taken by the Austrians, in 1757, but regained the same year. It was for some time besieged by the French, and surrendered to them in January, 1807, and again in 1813; but reverted to Prussia after the peace of 1814. It is 112 miles N. E. of Prague, and 165 N. of Vienna. Long. 17. 9. E. lat. 51. 3. N. The principality contains about 950 square miles of area, and 180,000 inhabitants.

Bresle, a river of France, which divides the department of Lower Seine from that of Somme, and enters the English Channel at Treport.

Bressay Sound. *See* Brassa.

Bresse, a late province of France, bounded on the N. by Burgundy and Franche Compte, E. by Savoy, S. by the Viennois, and W. by the Lyonnois. It now forms the department of Ain.

Bressuire, a town of France, in the department of Two Sevres, with a village; 35 miles N. W. of Poitiers. Pop. 2000.

Brest, a maritime town of France, in the department of Finisterre. Prior to 1631, it was an insignificant fishing town; but, having one of the most commodious and secure harbours in Europe, it was availed of by the French government, under the administration of Richelieu, in the reign of Louis XIV., for a marine station, and it is now the chief naval depôt of France. Situate on a promontory at the western extremity of the kingdom, it is equally convenient for the equipment of expeditions to all parts of the coast, or of the world. The English made an ineffectual attempt to take it in 1694; and during the twenty-three years' war, from 1793 to 1814, it compelled the English to maintain a large blockading squadron off the harbour, without doing the least possible injury to France. The extensive occupations attendant on the building, repairing, and equipment of a great national marine, necessarily gave rise to an extensive interchange and consumption of commodities of various kinds; and the town of Brest has consequently risen into importance proportionate to the consequence derived from its being the chief naval station of the kingdom; and it now contains a population of about 25,000. It has a marine academy, theatre, &c. It is 33 miles E. of Ushant Light, in the lat. of 48. 23. N. and 4. 29. of W. long.; being 27 miles S. and 6 deg. 49., or about 325 geographical miles, W. by S. of Paris.

Bretagne, or Brittany, a late province of France; 150 miles long and 112 broad. It is a promontory, united on the E. to Maine, Anjou, and Poitou. The air is temperate, and it has large forests. It now forms the departments of Finisterre, Cotes du Nord, Ille and Vilaine, Lower Loire, and Morbihan.

Breteuil, a town of France, in the department of Oise; 14 miles N. N. E. of Beauvais, and 8 S. of Amiens. Pop. about 2200.

Breton, Cape. *See* Cape Breton.

Bretten, a town of Germany, in the late palatinate of the Rhine, on the frontier of Wurtemberg; 20 miles S. of Heidelberg, and about 20 N. by W. of Stuttgard. Pop. 2500. It was the birthplace of Melancthon, and is now included in the territory of the duchy of Baden, circle of the Pfintz and Enz.

Brevard, or Brevoort, a strong town of Holland, in the county of Zutphen, with a castle; situate in a morass; 24 miles S. E. of Zutphen.

Brewood, a town in Staffordshire, with a market on Tuesday; 10 miles S. by W. of Stafford, and 129 N. W. of London.

Briansk, an interior town of Russia, in the province of Orel; situate on the Desna, an eastern branch of the Dnieper; about 250 miles S. W. of Moscow. Pop. about 4000. It has an annual fair, very numerously attended.

Briançon, a town of France, on the frontier of Piedmont, in the department of Upper Alps, with a castle on a craggy rock, and other fortifications. In its neighbourhood manna is gathered from a sort of ash-tree. It has a handsome church, and a noble bridge over the Durance; 20 miles N. of Embrun, and about 70 E. by S. of Turin. Pop. about 3000.

Briançonnet, a fortress of Savoy, near the town of Moustiers, situate on a rock inaccessible every way, except by the side of a river, where it is ascended by two or three hundred steps. The common passage from Savoy to Italy is by this fortress.

Briare, a town of France, in the department of Loiret; seated on the Loire, and has a canal between that river and the Seine. It is 40 miles E. S. E. of Orleans.

Bridgend, a town of Wales, in Glamorganshire, with a market on Saturday, and a woollen manufacture; seated on the Ogmore, a river abounding in trout and salmon; 7 miles W. by N. of Cowbridge, and 181 W. of London.

Bridgenorth, a borough in Shropshire, with a market on Saturday. It has two churches, and a free-school that sends and maintains eighteen scholars at the University of Oxford. It was formerly fortified with walls, and had a castle, now in ruins. Its trade both by land and water is considerable. It is seated on both banks of the Severn, over which is a handsome bridge of six arches. The upper part of the town is 180 feet above the bed of the river, and commands an extensive and delightful prospect. An annual fair, on the 29th of October, is very numerously attended, and the quantities of cattle, sheep, butter, cheese, and bacon, brought for sale, is very great. It had formerly some manufactures of worsted, which have declined. It returns two members to parliament, and is 23 miles S. E. of Shrewsbury, and 139 N. W. of London.

Bridgetown, the capital of the island of Barbadoes; situate in the inmost part of Carlisle Bay, which is large enough to contain 500 ships, but the bottom is foul, and apt to cut the cables. This city was burnt down in 1688, and suffered also greatly by fires in 1756, 1766, and 1767. Before these fires it contained 1500 houses; and it has since been rebuilt.

The streets are broad, the houses high, the wharfs and quays convenient, and the forts strong. The church is as large as some cathedrals. Here also is a free-school, an hospital, and a college; the latter erected by the Society for Propagating the Gospel, pursuant to the will of Colonel Codrington, who endowed it with 2000*l*. a year. The town had scarcely risen from the calamities already mentioned, when it was torn from its foundation by a hurricane, in 1780, in which many of the inhabitants perished. It is scarcely yet restored to its former splendour. Long. 59. 43. W. lat. 13. 5. N. *See* BARBADOES.

BRIDGETOWN, the capital of Cumberland county, in New Jersey. The county court is held in it quarterly. It is situated on Cohanzy-creek; 54 miles S. of Philadelphia, and 71 S. S. W. of Trenton.

BRIDGEWATER, a borough in Somersetshire, governed by a mayor, with a market on Thursday and Saturday. It is seated on the Parret, over which is a handsome bridge. It has a large handsome church with a lofty spire. The summer assizes are held here every other year. In the wars between Charles I. and the parliament, the forces of the latter reduced great part of the town to ashes; and the castle was then so far demolished, that few vestiges of it are now observable. The river is navigable up to the town, for vessels of 200 tons burthen, and for barges as far as Langport, and by the Thone to Taunton; and although a prevalence of westerly wind causes the tide, at times, to set into the river with great fury, its navigation contributes essentially to the interest of the town; its commercial intercourse, however, is principally confined to the coast. It returns two members to parliament; and is 31 miles S. S. W. of Bristol, and 138 W. by S. of London. It was the birthplace of Admiral Blake, the worthy antagonist of Van Tromp.

BRIDLINGTON, commonly called BURLINGTON; a seaport in East Yorkshire, with a market on Saturday. The harbour is commodious, and defended by two strong piers. Its mineral waters, and accommodations for sea-bathing, draw much company in summer; and its trade is considerable, owning about 6000 tons of shipping. It is seated on a creek S. of Flamborough-head; 40 miles E. N. E. of York, and 206 N. of London.

BRIDPORT, a borough in Dorsetshire, with a market on Saturday. It is seated about 3 miles from the shore of the British Channel between the rivers Brit and Bride, which unite just below the town, and form a convenient harbour, which, since 1822, has been improved so as to admit vessels of 200 to 300 tons burthen. It was formerly celebrated for its manufactures of cordage, sail-cloth, twine, and netting; and Henry VIII. granted it a monopoly for making all the cordage for the national marine, which it retained for about sixty years; but its maufactures are now inconsiderable. It builds and owns some shipping, and carries on a little external, as well as coasting trade. It returns two members to parliament. It is 12 miles W. of Dorchester, and 135 W. by S of London.

BRIEG, a fortified town of Silesia, capital of a principality of the same name, with a Lutheran cathedral, and several other churches for Protestants and Catholics. Here is a manufacture of cloth. It was taken by the Prussians in 1741, and its ancient castle burned down during the siege. It is seated on the Oder; 25 miles S. E. of Breslau. Pop. about 9000.

BRIEG, or BRIG, a handsome town of the Valais, seated on the Saltina river, which falls into the Rhone on the S. side, about 28 miles E. of Sion. It suffered much from an earthquake in 1755.

BRIEL, or BRILL, a fortified seaport of South Holland, capital of the island of Voorn. The Dutch took it from the Spaniards in 1572, which was the foundation of their republic. It was the birthplace of Van Tromp, and is seated at the mouth of the Maese; 20 miles W. S.W. of Rotterdam. Long. 4. 1. E. lat. 51. 48. N. Pop. about 3000.

BRIENNE, a small town of France, in the department of Aube, distinguished for its military school, at which Napoleon Buonaparte received his education. It is about 20 miles E. of Troyes.

BRIENTZ, a town of Switzerland, in the canton of Bern, famous for the cheese made in its neighbourhood. It is situate on a lake of the same name, (9 miles long and 3 broad;) 42 miles S. E. of Bern.

BRIEZEN, a small town of Brandenburg in the Middle Mark, on the frontier of Anhalt; about 25 miles S. of Potsdam.

BRIETZEN. *See* WRIEZEN.

BRIEUX, ST., a town of France, capital of the department of Cotes du Nord, and a bishop's see, with a small harbour. It is seated among hills, near the English Channel; 30 miles S. W. of St. Malo. Pop. about 6000.

BRIEY, a town of France, in the department of Moselle, near the river Manse; 12 miles N.W. of Metz. Pop. 1800.

BRIGG. *See* GLANDFORDBRIDGE.

BRIGA, LA, a town in the Col de Tende, on the frontier of Nice; a few miles S. of the town of Tende.

BRIGHTON, or BRIGHTHELMSTONE, borough of England, county of Sussex. It stands at the foot of the South Downs, and extends for a considerable distance along the coast. It was little noticed till sea-bathing was strongly recommended in several disorders; and, from its being nearer the metropolis than almost any other part of the sea-coast, it gradually increased in attraction as a watering-place, till it has become one of the principal resorts of gaiety and fashion in the kingdom.

In 1784, the Prince of Wales, afterwards George IV., erected at Brighton, for an occasional residence, an edifice, called a marine pavilion, which he afterwards converted into a splendid palace, where he spent a great portion of every year. Up to this period the buildings were comparatively mean; but since that time, the improvements have been such as to render Brighton a splendid town. It extends from

Kemp Town on the E. for upwards of 2½ miles, to Brunswick Square on the W. Midway between these places is the magnificent chain-pier, 1154 feet long and 13 wide, suspended by means of chains over four towers of cast iron. The parish church, situate on an eminence at the N. W., was formerly at a small distance from the town, which has now almost entrenched upon its sacred enclosure. The other places of worship, connected with the Establishment, are the Chapel Royal, St. James's Chapel, and Trinity Chapel, and four others situate on the eastern and western divisions of the town, besides the church of St. Peter's, recently erected, which is one of the most beautiful ornaments that Brighton has to boast of. Here are also a Roman Catholic chapel, a Jews' synagogue, and several meeting-houses for the different denominations of dissenters. Besides the accommodations for sea-bathing, warm, cold, and vapour-baths, of the most elegant and commodious construction, have also been erected; while the park furnishes a beautiful ride, and the spa all the varieties of artificial, mineral, and medicinal waters. Here are also two assembly rooms, a handsome theatre, (opened in 1807,) a celebrated race-ground, &c. It is connected with with the metropolis by means of the Brighton and South Eastern Railway. After the battle of Worcester, in 1651, Charles II. embarked at this place for France, in a vessel which is said to have been moored, after the restoration, in the Thames, opposite Whitehall. It sends two members to parliament. It is 17 miles W. by N. of Beachy Head, 50 E. by N. of Portsmouth, and 52 S. from London.

Brightside, Bierlow, the W. quarter of the parish of Sheffield; which see.

Brignais, a town of France, in the department of Rhone. During the summer season it is the favourite resort of the citizens of Lyons, who have here many elegant villas and country houses. It is seated on the small river Garron; 9 miles S. of Lyons.

Brignolles a town of France, in the department of Var, famous for its prunes. It is seated among mountains, in a pleasant country; 20 miles N. N. E. of Toulon. Pop. about 9000.

Brihuega, a town of Spain, in New Castile, with a manufacture of broad cloth, and a trade in wool. Here General Stanhope and an English army were taken prisoners, in 1710. It is seated on the Tajuna; 43 miles N. E. of Madrid.

Brillon, a town of the duchy of Westphalia, on the river Alme; 27 miles E. by S. of Arensberg.

Brindisi, (the ancient Brundusium,) a maritime and archiepiscopal city of Naples, in the province of Otranto, situate just within the entrance to the Adriatic, in the lat. of 40. 39. N. and 18. 20. of E. long. Its harbour at one period was the most commodious and secure in the Mediterranean; but during the commercial career of Venice, it became neglected and inaccessible, except for small vessels. Within the present century, efforts have been made to render it again convenient and useful; but, so long as the subduing and precluding line of policy of the present government of Naples prevails, all efforts at social improvement will be made in vain. The adjacent country, like the harbour, presents an aspect of desolation. It is surrounded by extensive forests of olive-trees, and some mulberries, from which silk is gathered. Pop. of the city about 6000. It is about 190 miles S. E. of Naples. Virgil died at Brindisi, B. C. 19.

Brioni, islands in the Gulf of Venice, opposite Pola, famous for their marble quarries.

Brionne, a town of France, in the province of Normandy; 32 miles from Rouen.

Brioude, a town of France, in the department of Upper Loire. Near it is a small town called Church Brioude, on account of a famous chapter. Brioude stands on the Allier, over which is a bridge of one arch, 173 feet in diameter. It is 32 miles N. W. of Puy, and 34 S. by E. of Clermont. Pop. about 5000. It was the birthplace of La Fayette, distinguished for his enthusiasm in the cause of the Americans to obtain their independence.

Brisach, Old and New. Old Brisach is on the E. bank of the Rhine, and was formerly the chief town of the Brisgau; but the fortifications were demolished in 1741, and the ordnance removed to Friburg, about 15 miles in the interior. New Brisach is a fortified town on the opposite bank of the river, in the French department of the Upper Rhine; about 40 miles S. of Strasburg, and 250 E. by S. of Paris. The fortification is one of those constructed under the superintendence of Vauban, in the reign of Louis XIV.

Brisago, a town of Switzerland, on the Lake Maggiore; 5 miles S. of Locarno.

Brisgau, a territory in the circle of Suabia, of about 1000 square miles in extent, intersected by the line of the 48th degree of N. lat., and 8. of E. long., extending eastward from the Rhine into the Black Forest. As a frontier district bordering on France, it has been exposed to ravage in all the wars between that nation and Austria, and has been the scene of several bloody contests. At an early period of the French revolution, in 1793, the French reduced nearly the whole of the town of Old Brisach to ashes, and in 1796, after a severe action, possessed themselves of Friburg, the capital, but which they were obliged to abandon the same year. After various changes of sovereignty, it was wholly ceded by Buonaparte to the grand duke of Baden, in 1805; confirmed by treaty with Austria; and, in the new subdivisions of the territory of the States of Baden, in 1810, the Brisgau was divided between the three circles of Wiesen, Treisam, and Kinzig, the names of three rivers by which the territory of Baden is intersected.

Bristino, a town of Naples, in Capitanata; 11 miles S. S. W. of Manfredonia.

Brissac, a town of France, in the department of Maine-et-Loire; seated on the Aubence; 13 miles S. of Angers.

Bristol, an ancient maritime and ecclesiastical city and county of England, situate at the S. W. extremity of the county of Gloucester, at the confluence of the little river Frome with the Lower Avon, which divides it from Somersetshire on the S., about ten miles above the confluence of the Avon with the Severn, into the arm of the sea called the Bristol Channel. Bristol was known at a very early period; and about the year 430, it is mentioned as one of the fortified cities of Britain. It was known to the ancient Britons by the name of *Caer Oder nant Baden*, or the city of Ostorius, in the valley of Bath; and by way of eminence it is sometimes called *Caer Brito*, the British city, and by the Saxons *Brightstowe*, pleasant place. It is adverted to both by Gildas and Nennius, in the fifth and seventh centuries, and from the period of Henry II. in the twelfth, to the middle of the eighteenth century, it ranked next to London, as the most populous, commercial, and important place in the kingdom. Since the latter period, although it has declined, it has been greatly exceeded in population, commerce, and importance by Glasgow, Liverpool, Manchester, Leeds, and Birmingham. As into all the rivers falling into the Bristol Channel the tides rise to a great height, and occasionally rush in with considerable fury, the spring tides at Bristol rising to the height of forty-two feet, the ebbs and neaps were consequently attended with great inconveniences and detentions. This circumstance, since the completion of the canal navigation of the inland counties communicating with Liverpool and London—neither of which ports are materially affected by the inequality of the tides—tended to divert a considerable portion of the West India trade and refining of sugar from Bristol. It, however, retains a certain portion: the importation of sugar, on an average of the six years 1819—1824, was about 27,000 hogsheads per annum. It also imports a considerable quantity of wool, fruit, and wine, direct from Spain, Portugal, and France; and maintains a partial intercourse direct with all other parts of the world, except the East Indies, to which, up to 1826, it had not sent more than one or two ships. From 1809 to 1822, about 600,000*l.* had been expended towards the improvement of the harbour. In the latter year another act was granted for its further improvement; and in 1825, numerous arbitrary and oppressive town dues were abolished, or duly regulated; all of which are as well calculated to revive and maintain its commercial prosperity, as to add to the comfort, interest, and character of the city at large. It has some extensive works in copper and brass, and manufactures of glass bottles, lead, painters' colours, &c. &c. The principal resort of visitors is the suburb of Clifton, about a mile W. of the city, the houses and terraces of which are magnificent, and are arranged on different acclivities above the Hot Well. There is a railway between this place and London, called the Great Western Railway; and from here, the steam navigation of the Atlantic has been permanently established. In addition to the advantages derived from its commerce, it is indebted to a hot well for a considerable portion of the increase of its population: the water being considered very efficacious in the cure of diabetes, phthisical, scorbutic, and inflammatory disorders, it renders it the resort alike of valetudinarians and of fashion. Besides the cathedral and the church of St. Mary Redcliffe, it has sixteen other churches, and five episcopal chapels, some of them beautiful, and most of them fine edifices. There are several dissenting meeting-houses, thirteen fellowship companies, some of whom have elegant halls, several hospitals, and other public buildings; and, being surrounded by a very fertile as well as picturesque country, its markets are abundantly supplied with every kind of fish, flesh, fowls, vegetables, and fruits, on Wednesdays, Thursdays, and Saturdays; and two annual fairs in March and September are very numerously attended. It has a distinct jurisdiction, and returns two members to parliament. It is 13 miles W. N. W. of Bath, 34 S. S. W. of Gloucester, and 114 W. of London. Long. 2. 36. W. lat. 51. 27. N.

Bristol, a maritime county of the state of Massachusets; bounded on the S. by Buzzards' Bay, and W. by the state of Rhode Island. Pop. 60,164. Taunton, the chief town, situate near the head of a river of the same name, nearly in the centre of the country, is 33 miles S. of Boston. New Bedford, on Buzzards' Bay, is the other principal town.

Bristol, a small maritime county of the state of Rhode Island; bounded on the W. by the upper part of the preceding county, and on the E. by Naragansett Bay. Pop. 6467. The chief town, of the same name, situate near the S. end of the county, was distinguished for the part which it took in the slave-trade previous to its abolition by the American government. It owns about 7000 tons of shipping. Pop. 3490.

Bristol, a town in the S. W. part of Ontario county, state of New York; 217 miles W of Albany. Pop. 1,953.

Bristol Bay, a spacious bay, formed by two projecting points of the W. coast of North America. The mouth of a river called Bristol River, falling into the head of the bay, is in the lat. of 58. 12. N. and 157. 33. W. long. and Cape Newnham, which forms the N. point of the bay, is in lat. 58. 34. N. and 161. 55. W. long.; and the island of Oonalaska, one of the Aleutian group, off the S. point of the bay, is in lat. 53. 54. N. and 166. 22. W. long.

Bristol Channel, an arm of the sea between the south coast of Wales and the north coast of the counties of Somerset and Devon, leading into the river Severn and Lower Avon, on which the city of Bristol is situate.

Britain, New, a country of North America, comprehending all the tract north of Canada, commonly called the Esquimaux country, including Labrador and New North and South Wales. It is subject to Great Britain; and lies between 50. and 70. N. lat. and 50. and 100. W. long. There are innumerable lakes and morasses, which are covered with ice and snow a great part of the year. The principal settlements belong to the English Hudson Bay Company. *See* Esquimaux, Hudson Bay, and Labrador.

Britain, New, an island in the South Pacific Ocean, to the east of New Guinea, explored by Dampier, who sailed through the strait which separates it from New Guinea; and Captain Carteret, in 1767, sailed through a channel, which divides it on the north-east from a long island, called New Ireland. New Britain lies in long. 152. 20. E. and 4. 0. S. The shores of both islands are rocky, the inland parts high and mountainous, but covered with trees of various kinds, among which are the nutmeg, the cocoa nut, and different kinds of palm. The inhabitants are black, and woolly-headed, like negroes, but have not their flat noses and thick lips.

Brittany. *See* Bretagne.

British America comprises the whole of the north part of the northern division of the western hemisphere, from the Atlantic to the Pacific Ocean, extending south in the long. of 83. W. to the lat. of about 42. N.; but further west it is bounded on the south by a conventional line dividing it from the United States of America, in the lat. of about 48. N., and the Columbia river. This extensive territory, of several millions of square miles, will be found more particularly elucidated under the ten heads, as specified under the head of British Empire.

British Empire, the most extensive, influential, and, with the exception of China, the most populous empire in the world. Its extent, influence, population, character, &c. &c., will be exhibited under the following heads, to each of which refer: viz.—

- Europe.
  - United Kingdom
    - Great Britain.
      - England
      - Scotland.
      - Wales.
    - Ireland.
    - Guernsey, Jersey, Man, and Scilly Isles.
  - Heligoland.
  - Gibraltar.
  - Ionian Isles.
- Asia.
  - Hindostan.
  - Ceylon.
  - Prince of Wales's Island.
  - Sincapore.
  - Bencoolen.
- Africa.
  - Isle of France.
  - St. Helena.
  - Cape of Good Hope.
  - Gold Coast.
  - Sierra Leone.
  - Malta.
- North America.
  - New Brunswick
  - Canada.
  - Cape Breton.
  - Hudson Bay.
  - Labrador.
  - New South Wales.
  - North West Coast.
  - Nova Scotia.
  - Prince Edward's Island.
- Islands and South America.
  - Bermudas.
  - Bahamas.
  - West Indies
    - Twelve Islands.
    - Jamaica.
  - Honduras.
  - Berbice.
  - Demerara.
- Australia.
- Van Diemen's Land.
- New Zealand, &c., &c.

Brive, a town of France, in the department of Correze, with manufactures of silk handkerchiefs, muslins, gauzes, &c. It is seated on the Correze, opposite the influx of the Vezere, in a delightful valley; 12 miles S. W. of Tulle. Pop. about 6000.

Brix, or **Brux**, a considerable town of Bohemia, at the north end of the circle of Saaz; about 8 miles S. W. of Bilin, and 40 N. W. of Prague. Pop. 2500.

Brixen, a principality of Germany, lately a bishopric, in the east part of Tyrol. It is extremely mountainous, but produces excellent wine.

Brixen, a town of Germany, capital of the principality of Brixen. Beside the cathedral, there are one parochial and six other churches. It was taken by the French in 1796, and again in 1797. It is seated on the Eysach, at the influx of the Rientz, 38 miles S. by E. of Inspruck. Pop. about 4000.

Brixham, a small seaport in Devonshire, on the W. side of Torbay, celebrated for its fishery. A quay has been built for the purpose of supplying the ships of war with water. The Prince of Orange, afterwards William III., landed here in 1688. It is 4 miles N. E. of Dartmouth, and 201 W. by S. of London.

Brizen, or **Britzen**, a town of Brandenburg, in the Middle Mark, on the Adab; 18 miles N. E. of Wittenberg.

Broach. *See* Baroach.

Broadalbin, a town of Fulton county, state of New York; 38 miles W. of Albany. Pop. 2738.

Broadstairs, a village in Kent, on the seashore; 2 miles N. of Ramsgate. It has a small pier, with a harbour for light vessels; and is a fashionable resort for sea-bathing, more retired than Ramsgate.

Broadwater, a village in Sussex, near the seacoast; 4 miles W. of Shoreham.

Brod, **Brodt**, or **Brodo**, a strong town of Sclavonia, on the river Saave, which divides it from the Turkish province of Bosnia, where the emperor gained a victory over the Turks, in 1688. It is 45 miles S. W. of Esseck, and about 120 W. of Belgrade. Long. 18. 30. E. lat. 45. 10. N.

Brod Hun, or **Hun Brod**, a town of Moravia, on the frontiers of Hungary; 10 miles E. S. E. of Hradisch. Pop. about 3000.

Brod, Bohmisch. *See* Bohmisch.

Brod, Deutsch, a town of Bohemia, on the river Sazawa; 20 miles S. by E. of Czazlau.

Brodera, a town and fortress of Hindostan, in Guzerat, celebrated for its linens, indigo, and lace. It is 62 miles S. S. E. of Ahmedabad. Long. 73. 11. E. lat. 22. 15. N.

BRODZIAC, a town of Lithuania, on the river Berezina; 100 miles S. of Polotsk, and 40 W. of Mohilow.

BROEK, a town of Westphalia, in the duchy of Berg, capital of a county of its name; seated on the Roer; 11 miles N. of Dusseldorf.

BROEK, a village of North Holland; 6 miles from Amsterdam. It is one of the most singular and picturesque places in the world. The streets are paved in mosaic work with variegated bricks; and no carriages ever enter them. The houses are painted on the outside, and each has a terrace and garden to the street, enclosed by a low railing; the garden adorned with China vases and shell-work, with borders composed of minute particles of glass, of different colours. Behind the houses are meadows full of cattle, in which the inhabitants carry on a great trade. Pop. about 700.

BROKEN BAY, a bay of New South Wales; 18 miles N. of Port Jackson. It is formed by the mouth of a great river, called the Hawkesbury, and is a good harbour. Long. 151. 27. E. lat. 33. 34. S.

BROMBERG, a town of Prussia, grand duchy of Posen, on the river Brahe. A canal which unites the Elbe, Oder, and Vistula rivers with this town, is of great importance to the interior trade of the country.

BROMLEY, a town in Kent, with a market on Thursday. Here is a college for 20 poor clergymen's widows; and near the town is a palace of the bishops of Rochester, where there is a chalybeate spring. Bromley is seated on the Ravensbourn; 10 miles S. by E. of London.

BROMLEY, a town in Staffordshire, with a market on Monday. It was formerly called Abbots-Bromley, and afterward Paget Bromley, being given to Lord Paget at the dissolution of the abbeys. It is 7 miles E. of Stafford, and 129 N. W. of London.

BROMSGROVE, a corporate town in Worcestershire, with a market on Tuesday. Here are manufactures of sheeting, nails, and needles; and a grammar-school, founded by Edward VI. It is seated on the Salwarp; 13 miles N. N. E. of Worcester, 13 S. W. of Birmingham, and 116 N. W. of London.

BROMWICH, WEST, a town in Staffordshire, contiguous to Wednesbury, and 7 miles W. by N. of Birmingham. Population extensively occupied in the various branches of the hardware manufacture.

BROMYARD, a town in Herefordshire, with a market on Tuesday; seated near the Frome, amid fine orchards; 13 miles N. E. of Hereford, and 125 W. N. W. of London.

BROON, or BRONI, a town of Italy, near the S. frontier of the Milanese, where the French defeated the Austrians in 1800. It is 10 miles S. E. of Pavia.

BRONTI, a town of Sicily, in Val di Demona, at the foot of Mount Ætna, on the W. side. It was conferred, with its territory, by the king of Naples, on Lord Nelson, for his naval services, after the battle of the Nile.

BROOKE, a frontier county, at the northern extremity of Virginia; bounded on the E. by Washington county, Pennsylvania, and W. by the Ohio river. Pop. 7948. Wellsburg, on the E. bank of the Ohio, 400 miles N. W. of Richmond, is the chief town.

BROOKFIELD, a township of Madison county, New York; 93 miles W. of Albany. Pop. 3695.

BROOKFIELD, a town of Massachusets, in Worcester county, Here are iron ore, and large quantities of stone which yield copperas. It is seated on the Quaboag; 17 miles W. by S. of Worcester. Pop. 2472. There are several other towns and villages named Brookfield, in different parts of the United States.

BROOKHAVEN, a township of New York, in Suffolk county, Long Island; 60 miles E. of New York. Pop. 7050.

BROOKLYN, a city of New York, in King's county; at the W. end of Long Island, near East River, which separates it from the city of New York. Here is a naval station of the federal government: it has four churches. Pop. 36,233.

BROOKLYN, a town of Massachusets, in Norfolk county, separated from Boston on the E. by a narrow bay. Large quantities of fruits and vegetables are produced here for the Boston market.

BROOKLYN, the chief tn. of Windham county, Connecticut; 46 miles E. of Hartford.

BROOKVILLE, the chief town of Franklyn county, state of Indiana. It is finely located between the E. and W. forks of the White Water river, which falls into the Miami, a little above its entrance into the Ohio; 71 miles S. E. by E. of Indianopolis.

BROOME, a south frontier county of the state of New York, bordering on Susquehannah county, Pennsylvania, and the S. E. corner borders on the Delaware river. It has some mountain districts. Pop. 22,338. Binghampton, on the N. bank of the Susquehannah, 148 miles W. by S. of Albany, is the chief town. Owega, Westville, Lisle, Colesville, and Oquago, are the other towns of the county.

BROOME is also the name of a township in Schoharie country, New York; 35 miles W. of Albany. Pop. 2404.

BROOM, LOCH, GREAT and LITTLE, two lakes or arms of the sea, on the W. coast of Scotland, in Ross-shire. They contain several good harbours, have been long noted for excellent herrings, and are esteemed as the best fishing stations on the coast. Ullapool, on the N. E. coast of the Great Loch, is a good harbour, and at the head is the town of Lochbroom.

BROOS, a town of Austria, province of Transylvania. Here is a large castle. Pop. 3300.

BRORA, a river of Scotland, in Sutherlandshire, which issues from a lake of the same name, and forms several cascades in its course to the town of Brora, where it enters the sea.

BRORA, a vill. of Scotland, on the S. E. coast of Sutherlandshire, with a small harbour at the mouth of the Brora; 14 miles N. E. of the Dornoch.

BROSELEY, a town of Shropshire, with a market on Wednesday; it is situate near the Severn, on the W. side, in a very interesting and important district, abounding in coal, iron, and lime. The celebrated iron-works of Colebrooke Dale are in the parish, and immediate vicinity of the town, on the banks of the river, over which there is an iron bridge of one arch, leading to Madely, on the opposite side, which was the first of its kind erected in the kingdom. It has also an extensive porcelain manufactory, and another of tobacco pipes. The coal of this district contains much bitumen, and in 1711, naphtha was discovered issuing from a spring of water, but which has totally disappeared since 1755. Brosely is 6 miles N. N. W. of Bridgenorth, and 146 N. W. of London.

Brouage, a town of France, in the department of Lower Charente. It has the most considerable salt-works in France, and stands near a bay of the sea; 17 miles S. of Rochelle.

Brouca, a town of Sicily, in Val di Demona, on the Gulf of Catania; 15 miles S. of Catania.

Brough, a town in Westmoreland, with a market on Thursday. Near it is a cotton spinning manufacture; at the foot of a mountain. It is 8 miles E. S. E. of Appleby, and 261 N. N. W. of London.

Broughton in Furness, a town of Lancashire. Considerable quantities of blue slate are exported from this place; 283 miles from London.

Broussa. *See* Bursa.

Browershaven, a seaport of Holland, on the N. side of the island of Schonen; 9 miles S. W. of Helvoetsluys. Long. 3. 50. E. lat. 41. 38. N.

Brown, a frontier county of the state of Ohio, bounded on the S. by the Ohio River, which divides it from Mason county, Kentucky. Pop. 22, 715. Ripley, seated on the bank of the river, 100 miles S. S. W. of Columbus, is the chief town.

Brownsville, a town of Pennsylvania, in Fayette county. The trade to Kentucky renders it a flourishing place, and many boats are built here. The vicinity abounds with monuments of Indian antiquity. It is seated on the Monongahela, at the mouth of Redstone Creek; 30 miles S. S. E. of Pittsburg. Pop. 3000 to 4000.

Bruc de Grignols, a town of France, department Dordogne; 10 miles S. W. of Perigueux. Pop. 1250.

Bruchshal, a town of the duchy of Baden, circle of Pfinz and Enz. It has a large saltwork, and is seated on the river Satz; 5 miles S. E. of Philipsburg. Pop. about 6000.

Bruck, a town of Saxony; 35 miles N. by W. of Wittenberg.

Bruck, a town of Austria, on the river Leyta; 20 miles E. S. E. of Vienna.

Bruck, or Brug, a town of Switzerland, in Argau, with a college; seated on the river Aar; 22 miles S. E. of Basel.

Bruck, or Pruck, a town of Bavaria, on the river Ammer; 12 miles W. of Munich. Another in the Palatinate; 22 miles N. N. E. of Ratisbon.

Bruck, or Pruck, a town of Germany, in Stiria, capital of a circle of its name. It stands on the river Muehr; 24 miles N. N. W. of Gratz, and 82 S. W. of Vienna.

Brue, a river in Somersetshire, which rises in Selwood Forest, on the borders of Wiltshire, and flows through the county, by Bruton and Glastonbury, into Bridgewater Bay.

Brug, or Brig, a town of Switzerland, in the Valais; seated on the Rhone; 39 miles E. of Sion.

Bruges, a city of Belgium, in West Flanders. It was once a great trading town; but in the 16th century the civil wars drove the trade first to Antwerp, and then to Amsterdam. The inhabitants are estimated at 47,000; but it is not populous in proportion to its extent. Its situation still commands some trade, for it has canals to Ghent, Ostend, Sluys, Nieuport, Furnes, Ypres, and Dunkirk. Bruges has been often taken. It is 14 miles E. of Ostend. Long. 3. 13½. E. lat. 51. 12. N.

Brugge, or Bruggen, a town of Lower Saxony, in the principality of Hildesheim, on the river Leyne; 12 miles S. W. of Hildesheim.

Bruggen, a town of Germany, in the duchy of Juliers; seated on the Schwalm; 6 miles N. E. of Ruremonde.

Brugneto, a town of the territory of Genoa, at the foot of the Appennines; 35 miles E. S. E. of Genoa.

Bruguiere, La, a town of France, in the department of Tarn; 5 miles S. of Cashes. Pop. about 4000.

Bruhl, a town of the Lower Rhine, in the electorate of Cologne; about 7 miles S. of the city of Cologne. Pop. about 2000.

Brumau, a town of Moravia, in the circle of Hradisch, at the foot of the Carpathian Mountains, on the frontiers of Hungary; 26 miles E. of Hradisch.

Brummen, a populous village of Holland, in Guelderland, on the road from Arnheim to Zutphen.

Brumt, or Brumeth, a frontier town of France, in the department of the Lower Rhine; 10 miles N. of Strasburg. Pop. 2800.

Bruneg, or Brunecken, a town of the Tyrol, situate in a fork of two branches of the river Rientz; it has medicinal baths in its vicinity, and is about 15 miles E. by N. of Brixen.

Brunn, or Brinn, a town of Moravia, capital of a circle of the same name, and a bishop's see. It is defended by a strong fortress, called Spilberg, built on an eminence; and has manufactures of cloth, velvet, and plush. The Prussians besieged it in 1742, but were obliged to raise the siege. It is seated at the confluence of the Zwittau and Schwartz; 33 miles S. W. of Olmutz. Long. 16. 38. E. lat. 49. 13. N. Pop. 24,000

Brunnen, a town of Switzerland, in the canton of Schweitz. Here the cantons of Uri, Schweitz, and Underwalden, formed the alliance which was the foundation of the republic of Switzerland. It is seated on the Waldstrædter See; 2 miles S. W. of Schweitz.

Brunsbuttle, a town of Germany, in Holstein, near the mouth of the Elbe; 13 miles N. W. of Gluckstadt.

Brunswick, Duchy of, a territory of Germany, in the S. part of the circle of Lower Saxony. This territory formed the patrimony of the family of Guelph, who trace their descent from the Marquis of Este, who died about the middle of the 10th century. In 1546, it was divided by Ernest, the then duke, between his two sons; one founding the dukedom of Brunswick Luneburg, and the other of Brunswick Wolfenbuttle; the former will be elucidated under the head of Luneburg and Hanover, and the other under that of Wolfenbuttle. They contain 208,700 inhabitants.

Brunswick, the chief town of the states of Brunswick Wolfenbuttle, is situate in the principality of Wolfenbuttle, on the banks of the river Ocker, which falls into the Aller. It is strongly fortified, and contains ten Lutheran churches, a cathedral dedicated to St. Blasius, one Calvinist, and one catholic church, a college, two academies, a mint, opera-house, town-hall, &c. The ducal palace was formerly a monastery. There is a large building appropriated as a public storehouse for wine. It has several manufactories, and claims the invention of the spinning-wheel; and is distinguished for its breweries of *mum*, made principally from wheaten malt, with a portion of oat and bean malt, tops of fir and birch, and various herbs; and, with the exception of Leipzic and Frankfort, the fairs of Brunswick are more numerously attended than in any other town in Germany. It formerly ranked as a free and independent city; and for the continuance of its freedom it long and strenuously contended; but towards the close of the 17th century, yielded all its pretensions, and became the ducal residence in 1764. It is 47 miles W. by N. of Magdeburg, 37 E. by S. of Hanover, and about 110 S. by E. of Hamburg; in the lat. of 52. 16. N. and 10. 30. of E. long. Pop. about 35,000.

Brunswick, New, a province of British America, extending from the Bay of Fundy S., in the lat. of 45., to the frontier of Canada, in the lat of 48. N.; bounded on the W., partly by the Schoodie river, and partly by a conventional line running from the head of tide-water in the above river, which divides it from the united state of Maine, in the long. of 67. 45. W., to the Gulf of St. Lawrence, in the long. of 64. It is joined to Nova Scotia, at the S. E. corner, by an isthmus about 15 miles in breadth, and contains an area of about 8500 square miles, and an aggregate population of about 60,000. It is intersected from the N. by the river St. John, which falls over a rapid into the Bay of Fundy; the rapid impedes the navigation from and into the bay; but above, it is navigable for vessels of 100 tons burthen for a hundred miles; and vast quantities of masts and logs of timber are floated down for shipment in the bay, which is spacious and secure. St. John's, the chief town of the province, is situated on the E. shore of the bay, immediately contiguous to the river of the same name. It has several rivers running from W. to E. into the Gulf of St. Lawrence, on which side of the province are several spacious bays, such as Chaleure, Miramichi, Richibucto, &c., from whence vast quantities of timber are shipped to Great Britain annually. A few tribes of native Indians are scattered over the province. It possesses in general a capable soil, but cultivation has made but little progress; the inhabitants depending more on the forests and the fishery, in obtaining a supply of manufactures and other foreign productions, than on agriculture. Besides St. John's, the other chief towns are St. Andrew's, on the E. bank of the Schoodie, and St. Ann's, or, as it is now called, Frederic Town, which is the seat of the provincial government; about 80 miles up the river St. John.

Brunswick, a S. frontier county of the state of Virginia, bordering on Northampton county, North Carolina. The S. W. corner jets upon the Roanoke river. Pop. 14,346 (two-thirds of whom are slaves). Meherrin, 63 miles S. by W. of Richmond, is the chief town.

Brunswick, a maritime and frontier county at the S. extremity of North Carolina. It is bounded on the N. and E. by Cape Fear River. It is a swampy and desolate district. Pop. 5265, of whom 2119 are people of colour. Smithville, near the mouth of Cape Fear river, 255 miles S. by E. of Raleigh, is the chief town. It has also a town of the same name about 30 miles up the river.

Brunswick, a seaport of the state of Georgia, chief town of Glynn county, with a safe harbour, capable of containing a numerous fleet of men-of-war. It is seated in a fertile country, at the mouth of Turtle River, in St. Simon Sound; 60 miles S. S. W. of Savannah, and 10 S. of Darien. Long 81. 0. W. lat. 31. 10. N.

Brunswick, New, a city of New Jersey, in Middlesex county. Its situation is low, but many houses are now built on a pleasant hill, which rises at the back of the town. It has a considerable inland trade; and, over the Rariton, one of the most elegant bridges in America. Queen's College was in this city, but is now extinct as a place of instruction. New Brunswick is 60 miles N. E. of Philadelphia, on the high road to New York. Pop. 8693.

Brunswick, a town of Rensselaer county, New York, 11 miles W. of Albany. Pop. 3051.

Brunswick, a town of the state of Maine, situate on a spacious plain on the S. bank of the Androscoggin river, which here falls over a succession of rapids, forming some beautiful scenery, as well as holding out great advantages for mill-sites. It has a college, founded by the legislature of Massachusets in 1794, called Bowdoin College, after the name of a liberal benefactor. It is about 30 miles N. E. of Portland.

Bruny Isle, an island off the S. E. point of Van Diemen's Land; about 30 miles in length, indented by Adventure Bay.

Brussels (*Bruxelle*), a deservedly celebrat

ed city of South Brabant, and capital of the kingdom of Belgium, situate on the banks of the Sienne, which affords a facility of communication by water to Antwerp. During the domination of Austria over this part of Europe it was the seat of the Austrian governor, and head quarters of the commissariat of the armed forces; and during the successful career of Napoleon Buonaparte it was the chief town of the department of the Dyle, annexed to the French empire, and adopted as a favourite station by that distinguished individual. On the Netherlands being annexed to Holland, at the peace of 1814, Brussels was made the seat of government of the two countries alternately, year by year, with the Hague. It has since that period undergone great improvements, and is now the seat of government, and residence of King Leopold. The city is about seven miles in circumference, surrounded by a wall, which, however, offers little or no security against the now efficient mode of warfare. It was bombarded by Marshal Villeroy in 1695, when about 400 houses and 14 churches were destroyed; a disaster, together with its having been exposed to the ravages of war in every contest that has prevailed in this part of Europe from that period up to 1814, it has not thoroughly recovered. During the career of Antwerp and Amsterdam, as the chief commercial cities of Europe, Brussels and the surrounding country was equally distinguished for the extent and excellence of its manufactures in linens, silks, &c., as well as in cottons, since the introduction of the manufacture into this part of Europe; and the carpets and lace of Brussels were proverbial for their fineness and superiority over the whole trading world; and although it has greatly declined from its former pre-eminence, partly in consequence of the frequent wars to which it has been exposed, but more from the manufacturing energy of the English, which, during the 23 years' war, from 1793 to 1815, attained an ascendancy in every branch over the manufactures of the whole world, it still retains some extensive and respectable establishments for the manufacture of lace, cambrics, and cottons, and for the printing of calicoes, &c. &c. The site of Brussels, selected by St. Gery, Bishop of Cambray, at the commencement of the 7th century, was very judicious, being at the foot of the first ascent from the great level called the *Pays de Bas*, or low countries. The buildings extend up the ascent to a height of 100 to 200 feet, affording to the upper part of the town an extensive and beautiful prospect over the surrounding territory; whilst the lower part possesses every advantage of traffic by the canals, which intersect the level country. It is also connected with Mechlin, and the system of railways with all parts of Belgium, which will also extend to the Rhine, eastward, and to Paris on the S., rendering it a chief centre for continental travellers. The market-place is a handsome square in the lower part of the town, surrounded on three sides by very stately houses, the window-frames of which, being gilt, produce a very imposing effect. On the S. side is the town-hall, a very ponderous edifice, with a long sloping roof, and a range of projecting windows. It has a beautiful spire, towering in the air to the height of 364 feet, surmounted with a figure of St. Michael, on copper, 17 feet in additional height. In the upper part of the town, overlooking the market-place, is a square, surrounded by ranges of very elegant and uniform buildings of stone, principally occupied as hotels; an avenue from the N. side of this square leads to the park, surrounded on all sides by very handsome buildings, among which are the residences of the ambassadors and the opulent classes; at the upper end are the king's palace and the house of assembly of the states-general of the kingdom. The park itself is a kind of public garden, intersected by beautiful alleys, bordered with trees, and ornamented with numerous statues of white marble. The cathedral, dedicated to St. Gudule, also in the upper part of the town, is a very ponderous edifice, which, like the town-hall, interests more by its magnitude than the beauty of its architecture, or justness of its proportions. The interior is disfigured by the exhibition of numerous collections of catholic mummery, and works of art, dispersed about the edifice without any regard to order or taste. It has sixteen chapels, or recesses; and were the numerous works of art judiciously arranged, as in the cathedral at Ghent, the whole is susceptible of being made to produce a very interesting and imposing effect. The church of the Capuchins, one of the finest of that order in Europe, and one or two others, are fine edifices. There are several squares of minor note; and several parts of the city are ornamented with fountains, which once were elegant, but have of late been neglected; the most celebrated is a representation of Neptune, the Tritons and the horses spouting the water from their nostrils; and another, which excites the curiosity of all strangers, is called, in the language of the country, *manikin pis*, which, if correctly translated and described, would, to the fastidious taste of an English reader, be deemed indelicate. The water for the supply of these fountains is raised from a lake about half a mile to the E. of the city, by means of machinery. It has a museum of works of art, and cabinet of natural productions, a botanic garden, an extensive public library, and several institutions for education, useful, scientific, and refined. The opera house, built in the year 1700, is a stately edifice, in the Italian style; and the theatre, erected in 1819, is worthy of notice. The ramparts within the walls, surrounding the high part of the town, being planted with rows of trees, afford agreeable promenades. The gates are seven in number, but have no claim to notice, except as affording ingress and egress. The palace of Laeken, a favourite residence of Napoleon, situate about two miles from the Antwerp gate, is a fascinating place, but not extensive. Brussels being situate in the bosom of a very fertile district, its markets are exceedingly well supplied with all the substantial articles of subsistence. In regard to the important considerations of salubrity and mildness of temperature, it is second to no city in Europe; and it has always been a favourite resort for the English. During the commonwealth it was the occasional abode of Charles II. and his brother the Duke of York. The inhabitants are Catholics, and speak the French language, but all religious tenets are tolerated. The population has increased considerably since 1814, and may be estimated at 90,000. It is 25 miles S. of Antwerp, about the same distance E. by S. of Ghent, and 148 N. by E. of Paris.

Bruton, a town in Somersetshire, with a market on Saturday. Here are manufactures of silk and hosiery; a free-school, founded by Edward VI.; and a stately alms-house, consisting of the ruins of a priory, with an income of nearly 3000*l.* per annum. It is seated on the river Brue; 12 miles S. E. of Wells and 100 W. of London.

Brutus, a township of Cayuga county, New York, lying between the S. shore of Lake Ontario and the Erie Canal; 172 miles W. by N. of Albany. Pop. 2044.

Brux, a town in the N. part of the circle of Saaz, Bohemia.

Bruyeres, a town of France, in the department of Vosges; 11 miles E. N. E. of Epinal. Pop. 1900.

Bryan, a small maritime county of the state of Georgia, bounded on the N. by the Ogeechee river, which divides it from Chattam county; the Cannouchee river intersects it from the S. W. corner, falling into the Ogeechee about the centre of the N. side. Pop. 897 whites, 7 free blacks, and 3,182 slaves. The court house of the county is about 15 miles S. of Savannah, and 206 S. E. by E. of Milledgeville.

Brzesc, or Polesia, Palatinate of, a district of Russian Poland, lying between the rivers Bug on the W., and Dnieper on the E., intersected by the line of the 52nd degree of N. lat.; and also from W. to E. by the Przsypiec or Pripet river, with numerous branches falling into the Dnieper. These rivers, from a total absence of all regard to free the obstructions of their currents, tend to make Brzesc a marshy and dreary district, which, under social and reciprocal arrangements, might easily be made to rank among the most fertile in Europe. The Pina, a branch of the Przsypiec, is united by a canal to the Machawiza, a branch of the Bug, falling into the Vistula, thereby uniting the waters of the Black Sea with those of the Baltic.

Brzesc Litov, the chief town of the above district, is situate at the confluence of the river Machawiza with the Bug, opposite to Therespol. It is a considerable place, the see of a Greek bishop, and celebrated for its being the chief place for the instruction of Jews destined for rabbinical pursuits, and its magnificent synagogue. It is strongly fortified, and has a castle on an eminence; about 100 miles E. by S. of Warsaw, and 250 S. E. of Dantzic.

Brzesc is also the name of another town, capital of another palatinate of the same name, lying between the rivers Wartha on the S. W. and Vistula on the N. E. The town, seated near the Vistula, is about 90 miles W. by N. of Warsaw, and 150 due S. of Dantzic.

Brzezany, a town in the S. E. part of Austrian Gallicia, seated near a small lake communicating with the Dneister river. Pop about 5000.

Brzesnitz, a town of Bohemia, in the circle of Saatz, on the frontier of the principality of Miessen, with manufactures of lace, fire-arms, and hardware; 24 miles W. N. W. of Saatz. Another, in the N. part of the circle of Prachin; 18 miles W. N. W. of Pisek.

Bshirrai, a village and district of Palestine, near the celebrated cedars of Lebanon, on the Nahr Kadesha, which falls into the Mediterranean.

Bu, a town of France, department Eure et Loire; 9 miles N. E. from Dreux.

Bu-Regreg, a river of Fez, North Africa, on which the town of Sla, or Salee stands.

Bua, an island in the Gulf of Venice, on the coast of Dalmatia, called likewise Partridge Island, because frequented by those birds. It is joined by a bridge to the town of Traon; about 20 miles W. S. W. of Spalatro.

Buarcos, a town of Portugal, in Beira, on the sea-coast, at the mouth of the Mondego; 27 miles S. of Aveira. It suffered greatly by the earthquake which destroyed the greater part of Lisbon in 1759.

Buccari, or Buchari, a seaport of the Austrian empire, on the coast of Morlachia, at the head of the N. E. part of the Gulf of Venice, declared by the emperor, in 1780, a free port for commerce with the East Indies; but the favour might just as well have applied to trading with the moon, for any advantage that has resulted from the declaration. It is 12 miles E. of Fiume. Pop. about 3000.

Buchaness, the most eastern promontory of Scotland, to the E. of Peterhead, in Aberdeenshire, in long. 1. 34. W. lat. 57. 27. N. Near this promontory are the Bullers of Buchan, and other stupendous rocks and precipices, much admired for their awful grandeur.

Bucharia. *See* Bokharia.

Buchau, a town of Suabia, with a nunnery, seated on a small lake, called Feyder See; 25 miles S. W. of Ulm.

Buchau, a town of Bohemia, in the circle of Saatz; 26 miles S. W. of Saatz.

Bucholz, a town of Brandenburg, in the Middle Mark, seated on the Dahme, near the frontier of Lusatia; 23 miles S. S. E. of Berlin.

Buchorest, (*Buckarest*, city of joy), a strong city of European Turkey, capital of Wallachia, where the hospodar commonly resides. The patriarchal church is large, adjoining to the palace of the archbishop; and in a square, near the centre of the town, is the great church of St. George, the patron saint of Wallachia. The inhabitants are estimated at 60,000. It is seated on the Domboriza, which falls into the Danube; 35 miles S. S. E. of Tergovist, and 200 N. by W. of Adrianople. Long. 26. 8. E. lat. 44. 37. N.

Buchorn, a town of Suabia, seated on the

N. bank of the Lake of Cónstance; 13 miles N. W. of Lindau.

BUCHOVINE, or BUKOVINA, a circle of Moldavia in Austria, a mountainous district, cold but salubrious. Pop. 130,000. Capital, Czernowitz. *See* BUKOWINE.

BUCHSWEILER, a town of France, department of Lower Rhine. Pop. 2500.

BUCKDEN, a village in Huntingdonshire; 5 miles S. W. of Huntingdon, and 61 N. of London. Here is a superb palace of the bishops of Lincoln, and several of the prelates have been interred in the church.

BUCKEBURG, a town of Westphalia, in the county of Schauenburg, with a castle, on the river Aa; 3 miles E. S. E. of Minden.

BUCKENHAM, OLD and NEW, two towns in Norfolk, with a market on Saturday; 12 miles E. by N. of Thetford, and 93 N. E. of London.

BUCKINGHAMSHIRE, an interior county of England, bounded on the S. by the river Thames, which divides it from Berkshire, E. by the counties of Middlesex, Hertford, and Bedford, S. by Northampton, and W. by Oxfordshire. The S. part is intersected by the Ouse river, running from W. to E. into Bedfordshire, working several corn and paper mills, but is not navigable within the county. The Lyssel runs from S. to N. into the Ouse, and the Coln, which divides the county from that of Middlesex, runs from N. to S. into the Thames. The Thame, which rises in the centre of the county, runs W. falling into the Thames in Oxfordshire. The N. part is intersected by a range of chalk hills, and the Grand Junction Canal runs through the S. E. part of the county, being carried over the river Ouse by an aqueduct three quarters of a mile in length. The county may be considered divided by the chalk hills into two extensive plains; the S. part producing wheat and beans of superior quality, and the N. part appropriated more to pasture. In addition to its chalk, which is distributed over all the inland counties for whitewashing, it has veins of fuller's earth and ochre.

This county has long been celebrated for its corn and cattle: formerly fine flocks of sheep were fed in the vale of Aylesbury, but the breeding of these useful animals has been for some time on the decline. At present this vale feeds oxen for the London market, to which it also sends immense supplies of butter weekly. There is a small proportion of arable land in the northern division of the county; and not much in any other part, except the Chiltern districts, which are usually cultivated with wheat, barley, oats, beans, and sainfoin. In the neighbourhood of Aylesbury, ducks are reared very early in the spring, and sometimes at Christmas, which, being sent to London, sell at a high price. The only manufactures of consequence in this county are those of bone lace and paper. The former is carried on at Olney, Newport Pagnell, and Hanslope, and the latter principally in the neighbourhood of Wycombe. At Amersham there is a manufacture of sacking and of white cotton goods; and at Marlow are some large works of copper, brass, and brass wire, and mills for making thimbles and pressing rape and linseed. This county is adorned with several magnificent seats, and in various parts Roman roads and military stations are traced; and Roman antiquities have been occasionally discovered. The principal towns are Aylesbury, Buckingham, Marlow; and, of a secondary class, Amersham, Wycombe, and Wendover. It sends three members to parliament.

BUCKINGHAM, a borough, and one of the principal towns in the preceding county, is situate on the N. bank of the Ouse, by which it is nearly surrounded, and over which there are three bridges. It is a place of considerable antiquity, having been fortified by Edward the Elder in 918, against the incursions of the Danes. It had formerly a castle in the centre of the town, on the site of which, towards the close of the last century, an elegant new church was erected. The summer assizes for the county are held here. The town hall is a spacious edifice of brick. A great number of calves are fattened, and large quantities of butter made for the London market, in this part of the county; lace is also made here. Market on Saturday. 16 miles N. of Aylesbury, 26 N. E. of Oxford, 23 S. W. of Northampton, and 55 N. of London.

BUCKINGHAM, an interior county of Virginia, forming nearly a square, the W. and N. sides of which are bounded by James River. Pop. 18,786. The court-house, in the centre of the county, is 64 miles W. of Richmond.

BUCKINGHAMSHIRE, a county of Lower Canada, in the district of Trois Rivieres, on the S. bank of the St. Lawrence.

BUCKS, a frontier county of the state of Pennsylvania, bounded on the N. E. and S. E. by the Delaware river, which divides it from New Jersey, and on the S.W. by Montgomery county, the S. W. corner jetting upon Philadelphia. It is divided into twenty-seven townships, containing together about 410,000 acres, and a population of 48,107. Bristol, the chief town, in the S. E. part of the county, on the bank of the Delaware, is 142 miles E. of Harrisburg, and 18 N. E. of Philadelphia.

BUDA, or OFEN, the capital of Lower Hungary, situate on the side of a hill, on the W. side of the Danube, over which is a handsome bridge to Pest. The inhabitants are estimated at 30,000. The churches and public buildings are handsome. In the adjacent country are vineyards, which produce excellent wine. Prior to 1526, when it surrendered to the Turks, it was the residence of the kings of Hungary. From that period, for 160 years, it was an object of jealousy and contention between the Turks and the Christian powers of Europe; when, in 1686, it surrendered to the latter, who strengthened the fortifications, by whom it has since been retained without interruption. It suffered greatly by fire in 1810, when 600 houses were destroyed; but their places have since been supplied with improved buildings. It is about 130 miles E. S. E. of Vienna, and 180 N. N. W. of Belgrade. Long. 19. 5. E. lat. 47. 30. N.

BUDANITZA, a town at the N. W. end of Sclavonia, near the south bank of the Drave; 23 miles S. W. of Funfkirchen.

Buddegaum, a town of Hindostan, in the province of Agra, with 4000 inhabitants.

Bude, a hamlet in Cornwall, on the Bristol Channel, with a lighthouse

Budelich, a town of Germany, in the territory of Treves; seated on the Traen; 12 miles E. N. E. of Treves.

Buderich, or **Burich**, a town of Germany, in the duchy of Cleves; seated on the Rhine; 22 miles S. E. of Cleves, and 4 S. E. of Wesel.

Budin, a town of Bohemia, in the circle of Rakonitz, with a castle; 9 miles S. by W. of Leutmeritz.

Budingen, a town of Germany, in Wetteravia, with a castle; situate on the Sambach; 25 miles E. N. E. of Frankfort on the Maine.

Budinze, a town of Sclavonia; 18 miles S. W. of Essey.

Budissen. *See* Bautzen.

Budoa, a strong seaport of Dalmatia, and a bishop's see. It sustained a siege by the Turks, in 1686; and is 30 miles S. E. of Ragusa. Long. 18. 58. E. lat. 42. 10. N.

Budrio, a town of Italy, in the Bolognese; 8 miles E. of Bologna.

Budweis, a fortified town of Bohemia, in the circle of Bechin, and lately a bishop's see. In the environs are mines of gold and silver. It is seated on the Muldau; 75 miles S. by W. of Prague.

Budweis, a town of Moravia, in the circle of Znain; 40 miles S. W. of Bunn, and 65 N.N.W. of Vienna.

Buen Ayre. *See* Bonair.

Buenos Ayres, a republic of South America, extending from the 13th to the 41st degree of S. lat., comprising an area of about 1,096,440 square miles: constituted a viceroyalty of Spain in 1778, but from the period of July, 1806, to July, 1821, it continued in perpetual collision, when at the latter period it was constituted an independent republic, by the title of the *United Provinces of South America*. It is sometimes called the *Argentine Republic*, in reference to Rio de la Plata, or Silver River. It is divided into 13 provinces, and is bounded on the N. by Bolivia, W. by Chili, S. by Patagonia, on the N. E. by Brazil, and E. by Uruguay. The valley of the Plata river comprehends the northern part, while to the S. are the level plains covered with tall grass, affording pasturage to numerous herds of wild cattle and horses, and which stretch away into the unpeopled districts of Patagonia, in the S., and are called pampas. The western part, at the foot of the Andes, is exceedingly cold in winter, while the heat is oppressive in summer. On the coast, violent and sudden winds are common. The soil is exceedingly various in such an extensive tract, but it is generally fruitful, and produces much valuable timber and fruits of numerous varieties. Gold and silver are found in the northern districts. The provinces are independent of each other, but are all subject to a governor, captain-general, and house of representatives; and all political disputes were settled by the treaty of August 27, 1828. The population may be considered as about 2,000,000, and the commerce of the interior is considerable, principally in the herb paraguay, or maté, used as an infusion resembling tea. The principal exports are hides, tallow, gold, and silver. The chief towns are Buenos Ayres, the capital, Santa Fe, Cordova, Mendoza, Tucuman, and Vera Cruz.

Buenos Ayres, city of, is seated on the S. bank of the La Plata, about 180 miles from its mouth, in the lat. of 34. 35. S. and 58. 24. of W. long., opposite to where the Uruguay forms its junction with the Parana. This city is justly esteemed as the finest, and as containing the most active and intelligent population of all South America. It was founded by Mendosa, in 1535, but afterwards abandoned; and in 1544 another colony of the Spaniards came here, who left it also; but it was rebuilt in 1582, and inhabited by Spaniards and the native Americans. It was, however, but little known to the world until the commencement of the last century, up to which period the intercourse of the country had been restrained by a rigorous monopoly, when, in 1748, the annual fleet of the monopolists sailed for the last time to Cadiz, the intercourse being thrown open to the whole of Spain. In 1774, the freedom of its intercourse was extended to the greater part of the ports of the other Spanish governments in America; and in 1778, when the provinces of Buenos Ayres, which had previously been under the government of Peru, were constituted a separate viceroyalty, and the city of Buenos Ayres made the seat of the viceroy, it gradually increased in extent, population, and importance, during the remainder of the last century; about which period the imperial French government, under Napoleon, sent emissaries for the purpose of rendering it subservient to the views and policy of France, which tended materially to retard its commercial career, on which alone the prosperity of the city depended. To counteract this influence, the English, in 1806, sent an expedition from the Cape of Good Hope against Buenos Ayres, which they took by surprise in the month of May of that year, but the whole force were compelled to surrender at discretion, after a few weeks, to a body of militia under the command of General Liniers, a partizan of the French government. In June of the following year, successive reinforcements having arrived from England, a renewed attack was made upon the city with a force of 10,000 men, under the command of General Whitelocke, but the inhabitants, animated by Liniers to the most determined resistance, and aided by the militia, converted every house into a fortress, from which they assailed the English troops at all points, with such disastrous effect as to compel the whole force to surrender prisoners of war. From this period, up to July, 1816, the city became the theatre of internal dissensions, when a declaration of independence was agreed upon; and it has since then remained comparatively tranquil, and been progressively recovering from the disasters of the preceding fifteen or twenty years. The buildings of Buenos Ayres are stately and uniform, and the streets regular. Among the public buildings are a stately cathedral, and two or three churches, town-hall, several convents, and other similar institutions. The public edifices are all built of stone of a whitish colour, and produce an imposing effect. Its commercial intercourse now extends to all parts of the world, and its export productions of hides and tallow, in addition to the silver and gold from the mines of Potosi, &c. enable it to command an abundant supply of all the manufactured productions of Europe and Asia, as well as of every other commodity, from every quarter of the globe. The population, which, at the commencement of the present century, was estimated at about 40,000, is now above 80,000.

Buffalo, a city of Erie county, state of New York, situate at the mouth of a small river of the same name, at the E. end of Lake Erie, about 20 miles S. of the great falls of Niagara, and 296 miles W. of Albany. Pop. 18,213.

Bug, a river of Poland, rising near Leopol, or Limberg, running N., dividing Austrian Gallicia from Russian Poland, to Brzesc. It then takes a westerly course, between Gallicia and Prussian Poland, falling into the Vistula a few miles below Warsaw.

Bugia, or Bujeia, a seaport of Algier, in the province of Constantina, at the mouth of the Major, on a bay of the Mediterranean. It has a strong castle, but Sir Edward Spragge destroyed several Algerine men-of-war under its walls in 1671. The harbour is safer and more capacious than that of Algier, but its entrance is equally dangerous. The principal trade is in instruments of agriculture, made of iron, obtained from mountains near the town. It is 90 miles E. of Algier. Long. 5. 28. E. lat. 36. 49. N.

Bugie, a town of Egypt, situate on the west shore of the Red Sea, almost opposite to Ziden, the port town of Mecca, and about 110 miles W. of it. Long. 36. 6. E. lat. 22. 15. N.

Builth, or Bualt, a town of Wales, in Brecknockshire, with a market on Monday and Saturday. Here was an ancient castle, whose keep, its last remains, was burnt down in 1690. In this neighbourhood the Welsh made their last stand for independence, and were defeated by Edward I. in 1283. Builth has a manufacture of stockings. It is seated on the Wye, over which is a bridge into Radnorshire; 12 miles N. of Brecknock, and 173 W. by N. of London.

Buis, a town of France, in the department of Drome; 40 miles E. of Orange, and 65. S .S. E. of Valence.

Buitrago, a fortified town of Spain, in New Castile, on the frontier of Segovia, celebrated for the wool collected in its environs. It is seated on the Lozoya; 40 miles N. of Madrid.

Bukharia Great. *See* Bokhara.

Bukharia Little. *See* Cashgur.

Bukowine, a district in the north-west part of the province of Moldavia, bordering on Gallicia, comprising about 4000 square miles, and 160,000 inhabitants of various nations, among whom are about 2000 gypsies. It is under the dominion of Austria.

Bulac, or Boulac a town of Egypt, on the Nile; 2 miles W. of Cairo, and the port of that city. On the north side of it is the Calisch, whose banks are cut every year, to convey the waters of the Nile, by a canal, to Cairo.

Bulam, or Boolam, an island on the west coast of Africa, at the mouth of the Rio Grande. The soil is good; and a settlement of free blacks was formed here in 1792, but abandoned the following year. Long. 14. 30. W. lat. 11. 0. N.

Bulgaria, a province of European Turkey; bounded on the north by the Danube, which divides it from Wallachia and Bessarabia; east, by the Black Sea; south, by Romania and Macedonia; and west by Servia. It is mountainous, but fertile in the intervening valleys. Sofia, or Sophia, on the frontier of Romania, 280 miles N. N. E. of Constantinople, is the capital.

Bullitt, a county of Kentucky, the west end of which jets upon the Ohio river. Pop. 6334. Shepherdsville, 69 miles W. S. W. of Frankfort, is the chief town.

Bullock, an interior county of the state of Georgia, lying between the Cannouche and Great Ogeechee rivers. Statesborough, in the centre of the county, 35 miles N. W. of Savannah, is the chief town. Pop. 3102.

Buncombe, a large dreary county, at the western extremity of North Carolina; bounded on the north by Tennessee, and south by South Carolina. Pop. 10,084, of whom 1199 are slaves. Ashville, in the centre of the county, 273 miles W. by S. of Raleigh, is the chief town.

Bundelcund, or Bundela, a circar of Hindostan, lying south of the Ganges, in the province of Allahabad; inhabited by a tribe of Rajpoots. It is a mountainous tract, and contains the celebrated diamond mines of Paunah, with some strong fortresses. Chatterpour is the capital. It was annexed to Benares in 1804.

Bungay, a town in Suffolk, with a market on Thursday, seated on the Waveney, which is navigable hence to Yarmouth. It has two churches, and the ruins of a nunnery and a castle. It is 36 miles N. by E. of Ipswich, and 106 N. E. of London.

Bungo, a kingdom of Japan, in the island of Ximo. The king of this country was converted to Christianity, and sent a solemn embassy to the Pope in 1583. The capital is Fumay. Long. 132. 0. E. lat. 32. 40. N.

Buniva, a mountain of Greece, between Janna and Livadia, extending to the Gulf of Zeiton. The ancient name was Æta; and it is famous for the pass of Thermopylæ, (so called from the hot baths in the neighbourhood) where Leonidas, and his 300 Spartans, resisted for three days the whole Persian army.

Bunkers Hill. *See* Breeds Hill.

Buntingford, a town in Hertfordshire, with a market on Monday; 31 miles N. by E. of London.

Buntwala, a town of Hindostan, in Canara, which has a great inland trade; situate near the Netrawari; 10 miles E. of Mangalore.

Buntzlau, a town of Silesia, in the principality of Jauer. It has a manufacture of brown pottery with gold and silver flowers; and is seated on the Bober; 23 miles W. by N. of Lignitz. Pop. 3300.

Buntzlau, a circle in the north part of Bohemia, between Leutmeritz and Konigingratz; bounded on the north by Lusatia, and south by the Elbe, which divides it from Kaurzem. It contains about 1850 square miles, and 280,000 inhabitants. The Iser intersects it from N. to S., falling into the Elbe.

Buntzlau, Alt, a town of Bohemia, seated on the Elbe; 16 miles S. S. W. of Jung Buntzlau.

Buntzlau, Jung, a town of Bohemia, capital of the circle of Buntzlau. It was a royal town under Rodolphus II., and is seated on the Iser; 28 miles N. N. E. of Prague.

Burdwan, a town of Hindostan, capital of a district in Bengal; seated on the north bank of the Dummooda; 57 miles N. W. of Calcutta. Pop. 45,000.

Burello, or Civita Burella, a town of Naples, in Abruzzo Citeriore; 20 miles S. of Lanciano.

Buren, a town of Holland, in Guelderland, with a fortified castle; 22 miles W. of Nimeguen. Pop. 3500.

Buren, or Bueren, a town of Westphalia, in the principality of Paderborn, seated on the Alme; 10 miles S. by W. of Paderborn.

Buren, a town of Switzerland, in the canton of Bern, seated on the Aar; 6 miles S. by W. of Soleure.

Burford, a town in Oxfordshire, with a market on Saturday. Here are manufactures of saddles, dussels, and rugs. It is seated on the Windrush; 17 miles W. by N. of Oxford, and 72 W. of London.

Burg, a town of Holland, in the county of Zutphen; seated on the Old Yssel; 18 miles E. by N. of Nimeguen.

Burg, a town of Lower Saxony, in the duchy of Magdeburg; on the river Ihle; 12 miles N. N. E. of Magdeburgh. Population about 7000.

Burg, or Borg, a town of Westphalia, in the duchy of Berg, with manufactures of gun-barrels and woollen stuffs; seated on the Wipper; 18 miles S. E. of Dusseldorf.

Burgau, a town of Suabia, with a castle which gives name to a marquisate, ceded to Bavaria in 1805, and now forms part of the circle of the Upper Danube. It is seated on the Mindel; 6 miles E. of Guntzburg, (the capital,) and 22 N. N. W. of Augsburg.

Burgdorf, a town of Switzerland, in the canton of Bern, with a castle, seated on an eminence, on the river Emmen; 8 miles N. E. of Bern.

Burgdorf, a town of Lower Saxony, in Luneburg, with a castle, on the river Awe; 15 miles S. of Zell.

Burgh, a village in Cumberland; 5 miles W. N. W. of Carlisle. Near it is a column, erected to denote the spot where Edward I. died, when preparing for an expedition against Scotland.

Burghaun, a town of Germany, in the principality of Fulda, on the river Haun; 8 miles N. N. E. of Fulda.

Burglengenfel, a town of Bavaria, in the principality of Neuburg, seated on the river Nab; 16 miles N. W. of Ratisbon.

Burgos, a city of Spain, capital of Old Castile, and an archbishop's see. It has an antique castle, once the abode of the kings of Castile; and the cathedral is one of the most magnificent Gothic fabrics in Europe. The squares, public buildings, and fountains, are fine. In 1812 the allied army, under Lord (now Duke of) Wellington, entered Burgos, after the battle of Salamanca, and besieged the castle near three months, during which they made several attempts to carry it by assault, but in vain; and the allies were ultimately obliged to raise the siege and retire into Portugal; but it surrendered the following year, without resistance. It is seated partly on a mountain, and partly on the river Aranzon; 95 miles E. by S. of Leon, and 117 N. of Madrid. Pop. about 9000.

Burgos d'Osma. *See* Borgo.

Burgu, or Berdoa, a territory of Zahara, in the desert of Libya, in the south of Augila and east of Fezzan. The capital is of the same name; 250 miles S. S. W. of Augila, and 430 E. S. E. of Mourzook. Long. 21. 40. E. lat. 26. 10. N.

Burgundy, or Bourgogne, a late province of France; 112 miles long and 75 broad; bounded on the E. by Franche Compte; W. by Bourbonnois and Nivernois; S. by Lyonois; and N. by Champagne. It is fertile in corn, fruits, and excellent wines; and is now formed into the three departments of Cote d'Or, Saone and Loire, and Yonne.

Burhampour, a town of Hindostan, capital of Candeish, and, at one period, of the Deccan also. It has a great trade in fine cotton for veils, shawls, &c. In the war with the Mahrattas in 1803 it surrendered to the British. It is situate in a delightful country, on the river Tapty; 225 miles E. by N. of Surat. Long. 76. 19. E. lat. 21. 25. N.

Buriano, a town of Tuscany, in the Siennese, near the lake Castiglono; 10 miles S. S. E. of Massa.

Burich. *See* Buderich.

Burka, a fortified seaport of Arabia, on the east coast, in the province of Oman; 45 miles W. N. W. of Muscat.

Burias, one of the Philippine islands, lying within the S. E. promontory of Luzon.

Burke, a western county of North Carolina, bounded on the west by the Blue ridge of the Allegany mountains, which divides it from Buncomb. The Great Catawah river rises from about twenty sources, at the foot of the mountains, within this county. Pop. 15,799. Morgantown, 205 miles W. of Raleigh, is the chief town.

Burke is the name of a frontier county in Georgia; bounded on the N. E. by the Savannah river, which divides it from South Carolina. It is bounded on the south by the Great Ogeechee. Pop. 13,176. Waynesborough, in the centre of the county, 104 miles E. of Milledgeville, and 75 N. W. of Savannah, is the chief town.

BURKEN, a town of Germany, in the territory of Mentz; 27 miles E. of Heidelberg.

BURKHAUSEN, a town of Bavaria, with an old fortified castle on a mountain. It is the seat of a regency, and stands on the river Salza, near its confluence with the Inn; 27 miles N. N. W. of Salzburg.

BURLINGTON, a town of England. *See* BRIDLINGTON.

BURLINGTON, a county of New Jersey, the S. E. point of which jets upon the Atlantic Ocean, at Little Egg Harbour, and the N. W. end is bounded by the Delaware river; it is divided into 12 townships, and contains a population of 32,831. The town, of the same name, is seated on the E. bank of the Delaware river; 17 miles above Philadelphia, and 10 below Trenton.

BURLINGTON, a town of Vermont, chief of Chittenden county. In 1791 a charter was granted for a richly endowed university to be established here. It is beautifully located on an eminence, at the head of a spacious bay, on Lake Champlain; 122 miles N. of Bennington. Pop. 4271.

BURLINGTON, a town in Otsego county, state of New York; 77 miles due west of Albany. Pop. 2154.

BURNHAM, a town in Norfolk, with a market on Monday and Saturday. It stands near the sea, on the river Burn, in which is a small harbour. Around it are five villages of the same name, with an addition; and that of Burnham Thorp is the birthplace of the celebrated Admiral Lord Nelson, whose father was the rector. Burnham is 29 miles N. W. of Norwich, and 117 N. E. of London.

BURNHAM, a town in Essex, at the mouth of the river Crouch, which is here called Burnham Water. The Walfleet and Burnham oysters are the product of the creeks and pits of this river. Burnham is 11 miles S. E. of Malden.

BURNLEY, a town in the parish of Whalley, Lancashire, situate at the foot of the range of hills which divide Lancashire from Yorkshire, in the centre of a very populous district, extensively occupied in the cotton manufacture, and abounding in coal. Immediately contiguous to Burnley there are eight extensive collieries, about thirty extensive cotton mills and manufactories, four calico printers, five or six machine makers, &c., &c. The Leeds and Liverpool Canal nearly encircles the town. It holds a market on Saturday, and is 24 miles due N. of Manchester, and 15 W. of Halifax.

BURNT ISLAND, an island near the S. coast of Newfoundland; 15 miles E. S. E. of Cape Ray. Long. 58. 50. W. lat. 47. 30. N.

BURNT ISLANDS, a cluster of islands in the Indian Ocean, W. N. W. from Goa. Long. 73. 30. E. lat. 16. 0. N.

BURNTISLAND, a town of Scotland, in Fifeshire, on the Frith of Forth, with an excellent harbour, and a trade in ship-building. It is seated at the foot of lofty hills; 9 miles N. of Leith.

BURRAMPOOTER, BRAHMAPUTRA, or MEGNA, a river of Asia, which rises in the mountains of Tibet, near the head of the Ganges, in the lat. of 34. N., and of 80. of E. long. These two rivers, issuing from opposite sides of the same ridge of mountains, direct their course toward opposite quarters, till they are more than 700 miles asunder; and afterwards meet in one point near the sea, each having performed a winding course of about 1400 miles. From its source the Burrampooter proceeds S. E. through Tibet, where it is named Sampoo, or Zancin, that is, *the river:* after washing the border of the territory of Lassa, it proceeds S. E. beyond the 95th degree of E. long. to within 220 miles of Yunan, the westernmost province of China; it then turns suddenly to the W., and passing through Assam, assumes the name of Burrampooter. It enters Bengal on the N. E., makes a circuit round the western point of the Garrow Mountains, and then, altering its course to S., meets the Ganges about 40 miles from the sea, in the lat. of 22. 40. N. During the last 60 miles before its junction with the Ganges, it forms a stream which is regularly from 4 to 5 miles wide.

BURSA, or BRUSA, a city of Asiatic Turkey, in Natolia, built by Prusias, king of Bithynia. It was the capital of the Ottoman empire, before the taking of Constantinople; and it now contains about 60,000 inhabitants. It stands upon several little hills, at the bottom of Mount Olympus, and on the edge of a fine plain full of fruit-trees. So many springs proceed from the mount, that every house has its own fountain; and at its foot are splendid hot-baths. The mosques are elegant, as are the caravanseras. The bezestine is a large structure full of warehouses and shops, containing all the commodities of the E., besides their own manufactures in silk. Here are the best workmen in all Turkey, who are excellent imitators of the tapestry of Italy and France. None but mussulmans are permitted to dwell in the city; but the suburbs, which are much finer, and better peopled, are filled with Jews, Armenians, and Greeks. Bursa is seated on the banks of the Nilifur, which falls into the Sea of Marmora; 68 miles S. by E. of Constantinople. Long. 29. 12. E. lat. 40. 12. N.

BURSLEM, a town in Staffordshire, with a market on Monday and Saturday. Till towards the close of the last century it was an inconsiderable place, but being intersected by the Trent and Mersey Canal, it has become one of the principal centres of the pottery, porcelain, or earthenware manufacture. It is 3 miles N. of Newcastle-under-Line, and 151 N. by W. of London.

BURTON-UPON-TRENT, a tn. in Staffordshire, with a market on Thursday. It has the remains of a large abbey; and is seated on the W. bank of the Trent, which here divides the counties of Stafford and Derby; there is an old bridge of thirty-six arches over the river, and on its banks are two extensive corn mills, one cotton mill, and six extensive breweries, the produce of which is distributed, and justly esteemed, over every part of the world. There are also six or eight employers in the manufacture of hats; the cotton spinning, at the commencement of the present century, was more extensive. It is 12 miles E. of Litchfield, 12 W. of Derby, and 123 W. of London.

Burwah, a town of Hindostan, in Bengal, on the borders of Orissa; 256 miles W. by N. of Calcutta.

Bury, a borough in Lancashire. Market on Thursday. Returns one member to parliament. It is extensively engaged both in the cotton and woollen manufacture, in all the operations of spinning, weaving scouring, fulling, dressing, bleaching, printing &c., in all the various branches of which there are nearly one hundred establishments, some of them very extensive. There are also iron foundries, machine makers, and six or eight employers in the manufacture of hats; it communicates with the Leeds and Liverpool Canal by a collateral cut, called the Bury Extension. It is seated on the banks of the Irwell; 9 miles N. of Manchester.

Bury St. Edmund, a borough in Suffolk, with a market on Wednesday and Saturday. It took its name from St. Edmund the king, who was buried here; and to his honour an abbey was founded, of which some noble ruins remain. Here are two parish churches, which stand in one churchyard; in St. Mary's lies Mary, queen of France, who was married to Charles Brandon, duke of Suffolk. At this town the barons met and entered into a league against king John. Henry VI. called a parliament here in 1446, when Humphry, duke of Gloucester, was imprisoned, and here he died, as supposed, by poison. The assizes for the county are held here; and it has a free-school, founded by Edward VI. It returns two members to parliament, and is seated on the Larke, a branch of the Ouse; 25 miles N. W. of Ipswich, and 71 N. N. E. of London.

Buryens, St., a village in Cornwall; 5 miles W. S. W. of Penzance. It was once of great note, and had a college founded by king Athelstan. The church is spacious, and contains many curious relics of antiquity. In its neighbourhood are nineteen large stones standing in a circle, 12 feet from each other, and in the centre is one much larger than the rest.

Buseo, a town of Turkey in Europe, pachalic of Wallachia; capital of a district of the same name. Pop. 6000.

Busheir, or Bushire, a town of Persia, in Farsistan, surrounded by a wall, with a few bastions. The English East India Company had formerly a factory here.. The trade with Shiraz, by caravans, is considerable. It is situate on a narrow neck of land, in the Gulf of Persia, 110 miles W. S. W. of Shiraz. Long. 51. 0. E. lat. 29. 20. N.

Bussorah. *See* Bassorah.

Bute, an island of Scotland, in the Frith of Clyde, separated on the N. from the peninsula of Cowal, in Argyleshire, by a narrow channel. It is 14 miles long, and 4 broad; the N. part hilly and barren, but the S. fertile and well cultivated. The coast is rocky, and indented with several safe harbours, chiefly appropriated to the herring fishery. Rothsay is the capital.

Buteshire, a county of Scotland, consisting of the islands of Bute, Arran, Great and Little Cumbray, and Inchmarnoc, which lie in the Frith of Clyde, between the counties of Ayr and Argyle.

Butgembach, a town of the Netherlands; 25 miles S. by E. of Aix-la-Chapelle.

Butler, an interior county in the W. part of Pennsylvania, the S. E. point jutting upon the Allegany river; 18 miles above Pittsburg. Pop. 22,378. The chief town, of the same name, in the centre of the county, is 242 miles W. by N. of Harrisburg. Pop. 861.

Butler, an interior county in the W. part of Kentucky, intersected from E. to W. by Green River, which falls into the Ohio. Pop. 3898. Morgantown, on the S. bank of Green River, 144 miles W. by S. of Frankfort, is the chief town.

Butler, a frontier county at the S. E. extremity of the state of Ohio, bordering on Indiana. It is intersected from the N. W. corner to the centre of the S. border, by the Miami river. Pop. 28,173. Hamilton, on the E. bank of the Miami, 107 miles W. S. W. of Columbus, and 12 N. of Cincinnati, is the chief town. Pop. 1409.

Butler is also the name of a newly-formed county in Alabama. The court-house is 47 miles S. E. by S. of Cahawba. Pop. 8685.

Butrinto, a seaport of European Turkey, in Albania, and a bishop's see; seated on the canal of Corfu, at the entrance of the Gulf of Venice; 30 miles S. of Chimæra. Long. 19. 9. E. lat. 39. 49. N.

Buttermere, a lake in Cumberland, 8 miles S. W. of Keswick. It is two miles long, and nearly half a mile broad. On the W. side it is terminated by a mountain, called, from its ferruginous colour, the Red Pike; a strip of cultivated ground adorns the E. shore; at the N. end is the village of Buttermere; and a group of houses, called Gatesgarth, is seated on the S. extremity, under an amphitheatre of mountainous rocks. Here Honister Crag is seen rising to a vast height, flanked by two conical mountains, Fleetwith on the E., and Scarf on the W. side. Numerous mountain torrents form never-failing cataracts, that thunder and foam down the rocks, and form the lake below. This lake is called the Upper Lake; and, near a mile from it, to the N. E., is the Lower Lake, called also Cromack-water. The river Cocker flows through both these lakes to Cockermouth.

Butterworth, an appendage to the town of Rochdale, in Lancashire. *See* Rochdale.

Buttevant, a town and parish of Ireland, in the county of Cork. The town is 4 miles N. of Mallow.

Button Bay, the north part of Hudson Bay through which attempts were made by Sir Thomas Button, to discover the N. W. passage to China, when he lost his ship, and came back in a sloop built in the country. It lies between 60. and 66. N. lat.

BUTTSTADT and BUTTELSTADT, two towns of Upper Saxony, in Thuringia, seated on the Loss; 16 miles W. of Naumburg.

BUTZBACH, a town of Germany, in Wetteravia, seated in a marshy but fertile plain; 10 miles S. of Giessen, and 25 N. of Frankfort. Pop. about 3200.

BUTZOW, a town of Lower Saxony, in Mecklenburg-Schwerin, seated on the Warna; 17 miles S. W. of Rostock.

BUXADEWAR, a strong fort of the country of Bootan, at the entrance of the mountains from Bengal. It stands on the top of a rock; 20 miles N. of Chichacotte.

BUXAR, a town and fort of Hindostan, in Bahar, on the S. bank of the Ganges; 72 miles W. of Patna.

BUXTEHUDE, a town of Lower Saxony, in the duchy of Bremen, on the river Este; 18 miles S. E. of Stade.

BUXTON, a village in Derbyshire, at the entrance of the Peak. It has nine wells that rise near the source of the river Wye, and they are deemed one of the seven wonders of the Peak. Their waters, noted in the time of the Romans, are hot and sulphureous, temperature about 82; much company resort to them in the summer. The building for the bath was erected by George, Earl of Shrewsbury; and here Mary, Queen of Scotland, was for some time. The Duke of Devonshire has erected a beautiful building in the form of a crescent, under which are piazzas and shops. A mile hence is another of the wonders, called Pool's Hole, at the foot of a mountain. The entrance is low and narrow, but it presently opens to a cave of considerable height, and 696 feet long, with a roof resembling a Gothic cathedral It contains many stalactitious concretions, and several curious representations both of art and nature, produced by the petrifying water continually dropping from the rock. Buxton is 32 miles N. W. of Derby, and 160 N. N. W. of London.

BUZANCOIS, a town of France, in the department of the Indre, on the E. bank of the river of that name; 12 miles S. E. of Chatillon. Pop. 3200.

BYCHOW, a town of Lithuania, on the W. bank of the Dnieper; 180 miles S. S. W. of Wilna, and 8 S. of Mohilon.

BYKER, an appendage to Newcastle-on-Tyne. *See* NEWCASTLE.

BYRON ISLAND, an island in the Pacific Ocean, discovered by Commodore Byron in 1765. It is low, full of wood, and very populous. The natives are tall, well proportioned, and clean, and their countenance expressive of a surprising mixture of intrepidity and cheerfulness. Long. 173. 46. E. lat. 1. 18. S.

C.

*** *Words that sometimes begin with C, and are not found under that letter, may be sought for under the letter K or S.*

CABARRAS, a small interior county of North Carolina, lying to the W. of the Yadkin river. Population, 9259, of whom 2179 are slaves. Concord, 143 miles W. S. W. of Raleigh, is the chief town.

CABECA DE VIDE, a town of Portugal, in Alentejo, with a castle; 12 miles S. W. of Portalegro.

CABELL, a large mountainous county of Virginia, bounded on the S. W. by the Big Sandy river, which divides it from Kentucky, and on the N. W. by the Ohio river, which divides it from the state of Ohio. It is about 50 miles in length from S. E. to N. W., and 25 in breadth. Pop. 8163. Guyando, at the mouth of a river of the same name, which intersects the county its whole length, falling into the Ohio, is the chief town.

CABELLO, or CAVELLO. *See* PORTO CABELLO.

CABENDA, a seaport on the W. coast of South Africa, subject to Portugal; 100 miles S. E. of Loango. Long. 12. 2. E. lat. 4. 5. S.

CABES, or GABES, a town of the kingdom of Tunis, near a gulf of the same name; 170 miles S. of Tunis. Magnificent ruins are at a short distance from this place. Long. 10. 55. E. lat. 33. 40. N.

CABOTIA, a name sometimes applied to the countries on the St. Lawrence, North America, comprising Canada, New Brunswick, &c., from their being first explored by the Cabots.

CABRA, a town of Spain, in Andalusia, with six convents, and a college for the study of philosophy and divinity. It is situate at the foot of a mountain, near the source of a river of the same name; 25 miles S. E. of Cordova.

CABRA, a town of the kingdom of Tombuctoo. It is a place of great trade, seated on the Niger, and serves as a port to the capital; 10 miles S. E. of Tombuctoo.

CABRERA, one of the Balearic Isles, in the Mediterranean; 7 miles S. of Majorca. It has a large harbour, on the N. side, defended by a castle. Long. 2. 55. E. lat. 39. 8. N.

CABUL, or CABOOL, a country of Asia, bounded on the W. by Persia, N. by the Hindoo-ko, E. by Cashmere and Lahore, and S. by Candahar. It was anciently a province of Persia; afterwards it was annexed to the Mogul empire till 1739, when it was restored to Persia by Nadir Shah. The country is highly diversified, consisting of mountains covered with snow, hills of moderate height, rich plains, stately forests, and innumerable streams. It produces every article necessary for human life, and the most delicate fruits and flowers. It is sometimes called Zabulistan, from Zabul, one of the names of Ghizni, which was the ancient capital of the country.

CABUL, the capital of the province of Cabul, and of the dominions of the sultan of the Afghans, (*see* AFGHANISTAN,) seated near the foot of the Hindoo-ko, on the river Attock, a branch of the Indus. It carries on a considerable trade, and is considered as the gate of India towards Tartary. In 1739 Nadir Shah took it by storm, and plundered it of great treasures. It is 170 miles N. E. of Candahar. Long. 68. 35. E. lat. 34. 30. N.

CABYNA. *See* CAMBYNA.

CACACA, or KASUSA, a town of the kingdom of Fez, with a fort upon a rock; 16 miles S. of Melilla, on the shores of the Mediterranean.

CACELLA, or TACELLA, a town of Portugal, on the S. E. coast of Algarva; 6 miles E. by N. of Tavira, and 8 W. S. W. of Castro Marim.

CACERES, a town of Spain, in Estremadura, seated on the Sabrot; 22 miles S. E. of Alcantara, on the road to Truxillo. Pop. about 8000.

CACERES, a town in the S. part of the island of Luçonia, East Indies, capital of the province of Camarines, and a bishop's see. Long. 124. 0. E. lat. 14. 33. N.

CACHAN, or KASHAN, a town of Persia, in Irac Ajemi, which has a considerable trade in silks, silver and gold brocades, and porcelain. Here are many Christians, and Guebres, or worshippers of fire. It is seated in a vast plain; 55 miles N. by W. of Ispahan.

CACHAO, or KESHO, the capital of the kingdom of Tonquin. It contains 20,000 houses, whose walls are of mud, and the roofs covered with thatch; a few are built with brick, and roofed with pantiles. The principal streets are very wide, and paved with small stones. The king has three palaces here, such as they are; and near them are stables for his horses and elephants. The house of the English factory is the best in the city; but the factories have been discontinued. It is seated on the river Hoti; 80 miles from the Gulf of Tonquin. Long. 105. 11. E. lat. 21. 10. N.

CACHOEIRA, a town of Brazil, in the government of Bahia. It is the mart for the northern gold mines, and stands on a small river; 42 miles N. W. of St. Salvador.

CACONGO, a town of the kingdom of Loango, on the W. coast of South Africa, seated near the mouth of a river; 40 miles S. S. E. of Loango.

CACORLA, a town of Spain, situate between two mountains on the frontiers of La Mancha, Murcia, and Granada; 15 miles E. N. E. of Ubeda.

CADENAC, a town of France, in the department of Lot, on the river Lot; 27 miles E. N. E. of Cahors.

CADENEL, a town of France, in the department of Mouths of the Rhone; 28 miles S. E. of Avignon.

CADER IDRIS, a mountain of Wales, in Merionethshire, to the S. of Dolgelly; the perpendicular height of which is 2914 feet above the level of the sea; and on it are several lakes, abounding in fish.

CADIAR, a town of Spain, in Granada; 28 miles S. E. of Granada.

CADILLAC, a town of France, in the department of Gironde, with a castle, seated on the E. bank of the Garonne; 15 miles S. E. of Bordeaux.

CADIZ, a town of Spain, in Andalusia; it is situate at the N. W. extremity of a promontory, jetting into the Atlantic Ocean, and running parallel with the coast, forming a bay twelve miles in extent, and five or six broad, defended at the entrance by two forts, which render the harbour secure, and, being edged by craggy rocks on the south, and strongly defended on the land side, enables it to defy whatever armed force may be brought against it, either by sea or land. It is supposed to have been first founded by the Phœnicians, and to have attracted the enlightened attention of the Romans at an early period of their career, several vestiges of their works of art still remaining to attest their supremacy, and refinement of taste. It was taken and pillaged by the English in 1596, who made another attempt upon it in 1626, and again in 1702, but in both instances without effect. During the domination of Spain in Mexico and South America, it was not only the chief station of the national marine, but the grand depôt of all the monopolized commerce of those extensive regions, and it consequently ranked, up to the period of 1778, among the most considerable and important of the commercial cities of Europe. In 1778, the commerce of the Americans was opened generally, to all the seaports of Spain, when Cadiz experienced some decline; it however retained a pre-eminence over all the other ports, and continued to hold a high commercial rank, until the events of the war growing out of the French revolution in 1793, led not merely to an interruption of the commerce of Cadiz, but to an almost total extinction of all external intercourse. It was bombarded by the English, without effect, in 1800. Its harbour was the rendezvous of the combined fleets of France and Spain, previous to the fatal battle with the English off Cape Trafalgar, in October, 1805. On the ebullition of the Spaniards in favour of the late king Ferdinand, in 1806, in opposition to the government established by Napoleon Buonaparte, under his brother Joseph, the wreck of the French fleet, then in the harbour of Cadiz, surrendered to the ebullitionists; and, on Seville being taken possession of by a French force in the following year, Cadiz became the seat of the Central Junta, and afterwards of the Cortes, the French maintaining a large armed force in its vicinity, occasionally bombarding it from that period up to 1812, when they finally withdrew, and it once again endeavoured to resume its wonted activity and importance in commerce; but during its suspension a revolution had taken place, more or less, over all South America; its commerce diverted into new channels; and, as such, the merchants of Cadiz found that every enterprise had to be formed anew. The time was unpropitious; and the commercial as well as social policy of Spain were incompatible with the time and circumstances, and Cadiz continued to droop, whilst distrust and dissatisfaction pervaded the whole country; to such a height had the spirit of distrust and disorder attained, that on the 10th of March, 1820, near 1000 of the inhabitants of Cadiz fell a prey to the fury of the soldiery. In the following year, when a party sprung up in Spain, demanding of the king the assembling of the Cortes, and the fulfilment of the constitution, the citizens of Cadiz identified themselves with the constitutional party; and, on a French army of 100,000 men entering the country in 1823, to protect the king in his absolute and despotic authority, the constitutionalists removed him and the court from Madrid, first to Seville, and ultimately to Cadiz, as to a place impregnable to all the force which the French could bring against it. A large French naval force now blockaded the harbour, and on the 1st of October of that year, treachery triumphed over patriotism, and accomplished what fleets and armies could not have effected. The French became masters of Cadiz, released Ferdinand from the shackles of the constitutionalists, and proscription and terror again reigned with uncontrolled sway over Cadiz and all Spain.

The aspect of Cadiz, viewed either from the harbour, or from the opposite shore of the bay, is very imposing; on entering it, however, the streets are narrow and the houses have a gloomy appearance; the great square of St. Antonio is, however, an exception. It has several churches, some of them spacious and fine edifices, numerous convents, and other religious houses, an extensive hospital, and custom-house. Its greatest inconvenience is its destitution of good water, with which essential commodity the city is supplied from a considerable distance, being conveyed in butts, at a great expense of labour and cost. Large quantities of salt are made in the vicinity. It has no manufacture deserving of notice; indeed, not only its prosperity and importance, but its subsistence, may be considered as depending altogether on its external commerce; and as such, it suffers in an equal or greater proportion than any other part of Spain, by the unsocializing policy which pervades that delightful country. Cadiz is about 60 miles S. of Seville, 45 N. W. of Gibraltar, and 320 S. by W. of Madrid; the observatory being in the lat. of 36. 32. N. and 6. 17. W. long.

Cadolzburg, a town of Bavaria, circle of Rezat; 8 miles W. of Nuremberg.

Cadore, a town of the Austrian Venetian territory, the birthplace of Titian, the painter. It is seated on the Piave; 15 miles N. of Belluno.

Cadsand, or Cassand, an island of Holland, on the N. coast of Flanders, at the mouth of the Scheldt. The land is fertile, and the inhabitants make a large quantity of excellent cheese. The chief town is Cassandria.

Caen, a city of France, capital of the department of Calvados. It has a celebrated university, and a castle with four towers, built by the English. The abbey of St. Stephen was founded by William the Conqueror, who was buried in it. The river Orne, which falls into the English Channel, runs through the city, to which the tide brings up large vessels. It exports large quantities of clover seed to England. It is 65 miles W. by S. of Rouen, and 125 W. by N. of Paris. Long. 0. 22. W. lat. 49. 11. N. Pop. 38,161.

Caerleon, a town of Monmouthshire, with a market on Thursday. Many Roman antiquities have been found here, and it has the ruins of a castle. It is seated on the Usk; 19 miles S. W. of Monmouth, and 146 W. by N. of London.

Caermarthenshire, a maritime county of South Wales, 48 miles long, and 25 broad. It is bounded on the S. by the Bristol Channel, on the W. by Pembrokeshire, on the N. by Cardiganshire, and on the E. by Brecknock and Glamorganshire. The air is wholesome, and the soil less rocky and mountainous than in most other parts of Wales, and consequently it is proportionately more fertile both in corn and pasture. It has also plenty of wood, and is well supplied with coal and limestone. The principal rivers are the Towy, Cothy, and Tave; of which the first abounds with excellent salmon. It has numerous ancient forts, camps, and tumuli. Near Caermarthen, towards the E., may be seen the ruins of Kastelk Karry, and several vast caverns, supposed to have been copper mines of the Romans. Near this spot is a fountain, which ebbs and flows twice in twenty-four hours. The county and city send each a member to parliament.

Caermarthen, a borough of Wales, capital of Caermarthenshire, with a market on Wednesday and Saturday. It is seated on the Towy, over which is a strong bridge, to which vessels of 200 to 300 tons burden may come up. It was fortified with a wall and a castle, now in ruins; and on the E. side of the town, near the river are the remains of a monastic building of considerable extent. Caermarthen is a county of itself, governed by a mayor. There are iron and tin mines in the neighbourhood. It is 24 miles S. E. of Cardigan, and 220 W. by N. of London.

Caernarvonshire, a county of North Wales, of an oblong form, the S. part projecting into St. George's Channel, the N. being bounded by the Irish Sea, or what would now more properly be called Liverpool Bay, from the celebrity of the town of that name: the Menai Strait divides it from the Isle of Anglesea on the N. W., and the river Conway divides it from Denbighshire on the E., whilst part of the S. E. side borders on Merionethshire. This county, being the most rugged district of North Wales, may be truly called the Cambrian Alps. Its central part is occupied by the famed Snowdon, rising to the height of 3571 feet above the level of the sea, and the prospects around are rude and savage in the highest degree, but not without a mixture of beauty, where the dimensions of the vales admit the varieties of wood, water, and meadows. The soil in the valleys, on the side of St. George's Channel, is pretty fertile, especially of barley; great numbers of black cattle, sheep, and goats, are fed on the mountains; and the sea, lakes, and rivers, abound with a variety of fish. Copper mines have been worked in various parts of these mountains, as well as lead; and quantities of stones, excellent for hones, are dug near Snowdon; to the dreary region of which the rich vale of Conway below forms a pleasing contrast. It sends one member to parliament

Caernarvon, a borough and seaport of Wales, capital of Caernarvonshire, with a market on Saturday. It is seated within the Menai Strait, near its entrance into Caernarvon Bay, and carries on a considerable trade with Ireland, and the principal English ports, to which it exports vast quantities of slates. It has a celebrated castle, built by Edward I., in which his son, Edward II., the first prince of Wales, was born. Caernarvon is governed by the constable of the castle who is always mayor. Here are salt-water baths, and elegant hot and cold baths, which are much frequented during the season. It is 7 miles S. W. of Bangor, and 244 N. W. of London. Long. 4. 20. W. lat. 53. 8. N. It sends one member to parliament.

Caerphilly, a town of Wales, in Glamorganshire, with a market on Thursday. The ruins of its celebrated castle more resemble that of a city than a single edifice; a circular tower, about 75 feet in height, inclines 11 ft. 6 in. from its base. It is seated between the Taafe and Rumney; 7 miles N. of Cardiff, and 160 W. of London.

Caerwent, a village in Monmouthshire; 4 miles S. W. of Chepstow, and about 2 miles from the bank of the Severn.

Caerwys, a town of Wales, in Flintshire, with a market on Tuesday; 5 miles W. of Flint, and 212 N. W. of London.

Caffa, or Theodosia, the largest town of the Crimea, with an excellent road and harbour. It was taken in 1266, by the Genoese, who made it one of the most flourishing towns in the E. of Europe. It was taken from the Venetians in 1297, but soon recovered; however, in 1474, the Tartars, assisted by the Turks, finally expelled them. It was the last post in the Crimea of which the Genoese retained the sovereignty. Caffa was the Theodosia of the ancients; a name which has been restored to it since the Russians became possessed of the Crimea, in 1770. It contains about 20,000 inhabitants, and is constantly well garrisoned. The trade consists in wax, furs, lambskins, leather, horses, and female slaves; most of the latter are brought from Circassia, and are here sold at from 400*l.* to 800*l.* each, in proportion to their charms. Caffa is seated on a bay of the Black Sea, at the foot of some high mountains; 65 miles E. by N. of Sympheropol, and 130 S. E. of Precop. Long. 35. 20. E. 40. 0. N.

Caffa, Strait of, the ancient Cimmerian Bosphorus; a strait that forms the communication between the Black Sea and the Sea of Asoph, and a separation between Europe and Asia.

Cafiristin, or Kettore, a mountainous country of Asia, lying between the N. E. part of Persia and Tartary. The valleys are inhabited by various independent tribes, possessing manners and speaking a language peculiar to themselves, but of which very little is known.

Caffraria, or Kaffraria, a country on the E. coast of South Africa, extending from the latitude of about 30 S. to the Great Fish River, in the latitude of about 34., which divides it from the country of the Hottentots: its western boundaries are not ascertained. The Caffres are tall and well proportioned, and, in general, evince great courage in attacking lions, and other beasts of prey. Their skin is a jet black, their teeth white as ivory, and their eyes large. The clothing of both sexes is the same, consisting entirely of the hides of oxen, which are as pliant as cloth. The men wear tails of different animals tied round their thighs, pieces of brass in their hair, and large ivory rings on their arms; they are adorned also with the hair of lions, and feathers fastened on their heads, with many other fantastical ornaments. They are fond of dogs, and have great pride in their cattle, which pay the most perfect obedience to their voice. Their exercise is hunting, fighting, or dancing. They are expert in throwing lances, and, in time of war, use shields made of the hides of oxen. They sometimes make incursions into the English territories of the Cape of Good Hope. The women are employed in the cultivation of their gardens and corn. They raise several vegetables which are not indigenous to the country, as tobacco, water-melons, kidney-beans, and hemp. Their huts are higher and more commodious than those of the Hottentots, and their lands more fertile, but their oxen, and almost all their animals, are much smaller. Industry is the leading trait in the character of the Caffres, who are distinguished from their neighbours to the S. by their fondness for agriculture. They have a high opinion of the Supreme Being, and of his power; they believe in a future state of rewards and punishments; but think that the world had no beginning, and will be everlasting. They have no sacred ceremonies, and, consequently, no priests; but they have a kind of conjurors, whom they greatly revere. They are governed by an hereditary king, whose power is very limited; but, being permitted to take as many wives as he pleases, he has a larger portion of land to cultivate, and a greater number of cattle to tend and feed. The distance of the different hordes makes it necessary that they should have inferior chiefs, who are appointed by the king. They are divided into several tribes, of which the Koozas are those to whom "Caffre" is now more specifically applied. They have continually threatened the eastern frontier of the colony, which has led to much warfare.

Cagayan Sooloo, an eastern island, lying off the N. E. point of Borneo, in the lat. of 7. N. and 118. 36. E. long. It is about 20 miles in circumference, and governed by a rajah.

Cagayan, a district, the most northern part of Luçonia, the chief of the Philippine islands. It is a fertile and populous district, in the lat. of 19. N.

Cagayan Isles, a group of small islands in the Mindoro Sea, between Borneo and the Philippines, in the lat. of 9. N. and 121. E. long.

Cagliari, a fortified city and seaport of Sardinia, capital of the island, and an archbishop's see, with a university and a castle. Here are numerous churches, beside the cathedral, three of which are collegiate. It stands on the S. part of the island, at the bottom of a gulf of its name, which forms a large and secure harbour, and exports considerable quantities of olive oil and salt. Long. 9. 8. E. lat. 39. 20. N. Pop. about 30,000.

CAGNETE, CANETE, or GUARCO, a town of Peru, capital of a district of the same name, extending about 24 leagues along the sea coast. It is situate near the sea; 80 miles S. E. of Lima. Long. 76. 16. W. lat. 13. 10. S.

CAHAWBA, the chief town of Dallas county, and once seat of the legislative government of the state of Alabama. It is seated at the junction of a river of the same name with the Alabama river; 915 miles S. W. of Washington, and about 180 N. of New Orleans.

CAHIR, a town and parish in the S. part of the county of Tipperary, in Ireland. The town is seated on the W. bank of the Suir; about 6 miles S. of Cashel, and 85 S. W. of Dublin.

CAHIR is also the name of a small island off the S. W. coast of the county of Mayo, in the lat. of 53. 44. N. and 9. 53. W. long.

CAHORS, a city of France, capital of the department of Lot, and a bishop's see, with a university. It is seated on a peninsula made by the river Lot, and built partly on a craggy rock. There are three bridges over the river. The cathedral is a Gothic structure, and has a large square steeple. The town has a manufacture of fine cloths and ratteens, and furnishes excellent wine, of the kind called *vin de grave*. It was taken by assault, in 1580, by Henry IV., by means of petards, which were first employed here. In one of the suburbs are the remains of a Roman amphitheatre. Cahors is 70 miles N. of Toulouse, and 315 S. by W. of Paris.

CAICOS, or CAYCOS, the southernmost of the Bahama Isles. *See* BAHAMAS.

CAI-FONG, a city of China, capital of the province of Ho-nan. It is situate on a plain, 6 miles from the river Hoanho, or Great Yellow River, above 300 miles above its entrance into the sea, which is higher than the plain, and kept in by raised dikes, that extend above 90 miles. When the city was besieged by the rebels, in 1642, they cut the dikes of the river, which drowned 300,000 of the inhabitants. Some of the ruins still remain, which show that its present state is far inferior to its former magnificence. Its jurisdiction comprehends four cities of the second class, and 30 of the third. It is 350 miles S. S. W. of Pekin, and about 850 N. by E. of Canton. Long. 114. 28. E. lat. 34. 53. N.

CAIFFA, or HAIFA, a seaport of Syria, in Palestine, defended by a wall and a citadel. It stands on the S. side of the bay of Acre; 8 miles S. W. of Acre. It is a place of some importance.

CAIMAN, or CAYMANS, three small islands lying to the N. W. of Jamaica, between it and the S. coast of Cuba. The N. E. point of Grand Caymans is in lat. 19. 12. N. and 81. 26. W. long. The inhabitants of Jamaica come hither to catch turtle.

CAIRNGORM, a mountain of Scotland, at the S. W. extremity of Banffshire, on the border of Inverness. It rises in a conical form 1750 feet above the level of a small lake near its base, which is the source of the Aven, and 4050 feet above the level of the sea; its sides clothed with firs, and its top generally covered with snow. It is famous for beautiful rock-crystals, much esteemed by lapidaries; about 30 miles E. of Fort Augustus.

CAIRO, (*El Kahira*, the victorious, Arabic,) or GRAND CAIRO, a large city, capital of Egypt. It consists of three towns, about a mile apart; Old Cairo, New Cairo, and the port termed Bulac. The population is estimated at 300,000. Old Cairo is now reduced to a small place. New Cairo is a mile from the river, and 7 miles in circumference. The streets are narrow; and the finest houses are built round a court, in which they make the best appearance, having few or no windows next to the street. The castle stands on a steep rock, and is surrounded by thick walls, on which are strong towers. Joseph's Well, made by a vizier of that name, about the year 1100, is the most curious part of the castle: it is sunk in the rock, 280 feet deep and 40 in circumference, with a staircase carried round; and a machine, turned by oxen, raises the water (which comes from the Nile) into a reservoir, whence it is again raised by a similar machine. There are many other reservoirs for water; and numerous bazaars, where each trade has its allotted quarter. There are several public bagnios, very handsome within, and used as places of refreshment and diversion, especially for the women, who go there twice a week; but the wives of great men have baths at home. The women have greater liberty here than in any part of the Turkish empire; and on Friday a mosque without the walls is frequented by them as a pilgrimage of pleasure. The Kaliss, a canal which conveys the waters of the Nile into the city, is 20 feet broad, and has houses on each side of it. As soon as the water begins to rise, they close the mouth of the canal with earth, and place a mark, to show the time when this and all other canals in the kingdom are to be opened, which is done with great solemnity. There are not less than 300 mosques in Cairo, the lofty minarets of which present a very picturesque appearance. It was a place of very great trade before the discovery of the Cape of Good Hope, and is still the centre of that of eastern Africa. The chief manufactures are sugar, sal ammoniac, glass lamps, saltpetre, gunpowder, red and yellow leather, and linen made of the fine Egyptian flax. This city was taken by the French, under Buonaparte, in 1798, and retaken by the British in 1801. It stands on the E. bank of the Nile, about 120 miles S. E. of Alexandria, and about the same distance from each of the two mouths of the river at Rosetta and Damietta. Lat. 30. 2. N. and 31. 20. of E. long.

CAIRO, a town of Piedmont; 25 miles W. of Genoa. It was the scene of a sanguinary battle between the French and Austrians in 1794, and in 1796 was taken by the French Pop. about 4000.

CAIRO, a town in Greene county, state of New York; about 5 miles W. of Hudson.

CAIROAN, or KAIRWAN, an interior town of the kingdom of Tunis, and next to the city of Tunis for trade and number of inhabitants. It is situate near a sandy desert, where are found many vestiges of former magnificence, and on the river Magrida; about 60 miles S. by E. of Tunis, and a few miles W. of Susa.

CAISTOR, a town in Lincolnshire, with a market on Monday. Near it are the remains of a monastery, and many Roman vestiges. It is 12 miles S. W. of Grimsby, and 156 N. of London.

CAITHNESS-SHIRE, a county at the S. E. extremity of Scotland; 35 miles long and 20 broad; bounded on the N. by Pentland Frith, which divides it from the Orkneys, E. and S. E. by the German Ocean, and W. by Sutherlandshire. The S. angle is occupied by mountains; and a vast ridge of hills forms the S. W. boundary, ending in a promontory, called the Ord of Caithness, which runs out into the sea, in the lat. of 58. 10. N. The rest of the county may be deemed an immense morass, interspersed with some fruitful spots, producing oats and barley, and others affording pasture for sheep and black cattle. Its other chief products are butter, cheese, yarn, skins, feathers, and kelp. It sends a member to parliament alternately with Buteshire. English is chiefly spoken on the coast, but in the highlands the Gaelic prevails. Thurso, on the N., and Wick, on the E. coast, are the chief towns.

CAJANA, or KAJANA, one of the seven principal towns of East Bothnia.

CAJAZZO, a town of Naples; 25 miles N. of the city of Naples.

CAJELI, BAY OF. *See* BOURO.

CALABAR, OLD and NEW, a territory at the eastern extremity of the coast of Guinea, on the W. coast of North Africa. Since the restriction of the slave trade to the S. of the Equator, this district has carried on a more extensive trade in palm oil and bar wood, and some elephants' teeth, than any other part of the coast. The town of New Calabar is situate at the mouth of a river of the same name, in the lat. of 4. 10. N. and 6. 42. of E. long. Duke's Town, the chief town of Old Calabar, is situate at the mouth of another river of the same name, falling into a bay, about 80 miles E. by N. of New Calabar. These rivers form part of the Delta of the mysterious Niger, which debouches at the River Nun, near to them.

CALABAZO, or CALABACO, an interior town of Colombia; about 150 miles S. of Caraccas. It contains about 5000 inhabitants.

CALABRIA, a promontory and province of Naples, forming the foot and southern extremity of Italy, extending from 37. 53. to 40. 5. of N. lat., and being about 40 miles in mean breadth, between the long. of 15. 40. and 17. 30. E. A ridge of mountains, the Appennines, intersects the whole territory from N. to S., and numerous streams fall into the sea on both coasts. It gives the title of Duke to the eldest son of the King of Naples. It is divided into two parts: Citra, N., bordering on the Basilicata, contains about 350,000 inhabitants, and Ultra, S., contains about 400,000. This country abounds in excellent fruit, corn, wine, oil, silk, cotton, and wool. In 1783, a great part of Calabria Ultra, as well as of Sicily, was destroyed by one of the most terrible earthquakes on record: beside the destruction of many towns, villages, and farms, above 40,000 people perished by this calamity. The principal towns are, Bova, at the S. extremity; Reggio, Rosarno, St. Eufemia, Castigiene, and Paula, on the W.; and Rossano, Cariato, Catanzaro, and Squillace, on the E. coast; and, in the interior, Cossano, Bisagnano, Cosenza (the capital), Policastro, Mileto, and Oppido.

CALAHORRA, an episcopal town of Spain, in Old Castile, on the side of a hill, which extends to the Ebro; 90 miles E. of Burgos. It was the birthplace of Quintilian. Pop. about 4300.

CALAIS, a seaport of France, in the department of Pas de Calais, with a citadel. It was taken by Edward III. of England, in 1347, after a siege of more than 11 months, which has given rise to some historical as well as dramatic fiction. In 1557 it was retaken by the Duke of Guise. It was bombarded by the English in 1696, without receiving much injury. The fortifications are good, but its greatest strength is its situation among the marshes, which may be overflowed at the approach of an enemy. In the centre of the town is a spacious square, surrounded by good buildings, and the church is a stately edifice; the harbour, which is formed of two wooden piers, running into the sea, only admits small vessels. On the N. pier is a pillar erected to commemorate the landing of Louis XVIII. from England, in 1814, after 23 years of exile. Calais derives all its importance from its contiguity to the English coast; being only 20 miles from Dover, with which a daily intercourse is maintained; several hundred persons passing to and from it weekly. It is 25 miles W. by S. of Dunkirk, 20 N. by E. of Boulogne, and 145 due N. of Paris. Pop. about 8000.

CALAIS, ST., a town of France, in the department of Sarte; 54 miles E. S. E. of Le Mans.

CALAMAS, a town of Persia, on the coast of Mekran; 60 miles E. of Guadal, and 290 W. of Tatta, on the western branch of the Indus.

CALAMATA, a town of European Turkey, at the head of the Gulf of Coron, in the Morea, on the river Spinarza; 36 miles W. S. W. of Misitra.

CALAMIANES, a cluster of islands, the most westerly of the Philippines, and to the N. of Borneo. They are 17 in number, and mountainous, but produce great quantities of wax, honey, and edible birds' nests. The principal island is Paragoa, in the lat. of 12 N. and 120. of E. long.

CALANORE, a town of Hindostan: 70 miles E. of Lahore; distinguished as the place where the emperor Akbar ascended the throne of India in 1556.

CALATAGIRONE, a large town in the interior of

Sicily; about 50 miles W. by N. of Syracuse; it has manufactures of earthenware. Pop. 15,000.

CALATAYUD, a city of Spain, in Arragon, with a castle on a rock. It stands at the foot of a hill, on the river Xalon, at the influx of the Xiloca; 42 miles S. W. of Saragossa. It has manufactures of soap. Pop. about 9000.

CALATANISETTA, a town of Sicily, in Val di Noto; 20 miles N. W. of Lentini. Pop. 5000.

CALATRAVA, a town of Spain, in New Castile, the chief place of the military order of the knights of Calatrava. It is seated near the Guadiana; 90 miles S. of Madrid. Long. 3. 10. W. lat. 39. 4. N.

CALBE, or KALBE, a town of Lower Saxony, in the duchy of Magdeburg, on the river Saale; 16 miles S. by E. of Magdeburg. Pop. about 3000.

CALBE, a town of Brandenburg, in the Old Mark, with a castle; seven miles south-west of Stendel.

CALBERGA, a town of Hindostan, in Golconda, formerly a vast city, and the residence of the sovereigns of the Deccan. It is 85 miles W. of Hydrabad, and 110. E. of Visiapour. Long. 77. 20. E. lat. 17. 25. N.

CALCAR, a town of Germany, in the duchy of Cleve; seated near the Rhine; eight miles S. E. of Cleves.

CALCASUI, a river in the western part of Louisiana, forming a considerable lake before it falls into the Gulf of Mexico.

CALCHAGUA. *See* COLCHAGUA.

CALCINATO, a town of Italy, in Bresciano, where a victory was gained over the Austrians by the French, in 1706. It is eight miles S. E. of Brescia.

CALCUTTA, the capital of Bengal, and the seat of the Governor-general of the British dominions in the East Indies, is situated on the eastern bank of the river Hoogley (the western arm of the Ganges), about 100 miles from the sea. Its name is derived from *Cutta*, a temple dedicated by the Hindoos to *Caly*, the goddess of time, which was situate between the villages of Chuttanutty and Gobindpore, where the agents of the English East India Comqany, in 1690, obtained permission of Aurungzebe to establish a trading factory, which, in 1696, in consequence of the disturbed state of the province of Bengal, they were allowed to fortify. In 1698, Prince Azeen Ooshan, grandson of Aurungzebe, granted a lease to the agents of the English company, of the villages above mentioned, in perpetuity, upon which they strengthened the fortification, and gave it the name of Fort William, in compliment to the English monarch of that time. From this period Calcutta gradually increased in population and importance up to 1756, when it was attacked by the soubah of Bengal, with an army of 70,000 horse and foot, and 400 elephants, when the besieged were forced to abandon their posts, and retreat into the fort; on which the enemy's troops entered the town, and plundered it for 24 hours. An order was then given for attacking the fort, the garrison of which defended themselves bravely for some time; but many of them being killed and wounded, and their ammunition almost exhausted, they were at last obliged to surrender, and were all, to the number of 146, crammed into the Black Hole prison, a dungeon about 18 feet square; from whence only 23 came out alive in the morning; the rest were all suffocated from want of air. Calcutta, however, was retaken the next year; and, after the victory of Plassey, the inhuman soubah was deposed, and put to death by his successor, and the whole of the province of Bengal transferred to the English East India Company. Immediately after this victory, the erection of a new fort, about a mile below the old one, was commenced, which is superior in extent and security to any fortress in India, containing commodious accommodation for 4000 men. From this period Calcutta rapidly increased in extent and population. In 1798 the number of houses was 78,760, exclusive of the forts, since which time they have increased more than one-half; the number of inhabitants, composed of people from all parts of the world, amouting to 600,000 or 700,000. The part inhabited by the English is elegantly built; but the greatest part is built after the general fashion of the cities of India. Their streets are exceedingly confined, narrow, and crooked, with a vast number of ponds, reservoirs, and gardens, interspersed. A few of them are paved with brick. The houses are built, some with brick, others with mud, and a still greater number with bamboos and mats, all which different kinds of fabrics, intermixed, form a very uncouth appearance, and are very readily destroyed by fire. The brick houses are seldom above two stories high, with flat and terraced roofs; those of mud and bamboos are only one story, and are covered with thatch. During the administration of the Marquis of Wellesley, at the commencement of the present century, a magnificent palace was erected at the distance of about a mile from the fort. The line of houses that surround two sides of the esplanade of the fort is also magnificent; they are all on a large scale, and detached from one another. From the necessity of having a free circulation of air in a climate so extremely hot, the approach to the houses is generally by a flight of steps, with great projecting porticoes, or surrounded by colonnades and arcades, which give them much the appearance of Grecian temples. Since the commencement of the present century, Calcutta has been greatly improved, both in appearance and in the salubrity of its air; the streets have been properly drained, and the ponds filled; thereby removing a vast surface of stagnant water, the exhalations of which were particularly hurtful. Contiguous to the old fort is the spacious square, on one side of which is the college, founded also under the administration of the Marquis Wellesley, in 1801; another side of the square is occupied by buildings appropriated to the use of the junior servants of the company, and the remainder is occupied by some of the principal traders. Calcutta is the residence of a bishop, who, assisted by three archdeacons, is entrusted with the ecclesiastical affairs of all the British possessions in Asia: the cathedral is a spacious edifice. Here is likewise a supreme court of judicature, in which justice is dispensed according to the laws of England, by a chief justice and three puisne judges. The natives of the province still retain their Hindoo laws, as well as religion, and courts are duly appointed for the administration of justice accordingly. The southern part of Calcutta is occupied almost entirely by Europeans, who have adopted a style of building at once magnificent in its appearance and well adapted to the climate. Every house is detached, enclosed with walls, and fronted with an elegant veranda, shading a flight of steps. The northern part is chiefly inhabited by natives, whose dwellings are, for the most part, mere mud or bamboo cottages. The mixture of European and Asiatic manners that may be observed in Calcutta is curious; coaches, phaetons, single-horse chaises, with the palanquins and hackeries of the natives, the passing ceremonies of the Hindoos, and the different appearance of the fakirs, form a sight more novel and extraordinary, perhaps, than any other city in the world can present. The Hoogly is navigable up to the town, for ships of 400 to 500 tons, but those of greater burden lie at Diamond Point, about 50 miles below, their cargoes being conveyed to and from the town by lighters. Independently of its commercial intercourse with England, Calcutta maintains an extensive intercourse with China, as well as with almost every port in Asia, and islands in the eastern seas, with which an interchange is effected in every commodity that mankind possibly can desire, either for subsistence and comfort, or to gratify the most refined and luxurious taste. Ship-building is also carried on to a great extent; there are several banking establishments to facilitate the operations of commerce, and insurance establishments for its protection. The control of the governor-general and council of Bengal, at Calcutta, extends over the presidencies of Madras, Bombay, and Bencoolen; the extent of the civil establishments attending the administration of so extensive an empire, in addition to the military and commercial affairs of the place, necessarily give an importance to Calcutta beyond that of any city in Asia, except those of China and Japan. The new fort is in the lat. of 22. 35. N., and 88. 28. E. long.; 1030 miles N. N. E. of Madras, and about 1100 E. N. E. of Bombay.

Caldas, the name of several small towns in different parts of Spain and Portugal, which, like the Badens of Germany, implies their contiguity to hot or medicinal springs: one 25 miles N. by E. of Lisbon, another 10 miles N. E. of Castel Branco; another contiguous to Montalegre, 60 miles N. E. of Oporto; another 15 miles N. of Barcelona; another 25 miles N. of Vigo.

Calder, a river which rises on the W. borders of Yorkshire, flows by Halifax to Wakefield, and, eight miles below, joins the Aire. It is navigable the greater part of its course. There are three or four rivers, and as many villages, named Calder, in different parts of Scotland.

Caldolzburg, a town of Franconia, in the principality of Anspach, with a castle; 18 miles N. E. of Anspach. It is now included in the Bavarian circle of Rezat.

Caldwell, an interior county in the western part of Kentucky, bounded on the S. W. by the great Cumberland river. Population, 10,365. Eddyville, on the N. bank of the river, about 30 miles above its entrance into the Ohio, and 200 S. W. of Frankfort, is the chief town.

Caldwell, the chief town of Warren county, state of New York; 43 miles N. of Albany. Pop. 693.

Caledon, a town in the parish of Aughloe, (sometimes called Caledon), S. part of the county of Tyrone, Ireland.

Caledonia, a county in the N. part of the state of Vermont, the S. E. part of which is bounded by the Connecticut river, which divides it from New Hampshire. Pop. 21,891. Danville, in the centre of the county, about 20 miles N. E. of Montpelier, is the chief town. Pop. 2633.

Caledonia, a town of Livingstone county, state of New York, lying to the W. of Genesee River, and S. of Erie Canal; 240 miles W. of Albany. Big Spring, remarkable for the abundance of its water, is in this township. Pop. 1987.

Caledonia, New, an island in the Pacific Ocean, to the E. of New Holland, discovered by Cook, in 1774. It is 260 miles from N. W. to S. E., and 70 broad. The inhabitants are strong, active, and well made; their hair is black, and much frizzled, but not woolly; their beards are crisp and thick; they besmear their faces with black pigment, and their only covering is a wrapper, made from the bark of a tree, or of leaves. Their houses are circular, like a bee-hive, formed of small spars and reeds, covered with long coarse grass, and the floor laid with dry grass. They deposit their dead in the ground, and decorate the graves of their chiefs with spears, darts, paddles, &c. They are of a pacific disposition, and their women chaster than those of the more eastern islands. They cultivate the soil with some art and industry, but subsist chiefly on roots and fish. Plantains and sugar-canes are not plentiful; bread-fruit is scarce, and cocoa-nut trees are but thinly planted; but yams and taras are in great abundance. The cape at the S. end, called Queen Charlotte Foreland, is in long. 167. 12. E. lat. 22. 15. S.

Calenberg, a principality of Lower Saxony, which constitutes a part of the duchy of Brunswick. It is divided into two parts by the principality of Wolfenbuttle. The S. part is intersected from E. to W. by the Werra, and the chief town is Gottingen. The Lene has its source in this part, near the banks of the Werra, and runs N. through the principality of Wolfenbuttle, then dividing the bishopric of Hildesheim from North Calenberg on the E., and afterwards intersects the N. part of North Calenberg. The Weser also intersects the S. part of North Calenberg from S. E. to N. W., the chief towns being Hanover, Neustadt, and Hameln. The aggregate extent of the surface may be estimated at about 1700 square miles. Pop. 139,230. The soil is generally fertile, and, under social and reciprocal arrangements, Calenberg might be made to yield a surplus produce sufficient to command an abundance of tropical and other luxuries, the consumption of which has hitherto been very limited.

Calhuco, a town at the S. extremity of Araucan, opposite the N. end of the Isle of Chiloe, in the South Pacific Ocean, inhabited by Spaniards, Mestees, and Indians; 180 miles S. of Valdivia. Long. 73. 37. W. lat. 41. 40. S.

Cali, a city of Colombia, in the valley of Popayan, on the W. bank of the river Cauca. The governor of the province generally resides here. It is 90 miles E. of Bonaventura, and 200 W. by S. of Santa Fe. Long. 77. 5. W. lat. 3. 15. N.

Calicut, a city of Hindostan, capital of a province of the same name, on the coast of Malabar. It was the first Indian port visited by European shipping; being discovered by the Portuguese, in 1498. Here is a manufacture of plain cotton goods. The name of calico, applied to cotton goods, was derived from this place. Much salt is made here, by the natural evaporation of the sea water. The principal exports are cocoa and betel nuts, black pepper, ginger, and turmeric. It is seated at the mouth of a river; 110 miles S.W. of Seringapatam, and 130 S.S.E. of Mangalore. Long. 75. 52. E. lat. 11. 12. N. It was formerly much more considerable, having been much encroached upon by the sea.

California, a promontory in the Pacific Ocean; separated from the W. coast of North America by the Vermilion Sea, or Gulf of California; extending N. W. from Cape St. Lucas, in the lat. of 22. 44. to lat. 33. N., being about 50 miles in average breadth. It was discovered by Cortes, in 1536; and is said to have been visited by Sir Francis Drake in 1578. Toward the close of the seventeenth century, the Jesuits formed several settlements here, and endeavoured to govern the natives with the same policy and authority that they exercised in their missions in Paraguay. They seem studiously to have depreciated the climate and soil of the country; but on their expulsion from the Spanish dominions, the court appointed Don Joseph Galvez to visit this peninsula. His account of the country was favourable: he found the pearl fishery on its coast to be valuable, and he discovered mines of gold of a very promising appearance. Divers nations or tribes inhabit the country, without acknowledging any chief. Each father is a prince over his own family; but his power ceases when the children are able to provide for themselves. Each tribe, nevertheless, has persons appointed, who call assemblies to divide the productions of the earth, regulate the fisheries, and march at their head when engaged in war. Want of provision obliges them often to change their abode; and in severe winters they retire into caves. A girdle and piece of linen round the body, some ornaments for the head, and a chain of pearls, serve them for dress and finery. Those who live towards the north, where they have no pearls, dress their heads with shells. The women commonly wear a kind of long robe, made of leaves of palms; though some wear nothing but a girdle. A range of mountains runs parallel with the coast, its whole extent, rising in some places to the height of about 4700 feet. The soil is in many places excellent; and it is reported that vines grow naturally in the mountains, and that the Jesuits, when they resided here, made abundance of wine, in taste approaching to that of Madeira. The chief town is St. Joseph, about 25 miles N. E. of Cape St. Lucas. The population of the whole territory is supposed not to exceed 15,000.

California, New, is an extension of territory along the coast, N. of the promontory of California, to the lat. of about 40. N., comprising the greater part of the coast formerly called New Albion. The same mountain ridge which intersects the promontory continues to run N., parallel with the coast, at a distance of 30 to 50 miles. The Jesuits, who extended themselves in this direction, found the soil somewhat more congenial for the general purposes of culture, and founded about twenty settlements upon and between the coast and the mountain ridge, each settlement dedicated to some saint of their holy order. The four principal settlements on the coast are St. Diego, in the lat. of 32. 42.; La Purissima, in 34. 32.; St. Carlos de Monterry, in 36. 36.; and St. Francisco, in 37. 48. N. The total population of this district is estimated at about 16,000.

Calimna, or Calimno, an island of the Grecian Archipelago, near the coast of Asia; 7 miles N. W. of Stanchio. Long. 26. 46. E. lat. 36. 56. N.

Calix, a town of Sweden, in West Bothnia, on a river of the same name, near its entrance into the Gulf of Bothnia; 22 miles W. of Tornea.

Callah, a town of Algier, in the province of Mascara, which has a considerable trade, and the greatest market for carpets in the country. It is 40 miles E. of Oran.

Callan, a town of Ireland, in the county of Kilkenny, on the frontier of Tipperary; 7 miles S. W. of the city of Kilkenny, and 65 from Dublin.

Callander, a town of Scotland, in Perthshire, with a considerable manufacture of muslin; seated on the river Teath; 30 miles W.S.W. of Perth.

Callao, a seaport of Peru, with the best harbour on the coast, and a large and safe roadstead, defended by the islands of Callao and St. Lawrence. In the port every commodity is to be procured that vessels may be in need of. The town was almost totally destroyed by an earthquake, in 1746. It is seated on a river of the same name; 5 miles W. of Lima, of which it is the port. Long. 76. 58. W. lat. 12. 2. S.

Calle, a town of Algier, in the province of Constantina, where the French have a factory established for a coral fishery, and trade for grain, wool, leather, and wax. It stands on a rock, almost surrounded by the sea; 36 miles E. of Bona.

Callianee, a town of Hindostan, in the province of Aurungabad; 30 miles N. E. from Bombay. It is populous, and has considerable trade. It is surrounded by ruined fortifications.

CALLINGER, a fortified town of Hindostan, in the province of Allahabad, formerly capital of Bundelcund. It was ceded by the Mahrattas to the English in 1793. It is 20 miles N. of the Diamond Mines of Punnah, and 150 W. by S. of Benares.

CALLINGTON, a town of Cornwall; market on Wednesday; situate on the Lynher; 12 miles S. of Launceston, and 216 W. by S. of London.

CALLOMA, or CAILLOMO, a town of Peru, celebrated for its silver mines; 50 miles N. by E. of Arequipa, and 170 S. of Cusco.

CALMAR, a strong seaport of Sweden, capital of Smaland, and a bishop's see. It is celebrated as the place where the deputies of Sweden, Denmark, and Norway were appointed to assemble for the election of a king, according to the Union of Calmar. On an eminence, half a mile from the town, is the ancient castle, now converted into a distillery. The chief exports are deals and tar. It is seated near the Baltic; 190 miles S. S. W. of Stockholm. Long. 16. 22. E. lat. 56. 41. N. Pop. 4200.

CALMUCS, or KALMUCS, a people of central Asia, in Mongolia, a branch of the Great Mongol or Mogul nation, and the only one that has retained the language and customs. *See* KALMUCS.

CALNE, a borough in Wiltshire; market on Tuesday. It has eight or ten extensive employers in the manufacture of woollen cloth, and in the vicinity are many fulling and corn mills. It is seated on a river of the same name; 25 miles E. of Bristol, and 88 W. of London. It returns one member to parliament.

CALPEE, a town of Hindostan, in the province of Agra, on the Jumna. It is a depôt for the transit of cotton, &c. from the S. W., and is famous for its paper and candy.

CALTURA, a town on the W. coast of Ceylon, with a fort. A great quantity of arrack is made here, and other manufactures carried on. It stands at the mouth of a large branch of the Muliwaddy; 28 miles S. by E. of Columbo. Long. 79. 56. E. lat. 6. 44. N.

CALVADOS, a maritime department of France, including part of the late province of Normandy, bounded N. by the English Channel. It is so called from a ridge of rocks of the same name, near the coast of what was heretofore called Normandy, extending 12 miles in length. It contains an area of about 2200 square miles, and 557,663 inhabitants. It is intersected from the S. to the sea by the river Orne. It is a fertile province, and exports a considerable quantity of clover seed. Caen, on the banks of the Orne, is the chief town.

CALVERT, a county of the state of Maryland, lying between the Patuxent river and Chesapeake Bay. Pop. 9229. St. Leonard's, on the shore of the Chesapeake, 71 miles S. of Annapolis, is the chief town.

CALVI, a town of Naples, in Terra di Lavoro; 8 miles N. of Capua.

CALVI, a town of Corsica, on a craggy mountain and gulf of the same name, with a strong fortress, and a good harbour. It was taken by the English in 1794. It is 38 miles W. S. W. of Bastia. Pop. 1500.

CALVISANO, a town of Bresciano; 12 miles S. by E. of Brescia. Pop. about 3000.

CALVISSON, a town of France, in the province of Languedoc; 9 miles from Nismes. Pop. 3000.

CALW, a town of Suabia, in the kingdom of Wirtemburg, with a porcelain manufacture, and a great trade in stuffs. It is 20 miles W. by S. of Stuttgard. Pop. 3500.

CAM, a river which rises in Hertfordshire, flows by Cambridge into the Isle of Ely, and there joins the Ouse, to which river it is navigable from Cambridge.

CAMANA, a town of Peru, capital of a jurisdiction; situate on a river of the same name, near the Pacific Ocean; 70 miles W. of Arequipa, in lat. 16. 10. N. and 73. 15. W. long.

CAMARAN, an island of Arabia, on the Red Sea, where there is a fishery for white coral and pearl oysters. Long. 42. 22. E. lat. 15. 6. N.

CAMARET, a town of France, in the department of Finisterre. In an expedition against Brest, in 1694, the English landed here, and lost a great number of men. It stands on a bay of the same name; 8 miles S. of Brest.

CAMARINES, the most southern province of the isle of Luzon, of which Caceres is the chief town.

CAMARGUE, an island, or cluster of islands, of France, in the mouths of the Rhone, separated by canals, and fortified. The whole contains 80 square miles; the land is fertile, but the air is unwholesome.

CAMBAT, the southernmost province of Abyssinia; inhabited by a people called Seb-a-adja, who are a mixture of Pagans, Christians, and Mahometans. It is abundant in fruits.

CAMBAY, a considerable city of Hindostan, in the province of Guzerat. It stands on a gulf of the same name, and was the Camanes of Ptolemy. Here are three bazaars, and four public cisterns, capable of supplying the whole town with water in times of the greatest drought. Its products and manufactures are considerable; for the country abounds in corn, cattle, and silk; and cornelian and agate stones are found in its rivers. The inhabitants are noted for embroidery. It is 100 miles N. of Surat, and 50 miles S. of Ahmedabad, of which it is the port. It belongs to the English, and is included in the presidency of Bombay. Long. 72. 34. E. lat. 22. 17. N.

CAMBERG, a town of Germany, on the southwest frontier of the electorate of Hesse; situate on a hill; 17 miles E. by S. of Nassau, and 20 N. W. of Frankfort on the Maine.

CAMBERWELL, a parish in Surrey, contiguous to London, on the south side; and to which it forms an appendage, being occupied principally by the private residences of the merchants, shopkeepers, and clerks employed in the several public establishments of the Bank, East India House, Customs, &c. &c. The church is 2½ miles S. of London Bridge; an additional church, after the model of one in Rome, was erected in 1825

CAMBODIA, CAMBOJA, or CAMBOYA, a kingdom or territory of Asia, extending from Cape Cambodia, in the China Sea, south, in the lat. of 8. 40., to Laotchua, or Laos, in the lat of about 17. N.; bounded on the east, at the south end, by Tsiompa; and further north, by the country of the Kemoys, which divides it from Cochin-China; and on the west, from the 8th to the 14th degree of latitude, by the Gulf of Siam; and further north, by the territory of Siam; being of an average breadth of about three degrees of longitude, between 101. and 106. E., comprising an aggregate extent of surface of about 100,000 square miles. As far as any knowledge of this country has been obtained, it appears to be exceedingly rich, alike in vegetable, animal, and mineral productions: whilst the unsocial habits of the people, who appear to be a mixture of Japanese, Cochin-Chinese, Malays, and natives of the Eastern islands, preclude nearly all intercourse with Europeans. In the 17th century, the Portuguese, Dutch, and English, each unsuccessfully endeavoured to establish an intercourse in this country; and all succeeding attempts, except to a trifling extent surreptitiously, appear to have met with disadvantageous results. It is intersected by a noble river of the same name, which rises in Chinese Tartary, runs through Thibet and the west side of Yun-nan, the south-west province of China, and Laos, and through the Cambodian territory, in a south-east direction, falling into the China Sea, by several channels, between the latitudes of 9. and 11. N. In Thibet this river is called the *Matchou*, in China the *Kiou Long*, and through Laos the *May Kung;* and the eastern channel, into the sea, is sometimes called the *Japanese*. The chief town of the country, called also *Cambodia*, is situate on the western bank of the river, about 240 miles above its entrance into the sea. Cambodia appears to be thinly peopled, but of the number of its inhabitants no estimate has been formed. They appear to manufacture both silk and cotton; and the country producing every possible article necessary for subsistence and comfort, and also to gratify the most luxuriant sense, either of taste, smell, or ornament, there is but little inducement on the part of the Cambodians to cultivate an intercourse with Europeans, more especially on the overbearing, higgling, and selfish principle which they seem to have exercised over all Asia. As far as the Cambodians do maintain an external commerce, sandal wood, elephants' teeth of the finest quality, camphor, and the gum called cambogia, or gamboge, from the name of the country, constitute the chief articles of export. It was divided, in 1820, into three parts, one of which is still independent; another became tributary to Siam, the third to Cochin-China. Saegon is the chief trading port. (*See* SIAM.)

CAMBORNE, a town in Cornwall. In the neighbourhood are some of the chief copper mines in the county; it is pleasantly situated, and is a neat town.

CAMBRAY, a fortified city of France, capital of the department of Nord. The linen manufacture is extensively carried on in this district, and the term *cambric* was derived from the finer qualities of linen, which were distributed from this city. It has since been applied by the English to the fine fabric of cotton as well as of linen. Cambray has also some manufactures of lace and leather. It is seated near the source of the Scheldt, which runs through the city; 18 miles S. by W. of Valenciennes, 35 S. by E. of Lisle, and 102 N. N. E. of Paris. The fortification was one of those retained by the allies for five years after the peace of 1815.

CAMBRIA, an interior county of Pennsylvania, lying W. of the main ridge of the Allegany mountains. The S. W. branch of the Susquehannah river rises in this county. Pop. 11,256. Ebensburg, in the centre of the county, 143 miles W. by N. of Harrisburg, is the chief town.

CAMBRIA, a town in the state of New York, near the great falls of Niagara; 310 miles W. by N. of Albany. Pop. 2099.

CAMBRIDGESHIRE, an interior county towards the S. E. part of England, being about 50 miles in extent from N. to S. and 20 to 25 from W. to E. It is bounded on the S. by a range of hills, which divide it from the counties of Bedford and Essex, having the counties of Suffolk and Norfolk on the E., and Bedford, Huntingdon, Northampton, and Lincoln on the W., the northern extremity jetting upon the Boston Wash. The river Ouse intersects it from E. to W., whilst the Nen forms the boundary between the counties of Northampton and Lincoln, and the Cam, which rises at the foot of the hills which form the southern boundary falls into the Ouse about the middle of the county. After descending the hills from the S., the country is one entire level, and that part was formerly little better than a swamp, which, by well-directed efforts in draining and embanking, since the middle of the last century, has been converted into rich and verdant pastures, which yield great supplies of butter and cream-cheese for the London market. It has no manufactures of any kind; but, in addition to its butter, it yields a surplus of calves, cattle, sheep, and wool, and large quantities of wild fowl. Its supply, however, of foreign and manufactured productions is obtained in exchange for the expenditure of the students at the university of the town of Cambridge, and rents abstracted from different parts of the country, on account of the endowments of the several colleges. The only other place in the county deserving of notice, besides the town of Cambridge, is the city of Ely. It returns three members to parliament.

CAMBRIDGE, the chief town of the preceding county, and seat of one of the universities of England, is situate in the S. part of the county; 17 miles S. of Ely, 23 E. of Bedford, 28 W. of Bury, and 51 N. by E. of London. It is a corporate town, governed by a mayor and thirteen aldermen; but its importance is derived from its university, which dates its foundation by Siegebert, King of the East Angles, in 630.

It acquired, however, but little celebrity until after the period of the collisions between the barons and the court had subsided, in the 13th century, from which period, to the close of the 16th century, twelve colleges and four halls were founded, by the names, and in the order of date as follows, viz.—

COLLEGES.

1. St. Peter's in	1257	7. St. John's in	1509
2. Gonville and Caius	1348	8. Magdalene	1519
		9. Trinity	1546
3. Corpus Christi	1350	10. Jesus'	1576
4. King's	1441	11. Emanuel	1584
5. Queen's	1448	12. Syd. Sussex	1598
6. Christ's	1505		

HALLS.

1. Clare in	1326	3. Trinity in	1350
2. Pembroke	1343	4. Catharine	1475

These institutions, founded in ages of monastic influence, and when architecture was the ruling passion of those who possessed the means of indulging either in acts of benevolence or vanity, claim the attention of the present age, some for their monastic features, some for the history of their foundations, and others for their architectural beauty. Most of them have chapels and libraries attached, some of them extensive and valuable, and the chapel of King's College is justly esteemed as the most beautiful Gothic edifice in the world. It is 304 feet in length, 71 broad, and 91 in height; the effect of its proportions, and beauty of its decorations, must be seen to be understood. In 1807 another college was founded, pursuant to the will of a Sir George Downing, whose name it bears; and, in 1810, Viscount Fitzwilliam bequeathed a very extensive and valuable cabinet of works of nature and art, and ample funds for the foundation of an observatory, and a building for the reception of his collection for the use of the university at large, which has been erected on a magnificent scale, and completed in 1842. This munificent donation excited a general spirit of improvement both in the town and university; several of the colleges have been enlarged, repaired, and beautified, several old buildings in the town taken down, judicious sites for the new buildings selected, and those edifices more particularly deserving of attention for their architecture laid more open to the view. In addition to the libraries attached to the several colleges and halls, there is also one common to the university, in a splendid building of recent erection, a senate-house, and schools for public examinations, which, together with fourteen parish churches, a county hospital, and other public buildings for county purposes, afford a very interesting extent of varied architectural display. There are also six bridges of stone over the river Cam, which, in addition to their convenience, add considerably to the general picturesque effect. The town and university each send two members to parliament. The town market is abundantly supplied on Wednesdays and Saturdays; and in a field called Sturbich, about two miles from the town, one of the largest fairs in England is held, for a fortnight, commencing on the 7th of September.

CAMBRIDGE is also the seat of the chief university in the United States of North America. The town is in Middlesex county, and contains a total pop. of 8409. The collegiate buildings are situate about four miles from BOSTON (which see,) at the N. E. end of a plain, similar in extent and aspect to Clapham Common, in the vicinity of London. The buildings consist of four uniform ranges, four stories high, of brick; in one of them is a library, containing 35,000 volumes of books, and some philosophical apparatus.

CAMBRILLA, a town of Spain, in Catalonia, surrounded by a wall, and seated near the sea; 14 miles W, by S. of Tarragona.

CAMBURG, a town of Saxony, on the E. bank of the Saal; 18 miles N. by E. of Jena, and 32 S. W. of Leipsic.

CAMBYNA, an island lying between the S. E. promontory of Celebes and the Isle of Bouton. It is about 60 miles in circumference.

CAMDEN, a county in the N. E. part of North Carolina, about 25 miles from N. to S., and 4 in breadth; the north end borders on Virginia, and forms part of the Great Dismal Swamp; and the south end jets upon Albemarle Sound, between Pasquotank and George Rivers. Pop. 5663, of whom 1661 are slaves. New Lebanon is the chief town.

CAMBDEN, a maritime county of the state of Georgia; bounded on the south by St. Mary's River, which divides it from East Florida. It is about 20 miles in extent each way, bounded on the west by the Great Swamp of Oke-fin-o-caw. The St. Illa river intersects it from the N. W. corner, running to the centre of the county, falling into the sea at the N. E. corner. It is very productive in rice and cotton. Pop. 6075, of whom 4049 are slaves, and 22 free blacks; beside the population of the town of St. Mary, and the town of Jefferson, in the centre of the county.

CAMDEN, a town on the west side of Penobscot Bay, state of Maine.

CAMEL, a river in Cornwall, which rises two miles north of Camelford, flows south almost to Bodmin, and then north-west to Padstow, where it enters the British Channel. Its banks were the scenes of some bloody battles between the Britons and Saxons.

CAMELFORD, a town in Cornwall; market on Friday. A great quantity of yarn is spun in this place and its neighbourhood. It is seated on the Camel; 14 miles W. of Launceston, and 228 W. by S. of London.

CAMERINO, a town of Italy, in the marquisate of Ancona, and an archbishop's see. It is seated on a mountain, near the river Chiento; 37 miles S. W. of Ancona.

CAMEROON'S PEAK, on the west coast of Africa, near the Old Calabar river, 13,000 feet high, and near a river of the same name, which flows into the bight of Biafra.

CAMILLUS, a township of Onandago county, state of New York, containing four towns, viz. Elbridge, Jordan, Camillus, and Ionia. The town of Camillus is 155 miles, and Jordan 167 miles W. of Albany.

CAMIN, a seaport of Further Pomerania, and once a bishop's see, which was secularized at the peace of Westphalia; but it still has a fine cathedral and a chapter; 25 miles N. of Stettin. Long. 14. 52. E. lat. 53. 54. N.

CAMINHA, a town of Portugal, in Entre-Douro-e-Minho, with a fort; seated at the mouth of the Minho; 12 miles N. of Viana.

CAMOROTA, one of the Nicobar isles off the west coast of Malay; in the lat. of 8. N.

CAMPAGNA, or CAMPANIA, a town of Naples, in Principato Citeriore; 40 miles S. E. of Naples.

CAMPAGNA DI ROMA, OR TERRITORY OF ROME, the most south-west province of the ecclesiastical states of Rome, extending from the river Tiber, for about 65 miles along the shore of the Mediterranean, to the Neapolitan province of Lavora, being about 50 miles wide; bounded on the east by Abruzzo. This extensive district, lying between the 41st and 42nd degree of north latitude, was the ancient Latium, and was once the most populous and fertile district in the world, but now presents one general scene of desolation. The Pontine marshes, which are constantly emitting the most noisome vapours, comprise a great portion of the south-east part of the province. Besides the city of Rome on the banks of the Tiber, at the northern extremity of the province, Albana, Velletri, and Piperno, all on the western side, still exhibit marks of former greatness; whilst the ruins of temples, baths, and other stately edifices, are seen scattered in all directions. (*See* ROME.)

CAMPAN, a town of France, in the department of Upper Pyrenees, on the river Adour; one of the most delightful spots in the south of France. Pop. 4300.

CAMPBELL, an interior county of Virginia; a fertile district. Pop. 21,030, nearly half of whom are slaves. The court-house, in the centre of the county, is 144 miles W. by S. of Richmond.

CAMPBELL, a frontier county in the north-east part of Tennessee. It contains an area of about 230 square miles, and a population of 6149. Jacksborough is the chief town.

CAMPBELL, a county of Kentucky, pop. 5214.

CAMPBELLTOWN, a town of New South Wales, 33 miles from Sydney. It has a church, court-house, and a considerable number of houses.

CAMPBELTON, a borough and seaport of Scotland, in Argyleshire, situate on a bay, toward the south extremity of the peninsula of Cantyre. It has a considerable trade in the distillation of whiskey, besides being the general rendezvous of the fishing vessels that annually visit the western coast. It is 65 miles S. S. W. of Inverary. Long. 5. 32. W. lat. 55. 28. N. Pop. in 1821, 6445.

CAMPDEN, a corporate town in Gloucestershire, with a market on Wednesday; 22 miles N. E. of Gloucester, and 90 W. N. W. of London.

CAMPEACHY, a town of Yucatan, on the west coast of the bay of Campeachy, in the Gulf of Mexico, defended by strong forts. The port is large but shallow, and has a good dock. It is noted for logwood, which, however, does not grow very near it. It was taken by the English in 1659; by the buccaneers in 1678; and by the freebooters of St. Domingo, in 1685, who burnt it and blew up the citadel. Long. 91. 30. W. lat. 19. 35. N.

CAMPEN, a town of Holland, in Overyssel, with a citadel, and a port almost choked up. It is seated near the mouth of the Yssel, on the Zuyder Zee; 8 miles W. N. W. of Zwoll. Pop. about 6000.

CAMPERDOWN, a seaport of Holland, about 25 miles S. of Texel Island; famous for the signal victory obtained by Admiral Lord Viscount Duncan, off its coast, over the Dutch fleet, on the 11th October, 1797.

CAMPO BASSO, a town of Naples, in the Molise. In 1805 it suffered greatly by an earthquake, and most of the inhabitants were destroyed. It has a considerable trade in articles of cutlery, and is 12 miles S. of Molise. Pop. about 6000.

CAMPO FORMIO, a village of Italy, in Friuli, with an elegant castle, where a treaty of peace was concluded between the Austrians and French, in 1797. It is 2 miles S. W. of Udina.

CAMPO MAYOR, a fortified town of Portugal, in Alentejo, on the frontier of Spain; 14 miles N. by E. of Elvas. Pop. about 5000.

CAMPO ST. PIETRO, a town and castle of Italy, in the Paduano, on the river Menson; 12 miles N. of Padua, and about the same distance N. W. of Venice. Pop. about 3000.

CAMPOLI, a town of Naples, in Abruzzo Ulteriore; 23 miles N. by E. of Aquila.

CAMPREDON, a town of Spain, in Catalonia, at the foot of the Pyrenees, and on the river Ter; 45 miles N. of Barcelona.

CAMPSIE, a village of Scotland, on the S. confines of Stirlingshire; 9 miles N. of Glasgow. It has some extensive printfields, and other manufactures.

CAMTOOS RIVER, a river in South Africa, in the province of Uitenhage, which falls into an extensive bay of the same name; in lat. 35. 50. S. long. 25. 25. E.

CANAAN. *See* SYRIA.

CANAAN, a town of Columbia county, state of New York, on the E. side of Hudson River; 25 miles W. by S. of Albany. Pop. 1957.

CANADA, a vast territory of North America, lying between the 42d and 54th degrees of N. latitude, and the 64th and 98th of W. longitude. This extensive country appears to have been first made known in 1535, by Jacques Cartier, commanding a fleet fitted out from St. Maloes, under the auspices of the French government. Three or four attempts, during the fifteen years from 1535 to 1550, were made to establish a colony upon it, but all proved unsuccessful. In 1607 the first permanent establishment was formed by M. de Champlain, from France, who founded the city of Quebec on the site of the Indian village Hochelaga; but for more than fifty years it remained without any laws or social arrangements, the settlers being little better than hordes of banditti, living in constant collision with the native Indians, with whom the most sanguinary conflicts frequently occurred, with alternate success. In 1663, at which period the European inhabitants did not exceed 7000, the French government affected to extend its paternal regard to the colony, and appropriated a train of civil officers to organize and administer a code of laws on the principle of those then prevailing in France. This arrangement produced some excitement and indications of improvement; but both were of short duration. The collisions with the natives were renewed, and their frequent incursions upon the lands of the settlers, which were often stained with acts of cruelty, operated as a check to all social enterprise; so that at the end of another half century, the number of settlers did not exceed 20,000. During the earlier part of the 18th century, the colony made some progress towards improvement; but the object of the French government seemed to be extension of territory rather than social arrangement, and as such, in addition to the collisions in which it was so frequently involved with the natives, it involved itself also with the outposts of the English, who then possessed the territory now forming the United States of North America; and, on war being declared between France and England in 1756, the English prepared to expel the French entirely from the North American continent, in which they completely succeeded in 1759. At this period the number of settlers in Canada amounted to about 70,000. During the first fifteen years after its surrender to the English, it made but little progress either in population or improvement; the prejudices of some of the older settlers being inimical to the English laws, introduced immediately after its surrender, led in 1775 to a revision of the civil code, more conformable to the usage and prejudices of the inhabitants. The revolt of the other Anglo-American provinces taking place about this time, occasioned a considerable accession of population to Canada, which progressively increased up to the period of 1792, when a further important arrangement took place in its internal administration: the territory was divided into two great parts, denominated Upper and Lower Canada, with separate jurisdictions, and a council, and an assembly of representatives established for each. But dissensions having sprung up between the two states, and which led to some warfare, they were declared, in 1840, to be be but one state, under the title of the *Vice-Royalty of Canada*, and will be governed by the same laws and customs in each, which were before different; but, for convenience, they will be described under their original denomination.

Canada, Lower, although the least favoured in climate of the two, is by far the most populous, owing to its nearer contiguity to the sea, and earlier settlement. This division extends from the United States territory, in the lat. of 45. to that of 52. N.; and W. from the 65th degree of long. to the Ottawa river; the part, however, which is inhabited and under cultivation, lies within much narrower limits, comprising a tract of territory about 700 miles in length, and 150 in mean breadth, lying in a N. E. direction, from the lat. of 45. N. and 74. 30. of W. long. The geographical bearing of this territory has been owing to the noble river St. Lawrence, which intersects it in that direction, its whole extent, falling into the Gulf of St. Lawrence at the N. E., the settlements extending along both banks of the river, and which are intersected on both sides by innumerable tributary streams and rivers, some of them of great magnitude. The most considerable of those on the S. side of the St. Lawrence, taking them in order from the W., are, 1st, the Chambly, which runs out of Lake Champlain, falling into the St. Lawrence about 60 miles below Montreal; 2nd, the Tortu; 3rd, the St. Francis; 4th, the Nicolet; 5th, the Becancour; 6th, the Beaurivage; and 7th, the Chaudiere, which falls into the St. Lawrence, about 20 miles below Quebec; E. of the Chaudiere, the waters chiefly flow to the S., or E. into the Gulf of St. Lawrence. The N. bank is intersected, at the distance of every fifteen to twenty miles, by rivers of greater or less magnitude; the most considerable is the Piekouagamis, which, after passing through a lake of considerable extent, is called the Saguenay, and falls into the St. Lawrence about 150 miles below Quebec. At the new organization of the government, in 1762, this territory was divided into the four districts of Montreal, Trois Rivers, Quebec, and Gaspé: the first three extend on both sides the river; and the latter, which is called the district and county of Gaspé, comprises all the S. E. part of the territory S. of the St. Lawrence, bounded on the E. by the Gulf of St. Lawrence, and S. by the province of New Brunswick: the first three districts were further subdivided into twenty counties, eleven on the S., and nine on the N. side of the river, as follows, beginning at the S. W. viz.—

On the south side.	On the north side.
1. Huntingdon.	12. York.
2. Bedford.	13. Effingham.
3. Montreal.	14. Leinster.
4. Richelieu.	15. Warwick.
5. Surrey.	16. St. Maurice.
6. Kent.	17. Hampshire.
7. Buckingham.	18. Orleans.
8. Dorchester.	19. Quebec.
9. Hertford.	20. Northumberland.
10. Devon.	
11. Cornwallis.	

Of these, the first eight, which all lie within, or S. W. of the river Chaudiere, are the most fertile, and afford the most favourable spots for agricultural and commercial enterprise. The counties of Cornwallis and Northumberland each extend from the lat. of about 47., the former to the district of Gaspé, and the latter borders on Labrador, all of which at present may be looked upon as one great wilderness.

With this subdivision of territory and new organization of the government of Canada in 1792, a more stedfast career of improvement seems to have been pursued than in any former period. Incidental circumstances, however, rather than any measures of foresight or well directed exertion, contributed to give it an interest and importance which it otherwise might never have obtained. For some years previous to 1807, England had been accustomed to draw a supply of timber, to the extent of 150,000 to 200,000 tons per annum, from the United States of America, when in that year the United States government adopted the most extraordinary policy ever before heard of, in proscribing its citizens from all external intercourse. This circumstance forced the English upon Canada and the other British American provinces, for a supply of that essential commodity; and in 1809, when the folly of the measure of the United States government became too apparent to be any longer continued, so reciprocal had an extensive intercourse between Canada and England, as well as between Canada and the West Indies proved, that, on the United States attempting to renew their intercourse, they found all the ports of the British West India islands completely shut against them, and in all the ports of England a duty on all sorts of wood from their territory, that amounted to an entire prohibition. Never did presumption so effectually recoil upon its authors as did that ridiculous pretension of proscription of the United States government, in 1808. It destroyed at once and for ever the employment of 100,000 to 200,000 tons of shipping annually, whilst it threw an advantage to a corresponding extent into the hands of the Canadians, and the other British American provinces; and it was not only the marine that was affected by the measure; a great number of the most active and intelligent of the citizens of the United States, living on or near the borders of Canada, moved within the British territory, and directed an extensive and valuable branch of commerce in pot and pearl ashes, and other commodities, through Canada, which would otherwise have found its way by the Atlantic coast. This extension of commercial intercourse brought a vast accession of population: the number of inhabitants which, in 1775, did not exceed 90,000, in 1814, according to a capitation tax, amounted to 335,000; and the number has since been gradually increasing, and was, according to the census of 1834, 549,005.

One of the most distinguishing characteristics of Lower Canada is its climate, in the intensity of cold in the winter, and of heat in summer, and the sudden transition from one to the other, without producing any injurious effect upon the constitutions either of the inhabitants or other parts of the animal creation. The frosts begin about the middle of October, the sun continuing to render the days mild and agreeable for three or four weeks, when the snow storms set in, which continue for about a month, with variable winds and hazy atmosphere, until about the middle or end of December; by which time the whole country is covered with an average depth of snow of three to five feet. An invariable season now commences; an uninterruptedly clear sky prevails for about twenty weeks, the thermometer ranging, the greater part of the time, from 20 to 25 below zero, sometimes descending more than 30 below, when the frost suddenly breaks, and, in the course of a few days, about the end of April, or middle of May, the snow as suddenly disappears. All the energies of the husbandman are now directed to prepare the earth for seed, and in the short space of a month the most luxuriant verdure and vegetation are spread over all Canada; the thermometer sometimes, in June, ranging as high as 95 or 100, prevailing through the summer from about 75 to 80. Although the severity of the winter precludes the earth from yielding any produce, yet it essentially facilitates the conveyance to market of its summer products: a track once beaten upon the snow, which is easily effected after the storms have ceased, enables a horse to drag, on a sledge, a twofold weight, twice or thrice the distance in a day, which he would be able to draw in the best constructed carriage, on the best possible road. In any country this facility of conveyance would be a great advantage; but in Canada especially, where the rapidity of vegetation, and the abundant produce of the summer, claim all the attention and all the energy of the population during that season, it more than counterbalances the severe and long duration of the winter, inasmuch as it supersedes the necessity of cost and labour in the construction of bridges and roads, and renders conveyance easy by routes and over tracts that would otherwise be impassable; and, so far from being deemed severe or inconvenient, it is regarded by the Canadians as the season of social intercourse and festivity. The basis of the commerce of Canada is in the produce of its forests, which, since 1817, have supplied England and the West Indies with an average of about 300,000 loads (of 50 cubic feet each) of timber annually. Its next source of supply for export is the skins of the innumerable wild animals which inhabit the forests, comprising the bear, stag, elk, deer, fox, martin, wild cat, and various others, including hare and rabbit, as well as a great variety of the weasel species; and the banks of the numerous lakes and rivers supply large quantities of otter and beaver skins. The aggregate value of this branch of commerce to Canada may be estimated at from 100,000*l.* to 150,000*l.* annually, varying in some measure according to the caprice of fashion. Fox and otter skins, which at one time sold in London for 10*l.* or 15*l.* a skin, at other times obtain only two or three to five pounds each; the others occasionally varying in nearly like proportion. Another great article of production for export is pot and pearl ash; which, with a few other articles of minor importance, constitute the whole of the exports; amounting, in the aggregate, including the freight of a portion of the wood in Canadian built vessels, to a money value of about 800,000*l.* The exclusion of a market for the surplus of grain, which would easily be supplied, is, however, more than counterbalanced to Canada by a large military force and civil establishment, which is maintained in that country out of the taxes levied on the people of England. These maintenances, in addition to its exports, enable the Canadians to draw from England a supply of manufactured and Asiatic productions to the amount, in money value, of about 1,400,000*l.* annually; whilst the direct intercourse of Canada with the British West India islands, enables it to obtain a liberal supply of the products of those luxuriant climes. From these circumstances, it is easy to conceive that Canada affords great advantage to agricultural enterprise and well-directed exertion. The inhabitants consist chiefly of the descendants of the original French settlers, and have preserved their language and customs to the present day. French is the general language; and the great subdivision of the estates under seignorial laws, is a remarkable feature in this part of Canada. The upper division of the vice-royalty has been the principal resort of later emigrants.

The legal establishment consists of a Court of Queen's Bench, Common Pleas, and Court of Appeal; and the civil and criminal law is administered by a chief justice and two puisne judges: the chief justice is also president of the legislative council. The ecclesiastical affairs of this country are under the superintendence of a Catholic bishop resident at Quebec, and an assistant bishop, nine vicars-general, and about 200 curés, who are supported chiefly out of grants of land made under the French government, and an assessment of one twenty-sixth part of all grain produced on the lands held by Catholics. The Protestant establishment consists of a lord bishop, also resident at Quebec, nine rectors, and several curates or clergymen, supported in part out of the civil list, and an appropriation of one-seventh of all the lands held by Protestants. The Protestant bishop has also a seat in the legislative council, by virtue of his appointment: no distinction is otherwise made on account of religious profession, Catholic and Protestant being alike eligible to a seat in the executive or legislative council and assembly, as well as to all other civil or military appointments. Numerous tribes of native Indians still inhabit all the western and interior parts of this vast country, though their number has been much reduced since 1780, about which period the small-pox raged with such destructive fury as to entirely depopulate several hundred thousand square miles of territory. Since the abatement of that dreadful catastrophe, and the conciliatory measures of the Canadian government towards them, although they still withhold themselves as much as ever from the society of the settlers, they have maintained a much more social intercourse, with but few attempts at open hostility; and it is the Indian population who contribute so essentially to the traffic in furs. The principal towns in Lower Canada are QUEBEC, MONTREAL, and TROIS RIVIERES, each of which see for more circumstantial details of their commerce, &c.

CANADA, UPPER, in its most comprehensive sense, comprises a tract of country extending from the *Ottawa*, or Grand River, which divides it from Lower Canada at its junction with the St. Lawrence, in the longitude of 74. 30. W. and 45. of N. lat., to the N. W. extremity of Lake Winnipeg, in the lat. of 59. N. and the 98th of W. long. bounded on the S. by a chain of lakes which discharge their waters into the sea by the great river St. Lawrence, and on the N. by the Ottawa River, in a N. W. direction, to the longitude of about 82., when it borders, by undefined limits, on the Hudson Bay and N. W. territories. However, like Lower Canada, the part under cultivation, and which at present more particularly merits attention, lies within comparatively narrow limits, in a S. W. direction, along the N. bank of the St. Lawrence and N. shores of Lakes Ontario and Erie, from the Ottawa River before mentioned, at its entrance into the St. Lawrence, to the Straits of Erie and St. Clair River, between the Lakes Erie and Huron, in the longitude of 82. 30. W.., being about 570 miles from N. E. to S. W., and 40 to 50 in breadth, including about 10,000,000 of acres of as fertile land as any in all North America. The S. W. extremity extending to the 42nd deg. of latitude, it is not subject to such severity of winter as the lower province; numerous streams, affording the most advantageous site for the erection of mills, fall into the lakes, and two considerable rivers in the eastern district fall into the Ottawa, and two others run in a S. W. direction, falling into Lake St. Clair, between the Strait of Erie and the St. Clair River. The southernmost of these rivers is called the Thames, with a London on its banks, destined, probably, at some future time, to rival in population and importance its namesake in Britain. Upper Canada is divided, for judicial and local purposes, into eight districts. About one-third of the lands were granted in free and common soccage, prior to 1825, about 500,000 acres of which are already under cultivation; one-third more being reserved for the crown and clergy, leaves about 4,000,000 of acres of fertile land, in the immediate vicinity of settlements already formed, for future grants; in addition to which, millions of acres in the rear, northward, covered at present with the finest timber of oak, hickory, beech, walnut, maple, pine, &c., &c., present a rich field for exertion, and the supply of future ages. The population of this province has increased, and continues increasing, in a greater ratio than the lower one. The population, which in 1783 did not exceed 10,000, in 1814 amounted to 95,000, in 1825 to double that number; according to the last census (1834) 336,461, and was estimated to be 450,000 in 1840. Its civil and religious institutions are similar to those of the sister province, with the exception of its being settled since the expulsion of the French; there are no feudal tenures or lands held in seignorage, which is the case with all those granted to the original French settlers in the lower province. The inhabitants also of Upper Canada, being emigrants from the United States, Scotland, and England, are principally protestants, and as such there are no special enactments or reservations for the catholics. The government and people of the United States of North America have long viewed this fine province with a longing and a jealous eye; and, immediately after their declaration of war against England, on the 18th of June, 1812, they landed an army from Detroit, of about 2000 men, under the command of General Hull, at its S. W. extremity, but who were immediately obliged to retreat, and, being pursued into their own territory by the English General Brock, the whole force surrendered prisoners of war on the following 16th of August. A second attempt, in October of the same year, proved equally unsuccessful. In the spring of the following year, however, the United States forces obtained some advantages, and, on the 10th of September, a British naval force, on Lake Erie, of five vessels carrying 69 guns, was completely defeated and captured by a United States squadron of nine vessels. This affair completely turned the tide of victory in favour of the United States; but it led to no ulterior advantages of any kind, though it probably presented them some disadvantages. The war terminated in 1815, without any object on the side of Canada having being obtained. Upper Canada participates in common in the commerce of the lower province; in addition to which, it has also the advantage of interchanging its surplus productions with the United States, as either one direction or the other may best promote its interest. As long, however, as the English government are enabled to afford the same protection to Upper Canada, and under the same circumstances as prevailed in 1826, and more especially so, should the English government qualify their present policy of excluding grain of foreign growth from importation into England, the interest of the Canadians will unquestionably lie on the side of England, and the Canadas afford the fairest field for agricultural exertion of any country in the world. Independent of its abundance of vegetable and animal food, the forests supply abundance of every variety of game and fowl, and the rivers and lakes afford a great variety of fish common to inland waters; and, by due attention to culture, the gardens may be made to yield abundance of delicious fruits.

The Canadas, in a general sense, may be considered a level country, beautifully undulated, but nowhere attaining an elevation exceeding 300 to 500 feet above the level of the waters of the great chain of lakes. A ridge of mountains skirts the northern boundaries of both provinces, from the 74th to the 98th degree of W. longitude; the altitudes have not been correctly ascertained, but they seem to claim the character only of a chain of broken hills rather than mountains. But little discovery of minerals has as yet been made: coals, copper, and iron, have been found: and, as population extends itself, and when necessity requires them, the mineral substances will, most probably, not prove deficient. The two principal towns are Toronto and Kingston, the capital, both of which see; and, for a more comprehensive and general view of the advantages which the Canadas are destined to derive from the facility of conveyance by water, see, under their respective heads, besides those previously mentioned, the following lakes and rivers, viz.:—

Winnipeg,	Miami,
Lake of the Woods,	Sandusky,
Red Lake,	Nipissing,
Sturgeon Lake,	Niagara,
Superior,	Ottawas,
Michigan,	Champlain, and
Huron,	Memphramagog.

Canajoharie, a town of New York, in Montgomery county. Its vicinity abounds with apple trees, from which is made cider of an excellent quality; 25 miles N. E. of Cooperstown, and 56 W. N. W. of Albany. Pop. 5146.

Canale, a town of Italy, in Piedmont. Pop. 3500

Canandaigua, a town of New York, chief of Ontario county, situate on the N. end of a lake of the same name, at its outlet into Canandaigua Creek, which runs E. into Seneca River. The lake is 20 miles long and 3 broad. The town stands on a pleasant slope from the lake. It has three churches, and a population of 5652, 90 miles E. S. E. of Niagara, and 208 W. by N. of Albany.

Cananore, a town of Hindostan, in Malabar, defended by a fortress, with other works after the European fashion, and the head quarters of the province. This town was taken in 1790 by the British, in whose possession it remains. It has several good houses, and carries on a good trade with other parts of the peninsula, and with Arabia and Sumatra. The country furnishes a large quantity of pepper, cardamoms, sandalwood, coir, sharks' fins, &c.; the imports are horses, benzoin, camphor, almonds, opium, sugar, and piece goods. It is governed by a native sovereign, who pays an annual tribute of 14,000 rupees to the English East India Company. It is seated on a small bay, one of the best on the coast; 56 miles N. N. W. of Calicut. Long. 75. 30. E. lat. 11. 53. N.

Canara, a province on the W. coast of Hindostan, formerly subject to the regent of Mysore, on whose defeat and death, in 1789, it came into the hands of the British. It is 180 miles in length, between the Concan and Malabar, and from 30 to 80 in breadth. The soil is fertile, and it produces abundance of rice, betel-nuts, and wild nutmegs. The principal port is Mangalore.

Canaries, or Canary Islands, anciently called the Fortunate Islands, are 13 in number; lying in the North Atlantic Ocean, off the W. coast of North Africa, between the latitudes of 28. and 30. N. Seven of them are considerable, namely, Palma, Ferro, Gomera, Teneriffe, Canaries, Fuerteventura, and Lancerota, each of which see; the other six are very small—Graciosa, Rocca, Allegranza, St. Clare, Inferno, and Lobos. They were formerly inhabited by a brave and independent race of people, called *Guanches*. Fuerteventura and Lauzerota, being the least populous, were taken possession of by John de Bethencourt, a Norman, about the commencement of the 15th century, in behalf of John, the then king of Castile: but it was not till towards the close of that century that the Spaniards, under whose sovereignty they still remain, obtained complete possession of the whole group, after the most determined resistance of the natives; the whole of whom, during the 16th century, fell victims to the cruelty of the Spaniards, either by the sword or the inquisition, which was established in these islands in 1532.

CANARY, GRAND, one of the principal of the above islands, lying between the E. side of Teneriffe, and the S. end of Fuerteventura. Next to Teneriffe, it is the most fertile and productive of the group. The surface near the coast is beautifully diversified with hill and dale, and well watered with streams issuing from mountains converging towards the centre of the island. The vine in all its varieties flourishes in this island in the utmost luxuriance. It is here that the most delicious wine or sack is made, and it was from hence that the English obtained their sack, so celebrated in the time of Shakspere. But under the proscriptive policy of Spain, nothing depending on human exertion prospers, and, though the Canary Islands are less exposed to its despotism than any other part of the Spanish dominions, every thing languishes. The extent of this island is about 30 miles from N. to S., and 28 in breadth. Palmas, or Canary, as it is sometimes called, the chief town, is situate on the coast, towards the N. E. end of the island, in the latitude of 28. 43. N. and 17. 46. of W. long., having a tolerable harbour for vessels of 100 to 200 tons burthen, sheltered by a promontory, jetting for about two miles into the sea, from the N. E. extremity of the island. Palmas was formerly the capital and seat of government, both civil and ecclesiastical, of the whole group of islands, but the governor now resides at Santa Cruz, on Teneriffe; the bishop continuing at Palmas, the population of which is estimated at about 25,000, and the remainder of the island at about the same number.

CANCALE, a town in France, in the department of Ille and Vilaine, seated on a bay of its name, and celebrated for oysters. The English landed here in 1758, and proceeded by land to burn the ships at St. Malo. It is nine miles E. of St. Malo, and 40 N. N. W. of Rennes. Pop. about 3000.

CANDAHAR, or KANDAHAR, a province of Afghanistan, lying between the 31st and 34th degree of N. lat., and the 65th and 70th of E. long.; the chief city, of the same name, is situate on the frontier of the Persian province of Segistan, in the lat. of 33. N. and 65. 30. of E. long. During the entirety of the Persian and Mogul empires, it was considered the most important barrier between the two territories, and it was formerly the capital and seat of government of the whole Afghan territory, which is now at Cabul. It is, however, still an important place, both as a fortress and of commercial intercourse. *See* AFGHANISTAN.

CANDEISH, a province of the Deccan of Hindostan, subject to the Poonah Mahrattas; bounded on the N. by Malwa, E. by Berar, S. by Dowlatabad, and W. by Baglana. The soil is fertile, though mountainous, and produces abundance of cotton. Burhampour, which surrendered to the British in 1803, is the capital.

CANDES, a town of France, in the department of Indre and Loire, at the confluence of the Vienne with the Loire; 30 miles W. S. W. of Tours.

CANDIA, an island in the Mediterranean, formerly Crete, lying to the S. of the Archipelago. It is 180 miles long, from W. to E., and 50 broad, and pervaded by a chain of mountains. The soil is fertile; and it abounds in fine cattle, sheep, swine, poultry, and game. The chief products are corn, wine, oil, wool, silk, and honey. It was taken by the Turks in 1669, after a war of 25 years. It was attempted to be retaken by the Venetians, in 1692, without effect. Mount Ida, so famous in history, is in the middle of this island; beside the capital of the same name, the other principal towns are Canea, Retimo, Nuovo, Legortino, and Setia. Total population, about 280,000, in nearly an equal proportion of Greeks and Turks.

CANDIA, the capital of the island of the same name, and the see of a Greek archbishop. Though populous formerly, little of it remains beside the walls and the market-place; and the harbour is now fit for nothing but boats. It is seated on the N. side of the island, about 240 miles S. S. W. of Smyrna. Long. 25. 18. E. lat. 35. 19. N. Pop. about 13,000.

CANDLEMAS ISLES, two islands in the Southern Ocean, near Sandwich Land. Long. 27. 13. W. lat. 57. 10. S.

CANDY, formerly a kingdom, comprising the greater part of the interior of the island of CEYLON, (which see;) the chief town, of the same name, is situate nearly in the centre of the island, on the banks of a river called the Malivaganga, which falls into the sea by several channels on the E. side. The town consists principally of one street about two miles in length, the principal buildings being the former king's palace and the temple of Boodh. It surrendered to a British force in March 1815, and was annexed, with the whole of the Island of Ceylon, to the British dominions. Candy is about 70 miles E. N. E. of Colombo, and 85 S. W. of Trincomalee.

CANEA, a strong town of the island of Candia, with a good harbour. The environs are adorned with olive-trees, vineyards, gardens, and brooks, bordered with myrtle and laurel roses. It was taken from the Venetians by the Turks, in 1645, after a defence of two months, in which the victors lost 25,000 men. It is seated on the N. coast of the island; 63

miles W. by N. of Candia. Long. 24. 7. E. lat. 35. 27. N.

Canelle, a town of Piedmont, at the S. extremity of Asti; 12 miles S. S. E. of the town of Asti. Pop. about 3000.

Canete. *See* Cagnete.

Caneto, a town of Italy, in the Mantuan, several times taken and retaken by the French and Austrians. It is seated on the Oglio; 20 miles W. of Mantua.

Canga, a town of the kingdom of Congo, on the river Zaire; 280 miles N. E. of St. Salvador. Long. 17. 10. E. lat. 2. 10. S.

Cangiano, a town of Naples, in Principato Citeriore; 40 miles E. by S. of Salerno.

Cangoxima, a strong seaport of Japan, on the most southern verge of the isle of Ximo, or Kiusiu, with a commodious harbour. At the entrance of the haven is a light-house, on a lofty rock; and at the foot of the rock is a convenient road for shipping. Here are large and sumptuous magazines, belonging to the emperor, some of which are proof against fire. Long. 132. 15. E. lat. 32. 10. N.

Canina, a town of European Turkey, in Albania, near the entrance of the Gulf of Venice; 8 miles S. E. of Avlona.

Canischa, a strong town of Lower Hungary. It was taken in 1600 by the Turks, who held it till 1690, when it was taken by the Austrians, after a blockade of two years, and ceded to the emperor by the peace of Carlowitz. It is seated on the bank of a small lake; 12 miles N. of the Drave River, and 85 miles S. S. W. of Raab. Long. 17. 10. E. lat. 46. 30. N.

Canna, one of the Hebrides of Scotland, S. W. of the Isle of Skye. It is four miles long and one broad: the high parts produce excellent pasture for cattle, and the low are tolerably fertile. Here are many basaltic columns. On the S. E. side of Canna is Sand Island, separated by a narrow channel; and between them is a well-frequented harbour. Long. 6. 38. W. lat. 57. 13. N.

Cannæ. *See* Canosa.

Cannes, or Cagnes, a small seaport at the S. E. extremity of France; distinguished as the place of debarkation of Napoleon from Elba, on the 1st of March, 1815. It is about six miles S. W. of Nice.

Cannobine, or Kanobine, a village of Syria, at the foot of Mount Lebanon, and near to the celebrated cedars, which are about 36 in number, besides a large number of minor ones, presenting a very picturesque appearance.

Cano. *See* Ghana.

Canobia, a town of Italy, in the Milanese, on the lake Maggiore; 35 miles N. N. W. of Milan.

Canoge, a town of Hindostan, in the province of Agra. It is said to have been the capital of all Hindostan, under the predecessor of Porus, who fought against Alexander; and that in the 6th century it contained 30,000 shops in which betel-nut was sold. It is now reduced to the size of a middling town, and seated on the Calini, near its conflux with the Ganges; 110 miles E. by S. of Agra. Long. 80. 13. E. lat. 27. 3. N.

Canonsburg, a town of Pennsylvania, in Washington county, on the W. branch of Chartier Creek; 4 miles above Marganza, and 15 S. S. W. of Pittsburg.

Canosa, a town of Naples, in Terra di Bari, which stands on part of the site of the ancient Canusium, one of the most magnificent cities of Italy. Between Canosa and the river Ofanto are still some traces of the ancient town of Cannæ, in the plain of which was fought the celebrated battle between Hannibal and the Romans, wherein the latter lost 45,000 men. Canosa is 4 miles W. by N. of Trani.

Canoul, a town of Hindostan, in Golconda; capital of a circar of the same name, seated on the S. bank of the Toombudra river; 110 miles S. S. W. of Hydrabad. Long. 78. 7. E. lat. 15. 48. N.

Canourgue, a town of France, in the department of Lozere, with a trade in cattle and woollen stuffs; seated near the Lot; 13 miles S. W. of Mende.

Canso, a seaport at the S. E. extremity of Nova Scotia. Near the town is a fine fishery for cod. Long. 60. 55. W. lat. 45. 20. N.

Canso, Gut of, a strait about 25 miles in length, and from a half to a mile wide, between the E. end of Nova Scotia and Cape Breton, leading from the Atlantic Ocean through Chedabucto Bay, into St. George's Bay, in the Gulf of St. Lawrence.

Canstadt, a town of Suabia, in the kingdom of Wirtemberg, with a manufacture of printed cottons. In the neighbourhood are some medicinal springs. It is seated on the Neckar, 3 miles N. E. of Stuttgard.

Cantal, an interior department in the S. of France, including part of the late province of Auvergne. It is so called, from a mountain near the centre of the department, whose summit is always covered with snow. The capital is St. Flour. Pop. about 250,000.

Cantazaro, a town of Naples, in Calabria Citeriore, near the sea; 26 miles S. W. of St. Severino. Pop. 10,000.

Canterbury, a city in Kent, capital of the county, and the see of an archbishop, who is primate of all England. It was the Durovernum of the Romans, and founded before the Christian era. The cathedral, a large structure, was once famous for the shrine of Thomas à Becket, a turbulent priest, who was murdered here in 1170, and afterwards made a saint. In this cathedral are interred Henry IV. and Edward the Black Prince. The city has likewise 14 parish churches, the remains of many Roman antiquities, and an ancient castle, with walls and a deep ditch; and a grammar-school founded by Henry VIII. It is a county of itself, governed by a mayor; and is noted for excellent brawn. The adjacent country produces abundance of hops. It has a market on Wednesday and Saturday, and is seated on the river Stour; 55 miles E. S. E. of London, on the high road to Dover, from which it is distant 17 miles.

Canth, a town of Silesia, on the river Weistritz; 15 miles S. W. of Breslau.

CANTIN, CAPE, a promontory of the Atlantic Ocean, on the coast of Morocco. Long. 9. 5. W. lat. 32. 33. N.

CANTON, a city, seaport, and capital of Quangtong, the most southern province of China, and the only port in that vast empire with which Europeans are permitted to hold any intercourse; it is finely located at the head of a bay, into which flow two large rivers, one from the westward, which by numerous collateral branches intersects all the southern part of the empire, and the other from the north, which, by a portage of only one day's journey, communicates with the great chain of inland waters that intersects every other province, thereby affording a facility of conveyance by water, which renders Canton peculiarly well adapted for the great outport of the empire. The harbour is very commodious, and, being sheltered by several small islands, it affords secure moorings for the innumerable barks or junks which navigate the inland waters; all the foreign ships anchor several miles distant from the town, not on account of the incapacity of the harbour to accommodate them, but from the peculiarly jealous policy of the Chinese, which seems to dread nothing so much as sociality of intercourse. Canton consists of three towns, divided by high walls, but so conjoined as to form almost a regular square. The streets are long and straight, paved with flag-stones, and adorned with triumphal arches. The houses in general have only one floor, built of earth or brick, some of them fantastically coloured, and covered with tiles. The better class of people are carried about in chairs, but the common sort walk barefooted and bareheaded. At the end of every street is a barrier, which is shut every evening, as well as the gates of the city. The Europeans and Americans occupy a range of buildings termed the factories, fronting a spacious quay along the bank of the harbour, without the city, which no foreigner is permitted to enter without the special permission of the viceroy, which is seldom or never obtained. The foreign trade of Canton resolves itself into a monopoly more peculiar and oppressive than any where else exists; it is vested in twelve persons, each paying a large premium for the privilege of trading, who are collectively amenable, as well to foreigners as to the government, for any default or mulct imposed upon any one or more of them individually. In addition to the external commerce of Canton, it also appears to be the seat of almost every branch of manufacture, more especially of silks and household gods. From the circumstance of there being no *public* worship in China, every house has its own collection of idols, the manufacture of which forms one of the most important branches of occupation. The main article of export from Canton is tea, which, since 1798, to England alone, has averaged about 25,000,000 lbs., whilst to America and other parts (since 1815 more especially) it has been gradually increasing, making an aggregate average quantity annually exported at the period of 1826, of about 40,000,000 lbs. The other principal articles exported to England are raw silk and nankeens; of the former, about 250,000 lbs. weight, and of the latter, about 600,000 pieces of four and seven yards each, annually; a few manufactured silks and crapes, fans, ivory chessmen, fancy boxes, and other toys, soy, and ink, constitute the remaining exports to England, which employs about 25 sail of ships annually, of about 1200 tons each; the reimbursement by the English for the above productions is made in cotton, wool, opium, and some other articles from Bombay and Bengal, and in woollen cloths, lead, &c. from England, to the amount of about 700,000*l.* annually. In addition to the trade direct to England, there is also an extensive traffic on English account between the different ports of India and Canton, which consists in a reciprocal interchange of the productions of the respective countries, and in which porcelain forms a considerable article of export from Canton. The intercourse of America with Canton is maintained on the part of America, with furs from the N. W. coast, sandal-wood, and the edible birds'-nests, collected among the eastern islands, and with dollars. A considerable portion of the tea exported in American ships, being on account and risk of the Chinese merchants, more especially the portion brought to Hamburgh, Antwerp, and other European ports, is wholly reimbursed in specie, the imposts of the government on its external commerce being levied on the length and breadth of the shipping entering and leaving the port. The following statement of the amount of duties returned to the Chinese treasury for the year 1822, will best show the extent and proportion of the three great branches into which the external commerce of Canton resolves itself: viz. 1st, that with the English East India Company; 2nd, that with the different ports of British India; 3rd, that with America:—

	On Import.	On Export.
English East Ind. Com.	395,112	460,042
Country Trade . . .	118,533	80,623
America	276,578	339,409
Total *Tale* . .	790,223	897,074

The *Tale* being only equal to 6s. 8d. of English money, the whole impost will be seen to amount, according to the above statement, to only £556,800, not equal to the amount levied on the single article of coals alone, at the port of London; and yet, such is the extent and insidious nature of the intermediate oppression of the Chinese *Hong* (or council, which is the term by which the twelve privileged merchants of Canton are collectively called), on one side, and the English East India Company on the other, that whilst the 25,000,000 lbs. of tea annually consumed in Great Britain and Ireland costs the *consumer*, on an average, at least 7s. per lb., it does not yield to the *producer*, including the inland conveyance to Canton, an average of 3½d. per lb. In 1823, several thousand houses in Canton were destroyed by fire, but the ground has since been rebuilt upon.

The population is estimated at about 1,500,000. It is in the lat. of 23. 8. N. and 113. 2. of E. long. being 16. 47. or about 1190 British statute miles S. by W. of Pekin, the metropolis of the empire.

CANTYRE, or KINTYRE, a peninsula of the W. coast of Scotland, in Argyleshire, 35 miles long and 7 broad; connected on the N. by an isthmus, scarce a mile broad, to the mountainous district of Knapdale. To the S. the peninsula terminates in a great promontory, surrounded by a group of dangerous rocks, called the Mull of Cantyre, on which is a lighthouse, in the lat. of 55. 17. N. and 5. 41. W. long. It is a mountainous district, with some fertile spots. The chief town is Campbelton. The other towns are Kirkmichael, Ballachintea, Killean, Kilcalmonil, and Skipness.

CANY, a town of France, in the department of Lower Seine; situate in a country which produces great quantities of corn and flax; 26 miles N. W. of Rouen.

CAORLO, a small island in the Gulf of Venice, on the coast of Friuli. It has a town of the same name; 20 miles S. W. of Aqueleia. Long. 12. 36. E. lat. 45. 42. N.

CAPACIO, a town of Naples, in Principato Citeriore; 20 miles S. E. of Salerno.

CAPE BRETON, an island forming part of the British dominions in America; lying between the N. end of Nova Scotia, from which it is separated by the GUT of CANSO (which see), and the S. W. point of Newfoundland, from which it is separated by the principal entrance into the Gulf of St. Lawrence. It extends, in a N. by E. direction, from the lat. of 45. 30. to 47. 6. N., and from the long. of 59. 45. to 61. 35. W., forming a barrier between the Atlantic Ocean and the gulf, which it completely landlocks, and forms into a vast inland sea; the passage between the N. E. end and Newfoundland being about 65 miles wide, intercepted, however, by the island of St. Paul, and, just within the gulf, by the Magdalen group of isles. Cape Breton is indented from N. to S. by spacious bays, dividing it into two islands joined together by a very narrow isthmus. The coast on all sides is also much indented by bays, making the figure of the land very irregular. Its area, however, amounts to about 40,000 square miles. The French first formed a settlement upon this island in 1712, which surrendered to a British force from New England, in 1745, and was confirmed, with all the other French possessions in North America, to England, by the treaty of 1763. Its most distinguishing property is its rich strata of coal of superior quality; with some dreary surface, it also presents some very fertile spots, well wooded, and containing a variety of wild animals, the skins of which forms a branch of its traffic. Louisburg, the chief town, is situate on the Atlantic coast, in the lat. of 45. 54. N. and 59. 55. W. long. The chief occupation of the people, not only of Louisburg but of the whole island, in addition to agriculture, is the cod fishery, which they pursue to some extent, for the West India and other markets. Total population of the island, about 4000. It was constituted a separate government in 1784, under a lieutenant-governor appointed by the king; but by a stretch of authority on the part of the legislative assembly and council of Nova Scotia, it has reverted as a province to that government, to which it was originally attached.

CAPE GIRARDIEU, a county of the state of Missouri, North America, lying between the St. Francis and Mississippi rivers, just above the junction of the Ohio with the Mississippi, in the lat. of 37. N. It is 40 miles in length, from N. to S. and about 20 in mean breadth. Pop. 9359. There is a town of the same name on the W. bank of the Mississippi; but Jackson, further N. in the interior, 80 miles S. S. E. of St. Louis, and about 600 N. N. W. of New Orleans, is the chief town.

CAPE OF GOOD HOPE, a territory comprising the whole southern extremity of Africa, discovered by the Portuguese navigator, Bartholomew Diaz, in 1493, who gave it the name of *Cabo Tormentoso*, from the boisterous weather which he met with near it; but Emanuel, king of Portugal, on the return of Diaz, changed its name to that of Cape of Good Hope, from the hope he entertained of finding a passage beyond it to India; and in this he was not deceived, for Vasco de Gama, having doubled this cape on the 20th November, 1497, proceeded to India, and landed at Calicut, on the 22nd of May, 1498. The Cape of Good Hope was first touched at by the Dutch in 1600, and in 1650 they established a settlement at this place, of which they held undisturbed possession for near 150 years. The cape or promontory, which gives name to the territory, is about 13 leagues W. N. W. of Cape Aguillas, which is the extreme S. point of the African continent; and the territory extends northward to the lat. of about 30. S., and eastward from the shore of the Atlantic Ocean in 18. to that of the Indian Ocean in 28. of E. long. This extensive territory was taken from the Dutch by the English, in 1795; but restored to Holland at the peace of Amiens, in 1802; retaken in 1806, and confirmed to Great Britain by the Congress at Vienna, in 1816; and it now forms part of the British dominions. From the southern extremity to the latitude of about 30. the ground rises, by three successive gradations, to the height of 5000 or 6000 feet above the level of the sea; the back mountain ridge in some places rising to the height of 9000 to 10,000 feet. This variation in altitude is subject to almost every variety of climate, and the surface is as various as the climate, there being much dreary and sterile district, some very fine pasture, and some exceedingly fertile arable land. The capriciousness of the seasons, however, is such as to render the pursuit of tillage exceeding hazardous, though, when the seasons are favourable, the produce is superabundant, The culture of the vine seems attended with less risk, and is likely to supersede the attention to agriculture, beyond what is necessary for the subsistence of the colony. The surplus produce of wine, exported during the eight years, 1817 to 1824, averaged about 4500 pipes per annum. In 1819, an attempt was made to establish a settlement at Algoa Bay, towards the eastern extremity of the southern coast, in the long. of 25. 42. E., about 450 miles E. of the settlement at the Hope Cape, but the seasons in succession cutting off all the crops, the settlers were all subjected to the extreme of privation. By due attention, however, to the nature of the climate, and application of the soil to purposes for which it is best adapted, the Cape territory, in the aggregate, is doubtless susceptible of being rendered subservient to the highest degree of comfort and enjoyment of the settlers, and reciprocally so to the inhabitants of Great Britain. For magisterial purposes, it is divided into the districts of the Cape, Stellenbosch, Clanwilliam, Tulbagh or Worcester, Zwellendam, Beaufort, Graff Reynet, George, Uitenhage, Albany, and Somerset, and also a tract called the Neutral Ground, to the east of Albany, which has been the subject of much dispute with the Koosas, a tribe of Caffres. The Cape district comprises the promontory which gives name to the territory. The promontory jets into the Southern Ocean, at the south-west extremity. On each side of this promontory is a bay, frequented alternately as the winds prevail; that on the east side, in the Southern Ocean, is called False Bay, availed of during the prevalence of north and north-west winds; and that on the west side, in the Atlantic Ocean, is called Table Bay, which affords tolerable shelter during the prevalence of south and south-east winds. They are, however, both destitute of convenient harbours. There are two other bays north of Table Bay; Saldanha, in the lat. of 33. 7. S., and St. Helens, in 32. 40., both of which have more convenient harbours than either of the other two; but, being deficient in fresh water, they are not much frequented. On the shore of Table Bay, in the lat. of 33. 56. S. and 18. 28. E. long., is the chief town of the colony, called *Cape-town*, rising in the midst of a desert, surrounded by black and dreary mountains. To the south-east of the town are some vineyards, which yield the famous wine called Constantia. The store-houses built by the Dutch East India Company are situate next the water, and the private buildings lie beyond them, on a gentle ascent toward the mountains. The castle, or principal fort, which commands the road, is on the east side; and another strong fort, called Amsterdam fort, is on the west side. The streets are broad and regular; and the houses, in general, are built of stone, and whitewashed. There are barracks for 2000 men, built on one side of a spacious plain, which serves for a parade. There are two other large squares, in one of which the market is held, and the other serves to assemble the numerous waggons and vehicles bringing in the produce from the country. There is another large building erected by the Dutch for a marine hospital, and a house for the accommodation of the government slaves; the government house, a town hall, and a Calvinist, and Lutheran church, constitute the remainder of the public buildings. The population, in 1826, amounted to about 20,000, more than one-half of whom were Hottentots, Negro, and Malay slaves, and people of colour. The Table Mountain, so called from the flatness of its main summit, rises from immediately behind the town, to the height of 3592 feet above the level of the sea, having a collateral peak on the east, 3315 feet in height, and another on the west, 2160 feet. The profitable productions of the colony, taken as a whole, are wine, grain, all the European and most of the tropical fruits, vegetables of every description, cattle, and sheep. At the foot of the Table Mountain are considerable plantations of the *protea argentea*, or silver tree, (a species of the protea peculiar to this spot), the stone pine, and the white poplar. Avenues of oak adorn the country houses; and this tree grows rapidly throughout the colony, but rarely to any perfection as timber. It is constantly cut down with the rest of the few forest trees of the Cape, for fuel, which is so scarce that most families in decent circumstances keep a slave employed entirely in collecting it. On the eastern side of the mountains that run northward from the Cape, and at the southern foot of the Zwartzberg, or Black Mountains, are some good pasture farms, and whole plains of the common aloe, which forms a considerable article of trade. The markets are well supplied with fish from the open sea, and from the numerous inlets of the coast.

Cape May, a maritime county, forming a promontory at the S. extremity of the state of New Jersey. The cape, at the extreme S. point, is in lat. 38. 57. N., the W. side being washed by Delaware Bay, and the E. to Great Egg Harbour, in the lat. of 39. 18. N., by the Atlantic Ocean, this side in its whole extent being flanked by a chain of islands. Pop. 5324. The court-house of the county is 91 miles S. of Trenton.

*** *For numerous other capes, see their respective names.*

Capelle, a town of France, in the department of Aisne; 10 miles N. E. of Guise.

Caper's Island, a island near the coast of South Carolina. Long. 79. 39. W. lat. 32. 55. N.

Capestan, a town of France, in the department of Herault, near the river Aude and the canal of Languedoc; 6 miles W. of Beziers.

Capitanata, a province of Naples, E. of the Appennines, bounded on the E. for about 70 miles by the Adriatic; varying in breadth from 40 to 80 miles; containing an area of about 3500 square miles, and 270,000 inhabitants. It is watered by several streams falling into the Adriatic. The chief town upon the coast is Manfredonia; and Lucera, 35 miles W. of Manfredonia, and 90 E. by N. of the city of Naples, is the chief town.

Capo Fino, a barren rock in the territory of Genoa, with a castle on its eastern peak. Near it is a port of the same name; 13 miles E. S. E. of Genoa. Long. 8. 56. E. lat. 44. 20. N.

Capo D'Istria, a town of Italy, capital of Istria, and a bishop's see. It stands on a small island in the Gulf of Trieste, connected with the continent by a causeway, which is defended by a castle. The principal revenue consists in wine and salt. It is 8 miles S. of

Trieste. Long. 14. 0. E. lat. 45. 40. N. Pop. about 5000.

CAPPEL, a town of Denmark, in the duchy of Sleswick, on the E. coast; 16 miles N. E. of Sleswick.

CAPPOQUIN, a town of Ireland, in the county of Waterford, on the Blackwater river, over which is an ancient bridge. Here is also an ancient castle built by the Fitzgeralds; 131 miles from Dublin.

CAPRARIA, an isle in the Mediterranean, to the N. E. of Corsica; 15 miles in circumference. It has a town of the same name, with a good harbour, defended by a castle. It is included in the Sardinian States. Pop. about 2000. Long. 9. 56. E. lat. 43. 5. N.

CAPRI, an island in the Mediterranean, at the entrance of the Gulf of Naples, nearly opposite Sorento. It is 5 miles long and two broad, with steep shores, accessible only in two places; and was the retreat of the Emperor Tiberius, who here spent the last ten years of his life in luxurious debauchery. A vast quantity of quails come here every year; and the tenth of what are caught forms a great part of the revenue of the bishop, who is hence called the Bishop of Quails. Pop. about 3600.

CAPRI, the capital of the island of the same name, and a bishop's see, with a castle. It was once a delightful place, embellished with magnificent works, which were demolished after the death of Tiberius. It is 27 miles S. S. W. of Naples. Long. 14. 10. E. lat. 40. 32. N.

CAPRYCKE, a town of the Netherlands; 18 miles E. of Bruges, on the road to Phillipina. Pop. about 3500.

CAPUA, a strong city of Naples, in Terra di Lavoro, and an archbishop's see, with a citadel. It is two miles from the ancient Capua, and was built out of its ruins. No city in Italy, except Rome, contains a greater number of ancient inscriptions. In 1803 it suffered much by an earthquake, and a number of cavalry were buried under the ruins of their barracks. It stands at the foot of a mountain, on the river Volturno; 20 miles N. of Naples. Long. 14. 19. E. lat. 41. 7. N.

CAPA, a river of Russia, which issues from the N. extremity of the Ural mountains, and flows into the Gulf of Karskoi, in the Arctic Ocean; forming the boundary between Europe and Asia, for the space of about 140 miles.

CARACCAS, a province of Colombia, South America, extending along the northern coast, between the 64th and 70th degree of W. long. It was first discovered by Columbus, on his third voyage in 1498. Several attempts were immediately after made by Spanish adventurers to form settlements, which being partially effected, it was sold by Charles V. of Spain to a company of German trading adventurers, who, by their intolerable oppressions, were expelled the country in 1550, when it was formed into a captain-generalship, under the command of a supreme governor appointed by the king of Spain, under whose sovereignty it remained in undisturbed possession up to 1806. When the events of the war, which had desolated Europe from 1793, had cut off all direct intercourse between Spain and her external possessions, a futile attempt was made by a General Miranda, to revolutionize this part of South America, which only served to expose those whom he seduced into his project to undergo the extreme of privation, and some of them the punishment of death. In 1810, however, when the French had obtained the entire possession of Spain, and proclaimed the sovereignty of all its external possessions, a congress was convened of deputies from all the provinces of the captain-generalship of Caraccas, to devise measures either for the establishment of an independent government, or for effecting some modification in the then existing one. This led to internal dissensions and inveterate hostility between the two parties; one advocates for maintaining the government as it then existed, which were supported by Spain on the reinstation of Ferdinand in 1812, and the other, who placed General Bolivar in the command of their armed forces, resolved upon acceding to nothing short of unqualified independence. The contest continued with alternate success up to the close of the year 1819, when on the 19th of December a union was effected between the provinces of the Caraccas and those of New Granada; and on the 24th of June, 1821, the last battle was fought, which decided the fate of the pretensions of Spain, and the final extinction of its authority over all this part of South America, which has since resolved itself into one great united republic under the denomination of Colombia, divided into three provinces, of which that of Venezuela comprises the greater part of the former captain-generalship of Caraccas. *See* VENEZUELA.

CARACCAS, LEON DE, the chief town of the new Venezuelean province of the republic of Colombia, is situated on an elevated plain, 2900 feet above the level of the sea, at a distance of about 8 miles from the shore, in the lat. of 10. 31. N. and 67. of W. long. Notwithstanding its altitude, it is watered by two or three streams, whilst by its elevation it enjoys a comparatively temperate and delightful climate. The town is regularly laid out, and has two or three squares, a cathedral, college, and several churches, but none remarkable for architectural beauty. The population in 1802 was estimated at 42,000, but an earthquake in March, 1812, destroyed 12,000 of the number, as well as great part of the town. Its markets are well supplied with almost every luxury as well as necessary of life; and, should the new government continue firm, discreet, and just, Caraccas de Leon will probably rank among the most important towns of the republic. *See* LA GUAYRA.

CARAMAN, a town of France, in the department of Upper Garonne; 20 miles S. E. of Toulouse. Pop. about 2300.

CARAMANIA, or KARAMANIA, a province of Asiatic Turkey, to the E. of Natolia. It comprehends the ancient Pamphylia, and a great part of Cilicia, Pisidia, and Cappadocia. It contains several lakes, which abound with fish, and furnish great quantities of salt, and the Kisil Irmak river intersects the eastern part of the province, running N. into the Black Sea. Cogni, or Konieh, in the lat. of 38. 10. N. and 32. 25. of E. long., is the capital. It is more specifically applied to the S. coast of Asia Minor, as the name is unknown to the Turks.

CARAMANTA, a district of Colombia. included in the S. part of the province of Magdalena; bounded on the W. by Ystmo, S. by Popayan, and E. by Zulia. It is a valley surrounded by high mountains, and there are waters whence the natives get salt. The capital, of the same name, is seated on the Cauca; 240 miles N. N. N. E. of Popayan. Long. 75. 15. W. lat. 5. 18. N.

CARANGAS, a town of Peru, capital of a district which contains valuable silver mines, and feeds a great number of cattle. It is 45 miles W. of Potosi.

CARARA, properly CARRARA, a town of Italy in the principality of Massa, celebrated for its quarries of marble of various colours. It is 5 miles N. N. E. of Massa.

CARASUI, a lake of European Turkey, in Bulgaria, 55 miles in circumference, containing several islands. It is formed by a branch of the Danube, not far from its entrance into the Black Sea.

CARAVAYA, a town of Peru, capital of a jurisdiction of the same name. It is 160 miles S. E. of Cusco. Long. 69. 36. W. lat. 14. 40. S.

CARBONNE, a town of France, in the department of Upper Garonne, on the E. bank of the river Garonne; 25 miles S. by W. of Toulouse. Pop. about 2000.

CARCAGANTE, a town of Valencia, on the S. bank of the river Xucar; 25 miles S. of the city of Valencia.

CARCASSONE, a city of France, capital of the department of Aude, and a bishop's see. It is situate on the line of the grand canal of Languedoc, and divided into the upper and lower town by the Aude, over which is a stone bridge. In the upper town, called the city, are a strong castle and the cathedral. The lower town is square, regularly built, and kept very neat, by means of an aqueduct which brings the water of the Aude to different fountains. Here are manufactures of all sorts of cloth. It is 35 miles W. of Narbonne, and 50 S. E. of Toulouse. Pop. about 15,000.

CARCULLA, or CARICUL, a town of Hindostan, in Canara, chiefly inhabited by shopkeepers. In an open temple here is the image of a naked man, 38 feet in height by 19 in thickness, made of one piece of granite. Much rice, ginger, turmeric, and betel-nut is raised in the vicinity. It is seated between two lakes, or tanks, which give source to two rivers; 26 miles N. by E. of Mangalore.

CARDIFF, a borough and seaport of Wales, capital of Glamorganshire with a market on Wednesday and Saturday. It is seated on the Taafe, over which there is a handsome bridge of five arches. Its castle was an elegant Gothic structure, but has undergone a motley repair. The town was formerly encompassed by a wall, and vestiges of its four gates yet remain. The constable of the castle is the chief magistrate, who is called mayor; and here the assizes for the county are held. Near the town are some iron works, and a canal extending 25 miles, to the great iron works at Merthyr Tydvil. In the castle died Robert Duke of Normandy, eldest son of William the Conqueror, after having been blinded, and confined 28 years, by his brother Henry I. Cardiff is 40 miles W. of Bristol, 47 E. of Swansea, and 160 W. of London. Long. 3. 12. W. lat. 51. 28. N. It sends, with its contributaries, one member to parliament.

CARDIGAN, a maritime county of South Wales, extending for about 50 miles along the shore of St. George's Channel, from the river Tievy, which divides it from Pembroke and Caermarthenshires on the S., to the Dovey, which divides it from Merionethshire, N.; being about 30 miles in mean breadth, bounded on the E. by the counties of Montgomery, Radnor, and Brecknock. The Rheidol, and one or two other rivers, intersect the country from E. to W. Parts of this county are very fertile, both in tillage and pasture, which enables the inhabitants to produce a considerable surplus of grain, and small black cattle, with which, and some few sheep and wool, they obtain a tolerable supply of manufactured and colonial productions. The principal towns besides Cardigan are Aberystwith and Llanbeder. It sends one member to parliament.

CARDIGAN, the chief town of the preceding county, is situated at the mouth of the Tievy, over which is a handsome bridge of seven arches, at the S. W. extremity of the county. It had formerly a strong and an extensive castle, of which but little now remains. It was from hence that the first descent upon Ireland was made by the English. The church is a spacious edifice; the county gaol and hall have been rebuilt within the present century. It is a corporate town, governed by a mayor, 12 aldermen, &c., and unites with Adpar, Aberystwith, and Llanbeder in returning one member to parliament. It is 25 miles E. N. E. of St. David's Head, 132 miles W. of Gloucester, and about the same distance due E. of Waterford in Ireland. Its commerce by sea is confined to the coast.

CARDIGAN BAY is formed by St. David's Head, the western point of Pembrokeshire S., in the lat. of 51. 44. N. and 5. 17. of W. long., and Bardsey Island, off the S. W. point of Caernarvonshire N., in the lat. of 52. 44. and 4. 39. of W. long.; the main coast of Caernarvonshire being in the long. of about 4.; it gives a stretch of about 40 miles from W. to E., and 50 from S. to N. within the bay.

CARDONA, a town of Spain, in Catalonia, with a castle. Near it is a mountain of solid rock salt, of which are made vases, snuff-boxes, and trinkets; and there are vineyards that produce excellent wine. It is seated on the Cardenero; 36 miles N. W. of Barcelona. Population about 3000.

CARELIA, or RUSSIAN FINLAND. *See* WIBURG.

CARENTAN, a town of France, in the department of Manche, with an ancient castle; 8 miles from the sea, and 21 W. of Bayeux. Pop. 2860.

CARES, or KAREIS, a town of European Turkey, in Macedonia, situate on Mount Athos; 17 miles S. E. of Salonica.

CAREW, a village of Wales; 4 miles E. by N. of Pembroke; noted for the noble and extensive remains of its castle; situate on a gentle swell above an arm of Milford Haven.

CARFAGNANO. *See* CASTEL NUOVO DI CARFAGNANO.

CARHAIX, a town of France, in the department of Finisterre, on the river Yer; 19 miles S. of Morlaix.

CARIACO, a city in Colombia, province of Venezuela, containing a population of about 6000. It is about 50 miles E. of Cumana.

CARIACOU, an island dependent on Grenada, between it and St. Vincent.

CARIATI, a town of Naples, on the sea coast, in Calabria Citeriore, near the Gulf of Taranto; 25 miles N. of Severino.

CARIBBEAN SEA, that part of the Atlantic Ocean lying between Cuba, St. Domingo, and Porto Rico, on the N., and the N. coast of the new republic of Colombia on the S., and extending W. from the 62nd to the 84th degree of W. long.

CARIBBEE ISLANDS, the most eastern islands of the West Indies, divided into Windward and Leeward Islands. *See* INDIES, WEST.

CARIBOU, a considerable island in Lake Superior, towards the E. end, claimed by the United States, as being wholly within their boundary line.

CARICAL, a town of Hindostan, in the Carnatic, where the French had a settlement, which was taken by the British in 1760. It stands at the mouth of a branch of the Cavery; 8 miles S. of Tranquebar.

CARIGNAN, or CARNIGNANO, a town of Piedmont, in a district of the same name, in the S. part of the province of Turin, with a castle; seated on the river Po; 12 miles S. of Turin. Pop. about 7000.

CARIMON, an island in the Straits of Malacca, at the entrance into the China Sea, in the lat. of 1. N. and 104. E. long.

CARIMON JAVA, a cluster of islands to the N. of Java, at the principal of which ships touch for refreshment, in their voyage to Borneo. Long. 110. 12. E. lat. 5. 56. S.

CARIN[illegible]OU, the chief of the Grenadilla Islands, in the West Indies; 16 miles N. N. E. of Grenada. It produces much cotton, and has a good harbour. *See* GRENADA.

CARINI, a town of Sicily, seated on a point of land near the sea; about 16 miles N. W. of Palermo; it was the birthplace of Lais.

CARINOLA, a town of Naples, in Terra di Lavoro; seated near Mount Massico; about 8 miles from the sea, and 25 miles N. W. of Naples.

CARINTHIA, DUCHY OF, an interior province or division of the Austrian empire, lying between the lat. of 46. 21. and 47. 6. N. and 12. 30. to 14. 50. of E. long., comprising an area of about 3500 English square miles; the W. end borders on the Tyrol, and it is bounded on the N. by the bishopric of Saltzburg and Upper Styria, E. by Lower Styria, and S. by Upper Carniola and the Venetian territory. The river Drave, which rises in the Tyrol and falls into the Danube at Belgrade, intersects Carinthia its whole extent from W. to E., receiving several tributary streams, both from the N. and S.; there are also several lakes. It is a mountainous and woody district, the mountains yielding abundance of iron, lead, and copper, as well as quicksilver, bismuth, and zinc, and also the purest marbles, and a variety of gems; whilst the forests abound with the finest timber, the valleys afford some excellent pasturage, as well as fertile lands for tillage; but, being edged in by mountains both on the N. and S., whilst the remoteness of the course of the Drave precludes it from being availed of as a channel of conveyance, the rich store of natural products which this district contains are of little advantage either to the inhabitants or to the world. It is divided, for local jurisdiction, into two parts, Upper, West; and Lower, East; the former containing about 175,000 inhabitants, and the latter about 105,000. The principal towns in the upper part are Gmund and Villach, and in the lower, Clagenfurt, (which is the capital of the duchy,) Wolfsberg, Wolfenmarck, Pleyburg, &c. The inhabitants, who speak chiefly the Sclavonian language, are of the Romish church, and contribute to the Austrian government an impost of about 250,000*l.* English per annum.

CARISBROOK, a village contiguous to Newport, in the Isle of Wight, remarkable for its castle and church, which are both very ancient. The church had once a convent of monks annexed, part of which is now a farm house, still retaining the name of the priory. The castle stands on an eminence, and was the prison of Charles I. in 1647, before he was delivered to the parliament forces. It is now nominally the seat of the governor of the Isle of Wight.

CARISTO, or CASTLE ROSSO, an episcopal town of Greece, at the S. extremity of the island of Negropont. Long. 24. 35. E. lat. 38. 34. N.

CARLEBY, OLD and NEW, two towns on the coast of West Bothnia; about 50 miles N. of Wasa.

CARLENTINI. *See* LENTINI.

CARLI, a town of Hindostan, in the province of Aurungabad; 32 miles N. W. of Poonah. There are some remarkable apartments hewn out of the rock; among others, a spacious temple dedicated to Buddha.

CARLINGFORD, a populous parish and town in the county of Louth, Ireland. The parish comprises a promontory between Dundalk and

Carlingford Bays. The town is situate on the S. shore of the bay of Carlingford, and is noted for its oyster fishery; it is a corporate town, and returned two members to the Irish parliament. It is 8 miles S. of Newry, and 52 N. of Dublin.

CARLISLE, a city, bishop's see, and capital of the county of Cumberland, England, is situate at the junction of three rivers, Calder, Petterill, and Eden, about six miles above the entrance of the united streams into Solway Frith, and 13 miles from the S. W. frontier of Scotland. Carlisle has held a distinguished rank among the cities of England in every period of British history, and is supposed to have been first founded by Luil, a native Briton, long before the irruption of the Romans into England. The contiguity of Carlisle to Scotland, during the less social habits and distinctiveness of interest of the people of that country, frequently exposed it to their depredations; to avoid which, the Romans, on their possessing themselves of this part of England, erected a wall from Solway Frith to the German Ocean, which included Carlisle on one side, and Newcastle on the other, within its southern limits. After the departure of the Romans from England, Carlisle was surrounded with a wall, by Egfrid, king of Northumberland; and after the Norman conquest it was further protected by a citadel and castle, built by William Rufus, having three gates, called the English, Irish, and Scottish, with reference to their bearing on the side of each respective country. These defences, however, did not prevent it from falling into the possession of the Scots, who held it alternately with the English, from the period of William Rufus to that of Henry VII. It was constituted a bishop's see by Henry I., destroyed by fire by the Scots in the reign of Henry III., and experienced the same disaster twice in the following reign. In 1568 the castle was made the prison-house of the unfortunate Mary of Scotland; in 1645 it surrendered, through famine, to the parliamentary forces, and in 1745 fell into the possession of the partisans of the Pretender, but was immediately after retaken by the Duke of Cumberland, who demolished the gates and part of the wall; and it has since that period enjoyed an uninterrupted tranquillity. Since the commencement of the present century it has undergone great improvements: on the site of the citadel two commodious court-houses have been erected, the county gaol rebuilt, a handsome stone bridge built over the Eden, with other improvements, which have contributed to render it one of the most agreeable and interesting cities of England. The castle is still kept in repair, and serves, with other purposes, for a magazine, and an armoury of about 10,000 stand of arms. The cathedral is a stately and venerable edifice, partly of Saxon and partly of Gothic architecture; there are two other churches, as well as several sectarian meeting-houses. The markets, on Wednesdays and Saturdays, are well supplied with every thing necessary for subsistence and comfort. The cotton manufacture has long been established here upon an extended scale, whilst the architectural and external appearances of the city indicate great prosperity. The conveyance of its commodities of commerce has been facilitated by a canal to the Solway Frith; it likewise participates in the advantages of the railways which now communicate with all parts of the kingdom ; and it is a point of union and interchange for the mails to all parts of England, Scotland, and Ireland. Its corporation consists of a mayor, twelve aldermen, &c. It returns two members to parliament, and is 101 miles S. E. of Glasgow, 91 S. by W. of Edinburgh, and 303 N. N. W. of London.

CARLISLE, a town of Schoharie county, state of New York. Pop. 1850; 40 miles W. of Albany.

CARLISLE, a town of Pennsylvania, capital of Cumberland county, with a college, and four edifices for public worship. It is situate near a creek of the Susquehannah; 100 miles W. by N. of Philadelphia.

CARLISLE BAY, on the S. coast of Jamaica, W. coast of Barbadoes, and island of Antigua.

CARLO, an island off the coast of East Bothnia; about 20 miles in circumference; it is opposite to the harbour of Leaborg.

CARLOPAGO, a town of Crotia, in the Adriatic Sea, at the foot of a craggy rock, near the channel that separates the island of Pago from the continent. The commerce consists chiefly of wood. Pop. about 10,000. It is 46 miles S E. of Buccari. Long. 15. 13. E. lat. 44. 55. N.

CARLO, ST., a city in the interior of Colombia, province of Venezuela, situate on one of the branches of the Apure river; about 85 miles S. W. of Valencia. The inhabitants are principally descendants of settlers from the Canary Isles; who are more industrious and social than those from Spain. Under the newly formed government of Colombia, St. Carlo promises to become a flourishing place, being situate in a very fertile country, affording great inducements to agricultural enterprise. Pop. in 1826, about 10,000; but since that period it has greatly increased.

CARLO DE MONTEREY, SAN, the principal settlement of New California, on the W. coast of North America, in the lat. of 36. 36. N., and 121. 34. of W. long. It is beautifully situated within a small bay of the same name, first discovered by Cabrillo in 1542. It was afterwards visited by the Count de Monterey, from whom it received its present name. The forests and mountains preclude much intercourse with the interior ; nor does it appear that there is any considerable river, either N. or S., for some distance, otherwise it would be an inviting spot for colonization.

CARLOW, an interior county in the S. E. part of Ireland ; it is bounded on the W. by the Barrow river, which divides it from the county of Kilkenny, and is intersected on the E. by the Slaney river, which falls into Wexford Haven: it is one of the smallest counties of Ireland, containing 211,440 acres, but exceedingly fertile; its butter is highly esteemed. There is a canal to Dublin, and the rivers Barry and Slaney are navigable. It returns two members to parliament. The only towns besides Carlow, the capital, are Tullow and Hacketstown.

CARLOW, the chief town of the preceding county, is situate on the E. bank of the Barrow river, at the N. W. extremity of the county, bordering on Queen's county. The ruins of a castle overhanging the river, the ruins of a very fine abbey, a convent, and Roman Catholic college, are the principal objects of interest in the town. It has also a respectable market house, county court house, gaol, and cavalry barracks, and manufactures some woollen cloths; it returns one member to parliament. It is 18 miles N. E. of the city of Kilkenny, and 39 S. W. of Dublin.

CARLOWITZ, a town of Sclavonia, where a peace was concluded between the Turks and Germans in 1669. It is seated on the S. bank of the Danube, just below Peterwarden; 38 miles N. W. of Belgrade. Pop. about 5600.

CARLSBAD, a town of Bohemia, in the circle of Saatz, celebrated for its hot baths, discovered by the Emperor Charles IV. as he was hunting. It is seated on the Topel, near its confluence with the Egra; 24 miles E. N. E. of Eger, and 70 S. E. of Dresden. Pop. about 3000.

CARLSBURG, a town of Lower Saxony, in the duchy of Bremen, on the river Geeste, at the mouth of the Weser; 30 miles N. by W. of Bremen. Long. 8. 45. E. lat. 53. 32. N.

CARLSBURG, a city of Transylvania. *See* WEISSENBURG.

CARLSCRONA, or CARLSCROON, a city and seaport of Sweden, in Blekingen. It was founded in 1680 by Charles XI., who removed the fleet from Stockholm to this place, on account of its centrical situation, and the superiority of its harbour, the entrance of which is defended by two strong forts. The greatest part of the town is built of wood, and stands upon a small rocky island, which rises gently in a bay of the Baltic. The suburbs extend over another small rock, and along the mole, close to the basin where the fleet is moored; and are fortified towards the land by a stone wall. Here are excellent docks for the repairing and building of ships, foundries for cannon, and manufactures of gunpowder, ropes, sails, &c. The admiralty board was transferred back to Stockholm in 1770. The inhabitants are estimated at 11,000. It is 220 miles S. S. W. of Stockholm. Long. 15. 26. E. lat. 56. 7. N.

CARLSHAVEN, or CARLSHAMM, a town of Sweden, in Blekingen, with a woollen manufacture, a forge for copper, and a timber-yard; 22 miles W. of Carlscrona.

CARLSRUHE, a town in the northern part of the territory of the grand duke of Baden, and recently adopted as the seat of government. It was first founded in 1715, but has not been of much importance until subsequent to the peace of 1814; it was taken possession of by the French in 1796; the streets are laid out in regular order; the ducal palace is in the centre of the town, and has a lofty spire, and being, as well as several other public buildings, and the houses generally, built of stone, the whole presents rather an imposing appearance. The population is 18,000. It is about 14 miles N. by E. of Strasburg, and about the same distance W. by N. of Stuttgard.

CARLSTADT, the capital of Croatia, with a fortress; seated on the Kulpa, a branch of the Save, at the influx of the Corona; 180 miles S. by W. of Vienna, and 45 E. N. E. of Fiume.

CARLSTADT, a town of Sweden, capital of Wermeland, and a bishop's see. It stands on the N. side of the lake Wenner, and on the island of Tingwalla, which is formed by two branches of the Clara. The houses are built of wood, and painted; the episcopal palace is also of wood, and has an extensive front. The inhabitants carry on a trade in copper, iron, and wood, across the lake. It is 55 miles W. of Stockholm. Pop. 2200.

CARLSTADT, a town of Franconia, in the principality of Wurtzburg, seated on the Maine; 13 miles N. by W. of Wurtzburg. It is now included in the Bavarian circle of the Lower Maine. Pop. about 2200.

CARMAGNOLA, a fortified town of Piedmont, with a citadel; seated on a small river, which runs into the Po; 14 miles S. of Turin. Pop. about 12,000.

CARMEL, a mountain of Syria, in Palestine, about 2000 feet above the level of the sea, on the N. side of the Bay of Acre; noted for having been the retreat of the prophet Elias, and for a monastery of Carmelites. It is 50 miles N. of Jerusalem. Lat. 32. 51. N. long. 34. 59. E.

CARMEL, a town of Putnam county, state of New York, on the E. bank of the Hudson river; 40 miles N. of the city of New York, and 108 S. of Albany. Pop. 2247.

CARMI. *See* WHITE.

CARMONA, a town of Italy, in Austrian Friuli, on a mountain near the river Indri; 7 miles N. W. of Goritz.

CARMONA, a town of Spain, in Andalusia, with many remains of ancient walls, inscriptions, &c. The gate toward Seville is one of the most extraordinary pieces of antiquity in all Spain; and its castle, now in ruins, was formerly of immense extent. It is seated on a high hill; 24 miles E. N. E. of Seville.

CARNATIC, a territory of Hindostan, extending along the E. coast from Cape Comorin, the southern extremity of Asia, in the lat. of 8. 4. N. to near the mouth of the Kistna, in the lat. of 16. N., varying in breadth from 50 to 100 miles; bounded on the W. by the Mysore, and on the E., for about two degrees of lat., by the Gulf of Manara and Palks Strait, which divides it from the N. end of the island of Ceylon, the remainder of its eastern boundary being better known by the name of the coast of Coromandel. The principal towns on the coast, beginning from the S., are Negapatam, Pondicherry, Madras, Pullicat, and Gangapatam, and those in the interior, beginning also from the S., are Tinevelly, Madura, Tritchinopoly, Tanjore, Arcot, Nellore, and Ongole.

Numerous streams and rivers from the westward intersect this territory, the principal of of which are the Cauvery, Cuddalore, Paliare, and Pennar. The soil is various in quality, being in some places exceedingly fertile, and in others sandy and barren, and the inhabitants occasionally exposed to great privation for want of water. Since 1801, it has been uninterruptedly possessed by the British, and included in the presidency of MADRAS, which see.

CARNAWL, a town of Hindostan, in the province of Delhi. Here, in 1739, Kouli Khan gained a victory over the army of the Great Mogul; and in 1761, the Seiks, under Abdalla, defeated the Mahrattas. It is seated at the junction of the Hissar canal with the Jumna. It is 80 miles N. W. of Delhi.

CARNESVILLE. *See* FRANKFORT.

CAR NICOBAR, an island in the Bay of Bengal; it is the most northern of the Nicobar Islands; about 40 miles in circumference, and covered with timber. The climate is very insalubrious. Lat. 9. 10. N. long. 93. 0. E.

CARNIOLA, DUCHY of, a territory of the Austrian empire, lying between the lat. of 45. 30. and 46. 30. N. and 13. 25. and 15. 40. of E. long., comprising an area of about 4600 square miles, and containing about 400,000 inhabitants. It is bounded on the N. by Lower Carinthia, the S. W. point jutting upon the Gulf of Trieste. It is intersected from the N. W. to the S. E. by the Save river, which receives several tributary streams, both from the N. and S. In feature, character, and productions, it is very similar to CARINTHIA (which see), somewhat more diversified and fertile, and, having the advantage of a nearer proximity to the sea, the inhabitants are somewhat more active and enterprising. It is divided into four parts, viz. Upper, N.; Inner, S. W.; Middle and Lower, S. E. Laybach, in the middle district, is the chief town. For commercial purposes it has the advantage of the port of Fiume, as well as Trieste.

CAROLATH, a town of Silesia, capital of a principality of the same name, seated on the Oder; 14 miles N. W. of Glogau.

CAROLINA, a town of Spain, in Andalusia, the chief of a new colony of the same name, in the Sierra Morena. It stands on a hill, towering above the whole settlement; 20 miles N. E. of Anduxar.

CAROLINA, NORTH, one of the United States of North America, lying between the lat. of 33. 53. and 36. 33. N. It is bounded on the E. by the Atlantic Ocean, and on the W. by a chain of the Allegany Mountains running in a N. E. direction: a conventional line of 36. 30. of N. lat. from the 76th to the 82nd of W. long. divides it from Virginia, and another conventional line, in a N. W. direction, from the long. of 78. 40. to 79. 50. and from thence due W., under the line of 35. of N. lat. to the long. of 84. W. divides it from South Carolina; its area, according to American computation, comprises 43,800 square miles. Although it has upwards of 200 miles of sea coast, besides being indented by several very large inlets, it does not afford one good harbour; indeed, a ledge of sand-banks flanks the coast its whole extent, rendering the navigation very dangerous in stormy weather, and almost inaccessible at all times; it consequently partakes more of the character of an interior than a maritime state. Some little external intercourse, however, is maintained through Wilmington, situate on Cape Fear river, which intersects the centre of the state from N. to S., falling into the sea in the lat. of 34. N.; and the productions of the western part of the state are facilitated in their conveyance to market, by the Yadkin and Catawba rivers, which intersect that part between the long. of 80. and 82. W., running S. into South Carolina. The Neuse, Tar, Roanoke, and Chowan, are other rivers which intersect the N. E. part of the state, falling into the great inlets of Pamtico and Albemarle Sounds, which it is proposed to connect with Chesapeake Bay by means of a canal through the Dismal Swamp. The coast for about 70 miles from the shore is level and swampy, but westward the ground gradually rises into a mountainous country, being in parts beautifully diversified. The gold-mines of this state, which have excited much interest, are on the Yadkin river, and the gold is found in the usual manner, by washing. The first mine was found in 1814, and produces annually between 200,000 and 250,000 dollars. The swamps are favourable to the growth of rice, and the pitch-pine flourishes in them in the utmost luxuriance, yielding an unbounded supply of timber, tar, and turpentine, whilst the upper country is favourable to the growth of every kind of grain, as well as to cotton and tobacco, and yields a variety of vegetables and plants, some of them of a medicinal nature, peculiar to itself; and as population increases, North Carolina will doubtless prove a country of great capability and resources. In 1820 it was divided into 62 counties, and the population, which in 1790 was only 393,751, is now 753,419, of whom 245,817 are slaves. Raleigh, nearly in the centre of the state, is the seat of the legislative assembly. Wilmington, Fayetteville, and Newburn, are the other principal towns.

CAROLINA, SOUTH, another of the United States of North America, being divided from North Carolina by a conventional line, as already described, extending S. S. W. along the Atlantic coast from the lat. of 33. 50. to the Savannah river, in the lat. of 32. 2. N. The Savannah river, in a N. N. W. direction, until it cuts the S. W. point of North Carolina, separates it from the state of Georgia, its area being 30,800 square miles. The general features, character of the soil, and productions of this state, are very similar to North Carolina; but having the advantage of several fine navigable rivers, and some tolerably good harbours, to facilitate an external commerce, whilst North Carolina ranks among the least, South Carolina ranks among the most important states of the union. The Yadkin river rising in North Carolina, which when it enters this state is called the Great Pedee, and after being joined by several tributary streams, falls into Georgetown Bay; and the Cahawba, which also rises in North Carolina, and in this state is first called the Wateree, and afterwards the Santee, is united by a canal to Cooper River, which falls into Charleston harbour. Numerous streams, intersecting all the N. W. part, unite with the Santee about the centre of the state, and between the Santee and the Savannah are the Edisto, Bigslake, and Coosahatchie Rivers; so that there is hardly five miles in the state without the advantage of water communication. Between the mouths of the Santee and Savannah Rivers the coast is flanked by a chain of islands, on which is produced the valuable cotton called Sea Island. The swamps produce vast quantities of the finest rice, the seed of which was first introduced from Madagascar at the close of the seventeenth century; and, previous to 1790, indigo was cultivated to a great extent, and with proportionate advantage; but since that period, the culture of the cotton plant in the upland country has superseded every other pursuit, and has been carried to an extent without any precedent. South Carolina is divided into thirty-six districts, and the population, which in 1790 was 240,073, is now 594,398, including 327,038 slaves. Gold is found in considerable quantities in this state. Columbia, nearly in the centre of the state, 507 miles S. W. by S. of Washington, is the seat of its legislative assembly. Charleston is, however, the chief and most important town of the state; the other principal towns are Beaufort and Georgetown.

Caroline, a county of the state of Maryland, bounded on the E. by Kent county, state of Delaware, and on the W. by the Tuckapo and Choptank rivers, which fall into Chesapeake Bay. Pop. 7806, of whom 752 are slaves. Denton, the chief town, is 65 miles E. by S. of Annapolis.

Caroline, an interior county in the E. part of Virginia, bounded on the N. E. by the Rappahannock river, and S. W. by the North Anna river. Its area is about 20 miles each way, or 400 square miles, and is tolerably fertile. Pop. 17,813, of whom 9314 are slaves. Bowling Green, 44 miles N. N. E. of Richmond, is the chief town.

Caroline is also the name of a town in Tioga county, state of New York, near the S. end of Cayuga Lake; 176 miles W. of Albany. Pop. in 1820, 1608.

Caroline Islands, a range of islands on the North Pacific Ocean, discovered in 1686 by the Spaniards, in the reign of Charles II. They lie to the E. of the Philippines, between 138. and 135. E. long. and 8. and 11. N. lat. They are about 30 in number, and populous; the natives resembling those of the Philippines. The most considerable island is Hogoleu, about 90 miles long, and 40 broad: the next is Yap, at the W. extremity of this chain, but not above a third part of that size. They have been little visited by recent navigators.

Caroon. *See* Cairoon.

Caroon Beled, extensive ruins in central Egypt—perhaps of the famous labyrinth of Egypt. The ruins of Kasr Caroon, near the lake of Caroon, about 2 distant, are very interesting.

Caroony, a river in South America, a tributary of the Oroonoco. It has a very rapid current, which renders it quite unnavigable.

Caroor. *See* Carura.

Carora, a city of Colombia, in the province of Venezuela; situate about 45 miles from the strait that separates the gulf from the lake of Maracaibo, and 150 miles W. of Valencia. It is intersected by a stream called the Morera, that runs E. into the Caribbean Sea. The inhabitants, about 6000 in number, subsist principally by means of cattle and mules, which they drive to the coast for transhipment to the West India islands. The surrounding country produces a variety of odoriferous balsams and aromatics, which, under social arrangements, may be made to constitute an extensive and reciprocal external commerce.

Carpathian Mountains, a grand chain which divides Hungary and Transylvania from Poland on the N. and N. E., and from Moravia on the N. W., extending about 500 miles.

Carpendolo, a town of the Bresciano, on the Chiese; 15 miles S. S. E. of Brescia. Pop. about 4000.

Carpentaria, a large bay on the N. coast of New Holland, discovered in 1618 by a Dutch captain, named Carpenter. That part of the country which borders on the E. side of the bay is also called Carpentaria. It has about 1200 miles of coast, which is but little known. It is frequented by Chinese junks, to fish for the biche-de-la-mar, or sea-slug, which superabound at the entrance of this bay.

Carpentras, a town of France, in the department of Vaucluse. It was formerly the capital of Venaissin, and a bishop's see. It is seated on the Auson, at the foot of a mountain; 14 miles N. E. of Avignon. Pop. 9000.

Carpi, a town of Italy, in the Modenese, with a fortified castle, and a good trade. It stands on a canal to the Secchia, 8 miles N. of Modena.

Carpi, a town of Italy, in the Veronese, where a victory was gained by the Austrians over the French in 1701. It is seated on the Adige; 24 miles S. E. of Verona.

Carrara. *See* Carara.

Carrick on Shannon, a town of Ireland, capital of the county of Leitrim. It is a small place, seated on the Shannon; 78 miles W. N. W. of Dublin.

Carrick on Suir, a town of Ireland, in Tipperary, famous for its woollen cloth, called ratteen. It is seated on the Suir; 22 miles S. E. of Cashel, and 10 W. N. W. of Waterford.

Carrickfergus, a borough and seaport of Ireland, chief town of the county of Antrim, with a castle. It is seated on a bay of its name, in the Irish channel; 88 miles N. by E. of Dublin, and 8 from Belfast.

Carrickmacross, a town of Ireland, in the county of M naghan; 19 miles E. S. E. of Monaghan, and 44 N. by W. of Dublin.

Carrion di los Gondes, a town of Spain, in Leon, on the frontiers of Old Castile. It has ten parish churches, ten convents, and two hospitals; and is seated on the river Carrion; 18 miles N. of Placentia, and 40 W. of Burgos.

Carrol, a newly formed county, at the western extremity of Tennessee, bordering on Wood Lake, contiguous to the Mississippi river.

Carron, a river of Scotland, in Stirlingshire, which rises on the S. side of the Campsey hills, and flows into the Frith of Forth, below Falkirk. Two miles from its source it forms a fine cascade, called the Fall of Auchinlilly; and near its mouth commences the Great Canal from the Forth to the Clyde.

Carron, a village of Scotland, in Stirlingshire, on the river Carron; 2 miles from Falkirk; celebrated for the greatest iron-works in Europe. These works employ about 3000 men; and, on an average, use weekly 800 tons of coal, 400 tons of ironstone, and 100 tons of limestone. All sorts of iron goods are made here, from the most trifling article to the largest cannon; and the short piece of ordinance called a carronade hence received its name. The trade in coke and lime is also considerable. These works were erected in 1761, and are carried on by a chartered company.

Carrouge, a newly erected town, duchy of Savoy; 2 miles S.E. from Geneva; manufactures watches, clocks, &c.

Carru, a town of Piedmont, in the province of Mondoni; 8 miles S. S. W. of Bene. Pop. about 4000.

Cart, two rivers in Scotland, in Renfrewshire, distinguished by the appellation of Black and White. The Black Cart issues from the lake Lochwinnoch ; the White Cart descends from the N. E. angle of the county; and they both flow into the Gryfe, a few miles before its confluence with the Clyde.

Cartago, a city and capital of Costa Rica in Guatimala, and a bishop's see. It stands on a river of the same name, 50 miles from its mouth, in the Pacific Ocean, and about the same from Lake Nicaragua. Long. 84. 10. W. lat. 10. 15. N.

Cartago is also the name of a town in Colombia, in the valley of Popayan; about 100 miles W. of St. Fe de Bogota. Pop. about 5000.

Cartama, a town of Spain, in Granada, at the foot of a mountain, near the river Guadala Medina; 8 miles N. W. of Malaga.

Carter, a frontier county at the N. E. extremity of Tennessee, bounded on the E. by the iron, yellow, and stone mountains, which divide it from North Carolina. It is intersected by the Watonga, a branch of the Tennessee river. It contains about 170 square miles, and a pop. of 5372. Elizabeth Town, on the W. side of the county, 284 miles E. by N. of Murfriesborough, is the chief town.

Carteret, a county of North Carolina, bordering on the Atlantic Ocean, S. of Pamtico Sound. It is a swampy and dreary district. Pop. 6591, of whom 1860 were slaves. Beaufort, 164 miles S. E. by E. of Raleigh, is the chief town.

Carteret Island, an island in the Pacific Ocean, seen by Captain Carteret in 1767. It is six leagues long, from E. to W. Long. 159. 14. E. lat. 8. 26. S.

Cartersville, a town of Virginia, in Powhatan county, seated on James River; 40 miles W. N. W. of Richmond.

Carthage, Cape, a promontory on the E. coast of the kingdom of Tunis, near which stood the famous city of Carthage, razed by the Romans; and some of the ruins are to be seen on the coast. It is 10 miles N. E. of Tunis. Long. 10. 20. E. lat. 36. 50. N.

Carthagena, a seaport of Spain, in Murcia, built by Asdrubal, a Carthaginian general, and named after the city of Carthage. It is the see of a bishop, and a great mart for merchandize. It has the best harbour in Spain; also the most considerable docks and magazines. The principal crops of barilla are produced in its vicinity; and a fine red earth, called almagra, used in polishing mirrors, and preparing tobacco for snuff. Carthagena was taken by Sir John Leake in 1706, but the Duke of Brunswick retook it. It is seated on a gulf of the same name; 27 miles S. of Murcia. Long. 1. 0. W. lat. 37. 35. N. and 240. S. S. E. of Madrid. Pop. 25,000.

Carthagena, a city of South America, in the New Colombian province of Magdalena, of which it is the capital. It is situate on an island off the shore of the Caribbean Sea, in the lat. of 10.25. N. and 75.27. of W. long.; about 70 miles S. S. W. of the mouth of the Magdalena, and 180 N. N. E. of the Gulf of Darien. It has a commodious and safe harbour, and for nearly three centuries has ranked among the most considerable cities of America. It was the port first resorted to by galleons from Spain, during the monopoly of the commerce of America with that country. It has experienced various alternations of fortune, having been several times captured, and was an object of severe contention between the royalist and republican forces, from 1815 down to the period of the final extinction of Spanish domination in America in 1823. The island is united to the main land by two wooden bridges. The houses are chiefly built of stone, and it has several churches and convents, some of which are elegant edifices. Its harbour will doubtless contribute towards its retaining its high rank among the cities and seaports of the new republic. Pop. about 24,000.

Cartmel, a town of Lancashire, with a market on Monday. It has a spacious old church, with a curious tower, being a square within a square, the upper part set diagonally within the lower. It is seated among the hills called Cartmel Fells, not for from the sea; 14 miles N. by W. of Lancaster, and 254 N. N. W. of London.

Carura, or **Caroor**, a town of Hindostan, in the province of Coimbetore, with a neat fort, in which is a large temple. Much sugar-cane is raised in the vicinity. It is seated on the Amarawati; 8 miles above its confluence with the Cavery, and 37 N. E. of Daraporam.

Carwar, a town of Hindostan, in the province of Canara, and a British settlement. It is seated near the mouth of the Aliga; 50 miles S. S. E. of Goa. Long. 74. 14. E. lat. 14. 52. N.

Carysfort, a town of Ireland, county of Wicklow: there is a free-school.

Casac, or Cazac, a country in the dominions of Persia, on the frontiers of Armenia, governed by princes of its own, nominally subject to Persia. The inhabitants are descended from the Cossacs, and represented as a rude and barbarous people. Casac, or Cazac Lora, is the name of the capital.

Casagrande, a town of New Mexico, in the N. part of New Navarre. Here is an immense edifice, supposed to have been built by the ancient Mexicans for a fortress: it consists of three floors, with a terrace above them; and the entrance is at the second floor; so that a scaling-ladder was necessary. Long. 113. 23. W. lat. 33. 40. N.

Casale, a town of Piedmont, lately the capital of Lower Montferrat, and a bishop's see. Its castle, citadel, and all its fortifications, have been demolished. It is seated on the river Po; 37 miles N. E. of Turin. Pop. about 15,000.

Casale Maggiore, a town of Italy, in the duchy of Milan, on the river Po; 20 miles E. S. E. of Cremona. Pop. about 4900.

Casale Nuova, a town of Naples, in Calabria Ulteriore. An earthquake happened here in 1783, by which upwards of 4000 inhabitants lost their lives. It stands near the sea; 11 miles N. by W. of Oppido.

Casandrino, a city of Naples; 4 miles from Naples. Pop. 3000.

Casbin, or Caswin, a town of Persia, in Irac Ajemi, where several of the kings of Persia have resided. Nadir Shah built a palace here, enclosed by a wall a mile and a half in circumference; and the town is surrounded by another, 4 miles in circuit. It carries on a great trade, and is seated near the S. shore of the Caspian Sea, in a sandy plain; 280 miles N. W. of Ispahan. Long. 50. 10. E. lat. 36. 8. N. Pop. estimated at 40,000.

Cascais, a town of Portugal, in Estremadura, at the mouth of the Tajo, on the N. bank, near the rock; 17 miles W. of Lisbon. Pop. 2500.

Caschau. *See* Cassovia.

Casco Bay, a bay of the state of Maine, between Cape Elizabeth and Cape Small Point, leading into the harbour of Portland. It is 25 miles wide, and interspersed with small islands. Long. 69. 30. W. lat. 43. 40. N.

Caserta, a town of Naples, in Terra di Lavoro. Here is a magnificent unfinished royal palace, and a grand modern aqueduct, which furnishes a great part of the city of Naples with water. Most of the buildings were greatly damaged by an earthquake in 1803. It is 15 miles N. of Naples. Pop. about 16,000.

Casey, an interior county of the state of Kentucky. Pop. 4939. Liberty, the chief town, is 68 miles S. of Frankfort.

Cashan. *See* Kasan.

Cashel, a borough of Ireland, capital of the county of Tipperary, and an archbishop's see. It had formerly a wall; and part of two gates are still remaining. The old cathedral is supposed to have been the first stone edifice in Ireland. A synod was held here by Henry I. in 1158, by which the kingdom of Ireland was confirmed to him. The new cathedral is an elegant edifice; it has several other public buildings, and barracks for infantry. It sends one member to parliament; and is seated on the east bank of the Suir; 43 miles N. N. E. of Cork, and 77 S. S. W. of Dublin.

Cashgur, or Little Bokharia, a country of Usbec Tartary, which commences on the north and north-east of Cashmere, in Hindostan (from which it is separated by the Himmaleh mountains), and extends to 41. N. lat. Great part of it is a sandy desert; the other parts are populous and fertile. Here are mines of gold and silver, which the natives do not work, because they are employed wholly in feeding cattle. The musk animals are found in this country. It likewise produces diamonds, and several other precious stones. Ireken is the capital.

Cashgur, a city of Usbec Tartary, formerly the capital of the country of the same name. It has a good trade with the neighbouring countries, and stands at the foot of the Himmaleh Mountains; 11 miles S. of Ireken. Long. 73. 25. E. lat. 41. 30. N.

Cashmere, a province of Hindostan, subject to the king of Candahar, or sultan of the Afghans; bounded on the W. by the Indus, N. by Mount Himmaleh, and E. and S. by Lahore. It is an elevated valley, 90 miles long and 50 broad, lying between the 34th and 35th degree of N. lat. and 73. to 76. of E. long., surrounded by steep mountains, which tower above the regions of snow. The periodical rains, which almost deluge the rest of India, are shut out of Cashmere by the height of the mountains, so that only light showers fall here; but these are sufficiently abundant to feed some hundreds of cascades, which are precipitated into the valley. The soil is the richest that can be conceived, and its productions those of the temporate zone. Numerous streams, from all quarters of the valley, bring their tribute to the Chelum, a large navigable river, running from east to west, falling into the Indus. It contains several small lakes, in some of which are floating islands. But the country is subject to earthquakes; and, to guard against their most terrible effects, all the houses are built of wood. Among other curious manufactures of Cashmere is that of shawls, 80,000 of which are annually produced; and the delicate wool of which the finest are made is the produce of a species of goat of this country, or of the adjoining Tibet. Here are bred a species of sheep called Hundoo, which are employed in carrying burdens. The Cashmerians are stout and well made, but their features are often coarse and broad: even the women are of a deep brown complexion; but they are gay and lively, and fond of parties of pleasure on their beautiful lakes. They have a language of their own, said to be anterior to that of the Sanscrit; and a religion too, it is thought, different from that of the Hindoos. The superstition of the inhabitants has multiplied the places of worship of Mahadeo, Beschan, and Brama. All Cashmere is holy land, and miraculous fountains abound. In addition to their shawls, in the manufacture of which about 16,000 looms are supposed to be employed, saffron, otto of roses, and some drugs, form the chief articles of commerce.

CASHMERE, or SERINAGHUR, a city of Hindostan, capital of the province or valley of Cashmere. Here are many fountains, reservoirs, and temples. The streets are narrow and dirty. The houses, many of them two and three stories high, are slightly built of brick and mortar, with a large intermixture of timber; and on the roof is laid a covering of fine earth, which is planted with a variety of flowers. This city is without walls, and seated on both sides of the Chelum; 285 miles E. by S. of Cabul. Long. 73. 11. E. lat. 33. 49. N.

CASPE, a town of Spain, in Arragon, where Ferdinand IV. was elected king of Arragon. It stands at the confluence of the Guadaloupe and Ebro; 35 miles S. of Balbastro, and 44. S. E. of Saragossa.

CASPIAN SEA, a large inland sea of Western Asia; bounded on the S. by the Persian province of Mazanderan, in the lat. of 36. 40., and N. by the Russian government of Astracan, in the lat. of 46. 50., thus being about 700 miles in length from S. to N.; its eastern and western boundaries are very irregular, extending from the long. of 46. 30. to 57., whilst the mean breadth does not extend 260 miles. The eastern coast is indented by several bays, the more prominent of which are Calkan, in the lat. of 39., Alexander, in 43., and Mertvoi, or Koultjouk, in 45. N. The Persian province of Korasan extends along the E. coast to the Bay of Balkan, and further N. the E. coast is occupied by the Turcomans, Kirgees, and other Tartar tribes; and the W. coast by the governments of Gilhan, Baku, Derbent, and the Caucasus. Numerous rivers flow into this sea from all points; the most important of which are the Oural and the Volga, the former at its N. extremity, and the latter at the N. W. It contains several islands near both the eastern and western coasts; and the depth is very irregular, being in some places unfathomable with a line of 450 fathoms, whilst in other places the navigation is difficult with vessels drawing only 10 feet of water; the water is as salt as that of the ocean, with a bitter taste, which taste is ascribed to the prevalence of the naphtha on the western coast. (*See* BAKU.) It is 25 feet below the level of the Black Sea. Its waters have no visible outlet; their equilibrium must therefore be maintained either by subterraneous channels, or by evaporation. Salmon, sturgeon, and other fish, abound in all parts of this sea, and seals are extremely numerous. Of birds properly aquatic, it contains the grebe, the crested diver, the pelican, the cormorant, and several species of gull; while geese, ducks, storks, herons, crows, &c., frequent the shores. The Russians are the only people who derive much benefit from this great natural basin, although so well calculated to facilitate an extensive and reciprocal intercourse between all its surrounding nations; and, were a communication to be effected with the Black Sea, by means of canals, Europe at large might participate in the advantages of an extended intercourse.

CASSANDRA, a town of Turkey in Europe, in the province of Macedonia, on a peninsula; 50 miles S. E. from Salonica.

CASSANDRIA, a town of Holland, on the S. W. side of the island of Cadsand, at the mouth of the Zwin; 3 miles N. of Sluys.

CASSANO, a town of Italy, in the Milanese, with a castle. Here Prince Eugene, in 1705, was checked in attempting to force the passage of the Adda; and in 1799 the French were defeated by the Austrians. It is seated on the Adda; 15 miles N. E. of Milan.

CASSANO, a town of Naples, in Calabria Citeriore; 24 miles N. W. of Rossano, and 50 E. S. E. of Policastro.

CASSAY, or MECKLEY, a country of Asia; bounded on the W. by Bengal, N. by Assam, E. and S. E. by Birmah, and S. W. by Aracan. The inhabitants are called Mugguloos, a tribe of rude mountaineers little known It is now subject to the Birmans. Munnypour is the capital.

CASSEL, a city of Germany, capital of Lower Hesse, and seat of the court and government of the electorate of Hesse. It is divided into the Old Town, Lower New Town, and Upper New Town; the former towns are chiefly built in the ancient style, but the last is very regular and handsome. The inhabitants are estimated at 25,000; and they have manufactures of linen cloth, hats, procelain, &c. Here is a college, founded by the landgrave in 1709. The castle or palace, the gardens, the arsenal, the foundery, and the cabinet of curiosities, deserve the attention of travellers. It was taken by the French in 1760, and restored at the peace, in 1763. It is seated on the Fulda; 40 miles S. E. of Paderborn. Long. 9. 25. E. lat. 51. 19. N.

CASSEL, a strong town in Germany, situate on the Rhine, opposite Mentz, with which it has a communication by a bridge of boats. It was taken by the French in 1792, and retaken by the Prussians, in 1793.

CASSEL, a town of France, in the department of Nord, with a fortified castle. It stands on a mountain, rising like a sugar-loaf from the centre of a vast plain, whence may be seen thirty-two towns, and the German Ocean, though 50 miles distant. It is 10 miles N. E. of St. Omer, on the road from Lisle to Dunkirk. Pop. about 3000.

CASSELLE, a populous town of Piedmont, about 6 miles N. of Turin, having a variety of manufactures; number of inhabitants about 9000.

CASSINA, or KASHNA, an extensive empire, in the interior of North Africa, to the W. o Bornou. It resembles Bornou in climate, soil, and natural productions, and in the colour, genius, religion, and government of the people. It is bounded on the S. by a large river, flowing to the eastward—the Yeu or Tchadda.

CASSINA, or KASHNA, the capital of the empire of the same name. The chief trade is in senna, gold dust, slaves, cotton cloths, goat skins, ox and buffalo hides, and civet. It is 750 miles W. S. W. of Bornou, and about the same distance E. of Tombuctoo, and N. by E. of Old Calabar, on the coast of Guinea. Long. 11. 35. E. lat. 15. 40. N.

CASSIQUIARE, a river of South America, in the Republic of Colombia, forming a communication between the Amazons and Oroonoco. It is a principal branch of the Rio Negro.

CASSIS, a town of France, in the department of Mouths of the Rhone, with a small port on the Mediterranean; 9 miles S. S. E. of Marseilles. Pop. 2300.

CASSOVIA, or KASCHAU, a strong town of Upper Hungary, with a fine arsenal, seated near the river Herat; 85 miles E. by N. of Schemnitz. Long. 20. 55. E. lat. 48. 40. N. Pop. about 8000.

CASTAGNOLA, a town of Piedmont, on the river Po, 8 miles S. of Turin.

CASTAMENA, or KASTAMONI, a town of Asiatic Turkey, in Natolia, formerly a large city, but now much reduced in size and magnificence. It is 240 miles E. of Constantinople. Long. 34. 22. E. lat. 41. 32. N.

CASTANOWITZ. *See* COSTAINITZO.

CASTEL A MARE, a town of Naples, in Principato Citeriore, where the ships of the royal navy are built. It stands on the site of the ancient Stabia, at the foot of a woody mountain, on the bay of Naples; 15 miles S. E. of Naples.

CASTEL A MARE, a town of Sicily, in Val di Mazara, on a bay on the N. coast; 30 miles W. by S. of Palermo.

CASTEL ARRAGONESE, or CASTEL SARDO, a fortified seaport of Sardinia, and a bishop's see. It was the first place taken in this island, at the end of the 13th century, by the Arragonese, whence its name; but in 1767 the king ordered it to be called Castel Sardo. It stands on the N. coast; 20 miles N. E. of Sassari. Long. 9. 1. E. lat. 40. 56. N.

CASTEL BALDO, a town of Italy, in the Paduan, on the river Adige; 30 miles S. W. of Padua.

CASTEL BRANCO, a strong town of Portugal, in the S. E. part of Beira, with a castle and two churches. In 1762 it was taken by the Spaniards. It is situated between the rivers Vereza and Poncal, about 15 miles above their entrance into the Tagus; 62 miles S. E. of Coimbra. Long. 7. 22. W. lat. 39. 52. N.

CASTEL DE VIDE, a town of Portugal, in Alentejo; 8 miles N. E. of Portalegre. Pop. about 6000.

CASTEL FOLIT, a town of Spain, in Catalonia, on an eminence near the river Fulvia; 15 miles W. of Gerona.

CASTEL FRANCO, a town of Italy, in Trevisano; 12 miles W. of Treviso.

CASTEL GONDOLFO, a town of Italy, in Campagna di Roma, near the lake Albano. Near this place is the villa Barberina, where are the ruins of an immense palace, built by the emperor Domitian. It is 10 miles S. by E. of Rome.

CASTEL JALOUX, a town of France, in the department of Lot and Garonne, with a considerable trade in wine, honey, and cattle; seated on the Avance; 20 miles E. by S. of Bazas, and 32 W. by N. of Agen.

CASTEL LEONE, a town of Italy, in the Cremonese; 18 miles N. of Placenza. Pop. about 8000.

CASTEL NUOVO, a town of Dalmatia, on the Gulf of Cattara; 12 miles N. by W. of Cattaro. Pop. about 2000.

CASTEL, or CASTRO NUOVA, a town of Sicily, in Val di Mazara, seated on a hill; 18 miles S. S. W. of Termini.

CASTEL NUOVO DI CARFAGNANA, a town of Italy, in the Modenese, with a strong fort; seated on the valley of Carfagnana, on the river Serchio; 18 miles N. of Lucca, and 37 S. S. W. of Modena.

CASTEL RODRIGO, a town of Portugal, in Beira; 11 miles N. of Pinhel.

CASTEL ROSSO, or KASTELORIZO, an island in the Mediterranean, near the coast of Karamania; 90 miles E. of Rhodes. It is 2 miles long, and has a secure road and harbour. Long. 29. 21. E. lat. 36. 7. N.

CASTEL SARASIN, a town of France, in the department of Upper Garonne; 30 miles W.N.W. of Toulouse. Pop. about 5000.

CASTEL VETERE, a town of Naples, in Calabria Ulteriore; 33 miles S. of Squillace.

CASTEL VETRANO, a town of Sicily, in Val di Mazara. Here is a palace, in which is a considerable collection of old armour. It is 8 miles E. by N. of Mazara.

Castel is prefixed to the names of many other towns in the several Italian states.

CASTELANE, a town of France, in the department of Lower Alps. Near it is a salt spring, from which the water issues in such abundance as to turn a mill at the very source. It is seated on the Verdon, in a hilly country; 20 miles S.E. of Digne. Pop. about 2000.

CASTELAUN, a town of Germany, in the county of Sponheim; 23 miles S. S. W. of Coblentz.

CASTELLANETTA, a town of Naples, in Terra d'Otranto; 19 miles W. N.W. of Taranto.

CASTELLARA, a town of Italy, in the Mantuan; 6 miles N. E. of Mantua.

CASTELLAZO, a town of Piedmont; 7 miles S. of Alessandria. Pop. about 4700.

CASTELLON DE AMPURIAS, a town of Spain, in Catalonia, at the mouth of a river, in the Gulf of Rosas; 8 miles W. by S. of Rosas.

CASTELLON DE LA PLANA, a town of Spain, in Valencia; 28 miles S. S. W. of the city of Valencia. It contains many vestiges of ancient grandeur, and is still populous, having upwards of 10,000 inhabitants.

CASTELNAUDARY, a town of France, in the department of Aude, on an eminence, at the foot of which is the grand basin of the Canal Royal. It is 15 miles W. of Carcassone. Pop. about 8000.

CASTER, a town of Germany, in the duchy of Juliers, seated on the river Erst; 9 miles E. of Juliers.

CASTIGLENO, a town of Tuscany, in the Siennese, on a lake of the same name, which communicates with the sea, and produces much salt. It is 12 miles S. by E. of Massa.

CASTIGLIONE, a fortified town of Italy, in the Mantuan, with a castle. It was taken by the Austrians, in 1701; and the French defeated them near it, in 1706, and again in 1796. It is 20 miles N. W. of Mantua. Pop. about 4000.

CASTILE, the principal and most opulent of the kingdoms into which Spain was formerly divided. It now forms the two provinces of Old and New Castile; the former having been recovered from the Moors some time before the latter.

CASTILE, OLD, a province of Spain, bounded on the N. by Asturias and Biscay, E. by Navarre and Arragon, S. by New Castile, and W. by Leon, being in extreme length from N. to S. about 240 miles, and 100 in mean breadth. It is subdivided into four inferior provinces, after the name of the four chief towns. The superficies and population of each province is as follows: viz.—

		Sq. Miles.	Inhab.
Burgos . .	N.	7,752	470,588
Soria . . .	E.	4,118	198,107
Segovia . .	S.	3,502	164,007
Avila .	S.W.	2,600	118,061
Old Castile . .		17,972	950,763

The Ebro rises on the N. part of Burgos, and forms the boundary of Old Castile, on the side of Biscay and Navarre. Several streams fall into the Ebro, but the waters of Old Castile run chiefly to the westward, into the Douro. The chief production of this part of Spain is wool, of which commodity about 6,000,000 lbs. are annually exported to England. The government, however, is a bar to all social exertion, in this as well as every other part of Spain.

CASTILE, NEW, lies to the S. of the preceding province, and is divided into five inferior provinces, as follows: viz:—

		Sq. Miles.	Inhab.
Guadalaxara	N.	1,970	121,115
Madrid .	N.W.	1,330	228,520
Cuenca . .	E.	11,410	294,290
Toledo .	S.W.	8,863	370,641
La Mancha	S.	7,620	205,548
New Castile .		31,193	1,220,114

The Tagus, Guadiana, and Lucar, all afford to New Castile the advantage of a facility of intercourse; but the chief riches of this province are its flocks of sheep, which, under the regulation of the "Mesta," preclude all agricultural improvements. *See each of the inferior provinces.*

CASTILLON, a town of France, in the department of Gironde; seated on the Dordogne; 25 miles E. of Bordeaux. Pop. 2600.

CASTINE, a seaport of the state of Maine, chief town of Hancock county, situate on Penobscot Bay; 65 miles W. S. W. of Machias. It was taken by the British in 1814, but restored at the peace in 1815. Long. 69. 0. W. lat. 44. 26. N.

CASTLE CARY, a town in Somersetshire, with a market on Tuesday; 12 miles S. E. of Wells, and 113 W. by S. of London.

CASTLE RISING, a town in Norfolk. The market is now disused. It is 5 miles N. E. of Lynn, and 103 N. N. E. of London.

CASTLE BLAYNEY, a town in Ireland, county of Monaghan; 68 miles from Dublin. Here is the magnificent seat of Lord Blayney.

CASTLE COMER, a town in Ireland, county of Kilkenny; 70 miles from Dublin. Near the town are some extensive collieries. It is a regularly built town, with a large church, town-hall, &c.

CASTLE CONNEL, a town in Ireland, county of Limerick, near the Shannon; 114 miles from Dublin.

CASTLE DERMOT, a town in Ireland, county of Kildare, on the river Lane; 43 miles from Dublin. In the vicinity are many ecclesiastical ruins.

CASTLE ISLAND, a town in Ireland, county of Kerry; 197 miles from Dublin. Here is an ancient castle.

CASTLE REAGH, a town in Ireland, county of Roscommon; 112 miles from Dublin.

CASTLEBAR, a parish and town in the county of Mayo, Ireland. A considerable portion of the inhabitants are employed in the linen manufacture. The town is also the seat of assize, and a chief place in the county, having a spacious church, a handsome court-house, gaol, and cavalry barracks. It is situate at the E. end of a small lake; 11 miles E. by N. of Westport, and 113 W. by N. of Dublin.

CASTLETON, a village on the Peak of Derbyshire; 5 miles N. of Tideswell. It is situate at the foot of a rock about 250 feet high, on which are the remains of a castle, ascribed to William Peveril, natural son of the Conqueror. Three of the seven wonders of the Peak are in its neighbourhood; the Devil's Cave, Mam Tor, and Elden Hole. The first is in a cavern in the rock above mentioned, whose arched entrance is 42 feet high and 120 wide, which becomes narrower as it proceeds, and the roof descends to within 2 feet of the surface of a brook; this being passed over, another large cavern succeeds, with several high openings in the roof, which descends again to a second brook; after which is a third cavern, called Roger Rain's House, because of the perpetual dropping: the length of the whole cavern is 617 yards. Mam Tor, a mile W. of the village, is a mountain, 1300 feet above the level of the valley, on the top and sides of which is a camp, supposed to be Roman: it overtops the whole Peak Country, and the vulgar story is, that this hill is continually crumbling, without being diminished. Elden Hole, a mile S. of Mam Tor, is a perpendicular gulf or chasm in a limestone rock, the depth of which is unfathomable, its sides being so very shelving and irregular; it has been plumbed from 192 to 295 yards, 70 of which seemed to be in water.

Castleton, a township in the parish of Rochdale, Lancashire. *See* Rochdale.

Castletown, the capital of the Isle of Man, near the S. coast, with a rocky and shallow harbour, which checks its commerce, and renders it inferior to Douglas in most respects. In the centre of the town, on a high rock, is Castle Rushen, a magnificent pile, built of freestone, in 960, by Guttred, a prince of the Danish line, who lies buried in the edifice. It is occupied by the governor of the island, and on one side of it are the chancery offices, and good barracks. Near the town is a fine quarry of black marble, whence the steps of St. Paul's church, in London, were taken. Long. 4. 38. W. lat. 55. 4. N.

Castletown, a town on Staten Island, at the entrance of New York harbour, where is the Quarantine Ground and Marine Hospital for that city. Pop. 4275.

Castres, a city of France, capital of the department of Tarn, and lately an episcopal see. In the reign of Louis XIII. it was a kind of Protestant republic; but in 1629 its fortifications were demolished. It is the birthplace of Rapin, Thoyras, and M. Dacier; has a good trade, and contains a number of beautiful edifices and about 12,500 inhabitants. In the vicinity turquoise stones have been found. It is seated in a fine valley, on the Agout; 36 miles E. of Toulouse.

Castries, Bay of, a bay on the N. E. coast of Chinese Tartary, in the strait of Saghalien, visited by Perouse. Long. 142. 1. E. lat. 51. 29. N.

Castro, a town of Italy, in the patrimony of St. Peter, capital of a duchy of its name. It is 56 miles N. W. of Rome.

Castro, a town of Naples, in Terra d'Otranto; 6 miles S. S. W. of Otranto.

Castro, a town of the island of Chiloe, with a castle, which commands the harbour. It is 180 miles S. of Valdivia. Long. 75. 5. W. lat. 42. 4. S.

Castro, the ancient Mytilene, a seaport, and capital of the island of Metelin, with two harbours, one of which will admit large vessels. There are two castles, the one ancient, the other modern, in each of which is a Turkish governor and commander. Considerable vestiges still remain of its former grandeur and magnificence. The chief trade is ship-building. It is 30 miles S. W. of Adramitti, and 60 N. W. of Smyrna. Long. 26. 39. E. lat. 39. 14. N.

Castro de Uriales, a town of Spain, in Biscay, with a castle and an arsenal, on the sea coast; 22 miles N. W. of Bilboa.

Castro Giovanni, a town of Sicily, in Val di Demona. It was the ancient Enna, famous for the worship of Ceres and Proserpine. It is 40 miles W. of Catania. Pop. about 12,000.

Castro Marim, a strong town of Portugal, in Algarve, seated near the mouth of the Guadiana; 15 miles E. N. E. of Tavira, and 62 S. by E. of Beja. Long. 7. 20. W. lat. 37. 12. N.

Castro Reale, a town of Sicily, in Val di Demona; 15 miles W. of Messina. Pop. 8000.

Castro Verde, a town of Portugal, in Alentejo, on the Corbes; 18 miles S. S. W. of Beja.

Castro Vireyna, a town of Peru, in the province of Guamanga, noted for good tobacco and fine wool. It is 125 miles S. E. of Lima. Long. 74. 45. W. lat. 13. 50. S.

There are several other towns in Italy, Spain, and Portugal, to the names of which *Castro* is prefixed.

Castria, a town of Austrian Istria, a few miles W. of Fiume.

Castrop, a tn. of Westphalia, in the county of Mark; 7 miles W. of Dortmund.

Castropol, a town of Spain, in Asturias; 14 miles N. E. of Mondonedo.

Caswell, a county of North Carolina, bordering on Pitsylvania county, Virginia. Pop. 14,693, of whom 7024 were slaves. The court-house, in the centre of the county, is 60 miles N. N. W. of Raleigh. The principal town is called Leesburg.

Cat Island. *See* Bahamas.

Catabamba, or Cotobamba, an interior town of Peru, in a district of the same name, in the 14th degree of S. latitude. The town is seated on the S. W. bank of the Apurimac river; about 60 miles S. of Cuzco.

Catabaw, properly Catawba, a river of the United States of North America, rising from numerous sources in the N. W. part of North Carolina, in the lat. of 36. N. and 82. of W. long. running in a S. S. E. direction into South Carolina, in which state it is called the Wateree, until it reaches the centre of the state, where it is joined by the Saluda, or Congaree, and numerous other streams from the S. W., where it is called the Santee, falling into the Atlantic Ocean, in the lat. of 33. 5. N. and 79. 15. of W. long.; about 40 miles N. of Charleston, with the harbour of which city it is connected by a canal from a point 50 miles above its entrance into the sea.

Catabaw, or Catawba, an Indian town on the banks of the preceding river, at its entrance into South Carolina. The native inhabitants amount to about 450, the remains of a once powerful nation, who have degenerated in physical energy, and progressively decreased in number, since their association with Europeans.

Catahoula, or Ocatahool, a parish of Louisiana; about 60 miles in extent from N. to S. and 30 in mean breadth; it is intersected by the Washita, and several other rivers and lakes. A town of the same name, on the W. bank of the Washita, is 260 miles N. W. of New Orleans, by the course of the Mississippi, and about 160 in a meridional line.

Catalonia, a province of Spain; lying along the shore of the Mediterranean, in a N. N. E. direction from the lat. of 40. 30. to 42. 30. N. separated from France on the N. by the Pyrenees, and bounded on the W. by Arragon, being in the shape of a right-angled triangle, of which the Pyrenees are the base, and the sea coast the hypothenuse. It contains 1003 square miles, and a population of 858,818. Barcelona is the chief town; the other towns of note being Tortosa, Lerida, Tarragona, Mantresa, Gerona, and Rosas. The river Ebro intersects the S. end of the province, and the united streams of the Pallaresa and Segre run from the Pyrenees into the Ebro, near the frontier of Arragon. The Lobregat, Ter, and several other streams of minor note, fall into the Mediterranean. The Catalonians are the bravest and least bigoted, and the most active and enterprising of the Spanish people; but the subduing tendency of the national policy of Spain precludes all advance towards social improvement. The chief surplus products of the soil of Catalonia are cork, nuts, and brandy; woollens, hardware, and cutlery, are manufactured for distribution over the other parts of Spain, and partially for exportation.

CATAMANDOO, or KHATMANDU, a city, and capital of Nepaul, containing about 50,000 inhabitants; 200 miles due N. of Patna. *See* NEPAUL.

CATANDUANES, one of the Philippine Islands, lying off the S. E. coast of Luzon; it is about 30 miles in extent from N. to S., and 20 in breadth; the inhabitants are much employed in building of boats for the neighbouring islanders.

CATANIA, a celebrated city on the E. coast of Sicily; it is a place of great antiquity, but has suffered greatly, as well by the eruptions of Mount Ætna, as by earthquakes; it was nearly overwhelmed with lava from the former, in 1669, and in 1693 an earthquake destroyed a great portion of the city, and buried 18,000 persons in its ruins; it appears, however, to have risen from each succeeding disaster with increasing splendour, and in 1825 ranked among the finest cities in Europe. It is the see of a bishop, and seat of the only university in Sicily. The principal square, formed by the cathedral, college, and town-hall, is very grand; it has about 30 convents and 50 churches, some of them fine edifices; a museum of natural history and antiquities, the remains of a Roman amphitheatre, and other vestiges of ancient splendour, render it a place of peculiar interest to an intelligent and inquiring traveller. It is situate at the foot of Mount Ætna, on the S. side; 35 miles N. of Syracuse, in the lat. of 37. 26. N. and 15. 15. of E. long. Pop. about 50,000.

CATANZARO, a city of Naples, capital of Calabria Ulteriore, and the see of a bishop. The chief manufacture is silks of various kinds, and these, with corn and oil, are the principal articles of trade. It is seated on a mountain, near the Gulf of Squillace; 43 miles S. E. of Cosenza. Long. 16. 48. E. lat. 39. 0. N.

CATARAUGUS, a county towards the W. extremity of the state of New York, bordering on Pennsylvania. The court-house of the county is 317 miles W. of Albany.

CATAUBA. *See* CATABAW.

CATAWISSA, or HUGHESBURG, a town of Pennsylvania, in Northumberland county, situate at the mouth of the Catawissa Creek, on the E. branch of the Susquehannah; 25 miles E. N. E. of Sunbury, and 100 N. W. of Philadelphia. Pop. about 2000.

CATEAU. *See* CHATEAU CHAMBRESIS.

CATHARINBURG, a town of Russia, capital of a province of the same name, in the government of Perm. The chief gold mines of Siberia are in its vicinity, and above 100 founderies, chiefly for copper and iron. It is seated at the foot of the Ural Mountains, on the E. side, near the source of the Iset; 310 miles W. S. W. of Tobolsk. Long. 61. 25. E. lat. 56. 45. N.

CATHARINENSLAF, a government of the Russian empire, divided into two provinces, namely, Catharinenslaf, which includes New Russia; and the late government of Asoph, and Taurida. which includes the Crimea.

CATHARINENSLAF, a town of Russia, capital of a government of the same name. It was built by the Empress Catharine, and is seated near the confluence of the Kiltzin and Samara with the Dnieper; 178 miles N. E. of Cherson. Long. 35. 15. E. lat. 47. 23. N.

CATHARINE, ST., the principal island on the coast of the S. part of Brazil, with a harbour defended by several forts. It is 27 miles long, but not more than six broad, but exceedingly fertile; it forms a part of the Brazilian republic. Pop. about 30,000. There is a town of the same name, the chief place on the island. Long. 49. 17. W. lat. 27. 35. S.

CATOCHE, CAPE, the N. E. promontory of Yucatan, where the English adventurers from Jamaica first attempted to cut log-wood. Long. 87. 30. W. lat. 21. 25. N.

CATRINE, a town of Scotland; 14 miles E. of Ayr, on the river Ayr. Here is a flourishing cotton manufacture.

CATSKILL, an incorporated town of Greene county, state of New York, situate on the W. bank of the Hudson river, nearly opposite to the town of Hudson; and 36 miles S. of Albany. Pop. 5339.

CATSKILL MOUNTAINS, North America, state of New York. They are a branch of the Apalachian chain, and are about 3000 feet in height, abounding in beautiful scenery.

CATTARO, a town of Dalmatia, with a castle, seated on a gulf of its name, in the Adriatic, which forms two extensive and secure harbours. The town is built at the extremity of the inner basin, surrounded by rocks, and strongly fortified. It is 24 miles S. of Scutari. Long. 19. 15. E. lat. 42. 12. N.

CATTEGAT, a gulf of the German Ocean, between Sweden and Jutland; extending for about 120 miles from N. to S., and 70 from E. to W., through which the Baltic Sea is entered by three straits, called the Sound, the Great Belt, and the Little Belt.

CATTAIO, a town of Italy, in the Paduan; 5 miles S. of Padua.

CATTERICK, a village in West Yorkshire, near Richmond. It has a bridge over the river Swale, and a Roman highway crossed the river here, on the banks of which are the foundations of great walls, and a mount cast up to a vast height.

CATWYCK, a village of South Holland, on the German Ocean, near which the river Rhine is lost in the sands. It is 6 miles N. by W. of Leyden.

CATZENELNBOGEN, a town and castle of Germany, in the circle of Upper Rhine, which gives name to a county. The town has an iron mine near it; and is 10 miles N. E. of St. Goar.

CAUB, a town of Germany, with a citadel; seated on the Rhine; 2 miles N. by E. of Bacharach.

CAUCA, a river of Colombia, rising near Popayan, in the lat. of 3. N., running N. through the valley of Popayan, between the second and third ridges of the Andes, falling into the Magdalena, about 120 miles above the entrance of that river into the Caribbean Sea, in the lat. of 11. N.

CAUCASIA, a government of Asiatic Russia, divided into the two provinces of Astracan and Caucasia. The province of Caucasia comprises the Cuban, and all that district to the E. and S., now in the possession of Russia, between the rivers Don and Cuban, and between the Black Sea and the Caspian, extending as far as the confines of Georgia.

CAUCASUS, a chain of mountains extending from the mouth of the Cuban, in the Black Sea, to the mouth of the Kur, in the Caspian. Their tops are always covered with snow; and the lower parts abound in honey, corn, wine, fruits, gum, hogs, and horned cattle. The Caucasian mountains are inhabited by seven distinct nations, each speaking a different language; namely, the Turcomans, the Abkahs, the Circassians, the Ossi, the Kisti, the Lesgius, and the Georgians.

CAUDEBEC, a town of France, in the department of Lower Seine; 18 miles W. by N. of Rouen. Pop. about 3000.

CAUDETTE, a town of Spain, on the frontiers of Murcia and Valencia; about 50 miles W. of Denia. Pop. about 6000.

CAUDHULLY, a town of Hindostan, in the province of Coimbetore. It is the first place of any note above the Gauts, and a principal thoroughfare between the country below and that above those mountains. The inhabitants are chiefly traders. It is 60 miles S. E. of Seringapatam.

CAUGHNAWAGA, a town of the United States, in Montgomery county, New York; situated S. of the river Mohawk; 30 miles W. by N. of Schenectady, and 206 N. N. W. of New York.

CAUGLINARY, a town of Hindostan, in Bengal, lying between the Ganges and Burrampooter; 30 miles N. W. of Dacca, and 146 N. E. of Calcutta.

CAULABAUGH, a town of the Afghan territory, on the W. bank of the Indus; 110 miles N. of Moultan.

CAUNE, a town of France, in the department of Tarn; 20 miles E. N. E. of Castres. Pop. 2500.

CAUNPOOR, a town of Hindostan, capital of a district of the same name, province of Allahabad. This district is a fertile plain between the Ganges and Jumna rivers, and produces much corn. The town is one of the principal thoroughfares in this part, and is the head military quarters of the neighbourhood. It is excessively hot in summer, and is well supplied with necessaries.

CAUTERES, a village of France, in the department of Upper Pyrenees, at the foot of the mountains; noted for its mineral water; 18 miles S. W. of Bagneres.

CAUVERY, or CAVERY, a considerable river of Hindostan, which rises among the western Gauts, flows by Seringapatam, Bhawanikudal, and Tritchinopoly, and enters the Bay of Bengal, by a wide delta of mouths, which embraces the province of Tanjore, in the lat. of 11. N.

CAVA, a town of Naples, in Principato Citeriore, at the foot of Mount Matelian; 3 miles W. of Salerno.

CAVAILLON, a town of France, in the department of Vaucluse; seated on the Durance; 20 miles S. E. of Avignon. Population about 7000.

CAVALIERI, an island in the Archipelago, between the S. W. point of the island of Negropont and the continent of Greece. Long. 24. 17. E. lat. 38. 7. N.

CAVALLA, a town of European Turkey, on the coast of Rumelia; about 90 miles E. of Salonica. Pop. about 3000.

CAVAN, an interior county of Ireland, in the S. part of the province of Ulster. It has several lakes; two on the S. side discharge their waters eastward by the Blackwater river into the Boyne, and others westward into Donegal Bay through Lough Erne, which jets upon the northern boundary of the county. The Lagan river, which falls into Dundalk Bay, also intersects its S. E. part; it partakes but partially of the linen manufacture. The chief town, of the same name, is situate in the centre of the county; 30 miles due W. of Dundalk, the same distance S. S. E. of Armagh, and 68 N. N. W. of Dublin. As the seat of assize for the county, it has a court-house, jail, and a free grammar-school, founded by Charles I. The county sends two members to parliament.

CAVARGERE, a town of the Venetian territory, on the S. bank of the Adige, near its entrance into the Gulf of Venice.

CAVERYPATAM, a town of Hindostan, in the Carnatic, seated on the Panaur; 80 miles W. S. W. of Arcot. There is another town of the same name at one of the mouths of the Cavery river, a few miles N. of Tranquebar.

CAVIANA, an island of South America, at the mouth of the river Amazon, 90 miles in circumference, and of a triangular form, with its base to the ocean. It lies under the equinoctial line, in long. 50. 20. W.

CAVITE, a seaport on the W. coast of the island of Luzon. *See* MANILLA.

CAVOR, a town of Piedmont, in the province of Pignerol; 8 miles S. by E. of the town of Pignerol. Pop. about 7000.

CAWOOD, a town in East Yorkshire, on the river Ouse; 12 miles S. of York. Here are the ruins of a very ancient castle, a manufacture for hop-bagging, and a good ferry over the river.

CAXAMARCA, a town of Peru, capital of a territory of its name, in the province of Truxillo. Here the Spanish general, Pizarro, in 1532, perfidiously seized the inca, Atahualpa, and the next year, after a mock trial, caused him to be publicly executed. It is 70 miles N. E. of the city of Truxillo. Long. 78. 20. W. lat. 7. S.

CAXAMARQUILLA, another considerable city of Peru, also in the province of Truxillo; about 40 miles S. S. E. of Caxamarca.

CAXATAMBO, another city of Peru, in the province of Tarma; about 200 miles S. by E. of Caxamarquilla, and 140 N. by E. of Lima.

CAXTON, a town of Cambridgeshire, with a market on Tuesday; 10 miles W. by S. of Cambridge, and 49 N. of London. It was the birthplace of Caxton, who introduced the art of printing into England; and also of Matthew Paris, the historian.

CAYAGAN SOOLOO. *See* CAGAYAN SOOLOO.

CAYAHOGA, or CUYAHOGA, a county of the state of Ohio, bordering for about 35 miles on the S. W. shore of Lake Erie, being about 8 miles in mean breadth. It is intersected by three or four streams or rivers, falling into the lake, the principal of which, of the same name as the county, enters the lake in the long. of 82. 20. W. It is deep enough to receive large sloops from the lake; and is navigable for boats to its source, whence there is only a short portage to the Tuscarawa branch of the Muskingum, which is also navigable, and runs S. into the Ohio, at Marietta. It is proposed to connect these two rivers by a canal, and thereby unite the waters of the great chain of lakes with the Gulf of Mexico. Pop. 26,506. Cleveland, at the mouth of the river, 174 miles N. E. of Columbus, is the chief town.

CAYAMBA, a town of Peru, in the province of Quito; 30 miles N. E. of Quito.

CAYENNE, a rich town and island on the coast of Guiana, capital of the French settlements there; bounded on the W. by the Dutch colony of Surinam. The island is about 50 miles in circumference, separated from the continent by a very narrow channel. The surface is low and marshy, and covered with forests. Cayenne pepper, sugar, coffee, cloves, and the singularly elastic gum called caoutchouc, are the principal commodities. The French settled here in 1625, but left it in 1654, and it was successively in the possession of the English, French, and Dutch; but the latter were expelled by the French in 1677. It surrendered to the English in 1809, but was restored to France at the peace of 1814. Long. 52. 15. W. lat. 4. 56. N. *See* GUIANA.

CAYTE, a town of Brazil, in the government of Para, near the mouth of the Cateypeyra; 105 miles N. E. of Para. Long. 48. 12. W. lat. 0. 56. S.

CAYUGA, a county of the state of New York, the N. end of which borders on Lake Ontario, extending S. about 50 miles, and about 10 miles in mean breadth. The population is 50,338. Auburn, the chief town, is 169 miles W. by N. of Albany.

CAYUGA LAKE bounds the W. side of the above county for about 25 miles, extending about 10 miles further S. into Tompkins county. It is 3 to 4 miles wide, and discharges its waters at the N. end through Seneca River into Lake Ontario, from which the N. end of Cayuga Lake is distant about 25 miles. The Erie canal runs past, near the N. end of Cayuga. There is a town of the same name on the E. bank, 5 miles W. of Auburn.

CAYUTA, a town of Tioga county, state of New York.

CAZAUBON, a town of France, department of Gers, on the banks of the Adour; 80 miles N. N. E. of Bayonne.

CAZENOVIA, the chief tn. of Madison county, state of New York, situate on the bank of a small lake, a few miles S. of the line of the Erie canal; 110 miles W. by N. of Albany. Pop. 4153.

CAZERES, a town of France, in the department of Upper Garonne; about 35 miles S. W. of Toulouse.

CECIL, a county of the state of Maryland, at the head of Chesapeake Bay, forming the N. E. extremity of the state; bounded W. by the Susquehannah river. Pop. 17,232, 1352 of whom were slaves. ELKTON is the chief town, which see.

CAZIMIR, a town of Little Poland, in the palatinate of Lublin, seated on the Vistula; 80 miles E. of Zarnaw. Long. 22. 3. E. lat. 51. 0. N.

CEDAR CREEK, a water of James River, in Virginia, in the county of Rockbridge; remarkable for its natural bridge, justly regarded as one of the most magnificent natural curiosities in the world. It is a huge rock, in the form of an arch, 90 feet long, 60 wide, and from 40 to 60 deep, lying over the river more than 200 feet above the surface of the water, supported by abutments as light and graceful as though they had been the work of Corinthian art. This bridge gives name to the county, and affords a commodious passage over a valley, which cannot be crossed elsewhere for a considerable distance. It is about 100 miles W. of Richmond, and 160 S. S. W. of Washington city.

CEDAR POINT, a seaport of Maryland, in Charles county. The exports are chiefly tobacco and maize. It is seated on the Potomac; 12 miles below Port Tobacco, and 40 S. by E. of Washington.

CEDOGNA, a town of Naples, in Principato Ulteriore, at the foot of the Appennines; 20 miles N. N. E. of Conza.

CEFALONIA, or CEPHALONIA, the most considerable of the Ionian Isles, in the Mediterranean, on the coast of Livadia, opposite the Gulf of Lepanto. It is 40 miles long, and from 10 to 20 broad. fertile in oil and muscadine wine. The capital is of the same name; on the S. E. coast. Long. 20. 56. E. lat. 38. 12. N. Pop. 63,200.

CEFALU, a seaport of Sicily, in Val di Demona, and a bishop's see, with a castle; seated on a promontory 40 miles E. by S. of Palermo. Long. 13. 58. E. lat. 38. 15. N. Pop. about 5500.

CELANO, a town of Naples, in Abruzzo Ulteriore, near a lake of the same name; 30 miles in circumference. It is 15 miles S. of Aquila.

CELAYA, or SILAO, a town of Mexico, situate on a spacious plain 6000 feet above the level of the sea; a few miles N. N. W. of the city of Guanaxuato.

CELBRIDGE, a town of Ireland, in the county of Kildare; 10 miles W. of Dublin.

CELEBES, or MACASSAR, a very irregular and singular-shaped island in the Eastern Sea, lying between Borneo and the Moluccas. The centre of the island is intersected by the line of 120. of E. long. and 2. of S. lat. From this centre four tongues of territory project, terminating as follows: viz.—

	Lat.	Long.
1st, At Bontham,	5. 34. S.	120. 32. E.
2nd, At Cape Lessen,	4. 54. S.	121. 28. E.
3rd, At Cape Talabo,	0. 48. S.	123. 57. E.
4th, At Cape Rivers,	1. 15. N.	120. 34. E.

5th, From Cape Rivers another tongue projects eastward, in nearly a straight line, wholly N. of the equator, to the long. of 125. 5. E. The centre from whence the tongues respectively diverge, comprises an extent of territory of about 150 miles from N. to S.; and 110 from W. to E.: the mean breadth of the projections, each being about 55 miles, gives an aggregate extent of surface of about 67,000 square miles. The Portuguese, who first doubled the Cape of Good Hope into the Eastern seas, in 1493, formed a settlement upon the S. W. point of Celebes in 1512. The Portuguese were expelled by the Dutch in 1667, by whom the possession was called *Macassar*, who held it undisturbed till after the commencement of the present century. It is divided into six kingdoms, viz.:—Goa, Selindrin, Mandar, Wayoo or Tuadjo, Bony, and Jopin. The total population of Celebes is supposed to amount to about 3,000,000, under the surveillance of several separate rajahs, among whom polygamy and the other sensualities of Mahometanism generally prevail. The principal river of the island, the Chrinrana, falls into the Bay of BONY or BUGGES, which see; and see also TOBO, TOMINIE, CAMBYNA, and BOUTON, other bays and islands connected with Celebes.

CELI, or MARIA ZELL, a town of Styria, with a celebrated abbey, seated on the Saltza; 17 miles N. N. E. of Bruck.

CENEDA, a town of Italy, in Trevisano; 18 miles N. of Treviso.

CENIS, a mountain of the Maritime Alps, in Savoy, which is a noted passage from the S. of France to Turin. The summit of the pass, which is about 9000 feet above the level of the sea, is 35 miles W. N. W. of Turin. The facility of intercourse by this route was much improved by Napoleon Buonaparte.

CENTRE, a county of Pennsylvania, being, in conformity with its name, in the centre of the state. Its shape is an irregular square, about 35 miles each way. The main ridge of the Allegany mountains terminates in a bluff towards the N. side of the county, near to which runs the W. branch of the Susquehannah river, a branch of which bounds all the W. side of the county, Bald Eagle Creek intersecting it from S. to N. eastward of the mountain ridge. Pop. 20,492. Bellfonte, 121 miles N. W. of Harrisburg, and 150 W. N. W. of Philadelphia, is the chief town.

CENTREVILLE, a town of Maryland, chief of Queen Anne county; 48 miles E. S. E. of Baltimore, and 95 S. S. W. of Philadelphia.

CEPHALONIA. *See* CEFALONIA and IONIA.

CERAM, one of the Molucca Isles, extending from 128. to 130. 51. of E. long., being about 35 miles in mean breadth, between the lat. of 2. 51. and 3. 55. S. The island of Amboyna, on which the Dutch have their principal spice plantations, lies off the S. W. end of Ceram, on which island, in the true spirit of their characteristic policy, they endeavoured to destroy all the spice trees, in which despicable attempt they succeeded to a very great extent. Sago is now the prominent production of Ceram. The *salangan*, whose edible nests command such an exorbitant price in China, is common in the island.

CERDAGNA, a district of the Pyrenees, partly in Spain, in the province of Catalonia, and partly in France, in the department of Eastern Pyrenees. Puycerda is the capital of the Spanish part, and Mont Louis of the French.

CERE, ST., a town of France, in the N. E. corner of the department of Lot; 37 miles N. E. of Cahors, and 280 S. of Paris. Pop. about 4000.

CERENZA, or GERCENZA, a town of Naples, in Calabria Citeriore, seated on a rock; 10 miles N. by W. of Severino.

CERET, a town of France, in the department of Eastern Pyrenees, with a magnificent bridge of one arch over the Tet. Here the commissioners of France and Spain met, in 1660, to settle the limits of the two kingdoms. In 1794 the French defeated the Spaniards near this town. It is 14 miles W. S. W. of Perpignan.

CERIGNOLA, a town of Naples, in Capitanata, celebrated by Horace for its excellent bread. Near this town is the ancient Salapia, the ruins of which are still called Salpe. It is 20 miles S. of Manfredonia. Pop. about 12,000.

CERIGO, (the ancient *Cythera,*) an island of the Mediterranean, lying off the S. E. promontory of the Morea: it formerly belonged to the Venetians: the French took possession of it in 1797, it surrendered to the English in 1809, and at the peace of 1815 was included in the Ionian republic, under the protection of England. It is about 17 miles long, from N. to S., and 10 in breadth, mountainous, and but little cultivated. The inhabitants are princi pally Greeks, whose chief occupation is in attending to their flocks of sheep and herds of goats. There is a town of the same name near the S. end of the island, containing about 1200 inhabitants; the extreme S. point of the island is in lat. 36. 9. and 22. 57. E. long.

Cerigotto, (the ancient *Ægilia,)* a small island, lying between the S. E. point of Cerigo and the N. W. point of Candia. Lat. 35. 51. N. and 23. 44. W. long. It is unproductive, and has but few inhabitants.

Cerilly, a town of France, in the department of Allier; 25 miles W. of Moulins, and 40 S. by E. of Bourges.

Cerina, a seaport, (the ancient *Cerynia)* on the N. coast of Cyprus, and a Greek bishop's see, with a castle on an immense rock. The chief exports are barley, silk, cotton, oil, and carob beans. It is 20 miles N. W. of Nicosia. Long. 32. 55. E. lat. 25. 45. N.

Cerne Abbas, a town in Dorsetshire, with a market on Wednesday. It is surrounded by high chalk hills, and on the side of one of them is cut the figure of a man, 180 feet in height, holding a club in his right hand, and extending the other. Here was formerly a stately abbey, and part of its remains is now converted into a house and barn. It is seated on the river Cerne; 7 miles N. N. W. of Dorchester, and 120 W. by S. of London.

Cernetz, a town of Switzerland, in the canton of Grisons, with a mineral spring; seated on the river Inn; 24 miles S. E. of Coire.

Cerrito, a town of Naples, in Terra di Lavoro, with a cathedral and collegiate church; 5 miles N. N. E. of Telesa.

Certosa, a town of Italy, in the Milanese, with a celebrated Carthusian monastery; 5 miles N. of Pavia.

Cervera, a town of Spain, in Catalonia, with a university; 34 miles N. by W. of Tarragona. Another on the borders of France and the Mediterranean; 8 miles N. of Rosas; and five or six others in different parts of Spain.

Cervia, a town of Italy, in Romagna, seated near the Gulf of Venice, whence canals are cut to admit sea water, from which much salt is made. It is 10 miles S. E. of Ravenna.

Cervin, Mont, the most conical point of the Alps, in Savoy, contiguous to Mont Blanc.

Cervinara, a town of Naples, in Principato Ulteriore; 12 miles S. W. Benevento.

Cesena, a town of Italy, in Romagna, seated on the Savio; 18 miles S. by E. of Ravenna.

Cesenatico, a seaport of Italy, in Romagna. In 1800 the inhabitants having arrested a messenger with despatches, the English set fire to the moles of the harbour, and destroyed sixteen vessels. It is seated on the Gulf of Venice; 16 miles S. E. of Ravenna, and 8 E. of Cesena.

Cessieaux, a town of France, in the department of Isere; 27 miles E. S. E. of Lyons.

Cette, a seaport of France, situate on a tongue of land stretching along the coast of the department of Herault, on the Gulf of Lyons. A considerable quantity of salt is made from the water of the inlet. It has a manufacture of soap, and sugar refinery, and exports a considerable quantity of brandy; the canal of Languedoc falling into the inlet, occasions Cette to be the medium of an extensive intercourse between the eastern and southern departments of France. Pop. about 8000. The lighthouse is in lat. 43 24. N. and 3. 42. W. long. and about 18 miles S. W. of Montpelier.

Ceuta, (the ancient *Abylo*), a town of Fez, at the N. W. extremity of Africa, opposite to Gibraltar, from which it is distant only 14 miles. It was taken from the Moors, by the Portuguese, in 1409; it fell into the hands of the Spaniards in 1640, was confirmed to them by the treaty of Lisbon in 1688, and in whose possession it still continues. The Moors besieged it in 1694, and maintained a close blockade before it, on the land side, for nearly thirty years, when they ultimately retired with great loss. Its fortress, like that of Gibraltar, to which it is considered a counterpart, may be regarded as impregnable; and, as such, they are poetically termed the Pillars of Hercules. It has a tolerable good harbour for vessels not of very large burthen; in the lat. of 35. 54. N. and 5. 16. W. long.

Ceva, a town of Piedmont, with a fort. It was taken by the French in 1796, and retaken by the Piedmontese peasants in 1799. It stands on the Tanaro; 8 miles S. E. of Mondovi. Pop. about 5500.

Cevennes, a late territory of France, in the province of Languedoc. It is a mountainous country, and now forms the department of Gard.

Ceylon, an island of the Indian Ocean, lying off the S. W. coast of the promontory of Hindostan, from which it is separated by the Gulf of Manara and Palk's Strait, about 90 miles in breadth. The form of Ceylon has not inaptly been compared to that of a pear, the N. part forming the stem. It is 270 miles in extreme length, from Point de Galle, in the lat. 6. 4., to Point Pedro, in 9. 50. N., and 120 in extreme breadth between the long. of 80. and 81. 52. E.

The early history of Ceylon is involved in obscurity; but supposing it to be the *Taprobane* adverted to by Strabo, Pomponius, Mela, and Pliny, it must have ranked high in population and influence among the nations of Asia, for ages antecedent to the Christian era, having sent an embassy overland to Rome in the reign of the Emperor Claudius. It appears to have been visited by some Nestorian missionaries, in the 9th century. About the middle of the 13th century it was visited by Marco Polo, a Venetian, who travelled over a great part of Asia, and afterwards published an account of his travels. The information, however, which he communicated being of a general, rather than of a circumstantial nature, but little was known of Ceylon, beyond its actual existence as an island, until after the discovery of the passage by the Cape of Good Hope, and its being visited by the Portuguese in 1505, who found it divided into several petty sovereignties, which subsequently merged into one, under the title of the kingdom of Candy. The Portuguese held settlements on different parts of the coast for upwards of 150 years, when they were expelled by the

Dutch, who possessed themselves of the entire circuit of the coast, for 10 to 20 miles from the sea, and the whole of the N. part of the island; confining the dominion of the king of Candy entirely to the interior. The Dutch possessions of the island all surrendered to the English in 1796, after sustaining a siege of three weeks; and in 1815 a British force marched into the interior, took the king of Candy prisoner, deposed him, and possessed his territory, thereby rendering the whole island a part of the British dominion. The entire revenues yielded by the island to our government have been estimated at 250,000*l.* The general character of the surface of the island of Ceylon is mountainous and woody, with an ample extent of soil; and sufficiently intersected by streams of water, to afford the most abundant means of subsistence and comfort to a population more than tenfold its present extent. The most lofty range of mountains divides the island nearly into two parts, and terminates completely the effects of the monsoons, which set in periodically from opposite sides of them. The seasons are more regulated by the monsoons than the course of the sun; for the coolest season is during the summer solstice, while the western monsoon prevails. Spring commences in October, and the hottest season is from January to the beginning of April. The climate, on the coast, is more temperate than on the continent of Hindostan, but in the interior of the country the heat is many degrees greater, and the climate often extremely sultry and unhealthy. The finest fruits grow in vast plenty; but there is a poisonous fruit called Adam's apple, which in shape resembles the quarter of an apple cut out, with the two insides a little convex, and a continued ridge along the outer edges; and is of a beautiful orange colour. Pepper, ginger, and cardamoms are produced in Ceylon, with five kinds of rice, which ripen one after another. One of the most remarkable trees in the island is the talipot, which grows straight and tall, and is as big as the mast of a ship; the leaves are so large as to cover 15 men; when dried, they are round, and fold up like a fan. The natives wear a piece of the leaf on their head when they travel, to shade them from the sun; and they are so tough that they are not easily torn. Every soldier carries one, and it serves for his tent; other trees and shrubs, some valuable for their timber, and others for their resin, gums, and flowers, are interspersed over every part of the island; but the most important of all its vegetable productions is the cinnamon tree, the bark of which is distributed over every part of the habitable globe.

Ceylon also abounds with topazes, garnets, rubies, and other gems; besides ores of copper, iron, &c., and veins of black crystal. Common deer, as well as Guinea deer, are numerous; but the horned cattle are both very small and scarce, six of them weighing altogether only 714lbs., and one of these only 70 lbs. Yet the island produces the largest and best elephants in the world, which occasionally form an extensive branch of traffic to different parts of Hindostan. The woods are infested by tigers: they abound also with snakes of a monstrous size, among which is the boa constrictor, one of which has been known to destroy a tiger, and devour him at one meal. Spiders, centipedes, and scorpions, also grow to an enormous size. Among the curiosities of the insect tribe, the mantis, or creeping leaf, is met with, having every member of common insects, though in shape and appearance it greatly resembles a leaf: it is of a green colour. The sea coasts abound with fish. Alligators, and all the lizard tribe, are also numerous.

The aborigines of Ceylon consist of two classes of people, the Cingalese, and the Veddahs. The latter are still in the rudest stage of social life; they live embosomed in the woods, or in the hollows of the mountains: hunting, their sole employment, and providing for the day, their only care. Some of them acknowledged the authority of the king of Candy, and exchanged with the Cingalese, elephants' teeth and deer flesh, for arrows, cloth, &c.; but this practice is not general, for two-thirds of them hold no communication with the Cingalese, and have an utter antipathy to strangers. They worship a particular god; and their religious doctrine seems to consist of some indistinct notions of the fundamental principles of the Braminical faith. In some places they have erected temples; but for the most part they perform worship at an altar constructed of bamboos, under the shade of a banyan tree. The Cingalese, the subjects of the kings of Candy during the existence of their reign, appear to have been, beyond time of memory, a race of Hindoos, instructed in all the arts of civil life, and maintaining, if not an ascendancy, a co-equality of influence and importance with their continental neighbours. The distinction of castes into nineteen grades, prevails among them as scrupulously as among the Hindoos. In their devotions they are Pagans; and, though they acknowledge a supreme God, they worship only the inferior deities, among which they reckon the sun and moon. In their temples are images, well executed, though their figures are monstrous; some are of silver, copper, &c. The different sorts of gods have various priests, who have all some privileges. Their houses are small and low, with walls made of hurdles, smoothly covered with clay, and the roofs thatched. They have no chimneys, and their furniture is only a few earthen vessels, with two copper basins, and two or three stools; none but their king having been allowed to sit in a chair. Their food is generally rice, and their common drink is water, which they pour into their mouths out of a vessel like a tea-pot, through the spout, never touching it with their lips. There are some inscriptions on the rocks, which must be very ancient, for they are not understood by any of the present inhabitants. The subversion of the native government of Ceylon, and the predilection of the English to force a distribution of the products of British labour over every part of the globe, are calculated to effect a great change in the taste and habits of the Cingalese. the result of which it is difficult to foresee. In addition to the various productions of Ceylon, previously enumerated, connected with it is the pearl fishery, in the Gulf of Manara, which is considered the richest source of that article in the world; and which, with cinnamon, to the amount of 300,000 to 400,000 lbs. weight annually, constitutes the basis of its commerce, in exchange for European productions. The population is estimated at about 1,500,000. The principal towns are Colombo, Negombo, and Arroboo, on the W. coast; Trincomalee and Batacolo, on the E. coast; Magane and Matura, at the S. end; and Candy, nearly in the centre of the island.

CHABEUIL, a town of France, in the department of Drome, with about 4000 inhabitants; 8 miles S. by E. of Valence.

CHABLAIS, a fertile province of Savoy, bounded on the N. by the lake of Geneva, E. by Valois, S. by Faucigny, and W. by the Genevois. Thonon, 22 miles E. N. E. of Geneva, is the capital.

CHABLAIS, a town of France, in the department of Yonne, celebrated for its excellent white wine. It is 12 miles E. by N. of Auxerre.

CHACAO, a sea-port at the N. E. end of the island of Chiloe, on the strait that separates it from the main land, in the lat. of 41. 53. S.

CHACHAPOYAS, a town of Peru, in the province of Truxillo, capital of a district lying E. of the main ridge of the Andes. It is seated on a river; 160 miles N. N. E. of Truxillo. Long. 77. 30. W. lat. 6. 20. S.

CHACO, or GRAN CHACO, an interior district of South America, bordering east on the Paraguay river, which, under the influence of the Incas, and more recently of the domination of the Spaniards, was a sort of country of refuge for the native Indians. Its length is estimated at 750, and its breadth 450 miles. It is well watered, and yields most of the productions of other parts of Peru: it is now merged into the United Provinces of Buenos Ayres.

CHADDERTON, a township in the parish of Oldham, Lancashire. *See* OLDHAM.

CHAFALIA, properly ATCHAFALAYA, a diverging branch of the MISSISSIPPI RIVER, which see.

CHAGANG, a city of Birmah, with a small fort. It is the principal emporium for cotton, which is brought from all parts of the country, and embarked here in boats up the river Irrawaddy into the province of Yunen. Here also is the only manufacture of marble idols, whence the whole Birman empire is supplied, none being allowed to be made in any other place. It is situate opposite Ava, the deserted capital, on the N. side of the Irrawaddy, which here turns N. and parts it from Ummerapoora, the present capital.

CHAGRE, a town of Central America, in the republic of Colombia, and intendancy of Panama, connecting the two great divisions of the western hemisphere, at the mouth of a river of its name, to the S. W. of Porto Bello, forming the easiest channel of communication between the Atlantic and Pacific Oceans, which it is proposed to do either by means of a canal or rail-road. The fort was taken by Admiral Vernon, in 1740. Long. 90. 17. W. lat. 9. 10. N.

CHAIS DIEU, a town of France, in the department of the Upper Loire, with a celebrated Benedictine abbey; 12 miles E. of Brioude.

CHALAIN NEW, a town of Asia, kingdom of Ava, and chief town of a district in Burmah. It is walled, and is very ancient.

CHALCO, a town of Mexico; 18 miles S. E. of the city of Mexico.

CHALEUR, BAY OF, a spacious bay on the W. side of the Gulf of St. Lawrence, which divides the district of Gaspe, Lower Canada, from the province of New Brunswick. Miscou Island, at the entrance of the bay, is in lat. 48. 4. N. and 64. 14. W. long.; from which point the bay runs about 80 miles further west, being about 20 miles in breadth, indented on the N. by Cascapedia, and on the S. by Nipisiguit Bay. It receives several rivers, the principal of which is the Ristigouche, at its head. Along the coast are numerous inhabitants whose occupation is fishing and ship-building.

CHALLANS, a town of France, in the department of Vendee; situate about 12 miles from the coast, and 21 miles N. of Sables d'Olonne.

CHALLONE, a town of France, in the department of Mayenne and Loire, situate on the S. bank of the Loire; 30 miles E. N. E. of Nantes. Pop. about 5000.

CHALONS SUR MARNE, a city of France, capital of the department of Marne, and lately an episcopal see. It contains several public buildings, and 12,000 inhabitants, who carry on a considerable trade in shalloons and other woollen stuffs. Here is an academy of the sciences, arts, and belles-lettres. Chalons is seated on the river Marne, over which there is one very handsome, and two other bridges. It is 25 miles S. E. of Rheims, and 95 E. of Paris.

CHALONS SUR SAONE, a city of France, in the department of Saone and Loire, with a citadel, and lately an episcopal see. It is the staple of iron for Lyon and St. Etienne, and of wines for exportation. Here are various indications of Roman magnificence, particularly the ruins of an amphitheatre. The city contains the old town, the new town, and the suburb of St. Lawrence. In the first is the court of justice, and the cathedral. Chalons is seated on the Saone; 70 miles N. of Lyons, and 170 S. E. of Paris. Pop. about 9000.

CHALUS, a town of France, in the department of Upper Vienne, with a castle. Richard I. of England, while preparing to besiege this place, received a wound in his shoulder, by an arrow, which proved mortal. It is 15 miles W. S. W. of Limoges.

CHAM, a town of Bavaria, seated on the river Cham, at its confluence with the Regen; 27 miles N. E. of Ratisbon. Pop. about 2000.

CHAMBERSBURG, a town of Pennsylvania, chief of Franklin county, with two presbyterian churches; situate in a hilly country; 30 miles S. W. of Carlisle.

CHAMBERTIN, a village of France, in the department of Cote d'Or, celebrated for its delicious wine. It lies to the S. of Dijon.

Chambery, the capital of Savoy, with a castle and ducal palace. It is fortified by walls and ditches, and watered by many streams, which run through several of the streets. There are piazzas under most of the houses, where people may walk dry in the worst weather. It has large and handsome suburbs; and in the neighbourhood are some baths, much frequented in summer. In 1742 the Spaniards made themselves masters of this capital, but it was restored by the peace of 1748. It was taken in 1792 by the French, who were dispossessed of it in 1799, but regained it in 1800. It is seated at the conflux of the Lesse and D'Albon; 27 miles N. E. of Grenoble, and 85 N. W. of Turin. Pop. about 12,000. Long. 5. 50. E. lat. 45. 33. N.

Chambly, a fort of Lower Canada, on the river Chambly, or Sorel, issuing from Lake Champlain. It was taken by the Americans in 1775, and retaken by the English in 1776. It is 15 miles E. of Montreal; and a little higher on the same river is the fort of St. John, which is a frontier garrison.

Chamneiskoi, a town of Asiatic Russia, lying S. of the S. end of Lake Baikal, near the frontiers of Chinese Tartary.

Chamouni, one of the elevated valleys of the Alps, about 3300 feet above the level of the sea. It is at the foot of Mont Blanc, on the N. side, and is watered by the Arve, and celebrated for its herds of goats. There is a village of the same name in the bosom of the valley, on the banks of the Arve; 42 miles E. N. E. of Chambery, and 35 S. E. of Geneva.

Chamond, St., a town of France, in the department of Rhone, with a castle; on the river Giez; 17 miles S. of Lyon.

Champagne, a late province of France, 162 miles long and 112 broad; bounded on the N. by Hainault and Luxemburg, E. by Lorrain and Franche Comte, S. by Burgundy, and W. by the Isle of France and Soissonnois. It now forms the departments of Ardennes, Aube, Marne, and Upper Marne.

There are several small towns and villages of the same name in different parts of France.

Champagne, an interior county of the State of Ohio; about 20 miles in length, from E. to W., and 10 broad; it is intersected from N. to S. by Mad River, a branch of the Great Miami. Pop. 16,721. Urbane, 50 miles W. N. W. of Columbus, is the chief town.

Champagnei, a town of France, department of Upper Saone; 8 miles from Lure. Pop. 2200.

Champion, a town of North America, United States, state of New York, at the Long Falls on Black River, with a trade in corn. Pop. 2206.

Champaneer, a city and capital of a district of the same name, in the province of Malwa, Hindostan; it was formerly the capital of the rajahs of Guzerat; ruins of temples and mosques remain to attest its former consequence. It is 45 miles due E. of Cambray.

Champlain, a lake of North America, which divides the N. part of the state of New York from that of Vermont. It is 90 miles long, in a direction due N., and 18 in its broadest part; the mean width is about 6 miles, and its depth is sufficient for the largest vessel. It contains many islands, the principal of which, called North Hero, is twenty-four miles long, and from two to four wide. It receives the waters of Lake George from the S. S. W. and sends its own waters a N. course, through Chambly River into the St. Lawrence. The land on its borders, and on the banks of its rivers, is good. During the war declared by the United States against England in 1812, each party maintained a naval force of three or four vessels, which came to an engagement on the 14th of September, 1814, when the British squadron was defeated and taken. Although this lake lies between the lat. of 45. and 47. it is frequently frozen over, so as to afford a passage on the ice for two or three months in the year; it is united with Lake Erie by a canal. *See* Albany.

Champlain, a town of New York, in Clinton county, situate on Lake Champlain, near its N. extremity. In 1777 a battle was fought here between the British, under General Carlton, and the Americans, under General Arnold, in which the latter were totally defeated. Pop. 3632. It is 92 miles due N. of Albany.

Champlemy, a town of France, in the department of Nievre, near the source of the Nievre; 25 miles N. N. E. of Nevers.

Chanac, a town of France, in the Province of Languedoc: 8½ miles from Mende. Pop. 2000.

Chanak Kalessi, a town and fort on the Dardanelles, Turkey in Asia. Pop. 2500.

Chancay, a seaport of Peru, capital of a district of the same name. It has a convenient port; 45 miles N. by W. of Lima.

Chanda, a town of Hindostan, in Berar, seated on a branch of the Godavery; 78 miles S. of Nagpour. Long. 79. 54. E. lat. 20. 2. N.

Chanderee, a town of Hindostan, capital of a district in the Malwa country, near the river Betwha. It is the residence of a rajah, and 170 miles S. of Agra. Long. 78. 43. E. lat. 24. 48. N.

Chandernagore, a town of Hindostan, in Bengal. It was the principal French settlement in the East Indies, and had a strong fort, which was destroyed by the English in 1757; and in 1793 they again dispossessed the French of this settlement. It is seated on the W. side of the Hoogly; 15 miles N. of Calcutta.

Chandor, a town of Hindostan, in the country of Baglana, taken by the English in 1804. It is 90 miles W. N. W. of Arungabad. Long. 74. 38. E. lat. 20. 8. N.

Chandraguti, a town of Hindostan, in Mysore, with a fort on a high peaked hill. The vicinity produces sandal-wood of a good quality. It is seated near the Varada, on the confines of the country; 110 miles N. by E. of Mangalore.

Chand begins the name of numerous other towns in different parts of Hindostan. It signifies the moon.

Chandui, a seaport of Colombia, near the N. point of the Gulf of Guayaquil, in the Pacific Ocean. Lat. 2. 23. S.; it is inconsiderable.

Chang-hai, a town of China, in the province of Kiang-nan. In this town, and the villages dependent on it, are more than 200,000 weavers of cloth. It is situated near the sea coast, 18 miles N. E. of Songkiang.

Chanmanning, a city of Tibet, which has been the residence of the grand lama. It is 130 miles W. of Lassa. Long. 89. 45. E. lat. 31. 0. N.

Chan-si, or Shan-see, a province of China, the N. end bordering on the great wall, and the S. on the Great Yellow River; bounded on the E. by the metropolitan province of Petcheli, and W. by Chensi, or Shen-see. The climate is salubrious and agreeable, and the soil generally fertile, though the N. part is full of mountains. Some of these are rough, wild, and uninhabited; but others are cultivated with the greatest care from top to bottom. They abound with coal, which the inhabitants pound, and make into cakes with water, a kind of fuel principally used for heating their stoves, which are constructed with brick, and in the form of small beds, so that the people sleep upon them. The country abounds with musk, porphyry, marble, lapis lazuli, and jasper, of various colours, and iron-mines, as well as salt-pits and crystals, are very common. Here are five cities of the first class, and eighty-five of the second and third. The capital is Tai-youen-fou.

Chantilly, a town of France, in the department of Oise, celebrated for a great pottery; also for a fine forest and magnificent hunting-seat. It is 17 miles N. by E. of Paris.

Chan-tong, or Shan-tung, a maritime province of the N. of China. It contains six cities of the first class, and 114 of the second and third; besides which there are, along the coast, several forts and villages of considerable note on account of their commerce; and a number of small islands in the Gulf of Leaotong, the greater part of which have very convenient harbours. This province has large manufactures of silk, and a kind of stuffs peculiar to this part of China. It is traversed by the Imperial Canal. The capital is Tsinan.

Chao-hing, a city of China, in the province of Tche-kiang, which has eight cities of the third rank under its jurisdiction. It is situate near the sea coast; 730 miles S. by E. of Pekin. Long. 120. 38. E. lat. 30. 10. N.

Chao-tcheo, a city of China, in the province of Quang-tong, situate between two navigable rivers, and celebrated for a monastery of the bonzes in its neighbourhood. It is 140 miles N. of Canton.

Chapala, a lake 15 miles in breadth, and 55 in length, in the province of Guadalaxara, Mexico, which discharges its waters by the Rio Grande de Santiago, into the Pacific Ocean; the E. end of the lake is about 200 miles N. W. of the city of Mexico.

Chaparang, or Desaprong, a city of Tibet, seated near the head of the Ganges; 90 miles westward from the Lake Mansaroar. It is 160 miles N. N. E. of Sirinagur. Long. 79. 22. E. lat. 38. 10. N.

Chapel-en-le-Frith, a town in Derbyshire, with a market on Thursday; seated on the confines of the Peak; 17 miles S. E. of Manchester, and 167 N. N. W. of London. In 1821 it had three establishments for spinning of cotton, and two for the manufacture of nails.

Chapel Hill, a town of North Carolina, in Orange county, with a university established by the state; seated on an eminence; 20 miles N. W. of Raleigh.

Chapel Izod, a village on the bank of the Liffey, on the W. side of Dublin.

Chapelle Blanche, a town of France, in the department of Maine et Loire. Pop. 3500.

Chapnier, a town of France, in the department of Lower Charente. Pop. 2800.

Charasm, or Kharism, a fertile country of Usbec Tartary, bounded on the N. by Turkestan, E. by Bokharia, S. by Chorasan, and W. by the Caspian Sea. It is divided among several Tartarian princes, of whom one takes the title of khan, with a degree of pre-eminence over the rest. Khiva is the capital, and the usual residence of the khan in winter; but during the summer he generally encamps on the banks of the river Amu.

Charcas, one of the United Provinces of South America, lying between the lat. of 18. and 21. S. and the 61st and 70th of W. long. Chuquisaca, or La Plata, is the chief town, near to which the main branch of the Pilcomayo has its source; it is bounded on the W. and S. by the province of Potosi, and is in the centre of the chief silver mining district.

Chard, a town in Somersetshire, with a market on Monday. It stands pre-eminent over all the country between the two seas; and has a copious stream, which might be easily conducted in a direction opposite that which it now takes. It is 12 miles S. S. E. of Taunton, and 139 W. by S. of London.

Charente, a department of France, including the late province of Angoumois. It is named from a river, which rises in Limosin, and runs by Angouleme, Saintes, and Rochefort, into the Bay of Biscay. Angouleme is the capital. Pop. about 325,000.

Charente, Lower, a maritime department of France, consisting of the two late provinces of Aunis and Saintonge. Rochefort, Rochelle, and Marennes on the coasts, and Saintes and St. Jean d'Angely, are the principal towns in this department, and in which the isles of Re and Oleron are included. It is a fertile district, and exports a considerable quantity of brandy. Pop. 395,000.

Charenton, a town of France, about 5 miles S. E. of Paris, celebrated for its iron-works. There is another town of the same name in the department of the Cher.

Charite, a town of France, in the department of Nievre, with manufactures of woollen and hardware. Here is a priory of Benedictine Clunistes, which once, in a season of scarcity, subsisted the whole town by its bounty; and hence it derives its name. It is seated on the E. bank of the Loire; 15 miles N. by W. of Nevers. Pop. about 4000.

Charkow. *See* Kharkoff.

Charlbury, a town 5 miles from Woodstock, in Oxfordshire, England. It holds four large cattle fairs annually. The greater part of the population are employed in the manufacture of gloves, and other articles of leather.

Charlemont, a tn. of Ireland, in the county of Armagh, seated on the river Blackwater; 6 miles S. of Dungannon, and 68 N. of Dublin.

Charlemont, a fortified town of France, on the frontier of the Netherlands, in the department of Ardennes; seated on a craggy mountain, by the river Meuse; 20 miles N. E. of Rocroy. Pop. about 4000.

Charleroi, a town of Belgium, in the county of Namur. It has been often taken. It is seated on the Sambre; 18 miles W. of Namur, and 32 S. of Brussels.

Charles, Cape, a promontory of Virginia, forming the N. point to the entrance of Chesapeake Bay. Long. 76. 14. W. lat. 37. 12. N.

Charles, Cape, the N. point of an island in the South Channel of Hudson's Strait, leading into Hudson's Bay. Long. 74. 15. W. lat. 62. 46. N.

Charles, a county in the S. W. part of the state of Maryland, lying between the Patuxent and Potomac rivers. Pop. 16,023, 9182 of whom were slaves. Port Tobacco, at the head of an inlet of the Potomac, 65 miles S. of Baltimore, is the chief town.

Charles City, a county of Virginia, extending for about 15 miles along the N. side of James River, being about 6 miles in mean breadth; bounded on the N. by the Chickahomino river. The court-house of the county is 30 miles S. E. by E. of Richmond. Pop. 4774, 2433 of whom were slaves.

Charles River, a small river of Massachusets, falling into the Boston Harbour, on the N. E. side of the town.

Charles, St., a parish of Louisiana, lying on both sides of the Mississippi; bounded on the N. by the lakes Maurepas and Pontchartrain; it is a swampy district, containing about 300 square miles. Pop. 4700. The court-house of the district is 45 miles W. of New Orleans. Also the name of a county in the state of Missouri, being a nook formed by the Missouri and Mississippi rivers, opposite to the junction of the Illinois with the latter. Pop. 7911. The chief town, of the same name, on the N. bank of the Missouri, is 21 miles N. W. of St. Louis.

Charleston, a maritime district of the state of South Carolina, extending for about 70 miles along the shore of the Atlantic Ocean, in a north-eastern direction, from the lat. of 32. 30. to 33. 5. N., and inland about 50 miles; it is bounded on the N. by the Santee river, and intersected by Ashley, Cooper, and one or two other rivers of inferior note. It contains a good deal of swampy land; but is, on the whole, very productive in maize, rice, and cotton. The coast is broken into numerous islands, which yield a cotton of very superior quality, known by the name of Sea Island. Pop. 82,661.

Charleston City, the chief place of the above district, and fifth in rank and importance in all the United States of North America; it is advantageously located on a point of land between the rivers Ashley and Cooper, which unite just below the city, forming a commodious harbour, protected from the swell of the ocean by Sullivan's Island, about 7 miles distant, and by three forts. The lighthouse, at the southern entrance of the harbour, is in lat. 32. 42. N. and 79. 46. W. long.; a sand-bar precludes the entrance of vessels of large burthen, there being only 16 ft. of water in the deepest channel, and the highest tides rising only 6 ft. The principal streets of the city run parallel to each other from river to river, intersected by others at right angles. It contains about 20 places of religious worship, a city hall, theatre, and several other public buildings. Independent of its being the focus of all the commerce of the state, and of part of North Carolina and Georgia, it is much resorted to by visitors from the northern states, and from the West Indies, who indulge greatly in gaming and dissipation. The population in 1790 was 16,360, and is now 29,261. For the extent of its commerce see Carolina, South.

Charlestown, a town of Massachusets, united to Boston by a wooden bridge, about 1500 feet in length, over Charles River. The marine hospital, state prison, and United States navy yard, are all on the Charlestown side of the river. It has six or seven places of religious worship; also some of the most commodious private wharfs of any belonging to the port; and, being the outlet of Boston to the states of New Hampshire and Maine, it constitutes a very important section of the port of Boston, which see. Breeds Hill, or Bunkers Hill, celebrated in the history of the revolutionary war, lies on the E. side of the town; it is merely an undulation of the soil, not exceeding 30 feet above the level of the sea. Pop. 11,484.

There are several other towns named *Charleston* and *Charlestown*, in different parts of the United States.

Charlestown is also the name of the principal town in the island of Nevis, and of a town of the island of Barbadoes.

Charlestown, a town of Scotland, in Aberdeenshire, much frequented by invalids, for the benefit of goats' whey. It is seated near the Dee; 28 miles W. by S. of Aberdeen.

Charleville, a town of Ireland, on the N. boundary of the county of Cork. It has a Roman Catholic school, supported by voluntary subscriptions; it has 11 other schools. It is situate on the high road from Limerick to Cork, about 20 miles distance from each, and 108 W. S. W. of Dublin.

Charleville, a town of France, in the department of Ardennes. Here is a magnificent square, and in the centre a handsome fountain. It has extensive manufactures of fire-arms, and is seated on the Meuse, opposite Mezieres; 25 miles W. N. W. of Sedan. Pop. about 8000.

Charlotte, a county of Virginia, extending

for about 25 miles along the N. side of the Roanoke river, being about 12 miles in breadth, intersected by several streams falling into the Roanoke. Pop. 11,595. Marysville, about 70 miles S. S. W. of Richmond, is the chief town.

CHARLOTTE, a town in Monroe county, New York, situate on the W. bank of the Genessee river, at its entrance into Lake Ontario; 240 miles W. by N. of Albany. Pop. about 2000. Also the name of a town in Vermont, on the E. bank of Lake Champlain.

Charlotte, and *Charlotteville*, is also the name of several other townships in the United States of North America.

CHARLOTTENBURG, a town of Brandenburg, in the Middle Mark, with a royal palace, and magnificent gardens. It was built by Sophia Charlotte, the first queen of Prussia, on the river Spree; 4 miles W. of Berlin.

CHARLOTTE-TOWN, the capital of the isle of St. John, (now Prince Edward Island,) in the Gulf of St. Lawrence. It stands on a point of land, on the S. W. side of the island, which forms two bays. Long. 62. 50. W. lat. 46. 14. N.

CHARLOTTE-TOWN, the capital of Dominica, formerly called Roseau. In 1806 it was nearly destroyed by a hurricane. It is 21 miles S. E. of Prince Rupert Bay. Long. 61. 28. W. lat. 15. 18. N.

CHARLTON. There are upwards of twenty villages of this name in England. It is also the name of a town in Saratoga county, New York; 24 miles N. of Albany, pop. about 2000, and of another town in Worcester county, Massachusets.

CHARLTON ROW, a township in the parish of Manchester. *See* MANCHESTER.

CHARMES, a town of France, in the department of Vosges, seated on the Moselle; 8 miles E. of Mirecourt.

CHAROLLES, a city of France, in the department of Saone and Loire, with a ruinous castle; seated on the Reconce; 24 miles W. N. W. of Macon. Pop. 2518.

CHAROST, a town of France, in the department of Indre, seated on the Arnon; 6 miles N. E. of Issoudun.

CHARROUZ, a town of France, in the department of Vienne; 25 miles S. of Poitiers.

CHARTRE, LA, a town of France, in the department of Sarthe; 13 miles S. W. from Calais. Pop. 1551.

CHARTRES, a city of France, capital of the department of Eure and Loire. The cathedral is one of the finest in France, and its steeple is much admired. The principal trade consists in corn. It is seated on the Eure, over which is a bridge, the work of the celebrated Vauban; 45 miles S. W. of Paris. Pop. about 13,000.

CHARYBDIS, a famous whirlpool, in the Strait of Messina, on the coast of Sicily, opposite the celebrated Scylla, in Italy. According to the theme of ancient poets, it was very formidable to mariners; but it is said to have been entirely removed by the great earthquake in 1783.

CHATAHOUCHEE, a rapid river of the state of Georgia, which rises in the Apalachian mountains, on the frontier of Tennessee, and runs S. for 300 miles to East Florida, where it is joined by the Flint, and then their united stream takes the name of Apalachicola. It separates the state of Alabama from that of Georgia, for about 100 miles before it enters Florida.

CHATEAUBRIAND, a town of France, in the N. part of the department of Lower Loire; 35 miles N. by E. of Nantes. Pop. about 3000.

CHATEAU CAMBRESIS, a town of France, in the department of Nord, with a palace belonging to the bishop of Cambray. A treaty was concluded here in 1559, between Henry II. of France, and Philip II. of Spain. It is seated on the Scille; 14 miles S. E. of Cambray. Pop. about 4000.

CHATEAU CHINON, a town of France, in the department of Nievre, with a considerable manufacture of cloth; seated near the source of the Yonne; 36 miles E. by N. of Nevers. Pop. 3300.

CHATEAU DAUPHIN, a strong castle of Piedmont, near the source of the Po; 16 miles W. by N. of Saluzzo.

CHATEAUDUN, a town of France, in the department of Eure and Loire, with a castle, built by the famous Count of Dunois; seated on an eminence near the Loire; 30 miles N. of Blois. It was entirely burnt down in 1723, but was speedily rebuilt. Pop. about 6000.

CHATEAU DU LOIR, a town of France, in the department of Sarte, famous for a siege of seven years against the Count of Mans. It is seated on the Loire; 22 miles S. S. E. of Mans.

CHATEAUGAY, a town of Franklin county, state of New York, situate midway between Lake Champlain and the St. Lawrence; 210 miles N. by W. of Albany. Population, 2824. There is a small river of the same name, falling into the St. Lawrence.

CHATEAU GONTIER, a town of France, in the department of Mayenne, with a castle, a mineral spring, and a trade in linens. It is seated on the Mayenne; 22 miles N. W. of Angers. Pop. about 5500.

CHATEAU LANDON, a town of France, in the department of Seine and Marne, with an Augustine abbey; seated on a hill; 30 miles S. of Melun.

CHATEAULIN, a town of France, in the department of Finisterre, with a considerable trade in slates; seated on the Auzon; 12 miles N. of Quimper.

CHATEAU MEILLANT, a town of France, in the department of Cher; 8 miles from La Chatre. Pop. 2281.

CHATEAU NEUF, a town of France, in the department of Charente, on the river Charente; 12 miles from Angouleme. Pop. 2300.

CHATEAU RENARD, a town of France, in the department of Bouches du Rhone; 10 miles from Tarascon. Pop. 3200.

CHATEAUROUX, a town of France, capital of the department of Indre, with a castle. It has a manufacture of cloth, and iron mines in its vicinity, and is seated in a pleasant plain, on the Indre; 35 miles S. W. of Bourges, and 148 S. by W. of Paris. Pop. about 8500.

CHATEAU SALINS, a town of France, in the department of Meurthe, with extensive salt-works; 16 miles N. E. of Nancy.

CHATEAU THIERRY, a town of France, in the department of Aisne, with a castle on an eminence. It is the birthplace of the celebrated Fontaine, and famous for a battle fought near it, in February, 1814, when a part of Marshal Blucher's army was defeated with great loss, and driven through the town by the French under Buonaparte. It is seated on the river Marne; 57 miles E. S. E. of Paris. Pop. about 4000.

The names of several other towns in France are preceded by *Chateau*, but there are none that merit any particular notice.

CHATEL, a town of France, in the department of Vosges, seated on the Moselle; 8 miles N. of Epinal.

CHATEL CHALON, a town of France, in the department of Jura; 25 miles E. N. E. of Lons le Saunier.

CHATELLERAULT, a town of France, in the department of Vienne, noted for its cutlery, watchmaking, and the cutting of false diamonds; seated on the Vienne, over which there is one of the finest bridges in France; 22 miles N. E. of Poitiers. Pop. about 8000.

CHATENOY, a town of France, in the department of Vosges; 6 miles S. E. of Neufchateau.

CHATHAM, a borough in the county of Kent, England, situate on the S. bank of the river Medway, about 8 miles above its confluence with the Thames. It is one of the stations for building, fitting, and victualling of the national marine; and the apparatus and accommodation for this purpose, in conjunction with its fortifications, and marine and artillery barracks, render it one of the most magnificent establishments of the kind in the world, and every way worthy of the distinguished character of the British nation. The local advantages of its situation are very great, whilst the lines of the fortifications command the segment of a circle from the river, of several miles in extent, and are as complete and efficient as art and execution can make them; there are six slips for building ships of the first rate, and four docks for repairing; and twelve to fifteen first-rate ships are generally lying off the town. The dockyard was first established in the time of Elizabeth; and the Dutch, in the hey-day of their valour, in 1667, ascended with a naval force up the river, and did considerable damage. In 1558, the fund for relieving the wounded in the naval service was established at Chatham; but the *chest* (the term by which the accounts of the fund was called) was transferred to Greenwich in 1802. In 1592 an hospital for decayed marines, shipwrights, and their widows, was founded by Sir John Hawkins. The hospital has been rebuilt within the present century, on a commodious and extensive scale. This town was very inconsiderable till after the peace with Holland in 1678. Chatham is 30 miles E. S. E. of London Bridge, on the road from London to Dover. It has a weekly market on Saturdays, and returns one member to parliament.

CHATHAM, an interior county of North Carolina, intersected by Cape Fear river. Pop. 16,242, of whom 5316 are slaves. Pittsborough, 36 miles W. of Raleigh, is the chief town.

CHATHAM, a maritime county of Georgia, bounded on the N. W. by the Savannah river, which divides it from South Carolina. Pop. (including the city of SAVANNAH, which see,) 18,081, of whom 11,331 are slaves, and 669 free blacks.

CHATHAM, a town in Colombia county, state of New York, on the E. bank of the Hudson river. Pop. 3662; 22 miles E. of Albany.

There are several other towns of the same name in different parts of the United States of North America.

CHATHAM ISLAND, an island of the Pacific Ocean, discovered by Captain Broughton in 1791, off the E. coast of New Zealand. It was attached to the government of those islands in 1840. It lies 450 miles E. by S. of Cook Strait, in New Zealand, in lat. 44. S. and long. 176. 0. E. It is 40 miles long by 28 broad, and is inhabited by a tribe of New Zealanders, who emigrated here in 1835.

CHATRAKAL, a fort and district of Mysore. *See* CHITTLEDROOG.

CHATRE, LA, a town of France, in the department of Indre, with a woollen manufacture; seated on the Indre; 22 miles S. S. E. of Chateauroux. Pop. about 4000.

CHATSWORTH, a village in the Peak of Derbyshire, near the river Derwent; 6 miles W. of Chesterfield. Here is a magnificent seat of the Dukes of Devonshire, which, for its fine situation, park, gardens, fountains, &c., is justly deemed one of the wonders of the Peak. In its first age it was the prison of Mary Queen of Scots, for 17 years, and afterwards of the French Marshal Tallard, taken prisoner at the battle of Blenheim.

CHATTERIS, a town of Cambridgeshire, England. It is 75 miles N. by E. of London, and 11 W. of the city of Ely.

CHATTERPOUR, a town of Hindostan, in the country of Allahabad, capital of the circar of Bundelcund. It is 130 miles W. S. W. of Allahabad. Long. 79. 56. E. lat. 25. 0. N.

CHATTILLON, a town of Piedmont; 10 miles S. E. of Aoust. There are several towns in France, called *Chattillon*, which implies a town, and as such is generally a prefix, as Chattillon-sur-Seine, sur-Loire, &c., &c., implying Chattillon, or the town, on the Seine, Loire, &c. There are none that merit any particular notice.

CHATTONNAY, a town of France, in the department of Isere; 12 miles E. of Vienne, an. 22 S. E. of Lyons.

CHAUDIERE, a river of Lower Canada, whic falls into the St. Lawrence, about 6 miles below Quebec; it rises on the frontier of the state o

Maine, and, 4 miles above the St. Lawrence, it forms a magnificent cataract of 360 feet, called the Chaudiere Falls.

CHAUMONT, a town of France, capital of the department of Upper Marne. Here is a manufacture of woollen cloth, and a trade in deer and goat skins. It is seated on a mountain, near the river Marne; 55 miles E. by S. of Troyes. Pop. about 6000. It is also the name of another town in the department of the Loire, about 5 miles E. by N. of St. Etienne. Pop. about 500. It is also the name of several other towns in different parts of France.

CHAUMONT, a town of Jefferson county, state of New York, beautifully located at the head of a small bay, at the E. end of Lake Ontario; 185 miles N. W. of Albany. Pop. about 1200.

CHAUNY, a town of France, in the department of Aisne, on the river Oise; 20 miles E. of Noyon. Pop. about 450.

CHAUTAUQUE, a county at the S. W. extremity of the state of New York, bordering on the S. on Pennsylvania, and W. on Lake Erie. There is a lake of the same name, about 10 miles in length and two broad, in the centre of the county, which discharges its waters, by the Allegany river, into the Ohio, although the N. W. end of the lake is within 6 or 7 miles of that of Erie. Pop. 47,975. The chief town, called also Chautauque, or Mayville, situate at the N. W. end of the lake, is 364 miles W. by S. of Albany.

CHAUX DE FONDS, a village of Switzerland, in the principality of Neufchatel. The inhabitants, about 3000, make numerous watches and clocks; and the women are employed in the lace manufacture. It is seated in a fertile valley; 9 miles N. N. W. of Neufchatel. Pop. about 3000.

CHAVES, a town of Portugal, in Tra los Montes, with two suburbs, and two forts. Between the town and the suburb Magdalena, is a Roman stone bridge. It stands near the confines of Spain, on the river Tamega; 26 miles W. of Braganza.

CHAZY, a small river in Clinton county, state of New York, which falls into Lake Champlain. A town of the same name, on the N. bank of the river, 186 miles due N. of Albany, contains about 2000 inhabitants.

CHEADLE, a town in Staffordshire, with a market on Saturday. Here is a large tape manufactory, and in the vicinity are several copper and brass works, and rich coal mines. 4 miles S. E. are the ruins of Croxden Abbey. It is seated in the most fertile part of the Moorland; 12 miles N. N. E. of Stafford, and 146 N. W. of London.

CHEBUCTO BAY, Nova Scotia. *See* HALIFAX.

CHEDABUCTO BAY, at the east end of Nova Scotia, opening into the Atlantic Ocean, at the entrance of the Gulf of Canso, in lat. 45. 20. N. and 61. of W. long. Salmon River, which abounds in the estimable fish of that name, falls into this bay.

CHEDDER, a village contiguous to Axminster, in Somersetshire, England. It is situate in a delightfully picturesque part of the county, on the S. W. side of the Mendip Hills, and is deservedly celebrated for the excellence of its cheese.

CHEDUBA, an island in the Bay of Bengal, on the coast of Birmah; 45 miles long and 10 broad. It yields abundance of rice, and the most western point is in long. 93. 35. E. lat. 18. 56. N.

CHEGO MUDDI, a town of Hindostan, in the country of Cutch, at the mouth of the Caggar; 23 miles S. W. of Bhooj, near the mouth of the eastern branch of the Indus.

CHEITORE, or CHITORE, a town of Hindostan, in the territory of Odipour. It was the capital of the ranna, or chief prince, of the Rajpoots, in the days of his greatness; and was a fortress and city of great extent, situate on a mountain; but it has been in ruins since the time of Aurungzebe, in 1681. It is 46 miles N. N. E. of Oudipour, and 88 S. S. W. of Agimere. E. long. 74. 50. and 24. 35. N. lat.

CHELICUT, a town of Abyssinia, in the province of Tigré, with one of the finest churches in the kingdom, ornamented with paintings, and has been the residence of the ras, or sovereign.

CHELM, a town of Poland, in Red Russia, capital of a palatinate of its name, and a bishop's see. In 1794 the Poles were defeated by the Prussians near this town. It is 100 miles E. S. E. of Warsaw. Long. 23. 29. E. lat. 51. 20. N.

CHELMSFORD, the county town of Essex, with a market on Friday. Here is a stately church, a magnificent shire-house, theatre, and barracks, an excellent conduit, and a free school, founded by Edward VI. It is situate at the confluence of the Can with the Chelmer; 29 miles E. N. E. of London.

CHELMSFORD, a town of Massachusetts, in Middlesex county, situate on the S. side of the Merrimac, over which is a curious bridge, at Patucket Falls, which connects this town with Dracut. It is 28 miles N. N. W. of Boston. A canal from the Merrimac to Boston harbour commences at Chelmsford, which contributes considerably to its importance and interest, having an extensive quarry of very fine granite in its vicinity. Pop. 1697.

CHELSEA, a parish lying along the N. bank of the Thames, to the S. W. of London, and to which it forms an integral part. This section of the metropolis is distinguished for its hospital for the support of decayed and maimed soldiers, founded in the time of Charles II.; its chief promoter was Sir Stephen Fox, who contributed 13,000*l.* towards the building; it was finished in the time of William and Mary. The building is a quadrangle, the wings extending towards the river; the base, which is nearly 800 feet in extent, is entered from the centre of the north front, into a noble vestibule; the E. side is appropriated to a chapel, and the W. to a hall, in which the inmates dine; the wings, which are divided into wards, are each 360 feet in length, 80 wide, and three stories high; the infirmary, and other outbuildings, and gardens, compose an area of nearly 50 acres. Sir Christopher Wren was the architect; and, in respect to proportion and convenience, the edifice is worthy of his high reputation, and the whole produces an imposing effect; but being built mostly of brick, it is inferior in magnificence to the marine hospital at Greenwich. The number of inmates is 336, exclusive of officers and the necessary attendants; there are about 20,000 out-pensioners. In 1801 a military asylum, contiguous to the hospital, was established for the education of 1000 children of non-commissioned officers and soldiers, towards the support of which the whole army contributes one day's pay per ann.; the building, which is principally of brick, cost about 150,000*l.* Chelsea is also distinguished for its botanic garden, formed by Sir Hans Sloane, and presented by him, in 1721, to the Apothecaries' Company of London, on condition of paying a quit-rent of 5*l.* per annum and presenting annually to the Royal Society fifty different specimens of plants grown in the garden, until the number of new specimens amounted to 2000. The hospital is about two miles W. S. W. of Westminster Abbey, and 4 miles in the same direction from the Royal Exchange.

Cheltenham, a borough in Gloucestershire, England, situate in a fertile vale near the foot of the Coldswold Hills; 94 miles N. W. of London, on the road to Gloucester. Till within the present century it was an inconsiderable place, participating partially in the woollen manufactures of the neighbouring district. It acquired some distinction by the discovery of a medicinal spring in 1740; and, being visited by George III. in 1788, it became somewhat celebrated; the population, however, in 1801 amounted only to 3076, since which it has greatly increased in numbers and importance, and is one of the chief resorts of gaiety and fashion in the kingdom. A theatre was erected in 1803; baths, assembly-rooms, libraries, public walks, and other attractions, have progressively been extended for the accommodation of an increasing population. Its waters, which increase in quantity in proportion to the demand for them, and increase of visitors, operate both as aperient and restorative, being impregnated with salts, sulphur, steel, and calcareous earth. The parish church is an ancient and venerable structure; there are several sectarian places of worship; its market, on Thursday, is well supplied with every necessary. It returns one member to parliament.

Chelum, or Jailum, a river of Asia, the westernmost of the five eastern branches of the Indus. It rises above Cashmere, flows through the province of that name into the Punjaub, and joins the Chunaub, 16 miles below Kooshaub. This river is the Hydaspes of Alexander.

Chelva, or Chulilla, a town of Spain, situate on the N. bank of the Guadalaviar; about 20 miles N. W. of Valencia.

Chemille, a town of France, in the province of Anjou; 20 miles S. S. E. from Angers. Pop. 3300.

Chemnitz, or Kemnitz, a town of Upper Saxony, in Misnia, surrounded by walls and ditches. It has four suburbs, and a castle about a mile from the town. Great quantities of cottons, and other fine stuffs, are made here; and the bleaching business is considerable. It is situate on a river of the same name, 38 miles S. W. of Dresden, and about the same distance S. E. of Leipsic. Pop. about 10,000.

Chemnitz, a town in the circle of Leutmeritz, in Bohemia; about 42 miles S. E. of Dresden.

Chenango, an interior county on the S. side of the state of New York; it is intersected by a river of the same name, which flows from N. to S. into the Susquehannah; the population is 40,785, the county being divided into seventeen townships. Norwich, 111 miles W. by S. of Albany, containing 4145 inhabitants, is the chief town; there is also a town of the same name at the entrance of the river into the Susquehannah, in the adjoining county of Broome, near the frontier of Pennsylvania; 148 miles W. S. W. of Albany.

Chenapatam, or Chinnypatam, a town of Hindostan, in Mysore, near which is a handsome stone fort. It has manufactures of sugar, glass, and excellent music-wire, and a great trade in the produce of the palm gardens in its vicinity. It is 40 miles E. N. E. of Seringapatam.

Chencour, or Chemkon, a town of Armenia, on the frontiers of Georgia, with a beautiful castle, grand caravansaries, and several mosques; 169 miles N. E. of Erivan.

Chen-si, or Shen-si, a western frontier province of China, lying between the lat. of 32. and 38. N. and 103. to 110. of E. long. It is bounded on the S. by the province of Setchuen, and on the E. partially by the province of Honan, but mainly by the Hoang-ho, or Great Yellow River which divides it from Chan-si, on the N., partly by the great wall which divides it from Chinese Tartary; and on the W. by the dreary country of the Monguls, containing an area of about 147,000 square miles. The Hoang-ho, in the eccentricity of its course, skirts the N. W. part of the province, running in a northerly direction; whilst on the E. it runs a course due S. Numerous streams intersect this province in all directions, some falling into the Hoang-ho on the W., and some into the same river on the E., and others into the Kiang Kien, or Great River, which intersects the province of Setchuen. A province so extensive, as may be expected, comprises much diversity of soil and features. It abounds with drugs, rhubarb, musk, cinnabar, wax, honey, and coals, of which last it contains inexhaustible veins. It has also rich gold mines, which, for political reasons, are not allowed to be opened. It produces little rice, but plentiful crops of wheat and millet; but it is occasionally subject to long droughts, when clouds of locusts, from the forests of Mongul Tartary, destroy the entire vegetation of extensive districts; the inhabitants, however, make food of the locusts, and esteem them as a delicacy. The population is estimated at upwards of 30,000,000.

Chen-yang, Chin-yan, or Mouk-den, a city of Eastern Tartary, capital of a province of the same name, otherwise called *Leaotong.* It is situate on the bank of a fine river, running S. into the Gulf of Leaotong. The walls are 10 miles in cicumference; and it is ornamented with several public edifices, and provided with arsenals and storehouses. It is 350 miles E. N. E. of Pekin. Long. 123. 5. E. lat. 41. 55. N.

CHEPELLO, an island in the Bay of Panama, about 20 miles from the city of Panama, which it supplies with provisions and fruit.

CHEPSTOW, a town in Monmouthshire, with a market on Saturday. It is seated on the side of a hill, on the Wye, near its confluence with the Severn. It was surrounded by a wall, traces of which are observable; and on a perpendicular rock are the remains of a large castle. Here was also a priory, part of which is converted into a church; and comparatively, it was in former times of much greater consequence than at present. It is now the port of entry for all the towns on the rivers Wye and Lug, and fits a few ships annually to the Baltic and British America, for timber, deals, &c.; ships coastway, a considerable quantity of timber, bark, &c. and has two ship-yards, where vessels of 500 to 600 tons are generally in a course of building. The spring tides rise to the height of 60 feet; which is consequently attended with great inconvenience, and preclude it from materially extending its commerce. There is a fine bridge of iron over the Wye, erected at the joint expense of the counties of Monmouth and Gloucester. It is about 10 miles N. of Bristol, and 130 W. N. W. of London.

CHER, an interior department in the centre of France, including part of the late province of Berry. It receives its name from a river which rises in Auvergne, and flows into the Loire, below Tours. Bourges, 126 miles due S. of Paris, is the capital. It contains about 3000 square miles, and 230,000 inhabitants.

CHERASCO, a fortified town of Piedmont, capital of a fertile territory of the same name, with a strong citadel. It is seated on a mountain, at the confluence of the Stura with the Tanaro; 24 miles S. S. E. of Turin. Pop. about 11,000.

CHERBOURG, a seaport of France, in the department of Manche, with an Augustine abbey. Here was a sea-fight between the English and French, in 1692, when the latter were beaten, and upwards of twenty of their men-of-war burnt near Cape la Hogue. The English landed here in 1758, took the town, with the ships in the basin, demolished the fortifications, and ruined the works for improving the harbour. These works were resumed on a stupendous scale by Louis XVI.; but their progress was interrupted by the revolution, resumed again under Napoleon Buonaparte in 1803, and the works destroyed by the fury of the elements in 1808; after which a new plan of operations was resolved upon, by excavating a basin out of the reach of the violence of the ocean, which, by 1813, was so far accomplished as to hold fifty sail of the line, having 50 feet depth of water. Other works of corresponding magnitude have since been carried on, and it now appears destined to become the chief naval station of France, and to rival in extent and magnificence every establishment of the like kind in the world. Its situation is very advantageous, either for dispatching a fleet to any part of the world, west or south; or for commanding the Channel between France and England, being about 70 miles due S. of the S. side of the Isle of Wight, and 190 W. N. W. of Paris; in N. lat. 49. 39. and 1. 37. W. long.

CHERIBON, a seaport on the N. coast of the Island of Java, about 150 miles E. of Batavia; it exports large quantities of coffee.

CHEROKEES, an Indian tribe, occupying an extensive tract of country between the Chattahoochee and Tennessee rivers, comprising the N. W. part of Georgia, and the N. E. of Alabama. The Cherokees were among the bravest and noblest of the American race; but they have progressively declined in numbers and influence, as that of the Europeans has increased.

CHERONISO, a town of European Turkey, on the N. E. coast of the island of Negropont, 25 miles E. of Negropont.

CHEROY, a town of France, in the department of Yonne; 10 miles W. of Sens.

CHERRYVALLEY, an incorporated and flourishing town of New York, in Otsego county, at the head of a creek of its name; 18 miles S. of Canajohary, and 53 W. by N. of Albany. Pop. 3923. It is a place of great intercourse, being situate at the intersection of several turnpike roads.

CHERSO, an island in the Gulf of Venice, between the coasts of Istria and Croatia. On the S. it is separated from Osero by a very narrow channel, and the two islands are united by a bridge. The soil is stony; but it abounds in cattle, wine, oil, and honey. It has a town of the same name, with a good harbour. Long. 14. 45. E. lat. 45. 10. N. The two islands contain together a population of about 11,000, and were ceded to Austria by the treaty of Campo Formio, in 1797, after having for nearly eight centuries formed a part of the Venetian republic.

CHERSON, the capital of New Russia, in the government of Catharineslaf, founded by Catharine II. on the N. bank of the Dnieper, 10 miles below the influx of the Ingulec. The church and many of the houses are built of stone. Here is a dock, from which several men-of-war and merchant-ships have been launched; but owing to some sand-banks in the river, the naval establishment has been transferred hence to Nicolaef, and its commerce to Odessa; the population, which at one time amounted to about 50,000, has progressively decreased to below 10,000. In 1787 the empress made a triumphant journey to this capital, and here met Emperor Joseph II. At this place, in 1790, the philanthropic Howard fell a victim to his indefatigable humanity; and a monument was erected to his memory by the Russian admiral. Cherson is 50 miles E. of Oczakow. Long. 32. 56. E. lat. 56. 58. N.

CHERTSEY, a town in Surrey, with a market on Wednesday. Here was formerly an abbey, of which only a part of the walls now remain;

it was the first burial-place of Henry VI., who was afterwards removed to Windsor. It is seated near the Thames, over which is a handsome bridge; 20 miles W. by S. of London.

CHESAPEAKE, the largest and safest bay in the United States. Its entrance is between Cape Charles, in Maryland, and Cape Henry, in Virginia; 12 miles wide. It extends 270 miles to the N.; is from 10 to 40 miles broad, and generally 9 fathoms deep; containing several islands and many commodious harbours. It receives the Susquehannah, Potomac, Rappahannoc, York, and James rivers, which are all large and navigable.

CHESHAM, a town in Buckinghamshire, with a market on Wednesday, and manufactures of lace and wooden ware. It stands in a vale, 27 miles N. W. of London.

CHESHIRE, a county palatine of England, bounded on the N. by the river Mersey, which divides it from Lancashire, N. E. by Yorkshire, E. by Derbyshire, S. E. by Staffordshire, S. by Shropshire, W. by the river Dee, which divides it from Denbighshire and Flintshire, and N. W. by the Irish Sea, into which projects a peninsula, 13 miles long and 6 broad, formed by the mouths of the Mersey and the Dee. This county extends 30 miles from N. to S., and 42 from E. to W., without including the peninsula just mentioned on the W., and a narrow tract of land, which stretches between Lancashire and Derbyshire, to Yorkshire on the N. E., and containing 673,280 acres. Antecedent to the invasion of Britain by the Romans, this part of the country was occupied by a tribe called the *Cornavii;* and Cheshire was constituted a county palatine by William the Norman, who conferred it upon his nephew, Hugh Lupus; but the succeeding palatines, exercising an authority incompatible with justice to other parts of the country, such as affording sanctuary, &c., Henry VIII. abrogated most of the privileges of this palatinate, the forms of which, however, it still retains. Its principal towns, besides the city of Chester, are Stockport, Macclesfield, Congleton, and Nantwich: Stockport, at the N. E. extremity of the county, and the surrounding country, participates largely in the cotton manufacture; Macclesfield and Congleton are extensively engaged in the silk manufacture; and Nantwich is celebrated for its salt springs; and ship-building is extensively carried on at the city of Chester.

In addition to the rivers Mersey and Dee, the county of Cheshire is intersected by the rivers Wever and Bollin, and contains several small lakes well stored with fish; it is also intersected by several canals, affording it a facility of communication with all parts of the kingdom. The river Dee is united by a canal of one entire level, about 14 miles in length, from the city of Chester, to the Mersey, about 12 miles above Liverpool; other canals diverge from the city of Chester, to Northwich, and into Wales. The Trent and Mersey Canal (see RUNCORN and PRESTON) intersects the heart of the county, whilst the Duke of Bridgewater's is carried nearly parallel with the Mersey to Manchester; and the Peak Forest Canal intersects the N. E. end of the county. The E. and N. E. parts of the county supply abundance of coal and various minerals; but the distinguishing characteristics of the county are its salt and cheese; the supply of the first is inexhaustible, and celebrated for its purity; whilst the cheese stands unrivalled for the excellence of its quality The salt is produced both in a rock or solid state, and by evaporation of the water from the numerous springs. The quantity consumed in Great Britain since 1779, has averaged about 55,000 tons per annum, produced chiefly by evaporation; and the quantity exported since that time has averaged about 250,000 tons per annum, in the proportion of about 35,000 tons of rock, and the remainder produced by evaporation. The S. and W. parts of the county are the most productive in cheese, and are those in which the salt springs abound. This part of the county is rather level than hilly, and subdivided by hedgerows, well stocked with timber, into comparatively very small enclosures, intersected by numerous paved roads; which imply either a Roman origin, or perhaps were found necessary on account of the sandy prevalence of the surface. On the N. and E. side of the county about 100,000 persons are employed in the silk and cotton manufacture. *See* CONGLETON, MACCLESFIELD, and STOCKPORT. It returns four members to parliament, two for each of the divisions, northern and southern.

CHESHIRE, a county of New Hampshire, bounded on the W. for about 50 miles by the Connecticut river, which separates it from Vermont; it is about 20 miles in mean breadth and is, upon the whole, a tolerably fertile district; the S. end borders on Massachusets. Pop. 26,429. Charlestown, on the E. bank of the Connecticut river, 65 miles W., and Keene, in the interior of the county, 60 miles S. W. by W. of Concord, are the chief towns.

Cheshire is also the name of a town in Berkshire county, Massachusets, and of another in Newhaven county, Connecticut.

CHESHUNT, a parish in Hertfordshire, England. Waltham Cross, at the entrance of the parish from London, is 11 miles from Shoreditch church, on the line of the great north road.

CHESTER, a city and county in itself, ecclesiastical see, and capital of the county of Cheshire, is situate on the banks of the river Dee, at the western extremity of the county; 183 miles N. N. W. of London, and 24 due E. of Liverpool. Chester is one of the most ancient and interesting cities of England; it is surrounded by a wall, nearly 2 miles in circumference, still kept in a good state of repair, the top affording, in its entire circuit, a delightful promenade. It has four gates, in the position of the four cardinal points, two of them very ornamental, and the whole interesting for their antiquity. Within the present century this city has undergone vast improvements: formerly, the houses in the principal streets projected over the foot-path, forming a covered way five or six feet wide; which, although agreeable enough in wet weather, rendered the shops and rooms on the ground-floor dark and disagreeable, and gave an uncouth feature to the city. This defect is now wholly, or nearly so, removed, whilst several public edifices, unequalled in the British dominions for their architectural taste and grandeur, ornament different parts of the city; the most distinguished of these is the county gaol, on the site of the old castle, and the county-hall, contiguous thereto; the porticoes of these two edifices, in their appropriateness of design, exactness of proportion, and grandeur of effect, have no parallel in Britain, and cannot be surpassed in any part of the world. They were erected about the commencement of the present century, under the superintendence of Mr. Harrison, a native of the city, whose refined and correct taste is also displayed in a public library, an exchange, &c. The cathedral is a venerable structure of reddish sand-stone, built in the 8th century; there are 8 other churches, and several dissenting places of worship, a county infirmary, and several schools. Its markets, on Wednesdays and Saturdays, are abundantly supplied with every necessary of life; and it holds two annual fairs, in July and October, each of which continues several days, and are very numerously attended, giving rise to great traffic in linens from Ireland, and woollen cloths and stuffs from Yorkshire, and for the accommodation of which, a commodious hall was erected in 1809, and another in 1815. The river Dee is navigable up to the city, for vessels of considerable burthen; and ships of 300 to 400 tons are always in a course of building, and occasionally eight or ten at a time; on the whole, however, Chester has more the character of a provincial, than of a sea-port town, the contiguity of Liverpool having superseded it in its latter character. Its local jurisdiction is vested in a mayor and 24 aldermen: it returns two members to parliament. It is one of the great centres of the post-office establishment, being on the line of the mail conveyance from London to Dublin. The Irish letters to and from Liverpool, Manchester, and the West Riding of Yorkshire, concentrate at and diverge from Chester. It derives great advantage from its canal navigation. *See* CHESHIRE. A new bridge, of a single arch of 200 feet in the span, has recently been erected over the Dee, at an expense of 40,000*l.*, from a design by Mr. Thomas Harrison. The old bridge, consisting of seven arches, has within the last few years been considerably widened and improved.

CHESTER, a county at the S. E. extremity of the state of Pennsylvania, bounded on the N. E. by the Schuylkill river, and intersected by the Brandywine, celebrated for the battle fought on its E. bank, on the 11th September, 1777, when the American army sustained a severe defeat. The county is about 35 miles from N. to S., and 15 in mean breadth. Pop. 57,515. West Chester, on the E. border of the county, 18 miles from Philadelphia, on the great western road to Pittsburg, is the chief town.

CHESTER DISTRICT, a county or district in the N. part of the state of South Carolina, bounded on the E. by the Catawba river, and W. by Broad River, distant from each other about 25 miles. This district is about 20 miles from N. to S.; and contains a population of 17,747. The chief town of the same name is 60 miles N. by W. of Colombia.

There are several other towns named Chester in different parts of the United States of North America, among which are the following, with their distance and bearing from the chief town of the state in which they are respectively situate, viz.:—In Rockingham county, New Hampshire, 20 miles S. by E.; Windsor county, Vermont, 70 S.; Hampden county, Massachusets, 70 W.; Orange county, New York, 110 S.; Warren county, New York, 86 N.; Morris county, New Jersey, 33 N.; Burlington county, New Jersey, 30 N.; Delaware county, Pennsylvania, 85 W. by N.; Shenandoah county, Virginia, 190 N. W.; Cumberland county, Virginia, 45 W.; Kent county, Maryland, 67 N. E. by E.

CHESTERFIELD, a borough in Derbyshire England, with a market on Saturdays. Next to Derby it is the most important trading town in the county, and situated in a fertile and most romantic district. It has mines of coal and iron in its vicinity, and a canal, communicating with the Trent below Gainsborough. Earthenware is manufactured in the neighbourhood to a great extent. It has also silk and other mills; net factories; and has recently been much improved by new streets. It has two churches, one very ancient, and noted for its crooked spire; four meeting-houses; also a handsome town-hall, a theatre, assembly rooms, baths, libraries, an ancient grammar school, and a very large market-place. It is 150 miles N. by W. of London, 12 from Sheffield, and 26 from Nottingham.

CHESTERFIELD DISTRICT, a frontier district of South Carolina, bordering on North Carolina; bounded on the E. by the Great Pedee river, and W. by Lynch's Creek; it contains 450 square miles, and a population of 8574. The chief town, of the same name, is 111 miles N. E. of Colombia.

Chesterfield is also the name of four towns in the United States of North America, viz.:—In Essex county, New York, 158 miles N.; St. Lawrence county, New York, 250 N. by W.; Cheshire county, New Hampshire, 70 S. W.; Hampshire county, Massachusets, 85 W. The bearing and distances are from the chief towns of the respective states.

CHESTERFIELD INLET, an inlet extending about 200 miles westward from the N. end of Hudson's Bay; the entrance to the inlet is in lat. 63. 30. N. long. 90. 40. W.; its mean breadth is about 15 miles.

CHESTER-LE-STREET, a parish in the county of Durham, containing 18 townships. The parish abounds in coal, and is intersected by the river Wear; the township of Chester-le-Street is situate on the W. bank of the Wear; 6 miles N. of Durham, and 18 S. of Newcastle.

Chestertown, a port of the United States, state of Maryland. Here is Washington College, incorporated in 1782; 45 miles E. S. E. of Baltimore.

Cheviot Hills, a ridge of mountains in England, which runs from N. to S. through Northumberland and Cumberland, famous for its free chase, formerly much used by the English and Scotch gentry. These hills are now chiefly wild and open sheep-walks; goats also are fed among them, and some of the finest cattle in the kingdom, in parts of the Scottish border. Near these many an obstinate battle has been fought between the English and Scots, before the two kingdoms were united; among which may be numbered the encounter between the Earls Percy and Douglas, celebrated in the ancient ballad called Chevy Chase. The altitude of the peak called Cheviot Hill, which is about 20 miles W. by N. of Alnwick, is 2658 ft. above the level of the sea; other peaks of the range rise 300 to 400 feet higher.

Chevres, a town of France, department of Charente; 8 miles from Rochefoucauld. Pop. 1300.

Chiapa, a province of the republic of Guatimala. This province extends from the lat. of 14. 50. to 17. 30. of N. lat., and lies between the long. of 90. 20. and 92. 50. W., being about 180 miles in extreme length, but the mean breadth not exceeding more than about 100 miles. The Andes run into this province in broken ridges at its S. E. extremity; but, towards its more western boundary, the grand mountain chain may be said to be completely divided. The Tabasco river rises at the foot of the termination of the mountain chain, runs first in a W. N. W. direction, and afterwards takes a northerly course through the province of Tabasco, into the Bay of Campeachy, thereby affording an advantageous opening with the Atlantic Ocean. Four or five other streams of inferior importance intersect the central and eastern side of the province, all uniting into one, near its northern frontier; afterwards running through the province of Tabasco, into the Bay of Campeachy, there being no river of any note running out of Chiapa into the Pacific Ocean. With the exception of the S. E. part, Chiapa may be considered a level rather than a mountainous country, and exceedingly fertile; and having hitherto been uncursed with the discovery of any gold or silver mine, the native inhabitants are proportionably more numerous, more social, and exhibit more primitive characteristics than in any other part of the western hemisphere. Nearly all the animated creatures and vegetable productions common to the tropical section of this division of the globe are common in Chiapa. The most prominent of the animal race is the horse, the breed of which, first introduced from Europe, is deservedly celebrated, and cherished with great care by the inhabitants, with whom the horse constitutes the most important branch of traffic, great numbers being constantly sent into Mexico. Its forests will supply abundance of cypress, cedar, pine, walnut, and other timber, whilst the cultivated parts will yield abundance of cotton, cocoa, coffee, sugar, and cochineal, with a boundless variety of aromatic resins, gums, and dyes, to constitute fit and ample equivalents to exchange for the varied useful productions of European art. Most of the domestic animals and fowls common to Europe, as well as the horse, have become naturalized in Chiapa, and in greater plenty and excellence than in almost any other part of America S. of the United States; and its climate, in reference to its geographical position, being of a congenial and mean, rather than of an extreme temperature, it affords as favourable a domicile for a portion of the population of the denser inhabited parts of Europe, as any part of the world. *See* Villa Hermosa.

Chiapa, the chief town of the preceding province, is situate on the W. side of the river Tabasco, near the N. W. extremity of the province, in the lat. of 17. 5. N. and 92. 40. of W. long. The number of inhabitants is estimated at 20,000, chiefly Indians; hence it is called *Chiapa dos Indios*, in contradistinction to another town about 20 miles W., called *Chiapa dos Espagnols*, in consequence of its being inhabited chiefly by persons of Spanish descent; the latter is sometimes called *Ciudad Real*, and is the see of a bishop, having a stately cathedral, and several monastic establishments; its population is, however, inconsiderable, not exceeding more than 2000.

Chiarenza. *See* Clarenza.

Chiari, a town of Italy, in Bresciano, wher the Austrians defeated the French in 1701. It is situate between two rivers which fall into the Oglio, on the E. side; 15 miles N. N. E. of Crema. Pop. 8000.

Chiaromonte, a town of Sicily, in Val di Noto, seated on a mountain; 25 miles W. of Syracuse; it gave the surname to the family of the virtuous and amiable Pope Pius VII.

Chiavari, a town of the territory of Genoa, situate at the mouth of a river falling into the gulf; about 20 miles S. E. of Genoa. It has several manufactures. Pop. about 8000.

Chiavenna, a town of North Italy, capital of a country of its name, subject to the Grisons. It is a trading place, especially in wine and delicate fruits, being the principal communication between the Milanese and Germany. The governor's palace and the churches are magnificent; and the inhabitants are Roman Catholics. Here are the ruins of a once celebrated fortress, on the summit of a rock; and close to the town is a rock of asbestos. It is seated on the banks of the river Maira, which falls into the N. end of the Lake of Como. Pop. about 3000. The district, which is mountainous, contains a population of about 18,000.

Chicasaws, or Chickasaws, a nation of American Indians, settled on the head branches of the Tombeckbe and Yazoo rivers, in the N. E. corner of the state of Mississippi; the N. W. extremity of their territory jets upon the river of that name; they have seven towns, the central one of which is in long. 89. 43. W. lat. 34. 23. N.

CHICHACOTTA, a fortified town of Bootan, on the S. frontier, frequently taken and relinquished by the British India troops, in the war with the Booteeas in 1772. It is 84 miles S. by E. of Tassasudon. Long. 89. 35. E. lat. 26. 35. N.

CHICHESTER, a city, and the capital of Sussex, and a county of itself, governed by a mayor, with a market on Wednesday and Saturday, and sends two members to parliament. It is a bishop's see, and has seven churches, beside the cathedral, a spacious edifice, 410 ft. in length, with a tower, surmounted by a spire rising to the height of 297 feet. The city is walled round, and had formerly four gates. It exports corn, malt, &c., has some foreign commerce, and a manufacture of needles. The haven affords fine lobsters. It is seated in a plain, on the river Levant, near its entrance into an arm of the English Channel; 12 miles E. N. E. of Portsmouth, and 61 S. W. of London.

CHIDLANA, a town of Spain, province of Andalusia; seated on a canal which is connected with the Cadiz harbour; 17 miles from Cadiz. Pop. 10,000.

CHIELEFA, a town of European Turkey, in the Morea, near the Gulf of Coron; 14 miles W. of Colokythia.

CHIEM-SEE, a lake of Bavaria, 35 miles in circumference. In the midst of it are two islands; on one of them is a convent of Benedictine nuns, and on the other an Augustine monastery. It lies 22 miles W. N. W. of Salzburg, and discharges its waters by the river Alza, in a northerly direction, into the Inn.

CHIERI, a town of Piedmont, surrounded by an ancient wall, in which are six gates. It has four grand squares; many churches and religious houses, and considerable manufactures of cloth and silk. It is 7 miles E. of Turin. Pop. about 11,000.

CHIETI. *See* CIVITA DI CHIETI.

CHIGWELL, a village in Essex; 10 miles N.E. of London. It is noted for a free-school, founded by Archbishop Harsnett, where William Penn was educated.

CHIHUAHUA, a city in the province of Cohahuila, situate in the lat. of 28. 50. N. on the high road from the city of Mexico to Santa Fe; about 700 miles N. N. W. of Mexico. Chihuahua is a considerable place, having several public buildings, and about 16,000 inhabitants. The principal church is a beautiful edifice: the surrounding country is productive in silver.

CHILCA, a small seaport of Peru; about 30 miles S. of Lima.

CHILI, or CHILE, a territory of South America, extending from the lat. of 24. 20. to 43. 50. S. and from 68. 50. to 74. 20. of W. long.; bounded on the W. by the Pacific Ocean, and on the E. by the Andes, which divide it from the United Provinces of Buenos Ayres; being about 1350 miles in length, from N. to S., and 130 in mean breadth, in a position from the S., of N. N. E. Antecedent to the irruption of the Spaniards into this part of the world, Chili was divided into several independent states, of whom the earliest information hitherto obtained respecting them is, that in 1450, Upanqui, the then Inca of Peru, made inroads upon the Chilian territory, and subdued the four northern provinces; at the southern boundary of which their progress was stayed by the bravery of a tribe called the Promancians. The Peruvians, however, remained masters of the four provinces, up to the period of 1535, when it was first visited by the Spaniards, who invaded it from Peru with a force of 570 Europeans and 15,000 Peruvians, under the command of Almagro, the coadjutor of Pizarro. Two-thirds of the number of this expedition perished with fatigue on the march; the remainder, however, succeeded in reaching the northern province of Chili, and the Spaniards were received by the inhabitants with cordiality and respect; but the perfidy and baseness of Almagro indulged in the wanton massacre of some of the chief men of the country, and thereby raised the indignation of the whole population against him; and having, in a general engagement with the Promancians, sustained a complete defeat, and dissatisfaction prevailing among his troops, he returned to Peru in 1538. In 1540, however, Pizarro dispatched another expedition, under the command of Valdivia, who, after much resistance, succeeded in extending his arms as far as Mapocho; and from that period the Spaniards maintained possession in the country, though not without repeated conflicts with the natives, and occasional reverse of fortune; and such has been the bravery of the Araucans, a tribe of Indians occupying the southern part of the territory, from the lat. of 37. to 42. S., that up to the present time they have never been subdued. The last conflict in which they were engaged with the Spaniards was in 1773, in which great slaughter ensued, without a decided triumph to either party. From that period, however, tranquillity has generally prevailed, the Araucans having since then had a resident at Santiago, more in the character of representative of an independent nation, than a conquered or dependent province. The more southern portion of the territory, to the lat. of 42. S., is occupied by the Araucans, and the Island of Chiloe, projecting into the Pacific Ocean, forms the southern extremity of the territory, which is separated from Peru on the N., by the dreary desert of Atacama. The Andes, which flank the whole eastern boundary, rise to an average altitude of 12,000 to 14,000 feet above the level of the sea, having, in the course of this range, 14 volcanoes in a state of constant eruption, and several others which emit occasionally. All of them are, however, too remote from the inhabited parts of the territory, either to occasion inconvenience, or inspire terror, by the violence of their eruption. It is now divided into three departments—Santiago, Coquimbo, and Concepcion, which are again subdivided into 13 provinces; and contains a population of 1,200.000, exclusive of the independent tribes of Indians. The several provinces are mostly divided from each other by ranges of hills, each intervening valley being intersected by one or more streams of water, contributing alike to the beauty and fertility of the country, which, as a whole, for diversity, beauty, and grandeur of feature, is unequalled in the world. Although the soil and climate of Chili are alike congenial to the culture and breed of all the fruits, grain, and animals conducive to the well-being, comfort, and enjoyment of society, its more distinguishing feature is the abundance of its mineral productions, in gold, silver, copper, tin, and iron. Such, however, for nearly three centuries, was the subduing and perverse policy of the Spaniards, that, with means to command every possible comfort, the inhabitants of this fine and fertile territory were kept in a state of barbarism, and on the verge of want. The ties of Spanish bondage, however, now appear broken, never to be united. The first movement of resistance to Spanish authority took place in 1809, which, for some time, appeared likely to succeed without interruption; but in 1814 a Spanish force from Peru subdued nearly the whole country, and held it again in subjection until 1817, when a force in the cause of independence, under the command of General San Martin, entered Chili from Buenos Ayres, and turned again the tide of victory against Spanish domination; and on the 12th of February, 1819, the Chilians formally renounced all obligation to Spanish authority, and declared themselves independent; which the battle of Maypa, in the following April, not only confirmed to them, but enabled them to extend their arms, in pursuit of their oppressors, into Peru. Santiago, or St. Jago de Chili, (as it is sometimes written,) in the province of Mapocho, in the lat. of 33. 20. is the chief city, and to which Valparaiso, distant 100 miles W., is the seaport. The other seaports are COPIAPO, COQUIMBO, CONCEPCION, and VALDIVIA, all of which see, under their respective heads; as well as those of the several provinces respectively, for a more ample elucidation of the nature and extent of the present state of their productions, commerce, &c. &c.

CHILKA, a lake in the Deccan of Hindostan, which bounds the five Circars on the N. It lies on the coast of the Bay of Bengal, and seems the effect of the breach of the sea over a flat sandy surface, whose elevation was something above the level of the country within. It communicates with the sea by a very narrow but deep opening, and is shallow within. It is 40 miles long and 14 broad, with a narrow slip of ground between it and the sea. It contains many inhabited islands. On the N. W. it is bounded by a ridge of mountains, a continuation of that which extends from the Mahanuddy to the Godavery river, and shuts up the Circars towards the continent.

CHILLAN, one of the inland provinces of Chili; it is inconsiderable, and the least important of them all. The chief town, of the same name, is about 105 miles N. W. of Concepcion. A river of the same name intersects the province from E. to W., falling into the Itata, in the maritime province of Puchacay

CHILLICOTHE, the chief town of Ross county, Ohio, and second in rank in the state; seated on a point of land formed by Point Creek, and the W. bank of the Scioto river, 70 miles, by the water-course, above its entrance into the Ohio; it has several mills and manufactures in its vicinity. The Grand Canal passes through the town, and adds much to its commerce. It is 45 miles S. of Columbus, the capital of the state, and 90 E. by N. of Cincinnati. Pop. 3977.

CHILLON, a town of Switzerland, in the canton of Berne, at the end of the lake of Geneva. On a rock in the lake is an ancient castle, which has lately been used as a state prison. It is 5 miles E. S. E. of Vevay.

CHILMARY, a town of Hindostan, in the district of Rungpoor, Bengal, on the Brahmaputra river. It has a trade in rice and cotton, and is a place of pilgrimage.

CHILOE, ISLAND AND ARCHIPELAGO OF. The Island of Chiloe forms the southern extremity of the territory of Chili; separated from the province of Araucan on the N. by a channel 4 to 5 miles wide. It is 140 miles in length, and about 50 in mean breadth; separated on the E. from the main land by a gulf about 50 miles wide, containing 46 small islands, 15 uninhabited, forming the Archipelago of Chiloe. The total population is about 30,000. Castro, seated at the head of a bay, opening into the Archipelago is the chief town.

CHILPANZINGO, a considerable town, 2500 feet above the level of the sea; 65 miles N. by E. of Acapulco, on the road to Mexico.

CHILQUES Y MASQUES, a district of the province of Cuzco, Peru, lying E. of the Apurimac river, having a ridge of the Andes for its E. boundary. It is a fertile district, containing about 16,000 inhabitants. Parino, in the lat. of 12. 45. S. and 71. 35. of W. long. is the chief town.

CHILTERN, a chain of chalky hills in England, passing from E. to W., out of Hertfordshire, through the middle of Buckinghamshire, to the Thames at Henley. This district formerly belonged to the crown, which, from time immemorial, has had the nominal office of steward of the Chiltern Hundreds, by the acceptance of which a commoner vacates his seat in parliament.

CHIMAY, a town of Belgium, in the forest of Thierarche. Near it are mines of iron, with founderies and forges. It is seated near the French frontier; 12 miles N. W. of Rocroy.

CHIMBORAZO, the highest peak of the Andes, in the province of Quito, Colombia; lat. 1. 30. S. On the 23rd of June, 1797, this mountain was ascended by the Prussian traveller, Humboldt, to the height of 19,300 feet above the level of the sea, when a chasm several hundred feet wide prevented the summit being attained; the extreme altitude of which is 21,440 feet. At the height attained, the cold was intense, and respiration rendered difficult by the extreme tenuity of the air. The peak is about 100 miles N. N. E. of Guayaquil, and presents a most magnificent spectacle for many leagues out at sea, in the Pacific Ocean.

Chimera, a town of European Turkey, in Albania, with a fort; seated on a rock, at the entrance of the Adriatic; 24 miles S. of Avlona.

China, an empire of Asia, extending from the lat. of 21. 30. to 41. N. and from 98 to 122. of E. long., giving an extreme length of about 1400 miles, and about the same number in an extreme breadth; but its boundaries being somewhat irregular, if resolved into a square it would comprise about 15½ degrees of lat. between 22. 30. and 38. N., and 18 degrees of long. between 102. and 120. E., thereby giving a superficial area of about 1,200,000 square miles, or more than twenty times the extent of England and Wales, exclusive of the eastern provinces of Leaotong and the Corea, and the vast territory of Tartary on the N. (each of which see, under their respective heads.) The above limits comprise what may be considered as constituting *China Proper*, which has about 1700 miles of sea-coast on the S., S. E., and E., from the long. of 108. E. in the lat. of 21. 30. N., to the long. of 120. E. in the lat. of 40. N., or from the Gulf of Tonquin to the Gulf of Leaotong. The N. and N. E. part of China Proper is bounded by a wall, which divides it from Mongol Tartary, and the W. by Kokonor and Sifan, provinces of Thibet, at present but little known; and the S. W. province of Yunnen borders on the Birman Empire, and the territory of Tonquin, or Tonkin. Every part of this extensive territory appears to be intersected by streams of water, falling into two grand rivers, both rising in Thibet, and falling into the sea, one in the lat. of 31. 30., and the other in lat. 34. N. The most northerly of these is called the Hoang-ho, or Great Yellow River, and the other the Kiang-keou, or the Great River, (each of which see under their respective heads.) There are also several lakes in the interior; two, S. of the Kiang-keou, called Tong-tong and Poyang, each contains about 300 square miles of surface; and in the latter are several islands. The coast, also, from the Gulf of Tonkin to the mouth of the Great River, is flanked by a chain of small islands; and, as forming an integral part of China Proper, are the islands of Hainan and Formosa; the former at the S. extremity of the empire, intersected by the lines of 19. of N. lat. and 113. of E. long., and the other intersected by the line of the tropic of Cancer, and the 121st of E. long.; and as dependent islands, are the Lekeyo, or Loo Choo Islands, the principal of which is about 150 miles in length, from N. to S., and 30. to 40. in breadth, in the long. of 129. E. and the lat. of 36. N. Between these and Formosa is another group, thirty or forty in number, nearly all of which are inhabited. Mountain ridges run in various directions over nearly every part of China Proper: but there are none remarkable for their altitude; and, in an aggregate sense, it may be considered a level, rather than a mountainous country.

Of all the communities at present existing, that of China is unquestionably the most ancient, and, from a very early period, had obviously made great progress in the arts of social life; but of the origin of the community nothing satisfactory is at present known; for although their records appear to have been preserved with great care, the peculiarity, and formerly supposed difficulty of acquiring a knowledge of the written characters of their language (being symbolic), together with the peculiarly jealous character of the people, had, antecedent to the close of the eighteenth century, precluded Europeans from obtaining any correct knowledge, either of the past or present extent and condition of the people; and, in the absence of all authentic and correct data on the subject, numerous vague and exaggerated statements, relating alike to their antiquity and extent of numbers, obtained current belief in Europe; but since the commencement of the nineteenth century, the supposed difficulty of acquiring a knowledge of their language has proved erroneous, and the details of the several local divisions and institutions of the country are becoming every year more extensively and accurately known.

Of their origin, the most rational supposition is, that the Chinese were among the first portion of the wandering tribes spread over the northern hemisphere, dispersed from some of the populous districts of that time, who formed themselves into a social community; whilst an examination of the localities and natural advantages of the territory of China Proper, as well with reference to the natural fertility of its soil, as the variety, and adaptation to the wants of a social community, of its indigenous productions, will sufficiently account for the numerical extent and peculiarity of manners of its population. By the writings of Confucius, (the only Chinese that appears to have obtained immortality among them,) who flourished 520 years before our era, China had then attained nearly, if not quite as high a degree of sociality and refinement as prevails there at the present time; and, indeed, the moral character of the people, which may be considered the surest foundation and best security for the permanence and well-being of every community, appears progressively to have increased in turpitude since the time of Confucius: and, that China has not experienced the fate (viz. subjection or dissolution) which has befallen every other nation, on the perversion of moral order, is to be ascribed entirely to the local barriers of deserts and mountains with which it is protected, and not to any efficiency or superior agency of the people. But, in fact, in the twelfth century China Proper may be considered as having been subjected to the arms of the Mongol Tartar chief, Genghis Khan, who subverted the then ruling power, and established a Tartar dynasty in the government of China; but notwithstanding this change in the ruling power, instead of the territory of China yielding itself up as a dependent province of Tartary, the superior fertility of China brought Tartary into its subservience; thereby reversing the usual result of conquest, in the conquering becoming the dependent: and the dynasty of Genghis also gradually declined in influence, until it became entirely supplanted again by one of Chinese origin, which ruled undisturbed until the commencement of the 17th century, when a host of Manchoo Tartars from the N. E. part of Asia poured down their arms, and by whom the ruling power in China was again subverted, but with the same result to the country as in the former instance, the revolution having only extended itself to the central government, and substitution of a Tartarian for a Chinese sovereign, Manchoo, like Mongol, becoming a dependent province on China; and, amid the various changes which have taken place in the ruling power, no material alteration appears to have been effected in the character, habits, or manners of the people, beyond that progressive change resulting from the increasing turpitude of their moral character, which necessarily tends to weaken their physical enegies.

According to an account furnished by an intelligent native of China to the agents of the English East India Company, in Canton, in 1823, the territory of China Proper was then divided into nineteen civil and military jurisdictions. Notwithstanding all the magnified impressions which have heretofore prevailed, in reference to the supposed populousness of China, relatively to the extent of territory in the two countries, its population is but little more than half that of England and Wales; and, although the numerical military force of China is represented as exceeding 1,200,000 men, the state revenues will be seen relatively not to amount to a hundredth part of those of England. Yet, notwithstanding the abject and servile condition to which centuries of severe rules have subjected them, the Chinese are, in general, a cheerful people; indeed, everything relating to and connected with China, in comparison with the communities and institutions of Europe, seems anomalous. With a soil of more than ordinary fertility, in which all the fruits and vegetable productions common to Europe flourish, and which abounds in a variety inestimably valuable, peculiar to itself, and a people proverbially and really industrious, famine frequently prevails extensively. To unfold, however, these mysteries, belongs more to the philosopher than to the geographer.

In some of the provinces of China, part of the exactions for the support of the government are levied in kind—in grain and rice. This fact, whilst it serves to show somewhat the nature of the soil in the respective provinces, leads to the consideration of a feature in the policy of China, peculiar at this time to itself, but which appears in past times to have been acted upon both in Egypt and in Rome; viz. that of storing of grain to meet the exigencies of occasional dearth. The average stock maintained in China for this purpose is about 30,000,000 of *Ski*, equal to about 2,000,000 of English tons, in the proportion of one-sixth rice, and the remainder in grain, chiefly maize and wheat; and although this quantity is not more than equal to two months' subsistence for the aggregate population, yet, when it is considered that China proper extends through 20 degrees of latitude, partly within the tropic of Cancer, and 25 degrees of longitude, in which extensive range it is not likely that a scarcity would, at most, pervade more than one-fifth part, if so much, at one time, it is probable that the quantity in question has proved, by the experience of centuries, adequate to its proposed object: and it is unquestionably a measure, if duly regulated, worthy the adoption of every social community.

As there is scarcely a town, or even a village in China, which has not the advantage either of an arm of the sea or a canal, navigation is so common, that almost as many people live on the water as on land. The Great Canal runs from N. to S., from the city of Canton to the extremity of the empire; and by it all kinds of foreign merchandise entered at that city are conveyed directly to Pekin, a distance of 825 miles. This canal is about 50 feet wide, passes through or near 41 large cities, and has 75 large sluices to keep up the water, besides several thousand bridges. China owes a great part of her riches to these numerous canals, which are cut through any kind of private property, not even excepting the gardens of the emperor.

Among the fruits peculiar to China, and in addition to the orange, lemon, lime, citron, pomegranate, and the vine, in great variety, are the tse-tse, a kind of fig; the li-tchi, of the size of a date, its stone covered with a soft juicy pulp, of an exquisite taste, but dangerous when eaten to excess; the long-yen, or dragon's-eye, its pulp white, tart, and juicy, not so agreeable to the taste, but more wholesome than the litchi. Of esculent plants they have an infinity unknown to Europe. They cultivate also the bottom of their waters; the beds of their lakes, ponds, and rivulets producing crops unknown to us, particularly of the pi-tsi, or water-chestnut, the fruit of which (found in a cover formed by its root) is exceedingly wholesome, and of a very delicate taste. Among the trees peculiar to China are the tallow-tree, the fruit of which is white, the size of a small walnut, and the pulp has the properties of tallow; the wax-tree, producing a kind of white wax, almost equal to that made by bees; the tsi-chu, or varnish-tree, which produces the admirable Chinese varnish; the tie-ly-mou, or iron-wood, the wood of which is so hard and heavy that it sinks in water, and the anchors of the Chinese ships are made of it; the camphire-tree; the bamboo reeds, which grow to the height and size of a large tree, and, besides being used as natural pipes to convey water, are employed for numberless other purposes; the tea-plant, &c., with cotton, betel, and tobacco: the flowering shrubs, flowers, herbs, and medicinal plants, are exceedingly numerous. In the mountains and forests are wild animals of every species: but that valuable quadruped, the musk-deer, is peculiar to this country. Of its birds, the most beautiful in China, and perhaps in the world, is the kin-hi, or golden fowl. Gold and silver are said to be common in several parts of the empire; but the working of the mines is interdicted, to prevent, as is pretended, the produce leading to a derangement of their general system of policy.

The mountains also, chiefly in the N. and W. parts of the empire, contain mines of iron, tutenag, copper, and quicksilver, as well as quarries of marble, coal, lapis lazuli, jasper, rock crystals, granite, and a kind of sonorous stones, of which musical instruments are composed; and here is potters' earth, of such various and superior kinds that the fine porcelain of China is unrivalled. The number of domestic animals appears to be very limited, and animal food, though not interdicted, either from state or religious scruples, as is the case over a great part of Hindostan, is very uncommon.

This paucity, or indeed it may be said entire destitution, of domestic animals, will suffice to explain various points of Chinese policy, and to account for various features in their economy. To substitute oxen for draught horses, and to subvert even the quadruped race of animals, for the purpose of leaving a more abundant supply of farinaceous and esculent food for the biped race of animals, is by no means a new idea among European speculators in political economy. It will be out of place here philosophically to expose the absurdity of such notions, which, once carried into practice, it requires no great stretch of philosophy to see that it will of necessity give a peculiar feature to the economy of every community that may act upon it. In China it at once accounts for the apparent universality of tillage, and redundancy of population contiguous to all their rivers; but it will doubtless prove, on a general survey of the country, that it is progressively less cultivated and less populous in proportion to its distance from the banks of rivers, or some artificial channel of conveyance; and although they appear to have availed themselves of sails, to aid and accelerate the force of their wheeled-carriages on land, and rotatory paddles, to accelerate the force of their boats on the water, as they seem equally unacquainted with tram-roads, and the application of steam as an agent of motion, all their contrivances partake more of the character of petty conceit or device, than of useful invention. Independent, also, of the obviously superior agency, in reference to motion and conveyance of bulky commodities, of the quadruped over the biped race of animals, the Chinese, like the speculative reasoners on political economy in Europe, appear totally ignorant of the fact, of quadrupeds possessing also a superior agency in refixing the gaseous or volatile matters, and thereby of refertilizing the earth; consequently, instead of adding to the supply of food for their biped race, by the subversion of the race of quadrupeds or of domestic animals, it led to the opposite result; and hence the anomaly is explained, of famine in a country naturally fertile, occasionally pervading extensive districts. This circumstance may also have led to a very sensible diminution in the number of its human inhabitants, in comparison with former periods, and may therefore account for the incongruity of the statements on that subject. The same destitution of knowledge in the first principles of the law of nature, in reference to all subjects, appears to be universal in China; and, as pretension and presumption universally predominate in a ratio inversely to the depths of ignorance that prevail, a solution is afforded to all that heretofore appeared enigmatical respecting China; in which all is bustle, parade, and pretension, excelling only in trifles; and, whilst their manufactures embrace every possible commodity to gratify artificial wants, and their fabrics in porcelain, silk, and paper more especially, cannot be surpassed, nor their carving in ivory, and other works of fancy, equalled in any other part of the world, in all that requires skill, combined with superior physical power, they are inferior to the least settled parts of Europe. Ignorant of the laws of geometry, as well as of the laws of nature, their fortifications for defence, their habitations, public edifices, and monuments, in which a display of taste has been aimed at, are ridiculously fantastic, and, when solidity has been the object, exceedingly clumsy; hence the water communication between the northern and southern parts of the empire, which has been adorned with the designation of *Grand*, and as surpassing any thing of the kind in the world, is a mere connexion of natural streams, displaying no evidence of genius or skill beyond that of finding the nearest level whereby to effect the union. The only work of art connected with China, having any claim to admiration, is the Great Wall, which separates the N. and N. W. parts of China Proper from Mongol Tartary, which was probably not the work of the Chinese, but of the Tartars themselves, soon after the conquest of Genghis Khan; but the accounts hitherto obtained of the period of its erection are too imperfect to justify any positive conclusion on the subject.

The most singular characteristic in the civil policy of China is the total absence of all state religion and priesthood, which is supposed to have been subverted for the two-fold purpose of preventing a priesthood from sharing in the influence of the government, and the people from congregating in too large numbers; and the latter notion seems also to have precluded the toleration of public theatres. Both religious worship and dramatic representations are, however, universal throughout the empire. Of the former, every house has its own altar and collection of gods, the form and number of which are generally in proportion to the taste of the head of the family to select, and of his ability to purchase; hence their religious worship may be said to resolve itself into one of their most extensive branches of manufacture. In like manner, the dramatic representations are all of a family nature, the performers consisting of strolling companies, who engage themselves for an evening to any one that can afford to pay them. Connected with the question of religion, the civil policy of China tolerates polygamy. It appears, however, not to be so extensively indulged in, as in other parts of Asia and Africa. Burials are not permitted in cities or towns, and their sepulchres are commonly on barren hills and mountains. They pretend to have a great veneration for their ancestors; and some keep images of them in their houses, to which they pay a sort of adoration. They have laws, which regulate the civilities and ceremonious salutations they pay to each other; for which reason they always appear to be extremely good-natured, whilst low cunning and deceit is their ruling passion: and yet, while infanticide is not unfrequent among them, they are not destitute of social affections in their families. In person, the complexion of the Chinese is a sort of tawny, and they have large foreheads, small eyes, short noses, large ears, long beards, and black hair; and those are thought to be the most handsome who are the must bulky. The women affect a great deal of modesty, and are remarkable for their little feet. The men endeavour to make a pompous appearance when they go abroad; and yet their houses are mean and low, consisting only of a ground floor. In conclusion it may be said, in point of aggregate efficiency, or in affording general examples of social policy worthy of imitation, China is inferior to the least important state of Europe; whilst the extent and grandeur of its natural features, the diversity, beauty, and interest of its productions, both natural and artificial, and the superlative excellence of many of its fabrics, both of utility and ornament, render research and development in the details of all these characteristics an object in the highest degree desirable. Peking, in the province of Petchelee, in the N. E. part of the empire, is the capital, and residence of the emperor. The other principal cities are Nan-king, and Canton—the only port where Europeans are allowed to trade or visit. For further particulars, see CANTON, MACAO, PEKING, &c. &c.

CHINABAKEER, a town of Pegu, situate in the marshes of the Irrawaddy, S. of Rangoon.

CHINABALABRAM, a town of the Mysore; 55 miles N. of Bangalore.

CHINAPATAM, or CHINYPATAM, another town of the Mysore; about 40 miles E. S. E. of Seringapatam.

CHINCHILLA, a town of Spain, in Murcia; 37 miles W. of Almanza, and 67 N.N.W. of Murcia. Pop. about 5000.

CHIN-CHI. *See* QUIN-NONG.

CHINGLEPUT, a town of the Carnatic, near the sea-coast; about 40 miles S. of Madras.

CHINACHIN, or CHEENYCHIN, the chief town of the district of Jenilah, in the N. W. part of Nepaul, at the foot of the Himalaya mountains.

CHINANT. *See* CHUNAUD.

CHINCHOOR, a town of Hindostan, in the province of Aurungabad, celebrated as the residence of an incarnation of the Deity—the residence of whom is a large mass of buildings thronged with Brahmins. Lat. 18. 38. N. long. 73. 55. E. Pop. 5000.

CHINON, a town of France, in the department of Indre and Loire, with a strong castle in which Henry II. of England expired. Chinon is the birth-place of Rabelais and of Quillet. It is seated on the Vienne; 10 miles N. of Richelieu, and 150 S.W. of Paris. It has some manufactures, and contains about 5500 inhabitants.

CHINE, LA, a town in Canada; 7 miles from Montreal, on the La Chine Canal, which connects the navigation and commerce of the two Canadas.

CHINSURA, a town of Hindostan, in Bengal, with a fortress belonging to Holland; seated on the Hoogly; 17 miles N. of Calcutta. It was formerly the principal settlement of the Dutch in Bengal.

CHINY, a town of Belgium, in Luxemburg, on the river Semoy; 40 miles W. by N. of Luxemburg.

CHIOURLIC, a town of European Turkey, in Romania; the see of a Greek bishop; seated on a river of the same name; 47 miles W.N.W. of Constantinople.

CHIOZZO, a town and island of Italy, in the Gulf of Venice. Much salt is made here. The town is built on piles, and has a harbour, defended by a fort; 18 miles S. of Venice. The island contains about 20,000 inhabitants.

CHIPIONA, a town in Spain, in Andalusia, situate on a rock, near the sea; 5 miles W. S.W. of St. Lucar de Barameda.

CHIPPENHAM, a borough in Wiltshire, with a market on Saturday. It has three establishments for the manufacture of fine woollen cloth, and sends two members to parliament. It is seated on the Lower Avon, over which is a bridge: 21 miles E. of Bristol, and 93 W. of London.

CHIPPEWAY, a river falling into the Missisippi, from the N. E., about 70 miles below the falls of St. Anthony. It has its source near one of the rivers falling into the W. end of Lake Superior, and will probably, at no distant day, be the channel by which a direct inland water communication will be opened between the two great Gulfs of St. Lawrence and Mexico.

CHIPPING, a Saxon word, signifying market or fair, precedes, in all formal proceedings, the names of several towns in England, such as those of Barnet, Norton, Ongar, &c. &c.; but the prefix is now fallen into disuse, in common parlance, except in the case of CHIPPING-NORTON, which is a neat town in Oxfordshire, with a market on Wednesdays. The church is an elegant structure of Gothic arhcitecture. It is 73 miles W. N. W. of London, on the road to Worcester.

CHIQUITOS, a division of Bolivia, in South America; inhabited by a tribe of independent Indians, and produces some honey and wax. A branch of the Andes traverses this district.

CHIRIQUI, a town of Colombia, on a river of the same name, 12 miles N. of its mouth, in the Pacific Ocean. Long. 83. 28. W. lat. 8. 30. N.

CHIRK, a town of Wales, in Denbighshire, on the top of a hill near Wrexham. It had formerly two castles, one of which seems to have been a magnificent structure. In the vicinity, the Ellesmere Canal is carried over the vale and river Ceiriog, by a magnificent aqueduct.

CHISME, a seaport of Asiatic Turkey, in Natolia, on the strait that parts the continent from the Isle of Scio. It was anciently called Cysus, was celebrated for the great victory which the Romans gained here over the fleet of Antiochus, in 191 B. C. and has been distinguished by the destruction of the Turkish fleet by the Russians, in 1770. It exports large quantities of raisins, and is 40 miles W. of Smyrna. Long. 26. 16. E. lat. 38. 24. N.

CHISWICK, a village in Middlesex, on the Thames; 7 miles W. by S. of St. Paul's, London. Here is a celebrated villa of the Duke of Devonshire; and in the churchyard is a monument of Hogarth.

CHITORE, the chief town of a district of the same name, in the province of Ajimere; about 100 miles S. by W. of the city of Ajimere.

CHITPOOR, a considerable town of Guzerat, about 30 miles N. E. of Mangalore, on the shore of the Arabian Sea. It has extensive manufactures of chintzes.

CHITRO, or KITRO, a town of European Turkey, Macedonia, on the W. shore, near the head of the Bay of Salonichi. Here the mother, wife, and son of Alexander were murdered by Cassander. It is 36 miles S. S. E. of Edessa.

CHITTAGONG, a province of Asia, lying between the Bay of Bengal and Arracan. It was conquered from Arracan by Aurungzebe, in 1666, and now belongs to the English East India Company. Islamabad is the chief town. Pop. 1,200,000.

CHITTELDROOG, or CHALTRAKAL, a strong fort and town of Hindostan, capital of the N. E. district of Mysore. The plain of Chitteldroog is 10 miles long and four broad, surrounded by rocky hills, on one of which stands the fort. The town formerly occupied a great portion of the plain, and is still a considerable place, but now confined entirely within the walls, which are near the foot of the rock. Hyder, who obtained possession of this place by treachery, strengthened the walls; and other works have been since added, so as to render it totally impregnable against any neighbouring power. Since the final defeat of Tippoo, in 1799, it belongs to the rajah of the Mysore; and the English keep a garrison here. It is 48 miles N. W. of Sera, and 117 N. by W. of Seringapatam.

CHITTENDEN, a county of Vermont; bounded on the W. for about 38 miles by Lake Champlain, between the lat. of 44. and 45. N. It is about 18 miles in mean breadth, and is divided into 24 townships. The population is 22,977. Burlington is the chief town.

CHITTENING, a town of Madison county, New York, situate near the line of the Erie Canal; 127 miles W. N. W. of Albany.

CHITTENINGO CREEK, a stream in Onandago county, New York, having, in the course of about 10 miles, a fall of 80 feet, into Oneida Lake.

CHITTORE, a town of Hindostan, in the Carnatic; 28 miles N. W. of Arcot, and 70 W. of Madras.

CHIVAS, or CHIVAZZO, a fortified town of Piedmont, on the river Po; 12 miles N. N. E. of Turin. Pop. about 5500.

CHIUSA, a strong town of Italy, in the Veronese, on the E. bank of the Adige, in a narrow pass; 14 miles N. N. W. of Verona. Also of another town in Piedmont, about 10 miles S. E. of Coni. Pop. about 6000.

CHIUSI, a town of Tuscany, in the Siennese, on the river Chiano; 35 miles S. E. of Sienna.

CHIUTAJA. *See* KIUTAIA.

CHMIELNIK, a town of Poland, in Podolia, on an island formed by the river Bog; 80 miles N. E. of Kaminieck. Long. 27. 50. E. lat. 49. 44. N.

CHOCO, a bay of Colombia, in the Pacific Ocean. There is a town named Buenaventura, at the mouth of a river falling into this bay, in the lat. of 3. 50. N.

CHOCO is also the name of a district in Colombia, lying between the two first western ridges of the Andes, between the 6th and 8th degrees of N. lat. The river Atrato intersects this district from S. to N., falling into the Gulf of Darien; the head waters of this river were united in 1788 by the Canal de Raspadura, with the river St. Juan, falling into the Pacific Ocean, about 20 miles N. W. of Buenaventura.

CHOCTAWS, a numerous and powerful tribe of Indians, in the states of Mississippi and Alabama. By a treaty with the United States of North America, in 1820, the boundaries of their territory were fixed as follows: viz. on the W. by the Tombecbee river, from the lat. of 32. N., to the mouth of Wolkey Creek, in the lat. of 33. 32. N.; then by a conventional line drawn in a N. W. direction, which divides the territory of the Choctaws from the Chicasaws, till it strikes the Mississippi river, and the S. W. corner of the state of Tennessee, in the lat. of 35. N.: the Mississippi river in a S. W. direction then forms the boundary on the N. W. to the mouth of the Arkansas river, in the lat. of 34. N.; then by a conventional line in a S. E. direction, to the lat. of 33. N., from whence it strikes in a direction due S., to the lat. of 31. 48. in the long. of 89. 30. W., from which point it is bounded on the S. by another conventional line, till it strikes the Tombecbee river, as before mentioned, in the lat. of 32. N. and 88. of W. long. These boundaries enclose about 17,000 square miles of territory, intersected by the Talahotchee, the Yazoo, and several other rivers; but so surrounded as to be completely subservient to any dictations which the United States Government may think proper to prescribe.

CHOCZIM, a town and fortress of Moldavia, situate on the S. bank of the Dneister; 110 miles N. N. W. of Jassy, and 15 S. W. of Kaminiec, in Podolia. Choczim was the seat of repeated conflicts between the Turks and Poles, during the integrity of Poland, and, since its dissolution, between the Turks and Russians, till it was finally ceded to the latter power in 1812; and it is now included in the government of Podolia. Pop. 25,000.

CHOISEUL, a town of France, in the department of Upper Marne; 12 miles N. E. of Langres.

CHOLLET, a town of France, in the department of Mayenne and Loire, with a castle; 27 miles S. S. W. of Angers. Pop. about 4800.

CHOLM, or KOLM, a town of Russia, in the government of Pskov, on the river Lovat; 180 miles S. of Petersburg.

Cholmogor, or **Kolmogor**, a town in the government of Archangel, situate on an island in the river Dwina; 30 miles S. of the city of Archangel.

Cholula, a city of Mexico, in the intendancy of Puebla, and about 7 miles W. of the city of Puebla. Previous to the irruption of the Spaniards into Mexico, Cholula was the seat of government of an independent state, which, in conjunction with three other adjoining republics, had resisted the authority of the Mexicans for several centuries. Cortes halted at Cholula, on his way to the city of Mexico, in 1519, at which time it contained about 200,000 inhabitants, who carried on extensive manufactures of cotton cloths, jewellery, and earthenware. It was also the chief place of religious resort in all Mexico, having a temple which vies with the Pyramids of Egypt in extent and magnificence; and had at that time not less than 400 other places of worship. Cholula is now comparatively an inconsiderable place, having only about 15,000 inhabitants, being eclipsed in splendour and importance by Puebla.

Chonad, or **Csonad**, an episcopal town of Hungary, and capital of a county of the same name. It is seated on the S. bank of the N. branch of the Marosch river, 25 miles above its entrance into the Theiss, at Zeged in.

Chonos, an island of the South Pacific Ocean; 20 miles long, and 5 broad; lying off the W. coast of Patagonia, and one of the Chonos Archipelago.

Chorasan, or **Korassan**, a province of Persia, extending from the lat. of 32. to 39. N., and from 54. 30. to 93. of E. long. containing an area of about 147,000 square miles. It is bounded on the W. by the Great Salt Desert, Mazenderan, and the Caspian Sea; N. by the Bay of Balkan and the Desert of Karakum; N. E. by the main branch of the Gihon Amu, or Oxus river, which divides it from Great Bucharia; E. by the territory of Balk; S. E. by the Lake of Zeresh, or Durra, which divides it from Segistan; and the extreme S. projects upon the Desert of Kerman. A ridge of the Gaur mountains intersects the E. side of the province, from S. to N.; and E. of this ridge is the Magrab river, which falls into the Oxus at Amol. Another river, with several tributary streams, rises near Herat, in the S. E. corner of the province, and runs in a N. W. direction into the Bay of Balkan. Meshid, in the lat. of 37. 35. N. and 57. 15. E. long., is the capital of the province; the other chief towns are Herat, Badkis, Zenzau, Abiverd, &c.

Chorley, a town in Lancashire, with a market on Tuesday. It is seated on the line of the Liverpool, Lancaster, and Leeds Canal; 22 miles N. W. of Manchester, on the road to Preston, from which it is distant 9 miles. It has a considerable manufacture of calico, muslin, and fustian. In the neighbourhood are quarries of ashler, flag, and millstone; and mines of coal, lead, and alum, and also carbonate of barytes. It holds four fairs annually.

Chorlton-Row, a township in the parish of Manchester, on the S. W. side of the town, distant about 3 miles. *See* **Manchester**.

There are five villages in different parts of England named *Chorlton*, all inconsiderable.

Chowbent, or **Atherton**, a township in the parish of Leigh, Lancashire. *See* **Leigh**.

Choubar, a town of Asia, in the province of Mukran, Beloochistan, on the Indian Ocean, at the mouth of a gulf of the same name. Lat. 25. 17. N. long. 60. 23. S.

Choule, a town of Hindostan, on the coast of Concan, with a harbour for small vessels, which is fortified. It is 24 miles S. of Bombay.

Chowan, a county of North Carolina, containing about 100 square miles; bounded on the E. by the Chowan river, at its influx into Albemarle Sound. Pop. 6690, of whom 3365 were slaves. Edenton, 183 miles E. by N. of Raleigh, is the chief town.

Christburg, a town of West Prussia, with a castle on a hill, situate on the Sorge; 15 miles S. E. of Marienburg.

Christchurch, a borough in Hampshire, with a market on Monday, and a considerable trade in knit silk stockings and watch-strings. It returns one member to parliament. Here are the remains of a castle and priory; and the church is a large and interesting structure. It is seated on the little Avon, opposite the influx of the Stour about half a mile above the entrance of the united stream into the British Channel; 25 miles S. of Salisbury, and 100 S. W. of London.

Christian, a western county of Kentucky, the S. end of which borders on Tennessee. It is watered by several streams, which after being united into one, run W. into Cumberland River. Pop. 15,587. Hopkinsville, in the centre of the county, 212 miles S. W. by W. of Frankfort, is the chief town.

Christiana, a town of Delaware, in Newcastle county. It stands on a navigable creek of its name, and is the greatest carrying place between the navigable waters of the Delaware and Chesapeake, which are here only 13 miles asunder. It is 4 miles S. W. of Newcastle.

Christianburg, a town of Virginia, chief of Montgomery county, situate on the W. side of the Allegany mountains, near a branch of the Kannaway; 170 miles W. S. W. of Richmond. Long. 80. 50. W. lat. 37. 5. N.

Christianburg, a fort of Guinea, on the Gold Coast, subject to the Danes. Long. 1. 55. E. lat. 4. 10. N.

Christianfeld, a town of Denmark, in the duchy of Sleswick, built by a society of Moravians, under the protection of Christian VII. All articles manufactured here are of excellent quality. It is 8 miles N. of Hadersleben.

Christiania, the capital of Norway, and an episcopal see, in the government of Aggerhuys, situate at the extremity of a fertile valley, forming a semicircular bend along the shore of the Bay of Biorning, which forms the N. extremity of the Gulf of Christiania. It is divided into the city, the suburbs of Waterlandt, Peterwigen, and Fierdingen; the fortress of Aggerhuys, and the old town of Opsloe. The city was rebuilt in its present situation by Christian IV. after a plan designed by himself. The streets are carried at right angles to each other, and uniformly 40 feet broad. It covers a considerable extent of ground, but has not more than 10,000 inhabitants. The castle of Aggerhuys is built on a rocky eminence on the W. side of the bay, at a small distance from the city. Opsloe was the site of the old city, burnt in 1624; it contains the episcopal palace. Christiania has an excellent harbour, and its principal exports are tar, soap, iron, copper, deals, and alum. It is 30 miles from the open sea, and 290 N. by W. of Copenhagen. Long. 10. 50. E. lat. 59. 50. N.

CHRISTIANOPEL, a strong seaport of Sweden, in Blekingen, seated on the Baltic; 13 miles N. E. of Carlscrona. Long. 15. 47. E. lat. 56. 26. N.

CHRISTIANSAND, a seaport of Norway, capital of a province of the same name, which is famous for iron mines. It is seated at the mouth of the Torrisdals, on the N. shore of the Scagerak, opposite the Isle of Fleckeren; 110 miles E.S.E. of Stavanger, and 120 S. S. W. of Christiania. Long. 8. 40. E. lat. 58. 25. N.

CHRISTIANSTADT, a fortified town of Sweden, in Blekingen, built by Christian IV. of Denmark, when the country was in the power of that crown. The chief trade is in alum, pitch, and tar; and it has manufactures of cloth, and silken stuffs. The town is seated in a marshy plain, on the river Helge, which is navigable only for small craft; 57 miles W. by S. of Carlscrona. Long. 14. 10. E. lat. 56. 25. N.

CHRISTIANSTADT, a seaport of Russian Finland, at the mouth of a river, on the Gulf of Bothnia; 155 miles N. by W. of Abo. Long. 21. 28. E. lat. 62. 40. N.

CHRISTIANSUND, a town of Norway, in the Island of Fossen, with a commodious harbour and wharf. The chief trade is in timber. It is 36 miles W. S. W. of Drontheim.

CHRISTINEHAM, a town of Sweden, in Wermeland, at the E. end of the lake Wenner; 30 miles S. E. of Carlstadt.

CHRISTINI, ST., the principal of the islands called Marquesas. *See* MARQUESAS.

CHRISTMAS ISLAND, an island in the Pacific Ocean, so named by Cook, who first landed here on Christmas day, 1777. It is 45 miles in circumference, uninhabited, and destitute of fresh water; but has abundance of fine turtle. Long. 157. 30. W. lat. 1. 59. N.

CHRISTMAS SOUND, a bay on the S. coast of Terra del Fuego, so named by Cook, who passed here the 25th December, 1774. The country is barren, and the refreshments to be got here are chiefly wild fowl. Long. 70. 3. W. lat. 55. 22. S.

CHRISTOPHE DE LAGUNA, ST., the capital of the Island of Teneriffe. Here the courts of justice are held, and the governor has a palace, but he commonly resides at St. Cruz. It stands on an eminence, in an extensive fertile plain, and has several fountains supplied with water from the neighbouring heights, by an aqueduct. The lake from which it has been supposed to take its name is now a very inconsiderable piece of water. Long. 16. 11. W. lat. 29. 29. N.

CHRISTOPHER, ST., or ST. KITTS, one of the Leeward Islands, in the West Indies; 60 miles W. of Antigua, the N. W. end being divided by a narrow strait from the small island of Nevis. It was formerly inhabited by the French and English; but in 1713 it was ceded to the latter; taken by the French in 1782, but restored to the English again in the following year. It is 15 miles long and 4 broad, with high mountains in the middle, whence rivulets flow. Between the mountains are dreadful rocks, horrid precipices, and thick woods, and, in the S. W. parts, hot sulphurous springs at the foot of them. Basseterre is the capital.

CHRISTORF, a town of Bohemia, in the N. part of the circle of Bunslau; 6 miles S. S. E. from Krottau.

CHROBERG, a town of Austrian Poland, in the palatinate of Sandomirz; 52 miles W. of Sandomirz.

CHRUDIM, a town of Bohemia, capital of a circle of the same name, which is remarkable for a great number of fish ponds, and an excellent breed of horses. It stands on the river Chrudinka, 10 miles above its entrance into the Elbe; 46 miles E. S. E. of Prague.

CHUCUITO, a town of Peru, in the diocese of Paz, on the W. side of Lake Titicaca, called also the Lake of Chucuito; 130 miles N. W. of Paz. Long. 70. 26. W. lat. 16. 20. S.

CHUDLEIGH, a town in Devonshire, with a market on Saturday. The neighbourhood is famous for its cider, and for a stupendous rock of bluish limestone, called Chudleigh marble, in which is a large cavern. This town was almost entirely destroyed by fire in 1807. It is seated near the Teign; 9 miles S. W. of Exeter, and 185 W. by S. of London.

CHUGANSERAI, a town of Hindostan, in the province of Cabul, on a river of the same name; 80 miles E. of Cabul. Long. 70. 8. E. lat. 34. 55. N.

CHUKOTSKIJA, or TCHONKCHI, a province of Siberia, and the most easterly of the dominions of Russia. It extends from 156. to 197. E. long. and from 63. to 73. N. lat.; and is separated from America by Behring's Straits.

CHUMLEIGH, a town in Devonshire, with a market on Thursday; seated on the river Taw; 21 miles N. W. of Exeter, and 194 W. by S. of London.

CHUMBUL, a considerable river of Hindostan, rising near Ougein, in Malwa, and, after a winding course of about 400 miles, falls into the Jumnah, about 90 miles below Agra.

CHUMLA, or SHUMLA, a city of Turkey in Europe, province of Bulgaria; 52 miles W. from Varna. Pop. 30,000. It was the scene of a sanguinary conflict between the Russians and Turks, in 1828, in which the Russians were victors.

CHUNAR, a fortress of Hindostan, in Allahabad, built on a rock, fortified all round by a wall and towers. It was unsuccessfully attempted by the English, in 1764; but in 1772 it was ceded to them by the nabob of Oude. It is seated on the S. bank of the Ganges; 15 miles S. of Benares, and 140 W. by S. Patna.

CHUNAUB, or CHINAUB, a river of Asia, the

chief of the five eastern branches of the Indus. It rises in the Tibetian mountains, runs through Cashmere, and joins the Indus 20 miles below Moultan. This river is the Acesines of Alexander.

CHUNG-KING, a city of China, of the first rank, in the province of Setchuen; it is beautifully located on a mountain, in the fork of a river, which runs from N. to S. into the Kiang-kiou.

CHUN-NING, another city of China, of the first-rank, in the province of Yun-nan. Chunning may be considered the frontier city of China on the side of the Birman empire; it is seated on a stream, which falls into the Kioulong, or Great River of Cambodia, and is only a few miles distant from another stream, which falls into the Maygue, or Great River of Siam. It is in lat. 34. 37. N. and 100. 15. of E. long.

CHUN-TE, a city of China, in Pe-tcheli, with nine cities of the third rank under its jurisdiction. It is 210 miles S. S. W. of Pekin.

CHUPRAH, a large town of Hindostan, in Bahar, on the N. bank of the Ganges; 28 miles W. N. W. of Patna. Pop. about 40,000.

CHUQUISACA. *See* PLATA.

CHUR. *See* COIRE.

CHURBAR, a seaport of Persia, on the coast of Mekran; it is seated on the E. shore, near the entrance of a bay of the same name, in the lat. of 25. 16 N. and 60. 24. E. of long.

CHURCH, STATES OF. *See* POPEDOM.

CHURCH. There are 30 towns and villages in different parts of England, the names of which are preceded by Church, but none that claim any particular notice; the most considerable are Church Staunton, in Devonshire, and Stretton, in Shropshire.

CHUSAN, an island on the E. coast of China, with a town called Ting-hai, and a much frequented harbour. It was taken by the British in 1840. Long. 122. 30. E. lat. 30. 0. N.

CHUSISTAN. *See* KUSISTAN.

CIAMPA, or TSIOMPA, a small kingdom of Asia bounded on the N. by Cochin-China, S. E. by the China Sea, W. and N. W. by Cambodia. It is more elevated than Cambodia, but not so fertile; having tracts of sand intersected with rocks. The productions are cotton, indigo, and bad silk; and the inhabitants are much employed in fishing. Cape St. James, at the S. E. extremity of the territory, is in lat. 10. 18. N. and 107. 10. E. long.; from this point the coast lies in a direction E. N. E. for about 200 miles. There are two or three small harbours along the coast, of which Ceeir Bay, about 140 miles E. N. E. of Cape St. James, is the most considerable.

CICACOLE, a town of Hindostan, capital of one of the Northern Circars. It is 150 miles N. E. of Rajamundry, and 308 E. N. E. of Hydrabad. Long. 84. 8. E. lat. 18. 16. N.

CICLUT, a frontier town of Dalmatia, on a rocky hill, on the W. bank of the Narenta. It was taken from the Turks by the Venetians, in 1694, and is 6 miles S. W. of Narenta. Long. 18. 22. E. lat. 43. 29. N.

CILLEY, a town of Austria, in Stiria, capital of a circle of the same name. It has a considerable trade in merchandise going to and from Vienna and Trieste; and is seated on the Saan, where it receives the Koding, and becomes navigable; 58 miles S. by W. of Gratz. Long. 15. 19. E, lat. 46. 21. N.

CIMBRISHAMN, a seaport of Sweden, in Schonen; 24 miles S. of Christianstadt. Long. 14. 21. E. lat. 55. 33. N.

CINALOA, or SINALOA, a province and town of Mexico, in the intendancy of Sonora, on the Gulf of California. The aborigines in this province are robust and warlike, and were with difficulty brought to submit to the Spaniards about the year 1771. This province produces abundance of maize, legumes, fruits, and cotton; and abounds in the richest gold mines. Pop. 60,000. The town is seated on a river of the same name, and contains about 9500 inhabitants. Long. 109. 35. W. lat. 26. 15. N.

CINCINNATI, the largest town of the state of Ohio, and the capital of Hamilton county. It is seated on the N. bank of the Ohio river, about two miles below the entrance of the Lecking, from the state of Kentucky, and 20 above the entrance of the Great Miami, and above 600 above the entrance of the Ohio in the Mississippi, in the lat. of 39. 7. N. and 7. 30. W. long. of Washington city. Cincinnati has increased in population and importance more rapidly than any other town in the North American Union. The population, which in 1805 did not exceed 500, amounts to above 46,338. It has extensive flour and saw mills, worked by steam, and various manufactures. It carries on a very extensive traffic with New Orleans, in exchanging the agricultural productions of the state of Ohio, principally flour and pork, for tropical and other foreign articles; and is the most important trading town of all the territory of America, west of the Allegany mountains. It has twenty-four places of public worship, and four banks for the circulation of a paper currency, and an office for the sale of public lands. The mean temperature of its climate, in 1819, was 56.89.

CINEFI, a town of Sicily, in Val di Mazara, in the neighbourhood of which excellent manna is collected. It is 20 miles W. of Palermo.

CINEY, a town of Belgium, in the territory of Liege; 17 miles S. E. of Namur, and 37 S. W. of Liege.

CINQUE PORTS, certain ports on the S. coast of England, opposite France; so called on account of their being five in number, when their first charter was granted by William I. in 1077. These were Dover, Hastings, Hythe, Romney, and Sandwich, to which were afterwards added Winchelsea, Seaford, and Rye. The king appointed a constable of Dover Castle (who is now called Lord Warden of the Cinque Ports,) and invested him with the command of these ports, whose inhabitants had considerable privileges and immunities, for which they were to supply the government with 57 ships, at forty days' notice, and to pay their crews during fifteen days. At that period, the opulent traders of London were styled barons; a privilege that was enjoyed likewise by the merchants of these ports; each of which formerly returned two members to parliament, the representatives being styled Barons of the Cinque Ports. Their other privileges are now become nominal. *See* each place under its respective head.

CINQUE VILLAS, a town of Portugal, in Beira; 6 miles N. E. of Almeida.

CINTEGABELLE, a town of France, in the department of Upper Garonne, on the frontier of Arriege; 17 miles S. of Toulouse. Pop. about 3000.

CINTRA, a town of Portugal, in Estremadura, situate between the mountains of Cintra, on the N. side of the entrance of the Tajo. Here was a palace built by the Moors, which was destroyed by an earthquake in 1655, and rebuilt by King Joseph. It is 12 miles N. W. of Lisbon, by the inhabitants of which place it is much frequented as an occasional retreat; and is distinguished for the convention concluded at it, on the 22nd Aug. 1808, between the English general, Dalrymple, and the French general, Junot.

CIOTAT, LA, a seaport of France, in the department of Mouths of the Rhone, defended by a strong fort. It is famous for muscadine wine, and seated on the Bay of Laquee; 14 miles S. E. of Marseilles. Pop. 6000.

CIRCARS, five provinces of the Deccan of Hindostan, on the Bay of Bengal. They were originally denominated Northern, from their position in respect to the Carnatic. Under the Mogul dynasty the government of these provinces was vested in the Nizam of the Deccan, and was assigned to the French in 1753, for arrears of pay claimed by them for auxiliary troops, with which they had supplied the Nizam. In 1759 they were conquered from the French by the English; and in 1765 were formally ceded by the Great Mogul, Shah Alum, to the English East India Company, during the governorship of Lord Clive. Four of these provinces, viz. Guntoor, Condapilly, Ellore, and Rajamundry, comprise about 7000 square miles of territory, between the mouths of the Kistna and Godavery rivers, and the line of 16. to 17. of N. lat.; and the fifth, Cicacole, extends in a N. E. direction along the shore of the Bay of Bengal, from the Godavery river, in the latitude of 17. N. for about 280 miles, to the lake Chilka, and is about 60 miles in mean breadth. This is the district from whence 500,000 to 600,000 pieces of cotton manufactured goods were formerly imported into England, under the name of long cloths, sallampores, and calicoes; and handkerchiefs, under the name of mazulipatams, &c.; it is also fertile in maize. Cicacole is now divided into two districts, viz. Ganjam, Vizgaapatam; and the other four Circars, resolved into three districts, viz. RAJAMUNDRY, MAZULIPATAM, and GUNTOOR; each of which see.

CIRCASSIA, a country of Asia, lying between the 44th and 45th degrees of N. lat., and longitudinally between the Black Sea, Sea of Azof, and the Caspian; its precise boundaries are very undefined: the Caucasian mountains, dividing it from the territories of the Abkhas, may be considered as forming its boundary on the S.; but the habits of the people being completely predatory, they acknowledge no boundary but that prescribed by the force of arms. It contains the districts of Great Cabarda, Little Cabarda, Beslen, Temirgoi Abasieh, Bseduch, Hatukai, and Bshani. It is now nominally subject to Russia; but they maintain their independence in defiance of the numerous attempts of the Russians to subdue them; and, from the peculiarly advantageous local circumstances of this country, and the extraordinary courage and military genius of its inhabitants, it might become very formidable were they united under one chief; but they are entirely a predatory people, divided into many different and hostile tribes, and want that spirit of unity necessary to make their power effectual. The Cabardians are the most powerful race, and their superiority has introduced a general imitation of their manners among their neighbours; so that from a description of these, an idea may be formed of all the rest. They are divided into three classes, the princes, the usdens or nobles, and the vassals or people. The people are divided into certain portions, who are each governed by a princely family, the eldest of whom is considered as chief, and the judge, protector, and father of the vassals. His person is sacred; but he cannot be a landholder. His property is nothing more than his arms, horses, slaves, and what tribute he can occasionally exact from foreign powers. In times of peace they are with difficulty distinguished from their subjects, their dress and food being the same, and their houses little better. The usdens are chosen by the princes from among the people, and are their officers, the executors of the law, and ministers of the legislature. Both the usdens and the people are proprietors of land. There does not appear to be any written law: the people are governed by a kind of common law, founded on a collection of ancient usages. They have a few manufactures; and their tillage produces scarcely sufficient for their own subsistence. The principal articles of commerce are sheep and horses, particularly the latter, which sell at a high price, being much esteemed. The balance of trade would, however, be considerably against them, were it not for the slaves they make in their predatory excursions. They have no money, and all their commerce is carried on by exchange. They almost universally subsist by robbery, being trained to it from their very cradle. This disposition naturally produces a bold adventurous spirit: they are expert horsemen and able warriors, being in general stout and well made. Their women are famed for their beauty, and chiefly supply the seraglios of Persia and Turkey. Those that are thus sold are, however, chiefly slaves, or their descendants. They sell at from 20*l.* to 100*l.* according to their beauty. The women participate in the general character of the nation, taking pride in the courage of their husbands, and loading them with reproaches when defeated.

They are kept extremely close; and the greatest reserve subsists between the married pairs. Their habitations are usually two huts, one for the husband, and the reception of strangers; and the other for the wife and family. The Circassians were formerly Christians; but, for want of instruction and written laws, they content themselves with a bare profession of being Christians or Mahometans. They have no letters of their own; and those who wish to write their language are obliged to make use of Arabian characters.

CIRENCESTER, commonly called CICITER, a borough in Gloucestershire, returning two members to parliament, with a market on Monday and Friday. The ruins of the walls are yet visible. It had also a castle and an abbey; and here three Roman roads, the Foss, Irmin, and Icknild, crossed each other. It is one of the greatest marts in the county for wool; and has a manufacture of curriers' knives, highly valued, and two public breweries; the church is a very stately edifice. It is seated on the banks of the little river Churn; 18 miles S. E. of Gloucester, and 89 W. of London. It communicates both with the Severn and the Thames, by a canal.

CIRIE, a town of Piedmont; seated on the Doria, near the foot of the Alps; 8 miles N. N. W. of Turin. Pop. 3500.

CIRTKNITZ. *See* CZIRNITZ.

CISMAR, a town of Lower Saxony, in Holstein; seated near the Baltic; 17 miles N. of Travemunde.

CITTADELLA, or CIUDADELLA, a seaport, and the capital of Minorca, surrounded by walls and bastions, with a good harbour at the N. W. point of the island. Long. 3. 11. E. lat. 39. 58. N.

CITTADELLA, an inland town of the Venetian territory; 25 miles N. W. of Venice. Pop. about 6000.

CITTA DI CASTELLO, a city of Italy, with a castle, capital of a district of the same name W. of the Appennines; seated on the Tiber; 27 miles S. W. of Urbino.

CITTA NUOVA, a town of Italy, in the marquisate of Ancona, on the Gulf of Venice; 10 miles S. of Loretto.

CITTA NUOVA, a seaport of Istria, and a bishop's see; seated on an isthmus, at the mouth of the Queto, which forms a good harbour; 26 miles S. S. W. of Capo d'Istria. Long. 13. 47. E. lat. 45. 32. N.

CITTA VECCHIA, a fortified city of Malta, formerly the capital of the island, and still the seat of the bishopric. The most remarkable edifices are the palace of the grand master and the cathedral. Here are extensive catacombs, about 15 feet below the surface of the rock in which they are cut; they contain streets formed with such regularity, that the title of Subterranean City has been given to this place. Near the city is the Grotto of St. Paul, divided into three parts by iron grates; in the furthest part is an altar, and a statue of the saint, in white marble. This old city was considerably larger than at present; for the new city, Valetta, being more conveniently seated, has drawn away the greater number of inhabitants. It stands on a hill, in the interior of the island 6 miles W. by S. of Valetta.

CITY POINT. *See* BERMUDA HUNDRED.

CIUDAD REAL, a town of Spain, capital of Mancha. The inhabitants are noted for dressing leather for gloves. It is 2 miles from the Guadiana, and 98 S. of Madrid.

CIUDAD REAL, a city of Chiapa. *See* CHIAPA DOS ESPAGNOLS.

CIUDAD RODRIGO, a town of Spain, in Leon, and a bishop's see; seated on the river Aguada, on the frontier of Portugal. It was taken by the French in 1810, and retaken by the English in 1811; 50 miles S. W. of Salamanca.

CIVITA CASTELLANA, a town of Italy, in the patrimony of St. Peter; seated on a high rock, at the foot of which is a river that flows into the Tiber; 25 miles N. of Rome.

CIVITA CHIETI, a city of Naples, capital of Abruzzo Citeriore, and an archbishop's see. It contains four churches and nine convents, and is situate on a mountain, near the river Pescara, a few miles above its entrance into the Adriatic; 28 miles E. of Aquila, and 96 N. of Naples.

CIVITA DI FRIULI, a town of Italy, in Friuli; seated on the Natisona; 10 miles E. of Udina.

CIVITA DI PENNA, a town of Naples, in Abruzzo Ulteriore, near the river Salino; 25 miles N. E. of Aquila.

CIVITA DUCALE, a town of Naples, in Abruzzo Ulteriore, on the river Velino; 10 miles W. of Aquila.

CIVITA MANDONIA, a town of Naples, in Calabria Citeriore, near which are the ruins of the famous city of Sibaris. It is seated on the Gulf of Tarento, at the influx of the Crati; 31 miles N. by E. of Cosenza.

CIVITA VECCHIA, a strong seaport of Italy, in the patrimony of St. Peter, with an arsenal. The chief exports are puzzolana, and a superior kind of alum, prepared at Tolfa. Here the pope's galleys are stationed, and it is a free port. It was taken by the French in 1798, and retaken by the Austrians and Russians in 1799. It is 35 miles N. W. of Rome. Long. 11. 46. E. lat. 42. 5. N.

CIVITELLA, a town of Naples, in Otranto; 5 miles N. of Taranto.

CIVRAY. *See* SIVRAY.

CLACKMANNANSHIRE, a county of Scotland, bounded on the S. and S. W. by the Forth, and on all other sides by Perthshire. It is 9 miles long, and 6 broad; produces good corn and pasture, and plenty of coal and salt. It has also veins of lead, cobalt, and antimony. Alloa is the principal town. Clackmannan and Kinross send one member to parliament.

CLACKMANNAN, a parish and town of the above county. The parish comprises nearly four-fifths of the county, and contains about 800 acres of woodland. The town is seated on an eminence, and has a harbour formed by the Devon, at its influx with the Forth. On the top of a hill, 190 feet above the level of the Forth, is a square tower which derives its name from the illustrious Robert Bruce, whose great sword and casque are here preserved. It is 27 miles W. N. W. of Edinburgh.

CLAGENFURT, a town of the Austrian empire, capital of Lower Carinthia. It has a strong wall, and contains six churches and three convents. Here is a manufacture of cloth, and a considerable one of white lead. This town was taken by the French in 1797, and again in 1809, when they demolished the fortifications. It stands on the river Glan, which falls into the Drave; 148 miles S. W. of Vienna. Pop. about 10,000.

CLAIR, ST., a lake of North America, between the Lakes Huron and Erie, 90 miles in circumference. It receives the waters of the Lakes Superior, Michigan, and Huron, and also of the river Thames, from Upper Canada, in the lat. of 42. 32. N., and discharges them through the strait called Detroit, into the Lake Erie.

CLAIR, ST., a county in the state of Illinois, the W. side of which borders on the Mississippi river, in the lat. of 38. 30. N. Pop. 7092. Cahokia, on the bank of the river, 81 miles S. W. by W. of Vandalia, is the chief town. St. Clair is also the name of a township in Allegany county, and another in Bedford county, both in Pennsylvania.

CLAIRAC, or CLAVRAC, a town of France, in the department of Lot and Garonne. Corn and tobacco are cultivated, and a great deal of wine and brandy made here. It is seated in a valley, on the river Dort; 13 miles N. W. of Agen. Pop. about 6000.

CLAIRBORNE, a county of the state Mississippi; bounded on the S. by the Big Black, and N. by the Yazoo rivers, and on the W., for about 25 miles, by the Mississippi river, between the lat. of 32. and 33. N. Pop. 13,078. Port Gibson, 118 miles N. W. by W. of Monticello, is the chief town.

CLAIRBORNE is also the name of another county, on the N. frontier of the eastern part of the state of Tennessee. Pop. 9474. Tazewell, N. of the Mountain Ridge, and 222 miles E. N. E. of Murfreesborough, is the chief town.

CLAMECY, a town of France, in the department of Nievre. Before the late revolution, the chapel of an hospital in the suburb was the provision for the bishop of Bethlehem, who was fixed here in 1180, after the Christians had been driven from the Holy Land. Clamecy is seated at the confluence of the Buevron with the Yonne; 35 miles N. N. E. of Nevers. Pop. about 5300.

CLANE, a town of Ireland, county of Kildare, on the Liffey.

CLAPHAM, a village in Surrey, an appendage to the British metropolis; 4 miles S. of London Bridge. It is composed of a number of very neat houses, built round an extensive common, presenting a very rural, picturesque, and interesting scene.

CLAPTON, UPPER and LOWER. *See* HACKNEY.

CLARA, ST., a small island of Peru, in the Bay of Guayaquil; 70 miles S. W. of Guayaquil. Long. 82. 20. W. lat. 2. 20. S.

CLARE, a town in Suffolk, with a market on Tuesday. Here are the ruins of a castle; also of a priory, the house of which is now occupied by a farmer, and the chapel is a barn. Clare has a manufacture of baize, and is seated near the Stour; 15 miles S. of Bury St. Edmund, and 56 N. E. of London.

CLARE, a maritime county in the province of Munster, on the W. coast of Ireland, bounded on the N. by Galway Bay, and S. by the Shannon. It contains a good deal of mountainous surface; the valleys, however, are very fertile; and it breeds more horses than any other county in Ireland, beside a great number of cattle and sheep. Ennis, 113 miles W. by S. of Dublin, is the capital. Although it has 70 miles of sea-coast, it has no frequented harbour, its principal outport being Limerick. It sends two members to parliament.

CLARE, a parish and town on the N. bank of the Shannon, in the preceding county. The town is at the head of a bay, in the Shannon; 3 miles S. of Ennis. There is also another parish of the same name in the county of Galway, intersected by the river Clare, which falls into Lough Corrib ; about 5 miles N. of the town of Galway.

CLAREMONT, a town of New Hampshire, in Cheshire county, situate on Surgar River, at its conflux with the Connecticut; 90 miles W. N. W. of Portsmouth.

CLARENDON, a village in Wiltshire; 3 miles E. of Salisbury. Here was once a royal palace, in which the parliament was several times convened; the first time by Henry II. in 1164, who enacted the laws called the Constitutions of Clarendon, by which the power of the clergy was restrained.

CLARENZA, or CHIARENZA, a small village and cape of Greece, N. W. part of the Morea. It gives the title to the English Dukes of Clarence—one of the Dukes of Chiarenza having married into the Hainault family, a descendant of which (Philippa) was queen to Edward III., whose third son, Lionel, bore the title, which has since been given to the third son of the kings of England.

CLARITZA, a town of European Turkey, in Janna, at the mouth of the Penco, in the Gulf of Salonica; 26 miles E. of Larissa.

CLARKE, the name of seven counties in different parts of the United States of North America, as follows, viz. with the number of inhabitants in each, and the distance and bearing of the chief town from the seat of government of each respective state :—

In Georgia	10,552	Watkinsville	63 N. by W.
Alabama	8640	Woodstown	75 S. W.
Kentucky	10,802	Winchester	40 E. S. E.
Ohio	16,882	Springfield	46 W.
Indiana	15,596	Charleston	121 S. by E.
Illinois	7453	Clark	110 E. N. E.
Arkansas	2309	Clarke	75 E. N. E.

CLARKESBURG, a town of Virginia, chief of Harrison county, situate on the Monongahela; 40 miles S. W. of Morgan-town, and 325 N. W. of Richmond.

CLARKSON, a town of Monroe county, New York; 255 miles W. by N. of Albany. Pop 3486.

CLARKSTOWN, a town of Rockland county, New York, on the W. bank of the Hudson river; about 40 miles above the city of New York.

CLARKSVILLE, a town of Tennessee, chief of Montgomery county; situate on Cumberland River, at the influx of the Red River; 45 miles N. W. of Nashville. Also another town in Otsego county, New York; 61 miles W. by S. of Albany.

CLATSOPS FORT, at the mouth of Colombia River, in the Pacific Ocean, named after a tribe of Indians inhabiting the banks of that river. *See* ASTORIA.

CLAUDE, ST., a town of France, in the department of Jura. It owes its origin to a celebrated abbey, which was secularized in 1742. The cathedral is extremely elegant; and here are many public fountains with large basins. It is seated between three high mountains, on the river Lison; 35 miles N. W. of Geneva. Pop. about 3700.

CLAVERACK, a town of New York, in Colombia county; seated in a large plain, near a creek of its name; 2 miles E. of Hudson. Pop. 3056.

CLAVO, a town of the island of Corsica; 8 miles E. S. E. of Ajaccio.

CLAUSEN, a town of Germany, in Tyrol, with a castle. The adjacent country produces a fine red wine. It stands near the river Eisack; 8 miles S. W. of Brixen.

CLAUSEN, a town of Germany, in the electorate of Treves ; 5 miles S. of Wittlick.

CLAUSENBURG, or COLOSWAR, a town of Transylvania, where the states of the province generally assemble. On one of the gates is an inscription in honour of Trajan. It suffered greatly by fire in 1798, at which period it contained about 13,000 inhabitants. It is seated on the Samos; 60 miles N. N. W. of Hermanstadt, and 225 E. S. E. of Vienna. Long. 23. 20. E. lat. 46. 55. N.

CLAUSTHAL, a town of Lower Saxony, in the principality of Grubenhagen, and immediately contiguous to Zellerfeld. Here is a mint for coining money; and near it are some rich silver mines. It stands in the Hartz mountains; 14 miles S. S. W. of Goslar, and 48 S. E. of Hanover. Pop. about 8000.

CLAUSZ, a town of Germany, in the Traun quarter of Upper Austria; 17 miles S. W. of Steyn.

CLAY, or CLEY, a village in Norfolk seated on an arm of the sea; 4 miles N. N. W. of Holt. It has some large salt-works, and is frequented for sea-bathing.

CLAY, an interior county in the S. E. part of Kentucky, containing about 1000 square miles of surface. Pop. 4607. The S. fork of the Kentucky river has its source in this county. Manchester, in the vicinity of which are some salt-works, about 100 miles S. S. E. of Frankfort, is the chief town.

CLAYDON. There are five villages of this name in different parts of England, all inconsiderable.

CLAYTON. There are eight townships and villages of this name in different parts of England, the most important of which is a township in the parish of BRADFORD, Yorkshire, which see; the others are unimportant.

CLEAR, CAPE, the S. point of a small island off the S. extremity of Ireland, in the lat. of 51. 20. N. and 9. 37. W. long. It generally forms the point of departure, or commencement of the reckoning, of vessels sailing out of St. George's Channel to the westward.

CLEARFIELD, an interior, large, but thinly inhabited county, in the W. part of Pennsylvania, in which the western branch of the Susquehannah and several creeks have their source. Pop. 7834. The chief town, of the same name, is about 200 miles N. N. W. of Philadelphia.

CLEGUEREC, a town of France, near the N. frontier of the department of Morbihan ; 11 miles N. W. of Pontivi. Pop. about 4000.

CLEMENTS, ST., a town in Spain, in the province of New Castile ; 40 miles from La Mancha. Pop. 4000.

CLEOBURY MORTIMER, a town in Shropshire, with a market on Thursday; seated on the river Rea; 28 miles S. S. E. of Shrewsbury, and 137 N. W. of London.

CLERKENWELL, one of the out parishes, forming an integral part of the British metropolis, lying on the N. side. A great portion of the inhabitants are employed as lapidaries, working jewellers, and in all the various branches of the manufacture of clocks, watches, and time keepers, which are here made in greater perfection than in any other part of the world. In this district are two or three extensive distilleries, several iron foundries, and various other manufactures, as also the works of the New River Company, which supply a great portion of the metropolis with water, conveyed by pipes into the several houses. Clerkenwell contains also a very elegant and spacious edifice, in which the sessions for the county of Middlesex are held; two extensive prisons, one appropriated as a house of correction for juvenile offenders, and the other, which has recently been much enlarged, to general purposes. It has a theatre for pantomime and aquatic exhibitions, called Sadler's Wells, and was formerly distinguished for an extensive establishment of the Knights of St. John of Jerusalem, which was destroyed by the rebels under Wat Tyler, in 1381, except the principal gate tower, which still remains entire, and forms one of the most interesting features of antiquity connected with the metropolis. It has four churches. The general aspect of this division of the metropolis is not in any way imposing to the eye; but, in the extent and value of its productions, it is entitled to rank among the most important.

CLERKE, or SINDE ISLES, two islands near the entrance of Behring's Strait, between the coasts of Kamtschatka and North America. They were seen by Cook in 1778, and so named in honour of Captain Clerke, his second in command. They were both inhabited, and not unknown to the Russians. Long. 169. 30. W. lat. 63. 15. N.

Clermont, a city of France, capital of the department of Puy de Dome, and a bishop's see. It is seated on an eminence, and sometimes called Clermont Ferrand, since the town Montferrand, about a mile distant to the N. E., was united under the name of a suburb. The cathedral, public squares, and walks, are very fine, but the streets are narrow, and the houses built of stone of a gloomy hue. In the neighbourhood are some mineral springs; and that of the suburb St. Allyre has formed a natural bridge over the brook into which it falls, so that carriages can pass over. Clermont is the birthplace of the celebrated Pascal, and has manufactures of ratteens, druggets, serges, and leather. It is 215 miles S. by E. of Paris, and 10 W. of Lyons. Pop about 16,000.

Clermont, a town of France, in the department of Meuse, on an eminence by the river Ayr; 12 miles W. by S. of Verdun.

Clermont, a town of France, in the department of Oise, on an eminence near the Bresche; 37 miles N. of Paris. *Clermont* is also the name of several other inconsiderable towns in different parts of France.

Clermont, a county in the state Ohio, the S. end of which is bounded by the Ohio river. It is about 30 miles from N. to S., and 20 from E. to W. The population is 23,106. Williamsburg, on a branch of the Miami river, about 18 miles from the Ohio, and 30 E. of Cincinnati, is the chief town.

Clermont, a town of New York, in Colombia county; 45 miles S. of Hudson, and 117 N. of New York. Pop. 1231.

Clermont de Lodeve, a town of France, in the department of Herault, with manufactures of cloth and hats; seated on an eminence near the Loguere; 80 miles S. S. E. of Lodeve, and 24 W. of Montpelier. Pop. about 5500.

Clery, a town of France, in the department of Loiret, once famous for the pilgrimages to our Lady of Clery. Here is the tomb of Louis XI., who appears in white marble as the saint and the patriot king. It is 9 miles S. S. W. of Orleans.

Cleveland. *See* Cayahoga.

Cleves, a duchy of Westphalia, bordering on the S. E. part of Holland, divided into two parts by the Rhine. It is a fine country, variegated with hills, woods, fields, towns, and villages, and the chief rivers are the Rhine, Lippe, and Roer. The capital is Wesel.

Cleves, a city of Germany, and the capital of the duchy of Cleves. It is seated on the eastern side of three hills, 2 miles W. of the Rhine; and has a castle, built in the time of Julius Cæsar. It is 70 miles N. N. W. of Cologne, and about the same distance E. by S. of Rotterdam. Pop. about 5000.

Cliff, a Saxon word implying a rock or high ground. There are eight villages in different parts of England, so named probably from their situation (in a relative sense) on high ground. There are three others named Clifford, in reference to their contiguity to a fordable stream; and 22 named Clifton, implying towns on a cliff, or high ground. None of these demand any particular notice, except Clifton, contiguous to Bristol, to which city it forms a beautiful and interesting appendage; as its name implies, it is built on an eminence, at the foot of which, on the N. bank of the Lower Avon, is a hot well, that contributes greatly to its advantage, by the numerous visitors who seek to avail themselves of the benefits of its restorative properties. The buildings of Clifton are in general elegant and commodious, and, from their elevated site, command extensive and beautiful prospects. *See* Bristol.

Clinton, a county at the N. E. extremity of the state of New York. It is bounded on the E. for about 35 miles by Lake Champlain, which divides it from Vermont. Plattsburg, on the shore of Lake Champlain, 170 miles N. of Albany, is the capital.

Clinton, an interior county in the S. W. part of the state of Ohio, in which one of the branches of the Little Miami river has its source. Pop. 15,719. Wilmington, in the centre of the county, is the chief town; 75 miles S. W. of Columbus.

Clinton is also the name of several townships in different parts of the United States of North America, named probably, as well as the preceding counties, in reference to George Clinton, who was vice-president of the United States from 1805 to 1813. The most considerable is in Duchess county, on the E. bank of the Hudson river, 70 miles N. of New York. Pop. 1830. At Clinton, in Oneida county, New York, 102 miles W. of Albany, is Hamilton College, endowed by the state, and which promises to become a flourishing seat of instruction.

Clithero, a borough in Lancashire, seated on the E. bank of the river Ribble, at the foot of Pendle Hill, on the confines of Yorkshire. It is a place of some antiquity, having the ruins of a castle, built by the Lacys in 1178. It communicates by a collateral cut with the Leeds and Liverpool Canal, which facilitates the conveyance of large quantities of lime, dug in the vicinity of the town. It has a spring of water impregnated with sulphur. It holds a market on Saturday, and four fairs annually, and returns one member to parliament. It is 30 miles N. by W. of Manchester.

Clogher, a parish in the county of Tyrone, Ireland. The city, now much decayed, was the see of a bishop, but is now united to Armagh. It is 20 miles W. by N. of Armagh, and 76 N. N. W. of Dublin.

Clon. There are 102 parishes and towns in Ireland beginning with *Clon*, among which the following are the most important, viz.—

Clonakilty, a town of the county of Cork, seated at the head of a bay on St. George's Channel. The principal part of the town is formed of a spacious square. It is 20 miles W. S. W. of Cork.

Clones, a town of Ireland, in the county of Monaghan; 85 miles N. by W. of Dublin. The parish of Clones extends into Fermanagh county.

Clonfert, formerly a bishop's see, on the eastern confines of the county of Galway, Ireland. It is a miserable place, containing only 31 houses; 36 miles E. of Galway, and 70 W. of Dublin.

Clonmel, a town partly in the county of Tipperary, and partly in that of Waterford, Ireland. It is seated on the banks of the river Suir, over which is a bridge of twenty arches; 22 miles W. N. W. of the city of Waterford, and 82 S. W. of Dublin. It is the assize town for the county of Tipperary, and returns one member to the parliament of the United Kingdom; it has considerable manufactures of woollens, a lunatic and orphan asylum, several schools, and other public buildings. It was the birthplace of Sterne.

Clontarf, a town on the N. shore of Dublin Bay, two miles E. of the city of Dublin. It has several neat residences in its vicinity, and is memorable in Irish history for the last battle fought between the native Irish and the Danes, in 1015, which led to the expulsion of the latter from Ireland.

Cloppenburg, a town of Westphalia, in the principality of Munster; 32 miles N. E. of Lingen.

Closter Neuburg, a town of Austria, with an Augustine convent of regular canons. It has a yard for ship-building, and is seated on the Danube; 7 miles N. N. W. of Vienna.

Closter Seven, or **Kloster Zeven**, a town of the Duchy of Bremen, memorable for a convention entered into between the Duke of Cumberland and the Duke of Richelieu, commander of the French armies, in 1758, by which 38,000 Hanoverians laid down their arms and were dispersed. It is 19 miles S. of Stade.

Cloud, St., a town of France, 5 miles E. of Paris; celebrated for its palace, which was the favourite residence of Napoleon Buonaparte.

Cloye, or **Clois**, a town of France, in the department of Eure and Loire; 5 miles S. W. of Chateaudun.

Cloyne, a town of Ireland, on the E. shore of Cork harbour, in the county of Cork, and a bishop's see; 16 miles E. of Cork.

Clundert, a town and fortress of South Holland, near an arm of the sea called Hollands Diep. In 1793 it was taken by the French, who were obliged to evacuate it soon after; but it surrendered to them in 1795. It is 9 miles S. E. of Williamstadt.

Cluny, a town of France, in the department of Saone and Loire, with a late famous Benedictine abbey, seated on the Grosne; 13 miles N. W. of Macon.

Cluses, a town of Savoy, in Faucigny, seated on the Arve; 22 miles S. E. of Geneva.

Clwyd, a river of Wales, which rises in the middle of Denbighshire, runs N. through a beautiful valley of the same name, and, having entered Flintshire, flows into the Irish Sea, 6 miles below St. Asaph.

Clyde, a river of Scotland, which rises in the S. part of Lanarkshire, passes by Lanark, Hamilton, Glasgow, Renfrew, Dumbarton, and Port Glasgow, to Greenock, where it enters an arm of the sea, called the Frith of Clyde. This river runs, for several miles, between high rocks, and in its course forms several cataracts: it is deservedly celebrated for its romantic and diversified scenery, and has several extensive cotton and other works on its banks. At Glasgow it becomes navigable; and, 6 miles below that city, it is joined by the Great Canal from the Forth.

Clyde, Frith of, an inlet of the sea, between the coast of Ayrshire and the Isle of Arran, which opens into the north channel, between the N. E. end of Ireland and Scotland.

Coango, a tributary stream of the great river Congo, in South Africa. It rises in Matamba, and runs a course nearly due N., falling into the Congo, about 100 miles above the Cataracts. It is supposed by some to be the main branch of the Congo.

Coanzo, a river of Africa, which rises in the interior parts, crosses the kingdoms of Matamba and Angola, and enters the Atlantic in lat. 9. 20. S.

Coast Castle, Cape, the principal settlement of the English on the coast of Guinea, with a strong citadel. The Portuguese first formed an establishment here in 1610, but were soon after dislodged by the Dutch, who, in their turn, surrendered it to the English in 1661. It is in the lat. of 57. N. and 152. of W. long.

Cobbe, the capital of the territory of Darfur, in Zahara, North Africa, situate on the borders of Nubia; 150 miles W. S. W. of Sennaar, and 500 S. E. of Mathan. Long. 28. 8. E. lat. 14. 11. N.

Cobham, a village in Surrey, on the river Mole; 7 miles S. W. of Kingston. It has several handsome villas, two medicinal springs, and a manufacture of iron and copper.

Cobi, called by the Chinese *Shamo*, a vast desert of Asia, extending from the 75th to the 110th degree of E. long., and lying between the 35th and 45th of N. lat. The western part of this vast district borders on Bucharia, and the S. W. on Thibet. The Chinese province of Kan-suh (which see) projects into this desert, and the N. E. part stretches towards the frontiers of Asiatic Russia; but its limits are on every side too imperfectly defined to admit of any precise description.

Cobija, a town of Peru, on the coast of the desert of Atacamas, with a good harbour for vessels carrying the metal from the neighbouring mines. It is 250 miles S. of Arica. Long. 34. 44. W. lat. 22. 20. S.

Coblentz, a strong city of Germany, in the circle of Lower Rhine, situate at the conflux of the Rhine and the Moselle; with a bridge of boats over the former, and a stone bridge over the latter. In the time of the Romans it was the station of the first legion, by whom it was called *Confluentes*, and after them, the residence of the successors of Charlemagne, and at a later period it was the capital of the Grand Duchy of Treves. It contains three large churches, two of which are collegiate, a college, eight convents, &c. It is memorable for having been the chief rendezvous of the French emigrant princes, at the commencement of the revolution. It was taken by the French in 1794, who retained it until the peace of 1814, when it was assigned to Prussia. It transmits large quantities of excellent wine, timber, and iron, by the Rhine, into Holland. It is 285 miles W.S.W. of Berlin, 420 W. N. W. of Vienna, and 260 E. S. E. of Paris. Long. 7. 32. E., lat. 50. 24. N. Pop. about 11,000.

Coblentz, a town of Switzerland, in the district of Baden, at the conflux of the Aar and the Rhine. It is ten miles N. N. W. of Baden.

Cobre, El, a town of the island of Cuba, 10 miles W. of St. Jago.

Coburg, Saxe, a principality, at the S. W. extremity of the circle of Upper Saxony, projecting into the circle of Franconia. It is one of the states of the Germanic confederacy. Its area is about 960 square miles; the population is 139,440. The feudal principles were abolished in 1809, and in 1826 the duke obtained the accession of the duchy of Gotha, and other minor states, to his dominions. It is a tolerably fertile district, intersected by the river Itsch, which runs from N. to S. into the Mayne, and contains, besides several villages, the towns of Hilburghausen, Eisfeld, Sonneberg, Schalkaw, Neustadt, Heldburg, Umerstadt, and Coburg; and Konigsberg, with several villages insulated in the bishopric of Wurzburg.

Coburg, the capital of the preceding principality, is seated on the banks of the Itsch, 95 miles S. S. W. of Leipsic, and has a college, a fort, and a castle. Here are manufactures of porcelain, and of petrified wood, with which the country abounds: it also carries on some trade in wool. The government offices and town-house form part of the sides of a spacious square. Pop. 8100.

Coca, a town of Spain, in Old Castile, with a strong castle for state prisoners; seated among mountains, on the river Eresma; 22 miles N. W. of Segovia.

Cochabamba, a district of South America, in Bolivia, lying between the 62nd and 68th degrees of W. long., and the 16th and 19th of S. lat. Cochabamba is watered by several streams, all running from S. to N., uniting, on the northern frontier, to form the river Mainore, running through the government of Moxos and Brazil, where, after the union of the Guapore, it is called the Madeira, falling into the Amazons. Cochabamba is an exceedingly fertile district; and the inhabitants, about 70,000 in number, seem to prefer the pursuits of agriculture, rather than of mining. The chief town, of the same name, is situate on the western confines of the province, in the lat. of 18. S. and about 200 miles E. of Arica.

Cocheim, a town of Germany, seated on the Moselle; 25 miles S. W. of Coblentz.

Cocherel, a town of France, in the department of the Eure; noted for a victory gained by Gueschlin over the king of Navarre, in 1564. It is 7 miles E. of Evreux.

Cochin, a province of Hindostan, on the coast of Malabar, towards the southern extremity of the peninsula; a chain of islands flanks the whole extent of the coast. It is a very fertile district, and yields abundance of rice, pepper, and cocoa nuts, and excellent timber for ship-building. It was the first part of India where the Portuguese, after passing the Cape of Good Hope, formed a settlement; but their intrigues and extortions soon occasioned them to be repulsed from the main land; but they were allowed, in 1503, to erect a fortification on one of the islands, in the lat. of 9. 57. N. The fort surrendered to the Dutch in 1663, who, by their toleration of all religious professions, occasioned it to increase greatly in population. The natives of the province successfully resisted the Mahometan arms up to the period of 1776, when Hyder Aly rendered them tributary; and the exaction being enforced with increased vigour, under Tippoo Saib, in 1791, the rajah sought the protection of the English; to whom the Dutch fort and town surrendered in 1795, and thereby the whole territory became subservient to the English. The town of Cochin is 120 miles S. by E. of Calicut.

Cochin China, a maritime kingdom of Asia, extending from Cape Varela-falsa, in the lat. of 12. 55. N., to Sinhoo Bay, in the lat. of 17. N.; it is bounded on the W. by a high mountain ridge, running parallel with the coast its whole extent, at the distance of 60 or 70 miles; this mountain ridge divides Cochin China from a vast desert, lying between the mountains and the great river Cambodia. The aborigines of Cochin China are called Moys, and reside chiefly on the western declivities of the mountains. To these strong holds they were driven, about the beginning of the 15th century, by the present possessors of the country. The aborigines are a savage people, very black, and in features resemble the Caffres. The present inhabitants bear evident marks of being derived from the same stock as the Chinese; their religion is also the same, and most of their manners and customs. They are a courteous, affable, inoffensive race, rather inclined to indolence. The women are by far the most active sex, and merchants often employ them as their factors and brokers. The cities and towns have gates at the end of each street, which are shut every night. The houses are mostly of bamboo, covered with rushes, or the straw of rice, and stand in groves of oranges, limes, plantains, and cocoa trees. Here is plenty of sugar, pepper, rice, yams, sweet potatoes, pumpkins, and melons; also ivory, musk, honey, and silk, and the edible birds'-nests. The climate is healthy, the summer heat being tempered by regular breezes from the sea. September, October, and November is the rainy season, when the low lands are suddenly overflowed by torrents of water from the mountains: the inundations happen generally once a fortnight, and continue three or four days. In the three following months there are frequent rains, brought by cold northerly winds, which distinguish this country by a winter different from any other in the east. The inundations render the land fruitful, many parts producing three crops of grain in the year. Gold is taken almost pure from the mines, and there are rich silver mines. The country is intersected by rivers, which are well calculated for promoting inland commerce, yet not large enough to admit vessels of great burden; but there are commodious harbours on the coast, particularly that of Turon, in the lat. of 16. 5. N. The vanity of the Chinese induces them to consider Cochin as a tributary province of their empire; but if any acknowledgment is made, it is merely nominal. The Cochin Chinese are the most brave and efficient of the eastern nations; they have hitherto held very little intercourse with Europeans, but carry on an extensive traffic with China and various parts of the eastern seas.

Cocke, a county of Tennessee, bounded on the S. E. by a ridge of the Allegany mountains, called the Smoky Mountains, which divides it from North Carolina. It is intersected by the Big Pigeon and French Bread rivers, which unite their streams toward the N. W. boundary of the county. Pop. 6992. Newport, 216 miles E. of Murfreesborough, is the chief town.

Cocker, a river which rises in the S. of Cumberland, flows through the Lakes of Buttermere, Cromack-water, and Lowes-water, and joins the Derwent below Cockermouth.

Cockermouth, a borough in Cumberland, with a market on Monday. It stands on the Cocker, at its conflux with the Derwent, and between two hills, on one of which is a handsome church, and on the other the remains of a stately castle. It has manufactures of shalloons, coarse linen and woollen cloths, leather, and hats. It returns two members to parliament, and is 36 miles S. W. of Carlisle, and 305 N. N. W. of London.

Coconato, a town of Piedmont, the birthplace of Columbus; 20 miles E. of Turin.

Cocos Islands, in the Bay of Bengal, occupied by some British settlers, and producing a large supply of cocoa nuts.

Cod, Cape, is the northern extremity of a peninsula, more than 120 miles in extent, and 10 to 15 in mean breadth, forming part of the state of Massachusets. Cape Cod and the main land form a very spacious bay, about 50 miles each way; and Cape Cod and Cape Ann are the S. and W. points which form the open bay called Massachusets Bay, leading to the harbour of Boston; the outer side of the peninsula forming Cape Cod is flanked by shoals, which render the navigation thereabouts dangerous. A lighthouse on the Cape Point is in lat. 42. 3. N., and 70. 6. W. long.

Codogno, a town of Italy, in the Lodesan, duchy of Milan, near the confluence of the Adda with the Po; 12 miles S. S. E. of Lodi.

Codomudi, a town of Hindostan, in Coimbetore, seated near the Cavery, a little above the influx of the Noyelar; 23 miles S. E. of Bhawanikudal.

Coepang, a seaport in the Asiatic archipelago, on the S. W. end of the Island of Timor. It is the principal port of the island, and a great resort of the Malays, who fish for the biche-de-la-mar off the N. coast of Australia; and also the chief place of export for the Timor ponies to Australia, and other ports. It lies W. of Port Essington, North Australia. Fort Concordia is in lat. 10. 13. S. and long. 123. 45. E.

Coesfeld, a town of Westphalia, in the principality of Munster, near the source of the Burkel; 18 miles W. of Munster.

Coevorden, a fortified town of Holland, on the confines of Drenthe, Westphalia, and Overyssel, and one of the strongest places in the whole country. It stands in a morass, on the river Aa; 33 miles S. by E. of Groningen. It is the capital of Drenthe.

Coeymans, a town in Albany county, New York, on the W. bank of the Hudson river; 14 miles S. of Albany. Pop. 3107.

Coggeshall, a town in Essex, with a market on Saturday, and a manufacture of baize; seated on the N. bank of the river Blackwater; 7 miles W. of Colchester, and 44 E. N. E. of London.

Cognac, or Coignac, a town of France, in the department of Charente, with a castle, where Francis I. was born. It is celebrated for excellent brandy, and seated on the Charente; 17 miles W. of Angouleme, and 40 E. by S. of Rochefort.

Cogne, a town of Piedmont, in a valley and on a river of the same name. The mountains which surround it are rich in mines of iron and copper. It is 6 miles S. of Aousta.

Cogni, or Konieh, a city of Turkey, capital of Caramania, and the see of a Greek archbishop. The walls have 108 square towers, at forty paces distant from each other; it has two large suburbs, into one of which the caravans and strangers retire. It has upwards of 100 mosques; and, though much declined of late years, it is still a place of great trade: it is seated on the E. side of a ridge of lofty mountains, in a country abounding in corn, fruit, pulse, and cattle; 280 miles S. E. of Constantinople, and about the same distance due E. of Smyrna.

Cohahuila, an intendancy of North America, republic of Mexico, bounded on the E. by the Texas. There are productive mines in this district. Pop. 160,000. Chief town, Chihuahua.

Cohasset, a town on the S. coast of Massachusets Bay, just without the entrance to Boston harbour; 25 miles S. W. of Boston. Cohasset has a tolerably good harbour; but a ledge of rocks at its entrance renders its approach dangerous.

Cohoes Falls, a village 8 miles due N. of Albany, in the state of New York; it is seated on the banks of the Mohawk river, over which is a bridge, about one mile and a half above its entrance into the Hudson; about three-quarters of a mile higher up, the Mohawk, being about 350 yards wide, pours down its waters over a precipice, in an unbroken sheet, a height of 70 feet perpendicular, and, next to Niagara, forms the grandest natural object in the state of New York.

Coimbetore, a province of the peninsula of

Hindostan, lying S. of Mysore, to which it was lately subject, but ceded to the English on the final defeat of Tippoo, in 1799. It is 110 miles long, and 70 broad; and is divided by the river Noyelar into two districts, N. and S., of which Bhawanikudal and Daraporam are the chief towns.

Coimbetore, a town of Hindostan, the ancient capital of the province of the same name. It was taken by General Meadows in 1790, and retaken in 1791 by Tippoo, who soon after destroyed the fort. It contains 2000 houses, an extensive mud palace, and a tolerable mosque, built by Tippoo, who sometimes resided here; but it has no large temple. The palace now serves as a barrack for a regiment of British cavalry. The chief manufactures are muslins and cotton cloths; and these, with cotton-wool and thread, tobacco, sugar, and betel-leaf, are the principal articles of trade. It is 100 miles S. by E. of Seringapatam. Long. 77. 6. E. lat. 11. 0. N.

Coimbra, a city of Portugal, capital of Beira, and a bishop's see, with a celebrated university, the only one in Portugal, transferred hither from Lisbon in 1306, where it was originally founded in 1290. The cathedral is magnificent; beside which there are nine churches and eight convents. It stands on a mountain, on the river Mondego, over which is an elegant bridge, about 25 miles above its entrance into the sea; 100 miles N. E. of Lisbon. It suffered considerably by the great earthquake in 1755. Pop. about 12,000.

Coioacan, a town of North America, republic of Mexico; 5 miles S. E. of Mexico, in a rich and fertile district; it has manufactures of woollen fabrics. Pop. 5200.

Coire, or Chur, a town of Switzerland, capital of the canton of the Grisons, and a bishop's see. It is surrounded by ancient brick walls, with square and round towers, and divided into two parts, the least of which is of the catholic religion, and the greatest of the protestant. The French surprised and defeated the Austrian army at this place in 1799. It is seated between two mountains, on the river Plessur, near the Rhine, 65 miles S. by W. of Constance, and contributes to render Coire a place of considerable traffic. It was the birthplace of Angelica Kauffman, the female painter.

Colabba, a town of Hindostan, on the coast; 19 miles S. of Bombay.

Colapoor, a small independent state of Hindostan, on the coast of the Concan, bounded on the S. by the Portuguese territory of Goa. The rajah of this district claims being descended from the founder of the Mahratta empire. The natives were formerly celebrated for their piracies; but their depredations were put an end to under the administration of the Marquis Wellesley, in 1804. Vingorla, the principal town, is in lat. 16. N.

Colar, or Coloram, a town of Hindostan, in Mysore, with a large mud fort, and the remains of a hill-fort. It is the birthplace of Hyder Aly, who erected here a handsome mausoleum for his father; and near it is a mosque, and a college of Mussulman priests. The chief manufactures are cotton cloths and muslins. It is 40 miles E. N. E. of Bangalore, and 140 W. of Madras. Long. 78. 9. E. lat. 13. 9. N.

Colbene, a town of Tripoli, on the S. W. part of the Gulf of Sidra; 90 miles S. S. E. of Messurata.

Colberg, a fortified seaport of Farther Pomerania. It has a collegiate church, good linen manufactures, and considerable salt-works. The Russians laid siege to this town in 1758 and 1760, without success; but it surrendered to them, after a long siege, in 1761, and was restored at the subsequent peace. It is seated at the mouth of the Persant, on the Baltic; 60 miles N. E. of Stettin. Long. 15. 36. E. lat. 54. 9. N.

Colchagua, a province of Chili, extending from the Pacific Ocean to the Andes, in the lat. of 34. 30. S. It is intersected by two or three rivers, falling into the Pacific; but it has no port or harbour of note. Pop. about 15,000. St. Fernando, about 50 miles from the sea, and 100 S. of St. Jago, is the chief town.

Colchester, a borough and market town in the county of Essex, pleasantly situate on a gentle eminence, on the W. bank of the river Coln, about 8 miles above its entrance into the English Channel. It is a place of antiquity, supposed to have been a Roman station; and was formerly surrounded by a wall, some vestiges of which still remain; and contained a castle of great strength, supposed to have been built by a son of Alfred the Great, the remains of which now serve for a house of correction for petty offenders. Prior to the civil war, in the time of Oliver Cromwell, the wall, castle, and fortifications were entire, and held out with great obstinacy against the parliamentary forces, until after Charles I. was beheaded in 1648, in which year it surrendered. The town sustained great damage during the siege. It is now by far the largest and most important town in the county, and has undergone great improvement within the present century: a spacious quay has been constructed, and the river made navigable up to the town for vessels of 90 to 100 tons burthen. It is a port of entry for vessels from foreign parts, and has a custom-house a little below the town; but its external commerce is very inconsiderable. Its chief traffic in export is in oysters and grain, which it sends to the London market in great quantities, and receives in return every description of shop goods for the supply of the town, and distribution over the surrounding country. It had formerly extensive manufactures of woollen stuffs *(baize)*, but the manufacture of Colchester is now trifling; no small share of its present importance is derived from the extensive intercourse of which it is a centre point between London, Harwich, Ipswich, Yarmouth, and Norwich. It is divided into 16 parishes, and has as many churches; but four of them are not used, and only three are entitled to notice for their architecture. It has three bridges over the Coln, a spacious market-place, town-hall, corn-exchange, and a theatre. It has also an hospital, free grammar-schools, water-works, two public libraries, a botanical and philosophical institution, and several dissenting meeting-houses. The town is governed by a mayor, recorder, town-clerk, 12 aldermen, 18 assistants, and 18 common-councilmen; and returns two members to parliament. Its markets are on Wednesdays and Saturdays. Pop. 16,167. It is 51 miles E. N. E. from London, 21 W. by S. of Harwich, and the same distance S. S. W. of Ipswich.

COLCHESTER, a township in Delaware county, New York; 91 miles S. of Albany. Pop. 1068.

COLCHESTER, a town of Virginia, in Fairfax county, on Ocquoquam Creek; 3 miles from its conflux with the Potomac, and 16 S. W. of Alexandria.

COLCHESTER, a town of Connecticut, in New London county; 20 miles N. W. of New London.

COLCHESTER, a town of Vermont, in Chittenden county, on a bay of Lake Champlain, at the influx of the Onion; 6 miles N. by E. of Burlington.

COLDING, or KOLDING, a town of Denmark, in Jutland, formerly the residence of many Danish kings, who adorned it with several edifices. The harbour is choked up, and its commerce nearly annihilated. It is seated on the Thueths, near its entrance into a bay of the Little Belt; 30 miles E. N. E. of Ripen.

COLDINGHAM, a town of Scotland, in the county of Berwick, anciently noted for a nunnery, rebuilt by Edgar, king of Scotland, in 1098. Ebba, one of the abbesses, renowned in tradition for her charity, gave name to the neighbouring promontory called St. Abb's Head. It is 9 miles N. N. W. of Berwick.

COLDITZ, a town of Upper Saxony, in Misnia, with manufactures of linen and stuffs; seated on the Mulda; 22 miles S. E. of Leipsic.

COLDSTREAM, a town of Scotland, in the county of Berwick. Here General Monk first raised the Coldstream regiment of guards, with which he marched into England, to restore Charles II. It is seated on the Tweed, over which is a handsome bridge; 13 miles S. W. of Berwick.

COLEAGARA, a town of Hindostan, in the province of Coimbetore. It has two large temples, and is a considerable mart for the traders between Seringapatam and the country below the eastern Gauts. It is 34 miles S. E. of Seringapatam.

COLEBROOK DALE, a village in Shropshire, on the banks of the Severn; 2 miles N. by E. of BROSELEY, which see.

COLERAIN, a town of the state of Georgia, in Camden county. A treaty was concluded here, in 1796, between the United States and the Creek Indians. It is seated on the St. Mary river, 35 miles W. by N. of the port of St. Mary, and 14 S. by E. of Louisville.

COLERAINE, a borough of Ireland, in the county of Londonderry; seated on the banks of the river Bann, about 4 miles above its entrance into the Atlantic Ocean. It participates largely in the linen manufactures, and its fabrics and bleaching are in the highest esteem. The fall of the river Bann precludes it from affording much commercial advantage to Coleraine; but this defect is in some measure compensated for by its salmon fishery, which is the most valuable in Ireland. Coleraine sends one member to parliament, and is 25 miles E. by N. of Londonderry, and 108 N. by W. of Dublin.

COLERAINE is also the name of a town in Hamilton county, Ohio, on the E. bank of the Miami river, about 15 miles above its entrance into the Ohio, and 10 N. of Cincinnati. There is also a township of the same name in Franklin county, Massachusets.

COLESHILL, a town in Warwickshire, with a market on Wednesday; seated on a hill, by the river Cole; 10 miles E. of Birmingham, and 105 N. W. of London. The church is an elegant structure.

COLFORD, a town in Gloucestershire, with a market on Tuesday; 5 miles E. S. E. of Monmouth, and 124 W. by N. of London. It has several iron forges in its vicinity.

COLIN. *See* KOLIN.

COLIMA, a town of Mexico, in the intendencia of Guadalaxara, on the frontiers of Valladolid; it is seated at the foot of a volcanic mountain, about 300 miles due W. of the city of Mexico, under the banks of a small river, about 30 miles above its entrance into the Pacific Ocean, in the lat. of 18. 40. N. The intervening country between the town and the sea is very fertile. Pop. of the town about 2500.

COLKING, a city of China, of the first rank, in the N. W. part of the province of Yun-nan; 1160 miles S. S. W. of Peking.

COLL, an island of Scotland, one of the Hebrides, to the W. N. W. of Mull; 13 miles long and 3 broad. The greatest part is covered with heath, and abounds with rabbits; and many black cattle are fed here. The castle of Coll is a strong square-built structure, and still in tolerable repair.

COLLAHUAS, a district of Peru, lying between Lake Titicaca and the Pacific Ocean. It is a very mountainous district; the Andes here diverging into several ridges, among which the Apurimac and other streams, forming the head waters of the noble river Amazon, have their source. Cailloma, in the lat. of 15. 40. S., is the capital.

COLLE, a town of Tuscany, on a hill near the river Elza; 10 miles N. N. W. of Sienna. There are five other towns of the same name in different parts of Italy, all inconsiderable.

COLLEDA, a town of Upper Saxony, in Thuringia, on the Unstrut; 19 miles N. by W. of Weimar.

COLLETON, a maritime district of South Carolina, S. of Charleston; it is intersected by the Eduto river, and is fertile in rice and cotton. Pop. 25,548, of whom 19,246 were slaves.

COLLIN, a town of Prussia, kingdom of Bohemia; 27 miles E. from Prague. Pop. 4400.

COLLIOURE, a town of France, in the department of Eastern Pyrenees, with a castle. It was taken by the Spaniards in 1793, but retaken the next year. It has a small port on the Mediterranean; 16 miles S. S. E. of Perpignan.

COLLON, a well-built town of Ireland, in Louth county, with a stocking manufactory, and an extensive bleach-field; 29 miles from Dublin.

COLLUMPTON, a town in Devonshire, with a market on Saturday, and a considerable trade in woollen cloth. It is seated on the river Culm; 12 miles N. by E. of Exeter, and 160 W. of London.

COLMAR, a town of France, capital of the department of Upper Rhine. It is surrounded by a wall, flanked with towers, near the river Ill; and has various manufactures; 42 miles S. by W. of Strasburg. Pop. about 15,000.

COLMAR, a town of Germany, in the duchy of Holstein; 5 miles S. E. of Gluckstadt.

COLMARS, a town of France, in the department of Lower Alps; 20 miles E. N. E. of Digne.

COLMITZ, a town of Austria; 4 miles S. S.W. of Drossendorf.

COLN, a river which rises near Clare, in Suffolk, passes by Halstead and Colchester in Essex, and, after a course of about 40 miles, enters the German Ocean, at the E. end of Mersey Island. In the inlets and pools at the mouth of this river are bred the famous Colchester oysters. There are several small rivers of the same name in England.

COLNBROOK, a town in Buckinghamshire, seated on the river Coln, which falls into the Thames; 17 miles W. of London, on the road to Bath.

COLN, a town in Lancashire, with a market on Wednesday. It is a place of great antiquity, having been selected for a Roman station by Agricola. It is situate near the border of Yorkshire, within about a mile of the Liverpool and Leeds Canal. It formerly participated in the woollen manufacture, which, within the present century, has given way to the cotton manufacture, in which branch, in 1821, there were seven large establishments for spinning and weaving, and twelve others for weaving only. The vicinity abounds in coals and slate. It is 21 miles N. by E. of Manchester.

COLOCYTHIA, a town of European Turkey, in the Morea, on the W. side of a bay to which it gives name; 36 miles S. of Mistra. Long. 22. 24. E. lat. 36. 38. N.

COLOCZA, or KALOTSHA, a town of Hungary, on the E. bank of the Danube, and an archbishop's see; 57 miles S. of Buda.

COLOGNA, a town of Italy, in the Paduan; 26 miles W. by S. of Padua. Pop. about 6000.

COLOGNE, a late archbishopric and electorate of Germany, in the circle of the Lower Rhine; bounded on the N. by the duchy of Cleves and Gelderland; on the S. by the archbishopric of Treves; and from the S., in a N. N. W. direction, for about 90 miles, by the Rhine, which divides it on the E. from the duchy of Berg; and on the W. it is divided by a very irregular boundary from the duchy of Juliers. It is not more than about 15 miles in mean breadth, and contains a good deal of forest, and some mines of coal and iron, and parts are very fertile in corn, wine, and flax. Pop. about 220,000. It held a distinguished rank in the Germanic confederacy, as early as the 4th century, and at the general partition in 1814, it was transferred to Prussia. Besides the city of Cologne, the other principal towns are Kemper, Lunne, Nuys, Brul, Meckennheim, Bonn, &c.

COLOGNE, the chief town of the preceding territory, and one of the most ancient and celebrated cities of Europe; it is seated on the W. bank of the Rhine, in the lat. of 50. 55. N. and 6. 55. of W. long.; 295 miles W. S. W. of Berlin, and 105 E. of Brussels. Antecedent to the ascendancy of the Romans over western Europe, the site of Cologne is supposed to have been the capital of a tribe called the Ubii; and at a subsequent period, to have given birth to Agrippina, the mother of Nero; in reference to whom the Romans named it *Colonia Agrippina*. It joined the Hanseatic league at an early period of its formation; and in the 13th century ranked high as a commercial city. After that period its commercial activity yielded to the influence of priestcraft and indolence. Persecution followed. In 1485 the Jews, and in 1618 the Protestants, were expelled the city; so that in 1794, when the French took possession of it, the ecclesiastics amounted to about 2000; and, besides the university, founded in 1388, nine collegiate churches, two abbeys, and an archiepiscopal seminary, it contained no less than 126 other monastic and religious establishments. The walls of the city are about seven miles in circumference, but a considerable portion of the area is now converted into gardens and vineyards; and although the perspective of the city on all sides is very imposing, on inspection it proves to be low and ill built. The town-hall, cathedral, and some of the churches, are, however, stately and fine edifices. Cologne is connected with Duytz, on the opposite bank of the river, by a bridge of boats, and contains within itself almost every branch of manufacture for domestic use; and still carries on some traffic up and down the Rhine, from the waters of which it is liable to inundation. The city was transferred, with the territory of Cologne, to Prussia, in 1814. Pop. about 40,000. It was the birthplace of Rubens.

COLOMBE, ST., the name of about 20 towns in different parts of France, all inconsiderable.

COLOMBEY AUX BELLES FEMMES, a town of France, in the department of the Meurthe, and chief place of a canton in the district of Veselize; 15 miles S. W. of Nancy.

COLOMBIA, REPUBLIC OF, an extensive territory, forming the whole northern part of the southern division of the western hemisphere, commonly called South America, and includes what, previous to 1811, constituted the viceroyalty of NEW GRANADA, and the captain-generalship of CARACCAS, or VENEZUELA, each of which see. In its extreme length from N.

to S. Colombia extends from the shores of the Caribbean Sea, in the lat. of 12. 30. N. to the Tungaragua, the main western branch of the great river Amazon, in the lat. of 5. S. and longitudinally from 59. to 83. W. From the 59th to the 68th of W. long., however, it extends only to 3. of N. lat., and its mean long. on the western side, or side of the Pacific Ocean, will not exceed the line of 79. W. These limits will give an aggregate extent of surface of about 1,200,000 square miles, or an area fourteen times the extent of Great Britain; but over this wide domain the human inhabitants are supposed not to exceed 3,000,000. In its north-western extremity, it includes the Isthmus of Panama, which alone includes an unbroken range of sea coast of nearly 3000 miles in extent, with several spacious and commodious harbours. On its eastern extremity it is bounded by the Essequibo river, which divides it from French Guiana and the English and Dutch settlements of Demerara, Berbice, and Surinam; from the 59th to the 65th degree of W. long., it is bounded on the S. by a mountain ridge, which divides it from Portuguese Guiana, the most northern part of Brazil; whilst the Tungaragua, or, as it is afterwards called, the Maranon river, divides it from Peru; the whole of its western boundaries being washed by the Pacific Ocean, and its northern by the Caribbean Sea, and the N. E. by the Atlantic Ocean. The earlier history of this territory will be found more particularly adverted to under the heads of NEW GRANADA and VENEZUELA. A futile attempt was made by a General Miranda to revolutionize Venezuela in 1806; but it was not till 1811 that the people generally exerted themselves in favour of independence: from which period up to 1819, various sanguinary conflicts ensued between the European Spaniards and the natives, with alternate success. It was on the 17th of December, 1819, that the two territories of New Granada and Venezuela became united under the title of the Republic of Colombia, and a popular representative government, divided into legislative, executive, and judicial. On the 6th of May, 1821, in conformity with the fundamental law, the installation of the general congress took place in the city of Rosario, of Cucuta, but the seat of government has since been established at St. Fe de Bogota; and it was at Curabobo, on the 24th of June of that year, when the last battle was fought, that decided the downfall of Spanish domination and the independence of the Colombian republic. The territory was at first divided into four parts; viz. Quito, Cundenamarca, Venezuela, and Spanish Guyana; but it has since been divided into twelve provinces.

The aggregate features of the Colombian territory are, in the highest degree, grand and imposing. The Andes, in a parallel ridge of about 200 miles in extent, between which is a valley 20 or 30 miles wide, at an elevation of about 9000 feet above the level of the sea, enter at the S. W. extremity, in which direction the peaks of Chimborazo, Cotopaxi, and Antisana, rear their majestic heads, all S. of the equator; and in the lat. of 2. N. the chain diverges into three ridges, the most easterly of which takes an E. N. E. direction towards the shores of the Caribbean Sea, with which it runs parallel through seven degrees of longitude to near the Delta of the Orinoco, opposite to the island of Trinidad. It is on the eastern declivity of this ridge, which is called the Venezuelan chain, at an altitude of 8000 feet above the level of the sea, in the lat. of 4. 45. N., that St. Fe de Bogota is situate; between this and the central ridge, which is called the Chain of Santa Martha, runs, for a course of 650 miles, the fine river Magdalena; and between the chain of Santa Martha and the main ridge, runs the river Cauca, which unites with the Magdalena at the foot of the Knol of the Santa Martha chain, about 150 miles above the entrance of the Magdalena into the Caribbean Sea. From the lat. of 6. N. the main ridge of the Andes takes a N. by W. direction into the isthmus that unites the two grand divisions of the western hemisphere, whilst another collateral ridge runs nearly due N. towards Carthagena; between these two ridges runs the Atrato, N. into the Gulf of Darien, the head waters of which river are contiguous to those of the St. Juan, which runs S. into the Bay of Choco in the Pacific Ocean; which rivers seem to form the most favourable means for effecting a water communication between the Atlantic and Pacific Oceans. *See* CHOCO. East of the Andes, the country is intersected by innumerable streams, those in the S. part running into the MARANON, or AMAZON, and those in the N. part into the ORINOCO, which see. From the extreme N. the country is indented by a spacious bay called the Gulf of Maracaibo, which leads by a narrow strait into a spacious lake of the same name. This lake, which is about 180 miles in length, and 70 in width, is bounded on the E. by the Venezuelan chain of the Andes, and on the W. by a ridge which diverges from it in the lat. of 8. N., and with the lake forms a very distinguishing feature of the country. Numerous islands flank the coast of the Caribbean Sea, from the long. of 61. to the Gulf of Maracaibo, in the long. of 70.: the most easterly and important of these is Trinidad, in possession of the English; and near the entrance of the Gulf of Maracaibo is Curacoa, in possession of the Dutch. The rest may be considered as forming part of the Colombian territory, the most important being Margarita. The principal seaports on the side of the Atlantic and coast of the Caribbean Sea, are Cumana, La Guayra (the outport of Leon de Caraccas,) Maracaibo, Carthagena, and Portobello; and, on the side of the Pacific Ocean, Panama, Bay of Choco, and Guayaquil; and the most important towns in the interior, besides St. Fe de Bogota, are Loja, Jean de Bracomoros, Cuenca, Rio Brambo, Quito, Popayan, Merida, and Angostura.

Colombia is not remarkable for any peculiar productions either animal or vegetable. Its capabilities for supplying all that can contribute to the comfort and enjoyment of man are, however, of the first order, while the elevated plains on the western side of the territory afford the most agreeable temperature of climate. The S. W. section of the territory is rich in minerals, including both gold and silver; but the most distinguishing feature of surplus production, hitherto, has been horses, mules, and horned cattle, which have been exported in large quantities to Jamaica, and all the other West India islands; these, with an inconsiderable supply of cotton, wool, cocoa (the best in the world), coffee, tobacco, and indigo, and some dye-woods, with silver to the amount of about 2,000,000 to 3,000,000 of dollars, making an average return of about 1,500,000*l.*, constitute about the collective extent of its external commerce.

COLOMBER, a town of France, in the department of the Upper Saone, and chief place of a canton in the district of Vesoul; 4 miles N. E. of Vesoul, and 10 W. of Lure.

COLOMMIERS, a town of France, in the department of Seine and Marne; 18 miles S. E. of Meaux, and 40 E. of Paris.

COLONNA, CAPE, the S. E. point of Livadia; 30 miles S. E. of Athens. The name also of another cape on the E. coast of Calabria, near the entrance to the Gulf of Tarento, in lat. 39. 6. N.

COLONSA, a fertile island off the W. coast of Scotland, to the W. of Jura. It is separated on the S. from that of Oronsa, by a narrow channel, which being dry at low water, they may be considered as one island; about 12 miles long and two broad.

COLOOR, a town of Hindostan, in the circar of Guntoor, near which is a diamond mine. It is situate on the S. side of the Kistnah; 13 miles N. W. of Condavir.

COLORADO, a river of Mexico, which falls into the Gulf of California, at its head, in the lat. of 33. N. The main branch, which is called the St. Rafael, has its source in the lat. of about 40. N., not far distant from those of the del Norte, the Arkansas, and the Platte, all of which flow S. and W. into the Gulf of Mexico. There are six other branches, all of which have their source N. of the 36th degree of N. lat., which fall into the St. Rafael, whose united stream may be considered the main branch of the Colorado; about 50 miles above its entrance into the Gulf of California, it is united by another stream, from the eastward, called the Gila. These rivers are said to afford several hundred miles of navigation for vessels of considerable burthen.

COLORADO, or RED RIVER, is also the name of another river, rising E. of the Andes, in the lat. 32. S., running in a S. S. E. direction, through the red loamy plains of Pampas and Buenos Ayres, into the South Atlantic Ocean, in the lat. of 40. S.

COLOURI, an island of Greece, formerly called *Salamis*, near the coast of Livadia; 7 miles long and two broad. The principal town is of the same name, on the S. side, with an excellent harbour; 17 miles W. by S. of Athens. It was in the strait between this island and the main land where Themistocles defeated the Persian fleet.

COLOSWAR. *See* CLUSENBURG.

COLSTERWORTH, a village in Lincolnshire, on the Witham; 8 miles S. of Grantham; celebrated for being the birthplace of the famous Sir Isaac Newton.

COLUMB MAJOR, ST., a town in Cornwall, with a market on Thursday, seated on a hill; 26 miles N. N. W. of Penryn, and 249 W. S. W. of London.

COLUMBIA, or OREGON, a river in the N. W. part of North America. It rises in the Rocky Mountains, in lat. 55. 0. N., and falls into the Pacific Ocean in lat. 46. 16. N., after a course of 1500 miles; 190 miles up it is obstructed by rapids, when it is navigable for 65 miles to the "long narrows" and falls, and then 150 miles to the embouchure of the Lewis river. It abounds with salmon, and the Indians, who inhabit permanent villages on the banks, live on the produce of its waters. Astoria, a commercial settlement, is at its mouth. It was first explored by Captains Lewis and Clarke, in 1805, who passed down it to the Pacific Ocean, into a bay of which it enters, by a mouth above three miles wide, in long. 123. 26. W., lat. 46. 19. N. *See* MISSOURI. The Spaniards claim the discovery of this river, and call it Entrada de Ceta, after the commander of the vessel. It gives its name OREGON to the adjacent territory.

COLUMBIA, a district of the United States of America, the seat of the federal city. Pop. 43,712, including 4694 slaves. *See* WASHINGTON.

COLUMBIA, a county of the state of New York, on the E. side of the Hudson river; bounded on the E. by Berkshire county, Massachusets. It is about 35 miles from N. to S., and 20 from W. to E. The pop. is 43,252. It is divided into 14 townships. It yields some iron at Ancram, in the S. E. part of the county. The city of HUDSON (which see) on the E. bank of the noble river of that name, 30 miles S. of Albany, and 110 N. of New York, is the chief place in the county.

COLUMBIA, a county in the state of Georgia, bounded on the E. by the Savannah river, which divides it from Edgefield county, South Carolina. It is nearly a square of about 25 miles each way; being on the verge of the upland district, it is a healthy, agreeable, and fruitful county. Pop. in 1840 was 11,356, of whom 7313 were slaves.

COLUMBIA, a city of South Carolina, capital of Kershaw county, and the seat of government of the state; but a branch of each of the public offices is retained in Charleston. It is the seat of a university, liberally patronized by the state; and is situate on the Congaree river, just below the conflux of the Saluda and Broad rivers; 110 miles N. N. W. of Charleston, 170 S. W. of Raleigh, and 507 S. W. by S. of Washington. Long. 81. 10. W. lat. 33. 58. N.

COLUMBIA, a town of Pennsylvania, in Lancaster county, situate on the Susquehannah, at

Wright's Ferry; 12 miles W. of Lancaster, and 70 W. by N. of Philadelphia.

COLUMBIA, a town of the district of Maine, in Washington county, situate on Pleasant River, near the Atlantic; 15 miles W. S. W. of Machias.

COLUMBIA is also the name of a township in Herkimer county, New York, and of a town in St. Lawrence county, in the same state; 227 miles N. W. of Albany. It is also the name of several other towns or townships in different parts of the United States.

COLUMBIA, REPUBLIC OF. *See* COLOMBIA.

COLUMBIANA, a county of the state of Ohio. It is a square of about 35 miles each way; the S. E. corner jets upon the Ohio river at the point where it divides the state of Ohio from that of Virginia, the E. side being bounded by Beaver county, in the state of Pennsylvania. It is intersected from the N. W. by Little Beaver River, which falls into the Ohio at the point of union with Beaver county. The fertility and local advantages of this county may be inferred from the increase of population since 1810, when it was 10,870, in 1820, 22,033, and is now 40,378. There is a town of the same name in the N. part of the county; but the chief town is New Lisbon, on the N. bank of Little Beaver River, in the centre of the county; 185 miles E. N. E. of Columbus.

COLUMBO, the maritime capital of Ceylon. In 1805 its site was the residence of a powerful native chief, on whose territory the Portuguese first settled in 1517, and founded the present town in 1638; the Portuguese, in 1658, were expelled by the Dutch, and they surrendered it to the English in 1796. The fort, upwards of a mile in circumference, stands on the extremity of a peninsula, and is strong both by nature and art. The town is built more in the European style than any other garrison in India, and nearly divided into four equal quarters by two principal streets, to which smaller ones run parallel, with connecting lanes between them. The natives, who are very numerous, live in the old town, without the walls of the new, like most of the maritime cities of the east. Its inhabitants comprise some of all nations, and the aggregate population is very considerable. Here is a school for the propagation of the Christian religion, and a botanical garden. Columbo is the chief place for the staple trade of the island. The articles exported are cinnamon, pepper, arrack, and coya rope, or cordage; also cocoa-nuts and oil, wax, honey, cardamoms, coral, ivory, fruit, &c. Columbo is situate in a rich district on the W. coast, towards the S. part of the island. Long. 79. 49. E. lat. 7. 4. N. It contains about 50,000 inhabitants.

COLUMBRETES, ISLES, off the coast of Spain, in the province of Valencia; 29½ miles from Cape Oropesa. They are fourteen in number, and the principal one, which has a harbour, is apparently the extinguished crater of a volcano; which has afforded shelter to the Moorish corsairs.

COLUMBUS, a small county in the S. E. part of North Carolina, in the swampy district, through which runs the line dividing N. from S. Carolina. Pop. 3941, of whom 1086 are slaves.

COLUMBUS, the chief town of Franklin county, in the state of Ohio, and seat of government of the state. It is pleasantly situate on a gentle eminence, on the E. bank of the Scioto river, just below the junction of the Whetstone; 45 miles above, or N. of, Chillicothe, and 418 W. by N. of Washington.

COLUMNA, a town of Russia, in the government of Moscow, and an archbishop's see; situate on the S. E. frontier of the province, at the confluence of the Moskwa with the Oka river, 50 miles S. E. of Moscow.

COLYTON, a town of Devonshire, with a market on Thursday; seated on the Cole, at its confluence with the Ax; 17 miles E. of Exeter, and 171 W. by S. of London.

COM, or KOM, a town of Persia, in Irac Ajemi, with several beautiful mosques, and some grand sepulchres, especially those of Seli I. and Abbas II. The trade is considerable; and the chief articles are fruit, both fresh and dry, the best soap in Persia, excellent sword blades, white porcelain, silks, and velvets. It is seated near the foot of a mountain, and on the banks of a river, in a fine plain; 110 miles N. N. E. of Ispahan. Pop. 15,000.

COMACCHIO, a town of Italy, in the Ferrarese, seated in a lake of the same name, lying between two mouths of the river Po; 27 miles E. S. E. of Ferrara.

COMANA. *See* CUMANA.

COMBE MARTIN, a town in Devonshire, with a market on Tuesday. It is seated on an inlet of the Bristol Channel, surrounded by lodes of iron and lead, the produce from which is shipped for Wales and Bristol. It is 6 miles E. of Ilfracomb, and 202 W. of London.

COMBOURG, a town of France, in the department of Ille and Vilaine; 25 miles S. S. E. of St. Maloes: it was the birth-place of Chateaubriand.

COMBICONUM, a town of Hindostan, situate on the banks of the Cavery river, about 20 miles above its entrance into the sea. It was the capital of the most ancient of the Hindoo dynasties; it is now inconsiderable, but several ruins still remain to attest its former greatness. It is about 15 miles N. by E. of Tanjore.

COMERCOLLY, a town of Bengal, near the S. bank of the main branch of the Ganges; about 100 miles N. by E. of Calcutta; it is one of the stations or factories of the English East India Company, for collecting of silk and cotton manufactures.

COMILLA, a town of Hindostan, in Bengal, and chief place of the country of Tippera. It is seated on a river that flows W. into the Burampooter; 58 miles E. S. E. of Dacca, and 185 E. N. E. of Calcutta.

COMINES, a town of France, in the department of Nord, on the river Lys; 8 miles N. from Lille. It has a trade in linen, &c. Pop. 2582.

Commendo or **Commani**, a kingdom of Guinea, on the Gold Coast, formerly a part of the kingdom of Fetu. The natives are of a warlike disposition, and so numerous that the king is said to be able to raise an army of 20,000 men. The capital, where the king resides, is called Grand Commendo, or Guffo; 4 miles to the S. of which, on the sea-coast, is Little Commendo, where the English and Dutch have forts. It lies to the W. of Cape Coast Castle, in the lat. of 4. 54. N. and 3. 34. W. long.

Commercy, a town of France, in the department of Meuse, with a castle seated on the Meuse; 16 miles E. of Bar le Duc. Pop. about 3600.

Commotau, or **Chomutou**, a town of Bohemia, in the circle of Saatz. Its alum pits, and the great quantities of fruit and vegetables raised here, are the principal part of its trade. It is 58 miles N. W. of Prague, on the road to Chemnitz.

Como, a town of Italy, in the Milanese, and a bishop's see. It is surrounded by a wall, backed by a conical eminence, on which are the ruins of a castle. The cathedral is a handsome edifice of white marble, hewn from the neighbouring quarries. The inhabitants have manufactures of cotton and silk, and carry on some trade with the Grisons. Pliny was born here, and, in his Letters, speaks of the delightful scenery of its environs. It stands at the S. W. end of the Lake of Como; 18 miles N. of Milan, and 80 N. E. of Turin. Pop. about 15,000.

Como, Lake of, a lake of Italy, in the Milanese, extending from the city of Como in a N. N. E. direction for about 35 miles: it varies in breadth from 1 to 6 miles, and receives from the N. the river Maira, and from the E. the Adda, both of which rivers fall into the lake at its N. E. end, and discharge their waters by an arm from near the centre, on the S. E. side; this arm extends for about 20 miles, from 1 to 2 miles wide, and is called Lake Lecco, when it again narrows, and resumes the name of the Adda, till it falls into the Po, after a further course of about 60 miles, a few miles above Cremona.

Comorin, Cape, the most southern point of Hindostan, in the lat. of 8. 4. N. and 77. 45. of E. long.

Comorn, a strong tower of Hungary, capital of a territory of the same name. It is seated on an island called Schut, formed by the confluence of the Wag with the Danube; 70 miles E. S. E. of Vienna. The citadel is deemed one of the strongest in Europe, and has never surrendered to any besieging force. The town was taken by the sultan Solyman, in 1543; and has since then been exposed to various conflicts and ravages, alike from war, fire, and earthquakes. In the third decennary of the 19th century it contained about 9000 inhabitants, who carry on a considerable traffic with the surrounding country.

Comoro Islands, five islands in the Indian Ocean, between the coast of Zanguebar and the N. end of the island of Madagascar. They are called Hinzeuan, Mahotta, Mohilla, Angezeia and Comora. *See* Hinzuan. Grand Comoro rises to the height of nearly 8000 feet above the level of the sea.

Compiegne, a town of France, in the department of Oise. Here is a palace, in which the kings of France often resided. The Maid of Orleans was taken prisoner here by the English, in 1430. It is seated near an extensive forest, on the E. bank of the river Oise, over which is an elegant bridge, a little below the confluence of the Aisne, and 45 miles N. E. of Paris.

Compostella, or **St. Jago de Compostella**, a city of Spain, capital of Galicia, and an archbishop's see, with a university. The public squares and churches are magnificent; and it has a great number of convents for both sexes. It is pretended that the body of St. James, the patron of Spain, was buried here; and pilgrims visit his wooden image, which stands on the great altar of the cathedral. From this city the military order of St. Jago had its origin. It is seated in a beautiful plain between the rivers Tambra and Ulla; 35 miles S. by W. of Corunna, and 300 N. N. W. of Madrid. Pop. about 12,000.

Compostella, a town of Mexico, in Guadalajara; capital of the district of Xalisco. There are several mines of silver in its neighbourhood. It is 110 miles W. Guadalajara, and about 50 from the shore of the Pacific Ocean, in the long of 105. 42. W. lat. 21. 15. N.

Concan, a low tract of country, on the W. coast of the Deccan of Hindostan. From this tract rises abruptly that stupendous wall of mountains, called the Gauts. It lies between the Portuguese settlement of Goa and Bombay, in the lat. of 16. and 19. N., and was formerly designated the Pirate Coast, in consequence of the frequent piracies committed upon it during the 17th and 18th centuries. The pirates were extirpated by a united British and Mahratta force in 1756, and the territory guaranteed to the Peishwa of the Mahrattas, in whose sovereignty it still continues. It is about 40 miles wide, and intersected by several small rivers; and the coast is indented by numerous bays and harbours, the principal of which are as follows, beginning at the N., viz.—Choul, Bancoote or Fort Victoria, Dabul, Zigar, Gheria, and Rajpoor: off Dabul lies the small island of Severndroog, which was the main point of rendezvous for the pirates.

Concarneau, a town of France, in the department of Finisterre, with a castle; seated on a small inlet of the sea; 16 miles S. E. of Quimper.

Conception, Bay and Town of, in Chili. The Bay of Conception is one of the most commodious on the whole western coast of South America. It is about 10 miles each way, open to the N. W., the entrance being divided into two channels by the small island of Quiriquina. Both channels have sufficient depth of water for the largest vessels; the eastern is about 2 miles wide, and the western about 1 mile and a half. The S. side of the island of Quiriquina affords very good anchorage; but the S. W. extremity of the bay is more convenient. On the shore of this part of the bay is the town of Talcahuana, nearly on the site of which the town of Conception was originally founded by Valdivia in 1550; and it was, for a conderable time, the capital of all Chili; but having repeatedly suffered from the attacks of the Araucanians, the seat of government was transferred to St. Jago; and, having suffered greatly by an earthquake in 1730, and totally destroyed in 1751, the town was rebuilt on the N. bank of the Biobio river, at a distance of about 6 miles S. E. of the site of the former town. Next to St. Jago, it is the most populous town in Chili, and in 1826, contained about 13,000 inhabitants. It is situate in the province of Puchacay, in the lat. of 36. 48. N., and 73. 8. of W. long.

CONCEPTION, a seaport of the province of Veragua; seated near the shore of the Caribbean Sea, on the river Veragua; 95 miles W. by S. of Portobello. Long 81. 40. W., 8. 48. N.

CONCEPTION DEL PAO, an interior town of Colombia, in the province of Venezuela, situate on the border of the great plain of Orinoco; about 140 miles S. S. W. of Cumana. The inhabitants drive considerable herds of cattle to Barcelona and Cumana, for exportation to the West Indies.

CONCEPTION, one of the large bays of the island of Newfoundland, at the S. E. end, in the lat. of 47. 30. to 48. N., and 52. 30. of W. long.

CONCHAS, a river of Mexico, in the intendancy of Durango, which has its source near St. Cruz, in the lat. of 28. 40. N.; runs S. for about 70 miles, then in a W. N. W. direction for about the same distance, and then due N. for about 160 miles into the Rio del Norte.

CONCIZE, a town of Switzerland, on the W. bank, near the S. end of the Lake of Neufchatel. Pop. about 2500.

CONCOBELLO, a town in the interior of South Africa, in Anziko, the residence of a prince; seated on the river Zaire, and borders of Congo; 150 miles S. W. of Monsol. Long. 15. 54. E. lat. 2. 5. S.

CONCORD, a town of New Hampshire, in Rockingham county; seated on the W. bank of the Merrimac, over which is a handsome bridge. It is the seat of the legislative government of the state; 54 miles W. N. W. of Portsmouth, 70 N. of Boston, and 502 N. E. of Washington.

CONCORD, a town of Massachusets, in Middlesex county, with a handsome court-house, and three bridges over the river Concord. This town was the seat of the provincial congress in 1774, and the spot where the first opposition was made to the British troops in 1775. It is 18 miles N. N. W. of Boston.

CONCORDIA, a town of Italy, in the duchy of Modena, on the river Sechia; 5 miles W. of Mirandola.

CONCORDIA, a town of Italy, in Friuli; 28 miles S. S. W. of Udina.

CONCORDIA, a parish of Louisiana, extending N. from the entrance of Red River, about 140 miles along the W. bank of the Mississippi; being about 15 miles in mean breadth. Pop. of this vast tract, only 9414, of whom 8003 are slaves.

CONDANORE, a town of Hindostan, in Golconda ; 24 miles E. of Adoni.

CONDAPILLY, a town of Hindostan, capital of one of the five Circars. It is situate near the bay of Bengal, N. of the Kistnah ; 80 miles S. S. E. of Rajamundry. Long. 80. 30. E. lat. 16. 37. N.

CONDAPOUR, a town of Hindostan, in Golconda ; 20 miles S. by W. of Hydrabad.

CONDATCHY, a town on the W. coast of the island of Ceylon, off which is the principal pearl fishery. It is S. of the island of Manar, in the lat. of 8. 45. N.

CONDAVIR, a town of Hindostan, and the principal post of Guntoor, one of the five Circars. It is strongly situate on a mountain ; 30 miles S. W. of Condapilly, and 65 N. N. W. of Ongole.

CONDE, a strong town of France, in the department of Nord, with a fortress. It surrendered to the allies, after enduring the rigours of famine in 1793 ; but was retaken in 1794. Conde is seated on the Scheldt, at the influx of the Haisne ; 7 miles N. by E. of Valenciennes, and 26 S. E. of Lisle. Pop. about 6000.

CONDE, a town of France, in the department of Calvados ; seated on the Noireau ; 28 miles S. S. W. of Caen.

CONDECEDO, or LA DESCONOCIDA, a cape of Yucatan, on the E. shore of the Bay of Campechy ; 100 miles W. of Merida. Long. 91. 27. W. lat. 20. 50. N.

CONDESUYAS, a town of Peru, capital of a district, in which is gathered a species of wild cochineal, that forms a great article of trade. It is 85 miles N. N. W. of Arequipa.

CONDOM, a town of France, in the department of Gers ; seated on the Baise ; 26 miles N. N. W. of Auch, and 28 S. E. of Bordeaux.

CONDORE, or PULO CONDORE, a fertile island in the China Sea, near the coast of Cambodia ; 9 miles long, and 2 where broadest ; and is surrounded by seven islets. Buffaloes, hogs, vegetables, and water are to be had here. The English had a settlement here in 1702 ; but the factors falling out with the natives, most of them were murdered, and the rest driven thence in 1792. It has a spacious bay on the E. side Long. 107. 20. E., lat. 8. 40. N.

CONDRIEU, a town of France, in the department of Rhone, celebrated for excellent wine ; seated near the Rhine ; 18 miles S. of Lyons. Pop. about 4000.

CONFLANS, a town of Savoy, near the confluence of the Isere and Doron ; 18 miles E. of Chambery.

CONFLANS, a town of France, in the department of Upper Saone ; 12 miles N. of Vesoul.

CONFOLENS, a town of France, in the department of Charente, on the river Vienne ; 30 miles N. E. of Angouleme.

CONG, a village of Ireland, in the county of Mayo ; 24 miles S. of Castlebar. It is seated on the N. bank of Lake Corr, and was formerly the residence of the kings of Connaught. The ruins of several churches and religious houses are yet visible.

Congaree, a river of S. Carolina. It is formed of the united waters of the Broad and Saluda rivers, which, after a course of about 40 miles, when united with the Wateree, in nearly the centre of the state, the united streams then take the name of the Santee.

Congleton, a town of England, in the county of Cheshire. It is seated on the banks of the river Dean; 161 miles N. W. of London, on the mail-coach road to Liverpool. In 1754 an extensive silk-mill was erected here; and in 1825 the number of mills for the like purpose exceeded thirty, with four or five for spinning of cotton: the weaving, also, both of cotton and silk, has been partially established in the town and neighbourhood. It has two tan-yards, and various other manufactures dependent on the process of spinning. It is 7 miles S. S. W. of Macclesfield.

Congo, a country on the W. coast of South Africa, between 4 and 15 deg. of S. lat., containing the kingdoms of Loango, Congo, Angola, Matamba, and Benguela. It was discovered by the Portuguese in 1481; and is bounded on the N. by Guinea, E. by parts unknown, S. by Bemba, and W. by the Atlantic. It is sometimes called Lower Guinea; and the Portuguese have many settlements on the coast, as well as in the inland country. There are many desert places within land, in which are elephants, tigers, leopards, monkeys, and monstrous serpents; but near the coast the soil is more fertile; and there are fruits of many kinds, beside palm-trees, from which wine and oil are made The greatest part of the inhabitants go almost naked; they worship the sun, moon, stars, and animals of different kinds; but the Portuguese have made many converts: they are skilful in weaving cotton cloth; and trade in slaves, ivory, cassia, and tamarinds. Congo, properly so called, is only 150 miles broad along the coast, but is 370 inland. From March to September is called the winter season, when it rains almost every day; and the summer is from October to March, when the weather is very hot. The principal rivers are the Zaire and Coanza. The capital is St. Salvador. *See* Zaire.

Congo, a town of Persia, in Laristan. It is a market for pearls, brought from Bahrein, and is seated on a river, which flows into the Persian Gulf; 90 miles W. by S. of Ormuz. Long. 54. 30. E., lat. 26. 36. N. Pop. about 7000.

Coni, a fortified town of Piedmont, capital of a territory of its name, with a strong citadel. Its trade is considerable, being the repository for all the merchandise from Turin and Nice, which is intended for Lombardy, Switzerland, and Germany. It is so strong by nature and art, that though frequently besieged by the French, they never could take it. In 1796 it was delivered up to the French after their victory at Mondovi, as a hostage for the performance of a treaty; and it surrendered to the Austrians in 1799. It fell again into the hands of the French in 1810, and was ceded to Sardinia at the general peace of 1814. It is seated on a rock, at the confluence of the Gezzo and Stura; 35 miles S. of Turin. Pop. about 10,000.

Conil, a town of Spain, in Andalusia, on a bay to which it gives name. The inhabitants are much engaged in fishing, especially for tunnies; and beautiful crystallized sulphur is found here. It is 13 miles N. of Cadiz.

Conisberg. *See* Konigsberg.

Conisbrough, a village in West Yorkshire, 5 miles S. W. of Doncaster. It was formerly a place of note, and has large remains of an ancient castle.

Coniston-mere, a lake in Lancashire, 6 miles long and nearly one broad. It is in some places 40 fathoms deep, and abounds in excellent char. Near the head of it, on the N. W. side, is the village of Coniston, 3 miles W. by S. of Hawkshead, and N. of the village rises the peak of Coniston Fell, to the height of 2577 feet above the level of the sea.

Conjeveram, a town of Hindostan, in the Carnatic. The streets are tolerably wide; and on each side is a row of cocoa-nut trees. The inhabitants are most of them Brahmins belonging to two large temples; there is also a small mosque of very neat workmanship. It is seated near the Palear; 24 miles E. of Arcot, and 44 W. S. W. of Madras.

Connaught, one of the four provinces of Ireland; bounded on the S. by Munster, E. by the river Shannon, which divides it from Leinster, N. by Donegal and Sligo Bays, and W. by the Atlantic Ocean, which indents it with numerous bays, giving it from 300 to 400 miles of sea-coast, flanked by numerous islands. It has a good deal of mountainous territory, and several lakes. It contains five counties, viz. Galway, Roscommon, Mayo, Sligo, and Leitrim; and 3,658,546 English acres.

Connecticut, one of the united states of North America; bounded on the E. by a conventional line, from the lat. of 41. 20. to 42. N., which divides it from the state of Rhode Island, N. by the line of the 42nd deg. of N. lat. from the long. of 71. 53. to 73.30. W.; this line divides it from the western part of the state of Massachusets; on the W. it is divided from the state of New York by another conventional line, in a direction nearly due S., to the lat. of 41. N., the whole of its southern boundary being washed by the waters of Long Island Sound: these limits give an area of about 4675 square miles—nearly 3,000,000 of acres. The surface of Connecticut is agreeably diversified by gently swelling hills and valleys, presenting to the eye of the traveller a constantly varying prospect; and in the western part of the state, the hills rise to a height to claim the denomination of mountains, more especially so in the county of Lichfield: and the state is intersected from N. to S. by three fine rivers; the most easterly is the Thames, the next the Connecticut, and the most westerly the Housatonick; these, with their numerous tributary streams, intersect every part of the state, contributing alike to the diversity and fertility of the country. The first settlements in Connecticut were made on the bank of the river of that name by a band of emigrants from Massachusets, in 1634. A short time after, another band of emigrants from England established themselves at Newhaven, at the head of a small bay, near the mouth of the Housatonick river. The two settlements were united under a charter granted by Charles II. in 1662. In 1673 Connecticut formed a confederacy with Massachusets and Plymouth, under the name of the United Colonies of New England. The early settlers experienced much interruption from the Indians, who have long since been driven far beyond the limits of the state. An attempt was early made to infringe upon the conditions of the charter, which occasioned continued contentions during the reign of the Stuarts ; but on the charter being confirmed by William and Mary, in 1688, the province continued to increase in population and prosperity, and contributed essentially and effectually to all the expeditions of the English against the French, in Canada, and other parts of America, especially towards the capture of Louisbourg in 1745. During the revolution of 1776—1783, although Connecticut manifested less virulence towards England than some of the other provinces, she acted a steady and determined part in favour of independence. To the war declared by the United States against England, in 1812, the state of Connecticut displayed a marked and decided opposition: and in 1814-15, a convention assembled at Hartford, the capital of the state, with the view, as is supposed, of proposing to secede from the confederacy ; but a treaty of peace being signed at Ghent, on the 24th of December, 1814, prevented the intentions of the assembly being announced.

The charter of 1662 continued to form the basis of the government of Connecticut until 1818, when a new constitution, resembling those of most of the other states, was adopted. (*See* UNITED STATES.) Although limited in extent of territory, Connecticut is a very efficient member of the United States confederacy ; the industry, well-directed exertion, and social order of the people, not being exceeded by any in the union ; and, while she exhibits no pre-eminent traits of character in any one pursuit, agriculture, manufactures, commerce, education, and the useful arts, display a rational medium of influence and effect over every part of the state. The supplies of its agricultural produce in horses, mules, Indian corn, beans, onions, butter, cheese, cider, beef, and pork, is considerable ; part of which is exchanged at New York and Boston for manufactured productions, and part in the southern states and the West Indies, for the production of those climes. In 1818 there were forty-eight iron forges, chiefly in the N.W. part of the state ; sixty-seven cotton factories, (into which improved machinery has been introduced ;) some considerable glass-works, several tanneries and distilleries, an extensive armoury, a powder-mill, sail-cloth manufactory, manufactures of tin-ware, and various other manufactures, as well for domestic use as for exchange in the neighbouring states. Yale College, at New Haven, next to Harvard, in Massachusets, is the most extensive and respectable in the United States, the number of students generally exceeding 400 ; whilst a sound and useful education is provided, at the expense of a fund under the control of the state, for the whole of its youth, without any exception. In 1820 Connecticut was divided into eight counties ; viz. Hartford, New Haven, New London, Fairfield, Windham, Lichfield, Middlesex, and Tolland. The population, next to that of Massachusets, is more dense than in any other part of the United States ; notwithstanding which, great numbers are constantly emigrating to Ohio, and other parts of the western territory. The climate of Connecticut varies from 91. above to 10. below 0. Fahrenheit, though the extremes seldom exceed 84. and 0. ; a variation, however, which may be considered extreme, considering its latitude. Pop. 301,015.

CONNECTICUT RIVER rises at the foot of the range of hills which divides New Hampshire from Lower Canada; and, for a course of about 170 miles in a S. S. W. direction, divides the state of New Hampshire from the state of Vermont, when it enters the western part of the state of Massachusets, through which it runs in a direction nearly due S., a distance of about 50 miles, when it enters the state of Connecticut, through which it runs in a S. by E. direction for about 60 miles into Long Island Sound dividing the state into nearly two equal parts. This river is navigable to Middletown, 36 miles from its mouth, for vessels drawing 10 feet of water ; and to Hartford, 14 miles further, for those drawing 8 feet : higher up, the navigation, except for boats, is impeded by a succession of rapids, which afford the most advantageous sites for mills. The scenery of its banks, nearly the whole of its course, is delightful, and in parts grand; and the soil exceedingly fertile. It is crossed by numerous bridges above Hartford.

CONNECUH, a south frontier county of the state of Alabama, bordering on West Florida. Pop. 5713. A river of the same name intersects the county, running S. through West Florida into the Bay of Pensacola. Sparta is the chief town.

CONNEMARA, a district of Ireland, in the province of Connaught, containing some of the best harbours in Ireland.

CONNOR, a parish in the county of Antrim, Ireland. There is a decayed town in the parish, formerly a bishop's see, now united to Down. It is 6 miles N. of Antrim.

CONQUET, a town of France, in the department of Finisterre, with a good harbour and road. It is 12 miles W. of Brest.

CONSELVE, a town of Italy; 12 miles S. of Padua. Pop. about 6000.

CONSIGLIONE, a town of Sicily, in Val di Mazara; 19 miles S. of Palermo.

CONSTADT, a town of Silesia, in the principality of Oels; 23 miles N. E. of Brieg.

CONSTANCE, a fortified city of Suabia, seated on the S. side of the Rhine, between the upper and lower lakes of Constance, or the lakes of Constance and Zell. Though once flourishing in commerce, and celebrated in history, it now scarcely contains 4000 inhabitants. Constance is famous for a council in 1514, which caused John Huss and Jerome of Prague to be burnt; and likewise condemned the doctrine of Wickliffe, and ordered his bones to be burned forty years after he was dead. It was formerly the capital of a secularized bishopric, extending on both sides of the Rhine; that on the S. is now included in the Swiss Canton of Thurgau; and that on the N., with the city itself, now forms part of the circle of the lake in the territory of the Grand Duke of Baden; 100 miles S. S. E. of Carlsruhe, 80 E. of Basle, and 42 N. N. E. of Zurich.

CONSTANCE, LAKE OF, the most considerable lake of Switzerland, which it separates from Suabia, that part excepted where the city of Constance is seated on its S. side. It is divided into three parts. The upper and largest part is called Boden See; the middle part is named Bodmer See; and the lower part Unter See, Zeller See, or the lake of Zell. The upper lake, from Bregentz, at its eastern extremity, to Constance, is 37 miles long, and 15 in its greatest breadth. Through this lake the Rhine flows, and then enters the Zeller See, which is 16 miles long, and 10 in its greatest breadth. It is in some places 350 fathoms deep, and 100 generally; and, like all the lakes in Switzerland, is deeper in summer than in winter; which is owing to the first melting of the snow from the adjacent mountains. It abounds with fish, and its trout are much esteemed; and besides the city of Constance, has many agreeable towns and villages on its banks.

CONSTANTINA, a town of Spain in Andalusia, with a castle on a mountain; 40 miles N. E. of Seville.

CONSTANTINA, the eastern province of the kingdom of Algier, and the largest and richest of the four. The greatest part along the coast is mountainous. In the mountains dwell free Arabian and Moorish tribes, of whom the Cabyls are deemed the most turbulent and cruel.

CONSTANTINA, a city of the kingdom of Algier, capital of the province of the same name. It is seated at the top of a steep rock, and there is no way to it but by steps cut out of the rock. The usual way of punishing criminals here is to throw them down the cliff. Here are many Roman antiquities, particularly a triumphal arch. Next to Algier, this is the most populous city in the kingdom. It is 190 miles E. by S. of Algier. Long. 6. 24. E. lat. 36. 24. N.

CONSTANTINOPLE, or STAMBOL, one of the largest cities in Europe, and the capital of the Turkish empire. It is of a triangular form, and seated between the Black Sea and the Sea of Marmora, on a neck of land that advances towards Natolia, from which it is separated by a strait a mile in breadth. The Sea of Marmora washes its walls on the S., and a gulf of the strait of Constantinople does the same on the N. E. It was anciently called Byzantium, but the name was changed in the year 330, by Constantine the Great, who made it the seat of the Roman empire in the East. It was taken in 1453 by the Turks, who have kept possession of it ever since. The grand seignior's palace, called the Seraglio, is on the sea side, surrounded by walls flanked with towers, and separated from the city by canals. It stands on the site of ancient Byzantium, the E. point of the present city, and is 3 miles in circumference, consisting of an assemblage of palaces and apartments placed by the side of one another, without symmetry and without order. The principal entrance of this palace is of marble, and is called Capi, that is, the Porte, or gate, a name used frequently to express the court, or the empire. The castle of Seven Towers is a state prison, and stands near the Sea of Marmora, at the W. point of the city from the seraglio; and at the N. W. point, without the walls of the seraglio, is the Atmeidan, the ancient Hippodrome. The number of houses in Constantinople is prodigious; but in general they are mean, and all of them constructed of wood, and the roofs covered with hollow tiles. The public edifices alone are built of masonry, in a very solid manner. The streets are narrow, badly paved, and dirty; and the people are infested with the plague almost every year. The inhabitants, who are variously said to amount to from 300,000 to 400,000, are half Turks, two-thirds of the other half Greeks or Armenians, and the rest Jews. Here are a great number of ancient monuments still remaining; particularly the superb temple of St. Sophia, built in the sixth century, which is converted into a mosque, and will contain 100,000 persons conveniently. Between the two mosques of Sultan Solyman and Bajazet is the old seraglio, in which are shut up the wives of the deceased sultans, and also such women as have displeased the grand seignior. The bazaars, or bezesteins, are large square buildings, covered with domes supported by arcades, and contain all sorts of goods, which are there exposed to sale. There is a market for slaves; the Jews are the principal merchants, who bring them here to be sold: great numbers of girls are brought from Hungary, Greece, Candia, Circassia, Mingrelia, and Georgia, for the service of the Turks, who generally buy them for their seraglios. The great square, near the mosque of Sultan Bajazet, is the place for public diversions. The gulf on the N. E. of the city is the harbour, which runs up from the point of the seraglio to the village of Aijub, about 4 miles in length and half a mile wide where broadest. Aijub may be reckoned one of the suburbs, and has a mosque, in which is the tomb of Sultan Othman, the founder of the empire. The suburbs of Galata and Pera are on the other side of the harbour. The former extends along the entrance of the harbour, and is chiefly occupied by merchants; and adjoining it, on the E., is a cannon foundry, called Tophana. Pera stands behind these, on an eminence, and is the place where the foreign ambassadors reside. It was burnt down some years since, and now presents a mass of blackened ruins. The palace of the British embassy is a fine brick building. On the opposite side of the Bosphorus, in Asia, is the suburb of Scutari, or Skoutari, which is surrounded with very extensive cemeteries. The circumference of this city is 14 miles, and 24 with the suburbs included; and as they are built on ground which rises gradually, there is a view of the whole town from the sea. The city is surrounded by walls of freestone, here and there mixed with bricks, and flanked with 250 towers. There are 22 gates, 6 on the land side, and the rest toward the harbour and sea. The palaces, mosques, bagnios, and caravansaries, are many of them magnificent. Constantinople is 780 miles in a meridional line S. E. of Vienna. Long. 28. 35. E. lat. 41. 1. N.

CONSTANTINOPLE, STRAIT OF, anciently the Thracian Bosphorus, and forming the communication between the Propontis, or Sea of Marmora, and the Euxine or Black Sea. It is 20 miles long, and a mile and a quarter where broadest; and forms the separation here between Europe and Asia. At its entrance on the W. side is situate Constantinople, and on the other Scutari. Both its banks are lined with villages, where are seen some very handsome houses, almost entirely built of wood, and variously painted; those belonging to the Turks are in white or red; those of the Greeks, Armenians, and Jews, are of a blackish brown, for they are not allowed to employ the colours of the Mussulmans. At its termination in the Black Sea are two forts opposite each other, to defend the passage. *See* BOSPHORUS.

CONSTANTINAW, a town of Poland, in Podolia, on the river Bog; 8 miles S. W. of Chmielnik, and 72 N. E. of Kaminieck.

CONSTANTINOW, another town of Poland, in Volhinia, on the river Sulucza; 30 miles W. by N. of the former.

CONTESSA, a seaport of European Turkey, in Macedonia, advantageously located at the head of a gulf of its name, at the influx of the Strimon; 60 miles E. by N. of Salonichi, and 246 W. of Constantinople. Long. 24. 8. E., and lat. 40. 52. N.

CONTRES, a town of France, in the department of Loir and Cher; 10 miles S. E. of Blois.

CONTY, a town of France, in the department of Somme; seated on the Seille; 14 miles S. S. W. of Amiens.

CONVERSANO, a town of Naples, in Terra di Bari; 12 miles S. E. of Bari.

CONWAY, (i. e. *Chief River*,) a river of Wales, which flows through a fertile vale of the same name, along the whole eastern border of Carnarvonshire, and enters the Irish Sea at Aberconway.

CONZA, a town of Naples, in Principato Ulteriore, and an archbishop's see. It suffered so much by an earthquake in 1694, that the place where the cathedral stood is hardly known. Its principal commerce is in marble. It is seated near the head waters of the Ofanti river; 52 miles E. of Naples.

COOCH BEYHAR, a district of Bengal on the frontier of Bootan, which exhibits a melancholy proof of two facts frequently united; the great facility of obtaining food, and the wretched indigence of the lower order of inhabitants. It became tributary to the English in 1772. Beyhar, the chief town, is 260 miles N. by E. of Calcutta.

COOK'S INLET, an extensive arm of the sea, on the N. W. coast of America, discovered in 1778 by Captain Cook, who traced it 70 leagues from its entrance, in long. 152. W., and supposed it to be the mouth of a large river; but it was further explored in 1794 by Captain Vancouver, who found its termination to be in long. 148. 43. W. lat. 61. 29. N.

COOK'S STRAIT, a strait dividing the two islands of which New Zealand is composed; it is about 4 or 5 leagues broad.

COOPER, a county of the state of Missouri, and on the western frontier of the United States territory. It lies S. of the Missouri river, and is bounded on the E. by a mountain ridge, which divides it from Wayne county, and is intersected from W. to E. by Orange river. Pop. 6959. Boonsville, on the S. bank of the Missouri, in the lat. of 39. S. is the chief town.

COOPERSTOWN, an incorporated town of New York, chief of Otsego county, situate at the S. W. end, and the outlet of Lake Otsego; 12 miles N. W. of Cherry Valley, and 64 W. by N. of Albany.

COOS, a county forming the whole of the N. part of the state of New Hampshire. It is about 90 miles in length from N. to S., and 28 in mean breadth; it is bounded on the E. by the state of Maine, and W. by the Connecticut river which divides it from Vermont, and N. by the ridge of mountains which divides the United States territory from Lower Canada. This county takes its name from a tribe of Indians who formerly inhabited these parts. On the southern confines of this county is a ridge of mountains called the White Mountains, which rises to the height of about 6500 feet above the level of the sea; through them is a pass in one place not more than 22 feet wide, which appears cloven down to its very base, in a perpendicular line on one side, and, on the other, in an angle of about 45 degrees; through this notch or gap, as it is termed, a turnpike road has been constructed from the banks of the Connecticut river to the Atlantic Ocean at Portland, a route much availed of for the conveyance of heavy produce on the sledges in the winter season; and thus, whilst it forms one of the grandest natural features of the world, it is rendered subservient to the medium of an extensive and an advantageous intercourse. Coos county is at present but thinly inhabited. The population, however, which, in 1810, was only 3991, is now 9849. Lancaster, on the E. bank of the Connecticut river, 117 miles due N. of Concord, is the chief town.

COOSAWATCHIE, a town of South Carolina, in Beaufort district. The courts formerly held at Beaufort are held here. It is seated on the Coosaw, over which is a bridge; 20 miles N. W. of Beaufort, and 60 W. S. W. of Charleston.

COOTEHILL, a town of Ireland, in the county of Cavan; 74 miles from Dublin. It has a good linen market.

Copenhagen, the capital of Denmark, built on a morass, and surrounded with several small lakes. It was founded by some wandering fishermen, in the 11th century, and is now accounted the best built city of the north of Europe. It became the seat of the court and government of Denmark in 1443. The streets are well paved, with a foot-way on each side. The greatest part of the buildings are of brick, and a few of freestone; the houses of the nobility are in general splendid, and built in the Italian style. The harbour is capable of containing 500 sail; and the streets are intersected by broad canals, which bring the merchandise close to the warehouses on the quays. Copenhagen contains four royal palaces, twenty-two churches, a great number of public buildings, and a university, and about 110,000 inhabitants. The palace, called Christiansburg, built by Christian VI. and burnt down in 1794, was an immense pile of building of hewn stone, the wings and stables of brick, stuccoed. The hospital of Warlow is large and convenient, containing 350 beds, occupied by as many poor. The church is so placed, that service may be heard by those who are confined to their bed. The exchange is a large Gothic building; vessels are brought very near it by means of canals; and here the merchants assemble. The new royal market is the largest square in the city, and almost entirely composed of stately buildings, as the academy of painting and sculpture, the theatre, the great hotel, the artillery-house, &c., and in the centre is a marble equestrian statue of Christian V. In the N. suburbs is an obelisk of reddish stone erected in 1793 by the city, to the honour of Christian VI. on his abolishing vassalage; and around its pedestal are four female figures of white marble. The citadel is a regular fortification, with five bastions, a double ditch full of water, and several advanced works. This city owes its present beauty to the fire of 1728, which destroyed five churches and sixty-seven streets, having been rebuilt in a better style. It suffered greatly by fire in 1794, and again in the following year. The new part of the town, raised by Frederic V., is extremely beautiful. It consists of an octagon containing four uniform and elegant buildings of hewn stone, and of four broad streets leading to it, in opposite directions. In the middle of the area stands an equestrian statue of Frederic V. in bronze, as large as life, which is justly admired. The round tower, built by Christian IV., and designed for an observatory, is a singular structure, not having a single step in it, though very lofty: its ascent is by a spiral road near 14 feet wide; and one of their kings has driven in his carriage up and down it. On the interruption to the commerce of Holland, by the events of the French revolution in 1793-4, Copenhagen became the principal entrepôt for the commerce of the north of Europe; for which no place can be more advantageously situated; but Denmark becoming involved in the contentions of that period, and joining in a confederacy with Russia and Sweden against the naval ascendancy of England, an English fleet, in March, 1801, was despatched to bombard Copenhagen, when, after considerable damage being done to the town, and 28 ships of war taken or destroyed, an armistice was entered upon, which led to a treaty of peace with all the northern powers; but not without operating as a severe check to the commercial enterprise of Copenhagen; and in 1807 the British Government, anticipating the designs of the French on the fleet and naval stores in the harbour of Copenhagen, sent a fleet of seventeen ships of the line, with frigates, &c., and a considerable army, to take possession of the island of Zealand, Copenhagen, &c., which the Danes opposed, and the city was bombarded for three days, when 300 houses, the cathedral, and part of the university were destroyed, and as many more buildings greatly damaged; and with this event, the ephemeral importance of Copenhagen, as a great commercial entrepôt, may be considered as terminating. Eighteen Danish ships of the line, fifteen frigates, six brigs, and twenty-five gun-boats, with all the naval stores in the arsenal of Copenhagen, were delivered up by capitulation, to Admiral Gambier and Lord Cathcart. The city is five miles in circumference, seated on the E. shore of the isle of Zealand, at the entrance into the Baltic Sea, about 25 miles within the strait called the Sound; 340 miles S. W. of Stockholm, and 500 N. E. of London. Long. 12. 35. E. lat. 55. 41. N. *See* Amak.

Copiapo, the most northern province of Chili; bounded on the N. by the great desert of Atacama, E. by the Andes, and W. by the Pacific Ocean; being about 260 miles from N. to S., from 24. 20. to 28. of S. lat., and about 90 miles in mean breadth, abounding in mines of gold, iron, copper, sulphur, tin, and lead. The chief town, of the same name, stands on the S. side of a river, also of the same name, at its entrance into the Pacific Ocean; 490 miles N. by E. of Valparaiso. Long. 70. 50. W. lat. 27. 20. S. On the Andes, in a parallel line with the town of Copiapo, is a volcano, called the Volcano of Copiapo.

Coppenbrugge, a town of Hanover, in the principality of Collenberg; 10 miles E. by N. of Hamelin.

Copper-Mine River, a river of North America, which runs from S. to N. into the Icy Sea, in the long. of 111. 5. W. and 69. 7. of N. lat.

Coppet, or **Copet**, a town of Switzerland, with a castle, on the W. bank of the Lake of Geneva; 10 miles N. of Geneva. The castle and barony became the property of M. Neckar, celebrated for his pretensions as a financier in the time of the French revolution; both he and his daughter, Madame de Stael, lie interred here in a fine mausoleum in the castle-garden.

Coquet, a river of England, which rises on the borders of Scotland, crosses the centre of Nothumberland, and enters the German Ocean at Warkworth. Opposite its mouth is a small island of the same name.

Coquimbo, or **Serena**, a seaport of Chili, near the mouth of a river of the same name, and the capital of a province also of the same name, rich in corn and mines of gold and silver. The streets are shaded with fig-trees, palms, oranges, olives, &c. always green. It is 260 miles N. by E. of Valparaiso. Long. 71. 19. W. lat. 29. 52. S.

CORACHIE, or KURACHEE, a seaport of Asia, at the mouth of a creek which communicates, in the rainy season, with the Indus, on the western side. It is supposed to be the *Sangada* of Arrian, or Port of Alexander, and is now the principal outport of the Afghans. The inhabitants are of an enterprising disposition, and it appears to afford a favourable opening for commercial adventure. It is about 100 miles W. of Tatta, in the lat. of 24. 30. N. and 67. 15. of E. long.

CORAH, a town of Hindostan, capital of a district of the same name, lying between the Jumna and the main branch of the Ganges; which came wholly into the possession of the English in 1801. It is a very fertile and productive district; the town is 98 miles N. W. of Allahabad.

CORBACH, a town in the electorate of Hesse, capital of the county of Waldeck. It is divided into the old and new town, and near it, on a mountain, is the castle of Eisenberg. The Hanoverians were defeated here by the French in 1760. It is seated on the Itter; 22 miles W. of Cassel. Long. 9. 1. E. lat. 51. 16. N.

CORBECK, a town of the Netherlands, in Brabant; 3 miles S. of Louvain.

CORBEIL, a town of France, in the department of Seine and Oise; seated on the Seine at the influx of the Juine; 17 miles S. of Paris.

CORBIE, a town of France, in the department of Somme, with a celebrated Benedictine abbey; seated on the Somme; 10 miles E. of Amiens.

CORBIERES, a town of Switzerland, in the canton of Friburg; 10 miles S. of Friburg.

CORBY, a town in Lincolnshire, with a market on Thursday; 13 miles N. of Stamford, and 102 N. by W. of London.

CORDILLERAS. *See* ANDES.

CORDOUAN, TOWER OF, a lighthouse built on a rock at the mouth of the Garonne river; 55 miles W. by N. from Bordeaux. It is 175 feet high, and of handsome proportions.

CORDOVA, an interior province of Andalusia, in the S. of Spain, comprising an area of about 5500 square miles, and contains a population of 252,028. It is divided into nearly two equal parts, by the Guadalquiver river, which intersects it from E. to W.: the N. W. part is mountainous, but the more southern part is exceedingly fertile in corn, fruit, wine, and olives. It was formed into an independent kingdom by Abderame, a Moorish general, about the year 695; besides the city of Cordova, the other principal towns are Bujalance and Montilla.

CORDOVA, CITY OF, the capital of the preceding province, is seated on the N. bank of the Guadalquiver, over which is a bridge of sixteen arches, built by the Moors. It was a considerable place in the time of the Romans, who surrendered it to the Goths in 572. In 692 it was taken by Abderame, a Moorish general, who soon after renounced the authority of the grand caliph of Damascus, and made the city of Cordova the capital of a kingdom. It is now a bishop's see, and one of the finest cities of Spain. The circumference is large, but there are many orchards and gardens within the walls. The palaces, church, and religious houses are superb, particularly the cathedral, which is 534 feet in length, and 387 wide, built by Abderame, for a mosque, and it still retains the same of Mezquita. The square, called the Plaza Major, is surrounded by fine houses, under which are piazzas. The trade consists in wine, silk, and leather; but it is not so considerable as formerly. In the neighbourhood are a vast number of orange and lemon trees; and here are the best horses in Spain. It was from hence that the leather called cordovan derived its name, the mode of manufacture being first introduced here by the Moors. Cordova is 130 miles N. E. of Cadiz, and 190 S. by W. of Madrid.

CORDOVA, a town of Mexico, in the intendancy of Vera Cruz, and a bishop's see. Here are upwards of thirty sugar-mills. It is seated on a river which flows into the Gulf of Mexico; 80 miles E. S. E. of Puebla de los Angelos, and 55 W. by S. of the port of Vera Cruz.

CORDOVA, one of the eight intendancies of the united provinces of South America, extending through nine degrees of latitude, from 29. to 38. S., and ten degrees of longitude, between 60. and 70. W.; it comprises nearly the whole of the vast plain lying between the great river La Plata and the Andes. The principal towns are St. Louis and Mendoza, both on the route from Buenos Ayres to Santiago in Chili. There is also a town of the same name in the N. E. part the province, in the vicinity of some salt lakes, and on the line of road from Buenos Ayres to Potosi. Some scattered tribes of Indians roam over parts of this extensive district, but the aggregate population is very limited.

COREA, a kingdom of Asia, bounded on the N. by Chinese Tartary, on the E. by the sea of Japan, on the S. by a narrow sea, which separates it from the Japanese islands, and on the W. by the Yellow Sea, which separates it from China. The W. coast is flanked by innumerable islands. It is a peninsula, being surrounded on every side by the sea, except towards the N. It is governed by a king, tributary to the emperor of China, and is divided into eight provinces, Hien king, Ping ngang, Hoang hai, Kiang-yuen, King-ki, Tchu-sin, King-chan, and Tchuen-so, which contains 33 cities of the first, 53 of the second, and 70 of the third rank. Pop. 8,000,000. The towns are exceedingly populous, and the inhabitants follow nearly the same customs, and are of the same religion, with the Chinese. The country abounds in corn and rice, of which last they have two kinds, one of which delights in water, and the other, which is the better sort, is cultivated on dry ground, like corn. There are mines of gold and silver in the mountains, and good pearl fisheries on the coast. The Coreans are well made, ingenious, brave, and tractable. They are fond of dancing and music, and show great aptness for acquiring the sciences, which they apply to with ardour. They are less fastidious and less ceremonious than the Chinese, but equally jealous of admitting strangers into the country. Men of learning are distinguished from other people by two plumes of feathers, which they wear in their caps. Their women are less confined than those in China, and have the liberty of appearing in company with the other sex. In China, parents often marry children without their consent, but in Corea they choose for themselves. They never bury their dead till three years after their decease, but keep them in coffins for that time. Corea extends from N. to S. from the lat. of 34. 30. to 42. 30. N., and from E. to W. from 125. to 129. of E. long. King-ki-tao, nearly in the centre of the kingdom, is the capital.

Corfe Castle, a town in Dorsetshire, with a market on Thursday. It is seated on a peninsula in the British Channel, called the Isle of Purbeck, on a river, between two hills, on one of which stands the castle, formerly a place of great importance. Great quantities of fine clay and stone are shipped here for the Staffordshire potteries. The town is governed by a mayor, and every alderman that has served the office has the title of baron. It is 18 miles S. by E. of Dorchester, and 116 W. by S. of London.

Corfu, an island in the Mediterranean, near the coast of Albania, at the entrance of the Adriatic. Here is made a great quantity of salt; and it abounds with vineyards, lemons, and olives. It was anciently known under the several names of *Scheria*, *Phacia*, and *Corcyra*. The Corcyrians were an independent people, coeval with the proudest epoch of the Greeks. In the 14th century the island became subject to the Venetians, in whose possession it continued until 1797, when it was ceded to the French, by the treaty of Campo-Formio. It capitulated to the Turks and Russians in 1729, and, with six other islands, was constituted independent, under the title of Ionian Republic (which see).

Corfu (the ancient *Corcyra*), the chief town of the preceding island, is situate on the E. side, on the shore of a spacious and secure harbour, for vessels of easy draught of water. The fortifications are very strong. It is the seat of government of the whole of the Seven Islands, or Ionian Republic, and contains about 15,000 inhabitants. Lat. 39. 36. N. long. 19. 50. E.

Coria, an episcopal town of Spain, in Estremadura; seated on the Alagon; 120 miles W. S. W. of Madrid.

Coringa, a town at the N. extremity of the coast of Coromandel, having a commodious harbour a few miles N. of the main channel of the Godavery river; in the lat. of 17. N.

Corinth, Isthmus of, a neck of land which joins the Morea to Livadia, and reaches from the Gulf of Lepanto W., to that of Ægina, E. The narrowest part of it is 6 miles over; and on a mount here, called Oneius, were formerly celebrated the Isthmian games. There are still the ruins of a town upon it, and of the temples dedicated to the Sun, Pluto, Diana, Neptune, Ceres, and Bacchus. Julius Cæsar, Caligula, and Nero in vain attempted to cut a channel through the isthmus; they therefore built a wall across it, called *Hexamilia*, because it was 6 miles in length. This was demolished by Amurath II., rebuilt by the Venetians, and levelled a second time by Mahomet II.

Corinth, a town of the Morea, situate on the northern declivity of a mountain, sloping towards the Gulf of Lepanto and the preceding isthmus, to which it gives name. During the zenith of Grecian glory, Corinth justly ranked among the most important and magnificent cities of Greece; its temples, theatres, and fountains were the admiration of every beholder; and in the proportions and richness of their columns and porticoes architecture was perfected, leaving nothing for after ages to perform in that noble art but to copy: and the Corinthian pillar or column now, more or less, adorns every city of the civilized world. Corinth fell a prey to the fury of the Roman arms under Mummius, in the year 146 B. C.; and although Julius Cæsar endeavoured to restore it to its former grandeur, in whose time it was visited by St. Paul, it has progressively sunk into a place of insignificance. It fell into the hands of the Venetians during their ascendancy, but the Turks became masters of it in 1715, and in their possession it continued till the Greek revolution. It had formerly a port on the Gulf of Ægina, called *Cenchrea*, as well as on that of Lepanto; but the former is now little used. The ancient citadel, *Acro-Corinthus*, still remains entire, and, to a well-disciplined garrison, may be considered impregnable. Corinth is the seat of a Greek metropolitan and bishop. Pop. about 3000. It is 65 miles E. by S. of Patros, and 48 W. by S. of Athens.

Cork, a maritime county, forming the S. W. extremity of Ireland, having upwards of 100 miles of sea-coast, indented with several very spacious and safe bays and harbours, opening into the Atlantic Ocean. It is about 35 miles in mean breadth from S. to N., and is intersected from E. to W. by two fine rivers, the Blackwater and the Lee, with five or six others of inferior note. The following are the principal bays and harbours, beginning at the west: viz. Bantry, Dunmanny, Baltimore, Glandore, Ross, Clonakilty, Kinsale, Cork, and Youghal. Besides the city of Cork, the principal towns in the interior are Charleville, Mallow, Doneraile, Michelstown, Bandon, Cloyne, &c. Bandon, Kinsale, Mallow, and Youghal, each return one, and the city of Cork and the county each two members to the parliament of the United Kingdom. The agriculture of this county, both in tillage and pasture, has been much improved since the middle of the eighteenth century, and, in conjunction with the adjoining interior county of Tipperary, supplies a great portion of the English marine with salt beef and pork, more especially the former, and exports vast quantities of butter; and since 1800, it has also exported a considerable quantity of grain. Some woollen manufactures are carried on for internal consumption in the eastern part of the county; and, during the third decennary of the 19th century, several efforts were made to establish the cotton manufacture over the county generally.

Cork, City of, and capital of the preceding county, supposed to have been founded by the Danes in the sixth century, is beautifully and advantageously situate on the banks of the river Lee, about 5 miles above its entrance into Cork harbour. Cork, in conjunction with Ross, is a bishop's see. The city is divided into twenty-two parishes. Next to Dublin, Cork is the largest and most important place in all Ireland. During the twenty-four years' war, from 1793 to 1815, Cork harbour was one of the chief rendezvous of the British navy; and the extensive demand which that war created for salt provisions, led to Cork becoming the largest and most celebrated market in Europe for that article, and it still continues to be the chief source of supply, not only of the national, but of the commercial navy of the United Kingdom; and, for long voyages, and tropical climates, is preferred by the ships of all nations. As the chief commercial town of the south-west of Ireland, it concentrates the surplus production, not only of the whole county, but of the greater part of those of Kerry and Tipperary, which it also supplies with such British and foreign productions as are received in exchange. Since the commencement of the war in 1793, the city has undergone great improvement, both in regard to public and private buildings. There are five bridges over the Lee; that of St. Patrick is a fine structure. The exchange, custom-house, and town-hall, are all fine edifices. It has two theatres, several hospitals, and other public buidings. The cathedral, erected between 1725 and 1735, is a stately edifice, and some of the parish churches are of a like character. The barracks, on the N. side of the city, situate on an eminence, present a very imposing aspect. Cork has a public brewery on a very extensive scale, and which makes also its own malt. Cork is 125 miles S. W. of Dublin, in the lat. of 51. 54. N. and 8. 28. of W. long.

Cork, Cove of, is that part of the harbour of Cork usually occupied as the anchorage ground. The harbour, which is entered by a deep and narrow channel, and defended by a strong fort on each side, is about 9 miles from the mouth of the river Lee, and about the same extent in breadth. At the upper end is an island, called Great Island, from 4 to 5 miles long from W. to E., and from 2 to 3 miles wide. At the W. end of this island is a town called *Cove*, and at the entrance of the channel between Great Island and the main land, are two small islands called Haulbowline and Rocky Islands, strongly fortified; and thus, whilst the natural positions of Cork harbour are such as to afford accommodation for the whole British marine, secure from the effects of the elements, the fortifications render the shipping and the town equally secure from the irruptions of an enemy; and, the surrounding shore being studded with neat and commodious residences, render the the whole as picturesque and agreeable as it is important in point of security and defence.

Corleone, a large and well-built town of Sicily, in the Val di Mazzara. It is 24 miles S. S. W. of Palermo. Pop. about 12,000.

Corlin, a town of Further Pomerania, with a castle. It has considerable woollen manufactures, and is seated on the Persant; 10 miles S. E. of Colberg.

Cormantin, a town of Guinea, on the Gold Coast, large and populous. Here the Dutch have a fort, which was taken by the English in 1665. Long. 0. 15. W. lat. 5. 30. N.

Cormery, a town of France, in the department of Indre and Loire, with a Benedictine abbey; seated on the Indre; 8 miles S. E. of Tours.

Corna, a town of Asiatic Turkey, in Irak Arabi; seated on the Tigris, near its conflux with the Euphrates; 35 miles W. N. W. of Bassora.

Corneto, a town of Italy, in the patrimony of Saint Peter; seated on the Marta; 3 miles E. of the sea, and 10 N. of Civita Vecchia.

Cornhill, a town of the county of Durham, in Norhamshire; seated near the Tweed over which it has a large bridge to Coldstream, in Scotland. It is 12 miles S. W. of Berwick, and 333 N. N. W. of London.

Cornigliano, a town of Italy, in the Milanese; 15 miles E. of Milan.

Cornwall, a county forming the S. W. extremity of England, projecting into the Atlantic Ocean. It is bounded on the E. N. E. by the river Tamar, which divides it from Devonshire, being washed on all its other sides by the sea. The S. coast, for about 70 miles, borders on the entrance to the English, and the N., for about 90 miles, on the entrance to the Bristol Channel. At its eastern, or E. N. E. extremity, it is about 42 miles wide, but gradually narrows towards the W. to about 15 miles, when it diverges, at a distance of about 60 miles, into two points; the most southerly called the *Lizard*, in the lat. of 49. 58. N. and 5. 11. of W. long., and the other the *Land's End*, in the lat. of 50. 4. N. and 5. 42. of W. long., the intermediate space being known by the name of *Mount's Bay*. It contains 849,286 acres, and returns two members to parliament for each of the divisions, Eastern and Western. The distinguishing characteristics of this county are its minerals, semi-metals, and clays, which are found here in greater variety than in almost any other part of the world. Gold, silver, iron, cobalt, antimony, manganese, and lapis calaminaris, are all found to a certain extent, and some in abundance; but the predominating productions are copper and tin, with which are mixed mundic and arsenic; in the supply of which upwards of 100 mines are in constant work. Some of the mines are worked to a vast depth; but the perfection of the means applied, as well in bringing the ores to the surface, as in smelting, &c., renders the operations comparatively easy, and the proceeds a source of great wealth to the parties engaged in them, and of general advantage to the county. The mining business is entirely regulated by a code called the Stannary Laws, enacted by a court of stannaters, or proprietors. These laws divide the tinmen into t● divisions, under the superintendence of one warden. A vice-warden is appointed every month; and there is a steward for each precinct, who holds his court every three weeks, where a jury of six persons decides disputes, with a progressive appeal, however, to the vice-warden, lord-warden, and lords of the Duke of Cornwall's council. The mines are under no other jurisdiction excepting in such cases as affect land or life. In addition to its minerals, a vein of soapy earth, and of potter's clay, estimable in the manufacture of porcelain, add considerably to the resources of the county. The shaping of granite for building, and moorstone for grinding of corn, give employment to great numbers; and, in addition to these resources, the coast of Cornwall is annually visited by shoals of pilchards, which, in fish and oil, yield an average produce of 50,000*l.* per annum. The occupations of mining and fishing, up to the middle of the eighteenth century, prevailed to such an extent in this county as to render agriculture almost entirely neglected, and to give it a rudeness and wildness of character distinct from that of every other part of the kingdom; but since that period agriculture has been progressively improving, and potatoes and grain are now included among its surplus productions, which, in the aggregate, may be considered as exceeding 500,000*l.* per annum in amount. What are denominated the duchy lands are very extensive, and the income derived from them, together with the duty on tin ore, form the only remaining parts of those immense hereditary revenues, which were anciently appropriated as a provision for the heir apparent to the crown. Previously to the invasion of Britain by the Romans, Cornwall was inhabited by a tribe called the *Danmonii*, with whom the Phœnicians are supposed to have traded largely for tin. The descendants of that tribe, and the succeeding inhabitants, continued longer to retain the language, manners, and customs of antiquity, than in any other part of England, and which, up to this time, can hardly be said to be extinct. The coast is, in many parts, extremely rugged, and ridges of granite intersect the western part of the county, whilst the valleys are beautifully diversified with verdure, shrubs, and plants, among which the myrtle is common, with several peculiar to the district. The coast abounds with marine vegetables, which are much used for manure. The blocks of broken granite appear in remote ages, according to the supposition of some persons, to have been much used in the construction of rude temples for religious worship. Near the Land's End is a block from 90 to 100 tons in weight, so nicely poised as to be moveable with the hand; there are several others of less magnitude similarly poised; these are termed *loggin stones.* The principal ports on the N. coast, are Padstow and St. Ives; on Mount's Bay, Penzance and Helstone; on the S. coast, Falmouth, Truro, Fowey, and Looe; Plymouth Sound, bounding the S. E. extremity of the county. The principal towns in the interior are Redruth, St. Austle, Penryn, Bodmin, Launceston, &c. The assizes, &c., for the county, are held alternately at Bodmin and Launceston. Streams of water intersect the county in all directions, and add considerably to its diversity and picturesque beauty. Some woollen, and a few other manufactures, are carried on in different parts of the county, but they are inconsiderable.

Cornwall Cape is about 5 miles N. by E. of the Land's End.

Cornwall, a township in Orange county, New York, situate along the W. bank of the Hudson river; 105 miles S. of Albany. Pop. 3,925. Also the name of a township in Addison county, Vermont; and of a town in Lichfield county, Connecticut.

Cornwall, a town of Stormont county, Upper Canada, situate on the N. bank of the St. Lawrence; about 50 miles above Montreal.

Cornwall, New, a county in the western part of North America, extending from Gardner's Canal, in lat. 53. 15., to Frederick's Sound, lat. 37. 6. N.

Cornwallis, a town of Nova Scotia, seated on the S. shore of the basin of mines at the head of the Bay of Fundy; about 10 miles N. W. of Windsor, and 45. N. W. of Halifax.

Cornwallis, a county of Lower Canada, extending for about 160 miles along the S. E. bank of the great river St. Lawrence; bounded on the N. E. by the district of Gaspe. It is at present but thinly inhabited.

Coro, a town of Colombia, in the province of Venezuela. It is advantageously situate at the entrance of an isthmus, at about an equal distance from the Caribbean Sea and the Gulf of Maracaibo. It contains about 10,000 inhabitants, who carry on a considerable trade in mules, cattle, &c., with Curacoa, and other islands in the Caribbean Sea. *See* Venezuela.

Coromandel, Coast of, the eastern coast of the peninsula of Hindostan, extending from Point Calymere, in the lat. of 10. 18. N. to the Kistnah river, in the lat. 16. N. There is not a port for large ships on the whole coast, which is an even, low, sandy country. Madras is the principal town, and the other places of note are Negapatam, Pondicherry, Pullicate, &c.

Coron, a seaport of European Turkey, in the Morea; seated on the W. side of a bay to which it gives name; 15 miles E. of Modon. Long. 21. 46. E. lat. 36. 55. N.

Coronation Gulf, in the Polar Seas, between Melville Sound and Duke of York's Archipelago. Lat. 68. 0. N. long. 112. 0. W.

Coronation, Cape, a cape of the island of New Caledonia, in the Pacific Ocean. Long. 167. 8. E. lat. 22. 5. S.

Corregio, a town of Italy, in the duchy of

Modena, with a castle; 9 miles N. N. E. of Reggio.

Çorreze, an interior department of France, containing the late province of Limousin. It takes its name from a river which runs into the Vezere, after having watered Tulles and Brives. Tulles is the capital.

Corrib, Lough, Ireland, county Galway, connected by a canal with Galway Bay; area 30,000 acres.

Corrientes, Cape, on the E. coast of South Africa, opposite the S. end of the island of Madagascar. Also the name of another cape on the W. coast of Mexico, in the Pacific Ocean, in the lat. of 20. N.

Corrientes, a town of Paraguay, with a fort, seated on the E. side of the Parana, at the influx of the river Paraguay; 490 miles N. of Buenos Ayres. Long. 59. 0. W. lat. 27. 30. S.

Corryvrekan, a dangerous whirlpool on the W. coast of Scotland, between the Isle of Scarba and the N. point of that of Jura. It is so named from a young Danish prince, who perished in this place. Its vortex extends above a mile in circuit.

Corsham, a town in Wiltshire, with a market on Wednesday, and a considerable woollen manufacture. It is 9 miles E. N. E. of Bath, and 97 W. of London.

Corsica, or Corse, an island in the Mediterranean, separated from that of Sardinia, on the S., by the Strait of Bonifacio. It is 150 miles from N. to S., and from 40 to 50 in breadth. It was known to the ancient Greeks by the names of Callista and Cyrnus, and to the Romans by its present appellation. On the coast are many excellent harbours. It is mountainous, but fruitful valleys are interspersed; and it has some fine lakes and rivers. In the earliest time it has been famous for its swarms of bees, and produces vast quantities of honey, which, however, is reckoned bitter, on account of the box and yew with which the country abounds. The mountains are rich in lead, iron, copper, and silver; and there are also mines of alum and saltpetre. The granite of Corsica is nearly equal to oriental; porphyries, jasper, talc, amianthes, emeralds, and other precious stones, are found scattered in the mountains, and the S. coast abounds with beautiful coral. This island was, for some centuries, under the dominion of the Genoese, whose tyranny was such, that the Corsicans were almost in a perpetual state of insurrection. In 1736, a German adventurer, Theodore Baron Newoff, brought some assistance to them; and, on his assurance of more powerful aid, they elected him king; but, as he could not substantiate his promises, he was obliged to leave the island. He went into England, was thrown into the Fleet Prison, released by an act of insolvency, (after having registered his kingdom of Corsica for the benefit of his creditors,) and suffered to die in extreme indigence. The Genoese, tired of the contest, sold the sovereignty to France, in 1767; and the celebrated Paoli, who had been elected to the chief command in 1755, was obliged to abandon the island in 1769. After the French revolution in 1789, Corsica was admitted as an eighty-third department of France, at the particular request of a deputation, of which Paoli was at the head. In consequence of some events which followed the revolution in 1792, Paoli revolted; the French, by the assistance of the English, were expelled from the island; and Corsica, in 1794, was declared annexed to the crown of Great Britain. In 1796, however, the English found it expedient to evacuate the island, of which the French immediately took possession, and again united it to France, of which country it now forms the eighty-sixth department. It is divided into four prefectures, viz. Bastia, Calvi, Corte, and Sartenne. Ajaccio, on the W. coast, is the principal seaport. Pop. about 180,000.

Corsoer, a town of Denmark, in the isle of Zealand, on a peninsula in the Great Belt, with a good harbour for light vessels. It is defended by a citadel, which serves also as a magazine for corn, and is 54 miles W. S. W. of Copenhagen. Long. 11. 12. E. lat. 55. 12. N.

Corte, a town of Corsica, situate in the centre of the island, on the side and foot of a rock, at the confluence of the Tayignano and Restonica. On the point of a rock, rising above the rest, is the castle, to which there is but one winding passage, that will admit only two persons abreast. While the island was in the possession of the English, Corte was made the seat of the viceroy; and it has been enlarged and fortified by the French. It is 27 miles N. E. of Ajaccio, and 90 S.W. of Bastia. Pop. 2735.

Cortemiglia, a town of Piedmont, in Montferrat, situate on the Bermida; 16 miles E. of Cherasco.

Cortlandville, a town of North America, state of New York; 40 miles N. of New York, in a populous and fertile country. Pop. 3799.

Cortona, a fortified town of Tuscany, and a bishop's see, with a famous academy. It stands on a mountain, on the frontiers of the Ecclesiastical States; 32 miles E. of Sienna.

Corunna, a seaport at the N. W. of Spain, in Galicia, with a large and safe harbour, called the Groyne, defended by two castles. The town is of a circular form; but the poverty of the surrounding country affords few resources for trade. A British army of 13,000 were, on the 16th Jan. 1809, near being driven into the sea by a French force of 30,000 men. It is 20 miles S. W. of Ferrol, and 35 N. by E. of Compostella. Long. 8. 19. W. and lat. 43. 33. N.

Corvey, a town and small principality of Westphalia, with a celebrated abbey; situated on the Weser; 27 miles E. by N. of Paderborn. Long. 9. 35. E. lat. 51. 46. N.

Corvo, the smallest and most northerly island of the Azores, so called from the abundance of crows found upon it. The inhabitants cultivate wheat, and feed hogs. Long. 31. 6. W. lat. 39. 42. N.

Corwru, a town in Wales, county of Merioneth; 10 miles N. E. of Bala, and 194 W. N. W.

of London. It is situate on the S. bank of the Dee.

Corydon, a flourishing town of Harrison county, Indiana, situate on the base line of a bend of the Ohio river; from which it is distant about 15 miles both E. W. and S.

Cosel, a town of Prussia, province of Silesia, on the Oder. It is fortified, and contains a population of 3600.

Cosenza, a city of Naples, capital of Calabria Citeriore, and an archbishop's see, with a strong castle. The environs produce abundance of corn, fruit, oil, wine, and silk. It is situate on several small hills, at the foot of the Appennines on the E. side, and by the river Crati; 155 miles S. E. of Naples. Pop. about 16,000.

Coshocton, an interior county of the state of Ohio. Several streams of considerable magnitude unite in this county to form the Muskingum river, which river it is in contemplation to unite with the Cayahoga, and thereby open a direct water communication between the Ohio and Lake Erie. The chief town, of the same name, is situate on the E. bank of the Muskingum, 65 miles N. N. E. of Columbia, the capital of the state. Pop. of the county, 21,590.

Coslin, or **Koeslin**, a town of Further Pomerania, Prussia, which has good woollen manufactures, excellent fisheries, and fine cattle. It is seated on the Nesebach; 18 miles E. of Colberg.

Cosne, a town of France, in the N. W. part of the department of Nievre. Anchors for ships are forged here; and its cutlery and gloves are much esteemed. It is seated on the E. bank of the Loire, at the influx of the Noain; 34 miles N. by W. of Nevers, and 110 S. by E. of Paris. It is the seat of a prefect. Pop. 5823.

Cospour, a town of Hindostan, province of Cachar, now much decayed; 276 miles E. of Patna. Long. 92. 57. E. lat. 24. 56. N.

Cossacks, a people inhabiting the confines of Poland, Russia, Tartary, and Turkey. They are divided into the Kosakki-sa-Parovi, the Kosakki-Donski, and the Uralian Cossacks. The men are large and well made, have blue eyes, brown hair, and aquiline noses; the women are handsome, well shaped, and complaisant to strangers. The Uralian Cossacks dwell in villages along the banks of the Ural, and their chief town is Uralsk. The country which the Kosakki-sa-Parovi inhabit is called the Ukraine, and their towns are built of wood, after the manner of the Russians. The Kosakki-Donski dwell on both sides of the Don, are under the protection of Russia, and profess the same religion. *See* Ukraine and Uralian Cossacks.

Cosseir, a town of Egypt, on the Red Sea, and the chief place of trade across that sea, between Egypt and Arabia. It is 280 miles S. by E. of Suez. Long. 33. 50. E. lat. 26. 8. N.

Cossimbazar, a river of Hindostan, in Bengal; the most western arm of the Ganges, from which it separates 35 miles below Rajemal. It passes by Moorshedabad, Cossimbazar, &c. to Nuddea, where it is joined by the Jellingy, another arm of the Ganges; and their united streams form the Hoogly.

Cossimbazar, a town of Hindostan, in Bengal. It has been at all times the residence of the different European factors, this being the centre of their trade. It is seated on the river of the same name, by which it is surrounded; 7 miles S. of Moorshedabad, and 105 N. of Calcutta.

Cossimcotta, a town of Hindostan, in the circar of Cicacole, on a river that flows into the Bay of Bengal; 74 miles S.W. of Cicacole. Long. 83. 7. E. lat. 17. 42. N.

Cossipour, a town and fortress of Hindostan, in Delhi, on the N. E. border of the province; 100 miles E. N. E. of Delhi. Long. 79. 18. E. lat. 29. 14. N.

Costa Rica, a province of Guatimala, central America; bounded on the N. by Lake Nicaragua, and on the S. E. by Veragua. It has rich mines of gold and silver, but in other respects is mountainous and richly wooded. Cartago is the capital.

Costalnitza, a town of Croatia, on the river Udda, and borders of Bosnia; 57 miles E. S. E. of Carlstadt. Long. 17. 8. E. lat. 45. 20. N.

Coswick, a town of Upper Saxony, in the principality of Anhalt, with a castle, situate on the Elbe; 10 miles W. by N. of Wittenburg.

Cotabamba, a town in the province of Cuzco, Peru; seated on the W. bank of the Apurimac river; 75 miles S. of the city of Cuzco.

Cotbus, a town and district of Lower Lusatia. The castle stands on an eminence on the E. side of the town. Here are a great number of French protestants, who have introduced their manufactures; and it is noted for excellent beer, pitch, and flax. It is seated on the river Spree; 60 miles E. by S. of Wittenburg. Long. 14. 24. E. lat. 51. 46. N.

Cote d'Or, an interior department in the E. part of France, which has its name from a mountain situate to the S. of Dijon. It contains part of the late province of Burgundy. Dijon is the capital. Pop. estimated at 400,000.

Cotes du Nord, a department of France, so named from its northern maritime position. It contains part of the late province of Bretagne. St. Brieux is the capital.

Coteswold Hills, a long tract of high ground in the E. part of Gloucestershire. It affords, in many places, a fine short grass for the feed of sheep; and others are devoted to the growth of corn. The sides of this long range are beautiful as they sink into the vale, from the hills of Stinchcomb and Nibley in the S., to that of Bredon in the N., which has been celebrated in ancient rhyme.

Cothen, a town of Upper Saxony, capital of the principality of Anhalt-Cothen, with a castle. It is 12 miles S. W. of Dessau. Long. 12. 9. E. lat. 51. 48. N.

Cotignac, a town of France, in the department of Var, on the river Argens; 33 miles N. N. E. of Toulon.

Cotignola, a fortified town of Italy, in the Ferrarese; 25 miles S. S. E. of Ferrara.

Cotopaxi, one of the highest peaks of the

Andes, remarkable for the frequency and violence of its volcanic eruptions, at a height of 18,898 feet above the level of the sea. It is about 35 miles S. E. of the city of Quito.

Cotrona. *See* Crotona.

Coulan, a seaport of Hindostan, in Travancore, with a good harbour, and a navigable river. It stands on a peninsula; 60 miles N. W. of Travancore. Long. 76. 24. E. lat. 8. 51. N.

Coulommiers, a town of France, department of Seine and Marne. Trades in cheese, corn, horses, and cattle; 31 miles E. from Paris. Pop. 3300.

Coulonges les Royaux, a town of France, department of Sevres, with a manufacture of leather. Pop. 2000.

Coumassie, or Coomassie, a town of West Africa, capital of Ashantee. Pop. 18,000. Here the monarch of Ashantee lives in barbaric splendour. An active trade is probably carried on with the interior.

Council Bluff, an important military station belonging to the United States of America, on the W. bank of the Missouri river: it is the highest station on that river. Lat. 41. 31. N. long. 96. 42. W.

Courland, a duchy of European Russia; bounded on the W. and N. by the Baltic, E. by Livonia, and S. by Poland. It is divided into Courland Proper, and Semigallia, and is 250 miles long and 40 broad. The country swells into gentle hills, and is fertile in corn, hemp, and flax. It is mostly open, but in some parts there are forests of pine and fir, and groves of oak. It was formerly a feudatory province of Poland, but was annexed to the dominions of Russia in 1795, by an act of the states. Mittau is the capital. Pop. 581,300.

Courtlandt, or Cortland, an interior county of the state of New York. Pop. 24,607. Also, the name of a town in West Chester county, New York, on the E. bank of the Hudson river; 121 miles S. of Albany, and 21 N. of the city of New York.

Courtray, a town of Belgium, in West Flanders, celebrated for its trade and manufactures of table linen and woollen cloths. It is seated on both sides the river Lis; 12 miles E. of Ypres.

Coutances, a seaport of France; capital of the department of Manche, and a bishop's see, with a fine cathedral. It is 37 miles S. W. of Bayeux, and 185 W. of Paris. It is the seat of a prefect. Pop. 9015.

Coutras, a town of France, in the department of Gironde, at the conflux of the Ille and Dronne; 25 miles N. E. of Bordeaux.

Cove. *See* Cork, Cove of.

Coventry, City and County of, is insulated within the county of Warwick. It is a place of considerable antiquity, and was formerly surrounded with strong walls, which were three miles in circumference, having twenty-six towers and twelve gates; but few vestiges of which now remain, having been demolished by order of King Charles II. in 1662, in despite for the resistance made to the troops of his predecessor. A parliament was held here in the reign of Henry IV. called ***Parliamentum Indoctum***, or the unlearned parliament, because the lawyers were excluded. Leofric, Earl of Mercia, who was lord of the place about 1040, is said to have loaded the inhabitants with heavy taxes, on account of some provocation he had received from them; and that, being importuned by his lady, Godiva, to remit them, he consented, upon condition that she would ride naked through the town, which condition she accepted and performed; for, being possessed of a long flowing head of hair, she contrived to dispose of her tresses so as to preserve her decency; and at the same time enjoined the citizens, on pain of death, not to look out as she passed. The curiosity of a poor tailor, however, prevailed over his fears, and he ventured to take a single peep, but was struck blind, and was ever after called Peeping Tom. This improbable story is annually commemorated by the citizens of Coventry, with great splendour, and a female, closely habited in fine linen of flesh colour, rides through the town, attended by a very numerous and elegant procession. The window through which the tailor is said to have gratified his curiosity is still shown, with his effigy always newly dressed for the occasion of the procession, on the Friday preceding Trinity Sunday.

It had formerly extensive manufactures of woollen and worsted stuffs, now quite discontinued in this part of the country, they having been supplanted by the manufacture of ribbons, of which it is the focus for the produce of from 17,000 to 18,000 looms. It has, also, two tolerably extensive establishments for the manufacture of watches, and four or five others of inferior importance. It has a canal communicating with the grand line of canal navigation between London, Liverpool, and Manchester. It is situate on the verge of the great coal strata, running through all the northern part of the country. The vein is worked in abundance within five miles of the city of Coventry. The city is divided into two parishes, and the churches, contiguous to each other, are both fine structures; more particularly so that dedicated to St. Michael, which was twenty-two years in building, and finished in 1394. The spire is 303 feet high, and deservedly ranks among the most beautiful specimens of architecture in the kingdom. There is a third spire, the church to which has long since been demolished; but there is a third church with a stately tower, which serves as a chapel of ease to St. Michael. The three spires form beautiful and interesting objects in the perspective from the surrounding country, for many miles, on all sides. The corporation consists of a mayor and nine other aldermen. St. Mary's Hall, in which the archives of the city are kept, and its business transacted, is an ancient and venerable edifice: the county hall is a neat Doric structure. It has a free school and two hospitals, and had formerly a very extensive establishment of Carmelites, or White Friars, whose house, after lying in ruins many years, was converted into a workhouse in 1806, at which period the two parishes were united for parochial purposes. Coventry is united with Lichfield, as a bishop's see, but does not exhibit any ecclesiastical parade. It returns two members to parliament. Its market, on Fridays, is well supplied, and it has three fairs annually; one, on the Friday preceding Trinity Sunday, on the occasion of the procession of Lady Godiva, is numerously attended, and continues till the Friday following. Since 1820 the city has undergone considerable improvements in the widening, cleaning, and lighting the streets, and several new buildings have been erected. It is 10 miles N. by E. of Warwick, 18 E.S.E. of Birmingham, and 91 N.W. of London.

COVENTRY is also the name of four townships in the United States of North America.

1st. in Kent county, Rhode Island.

2nd. in Tolland county, in Connecticut.

3rd. in Chester county, Pennsylvania.

4th. in Portage county, Ohio.

The latter is on the line of the portage between the Cayahoga and the Tuscarawa branch of the Muskinghum river, by which the waters of Lake Erie and the River Ohio are proposed to be united.

COVERDEN. *See* COEVORDEN.

COVERIPORUM, a town and fortress of Hindostan, in Mysore, on the S. bank of the Cavery; 60 miles S. E. of Mysore. Long. 77. 38. E. lat. 11. 51. N.

COVILHAM, a town of Portugal, in Beira. It has a manufacture of woollen cloth, and is 18 miles S. W. of Guarda.

COVINGTON, a county of the state of Mississippi, bounded on the N. by the territory of the Choctaw Indians, and intersected by the line of road from the Tennessee river to Lake Portchartrain. Pop. 2717. Also the name of a newly-formed county, in the state of Alabama, bordering on West Florida.

COWBRIDGE, a corporate town of Wales, in Glamorganshire, with a market on Tuesday. It is called by the Welsh Pont-faen, from the stone bridge over the river, which soon after enters the British Channel. Near it are the remains of Llanbithian Castle, of which a massive gateway is now converted into a barn; and about a mile distant, on a lofty hill, are the ruins of Penline Castle. It joins with Cardiff, Llantrissent, Aberdare, and Llandaff, in sending one member to parliament. Cowbridge is 12 miles W. of Cardiff, and 173 of London.

COWES, WEST, a seaport on the W. side of the Isle of Wight, at the mouth of the Medina, or Cowes. On the opposite side is the village of East Cowes, and at each place is a fort built by Henry VIII. for the security of the island and road. Cowes has an excellent harbour, which is much frequented by ships to repair damages sustained at sea, and to water; and also a good trade in provisions, &c., for the use of the shipping. During the summer it is much frequented for the purpose of sea-bathing; and here are a number of genteel lodging-houses, and an assembly-room. It is 12 miles S. by E. of Southampton, 12 W. S. W. of Portsmouth, and 86 S. W. of London.

COWLDURGA, a town of Hindostan, in Mysore, with a strong hill fort. It is surrounded by hills and forests, and stands 12 miles S. of Nagara.

COYLAN. *See* QUILON.

COZUMEL, or COSUMEL, an island on the E. coast of Yucatan, where Cortes landed and refreshed his troops, before he attempted the conquest of Mexico. It abounds with fruit, pulse, cattle, and fowls, and is inhabited principally by native Indians. Long. 87. 19. W. lat. 19. 40. N.

CRAB ISLAND. *See* PORTO-RICO.

CRACATOA, the southernmost of a cluster of islands in the entrance of the Strait of Sunda. It consists of elevated land, gradually rising on all sides from the sea, and is covered with trees except a few spots, which have been cleared by the natives for the purpose of forming rice fields; and its coral reefs afford small turtle in abundance. The inhabitants are not considerable; and their chief, like those of the other islands in the strait, is subject to the king of Bantam.

CRACOW, a city and republic of Poland, capital of a palatinate of the same name, and a bishop's see, with a university. It was formerly the capital of Poland, where the kings were elected and crowned, and nearly in the centre of the Polish dominions. On a rock near the Vistula is the ancient royal palace, surrounded by brick walls and old towers, which form a kind of citadel. Adjoining is the cathedral, within the walls of the citadel, in which most of the sovereigns of Poland are interred. Though the city and suburbs occupy a vast tract of ground, they scarcely contain 26,000 inhabitants. The great square is spacious and well built, and many of the streets are broad and handsome; but almost every building bears the mark of ruined grandeur. This devastation was begun by the Swedes in 1702, when it was taken by Charles XII.; but it has since experienced greater calamities, having been retaken by the Russians and the confederates. When the general insurrection broke out in 1794, against the Prussian and Russian usurpers of the Polish territory, Kosciusko, the chief of the patriotic insurgents, expelled the Russian garrison from this city, on the 24th of March, 1794; but, having marched in the sequel to the protection of Warsaw, Cracow surrendered to the Prussians on the 15th of June. By the Congress of Vienna it was restored to independence, with 487 square miles of territory, and now forms a republic under the protection of Russia, Austria, and Prussia, who, however, have some authority in the legislature. It is seated on the Vistula 130 miles S. S. W. of Warsaw. Long. 9. 50. E. lat. 40. 50. N.

CRAIL, a borough of Scotland, in Fifeshire, seated on the Frith of Forth; 7 miles S. E. of St. Andrew's. It is an ancient town, and unites with Cupar, &c., in sending one member to parliament.

CRAINBURG, a town of Germany, in Carniola, with a castle on the river Save; 18 miles N.W. of Laubach.

CRAMOND, a village of Scotland; 3 miles

N.W. of Edinburgh, at the mouth of the Amond, in the Frith of Forth. It has a commodious harbour, and considerable iron-works.

CRANBOURN, a town in Dorsetshire, with a market on Wednesday. It stands near a fine chase, which extends almost to Salisbury; 38 miles N. E. of Dorchester, and 93 W. of London.

CRANBROOK, a town in Kent, with a market on Saturday. Here is a free grammar-school, and a free writing-school for poor children, the former endowed by Queen Elizabeth. It is 13 miles S. of Maidstone, and 49 S. E. of London.

CRANGANORE, a town and fort of Hindostan, on the coast of Cochin. It was taken from the Portuguese in 1662, by the Dutch, who sold it in 1789 to the rajah of Travancore. It is seated at the mouth of a river; 30 miles N. by W. of Cochin. Long. 75. 58. E. lat. 10. 23. N.

CRANSAC, a village of France, in the department of Aveiron, celebrated for its mineral waters; 15 miles N. W. of Rhodez.

CRAON, a town of France, in the department of Mayenne, near the river Oudon; 17 miles S. by W. of Laval.

CRATO, a town of Portugal, in Alentejo, with a priory belonging to the order of Malta; 14 miles W. of Portalegre.

CRAVEN, a county of North Carolina, the east end of which borders on Pamtico Sound. It is intersected by the Neuse river. Pop. 13,348, of whom 5702 were slaves. Newbern, on the W. bank of the Neuse, 119 miles S. E. by E. of Raleigh, is the chief town. Pop. 3690.

CRAWFORD. There are five counties of this name in different parts of the United States of North America, named probably in reference to W. H. Crawford, who was secretary to the treasury during the presidency of James Munroe, from 1807 to 1825:—

1. At the N. W. extremity of Pennsylvania, bordering on the state of Ohio, intersected by French Creek, falling into the Allegany river. Pop. 31,724. Meadville, 286 miles W. N. W. of Harrisburg, is the chief town.

2. In the state of Indiana, bounded on the E. by Big Blue river, the S. end jetting upon the Ohio. Pop. 5282. Fredonia, on the N. bank of the Ohio, 130 miles S. by W. of Indianopolis, is the chief town.

3. In the state of Illinois, extending westward from the Wabash river for about 80 miles, being about 35 miles in breadth. Pop. 4422. Palestine, on the W. bank of the Wabash, 80 miles E. of Vandalia, is the chief town.

4. In the interior of Ohio, intersected by the Sandusky river, which falls into Lake Erie; the Scioto, falling into the Ohio, rises in the adjoining county. Pop. 13,152.

CRAYFORD, a village in Kent, on the river Cray; 2 miles W. by N. of Dartford. Here are some calico-printing grounds, and a manufacture of iron hoops.

CRECI-EN-PONTHIEU, a town of France in the department of Somme, province of Picardy, on the river Maye. Pop. 1587. 15 miles E. from Montreuil. Here the French, under Philip VI., were defeated by Edward III. of England, in the famous battle of Crecy, on August 26, 1346.

CREDITON, a town in Devonshire, with a market on Saturday, and a considerable manufacture of serges. The church is a noble structure, and was formerly a cathedral. The town was almost all destroyed by fire in 1769. It is seated between two hills; 8 miles N. W. of Exeter, and 180 W. by N. of London.

CREE, a river of Scotland, which rises in the northern parts of the counties of Wigton and Kirkcudbright, forms the boundary between them, and enters the head of Wigton Bay.

CREEK, or MUSKOGEE INDIANS, the most numerous tribe of Indians of any within the limits of the United States of North America. They inhabit an extensive tract of country between the states of Georgia and Alabama; their principal towns are in long. 86. 30. W. lat. 30. 0. N. Their country abounds with creeks and rivulets, and hence they derive their name.

CREETOWN, or FERRYTOWN, a small post of Scotland, in Kirkcudbrightshire. Here several sloops are constantly employed in the coasting trade. It stands on Wigton Bay, near the influx of the Cree; 12 miles W. by N. of Kirkcudbright.

CREGLINGEN, a town of Franconia, in the principality of Anspach, on the Tauber; 22 miles S. of Wurtzburg, and 30 N. W. of Anspach, now included in the Bavarian circle of the Lower Mayne.

CREIL, a town of France in the department of Oise, on the river Oise; 5 miles E. of Senlis.

CREILSHEIM, a town of Franconia, in the principality of Anspach, on the river Jaxt; 22 miles S. W. of Anspach; now included in the Bavarian circle of the Rezat.

CREMA, a fortified town of Italy; capital of Cremasco, a bishop's see. It is well built, and populous, and seated on the Serio; 30 miles S. of Bergamo. Pop. 4000.

CREMASCO, a small territory of Italy, in the S. part of the province of Bergamasco. It is nearly surrounded by the Duchy of Milan, and fertile in corn, wine, flax, and hemp. Crema is the capital.

CREMIEU, a town of France, in the department of Isere, at the foot of a mountain near the Rhone; 20 miles N. E. of Vienne.

CREMNITZ, a town in the N. part of Lower Hungary, noted for its gold and silver mines; 17 miles N. of Schemnitz. The silver mine of Bacherstollen is one of the principal mines of Austria. Pop. about 10,000.

CREMONA, a city of Italy, capital of the Cremonese, and a bishop's see, with a castle and a university. The streets are broad and straight, adorned with some small squares, a few palaces, 40 parish churches, and 43 convents of both sexes. It stands in a delightful plain, watered by the Oglio, about a quarter of a mile from the Po, over which is a bridge of boats, defended by a fort. A canal passes through the town, and forms a communication between the two rivers. Cremona has been several times taken. It has considerable manufactures of silk, and is peculiarly celebrated for the manufacture of violins.

A tower, 372 feet in height, forms a prominent object over all the surrounding country. The Romans established themselves here in 291, B. C. It is 48 miles S. E. of Milan, and about the same distance S. by W. of Mantua. Pop. 24,000.

CREMONESE TERRITORY, in the Lombardo-Venetian kingdom, subject to Austria, extends from the S. in a W. N. W. direction, for about 45 miles, between the river Po on the S., which divides it from the duchy of Parma, and the Oglio on the N., which divides it from Bresciano; the E. end borders on the duchy of Mantua, and the W. on the small district of Cremasco. It is a very fertile country.

CREMSIER, a town of Moravia, with a fine castle and a convent, seated on the W. bank of the river Marsch; 18 miles S. S. E. of Olmutz.

CREPY, a town of France in the department of Oise; 17 miles S. of Compeigne.

CRESCENTINO, a fortified town of Piedmont, on the N. bank of the river Po; 20 miles N. E. of Turin.

CREST, a town of France in the department of Drome, on the river Drome; 16 miles S. S. E. of Valence.

CREVELDT, a town of Germany, at the N. extremity of the territory of Cologne. Near this place the French were defeated by the Hanoverians in 1758. It has considerable manufactures of linen. It it 32 miles N. N. W. of Cologne, and 7 from Dusseldorf. Pop. about 7000.

CREUSE, an interior department, nearly in the centre of France, so named from a river, which crosses from S. to N., and flows into the Vienne. It contains the late province of Marche. Gueret is the capital.

CREUSEN, a town of Franconia, in the principality of Bayreuth, 7 miles E. of the city of Bayreuth.

CREUTZBURG, a town of Silesia, in the principality of Brieg, with a castle. It has a great trade in honey, wax, leather, and flax; and is seated on the Brinnitz; 35 miles E. by N. of Brieg.

CREUTZNACH, a town of Germany, in the circle of Upper Rhine. It has a trade in wine, salt, corn, wool, and tobacco. On December 2, 1795, this town was taken three times; first, by the French, then by the Austrians, and again by the former. It is seated on the Nahe; 25 miles S. W. of Mentz.

CREWKERNE, a town in Somersetshire, with a market on Saturday. It has considerable establishments for the manufacture of sail-cloth. It is seated near a branch of the Parret; 25 miles S. of Wells, and 132 W. S. W. of London.

CRICKEITH, or CRICCAETH, a town of Wales, in Caernarvonshire, with a market on Wednesday; 18 miles S. S. E. of Caernarvon, and 244 N. W. of London. It contributes with Caernarvon in sending one member to parliament.

CRICKHOWELL, a town of Wales, in Brecknockshire, with a market on Thursday. Near it are the ruins of an ancient castle. It is seated on the Usk; 10 miles S. E. of Brecknock, and 153 W. by N. of London.

CRICKLADE, a borough in Wiltshire, with a market on Saturday; seated near the Thames, and the Stroud Canal; 25 miles W. by S. of Oxford, and 84 W. by N. of London.

CRIEFF, a town of Scotland, in Perthshire, with manufactures of paper and thin linen; seated on the Erne; 18 miles W. of Perth.

CRIM, a town of the Crimea, supposed to be on the site of an ancient city that once gave its name of Crim Tartary, or Crimea, to the whole peninsula of the Taurida; after having, under the name of Cimmerium, been the capital of a famous people, who gave laws to the greatest part of Europe. The modern town called, Eski Krim (Old Crim) by the Tartars, is seated at the foot of an insulated mountain; 10 miles W. of Caffa.

CRIMEA, or TAURIDA, the ancient Taurica Chersonesus, a peninsula of Europe, bounded on the S. and W. by the Black Sea, N. by the province of Catharinenslaf, with which it communicates by the Isthmus of Prekop, and E. by the Sea of Asoph and the Strait of Caffa. Towards the end of the 11th century the Genoese settled in this country; but they were expelled by the Crim Tartars, in 1474. *See* CAFFA. These Tartars had been settled in the Crimea above two centuries before the expulsion of the Genoese. They were subjects to Batu Khan, grandson of Lingis: and their conquest was annexed to the kingdom of Kusan, till the death of Tamerlane, in 1400, when Edegai Khan, an officer of that prince, took possession of it, and was succeeded by Duelet Cherai, in whose family the sovereignty continued till the 18th century. The Khans, however, were vassals, or tributary to the Turks, till the year 1774, when their independence was stipulated in the treaty of Cainargi. In 1783, the Russians took possession of the country with an army; the following year it was ceded to them by the Turks; and the peaceable possession of the whole was secured to them in 1791, by the cession of the fortress of Oczakow. The Crimea is divided into two parts by the river Salgir, which runs from W. to E. The N. division is flat, poor, and fit for pasturage only. It has neither tree nor hillock; salt-lakes and flocks of sheep are its greatest riches. This district is bleak and cold in winter, and sultry and scorching in summer. The S. part is mountainous; but the valleys are astonishingly productive, and the climate extremely mild, from the exclusion of those violent winds by which the N. division is frequently incommoded. The lower hills, extending from Caffa to the E. extremity of the country, are principally used in gardening, and produce excellent fruit. Besides the port of Kertch, the road of Caffa, and the harbour of Balaclava, there is, near Sebastopol, one of the finest harbours in the world. The principal articles of export are corn, salt, honey, wax, butter, horses, female slaves, hides, and furs, especially the Tauric lamb-skins, which are in high esteem. The Crimea now forms one of the two provinces of the government of

Catharinenslaf, under the name of Taurida. Sympheropol is the capital. *See* Russia.

Croagh-Patrick, a mountain in Ireland, in the county of Mayo, 2528 feet above the sea.

Croatia, a province of the Austrian empire; bounded on the N. by the river Drave, which separates it from Lower Hungary, extending S. for about 160 miles to the Adriatic: the Save intersects it from the W. in an E. S. E. direction, parallel with the Drave, at a distance of about 45 miles; the part N. of the Save is bounded on the E. by Sclavonia, and on the W. by Lower Syria, and the part S. of the Save is bounded on the E. by the Turkish province of Bosnia, and on the W. by Lower Carniola; this part was ceded to France at the peace of Vienna in 1809, but restored to Austria at the general peace of 1815. The mean breadth of Croatia is about 60 miles, and its superficial area 9420 square miles, containing a population of about 800,000. It was called by the Romans *Liburnia*, and subsequently formed part of Illyria and Sclavonia; and at a somewhat later period became an independent kingdom under the protection of the eastern emperors. In 1087 it was conquered by Ladislaus, king of Hungary, and passed into the hands of Austria by its being made an integral part of Hungary in 1102. It is now divided into six counties, and the S. E. part into six districts. It is in general a mountainous country; containing some mines of iron and copper, and the best timber in Europe. The valleys are tolerably fertile, and the mulberry, prune, vine, and olive are interspersed over most parts of the country, and, in parts, flourish luxuriantly. Honey is collected in great quantities on the banks of the Drave. The port of Fiume, at the S. W. extremity of the province, supplies the interior with such foreign productions as the inhabitants can command, in exchange for their surplus produce, which is limited both in value and extent. The capital of the country is Carlstadt, and the other principal towns are Warasden, Agram, Petrinia, Ogulia, Zettin, &c. &c. *See* Morlachia.

Croce, St., Croix, St., or Cruz, Santa. There are several towns, villages, and rivers of this name both in Europe and America, but all inconsiderable.

Croisic, or Croisil, a town of France, in the department of Lower Loire, seated on the Bay of Biscay, between the mouths of the Loire and Vilaine; 35 miles W. of Nantes.

Croix, St., a river of North America, which forms the N. E. boundary of the United States, and runs into the Bay of Passamaquoddy, in the lat. of 45. 0. N. and 67. 0. of W. long.

Croix, St., one of the Virgin Islands, in the Caribbean Sea; 30 miles long, and 8 where broadest; lying 40 miles E. by S. of St. Thomas, and about the same distance E. S. E. of Crab Island, off the S. E. end of Porto Rico. Columbus landed upon this island in one of his early voyages. It was successively held by the Spaniards, English, and Dutch. In 1651 it was bought for the knights of Malta, who sold it in 1664 to the French West India Company, by whom it was sold to the Danes in 1696; who held it till 1801, when it was taken by the English, and restored after the naval action off Copenhagen in the same year; retaken in 1807, and restored again at the general peace of 1815. It is divided into about 350 plantations, yielding about 25,000 hogsheads, or 16,000 tons, of sugar annually. The population amounted to 31,387, of whom 28,000 were slaves. The chief town is Christianstadt, on the N. coast, with a fine harbour, defended by a fortress. Long. 65. 28. W. lat. 17. 45. N.

Croja, a town of European Turkey, in Albania, seated near the Gulf of Venice; 13 miles N. by E. of Durazzo. It was once the residence of the kings of Albania.

Cromack-water, or Crumack-water, a lake in Cumberland, between Buttermere-water and Lowes-water, receiving the former at its S. end, by the river Cocker, and the latter at its N. end. It is four miles long, and half a mile over; with three small isles, one of them a rock, and the other covered with wood. Half a mile from the S. W. end is a waterfall, called Scale Force, between the mountains of Mellbreak and Bleacragg. At the N. E. corner is a stone bridge over its outlet, the Cocker. It abounds with char and red trout.

Cromarty, a county of Scotland, sixteen miles long and six broad, comprehending part of a peninsula on the S. side of a frith, to which it gives name. On the S. and W. it is bounded by Ross-shire. It is divided into five parishes. The highlands are healthy, and on the coast it is fertile and well cultivated. It sends one member to parliament in conjunction with Ross. The towns are Cromarty, Kirkmichael, Resolis, and Urquhart.

Cromarty, a seaport of Scotland, and capital of the preceding county. The harbour is one of the finest in Great Britain, and has a commodious quay. Here is a considerable manufacture of hempen cloth, and a coasting trade in corn, thread, yarn, fish, and skins of various sorts. It stands at the mouth of the Frith of Cromarty; 16 miles N. N. E. of Inverness. It joins with Kirkwall and four other places in sending one member to parliament. Long. 3. 50. W. lat. 57. 38. N.

Cromer, a town in Norfolk, with a market on Saturday. It formerly had two churches, one of which, with several houses, was swallowed up by the sea. The inhabitants are chiefly fishermen; and the best lobsters on this part of the coast are taken here. It is seated on the German Ocean; 22 miles N. of Norwich, and 129 N. E. of London, and is frequented in the summer season for sea-bathing.

Cromford, a village in Derbyshire, on the river Derwent; 2 miles N. of Wirksworth. The Arkwrights have erected an extensive cotton-mill at this place, and connected it by a canal with the Erwash and Nottingham canals, and thereby with the river Trent.

Crompton, a township in the parish of Oldham, Lancashire. *See* Oldham.

Cronach, a town of Bavaria, in the principality of Bamberg, near which is a mountain-fortress called Rosenberg. It is seated near the river Cronach; 11 miles N. of Culmbach.

CRONBORG, a strong fortress of Denmark, on the Isle of Zealand, near Elsinore, which guards the passage of the Sound. It is situate on the point of a peninsular promontory, opposite Helsingburg in Sweden, little more than 2 miles distant. In 1658 it was taken by the king of Sweden, and restored in 1660. In this fortress is a palace where Queen Matilda was imprisoned till she was permitted to retire to Zell. Not far from this, at Barienfelt, is Hamlet Garden, said to be the spot where the murder of his father was perpetrated.

CRONENBERG, or KRONBERG, a town of Germany, in the late electorate of Mentz; seated on a mountain; 9 miles N. W. of Frankfort.

CRONSTADT, a seaport and fortress of Russia, on the island of Retusari, in the Gulf of Finland. The harbour is the chief station of the Russian fleet. Here are great magazines of naval stores, docks and yards for building ships, a foundry for casting cannon balls, and an extensive marine hospital. The Man of War's Mole is enclosed by a strong rampart, built of granite, in the sea, and Peter's Canal, lined with masonry, is 1050 fathoms long, 60 broad at the bottom, and 100 at the top; it is 24 fathoms deep, and in this manner stretches 358 fathoms into the sea. At the end of the canal are two pyramidal columns, with inscriptions relative to this great work. The town occupies the E. part of the island, and the inhabitants are estimated at 54,717. It is 22 miles W. of Petersburg, of which it is the outport. Long. 29. 26. E. lat. 59. 56. N.

CRONSTADT, a town of Transylvania. *See* BRASSAU.

CROOKED ISLAND. *See* BAHAMAS.

CROPANI, a town of Naples, in Calabria Ulteriore; 9 miles E. N. E. of St. Severino.

CROSNE, a town of Austrian Poland, in the palatinate of Lemberg; 80 miles W. S. W. of Lemberg.

CROSSEN, a town of Brandenburg, in the New Mark, capital of a duchy of the same name, with a strong castle. It is seated on the frontiers of Silesia, near the conflux of the Bober with the Oder, in a country abounding with wine and fruit; 23 miles S. E. of Frankfort.

CROSS-FELL, a mountain in Cumberland, 8 miles E. S. E. of Kirkoswold. Its extreme altitude is 2902 feet. At different elevations there are two extensive plains; and a third on the summit contains several hundred acres covered with moss and other vegetable productions. The view from this height comprehends a great part of six counties. A few yards below the summit is a spring called the Gentleman's Well.

CROSSMALINA, a town in Ireland, county of Mayo; about 90 miles from Dublin.

CROTONA, or CROTON, a seaport of Naples, on the E. coast of Calabria Ulteriore, and a bishop's see, with a citadel. It has a trade in grain, cheese, oil, and silk, and is 15 miles S. E. of St. Severino. Long. 17. 27. E. lat. 39. 9. N.

CROTOY, a town of France, in the department of Somme, on the E. side of the mouth of the Somme; 35 miles N. W. of Amiens.

CROUCH, a river in Essex, which rises near Horndon, and enters the German Ocean between Burnham and Foulness Island. The Walfleet and Burnham oysters are the produce of its creeks and pits.

CROWLAND, a town in Lincolnshire, with a market on Saturday. Here was formerly an abbey of great note; and some stately ruins yet remain. The town consists of four streets, which are separated by watercourses, and connected by a curious triangular bridge for foot passengers. The chief trade is in fish and wild ducks, which are plentiful in the adjacent pools and marshes. It is 11 miles N. of Peterborough, and 93 N. by W. of London.

CROWLE, a town in Lincolnshire, with a market on Monday; seated on the Isle of Axholm, near the river Dun; 18 miles N. of Gainsborough, and 167 N. N. W. of London.

CROWN POINT, a fort and town of New York, in Essex county. The fort was erected by the French in 1731, on a point that runs N. into Lake Champlain. It was reduced by the English in 1759, taken by the Americans in 1775, and retaken by the English the year after. It is 123 miles N. of Albany. Pop. 2212.

CROYDON, a town in Surrey, with a market on Saturday. It has an hospital and free-school, founded by Archbishop Whitgift; and in the church are some monuments of the archbishops of Canterbury, who had here an ancient palace, which was alienated from the see in 1780: the building and adjoining premises are now occupied by some cotton manufactures. The summer assizes are held here and at Guildford alternately. Croydon is seated near the source of the Wandle; 10 miles S. of London. A railroad is now established from London to this place, from whence the Brighton and South-eastern lines are continued.

CROZEN, a town of France, in the department of Finisterre, situate on the promontory which forms the S. boundary of Brest Harbour, 16 miles N. W. of Chateaulin. Pop. about 8000, mostly sailors and fishermen.

CRUACHAN-BEN, a mountain of Scotland, between Loch Etive and the N. end of Loch Awe, in Argyleshire. It has two conical peaks, one of which is 3962, and the other 3390 feet above the level of the sea.

CRUCES, a small seaport in the Gulf of Mexico, about 15 miles W. S. W. of Porto Bello.

CRUMLAU, or CRUMAU, a town of Bohemia, in the circle of Bechin, with a castle; seated on the Muldau; 12 miles S. by W. of Budweis.

CRUMLAW, or CROMAU, a town of Moravia, in the circle of Znaim, with a castle; 10 miles N. N. E. of Znaim.

CRUZ, ST., a seaport of Morocco. The Portuguese had a fortress here, which was taken from them by the Moors in 1536, and the emperor caused it to be destroyed in 1773. The harbour is safe and commodious. It is seated on a bay of the Atlantic; 130 miles W. S. W. of Morocco, and 65 S. of Mogador. Long. 9. 30. W. lat. 30. 28. N.

CRUZ, ST., a seaport on the south-east side of Teneriffe, and the general residence of the governor of all the Canary Islands. It has a well-built pier and quay, and is defended by several forts and batteries. Long. 16. 16. W. and lat. 28. 27. N.

CRUZ, ST., a town of Bolivia, capital of a jurisdiction, and a bishop's see. The country is woody and mountainous; but the town stands in a fertile valley, near the river Guapaix; 160 miles N. N. E. of Plata. Long. 65. 15. W. lat. 17. 26. S.

CRUZ, ST., a town on the N. side of the island of Cuba; 50 miles E. of Havannah.

CRUZ, ST., an island in the Pacific Ocean. *See* CROCE, ST.

CUBA, an island in the West Indies, lying between the lat. of 19. 40. and 23. 10. N., and extending from 74. to 85. of W. long. The E. end is bounded by a strait called the Windward Passage, about 65 miles wide, which divides it from the N. W. end of Hispaniola; and the W. end projects into the Gulf of Mexico, being about 100 miles from the promontory of Yucatan on the S., and the same distance from the promontory of East Florida on the N. Its mean breadth, however, does not exceed 75 miles, comprising an area of about 52,000 square miles, or a superficies nearly equal to that of England and Wales. The island was first made known to Europeans by Columbus, in 1492; and, from the great extent of its coast from E. to W., was at first supposed to form part of the western continent. It was, however, ascertained to be an island, in 1508, by Nicholas Ovando, who sailed round it in that year; and in about three years after, it was taken possession of by a Spanish force from Hispaniola, under the command of Don Jago de Velasquez, who took the native chief prisoner, and roasted him alive, and afterwards extirpated the natives; after which, the island remained, with but little interruption, in possession of the Spaniards until 1741, when an unsuccessful attempt was made upon it by the English; to whom, however, it surrendered on the 13th of August, 1762, after a desperate resistance of the Spaniards, for about two months. *See* HAVANNAH. It was restored to Spain in the following year, and has remained in their quiet possession up to the present time, having been but little affected by the events which led to the entire subversion of Spanish domination over every part of their continental possessions in the western hemisphere. Since the period of 1791, when the mania of the French revolution extended to the neighbouring island of Hispaniola, numerous planters of that island fled to Cuba, which has ever since continued to improve in cultivation and increase in population, and its produce in sugar, coffee, and tobacco, since the commencement of the present century, has been very great and progressively increasing. The tobacco is unequalled in quality, and is chiefly made into cigars.

Mountain ridges pervade the whole island, rendering the face of the country exceedingly picturesque. It is tolerably well watered; and, by social arrangements and well directed exertion, it is capable of subsisting twenty millions of people, in the highest degree of earthly enjoyment. In the woods are some valuable trees, particularly cedars of a large size; and birds abound here, both in variety and number, more than in any of the other islands. The soil is fertile, and cattle, sheep, and hogs are numerous. There are copper mines in the mountains, and forests full of game. The principal ports are the Havannah and Matanzas, on the N. coast, near the W. end; and St. Jago de Cuba and St. Salvador, on the S. coast, near the E. end; and, in addition to its staple productions of sugar, coffee, and tobacco, ginger, long pepper, cassia, tamarinds, wild cinnamon, mastic, aloes, honey, &c. &c. are abundant.

CUBA, a town of Portugal, in Alentejo; 30 miles S. by E. of Evora.

CUBAGUA, a small island off the N. coast of Colombia, between that of Margarita and Cumana. Here the Spaniards, in 1509, established a fishery of pearl; but the banks disappeared in 1524. The island is barren and nitrous. Long. 64. 10. W. lat. 10. 56. N.

CUBAN, a river which issues from the N. side of the Caucasian mountains, divides Circassia from part of Taurica, and flows into the N. extremity of the Black Sea, near the entrance to the Sea of Asoph. It receives several tributary streams from the S.

CUBAN, or CUBAN TARTARY, a county in the Russian province of Taurica; bounded on the W. by the Sea of Taurica; N. by the river Don, which separates it from Europe, E. by the desert of Astracan, and S. by the river Cuban, which divides it from Circassia.

CUCKFIELD, a town in Sussex, with a market on Friday; 13 miles N. W. of Lewes, and 39 S. by W. of London.

CUDDALORE, a town of Hindostan, on the coast of Carnatic, near the place where Fort St. David once stood. It was taken by the French in 1758, and again in 1783. It is 20 miles S. S. W. of Pondicherry. Long. 79. 55. E. lat. 11. 41. N.

CUDDAPA, a town of Hindostan, capital of a circar of the same name, ceded by Tippoo, in 1792, to the Nizam of the Deccan. It is 133 miles N. W. of Madras. Long. 78. 57. E. lat. 14. 23. N.

CUDREFIN, a tn. and bailiwick of Switzerland, in the canton of Bern; 21 miles W. of Bern.

CUENZA, a province of Spain, on the E. side of New Castile, intersected by the river Xucar. It is cultivated in the southern part, and produces corn, hemp, &c.; while the northern and eastern portions are devoted to pasturing sheep. The principal produce is wool. Pop. 296,750.

CUENZA, a city and bishop's see, capital of the preceding province. It is seated on a high and craggy hill, on the banks of the Xucar, over which is an elegant stone bridge of five arches. The cathedral is a stately edifice; besides which there are several churches and six monasteries. It is 90 miles E. by S. of Madrid. Pop. about 6000.

CUENCA, a town of Colombia, and capital of a jurisdiction of the same name, in the province of Quito; bounded on the W. by the shore of the Bay of Guayaquil, and E. by the Andes. The town is situate in a valley, about midway from the foot of the Andes and the shore of the bay, and 176 miles S. by W. of the city of Quito. Pop. about 18,000.

CUERNAVACCA, a town of Mexico; 40 miles S. by W. of the city of Mexico, on the road to Acapulco. In the time of Cortes it was the capital of an independent state. It is situate on the southern declivity of the Cordilleras, 5,400 feet above the level of the sea. The climate is delightful.

CUIABA, a town of Brazil, in the province of Matto Grosso; seated on the W. bank of the river Cuiaba, which falls into the Paraguay, in the long. of 56. W. and lat. of 15. 35. S. The population is estimated at 30,000. There is a tolerably productive gold mine in the vicinity of the town.

CUILLY, a town of Switzerland, in the canton of Bern, on the N. E. side of the Lake of Geneva; 8 miles E. S. E. of Lausanne.

CULENBURG, or KARLENBOURG, a town of Holland, in Gelderland, on the S. bank of the river Leck; 16 miles S. S. E. of Utrecht.

CULIACAN, a town of Mexico, seated near the source of a river of the same name, which after a course of about 50 miles, falls into the Gulf of California, in the lat. of 24. 20. N. It is celebrated in Mexican history under the name of *Hueicollinacan*, and as the capital of a populous and fertile district.

CULLEN, a town of Scotland, in Banffshire, at the mouth of the Culan or Cullen. It has manufactures of linen and damask, and a trade in fresh and dried fish. Near it are seen three lofty spiring rocks, formed of flinty masses, called the Three Kings of Cullen. It is 13 miles W. by N. of Banff.

CULLFRA, a town of Spain, in Valencia, at the mouth of the Xucar; 21 miles S. of Valencia. Pop. about 4000.

CULM, a city of Prussia, capital of a palatinate of the same name, and a bishop's see, with a Catholic university. It is seated on the E. bank of the Vistula; 85 miles S. of Dantzic. Long. 18. 30. E. lat. 53. 24. N.

CULM is also the name of a town in Bohemia, in the W. part of the circle of Saaz. It was near this place where the French general Vandamme was defeated by a corps of Austrians and Prussians, in August 1813.

CULMBACH, a town of Franconia, formerly the capital of a principality of the same name. Near it, on a mountain, stands the fortress of Plassenburg, where the archives of the principality were preserved; but they were removed to Bayreuth in 1783. Culmbach is seated near the Weiss branch of the Maine; 13 miles N. N. W. of Bayreuth. Pop. about 3800.

CULMORE, a town of Ireland, in the county of Londonderry, on the coast of Lough Foyle; 5 miles N. by E. of Londonderry. It is stated, in a return made to parliament in 1821, to be extra-parochial, and exempt from tithe, and parish, and county rate.

CULNA, a town of Hindostan, in the presidency of Bengal, on the Hoogly. It is the port of the Burdwan district; 48 miles N. W. of Calcutta.

CULPEC, a town of Hindostan; an unhealthy station on the Hoogly; 33 miles S. of Calcutta.

CULPEPER, a county of Virginia, bounded on the N. W. by the Blue ridge of the Allegany mountains, and on the E. by the Rappahannock river. Fairfax, 72 miles N. by W. of Richmond, is the chief town. Pop. of the county 11,393.

CULROSS, a borough of Scotland, in Perthshire, in a district almost surrounded by Clackmannanshire. Here is a princely abbey, built in 1217. It is situate on the Frith of Forth; 20 miles S. of Perth; and 21 W. N. W. of Edinburgh.

CUMANA, a seaport of Colombia, and capital of the province of Orinoco. It is seated on an arid sandy plain, at the entrance of a spacious inlet of the Caribbean Sea, in the lat. of 10. 12. N. and 64. 24. W. long. Cumana has suffered much both by inundations and by earthquakes. On the 14th of December, 1797, about four-fifths of the town was destroyed. It is otherwise advantageously situate for external commerce, which it carries on to some extent in cotton, cocoa, mules, cattle, &c., in exchange for the manufactures of Europe generally. Pop. about 20,000.

CUMBER, or COMBER, a parish and town in the county of Down, Ireland. The town is pleasantly seated at the head of a small bay of Strangford Lough.

CUMBERLAND, a maritime and mountainous county of the N. of England; bounded on the N. by the river Liddel, which separates it from Scotland, and on the E. by the counties of Northumberland and Durham, S. by those of Westmoreland and part of Lancashire, and E. by the Irish Sea. It contains 974,720 acres, and is divided into the eastern and western divisions, for each of which it sends two members to parliament. This county contains a good deal of dreary moor, but some of the valleys, intersected by streams of water and interspersed with lakes, are exceedingly picturesque, and very fertile. The two principal rivers are the Eden and Derwent, which abound with salmon and char. The mountains and moors are rich in minerals, especially coals and lead. It has also a very valuable bed of plumbago, or black lead. Sea Fell, the highest peak of the mountains, rises to a height of 3166 feet above the level of the sea. Skiddaw and Helvellyn also each rise to heights exceeding 3000 feet, and five or six others approximate to 3000 feet. Carlisle is the capital, where some considerable manufactures of cotton are carried on. The county also yields a surplus of cattle, and about 200,000 chaldrons of coals annually. The seaports are Whitehaven, Workington, and Maryport; and the principal towns in the interior, Aldston, Cockermouth, Penrith, and Wigton.

CUMBERLAND is also the name of several counties in different parts of the United States of North America, viz.

1st. In the state of Maine, of which Portland

is the chief town, and seat of government of the state. (*See* PORTLAND.) It is a maritime county. its area not exceeding 700 square miles, comprising a considerable surface of lakes. The N. E. corner of the county is bounded by the Kenebec river. Pop. 68,658.

2nd. At the S. extremity of the state of New Jersey, bordering on Delaware Bay, in the lat. of 39. 15. to 39. 30. N. Pop. 14,374. Bridgetown is the capital.

3rd. In Pennsylvania, bounded on the N. by the Blue ridge of the Allegany mountains, and on the E. by the Susquehanna river. It is about 35 miles in extent from E. to W., and 15 in mean breadth. Pop. 30,953. Carlisle, 18 miles W. of Harrisburg, is the chief town.

4th. In Virginia, extending S. from James River for 28 miles, to the Appomattox River. The mean breadth of this county does not exceed 8 miles. Carterville, the chief town, on the S. bank of James River, is 32 miles W. by N. of Richmond. Pop. of the county 10,399, of whom 6781 are slaves.

5th. In the interior of North Carolina, intersected by Cape Fear River. Pop. 15,284, of whom 5392 are slaves. Fayetteville, 48 miles S. by W. of Raleigh, is the chief town.

6th. In Kentucky, bordering on Tennessee, intersected by the Cumberland river. Pop. 6090. Burkesville is the chief town.

CUMBERLAND RIVER, which gives name to the preceding county, rises on the W. side of the Cumberland ridge of mountains, which divide the S. E. end of the state of Kentucky from that of Virginia, in the lat. of 37. N., runs W. for about 120 miles, when it leaves the state of Kentucky in a southerly direction, at the S. W. corner of Cumberland county, into the state of Tennessee, through which it runs a course of about 150 miles, when it re-enters the state of Kentucky in a N. W. direction; and, after a further course of about 60 miles, falls into the Ohio about 50 miles above the entrance of that river into the Mississippi. From the source of the Cumberland River, to its conflux with the Ohio, the distance in a direct line is 300 miles, being 6 deg. of long. between 82. 15. and 88. 15. in the lat. of 37. N.; but the distance by the course and windings of the stream is near 600 miles, 500 of which it is navigable for batteaux of 14 or 15 tons burthen.

CUMBERLAND RIDGE is the most westerly of the Allegany chain of mountains, and extends from the frontier of Georgia, in the lat. of 35. N. in an E. N. E. direction, through the state of Tennessee, flanking the S. E. end of the state of Kentucky, into Tazeville county, in the state of Virginia, in the lat. of 37. 20. N., where it terminates in several knolls, which give rise to several streams that form the Big Sandy River.

CUMBERLAND, an island on the coast of Georgia; the most southern territory of the United States on the Atlantic Ocean, previous to their possession of the Floridas, in July 1821. It is 15 miles long and 2 broad. Opposite its S. extremity is the island Amelia, and between them is the entrance to St. Mary's River, in the lat. of 30. 39. N.

Cumberland is also the name of two or three townships in different parts of the United States of North America.

CUMBERLAND, a town and fort of British America, in a county of the same name, forming the isthmus which unites Nova Scotia to New Brunswick. The fort is situate at the head of the Bay of Fundy, on the E. side of its northern branch, called Chignecto Bay. The isthmus is here about 15 miles across, easily admitting a canal to unite the Bay of Fundy with the Gulf of St. Lawrence. Long. 64. 10. W. lat. 45. 45. N.

CUMBERLAND HOUSE, a station of the Hudson Bay Company, in the country of the Knistineaux Indians, on the S. W. side of Pine Island Lake, in the lat. of 54. N. and 102 of W. long.

Cumberland is also the name of several other islands, bays, and capes in different parts of the world.

CUMBO, or COMBO, a kingdom on the W. coast of Africa, S. of the river Gambia. The Portuguese have a settlement at Cacheo.

CUMBRAY, GREAT AND LITTLE, two islands of Scotland, at the entrance of the Frith of Clyde, to the S. E. of the Isle of Bute. The former is 6 miles in circumference, has excellent freestone quarries, and the ruins of a cathedral dedicated to St. Columba. The latter lies a little to the S. of the other, and on it is a lighthouse. Long. 4. 47. W. lat. 55. 45. N. They are included in the county of Bute.

CUMIRNA, a town of Piedmont; 12 miles S. W. of Turin. Pop. about 4500.

CUMLY, a fort and town of Hindostan, in Canara, seated between two rivers, at their entrance into a salt water lake, which is separated from the sea by a spit of sand. On the opposite side of the S. river is the town of Kanyapura, to which it was formerly joined by a bridge. It is 15 miles S. by E. of Mangalore.

CUNDINAMARCA, one of the four great divisions into which the new republican territory of Colombia was first divided; but since the division of 1823, when the country was divided into twelve provinces, it forms the central and metropolitan province of the republic. *See* BOGOTA, ST. FE DE.

CUPAR OF FIFE, a borough of Scotland, capital of Fifeshire. Here are manufactures of coarse linens, and a considerable tannery. It is seated in a rich valley, on the N. side of the Eden; 8 miles W. by S. of St. Andrews, and 30 N. N. E. of Edinburgh. It joins with St. Andrews, &c., in sending one member to parliament.

CUPAR OF ANGUS, a town of Scotland, partly in Forfar, but chiefly in Perthshire, with a considerable linen manufacture and tannery. It is seated on the Isla; 12 miles N. W. of Dundee, and 13 N. N. E. of Perth.

CURACAO, an island in the Caribbean Sea, lying off the coast of Colombia, near the entrance to the Gulf and Lake of Maracaibo, 35 miles long and 12 broad; subject to the Dutch. It produces sugar, tobacco, and salt; has numerous warehouses, which used formerly to supply the adjacent coast with the productions of Europe and Asia, and which still continue to do so to some extent. In 1800 some French having settled on part of the island, and becoming at variance with the Dutch, the latter surrendered the island to a single British frigate. It was restored to the Dutch by the peace of 1802, and taken from them by a British squadron in 1807, and again restored by the peace of 1814. The principal town is St. Peter, at the N. E. extremity of the island. Long. 69. 15. W. lat. 12. 22. N.

CURICO, the tenth in order of the provinces of Chili; the chief town, of the same name, is about 100 miles from the sea, in the lat. of 35. S. on the road from Conception to Santiago.

CURIA MURIA, an island on the coast of Arabia Felix, opposite the mouth of the river Prim. Long. 55. 25. E. lat. 17. 0. N.

CURISCH HAFF, a lake or bay of Prussia, separated from the Baltic Sea by a tongue of land 70 miles in extent, in a N. N. E. direction, but not more than 2 or 3 miles wide; the Haff is about 30 miles wide at the S. end, progressively narrowing to about a mile only at its outlet into the sea at Memel.

CURNOUL, or KURNOUL, a town of Hindostan, district of Balaghaut, the ancient capital of the Deccan, and defended by a strong fort. It was taken by the British in 1815, and again in 1839. It is 279 miles from Madras, on the river Toombudra.

CURRAH, a town of Hindostan, in Allahabad, on the S. bank of the Ganges; 36 miles N. W. of Allahabad.

CURRITUCK, a maritime county at the N. E. extremity of North Carolina, the N. end bordering on the great Dismal Swamp of Virginia, and the S. end on Albemarle Sound. This was formerly a very dreary district, but some of the land, within the present century, has been rendered very productive in rice. Pop. 6703, of whom 2100 are slaves. The county gives name to one of the inlets into Albemarle Sound.

CURUPA, a town of Brazil, in the government of Para, seated on the S. bank of the main channel of the Amazon; 250 miles W. of Para. Long. 53. 10. W. lat. 1. 50. S.

CURZOLA, an island in the Gulf of Venice, on the coast of Dalmatia; about 26 miles long. It abounds in wood proper for building ships, and produces good wine. At the E. end is a fortified town of the same name, with a good harbour. Long. 17. 10. E. lat. 43. 6. N.

CUSCO, or CUZCO, a city of Peru, and a bishop's see, formerly the capital of the incas; supposed to have been first founded by Manca Capac, in 1043. The Spaniards, under Pizarro, took possession of it in 1534. On a mountain contiguous to the N. part of the city are the ruins of a fort and palace of the incas, the stones of which are of enormous magnitude. Cusco is built in a square form, in the middle of which is the best market in all America: four large streets, which are perfectly straight, terminate in the square. It contains nine churches besides the cathedral, which is a noble structure. The number of inhabitants is about 30,000, of which one-half are original Americans. Streams of water run through the town, which are a great conveniency in a country where it seldom rains. It is seated near the source of a river falling into the Velcomayo, on the E. side of the first collateral ridge of the Andes; 350 miles E. by S. of Lima. Long. 71. 47. W. lat. 13. 20. S.

CUSSET, a town of France, in the department of Allier; 37 miles S. by E. of Moulins. Pop. about 4000.

CUSTEE, a town of Bengal on the S. bank of the main branch of the Ganges; 100 miles N. by E. of Calcutta. It has considerable manufactures of silk.

CUSTRIN, a fortified town of Brandenburg, capital of the New Mark, with a castle. In 1760 it was bombarded and almost destroyed by the Russians, and in 1806 it was taken by the French. It is seated amid morasses, at the conflux of the Warta with the Oder; 46 miles E. by N. of Berlin.

CUTAIS, or KOTATIS, the chief town of Imeritia, Russian Asia, government of Georgia. The remains of the cathedral seem to prove that it was once a considerable place. It is seated on the Riona; 120 miles W. by N. of Tefflis. Long. 43. 0. E. lat. 42. 25. N.

CUTCH, a country of Hindostan, governed by a rajah, and situate on the S. E. of Sind; the E. branch of the Indus separating the two countries. It extends along the N. coast of the Gulf of Cutch, and is separated from Guzerat by river Ban. It abounds with hills, woods, an sandy wilds. The capital is Bhooj, in the lat. of 23. 16. N., and 69. 2. of E. long. The Runn, or Rin of Cutch, is an extensive tract of 8000 square miles to the N. of the district, which is alternately a muddy plain, or a dry sandy desert, covered with saline deposits, from which much salt is manufactured.

CUTTACK, a maritime district of Hindostan, extending from Lake Chilka in the lat. of 19. 30. N., to the Subunreeka river, which separates it from Bengal in the lat. of 21. 30. N., being bounded on the W. by the province of Orissa. The rivers Coyle, Nuddy, and Mahanuddy intersect it from W. to E. It is a very fertile district, and has numerous and extensive manufactures of cotton; but is more particularly celebrated as the chief district of Hindoo devotees, and containing the temple of Jagarnaut. The chief town, of the same name, sometimes called,

CUTTACK BENARES, is seated on an island formed by the Mahuddy river, about 50 miles from the sea, in the lat. of 20. 30. N., and 86. 10. of E. long. Besides Jagarnaut, the other places of note are Balasore, Masulipatam, and Jagepoor. This district was familiar to the Mahomedans as early as the commencement of the 13th century, but continued in possession of the Hindoos till 1569, when it surrendered to Solyman Kerang, who annexed it to Bengal. In 1757, it was ceded to the Nagpore Mahrattas, and fell into the possession of the English in 1803. Pop. about 1,200,000.

CUTTERAH, a town of Hindostan, in the province of Oude; 25 miles S. by E. of Bareilly; celebrated for a decisive battle fought in its vicinity on the 18th of April, 1774, between the Rohillas and the British.

CUTTUB, a town of Hindostan, in the province of Delhi; 13 miles S. from Delhi: near the town is a remarkable column, 242 feet high, erected in the 11th century.

CUXHAVEN, a seaport of Lower Saxony in the Duchy of Bremen; situate near the point of the promontory formed by the mouths of the rivers Weser and Elbe. It is an insignificant place, but rendered of some importance as the station of the post-office packets between England and the N. of Europe. It is 60 miles N. N. W. of Hamburg. Lat. 53. 50. N. and 8. 40. of E. long.

CUYAHOGA. *See* CAYAHOGA.

CYCLADES, the ancient name of ten islands at the entrance of the Grecian Archipelago, between 36. and 38. of N. lat.

CYPRUS, an island at the eastern extremity of the Mediterranean Sea, lying off the coast of Syria, from which the eastern extremity of the island is distant 70 miles. It is 165 miles in extreme length, and 50 wide in its broadest part, but its mean breadth does not exceed 30 miles, giving an area of about 5000 square miles, in 35. of N. lat. It is intersected by mountains and streams of water. The mountains are of considerable elevation, and the tops of some of them are covered with snow a great part of the year. The principal river runs from W. to E. and is called the Pedia. During the national career of Egypt, Persia, Greece, and Rome, Cyprus was the resort of the learned, gay, refined, and vicious of those nations. Its pre-eminence declined with the fall of the Roman empire, and, from its being the abode of all that was refined in art, and voluptuous in every species of indulgence—yielding to a numerous population abundance of every thing necessary to subsistence, and a variety of the most delicious fruits—it rapidly became a wilderness in comparison with its previous fertility, overrun by tribes of Arabs, who were driven from the island during the crusades, at the close of the twelfth century, by Richard I. of England, who assumed the title of king of Cyprus. In 1480 it fell into the hands of the Venetians, at which period it is made the place and scene of a drama by the English dramatic poet, Shakspere. The Venetians surrendered it to the Turks in 1570, in whose possession, up to 1826, it still continued. Its present population is supposed not to exceed 70,000, about one-third of whom are Turks, and the remainder Greeks, who have three bishops and one archbishop. The principal towns are Pafo, or Baffo, at the W. end, Massarea and Mancorta, or Famagousta, at the mouth of the Pedea, towards the end, and Cerina, on the N. coast of the island, and Lesscossia, or Viconia, the capital, in the interior. Cyprus is still rich by nature, in mineral, animal, and vegetable productions: the vine and olive, with a variety of other plants and flowers, esculent, ambrosial, and medicinal, luxuriate in a perfection equal to any part of the world, and superior to most parts. The wines possess a strong aperient quality, and require forty years to duly qualify them for the palate. The inhabitants carry on various manufactures in silk, cotton, and wool, and their carpets are deservedly esteemed for the variety, richness, and beauty of their colour.

CYR, ST., a village of France, 2 miles from Versailles; celebrated for an abbey founded by Madame de Maintenon, who was the abbess till her death, in 1719.

There are a number of towns and villages of this name in different parts of France, but all inconsiderable.

CZ. For places sometimes written with Cz, *see* CS, and TSCH.

CZASLAU, or TCHASLAU, a circle of Bohemia, bordering on Moravia, the N. end jetting upon the Elbe; containing about 800 square miles of territory. It is intersected from E. to W. by the Yasawa, which river falls into the Moldau, and from N. to S. by another river which falls into the Elbe. Pop. about 180,000, chiefly agricultural. The chief town, of the same name, is seated in the N. part of the circle, 8 miles S. of the Elbe, and 45 E. N. E. of Prague. The church has the highest tower of Bohemia. Near this place the king of Prussia gained a victory over the Austrians, in 1742.

CZENSTOCHOW, or CZESTOCHOW, a town of Prussian Poland, near the frontier of Silesia and the source of the Warta; near which there is a celebrated convent, fortified and garrisoned. It sustained a siege against the Swedes in 1657, and near it a battle was fought in 1665, between the royal army of Poland and Lubomirski, to the disadvantage of the former. It was garrisoned by the French in 1812. It is 50 miles N. N. W. of Cracow.

CZERCOSSI, or ST. CZYRKOSSY, a town of Russia, in the Ukraine, with a castle; seated near the Dnieper; 85 miles S. E. of Kiow. Long. 32. 5. E., lat. 49. 20. N.

CZERNETZ, a town of European Turkey, in Walachia, near the Danube; 140 miles W. by N. of Bucharest.

CZERNITZ, or KASCHAU, a town of Carniola, remarkable for its lake, which produces grass and corn every year. The lake is surrounded by mountains, and in dry seasons is from 20 to 25 miles in circumference; but when full it is 40 miles round, and contains several islands, on the largest of which is a village. When the water subsides, buck-wheat is sown on the dry parts, and becomes ready for the sickle in six weeks; and the pasturage is not hurt by the water if it does not stay too long. The town is situate at the N. part of the lake; 20 miles S. by W. of Laybach.

CZERNIGOV, or TCHERNIGOV, a government of European Russia; bounded on the W. by the Dniester. The chief town, of the same name, is seated on the N. bank of the Desna, which falls into the Dniester; 450 miles S. S. W. of Moscow, and 75 N. by E. of Kiov. Pop. about 5000.

CZERSKO, a town of Prussian Poland, in the palatinate of Masovia; seated on the W bank of the Vistula ; 30 miles S. S. E. of Warsaw.

CZERWENIZA, a town of Upper Hungary, famous for mines of opal, a noble gem not yet discovered in any other region of the globe. It is 15 miles N. of Cassovia.

CZONORSDT, or ALT-CZONGRAD, a town of Hungary, at the conflux of the Theiss and Korosh ; 18 miles N. of Zegedin.

Cz begins the names of several other towns in Poland, Russia, and Austria.

D

DABER, a town of Hither Pomerania, in a circle of its name ; 16 miles N. N. E. of Stargard.

DABUL, a town of Hindostan, on the coast of CONCAN, (which see,) with a trade in pepper and salt ; seated at the mouth of a river ; 75 miles S. by E. of Bombay. Long. 72. 53. E. lat. 17. 50. N.

DACCA, a district of Bengal, lying between the main branch of the Ganges and the Burrampooter rivers. The chief town, of the same name, is seated on the banks of a small river, which communicates with the Burrampooter. It was once the capital of Bengal, and defended by a strong fortress, the remains of which appear. It has a vast trade in muslins and other cotton manufactures of the most delicate texture, manufactured from the cotton produced in the province. The country round Dacca lies low, and is always covered with verdure during the dry months. It is 150 miles N. E. of Calcutta. Long. 90. 32. E. lat. 23. 42. N.

DACHAU, a town of Bavaria, where the king has a palace ; seated on a hill near the river Ammer ; 10 miles N. N. W. of Munich.

DAGELET'S ISLAND, an island about 9 miles in circumference, in the Japanese Sea, at about an equal distance from the Isle of Niphon and the coast of the Corea, in the lat. of 37. 25. N. It was visited by La Perouse. It abounds with timber, which the Coreans are supposed to use in the building of boats.

DAGENHAM, a village of Essex, England, on the N. bank of the Thames, from the tide-waters of which it is secured by an embankment. In 1703 the embankment gave way, and inundated 5000 acres of ground, which were reclaimed in 1715.

DAGHISTAN, a province of Georgia, lying between the W. shore of the Caspian Sea and the Caucasian mountains. It is intersected by several small rivers falling into the Caspian. The inhabitants are a brave and hardy race, and successfully resisted the arms of Nadir Shah in 1743. It sovereignty is claimed by Russia, but the resoluteness of the inhabitants renders it nominal rather than real. It has two considerable towns, Tasker and Derbent, on the shores of the Caspian. It is a fertile district, and, under social institutions, might be made an agreeable country. It is intersected by the line of 42. of N. lat.

DAGO, or DAGOE, an island in the Baltic, on the coast of Livonia ; 7 miles N. of the Isle of Oesel, near the entrance to the Gulf of Finland. It is 20 miles in circumference, and has two castles called Dagerwort and Paden. Long. 22. 56. E. lat. 58. 44. N.

DAGON. *See* RANGOON.

DAHL, the finest river of Sweden, which flows through Dalecarlia, or Dalarne, and on the S. confines of Gastricia, and enters the Gulf of Bothnia south of Gefle. Near Escarleby, not far from its mouth, it forms a celebrated cataract, little inferior to that of the Rhine at Lauffen.

DAHLAK, an island in the Red Sea, near the N. end of the coast of Abyssinia ; 40 miles long and 6 broad. It is fertile, populous, and remarkable for a pearl fishery. The inhabitants are blacks, and great enemies to the Mahometans. Long. 40. 10. E. lat. 15. 44. N.

DAHOMY, a kingdom of Guinea, supposed to reach 180 miles inland, though no European has penetrated above half the distance. The country is fertile, yielding a plentiful supply of farinaceous vegetables and tropical fruits ; also indigo, cotton, sugar-cane, tobacco, palm oil, and a variety of spices. The religion of Dahomy consists of a jumble of superstitious ceremonies, of which it is impossible to convey any satisfactory idea. The government is perhaps the most perfect despotism in the world ; for the polity admits of no intermediate degree of subordination between king and slave, at least in the royal presence, where the prime minister prostrates himself with as much abject submission as the meanest subject. The king maintains a considerable standing army, commanded by an agaow, or general, and their subordinate officers, who must hold themselves in readiness to take the field at the command of the sovereign. On extraordinary occasions, all the males able to bear arms are obliged to repair to the general's standard ; every caboceer marching at the head of his own people. Sometimes the king takes the field at the head of his troops ; and, on very great emergencies, at the head of his women. In the different royal palaces in Dahomy, are immured not less than 3000 women ; several hundreds of whom are trained to arms, under a female general and other officers. The general character of the Dahomans is marked by a mixture of ferocity and politeness ; the former appears in the treatment of their enemies ; the latter they possess far above the African nations with whom Europeans have hitherto had any intercourse. The leopard and hyæna are common in this part of Africa, and commit great ravages, as sometimes do also a species of white ant. Grewhe, or Griwhee, in the lat. 6. 17. N. and 3. 6. of E. long. is the principal seaport. Pop. about 6500. Abomey, about 90 miles inland, is the capital.

Dalebu, a town of Sweden, capital of Dalia; situate on the S. W. side of Lake Wenner; 60 miles N. by E. of Gotheburg.

Dalecarlia, or **Dalarne**, (signifying the valley,) an interior province of Sweden, in the division of Sweden Proper, between Nordland and the mountains of Norway. It is 270 miles long, and from 40 to 120 broad. The principal productions are wood, corn, and hemp, and it contains many mountains, in which are mines of silver, copper, and iron. The capital is Fahlun. The manners of the people are distinct from those of other parts of Sweden.

Dalheim, a town of the Netherlands, in the duchy of Limberg, capital of a territory of the same name, seated near the Meuse; 15 miles N. W. of Limberg.

Dalen, a town of Germany, in the duchy of Juliers, situate on the Bervine, which falls into the Meuse; 15 miles N. N. W. of Juliers. Pop. about 3700.

Dalia, **Daland**, or **Dalsland**, a province of Sweden, in Gothland, to the W. of Wermeland and Lake Wenner. It is 85 miles long and 40 broad. The N. part is full of mountains, forests, and lakes; but to the S. it produces corn sufficient for the inhabitants. Cattle, fish, butter, and cheese are the chief articles. The capital is Daleburg, or Amal, on the shore of the lake.

Dalkeith, a town of Scotland, in Edinburghshire, with a great market on Thursday for corn and oatmeal. Here is Dalkeith-house, the magnificent seat of the Duke of Buccleugh. It is seated on a strip of land between the North and South Esk; 6 miles S. E. of Edinburgh.

Dalla, or **Della**, a district of low land at the delta of the Irawaddy river; a town of the same name on the E. bank of the main branch of the river, about 40 miles W. S. W. of Rangoon, manufactures a great quantity of salt. The soil is capable of being rendered very productive. It is at present much infested with wild animals.

Dalmatia, a country of Europe, stretching, in a N. W. direction, from the lat. of 42. to 44. N., along the E. shore of the Adriatic Sea. It is a country of great antiquity, and formerly extended inland to the lat. of 45. 39. N., and included parts of Croatia, Bosnia, and Albania; the whole was incorporated with Hungary in the 12th century. The Venetians afterwards made inroads upon the sea-coast, and in the 15th century the whole country, now commonly called Dalmatia, became subject to that republic. It was ceded to Austria by the treaty of Campo Formio, in 1797; Austria ceded it to France in 1805. It fell again into the possession of Austria at the general partitioning of 1814. This portion of Dalmatia, which is all now understood by that name, has 200 miles of sea-coast, within the latitude above-mentioned, with an area of about 5800 square miles, and is supposed to contain 350,000 inhabitants. It is bounded on the E. by the Bocana river, which separates it from Albania, on the N. by Bosnia and Croatia, and W. by Morlachia, (which see). It has several islands lying off the coast, the principal of which are Brazza, Lessins, Curzola, Sabbioncello, and Meleda. It has some mountainous territory, containing marble, gypsum, iron, and other minerals; but parts are very fertile, and the mulberry, vine, and olive flourish in considerable luxuriance. The principal river is the Narenta, which rises in Bosnia; and either this or the Bocana might easily be united with collateral branches of the Save, near its union with the Danube, and thereby open a water communication by means of the latter, with the Black Sea on one side, and the interior of Germany on the other; but military despotism and catholic subjugation are incompatible with social improvements. The principal towns on the coast are Cattaro, Ragusa, and Spalatro, and in the interior Krin and Mostar.

Dalme, a town of Prussia, at the S. extremity of the Middle Mark; 45 miles S. of Berlin. Pop. about 3000.

Dalry, a village of Scotland, in Ayrshire, 7 miles N. N. W. of Irvine. It has a cotton manufacture, and near it are valuable coal mines, and a strong sulphurous spring.

Dalsland. *See* Dalia.

Dalton, a town in Lancashire, with a market on Saturday. Here are the remains of an ancient castle, and near it are the magnificent ruins of Furness Abbey. It is seated in a champaign country, not far from the sea; 6 miles S. W. of Ulverston, and 265 N. N. W. of London.

Damanhur, a town of Egypt, near the canal of Alexandria; 32 miles E. S. E. of Alexandria.

Damar, a town of Arabia Felix, in Yemen, with a university; 60 miles S. by E. of Sana.

Damascus, or (as it is called by the Arabs) **Sham**, a city of Syria, capital of a Turkish pachalic, and the see of a Greek archbishop. The form is an exact square, each side being a mile and a half long, and is supposed to contain from 200,000 to 250,000 inhabitants, among whom are great numbers of Christians and Jews. It has three walls, now almost entirely ruined; and, of the several suburbs which it formerly had, there remains only one, which extends 3 miles in length. Several streams flow across the fertile plains of Damascus, which water all the gardens, supply the public fountains, and are carried into every house. The houses are built of wood, with their fronts inward, where there is a court; in the streets there are only walls to be seen, but the insides are richly adorned. The most remarkable buildings are the caravansaries, which consist of long galleries supported by marble pillars, and surrounding a large square court. The castle is like a little town, having its own streets and houses; and the famous Damascus steel was kept here in a magazine. The mosques, of which there are about 200, are extremely handsome edifices, the most stately of which was a Christian church. One street runs across the city and suburbs in a direct line, on each side of which are shops, where all sorts of rich merchandise are sold. Several manufactures are carried on here, among which that of sabres and knives has been the most famous. Damascus is one of the most ancient places existing: it is mentioned by Abraham 1917 years before the Christian era, as the place near which he encountered the forces of Chedorlaomer, king of Elam, *(Persia,)* and rescued his nephew Lot, with considerable treasure, which the Elamites had taken from the cities of the plain. It afterwards became the capital of an independent kingdom, and at a later period became subject to the Jews. It was conquered by the Romans; and, after the fall of the Roman empire, Damascus became the seat of the grand caliph of the Saracens, who surrendered it to the Turkish emperor Selim, the third of the Ottoman dynasty, about 1515. It has continued subject to the Turks since tnat time. The pachalic, which extends from the Desert of Arabia, through five degrees of latitude, to Aleppo, is considered the most valuable and important of all the Turkish possessions. The pacha makes an annual journey to Mecca, as the representative of the grand seignior. *See* SYRIA. Damascus is seated 60 miles from the sea, at Beirut, in the lat. of 33. 30. N.; 130 miles N. N. E. of Jerusalem, and 170 S. by W. of Aleppo.

DAMAUN, a seaport of Hindostan, in the country of Baglana, at the entrance of the Gulf of Cambay. Aurungzebe besieged it about the middle of the 17th century, with an army of 40,000 men; but the garrison sallying out on a part of his camp, guarded by 200 elephants, so terrified those animals by their fire-arms, that they turned on their masters, and trampled to death half his army. The Parsees (*see* BACHU) ·ve a celebrated temple here. It is subject to the Portuguese, and 60 miles S. of Surat. Long. 72. 47. E. lat. 20. 18. N.

DAMBOOLLOO, a town of the island of Ceylon; 34 miles N. of Candy; celebrated for its cavern temples, which are in excellent preservation.

DAMEGAN, or DAMGAN, a town of Persia; seated near the S. shore of the Caspian Sea, in the district of Mazanderan. It is supposed once to have been the seat of government of the Parthian empire. It is 90 miles E. by S. of Ferrabad, and 300 N. by E. of Ispahan.

DAMGARTIN, or DAMGARD, a town of Hither Pomerania, with a castle seated at the mouth of the Recknitz; 18 miles W. of Stralsund.

DAMIETTA, a town of Egypt, and a Greek archbishop's see, with a good harbour, at one of the eastern mouths of the Nile. It has several squares, various grand mosques, and public baths faced with marble. The rice mezelaoui, the finest in Egypt, is cultivated in the neighbouring plains. Here are likewise Indian stuffs, silks, sal ammoniac, wheat, &c. The Christians of Aleppo and Damascus carry on the principal trade, the Turks being indolent, and contenting themselves with occasional extortions. During the crusades, Damietta was frequently an object of contention. It surrendered to the French in 1798, since which period it has been on the decline. It is about 90 miles E. of Alexandria, the same distance N. by E. of Cairo, in the lat. of 31. 26. N. and 31. 50. of E. long. Pop. about 30,000.

DAMM, a town of Further Pomerania, which has a considerable trade in steel manufactures. It is seated on the S. end of a lake of the same name, near the mouth of the Oder; 8 miles E. S. E. of Stettin. Pop. about 2000.

DAMME, a town of Belgium, in West Flanders; seated on the canal between Sluys and Bruges; 5 miles N. by E. of Bruges.

DAMME, or APPINGEDAM, a town of Holland, in Groningen; seated on the Damster, near the mouth of the Ems; 14 miles N. E. of Groningen.

DAMPIER'S LAND, in the lat. of 19. S., on the W. coast of Australia; so called from the navigator of that name, who visited it in 1688.

DANBURY, a village in Essex, England, 5 miles E. of Chelmsford, and 16 W. of the sea. It stands on the highest ground in the county, and the spire of the church serves as a seamark.

DANBURY, a town of Connecticut, in Fairfield county, with two churches. This town, with a large quantity of military stores, was burnt by the British in 1777. It is 20 miles N. N. W. of Fairfield, and 65 N. N. E. of New York.

DANCALI, a country in the E. part of Abyssinia, at the entrance to the Red Sea. The soil is unproductive; and its chief riches consist in fossil salt, and honey. It is governed by a prince nominally tributary to the negus, or emperor of Abyssinia. Bailur is the principal town.

DANGALA. *See* DONGOLA.

DANGER, ISLES OF, three islands in the Pacific Ocean, seen by Byron in 1765, but so surrounded by rocks and breakers, that it was unsafe to land. Long. 169. 28. W. lat. 10. 15. S.

DANNEMORA, or DAMMORA, the most celebrated iron mine in Sweden. It produces from four to five thousand tons of iron, of the very best quality, annually. It is about 30 miles N. of Upsal.

DANNENBURG, a town of Lower Saxony, in the duchy of Luneburgh; capital of a district of the same name; seated on the Jetze, near the Elbe; 30 miles E. by S. of Luneburg.

DANZIC, or DANTZIG, a city of Europe, very advantageously located on the W. bank of the Vistula, about 5 miles above its entrance into the Baltic Sea, in the lat. of 54. 21. N. and 18. 38. of E. long. It is supposed to have been first founded by the Danes in the 12th century, and for some time continued a free and independent city. In 1454 it became subject to Poland, retaining, however, all its municipal institutions, and long continued to rank as the chief commercial city of the N. of Europe, included in the Hanseatic league. At the commencement of the 18th century it contained upwards of 100,000 inhabitants, more than 20,000 of whom were carried off by a pest, in 1709. In 1734 it offered protection to Stanislaus, king of Poland, when it was besieged by the Russians and Saxons, to whom it was obliged to surrender. In 1793 it was taken possession of by a Prussian force, who held it till 1807, when, after a long siege, it surrendered to the French, who, in their turn, were forced to surrender it to a united Russian and Prussian force, after the disastrous campaign of 1812-13; and in the following year

(1814) it was confirmed in full sovereignty to Prussia. The easy navigation of the Vistula, and three or four considerable collateral rivers which intersect an extensive and fertile country, affords to Danzic great commercial advantages. The chief product of the interior country is grain, of which article Danzic has occasionally exported 500,000 quarters per annum ; and the vicinity of the city contains very extensive granaries. It is also capable of affording very extensive supplies of timber, pearl-ash, flax, and hemp. It has several yards for ship-building, but its commercial activity has of late years very much declined. It has upwards of twenty churches, chiefly Lutheran, and several other public buildings. It is nearly surrounded by water, and two streams intersect the city, dividing it into three parts. The fortifications are very strong by nature, and rendered formidable by art. It is 90 miles W. S. W. of Konigsberg, 250 N. E. of Berlin, and 190 N. by W. of Warsaw. Pop. 52,820.

Danube, German, "Duna," *i. e.* deep water, (the lower part called *Ister* by Strabo,) the noblest river of Europe ; has its source in the territory of the grand duke of Baden, on the eastern confines of the Black Forest, in the lat. of 48. N. and 8. 15. of E. long. It pursues a winding course in a N. N. E. direction to Ulm, where it receives the Iller from the S., and becomes navigable. From Ulm it bears N. into Bavaria, to the lat. of 49. at Ratisbon, previously receiving the united waters of the Wartasch and Lech from the S.; and, before passing Ratisbon, it receives the waters of the Altmucht and of the Nab from the N. From Ratisbon it bears to the S., past Ilstadt into Austria, previously receiving the Iser, Inn, and Salza, all from the S.

Its course through the archduchy of Austria, past Vienna to Presburg, is rather circuitous: from Presburg it runs E. by N. for about 100 miles, receiving several streams from the Carpathian mountains, when it takes a course due S. through the heart of Lower Hungary, past Buda, for 160 miles, to the lat. of 45. 35., when it receives the waters of the Drave from the W., and again bears to the E., receiving the Theis, which divides Upper and Lower Hungary from the N., and the Save from the W. at Belgrade; from Belgrade it forms the boundary between Hungary and Servia, then bears S., separating Bulgaria from Wallachia, receiving numerous streams, both from the N. and S. It again bears N. to Galats, near which it receives the waters of the numerous rivers of Moldavia and Bessarabia, falling into the Black Sea on the E., by several channels between the lat. of 44. 40. and 45. 30. N. in 29. 20. of E. long. The meridional distance from the source to the mouth of this river is 21 degrees of long., between the lat. of 45. and 49., equal to about 1000 English miles, but the course of the stream, by its continued windings, may be estimated at from 1500 to 1600 miles. It is navigable to Ulm, within 150 miles of its source, and has a number of steam vessels communicating with the Black Sea and its ports, constantly navigating it. In the archduchy of Austria it forms several islands. Under the head of Dalmatia it is shown that it might easily be made to communicate with the Adriatic. It contains a great variety of fish, and is celebrated for its sturgeon, which ascend the river several hundred miles.

Danube, Upper, Circle of, from the S. E. part of the kingdom of Bavaria, lying between 48. and 49. of N. lat. and 10. and 11. of E. long., and comprises the S. part of the circle of Suabia, the county of Pappenheim, and the principality of Neuberg. It is watered by the Iller, Mindel, Wertach, and the Lech, all running from S. to N. into the Danube, which gives name to the circle. The Iller might readily be united with the Lake of Constance, and thereby open a water communication between the Danube and the Rhine. It is a district of capability and of resource, under a well-directed exertion of agricultural pursuit. The principal towns are Gunsburg, Dillengen, Hochstadt, Donauwert, Pappenheim, Neuberg, Eichstadt, Nordlingen, &c. &c.

Danube, Lower, Circle of, another circle of the kingdom of Bavaria, comprises the E. part of Lower Bavaria, and the bishopric of Passau. It lies on both sides of the Danube, between the lat. of 12. 30. and 13. 40. E., in the same parallel of lat. as the Upper Circle. The Iser and the Inn intersect the S. part, which is considered the most fertile district of all Bavaria. Passau is the capital; and the other principal towns are Straubing, Landau, Deckendorf, Osterhofen, Wilshofen, &c. Pop. about 400,000.

Danube, Circle of. The source of the Danube also gives name to a circle in the territory of the grand duke of Baden, comprising part of the Black Forest. Willengen, 20 miles E. by N. of Friburg, is the capital. Pop. about 75,000.

Danville, a town of Kentucky, in Mercer county, situate in a fertile plain; 35 miles S. S. W. of Lexington, and 70 S. E. of Louisville. Danville is also the name of three or four other townships in different parts of the United States of North America.

Darabgherd, a town of Persia, in Fars, said to have been founded by Darius. It is large, but not populous, and surrounded by luxuriant groves of orange and lemon trees. Near it salt is found of various colours—white, black, red, and green. A considerable manufacture of glass is carried on here. It stands 140 miles E. S. E. of Shiraz, on the road to Ormus. Long. 54. 56. E. lat. 28. 56. N.

Darah, or Drass, a country of Barbary, bounded on the N. by Sus, E. by Tafilet, S. by Zahara, and W. by the Atlantic. A river of the same name flows through it, which enters the Atlantic on the S. side of Cape Non. The principal produce is indigo and dates. The inhabitants are Arabs and Mahometans; and some of the districts are dependent on Morocco.

Daraporam, a town of Hindostan, capital of the S. part of Coimbetore. It has a large mud fort, and straight and wide streets. Much cotton and tobacco are cultivated in the vicinity, and the garden and rice grounds are considerable.

It is seated at about an equal distance from the Malabar and Coromandel coasts; 42 miles E. S. E. of Coimbetore, and 106 W. of Tanjore. Long. 77. 40. E. lat. 10. 47. N.

DARDA, a town and fort of Lower Hungary, built by the Turks in 1686, and taken by the Austrians the next year. It is seated near the Drave, at the end of the bridge of Esseck; 8 miles S. of Barany.

DARDANELLES, two castles of Turkey, the one called *Sestos*, seated in Rumelia, the other called *Abydos*, in Natolia. They command the S. W. entrance of the Hellespont, leading from the Grecian Archipelago into the sea of Marmora, which separates Europe from Asia. The name is sometimes, but erroneously, applied to the strait itself.

DARFOOR, a kingdom of North Africa, on the borders of Nubia and Negroland, governed by a chief who calls himself sultan, and assumes the most extravagant titles. The wild animals are the lion, leopard, hyæna, wolf, and buffalo. The domestic animals are camels, goats, sheep, and horned cattle. Considerable quantities of grain of different sorts are raised, and, after the tropical rains, the fertility is sudden and great. The people are very barbarous, consisting of native tribes, of a deep black complexion, and woolly hair, though with features different from those of the Negroes, and of Arabs of various tribes. Polygamy is not only established, but the intercourse of the sexes is totally destitute of decency. The most severe labours of the field are left to the women; and the houses, which are of clay covered with thin boards, are chiefly built by them. Salt is the general medium of commerce here, as gold-dust is in many other parts of Africa. Caravans travel between this country and Egypt. Cobbe is the capital, in the lat. of 13. 40. N. and 28. 30. of E. long.

DARIEN, GULF OF, at the N. W. extremity of the territory of Colombia, opening into the Caribbean Sea. It runs inland about 80 miles, and is from 20 to 30 miles wide. Under the domination of Spain in South America, this gulf gave name to a province on the E. side, in the vice-royalty of New Granada, now comprised in the Colombian province of the Ystmo, or Isthmus. On the W. shore of the gulf, at the mouth of the river Atrata, are the remains of a town founded by a company of Scotch adventurers in 1699; and, although the most favourable spot in all South America, on the Atlantic side, for opening a water communication with the Pacific (see CHOCO), the project for forming a permanent establishment completely failed. It has been usual to confound the narrowest part of the chain of territory which unites the two grand divisions of the western hemisphere, under the name of the Isthmus of Darien, but which is 200 miles W. of the Gulf of Darien. It is itself about 700 miles in length, and generally about 60 miles wide; but at the narrowest part, between Porto Bello and Panama, called the Isthmus of Panama, it is about 37 miles, and which offers no great obstacle to the formation of a railroad, which would unite the Atlantic with the Pacific, and which will probably be carried into execution.

DARIEN, a town of the state of Georgia, in Liberty county, seated on the Alatamaha, not far from its mouth, and 47 miles S. S. W. of Savannah. Long. 81. 14. W. lat. 31. 23. N.

DARKE, a frontier county of the state of Ohio, bordering on Indiana. It is about 33 miles from N. to S., and 22 wide. Pop. 13,282. Chief town, Greenville; 70 miles W. by N. of Columbus. Pop. 2006.

DARLASTON, a parish of Staffordshire, England, contiguous to the great coal district of WEDNESBURY, which see.

DARLINGTON, a town in the county of Durham, with a market on Monday. Here are manufactures of huckabacks, camlets, small wares of the Manchester kind, and leather; also a curious water-machine for grinding optical glasses, the invention of a native, and another for spinning linen yarn. The railroad from Wilton Park colliery to Stockton passes near Darlington. It is seated on the Skerne; 19 miles S. of Durham, and 241 N. by W. of London.

DARMSTADT, the capital and seat of government of the landgrave of Hesse Darmstadt, in the circle of the Upper Rhine. It is seated on the banks of the river Darm, contains several public buildings, and a population of about 20,000. It is about 18 miles S. of Frankfort-on-the-Maine, and the same distance S. E. of Mentz.

DARNEY, a town of France, in the department of Vosges; 21 miles W. S. W. of Epinal.

DAROCA, a town of Spain, in Arragon, with seven parish churches, one of which is collegiate It stands between two hills, on the Xiloca; 48 miles S. S. W. of Saragossa.

DARRAWAY, a town of Hindostan, in the country of Tatta, at the mouth of a river of the same name, a branch of the Indus; 74 miles W. S. W. of Tatta. Long. 67. 31. E. lat. 24. 32. N.

DART, a river in Devonshire, which rises at the foot of Dartmoor Hills, crosses Dartmoor to Ashburton and Totness, where it is navigable for small vessels, and enters the English Channel at Dartmouth.

DARTFORD, a town in Kent, with a market on Saturday; seated on the river Darent. Here was a celebrated nunnery, which Henry VIII. converted into a royal palace, and is now become a gentleman's seat. The first paper-mill in England was erected here by Sir John Spilman, to whom Charles I. granted a patent, with 200*l*. a year to encourage the manufacture. On this river was also the first mill for slitting iron bars to make wire. Dartford is distinguished in English history as the place where, in 1391, the insolence of a taxgatherer to the daughter of Wat Tyler provoked the father's resentment to such a degree, as led to his exciting 100,000 men to arms, who threatened the subversion of the government of Richard II. Tyler was killed by the treachery of the lord-mayor of London. It is 15 miles E. S. E. of London, on the great high road to Dover.

DARTMOOR, an extensive forest in Devonshire;

bounded on the N. by bleak hills, comprising about 53,000 acres, and is watered by the river Dart. Many sheep are bred here, but of a small kind, and black cattle, which thrive well on the coarse herbage.

DARTMOUTH, a borough and seaport in Devonshire; market on Friday. It stands on the side of a craggy hill, by the river Dart, near its entrance into the sea, and has a spacious bay, defended by a castle and strong battery. The dock-yards and quay project into the river, and the rocks on each side are composed of a purple-coloured slate. The town contains three churches, and has a considerable trade to the south of Europe and to Newfoundland, as well as a share in the coasting traffic. It was burnt in the reigns of Richard I. and Henry IV. by the French; but they were repulsed in a third attempt afterwards, chiefly by the valour of the women, who fought so bravely, that, after a great slaughter, they took M. Castel, the French general, three lords, and twenty-three knights, prisoners. It is 25 miles S. of Exeter, 204 W. S. W. of London, and returns one member to parliament.

DARTMOUTH, a seaport in Massachusets, in Bristol county; situate on the Accushnet, falling into Buzzard's Bay; 70 miles S. of Boston. Long. 70. 52. W. lat. 41. 37. N.

DARTON, a town in Yorkshire; 3 miles N. of Barnsley, and 175 from London.

DARWAR, a fortress of Hindostan, in the country of Sanore; taken from Tippoo by the British in 1791, and afterwards restored to the Mahrattas. It is 45 miles W. N. W. of Sanore, and 90 E. of Goa.

DARWEN, UPPER and LOWER, two townships in the parish of, and contiguous to, Blackburn, Lancashire. *See* BLACKBURN.

DASSEL, a town of Germany, in the principality of South Calenburg; 48 miles S. by W. of Hanover.

DAUPHIN, an interior county of Pennsylvania; bounded on the W., for about 40 miles, by the Susquehanna river, being about 20 miles in mean breadth. The Blue Mountain ridge intersects this county from W. to N. by E. Pop. 30,118. Harrisburg, 97 miles W. N. W. of Philadelphia, is the chief town and seat of government of the state.

DAUPHINY, a late province of France, extending 40 leagues from N. to S., and 36 from E. to W.; bounded on the W. by the Rhone, N. by the Rhone and Savoy, S. by Provence, and E. by the Alps. The heir apparent of the kings of France derives the title of dauphin from this province. Two-thirds of Dauphiny are intersected by mountains, which afford good pasturage; plenty of timber, fir-trees in particular, for the building of ships; and very scarce simples. In these mountains, which are branches of the Alps, are bears, chamois, marmots, eagles, hawks, &c., and mines of iron, copper, and lead. The valleys afford wheat, and the hills in the vicinity of the Rhone, excellent wines, olives, and silks. The principal rivers are the Rhone, Durance, Isere, and Drome. It now forms the departments of Drome, Isere, and Upper Alps.

DAVENTRY, a town in Northamptonshire, governed by a mayor; with a market on Wednesday, and a manufacture of whips. It stands on the Roman highway called Watling-street, on the side of a hill; 16 miles W. of Northampton, and 72 N. W. of London, on the mail-coach road to Birmingham and Liverpool. It is distinguished for its cheese fairs, in April and October.

DAVID'S, ST., a city of South Wales, in Pembrokeshire, with a market on Wednesday. It was formerly an archbishop's see, and, in King Arthur's days, the metropolitan of the British church, and continued so till King Henry I., at which time Bernard, who was the forty-seventh archbishop of St. David's, became suffragan to the see of Canterbury. The situation of the town being very unhealthful, and the soil of the adjacent country very barren, it has nothing now to boast of but its cathedral, which is 300 feet long, and about 127 high, and supposed to be the highest in Britain; though the E. end is in ruins, the western part and choir are in good repair. St. David's is at present a bishop's see, yet only a single street of miserable cottages. It is seated on the Illen, near the coast; 24 miles N. W. of Pembroke, and 255 W. by N. of London.

DAVID, ST., a village of Scotland, in the parish of Dalgety, Fifeshire, with a harbour in Inverkeithing bay. It has a considerable manufacture of salt, and exports an immense quantity of coal.

DAVID, FORT ST., an English fort on the coast of Coromandel, which was taken and destroyed by the French in 1758, and has not yet been rebuilt. It is 80 miles S. of Fort St. George.

DAVIDSON, an interior county of the state of Tennessee, about 30 miles square. It is intersected, from E. to W., by Cumberland River, and contains a population of 30,509. Nashville, on the S. bank of the river, is the chief town.

DAVIESS, an interior county of the state of Indiana; 25 miles from S. to N., and 15 wide, intersected by White River, which falls into the Wabash. Pop. 6720.

DAVIESS, another county in the western part of Kentucky; bounded on the S. and W. by Green River, and on the N. by the Ohio, which separates this county from the state of Indiana. Owenboro', on the S. bank of the Ohio, is the chief town. Another town, called Vienna, is seated on the N. bank of Green River. The extent of this county is about 25 miles each way. Pop. 8331.

DAVIS' STRAITS, an arm of the sea between Greenland and North America, discovered by Captain Davis in 1585, when he attempted to find a N. W. passage. This sea comprises a space between the lat. of 58. and 68. N., and from 50. to 70. of W. long., and is the entrance to Baffin's Bay.

DAVOS, a town of Switzerland in the canton

of Grisons, capital of a district in which are mines of copper, lead, and silver. It is 14 miles E. of Coire.

Dawlish, a village pleasantly situate near Teignmouth, on the shore of the English Channel, in Devonshire. It is a good deal frequented in the summer season for sea-bathing.

Dax, or Dacqs, a town of France, in the department of Landes; and lately a bishop's see. Here are some famous hot baths, the spring of which discharges 36 cubic feet of water in a minute. It is surrounded by walls, flanked with towers, and seated on the Adour; 24 miles N. E. of Bayonne. It is the seat of a prefect, and contains 4849 inhabitants.

Dead Sea, a lake or inland sea of Palestine, into which the river Jordan runs. It is 60 miles long and 15 broad, enclosed on the E. and W. by high mountains. Mines of fossil salt are found in the sides of the mountains, which supply the neighbouring Arabs and the city of Jerusalem; also fragments of sulphur and bitumen, which the Arabs convert into trifling articles of commerce. It is called by the Arabs *Bahr Lout*, or the Sea of Lot, from its having been the site of the cities of the plain, Sodom, Gomorrah, Zeboim, &c. Large masses of asphaltum are found floating on its surface. The scenery around it is of a most extraordinary character of desolation and wildness. It has been asserted that neither fish inhabit its waters, nor birds fly over it, both of which are founded in error. One most extraordinary circumstance attending it is the depth of the valley which contains it. From Jericho, towards the W. side, the whole way is a succession of terraces, which fall towards it; and it is supposed by some to be as much as 1500 feet below the surface of the Mediterranean. The probability is, that it is between 1100 and 1200 feet. It is 17 miles W. of Jerusalem, and may be discerned from that city.

Deadman s Head, a cape on the S. coast of England in Cornwall, between St. Mawes and Fowey,

Deal, a town in Kent, with a market on Thursday. It is seated between the North and South Foreland, and is a member of the cinque port of Sandwich; governed by a mayor. It has no harbour, but the sea between the shore and the Goodwin Sands, called the *Downs*, is generally a secure road for ships, where they usually ride at their leaving or entering the river Thames. The port is defended by two castles, Deal, or Walmer Castle, to the S., and Sandown Castle to the N.; and also by several batteries. Deal has long been famed for its intrepid and skilful pilots. The Goodwin Sands are an extensive and very dangerous quicksand, lying off this town, and which, with westerly winds, are a serious obstruction to the navigation. Two life beacons have lately been erected on them, for those who may be unfortunately shipwrecked. The town of Deal is 9 miles N. of Dover, and 74 E. by S. of London.

Dean, a celebrated forest in Gloucestershire, which originally included all that part of the county which lies between the Severn and the shires of Monmouth and Hereford, and contained 4 market towns and 23 parishes. It is fertile in pasture and tillage; bears very fine oaks, and has rich mines of iron and coal. It was once reckoned the chief support of the English navy; but, having been much thinned by frequency of felling, and narrowed by increase of cultivation, it was near losing all features of its former character, until within the present century, when a still extensive tract, containing a population exceeding 7000, has been replanted and replenished with deer, and divided into six walks, extra-parochial, over which proper rangers have been appointed. There is a village without the boundary of the present forest, 1 mile N. of Newnham, called *Little Dean*, and contiguous is *Mitchel Dean*, at which a market was formerly held on Mondays.

There are 10 other villages in different parts of England named *Dean*, all inconsiderable.

Dearborn, a frontier county at the S. E. extremity of the state of Indiana. Lawrenceberg, the principal town, is seated on a point of land formed by the junction of the Miami with the Ohio river. The county is about 30 miles from S. to N., and 15 in mean breadth. The N. E. part borders on the state of Ohio, and the S. E. on that of Kentucky. Pop. 19,327.

Dearborn. This name, after one of their military officers, the United States government have also given to one of the head water branches of the Missouri river, in the lat. of 46. N. and 34. to 36. of long. W. of Washington.

Deba, a town of Thibet, Asia, standing 14,924 feet above the level of the sea; it contains many temples. The houses are built of stone.

Debalpoor, a town of Hindostan, capital of a district in the country of Moultan. It is situate on the great road from Delhi to Moultan, near the river Setlege; 80 miles S. of Lahore, and 170 E. by N. of Moultan. Long. 73. 32. E. lat. 30. 5. N.

Deben, a river in Suffolk, which rises near Debenham, and flows to Woodbridge, where it expands into a long narrow arm of the German Ocean, a little to the N. of Harwich.

Debenham, a town in Suffolk, with a market on Friday; seated on the side of a hill, near the the source of the Deben; 24 miles E. of Bury St. Edmunds, and 83 N. E. of London.

Debretzin, a town of Upper Hungary, capital of a district of the same name, and one of the most populous and important trading towns in all Hungary. It was taken by the Turks in 1684, and the Austrians retook it the same year. It is 107 miles E. of Buda. Long. 21. 38. E. lat. 47. 34. N.

Decatur, a frontier county of the state of Alabama, lying between Tennessee river and the state of Tennessee.

Deccan, an extensive tract in Hindostan, which, from the signification of its name, the *South*, has been supposed to include the whole region S. of Hindostan Proper. But, in its more accepted sense, it contains only the countries situate between Hindostan Proper and what is termed the Peninsula; namely, the provinces of Candeish, Dowlatabad, Visiapour, the N. part of Golconda, Berar, Orissa, and the Circars. It is bounded on the N. by the river Nerbudda, by Bengal, and by Bahar; and the river Kistna forms its separation on the S. from what is called the peninsula of Hindostan. All this vast country was once the southern province of the Moguls, who did not pass the Kistna till a recent period. Candeish, Visiapour, and a part of Dowlatabad, Berar, and Orissa are subject to the Mahrattas. The English have part of Orissa and of the Circars, the dominions of the Nizam of the Deccan comprising Golconda, the principal part of Dowlatabad, and the western part of Berar. His territories are bounded on the N. W. by the Poonah Mahrattas, N. by the Berar Mahrattas, E. by the Circars, and S. by the Carnatic and Mysore. By a family succession in 1780, the Nizam became possessed of the districts of Adoni and Tachore, and of the Gunto or Circar; and by the peace of 1792, and partition of 1799, he had a share of the countries belonging to Tippoo Sultan, including Kopaul, Cuddapa, Gangecoha, Gooty, and Gurrumconda. His dominions, without including the cessions, are supposed to be 430 miles from N. W. to S. E. by 300 wide. The capital is Hydrabad.

Decize, town of France, in the department of Nievre; seated on an island, at the conflux of the Airon with the Loire; 16 miles S. E. of Nevers.

Deckendorf, a town of Lower Bavaria; seated on the Danube; 27 miles N. W. of Passau.

Deddington, a town in Oxfordshire, with a market on Saturday; 16 miles N. of Oxford, and 69 W. N. W. of London.

Dedham, a town in Essex, with a market on Tuesday, and a manufacture of baize. It has an ancient large church, with a curious steeple, and a free grammar-school, endowed by Queen Elizabeth. It is seated on the Stour; 8 miles N. N. E. of Colchester, and 58 N. E. of London.

Dedham, a town of Massachusets, chief of Norfolk county; seated on Charles River; 11 miles S. W. of Boston.

Dee, a river of Wales, held in great veneration by the ancient Britons, and the theme of many a poet since. It issues from the Lake of Bala, in Merionethshire, whence it flows through a fine vale across the S. part of Denbighshire to the N. W. part of Shropshire, visits the W. border of Cheshire, passes on to Chester, and flows thence to the Irish Sea, making a broad estuary, which separates Cheshire from Flintshire. The Dee is navigable from near Ellesmere, in Shropshire, to Chester, where the continuity of the navigation is broken by a ledge of rocks, running across the river: but by embankments made here, much land has been gained from the tide; and a narrow channel, fitter for navigation, has been formed from Chester half-way to the sea. *See* **Chester**.

Dee, a river of Scotland, which rises on the W. border of Aberdeenshire, amid the mountains of Mar forest, and flows E. through a wild country till it reaches the fertile vale of Braemar, whence it proceeds to Aberdeen, below which it enters the German Ocean.

Dee, a river of Scotland, which rises in the W. part of Kirkcudbrightshire, receives the Ken below New Galloway, and runs into the Irish Sea, 5 miles below Kirkcudbright.

Deeping, or Market Deeping, a town in Lincolnshire, with a market on Thursday, seated on the banks of the river Welland, in a fenny county; 6 miles E. of Stamford, and 90 N. of London.

Deeping, St. James's, contiguous to the above.

Deer, a town of Scotland, in Aberdeenshire, on a river of its name; 10 miles W. of Peterhead. It has a trade in fine yarn, and near it are the remains of the abbey of Deer.

Deerfield, a town of Massachusets, in Hampshire county; seated on the Connecticut, near the influx of the river Deerfield; 15 miles N. of Northampton, aud 80 W. by N. of Boston.

There are five other towns of the same name in different parts of the United States of North America.

Deerhurst, a village in Gloucestershire; 3 miles S. of Tewkesbury; subject to frequent inundations from the Severn. Here was a celebrated monastery, which was afterwards made a cell to Tewkesbury Abbey.

Deer Island, in Penobscot Bay, state of Maine, containing about 1100 inhabitants.

Deizabad, a town of Persia, in Irac Ajemi; 90 miles N. of Ispahan.

Delagoa, a bay on the E. coast of South Africa, at the N. end of the country of Natal. The adjacent country abounds in cattle and poultry, which may be purchased for a trifle; and it is frequently visited by vessels employed in whale fishery. Long. 32. 0. E. lat. 26. 0. S.

Delawar, a town of Virginia, in King William county; seated on the broad peninsula formed by the confluence of the Pamunky and Mattapony, whose united streams hence assume the name of York River. It is 20 miles N. by W. of Williamsburg, and 45 W. of Richmond.

Delaware, a river of the United States, formed of two streams in the state of New York, in the lat. of 42. 30. N. In its course S. it separates, for about 50 miles, the N. E. part of Pennsylvania from New York, and afterwards, for about 100 miles in a direction nearly due S., it separates Pennsylvania from New Jersey, and, a few miles below Philadelphia, the state of Delaware from New Jersey, till it enters the head of Delaware Bay, at Bombay Bar, in the lat. of 39. 15. N., where it is about 5 miles wide. At Philadelphia it has sufficient depth of water for a 74 gun ship; is navigable thence for sloops up to the Falls of Trenton, a distance of about 30 miles; for boats that carry 8 or 10 tons, 40 miles higher.

Delaware Bay, into which the preceding river falls, is formed by Cape Henlopen, on the W., on which is a light-house, in the lat. of 38. 45., and Cape May on the E., in the lat. of 39. N. the two capes being about 18 miles distant, narrowing to about 10 miles, at Bombay Bar, which is considered as forming the entrance to the river. The bay, and its entrance, is interspersed with numerous shoals, the ship channel being on the side of Cape Henlopen; and, about midway between Bombay Hook and Philadelphia, the ship channel runs between two small islands, called *Pea Patch*, on which are two strong forts.

Delaware, State of, one of the united states of North America, extends from the lat. of 38. 27. to 39. 50. N., being bounded on the E. by the Atlantic Ocean, and Delaware Bay, and separated on the S. and W. by conventional lines from the state of Maryland, and on the N. by another conventional boundary from the state of Pennsylvania. At its southern boundary it is about 30 miles wide; but its mean breadth does not exceed 20 miles, giving an area of about 2000 square miles. It is divided into three counties, Newcastle, Kent, and Sussex; Kent subdivided into five, and the other two counties each into ten (hundreds, or) townships. The first permanent settlers from Europe on this part of the western continent were Swedes, who emigrated in 1627, and who made considerable progress in colonization, the Indians receding westward into Indiana, (*see* Delaware County, Indiana,) when, in 1655, their authority was extinguished by the Dutch, who, in their turn, surrendered to the English in 1664. The Dutch, however, regained an ascendancy in 1673, but in the following year the three counties were confirmed to England by treaty. In 1682, it was granted by Charles II. to the then Duke of York, who in the same year transferred it to William Penn, who landed at Newcastle on the 24th of October, and, from that time to the period of the American revolution, it formed part of the state of Pennsylvania, under the title of the *Three Lower Counties upon Delaware.* In 1704, however, a separate house of assembly was established, but under the same government as Pennsylvania. It was one of the first sections of the then British possessions to assert its independence, which was established in 1776 under the executive authority of a president and privy council of four members. In 1792, a new constitution was adopted similar to the other states, of a governor, senate, and house of assembly. The population, which in 1790 was 59,094, is 78,058, of whom 2605 are slaves; at the former period there were 8887 slaves, and 3889 free blacks. Dover, nearly in the centre of the state is the seat of government. For other towns, rivers, local relations, productions, manufactures, &c. &c., see each of the three counties, under their respective heads.

Delaware is also the name of four counties in the different states of North America, as follows—

1. In the state of New York, bordering on Pennsylvania, in which the Susquehanna, as well as the Delaware rivers, both have their source. It is a somewhat mountainous district, but its fertility and local advantages may be inferred from its increase of population, which in 1800 was 10,281, is 35,390. Delhi is the chief town.

2. In Pennsylvania, bounded on the S. by the state of, and E. by the river, Delaware, and N. by the county of the city of Philadelphia. It is the smallest county in the state. Pop. 19,791. Chester, 15 miles S. W. of Philadelphia, is the chief town.

3. In the centre of the state of Ohio, intersected by the Scioto river, and Walnut, Alum, and Whetstone creeks. It is a square of about 28 miles each way. The pop., which in 1810 was only 2000, is 22,060. The chief town, of the same name, is seated between the main branch of the Scioto and Whetstone Creek, 25 miles N. of Columbus.

4. An extensive tract in the centre of the state of Indiana, extending 100 miles from S. to N., and 70 from E. to W. White River, the head waters of which are occupied by the Delaware Indians, has its source in the N. part of this county, and Indianopolis, nearly in its centre, has been adopted for the seat of government of the state. Pop. 9683.

Delft, a town of South Holland, well built, with canals in the streets, planted on each side with trees. Here are two churches, in one of which is the tomb of William I. Prince of Orange, who was assassinated. It has a fine arsenal, and a considerable manufacture for earthenware. Delft is the birth-place of the renowned Grotius. It is seated about midway between Rotterdam and the Hague.

Delftshaven, a fortified town of South Holland, on the N. side of the Maese, with a canal to Delft. It is between Rotterdam and Schiedam, about 3 miles from each.

Delftzyl, a town and fortress of Holland, in Groningen, with a good harbour. It is seated on the Demster, at its entrance into the mouth of the Ems; 12 miles W. by S. of Emden. Long. 6. 58. E. lat. 58. 18. N.

Delhi, a province of Hindostan; bounded on the N. W. by Lahore, N. E. by Serinagur, E. by the Rohilla country, S. by Agra, and W. by Moultan. Having been the seat of continual wars above 60 years previous to 1806, when it fell under the influence of the English, it had become almost depopulated; and a tract of country that possessed every advantage that could be derived from nature, contained the most miserable of inhabitants. It is now all that remains to the Great Mogul of his once extensive empire; but since his alliance with the English, the country has been progressively improving.

Delhi, the capital of the province of the same name. It is the nominal capital of all Hindostan, and was actually so during the greatest part of the time since the Mahometan conquest in 1193. In 1738, when Nadir Shah invaded Hindostan, he entered Delhi, and dreadful were the massacres and famine that followed: 100,000 of the inhabitants perished by the sword; and plunder to the amount of 62,000,000*l.* sterling was said to be collected. The same calamities were endured in 1761, on the invasion of Abdalla, king of Candahar. In 1803 the Mahrattas, aided by the French, got possession of this place; but they were afterwards defeated here by General Lake, and the aged Shah Aulum, emperor of Hindostan, was was restored to his throne. Delhi may be said to be now in ruins; but there are many splendid remains of palaces, with baths of marble. The grand mosque is a magnificent edifice of marble and red free stone, with high minarets, and domes richly gilt. At Cuttab Minor, 15 miles S. W. of the city, is a noble monument, 242 feet high, built by the khan Cuttabaddeen, in 1194, to commemorate his conquest of Delhi, which is seated on the W. bank of the Jumna, 350 miles N. W. of Allahabad, and 1500 N W. of Calcutta. Long. 77. 40. E. lat. 28. 37. N.

Delhi, the chief town of Delaware county, in the state of New York, seated on the N. bank of the Mohawk branch of the Delaware river; 70 miles W. S. W. of Albany. Pop. 2554.

Delitz, a town and castle of Upper Saxony, in Misnia. Great quantities of worsted stockings are made here. It is 15 miles N. by E. of Leipsic.

Dellamcotta, a fortress of the country of Bootan, which commands the principal pass over the mountains. It was taken by storm in 1773, by a detachment under the command of Captain John Jones. It is 55 miles S. S. W. of Tassasudon, and 200 N. of Moorshedabad. Long. 88. 46. E. lat. 27. 2. N.

Delmenhorst, a town of Westphalia, capital of a district in the duchy of Oldenburgh; seated on the Delm, near the Weser; 8 miles S. W. of Bremen.

Delos, or Dili, an island of the Grecian Archipelago, formerly celebrated for the temples of Diana and Apollo, whose birthplace it is said to be. It is 6 miles in circumference, but now little more than a desert rock, covered with ruins, and uninhabited. Long. 25. 12. E. lat. 37. 38. N.

Delphi, or Delphos, a town of European Turkey, in Livadia, once famous for the oracle of Apollo, which people came from all parts to consult. It is seated in a valley near Mount Parnassus; 18 miles W. S. W. of Livadia, and now called *Castri*.

Del Rey, a tract of country on the coast of Brazil; about 100 miles wide, and 800 from N. to S., between the mountains of Paraguay and the Atlantic Ocean. At its S. extremity are two lakes, called De los Patos and Mini, each about 160 miles long, and from 10 to 50 broad, with a fort at each end. The principal place on this extensive coast is the island of St. Catherine, in the lat. of 27. 30. S. This coast is now principally included in the province of Rio Grande.

Delsburg, a town of Switzerland, in the late bishopric of Basil, on the river Birs; 10 miles N. W. of Soleure.

Delta, a part of Lower Egypt, enclosed between the mouths of the Nile and the Mediterranean; so called, it is supposed by some, from its triangular form, resembling the Greek letter of that name, and by others, as implying a maritime and swampy district; hence the term *Delta* is now generally applied to the mouths of all great rivers having diverging branches, such as the Indus, Ganges, Mississippi, &c.

Delvino, a town of Lower Albania, seated about 15 miles from the coast of the Adriatic, opposite Corfu. It is the residence of a pacha, and is populous.

Dembea, an interior province of Abyssinia, of which Emfras is the capital, in the lat. of 12. N. and 37. 30. E. long. In the centre of the province is a lake, supposed to be 450 miles in circumference, and containing many islands, one of which is a place of confinement for state prisoners. Its waters appear to form one of the principal sources of the Nile, the Bahr-el-Azrek; but this part of Africa is at present very little known.

Demerara, a river and plantation of South America, in British Guaiana. The entrance to the river is in the lat. of 6. 48. N. and 58. 2. of W. long. It is navigable for about 100 miles inland, and at its entrance forms a very commodious harbour, impeded, however, by a bar, not admitting vessels drawing more than 18 feet of water. The plantations lie on both banks of the river. They were originally formed by the Dutch, but fell into the hands of the English in 1796; restored at the peace of Amiens in 1802; retaken on the renewal of the war in the following year, and confirmed to England at the general peace in 1814; since which the cultivation has been greatly extended, and, next to Jamaica, is now the most populous and productive of all the British colonies in the West Indies and South America.

Demianskoi, a town of Siberia, in the government of Tobolsk; seated on the Irtysh, at the influx of the Demianha; 100 miles N.N.E. of Tobolsk.

Demmin, a fortified town of Anterior Pomerania, seated on the banks of the Ribnitz; 27 miles S. of Stralsund. Pop. about 3,000.

Demona, a town and fort of Piedmont, on the river Stura; 10 miles S. W. of Coni.

Demona Val. *See* Dimona.

Demotica, or Domotica, a town of European Turkey, in Roumelia, where a Greek archbishop resides. It was the residence of Charles XII. for some years; and is situate near the Marisca; 12 miles S. of Adrianople.

Denain, a village of France, in the department of Nord, where a victory was gained over prince Eugene, by Marshal Villars, in 1712. It is seated on the Scheldt; 6 miles S. W. of Valenciennes.

Denbigh, a borough of North Wales, capital of Denbighshire, with a market on Wednesday. Its ruined castle, with its vast enclosure crowning the top of the hill, forms a striking object. Denbigh has a considerable manufacture of gloves and shoes. It is situate on the side of a rocky hill, above the vale of Clwyd, on a branch of the river of that name; 27 miles W. of Chester, 5 S. of St. Asaph, and 218 N. W. of London. It returns one member to parliament, in conjunction with Ruthin, Wrexham, &c.

DENBIGHSHIRE, a county of North Wales, bounded on the N. by the Irish sea, N. E. by Flintshire, E. by Cheshire, S. by Salop, Merioneth, and Montgomeryshires, and W. by the river Conway, which separates it from Caernarvonshire. It is 48 miles long from S. to W., and 20 in its broadest part, but its mean breadth does not exceed 14 miles. This county contains some picturesque and beautiful scenery: besides the Conway, the Clwyd and Elwy also fall into the Irish sea, whilst the Dee, running in a meandering course from E. to W., intersects all the S. part of the county; and the vale of Clwyd, for 20 miles in extent, is deservedly celebrated for its fertility as well as for its picturesque beauty. Its surplus products consist principally of cattle and butter, a partial supply of grain, some wool, &c. &c. It contains veins of both coal and lead, but the mines are very partially worked. Besides the borough of Denbigh, the other principal towns are Wrexham, Ruthin, Abergely, and Llangollen. It sends two members to parliament.

DENDER, a river of the Netherlands, which rises in Hainault, flows by Leuze, Ath, Lessines, Grammont, Ninove, and Alost, and joins the Scheldt at Dendermond.

DENDERA, a town of Egypt, the residence of an Arabian prince, who takes the title of Emir. It was anciently called Tentyra, and, from the ruins that are seen, appears to have been a large city: they consist principally of three temples, whose beautiful remains are the finest in Lower Egypt, and are the first seen in ascending the hill. This place supplies most part of Egypt with charcoal. It is seated near the W. bank of the Nile; 260 miles S. by E. of Cairo. Long. 31. 58. E. lat. 26. 15. N.

DENDERMOND, a fortified town of the Netherlands, in Flanders, with a strong citadel. It was taken by the allies in 1706, and the Dutch put a garrison into it as one of the barrier-towns. The French took it in 1745, and again in 1794. It is surrounded by marshes and fine meadows, which can be covered with water: it is seated at the conflux of the Dender with the Scheldt; 16 miles E. of Ghent. Pop. about 6,000. Its name is rendered immortal by Sterne, in his tale of Lefevre.

DENIA, a seaport of Spain, in Valencia. The entrance into the harbour is difficult, and the chief trade is in almonds and raisins. It stands at the foot of a mountain; 47 miles N. E. of Alicant. Long. 0. 2. E. lat. 38. 50. N.

DENIS, ST., or ST. DENY'S, a town of France, in the department of Paris. The abbey of the Benedictines, to which the town owes its rise, has the appearance of a palace. Here is an ancient and magnificent church, in which were the tombs of many of the French kings; and in the treasury, among other curiosities, are the swords of St. Louis and the Maid of Orleans, and the sceptre of Charlemagne. In 1793, after the abolition of royalty, the royal tombs in the church were all destroyed; and the name of the town was changed to that of Francade; but, since the re-establishment of the monarchy and Catholic religion, St. Denis has resumed its former celebrity. It is the seat of a prefect, and seated on the river Crould, near the Seine; 5 miles N. of Paris. Pop. 5569.

DENMARK, a kingdom of the N. of Europe, lying between the lat. of 53. 34. and 57. 43. N. partly continental and partly insular. The continental part comprises North and South Jutland, and Holstein Lunenburg; and the insular part, the islands of Zealand, Funen, Laaland, Falster, Bornholm, Femern, &c., all lying between the E. coast of Jutland and Sweden; and, in the Atlantic Ocean, in the lat. of 62., are the Ferro Isles; and, in the lat. of from 64. to 66., Iceland, and several other islands lying off the W. coast of Jutland—all forming a part of the European dominions of the kingdom of Denmark; comprising together an area of about 22,000 square miles of surface. In addition to these, the islands of St. Croix, St. Thomas, and St. John, in the West Indies, are also subject to Denmark. *See each part of the kingdom under its respective head.* The aspect of the continental part of Denmark is flat and undiversified, containing neither mountains nor rivers of any magnitude. It is largely indented by the sea, and possesses numerous creeks and bays, as well as internal lakes. The only canal of importance is that of Kiel, which will admit vessels of 120 tons burden, and extends from the Baltic to the Eyder at Rendsburg, where the river becomes navigable, thus opening a communication between the two seas, or through 105 miles of territory: it is 22 English miles in length, and 10 feet deep; its breadth at the top is 100 feet, at bottom 54 feet. It was begun in 1777, and completed in 1785, at an expense of 800,000*l.* During the last war, between 3,000 and 4,000 vessels annually passed through it; but in the time of peace the number is much smaller. The lands are in general in an excellent state of cultivation, and the pasturage is rich: the climate bears a great resemblance to that of Britain.

The Danish community, although its early history is involved in considerable obscurity, appears to have been of Scandinavian origin, and its monarchy ranks among the most ancient, perhaps the most so of any, in Europe, having been contemporary with the proudest epoch of the Roman empire; and their advancement in discipline and arms in the tenth century may be inferred from their irruption into England, in the ninth decennary of that era, and their complete subjection of the country in the early part of the following century. It was, not, however, till towards the close of the fourteenth century, that Denmark appears to have obtained a respectable and commanding position in the great European compact, when Norway by inheritance, and Sweden by conquest and cession, in 1397, became united with Denmark under Queen Margaret, whose heroism obtained for her the appellation of the Semiramis of the North; and further, when, in 1448, the royal race of Skioldung became extinct, Christian of Oldenburg succeeded to the crown, by whom Holstein and Sleswick, the southern province of Jutland, also became annexed to the dominions of Denmark. Sweden, however, re-established her independence in 1523, which she has ever since maintained. The doctrines of Luther were early promulgated in Denmark. In 1522 the inhabitants embraced the Confession of Augsburg, and in 1536 the bishops were deprived of their temporal power, and placed on a footing similar to those of England, with the exception of the Danish bishops having no legislative voice. Previously to 1660, Denmark was a limited and elective monarchy, in which year it was made absolute and hereditary, by a revolution almost unparalleled in history. The avarice and contentions of a rival aristocracy led to such oppressions of the people, as induced them voluntarily to resign their liberties into the hands of their sovereign. The turbulent and martial spirit of Charles XII. of Sweden involved Denmark in a state of continual warfare, during the first twenty years of the eighteenth century, which contention terminated in 1720; in which year a treaty of peace was concluded, that continued with but little interruption for about eighty years; during which period the inhabitants of Denmark directed much of their attention to external commerce, which they pursued with considerable success, purchasing from a company of French adventurers the island of St. Croix in the West Indies: formed settlements in the East, at Tranquebar on the Coromandel coast, and at the Nicobar Isles; and a factory at Canton, in China; and, at the close of the century, her commercial navy exceeded 250,000 tons, with a proportionate national marine for its protection. The interruption to the external commerce of Holland and France, by the events of the war with England, commencing in 1793, promised for a time to make Denmark the emporium for all the external commerce of the N. of Europe, which her local and advantageous maritime position at the entrance to the Baltic Sea tended much to favour. But unhappily for the Danes, Denmark became involved in the general contention of the time, and in 1801, a British armament frustrated their commercial career by the almost total destruction of their national marine. *See* COPENHAGEN. The peace of Amiens, and the almost immediate renewal of war, tended to revive the hopes of Denmark, for regaining their commercial importance, and great exertions were made to replenish and strengthen her national marine; but the spirit and circumstances of the times were such as to admit of no neutrality; and in 1807, another armament from England annihilated her commercial career, and her power for resuming it. Her possessions both in the East and West all fell into the hands of the English in that year, and Norway was offered to Sweden as a boon to induce that power to join the confederacy against France, with which Denmark had coalesced. This proposal being assented to by Sweden, involved Denmark in the political necessity of endeavouring to resist the transfer; but, although the efforts made were not inconsiderable, they proved ineffectual. After the battle of Leipsic, however, in October, 1813, which changed the relations of all the states of Europe, it was endeavoured to reconcile Denmark to the transfer of Norway to Sweden, by proposing to cede to Denmark the island of Rugen and Swedish Pomerania; but in the general partitioning which took place after the peace of Paris, in 1814, Norway was confirmed to Sweden, the island of Rugen and Pomerania to Prussia; whilst Denmark was confirmed in the possession of Holstein of Lunenberg, and reinstated in her former possessions in the West Indies.

As sovereign of Holstein-Lunenberg, Denmark is a member of the Germanic confederation, her quota of troops being 3600, occupying the tenth place in the diet, and having three votes.

Since the general peace in 1815, Denmark has excited little or no interest in the considerations of the relations of Europe; like most of the other states she has been occupied in attempting to repair her finances, so extensively deranged by the events of so protracted a state of warfare, and the speculative experiments to which it gave rise. In 1826 the national marine of Denmark consisted of three ships of the line, four frigates, and three brigs: her commercial navy has increased since the termination of the war, but not equal to its extent in 1800, when she possessed above 2000 merchantmen, 20,000 seamen, and 250,000 tons of shipping. The nature and extent of her commerce and capabilities will be found more particularly elucidated under the heads of HOLSTEIN, JUTLAND, and ZEALAND. The manufactures of Denmark are very limited. The ancient literature of Denmark is rich in the elucidation of Scandinavian antiquity, and their traditions, whilst they vie with the heathen nythology in preposterousness, are exceedingly amusing for their quaintness. For the higher order of mental cultivation, at the present time, there is a university at Copenhagen, on an extensive scale, and under liberal regulations; another at Kiel, in Holstein, and a college at Ovensee, in the Island of Funen. The manners and customs of the superior classes differ but little, whilst the manners of the people at large are more social and orderly than in most parts of Europe. For some time after the adoption of the tenets of Luther, the penal statutes against dissenters were very severe, bu the most complete toleration in reference tc religious pretensions now prevails.

DENNEWITZ, a village of Brandenburg, where the French experienced a severe defeat in 1813; 2 miles from Juterbock.

DENNY, a town of Scotland, Stirlingshire; 30 miles from Edinburgh: it possesses abundance of coal and free-stone, and manufactories of woollen cloth and paper.

Dentila, a country of Western Africa, situated to the W. of Konkodoo. It is famous for its iron, in preparing which the natives employ as a flux the ashes of the bark of the kino tree.

Denton, a town of Maryland, capital of Carolina county; suated on the E. side of Choptank river; 37 miles S. S. E. of Chester.

D'Entrecasteaux's Channel, a strait on the S. E. coast of Van Dieman's Land; about 30 or 40 miles long.

D'Entrecasteaux's Port, or **Port North**, a harbour near the S. extemity of Van Diemen's Land.

Deogur, (the mansion of the Gods,) a town in the province of Bahar, Hindostan; 170 miles N. N. W. of Calcutta. The name is applied to several hill-forts in different parts of India.

Deounella, a town of the Mysore, supposed to have been the birth-place of Hyder Ali; it surrendered to the English under Lord Cornwallis, in 1791. It is 20 miles N. by E. of Bangalore.

Deptford, an appendage to the metropolis of England; situate in the county of Kent, on the S. bank of the Thames; the market-place is 4½ miles E. of London Bridge. The town is intersected by a stream called the Ravensbourne, on the banks of which are some extensive flour mills; a handsome bridge over this river, near its entrance into the Thames, connects Deptford with Greenwich on the E. It contains the principal storehouse for victualing the national marine, and also several slips for building and repairing the largest ships of war. It has also two floating docks, a basin, and two ponds for masts, and extensive workshops for the manufacture of cables, anchors, and blocks. In the reign of Henry VIII. a society was incorporated here under the title of the Master, Warden, and Assistants of the Guild of the most glorious and undivided Trinity; which society was invested with the power of examining the masters of the king's ships, the appointment of all pilots, ballasting of all ships in the port of London, and the erecting and maintaining light-houses, buoys, beacons, &c., in the river Thames, and within certain limits on the E. coast of England. The business of this society was transferred to an elegant edifice in the vicinity of the Tower in London, in 1788; but in 1685 an hospital with 56 apartments, and another in 1788, with 25 apartments, was endowed here for decayed masters of vessels and pilots, and their widows, with very comfortable allowance. Deptford is divided into two parishes, St. Nicholas and St. Paul; the church of the latter, erected in 1730, is an elegant and spacious structure. With the exception of the importance which Deptford derives from its extensive government establishments, it is an uninviting part of the metropolis.

Derbent, a district or khanship in the province of Daghestan, Persia, extending about 20 miles along the W. shore of the Caspian Sea, and 15 miles inland; the chief town, of the same name, which implies a door locked, or an inpassable place, is supposed to have been built by order of Alexander of Macedon, as the portal of Persia from the north. The town extends from the shore of the Caspian to the foot of a lofty mountain, and is surrounded by a a strong wall flanked with numerous towers; and, to a well organized garrison, might defy any assault. It surrendered to the Russians in 1722, when it was defended by 230 pieces of ordnance; the Russians held it till 1735, since when it has several times changed masters, and, since 1806, has again been occupied by the Russians: the inhabitants of the district, however, acknowledge no sovereignty but their own will, and the town is now deemed but of little importance: it is inhabited by about 900 families—Persians, Tartars, and Armenians: the harbour is nearly choked up. It is in the lat. of 42. 8. N. and 48. 10. of E. long.

Derbyshire, an interior county of England, extending about 56 miles from N. to S., and 20 in mean breadth, and contains 720,640 acres. The greater part of its W. side is bounded by the river Dove, which divides it from Staffordshire; the N. W. corner is bounded by the county of Chester, and the N. by the county of York; and the counties of Nottingham and Leicester bound it on the E. and S. The noble river Trent, and the Trent and Mersey Canal, intersect the S. end, whilst the Derwent, falling into the Trent, intersects the heart of the county from N. to S.; the N. W. part of the county is mountainous, several of the peaks rising to the height of upwards of 1700 feet; and Holme Moss, the highest point, to 1859 feet above the level of the sea. Near the centre of the county is a rich vein of lead ore (*see* Wirksworth); it also contains several veins of iron; in the mountainous district of the N. W. corner of the county are several extensive caverns, which attract numerous visitors, and produce a beautiful variety of spar and petrifactions, which are extensively wrought into vases and other ornaments. *See* Peak. It abounds also in numerous mineral springs, (*see* Buxton & Matlock,) and parts of the county are esteemed as the most beautifully picturesque of any in the kingdom: the S. part of the county is rich in pasture, and yields a very considerable surplus of cheese and cattle, and other agricultural produce. The county also contains several tan-yards, participates partially in the cotton, silk, and hosiery manufactures, and extensively in the manufacture of nails. *See* Belper. Besides the Trent and Mersey Canal, already mentioned, another extends from the S. extremity of the county into Warwickshire. Two others, the Derby and Erewash, intersect the S. E. part of the county, another extends from Chesterfield in the N. E. into Yorkshire, and another intersects the mountainous district of the N. W., running through Cheshire into Lancashire. The happy combination of agriculture, mines, and manufactures of the most useful and valuable description in this county with the great facility of conveyance afforded by its several canals, tend to render it one of the least demoralized and deranged parts of the country. The principal towns in Derbyshire, besides those previously mentioned, are

Derby, the county town, Alfreton, Ashborne, Bakewell, Chapel-in-le-frith, Dronfield, and Tideswell. It sends 4 members to parliament, for the northern and southern divisions.

DERBY, the chief town of the preceding county, is situate on the W. bank of the river Derwent, about 10 miles above its entrance into the Trent; 28 miles N. of Leicester, 15 W. of Nottingham, about 30 E. of Stafford, and 126 N. N. W. of London, on the mail coach road to Manchester, from which it is distant 60 miles. Derby is a place of considerable antiquity, and was created a royal borough by Edward I., in 1305. It consists of five parishes. The church of All Saints is a stately and elegant structure, having a beautiful Gothic tower 178 feet in height. About the year 1735, an extensive silk-mill was erected here, the model of which was surreptitiously obtained from Italy; it was for many years the only establishment of the kind in England, and is still one of the most extensive; and, in 1750, a porcelain manufacture was established, which is now in high repute for the elegance of its productions. In 1803 a military depôt was established here, suitable for the arming and equipment of 15,000 men; and in 1810 a county infirmary was erected on an extensive scale, and rendered very complete in all its interior arrangements. Besides the original silk-mill, Derby has now three others, and two for spinning of cotton, on a tolerably extensive scale; four paper-mills, five tan-yards, fourteen malting-houses, and two public breweries; five establishments for the manufacture of silk-stuffs, and six for small wares of cotton, &c.; five for the manufacture of hats, eleven for hosiery, two bleach-grounds, nine manufactures of shot, white-lead, and painters' colours; three soap-houses, five foundries, two watch manufacturing establishments, and seven for working of spar and petrifactions into chimney ornaments; with some of almost every other occupation attendant on an active and social state. This variety of occupation, since the commencement of the present century, has rendered Derby one of the most flourishing towns in the kingdom. A public promenade, or arboretum, has lately been presented to the town, and was opened in 1840. But the principal improvement is its magnificent railway station on the North Midland Railway, which is the largest in England: the covered way for the carriages is nearly a quarter of a mile in length, and its other arrangements in a corresponding style of magnitude. The general aspect of the town is respectable, and in its principal part assumes a feature of importance; the county hall, and other county buildings, are stately; it has a spacious assembly-room, and a literary and philosophical society; a range of alms-houses for clergymen's widows, two others for lay persons, and several dissenting places of worship. Derby was formerly surrounded by a wall, and contained a castle and three monasteries, no vestiges of any of which now remain. The Pretender's army from Scotland entered the town in 1745, but withdrew after a very short stay. Derby returns two members to parliament, and holds seven fairs annually, and a weekly market for corn, &c., on Fridays. The river Derwent is navigable from the Trent up to Derby, in a N. N. W. direction, but the town communicates with the Trent and Mersey Canal, by a cut in a direction due S., and with the Erewash Canal (*see* EREWASH,) in a direction nearly due E., which affords an easy conveyance to all the S. E. parts of the county.

DERBY, WEST, a township, 4 miles N. of Liverpool, Lancashire. *See* WALTON and LIVERPOOL.

DERBY, a town of Connecticut, in Newhaven county; seated on Housatonic, which is navigable hence to the sea; 14 miles N. W. of Newhaven.

DERBY, a town of Pennsylvania, in Dauphin county. Here is a cave divided into several apartments, and adorned with stalactites. It is situate on the Swatera, 2 miles above its conflux with the Susquehanna, and 10 S. E. of Harrisburg.

DERBY is also the name of a township in Vermont, on the E. side of Lake Memphramagog, and bounded on the N. by the conventional line which divides the United States territory from Lower Canada.

DEREHAM MARKET, a town in Norfolk, with a market on Friday. The church is a very ancient structure, with four chapels, and a curious stone font. The poet Cowper is interred here. It is 16 miles W. of Norwich, and 101 N. N. E. of London.

DERKUS, a town of European Turkey, in Romania, on the coast of the Black Sea; 30 miles N. N. W. of Constantinople. At some former period a wall appears to have extended from this place to Erekli, 100 miles W. of Constantinople, on the coast of the sea of Marmora.

DERBY. *See* LONDONDERRY.

DERVEL, a town of Ayrshire, Scotland. Here are extensive lime-works, collieries, and manufactories.

DERWENT, the name of four rivers, in different parts of England: 1st, rising in the Peak district of Derbyshire, and, after a course of about 50 miles, in a direction S. E. by E., falls into the Trent, about 10 miles below the town of Derby, from whence it is navigable; 2nd, rises near Whitby, in the N. Riding of Yorkshire, and, after a winding course of about 25 miles, is joined by the Rye, when the united stream runs nearly due S. for about 35 miles, falling into the Ouse, about 6 miles below Selby; 3rd, rises at the foot of Kilhope Law Mountain, and for about 15 miles, in an irregular course, forms the boundary between the counties of Durham and Northumberland, when it intersects, for about 7 miles, the N. W. corner of the former county, falling into the Tyne about 5 miles above Newcastle; 4th, rises on the border of Westmoreland, intersects the S. E. part of the county of Cumberland, and after a course of about 30 miles, through Derwent and Bassenthwaite waters, and past Cockermouth, falls into the Solway Frith at Workington: this river abounds in excellent fish.

DERWENT-WATER, near to Keswick, in Cumberland, is of an oval form, 3 miles in length, and a mile and a half wide. It is surrounded by rocky mountains, broken into many fantastic shapes. The precipices seldom overhang the water, but are arranged at some distance; and the shores swell with woody eminences, or sink into green pastoral margins. The lake contains five islands; one of which, near the centre, is famous for having been the residence of St. Herbert, the ruins of whose hermitage are yet remaining.

DESAGUEDERO, a river and lake of the La Paz, Upper Peru, communicating with the S. end of the lake Titicaca.

DESAGUEDERO CHAHALGE is the name applied to part of the channel of waters concentrating in the great plains E. of the Andes, between the lat. of 36. and 41. S., whose outlet is into St. Matthias's Bay.

DESEADA, a small island, 12 miles E. of Point Chateau, the eastern extremity of Guadaloupe, to which it is dependent; it is about 25 square miles in extent, and contains about 300 white inhabitants and 600 slaves; it was the first landmark of Columbus on his second voyage. Lat. 16. 40. N. and 61. 20. of E. long.

DESEADA, CAPE, the N. W. point of Terra del Fuego, forming the S. W. point of entrance into the Straits of Magellan from the Pacific Ocean. Lat. 53. 48. and 74. 18. of W. long.

DESEADA RIVER. *See* PORT DESIRE.

DESSAU, a strong town of Upper Saxony, capital of the principality of Anhalt-Dessau. It has manufactures of cloth, stockings, and hats; and is seated on the Mulda, at its conflux with the Elbe, 37 miles N. of Leipsic. Pop. about 9500.

DETMOLD, a town of Westphalia, in the county of Lippe, with a fortified castle; seated on the river Wehera; 17 miles N. N. W. of Paderborn. Pop. about 2400.

DETROIT, a town of the state of Michigan, with a strong fort. It surrendered to the English, 16th August, 1812. *See* MICHIGAN. Its trade consists in a barter of coarse European goods with the Indians, for furs, deer-skins, tallow, &c. It is situate in a fruitful country, on the W. side of the strait or river that forms the communication between the lakes of St. Clair and Erie, and the boundary line between the United States territory and Canada. Pop. 2222. Long. 83. 0. W. lat. 42. 40. N.

DETTENHEIM, a small town of Bavaria, in the district of Pappenheim, in the circle of the Upper Danube; it is seated on the E. bank of the Altmuhl, and is remarkable as the place from near which Charlemagne, in the 8th century, undertook to unite by a canal the waters of the Altmuhl with the Rednitz, and thereby the Danube with the Rhine.

DETTLEBACH, a town of Franconia, in the principality of Wurtzburg, now included in the kingdom of Bavaria, circle of the Lower Maine; seated on the Maine; 8 miles E. of Wurtzburg.

DETTINGEN, a village of Bavaria, in the territory of Hanau, circle of the Lower Maine; 4 miles S. E. of Hanau. Here George II. gained a victory over the French, in 1743.

There are three small towns of this name in the Duchy of Wurtemberg.

DEVA, a considerable town of Transylvania; seated on the S. bank of the Marosch; about 12 miles S. W. of Carlsburgh.

DEVAL COTTY, a town of Upper Hindostan, on the E. bank of the main branch of the Ganges; 10 miles S. of Gangotry, in the lat. of 32. 40. N.

DEVAPRAYAGA, or DEUPRAG, another town of Upper Hindostan, on the E. bank of the Ganges; a few miles S. of SIRINAGUR, (which see,) and near the junction of four united streams from the N., with the Ganges, and where the water is esteemed most sacred by the Hindoos. The town contains the celebrated temple of Ramachandra, the resort of numerous pilgrims, who contribute to the support of numerous Brahmins who form the principal population of the town. It suffered considerably by an earthquake in 1803.

DEUCAR, a district of Nepaul, bordering on the province of Oude; a town of the same name is about 90 miles N. of the city of Oude.

DEVELTO, or ZAGORA, a town of European Turkey, in Romania, the see of a Greek archbishop; situate on the Paniza, near its entrance into the Gulf of Forus, in the Black Sea; 58 miles N. E. of Adrianople, and 106. N. N. W. of Constantinople. Long. 27. 22. E. lat. 42. 35. N.

DEVENISH, a parish of Ireland, county of Fermanagh, situate on Lough Erne, or Holy Island; in this parish stands the most perfect of the ancient Irish pillar towers, 70 feet high, and the ruins of two churches.

DEVENTER, a city of Holland, the capital of Overyssel, with a college. It is surrounded by strong walls, and seated on the Yssel; 50 miles E. of Amsterdam. Pop. about 10,000.

DEVERON, a river of Scotland, which rises in the S. E. of Banffshire, and enters the ocean at Banff. It forms the boundary between the counties of Aberdeen and Banff for about 50 miles.

DEVICOTTA, a town on the coast of the Carnatic, at the mouth of the Colran, or N. branch of the Cavery river, in the lat. of 11. 40. N. This place surrendered to the English in 1749, and for several years was one of the principal factories of the East India Company on that coast; the entrance to the harbour is impeded by shoals.

DEVIL'S BASON, a harbour in Christmas Sound, at the S. W. extremity of Terra del Fuego, opening into the South Pacific Ocean, in the lat. of 55. 25. S.; the harbour is surrounded by rugged rocks of such a repulsive aspect, and so lofty, as to preclude the rays of the sun from ever beaming on its waters; hence its name.

DEVIL'S ISLAND, KEY, AND RACE, names given to several small islands in the West Indies, and off the E. coast of South America, generally of rugged aspect and difficult to approach.

DEVIL'S-ASS-O-THE-PEAK, a cavern in the N. W. part of the county of Derby. *See* PEAK.

DEVIZES, a borough town, in the centre of the county of Wiltshire, England; 88 miles W. by S. of London, on the road to Bath from which it is distant 18 miles. It was a Roman station, and, at a more recent period, had considerable manufactures of worsted stuff; but two public breweries, on no very extensive scale, are now the only source of surplus production. Its corn market, on Thursday, is the most considerable in the county. It is divided into two parishes; has a town-hall and gaol; and sessions for the county are held here annually in January; it returns two members to parliament, and is passed by the Kennet and Avon canal, but is a declining rather than a prosperous place.

Devonport, the principal station of the national navy of England, formerly called Plymouth Dock, (*see* Plymouth;) but received its present name by mandate of the king, Geo. IV., on January 1st, 1824; it is situate on the S.W. extremity of the county of Devon, at the mouth of the Tamar river, which here forms one of the most commodious harbours in the world. It is a borough, and sends two members to parliament. This spot was first availed of for a marine station at the close of the 17th century, previous to which it was a mere fishing village, and it was not till after 1760 that it assumed any thing like importance, whilst during the long war, from 1793 to 1815, it progressively rose to be the most extensive and complete arsenal in the world, the natural advantages having been rendered as convenient as labour and skill could make them. The natural accommodations of Devonport consist of a triple harbour; the outer one is called the Sound, the first inner one, Catwater; and the upper one, Hamoaze; the Sound was formerly open and exposed to the swells of the Atlantic Ocean, which, during a continuance of S. W. winds, used to subject the anchorage to much inconvenience, and sometimes to danger; but in August, 1812, the first stone was sunk of a breakwater pier, or mole, 5100 feet in length, 4000 feet in a straight line, with an angle inclining into the Sound at each end; this stupendous work is composed of upwards of two million tons of stone, blasted from the adjoining rocks, in pieces of 1½ to 5 tons each, sunk indiscriminately into the water, to work their own position; it is carried up 10 feet above high water mark at spring tides, 30 feet broad at the top, on which it is proposed to erect store houses at intervals, and lights along its whole extent. The space within the pier is about 3 miles each way, affording anchorage for 2000 sail of the largest ships, secure from the fury of the ocean, however tempestuous; the ingress and egress being safe and easy at either end of the pier, defended from the land side on the W. by the rock of St. Carlos, and on the E. by the Shovel rock. The Catwater is formed by the estuary of the little river Plym with the Tamar, and may be regarded as the harbour of the town of Plymouth, and applicable to the commercial intercourse of the port; whilst the Hamoaze extends inland for about 4 miles, in a direction nearly due N., and about half a mile wide, forming one of the most convenient and beautiful natural basins known in the world, affording moorings for 100 of the largest ships of war, without interruption to the anchorage and movement of numerous other vessels, and with sufficient depth of water to enable ships of the largest burden to take in their stores directly off the quays and jetties that range along its eastern shore; the dock yard extends 3500 feet along the shore, and comprises 96 acres, containing a basin 250 feet by 180, in which are kept the boats and launches belonging to the yard; also two mast ponds and a canal, which enables vessels bringing stores, to land them at the door intended for their reception; slips and dry docks, for building and repairing of the largest ships of war, range along the shore of Hamoaze, and communicate with the dock basin, by a block of store houses built of stone, 450 feet long, and 300 wide; two roperies, 1200 feet in length, three stories high, and a smithery containing forty-eight forges, are all included within the yard; the bakehouse, brewhouse, cooperage, slaughter house, hospital, and barracks for 3000 men, are without the yard, but contiguous thereto; all defended on the land side by several batteries and a line of circumvallation mounted with numerous cannon, and an outer trench excavated 12 to 20 feet deep, out of the solid rock, forming altogether the most complete and magnificent display of human art and exertion in the world. The parish church is at Stoke, about a mile distant, but the town contains two chapels of ease, and numerous dissenting meeting-houses. Here are also a commodious town-hall, and a public library, besides several other handsome buildings. The column erected to commemorate the name of the town is a prominent and interesting object. The streets are mostly at right angles, and are well paved. In the census of 1821, the population of Devonport, then Plymouth Dock, was returned with Plymouth, (which see;) the post-office at Devonport is 217½ miles S. W. of Hyde Park Corner, London, by way of Salisbury and Exeter; distant from the latter 45 miles. The block-house flag-staff of the garrison is in the lat. of 50. 22. 56. N. and 4. 9. 11. long. W. of Greenwich.

Devonshire, a maritime county in the S. W. of England, bounded on the N. E. by the county of Somerset, N. W. by the entrance to the Bristol Channel, W. S. W. by the Tamar river, which divides it from the county of Cornwall, and S. by the English Channel. Its extreme length from the Start point in the English Channel to Ilfracomb, on the shore of the Bristol Channel, is about 70 miles, but its mean length and breadth is about 50 miles, giving the largest area of any county in England, except those of York and Lincoln. It contains 1,654,400 acres, and sends four members to parliament for the northern and southern divisions. It is the fourth county in order of population, and the most agricultural of any in the kingdom; although it has the finest harbour in the world, and several other convenient ones, and intersected by numerous streams, favourable for mill sites, and other manufacturing operations, relatively it is one of the least commercial and manufacturing counties in the kingdom. The S. W.

part of the county contains a dreary tract called Dartmoor, containing upwards of 53,000 acres; the highest elevation of this moor is 1549 feet above the level of the sea; the other parts of the county, more particularly the S. and W., are exceedingly fertile. Its principal surplus produce is cattle, of a remarkably fine breed, either for dairying or for feeding, and of beautiful symmetry; the N. E. part of the county contains veins of copper, lead, manganese, gypsum, and of loadstone; antimony, bismuth, and cobalt are also found in small quantities; it has also quarries of beautiful marble and granite, none of which, however, are worked to any great advantage. The principal manufactures of the county are serges, kerseys, shalloons, broadcloth, blond-lace, and porcelain; there is also a considerable ship-building trade at Barnstaple. The woollen cloth manufactures at Tiverton and Great Torrington, and the wool-combing at Chumleigh, were formerly extensive, but have now much decayed or vanished. Besides the Tamar, which divides the county from Cornwall on the S. W., the other principal rivers falling into the English Channel are the Dart and the Exe, and into Bideford Bay, on the side of the Bristol Channel, the Torridge and the Taw; Devonshire contains one city, Exeter; and eight boroughs, viz. Ashburton, Barnstaple, Dartmouth, Honiton, Plymouth, Tavistock, Tiverton, and Totness, which each return two members to parliament. It contains twenty-five other market towns, and upwards of 400 villages. EXETER, which see, is the seat of assize and other local business of the county.

DEVON, a river of Scotland, which rises in the S. E. part of Perthshire, and, after a course of 40 miles, enters the Forth at Clackmannan, only 8 miles distant from its source. In Perthshire it forms some romantic waterfalls, called the Devil's Mill, the Rumbling Bridge, and the Caldron-linn.

DEUREN, a town of the Prussian states, in the duchy of Juliers, with manufactures of cloth and paper, and some iron works. It is 14 miles E. of Aix-la-Chapelle. Pop. about 3500.

DEUTZ. *See* DUYTZ.

DEUX PONTS, a late duchy of Germany, lying W. of the Rhine; it is about 30 miles in length from N. to S., and 12 in mean breadth, and tolerably fertile. It was ceded to France at the peace of Luneville, in 1802, assigned to Austria, at the general partitioning after the peace of Paris, in 1814, and by Austria exchanged with Bavaria for other districts on the E. It now forms part of the Bavarian circle of the Rhine, and is supposed to contain from 50,000 to 60,000 inhabitants; besides the chief town of the same name, the other principal towns are Kussel, Honiburg, and New Hornbach.

DEUX PONTS, the chief town of the preceding district or duchy, is seated at the confluence of the Hornbach with Erlbach, a short distance above the entrance of the united stream into the Blise, near the S. end of the duchy. Its castle, the former residence of the grand duke, is a stately edifice; and it has two spacious churches, an academy, and an orphan house, and was formerly celebrated for a printing establishment, since removed to Strasburg, which produced a valuable edition of the Greek and Latin classics. Pop. about 5000; Deux Ponts is 55 miles E. by N. of Metz, and 65 N. W. by N. of Mentz. Lat. 49. 15. N. and 7. 22. of E. Long.

DEWANGUNGE, a town of Bengal, on the W. bank of the Burhampooter; 110 miles N. N. W. of Dacca.

DEWARCOTE, a town and district of North Hindostan, between the Ganges and the Jumna; the town is seated on the W. bank of the main branch of the Ganges; 175 miles N. by W. of Delhi, and 90 N. W. of Sirinagur.

DE WITT'S LAND, the name given to about 10 degrees of lat. of the N. W. part of Australia, after the Dutch navigator of that name, who first made it known to Europeans.

DEWSBURGH, or DEWSBURY, a parish and town in the West Riding of Yorkshire, England. The parish, which includes the townships of Osset, Soothill, and Clifton-cum. The town of Dewsbury is a place of great antiquity, being mentioned as early as 626, when Paulinus, the first archbishop of York, preached Christianity to the inhabitants of the surrounding country; it is now distinguished as the seat of an extensive commerce, having upwards of 50 establishments for the manufacture of blankets, carpets, and other heavy woollen fabrics; and Heckmondwike, adjoining, has 40 other establishments for the like purpose, chiefly blankets. Dewsbury is seated near the N. bank of the Calder river; 5 miles W. by N. of Wakefield, on the road to Halifax.

DEYNSE, a town of Flanders; seated on the S. bank of the Lys; 9 miles W. S. W. of Ghent.

DEYRAH, a town of Upper Hindostan, on the frontier of Delhi, in the province of Sirinagur.

DESAIGNE, a town of France, in the N. part of the department of L'Ardeche; 25 miles W. N. W. of Valence. Pop. about 3500.

DEZENSANO, a town of Bresciano, situated at the S. end of Lake Garda; 15 miles E. of Brescia. Pop. about 3500.

DEZFUL, a populous town of Persia, in the province of Kurdistan; seated on the banks of the Abzal, over which is an elegant bridge of twenty-two arches. Dezful is 130 miles N. by E. of Bassora; the Abzal falls into the Ahwas, which joins the Tigris, at its junction with the Euphrates.

DHAR, a town of Hindostan, in the province of Malwa, surrounded by a mud wall. Pop. 37,865.

DHOLPOOR, a considerable town in the province of Agra, Hindostan, on the river Chambul, between Agra and Delhi.

DIADIN, a town of Armenia; seated near the source of the Euphrates, and frontier of Persia; 80 miles S. S. W. of Erwan.

DIAKOVAR, a town of Sclavonia; about 20 miles S. S. E. of Essig, on the road to Brodo. Pop. about 3000.

DIAMOND HARBOUR AND POINT, on the Hoogly river. *See* CALCUTTA.

DIAMOND ISLE, a small island lying off the

S. W. point of Pegu, and S. E. point of the Bay of Bengal, in the lat. of 15. 51. N. and 94. 12. of E. long.

Diamond Point, the N. E. point of the island of Sumatra, at the entrance to the Strait of Malacca, in the lat. of 5. 18. N. and 97. 43. of E. long.

There is a river of Sumatra, called Diamond River, falling into the strait a little S. of the point. The S. W. part of the island of Martinique in the West Indies, in the lat. of 14. 25. N. and 61. 9. of W. long., is also called Diamond Point.

Diano, a town of Naples W. of the Appennines, in Principato Citra; 15 miles N. by E. of Policastro. Pop. about 4500.

Diarbekir, a district of Asiatic Turkey, in the province of Algezira, the whole of which, extending from 33. 20. to the lat. of 39. N., was formerly called Diarbekir; and the pasha, or governor of the province, is still called the Pasha of Diarbek. It formed the ancient kingdom of Mesopotamia; but the district of Diarbekir is now confined between the 37th and 38th degrees of N. lat.; it lies E. of the Euphrates, and is intersected by numerous streams, forming the head waters of the Tigris. It is beautifully diversified with mountains and valleys, and, to a social people, would form a most delightful residence.

Diarbekir, the chief city of the preceding district, or, as it is called by the Turks, *Kara Amid*, which signifies a black wall, in reference to a lofty wall of black stone, with which the city was formerly surrounded, is seated on the banks of the main branch of the Tigris, in the lat. of 37. 55. N., and 39. 22. of E. long.; 570 miles E. S. E. of Constantinople, and 180 N. E. of Aleppo. The pasha resides in an extensive castle on the N. side of the city. Extensive manufactures of silk, wool, cotton, and leather, and in metals, are carried on at Diarbekir; and their dyed fabrics in wool and cotton are justly esteemed for the beauty of their colours; as in most eastern cities, the streets are narrow and dirty, but many of the houses are spacious and elegant within. It contains several commodious bazaars, a magnificent mosque, and also a noble cathedral belonging to the Armenians. As a place of residence to Europeans, it is considered among the most agreeable of all the Turkish cities. The population is estimated at 50,000, consisting of Armenians, Kurds, Christians, Jews, and Turks.

Dickson, an interior country in the western part of Tennessee, about 28 miles from N. to S. and 25 in breadth. Duck River, which falls into the Tennessee, washes all the S. part of the country, whilst the E. and W. corners of the N. side jet upon the great Cumberland river; a collateral ridge of the Allegany mountains intersects the county from the S. E. to the N. W. Pop. 7074. Charlotte, N. of the mountain ridge, 72 miles W. N. W. of Murfreesboro, is the principal town.

Didier, St., a town of France, at the N. E. extremity of the department of Upper Loire; 40 miles S. S. W. of Lyons. Pop. about 3200. There are three other small towns, of the same name in different parts of France.

Die, a town of France, in the department of Drome; situate on the N. bank of the river Drome: it is the seat of a prefect, and contains 3509 inhabitants. It produces excellent wine, and has a mineral spring in its vicinity. It is 30 miles S. W. of Grenoble, and 80 S. S. E. of Lyons.

Dieburgh, a town of Hesse Darmstadt; seated on the N. bank of the Gerspienz river; 7 miles E. by N. of Darmstadt, and 18 S. S. E. of Frankfort-on-the-Maine.

Diego, St., a town on the coast of New California, republic of Mexico, in the North Pacific Ocean, capital of a jurisdiction of its name. It stands in so barren a country, that in the dry season cattle are sent upwards of 20 miles for pasturage. The port affords excellent anchorage. Long. 116. 53. W. lat. 33. 12. N.

Diekirch, a town of Belgium, in the grand duchy of Luxembourg, on the river Saure; 17 miles N. from Luxembourg. Pop. 3100.

Diemen, a town of Holland, in the province of North Holland; 5 miles S. E. from Amsterdam. Pop. 1000.

Diepholtz, a town and castle of Westphalia, capital of a county of the same name. It has manufactures of coarse wollen and linen cloth, and stands on the river Hunte, near the lake Dummer; 30 miles N. W. of Minden, and 38 S. S. W. of Bremen; the county comprises about 265 square miles, and contains about 15,000 inhabitants; and now forms part of the kingdom of Hanover; the inhabitants subsist chiefly by breeding of cattle, which they drive down to the markets of Holland.

Dieppe, a seaport town of France, in the department of Lower Seine, with a good harbour, formed by the mouth of the river Arques, an old castle, and two piers. The principal trade consists in fish, ivory toys, and laces. It was bombarded by the English in 1694, and is not so considerable as formerly. It is situated on the coast of the English Channel, opposite to Brighton, from whence packets sail. Dieppe is 50 miles N. N. E. of Havre, 35 N. of Rouen, and 96 in a meridional line N. N. W. of Paris; the lighthouse at the entrance of the harbour is in lat. 49. 55. 34. N. and 1. 4. 29. of E. long. It is the seat of a prefect, and contains a population of 18,248.

Dierdorf, a town of Westphalia, capital of the upper county of Wied, with a castle situate on the Wiedbach; 10 miles N. N. W. of Coblentz.

Diernstein, a town of Austria, with an Augustine convent, and the ruins of a castle, in which Richard I. of England was imprisoned. The French were repulsed here by the Austrians and Prussians in 1805. It is seated on the N. bank of the Danube; 17 miles N. of St. Polten, and 45 W. by N. of Vienna.

Diesen, a town of Bavaria, on the W. side of the lake Ammersee; 10 miles S. E. of Landsberg.

Diesenhofen, a town of Switzerland, in Thurgau; seated on the Rhine; 5 miles E. of Schaffhausen.

Diest, a town of Belgium, in South Brabant, with considerable manufactures of cloth, stockings, &c. ; seated on the Demer ; 32 miles E. N. E. of Brussels. Pop. about 6000.

Dietz, a town of Germany, in the Westerwald, capital of a county of the same name, with a strong castle. It is seated on the Lahn, 18 miles above its entrance into the Rhine, near Coblentz.

Dieuze, a town of France, in the department of Meurthe, with wells of salt water, which produce much salt. It is seated on the Seille ; 22 miles N. E. of Nancy, and 50 W. N. W. of Strasburg. Pop. about 3600.

Diez, St., a town of France, in the department of Vosges. It had lately a celebrated chapter, whose canons were obliged to produce proofs of nobility. It is seated near the source of the Meurthe ; 30 miles S. E. of Luneville, and 45 S. W. of Strasburg. It is the seat of a prefect, and contains 6823 inhabitants.

Dighton, a town of Massachusets, in Bristol county ; situate near Taunton river ; 7 miles S. S. W. of Taunton.

Digne, a town of France, capital of the department of Lower Alps, and a bishop's see. It is famous for its hot baths, and seated on the Bleone ; 30 miles S. by W. of Embrun, and 70 N. E. of Marseilles. Pop. 3621.

Dihong, a river of Upper Assam, East Asia, the W. branch of Brahmaputra ; the navigation is intercepted by rapids, and its source is unknown.

Dijon, a city of France, capital of the department of Cote d'Or. The public structures, and particularly the churches, are very fine. The spire of St. Benigne is 370 feet in height. In front of the Palace Royale is the ancient palace of the dukes of Burgundy ; and at the gates of Dijon is a chartreuse, in which some of those princes are interred. Dijon is seated in a pleasant plain, which produces excellent wine, between two small rivers ; 48 miles N. E. of Autun, and 175 S. E. of Paris. Pop. 22,397.

Dili. *See* Delos.

Dillenburg, a town of Germany, in the Westerwald, capital of a county of the same name, rich in mines of copper and iron. It has a fortress, on a mountain, the usual residence of the Prince of Nassau-Dillenburg ; and is seated on the Dillen ; 14 miles N. N. W. of Wetzler. Long. 8. 27. E. lat. 50. 42. N.

Dillingen, a town of Suabia, with a Catholic university; seated on the Danube ; 17 miles N. W. of Augsburg. Now included in the Bavarian circle of the Upper Danube.

Dimotuc, or **Domotica**, a town of European Turkey, in Romania, and a Greek archbishop's see ; seated on a mountain, surrounded by the Meriza ; 12 miles S. W. of Adrianople.

Dinagepoor, the capital of a district, N. of the Ganges, in Bengal ; 100 miles N. of Moorshedabad.

Dinan, a town of France, in the department of Cotes du Nord ; seated on a craggy mountain, by the river Rance ; 20 miles S. of St. Malo. It is the seat of a prefect. Pop. 6280.

Dinant, a town of Belgium, in the province of Namur, with a castle and eight churches. The chief trade is in leather, and in the vicinity are quarries of marble and mines of iron. It is seated near the Meuse ; 15 miles S. by E. of Namur, and 44 S. W. of Liege.

Dinapore, or **Dinapoor**, a military cantonment of Hindostan ; 11 miles W. of Patna, on the S. bank of the Ganges.

Dinasmouthy, or **Dinas Mowdda**, a town of Wales, in Merionethshire ; governed by a mayor ; with a market on Friday. It stands at the foot of a high precipice, on the river Dysi ; 18 miles S. by W. of Bala, and 196 N. W. of London.

Dindigul, a province of the peninsula of Hindostan, 86 miles long, and 40 broad, lying between Coimbetore and Travancore, and chiefly fertile in rice. On the defeat of Tippoo, in 1799, it became subject to the British.

Dindigul, a town of Hindostan, capital of the province of the same name, with a fortress on a rock. It is 40 miles N. by W. of Madura, and 77 S. E. of Coimbetore. Long. 78. 2. E. lat. 10. 24. N.

Dingelfingen, a town of Bavaria ; seated on the Iser ; 20 miles E. N. E. of Landschut.

Dingle, a seaport and borough of Ireland, in the county of Kerry. The chief exports are butter, beef, corn, and linen. It is seated at the head of an inlet, on the N. side of Dingle Bay ; 28 miles W. S. W. of Tralee, and 164 S. W. of Dublin. Long. 10. 38. W. lat. 51. 58. N.

Dingwall, a borough of Scotland, in Rossshire. Some linen yarn is manufactured here, and there is a lint-mill in the neighbourhood. It is seated at the head of the Frith of Cromarty; 18 miles W. of Cromarty. In conjunction with Kirkwall, &c., it returns one member to parliament.

Dinkelsbuhl, a town of the S. E. extremity of the circle of Suabia. It has a foundation of Teutonic knights, and a trade in cloth and reaping-hooks. It is seated on the Wernitz ; 25 miles S. S. W. of Anspach, and is now included in the Bavarian circle of the Rezat. Pop. about 6500.

Dinwiddie, a county of Virginia, lying between Appomattox and Nottoway Rivers. It is about 18 miles square. Pop. 22,558. Petersburg (which see) is the chief town.

Dippoldiswalda, a town of Saxony, 12 miles S. by W. of Dresden.

Disentis, a town of Switzerland, in the canton of Grisons, with an abbey founded in the seventh century. It is situate near the source of the Lower Rhine ; 10 miles W. by S. of Ilantz.

Dishley, a village in Leicestershire ; 2 miles N. W. of Loughborough, rendered famous by a native grazier and farmer, Robert Bakewell, (who died in 1795,) from his successful experiments and practices in the improvement of live stock, more particularly sheep.

Dismal Swamp, Great, extends about 30 miles from N. to S., and 10 broad, between the Chesapeake and Albemarle Sound, partly in Virginia, and partly in North Carolina. It dorived its name from its dismal aspect, being impervious in most parts, from trees and brushwood; there is a pond in the centre, about 15 miles in circumference. The territory abounds with noxious reptiles and wild animals. Within the present century a canal has been cut through it from the Elizabeth river, falling into the Chesapeake, to the Pasquotank, falling into Albemarle Sound; this is calculated to change the face and character of the whole territory, but its original dismal features are immortalized by the Irish bard Moore, in his Epistles from America. There is another swamp between Albemarle and Pamtico Sounds, called the Little Dismal Swamp.

DISS, a town of Norfolk, on the border of Suffolk, with a market on Friday. It is seated on the river Waveney, on the side of a hill; 19 miles S. of Norwich, and 85 N. N. E. of London.

DISSEN, or TISSEN, a town of Westphalia, in the principality of Osnaburgh, where are salt works, which belong to Hanover. It is 16 miles S. E. of Osnaburg.

DITMARSON, a district of the duchy of Holstein, lying on the coast of the German Ocean, between the rivers Eyder and Elbe; it contains no towns of importance.

DITTEAH, a town and fortress of Hindostan, in Bundelcund, on the frontier of Agra; about 120 miles S. by E. of the city of Agra.

DIU, an island of Hindostan, making the S. point of Guzerat, at the entrance of the Gulf of Cambay, three miles long and one broad. On it is a fortified town, of the same name, built of freestone and marble; and it contains some fine churches, erected by the Portuguese, about the time they took possession of the island in 1515. The trade of the town, once so important, is almost entirely removed to Surat. It is 180 miles W. by S. of Surat, and 200 N. W. of Bombay. Long. 71. 5. E. lat. 20. 45. N.

DIXAN, a town of Abyssinia, in Tigre, seated on the top of the conical hill, and inhabited by Moors and Christians. Their chief trade is stealing children, and carrying them to a market at Masuah, whence they are sent to Arabia or India. It is 34 miles S. of Masuah.

DIX COVE, a British fort on the Gold Coast of N. Africa; 40 miles S. W. of Cape Coast Castle.

DIXMUIDE, a fortified town of Belgium, in Flanders, celebrated for its excellent cheese and butter. It is seated on the Yperlee; 13 miles N. of Ypres, and 11 S. of Ostend.

DIZIER, ST., a town of France, at the N. extremity of the department of the Upper Marne, seated on the Marne; 13 miles N. N. E. of Joinville, and 120 E. of Paris. The Marne is navigable from here to Paris, which renders St. Dizier a place of considerable commerce. Pop. about 6000.

DJEBAIL, GEBAIL, or GEBILER, a town of Syria, seated near the coast, on the site of the ancient *Biblos*, about 25 miles N. of Berus. It was a place of some importance during the reign of Solomon, the *Biblos* having had at that time several vessels employed in the conveyance of wood for the building of the temple. The town was taken possession of by the crusaders in 1100, and at present contains from 5000 to 6000 inhabitants.

DJEBEL, or GEBEL HADDA, GEBEL SAADE, and GEBEL AMER KEMIR, places of Mahometan devotion, S. of Mecca.

DNEPER, or DNIEPER, a river of European Russia, (the ancient *Borysthenes,*) rising near the northern frontier of the government of Smolensk, in the lat. 56. 20. N., and, after a course of about 800 miles in a direction nearly due S., falls into the Black Sea, at Otchakov, in the lat. of 46. 30. N. It is navigable from above the city of Smolensk, the whole of its remaining course, but is impeded by rapids within about 200 miles of its entrance into the Black Sea; it receives a great number of tributary streams both from the E. and W.; the principal of those on the E. are the Sotz, the Uiput, and the Deszna; and from the W. the Berezyna, and the Przypiec; by the latter, and a canal, the waters of the Black Sea, are made to communicate with the Baltic. *See* BRZESC.

DNIESTER, a river of Europe, (the ancient *Tyras,*) rising on the N. side of the Carpathian Mountains in Austrian Gallicia, in the long. of 23. E.; and from the long. of 26. 20. to 29. E., in a direction S. S. E., it divides the Polish palatinate of Podolia from Moldavia, when it takes its course nearly due S. for about 100 miles past Bender, and dividing Bessarabia from the Russian province of Catharinenslaf, falls into the Black Sea at Akerman, 100 miles W. of Otchakov; it is navigable the greater part of its course.

DOBRZIN, a town of Poland, in the palatinate of Ploczko, or Polock; seated on a rock near the Vistula; 14 miles N. W. of Ploczko.

DOCKUM, a town of Holland, in West Friesland, near the mouth of the river Ee; 10 miles N. E. of Lewarden.

DODBROOK, a town of Devonshire, with a market every third Wednesday, and noted as being the first place where white ale was brewed; 208 miles W. S. W. of London.

DOEBELN, a town of Saxony; 35 miles S. E. of Leipsic. Pop. upwards of 4000, chiefly employed in manufactures.

DOEL, a town of Belgium, in Flanders, on the river Scheldt, opposite Lillo; 7 miles N.W. of Antwerp.

DOESBURG, a town of Holland, in Gelderland. It has been often taken; and the reduction of it, in 1586, was the first exploit of the English forces sent by Queen Elizabeth to the assistance of the Dutch. It is seated on the Yssel; 10 miles S. S. W. of Zutphen.

DOFAR, a town on the coast of Arabia, in the Indian Ocean, seated on the E. shore of a bay of the same name: it is the residence of a sheik, and exports some gum, olibanum, and other drugs. Lat. 16. 16. N. and 54. of E. long.

DOGGER BANK, a sand bank in the German Ocean, between Flamborough Head and the coast of Jutland; it is about 200 miles from W. to E., and 30 to 50 broad, having from 15 to 30 fathoms depth of water; it yields abundance of excellent cod to the English and Dutch fishermen. A sanguinary, but undecisive sea fight, between the Dutch and English, took place on this bank, on the 8th August, 1781.

DOGLIANI, a populous town of Piedmont; 18 miles N. by E. of Mondovi.

DOL, a town of France, in the department of Ille and Vilaine, situate in a morass; 5 miles from the sea, and 11 S. E. of St. Malo. Pop. about 3500.

DOLCE AQUA, a town of Piedmont, in the county of Nice, with a castle, seated on the Nervia; 5 miles N. of Vintimiglia.

DOLE, a town of France, in the department of Jura, on the river Doubs. It contains several public buildings, evidences of Roman magnificence. Under the ancient regime of France, it was the capital of Franche Compte, until 1674, when Besancon was made the capital. It is now the seat of a prefect; and contains 9647 inhabitants. It is 70 miles N. by W. of Geneva, and 30 S. E. of Dijon.

DOLE, LA, one of the loftiest peaks of the Jura chain of mountains, rising to the height of 5600 feet above the level of the sea.

DOLGELLY, a town of Wales, in Merionethshire, with a market on Tuesday, and a manufacture of coarse woollen cloth, undyed, called webbing. It is seated on the river Avon, at the foot of the mountain Cader Idris; 12 miles S.E. of Harleigh, and 208 N. W. of London, on the road to Caernarvon, from which it is distant 39 miles. The summer assizes for the county are held here.

DOLLART BAY, a bay or lake separating East Friesland, in Germany, from Groningen, in Holland. It was formed by an inundation of the sea, in 1277, when 33 villages are said to have been destroyed.

DOMFRONT, a town of France, in the department of Orne, seated on a craggy rock, by the river Mayenne; 35 miles N.W. of Alencon, and 65 E. of St. Maloes. It is the seat of a prefect. Pop. 1670.

DOMINGO, ST., or HISPANIOLA, or HAYTI, an island of the West Indies, extending from Cape Engagno, in the long. of 68. 20. W., to Cape Donna Maria, in 74. 26 W.; the length is 408 English statute, or 346 geographical miles, between 18. and 20. of N. lat., or a breadth of 135 statute miles: these limits give an area of 37,125 square miles, or 43,760,000 English statute acres, being about three-fourths the extent of England exclusive of Wales. The E. end of the island is separated from Porto Rico by the Mona, or Porto Rico Channel, about 120 miles wide; and the northern promontory of the W. end is separated from the Island of Cuba by the windward passage, about 60 miles wide; and the southern promontory of the W. end is about 100 miles distant from the E. end of the Island of Jamaica; a chain of mountains extends from the extremity of the northern promontory of the W. end to the S. E. end of the island, and about the centre rises to the height of about 6000 feet above the level of the sea. This island was discovered by Columbus, on the 6th of December, 1492, after having touched on the Bahamas on his first voyage, and is memorable for being the first spot in America which was colonized by Europeans. Columbus landed at St. Nicholas-le-mole, at the extremity of the N. W. promontory, where he left 38 of his comrades; returning to Spain the following month. At this time the country was called *Hayti* by the natives; Columbus gave it the name of *Espanola*, or little Spain; hence *Hispaniola*. The avarice of the settlers soon excited the just indignation of the native inhabitants, whose resentment, however, was readily subdued by the more ample and destructive means of warfare of the Spaniards. Columbus returned to Spain in 1496, leaving his brother Bartholomew in command of the settlement, who soon after removed to the southern coast, and founded the city of St. Domingo, which afterwards gave name to the whole island. The number of settlers from Spain increased rapidly, by whom the natives were compelled to the severest labour, which soon brought on disease and premature death; and so fatal to life was the cruel policy of the Spaniards, that after a lapse of 20 years, an efficient labourer scarcely remained on the island; under this exigency about 40,000 of the inhabitants of the Bahama Isles were decoyed from their homes to become labourers or slaves in St. Domingo: but such was the perverse policy of the Spaniards, that notwithstanding this acquisition, and 1,000,000 of native inhabitants—and some historians carry the number as high as 3,000,000—which the island was supposed to contain on its first discovery in 1492, by the middle of the following century scarcely 150 remained alive; whilst the Spaniards had progressively sunk into indolence, and the island reduced again to a wilderness. The French obtained a footing on the W. end of the island about the middle of the 17th century, and resumed the culture of the sugar-cane, which had been early introduced by the Spaniards from the Canary Islands, but had been entirely neglected by them. By the treaty of Ryswick, in 1691, Spain ceded to France all the W., or about a third part of the island. After this period the French plantations progressively increased in number and importance, and, in 1789, the population of the French part of the island had increased to 534,830 inhabitants, whilst the total population of the Spanish part did not exceed 155,000. From this period a new and important era in the history of St. Domingo commences; the desolating mania of the French revolution had extended to this island; an insurrection ensued, in which upwards of 2000 of the white oppressors fell a prey to the fury of their slaves. In 1792, the national assembly of France proclaimed the political equality of the negroes and whites; in the following year three commissioners were despatched from France, who, on their arrival in St. Domingo, proclaimed the emancipation of the slaves; this served as a signal for the slaves to wreak their vengeance on their white oppressors, and, on the 21st of June, 1793, a force of 3000 blacks entered Cape François, and worked an indiscriminate slaughter among the white inhabitants, whilst the most cruel vengeance displayed itself over all the French part of the island. In the midst of this confusion, the English attempted to establish an authority, and a force from Jamaica succeeded in taking possession of Port au Prince; but, after suffering much from disease and resistance of the blacks, they abandoned the island in 1798; by which time the whole of the white population had become nearly extirpated, whilst the blacks, under the command of Rigaud and Toussaint L'Ouverture, had effected considerable progress in military discipline; and, on the 1st of July, 1801, the independence of the island was formally proclaimed in the name of the republic of Hayti, when Toussaint L'Ouverture was appointed governor for life, with the power of naming his successor. On the 6th of October, 1801, the French concluded a peace with England, and, in the December following, despatched a squadron with 20,000 men, under the command of General Le Clerc, to attempt the subjugation of St. Domingo. Le Clerc commenced the campaign in February, 1802, and fought with varied success until the following May, when a truce was concluded upon; pending which, Toussaint was inveigled on board a vessel, and conveyed to France, where he died in prison, in April, 1803. Hostilities recommenced with greater animosity than ever; the command of the black troops devolved on Dessalines; and the English being now regarded as auxiliaries against the French, on the 30th December, 1803, the whole of the remaining French forces surrendered prisoners of war to the English; and thus St. Domingo was again freed from all European oppression; but new calamities now awaited it. On the 1st of January, 1804, the generals and chiefs of the army entered into a solemn compact, in the name of the people of Hayti, renouncing for ever all dependence on France, at the same time appointing Dessalines governor for life, invested with extensive powers; in September following, he assumed the imperial title of Jacques the 1st, Emperor of Hayti. His ambition and tyranny brought upon him the detestation of the people, and he was slain by a military conspiracy in October, 1806. He was succeeded by Christophe as "chief of the government," but Petion starting as a rival candidate for the supreme authority, a severe battle was fought between the forces of Petion and Christophe, on the 1st of January, 1807, in which Petion was defeated. In the same year Christophe was appointed chief magistrate for life, with the power of appointing his successor; but, like his predecessor Dessalines, he was not content with conditional power, and, in 1811, he assumed the regal title of Henry I., king of Hayti, making the title hereditary in his family, and *Sans Souci*, a village about 15 miles from Cape Francois, now called Cape Henry or Cape Hayti, the seat of his court and government. King Henry was both avaricious and cruel, and, like Dessalines, fell a prey to his own soldiery, who dragged him from his palace by force, and massacred him in October, 1820. In the mean time, from 1810 to 1818, Petion, after his defeat in 1807, retreated to the S. of the W. part of the island, and remained at the head of a considerable military force, and ruled over a great portion of the country. In 1816 he was appointed president for life, but died in May, 1818, universall lamented by all who had espoused his cause; he was succeeded by Boyer, who, on the death of Christophe, succeeded also to the command and government of the whole of what was formerly the French part of the island. In 1794 Spain ceded the whole of the remaining part of the island to France; but the troubles which ensued rendered the cession nominal, the French never having been able to take possession; and the Spanish flag continued to wave over the fortress of the city of St. Domingo until the 1st of December, 1821, when the inhabitants issued a formal declaration of independence, and made overtures to the republic of Columbia, to be admitted as an integral part of its confederacy; which proposition, however, was not acceded to. Such was the political state of St. Domingo at the period of 1822; about which time the French endeavoured again to regain an ascendancy in the island; and, conceiving all attempts by force of arms likely to prove ineffectual, they succeeded in inducing the Haytians to agree to a pecuniary indemnity, for the loss of the plantations at the commencement of the revolution; this, after several years' negotiation, in 1825 was settled at 120,000,000 francs, or about 5,000,000*l.* sterling, payable by instalments, and under regulations calculated to divert a great portion of the produce of the island into the lap of France, on better terms than though she held the island in colonial possession.

Under the mild and judicious administration of President Boyer, Hayti promises to advance in prosperity and social influence; a college has been founded and liberally endowed at Cape Hayti, in which provision is made for instruction in all the languages, arts, and sciences usually taught in the European establishments of the like kind; public schools have been established in most of the principal towns of the W. part of the Island. The indigenous vegetable productions of St. Domingo are various, beautiful, and valuable; its mahogany is unrivalled for its texture and beauty, and there is a satin wood proportionably superior to that of other parts of the world; the flowering shrubs are various, and nowhere surpassed in beauty and fragrance; vanilla and the plantain both luxuriate; pine for ship-building and house-carpentry is abundant; whilst the cotton tree supplies the means of capacious canoes. Of quadrupeds one only is known peculiar to the island—the agouti, in size less than the common cat of Europe; all the domestic animals of Europe have, however, been introduced, and thrive exceedingly; swine, horses, and horned cattle, all running wild in considerable numbers. The feathered race is numerous and beautiful in plumage, and more melodious than common with birds of tropical climates. There is a salt water lake of considerable extent, between the French and Spanish part of the island, on the S. side, which, as well as the plains and rivers of that side, abound in alligators and other reptiles of great size, and also of such noxious insects as are common to the situation and climate. The land tortoise is common, and the coast abounds in turtle and other fish.

Domingo, St., City of, is situate on the W. bank of a river called the Ozama, in lat. and long. as previously laid down. The city was originally founded in 1496, on the opposite bank of the river, but afterwards moved to its present site. It is regularly laid out, and, like most of the cities built by the Spaniards in this part of the world, the private houses have interior courts and flat roofs. The cathedral, finished in 1540, is a ponderous edifice; the government house, hall of justice, barracks, and arsenal, are all respectable buildings; it has also several convents, which have been mostly deserted by their inmates since 1794. The harbour is capacious, but exposed to the tempests from the S. W. The population, which at one time amounted to 25,000, is now reduced to half that number, and indicates decline rather than prosperity. It was sacked by the English Admiral Drake, in 1586, who obtained a ransom from the inhabitants of 7000*l.*, to prevent further devastation: it has not experienced any marked vicissitude since that period.

There are several other towns called St. Domingo, in different parts of America, settled by the Spaniards, but all inconsiderable.

Dominica, one of the West India Leeward islands, lying N. of Martinico, and S. of Guadaloupe, being about 34 miles from N. to S. and 10 in mean breadth. It was discovered by Columbus on Sunday, November 3, 1493. A party of Frenchmen settled upon it about the beginning of the 17th century, who, by cultivating the friendship of the natives, succeeded in the culture of the soil. At the treaty of Aix-la-Chapelle, in 1748, it was agreed that it should be neutral, but the English took possession of it in 1759, and it was confirmed to them at the peace of 1763. It was captured by a French force from Martinico in 1778, but restored to the English in 1783, since when it has remained in their possession. It is very productive of coffee of a choice quality, and yields some sugar. Charlotte Town, at the mouth of a river towards the S. end of the island, on the W. side, is in lat. 15. 18. N. and 61. 28. of W. long.

Dominica, the largest of the islands of the Pacific Ocean called the Marquesas. Long. 139. 2. W. lat. 9. 41. S.

Domino, St., one of the Tremiti islands, in the Gulf of Venice; 15 miles from the coast of Naples, in the lat. of 42. 10. N.

Domitz, a town of Lower Saxony, in Mecklenburg-Schwerin, with a fort seated at the confluence of the Elde and Elbe; 25 miles S. of Schwerin.

Dommel, a river of Dutch Brabrant, which receives the Aa below Bois le Duc, and then flows into the Meuse.

Domo d'Ossola, a town of Italy, in the Milanese, with a castle, seated near the frontier of the Valois, on the Tossa; 20 miles N. of Varallo. The famous road of the Simplon passes this place.

Domotica, or Dimotice, a large town of European Turkey, situate on the W. bank of the Marissa; 12 miles S. by W. of Adrianople. Pop. about 8000.

Dompaire, a town of France, in the department of Vosges; 10 miles W. N. W. of Epinal.

Domremy, a town of France, in the department of Meuse, the birthplace of the celebrated Joan of Arc, the Maid of Orleans. It is seated on the Meuse; 5 miles N. of Neufchateau.

Domvillers, or Danvillers, a town of France, in the department of Meuse; 14 miles N. of Verdun.

Don, a river of Europe, (the *Tanais* of the ancients,) which intersects the S. E. provinces of Russia. It issues from the Lake St. John, in the government of Tula, and, after a very circuitous course of several hundred miles, flows into the Sea of Asoph. This river has so many windings, and such numerous shoals, as to be scarcely navigable, except in the spring, on the melting of the snows; and flat-bottomed boats only, except in the same season, can pass into the Sea of Asoph.

Don, a river of Scotland, which rises in the W. part of Aberdeenshire, receives the Urie-water at Inverary, passes by Kintore, and enters the German Ocean, at Old Aberdeen.

Don, a river in Yorkshire, which rises on the borders of Cheshire, flows by Penistone, Sheffield, Rotheram, Doncaster, and Thorn, and joins the Ouse near its termination in the Humber.

Donaghadee, a town and parish of Ireland, in the county of Down; it is seated on the coast, 35 miles W. N. W. of the Isle of Man, and 23 W. by S. of the Mull of Galloway. It is the mail-packet station between Ireland and Scotland. *See* Port Patrick. It has a custom-house, and exports some cattle and other live stock to Scotland, but in other respects its commerce is very inconsiderable, the receipt of customs not equalling the expense. On Mew Island, at the entrance of the harbour, which has been made convenient for the packets, is a lighthouse in the lat. of 54. 37. N. and 5. 24. of W. long.

Donaghmore, the name of 13 extensive parishes and townships in Ireland.

Donaghmore, a town of Ireland, county of Cork, giving the title of earl to the Hely Hutchinson family.

Donaueschingen, or Doneschingen, a town of Suabia, on the E. border of the Black Forest, in the principality of Furstenburg. It is the chief residence of the prince; in the court-yard of whose palace are some springs, collected in a reservoir about 30 feet square, which has the honour of being called the head of the Danube. It is 13 miles N. N. W. of Schaffhausen.

Donawert, a strong town of Bavaria,

seated on the N. bank of the Danube, at the influx of the Wernitz; 25 miles N. by W. of Augsburg; here is a bridge over the Danube, which causes Donawert to be a place of considerable intercourse. Pop. about 2500.

DONCASTER, a handsome town in the S. E. part of the West Riding of Yorkshire; it is situate on the great high road from London to York and Edinburgh, on the S. bank of the river Don, over which are two handsome bridges. It is a corporate town, with considerable funds, governed by a mayor, recorder, and common council, and formerly sent members to parliament. The principal street is about a mile in length; the mansion-house, in which the mayor and justices hold their sittings, is a spacious and elegant building; there is also a town hall, theatre, dispensary, hospital, and two or three other public buildings, and the church dedicated to St. George is a noble edifice. Doncaster has five tan-yards, several flax dressers, and some manufactures of sacking, carpets, nails, &c., and its trade in corn is considerable; but the agreeableness of its locality renders it more celebrated as a place of gaiety and fashion, than as a manufacturing or trading town. The annual races are about the gayest in the kingdom, and the frequent balls and concerts held in the mansion-house make it the resort of all the fashion and gaiety of the surrounding country; which, with its constant thoroughfare, tend to render it an agreeable residence. It is 158 miles N. from London, 18 N. E. of Sheffield, 20 S. E. of Wakefield, and 37 S. of York. Market on Saturday.

DONDRA HEAD, the southern point of the island of Ceylon, in the lat. of 5. 55. 30. N. and 80. 42. of E. long. The land is low and densely populated, but appears to have been of greater importance than at present, there being the ruins of a magnificent Hindoo temple in the vicinity. *See* MATURA.

DONEGAL, a maritime county forming the N. W. extremity of Ireland; it is about 70 miles in extreme length, but, being indented by numerous bays and harbours, it has about 150 miles of sea coast; the principal bay is called Lough Foyle, and divides Donegal from the county of Londonderry, opening by a narrow strait into the N. channel. Lough Swilly is another capacious bay, opening into the Atlantic Ocean, and Donegal Bay forms the southern boundary of the county, which is bounded on the E. and S. E. by the counties of Tyrone and Fermanagh. The river Finn intersects the centre of the county from W. to E., and then takes a northern course into Lough Foyle. Donegal is a mountainous and rather dreary district, and its inhabitants may be considered the rudest in Ireland, the greater portion speaking only their vernacular language. The mountains contain various minerals; kelp is made upon the coast, which yields also a siliceous sand used in the manufacture of glass; the spinning of flax, the linen manufacture, and distillation of spirits, prevail over the greater part of the county; the principal towns are Lifford, Raphoe, Johnstown, Letterkenny, Ballyshannon, Donegal, and Killibegs; at Ballyshannon is a valuable salmon fishery. It contains the ruins of several castles and other works of antiquity; and returns two members to parliament.

DONEGAL, a town and parish of the preceding county; seated at the head of a bay 111 miles N. W. of Dublin, and 25 S. W. of Lifford.

There are four townships called Donegal in the state of Pennsylvania.

DONERAILE, a town and parish of Ireland, in the county of Cork. Near it are quarries of beautiful variegated marble. It is situate on the Awbeg, which falls into the Blackwater; 19 miles N. W. of Cork, and 113 S. W. of Dublin.

DONGA, a country in central Africa, on the N. side of the Donga Mountains, and watered by the Bahr-el-Abiad, or White Nile.

DONGOLA, or DUNGALA, a town of Nubia, capital of a province of the same name. It contains 10,000 houses of wood, and is seated on the Nile, among mountains; 500 miles N. by W. of Sennaar. The country is celebrated for a fine breed of horses, and the inhabitants for their skill in horsemanship. Long. 32. 5. E. lat. 19. 25. N.

DONJON, a town of France, in the department of Allier; 24 miles S. E. of Moulins.

DONNINGTON, a town in Lincolnshire, with a market on Saturday. Much hemp is cultivated in the neighbourhood. It is 8 miles W. S. W. of Boston, and 106 N. of London.

There are seven villages of the same name in different parts of England—the principal one in Leicestershire.

DONNYBROOK, a village in Ireland, county of Dublin, 2½ miles from Dublin, celebrated for its annual saturnalia or fair.

DONZY, a town of France, in the department of Nievre; 22 miles N. of Nevers.

DOOAB, a term applied by the Hindoos to tracts of land lying between two rivers; the most celebrated tract is that lying between the Ganges and Jumna, in the provinces of Allahabad, Agra, and Delhi.

DOON, a river of Scotland, which issues from a lake of the same name in Ayrshire, and enters the Frith of Clyde, 2 miles S. of Ayr.

DOORNSPYK, a town of Holland, in the province of Gelderland, on the Zuyder Zee. Pop. 2100.

DOOSHAK, or JULALABAD, a town of Asia, empire of Cabool, province of Seistan, on the river Elmuud. It is principally built of brick, and there are extensive ruins of an ancient city of the same name; 280 miles S. W. of Candahar.

DORAN, a town of Arabia, in Yemen, on the side of a mountain; 28 miles S. of Sana.

DORAT, a town of France, in the department of Upper Vienne; seated on the Abran, near its junction with the Sevre; 25 miles N. of Limoges.

DORCHESTER, a borough and the capital of Dorsetshire, England, governed by a mayor; with a market on Wednesday and Saturday; it sends two members to parliament. It was formerly much larger, and the ruins of the walls are still to be seen in some places. It has three churches, and a fine terrace-walk, planted with trees, almost surrounds the town, which has no manufactures, but is famous for excellent ale. A little to the S. is a Roman amphitheatre, constructed of chalk and turf, supposed to be the most perfect in the kingdom. One mile to the S. W. is Maiden Castle, another work of the Romans. There are three ramparts and ditches, nearly oval, and the whole area is 115 acres. Dorchester is seated on the river Frome, about 10 miles from the sea at Weymouth, 53 miles E. of Exeter, and 120 W. by S. of London.

DORCHESTER, a town in Oxfordshire, which was a station of the Romans, and ruined in the wars with the Danes. It was a bishop's see till 1086, when William the Conqueror translated it to Lincoln; and it had five churches, though now but one, which was the cathedral; 10 miles S. E. of Oxford, and 49 W. N. W. of London.

DORCHESTER, a county of the state of Maryland, lying between the Nanticoke and Choptank Rivers, on the E. side of Chesapeake Bay. Pop. 18,843. The chief town is Cambridge, on the S. bank of the Choptank; 60 miles S. S. W. of Baltimore.

There is also a town of the same name contiguous to Boston, Massachusets, on the S. side of the town, and another on Ashley River, South Carolina, and two or three others in different parts of the United States.

DORDOGNE, an interior department in the S. W. of France, comprising the late province of Perigorde, and part of the Limousin; a river of the same name intersects the S. part of the department; the Vizere, Ille, and La Drome, all falling into the Dordogne, in its course to the Garonne at Bourg, intersects other parts of the department, which is in general fertile, and yields some delicious wines. It is divided into five arrondissements, the principal towns of which are Perigueux, the capital, Bergerac, Nontron, Riberac, and Sarlat; the other principal towns are Belves, Monpont, and Eaciderfil. Pop. 453,360.

DORESTRO. *See* SILISTRIA.

DORKING, a beautifully picturesque town in Surrey, England, with a market on Thursdays; celebrated for a remarkably fine breed of poultry; a vast quantity of lime is burnt in the neighbourhood. It is 23 miles S. S. W. of London Bridge.

DORN, a village in a detached part of Worcestershire; 3 miles S. E. of Camden in Gloucestershire. The Roman fossway runs through it, and abundance of coin, both Roman and British, have been found here.

DORNBURG, a town of Upper Saxony, in the principality of Weimar, with a castle; situate on a hill, by the river Saale; 14 miles E. of Weimar, and 40 S. W. of Leipsic.

DORNOCH, a borough on the E. coast of Scotland, capital of Sutherlandshire, at the entrance of a frith of the same name, over which it has a ferry to Tain. It is a small place, and half in ruins, but was formerly the residence of the bishops of Caithness; and part of the cathedral is kept up as the parish church. It is 40 miles N. of Inverness. Long. 3. 48. W. lat. 57. 52. N. It unites with Kirkwall, &c., in sending one member to parliament.

DORPT, DORPAT, or DORFAT, a town of Russia, in the government of Riga, with a university; seated on the Ember, between the lakes Wosero and Pepas; 60 miles S. of Narva, and about 50 E. of Pernau. Pop. 12,203.

DORSETSHIRE, a maritime county of England, having about 70 miles of coast in the British Channel; bounded on the W. by Devonshire, N. by the counties of Somerset and Wilts, and E. by Hampshire; it is of an irregular form, having an extreme length of 55 miles from W. to E., and 35 in extreme breadth; but the mean lines do not much exceed half that extent, the superficial area being only 720,000 acres. The soil is generally rich and fertile, though in some parts very sandy; the northern part, which is divided by a range of chalk-hills from the southern, affords good pasturage for cattle; while the southern part chiefly consists of fine downs, and feeds incredible numbers of sheep. The chalk-hills, which run through every county from the S. E. part of the kingdom thus far, terminate at the further extremity of this; but, on the coast, chalk-cliffs extend beyond it into Devonshire, 10 miles W. of Lyme. From the Hampshire border to the neighbourhood of Blandford a heathy common extends, which causes an exception to the general character of fertility which this county merits; but the rich vales to the S. W. make ample amends. The greatest altitude of the county is 669 feet above the level of the sea; the climate is mild and congenial. The principal rivers are the Stour, Piddle, and Frome. Here is plenty of poultry of all sorts, swans, woodcocks, pheasants, partridges, fieldfares, &c. The principal towns on the coast are Lyme Regis, Melcombe Regis, Weymouth, Bridport, Wareham, and Poole; at the two latter some ships are built, and some foreign trade carried on; and Poole was formerly celebrated for its extensive interest in the Newfoundland fishery; and considerable manufactures of cordage, twine, and coarse woollens were formerly carried on in the vicinity of Bridport and Poole; but the commercial and manufacturing concerns of the county have of late years declined, and are now relatively insignificant, the shipping being principally employed in carrying; and the rental, taxes, and supply of shop goods for the consumption of the county, are now paid out of the surplus produce of sheep and lambs for the London market, some cattle, wool, and stone, from the quarries of Portland and Purbeck, and freight of shipping; some trifling manufactures also contribute to constitute an exchange; and the western part of the coast abounds in mackerel during the season. The principal towns in the interior are Dorchester (the capital,) Corfe-castle, and Shaftesbury. It returns three members to parliament. There are thirteen other market towns, and upwards of 200 villages, in this county.

Dorsten, a fortified town of Westphalia, in the county of Recklinghausen; seated on the Lippe; 15 miles E. by N. of Wesel.

Dort, or Dordrecht, a city of Holland, province of South Holland, on an island formed by the Meuse, which is here called the Merwe. The island was formed in 1421, in November of which year an inundation destroyed 72 villages, and drowned 100,000 persons. In 1457 Dort was nearly destroyed by fire, and is further celebrated for an assembly of Protestant clergy from all parts of Europe, in 1618-19, called the Synod of Dort, which condemned the tenets of Arminius. Here are several Lutheran and Calvinist churches, a fine council-house, an excellent academy, and the mint of South Holland. It has a good harbour, and a great trade in corn, wine, and timber; of the latter immense rafts are floated hither from Andernach, in Germany. It was formerly the chief depository of Rhenish wines; but its commerce has much declined of late years, having been transferred to Rotterdam. The father of the celebrated De Witt was burgomaster of Dort, and Vossius was once superintendent of its academy. The natural situation of Dort is such that it has never been taken by an enemy; but it surrendered to the French in 1795. It is 10 miles S. E. of Rotterdam. Long. 4. 45. E. lat. 51. 54. N. Pop. about 20,000.

Dortmund, a strong town of Westphalia, in a nook at the S. extremity of the upper bishopric of Munster. It was lately imperial, and is seated on the Emster; 15 miles S. W. of Ham, and 30 S. by W. of the city of Munster. Pop. about 4000.

Dotekom, or Duetckom, a town of Holland, in Gelderland, with a foundry for bombs and cannon-balls; seated S. of Yssel; 10 miles S. E. of Doesburg.

Douarnenez, a town of France, in the department of Finisterre; seated on a bay of the same name, at the entrance of the English Channel; 8 miles N. W. of Quimper.

Douay, a city of France, formerly the capital of the department of Nord, with a fine arsenal, a foundry for cannon, a military school, a citadel, and three famous colleges; to which a great number of the Catholic youths of England and Ireland are sent for education. It was taken by the Duke of Marlborough in 1710, and retaken by the French in 1712, after the suspension of arms. It is 110 miles N. by E. of Paris, 70 E. S. E. of Boulogne, and 18 S. of Lisle, to which it is connected by a canal. It is the seat of a prefect, and contains 19,500 inhabitants.

Doubs, a department of France, on the frontier of Neufchatel, in Switzerland. It comprises the eastern part of the late province of Franche Compte, and is watered by a river giving name to the department, which falls into the Saone a little above Chalans. Doubs is a woody and mountainous district, interspersed with fertile valleys; the mountains yield a considerable supply of iron, the forests abundance of timber, whilst sheep and black cattle abound in the valleys, yielding a considerable supply of butter and cheese; the latter is celebrated by the name of grueyere. The vine is also cultivated with success, and to some extent; it has been proposed to unite the river Doubs with the Ille, falling into the Rhine, and thereby unite the waters of the North Sea with the Mediterranean. The department of Doubs is divided into four arrondissements; Besançon, 210 miles S. E. of Paris, is the capital; and the chief towns of the other three arrondissements are Baume, Pontarlier, and Montbelliard; there are two other considerable towns, viz., Quingey and Ornans. Pop. 230,000.

Doue, a town of France, in the department of Mayenne and Loire, with a considerable manufacture of druggets and tammies. Near it is a vast Roman amphitheatre, cut out of the solid rock. It is 9 miles S. W. of Saumur.

Douglas, a village of Lanarkshire, Scotland, seated on a river, of the same name, falling into the Clyde; 29 miles S. S. E. of Glasgow, on the road to Carlisle.

Douglas, the chief town of the Isle of Man, seated at the mouth of two united streams, on the E. side of the island, in the lat. of 54. 4. N. and 4. 36. of W. long. *See* Man.

Douglas, Cape, a promontory on the W. coast of America, the W. point of the entrance of Cook's Inlet. Its summit forms two very high mountains. Long. 153. 30. W. lat. 58. 56. N.

Doulaincourt, a town of France, in the department of Upper Marne; 10 miles S. W. of Joinville.

Doullens, a town of France, in the department of Somme, with two citadels; seated on the Antie; 15 miles N. of Amiens; it is the seat of a prefect. Pop. 3504.

Doune, Doun or Donne, a town of Scotland, in the parish of Kilmadock, Perthshire, with the ruin of a huge square castle, whose tower is full 80 feet in height. Here is a manufacture of pistols; also an extensive work called the Adelphi cotton-mill. It is seated on the Teith; 8 miles N. W. of Stirling, and 32 S. W. of Perth.

Dourdan, a town of France, in the department of Seine and Oise, with a manufacture of silk and worsted stockings; seated on the Orge; 25 miles S. W. of Paris.

Douro, a river of Spain, rising near Soria, in Old Castile, in the long. of 2. 30. W. It rises to the W. of Soria, and from thence runs S. for about 20 miles, when it takes a course nearly due W. past Aranda into Leon, past Zamora to the frontier of the Portuguese province of Traz os Montes; it then takes a course S. S. W. past Mirandi, and for about 60 miles forms the boundary between Leon in Spain, and Traz os Montes; it then takes a course N. by W. dividing the latter province and Entre Douroe Minho from Beira, falling into the sea a short distance below Oporto. The meridional distance from its source to its entrance into the sea, is about 300 miles, while the course of the stream will be near 400 miles; it receives numerous tributary streams both from the N. and S.

DOVE, a river of Derbyshire, which rises in the Peak, near Buxton, parts the county from Staffordshire, and, after a course of about 40 miles, joins the Trent, 4 miles below Burton.

DOVER, STRAITS OF, between the S. E. point of England and the N. W. extremity of France, leading from the Atlantic Ocean, through the English Channel into the North Sea: the narrowest part of the strait is about 20 English statute miles, and the two usual points of intercourse about 23 miles, Dover Castle being in l. 19. 7., and Calais lights in l. 51. l. of E. long., being a difference of 32 miles of long., which in the lat. of 51. is equal to 19 geographical, or 23 English statute miles. The straits extend from the S. W. in a direction N. N. E. for about 45 miles, intersected by the line. of 51. of N. lat.

DOVER, TOWN OF, which gives name to the preceding strait, is seated on the English coast, in the county of Kent, and is celebrated in every period of English history; by the ancient Britons it was called *Dour*, by the Romans *Dubris*, and by the Saxons *Dovre;* and the Romans regarded it as *clavis et refragulum totius regni*—the lock and key of the whole realm. It is sometimes spelt *Dovor*, but without authority. Dover may doubtless still be regarded as the great outlet and portal of the realm on the side of northern Europe, and, from its peculiar local situation and advantages, to be still entitled to high consideration. But as navigation has advanced towards perfection, and England advanced in her maritime ascendancy, in a relative sense, Dover has become an inconsiderable place, and, in point of security and defence, is very insignificant compared with either Portsmouth or Devonport; while Southampton and Falmouth vie with it, as points of egress and ingress to and from foreign parts; and, since the application of steam to purposes of navigation, numerous visitors to and from France now proceed and arrive direct from and to the Thames at London, who used formerly to pass by way of Dover. Dover is, however, still the medium of conveyance for the mails, and of all messengers and travellers intent on dispatch, between England and France, for whose accommodation packets proceed to and from Calais with every tide; and the intercourse is still very great, constituting the chief support of the town, which extends for near a mile along the shore, and is divided into two parts; the eastern part is called *the town*, at the extremity of which, on an eminence, is the castle, supposed to have been first founded by Julius Cæsar; the west part is called the pier, and is overhung by a range of chalk cliffs, which seem to threaten an immediate overwhelming of all below. The heights to the N. W. of the town, 300 to 350 feet above the level of the sea, are fortified with trenches, subterraneous works, and casements for the accommodation of 2000 men, and in clear weather presents fine prospects of the coast of France. Dover is one of the (five) cinque ports vested with peculiar privileges by the 32 Henry VIII. cap. 48, on condition of furnishing a certain number of ships equipped and manned for the national defence: one of the privileges was, each port returning two members to parliament, by the title of Barons of the Cinque Ports. Dover post office is 71 miles S. S. E. of London Bridge, by way of Canterbury, from which it is distant 16 miles; it is divided into two parishes; it holds two weekly markets on Wednesdays and Saturdays. The castle is a very extensive edifice, and interesting from its antiquity, and the historical events connected with it; it occupies 35 acres; besides the castle and two churches, the other public buildings are a town-hall, theatre, and military hospital, victualling office, and custom-house; the business of the latter is confined almost exclusively to the inspecting the baggage of the passengers arriving by the packets. The harbour will admit ships of 500 tons burthen, but the town carries on little or no foreign trade. To the W. of the town is the celebrated cliff mentioned by Shakspere in King Lear, which is now cut through by a double tunnel, for the South Eastern Railway.

There are several towns called Dover in different parts of the United States of North America.

1. In Duchess county, New York.
2. In Stafford county, New Hampshire.
3. In Kent county, Delaware.
4. In York county, Pennsylvania, &c.

DOVRAFIELD MOUNTAINS, a chain of mountains dividing Norway into the N. and S. divisions, and also separating it from Sweden. Their greatest altitude is about 800 feet.

DOWLATABAD, formerly called Amednagur, a province of the Deccan of Hindostan; intersected by the Godavery river; bounded on the N. by Candeish, W. by the Gauts, S. of Visiapour and Golconda, and E. by the Berar. Aurungabad is the capital.

DOWLATABAD, one of the celebrated hill-forts of Hindostan, and formerly the capital of the preceding province. The fort is 420 feet above the level of the plain. In the beginning of the 14th century, the Emperor Mahomet III. caused a great number of the inhabitants of Delhi to emigrate S. of the Godavery river, and attempted to make Dowlatabad the seat of government of his empire; but the project did not succeed, and his successor returned to the ancient capital. Dowlatabad, nevertheless, continued an important place, and capital of the province, until the time of Aurungzebe, who fixed his residence at AURUNGABAD (which see), about 10 miles to the S; it is now included in the territories of the nizam of the Deccan.

DOWN, a maritime county on the N. E. coast of Ireland, opposite to the Isle of Man; it is bounded on the N. by the Lough of Belfast, which divides it from the county of Antrim; S. by Carlingford Bay, which divides it from the county of Louth; and on the W. it is bounded by the county of Armagh. It is 53 miles in extreme length from S. W. to S. E., and about 25 in mean breadth, the N. E. being indented by Strangford Lough, containing about 100 square miles of surface; a canal from Carlingford Bay to Lough Neagh, bounds the W. end of the county, and the river Lagan, falling into Belfast Lough, waters the northern side, the river Bann intersecting the S. W. Down is the fifth county in Ireland, in order of population, both collectively and relatively, and although it is one of the least productive counties in the country, a great portion of its surface being occupied as bleach grounds, the industry of the inhabitants in the linen manufactures, enables it to command an equal or greater share of comforts than in most other parts of Ireland; the S. part of the county is mountainous, Slieve Donard Peak rising to the height of 2800 feet above the level of the sea; various minerals are found in different parts of the county, but none are worked to advantage, the linen manufactures absorbing all the labour and exertion of its inhabitants, about an equal portion of whom are Protestants, emigrants, or descendants of emigrants, from Scotland. Remains of antiquity are common in every part of the county. The principal towns are Downpatrick (the capital and a bishop's see), Newton Ardes, Bangor, Donaghadee, Killyleagh, Hillsborough, Dromore (another bishop s see), and Newry, at the head of Carlingford Bay, which is the largest and most considerable trading town in the county. It sends two members to parliament.

DOWN, or DOWNPATRICK, the chief town of the preceding county, is pleasantly located on the banks of a stream falling into the S. end of Strangford Lough; 74 miles N. N. E. of Dublin, and 23 S. by E. of Belfast: it is a bishop's see, in conjunction with Connor, in the county of Antrim, and, besides the cathedral, has three other places of religious worship; its other public buildings consist of a diocesan school, hospital, town-hall, court-house, and gaol. Down is celebrated as the supposed place of interment of Ireland's adopted saint, St. Patrick, and a well in the vicinity, dedicated to that saint, is held in high veneration. Down participates in the linen manufacture. It returns a member to the parliament of the United Kingdom.

DOWNHAM, MARKET, a town in Norfolk, with a market on Saturday; seated on the side of a hill, about a mile from the river Ouse. It has a great trade in butter, which is sent up the river in boats to Cambridge, and thence conveyed in waggons to London, under the name of Cambridge butter. It is 11 miles S. of Lynn, and 86 N. by E. of London.

There are four villages of the same name in different parts of England.

DOWNS, a famous road for shipping, on the E. coast of Kent, between the North and South Foreland. *See* GOODWIN SANDS, and DEAL.

DOWNTON, a town in Wiltshire, which has now no market; seated on the Avon; 6 miles S. E. of Salisbury, and 88 W. S. W. of London.

DRAABURGH, a town of Carinthia, on the river Drave, near the frontier of Tyrol.

DRACUT, a town of Massachusets, in Middlesex county, on the N. bank of the Merrimac, at Patucket Falls; 28 miles S. W. of Exeter, and 30 N. N. W. of Boston.

DRADATE, or DORHO, a town of Nubia, with a harbour, on the Red Sea, and wells of good water in the vicinity. It is 36 miles N. N. W. of Suakem.

DRAGUIGNAN, a town of France, capital of the department of Var; 10 miles N. W. of Frejus, 40 N. E. of Toulon, and 420 S. S. E. of Paris. Pop. 9300.

DRAKENSTEIN, an extensive valley in the Cape of Good Hope territory. *See* STELLENBOSCH.

DRAME, a town of Macedonia, near the ruins of Philippi, and about 20 miles N. N. E. of Emboli.

DRAMBURG, a town of Brandenburg, in the N. part of the New Mark; seated on the Drage; 15 miles E. by N. of New Stargard.

DRAMMEN. The two towns of Stromsoe and Bragnas, on each side of the Drammen river, falling into the Bay of Christiana, in Norway, are called Drammen. *See* STROMSOE.

DRAS. *See* DARAH.

DRAVE, a river which rises in Germany, at Innichen, in Tyrol, flows through Carinthia and Stiria, then along the confines of Sclavonia and Lower Hungary, and, after a course of about 300 miles, joins the Danube a little below Essig.

DRAYTON, a town in Shropshire, England, with a market on Wednesday; it is seated on the banks of the river Tern, at the N. E. end of the county, on the road from Shrewsbury to Newcastle. It has three tan yards, two paper-mills, and two manufactures of haircloth; 151 miles N. W. of London.

DRESDEN, a city of Germany, and the capital of the kingdom of Saxony. It is divided by the Elbe into the old and new town, which are united by a grand bridge, and surrounded by strong fortifications. It has a castle, an academy of painting and sculpture, and a magnificent church for the Roman Catholics, with a tower 300 feet in height, one Calvinist, and eleven Lutheran churches. The houses are built of freestone, almost all of the same height; and, though the palaces are few, it is deemed the handsomest city in Germany. The palaces of Holland and Japan are full of curiosities from that country and China: and the picture gallery may claim precedence over every individual gallery in Italy. The royal palace has a tower 355 feet in height Dresden is deservedly celebrated for its manufacture of porcelain; the repository for which is in the castle. Here are also manufactures of gold and silver lace, jewellery, paper hangings, and wind instruments of music, &c. &c. The arsenal contains specimens of the first invented fire-arms, and a curious collection of arms of all ages and countries. The other public buildings of Dresden are the house of assembly of the Saxon diet, an academy for the young nobility, a military school, and several edifices for charitable institutions. It was taken by the king of Prussia, in 1745, and again in 1756, but retaken in 1759; and it was bombarded by him in 1760, for nine days, when he was obliged to raise the siege. Dresden is further rendered memorable for its neighbourhood being the principal theatre of operations between the allied and French armies, during the greater part of the year 1813. The Russian and Prussian troops having entered it in the month of March, were obliged to quit it in May, after the battle of Lutzen; and Buonaparte afterwards held his head quarters here for a long time. On the 26th and 27th of August of the same year, the allied army, 200,000 strong, under Prince Schwartzenburg, attempted to carry the town by assault; but Buonaparte having arrived from Silesia, with his guards, the night before the attack, repulsed them with great loss in killed, wounded, and prisoners. It was at this time the celebrated General Moreau received a mortal wound, while in conversation with the Emperor of Russia. The allies, in consequence of this disaster, immediately commenced their retreat into Bohemia; and the French being too eager to profit by their success, had sent General Vandamme with about 30,000 men, into the mountains of that country, to cut off their retreat. But on their arrival near Culm, they were assailed on all sides; and, after a furious conflict, the whole army was nearly destroyed, and the commander, with the whole of his staff, were made prisoners; and on the 6th of November, after the battle of Leipsic, Marshal St. Cyr, who remained in Dresden with a French force of 39,000 men, after a fruitless attempt to negotiate a retreat, was compelled to yield to an unconditional surrender. Prior to the spoliation by Prussia in 1756, Dresden contained about 65,000 inhabitants; from which period it progressively declined down to 45,000 in 1810; but since the restoration of peace in 1814, it has gradually increased, and now contains a population of 60,000. In the vicinity are several fine gardens and public promenades, which serve to render Dresden one of the most agreeable abodes in the north of Europe. It is in the lat. of 51. 2. 50. N. and 13. 43. of W. long.; 230 miles N.N.W. of Vienna, 240 N.N.E. of Munich, 100 S. by E. of Berlin, 190 E. of Cassel, by way of Leipsic, from which it is distant 55 miles. *See* Pilnitz and Saxony.

Dreux, a town of France, in the department of Eure and Loire, with a considerable manufacture of cloth for the army. It is seated on the river Blaise, at the foot of a mountain; 48 miles W. by S. of Paris. It was burnt by Henry II. of England, in 1186, taken by Henry V. in 1421, and is further celebrated for a battle fought in its neighbourhood on the 18th of December, 1562, between the army of the King of France and the Protestants under the Prince of Conde, when the latter were defeated. It surrendered to Henry IV. of France in 1593, and is now the seat of a prefect, with a population of 6032.

Driesen, a town of Brandenburg, in the New Mark; seated on an island formed by the river Netze, near the Polish frontier; 20 miles E. of Landsberg.

Driffield, a town in East Yorkshire, with a market on Thursday, and a considerable trade in corn, by a canal to the river Hull. It is 28 miles E. by N of York, and 22 N. by W. of Hull. The neighbourhood is very productive in corn, but thinly inhabited.

Drino, a river of Albania, formed of two streams, one flowing from the frontier of Bosnia, on the N., is called the White Drino, and the other from the frontier of Macedonia in the S., is called the Black Drino; after each running a course of about 100 miles, the united stream, after a further course of about 50 miles, falls into the Gulf of Drino in the Adriatic, by several mouths, at Alessio.

Drino, or Drinizza, another river which rises in the N. part of Albania, and runs parallel with the White Drino for a considerable distance in a contrary direction into Bosnia, and, after dividing Bosnia from Servia for about 30 miles, and a course of about 150 miles, falls into the Save, about 70 miles above Belgrade; this river seems to afford a favourable opportunity for uniting the waters of the Save, and thereby the Danube, with the Adriatic. *See* Dulcigno.

Drissa, a town of Russia, in the government of Polotsk, at the conflux of the Drissa with the Dwina; 20 miles W. N. W. of Polotsk, and 272 S. of Petersburg.

Drista. *See* Silistria.

Drivastro, a town of European Turkey, in Albania; 20 miles N. E. of Dulcigno.

Drogheda, a sea-port on the E. coast of Ireland; seated at the head of a bay on the banks of the river Boyne, which here divides the counties of Meath and Louth; Drogheda being a town and county of itself, with a separate jurisdiction. It is a respectable town, and carries on a considerable trade in butter, grain, and coarse linens; the harbour is tolerably commodious, but its entrance is impeded for ships of large burthen, by a bar. It is divided into three parishes. Oliver Cromwell took it by storm in 1649; and it was near here where the decisive battle was fought between the forces of William and James, in 1691, when the latter were defeated. *See* Boyne. Drogheda is 24 miles N. of Dublin. It returns a member to the parliament of the United Kingdom.

Droitwich, a borough in Worcestershire; market on Friday. Here are famous salt springs, which were in great celebrity at the period of the Norman conquest, from which is made much peculiarly fine white salt. It is seated on the Salwarp; 7 miles N. N. E. of Worcester, and 116 W. N. W. of London. It is connected with the river Severn by a canal 7 miles in length, and the Birmingham and Worcester canal runs at a short distance, and by this means the salt is distributed over all parts of the kingdom. Droitwich is divided into four parishes, and returns one member to parliament.

Drome, an interior department in the S. E. of France; bounded on the W., for 65 miles, by the Rhone, which divides it from Ardeche; it is about 35 miles in mean breadth, bounded on the N. and E. by the departments of Isere and Upper Alps, and S. by Vaucluse. It derives its name from a river which intersects its centre, and falls into the Rhone. The Isere intersects the N., and the Argues the S. part of the department, which is comprised of the western part of the late province of Dauphiny. It is divided into four arrondissements, the chief towns of which are Valence, Die, Montelimart, and Nyons; the other principal towns are Romans, Le Crest, and Le Buis; Valence is the capital.

Dromore, a town and parish in the county of Down, Ireland; the town is a bishop's see; the palace of the prelate is a stately edifice. It is 20 miles W. by N. of Downpatrick, and 66 N. of Dublin, on the road to Belfast.

Dronero, a town of Piedmont, at the foot of the Alps, on the river Maira; 14 miles S. S.W. of Saluzzo, and about the same distance W. by N. of Coni. It contains six churches, and has a fine bridge across the river. Pop. about 6500.

Dronfield, a town in Derbyshire; 156 miles from London. Here is a free grammar-school, and a chalybeate spring.

Drontheim, the most northerly of the four great dioceses of Norway, extending from the lat. of 62. 5. to 65. 20. N., being about 80 miles in mean breadth; it is intersected by several small streams, and the coast is indented with numerous inlets and bays, and flanked with numerous islands; although a dreary district, the industry of the inhabitants counteracts, in a considerable degree, the inhospitality of its position and climate. It is divided into 80 parishes, containing a population of about 250,000, having considerably increased during the last and present century. The chief town, of the same name, is seated on a point of land, formed by a deep inlet, about 40 miles from the open sea, in the lat. of 63. 26. N. and 10. 22. of E. long.; 253 miles N. E. of Bergen, about the same distance due N. of Christiania, and 360 N. W. of Stockholm. It was the residence of the ancient kings of Norway, and is now the principal trading town of the diocese, and exports a very considerable quantity of fir timber and deals, some pitch, tar, peltry, &c. It is the residence of the bishop of the diocese; the cathedral is a stately edifice; the houses are mostly built of wood, but the streets are commodious, and in the summer season it is not an unpleasant residence. Pop. about 9000.

Drosendorf, a town of Austria, with an ancient castle; seated on the Teya, on the frontier of Moravia; 10 miles N. of Horn.

Drossen, a town of Brandenburg, in the New Mark; 14 miles S. E. of Custrin.

Drum, the name of two parishes in Ireland, one in the county of Mayo, and the other in Roscommon; there are also about thirty other parishes and several villages in different parts of Ireland beginning with *Drum*, such as Drumara, Drumboe, Drumcannon, &c. &c

Drumsna, a town of Ireland, in the county of Leitrim; seated on the E. bank of the Shannon; 4 miles S. E. of Carrick, and 73 from Dublin; it is rather a neat town.

Drusenheim, a town of France, in the department of Lower Rhine; seated on the Motter, near the Rhine; 15 miles N. by E. of Strasburg.

Druses, a community of people in Syria, which had its origin in a fanatical persecution of a caliph of Egypt, against the Mahomedans. About the beginning of the 11th century, the caliph and his prophet (a native of Persia) both met a violent death, and such of their disciples (the Druses) as adhered to their tenets, fled for a refuge to the mountains of Lebanon and Antilibanus; from whence they successively made war against the crusaders, the sultans of Aleppo, the Mamelukes and Turks; they were effectually subdued by Amurath III., in 1588, who imposed a regular tribute upon them, appointing an emir, or chief, whom he invested with executive power, and held him responsible for the payment of the tribute; this organization, however, the Druses soon turned against the Turks, with whom they have since been involved in repeated conflicts, with alternate success; they still maintain a nominal independence, occupying about 70 miles of coast from Saide, the ancient Sidon, to Gebail or Djebail; **Bairout**, or **Berut** (which see) being their chief station. Their number is estimated at about 120,000, all the males being trained to arms. Their language is the Arabic; and they now appear to have but little religion of any kind, praying indifferently in Christian churches or Turkish mosques.

Dryburg, or **Driburg**, a tn. in the Prussian States, seated near the source of a stream falling into the Weser, in the principality of Paderborn; it is pleasantly located, and distinguished for its baths; 10 miles E. of the town of Paderborn.

Dublin, a maritime and fertile county on the E. coast of Ireland, being about 30 miles in extreme length, and 13 in mean breadth, of which a city of the same name is the capital of all Ireland, and in extent of population and architectural display, is the second city of the British dominions in Europe; but in other respects inferior to either Liverpool, Manchester, Glasgow, or Edinburgh.

Dublin City is seated on the banks of the river Liffey, at its entrance into a bay of about 40 square miles in surface. It is an archiepiscopal see, and seat of the only university in Ireland, and also its principal centre of commerce; the banks of the river are faced with cut stone for nearly 3 miles in extent; forming spacious quays on both sides, and connected at convenient distances by six elegant bridges. The other public edifices deserving notice, are the castle, the residence of the viceroy, built about the beginning of the 13th century; the university (the only one in Ireland), the cathedral of Christ Church, and the collegiate church of St. Patrick, and the churches of St. George and St. Werburgh; the custom house, stamp and post offices, courts of law, and king's inns, the bank of Ireland (formerly the parliament house), linen hall, royal exchange, and commercial buildings; the royal barracks, several hospitals, 18 parochial, 26 Roman catholic, and 10 sectarian places of worship, and an elegant theatre. The harbour is formed by a pier, run from the S. bank of the river, for near 3 miles into the bay, terminated by an elegant light-house. The entrance of the harbour is, however, impeded by sand-banks, which preclude the entrance of ships exceeding

200 tons burthen, except at spring tides; two canals facilitate the commerce of the city with the interior; the royal canal from the N. side of the city is carried into the county of Meath, and the grand canal, from the S. W. quarter of the city, extends into the centre of the county of Kildare, where it diverges, one branch to the Shannon, and the other to the Barrow, thereby uniting the ports of Limerick and Waterford with Dublin; a railroad now connects the harbour of Kingstown, formerly Dunleary, with the city, and which obviates much of the inconveniences of the port. On the N. W. side of the city is the Phœnix Park, a royal demesne, about 7 miles in circumference, containing a residence for the viceroy, and another for the chief secretary; and also an observatory; and, on an eminence on the S. bank of the river is Kilmainham hospital, for the invalids of the army. The city is bounded by a fine road, called the Circular, about 10 miles in its course, similar to the Fauxbourgs of Paris; within the city are five spacious squares, three on the S. and two on the N. side of the river; and the principal street, called Sackville Street, 170 feet wide, is entitled to rank among the finest in Europe; in the centre is a pillar 130 feet in height, to commemorate the naval achievements of Nelson. Prior to the union of Ireland with England, Dublin was the seat of the legislature, and most of the nobility and members of parliament had residences there; some of them, very extensive and elegant, have since been converted into hotels, hospitals, and to other public purposes. The local government of Dublin consists of a lord mayor, 24 aldermen, and 96 common councilmen; it has a considerable manufacture of broad silks, and some woollen manufactures are also carried on within the city, with various other manufactures for domestic purposes. There does not appear to have been any authentic return of the population of Dublin prior to 1811, but it is supposed to have decreased since the union of the legislature with that of England in 1801. The university returns two, and the city and county each two, members to the parliament of the United Kingdom. The general exterior aspect of Dublin is grand and imposing, and the general character of its inhabitants frank, hospitable, and prepossessing. On close investigation, however, it proves to contain more abodes of wretchedness and misery than is to be found in any other city of the like extent, in any other part of the world. Dublin, in its most comprehensive sense, contains 26 parishes, 17 within the city boundaries, and 9 between the city boundaries and the Circular road. The civil government is vested in the lord mayor, recorder, 2 sheriffs, 24 aldermen, and a common council composed of representatives from the 15 guilds. It is divided into four districts, each submitted to the care of a police magistracy, who have an office and court within their respective districts. Police stations are established at convenient distances, and a horse patrol is in constant motion during the greater part of the night, to a distance of 7 miles from the city. The observatory in the Phœnix Park, about 4 miles W. of the custom house, on the N. bank of the river, near its entrance into the bay, is in the lat. of 53. 23. 7. N., and 6. 20. 30. of W. long. The bay is formed by HOWTH HILL on the N. and DUNLEARY on the S. See each, under their respective heads, for distance from Holyhead, the nearest point of communication with the British coast, &c. &c.

There are four townships called Dublin in the United States of North America; three in Pennsylvania, and one in New Hampshire.

DUBRO, a town of Russian Poland, in the province of Volhynia; seated on the banks of a branch of the Przypiec, near the frontier of Galicia; it was formerly celebrated for its great annual fair. It is 24 miles S. E. of Lucko. Pop. about 6500, chiefly Jews.

DUCKENFIELD, a township in the parish of Stockport, Cheshire. *See* STOCKPORT.

DUDDINGSTON, a pleasant village on the S. side of Edinburgh, Scotland.

DUDERSTADT, a town of Germany, in the territory of Eichsfeld; 18 miles E. of Gottingen. Pop. about 4000.

DUDLEY, a borough of Worcestershire, England, insulated in the county of Stafford; 10 miles W. by N. of Birmingham, and 128 from London. It is a place of antiquity, having the remains of a castle, built about the year 700; the neighbourhood abounds in coal, iron, and limestone, and the town participates largely in the manufactures of the district, having about 20 establishments for the manufacture of nails, anvils, vices, tracery, and other heavy iron work; 10 other establishments for the manufacture of fenders and fire irons, 5 glass-houses, and 2 other establishments for glass cutting; 3 malt and coffee-mill makers, 20 malting-houses, &c. &c. It has 2 churches; that of St. Thomas is a beautiful structure, with a lofty spire. Market on Saturday. It returns one member to parliament.

DUDLEY, a town in Worcester county, Massachusets, near the frontier of Connecticut; 20 miles S. of Worcester.

DUFFEL, a town of the Netherlands, a few miles N. of Malines. Pop. about 3000.

DUISBURG. *See* DUYSBURG.

DUKE OF YORK ISLAND, an island in the Pacific Ocean, discovered by Commodore Byron, in 1765, lying N. of the Friendly Islands. Long. 172. 30. W. lat. 7. 56. S.

DUKE OF YORK ISLAND, an island in the Pacific Ocean, lying between New Britain and New Ireland; so named by Captain Carteret, in 1767. The natives go entirely naked; are stout, well made, and of a light copper colour; their hair is woolly, but they dress it with grease and powder, and make it hang straight. Their huts are made chiefly of bamboo, and placed under the shade of cocoa-nut trees with a fence before them, within which the plaintain, banana, yam, sugar-cane, &c., are cultivated. The island produces, besides the plants above mentioned, betel-nuts, mangoes, bread-fruit, and guavas. Here are also dogs, hogs, poultry, and some spices. The nutmeg was seen by Capt. Hunter, who anchored in Port Hunter Bay, in this island, in 1791. Long. 151. 20. E. lat. 4. 7. S.

DUKE'S COUNTY, in the state of Massachusets. *See* MARTHA'S VINEYARD.

DULAS, a village of Wales, in the Isle of Anglesea; 10 miles N. W. of Beaumaris. It stands on the Irish Sea, at the mouth of a river of the same name; and is much frequented on account of the corn and butter trade, and for fern ashes and kelp.

There are several small rivers in different parts of Wales, named *Dulas*, and also a village in Herefordshire.

DULCIGNO, a town of European Turkey, in Albania; seated at the mouth of the river Bosnia; 15 miles S. W. of SCUTARI (which see). Long. 18. 56. E. lat. 42. 23. N. Pop. about 8000.

DULEEK, a town of Ireland, in the county of Meath, formerly the see of a bishop, but now an inconsiderable place. It is seated near the S. bank of the river Boyne; 3 miles S. W. of Drogheda, and 21 N. by W. of Dublin.

DULKEN, a town of the Prussian states, lying about midway between the Rhine and the Maese; 20 miles N. by W. of Juliers. Pop. about 4000.

DULMEN, a town of Westphalia, in the principality of Munster; 14 miles S. W. of Munster. Pop. about 1800.

DULVERTON, a town in Somersetshire, with a market on Saturday, and manufactures of coarse woollen cloths and blankets. It is seated near the Ex; 20 miles S. of Minehead, and 165 W. by S. of London.

DULWICH, a beautifully sequestered village in Surrey; 4 miles S. of London. It is famous for a college, founded by Edward Alleyn, a comedian, called the College of God's Gift; to which is attached a gallery, containing a beautiful collection of paintings; the village is seated in a vale.

DUMARING, a town of the island of Borneo, on the E. coast. Long. 117. 30. E. lat. 2. 10. N.

DUMBARTON, COUNTY OF, sometimes called Dunbarton, formerly Lennox, formed of a narrow strip of territory between the lowlands and the highlands of Scotland, extending W. from near the Frith of Forth, for about 25 miles, to the mouth of the Clyde, and then N. for about 25 miles more, between Loch Long and Loch Lomond, the mean breadth not exceeding 5 miles; the Grand Canal from the Clyde to the Forth runs along the E. part of the county, which is divided into 12 parishes: the principal towns and villages are Cumbernald and Kirkintilloch, in the E. part, Kirkpatrick, Kilpatrick, Dumbarton, Cardcross, Bonhill, and Kilmarnock, in the centre; and Roseneath, Row, Lup, and Aroquhar, in the N. It returns one member to parliament. The cotton manufacture is carried on in the central part of the county, and illicit distillation in the N.

DUMBARTON, the chief town of the preceding county, is a royal burgh; seated on the N. bank of the Clyde, at the junction of the Leven, the outlet of Loch Lomond: on a point of land formed by the junction of the two rivers is a castle, occupying a very commanding position, and formerly deemed the key of the passage between the lowlands and the highlands, on the W., as well as commanding the navigation of the Clyde. The town consists principally of one long street, in the form of a crescent, parallel with the Leven, over which is a handsome bridge of five arches. It has a handsome church, with a lofty spire, erected at the close of the last century. Its principal manufacture is glass; a portion of the inhabitants are employed in the cotton manufacture in connexion with Glasgow. It has a convenient port for small vessels, and a quay, but no custom-house, being included in the port of Greenock; and, with Renfrew, &c. it sends one member to parliament. It is 12 miles W. N. W. of Glasgow.

DUMBOOC, or DOMBOO, a salt lake on the north frontier of Bournou, in the interior of North Africa, from whence much salt is carried to Agades and other parts of western Africa; there is a considerable town, of the same name, on the W. side of the lake, which is S. of the tropic of Cancer, in the long. of 21. 50. E.

DUMFRIES, a county of the S. of Scotland, being about 65 miles in extreme length from E. to W., and 30 in mean breadth, its superficial area being 672,000 Scotch acres; it is bounded on the N. by the counties of Ayr, Lanark, Peebles, Selkirk, and Roxburgh; E. S. E. by the English border, W. S. W. by Kirkcudbrightshire, and S. by the Solway Frith; it is intersected from N. to S. by three considerable rivers, abundant in salmon and trout, viz. the Nith, Annan, and Esk, all running from the N. into Solway Frith, and is divided into 44 parishes, including four royal burghs, viz. Dumfries, Annan, Lochmaber, and Sanquhar, and sends one member to parliament. A great part of this county is mountainous, overspread with heath, well stocked with game, and affording pasture to numerous herds of sheep and black cattle, which are driven into England in great numbers; the valleys, watered by the three rivers before mentioned, and the coast bordering on the Frith, are fertile both in pasture and tillage; the mountains in the N. W. part of the county contain a bed of rich lead ore, yielding a small portion of silver; coal and lime abound over the greater part of the county, and on the English border both copper and iron have been found; the county also contains a vein of antimony, and two mineral springs. It has no manufactures of importance.

DUMFRIES, a royal burgh, and chief town of the preceding county; seated on the E. bank of the river Nith, where that river forms the boundary between the counties of Dumfries and Kirkcudbright, and about 9 miles above its entrance into Solway Frith. Dumfries is a port of entry, but its external commerce is inconsiderable (except coastwise); it derives its chief importance from being the assize town for the county of Kirkcudbright, as well as for Dumfries, and from being the seat of the commissary and sheriff court, and of the presbytery and synod, while the agreeableness of its locality renders it the focus of gaiety and fashion for all the S. W. part of Scotland. It has two bridges over the Nith, one of them ancient, the other modern and elegant, two churches, a catholic chapel, and four dissenting places of worship. Its other public buildings are the town house, guildhall, infirmary, house of correction, and lunatic asylum. In conjunction with Sanquhar, &c., it sends one member to parliament. Dumfries is 38 miles W. N. W. of Carlisle, 75 S. W. of Edinburgh, 79 S. S. E. of Glasgow, and 80 E. N. E. of Port Patrick. It is the place of interment of Burns.

DUN, a town of France, in the department of Meuse, on the river Meuse; 15 miles N. N. W. of Verdun.

DUN LE ROI, a town of France, in the department of Cher, on the river Auron; 15 miles S. of Bourges.

DUNAGHY, a town of Ireland, county of Antrim, on the Ravel water; here is a chalybeate spa.

DUNAMUNDE, a town of Russia, in the government of Riga. It formerly belonged to the duchy of Courland, but was taken by the Swedes in their wars with the Poles. In 1700 it was taken by the Poles, and retaken the next year by Charles XII. In 1710 it was taken by Peter the Great. It is situate at the mouth of the Dwina; 15 miles N. W. of Riga, to which it is the outpost, and 20 N. of Mittau. Long. 23. 41. E. lat. 57. 5. N.

DUNABURGH, a town of Russia, in the government of Vitepsk; seated on the E. bank of the Divena, about 100 miles above Riga. The Russians formed extensive entrenchments near this place in 1812, but abandoned them on the approach of the French towards Moscow. Pop. about 6000.

DUNBAR, a town of Haddingtonshire, on the S. E. coast of Scotland; seated on the shore of a bay opening into the German Ocean: the harbour, defended by a battery, is difficult of access, but safe and commodious when attained. It is a port of entry, but its foreign commerce is inconsiderable; it has a yard for ship-building, a ropery, soap-work, and one or two iron foundries; it exports a considerable quantity of corn to the London market, and the inhabitants in the season pursue the herring fishery with much industry. Here was anciently a castle, now in ruins, which stood on a rock, and, before the use of artillery, was deemed impregnable. Under the rock are two natural arches, through which the tide flows; and between the harbour and the castle is a stratum of vast basaltic columns of red stone, interspersed with veins of jasper. Dunbar is distinguished in various periods of Scottish history through several centuries, and was formerly deemed of much greater importance than at present. It was created a royal burgh about the middle of the 14th century, and contributes, with Haddington, &c. in sending one member to parliament. The parish extends for about 9 miles along the coast. It is 27 miles E. of Edinburgh, and 29 N. W. of Berwick-on-Tweed. Lat. 56. N. and 2. 30. of W. long.

DUNBARTON. *See* DUMBARTON.

DUNBLANE, or DUMBLANE, a town of Scotland, in Perthshire, formerly a bishop's see, with a magnificent cathedral; it is 6 miles N. of Stirling.

DUNCANSBY, or DUNGISBY HEAD, the extreme N. E. point of Great Britain, in the lat. of 58. 40. N. and 3. 8. of W. long.

DUNCHURCH, a village in Warwickshire; 80 miles N. W. of London. It derives its name from its situation on the border of what was formerly an extensive heath called *Dunsmore* heath, celebrated for a legendary tale of a cow of enormous size, which roamed upon it.

DUNDALK, a parish and town on the E. coast of Ireland, in the county of Louth, and of which it is the assize and chief town. The town is seated at the mouth of a small river, falling into a bay of the same name. It participates largely in the linen manufacture, and is distinguished for a manufacture of fine cambrics, established in 1737. It has a custom-house, and an elegant town-hall, and other public buildings. It is 18 miles N. of Drogheda, and 12 S. of Newry. It returns a member to the parliament of the United Kingdom.

DUNDEE, a seaport of Scotland, seated at the S. extremity of Angus, or Forfarshire, on the N. shore of the Frith of Tay, which forms a convenient and commodious harbour for ships of large burden. Next to Edinburgh and Glasgow, Dundee is the most manufacturing and commercial town in Scotland; independent of its extensive coasting trade, it imports a large quantity of flax and other products direct from the Baltic, and employs several ships in the Greenland whale fishery. Its manufactures consist of sail-cloth, cotton, bagging, osnaburgs, and other heavy linen fabrics, and coloured sewing threads. The town consists of four principal streets, diverging from a square in the centre; the public buildings are a town-house, trades-hall, infirmary, orphan and lunatic asylum, three churches, and a theatre, and is the commencement of the Dundee and Arbroath Railway. Dundee was erected into a royal burgh in 1165, and has been exposed to the repeated ravages of the contending parties which have prevailed in Scotland since that period; the last time it suffered from such cause was in the time of Cromwell, when it was taken by assault, and given up to pillage by the troops under General Monk, who shared 60*l*. a man from the booty they obtained. It is 22 miles E. of Perth, and 42 N. E. of Edinburgh. Lat. 56. 27. N. and 3. 3. of W. long.

DUNDONALD, a village S. of Irvine, in Ayrshire, Scotland, abounding in excellent coal. The cotton manufacture is also carried on in the village.

DUNFERMLINE, a royal burgh of Scotland, in Fifeshire; seated near the S. W. extremity of the county; about 3 miles from the N. shore of the Frith of Forth. It is celebrated for its once magnificent abbey, which fell a prey to the plundering army of Edward I., and as the place of interment of Malcolm Canmore, the founder of the abbey, seven other Scottish monarchs, five queens, and several of the most eminent persons who figure in Scottish history. Dunfermline has been celebrated in later times for its extensive manufacture of fine table linen, and still ranks among the most important manufacturing towns of Scotland. The town is well built on an eminence, and commands some beautiful prospects of the surrounding country; its public buildings consist of a town-house, an elegant guildhall, &c. It returns one member to parliament, and is 17 miles N. W. of Edinburgh.

Dungannon, a town of Ireland, in the S. E. part of the county of Tyrone. It returns a member to the parliament of the United Kingdom. It is 11 miles N. by W. of Armagh, and 73 from Dublin.

Dungarvon, a town of Ireland, seated at the head of a bay, in the county of Waterford; although the harbour is safe and convenient, it is not a port of entry; its principal trade consists of potatoes and fish, for the Dublin market. It returns one member to the parliament of the United Kingdom, and is frequented, in the summer season, for sea-bathing; the principal object of the town is the ruin of an ancient castle; 17 miles W. by S. of Waterford, in the lat. of 52. 2. N. and 7. 35. of W. long.

Dungeness, a celebrated promontory, forming the S. E. point of the county of Kent, England, at the entrance to the Straits of Dover; the light-house is in the lat. of 50. 55. 1. N. and 0. 57. 48. of E. long.

Dungiven, a town in Ireland, county of Londonderry. Here are the ruins of a very ancient church, and also of a castle; 183 miles from Dublin.

Dunkeld, a town of the highlands of Scotland, seated on the N. bank of the river Tay, in a delightfully romantic part of the county of Perth. It was the capital of ancient Caledonia; and, at an early period, a Pictish king founded here a monastery of Culdees, which was converted into a bishopric by David I., in 1130, and, for a length of time, held the first rank in Scotland. The choir of the cathedral is still entire, and serves for the parish church. At a more recent period it was much frequented as a place of fashionable retreat, and for obtaining goats' whey; but this practice has ceased. The town and surrounding country is claimed by the Duke of Argyle, as his exclusive property; and as such, he has converted the whole of the adjacent vicinity to his own immediate purpose and gratification; there is an elegant bridge of seven arches over the Tay. Dunkeld is the chief market town of the highlands; it is 15 miles N. of Perth, on the line of the military road to Fort Augustus and Inverness.

Dunkirk, a sea port of France, in the department of Nord. It was taken from the Spaniards by the English and French in 1658, and put into the hands of the English, but sold to the French by Charles II., in 1662. Louis XIV. made it one of the best fortified ports in the kingdom; but all the works were demolished, and the basins filled up, in consequence of the treaty of Utrecht, in 1713. The French afterwards resumed the works; but they were ordered to be demolished at the peace of 1763. They continued thus till the peace of 1783, when the works were again resumed; and the next year it was declared a free port. The English attempted to besiege this place in 1793, but were obliged to retire with loss. Dunkirk is divided into the old and new town, is well built, has a spacious market-place, and an elegant modern built church; as a sea port it is now but of little note. It is the seat of a prefect; 16 miles E. by N. of Calais. Pop. 28,000

Dunleary. *See* Kingstown.

Dunmow, a corporate town in Essex, with a market on Saturday. It is seated on a hill; 13 miles N. N. W. of Chelmsford, and 38. N. E. of London.

Dunmow, Little, a village, 2 miles from Dunmow. It had once a monastery, built in 1103, and part of the priory now forms the parish church. This place is famous for the tenure of its manor; namely, that whatever married couple will go to the priory, and swear they have not repented of their marriage, within a year and a day after it took place, shall receive a flitch of bacon. The first grant of this description took place in the reign of Henry VI., and the last in 1751.

Dunnet Head, an extensive promontory of Scotland, in the county of Caithness. Its N. extremity, in the Pentland Frith, is the most northern point of Great-Britain. Long. 3. 29. W. lat. 58. 42. N. It gives name to a bay on the W.; on the E. shore of which is a village of the same name. *See* Thurso.

Dunning, a town of Scotland, in Perthshire; 59 miles from Edinburgh. It has an extensive linen manufactory.

Dunnose, a cape in the English Channel, on the S. E. side of the Isle of Wight. Long. 1. 12. W. lat. 50. 37. N.

Dunse, a town of Scotland, the largest in Berwickshire. Here is a woollen manufacture, and celebrated mineral well, similar to that of Tunbridge in England. It is situate under a hill, near the river Whiteadder; 14 miles W. of Berwick, and 40. E. S. E. of Edinburgh. It is distinguished as the birth-place of Joannes Duns Scotus, in 1274.

Dunsinane, or Dinsinnan, a hill, 6 miles N. E. of Perth, in Scotland, 1024 feet above the level of the sea; immortalized by the English poet Shakspere, in his drama of Macbeth.

Dunstable, a town in Bedfordshire, with a market on Wednesday. It is of great antiquity, having been ruined by the Danes, and restored by Henry I., who made it a borough, but no members were ever sent to parliament. The church is the remainder of a priory, and opposite to it is a farm house, once a royal palace. Dunstable consists principally of one long street, and is celebrated for its manufacture of straw for bonnets, &c. It is seated on the verge of a range of chalk hills, which extend across the counties of Bedford, Buckingham, and Oxford; and large quantities of larks are caught in its vicinity, and sent to the London market. It is 33 miles N. N. W. of London.

Dunstaffnage, a castle of Scotland, in Argyleshire, one of the first seats of the Pictish and Scottish monarchs. Here was long preserved the famous stone, used as the coronation seat of the Scottish monarchs, which was removed to Scone by Kenneth II., and thence by Edward I., in 1206, to Westminster Abbey, where it now remains as an appendage to the coronation chair. Some of the ancient regalia still continue in the castle; and near it is a small roofless chapel, of elegant architecture, where several of the kings of Scotland are said to be interred. It stands on a promontory, almost insulated, at the entrance of Loch Etive; 24 miles N. W. of Inverary.

DUNSTER, a town in Somersetshire, with a market on Friday. It has a castle, on a steep knoll; and at one corner of the terrace is an ancient turret, supposed to be part of the original castle, built in the time of William I. A priory stood on the N. W. side of the castle, part of which now serves for the parish church. It stands on the edge of a vale, near the Bristol Channel; 20 miles N. W. of Taunton, and 161 W. of London.

DUNWICH, a village in Suffolk. It was formerly a bishop's see, and had many churches, which have been swallowed up by the sea; 24 miles S. of Yarmouth, and 100 N. of London.

There are numerous other towns and villages in England, the names of which begin with *Dun*, a Saxon word signifying a down, or level place, or country.

DUPLIN, an interior county in the S. E. part of the state of North Carolina, watered by the N. E. branch of Cape Fear River. Pop. 11,182.

DUQUELLA, a province of Morocco, about 80 miles long and 60 broad, exceedingly fertile in corn and pasture.

DURANCE, a river in the S. E. of France, which is formed near Briançon, of the rivulets Dure and Ance, and flows by Embrun, Tallard, Sisteron, Manosque, Cavaillon, and Avignon, into the Rhone.

DURANGO, a town of Spain, in Biscay; 14 miles S. E. of Bilboa.

DURANGO, a division of Mexico, extending from the lat. of 24. to 32. N., comprising the greater portion of the late province of New Biscay; intersected from S. to N. by the main ridge of the Andes. Its superficial area is computed at 129,247 square miles, and a population of 159,700. The chief town, of the same name, is seated near the S. end of the province, in the lat. of 24. 10. N. and 104. of W. long., at an elevation of 6854 feet above the level of the sea. It is about 520 miles N. W. of the city of Mexico. Pop. about 12,000.

DURAZZO, a town of European Turkey, capital of Albania, and a Greek archbishop's see. It has a ruined fortress, and a good harbour on the Gulf of Venice; 50 miles N. of Avlona. Long. 19. 36. E. lat. 41. 25. N. Pop. 9000.

DURBUNGA, a town of Hindostan, in Bahar, near the Gogary; 50 miles N. E. of Patna.

DURBUY, a town of Holland, in Luxemburg; seated on the Ourthe; 25 miles S. by W. of Liege, and about the same distance E. by S. of Namur.

DUREN, or DEUREN, a town of the Prussian states of the Rhine, on the E. bank of the Roer, in the duchy of Juliers; 15 miles E. of Aix-la-Chapelle. Pop. about 4700.

DURHAM, a maritime county, on the N. E. coast of England; bounded on the S. and S.W. by the river Tees, which divides it from Yorkshire. The western extremity of the county jets upon Westmoreland and Cumberland, and the rivers Derwent and Tyne divide it from Northumberland on the N. The line of coast from the mouth of the Tees to the Tyne is about 32 miles; but in its extreme extent from N. to S. the distance is 36 miles, and from E. to W. about 40 miles and contains 610,000 acres. All the W. part of the county is mountainous, some of the peaks rising upwards of 2000 feet above the level of the sea; from these mountains rises the river Wear, which, by its circuitous course and collateral streams, waters all the interior parts of the county. The chief characteristic of this county is its coal mines, which yield about two million tons annually, chiefly for the supply of London, and the E. and S. E. parts of England. The rivers and coasts abound in salmon and other excellent fish, while the E. and S. E. parts of the county yield a surplus of agricultural produce, both in grain and cattle; it owns also a considerable extent of shipping, employed chiefly in the conveyance of its coal, the value of which, including the freight and its supply of agricultural produce, together with some lead, iron, and mill-stones, constitute an exchangeable amount, exceeding 1,000,000*l*. per annum. The principal towns besides the capital, of the same name, are Stockton, Darlington, and Bernard Castle, on the N. bank of the Tees; Gateshead and South Shields, on the S. bank of the Tyne; Monk Wearmouth, Bishop's Wearmouth, and Sunderland, at the mouth of the Wear; Bishop's Auckland, Chester-le-Street, &c., in the interior. It is divided into the North and South divisions, and returns two members for each.

DURHAM CITY, the chief place and capital of the preceding county, is seated on the banks of the river Wear, about the centre of the county, on the line of the great high road from London to Edinburgh; 10 miles from the sea in a direct line, about 20 from the mouth of the Wear, by the course of the stream, 14 from the Tyne at Newcastle, 19 from the Tees at Darlington, 242 in a meridional line, and 255 by the line of road N. by W. of London. It was created a bishop's see by a king of Northumberland, prior to the conquest; who, out of devotion, conferred the whole county of Durham upon St. Cuthbert, a monk of Lindisfarne, its first bishop, and his successors for ever. This grant was confirmed by William, the Norman conqueror, who constituted it a principality, or county palatine; hence the county is sometimes designated the principality of Durham. The cathedral was founded towards the close of the 11th century, and is a magnificent edifice, upwards of 400 feet in length, seated on an eminence, 80 feet above the surface of the river; the principal tower is 214 feet in height. Besides the cathedral there are six other churches, three of them fine edifices; two Roman Catholic, and several dissenting places of worship. Durham has also a stately castle, founded by William the Norman, now the bishop's palace, and several public buildings more immediately belonging to the city; while the gaol, house of correction, courts, and governor's house for county purposes, have all been recently rebuilt in a handsome style. The university of Durham, recently founded, is endowed with ample revenues, derived from the cathedral bishopric. There are three bridges over the river; and, on the whole, the city of Durham presents a very interesting and imposing aspect, and is celebrated in English history. It returns two members to parliament; market on Thursday; it has no manufacture of importance.

There are several towns named *Durham* in different parts of the United States of North America; the only one deserving of notice is in Stafford county, New Hampshire. Near it is a rock, computed to weigh 60 tons, so exactly poised on another rock, as to be easily moved with a finger. It is situate on Oyster River, near its junction with the Piscataqua; 16 miles W. of Portsmouth.

DURKHEIM, a town of Germany, in the palatinate of the Rhine; seated on the river Hardt; 17 miles S. W. of Worms.

DURKHEIM, or TURKHEIM, a town of France, in the department of Upper Rhine, where the French gained a victory over the Austrians in 1675. It is 4 miles N. W. of Colmar.

DURLACH, a town of Suabia, capital of Baden-Durlach, with a castle. It was formerly the seat of government of the grand duke of Baden, who transferred his residence to Carlsruhe, since the peace of 1814. Here are manufactures of porcelain, cloth, and stuffs. It is seated on the Giessen; 15 miles N. N. E. of Baden. Long. 8. 35. E. lat. 48. 58. N. Pop. 5100.

DURSLEY, a corporate town in Gloucestershire, with a market on Thursday. In 1821 it had three establishments for drawing of wire, four for the manufacture of carding machines, and four for the manufacture of woollen cloths; it had formerly a castle. It is 13 miles S. W. of Gloucester, 20 W. of Cirencester, and 108 from London.

DURTAL, a town of France, in the department of Mayenne and Loire. The chief trade is tanning. It is 16 miles N. E. of Angers.

DUSKY BAY, a bay on the S. W. coast of New Zealand, in the Pacific Ocean. The country here is steep, and the hills near the seaside are covered with intricate and impenetrable forests. Abundance of excellent refreshments are found here; and it contains several coves and harbours. Long. 166. 18. E. lat. 45. 47. S.

DUSSARAH, a town of Hindostan, province of Guzerat. Pop. 7000.

DUSSELDORF, a strong city of Westphalia, capital of the duchy of Berg. Contiguous to the palace is a celebrated gallery of paintings. Dusseldorf was taken by the French in 1795. It is seated on the river Dussel, near the Rhine; 25 miles S. of Wesel. It was included in the cessions to Prussia in 1815, and is now the capital of a circle, with about 365,000 inhabitants; those of the town 20,000. Long. 6. 40. E. lat. 51. 12. N.

DUCHESS, a county of New York, extending for 45 miles along the E. bank of the Hudson river, and 22 in breadth. Poughkeepsie, the chief town, seated near the banks of the river, is 60 miles N. of the city of New York, and 73 S. of Albany. Pop. 52,398.

DUXBURY, a town of Massachusets, in Plymouth county, on the W. shore of Massachusets Bay, with a harbour for small vessels, and a lighthouse at the S. extremity of the beach. It is situate S. by E. of Plymouth, 3 miles across Plymouth Bay.

DUYSBURG, a fortified town of Westphalia, in the duchy of Cleve, with a Calvinist university. It has a considerable trade with Holland, and is seated on the Roer, near the Rhine; 12 miles S. by E. of Wesel.

DUYTZ, a town of Westphalia, in the duchy of Berg, with a Benedictine abbey It is inhabited chiefly by Jews, and seated on the Rhine, opposite Cologne.

DUYVELAND, one of the islands of Zealand, in Holland, E. of Schowen, from which it is separated by a narrow channel.

DWINA, a river of Russia, which runs from S. to N. into the White Sea, at Archangel.

DWINA, another river of Russia, which issues from two lakes; one in the government of Twer, and the other in the government of Pskov, runs S. by W. to Vitepsk, then W. N. W. past Polotsk and Dunabourg, dividing the ancient province of Livonia on the N. from Samigalia on the S., and, after a course of 450 miles in a meridional line, and upwards of 600 by the course of the stream, falls into the Gulf of Riga at Dunamunde, a few miles below the city of Riga.

DYNAPOOR, a town and fort of Hindostan, in Bahar, near which is a diamond mine. It is seated on the Ganges; 10 miles W. of Patna.

DYSART, a borough of Scotland, in Fifeshire, with a good harbour. It has a considerable trade in coal, a salt work, a manufacture of checks, and some employment in ship-building. It joins with Kirkaldy, Kinghorn, and Burntisland, in returning one member to parliament, and is seated on the N. shore of the Frith of Forth; 16 miles N. by E. of Edinburgh, and 20 S. W. of St. Andrews.

E.

Eaglseham, a village of Scotland, in Renfrewshire; 9 miles S. W. of Glasgow. It has bleaching-grounds, and a considerable cotton manufacture.

Ealing, with Old Brentford, a village in Middlesex, having a great number of private schools for the education of the youths of the metropolis.

Eaoowe, one of the Friendly Islands, in the Pacific Ocean, discovered by Tasman in 1643, and by him named Middleburgh. The land gently rises to a considerable height, presenting a beautiful prospect of extensive meadows, adorned with tufts of trees, and intermixed with plantations. Long. 174. 30. W. lat. 21. 24. S.

Earlston, a town of Scotland, in Berwickshire. Near it, on a rocky bank, stands Cowdenknows, an old building, now somewhat modernized; and on the adjacent knolls may be seen the remains of its broom, so renowned in Scottish ditty. Earlston is seated on the river Leader; 35 miles S. E. of Edinburgh.

Earn. *See* Erne.

Easdale, a small island of Scotland, near the coast of Argyleshire, to the S. E. of Mull; celebrated for its slate quarries, which abound throughout the whole island: it is also traversed in many places with basaltic veins and thin layers of quartzose and calcareous stones.

Easingwold, a town in the North riding of Yorkshire, with a market on Friday, and a great trade in bacon and butter. It is 13 miles N. N. W. of York, and 208 N. by W. of London.

Eastbourn, a town in Sussex, noted for plenty of the birds called wheatears, and as a place of resort for bathing. Near it is a chalybeate spring. In 1707 a tessellated pavement and a Roman bath were discovered here. It is seated near Beachy Head, in the English Channel; 15 miles E. S. E. of Lewes, and 61 S. S. E. of London.

East Cape, the most eastern extremity of Asia, on the W. side of Behring Strait, nearly opposite Prince of Wales Cape, on the continent of America. Long. 92. 20. E. lat. 59. 17. N.

East Looe. *See* Looe, East; and so with other places, the names of which are preceded by *East*.

Easter Island, or Teapy, an island in the Pacific Ocean; 12 leagues in circuit. It has a hilly and stony surface, is naturally barren, and affords neither safe anchorage, fresh water, nor wood for fuel. Rats are the only quadrupeds, and there are but few birds. The natives are industrious, and plant paper-mulberries and bananas, with regular fields of potatoes and yams. This island was seen by Davis in 1686; it was visited by Roggewin in 1722, and by Cork in 1774. Long. 109. 47. W. lat. 27. 6. S.

Easton, the name of several towns in North America:—

1. In Northampton county, Pennsylvania.
2. In Talbot county, Maryland.
3. In Bristol county, Massachusets, &c.

Eastport, the most eastern point of the United States of North America. The town is beautifully located on Moose Island, in Passamaquody Bay, and is favourably situate for carrying on an extensive traffic up the Passamaquody, and other rivers falling into the Bay of Fundy. Lat. 44. 43. N. and 10. 5. or about 530 statute miles in a meridional line N. E. of Washington, in the long. of 67. 14. W. of Greenwich.

Eastwood, a parish of Renfrewshire, Scotland, seated on the border of Lanarkshire; participating largely in the cotton manufacture.

Eaton Socon, a town in Bedfordshire, England; united with St. Neot's, in Huntingdonshire, by a handsome bridge over the river Ouse; 55 miles N. of London.

Eause, a town of France, in the department of Gers; 17 miles S. W. of Condom. Pop. 4000.

Ebeltoft, a town of Denmark, in Jutland with a good harbour, on a bay of the Cattegat; 16 miles N. E. of Aarhus.

Ebenezer, a town of the state of Georgia, capital of Effingham county, situate on the Savanna; 25 miles N. N. W. of Savanna.

Ebenfurth, a town of Austria, on the Leyta; 22 miles S. of Vienna.

Eberbach, a town of Germany, in the Lower Rhine, with a Cistertian abbey; seated on the Neckar; 11 miles E. by N. of Heidelberg; now included in the territory of Baden.

Ebermanstadt, a town of Franconia, in the principality of Bamberg, on the Wisent, near its entrance into the Rednitz; 13 miles S. S. E. of Bamberg.

Eberstein, a town and castle of Suabia; 8 miles S. by E. of Baden.

Eberville, a town of France, in the department of Puy de Dome, with a Benedictine abbey; seated on the Scioule; 8 miles N. of Riom.

Ebingen, a town of Wirtemberg, noted for its cheese; 7 miles S. of Hohenzollern. Pop. 3800,

Ebro, a river of Spain, the ancient Iberu, which rises in the mountains of Asturias, on the confines of Leon, about 60 miles from the shore of the Bay of Biscay, runs E. across the N. part of Old Castile, and afterwards, in a direction E. S. E., forming the boundary between that province and those of Biscay and Navarre: it then, in a S. E. direction, divides Arragon into nearly two equal parts, intersecting the S. part of Catalonia, and, after a course of 300 miles in a meridional line, and about 400 by the course of the stream, past Logrono, Calahorra, Tudela, and Saragossa, falls into the Mediterranean, a few miles below Tortosa;

There are several islands off its mouth, and a canal runs parallel with it through Arragon, used more for irrigation than navigation. The river is but little used for navigable purposes, on account of its numerous shoals and rapids.

ECCLES, a parish of Lancashire, consisting of five townships, on the W. side of MANCHESTER, (which see.)

ECCLESALL BIERLOW, a township in the parish of, and contiguous to Sheffield, on the S. W. side. *See* SHEFFIELD.

ECCLESFIELD, a town and parish; 5 miles N. of Sheffield. *See* SHEFFIELD.

ECCLESFECHAN, a town of Scotland, in Dumfriesshire, noted for its great monthly market for cattle; 5 miles N. of Annan, and 15 E. of Dumfries.

ECCLESHALL, a parish and town in Staffordshire, with a market on Friday. The bishop of Lichfield and Coventry has a castle here. It is seated on the river Sow; 7 miles N. W. of Stafford, and 148 of London. The parish consists of 21 small townships.

ECCLESIASTICAL STATE, or STATES OF THE CHURCH. *See* POPEDOM, &c.

ECHTERNACH, a town of the Netherlands, in Luxemburg, on the river Sour, surrounded by mountains; 18 miles N. E. of Luxemburg.

ECIJA, an episcopal and populous town of Spain, in Andalusia, with manufactures of leather and shoes, and a trade in wool and hemp. It is seated on the Xenil; 62 miles E. N. E. of Seville.

ECKARDSBERG, a town and castle of Upper Saxony, in Thuringia; 10 miles S. W. of Naumburg.

ECKERNFORDE, a seaport of Denmark, in South Jutland, on a bay of the Baltic. Near the town is a fresh-water lake, which is connected with the bay. It is 14 miles N. W. of Kiel, in Holstein. Long. 10. 1. W. lat. 54. 33. N.

ECKMUHL, a small town of Bavaria, near to which Buonaparte defeated the Austrians, in April, 1809; it is 13 miles S. by E. of Ratisbon, and about the same distance W. of Straubing, S. of the Danube.

EDAM, a town of North Holland, famous for its red rind cheeses; seated on the Ey, near the Zuyder Zee; 11 miles N. N. E. of Amsterdam.

EDDYSTONE, the name of some rocks in the English Channel, lying S. S. W. from the middle of Plymouth Sound, at the distance of 14 miles. On the principal rock (for the rest are under water) Mr. Winstanley built a lighthouse, in 1700, which was destroyed by a storm in 1703, and the projector perished in it. In 1709, another, built of wood, was erected by Mr. Rudyard, which was consumed by fire in 1755. Within four years after, one was built by Mr. Smeaton, which also was burnt down in 1770; and another, of stone, was completed by him in 1774, which has hitherto withstood the fury of the elements. The building, to the height of 33 feet from the foundation, is a solid mass of stones, engrafted into each other; above this are four rooms, one over the other, and at the top a gallery and lantern. It is nearly 80 feet high; and its distance from the Ram Head, the nearest point of land, is 12 miles. Long. 4. 24. W. lat. 50. 8. N.

EDEN, or EHDEN, a vill. on Mount Lebanon, pach. of Tripoli, in Syria, near the celebrated cedars. *See* BSHIRRAI.

EDEN, a river of Scotland, which rises in Perthshire, on the confines of Fifeshire, and flows through the latter county, by Cupar, into the German Ocean, at the bay of St. Andrew. Also another river in Scotland, in Berwickshire, falling into the Tweed; and another, which rises in Westmoreland, on the confines of Yorkshire. It runs N. by Appleby into Cumberland, and thence flows by Kirkoswald and Carlisle, into Solway Frith.

EDENTON, a town of North Carolina, capital of Chowan county: it formerly gave name to an extensive district, now divided into eight or nine counties, in the N. E. corner of the state. It is situate on Albemarle Sound, at the mouth of the Chowan; 110 miles E. by N. of Raleigh. Long. 77. 5. W. lat. 35. 38. N.

EDESSA, or VODENA, a town of European Turkey, in Macedonia, once the residence of the Macedonian kings. It is seated near the Viestrieza; 44 miles W. N. W. of Salonichi. Long. 22. 3. E. lat. 40. 50. N.

EDFOU, or EDFU, a town of Upper Egypt, the ancient Apollinopolis Parva, of which the principal remains are the ruins of two splendid temples, which are sumptuous specimens of the ancient Egyptian architecture.

EDGARTON. *See* MARTHA'S VINEYARD.

EDGBASTON, an out-parish of the town of BIRMINGHAM (which see).

EDGECOMBE, MOUNT, a hill on the W. side of the harbour of Devonport, from the summit of which is an enchanting prospect of the surrounding country, and the English Channel.

EDGECOMBE, an interior county on the E. part of N. Carolina, intersected by Tar river. Pop. 14,993. Tarborough, 60 miles E. of Raleigh, is the chief town.

EDGEFIELD, a district of S. Carolina, bounded on the S. W. by the Savannah river, comprising about 1500 square miles of surface. Pop. 32,852. The chief town, of the same name, in the centre of the county, is 63 miles E. S. E. of Colombia, and 140 S. S. E. of Savannah.

EDGEHILL, a village in Warwickshire, 14 miles S. of Warwick, memorable for the first battle fought between Charles I. and the parliament, in 1642: from the brow of the hill there is an extensive and delightful prospect over the vale of Redhorse.

EDGEWARE, a town in Middlesex; market on Thursday. It stands on the Roman road leading to St. Albans; 8 miles N. W. of London.

EDGEWORTHSTOWN, a town of Ireland, in the county of Longford; 66 miles from Dublin. This is the birth-place of Maria Edgeworth, and the residence of her father, Lovel Edgeworth, well known in the literary world.

EDINBURGHSHIRE; or MID LOTHIAN, a county of Scotland, bounded on the N. by the Frith of Forth, E. by the shires of Haddington, Berwick, and Roxburgh, S. by those of Selkirk, Peebles, and Lanark, and W. by Linlithgowshire. It is divided into 31 parishes, comprising an area of 230,000 acres, and sends one member to parliament. The soil is fertile, and produces corn of all sorts, with plenty of grass; also coal, iron, limestone, and black marble. The principal rivers are the N. and S. Esk, Leith, Amond, and Gala, all flowing into the Frith of Forth. *See* SCOTLAND.

EDINBURGH CITY, the chief place of the preceding county, and metropolis of Scotland, is seated about 1½ mile from the S. shore of the Frith of Forth, in the lat. of 55. 58. N., and 3. 13. of W. long.; 341 miles in a meridional line, and 398 by the mail line of road N. N. W. of London. It is surrounded by hills on every side but the N., and which form a magnificent amphitheatre; on the E. are Arthur's Seat and Salisbury Craigs—a range of almost perpendicular rocks—and the Calton hill, on the summit of which is erected a temple—a model of the Pantheon at Athens—a column to the memory of Lord Nelson, and an observatory; a road entering the town from the E. was cut through this rock in 1814. On the S. are the Pentland hills, and the hills of Braid; and on the W., are the Corstorphine mountains. The improvements of Edinburgh date from 1753, previous to which it had remained stationary for centuries, since that time the increase of handsome edifices, and its fine situation, have acquired for it the designation of the Modern Athens. Edinburgh is divided into three parts, standing on as many hills, which run from E. to W. in a direction almost parallel. On the middle ridge, which is narrow and steep, stands the Old Town; the North Town is seated on an elevated plain, gently sloping on every side; and the South Town stands also on a similar sloping eminence. The main or High-street of the Old Town is built along the centre ridge, 5570 feet in length, terminated at one end by Holyrood House, and at the other by a castle, seated on a high, craggy, and precipitous rock, 300 feet high, with a drawbridge on the only accessible side: here is shown the apartment in which was born James VI., of Scotland, afterwards James I. of England. In the High-street is the collegiate church of St. Giles, a fine Gothic structure, which has four places of public worship under its roof. Near this is the building in which the Scotch parliament were convened: it is now occupied by the courts of justice; and has a magnificent lofty hall. The palace of Holyrood House forms a grand quadrangle, with a court in the centre surrounded by piazzas: the N. W. towers were built by James V., and the whole was completed in the reign of Charles II. A spacious gallery here is hung with the pictures of 111 monarchs, from Fergus I., who reigned in 403, to James VI.—the greatest part of them imaginary. In the N. W. tower is shown the chamber where Queen Mary sat at supper, when Rizzio was dragged from her side and murdered, and the private staircase by which Ruthven entered with the assassins, to perpetrate the savage deed. Adjoining are magnificent ruins of an abbey, founded by David I., and converted by Charles II. into a royal chapel. The university, which was founded by James VI., in 1580, is celebrated throughout the world; and its medical school in particular is entitled to the first rank. The high school of Edinburgh has also been long famous for the scholars it has produced. Of the other buildings a few only can be noticed; the royal exchange, the register office, the physicians' hall, Heriot's hospital, for the education of 140 poor boys, Watson's hospital, for the support of decayed merchants, the royal infirmary, the public dispensary, and some other public charities. The city of Edinburgh is divided into 11 parishes, and 4 in the suburbs, and returns two members to parliament. The churches, both presbyterian and episcopal, and other places of worship, of various denominations, are numerous, and some of them beautiful edifices. It is now nearly united by its suburbs to the port of Leith, on the Frith of Forth, the principal residence of the merchants. There are two mineral springs near the village of Stockbridge, on the N., much frequented for scrofulous diseases, &c., one called St. Bernard's Well, surmounted by a beautiful temple erected by Lord Gardenstone; the other, the Jubilee Well. Edinburgh, as a whole, is a beautiful, picturesque, and interesting place. It is governed by a lord provost, a dean of guild, a guild council, and 25 common council. Here are 14 incorporated trades, each having its deacon or warden. Its principal importance is derived from the courts of justice, and the university and medical schools, which render it the focus of science and literature, and of polite society. Its manufactures are inconsiderable. Two miles to the S. are the remains of Craigmillar Castle, the residence of James V., during his minority, and of Queen Mary, after her return from France in 1562.

EDISTO, a river of South Carolina, which, after a course of about 140 miles, falls into the Atlantic Ocean by two channels, about 40 miles S. of Charleston. The island, formed by the divergence of the stream, contains about 3000 inhabitants, the greater part of whom are slaves.

EDKO, a lake and town of Lower Egypt, 15 miles S. W. from Rosetta.

EDMONTON, a village of Middlesex, England; 6 miles N. of Shoreditch church, London, on the great high road to Edinburgh. It has nothing but its thoroughfare to entitle it to notice.

EDWARDS, a county on the E. frontier of the state of Illinois; bounded by the great Wabash river; 35 miles from S. to N. and about 30 in mean breadth: the little Wabash intersects the W. side of the county; and, towards the S. part, between the two rivers, 40 miles above their entrance into the Ohio, is an English settlement, founded by an adventurer of the name of Birkbeck, in 1813; being a level country, the settlement is designated *Birkbeck's Prairie.*

EECLOO, a populous town of Belgium; 11 miles N. by W. of Ghent.

EFFERDING, a town of Austria, with a castle; seated near the S. bank of the Danube; 12 miles W. of Lintz.

Effingham, a village in Surrey; 12 miles N. E. of Guildford. It was once a much larger place, and supposed to have contained sixteen churches; wells, cavities like cellars, having been frequently found in the neighbouring fields and woods; and in the present church are some ancient stalls and monuments.

Effingham, a county in the state of Georgia, bordering on the Savannah river; its area comprises about 500 square miles. Pop. 3075, of whom 1433 are slaves. Springfield, the chief town, is 20 miles N. W. of the city of Savannah.

Egeln, a town and castle of Germany, in the duchy of Magdeburg, on the river Bode; 16 miles S. S. W. of Magdeburg.

Egenburg, a town of Austria, noted for good wine; 13 miles S. W. of Znaim in Moravia.

Eger, a river in Germany, which rises in the principality of Culmbach, running in an E.N.E. direction through the circle of Saaz, and, after a course of about 120 miles, falls into the Elbe, near Leutmeritz.

Eger, a fortified town at the western extremity of Bohemia, in the circle of Saaz, with a castle and college. It was taken by the French in 1742, but they were forced to evacuate it the next year, through famine. Here are manufactures of leather, hats, cloths, and stuffs; and its mineral waters are famous. It is seated on the Eger; 90 miles W. by N. of Prague. Long. 12. 27. E. lat. 50. 5. N. Pop. about 8000.

Egerseg Szala, a town of Lower Hungary; seated on the banks of the Szala, which falls into the S. end of Lake Balaton.

Egg, an island of Scotland, one of the Hebrides, to the S. of Skye, 5 miles in length, and from 2 to 3 in breadth. It is partly flat, and partly hilly and rocky, with some basaltic pillars. The low grounds are fertile.

Egg Harbour River, and Harbour, Great and Little, the former forming the S., and the other the N. boundary of Gloucester county, New Jersey; the harbours opening into the Atlantic Ocean, in the lat. of 39. 17. and 39. 30. N.

Egham, a village of England, in Surrey; 18 miles from Hyde Park Corner, London, on the great western road. On a plain, adjoining the river Thames, in this parish, known as Runnymede, the barons of England conferred with King John, and compelled him to sign Magna Charta, 19th June, 1215; which was done on a small island, still called Magna Charta Island.

Eglingen, a town of Suabia, capital of a lordship of the same name; 8 miles N. of Dillengen.

Eglisau, a town and castle of Switzerland, in the canton of Zurich; seated on the Rhine; 13 miles N. of Zurich.

Egmont op den Hoef, a village of Holland, in the province of North Holland; 3 miles W. by S. of Alkmaer. It appears to have been a considerable town, but was destroyed in 1573, by the enraged Spaniards, after their failure before Alkmaer. It now exhibits extensive and picturesque ruins, perhaps the only ruins in all Holland. Near it are two other villages: Egmont op Zee, a mile to the W. on the sea-coast; and Egmont Binnen, nearly two miles to the S., where a bloody but undecisive battle was fought in 1799, between the allied English and Russian army, and the French and Dutch.

Egremont, a town in Cumberland, with a market on Saturday. On the W. side is an artificial mount, with the ruins of a castle; and 3 miles S. E. of the town, in the wooded vale of the Calder, are the remains of the Calder abbey. Egremont is seated near the Irish Sea, on the river Eden; 5 miles S. S. E. of Whitehaven, and 289 N. W. of London.

Egypt, a country comprising the N. E. extremity of Africa, having about 400 miles of coast, between Alexandria and El Arisch, including the indentations of lakes and bays. Cape Bourlos, its N. extremity, is in lat. 31. 36. N., from which point it extends inland to the frontier of Nubia, in the lat. of about 24. 30., giving a length of about 500 miles, while its boundaries E. and W. are very undefined. It is divided from Asia, at its N. E. extremity, by an extensive desert, and further S. by the Gulf of Suez, and the Red Sea. *See* Suez. It is bounded on the W. by the deserts of Barca and Libya, and parts of Africa but little known, and in its extreme limits from W. to E. may be considered as comprising about 2 degrees of long. or 122 statute miles, between 31. and 33. E.; the inhabited parts, however, do not exceed more than 15 to 25 miles on each side of the Nile, which runs in a direction N. by W. through the whole extent of Egypt, except for about 120 miles above its entrance into the Mediterranean, where it diverges into two main, and numerous collateral channels. This is called the *Delta of the Nile;* comprising an area of about 12,000 square miles, studded, over the greater part, with towns and villages. This country, so celebrated in history for its fertility, its policy and arts, appears first to have obtained pre-eminence under the renowned Sesostris, about 1720 years antecedent to the Christian era. For nearly four centuries prior to this period, Egypt appears to have been divided into several petty sovereignties, under what were then termed *Hycsos*, or Shepherd Kings, of whom Amasis al Thetmosis was the first who gained an ascendancy over his compeers: this ascendancy was acquired about 100 years prior to that of Sesostris; and it appears to have been the descendants of Amasis who were ruling in Egypt at the time of the dearth in western Asia, when Jacob and his family established themselves in the valley of Gessen, or Goshen, E. of the Nile. From the descendants of Amasis and Sesostris sprung the race of the Pharaohs, who ruled over Egypt for twelve centuries, until Cambyses, king of Persia, became master of it, 525 years B. C.; and in their time all those wonderful structures were raised, and works perfected, which we cannot behold without astonishment. These are the pyramids, the labyrinths, the immense grottoes in the Thebaid, the obelisks, temples, and pompous palaces, the lake Mœris and the vast canals which served both for trade and to irrigate the land. After this conquest, Cambyses demolished the temples, disinterred the remains of Amasis, and burnt them, and persecuted the priests. This country continued under the Persian yoke till the time of Alexander of Macedon, who, having conquered Persia, built the city of Alexandria. He was succeeded by Ptolemy, the son of Lagos, 324 years B. C. Ten kings of that name succeeded each other, till Cleopatra, the sister of the last Ptolemy, ascended the throne; when Egypt became a Roman province, and continued so till the reign of Omar, the second caliph of the successors of Mahomet, who drove out the Romans after it had been in their hands 700 years. When the power of the caliphs declined, in the 13th century, Saladin set up the empire of the Mamelukes, which in time became so powerful, that they extended their dominions over a great part of Africa, Syria, and Arabia. Next, about 1570, Egypt yielded to the arms of Selim, the second emperor of the Turks. The present inhabitants are composed of four different races of people; the Turks, who assume to be masters of the country; the Saracen Arabs, who were conquered by the Turks; the Copts, who are descended from the first Egyptians that became Christians; and the Mamelukes, who were originally Circassian or Mingrelian slaves, and, being the only military force, continued for centuries to be the real masters of the country; and Egypt had been for many years distracted by the civil wars between the different contending beys, by which its twenty-four provinces were governed. The famous Hassen Ali, the Turkish admiral, gained several victories over them in 1786; but though he repressed, he could not totally subdue them. The French invaded Egypt in 1798, under Gen. Buonaparte, who defeated the beys in several engagements; but after the departure of Buonaparte, and a strong British force arriving to aid the country, the French were expelled in 1801. But the Turkish pacha, Mehemet Ali, finding the power of the Mamelukes broken by their conflicts with the French, invited them to his palace, under pretext of an entertainment, and then commenced a general slaughter of them. A few escaped, but the power of these tyrants of Egypt, and the possessors of nearly all the land, was broken, and has now been reduced to insignificance. The complexion of the Egyptians is of a dusky brown; they are generally indolent and cowardly; and the lower class are disgustingly filthy in their persons: the richer sort do nothing all day but drink coffee, smoke tobacco, and sleep; and they are ignorant, proud, haughty, and ridiculously vain. But the Copts are an ingenious people, and have great skill in business. From March to November, the heat, to a European, is almost insupportable; but the other months are more temperate. The south winds, which occur at intervals, from February to the end of May, are by the natives called poisonous winds, or the hot winds of the deserts; they are of such extreme heat and aridity, that no animated body exposed to them can withstand their fatal influence; and for the three days that they generally last, the streets are deserted. The sands are so subtle, that they penetrate into the closets, chests, and cabinets; which, with the hot winds, are probably the cause of sore eyes being so very common here. It rains very seldom in Egypt; but that want is fully supplied by the annual inundation of the Nile. When the waters retire, all the ground is covered with mud; then the corn is harrowed into it, and in the following March there is usually a plentiful harvest. But some lands are never fallow, and yield three harvests annually; particularly in Lower Egypt, where sowing and reaping are going on incessantly, wherever the water of the river can be obtained for irrigation. There is no place in the world better furnished with corn, flesh, fish, sugar, fruits, and all sorts of garden vegetables; and, in Lower Egypt, oranges, lemons, figs, dates, almonds, cassia, and plantains, are produced in great plenty. The ancient fertility of Egypt has been much extolled; that it was more so than at present, is problematical. The fact has lately been elicited, that the valley of the Nile, and the breadth of the cultivable land, has considerably and progressively increased, from the deposits of the Nile, which have in some places covered the ancient remains to the depth of seven feet; thus widening the ancient valley in proportion to the depth of the deposit. Lentiles form a considerable article of food to the inhabitants of Upper Egypt, who rarely enjoy the luxury of rice; and onions, remarkably mild, and of the purest white, continue to be a favourite diet among all classes. The animals of Egypt are tigers, hyenas, antelopes, apes, black cattle, fine horses, large asses, crocodiles, hippopotami, the camelion, the cerastes, or horned viper, and a kind of rat called ichneumon; eagles, hawks, pelicans, water-fowls of all kinds, and the ibis, which resembles a duck, and was deified by the ancient Egyptians, on account of its destroying serpents and noxious insects. The pyramids of Egypt, so justly celebrated as evidences of human labour and art, are all built on rocky and sandy plains; the largest is 500 feet in height, and covers 11 acres of ground. They are situate in the south part of the Delta, or Lower Egypt, on the W. bank of the Nile. Egypt is now spoken of as divided into three parts—Lower, or the Delta, Middle, and Upper. During the reign of some of the Pharaohs, Thebes in Upper Egypt, in the lat. of 25. 25., appears to have been the capital of the whole country; afterwards transferred to Memphis, in the lat. of 29.; and during the reign of the Ptolemies the seat of empire was transferred to Alexandria; whilst at the present time Cairo is the seat of government. Under the present pacha, Mehemet Ali, who has ruled since 1798, Egypt has made advances in enterprise and cultivation, almost without a precedent; and cotton, wool, indigo, sugar, and grain, are again forming the basis of an extensive external commerce. His government. however, is despotic, and his system monopoly; all the commerce is in his own hands; the manufacturer and the agriculturist deposit their produce in the public stores, and receive a moderate remuneration for them. The pacha then retails them for his own profit. He has instituted European tactics in his army, and the usages and sciences of more civilized life into his government; and has introduced many European men of science into the principal offices of the government. He is open to any suggestions, formerly thought incompatible with the Mussulman character. He has asserted his independence of the Ottoman Porte, but which has been disputed, and has led to warlike operations against him. Respecting the extent of the population of Egypt, information is very imperfect, both in reference to the past, as well as at the present time, being now variously estimated at from two to four millions: conjecture has hardly ever offered an opinion as to the number in former times. In further illustration of this very interesting section of the globe, *see* NILE, SUEZ, and THEBES.

EHINGEN, a town of Suabia, near which the Austrians were defeated by the French, in 1805. It is seated on the Danube; 12 miles S. W. of Ulm.

EHINGEN, another town of Suabia; seated on the Neckar, opposite Rotenberg; 6 miles W. by S. of Tubingen, and 25 S. S. W. of Stutgard; both these towns are in the dominions of the king of Wurtemberg, and contain each about 4000 inhabitants.

EHRENBREITSTEIN, a fortress of Germany, in the circle of Lower Rhine, on the E. bank of the river Rhine, opposite Coblentz. It stands on the summit of a stupendous rock, not less than 800 feet above the level of the river, and is deemed to be impregnable. It has a communication with Coblentz by a subterraneous passage, cut out of the solid rock, and is plentifully supplied with water from a well 280 feet deep. In the vale of Ehrenbreitstein is an old palace which belonged to the Elector of Treves. This fortress surrendered to the French through famine, in 1799, after a blockade of above 20 months.

EIBENSTOCK, or EYBENSTOCK, a town of Upper Saxony, in the circle of Erzeberg, near the N. W. frontier of Bohemia 60 miles S. by E. of Leipsic. Pop. 3200.

EICHSFELDT, a territory of Germany, at the N. E. extremity of the circle of the Lower Rhine; surrounded by Brunswick, Thuringia, and Hesse. It produces much flax and tobacco. Heiligenstadt is the capital. It is now divided between Prussia and Hanover: it formerly belonged to the Elector of Mentz, and contained a population of 90,000, on a surface of about 600 square miles. Stadt Worbis and Mulhausen are the other principal towns.

EICHSTADT. *See* AICHSTADT.

EIL LOCH. *See* LINNHE, LOCH.

EILENBURG, a town of Upper Saxony, in Misnia, situate on the Mulda; 12 miles N. E. of Leipsic.

EIMEO, one of the Society Isles, in the Pacific Ocean; lying 12 miles W. of Otaheite. The products of the two islands, and the manners of the people, are much the same. Eimeo has steep, rugged hills, running in different directions, leaving large valleys, and gently rising ground about their sides. The hills, though rocky, are generally covered with trees almost to the tops.

EINBECK, a fortified town of Lower Saxony, in the principality of Calenberg. It has manufactures of cloth, and all kinds of stuffs; and in the mountains near it are mines of silver, iron, copper, and lead. It is situate 17 miles N. of Gottingen, and 45 S. of Hanover. Pop. about 5000.

EISENACH, or EYSENACH, a town of Upper Saxony, at the western extremity of Thuringia, capital of a principality of the same name, with a celebrated college. The duke resides in a castle within the town; and there is another on a mountain out of it, called Wartburg, which, in 1521, was for some time the asylum of Luther. It is seated on the Nesse, at its conflux with the Horsel; 16 miles W. of Gotha. Long. 10. 21. E. lat. 51. 0. N. Pop. about 8000.

EISENARTZ, or EISENITZ, a town of Germany, in Styria, famous for its iron miles; 34 miles N. N. W. of Gratz.

EISENBERG, another town in Thuringia; 35 miles S. W. of Leipsic. Pop. 3500.

EISENSTADT, a town of Hungary, with a magnificent palace; 5 miles N. W. of Oldenburg, and 27 S. of Vienna.

EISLEBEN, a town of Upper Saxony, capital of the county of Mansfield, with a decayed castle. The celebrated Luther was born and died here. In the churches of St. Andrew and St. Ann are the superb burial places of the ancient counts of Mansfield. Eisleben contains many breweries, and derives much profit from the neighbouring iron mines. It is 28 miles N. N. W. of Naumburg. Long. 11. 47. E. lat. 51. 32. N.

EISSFELD, a town of Upper Saxony, in the principality of Coburg, with a castle. It has manufactures of vitriol, &c., and stands on the Werra, near its source; 7 miles E. of Hildburghausen.

EKATERINBURG. *See* CATHARINBURG.

ELBA, an island in the Mediterranean Sea, between Italy and the island of Corsica, and separated from Tuscany by the channel of Piombino. It was known to the Greeks by the name of Æthalia, and to the Romans by that of Ilva. The form of the island is very irregular; the length from E. to W. is about 14 miles, and the greatest breadth, which is at the W. end, is between 8 and 9 miles: it contains a population of about 14,000 souls. The whole island presents numerous mountains, separated by deep valleys, and some plains of considerable extent; the S.W. part is the most elevated, and is composed of black and white granite, susceptible of a fine polish. Elba has been renowned for its mines of iron and loadstone, for a period beyond the reach of history. Aristotle speaks of them as opened from time immemorial: it has also quarries of fine marble. On the N. E. part is the mountain, or mine of iron ore, which supplies most of the forges of Italy. The tower of Voltorajo stands on this mountain, on a shaggy rock. The view from this tower is wonderfully fine every way, as the eye overlooks the whole island, that of Corsica, many scattered islets, the channel of Piombino, and a great range of continent. On the E. side of the mountain stands Rio, a village inhabited by miners. Under it breaks out the only rivulet in Elba, which does not run above a mile before it falls into the sea; but the water gushes out of the rock in such abundance, that it turns seventeen mills in that short course. The soil of Elba is very shallow, with scanty room for cultivation, and few places level enough for corn, producing little more than six months' provisions for its inhabitants: but the island is so situated that it can, in spite of a blockading fleet, be always supplied with provisions, and the garrison with reinforcements. The wine is good, if made with care, and properly kept; the fruit of its standard trees are excellent, though not in great plenty; orange and lemon trees thrive very well in the sheltered valleys and narrow plains near the sea. There are several springs of excellent water in the island; and the climate is much milder than the adjacent continent, for it produces many fruits and plants that cannot stand the Tuscan winters. Among the animals and birds are wild boars, hedgehogs, partridges, quails, canary-birds, nightingales, ortolans, &c. This island was held with Piombino, by the Appiani, as a fief of the empire, till Charles V. thought proper to transfer it to Cosmo I. duke of Florence, that he might rescue it and the adjacent coast from the Turks and French. Before the French Revolution, it was subject to the Prince of Piombino, except Porto Ferrajo and Porto Longone, the former belonging to the Duke of Tuscany, and the latter to the king of Naples; but in 1801 the French became possessed of the whole island, which owes its celebrity to the circumstance of its having been ceded by the powers of Europe in full sovereignty to Napoleon Buonaparte, after the surrender of Paris to the allies in March, 1814. He landed at Porto Ferrajo, the capital of the island, on the 4th of May in that year, but on the 26th of February following, he embarked again for France, and reached Paris without encountering the least obstruction; since when, the island has been wholly ceded to the Grand Duke of Tuscany. Porto Ferrajo, on the N. side of the island, is in lat. 42. 50. N. and 10. 15. of E. long.

Elbassano, a town of European Turkey, in Albania; 45 miles S. E. of Durazzo.

Elbe, a river of Europe, rising on the N. E. frontier of Bohemia, bordering on Silesia, in the lat. of 50. 30. N. and 15. 35. of E. long., flows S. for about 40 miles past Konigingratz to Pardubitz, in the circle of Chrudim, from whence it takes a meandering course in a N. W. direction to Melnick, where it receives the Moldau from the frontiers of Austria on the S.: from Melnick it continues a winding course through the circle of Leutmeritz, in which it receives the Eger from the frontier of Franconia, on the W. S.W., and then enters the circle of Meissen in Upper Saxony, still running in a N. W. direction past Dresden into the duchy of Saxony to Magdeburg; from whence it takes a direction N. by E. to Havelberg, where it receives the Havel; from Havelberg it intersects, in a N.W. direction, the Old Mark of Brandenburg, and then divides Mecklenburg Schwerin, and the duchy of Saxe Lauenburg on the N., from Luneburg Zell to Hamburg; from whence it becomes navigable for ships of the largest burthen, dividing for about 70 miles the duchy of Holstein on the N. from Bremen on the S., and, after a course of 380 miles in a meridional line, and upwards of 500 miles by the course of the stream, falls into the North Sea at Cuxhaven, in the lat. of 53. 52. N. and 8. 46. of E. long. The Elbe is rendered subservient to the purposes of navigation, and, by itself and numerous collateral branches, receives and distributes produce along various lines of country several hundred miles in extent. *See* Lubec.

Elberfeldt, or Elverfeldt, a town of the grand duchy of Berg; seated on the banks of the Wipper, which falls into the Rhine between Cologne and Dusseldorf. It has extensive manufactures of linen, silk, and wool, and a population of near 20,000. It is 18 miles due E. of Dusseldorf.

Elbeuf, a town of France, in the department of Lower Seine. It has extensive manufactures of cloth, and is seated on the Seine; 10 miles S. of Rouen, and 65 N. W. of Paris.

Elbert, a county of the state of Georgia; lying between the Savannah and Broad Rivers. Population, 11,125, of whom 4975 were slaves. Elbert, the chief town, is 190 miles N. W. of the city of Savannah.

Elbing, a strong town of West Prussia, in the palatinate of Marienburg, with a considerable trade in butter, cheese, and corn. It is seated on a river of the same name, near its entrance into the Frische Haff; 30 miles E.S.E. of Dantzic. Long. 19. 30. E. lat. 54. 18. N. Pop. about 18,000.

Elbogen, a town of Bohemia, in the circl of Saatz, with a citadel, seated on a mountain, by the river Eger; 10 miles N. E. of Egra.

Elburg, a town of Holland, in Gelderland, on the E. coast of the Zuyder Zee; 10 miles N. E. of Harderwick.

Elche, Albufera de, a town of Spain, in Valencia; 10 miles W. S. W. of Alicant.

Elchingen, a village of Suabia, on the N. bank of the Danube, about 5 miles N. E. of Ulm, where a battle was fought between the French and Austrians, in 1805, which obtained for Ney, one of Buonaparte's generals, the title of Duke of Elchingen.

Elda, a town of Spain, in Valencia; 20 miles W. N. W. of Alicant.

Elephanta, called by the natives *Gharipoor*, an island on the W. coast of Hindostan; 5 miles from Bombay. It contains one of the most celebrated temples of the Hindoos. The figure of an elephant, of the natural size, cut coarsely in stone, appears on the landing-place, near the foot of a mountain. An easy slope then leads to a subterranean temple, hewn out of the solid rock, 80 feet long and 40 broad, the roof supported by rows of pillars 10 feet high. At the further end are gigantic figures of the three Hindoo deities, Brahma, Vishna, and Seva, which were mutilated by the zeal of the Portuguese, when this island was in their possession. Elephanta was ceded to the English by the Mahrattas.

ELEPHANTINA. *See* SYENE.

ELEUTHS, a kingdom of Tartary, lying to the N. W. of Chinese Tartary. It was conquered in 1759 by the Emperor of China. *See* KALMUCKS.

ELEUTHERA, or ETHERA, an island in the West Indies, one of the principal on the Bahama bank. It produces abundance of pineapples, and there is a magnificent tunnel piercing the island from end to end, formed by the sea.

ELGIN, a borough of Scotland, capital of Murrayshire, and formerly the see of a bishop. Here are many large old buildings over piazzas. Its cathedral was one of the most magnificent structures in Scotland; of which its ruins are a sufficient proof. Two miles to the N. E., on the banks of a lake, is the palace of Spynie, formerly the residence of the bishop, of which some rooms are still pretty entire. Elgin stands on the Lossie, 5 miles from its port at Lossiemouth, where there is a tolerable harbour, whence much corn is exported. It sends, in conjunction with Cullen, &c. one member to parliament. It is 38 miles E. N. E. of Inverness, and 163 N. of Edinburgh.

ELGINSHIRE. *See* MURRAYSHIRE.

ELINGE, a village of Hampshire, at the head of Southampton Bay, 5 miles W. of Southampton. Here are docks for building and repairing ships, and store-houses for merchandise and corn, in which last it carries on a considerable trade.

ELIZABETH CITY, a small county of Virginia, forming the promontory between the mouths of York and James Rivers, into Chesapeake Bay. Pop. 3706. The town is called Hampton, and gives name to the celebrated anchorage ground, called Hampton Roads, at the entrance of James River. A town of the same name is seated on the Pasquotank river, in North Carolina, which is united with Chesapeake Bay, by the canal cut through the Great Dismal Swamp.

ELIZABETH ISLANDS, small islands near the coast of Massachusets, bearing N.W. of Martha's Vineyard, and belonging to Duke's county. They are about 16 in number; the chief of which are Nashawn, Pasqui, Nashawenna, Pinequese, and Chatahunk. Nashawn, the largest, supports a considerable number of cattle and sheep, and is famous for excellent cheese and wool. It is 2 miles from the continent, and the N. point 6 miles W. S. W. of Falmouth. Long. 70. 38. W. lat. 41. 34. N.

ELIZABETHTOWN, a town of New Jersey, in Essex county, with a handsome Presbyterian church, an episcopal church, and an academy. It is situate on a creek of Newark Bay; 14 miles W. S. W. of the city of New York.

ELIZABETHTOWN, a town of North Carolina, chief of Bladen county; seated on the W. bank of Cape Fear River; 36 miles S. by W. of Fayetteville, and 48 N. W. of Wilmington.

ELIZABETHTOWN, or HAGERSTOWN, a town of Maryland, chief of Washington county. It has a considerable trade with the western country, and the neighbourhood produces the finest Oroonoko tobacco. It is situate in a valley; 70 miles W. N. W. of Baltimore, and 80 N. N. W. of Washington.

There are several other places so called in different parts of the United States of North America; one in Allegany county, Pennsylvania, on the E. bank of the Monangahela; another in Pleasant Valley, Essex county, New York, near the W. shore of Lake Champlain.

ELK, a river of Maryland, which falls into the head of Chesapeake Bay; which is proposed to be united with the Delaware, by the Elk river.

There are several other rivers and creeks so called, as well as *Elk-horn*, *lick*, and *ridge*, in different parts of the United States of North America.

ELKTON, a town of Maryland, chief of Cecil county, with a considerable trade, particularly in wheat. It is situate at the conflux of the head branches of the Elk, 13 miles from its mouth in Chesapeake Bay, and 47 S. W. of Philadelphia. Long. 76. 20. W. lat. 39. 40. N.

ELLESMERE, a town in Shropshire, with a market on Tuesday, and a considerable trade in malt. It has a canal from Shrewsbury, which passes hence, by Wrexham and Chester, to the estuary of the Mersey. The town is seated on a large mere; 16 miles N. N. W. of Shrewsbury, and 178 N. W. of London.

ELLICHPOUR, or ELLISHPOOR, a town of Hindostan, in Berar, capital of a circar of the same name, subject to the nizam of the Deccan. It was formerly the capital of Berar, and is 154 miles N. E. of Aurungabad. Long. 78. 5. E. lat. 21. 12. N.

ELLORE, a town of Hindostan, capital of one of the circars, on the Bay of Bengal. It is 32 miles N. of Masulipatam. Long. 81. 15. E. lat. 16. 43. N.

ELMINA, or ST. GEORGE DEL MINA, a town of West Africa, on the Gold Coast, founded by the Portuguese in 1481. It is seated on a peninsula, near a navigable river, and trades in gold-dust and ivory. It was taken in 1637 by the Dutch, and was formally ceded to them.

ELMSHORN, a town of Denmark, in the duchy of Holstein; 20 miles N. W. of Hamburgh.

ELNBOGEN, a town of Bohemia, capital of a territory in the circle of Saatz, with a castle on a rock, by the river Egra; 38 miles W. S. W. of Saatz. Long. 12. 50. E. lat. 50. 10. N.

ELNE, a town of France, in the department of Eastern Pyrenees. It suffered greatly in the civil wars, during the reign of Louis XI. It is 8 miles S. by E. of Perpignan.

ELORA, a town of Hindostan, in Dowlatabad, celebrated for its wonderful temple, cut out of the natural rock. It is 15 miles N. of Aurungabad.

ELPHIN, a town of Ireland, in the county of Roscommon, and the see of a bishop; 16 miles N. of Roscommon.

ELRICH, a town of Upper Saxony, in Thuringia; the capital of the county of Hohenstein.

It stands on the river Zorge; 12 miles N. N. W. of Nordhausen. Long. 10. 43. E. lat. 51. 38. N.

ELSFLET, a town of Westphalia, at the conflux of the Huntorf with the Weser; 13 miles E. N. E. of Oldenburg, and 12 N. W. of Bremen.

ELSINBURG. *See* HELSINBURGH.

ELSINORE, a town of Denmark, seated on the Sound, in the Isle of Zealand. It is the most commercial place in Denmark, next to Copenhagen, being the residence of a considerable number of foreign merchants, and the consuls of the principal nations trading to the Baltic. A little to the E. is the fortress of Cronborg, which guards the Sound. Every vessel, as it passes, pays a toll at Elsinore; in return for which, the crown takes the charge of constructing lighthouses, and erecting signals to mark the shoals and rocks, from the Categat to the entrance into the Baltic. Elsinore has no harbour, but a good and safe road. It is 22 miles N. of Copenhagen. Long. 12. 35. E. lat. 56. 0. N. *See* CRONBORG.

ELSTER, WHITE and BLACK, two rivers of Upper Saxony: the first rises near the northern frontier of Franconia, and runs N. nearly parallel with, and E. of the Saal, into which it falls about 18 miles N. W. of Leipsic; this river proved very disastrous to the French troops, on their retreat after the battle of Leipsic, in October 1813. The Black Elster rises near the Spree in Upper Lusatia, and after a winding course E. of the Elbe, falls into that river in the duchy of Saxony.

ELSTERBERG, a town on the W. bank of the White Elster, near its source; 7 miles N. of Plauen.

ELSTERWERDA, a town and castle of Upper Saxony, in Misnia, on the E. bank of the Black Elster; 24 miles N. by W. of Dresden.

ELTHAM, a town in Kent, with a market on Monday. Here are the remains of a palace, in which Edward II. often resided, and his son, John of Eltham, was born; it is now in part converted into a farm-house, and the stately hall forms the barn. It is 8 miles S. W. of London Bridge.

ELVAS, a strong frontier town of Portugal, in Alentejo, and a bishop's see, with a castle. Here is a cistern so large, that it will hold water enough for the town for six months. The water is brought by a Moorish aqueduct, 3 miles in length, which, in some places, is supported by several stories of arches. On the side of it is a forest of olive-trees, among which are walks and fine mountains. Elvas was bombarded by the French in 1706. A royal academy for young gentlemen was founded here in 1733. It is seated near the Guadiana; 15 miles W. of Badajos, and 118 E. of Lisbon. Pop. about 16,000.

ELWANGEN, a town of Suabia, near the S. frontier of Franconia, with a castle on a mountain; seated on the Jaxt; 18 miles N. W. of Nordingen.

ELY, a city in Cambridgeshire, and a bishop's see, with a market on Saturday. It is seated on the Ouse (which is navigable hence to Lynn), in the fenny tract called the Isle of Ely. The spring assizes are held here. It is a county of itself, including the territory around it, and has a distinct civil and criminal jurisdiction, of which the bishop is the head. It has a fine cathedral, and an episcopal palace. It is 17 miles N. of Cambridge, and 67 N. by E. of London.

ELY, or ELIE, a town of Scotland, on the S. E. coast of Fifeshire, with a good harbour. with upwards of 20 feet water at common tide, but has little trade. It is opposite to North Berwick, and forms the N. point of entrance to the Frith of Forth.

ELZE, a town of Lower Saxony, in the principality of Hildesheim; seated on the Leina; 12 miles S. W. of Hildesheim, and 20 S. of Hanover.

EMBOLY, or JEMBOLI, a town of European Turkey, in Macedonia, and a Greek archbishop's see. It is the ancient Amphipolis, and is sometimes called Christopolis. It is seated on the Strumona, at its entrance into the Gulf of Contessa. Long. 23. 55. E. lat. 40. 59. N.

EMBRUN, a city of France, in the department of Upper Alps. It has a fortress built by Louis XIV., and is seated on a craggy rock, near the river Durance; 17 miles E. of Gap. It is the seat of a prefect, and contains 3002 inhabitants.

EMDEN, a strong town of Westphalia, capital of E. Friesland. It has a good harbour and a safe road at the mouth of the Ems; and considerable manufactures of stockings, soap, leather, and cotton. The greatest part of the inhabitants are Calvinists, but there are some Lutherans, Papists, and Jews. It was a free port under the protection of the United Provinces, but in 1744 they sold their right to the King of Prussia. It was a neutral port during the early part of the war between England and France, which began in 1793. It is now included in the kingdom of Hanover; population, about 12,000. It is 28 miles E. N. E. of Groningen, and 47 W. N. W. of Oldenburg. Long. 7. 8. E. lat. 53. 20. N.

EMMENDINGEN, a town of Suabia, in Brisgau, and chief town in the marquisate of Hochberg: seated on the river Ens; 10 miles N. by W. of Friburg.

EMMERICK, a strong town of Germany, in the duchy of Cleve. It has a considerable trade with Holland, and is seated on the Rhine; 22 miles N. W. of Wesel.

EMS, a river of Westphalia, which rises in the territory of Paderborn, and, after a course of about 150 miles in a N. N. W. direction, flows, at Emden, into the Dollart, a bay of the German Ocean.

EMS, or EMBS, a town of Germany, in Tyrol, near which are some baths impregnated with sulphur. It is 10 miles S. E. of the Lake of Constance.

ENCHUYSEN, or ENKHUYZEN, a town of North Holland, on the Zuyder Zee. It was once a flourishing place; but, its harbour being now obstructed by sand, it has lost its former consequence. It was taken by the English in 1709. It is 27 miles N. E. of Amsterdam.

Endeavour Strait, a strait of the South Pacific Ocean, which separates New Guinea from the N. E. point of New Holland. It received its name from Captain Cook, who explored it in 1770. Its length is 10 leagues, and its breadth about 5, except at the N. E. entrance, where it is contracted to less than 2 miles, by the islands called Prince of Wales Islands.

Endingen, a town of Suabia, in Brisgau, near the Rhine; 7 miles N. N. E. of Old Brisach.

Enfield, a town in Middlesex, with a market on Saturday. It was once famous for an extensive royal chase, disforested in 1779; and had a royal palace, of which little now remains, the front having been taken down in 1792, and its site occupied by some houses. It is 10 miles N. of London.

Enfield, a town of Connecticut, in Hartford county, situate on the E. bank of the Connecticut; 16 miles N. by E. of Hartford. Also the name of another town in Grafton county, New Hampshire.

Engadine, or **Inthal**, a delightful valley of Switzerland, in the canton of Grisons, extending along the banks of the river Inn, from its source to Tyrol. It is divided into Upper and Lower; the chief towns are Zurz and Cernetz.

Engelberg, a valley of Switzerland, in the canton of Underwalden; 10 miles long; surrounded by mountains. It is subject to the abbot of a Benedictine monastery of the same name, whose revenues arise principally from a commerce in cheese The country contains extensive glaciers, on the side of fertile mountains; fine black marble, white veined, small crystals called Swiss diamonds, silver, and vitriol. The abbey is 12 miles S. W. of Altdorf.

Engelholm, a seaport of Sweden, in Schonen, on a bay of the Categat, with good anchorage near the entrance to the Sound. In 1678 it was taken by the Danes, after an obstinate defence. It is 44 miles N. by W. of Lund. Long. 12. 57. E. lat. 56. 22. N.

Engers, a town of Germany, in the Westerwald; capital of a county of its name; seated near the Rhine; 5 miles N.W. of Coblentz.

Enghein, a town of Belgium, in Hainault, 15 miles S. W. of Brussels, on the road to Tournay. It gave the title of duke to one of the Bourbon family.

Enghia, **Egina**, or **Ægina**, (its ancient name,) an island of European Turkey, in the Gulf of Egina, between Livadia and the Morea. It has a town of the same name; 22 miles S. S. W. of Athens. Long. 23. 39. E. lat. 37. 45. N.

England, the southern part of the island of Great Britain, is a very irregularly shaped territory, extending, in its extreme length, from the Land's End in Cornwall, in the lat. of 50. 4. 7. and long. of 5. 41. 31. to Berwick, at the mouth of the Tweed, which divides it from Scotland, in the lat. of 55. 46. 21. N., and 1. 59. 41. of W. long. The meridional distance between these two points is 366 geographical, or 425 English statute miles; this line, however, intersects the entrance to the Bristol Channel, South and North Wales, and the Irish Sea; the extreme meridional line that could be drawn on English ground from N. to S., would be from Berwick to St. Alban's Head, in the county of Dorset: this line would measure 366 statute miles; and the extreme length from W. to E. would be from the Land's End, Cornwall, to the Dudgeon light, on the N. E. coast of Norfolk, which would measure 359 statute miles. The four S. E. counties of Somerset, Dorset, Devon, and Cornwall, however, form a promontory; and, as the superficial area of England, by actual survey, proves to be 50,535 square miles, taking the length from N. to S. to be 306 miles, the mean breadth from W. to E. will be within 150 miles. The sea on the S. is called the English Channel, and which divides England from the N. W. coast of France: the sea at the S. E. point is called the Straits of Dover, and divides England from the N. W. point of France and the Netherlands; the sea on the E. coast of England is called the North Sea, or German Ocean, and divides England from Holland, Germany, and Denmark; the sea on the N.W. coast of England is called the Irish Sea, and divides England from the N. E. coast of Ireland. Wales, North and South, bound the centre of its western side; and the four S. W. counties before mentioned project into the Atlantic Ocean. England, for local purposes, is divided into 40 counties; viz. Bedford, Berks, Bucks, Cambridge, Chester, Cornwall, Cumberland, Derby, Devon, Dorset, Durham, Essex, Gloucester, Hants, Hereford, Huntingdon, Hertford, Kent, Lancaster, Leicester, Lincoln, Middlesex, Monmouth, Norfolk, Northampton, Northumberland, Nottingham, Oxford, Rutland, Salop, Somerset, Stafford, Suffolk, Surrey, Sussex, Warwick, Westmoreland, Wilts, Worcester, and York; each of which is subdivided into hundreds and parishes. For judicial purposes it is divided into six circuits; and for ecclesiastical purposes into two archiepiscopal and 23 episcopal sees, or jurisdictions. The extent, relations, &c., of each of the several counties, towns, &c., are noticed in their alphabetical place in this work.

The face of the country affords all that beautiful variety which can be found in the most extensive tracts of the globe; not, however, without romantic, and even dreary scenes, lofty mountains, craggy rocks, black barren moors, and wide uncultivated heaths; and yet, few countries have a smaller proportion of land absolutely sterile and incapable of culture. The richest parts are, in general, the midland and southern. Towards the N. it partakes of the barrenness of the adjoining parts of Scotland. The E. coast is, in many places, sandy and marshy. A range of rude and elevated land, sometimes rising into mountains 3000 feet in height, extends from the borders of Scotland to the very heart of England, forming a natural division between the E. and W. sides of the kingdom. Cornwall is also a rough hilly tract; and a similar character prevails in part of the adjacent counties. These mountainous tracts abound with various mineral treasures, more particularly coal, iron, copper, lead, and tin.

The rivers of England are numerous, and contribute essentially to the beauty and fertility of the country, as well as to facilitate the conveyance of its products from one part of the kingdom to another: the four most deserving of notice for their magnitude and utility, are the Trent, Mersey, *Severn, and Thames. These four rivers rise in the interior of the country, and flow in contrary directions; the first to the N. E., the next to the N. W., the Severn to the S.W., and the Thames to the S. E.; and, being rendered navigable, and united to each other by canals, they afford an admirable facility of conveyance over all parts of the country. In addition to these, the great Ouse and the Nen flow from the centre of the country in a N. E. direction, into the North Sea, between the Thames and the Trent, and the Nen is united to the line of canal which unites those two rivers, and thereby with the Mersey and Severn. Further N. is the Humber, *Tees, Wear, *Tyne, and the *Tweed, which divides England from Scotland, all flowing from W. to E. into the North Sea: and on the other side is the *Eden, *Derwent, Ribble, and the *Dee, flowing into the Irish Sea: the tributary rivers deserving of notice are the Medway and Lea, falling into the Thames; the Soar and Derwent falling into the Trent; the Don, Aire, and Ouse, falling into the Humber; the Irwell into the Mersey; and the Upper and Lower Avon and Wye into the Severn; all of which are navigable, and yield a variety of fish; those noted with a * yielding an abundance of delicious salmon. The Tamar, Torridge, Tame, Exe, Arun, and a few other rivers of inferior note, intersect the S. and S.W. parts of the country, falling into the Bristol and English Channels. The lakes are neither numerous nor extensive, and are chiefly in the N.W. counties: those of Westmoreland and Cumberland, in particular, exhibit such varieties of beautiful scenery, as to become the object of summer excursions from every part of the country. With respect to climate, England is situate in the N. part of the temperate zone, so that it enjoys but a scanty share of the genial influence of the sun. Its atmosphere is inclined to chilliness and moisture, subject to frequent and sudden changes, and is more favourable to the growth, than to the ripening of the products of the earth. No country is clothed with so beautiful and lasting a verdure; but the harvests, especially in the northern parts, frequently suffer from unseasonable rains. The country, nevertheless, in general, affords an abundant supply of grain, and all the other necessaries of life, and the rigours of winter, and the heats of summer, are felt here in a much less degree than in parallel climates on the continent; a circumstance common to all islands. The whole country, some particular spots excepted, is sufficiently healthy; and the longevity of its inhabitants is equal to that of almost any region. All its most valuable productions, both animal and vegetable, have been imported from foreign countries, and have been kept up and improved by constant attention. England has now no other wild quadrupeds than those of the smaller kind, as the fox, badger, marten, otter, hare, rabbit, squirrel, &c. On the other hand, every kind of domestic animal, imported from abroad, has been reared to the greatest degree of perfection. The horse has been trained up for all the various purposes of strength and swiftness, so as to excel in those qualities the same animal in every other country. The breeds of cattle, in various parts of the kingdom, have also been cultivated with much care, and have been brought to the largest size and greatest justness of shape. The different races of sheep are variously distinguished, either for uncommon size, goodness of flesh, or plenty or fineness of wool. The deer of its parks, which are originally a foreign breed, are superior in beauty of skin, and delicacy of flesh, to those of most countries. Even the several kinds of dogs have been trained to degrees of courage, strength, and sagacity, rarely to be met with elsewhere. Domestic poultry, as well as wild birds, are numerous; the shape and beauty of plumage of the pheasant, and delicious note of the nightingale, cannot be surpassed. The improvement in the vegetable products of this island is not less striking than in the animal. Nuts, acorns, crabs, and a few wild berries, were almost all the variety of vegetable food which its woods could boast. To other countries, and to the efforts of culture, it is indebted for corn, esculent roots, plants, and all its garden fruits. The seas, as well as the rivers of England, are stocked with a great variety of fish, which yield a plentiful article of provision to all ranks of people.

Of the early history of England but little is known prior to its becoming a province of the Roman empire, during the first century of the Christian era. The first invasion of England by the Romans was under Julius Cæsar, in the year 35, at which period the country was inhabited by a very numerous but hardy and rude race of people, denominated Britons, living in tribes and subject to an austere and rigorous priesthood; about the year 86, the whole country, after numerous conflicts, was subdued under Agricola. During a period of nearly 400 years, from the time of Agricola to the year 447, when the Romans finally quitted the island, they had effectually succeeded in reconciling the natives to a dependence on their government, and in diffusing a taste and desire to cultivate and practise the arts of social life; they had, however, so implicitly yielded to Roman government and protection, that, on being left to govern and protect themselves, they were unable to withstand the rude and vigorous attacks of the Picts and Scots, who poured into the country from the N.; and the Romans, on being applied to by the Britons, declining, from inability, to render them assistance, the Britons invited the assistance of the Saxons, a people who had acquired celebrity for their valour in the N. of Europe. In the year 449, Hengist and Horsa, two Saxon leaders, arrived with a force of 1600 men, who succeeded in speedily subduing the Scots and Picts; but, perceiving the inefficiency of the

Britons, the Saxons obtained a succession of reinforcements, made allies of the Scots and Picts, and turned their whole force to the subjugation of England; and, in the progress of time, the country became divided into seven monarchies, some one of which, however, in its turn, maintaining an ascendancy over the rest, the ascendant monarch being regarded as king of England. The following is a list of the seven monarchies, with the dates of their foundation and extinction: viz.—

Kent	founded in	454	extinct	823
South Saxons .	„	491	„	685
East Saxons . .	„	527	„	827
Northumberland	„	547	„	827
East Angles . .	„	575	„	792
Mercia . . .	„	582	„	827
West Saxons .	„	592	„	828

This period is denominated the Heptarchy, which merged into an undivided sovereignty under Egbert, the 17th king of the West Saxons, in 828. In 860 the Saxon dynasty in its turn was assailed by the Danes, and, after repeated conflicts and aggressions, Sweyne, a Dane, was crowned king of England in 1013. The crown reverted again to the Saxons in Edward, surnamed the Confessor, in 1042; but on the 14th of October, 1066, the destinies of England were placed in the hands of William of Normandy, surnamed the Conqueror, from the decisive victory he gained on that day over Harold II., king of England. From that period to the present time, the whole country has been under the rule of a successive line of kings, except for 11 years, from 1649 to 1660, when it was under a protectorate, in consequence of the arbitrary measures of the monarch having led to his decapitation on the 30th of January, 1649.

ENGLAND, NEW, the N. E. part of the United States of North America, extending from the lat. of 41. to 48. N., thus first named by Captain Smith, in 1614. It is bounded on the N. by Canada, on the E. by New Brunswick and the Atlantic, on the S. by the Atlantic and Long Island Sound, and on the W. by New York. It comprises the states of MASSACHUSETS, MAINE, NEW HAMPSHIRE, VERMONT, RHODE ISLAND, and CONNECTICUT; each of which see under its respective head.

ENKIOPING, a town of Sweden, in Upland, on the N. side of Lake Maeler; 21 miles S. W. of Upsal.

ENNIS, a town in the parish of Drumcliff, Ireland; capital of the county of Clare. It is seated near the head of a bay, on the N. side of the river Shannon. It is 19 miles N. N. W. of Limerick, and 113 S. S.W. of Dublin. It returns a member to the parliament of the United Kingdom.

ENNISCORTHY, a town of Ireland, in the county of Wexford, with a manufacture of coarse woollen cloth, and some iron-works. It is situate on the Slaney; 10 miles N. of Wexford, and 27 N. E. of Waterford.

ENNISKILLEN, a borough of Ireland, capital of the county of Fermanagh. It is seated on an island in Lough Erne, where that lake is contracted, for about 6 miles, to the width of an ordinary river, and has a strong fort, it being a pass of great importance between the N. and S. of Ireland. In 1595 it made an obstinate defence against the army of Queen Elizabeth, and again in 1680 against James II. It is 80 miles N. W. of Dublin. It returns one member to the parliament of the United Kingdom.

ENO, or ENOS, a town of European Turkey, in Rumelia, and a Greek archbishop's see; seated near a gulf of the Archipelago, at the influx of the Marissa; 90 miles S. by W. of Adrianople, and 145 W. S. W. of Constantinople. Long. 28. 15. E. lat. 40. 46. N.

ENS, a town of Austria, on a river of the same name, at its conflux with the Danube; 12 miles E. S. E. of Lintz.

ENSENE, a town of Egypt, on the E. side of the Nile. Here are considerable ruins of the ancient Antinoe. It is 120 miles S. of Cairo. Long. 30. 54. E. lat. 28. 5. N.

ENSISHEIM, a town of France, in the department of Upper Rhine, on the river Ille; 10 miles S. of Colmar.

ENSKIRKEN, a town in the duchy of Juliers; 15 miles S. W. of Cologne.

ENSTORF, a town of the palatinate of Bavaria; 22 miles N. of Ratisbon.

ENTLIBUCH, a town of Switzerland, in the canton of Lucern; 14 miles W. S. W. of Lucern.

ENTRE DOURO E MINHO, the most N. W. province of Portugal, lying on the sea coast, between the rivers Douro and Minho, and bounded on the E. by Tra los Montes. It is 68 miles from N. to S., and 40 broad; and contains a population of 907965. Braga, 30 miles N. N. E. of Oporto, is the capital. It is watered by two other rivers, falling into the Atlantic Ocean, viz. the Lima and Cavado; the other principal towns are, Lagos, Lapeda, and Moncao, on the S. bank of the Minho, which divides the province from the Spanish province of Galicia; Port de Lima and Viana, near the mouth of the Lima, Barcellos, between Braga and the mouth of the Cabado, Guimaraens and Amarante on the S. E., and Oporto on the N. bank, near the mouth of the Douro, which separates the province from Beira.

EPERIES, a town of Upper Hungary, capital of the county of Saros, celebrated for its mines of salt. It is seated on the Tatza; 20 miles N. E. of Cassovia. Long. 21. 13. E. lat. 48. 50. N. Pop. about 7500.

EPERNAY, a town of France, in the department of Marne. It was taken by Henry IV. in 1592, when Marshal Biron was killed while the king's hand was on his shoulder. The wines produced in its neighbourhood are excellent. It is 17 miles N. W. of Chalons, and the seat of a prefect, with a population of 4997.

EPERNON, a town of France, in the department of Eure and Loire; 15 miles N. N. E. of Chartres.

EPHESUS, a village of Asiatic Turkey, in Natolia, anciently one of the most splendid cities of Asia Minor, and the most frequented emporium of that continent. Of its former splendour there is nothing to be seen but heaps of marble, overturned walls, columns, capitals, and pieces of statues. The fortress, which is upon an eminence, seems to have been the work of the Greek emperors; and also the aqueduct, part of which is yet standing, supported by pillars of fine marble. The eastern gate has three basso-relievos, taken from some ancient monuments; that in the middle was constructed by the Romans. The most remarkable structure was the Temple of Diana, deemed one of the seven wonders of the world, and which the primitive Christians had converted into a church; but it is now so entirely ruined, that it is not easy to find the ground plot. Ephesus is seated near the mouth of the Cayster, which formerly afforded a good harbour for ships, but is now almost choked up with sand. The present inhabitants are only Greek peasants, who live in extreme wretchedness and insensibility. It is 30 miles S. S. E. of Smyrna. Long. 27. 23. E. lat. 38. 8. N.

Ephrata, or Tunkerstown, a town of Pennsylvania, in Lancaster county, and the principal settlement of a sect called Tunkers (Dippers), who are of German extraction, and first appeared in America in 1719. It is 22 miles N. of Lancaster.

Epinal, a town of France, capital of the department of Vosges. It is famous for its paper-mills: it is seated on the river Moselle, near the mountains of the Vosges: 65 miles S. W. of Strasburg, and 195 E. by S. of Paris. Pop. 7941.

Epingen, a town of South Germany, in the grand duchy of Baden; 20 miles S. E. of Heidelberg. Pop. 3000.

Epirus, a sandjak of Turkey in Europe, in the pachalic of Albania. It is inhabited principally by Arnauts.

Epping, a town in Essex, with a market on Friday. It is famous for excellent butter; it is seated at the N. end of a forest of the same name; 17 miles N. N. E. of London.

Epsom, a town in Surrey, which has, from the number of opulent people residing in and near it, a daily market. It is celebrated for its mineral waters and salts; and on its neighbouring downs are annual horse-races. It is 15 miles S. S. W. of London.

Epworth, a town in Lincolnshire, in the isle of Axholm, with a market on Friday, and a manufacture of sacking. John Wesley, the founder of the Arminian sect of Methodists, was born here. It is 11 miles N. of Gainsborough, and 106 N. N. W. of London.

Erbach, a town of Wirtemberg, capital of a county of the same name, with a castle. It is 22 miles W. by S. of Wertheim, and 35 S. S. E. of Frankfort.

Erbil, a town of Asiatic Turkey, pach. of Kurdistan. It occupies a hill in the midst of fruitful plains, near the ancient Arbela, the scene of the defeat of Darius by Alexander the Great, B. C. 331.

Erekli, a town of European Turkey, on the N. shore of the Sea of Marmora 55 miles W. of Constantinople. It was the ancient Heraclia, and contains the ruins of an amphitheatre, built by the emperor Severus; and a wall at some former time extended from this place to Derkus, on the shore of the Black Sea, a distance of about 55 miles, the object of which seems to have been the protection of Constantinople from the northern barbarians.

There is another town of the same name, on the S. W. shore of the Black Sea; 130 miles E. by N. of Constantinople.

Erfurt, a city of Upper Saxony, sometimes accounted the capital of Thuringia, with a university and two strong forts. The principal magistrate is sometimes a protestant and sometimes a papist; but the greatest part of the burghers are protestants. It has three fine libraries, one of which belongs to the papists, another to the university, and a third to the protestant ministers. The inhabitants are computed at 15,000. A fire happened here in 1736, which burnt down 180 houses, and several churches. In 1806 it was taken by the French; and in 1814 it surrendered to the allies. It is seated in a fertile country, on the river Gerar; 58 miles W. S. W. of Leipsic.

Eribol, Loch, in Scotland, an arm of the sea, on the N. coast of Sutherlandshire, in the long. of 4. 30. W., capable of affording a safe retreat to the largest vessels. It receives several streams: particularly that which flows from a lake called Loch Hope.

Ericht, Loch, a lake of Scotland, lying in the counties of Inverness and Perth. It is 24 miles in length, and one in breadth, surrounded by lofty mountains and rugged cliffs, and its banks covered with heath and a few straggling birches and alders. Its outlet, at the S. extremity, is the river Ericht, which flows into Loch Rannock.

Erie, Lake, one of the great chain of lakes in North America, lies between 79. and 84. W. long. and 41. and 43. N. lat. Its length is 230 miles, and 40 its medium breadth. It is upwards of 650 miles in circumference, and navigable for ships of any burden. Its depth in the centre is 120 feet, and it is 330 feet above the level of Lake Ontario, into which it discharges its waters by the falls of Niagara. The coast on both sides is generally favourable for batteaux and canoes; yet in some places, chiefly on the S. side, there are rocks that run several miles in length. Some of these, near the mouth of the Cayahoga, rise 40 or 50 feet perpendicular out of the water, and project over the lake so as to inspire dread in the boldest breast, when they are approached. The heathen Indians, when they pass this impending danger, offer a sacrifice of tobacco to the water. The islands and banks, towards its W. end, are so infested with rattlesnakes, as to render it dangerous to land on them. The lake is covered, near the banks of the islands, with a large pond lily, the leaves of which are thickly spread on the surface of the water, to an extent of many acres: on these, in the summer, lie myriads of watersnakes, basking in the sun. This lake, at its N. W. end, receives the waters of the great chain from the N. W. by the river

Detroit, and discharges them by the river Niagara, over the great falls at its N. E. end, into Lake Ontario. It forms the boundary line between the United States and British North American territories, both parties claiming an equal right of navigation. During the war of 1812–1815, the Americans had a squadron of 9 vessels, carrying 56 guns, and the British, one of 6 vessels, carrying 69 guns; on the 10th of September 1813, after an action of three hours, the whole of the British squadron surrendered to the American Commodore Perry. The English have a fort, called Fort Erie, at the N. E. extremity of the lake, where it narrows into the river Niagara, in the lat. of 42. 57. N. and 78. 20. of W. long.; and the United States have two counties named after the lake: viz.—1st. At the N. W. extremity of the state of Pennsylvania, the W. N. W. side is washed by the waters of the lake, the W. end borders on the state of Ohio, and the E. end on that of New York. Its area is about 750 square miles. Pop. 31,344. A town of the same name, seated near the shore of the lake, is 315 miles in a meridional line N. N. W. of Philadelphia. 2nd. At the N. W. extremity of the state of New York, bordering on the E. end of the lake and Niagara River, bounded on the N. by the Tonnewanta, and S. by the Cattaraugus River; this county was divided off from Niagara county since 1810, and contains a population of 62,465. Buffalo, opposite the British Fort Erie, is the chief town; 265 miles W. of Albany.

Eriskay, a small island of the Hebrides of Scotland, at the S. end of South Uist; noted for being the first place upon which Charles tuart landed, in his wild attempt to gain the British crown.

Erith, a village in Kent, on the Thames; 5 miles E. by S. of Woolwich. Great quantities of corn and wood are shipped hence, and here the East India ships, in their passage up the river, generally discharge a part of their cargoes.

Erivan, the capital of Persian Armenia, in a province of the same name, and the seat of an Armenian patriarch. The city is defended by a fortress, in which is the governor's palace, and by a castle, on the river Zuengui, near the lake of Erivan, which is very deep, and 60 miles in circumference. The Meidan is an open square, 400 paces over, in which are very fine trees. The baths and caravansaries have their beauties, but the churches of the Christians are small, and half under ground. It is seated on the banks of the Arus river, which runs past Shirvan into the Caspian Sea, from which it is distant about 130 miles, and about the same distance from Gonieh, on the S. E. shore of the Black Sea. The Russians attempted to take this place by storm in 1808, but were repulsed with great slaughter. Long. 44. 10. E. lat. 40. 20. N.

Erkelens, a town of Germany, in the duchy of Juliers; seated on the Roer; 10 miles N. W. of Juliers. Pop. about 2300.

Erlan, or Erlau, a populous town on the frontiers of Lower and Upper Hungary; 60 miles E. N. E. of Buda. It is the see of an archbishop. The cathedral and archiepiscopal palace are stately edifices.

Erlangen, a town of Bavaria, with a university and a palace. It is divided into the old and new town; and the latter is one of the handsomest towns in Germany. The principal manufactures are hats, gloves, and stockings. It is seated on the Rednitz, 12 miles N. of Nuremberg, and is now included in the dominions of the king of Bavaria. Long. 11. 2. E. lat. 49. 38. N.

Erne, a river of Scotland, which issues from a lake of the same name, in Perthshire, flows by Crief, and joins the Tay, a little below Abernethy.

Erne, a river of Ireland, which issues from a small lake on the N. border of the county of Longford, flows N. through that of Cavan, and N. W. through Fermanagh into Donegal Bay. In the latter county it forms a lake, called Lough Erne, 30 miles in length, containing several islands; and on one in the middle part, where the lake is very narrow, stands the town of Enniskillen.

Ernee, town of France, in the department of Mayenne, on a river of the same name; 15 miles N. N. W. of Laval.

Erodu, or Erroad, a town of Hindostan, in the province of Coimbetore, with a large mud fort. Much coarse cotton cloth is made here and in the vicinity. It is seated on a canal from the Bhawani, E. of the Cavery river; 75 miles W. N. W. of Tritchinopoly.

Errol, a town in Perthshire, Scotland, 43½ miles from Edinburgh. The population are employed in the making of linen, and the salmon fishery. Grain is also exported hence in large quantities.

Erromango, one of the New Hebrides in the S. Pacific Ocean; 70 miles in circumference, with low shores. On the W. side is a promontory that separates two bays; and Captain Cook, from the treacherous behaviour of the inhabitants, named it Traitor's Head. Long. 169. 19. E. lat. 18. 47. S.

Ervy, a town of France, in the department of Aube; 17 miles S. by W. of Troyes.

Erzerum, or Arz Roum, the capital of Turkish Armenia, with Armenian and Greek episcopal sees. It is surrounded by double walls, defended by strong towers, and estimated to contain 125,000 inhabitants. The Armenians have two churches, the Greeks but one; the latter are mostly braziers, and live in the suburbs. A great trade is carried on in furs, Persian silks, cottons, calicoes, and drugs. This city is a thoroughfare, and a resting-place for the caravans to the East Indies. It is situate between the two sources of the Euphrates, at the foot of a chain of mountains; 104 miles S. E. of Trebisond, on the S. E. shore of the Black Sea. Long. 41. 36. E. lat. 39. 57. N.

Erzgeberg, Circle of, a populous district of Upper Saxony, forming the S. W. part of the margraviate of Meissen, or Misnia; bounded on the S. by the Bohemian mountains. It abounds in valuable minerals. Freyburg, Altenburg, and Chemnitz, are the principal towns.

ESCALONA, a town of Spain, in New Castile; surrounded by walls. It is situate on an eminence, in a fertile country, near the Albreche, a tributary of the Tagus; 20 miles N. W. of Toledo, and 32 S. W. of Madrid.

ESCHWEGEN, a town and castle of Germany, in the landgravate of Hesse Cassel; seated on the Werra; 25 miles E. S. E. of Cassel.

ESCURIAL, a village of Spain, in New Castile; seated on the Guadara; 15 miles N. W. of Madrid. It takes its name from a noble structure, founded by Philip II., in memory of the victory gained over the French near St. Quentin, in 1557. This edifice consists of a royal palace, a church, a monastery, a college, a library, shops of different artists, apartments for a great number of people, beautiful walks, large alleys, an extensive park, and fine gardens. It is built of grey stones, found in the neighbourhood, and in the form of a gridiron, because St. Lawrence, on whose day the victory was gained, suffered martyrdom by being broiled on such an instrument. It is a long square of 740 feet by 580, and four stories high, with a tower at each angle 200 feet high; and the palace forms the handle of this imaginary gridiron. The most remarkable part is the arched chapel; in which is a magnificent sepulchre, called the Pantheon, being built in imitation of that church at Rome; it is the burying-place of the kings and queens of Spain; and is thought by some to be the most curious piece of architecture in the world. The church is built after the model of St. Peter's at Rome.

ESGUEYRA or ESGUERIA, a town of Portugal, in Beira; 3 miles S. of Aveiro.

ESK, a river which rises in Scotland, in the N. E. part of Dumfriesshire, and flows S. E. through a dale to which it gives name, to the edge of the county. It there receives the Liddel from Roxburghshire, and enters Cumberland, flowing S. by Longtown, into the N. E. extremity of Solway Frith.

ESK, a river of Scotland in Edinburghshire, formed by the junction of two streams called North and South Esk. They almost encircle the town of Dalkeith, passing on each side of the eminence on which it stands, and unite a little below the town. The river enters the Frith of Forth, at Musselburgh.

ESK, NORTH and SOUTH, two rivers of Scotland, in Angusshire, which descend from the hills called the Braes of Angus. The former divides the county from Kincardineshire, for several miles, and reaches the ocean a little to the N. of Montrose: the latter, after traversing the whole breadth of the county, enters the bay on the W. of the same town.

ESKI SHEHR, a town of Asiatic Turkey, in Natolia, on the river Sakaria, which falls into the Black Sea; 80 miles E. S. E. of Brusa. Long. 31. 18. E. lat. 39. 48. N.

ESMERALDAS, a department of S. America, republic of Colombia. The chief town, of the same name, is situated on a neck of land, at the mouth of a river discharging itself into the Pacific Ocean.

ESNE, ASNA, or ESNAY, a town of Egypt, supposed to be the ancient Latopolis. Here is an ancient temple, with walls on three sides, and in the front 24 columns well preserved: within it are three stories of hieroglyphics, of men about three feet high; and the ceiling is adorned with animals, painted with beautiful colours. On the N. side of the town is another temple, richly carved with hieroglyphics, crocodiles, &c.; and a mile to the S. is the monastery of St. Helena, which contains many magnificent tombs. Esne stands on the Nile; 300 miles S. of Cairo. Long. 31. 40. E. lat. 24. 46. N.

ESOPUS. *See* KINGSTON.

ESPALION, a town of France, in the department of Aveiron, on the river Lot; 14 miles N. N. E. of Rhodez. It is the seat of a prefect, and contains 3261 inhabitants.

ESPOSENDA, or ESPONDENDA, a seaport of Portugal, in Entre Douro e Minho, at the mouth of the Cavado; 22 miles N. of Oporto. Long. 8. 21. W. lat. 41. 32. N.

ESQUIMAUX, a people of North America, chiefly inhabiting Labrador and the shores of Hudson's Bay; each of which see.

ESQUIMAUX BAY, a bay on the S. coast of Labrador, at the entrance to the Straits of Belleisle from the Gulf of St. Lawrence. Long. 57. 59. W. lat. 51. 30. N.

ESQUIMAUX ISLANDS, a cluster of small islands in the Gulf of St. Lawrence, off the entrance to the bay.

ESSEG, or ESZEK, a trading town of Austria, in Sclavonia, with a strong castle. It has a wooden bridge over the Drave, into Lower Hungary, and the marshes, 8 miles in length, and 80 feet in breadth, with towers at a quarter of a mile distant from each other. It is a difficult pass, and several battles have been fought here, between the Turks and Germans. Esseg was taken from the Turks in 1687, since which time it has continued in the hands of the House of Austria. It is seated on the river Drave; 100 miles W. N. W. of Belgrade, and 136 S. of Buda. Long. 19. 16. E. lat. 45. 30. N. Pop. about 9000.

ESSEN, a town of Westphalia, in the duchy of Berg. Here are several Catholic churches and convents, but the inhabitants are chiefly Lutherans. It is 8 miles E. of Duysburg.

ESSENS, a town of Westphalia in East Friesland, near the German Ocean; 20 miles N. N. E. of Emden.

ESSEQUIBO. *See* ISSEQUIBO.

ESSEX, a maritime and fertile county of England. It is bounded on the S. by the river Thames, which divides it from the county of Kent, and N. by the Stour, which divides it from the county of Suffolk, and W. by the Stort and Lea, dividing it from the counties of Hertford and Middlesex: the E. boundary is washed by the German Ocean, and the N. W. corner borders on the county of Cambridge: the Colne and two other rivers, the Chelmer and Blackwater, intersect the interior parts of the county, and the united streams of the two latter, at Maldon, form a beautiful estuary to the German Ocean. The county is nearly a square, the area of which is 1,240,000 acres. It possesses a variety of soil and face of country. The S. W. part is occupied principally by the two forests of Epping and Hainault, and is noted for its butter. The N. W. part, from Saffron-Walden to Cambridge, is famous for the growth of saffron, and for a kind of triple crop of coriander, caraway, and teazle, which are all sown together, but come to maturity at different periods. The middle part is a fine corn country, varied with gentle inequalities of surface, and sprinkled with woods. The part bordering on the Thames and the sea consists chiefly of marshy grounds, which afford excellent pasturage, being secured from the inroad of the tides by embankments. Its contiguity to the metropolis affords it a facile and advantageous market for its surplus produce of grain, seeds, calves, butter, poultry, potatoes, fruit, wild fowl, and oysters, all of which it supplies in a greater proportion than any other county in the kingdom ; yet notwithstanding all the advantages of fertility, abundance, and contiguity to market, pauperism and crime prevail to an equal extent to any, and to a much greater extent than in most other parts of the kingdom. The manufacture of baize, and other worsted stuffs, was formerly carried on over the greater part of this county, but since the middle of the 18th century it has progressively declined, and is now almost extinct. It has large establishments for the printing of calico, and mills for making sheet lead. The assize town for Essex is Chelmsford ; and the other principal towns are Colchester, Saffron-Walden, Romford, Harwich, &c. It returns four members to parliament, for the north and south divisions.

Essex is also the name of a county in Upper Canada, forming a promontory at the southern extremity of the province, and nearly surrounded by Lakes Erie and St. Clair, and Detroit River.

Essex is also the name of five counties in different parts of the United States of North America ; viz.

First, In Vermont, bounded on the E. for about 45 miles by the Connecticut river, and bounded on the N. by Lower Canada ; its mean breadth is about 20 miles. Pop. 4226, chief town, Guildhall.

Second, Forming the N. E. part of the state of Massachusets, bordering on New Hampshire and the Atlantic Ocean : it is intersected by the Merrimack river, and contains several considerable towns ; viz. Newbury Port, Ipswich, Glocester, Marblehead, Salem, and Beverley, &c. Pop. 94,987. Salem, 15 miles N. E. of Boston, is the chief town.

Third, In New York, bounded on the E. for 52 miles, by Lake Champlain. Pop. 23,634. The court-house at Elizabeth town, in Pleasant Valley, is 130 miles N. of Albany.

Fourth, In New Jersey, bounded on the W. N. and E. by the Passiac river: its area is only about 150 square miles. Pop. 44,621. Newark, 10 miles W. of New York, is the chief town its contiguity to which renders it the most populous and important part of the state.

Fifth, In Virginia, on the S. W. bank of the Rappahannoc river, along which it extends about 30 miles, being about 8 miles in mean breadth. Pop. 11,309. Rappahannoc, 46 miles N.N.E. of Richmond, is the chief town.

There are two or three towns named Essex in different parts of the United States of North America.

Essington, Port, a remarkably fine harbour in Coburg Peninsula, on the N. coast of Australia, on the W. shore of which is the British settlement of Victoria, founded in October, 1838. It is seated on a rising ground, on the inner harbour, and has a pier. It is the third settlement that has been formed in this neighbourhood ; the first in 1824, in Apsley Straits ; and the next in 1827, in Raffles Bay, Coburg Peninsula. They were founded for the purpose of opening a trade in British merchandise with the Malays, who visit these parts to fish for trepang, or sea-slug, which is sent to China. These two settlements were abandoned from misrepresentation, and the last has been formed for the same purposes of trading. The climate is tropical, and produces many of the vegetables common in those regions. The natives are friendly and useful, and the climate is very salubrious. Victoria is in 11. 20. 30. S. lat. and 132 9. E. long.

Essling, a village of Austria, on the N. bank of the Danube, about 6 miles E.S.E. of Vienna; between which and Aspern a sanguinary battle was fought between the French and Austrians, on the 21st and 22nd May, 1809.

Esslingen, a town of Suabia, in the kingdom of Wirtemberg. Here are several convents, but the inhabitants are chiefly Lutherans. It has three extensive suburbs, and its district yields good Neckar wine. It is seated on the Neckar; 8 miles S. E. of Stutgard. Pop. 7000.

Estain, a town of France, in the department of Meuse ; 12 miles E.N.E. of Verdun.

Estakar, a town of Persia, in Farsistan ; capital of a district of the same name. Near it are the magnificent ruins of ancient Persepolis. It is 50 miles N.E. of Shiras. Long. 53. 40. E. lat. 30. 5. N.

Estavayer, a town and bailiwick of Switzerland, in the canton of Friburg, with a fine castle. seated on the lake of Neufchatel ; 13 miles W. of Friberg.

Este, a populous town of the Venetian territory ; 14 miles S. S. W. of Padua.

Estella, an episcopal town of Spain, in Navarre, with a castle and university ; seated on the Ega ; 15 miles W.S.W. of Pamplona. Long. 2. 2. W. lat. 42. 38. N.

Estepa, a town of Spain, in Andalusia, with an ancient castle on a mountain; 18 miles S. of Ecija, and 58 E. of Seville.

Estepona, a town of Spain, in Granada, near the coast; 20 miles W.S.W. of Marbella.

Esterabad. *See* Asterabad.

Esthonia, or Revel, a government of the Russian empire, bounded on the W. by the Baltic, N. by the Gulf of Finland, E. by Ingaria, and S. by Livonia. After having been long an object of bloody contention between the Russians, Poles, and Swedes, it was confirmed to the latter by the peace of Oliva, in 1660; but it was subdued by Peter the Great, in 1710, and finally ceded to Russia in 1721 It is divided into four circles. Revel is the capital.

ESTHWAITE-WATER, a lake in Lancashire, between Hawkshead and Windermere-water. It is two and a half miles long, and half a mile broad, intersected by a peninsula from each side, jutting far into the lake. On the banks are villages and scattered houses, pleasantly situate under woods and hanging grounds clothed with verdure, all heightened by the strong back ground of rocky mountains. No char are are found in this lake, though it is connected with the Windermere-water.

ESTILL, an interior county in the E. part of the state of Kentucky, intersected by the Kentucky river; its area is about 500 square miles. Irvine is the chief town.

ESTRAMADURA, a province in Spain extending from the lat. of 37. 56. to 40. 15. of N. lat., bounded on the W. by the Portuguese province of Alentejo and part of Beira. It is about 90 miles in mean breadth, giving an area of 14,400 square miles. Pop. 428,493. The N. end is intersected by the Tagus, and the S. by the Guadiana; it seems a county of great capability. The vine, olive, and corn, all luxuriate within its limits. Cattle and fine wool are the chief articles of trade; and great herds of black swine are fed on the hills, which are covered with oaks. Badajoz, near the Portuguese frontier, is the capital, and the other principal towns are Plazencia, Coria, Alcantara, Albuquerque, Truxillo, Marida, Olivenzia, Xeres, and Llerena.

ESTRAMADURA, the metropolitan province of Portugal, lying on both sides of the Tagus: its area is about 700 square miles. Pop. 826,680. The part S. of the Tagus is mountainous and unproductive, whilst the N., although in parts mountainous, is exceedingly fertile; the vine, olive, orange, lemon, and other delicious fruits, as well as corn, millet, and legumes, abound; besides Lisbon, the capital of the province, and of all Portugal, the other principal towns are Leyria, Thomar, Abrantes, Santarem, and Alenquer, all N. of the Tagus, and Setuval, near the coast on the S.

ESTREMOZ, a town of Portugal, in Alentejo, and one of the strongest in the kingdom, being surrounded by ten bastions. An earthenware is made here, greatly esteemed for its beauty; and in the vicinity are quarries of beautiful marble. It is 18 miles W. of Elvas, and 100 E. of Lisbon. Pop. about 6500.

ESZEK, or ESZEG. *See* ESSEG.

ETAMPES, a town in France, in the department of Seine and Oise; seated on the river Loet, or Etampes; 15 miles E. of Chartres. It is distinguished for the murder of its prefect, on the 1st of March, 1792. Pop. 9400.

ETAPLES, a town in France, in the department of Pas de Calais; situate on the English Channel, near the mouth of the river Canche; 13 miles S. of Boulogne.

ETAYA, or ETAWEH, a town of Hindostan, in the province of Agra; situate on the E. bank of the Jumna, which is here 60 feet high. On the top, near the river, are the remains of a fort. It is 62 miles S. E. of Agra. Long. 79. 16. E. lat. 26. 45. N.

ETHIOPIA, a name by which a vast region of Africa has been distinguished by some geographers, who have divided it into Upper and Lower Ethiopia. The first includes Nubia, Abyssinia, and part of Guinea; the second all the countries S. of the equinoctial line, as Congo, Monumugi, Monomotapa, &c. Ethopia appears to have once been a great and powerful empire, but the details of its history are lost in the vortex of time. The Egyptian empire was probably founded on the ruin of that of Ethiopia.

ETIENNE, ST., a town of France in the department of Loire. Besides the manufactures of arms, hardware, and cutlery, (the most considerable in France,) the weaving of ribbons forms a considerable article of commerce. Coal is found in the neighbourhood, and also a soft stone, fit for grindstones. It is the seat of a prefect; 20 miles S. E. of Montbrison, and 32 S. W. of Lyons. Pop. 21,000.

There are about a dozen other towns in different parts of France, named after Saint Etienne (Stephen), all inconsiderable.

ETIVE LOCH, a navigable inlet of the sea, on the W. coast of Scotland, in Argyleshire. It is 20 miles in length, but of very unequal breadth; and its banks are indented with creeks, which afford safe anchorage. About 7 miles from the entrance it contracts into a narrow channel, called Connel, where a ridge of rocks occasion, at particular times of the tide, a violent current. About 2 miles below is the ancient castle of Dunstaffnage.

ETNA. *See* ÆTNA.

ETON, a town in Buckinghamshire, England; seated on the N. bank of the Thames, opposite to Windsor, to which it is united by an elegant stone bridge over the river. Eton is celebrated for its school, founded by Henry VI. in 1440, for the education of 70 scholars, a portion of which, when duly qualified, are annually elected to King's College, Cambridge. In addition to the 70 foundation scholars, there are generally 300 to 400 of the sons of the opulent classes, receiving their education at Eton. The buildings are commodious and elegant; their light Gothic turrets form a beautiful and interesting contrast to the massive and majestic towers of Windsor Castle, from which Eton is separated only by the river. Eton is 22 miles N. W. of London.

ETRURIA. *See* TUSCANY, *and* STOKE-UPON-TRENT.

ETTENHEIM, a town in the territory of the Grand Duke of Baden, distinguished as the residence of the illustrious Duke D'Enghein. Buonaparte, in violation of the established law of nations, sent a military force into the territory of Baden, then at peace, and arrested the Duke D'Enghein, who was dragged to Paris and shot. Ettenheim is 25 miles S. by E. of Strasburg.

ETTLINGEN a town of Suabia, in the duchy

of Baden, on the river Albe; 4 miles S. S. W. of Durlach.

EU, a town of France, in the department of Lower Seine, with a strong castle, and a harbour for small vessels at Treport. The principal trade is in serges and lace. It is seated on the river Bresle, near the English Channel; 15 miles N. E. of Dieppe.

EU-HO, or PRECIOUS-RIVER, a river of China, in Pe-tche-li, which flows N. E. into the Pei-ho, at Tien-sing. Much grain is conveyed by this river for Pekin, and it is also important for its connexion with the N. extremity of the Grand Canal.

EULE, a town of Bohemia, in the circle of Kaurzim, with a gold mine; 11 miles S. by E. of Prague.

EUPATORIA, or KOSTOF, a town of Russia, in the Crimea, or government of Taurida, situate on the W. side of a salt lake, and near the Black Sea, 68 miles S. by W. of Perecop. Long. 33. 16. E. lat. 45. 12. N.

EUPEN. *See* OEPEN.

EUPHEMIA, ST., a town of Naples, on the W. coast of Calabria Ulteriore, on the gulf of the Mediterranean to which it gives name; 27 miles S. by E. of Cosenza.

EUPHRATES, a noble river of Western Asia, which rises from three sources in Turkish Armenia. The principal head is about 35 miles S. E. of Erzerum, and is called by the Turks Binggheuil Frat, or 1000 springs; and on the opposite side of the mountains from whence these springs flow, the Raksi, a branch of the Aras, which falls into the Caspian Sea below Shirvan, also has its source: another branch of the Euphrates rises about 35 miles N. by W. of Erzerum; these two branches unite in the long. of 40. E. and lat. of 39. 50. N., and about 40 miles W. by S. of Erzerum, from whence the united stream becomes navigable for boats. Another branch rises on the frontier of Persia, in the long. of 43. 40. E., and runs a course nearly due W. to the long. of 39. 25. and lat. of 39.; the united streams are then called the Frat, and flow in a direction S. S. W. to Semisat, in the lat. 37. 8. N. and long. of 37. 20. E., being within 60 miles of the Gulf of Iskenderun, at the N. E. extremity of the Mediterranean; from this point the Euphrates flows in a S. E. direction through twelve degrees of longitude in Asiatic Turkey, falling into the Gulf of Persia, in the lat. of 30. N. and long. of 48. 40. E. The meridional distance from the source to the mouth of this noble river is about 800 miles, but the course of the stream to its junction with the Tigris is about 1350 miles. It is navigable for ships of the largest burthen to Bassorah, 35 miles from its mouth, and for steam-vessels, properly constructed, as far as Bir, a distance of 1150 miles. It will probably become a great means of communication between Europe and Western Asia. Babylon was seated on its banks. *See* SYRIA, IRAC-ARABI, ROUM, and TIGRIS.

EURE, a department of the North of France, so named from a river which intersects the E. part, falling into the Seine, about 15 miles above Rouen: the Seine then forms its northern boundary to its entrance into the sea. Eure, however may be considered a manufacturing and agricultural, rather than a maritime department. It is divided into five arrondissements. Pop. 416,718.

EURE and LOIRE, an interior department of France, bordering on the preceding province, on the S. It is so named from the two rivers, the Eure and the Loire, both of which rise within the department; the Loire flowing to the S., and the Eure to the N., as described in the preceding article. Pop. 264,448.

EUROPE, one of the five grand divisions of the globe; the extreme limits of which are as follow: viz. Cape Matapan, S. in 36. 23. N. and 22. 29. E.; Cape St. Vincent, W. in 37. 3. N. and 9. 2. W.; Cape North, N. in 71. 10. N. and 25. 50. E.; Kara River, E. in 66. 30. N. and 63. 30. E. The longest meridional line that could be drawn across Europe, would be from Europa Point, in the straits of Gibraltar, which divides Europe from the N. W. extremity of Africa, in the lat. of 36. 7. N. and 5. 20. of W. long., to the Kara River, in the long. of 63. 30. E., in the lat. of 66. 30. N. This line, the angle of which is N. E. bearing E., would intersect the gulfs of Dantzig, Riga, and Finland, and the lakes Ladoga and Onega; and its length would be 3055 geographical, or 3546 English statute miles. The longest line that could be drawn from S. to N. would be from Cape Matapan, at the S. extremity of the Morea, to Cape North, at the northern extremity of Finmark; this line would intersect the Gulf of Riga, the entrance to the Gulf of Finland, and the N. E. shore of the Gulf of Bothnia; and its length would be 3090 geographical, or 2423 English statute miles. Europe is estimated to contain 3,387,019 square miles, and a population of 210,000,000. It is bounded on the N. by the Arctic Sea, W. by the Atlantic Ocean, S. from the long. of 5. W. to 35. E. by the Mediterranean Sea. For its boundary on the E. *see* ASIA. The predominating feature of Europe is variety; mountain ridges run in all directions; but, with the exception of the Alps and the Pyrenees, there are none remarkable for their altitude. The Appennines, Carpathian, Hartz, Oural, and other mountains of inferior note, abound in every species of metallic and semi-metallic ores, which are worked, wrought, and distributed over every part of the world. The rivers are numerous, and flow in every direction; their courses, extent, &c. will be elucidated under the heads of their respective names, as will also the several countries through which they flow.

EURVILLE, a town of France, in the department of Upper Marne; 6 miles S. E. of St. Dizier.

EUSKIRCHEN, a town of the Prussian states; 23 miles S. E. of Juliers.

EUSTACE, an island which forms, with a long point of land, the entrance to the harbour of St. Augustine, in East Florida.

EUSTATIA, ST., one of the least of the Leeward Islands, in the West Indies; 10 miles N.W. of St. Christopher. It is a mountain in the form of a sugar-loaf, whose top is hollow; yet, for its size, it is one of the most valuable of all the Caribbees. Tobacco is cultivated on its sides, to the very summit; and hogs, kids, rabbits, and all kinds of poultry, are in great abundance. It has a town of the same name, with a good fort. It was taken by the English in 1781, who pillaged the inhabitants, and confiscated all private property; it was soon after retaken by the French, and restored to the Dutch, in 1783; again taken by the English in 1801, and again restored to the Dutch at the general peace of 1814.

Eutin, a town of Lower Saxony, in Holstein, near the side of a lake; 20 miles N. N. W. of Lubec.

Euxine, or Black Sea, a large inland sea, dividing Europe from Asia, between the latitudes of 41. and 47. N. extending E. from the long. of 28. to 41. 25., giving an extreme length from W. to E. of 606 geographical, or 702 British statute miles: on the W. it washes the coasts of Romania, Bulgaria, and Bessarabia; and on that side receives the waters of the Danube: at the N. W. corner it receives the waters of the Dniester and the Dnieper, which flow through the southern provinces of European Russia; and from the N., between the longitudes of 33. and 37. E., projects the peninsula of the Crimea, or Russian province of Taurida. A narrow strait at the eastern extremity of this peninsula, leads into the Sea of Azof, into which flows the river Don: the N. E. part of the Euxine washes the coast of Circassia and the territory of the Abkhas; the eastern extremity washes the coast of Mingrelia, which contributes to the waters of the Euxine by several streams, the most important of which is the Roni or Phasis: the S. part washes the coasts of the Turkish provinces of Armenia, Roum, and Natolia, which contribute the waters of the Kisil-Irmak, and numerous other rivers of inferior note. The Euxine communicates with the Mediterranean, first by the narrow Strait of Constantinople into the Sea of Marmora, and from thence by the Dardanelles, the ancient Hellespont, or Thracian Bosphorus, into the Grecian Archipelago. The navigation of the Euxine appears to have been more general in past than at the present time, the Phœnicians, Egyptians, Greeks, Romans, Venetians, and Genoese all appearing to have maintained an extensive intercourse with the inhabitants on its shores. In 1476, when the Turks drove the Genoese from the Crimea, they precluded all intercourse through the Straits of Constantinople, and claimed an exclusive right of navigation within. In 1774 the Russians, and in 1784 Austria, obtained by treaty an equal right of navigation, which at the peace of Amiens was extended to all nations; and, since the peace of 1814, a considerable traffic has been carried on from the port of Odessa, between the rivers Dniester and Dnieper, with the Mediterranean and with England; but the other parts of its extensive shores are but little frequented, and but little known, though doubtless susceptible of affording a rich field for well-directed enterprise and exertion.

Euzet, town of France, in the department of the Gard, and chief place of a canton, in the district of Uzes; 9 miles W. N. W. of Uzes.

Evaux, a town of France, in the department of Creuse, near which is a mineral spring, and baths. It is 25 miles E. of Gueret.

Everding. *See* Efferding.

Everfeld, or Elverfeld, a town of Westphalia, in the duchy of Berg, near the river Wipper; 18 miles E. of Dusseldorf.

Everghem, a populous town of the Netherlands; 7 miles N. of Ghent.

Evesham, a borough in Worcestershire, England, governed by a mayor, with a market on Monday. Here are three churches, and it had formerly an abbey, of which some remains are still visible. A remarkable battle was fought here in 1265, between Prince Edward, afterward Edward I., and Simon de Montfort, earl of Leicester, in which the earl and most of his adherents were slain. Evesham is seated in a fertile vale, and is nearly surrounded by the Avon. The vale is mostly appropriated to gardens, and supplies vast quantities of fruit and vegetables for the Worcester, Bath, Bristol, and other markets. It has also some extensive flour-mills, worked by the water of the Avon, over which there is here a bridge of seven arches. It is 14 miles S. E. of Worcester, and 100 N. W. of London. It returns two members to parliament.

Evora, a fortified city of Portugal, capital of Alentejo, and a bishop's see, with a university. Some remains of the ancient Roman wall are visible; part of a temple of Diana, of which there are seven entire pillars standing, is now converted into butchers' shambles; and the famous aqueduct built by Sertorius still conveys a noble stream of water to the city. Evora is seated in a pleasant country, surrounded on all sides by mountains; 65 miles E. by S. of Lisbon. Long. 7. 50. W. lat. 38. 28. N.

Evoramonte, a town of Portugal, in Alentejo, situate on a rock; 8 miles W. S. W. of Estremoz, and 23 N. N. E. of Evora.

Evereux, a town of France, capital of the department of Eure, and a bishop's see. The cathedral is a handsome structure. The trade consists in corn, linen, and woollen cloth; and it has manufactures of cotton, velvets, and tick. It is seated on the Iton; 25 miles S. of Rouen, and 55 N. W. of Paris. Pop. 10,250.

Ewell, a town in Surrey, contiguous to Epsom, with a market on Thursday; 6 miles W. of Croydon, and 13 S. S. W. of London.

Ex, a river rising in the forest of Exmoor, in Somersetshire, and, leaving that county, below Dulverton, runs through Devonshire, by Tiverton, Exeter, and Topsham, whence it forms an estuary to the English Channel, at Exmouth.

Exeter, a city and county of itself, and the capital of Devonshire, on the river Ex, with a market on Wednesday and Friday. It was formerly the seat of the W. Saxon kings, who resided in the castle, called Rougemont, from the colour of the hill on which it is built. It was encompassed by walls, and had four gates, two of which are now pulled down. With its suburbs it contains 19 churches, beside the cathedral, which is a magnificent fabric. It is governed by a mayor, has thirteen companies of tradesmen, and formerly carried on an extensive commerce in woollen stuffs to Spain, &c.; but its commerce and manufactures have materially declined since the close of the 18th century, and its present importance is derived from the agreeableness of its locality, occasioning it to be much resorted to by the neighbouring gentry. An elegant bridge crosses the river. The public buildings consist of a guildhall, county hall, hospital, lunatic asylum, &c. &c. It returns two members to parliament. It is situate 9 miles above the entrance of the river into the sea; 43 miles E. of Plymouth, 87 S. W. of Bath, and 168 W. S. W of London, by way of Salisbury.

EXETER, a town of New Hampshire, in Rockingham county, with a good harbour on Exeter River, a branch of the Piscataqua. It has several manufactures, and the saddlery business is carried on to a great extent. Some vessels are built here, the river being capable of floating down those of 500 tons. The public edifices are two congregational churches, a celebrated academy, and a court-house. It is 15 miles S. W. of Portsmouth, and 54 N. of Boston. Pop. 2925.

EXETER, a town in North Carolina, in New Hanover county, on the N. E. branch of Cape Fear River; 30 miles N. of Wilmington.

EXIDEUIL, or EXCIDERFIL, a town of France, in the department of Dordogne; 20 miles N. E. of Perigueux, and 32 S. of Limoges.

EXILLES, a strong town of Piedmont, with a fortified castle on a mountain, which guards one of the passes into the country. It is seated on the river Doire; 37 miles W. N. W. of Turin.

EXMOUTH, a town in Devonshire, on the E. side of the mouth of the river Ex; 10 miles S. S. E. of Exeter. It is much frequented for the benefit of sea-bathing.

EYBENSCHITZ, a town of Moravia, in the circle of Znaim, on the river Ollawa; 12 miles S. W. of Brunn.

EYDER, a river and canal that separates Jutland from Holstein. The river rises in Holstein, and flows W. by Rendsburgh, Fredericstadt, and Tonningen, into the German Ocean. The canal passes E. from Rendsburgh to a bay of the Baltic, a little N. of Kiel. These jointly afford a safe inland navigation across the country, between the Baltic Sea and German Ocean.

EYE, a borough in Suffolk, with a market on Saturday. Here are the ruins of a castle and a Benedictine abbey. It is a mean place; 20 miles N. of Ipswich, and 89 N. E. of London. It returns one member to parliament.

EYEMOUTH, a town of Scotland, in Berwickshire, with a harbour for vessels of small burden, and a trade in corn and meal. It is seated at the mouth of the Eye; 8 miles N. by W. of Berwick.

EYLAU, DUTCH, a town of Prussia, in the province of Oberland, at the S. end of a lake; 47 miles E. by N. of Culm, and 90 S. S. W. of Konigsberg.

EYLAU, PRUSSIAN, a town of Prussia, in the province of Natangen. On February 8, 1807, a most bloody battle was fought here between the French and Russians, which terminated in favour of the former. It is 24 miles S. by E. of Konigsberg.

EYMOUTIERS, a town of France, in the department of Upper Vienne, with a considerable trade in skins, leather, and rags; seated on the Vienne; 20 miles N. of Limoges.

EYNDHOVEN, a town of Holland, in North Brabant, at the conflux of the Eynds with the Dommel; 13 miles S. E. of Bois le Duc.

EYRECOURT, a town of Ireland, in the county of Galway; 89 miles from Dublin. Here are the ruins of a castle.

EYWANOWITZ, a town of Moravia, in the circle of Olmutz; 23 miles S. S. W. of Olmutz.

EZAGEN, a rich and ancient town in the kingdom of Fez; 60 miles S. of Tetuan.

EZEL, an island of Russia, in the Baltic Sea, of a triangular form, about 8 miles in circumference. Long. 40. E. lat. 58. 20. N.

EZY, a town of France, in the department of the Eure; 15 miles S. E. of Evreux.

F.

FAABORG, a seaport town of Denmark, on the S. coast of the island of Funen, in a flat but fertile country. The principal trade is in provisions. It is 17 miles S. of Odensee. Long. 10. 16. E. lat. 55. 12. N.

FABRIANO, a town of Italy, in the marquisate of Ancona, famous for its excellent paper. It is 25 miles N. E. of Foligno.

FAENZA, a city of Italy in Romagna, and a bishop's see, with an old fortress. The cathedral stands in the great square, and has a steeple five stories high, with balustrades. In 1796 it was taken by the French, and afterwards taken by the troops of the pope. In 1797 the pope's troops were defeated and expelled. Faenza is famous for fine earthenware. It is seated on the Amona; 20 miles W. S. W. of Ravenna.

FAHLUN, a town of Sweden, capital of Dalecarlia. Near it is a large copper mine, deemed the most ancient in Europe; also a manufacture of green and blue vitriol. It is situate in the midst of the rocks and hills, between the lakes Run and Warpen; 110 miles N. W. of Stockholm. Pop. about 4000.

FAIFO, a town of Cochin-China, and a place of great trade; situate on a river that flows into the Bay of Turon; 30 miles S. E. of Turon.

FAIRFAX, a county of Virginia, lying W. of the Potomac river; bounded on the E. by the federal district of Columbia. Its area is about 400 square miles. Pop. 9370.

FAIRFIELD, a county at the S. W. extremity of Connecticut; bounded in a W. S. W. direction by Long Island Sound, and N. N. E. by the Housatonick River. It is divided into 18 townships. Pop. 49,917. The chief town, of the same name, is seated on the W. bank of a creek in Long Island Sound; 22 miles W. S. W. of Newhaven. It was burnt by a party of Tories and British, in 1777.

FAIRFIELD is also the name of an interior county in the S. part of Ohio, in which the Hockhockings river and a tributary of the Scioto have their sources; it extends about 20 miles from N. to S., and 15 in mean breadth. Pop. 31,924. Lancaster, the chief town, is 30 miles S. E. of Columbus.

FAIRFIELD, a district of South Carolina, lying between the Catawba and Broad Rivers. Pop. 20,163. Winnsborough, 30 miles N. by W. of Columbia, is the chief town.

There are seven or eight towns named *Fairfield*, in different parts of the United States of North America.

FAIRFORD, a town of Gloucestershire, with a market on Thursday. The church was founded in 1493, by John Tame, a merchant of London, purposely for the reception of some glass, taken by one of his vessels, in a ship going to Rome; it has 28 windows, beautifully painted, with subjects chiefly scriptural, designed by the famous Albert Durer. It is seated near the Coln; 25 miles S. E. of Gloucester, and 80 W. by N. of London.

FAIRHEAD, the N. E. point of Ireland, rising 636 feet above the level of the sea, in lat. 55. 3. N. and 6. 10. of W. long. It is opposite to Raughlin Island.

FAIR ISLE, a small island in the Northern Ocean, between the Shetland and Orkneys, from both of which its high towering rocks are visible. On the E. side, the duke of Medina Sidonia, admiral of the Spanish armada, was wrecked in 1588.

FAISANS, an island in the river Bidassoa, which separates France from Spain. It is also called the Isle of Conference, because Louis XIV. and Philip IV. here swore to observe the peace of the Pyrenees, in 1660, after twenty-four conferences between their ministers. It is considered as a neutral place, and situate between Andaye and Fontarabia.

FAKENHAM, a town in Norfolk, with a market on Thursday, situate on a hill, by the river Yare; 9 miles from the coast; 20 N. W. of Norwich, and 108 N. N. E. of London.

FALAISE, a town of France, in the department of Calvados, with a castle, and one of the finest towers in France. It is the birthplace of William the Conqueror, and has a good trade in serges, linen, and lace. It stands on the river Ante; 20 miles S. E. of Caen, and 115 W. of Paris: it is the seat of a prefect. Pop. 14,575.

FALE, a river in Cornwall, which flows by Grampound and Tregony to Falmouth, where it forms a fine haven in the English Channel.

FALKENAU, a town in Bohemia, in the circle of Saatz, with manufactures of alum, sulphur, and vitriol; seated on the river Egra; 12 miles N. E. of Egra.

FALKENBERG, a town of Sweden, in Holland, at the mouth of the Athran, on the Categat, opposite to the Isle of Anholt; 17 miles N. by W. of Halmstadt.

FALKENBERG, a town of Brandenburg, in the New Mark, with a castle, seated on the Drage; 32 miles E. by N. of New Stargard.

FALKENBERG, a town of Silesia, in the principality of Oppeln, with a castle; 14 miles S. by E. of Brieg.

FALKENSTEIN, a town in Germany, in a county of the same name. It stands a little to the N. of Winweiler; 24 miles W. by S. of Worms.

FALKENSTEIN, a town in the Vogtland, near the N. W. frontier of Bohemia.

FALKIOPING, a town of Sweden, in W. Gothland; 56 miles E. of Uddevalla. It is memorable for a battle fought in 1388, between Margaret, Queen of Denmark, and Albert, King of Sweden, when the latter was defeated and taken prisoner, with his son.

FALKIRK, a populous town of Scotland, in Stirlingshire, famous for its trysts held thrice a year; at which 60,000 head of black cattle have been sold at one tryst, besides a great number of sheep and horses. It is seated near the Carron and the Great Canal; 12 miles S. E. of Stirling. The royal army was defeated near this place in 1746.

FALKLAND, a town of Scotland, in Fifeshire, with some linen manufactures. Here are the ruins of the royal palace in which James V. died in 1582; some of its apartments are still inhabited. It is 20 miles N. of Edinburgh.

FALKLAND ISLANDS, two large islands, surrounded by a great number of smaller, lying in the Atlantic Ocean, to the E. of the Strait of Magellan. The smaller of the two large islands lies E. of the other, from which it is separated by a channel called Falkland Sound. These islands were probably seen by Magellan, but Davis is deemed the discoverer of them, in 1592. They were visited by Sir Richard Hawkins, in 1594; and in 1765, Commodore Byron made a settlement here; but in 1770, the Spaniards forcibly deposed the English. This affair was settled by a convention, and the English regained possession; but in 1774 it was abandoned, and the islands ceded to Spain.

FALMOUTH, a seaport on the E. coast of Cornwall, governed by a mayor, with a market on Thursday. It has a noble and extensive harbour, communicating with a number of navigable creeks, and its entrance is defended by the castles of St. Mawes and Pendennis. It is a town of great traffic, much improved by its being the station of the post-office packets to the S. of Europe, the West Indies, and America. It stands on the Fale, at its entrance into the English Channel, 14 miles N. N. E. of the Lizard Point, 10 S. of Truro, and 269 W. S.W. of London. Long. 5. 2. W. lat. 50. 8. N.

FALMOUTH, a town of the island of Jamaica, on the N. coast, and on the S. side of Martha Brae Harbour. Long. 77. 33. W. lat. 18. 31. N.

FALMOUTH, a town of the island of Antigua, on the S. coast, with a fortified harbour. Long. 62. 0. W. lat. 16. 55. N.

FALMOUTH, a seaport of Massachusets, in Barnstable county. In 1775 this town was burned by the British. It is situate on the W. side of a small bay; 70 miles S. S. E. of Boston. Long. 70. 32. W. lat. 41. 36. N.

There are two or three other towns named *Falmouth*, in different parts of the United States.

False Bay, a bay between the Cape of Good Hope and Cape False, frequented during the prevalence of the N. W. winds in May. Long. 18. 53. E. lat. 34. 10. S.

False Cape, a promontory 20 miles E. of the Cape of Good Hope. Long. 18. 44. E. lat. 34. 16. S.

Falster, a fertile island of Denmark, 60 miles in circumference, near the entrance of the Baltic, off the N. end of Zealand, and between the islands Moen and Laland. Nykoping is the capital. Its area is about 185 square miles; and population 16,500.

Falsterbo, a town of Sweden, in Schonen, chiefly known for its lighthouse, at the entrance of the Baltic from the Sound; 22 miles S. S.W. of Lund. Long. 12. 48. E. lat. 55. 22. N.

Famagusta, a town on the S. E. coast of the island of Cyprus, and a Greek bishop's see, with a harbour defended by two forts. It was taken by the Turks in 1570, after a siege of 10 months, when they flayed the Venetian governor alive, and murdered the inhabitants, though they surrendered on honourable terms. It is 62 miles S. by E. of Nicosia. Long. 33. 35. E. lat. 35. 10. N.

Famars, a village of France, in the department of Nord; near which the French were defeated by the allies in 1793. It is 3 miles S. of Valenciennes.

Fano, a fortified town of Italy, in the duchy of Urbino, and a bishop's see. Here are an ancient triumphal arch, handsome churches, and fine palaces. It is seated on the Gulf of Venice; 18 miles E. of Urbino, and 32 N.W. of Ancona. Pop. about 7500.

Fanoe, an island of Jutland, at the entrance of the Little Belt from Categat.

Fantees, Fantin: the Gold Coast of Africa, from Cape Three Points to Anconah, was formerly called Fantin; but, since 1811, it has more commonly been called Ashantee. The Fantees occupy the coast, and the Ashantees the interior. *See* Ashantee.

Faoua. *See* Foue.

Faouet, a town of France, in the department of Morbihan; 21 miles N. by W. of L'Orient.

Fareham, a town in Hampshire, with a market on Wednesday. Sloops and smaller vessels are built here; and it has a considerable trade in coal, corn, canvas, and ropes. It is seated at the N. W. point of Portsmouth Harbour; 5 miles N. N. W. of Gosport, and 73 W. by S. of London.

Farewell, Cape, the most southerly promontory of Greenland, at the entrance of Davis Strait. Long. 42. 42. W. lat. 59. 38. N.

Farewell, Cape, a promontory of the N. end of the island of New Zealand. Long. 172. 41. E. lat. 40. 37. S.

Fargeau, St., a town of France, in the department of Yonne, with a castle; 10 miles S. E. of Auxerre.

Farim, a country of Africa, to the S. of the river Gambia. It has a town of the same name, on the river St. Domingo, about 130 miles above its entrance into the sea. Long. 14. 30. W. lat. 12. 10. N.

Farmington, a town of Connecticut, in Hartford county, with a large congregational church, situate on the river Farmington, which below the town receives the Cambridge, and then acquires the name of Windsor River. It is 10 miles W. S.W. of Hartford, and 22 E. of Lichfield.

Farnham, a town in Surrey, on the border of Hampshire, with a market on Thursday. It has a castle, situate on an eminence, belonging to the bishop of Winchester. Farnham is celebrated for its plantations of hops, and has a great trade in corn. It is seated on the Wey; 12 miles W. of Guildford, and 38 W. S. W. of London.

Farn Islands. Two clusters of islands, about 17 in number. They are much frequented by wild fowls and seals, which are caught in great abundance; some kelp is also made. A lighthouse has been erected on the principal island.

Faro, an island of Sweden, in the Baltic, off the N. E. end of the island of Gothland; about 30 miles in circumference, populous and fertile. The principal town has the same name, and is situate on the S. E. coast. Long. 19. 27. E. lat. 57. 50. N.

Faro, a town of Portugal, in Algarve, and a bishop's see. It has some trade in almonds, figs, oranges, and wine; and is seated on the Gulf of Cadiz; 20 miles S. W. of Tavira. Long. 7. 54. W. lat. 36. 52. N.

Faroer Islands. *See* Feroe Islands.

Faro of Messina, the straits between Italy and Sicily, remarkable for having the tide ebb and flow every six hours, with great rapidity, though it is but 7 miles over. It is so named from the faro, or lighthouse, on Cape Faro, and its vicinity to Messina.

Farr, a town of Scotland, in Sutherlandshire, at the head of a bay of its name, on the N. coast; 52 miles N. by W. of Dornoch.

Farringdon, a town in Berkshire, with a market on Tuesday; seated on an eminence: vast quantities of hogs are fattened in its neighbourhood. It is 15 miles W. of Abingdon, and 68 W. by N. of London.

Fars, or Farsistan, a province of Persia, bounded on the E. by Kerman, N. by Irac-Ajemi, W. by Kuzistan and the Gulf of Persia. It is very fertile in the centre; mountainous on the N., where are a great number of wild-swine; and the land so sandy on the S. as to produce little else than palm-trees. In the forests is a tree from which mastic is gathered; and emeralds are common. Shiras (which see) is the capital.

Fartash, a town of Arabia Felix, in Hadramaut, at the foot of a cape of the same name, in the Indian Ocean; 150 miles E. of Shibam. Long. 51. 50. E. lat. 15. 30. N.

Fasano, or **Fasiano**, a populous town of Naples, near the coast of the Adriatic, in Terra di Bari; 15 miles S. S. E. of Polignano.

Fattipour, a town of Hindostan, in the province of Agra. Here the emperors of Hindostan, when in the zenith of their power, had a palace, which is now in ruins; and on a hill is a grand mosque, built by the emperor Acbar. It is 22 miles W. by S. of Agra.

Faucigny, a town and castle of Savoy, in a district of the same name; seated on the Arbe; 14 miles S. E. of Geneva.

Fauquemont. *See* Valkenburg.

Fauquire, a county of Virginia, bounded on the W. by the Rappahannock river, and N. W. by the Blue Mountains: it is about 35 miles in length, and 12 in mean breadth. Warrenton, the chief town of the county, is 124 miles N. by W. of Richmond.

Faverney, a town of France, in the department of Upper Saone; 8 miles N. of Vesoul.

Favignana, an island 15 miles in compass, off the W. end of Sicily, with a fort and a good harbour. Long. 12. 25. E. lat. 38. 16. N.

Fay, a town of France, in the department of Lower Loire; 18 miles N.W. of Nantes. Pop. 3500.

Fayal, one of the Azores, or Western Islands, which suffered greatly by an earthquake in 1764. Its capital is Villa do Horta, the S. E. point of the island: it is in lat. 38. 31. N. and 28. 42. of W. long. It is very fertile, and exports large quantities of wine.

Fayette, the name of five counties in the United States of North America, so called after a French officer, the Marquis de la Fayette, who volunteered his services against the English in America, during the revolutionary war:—

1st. At the S. W. corner of Pennsylvania; bounded on the E. by the Laurel Ridge of the Allegany Mountains: W. by the Monangahela river, and S. by Monangahela county, Virginia. It is nearly a square of about 32 miles each way. Pop. 33,574. Union, 186 miles W. by S. of Harrisburg, is the chief town.

2nd. In Georgia; bounded on the W. by Flint River, which divides it from the territory of the Creek Indians. This county has been recently formed. Pop. 6191.

3d. In the S. W. part of Ohio, W. of the Sciota river. Pop. 10,984. Washington, the chief town, is 40 miles S. W. by S. of Columbia, and 35 N. W. of Chillicothe.

4th. In the interior of Kentucky, E. of Kentucky River. Pop. 22,194. Lexington (which see) is the chief town.

5th. In the E. part of Indiana. Pop. 9837. Connersville, 65 miles S. E. by E. of Indianopolis, is the chief town.

Fayetteville, a town of North Carolina, in Cumberland county, capital of a district, formerly called Fayette, but now divided into several counties. Its trade with Wilmington is very considerable, to which it sends tobacco, wheat, hemp, cotton, lumber, staves, naval stores, &c., and has a return of European and Indan goods. It is situate on the N. W. branch of Cape Fear River; 50 miles S. by W of Raleigh, and 90 N. W. of Wilmington.

Fayoum, or **Fium**, a town of Egypt, capital of a province of the same name. It has a trade in flax, linen, mats, raisins, and figs; and is seated on a canal, which commuicates with the Nile; 49 miles S. S. W. of Cairo. Long. 30. 39. E. lat. 29. 27. N.

Fe, St., a town of Spain, in the province of Granada, near the river Xenil; 6 miles W. by N. of Granada.

Fe, St., a city of Paraguay, in the province of Buenos Ayres. The environs abound in silk, corn, wine, fruit, game, and cattle. It is seated on the Parana, at the influx of the Salado; 240 miles N. N. W. of Buenos Ayres. Long. 61. 10. W. lat. 31. 30. S.

Fe, St., the capital of New Mexico, and a bishop's see, with a fortress. The environs are rich, and it stands on a river, which, 57 miles below, enters the Rio del Norte. Long. 108. 48. W. lat. 36. 50. N.

Fe de Bogota, St. *See* Bogota.

Fear, Cape, a cape of North Carolina, where there is a dangerous shoal, called, from its form, the Frying Pan, lying at the entrance of Cape Fear River. This river is formed by two branches, called the N. W. and N. E. branches, which unite above Wilmington; and it enters the Atlantic below Brunswick. Long. 77. 45. W. lat. 33. 40. N.

Fecamp, a town of France, in the department of Lower Seine, with a trade in linen, serges, lace, leather, and hats; seated near the English Channel; 24 miles N. E. of Havre de Grace.

Feckenham, a parish in Worcestershire, with an extensive manufacture of needles.

Feejee, **Fidjee**, or **Viji Isles**, South Pacific Ocean, an extensive group of islands discovered by Tasman, in 1643. The principal island, called Viji, is high and fruitful, and abounding in hogs, fruits, and roots of all kinds. The inhabitants are very ferocious, and are addicted to cannibalism; they are tall, well-formed, and dark, with hair approaching to woolly, and are of Malay origin.

Feira, a town of Portugal, in Beira; 10 miles S. E. of Oporto, and 30 N. by E. of Aveiro.

Feldkirch, a town of Germany, in Tyrol, capital of a county of the same name. It is seated on the river Ill, near its entrance into the Rhine; 19 miles S. of the Lake of Constance.

Feldsburg, a town and castle at the N. E. extremity of Lower Austria, with a fine palace; seated on the Teya; 18 miles E. of Laab.

Felicuda, one of the Lipari islands in the Mediterranean; 28 miles W. of Lipari.

Felipe, St. *See* Xativa.

Felippe, St., a populous town of Colombia; seated on the banks of a river falling into the Caribbean Sea, about 100 miles W. of Caraccas.

Felix, St., an island in the Pacific Ocean, N. N. W. of Juan Fernandez. Long. 86. W. lat. 26. S.

Felletin, a town of France, in the department of Creuse, with a manufacture of tapestry.

It is 20 miles S. S. W. of Evaux, and 21 S. S. E. of Gueret.

FELLIN, a town of Russia, in Livonia, on the river Pernau; 62 miles S. E. of Revel.

FELSBERG, a town of Germany, in Hesse-Cassel, with an ancient castle on a rock; 12 miles S. of Cassel.

FELSO-BANYA, a village of Upper Hungary, near the frontier of Transylvania; celebrated for a gold mine in its vicinity.

FELTRI, a town of Italy, capital of Feltrino, and a bishop's see. It is fortified, and seated on the Asona, a small stream, falling into the Piave from the W.; 30 miles N. W. of Treviso. Long. 11. 55. E. lat. 46. 3. N. Pop. about 5000.

FELTRINO, a district of Italy, lying between Belunese, Trevisano, Vicentino, and the principality of Trent. It abounds in mountains, in which are iron mines. Feltri is the only place of note.

FEMERN, a fertile island of Denmark, at the entrance of the Baltic, from the passage of the Great and Little Belt. It is 10 miles long and 5 broad, separated from the coast of Holstein by a narrow channel, called the Femern Sound. Borg is the chief town. population of the island about 7500.

FENNESTRANGE, or ENESTRANGE, a town of France, in the department of Meurte, on the river Sarre; 40 miles E. by N. of Nancy.

FENESTRELLE, a town and fort of Piedmont; seated on the Cluson; 18 miles W. of Turin.

FERABAD, a town of Persia, capital of the province of Mazenderan. The environs produce sugar, cotton, and silk. The inhabitants, about 16,000, are principally descendants of Georgians and Armenians. It is seated among the mountains which bound the Caspian Sea to the S.; 12 miles from that sea, and 280 N. of Ispahan. Long. 52. 21. E. lat. 36. 54. N.

FERCALA, or FORCULA, a town of the kingdom of Tafilet, E. of Morocco, and the principal place of a district. It is 50 miles W. of Sigilmessa. Long. 4. 30. W. lat. 31. 40. N.

FERE, a town of France, in the department of Aisne, famous for its powder-mill and school of artillery. Near it is the castle of St. Gobin, in which is a manufacture of fine plate-glass. Fere is seated at the conflux of the Serre with the Oise; 20 miles N. of Soissons, and 75 N. E. of Paris.

FERENTINO, or FIORENZO, a town of Italy, in Campagna di Roma; 3 miles W. of Alatri, on the high road from Rome to Naples.

FERETTE, a town of France in the department of Upper Rhine, on the river Ill, near its source; 40 miles S. of Colmar.

FERGUS, a river in Ireland, county of Clare, tributary to the Shannon.

FERMANAGH, a county of Ireland, in the province of Ulster; bounded on the N. by the counties of Donegal and Tyrone, E. by Monaghan, S. by Cavan, and W. by Leitrim, the N. W. end jetting upon Donegal Bay; it extends from the S. in a N. W. direction about 36 miles, being about 24 in mean breadth. One-sixth of its area in summer, and one-fifth in winter, is occupied by Lough Erne, which discharges its waters into Donegal Bay, dividing the county into nearly two equal parts. In the centre of the county, the water narrows so as to admit of the two parts being united by a bridge. *See* ENNISKILLEN. The linen manufacture, and the raising of cattle and hemp, are the chief employ of the inhabitants. The county is navigable throughout by means of Lough Erne, but its uneven surface and numerous bogs render it difficult for travelling. Enniskillen is the capital and only town of importance in the county. It returns two members to parliament.

FERMO, a town of Italy, in the marquisate of Ancona, and an archbishop's see, with a good trade in corn, wool, &c. It has a harbour on the Gulf of Venice, and is 17 miles S. E. of Macerata. Long. 13. 50. E. lat. 43. 7. N. Pop. about 7000.

FERMOSELLA, or FORMOSELLA, a town of Spain, in the province of Leon; seated on the N. bank of the Tormes, near its entrance into the Douro.

FERMOY, a town of Ireland, in the county of Cork; seated on the banks of the Blackwater; 142 miles N. W. of Dublin, on the road to Cork, from which it is distant 17 miles. This place has risen from an inconsiderable village, since the commencement of the war in 1793.

FERNANDEZ. *See* JUAN FERNANDEZ.

FERNANDO NORONHA, an island in the S. Atlantic; 100 leagues from Cape St. Roque, the N. E. point of the province of Pernambuco. Long. 32. 33. W. lat. 3. 56. S.

FERNANDO PO, an island of Africa, on the coast of Benin; 30 miles long and 20 broad. Long. 7. 36. E. lat. 3. 6. N.

FERNEY, a village of France, in the department of Ain, a few miles N. W. of Geneva, celebrated as having been the residence of Voltaire.

FERNS, a town of Ireland, in the county of Wexford, and a bishop's see united to Leighlin. It is seated on the Bann, near its conflux with the Slaney; 17 miles N. of Wexford, and 30 S. S. W. of Wicklow.

FEROE ISLANDS, a cluster of 22 small islands in the Northern Ocean, between the Shetland Islands and Iceland, in 5. and 8. W. long. and 61. and 63. N. lat.; subject to Denmark. Seventeen are habitable, each of which is a lofty mountain, divided from the others by deep and rapid currents. Some of them are deeply indented with secure harbours, all of them steep, and most of them faced with tremendous precipices. They produce agate, jasper, and beautiful zoolites. The surface consists of a shallow soil of remarkable fertility, yielding plenty of barley and fine grass for sheep. No trees above the size of a juniper, or stunted willow, will grow here; and the only quadrupeds are sheep. Vast quantities of sea-fowls frequent the rocks, and the taking of them furnishes a perilous employment for the inhabitants. The exports are salted mutton, tallow, goose-quills, feathers, eider down, knit woollen waistcoats, caps, and stockings. To the S. of these islands is a considerable whirlpool. Pop. 5265.

FEROZABAD, or FIRUZABAD, a city of Persia,

in Farsistan, formerly of considerable repute, and yet contains a number of fine tombs, gardens, and buildings. It is seated in a fertile county; 60 miles S. by W. of Shiras, on the route to Ormus. Long. 53. 0. E. lat. 28. 50. N.

FERRARA, a city of Italy, capital of a duchy of the same name, and an archbishop's see, with a strong citadel, and a university. Its broad streets, and number of fine buildings, evince that it was formerly a flourishing place, but the present inhabitants are few, in proportion to its extent. In the middle of the city is a palace, surrounded by walls flanked with towers and ditches. The cathedral is remarkable for its antiquity. In the Benedictine church, Ariosto the poet is interred. Ferrara was taken by the French in 1796; in 1799 it was retaken by the Austrians, but shortly after surrendered to the French. It is seated near the Po; 25 miles N. E. of Bologna. Long. 11. 36. E. lat. 44. 50. N.

FERRARA, or FERRARESE, a duchy of Italy; bounded on the N. by the Po, which divides it from Polesino di Rovigno, W. by the Mantuan, S. by the Bolognese and Romagna, and E. by the Gulf of Venice. It had its own dukes till 1597, when Clement VIII. united it to the apostolic chamber. The air is unwholesome, on account of the marshes, which the abject condition of the inhabitants precludes from draining. Ferrara is the capital.

FERRENDINA, a town of Naples, in Basilicata, near the river Basianto; 25 miles S. W. of Matera.

FERRINTOSH, a village of Scotland, shire of Ross, whose inhabitants possessed the privilege of distilling whisky duty free, till 1786, when it was abolished.

FERRO, or HIERO, the most westward of the Canary Islands; about 18 miles in circumference. It is not fertile, but produces some corn, sugar, fruit, and legumes. The inhabitants make use of water collected in cisterns during the rainy season, for there is no spring in the island. Voyagers speak of a fountain tree in the middle of the island, and that in the night much water distils from its leaves. Ancient geographers have taken their first meridian from the W. extremity of this island. Long. 17. 52. W. lat. 27. 47. N.

FERROL, a seaport of Spain, in Galicia, on a bay of the Atlantic. Its harbour is one of the best in Europe, and here the Spanish squadrons frequently rendezvous in time of war. The town is surrounded on three sides by the sea, and strongly fortified on the other. In 1800 the English made an unsuccessful attempt on this place. It is 20 miles N. E. of Corunna, and 305 N.W. of Madrid. Long. 8. 4. W. lat. 43. 28. N.

FERRYBRIDGE, a large village in West Yorkshire, on the S. side of the Aire, over which is a noble bridge; 21 miles S. by W. of York, and 174 N. by W. of London.

FERRYPORT, a village of Scotland, in Fifeshire, on the Frith of Tay; 4 miles below Dundee, and 9 N.N.W. of St. Andrews. It has a considerable manufacture of brown linens, and a ferry over the Tay, well frequented before the bridge at Perth was built.

FERRYTOWN. *See* CREETOWN.

FERTE SUR AUBE, a town of France, in the department of Upper Marne; seated on the Aube; 22 miles W. by S. of Chaumont, and 33 E.S.E. of Troyes.

There are seven or eight towns in France named *Ferte*, all prefixed to some other name, as in the case of Aube, to distinguish them from each other.

FESTENBERG, a town of Silesia, in the principality of Oels; 14 miles N. W. of Wartenburg.

FESTINIOG, a hamlet in North Wales, county of Merioneth. It is near the junction of the rivers Dwyrhyd and Cynfoel, on which are several beautiful cascades.

FETHARD, a town of Ireland, in the county of Tipperary: 8 miles S. E. of Cashel, and 86 S.S.W. of Dublin. It was formerly fortified, but the walls are now ruined: it was, also, anciently a borough.

FETHARD, a town of Ireland, in the county of Wexford, on the W. side of Bannow Bay; 14 miles S. by E. of New Ross.

FEVERSHAM, or FAVERSHAM, a town in Kent, on a creek falling into the mouth of the Thames, much frequented by small vessels. It is a member of the port of Dover, and governed by a mayor. The church is in the form of a cross, and the interior well worthy of observation; and here is a free grammar-school founded by Queen Elizabeth. It has a market on Wednesday and Saturday; is famous for the best oysters for laying in stews; and has several gunpowder mills in its neighbourhood. Here are the remains of a stately abbey, built by King Stephen, who was interred in it with his queen and son. James II. embarked here in disguise, after the success of the prince of Orange; but the vessel was detained by the populace, and the king conveyed back to London. Feversham is 9 miles W. of Canterbury, and 47 E. by S. of London.

FEURS, a town of France, in the department of Loire, seated on the Loire; 13 miles E.N.E. of Montbrison.

FEYSTRITZ, or WINDISCH FISTRITZ, a town and castle of Germany, in Lower Styria, on a river of the same name; 17 miles N.N.E. of Cilley.

FEZ, a kingdom of Barbary, at the N. W. extremity of North Africa; bounded on the W. by the Atlantic, N. by the Mediterranean, E. by Algier, and S. by Morocco and Tafilet. It extends upwards of 400 miles from E. to W. and is about 150 in breadth, is divided into 9 provinces, and forms part of the empire of Morocco. The country is full of mountains, particularly to the W. and S. where Mount Atlas lies; but it is populous and fertile, producing citrons, lemons, oranges, dates, almonds, olives, figs, raisins, honey, wax, cotton, flax, pitch, and corn in abundance. The inhabitants breed camels, beeves, sheep, and the finest horses in Barbary. At the extreme N point is the town and fortress of Ceuta, garrisoned by the Spaniards. *See*

CEUTA. The principal places on the Atlantic coast are Salee and Laranche; Melitta and Tangier, on the coast of the Mediterranean; and in the interior, Mequinez, Fez, and Teza.

FEZ, the capital of the kingdom of Fez, and one of the largest cities in Africa. It is composed of three towns called Beleyde, Old Fez, and New Fez. Old Fez is the most considerable, and contains about 80,000 inhabitants. New Fez, founded about the 13th century, is principally inhabited by Jews, who trade with the Moors, notwithstanding the contempt with which they are treated by them. Old Fez was founded in 793, by Sidy Edris, a descendant of Mahomet and Ali, whose father fled from Medina to avoid the proscriptions of the caliph Abdallah. The palaces are magnificent; and there are numerous mosques, one of which, called Carubin, is one of the finest edifices in the empire. The houses are built of brick or stone, and adorned with mosaic work: those of brick are ornamented with glazing and colours like Dutch tiles, and the wood-work and ceilings are carved, painted, and gilt. The roofs are flat; and every house has a court, in which is a square marble basin. Here are two colleges for students, finely built of marble, and adorned with paintings. The hospitals and public baths are numerous, many of which are stately structures. All the traders live in a separate part of the city; and the exchange, full of all sorts of rich merchandise, is as large as a small town. The gardens are full of all kinds of fragrant flowers and shrubs. The Moors of Fez are clothed like the Turks; and, though more polished than their countrymen, are vain, superstitious, and intolerant. The saints, whom they pretend to have been buried in the city, serve them for a pretext to forbid its entrance to Jews and Christians; and an order from the emperor is necessary to gain admission. Arabic is better spoken here than in other parts of the empire; and the rich Moors send their children to the schools at Fez, where they gain more instruction than they could do elsewhere. Fez is the centre of the trade of this empire; and hence caravans go to Mecca, carrying ready-made garments, leather, indigo, cochineal, and ostrich feathers, for which they bring in return silks, muslins, and drugs. Other caravans go to Tombuctoo, and the river Niger. They travel over such dry barren deserts, that every other camel carries water. Their commodities are salt, cowries, wrought silk, British cloth, and the woollen manufactures of Barbary. Fez is seated in a circular valley, watered by a river, and surrounded by mountains; 160 miles S. S. W. of Gibraltar, and 240 N. E. of Morocco. Long. 4. 45. W. lat. 33. 40. N.

FEZZAN, an interior kingdom of North Africa, lying between the great deserts of Zahara and Libya; bounded on the N. by Tripoli, to the bashaw of which province Fezzan pays an annual tribute of 4000 dollars. It is an extensive plain, encompassed by mountains, except to the W.; and to the influence of these heights it may be owing, that here, as well as in Upper Egypt, no rain is ever known. Though the character of the surface (which in general is light sand) and the want of rain, may seem to announce sterility, yet the springs are so abundant, that few regions in the N. of Africa exhibit a richer vegetation. The greatest length of the cultivated part is about 300 miles from N. to S. and 200 from E. to W. From wells of 10 or 15 feet deep, with which every garden and field is furnished, the husbandman waters the productions of his land; among these are the date-tree, the olive, lime, apricot, pomegranate, fig, maize, barley, wheat, pompions or calabash, carrots, cucumbers, onions, and garlic. Among the tame animals are the sheep, cow, goat, camel, ass, and a species of the domestic fowl of Europe. The wild animals are the ostrich and antelopes of various kinds. A multitude of noxious animals infest the country; adders, snakes, scorpions, and toads swarm in the fields, gardens, and houses; the air is crowded with mosquitos; and persons of every rank are overrun with vermin. The heat of the climate in summer is intense, and the S. wind is scarcely supportable even by the natives; and in winter a penetrating N. wind prevails, which drives to the fire even the natives of the northern country. Tempests of wind are frequent, which whirl up the sand and dust so as to give a yellow tinge to the atmosphere. The towns are chiefly inhabited by husbandmen and shepherds; for, though they also contain merchants and artificers, yet agriculture and pasturage are the principal occupations. The houses are built of clay with a flat roof composed of boughs of trees, on which a quantity of earth is laid. The natives are of a deep swarthy complexion; their hair is a short curly black; their lips thick, their noses flat and broad, and their skin emits a fetid effluvia; they are tall, and well shaped, but weakly, indolent, and inactive. Their dress is similar to that of the Moors of Barbary. In their common intercourse, all distinctions of rank seem forgotten; the shereef, or governor, and the lowest plebeian, the rich and the poor, the master and the servant, converse familiarly, and eat and drink together. Generous and hospitable, let his fare be scanty or abundant, the Fezzaner is desirous that others should partake of it; and if twenty persons were unexpectedly to visit his dwelling, they must all participate as far as it will go. When they settle their money transactions, they squat upon the ground, and, having levelled a spot with their hands, make dots as they reckon: if they are wrong, they smooth the spot again, and repeat the calculation. Gold dust constitutes the chief medium of payment; and value in that medium is always expressed by weight. In religion they are rigid but not intolerant Mahometans. The government is monarchical; and its powers are administered with such a temperate hand, that the people are ardently attached to their sovereign. MOURZOUK (which see) is the capital.

FIANO, a town of Italy, in the patrimony of St. Peter. It is seated on the Tiber; 15 miles N. of Rome.

FIANONO, a town of Istria, on the S. W. coast; 17 miles N. of Pola.

Fiascone, a town of Italy, in the patrimony of St. Peter; noted for fine muscadine wine; seated on a mountain near Lake Bolsena; 12 miles N. W. of Viterbo.

Ficherulolo, a fortified town of Italy, in the Ferrarese; seated on the Po; 12 miles W. of Ferrara.

Fichtelberg, a mountain in Franconia, one of the highest mountains in Germany. It extends from near Bayreuth, to Eger in Bohemia, about 16 miles, and is covered with pines and other trees.

Fielewier, an island near the W. coast of Norway; 22 miles long and 4 broad, with a town of the same name; 48 miles W. N. W. of Drontheim. Long. 10. 40. E. lat. 63. 44. N.

Fife, a maritime county on the coast of Scotland, forming a peninsula between the Friths of Forth and Tay: it extends from the mouth of the river Forth, in a N. N. E. direction, about 40 miles, and is about 12 miles in mean breadth; it is watered by numerous streams, the principal of which is the Eden, flowing through the centre of the county in a N. E. direction, into St. Andrew's Bay. From the earliest period, the security afforded by its peninsular position appears to have occasioned it to have been the most densely populated part of Scotland; it seems to have constituted the stronghold of the Picts, during their conflicts with the Cimbri, or more ancient Scots. But it attained its greatest distinction in the early part of the 16th century, when its advantageous position obtained for it the special favour of James V., who incorporated several of its towns, and conferred upon them royal privileges: 13 of these royal burghs still continue incorporated, but most of them are now become inconsiderable, and several others have become dissolved, from their inability to sustain the expense of civic parade; and, since the commencement of the 18th century, the whole county has declined in importance, relative to other counties of Scotland; and, whatever benefit the county of Fife may have derived at former periods from royal favour, it now obviously militates against its social advancement. Some linen manufactures are carried on in the S. W. parts of the county, (*see* Dunfermline,) but as a whole, it is an agricultural rather than a manufacturing district; it produces coal and lime in abundance, and copper, lead, iron, and other minerals are also found in different parts of the county, though but partially worked; a beautiful grey marble, cornelian, agates, and jasper, are occasionally met with, and fishing on its coasts and its rivers is assiduously pursued by the inhabitants. It returns one member to parliament. Cupar is the assize town.

Figarnolo, an island in the Gulf of Venice, near the coast of Istria. Long. 13. 47. E. lat. 45. 18. N.

Figeac, a town of France, in the department of Lot, with a Benedictine abbey; seated on the Selle; 22 miles E. of Cahors. It is the seat of a prefect, and contains 6153 inhabitants.

Fighig, or Fihig, a town of Barbary, in Biledulgerid, at the foot of Mount Atlas, on the S. The inhabitants carry on a great trade with the merchants of Morocco and Fez, and with the negroes. It is 240 miles E. S. E. of Mequinez. Long. 1. 5. W. lat. 32. 20. N.

Figueras, or St. Fernando de Figueras, a strong town and important fortress of Spain, in Catalonia. It surrendered to the French in 1794, without firing a shot. It is 10 miles S. by W. of Rosas, and 25 due S. of Perpignan.

Figuero dos Vinhos, a town of Portugal, in Estramadura, much celebrated for its wine; seated among mountains, near the frontier of Beira and the river Zezere; 22 miles N. of Thomar.

Filey, a town in Yorkshire. Off the shore of this parish is a lobster fishery.

Finale, a sea-port of Genoa, with a strong citadel, two forts, and a castle. It was the capital of a marquisate, and annexed to the duchy of Milan in 1602, but sold to the Genoese in 1713. In 1746 it was taken by the king of Sardinia, and restored in 1748. It is 30 miles S.W. of Genoa. Long. 8. 25. E. lat. 44. 14. N. Pop. about 7000.

Finale, a town of Italy, in the Modenese, on an island formed by the river Penaro; 22 miles N. E. of Modena.

Finchley, a parish in Middlesex, 8 miles from London. General Monk here drew up his forces in 1660, to effect the restoration.

Findhorn, a town of Scotland, shire of Elgin. It possesses a thriving foreign and coasting trade in corn, salmon, yarn, &c.

Finisterre, Cape, a cape of Spain, forming the extreme N.W. point of that country, projecting into the Atlantic Ocean, from the province of Galicia. It was thought by the ancients to have no country beyond it, and therefore they gave it a name which signifies the land's-end. Long. 9. 17. W. lat. 42. 54. N.

Finisterre, a maritime department of France, which includes part of the late province of Bretagne. It is the most westerly part of France, and bounded on three sides by the sea. On the N. it forms the boundary to the entrance of the English Channel. It is divided into five arrondissements, of which Quimper, Brest, Morlaix, Chateaulin, and Quimperle, are the seats of the prefects. The other principal towns are Lesneven, Landerneau, and Carhaix.

Finland, a principality of European Russia, extending from the lat. of 60. to 66. 30. N., and in its extreme breadth from the long. of 21. to 31. 30. E. It is bounded on the S. by the Gulf of Finland, and W. by the Gulf of Bothnia, N. by Lapland, and E. by the Russian provinces of Wiburg and Olonetz; it formerly belonged to Sweden, and was divided into two great parts, the N. called East Bothnia, (*see* Bothnia,) and the S., Finland Proper, which contains several considerable towns, of which Abo is the chief, and capital of the whole country (*see* Abo.) The other towns are Nystadt, Raumo, and Biorneborg, on the shore of the Gulf of Bothnia, and Helsingfors, Borgo, and Louisa, on the shore of the Gulf of Finland. There are also four or five considerable towns in the interior. About one-third of the area of Finland Proper is composed of lakes. The contiguity of Finland to the maritime capital of the Russian empire had long rendered it an object of jealousy to that power, and in 1808 they overran it with so formidable a force as to compel the Swedes to consent to a formal cession of the whole country, and it now forms one of the fifty governments of the Russian empire. It is divided into thirteen districts, containing together a population of 1,378,500, who contributed a revenue of 3,200,000 rubles, equal to about 130,000*l*.

FINMARK, the most northern section of Europe, jetting into the Arctic Ocean: it formerly belonged to Denmark, but with Norway was ceded to Sweden, in 1815. The coast is flanked with islands, and indented with bays. It comprises about 400 square miles of surface, but the inhabitants, a mixed race of Fins and Laplanders, do not exceed 26,000, who principally inhabit the coast, fishing and hunting constituting their chief employment; the S. part, bordering on Lapland, is mountainous. North Cape, its extreme northern limit, and also of Europe, is in the lat. of 71. 10. N. and 25. 50. of E. long.

FINOW, a town of Brandenburg, in the Ucker Mark. It has a canal, by which the Oder and Havel are united. It is 28 miles N. W. of Custrin.

FIONDA, a town of Asiatic Turkey, in Natolia, and a bishop's see; on the Gulf of Satalia; 25 miles S. W. of Satalia.

FIORENZO. *See* FERENTINO.

FIORENZO, ST., a seaport on the N. W. coast of Corsica, defended by walls and a tower. It was taken by the English and Corsicans, from the French, in 1794. It is 7 miles W. of Bastia.

FIROSEPOUR, a town of Hindostan, in Moultan; seated on the Setlege, at the influx of the Beyah; 20 miles W. of Depalpour, and 150 E. by N. of Moultan.

FISCHHAUSEN, a town of Prussia, with a royal castle; seated on the Frische Haff; 21 miles W. of Konigsberg, and 5. N. N. E. of Pillau.

FISH RIVER, GREAT, a river of Africa, which rises in the unknown interior regions, divides Caffraria from the country of the Hottentots, and enters the Indian Ocean in long. 28. 22. E. lat. 33. 24. S.

FISHER-ISLAND, in Long Island Sound, opposite to Stonington harbour in Connecticut. It is 10 miles long and 2 broad, with a fertile soil, and is annexed to the township of Southold, in Long Island.

FISHERROW, a town of Scotland, Edinburghshire. It is separated from the town of Musselburgh by the river Esk, over which is an ancient bridge.

FISHGUARD, OR ABERGWAYN, a town of Wales, in Pembrokeshire, governed by a mayor, with a market on Friday. Here is a good harbour, which has been lately improved, with every convenience for ship-building, and a considerable trade in herrings, corn, and butter. It is situate on a steep cliff, on a bay of St. George's Channel; 16 miles N. E. of St. David, and 249 W. by N. of London.

FISHKILL, a town of New York, in Duchess county, on a creek of the same name; 5 miles E. of Hudson River, and 66 N. of New York. Pop. of the township 10,437.

FISINES, a town of France, in the department of Marne; 20 miles S. of Laon, a town of great antiquity, and has a trade in wool, corn, and wine. Pop. 2500.

FISSATO, a seaport of Barbary, in the province of Tripoli; 90 miles N. W. of Tripoli. Long. 12. 10. E. lat. 33. 50. N.

FISTELLA, a fortified town in Morocco. The inhabitants carry on a great trade in fine garments. It is 125 miles N. E. of Morocco. Long. 5. 55. E. lat. 32. 27. N.

FIUM. *See* FAYOUM.

FIUME, a seaport of Austrian Istria, with a castle, and many fine churches and convents. It is noted for wine, good figs, and other fruits; and has a sugar refinery, and a wax manufacture. The harbour is formed by the river Fiumara, which enters the Bay of Carnero, at the extremity of the Adriatic. It is 37 miles E. of Capo d'Istria. Long. 14. 12. E. lat. 45. 38. N. Pop. about 12,000.

FLADSTRAND, a seaport of Denmark, in North Jutland, with a harbour defended by three forts, just within the entrance to the Cattegat. It is 30 miles N. N. E. of Alburg. Long. 10. 29. E. lat. 57. 33. N.

FLAMBOROUGH, a factory of the Hudson Bay Company, on Hayes River, 70 miles from its mouth, on the W. side of Hudson Bay. Long. 90. 5. W. lat. 56. 8. N.

FLAMBOROUGH HEAD, a lofty promontory, on the coast of Yorkshire, whose snow-white cliffs, rising from 300 to 450 feet above the level of the sea, and are the northern extremity of the chalk cliffs of Albion, afford shelter to innumerable multitudes of sea-fowls. The lower parts contain vast caverns, and on the summit is a lighthouse; 5 miles E. N. E. of Burlington. Long. 0. 2. W. lat. 54. 8. N. There is a village of the same name, contiguous to the cliffs.

FLAMSTEAD, a village in Hertfordshire, England. It was a place of some importance in the time of the Romans being in possession of England.

The house in Greenwich Park, in which is the Royal Observatory, and from whence the English meridional line of longitude is drawn, is commonly called *Flamstead House*, after the name of its first astronomer. *See* GREENWICH.

FLANDERS, a country of Europe; bounded on the N. by the mouth of the Scheldt, and N. W. by the North Sea or German Ocean, lying between the lat. of 50. 40. and 51. 20. N. and 2. 15. to 4. 15. of E. long. The early history of this country is involved in considerable obscurity; it has, however, for several centuries ranked among the most fertile, populous, and civilized parts of Europe; it was formerly known under three divisions of French, Austrian, and Dutch Flanders; the French, or S. part was comprised in the late province of Artois, now the department du Nord, or North. The Austrian comprised the centre, from E. to W.; and the Dutch the coast of the mouth of the Scheldt; the whole country was overrun by the French in the early part of the war, which commenced in 1793, and confirmed to them by the treaty of Campo Formio, in 1797. After the treaty of Luneville, in 1801, Austrian and Dutch Flanders was divided into two departments—Lys, on the W., and Scheldt, on the E., and incorporated with the French empire. At the general partitioning of this part of Europe, which followed the peace of 1814, these two departments were ceded to the new kingdom of the Netherlands, and were included in the kingdom of Belgium on the erection of that state in 1831, and are now called the provinces of East and West Flanders. The area of the E. part comprises about 1260 square miles, and contains about 700,000 inhabitants. It is divided into four circles, of which Ghent. Dendermonde, Oudenarde, and Eecloo, are the chief towns; the other places of note are Sluys, Ardenberg, Phillipina, and Sas Van Ghent, on the shore of the mouth of the Scheldt; and Deynse, Renaix, Grammont, Sotteghem, Alost, and Watteren, in the S. The river Scheldt, which rises in the French department of Aisne, enters the S. W. corner, running N. by E. to Ghent in the centre of the province, and then nearly due E. till it changes its course to the N., forming the boundary of the province on the side of Brabant; towards the S. the surface is slightly undulated, but northward it is an entire level, intersected by canals, communicating both with the North Sea and the mouth of the Scheldt.

Flanders, West, is bounded on the S. and S. W. by the French department, on the N. and N.W. by the North Sea; the area of this province is about 1500 square miles, containing 557,871 inhabitants. It is also divided into four circles, of which Bruges, Furnes, Ypres, and Courtray are the chief towns; the other places of note are the seaports of Nieuport and Ostend: the latter is regarded as the maritime portal of this part of Europe; this, like East Flanders, is a level country; in the S. E. part fine thread, lace, and linen cambrics are manufactured to a great extent for exportation; over all the other parts of the two provinces, fishing, agriculture, and manufactures are assiduously pursued, and tend to render the inhabitants among the most social and best conditioned in Europe. The language of the common people is peculiar—a mixture of Dutch and French; but in the towns the French is most generally spoken. The Roman Catholic religion prevails through both provinces: the clergy are, however, a tolerant and respectable body.

Flatbush, a town of New York, chief of King's county, Long Island. The Americans were defeated near this place by the British, in 1776. It is situate amid garden grounds; 5 miles S. by E. of New York.

Flattery, Cape, on the W. coast of North America, discovered by Cook, in 1778; and so named because he was disappointed at not finding a harbour. Long. 124. 57. W. lat. 48. 25. N.

Flavigny, a town of France, in the department of Cote d'Or, with a Benedictine abbey; seated on a mountain, by the river Ozerain; 27 miles W. N. W. of Dijon.

Fleche, La, a town of France, in the department of Sarte. Here was a noble college built by Henry IV., at which Descartes was educated, the centre is now converted into a town-house, and one of the wings rebuilt as a prytaneum, or military school for soldiers' children. It is seated on the N. bank of the Loire, and is the seat of a prefect. Population 5387. It is 80 miles E. N. E. of Nantes.

Fleckeroe, Justeroe, or Fleckeren, an island in the Scaggerac, near the coast of Norway; a few miles E. of Christiansand. Between the island and the continent is a most excellent harbour, defended by a fortress. Long. 8. 18. E. lat. 58. 4. N.

Fleet, a river of Scotland, in Kircudbrightshire, which issues from a small lake of the same name, and enters Wigton Bay, below Gatehouse. On its W. side are the vestiges of a camp, a druidical circle, and a vitrified fort.

Fleetwood, Port, a new town at the mouth of the Wyre river, Lancashire. Piers to form a harbour and a lighthouse have been erected here, 15 miles S. of Lancaster, to which it is connected by the Preston and Wyre railway, a branch of the Liverpool and Manchester railway.

Flensburg, a seaport of Denmark, in the duchy of Sleswick, with a strong citadel, and a harbour at the head of a bay in the Little Belt, at its entrance into the Baltic. It is a place of great commerce; 15 miles N. N. W. of Sleswick. Long. 9. 47. E. lat. 54. 52. N. Population about 15,000.

Fleurance, a town of France, in the department of Gers, on the river Gers; 3 miles N. of Auch.

Fleurus, a town of Belgium, in Namur; 6 miles N. E. of Charleroi. Here, in 1690, a victory was gained by the French over the allies; and in 1794 the Austrians were defeated in a general attack of the French posts.

Flie, or Vlieland, an island on the coast of Holland, N. of the Texel, at the middle of the entrance of the Zuyder Zee.

Flint, a county at the N. E. extremity of Wales; bounded, in a N. W. direction, by the estuary of the river Dee, and N. by W. by the Irish Sea. It is the smallest county in Wales, its superficies being only 243 square miles. It is, however, rich in coal, copper, and lead, and, since the commencement of the present century, the cotton manufacture has been introduced. It returns one member to parliament. The principal towns are Mold, Holywell, Hawarden, and St. Asaph.

Flint, formerly the chief town of the county, though now a small place. It has the county gaol, but the assizes are held at Mold. Here are the remains of a royal castle, in which Richard II. took shelter on arriving from Ireland; but on leaving it he was delivered into the hands of his rival, afterward Henry IV.: it stands on a rock close to the sea, and is governed by a constable, who is also mayor of the town. Flint has no market, but is well frequented as a bathing-place. It is seated on the estuary of the Dee; 12 miles W. N. W. of Chester, and 195 N. N. W. from London, and contributes, with Holywell, &c. in sending one member to parliament.

Flint, a river of the state of Georgia, which rises in the country of the Creek Indians, runs S. W., and joining the Catahoochee, at its entrance into East Florida, forms the Apalachicola.

Flix, a town of Spain, in Catolonia, strong both by nature and art. It stands on a peninsula formed by the Ebro, and the side where the river does not pass is covered by mountains, and defended by a castle. It 23 miles N. of Tortosa.

Flodden, a field in the parish of Kirknewton, Northumberland, 5 miles N. N. W. of Woller, on which a battle was fought between the English and Scots, in 1513, in which James IV. was killed, with many of his nobility, and 10,000 men.

Florac, a town of France, in the department of Lozere; 13 miles S. of Mende, and 55 N. of Montpelier. It is the seat of a prefect. Pop. 2450.

Florence, a celebrated city of Italy, capital of Tuscany, and an archbishop's see, with a citadel and a university. It was first founded by the soldiers of Sylla, embellished and enlarged by the triumvirs, destroyed by Totila, and rebuilt by Charlemagne. The circumference is about six miles, and the fortifications consist of only a wall and a ditch, with two or three forts which command a part of the town. It is divided into two unequal parts, by the river Arno, over which are four handsome bridges. The quays, the buildings on each side, and the bridges, render the part through which the river runs by far the finest; but every part is full of wonders in the arts of painting, statuary, and architecture. The environs are beautiful, rich, and populous. Some of the Florentine merchants, formerly, were men of great wealth; and one of them, in the middle of the fifteenth century, built that noble fabric, which, from the name of its founder, is still called the Palazzo Pitti. It was afterwards purchased by the Medici family, who made some enlargements; and it thence became the residence of the grand dukes of Tuscany. The Palazzo Vecchio, or old palace, contains a room 172 feet long and 70 wide, for public entertainments. The beauties and riches of these palaces, in all that is masterly in architecture, literature, and the arts, especially those of painting and sculpture, have been often described; but before they were plundered by the French, in 1800, all description fell short of their contents. The celebrated Venus of Medici, the standard of taste in female beauty and proportion, stood in a room called the tribune; this, with other masterpieces of sculpture, was carried away to Paris, but restored, with most of the other works of art, at the general peace in 1815. There are other rooms, whose contents are indicated by the names they bear; as the cabinet of arts, of astronomy, natural history, medals, portraits, porcelain, antiquities, &c. Beside the Medicean library, begun by Julius de Medici, and greatly augmented by Duke Cosmo I., there are several other copious libraries, especially those in the two Benedictine and Carmelite convents. The Florentine Academy, and the Academia della Crusca, were instituted to enrich the literature and improve the language of Tuscany; the latter is so named becase it rejects, like *bran*, all words not purely Tuscan. The cathedral, the churches, and other public buildings, contain paintings and sculptures by the first masters in Italy; and the chapel of Lorenzo is, perhaps, the most expensive habitation that ever was reared for the dead, being incrusted with precious stones, and adornedwith the workmanship of the best modern sculptors. The manufactures of Florence are chiefly silks, satins, gold and silver stuffs, and damask tablecloths; and it has a considerable trade in fruits, oil, and excellent wines. Florence is 45 miles E. N. E. of Leghorn, which is its outport, and 125 N. W. of Rome. Long. 11. 3. E. lat. 43. 46. N. Pop. 80,000.

Florent, St., a town of France, in the department of Mayenne and Loire, with a Benedictine abbey; seated on the Loire; 20 miles W. S. W. of Angers.

Florentin, St., a town of France, in the department of Yonne, at the conflux of the Armance and Armancon; 15 miles N. E. of Auxerre, and 80 S. E. of Paris.

Florentino, one of the three provinces of Tuscany; bounded on the N. W. by the republic of Lucca and the Modenese, N. E. by the Apennines, and S. by the Siennese. Population, about 580,000: besides Florence, the capital, the other principal towns are Leghorn, Pisa, and Pistoia.

Flores, or Mangeyle, an island of the East Indies, one of the chain that forms the S. boundary of the Java and Banda seas; 180 miles long and 45 broad; lying to the E. of that of Sumbawa. On the S. side, near the E. end, is a town named Larantuca. Long. 121. 56. E. lat. 8. 20. S.

Flores, a fertile island, one of the Azores; so called from the abundance of flowers found upon it. Lagens is the most populous town, but St. Cruz is the capital. Long. 31. 0. W. lat. 39. 34. N.

Florida, a country of North America, forming a promontory extending from St. Mary's River, which divides it from Georgia, in the lat. of 30. 40. to Cape Sable, in 25. 2. N., between 80. and 83. of W. long.. This part of America was first made known to Europeans by Cabot, in 1496. It appears, however, not to have been revisited until 1512, when Ponce de Leon drew so flattering a picture of its fertility and capabilities as to render it an object of considerable attraction to all the maritime states of Europe; and it was, for upwards of two centuries, an object of repeated contention between the French, Spaniards, and English. In 1763, it was ceded by treaty to England, in whose possession it continued until 1779, when it was overrun by a Spanish force from Louisiana; and in 1783 it was ceded back to Spain, between which power and the United States of North America it continued an object of contention until 1819, when it was ceded to the latter power: the cession being ratified in 1821, it was taken possession of by the United States in July of that year, and now forms the Florida Territory, being the 27th state of the republic.

Florida, East, comprises the promontory: the outline of which has been already described, its western shore is washed by the waters of the Gulf of Mexico, and the eastern by the Atlantic Ocean. It is divided on the N. from the state of Georgia by a conventional line, drawn from St. Mary's River, about 45 miles above its entrance into the Atlantic Ocean, across the Oke-fin-o-con swamp, to the point where the Flint unites with the Chattahochee River, to form the Apalachicola, which forms the western boundary of the province, in the long. of 85. 30.W. There are numerous streams which discharge their waters into the Gulf of Mexico, and some into the Atlantic, and a river of considerable magnitude, rising from a lake 50 miles in circumference, in the lat. of 26. N., flows parallel with the Atlantic coast, at a distance of about 30 miles, and falls into the Atlantic, in the lat. of 30. 10. N. This river is at intervals two to five miles wide, and is navigable for vessels drawing eight or nine feet water, 150 miles from its mouth. The area of this territory comprises about 45,000 square miles; and its aggregate population is 13,651, the greater portion of whom are concentrated at St. Augustine, the principal town, seated on the Atlantic coast, in the lat. of 29. 48. N. East Florida produces some of the finest timber in all America, either for ship-building, or for carpentry purposes: at present it forms the chief article of commerce; but, as population increases, cotton and other products common to the tropics will probably be cultivated with success, and, to an industrious and enterprising people, it will doubtless yield an abundance of all the necessaries of life. It is, generally speaking, a level country; but in the centre, during its whole extent from N. to S., the land rises into gentle hills, but in no instance to come under the denomination of mountainous. Cape Sable, the southern extremity of the territory, is 135 miles N. N. W. of Havannah. A chain of islands, or rather sand-banks, flank nearly the whole line of coast, both on the side of the Atlantic and the Gulf of Mexico, and extensive shoals and reefs of sand bound the southern extremity. There are two or three commodious harbours on the W. coast, within the Gulf of Mexico; viz. St. Juan, Charlotte Harbour, and Spirito Santo, or Hillsborough.

Florida, West, extends W. 140 miles from the Apalachicola to the Perdida river, which divides it from the S. W. part of the state of Alabama. It is bounded on the S. by the Gulf of Mexico, and N. by a conventional line, which divides it from the S. E. part of Alabama. The mean breadth is about 55 miles, giving an area comprising 7700 square miles. The aggregate population is 5454; but as Pensacola, the chief town, has the best harbour in the Gulf of Mexico, with sufficient depth of water for ships of the largest class, under the influence of the enterprising and migratory disposition of the people of the United States, both West and East Florida may fairly be anticipated rapidly to increase in population, productions, and importance.

Florida Cape is on the E. coast of East Florida, in the gulf of the same name, in the lat. of 25. 41. N. and 80. 5. of W. long; 90 miles N. E. of Cape Sable, and about 30 W. of the N. W. end of the Great Bahama bank.

Florida, Gulf of, is the passage out of the Gulf of Mexico into the Atlantic Ocean, between the N. W. coast of the Island of Cuba, and the Bahama bank and islands on the E., and the promontory of East Florida on the W. Through the passage the great body of waters, flowing into the Gulf of Mexico from the Mississippi, Colorado, and Rio del Norte, set, in a continual stream, running at the rate of 4 to 5 miles per hour: the stream continues to run along the eastern coast of North America, to the lat. of 42. when the current is dispersed by the great bank of Newfoundland. The gulf passage is from 30 to 130 miles wide, the narrowest part being between Cape Florida and the Great Bahama bank before mentioned.

Florida Keys, or Martyrs Islands and Reefs, are the shoals and sand-banks flanking the southern extremity and E. coast of the promontory of East Florida, as previously described.

Flour, St., a city of France, in the department of Cantal, and a bishop's see. Good knives are made here, and it has a considerable trade in corn. It is seated on a mountain; 53 miles S. of Clermont, and 108 N. by W. of Montpelier. It is the seat of a prefect. Pop. 7500.

Flushing, a strong seaport of Dutch Zealand, in the island of Walcheren, on the N. side of Western Scheldt, the entrance of which it defends. It has a good harbour, and a great canal, which is deep enough to admit loaded vessels, runs through the town. The stadthouse is a superb building, after the model of that of Amsterdam. Flushing was the birthplace of Admiral De Ruyter, and has a capacious harbour and basin for ships of the largest burthen. It is one of the naval depôts of the Netherlands. Its trade consists chiefly of smuggling. Pop. 6000. It is in lat. 51. 27. N. and 3. 34. of E. long.

Flushing, a town of New York, in Queen's county, Long Island, situate on the E. side of Hell-gate; 7 miles E. by N. of New York. Pop. 4124.

Fluvanna, a county of Virginia, N. of James River, at the foot of the first ridge of the Allegany mountains. The population is 8812. Columbia, the chief town, at the S. E. corner of the county, is 52 miles W. by N. of Richmond.

Fochabers, a town of Scotland, belonging to Murrayshire, though seated on the E. side of the river Spey. It is 8 miles E. by S. of Elgin, and 22 W. of Banff.

Fochan, a populous village of China, in the vicinity of Canton.

Fochea, or **Foggia**, a seaport of Asiatic Turkey, in Natolia, with a castle. The Venetians beat the Turkish fleet near this place, in 1650. It is seated on the Gulf of Smyrna, at the influx of the Hermus; 28 miles N.W. of Smyrna. Long. 26. 39. E. lat. 38. 44. N.

Foedwar, a town of Hungary; seated on the W. bank of the Danube, opposite Colocza; 40 miles S. of Buda. Pop. 2500.

Fogaras, a town and castle of Transylvania, on the river Alauta; 30 miles N. by E. of Hermanstadt.

Foggia, a town of Naples, in Capitanata. It is a staple for corn and wool, and seated near the Cerbero; 20 miles S. of Manfredonia. It suffered greatly by an earthquake, in 1732. Pop. about 17,000.

Foglia, a river of Italy which rises on the confines of Tuscany, crosses the duchy of Urbino, and enters the Gulf of Venice at Pesaro.

Foglizzo, or **Foglino**, a town of Piedmont; 5 miles N.W. of Chivasso, and 13 W. of Crescentino.

Fogo. *See* Fuego.

Fohr, or **Fora**, an island of Denmark, about 12 miles in circumference, near the coast of Sleswick, in the German Ocean; 65 miles N. of Heligoland. Pop. about 5500. Long. 8. 31. E. lat. 54. 44. N.

Foix, a late district of France, in Languedoc, adjoining the Pyrenees. It now forms, with Couserans, the department of Arriege.

Foix, a town of France, capital of the department of Arriege. Here is a manufacture of coarse woollen cloths, and some copper-mills. It is seated on the Arriege, near the foot of the Pyrenees; 42 miles S. by E. of Toulouse.

Fo-kien, a maritime province in the S. of China; bounded on the N. by Tche-kiang, W. by Kiang-si, S. by Quang-tong, and E. by the China Sea. The climate is warm; and yet the air is so pure, that no contagious diseases ever prevail. It produces musk in abundance, precious stones, quicksilver, iron, and tin; also gold and silver, but it is forbidden to dig for these. It has fine plains; and industry fertilizes even the mountains, the greater part of which are cut into terraces, rising above each other. Its valleys are watered by springs and rivers from the mountains, which the husbandman distributes with great skill, to refresh his rice: he has even the art to raise his water to the tops of the mountains, and to convey it from one side to the other, by pipes made of bamboo. The people speak a different language in most of the cities, each of which has its particular dialect. The language of the mandarins is that which is spoken everywhere; but few understand it in this province; however, it produces a great number of literati. It contains nine cities of the first, and sixty of the third class. Fou-tcheou is the capital.

Foleshill, a parish in the county of the city of Coventry, lying on the N. side of the city, and intersected by the Coventry canal. Population almost exclusively employed in the ribbon manufacture.

Foligno, a town of Italy, in the duchy of Umbria; famous for its sweetmeats, paper-mills, and silk manufactures. It is seated on the W. side of the Appennines, near a fertile plain; 69 miles N. of Rome.

Folkingham, a town in Lincolnshire, with a market on Thursday. Here are the ruins of an ancient castle. It is seated on a rising ground; 18 miles W.S.W. of Boston, and 106 N. of London. Pop. 744.

Folkstone, a town in Kent, with a market on Thursday. It had once five churches, of which four have been destroyed by the incursions of the sea. The inhabitants are chiefly employed in fishing. Dr. Wm. Harvey, the far-famed discoverer of the circulation of the blood, was born here in 1578. It is a member of the port of Dover, governed by a mayor; and a little to the W. is Sandgate Castle, built by Henry VIII. It is seated on the English Channel; 8 miles S.W. of Dover, and 72 E. by S. of London.

Fondi, a town of Naples, in the Terra di Lavora; seated on the Appian Way, near the sea-coast; 65 miles S.S.W. of Rome.

Fong-tsiang, or **Fontcheou**, a city of China, in the province of Chen-si. Its district contains eight cities of the second and third class. It is seated on the Hoie Ho, which falls into the Yellow River; 500 miles S.W. of Peking. Long. 106. 57. E. lat. 34. 36. N.

Fong-yang, a city of China, in the province of Kiang-nan. It encloses within its walls several fertile little hills; and its jurisdiction comprehends five cities of the second, and thirteen of the third class. It is seated on a mountain which overhangs a river falling into the Hongts Hou; 70 miles N.E. of Nankin. Long. 116. 58. E. lat. 32. 52. N.

Fons, a town of France, in the department of Lot; 5 miles N.W. of Figeac.

Fontainbleau, a town of France, in the department of Seine and Marne; celebrated for its fine palace, and a hunting seat of the sovereigns of France. It stands in the midst of an extensive forest; 35 miles S.S.E. of Paris. It is the seat of a prefect. Pop. about 8000.

Fontaine l'Eveque, a town of the Netherlands, in the territory of Liege; 6 miles W. of Charleroi.

Fontanetto, a town of Piedmont; 7 miles E. of Crescentino.

Fontarabia, a seaport of Spain, in Biscay, on the frontiers of France, from which it is separated by the river Bidassoa, which forms a harbour at its mouth, in the Bay of Biscay. It stands on a peninsula, at the foot of the Pyrenean mountains, and is so strong, both by nature and art, as to be accounted the key of Spain on that side; but it opened its gates to the French in 1794. It is 22 miles S.W. of Bayonne, and 62 E. by N. of Bilboa. Long. 1. 47. W. lat. 43. 23. N.

Fontenay le Compte, a town of France, in the department of Vendee. It has a woollen manufacture, and its fairs are famous for cattle. It is seated on the Vendee; 25 miles N.E. of Rochelle, 55 W. by S. of Poitiers, and 215 S.E. of Paris. It is the seat of a prefect. Pop. 7470.

Fontenoy, a town of Belgium, in Hainault; 4 miles S. E. of Tournay. It is celebrated for a battle between the allies and the French, in 1745, in which the former were defeated.

Fontevrault, a town of France, in the department of Mayenne and Loire. Here is a famous abbey, in the church of which several kings and queens of France lie interred. It is 7 miles S. E. of Saumur.

Fora, an island of Denmark, on the W. coast of S. Jutland, between those of Sylt and Nordstrand. It is of an oval form, 20 miles in circumference, and the chief place is Utersen. *See* Fohr.

Forcheim, a strong town of Franconia, in the principality of Bamberg, with a fine arsenal. It surrendered to the French in 1796, but the Austrians compelled them to abandon it soon afterward. It is seated at the conflux of the Wisent and Rednitz, 16 miles S. S. E. of Bamberg, and is now included in the territory of the king of Bavaria.

Fordingbridge, a town in Hampshire, with a market on Saturday, and a manufacture of checks and bed-ticks; seated on the Little Avon; 10 miles S. of Salisbury, and 88 W. by S. of London.

Foreland, North, a promontory of Kent, the E. point of the isle of Thanet. It is the most southern point of the port of London; and a line thence extended N. to the point called the Nase, in Essex, forms the mouth of the Thames. Here is a lighthouse upwards of 100 feet high. Long. 1. 29. E. lat. 51. 22. N.

Foreland, South, another promontory of Kent. It is called South, in respect to its bearing from the other Foreland, which is 13 miles to the N. Between these two capes is the noted roadstead, called the Downs.

Forest Towns, four towns of Suabia, in Brisgau, situate on the Rhine and the confines of Switzerland, at the entrance of the Black Forest. Their names are Waldschut, Lauffenburgh, Seckingen, and Rheinfelden.

Forfar, a borough of Scotland, capital of Angusshire. It contains many neat modern houses, and has manufactures of coarse linens and shoes. It is situate in an extensive plain, nearly in the centre of the country; 14 miles N. by E. of Dundee. It contributes, with Inverbervie, &c., in sending one member to parliament, and has a railway to Arbroath.

Forfarshire. *See* Angusshire.

Forges, a town of France, in the department of Lower Seine; celebrated for its mineral waters. It is 24 miles N. E. of Rouen.

Forio, or **Fontario**. *See* Ischia.

Forli, a town of Italy, in Romagna; seated on the frontier of Tuscany, in a fertile country, near the river Rones; 11 miles S. S. W. of Ravenna.

Formentera, an island in the Mediterranean, belonging to the crown of Spain. It is situated to the S. of Ivica, from which it is separated by a channel 4 miles wide.

Formosa, Tae-wan, or **Taiouan**, an island in the China Sea, lying between 120. and 122. E. long. and 22. and 25. N. lat., and separated from the province of Fo-kien, in China, by a channel about 80 miles wide where narrowest. It is 280 miles from N. to S., and 70 in its broadest part, but is greatly contracted at the S. extremity. It is subject to the Chinese, who, however, did not know of its existence till the year 1430. A chain of mountains, running its whole length, divides it into two parts, the E. and W. The Dutch built the fort of Zealand, on the W. part, in 1643. They were driven thence in 1661, by a Chinese pirate, who made himself master of all the W. part. In 1682 the whole island submitted to the emperor of China. It contains extensive and fertile plains, watered by a great number of rivulets from the mountains. It produces abundance of corn and rice, most of the Indian fruits, many of those of Europe, tobacco, sugar, pepper, camphire, and cinnamon. Wholesome water is the only thing wanting in Formosa. The inhabitants rear a great number of oxen, which they use for riding, from a want of horses. This island was almost totally destroyed by a furious hurricane and dreadful inundation of the sea. Taiouan, at the S. W. end of the island, is the capital.

Formosa, Cape, the point of land between the Bights of Benin and Biafra, in the Gulf of Guinea. Lat. 4. 15. N. and 5. 10. of E. long. One of the Bissagos Isles, on the W. coast of North Africa, is also called Formosa. Lat. 11. 30. N. long. 16. 10. W.

Fornovo, a town of Italy, in the duchy of Parma; near which, in 1495, Charles VIII. of France obtained a victory over the princes of Italy. It is 8 miles W. S. W. of Parma.

Forres, a royal burgh of Scotland, in Murrayshire, neatly built on an eminence, on the river, and near the Bay of Findhorn, which is its port. It has manufactures of linen and thread, and a valuable salmon fishery. A little W. of the town is a column, called Sweno's stone, covered with antique sculpture, and said to have been erected in memory of a victory obtained over the Danes in 1008; Forres is 12 miles W. by S. of Elgin, and 12 E. of Nairn. It is contributory, with Fortrose, &c., in sending one member to parliament.

Forsta, a town of Lusatia, with a castle. It has manufactures of woollen and linen cloths and carpets, and stands on a little island in the Neissa; 15 miles S. S. W. of Guben, and 54 N. E. of Dresden.

Fort is prefixed to numberless fortresses and towns in different parts of the world, all the most important of which will be found in order of their substantive names.

Forteventura, or **Fuerteventura**, one of the Canary Islands, 65 miles in length, and of a very irregular breadth, consisting of two peninsulas, joined by an isthmus 12 miles in breadth. Its chief product is the barilla plant; it also produces some wheat, barley, beeves, and goats. The S. W. point is in long. 14. 31. W. lat. 28. 4. N. Pop. about 14,000.

Forth, a river of Scotland, which rises in the mountain Benlomond, in Dumbartonshire, flows E., in a sinuous course, by Stirling and Alloa, and meets the German Ocean a little below

Alloa, where it forms a noble estuary, called the Frith of Forth. The Forth is navigable for vessels of 80 tons, as far as Stirling Bridge, and for merchant vessels of any burthen, as far as Grangemouth, where there is a communication between this river and the Clyde, by a canal.

FORTH, FRITH OF, the estuary above mentioned, is about 10 miles in mean breadth, that is, reckoning the entrance from North Berwick, on the S., to Elie Ness, on the N., the distance from which two points is about 8 miles; from this line to the Queensferry, where it narrows to a mile and a half, the distance is about 28 miles, and from Queensferry to Grangemouth the distance is about 12 miles, the water spreading again to the extent of 3 to 4 miles. Between Queensferry and the line of Elie Ness are a number of islands, the most celebrated of which are Inch Garvie, Inch Colm, and Inch Keith: on the latter, and on the Isle of May, without the line of Elie Ness, are lighthouses, and these, as well as most of the other islands, contain ruins of castles or religious houses. St. Abb's Head on the S. and Fife Ness on the N., distant from each other 35 miles, are by some considered as forming the points of entrance to the Frith of Forth.

FORTROSE, a borough of Scotland, in Ross-shire situate on the Murray Frith, nearly opposite Fort George, to which there is a regular ferry. It is composed of two towns, Rosemarkie and Chanonry; the former a very ancient borough, and the latter one a bishop's see. Two small parts of the ancient cathedral remain; one used as a burial-place, the other as a court-house and prison. It contributes, with Inverness, Forres, and Nairn, in returning one member to parliament. It is 9 miles S. S. W. of Cromarty.

FORT-ROYAL, the capital of Martinico, on the W. side of the island, with one of the best harbours in the West Indies, defended by a strong citadel. Long. 61. 9. W. lat. 14. 36. N.

FORT-ROYAL, the capital of the island of Granada. *See* ST. GEORGE.

FOSSANO, a town of Piedmont, with citadel; seated on the Store; 10 miles N. E. of Coni. It has manufactures of silk.

FOSSE, a town of the Netherlands, in Namur, situate between the Sambre and Meuse; 7 miles N. W. of Namur.

FOSSOMBRONE, a town of Italy, in the duchy of Urbino, with a castle on a mountain; near the river Metro; 10 miles S. E. of Urbino. The vicinity is very productive of silk.

FOSSUM, a town of Norway, in the government of Aggerhuys, noted for rich mines of cobalt; 35 miles W. of Christiania.

FOTHERINGAY, a village in Northamptonshire; 3 miles N. of Oundle, near the Nen. Here are the ruins of a castle in which Richard III. was born, and Mary, Queen of Scots, tried and beheaded. In the church are interred two dukes of York; Edward, killed at Agincourt in France, and Richard, slain at Wakefield.

FOUE, or FAGUA, a town of Lower Egypt; seated on the W. branch of the Nile; 25 miles S. by E. of Rosetta.

FOUGERES, a town of France, in the department of Ille and Vilaine, with an ancient castle. In 1302 it was taken by John, king of England. It is seated on the Coesnon; 25 miles N. E. of Rennes, and 150 W. by S. of Paris. It is the seat of a prefect.

FOULA, or FOWLA. *See* FULA.

FOULI, PHOLEY, or FOULAH, a country of Africa, extending on both sides of the river Senegal, about 500 miles from E. to W.; the boundaries from N. to S. are unknown. It is populous and fertile. The Foulahs are, in general, of a tawny complexion, though many of them are entirely black. Some lead a wandering life, and roam about the country with large droves of cows, sheep, goats, and horses; others are dexterous at hunting wild beasts; the teeth of elephants, and the skins of lions, leopards, and tigers, being articles of trade. Their arms are bows and arrows, lances, swords, daggers, and occasionally a kind of small fusee. They are praised by travellers for their hospitality: nor is their humanity in other respects less commendable; for if one of their countrymen have the misfortune to fall into slavery, the rest join stock to redeem him. The king of this country is called the Siratick; and, though he seldom appears with the badges of majesty, he has great authority, and is as much respected as any one on the coast.

FOULNESS, a small island on the S. E. coast of Essex, formed by the river Crouch at its entrance into the mouth of the Thames.

FOULSHAM, a town in Norfolk, with a market on Tuesday; 16 miles N. W. of Norwich, and 111 N. E. of London.

FOUR CANTONS, LAKE OF THE. *See* WALDSTÆDTER SEA.

FOURNEAUX ISLAND, a small island in the Pacific Ocean. Long. 143. 2. W. lat. 17. 11. S.

FOU-TCHEOU, a city of China, in Fo-kien, and the most considerable in that province, on account of its trade, the convenience of its rivers and port, and the number of its literati. It is the residence of a viceroy, and has under its jurisdiction nine cities of the third class. It is seated near the mouth of a river falling into the China Sea; 435 miles N. E. of Canton, and 1030 S. by E. of Peking. Long. 119. 4. E. lat. 26. 4. N.

FOU-TCHEOU, another city of China, in Kiang-si, formerly one of the most beautiful cities of China, but almost ruined by the invasion of the Tartars. It is 240 miles N. W. of the other Fou-tcheou, and 835 miles S. of Peking. Long. 115. 56. E. lat. 27. 55. N.

FOWEY, or FAWY, a river in Cornwall, which rises 4 miles S. E. of Camelford, passes by Lostwithiel, and after a winding course of about 40 miles, enters the English Channel at Fowey.

FOWEY, a seaport in Cornwall; market on Saturday, and a considerable trade in the pilchard fishery. It is seated at the mouth of the Fowey, which forms a capacious harbour; 11

miles S. of Bodmin, and 239 W. by S. of London. Long. 4. 37. W. lat. 50. 19. N.

FOX ISLANDS, or ALEUTIAN ISLANDS, a group of islands in the Northern Archipelago. They are 16 in number, between the coast of Kamtschatka and the W. coast of America; between 52. and 55. N. lat.. Each island has a peculiar name; but this general name is given to the whole group, on account of the great number of black, grey, and red foxes with which they abound. The dress of the inhabitants consists of a cap and a fur coat, which reaches down to their knees: some wear a cap of a party-coloured bird-skin, upon which is left part of the wings and tail. On the forepart of their hunting and fishing caps they place a small board, like a screen, adorned with the jawbones of sea-bears, and ornamented with glass beads, which they receive in barter from the Russians. They feed upon the flesh of all sorts of sea animals, and generally eat it raw. The provision intended for keeping is dried without salt, in the air. Their weapons are bows, arrows, and darts; and, for defence, they use wooden shields. The most perfect equality reigns among them: they have neither chiefs nor superiors, neither laws nor punishments. They live together in families, and societies of several families united, which form what they call a race, who, in case of attack or defence, mutually aid each other. They have a good share of plain natural understanding, and seem cold and indifferent in most of their actions; yet if an injury, or mere suspicion, rouse them from this phlegmatic state, they become furious and revengeful. The Russians call these islands the Lyssie Ostrova.

There is a cluster of small, but beautifully fertile and romantic islands, called Fox Islands, on the coast of the state of Maine, North America.

FOXFORD, a town of Ireland, in the county of Mayo, on the river Moy; 8 miles E. N. E. of Castlebar.

FOY, ST., a town of France, in the department of Gironde, on the river Dordogne; 38 miles E. of Bordeaux.

FOYERS, or FYERS, a river of Scotland, in the county of Inverness, which rises a few miles E. of Fort Augustus, and flows into Loch Ness. About 2 miles before its entrance into the lake is the fall of Foyers, one of the highest in the world, being 207 feet in height, in one unbroken stream.

FOYLE, a river of Ireland, formed by the conflux of the Fin and the Mourne, at Lifford, in the county of Donegal. It passes by St. Johnstown and Londonderry, and, four miles below, expands into a bay, called Lough Foyle, of an oval form, 14 miles long and 8 broad, which communicates with the ocean by a short and narrow strait.

FRAGA, a town of Spain, in Arragon, strong by situation, having the river Cinca before it, whose high banks are difficult of access, and at its back a hill, which cannot easily be approached with cannon. Alphonso VII., king of Arragon, was killed here by the Moors, in 1134, when he besieged this town. It is 63 miles E. S. E. of Saragossa.

FRAGOAS, a town of Portugal, in Estramadura; 7 miles N. W. of Santarem.

FRAMLINGHAM, a town of Suffolk, with a market on Saturday. It has the remains of a castle. To this place the Princess Mary retired, when Lady Jane Grey was proclaimed queen; and here she found that powerful support, which soon seated her on the throne. It is 30 miles E. of Bury, and 87 N. E. of London.

FRANCAVILLA, a town of Naples, in Terra de Otranto, with a trade in oil, cotton stockings, and snuff; 15 miles E. N. E. of Tarento.

FRANCAVILLA, a town in Naples, in Basilicata, on the river Sino; 20 miles W. S. W. of Trusi.

FRANCE, a country of Europe, extending in its extreme limits from the village of Peats de Mello, at the foot of the Eastern Pyrenees, in the lat. of 42. 25., in nearly a perpendicular line to Dunkirk, in the lat. of 51. 2. N.; this line gives a distance of 517 geographical, or 593 British statute miles: the most important extreme point on the W. is Brest, in the long. of 4. 29. W., and 48. 23. of N. lat. and on the E. Strasburg, in the long. of 7. 45. E., and lat. of 48. 35.; the distance between these two points is 12. 14. of W. long., which, in the mean lat. of 48. 29., is equal to 490 geographical, or 576 British statute miles; but a line exceeding this by about 40 miles might be drawn in this direction within the French territory, from Point Ras, 28 miles S. of Brest, to the extreme eastern limit, 45 miles S. by E. of Strasburg: the mean line, however, from N. to S., does not exceed 470, and from W. to E. 420 British statute miles: these limits give a superficies of 197,400 square miles, equal to 126,336,000 British statute acres. A report made to the French government in 1817, computed the superficies to be equal to 128 millions of acres, of which about 92 millions were in a state of cultivation, and about 36 millions of acres reported as unproductive, and unfit for cultivation. This fine territory is bounded, from Dunkirk to the Rhine, in the lat. of 49. N., a distance of 290 miles in a direction E. S. E., by the Prussian provinces of the Rhine: about 100 miles of this frontier, nearest to Dunkirk, is an open plain, without any natural barrier; further south the inroad is more or less impeded by forests. From the lat. of 49. the Rhine, in a direction S. by W. for about 110 miles, divides France from the territory of the Grand Duke of Baden; from the lat. 47. 40. to 43. 42., it is divided from Switzerland, Savoy, and Piedmont, by collateral ridges of the Alpine mountains; the S. E. extremity is bounded by the little river Var, which divides France from the county of Nice: the meridional distance from this point to the eastern extremity of the Pyrenees is 200 statute miles, but the identations of the Mediterranean Sea give an extent of sea-coast on that side of France, near to, if not exceeding 300 miles. The Pyrenean mountains, in a direction W. by N. for 250 miles, next form the southern boundary of France, dividing it from the Iberian peninsula of Spain and Portugal: the little river Bidassoa forms the boundary at the S. W. extremity; and W. from the mouth of this river, in the lat. of 43. 22. and 1. 47. of W. long. to the Isle of Ushant, in the lat. of 48. 28. and 5. 3. of W. long., France is bounded by the Atlantic Ocean, and N. W. from the Isle of Ushant to Dunkirk by the English Channel: the meridional distance from the Bidassoa to Ushant is 390 miles, and from Ushant to Dunkirk, 380 miles; but the identations of the sea will give about 500 miles of coast on each side of the Isle of Ushant, and, with the S. E. boundary on the Mediterranean, an aggregate extent of sea-coast of about 1300 miles, and a circumference of about 2200 miles. The seaports are Dunkirk, Calais, Boulogne, Dieppe, Fecamp, Havre, Caen, Cherburg, St. Maloes, and Morlaix, on the coast of the English Channel; Brest, Quimper, L'Orient, Nantes, Rochelle, Rochefort, Bordeaux, and Bayonne, on the coast of the Bay of Biscay, or Atlantic Ocean; and Marseilles and Toulon in the Mediterranean. Cherburg, Brest, Rochefort, and Toulon, are the chief stations of the French national marine. Every part of France is intersected by rivers flowing in all directions: taking them in geographical order the N., the first entitled to notice are the Moselle and the Meuse, both of which rise in the N. E. part of France, and take circuitous courses northerly into the Netherlands, the former falling into the Rhine, and the latter into the North Sea: the Somme is an inconsiderable river, running W. N. W. into the English Channel; the next in order and importance is the Seine, which also runs in a W. N. W. direction into the English Channel, being joined in its course by the Marne, Aube, and the Oise, on the N., and by the Yonne and the Eure on the S.; the Orne, and two or three other rivers of inferior note, also fall into the English Channel. The noblest river in all France is the Loire, which rises in the S., and flows in a direction N. by W., for about 250 miles, when it takes a direction nearly due W. for about 250 miles more, falling into the Atlantic Ocean, receiving in its course numerous tributary streams; the most considerable of which are the Allier, running parallel with it from the S. for about 180 miles, and the Cher, Indre, Creuse, Vienne, and Sevre, all from the S.; and from the N. it receives the Lower Loire, Sarthe, Mayenne, and a few others of inferior note; in the S. the united streams of the Lot, the Tarn, and Garonne, with several others of inferior note, form the Gironde, which falls into the Bay of Biscay, being joined from the E. below Bordeaux by the Dordogne and Ille: between the Loire and the Gironde, the Charente, and between the Gironde and the Pyrenees the Adour, each with numerous tributary streams, also fall into the Bay of Biscay. The Rhone, rising near Mount St. Gothard, in Switzerland, after forming the Lake of Geneva, enters France on the S. E., and, after a course of about 80 miles to Lyons, first S. and then W., it takes a course nearly due S. from Lyons, for about 150 miles, falling into the Mediterranean; being joined at Lyons by the Saone from the N., and below Lyons from the E. by the Isere, the Drome, and the Durance: the Herault, the Aude, and one or two other rivers of inferior note, run also into the Mediterranean, between the Rhone and the Pyrenees: the Seine is united with the Loire by a canal, as is the Garonne with the Mediterranean Sea. The canals are executed by government, and consist of seven principal lines, comprising about 80 large branches. The principal roads are also under government control, of which there are 28 royal roads, of the first class, and 97 of the second. Railroads have made but little progress: the first in operation was that from Paris to Versailles.

Since the revolution which commenced in 1789, France has been divided into 86 departments, each department into three to six arrondissements, the total being 368; the arrondissements into 2669 cantons, and the cantons into 38,990 communes. The population taken in 1789, the numbers were 26,300,000, and in 1820, 30,451,187, or 202 to the square mile, and at present is upwards of 32,000,000; this number, taken in reference to the extent of surface over which it is spread, renders France, relatively, more than one-third less populous than England and Wales. This territorial division is principally dependent on the rivers which intersect the country, and superseded the former division into 35 provinces; for military purposes it is now divided into 22 governments. With the exception of the S. E. departments bordering on the Alpine territories of Switzerland, Savoy, and Piedmont, France may be regarded as a level, rather than a mountainous country, and in many respects, alike in a geographical, political, and social sense, as bearing a similar relation to Europe as the fine and fertile plains and people of China do to Asia. Over all the S. E. part of the country the vine, almond, olive, and mulberry flourish and bring forth fruit in the highest degree of perfection, and the vine and a variety of delicious fruits luxuriate over the greater part of the country, to the 49th degree of lat. The N. and N. W. departments are productive in every kind of grain, pulse, and legumes; manufactures of silk, wool, linens, leather, and metals are carried on over all the parts of the country; and, since the termination of the war in 1814, the cotton manufacture has been progressively increasing, and is now carried on to a great extent. In addition to these internal resources, France exclusively enjoys the abundant produce of the islands of Martinique, and Guadaloupe, in the West Indies; she also holds in colonial possession Algeria, in Africa; Cayenne, in S. America; Goree and Senegal, on the coast of Africa; and the Isle of Bourbon, in the Indian Ocean; and draws considerable produce from the Brazils, the United States of North America, parts beyond the Cape of Good Hope, the Levant, and other parts of the world, in exchange for her surplus produce of wines, brandy, silks, and various manufactures. Exempt from all those extremes of climate, which in several parts of the world militate against physical exertion, as well as vegetation, France may be considered as possessing within itself all the means of commanding a higher degree of human enjoyment than can be obtained in any other part of Europe, and equal to what can be obtained in any other part of the globe; yet, notwithstanding her superior natural advantages and aggregate means exceeding those of Great Britain in the proportion of three to one, in point of efficiency, in everything calculated to promote a high degree of social existence and enjoyment, France is incomparably deficient. The cause of this disparity in the efficiency of character of the two nations will perhaps be more apparent as the history of the rise and progress of their several institutions and relations are elucidated and examined.

For centuries prior to the Christian era, this part of Europe appears to have been inhabited by a numerous and hardy race of people, those occupying the interior being denominated Celts. The first important notice which history furnishes of them is in 225 B.C., when the Gauls, who inhabited part of Piedmont and the N. of Italy, invited the people then occupying the banks of the Rhone to aid them in repelling the aggressions of the Romans; and from thus being brought in contact with that powerful and enlightened people, they acquired the name of Transalpine Gauls, in reference to their territory lying W. of the Alps, and in contradistinction to the ancient Gauls, who were designated the Cisalpines. In 106 B.C. the Cimbri and Teutones, from the N. of Germany, marched through Transalpine Gaul into Spain, ravaging the country on their way; but being driven back by the Celtiberians, they divided their forces with the view of penetrating into Italy in two directions; the Teutones directed their course to the S. E. when they were opposed by Marius, between the mouths of the Rhone and the Durance, and experienced a complete defeat, losing 200,000 men on the field of battle, and 80,000 more taken prisoners. From this period the Romans extended their arms and their arts over the greater part of the country, and in the year 59 B.C. the Roman senate conferred on Julius Cæsar the government of all Transalpine Gaul, for five years; two years after this, the whole western coast, from the Seine to the Loire, became effectually subdued to Roman control, and in five years more, by awarding honorary distinctions to the principal cities, and distributing bribes to the leading chiefs, the whole country became reconciled to the Roman government. It was afterwards divided into 17 military divisions.

As the power of the Romans declined, Transalpine Gaul again became exposed to the inroad of the different tribes on the N. E. In the year 406 a tribe of Burgundians, from the banks of the Vistula, crossed the Rhine and took possession of all that part of the country afterwards named Burgundy; and in 420 another tribe from Franconia, under the command of Pharamond, entered from the N. E. From 450 to 452 it was ravaged by the Huns, under Attila, who, on laying siege to Orleans, was brought to battle by Maroveus, who defeated Attila with a loss of 200,000 men. In 482 Clovis, a Franconian and descendant of Maroveus, possessed himself of all the places in Transalpine Gaul previously held by the Romans, and in 492, marrying Clotilda, daughter of Chilperic, king of the Burgundians, became king of the whole country now called France. Clotilda at the time of her marriage had embraced Christianity, and in 496 Clovis initiated himself in its mysteries, through the means of St. Remi, and was baptized at Rheims on Christmas-eve of that year: hence the coronation at Rheims of the kings of France, through a period of more than 1300 years. Clovis was the first of a race of seventeen kings who reigned over France in regular succession, denominated the *Merovingian* race, in reference to their descent from Maroveus. In 732 France was ravaged by the Saracens, under the command of Abdalrahman, when Eudes, duke of Aquitaine, implored the assistance of Charles Martel, duke of Austrasia, who brought Abdalrahman to battle between Tours and Poitiers, and defeated him, as history informs us, with the loss of 375,000 men, Abdalrahman himself being slain on the field of battle. In 737 the crown of France devolved to Charles Martel, whose manly spirit, however, disdained regal parade; he ruled France for four years, under the title of duke; he died in 741, and was succeeded by an imbecile named Childeric, whose authority in 752 was superseded by Pepin, who became the first of a race of 13 kings denominated *Carlovingians.* Pepin died in 768, and was succeeded by Charlemagne the renowned, crowned emperor of the Romans, or of the West, at Rome, in 800. On the death of Louis V. in 986, after a reign of one year, the crown of France descended to Charles, an uncle of Louis; but in consequence of his having vassalated himself to the emperor Otho III. he was precluded from its accession, and the crown was conferred, by election, on Hugh Capet, who became the first of another race of 14 kings termed the *Capetian.* Charles IV., the last of the Capets in regular succession, dying in 1334, without male issue, the crown devolved on Philip of *Valois*, who was the first of 7 kings of that race. In 1498 it devolved on the duke of Orleans, who became Louis XII. and was the first of another race of 6 kings. On the death of Henry III. in 1589, the succession was again broken, when the crown devolved on Henry of Bourbon, in whose line it continued until the decapitation of Louis XVI. on the 21st of January, 1793.

For some centuries antecedent to this period, France had been divided into 32 provinces of very unequal extent, each with a distinct local administration. The period of their formation does not appear: at the time the Romans first entered France it was divided into four great parts, viz. Narbonensis, comprising the S. E., Aquitaine the S. W., Celtica the interior, and Gallia Belgica the N. The division into 17 provinces took place under Augustus, the first emperor of Rome, and some of the Roman names continued as late as the 13th century.

John, king of England, in the preamble to Magna Charta, being styled Duke of Normandy and Aquitaine; Austrasia, over which Charles Martel presided in the 8th century, appears to have comprised part of the N. E. of France, and what now forms part of the Prussian Provinces of the Rhine. Subsequent to the period of the accession of Clovis, in 481, the country appears to have been exposed to a continuity of internal dissensions; and when these had subsided, the vain glory which France acquired under Charlemagne increased the jealousy of the neighbouring powers, and excited external broils. In 912 the N. W. coast was invaded by a northern tribe called Normans, who retained possession of that part of the country, afterwards called Normandy; and in 1060, William, the duke of this province, invaded, conquered, and became king of England. This event subsequently led to violent contests between England and France. Louis VII. in 1137, embarked in the crusading mania of that period; and in 1334, on Charles IV., the last of the Capets, dying without male issue, Edward III. of England set up his claim for the French crown. The battles of Cressy and Poitiers, in 1346 and 1355, resulted from this pretension. At the battle of the Poitiers, John, king of France, was taken prisoner, but afterwards ransomed for 3,000,000 crowns of gold, equal to 1,500,000*l.*; a respite from external war followed this negotiation, but internal broils again ensued, and in 1415, Henry V., king of England, availed himself of prevailing dissensions, to renew the claim of Edward to the French crown; and on the 25th of October of that year, the French forces experienced a decisive defeat at Agincourt. Henry followed up his victory by the capture of several of the most important towns in Normandy, and in 1420 the succession to the crown was ceded to him by treaty. In 1422 he assumed the regency of France; but he dying at Vienne, on the 30th of August of that year, his brother succeeded him in the regency, during the minority of his son Henry VI. who was crowned king of France at Paris, on the 7th of December, 1431. The English influence had, however, previously experienced a considerable check, by the singular and daring exploits of Jeanne of Arc, celebrated as the Maid of Orleans; and, by 1451, Calais was the only place in France held by the English. Her kings, however, retained the title of king of France, until the peace of Amiens, in 1801-2. After having succeeded in driving the English from the French territory, France embroiled herself in the contentions of her northern and eastern neighbours; but a general peace pervading all Europe during the latter part of the 16th century, by the treaty of Cambray, in 1559, the restless spirit of the French government, during the reigns of Francis II., Charles IX., and Henry III., the three last kings of the Orleans race, directed their wantonness and cruelty against their own Protestant subjects. This persecution was allayed for a time by Henry IV., the first of the Bourbons, who ascended the throne in 1589, under whose conciliatory policy the interests of France became more consolidated than at any former period. Henry, however, was assassinated by a fanatic, in 1610, when fresh disorder ensued, and France again is seen involved in all the contentions of the European states, and of England with her American colonies, which took place in the interval of that period.

It was immediately after the general peace of Europe, in 1783, when the English American colonies obtained an honourable independence, that the triple oppression of the crown, the nobles, and the clergy, became intolerable to the French people, whilst the division of the country into 32 provincial governments aggravated the evils by retarding that relief which the exegincies of one part of the country occasionally required, at the expense of the others; consequently, in May, 1788, a convocation was assembled, which led to the division of the country into 86 departments, as previously mentioned, and also of the formation of a new constitution, in which the equality of all ranks to the rights of government formed the basis. The internal convulsions of the kingdom, after this event, usually termed the French revolution, forms the most tragic and bloody page in the whole volume of modern history; and a standing lesson to all ages, that a settled government, in almost its worst forms, is preferable to the domination of mobs, and regicides, and political clubs, whose march up to the seat of authority is effected by trampling upon the rights, the liberties, and the lives of their fellow subjects. Among those who contributed more especially to the eclât of the French armies was a young officer, of the name of Napoleon Bonaparte, who, on his return to Paris, after his successful campaign in Italy, was entrusted with the command of a vast armament to the shores of Egypt, and, when he returned in 1799, was mainly instrumental in forming a new constitution under a triune consulate, senate, and legislative body, in which he himself was appointed one of the consuls. In October, 1801, a peace was signed with England, which proved, however, of short duration. War was renewed in 1803, when Bonaparte was appointed consul for life, with power to nominate his successor; this, however, fell short of his ambition, and in May of the following year he was proclaimed emperor of France. On the 1st of October, 1805, he again headed a powerful army against the German States; detached the minor powers from the Germanic confederacy, and united them to his own interest, under the new title of the Confederation of the Rhine. In 1808 he marched an army of 80,000 men into Spain, and placed one of his brothers on the throne of that country; another brother he had caused to be crowned king of Holland; another king of Westphalia; and a brother-in-law king of Naples. The whole of the Netherlands he had annexed to France, in 16 departments; and, on the king of Holland resigning his crown in 1809, the whole of that country, with the coast of Germany, as far as the Elbe, the states of the papal church, and the greater part

X

of the N. of Italy, were also decreed integral parts of the French empire, in 28 additional departments.

The emperor of Austria, imagining that the division of the French forces into Spain afforded him an opportunity of avenging the repeated defeats he had sustained, provoked a new contest in 1809, when Napoleon again broke the field against the Austrians, and on the 5th of July completely defeated them. A treaty of peace followed, in which the daughter of the emperor of Austria was ceded in marriage to the conqueror of her father's capital. The birth of a son, in 1811, seemed for a time to render permanent the fortunes of Napoleon and his family; but an ill-fated ambition led him, in 1812, to march an army of 300,000 men into Russia, which after repeated and severe conflicts reached Moscow, the ancient capital of that empire, on the 14th of September. By the order of the governor this city was secretly set on fire, and the desolation by which Napoleon found himself surrounded induced him to withdraw his forces, which were overtaken with snow storms before they could reach the frontiers, whilst the Russians on their rear subjected them to continued disasters, and in the end destroyed the finest army which ever assembled in Europe. In the meantime the French troops in the peninsula were exposed to frequent defeats; and by 1814 Napoleon and his troops had not only been driven within their own frontier, but whilst a united Russian, Prussian, and Austrian army entered France from the N. E., the British, Spanish, and Portuguese armies entered it from the S. W.: and Napoleon, seeing the tide of fortune completely set against him, immediately abdicated the sceptre. The island of Elba was assigned to him as a residence in full sovereignty for life, with an income of about 200,000*l.* per annum. On the 3rd of May, 1814, Louis XVIII., who had been exiled in England during the consular and imperial dynasty, arrived in Paris, to resume the throne of his ancestors. On the 5th of March, 1815, Napoleon secretly landed at Frejus, and marched without interruption to Paris, from which Louis fled at midnight on the 20th. Napoleon arrived the same evening; on the 27th the national council annulled his abdication, and called upon him to resume his imperial functions. On the 29th he abolished the African slave trade; on the 12th of June he left Paris to take the command of an army on the N. E. frontier; but after a whole day's severe fighting, on the 18th his line was broken, his troops thrown into confusion, and the palm of victory left with the allies, who marched again upon Paris, which they reached on the 6th of July. Napoleon again abdicated the imperial sceptre, and on the 29th of June quitted Paris never to return. Louis again resumed the sovereignty on the 18th of July; on the 25th of the same month Napoleon surrendered to the commander of a British ship of war, and was afterwards carried to the island of St. Helena, in the Atlantic Ocean, where he died on the 5th of May, 1821.

Louis XVIII. died in September, 1824, and was succeeded by his brother Charles Philip, (Count d'Artois,) under the title of Charles X.; whose increasing infringement of the rights of the people at length aroused universal indignation, and expelled him from the throne he had so unworthily filled, and the country he had laboured to enslave. The form of government since 1814 resembles that of Britain—the power being vested in the king, the chamber of peers, and the chamber of deputies. To strengthen himself in the chamber of peers, Charles X. increased it by creations; to weaken the people he invaded the elective franchise and shackled the press. In August, 1829, he dismissed M. Martignac's administration, because it would not go all lengths against the people, and appointed another of ultra-royalists, under his natural son, Prince Polignac. The first act of the deputies, on the meeting of the chambers, in March 1830, was an address praying for the dismission of the ministers. The king answered it haughtily, and dismissed the chambers. Finding that the new chamber was likely to thwart his views still more than the former, he determined to strike a decisive blow, and on Sunday, July 25, he signed three ordinances; the first abolishing the freedom of the press; the second dissolving the chamber of deputies, which had never assembled; and the third abrogating the most important rights of the elective franchise. This, however, was the last act of his misrule. A revolution ensued. The people were victorious. The government of Charles was overturned, and himself left to drag out the remains of his days in ignominious and unpitied banishment; while the sceptre was placed in the hands of a constitutional monarch, Louis Philippe I., formerly the Duke of Orleans.

A distinguishing feature of the present order of government is its perfect toleration in religious matters. The religion of the sovereign and the court is the Roman Catholic, but the teachers of all other sects of Christians are now supported by government. The establishment of the Roman Catholic church consists of 14 archbishops, 66 bishops, 1 royal chapter (St. Denis), 174 vicars-general, 660 titular canons, 2917 rectors, and 22,316 curates.

France contains 26 universities, and 36 lyceums or royal colleges; and the military establishment is a standing army of 231,608; and military parade is the principal amusement of the French. The manufactures principally excel in fabrics where taste and elegance is required, as in silk weaving, and the manufacture of jewellery; the total annual value of the manufactures may be estimated at 2,000,000,000 francs.

France exhibits an imposing picture of physical, moral, and social power, which the philosopher and philanthropist will view with hope that she will henceforward be as assiduous to acquire glory in pursuing the arts of peace, and the attainment of social order, as she has heretofore been in the pursuit of conquest and political aggrandizement.

FRANCE, ISLE OF, a late province of France, so called because it was bounded by the rivers Seine, Marne, Oise, Aisne, and Ourque. It now forms the four departments of Oise, Seine and Oise, Seine and Marne, and Seine, or Paris.

France, Isle of, or Mauritius, an island in the Indian Ocean; 400 miles E. of Madagascar. It was discovered by the Portuguese; but the first who settled here were the Dutch, in 1598. They called it Mauritius, in honour of the prince Maurice, their stadtholder; but, on their acquisition of the Cape of Good Hope, they deserted it; and it continued unsettled till the French landed here in 1720, and gave it the name of one of the finest provinces in France. It is 150 miles in circumference. The climate is healthy, but the soil not very fertile. There are many mountains, some of which are so high, that their tops are covered with snow; they produce the best ebony in the world. The valleys are well watered with rivers, and are made very productive by cultivation, of which sugar is the principal object. The town and harbour, called Port Louis, are strongly fortified; but in the hurricane months the harbour cannot afford shelter for more than eight vessels. Here are large storehouses, and every thing necessary for the equipment of fleets. This island was taken by the British in 1810, and confirmed to them by the treaty of Paris, in 1814. According to an account presented by the colonial department to the British parliament, the island was divided into eight districts, containing a population of 87,603, in the proportion of 63,769 slaves, 13,475 free blacks, and 10,359 whites, exclusive of 1310 troops. Port Louis, on the N. W. coast of the island, is in lat. 20. 10. N. and 57. 29. of E. long. *See* Bourbon.

Franche Compte, a late province of France; bounded on the N. by Lorraine, E. by Alsace and Switzerland, W. by Burgundy, and S. by Bresse. It is 125 miles long and 80 broad, and abounds in corn, wine, cattle, horses, mines of iron, copper, and lead. It now forms the three departments of Doubs, Jura, and Upper Saone.

Franchemont, a town of the Netherlands, in the territory of Liege; 12 miles S. E. of Liege.

Franciade. *See* Denis, St.

Francis, St., a tributary stream of the great river Mississippi, rising in the state of Missouri, in the lat. of 37. 45. N., running parallel with the Mississippi on the W., at the distance of about 40 miles, and enters it after a course of about 220 miles, 45 miles above the entrance of the Arkansas.

Francis, St., a river of Lower Canada, rising in the lake Memphramagog, which spreads into the state of Vermont. The St. Francis, after a course of about 200 miles, falls into the St. Lawrence, about midway between Montreal and Quebec, and will probably, some future day, be united by a canal with the Connecticut.

Francis, St., a river of Brazil, which rises W. of the Brazilian Andes, in the province of Minaes Geraes, in the lat. of 20. S., runs N. through the province of Bahia to the frontier of Pernambuco, when it takes a course E. by S., dividing that province from Bahia, and, after a course of near 1000 miles, falls into the Atlantic Ocean, in the lat. of 11. 20. S. It has a number of towns and settlements, chiefly on its head waters.

Francisco, St., a seaport of New Albion, capital of a jurisdiction of its name, with a citadel. Long. 122. 8. W. lat. 38. 18. N.

There are a number of other rivers, bays, towns, and settlements, in different parts of America, named after St. Francis by the Spaniards, Portuguese, and French.

Franckenau, a town of Germany, in Upper Hesse; 26 miles S. W. of Cassel.

Francois, Cape, now called Cape Henry, or Cape Hayti, the principal seaport and city of what was formerly the French part of St. Domingo. It is seated on the N. coast of the island, in the lat. of 19. 46. N. and 72. 15. of W. long. Before the sanguinary revolt of the negroes in 1793, it contained 800 to 900 houses of stone or brick, and 8000 free inhabitants, exclusive of about 12,000 slaves: but in 1793 the whole of the white inhabitants, who could not effect their escape, were massacred by the blacks. It was named Cape Henry by Christophe, in 1811, and during his reign it was deemed the principal port of the island, though inferior to Port au Prince in commercial importance. Its quota of the contribution towards the 30,000,000 of dollars to be paid to France in ten years, from the 1st of January, 1827, as an indemnity for the sacrifice of their plantations by the revolt in 1793, is 208,451 dollars annually. It is 84 miles due N. of Port au Prince, and 134 W., 30 degrees N. of the city of St. Domingo. The harbour is secure and commodious, and the environs rich in tropical productions.

Franconia, one of the ten circles into which the German empire was formerly divided, lying between the lat. of 48. 45. and 50. 55. N. It is bounded on the N. by Upper Saxony, E. by Bohemia and the palatinate of Bavaria, S. by Suabia, and W. by the circles of the Rhine. The middle is fertile in corn, wine, and fruits; but the borders are full of woods and barren mountains. The Franks, who conquered France in the early part of the 5th century, came from this province, and gave their name to that country. It comprises about 11,000 square miles, and was formerly divided into two principalities, three bishoprics, seven counties, and three lordships; but at the general partitioning of this part of Europe, after the peace of Paris in 1814, the greater part of Franconia was assigned to Bavaria, and the remainder to Wirtemberg, Baden, Hesse, and Saxe Coburg. The river Mayne, which falls into the Rhine, intersects it from E. to W.; the Rednitz from S. to N. falling into the Mayne; and the Altmuhl, falling into the Danube, intersects the S. E. Nuremberg was considered the capital.

Frankenburg, another town in Hesse; 5 miles W. S. W. of Franckenau.

Franeker, a town of Holland, in Friesland, with a castle and a university. The public buildings and palaces are magnificent, and it has two navigable canals, communicating with the

Zuyder Zee and Leewarden: it is 5 miles E. of Harlingen. Population about 4000.

FRANKENBERG, a town of Upper Saxony, in Misnia, with a considerable manufacture of woollen stuffs; 7 miles N. N. E. of Chemnitz.

FRANKENTHAL, a town of Germany, in the palatinate of the Rhine. It has rich manufactures of stuffs, silks, cloths, &c.; and a canal to the river Rhine. It was taken by the French in 1793, and retaken by the allies in 1794. It is seated 2 miles W. of the Rhine, and 7 S. of Worms.

FRANKENHAUSEN, a town of Upper Saxony, in Thuringia, with some extensive salt-works; situate on a branch of the Wipper; 26 miles N. of Erfurt. Pop. about 3000.

FRANKENSTEIN, a town of Germany, in the palatinate of the Rhine; 9 miles S. E. of Kayserslautern.

FRANKENSTEIN, a town of Silesia, in the principality of Munsterberg, on the river Bautze; 12 miles W. S W. of Munsterberg.

FRANKFORD, a town of Ireland, King's County. Here was a Carmelite friary.

FRANKFORT ON THE MAINE, a fortified city of Germany, in the circle of the Rhine. It is divided by the river Maine, 25 miles above its entrance into the Rhine, into two parts, which communicate by means of a stone bridge; the larger part, on the N. side, is called Frankfort, and the smaller Sachsenhausen. It contains several palaces and courts belonging to princes and counts; and here the kings of the Romans have generally been elected and crowned. The chief structure is the town-house, in which is preserved the golden bull, the origin of the fundamental laws of the empire. All religions are tolerated at Frankfort, under certain restrictions; but Lutheranism is the established faith, through the principal church is in the possession of the Roman Catholics. The Jews, 8000 to 9000 in number, were formerly confined to a particular corner of the city; but since 1796 they have resided indiscriminately in all parts. Frankfort is one of the most considerable trading places in Europe, and has two great fairs every year. It was taken, in 1759, by the French, who evacuated it in 1763; and was several times taken and retaken by the French and Austrians, in the war of 1793—1814. Since the peace of the latter year, it has been declared the permanent seat of the Germanic Diet; and as such, most of the European states have a minister resident here. It was the birthplace of Goethe, and also of the family of the Rothschilds, who, during the war between 1807 and 1815, and ten years subsequent thereto, became the greatest money-jobbers in Europe. Frankfort is in lat. 50. 7. N. and 8.82. of E. long. Pop. about 46,000.

FRANKFORT ON THE ODER, a town of Brandenburg, in the Middle Mark, with a famous university and a noble academy. It has three great fairs, and the exclusive right of navigation up the Oder to Breslau. Here are two suburbs, called Lebus and Guben, and a bridge over the Oder. In 1759 it was taken by the Russians and Austrians, and in 1806 it fell into the hands of the French; but fell to Prussia on the retreat of the French army from Moscow, in 1812. It is 45 miles E. by S. of Berlin, and 72 S. of Stettin. Pop. 16,000.

FRANKFORT, the chief town of Franklin county, Kentucky, and seat of the legislative assembly of the state. It is regularly laid out, and stands on the E. bank of the Kentucky; 60 miles from its conflux with the Ohio, and 415 miles W. by S. of Washington. Pop. 1917.

Frankfort and *Frankford* are the names of several other towns and townships in different parts of the United States.

FRANKLIN, the name of 15 counties, in different parts of the United States of North America, named after Benjamin Franklin, an American sage, who died at Philadelphia in the 85th year of his age, on the 17th of April, 1790. The following are the states, in geographical order, which have commemorated his name in one of their counties, with the population of each, and name of its chief town, and distance from the capital of the state.

Vermont, 24,531, St. Albans, 52 N. W.
Massachusets, 28,812, Greenfield, 95 W.
New York, 16,518, Malone, 264 N.
Pennsylvania, 37,793, Chambersberg, 49 S. W.
Virginia, 15,832, Rockymount, 210 W.
North Carolina, 10,980, Lewisburg, 32 N. E.
Georgia, 9886, Cornesville 110 N.
Alabama, 14,270, Russelville, 249 N. W.
Mississippi, 4775, Franklin, 70 W.
Tennessee, 12,033, Winchester, 60 S. E.
Kentucky, 9420, Frankfort.
Ohio, 25,949, Columbus.
Indiana, 13,349, Crookville, 71 S. E.
Illinois, 3682, Franklin, 97 S.
Missouri, 7575, Newport, 40 S. W.

There are also a number of towns named *Franklin*, in different states of the Union; but none require particular mention.

FRASCATI, a town of Italy, in Campagna di Roma; seated on the side of a woody mountain: it is a bishop's see, always possessed by one of the six eldest cardinals; and in its neighbourhood are some of the most magnificent villas in Italy, and a seminary richly endowed by Cardinal York. The ancient city of Tusculum is supposed to have stood above Frascati; and between the ruins and the town, it is generally believed, was the Tusculum of Cicero, where some Greek monks, in the 11th century, built a convent on the ruins of his house. Frascati is 12 miles S. E. of Rome. Pop. about 9000.

FRASERBURG, a town of Scotland, in Aberdeenshire, with a small but excellent harbour, and a manufacture of linen yarn. It is seated on the German Ocean, a little S. of the point of Kinnaird Head; and 38 miles N. of Aberdeen.

FRATTA MAGGIORE, a populous village in the vicinity of Naples.

FRAUENBURG, a town of E. Prussia, in the bishopric of Ermland, on the Frisch Haff; 14 miles N. E. of Elbing, and 4 miles W. of Braunsberg. Copernicus died here in 1543.

FRAUENFELD, a town of Switzerland, capital of the canton of Thurgau, with a good castle. It is seated on an eminence, by the river Murg; 19 miles N. E. of Zurich, and 8. W. of Constance.

Frauenstein, a town of Upper Saxony, in Misnia, on the river Boberisch; 20 miles S. S. W. of Dresden.

Fraustadt, a tn. of Poland, in the palatinate of Posen, which has a great trade in wool and oxen. Near this town a battle was gained by the Swedes over the Saxons, in 1706. It stands on the frontiers of Silesia; 20 miles N. W. of Glogau, and 55 S. S. W. of Posen.

Fredeberg, a town of the duchy of Westphalia, on the river Wenne; 23 miles S. S. E. of Arensberg.

Frederica, a town of the state of Georgia in Glynn county, and on the W. side of St. Simon Island, with a safe and commodious harbour; 64 miles S. W. of Savannah. Long. 80. 56. W. lat. 31. 6. N.

Fredericia, or **Fridericia**, a town and fortress of Jutland, at the entrance of the Little Belt from the Categat, in the lat. of 55. 35. N. and 9. 44. of E. long. All ships entering the Little Belt are here brought to, and a contribution levied towards the lights and buoys on the coast of Denmark. Pop. about 3500.

Frederick, a county of the state of Maryland bounded on the N. by the conventional line which divides Maryland from Pennsylvania, and on the S. by the Potomac river, which divides it from Virginia: it is about 35 miles in length from N. to S. and 25 miles in mean breadth ; it it intersected from N. to S. by the Monocoey river, which springs from several sources in Pennsylvania, and falls into the Potomac. Pop. 36,405, of whom 4345 are slaves. Fredericktown, the chief town, with a population of 5182, W. of the Monocoey, is 120 miles N. W. of Annapolis.

Frederick, a county in the N. part of Virginia, between the Blue and North ridges of the Allegany mountains ; the Shenandoah river skirts the foot of the Blue Mountains on the E. side of the county, running from S. to N. into the Potomac. Pop. 14,242. Winchester, the chief town, is 130 miles N. by W. of Richmond.

Fredericsburg, a town of Virginia, capital of Spotsylvania county, and a place of considerable trade. It is situate on the S. side of the Rappahannoc ; 85 miles above its entrance into the Chesapeake, and 60 N. of Richmond.

Fredericsburg, a Danish fort, on the Gold-coast of Guinea, near Cape Three-points ; 62 miles W. S. W. of Cape Coast Castle. Long. 1. 5. W. lat. 4. 30. N.

Fredericsburg, a town of Further Pomerania ; 23 miles N. of Stargard, and 33 S. S. W. of Colberg.

Fredericsburg, an interior tn. of Denmark, in the isle of Zealand, with a castle and palace ; 15 miles N. N. W. of Copenhagen.

Fredericshall, or **Fredericstadt**, a seaport of Norway, in the province of Aggerhuys ; situate at the mouth of the river Tiste, in a bay called the Swinesund. The harbour is safe and commodious ; but the large quantity of saw-dust brought down the river, from the different saw-mills, occasions an annual expense to clear it away. On the summit of a rock, which overhangs the town, stands the hitherto impregnable fortress of Fredericstein ; at the siege of which, in 1718, Charles XII. of Sweden was killed by a musket-ball. It is 51 miles S. E. of Christiania. Long. 10. 55. E. lat. 59. 12. N. Pop. about 4000.

Fredericsham, a tn. and fortress of Russia, in Carelia. It is neatly built, the streets going off like radii from a centre. Here, in 1783, an interview was held between the Empress of Russia and the king of Sweden. It is seated near the Gulf of Finland ; 68 miles W. S. W. of Wiburg. Long. 28. 18. E. lat. 60. 36. N.

Fredericstadt, a town of Denmark, in S. Jutland ; seated at the conflux of the Tren with the Eyder ; 17 miles S. W. of Sleswick, and 6 N. E. of Tonningen.

Fredericstadt, or **Fredericstein**, a town of Norway, in the province of Aggerhuys, and the most regular fortress in this part of Norway. It has a considerable trade in deal timber, and is seated on the Glomme; 26 miles W. of Fredericshall.

Frederictown, the capital of New Brunswick, on the river St. John, which is thus far navigable for sloops; 90 miles above the city of St. John. Long. 66. 30. W. lat. 46. 20. N.

Freehold, or **Monmouth**, a town of New Jersey, chief of Monmouth county. Here, in 1778, General Washington attacked Sir Henry Clinton, on his retreat from Philadelphia, and the latter lost 300 men. It is 20 miles S. by E. of Brunswick, and 30 E. of Trenton.

Freetown, the capital of the colony of Sierra Leone. The harbour has three wharfs, and is protected by a battery. It stands on the S. side of the river Sierra Leone, near its entrance into the Atlantic Ocean. Long. 12. 56. W. lat. 8. 30. N.

Frehel, a cape of France, in the department of Cotes du Nord ; 13 miles W. of St. Malo. Long. 2. 15. W. lat. 48. 41. N.

Frejus, a town of France, in the department of Var. By the Romans it was called Forum Julii; and had then a port on the Mediterranean, from which it is now 2 miles. It is the birthplace of that great Roman general and philosopher, Agricola ; and near it some fine remains of antiquity are still visible. It is celebrated in later times as the place where Napoleon landed on his return from Egypt, in the autumn of 1799, and again in March, 1815, from the Island of Elba. It is seated near the river Argens, in a morass ; 40 miles N. E. of Toulon. Long. 6. 44. E. lat. 43. 26. N.

Frenay le Vicomte, a town of France, in the department of Sarte ; 9 miles S. S. W. of Alençon.

Freudenberg, a town of Franconia, on the river Maine ; 8 miles W. of Wertheim.

Freudenberg, a town of Westphalia, in the county of Hoya ; 14 miles S. by W. of Bremen.

Freudenstadt, a strong town of Suabia, in the Black Forest, built to defend the passage into that forest. In 1796 it was taken by the French. It is 23 miles S. by E. of Baden.

Freudenthal, a town of Austrian Silesia, in the principality of Troppau ; celebrated for its breed of horses, and manufacture of fine linen; seated near the Mohra; 24 miles W. of Troppau.

FREYBERG, a town of Upper Saxony, in Misnia, with a castle. In the environs are mines of copper, tin, lead, and silver, which employ a great number of workmen. Here is the usual burying-place of the princes of the house of Saxony. It is situate on a branch of the Muldau; 15 miles W. S. W. of Dresden. Pop. about 9000.

FREYBERG, a town of Moravia, in the circle of Olmutz; 16 miles S. W. of Teschen, and 48 E. of Olmutz. Pop. about 3500.

FREYBURG, a town of Silesia, in the principality of Schweidnitz, near the river Polsnitz: 7 miles N. W. of Schweidnitz.

FREYENSTEIN, a town of Brandenburg, in the Mark of Pregnitz, on the frontiers of Mecklenburg; 22 miles N. E. of Perlberg.

FREYENWALDE, a town of Brandenburg, in the Middle Mark, near which are mineral springs and extensive alum works. It is seated on the Oder; 36 miles N. E. of Berlin.

FREYSINGEN, a town of Bavaria, capital of a principality of the same name. The cathedral and palace are beautiful structures. It was taken by the French in 1796. It is seated on a mountain, near the Iser; 20 miles N. N. E. of Munich. Long. 11. 50. E. lat. 48. 21. N.

FREYSTADT, a town of Hungary with a castle; seated on the Waag, opposite Leopoldstadt.

FREYSTADT, a town of Moravia, in the principality of Teschen, with a castle on the river Elsa; 8 miles N. N. W. of Teschen.

FREYSTAT, a town of Silesia, in the principality of Glogau, with an ancient castle; 14 miles N. E. of Sagan.

FREYSTAT, a town of Austria, which has a great trade in worsted; 17 miles N. of Ens.

FRIBURG, one of the cantons of Switzerland, surrounded on all sides by the canton of Bern. It is fertile in corn, fruits, and pastures, and the cheese made in this canton is deemed the best made in Switzerland. The inhabitants, 70,000 in number, are papists; quota of troops, 1240.

FRIBURG, a fortified town of Switzerland, capital of the canton of the same name. It is seated in a mountainous country, on the river Sanen, which divides it into two parts; that on the W. side standing on plain ground, and the other among rocks and hills. The public buildings, especially the cathedral, are very handsome; and the bishop of Lausanne resides here. Three miles from this town is a celebrated hermitage, cut in a rock, said to be the work of one man, with his servant, who performed it in 25 years. Friburg was taken by the French in 1798. It is 18 miles S. W. of Bern, and 30 N. E. of Lausanne. Long. 7. 15. E. lat. 46. 43. N.

FRIBURG, a town of Suabia, capital of Brisgau. The steeple of its great church is the finest in Germany; and here is a university, a college formerly belonging to the Jesuits, and several convents. The inhabitants are famous for polishing crystal and precious stones. It has been often taken. It is seated on the Triser; 53 miles S. by W. of Baden, and 10 E. of Brisach, on the Rhine. Long. 7. 58. E. lat. 48. 3. N. Pop. about 10,000.

FRIBURG, a town of Upper Saxony, in Thuringia, with a castle on a mountain, situate on the Unstrut; 5 miles N. N.W. of Naumberg.

There are numerous other towns and villages beginning with *Fri* or *Frey*, in different parts of Germany, and *Fri* and *Frey* are indiscriminately written.

FRIDECK, a town of Silesia, in the circle of Teschen, on the frontier of Moravia; 12 miles S. by W. of Teschen.

FRIDINGEN, a town of Suabia, on the Danube; 50 miles S. W. of Ulm.

FRIEDBERG, a town of Germany, in Wetteravia. It is seated on a mountain by the river Usboch; 15 miles N. by E. of Frankfort.

FRIEDBERG, a town of Bavaria, with a castle, situate on the Lechfeld; 6 miles E. of Augsburg, and 30 N. W. of Munich.

FRIEDBERG, a town of Silesia, in the principality of Schweidnitz. A little N. of the town a battle was gained by the King of Prussia over the Austrians, in 1745. It is 7 miles N. W. of Schweidnitz.

FRIEDBERG, a town of Germany, in Styria, on the river Pink and frontiers of Hungary; 33 miles N. E. of Gratz.

FRIEDBURG, a town of Westphalia, in East Friesland, with a castle; 25 miles E. of Emden.

FRIEDLAND, a town of Silesia, in the principality of Oppelen, on the river Steina; 12 miles E. of Neisse.

FRIEDLAND, a town of Lower Saxony, in Mecklenburg; seated in a swampy country, on the frontiers of Pomerania; 16 miles S. S. W. of Anclam.

FRIEDLAND, a town of Bohemia, on the confines of Lusatia; 7 miles E. S. E. of Zittau.

FRIEDLAND, a town of Prussia, where the French, under Buonaparte, gained a complete victory over the Russians, June 14, 1807. It is seated on the Alla; 28 miles S. E. of Konigsberg.

FRIENDLY ISLANDS, a group of islands in the South Pacific ocean, so named by Cook, in 1773, on account of the friendship that appeared to subsist among the inhabitants, and their courteous behaviour to strangers. Tasman, a Dutch navigator, first touched here in 1653, and gave the names of New Amsterdam, Rotterdam, and Middleburg, to three of the principal islands. Cook explored the whole cluster, which he found to consist of more than 20 islands, the principal of which are Tongataboo, or Amsterdam; Eaoowe, or Middleburg; Annamooka, or Rotterdam; Hapaee, and Lefooga. The first, which is the largest, lies in 174. 46. W. long., and 21. 9. S. lat. The general appearance of these islands conveys an idea of the most exuberant fertility; the surface, at a distance, seems entirely clothed with trees of various sizes, some of which are very large, particularly the tall cocoa-palm, and a species of fig, with narrow-pointed leaves. On closer examination, they are almost wholly laid out in plantations, in which are some of the richest productions of nature, such as bread-fruit and cocoa-nut trees, plantains, yams, sugar-canes, and a fruit like a nectarine. The stock of quadrupeds is scanty; but they received from Cook some valuable additions, both to the animal and vegetable kingdom. Their domestic fowls are as large as those of Europe. Among the birds are parrots and paroquets of various sorts, which furnish the red feathers so much esteemed in the Society Isles. The numerous reefs and shoals afford shelter for an endless variety of shell-fish. These islands are all inhabited by a race of people who cultivate the earth with great industry; and nature, assisted by a little art, appears no where in greater splendour. Agriculture, architecture, boat-building, and fishing, are the employments of the men; and to the women is confined the manufacture of cloth.

Friesach, a town of Germany, in Carinthia, with a strong castle on a mountain; seated on the Metnitz; 17 miles N. N. E. of Clagenfurt.

Friesland, one of the provinces of Holland; bounded on the N. by the German Ocean, W. by the Zuyder Zee, S. by the same and Overyssel, and E. by Overyssel and Groningen. This country much resembles the province of Holland in its soil, canals, and dikes. Leewarden is the capital. Harlingen, on the shore of the Zuyder Zee, is the principal seaport.

Friesland, East, a province of Hanover; so called from its situation with respect to the Dutch province of Friesland. It is 45 miles long, and 43 broad; bounded on the N. by the German Ocean, E. by Oldenburg, S. by Munster, and W. by Groningen and the German Ocean. The country being level and low, is obliged to be secured against inundations by expensive dikes. The land is fertile; and the pastures feed horned cattle, horses, and sheep of an extraordinary size. On the death of Prince Charles Edward, in 1744, it became subject to the king of Prussia. It was taken possession of by Buonaparte, in 1806, and at the general partitioning of Europe, subsequent to the peace of Paris in 1814, it was relinquished by Prussia, and ceded to Hanover. Emden is the principal seaport; and the principal towns in the interior are Aurich, Essens, and Friedeburg. The aggregate population is estimated at 120,000, spread over a surface of about 1150 square miles.

Frio, Cape, a promontory of Brazil, in the province of Rio Janeiro. Long. 41. 31. W. lat. 22. 54. S.

Frisch Haff, a lake or bay of Prussia, from 3 to 9 miles broad, and extending 70 in length, along the Baltic Sea, with which it communicates by a narrow passage, at Pillau; it receives the Pregel at the N. E. end, the Passarges from the S., and the E. branch of the Vistula at the W. end; the principal seaports within the Haff are Elbing, Braunsberg, Brandenburg, and Konigsberg.

Fritzlar, a fortified town of Germany, in Lower Hesse, with two colleges and a convent; seated on the Eder; 20 miles S. W. of Cassel.

Friuli, Austrian, a district of Austria, comprising about 400 square miles; bounded on the N. and E. by Upper and Inner Carniola, and W. by Venetian Friuli, while a strip of the Venetian territory shuts it in from the Gulf of Trieste. Trieste is the capital. Population, 125,000.

Friuli, a province of Italy; bounded on the N. by Carinthia, E. by Carniola and Austrian Friuli, S. by the Gulf of Venice, and W. by the Trevisano and Bellunese. It is rich in timber, cattle, silk, wine, and fruit. It is watered by the Tagliamento, and several other rivers falling into the Gulf of Venice, and contains about 370,000 inhabitants. Udina, in the centre of the province, is the chief town.

Friuli, or Citta di Friuli, a town of Italy, in Friuli, with a collegiate church, and five convents. It stands at the foot of the mountains which separate Friuli from Carniola, on the river Natisone; 15 miles N. E. of Udina.

Frodsham, a town in Cheshire, with a market on Wednesday. Here is a graving dock and yard for building and repairing vessels. It is seated on the Weever, near its entrance into the estuary of the Mersey; 11 miles N. E. of Chester, and 192 N. N. W. of London. It has some extensive salt-works in the town and neighbourhood, and partakes partially of the cotton manfacture.

Frome, a river which rises in the N. W. part of Dorsetshire, near Beaminster, flows by Frampton, Dorchester, and Wareham, and enters the bay that forms the harbour of Poole. There is another river of the same name, which rises on the border of Worcestershire, and falls into the Lug, a little above its entrance into the Wye, near Hereford; and another, rising on the border of Wilts, flows through Somersetshire, and falls into the Lower Avon, near Bath.

Frome Selwood, a borough of Somersetshire; seated on the banks of the last of the preceding rivers, over which is a bridge of five arches; it has three churches, one of them ancient and elegant, another erected in 1817, several schools, almshouses, five meeting-houses, new market-house, &c. Frome is the seat of an extensive manufacture of fine woollen cloth, there being about 50 establishments engaged therein, 6 extensive dealers in wool, as many dyers, 3 dressers, 4 wire-drawers, and 7 for the manufacture of cards; its markets on Wednesdays and Saturdays are well supplied. It is 12 miles S. of Bath, and 104 W. by S. of London. It returns one member to parliament.

Frontignan, a town of France, in the department of Herault; celebrated for its muscadine wine, generally called Frontignac. It is seated on the Lake Magulcone; 12 miles S. S. W. of Montpelier.

Froyen, an island in the North Sea, near the coast of Norway; about 35 miles in circumference. Long. 9 0. E. lat. 63. 45. N.

Frozen Ocean, or Icy Sea, washing the northern shore of Asia It is frozen over during the greatest part of the year, and its shores are covered with drift-wood, brought down by the river Kovima, and other rivers of magnitude, which discharge themselves into it. There are no sensible tides, but violent currents are at times felt, from the breaking up of the ice. The delta of the river Lena consists of turf hills on a foundation of ice, and the numerous isles composing it are inhabited by rein-deer and bears. Farther E. off the coast lie the large islands of Kotelnoi, Fadeefskoi, &c., collectively called New Siberia. On the shores of the lakes in these islands are found innumerable remains and entire skeletons of elephants, rhinoceroses, and other inhabitants of tropical regions, imbedded in soft friable earth, the ivory of which is perfectly white and fresh.

FRUTINGEN, a town of Switzerland, in the canton of Bern; 30 miles S. of Friburg.

FUEGO, one of the Cape Verd Islands, in the Atlantic Ocean, with a volcano, which burns continually. It is much higher than any of the rest, and seems to be a single mountain, at sea, but on the sides there are deep valleys. It has no river, and is almost destitute of fresh water; but is fertile in maize, gourds, wild figs, oranges, and apples, and has a great number of wild goats. It is 300 miles W. of Cape Verd. Long. 24. 30. W. lat. 14. 54. N.

FUEN-TCHEOU, a city of China, in the province of Chan-si. Here are hot baths, which attract a great number of strangers. Its district contains one city of the second, and seven of the third class. It is seated on the river Fuen; 280 miles S. W. of Peking. Long. 111. 20 E. lat. 37. 20. N.

FUENTE DUENNA, a town of Spain, in New Castile; seated on the Tagus; 35 miles S. E. of Madrid.

FUENTE GINALDO, a town of Spain, in Estramadura. In 1734 it was taken and plundered by the Portuguese. It is 16 miles N. W. of Coria.

FUESSEN, a town of Suabia, in the principality of Augsburg, with an ancient castle, and a Benedictine abbey. It commands the pass into Bavaria and Tyrol, and is seated on the Lech; 50 miles S. of Augsburg. Long. 10. 45. E. lat. 47. 34. N.

FULA, or FOULA, the most western of the Shetland Islands; supposed to be the Ultima Thule of the ancients. It is 3 miles in length, and half as much in breadth, and affords pasturage for sheep. The only landing-place, which is called Ham, lies on the E. side. Long. 1. 37. W. lat. 60. 27. N.

FULDA, a bishopric of Germany, in the electorate of Hesse, circle of Upper Rhine; bounded on the E. by the county of Henneberg and Wurtzburg, and on the other sides by Wetteravia and Hesse. This country, containing 760 square miles, is very bleak and mountainous, but contains numerous towns and villages, and an aggregate population of about 65,000. The river Fulda, running from S. to N., intersects the N. W. part of the district, and falls into the Weser, about 3 miles S. of Cassel.

FULDA, a town, capital of the preceding bishopric, contains several very fine buildings, among which are a palace, three churches, a college, and a university. It is seated on the E. bank of the Fulda; 55 miles S. by E. of Cassel; in the lat. of 50. 34. N. and 9. 48. of E. long. Pop. 8800.

FULHAM, a village of Middlesex; seated on the N. bank of the Thames; 4 miles W. by S. of Hyde Park Corner. Here is a wooden bridge over the Thames, erected in 1729, at an expense of 23,975*l.*, to defray the interest of which a toll is still levied. Fulham has been the demesne of the bishops of London ever since the conquest; here they have a palace and very fine gardens, and in the churchyard are the tombs of several of the prelates. The situation of the village is rather secluded, and as such has been selected for the residence of a number of the retired traders of the metropolis.

FULNEK, a town and castle of Moravia, on the frontiers of Silesia; 26 miles E. N. E. of Prerau.

FUNCHAL, the capital of Madeira; situate round a bay, on the gentle ascent of some hills, in form of an amphitheatre. An old castle, which commands the road, stands on the top of a steep black rock, called the Loo Rock, surrounded by the sea at high water; there are also three other forts, and several batteries. The streets are narrow and dirty, though streams of water run through them. The houses are built of freestone, or of bricks; but they are dark, and only a few of the best are provided with glass windows; all the others have a kind of lattice work in their stead, which hangs on hinges. The beams and roof of the cathedral are of cedar; but the chief curiosity here is a chamber in the Franciscan convent, the walls and ceiling of which are covered with human skulls and thigh bones, said to be the relics of holy men who have died on the island. The town contains about 11,000 inhabitants. Long. 17. 6. E. lat. 32. 38. N.

FUNDY, a bay of North America, between New Brunswick and Nova Scotia; remarkable for its tides, which rise from the height of 30 to 60 feet, and flow rapidly. It extends about 200 miles in an E. N. E. direction; and, with Vert Bay, which pushes into the land in a N. W. direction from Northumberland Strait, forms an isthmus of only 12 miles wide, which unites Nova Scotia to New Brunswick.

FUNEN, an island of Denmark; 150 miles in circumference; separated from Jutland by a strait called the Little Belt, and from Zealand, by the Great Belt. It is fertile in pasture and grain, and exports to Norway, barley, oats, rye, and peas. Population about 110,000. Odensee, on a bay at the N. end of the island, is the capital.

FUNFKIRCHEN, or FIVE CHURCHES, an episcopal town of Hungary; situate in a fertile country, between the Drave and the Danube; 85 miles S. S. W. of Buda. Long. 18. 13. E. lat. 46. 12. N. Pop. 10,000.

FUORLI, a town of Naples, in Abruzzo Citeriore; 21 miles S. S. E. of Solomona.

FURNES, a town of Belgium, in Flanders

seated near the German Ocean, on the canal from Bruges to Dunkirk. It was one of the barrier towns; but in 1781, Emperor Joseph II. expelled the Dutch garrison. It was taken by the French in 1793: it is 12 miles E. of Dunkirk.

FURRUCKABAD, a town of Hindostan, in the territory of Rohilcund; capital of a small district, about 30 miles in length, on the W. bank of the Ganges, which belongs to a chief of the Patan Rohilla tribe. Holkar was defeated here by the British in 1804. It is seated on the Ganges; 70 miles E. of Agra, and 76 N. W. of Lucknow. Long. 79. 30. W. lat. 27. 28. N.

FURSTENAU, a town of Westphalia, in the principality of Osnaburg; 13 miles S. W. of Quakenburg.

FURSTENBERG, a principality of Suabia, between the Black Forest and the principality of Constance. In this state the river Danube takes its rise.

FURSTENBERG, a town of Suabia, in the principality of the same name, with an ancient castle on a mountain, near the Danube; 27 miles E. by S. of Friburg. Long. 8. 35. E. lat. 47. 53. N.

FURSTENBERG, a town of Upper Saxony, in Lusatia, on the river Oder; 11 miles S. by E. of Frankfort.

FURSTENBERG, a town of Lower Saxony, in Mecklenburg-Strelitz, on the river Havel; 10 miles S. of Strelitz.

FURSTENFELD, a town of Germany, in Styria, with a castle, on the frontier of Hungary; 39 miles E. by S. of Gratz.

FURSTENWALD, a town of Brandenburg, in the Middle Mark; seated on the Spree; 32 miles E. S. E. of Berlin.

FURSTENWERDER, a town of Brandenburg, in the Ucker Mark; 12 miles N. W. of Prenlzo.

FURTH, a town and castle of Lower Bavaria, on the river Cham; 10 miles N. E. of Cham.

FURTH, a town of Franconia, in the principality of Anspach; seated on the Rednitz; 5 miles N. W. of Nuremberg. It is a populous place, and the seat of extensive manufactures, which the exclusive privileges of Nuremberg prevent from being carried on in that city. Pop. about 13,000.

FUTTEHABAD, a town of Hindostan, in the province of Ajmeer. It has a fort, and is surrounded by lofty brick walls. It is seated in a country infested with lions and phatty thieves, who inhabit the jungle. Pop. 5000.

FUTTEHGHUR, a town of Hindostan, in the province of Agra. It has an arsenal, fort, and theatre, and a manufacture of tents.

FUTTEHPOUR, or FATTIPOOR, a town of Hindostan, in the province of Agra; 24 miles W. of the city of Agra. It was a favourite place of Akbar.

FYERS. *See* FOYERS.

FYNE, LOCH, in Scotland, an inlet of the Atlantic, in Argyleshire; nearly 40 miles in length. It receives and returns a tide on each side of the Isle of Arran, which is opposite its entrance. It is indented with bays; and, in the herring season, is the resort of numerous fishing vessels.

FYZABAD, a city of Hindostan, in the territory of Oude, of which it was once the capital. Here are the remains of a vast building, the palace of the nabob Sujah Addowlah, which, at the time of his death, is said to have contained 1000 women and upwards of 50 of his children. The city is populous; but, since the removal of the court of Oude to Lucknow, it has greatly declined in wealth. It is seated on the Gogra; 76 miles E. of Lucknow. Long. 82. 26. E. lat. 26. 46. N.

G.

GABARET, a town of France, in the department of Landes; seated on the Gelisse; 16 miles W. of Condom.

GABEL, a fortified town of Bohemia, which commands the pass into Lusatia. It is 8 miles S. of Zittau.

GABES, or GABS. *See* CABES.

GABIAN, a village of France in the department of Herault; 9 miles N. W. of Beziers. It has a mineral spring; and near it is a rock from which issues petroleum.

GABON, a county of Guinea; bounded on the N. by Majombo, E. by Anziko, S. by Loango, and W. by the Atlantic. It has a river of the same name, which enters the Atlantic a little N. of the equinoctial line. The chief town is Sette.

GADAMIS, a town of Barbary, in Biledulgerid; capital of a country of the same name. It is 170 miles S. W. of Tripoli. Long. 10. 40. E. lat. 30. 40. N.

GADEBUSCH, a town of Lower Saxony, in Mecklenburg, near which the Swedes defeated the Danes and Saxons, in 1712. It is 16 miles N. N. W. of Schwerin.

GAETA, a strong town on the W. coast of Naples, in Terra di Lavoro, with a fort, a citadel, and a harbour. Near this town was the Formian villa of Cicero; tradition points out its site, and the very spot where he was butchered. It was taken by the Austrians in 1707, by the Spaniards in 1734, and by the French in 1806. It is seated at the foot of a mountain, on the Gulf of Gaeta; 30 miles N. W. of Capua. Long. 13. 47. E. lat. 51. 30. N.

GAILDORF, a town of Franconia, in the lordship of Limburgh, with a castle near the river Koeher; 13 miles W. of Elwangen.

GAILLAC, a town of France, in the department of Tarn, celebrated for its wine. It is seated on the Tarn, which is here navigable; 10 miles S. W. of Alby. It is the seat of a prefect, and contains 7310 inhabitants.

GAILLON a town of France in the department of Eure, with a magnificent palace, belonging to the archbishop of Rouen. It is 11 miles N. E. of Evreux, and 22 S. S. E. of Rouen.

Gainsborough, a town in Lincolnshire, with a market on Tuesday; seated on the Trent, over which is a handsome stone bridge. It is a riverport of some consequence, being accessible to vessels of sufficient size to navigate the sea; and serves as a place of export and import for the N. part of the county, and for Nottinghamshire. It is 17 miles N. W. of Lincoln, and 149 N. by W. of London.

Gairloch, a large bay of Scotland, on the W. coast of Ross-shire, which gives name to a tract of land near it. The fishing of cod, and other white fish, is here very considerable.

Galacz or Gala, a town of European Turkey, in Moldavia. In 1790 it was taken by the Russians, after a bloody battle. It is seated on a lake, near the conflux of the Pruth with the Danube; 55 miles W. of Ismail, and 120 S. S. W. of Bender. Long. 28. 24. E. lat. 45. 24. N.

Galashiels, a town of Scotland, in Selkirkshire, with a manufacture of woollen cloth known by the name of Galashiels grey. It is seated on the Gala, near its conflux with the Tweed; 5 miles N. of Selkirk.

Galata, a suburb of Constantinople, (which see.)

Galicia, a late province in the S. W. part of Poland, lying between the lat. of 48. and 51. N., and 19. and 26. of E. long. It is bounded on the S. in a direction W. by N. by the Carpathian mountains, which divide it from Hungary; the W. end jets upon Silesia; the Vistula river forms part of its northern, and the Bug part of its eastern boundary; the S. E. extremity is divided by the Bukowine district from Moldavia, and the Dniester river intersects the S. E. part. This territory was forcibly seized by the Austrians in 1772, and incorporated into the Austrian dominions, under the appellation of the kingdom of Galicia and Lodomeria. The mountainous parts produce fine pasture; the plains are mostly sandy, but abound in forests, and are fertile in corn. The principal articles of traffic are cattle, hides, wax, and honey; the country also contains mines of copper, lead, iron, and salt, of which the latter are the most valuable. Its limits comprise upwards of 32,000 square miles; the population about 4,500,000. It is divided into East Galicia and West Galicia, of which the capitals are Lemburg and Cracow.

Galicia, a province of Spain, forming the N. W. extremity of the peninsula; bounded on the N. and W. by the Atlantic Ocean, on the E. by Asturias and Leon, on the S. by the Portuguese province of Traz-os-Montes, and on the S. W. by the river Minho, which divides it from the Portuguese province of Entre-Douro-e-Minho; its extreme length from the mouth of the Minho river, in 41. 52., to Cape Ortegal, the extreme northern limits of Spain, in 43.46. N., is 133 statute miles; and its extreme width, from the frontier of Leon to Cape Finisterre, the extreme western limit of Spain, in the lat. of 42. 56. N., and 9. 17. of W. long. is about 120 miles, but the mean length and breadth does not much, if at all, exceed 100 miles; its area, therefore, comprises about 10,000 square miles; the population about 2,000,000. It is one of the most mountainous districts in Spain, yielding abundance of fine timber, and various minerals. The whole extent of its coast is indented with fine bays and harbours. Ferrol, 25 miles S. S. W. of Cape Ortegal, is one of the principal stations of the Spanish national marine; the port of Corunna is on the S. W. side of the same bay in which the harbour of Ferrol is situate: the most important harbour on the W. coast is Vigo Bay, about 50 miles S. of Cape Finisterre, and a few miles N. of the mouth of the Minho. Santiago, or St. Jago de Compostella, 35 miles S. of Corunna, and 300 N. W. of Madrid, is the capital of the province; the other principal towns are Mondoneda and Betanzos, in the N. E., Lugo, 35 miles E. of Santiago, Orense on the S., and Ciudad Tuy on the N. bank of the Minho, and Bayona on a southern inlet of Vigo Bay.

Galitsch, a town of Russia, in the government of Kostroma, on the S. side of a lake of its name; 56 miles E. N. E. of Kostroma. Long. 42. 54. E. lat. 57. 56. N.

Gall, St., a small but populous canton of Switzerland; the E. end bordering on the lake of Constance, between the cantons of Thurgau and Appenzel. Its population amounts to 134,000; its quota of trorps, 2630.

Gall, St., or St. Gallen, a town of Switzerland, capital of the canton of St. Gall. It has a rich abbey, whose abbot formerly possessed the sovereignty of the town. The town is entirely protestant; and the subjects of the abbot, whose territory is distinct, are mostly catholics. The abbey is situate close to the town; and in its library are many curious manuscripts. The town has an extensive trade, arising chiefly from its linen and cotton manufactures and bleaching grounds. It is seated in a narrow valley, on two small streams; 35 miles E. of Zurich. Long. 9. 18. E. lat 47. 21. N. Pop. about 10,000.

Galla, an extensive territory of Africa, comprising all the S. part of Abyssinia: the limits on the S. and W. are very undefined: the inhabitants are among the rudest and most uncivilized of any in Africa.

Gallam, a town of Negroland: capital of a kingdom of the same name, on the river Senegal. The French built a fort here, which was ceded to the English in 1763. During the American war it was taken by the French, but restored in 1783. Long. 10.0. W. lat. 14.35.N.

Gallapagos, a number of islands in the Pacific Ocean, discovered by the Spaniards, to whom they belonged. They are not inhabited; but the South Sea fishermen touch here for fresh water and provisions. Here are a great number of birds, and excellent tortoises. They lie under the equator, the centre island in long. 85. 30. W. about 9 degrees W. of the coast of Columbia.

GALLATIN, a county of Kentucky; bounded on the N. for about 35 miles by the Ohio river, which divides it from the state of Indiana. Population 4,003. Port William, on the E. bank of the Kentucky river, at its entrance into the Ohio, 45 miles N.N.W. of Frankfort, is the chief town.

GALLATIN is also the name of another county in the state of Illinois. Population, 10,760. It is celebrated for its salt springs, from which vast quantities of salt are made. Shawnee town, on the W. bank of the Ohio, 12 miles below the junction of the Wabash, is the chief town.

GALLATIN'S RIVER, one of the head water streams of the Missouri, rising in the lat. of 44. N. and 110. 5. of W. long., upwards of 3000 miles, by the course of the river, above the entrance of the Missouri into the Mississippi.

GALLIA, a county on the S. E. border of the State of Ohio; bounded by the Ohio river, where it receives the great Kanhawa from Virginia. Population, 13,444. Gallipolis, on the bank of the Ohio, 104 miles S.S.E. of Columbia, is the chief town.

GALLE, or POINT DE GALLE, a seaport on the S. coast of Ceylon, in a rich and beautiful district, with a strong fort, and a secure harbour. It is populous, and, in point of trade, ranks next to Colombo. The chief branch of its traffic consists in the exportation of fish to the continent; but a great part of the products of the island are also shipped here for Europe. It is 85 miles S. by E. of Colombo. Long. 80. 10. E. lat. 6. 0. N.

GALLIPOLI, a strait between European and Asiatic Turkey—the ancient Hellespont. It forms the communication between the Archipelago and the Sea of Marmora, and is defended at the S.W. entrance by two castles. It is here 2 miles over, and is 33 miles long. *See* DARDANELLES and HELLESPONT.

GALLIPOLI, a town of European Turkey, which gives name to the preceding strait, is seated next its opening into the Sea of Marmora. It is the residence of a pacha, and the see of a Greek bishop. It contains about 10,000 Turks and 3500 Greeks, besides a great number of Jews, amounting together to about 20,000. It is an open place, with no other defence than a sorry square castle. It was the first place in Europe possessed by the Turks; 100 miles S. W. of Constantinople. Long. 26. 59. E. lat. 40. 26. N.

GALLIPOLI, a seaport of Naples, in Terra d'Otranto, and a bishop's see. This place is a great mart for olive oil, and has a manufacture of muslins. It is seated on a rocky island, on the E. shore of the Bay of Tarento, and joined to the main land by a bridge protected by a fort; 23 miles W. of Otranto. Long. 18. 5. E. lat. 40. 20. N. Pop. about 9000.

GALLOWAY, a district of Scotland, now divided into East and West Galloway, or KIRKCUDBRIGHTSHIRE and WIGTONSHIRE. It was famous for a particular breed of small horses called galloways.

GALLOWAY, MULL OF, the extreme S. W. point of Scotland, in the lat. of 59. 38. N., and 4. 50. of W. long. It forms the W. point of entrance to Luce Bay, and the E. point of entrance to the North Channel, between the Irish Sea and the Atlantic Ocean.

GALLOWAY, NEW, a borough of Scotland, in Kirkcudbrightshire, on the river Ken; 18 miles N. of Kirkcudbright, and 80 S.W. of Edinburgh. In conjunction with Wigton, &c. it sends one member to parliament.

GALMIER, ST., a town of France in the department of Loire, with a medicinal spring of a vinous taste; 18 miles E. of Montbrison.

GALSTON, a populous village of Ayrshire, Scotland; seated on the banks of the river Irvine; 3 miles S. S. E. of Kilmarnock.

GALTEE MOUNTAINS, in the county of Tipperary, Ireland; the highest of which, Galteemore, is 3000 feet high.

GALWAY, a maritime county, in the province of Connaught, on the W. coast of Ireland, being about 100 miles in extreme length from E. to W.; the W. part, projecting into the Atlantic Ocean, is a mountainous and dreary district, but the inland part is in general fertile both in grain and pasture. Next to Cork, it is the largest county in Ireland, comprising 1,255,362 acres. It is bounded on the E. by the river Suck, which divides it from Roscommon; the Shannon on the S. E. divides it from Tipperary; Lough Corrib divides the W. from the E. part of the county. Beside the county town, of the same name, the other principal towns are Tuam, Athenry, and Loughrea.

GALWAY, the chief town of the preceding county, is seated on the banks of the outlet of Lough Corrib into Galway Bay; 126 miles due W. of Dublin. It was formerly surrounded by strong walls; the streets are large and straight, and the houses are generally well built of stone. The harbour is defended by a fort. Here is a coarse woollen and linen manufacture, and a considerable trade in kelp. The salmon and herring fishery is also considerable. It is divided into three parishes, and is a county of itself, having a separate jurisdiction. The principal church, which is collegiate, is a spacious Gothic edifice; it has several catholic establishments of friars and nuns, a county infirmary, exchange, and several other public buildings. It returns two members to parliament.

GALWAY BAY extends about 20 miles from W. to E., and is from 7 to 10 miles wide; the South Arran Isles stretch across the entrance.

GAMBIA, a noble river of Africa, falling into the Atlantic Ocean by several channels between the lat. of 12. and 13. 45. N. Cape St. Mary, the S. point of entrance to the main channel, is in the lat. of 13. 8. N., and 16. 33. of W. long. The banks, for about 100 miles from the mouth, are low and swampy, but, higher up, the river flows through a delightfully fertile country, interspersed with numerous towns and villages. At a distance of about 400 miles from its mouth, the navigation is impeded by falls.

GAMBRON. *See* GOMBROON.

GAN, a town of France, in the department of

Lower Pyrenees; 3 miles S. of Pau. Pop. 3000.

GANA, GANARA. *See* GHANA.

GANATT, a town of the empire of Cassina, in the interior of North Africa; 280 miles N. by E. of Agades. Long. 14. 30. E. lat. 24. 40. N.

GANDERSHEIM, a town of Lower Saxony, in the duchy of Brunswick-Wolfenbuttle, with a celebrated convent; 17 miles S.W. of Goslar.

GANDIA, a town of Spain, in Valencia, with a small university; seated on a river near its entrance into the Gulf of Valencia; 32 miles S. by E. of Valencia, and 48 N. by E. of Alicant. Population, about 6000.

GANDICOTTA, or WANDICOTTA, a town and fortress of Hindostan, in the circar of Cuddapa, near which is a diamond mine. It is seated on a lofty mountain by the river Pennar; 33 miles W. N. W. of Cuddapa.

GANGAPATNAM, a town of Hindostan, in the Carnatic, at the mouth of the Pennar: 94 miles N. of Madras. Long. 80. 12. E. lat. 14. 24. N.

GANGEA, or GANJA, a town of Persia, in the province of Erivan; 105 miles S. by E. of Teflis. Long. 45. 50. E. lat. 41. 10. N.

GANGES, a celebrated river of Asia, which has its source in two springs, on the W. side of Mount Kentaiffe, in Tibet, in the lat. of 34. N. and 82. of E. long. The two streams take a W. direction for 300 miles, when, meeting the ridge of Himmaleh, they turn S., unite their waters, and form what is properly called the Ganges, from the Hindoo word *ganga*, which signifies a river; a term given it by way of eminence. The great body of water now forces a passage through the ridge of Himmaleh, at the distance of 400 miles below the place of its first approach, and, rushing through a cavern, precipitates itself into a vast basin, at the hither foot of the mountain. The Ganges thus appears, to incurious spectators, to have its source from this chain of mountains. Superstition has given to the mouth of the cavern the form of the head of a cow, an animal held by the Hindoos in great veneration; and it is therefore called the Gangotri, or the Cow's Mouth. From this place it takes a S. E. direction through the country of Sirinagur, until, at Hurdwar, it finally escapes from this mountainous tract, in which it has wandered 800 miles. From Hurdwar, where it gushes through an opening in the mountains, and enters Hindostan, it flows 1200 miles with a smooth navigable stream through delightful plains to the Bay of Bengal, which it enters by several mouths, that form an extensive delta, in the lat. of 22. N. and between 88. and 91. of E. long. In its course through these plains, it receives 11 rivers, some of them larger and none smaller than the Thames, besides many of inferior note; the principal of which are the Gogra, Coosy, and the Burrampooter, from the N., and the Jumna, Soane, and Dummooda, from the S. In the annual inundation of this river, which on an average rises 31 feet, the country is overflowed to the extent of more than 100 miles in width. The Ganges is, in every respect, one of the most beneficial rivers in the world; diffusing plenty immediately, by means of its living productions, and, by enriching the lands, affording an easy conveyance for the production of its borders, and giving employment to many thousand boatmen. It is no wonder, therefore, that the Hindoos regard this river as a kind of deity, that they hold its waters in high veneration, and that it is visited annually by a prodigious number of pilgrims from all parts of Hindostan. *See* HOOGLY.

GANGOTRI, a town of the country of Sirinagur, 10,073 feet above the sea, and a celebrated place of pilgrimage; seated on the Ganges, where that river rushes through a cavern of the Himmaleh mountains; 170 miles N. N. W. of Sirinagur. Long. 76. 35. E. lat. 38. 8. N.

GANGPOUR, a town of Hindostan, in Orissa; capital of a circar of its name. It is 50 miles N. N. E. of Sumbulpour, and 160 N. W. of Cuttack. Long. 84. 10. E. lat. 22. 2. N.

GANJAM, a town of Hindostan, in the circar of Cicacole, on the Bay of Bengal, at the mouth of a river which is rarely navigable; near the S. end of lake Chilca, 110 miles N. E. of Cicacole. Long. 85. 20. E. lat. 19. 22. N.

GANNAT, a town of France, in the department of Allier; 30 miles S. of Moulins. It is the seat of a prefect. Pop. 5000.

GAP, a town of France, capital of the department of Upper Alps, and lately a bishop's see. It has a fort called Puymore, and is seated on the small river Bene, at the foot of a mountain, in which some mineral waters are found; 348 miles S. S. E. of Paris, and 82 N. N. W. of Nice. Pop. 9000.

GAPSAL, a town of Russia, in the government of Revel, on a small gulf of the Baltic; 36 miles W. S. W. of Revel.

GARAK. *See* KAREK.

GARD, a department of the S. of France, including part of the late province of Languedoc. It has its name from a rapid river, which rises in the department of Lozere, flows S. E. through this department, and enters the Rhone, above Beaucaire. It is bounded on the E. by the Rhone; the S. point jets upon the Mediterranean; it partakes, however, more of the character of an interior than a maritime district. It is rich in mines of lead, calamine, antimony manganese, gypsum, &c. The vine and olive, and especially the latter, flourish luxuriantly. Pop. 334,164.

GARDA, a town of Italy, in the Veronese; seated on the E. shore of a lake of its name: 17 miles N. W. of Verona.

GARDA, LAKE OF, one of the largest lakes in Italy, lying between the territories of Verona and Brescia. It is 30 miles long, and 10 where broadest; but not above 4 towards its northern extremity, which enters the principality of Trent: its outlet is by the Mincio, which runs past Mantua into the Po.

GARDEFAN, or GUARDAFUI, a cape in the Indian Ocean, the most easterly point of Africa. Long. 51. 10. E. lat. 11. 40. N.

GARDELEBEN, a town of Brandenburg, in the Old Mark, with manufactures of cloth, and a trade in hops and excellent beer; seated on the river Beise; 15 miles W. of Stendal. Pop. 4000.

GARDINER, a town of the United States, state of Maine, on the Kennebeck river, opposite Pittstown. Here is an establishment for instruction in natural science. Pop. 5042.

GARCNANO, a town of the Bresciano; seated on the W. shore of Lake Garda; 26 miles N. E. of Brescia.

GARMOUTH, a town of Scotland, in Murrayshire, at the mouth of the Spey, with a good harbour. Great quantities of ship-timber are floated down the river to the town, and many small vessels are built here. Wood is also a considerable article of commerce. It is 8 miles E. of Elgin.

GARONNE, a river of France, which rises in the Pyrenees, and flows N. N. E. of Toulouse, and from thence N. W. past Valence, Agen, Marmande, and Bordeaux, into the Bay of Biscay, receiving in its course from the E. the Tarn, Lot, Vezere, and Dordogne; from whence it is called the Gironde, and is united with the Mediterranean by a canal from Toulouse, called the canal of Languedoc.

GARONNE, UPPER, a department of the S. of France, containing part of the late province of Languedoc. The S. end extends to the Pyrenees, and it is intersected its whole extent from S. to N. by the Garonne. It is fertile both in tillage and pasture; the vine is also cultivated to a great extent. It is divided into four arrondissements, of which Toulouse (the capital), Villefranche, and St. Gaudens are the chief towns. Pop. 391,000.

GARSIS, a town of the kingdom of Fez, surrounded by walls, and the houses are built with black stone. It stands in a fertile country, on the Mulu; 56 miles S. E. of Melilla.

GARSTANG, a parish and corporate town of Lancashire, with a market on Thursday. Here are the ruins of Greenhough Castle; and in the neighbourhood are several cotton works. The town is seated on the river Wyre; 10 miles S. of Lancaster, and 229 N. N. W. of London.

GARTZ, a town of Hither Pomerania; seated on the Oder; 13 miles S. by W. of Stettin.

GASCONY, a late province of France; bounded on the W. by the Bay of Biscay, N. by Guienne, E. by Languedoc, and S. by the Pyrenees. The inhabitants are of a lively disposition, famous for boasting of their exploits, which has occasioned the name of *gasconade* to be given to all bragging stories. This province, with Armagnac, now forms the departments of Landes, Gers, Upper Pyrenees, and parts of the Upper Garonne, and Arriege.

GASPE, an extensive district of Lower Canada, lying between the river St. Lawrence on the N. and Bay of Chaleur on the S.; bounded on the E. by the Gulf of St. Lawrence. It is at present but thinly inhabited (pop. about 5000); the population is, however, progressively increasing along the shore of the Bay of Chaleur, which supplies abundance of fine timber. The Bay of Gaspe is at the eastern extremity of the district.

GASTEIN, a town of Bavaria, in the duchy of Salzburg, near the frontier of Carinthia; celebrated for its warm baths, and mines of lead, iron, and gold. It is 45 miles S. of Salzburg.

GASTOUNI, a town of Greece, in the Morea, opposite the Island of Zante, and 11 miles E. from Clarenza. Pop. about 3500, employed in raising cotton and wine.

GATA, CAPE, a promontory of Spain, on the coast of Granada, consisting of an enormous rock of a singular nature and appearance, 24 miles in circuit. Long. 2. 22. W. lat. 36. 43. N.

GATEHOUSE, a town of Scotland, in Kirkcudbrightshire, near the mouth of the river Fleet. Here are considerable cotton works, and an extensive tannery. It is 9 miles N. W. of Kirkcudbright.

GATES, a frontier county of North Carolina, bordering on the Great Dismal Swamp, and bounded on the W. by the Chowan river: it comprises about 200 square miles.

GATESHEAD, a borough in the county of Durham, seated on the Tyne, over which is a handsome bridge to Newcastle. It appears like a suburb to Newcastle, and is celebrated for its grindstones, which are exported to all parts of the world. It is 13 miles N. of Durham, and 269 N. by W. of London, and returns one member to parliament.

GATTON, a village in Surrey. It is 2 miles N. E. of Ryegate, and 19 S. by W. of London.

GAUDENS, ST., a town of France, in the department of Upper Garonne; seated on the Garonne; 13 miles E. N. E. of St. Bertrand: it is the seat of a prefect.

GAUKARNA, a town of Hindostan, in the province of Canara, on the sea-coast, and principally occupied by Brahmins. Pop. 2000.

GAVI, a town of the territory of Genoa; an important frontier place toward Montserrat and the Milanese; seated on the Lemo; 22 miles N. W. of Genoa.

GAUR, or ZOUF, a city of Usbec Tartary; capital of the province of Gaur; seated on the river Zouf; 120 miles S. by W. of Balk. Long. 64. 40. W. lat. 35. 5. N.

GAUTS, stupendous mountains of Hindostan, extending along the E. and W. coasts of the peninsula. The W. ridge, called by the natives the mountains of Sukheim, extends from Cape Comorin to the river Tapty, in the lat. of 21. N., at the distance of from 40 to 70 miles from the shore, except a gap, opposite Paniany, about 16 miles in breadth, chiefly occupied by a forest. They rise abruptly from the low country, supporting, in the nature of a terrace, a vast extent of fertile and populous plains, which are so elevated as to render the air cool and pleasant. *Gaut*, according to the original import of the word, signifies a pass through or over mountains; and, by an extended sense, is applied to the mountains themselves.

GAWELGHUR, a town of Hindostan; capital of a fruitful district of the same name, in the province of Berar. It is a strong fortress, and was taken by storm, in 1803, by Gen. Wellesley.

GAYA, a city of Hindostan; the modern capital of Berar; 55 miles S. from Patna. It is divided into two parts. It is one of the most celebrated places of Hindoo pilgrimage, it having been the birthplace of Budha, who has a temple here, with an image very rudely carved. The ceremonies are directed by the resident priests, and are very numerous. It has also a cantonment for native troops.

GAZA, a town of Syria, in Palestine ; 2 miles from the Mediterranean ; with a harbour and a castle. It is now very small ; but, from the appearance of the ruins, it was formerly a considerable place. Here are manufactures of cotton ; but the principal commerce is furnished by the caravans between Egypt and Syria. It stands in a fertile country ; 50 miles S. W. of Jerusalem. Long. 34. 45. E. lat. 31. 28. N.

GAZYPOOR, capital of a fertile and populous district of Hindostan ; seated on the N. bank of the Ganges ; 45 miles N. E. of Benares.

GEARON, or JARON, a town of Persia, in Farsistan, in whose territory the best dates of Persia are produced. It is 80 miles S. by E. of Shiras. Long. 51. 17. E. lat. 28. 15. N.

GEAUGA, a county in the N. E. of Ohio ; the N. end borders on Lake Erie: it comprises about 600 square miles. Pop. 15,813. Chardon, in the centre of the county, 145 miles N. E. of Columbus, is the chief town.

GEASHILL, a village in King's County, Ireland ; 65 miles from Dublin.

GEFLE, a seaport of Sweden ; capital of Gestricia ; seated on an arm of the Gulf of Bothnia, which divides the town, and forms two islands. The exports are principally iron, pitch, tar, and deals. It is 90 miles N. N. W. of Stockholm. Long. 17. 20. E. lat. 60. 40. N. Pop. 6000.

GEHOL, or ZHEHOL, a town of Chinese Tartary, with a large palace, and a magnificent temple of Budha. Here the emperor of China received the British embassy in 1793. It is 136 miles N. of Peking.

GELDERLAND, one of the provinces of Holland, and the largest of them all. It lies between the Zuyder Zee, the provinces of Holland, Utrecht, and Overyssel, the principality of Munster, the duchy of Cleve, and Dutch Brabant; and is divided into three quarters, or counties, called Nimeguen, Arnheim, and Zutphen, from the principal towns. It is fertile in fruit and corn, and in many parts abounds in wood.

GELDERLAND, UPPER, a territory of the Netherlands, lying in detached parts, on both sides of the river Meuse ; divided into Austrian, Dutch, and Prussian Gelderland. The Austrian part includes Ruremonde and its dependencies; the Dutch comprehends the lordships of Velno and Stevenswert ; and the Prussian contains the capital, Gueldres, and its district, which is reckoned as a part of the circle of Westphalia ; the Austrian and Dutch part, at the peace of 1814, were included in the kingdom of the Netherlands, and the remainder assigned to Prussia.

GELDERS, a town of Prussia, in the province of Cleves, and formerly the capital of Prussian Gelderland. Here is a palace, the residence of the former dukes. It was taken in 1702, by the king of Prussia ; and in 1713 the town and its district was ceded by France to that prince, in exchange for the principality of Orange. In 1757 it surrendered to the French, who restored it in 1764, after demolishing the fortifications ; and in 1794, it again surrendered to them, and, at the peace of 1814, was assigned to Prussia. It is 20 miles S. S. E. of Cleves. Long. 6. 16. E. lat. 51. 31. N.

GELNHAUSEN, a town of Germany, in the electorate of Hesse, with a castle ; seated on the Kintzig ; 18 miles N. E. of Hanau.

GEMAPPE, a town of Belgium, in the province of Hainault ; 3 miles from Mons. A decisive victory was gained in the revolutionary war, on November 6th, 1792, by the French army, over the Austrians. It also was the site of some warfare at the period of the battle of Waterloo. Pop. 2700.

GEMARKE, a town of Prussia, in the province of Lower Rhine. It has an extensive commerce in linen, &c.; 18 miles S. E. of Dusseldorf. Pop. 5500.

GEMBLOUX, a town of the Netherlands, in Brabant, with an ancient abbey ; seated on the Orneau ; 22 miles S. E. of Brussels, on the road to Namur.

GEMINIANO, ST., a town of Tuscany, in the Florentino ; seated on a mountain, in which is a mine of vitriol ; 25 miles S. S. W. of Florence.

GEMISHKHANA, a town of Asiatic Turkey, in the pach. of Trebisonde. It derives its name (Silver House) from a neighbouring silver mine ; 45 miles S. from Trebisonde. Pop. 6500.

GEMONA, a town of Italy, in Friuli, near the river Tagliamento ; 20 miles W.N.W. of Friuli.

GEMUND, a town of Suabia ; seated on the Rems ; 24 miles N. by W. of Ulm, and 25 E. by S. of Stutgard.

GEMUND, a town of Germany, in the duchy of Juliers ; seated on the Roer ; 24 miles S. W. of Cologne.

GEMUND, a town of Upper Carinthia, with manufactures of iron and steel ; 16 miles N.W. of Villach.

GEMUNDEN, a town of Franconia, in the principality of Wurtzburg, on the river Maine ; 22 miles N. of Wurtzburg.

GEMUNDEN, a town of Austria, famous for its salt-works ; seated at the N. end of a lake of the same name, on the river Traun ; the outlet of the lake is 40 miles S. S. W. of Lintz, on the Danube.

GENESSEE, a river of the United States, which rises on the N. border of Pennsylvania, and runs N. N. E. through the state of New York into Lake Ontario. It has three falls, which furnish excellent mill seats ; and on its borders are the Genessee flats, 20 miles long and 4 broad, the soil rich, and clear of trees.

GENESSEE, a county in the state of New York ; the N. end of which borders on Lake Ontario ; it comprises about 1600 square miles, and is intersected by the canal from Lake Erie to the Hudson river. Pop. 59,587. Batavia, 225 miles W. of Albany, is the chief town.

GENEVA, a fortified city, capital of a territory of the same name, surrounded by the duchy of Savoy, of which it was formerly a part, and the see of a bishop, now resident at Annecy. In 1584 Geneva concluded an alliance with Zurich and Bern, by which it was an associate with Switzerland. During the greater part of the 18th century, there were frequent contests between the aristocratic and the popular parties; and the years 1768, 1782, 1789, and 1794, were distinguished by great revolutions. The last was effected entirely by the influence of the French; and, not long after, this city and its territory was made a department of France, under the name of Leman; but in 1814, after the expulsion of the French, it was annexed to Switzerland. Geneva, which stands partly on a plain at the W. end of a lake, and partly on a gentle ascent, is irregularly built. It had a good arsenal, and a university, founded in 1368. The houses are lofty; and many in the trading part of the city have arcades of wood, which are raised even to the upper stories. The inhabitants, estimated at 26,000, carry on a great trade; and, among others, the watchmaking business is particularly flourishing. The population of the district is 41,560. Geneva is 40 miles N. E. of Chambery, 135 N. W. of Turin, and 256 S. E. by S. of Paris. Long. 6. 0. E. lat. 46. 12. N.

Geneva, a town of New York.

Geneva, Lake of, or Lake Leman, a large expanse of water, between Savoy and Switzerland, in a valley which separates the Alps from Mount Jura. Its length, from the city of Geneva to Villeneuve, is 54 miles, and the breadth in the widest part is 12. The water near Geneva is shallow: in other parts the depth is various: the greatest yet found by sounding is 160 fathoms. The river Rhone runs through it from the E. to the W. extremity.

Genevieve, St., a county in the state of Missouri, on the W. bank of the Mississippi river, comprising about 1100 square miles of territory; the St. Francis river intersects the S. W. part of the county, which contains an exceedingly rich bed of lead ore.

Gengenbach, a town of Suabia, in Brisgau, with a Benedictine abbey; seated on a rivulet of the same name, which flows into the Kintzig; 20 miles N. of Friburg.

Genoa, a celebrated city and seaport of Italy, distinguished for its trading importance, as far back as the 11th century, about which period it began to take under its protection the towns and territory of the adjoining coast; but the most celebrated period of its history is from the close of the 13th to the middle of the 15th century, when the Genoese divided with the Venetians the exclusive commerce of Europe in the productions of Asia. Their success, however, in commerce and banking, excited the jealousy of the Venetians, and ultimately involved them in open hostilities; and in 1746 it surrendered to the Austrian power, whose oppression of the inhabitants was such, that the latter suddenly rose and expelled their conquerors, who again besieged the city the next year, but without effect. In 1798 the French became masters of this city. In 1800 it sustained a siege by a British fleet and Austrian army, till literally starved, and was evacuated by capitulation; but soon afterwards it was again delivered up to the French, on their victory at Marengo. Early in 1814 it was taken by the British, under Lord Bentinck; but at the general partitioning of Europe, which followed the peace of Paris in that year, the city and territory of Genoa was assigned to the king of Sardinia, and incorporated as a state into his dominions. The harbour is commodious, protected by two moles of considerable length; the city is about six miles in circumference, surrounded on all sides by a strong wall, and on the land side is defended by a double fortification; most of the streets are narrow and irregular, but the Balbi, New Street, and Strada Nuovissima, are spacious and elegant. Prior to the French revolution it had upwards of 30 churches, and 70 religious houses, three theatres, and several other public buildings. Many of the houses in the principal streets are adorned with marble porticoes, and several of the churches are beautiful specimens of architecture, and their interior decorations exceedingly tasteful and rich. The bank of Genoa, established in 1345, considerably extended at the commencement of the following century; in 1751 it became insolvent for a large amount, and in 1798 was finally abolished by Bonaparte. Although Genoa now holds an inferior rank, from its relatively advantageous local position, and maritime accommodation, as the outport and depôt for the whole of Piedmont and Sardinia, it must necessarily continue a place of considerable importance. Genoa is the see of an archbishop, and the seat of a university with a valuable library, a nautical and other public schools; has several manufactures of silks and jewellery, and is particularly distinguished for its manufacture of silk velvets. It is seated at the head of a spacious gulf of the Mediterranean, in the lat. of 44. 25. N. and 8. 58. of E. long. 80 miles in a meridional line S. E. of Turin, about the same distance S. by W. of Milan, 86 N. W. of Leghorn, 95 N. E. of Nice. The territory which formed the republic of Genoa extends along the shore of the gulf for about 120 miles.

Gentiah, or Jaintuja, the capital of a principality of Hindostan, province of Bengal, and adjoining the district of Silhet. The chief produce of the district is rice and cotton, and some ivory is also exported. The natives are barbarous, and their religion Brahminism.

Gentilly, a town of France; 5 miles S. of Paris: it was the residence of the earlier kings of France. Pop. 5000.

George, Fort, a fortress of Scotland, in Inverness-shire, which has several handsome streets of barracks. It is seated on the point of a peninsula, forming the point of entrance into the Murray Frith, and completely commands the entrance into the harbour of Inverness. It is 10 miles N. E. of Inverness.

George, St., a small island in the Gulf of Venice, to the S. of Venice, to which it is subject. Here is a Benedictine monastery, whose church is one of the finest in Italy.

George, St., one of the Azores, which produces much wheat. In 1808 a volcano broke out here, which destroyed the town of Ursulina, several farming-houses, &c. The chief town is Vellas. Long. 28. 0. W. lat. 38. 39. N.

George del Mina, St., or Elmina, a fort of Guinea, on the Gold Coast, and the principal settlement of the Dutch in those parts. The town under it, called by the natives Oddenna, is very long, and pretty broad. The houses are built of stone, which is uncommon, for in other places they are composed only of clay and wood. It is 10 miles W. S. W. of Cape Coast Castle. Long. 0. 8. W. lat. 4. 56. N.

George Fort, St. *See* Madras.

George, Lake, in the state of New York, lies to the S. W. of Lake Champlain, and is 35 miles long, but is narrow. The adjacent country is mountainous, presenting some beautiful romantic scenery; the valleys are tolerably fertile. The remains of Fort George, 48 miles N. of Albany, are at the S. end of the lake, and those of the fort of Ticonderoga at the N. end, at its outlet into Lake Champlain.

George, St., the largest of the Bermudas Islands. It is in the form of a hook; about 40 miles in length, but seldom 2 in breadth. It has a town of the same name, containing 500 houses built of freestone; it is the capital of all the islands. Long. 63. 35. W. lat. 32. 45. N.

George, St., the capital of the island of Granada, formerly called Fort-royal, which name the fort still retains. It is situate on the W. coast, not far from the S. end of the island, and has a safe and commodious harbour. Long. 61. 45. W. lat. 11. 50. N.

George, St., an island of the United States, in the Strait of St. Mary, which forms the communication between Lake Superior and Lake Huron.

George, St., an island in the Gulf of Mexico, opposite the mouth of the Apalachicola. Long. 84. 50. W. lat. 29. 30. N.

George's Key, St., a small island in the Bay of Honduras, on the E. coast of Yucatan. It is likewise called Casina, or Cayo Casigo. By a convention in 1786, the English logwood-cutters were permitted, under certain restrictions, to occupy this island. Long. 88. 35. W. lat. 17. 40. N.

Georgetown, a maritime district of South Carolina; bounded on the S. by the Santee river, which divides it from Charlestown district: it has 34 miles of sea coast, indented with several small inlets. Black River, Cedar and Lynches Creeks, the Great and Little Pedee, and the Waccamaws river, all unite their waters in this district, which comprises a surface of about 900 square miles, exceedingly fertile in rice and cotton.

Georgetown, a town of the district of Columbia, county of Washington, with a college for the promotion of general literature, founded by the Roman Catholics. It is situate on the E. bank of the Potomac, opposite Mason's Island, and on the W. side of Rock Creek, which separates it from the city of Washington; 3 miles W.N.W. of the capital, and 46 S. W. of Baltimore. Georgetown may be regarded as a suburb and the commercial quarter of the city of Washington. It owns about 7000 tons of shipping The population is 7312.

Georgetown, a town of the state of Maine, and the oldest in Lincoln county. It is the spot where the English first attempted to colonize New England, in 1607, and stands near the mouth of the Kennebec; 15 miles S. by W. of Wiscasset.

Georgetown, a small town of Van Diemen's Land, in Dorset county, near the mouth of the Tamar, or Port Dalrymple. It has declined since Launceston has become prosperous: 32 miles N. of Launceston, and 152 from Hobart Town.

There are several other towns named *Georgetown* in different parts of the United States of North America.

Georgia, a country of Asia, called by the Persians Kurdistan, and by the Turks Gurtshi. It is one of the seven Caucasian nations, in the countries between the Black Sea and the Caspian, and the lat. of 39. and 43. N., and comprehends the ancient Iberia and Colchis. It is bounded on the N. by Circassia, E. by Daghestan and Schirvan, S. by Armenia, and W. by Cuban, or the new Russian government of Caucasia. It is divided into nine provinces. Of these, five form what is commonly called the kingdom of Georgia; and four the kingdom or principality of Imeritia. The last reigning prince, Heraclius, ceded this country to Russia on his death, which happened in 1800. The hills of Georgia are covered with forests of oak, ash, beech, chesnuts, walnuts, and elms, encircled with vines, growing perfectly wild, but producing vast quantities of grapes, from which much wine and brandy are made. Cotton grows spontaneously, as well as the finest European fruit trees. Rice, wheat, millet, hemp, and flax are raised on the plains, almost without culture. The valleys afford the finest pasturage, the rivers are full of fish, the mountains abound in minerals, and the climate is healthy. The rivers of Georgia, the principal of which is the Kur, falling into the Caspian Sea, being fed by mountain torrents, are always either too rapid or too shallow for the purposes of navigation. The Georgians are Christians of the Greek communion, and appear to have received their name from their attachment to St. George, the tutelary saint of these countries. Their dress nearly resembles that of the Cossacks; but men of rank frequently wear the habit of Persia. They usually dye their hair, beards, and nails with red. The women employ the same colour to stain the palms of their hands. On their head they wear a cap or fillet, under which their black hair falls on their forehead; behind, it is braided into several tresses: their eyebrows are painted with black, in such a manner as to form one entire line, and the face is coated with white and red. They are celebrated for their beauty; but their air and manners are extremely voluptuous. The Georgians have great skill in the use of the bow, and are deemed excellent soldiers; but the men have no virtue, except courage: fathers sell their children, and sometimes their wives. Both sexes are addicted to drunkenness, and are particularly fond of brandy. The other inhabitants of Georgia are Tartars, Ossi, and Armenians. These last are found all over Georgia, sometimes mixed with the natives, and sometimes in villages of their own. They speak among themselves their own language, but all understand and can talk the Georgian. Besides these there are a considerable number of Jews, some having villages of their own, and others mixed with the Georgian, Armenian, and Tartar inhabitants, but never with the Ossi; the aggregate number amounts to 320,000. The Christians of the country in part follow the rites of the Armenian, and in part that of the Greek church; and they are represented as the most tractable Christians in the East. Teflis is the capital. *See* IMERITIA.

GEORGIA, one of the states of North America, originally extended from the Atlantic Ocean to the Mississippi; but since the formation of the federal government, in 1776, the states of Mississippi and Alabama have been divided off on the W. from Georgia, which, in its present extent, has 95 miles of sea-coast, between the entrance to St. Mary's River, in the lat. of 30. 40., and entrance to the Savannah river in the lat. of 32. N.; the Savannah river, for 225 miles in a N.W. direction, divides Georgia from South Carolina; on the N. the line of the 35th degree of N. lat. for 140 miles then divides Georgia from Tennessee; another conventional line, from the 35th degree of N. lat., bearing S. by E. till it cuts the Chatahoochee river at Fort Mitchel, in the lat. of 32. 20., and then that river, till it joins the Flint, in the lat. of 30. 40., divides Georgia from the state of Alabama; and another conventional line for 185 miles divides it on the S. from East Florida: these limits give a length, from N. to S., of 300 miles, and a mean breadth of 195 miles. The St. Mary and Savannah rivers form the northern and southern boundaries of the state: the Alatamaha, with several tributary streams, intersects all the inferior parts, and, with the great Ogeechee, falls into the Atlantic Ocean. The S. part of the state is divided into three large counties, Appling, Early, and Irwin, which, as cultivation is extended, will probably be subdivided; the remainder of the state is divided into 44 other counties, averaging about 3800 square miles each, and 8 counties of towns. The coast, for about 7 miles from the sea, is indented by rivers, creeks, and inlets, which form a chain of islands in which is produced the fine green-seeded cotton, commonly called Sea Island. The mouths and banks of all the rivers are in general exceedingly fertile in cotton and rice, and the forests supply abundance of fine timber, both pine and oak, which form an extensive external traffic, while the fig, orange, lemon, pomegranate, olive, and melon, supply luxurious repasts to the inhabitants. The government of Georgia, as established in 1798, being the third constitution since 1776, consists of a governor, senate, and house of representatives; the judicial power consists of a supreme court of four judges, and an inferior court of five judges, in each county, and subordinate justice courts of one justice of the peace, assisted by seven jurors. The religious denominations of Georgia are principally baptists and methodists: the latter were established in Georgia by Mr. John Wesley. In the value of its productions, Georgia holds the sixth rank in the Union of the North American States; the value of the cotton and rice exported in 1820, was 6,954,623 dollars, since when, cultivation has been gradually extended. The imports from foreign countries, direct into Georgia, are very limited; the excess of exports being equalized principally through New York and Boston. The population is 516,823, of whom 280,944 are slaves, and 2,753 free blacks. The seat of the legislative assembly is at Milledgeville, nearly in the centre of the state; but the principal town is Savannah, seated on the S. W. bank of the river of the same name.

GEORGIA, or SOUTH GEORGIA, an island in the South Atlantic Ocean, visited by Cook in 1775. It is 64 miles long, and 30 in its greatest breadth. It abounds in bays and harbours, which the vast quantities of ice render inaccessible the greatest part of the year. Here are perpendicular ice cliffs, of considerable height, like those of Spitzbergen; from which pieces were continually breaking off and floating out to sea. The valleys were covered with snow; and the only vegetation observed was bladed grass, wild burnet, and a plant like moss, which sprung from the rocks. Not a stream of fresh water was to be seen on the whole coast.

GEORGIA, GULF OF, a gulf of the North Pacific Ocean, between the continent of North America and Quadra and Vancouver Islands; about 120 miles in length, from N. to S., but the breadth varies in its different parts from 6 to 20 miles. It contains several clusters of islands, and branches off into a great number of canals, most of which were examined by Captain Vancouver and his officers.

GERA, a town of Upper Saxony, in Thuringia. It has a castle about a mile from the town, on a mountain, in a wood, and is called Osterstein. It is seated on the Elster; 32 miles S. S. W. of Leipsic.

GERAU, a town of Germany, in Hesse-Darmstadt; 8 miles W. N. W. of Darmstadt.

GERBSTADT, a town of Upper Saxony, in the county of Mansfield, Thuringia; 7 miles N. E. of Mansfield.

GERDAVEN, a town of Prussia, defended by two castles, and seated on the Omet, near a considerable lake; 50 miles S. E. of Konigsberg.

GERMAIN, ST., a town in Cornwall; market on Friday. It was once the largest town in the county, and a bishop's see. It stands near the sea; 10 miles W. of Plymouth, and 228 W. by S. of London..

GERMAIN, St., a town of France, in the department of Seine and Oise, with a magnificent palace, in which Louis XIV. was born. Here James II. found an asylum, when he fled to France. It is seated on the Seine, near a fine forest; 10 miles N. W. of Paris, to which there is a railroad.

GERMAN, and GERMAN TOWN. There are several towns of these names, in different parts of the United States of North America.

German Ocean, or **North Sea**, is the sea between the E. coast of England, from the Straits of Dover to the Shetland Isles, and the coast of Jutland and Norway: it comprises about 8 degrees of latitude, and 10 of longitude.

Germano, St., a town of Piedmont, on the River Naviglio; 9 miles W. of Vercelli, on the line of the canal to Ivrea.

Germano, St., a town of Naples, in Terra di Lavoro, at the foot of Monte Cassino; 17 miles S. S. E. of Sora.

Germany, an extensive country of Europe, lying between the 45th and 54th degree of N. lat. and 6. to 19. of E. long.; the mean length, however, from N. to S. does not exceed 530 British statute miles, and the mean breadth 460 miles, comprising an area of about 245,000 square miles. It is bounded on the E. by Hungary and Poland, N. by the Baltic Sea and Denmark, W. by the Netherlands and France, and S. by Switzerland and Italy. The extreme S. point jets into the Gulf of Venice. Prior to the French revolutionary war, which commenced in 1793, Germany had geographically been divided into 9 circles, politically subdivided into 206 archbishoprics, bishoprics, principalities, dukedoms, marquisates, lordships, provinces, &c., under the government of nearly as many sovereign potentates; but the whole of them formed a great confederacy, governed by political laws, at the head of which was an emperor, whose power in the collective body, or diet, was not directive, but executive. The western Roman empire, which had terminated in the year 475, in the person of Augustulus, the last Roman emperor, and which was succeeded by the reign of the Huns, the Ostrogoths, and the Lombards, was revived by Charlemagne, king of France, on Christmas-day, in the year 800. This prince being then at Rome, Pope Leo III. crowned him emperor, in St. Peter's church; and Nicephorus, who was then emperor of the east, consented to this coronation. The French kept the empire under eight emperors, till the year 912, when Louis III., the last prince of the line of Charlemagne, died without issue male. Conrad, Count of Franconia, the son-in-law of Louis, was then elected emperor. Thus the empire went to the Germans, and became elective, having been hereditary under the French emperors. The emperor was chosen by the princes, the lords, and the deputies of cities, till the year 1239, when the number of the electors was reduced to seven; one more was added in 1649, and another in 1692; these nine electors continued to the year 1798, when, in consequence of the alterations made in the constitution of the empire, under the influence of France and Russia, they became ten in number; namely, the elector and archbishop of Ratisbon, the elector and King of Bohemia, (the then emperor,) the elector of Bavaria, the elector of Saxony, the elector of Brandenburg, (king of Prussia,) the elector of Hanover, (king of England,) the elector of Wurtzburg, (late Grand Duke of Tuscany,) the elector of Wirtemberg, the elector of Baden, and the elector of Hesse. On the death of Charles VI. of Austria, in 1740, an emperor was chosen from the house of Bavaria, by the name of Charles VII. On the death of this prince, in 1745, Francis, grand duke of Tuscany, was elected emperor; whose grandson, Francis II. enjoyed the dignity of emperor of Germany till 1806, when he formally resigned the title and office, transferring his title of emperor to his hereditary dominions of Austria. At the close of the Saxon race, in 1024, the prerogatives of the emperor were very considerable; but in 1437 they were reduced to the right of conferring all dignities and titles, except the privilege of being a state of the empire; of granting dispensations with respect to the age of majority; of erecting cities, and conferring the privilege of coining money; of calling the meetings of the diet, and presiding in them. But, after all, there was not a foot of land annexed to this title; for, ever since the reign of Charles IV., the emperors depended entirely on their hereditary dominions, as the only source of their power, and even of their subsistence. To prevent the calamities of a contested election, a king of the Romans was often chosen in the lifetime of the emperor, on whose death he succeeded to the imperial dignity, of course. The emperor (always elected and crowned at Frankfort on the Maine) assumed the title of august, and pretended to be successor to the emperors of Rome. Although he was chief of the empire, the supreme authority resided in the diet, which was composed of three colleges—the college of electors, the college of princes, and the college of imperial towns. The diet had the power of making peace or war, of settling general impositions, and of regulating all the important affairs of the empire; but the decisions had not the force of law till the emperor gave his consent. When a war was determined on, every prince contributed his quota of men and money, as valued in the matriculation roll; though, as an elector or prince, he might espouse a different side from that of the diet. All the sovereigns of Germany had, and still have, an absolute authority in their own dominions, and can lay taxes, levy troops, and make alliances, provided they do not prejudice the empire. They determine all civil causes definitely, unless in some particular cases in which an appeal may be made. These appeals were to two courts, called the Imperial Chamber, at Wetzlar, and the Aulic Council, at Vienna. The three principal religions are the Roman Catholic, the Lutheran, and the Calvinistic; but Christians of all denominations are tolerated, and there is a multitude of Jews in all the towns. Germany is watered by numerous rivers, the three principal of which are the Rhine, the Danube, and the Elbe; the first of these rises in Switzerland, and forms the S. W. boundary of the empire, dividing it from Switzerland and France; it afterwards intersects the N. W. part of Germany and Holland, and falls into the Meuse, near Rotterdam. The

Danube rises in Suabia, the S. W. circle of the empire, and, by itself and several tributary streams of inferior note, intersects a great portion of the southern part of Germany; it afterwards runs through Hungary and European Turkey into the Black Sea. The Elbe rises near the centre of the eastern frontier, and runs in a N. W. direction into the North Sea. The Oder intersects all the N. E. part of Germany, and falls into the Baltic Sea. The Weser, the Embs, the Adije, the Drave, and other small rivers are navigable, and afford admirable means of facilitating an interchange of productions from one part of the country to the other; but the Oder and the Elbe are the only two that are united by art. The mountains of the south are rich in every kind of metal and semi-metal. The forests supply abundance of the finest timber, and the vine, olive, and mulberry only require common attention to yield fruit in abundance; while the plains of the north yield a surplus of grain and cattle for exportation, and of wool and flax to furnish materials for extensive manufactures, especially of linens, which are exported in considerable quantities to almost every part of Europe, Africa, and America.

In 1806 the Germanic Confederacy was dissolved by Napoleon Bonaparte, and several of the minor states formed into a new confederacy, under the title of the Confederation of the Rhine; while Westphalia, Wurtemberg, and Bavaria, were constituted new and independent kingdoms, Prussia and Austria retaining their respective hereditary dominions; but at the general pacification of Europe, in 1815, the Rhenish confederacy was dissolved, and that of Germany again re-established, with some variations and modifications; and in 1825 the confederacy consisted of 35 sovereignties, exclusive of the four free towns of Hamburg, Bremen, Lubec, and Frankfort. No people apply themselves more closely to their studies than the Germans; and the Hebrew is no where so generally learnt, or better understood. Printing is most extensively encouraged; every man of letters is an author; they multiply books without number; thousands of suppositions and disputations are annually published, with which they overstock the fairs of Frankfort and Leipsic; for no man can be a graduate in the university, who has not published one disputation at least. The language of Germany is a dialect of the Teutonic, which succeeded that called the Celtic. The population is estimated at 30,000,000. Vienna is the principal city.

Gerona, a fortified town of Spain, in Catalonia, and a bishop's see; seated on the Ter; 20 miles from its entrance into the Mediterranean, and 47 N. E. of Barcelona.

Gers, an interior department in the S. W. of France: it is watered by numerous streams, running from S. to N. into the Garonne; the principal of them is the Gers, which gives name to the department. It contains a strata of pit-coal, and has manufactures of wool, linen, and saltpetre; its chief vegetable productions are flax the vine, and pears. It is divided into four other arrondissements; the chief towns of which are Condon, Lecture, Lombez, and Mirande.

Gersau, a town of Switzerland, on the lake of Schweitz, at the foot of the Righi; 12 miles S. W. of Schweitz.

Gertruydenburg, a fortified town of South Holland, with a good harbour and salmon fishery on a large lake, called Biesbosch. It has been often taken; the last time by the French, in 1793. but soon recovered. It is 7 miles N. by E. of Breda. Long. 4. 52. E. lat. 51. 42. N.

Gerumenha, or Jurumenha, a town of Portugal, in Alentejo, with a strong castle; seated on a hill, near the river Guadiana; 18 miles below Badajoz.

Gervais, St., a town of France, in the department of Auvergne; 10 miles S. from Montagne. Pop. 2450.

Gerzat, a town of France, in the department of Puy de Dome; 7 miles N. E. from Clermont. Pop. 2500.

Gesecke, a town of Germany, in the duchy of Westphalia, seated on the Weyck; 11 miles W. S. W. of Paderborn.

Gessenay. *See* Sanen.

Gestricia, a province of Sweden, the S. part of Nordland, between Dalecarlia on the W. and the Gulf of Bothnia on the E.. It is 100 miles long and 60 broad, diversified by forests, rocks, hills and dales, lakes and rivers; and there are numerous mines and forges. Gefle is the capital.

Getafe, a town of Spain; 7 miles S. of Madrid. It is a decayed town, on the road to Toledo. Pop. 5250.

Gettysburg, a town of Pennsylvania, in York county; situate at the head of Rock Creek; 30 miles W. by S. of York.

Gewicz, a town of the Austrian empire, in the province of Moravia; 25 miles W. from Olmutz. Pop. 2320, of whom 900 are Jews.

Gex, a town of France, in the department of Ain; noted for excellent cheese; seated at the foot of Mount St. Claude, between the Rhone, the Lake of Geneva, and Switzerland; 10 miles N. W. of Geneva. It is the seat of a prefect.

Geyss, a town of the electorate of Hesse, in the principality of Fulda; seated on the Ulster; 17 miles N. E. of Fulda.

Gezan, or Ghezan, a seaport of Arabia Felix, which has a considerable trade in senna and coffee; seated on the Red Sea; 90 miles N. W. of Loheia. Long. 43. 15. E. lat. 16. 25. N.

Gezira, a town of Asiatic Turkey, in Diarbek, on an island formed by the river Tigris; 70 miles N. W. of Mosul. Long. 40. 50. E. lat. 37. 16. N.

Gezula, a province of Morocco, which is very productive, and contains mines of iron and copper. The inhabitants are numerous, and considered as the most ancient people of Africa: they live in tents, and are so independent that they are rather the allies than the subjects of the emperor of Morocco.

Ghana, or Gana, a city of Negroland, capital of a country of the same name, governed by a sultan. It stands on the S. side of a large lake at its outlet, which separates the city into two parts, and soon after joins the river Niger, which is here called Neel il Abeed, or Nile of the Negros. It is 100 miles E. by S. of Cassina.

GHAUTS. *See* GAUTS.

GHEELEN, a town of Belgium, in the province of Antwerp; 7 miles E. from Turnhout. Here are extensive distilleries and lace manufactures. Pop. 7350.

GHENT, or GAND, a city of Belgium, formerly the capital of Austrian Flanders, now the capital of the department of East Flanders, and a bishop's see. It contains 60,000 inhabitants; but it is not populous in proportion to its extent, being 15 miles in circumference. The city is intersected by many canals, which divide it into 26 isles, and over the canals are 300 bridges. It has also two navigable canals; the one to Sas van Ghent, the other to Bruges and Ostend. Here are several linen and woollen manufactures, and it has a great trade in corn. The cathedral of St. Bavon, and the abbey of St. Peter, are magnificent edifices; in which, as also in the churches, are some capital paintings by the best masters: the cathedral in particular contains one of the most magnificent collections of works of art in fresco, mosaic work, painting, and sculpture in the world. Charles V. was born here; but the inhabitants have no reason to respect his memory; for he repeatedly loaded them with heavy exactions, and built a citadel to awe them. Here, in 1576, was concluded the famous treaty, called the Pacification of Ghent, the first commencement of the separation of seven provinces from the seventeen which then formed the Netherlands; and it was the seat of the negotiation of the treaty of peace between England and the United States of North America, in 1814-15. Ghent was often taken and retaken in the wars of 1793—1815. It is seated on the Scheldt, at the influx of the Lis, Lieve, and Moeze; 26 miles N. W. of Brussels. Long. 3. 44. E. lat. 51. 3. N.

GHERGONG, a city and formerly the capital of the kingdom of Assam. It is seated on the Degoo, near its conflux with the Burrampooter; 400 miles N. E. of Calcutta. Long. 93. 36. E. lat. 25. 35. N.

GHERIAH, a seaport of Hindostan, on the coast of Concan. It was the capital of Angria, a famous piratical prince, whose fort here was taken by the English and Mahrattas, in 1756, and his whole fleet destroyed. It is 165 miles S. by E. of Bombay. Long. 73. 8. E. lat. 16. 45. N.

GHILAN, a province of Persia, on the S. W. side of the Caspian Sea; supposed to be the Hyrcania of the ancients. On the W. side are high mountains, which are covered with many sorts of trees, and in the highest parts of them are deer, bears, wolves, leopards, and tigers. It produces abundance of silk, oil, wine, rice, tobacco, and excellent fruit. This province was ceded to Russia, by a treaty concluded at Petersburg in 1724, but not possessed by Russia till 1780. Reshd is the capital.

GHIZNI, or GHUZNEE, a town of the country of Cabul, once the capital of a powerful empire of the same name. It is called the second Medina, from the great number of illustrious persons who have been interred here. It is 54 miles S. of Cabul. Long. 68. 20. E. lat. 38. 40. N.

GHOURBOND, a town of the country of Cabul; 42 miles N. W. of Cabul.

GIANT'S CAUSEWAY, a remarkable basaltic headland in the county of Antrim, Ireland; probably a continuation of a similar formation on the opposite shore of Scotland.

GIBELLO, a town of Italy, in the duchy of Parma, on the river Po; 16 miles N. W. of Parma.

GIBRALTAR, a town of Spain, in Andalusia, near a mountain of the same name, formerly called Calpe, which, with Abyla (now Ceuta), on the opposite shore of Africa, were called the Pillars of Hercules. Tarick, a general of the Moors, built a fortress here, which he called Gebel-Tarick, that is, Mount Tarick. Since that time a town has been built at the foot of this rock, which is strongly fortified. It can be approached only by a narrow passage between the mountain and the sea, across which the Spaniards have drawn a line and fortified it, to prevent the garrison from having any communication with the country. The rock abounds in partridges: and on the E. side, amid the broken precipices, is a stratum of bones, belonging to various animals, encased in a reddish calcareous stone. Gibraltar was taken from the Moors in 1462, and in 1704 it fell into the hands of the English. The Spaniards attempted to retake it the following year; and they besieged it again, in 1727, with as little success. It sustained a siege from July, 1779, to February, 1783, when the siege was finally raised, on advice being received that the preliminaries of peace were signed; but it may be considered as terminated on September 13, 1782, on the failure of a grand attack made by the Spaniards, whose floating batteries were destroyed by red-hot shot from the garrison. The number and strength of the military works, and the vast galleries opened in the calcareous rock, excite admiration; and the fortress, in the opinion of most engineers, is absolutely impregnable. The garrison here is cooped up in a very narrow compass, and in a war with Spain has no provisions but what are brought from Barbary and England. The Strait of Gibraltar is 24 miles long, and 15 broad, and a strong current always sets into the Mediterranean through the strait to the Atlantic Ocean. The rock at the foot of which the town is situate, forms a promontory, and the E. boundary of a spacious bay, which affords tolerably good anchorage for the largest ships of war. The English garrison generally consists of from 2000 to 3000 men, and the population of the town amounts to about 12,000, who carry on an extensive commerce. The value of the merchandise exported from England to Gibraltar during the 10 years 1816—1825, averaged about 1,700,000*l*. per annum, about two-fifths of which amount is reimbursed by bills drawn against fruit, wine, and wool from Spain, and the remainder by bills drawn on the British treasury or government agents.

GIBRALTAR, a town of Colombia, in the province of Zulia; defended by some fortifications. The air is so unhealthy in the rainy season, that the town is now reduced to an insignificant hamlet.

GIBSON, a county of the state of Indiana; bounded on the N. by White River, and W. by the Wabash, which divides it from the state of Illinois. The S. W. point of the county is 30 miles above the entrance of the Wabash into the Ohio. Pop. 8,977.

GIEN, a town of France, in the department of Loire. It is seated on the N. bank of the Loire; 40 miles E. by S. of Orleans. It is the seat of a prefect.

GIENGEN, a town of Suabia, on the river Brentz; 18 miles N. N. E. of Ulm; now included in the kingdom of Wirtemberg.

GIERACE, a town of Naples, in Calabria Ultra; seated on a mountain, near the sea; 34 miles E. N. E. of Reggio.

GIESSEN, a fortified town of Germany, in Upper Hesse, with a citadel and a university. It is seated on the Lahn; 16 miles W. S. W. of Marburg. Long. 8. 43. E. lat. 50. 35. N.

GIGA, or GIGHA, a small island, one of the Hebrides, lying on the W. coast of Scotland.

GIGLIO, a small island, on the coast of Tuscany, with a castle; 15 miles W. S. W. of Orbitello.

GIGNAC, a town of France, in the department of Herault, on the river Herault; 14 miles W. of Montpelier.

GIHON. *See* AMU.

GIJON, or GYON, a seaport of Spain, in Asturias, with an ancient castle; seated on the Bay of Biscay; 18 miles N. E. of Oviedo. Long. 5. 36. W. lat. 43. 34. N.

GILES, an interior county in the W. part of Virginia; bounded on the E. by the great Kenhawa river. It contains about 2000 square miles of surface, inhabited by 5307 persons.

GILES, another county in the state of Tennessee, bordering on Alabama; intersected by the Elk river, which flows S. into the Tennessee; it comprises about 600 square miles of surface, inhabited by 21,494 persons. Pulaski, 60 miles S. W. of Murfreesboro' is the chief town.

GILFORD, a town of Ireland, in the county of Down; 82 miles from Dublin; with manufactures of linen. Here is a chalybeate spa.

GILLES, ST., a town of France, in the department of Gard; 10 miles S. of Nismes. Pop. 5600.

GILLINGHAM, a town in Kent, on the E. bank of the Medway, near its entrance into the Thames; it is strongly fortified, forming the outport of the arsenal of Chatham. It is a place of considerable antiquity.

GILOLO, an island, the largest of the Moluccas. It is 130 miles from N. to S., but is intersected by several large bays; the breadth of any limb seldom exceeds 40 miles. The shores are in general low, and the interior rises in high peaks. It does not produce any fine spices, but has a great deal of rice, and abounds with oxen, buffaloes, goats, deer, and wild hogs. The sultans of Ternate and Tidore shared this island between them, but it is entirely under Dutch influence. The natives are industrious, particularly in weaving. One of the chief towns is Tatany, on a small promontory of the eastern limb, and only accesssible by ladders.

GILZEN, a town of Holland, in the province of North Brabant; 7 miles S. E. from Breda. Pop. 2000.

GIMONT, a town of France, in the department of Gers; 16 miles E. of Auch.

GINJEE, a town of Hindostan, in the Carnatic, strong both by nature and art, being seated on a mountain, whose top is divided into three points, on each of which is a castle. It is 38 miles N. W. of Pondicherry. Long. 79. 35. E. lat. 12. 15. N.

GIORGIEV, or GIURDESOV, a town of European Turkey, in Wallachia, near which the Russians gained a victory over the Turks, in 1771. It is seated on the Danube; 40 miles S. W. of Bucharest.

GIOVANNI, ROTONDO, ST., a town of Italy, in the kingdom of Naples, on Mount Gargano; 12 miles N. W. from Manfredonia. Pop. 1800.

GIOVENAZZO, a town of Naples, in Terra di Bari, with a castle. It has high houses and towers, built of polished stone, with flat roofs, which give it a very singular appearance. It is seated near the sea. It is 10 miles N. W. of Bari.

GIRARDEAU, CAPE, a county of the state of Missouri, lying between the St. Francis and Mississippi rivers; it contains about 1200 square miles of surface. The chief town, of the same name, is seated on the W. bank of the Mississippi, about 30 miles above the entrance of the Ohio.

GIREST, a town of Persia, in Kerman, with a trade in wheat and dates; 100 miles E. by N. of Gombroon.

GIRGE, a town of Egypt, about three miles in circumference, and contains several mosques, bazaars, and squares, but no marble buildings, or remains of ancient structures. It stands near the left bank of the Nile; 40 miles N. of Esne, and 200 S. of Cairo. Long. 31 12. E. lat. 28. 35. N.

GIRGENTI, an episcopal town, on the S. W. coast of Sicily, in Val di Mazara, with a castle. It is part of the ancient Agrigentum, and in the vicinity are numerous remains of temples, &c.; great quantities of sulphur are exported from this place. It stands on a hill, near the river St. Blaise; 62 miles S. of Palermo. Long. 13. 33. E. lat. 37. 14. N.

GIRONDE, a river of France, formed by the union of the Garonne and Dordogne; 12 miles N. of Bordeaux.

GIRONDE, a maritime department of France, which includes part of the late province of Guienne. It lies on both sides of the Garonne, and it is the largest of the 86 departments, containing about 1,022,000 hectares; it yields abundance of wine, and is fertile in every kind of grain and cattle, whilst the rivers and coast supply abundance of fish. Its principal manufactures are in founderies, glass, earthenware, dye-stuffs, liqueurs, (aniseed,) and salt; it contains some seams of pit coal, and beds of peat. It is divided into six arrondissements, of which Bordeaux (the capital), Bazas, Blaye, Lesparre, Libourne, and Reole are the chief towns. Pop. 522,040.

GIRONS, ST., a town of France, in the department of Arriege; 4 miles S. by E. of St. Lizier.

GIRVAN, a town of Scotland, in Ayrshire, at the mouth of the river Girvan, which forms a tolerable harbour. It is 16 miles S. S. W. of the borough of Ayr.

GISBOROUGH, or GUISBOROUGH, a town in North Yorkshire, with a market on Monday. It is celebrated for being the first place where alum was made, as it was formerly for its fine abbey. It is 22 miles N. W. of Whitby.

GISORS, a town of France, in the department of Eure; seated on the Ept; 28 miles S. E. of Rouen.

GITSCHIN, a town of Bohemia, which suffered greatly during the long war of the Swedes in Germany. It is 22 miles S. W. of Koningsgratz.

GIULA, or GULIEST, a strong town of Upper Hungary, on the frontiers of Transylvania and the river Keresblau; 30 miles E. of Great Waradin. Long. 20. 40. E. lat. 46. 40. N.

GIULA NUOVA, a town of Naples, in Abruzzo Ulteriore; near the Gulf of Venice; 13 miles N. of Atri.

GIULIANI, a town of Sicily, in Val di Mazara, on a craggy rock; 12 miles N. N. E. of Xacca, or Siacca.

GIUSTENDIL. *See* KOSTENDIL.

GIVET, a fortified and frontier town of France in the department of Ardennes; divided by the Meuse into two parts, Givet Saint Hilaire, and Givet Notre Dame; the former situate at the foot of a mountain close by Charlemont, and the other on the opposite side of the river. It is 15 miles N. E. of Rocroy. Pop. 3533.

GIZEH, a fortified town of Egypt, with a palace, several mosques, a cannon foundery, and a manufacture of coarse earthen pots and tiles. A few miles to the S. W. are the largest pyramids in the country. Gizeh was taken from the French, by the British, in 1801. It stands on the left bank of the Nile, nearly opposite Cairo.

GLADBACH, a town of Germany, in the duchy of Juliers, with a Benedictine abbey. It has manufactures of fine strong linen, and is seated on the Ners; 13 miles N. of Juliers. Pop. about 6000.

GLADENBACH, a town of Germany, in Upper Hesse; 12 miles N. of Giessen.

GLAMMIS, a town of Scotland, in Angusshire, with manufactures of yarn and linen cloth. Near it, on the banks of the Dean, is Glammis Castle, a large edifice, in which Malcolm II. was murdered.

GLAMORGANSHIRE, the extreme S. E. county of Wales; bounded on the S. for about 50 miles by the Bristol Channel, on the E. by the county of Monmouth, N. by Brecknock, and W. by Carmarthenshire. It contains 792 square miles of surface, or about 506,880 acres; is divided into ten hundreds, and 124 parishes; has one city, and five market towns; and sends two members to parliament. On the N. side it is mountainous; but, being more level on the S. side, it there bears large crops of corn and very sweet grass. Cattle abound in all parts, there being fruitful valleys among the mountains, that yield very good pasture. The quantity of butter with which it supplies the Bristol market is very considerable. In the N. part of the county are the most extensive iron works in the world, (*see* MERTHYR TYDVIL;) copper and lead also abound, (*see* SWANSEA.) The county is intersected from N. to S. by several streams of water, and by three canals, and numerous railroads, by which the heavy products of the mines and forges are conveyed to the coast. Cardiff is the assize town, but Merthyr Tydvil is the most populous, and Swansea the most important town in the county; the other towns of note are Neath, Lantrissant, Cowbridge, and Llandaff.

GLANDFORDBRIDGE, or BRIGG, a town in Lincolnshire, with a market on Thursday, and a good trade in corn, coal, and timber. It is seated on the Ancholm, which is navigable for sloops to the Humber; 23 miles N. of Lincoln.

GLANWORTH, a town in Ireland, county of Cork. Five fairs are held here annually.

GLARIS, or GLARUS, a canton in Switzerland; bounded on the N. by the rivers Linth, Grisons, and lake of Wallenstadt; E. by the canton of Sargans, the canton of Uri, and W. by that of Schweitz. It is a mountainous country; and the chief trade is in cattle, cheese, and butter. The inhabitants, amounting to 22,800, are partly protestants and partly catholics; and both sects live together in the greatest harmony. Glarus is surrounded by the Alps, except toward the N.; and there is no other entrance but through this opening, which lies between the lake of Wallenstadt, and the mountains separating this canton from that of Schweitz.

GLARIS, a town of Switzerland, capital of the preceding canton, is surrounded by mountains, and seated on the river Linth. It has manufactures of cloth, and a trade in cattle, horses, cheese, slates, and wooden ware; 32 miles S. E. of Zurich.

GLASGOW, a large and populous city of Scotland, in Lanarkshire. From its extent, beauty, regularity, and modern improvements, it is undoubtedly the second, if not the first city in North Britain. The four principal streets, which intersect each other at right angles, divide the city nearly into four equal parts. The high church, the most magnificent Gothic structure in Scotland, St. Andrew's church, St. Enoch's church, the Tron church, the college, the tontine, and trades'-hall, are some of the principal buildings in Glasgow. The town-house is an elegant building, with a piazza in front; and opposite to it is the exchange, a square building, with an equestrian statue of William III. in the centre. The toll-booth, the guild-hall, and the theatre, are also worthy of notice. There are several charitable establishments; particularly the Merchants' Hospital, and that of the town, and a large infirmary. Here is also a monument, 145 feet high, in the Green of Glasgow, to the memory of the gallant Nelson. The university, instituted in 1450, is constantly increasing in reputation. It consists of a chancellor, rector, dean of faculty, a principal, and 16 professors, of which one is for law, four for theology, five for the study of medicine and subjects connected therewith, and the others for the faculty of arts. It has been greatly enriched in the mathematical department, by the library of the late celebrated Dr. Robert Simson, author of the translation of Euclid, and has received an important addition, by a collection of rare books and manuscripts, in every department of science, but particularly in medicine, bequeathed by the late Dr. William Hunter, who has also left his extensive museum to the university of Glasgow. Besides the anatomical preparations, the museum, for which an elegant building has been erected, contains a collection of shells, corals, insects, and fossils, made by the late Dr. Fothergill, and a cabinet of medals and coins, ancient and modern, the most complete of the kind in Europe. The observatory is well fitted up and supplied with the most improved instruments for the use of the professor of practical astronomy; but, being mainly dependent on private aid for support, since the novelty of its erection has ceased, it is not maintained without difficulty. Glasgow, next to London and Liverpool, is the most commercial place in the British dominions, and in manufacturing extent and importance, it is only exceeded by Manchester and Leeds; the cotton manufacture employs a large number of looms, with all the attending operations of staining, dyeing, glazing, &c. &c.; which support numerous iron foundries, machine makers, &c. &c.; in addition to which, it has several glasshouses, sugar refineries, &c. Glasgow was originally one parish, but is now, for the benefit of the poor and ease of ministers, divided into 12, with as many churches, and several chapels of ease, and numerous meeting houses for Dissenters. The city of Glasgow is seated on the N. bank of the Clyde, the suburbs extending to the opposite side, connected by three elegant bridges of stone. The river is navigable for vessels of eight feet water, as far as the bridge; but larger vessels stop at Port Glasgow, or Greenock, at the mouth of the river, to unload. There is a railway to Paisley, Kilmarnock, and Ayr. It has also the advantage of two canals, beside the great canal that joins the Clyde to the Forth. Glasgow is 44 miles W. of Edinburgh, and 60 S. W. of Perth: the mean distance from London is only 348 miles, the route of the mail, 404.

GLASGOW PORT. *See* PORT GLASGOW.

GLASTONBURY, a town of Somersetshire, with a market on Tuesday; it is seated near a high hill, called the Tor, and famous for an abbey, that occupied an area of 60 acres, of which some considerable ruins still remain; particularly the kitchen, which is the most entire, and of a very unusual contrivance. The George Inn was formerly an hospital for the accommodation of pilgrims who came to the abbey, and to the thorn, which, it is pretended, was planted by Joseph of Arimathea, and blossomed on Christmas eve. It was also pretended, that the bodies of Joseph of Arimathea, of King Arthur, and of Edward the Confessor, were buried here. The last abbot of this place was hanged on the top of the Tor, by order of Henry VIII., for not acknowledging his supremacy; and on this hill is a tower, which serves as a landmark to seamen. Glastonbury has two churches, and a manufacture of worsted stockings. It is seated on the river Brue; 6 miles S. W. of Wells, on the road to Exeter, and 124 W. by S. of London.

GLATZ, a sovereign county of Germany, lying between Silesia, Bohemia, and Moravia; surrounded by mountains. It is 40 miles long and 25 broad; has mines of coal, copper, and iron, good quarries of marble and stone, and fine springs of mineral waters. In 1742 it was ceded to the King of Prussia, by the Queen of Hungary, and is now deemed a part of Silesia.

GLATZ, a strong town of Silesia, capital of the county of Glatz; seated on the side of a hill, by the river Neiss. On the top of the hill is an ancient castle, and a new citadel. In 1742 the Prussians took the town by capitulation; and in 1760 the Austrians took it by storm, but restored it in 1763. It is sixty miles S. S. W. of Breslau, and 90 E. N. E. of Prague. Long. 16. 32. E. lat. 50. 18. N.

GLAUCHAU, a town of Upper Saxony, in Misnia, with considerable manufactures of cotton and other stuffs; seated on the Mulda; 36 miles S. by E. of Leipsig.

GLEIWITZ, a town of Silesia, noted for the culture of hops and the weaving of cloth; 34 miles S. E. of Oppelen.

GLENARM, a town of Ireland, county of Antrim; 133 miles from Dublin. Here are the ruins of a Franciscan friary.

GLENDALOUGH, a parish of Ireland, county of Wicklow. This magnificent glen is celebrated for the ruins of its seven churches, and a noble pillar tower; for the beautiful scenery of lake, mountain and wood, overhung by lofty summits, and the interesting legendary history.

GLENELG, a parish in Scotland, shire of Inverness, giving the title of baron to the family of Grant.

GLENLUCE, a town of Scotland, in Wigtonshire, with a harbour for small vessels.

GLOGAU, or GNOSS GLOGAU, a town of Silesia, capital of a principality of the same name, which is very fertile, and produces wine. The town is well fortified, and formerly stood close by the Oder, which has since changed its course, and now flows above a mile from it. Besides the Papists, there are a great number of Protestants and Jews. It was taken by the king of Prussia, in 1741. It is 60 miles N. W. of Breslau. Long. 16. 14. E. lat. 51. 38. N.

GLOGAU, LITTLE, a town of Silesia, with a collegiate church and Minorite convent; 23 miles S. of Oppeln.

GLOMMEN, the largest river of Norway, in the bishopric of Aggerhuys, which flows into the North Sea at Frederickstadt. At least 50,000 trees are annually floated by this river to Frederickstadt.

GLOSSOP, a parish of Derbyshire, which contains 18 townships and hamlets. It is 8 miles N. of Chapel-in-le-frith.

GLOUCESTERSHIRE, a county of England; 60 miles long and 29 broad; bounded on the W. by Herefordshire and Monmouthshire, N. by Worcestershire, E. by Warwickshire and Oxfordshire, and S. by Wiltshire and Somersetshire. It contains 805,120 acres; is divided into 23 hundreds, has two cities, and 23 market-towns. The air is sharp in the E. or hilly part, called the *Coteswold;* but very mild in the rich vale that occupies the centre, through which the river Severn flows. The W. part, which is the smallest district, is varied by hill and dale, and is chiefly occupied by the forest of *Dean.* The staple commodities of the county are its woollens and cheese. Its principal rivers are the Severn, Warwickshire Avon, Lower Avon, Wye, Thames, Coln, and Lech; the Severn and Thames are united by a canal. The principal manufacturing towns are Stroudwater, Tewkesbury, and Wootton-under-edge, and the other places of note, besides the capital and city of Bristol, are Cheltenham, Cirencester, and Dursley. The county sends four members to parliament for the E. and W. divisions.

GLOUCESTER, a city and capital of the preceding county, with a market on Wednesday and Saturday. It sends two members to parliament. It is a county of itself, governed by a mayor, and seated on the E. side of the Severn, where, by two streams, it makes the isle of Alney. It was fortified with a wall, which Charles II. after the Restoration ordered to be demolished. The four principal streets have their junction in the centre of the town. It once contained 11 churches, but now has only two beside the cathedral, in which is a large cloister, a whispering gallery, and the tombs of Robert, duke of Normandy, and Edward II. It has five hospitals, two free-schools, and a large county jail. It has four extensive establishments for the manufacture of pins, and is a great mart for wool, and there are 12 incorporated trading companies. Ships come up the Severn to the bridge; but the navigation being circuitous and difficult, a canal is made hence to Berkeley, with sufficient depth of water for ships of 400 tons burthen, at the head of which is a basin, fit for the reception of 100 vessels. Berkeley is distant from Gloucester 15 miles. The city and neighbourhood contain many remains of abbeys; and those of Lantony Abbey, in the S. suburb, are converted into outhouses belonging to adjacent farms. Gloucester is 24 miles N. E. of Bristol, and 104 W. by N. of London.

GLOUCESTER, a county of the state of New Jersey, extending from the Atlantic Ocean to Delaware River, a distance of 60 miles, and is about 20 in mean breadth, giving a superficies of 1200 square miles. It is divided into 12 townships. Pop. 25,438.

GLOUCESTER, a maritime county of Virginia; bounded on the S. W. by York River and Chesapeake Bay. It contains about 300 square miles. Population, 10,715. The chief town, of the same name, stands on a point of land on the N. side of the mouth of York River; 17 miles N. E. of York town, and 70 E. by S. of Richmond.

GLOUCESTER, a seaport of Massachusets, in Essex county, and on the peninsula of Cape Ann, which forms the N. side of Massachusets Bay. The harbour is accessible for large ships, and defended by a battery and citadel. It is one of the most considerable fishing towns in the United States: it is 16 miles N. E. of Salem. Long. 70. 40. W. lat. 42. 36. N. Pop. 6350.

GLUCKSTADT, a seaport of Lower Saxony, capital of the duchy of Holstein, with a strong castle. It has a considerable foreign trade, the principal branch of which is the whale fishery. It is seated on the Elbe, near its mouth; 28 miles N. W. of Hamburgh. Long. 9. 20. E lat. 53. 51. N.

GLYNN, or GLINN, a town of Ireland, county of Limerick; seated on the river Shannon.

GLYNN, a maritime county of the state of Georgia, comprising about 350 square miles of territory. Brunswick, the chief town, is 70 miles S. by W. of Savannah.

GNESEN, or GNESNA, in Prussian Poland, contains an archbishop's see, whose prelate was primate of Poland. It was the first town built in the kingdom, and formerly more considerable than at present. It is 98 miles N. by E. of Breslau, and 145 W. by N. of Warsaw. Long. 17. 40. E. lat. 52. 28. N.

GOA, a city of Hindostan, in the Concan, and the capital of the Portuguese settlements in India. It stands on the N. side of an island, 22 miles long and 6 broad, formed by the river Mandova, which is capable of receiving the largest ships. The viceroy's palace was a noble building; but this, as well as the city at large, is very much on the decline. The inhabitants are contented with greens, fruits, and roots, which, with a little bread, rice, and fish, is their principal diet, though they have hogs and fowls in plenty. Their religion is the Roman Catholic, and the clergy are numerous and illiterate. In this place was one of the last refuges of the inquisition; a description of which is given in Dr. Buchanan's Christian Researches. Goa has few manufactures or productions, the best trade being in arrack, which is distilled from the sap of the cocoa-nut tree. The harbour is defended by several forts and batteries. It is 250 miles S. by E. of Bombay. Long. 73. 45. E. lat. 15. 31. N.

GOALPARA, a town of Hindostan, at the N. E. extremity of Bengal, where the Europeans have factors, who carry on a great trade with Assam, Bootan, Thibet, &c. It stands on the E. bank of the Brahmapootra; 38 miles E. of Rangamatty.

GOAR, St., a small town of Germany, formerly the capital of the lower county of Catzenellenbogen. It is seated on the Rhine, under the stupendous rock and castle of Rheinfels, which it surrendered to the French, in 1794. It is 25 miles S. of Coblentz.

GOAVE, GRAND, a town of St. Domingo, near the sea-coast. It is 10 miles S. S. W. of Leogane.

GOAVE PETIT, a seaport of St. Domingo, in the Gulf of Gonaves, and the mart to which the traders in Grand Goave, and other places, send their commodities. It is 31 miles W. S. W. of Port au Prince.

GOBBI, a country of South Africa, on the coast of the Atlantic, between the country of Cawma and Cape Lopez Gonsalvo, under the equator. The chief town is situated about a day's journey from the sea. The principal trade of the inhabitants consists in elephants and ivory.

GOBIN, ST. *See* FERE.

GOCH, a town of Germany, in the duchy of Cleves; seated on the Niers; 6 miles S. of Cleves.

GOCHSHEIM, or GOCHEN, a town of Suabia, lately belonging to Wirtemberg, but ceded to Bavaria, in 1802; 21 miles S. of Heidelberg, and 34 N. W. of Stutgardt.

GOCIANO, a town of Sardinia, capital of a county of the same name, with a castle; seated on the Chirso; 25 miles E. of Algheri.

GODALMING, a town in Surrey, with a market on Saturday, and manufactures of stockings and coarse woollen cloths. It is seated on the Wye, where it divides into several streams; 4 miles S. W. of Guildford, and 34 of London.

GODAVERY, a river of Hindostan, which has its source in the Suckhein mountains; 70 miles to the N. E. of Bombay. In the upper part of its course it is esteemed a sacred river by the Hindoos, who call it Gonga, a term for a river in general. After crossing Dowlatabad and Golconda, from W. to E., it turns to the S. E., and, receiving the Bain about 90 miles above the sea, divides into two principal channels at Rajamundry; and these subdividing again, form altogether several tide harbours, for vessels of moderate burden, at its different mouths, in the Bay of Bengal. Its course is estimated to be above 700 miles; and extensive forests of teak timber border on its banks, within the mountains.

GODING, a town of Moravia, with a fine castle; seated on a branch of the Marsche; 38 miles S. E. of Brunn.

GODMANCHESTER, a corporate town in Huntingdonshire, parted from Huntingdon by the river Ouse. It is seated in a rich fertile soil, which yields great plenty of corn. When James I. came through it from Scotland, the inhabitants met him with 70 ploughs, drawn by as many team of horses; for which novel sight he granted them a charter. Here is a school called the free grammar-school of Queen Elizabeth. It is 59 miles N. by W. of London.

GODSTONE, a parish in Surrey; 20 miles from London. Here is a quarry of freestone.

GOES, or TER GOES, a small town of the Netherlands, in the island South Beveland. It has a considerable trade, particularly in salt and corn. The great church was burnt down in 1648, and another was built, which is a handsome structure. It communicates with the Scheldt by a canal, and is 10 miles E. of Middleburg. Long. 3. 50. E. lat. 51. 33. N.

GOGARD, a town of Sweden, in E. Gothland, near the Lake Wetter; 23 miles N. N. W. of Linkioping.

GOGO, a town of Hindostan, in Guzerat, with a good tide harbour, at the mouth of a river, in the Gulf of Cambay; 100 miles S. by W. of Ahmedabad. Long. 71. 53. E. lat. 21. 45. N.

GOGGRA, or SARFEW, a river which issues from Lake Lankee, in Tibet, and, forcing its way through Mount Himmaleh, pervades the province of Oude, in Hindostan, where it takes a S. E. direction, and unites with the Ganges, above Chuprah, in the province of Bahar.

GOHUD, a town of Hindostan, capital of a circar of the same name, in the province of Agra; 63 miles S. S. E. of Agra. Long. 78. 44. E. lat. 26. 24. N.

GOITO, a town of Italy, in the Mantuan; seated on the river Mincio, between the Lake of Mantua and that of Garda; 15 miles N.W. of Mantua.

GOLCONDA, a province of Hindostan, now called Hyderabad, between the lower parts of the rivers Kistna and Godavery, and the principal part of Dowlatabad. It was formerly called Tellingana, or Tilling, and is subject to the nizam of the Deccan. The king of Golconda, at one time, maintained in his pay above 500,000 soldiers; but in 1667 the reigning prince became tributary to Aurengzebe. The kings had vast revenues, arising from the properties of land, customs of merchandises, and provisions. It has been supposed that this is the country of diamonds; but this is erroneous. It is the depôt for diamonds that are brought from Balaghaut, and other districts, and cut for sale by the Golconda merchants: hence the commonly received opinion, that the mines themselves are in this district. In some districts the inhabitants have, yearly, two crops of rice, and several other kinds of grain. Hyderabad is the capital.

GOLCONDA, a fortress of Hindostan, in the country of the same name; 6 miles W. N. W. of Hyderabad, and joined to that city by a wall of communication. It occupies the summit of a conical hill, and is deemed impregnable.

GOLDAP, a town of East Prussia, in the province of Gumbinnen; 20 miles S. of Gumbinnen, with a manufacture of cloths, and a remarkable aqueduct. Pop. 3000.

GOLD COAST, a maritime country of Guinea, where the Europeans have several forts and settlements. It is about 220 miles in length from W. to E., between the rivers Ancobar and Volta; and includes several districts in which are two or three towns or villages, lying on the sea shore. Seven of the districts are dignified with the title of kingdoms, though they contain but a small extent of land along the coast: the chief is Ashantee. The natives are generally very rich, as they carry on a great trade with the Europeans for gold; and many of them are employed in fishing, and cultivating rice, which grows in incredible quantities. This they exchange with others for maize yams, potatoes, and palm oil. Most of the inhabitants go naked, and those who are best clothed have only some yards of stuff wrapped about their middle.

GOLDBERG, a town of Silesia, in the principality of Lignitz. It has manufactures of woollen and linen, and is seated at the foot of a mountain, on the river Katzbach; 11 miles S.W. of Lignitz, and 50 W. of Breslau. Pop. about 6000.

GOLDINGEN, a town of the duchy of Courland, with a castle, formerly the residence of the dukes. It is seated on the Wela, about 18 miles from the shore of the Baltic, and 60 miles W. of Mittau. Long. 22. 21. E. lat. 56. 48. N.

GOLETTA, or GOULETTE, a fortress of Tunis, on a narrow channel, between the Lake of Tunis and the sea. In 1536 it was taken by Charles V. when he attempted the siege of Tunis, and kept by the Spaniards till 1574, when it was taken from them by Selim II.

GOLLING, a town of Germany, in the duchy of Salzburg; 14 miles S. by E. of Salzburg.

GOLNITZ, or GŒLANITZ, a populous town of Upper Hungary; 25 miles N. N. W. of Raschan.

GOLNOW, a town of Pomerania; seated on the Ihna; 14 miles N. E. of Stettin.

GOLSPIE, a town of Scotland, Sutherlandshire; principally inhabited by fishermen and manufacturers of kelp; 288 miles from Edinburgh.

GOMBROON, or GAMBROON, a seaport of Laristan, in Persia, called by the natives Bunder Abbasi. The best houses are built of brick, flat at the top, with a square turret; but the common people have huts, made with the boughs of palm-trees, and covered with leaves. It is now reduced to a low condition. Long. 56. 10. E. lat. 27. 18. N.

GOMERA, one of the Canary Islands; 20 miles long and 10 broad. It has a town of the same name, with an excellent harbour, where the Spanish ships often take in refreshments. Long. 17. 8. W. lat. 28. 6. N.

GOMMERN, a town of Upper Saxony, with a castle, situate near the Elbe; 7 miles S. E. of Magdeburg.

GOMMERSAL, a town of Yorkshire; 6 miles W. of Huddersfield.

GONAVE, a seaport of the island of St. Domingo, in the Gulf of Gonaves, with an excellent harbour. Here is a medicinal spring, with baths, and accommodations for visitors. It is 30 miles S. E. of St. Nicholas-le-Mole. Long. 72. 26. W. lat. 19. 36. N.

GONAVES, GULF OF, is formed by two promontories, jutting from the W. end of the island of St. Domingo; it is about 100 miles wide at its entrance between Capes St. Nicholas-le-Mole and Donna Maria, and extends eastward about 100 miles, terminating in Port-au-Prince Bay, which is formed by the island of Gonave, about 35 miles from E. to W. and 5 to 7 wide; the N. side into Port-au-Prince Bay is called St. Mark's Channel, and the S. Gonaves Channel.

GONDAR, ... on a hill of considerable height. The palace of the neguz, or king, is at the W. end, flanked with square towers. The houses are chiefly of clay; the roofs thatched in the form of cones. The inhabitants are estimated at 40,000. They have no shops, but carry on their trade in a large square, where they expose their merchandise upon mats. There are numerous churches, and the patriarchate depends upon that of Alexandria. It is 180 miles S. E. of Sennaar. Long. 37. 33. E. lat. 12. 34. N.

GONDEGAMA, or GONDLACOMMA, a river of Hindostan, which rises near Combam, forms the nominal boundary of the Carnatic, on the N., and enters the Bay of Bengal at Mootapilly.

GONDRECOURT, a town of France, in the department of Meuse; seated on the Ornain; 20 miles S. of St. Michael.

GONDREVILLE, a town of France, in the department of Meurthe, with a castle and a magnificent hospital. It is seated on a hill on the river Moselle; 8 miles W. of Nancy.

GONESSE, a town of France in the department of Seine-et-Oise; seated on the Crould; 10 miles N. E. of Paris.

GONIEH, a town of Asiatic Turkey, at the S. E. extremity of the Black Sea, in the lat. of 41. 25. and 41. 15. of E. long.

GONJAH, a kingdom of Africa, between the coast of Guinea on the S. and Tombuctoo on the N. Gonjah, the capital, is 870 miles W. by S. of Cassina. Long. 6. 10. W. lat. 13. 20. N.

GONONG API, an island of the South Pacific, in the Banda group. It has an active volcano with two peaks, 1510 feet high, and is fertile.

GOOCHLAND, a county of Virginia, on the N. bank of the James river, above Richmond.

GOOD HOPE. *See* CAPE OF GOOD HOPE.

GOODWIN SANDS, sand-banks off the coast of Kent, between the N. and S. Foreland. They run parallel with the coast for 10 miles, at about 7 miles distance, and add to the security of the capacious road, the Downs; and on them two life beacons have been erected by Captain Bullock, 1840—1842.

GOOMSUR, a town of Hindostan, North Circars; 60 miles W. of Juggernauth, in an unhealthy district of the same name. Pop. 70,000.

GOOMTY, a river of Hindostan, which rises in the Rohilla country, flows S. E. by Lucknow and Joanpore, and enters the Ganges a little below Benares.

GOORACPOOR, a town and district of Hindostan, in the province of Oude; 65 miles E. of Fyzabad.

GOOTY, a town and fortress of Hindostan; capital of a district of the same name, on the N. side of the Pennar; formerly subject to the regent of Mysore, but ceded to the nizam of the Deccan in 1796. It is 46 miles S. S. W. of Canoul. Long. 77. 48. E. lat. 15. 15. N.

GOPPINGEN, a town of Suabia, in the kingdom of Wirtemberg, with a castle, a woollen manufacture, and a celebrated medicinal spring. It stands on the rivulet Vils; 22 miles S. E. of [illegible] Pop. upwards of 4000.

Goragot, a town of Hindostan, in Bengal; 94 miles N.E. of Moorshedabad. Long. 89. 22. E. lat. 25. 14. N.

Gorbals, a parish of Scotland, Lanarkshire. It abounds in coal, and is a suburb of Glasgow, and is connected with it by a bridge.

Gorcum, a town of South Holland, which has a small trade in corn, cheese, and butter. It is seated on the Linghe, at its junction with the Wahal; 20 miles E. of Rotterdam, and 38 S. of Amsterdam.

Gore Island, an island in the Pacific Ocean, so named by Captain Cook, who discovered it in 1778. It is 30 miles long, and appears to be barren and uninhabited. Cape Upright, the S.E. extremity, is in long. 172. 50. W. lat. 60. 30. N.

Goree, a small island of Africa, near to and S. of Cape Verd, of importance only as an almost impregnable military position. The French surrendered it to the British in 1800; it was taken in January 1804, by the French; and they were compelled to surrender it again in March following; but it was given up to them at the general peace of 1814. Long. 17. 25. W. lat. 14. 40. N.

Goree, or Goeree, a town of Holland; capital of an island of the same name, at the southern mouth of the Maese. It is 12 miles S. S. W. of Briel. Long. 3. 56. E. lat. 51. 44. N.

Gorey. *See* Newborough.

Gorgona, a small island of Italy; 16 miles from the coast of Tuscany, opposite to Leghorn, near which large quantities of anchovies are taken.

Gorgona, an island in the Pacific Ocean; 18 miles from the coast of Colombia. It is high land, very woody, and about 10 miles in circumference. Long. 77. 50. W. lat. 3. 6. N.

Goritz, or Goritia, a town of the Austrian empire; capital of a county of its name, with a castle. Here are considerable manufactures of leather, and the environs produce wine, fruit, corn and silk. In 1797 it was taken by the French. It stands on the Isonzo, on the frontiers of Friuli; 12 miles N. E. of Palma, and 40 W. of Laubach. *See* Gradisca.

Gorkah, the capital of a country of the same name, in Asia, on the borders of Nepaul; 35 miles N. W. of Catmundu, and 200 N. of Benares. Long. 84. 36. E. lat. 28. 25. N.

Gorlitz, a strong town in Upper Lusatia, with a celebrated academy. The inhabitants are above 12,000, and carry on a considerable trade in linen and woollen cloth. It is seated on the Neissa; 50 miles E. by N. of Dresden.

Goroditchi, a town of Russia, in the government of Penza; 30 miles E. S. E. of Penza.

Gort, a town of Ireland, in the S. part of the county of Galway; 124 miles from Dublin. In its neighbourhood are the ruins of Kilmacduagh monastery, and a pillar tower. It has a considerable trade.

Goschutz, a town of Silesia, with a castle; near the frontiers of Poland; 14 miles N. of Oels.

Goshen, a town of New York, chief of Orange county; 56 miles N. of the city of New York.

Goshen, a town of Connecticut, in Lichfield county, famous for excellent cheese; 7 miles N. N. W. of Lichfield.

There are two or three other towns of the same name, in different parts of the United States of North America.

Goslar, a city of Lower Saxony, in the territory of Brunswick. It derives its principal subsistence from the neighbouring iron mines, manufactures of brass and copper, and brewing. Here the art of making gunpowder is said to have been discovered by a monk. It is seated on the river Gose, at the foot of a mountain, called Rammelberg; 28 miles S. of Brunswick. Long. 10. 31. E. lat. 51. 57. N. Population about 6000.

Gosport, a fortified town in Hampshire, on the W. side of the harbour of Portsmouth, over which is a ferry. It has a market on Saturday, and a considerable trade, especially in times of war, from its contiguity to the naval arsenal at Portsmouth. Here are several breweries, an extensive iron-foundry, and a royal hospital, called Haslar Hospital, for the sick and wounded of the royal navy. It is 15 miles S. E. of Southampton, and 73 S. W. of London.

Gossweinstein, or Gossmanstein, a town of Franconia, in the principality of Bamberg, on the Putlach; 20 miles E. S. E. of Bamberg.

Gotha, Saxe, a principality in Central Germany, Saxony, comprising the greatest part of the ancient Thuringia, and is the thirteenth in order of the Germanic Confederation. It produces corn, flax, coal, manganese, iron, cobalt, woollen stuffs, spinning flax, and wool. It maintains a small military force, and has the usual appurtenances of an independent state, as an exchequer, &c. The religion is Lutheran. Area, 582 square miles. Population, 83,000. It formerly consisted of this duchy, and great part of the principality of Altenburg: but on the death of Frederic IV., in 1825, the duchy of Gotha went to the Duke of Saxe Coburg, and the principality of Altenburg to the Duke of Saxe Hildburghausen.

Gotha, a town of Upper Saxony; capital of a principality of the same name. It is the residence of the Duke of Saxe Gotha, whose palace contains a fine library of 150,000 volumes, and a rich cabinet of coins. Near it is the ducal observatory of Seeberge, the most beautiful and useful in Germany. Gotha has a foundry for cannon, a porcelain manufacture, and a considerable trade in woollens, wood, and beer. It is seated on the Leine; 16 miles W. by S. of Erfurt, and 75 from Leipsic. Long. 10. 48. E. lat. 50. 51. N. Population about 12,000.

Gotha, a river of Sweden, which issues from the S. W. extremity of Lake Wener, flows by Trolhatta (where it forms a cataract) and Bahus, and enters the Cattegat at Gottenburg.

Gothard, St., a celebrated mountain of Switzerland, in the canton of Uri. Its highest point is 10,600 feet from the sea: it is 22 miles S. of Altorf. Though not the highest mountain, it is deemed the principal summit of the

Helvetian Alps; for in its vicinity rise the rivers Tesino, Aar, Reuss, and Rhone, which flow hence in every direction.

Gotheburg, or **Gottenburg**, a city of Sweden, capital of West Gothland; seated at the mouth of the Gotha, which forms an excellent harbour; the best situated for foreign trade of any in the kingdom, as it lies on the Cattegat. Here is a considerable herring fishery, and a great trade in salt, iron, and fir planks; and from this port the Swedish East India ships take their departure. The inhabitants are computed at 20,000. Its environs present a uniform scene of barren rocks, on the sides of which part of the suburbs are built. The interior of the city resembles in some respects the towns of Holland, having canals with rows of trees along their margin. In 1802 nearly a fourth part of the city was consumed by a fire. It obtained great importance as a commercial depôt, during the proscription of Bonaparte in 1807—1811. It is 130 miles S. W. of Orebro. Long. 11. 39. E. lat. 57. 42. N.

Gothland, one of the five general divisions of Sweden; bounded on the N. by Sweden Proper, E. and S. by the Baltic, and W. by the Sound and the Cattegat. This country is inhabited by a nation celebrated for their excursions and invasions of other countries, which had its origin from the Getæ, or Tartars of the Crimea. The Goths had kings of their own till 1132, when they were united to Sweden. It was formerly divided into East, West, and South Gothland, but now into nine provinces and the isles of Gothland and Œland.

Gothland, an island of Sweden, in the Baltic; 70 miles from N. to S. and 25 in its greatest breadth. From its form and situation it has obtained the name of the *Eye of the Baltic.* The soil is fertile, and remarkable for an excellent breed of sheep. Here are fine woods of oak and pine, quarries of excellent stone, and very good limestone. Wisby is the capital.

Gottesberg, a town of Silesia, where great quantities of worsted stockings are knit; 16 miles S. W. of Schweidnitz.

Gottingen, a city of Lower Saxony, in the duchy of Brunswick. Here George II., of Great Britain, founded a university, which has acquired a very distinguished reputation: and it contains one of the most capital libraries in Europe. There are also many other literary institutions, and a commandery of the Teutonic order. The woollen manufactures are the principal support of the inhabitants. It is seated on the Leine; 58 miles S. of Hanover. Long. 9. 53. E. lat. 51. 32. N. Population about 9000.

Gottlenbe, a small town of Upper Saxony, in Misnia, on a river of the same name; 18 miles S. S. E. of Dresden.

Gottorp, a castle of Denmark, formerly the ducal residence, from which the ducal line, formed by Adolphus, son of Frederic I., was denominated Holstein-Gottorp, which still subsists in the person of the emperor of Russia.

Gottschee, a town of Lower Carniola, with a castle: 17 miles N. N. E. of Fiume.

Govan, a town of Scotland, in Renfrewshire, near the river Clyde; 5 miles W. of Glasgow, in the manufactures of which it participates.

Gouda, or **Tergouw**, a strong town of South Holland, celebrated for its noble church and painted glass windows, supposed to be the finest in Europe. Great quantities of yarn and tow are made here, also good cheese, and tobacco-pipes. It is seated on the Issel, at the influx of the Gouw; 10 miles N. E. of Rotterdam.

Goudhurst, a parish in Kent; 48 miles from London. It was formerly a market town, but has fallen to decay.

Gour, the ruins of a city in the province of Bengal; it was the seat of government of Hindostan, during the Afghan dynasty, from 1204 to 1564. It is on the E. bank of the Ganges; 160 miles N. of Calcutta.

Gourdon, a town of France, in the department of Lot; 25 miles N. of Cahors. It is the seat of a prefect.

Gournay, a town of France, in the department of Lower Seine; seated on the Epte; 24 miles E. of Rouen.

Gowran, a town of Ireland, in the county of Kilkenny; 66 miles from Dublin.

Gozi, or **Gozzo**, an island in the Mediterranean, the ancient Clauda, under which St. Paul sailed on his voyage to Rome. It is 24 miles from the S. W. coast of Candia, and vessels often put in here for water and provisions. Long. 23. 46. E. lat. 34. 50. N.

Gozo, a fortified island of the Mediterranean; 5 miles N. W. of Malta, and dependent on that island. It is 8 miles long and 4 broad, and more equally fertile than Malta.

Grabow, a town of Lower Saxony, in the duchy of Mecklenberg, with a castle; seated on the Elde; 24 miles S. by E. of Schwerin.

Graciosa, one of the Azores; 10 miles long and 8 broad. Its produce is wheat, wine, butter, and cheese. The principal place is Plata. Long 27. 58. W. lat. 39. 2. N.

Gradisca, a fortified town of Sclavonia, on the frontiers of Croatia; seated on the Save; 20 miles S. W. of Posega. Long. 18. 39. E. lat. 45. 21. N.

Gradisca, a strong town of Friuli, on the confines of Carinthia; capital of a county united with Goritz, and a bishop's see. It is seated on the Lisonzo; 6 miles S. W. of Goritz. Long. 13. 32. E. lat. 46. 2. N.

Grado, a town of Italy, in a small island of the same name, on the coast of Friuli; 50 miles E. by N. of Venice. Long. 13. 10. E. lat. 45. 46. N.

Graff Reynet, a district in the territory of the Cape of Good Hope; bounded on the E. by Somerset, N. by that of the Hottentots, S. by Uitenhage, and W. by Beaufort. Population 16,000, principally occupied in rearing cattle.

Grafton, a county of the state of New Hampshire; bounded on the W. 55 miles by the Connecticut river, which divides it from the State of Vermont; it is about 28 miles in mean breadth, and contains a population of 42,311. Haverhill, on the E. bank of the Connecticut, is the chief town.

GRAHAM'S ISLAND, a volcano that appeared in July, 1831, off the S. coast of Sicily, from the sea, and, after raging for some time, left an island of cinders and scoriæ, 120 feet in height at the W. end, which, gradually subsiding, disappeared beneath the waves, forming a shoal of 9 feet: this remained for 4 or 5 years, when that also dispersed.

GRAIN COAST, a maritime country of Guinea, extending along the Atlantic about 300 miles, between the Sierra Leone country on the W. and the Ivory coast on the E. The productions are peas, beans, gourds, lemons, oranges, dates, and palm wine; but the chief article is the abundance of Guinea pepper, or grains of paradise, which draws a great interior and export trade. Cows, hogs, sheep, and goats, are numerous. The Portuguese had formerly the whole commerce of this coast, but it has long been chiefly in the hands of the English and Dutch.

GRAITZ, or GREITZ, a town of Upper Saxony, with a castle on a rocky mountain, and another in the town. It has manufactures of snuff, and is situate on the Elster, between mountains and woods; 10 miles N. of Plauen, and 50 S. of Leipsic. Population, about 6000.

GRAMAT, a town of France, 28 miles N. N. E. of Cahors. Pop. 3295.

GRAMMONT, a town of Belgium; seated on both sides of the Dender; 12 miles N. E. of Tournay.

GRAMPIAN HILLS, a chain of hills in Scotland, which extends, in a N. E. direction, from the mountain Benlomond, in Dumbartonshire, through the counties of Perth, Angus, and Kincardine, to Aberdeen, and thence, in a N. W. direction, through the counties of Aberdeen, Banff, and Murray, to the borders of Inverness. They take their name from a single hill, the Mons Grampius of Agricola, where Galgacus waited the approach of Agricola, and where the battle was fought so fatal to the brave Caledonians.

GRAMPOUND, a town in Cornwall, governed by a mayor, with a market on Saturday, and a manufacture of gloves; seated on the Fal; 40 miles S. W. of Launceston, and 244 W. by S. of London; it formerly returned two members to parliament, but was disfranchised at the general election in 1820.

GRAN, a town of Lower Hungary, and an archbishop's see; seated near the conflux of the Gran with the Danube; 70 miles E. S. E. of Presburg. Long. 18. 46. E. lat. 47. 46. N.

GRAN, or GREEN, a seaport of Arabia, in the province of Bahrin, at the N. W. end of the Gulf of Persia, and on the borders of Irac Arabi; 40 miles S. of Bassora. Long. 47. 45. E. lat. 29. 56. N.

GRANADA. *See* GRENADA.

GRANADA, a maritime province, formerly a kingdom of Spain, part of Andalusia, having about 270 miles of sea-coast, on the Mediterranean; the mean length of the province from W. to E. being about 234 miles, the extreme breadth at the E. end is about 95 miles, but the W. part not more than 30, its superficies not exceeding 805 square leagues. Population 700,000. It is bounded on the E. by the kingdom of Seville, N. by those of Cordova and Jaen, and W. by Murcia. Though a mountainous country, the soil is good; but it has not been well cultivated since the Moors were expelled in 1492. However, it produces corn, wine, oil, sugar, flax, hemp, excellent fruits, honey, wax, and mulberry-trees, which feed a great number of silk-worms. The forests produce gall-nuts, palm-trees, and oaks. It is intersected by several streams falling into the Mediterranean, but the principal rivers run from E. to W. into the Guadalquiver through Cordova and Seville. Granada was the last province in Spain occupied by the Moors. The principal towns on the coast of the Mediterranean, beginning at the W., are Marbella, Malaga, Almunacar, Motril, Adra, Almeria, and Vera, and in the interior, Granada (the capital), Ronda, Velez, Malaga, Santa Fe, Guadix, Baza, Huescar, and Purchena.

GRANADA, a city of Spain, capital of the preceding province, and an archbishop's see, is built on four hills, and divided into four parts, in one of which is the large church containing the tombs of Ferdinand and Isabella, who took this place from the Moors in 1492. In another is the palace of the kings of Spain, and the Alhambra, an ancient palace of the Moorish kings, with so many rooms that it is like a labyrinth. In the third is the university; the fourth has nothing considerable; but all the public buildings are magnificent, and the cathedral and convents contain excellent pictures by Spanish masters. The walls and gates, and the aqueducts, are mostly destroyed; and its trade is feebly carried on, without encouragement or protection. The inhabitants are not more than 66,000, and half of them are lawyers, ecclesiastics, and mendicants. It is seated on the Xenil, near the influx of the Oro; 220 miles due S. of Madrid, and 63 N. E. of Malaga.

GRANADA, NEW, an extensive territory of South America, which comprised all the western part of the new republic of Colombia, from the great river Maranon, or Amazons, to the Caribbean Sea. This part of the western hemisphere was first explored by Ojeda and Americus Vespucci, in 1508, and became completely subdued to Spanish rule under a captain-general, in 1547. It 1718 it was formed into a viceroyalty; restored to a captain-generalship in 1724; but in 1740 the viceroyalty was re-established, and continued until 1816. In December, 1819, a union was effected with Venezuela, into one republic, under the name of COLOMBIA (which see).

GRANARD, a neat town of Ireland, in the county of Longford; 16 miles E. N. E. of Longford.

GRANBY, a small town of South Carolina; seated on the Congaree, on the contrary side to Colombia, about a mile below that city. It is noted for a curious bridge, whose centre arch is 100 feet wide, to give passage to large trees which are brought down by the floods.

GRANDMONT, a town of France, in the department of Upper Vienne. Near it was a celebrated abbey, suppressed in 1769, after the death of the then professed members. It is 15 miles N. N. E. of Limoges.

Grand Manan, an island at the entrance of the Bay of Fundy, the S. end of which is in lat. 44. 43. N. and 67. of W. long.: it is included in the province of Nova Scotia.

Grandpre, a town of France, in the department of Ardennes; seated on the Ayre; 32 miles E. of Rheims.

Grangemouth, a village of Scotland, in Stirlingshire, at the junction of the Great Canal with the river Carron; 4 miles N. E. of Falkirk, in which parish it is included. Upwards of 40,000 tons of shipping are annually entered here, belonging either to the foreign or coasting trade.

Gransee, a town of Brandenburg, in the Middle Mark; 30 miles N. of Berlin.

Granson, a town of Switzerland, in the Pays de Vaud. It stands near the S. end of the lake of Neufchatel; 16 miles W. S. W. of Neufchatel.

Grant, a newly formed county of Kentucky, E. of the Kentucky river. Pop. 1805.

Grantham, a borough in Lincolnshire, with a market on Saturday. The church is an elegant structure, with a very lofty spire. A canal passes hence to the Trent, at Nottingham. Grantham is seated on the Witham; 20 miles S. by W. of Lincoln, and 110 N. by W. of London. It returns two members to parliament.

Granville, a town of France, in the department of Manche; seated on the English Channel, in the bay of St. Malo, partly on a rock, and partly on a plain; 15 miles S. by W. of Coutances, and 25 N. E. of St. Malo. Pop. 7030. It carries on a considerable traffic with the Island of Jersey.

Graslitz, a town of Bohemia, in the circle of Saaz; famous for its manufacture of brass; 15 miles N. W. of Elbogen.

Grasmere-water, a small lake of Westmoreland, to the W. of Ambleside. Its margin is hollowed into small bays, with bold eminences, some of rock, some of turf, that half conceal and vary the figure of the lake. A low promontory projects far into the water, and on it stands a white village.

Grason, an island in the Gulf of Bothnia, near the coast of Sweden; 15 miles long and 2 broad. Long. 18. 20. E. lat. 60. 12. N.

Grasse, a town of France, in the department of Var, and lately a bishop's see. It has a trade in dry fruit, oil, perfumes, and tanned leather, and is seated on an eminence; 11 miles W. N. W. of Antibes, and 20 W. by S. of Nice. It is the seat of a prefect. Pop. 12,553.

Grasse, La, a town of France, in the department of Aude, on the river Othieu. Pop. 1244.

Gratz, a fortified town of Germany, capital of Lower Styria, and a bishop's see. Here are many churches, and a fine arsenal. The castle stands on a rock, and is a strong place. Gratz is seated on the W. side of the Muer, over which is a bridge to an extensive suburb. The inhabitants are estimated at 35,000. In 1797 it was taken by the French. It is 88 miles S. S. W. of Vienna. Long. 15. 26. E. lat. 47. 4. N.

Graudenz, a town of Prussian Poland, on the E. bank of the Vistula; 18 miles N. of Culm, and 55 S. of Dantzic. Population about 8000.

Grave, a strong town of Dutch Brabant, on the left bank of the Maese, beyond which there is a fort. It has been often taken. It is 8 miles S. S. W. of Nimeguen.

Gravelines, a small seaport of France; seated at the mouth of the Aa, defended by Fort Philip; 12 miles E. of Calais. Pop. 2570.

Gravenmachem, a town of Belgium, province of Luxemburg; 13 miles S. W. of Treves. Pop. 2500.

Gravenau, or Grayenau, a town of Bavaria, in the principality of Passau, on the river Sag; 16 miles N. of Passau.

Gravenwert, a town of Bavaria, in the upper palatinate; 17 miles N. of Amberg.

Gravesande, a town of South Holland, where the ancient counts of Holland formerly resided. It is about 4 miles from the sea, and 6 W. by S. of Delft.

Gravesend, a town in Kent, with markets on Wednesday and Saturday. It stands on the S. bank of the Thames, and is the common landing and embarking place for seamen and passengers to and from London; and here all outward bound vessels stop to be examined by the custom-house officers, and to receive their clearances; and inward bound vessels deliver in their manifests, it being the boundary of the port of London. A great part of it was burnt down, with the church, in 1727; the latter was rebuilt as one of the 50 new churches. It is called the corporation of Gravesend and Milton, these two places being united under the government of a mayor. The latter place is a mile E. of the other, and has a blockhouse over against Tilbury Fort. They were incorporated by Queen Elizabeth; but, long before, Richard II. had granted them the exclusive privilege of conveying passengers to London in boats. This privilege, however, since the application of steam, as a propelling power in navigation, has become obsolete; and since 1825, in consequence of the facility of intercourse which steam-boats afford, Gravesend has greatly extended on the W. side, for the accommodation of an increasing number of visitors from the metropolis, the bank of the river being here favourable for bathing. It is 22 miles E. S. E. of London.

Gravina, a town of Naples, in Terra di Bari; 32 miles W. S. W. of Bari. It has nine churches, and a population of about 2000.

Gray, a town of France, in the department of Upper Saone. It has a trade in iron, and is seated on the Saone; 25 miles N. E. of Dijon. It is the seat of a prefect. Population 6584.

GRAYSON, an interior county of Kentucky; bounded on the S. by Green River. Population about 4461. Lichfield, the chief town, is 114 miles S. W. of Frankfort.—Also a frontier county of Virginia, bordering on North Carolina; it is intersected by New River, which runs from S. to N. into the Ohio. Population 9087. Greensville, the chief town, is 180 miles W. S. W. of Richmond.

GREAT BRITAIN, an island of the Atlantic Ocean, off the W. coast of Europe, extending from the lat. of 49. 58. to 58. 40. N., a distance of about 605 British statute miles, varying in breadth from 60 to 260 miles; the superficies not exceeding 88,000 square miles, the mean breadth will not exceed 142 miles. It is divided into three great parts, ENGLAND, SCOTLAND, and WALES, each of which see.

GREBENSTEIN, a town of Germany, in Lower Hesse, on the river Esse; 12 miles N. N. W. of Cassel.

GREECE, a territory of the S. E. extremity of Europe, and, 2000 years ago, the most celebrated portion of that quarter of the globe, it having successfully combated the myriad armies of Persia and the East, and extended its arts and its arms eastward to the banks of the Indus. As the glory of Egypt declined, that of Greece rose to its meridian, to be eclipsed in its turn by the ascendancy of Rome, till, in the 15th century, it became tributary to, and dependent on, the government of the Turks. The main land of Greece extends from the lat. of 36. 25. to 39. 0. N., and is about 110 miles in mean breadth. In the days of Grecian celebrity, it was divided into four great parts, viz. Macedonia, Thessaly, Livadia, and the Peloponnesus, exclusive of the island of Candia and the Archipelago. Under the Turks it was divided into four pachalics, viz. Salonica, Joannina, Egripos or Negropont, and Tripolizza; and for four centuries was subject to their misrule and oppression, till the Greeks rose with one accord against their tyrants, in 1821, and the whole territory became one scene of slaughter and conflicts the most barbarous, till America, aided by the great powers of Europe, interfered; and, after the fortunate mistake of the destruction of the Turkish fleet, at Navarino, the sultan gave up what he was no longer able to maintain, and the choice of a Christian prince was left to the Greeks, who placed the sovereignty, in 1832, on Otho I. son of the king of Bavaria. In the new divisions of the kingdom, the ancient boundaries have been followed. *See* LIVADIA, MACEDONIA, MOREA, THESSALY, and SPORADES.

GREENBRIER, an interior county of Virginia, bounded on the W. by the great Kenhawa river. It is intersected by collateral ridges of the Allegany mountains; it contains about 1200 square miles, and a population of 8695.

GREENE RIVER, a river of Kentucky, which runs from E. to W., and, after a course of about 200 miles, falls into the Ohio, about 30 miles above the entrance of the Wabash. It is navigable 150 miles; and near it are a number of salt springs, and three ponds of bitumen. Quantities of nitre are found in the caves on its banks, and many of the settlers make gunpowder.

GREENE, an interior county of Kentucky, intersected by the above river; it contains about 450 square miles of surface. Population 14,212. Greensbury, the principal town, on the N. bank of Greene River, is 70 miles S. S. W. of Frankfort.

There are eight other counties of the same name, so called probably in commemoration of Major-general Greene, who died in 1786; viz.:—

State.	*sq. mi.*	*Pop.*	*Chief Towns.*
New York	600	30,446	Catskill.
Pennsylvania	220	19,147	Weynesboro'.
N. Carolina	350	6,595	Snow Hill.
Georgia	400	11,690	Greensboro'.
Alabama	900	24,024	Erie
Mississippi	700	1,636	Leakeville.
Tennessee	700	16,076	Greenville.
Ohio	400	17,528	Xenia.

GREENLAND, an extensive region stretching towards the north pole, which, whether continental or insular, is regarded as belonging to North America. This country was discovered in the tenth century, by the Norwegians, who planted a colony on the south-western coast; and the intercourse between this colony and Denmark was continued till the beginning of the 15th century; in that century, by the gradual increase of the arctic ice, the colony became completely imprisoned by the Frozen Ocean; while on the W. a range of mountains and plains, covered with perpetual ice, precluded all access. This settlement contained several churches and monasteries, and is said to have extended about 200 miles, in the S. E. extremity. They have been sought for without success on the E. coast, which has thus been first explored by Captain Graah, who found the few inhabitants of this inclement region of a class somewhat superior to those on the W. coast. It is, therefore, probable that the lost colonies occupied the same site as the present. In more recent times the western coast, washed by the waters of Davis' Straits and Baffin's Bay, was chiefly explored by Davis and other English navigators; but there was no attempt to settle a colony. In 1721 a Norwegian clergyman, named Egede, proceeded to this dreary country, where he continued till 1735, preaching to the natives; and his benevolent example has been since followed by several missionaries. The country is said to be inhabited as far as 76. N. lat., but the Danish and Moravian settlements are chiefly in the S. W. extremity. The short summer is very warm, but foggy; and the northern lights diversify the gloom of winter, which is very severe. The Esquimaux of America perfectly resemble the Greenlanders in their aspect, dress, mode of living, and language. The quadrupeds are deer, bears, foxes, hares, and some dogs resembling wolves. Cape Farewell, the S. W. point, is in long. 42. 42. W. lat. 59. 38. N.

GREENLAW, a town of Scotland, capital of Berwickshire. Though a small place, here are the remains of two religious houses. It is seated on the Blackadder; 8 miles S. W. of Dunse, and 36. S. E. of Edinburgh.

GREENOCK, the chief sea-port of Scotland, in Renfrewshire, at the mouth of the Clyde, with a fort for the defence of the harbour. Here are several dry docks, and the building and rigging of ships is much followed. It has a great trade; and the fisheries, particularly for herrings, and the Newfoundland fishery, are carried on to a great extent. It is 24 miles W. by N. of Glasgow, of which it is the port. Long. 4. 47. W. lat. 55. 56. N.

GREENSTED, a village in Essex, one mile W. of Ongar, remarkable for its little church, (built prior to the Conquest,) the walls of which are formed of the trunks of trees.

GREENSVILLE, a frontier county of Virginia; bounded on the N. by the great Nottoway River, and S. by North Carolina; superficies about 300 square miles. Pop. 6366. Hicksford, the chief town, is 69 miles S. of Richmond.

GREENUP, a frontier county, the extreme N. E. point of Kentucky, with a superficies of about 800 square miles. Greensboro' is the chief town.

GREENEVILLE, a frontier county or district at the N. W. extremity of South Carolina; superficies about 600 square miles. The chief town, of the same name, in the centre of the county, is 95 miles W. N. W. of Columbia. Population, 17,839.

There are several towns of the same name in different parts of the United States.

GREENWICH, formerly a distinct town, but now an appendage to the British metropolis. It is seated in the county of Kent, on the S. bank of the Thames, 5 miles below London Bridge. It is celebrated for its hospital for wounded and decayed seamen of the national marine, which is one of the finest architectural edifices in the world. The buildings consist of four distinct piles, two along the bank of the river, with a noble terrace in front, 860 feet in length; between these two piles is a lawn 270 feet wide; the two other piles are built behind, projecting into the square or lawn, so as to form a quadrangle with an opening in the centre, which is terminated by a elegant building, more recently erected, for a naval school; behind this, on the summit of a hill, is the royal observatory, from whence the English mariners reckon their longitude; a beautiful colonnade adjoins the buildings in the interior of the quadrangle, and immediately contiguous is a spacious park, most beautifully undulated and planted with trees, affording the most delightful promenades and interesting prospects; whilst the liberality and economy of the establishment is in every way worthy of the celebrity it has acquired, and the interest inspired by the beauty and magnificence of the edifice and its surrounding objects. Here was once a royal palace, in which Edward VI. died, and Queen Mary and Queen Elizabeth were born: it has long been pulled down, and on part of its site now stands the house belonging to the ranger of the park. Here is a college, called the Duke of Norfolk College, for the maintenance of 20 decayed housekeepers; and another called Queen Elizabeth College. In 1799 the chapel of the hospital, the dining-hall, and eight wards, were destroyed by fire; but the whole were soon re-built. The town is irregularly built, and, with the exception of the church, which is a noble structure, and the hospital, has nothing to recommend it to particular notice. There is a railroad between this place and London Bridge. It is a borough, and returns two members to parliament. The observatory is in the lat. of 51. 29. N. *See* BLACKHEATH and DEPTFORD.

GREENWICH, a seaport of Rhode Island, chief town in Kent county. It is noted for making good cider, carries on the fisheries to advantage, and sends some vessels to the West Indies. It stands on the N. W. part of Narraganset Bay; 16 miles S. of Providence.

The are ten or twelve other towns in different parts of the United States of North America named *Greenwich*, but none merit any particular notice.

GRIEFFEN, a town of Switzerland, on a small lake of its name; 9 miles E. S. E. of Zurich.

GREIFFENBERG, a town of Brandenburg, in the Ucker Mark, on the river Sernitz; 13 miles S. S. E. of Prenzlo, and 48 N. N. E. of Berlin.

GREIFFENBERG, a town of Silesia, in the principality of Jauer, with a fortress on a mountain. It is celebrated for its linen manufactures, and seated on the Queiss; 23 miles W. S. W. of Lignitz.

GREIFFENHAGEN, a town of Further Pomerania, on the river Oder; 12 miles S. of Stettin.

GREIFSWALDE. *See* GRIPSWALDE.

GREIN, a town of Austria, on the Danube; 28 miles E. of Lintz.

GREITZ. *See* GRAITZ.

GRENADA, an island in the West Indies, the last of the Windward Carribbees, and 30 leagues N. W. of Tobago. It is 20 miles long, and 13 broad, finely wooded, and the soil suited to produce sugar, tobacco, and indigo. It was taken from the French in 1762, confirmed to the English in 1763, taken by the French in 1779, and restored to the English in 1783. In 1795 the French landed some troops, and caused an insurrection in this island, which was not finally quelled till June, 1796. St. George is the capital.

GRENADILLAS, or GRENADINES, a cluster of islands in the West Indies, dependent on Grenada, and situate between that island and St. Vincent. They are upwards of twenty in number, most of them fertile, and capable of producing cotton, coffee, indigo, and sugar. The most considerable is Cariacou.

GRENADE, a town of France, in the department of Upper Garonne; seated at the junction of the Save with the Garonne; 17 miles N. W. of Toulouse. Pop. 3925.

GRENOBLE, a city of France, capital of the department of Isere, and a bishop's see, with a fortified castle. The leather and gloves that are made here are highly esteemed. It is seated on the Isere, over which are two bridges to pass into that part called Pernere, a large street on the side of the river. It is the head-quarters of the 7th military division, and seat of the Cour-Royale for the departments of the Upper Alps, Drome, and Isere; 300 miles S. S. E. of Paris, 60 from Lyons, and 100 due W. of Turin. Pop. 24,500.

GRETNA-GREEN, a village of Scotland in Dumfries-shire, near the mouth of the Esk, and on the borders of Cumberland. It has long been famous for the clandestine marriages of fugitive lovers from England, which are usually performed by two illiterate and drunken mechanics in the village, who have no form in the operation, excepting the entry of the names of the parties in a school-boy's copy-book. All their inquiries turn upon the length of the applicant's purse, that they may know how to regulate their demand; as they are not usually nice as to fees, any sum, from half-a-crown to 100 guineas, will be accepted, provided in all cases it is as much as they can get. It is 10 miles N. of Carlisle.

GREUSSEN, a town of Uppor Saxony, in Thuringia, on the river Elbe; 15 miles N. of Erfurt.

GRIMAUD, a town of France, in the department of Var; 12 miles S. W. of Frejus.

GRIMBERGEN, or GRUMBERGHEN, a town of Belgium, in Brabant, with an abbey and a castle; 6 miles N. of Brussels.

GRIMMA, or GRUMMA, a town of Upper Saxony, in Misnia, with a trade in wool, linen, thread, and flannel; seated on the Mulda; 14 miles S. E. of Leipsic.

GRIMMEN, a town of Hither Pomerania; 16 miles S. of Stralsund.

GRIMSBY, GREAT, a borough in Lincolnshire, with a market on Wednesday. It has a large church, like a cathedral, and a good trade in coal and salt. The harbour, at the mouth of the Humber, has been improved. It is 35 miles N. E. of Lincoln, and 168 N. of London. It returns one member to parliament.

GRINDENWALD, a village of Switzerland, in the canton of Bern; seated among mountains, at the foot of a celebrated glacier; 5 miles S. E. of Thun.

GRINDON, a village in that part of Durham called Norhamshire; 6 miles S. W. of Berwick. To the S. of it, at a place called Grindon Rigg, are four upright stone pillars, funeral monuments of the chieftains slain in a famous victory gained here over the Scots, in 1558, by the earl of Northumberland and his brother.

GRINSTEAD, EAST, a town in Sussex, with a market on Thursday. Here is Sackville College, a large stone building, founded by the duke of Dorset, in 1616, for 24 aged persons of both sexes. It is seated on a hill; 20 miles N. of Lewes, and 29 S. of London.

GRINTON, a mountainous and mineral parish in the North Riding of Yorkshire, comprising the four townships of Grinton, Melbecks, Muker, and Reith; seated near the head waters of the Swale river. Grinton is 8 miles, and Muker about 20 miles, W. of Richmond.

GRIPSWALD, or GRIEFSWALDE, a strong town of Hither Pomerania, with a good harbour and a university. It is seated on the river Rik, which is navigable to the Baltic; 14 miles W. of Wolgast, and 22 S. E. of Stralsund.

GRISONS, a new canton of Switzerland; bounded on the S. by Milan and Venice, E. and N. by Tyrol, and W. by the cantons of Glaris, Uri, and Tessin. It formerly included the Valteline, and the counties of Chiavenna and Bormio, now included in the Austrian dominions. The country was formerly divided into three leagues, namely, the Grey League, the League of God's House, and the League of the Ten Jurisdictions; each of them had a distinct internal government, and they were connected as one republic, by an annual diet held alternately at the towns of Coire, Ilantz, and Davos. But in 1803 the constitution was changed by the French, and the country made an additional canton of Switzerland. The inhabitants, amounting to about 73,000, are partly Calvinists and partly Catholics; but the former are most numerous. The principal subsistence of the peasantry is by breeding oxen, most of which are sent to Milan. The capital is Coire. The Rhine and the Inn both have their source in the Grisons.

GRODNO, the principal town, though not the capital, of Lithuania. It has the appearance of a decayed town, containing a mixture of wretched hovels, falling houses, and ruined palaces, with magnificent gateways, remains of its ancient splendour. A few habitations in good repair make the contrast more striking. Here is a college and physic garden. In the new palace, built by Augustus III., the diets were sometimes held; particularly the last, in 1793, which was compelled, at the point of the bayonet, to consent to the second partition of Poland; and here, in 1795, Stanislaus III. formally resigned his crown. Grodno is now subject to Russia. It is seated partly in a plain, on the river Niemen, and partly on a mountain, 140 miles N. E. of Warsaw. Long. 24. 25. E. lat. 53. 28. N. Pop. about 5000.

GROHNDE, a town of Hanover, near which is a monument of stone, erected in memory of a battle fought here in 1421. It is seated on the Weser, 9 miles S. of Hameln.

GROLL, a small town of Holland, in Gelderland. A duty is collected here on all merchandise passing through it for Germany. It is seated on the Slink; 20 miles E. by S. of Zutphen.

GRONINGEN, the most N. E. province of Holland; bounded on the E. by East Friesland, W. by Friesland, N. by the German Ocean, and S. by Drenthe. It is divided into two parts, called Groningen and Omelands. The excellency of this country consists in pastures, which feed a great number of large horses.

GRONINGEN, a city of Holland, capital of the province of the same name, with a citadel and a university. It is seated on the rivers Hunse and Aa, and has a communication, by a canal, with a bay of the German Ocean, at the distance of 10 miles, by which large quantities of butter are exported. The inhabitants are computed at 20,000. It is 96 miles N. E. of Amsterdam. Long. 6. 35. E. lat. 53. 12. N.

GROSSA, an island in the Gulf of Venice, near the coast of Dalmatia; 25 miles long, and 2 broad. Long. 15. 7. E. lat. 44. 18. N.

GROSSENHAYN, or HAAN, a town of Upper Saxony, in Meissin, with manufactures of cotton and woollen cloths, seated on the Roder; 8 miles N. of Meissin.

GROSSETTO, a town of Tuscany, in the Siennese, with a castle, situate near the sea; 30 miles S. W. of Sienna.

GROTKAU, a town of Silesia, in the district of Neisse. The forests round this town are the joint property of all the inhabitants. It is 16 miles N. N. E. of Neisse, and 30 S. of Breslau.

GROYNE. *See* CORUNNA.

GRUBENHAGEN, a town and castle of Hanover. The castle is now in ruins. It is 7 miles S. by W. of Einbeck.

GRUBENHAGEN, a principality of Hanover, at the S. extremity of the circle of Lower Saxony, comprising a portion of the Hartz mountains. The principal towns are Osterode, Grund, Clausthal, Cellerfeld, &c.

GRUNBERG, a town of Germany, in the electorate of Hesse, where the kings of the Merovingian race, and Charlemagne, held their court. It is 10 miles E. of Giessen.

GRUNBERG, or GRUMBERG, a populous town of Silesia, in the principality of Glogau, surrounded with vineyards. Here is a manufacture of cloth, and a great trade in vinegar and dried fruits. It is 30 miles N. W. of Glogau.

GRUNDE, a town of Hanover, in the mountains of Hartz; 4 miles W. of Clausthal.

GRUNHAYN, a town of Upper Saxony, in Misnia, with a trade in copper and lead; 16 miles S. by W. of Chemnitz.

GRUNINGEN, a town in the canton of Zurich, Switzerland, with a castle on an elevated rock; 10 miles S. E. of Zurich.

GRUNSTADT, a town of Germany, in the circle of Upper Rhine, county of Leiningen; 22 miles N. N. W. of Spire, and 25 S. of Mentz.

GRUYERES, a town and bailiwick of Switzerland, in the canton of Friburg, with a castle on a hill. It has a great trade in cheese, and is 15 miles S. W. of Friburg.

GRYFE, a river of Scotland, which rises in the S. W. angle of Renfrewshire, runs over several precipices into the lower country, fall- into the Black Cart, near the town of Paisley.

GUADALAXARA, an interior province of Spain, forming the N. W. part of the kingdom of New Castile. Superficies, 1250 square miles, with a population of 126,115. The chief town, of the same name, is seated on the banks of the river Henares; 30 miles N. E. of Madrid. It has a woollen manufacture. Pop. about 12,000.

GUADALAXARA, a division of Mexico, bounded on the W. by the Pacific Ocean. Superficies, 73,628 square miles, with a population of 630,500. It is intersected by the Santiago river, or Rio Grande. The chief town, of the same name, is seated on the W. bank of the Santiago, in the lat. of 21. 19. N.; 70 miles N. of Lake Chapala, and 275 N. W. of the city of Mexico. Pop. about 20,000.

GUADALOUPE, a town of Spain, in Estramadura, with a celebrated convent; seated on a rivulet of the same name; 34 miles E. by N. of Truxillo.

GUADALOUPE, one of the Leeward Caribbee Islands, in the West Indies, between Antigua and Dominica. It is divided into two parts by a strait, called the Salt River. At this place the land on each side is not above four miles broad, and by this strait the sea on the N. W. communicates with that on the S. E. The S. W. part is 60 miles long and 24 broad; and the N. E. part is much the same. The soil is exceedingly good, and well watered near the sea by rivulets which fall from the mountains, and produces large quantities of sugar, cotton, and coffee. On this island is a volcano, called the Mountain of Sulphur; and on its E. side are two mouths, which open into a pit of sulphur: the blacks who sell brimstone fetch it from this pit. The French settled on this island in 1635. It was taken by the English in 1759, but restored in 1763; again taken by the English in 1794, but evacuated the next year. The English again took it in 1810, and, in order to allure the Swedes into the late coalition against France, gave them this island. It was, however, by the consent of Sweden, restored to France in 1814. Basseterre, at the S. W. extremity of the island, is the capital. Lat. 16. N. 61. 48. W. long.

GUADALQUIVER, a river of Spain, which rises in the S. part of New Castile, flows through the kingdoms of Jaen, Cordova, and Seville, and enters the Bay of Cadiz at San Lucar, after a course of about 300 miles.

GUADARRAMA, a town of Spain, in Old Castile. It has a great trade in cheese, and is seated on the Guadarrama; 25 miles N. W. of Madrid.

GUADIANA, a river which rises in New Castile, in Spain, crosses Estramadura into Portugal, and, separating Algarve from Andalusia, enters the Bay of Cadiz at Ayamonte.

GUADIX, a town of Spain, in Granada, and a bishop's see. It contains three parishes and six convents, and is situated in a rich country, on a river of the same name; 36 miles E. N. E. of Granada.

GUAM, the chief of the Ladrone Islands, in the Pacific Ocean; 100 miles in circumference. The Spaniards have a garrison here: but the inhabitants are almost all natives of the country, and reputed to be skilful in building boats. It abounds with excellent fruit, and has several good harbours. Umata is the capital. Long. 143. 15. E. lat. 13. 10. N.

GUAMANGA, a city of Peru, capital of an interior province of the same name. It is famous for its mines of silver. It is 180 miles E. S. E. of Lima. Long. 74. 5. W. lat. 13. 20. S.

GUANAHANI, or CAT ISLAND, one of the Bahama Islands, the first land of America discovered by Columbus in 1491, and named by him St. Salvador.

Guanore, an interior town of Columbia, seated on a branch of the Apure river; 195 miles S. W. of Caraccas, and 130 E. of Merida. Pop. estimated at 12,000.

Guanaxuato, a small interior province of Mexico, containing only 6878 square miles, but a population of 517,300. It is the most densely populated part of the country, and is considered the most productive mineral district in Mexico. The chief city, of the same name, is seated on the eastern declivity of the Cordilleras, upwards of 6800 feet above the level of the sea, in the lat. of 21. N. and 101. 55. of W. long., giving a mean distance from the city of Mexico of 190 geographical, or 214 British statute miles. Population about 40,000, exclusive of about 30,000 more, employed in, or dependent on, the mines in its immediate vicinity.

Guancavelica, an interior province of Peru, E. of the maritime range of the Andes, extending about 190 miles from N. to S. between the lat. of 12. 20. and 14. 30. S., and is about 50 miles in mean breadth; it is thinly populated. The chief city, of the same name, is seated in an elevated glen of the Andes, in the lat. of 13. 5. S. and 74. 35. of W. long.; 170 miles S. E. of Lima.

Guanuco, a town of Peru, capital of a fruitful district of the same name. It is 172 miles N. N. E. of Lima.

Guarco. *See* Cagnete.

Guarda, a town of Portugal, in Beira, and a bishop's see. It is strong by nature and art, and has a stately cathedral; 138 miles N. E. of Lisbon.

Guardafui. *See* Gardefan.

Guastalla, a fortified town of Italy, capital of a small duchy included in that of Parma, with an ancient decayed castle. It is seated near the river Po, 19 miles N. E. of Parma.

Guasteca. *See* Panuco.

Guatimala, a republic of South America, having about 400 miles of seacoast on the shore of the Pacific Ocean, between the lat. of 14. and 17 N., being from 30 to 50 miles in breadth; it forms part of the chain of territory which connects the two great divisions of the western hemisphere, commonly called North and South America, and was formerly, with several other provinces, included in the government of Mexico; but since the subversion of the Spanish authority in the western world, the provinces of this territory have formed themselves into an independent republic, which was guaranteed by the other republics of America at the congress held at Panama in 1826. The indigo of Guatimala is the most esteemed of any in the world.

Guatimala, the chief city of the preceding republic, is seated on a small bay of the Pacific Ocean, in the lat. of 13. 54. N. and 90. 53. of W. long. A city of this name was first founded in 1524, which suffered greatly from an earthquake, and was afterwards rebuilt; the second city was totally destroyed by a similar cause in 1773, after which the present city was built at some distance from the site of the former one. It contains several churches, a monastic house, and a university. Pop. 30,775.

Guaxaca, or **Oaxaca**, a district of the chain of territory now forming the republic of Guatimala, comprising about 28,000 square miles, extending from sea to sea. Pop. 534,800. The chief city, of the same name, is seated on the banks of a river, which falls into the Gulf of Mexico, in the lat. of 17. 15. N. and 96. 20. of W. long. 450 miles N. W. of the city of Guatimala. Pop. 24,000.

Guayaquil, an intendancy of Colombia, bordering on the Pacific Ocean, comprising the S. W. part of the republic. The capital, or chief town, of the same name, is seated on the W. bank of a river falling into a gulf or bay of the same name; about 20 miles from the sea. Guayaquil is the seaport of Quito, from which it is distant about 150 miles S. S. W. The surrounding country produces an abundance of the finest cocoa, of which large quantities are exported to all parts of Europe. Lat. 2. 11. S., W. long. 79. 40. Pop. about 18,000.

Guayra, La, or **Laguira**, a seaport of Colombia, on the shore of the Caribbean Sea, and in the new province of Venezuela. It is in lat. 10. 37. N. and 66. 58. of W. long.; 7 miles N. of the city of Leon de Caraccas, of which it is the seaport; it exports large quantities of cocoa to Europe, and mules and cattle to the West India Islands; and, although the harbour is inconvenient, the traffic is considerable. Pop. 600.

Guben, a town of Lusatia; capital of a circle of its name, which yields great quantities of excellent red wine. It is seated on the Lubst, near its conflux with the Neisse; 24 miles N. E. of Cotbus, and 68 S. E. of Berlin. Pop. 6000.

Gudensberg, a town of Germany, in Lower Hesse; 10 miles S. S. W. of Cassel.

Guerande, a town of France, in the department of Lower Loire, with a considerable trade in salt. It is three miles from the Atlantic, and 40 W. by N. of Nantes. Pop. 7252.

Guerche, a town of France, in the department of Ille and Vilaine; 20 miles E. S. E. of Rennes. Pop. 3980.

Gueret, a town of France; capital of the department of Creuse. It is seated on the river Creuse; 35 miles N. E. of Limoges, and 190 S. by W. of Paris. Pop. 4014.

Guernsey, an island in the English Channel; 35 miles S. W. of Cape La Hogue, a promontory of the N. coast of France. It formed part of the dukedom of Normandy; but Henry I. of England annexed it to Great Britain, to which it has ever since continued an appendage, although the language, dress, manners, and form of government of the ancient Normans still continues. The island is about 86 miles in circumference, well defended by natural rocks; the surface is considerably varied, generally fertile, and breeds a considerable number of small cattle. It is divided into 10 parishes. St. Peter's Port, on the E. side of the island, in lat. 49. 33. N. and 2. 40. of W. long., is the chief place of the island, containing more than one half of the total population. The principal point of intercourse with England is Weymouth, from which it is distant 72 miles.

GUERNSEY, an interior county in the E. part of Ohio, containing about 650 square miles. It is intersected by Will's Creek, a branch of the Muskingum. The population, which in 1810 was only 3051, has increased to 27,748. Cambridge, the chief town, in the centre of the county, is 85 miles due E. of Columbus.

GUETA, or HUETA, a town of Spain, in New Castile; 52 miles E. by S. of Madrid.

GUGLINGEN, a town of Suabia, in the kingdom of Wirtemberg; situate on the Zaber; 20 miles N. of Stutgard.

GUIANA, or GUAYANA, an extensive territory of South America, comprising the whole country between the two great rivers Amazons and Orinoko, extending W. from the Atlantic Ocean, through 16 deg. of long. Prior to the war between England and France, which commenced in 1793, this extensive territory was divided between Portugal, Spain, France, and Holland; the Portuguese claimed the whole country lying N. of the Amazons, to about 1. 40. of N. lat. By a treaty in 1801, a line of demarcation was agreed upon between France and Portugal; this line extended from the island of Carpory, in the lat. above mentioned, through about 8 degrees of long. From this line *French Guiana* extends along the coast to the Maroni river, in the lat. of 5. 44. N. giving about 300 miles of seacoast, but westward it is not more than 130 miles wide. *Dutch Guiana* next extends along the coast, from the river Maroni, in 5. 44. of N. lat. and 53. 55. of W. long., to Cape Nassau, in 7. 34. N. and 58. 54. of W. long., giving about 360 miles of seacoast, and a mean breadth of about 170 miles; and *Spanish Guiana* comprised the coast from the river Maroni to the delta of the Orinoko, and all the country W. of Dutch and French Guiana, as far as the 68th degree of W. long. *Portuguese Guiana* now forms part of the republic of Brazil. French Guiana surrendered to the English in 1809, but was restored at the peace of 1814. *See* CAYENNE. The Dutch had formed four settlements upon their portion of the territory, viz. Surinam, Berbice, Demerara, and Essequibo, along the banks of four several rivers of those names, which also surrendered to the English during the war. At the peace of 1814, Surinam was restored to the Dutch, and all the rest confirmed to England by treaty. The greater portion of this vast territory is comprised of extensive swamps, and low lands of unbounded fertility, of which various kinds of animals, reptiles, and insects are the chief denizens, the human inhabitants being very limited, except upon the rivers SURINAM and DEMERARA, each of which see.

GUIENNE, a late province of France, 220 miles long and 85 broad, on the S. W. coast, of which Bordeaux was the capital. It now forms the departments of Gironde, Lot and Garonne, Dordogne, Lot, and Aveyron.

GUILDFORD, a borough in Surrey, governed by a mayor, with a market on Saturday. It is seated on the Wey, on the side of a hill, and had a castle and a palace, now in ruins; here is also part of a monastery, which is still occupied. The summer assizes are alternately held here and at Croydon; but the election of members for the county is always held here. It is a well built town, with two churches, and an elegant town-hall. The Wey is navigable to the Thames, and the trade in timber and corn is considerable. It is 23 miles W. S. W. of Croydon, and 29 S. W. of London. It returns two members to parliament.

GUILFORD, an interior county of North Carolina, a square of about 25 miles each way: it is well irrigated by the head waters of Cape Fear River, and contains a population of 19,175. Martinville, the chief town, is 70 miles W. N. W. of Raleigh.

GUILFORD, a town of Connecticut, in Newhaven county; situate on a bay in Long Island Sound; 17 miles E. by S. of Newhaven.

GUILLAC or GAILLAC, a town of France; seated on the N. bank of the river Tarn, in the department of Tarn: it is the seat of a prefect. Pop. 7310. It is 35 miles N. E. of Toulouse, and 15 W. by S. of Alby.

GUIMARAENS, a town of Portugal, in Entre-Douro-e-Minho, which has formerly been the residence of its kings. It is divided into the Old and New town; the former situate on an eminence, surrounded by walls. Here is a manufacture of linen, in high estimation. The public buildings are magnificent, and the collegiate church is said to be founded on the ruins of a temple of Ceres. It is 10 miles S. E. of Braga, and 25 N. E. of Oporto.

GUINEA, UPPER, an extensive region of North Africa, comprising about 1500 miles of seacoast, from Cape Mesurado, in the lat. of 6. 26. N. and 10. 30. of W. long., to the Calabar river, in 4. 10. N. and 6. 42. of E. long., and from thence S. to the equator. Of the interior parts of this country, either N. or S., very little is known. The coast of Upper Guinea, from Cape Mesurado to Cape Palmas, a range of 240 miles, is called the Grain Coast, from the vast quantity of grains of paradise, or Guinea pepper, which it was found to produce, on first being visited by Europeans; further E. for upwards of 200 miles is called the Tooth or Ivory Coast, from the large quantity of fine elephants' teeth which are brought to its markets; eastward of the Ivory Coast, to the meridional line, is called the Gold Coast, from the gold dust which is found in its rivers; and eastward of the meridional line is called the Slave Coast, from the extensive traffic in slaves, which was formerly carried on from thence by the English, Spaniards, French, and Americans, to the West Indies and America. This extensive tract of territory is occupied by various tribes and communities of negroes; the most numerous are the Fantees, who occupy the coast from Cape Mesurado to the meridional line. From a long continued intercourse with Europeans, the Fantees, have acquired strong trading habits, and among them most of the trading nations of Europe have formed settlements, protected by forts. In the rear of the Fantees are the Ashantees, who, although they appear to be one people, live in continued hostility with each other. North of the Ashantees is a tribe called the Chambas, who are represented as an amiable and industrious people, diligent in the pursuit of agriculture; and it was from this peaceful and social occupation, from which the Ashantees were wont to drag the people to the coast as slaves, when that traffic was carried on by the English; and the cessation of this traffic seems to be the cause of the revenge of the Ashantees, who acted as robbers and drovers to the inhabitants on the coast, their enmity being extended to the English, whom they regard as the cause of the cessation; and in 1823, and 1826, they waged, for a time, successful war against the discipline and skill of the British arms. The principal towns, or trading stations, on this part of the coast, westward of the meridional line, are Cape Coast Castle, Annamaboe, and Aconah: eastward of the meridional line is the kingdom of Dahomey, the principal town of which, on the coast is Griwhee, and in the interior Abomey, distant about 90 miles. The people of Dahomey are represented as fine looking, and industrious, their fields being productive in maize, legumes, and yams, and their pastures well stocked with sheep, goats, and cattle. Great ravages are frequently committed among them by leopards and hyenas, whilst the termes, or white ant, insidiously intrude, in such vast numbers, into the habitations of the people, as to commit the most destructive ravages, before resistance can be applied; there have been instances of their devouring an ox in a single night; and persons debilitated by disease are liable to be attacked by them. Another remarkable animal of Dahomey is a bat of enormous size, which suspend themselves in thousands by their claws, to the branches of trees, immediately contiguous to the habitations of the people. Eastward of Dahomey, on the banks of a river, about 25 miles from the sea, is the town of Ardrah, with a population of from 7000 to 10,000, which seems an independent, or free town, under the protection of the Hios, a powerful and numerous people, whose country extends 180 to 300 miles into the interior. The country around Ardrah is represented as exceedingly beautiful, and productive in every variety of tropical vegetation; further E. is the town of Lagos, the country to the northward of which is inhabited by the Jaboos, a very industrious people, who manufacture great quantities of cotton cloth, and whose country is well cultivated, and rich in all the products of agriculture; E. of the Jaboos is the kingdom of Benin, supposed to be very extensive: the capital, of the same name, is about 40 miles from the coast, the seaport being Gatto; further E., extending to the 10th degree of longitude, near the kingdom of Warre, and Old and New Calabar. It was from this part of the coast from whence the most active slave trade was carried on by the English, a people from the interior, called the Heebos, being the principal victims, and the town of Bonny the principal market; since the abandonment of this traffic in slaves by the English, the inhabitants of this coast have directed their attention to agriculture and commerce, and now export large quantities of palm oil, ivory, and dye-woods. From Old Calabar the coast extends to the S. which is commonly called Lower Guinea, comprising the kingdoms of Biafra, Calbonga, Gabon, Lopez, Malemba, Loango, Congo, Benguela, &c.: it is from this part of the coast from whence the Brazilians still continue to draw 30,000 or 40,000 slaves annually. Malemba, in the lat. of 5. 24. S. and 12. 20. of E. long. is represented as having a very salubrious climate, and as affording the most favourable spot on the whole western coast of Africa for the residence of Europeans. Off this coast, N. of the equator, are the islands of Fernando Po, Princes, and St. Thomas; which also afford favourable situations from whence to dispense the blessings of civilization and social order.

Guinea, New, or Papua, an island of the South Pacific Ocean, to the N. of New Holland, from which it is separated by Endeavour Strait: it is next in size to New Holland, extending S. E. from the equator to 12. S. lat., and from 131. to 153. E. long., a length of more than 1200 miles, by a medial breadth of perhaps 300; the coasts of the eastern part having been but recently investigated. The northern part is said to have been discovered by the Spaniards, in 1528, who had sailed from Mexico to explore the Spice Islands. The coasts are generally lofty, and, in the interior, mountain rises above mountain; but the whole appears covered with such luxuriance of wood and herbage, as can scarcely be conceived. The cocoa, sago, bread-fruit, and plantain-tree, beside most of the trees, shrubs, and plants common to the islands in the South Pacific Ocean, are found here in great perfection. This island is the chosen residence of the singular birds of paradise, which breed here during the wet monsoon, and, in the dry, migrate in flocks westward, to the smaller islands, particularly Arroo. Here are also elegant parrots, and pigeons that almost equal a turkey in size. The inhabitants of the northern part are called Papuas; whence the name of the country. They seem to have the true Malay complexion and features, but in general of horrible appearance, and great ferocity. Their language and habitations resemble those of Borneo, &c. On the W. the women seems the most industrious in making mats and pots of clay, which they afterward burn with dry grass or brushwood; and they even wield the axe, while the men are indolent, or engaged in the chace of wild hogs. In the interior is a race called Arafouras, who live in trees, which they ascend by a notched pole, drawing it after them, to prevent surprise. On this extensive territory, so favoured by nature, there is no European settlement. The chief commerce is with the Malays and Chinese, from whom they purchase blue and red cloth, axes, knives, and other instruments. Their returns are ambergris, tortoise-shell, small pearls, birds of paradise, and other birds, which the Papuans dry with great skill. Some slaves are also exported, probably captives taken in intestine wars.

GUINGAMP, a town of France, in the department of Cotes du Nord; seated on the Trieu; 18 miles S. of Treguier, and 23 W. by N. of St. Brieux. It is the seat of a prefect.

GUIPUZCOA, a district of Spain, forming the N.W. part of Biscay; comprising a superficies of 52 square leagues. Pop. 104,491. St. Sebastian is the capital.

GUISBOROUGH. *See* GISBOROUGH.

GUISE, a town of France, in the department of Aisne, with a castle; seated on the Oise; 18 miles E. of St. Quentin, and 95 N. E. of Paris.

GUISLAIN, ST., a town of the Netherlands, in Hainault; seated in marshy land, on the river Haine; 6 miles W. of Mons.

GUJUNAT, or GUJURAT, a town of Hindostan, in Lahore: 60 miles N. by W. of Lahore, on the road to Benares.

GUMBINNEN, a town of Prussia, capital of a government of the same name in Lithuania. It has manufactures of cloth, and is seated on the Pissa, which falls into the Pregel; 75 miles E. by S. of Konigsberg. The superficies of the government of Gumbinnen comprises upwards of 6000 square miles, with a population of about 350,000. Population of the town about 5000.

GUMURGINIA, a populous town of European Turkey, in Rumelia, near the seacoast; 190 miles due W. of Constantinople.

GUNDELFINGEN, a town of Bavaria, situate on the Brenz, near the Danube; 17 miles W. S. W. of Donawert.

GUNTOOR, a district of Hindostan, formerly the most southern of the circars, intersected by the river Kistnah, on the western coast of the Bay of Bengal. The chief town, of the same name, is seated S. of the Kistnah; 45 miles W. by N. from Masulipatam. *See* CIRCARS.

GUNTZBURG, a town of Suabia, with a castle. It stands on the river Guntz, near its conflux with the Danube; 6 miles W. of Burgau, and 14 E. of Ulm.

GUNZENHAUSEN, a town of Franconia, in the principality of Anspach; seated on the Altmuhl, near a forest; 16 miles S. S. E. of Anspach.

GURAU, a town of Silesia, in the principality of Glogau, with good cloth manufactures, and a great trade in corn. In 1759 it was reduced to ashes by the Russians. It stands on an eminence, by the river Bartch; 19 miles E. of Glogau.

GURCK, a town of Germany, in Carinthia, and lately a bishop's see; seated on the river Gurck; 20 miles N. by W. of Clagenfurt.

GURCKFELD, a town of Germany, in Carniola, with a castle on a hill; situate on the Save; 28 miles S. E. of Cilley.

GURGISTAN. *See* GEORGIA.

GURIEF, or GOURIEV, a town of Russia, in the government of Astracan, with a good harbour; seated near the Caspian Sea, between the mouths of the Ural; 210 miles E. by N. of Astracan. Long. 51. 56. lat. 47. 37. N.

GURRAH, a town of Hindostan, in the province of Allahabad; situate near the river Nerbuddah; 190 miles S. S. W. of Allahabad. Long. 80. 23. E. lat. 23. 9. N.

GURRUMCONDA, a town of Hindostan, lately subject to the regent of Mysore, but ceded by the nizam to the British, in 1799. It is 73 miles N. E. of Bangalore, and 112. W. N. W. of Madras. Long. 78. 36. E. lat. 13. 47. N.

GUSTROW, a city of Lower Saxony, in the duchy of Mecklenburg-Schwerin. The chief courts of judicature for the duchy are held here; and it has an elegant ducal palace. It is situate on the Nebel; 29 miles E. N. E. of Schwerin. Long. 12. 13. E. lat. 53. 47. N.

GUTTA, a town of Hungary, seated on the Wag, in the island of Schut; 16 miles N. W. of Comorn.

GUZERAT, a province of Hindostan, which is a peninsula, 200 miles long and 140 broad, formed by the Arabian Sea and the gulfs of Cambay and Cutch. The W. part is mountainous and woody, and inhabited by a wild hardy race, governed by rajahs of their own; but the largest and finest part is included within the extensive empire of the Mahrattas. Amedabad is the capital.

GWALIOR, a fortress of Hindostan, in a district of the same name, in the province of Agra, situated on a rock about 4 miles in length, but narrow, and nearly flat on the top, with sides almost perpendicular, from 200 to 300 feet above the surrounding plain. The rampart conforms to the edge of the precipice all around; and the only entrance is by steps running up the side of the rock, defended on the side next the country by a wall and bastions. The area within is full of noble buildings, reservoirs of water, wells, and cultivated land; so that it is a little district within itself. At the N. W. foot of a mountain is the town, which is well built. This fortress is considered as the Gibraltar of the east; but in 1780 Major Popham took it by an unexpected nocturnal escalade, and in 1804 it capitulated after a practicable breach was made through its walls by Colonel Henry White. It was afterwards given up to the Mahrattas by Lord Cornwallis. It is 80 miles S. of Agra. Long. 78. 28. E. lat. 26. 15. N.

GY, a town of France, in the department of the Upper Saone. Pop. 2701.

GYFHORN, a town of Lower Saxony, in the duchy of Luneburg; seated near the junction of the Iser with the Aller; 29 miles N. of Brunswick.

GYON. *See* GIJON.

GYONGYOS, a town of Hungary; 21 miles W. S. W. of Erlau. Pop. 8000.

GYULA, or JULIA, a town of Hungary; situated on an island in the river Kores, or Korash, with a castle. Population about 2000. It is 92 miles W. S. W. of Colosvar.

GZAT, or GHJAT, a town of Russia, in the government of Smolensk; 140 miles E. N. E. of Smolensk.

H.

Haa, a small island in the North Sea, near the N. coast of Scotland; 3½ miles S. E. of Farout Head.

Haag, a town of Bavaria, capital of a county of the same name. It is seated on a hill; 26 miles E. by N. of Munich. Long. 12. 15. E. lat. 48. 7. N.

Haarlem, or Haerlem. *See* Harlem.

Haastrecht, a village of South Holland; 3 miles E. of Gosida. Population about 1200.

Habelschwerdt, a town of Silesia, in the county of Glatz, on the river Neisse; 9 miles S. of Glatz.

Hacha. *See* Rio de la Hacha.

Hachenburg, a town of Germany, in the county of Sayn, with a castle; 20 miles N.N.E. of Coblentz.

Hacketstown, a town of New Jersey, in Sussex county; seated on the Musconekunk; 22 miles W. of Morristown.

Hackinsack, a town of New Jersey, chief of Bergen county, with a Dutch and episcopal church, and a flourishing academy. It is situate on a river of the same name; 20 miles N. W. of New York.

Hackney, a village and parish of Middlesex, an appendage to the metropolis; 2 miles N.E. of Shoreditch church. It has several hamlets, the principal of which are Upper and Lower Clapton, on the N.; Dalston, Shacklewell, and Kingsland, on the W.; and Homerton, on the E. It has a handsome modern church, begun in 1792, and a chapel of ease erected in 1810. The term *Hackney Coaches* was derived from the circumstance of this village being the first near the metropolis, that was accommodated with carriages of that description. It has a receptacle for lunatics. St. John's palace, an ancient edifice in Well Street, is said to have been the residence of the prior of the order of St. John of Jerusalem. In this parish, S. of Lea Bridge, are the Temple Mills, so called from having formerly belonged to the Knights Templars.

Haddam, a tn. of Connecticut, in Middlesex county, on the E. side of Connecticut River: 18 miles N. by E. of Saybrook.

Haddington, a royal borough of Scotland, capital of the county of the same name, on the Tyne; 17 miles E. of Edinburgh, and the first stage on the road to London. It consists of four principal streets, which intersect each other at nearly right angles: it has a considerable manufacture of coarse woollen cloth. Part of a monastery here is occupied as a parish church, which is a large and venerable building. It has a town-house and county hall; there are also two bridges over the Tyne. The site of the ancient abbey of Haddington is about a mile E. of the town; it was founded in 1178. In conjunction with Dunbar, North Berwick, Jedburgh, and Lauder, it sends a member to parliament. Here the celebrated John Knox was born.

Haddingtonshire, or East Lothian, of which the preceding is the capital, a county of Scotland, 25 miles long, and 15 where broadest; bounded on the W. by Edinburghshire, N. by the Frith of Forth, E. by the German Ocean, and S. by Berwickshire, and comprises an extent of about 297 square miles. It is divided into 24 parishes. The soil is in many places doubly productive; rich crops are raised on the surface, and mines of coal are inexhaustible. The southern part is mountainous, comprehending the N. side of Lammermuir hills; but these high grounds feed many sheep. It is intersected by numerous streams, but the principal river is the Tyne. The chief towns are the three royal burghs of Haddington, North Berwick, and Dunbar. It sends one member to parliament.

Hadersleben, a town of Denmark, in Sleswick, with a citadel, on a small island, in a narrow bay of the Baltic; 30 miles E. by S. of Ripen.

Hadit, or Hadice, a town of Syria, on the Euphrates; 115 miles W. of Bagdad.

Hadley, or Hadleigh, a town of Suffolk, with a market on Monday. It is seated on the Bret: 20 miles S. E. of Bury, and 64 N. E. of London.

Hadramaut, a province of Arabia Felix, on the seacoast, between Yemen on the W. and Oman on the E. Some parts are dry and desert, others are extremely fertile, with well watered valleys. The chief products are frankincense, gum-arabic, dragon's-blood, myrrh, and aloes. Shibam is the capital.

Haerlebecke, a town of the Netherlands, in Flanders, on the Lys; 23 miles S. W. of Ghent, on the road to Courtray, from which it is distant 3 miles. Pop. about 3000.

Haff, a lake or bay of Prussia, in Pomerania, divided into Great and Little; at the mouth of the Oder, between which and the Baltic are situated the islands of Usedom and Wallen. It is 36 miles in length, and its greatest breadth 9 miles.

Hagartstown. *See* Elizabethtown.

Hagen, a town of Westphalia, in the county of Mark. It has manufactures of cloth, and stands on the Vollme; 13 miles S. of Dortmund.

Hagetman, a town of France, in the department of Landes; 18 miles S. of Mont de Marsan, in the vicinity of which are some silver mines, Pop. about 2350.

Hagiar, a town of Arabia Deserta; 160 miles N. by W. of Medina.

Hague, a town of Holland, province of South Holland, which may compare with the handsomest cities in Europe, in the magnificence of its palaces, the beauty of its streets, the pleasantness of its situation, and the politeness of its inhabitants. It is seated 2 miles from the sea, and there is a pavement across the sand hills, with trees on each side, which leads to Scheveling on the sea-shore. There are 14 churches, and some charitable institutions. The castle of Ryswick, from which the treaty known by that name received its appellation, is about a mile an half S. E. of the town. It was, with Brussels, the alternate seat of government previous to the Belgic revolution, and has since been the residence of the king of Holland. It suffered greatly by the revolution under Bonaparte, but the inhabitants threw off the French yoke in 1813. It is 30 miles S. W. of Amsterdam, and 7 S. by W. of Leyden. Pop. 44,550.

HAGUENAU, a fortified town of France, in the department of Lower Rhine, with a citadel; seated on the Motter; 15 miles N. of Strasburg. There are manufactures of tobacco, madder, and earthenware.

HAILSHAM, a town in Sussex, 59 miles from London. Here are the ruins of Michaelham Priory.

HAIMBURG, a town of Austria, with a castle on a mountain, near the S. bank of the Danube; 27 miles E. by S. of Vienna. Pop. about 2700.

HAINA, or IAINA, a river of St. Domingo, which falls into a bay of the same name; 12 miles W. of St. Domingo.

HAI-NAN, an island in the China Sea, to the N. of the Gulf of Tonquin, and to the S. W. of the province of Quangtong, from which it is 12 miles distant. It is 400 miles in circumference. The soil of the N. part is level: but in the S. and E. are mountains, among which are valleys that produce two crops of rice every year. There are mines of gold and lapis lazuli, which last is carried to Canton, to paint the porcelain. There are also several kinds of woods, the most valuable of which is that called by the natives hoali, and by Europeans rose or violet wood. It produces the same fruits as China, beside sugar, tobacco, cotton, and indigo. Among the animals is a great black ape, with features resembling those of the human face; but the common sorts of apes are grey, and very ugly.

HAINAULT, a province of Belgium; bounded on the N. E. by Brabant, N. W. by Flanders, S. W. by France, and E. by the territories of Liege and Namur; it comprises an extent of 1700 square miles, and is intersected by the Scheldt, the Sambre, and the Haine. Its mineral productions are considerable, and there are several manufactures. The chief towns are Tournay, Mons, and Charetroi. It was formerly divided into Austrian and French Hainault, and in 1814 was ceded by Austria to the Netherlands: in 1815 it received an accession of Beaumont, Merbe, Le Chateau, and Dour, formerly belonging to French Hainault.

HAJOSH, a town of Hungary, in Cumania Minor; 65 miles S. by E. of Pest.

HAJYPOOR, the chief town of the district of the same name; seated on the N. E. bank of the Ganges, at its confluence with the Guxduck.

HALASZ, a town of Hungary, in Cumania Minor; 17 miles E. of Hajosh. Pop. about 8700.

HALBERSTADT, a town of Prussia, in Lower Saxony; capital of a principality of the same name, which was formerly a bishopric. The cathedral is a superb structure; here are three regular abbeys, and two nunneries, and the Lutherans have five churches. It is seated on the Hotheim; 32 miles S. E. of Brunswick, on the road to Leipsic.

HALDENSLEBEN NEW, a town of Prussia, in Lower Saxony, in the duchy of Magdeburg, on the river Ohra; 14 miles N. N. W. of Magdeburg.

HALDENSTEIN, a town of Switzerland, in the country of Grisons; seated near the Rhine; 4 miles N. of Coire.

HALEN, a town of Belgium, in Brabant; seated on the river Geet; 17 miles E. N. E. of Louvain.

HALES, a village in Gloucestershire; 2 miles N. E. of Winchcomb; noted for the remains of its abbey, which formerly was very magnificent, and had great privileges.

HALESOWEN, an insulated town of Shropshire, in Worcestershire, with a market on Monday, and a manufacture of nails, and pearl and horn buttons. The poet Shenstone was born and buried here; and near it is the Leasows, in the decoration of which his whole fortune was spent. It is 10 miles N. E. of Kidderminster, and 127 N. W. of London.

HALESWORTH, a town in Suffolk. Market on Tuesday. It has a canal to Southwold, and is seated near the river Blyth; 23 miles N. E. of Ipswich, and 101 of London.

HALIBUT ISLAND, an island in the Pacific Ocean, off the coast of Alaska; so named by Cook on account of the number of fish of that name caught here. It is 7 leagues in circumference, and very low and barren. Long. 164. 15. W. lat. 54. 48. N.

HALIFAX, a borough in the West Riding of Yorkshire. Market on Saturday. It returns two members to parliament. It is a very large parish, and the inhabitants are principally employed in the woollen manufacture. This town is the great mart for shalloons and worsted stuffs, in great variety. It has a market-house, called the Piece Hall, and various others for particular goods. The church is a venerable building, and contains a number of ancient monuments. A handsome new church was built in 1798. It is about three quarters of a mile long, and is seated in a hilly country, near a branch of the Calder; 40 miles W. S. W. of York, and 197 N. by W. of London. Pop. 15,382.

HALIFAX, a city, and the capital of Nova Scotia. It stands on the W. side of Chebucto Bay, which is large enough to shelter 1000 men of war. An island at the mouth of the harbour is so strongly fortified, as to bid defiance to all attack, and the town is protected on the land side by a fort, and several batteries, which render it impregnable. The streets are parallel and at right angles. At the N. extremity is the king's yard, supplied with stores of every kind for the royal navy. The inhabitants are estimated at above 15,000. It is 600 miles N.E. by E. of New York, and 90 E. of Annapolis. Lat. 44. 44. long. 63. 36.

HALIFAX, an interior county of N. Carolina; bounded on the N. E. by Roanoke, near the northern boundary. The chief town, Halifax, is 103 miles N. E. by E. of Raleigh.

HALIFAX, a county of Virginia, bordering on North Carolina, and bounded on the N. E. by the Roanoke. Its chief town, Bannister, is 143 miles S. W. by W. of Richmond.

Halifax is also the name of several townships of the United States.

HALITZ, a town of Poland, in the palatinate of Lemberg, with a castle. Since 1773 it has been included in the new kingdom of Galicia. It is seated on the Dniester; 60 miles S. S. E. of Lemberg.

HALLAND, a province of Sweden, on the W. coast of Gothland. It is 60 miles along the coast, but not above 18 in breadth. The country is in general mountainous, with considerable woods of oak and birch. Halmstadt is the capital. Population 75,000.

HALLATON, a town in Leicestershire, with a market on Thursday; 12 miles E. S. E. of Leicester, and 90 N. by E. of London.

HALLE, a town of Lower Saxony, in the duchy of Magdeburg, with a famous university. It has large salt-works, and manufactures of starch, linen, and flannel. It is seated on both sides of the Saale, over which there are five bridges; 18 miles N. N. W. of Leipsic, and 46 S. S. E. of Magdeburg.

HALLE, a town of Suabia, noted for its salt-pits, and the famous protestant league concluded here in 1610. It is seated on the Kocher, among rocks and mountains; 32 miles N. E. of Stutgard.

HALLE, a town of Germany, in Tyrol, famous for its salt-mine: seated on the Inn; 6 miles E. N. E. of Inspruck.

HALLE, a town of the Netherlands, in Hainault: seated on the Senne; 10 miles S. S. W. of Brussels.

HALLEIN, a town of Bavaria, in the duchy of Salzburg; seated on the Salza, among mountains that abound in mines of salt; 8 miles S. by E. of Salzburg.

HALLERSPRING, a town of Lower Saxony, in the principality of Calenberg, at the source of the Haller; 16 miles S. S. W. of Hanover.

HALMSTADT, a seaport of Sweden, capital of Halland. Here are flourishing woollen manufactures, and a profitable salmon fishery. It stands at the mouth of the Nissa, on a bay of the Cattegat; 82 miles S. S. E. of Gothenburg. Long. 12. 52. lat. 56. 40.

HALSALL, a parish in Lancashire. In this parish is a large morass, called Halsall Mere, containing a bituminous turf.

HALSTEAD, a town in Essex, with a market on Friday; seated on the side of a hill, on the river Coln; 15 miles N. of Chelmsford, and 46 N. E. of London.

HALTEREN, a town of Westphalia, in the principality of Munster; seated on the Lippe; 22 miles S. W. of Munster.

HALTON, a town in Cheshire, with a market on Saturday. It had a stately castle, belonging to the duchy of Lancaster, which maintained a large jurisdiction round it, by the name of Halton Fee; but all that remains is now a prison. It is near the Mersey; 13 miles N. E. of Chester, and 195 N. N. W. of London.

HALTWHISTLE, a town of Northumberland, with a market on Thursday; seated on a hill on the S. branch of the Tyne, near the Newcastle and Carlisle railway; 35 miles W. of Newcastle, and 315 N. by W. of London.

HAM, a strong town of Westphalia, capital of the county of Mark. It is a place of good trade, and has extensive bleaching-grounds. In 1761 the French were defeated near this place by the troops of Brunswick. It is seated on the Lippe; 20 miles W. of Lipstadt. Long. 7. 57. E. lat. 51. 40. N.

HAM, WEST, a village and parish of England, in the county of Essex, on the river Lea; 5 miles from London.

HAM, a town of France, in the department of Somme, with a strong castle, now used as a state prison; seated on the Somme; 70 miles N. N. E. of Paris.

HAMADAN. *See* AMADAN.

HAMAH, a town of Syria, the residence of the scheik, with the title of emir. The best houses, the mosques, and the castle, are built of black and white stones. The river Aaszi, formerly called Orontes, runs close by the castle, and fills its ditches, which are cut deep into the solid rock. The inhabitants have a trade in linen of their own manufacture. It is seated among hills; 78 miles S. S. W. of Aleppo.

HAMAMET, a town of the kingdom of Tunis, on a gulf of the same name; 37 miles S. of Tunis. Long. 10. 15. E. lat. 36. 13. N.

HAMBLEDON, a town in Hampshire, with a market on Monday; 15 miles S. E. of Winchester.

HAMBURG, a free and imperial city of Germany, in Lower Saxony; seated on the north bank of the Elbe, about 55 miles from its mouth; consisting of the old and new town, both nearly of an equal size. Most of the houses are built after the manner of the Dutch, and richly furnished within. The principal streets of the old town have long and broad canals, which are filled by the tide. It is seated on the rivers Elbe and Alster, and the latter, a tributary stream of the Elbe, before it enters the town by sluices, forms a fine basin. Here is a celebrated college, an arsenal, a bank, and a handsome exchange. The established religion is Lutheran, but all denominations are tolerated. Beside the five principal churches there are eleven smaller ones for particular occasions, some of which belong to hospitals, of which there are a great number. It has a library containing about 100,000 volumes. The cathedral of Our Lady is a very fine structure; it is well fortified, and on the ramparts are handsome walks, planted with rows of trees. On the east is the suburb of St. George, and on the west the Hamburger Berg. On May 5th and 6th, 1842, the central and older portion of the city was destroyed by fire, comprising above 60 streets and 2000 houses, &c., or three-eighths of the town. Among other public buildings thus burnt were the beautiful churches of St. Michael, St. Nicolai, and St. Peter's, the admiralty, exchange, bank, post office, and prisons. This portion of the town will probably be rebuilt on an improved system. Hamburg, from its situation, has all possible advantages for foreign and domestic trade; particularly from its communication, by the Elbe, with some of the principal navigable rivers of

Germany; and hence it is one of the most commercial places in Europe. The number of vessels that frequent its port is about 2000. It is distinguished for its sugar-refinery, and it has manufactures of cotton stockings, gold and silver lace, silk, linen, handkerchiefs, sail-cloths, thread, ribbons, and velvets. The commerce, however, received, a severe shock in 1807; and since that, the city itself has been almost reduced to ruin. Previous to the year 1806, this city became the depôt of all the continental commerce, and numbers of merchants flocked here from every part of Europe, bringing their property along with them, as to a place free from military sway, and secure from the warlike commotions which then agitated Europe; but after the defeat of the Prussians at the battle of Jena, the French took possession of it, and afterwards annexed it to the empire. In 1813, on the advance of the Russians into Germany, the French evacuated the town, and the Russians immediately entered. In May following, the French laid siege to it for more than a month, when the Russians, finding it impossible to defend it any longer, retired. The French, on re-entering, began to strengthen the fortifications; and, after the battle of Leipsic, and the commander, Marshal Davoust, hearing of the approach of the allies, made great preparations for a long siege. For this purpose he destroyed the suburbs and gardens, and expelled all the inhabitants who were not able to provide provisions for six months. On the restoration of the Bourbons, however, the French garrison was withdrawn, and the place delivered up to the allies in May, 1814; since which it has recovered its former independence and activity. It is 55 miles N. E. of Bremen, and 40 S. W. of Lubeck. Pop. about 115,000. Lat. 53. 34. long. 9. 58.

Hamelburg, a town of Franconia, in the principality of Fulda; seated on the Saale; 20 miles W. N. W. of Schweinfurt.

Hameln, a strong town of Lower Saxony, at the extremity of the duchy of Brunswick, of which it is the key. Here are manufactures of stuffs, silks, and stockings. The fortress surrendered to the French in 1806. It is situate at the confluence of the Hamel with the Weser; 28 miles S. W. of Hanover.

Ha-mi, a province of Western Tartary, surrounded by deserts, yet accounted one of the most delightful countries in the world. Its rice and fruits, particularly the melons and dried raisins, are in high esteem in China. It is tributary to that country; and its capital of the same name. Long. 91. 44.E. lat. 42. 55. N.

Hamilton, a county in the state of Tenessee; bounded on the S. E. by the river Tenessee. Population 8175. The chief town, Brainerd, is 102 miles S. E. of Murfreesborough.

Hamilton, a county in Ohio; bounded on the S. by the river Ohio, and intersected by the great Miami river. Pop. 31,764. Cincinnati, its chief town is 109 miles S. W. of Columbus.

Hamilton is also the name of a county in New York, containing 80,145 inhabitants. The court-house, in the centre of the county, is 80 miles N. W. by N. of Albany. There are several townships of the same name.

Hamilton, a town of Scotland, in Lanarkshire, with a noble seat belonging to the duke of that name. It has a trade in cabinet-work and the making of shoes; and the women are famous for the spinning of linen yarn, and making thread lace. It is seated on the Avon, near its conflux with the Clyde. It has a handsome parish church, an elegant town-house and prison, and a commodious market-place. It was made a royal burgh in 1548, by Queen Mary, and is contributory, with Linlithgow, &c., in sending one member to parliament. It is 11 miles S. E. of Glasgow, and 36 W. S. W. of Edinburgh.

Hammerfest, a town of Norway, 60 miles S. W. from the North Cape. It is the most northern town of Europe, and was founded in 1819 by Mr. Crowe, an English merchant. It is seated on a very secure harbour on Qualoen S., and has a considerable export trade in fish, oil, &c. Pop. 200.

Hammersmith, a large village in Middlesex; seated on the north bank of the Thames, over which is a handsome suspension bridge, and one of the appendages of the metropolis; 3½ miles west of Hyde Park Corner. Here also is a nunnery, established originally as a boarding school for young ladies of the Roman Catholic persuasion; and toward the river are a number of handsome seats and villas. Here is a charity school, a workhouse, and several places of worship for dissenters. The chapel is near the centre of the town. Here also was the celebrated villa of Brandenburg House, in which her late Majesty Queen Caroline died.

Hamont, a town of the Netherlands, in the late bishopric of Liege; 20 miles W. by N. of Ruremonde.

Hampshire, or County of Southampton, a maritime county of England; bounded on the N. by Berkshire, E. by Surrey and Sussex, S. by the English Channel, and W. by Dorsetshire and Wiltshire. It is nearly square, except a projection the S. W.; and contains 1,212,000 acres. This county has a great variety of soils, but the principal part is chalk. The Dorsetshire border has large tracts of heath; and toward the sea are great quantities of marsh land, but very fertile; and all the remainder is excellent land. It is one of the most fertile and populous counties in England. On the downs, of which a ridge runs almost across the county, are fed plenty of sheep; but the stock is considerably decreased, owing to enclosures. Besides wheat, barley, and hops, it is famous for bacon, honey, and timber; the last in particular, on account of its great woods, of which the principal are the New Forest, and the forest of Bere. The principal harbours, of which there are a great number along the coast, are Portsmouth and Yarmouth. Southampton is deemed the county town, but the assizes are held at Winchester. It sends 2 members to parliament for each of its divisions, N. and S., and one for the Isle of Wight.

Hampshire, New, one of the United States of North America; bounded on the E. by the

Atlantic Ocean, the Salmon Fall river, and a conventional line, extending to 45. 13. of N. lat., which divides it from the state of Maine; on the S. by a conventional line, in the lat. of 42. 40., which separates it from Massachusets; on the W. by the Connecticut river, which divides it from Vermont; and on the northern extremity, by Lower Canada. It lies between 71. 0. and 72. 39. W. long. It comprises a a superficies of about 9280 square miles, or 5,939,200 acres. The land, for 20 or 30 miles from the coast, is generally low; but, advancing into the country, it rises into hills, which in some parts of the state are entitled to the denomination of lofty mountains. From the vicinity of some mountains, whose summits are covered with snow most of the year, this country is intensely cold in winter, but cool and pleasant in summer. The chief lakes are Umbagog, Winnipiseogee, Sunapee, and Squam; and the principal rivers, the Androscoggin, Saco, Piscataqua, Merrimac, Connecticut, Upper and Lower Amonoosuck. The manufactures of this state have of late rapidly increased: they consist of cotton and woollen, glass and iron. The principal exports are pot and pearl ashes, fish, beef, live cattle, pork, flax, and hemp. Among the curiosities of this state, the Notch or Gap, which fell in September, 1826, is worthy of notice: it is on the W. side of the White Mountains, near the source of the Saco. It is a deep and narrow defile, twenty-two feet wide. The mountain appears as if cloven down to its base.

New Hampshire is divided into six counties, viz. Coos, Cheshire, Grafton, Hillsborough, Rockingham, and Strafford. The present constitution was adopted in 1792. The legislative power is vested in a senate and house of representatives, the former consisting of 13 members, chosen annually by the people, and the latter of delegates from the different towns. Population, 284,574.

Hampshire, a county in Massachusets; intersected by the Connecticut river; bounded by the counties of Hambden, Berkshire, Franklin, and Worcester. Its chief town, Northampton, 94 miles W. of Boston, is seated on the W. side of the Connecticut. Pop. of the county, 30,897.

Hampshire, a county of Virginia; bounded on the N. E. by the river Potomac, and by the counties of Morgan, Frederic, and Hardy. Pop. 12,295. Its chief town, Romney, is 214 miles N. W. by N. of Richmond.

Hampstead, a village of Middlesex, four miles N. N. W. of London, formerly famous for its medicinal waters. It may be considered one of the appendages of the metropolis, being a favourite residence of the merchants and citizens. It is seated on the side of a hill, on the top of which is a fine heath that commands a delightful prospect; and in the vicinity are many elegant seats and villas. In the windows of an ancient edifice, called the Chicken House, are painted, in stained glass, portraits of King James I., and the Duke of Buckingham, of the former of whom it is said to have been a hunting seat.

Hampton, a seaport of Virginia, in Elizabeth county, near the mouth of James River; 29 miles S. E. of Williamsburg. Long. 76. 17. W. lat. 37. 5. N

Hampton, a seaport of New Hampshire, in Rockingham county, on a river of its name, near the sea. It has a canal to the Merrimac, at Salisbury; and is 14 miles S. by W. of Portsmouth. Long. 70. 45. W. lat. 42. 55. N.

Hampton, a village in Middlesex, on the N. bank of the river Thames; 13 miles S. W. of London. It is famous for a royal palace, called Hampton Court, originally and magnificently built by Cardinal Wolsey, who gave it to Henry VIII. The remains of the old palace are only some of the domestic offices, the principal part being taken down in 1690, and the present palace erected by William III. The buildings, gardens, and parks, are four miles in circumference.

Hampton, Little, a town on the coast of Sussex. It is a small seaport; seated near the mouth of the river Arun.

Hanau, a strong town of Germany, in Hesse Cassel, capital of a fertile county of the same name. It is divided into the Old and New Town, and in the former is a magnificent castle. It has manufactures of woollen stuffs, stockings, porcelain, and tobacco; and a trade in corn, iron, and timber. It is seated on the Kintzig, near its conflux with the Maine; 13 miles E. N. E. of Frankfort-on-the-Maine. Population about 12,000.

Hang-tcheou, a city of China, of the first class, capital of the province of Tche-kiang. It is 12 miles in circumference, exclusive of its suburbs, contains more than a million of inhabitants, and is the general emporium of all articles that pass between the northern and southern provinces. Here are extensive shops and warehouses; and it has a great trade in dyed cottons and nankins, silks, rice, and other grain. It is seated between a large basin, that forms the S. extremity of the Grand Canal, and a small lake called See-hou; 700 miles S. by E. of Peking. Long. 120. 20. E. lat. 30. 20. N.

Hanover, a kingdom in the N. of Germany; bounded on the N. E. by the river Elbe, N. W. by the German Ocean, S. W. by Dutch Friesland and Prussian Westphalia, and S. E. by Saxony. Since 1815 it has been divided into the provinces of Calemberg, Gottingen, Luneburg, Hoya and Diepholtz, Hildesheim, Osnaburg, Verden, Duchy of Bremen, Bentheim, East Friesland, Lingen, and the lordship of Meppen. The chief towns are Hanover, the capital, Embden, Hildesheim, Luneburg, Osnaburg, Gottingen, Zell, Clausthal, Goslar, Eimbeck, and Hameln. In the S. is the mountainous tract of the Hartz, covered with forests, and with the exception of which the whole country is a vast plain. (*See* Hartz.) Towards the N. are numerous barren heaths; but the valleys in the S. are very fertile. This country abounds in extensive mines of silver, iron, copper, and lead. The iron mines are the most valuable, and bring annually to the revenue about 115,000*l.* sterling. The principal rivers are the Elbe, the Weser, and the Embs, with their tributary streams, and the chief lakes, Steinheim and Dummer.

The corn cultivated is much the same as in Britain. The extensive heaths of Luneburg produce honey annually to the amount of 40,000*l.* The chief manufactures are thread, linen, woollens, paper, and glass. The exports are linen, iron, copper, timber, horses, and black cattle. The imports are linen, broad cloth, silk, and jewellery.

The revenue of Hanover is about 1,000,000*l.* The prevailing religion is the Lutheran; but all denominations are tolerated. The Catholics amount to 150,000, and the Calvinists to 40,000. In every village elementary schools are established, and in more populous places acadamies, or high schools, which are well conducted; as well as the university of Gottingen. The frankness, simplicity, and hospitality, mentioned by Tacitus as characteristic of the ancient Germans, is still a prominent feature in the manners of the Hanoverians, particularly the inhabitants of the heaths.

Hanover, though under the government of Great Britain for more than a century, has undergone no political incorporation. At the diet of Germany, the King of Hanover occupies the fifth rank, and has four votes at the general assembly. The king's power is limited, having a counterpoise in the nobility of Wolfenbuttle, the heads of the church, and deputies of the towns. The only order of knighthood is that of the Guelf, instituted in 1815.

Hanover was taken possession of by the king of Prussia, in 1801, and invaded by Bonaparte in 1803, and in 1806 partly ceded to the Prussians; but on the expulsion of the French in 1813, the whole electorate was restored to the king of Great Britain; and the electoral office having been annulled, he assumed, in 1815, the title of King of Hanover. On the accession of our present Queen Victoria, the sovereignty passed to Ernest, Duke of Cumberland, the Salic law not permitting a queen. Population of the whole territory, about 1,600,000, of whom about 8000 are Jews.

HANOVER, a city of Germany, and capital of the above kingdom. It is built in the form of a half-moon, and divided by the river Leine, into the Old and New Town. The Old Town presents an antiquated appearance, but the buildings in the New Town are in a better style. Hanover contains a considerable number of public buildings, among which are the elector's palace, and the public library; the latter founded by Leibnitz, to whom an elegant monument has been erected in the town. There are five Lutheran churches, besides the chapels of the Calvinists and Catholics, and a Jewish synagogue. There are small manufactures of gold and silver lace, printing of cotton, linen, brewing, vinegar, &c. Pop. about 25,000. 41 miles W. by N. of Brunswick, and 154 W. of Berlin.

HANOVER, a town of Virginia, in a county of the same name; situate on the Pamunky, the S. branch of York River; 22 miles N. N. W. of Richmond. Pop. of the county, 14,968.

HANOVER, NEW, a large island in the South Pacific Ocean, opposite the N. W. extremity of New Ireland. It is high and covered with trees, among which are many beautiful plantations. Lat. of W. end, 2. 25. long. 149. 6. E.

HAN-SAN. *See* TURON.

HANSE TOWNS, the name of certain free towns of Germany, which, being infested with pirates and robbers, entered into a mutual league for their protection. This association is supposed to have continued from the 13th to the 16th century. It consisted at first of only two towns, but it so increased in strength and reputation, that at last it consisted of 66 cities. Having at length proclaimed war against Waldemark, king of Denmark, with 40 ships, and 12,000 troops, several merchants were ordered, by the princes of their respective kingdoms, to withdraw their effects, and the association for the most part was dissolved. Several towns in Germany still retain the name, though the laws by which they are governed are disannulled.

HAN-TCHONG, a city of China, of the first class, in the province of Chen-si; on the river Han; surrounded by mountains and forests. The articles of trade are honey, wax, musk, and cinnabar. Long. 106. 35. E. lat. 32. 58. N.

HANUYE, or HANNUT, a town of Belgium, Brabant, on the frontiers of Liege and Namur; 20 miles N. N. E. of Namur.

HAN-YANG, a city of China, of the first class; in the province of Hou-quang. It is seated at the conflux of the Han with the Kian-ku. Long. 113. 44. E. lat. 30. 36. N.

HAPAEE, the name of four of the Friendly Islands, in the Pacific Ocean. They are of similar height and appearance, and connected by a reef of coral rocks, dry at low water. The plantations are numerous and extensive. These islands extend from N. to S. about 19 miles, and lie between 174. 24. and 174. 15. W. long. and lat. 19. 39. and 19. 53. S.

HAPSAL, a town of Russia, in the government of Revel; seated on the Baltic, opposite the island of Dago; 45 miles S. W. of Revel.

HAPSBURG, an ancient castle of Switzerland, on a lofty eminence, near Schintznach. What is left of it is now inhabited by the family of a peasant. This castle was the cradle, as it were, of the House of Austria, whose ancestors may be traced back to the beginning of the 13th century, when Rodolph, Count of Hapsburg, was elevated to the empire of Germany and archduchy of Austria.

HARAN, or CHARAN, a town of Asiatic Turkey, in Diarbek, known in scripture as the country of Laban. To this place Crassus retired after his defeat by the Parthians, and not far from it he was killed. It is 25 miles E. by S. of Orfa.

HARBOROUGH MARKET, a town in Leicestershire, with a market on Tuesday. It is seated on the Welland; 15 miles S. of Leicester, and 83 N. by W. of London.

HARBURG, a town of Hanover, in the duchy of Luneburg, with a strong castle. It has manufactures of silks, stockings, wax, and tobacco; and a great trade in timber with Holland. In

1757 it was taken by the French, but retaken the same year by the Hanoverians. It is seated on the Seeve, at its conflux with the Elbe, opposite Hamburg; 29 miles N. W. of Luneburg.

HARCOURT, a town of France, in the department of Calvados; 12 miles S. by W. of Caen.

HARDBERG, a town of Germany, in Styria; 12 miles S. S. W. of Friedberg, and 25 E. S. E. of Gratz.

HARDEGSEN, a town of the province of Calenberg, with a considerable manufacture of leather; 10 miles N. W. of Gottingen.

HARDENBURG, a town of Westphalia, in the duchy of Berg; 17 miles E. N. E. of Dusseldorf.

HARDENBURG, a town of Holland, in Overyssel; situate on the Vecht; 10 miles S. W. of Covoerden.

HARDERWYCK, a fortified town of Holland, in Gelderland, with a university. It has a trade in corn and wood, and is seated on the Zuyder Zee; 30 miles N. N. E. of Arnheim, and 33 E. by S. of Amsterdam. Long. 5. 8. E. lat. 52. 20. N.

HARDY, a county of Virginia, bordering on Maryland. Population, 7,622. Its chief town, Moorfields, is 228 miles N. W. by N. of Richmond.

HAREWOOD, a village in West Yorkshire, on the river Wharf; 8 miles N. of Leeds, and 204 from London. Here are the remains of an ancient castle; and in the church is the monument of Sir William Gascoyne, who committed Henry, prince of Wales, to prison, for affronting him while he sat administering justice. Near it is Harewood-house, the noble seat of Lord Harewood.

HARFLEUR, a town of France, in the department of Lower Seine. Its fortifications have been long demolished, and its harbour nearly choked up. It stands on a small river, near the mouth of the Seine; 36 miles N. W. of Rouen. Long. 0. 12. E. lat. 49. 30. N.

HARFORD, a town of Maryland, in a county of the same name; situate on Bush River; 25 miles E.N.E. of Baltimore. Population of the county, 17,120.

HARIHARA, or HURRYHUR, a town of Hindostan, in Mysore, with a fort, in which is a celebrated temple. It stands on the E. side of the Toombuddra, which here separates Mysore from the country of the Mahrattas. In the vicinity much cotton wool is cleaned and spun into thread. It is 130 miles N. E. by N. of Mangalore.

HARLEIGH, or HARLECH, a town of Wales, capital of Merionethshire, with a market on Saturday. It is a poor place, though governed by a mayor, and has a castle, built by Edward I., almost entire, on a rock projecting into St. George's Channel. It is 26 miles S. E. of Caernarvon, and 231 N. N. W. of London.

HARLEM, HAARLEM, or HAERLEM, a fortified city of North Holland, memorable for the siege it held out against the Spaniards in 1573, for 10 months, before it capitulated. It has broad regular streets, and many canals; and it is noted for its velvets, damasks, worsted stuffs, and bleaching-grounds. A communication has been opened with the Lake of Harlem, Amsterdam, and Leyden, by means of navigable canals. It was formerly strongly fortified, but public promenades have been formed of the ramparts The chief public buildings are the stadthouse, the royal palace, and some charitable institutions. It has fifteen churches, one of which, called the great church, is the largest in Holland, and has the grandest organ in Europe: it contains 8000 pipes, and 68 stops. Harlem is seated near a lake of the same name; 12 miles W. of Amsterdam. Long. 4.37. E. lat. 52. 22. N.

HARLESTON, a town in Norfolk, with a market on Wednesday; seated on the Wavenay; 16 miles S. of Norwich, and 99 N. E. of London.

HARLING, EAST, a town of Norfolk, 89 miles from London. Linen, cloth, and yarn are manufactured here.

HARLINGEN, a fortified seaport of Holland, in Friesland, of which, next to Lewarden, it is the largest and most populous. It has flourishing manufactures of paper and canvas, and is seated on the Zuyder Zee; 66 miles N. N. E. of Amsterdam, and 15 W. of Lewarden. Long. 5. 20. E. lat. 53. 10. N.

HARLOW, a town in Essex. On a common, 2 miles from the town, is a famous fair, on the 9th of September, called Harlow Bush Fair, much resorted to by the neighbouring gentry. It is 23 miles E. of London.

HARMONY, a town of Pennsylvania, in Lucerne county, on the N. side of Starucca Creek, a water of the E. branch of the Susquehannah. Between this place and Stockport, on Delaware River, distance 18 miles E S.E., there is a portage. It is 130 miles N. W. of New York, and 140 N. by W. of Philadelphia.

HARPONELLY, a town of Hindostan, capital of a district of the same name, in the Mysore country. At the partition of this country, in 1799, Harponelly was ceded to the Mahrattas. It is 28 miles S. S. W. of Bijnagur.

HARRINGTON, a small port in Cumberland, on a creek of the Irish Sea, which admits vessels of 120 tons burden up to the houses. Coal, lime, iron-stone, and fire-clay, are sent hence to Ireland and Scotland. It is 6 miles N. of Whitehaven, and 8 W. S. W. of Cockermouth.

HARRIORPOUR, a town of Hindostan, in the eastern extremity of Orissa; capital of the district of Mohurbunge. It is 90 miles N.N.E. of Cuttack, and 130 W. S. W. of Calcutta.

HARRISBURG, a town of Pennsylvania; capital of Dauphin county; situate on the E. bank of the Susquehannah; 86 miles W.N.W. of Philadelphia.

HARRODSBURG, a town of Kentucky, in Mercer county; at the head of Salt River; 30 miles S. of Frankfort.

HARROW-ON-THE-HILL, a village in Middlesex, on the highest hill in the county, commanding a delightful prospect of the metropolis; 10 miles W. N. W. of London. It has a celebrated free school.

Harrowgate, a village in the West Riding of Yorkshire; 2 miles W. of Knaresborough. It is famous for medicinal springs, one of which is chalybeate, and the other the strongest sulphurous water in Great Britain. Here are several large buildings, with a theatre, &c., for the accommodation of the numerous visitants in the summer. It is 211 miles N. by W. of London.

Hartenstein, a town and castle of Upper Saxony, in Misnia; 6 miles S. of Zwickau.

Hartford, a city of Connecticut; capital of a county of its name, and a place where the half-yearly assembly of the state is held in May. It stands on the W. side of the river Connecticut, 50 miles from its mouth. The inhabitants enter largely into the manufacturing business. On the opposite side of the Connecticut is the town of East Hartford, where are iron and glass-works. The city is divided by a small stream, called Little River, with high romantic banks, over which is a bridge; and the streets intersect each other at right angles. It is 35 miles N. N. E. of Newhaven. Population of the county, 55,629.

Hartland, a town in Devonshire, with a market on Saturday. Near it is Hartland Abbey, which includes the site and some portion of the ancient abbey. It is seated near the Bristol Channel, on a promontory called Hartland Point; 28 miles W. S. W. of Barnstaple, and 217 W. by S. of London. Lat. of the Point, 51. 1. long. 4. 30.

Hartlepool, a seaport in the county of Durham, about 6 miles N. of the mouth of the Tees; governed by a mayor, with a market on Monday. In the vicinity are several coal-mines, and a large flour manufacture. It is seated on the German Ocean, partly surrounded by rocks and hills; 19 miles E.S.E. of Durham, and 258 N. by W. of London. Long. 1. 10. W. lat. 54. 41. N.

Hartley, a seaport of Northumberland; 6 miles N. W. of Tynemouth. Its prosperity is chiefly owing to the mineral productions of the neighbourhood. A haven has been constructed half a mile to the N., whence coal is shipped to London; and a canal is cut through a solid rock to the harbour. Here are also large salt, copperas, and glass-works. About a mile to the N. W. stands Seaton Delavel, a magnificent modern structure, equalled by few in the kingdom; the interior of which was destroyed by fire a few years ago.

Hartz, a mountainous tract lying chiefly in the S. of Hanover, extending from Goslan to Hartzgerode; 70 miles long and 20 broad. It is part of the ancient Sylva Hercynia, and still covered with large forests, the timber of which is of great importance in supplying the numerous mines and forges with fuel. *See* Hanover. There are many natural curiosities in the Hartz: the caverns of Scharsfeld and Baumann are the most interesting. The magnetic rocks of Ilsenstein, and the Brocken or Blocksberg mountain also deserve notice; the latter of which commands a prospect of about 8000 square miles.

Hartzgerode, or **Harzgerode**, a town of Upper Saxony, in the principality of Annalt-Bernburg; situate near the Hartz mountains. It has a mine-office and a castle, and is 23 miles S. W. of Brenburg. Population about 1800.

Harwich, a seaport and borough on the coast of Essex, governed by a mayor; with a market on Tuesday. It has a capacious harbour, in which a great number of the largest ships may anchor, and a convenient dock for the building of men-of-war. Since the advancement of steam navigation this town has much declined, it having been formerly the port from which all Dutch and German packets sailed. The entrance into the harbour is defended by a battery, and Languard Fort. The town is seated on a tongue of land, opposite the united mouths of the Stour and Orwell, which are navigable 12 miles above the town; 42 miles E. by N. of Chelmsford, and 72 E. N. E. of London. Long. 1. 13. E. lat. 51. 56. N.

Haslemere, a town in Surrey; market on Tuesday; 14 miles S.W. of Guildford, and 42 of London.

Haslingden, a town in Lancashire, with a market on Wednesday, and considerable manufactures of linen, woollen, and cotton. It is 16 miles N. by W. of Manchester, and 204 N. N.W. of London.

Hasselt, a fortified town of Holland, in Overyssel; seated on the Vecht; 6 miles N. of Zwoll.

Hasselt is also the name of a town of Belgium, in the province of Liege; 15 miles W.N.W. of Maestricht. Population about 6000.

Hasser, or **Aseerghur**, a town and fortress of Hindostan, province of Candeish; 20 miles N. of Burhampoor.

Hassfurt, a town of Franconia, in the principality of Wurtzburg, on the N. E. bank of the river Maine; 8 miles E. of Schweinfurt. Population about 1300.

Hasslach, a town of Suabia, in the Brisgau, on the river Kintzig; 14 miles S. S. E. of Gengenbach, and 20 N. E. of Friburg.

Hastenbeck, a town of Lower Saxony, in the duchy of Brunswick, near which the French gained a victory over the duke of Cumberland, in 1757. It is 5 miles S. E. of Hameln.

Hastings, a borough on the eastern extremity of Sussex; governed by a mayor; with a market on Wednesday and Saturday. It is one of the Cinque Ports, and had once a castle, now in ruins. The harbour, formerly of much consequence, is now only an indifferent road for small vessels. The town is commanded by a strong fort, has two churches, and is a fashionable watering place, which is now the chief source of its prosperity. In 1066 a bloody battle was fought here, between Harold II. of England, and William, duke of Normandy, in which the former lost his life and kingdom. Hastings sends two members to parliament: it is seated between a high cliff towards the sea, and a high hill towards the land side; 24 miles of Lewes, and 64 S. S. E. of London. Long. 0. 38. E. lat. 50. 52. N.

HATCHY, a tributary stream of the Missisippi, which it joins in Tennessee.

HATFIELD, a town of Massachusets, in Hampshire county, on the W. side of the Connecticut, nearly opposite Hadley, to which place there is a ferry. It is 5 miles N. of Northampton.

HATFIELD, a town of Hertfordshire, with a market on Thursday. It formerly belonged to the bishop of Ely, in whose place Elizabeth resided, and was thence conducted, on the death of Mary, to ascend the throne. She procured the alienation of this manor; and James I. exchanged it with Sir Robert Cecil, afterwards earl of Salisbury, for Theobald; and on the site of the episcopal palace that nobleman built the magnificent seat called Hatfield-house. It is seated on the river Lea; 20 miles N. by W. of London.

HATHAZ, a town of Hungary, in the county of Szaboltz; 11 miles N. of Debretzin. The number of inhabitants are about 4000, and chiefly Calvinists.

HATHERLEY, or HATHERLEIGH, a corporate town in Devonshire, with a market on Friday, and a woollen manufacture. It is seated on the river Oke; 28 miles N.W. of Exeter, and 200 W. by S. of London.

HATRAS, a fort and tower of Hindostan, province of Agra; 18 miles S. S. W. of Coel, and 35 N. E. of Agra.

HATTEM, a town of Holland, in Gelderland: seated on the Yssel; 4 miles S. W. of Zwoll. Pop. about 2400.

HATTERAS, a cape on the coast of North America. It extends far into the ocean, from the coast of North Carolina, in the lat. 35. 7. N. and long 75. 30.

HATTINGEN, a town of Westphalia, in the county of Mark; seated on the Roer; 22 miles E. N. E. of Dusseldorf. Pop. about 2000.

HATVAN, a town and fort of Upper Hungary; seated on a mountain; 28 miles E. N. E. of Buda.

HATZFELD, a town and castle of Germany, in Upper Hesse, capital of a county of its name; seated on the Eder; 17 miles N. N. W. of Marburg, and 60 N. E. of Coblentz.

HAUSEN, a town of Suabia, in Brisgau; on the river Kintzig; 22 miles N. N. E. of Friburg.

HAUSRUCKVIERTEL, on the quarter of Hausruck, a circle of Upper Austria; bounded on the N. E. by the Danube, S. E. by the quarter of Traun, S. W. by Bavaria, and N. W. by the quarter of Ihn, comprising a superficies of 733 square miles. Pop. about 109,000. The chief town is Lintz.

HAUTERIVE, a town of France, in the department of Upper Garonne; seated on the Arriege; 18 miles S. of Toulouse.

HAVANNAH, a city and seaport on the N. W. part of Cuba, two miles in circumference, and the capital of the island. The houses are elegant, built of stone, and there are 11 churches richly ornamented, 2 hospitals, a dock-yard, lazaretto, and other public buildings. The harbour is capable of containing upwards of 1000 vessels, and the entrance, which is so narrow that only one ship can enter at a time, is defended by two strong forts, called the Moro and the Puntal; there are also many other forts and platforms, well furnished with artillery. A citadel of great strength is erected near the centre of the town, which contains the captain-general's palace, and where the treasure is deposited. Here, all the ships that come from the Spanish settlements rendezvous on their return to Spain. This city was taken by the English in 1762, but restored to the Spaniards in 1763. It is seated on the W. side of the harbour, and watered by two branches of the river. This town exceeds, in point of commerce, every other town in Spanish America. Pop. about 70,000. Lat. of Fort Moro, 23. 9. long. 82. 15.

HAVANT, a town in the S. E. extremity of Hampshire, with a market on Saturday; 7 miles N. E. of Portsmouth, and 66 S. W. of London.

HAVELBERG, a town of Prussia, in Brandenburg, in the Mark of Pregnitz; seated on the Havel, near its conflux with the Elbe. Many vessels, for the navigation of the Elbe, are built here, and great quantities of wood sent hence to Hamburg. It is 37 miles N. N. W. of Brandenburg. Pop. about 2000.

HAVERFORDWEST, a borough of Wales, in Pembrokeshire; seated on the side of a high hill; with a market of Tuesday and Saturday. It is a county of itself, governed by a mayor, contains three parish churches, and has a considerable trade, and sends one member to parliament. The assizes and county gaol are kept here; and it had once a wall and castle, now in ruins, the latter built in the reign of Stephen. It is seated on the Cleddaw, which is navigable for vessels of small burthen, as high as the bridge, and which soon after enters a creek of Milford Haven: 15 miles E. S. E. of St. David, and 263 W. by N. of London. Long. 5. 0. W. lat. 51. 50. N.

HAVERHILL, a town of New Hampshire, chief of Grafton county; situate on the E. bank of the Connecticut; 32 miles N. by E. of Hanover, and 110 W. N. W. of Portland.

HAVERHILL, a town of Massachusets, in Essex county, with two churches; on the N. bank of the Merrimac, over which there is a bridge. Some vessels are built here, and it has a manufacture of canvas. It is 12 miles W. S. W. of Newbury Port, at the mouth of the river, and 32 N. by W. of Boston. Pop. 4336.

HAVERIL, a town in Suffolk, on the borders of Essex, with a market on Wednesday, and a manufacture of checks, cottons, and fustians. It is 16 miles S. W. of Bury, and 59 N. E. of London.

HAVRE DE GRACE, a very important and commercial seaport of France, in the department of Lower Seine, with a strong citadel, a good arsenal, and storehouses for the construction and arming of ships. It is surrounded by lofty walls, and large ditches filled with water. The harbour has particular advantages above all others on the coast; for the water does not begin to ebb till near three hours after the full tide. It is capable of containing a great number of the largest vessels. This town was bombarded by the English, in 1694 and 1759. It is seated at the mouth of the Seine; 45 miles W. of Rouen, and 112 N. W. of Paris, of which it is the seaport. Long. 0. 6. E. lat. 49. 29. N. Pop. 21,000.

Havre de Grace, a town of Maryland, in Hartford county, on the W. side of the Susquehanna, at the head of Chesapeake Bay; 37 miles N. E. of Baltimore.

Hawaii. *See* Owhyee.

Hawarden, a town of Wales, in Flintshire, with a market on Saturday, a considerable maufacture of earthenware, and a foundry for cannon. On an eminence, between the town and the river Dee, are the remains of an ancient castle. It is 7 miles W. of Chester, and 196 N. W. of London.

Hawick, a town of Scotland, in Roxburghshire, with manufactures of carpeting, woollen stockings, and tape. It is seated on the Tiviot, where it receives the small river Slitridge, by which it is divided into two parts, and over which there are two bridges. It has a parish church, and three chapels for dissenters. It is 21 miles S. W. of Kelso, and 47 S. S. W. of Edinburgh.

Hawkesbury, a river of New South Wales, which empties itself into Broken Bay, on the eastern coast. It is navigable upwards of 100 miles, for small vessels. *See* Broken Bay.

Hawkshead, a town in Lancashire, with a market on Monday. Here is a neat townhouse, and an excellent free school, founded by Archbishop Sandys, a native of this place. It 24 miles N. N. W. of Lancaster, and 276 N. N. W. of London.

Hawkins, a county of Tennessee, bordering on Virginia; watered by the rivers of Holston and Clinch. Pop. 15,035. Rogersville, its chief town, is 230 miles E. by N. of Murfreesborough.

Haws-water, a lake in Westmoreland, S. of Penrith; three miles long, and half a mile over in some places. It is almost divided in the middle by a promontory of enclosures; so that it consists of two sheets of water.

Hay, a town of Wales, in Brecknockshire, with a market on Saturday. It had a fine castle, now demolished; and, about two miles below, is the ruin of Clifford Castle, where fair Rosamond was born. Hay is seated on the Wye, over which there is a bridge; 15 miles N. E. of Brecknock, and 156 W. N. W. of London.

Haye, a town of France, in the department of Indre and Loire. It is the birth-place of Des Cartes, and seated on the Creuse; 25 miles S. of Tours.

Hayn. *See* Grossenhayn.

Hayniehen, a town of Upper Saxony; 30 miles W. by S. of Dresden. Pop. about 2450.

Hayti. *See* Domingo, St.

Hazebrouck, a town of France, in the department of Nord; 18 miles W. of Lisle, and 19 S. of Dunkirk. Pop. 7000.

Headfort, a town of Ireland, in the county of Galway; 12 miles N. of Galway.

Hean, a town of Tonquin, on the river Hoti; 20 miles S. E. of Cachao, and 60 N. W. of the Gulf of Tonquin.

Hebrides, or Western Islands, a large cluster of islands, situated in the Atlantic Ocean, on the W. coast of Scotland, extending from the lat. of 55. 17. N. to 58. 29. They are upwards of 300 in number, and contain about 2,000,000 acres. The chief of these are Lewis and its circumjacent islands, belonging to Rossshire; Harris, N. and S. Uist, Benbecula, St. Kilda, Bara, Sky Raaza, and Egg, attached to Inverness-shire; Canna, Rum, Muck, Coll, Tirey, Mull, Jura, Colonsay, Isla, Gigha, and Cara, belonging to Argyleshire; and Bute, Arran, Greater and Less Cambray, and Inchmarnock, which compose the shire of Bute. The ancient history of the Hebrides is involved in much uncertainty. They were governed by independent princes of their own, until the destruction of the Picts by Kenneth II., and for several centuries were the resort of pirates; and their chieftains were long lawless and seditious, till they were at last brought under the control of the royal power. The influence of the independent chieftains of the Western Isles was completely destroyed by the act of parliament in 1748, which abolished all heritable jurisdictions. About 86 are inhabited.

Hebrides, New, islands in the South Pacific Ocean, lying between 14. 29. and 20. 4. S. lat. and 166. 41. and 170. 21. E. long. They were discovered by Quiros, in 1606, and considered as part of a southern continent under the name of Tierra Australia del Espiritu Santo. Bougainville visited them in 1768, and found that the land was not connected, but composed of islands, which he called the Great Cyclades. Cook, in 1774, ascertained the extent and situation of the whole group, and gave them the name they now bear. The principal islands are Tierra del Espiritu Santo, and Mallicollo, beside several of less note, some of which are from 18 to 25 leagues in circuit. In general they are high and mountainous, abounding with wood, water, and the usual productions of the tropical islands. The inhabitants are of very different appearances at different islands; but are chiefly of a slender make and dark colour, and most of them have frizzled hair. Their canoes and houses are small, and poorly constructed; and, except their arms, they have scarcely any manufacture, not even for clothing. They are, however, hospitable and good-natured, when not prompted to a contrary conduct by the jealousy which the unusual appearance of European visitors may be supposed to excite.

Hebron, a town of Syria, in Palestine, with a Christian church, said to contain the tombs of Abraham and Sarah, to which the Mahometans, as well as Christians, come on pilgrimage. Constantine built a church here, the walls of which are still standing. It is 25 miles S. of Jerusalem.

Hechingen, a town and castle of Suabia, which gives name to a branch of the family of Hohenzollern, and is the residence of the prince. It is seated on the Starzel; 4 miles N. of Hohenzollern, and 30 S. of Stutgard. Pop 2600.

Hecla, Mount. *See* Iceland.

Hedemora, a town of Sweden, in Dalecarlia

with a manufacture of gunpowder: seated on the Dahl; 30 miles S. S. E. of Fahlun.

HEDON, a town in East Yorkshire. Market on Thursday. Seated on a creek of the Humber; 6 miles E. of Hull, and 179 N. by W. of London.

HEDJAZ, or HEJAZ, a division of Arabia, extending along the Red Sea, from Arabia Petræa to Yemen. It contains Mecca, the capital, and Medina.

HEERMUND, or HINDMEND, a river of Persia, in the province of Segistan, which, after a westerly course of about 400 miles, falls into the Lake of Zereh, or Durrah.

HEIDELBERG, a city of Germany, in the circle of Lower Rhine, with a celebrated university. It has manufactures of woollen stuffs, carpets, silk stockings, velvet, and soap. It was the capital of the palatinate, and celebrated for a great tun, which held 800 hogsheads. It has undergone so many calamities by war and fire, that it is not so large as formerly. The protestant electoral house becoming extinct in 1693, a bloody war ensued, in which the castle was ruined, and the elector removed his residence to Manheim. The French took possession of this town in 1800, and in 1803 it was given to the elector of Baden. It is seated on the Neckar, over which is a bridge; 12 miles S. E. of Manheim, and 52 S. of Frankfort. Pop. about 10,000.

HEIDELSHEIM, a town of Germany, in Lower Rhine; 17 miles S. of Heidelberg. Pop. about 1800.

HEILBRONN, a town of Suabia, in the kingdom of Wirtemberg. It is a handsome place, situate in a country yielding good wine, and derives great advantages from its baths. It stands on the Neckar, 25 miles N. of Stutgard. Pop. about 6000.

HEILBRUNN, a town of Franconia, in the principality of Anspach, with a medicinal spring; 10 miles E. N. E. of Anspach.

HEILIGENBEIL, a town of Prussia, in the province of Natangen. It is famous for fine beer and white bread, and seated on a small river, which soon after enters the Frisch Haff; 32 miles S. W. of Konigsberg.

HEILIGENBERG, a town of Suabia, in the principality of Furstenberg; 12 miles N. N. E. of Constance.

HEILIGENHAFEN, a town of Lower Saxony, in Holstein; seated on the Baltic, opposite the island of Femeren, 40 miles N. of Lubec. Lat. 54. 27. N. long. 10. 48. E.

HEILIGENSTADT, a town of Lower Saxony, capital of the territory of Eichfeld, with a castle and a college. It is seated at the conflux of the Geisland with the Leine, 17 miles S. E. of Gottingen.

HEILSBERG, a town of Prussia, in the province of Ermeland. In 1703, Charles XII. of Sweden fixed his head-quarters there. It is seated on the Alla, 45 miles S. of Konigsberg.

HELDER, a town of North Holland, with a strong fort which defends the entrance of the Texel. In September, 1799, the fort was taken by the English, and the whole of the Dutch fleet lying in the Texel surrendered to them, for the service of the prince of Orange; but the English abandoned the fort in November following. It is situate on the N. W. point of the province, opposite the W. end of Texel Island; 24 miles N. of Alcmaer, and 45 N. by W. of Amsterdam. Long. 4. 34. E. lat. 53. 0. N.

HELENA, ST., an island in the Atlantic Ocean, 27 miles in circuit, belonging to the English East India Company. It lies between the continents of Africa and South America, about 1200 miles W. of the former, and 1800 E. of the latter, and was discovered by the Portuguese in 1501, on St. Helena's day. Afterward the Dutch were in possession of it till 1600, when they were expelled by the English. In 1673 the Dutch retook it by surprise; but it was soon after recovered. It has some high mountains, particularly one called Diana Peak, which is covered with wood to the very top. There are other hills also, which bear evident marks of a volcanic origin, and some have huge rocks of lava, and a kind of half vitrified flags. The climate of St. Helena is temperate, being exempt from the extremes of heat and cold, from thunder and lightning, and hurricanes. It is moist, however, and only about one day in three is illumined by sunshine. The interior valleys and little hills are covered with verdure, and interspersed with gardens, orchards, and various plantations. There are also many pastures, surrounded by enclosures of stone, and filled with a fine breed of small cattle, and with English sheep; goats and poultry are likewise numerous. The inhabitants do not exceed 3000, including near 500 soldiers, and 1600 blacks, who are supplied with corn and manufactures by the Company's ships, in return for refreshments. The town, called James-town, is small, situated at the bottom of a bay on the S. side of the island, between two steep dreary mountains. The principal street is well built, and contains about 30 houses, at the top of which two other streets branch off to the E. and W. In the latter are the barracks, the hospital, and several shops, stored with every kind of commodities. On the left side of the parade are situated the government-house and the main guard-room, in the former of which the governor and public officers reside. The church is situated in front of the gateway by which the town is entered, and near it there is a small theatre. St. Helena is particularly celebrated for having been the prison of Bonaparte, the late emperor of France, and for being the place in which he breathed his last, and where his mortal remains were deposited, till their removal to the chapel of the Invalides in Paris, October, 1840. He died in May, 1821. Lat. of James-town, 15. 55. S. long. 5. 43.

HELENA, ST., one of a cluster of islands on the coast of South Carolina, composing the parish of St. Helena in the district of Beaufort.

HELENS, ST., a village in Hampshire, at the E. end of the Isle of Wight; 2 miles N. E. of Brading. It has a bay or road, called Spithead, of considerable note, as a rendezvous for ships that are outward bound.

Helens, St., a town in Lancashire, 3 miles N. E. of Prescot, on the Liverpool and Manchester railway. In and near it are a variety of manufactures, particularly an extensive copper-work, and a still larger one at Ravenhead, for casting plate-glass. The Sankey canal begins at the coal mines here, and takes a circuitous course by Newton to the Mersey, below Warrington.

Helier, St., the capital of the island of Jersey; seated on the E. side of the Bay of St. Aubin, with a harbour, and a stone pier. It has of late rapidly increased from a small village to a respectable town. The inhabitants are computed to be 10,000, and have manufactures of woollen, stockings, and caps. At the top of the market-place is the statue of George II., and in the church, where prayers are read alternately in English and French, is a monument to the memory of Major Pierson, who fell here in the moment of victory. Besides the church, there are chapels for dissenters. There are three gazettes published weekly in French, and one in English. Long. 1. 58. W. lat. 49. 11. N. *See* Jersey.

Helier, St., a little island near the town of the same name, in the Bay of St. Aubin, on the S. side of Jersey. It took its name from Elerius, or Helier, a holy man who lived in this island, and was slain by the pagan Normans. His cell, with the stone bed, is still shown among the rocks; and, in memory of him, a noble abbey was founded here. On the site of this abbey now stands Elizabeth Castle, the residence of the governor, and garrison of Jersey. It occupies the whole island, which is near a mile in circuit, and is surrounded by the sea at every half flood; and hence, at low water, is a passage to the town of St. Helier, called the Bridge, half a mile long, formed of sand and stones.

Heligoland, or Helgoland, a group of small islands in the German Ocean, off the coast of Denmark, to which they formerly belonged; but now to Great Britain. They are situated about 28 miles from the Weser, the Elbe, and the Eyder. The principal island, which is divided into the Cliff and Lowland, is about 2½ miles in circumference, and on it is erected a lighthouse, which is visible nearly 30 miles distant. Heligoland has two good harbours, and to the E. of the smaller island, called the Downs, is good anchorage in 48 feet of water. The number of inhabitants is about 2000, who live chiefly by fishing and acting as pilots. Lat. of the lighthouse, 54. 11. N. long. 7. 55.

Heliopolis, or Matèrea, a village of Egypt, 4 miles E. N. E. of Cairo, where the French gained a decisive victory over the Turks in 1800. Here is a celebrated spring of fresh water, said to be the only one in Egypt; and, according to tradition, the Holy Family came here on their flight from Herod, and bathed the child Jesus in this fountain.

Helleh, or Hillah, a town of Asiatic Turkey, in Irak Arabi, situate on both sides of the Euphrates, with a bridge of communication. The surrounding gardens are so covered with fruit trees, particularly palms, that the town appears as if seated in a wood. From the extensive ruins around, it appears to occupy the site of the ancient Babylon. The most remarkable of these is what at first appears to be a hill, but is in reality the ruins of a pyramid of sun-dried brick, cemented with bitumen. It is called the Mujelibah, and is about 660 feet long, 450 broad, and 170 high. South from this is the kasr, or palace, of fine bricks, cemented with lime, 2100 feet square; near this is another mound, 55 feet high, 3360 feet long, and 2250 feet broad, called the Mound of Amran; another, called the Birs Nemrood, an oblong mound of the finest bricks cemented with lime, of a pyramidal form, and 200 feet high, surmounted by a tower 40 feet high. These are the only vestiges remaining of the once powerful Babylon. It is 72 miles S. by E. of Bagdad.

Hellgate, a strait near the W. end of Long Island Sound, 8 miles N. by E. of New York. It is narrow and crooked, with a bed of rocks extending quite across; but, at proper times of the tide, ships of any burden may pass through this strait.

Hellin, a town of Spain, province of Murcia, 44 miles N. W. of Murcia. Pop. about 6000.

Helmershausen, a town of Germany, in Lower Hesse, on the river Diemel; 20 miles N. of Cassel.

Helmont, a town of Dutch Brabant, with a strong castle; seated on the Aa, 17 miles S. E. of Bois-le-Duc. Pop. about 2500.

Helmsdale, a town of Scotland, in the shire of Sutherland. It stands on the river Helmsdale, which issues from several mountain lakes in Sutherlandshire, and rolls over its rocky bottom to the Ord of Caithness. At its mouth, in the German Ocean, is a good salmon fishery.

Helmsley, a town in the North Riding of Yorkshire, with a market on Saturday. It has the remains of a castle, and is seated on the Rye; 20 miles N. of York, and 218 N. by W. of London.

Helmstadt, a town of Lower Saxony, in the duchy of Brunswick, with a university; 22 miles E. of Brunswick. Pop. 5300.

Helsinburgh, a seaport of Sweden, in Schonen, seated on the Sound, nearly opposite Elsinore. Here is a ferry across the Sound to Denmark. It has manufactures of ribbons, hats, and boots. It is 5 miles N. E. of Elsinore, and 32 N. W. of Lund. Pop. about 2500. Long. 12. 48. E. lat. 56. 3. N.

Helsingfors, a seaport of Russia, in Finland, and the chief town in the province of Nyland. It has a commodious harbour in the Gulf of Finland, and an immense fortress. It is 110 miles E. S. E. of Abo. Long. 25. E. lat. 60. 5. N. Pop. 12,725.

Helsingia, or Helsingland, a province of Sweden, in Nordland, 210 miles in length, between Dalecarlia and the Gulf of Bothnia, and from 50 to 80 in breadth, and comprises a superficies of about 4470 square miles. It has extensive forests, and many iron mines. The articles of trade are iron, flax, linen, tallow, butter, tar, deal, and timber. Population about 52,000. The principal town is Hudwickswald.

HELSTON, a borough in Cornwall; market on Monday. It stands on the river Loe, near its entrance into Mount Bay, and is one of the towns appointed for the coinage of tin. A little below it is a harbour, where vessels take in their lading. It sends one member to parliament. It is 12 miles S. W. of Falmouth, and 274 W. by S. of London. Long. 5. 15. E. lat. 50. 7. N.

HELVETIA. *See* SWITZERLAND.

HELVOETSLUYS, a strong seaport of South Holland, on the S. side of the island of Voorn. Here some of the Dutch men-of-war are laid up in ordinary; and it was the general port for the English packets from Harwich to Holland. It surrendered to the French in 1795. It is 7 miles S. by W. of Briel. Long. 4. 0. E. lat. 51. 46. N.

HEMPSTED, or HEMEL HEMPSTED, a corporate town in Hertfordshire, with a market on Thursday; seated among hills; on the river Gade; 18 miles W. of Hertford, and 23 N.W. of London.

HEM, a city of Syria, surrounded by walls three miles in circuit; but the present buildings only take up about a quarter of the area in the N. W. quarter. To the S. of the town is a large ruined castle, on a high round mount, faced with stone. It is seated on a small river, which runs into the Orontes; 100 miles S. of Aleppo.

HENDERSON, a county of Kentucky, North America, on the S. E. bank of the Ohio, and intersected by the Green River. Pop. 9548. Its chief town, of the same name, is 183 miles W. by S. of Frankfort.

HENEAGAS, or INAGUA, GREAT and LITTLE, two of the most southern of the Bahama Islands. Lat. of the former, S. W. point, 20. 56. N. long. 73. 40. W.; lat. of the latter, W. point, 21. 29. N. long. 73. 6. W.

HENG-TCHEOU, a city of China, of the first rank, in the province of Hou-quang. The chief manufacture is paper. It is seated on the river Heng; 265 miles N. by W. of Canton.

HENIN LEITARD, a town of France, department of Pas-de-Calais; 6 miles N. W. of Douay. Pop. about 2400.

HENLEY-UPON-THAMES, a town in Oxfordshire, governed by a mayor; with a market on Wednesday, Friday, and Saturday. The church is a large ancient building, the tower of which was built by Cardinal Wolsey; the houses are modern, and the streets spacious. The principal trade is in corn, flour, malt, and beech wood. It is seated on the Thames, over which is an elegant stone bridge; 24 miles S. E. of Oxford, and 35 W. of London.

HENLEY, or HENLEY-IN-ARDEN, a town in Warwickshire, with a market on Tuesday; seated on the Alne; 15 miles S. by E. of Birmingham, and 101 W. N. W. of London.

HENLOPEN, CAPE, the S. W. side of the entrance of Delaware Bay. Lat. 38. 46. N. long. 75. 12. W.

HENNEBERG, a town in Upper Saxony, in a county of the same name. Some ruins of the castle of its ancient counts are yet to be seen. It is 12 miles S. S. W. of Meinengen. Population of the county, which comprises a surface of 850 square miles, about 100,000.

HENNEBON, a town of France, in the department of Morbihan, with a great trade in corn, iron, honey, &c. It is seated on the Blavet; 6 miles N. E. of L'Orient. Population about 5000.

HENRICHEMONT, a town of France, in the department of Cher; seated on the Saudre; 16 miles N. N. E. of Bourges. Pop. 2987.

HENRICO, a county of Virginia; bounded on the S. W. by James River, N. by Hanover, and E. by Charles City. Population 33,076. Its chief town, Richmond, is 123 miles S. S. W. of Washington.

HENRY, a county of Virginia, bordering on North Carolina; intersected by Irvine, or Smith's River, and the N. and S. branches of Mayo River. Population 7335. Its chief town, Martinsville, is 135 miles W. S. W. of Richmond.

HENRY, a county of Kentucky; bounded on the N. W. by the Ohio, and on the E. by Kentucky River. Population 10,015. Newcastle, its chief town, is 26 miles N. W. of Frankfort.

HENRY is also the name of a county in Alabama; bounded on the E. by Chattahooche River, which separates it from Georgia, and watered by the Choctaw and Yellow Water. Pop. 5787. Centre of the county, 190 miles S. E. of Cahawba.

HENRY, CAPE, the south cape of Virginia, at the entrance of Chesapeake Bay. Long. 76. 21. lat. 36. 57.

HEPPENHEIM, a town of Germany, in the circle of Lower Rhine; situate on the Eisbach; 12 miles E. of Worms. Pop. 3200.

HEPTONSTALL, a township in the West Riding of Yorkshire; 8 miles W. of Halifax.

HEPWORTH, a township in Yorkshire, West Riding.

HERAKLI. *See* EREKLI.

HERAT, a city of Persia, in Chorasan, or Khorassan, of which it was formerly the capital. The neighbouring country produces excellent fruit; and roses are in such plenty, that it is called Surgultzar, or the City of Roses: it has a considerable manufacture of carpets. It is situate on a river of the same name, 300 miles S. E. of Mesched, on the high road from Persia to Hindostan.

HERAULT, a maritime department of France, so named from a river which runs into the Gulf of Lyons, in the Mediterranean. It is part of the late province of Languedoc, and the capital is Montpelier. It contains 2830 square miles. Pop. 324,126.

HERBEMONT, a town of Belgium, in Luxemburg, with a castle on a mountain, near the river Semoy; 3 miles N. N. W. of Chiny.

Herbiers, Les, a town of France, in the department of La Vendee; 25 miles N. E. of La Roche.

Herborn, a town of Germany, in the circle of Upper Rhine, with a celebrated Calvinist academy, and manufactures of iron; seated on the Dille; 8 miles S. S. E. of Dillenburg. Pop. about 2000.

Herculaneum, an ancient city of Naples, totally overwhelmed by an eruption of Mount Vesuvius, in the beginning of the reign of the emperor Titus. Its situation was long doubtful, till 1711, when something of this city was discovered by a peasant digging a well in his garden; and, from 1738 to the present time, researches being frequently made by digging, a great number of manuscripts, paintings, statues, busts, domestic utensils, instruments of husbandry, &c., have been found. The village of Portici now stands on part of its site. It is 5 miles E. by S. of Naples.

Hercyna, a river of Greece, in Bœotia, with two streams, the larger called by the ancients Lethe, and the smaller Mnemosyne.

Herefordshire, a county of England, bordering on Wales, and bounded on the N. by Shropshire, E. by Worcestershire, S. by Monmouthshire and Gloucestershire, and W. by the counties of Brecknock and Radnor. It contains 556,400 acres, and is divided into 11 hundreds, and 221 parishes. It has one city, Hereford, and seven market towns, Leominster, Ross, Weobly, Ledbury, Kingston, Bromyard, and Pembridge, and sends seven members to parliament; two for the city of Hereford, two for the borough of Leominster, and three for the county. Herefordshire is almost entirely an agricultural county. About nine-tenths of the land are in a state of cultivation, and it excels in almost every department of husbandry. The face of the county is rich and picturesque, the climate is mild, and the soil is extremely fertile, which arises from the subsoil of lime-stone on which it rests. Hops are cultivated, and the apples producing the cider, for which Herefordshire is celebrated, grow in greater plenty than in any other county. Red and yellow ochres are often met with; fullers'-earth is dug near Stoke, and on the borders of Gloucestershire iron ore is found. It is watered by several streams, the chief of which are the Wye, the Monnow, and the Lug. Before the invasion of the Romans, Herefordshire was inhabited by the Silures, a brave people, who long checked the progress of the Roman arms; but being at last overcome, they retired into the fastnesses of Wales. It was a part of Mercia, one of the kingdoms of the Saxon Heptarchy.

Hereford, an ancient city, and chief town of Herefordshire; seated on the N. bank of the Wye, over which there is a stone bridge of six arches. It has manufactures of gloves, flannels, and hats. It was anciently defended by a castle, which is now destroyed, and only part of the walls remain. It has four churches, the principal of which is the cathedral, a large and venerable structure; and there are also several places of worship for dissenters. It has also an infirmary, a county gaol, a house of correction, a lunatic asylum, and a free grammar school. The city is in general well built, the streets wide, and the environs delightful. It is governed by a mayor, six aldermen, a common council of 31, a high steward, and a recorder. It sends two members to parliament. Hereford, from its situation on the borders of Wales, suffered much from the wars between that country and England, and, in later times, from the contests between the houses of York and Lancaster, and the civil broils in the time of Charles I. It has six fairs, and a market every Wednesday, Friday, and Saturday. It is 135 miles W. N. W. of London, and 30 N. W. of Gloucester.

Herenthals, a town of Belgium, in Brabant, on the river Nethe; 20 miles N. E. of Louvain.

Herford, or **Herforden**, a town of Westphalia, in the county of Ravensberg, with a nunnery belonging to the Protestants of the confession of Augsburg. It has a trade in ale and linen. It is seated on the Werra, at the influx of the Aa; 20 miles S. W. of Minden, and 11 miles E. N. E. of Ravensburg. Pop. about 6000.

Hericourt, a town of France, in the department of Upper Saone; 15 miles S. E. of Lure, and 27 E. of Vesoul.

Herjadalen, a district on the N. of Sweden, now included in Gefleborgstæn, and bounded on the W. by Norway, and N. by Jamptland. It consists of an extensive valley, watered by the Ljusna and Ljunga. It is mostly covered with wood, and abounds in cattle, game, and fish. Territorial extent, 3200 square miles, with a population of only 4000.

Herinnes, a town of South Brabant, with 3300 inhabitants; 17 miles S. W. of Brussels.

Herisau, a town of Switzerland, in the canton of Appenzel, with manufactures of fine linen and muslin; 12 miles N. W. of Appenzel, and 8 S. W. of St. Gall. Pop. about 6500.

Heriura, a town of Hindostan, in Mysore; seated on the Vedawati; 22 miles W. N. W. of Sera.

Herkimer, a town of New York, chief of a county of the same name; situated on the N. side of Mohawk River; 81 miles W. N. W. of Albany. Population of the county 55,869.

Hermanstadt, a strong city of Transylvania, and a bishop's see. It has a large church, built by Maria Theresa, with a globe and steeple not easily described. In the great square is the house of the governor, in the best German style, containing many good pictures. It is seated on the Szeben; 230 miles E. S. E. of Buda, and 67 S. S. E. of Colosvar. Pop. 13,500.

Hermsdorf, two large villages of Silesia, the one 38 miles N. by W. of Breslau, and the other 40 miles W. by S. of the same place.

Hermstadt, a town of Silesia, in the principality of Wolau, on the river Bartch; 10 miles N. W. of Trachenberg, and 38 N. by W. of Breslau.

HERMUND, or HELMUND, a river of Central Asia, province of Afghanistan, Cabool. It is fordable during the summer, but in winter becomes a considerable river, half a mile broad. It flows into the Sea of Zerra, after a W. course of 350 miles.

HERNE BAY, a hamlet in the parish of Herne, county of Kent, at the mouth of the river Thames, which has arisen, in a few years, to be an attractive watering place. A pier was erected in 1831, upwards of 3000 feet in length; and other accommodations, requisite for a considerable population, have sprung up with great rapidity. It is 8 miles N. of Canterbury.

HERNGRUND, or HERRENGRUND, a town of Upper Hungary; seated among mountains with rich mines of copper; 28 miles N. by E. of Schemnitz, and 4 miles N. N. W. of Neushol.

HERNHUT, a village in Lusatia; 12 miles N. N. W. of Zittau. It was founded in 1722, by some persecuted Moravian brethren, in the fields belonging to Count Zinzendorf, whom they considered as their bishop and father, and they were for some time called Hernhutters, as this place continued their principal nursery.

HERNOSAND, a seaport of Sweden, in Angermania; situated on an island in the Gulf of Bothnia, which is joined to the continent by a bridge. It was formerly a staple town, and has still a considerable trade in linen. In 1710, 1714, and 1721, it was burned by the Russians, It is 240 miles N. by W. of Stockholm, Long. 17. 53. E. lat. 62. 38. N.

HERNOSAND is also the name of an extensive government of Sweden, of which the preceding is the capital; comprising the provinces of Angermannland, Jamptland, and Medelpad, containing 18,000 square miles, with only 100,000 inhabitants.

HERO, NORTH and SOUTH, two islands in Lake Champlain, North America.

HERSTAL, or HERISTAL, a town of Belgium, in Liege; seated on the Maese; 4 miles N. of Liege. Pop. 4750.

HERTFORDSHIRE, an interior county of England, extending, in a north-easterly direction, about 32 miles in length, and 16 in mean breadth; bounded on the S. by Middlesex, E. by Essex, N. by Cambridge and Bedford, and W. by Buckingham, and part of Bedford. It contains 337,920 acres, is divided into eight hundreds, 135 parishes, and has 19 market towns, the chief of which are St. Albans, Hertford, Ware, and Royston. It sends seven members to parliament, three for the county and two for each of the two boroughs. The N. part is hilly, forming a scattered part of the chalky ridge, which slopes towards London. A number of clear streams take their rise from the S. side. Flint stones are scattered in great profusion over the face of this county, and beds of chalk are frequently to be met with. The soil, however, with the aid of proper culture, is favourable to wheat and barley, which come to as great perfection here, as in any part of the kingdom. The W. part is, in general, a tolerably rich soil, and under excellent cultivation. The principal rivers are the Lea, Stort, and Coln, and the artificial one called the New River. The Grand Junction Canal passes through the S. extremity of the county. Corn is the principal object of agriculture, and a great trade in malt is carried on. The manufactures are inconsiderable.

HERTFORD, or HARTFORD, a borough, and the capital of Hertfordshire, with a market on Saturday. It is seated on the Lea, which is navigable for barges, as it was once for ships. In 879 the Danes erected two forts here, for security of their ships; but Alfred turned the course of the river, so that their vessels were left on dry ground. Edward, the eldest son of Alfred, built a castle here, which has been often a royal residence. The town is governed by a mayor, and had formerly five churches, but now only two. Here is a fine hospital, belonging to Christ's Hospital, London; also a noble shire hall, and a large county gaol. About a mile to the E. is a basin of water called Chadwell, which is the head spring of the New River; and, at the distance of 2½ miles on the London road, is the East India College, for the education of 100 students. Hertford is 21 miles N. of London: it sends two members to parliament.

HERTFORD, a county of North Carolina, bordering on Virginia, and bounded on the N. E. by Chowan River. Pop. 7434.

HERTZBERG, a town of Lower Saxony, in the principality of Grubenhagen; with manufactures of arms and iron tools; steated near the Hartz mountains; 21 miles S. S. W. of Goslar.

HERTZBERG, a town of the duchy of Saxony, with a trade in saltpetre, wool, and cloths; seated on the Elster; 14 miles N. N. E. of Torgau, and 28 S. E. of Wittemberg.

HERVE, a town of Belgium, in the province of Liege; 8 miles W. N. W. of Limburg.

HERZEGOVINA, a large tract of country, stretching along the E. shore of the Adriatic, from N. W. to S. E. The southern part belongs to the Turks, and the rest to the Austrians.

HESDIN, a strong town of France, in the department of Pas de Calais; seated on the Canche; 12 miles S. E. of Montreuil. Population, including the suburbs, 5000.

HESSE CASSEL, an electorate in the W. of Germany; bounded by Hanover, the Prussian States, Franconia, Nassau, and Hesse Darmstadt; comprising an extent of 4350 square miles. The chief towns are Cassel, the capital, Marburg, Fulda, and Hanau. It is chiefly composed of Upper and Lower Hesse, the grand duchy of Fulda, the district of Hanau, and the lordship of Schmalchalden. The country is rather mountainous, and produces abundance of wood and minerals, among which are copper, silver, iron, cobalt, salt, pit-coal, and marble. Population 602,700, of whom the greater number are Calvinists.

HESSE DARMSTADT, or the grand duchy of Hesse, a district of Germany, belonging to Hesse Cassel; like which, it is far from being compact; being divided by a strip of land into two parts, stretching from E. to W. It contains about 4000 square miles. The chief towns are Darmstadt and Giessen. Its acquisitions by the French revolution were considerable. It is mountainous, like Hesse Cassel, and is equally productive of minerals. The principal rivers are the Rhine, Maine, Lahn, Niddu, and the Ietir. Pop. 781,900, of whom the greater number are Lutherans.

HESSE HOMBURG, a small principality of Germany, near Frankfort, belonging with the title of landgrave, to the younger branch of the House of Hesse Darmstadt. Pop. 21,000.

HETTON-LE-HOLE, a township in the parish of Houghton-le-Spring, county of Durham: it contains extensive collieries.

HETTSTADT, a town of Upper Saxony, on the Wipper; 9 miles N. of Eisleben.

HEUKELEM, or HOEKELUN, a town of South Holland; seated on the Linghe; 5 miles N. E. of Gorcum.

HEUSDEN, a strong town of South Holland; seated on the Meuse; with a castle. It was taken by the French in 1705: it is 8 miles N. W. of Bois le Duc.

HEXHAM, a town of Northumberland, with a market on Tuesday, and a trade in tanned leather, shoes, and gloves. It had formerly a famous abbey, some parts of which yet remain. Near this place, in 1463, was fought a battle between the Houses of York and Lancaster, in which the latter was defeated. Hexham is seated on the river Tyne, a little below the junction of the North Tyne with the South, and on the Newcastle and Carlisle railway; 22 miles W. of Newcastle, and 285 N. N. W. of London.

HEYDENHEIM, a town of Suabia, in the duchy of Wirtemberg, with a castle; on the river Brenz; 16 miles N. N. E. of Ulm.

HEYDENSFELD, a town of Franconia, on the river Maine; 3 miles S. of Wurtzburg.

HEYMERTSEN, a town in the circle of Lower Rhine; situate on the Erfft; 11 miles S. of Cologne.

HEYST-OB-DEN-BERG, a town of Belgium, in South Brabant; on the Nethes; 11 miles N.E. of Mechlin. Pop. 5300.

HEYTESBURY, a town of Wiltshire, England; 17 miles W. N. W. of Salisbury, and 92 from London. The town consists of one well-built street, and has a large woollen manufacture.

HICKMANS, a county of Tennessee; bounded on the N. by Duck River.

HIELMAR, a lake in Sweden, 40 miles in length.

HIERES, a town of France, in the department of Var; seated near the Mediterranean Sea; but its harbour being choked up, it is now much decayed. It is 9 miles E. of Toulon. Lat. 43. 7. N. long. 6. 7. E.

HIERES, a cluster of islands in the Mediterranean, on the coast of France, opposite the town of Hieres. The four principal ones are called Porquerolles, Porteros, Bagneau, and Titan.

HIERO. *See* FERRO.

HIGHAM FERRERS, a town in Northamptonshire; market on Saturday. It had formerly a castle, now in ruins; 15 miles E. N. E. of Northampton, and 65 N. N. W. of London.

HIGHGATE, a village in Middlesex, contiguous to the metropolis; seated on a hill $5\frac{1}{2}$ miles N. W. of St. Paul's Cathedral. Here Lord Chief Baron Cholmondely built a free school in 1562, which was enlarged in 1570 by Sandys, bishop of London, who also added a chapel. In the vicinity are several elegant villas, the residences of wealthy citizens.

HIGHLANDS, an appellation applied to the mountainous tract in the N. and N. W. part of Scotland, by which it is distinguished from the Lowlands in the E. and S. E. It is divided into W. and N. Highlands; the former comprehending the shires of Argyle and Bute, and part of Perth and Dumbarton, with the islands attached to them; and the latter containing the shires of Inverness, Ross, Sutherland, the districts of Atholl, Rannoch, and the isles of Sky, Lewis, and those annexed to Inverness, and Ross. Its extent is 200 miles in length, and 90 in mean breadth. The proportion of arable land is small, and is found chiefly on the borders of the lakes and rivers.

HIGHWORTH, a town in Wiltshire; 77 miles from London; situated near the vale of the White-horse.

HIGUEY, a city on the E. part of the island of St. Domingo; formerly of some importance, but now greatly decayed. It is situated on a river of the same name; 90 miles E. by N. of St. Domingo.

HIJELLEE, the chief town of a district of the same name in Bengal; seated on an island near the western bank of the river Hoogly, near its mouth. It has an extensive salt manufactory. Lat. 21. 51. N. and long. 88. 7.

HILBURGHAUSEN, a town of Upper Saxony, in the principality of Coburg. It is subject to the Duke of Saxe-Hilburghausen, who has a palace here: it is seated on the Werra; 20 miles N. N. W. of Coburg.

HILDESHEIM, a city of Hanover; capital of a principality of the same name. It was lately an imperial city, and a bishop's see. It is divided into the Old and New town: it is seated on the Irneste; 20 miles S. E. of Hanover.

HILLAH. *See* HELLEH.

HILLSBOROUGH, a county of the United States of North America, in New Hampshire; bordering on Massachusets. Pop. 53,884.

HILLSBOROUGH, the chief town of Orange county, North Carolina; 41 miles N. W. of Raleigh. It is also the name of several townships.

HILLSBOROUGH, a town of Ireland, in the county of Down; 20 miles S. W. of Belfast.

HIMMALEH, HIMALAYA, or SNOWY MOUNTAINS, a vast chain of mountains, extending from the 73rd degree of E. long. to the borders of China, and separating Hindostan from Tibet and Tartary. They are the Imaus and Emodus of the ancients, and are said to exceed the Andes in height, in some places. The highest points are Dhawalagiri, 27,000 feet; Jumnautri, 25,500 feet; the Letghur peak, 24,261 feet, and several above 22,000 feet. The general formation of them is gneiss.

HINCHINBROOK ISLE, an island on the W. coast of America, in Prince William's Sound. Lat. 60. 24. N. and long. 145. 36. to 146. 10. W.

HINCHINBROOK ISLE, one of the New Hebrides, in the Pacific Ocean. Long. 168. 38. E. lat. 17. 25. S.

HINCKLEY, a town in Leicestershire, governed by a mayor, with a market on Monday. It has a large church, with a lofty spire; and had formerly a castle and walls, traces of which are still to be seen. Here is a considerable manufacture of common stockings, thread, and worsted. It is seated on an eminence; 12 miles S. W. of Leicester, and 99 N. N. W. of London.

HINDELOPEN, a town of the Netherlands, in Friesland; seated on the Zuyder Zee; 21 miles S. S. W. of Lewarden.

HINDIA, a town of Hindostan, a capital of a country of the same name, in Candeish; situate on the S. bank of the Nerbudda; 90 miles N. N. E. of Burhampour.

HINDON, a town in Wiltshire, England; market on Thursday; 15 miles W. of Salisbury, and 97 S. by W. of London.

HINDOSTAN, (Persian, *hindoo*, black, and *stan*, a place or country,) or INDIA, and by the aborigines called Bharatta, a region of Asia, which comprises all the countries between the mountains of Tartary and Tibet on the N., Bootan, Assam, and the Bay of Bengal on the E., the Indian Ocean on the S., and the same ocean and Persia on the W. But this country must be considered under the three grand divisions of Hindostan Proper, the Deccan, and the Peninsula. Hindostan Proper includes the provinces of Bengal, Bahar, and all those that lie to the N. of the river Nerbudda; the principal of which are Agimere, Agra, Allahabad, Cashmere, Delhi, Guzerat, Lahore, Malwa, Moultan, Oude, and Sindy. The Deccan has been extended to the whole region S. of Hindostan Proper; but, in its most restricted sense, it means only the countries situate between Hindostan Proper and the river Kistna. *See* DECCAN. The tract S. of the river Kistna is generally called the Peninsula; although its form does not authorize that appellation: it includes a small part of Golconda, Mysore, and the Carnatic, with Madura, and other smaller districts; the W. coast being called that of Malabar, and the E. that of Coromandel. The sikhs possess Lahore, part of Moultan and Delhi; the King of Candahar, Cashmere, Cabul, Sindy, and part of Moultan; Berar and Orissa, Malwa, Candeish, Visiapour, and part of Agimere and Guzerat, are in the possession of the Mahrattas; and the nizam of the Deccan possesses Golconda, part of Dowlatabad, and Berar.

The British possessions are Bengal, Bahar, part of Allahabad and Orissa, the Northern Circars, the Jaghire in the Carnatic, the countries north and south of Calicut, Bombay, and the island of Salsette. The allies of the British are the rajahs of Mysore, Tanjore, Madura, Travancore, Trichinopoly, the nabobs of Oude and Arcot, and the district of Cochin. The principal rivers are the Ganges, the Indus, Nerbudda, Puddar, Taptee, Caggar, Mahanuddy, Godavery, Kistna. The chief mountains are the Himmaleh, the western and eastern Gauts, and those which divide Bengal from Ava. The number of inhabitants is about 134,000,000, of which the greater proportion are idolaters, and are divided into three great sects: the first worship the Triad, Brahma, Vishnu, and Siva; the second are the followers of Boodh, whose principal tenet is the doctrine of transmigration; the Jains are the third, who chiefly worship Pariswanath; the other class of inhabitants are Mahometans, of whom there are about the eighth part of the number Hindoos. To give an idea of the modern revolutions in the empire of Hindostan, it is proper to observe, that from a pure Hindoo government, it became, at last, a Mahometan state, and continued to be so, under various dynasties, till the beginning of the 18th century. The first irruption of the Mahometans was in the year 1000. From this period the provinces of Hindostan were held rather as tributary kingdoms, than as provinces of the same empire; and the conquest of the Deccan, in particular, was for ages an object of considerable importance to the emperors. In 1389 the Mogul Tartars, under the conduct of Timur, or Tamerlane, invaded Hindostan; but the conquest of the country was not effected till 1525, by Sultan Baber, one of his descendants, who, from this circumstance, was the founder of the Mogul dynasty; and hence Hindostan has been called the Mogul Empire, and its chief, the Great Mogul. The illustrious Acbar, his son, failed in his attack upon the Deccan; an attempt in which many of his successors were equally unfortunate, and which tended, in the sequel, to the decline and dissolution of the empire. In 1615, emperor Jehanguire, his son, received Sir Thomas Roe, as the first English ambassador, and the Portuguese had by this time acquired considerable settlements in Bengal and Guzerat. In the reign of his grandson Arungzebe, which lasted from 1660 to 1707, the empire attained its full extent; his authority reached from 10 to 35 degrees in lat. and nearly as much in long., and his revenue exceeded 32,000,000*l.* sterling. But in the course of 50 years after his death, a succession of weak princes and wicked ministers reduced this astonishing empire to very narrow limits, and deprived it of all its power and splendour. In consequence of the intrigues of the nizam of the Deccan, Nadir Shah, the Persian usurper, invaded Hindostan in 1738. In the reign of Achmed Shah, successor of Mahomed Shah, the entire division of the empire took place; nothing remaining to the House of Tamerlane but the city and small territory of Delhi. The last imperial army was defeated by the Rohillas, in 1749. The Jats, a Hindoo tribe, founded a state in Agra; Oude was seized by Mahomed Kooli; and the Mahrattas, beside their ancient domains in the Deccan, obtained great part of Malwa, Guzerat, Berar, and Orissa. The Mogul empire was now become nearly nominal; and the emperors, from this period, must be regarded as of no political consequence, otherwise than as their names and persons were made use of, by different parties, to promote their own views; for the name and person of the emperor retains a considerable degree of veneration among the bulk of the people of Hindostan. Achmed was deposed in 1753, and his successor was deposed and murdered in 1760. He was succeeded, however, by his son Shah Ahlum, who was alternately dependent on the contending powers, and more particularly upon the English, who obtained from him a grant of the provinces of Bengal, Bahar, Orissa, and the Circars. This prince died in 1806, and was succeeded by his second son, Acbar Shah. The Mahometans or Mussulmans, whom the English improperly call Moors, are represented to be of a detestable character. The Hindoos, or Gentoos, are of a black complexion; their hair is long, their person straight and elegant, and their countenance open and pleasant. They differ materially from all other nations, by being divided into tribes or castes. The four principal tribes are the Brahmins, Soldiers, Labourers, and Mechanics; and these are subdivided into a multiplicity of inferior distinctions. There are Brahmins of various degrees of excellence, who have the care of religion allotted to them, and are held sacred by the rest; some of these acknowledge the errors that have crept into their religion, own one Supreme Being, and laugh at the idolatry of the multitude, but insist upon the necessity of working upon the weaknesses of the vulgar; yet the generality of them are as ignorant as the laity. Such as are not engaged in worldly pursuits are a very superstitious, innocent people, who promote charity as much as they can, both to man and beast; but those who engage in the world are generally the worst of all the Gentoos; but, persuaded that the waters of the Ganges will purify them from their sins, and being exempt from the utmost rigour of the courts of justice, (under the Gentoo governments,) they run into much greater excesses. The soldiers are commonly called rajah-poots; that is, descended from rajahs. They are much more robust than the rest, have a great share of courage, and a nice sense of military honour, which consists, among them, in fidelity to those they serve. Fighting is their profession; they readily enter into the service of any that will pay them, and will follow whereever he leads; but should their leader fall in the battle, their cause is at an end, and they run off the field, without any stain on their reputation. The English East India Company have many battalions of them in their service; they are called sepoys, and are clothed and are disciplined in the European manner. The Labourers include farmers, and all who cultivate the land. The Mechanics include merchants, bankers, and all who follow any trade; these again are subdivided into each profession. Beside these, are the Hallachores who cannot be called a tribe, being rather the refuse of all the tribes. They are a set of unhappy wretches, who perform all the vilest offices of life, bury the dead, and carry away every thing that is polluted. All the different tribes are kept distinct from each other by insurmountable barriers: they are forbidden to intermarry, to cohabit, to eat with each other, or even to drink out of the same vessel with one of another tribe. Every deviation from these points subjects them to be rejected by their tribe, renders them polluted for ever, and obliges them, from that instant, to herd with the Hallachores. The members of each caste adhere invariably to the profession of their forefathers; from generation to generation the same families have followed, and still continue to follow, one uniform manner of life. To this may be ascribed that high degree of perfection conspicuous in many of the Indian manufactures; and also that striking peculiarity in the state of Hindostan, the permanence of its institutions, and the immutability in the manners of the inhabitants. The Hindoos vie with the Chinese in respect to the antiquity of their nation. Their institutions of religion form a complete system of superstition, upheld by every thing which can excite the reverence of the people. The temples consecrated to their deities are magnificent; their religious ceremonies splendid; and the absolute dominion which the Brahmins have obtained over the minds of the people is supported by the command of the immense revenues with which the liberality of princes, and the zeal of pilgrims and devotees, have enriched their pagodas. The dominion of religion extends to a thousand particulars which, in other countries, are governed by the civil laws, or by taste, custom, and fashion. Their dress, their food, the common intercourses of life, their marriages, and professions, are all under the jurisdiction of religion. The food of the Hindoos is simple, consisting chiefly of rice, ghee (a kind of imperfect butter), milk, vegetables, and oriental spices. The warrior caste may eat of the flesh of goats, sheep, and poultry. Other superior castes may eat poultry and fish; but the inferior castes are prohibited from eating flesh or fish of any kind. Their greatest luxury consists in the use of the richest spiceries and perfumes, of which the great people are very lavish. They esteem milk the purest of food, because they think it partakes of some of the properties of the nectar of their gods, and because they esteem the cow itself almost as a divinity. Their manners are gentle. They are taught by their religion that matrimony is an indispensable duty in every man who does not entirely separate himself from the world from a principle of devotion; and, as none but male descendants can perform the obsequies to the manes of their ancestors, it is thought an irreparable calamity to die without male issue. Scarcely any state can be more degrading than that of Hindoo females. Till three years after the nuptial age, a girl is entirely at the disposal of her father. When married, she is immured in her husband's dwelling; her dependence upon him is perpetual and entire; she is not permitted to eat in his presence, and is considered, not as a companion to aid him in enduring the evils of life, but as a slave to bear children, and be subservient to his rule. Polygamy is tolerated; but the females, except among the Nairs, are not permitted to marry a second time. A husband can dismiss his wife at any time; but there is nothing that can dissolve the wife from her matrimonial engagement. The inhuman custom of women burning themselves on the funeral pile of their deceased husbands has, however, been recently prohibited in the presidencies of Fort William and Madras; and the progress of Christianity affords reason to hope for the speedy abolition of other revolting practices. The code of Gentoo laws, with their sacred books, the Veidam and the Shaster, are written in the Sanscrit language, which is very copious and nervous, although the style of their best authors is wonderfully concise. Hindostan, towards the N., is pretty temperate, but hot towards the S.; and it rains almost constantly for three months in the year. Its products are diamonds and other precious stones, silks, spices, aromatics, drugs, maize, rice, and sugar; and the chief manufactures are muslins and calicoes. But these and various other particulars will be found under the names of its different provinces, cities, towns, mountains, and rivers, described in this work.

HINGHAM, a town in Norfolk, with a market on Thursday; 14 miles W. of Norwich, and 99 N. E. of London.

HINGHAM, a town of Massachusets, in Suffolk county, with two churches; seated on a small bay; 19 miles S. E. of Boston.

HING-HOA, a city of China, of the first rank, in the province of Fo-kien. The vicinity furnishes abundance of rice, li-chi, and silk.

HINTERGERSDOF, a town of Saxony, in Meissen; 8 miles E. of Freyberg.

HINZUAN, JOANNA, or ANJOUAN, one of the largest of the Comorro Islands; situated off the eastern coast of Africa. It is of a triangular form; and the whole island appears to have undergone the action of a volcano, the rocks being every where volcanized. It is entirely mountainous, but is covered with vegetation, which even reaches to the summit of the highest conical hill. The coasts can be approached with safety. The sovereign of Hinzuan takes the title of sultan, and formerly ruled over the whole group of the Comorro Islands. His subjects view him with the most profound respect, and never approach him without kneeling, and touching the earth with their forehead. The nobles are on a familiar footing with the king, and must be consulted on many occasions. The natives are in general tall, robust, and well made; they have long black hair, piercing eyes, and are of a colour between olive and black. They profess Mahomedism; but the native African worship of fetiches is still very prevalent. They are courteous and hospitable, and all shipwrecked mariners have been received with the greatest kindness. The pine-apples are most delicious, and the other fruits are excellent. Yams and sweet potatoes are in abundance; also goats and poultry. The bullocks are of a moderate size, and are excellent food. This island is often frequented by Europeans, and particularly by English vessels, for the sake of procuring water and provisions. The commodities in demand are arms, toys, looking-glasses, shirts, and blue and red cloth. Saltam is the capital. Long. 41. 30. E. lat. 12. 54. S.

HIO, a town of Sweden, in Gothland; seated on the Lake Wetter; 145 miles S. W. of Stockholm.

HIORRING, a decayed town of Denmark, in North Jutland; 27 miles N. N. W. of Aalborg.

HIRSCHBERG, a town of Prussian Silesia, in the principality of Jauer; famous for its mineral baths. In the neighbourhood are extensive bleaching-grounds; and, next to Breslau, it is the most considerable trading town in Silesia. It is seated on the Bober; 23 miles S. W. of Jauer.

HIRSCHFELD, a town of Germany, in Lower Hesse; capital of a principality of the same name, depending on a famous abbey, which was secularized in favour of the House of Hesse Cassel. It is seated on the Fulda; 34 miles S. by E. of Cassel. Long. 9. 42. E. lat. 50. 50. N.

HIRSCHOLM, a town of Denmark, in the island of Zealand, with a castle; 12 miles N. of Copenhagen.

HIRSCHORN, a town of Hesse Darmstadt, with a castle; seated on the Neckar; 7 miles E. of Heidelberg.

HISPANIOLA. *See* DOMINGO, ST.

HISSAR, a town of Hindostan, in the country of Delhi; capital of a district of the same name; seated near the river Sursoory; 112 miles W. N. W. of Delhi. Long. 75. 40. E. lat. 29. 5. N.

HIT, a town of Syria, near which is a spring of naphtha and bitumen. It stands on a river of the same name, which soon after joins the Euphrates; 100 miles W. by S. of Bagdad.

HITCHIN, a town in Hertfordshire, with a market on Tuesday, and a great trade in malt. It has a handsome parish church, and several meeting-houses; 15 miles N. N. W. of Hertford, and 34 N. W. of London.

HOAI-KING, a city of China, of the first rank, in Ho-nan; 320 miles S. W. of Peking. Long. 112. 34. E. lat. 35. 6. N.

HOAI-NGAN-FOO, a city of China, of the first rank, in Kiang-nan. It is seated in a marsh, and enclosed by a triple wall. The suburbs extend to the distance of a league on each side of a canal, and form, at their extremity, a kind of port on the Hoang-ho. The canal, being above the level of the city, occasions perpetual danger of inundation; 515 miles S. S. E. of Peking. Long. 118. 47. E. lat. 53. 30. N.

HOANG-HO, a large river of Asia, also called the Yellow River, from the quantity of clay which it devolves. Its sources are two lakes, situate among the mountains of that part of Tartary known by the name of Kokonor, in about 35. N. lat. It pursues a N. E. direction to about 42. N. lat.; and, after running due E. it suddenly bends S., penetrating China to a latitude nearly parallel to its source; and then it pursues an easterly direction till it enters the Eastern Ocean, 100 miles to the N. of the mouth of the Kian-ku. The length of its course is estimated at 2000 miles. At 70 miles from the sea, where it is crossed by the Great Canal, the breadth is little more than a mile; but it is so rapid and shallow as to be scarcely navigable.

HOBART-TOWN, or HOBARTON, the capital of Van Diemen's Land, in Buckingham county. It is seated near the mouth of the river Derwent, which is here about 2 miles wide. The city, is about 1½ mile square; seated at the foot of Mount Wellington, which is 3750 feet high. The streets are straight, and cross each other at right angles, and have a number of handsome houses. The public buildings are numerous, and some of them are handsome. The government-house is near the harbour, or Sullivan's Cove; it is an irregular building, without architectural pretensions. The other principal buildings are the court-house, church, colonial hospital, barracks, &c. The view of the city, &c. from the harbour is magnificent, and the trade is prosperous. Population, about 11,000 or 12,000, including 3500 convicts. Lat. 42. 56. S. long. 147. 27. E.

HOCHBERG, a castle of Baden; situate on a mountain; 2 miles N. E. of Emmeddingen.

HOCHHEIM, a town of Central Germany, in the duchy of Nassau; surrounded by vineyards, and famous for its wine called Hock; 15 miles S. W. from Frankfort. Pop. 1910.

HOCHST, a town of Germany, in Nassau, with an extensive tobacco manufacture; seated on the Maine; 6 miles W. of Frankfort, and 17 N. E. of Mentz.

HOCHSTAT, a town and castle of Bavaria, famous for a signal victory gained near it by the Duke of Marlborough, in 1704, and which the English call the battle of Blenheim, from a village three miles S. W. of this place. It is seated on the Danube; 17 miles S. W. of Donawert.

HOCHSTAT, a town and castle of Bavarian Franconia, in the principality of Bamberg; on the river Aisch; 23 miles S. S. W. of Bamberg.

HOCKHOCKING, a town of the United States, Ohio, in the county of Fairfield. Pop. 3079.

HODDESDON, a town in Hertfordshire, with a market on Tuesday; seated near the river Lea; 4 miles S. E. of Hertford, and 17 N. by E. of London.

HODEIDA, a town of Arabia, in Yemen, with a harbour for small vessels, on the Red Sea; 90 miles N. N. W. of Mocha. Long. 43. 30. E. lat. 14. 10. N.

HOEI-TCHEOU, a city of China, of the first rank, in Kiang-nan; famous for its tea, varnish, and japanned wark; 625 miles S. of Peking.

HOEI-TCHEOU, a city of China, of the first rank, in Quang-ton; 1010 miles S. of Peking.

HOEKELM. *See* HEUKELUM.

HOFF, a town of Bavaria, in the principality of Bayreuth, with manufactures of cotton, linen, and fine paper. The adjacent country has quarries of excellent marble. It stands on the Saale; 32 miles N. N. E. of Bayreuth.

HOFF, a town of Moravia, in the circle of Olmutz, with a great trade in wool; 23 miles N. E. of Olmutz.

HOG ISLAND, one of the smaller Shetland Islands, near the E. coast of the Mainland.

HOG ISLAND is also the name of several other islands. One in Pamtico Sound, near the coast of North Carolina; long. 76. 36. W. lat. 34. 56. N. On the E. side of Lake Champlain; 9 miles long, and about 3 broad. Near the coast of Virginia; long. 75. 42. W. lat. 37. 30. N. In Rhode Island, in Naraganset Bay; 2 miles in circumference. In the Eastern Sea, near the coast of Palawan; long. 11. 36. E. lat. 10. 18. N. In the Eastern Sea; 40 miles in length, and 3 in breadth, 60 miles W. of Sumatra; long. 95. 50. E. lat. 2. 30. N. In the Eastern Sea, lying off the N. E. extremity of Java; 20 miles in circumference; long. 114. 55. E. lat. 7. 5. S. In the Eastern Sea, near the W. coast of Saleyer; 15 miles in length, and 6 in breadth; long. 120. 45. E. lat. 6. 12. S. On the W. coast of India, not far from Pigeon Island; long. 74. 36. E. lat. 14. 2. N.

HOG ISLANDS, a cluster of small islands near the S. W. coast of Ireland, and county of Kerry, between Ballinaskelling Bay and the mouth of Kenmare river; 4 miles from Hog's Head.

HOGUE, CAPE LA, the N. W. point of Normandy, near which Admiral Rooke burnt 13 French men-of-war, in 1692. Long. 1. 52. W. lat. 49. 45. N.

HOHENBERG, an ancient castle of Suabia, in a county of its name, now belonging to Wirtemberg; situate near the source of the Neckar; 10 miles S. E. of Rothweil.

HOHENLINDEN, a town of Bavaria, near which the French gained a great victory over the Austrians, in 1800. It is 22 miles E. of Munich.

HOHENLOHE, or HOLACH, a district of Franconia, abounding in wine, corn, wood, and cattle. It now belongs to the kingdom of Wirtemberg. The castle of its ancient counts stood close by the village of Holach, near Uffenheim. The chief town is Ohringen.

HOHENMAUT, a town of Bohemia, on the river Meyta; 13 miles E. of Chruddin.

HOHENSTEIN, an ancient castle of Saxony; situate on a mountain, at the foot of which is the village of Neustadt; 5 miles N. N. E. of Nordhausen.

HOHENTWIEL, a fortress of Wirtemberg, surrounded by the county of Nullenburg. Its fortifications were destroyed by the French, in 1800. It stands on a mountain; 9 miles E.N.E. of Schaffhausen.

HOHENZOLLERN, a town of Germany, in a principality of the same name, with a castle on a mountain, the seat of the ancient counts of Hohenzollern. It is seated on a branch of the Neckar; 16 miles S. by W. of Tubingen. Long. 9. 8. E. lat. 48. 28. N.

HOHNSTEIN, a town of Saxony, on the river Mulda; 11 miles N. E. of Zwickau.

HO-KIEN, a city of China, of the first rank, in the province of Pe-tcheli; situate between two rivers; 85 miles S. of Peking. Long. 116. 23. E. lat. 38. 40. N.

Hola, a town of Iceland, and a bishop's see; at the mouth of a river, on the N. coast. Long. 19. 20. W. lat. 65. 40. N.

Holbeach, a town in Lincolnshire, with a market on Saturday, and a considerable trade in corn and wool; 12 miles S. by E. of Boston, and 109 N. by E. of London.

Holbeck, a seaport of Denmark, in the island of Zealand, with a good harbour, from which great quantities of corn are annually exported; 30 miles W. of Copenhagen.

Holdsworthy, a town in Devonshire, with a market on Saturday; seated near the canal from Bude Harbour; between two branches of the Tamar; 43 miles W. by N. of Exeter, and 214 W. by S. of London.

Holland, kingdom of. *See* Netherlands.

Holland, an important province of the kingdom of Holland, which has often given name to the Seven United Provinces; but these appellations have been merged in the title of the kingdom, and Holland is now, properly, the maritime peninsula of that name. It is divided into two parts, North and South Holland; and is bounded on the N. and W. by the German Ocean, on the E. by the Zuyder Zee and the ci-devant state of Utrecht, and on the S. by the Meuse and Dutch Brabant; extending from lat. 51. 40. to 53. 10. N.; its long. is about 180 miles E. of London. It contains 90 walled towns, besides many others, and above 400 villages. Before the Revolution, in 1795, six large cities had seats in the states-general; viz. Dort, Haerlem, Delft, Leyden, Amsterdam, and Gouda. The number of inhabitants was estimated at 800,000. They also reached this number in 1801; but in 1817 they had been reduced by the war to 748,000. The division into the two governments of South and North Holland is recognized by the constitution of 1814; the former contains 1170 square miles, with 438,202 inhabitants, and is divided into the six districts of the Hague, Leyden, Rotterdam, Dort, Gorcum, and the Briel; while North Holland, which, in official papers, is called by its ancient name of West Friesland, contains 930 square miles, with 393,916 inhabitants, and is divided into the four districts of Amsterdam, Haerlem, Hoorn, and Alkmaar. The whole province is a continued flat; and, but for the constant care in forming ditches and canals, it would be hardly capable of cultivation. Some part of it lies even lower than the sea, from which it is secured by dikes, 25 or 30 feet high, and as many broad at top. The climate is moist and variable, and in various places, particularly in North Holland, unfavourable to health. The winters are severe, and the rivers are almost every season rendered unnavigable, for several weeks together, by the ice. The soil is rich, consisting of a deep fat loam; but, owing to the humidity of both soil and climate, tillage is very limited. Wheat, madder, tobacco, hemp, and flax are raised, but the chief agricultural wealth of the country consists in the pastures, which feed great numbers of cows; the making of butter and cheese being a principal occupation. The meadows are generally under water during the winter, and the inhabitants only discharge them from it by mills adapted, as in the fenny parts of England, to this particular purpose. The Hollanders are affable, industrious, laborious, absorbed in trade, excellent sailors, moderate politicians, and lovers of liberty. Holland is said to have derived its name from the vast and thick forests of wood with which it was at one time covered; *Holtlant*, in German, signifying woodland. In the middle ages it was governed by its counts or earls; in the 15th century it became subject to the House of Burgundy; it passed afterwards to Austria; and, finally, joined the other provinces that declared for independence. On the invasion of Holland by the French, in the beginning of 1795, the stadtholder with his family took refuge in England. Holland was subsequently under various forms of French domination. At length the people became weary of this connexion. The events of 1813 had weakened the power that bound them; the people rose; their fetters were broken; and "Orange boven," (up with the House of Orange,) resounded through the country. A provisional government was formed at Amsterdam, on the 18th of November. William Frederick, of Nassau and Orange, landed from England at the close of the same month, entered Amsterdam on the 2nd of December, and was proclaimed Sovereign Prince of the United Netherlands, on the following day. By the act of congress, signed at Vienna on the 31st May, 1815, the seventeen provinces of the Netherlands, which had formerly been subject to the dukes of Burgundy, were re-united under the Prince of Orange, as William I., king of the Netherlands. *See* Netherlands.

Holland, a strong town of E. Prussia; seated near the river Weeske; 14 miles S. S. E. of Elbing.

Holland, New. *See* Australia.

Hollodale, a river of Scotland, in the county of Sutherland, which rises in the mountains on the borders of Caithness, and flows N. into a bay of the North Sea, forming, for several miles, in the latter part of its course, the boundary between the two counties.

Hollywood, a town of Ireland, in the county of Down; situate on Belfast Lough; 105 miles from Dublin.

Holm Cultram, a town in Cumberland, sometimes called Holm-Abbey, from the celebrated abbey that formerly stood here, the remains of which have been converted into the parish church. It is seated near the mouth of the Waver; 12 miles N. of Cockermouth, and 310 N. N. W. of London.

Holmsworthy, a town in Devonshire; seated between two branches of the river Tamar; 214 miles from London.

Holstebroe, a town of Denmark, in North Jutland; situate on a shallow river which runs into the North Sea. The principal trade is in corn, oxen, and horses. It is 24 miles W. of Wiburg, and 68 N. of Ripen.

Holstein, a duchy at the N. extremity of

Germany, belonging to Denmark; 100 miles long, and 50 broad; bounded N. by Sleswick, E. by the Baltic and the duchy of Saxe-Lawenburg, S. by the duchies of Bremen and Luneburg, and W. by the German Ocean. Its principal rivers are the Elbe, the Eyder, and the Stor. It is a fruitful country, and well seated for trade, having some considerable harbours, particularly those of Hamburg, Lubec, and Kiel; and from the latter is a canal to the Eyder, at Rensburg, by which there is a free navigation from the Baltic to the German Ocean. Population, 360,000, most of whom are Lutherans.

Holston, a river of the United States, which rises in the Allegany mountains, in Virginia, and flows S. S. W. into the state of Tennessee, where it takes a more southerly course to Knoxville, and 35 miles below that town is joined by the Clinch, when their united waters take the name of Tennessee. It is navigable for boats of 25 tons upwards of 100 miles. On its banks are several iron-works; and the adjacent country abounds with iron ore, and has sundry lead mines.

Holt, a town in Denbighshire, North Wales; on the river Dee.

Holt, a town in Norfolk, with a market on Saturday, and an excellent free school, founded by Sir John Gresham. It is situate in a fertile district; 24 miles W. N. W. of Norwich, and 119 N. E. of London.

Holy Cross, a village in Ireland, county of Tipperary; on the river Suir. Here are the ruins of a beautiful Cistercian abbey.

Holy Island, an island on the coast of England; 8 miles S. E. of Berwick-upon-Tweed, but belonging to the county of Durham. It is three miles long and two broad; the soil rocky and full of stones; and at low water it is accessible by horses and carriages. It has a town called Kilo, and a castle on a high rock, under which is a commodious harbour, defended by a blockhouse. On this island are considerable remains of a stately monastery, called Lindisfarne; and here was anciently a bishop's see, removed, with the body of St. Cuthbert, first to Chester-le-Street, and afterwards to Durham.

Holyhead, a seaport and cape of Wales, in the isle of Anglesey. It derives its principal support from the expenditure of passengers to and from Ireland, being the usual place of embarkation for Dublin, and the station of the government packets to and from that city, distant about 20 leagues. In the neighbourhood is a large vein of white fullers'-earth, and another of yellow. Among the principal objects of interest are the venerable ruins of a hermitage, two chapels, and the remains of a Dutch wall; these, with the lighthouse and suspension bridge, attract the attention of strangers. The church, near the verge of the cliff, is a handsome structure of the 13th century: here are also four chapels for dissenters, a free school, and some almshouses. Market on Saturday. It is 86 miles W. by N. of Chester, and 267 N.W. of London. Long. 4. 40. W. lat. 53. 23. N.

Holywell, a town of Wales, in Flintshire, the best in North Wales. It has a neat parish church, and four places of worship for dissenters. From its vicinity to the mines, and the extensive manufactures carried on in the neighbourhood, it is become the most flourishing town in the county. Its name was derived from the famous well of St. Winifred, concerning which so many fables and superstitious notions have prevailed, but which is certainly a very remarkable spring, bursting out of the ground with great impetuosity, at the foot of a hill, and discharging upwards of 20 tons of water every minute. The waters have long since lost their reputation for miraculous healing powers, but are much esteemed by the manufacturer, being now applied to the purpose of turning several mills for the working of copper, making brass wire, paper, and snuff, and spinning cotton. It is 10 miles E. of St. Asaph, and 207 N. W. of London.

Holzapfel, a tn. of Germany, in the duchy of Nassau. It is situate on the Lahn, at the foot of a mountain, on which is the tower of an ancient castle, the original seat of the princes of Nassau; 4 miles N. E. of Nassau.

Holzminden, a town of the states of Brunswick, in Wolfenbuttel, with considerable ironworks. It is seated at the conflux of the Holz with the Weser; 28 miles N. W. of Gottingen.

Homburg, a town of Germany, in Hesse-Cassel, with an iron forge and a glass manufacture; 20 miles S. of Cassel.—Also a town of Prussia, in the duchy of Berg; 48 miles S. E. of Dusseldorf.—And a town of Bavaria, in Deux Ponts, seated on a mountain; 5 miles N. W. of Deux Ponts.

Ho-nan, a province of China; bounded on the N. by the provinces of Pe-tcheli, and Chan-si, E. by Kiang-si and Chantong, S. by Hou-quang, and W. by Chensi. As every thing that can contribute to render a country delightful is found in this province, that as it is situate almost in the centre of the empire, the Chinese call it Tong-hoa, the Middle Flower. Besides Caifong, its capital, it contains 8 cities of the first class, and 102 of the second and third.

Ho-nan, a city of China, of the first class, in the province of Ho-nan; 360 miles S. W. of Peking. Long. 112. 9. E. lat. 34. 44. N.

Honawera, or Onore, a town of Hindostan, in Canara; seated in an inlet of the sea, which spreads into a lake, and includes a number of islands. It was formerly a place of great commerce, but was demolished by Tippoo after he had recovered it by the treaty of Mangalore. Here is now a custom-house, and a few shops; also some merchants who live scattered near the banks of the lake, and sell rice, pepper, cocoa, and betelnuts, &c., to the trading vessels that come from Goa, Rajapura, and Bombay. It is 50 miles N. by W. of Kundapura, and 84 S. S. E. of Goa.

Hondtchoote, a town of France, department of Nord, near which a part of the allied troops were surprised and defeated in 1793. It is 7 miles S. E. of Dunkirk.

Honduras, a province of the republic of Guatimala; 400 miles long, and 150 broad; bounded on the N. by a bay of its name, E. by the Atlantic,

S. by Nicaragua, and W. by Guatimala and Vera Paz. The country consists of mountains, valleys, and plains, watered by numerous rivers; and is exceedingly fertile, but unhealthy to Europeans. The vineyards bear thrice a year; and the soil, in many parts, yields three crops of maize: other productions are wheat, peas, cotton, wool, logwood, with excellent pastures, honey, wax, and provisions of all kinds. Honduras was formerly one of the most populous countries in America, but at present, though so fertile, is almost deserted. The capital is Valladolid, or Comayaguas.

Honduras Bay, is that gulf of the Caribbean Sea between the peninsula of Yucatan and Cape Honduras. It is well known, from the colonies settled on it by the British for the cutting down of mahogany and dye-woods. The trees are cut at the wet season of the year, and after being dragged from the forest to the banks of the rivers, they are made into rafts and floated to the shore. The growth of the logwood here is extremely rapid; so much so, that it is said to attain maturity in five or six years, when it is cut and sent to Europe in logs. Besides the mahogany and logwood tree, Honduras Bay produces two or three kinds of the mangrove, as the red, white, and black. Cedars are large and abundant, and are commonly used in ship-building. The palmetto, the sapadilla, and the sea-grape trees, are all found very useful; as are also the bullet-tree, the iron-wood-tree, the calabash-tree, and the button-wood-tree. The althea grows at a considerable distance from the coast, and is generally made into rafts for floating the log-wood to the sea. The tree that exudes the resinous substance called caouchouc, or elastic gum, from which Indian-rubber is made, grows plentifully in several provinces of Guatimala, particularly in various parts of Honduras. In addition to these may be enumerated the locust-tree, the fustic, the cocoa-nut-tree, the cabbage, and the silk-cotton trees; besides which, both trees and shrubs of a medicinal nature grow in great variety and profusion. The soil which has been brought under cultivation is extremely fertile, and the climate is superior to a great part of the American continent. The shores abound with aquatic birds of different kinds. Myriads of swallows are found in some parts, particularly in Honduras, during the periodical rains. The humming-bird is seen, in most of its splendid varieties, and the oxilis, one of the most minute and beautiful of this elegant tribe, is very common. The number of fish, insects, and reptiles, is also great.

Honfleur, a seaport of France, in the department of Calvados. The harbour is very capacious, at the mouth of the Seine: and its principal trade is in lace. It is 8 miles N. of Pont l'Eveque, and 110 N. W. of Paris. Long. 0. 15. E. lat. 49. 24. N.

Hong Kong, an island near Canton, on the S. coast of China. It consists of high conical mountains, composed of primitive rocks, principally of trap and basalt; the only produce being a small quantity of rice and fruits; the vegetation consist of ferns, and some other plants of small growth, giving it, at a distance, an appearance of fertility, though it is in reality remarkably barren. It is inhabited by a few fishermen, and is described as having been the resort of Chinese pirates; thus giving the name of "Ladrones," which is applied to the group of which it forms a part. It was one of the first places resorted to by the Portuguese, and was ceded to Britain as a trading port in 1842.

Honiton, a borough in Devonshire, celebrated for the manufacture of broad lace. The church is half a mile from the town; but it has also a chapel belonging to the Establishment, and three meeting-houses for Independents, Baptists, and Presbyterians. A fire happened here in 1747, which consumed three-fourths of the town; and another in 1765, destroyed nearly 180 buildings. It is situated in a delightful vale, on the river Otter; 16 miles E. of Exeter: it sends two members to parliament. Market on Saturday.

Hooghly, a river of Hindostan, formed by the two westernmost branches of the Ganges, named the Cossimbazar and Jellinghy, which unite at Nuddea. It flows by Hooghly, Chinsura, Chandernagore, and Calcutta, to the Bay of Bengal, and is the only branch of the Ganges that is commonly navigated by ships.

Hooghly, a river of Hindostan, in Bengal, now nearly in ruins, but possessing many vestiges of former greatness. In the beginning of the 18th century it was the great mart of the export trade of Bengal to Europe. It is seated on the river Hooghly; 25 miles N. of Calcutta.

Hoogstraten, a tn. of Belgium, in Brabant; 15 miles N. of Herentals.

Hoorn, or Horn, a seaport, of North Holland, on the Zuyder Zee; with manufactures of woollen cloths and carpets, and a considerable trade in cattle, butter, cheese, herrings, and other fish. It is 20 miles N. N. E. of Amsterdam.

Hope, East, a village of Wales, in the county of Flint; contributory, with Flint and Caergurle, in returning one member to parliament. Here are the ruins of a castle.

Hope, a village of the United States, in New Jersey. It is 20 miles N. E. of Easton—Also a Moravian settlement of North Carolina, in Surrey county.

Hope, a river of the island of Jamaica, which runs into the sea, 5 miles S. of Kingston.

Hope Advance Bay, a bay in Hudson's Strait; 100 miles W. of Cape Chidley.

Hope Bay, a bay at the N. E. corner of Nootka Sound.

Hope Cape, a cape of Hudson's Bay, at the entrance of Repulse Bay.

Hope Islands, two small islands on the coast of New Holland. Lat. 15. 41. S.

Horaidan, a town of Persia, in the province of Farsistan; 76 miles N. W. of Shiras.

Horb, a town of Wirtemburg, with a considerable trade in woollen goods; seated on the Neckar; 21 miles W. S. W. of Tubingen.

Horeb, a mountain of Arabia Petrea, a little to the W. of Mount Sinai. Here are two or three fine springs, and a great number of fruit-trees.

Horn, a town of Austria, with a trade in beer made of oats; seated on the Tiffer; 48 miles W. N. W. of Vienna.

Horn, a town of the Netherlands, in the province of Liege; 3 miles W. N. W. of Ruremonde.

Horn, Cape, the southern extremity of South America, forming part of Hermite Island; on the coast of Terra del Fuego. Long. 67. 30. W. lat. 55. 46. S.

Hornachos, a town of Spain, in Estremadura, near the river Malachel; 30 miles S. S. E. of Merida.

Hornberg, a town of Baden, in the Black Forest, with a fortress on a mountain; seated on the Gutlash; 12 miles N. W. of Rothweil.

Hornburg, a town of Prussian Saxony, on the Ilse; 8 miles S. of Wolfenbuttel.

Hornby, a small town in Lancashire; situated on the bank of the Wenning; 9 miles N. E. of Lancaster. The principal object of attraction is Hornby Castle, erected, as it is supposed, by Nicholas de Mont Begons, soon after the Conquest. Here was formerly a weekly market on Friday, which has merged in the fair for cattle every alternate Tuesday.

Horncastle, a tn. in Lincolnshire; situated in an angle formed by the confluence of the Bane and the Waring; with a market on Saturday It was a Roman station, and part of the wall of the castle is still remaining. Here are a church, four meeting-houses, a dispensary, &c. It is 21 miles E. of Lincoln, and 136 N. of London.

Hornsey, a town in East Yorkshire, nearly surrounded by an arm of the sea, and much resorted to during the bathing season. Near it is a mere, two miles long and one broad, famous for its pike and eels. It is 16 miles N. of Hull, and 193 N. of London.

Hornsey, a village in Middlesex; 5 miles from London. Here was anciently an episcopal palace, and the manor has belonged to the see of London for many ages.

Horsens, a seaport of Denmark, in North Jutland, on the Cattegat, having manufactures of woollen goods, and a considerable trade. It is 20 miles S. S. W. of Arhusen.

Horsforth, a township in Yorkshire, with a manufacture of woollen.

Horsham, a borough in Sussex. Market on Saturday, noted for fine poultry. Here is the county gaol; and the spring assizes are held here. It returns one member to parliament. It is seated on the Adur; 20 miles N. W. of Brighton, and 36 S. of London.

Horstmar, a town of Westphalia, with a castle and a collegiate church; seated on an eminence; 15 miles N. W. of Munster.

Hospital, a town of Ireland, in the county of Limerick. The ruins of a castle are still visible, which was built on the site of a commandery of the Knights Hospitallers.

Hottentots, Country of the, or **Hottentotia**, a large region in the S. extremity of Africa, extending N. from the Cape Colony, beyond the mouth of Orange River, and westward to about the meridian of 27. 30. which divides it from Caffraria. The Hottentots are as tall as most Europeans, but are more slender; and the characteristic mark of this nation is the smallness of their hands and feet compared with the other parts of their body. Their skin is of a yellowish brown hue, resembling that of a European who has the jaundice in a high degree. There are not such thick lips among the Hottentots as among their neighbours the Negroes, the Caffres, and the Mozambiques; and their mouth is of the middling size, with the finest set of teeth imaginable. Their heads are covered with hair more woolly, if possible, than that of the negroes. With respect to shape, carriage, and every motion, their whole appearance indicates health and content. They are excellent swimmers and divers, and practise bathing several times in the day. The women braid or plait their hair as an additional elegance, and adorn themselves with necklaces of shells. Both the men and women generally go bareheaded, and seldom wear any shoes. Both sexes wear rings on their arms and legs, chiefly made of thick leather straps, cut in a circular shape; but rings of iron, copper, or brass, of the size of a goose-quill, are considered more genteel. Girls are not allowed to use any rings till they are marriageable. Their habitations are adapted to their wandering pastoral life: they are merely huts, resembling a round beehive, from 18 to 24 feet in diameter, and so low that a middle-sized man cannot stand upright in them. The fire-place is in the middle, and they sit or lie round it in a circle. The low door is the only place that admits the light, and the only outlet that is left for the smoke. The order of these huts, in a craal, or clan, is most frequently in the form of a circle, with the doors inward; by which means a kind of yard is formed, where the cattle are kept at night. From the atrocious system of indiscriminate slaughter practised toward them by their oppressors, the Dutch boors, or settlers, their numbers have been much reduced: they do not number more, at present, than about 12,000. Their condition has also been much degraded, from their hardships. They are now considered to be admirably adapted for agricultural pursuits, and are found dispersed among the British colonists as menial servants. Their appearance has more of the Tartar than of the African race, and their language is very peculiar, differing from all other languages, in the singular clucking sound in most of their words. They are now under the protection of the British government, and their condition is gradually ameliorating. Among the tribes inhabiting their territory is that of the Boschmen, Bosjesmans, or Bushmen, who leads a predatory life, and are thought to be of the same stock as the Caffres. They differ from the Hottentots considerably in their stature and appearance: they are about 4 ft. 6 in. to 4 ft. 9 in. in height, and are perfectly black. Their principal town is Lattakoo, or Litakun, in lat. 27. 10. S. long. 24. 30. E. They excel the Caffres in their arts, and are accustomed to the chase from their earliest infancy; and acquire surprising dexterity in the use of the bow and poisoned arrow. They are governed by hereditary chiefs, who have but little authority.

The other tribes are the Namaquas, Griquas, &c. - In 1778, Lieutenant Paterson visited a Hottentot village, in Little Namaqua Land, in the N. W. part of the country; it consisted of 19 huts, and about 150 inhabitants. The ensign of authority worn by their chief was a cane with a brass top, given to him by the Dutch East India Company. The Hottentots amused them, part of the night, with music and dancing; their visitors, in return, treated them with tobacco and dacka, or hemp leaves, which they prefer even to tobacco. Their music was produced from flutes, made of the bark of trees, of different sizes. Another tribe of Hottentots, near the mouth of Orange River, were observed by Lieutenant Paterson, in his journey to the N. W. in 1799. Their huts were loftier, and thatched with grass, and were furnished with stools made of the back-bones of the grampus. Their mode of living was in the highest degree wretched, and they were apparently the most dirty of all the Hottentot tribes. Their dress was composed of the skins of seals and jackals, the flesh of which they eat. Since these periods there have been many travellers in most parts of this regions; particularly Mr. Campbell, a missionary, who made a large portion of the N. E. quarter of this territory known to Europeans; and, more recently, by Dr. Smith and others, in the N.; and Sir J. Alexander, who travelled along the W. coast of Africa as far as Walvisch Bay. To the E., and on the banks of Orange River, is another tribe, called Koras, who may be reckoned to rank higher than any of the other Hottentots known in the S. of Africa. Their features are of a superior cast; they are more cleanly in their appearance, and neater in their dress and domestic utensils; their huts are also constructed with greater care, and with a view of being more durable. They seem to be a mixed breed, between the Hottentot and Caffre. The Hottentots, in general, are described as a mild, simple, affectionate, and inoffensive race; but extremely indolent in their habits, and limited in their faculties. But Christianity has been introduced through the exertions of the Moravians and other missionaries, who have endeavoured, with some degree of success, to ameliorate the condition even of some of the wilder tribes. Of the seventy species of antelope enumerated by naturalists, 50 belong to Africa, and nearly 30 are found on the Karroos, or steppes of this territory: they are principally gregarious, and are extremely cautious. Among the species are the spring-bok, which migrates in countless multitudes in search of pasturage; the gemsbok, which has remarkably long sharp horns, and, when attacked by dogs, will sit on its hind quarters, and defend itself; the koedo, an animal rather larger than a deer, of a mouse-colour, with three white stripes over the back, and the male having very large twisted horns. Three species of the horse genus, the zebra, the dauw, and the quagga, are found on the arid plains; and the graceful zerapha, or camelopard, is occasionally found in small herds, feeding on the prickly acacias of the desert. Lions are abundant and formidable; the leopard and cheetah, the lynx, and the hyæna, prey on the numerous antelopes, and other animals. Among other species may be enumerated the rhinoceros, horse, domestic horned cattle, common sheep, and a peculiar species of sheep covered with hair instead of wool. The hippopotamus, or river-horse, is frequently seen here. Among the birds are vultures, ostriches, (whose eggs are excellent food,) and the loxia, a species of gregarious bird. Among the insects are a species of termites, which do no injury to wood, as in the East Indies, but, by raising a number of hills, they impede the progress of vegetation. The black, or rock scorpion, is nearly as venomous here as any of the serpent tribe, of which there are numerous kinds.

Houat, an island of France, between Belleisle and the Continent. It is 10 miles in circumference, and is defended by a fort.

Houdain, a town of France, department of Pas de Calais; 6 miles S. of Bethune.

Houdan, a town of France, department of Seine-et-Oise; 21 miles W. of Versailles.

Houghton-le-Spring, a town in the county of Durham; 260 miles from London. There is a chalybeate spring in the vicinity; from which it derives its name.

Houghton, West, a township in Lancashire, a manufacturing place of great trade.

Hounslow, a town of Middlesex, with a market on Thursday; situate on the edge of a heath, of the same name, on which are many vestiges of ancient encampments; 10 miles W. by S. of London.

Hou-quang, a province of China, which occupies nearly the centre of the empire, and is divided into two parts, the N. and S., by the river Kian-ku. It is a flat, open country, watered by lakes, canals, and rivers; and has plenty of wild fowl and cattle. The soil is remarkably fertile; gold is found in the sands of the rivers; and there is such a variety of all sorts of commodities, that it is called, by the Chinese, the storehouse of the empire. It contains 15 cities of the first class, and 114 of the second and third. Vou-tchang is the capital.

Hourn, Loch, an arm of the sea, on the W. coast of Scotland, in Inverness-shire, extending 20 miles inland from the Sound of Skye.

Houssa, a considerable town of Negro-land; capital of a country of the same name, extending along the N. side of the Niger. It is 200 miles E. of Tombuctoo. Long. 4. 20. E. lat. 16. 10. N.

Hou-tcheou, a city of China, of the first class, in the province of Tche-kiang. The quantity of silk manufactured here is almost incredible, and it is the chief place for making writing pencils. It stands near a large lake, called Tai; 110 miles S. E. of Nan-king. Long. 120. 15. E. lat. 30. 55. N.

Howden, a town in E. Yorkshire, with a market on Saturday. It gives name to a small district called Howdenshire. The bishops of Durham had formerly a palace here, the remains of which are now occupied as a farmhouse. Here is a large church, like a cathedral, part of which is in ruins. It is seated near the Ouse, and the Hull and Selby railway; and surrounded by a level country in a high state of cultivation; 21 miles S. S. E. of York, and 175 N. by W. of London.

Howe, Cape, the promontory at the S. E. end of New Holland.

Howth, a village in Ireland, county of Dublin; seated on a peninsula called the Hill of Howth, on the N. side of Dublin Bay, and which has a fine harbour for a packet station.

Hoxter, a fortified town of the Prussian states, on the Weser; 23 miles E. by N. of Paderborn.

Hoy, one of the Orkney Islands, situate between the island of Pomona and the N. coast of Caithness-shire. It is 9 miles long and 6 broad. Here is a stupendous rock, called the Beary; and on the W. coast is a great conic hill, called Hoy Head, which is a seamark. Long. 3. 9. W. lat. 58. 46. N.

Hoya, a town of Hanover, capital of a county of the same name. It is seated on the Weser; 37 miles N. W. of Hanover. Long. 9. 20. E. lat. 52. 47. N.

Hoyer, a town of Denmark, in the duchy of Sleswick; celebrated for its oyster-fishery; 4 miles W. of Tonderen.

Hoyerswerda, a town and castle of Lusatia, on the Black Elster; 17 miles N. N. W. of Bautzen.

Hoym, a town and castle of Saxony, in the principality of Anhault; seated on the Godel, at its junction with the Selke; 7 miles E. of Quedlingburg.

Hradisch, a town of Moravia, capital of a circle of the same name, which produces excellent wine. It is a frontier fortress towards Hungary, and stands on an island in the river Moraw; 30 miles S. S. E. of Olmutz. Long. 17. 30. E. lat. 49. 7. S.

Huahine, one of the Society Islands, in the South Pacific; 30 leagues from Tahiti. It is 21 miles in compass, and has a commodious harbour, called Owharra Bay, on the W. coast. Long. 151. 8. W. lat. 16. 44. S.

Hubert, St., a town of the Netherlands, in Luxemburg, with a celebrated abbey; seated in the forest of Ardennes, on the rivulet Homme; 14 miles W. of Bastogne.

Hubertsberg, a town of Saxony, in Meissen, with a magnificent hunting-seat, built by Augustus III., then electoral prince. It is 22 miles E. of Leipsic.

Huddersfield, a borough in West Yorkshire, with a market on Tuesday. Here is a large circular hall, in which narrow and broad cloth, serges, kerseymeres, &c., manufactured in the town and neighbourhood, are weekly exposed to sale. It stands on the Colne, 3 miles from the Calder, from which it has a canal to Ashton-under-Line. In addition to the parish church, two others have been erected—Trinity Church, in 1819, and Christ Church, completed in 1824; and there are several meeting-houses for the different denominations of dissenters. The charitable institutions are numerous, and a mechanics' institute was established in 1825, to which a valuable library has since been attached. It returns one member to parliament. It is 41 miles S. W. of York, 25 N. E. of Manchester, and 189 N. N. W. of London.

Hudson, a city of New York, in Columbia county. The streets are spacious, and cross each other at right angles; and the houses are supplied with water brought in pipes from a spring 2 miles distant. The trade is considerable, and vessels of the largest size can unload here. It is seated on an eminence, on the E. side of Hudson River; 30 miles S. of Albany, and 120 N. of New York.

Hudson, a river of the United States, which passes its whole course of 250 miles in the state of New York. It rises between the Lakes Ontario and Champlain, flows S. by Lausenburg, Albany, and Hudson, and enters the Atlantic Ocean at New York. It is navigable for ships to Hudson, and for sloops to Albany.

Hudson's Bay, a bay of North America, lying between 51. and 69. N. lat.; discovered in 1610 by Captain Henry Hudson. The entrance of the bay from the ocean is between Resolution Isle on the N., and the Labrador coast on the S., forming the extremity of the strait distinguished by the name of its great discoverer. On the S. is James Bay: on the E. side it is bordered by Labrador, on the S. W. by New South Wales, and on the N. W. by New North Wales. In 1670 a charter was granted to a company, for the exclusive trade of this bay. The territories claimed by this company extend from 70 to 115. of W. long., and as far as 49. N. lat.; thus comprehending a length of 1300 or 1400 geographical miles, by a medial breadth of 350 miles. Over this large extent of country are established a number of forts, or houses, for the purpose of trading with the thinly scattered tribes of Indians, for furs and peltry, in exchange for blankets, ammunition, &c. These furs, &c. are exported principally to Britain. The Indians, who subsist entirely on the produce of the chase, have preserved their characteristics and habits much more than those of the more southern regions. The Esquimaux are a different and widely extended race, inhabiting the shores and islands of the Arctic Ocean and Greenland. The principal settlement of the Company is Fort Churchhill, on the W. shore of the bay. In December, 1770, Mr. Hearne set out from Prince of Wales Fort, to explore the Copper-mine River; he arrived at this river in June, 1771, and traced it to the Arctic Ocean, in long. 119. W. lat. 72. N. In 1789 Mr. Mackenzie explored the Mackenzie river to its mouth, in long. 135. W. lat. 71. N. In 1839-40 the extreme N. W. coast of America, and also the coasts between the Copper-mine and Back rivers, have been explored for the Company, by Messrs. Dease and Simpson, who have thus completed our knowledge of the northern boundaries of the continent.

HUDWICKSWALD, a seaport of Sweden, the chief town of Helsingia, with a good harbour, on the Gulf of Bothnia. The inhabitants carry on an advantageous trade in timber, flax, linen, butter, fish, &c. It is 185 miles N. by W. of Stockholm. Long. 17. 46. E. lat. 62. 6. N.

HUE, or HUEFO, the capital of Cochin China, with a royal palace. The inhabitants blacken their teeth, thinking it a shame to have them white, like dogs'. It is seated in a beautiful plain, and divided into two parts by a large river, 30 miles from its mouth, in the China Sea. Long. 107. 25. E. lat. 16. 25. N. Pop. 20,000.

HUELVA, a town of Spain, in Andalusia, on the coast of the Atlantic, between the mouths of the Odiel and Tinto; 53 miles W. of Seville.

HUEN, or HVEEN, an island in the Baltic, with one scattered village; 3 miles from the coast of Sweden, and 9 miles S. S. E. of Elsinore. It is 6 miles in circumference, and was ceded by the Danes to the Swedes, in 1658. *See* URANIBURG.

HUESCA, an old fortified town in the N. of Arragon, in Spain; situated in a plain on the Isuela. Its works have gone into ruins, but it is still a bishop's see, has a university, two large schools, a cathedral, and 6800 inhabitants, with manufactures of cloth and leather. It is 30 miles N. E. of Saragossa.

HUESCAR, a town of Spain, in Granada, with a castle; 42 miles N. E. of Guadix.

HUESSEN, a town of Holland, in Gelderland, seated on the Rhine; 7 miles N. E. of Nimeguen.

HUETA. *See* GUETA.

HUETINBERG, a town of the Austrian States, in Carinthia; 20 miles N. N. E. of Clagenfurt.

HUFFINGEN, a town of Baden, in the principality of Furstenburg; 4 miles N. N. W. of Furstenburg.

HUGHESBURG. *See* CATAWISSA.

HULL, or KINGSTON UPON HULL, a borough and seaport in East Yorkshire, with markets on Tuesday, Friday, and Saturday. The foundation of this town is now satisfactorily proved to have been long anterior to the date commonly ascribed to it, viz. that of the period when Edward I. gave it the appellation of King's-Town-upon-Hull: its more ancient name was Wyke. The principal streets are broad, well paved, and lighted with gas. It is a county of itself, governed by a mayor, recorder, twelve aldermen, &c.; and, including the parish of Sculcoates, has six churches, ten meeting-houses for dissenters, and a Jews' synagogue. It was the first town that shut its gates against Charles I. The commerce of this place is considerable, and it is deemed the fourth port in the kingdom. Besides its communication with the Yorkshire rivers and canals, it has access also to the Trent, and all its branches; and is connected with the grand chain of railways, by the Selby and Leeds railways; so that it has the import and export trade of many of the northern and midland counties. The foreign trade is chiefly to the Baltic; but it was also one of the privileged ports for trading to the East Indies, and has traffic with the southern parts of Europe, and with America. More ships are sent hence to Greenland than from any other port, that of London excepted. The harbour is artificial; and here are docks for building and repairing ships. Among the public buildings are the Trinity-house, for the relief of seamen and their widows, an armoury, a naval store-house, a custom-house, and an exchange. It is seated on the northern side of the Humber, about 20 miles from its mouth, the town extending almost in a direct line along the river Hull, and lying on a level tract of ground, washed on two of its sides by the Hull and the Humber. It is now well secured from inundations, by embankments. It is 38 miles S. E. of York, and 171 N. of London.

HULLEDYPURA, a town of Hindostan, in Canara; seated in a plain of rice-ground to the E. of a considerable creek, which runs N. from the entrance into Honawera Lake; 54 miles N. by W. of Kundapura.

HULPEN, a town of Belgium, in Brabant; 10 miles S. E. of Brussels.

HULST, a town of the Netherlands, in Dutch Brabant, strong by its situation and fortifications. It was shamefully surrendered to the French in 1747, and taken by them in 1794. It is seated on a plain, which may be overflowed, and on a canal that communicates with the Scheldt; 15 miles W. N. W. of Antwerp.

HULTSCHIN, a town of Silesia, near the river Oppa; 13 miles E. of Troppau.

HUMBER, a river formed by the junction of the Trent and Ouse. It is a large estuary, which divides Yorkshire from Lincolnshire, and enters the German Ocean at Spurn Head.

HUMMELSTOWN, a town of Pennsylvania, in Dauphine county, on the S. side of the Swetara; 10 miles E. by N. of Harrisburg, and 110 miles N. of Washington.

HUNDSMARCK, a town of the Austrian States, in Styria, near the river Muehr; 17 miles W. by S. of Judenburg.

HUNEFELD, a town of Germany, in the district of Fulda, with a collegiate church; 10 miles N. of Fulda.

HUNGARY, a country of Europe, forming an important part of the Austrian dominions. At different periods this name has been applied with a very different signification. In the fourteenth and fifteenth centuries Hungary comprised part of modern Poland and European Turkey, and was divided into ten separate governments, or kingdoms, viz. Hungary Proper, Croatia, Sclavonia, Dalmatia, Bosnia, Bulgaria, Moldavia, Galicia, and Lodomeria, besides the principality of Transylvania. Several of these provinces have long since been detached from Hungary; but that country has still a close political and military connexion with the Austrian provinces of Sclavonia, Croatia, and Dalmatia. This kingdom (for such it is still termed) is surrounded by mountains, except on the S., where its frontier is along the Danube and the Drave. It is bounded on the W. by part of Germany, N. by Galicia, E. by Transylvania and Walachia, and S. by Turkey, Sclavonia, and Croatia; and has a territorial extent of 84,500 square miles. It was formerly divided into Upper and Lower Hungary; but this division has been superseded by that of the following circles:—1. Circle this side the Danube; 2. Circle beyond the Danube; 3. Circle this side the Theiss; 4. Circle beyond the Theiss; 5. Province of Sclavonia; 6. Province of Croatia. These are divided into counties, of which there are thirteen in the first circle, and eleven in each of the others. The principal rivers are the Danube, the Drave, the Marosch, the March, the White Koresch, the Izamos, the Theiss, the Waag, and the Temes. The chief lakes are Balaton and Nieusied, W.; Palitsch on the S. W., and Grunsee, or the Gun Lake, among the Carpathians. There are also several extensive marshes here, as that of the Isle of Schut on the W., and that of Saxetje on the E. of the kingdom. The climate among the mountains is of course bleak; but in the S. it is in general mild; in the sandy districts extremely hot; on the banks of the rivers and near the marshes there is much humidity: indeed, this is a prevailing characteristic of the climate of the level part of Hungary. The country abounds in all the necessaries of life, and the wine, especially that called Tokay, is excellent. There are mines of gold, silver, copper, and iron; and also of opal, at Czerweniza, which gem is peculiar to this country. There is such plenty of game that hunting is allowed to all. The trade principally consists in cattle, hogs, sheep, flour, wheat, rye, wool, and wine; and these are almost wholly sent to the Austrian provinces. The commerce of the country is fettered by no internal taxes, a circumstance of which the Hungarians are very proud; but the Austrian government has environed it with custom-houses, where a duty of one and one-third per cent. is gathered on all goods that pass into it from the other Austrian states. We may thus see that the encouragement of manufactures within the kingdom will never, voluntarily, become the policy of that government. The kingdom of Hungary can easily raise an army of 100,000 men. The horsemen are called Hussars, and the foot Heydukes. The government is hereditary in the house of Austria, and the established religion is popery, though there are a great number of Protestants. No country in the world is better supplied with mineral waters and baths; and those of Buda, when the Turks were in possession of it, were reckoned the finest in Europe.

HUNGERFORD, a town in Berkshire, with a market on Wednesday, and a good trade by its canal navigation. John of Gaunt granted a charter by the gift of a brass bugle horn, which is blown annually for the inhabitants to elect the constable, who is the chief officer. It is seated on the Kennet; 22 miles S. S. W. of Abingdon, and 64 W. of London.

HUNINGUEN, a town of France, in the department of Upper Rhine; seated on the Rhine. The strong fortress of Huninguen, which for a long time held out against the allies in 1815, was afterwards demolished in consequence of a stipulation in the treaty of Paris; 2 miles N. of Basel, and 14 E. of Altkirch.

HUNMANBY, a town in East Yorkshire, with a market on Tuesday. The town is pleasantly situated on a rising ground, surrounded by a fine wood on the N. W. within 2 miles of the sea, and contains many good houses; 39 miles N. E. of York, and 207 N. of London.

HUNTINGDON, a town of New York, in Suffolk county, Long Island. It is situate on a bay, in the sound; 38 miles E. by N. of New York.

HUNTINGDON, a town of Pennsylvania, capital of a mountainous county of the same name, which abounds with lime-stone, iron, and lead. It is situate on the Juniatta, at the mouth of Standing Stone Creek; 23 miles W. S. W. of Lewistown.

HUNTINGDON, a borough, returning two members to parliament, and the capital of Huntingdonshire; governed by a mayor; with a market on Saturday, and a great trade in corn, coals, wood, &c. It was once a large place, said to have had 15 churches, which are now reduced to two; and there are the cemeteries of two other parishes, in one of which is an ancient steeple. Huntingdon is the birthplace of Oliver Cromwell. It is seated on the river Ouse, over which is a stone bridge to Godmanchester; 16 miles W. N. W. of Cambridge, and 59 N. by W. of London.

HUNTINGDONSHIRE, a county of England, 25 miles long and 20 broad; bounded on the N. W. and N. by Northamptonshire, E. by Cambridgeshire, and S. W. by Bedfordshire. It contains 241,690 acres; is divided into four hundreds, and 107 parishes; and has six market towns. It sends two members to parliament. The principal rivers are the Ouse and Nen. The S. E. part consists of beautiful meadows. The middle and western parts are fertile in corn, and adorned with woods; and the upland part was anciently a forest, peculiarly adapted for hunting. The N. E. part consists of fens, which join those of Ely; but they are drained, so as to afford rich pasturage, and even large crops of corn. In the midst of them are some shallow pools, abounding with fish; and a lake, 6 miles long, and 3 broad, called Whittleseamere. The principal commodities are corn, malt, and cheese; and it fattens abundance of cattle.

HUNTLEY, a town of Scotland, in Aberdeenshire; with a manufacture of linen cloth seated on the Bogie, near its conflux with the Deveron; 35 miles N. W. of Aberdeen.

HUNTSPILL, a town in Somersetshire; 7 miles N. of Bridgewater, and 143 W. by S. of London.

HUNTSVILLE, a town of North Carolina, on Yadkin River; 30 miles N. of Salisbury, and 90 W. of Hillsborough.

HURDWAR, a town of Hindostan, in the province of Delhi, where the Ganges first enters the country. The holy bathing place, in the Ganges, is much resorted to by pilgrims; and in 1819 upwards of 400 were crushed to death in the struggle to reach it. The fairs for the disposal of merchandize are sometimes attended by half a million of people. It is 100 miles N. by E. of Delhi. Long. 78. 23. E. lat. 29. 55. N.

HURON, a lake of North America, which lies between 80. and 85. W. long. and 43. and 48. N. lat. It has a communication with Lake Michigan and Lake Erie. Its shape is nearly triangular; 250 miles in length, and its circumference 800 miles. On the W. side is a chain of islands 150 miles long, called Manitoulin by the Indians, who consider them as sacred; on the S. W. is Saguina Bay, and a little more to the N. W. is Thunder Bay, so called from the frequent thunder that is heard there.

HURST CASTLE, a fortress of Hampshire, 4 miles S. of Lymington. It stands on the extreme point of a neck of land, about a mile distant from the Isle of Wight. In this castle Charles I. was confined previously to his being brought to trial.

HUS, or HUSSU, a town of European Turkey, in Moldavia; the see of a Greek bishop. Here Peter the Great made peace with the Turks in 1711. It is situate on the Pruth; 70 miles S. W. of Benda. Long. 28. 34. E. lat. 46. 35. N.

HUSSINGABAD, a town of Hindostan, in the province of Malwah, on the S. side of the Nerbuddah; 140 miles N. W. of Nagpore. Long. 77. 54. E. lat. 22. 42. N.

HUSUM, a seaport of Denmark, in the duchy of Sleswick, with a strong citadel. It has a trade in horses and oxen, and manufactures of leather, cotton, and linen. It stands on the river Ow or Aue, near the German Ocean; 16 miles W. of Sleswick. Long. 9. 20. E. lat. 54. 36. N.

HUTTANY, a town of Hindostan, in the province of Visiapour. It is surrounded by mud ramparts, and has a citadel, and a spacious caravansera; 30 miles S. S. W. of Visiapour. Long. 75. 6. E. lat. 17. 5. N.

HUY, a town of Belgium, in the territory of Liege, with many paper mills, and iron foundries. It is seated on the Maese; 12 miles W. S. W. of Liege.

HYDE, a township in Cheshire; 3 miles from Stockport. The neighbourhood abounds in coals.

HYDERABAD, a populous city in Hindostan, capital of Golconda, and the metropolis of the Deccan. The suburbs, which are very large, are occupied by merchants and tradesmen. It stands in a plain, on the river that runs into the Kistna; 310 miles N. N. W. of Madras. Long. 78. 52. E. lat. 17. 16. N.

HYDERADAD, a fort of Hindostan, in the province of Sinde, and the usual residence of the prince of Sinde; situate near the Indus; 6 miles E. of Nusserpour, and 62 N. E. of Tatta.

HYDRA, an island of the Grecian archipelago, but little better than a sterile rock, the inhabitants of which are all mariners, and derive wealth from commercial enterprise. The port is fortified, and the houses are built on the side of a steep acclivity. Pop. 30,000. It is 11 miles long, and 2 broad.

HYPOLITE, ST., a town of France, in the department of Gard; seated on the Vidourle, near its source; 12 miles S. W. of Alais.

HYPOLITE, ST., a town of France, in the department of Doubs, on the river Doubs; 40 miles E. by N. of Besançon.

HYS, a town of Asiatic Turkey, in the Arabian Irak, on the Euphrates; 120 miles S. of Bagdad.

HYTHE, a borough in Kent; market on Thursday. It is one of the principal cinque ports, and returns one member to parliament. The church is of great antiquity, and contains in a vault a remarkable pile of bones, 28 feet long, 6 broad, and 9 high, the remains of Danes and Britons, killed in a battle on the beach, in A. D. 824. There are extensive barracks adjoining the town, and the remains of Saltwood Castle, about 2 miles distant. It is 12 miles W. S. W. of Dover, and 71 from London.

I.

IBARRA, the capital of a fertile province of the same name, in South America, republic of Colombia, is situated on an extensive and delightful plain, watered on the E. by the river Taguando, and W. by Ajavi. The streets are wide and convenient, and the buildings of good construction; 42 miles N. E. from Quito.

IBBERVILLE, an outlet for the overflowing waters of the Mississippi, during the seasons of inundation, entering Lake Maurepas.

IBERIA, NEW, a village of Louisiana, in the district of Attacapas; 200 miles W. of New Orleans.

IBERIAN MOUNTAINS, the most extensive mountain range of Spain, beginning to the W of Ebro, and extending to the shore of the Mediterranean.

IBIZA. *See* IVICA.

IBURG, a small town of Hanover, in the principality of Osnaburg; 10 miles S. W. of Osnaburg.

ICELAND, an island of the North Atlantic Ocean, belonging to Denmark; extending, according to Henderson, from lat. 63. 20. to 67. 20. and between 15. 30. and 22. 30. W. long. It is of an irregular oval figure, about 380 miles in length, and 230 miles in its greatest breadth. For two months together the sun never sets; and in the winter it never rises for the same space, at least not entirely. The coast is indented all round with numerous deep gulfs, bays, and creeks, several of which form excellent harbours. The island is mountainous, stony, and barren; but in some places there are excellent pastures. The chief rivers are in the E. part; the Skalfanda, Oxarfiord, and Bruna, all flowing from S. to N. Some are white with lime, others smell of sulphur. The principal mountains, clothed with perpetual snow, are called Yokuls; and of these Snafial, hanging over the sea on the S. W. coast, is esteemed the highest, being computed at 6860 feet. Mount Hecla, about 5000 feet in height, is the most noted, and is a volcano: there are also several other volcanoes, and the convulsions caused by them in 1783 were so dreadful and multiplied, that it was feared the island would fall to pieces; the eruptions were the most tremendous of any recorded in history. The last eruption, which was less terrific in its consequences, occurred in December, 1821. Hot springs abound, and the most remarkable are those about 30 miles N. W. of Hecla, called the Geysers. The principal of these sends up, at intervals of about 6 hours, an immense jet or column of boiling water, of about 10 feet in diameter, to the height of 60, 100, or even 212 feet. The climate is not extremely cold, but the seasons are variable. The sea, at a small distance from the shores, is seldom frozen; and very little ice is ever seen near the W. coast, notwithstanding its proximity to Greenland. Iceland is governed as a dependency of Denmark, and is divided into four provinces, 19 shires, and 184 parishes. The inhabitants were estimated at 50,092, in 1824. Their houses are at a distance from each other, and many of them deep in the ground; but they are all miserable hovels of turf, without windows, and those of the common class are such wretched dens, that it is wonderful how any thing in the human form can breath in them. The Danes trade with the natives for hides, tallow, train oil, whalebone, and sea-horses' teeth, which are as good as ivory. The established religion is the Lutheran, and there are 300 churches in the island. The distressing scarcity of Bibles, which had long prevailed, was relieved in 1815, by a liberal distribution from Britain, which were received with the greatest thankfulness. The principal school, held at a place called Bessestadt, near the W. coast, has three masters, who teach the classics, theology, and the Danish language; and societies have been formed for the cultivation of literature.

ICOLMKILL, or IONA, one of the Hebrides, near the S. W. point of the isle of Mull; only three miles long and one broad. Here are the ruins of an august nunnery, monastery, and cathedral, said to have been founded by St. Columba, about the year 735; also a small chapel, dedicated to St. Oran, containing many marble tombstones of the great lords of the isles; and adjoining it is a cemetery, in which many ancient kings of Scotland, Ireland, and Norway, are buried. Other ruins of monastic and druidical edifices can be traced; and many places are pointed out, noted for particular acts of St. Columba. This island was the retreat of learning, during the Gothic ignorance which pervade Europe, after the overthrow of the Roman empire; and the seminary whence issued those pious monks and laymen who again revived learning, and propagated Christianity through many kingdoms of Europe.

IDA, a lofty and pointed mountain, in the middle of the island of Candia; famous in ancient times as being the place on which Jupiter was brought up, and where there was a temple dedicated to Cybele.

IDA, a mountain of Asiatic Turkey, in Natolia; 140 miles to the W. of Olympus.

IDANHA A NEUVA, a town of Portugal, in Beira; 3 miles S. W. of Idanha a Vella.

IDANHA A VELLA, a town of Portugal, in Beira. The French took it by assault, in 1704. It is seated on the Ponsul; 25 miles E. of Castel Branco. Long. 6. 14. W. lat. 39. 39. N.

IDRIA, a town of the Austrian states, in Carniola; celebrated for its rich quicksilver mines; 20 miles E. N. E. of Gorz.

IDSTEIN, a town of Germany, in the duchy of Nassau, with a castle, the residence of the duke; situate in a district containing several forests, and iron-works. It is 16 miles N. of Mentz, and 22 S. W. of Wetzlar.

IF, an island in the Mediterranean, on the coast of France, the most eastern of the three before the harbour of Marseilles, and well fortified.

IGLAU, a fortified town of Moravia, capital of a circle of the same name, with two convents and a college. Good cloth is manufactured here, and the commerce in corn and hemp is considerable. It is seated on the Igla; 40 miles W. N. W. of Brinn. Long. 15. 32. E. lat. 49. 28. N.

IGLESIAS, a town of the island of Sardinia, and a bishop's see; 37 miles W. S. W. of Cagliari. Long. 8. 39. E. lat. 39. 18. N.

IGUALADA, a town of Spain, province of Catalonia; 35 miles N. W. from Barcelona; with manufactures of printed calicoes, fire-arms, and paper. Pop. 12,575.

IHOR. *See* JOHORE.

IKERY, a town of Hindostan, in Mysore; formerly the capital of a principality. It was of a great size, surrounded by three concentric walls; but, the court being removed to Nagara, the inhabitants willingly followed, and devastation succeeded.

ILA. *See* IDA.

ILAK, or JALAK, a town of Nubia, on the Nile, supposed by some to be the ancient Meroe. Long. 34. 30. E. lat. 18. 48. N.

ILANZ, a town of Switzerland, in the Grisons, capital of the Grey League. It is seated on the Rhine, 23 miles S. W. of Coire.

ILCHESTER, or IVELCHESTER, a town in Somersetshire, market on Wednesday. It is a place of great antiquity, and the birthplace of the celebrated Roger Bacon. Here also is the county gaol. It is seated on the Ivel; 16 miles S. by W. of Wells, and 122 W. by S. of London.

ILDEFONSO, ST., a town of Spain, in New Castile; noted for a magnificent summer palace, built by Philip V., and for a large manufacture of glass, belonging to the crown. It is 5 miles N. of Uzeda, and 40 N. W. of Madrid.

ILDEFONSO, ST., a town of Mexico, in the province of Guaxaca; seated on a mountain 70 miles E. N. E. of Guaxaca.

ILDERTON, a village in Northumberland, four miles S. of Wooler. On a hill near it is a semicircular encampment, defended by two high rampires of earth, and a deep fosse, with an inner circle of stones, which appear uncemented. The area is about 100 yards in diameter, and contains many remains of buildings.

ILFORD, ward and chapelry, county of Essex; 7½ miles from London.

ILFRACOMB, a seaport in Devonshire, governed by a mayor, with a market on Saturday. It has a spacious natural basin, with a good pier and quay, projecting into the Bristol Channel. This port employs a number of brigs and sloops, chiefly in carrying ore from Cornwall, coals from Wales, and corn from Bristol; also a number of fishing skiffs. It is 49 miles N. N. W. of Exeter, and 202 W. of London.

ILHEOS, a province of Brazil, S. of that of All Saints' Bay. Its chief town, of the same name, is seated at the mouth of the river Ilheos; 130 miles S. S. W. of St. Salvador. Long. 40. 15. W. lat. 14. 55. S.

ILKUCH, a town of Poland, in the palatinate of Cracow, remarkable for its silver and lead mines; 15 miles N. W. of Cracow.

ILLE, a town of France, in the department of Eastern Pyrenees, on the river Teck; 10 miles W. of Perpignan.

ILLE-ET-VILAINE, a department of France, containing part of the late province of Bretagne. It takes its name from two rivers, which unite at Rennes, the capital of the department.

ILLER, a river of Germany, which rises in Tyrol, runs N. through Bavaria, and joins the Danube near Ulm.

ILLESCAS, a town of Spain, in New Castile; 15 miles S. S. W. of Madrid, and 15 N. N. E. of Toledo.

ILLINOIS, a river of North America, formed by the junction of several streams near the S. end of Lake Michigan: after taking a S. W. course of 250 miles, it enters the Mississippi, 30 miles above the influx of the Missouri.

ILLINOIS, a state of North America, in the United States, containing 476,183 inhabitants; also about 6000 Indians, of various tribes. It has an abundance of most fertile land, and of various qualities, adapted either for pasturage or tillage. In the N. W. angle, at Galena, are productive lead mines. It was first settled in 1720, by a few emigrants from Canada, and was admitted into the Union in 1818, with a population of 35,220. Capital, Vandalia, on the Kaskasia river, nearly in the centre of the state. It is bounded on the E. by Lake Michigan and Indiana, S. by Kentucky, W. by the Mississippi and the state of Missouri. Area, 50,000 square miles.

ILLOGAN, a parish of Cornwall, 264 miles from London. One of the richest copper mines in the county is in this parish.

ILM, a town of Saxony, on a river of its name; 13 miles N. W. of Rudolstadt, and 14 S. by E. of Erfurt.

ILMEN, a lake of Russia, in the government of Novogorod; 48 miles long, and from 12 to 18 broad. Near it stands the city of Novogorod. It communicates with Lake Ladoga by the river Volkhof.

ILMENAU, a town of Saxe-Weimar, in Henneberg. Near it is a mineral spring, also a copper and silver mine. It is seated near the source of the Ilm, 17 miles E. S. E. of Smalkalden.

ILMINSTER, a town in Somersetshire, with a market on Saturday, and a manufacture of narrow cloths. It is seated among hills, near the river Ille; 26 miles S. W. of Wells, and 136 W. by S. of London.

ILSLEY, a town in Berkshire, with a market on Wednesday; seated between two hills, 14 miles N. W. of Reading, and 54 W. of London.

ILST, a town of the Netherlands, in Friesland, seated on the Weymer, 12 miles S. of Lewarden.

ILSTROP, a town of Sweden, in W. Gothland, 27 miles S. S. E. of Gotheburg.

ILTEN, a town of Hanover, in the province of Luneberg, 16 miles S. S. W. of Zell.

ILTZHOFEN, a town of Prussian Saxony, 8 miles N. E. of Halle.

IMBRO, an island in the Grecian Archipelago, about 20 miles in circumference. It is mountainous and woody, and affords plenty of game. Long. 25. 44. E. lat. 40. 10. N.

IMERITIA, a county of Asia, lying E. of the Black Sea; bounded on the S. by Turkey, W. by Mingrelia, N. by Ossetia, and E. by Georgia, of which it is, properly speaking, a part. The inhabitants, estimated at not more than 20,000 families, are scattered over the country in small hamlets. They send yearly considerable quantities of wine to the neighbouring parts of Georgia, in leathern bags, carried by horses; but they are without manufactures, very poor and miserable, and cruelly oppressed by their landlords. Cutais, or Cotatis, is the capital.

IMMENSTADT, a town of Bavaria, in the circle of the Upper Danube; situate on a small river which soon after joins the Iller; 12 miles S. of Kempton.

IMOLA, an episcopal town of Italy, in the delegation of Ravenna, with a strong citadel. It is surrounded by walls, towers, and ditches; contains 16 churches and 17 convents, and is seated on the Santerno; 13 miles W. by S. of Ravenna, and 45 N. N. E. of Florence.

INCH, a town of Scotland, in Aberdeenshire; a parish of great fertility.

INCHBRAYOCK, a small island of Scotland, in Forfarshire, within the mouth of the South Esk, near Montrose, with which it communicates by a drawbridge. It has also a large and convenient dry dock.

INCHCOLM, a small island of Scotland, in the Frith of Forth, near the village of Aberdour, on the coast of Fife. Here is the ruin of a famous monastery, founded by Alexander I., in 1123, to commemorate the hospitable treatment he received here from a hermit.

INCHGARVIE, a small island of the Frith of Forth, nearly in the middle of the passage over the Queensferry.

INCHKEITH, a small island of the Frith of Forth, lying midway between the ports of Leith and Kinghorn. Here is a lighthouse, and also a ruinous fort.

INCHMARNOCK, a small island of Scotland, on the S. W. side of Bute. The ruins of a chapel dedicated to St. Marnock are still to be seen; and on the W. side are vast strata of coral and shells.

INDAL, a town of Sweden, in Medelpadia, on a river of the same name, near its entrance into the Gulf of Bothnia; 16 miles N. by W. of Sundiswald.

INDAPOUR. *See* INDRAPOUR.

INDEN HOTUN, a town of Chinese Tartary, capital of the Mantcheou Tartars; 420 miles E. N. E. of Peking.

INDIA, or HIND, a contraction of Hindostan, is a name often given to that region of Asia lying to the S. of Tartary, and between Persia and China, with its independent islands. It contains, besides Hindostan, the Birman Empire, Siam, Cochin China, Tonquin, Thibet, Japan, and Ceylon, but is now, in its geographical features, more usually, and far more properly, described under those respective heads, which see.

INDIANA, one of the United States of North America, formed in 1816. It is bounded N. by the N. W. territory, Michigan Lake and territory; E. by the state of Ohio; S. by Ohio River, which separates it from Kentucky; and W. by the state of Illinois. The most considerable towns are Indianapolis (the seat of government), N. Albany, the largest town, Madison, Richmond, Vincennes, Vevay, Brookville, and Jeffersonville. All these, with the exception of Vincennes, are new, and have risen suddenly into notice. The principal rivers are the Ohio, Wabash, White River, Whitewater, Tippecanoe, Illinois, Plein, Theakiki, St. Joseph's, and St. Mary's. The climate is generally healthy and pleasant: the principal productions are wheat, Indian corn, rye, oats, barley, buck-wheat, potatoes, pulse, beef, pork, butter, whisky, and peach-brandy. Population 685,866.

INDIES, EAST, the name given by Europeans to that vast tract of country in Asia which is situated to the S. of Tartary, between Persia and China (*see* HINDOSTAN), as well as to a great number of islands in the Indian Ocean, extending from the peninsula of Hindostan as far E. as New Guinea, and from the Bay of Bengal and the China Sea as far S. as New Holland. The most western of them are the Maldives, and the most eastern the Moluccas; between which are several very large ones, as Ceylon, Sumatra, Java, Borneo, and Celebes; besides many others of considerable importance as to riches, though much inferior as to extent.

INDIES, WEST, a denomination under which is comprehended a large chain of islands, extending in a curve from the Florida shore, on the northern peninsula of America, to the Gulf of Venezuela on the southern. Columbus gave this name to them, under the notion that they formed part of the Indian continent, which it was his object, in his first voyage, to find; and this opinion was so general, that Ferdinand and Isabella, king and queen of Castile, in their ratification of an agreement granted to Columbus, upon his return, gave them the name of Indies. Even after the error which gave rise to this opinion was detected, and the position of the New World was ascertained, the name has remained, and the appellation of West Indies is given by all the people of Europe to these islands, and that of Indians to the inhabitants, not only of these islands, but of the continent of America. The principal of these islands are Curazao, Trinidad, Tobago, Grenada, St. Vincent, Barbadoes, Martinico, Dominica, Marie-Galante, Guadaloupe, Antigua, Barbuda, St. Christopher, St. Eustatius, St. Bartholomew, St. Martin, Anguilla, St. Thomas, Porto-Rico, St. Domingo, Jamaica, Cuba, and the Bahamas; a full description of which will be found under their respective denominations.

INDORE, a town of Hindostan, in the province of Malwah; capital of one of the Poonah Mahratta chiefs, who was defeated by the British in 1804, and his successor compelled to enter into an engagement to renounce all connexion with the enemies of the British, and to furnish, when required, 3000 cavalry. It is seated on a river that flows into the Nerbuddah; 28 miles S. S. E. of Ougein. Long 76. 11. E. lat. 22. 5. N.

INDRAPOUR, a seaport on the W. coast of Sumatra; capital of a district of the same name. 160 miles N. W. of Bencoolen.

INDRE, a department of France, including part of the ci-devant province of Berry. It has its name from a river which rises in this department, flows into that of Indre-et-Loire, and joins the Loire 4 miles below the influx of the Cher. Its area is estimated at 2860 square miles; its population 205,000. Chateauroux is the capital.

INDRE-ET-LOIRE, a department of France, including almost the whole of the province of Touraine, and bounded by the department of the Loire-et-Cher, the Indre, the Vienne, and the Maine. It consists mostly of fine plains, interspersed, however, with small hills. The principal rivers are the Loire, the Vienne, the Cher, and the Indre. Tours is the capital.

INDUS, or SINDE, a great river of Asia, having its source in a range of the mountains of Tartary, between 38. and 39. of N. lat From Thibet it takes a S. W. course, and enters Hindostan in about 35. N. lat. It has always been considered as the western barrier of Hindostan: 60 miles from its source it is joined by the Cabul, when it is no longer fordable. Between lat. 25. and 26. it enters the province of Sinde, and here we find it again divided into two considerable branches; the principal, or western, divides into numerous streams, which form a delta similar to that of the Nile, or Ganges: they are, however, very shallow, and only navigable by boats. It is said to be 1350 miles in length, and some parts of it are capable of bearing vessels of 200 tons; but there is very little commerce transported by it. Its water is very wholesome. On the E. of this river is a great sandy desert, extending nearly 500 miles in length, and from 60 to 150 in breadth.

Ingatestone, a small town in Essex; 23 miles from London.

Inglefingen, a town of Wirtemberg, on the Kocher; 20 miles S. S. W. of Mergentheim.

Ingelheim, a town of Germany, in Hesse Darmstadt; seated on an eminence, on the river Salva; 9 miles E. of Bingen.

Ingleborough, one of the highest mountains of England, in Yorkshire; 8 miles N.N.W. of Settle. It is 2361 ft. above the level of the sea.

Ingleton, a village in West Yorkshire, at the foot of Ingleborough mountain. It is tolerably well built, and has manufactures of cotton yarn. Near it are several collieries, which supply the surrounding country to a considerable distance with coals; 10 miles W. N. W. of Settle, and 245 N. W. of London.

Inglis Island, an island on the N. coast of New Holland, near the entrance of the Gulf of Carpentaria.

Ingolstadt, a town of Bavaria. It is one of the strongest places in Germany; surrounded by a morass. The houses are built of stone, and the streets are large. Here was formerly a university, which, in 1800, was transferred to Landschut. It is seated on the Danube; 9 miles E. of Neuburg, and 45 N. by W. of Munich. Long. 11. 25. E. lat. 48. 46. N.

Ingraham Islands, a cluster of islands, seven in number, in the Pacific Ocean, discovered by Captain Ingraham, of Boston, in 1791, and named Washington, Adams, Lincoln, Federal, Franklin, Hancock, and Knox. Federal Island, (or Nooheva,) is considered the largest, most populous, and fertile. They appear generally to be diversified with hills and valleys, and to be well wooded. Most of them are inhabited, and the people resemble those of the Marquesas.

Ingrande, a town of France, department of Maine-et-Loire; situate on the Loire; 15 miles W. S. W. of Angers.

Ingre, a town of France, department of the Loiret; 4 miles N. W. of Orleans.

Inishannon, a town of Ireland, in the county of Cork, with a considerable linen manufacture; seated on the Bandon; 7 miles N. W. of Kinsale.

Inistioge, a town of Ireland, in the county of Kilkenny; 80 miles from Dublin. The lace manufacture is carried on here, and it has a salmon fishery.

Inn, a large river of Austria, which rises in the Swiss canton of Grisons, flows N.E. through Tyrol and Bavaria, and joins the Danube at Passau, where it is nearly 900 feet wide. It becomes navigable at Hall, in the Tyrol, and its whole course is more than 250 miles.

Innaconda, a fortress of Hindostan, in the Guntoor circar; situate on a hill; 46 miles N. W. of Ongole.

Insch, a town of Scotland, in Aberdeenshire; 26 miles W. N. W. of Aberdeen.

Inspruck, a fortified town of Austria, capital of Tyrol, with a strong castle, formerly the residence of the archdukes of Austria. The principal manufacture is that of cotton, but it has also maufactures of silk and woollen stuffs, and all kinds of glass wares; and the transit trade from Germany to Italy is considerable. Inspruck was entered by the French, in 1805, and was the scene of several heroic efforts of the Tyrolese against the French and Bavarians, in 1809. It is seated in a pleasant valley, on the river Inn; 62 miles S. of Munich.

Insterburg, a town and circle of East Prussia, on the Angerap, in the government of Gumbinnen. Its chief trade is in corn and linseed. The circle is of great extent, comprehending a population of 150,000. Part of it is covered with forests; but the soil of the rest is fertile, and the pastures here are extensive: manufactures are hardly known. The town is 50 miles E. of Konigsberg. It contains 5300 inhabitants.

Interlachen, a town of Switzerland, capital of a bailiwick of the same name, in the canton of Bern; 28 miles S. S. W. of Lucern, and 32 S. E. of Bern.

Inverary, a borough of Scotland, and the county town of Argyleshire; situate on the N. W. side of Loch Fyne, at the influx of the Aray. It has some manufactures, and a trade in wool, timber, and oak bark; but its chief support is from the herring fishery. It is contributory, with Campbeltown and Irvine, in returning one member to parliament. Near the town is Inverary Castle, the seat of the Duke of Argyle; and in the neighbourhood is a considerable iron-work. The planting around Inverary is very extensive and admirably variegated; 45 miles N. W. of Glasgow, and 75 W. N. W. of Edinburgh.

Inverbervie. *See* Bervie.

Invergordon, a village of Scotland, in Ross-shire, at the mouth of the Frith of Cromarty; 8 miles S. S. E. of Tain. It has a good harbour, and a regular ferry over the Frith to the town of Cromarty.

Inverkeithing, a borough and seaport of Scotland, in Fifeshire, with a considerable trade in coal and salt. Before the entrance of the harbour is a bay, which affords safe anchorage for ships of any burden, in all winds. The harbour itself is commodious, and has two quays. It is situate on the N. side of the Frith of Forth, 18 miles N. W. of Edinburgh, and contributes, with Stirling, &c. in returning one member to parliament.

INVERLEITHEN, a village of Scotland, on the river Tweed, at the influx of the Leithen; 5 miles E. of Peebles. Here is an extensive woollen manufacture; and near it is a sulphurous spring.

INVERNESS, a borough of Scotland, capital of a county of the same name; situate on both sides the river Ness, near its entrance into the Frith of Murray. It has a commodious harbour, and a good salmon fishery. The trade is very considerable, and the town is rapidly improving. The principal manufactures are those of hemp and flax; and there are also woollen and other manufactures, tanneries, brick-works, &c., which furnish employment to many of the inhabitants. On an eminence are the ruins of the old castle, demolished by the rebels in 1746; and over the Ness is a stone bridge of seven arches. The court-house, nearly in the centre of the town, is a handsome modern building, with a fine tower, terminated by an elegant spire, which sustained considerable injury from the earthquake in 1816. It contributes, with Fortrose, Nairn, and Forres, in returning one member to parliament. Near this town, on Culloden Heath, the Duke of Cumberland gained a decisive victory over the rebels, in 1746. To the W. of the town is the hill of Craig Phatric, on the summit of which are the extensive remains of a vitrified fort, so called from the marks of fusion which the cement and stones exhibit. Inverness is 50 miles N. E. of Fort William, and 156 N. of Edinburgh.

INVERNESS-SHIRE, the most extensive county of Scotland; bounded on the N. by Ross-shire; E. by the counties of Nairn, Murray, and Aberdeen; S. by those of Perth and Argyle; and W. by the Atlantic Ocean. It also includes several of the Hebrides. Independent of the islands, it is 80 miles long, and 50 broad. It comprehends the districts of Badenoch, Lochaber, and Glenaly, which are subdivided into 31 parishes. The principal towns are Inverness, Fort William, (or Inverlochy,) and Fort Augustus. The N. part is mountainous and barren, and is the most elevated ground in Scotland, Ben-Nevis rising to the height of 4370 feet above the sea. This county has several considerable lakes, and is divided, in a manner, into two equal parts, by those of Ness, Oich, Lochy, and Lochiel, united by the Caledonian Canal, which forms a communication between the two seas. The extensive plains which surround the lakes are, in general, fertile; the high grounds feed many sheep and black cattle, and numerous herds of goats are found in every district. The mountains and forests are inhabited by great numbers of red deer; the alpine and common hare, and other game, are also abundant. Limestone, iron-ore, and some traces of different minerals, have been found in this county, with beautiful rock crystals of various tints; but no mines have hitherto been worked with much success. The principal rivers are the Spey, the Beauly, the Ness, and the Lochy.

INVERUGIE, or ST. FERGUS, a village of Scotland, on the E. coast of Aberdeenshire, at the mouth of the Ugie; 1 mile N. of Peterhead. It has an extensive bleach-field, and a considerable brewery. Near it are the ruins of Inverugie Castle.

INVERURY, an ancient burgh of Scotland, in Aberdeenshire; seated at the conflux of the Don and the Ury. It has much improved within a few years, and joins with Elgin, Banff, &c., in returning one member to parliament; 15 miles W. N. W. of Aberdeen.

IONA. *See* ICOLMKILL.

IONIAN ISLANDS, a recently constituted republic of Europe; comprising, besides a number of islets, the seven principal islands of Corfu, Cephalonia, Zante, Santa Maura, Ithaca or Thiaki, Cerigo, and Paxo; of which Corfu, lying opposite to Albania, is the most northerly. The territorial extent of this small state is estimated at about 1500 square miles. The climate is in general mild, but the transitions from heat to cold are sudden: hot and scorching winds are sometimes destructive to vegetation; and, at certain seasons, there are violent rains and thunder. They are all subject to slight earthquakes, which are sometimes confined to a single island. The soil in the plains and valleys is fertile in vines, corn, olives, currants, cotton, honey, wax, &c. Pasturage is in general scanty; goats and sheep are reared in considerable number; but horses and cattle are brought from the continent. The wild animals are foxes, hares, and rabbits. Prior to the French revolution these islands were subject to Venice, but were ceded to France by the treaty of Campo Formio (1797). After repeatedly changing masters, the republic was placed under the protection of Great Britain, by the arrangements of the Congress of Vienna; and a constitution for this small state was drawn up and ratified by the British government in July, 1817.

IPS, a town of Austria, near the conflux of the Ips with the Danube; 22 miles W. of St. Polten.

IPSALA, a town of European Turkey, in Romania, and a Greek archbishop's see. Near it are mines of alum; and red wine is an article of commerce. It is seated on the Marissa; 43 miles S. of Adrianople.

IPSARA, an island of the Grecian Archipelago; 15 miles N. W. of the island of Scio. To the W. is another small island, called Anti-Ipsara.

IPSHEIM, a town of Franconia, in the principality of Bayreuth; 17 miles N. N. W. of Anspach.

IPSWICH, a borough and principal town of Suffolk; governed by two bailiffs, a high steward, recorder, &c.; with a market on Wednesday, Friday, and Saturday. It returns two members to parliament. It was once surrounded by a wall, traces of which are yet to be seen. It is irregularly built, and has declined from its former consequence: it now contains 12 parish churches, several meeting-houses for dissenters, a library, several hospitals, a free school, a commodious market-place, a guildhall, a custom-house, and a county jail. Much corn and malt is sent hence to London, and great quantities of timber were formerly sent to the king's dock-yard at Chatham. It has a considerable coasting trade, a small share of foreign commerce, and sends ships to Greenland. Vessels of large burden are obliged to stop at some distance below the town. It is the birthplace of Cardinal Wolsey. It is seated on the Orwell; 26 miles S. E. of Bury St. Edmund, and 69 N. E. of London.

Ipswich, a township and town of the United States, in Massachusets: situated on a river of the same name, about a mile from the sea; 23 miles N. E. of Boston.

Irabatty. *See* Irrawaddy.

Irac, a province of Persia, comprehending the greater part of the ancient Media. It is bounded S. by Fars and Khuzistan; E. by Khorassan and the Great Salt Desert; W. by Kurdistan, and N. by Azerbijan, Ghilan, and Mazanderan, and divided into five districts, Ispahan, Tehraun, Naen, Mullager, and Kermanshah.

Irac-Arabi, (the ancient Chaldea,) a province of Turkey in Asia; bounded W. by the desert of Arabia, N. by Kurdistan and Diarbeck, E. by Khuzistan, and S. by the Gulf of Persia and Arabia. Bagdad is the capital.

Irbit, or Irbitskaia, a town of Russia, in the government of Perm, on the river Irbit, and the frontiers of Siberia. In the vicinity is a large iron-work, which yields nearly 2000 tons of iron a year; 142 miles N.E. of Ekaterinenburg.

Ireby, a town in Cumberland, with a market on Thursday; seated in a valley, at the source of the Ellen; 10 miles N. E. of Cockermouth, and 303 N. N. W. of London.

Ireland, the second in magnitude of the British Isles, is situated to the W. of Great Britain, in the Atlantic Ocean. It is bounded on the N. W. and S. by the Atlantic, and on the E. by the North Channel, the Irish Sea, and St. George's Channel, which separate it from England. Its greatest length from N. E. to S. W. is 306 miles, and its greatest breadth is 207 miles: it contains 18,484,343 English acres, or 288,818 square miles. Ireland is divided into four provinces; namely, Ulster, to the N.; Leinster, to the E.; Munster, to the S.; and Connaught to the W.; and these are subdivided into 32 counties. Ulster contains the counties of Down, Armagh, Monaghan, Cavan, Antrim, Londonderry, Tyrone, Fermanagh, and Donegal: Leinster has those of Dublin, Louth, Wicklow, Wexford, Longford, East Meath, West Meath, King's county, Queen's county, Kilkenny, Kildare, and Carlow: Munster includes Clare, Cork, Kerry, Limerick, Tipperary, and Waterford; and Connaught has Leitrim, Roscommon, Mayo, Sligo, and Galway. These are again subdivided into 252 baronies, and these into 2436 parishes. The climate of Ireland is mild and temperate, but more humid than in England. It is, on the whole, of a mountainous character, but well watered with lakes and rivers; and the soil, in most parts, is very good and fertile: even in those places where the bogs and morasses have been drained, there is good meadow ground. It produces corn, hemp, and flax, in great plenty; and there are so many cattle that beef and butter are exported to foreign parts; and not only the English, but other ships, frequently come to be victualled here. The other commodities are hides, wool, tallow, wood, salt, honey, and wax. The commerce and manufactures have for many years been greatly on the increase: the staple branch of industry is the manufacture of fine linen cloth, which is brought to great perfection. This country is well situated for foreign trade, on account of its many secure and commodious bays and harbours. Its principal lakes are Lough Lean, Lough Ern, Lough Neagh, and Lough Coribb; and its chief rivers are the Shannon, Liffey, Boyne, Suire, Nore, Barrow, Blackwater, and Lee. The mountains are Sliebh Donard, 2809 feet, county of Down; Croagh Patrick, county of Mayo, 2510 feet; Carran Taal, 3410 feet, and Mangerton, 2550 feet, county of Kerry; Lagnoquilla, 3070 feet, county of Wicklow; and numerous others. The mineral productions of Ireland, which were little known till of late, are now fast rising into importance. The mining companies recently formed are nearly all of them eminently successful: copper, lead, iron, antimony, and molybdenum, are now obtained; and some of the mines are very productive. In the royalty of Glendalough, in the county of Wicklow, are two veins of rich lead ore, at one of which the lead is raised at an expense of 1*l.* 5*s.* per ton; and, within twelve fathoms, two parallel veins, equally rich, were discovered in 1827. Gold has been found in this county. There are likewise productive collieries, and quarries of marble, slate, and freestone; and numerous mineral springs, chiefly chalybeate. Formerly this kingdom had a parliament, which was subordinate to that of Great Britain; but in 1800 it was deemed expedient, for the welfare of Ireland, that it should be united to Great Britain. The two parliaments passed acts for that purpose, and the two kingdoms, at the commencement of 1801, were styled the United Kingdom of Great Britain and Ireland; and 32 peers (four of them bishops) and 105 commoners of Ireland, are elected to represent that country in the Imperial Parliament, assembled in England. The lord lieutenant of Ireland, as well as the council, is appointed, from time to time, by the king. General education has been much neglected, and still continues to be discountenanced by the Catholic clergy. Great efforts have been made, for some years past, to remove this, chiefly by two societies established in Britain, who have under their patronage a great number of schools, in a highly prosperous state. The established religion is the same as in England. The Irish protestant church is under the government of four archbishops, viz. of Armagh, primate of *all* Ireland; Dublin, primate of Ireland, Cashel, and Tuam; and eight bishops, viz. Meath, Down, Kilmore, Derry, Ferns, Limerick, Cloyne, and Killaloe; but the great majority of the people are catholics. The latter were long excluded all civil and military distinctions. This system, however, no longer exists.

Ireland, New, a long narrow island of the Eastern Seas, N. of New Britain, extending from N. W. to S. E. about 190 miles, and in general very narrow. The natives are Papuas, who go entirely naked, smearing their faces and powdering their heads with white clay; their huts have only an opening to crawl in on their hands and knees. Their canoes, however, are neatly formed of a single tree, sometimes 90 ft. long, and furnished with outriggers. *See* Britain, New.

Irishtown. *See* Kilkenny.

Irjab, a town of Afghanistan, in Cabul; seated near a western branch of the Indus; 110 miles S. S. W. of Cabul.

Irken, or Ibrien. *See* Yarkan.

Irkutsk, the largest and least populous government of the Russian empire; comprising all the E. part of Siberia, from the Northern Ocean to the frontiers of Chinese Tartary, and from the boundaries of the government of Tobolsk to the Eastern Ocean. This large territory was gradually conquered, and appropriated by the Russians in their desultory excursion from Tobolsk. It is divided into the four provinces of Irkutsk, Nertchinsk, Yakutsk, and Okhotsk. Pop. 400,000.

Irkutsk, a town of Siberia; capital of the government of the same name, and the see of a bishop. It is a place of considerable commercial importance, from the caravans passing through it, which trade to China, and from its being the seat of supreme jurisdiction over Eastern Siberia. There are several churches and other edifices of stone, and the wooden houses are large and convenient. The inhabitants are estimated at 12,000. It stands on the river Angara, near the Lake Baikal; 900 miles E. S. E. of Tobolsk. Pop. 20,000.

Iroquois. *See* Lawrence, St.

Irrawaddy, or Irabatty, a considerable river of Asia, which rises in Thibet, flows S. through the kingdom of Birmah and Pegu, and enters the Bay of Bengal by several mouths. On its banks are produced great quantities of the finest teak timber, so much esteemed in ship-building. The principal market for this valuable timber is Rangoon, at the most eastern mouth of the river.

Irtysch, a river of Siberia, which issues from the Lake Saisan, in Chinese Tartary, runs N. W. between the two countries, above 300 miles, then flows by Omsk, Tobolsk, and Samarof, below which it joins the Oby.

Irvine, a river of Scotland, in Ayrshire, which passes by Newmills and Kilmarnock, to the town of Irvine, below which it enters the Frith of Clyde.

Irvine, a borough of Scotland, in Ayrshire; contributory, with Ayr, &c., in sending one member to parliament. The chief trade is the exporting of coals to Ireland. Here is a dockyard, a large tan-work, and manufactures of carpets, muslins, silks, lawns, &c. It is seated near the mouth of the river Irvine; 1[illegible] miles N. of Ayr, and 24 S. W. of Glasgow.

Irwell, a river in Lancashire, which rises above Bolton, flows thence to Manchester, and joins the Mersey, below Flixton.

Is sur Tille, a town of France, in the department of Cote d'Or; seated on the Tille; 12 miles N. of Dijon.

Isabella, a town on the N. coast of Hispaniola; founded by Christopher Columbus, in 1493. Long. 71. 2. W. lat. 19. 55. N.

Ischia, an island of Naples, 15 miles in circuit, lying 3 miles off the coast of Terra di Lavoro. It is mountainous; but abounds in minerals, sulphur, fruits, and excellent wines. It was taken by a British and Sicilian force in 1807. Fresh water is scarce, and the rain is collected in cisterns; but the air is healthy; and there are several hot baths, on which account it is much resorted to by invalids.

Ischia, an episcopal city of Naples, capital of the above island; with a strong fort. It stands upon a rock, which is joined to the island by a bridge, and is like a pyramid of houses piled one upon another. At the end of the bridge, next the city, are iron gates, which open into a subterranean passage, through which the city is entered. Long. 14. 2. E. lat. 40. 41. N.

Isenburg, Upper, a principality of Germany, on the borders of Hanau; subject partly to Hesse-Cassel, partly to Hesse-Darmstadt. It is generally fertile, and contains 217 square miles, and 47,500 inhabitants.

Isenburg, New, a small town in the foregoing principality; 3 miles S. of Frankfort-on-the-Maine.

Isco, a town of Italy, in Bresciano, on the S. E. side of a lake of the same name; 10 miles N. W. of Brescia.

Iser, a river of Bavaria, which rises on the confines of Tyrol, and, passing by Munich and Landschut, joins the Danube between Straubing and Passau.

Iser, or Isar (Circle of), one of the modern divisions of Bavaria; bounded partly by the circles of the Regen and the Upper Danube, and partly by the Austrian states. It comprises most of the southern part of the old duchy of Bavaria, and is divided into 26 districts; its chief town, Munich, being the capital of the kingdom. The S. is mountainous, and consequently cold; the N. forms a large plain, with few elevations, possessing great fertility. The principal rivers are the Inn, the Iser, and the Lech.

Isere, a department of France, including part of the late province of Dauphiny. It is so named from a river which rises in Savoy, crosses this department by Grenoble, Moirans, and St. Marcellin, and joins the Rhone, above Valence. Grenoble is the capital.

Iserlohn, a town of Prussian Westphalia, in the county of Mark, with manufactures of iron, tin, velvets, silks, and stuffs. It is seated on the Buaren; 41 miles E. by N. of Dusseldorf.

Isernia, a town of Naples, in the Molise, at the foot of the Appennines. In 1805 it suffered much by an earthquake. 12 miles W. of Molise.

Isigny, a town of France, in the department of Calvados; 15 miles W. by N. of Bayeux.

Isis. *See* Thames.

Iskenderoon. *See* Alexandretto.

Isla, or **Ila**, an island of Scotland, one of the Hebrides, to the S. W. of Jura, from which it is separated by a narrow channel, called the Sound of Isla. It is 21 miles long, and 15 broad. On the E. side the surface is hilly, and covered with heath, but the greater part of the island is flat, and, when uncultivated, covered with a fine green sward. In the centre of the island is Loch Finlagan, about 3 miles in circuit, with an islet of the same name in the middle, where the great lord of the isles resided; but the palaces and offices are now in ruins. Isla has mines of iron, lead, copper, emery, quicksilver, and black-lead; with immense stores of limestone, marl, coral, and shell-sand for manure. Much flax is raised here, a great number of cattle fed, and a large quantity of whiskey distilled. The principal village is Bowmore, which has a convenient harbour and quay.

Islamabad, a town of Hindostan, in Bengal; capital of the country of Chittigong; situate on the Currumpooly, near its entrance into the Bay of Bengal. Long. 91. 55. E. lat. 22. 22. N.

Islands, Bay of, a bay of New Zealand, at the N. extremity of the most northern of the three islands that go under that name. In 1772 M. Dufresne Marion, with two French sloops, put into this bay, and, with 28 of his crew, was murdered by the natives. It contains Russell, the temporary seat of government, and several missionary and emigrant stations.

Isle Adam, a town of France, in the department of Seine-et-Oise; seated on the Oise; 20 miles N. by W. of Paris.

Isle Bouchard, a town of France, in the department of Indre-et-Loire; surrounded by the Vienne; 21 miles S. S. W. of Tours.

Isle Dieu, a small island of France; 14 miles from the coast of Poitou. It was taken by the English in 1795, but soon after evacuated.

Isle de France. *See* France, Isle of.

Isle Jourdain, a town of France, in the department of Gers; seated on an island in the river Save; 8 miles N. of Lombez.

Isleworth, a village in Middlesex; seated on the Thames; 9 miles W. of London. Here are many elegant villas; and near it is Sion-house, the magnificent seat of the Duke of Northumberland.

Islington, a large village in Middlesex, N. of London, to which it is now contiguous. The New River is received at the S. W. end of it into a large reservoir, whence its water is conveyed, in pipes, to all parts of the metropolis.

Ismail, a strong town of European Turkey, in Bessarabia. The Russians took it by storm in 1790; and it is said that the long siege, and the capture, did not cost them fewer than 20,000 men. The brave garrison merited the highest honours, but they were massacred by the Russians; and the city was abandoned to the fury of the brutal soldiery. Ismail is seated on the N. side of the Danube; 140 miles S. by W. of Bender. Pop. 10,000.

Ismid, or **Nikmid**, (ancient **Nicomedia**,) a town of Asia Minor, on the side of the hill over looking the Gulf of Nicomedia. Long. 29. 34. E. lat. 40. 39. N.

Isnik, a town of Asiatic Turkey, in Natolia, and a Greek archbishop's see. It is the ancient Nice, famous for the general council held here in 325. Nothing remains of its ancient splendour but an aqueduct. The Jews inhabit the greater part of it; and silk forms the principal article of trade. It is seated in a country fertile in corn and wine; 60 miles S. E. of Constantinople. Long. 30. 2. E. lat. 40. 22. N.

Isny, a town of Wirtemberg; with an abbey, called St. George. It is seated on the Isny; 18 miles N. E. of Lindau.

Isordskick, or **Kroczka**, a town of Servia; 14 miles S. E. of Belgrade.

Ispahan, a city of Persia, long the capital of the Persian monarchy, which is now removed to Tehran. It is situated in the province of Irac, and was formerly celebrated as the finest city in the East. It stands in the middle of a plain, surrounded on all sides by mountains at 8 miles distance, which rise gradually in the form of an amphitheatre. There is no river except a small one, called Sanderut, which supplies almost all the houses with water, and over which are several fine bridges. There are 168 marques, 1800 large caravanseras, and above 268 public baths. The streets are not paved, but are generally clean, on account of the dryness of the air; for it seldom rains or snows here. The inhabitants are computed at not more than 200,000, having been greatly depopulated by the intestine broils and civil wars with which this kingdom has been almost torn to pieces. This city is the emporium of the inland commerce of Persia, being the medium of communication with India, Cabul, and Turkey. It is 265 miles N. E. of Bassorah, and 300 S. of the Caspian Sea.

Issel. *See* Yssel.

Issengeaux, a town of France, in the department of Upper Loire; 17 miles N. E. of Puy.

Issequibo, or **Essequebo**, a settlement extending along the banks of a river of the same name, in British Guiana, and contiguous to that of Demerara, from which it is separated by the river Borassieri. It was taken from the Dutch during the late wars, and was finally ceded to Britain in 1814. It is extremely fertile, and is well cultivated. The Issequibo river is 20 miles wide at its mouth, and more than 300 in length.

Issoudun, a town of France, in the department of Indre, with a brisk trade in wood, cattle, cloth, hats, and stockings. It is seated on the Theole; 17 miles S. W. of Bourges, and 135 S. of Paris.

Istapa, a town of Mexico, in the province of Culiacan; 40 miles E. by S. of Culiacan.

Istria, a peninsula of Italy, between the Bay of Trieste, and the Quarnaro Isles; bounded by

Friuli on the W. and Carniola on the N.; being 200 miles in circumference. The air is unwholesome, especially near the coast; but the soil is fertile. Oil and wine are abundant, and there are some productive quarries of fine marble. The chief riches of the country, however, consist in its vast and valuable forests. One part of it belonged formerly to the Venetians; but the whole was ceded to the emperor by the treaty of Presburg, in 1805. In 1809 it fell into the hands of Napoleon, but was reconquered by the Austrians in 1814, and now forms the southern division of Austrian Illyria. The inhabitants (about 140,000) are chiefly occupied in agriculture, rearing bees, fishing, and the manufacture of silk, leather, tallow, and salt.

ITALY, one of the finest and most celebrated countries of Europe; lying between 7. and 10. E. long. and between 37. and 46. N. lat. On the N. N. W. and N. E. it is bounded by France, Switzerland, the county of the Grisons, and Germany; on the E. by the Adriatic Sea; and on the S. and W. by the Mediterranean; its figure bearing some resemblance to a boot.' Its length from Aosta, at the foot of the Alps, in Savoy, to the utmost verge of Calabria, is about 600 miles; but its breadth is very unequal, being in some places nearly 400 miles, in others not above 25 or 30. It was formerly the seat of the Roman empire, and, afterwards, of that more astonishing usurpation, the dominion of the pope. In the middle ages the kingdom of Lombardy and that of Naples held the two extremes, and the Ecclesiastical and Tuscan states occupied the centre. In more modern times the northern part became divided into a great number of states, differing considerably in their extent and importance. By the treaty of Campo Formio, in 1797, the Venetian territories to the E. and N. of the river Adige were ceded to Austria; and the remainder of the Venetian states, with the duchies of Modena, Milan, and Mantua, the principality of Massa, and the three legations of Ferrara, Bologna, and Romagna, in the pope's dominions, were erected into a government by the French, and called the Cisalpine Republic. This republic was overturned in 1799, but restored after the battle of Marengo, in 1800. In 1802 it received a new constitution, under the name of the Italian Republic, and Bonaparte, then first consul of France, was elected president. In 1805 the Italian Republic was erected into a kingdom, and the emperor of France assumed the title of King of Italy. In December following, the Austrian part of the Venetian states was added to its territories, by the treaty of Presburg. The kingdom was divided into departments, and the city of Milan was the capital. But the subsequent changes which took place in Europe again deranged the political situation of this country. The kingdom of Italy was overturned; and the country is now divided into the following states:—The Lombardo-Venetian kingdom, the kingdom of Sardinia, the States of the Church, or pope's dominions, the kingdom of the two Sicilies, the grand duchy of Tuscany, the states of Modena, the states of Parma, the duchy of Lucca, and the republic of San Marino. Italy, as to climate, has been divided into four separate regions. The first of these embraces the basin of the Po, extending about 260 miles in length, and 150 in its greatest breadth; being bounded by the Alps and Appennines on the N. W. and S., and open to the Adriatic on the E. Here the atmosphere is uniformly serene and bright; and, being tempered by refreshing breezes from the adjacent heights, the climate is altogether one of the most salubrious and delightful in the whole world. The second region includes the Tuscan and Roman Territories, being screened on the N. by the Appennines, and more exposed to the heats of summer than to the rigours of winter. Frost and snow are here experienced; but the temperature is sufficient to mature the orange, the fig, and similar fruits. The third district contains Campania Felix, and its dependencies, where the vegetable treasures of nature are also found in the greatest perfection: the air is uniformly mild and serene, and a peculiar glow of beauty pervades the landscape. The fourth division extends from the Appennines to the Adriatic, and embraces the southern districts of the peninsula. Here the aloe, the palm, and other productions of a southern climate flourish; but, when the sirocco blows, the heats are overcoming to a stranger from almost any other part of Europe. The climate of Italy also experiences much diversity from elevation and local circumstances. The general aspect of the country is highly beautiful and picturesque. The Alps and Appennines diversify this peninsula with almost every possible combination of hill and valley, rivers, lakes, and romantic scenery. Northern Italy is broken into bold and rugged acclivities by the former, from the southern face of which descend the streams that form the Po, and various other classical rivers. Towards the southern extremity of Italy, the Appennines diverge into two branches, one of which advances eastward to Capo di Leuca, and the other southward to the Straits of Messina. Several detached mountains, among which is the celebrated Vesuvius, here overhang the Gulf of Naples, and discharge their liquid fires into its waters. The Appennines are, in many parts, clothed with trees to their summits; in other places they are more precipitous, and attain the altitude of ice and snow. The principal rivers are the Po, Tiber, Adige, Brenta, Piave, and Tagliamento; and there are several fine lakes, as the Maggiore, Lugano, Como, Garda, Perugia, Bracciano, and Celano. The soil, in general, is very fertile. It produces a great variety of wines, and the best oil in Europe; excellent silk in abundance; corn of all sorts, but not in such plenty as in other countries; oranges, lemons, citrons, pomegranates, almonds, raisins, sugar, figs, peaches, apricots, pears, apples, filberts, chestnuts, &c. This country also yields good pasture, and abounds with cattle, sheep, goats, buffaloes, wild boars, mules, and horses. The forests are well stored with game, and the mountains have not only mines of iron, lead, alum, sulphur, marble of all sorts, alabaster, jasper, porphyry, &c., but also gold and silver, with a great variety of aromatic herbs, trees, shrubs, and evergreens. Wine, oil, perfumes, fruits, and silks, are the principal articles of exportation, and great sums of money are expended by travellers in the purchase of pictures, curiosities, relics, antiquities, &c. No country has produced better politicians, historians, poets, musicians, painters, and sculptors; that is, since the revival of the arts and sciences, exclusive of those of ancient times. The Italians are generally well proportioned, but of their complexion they cannot boast. With respect to dress, they follow the fashions of the countries on which they border, or to which they are subject. They are very affable, courteous, ingenious, sober, and ready-witted; but extremely jealous, vindictive, lascivious, ceremonious, and superstitious. Masquerades, gaming, horse-races, and conversations or assemblies, are the chief diversions of the Italians, excepting religious exhibitions, in which they are pompous beyond all other nations. The established religion is the Roman Catholic, but all other sects are now tolerated. The number of archbishops in the whole country is 38, and that of the suffragans indefinite, as may be truly added of the inferior ecclesiastics. Their language, a corruption of the Latin, is remarkable for its smoothness, and is said to be spoken in its greatest purity at Florence. Further particulars of this country will be found under the names of its particular divisions, as NAPLES, &c.

ITALY, AUSTRIAN. *See* LOMBARDO-VENETIAN KINGDOM.

ITAMARCA. *See* TAMARICA.

ITCHEN, or ALRE, a river in Hampshire, which enters the Bay of Southampton at the town of that name.

ITZEHOE, a town of Germany, in Holstein, belonging to Denmark, with a fortress. A duty is exacted here from all ships coming up the Stoer, on which river it is seated; 12 miles N. N. E. of Gluckstadt, and 31 miles N. W. of Hamburg.

IVANGOROD. *See* NARVA.

IVANITZ, a town of Croatia, seated on the Lonia; 42 miles N. E. of Carlstadt.

IVELCHESTER. *See* ILCHESTER.

IVES, ST., a borough in Cornwall, sending one member to parliament; seated on a bay of the same name, celebrated for its extensive pilchard fishery. Market on Wednesday. The church is a handsome building, close to the sea. Here are also meeting-houses for Independents and Methodists, and a good grammar-school, founded by Charles I. In the vicinity of the town is Treganny Castle, and one mile from this mansion, on the summit of a lofty hill, is a pyramid, erected by the late J. Knoll, Esq. who died in 1811, and directed, by will, that at the end of every five years an old woman, and 10 girls under 14 years of age, dressed in white, and accompanied by music, should walk in procession from the market-house to this pyramid, where they should dance, and sing the 100th Psalm. For this he bequeathed certain freeholds, and vested them in the minister, to whom, and the port collector, he bequeathed 10*l*. for a dinner; 8 miles N. E. of Penzance, and 277 W. by S. of London.

IVES, ST., a town in Huntingdonshire, with a market on Monday; seated on the river Ouse, 6 miles S. E. of Huntingdon, and 59 N. by W. of London.

IVICA, an island of the Mediterranean, 56 miles S. W. of Majorca. It is about 60 miles in circumference, and mountainous, but fertile in corn and fruits. A great quantity of salt is made here, highly esteemed for its whiteness. The capital, of the same name, which stands on the S. side of the island, is well fortified, and has a convenient harbour. Long. 1. 25. E. lat. 38. 52. N.

IVINGHOE, a town in Buckinghamshire, with a market on Saturday, and manufactures of bone-lace. It is 6 miles S. W. of Dunstable, and 33 N. W. of London.

IVREA, an ancient town of Piedmont, with a fort, citadel, and castle. It is a bishop's see, and contains a cathedral, four other churches, and several religious houses. It is seated on the Doria, between two hills; 20 miles N. of Turin. Long. 7. 48. E. lat. 45. 22. N.

IVRY, a town of France, in the department of Eure, with a late Benedictine abbey; seated on the Eure, 12 miles S. E. of Evreux, and 50 N. W. of Paris.

IVRY, a town of France, in the department of Cote d'Or; 9 miles S. E. of Arnay le Duc.

IXWORTH, a town in Suffolk, with a market on Friday; 7 miles N. E. of Bury St. Edmund, and 77 N. E. of London.

IZERY, ST., a town of France, department of Aveiron; 6 miles N. W. of Vabres.

IZERON, a town of France, in the department of Rhone, 10 miles S. W. of Lyons.

IZIGINSK, a town of Siberia, in the province of Okhotsk; defended by lofty palisades, and wooden bastions, provided with cannon and military stores. The commerce consists of furs and the skins of reindeer. It is seated on the Izingin, 15 miles from its mouth, and 520 N. E. of Okhotsk.

IZQUINTENANGO, a town of Mexico, in the province of Chiapa. The country about it produces cotton, and a great number of pine-apples. It is 100 miles S. E. of Chiapa.

J.

JAALONO, a town of France, in the department of Marne, 9 miles W. of Chalons.

JABAZ, a town of Asiatic Turkey, in Natolia 20 miles N. W. of Angura.

JABLUNKAU, a town of Silesia, in the principality of Teschen, on the river Elsa; with a fort near it, called Jablunkau Schanz, which defends a defile towards Hungary. It is seated between high mountains, 11 miles S. S. E. of Teschen.

JACCA, a town in Spain, formerly the capital of Arragon; seated on a river of the same name among the Pyrenees. It is a bishop's see, and is defended by a citadel; 45 miles N. by E. of Saragossa.

JACI D'AQUILA, a town of Sicily, in Val di Demona; 10 miles N. N. E. of Catania.

JACKSON, a county of the United States, in Indiana, laid out in 1815. It is bounded by Clark, Jefferson, Washington, Orange, and Indian counties, and watered by White River.

JACKSONBOROUGH, a town of South Carolina, on the E. side of the Edisto; 35 miles W. of Charleston.

JACOBSDORF, a town on the Prussian states, in Pomerania, 3 miles S. E. of Jacobshagan, and 8 E. of Zachan.

JACOBSHAGAN, a town of the Prussian states, in Pomerania, 14 miles S. of Daber.

JACOBSTADT, a town of Russia, in Finland, with a convenient harbour, and a thriving trade. 50 miles N. N. E. of Wasa.

JACURSO, a town of Naples, in Calabria Ultra, 8 miles W. of Squillace.

JAEN, a province of the eastern part of Andalusia, surrounded by the provinces of La Mancha, Murcia, Granada, and Cordova. Its erritorial extent is 4730 square miles, and its population about 207,000. This province, though badly cultivated, produces wine, oil, silk, and corn, especially along the Guadalquiver, which is the largest river in the province. Jaen was formerly a kingdom, and the king of Spain still takes the title of king of Jaen, although it is now included in the government of Andalusia.

JAEN, a fortified city of Spain, in Andalusia, capital of the above province. It is a bishop's see, and the residence of the magistracy of the province. It is seated at the foot of a mountain, on the river Guadalbulon; 36 miles N. of Granada.

JAFA, a fertile country of Arabia, N. W. of Aden and of Hadramaut; it was formerly under the dominion of the imam, but in the end of the seventeenth century the inhabitants made themselves independent, and are now governed by three petty chiefs, who have also conquered a part of the province of Hadramaut.

JAFFA, anciently called Joppa, a town of Asia, in Palestine, situated near the coast of the Mediterranean, with a small citadel. It was formerly a celebrated city, and is frequently mentioned in the scriptures. It has long been inhabited by Turks and Arabs, with a mixture of Greeks, Maronites, and Armenians. The houses are small, and surrounded with the ruins of the ancient walls and towers. The Franks, Greeks, and Armenians have small convents for the reception of pilgrims of different nations. The principal commerce is in grain, particularly rice from Egypt. Jaffa was laid waste in the crusades, and afterwards destroyed by an earthquake. In profane history it is said to be the place whence Perseus delivered Andromeda. It was taken by the French under Bonaparte in February, 1789, but they held possession 40 days only. It is 21 miles N. W. of Gaza, and 33 W. of Jerusalem, of which it is the port.

JAFFNA, a town of Ceylon, capital of Jaffnapatam, from whence are exported great quantities of tobacco, and some elephants, which are accounted the most docile of any in the world. The Dutch took it from the Portuguese in 1658, and it was taken by the English in 1795. It is seated on a river navigable for large boats, 100 miles N. of Candy. Long. 80. 10. E. lat. 9. 45. N.

JAFFNAPATAM, a district in the N. part of Ceylon, fertile in fruits and vegetables, and said to be the most populous and healthy in the island. Several small islands are politically connected with this district, and between it and the Candian provinces are numerous woods, inhabited by a savage race called Veddahs, supposed to be the aborigines of the country.

JAFFRABAD, a town of Hindostan, in Guzerat, near the mouth of a river, noted for large oysters; 37 miles E. N. E. of Diu.

JAGERNAUT. *See* JUGGERNAUT.

JAGERNDORF, a town and castle of Silesia, seated on the Oppa, 13 miles N. W. of Troppau. Long. 17. 44. E. lat. 50. 0. N.

JAGO, ST., the most fertile province of Chili, extending 45 miles in length from E. to W. and 36 in breadth from N. to S. It is bounded on the E. by the Andes, W. by Melipilla, N. by the province of Aconcagua, and S. by the river Maypo. Corn, wine, and fruits are produced here in great quantities. The mountains abound in the precious metals, and here are also mines of copper, tin, and lead. The province is watered by the Mapacho, the Colina, and several other fine streams.

JAGO, ST., the capital of the above province, and a bishop's see. Besides the cathedral, there are three parish churches, and eight monasteries. The inhabitants, about 46,000, are chiefly native Americans and Spaniards. Here are several canals, and a dike, by means of which they water the gardens and cool the streets. It is seated in a beautiful plain, at the foot of the Andes, on the river Mapacho, over which is a handsome bridge, which connects several suburbs with the city. The commerce is considerable, and the markets are well supplied with all kinds of provisions. 53 miles E. S. E. of Valparaiso. Long. 69. 48. W. lat. 33. 15. S.

JAGO, ST., a handsome town of Mexico, capital of Veragua. It has an elegant hospital, and stands in a fertile country, which produces maize, plantains, &c., with abundance of cattle. 110 miles S. W. of Porto Bello.

JAGO, ST., a fortified seaport on the S. coast of Cuba, and a bishop's see, with a good harbour; situate on a bay, about 6 miles from the sea. Long. 76. 10. W. lat. 20. 5. S.

JAGO DE LOS CAVALLEROS, ST., a town of Hispaniola, in a fertile soil; on the river St. Jago, 70 miles from its mouth, and 90 N. N.W. of St. Domingo.

JAGO DE COMPOSTELLA, ST. *See* COMPOSTELLA.

JAGO DE LOS VALLES, ST., a town of Mexico, in the province of Guasteca; seated on the river Panuco; 170 miles N. by E. of Mexico.

JAGO DE LA VEGA, ST. *See* SPANISH-TOWN.

JAGODINA, a town of European Turkey, in Servia; seated on the Morava; 60 miles S. S. E. of Belgrade.

JAISZA, a town of European Turkey, in Bosnia, with a strong citadel; seated on the Plena; 50 miles N. E. of Serai.

JAJGUR, a town and fortress of Hindostan; capital of a district of the same name, in the province of Agimere. The district contains upwards of 80 villages, chiefly inhabited by a predatory tribe of Hindoos called Meena.

JAKUTSKOI. *See* YAKUTSK.

JALALABAD, a town of Hindostan, in the country of Cabul; situate on the Kameh; 60 miles E. S. E. of Cabul.

JALLINDAR, a town of Hindostan, capital of a district of the same name, in the country of Lahore; 80 miles E. by S. of Lahore. Long. 74. 10. E. lat. 30. 50. N.

JALOFFS, or OUALOFFS, a people of Africa, who occupy great part of the country between the lower part of the Gambia and that of the Senegal. Their territory is estimated at 4800 square miles. They are celebrated as hunters and warriors; and the cotton cloth which they manufacture is superior, both in quality and colour, to that of the Mandingos.

JALONITZA, a town of European Turkey, in Walachia, on a river of the same name; 95 miles S. W. of Ismail.

JALOUR, a town of Hindostan, in the country of Agimere; situate on a mountain difficult of access; 85 miles W. N. W. of Cheitore.

JAMAGORD, a town of Russia, in the government of Petersburg; with a strong fort; seated on the Jama; 12 miles N. E. of Narva.

JAMAICA, the most considerable and valuable of the British West India Islands; discovered by Columbus, in 1494. It lies 30 leagues W. of St. Domingo, nearly the same distance S. of Cuba, and is of an oval figure, 150 miles long and 40 broad, containing 4,080,000 acres. An elevated ridge, called the Blue Mountains, runs lengthwise from E. to W., whence numerous rivers take their rise on both sides; and, though none of them are navigable for barges, yet the sugars are carried upon many of them in canoes, from the remote plantations to the seaside: some of them run underground for a considerable space, particularly the Cobre and Pedra. The year is distinguished into two seasons, the wet and dry; but the rains are not so frequent as formerly, which is supposed to be owing to the cutting down of the woods. About nine in the morning it is so extremely hot that it would be almost intolerable if the easterly breeze did not rise to cool the air. Sometimes the nights are pretty cool, and there are great dews, which are deemed unwholesome, especially to new comers. The months of July, August, and September, are called the hurricane months, because then they are the most frequent; and there is lightning almost every night. The best houses are generally built low, on account of the hurricanes and earthquakes; and the negroes' huts, made of reeds, will hold only two or three persons. The valleys are embellished with plantations, so well laid out, and with such a variety of fruit-trees, as to make the country look like a paradise. Horned cattle, hogs, and sheep are plentiful; but the servants generally feed upon Irish salt beef, and the negroes have herrings and salt fish. The general produce of this island is sugar, rum, molasses, ginger, cotton, indigo, pimento, cocoa, coffee, several kinds of wood, and medicinal drugs. It has some tobacco, but not good, and used only by the negroes; also maize, Guinea corn, and peas of various kinds, with variety of roots. Fruits are in great plenty, such as oranges, lemons, shaddocks, citrons, pomegranates, pine-apples, prickly-pears, melons, pompions, guavas, and many others. Jamaica can boast of a botanical garden, containing the rarest collection of curious trees and plants, perhaps in the world. The whole island is divided into three counties, Middlesex, Surrey, and Cornwall; and these into 20 parishes, or districts, six towns, and 27 villages. The legislature is composed of the governor, a council of 12 nominated by the Crown, and a house of assembly consisting of 43 members elected by the freeholders. The first settlement on this island was made in 1509, by the Spaniards, who were cruel to the natives; but it was taken by the English in 1656, and a colony soon after formed by disbanded soldiers from the parliamentary army, who were governed by military laws till the restoration. The tranquillity of this colony has been occasionally disturbed by the inroads of the Maroons, or original natives, who, however, were completely quelled in 1796; and since that period the colony has rapidly increased in importance. There is an ecclesiastical establishment in this island, consisting of 19 beneficed clergymen; but the state of religion has long been deplorable. Within the last few years, however, considerable efforts have been made by missionaries and others; and, though the principal men of the island have manifested much opposition, yet these efforts have already been crowned with very considerable success. The government of Jamaica is one of the richest places, next to that of Ireland, in the disposal of the crown: the standing salary is 2000*l.*, and the assembly commonly vote as much more to the governor, which, with other perquisites, make it little less than 10,000*l.* a year. Spanish Town is the seat of government, but Kingston is the capital.

JAMAICA, a town of New York in Queen's County, with three churches; 12 miles E. by S. of New York.

JAMALABAD, a town of Hindostan, in Canara, with a fort on the summit of an immense rock, which is accessible only by one narrow way. The town stands on the banks of a river; 30 miles E. N. E. of Mangalore.

JAMAMA, a town of Arabia, capital of a district of the same name, lying W. of the province of Bahrein. It is seated on the river Astan; 140 miles S. W. of Lachsa.

Jambi, the capital of a district of the same name, on the N. E. coast of the island of Sumatra; with a trade in gold dust, pepper, and canes. The town is large, and situate inland, on a river navigable for boats; 160 miles N. by E. of Bencoolen.

Jambo, a town of Arabia Deserta, with a good harbour on the Red Sea; 72 miles S. S. W. of Medina.

James, a river of Virginia, which rises on the W. side of the Blue ridge of the Allegany Mountains, and, flowing E. through the state, enters Chesapeake Bay, near Hampton.

James Bay. *See* Hudson's Bay.

James Island, an island of Africa; 30 miles up the river Gambia, and 3 miles from its nearest shore. Here the English have a fort and factory. Long. 16. 0. W. lat. 13. 15. N.

James Island, an island of South Carolina, on the S. side of Charleston harbour, opposite Charleston.

Jamestown, a town of Virginia, seated in a peninsula, on the N. side of James River; 5 miles S. S. W. of Williamsburg.

Jamestown, a town of Ireland, in the county of Leitrim; seated on the Shannon; 5 miles S. by E. of Carrick, and 73 N. W. of Dublin.

Jamets, a town of France, in the department of Meuse; 72 miles S. of Stenay.

Jamtland, a province of Sweden, bordering on Norway, nearly of a circular form; about 70 miles in length, and 60 in breadth. The western part is mountainous; the eastern is a fine champaign country, watered with several lakes and rivers, which abound with fish. The country produces excellent oats, and abounds in good turnips. The pastures are extensive, and of excellent quality, but are much neglected. It contains alum quarries, sandstone, slate, the lapis ollarius, fine rock crystal, and lead ore. The inhabitants carry on a considerable trade with the Norwegians.

Janeiro. *See* Rio Janeiro.

Janna, a province of European Turkey; bounded on the N. by Macedonia, E. by the Archipelago, S. by Livadia, and W. by Albania. It is the Thessaly of the ancients, and Larissa is the capital.

Janville, a town of France, department of Eure-et-Loire; 20 miles S. E. of Chartres.

Japan, an extensive empire in the most eastern part of Asia; extending from long. 131. to 142. E. and from lat 30. to 41. N. It consists of three large islands (the superficial extent of which is estimated at 90,000 square miles), and several smaller islands. The whole empire is divided into seven principal districts, which are subdivided into 70 provinces; and the population is, in proportion to extent, deemed equal to that of China, being about 17,000,000. It is the richest country in the world for gold; there are also rich silver mines, and fine copper is the main source of the wealth of many provinces. It produces a great deal of rice, which is the principal article of subsistence; millet, wheat, and barley are also cultivated to a small extent. Turnips, carrots, melons, cucumbers, &c., all grow spontaneously. Cedars are common, and so large that they are proper for the masts of ships, and columns for temples. The mulberry tree, the laurel, the tree shrub, and camphire tree are also common; but the most remarkable is the varnish tree (rhus vernix), the juice of which is used to varnish, or (as we call it) japan their furniture. The rocks and most barren places are cultivated, and produce a variety of fruits, plants, and roots. The woods and forests, and long ridges of mountains, with which the country is intersected, produce good pasturage, and are stocked with deer, oxen, buffaloes, and a few horses; but there are no sheep nor goats. Here are large quantities of fine porcelain, silk, and skins, as also red pearls, which are not in less esteem than the white. The Japanese are of a yellowish complexion all over; their heads are in general large, their necks short, and their hair, which is naturally black and thick, is rendered shining by the use of oils; their eyes are small, of a dark brown colour, and sunk deep in the head, and the eyelids form, in the great angle of the eye, a deep furrow, which discriminates them from other nations; their eyebrows are also placed somewhat higher; and their noses, though not flat, are thick and short. They are naturally ingenious, and have a high character for honesty and veracity. Their common drinks are all hot; they uncover their feet, out of respect, are fond of black teeth, and get on horseback on the left side. Their houses are of wood, coloured white, and never exceed two stories in height. The interior is divided into apartments, at pleasure, by movable partitions sliding in grooves. They have neither tables, beds, nor chairs, but sit and lie on carpets and mats. The dress consists of trowsers, and a loose robe of silk or cotton, fastened by a girdle; the number being increased according to the coldness of the weather: stockings are not used; and the shoes are commonly of rice straw. The mathematical and physical sciences are yet in their infancy, but are highly esteemed among them, and they have several schools at different places, in which are taught arithmetic, rhetoric, poetry, history, and astronomy. Some of their arts and manufactures even surpass those of Europe. They formerly carried on a considerable trade with the neighbouring countries; but now all communications are forbidden, except with the Chinese and Dutch; and with them only at the port of Nangasaki. The merchandise brought by the Dutch are spices, sugar, linen and woollen cloth, elephants' teeth, and haberdashery wares; for which they receive gold, silver, copper, rice, tea, fine porcelain, cabinets, and other japanned and lackered wares. Japan was formerly divided into a great many small kingdoms, which still retain their ancient names; but they were at length swallowed up in one, to which all the rest are become either subject or tributary. The tributary princes, amounting to between 50 and 60, are vested with the regal dignity, and are absolute in their respective territories; but they are entirely subject to the emperor, who can depose or even condemn them to death, if he think proper. The laws are extremely severe and cruel; and the people are doubly slaves, first to their own princes, and then to the emperor, who has power of life and death over them all. Anciently the emperor was likewise sovereign pontiff, under the title of dairo, and in fact worshipped by all his subjects; but in the civil wars which occurred on the minority of one of them, in 1150, one of the competitors for the crown assumed the ecclesiastical government, retaining the same title; while the other, who ruled in civil affairs, was called cubo. From that time, the dairo has only been at the head of religious matters, while the cubo, or secular emperor, bears an absolute dominion over all civil and military affairs. The former still lives in great state and grandeur, at Miaco; and the latter pays him a kind of homage, as if he acted only as his deputy or viceroy; but, in reality, the cubo is now the real monarch of Japan, and the dairo only his high priest. The Japanese are as fabulous as the Chinese in the antiquity of their empire; but the certain period begins with the hereditary succession of the ecclesiastical emperors, from the year 660 before the Christian epoch. The religion of the country is paganism; but there are two different sects. There was once a great number of Christians in different parts of the empire; but in 1638 they underwent great persecutions, and all who professed Christianity were either put to death or forced to revert to paganism. The capital of the empire is Jeddo.

JAPARA, a seaport on the N. coast of the island of Java, with a good harbour. It was the capital of a considerable kingdom, till the Dutch made themselves masters of it; and now they have a colony here, and a considerable trade; 253 miles E. by S. of Batavia. Long. 110. 45. E. lat. 6. 20. S.

JAQUEMEL, a town of St. Domingo, on a bay of its name, on the S. coast; 32 miles S. S. W. of Port au Prince.

JAQUES, a navigable river of Louisiana, which falls into the Missouri.

JAQUES CARTIER, a river of Canada, so called from the navigator who first explored the St. Lawrence, into which it falls in long. 71. 41. W. lat. 46. 38. N.

JARGEAU, a town of France, in the department of Loiret. It was taken by the English in 1438, and retaken by Joan of Arc, the next year. It is seated near the Loire; 10 miles E. S. E. of Orleans.

JARISBERG, a town of Norway; capital of a district abounding in mines; in the diocese of Aggerhuys; 5 miles N. of Tonsberg.

JARNAC, a town of France, in the department of Charente. Near this place the duke of Anjou, afterwards Henry III., obtained a victory over the Huguenots, in 1569. It is seated on the Charente; 20 miles W. of Angouleme.

JAROMITZ, a town of Bohemia; seated on the Elbe; 9 miles N. of Konigingratz.

JARON, a town of Persia, in Farsistan; celebrated for abundance of palm-trees and their excellent fruit; 89 miles S. by E. of Shiras. Long. 53. 10. E. lat. 28. 15. N.

JAROSLAU, a town of Poland, in Red Russia, with a strong citadel. A battle was gained here by the Swedes, in 1656, after which they took the town. It is included in the kingdom of Galicia, and seated on the Saine; 55 miles W. of Lemberg. Long. 22. 43. E. lat. 50. 4. N.

JAROSLAUL, or JAROSLAV, a government of Russia, formerly a province of the government of Moscow. Its territorial extent is estimated at about 14,000 square miles, and its inhabitants at 800,000. It is divided into 10 circles, exclusive of the level called the Steppes of Jaroslav. The principal rivers are the Wolga, the Schekna, and the Mologa. The chief trade is in cattle and wood. The capital, of the same name, is a large commercial place, and a bishop's see, with numerous manufactures. It is seated on the Wolga; 145 miles N. N. E. of Moscow.

JASENITZ, a town of Hither Pomerania; seated on the Oder; 10 miles N. of Stettin.

JASQUE, a town of Persia, in the province of Mecran; which gives name to a cape in the Gulf of Ormus. Long. 57. 4. E. lat. 25. 40. N.

JASSY, a town of European Turkey; capital of Moldavia, and an archbishop's see; with a trade in flax, corn, hides, wool, wax, honey, tallow, and canvas, large quantities of which are made in the town, and sent to Constantinople. In 1753 it was destroyed by fire; it was subsequently rebuilt and well fortified; but in 1788 the fortifications were demolished, excepting a small fort. The inhabitants are estimated at 12,000. It has been several times taken in the wars between the Turks and the Russians or Austrians. It is seated on the Pruth; 170 miles N. N. E. of Bucharest, and 370 N. of Constantinople.

JAUER, a town of Silesia, capital of a principality of the same name, with a citadel, and a large square, surrounded by piazzas. It has manufactures of woollen and cotton, and a trade in flax and yarn. It is seated in a fine country, on the rivulet Jauer; 35 miles W. by S. of Breslau. Long. 16. 23. E. lat. 51. 2. N.

JAULNAIS, a town of France, in the department of Vienne; 6 miles N. of Poitiers

JAURU, a river of Brazil, in Matto-Grosso, which rises in the plains of Parexis, in long. 58. 30. W. lat. 14. 42. S., and, after a long S. and S. E. course, falls into the Paraguay, in lat. 16. 24. S. At its mouth is erected a beautiful pyramid of marble, bearing inscriptions commemorative of the treaty between Spain and Portugal, which defined the boundaries of their respective territories. On its banks are extensive salt-pits, from which the province of Matto-Grosso derives large quantities of salt.

JAVA, an island of the East Indies, lying to the S. of Borneo, and separated, at its W. end, from Sumatra, by the Strait of Sunda. It is sometimes called Great Java, to distinguish it from Bali, by some named Little Java. It is 640 miles in length, and of various breadth, extending from 105. to 116. E. long. and 6. to 9. S. lat. The land is low, and in some places marshy, near the shore, which renders the air unhealthy; but it rises in a gradual slope towards the interior of the country, admitting in its ascent every variety of situation and verdure. Rice is the staple production of the island, and is exported in considerable quantity. Sugar, pepper, cotton, and coffee are produced in abundance; indigo, of a very superior quality, is also cultivated; and wheat, barley, oats, and Bengal grain, thrive well, and might be produced in great abundance, if due attention were bestowed on their culture. The N. coast has a great many commodious creeks, bays, harbours, and towns, with many little islands near the shore. The inhabitants are chiefly Javanese; next to these are the Malays; and in the seaports a considerable number of Chinese are settled. The Javanese inhabit all the interior parts of the island, and are in general the cultivators of the soil. They are described as a barbarous, proud, and fierce people; of a brown complexion, short, coal-black hair, large cheeks, small eyes, and large eyebrows. The men are very robust and strong limbed; the women are small, but of pleasing countenance, and in some districts they are really beautiful. The men wear a piece of calico, which is the principal manufacture of the island, wrapped two or three times round their middle; and the women wear them from their armpits down to their knees; but all other parts are bare. The men have two or three wives, and several concubines, according to their circumstances. The Javanese appear, from the remains of temples and inscriptions, to be of Hindoo descent, and their language is quite distinct from that of the Malays; but the professed religion of both is Mahomedism. The Malays principally inhabit along the coast; they are not so well featured as the Javanese; but the men are often very muscular and well made. They are generally indolent, but at the same time restless, vindictive, and treacherous. The Chinese are distinguished by their habits of industry, and generally by their wealth. Many of them carry on a considerable trade with their native country, and the several islands of the eastern archipelago. They intermarry with the Javanese and Malays, and purchase female slaves for wives and concubines. This island has very high mountains, particularly the Pepper Mountain, on the S. side; it has, likewise, impassable forests and wildernesses; but to the N., between Batavia and Bantam, is a very populous country, full of rice fields, and plenty of salt and pepper, besides most sorts of fruits proper to the climate. Here are also plenty of hogs, beeves, and sheep, with other tame animals; and likewise fowl, both wild and tame, in great abundance. In the woods are large tigers, rhinoceroses, and other wild beasts; and in the rivers are crocodiles. The serene season is from May to November; and then the rains begin, which lay the low grounds under water, kill the insects, and continue till March, when they commence sowing, and in July the sugar and rice begin to ripen; but September and October are the best months for all sorts of fruits. Java has a river which rises in the mountains, and, dividing itself into many branches, waters the circumjacent country: these afterwards reunite, and pass through Batavia, dividing it into two parts. For more than a century Java was under the dominion of the Dutch. In 1811 it was captured by the British, under Sir Samuel Auchmuty, and many important improvements were adopted in its internal administration. Government also did much to promote agricultural improvements, and the country prospered and enjoyed tranquillity. Since it has been restored to the Dutch, they appear, however, to have reverted to their former wretched system, as they have been engaged in quelling insurrections, which there is little doubt were provoked by their arbitrary and vexatious exactions. Batavia is the capital.

Jaxt, one of the four circles, or departments, of Wirtemberg, deriving its name from the river Jaxt; having Baden on the W., and Bavaria on the E. It comprises a superficial area of above 1400 square miles, with a population of about 260,000: the name was formerly given to a province not half the extent.

Jaxt, a river of Germany, in Wirtemberg, which rises in the county of Oettingen, and, after flowing through the principality of Ellwangen, falls into the Neckar, opposite to Wimpfen, in Hesse-Darmstadt.

Jaxtberg, a small town of Wirtemberg, on the river Jaxt; 10 miles S. E. of Mergentheim.

Jean, St., a town of France, in the department of Moselle; seated on the Sarre; 12 miles W. of Deux Ponts.

Jean d'Angely, St., a town of France, department of Lower Charente; famous for its brandy. It was taken from the Huguenots, in 1621, by Louis XIII., who demolished the fortifications. It is seated on the Bontonne; 17 miles N. E. of Saintes, and 37 S. E. of Rochelle.

Jean de Losne, St., a town of France, department of Cote d'Or; celebrated for the bravery of its inhabitants in opposing the imperial Count Gallas, at the head of a numerous army, in 1635. It is seated on the Saone; 15 miles S. S. E. of Dijon.

Jean de Luz, St., a town of France, in the department of Lower Pyrenees—the last next Spain; with a harbour. It owes its opulence to the cod and whale fishery. It is seated on a small river, near the Bay of Biscay; 14 miles S. W. of Bayonne. Long. 1. 40. W. lat. 43. 25. N.

Jean de Maurienne, St., a town of Savoy; capital of the province of Maurienne, and a bishop's see. It is seated on the river Arc; 25 miles E. N. E. of Greenoble. Long. 6. 20. E. lat. 45. 17. N.

Jean de Pied de Port, St., a town of France, department of Lower Pyrenees; defended by a citadel; upon an eminence, at the entrance of those passages, or defiles, in the Pyrenees, which, in this country, are called Ports. It is seated on the river Nive; 20 miles S. S. E. of Bayonne, and 30. N. E. of Pampeluna.

Jed, a river of Scotland, in Roxburghshire, which rises on the borders of England, and joins the Teviot, a little below Jedburgh. On its banks are several large caverns, which were the hiding-places of ancient border warriors.

JEDBURGH, a borough of Scotland; capital of Roxburghshire; with a market on Tuesday. Here is the ruin of a fine abbey, part of which has been made the parish church. A variety of woollen manufactures are carried on here, and the vicinity is noted for its orchards. It is situate on the Jed, near its conflux with the Teviot; 42 miles S. E. of Edinburgh.

JEDO, or JEDDO, the capital of the empire of Japan; situate on the S. E. side of Niphon, the largest of the Japanese islands. The city has neither walls nor ramparts, is 9 miles in length and 6 in breadth, and contains 1,000,000 inhabitants. The houses are built of earth, and boarded on the outside, to prevent the rains from destroying the walls. In every street is an iron gate, which is shut up at night, and a kind of custom-house, or magazine, for merchandise. The imperial palace is surrounded by walls and ditches, with drawbridges, forming of itself a considerable town, in the middle of the city. Where the emperor resides are three towers, nine stories high, each covered with plates of gold; and the hall of audience is supported by pillars of massy gold. Near the palace are several others, where the relations of the emperor live. The empress has a palace of her own, and there are twenty small ones for the concubines; besides which, all the printers of the empire, who are obliged to make it their residence during half the year, have each a palace in the city, with a handsome garden. The houses of the common class are nothing but ground floor, the rooms parted by folding screens, so that they can be made larger or smaller at pleasure. Jedo is seated in a plain at the head of a fine bay, and a river which passes through it supplies several canals. Long. 139. 30. E. lat. 36. 10. N.

JEFFERSON, the name of three counties in the United States, viz. one in the state of Indiana, one in Kentucky, and one in Ohio.

JEFFERSON, a town of Virginia, on the N. side of Roanoke River; 19 miles below the Oeconeachey Islands.

JEFFERSONVILLE, a post town of the United States, in Indiana; seated on the Ohio, nearly opposite Louisville.

JEGNI-KEVI, a town of Asiatic Turkey, in Natolia; 24 miles N. N. W. of Degnizlu.

JEGNIPANGOLA, a town of European Turkey, in Bulgaria; 70 miles E. S. E. of Distra.

JEHUD, or JOUD, mountains in the N. W. part of Hindostan, extending eastward from Attock to Behnbur. They are part of the territory of the mountaineers called Gickers, Gehkers, or Kakares.

JEKYL, a small island of North America, on the coast of Georgia; S. of the island of St. Simon.

JELLASORE, a town of Bengal; seated on the Sabaureeka; 50 miles S. by W. of Midnapour.

JELLINGHY, a town of Bengal; on the right bank of the Ganges, where a branch, called the Jellinghy River, separates from the main stream; 25 miles E. by S. of Moorshedabad.

JEMARROW, a kingdom of Africa, on the S. side of the Gambia; about 120 miles from the sea. The inhabitants are chiefly Mahomedans.

JEMME, EL, a town of Tunis, North Africa, 95 miles S. of Tunis; where there are the remains of a splendid Roman amphitheatre, and other ruins.

JENA, a strong town of Germany, in the grand duchy of Saxe-Weimar; with a castle and a university. Near this place, in 1806, there was a general action between the French and Prussians, in which the latter were defeated with immense loss. It seated on the Saale; 10 miles S. S. E. of Weimar. Long. 11. 34. E. lat. 50. 55. N. Pop. 61,000.

JENIKALE, a fortress of European Russia, in the government of Taurida. It was built in 1703, by the Turks, to prevent the Russians entering the Black Sea. It commands the narrowest part of Taman Strait.

JENISA. *See* YENISEI.

JENISKOI. *See* YENISEISK.

JENITZ, a town of Germany, in the principality of Anhalt-Dessau; situate on the Muldau; 2 miles N. E. of Dessau.

JENITZ, a town of European Turkey, in Macedonia; situate on a lake which communicates with the Gulf of Salonichi, by a canal 12 miles long. It is 24 miles N. N. W. of Salonichi.

JEREMIE, a town and cape on the N. side of the southern peninsula of the island of St. Domingo. The town is situate on an eminence, in a fertile soil, particularly excellent for the culture of coffee; 5 miles W. of St. Domingo. Long. 73. 14. W. lat. 18. 42. N.

JERICHO, a town of Syria, in Palestine, once a famous city. It is now called Herubi by the Arabs, and contains only a few wretched huts, where some beggarly Arabs reside. It is 5 miles W. of the river Jordan, and 20 E. by N. of Jerusalem.

JERICHO, a town of Prussian Saxony, in the government of Magdeburgh: situate on the Elbe; 32 miles N. N. E. of Magdeburg.

JERMAH, a town of the kingdom of Fezzan; distinguished by the numerous herds of sheep and goats that feed around it, and by many majestic ruins, that exhibit to the inhabitants of its clay-built cottages vestiges of greatness to which they are perfectly indifferent; 60 miles S. E. of Mourzouk.

JERSEY, an island in the English Channel; 18 miles from the coast of Normandy, in France, and 84 S. of Portland, in Dorsetshire. It is subject to the English, but is still governed by the ancient Norman laws. It is 30 miles in circumference, and difficult of access, on account of rocks, sands, and the forts erected for its defence. It produces excellent butter and honey, and the S. part of the island is nearly covered with apple-trees, for cider. The commerce of Jersey extends to almost every European nation, and also to America. It exports to England great quantities of cider; also fruits, potatoes, and cattle; and in return imports corn, flour, seeds, coals, cloth, linen, glass, &c. A number of ships are engaged in the Newfoundland fishery. In 1812, 59 vessels, altogether of 6000 tons burden, and navigated by 550 seamen, belonging to the island. The French have made various unsuccessful attempts to capture the island: the most remarkable one was in 1731, when a body of French troops landed, surprised the lieutenant-governor, made him prisoner, and obliged him to sign a capitulation; but they were repulsed, and compelled to surrender prisoners of war, by the English troops under the brave Major Pierson, who was unfortunately killed in the moment of victory. *See* HELIER, ST.

JERSEY, NEW, one of the United States of America; 145 miles long, and 66 broad; bounded on the E. by Hudson River and the Atlantic Ocean, S. by Delaware Bay and River, W. by Pennsylvania, and N. by the state of New York. It is divided into 13 counties; namely, Cape Mary, Cumberland, Salem, Gloucester, Burlington, Huntingdon, Sussex, Bergen, Essex, Middlesex, Monmouth, Somerset, and Morris; the last two are mountainous, and one-fourth of the others are sandy and barren. It contains 5,324,000 acres, and the hilly country feeds great quantities of cattle; the barren parts produce little else but shrub-oaks and yellow pines; and the sandy lands yield an immense quantity of bog-iron ore, which is worked up to great advantage in the numerous iron-works in this state; the soil in other parts is fertile, producing plenty of corn, and fruits of all kinds common to the climate. The principal rivers, besides the boundary ones, are the Hackinsack, Passaick, and Rariton. Trenton is the capital.

JERUSALEM, (modern name *El Kods*, the holy city,) an ancient and famous town of Asia, formerly capital of Judea. It was taken by Nebuchadnezzar, in the 11th year of Zedekiah, when the Jews were led captive to Babylon. It was afterwards taken by the Romans, and destroyed together with the temple, 70 years after the birth of Christ, after sustaining one of the most remarkable sieges in history. The emperor Adrian built a new city near its ruins. It was taken by the Persians in 614, and by the Saracens in 636. In 1099 it was retaken by the crusaders, who founded a new kingdom under Godfrey of Bouillon, which lasted 88 years, under nine kings. Saladin, king of Egypt and Syria, obtained possession of it in 1187. The Turks, who drove away the Saracens in 1217, have retained it ever since. It is now of an irregular oval form, about three-fourths of a mile in its greatest length from N. E. to S. W., and four-sevenths of a mile in its greatest breadth, from the mosque of Omar to the Damascus gate on the N. W. The northern portion of the city is in ruins, from a fire which destroyed it, and has never been rebuilt. The mosque of Omar, (or Great Sahara,) is the principal building in Jerusalem, and occupies the S. E. portion of the city. The outer walls enclose a parallelogram facing the cardinal points, of 1500 feet from N. to S., and 900 from E. to W.; in the western part of this enclosure is a raised platform of 450 feet by 600 feet, with 8 gateways, and on which stands the splendid mosque of Omar, a Saracenic building of exquisite beauty, of an octagonal form, and of great height, surmounted by a dome. It is built of marble, and it is of a pale blue colour: the platform on which it stands is of a dazzling white. The interior is plain, and contains but few objects of interest, though the architecture is of great beauty. It is surrounded by a great number of praying places, and on the S. side of the enclosure stands the mosque el Aksa, once the church of the purification; on the W. side is an extensive range of buildings, containing the college of Dervishes, court of justice, &c.; and at the N. W. angle is the Turkish governor's residence, or Pilate's house, according to the traditions; and the terrace of which affords a fine view of the mosque. It is precipitous from the walls on the eastern and southern sides, and there are some subterranean vaults built with immense stones on the S. E. side, which are of great antiquity, probably coeval with the temple of Solomon, the site of which is undoubtedly occupied by the present mosque. The city is well-built, and all the houses have flat roofs, with a dome over the principal chamber, and on which the inhabitants spend the chief part of their time, and from the parapets can view what is passing below. The streets are narrow, and regularly built. The Via Dolorosa, along which our Saviour passed to Calvary, is about three-fourths of a mile long. The Jews live in the southern quarter, near to the mosque of Omar. The principal object of veneration is the church of the holy sepulchre, a very handsome building, 300 feet long and nearly 200 broad. It is supposed to comprehend within these limits the scene of all the great events of the crucifixion, entombment, and resurrection of Christ. The chapel is cut out of the rock, and lamps are kept constantly burning in it. The whole is covered with white marble, both within and without; and on the outside there are ten fine columns of the same. It is covered with a platform, the middle of which forms a small dome, six feet in height, covered with lead, and supported by 12 columns of porphyry, placed by pairs on the platform, and forming 6 arches, which have three lamps under each. On Good Friday, all the parts of our Saviour's passion are solemnized in this church. Pilgrims flock here from various parts, and the inhabitants accommodate them with lodging and provisions, which is their chief business; and a bashaw, with a guard of janissaries, always resides here to protect them from the insults of the Arabs. The Greek convent, of which the church of the sepulchre forms a part, occupies the sight of Mount Calvary, which is but a slight elevation, now within the walls which have been built to enclose it. It lies on the W. side of the city, and S. of it is the city castle, and the immense building of the Armenian convent. Mount Sion is just outside the S. wall and is crowned with the tomb of David.

Eastward is the valley of Jehoshaphat, in which the Moslems believe the world will be assembled on the final day, to be judged by Mahomet, from a spot in the enclosure of the mosque above. The whole neighbourhood is full of objects connected with sacred history, most of which owe their present form to the piety of the Empress Helena, mother of Constantine; but whether they occupy the sites they commemorate, is a matter of conjecture in most instances. The population may be stated as 25,000, which is much augmented at the time of the Greek Easter, by the immense number of pilgrims who come to witness the farce of the descent of the sacred fire in the Greek convent, and from whom great part of the Turkish revenues are derived. The manufactures of Jerusalem are almost confined to one branch, that of beads, crosses, shells, and other objects supposed to derive their sanctity from their local origin. These articles receive a species of benediction in the church of the sepulchre; and they are bought even by those who are more sensible of their insignificance, as they form acceptable presents to all the inhabitants of Greek and Catholic countries. Jerusalem is politically included in the pachalic of Damascus; 112 miles S. W. of Damascus, 45 from the Mediterranean. Lat. 31. 47. 47. N. long. 35. 21. E.

Jesi, a town of Italy, in the states of the church; seated on the river Eisno; 10 miles W. S. W. of Ancona.

Jessamine, a county of Kentucky, with 10,000 inhabitants. Chief town Nicholasville.

Jasselmere, a town of Hindostan, in a district of the same name, in the province of Agimere; governed by an independent chief; 70 miles W. by N. of Bickaneer.

Jesso, a large island, lying between those of Niphon and Saghalien. It is 150 miles in length, and from 80 to 220 in breadth: the narrow part is in the S. towards Niphon. It is full of woods, and the natives, who live by fishing and hunting, are strong, robust, savage, and slovenly, when compared to the Japanese. Here are some Japanese colonies, and the island is generally deemed subject to Japan; but it may be rather considered as a foreign conquest, than as a part of the civilized empire. Matsmai is the capital. The S. point is in long. 142. 30. W. lat. 40. 50. N.

Jessore, a town of Hindostan, in Bengal; capital of a district of the same name. It is seated on the river Boirub, and on the high road from Calcutta to Dacca.

Jever, a small district of Germany; situated between East Friesland and the duchy of Oldenburg. Though surrounded by Westphalia, it was never included in any circle of the empire. It was ceded to Oldenburg in 1814.

Jever, a town of Germany, in the grand duchy of Oldenburg; 34 miles N. by W. of Oldenburg.

Jidda, a seaport of Arabia Felix, on the Red Sea, in a barren, sandy district, destitute of fresh water. A very considerable trade is carried on here, this city being a mart between Egypt and India. The ships from Suez seldom proceed further than this port, and those from India were not suffered to advance to Suez. The English are permitted to trade here; but, in consequence of the numerous exactions to which they are subjected, the trade has greatly declined; 34 miles W. S. W. of Mecca, of which it is the port. Long. 39. 15. E. lat. 21. 29. N.

Jillifree, a town of West Africa, kingdom of Bana; near the mouth of the river Gambia, where the duties of the exports and imports are levied.

Jinbala, a town of Negroland, capital of an island so called, which is formed by two branches of the Niger, that separate at leaving the Lake Dibbie, and unite again about 15 miles from Tombuctoo. The town is a resting place for traders between Tombuctoo and the western parts of the country. It stands on the W. branch of the Niger; 80 miles S. W. of Tombuctoo. Long. 0. 16. E. lat. 16. 4. N.

Jionpour, a town of Hindostan, capital of a circar of the same name, in Allahabad. It is seated on the Goomty; and, not far from the conflux of that river with the Ganges, is the fort of Jionpour, on a high bank commanding the bridge over the Goomty. This place was at one time the seat of an empire; and sultan Shirki built the great musjud, or mausoleum, which is still remaining. The stone bridge over the Goomty consists of sixteen pointed arches; and on the top of it are many little shops on both sides. Jionpour is 18 miles N. W. of Benares. Long. 82. 55. E. lat. 25. 45. N.

Joachimsthal, a town of Bohemia, in the circle of Saatz; noted for its mines and a manufacture of lace; 15 miles N. by E. of Elnbogen.

Joachimsthal, a town of Brandenburg, in the Ucker Mark; 36 miles N. N. E. of Berlin.

Joanna. *See* Hinzuan.

Joannina, a town of European Turkey; capital of the pachalic of Albania. It consists of two principal streets crossing each other, and contains a palace, and several mosques and churches. Its chief manufacture is leather. It was the capital of the rebel Ali Pacha, during the early part of the present century, who declared himself independent of the porte, but was ultimately subdued and beheaded. Pop. about 38,000.

Jockgrim, a town of Bavaria, province of the Rhine; situate on an eminence near the Rhine; 9 miles S. E. of Landau.

Johan-Georgen-Stadt, a town of Saxony, in the circle of Erzgebirge; celebrated for its mines, and for a considerable manufacture of lace. It is 18 miles E. S. E. of Zwickau.

Johannesburg, a town of Germany, in the duchy of Nassau; celebrated for the vineyards in its environs, which were bestowed by the emperor on Prince Metternich, in 1816. It has a citadel, and is seated on the river Pych, near the Lake Spirding; 95 miles S.E. of Konigsberg, and 18 W. of Mentz. Long. 22. 39. E. lat. 53. 16. N.

John, St., one of the Philippine islands, E. of Mindanao. Long. 126. 32. E. lat. 9. 30. N.

John, St., a small island in the West Indies, N. of St. Croix, belonging to the Danes. It has a town and spacious harbour.

John, St., or **Prince Edward**, an island in the S. part of the gulf of St. Lawrence, having New Brunswick on the W., Nova Scotia on the S., and Cape Breton on the E. It is 60 miles long and 30 broad, and fertile, with several streams. In 1745 it surrendered, with Cape Breton, to the English. Pop. in 1841, 32,292. The capital is Charlotte Town. Pop. 1965.

John, St., a river which rises in the N. W. part of the district of Maine, flows N. E. into New Brunswick, where it soon takes a S. S. E. course, and enters the Bay of Fundy, at the city of St. John. It is navigable 60 miles for sloops of 50 tons, and about 200 for boats; and affords a common and near route from the province of New Brunswick to Quebec.

John, St., a city of New Brunswick; situate at the mouth of the River St. John, in the Bay of Fundy. Long. 65. 15. W. lat. 45. 12. N.

John, St., the capital of Newfoundland; situate on the E. side of the island. It has a good harbour, entirely land-locked, and defended by several forts, in one of which the governor of the island resides. This city has suffered very severely by repeated fires. It is now the seat of the bishop of Newfoundland and Bermuda.

John, St., the capital of Antigua. It is one of the most regular towns in the West Indies, and has the most commodious harbour in the Leeward islands. Long. 62. 4. W. lat. 17. 4. N.

John, St., a town and fort of Lower Canada, on the W. bank of Chambly or Richelieu River, at the N. end of Lake Champlain. In 1796 it was made the sole port of entry and clearance for all goods imported from the United States into Canada. It is 20 miles E. by S. of Montreal, and 110 N. by E. of Crown Point. Long. 73. 20. W. lat. 45. 25. N.

John d'Acre, St. *See* Acre.

Johnshaven, a village of Scotland, in Kincardineshire, with a harbour for small vessels; 4 miles S. S. W. of Bervie. It was formerly a great fishing town, but is now more noted for an extensive manufacture of canvas.

Johnston, a town of New York, chief of Montgomery county; on the N. bank of Mohawk River; 24 miles W. N. W. of Schenectady.

Johnstown, a town of Upper Canada, extending nearly a mile on the river St. Lawrence. It is 50 miles N. E. of Kingstown, and 100 S. W. of Montreal. Long. 75. 10. W. lat. 44. 42. N.

Johnstown, St., a borough of Ireland, in the county of Donegal, on the river Foyle; 5 miles S. S. W. of Londonderry.

Johor, or **Jor**, a town of the peninsula of Malaya, destroyed by the Portuguese in 1603, but subsequently rebuilt: it is seated near the S. coast; 150 miles S. E. of Malacca. Long. 103. 30. E. lat. 1. 35. N.

Joigny, a town of France, in the department of Yonne; surrounded by thick walls, and seated near the Yonne; 17 miles S. S. E. of Sens. Pop. 5750.

Joinville, an ancient town of France, in the department of Upper Marne; situate on the Marne; 25 miles S. W. of Bar-le-Duc, and 125 S. E. of Paris. Long. 5. 20. E. lat. 48. 20. N. Pop. 3350.

Jolucar, a town of Spain, in Granada; 7 miles N. E. of Motril.

Jonesborough, a town of Tennessee; capital of the district of Washington; seated near the foot of the iron mountains; 86 miles E. by N. of Knoxville. Long. 82. 40. W. lat. 36. 8. N.

Jonkioping, a town of Sweden, in Smaland, and the seat of justice for Gothland. It has a strong citadel, and a manufacture of arms. The houses are chiefly of wood; and on the roof are spread layers of birch bark, covered with turf or moss, many of them producing herbage, and some ornamented with flowers. It is seated near the S. end of the Lake Wetter; 80 miles W. N. W. of Calmar.

Joodpour, a town of Hindostan; capital of a district of the same name, in the province of Agimere. It carries on a considerable trade by means of caravans, with Guzerat and the Deccan. The rajah is now one of the British allies. It is seated near a branch of the Pudda; 100 miles W. S. W. of Agimere. Long. 73. 18. E. lat. 26. 8. N.

Jordan, a river of Syria, which rises at Baneas, (ancient Panias,) at the foot of Djebel Essheikh, (Mount Lebanon,) but which is probably derived from Lake Phiala, a round bowl to the northward, which has no apparent discharge. It flows southward through the Lake Tabariah, (Tiberias,) and continues its southward course to the Dead Sea. It is about 200 or 300 feet wide, and the water is turbid from the sand it flows over. It has been supposed that before the destruction of Sodom and Gomorrah, and the formation of the Lake Asphaltitis, that it flowed into the Gulf of Suez and the Red Sea: but the great depth of the level of the Dead Sea below the surrounding country, and the elevation of the valley southward, which has lately been asserted, will contradict such a theory. The margin is generally covered with a thicket of oleander and willow, the lurking-place of wild animals. Near Jericho it is clear and rapid, and is much frequented by pilgrims for bathing. The Arabic name is El Sheriat (the river).

Jorehaut, a town of Eastern Asia; capital of Upper Assam. It was made the capital of the province, in 1794. The tea shrub has been found growing in its vicinity, and a manufacture of tea has been established.

Jorjan, or **Korgan**, a town of Persia, in Asterabad; bordering on the Caspian Sea. It is 60 miles E. by N. of Asterabad, and 320 W. of Mesched. Long. 56. 5. E. lat. 15. 56. N.

Jorkau, a town of Bohemia, in the circle of Saatz; celebrated for its breweries. On a mountain by the town is the magnificent castle of Rothenhaus; 5 miles N. of Commotau.

Josselin, a town of France, in the department of Morbihan; 25 miles N. N. E. of Vannes.

JOUARRE, a tn. of France, in the department of Seine-et-Marne; 10 miles S. E. of Meaux, and 35 E. of Paris. Pop. 2570.

JOUD. *See* JEHUD.

JOUE, a town of France, in the department of Indre-et-Loire; 3 miles S. of Tours.

JOUE DU PLAID, a town in the department of Orne; 5 miles S. W. of Argentan.

JOUGUE, a town in the department of Doubs, 8 miles S. of Pontarlier, and 22 E. S. E. of Salins.

JOUGUES, a town in the department of Mouths of the Rhone; 12 miles N. E. of Aix.

JOURA, an island in the Grecian Archipelago, 10 miles in circuit; 12 miles S. W. of Andros.

JOUY, a town of France, in the department of Seine-et-Oise; 3 miles S. of Versailles.

JOUY LE CHATEL, a town in the department of Seine-et-Marne; 10 miles N. W. of Provins.

JOUY SUR MORIN, a town in the department of Seine-et-Marne; 15 miles S.E. of Meaux.

JOUX, MOUNT. *See* JURA, MOUNT.

JOYEUSE, a town of France, in the department of Ardeche; seated on the Beaune; 17 miles S. W. of Privas.

JUAN, ST., or DESAGUADERO, a river of Mexico, which is the outlet of the Lake Nicaragua. It flows from the S. E. corner of the lake, in an easterly direction, between the provinces of Nicaragua and Costa Rica, into the Caribbean Sea.

JUAN, ST., a town of Mexico, in the province of Nicaragua, situate at the head of the river St. Juan; 110 miles E. of Nicaragua. Long. 84. 45. W. lat. 11. 15. N.

JUAN DE FUCA, STRAIT OF, a large bay or gulf of Pacific Ocean, on the W. coast of North America. The entrance is in long. 124. 55. W. lat. 48. 25. N.

JUAN DE LA FRONTERA, ST., a town of Chili. Its territory contains mines of gold, and a kind of almonds that are very delicate. It is seated near the Lake Guanacho, on the E. side of the Andes; 150 miles N. of Mendoza. Long. 68. 40. W. lat 31. 20. S.

JUAN DE PORTO RICO, ST., the capital of the island of Porto Rico; with a good harbour, defended by several forts. It is a bishop's see, and is well built, and better inhabited than most of the Spanish towns. It was taken by Sir Francis Drake, and afterwards by the Earl of Cumberland; who, losing most of his men by sickness, was obliged to abandon it. In 1615 the Dutch took and plundered this city, but could not retain it. It stands on a peninsula, on the N. coast of the island. Long. 66. 45. W. lat. 18. 29. N.

JUAN DE ULHUA, ST., a small island in the Gulf of Mexico. *See* VERA CRUZ.

JUAN FERNANDEZ, an island in the Pacific Ocean; 38 leagues eastward of the island of Massafuero, and 390 W. of the continent. It is supposed to have been inhabited by a Spaniard, whose name it retains; but it is more remarkable for having been the residence of Alexander Selkirk, a Scotchman, whose life and adventures furnished De Foe with the ground-work of that admirable novel, Robinson Crusoe. The island is about 30 miles in circumference, and at a distance appears like a naked rock; but there are intersecting valleys covered with wood, and a great number of goats on the sides of every hill. In 1766 a settlement was made by the Spaniards, on the N. and highest part of this island, at Cumberland Bay, which is defended by batteries. The town is situate in a fine valley, between two high hills, and every house has a garden, with harbours shaded with vines. Long. 78. 52. W. lat. 33. 40. S.

JUBO, a kingdom of Africa, on the coast of Ajan, with a capital of the same name; subject to the Portuguese. Long. 43. 20. E. lat. 0. 50. N.

JUCATAN. *See* YUCATAN.

JUDENBURG, a town of Upper Styria, capital of a circle of the same name; with a handsome castle. The public buildings, with the square, are magnificent. This town was taken by the French, in 1797. It suffered dreadfully from fire in 1807 and 1818. It is seated on the Muer; 40 miles W. of Gratz. Long. 14. 24. E. lat. 47. 10. N.

JUDOIGNE, a town of Belgium, in South Brabant, near which are the ruins of an ancient castle. It is seated on the Geele. 13 miles S. S. E. of Louvain.

JUGDISPORE, a town of Hindostan, in the province of Bahar; 20 miles from Patna.

JUGGERNAUT, a place of Hindoo worship, on the coast of Orissa, district of Cuttack; with a population estimated at 30,000. It is one of the most celebrated places in India. All the land within 20 miles is considered holy; but the most sacred spot is enclosed with a stone wall 21 feet high, and forms nearly a square, being 656 feet long and 626 feet wide. Within this area are about 50 temples, dedicated to various idols; but the most conspicuous buildings consist of one lofty stone tower, 184 feet high and 28½ feet square inside, and two adjoining stone buildings with pyramidical roofs. The tower is occupied by the idol Juggernaut, his brother Bulbudra, and his sister Subudra; and the other buildings are used for purposes connected with the worship. Adjoining is also a low building on pillars, (with a fabulous animal in the centre,) which is intended as an awning to shelter the entrance from the rays of the sun; and after this is another, where the food prepared by the pilgrims is daily brought, previous to distribution. The temple of Juggernaut was erected by rajah Anung Bheem, in A. D. 1198: it was taken by the British, together with the town, in 1803. The roofs are ornamented in a singular style, with representations of monsters; the walls of the temples, which are not visible beyond the enclosure, are covered with statues of stone. Each side of the boundary wall has a large gateway in the centre; but the grand entrance is in the eastern face. The idol Juggernaut is made of wood, and is probably the coarsest image in the country, having a frightful black visage, with a distended mouth. The figure does not extend below the loins, and it has no hands, but two stumps in lieu of arms, on which the priests occasionally fasten hands of gold: a Christian is almost led to think that it was an attempt to see how low idolatry could debase the human mind. When two new moons occur in Assaur (part of June and July), which is said to happen about once in 17 years, a new idol is always made. After the wood is made into a proper form by common carpenters, it is entrusted to certain priests, who are protected from all intrusion. The process is a great mystery. One man is selected to take out of the old idol a small box, said to contain the spirit, which is conveyed inside the new; and the man who does this is always removed from the world before the end of the year. On certain festivals the images of Juggernaut, Bulbudra, and Subudra, are superbly dressed, and placed in an immense moveable tower, which the pilgrims drag to a certain distance, and then return to the temple. During these processions many of the infatuated devotees fall under the wheels of the machine, and are crushed to death. There are two principal festivals (the Swinging and Car festivals) and eleven minor ones annually. The concourse of pilgrims to this shrine is immense; and the revenue derived from them by the British government is said to exceed 12,000*l.* per annum. A road has been recently completed from Calcutta to Juggernaut, great part of the expense being paid by a rich Hindoo (rajah Sookmoy Roy) on condition that the road should be named after him. Juggernaut is seated a few miles N. E. of the Chilka Lake; 300 miles from Calcutta. Long. 85. 54. E. lat. 19. 49. N.

JULALABAD. *See* DOOSHAK.

JULFAR, a town of Arabia, in the province of Oman; situate on a bay of the Gulf of Persia; 100 miles N. W. of Oman. Long. 56. 14. E. lat. 25. 55. N.

JULIAN, PORT ST., South America, E. coast of Patagonia. The entrance is dangerous: it is situated at the foot of some high mountains.

JULIEN, ST., a town of France, in the department of Jura; 18 miles S. by W. of Lons le Saulnier.

JULIEN DU SAULT, ST., a town of France, in the department of Yonne; seated between two mountains, covered with vines, near the river Yonne; 6 miles N. W. of Joigny.

JULIERS, a very fertile duchy of Westphalia, now forming part of the Prussian province of the Lower Rhine, adjacent to the territories of Aix-la-Chapelle, Liege, and Cologne. It contains 1600 square miles, and 222,000 inhabitants. Flax is cultivated, and made into fine linen, which is sent to Holland, and afterwards sold as the fabric of that country; there are also manufactures of cloth, ribbons, brass, iron, and wire. This duchy was ceded, in 1648, to the palatine of Neuburg, in whose family it continued down to the peace of Luneville, when it was given to France; but in 1815 it was transferred to Prussia.

JULIERS, a small town of the Prussian states, in the government of Aix-la-Chapelle, and formerly capital of the preceding duchy; seated on the Roer; 22 miles W. of Cologne. Long. 6. 25. E. lat. 50. 55. N.

JULIUSBURG, a town of Prussian Silesia, with a castle; 4 miles N. of Oels.

JUMELLA, a town of Spain, in the province of Murcia; 22 miles S. W. of Murcia.

JUMIEGE, a town of France, in the department of Lower Seine; with a late celebrated Benedictine abbey; seated on the Seine, 12 miles S. W. of Rouen.

JUMMOO, or JUMBO, a town of Hindostan; capital of a flourishing district of the same name, which is governed by an independent Hindoo chief. It is a place of considerable trade, being seated on the banks of a small river on the high road from Cashmere to Delhi; 80 miles N. E. of Lahore.

JUMNA, a river of Hindostan, which rises in the mountains of Serinaghur, flows S. E. by Delhi and Agra, and joins the Ganges at Allahabad.

JUNAGUR, a town and fortress of Hindostan, in Guzerat; 170 miles S. W. of Amedabad. Long. 70. 33. E. lat. 21. 48. N.

JUNIEN, ST., a town of France in the department of Upper Vienne; with manufactures of woollens, leather, hats, &c. It is seated on the river Vienne; 20 miles W. of Limoges.

JUNKSEILAN, or JUNKSEYLON, an island in the Indian Ocean, near the S. W. coast of Siam, about 60 miles long, and from 10 to 20 broad. The soil is luxuriant, and it has a considerable trade in ivory and tin. The principal town, of the same name, is situate on the N. part of the island, and has a harbour capable of receiving vessels of a moderate size. Long. 98. 0. E. lat. 8. 10. N.

JURA, one of the western isles of Scotland; N. E. of the Island of Islay, on the coast of Argyleshire. It is 26 miles long and 7 broad, and is composed of huge naked rocks piled on one another in the utmost disorder. The mountainous ridges occupy the centre of the island, extending along its whole length, and terminating in four mountains, called the Paps of Jura, which are of a conic form and of stupendous height. The W. side of the island is uninhabited. The whole of the E. side forms a pleasing scene, and the coast is indented with bays and harbours. The only products are oats, barley, potatoes, and flax. A few wild roses are still seen here.

JURA, a department of France, including part of the late province of Franche Comte. It contains mines of iron of a superior quality, mines of copper and lead, and many quarries of black marble, jasper, and alabaster. It takes its name from Mount Jura. Lons le Saulnier is the capital. Pop. 301,768.

JURA, MOUNT, a chain of mountains which begins in the canton of Zurich, in Switzerland, extends along the Rhine, into the canton of Soleure and the principality of Neufchatel, branches out toward the Pays de Vaud, separates that country from France, and continues beyond the frontiers of the Genevois, as far as the Rhone. In the Pays de Vaud this chain forms many elevated valleys, particularly one on the top of that part called Mount Joux, which is watered by two picturesque lakes, the largest called Joux, and the other Brenet. These mountains have different names in different parts of their course in Switzerland. The highest, Reculet, is 5633 feet.

JUSSEY, a town of France, in the department of Upper Saone; situate on the Amance; 17 miles N. W. of Vesoul.

JUSSY, a town of France, in the department of Yonne; 5 miles S. of Auxerre.

JUSTIN, ST., a town of France, in the department of Landes; 27 miles W. of Condom.

JUTERBOCK, a town of the Prussian province of Bradenburg, where, in 1813, a battle was fought between the French and the allies. It is seated on the Rohrbach; 27 miles N. E. of Wittenberg.

JUTHIA. *See* SIAM.

JUTLAND, a province of Denmark; bounded on all sides by the sea, except towards the S., where its boundary is the duchy of Sleswick. The name of Jutland was formerly applied to the whole peninsula forming the mainland of the Danish dominions, but it is now confined to the northern part of the peninsula, extending from 55. to 58. N. lat. It is about 180 miles in length, and from 70 to 90 in breadth; and is divided into four dioceses or districts, each of which has a bishop and governor. The prevailing religion is the Lutheran. The country is generally low, and, except the rocks on the E. coast, presents little picturesque scenery. In the E. are fine woods of oak, beech, fir, &c. The middle part consists of heaths and moors, with some arable land; it affords good pasture for oxen, sheep, and goats. The other parts are fertile, and yield large crops of grain, (principally rye,) which, together with horses, are annually exported to Sweden, Norway, and Holland. The air is cold, especially towards the North Sea, but the inhabitants are vigorous and robust. It is the only province of Denmark which contains useful minerals; and even here they are confined to iron, limestone, and marble.

JYENAGUR, or JYEPOUR, a fortified town of Hindostan, capital of a district of the same name, in the province of Agimere. It is a place of great wealth, being the staple for goods that are brought from the neighbouring provinces; and is reckoned one of the handsomest and most regular towns of Hindostan; 120 miles W. by S. of Agra. Long. 75. 40. E. lat. 26. 56. N.

K

KAATS' BANN, a town of New York, on the W. bank of Hudson's River; 7 miles S. of Kaats' Kill, and 11 N. E. by N. Esopus.

KADHEMA, a seaport of Arabia, in the province of Bahrein. The inhabitants are chiefly employed in the pearl fishery. It is seated on a bay of the Gulf of Persia; 170 miles N. by W. of Lachsa. Long. 47. 36. E. lat. 28. 40. N.

KAFFRARIA. *See* CAFFRARIA.

KAHLA, a town of Germany, in Altenburg; seated on the Saale; 8 miles S. of Jena.

KAHLENBERG, a mountain of Austria, extending along the Danube to the W. of Vienna, and forming the commencement of the Kahlengebirge range, which is a branch of the Noric Alps.

KAHONE, a town of Western Africa; capital of the kingdom of Bur-Salum. It is seated on a small river which falls into the Atlantic.

KAIA, a small village of Prussian Saxony, near Lutzen; celebrated as the scene of much fighting on the 2nd of May, 1813, between the French and the allied Russian and Prussian army.

KAIN. *See* KIN.

KAIRWAN. *See* CAIROAN.

KAISARIEH, or KAISARIYEH, a town of Asia Minor; the ancient capital of Cappadocia, then called Cesarea. It is surrounded with walls five miles in circumference, and defended by a castle. The inhabitants, estimated at 25,000, carry on an extensive trade, and it is the resort of merchants from all parts of Asia Minor and Syria. It is situate at the foot of a mountain, always capped with snow; 130 miles E. N. E. of Konieh.

KAKET, a town of the country of Georgia, in a province of its name, which comprehends a part of the ancient Iberia. It is situate near Mount Caucasus; 45 miles N. N. E. of Teflis, and 120 N. W. of Derbend.

KALAU, a town of Prussia, in Lusatia; with a great trade in wool; 11 miles S. E. of Luckau.

KALGUEV, an island in the Frozen Ocean, S. of Nova Zembla; inhabited by a few Samoiedes. In the government of Archangel.

KALHAT, a town of Arabia, on a river of the same name, at its entrance into the Gulf of Ormus; 80 miles S. E. of Mascat.

KALISCH, one of the eight palatinates of Russian Poland; bounded on the W. by Prussian Poland, and on the three other sides by the palatinates of Sendomir, Cracow, and Masovia.

KALISCH, a city of Poland, capital of the above palatinate, with manufactures of cloth, linen, and leather. It is surrounded by morasses and walls; has a collegiate and ten other churches, four religious houses, and a Catholic high school; 66 miles N. W. of Breslau.

KALKA PIRA, a river of Chinese Tartary, which gives name to a tribe of Monguls, and is nearly 300 leagues in extent from E. to W.

KALLINBURG, a seaport of Denmark, in the isle of Zealand; seated on an inlet of the Great Belt; with the best harbour, next to Copenhagen, on the island 55 miles W. by

N. of Copenhagen. Long. 11. 11. E. lat. 55. 47. N.

Kalmucs, a nation of Tartars, inhabiting that part of the Russian government of Caucasia which lies between the Volga and the Ural, towards the Caspian Sea. They all live in tents, and remove from place to place in quest of pasturage for their numerous cattle, consisting of horses, camels, cows, and sheep. They neither sow nor reap, nor make hay for their cattle, so that they live without bread, or any sort of vegetable; and, in winter, their cattle fare like the wild beasts. Their food is flesh, (especially that of horses,) fish, wild fowl, and venison; and they have great plenty of milk, butter, and cheese; but mare's milk is the most esteemed, and from it they make a strong spirit, to which they are partial. They are divided into a number of hordes or clans, each under its own particular khan, and all acknowledge the authority of one principal khan, who is called Orchicurtikhan, or the king of kings, and derives his pedigree from the great Tamerlane. All of them, however, have submitted to the government of Russia, or live under its protection. They are pagans, and believe in the transmigration of souls. In person, manners, and customs, they resemble the ancient Scythians, from whom they are descended. *See* Tartary.

Kalpaki, a town of Morea, Greece; 13 miles N. from Tripolizza; with the ruins of a Doric temple, and near the ancient Orchomenos.

Kaluga, a government of the Russian empire, formerly a province in the government of Moscow. Pop. 1,180,000. Its principal town, of the same name, is seated on the Occa; 107 miles S. S. W. of Moscow. Pop. 26,500.

Kamakura, an island of Japan, 3 miles in circumference; lying on the S. coast of Niphon. It is surrounded with very high and steep rocks, and is used as a place of exile for state prisoners.

Kamalia, a town of Negroland, in the country of Mandingo. The inhabitants are partly Pagans and partly Mahomedans, and have manufactures of cotton, leather, and iron.

Kambala, a ridge of mountains in Tibet, between the Lake Palte and the river Burrampooter.

Kamenitz, a town of Bohemia, in the circle of Bechin; 27 miles E. by N. of Bechin.

Kaminieck, a strong town of Russian Poland; capital of Podolia, and a bishop's see, with a castle. When the Russians seized part of the Polish territories, in 1793, this fortress held out a long time, but at last surrendered to their arms. The castle is seated on a craggy rock; 85 miles W. of Braclaw. Pop. 5450.

Kamnitz, a town of Bohemia, with manufactures of stockings, glass, and linen; also several bleach-fields; 21 miles N. N. E. of Leitmeritz.

Kamtschatka, a peninsula on the eastern coast of Asia, extending from 52. to 63. of N. lat., the long. of its extremity to the S. being 156. 45. E. The isthmus joining it to the continent on the N. lies between the Gulf of Olutorsh and Penshink; and its extremity to the S. is Cape Lopatka. Its greatest breadtn is about 150 miles, being from the mouth of the river Tigril to that of the river Kamtschatka; and towards each extremity it gradually becomes narrower. It is bounded by the North Pacific Ocean to the S. and E.; and by the sea of Okhotsk to the W. A chain of high mountains from N. to S. extends the whole length of the peninsula, and almost equally divides it; whence several rivers rise, and take their course into the Pacific Ocean, and the sea of Okhotsk. Stunted trees are thinly scattered over the whole face of the country, whose bottoms are mossy, with a mixture of low heath; the whole resembling Newfoundland in a most striking degree. The severity of the climate is in proportion to the sterility of the soil. Four months, commencing at midsummer, may be considered as forming their spring, summer, and autumn; the rest of the year is all dreary winter. They have great quantities of wholesome vegetables, in a wild state; such as chervil, garlic, onions, angelica, and wild celery, with some excellent turnips, and turnip radishes, upon a few spots of ground in the valleys; and this is the utmost extent of their garden cultivation. A variety of wild berries, which are gathered at proper seasons, and preserved by mashing them into a thick jam, constitute a considerable part of the winter provisions, serving as a general sauce to their dried fish, the main article of food. The forests abound in wild animals, particularly the bear; and wild fowl are also plentiful. The people of Kamtschatka may be said to consist of three sorts, the Kamtschadales, the Russians, and Cossacks, and a mixture produced by their intermarriages. The habitations of the natives consist of three different kinds, which they call jourts, balagans, and log-houses. They inhabit the first in winter, and the second in summer; in the third, introduced by the Russians, only the wealthy people reside. The external appearance of a jourt resembles a round, squat hillock; a hole serving for a chimney, window, and door, is left in the centre, and the inhabitants go in and out by the assistance of a long pole, having notches deep enough to afford a little security for the toe. The upper garment of the Kamtschadales resembles a wagoner's frock; if for summer wear, it is made of nankeen; if intended for winter, it is made of a skin, having one side turned, and the hair preserved on the other, which is worn innermost; a close jacket of nankeen, or other cotton stuff, is the next under this; and, beneath that, a shirt made of thin Persian silk, of any colour. They wear long breeches and boots, made of skins, with the hair innermost. They have also a fur cap, with two flaps, that are usually tied up close to the head, but are allowed to fall round the shoulders in rough weather. A species of dog, resembling the mountain or shepherd dogs of Europe, is used for the purposes of labour and draught. None of the inhabitants keep fewer than five of these dogs, which in winter are fed upon offals or decayed fish: in summer, when their services are not required, they are left to range over the country and provide for themselves; but, on the approach of winter, they return home in the most punctual manner. They are harnessed to a sledge, two abreast, with one well trained in front as a leader, and are used both for travelling and for conveying all sorts of commodities from place to place. The Russians made themselves masters of the whole of this peninsula in 1706; but the government they have established is exceedingly mild, the inhabitants being permitted to choose their own magistrates. Skins and furs form the only articles of trade; in return for which they import brandy (the introduction of which has been attended with the most destructive effects), nankeens, and other Chinese stuffs, together with various commodities of Russian and European manufacture.

KAMTSCHATKOI, NIZNEI, a town of Siberia, capital of Kamtschatka; with a citadel, arsenal, and barracks. It is seated on the N. side of the river Kamtschatka, 20 miles from it mouth. Long. 161. 50. E. lat. 56. 30. N.

KAMTSCHATKOI, VERCHNI, a town of Siberia, in Kamtschatka, on the river Kamtschatka; 120 miles S. W. of Niznei Kamtschatkoi.

KAMYSCHIA, a town of European Russia, government of Saratov; on the Volga, near a canal which communicates with the Don. It has a manufacture of salt. Pop. 2250.

KANDAHAR. *See* CANDAHAR.

KANEM, a town of the empire of Bornou, in a province of the same name, where are bred multitudes of cattle and horses. It is seated on the Gazel; 150 miles N. N. W. of Bornou.

KANGAROO ISLAND, an island on the S. coast of Australia; it was discovered by Captain Flinders, and so named from the number of kangaroos found on it, which were extremely tame. Kangaroo Head is in long. 137. 58. E. lat. 35. 43. S.

KANISCA, a strong town of Lower Hungary; capital of the county of Salawar; seated on the Drave; 100 miles S. by E. of Vienna. Long. 17. 40. E. lat. 46. 55. N.

KANSAS RIVER, North America, a tributary of the Missouri; it is about 1450 miles long, and is navigable for 900 miles. It is salt in some parts of its course.

KAN-TCHEOU, a city of China, of the first rank, in the province of Kiang-si. Its district contains 12 cities of the third class; and the soil produces a great number of trees, whence distils a fine varnish, reckoned the best in China. It is seated on the Kan-kiang; 840 miles S. of Peking. Long. 115. 2. E. lat. 25. 52. N.

KAO-TCHEOU, a city of China, of the first rank, in the province of Quangtong. In its vicinity is found a kind of marble, that represents, naturally, rivers, mountains, landscapes, and trees; it is cut into leaves, and made into tables, &c. Kao-tcheou stands on a navigable river; 36 miles from the sea, and 1130 S. S.W. of Peking.

KAPOSWAR, a fort of Lower Hungary, on the river Kapos, which washes its walls. It is 55 miles W. of Tolna. Long. 18. 13. E. lat. 46. 31. N.

KARAHISSAR. *See* APHIOM.

KARAMANIA. *See* CARAMANIA.

KARASUBAZAR, a town of the Crimea; noted for its noble antique bath, and an ancient manufacture of leather from the skins of Tauric goats. It is situate on the Karasu, in a delightful valley; 34 miles W. of Caffa.

KAREK, or GARAK, an island in the N. E. part of the Gulf of Persia; 5 miles long and 2 broad; where ships bound for Bassora generally call for pilots. Long. 50. 26. E. lat. 29. 15. N.

KARLEBY GAMLA, a seaport of Sweden, in East Bothnia; with a trade in hemp, salt, and ship-building; seated on the Gulf of Bothnia, near the influx of the river Karleby; 90 miles N. by E. of Christianstadt. Long. 22. 20. E. lat. 63. 56. N.

KARLEBY, NY, a town of Sweden, in East Bothnia, on the river Lappojock; 6 miles from the sea, and 20 S. of Gamla Karleby.

KASAN, the ancient Bulgaria; a government of European Russia; lying on both sides the Volga, between 46. 20. and 49. 40. of E. long., and 54. and 57. of N. lat., and bounded by the governments of Viatka, Orenburg, Niznei-Novgorod, and Simbirsk. Its extent is 22,000 square miles; its population about 850,000, partly Russians and partly Tartars, though of very mixed origin. It is watered by the Volga, the Kama, the Sura, the Viatka, and the Kasanka, besides smaller streams and a great number of lakes. It was formerly an independent kingdom, belonging to the Kalmucs, to whom the dukes of Moscow, with other petty principalities of Russia, were tributary. But in 1552 it was conquered by Ivan Basilowitz II., and annexed to Russia.

KASAN, a city of Russia, capital of the foregoing government, and an archbishop's see. It has an antique Tartar fortress, built of stone; several churches, and 11 convents; and there are several suburbs, one of them inhabited by Tartars. At one end of the city is a manutures of woollen, cotton, lace, and earthenware, with large soap-works and tanneries: it carries on an extensive trade. At a short distance from Kasan is a new admiralty establishment, with a navigation school, magazines, and a dock-yard, where galliots are constructed, and sent down the Volga to the Caspian Sea. It is seated on the rivulet Kasanka, where it enters the Volga; 420 miles E. of Moscow. Pop. 41,304. Long. 49. 20. E. lat. 55. 48. N.

KASKASIA, a town and river of the United States, in Illinois; one of the first settlements made by the French in the valley of the Missisippi. It has declined from its former importance.

KATABA, a town of Arabia, in Yemen, with a citadel; situate in a fertile country, near a river, which runs into the sea at Aden; 75 miles N. of Aden. Long. 44. 39. E. lat. 13. 54. N.

KATIF, a town of Arabia, in the province of Bahrein. It is built of rock-salt, and stands on the Gulf of Persia; 95 miles N. of Lachsa. Long. 48. 38. E. lat. 27. 40. N.

KAUFBEUREN, a town of Germany, in Bavaria; with manufactures of cotton, linen, fustian, and leather. It is seated on the Wertach; 38 miles S. by W. of Augsburg. Pop. 4350.

KAUGA, the capital of a kingdom of the same name, in the empire of Bornou. It is seated on a large lake; 280 miles S. by E. of Bornou. Long. 23. 30. E. lat. 15. 50. N.

KAUKEBAN, a town of Arabia, in Yemen; situate on an almost inaccessible mountain; 20 miles W. of Sana.

KAUNITZ, a town and castle of Moravia, on the river Igla; 6 miles S. S. W. of Brinn.

KAURZIM, a town of Bohemia; capital of a circle of the same name, which produces much timber. It stands on a river which runs into the Elbe; 26 miles E. S. E. of Prague.

KAYE ISLAND, an island in the Pacific Ocean, near the W. coast of North America; 30 miles long and 4 broad; discovered by Cook, in 1778. Long. 144. 48. W. lat. 59. 56. N.

KAYSERSLAUTERN, a town of Germany, in the palatinate of the Rhine. In 1793 it was taken by the French, who the year following were surprised in their intrenchments near it, by the Austrians, and defeated. It is seated on the Lauter; 28 miles S. W. of Worms. Long. 7. 50. E. lat. 49. 27. N.

KAYSERSTUHL, a town of Switzerland, in the county of Baden, with a castle; seated on the Rhine; 8 miles S. E. of Zurzack.

KAYSERSWERT, a town of Germany, in the territory of Cologne; seated on the Rhine; 7 miles N. N. W. of Dusseldorf.

KAZIMIERS, a town of Poland, in the palatinate of Lublin, with a castle; situate on a hill; on the Vistula; 25 miles W. S. W. of Lublin.

KAZROON, a town of Persia, in Farsistan, of considerable extent; but many parts of it are in ruins; 70 miles W. S. W. of Shiras.

KESHO. *See* CASHAO.

KEDGE, or KEJ, a town of Central Asia, in the province of Mukran, Beloochistan; on the River Dustee; in the midst of an arid, sterile conntry. The fort is on an eminence, and is very strong.

KEDLESTON, a village in Derbyshire; noted for its medicinal spring, much resorted to in summer, and for the elegant seat of the Earl of Scarsdale; 5 miles N. N. W. of Derby.

KEENE, a town of New Hampshire, in Cheshire county; 25 miles S. by E. of Charlestown, and 95 W. by S. of Portsmouth.

KEFF, or KEFFTS, a town of the kingdom of Tunis, witn a citadel; situate on the side of a hill; with a plentiful source of water; 70 miles W. S. W. of Tunis.

KEFIL, a village of Asiatic Turkey, in Irac Arabi; 14 miles S. of Hillah; celebrated for the tomb of the prophet Ezekiel, which is annually visited by a number of Jews.

KEHL, a strong fortress of Germany, seated on the Rhine, over which is a bridge to Strasburg; it is an important pass between France and Germany. It was ceded by France at the peace of Ryswick, 1697, and conferred on the margrave of Baden. During the war with Germany, the French repeatedly besieged and took it: in 1798 it fell into their hands, and they retained possession till 1804, when it was restored to the Grand Duke of Baden. Pop. 1000.

KEIGHLEY, a town of West Yorkshire; with a market on Wednesday, and manufactures of woollen cloths, cottons, and lindseys. The town is nearly all built of stone; and the church, which was rebuilt in 1805, is a spacious and handsome structure. Here is a free grammar-school, founded in 1716. The town is well supplied with water from two fine springs to the E. and W., under an act obtained in 1816. It is seated in a deep valley; 12 miles N. of Halifax, and 202 N. by W. of London.

KEITH, a town of Scotland, in Banffshire; with manufactures of flax; 12 miles S. S. W. of Cullen, and 46 N. W. of Aberdeen.

KELAT, a city of Central Asia, surrounded by a mud wall, with bastions; in the province of Beloochistan, of which it is the capital: it is inhabited by a mixed race: the Hindoos are the chief merchants; 80 miles E. from Sarowan. Pop. 25,000. Lat. 29. 6. N. long. 65. 50. E.

KELBRA, a town of Prussian Saxony, near the river Helm; 10 miles S. of Stolberg.

KELHEIM, a town and castle of Bavaria; with a Franciscan convent, a considerable brewery, and extensive magazines of salt. It is situate at the conflux of the Altmuhl and Danube; 10 miles S. S. W. of Ratisbon.

KELLS, a town of Ireland, in East Meath, on the river Blackwater; 12 miles N. by W. of Trim.

KELSO, a town of Scotland, in Roxburghshire; with a bridge over the Tweed, below the influx of the Teviot. The abbey, magnificent ruins of which still remain, was founded by David I. Here are manufactures of carpeting, flannels, leather, linen, and shoes. It is 10 miles N.N.E. of Jedburgh, and 20 S. W. of Berwick.

KEMI, or KIEMI. *See* KIMI.

KEMMO, a town of Negroland; capital of a country lying to the W. of Bambarra. It is 340 miles W. of Sego. Long. 7. 46. W. lat. 14. 15. N.

KEMPTEN, a town of Germany, in Bavaria, with a late princely abbey of the Benedictine order. It has a great trade in linen, and is seated on the Iller; 45 miles S. by W. of Augsburg, and 50. S. by E. of Ulm.

KEN, a river in Westmoreland, which flows by Kendal, and enters the sandy wash of Lancashire, called Morecambe Bay It has a cataract near its mouth, which obstructs the navigation.

KEN, a river of Scotland, which rises in the N. W. part of Kirkcudbrightshire, flows to New Galloway, thence expands into a lake, 4 miles long and a mile broad, and then joins the river Dee.

KENDAL, a borough in Westmoreland; market on Saturday: it returns one member to parliament. It is seated on the Ken, over which are two stone bridges, and one of wood leading to the castle, which is now in ruins. It has a spacious church, and two chapels belonging to the establishment, and no fewer than 10 meeting-houses for dissenters. Besides the free-school, which is well endowed, and has some exhibitions to Queen's College, in Oxford, there is a large national school, and also a school of industry, &c. Here are manufactures of kerseymeres, linsey-woolsey, serges, baizes, knit woollen caps, and jackets, carpetings of various textures, waistcoatings, &c.; and in the neighbourhood are gunpowder works, corn and paper mills, dye-works, &c. It has seven trading companies, who have each a hall; and the trade, notwithstanding the disadvantage of its river for water carriage, is very considerable. It is 44 miles S. of Carlisle, and 261 N. of London. Long. 2. 52. W. lat. 54. 15. N.

KENILWORTH, a town in Warwickshire; with a market on Wednesday. Its church is an ancient edifice; and there are two dissenting meeting-houses, a free-school, and a school of industry. Here was a famous castle, the remains of which form one of the most picturesque objects in the kingdom. It is 5 miles N. of Warwick, and 96 N. W. of London.

KENMARE, a town of Ireland, in the county of Kerry; at the head of a river, or bay of the same name; 26 miles S. S. E. of Tralee.

KENNEBEC, a county of the United States, state of Maine; chief towns, Augusta and Hollowell. Pop. 55,823. The Kennebec river runs through this county.

KENNET, a river of England, which rises among the chalky hills in Wiltshire, becomes navigable at Newbury, in Berkshire, and joins the Thames at Sunning.

KENSINGTON, a village in Middlesex, one mile W. of London. Here is a royal palace, which, until the reign of George III., was a favourite residence of our monarchs: King William, Queen Mary, Queen Anne, and George II. died here. The gardens now form a fashionable and extensive promenade, having been gradually augmented to 3½ miles in circumference.

KENT, a county of England; 55 miles long and 28 broad; bounded on the N. by the Thames and the German Ocean, E. by the same ocean. S. E. and S. by the English Channel and Sussex, and W. by Surrey. It contains 935,600 acres; is divided into 63 hundreds, and 414 parishes; has two cities, Canterbury and Rochester, and 24 market towns. In the soil and face of the country there is a great diversity. The banks of the Thames are low and marshy, but backed by a range of chalky eminences, sometimes rising to a moderate height. This kind of hard chalky soil, inclining to barrenness, extends to the N. E. extremity of the county, and thence round to Dover, exhibiting its nature in the lofty white cliffs which here bound the island, and produce that striking appearance at sea which gave it the name of Albion. The S. W. part of Kent, called the Weald, is a flat and woody tract, of a clayey soil, and fertile. The midland and western districts are a mixture of hill and vale, arable and pasture, equal in pleasantness to any part of England. The minerals of this county consist chiefly of chalk, flint, ragstone, and pyrites; and the only mineral water of any note is that of Tunbridge Wells. The manufactures are few; but every branch of agriculture is extensively prosecuted with ability and success. Besides the usual objects of agriculture, the county produces large quantities of hops, (for which it is famous,) fruit of various kinds (especially cherries and apples, of which there are large orchards for the London markets). In the S. W. angle of the county is Romney-marsh, celebrated for its rich meadows, affording pasturage to vast flocks of sheep. Few counties in Britain abound more in antiquities and noblemen's seats, than Kent. It is divided into the Eastern and Western divisions, each of which returns two members to parliament. The principal rivers, besides the Thames, are the Medway, Darent, Stour, Cray, and Rother.

KENT is also the name of three counties in the United States; one in Rhode Island, on the W. side of Narraganset Bay; another in Delaware, the soil of which is esteemed the richest in the state; and a third in Maryland, on the eastern shore of Chesapeake Bay.

KENTUCKY, one of the United States of America; 328 miles long, and from 30 to 190 broad. It is bounded on the N. by the Ohio, E. by Virginia, S. by Tennessee, and W. by the Mississippi; has an area of 40,110 square miles; and is divided into 54 counties. The soil is amazingly fertile in the central part; to the E. and W. it is mountainous, and the S. is principally composed of the Barrens, a sterile country destitute of water. Tobacco, hemp, cotton, and the different grains of Europe, but particularly maize and wheat, are cultivated. The trees are numerous, but of comparatively small size: the oak, beech, poplar, sugar-tree, mulberry, and ash are common; and here are also the pawpaw, cucumber, black mulberry, wild cherry, buck-eye, and some other kind of trees not common elsewhere. The mountainous parts produce a great quantity of ginseng. Iron ore and lead are found in abundance; and there are many large caves, some of which extend above a mile under a limestone rock, supported by curious arches and pillars. The waters produce plenty of fish and fowl; especially geese and ducks, which are amazingly numerous on the Ohio. The land fowls are turkeys; a specie of grouse which the inhabitants call pheasants; and quails to which they give the name of partridges. Among the native animals are deer, bears, wild cats, wolves, beavers, otters, foxes, rabbits, squirrels, racoons, and opossums. Most of the species of domestic quadrupeds, such as horses, cows, sheep, and hogs, have been introduced since the settlement. The manufactures of this state, which are considerable, consist of cloth and stuffs, bagging for cotton and hemp, iron castings, nails, earthenware, glass, leather, cordage, paper, distilled spirits, oil, salt, saltpetre, gunpowder, and maple sugar. Population, 779,828, including 182,258 slaves.

KENTUCKY, a river in the foregoing state, which rises in the Laurel Mountains, and after a general N. W. course of 200 miles, enters the Ohio in lat. 38. 42. N. It is navigable for boats

150 miles; but the stream in some places is rapid and dangerous, and its banks may rather be called precipices.

KEPPEL BAY, a bay on the E. coast of Australia, which communicates with Port Curtis.

KERBELAH, or MESJID HOSSEIN, a town of Asiatic Turkey, pach. of Irac Arabi, near the W. bank of the Euphrates. There is a splendid mosque and tomb of Hessein, grandson of the prophet, much resorted to by pilgrims; 55 miles S. W. from Bagdad.

KERCOLANG, an island in the Indian Ocean; about 80 miles in circumference. The face of the country is diversified with steep hills and extensive valleys, and is everywhere covered with trees and verdure. The inhabitants are Malay. Long. 126. 30. E. lat. 4. 28. N.

KERGUELEN LAND, an island in the Southern Ocean, which, on account of its sterility, Captain Cook, who visited it in 1779, would have denominated the Island of Desolation, but that he was unwilling to rob M. Kerguelen of the honour of its bearing his name. On the N. E. coast is a good and safe bay, named Christmas Harbour. Long. 69. 30. E. lat. 49. 20. S.

KERKUCK, a town of Kurdistan; the capital of a government, and residence of a pacha. It is surrounded by walls, and defended by a castle; 135 miles S. S. E. of Betlis. Pop. 14,500.

KERMAN, the ancient Caramania; a province of Persia, lying on the Gulf of Persia. The northern part is barren, but towards the S. the land is fertile.

KERMAN, or SIRJIAN, a city of Persia; capital of the foregoing province; celebrated for its beautiful pottery, carpets, and stuffs. It is 120 miles N. by W. of Bunder Abbas. Long. 55. 15. E. lat. 29. 20. N. Pop. 21,000.

KERPEN, a town of Prussian Westphalia, in the duchy of Juliers. It has a collegiate church; it is seated on the Erft; 10 miles E. S. E. of Juliers.

KERRY, a county of Ireland, in the province of Munster; bounded on the E. by the counties of Limerick and Cork; W. by the Atlantic Ocean; N. by the Shannon, which separates it from Thomond; and S. by Desmond and the Ocean. Its greatest length is about 67 miles, and its maximum breadth 62, comprising about 1,040,487 statute acres, or 1639 square miles. The southern part is plain, and fertile in corn; but the greater part is mountainous, and chiefly adapted for grazing. Considerable quantities of beef, butter, hides, and tallow, are exported from its excellent harbours. Tralee is the capital. It sends two members to parliament.

KERRY, a parish of Wales, in Montgomeryshire; situate in a beautiful vale of the same name; 3 miles from Newton.

KERTSCH, a seaport and fortress on the E. coast of the Crimea. The fortress is of great importance, as one of those commanding the passage which forms the communication between the Black Sea and Sea of Asoph. It is 60 miles N. N. E. of Caffa. Long. 36. 24. E. lat. 45. 15.

KESH, or SEBS, a town of Usbec Tartary, in Bukharia; once the ordinary summer residence of Timur, who surrounded it with walls, and built a new palace, in 1379. It is 30 miles S by W. of Samarcand.

KESSEL, a town of the Netherlands, in the province of Antwerp; with a handsome castle. It is seated on the Maese; 7 miles N. of Ruremonde.

KESSELDORF, a village of Saxony, 7 miles W. of Dresden; celebrated for a victory gained by the king of Prussia over the Saxons, in the year 1745.

KESWICK, a town in Cumberland, with a market on Saturday; seated in a vale of its name, near the rapid river Greta. This vale is much visited by the admirers of nature: here is the Lake of Keswick, or Derwent-water; and to the N. of this soars the lofty mountain Skiddaw, one of the most distinguished in England. Keswick has manufactures of cotton, linen, and coarse woollen goods; and an establishment for making some of the finer textures has been recently opened. About a mile and a half to the S. of the town is a remarkable arrangement of rude granite stones, which form a circle, called the Druids' Temple. It is 25 miles N. W. of Kendal, and 293 N. N. W. of London.

KETTERING, a town in Northamptonshire, with a market on Saturday, and manufactures of woollen articles, &c. It is 12 miles N. E. of Northampton, and 74 N. W. of London.

KEUSCHBERG, or KIADE, a town of Prussian Saxony; 6 miles S. E. of Mersburg.

KEW, a village in Surrey; 6 miles W. by S. of London. The royal palace of Kew was a favourite retreat of George III., who enlarged the gardens, and united them with those of Richmond. The botanic garden, chiefly for exotics, is one of the finest in the world.

KEXHOLM. *See* WIBURG.

KEXHOLM, a town of Russia, in Finland, formerly the capital of the Swedish province of Carelia, and now of a Russian government. It is seated on two islands, in the river Woxon, which here flows into Lake Ladoga; 90 miles N. of Petersburg. Long. 30. 25. E. lat. 61. 3. N.

KEYNSHAM, a town in Somersetshire, with a market on Thursday, and a trade in malt; seated on the Chew, at its conflux with the Avon; 5 miles S. E. of Bristol, and 114 W. London.

KHARKOFF, or CHARKOW, a town of European Russia, capital of a government of the same name, seated on the small rivers Kharkoff and Lapan; 400 miles S. by W. of Moscow.

KHORASSAN. *See* CHORASSAN.

KHUM. *See* COM.

KIA-KING, a city of China, of the first rank, in the province of Tche-kiang. Canals are cut through most of the streets, and passengers are sheltered from the sun and rain by beautiful piazzas. The silk manufactures are very extensive, and the trade considerable. It is 590 miles S. S. E. of Peking. Long. 120. 14. E. lat. 30. 50. N.

KIAKTA, or KIACHTA, a town of Asiatic Russia, in the government of Irkutsk. It has a considerable fur trade, and is the centre of the Russian and Chinese commerce. It stands on a small river, near its conflux with the Selenga, 75 miles S. S. W. of Selenginsk. Long. 106. 30. E. lat. 50. 20. N. Pop. 4000.

KIANGARI, a town of Asiatic Turkey, in Natolia, chief place of a sangiac; with a castle on a rock; 230 miles E. of Brusa. Long. 34. 47. E. lat. 39. 56. N.

KIANG-NAN, a province of China, bounded on the W. by Ho-nan, S. by Tche-kiang, and Kian-si, E. by the Gulf of Nan-king, and N. by Chantong. It is of vast extent, and contains 14 cities of the first rank, and 93 of the second and third, which are all places of considerable trade, the whole country being intersected by lakes, rivers, and canals. Its silks, cottons, japanned goods, and paper, are in high esteem. Nan-king is the capital.

KIANG-SI, a province of China, bounded on the N. by Kiang-nan. W. by Houquang, S. by Quang-tong, and E. by Fokien and Tche-kiang. The N. part contains the great Po-yang Lake, and some extensive morasses; the middle and S. parts are mountainous, but intermixed with fertile and well cultivated valleys. It contains 13 cities of the first rank, and 78 of the second and third. It is celebrated for its porcelain, which is the finest and most valuable of the empire. Nan-tchang is the capital.

KIAN-KU, or YANG-TSE-KIANG, the largest river of Asia. It flows E. during the first part of its course along the borders of China, after which it enters the empire, and, passing through the grand central provinces, falls into the Gulf of Tong-ming, in the eastern sea.

KIBURG, a town of Switzerland, in the canton of Zurich, with a castle; seated on the Theoff, 14 miles E. N. E. of Zurich.

KIDDERMINSTER, a borough in Worcestershire, with a market on Thursday, and another, recently established, on Saturday. It has long been celebrated for its carpet manufacture, which has been brought to great perfection: it has also manufactures of poplins, crapes, bombazeens, &c. A fine specimen of carpet-weaving, delineating the descent from the cross, is placed over the altar in St. George's chapel, recently erected. The Staffordshire and Worcestershire canal passes this place. It returns one member to parliament. It is seated on the river Stour, 14 miles S. E. of Bridgenorth, and 126 N. W. of London.

KIDWELLY, a town of Wales, in Caermarthenshire, governed by a mayor, with a market on Tuesday. It stands on a creek of the Bristol Channel, and has a canal to some collieries, whence coal is brought down and exported. Here are also an iron-foundry and a tin-mill. On the opposite bank of the creek, where the old town formerly stood, are the remains of a castle. It is 8 miles S. of Caermarthen, and 226 W. by N. of London.

KIEL, a strong town of Denmark, capital of the duchy of Holstein, with a castle and a university. It stands on a peninsula, in a bay of the Baltic, and has a commodious harbour for ships of the largest size. It is one of the most commercial places in Holstein, and its trade is augmented by means of the Eyder canal to Rendsburg. Kiel is 37 miles N. W. of Lubec, and 46 N. by E. of Hamburg. Long. 10. 16. E. lat. 54. 21. N. Pop. 7500.

KIEN-NING, a city of China, of the first rank, in the province of Fo-kien. At the time of the conquest of China by the Tartars, it sustained two sieges, and was at last taken, and all the inhabitants put to the sword. It was afterwards re-established by the Tartars, and is now a place of considerable trade. It stands on the river Min-ho, 260 miles S. E. of Nan-king. Long. 117. 2. E. lat. 27. 5. N.

KIEN-TCHANG, a city of China, of the first rank, in the province of Kiang-si; seated in a fertile country, 340 miles S. S. W. of Nan-king. Long. 118. 20. E. lat. 27. 35. N.

KIEOU-KIANG, a city of China, of the first rank, in the province of Kiang-si; situate on the Kian-ku, immediately above the influx of the Poyang-hou. It is the rendezvous of all the barks which pass to and from other places in this province, and the provinces of Kiang-nan and Hou-quang. It is 250 miles S. W. of Nan-king. Long. 116. 0. E. lat. 20. 51. N.

KIEV. *See* KIOV.

KILBARCHAN, a village of Scotland, on the W. side of Loch Winnoch; 5 miles S. W. of Renfrew. It is inhabited chiefly by weavers, and has extensive bleach-fields.

KILBEGGAN, a town of Ireland, in the county of Westmeath, 56 miles from Dublin.

KILBRIDE, a town of Scotland, in Lanarkshire, noted for its cotton manufactures, and for being the birthplace of Dr. William Hunter and his brother John, two celebrated anatomists. It is 6 miles S. by E. of Glasgow.

KILCALMONELL, a town of Scotland, in Argyleshire, 17 miles N. of Campbelton.

KILCONQUHAR, a town of Scotland, Fifeshire. The vicinity abounds in coal and limestone. It is situated on the north shore of the Frith of Forth.

KILDA, ST., one of the Hebrides, 28 miles to the W. of North Uist. It is 3 miles long and 2 broad, fenced about with one continued perpendicular face of rock, of prodigious height, except at the landing-place on the S. E., where there is a narrow and steep passage to a village on the top of a rock. The surface of the island is hilly, but it feeds many sheep, and produces plenty of barley and potatoes. Many of the inhabitants live chiefly by fishing, and catching wild fowls. In the latter employment they are incredibly adventurous. Being let down by a rope from the summit of the precipitous rocks, they clamber along their fronts, in search of the eggs and nests of various birds. St. Kilda is the most remote of the Hebrides, and is about 140 miles from the nearest point of the main land of Scotland. Long. 8. 23. W. lat. 57. 43. N.

KILDARE, a county of Ireland, in the province of Leinster, about 37 miles long and from 12 to 20 broad; bounded on the E. by Dublin and Wicklow, W. by King's county and Queen's county, N. by East Meath, and S. by

Carlow. The principal rivers are the Liffey, Barrow, and Boyne. It is a very fertile and arable country, much interspersed with bog, amounting to 36,480 acres, including the bogs of Allen, Lullymore, &c., part of which have been reclaimed. It sends two members to parliament.

KILDARE, a town of Ireland, capital of the foregoing county, and a bishop's see. It is chiefly supported by frequent horse-races on what is called the Curragh, a fine turfy plain, containing upwards of 5000 acres, which feeds a great number of sheep; 27 miles S. W. of Dublin. Long. 6. 57. W. lat. 53. 9. N.

KILFENORA, a small town of Ireland, in the county of Clare, and a bishop's see united with Killaloe. 12 miles N. W. of Ennis.

KILIA, a fortified town of European Russia, in Bessarabia; with a good trade in wool, goats' hair, tallow, wine, corn, &c. It is situated on the most northern branch of the Danube, 86 miles S. W. of Bialogorod.

KILKENNY, a county of Ireland, in the province of Leinster, about 40 miles long and 20 broad, containing 510,882 acres; bounded on the E. by Carlow and Wexford, W. by Tipperary, N. by Queen's county, and S. by Waterford. It sends two members to parliament. The surface is in general level, and the soil fertile It is particularly noted for its coal, which makes no smoke in burning. The principal rivers are the Barrow, Suire, and Nore.

KILKENNY, a city of Ireland, capital of the above county, situate on the river Nore, over which are two bridges. Irishtown, on the E. side of the river, is joined to it, and both together form a large and pleasant place. It had formerly a bishop, and the cathedral, which stands in Irishtown, belongs to the bishop of Ossory. The chief manufactures are coarse woollens and fine blankets. It sends one member to parliament; 26 miles N. of Waterford. Long. 7. 32. W. lat. 52. 36. N.

KILLALA, a seaport of Ireland, in the county of Mayo, and formerly a bishop's see united with Achonry, now united with Tuam. It stands on a fine bay of the Atlantic, to which it gives name; 24 miles N. of Castlebar. Long. 9. 4. W. lat. 54. 8. N.

KILLALOE, a town of Ireland, in the county of Clare, and formerly a bishop's see united with Kilfenora, now united with Tuam. It is seated on the Shannon, over which is a bridge of 19 arches; 10 miles N. N. E. of Limerick.

KILLARNEY, a town of Ireland, in the county of Kerry, with an extensive manufacture. It is much frequented on account of the adjoining lake; 14 miles S. E. of Tralee.

KILLARNEY, a beautiful lake of Ireland, in the county of Kerry, otherwise called Lough Lean, from its being surrounded by high mountains. It is divided into three parts, called the Lower, Middle, and Upper Lake. The northern, or lower lake, is 6 miles long and 3 broad. On the side of one of the mountains is O'Sullivan's Cascade, which falls above 70 feet into the lake with a tremendous roar; and opposite this cascade is the island of Innisfallen. The promontory of Mucruss divides the upper from the lower lake, and on passing round its extremity into the upper lake, there is a celebrated rock, called the Eagle's Nest, which produces wonderful echoes. The upper lake is 4 miles long and 2 broad; and from the mountains descend a number of beautiful cascades. The islands in this lake are numerous, and afford an amazing variety of picturesque views. The centre lake is small in comparison with the other two, and cannot boast of equal variety; but the shores are indented with bays, surrounded by dark groves of trees. The E. boundary is formed by the base of Mangerton, down the steep side of which descends a cascade, visible for 150 yards; this fall of water is supplied by a circular lake, near the summit of the mountain, called the Devil's Punch-bowl, which is considered one of the greatest curiosities of Killarney.

KILLCULLEN, a town of Ireland, in the county of Kildare, on the river Liffey, over which is a bridge; 9 miles E. S. E. of Kildare, and 25 S. W. of Dublin.

KILLINGLEY, a township of Windham county, Connecticut, seated on the Quinabaug; 18 miles N. E. of Windham.

KILLONY, a town of Ireland, in the county of Sligo, 6 miles S. of Sligo.

KILLOUGH, or PORT ST. ANN, a seaport of Ireland, in the county of Down, to the N. of St. John's Point, in the Irish Sea. A rock stands in the middle of the entrance of its harbour, covered at half flood. Here is a manufacture of salt; 6 miles S. S. E. of Downpatrick. Long. 5. 40. W. lat. 54. 14. N.

KILLRUSH, a town of Ireland, in the county of Clare, near the river Shannon; it is a modern town, and has a considerable trade in grain, butter, slates, &c.

KILLYBEGS, a town of Ireland, in the county of Donegal, with a spacious harbour on the N. side of Donegal Bay; 12 miles N. W. of Ballyshannon.

KILLYLEAGH, a town of Ireland, in the county of Down; with a linen and thread manufacture. The celebrated Sir Hans Sloane was born in this town; it is seated on an arm of Strangford Lough; 35 miles N. E. of Newry.

KILMACTHOMAS, a town of Ireland, in the county of Waterford; 12 miles W. S. W. of Waterford.

KILMAINHAM, town of Ireland in a valley; about half a mile W. of Dublin. It has a session-house, a gaol, a foundling hospital, and an hospital for invalid soldiers. Here the knights for the county of Dublin are elected; and it was the seat of government before the castle at Dublin was appropriated to that purpose.

KILMALLOCK, a town of Ireland, in the county of Limerick; 140 miles from Dublin. It is a place of considerable antiquity, and formerly of much importance, as its numerous ruined mansions, castles, &c. indicate.

KILMARNOCK, a populous and flourishing town of Scotland, in Ayrshire; with a market on Friday. In conjunction with Renfrew, &c. it sends one member to parliament. It is the principal manufacturing town in the county and carries on an extensive trade: its chief manufactures are carpets, serges, blankets, tartans, and other woollen goods, saddlery, leather, &c. Near it are the remains of Dean Castle, the seat of the earls of Kilmarnock, in the desolate condition to which it was reduced by fire in 1735. It is seated near the Irvine, on the Glasgow and Ayr railway; 11 miles N. N. E. of Ayr, and 20 S. S. W. of Glasgow. Long. 4. 28. W. lat. 55. 40. N.

KILMAURS, a town of Scotland, in Ayrshire; formerly celebrated for its cutlery; 2 miles N. W. of Kilmarnock.

KILMORE, a town of Ireland, in the county of Cavan, and, with Armagh, a bishop's see; 3 miles S. W. of Cavan.

KILRENNY, a parish of Scotland, in Fifeshire; on the Frith of Forth.

KILSYTH, a village of Scotland, in Stirlingshire; inhabited chiefly by weavers employed by the Glasgow manufacturers; it is situate on the Great North Road from Edinburgh and Stirling to Glasgow; 15 miles S. W. of Stirling, and 13 N. E. of Glasgow.

KILWINNING, a town of Scotland, in Ayrshire. Here is the elegant seat of the Montgomery family, Eglintoun Castle; also some remains of a magnificent monastery, which was erected here in 1140. The vicinity abounds in limestone and coal. It is seated on the Garnock, over which is a stone bridge; 5 miles N. N. W. of Irvine.

KIMBOLTON, a town in Huntingdonshire; with a market on Friday. Here is a castle, the seat of the Duke of Manchester, where Queen Catherine resided for some time after her divorce from Henry VIII.; 63 miles N. by W. of London.

KIMI, or KIEMI, a town of Russian Lapland; on a river of the same name, near its entrance into the Gulf of Bothnia; 10 miles E. of Tornea.

KIN, or KAIN, a town of Persia, in the province of Seistan; situate at the foot of a mountain; 60 miles S. S. W. of Herat.

KINBURN, a fortress of Russia, in the government of Taurida, on the S. side of the estuary of the Dnieper. It has been frequently attacked by the Turks, by land and sea, but without success; 18 miles S. S. E. of Oczakow, on the opposite side of the Dnieper.

KINCARDINE, a town of Scotland, in Perthshire; with a commodious harbour, and a good road in the Frith of Forth. Ship-building is carried on to a great extent, and the coasting and foreign trade is considerable; 5 miles S. E. of Alloa, and 22 S. by W. of Perth.

KINCARDINE, a town of Scotland, in Ross-shire, with a small harbour on the Frith of Dornoch; 14 miles W. by N. of Tain.

KINCARDINE O'NEIL, a town of Scotland, in Aberdeenshire; seated on the river Dee; 23 miles W. by S. of Aberdeen.

KINCARDINESHIRE, or MEARNS, a county of Scotland; bounded on the N. W. and N. by Aberdeenshire, E. by the German Ocean, and S. and W. by Angusshire. Its length along the coast, is 30 miles; and its greatest breadth about 24. The N. W. part is mountainous, and chiefly adapted for pasture; but to the S. of the Grampians, the surface is in general fertile. The small village of Kincardine, 9 miles S. W. of Stonehaven, was formerly the capital, but Stonehaven is now the county town. It sends one member to parliament.

KINDERHOOK, a town of New York, in Columbia county, on the E. side of Hudson River; 13 miles N. of the city of Hudson.

KINETON. *See* KINGTON.

KING GEORGE SOUND, a harbour on the S. W. coast of Australia; discovered by Captain Vancouver, in 1791. It is safe, and easy of access any where between its outer points of entrance, Bald-head and Mount Gardner, about 11 miles distant from each other. Long. 118. 17. E. lat. 35. 5. S.

KING GEORGE SOUND, the name given by Captain Cook, in 1778, to the bay which he discovered on the W. coast of North America, in long. 126. 48. W. and lat. 49. 33. N. But the natives call it Nootka, the name now generally adopted by the English. It is not situate on the continent, as Cook had reason to suppose, but on an island, to which Captain Vancouver, in 1792, gave the name of Quadra and Vancouver Island.

KIN-GAN, a city of China, of the first rank, in the province of Kiang-si; seated on the Kan-kiang; 800 miles S. of Peking. Long. 115. 10. E. lat. 27. 16. N.

KINGHORN, a borough of Scotland, in Fifeshire; on the Frith of Forth, nearly opposite Leith. It joins with Burntisland, Kirkaldy, and Dysart, in returning one member to parliament. It has two harbours, one below the town and the other half a mile W. at Pettycur, for the passage-boats between this place and Leith; 9 miles N. by W. of Leith.

KING'S COUNTY, a county of Ireland, in the province of Leinster; 43 miles long, and about 39 in its greatest breadth; bounded on the N. by West Meath, E. by Kildare, S. by Queen's County and Tipperary, and W. by the Shannon, which separates it from Galway and Roscommon. It is divided into 52 parishes, contains 453,370 acres, and sends two members to parliament. The principal rivers are the Shannon, and the Greater and Little Brosna; and the Grand Canal crosses the N. part of the county. It is not so well cultivated as some of the other counties, but the soil is tolerably fertile. The capital was Philipstown; but it has been abandoned for Tullamore.

KING'S LANGLEY, a village in Hertfordshire, where Henry III. occasionally resided. It is seated on the river Gade; 5 miles S. W. of St. Albans.

KINGSBRIDGE, a town in Devonshire, with a market on Saturday; seated on a branch of the Salcombe river, over which is a bridge to Dodbrook; 34 miles S. by W. of Exeter, and 208 W. S. W. of London.

KINGSCLERE, a town in Hampshire; with a market on Tuesday, and a great trade in malt. It was the residence of some of our Saxon kings; 54 miles W. by S. of London.

Kingscliff, a parish in Northamptonshire; 12 miles W. of Peterborough.

King's Lynn. *See* Lynn Regis.

Kingstein, a strong fortress of Norway. *See* Fredericstadt.

Kingston upon Thames, a corporate town in Surrey, with a market on Saturday. At a national council held here in the year 838, King Egbert, and his son Athelwolf, were present; and several of the Saxon monarchs were crowned here. This town sent two members to parliament in the reigns of Edward II. and III., but was disfranchised by the desire of the inhabitants. Queen Elizabeth founded here a free school; and the spring assizes are held at this place. It is seated on the river Thames, over which it had an ancient wooden bridge, now replaced by one of stone. It is 10 miles S. W. of London. The South Western railway passes near this town.

Kingston, a seaport of Jamaica, in the West Indies; situate on the N. side of Port Royal Bay. It was built in 1698, after the great earthquake which destroyed the town of Port Royal, and in 1803 was incorporated as a city. It is a place of good trade, being much resorted to by ships coming to load and unload their cargoes; and of late years it has been greatly enlarged by the addition of many handsome houses. Pop. 34,500. It is 10 miles E. of Spanish Town. Long. 76. 40. W. lat. 18. 3. N.

Kingston, the capital of St. Vincent, in the West Indies, situate at the head of a bay of the same name, on the S. W. shore of the island.

Kingston, or **Esopus**, a town of New York, in Ulster county. It was destroyed by an English fleet, in 1777, but has been rebuilt on a regular plan. It stands on Esopus Creek, near its entrance into Hudson River; 76 miles N. of New York. Long. 74. 3. W. lat. 41. 54. N.

Kingston, a town of North Carolina, chief of Lenoir county; on the N. side of the Neus; 40 miles W. by N. of Newbern, and 50 S. E. of Raleigh.

Kingston, a town of South Carolina, in Georgetown district; on the Wakkamaw; 30 miles N. N. E. of Georgetown.

Kingston, the largest and most populous town of Upper Canada; with a good harbour. Here the queen's stores are kept and guarded. Vessels from Lower Canada go no farther than this place; and hence to York, Niagara, &c., stores and merchandise are conveyed in boats. It is seated on Lake Ontario, at its outlet into the St. Lawrence; 190 miles W. of Montreal. Long. 76. 41. W. lat. 44. 8. N.

Kingston on Hull. *See* Hull.

Kingstown, or **Dunleary**, a town in Ireland, county of Dublin; 6½ miles from Dublin, to which it is connected by a railway, from which it has derived much advantage. It is an agreeable watering-place, and possesses an excellent asylum harbour, commenced in 1817, enclosed by two piers, each upwards of 4000 feet in length, and a lighthouse; area 260 acres.

King-tcheou, a city of China, of the first rank; in the province of Hou-quang. It is considered one of the keys of the empire, is well fortified, and has a large Tartar garrison. It stands on the Kian-ku; 620 miles S. S. W. of Peking. Long. 111. 37. E. lat. 30. 26. N.

King-te-tching, a town of China, in the province of Kiang-si; famous for its beautiful porcelain. It is computed to contain above 1,000,000 of inhabitants, and extends 4 miles along the banks of a river, which here forms a kind of harbour; 655 miles S. of Peking. Long. 115. 54. E. lat. 29. 25. N.

Kington, or **Kineton**, a town in Warwickshire, with a market on Tuesday. King John kept his court in a castle he erected here. It is 85 miles N. W. of London.

Kington, or **Kyneton**, an ancient town in Herefordshire; with a market on Wednesday, and a considerable clothing trade. It is seated on the Arrow, under Bradnor Mountain; 19 miles N. W. of Hereford, and 154 W. by N. of London.

Kin-hoa, a city of China, of the first rank; in Tche-kiang, on the banks of a fine river. It has a great trade in dried plums and hams; and it is famous for good rice-wine, and very white candles: the latter are made of a substance obtained from little shrubs with a white flower, not unlike jessamine. It is 190 miles S. by E. of Nan-king. Long. 119. 10. E. lat. 29. 16. N.

Kinnaird Head, a lofty promontory on the E. coast of Scotland, in Aberdeenshire; about a mile to the N. of the town of Fraserburg. Here is a castle four stories high, on the top of which is a lighthouse. Long. 1. 46. W. lat. 57. 39. N.

Kinross, a town of Scotland, the capital of Kinross-shire; seated in a plain, screened on the N. by the Ochill Hills; and on the river Leven, before it enters Loch Leven. It has a manufacture of cotton and coarse linens. It is 23 miles N. N. W. of Edinburgh. Long. 3. 9. W. lat. 56. 7. N.

Kinross-shire, a county of Scotland, surrounded by the shires of Perth and Fife, and almost circular; about 30 miles in circumference. It is divided into four parishes. The central part is occupied by Loch Leven, and the country around has a rich appearance. It sends one member to parliament alternately with the county of Clackmannan.

Kinsale, a seaport and borough of Ireland, in the county of Cork; returning one member to parliament. It is a maritime arsenal, and has an excellent harbour, defended by a strong fort. In times of war it is very much frequented by East and West India fleets, on which account the leases of the inhabitants oblige them to pay double rent during these seasons. It is seated at the mouth of the Bandon; 14 miles S. of Cork. Long. 8. 28. W. lat. 51. 42. N.

Kin-tching, the capital of the island of Loo-choo, in the China Sea, and of all the islands under that appellation. The king's palace, reckoned to be four leagues in circumference, is built on a neighbouring mountain. Long. 127. 30. E. lat. 26. 2. N.

KIN-TONG, a city of China, of the first rank; in the province of Yun-nan. The surrounding country is mountainous, but the valleys yield abundance of rice. It is seated on the Papien; 750 miles W. by N. of Canton. Long. 100. 40. E. lat. 24. 30. N.

KINTORE, a borough of Scotland, in Aberdeenshire; on the river Don; 13 miles W. by N. of Aberdeen. It sends, in conjunction with Elgin, &c., one member to parliament.

KINTYRE. *See* CANTYRE.

KIN-YANG, a city of China, of the first rank; in Chen-si. It has always been deemed as a barrier against the incursions of the Tartars, and is strongly fortified. The country around is very fruitful. It is 560 miles S. W. of Peking. Long. 107. 30. E. lat. 36. 6. N.

KIN-YUEN, a city of China, of the first rank, in Quang-si. It is seated on a fine river, but surrounded with craggy mountains, inhabited by a rude and savage race of people. It is 310 miles W. by N. of Canton. Long. 108. 15. E. lat. 25. 28. E.

KIOV, or KIOW, a government of the Russian empire, being part of the Ukraine, or Little Russia. It was once a duchy, belonging to the great dukes of Russia, and Kiov was their capital. This country was conquered by the Tartars, and came again into the possession of the great dukes, but was overrun and possessed by the Cossacks, under the protection of Poland. In 1664, the natives, discontented with John Casimir, king of Poland, submitted to Russia, and have ever since remained subject to that empire. This government is divided into twelve circles, and contains about 975,000 inhabitants.

KIOV, KIOW, KIOF, KIVA, or KHIVA, a town of European Russia; capital of the foregoing government, and a Greek archbishop's see; with a castle. It is divided into the Old Town, the Lower Town, and the Fortress of Petscherski, all connected by intrenchments. Here are catacombs of considerable extent, dug, as it would seem, through a mass of hardened clay. It is seated on the Dnieper; 180 miles N. E. of Kaminieck, and 335 E. S. E. of Warsaw. Pop. 47,424.

KIO-FEOU, a city of China, in the province of Chan-tong, and district of Yen-tcheou. It was the birthplace of Confucius, several monuments to whose memory are still to be seen here.

KIOGE, or KOGE, a seaport of Denmark, in the isle of Zealand. The English defeated the Danes here, and took the town in 1807. It is 10 miles S. W. of Copenhagen. Long. 12. 15. E. lat. 55. 30. N.

KIOPING, or KOPING, a town of Sweden, in the government of Westeraas; 18 miles N. by W. of Westeraas.

KIPPEN, a town of Scotland, in Stirlingshire; on the S. bank of the Forth; 9 miles W. of Stirling.

KIRBY, or KIRKBY LONSDALE, a town in Westmoreland; with a market on Thursday, and manufactures of carpets and blankets. It is seated on the Loyne, over which is a curious ancient stone bridge of three arches. It is 12 miles S. E. of Kendal, and 252 N. W. of London.

KIRBY, or KIRKBY MOORSIDE, a town in N. Yorkshire, with a market on Wednesday. There are several interesting ruins in the neighbourhood; and in the village of Kirkdale, 2 miles hence, many fossil animal remains were discovered in 1820. It is seated on the river Dow; 29 miles N. of York, and 221 N. by W. of London.

KIRBY, or KIRKBY STEPHEN, a town in Westmoreland, with a market on Monday. The woollen manufacture is the chief trade here. It is seated on the river Eden; 3 miles S. S. E. of Appleby, and 266 N. N. W. of London.

KIRCHBERG, a town and castle of Wirtemberg, in a district of the same name; seated on the Iller; 9 miles S. of Ulm.

KIRCHBERG, a town of Wirtemberg, with a castle on a hill, by the river Jaxt; 12 miles S. S. W. of Rotenburg.

KIRCHBERG, a town in the Prussian province of the Lower Rhine; 41 miles W. of Mentz.

KIRCHEIM, a town of Bavaria, on the Mindel; 29 miles E. S. E. of Ulm.

KIRCHHAYN, a town of the Prussian states, in Lusatia; seated on the Bober; 18 miles S. of Luckau.

KIRCHHEIM, a town of Wirtemberg, with a castle; seated on the river Lauter; 1 mile S. E. of Stutgard.

KIRDORF, a town of Germany, in Hesse-Darmstadt; 42 miles S. S. W. of Cassel.

KIRGUIS, a country of West Asia, in Independent Tartary; inhabited by three hordes of Cossacks, or Kirguises, considered to be the descendants of the ancient Mongolians; on the N. frontier of China. They are nominally under the dominion of Russia, and are about 650,000 in number.

KIRIN, a government of Eastern Tartary; enclosed between the sea of Japan, the northern frontier of Corea, and the river of Saghalien. The emperor of China sends hither the criminals banished by the laws.

KIRIN, a city of Eastern Tartary; capital of the foregoing province, and the residence of a Mandshur general, who is invested with the authority of a viceroy. It is situate on the river Songari, which is here called Kirin; 540 miles E. N. E. of Peking. Long. 126. 20. E. lat. 43. 20. N.

KIRKCALDY, a borough of Scotland, in Fifeshire, with a good harbour. Here are a dockyard for small vessels, and manufactures of checks, ticking, cotton, and leather. This was the birthplace of the celebrated Dr. Adam Smith, author of the "Wealth of Nations." It sends, with Dysart, &c., one member to parliament. It is seated on the N. side of the Frith of Forth; 11 miles N. of Leith.

KIRKCUDBRIGHT, a borough and seaport of Scotland, capital of the county of its name; with a castle; contributory, with Dumfries,

&c., in sending one member to parliament. The harbour will admit ships of any burden to come up to the town, and yet it has no considerable trade or manufacture. It is seated at the mouth of the Dee; 28 miles S. W. of Dumfries.

KIRKCUDBRIGHTSHIRE, or EAST GALLOWAY, a county of Scotland, 45 miles long and 30 broad; bounded on the N. W. by Ayrshire, N. E. and E. by Dumfries-shire, S. by Solway Frith and the Irish Sea, and W. by Wigtonshire. It is divided into 28 parishes, and sends one member to parliament. The northern parts are mountainous and uncultivated; but there is some fertile land on the sides of the rivers, and it feeds a great number of cattle and sheep. The chief rivers are the Dee, Fleet, Cree, and Orr.

KIRKHAM, a town in Lancashire, with a market on Thursday. The ancient church was taken down in 1822, except the tower. The manufactures are sail-cloth, cordage, coarse linens, cottons, &c. It is situated near the mouth of the Ribble, on the Preston and Wyre railway; 23 miles S. of Lancaster, and 226 N. N. W. of London.

KIRKINTILLOCH, a town of Scotland, in Dumbartonshire, with manufactures of linen and cotton; seated near the junction of the Luggie with the Kelvin; 7 miles E. N. E. of Glasgow.

KIRKLESS, a village in W. Yorkshire; situate on the Calder; 3 miles from Huddersfield. In the park near it is the monument of the famous Robin Hood.

KIRKOSWALD, a town in Cumberland, with a market on Thursday. On an elevated spot, a little E. of the town, are the ruins of a castle, and on another eminence, 3 miles to the S., is the famous Druidical monument called Long Meg and her Daughters. Kirkoswald is seated at the conflux of the Croglin with the Eden; 9 miles N. by E. of Penrith, and 292 N. W. of London.

KIRKPATRICK, a village of Scotland, in Dumbartonshire; 5 miles E. S. E. of Dumbarton. The vestiges of the Roman wall, built by Antonius, extend from the Clyde at this place to Abercorn on the Frith of Forth. It is called, by the country people, Graham's Dike.

KIRKTON, or KIRTON, a town in Lincolnshire, with a market on Saturday; situate on the top of a hill; 20 miles N. of Lincoln, and 147 N. by W. of London.

KIRKWALL, a borough of Scotland; capital of Pomona, the principal island of the Orkneys. It is contributory in sending one member to parliament. It is built on a neck of land on the E. side of the island; and the most striking object is the stately cathedral of St. Magnus, opposite which is the bishop's palace, now called a castle.. The harbour is excellent, with a good outer road, defended by a fortification. Here are manufactures of linen and cotton; and great quantities of kelp are exported. It is 30 miles N. E. of Thurso, in Caithness-shire.

KIRN, a town of the Prussian province of Lower Rhine; situate on the Nahe; 42 miles S. by W. of Coblentz.

KIRRYMUIR, a town of Scotland, in Forfarshire; with considerable manufactures of brown and coarse linens. It is 5 miles N. W. of Forfar, and 16 N. of Dundee.

KIRSHEHR, a town of Asiatic Turkey, in Natolia; formerly a considerable city, called Diocæsarea. Salt is made in the neighbourhood. It is 84 miles N. E. of Konieh. Long. 34. 15. E. lat. 39. 10. N.

KIRSOVA, a town of European Turkey, in Bulgaria; seated on the Danube; 76 miles S. W. of Ismael. Long. 28. 4. E. lat. 44. 47. N.

KISMICH, or KISHM, a fertile island at the entrance of the Gulf of Persia; 60 miles long, and 12 broad; separated by a narrow channel from the continent of Persia. Its E. end is 12 miles S. of Bunder Abbas.

KISSINGEN, a town of the Bavarian states, in Franconia, in the environs of which are some medicinal and salt springs. It is 32 miles N. of Wurzburg.

KISTNA, or KRISHNA, a river of Hindostan, which rises in the Sukhein Mountains, not far to the S. of Poonah, flows E. about 500 miles, forming the boundary between the Deccan and the Peninsula, and enters the Bay of Bengal by several mouths, to the S. of Masulipatam. Owing to the accumulation of sand at its mouths, it is not navigable for ships; but its inundations are of the greatest importance to the fertility of the country through which it passes.

KISTNAGHERI, a town and fortress of Hindostan; in the province of Barramaul. Since it came into the possession of the British, in 1792, it has been dismantled, to save the expense of a garrison. It is situate on a rock nearly 700 feet in height; 54 miles S. E. of Bangalore, and 66 W. S. W. of Arcot.

KITTERY, a town of the district of Maine, in York county, on the Piscataqua; 16 miles S. W. of York. Pop 2022.

KITZBICHL, a town of the Austrian states, in Tyrol, in the vicinity of which are mines of copper and silver. It is seated on the river Acha; 11 miles S. E. of Kufstein.

KITZINGEN, a town of Bavarian Franconia; on the river Maine; 10 miles E. S. E. of Wurzburg. Pop. 4100.

KIUN-TCHEOU, a city of China of the first rank; capital of the island Hainan, on the N. cost, at the mouth of the Limou. It stands on a promontory, and ships often anchor under its walls. Long. 109. 38. E. lat. 20. N.

KIUTAJA, or KUTAIAH, a town of Asiatic Turkey; capital of Natolia. Near it are some warm baths, much esteemed in several disorders. It is situate at the foot of a mountain, near the river Pursak; 136 miles S. S. E. of Constantinople. Pop. 55,000.

KIZIL IRMAK, the principal river of Asia Minor (the ancient Halys). It takes its rise in the pandjak of Sivas, and flows westward to long. 34., when it takes a N. course, and afterwards N. E., and falls into the Euxine near Bafra.

KLADRAU, a town of Bohemia, in the circle of Pilsen, near the river Misa; 20 miles W. of Pilsen.

KLATTAU, a town of Bohemia; capital of a circle of the same name; with a considerable woollen manufacture. Part of it was destroyed by fire in 1819. It is 69 miles S. W. of Prague. Pop. 3850.

KLINGNAU, a town of Switzerland, in the district of Baden, on the River Aar; 7 miles N. of Baden.

KNAPDALE, a district of Argyleshire, Scotland, about 20 miles long, and 16 broad. It is situate between the isthmus of Crinan and Tarbert, and is divided into the parishes of N. and S. Knapdale.

KNARESBOROUGH, a borough in West Yorkshire, with a market on Wednesday. It sends two members to parliament. It is the ancient seat of the linen manufacture, which is now carried on to a great extent. Here is a famous spring, of a strong petrifying quality, called the Dropping Well, which falls in drops from the top of a rock. The town is situate at the top of a rocky mountain, at the foot of which runs the river Nidd; 19 miles W. by N. of York, and 197 N. by W. of London.

KNIGHTON, a town of Wales, in Radnorshire, with a market on Thursday; seated on the Teme; 10 miles N. E. of Radnor, and 158 N. W. of London.

KNIGHTSBRIDGE, a village of Middlesex, now forming part of the suburbs of the metropolis.

KNIPHAUSEN, a seaport of Germany, in the grand duchy of Oldenburg; seated on the Jade; 39 miles E. of Embden.

KNOTTINGLEY, an extensive and populous village in West Yorkshire; on the river Aire; noted for its great production of limestone; 3 miles E. N. E. of Pontefract.

KNOXVILLE, a town of Tennessee; capital of Knox country. Here is a college, established by government, called Blount College. It stands on the river Holston; 22 miles above its junction with the Tennessee, and 200 S. by E. of Frankfort. Long. 84.8.W. lat. 35.58.N.

KNUTSFORD, a town of Cheshire, with a market on Saturday. Here are some cotton-mills, and manufacture of shag, velvets, &c. it is seated on a branch of the Birken; 25 miles E. by N. of Chester, and 175 N. W. of London.

KOANG-SIN, a city of China, of the first rank; in Kiang-si. Here are manufactures of good paper, and the best candles in the empire. It is 250 miles S. by W. of Nan-king. Long. 118. 20. E. lat. 28. 30. N.

KOEI-TCHEOU, a province of China, near the S. W. extremity of the empire. It is almost a desert, and full of precipitous mountains, inhabited by barbarous races, whom the Chinese have never been able fully to subdue. In the mountains there are mines of gold, silver, copper, and mercury. The horses are the best in China; and excellent game abound. Stuffs are made of a certain herb which resembles hemp, and are very much suited for summer clothes. The capital is Koei-yang.

KOEI-TCHEOU, or QUEI-CHOO, a city of China, of the first rank; in Se-tchuen. It is very rich, and carries on a great trade. It stands on the great river Kian-ku; 637 miles S. S. W. of Peking. Long. 109. 50. E. lat. 31. 10. N.

KOEI-YONG, a city of China; capital of the province of Koei-tcheou. It is built partly of earth and partly of bricks, and is surrounded by steep mountains. Long. 108. 30. E. lat. 27. 40. N.

KOGE. *See* KIOGE.

KOHISTAN, a district of Persia, in the province of Mecran; possessed by a powerful chief, who resides at Bunpoor.

KOHKELAN, a mountainous district of Hindostan, in the province of Lahore, on the western side of the Jhylum river; possessed by petty chiefs, who are subject either to the Seiks or Afghans.

KOKONOR, or HOHONOR, a country of Tartary, on the borders of China; inhabited by a tribe of Kalmucs called Sifans. It contains a large lake, of the same name.

KOLA, a town of Russian Lapland; in the government of Archangel. It has a good harbour on the River Kola, near a bay of the same name in the Frozen Ocean. Long. 32. 30. E. lat. 68. 20. N.

KOLIN, a town of Bohemia, in the circle of Kaurzim; with a castle. A little to the W. of this place, in 1757, the Austrians gained a victory over the Prussians; 26 miles E. S. E. of Prague.

KOLIVAN, or KHOLYVAN, a town of Asiatic Russia; capital of a district of the same name, in the government of Tomsk. In the neighbourhood are some very productive copper mines, with some silver and gold. It is seated on the river Berd, at its conflux with the Oby; 480 miles E. S. E. of Tobolsk. Long. 81. 20. E. lat. 55. 28. N.

KOLOMNA, a town of Russia, in the government of Moscow, and a bishop's see; with a trade in corn, tallow, salt beef, &c. It is seated on the Occa, near the influx of the Moskwa; 65 miles S. E. of Moscow.

KOM. *See* COM.

KONG, a kingdom of central Africa, on the borders of Guinea, from which it is separated by a ridge of mountains. The country is populous, and abounds in horses and elephants.

KONG, a town of Africa; capital of the above kingdom; 230 miles S. S. W. of Sego. Long. 3. 20. W. lat. 11. 20. N.

KONGSBERG, a town of Norway, in the government of Aggerhuys; formerly celebrated for the richest silver mines in Europe. It is situate on both sides of the river Lowe; 36 miles S. W. of Christiania. Long. 10. 0. E. lat. 59. 40. N.

KONGSWINGER, a town of Norway, on the frontiers of Sweden, near the river Glomme; at the foot of a steep rock, on which is a strong citadel; 42 miles N. E. of Christiania. Long. 12. 8. E. lat. 60. 12. N.

KONG-TCHANG, a city of China, of the first rank; in the province of Chen-si. It stands on the river Hoei, surrounded by high mountains, where a tomb is seen, which the Chinese pretend to be that of Fo-hi. Long. 104. 20. E. lat. 34. 56. N.

KONIEH, or KOINEH. *See* COGNI.

KONIGINGRATZ, a fortified town of Bohemia; capital of a circle of the same name, and a bishop's see. It has a spacious handsome market-place, an elegant cathedral, and many other handsome buildings. In 1762 a body of Prussian troops entered the town, and laid the greater part of it in ashes. It is seated on the Elbe; 44 miles E. of Prague. Long. 15. 40. E. lat. 50. 10. N. Population of the circle, 270,000; of the town, 6000.

KONIGSBERG, a government of the Prussian states; comprehending the N. and W. parts of the province of East Prussia, and corresponding nearly to East Prussia Proper. It comprises a superficial area of 8960 square miles, with 491,000 inhabitants.

KONIGSBERG, the capital of East Prussia; with a university, a magnificent palace, and a public library. The town-house, the exchange, the royal mint, and the cathedral, are fine structures. The tower of the castle is very high, whence there is a beautiful prospect. The wall which encloses the city and suburbs is 9 miles in circumference; but more than half this space consists of gardens and corn-fields, the population of the whole not exceeding 55,000, who are principally of the Lutheran religion. Many of the houses are large and elegant; and the trade is very considerable. No ships drawing more than 8 feet water can pass the bar of the river; so that large vessels anchor at Pillau, a small town on the Baltic. Konigsberg, though fortified, is not capable of making any serious resistance. It was taken by the Russians in 1758; and in June, 1807, it fell into the hands of the French; but, since the overthrow of Bonaparte, it has been under the dominion of Prussia. It is seated on the Pregel, near its entrance into the Frisch Haff; 170 miles N. of Warsaw. Long. 20. 45. E. lat. 54. 42. N.

KONIGSBERG, a town of Germany, in Hesse-Cassel; 46 miles N. N. E. of Mentz.

KONIGSBERG, a town and castle of the Bavarian states, in Franconia; 14 miles N. W. of Bamberg.

KONIGSBERG, a town of Hungary; seated on the river Gran; 70 miles E. by N. of Presburg.

KONIGSBERG, a well built town of Prussia; 59 miles N. E. of Berlin.

KONIGSHOF, a town and castle of Bohemia; eated on the Elbe; 14 miles N. of Koniginratz.

KONIGSHOFEN, a town of Bavarian Franconia; on the river Saale; 30 miles N. W. of Bamberg.

KONIGSLUTTER, a town of Germany, in the duchy of Brunswick, with a celebrated abbey. It is seated on the rivulet Lutter; 16 miles E. of Brunswick.

KONIGSTEIN, a town of Saxony, on the frontiers of Bohemia. A garrison is constantly maintained in the fort, which stands on a mountain, and is deemed impregnable. The town has manufactures of woollen and linen, and is seated on the Elbe; 16 miles S. E. of Dresden. Long. 14. 14. E. lat. 50. 54. N.

KONIGSTEIN, a town of Germany, in the duchy of Nassau; with a castle on a rock; 11 miles N. W. of Frankfort.

KONITZ, a town of West Prussia; 10 miles N. W. of Culm.

KONKODOO, a county of West Africa, bordering on Jallonkadoo, Satadoo, and Dentila. It is full of steep mountains, which, however, are cultivated even to the summit. The streams which descend from these mountains impregnate the sand and earth with gold dust, which the natives separate by a mechanical process.

KOONJOOR, a town of Hindostan; capital of a circar, in the province of Orissa; 86 miles N. N. W. of Cattack, and 163 W. S. W. of Calcutta. Long. 85. 38. E. lat. 21. 52. N.

KOOSHAUB, a town of Hindostan, in Lahore; seated on the Belut; 88 miles W. of Lahore. Long. 71. 20. E. lat. 30. 55. N.

KOPYL, a fortified town of European Russia, in the government of Mohilef; seated on the Dnieper; 28 miles N. of Mohilef.

KORDOFAN, a county of Central Africa; situate to the W. of the Bahr-el-Abiad, between the kingdom of Darfur and that of Sennaar. It is sometimes independent, and sometimes subject to the one or the other of these states. The inhabitants are said to be extremely licentious in their manners, and cherish a most inveterate enmity against those of Darfur. Ibeit is the capital.

KORFAKAN, a town of Arabia, in Oman; on a bay of the Gulf of Ormuz; 110 miles N. by W. of Rostak.

KORGAN. *See* JORJAN.

KORIACS, a people of Siberia, who inhabit that part of the government of Okhotsk which lies around the Gulf of Penginskaia, and N. as far as the banks of the Anadir. They are divided into two sorts. Those called simply Koriacs have a fixed residence, and the resemblance between them and the Kamtschadales is very striking. The others are wanderers, and are known by the appellation of Reindeer Koriacs; they roam in detached parties over these vast deserts, and are noted hunters and robbers. Their only property consists in their herds of reindeer, which they maintain by conducting them to those cantons that abound with moss; and, when these pastures are exhausted, they wander in search of others. The number of fixed Koriacs scarcely exceeds 900; and, though it is not easy to calculate that of the wandering Koriacs, it is imagined that they do not much exceed this amount. The features of the majority of the Koriacs are not Asiatic; and they might be considered as Europeans, but for their low stature, their ill shape, and the colour of their skin. In general the women have sunk eyes, flat noses, and prominent cheeks; and, in going about, they carry their children in a kind of net or basket arched over, in which the infant is placed in a sitting posture, and sheltered from the weather. They acknowledge a Supreme

Being, the creator of all things. He is supposed to inhabit the sun, whose burning orb they consider as the throne or palace of the Lord of Nature. They neither fear nor worship him: goodness, they say, is his essence; and it is impossible he should do any injury. The principle of evil they consider as a malignant spirit, who divides with the good Being the empire of Nature. As the one is intent on the happiness of mankind, the other endeavours to render them unhappy. Diseases, tempests, famine, calamities of every kind, are his works, and the instruments of his vengeance. To pacify his wrath, they offer to him various animals, the first fruits of their hunting and fishing, and whatever they possess that is most valuable; but there is no temple set apart for his votaries, who conceive that they render him propitious by piously getting drunk in their jourts; for drunkenness is become with these people a religious practice, and the basis of all their solemnities.

KORINCHI, a valley in the island of Sumatra, behind the range of mountains which forms the boundary of the countries of Anak, Sungei, and Indrapoor. It contains a fine lake, which abounds with fish, and its banks are covered with villages.

KOROS, BLACK, a river of Hungary, which rises in the palatinate of Bihar, and falls into the Thesis, near Czongrad, in the palatinate of Bel esch.

KOROTSCHA, a town of European Russia, in the government of Koursk; on a river of the same name; with a manufacture of saltpetre; 44 miles S. E. of Koursk.

KORSOR. *See* CORSOER.

KOSEL, or KOSTA, a fortified town of Prussia, in Silesia; on the river Oder; 17 miles N. of Ratibor.

KOSIE, a considerable kingdom of Western Africa; situated on the E. side of the river Lagos, about 60 miles from its mouth. The capital, of the same name, is said to be of great extent, and its buildings are described as much resembling those of Coomassie, the capital of Ashantee.

KOSLOF. *See* EUPATORIA.

KOSTENDIL, or GIUSTENDIL, a city of Turkey in Europe, and capital of the sandjak of the same name, pachalic of Roumelia. Near it are gold and silver mines, and a hot sulphureous spring; 85 miles S. W. of Sophia. Pop. 8500.

KOSTROMA, a town of Russia; capital of a government of the same name, and a bishop's see. It is surrounded by a strong wall, and situate on a river of the same name, at its entrance into the Volga; 380 miles E. S. E. of Petersburg. Long. 41. 14. E. lat. 57. 40. N. Population of the district, 1,200,000, and of the town, 9500.

KOTTA, a town and fortress of Hindostan, in the province of Agimere; seated on the Chumbul. Long. 75. 49. E. lat. 25. 15. N.

KOTUN, a city of Usbeck Tartary, in Cashgur; 110 miles S. E. of Ireken. Long. 81. 36. E. lat. 37. 50. N.

KOUE-TE, a city, of China, of the first rank; in the province of Ho-nan. It is seated in a vast plain, between two large rivers; 312 miles S. of Peking. Long. 115. 29. E. lat. 34. 30. N.

KOUS, or COSS, a town of Egypt, (the ancient Apollinopolis Parva,) on the E. bank of the Nile; once a place of great wealth and trade, being the staple of commerce between the Nile and the Red Sea; 18 miles S. of Dendera, and 45 N. N. E. of Esne.

KOWNO, a town of Russian Lithuania; with a brisk trade, particularly in corn, honey, wax, &c. It is seated at the conflux of the Wilna and Niemen; 66 miles W. N. W. of Wilna. Pop. 3650.

KOZLOV, a large town of European Russia, in the government of Tambov. The chief trade is in cattle, which are sold to the Don Cossacks, and in tallow and salt meat, which are sent to Moscow. It is seated on the Voronet; 48 miles W. N. W. of Tambov. Pop. 7350.

KRAINBURG, a town of Bavaria; seated on the Inn; 5 miles N. E. of Burkhausen.

KRAINBURG, a town of Austrian Illyria, in Carniola; with a castle; seated on the Save; 20 miles N. W. of Laubach.

KRANICHFELD, a town of Germany, in the principality of Saxe-Gotha; on the river Ilm; 12 miles S. E. of Erfurt.

KRAPPITZ, a town of Prussian Silesia, with a castle at the conflux of the Prudnitz with the Oder; 14 miles S. of Oppelen.

KRASNOIARSK, a flourishing town of Asiatic Russia, in the government of Tomsk; with a trade in furs, and a considerable transit of commodities for the trade with China and Siberia, the great road from Tomsk to Irkutsk passing through it. It is seated on a small river, which falls into the Yenisei. Pop. 3500.

KRASNOIARSK, a town and capital of a district in the government of Astracan, Asiatic Russia. It is situated on an island formed by branches of the Volga. Long. 48. 30. E. lat. 46. 30. N. Pop. 2150.

KRASNOSLAW, a town of Poland, in the palatinate of Lublin; 26 miles S. S. W. of Chelm.

KRAUPEN, a town in Bohemia, in the circle of Leutmeritz. It has considerable tin mines in its vicinity. It is 17 miles W. N. W. of Leutmeritz. Pop. 1750.

KREMPE, a town of Denmark, in Holstein; seated on a river of the same name; 5 miles N. of Gluckstadt.

KREMS, or CREMS, a town of Austria; with alum-works, and manufactures of velvet, silk stuffs, and excellent thread. It is seated on a river of the same name, at its conflux with the Danube; 38 miles W. N. W. of Vienna. Long. 15. 36. E. lat. 48. 24. N.

KRONBERG. *See* CRONENBERG.

KROTOSCHIN, a town and castle of Prussian Poland, near the borders of Silesia; 28 miles W. of Kalisch. Pop. 4350.

KRUMLAU, *See* CRUMLAU.

KRUSZWICA, a town of Russian Poland, in the palatinate of Brzesc; with a castle; noted for being the birthplace of Piast, who, from the station of a private citizen, was elected king of Poland, in the year 842. It is seated on a lake called Goplo, which supplies, the Netz with a great part of its water; 28 miles W. of Brzesc Litov.

KTEIFA, a small town of Syria, on the borders of the desert; supposed to be the ancient Adarisi; 22 miles E. N. E. of Damascus.

KUARA, a province of Abyssinia; situated near the banks of the Bahr-el-Abiad. It is very mountainous and unwholesome, but abounds in gold, which is brought from the neighbouring countries. The governor is one of the great officers of state, and has absolute power in his own province.

KUBBEES, a city of Persia, in Seistan, in the midst of a great sandy desert, on the road from Kerman to Herat; 160 miles S. E. of Yezd.

KUBIN, a town of Hungary, in the Bannat, opposite Semendria; with 2400 inhabitants, who carry on a brisk trade with Turkey.

KUBIN, a town of Hungary, in the district of the Tsaikists. Long. 19. 18. E. lat. 49. 14. N. Pop. 2120.

KUFSTEIN, a strong town of Austria, in the Tyrol, with a castle on a rock. It surrendered to the French and Bavarians in 1805. It is seated on the Inn, on the frontiers ot Bavaria; 46 miles S. S. E. of Munich. Long. 12. 15. E. lat. 47. 30. N.

KULLA, a country of Central Africa, to the S. E. of Wangara; traversed by a river of the same name. It was represented to Browne as an important state, but he did not enter it.

KULSHEIM, or KULZHEIM, a town of Baden, in the principality of Leiningen; 40 miles E. S. E. of Heidelberg.

KUMANIA, GREAT AND LITTLE, two districts in the central part of Hungary, separated from each other by a considerable tract of country, as well as by the river Theiss. Great Kumania comprises a superficial extent of 420 square miles, with 13,000 inhabitants. Little Kumania is, however, the more extensive district, comprising an area of 1000 square miles, and a population of 41,000. The Calvinist is the prevailing religion in both districts.

KUNDAPURA, a town of Hindostan, in Canara, and the chief place in the northern part of the province. It is seated near the mouth of a river of the same name, which here expands into a lake, and form a number of islands. It is the port for all goods coming from or going to Nagara; but the bar will not admit vessels that draw more than 12 feet. It is 30 miles W. S. W. of Nagara, and 54 N. N. W. of Mangalore. Long. 74. 45. E. lat. 13. 34. N.

KUNERSDORF, a village of Bradenburg, in the Middle Mark; 3 miles E. N. E. of Frankfort, on the Oder. Here, in 1759, was fought one of the most bloody battles on record, between the Prussians and Russians, in which the king of Prussia, after a great slaughter of the enemy, for upwards of six hours, was in the end obliged to quit the field, with the loss of all his cannon, and 20,000 men.

KUNKA, a district of Hindostan, in the province of Orissa; situate on the seacoast, near to Point Palmyras. Being much intersected by rivers, the rajah successfully maintained his independence against the Mahrattas, but surrendered to the British in 1805.

KUNKAGUR, the capital of the above district, and the residence of the rajah; situate on the coast. Long. 87. 5. E. lat. 20. 50. N.

KUNTING, a town of Bavarian Franconia, in the principality of Eichstadt, at the conflux of the Schwarzach with the Altmuhl; 12 miles N. E. of Eichstadt.

KUNNEE, a town of Hindostan, in the province of Delhi, and district of Sirhind. It is surrounded by a mud wall and deep ditch; but it was taken by the British, in 1809, without resistance.

KUNO, a fortress of Japan, in the island of Niphon; 60 miles W. S. W. of Jeddo.

KUNOWITZ, a town of Moravia, on the Olschowa; 37 miles S. by E. of Olmutz.

KUOPIO, a town of Sweden, in Finland; capital of Savolax, and that part of Carelia remaining to Sweden. It is situate on the W. side of an extensive lake; 200 miles S. E. of Ulea. Long. 29. 10. E. lat. 63. 20. N.

KUPFERBERG, a mine-town of Prussian Silesia in the principality of Jauer; on the river Boher; 17 miles S. W. of Jauer.

KUR, (the ancient Cyrus,) a river of Persia, which rises in the Caucasian Mountains, passes by Tefflis, and flows S. E. to the Caspian Sea. At its mouth are several islets, liable to be overflowed in the spring.

KURDA, a town of Hindostan, in the province of Guzerat, near the N. W. frontier; about three miles S. of Theraud.

KURDISTAN, a country lying partly in Armenia, and partly in Persia, along the eastern bank of the river Tigris, and comprehending great part of ancient Assyria. Its limits are not precisely ascertained; but it may be viewed as bounded on the N. by Armenia, on the E. by Persia, on the S. by Arabian and Persian Irak, and on the W. by Diarbekir, or, as it is sometimes called, Algezira. It is divided into two parts, viz. Lower Kurdistan, or the western division, which is included in the pachalic of Bagdad, and corresponds nearly to the whole of ancient Assyria Proper: and Ardelan, which extends from the small river Sharook to the Turkish district of Zohaub. The surface is diversified by mountains and valleys: and the soil is in some places fertile and well cultivated; but it abounds with deserts, and, except in the neighbourhood of the towns, is barren and desolate. Wheat and barley are the grains most commonly raised. The inhabitants are not subject either to the Turks or Persians. Some live in towns and villages, and others rove from place to place, having tents like the wild Arabs, and being robbers like them. The tribes are ruled by a number of their own princes, or chiefs. They are proud of their descent, and demand a premium for their daughters, on giving them in marriage. Their character and circumstances seem to have undergone little change since the most remote times. Xenophon is supposed to refer to them under the name of Carduchai, a people who opposed the retreat of the 10,000 Greeks. Their religion is partly Christianity, and partly Mahometlism. Altunkupri is the capital. The chief towns are Kerkook, Solymania, Beltis, Erbile, Amadia, Sennah, &c.

KUREH, a town of Asiatic Turkey, in Natolia; 34 miles W. of Sinub.

KURILES, a long chain of islands at the eastern extremity of Asia; extending from the southern point of Kamtschatka to the isles of Jesso, or Matsmai, an island of Japan. They lie between 42. and 51. of N. lat., and the whole length of the range is said to be nearly 900 miles. Exclusive of the very small ones, they are 22 in number. They are annexed to the government of Irkutsk, and pay a tribute of furs and sea-calves, which is collected every three years: the Russian authority, however, can only be considered as extending over 19, the three most southerly belonging rather to Japan. The northernmost, called Shoomska, is three leagues from Cape Lopatka; the next, named Paramousic, is considerably larger than Shoomska. These two islands were first visited by the Russians, in 1713, and the rest have been gradually discovered since that period. Some of these islands are fertile, wooded, and abound in fish and game; while others are destitute of water, and uninhabitable, but are occasionally visited by the islanders, for the sake of hunting foxes and otters. The natives are very hairy, wear long beards, and live entirely upon seals, fish, and the produce of the chase. They are hospitable and docile; but pusillanimous, and unable to support misfortune with fortitude. Their houses and customs resemble those of the Kamtschadales. They have some trade with the Chinese, Japanese, and Russians.

KURNOUL. *See* CURNOUL.

KURSK, or KOURSK, a considerable town of European Russia; capital of a government of the same name. It has 17,000 inhabitants, a Protestant consistory, and 16 churches. The export trade is very considerable, amounting to about 150,000*l.* sterling per annum. It is seated on the river Tuskara; 240 miles of Moscow. Long. 37. S. E. lat. 51. 40. N.

KUSISTAN, or CHUSISTAN, a province of Persia; bounded on the N. by Irac-Agemi, E. by Farsistan, S. by the Gulf of Persia, and W. by Irac-Arabi. The N. part is mountainous, the S. flat and marshy. Tostar is the capital.

KUTTENBERG, a town of Bohemia; seated near a mountain, in which are silver mines. It is situate 5 miles N. W. of Czaslau. Pop. 6420.

KUTTORE, a celebrated town and fortress of the N. of India; capital of a district of the same name, in the province of Cafiristan. It is situate on the summit of a perpendicular rock, and was with great difficulty taken by Timur, in the end of the 14th century; 100 miles N. E. of Cabul, and 280 N. W. of Lahore. Long. 70. 17. E. lat. 35. 27. N.

KUTY, a town of Austrian Poland, in Galicia, on the Czeremosz; with extensive manufactures of russia leather; 61 miles S. S. E. of Halicz. Pop. 4250.

KUYNDER, a town and fortress of the Netherlands, in Friesland; situated on a river of the same name, at its entrance into the Zuyder Zee; 23 miles S. of Lewarden. Long. 5. 32. E. lat. 52. 41. N.

KUZNECK, a town of Siberia; capital of a province of the same name, in the government of Kolivan. It has manufactures of iron, and stands on the Tom, at the influx of the Kondoma; 230 miles S. S. E. of Kolivan. Long. 85. 50. E. lat. 54. 16. N.

KYBURG, a bailiwick of Switzerland, including the whole of the N. E. part of the canton of Zurich. It is divided into 47 parishes, and is very productive, particularly in fruit and wine.

KYLBURG, a town in the Prussian province of the Lower Rhine; situated on the River Kyll; 30 miles N. N. E. of Luxemburg.

KYLL, a small river of Germany, which rises between the frontiers of Limburg and Juliers, and falls into the Moselle; 4 miles below Treves.

KYMMENEGARD, an extensive province of Finland, equal in extent to the half of Scotland, but containing only 115,000 inhabitants. It extends along the river Kymmene.

KYN, a small inland in the Baltic, on the coast of Russia; about 5 miles in length; 40 miles N. by E. of Riga.

KYNDEE, a town of Hindostan, in the province of Bahar, and district of Ramgur. Long. 86. 5. E. lat. 24. 15. N.

KYNETON. *See* KINGTON.

KYRAGUR, a town and fortress of Hindostan, in the province of Gundwaneh. It belongs to one of the Goand chiefs, who is tributary to the rajah of Nagpore. It is situate near the Lucknow Hills; 95 miles S. E. of Ruttunpore. Long. 81. 32. E. lat. 21. 27. N.

KYRANTY, a town of Bengal, in the district of Cooch Bahar, on the Durlah river. Long. 88. 50. E. lat. 26. 45. N.

KYRAUT, a district of Hindostan; bounded N. by the Himalaya Mountains, E. by Bootan, S. by Morung, and W. by Nepaul. It was conquered by the rajah of Nepaul in 1769, but is very little known to Europeans.

KYRITZ, a town of the Prussian states, in Brandenburg; 46 miles N. W. of Berlin.

L.

LAAB, a town of Lower Austria, on the river Teya: 39 miles N. by W. of Vienna. Long. 16. 20. E. lat. 48. 43. N.

LAAS, a town of Austria Illyria, in Carniola, with a trade in salt, leather, and horses; 12 miles S. of Laubach.

Laasphe, or Lasphe, a town of Germany, in the Prussian states; seated on the Lahn; 75 miles E. of Cologne.

Labadia, a town of Austrian Italy; seated on the Adige; 20 miles N. N. W. of Ferrara.

Laber, a river of Bavaria, in Franconia, which rises near Neumark, and falls into the Danube, at Sinzing, above Ratisbon.

Labes, a town of Prussia, in Pomerania; with manufactures of cloth; seated on the Reca; 35 miles N. E. of Stargard.

Labia, a town of European Turkey, in Servia; 70 miles S. W. of Nissa.

Labiau, a town of East Prussia, with a strong castle; seated at the mouth of the Deine, near the Curische Haff; 25 miles N. E. of Konigsberg.

Labrador, a country of North America, on the E. side of Hudson Bay. The general aspect of the country is most dreary: the surface is mountainous and rugged, and covered with large stones, and the soil is poor. Coarse plants, adapted to the nourishment of deer and goats, and other wild animals, are its chief productions. The climate, in only lat. 57. N., is excessively cold during winter. The ice begins to disappear in May; and, about the middle of July, commences hot weather, which at times is such as to scorch the faces of the hunters. Mock suns and halos are not unfrequent; and the night is enlivened by the aurora borealis, which spreads over the whole sky. No country is better furnished with large, safe, and convenient harbours, or supplied with better water. The numerous islands along the E. coast abound with eider-ducks and other water-fowl, and also with hares, foxes, and deer. The animals are not numerous; the most common are reindeer, bears, wolves, tigers, foxes, beavers, otters, lynxes, martens, ermines, and wild cats. Eagles, hawks, owls, geese, bustards, ducks, partridges, and all kinds of wild fowl, are numerous. The fishes are whales, morses, seals, cod, and a white fish preferable to herrings; and in the rivers and fresh waters are pike, perch, carp, trout, &c. During the three months of summer, there is a variety in the colour of the several animals, but in winter every thing, animate and inanimate, is white. The trees of Labrador are mere shrubs, with the exception of the black, white, and red spruce, silver-fir, birch, and aspen. A few vegetables are produced, and various kinds of fruit. A beautiful spar, called Labrador feldspar, was discovered by the Moravian missionaries, who have successfully exerted themselves in improving the condition of the natives. They have now three settlements on these inhospitable shores, the total population of which is about 600. The natives are called Esquimaux. They have no fixed abode, but rove from place to place, and sometimes come as far as Newfoundland. They are of a different race from other native Americans; for the other tribes have no beards, but these have them so thick and large, that it is difficult to discover any feature of their faces; they are likewise the only savages that eat their food in a raw state. They are of a middling stature, generally robust, lazy, and of a brown colour. Their head is large, and their face round and flat; they have thick lips, a flat nose, long black hair, large shoulders, and uncommonly small feet. They are always well clothed; for there is nothing to be seen but part of their faces and their hands. They have a sort of shirt, made of the guts of fish, with a coat of bear or bird skins, and a cap on their head. They have likewise breeches made of skins, with the hair inwards, and covered with furs without; also two pairs of boots, one over another, of the same sort of skins. In summer, they have nothing to cover them in the night; and in winter they lodge in tents made of hides, or in caves. The dress of the women is nearly the same as that of the men. They are very superstitious, and have some sort of sacrifices. They acknowledge two invisible essences: the one as the origin of good; the other, to whom they pay the most homage, as the origin of every species of evil. Their chief employment is hunting and fishing. They are very covetous; and pay so little regard to private property as to take every advantage of bodily strength to rob their neighbours, not only of their goods, but their wives. In other respects they are the mildest tribe, or nation, that is to be found on the borders of Hudson Bay. Murder, which is so common among all the tribes of southern Indians, is seldom heard of among them. A murderer is shunned and detested by all the tribe, and is forsaken even by his relations and former friends. The women perform the most laborious offices; they pitch the tents, carry or haul burdens, make or mend clothes, and prepare the victuals. When any thing is prepared for eating, the wives and daughters are never served till all the males have taken what they think proper.

Laby, a considerable town of Western Africa, in the kingdom of Foota Jalloo. It is upwards of 2 miles in circumference, and contains 5000 inhabitants, who are employed in the manufacture of narrow cloths, and various articles in iron, silver, wood, leather, &c., and carry on a good trade with Timbuctoo, which is four months' journey beyond.

Laccadives, or Lakdivas, a group of small islands in the Indian Sea, lying W. of the coast of Malabar; discovered by Vasco de Gama, in 1449. They are 32 in number, and are inhabited by a race of Mahomedans called Moplays, whose chief traffic is in the produce of the cocoa palm, such as oil, cables, and cordage; and in dried fish. These are sent to the continent of India, whence they get rice, &c., in return; and also to Mascat, in large boats, which bring back dates and coffee. Calpeny, one of the largest, is 170 miles W. of Cochin. Long. 73. 32. E. lat. 10. 0. N.

Lacedogna. *See* Cedogna.

Lacepedes Islands, a group of islands on the N. W. coast of Australia: the largest is about 9 miles long. A long chain of rocky reefs and great sand-banks proceed from their termination. Many whales, sea serpents, and fishes of different kinds, are seen in the surrounding sea. Long. 117. 8. E. lat. 16. 43. S.

LACFODERY, mountains of Ireland, on the E. side of the county of Kerry; 12 miles E. of Tralee.

LACHEN, a town of Switzerland, in the canton of Schweitz, near which are some mineral springs, and petrifactions: it is seated on the lake of Zurich.

LACHEN, a large village of the Bavarian circle of the Rhine, district of Spire; 3 miles S. E. of Neustadt.

LACHSA, or LASCHA, a division of Arabia, occupying nearly the whole of the south-western coast of the Persian Gulf, and extending to a considerable distance inland. Great part of the interior consists of sandy plains; but the coast is fertile and well peopled. The chief productions are dates, rice, and cotton. The asses and camels are esteemed to be of an excellent breed, and some thousands of the latter are annually exported to Syria. The extensive piracies committed by the inhabitants of this country were so intolerable, that in 1809 the British fitted out an expedition for the purpose of chastising them. They sailed to Ras-el-Khima, the principal port on this coast, which they took by assault, burned 70 vessels, and made considerable plunder. Lachsa was formerly subject to Turkey, but the inhabitants have now shaken off the yoke, and their sheik is one of the most powerful princes of Arabia.

LACHSA, a city of Arabia, capital of the above province, and the residence of the sheik. It is well built, and seated on the Astan, which flows into a considerable bay of the Gulf of Persia, opposite the isle of Bahrein. Long. 48. 40. E. lat. 26. 20. N.

LADAK, or LEH, a town of Tibet; capital of a district of the same name, with a considerable trade in the wool of the Cashmere goat, for the shawl manufacture. The religion is Buddhism.

LADENBURG, a town of Germany, in Baden; seated on the Neckar; 8 miles N. W. of Heidelberg.

LADOGA, a lake of Russia, between the Gulf of Finland and the lake Onega. It is 140 miles long and 80 broad. The shores of the lake are flat, but the navigation is very dangerous, on account of quicksands. This induced Peter I. to cause a canal to be cut from the S. W. extremity of this lake to the river Neva, by which it has a communication with the Gulf of Finland. It was begun in 1718 and finished in 1732: it is 67 miles long, and 70 feet broad.

LADOGA, NEW, a town of Russia, in the government of Petersburg; seated on the Volkhof, between the lake and canal of Ladoga. Old Ladoga, an inconsiderable place, is higher up the Volkhof. New Ladoga is 56 miles E. of Petersburg. Long. 31. 42. E. lat. 60. 0. N.

LADRONES, or MARIAN ISLANDS, islands of the Pacific Ocean, lying between 145. and 148. E. long., and between 13. and 22. N. lat. They were discovered by Magellan, in 1521. He touched first at the island of Guam, where the natives stole some of his goods, which caused him to name these islands the Ladrones, or Islands of Thieves. Besides the other fruits natural to the soil and climate, here is the bread-fruit tree in abundance. The names of the principal islands are Saypan, Tinian, Guam, and Rota.

LADRONES is also the name of a cluster of small islands in the Gulf of Sa, at the southern extremity of China. They are the resort of pirates, who have long set the naval power of China at defiance. It 1805 they had acquired possession of the whole island of Hainan and the southern part of Formosa.

LAGNASCO, a town of the Sardinian states, in Piedmont; 24 miles S. of Turin.

LAGNY, a town of France, in the department of Seine-et-Marne; with a late famous Benedictine abbey; seated on the Marne; 15 miles E. of Paris.

LAGOS, a seaport of Portugal, in Algarva; with a castle. Off the cape, near this town, in 1759, Admiral Boscawen defeated a French fleet. It is 130 miles S. S. E. of Lisbon.

LAGUNA. *See* CHRISTOPHE DE LAGUNA, ST.

LAGUNES OF VENICE, the marshes or lakes in Italy on which Venice is seated. They communicate with the sea, and are the security of the city. There are about 60 islands in these Lagunes, which together make a bishop's see. Eurano is the most considerable, next to those on which Venice stands.

LAHN, a river of Germany, which rises in Hesse-Cassel; and, flowing by Marburg, Wetzlar, and Nassau, falls into the Rhine above Coblentz.

LAHN, a town of the Prussian states, in Silesia, near which is the castle of Lahnhaus: it is seated on the Bober; 10 miles N. N. W. of Hirschberg.

LAHOLM, a seaport of Sweden, in Halland, with a castle; seated on the Laga, near its entrance into the Cattegat; 12 miles S. S. E. of Halmstadt. Long. 12. 56. E. lat. 56. 31. N.

LAHORE, a province of Hindostan; bounded on the W. by Candahar, N. by Cashmere, E. by Sirinagur and Delhi, and S. by Moultan. It is called Panjab, or the country of Five Rivers. It is extensive and fertile; affording, in addition to all the necessaries of life, wine, sugar, and cotton wool. In the tract between the Indus and the Chelum are salt mines, which afford pieces of rock salt, hard enough to be formed into vessels, &c. *See* PANJAB.

LAHORE, a city of Hindostan, capital of the above province, and of the country of the Seiks. It was the residence of the Mahomedan conquerors of Hindostan, before they had established themselves in the central parts of the country; and owes its chief improvements to Humaioon, the father of Acbar, who made it his residence during a part of his troublesome reign. The city and suburbs form a circumference of 7 miles. It is surrounded by walls of brick, and adorned with beautiful edifices and gardens. Here are manufactures of cotton cloths and stuffs of all kinds, and of very curious carpets: it is situate on the S. bank of the Rauvee; 210 miles S. of Cashmere.

LAHR, a town of Germany, in the grand duchy

of Baden, which was only a village in 1780; but is now an active manufacturing town. The manufactures are of woollens, linens, cotton, tobacco, and leather; 18 miles S. S. E. of Strasburg. Pop. 4550.

LAINO, a town of Naples, in Calabria Citra; near a river of the same name; 19 miles W. N. W. of Cassano.

LAI-TCHEOU, a city of China, of the first rank, in the province of Chang-tong; with a convenient harbour on the Yellow Sea. It stands on a promontory; 255 miles S. E. of Peking.

LALAND, an island of Denmark; situated at the entrance into the Baltic, near the coast of Zealand. It is about 60 miles in length by 14 in breadth, and is reckoned the most fertile spot in the Danish dominions. It produces peas, and plenty of all sorts of grain, particularly wheat. The climate, however, is considered unhealthy, on account of the damp. Laland forms a part of the bishopric of Funen. Naskow is the capital. Pop. 35,500.

LALANG, an island near the N. coast of the island of Sumatra, in the strait of Malacca. Long. 90. 20. E. lat. 1. 45. N.

LAMBACH, a town of Austria, on the Traun; 24 miles S. S. W. of Laintz.

LAMBALLE, a town of France, in the department of Cotes du Nord; with a good trade in cattle, linen, and parchment; 11 miles E. S. E. of St. Brieux.

LAMBAYEQUE, a town on the coast of Peru, with upwards of 10,000 inhabitants, the generality of whom are poor Spaniards, Mulattoes, and Indians. It is 95 miles N. N. W. of Truxillo. Long. 79. 35. W. lat. 6. 45. S. Pop. 8500.

LAMBESC, a town of France, in the department of Mouths of the Rhone; 12 miles N. of Aix.

LAMBETH, a parish of Surrey, on the river Thames, opposite Westminster; one of the metropolitan boroughs. It returns two members to parliament. Here the archbishop of Canterbury has an ancient palace. By the vast increase of buildings, Lambeth is now joined to the metropolis. *See* LONDON.

LAMBOURN, a town in Berkshire, with a market on Friday; seated on a river of the same name; 15 miles S. W. of Abingdon, and 65 W. of London.

LAMEGO, a town of Portugal, in Beira, and a bishop's see; with a strong citadel, two cathedral churches, and four convents. Here the states assembled to confirm the election of Alfonzo Henriquez, the first king of Portugal, and enacted the fundamental laws now forgotten. It is seated on the Balsamao; 50 miles E. of Oporto. Long. 7. 30. W. lat. 41. 12. N. Pop. 6750.

LAMMERMUIR, a mountainous ridge in Scotland, which divides the county of Berwick from that of Haddington, for above 20 miles, and terminates on the W. at Soutra Hill, which is elevated 1000 feet above the sea level. These hills are bleak and barren, affording but scanty

LAMLASH, a town of Scotland, on the S. E. coast of the isle of Arran; on a bay of its name, which forms an excellent harbour for vessels of any size. It is sheltered from the sea by a lofty islet, 2 miles long, called Holy Isle.

LAMPA, an extensive and mountainous district of Peru, in the intendancy of Cuzco. The climate is cold, and it is chiefly valuable for its pastures. The chief town, of the same name is 90 miles S. of Cuzco. Long. 81. 44. W. lat. 15. 55. S.

LAMPANGUI, a lofty mountain of the Chilian Andes, celebrated for its rich mines; 240 miles from Valparaiso.

LAMPEDOSA, an island in the Mediterranean, between the coast of Tunis and the island of Malta. It is about 21 miles in circuit, and is pleasant and fertile; but it is uninhabited. It has an excellent harbour, sheltered from all winds except the N. Long. 12. 24. E. lat. 35. 40. N.

LAMPERTHEIM, a village of Germany, in Hesse-Darmstadt, 2 miles S. E. of Worms.

LAMPON, a town of Sumatra, capital of a district belonging to the king of Bantam. The Dutch have a resident here. It is situate on a bay of the same name, in the Strait of Sunda, 180 miles S. E. of Bencoolen. Long. 104. 15. E. lat. 5. 40. N.

LAMPSAKI, (the ancient Lampsacus,) a town of Asiatic Turkey, in Natolia; celebrated for its wine; seated on the Sea of Marmora; 6 miles from the Dardanelles.

LAMSPRINGE, a town of Hanover, in the principality of Hildersheim; situate at the source of the rivulet Lame; 17 miles S. of Hildersheim. Pop. 1230.

LANARK, a borough of Scotland, and the county town of Lanarkshire. It is contributory, with Linlithgow, in sending one member to parliament. Since the introduction of the cotton manufacture, many new houses have been built. It is seated on an eminence, near the river Clyde; 22 miles S. E. of Glasgow, and 30 S.W. of Edinburgh. Long. 3. 43. W. lat. 55. 42. N.

LANARKSHIRE, a county of Scotland; bounded N. and N. W. by Renfrew, Dumbarton, and Stirling; N.E. by Linlithgow and Edinburgh; E. by Peebles; S. by Dumfries; and S.W. by Ayrshire. It is 52 miles in its greatest length, and 33 in its greatest breadth, comprising a superficial extent of 870 square miles, or 556,800 English acres. On the whole, it is mountainous and heathy, but pleasant, and agreeably diversified, exhibiting landscapes intermingled with wood and water, hill and dale. It contains as much curious, romantic, and varied scenery, as any in Scotland; but the falls of the Clyde are particularly interesting to a stranger. The climate is rather moist, and the S. W. wind is the most prevalent. The county is divided into three districts, called the Upper, Middle, and Lower wards, and contains 41 parishes. It sends one member to parliament. The river Clyde runs through the whole extent of the county, dividing it into two nearly equal parts. It abounds in lead, iron, and coal.

...time county of England;

bounded S. by Cheshire, E. by Yorkshire, N. by Westmoreland, and W. by the Irish Sea. It is 74 miles from N. to S. and its greatest breadth is 44 miles. It contains 1,155,840 acres, and sends four members to parliament for the northern and southern divisions. It is a county-palatine, under the title of the Duchy of Lancaster: the only duchy of England (that of Cornwall excepted) which is not merely titular. This county comprises a variety of soil and face of country; but, upon the whole, is one of the least favoured by nature. The Hundred of Furness, which is separated from the rest by Morecambe Bay, is a wild and rugged region, stored with quantities of iron ore and slate, and covered with a growth of underwood, which is cut in succession, and made into charcoal. The E. part, between the Ribble and the Mersey, comprising the ancient forests of Wyresdale and Bowland, is mountainous and generally barren; but the S. part of the tract between these two rivers is flat. Much of this is a fertile country, though occasionally deformed by black turf bogs, here called mosses, some of which are of large extent, and impassable in wet seasons. In the N. E. part of this division are some lofty hills, the most noted of which is Pendle Hill. The remaining part is varied with hill, dale, and moor. Among its products is a species of coal, called cannel, highly valuable as fuel, and capable of being manufactured into candlesticks, cups, snuff-boxes, &c. As a commercial and manufacturing county, it is superior to any other in the kingdom. Its principal manufactures are linen, silk, woollen, and cotton goods, shalloons, baize, serges, tapes, hardware, plate-glass, &c. Of the commerce of this county it may suffice to observe, that Liverpool is the second port in the kingdom. The principal rivers are the Mersey, Irwell, Ribble, Loyne, Leven, Wyre, Hodder, Roche, Duddon, Winster, and Ken; and it has two considerable lakes, Windermere and Coniston-mere. It has also numerous canals, and had the honour of exhibiting the first regular one in the kingdom, which was begun by the Duke of Bridgewater, in 1758.

Lancaster, a borough, and the capital of Lancashire; governed by a mayor; with markets on Wednesday and Saturday. It is seated on the Loyne, or Lune, which forms a port for vessels of moderate burden. The parish church of St. Mary is a fine structure, on the side of a hill, on the summit of which is a noble castle, serving both as the shire-house and the county gaol. Here are also two chapels belonging to the Establishment, and several dissenting meeting-houses. On the top of the castle is a square tower, called John of Gaunt's Chair, whence there is an extensive prospect. Among the modern improvements are an extensive quay, with large warehouses, and a commodious and elegant bridge over the river, in place of the old one, now in ruins. The canal from Kendal winds round the E. part of the town, and is conveyed over the river by an aqueduct of five arches, each of 70 feet span. Besides numerous other charities, there is a county lunatic asylum, a handsome stone erection, on Lancaster Moor, opened in 1816. It has a chapel attached, and the hospital is capable of accommodating 300 patients. Five miles from this place in Dunald-mill-hole, a cave at the foot of a mountain, into which a large brook runs and passes two miles under ground before it appears again: some of its vaults are so high that they resemble the roof of a church, and in other parts so low that they can be passed only by creeping on the hands and feet. Lancaster depends for its support principally on its trade and manufactures, and the county business. The merchants trade chiefly to America, the West Indies, and the Baltic. It is noted for the making of mahogany cabinet ware, and has manufactures of sail-cloth, cordage, linens, &c. The cotton manufacture is also gaining ground, and ship-building is carried on to a considerable extent. It returns two members to parliament. It is 53 miles N. W. of Manchester, and 240 N. N. W. of London.

Lancaster, a handsome town in Pennsylvania; capital of a county of the same name. It is a pleasant and flourishing place, situate in a fertile and well cultivated country; and contains a court-house, a gaol, two banks, and nine places of worship. A college was founded here in 1787, but the buildings are now appropriated to schools. Here are manufactures of guns and other hardware; and about a mile distant is a large cotton manufactory. The town has considerable trade, which increases with the population of the surrounding country. It is seated near Conestoga Creek, which runs into the Susquehanna, 61 miles W. by N. of Philadelphia. Long. 76. 32. W. lat. 40. 2. N. Population of the county, 84,203; and of the town, 8417.

Lancaster, a town of Massachusets, in Worcester county; with a large cotton manufactory. In its vicinity is a quarry of excellent stones for tombs, and the best slates for houses. It is situate on a branch of the Nashua, which runs into the Merrimac; 14 miles N. by E. of Worcester, and 35 W.N.W. of Boston. Pop. 2019.

Lancaster, a town of Fairfield county, Ohio. seated on the Hockhocking; 50 miles W. of Marietta.

Lançerota, one of the Canary isles, 30 miles long and 10 broad. It is very high, and has a good harbour at the N.E. end. Long. 13. 26. W. lat. 29. 14. N. Pop. 10,500.

Lanciano, a town of Naples, in Abruzzo Citra; on a river of the same name. It is an archbishop's see, and has a good trade, and two great annual fairs; 84 miles N. by E. of Naples. Long. 14. 30. E. lat. 42. 16. N. Pop. 9750.

Landau, a small but strong town of the Bavarian circle of the Rhine; well known in military history. It was formerly imperial, but was ceded to Louis XIV. in 1680, and afterwards fortified by Vauban. In 1702, 1703, 1704, and 1713, it was alternately taken by the Austrians and French, but was confirmed to France at the peace of 1713. In 1793 it was attacked, but without success, by the Prussians and Austrians. The French ceded it to Bavaria in 1815. It is seated on the Queich; 56 miles N. N. E. of Strasburg, and 347 N. E. of Paris. Long. 8. 7. E. lat. 49. 12. N. Pop. 4500

LANDAU, a town of Lower Bavaria; situate on an eminence on the Iser. Long. 12. 37. E. lat. 48. 36. N.

LANDAU, a small town of Germany, in Westphalia, near the Watter. Long. 9. 5. E. lat. 51. 12. N.

LANDECK, a town of Prussian Silesia, in the county of Glatz; 27 miles S. W. of Neisse.

LANDELLES, a town of France, in the department of Calvados; seated on the Vire; 28 miles S. W. of Caen.

LANDEN, a town of Belgium, in South Brabant; famous for an obstinate battle fought near it in 1693, in which the French, under Marshal Luxemburg, defeated the allies, commanded by William III. of England; and also a battle in 1793, in which the French were defeated by the Austrians. It is seated on the river Becke; 19 miles S. E. of Louvain. Pop. 4550.

LANDERNAU, a seaport of France, in the department of Finisterre; with considerable manufactures of linen, leather, and paper. It is seated at the mouth of the Elhorn; 23 miles N. E. of Brest.

LANDERON, a town of Switzerland, in the canton of Neufchatel, at the S. W. extremity of the lake Neufchatel; 7 miles N. E. of Neufchatel.

LANDES, a department of France; bounded W. by the Atlantic, and on its other sides by the departments of Gironde, Lot-et-Garonne, Gers, and Lower Pyrenees. It is divided into the three arrondissements of Mont de Marsan, Dax, and St. Sever, and has an area of 3700 square miles, with 256,311 inhabitants. The principal rivers are the Adour and the Douze, which traverses it from E. to W. To the S. of these rivers the soil is tolerably fertile, producing wine, fruit, and corn, but on the N. it is perfectly sterile. The forests are extensive, and the climate is generally warm. The exports are wood, turpentine, tar, wax, cattle, wool, and brandy.

LANDRECY, a strong town of France, in the department of Nord. It was besieged in vain by Prince Eugene, in 1712. In 1794 it was taken by the allies; but shortly after evacuated. It was one of the barrier fortresses occupied by the allies after the second treaty of Paris. It is seated on the Cambre; 18 miles E. by S. of Cambray, and 19 S. by E. of Valenciennes.

LANDRIANO, a town of Italy, in the Milanese; 11 miles S. S. E. of Milan.

LANDSBERG, a town of Brandenburg, in the New Mark; with a considerable trade in cloths and wool. In 1758 it was taken by the Russians. It is seated on the Warta; 23 miles N. E. of Custrin.

LANDSBERG, a town of Upper Bavaria, with a castle; near the river Leech; 20 miles S. of Augsburg.

LANDSCRON, a town and fort of Poland, in the palatinate of Cracow; 24 miles S. of Cracow.

LANDSCRONA, a fortified seaport of Sweden, in Schonen; seated on an island, near the Sound; with a good harbour between the continent and a small island. It is 20 miles N.W. of Lund, and 21 N. N. E. of Copenhagen. Long 12. 51. E. lat. 55. 53. N.

LANDS-END, a promontory in Cornwall, and the most westerly point of Great Britain. It is a vast aggregate of morestone; and on the outermost rocks, at low water, are to be seen veins of lead and copper. Long. 5. 42. W. lat. 50. 4. N.

LANDSHUT, a town of Bavaria; with a palace, a collegiate church, and a beautiful convent; the last is now occupied by the university, which was removed thither from Ingoldstadt, in 1800. Brewing and distilling are carried on here to a considerable extent, and there are manufactures of cloth, leather, and watches. Upon an adjoining mountain is the ancient castle of Trausnitz. It is seated on an island in the river Iser, 32 miles N. E. of Munich. Long. 12. 6. E. lat. 48. 30. N. Pop. 8350.

LANDSHUT, a town of Prussian Silesia, in the principality of Schweidnitz. It has a flourishing linen trade: it is seated on the Bober; 22 miles S. W. of Schweidnitz.

LANDSHUT, a town of Moravia; seated on the Morau, on the confines of Hungary and Austria; 36 miles S. E. of Brunn.

LANDSTRAAS, or LANDTROST, a town of Austrian Illyria, in Carniola; with a castle and a Cistercian convent; situate on an island in the river Gurk; 30 miles S. by W. of Cilley.

LANE, an island in the Atlantic; near the coast of Maine, a little to the E. of Scuttock Point; belonging to the United States. Long. 67. 56. W. lat. 44. 18. N.

LANE, a river of Ireland, in the county of Kerry, whose waters, being confined by a great ledge of rocks, from the Lake of Killarney. It runs from Lough Lane into Castlemain Bay.

LANEBOURG, a town of the Sardinian states, in Savoy, in the province of Marienne. It stands on the Arve, at the foot of Mont Cenis, and is so shut up with hills that the sun is scarcely visible from November to January. It is 20 miles N. N. W. of Susa.

LANE-END, a town in Staffordshire, with markets on Wednesday and Saturday; noted for its extensive potteries, by which it has greatly increased of late years. It contains two good market-houses, two churches, several meeting-ing-houses for dissenters, a catholic chapel, an English charity school, a mechanics' institute, &c. It is 5 miles E. by S. of Newcastle-under-Lyne.

LANEMEZAN, a town of France, in the department of Upper Pyrenees; 15 miles S. E. of Tarbe.

LANEPAX, a town in the department of Gers; 11 miles S. S. W. of Condom.

LANERCOST, a parish of England, in the county of Cumberland; situate in a romantic valley; 13 miles N. E. of Carlisle.

LANESBOROUGH, a town of Ireland, in the county of Longford, situate on the Shannon, over which is a fine stone bridge; 7 miles S. of Longford, and 62 W. N. W. of Dublin.

LANGANICO, (the ancient Olympia,) a town of Greece, in the Morea; situate on the small river Carbon, the ancient Alpheus.) It was once a city of great note, near which the famous Olympian games were celebrated; and here was a fine temple of Jupiter Olympus, with a celebrated image of that god, 50 cubits high, which was reckoned one of the seven wonders of the world. It is now an inconsiderable place. It is 32 miles S. S. E. of Chiarenza, and 60 S. W. of Corinth.

LANGEAC, a town of France, in the department of Upper Loire; seated near the Allier, 12 miles S. of Brioud. Pop. 1920.

LANGEAIS, a town of France, in the department of Indre-et-Loire; noted for the culture of melons; seated on the Loire; 12 miles W. of Tours. Pop. 2520.

LANGELAND, a fertile island of Denmark, in the S. part of the Great Belt. It is 33 miles long, but scarcely 5 broad. The principal town is Rudkioping.

LANGENAU, a town of Bohemia, in the circle of Konigingratz, on the Little Elbe; with some extensive manufactures of cambric and gauze.

LANGENAU, UPPER and LOWER, two populous villages of Prussia, in Silesia; 11 miles S. of Glatz.

LANGENAU, a long and straggling village of Germany, in Wirtemberg. It contains 3600 inhabitants, who are mostly weavers. It is 10 miles N. N. E. of Ulm.

LANGENBERG, a tn. of the Prussian province of Cleves and Berg. It is 15 miles N. E. of Dusseldorf.

LANGENBURG, a town of Germany, in Wirtemberg, with a magnificent castle; seated on the river Jaxt. It is 32 miles W. of Anspach.

LANGENSALZA, a town of Prussian Saxony, capital of Thuringia; with a castle, and manufactures of silk, woollen, cotton, &c. It stands on the Salza, near its conflux with the Unstrut; 14 miles W. by N. of Erfurt. Long. 10. 42. E. lat. 51. 5. N.

LANGENTHAL, a town of Switzerland, in the canton of Bern, in the neighbourhood of which are some medicinal springs. It is 18 miles N. E. of Bern.

LANGENZENN, a town of Germany in Bavaria, on the river Zenn, and near the Rednitz; 20 miles N. E. of Anspach.

LANGHOLM, a town of Scotland, in Dumfriesshire; with an extensive cotton manufacture; seated on the Esk, on the borders of England; 20 miles N. by W. of Carlisle.

LANGOGNE, a town of France, department of Lozere; 21 miles N. E. of Mende.

LANGON, a town of France, in the department of Gironde; with an extensive trade in wine and brandy. It has a good harbour, and is seated on the Garonne; 10 miles N. of Bazas. Pop. 3310.

LANGPORT, a town in Somersetshire, with a market on Saturday; situate on a hill, by the river Parrett, which is navigable for barges to the Bristol Channel. It is 10 miles S. E. of Bridgewater, and 128 W. by S. of London.

LANGRES, a town of France, in the department of Upper Marne. Its cutlery wares are in high esteem. It is seated on a mountain, near the source of the Marne; 40 miles N. E. of Dijon. Long. 5. 19. E. lat. 47. 52. N.

LANDGUARD FORT, a strong fort of England; situate on a sandy point of land, on the Suffolk side of the harbour of Harwich, but within the limits of Essex. At high water it is surrounded by the sea, and becomes an island nearly a mile from the shore. It was erected for the defence of the port of Harwich, and has a garrison, under the command of a governor.

LANGUEDOC, a province of the S. of France; divided, at the revolution, into the departments of Upper Garonne, Aude, Herault, Gard, Lozere, and Ardeche. It extends on the E. to the Rhone, and W. to the borders of Gascony, and comprises a superficial extent of 16,000 square miles, and a population of about 2,000,000. The Upper, or Western Languedoc, had Toulouse for its capital; and the Lower, or Eastern, Montpelier. The celebrated canal of Languedoc, constructed by Louis XIV., is 140 miles long, and connects the Mediterranean with the Atlantic. It commences at Cette, and joins the Garonne at Toulouse.

LANJAN, or LANCHANG, a city, and the capital of the kingdom of Laos; S. of China, at least of the southern part, to which it gives name. The king's palace is said to be of vast extent, and the houses of the grandees are also large, and highly ornamented. It is situate on the W. side of the river Menamkong; 400 miles N. N. W. of Cambodia. Long. 101. 38. E. lat. 18. 30. N.

LANMEUR, a town of France, in the department of Finisterre; 6 miles N. E. of Morlaix.

LANNILIS, a town of France, in the department of Finisterre; 19 miles N. of Brest.

LANNION, a town of France, in the department of Cotes du Nord; with a trade in wine, hemp, and butter. In the neighbourhood are mines of iron and silver. It is seated on the Guer; 39 miles W. N. W. of St. Brieux. Long. 3. 27. W. lat. 48. 44. N.

LANNOY, a town of France, in the department of Nord; 8 miles E. N. E. of Lisle.

LANSARGUES, a town of France, in the department of Herault; 19 miles W. of Montpelier. Pop. 1120.

LANSDOWN, a mountain in Somersetshire; 4 miles from Bath; 813 feet high.

LANSINBURGH, a village of New York, in Rensselaer county. It contains four churches, a court-house, a jail, and an academy; and is seated on the E. side of the Hudson, opposite the S. branch of the Mohawk; 9 miles N. N. E. of Albany. Long. 74. 8. W. lat. 42. 43. N. Pop. 3330.

LANZO, a town of the Sardinian states, in Piedmont, on the river Stura, over which is an elegant bridge. It is 12 miles N. W. of Turin. Pop. 2225.

LAO, a town of the island of Cuba; 25 miles W. of Havannah.

LAO, or LEAO, a city of China, of the second rank, in the province of Chan-si. Long. 112. 57. E. lat. 37. 4. N.

LAON, a decayed town of France, capital of the department of Aisne; with a castle. The principal trade consists in corn and wine. It is celebrated for a battle fought under its walls, between the French and allies, in March 1814.

It is seated on a mountain, near Ardon; 77 miles N. E. of Paris. Long. 3. 43. E. lat. 49. 34. N

Laos, a kingdom of India beyond the Ganges; extending from 12. to 18. N. lat., and bounded by Laktho, Siam, Cambodia, Tunquin, and Cochin-China, to the last of which it is nominally subject. It is surrounded by mountains covered with forests; but the country is in general flat, and the soil fertile, being watered by numerous rivulets from the mountains, and a number of canals from the Mecon, which flows from N. to S. through the whole region. It abounds in rice, fruit, honey, wax, and cotton; and the principal drugs are benzoin and lac. Gold and silver are found in certain places of the river; and it has mines of iron, lead, and tin. It is very thinly inhabited, the greater part of the population consisting of migrating tribes, who wage an almost constant internal warfare. The religion, language, and manners, are much the same as in Siam. Lanjan is the capital.

Lapland, a northern region of Europe, now belonging to Russia and Sweden; bounded on the N. by the Arctic Ocean, E. by the White Sea, S. by Sweden, and W. by Norway and the Atlantic. It was formerly divided into three parts, Russian, Swedish, and Danish, or (Norwegian) Lapland. The first, the most dreary region of the whole, consisted of three districts, Bellamoreskoi, Maremanskoi, and Terskoi; but these are now all included in the general appellation of the circle of Kola, which includes also the tract on the E. of the Torneo, called Kemi-Lapmark, which was ceded by Sweden in 1809. Swedish Lapland, or Lapland Proper, is subdivided into six provinces, now comprised in the government of Umea. Norwegian Lapland, or Finmark, the most northerly of all, now belongs also to Sweden. The general aspect of Lapland is mountainous. The principal rivers are the Torneo, which issues from a lake of the same name, and, after a course of 300 miles, falls into the Gulf of Bothnia; the Tana, and the Alten, both of which fall into the Frozen Ocean. The lakes are numerous, and many of them very extensive. The maritime districts are of uniform and rather mild temperature; but in the interior, the winter is intensely cold: in the most northern parts the sun remains below the horizon from the 20th of November to the 10th of January; and the whole country is covered with snow and ice, from the beginning of September to the middle of March. In summer the sun continues two months above the horizon; and in the valleys and plains the heat is excessive, favouring the production of numerous insects, particularly musquitoes, which greatly infest the inhabitants. Barley is the common grain, but rye and oats are also cultivated in some places, and a few culinary vegetables are raised. The trees are fir, birch, larch, and small beech, which form vast though not thick forests. Metals and minerals are found in abundance: gold has been found at Suappavara; copper, iron, lead, zinc, and plumbago are found in various places; and in the S. of Swedish Lapland several mines are wrought. Among the other internal productions of this country are limestone, marble, gypsum, rock-crystal, jasper, amethysts, and garnets. The animals of this country are much the same as those of Norway; but the rein-deer may more properly be said to belong to Lapland. The singular usefulness of this animal in a great measure recompenses the Laplander for the privation of the other comforts of life. The rein-deer in summer live upon leaves and grass, and in winter upon moss, which they dig up from under the snow; yet upon such scanty fare they will perform a journey of inconceivable length. The animal is fixed to a kind of sledge, shaped like a small boat, in which the traveller, well secured from cold, is laced down; and, taking the reins, which are fastened to the horns of the animal, in one hand, and a kind of bludgeon, to keep the carriage clear of ice and snow, in the other, he sets out, and continues his journey with incredible speed, the animals choosing the road and directing their course with very little trouble to the traveller. Their milk and cheese are nutritive and pleasant; their flesh is well tasted food, whether fresh or dried; their skin forms excellent clothing, both for the bed and body; and their intestines and tendons supply their masters with thread and cordage The Laplanders are rather lower in stature than the more southern Europeans. The men are of a swarthy and dark complexion; their hair is black and short, their mouth wide, and their cheek hollow, with a longish pointed chin. The women are in general well made, complaisant, chaste, and extremely nervous. In their manner of life the Laplanders are divided into fishers and mountaineers. The former, in summer, fix their habitations in the neighbourhood of some lake, from which they draw their subsistence, and in winter live in the woods. The latter seek their support on the mountains, and possess herds of rein-deer, more or less numerous. They are active and expert in the chase; and the introduction of fire arms has almost abolished the use of the bow and arrow. Besides looking after the rein-deer, the fishery, and the chase, the men are employed in making canoes, sledges, harness, cups, bowls, &c.; and the women in making nets, drying the fish and meat, milking the deer, making the cheese, and tanning hides. Like the Icelanders, they consider their country the finest in the universe. They live in tents composed of several poles or beams of wood, which meet at the top and support each other; the fire-place consists of a few stones, and is always in the middle of the hut, a hole being at the top for the smoke to pass. When travelling, and exposed to the inclemency of the weather, they throw a covering over the head, neck, and shoulders, leaving only a small opening, through which they see and breathe. In their dress they use no kind of linen. The men wear close breeches, reaching down to their shoes, which are made of untanned leather, pointed and turned up before. Their doublet is made to fit their shape; it is open at the breast, and over it they wear a close coat with narrow sleeves, the skirts of which reach down to the knees, and are fastened round them by a leathern girdle, ornamented with plates of tin and brass. To this girdle they tie their knives, instruments for making fire, pipes, and other smoking apparatus. The dress of the women is the same as that of the men, with the exception of a few ornamental peculiarities. All the Swedish and Norwegian, as well as the greater number of the Russian Laplanders, bear the name of Christians; but their religion is full of superstition, and a compound of Christian and Pagan ceremonies. Their language has an affinity with the Finnish, but is greatly intermixed with others. They trade with the Swedes and Norwegians, whom they supply with the skins and furs of quadrupeds, such as ermines, sables, martens, squirrels, foxes of various colours, bears, lynxes, and wolves; and receive in return meal, cloth, spirituous liquors, tobacco, and various utensils.

Lar, a town of Persia, capital of Laristan; with a castle on a rock; chiefly celebrated for the manufacture of muskets and cotton cloth. It was once a magnificent city, but is now in ruins. Some handsome houses still remain, and the bazaar is said to be the noblest structure of the kind in Persia. Pop. 12,500. Long. 43. 40. E. lat. 27. 30. N.

Laracha, or Laraish, a strong town in the kingdom of Fez; with a castle, and a good harbour. Here are magazines for the refitting of vessels, but no docks for building. It is seated near the mouth of the Lucos; 46 miles S. by W. of Tangier.

Laredo, a town of Spain, in Biscay; with a good harbour; 30 miles W. N. W. of Bilboa.

Largo, a town of Scotland, in Fifeshire; on a bay of its name, at the opening of the Frith of Forth, which is a safe roadstead for ships of all descriptions. The town has a manufacture of linen and checks. It is 9 miles S. S. W. of St. Andrew.

Largs, a town of Scotland, in Ayrshire; with a small harbour on the Frith of Clyde. It is memorable for the defeat of the Norwegians, in their last invasion of this country, in 1263. It is 15 miles N. W. of Irvine.

Larino, a town of Naples, in the Molise; 25 miles E. N. E. of Molise.

Larissa, a town of Greece; capital of Thessaly, and an archbishop's see; with a palace, and some handsome mosques. It was famous as the residence of Achilles, and retains its ancient name. The inhabitants, estimated at 25,000, carry on a large trade in dyeing yarn, tanning leather, &c. It was the centre of the military operations by the Turks against Ali Pacha. It is seated on the Peneus; 75 miles S. by W. of Salonica. Long. 22. 47. E. lat. 39. 48. N.

Laristan, a small province of Persia, extending along the northern shore of the Persian Gulf. The soil is so impregnated with acrid substances, and so destitute of water, that it is the most unproductive province of the kingdom. Those who inhabit the coast are addicted to piracy, and live under their own sheiks, paying the king only a trifling tribute. Lar is the capital.

Larne, a town of Ireland, in the county of Antrim; at the mouth of a river of the same name; 8 miles N. of Carrickfergus.

Larnica, a town of Cyprus; the second in the island, and the emporium of its commerce, the bay on which it is situated forming one of the best roadsteads in the island. It has no good water, but is supplied from a distance by an aqueduct. Long 33. 45. E. lat. 34. 56. N. Pop. 5250.

Larry Bundar, a town of Hindostan, on the N. branch of the Indus, called the Pitty; 56 miles W. by S. of Tatta. Long. 66. 42. E. lat. 24. 43. N.

Larta. *See* Arta.

Larvigen, or Laurwig, a seaport of Norway, in the bishopric of Christiania. It is a place of considerable trade, and has productive iron-works. It stands at the conflux of two rivers, near the sea; 74 miles S. S. W. of Christiania.

Lasnebourg, a town of Savoy; on the river Arc; at the foot of Mount Cenis, the passage of which is the principal support of the inhabitants. The sun is hidden from the inhabitants of this town, by the mountains, during two months in the year. It is 20 miles N. N. W. of Susa.

Lassa, or Lahassa, a city of Asia; capital of Great Tibet. It is not large, but the houses are spacious, and built of stone. About 7 miles to the E. of the city is the mountain of Putala, on the summit of which is the palace of the grand Lama, the high priest of Tibet; whose authority is as great over almost all the regions of Tartary and Tibet, as that of the pope was formerly over Europe. Lassa is seated on a spacious plain, on a river that flows S. into the Sanpoo; 680 miles N. N. E. of Calcutta. Long. 91. 25. E. lat. 29. 30. N.

Lassahn a town of Prussia, in Pomerania; on a lake of the same name; 38 miles S. S. E. of Stralsund.

Lassam, a town of Java, on the N. coast; through which flows a fine navigable river. It has a considerable trade; 419 miles E. of Batavia.

Lassay, a town of France, in the department of Mayenne; 12 miles E. N. E. of Mayenne.

Lastres, a town of Spain, in Asturias; near a cape of the same name, on the Bay of Biscay; 35 miles E. N. E. of Oviedo.

Laswaree, a town of Hindostan, in the province of Delhi; where a desperate battle was fought in 1803, between the British, under Lord Lake, and the Mahrattas, under Dowlat Row Scindia, in which the latter were totally defeated.

Latacunga, a town of Peru; capital of a district of the same name. The streets are broad and straight; the houses only one story high, and arched, on account of the frequency of earthquakes, one of which overturned the whole place in 1698. It contains manufactures of cloth and baize, &c., and exports great quantities of salt pork; the vicinity is noted for making fine red earthenware. It is situated 50 miles S. of Quito. Long. 78. 16. W. lat. 0. 56. S. Pop. 11,500.

LATAKIA, or LADIKIEH, (the ancient Laodicea,) a seaport of Syria, and a bishop's see. It has beautiful remains of antiquity, and a considerable trade, especially in tobacco, though the harbour is become too shallow for large vessels. It stands on the S. side of a small peninsula; 75 miles S. W. of Aleppo. Long. 34. 30. E. lat. 35. 40. N.

LAUBACH, a town of Germany, in Hesse-Darmstadt; with a castle; 10 miles E. by S. of Giesen.

LAUBACH, one of the two governments of Austrian Illyria, containing nearly 640,000 inhabitants. It is divided into the circles of Laubach, Neustadtel, Adelsberg, Clagenfurt, and Villach.

LAUBACH, or LAYBACH, a strong town of Austrian Illyria; capital of the preceding government. The castle, called the Old Fort, stands on a mountain, and is now used only for a prison. It has manufactures of silk, leather, and excellent cloth. In 1821 a congress was held here for deliberating on the affairs of Italy, and attended by the emperors of Russia and Austria. It is seated on a river of the same name; 38 miles S. E. of Clagenfurt. Long. 14. 35. E. lat. 46. 11. N. Pop. 11,500.

LAUBAN, a walled town of Upper Lusatia; on the frontiers of Silesia. It has a good trade in cloth, yarn, and linen. It is seated on the Queiss; 14 miles E. S. E. of Gorlitz.

LAUDA, a town and castle of Germany, in Baden; on the river Tauba; 18 miles S. W. of Wurtzburg.

LAUDER, an ancient royal burgh of Scotland, in Berwickshire; sending, in conjunction with Haddington, &c., one member to parliament. The castle, originally built by Edward I. as a fortress, is now the seat of the Earl of Lauderdale. It is seated on a river of the same name; 21 miles S. E. of Edinburgh.

LAUENBURG, a duchy in the N. of Germany; on the right bank of the Elbe, adjacent to Hamburg, and included, since 1815, in the Danish dominions, of which it forms the southern extremity. Pop. 32,000.

LAUENBURG, the capital of the foregoing duchy. There is only one wing of the ancient castle, where the dukes resided, now remaining. Great quantities of merchandise are sent hence to Lubec, by means of the Steckenitz. It stands on the Elbe and Steckenitz; 35 miles E. S. E. of Hamburg. Long. 10. 50. E. lat. 52. 22. N. Pop. 2500.

LAUENBURG, a town of Prussia, in Pomerania; on the Leba; 37 miles W. by N. of Dantzic. Long. 17. 48. E. lat. 54. 27. N.

LAUFFEN, a town of Austria, in the duchy of Salzburg; with a fine castle; seated on the Salza; 12 miles N. N. W. Salzburg.

LAUFFEN, a town of Switzerland, in the canton of Zurich; with a castle. Here is a celebrated cataract of the Rhine, the perpendicular height of which is about 60 feet, and the breadth 300. It is 3 miles S. by W. of Schaffhausen.

LAUFFENBURG, a strong town in the S. W. extremity of Germany; with a castle. It is seated on a rock, on the Rhine, which divides it in two parts. Here is a small cataract, noted for the beauty of the scenery; 26 miles W. of Schaffhausen. Long. 8. 2. E. lat. 47. 35. N.

LAUGHARNE, a town of South Wales, county of Caermarthen; on an arm of the sea, at the mouth of the Tave river; 245 miles from London.

LAUINGEN, a town of Bavaria, in the principality of Neuberg; seated on the Danube; 3 miles W. of Dillingen.

LAUNCESTON, a borough, and the capital of Cornwall; market on Wednesday and Saturday. It had a strong castle, now in ruins, but the tower serves as a prison; and a little without the town stands the old priory. The spring assizes are held here; the summer assizes at Bodmin. It returns one member to parliament. Here is a free school, founded by Queen Elizabeth, and two charity schools. It is seated on the side of a hill, on the Attery, which falls into the Tamar, 3 miles below the town; 28 miles N. N. W. of Plymouth, and 214 W. by S. of London. Long. 4. 21. W. lat. 50. 38. N.

LAUNCESTON, a town of Van Diemen's Land, seated at the junction of the Esk and Tamar, at the head of Port Dalrymple, or River Tamar, which will allow vessels of considerable burden to approach the town; but the navigation is intricate. It contains a church, government house, barracks, court-house, &c., and is a thriving and improving place; to the N. E. is a race-course, and to the S. W. is a beautiful cascade on the South Esk. The town has but a limited supply of water, which is principally brought from the South Esk. It is 121 miles N. from Hobart Town. Lat. 41. 30. S. long. 147. 15. E. This town contains, according to the last census, the following number of inhabitants:—Free males, 2348; females, 1524; bond males, 476; females, 112. Total, 4460.

LAUNY, a town of Bohemia, near the river Eger; 10 miles E. N. E. of Saaz.

LAUPEN, a town of Switzerland, in the canton of Bern, at the conflux of the Sannen and Sense; 5 miles S. W. of Bern.

LAURINGEN, a town of Germany, on the river Laur; 11 miles N. E. of Schweinfurt.

LAUSANNE, a city of Switzerland, capital of the canton of Pays de Vaud, and a bishop's see, with a famous college. It stands on a very uneven tract of land, formed by three small hills; and the lofty parts afford the most sublime views in nature. The cathedral, the town-house, and other public buildings, are magnificent; 30 miles N. E. of Geneva, and 42 S. W. of Bern. It is much frequented by visitors, and has been the residence of Voltaire, Gibbon, and Haller. Long. 6. 45. E. lat. 46. 31. N. Pop. 16,000.

LAUTENBURG, a town of West Prussia, in the palatinate of Culm. It is 4 miles E. by S. of Culm.

LAUTER, a river which rises in the Vosges mountains, and forms the boundary between France and Germany, on the W. of the Rhine, into which it falls at Lauterburg.

LAUTERBACH, a town of Bohemia, in the circle of Saatz, noted for excellent tin-mines; 9 miles S. S. W. of Carlsbad.

LAUTERBACH, a town of Germany, in the grand duchy of Saxe Weimar, with a trade in linen and woollen cloths; seated on the Vogelsberg, 15 miles W. N. W. of Fulda.

LAUTERBRUNN, a village of Switzerland, in the canton of Bern, 6 miles S. of Interlachen. It is seated in a romantic valley of the same name, celebrated for its cataract, called Staubbach.

LAUTERBURG, a town of France, in the department of Lower Rhine. It stands on the Lauter, near its conflux with the Rhine; 14 miles S. of Landau.

LAUZERTE, a town of France, in the department of Lot; 20 miles S. W. of Cahors.

LAUZUN, a town of France, in the department of Lot-et-Garonne, 17 miles N. E. of Marmande. Pop. 1250.

LAVAL, a town of France, capital of the department of Mayenne. It is surrounded by an old wall, and has two old castles, five churches, and three hospitals, with a monastery established in 1815. Linen of all kinds and qualities is manufactured here, and the neighbouring quarries produce green marble, or black veined with white. It is seated on the Mayenne, 40 miles W. of Mans. Long. 0. 45. W. lat. 48. 5. N. Pop. 15,167.

LAVAMUNDE, a small town of Austrian Illyria, in Lower Carinthia, seated on the Drave, 23 miles E. of Clagenfurt.

LAVELD, or LAFELD, a village of the Netherlands, in the province of Liege, 4 miles W. of Maestricht. In 1747 the French obtained a victory here over the allies, commanded by the Duke of Cumberland.

LAVELLO, a town of Naples, in Basilicata, 90 miles E. by N. of Naples.

LAVENHAM, a town in Suffolk, with manufactures of hempen cloth and woollen yarn. Here is a spacious market-place, with a cross in the centre; but the market has long been disused. The town is situate on an eminence, at the foot of which runs the river Breton; 12 miles S. by E. of Bury St. Edmund, and 62 N. E. of London.

LAVENZA, a town of Italy, in the principality of Massa, with a citadel; seated at the mouth of the Lavenza, on the Gulf of Genoa, 6 miles W. N. W. of Massa.

LAVINGTON, a town in Wiltshire, with a market on Monday and Wednesday, 4 miles S. of Devizes, and 90 W. by S. of London.

LAVIS, a town of the Austrian states, in Tyrol, at the conflux of the Lavis with the Adige; 7 miles N. of Trent.

LAVORO, TERRA DI, a province in the N. W. part of Naples; bordered on the W. by the Tuscan Sea, and containing 1720 square miles, with 625,000 inhabitants. It is proper for tillage, whence it took its name, and is fertile in excellent wines and fruits. There are also mineral springs and mines of sulphur. Capua is the capital, and Gaeta is the chief seaport.

LAWRENCE, ST., a large river of North America, proceeding from Lake Ontario, from which it runs 700 miles to the Gulf of St. Lawrence, in the Atlantic. Its mouth is 100 miles wide, and it is navigable for ships of war as far as Quebec, which is 360 miles; and vessels from Europe ascend to Montreal, which is 180 miles further. In its course it forms a great variety of bays, harbours, and islands, many of which are fruitful, and extremely pleasant. The navigation of this river is closed from December to April by the ice; but it then forms a medium of communication, by roads being marked on it and its tributaries; and goods are then transported on it, by means of sleighs and other vehicles. *See* QUEBEC, MONTREAL, &c.

LAWRENCE, ST., GULF OF, is formed between the western part of Newfoundland, the eastern shores of Labrador, the eastern extremity of the province of New Brunswick, part of the province of Nova Scotia, and the island of Cape Breton. It communicates with the Atlantic Ocean by three different passages.

LAWRENCE-KIRK, a town of Scotland, in Kincardineshire, with manufactures of lawn, cambric, thread, &c., and a large bleach-field. It is seated on the small river Leuther, 8 miles N. of Montrose.

LAXEMBURG, a town of Austria, with a palace; seated on the Suechat, 17 miles S. of Vienna.

LAYBACH. *See* LAUBACH.

LAZIZE, a town of North Italy, in Lombardy, on Lake Guarda. Here is a castle, and a port on the lake; 23 miles N. from Mantua. Pop. 8500.

LEA, a river of England, which rises near Luton, in Bedfordshire, flows to Hertford and Ware, and, dividing Essex from Hertfordshire and Middlesex, enters the Thames below Blackwall.

LEADHILLS, a village of Scotland, in Lanarkshire, situate amid mountains, in which are rich mines of lead. It is supposed to be the highest inhabited place in Britain, being about 2000 feet above the level of the sea. It is situate on the road from Glasgow to Dumfries, 18 miles S. of Lanark, and 44 S. of Glasgow.

LEAMINGTON PRIORS, a town in Warwick shire, with a market on Wednesday. Here are some saline springs, with warm and cold baths, a pump-room, and other accommodations for genteel company. It is seated on the river Leam, near its confluence with the Avon, 2 miles E. of Warwick, and 89 N. W. of London.

LEAO-TONG. *See* CHEN-YANG.

LEATHERHEAD, a town in Surrey, which had formerly a market. Here is a bridge of 14 arches over the river Mole, which a little above is said to make its reappearance above ground; 18 miles S. S. W. of London.

Leathes-water, or Withburn, a fine lake in Cumberland, lying S. E. of Keswick. It is narrow and irregular, about 4 miles in length, skirting the foot of Kelvellyn, and receiving numerous torrents from that huge mountain. The singular beauty of this lake is its being almost intersected in the middle by two peninsulas, which are joined by a neat wooden bridge. Its outlet, at the N. end, joins the river Greta, which runs into the Derwent below Keswick.

Leba, a town of Prussia in Pomerania, on a river of the same name, which, after forming a lake 15 miles in circumference, enters the Baltic Sea; 16 miles N. N. W. of Luenburg.

Lebanon, a town of Pennsylvania, capital of a county of the same name. It has considerable trade, and in the vicinity are copper and iron mines. It is seated on the Quitaphilla Creek, 80 miles W. N. W. of Philadelphia. Population of the county, 21,872; of the town, 1860.

Lebanon is also the name of several townships of the United States. 1. A post township in York county, Maine. 2. In Grafton county, New Hampshire. 3. In Windham county, Connecticut. 4. In Madison county, New York. 5. In Hunterdon county, New Jersey. 6. In Warren county, Ohio, 25 miles S. of Dayton. 7. The capital of Wilson county, Tennessee, 25 miles E. of Nashville.

Lebanon, New, a town of New York, in Columbia county, noted for its medicinal spring; 30 miles N. E. of Hudson. It is also the name of a township in Camden county, North Carolina.

Lebida, a seaport of Africa, in the territory of Tripoli, with a good harbour and an old castle. Here are the ruins of a temple and other splendid buildings, It is seated on the Mediterranean, 30 miles S. E. of Tripoli.

Lebrixa, or Lebrija, a town of Spain, in Andalusia, with a castle, seated in a territory abounding in olive-trees, that produce the best oil in Spain; 20 miles S. by W. of Seville. Pop. 6250.

Lebus, a town of Prussia, in Brandenburg, seated on the Oder, 5 miles N. of Frankfort.

Lecasello, a town in the state of Genoa; 23 miles N. E. of Genoa.

Lecce, a city of Naples, in Otranto, and a bishop's see. It is the residence of the governor of the province, which by some is called Lecce, instead of Otranto; 17 miles N. W. of Otranto, and 195 E. S. E. of Naples. Pop. 13,735. Long. 18. 20. E. lat. 40. 36. N.

Lecco, a town of Austrian Italy, in the Milanese, with several flourishing manufactures. It is seated on the E. branch of the lake Como, 15 miles E. N. E. of Como. Long. 9. 23. E. lat. 45. 5. N. Pop. 4250.

Lech, a river of the Bavarian states, which rises in Tyrol, divides Suabia from Bavaria, and enters the Danube below Donawert.

Lechlade, or Letchlade, a town in Gloucestershire, with a market on Tuesday. A canal from the Severn joins the Thames near this town, and the traffic here on both is considerable in cheese, corn, and coal. It is seated at the confluence of the Lech with the Thames, 28 miles E. by S. of Gloucester, and 76 W. by N. of London.

Lechnits, a town of Prussian Silesia, in the province of Oppeln. Near it is the convent of St. Annenberg, much resorted to by pilgrims. It is seated near the Oder, 17 miles S. S. E. of Oppeln.

Leck, a river of the Netherlands, which branches off from the Rhine at Deurstede, and enters the Maese; 10 miles E. of Rotterdam.

Lectoure, a strong town of France, department of Gers, with manufactures of leather, and some trade in corn and wine. It is situate on a mountain, near the river Gers; 16 miles N. of Auch. Long. 0. 37. E. lat. 43. 56. N. Pop. 6630.

Ledbury, a town of Herefordshire, with a market on Tuesday, and a considerable manufacture of ropes and sacking. The navigable canal from Gloucester to Hereford passes by this town, which is situate near the S. extremity of the Malvern hills, 16 miles E. of Hereford, and 120 W. N. W. of London.

Ledesma, a small but strong town of Spain, in Leon; seated on the Tormes; 20 miles S. W of Salamanca.

Lee, a river of Ireland, which rises on the confines of Kerry, flows E. to Cork, and falls into Cork Harbour.

Leeds, a borough in West Yorkshire; markets on Tuesday and Saturday. It returns two members to parliament. It stands on the river Aire, over which is a stately stone bridge. It is the principal of the clothing towns in Yorkshire, and the mart for the coloured and white broad cloths, of which vast quantities are sold in its two cloth halls, within the space of an hour, without the least confusion. Leeds has a flourishing manufacture of carpets; also some mills for the cutting of tobacco, and several potteries. In the neighbourhood are numerous collieries, and great quantities of coal are sent to York and Hull. Three miles N. N. W. of the town, on the river Aire, stands the remains of that venerable pile, Kirkstal Abbey, embowered in groves of oak. Leeds has seven churches, two of which were erected under the new act; and here are twelve meeting-houses, a general infirmary, an hospital, three almshouses, a free school, charity school, and a large national school, opened in 1813. The most handsome building in the town is the court-house and prison, erected in 1812. A canal passes hence to Liverpool, by which, and the river, this town has a communication with the Irish Sea and the German Ocean; and it is connected with London, Birmingham, &c., by means of the North Midland railway; 24 miles S. W. of York, and 189 N. W. of London Long. 1. 34. W. lat. 53. 48. N.

Leeds, a parish in Kent, with a castle and a priory: some ruins of the latter still remain; 5 miles S. W. of Maidstone, and 40 from London.

Leeds, a town of Virginia, in Richmond county, on the N. side of the Rappahannoc; 34 miles S. E. of Falmouth.

Leefogo, the most fertile of the Hapaee Islands, in the South Pacific. It is not above 7 miles in length, and only 2 or 3 in breadth, but is superior in many respects to Annamooka. The inhabitants are treacherous, and have frequently attempted to seize European vessels. Long. 185. 40. E. lat. 19. 49. S.

Leek, a town in Staffordshire, with a market on Wednesday. It has a brisk trade, and manufactures of bandana and other handkerchiefs, ribbons, twist, and buttons. It is seated on the Churnet; 21 miles N. of Stafford, and 154 N. N. W. of London.

Leer, or **Lehr**, a town of Hanover, in East Friesland, on the river Leda, which soon after joins the Ems; 14 miles S. E. of Emden.

Leerdam, a town of the Netherlands, in South Holland; seated on the Linghe; 11 miles S. of Utrecht. Pop. 2225.

Leerort, a fortress of Hanover, in East Friesland; seated at the conflux of the Leda with the Ems; 10 miles E. by S. of Emden.

Leers, or **Liers**, a town of Belgium, in the territory of Liege, near which the allies were defeated by the French in 1746; 4 miles N. of Liege.

Leesburg, a town of Virginia, in London county, near the Potomac; 35 miles N. W. of Washington.

Leesburg, a town of Ohio, in Highland county.—Also a township of Harrison county, Kentucky.

Leetakoo, or **Lattakoo**, a town of Southern Africa. The old town of this name was, until lately, the most remote place known in the Boshuana county. The inhabitants, when visited by Mr. Campbell and others, in 1813, appeared to have made considerable progress in the arts and civilization. Soon after, they removed to a more suitable situation, about 40 miles distant in a southern direction, and founded New Leetakoo. On his return, in 1820, he found this new town occupied by about 8000 persons, collected from various tribes. The women perform most of the agricultural labour; while the men milk the cows, make the clothes, and go to war. New Leetakoo is 900 miles N. E. of Cape Town.

Leeuwarden. *See* Lewarden.

Leeuwe, a fortified town of Belgium, in South Brabant. It is seated in a morass, on the river Geete; 12 miles E. of Louvain.

Leeward Islands, such of the Caribbee Islands, in the West Indies, as commence at Porto Rico, and extend to Dominica.

Leefooga. *See* Leefogo.

Leghorn, or **Livorno**, a strong city of Italy, in the grand duchy of Tuscany, and a bishop's see. It has a good harbour, and is the greatest commercial depôt of Italy. The Jews, who are numerous and rich, have a handsome synagogue and schools; the Greeks and Armenians have churches of their own; and no religion is disturbed. The inhabitants are 65,355, including 20,000 Jews. The town is supplied with excellent water, brought from the mountains of Colognole by means of a long and expensive aqueduct, constructed by government. The streets are wide and straight, and almost all the houses of the same height. There are so many canals, that some have given it the title of New Venice. At a little distance is a lighthouse, on a small island. The trade consists of foreign goods, as cotton, sugar, cocoa, spices, sulphur, and alum; and in home productions, as essences, oils, wine, straw hats, cloth, juniper-berries, oranges, lambs' and goats' skins, and coral. In 1741 this city suffered greatly by an earthquake. The neighbouring marshes have been rendered fit for culture by means of canals, which have also been useful in dissipating the noxious effluvia: but the air is still far from healthy; 140 miles N. W. of Rome, and 46 W. of Florence. Long. 10. 17. E. lat. 43. 33. N.

Legnano, a town of Austrian Italy, in the Veronese; with a fortress regularly constructed. The town is populous, and carries on a considerable trade, particularly in grain, which is greatly facilitated by means of a canal from the Adige to the Po. It is seated on the Adige; 22 miles S. E. of Verona. Pop. 6500.

Leibnitz, a town of the Austrian empire, in Lower Styria; seated on the Sulm; 16 miles S. of Gratz.

Leicester, a town of Massachusets, in Worcester county; with a considerable manufacture of wool cards; 6 miles W. N. W. of Worcester.

Leicester, a borough, and the capital of Leicestershire: it is governed by a mayor; with a market on Saturday: it returns two members to parliament. In the civil wars the walls were in a great measure demolished; the castle was also dismantled, the hall and kitchen being the only parts that are left entire. It has 6 churches, 18 meeting-houses for the different denominations of dissenters, several hospitals, a free school, and three charity schools. In 1821 an act was passed for lighting the town with gas. The principal manufacture is that of stockings, of which, several years ago, the value amounted to 60,000*l.* annually, and it has of late much increased. A canal passes hence by Loughborough to the river Trent, and the Midland Counties railway passes this town. At a parliament held here in the reign of Henry V., the first law was made for the burning of heretics. In the meadows near the town are the ruins of an abbey in which Cardinal Wolsey died. It is seated on the Soar; 28 miles S. by E. of Derby, and 96 N. N. W. of London. Long. 1. 8. W. lat. 52. 38. N.

Leicestershire, a county of England; bounded on the N. by Derbyshire and Nottinghamshire, E. by the counties of Lincoln and Rutland, S. by Northamptonshire, and W. by Warwickshire and Staffordshire. It is about 45 miles long, and 30 broad; contains 514,560 statute acres, is divided into six hundreds, and 196 parishes; has 12 market towns; and sends four members to parliament, for the Northern and Southern divisions. The climate is temperate, and the country is well watered. The chief rivers are the Avon, Soar, Swift, Wreke, Anker, and Welland; it has three distinct lines of canal navigation, and is traversed by the Midland Counties railway. The soil, in general, affords great quantities of rich grazing land, and is peculiarly fitted for the culture of beans. Towards the N. W., the Bardon Hills rise to a great height; and in their neighbourhood is Sherwood Forest, a rough and open tract; further to the N. W. are valuable coal mines. The manufacture of stockings, the principal one in the county, is very considerable; but it may be considered rather an agricultural than a manufacturing county. It is famous for its breed of large black cart horses, numbers of which are continually sent to London; and for its fine neat cattle and sheep: the latter, owing to the great care paid to crossing the breeds, and other modes of improvement, have been brought to an astonishing degree of excellence. More than half the land is constantly in pasture, and most of the rest, maintained in tillage, is also rendered subservient to the rearing of cattle. The principal object of the graziers here is to fatten their cattle for the butcher; but the dairy is also in some places attended to; and great quantities of cheese are annually exported. The Stilton cheese is made in this county.

LEIGH, a town in Lancashire; with considerable manufactures, particularly of fine jeans, in imitation of those of India; fustians, and other cotton articles; and a great traffic by its canal navigation, which communicates with the Mersey, Dee, Avon, Ribble, Ouse, Severn, Humber, Thames, &c. It is 12 miles W. of Manchester, and 198 N. W. of London.

LEIGH, a small seaport of Essex, opposite the E. extremity of Canvey Island. It is noted for oysters; and has a good road for shipping. It is 18 miles S. S. E. of Chelmsford, and 39 E. of London.

LEIGHLIN, OLD, a decayed town of Ireland; in the county of Carlow. It is 9 miles N. E. of Kilkenny.

LEIGHLIN BRIDGE, a town of Ireland, in the county of Carlow; with the ruins of an ancient abbey, and also of a strong castle; seated on the river Barrow; 7 miles S. of Carlow.

LEIGHTON BUZZARD, a town in Bedfordshire; with a market on Tuesday. The trade consists in corn, cattle, lace, platted straw, &c. About half a mile distant are the remains of a Roman camp. It is seated on the Ouse; 18 miles S. of Bedford, and 41 N. W. of London.

LEIN, a town of Germany, in the duchy of Nassau; 4 miles N. E. of Welburg.

LEININGEN, a small town of the Bavarian circle of the Rhine; 30 miles S. of Mentz.

LEINSTER, a province of Ireland; 104 miles long, and 55 broad: it contains 4,270,213 acres; bounded on the E. and S. by St. George's Channel, W. by Connaught and Munster, and N. by Ulster. It contains the counties of Carlow, Dublin, Kildare, Kilkenny, King's County, Queen's County, Longford, Lough, East Meath, West Meath, Wexford, and Wicklow. Dublin is the capital. The principal rivers are the Boyne, the Barrow, the Liffey, the Noir, and the May.

LEINSTER, NEW. *See* ZEALAND, NEW.

LEIPA, a town of Bohemia; with manufactures of porcelain, glass, fine cloth, and cotton. It is 47 miles S. E. of Dresden. Pop. 4925.

LEIPNIC, a walled town of Moravia; near the river Beczwa; 14 miles E. S. E. of Olmutz.

LEIPSIC, CIRCLE OF, a province of the kingdom of Saxony; bounded E. by the circle of Meissen, S. by that of the Erzgebirge and the principality of Altenburg, and W. and N. by the Prussian part of Saxony. It comprises 14 bailiwicks, and is the seat of considerable manufactures. Pop. 218,500.

LEIPSIC, a city of Saxony, in the circle of Meissen; with a famous university, and a strong citadel, called Pleyssenburg. It carries on a considerable trade, and has three great fairs every year, which last a fortnight each. The number of inhabitants is about 41,000; and the principal manufactures are silk, gold and silver stuffs, linen and cotton printing, leather, and paper. There are six handsome colleges, belonging to the university, besides the private colleges; and the exchange is a fine structure. Leipsic was taken by the Prussians in 1745 and 1756. The Austrians, in 1756, besieged it in vain; they took it two years after, but were soon obliged to give it up. Leipsic is celebrated for two of the greatest battles recorded in history having been fought in its vicinity, between the French and the allied armies, on the 16th and 18th of October, 1813, which were followed by the capture of the town, and the rear-guard of the French army, on the following morning, and also the king of Saxony and his family, who were made prisoners. It is seated in a plain, on the river Pleysse; 64 miles W. N. W. of Dresden, 90 S. by W. of Berlin, and 180 N. E. of Frankfort-on-the-Maine. Long. 12. 21. E. lat. 51. 19. N.

LEIRA, a town of Portugal, in Estremadura, and a bishop's see; with an ancient castle on an eminence. Pop. 4600. It is 77 miles N. N. E. of Lisbon. Long. 8. 34. W. lat. 39. 48. N.

LEISZNIG, a town of Saxony, in Meissen; with manufactures of cloth, lace, stockings, &c. It is seated on the Mulda; 24 miles E. S. E. of Leipsic, and 32 N. W. of Dresden.

LEITH, a seaport of Scotland, on the Frith of Forth; 2 miles N. N. E. of Edinburgh, of which it is the port. It is situate at the mouth of the river Leith, which forms the harbour and divides the town into N. and S. Leith, which communicate by two draw-bridges. The harbour is secured by a noble stone pier, and it is accommodated with wet and dry docks, and other conveniences for ship-building, which is carried on to a considerable extent. Here are also manufactures of ropes, canvas, carpets, glass, shoes, leather, soap, and candles, and several iron forges. There are three churches, an episcopal chapel, three meeting-houses, a magnificent banking-house, an hospital for disabled seamen, rebuilt in 1817, and numerous charities A little to the east of the town are the baths, which are constructed upon a grand scale, and in a style of great elegance. The harbour is defended by a martello tower, and to the W. of the citadel is a battery for the protection of the shipping. The commerce of Leith is very considerable; and the vessels employed in the London trade are, in general, of a large size; but the largest ships are those employed in the Greenland whale fishery. To foreign parts are exported lead, glass ware, linen, woollen stuffs, and a variety of other goods. It returns, with Portobello, &c. one member to parliament. Long. 2. 56. W. lat. 55. 54. N.

LEITMERITZ. *See* LEUTMERITZ.

LEITOMISCHEL. *See* LEUTMISCHEL.

LEITRIM, a county of Ireland, in the province of Connaught; bounded on the N. by Donegal Bay, N. E. by Fermanagh, E. by Cavan, S. E. by Longford, S. W. by Roscommon, and W. by Sligo. Its greatest length is about 54 English miles, and its maximum breadth 20. It contains 21 parishes, and an area of 407,260 English acres. The northern parts are mountainous and uncultivated, but they abound with inexhaustible veins of lead, iron, and copper ore, and have likewise some coal mines. The S. is level and fertile. The county is traversed by the river Shannon, and abounds with small lakes and rivers, has some productive iron-works, and feeds great herds of cattle. It returns two members to the imperial parliament. Carrick is the capital.

LEITRIM, a village of Ireland, from which the preceding county has its name. It is seated on the Shannon; 4 miles N. of Carrick, and 82. W. N. W. of Dublin.

LEIXLIP, a town of Ireland, in the county of Kildare. It has a noble castle, with large gardens, on one side of which is a fine waterfall, called the Salmon Leap. Near it are the ruins of the church and castle of Confy. It is seated on the Liffy; 8 miles W. of Dublin.

LEMBURG, or LEOPOLD, a town of Austrian Poland; formerly the capital of Red Russia and now of Galicia and Lodomeria. It is well fortified, and defended by two citadels, one of which is on an eminence without the city. The cathedral, churches, and public building, are magnificent; and the inhabitants, computed at 47,000, of whom 14,000 are Jews, carry on a considerable trade. It is the see of a Roman Catholic archbishop, and has also an Armenian and Russian bishop. It is seated on the Peltan; 72 miles S. S. E. Chelm, and 156 E. of Cracow. Long. 24. 26. E. lat. 49. 51. N.

LEMGOW, a town of Prussia, in Westphalia, and in the principality of Lippe-Detmold; with some cloth and stuff manufactures, and a considerable trade in printing and bookselling. It is seated on the Beya; 17 miles S. of Minden. Pop. 3650.

LEMNOS, or STALIMENE, an island of the Archipelago, lying near the Strait of Gallipoli; 15 miles long and 11 broad. The poets made it sacred to Vulcan, who was hence called Lemnius Pater. It was also celebrated for its labyrinth, of which not a trace remains. The air is pure, and the produce consists of corn, oil, cotton, and a variety of fruits. It has two harbours on the S. coast, and an extensive roadstead on the N. Its capital is of the same name, and is a metropolitan see. Long. 25. 28. E. lat. 40. 3. N.

LENA, a river of Asiatic Russia, in the government of Irkutsk, which rises in the mountains to the N. W. of the lake Baikal, flows N. and N. E. to Yakutsk, where it is 5 miles wide, and, proceeding N. N. W. enters the Frozen Ocean, by several mouths, forming an archipelago of two islands, on a basis of ice, which are the resort of bears and animals valuable for their fur.

LENCZICZ, a strong town of Poland, with a fort on a rock. It stands in a morass on the river Biusa; 77 miles W. of Warsaw, and 110 N. by W. of Cracow. Pop. 2340.

LENHAM, a decayed town in Kent; seated on an eminence, at the source of the Len; 10 miles E. of Maidstone, and 44 S. E. of London.

LENNEP, a town of the Prussian states, in the province of Cleves and Berg; on a river of the same name; 20 miles E. S. E. of Dusseldorf.

LENNOX. *See* DUMBARTON.

LENS, a town of France, department of Pas de Calais; 10 miles N. W. of Douay.

LENTINI, an ancient town of Sicily, in Val di Noto. It is a small remainder of the ancient Leontium, and situate at the foot of a height, on the top of which Charles V. built a new town, called Carlentini. Lentini was greatly damaged by an earthquake, in 1693. It is seated on a river of the same name; 17 miles S. W. of Catania. Pop. 5225.

LENTZBURG, a town of Switzerland, in the canton of Aargau; with a castle, and manufactures of linen, cotton, tobacco, &c. It is seated on the Aa; 6 miles E. of Aargau.

LENTZEN, a town of the Prussian province of Brandenburg, near the Elbe; 74 miles N. W. of Berlin.

LEUBEN, a town of the Austrian states, in Upper Styria; situate on the Muhr; 20 miles N. W. of Gratz.

LEOBSCHUZ, a town of Prussian Silesia; with a trade in corn and yarn; 10 miles N. N. E. of Jagerndorf.

LEOGANE, a town and fort, with a good harbour, on the N. side of the peninsula of St. Domingo. It was taken by the British in 1796; 26 miles S. S. W. of Port au Prince. Long. 72. 37. W. lat. 18. 38. N.

LEOMINSTER, a borough in Herefordshire, with markets on Tuesday and Friday, and a trade in cloth, gloves, hats, hops, leather, cider, &c. It sends two members to parliament. The church is spacious, and has a beautiful altar-piece by Rubens. Here are also four meeting-houses, two charity schools, and two free schools, one of them endowed by Queen Mary. It is seated on the Lug; 26 miles W. of Worcester, and 137 N. W. of London.

LEOMINSTER, a town of Massachusets, in Worcester county; with a manufacture of combs; 19 miles N. of Worcester, and 46 W. N. W. of Boston.

LEON, an important N. W. division of Spain, still retaining the title of a kingdom; bounded on the N. by Asturias W. by Galicia and Portugal, S. by Estremadura, and E. by Old Castile. It is 200 miles long, and 170 broad, and divided into about two equal parts by the river Douro. It is divided into the districts of Leon, Salamanca, Palencia, Zamora, Toro, and Valladolid. It is fertile, and produces some wine, and in the mountains copper and iron are found. Area, 21,000 square miles. Pop. 1,216,000.

LEON, capital of the above province, and a bishop's see, was formerly richer and more populous than at present. Its cathedral, which is admired for its elegant lightness, contains the tombs of 37 kings and one emperor; 174 miles N. by W. of Madrid. Long. 5. 38. W. lat. 42. 36. N. Pop. 6000.

LEON, ISLE OF, an insulated tract on the S. W. coast of Spain; separated from the mainland by a canal and river, 10 miles in length, and from 20 to 30 feet in depth. The defence thus afforded against an enemy in possession of the mainland (as was the case of the French in 1810) is farther strengthened by the salt marshes, which extend to the eastward, and are impassable, except along a causeway. *See* CADIZ.

LEON, a town on the above island. The population including St. Carlos, is said to amount to 40,000, whose chief support arises from the works carried on at the neighbouring arsenal and dockyard of Caraccas; 11 miles S. E. of Cadiz. Long. 6. 12. W. lat. 36. 27. N.

LEON, or LEON DE NICARAGUA, a city of Mexico; capital of the province of Nicaragua. In the vicinity is a mountain with a volcano, which sometimes occasions earthquakes. It is a commercial place; seated near the N. W. extremity of the lake Nicaragua; 30 miles from the Pacific Ocean. Pop. 6000. Long. 87. 20. W. lat. 12. 30. N.

LEON, NEW, a province in the S. part of the republic of Mexico, having the Gulf of Mexico on the E., Panuco on the S., and New Biscay on the W.

LEONARD, ST., an ancient town of France; department of Upper Vienne; with manufactures of paper and cloth; seated on the Vienne; 10 miles N. E. of Limoges and 195 S. of Paris. Pop. 5000.

LEONARDS, ST., ON SEA, a new town on the coast of Sussex, adjoining the town of Hastings, to which it has become a suburb, and is much frequented by visitors, for sea-bathing.

LEONARDTOWN, a town of Maryland, chief of St. Mary county: situate on Briton Bay, 5 miles from its mouth, in the Potomac; 60 miles S. S. E. of Washington.

LEOO-KEOO. *See* LOO-CHOO.

LEOPOLD. *See* LEMBURG.

LEOPOLDSTADT, a town and fortress of Hungary; seated on the Waag; 56 miles E. of Vienne.

LEPANTO, a seaport of Greece, in Livadia, and an archbishop's see. It is surrounded with high walls, and defended by a castle on an eminence. The produce of the adjacent country is wine, oil, corn, rice, leather, and tobacco. It is seated at the entrance of a gulf of the same name; 100 miles W. N. W. of Athens, and 360 S. W. of Constantinople. Long. 22. E. lat. 38. 30. N. Pop. 2000.

LEPER'S ISLE, one of the New Hebrides, in the Pacific Ocean. Long. 168. 5. E. lat. 15. 23. S.

LERENA, or LLERENA, a town of Spain, in Estremadura, at the foot of a mountain, and the source of Malachel; 50 miles S. of Merida, and 63 N. of Seville. Long. 5. 59. W. lat. 38. 7. N.

LERIDA, (the Ilerda of Lucan,) an ancient town of Spain, in Catalonia, and a bishop's see; with a university and a castle. Near this place are the remains of a palace of the kings of Arragon. It is seated on a hill, on the river Segra; 69 miles S. S. E. of Saragossa, and 200 N. W. of Madrid. Long. 0. 25. E. lat. 41. 32. N.

LERINS, two islands in the Mediterranean, on the coast of France; 5 miles from Antibes. That nearest the coast, which is the larger island, is called St. Margaret; the smaller is called St. Honorat, and has been a Benedictine abbey.

LERMA, a town of Spain, in the province of Burgos: with a palace; seated on the Arlanza; 23 miles S. of Burgos.

LERWICK, a town of Scotland; capital of the Shetland Islands; situate on the spacious harbour called Brassa Sound. It is the rendezvous of the fishing busses and vessels employed in the herring fishery. Near the N. end of the town is Fort Charlotte, which commands the N. entrance to Brassa Sound. Long. 0. 56. W. lat. 60. 12. N.

LESCAR, a town of France, department of Lower Pyrenees; seated on a hill; 3 miles N. W. of Pau, and 42 S. E. of Bayonne.

LESIGNAU, a town of France, department of Ande; 11 miles W. of Narbonne.

LESINA, an island in the Gulf of Venice, on the coast of Dalmatia, 65 miles long and 14 broad. It contains great quantities of different kinds of marble, and produces wine, oil, figs, almonds, oranges, saffron, aloes, honey, &c., in great abundance; but salt fish is the chief article of commerce. The capital, of the same name, has a good harbour; it contains 1200 inhabitants; 20 miles S. of Spalatro. Long. 16. 20. E. lat. 43. 33. N.

LESKEARD, or LISKEARD, a borough in Cornwall; market on Saturday, and manufactures of leather and yarn. It is one of the largest and best built towns in the country; had formerly a castle, now in ruins, and is one of the coinage towns for tin. Besides the church, which is a large and noble edifice, here are three places of worship for dissenters, a free grammar school, two national schools, and a charity school for poor children. In the vicinity are several extensive sheep-walks. It returns one member to parliament. It is 16 miles W. N. W. of Plymouth, and 225 W. by S. of London. Long. 4. 42. W. lat. 50. 27. N.

LESSINES, a town of Belgium, in Hainault, famous for its linen manufacture; seated on the Dender; 28 miles S. W. of Brussels.

LESTWITHIEL, or LOSTWITHIEL, a town in Cornwall, governed by a mayor, with a market on Friday, and a tolerable woollen manufacture. Here is a stannary gaol; and the county courts are held here. It is seated on the river Fowey, which was formerly navigable, but is now choked up with sand; 22 miles N. E. of Truro, and 232 W. by S. of London.

LETTERE, a town of Naples, seated at the foot of a mountain; 12 miles N. W. of Salerno.

LETTERKENNY, a town of Ireland, county Donegal, on the river Swilly; 150 miles from Dublin.

LEUBUS, a town of Prussian Silesia, with a celebrated Cistercian abbey; seated on the Oder, 30 miles N. N. W. of Breslau.

LEUCATE, a town of France, department of Aude; situate near the Mediterranean, on the N. side of the lake of the same name; 20 miles N. E. of Perpignan.

LEUCH, or LEUK, a town of Switzerland, in the Vallais; much frequented on account of its hot mineral springs. It is seated on an eminence near the Rhone; 20 miles E. S. E. of Sion.

LEUSE, a town of Belgium, in Hainault; seated on the Dender; 14 miles N.W. of Mons.

LEUTKIRCH, a town of Germany, in Wirtemberg; with two suburbs, and a good linen trade. It is seated on the Eschach, which runs into the Iller; 22 miles N. E. of Lindau.

LEUTMERITZ, or LEITMERITZ, a town of Bohemia; capital of a circle of the same name. The circle is such a delightful country, that it is called the Bohemian Paradise; it produces excellent wine, and contains warm baths, tin-mines, and precious stones. The town is well built and populous: it is seated on the Elbe; 36 miles N. E. of Prague. Pop. 3750; of the circle, about 300,000. Long. 14. 17. E. lat. 50. 32. V.

LEUTOMISCHEL, a town of Bohemia, in the circle of Chrudim; with manufactures of cloths and dye-stuffs, and extensive distilleries; 20 miles E. S. E. of Chrudim.

LEUTSCH, a town of the Austrian states, in Carniola; 8 miles S. S. E. of Idria.

LEVANT. This word properly signifies the East (Italian), but it is used, when speaking of trade, for Turkey in Asia, comprehending Natolia, Syria, the island of Cyprus, &c. The Levant Sea means the E. part of the Mediterranean.

LEVEK. *See* CAMBODIA.

LEVEN, a river in Lancashire, which issues from the S. extremity of Windermere-water, and flows into Morecambe Bay.

LEVEN, a river of Scotland, in Dumbartonshire, which issues from Loch Lomond, and enters the estuary of the Clyde, below Dumbarton.

LEVEN, a river of Scotland, which rises in Kinross-shire, flows through Loch Leven, and crosses Fifeshire, to the town of Leven, where it enters Largo Bay.

LEVEN, a town of Scotland, in Fifeshire; with a good harbour, and some share in the coasting and Baltic trade. It stands on the W. side of Largo Bay, at the influx of the river Leven; 7 miles N. E. of Dysart.

LEVEN, LOCH, a lake of Scotland, in Kinross-shire, upwards of 10 miles in circumference, and somewhat of a circular form. It has several small islands, on one of which is a ruinous castle, where Mary, queen of Scots, was confined by the confederate lords, after she had separated from Bothwell; and on another, named St. Serf's Isle, is the ruin of a priory. On the E. side of the lake, near its outlet, stands the ruinous monastery of Portmoak.

LEVENZO. *See* ÆGADES.

LEVROUX, a town of France, department of Indre; 11 miles N. of Chateauroux.

LEWARDEN, or LEEUWARDEN, a strong town of the Netherlands, capital of Friesland. It has several canals in the streets, which, being continued to the sea, and to the most considerable towns in the province, are a great assistance to its trade. Many of the buildings, as well public as private, are magnificent. It is seated on the Ee; 28 miles W. of Groningen. Long. 5. 48. E. lat. 53. 13. N.

LEWENTZ, a town of Hungary, on a river of the same name; 25 miles N. E. of Gran.

LEWES, a borough in Sussex, with a market on Saturday; it returns two members to parliament. It had formerly twelve parish churches, now reduced to six, including those of the adjoining villages of Southover and Cliff. It is a very ancient place, and vestiges of its walls and castle, and of an extensive priory, still remain. Here are seven meeting-houses for dissenters; also a handsome county-hall, a free grammar school, a good charity school, and several charitable institutions. On a hill, about a mile from the town, is the race ground, which is accounted one of the best in England. Near this town was fought a battle, in 1263, when Henry III. and his son (afterward Edward I.) were made prisoners by the Earl of Leicester. Lewes is situate at the edge of the South Downs, 8 miles N. E. of Brighton, and 49 S. of London. Long. 0. 2. E. lat. 50. 55. N.

LEWES, a town of Delaware, in Sussex county, situate on Lewes Creek, 5 miles from its mouth in Chesapeake Bay, and 16 N. N. E. of Georgetown.

LEWIS, one of the most considerable of the Western Islands of Scotland, parted by two arms of the sea into two divisions, the southern of which is called Harris, and the northern Lewis: the former is annexed to the county of Inverness, but Lewis belongs to Ross-shire. It is about 60 miles in length from N. to S., and from 10 to 15 in breadth. The country in general is wild, bleak, bare of wood, and little fitted for cultivation; and the poorer inhabitants are the most wretched in the British dominions. Barley, oats, peas, rye, and potatoes, are the products of the soil. The hills are covered with heath, which affords shelter for various sorts of game. The lakes and streams abound with salmon, large red trout, &c., and there are good fisheries on the W. coast, which is annually visited by millions of herrings. There are several small villages, but Stornaway is the only town. The promontory at the N. extremity of the island is called the Butt of Lewis. Long. 6. 32. E. lat. 58. 33. N.

LEWIS, a county of New York, erected from Oneida county, in 1805. It is 54 miles in length, and 33 in breadth, and is nearly equally divided by Black River. Chief town, Martinsburg.

Lewis, a county of the N. W. part of Virginia, formed out of Harrison county, in 1816. This name is common to several townships and rivers of North America.

Lewisburg, a town of Pennsylvania, in Northumberland county, on the W. branch of the Susquehanna; 17 miles N. N. W. of Northumberland.

Lewisburg, a town of Virginia, chief of Greenbrier county, on the N. side of Greenbriar River; 250 miles W. N. W. of Richmond. Long. 81. 15. W. lat. 38. 10. N.

Lewisham, a village in the county of Kent, which, from it pleasant situation, and its proximity to the metropolis, has become the residence of several opulent citizens, who have many elegant houses here. It is 5 miles S. E. of London.

Lewistown, a town of Pennsylvania, chief of Mifflin county, seated on the Juniatta; 160 miles W. N. W. of Philadelphia. Long. 78. 13. W. lat. 40. 35. N.

Lewiston, a town of Delaware, in Sussex county, with considerable salt-works for manufacturing salt by the heat of the sun. It is seated on Lewis Creek, 3 miles above its entrance into Delaware Bay, and the same distance N. N. W. of the lighthouse on Cape Henlopen.

Lexington, a town of Kentucky, chief of Fayette county, and formerly the capital of the state. It has six edifices for public worship, a university, and a large court-house; and has a railway to the Ohio. The trade is considerable, and the manufactures numerous and flourishing. Three newspapers are published weekly. Near this town are to be seen curious sepulchres, full of human skeletons, which are fabricated in a method totally different from that now practised by the Indians. In the neighbourhood are the remains of two ancient fortifications, with ditches and bastions; one containing about six acres of land, and the other nearly three. Pieces of earthen vessels, a manufacture with which the Indians were never acquainted, have also been ploughed up near Lexington. These, with the fortifications and the sepulchres, have been urged as an argument that this country was formerly inhabited by a people farther advanced in the arts of life than the present Indians. Lexington stands in a fine tract of country, on the head waters of Elkhorn River; 24 miles E. S. E. of Frankfort, the present capital. Pop. 6997. Long. 84. 55. W. lat. 38. 15. N.

Lexington, a town of Virginia, chief of Rockbridge county; situate near the N. branch of James River; 150 miles W. by N. of Richmond.

Lexington, a town of Massachusets, in Middlesex county, celebrated for being the place where hostilities commenced between the British troops and the Americans, in 1775. It is 10 miles N. W. of Boston.

Leyden, a city of the Netherlands, in South Holland, seated on the ancient bed of the Rhine, which here almost expires in a number of small channels. It is famous for the long siege it sustained in 1574, against the Spaniards, during which 6000 of the inhabitants died of famine and pestilence. In honour of this siege a university was founded in 1575, celebrated for its colleges, botanical garden, anatomical theatre, astronomical observatory, cabinet of natural history, and valuable library; in 1807 it was almost destroyed by the blowing up of a vessel loaded with 40,000 lbs. of gunpowder. The principal church is a superb structure, and the old castle, town-house, custom-house, and house for orphans, deserve notice. Here are excellent manufactures of soap and indigo; and the vicinity produces the best Dutch butter and cheese. It stands on 50 islands, and has 145 bridges, the greater part built of freestone. The inhabitants are 28,600. Leyden is 4 miles E. of the German Ocean, and 20 S. W. of Amsterdam. Long. 4. 28. E. lat. 52. 8. N.

Leypa, a town of Bohemia, in the circle of Leutmeritz; seated on the Pubietz; 23 miles E. N. E. of Lumeritz.

Leyta, one of the Philippines; about 40 leagues in length, and 95 in circumference. Its soil, on the E. side, is very fertile; but the high mountains that intersect it from E. to W. occasion so great an alteration in the climate, that, when the inhabitants of one part of the island reap, the others sow; and they have two plentiful harvests in the year, to which the rivers descending from the mountains not a little contribute. The island contains 9000 inhabitants, who pay tribute in rice, wax, &c. Long. 124. 40. E. lat. 10. 50. N.

Liam-po. *See* Ming-po.

Libanus, or **Lebanon**, (Djebel el Sheikh,) a lofty ridge of mountains of Syria, extending from the vicinity of Tripoli to the borders of Palestine, about 30 or 40 miles from the sea. The highest point is 9600 feet above the sea, the summit being covered with snow a great part of the year. It is inhabited by the Druses, who pay tribute to the émir of Tripoli. The cedars, for which it was once so celebrated, have now almost disappeared, with the exception of one group, near the village of Eden, and which are believed by the Maronites and Greek Christians to be coeval with King Solomon. They are of great antiquity, and exceedingly picturesque, and surrounded by a grove of smaller ones. Near Damascus there are immense caverns, one of which can contain 4000 men. To the E. is a parallel chain called Antilibanus.

Libatta, a town of Guinea, in the country of Gabon; seated near the mouth of a river of the same name; 120 miles N. W. of Sette. Long. 8. 54. E. lat. 0. 58. S.

Libau, a town of Courland, on the Baltic; with a harbour for small ships. The chief articles of commerce are hemp and linseed. It is seated on a peninsula; 50 miles N. of Memel; and 80 W. of Mittau. Long. 21. 25. E. lat. 56. 30. N.

Liberia, a district on the coast of Africa; so named from its being colonized by liberated captives and free people of colour. Under the auspices of a colonization society, in America, the first settlers proceeded to Africa in 1822. Cape Mesurado, in lat. 6. 18. N., was purchased of the natives; the plan of a town, afterwards called Monrovia, was formed; and, as fresh emigrants arrived, they purchased additional tracts of country. The greater part of the early settlers from America were men of decided piety; and their just, humane, and benevolent policy, has given them an astonishing influence over the native tribes. In 1827 this sable community had risen completely above the pressure of urgent necessities. Monrovia was rapidly improving in accommodations and increasing in magnitude, and several fresh towns were already springing up. The soil is extremely fertile; the natives of the country, without tools, without skill, and with little labour, raising more grain and vegetables than they can consume, and often more than they can sell. Cattle, swine, fowls, ducks, goats, and sheep, thrive without feeding, and require no other care than to keep them from straying. Cotton, coffee, indigo, and sugar-cane, are all the spontaneous growth of the forests, and may be cultivated at pleasure, to any extent, by such as are disposed. The same may be said of rice, Indian corn, Guinea corn, millet, and too many species of fruits and vegetables to be enumerated. Add to all this, that winter is here unknown; the hills and plains are covered with perpetual verdure, and Nature is constantly pouring her treasures, all the year round, into the laps of the industrious. The trade and commerce extend to the coast, to the interior parts of the continent, and to foreign vessels, and is already valuable, and fast increasing. The chief exports are rice, palm oil, ivory, tortoiseshell, dye-woods, gold, hides, wax, and a small amount of coffee. The imports consist of the products and manufactures of the four quarters of the world. The harbour is seldom clear of European and American shipping, and the bustle and thronging of the streets show something already of the activity of the smaller seaports of the United States. Mechanics of nearly every trade are carrying on their various occupations, and not a child or youth in the colony but is provided with an appropriate school. The piety of the first settlers has continued to spread, and the standard of morals consequently remains high. The Sabbath is carefully regarded, and Sunday schools have been established for the benefit of the native children. The cheerful abodes of civilization and happiness—the flourishing settlements—the sound of Christian instruction, and scenes of Christian worship, which are heard and seen in this land of brooding pagan darkness—a thousand contented freemen, united in founding a new Christian empire, happy themselves, and the instrument of happiness to others—while they refresh the hearts, cannot fail to encourage the brightest anticipations of Christian philanthropists.

Liberty, a county in the E. part of the state of Georgia, North America; the chief towns are Sunbury and Riceborough.

Liberty, a town of Kentucky, in Mason county; with a ship-yard; seated on the Ohio; 1 mile above Limestone, and 5 miles N. N. E. of the town of Washington. There are several townships of this name in the United States.

Liberthen, a town of Hungary; with rich mines of copper and iron, and productive springs of blue vitriol; 122 miles E. by N. of Vienna. Pop. 1420.

Libongo, a town of Africa: on the Lufuna; near the sea; 50 miles S. S. W. of Bombi.

Libourne, a town of France; department of Gironde; with manufactures of light woollen stuffs, and a trade in wine and brandy; it is seated at the conflux of the Iller with the Dordogne; 20 miles E. N. E. of Bordeaux. Pop. 8520.

Lichfield. *See* Litchfield.

Lichstall, or Lichtollen, a town of Switzerland, in the canton of Basel; seated on the Ergetz; 7 miles S. E. of Basel.

Lichtenau, a town of Germany, in Hesse-Cassel; 15 miles S. E. of Cassel. Pop. 1150.

Lichtenau, a town of Franconia, in the territory of Nuremberg; with a fortress on the Rezel; 6 miles E. of Anspach.

Lichtenberg, a town of Franconia, in the principality of Bayreuth. In the neighbourhood are medicinal springs, quarries of marble, and mines of copper and iron; it is seated on the Selbnitz; 18 miles N. E. of Culmbach.

Lichtenfels, a town of Bavarian Franconia; with a trade in timber; seated on the Maine; 15 miles N. E. of Bamberg.

Lichtensteig, a town of the Swiss canton of St. Gall; seated on the Thur; 27 miles E. S. E. of Zurich. Long. 9. 5. E. lat. 47. 16. N.

Lichtenstein, a town of Saxony, in the circle of Erzgebirge; with a castle on a mountain; 6 miles N. E. of Zwickau. Pop. 2000.

Lichtenvord, a town of the Netherlands, in Guelderland; 42 miles S. of Leipsic.

Licola, a lake of Naples, formerly famous for excellent fish; but, in 1538, an earthquake happened, which changed one part of it into a mountain of ashes, and the other in a morass. It was anciently known by the name Lucrino, or the Lucrine Lake.

Lida, a town and castle of Lithuania, in the government of Grodno; 56 miles S. of Wilna. Long. 25. 34. E. lat. 53. 50. N.

Liddel, a river of Scotland, in Roxburghshire, and the only one in the county that flows southward. It forms the boundary with England, for 5 miles, till it enters the Esk, from Dumfries-shire, 3 miles above Longtown in Cumberland.

Lidford, a village in Devonshire, formerly a borough; with a castle. It is seated on the river Lid, at the edge of Dartmoor Forest; 7 miles N. of Tavistock.

Lidkioping, a town of Sweden, in W. Gothland, on the S. side of the lake Wenner, at the mouth of the Lida; 80 miles N. E. of Gotheburg. Pop. 1640.

LIEBENWALD, a town of Prussia, in Brandenburg, near which commences the Finow Canal, that unites the rivers Oder, Finow, and Havel. It is seated on the Havel; 25 miles N. of Berlin.

LIEBENWERDA, a town of Prussian Saxony; with a castle; seated on the Elster; 38 miles N. N. W. of Dresden.

LIEBENZELL, a town of Wirtemberg, near which is the bath of Zell: it is seated on the Nagold; 17 miles W. by N. of Stutgard.

LIEBEROSE, a town of Lusatia; with a castle. It is seated on the Spreewald; 20 miles W. of Guben.

LIEBSTADT, a town of W. Prussia; with a castle; 45 miles S. S. E. of Marienburg.

LIEGE, a province of Belgium; bounded by the grand duchy of Luxemburg, the Belgic provinces of Namur, S. Brabant, and Limburg, and the Prussian province of the Lower Rhine. It is fertile in corn and fruits, and contains mines of iron, lead, and coal, besides quarries of marble. Pop. 354,000.

LIEGE, a large, ancient, and strong city of the Netherlands; capital of the above province. Here the river Meuse is divided into three branches, which, after passing through the city, under several bridges, unite again. Liege is 4 miles in circumference, and has 16 gates: it has also 10 large suburbs, in which, and the city, there were formerly a great number of churches and religious houses, part of which are suppressed. The magnificent cathedral contains many relics; and the other public structures are the castle, the council-house, the hotel de ville, and the arsenal. There are manufactures of arms, clock-work, nails, cloth, leather, glass, &c., and a brisk trade. In 1792 the French took the city; they were driven thence in 1793, but entered it again in 1794; and it was afterwards annexed to France. In 1814, however, Liege, with its district, was delivered up to the allied forces. It 60 miles W. S. W. of Cologne. Pop. about 47,000. Long. 5. 35. E. lat. 50. 38. N.

LIEGNITZ. *See* LIGNITZ.

LIEN-TCHEOU, a city of China, of the first rank; in the province of Quang-tong. Its territories border on the kingdom of Tonquin, from which it is separated by inaccessible mountains. It is seated on the Lien-kiang, which forms a convenient harbour for Chinese barks; 325 miles W. S. W. of Canton. Long. 108. 40. E. lat. 21. 40. N.

LIERRE, a town of Belgium, in the province of Antwerp; with manufactures of woollen and cotton, besides extensive breweries and distilleries, and a trade in cattle. It is seated at the junction of the Great and Little Nethe; 10 miles S. E. of Antwerp.

LIESSE, a town of France, department of Aisne, famous for an image of the Virgin, to which a great number of pilgrims used to resort; 7 miles E. of Laon.

LIFFEY, a river of Ireland, which rises in the county of Wicklow, runs W. into Kildare, turning N. E. passes through the county and city of Dublin, below which it enters the Irish Sea.

LIFFORD, a town of Ireland, in the county of Donegal; situate on the Foyle; 11 miles S. S. W. of Donegal.

LIGNEROLLES, a town of France, department of Allier; 4 miles S. of Montluçon

LIGNIERES, a town of France, department of Cher; with a collegiate church, and a castle; 24 miles S. of Bourges. Pop. 2000.

LIGNITZ, or LEIGNITZ, a government of Prussian Silesia; including the former principalities of Glogau, Sagan, Lignitz, Karolath, with part of those of Jauer and Upper Lusatia. It is divided into the circles of Lowenburg, Bunslau, Goldberg, Lignitz, Luben, Glogau, Sprottau, Sagan, Friestadt, Grunburg, Gorlitz, Rothenburg, and Lauban. The climate is mild, and the soil in many places fertile: it is necessary, however, to import corn.

LIGNITZ, an ancient town of Prussia Silesia, and capital of the government of the same name; with a considerable trade in cloth and madder. It is surrounded by an earthen mound, and has four gates, but is not fortified. The old palace of the princes, though within the town, is surrounded with a distinct moat and high wall. The other remarkable objects are the castle, the council house, the two Lutheran churches, the Catholic church of St. John, and the superb chapel where the dukes of Lignitz and Brieg were buried. Here is also an academy founded by Joseph I., for the education of the sons of Silesian gentlemen, whether Protestants or Catholics. It is seated at the confluence of the Katzbach and the Schwartzwasser; 39 miles W by N. of Breslau, and 110 N. E. of Prague. 9600. Long. 16. 12. E. lat. 51. 12. N.

LIGNY, a village of Belgium, in the province of Namur; celebrated for a sanguinary engagement between the French and Prussians, on the 16th June, 1815, which was the prelude to the battle of Waterloo; 3 miles N. E. of Fleurus, and 11 W. N. W. of Namur.

LIGNY, a town of France, department of Meuse; with a castle and a collegiate church. The inhabitants are estimated at about 3000. It is seated on the Orney; 9 miles S. E. of Bar-le-Duc.

LIGORE, a town of the Malay peninsula; subject to Siam; situate on a river of the same name. Long. 100. 35. E. lat. 8. 18. N.

LIGUEIL, a town of France; department of Indre-et-Loire: 21 miles S. of Tours.

LIHONS, a town of France; department of Somme; 18 miles E. of Amiens.

LILIENTHAL, a town of Saxony; on the river Warp; 10 miles N. N. E. of Bremen.

LILLE. *See* LISLE.

LILLERS, a town of France; department of Pas-de-Calais; seated on the Navez; 17 miles N. W. of Arras. Pop. 4250.

LILLO, a fort of Belgium, in Brabant; on the N. side of the Scheldt; 9 miles N. N. W. of Antwerp.

LIMA, an intendancy of the republic of Peru;

bounded N. by Truxillo, E. by the Andes, S. by Arequipa, and W. by the Pacific Ocean.

LIMA, the capital of Peru, and an archbishop's see; with a university. This city was founded in 1534, by Pizarro, who gave it the name of Ciudad de los Reyes, or City of the Kings. This Spanish name it retains in all legal deeds, but is better known to foreigners by that of Lima. It is 4 miles long, and 2 broad, and surrounded by brick walls with ramparts and bastions. The streets are handsome and straight: the houses are generally only one story high, in consequence of the earthquakes. They have flat roofs, and trees are planted round them to keep off the heat of the sun. The river forms canals in the streets, which run to most of the houses, and serve to water the gardens, &c. The churches and convents are extremely rich; and many images of the saints are of gold, adorned with jewels. Here are the courts of the viceroy and the archbishop, the royal mint, and the court of the municipal body. All the provinces remit their products and manufactures to Lima, and are supplied hence with the necessary commodities. The inhabitants, estimated at 50,000, are rich, fond of dress and splendid retinues, and extremely superstitious. Lima is 90 miles from the Cordilleras, and 850 S. by E. of Quito. Callao is its port. Long. 76. 49. W. lat. 12. 1. S.

LIMALE, a town of Belgium, in Brabant; seated on the Dyle; 13 miles S. E. of Brussels.

LIMAVADY. *See* NEWTOWN LIMAVADY.

LIMBURG, a province of Belgium; bounded by Prussia, and the provinces of South and North Brabant, Liege, and Antwerp. It contains an area of 1600 square miles with 293,000 inhabitants. It has good arable ground, abounds in a fine breed of cattle, and contains mines of iron and lead. Maestricht is the capital.

LIMBURG, a town of Belgium, in the province of Liege; with a castle built of marble. Here is a manufacture of woollen cloths, and it is famous for excellent cheese. In the neighbourhood are quarries of different kinds of marble, and good mines of calamine and coal. Limburg was taken by the French, in 1793; but in 1814 they delivered it up to the allies. It is seated on a mountain near the river Weze; 20 miles E. of Liege. Long. 6. 3. E. lat. 50. 38. N.

LIMBURG, a town of Germany, in the duchy of Nassau; with a fine cathedral. The Austrians defeated the French on the heights near this place, in 1796. It is seated on the Lahn; 26 miles N. W. of Frankfort.

LIME, a town of Dorsetshire. *See* LYME REGIS.

LIMEKILNS, a town of Scotland, in Fifeshire; on the coast of the Forth. It is famous for great lime-works, and has a good tide harbour for small vessels; 3 miles S. of Dunfermline.

LIMERICK, a county of Ireland, in the province of Munster; bounded on the N. by the river Shannon, which separates it from the county of Clare; W. by Kerry; S. by Cork, and E. by Tipperary. It is 50 English miles long from E. to W., and 32 broad from N. to S., and contains an area of 622,975 acres. It is divided into 10 baronies, and 125 parishes, and sends two members to parliament. The principal rivers are the Deel, Maig, Comogue, Feale, Gal, and Blackwater, besides the noble river Shannon, which may rather be said to flow by the county. The surface of the county is tolerably level, but sheltered on the S. E. by a range of mountains called the Galtees; and the fertility of the soil is proverbial. To the N. of the Galtees lies the tract of land denominated, for its fertility, the Golden Vein; and on the banks of the Shannon lie the carlaghs, or swamps, on which a quantity of manure is annually deposited by the overflowing of the river.

LIMERICK, a city of Ireland; capital of the above county, and generally considered the metropolis of the province of Munster. It was formerly well fortified, and reckoned the second city in the kingdom, but has long since yielded that rank to Cork. Limerick is a county of itself, and a bishop's see, and is divided into the Irish and English towns, the latter being built on an island of the Shannon, called King's Island. It sends two members to parliament. The linen, woollen, and paper manufactures are carried on to a great extent; and the exports of provisions is considerable. Besides the cathedral and other churches, it has a modern episcopal palace, many hospitals, and other handsome public structures. King William was obliged to raise a siege of this city in 1690; but in 1691 the garrison surrendered on a very honourable capitulation. It is 40 miles S. S. E. of Galway, and 94 W. S. W. of Dublin. Long. 8. 54. W. lat. 52. 42. N.

LIMESOL, a town of the island of Cyprus; in the Mediterranean Sea. It is built of unburnt bricks, and is in a beautiful country. It is the see of a bishop.

LIMESTONE, or MAYSVILLE, a town of Kentucky, in Mason county; with a glass manufactory, a printing office, &c. It is seated on the S. side of the Ohio; 4 miles N. by E. of the town of Washington, and 500 by the river, below Pittsburg.

LIMMAT, a river of Switzerland, formed by the junction of the Mat and the Linth; the former issuing from the N. W. extremity of the Lake Wallenstadt, and the latter flowing from the S. The Limmat flows N. W., passes through the Lake of Zurich, and unites with the Aar below Baden.

LIMOGES, an ancient town of France, department of Upper Vienne. It is a trading place, and the inhabitants are estimated at 26,612. It is seated on the Vienne; 110 miles E. of Bordeaux. Long. 1 20. E. lat. 45. 50. N.

LIMOSIN, or LIMOUSIN, a late province of France, divided into Upper and Lower Limosin, the former of which is cold and hilly, but the latter is temperate and fertile. It contains mines of lead, copper, tin, and iron. It now forms the departments of Upper Vienne and Correze.

LIMOUX, a town of France; department of

Aude; with manufactures of woollen, leather, and soap. It is seated on the Aude; 50 miles S. E. of Toulouse. Pop. 5350.

LINCOLN, a maritime county of the United States; in the district of Maine; 200 miles in length, and 54 in breadth. It is bounded on the E. by Hancock county, W. by Cumberland, N. by Canada, and S. by the ocean. Wiscasset is the chief town.

LINCOLN, a town of Kentucky; in Mercer county, on the E. side of Dick River, a branch of the Kentucky; 12 miles S. E. of Danville. Chief town, Stamford.

LINCOLN, a city, and the capital of Lincolnshire; with a market on Friday. It is situate on the river Witham, is divided into the Upper and Lower Town, and has two suburbs. Formerly it contained 52 churches, now reduced to 15. It is a bishop's see. The cathedral stands on the brow of the hill, and is admired for its rich and light architecture. The great bell of the cathedral, called *Tom of Lincoln*, required 15 able men to ring it: it was broken while under repairs, in 1831. Here are several meeting-houses for the different denominations of dissenters, a catholic chapel, a national school, erected in 1814, and several other schools and charitable institutions. Of the castle, built by William I., few vestiges remain; but the ruins of religious houses are so numerous, that the very barns, stables, &c., are built with arched doors and windows. Newport Gate, on the N. side of the city, still remains, and is one of the noblest remnants of Roman architecture left in Britain. Lincoln is a county of itself, governed by a mayor. The chief trade is in coal, brought by the Trent and Fossdike; and oats and wool, which are sent by the Witham. Here is a small manufacture of camlets. It returns two members to parliament: it is 32 miles N. E. of Nottingham, and 131 N. by W of London. Long. 0. 25. W. lat. 53. 15. N.

LINCOLNSHIRE, a large maritime county of England; bounded on the N. by the Humber, which divides it from Yorkshire, E. by the German Ocean, S. E. by the Wash and Norfolk, S. by Cambridgeshire and Northamptonshire, S. W. by Rutlandshire, and W. by the counties of Leicester and Nottingham. It contains 1,893,100 acres; is divided into 38 hundreds, and 630 parishes; has one city, and 31 market towns: it sends four members to parliament, for the Lindsey and Kesteven divisions. The coast is flat, and, at low water, may be seen the submarine relics of a forest, which is a great natural curiosity. The principal rivers are the Humber, Trent, Witham, Welland, and Ancholm. This county is divided into three districts, called Holland, Kesteven, and Lindsey. The air is various. The soil, in many places, is very rich, the inland part producing corn in great plenty, and the fens, coleseed, and very rich pastures; whence their breed of cattle is larger than that of any other county of England, except Somersetshire; their horses are also excellent, and very large; their sheep are not only of the largest breed, but are clothed with a long thick wool, peculiarly fitted for the worsted and coarse woollen manufacturers; and many of the unimproved fens are devoted to the rearing of geese, the quills and feathers of which are sent in immense quantities to the London and other markets. In the N. W. part, the rivers Trent, Dune, and Idle, form an island, called Axholm, which is a rich tract, and produces much flax. To the N. E. is a large tract of heathy land, called the Wolds, in which great flocks of sheep are bred. The southern portion is, for the most part, enclosed and well inhabited. Lincolnshire has no considerable manufactures, and its trade is almost confined to the exchange of its produce for manufactured and grocery goods, and other considerable commodities.

LINCOLNTON, a town of North Carolina; chief of Lincoln county; 33 miles E. by S. of Morgantown, and 35 W. of Salisbury.

LINDAU, a town of Bavaria; with a castle and wall, deemed to be Roman works. The French took possession of this city in 1796; and it became subject to Bavaria in 1805. It is a trading place; seated on an island of the Lake of Constance, joined to the mainland by a long bridge; 25 miles E. S. E. of Constance, and 75 S. W. of Augsburg. Long. 9. 41. E. lat. 47. 32. N.

LINDAU, a town and castle of Germany, in the principality of Anhalt-Kothen; 5 miles N. of Zerbst.

LINDESNESS. *See* NAZE.

LINDENFELS, a town of Germany, in Hesse-Darmstadt; 22 miles N. N. E. of Manheim.

LINDISFARNE. *See* HOLY ISLAND.

LINGEN, a county of Germany, in Westphalia; divided into Upper and Lower; partly belonging to Prussia, and partly to Hanover.

LINGEN, a town of Hanover; with an excellent Calvinist academy. A little to the N. of it is a passage over the Elbe, called the Lingen Ferry. It is seated on the Elbe; 40 miles N. N. W. of Munster.

LIN-KEANG, a city of China, of the first rank; in the province of Kiang-si. It is thinly inhabited; but is of some note, on account of one of its villages being the general mart for all the drugs sold in the empire. It is seated on the Yu-ho; 410 miles N. by E. of Canton. Long. 115. 0. E. lat. 27. 58. N.

LINKIOPING, a government of Sweden, corresponding nearly to the old province of East Gothland. It lies along the Baltic, and contains 3280 square miles, with 160,000 inhabitants.

LINKIOPING, a town of Sweden; capital of the foregoing government, and a bishop's see. It is defended by a castle, and stands on the river Stoeng, near the lake Roxen; 112 miles S. W. of Stockholm.

LINLITHGOW, a borough of Scotland; capital of Linlithgowshire; seated on a rising ground, overlooking a lake at its E. end. It returns, with its contributories, one member to parliament. It has manufactures of leather, and in the neighbourhood are an extensive printfield, bleachfield, and two distilleries. Here the kings of Scotland had one of their noblest palaces, now in ruins; but the room is still shown in which Queen Mary was born. Linlithgow is

16 miles W. of Edinburgh. Long. 3. 35. W. lat. 55. 58. N.

LINLITHGOWSHIRE, or WEST LOTHIAN, a county of Scotland; 20 miles long, and 12 broad; bounded on the N. by the Frith of Forth, S. E. by Edinburghshire, S. W. by Lanarkshire, and N. W. by Stirlingshire. It is divided into 13 parishes. The surface is finely diversified with hill and dale: it is fertile in corn and pasture, and produces coal, iron, limestone, and lead. It is passed by the Edinburgh and Glasgow railway. The chief rivers are the Avon and Amond. It returns one member to parliament.

LINNHE, LOCH, an arm of the sea, on the W. coast of Scotland, which separates the counties of Argyle and Inverness. It extends in a N. E. direction from the Sound of Mull to Fort William, where it takes a northerly direction, and acquires the name of Loch Eil. Another branch, in a south-easterly direction, is called Loch Leven. This lake is bounded on each side by lofty mountains. The island of Lismore lies at its entrance, and in it are interspersed several smaller ones.

LINNICH, a town of the Prussian states; in the duchy of Juliers; seated on the river Roer; 5 miles N. N. W. of Juliers.

LIN-TCHEIN, a city of China, of the second rank; in the province of Chan-tong; seated on the great canal. Here is an octagonal tower, divided into eight stories, about 135 feet high, the walls of which are covered on the outside with porcelain; 187 miles S. of Peking.

LINTON, a town in Cambridgeshire; with a market on Thursday; seated on the river Granton; 10 miles S. E. of Cambridge, and 40 N. by E. of London.

LINTZ, the capital of Upper Austria, and a bishop's see: it has two castles, and considerable woollen manufactures. The French became masters of it in 1741, and again in 1800. It is seated on the right bank of the Danube, over which is a wooden bridge; 96 miles W. of Vienna. Long. 14. 16. E. lat. 48. 21. N. Pop. 17,000.

LINTZ, a town and citadel of the Prussian states; in the late electorate of Cologne; seated on the Rhine; 23 miles S. S. E. of Cologne.

LIPARI ISLANDS, a cluster of islands in the Mediterranean, lying to the N. of Sicily, to which they politically belong. They are all of volcanic origin, were feigned to be the residence of Æolus and Vulcan, and formerly called Æolian Islands. They are 12 in number, and nearly as follows, in the order of their size; Lipari, Stromboli, Volcano, Salini, Felicuda, Alicuda, Panaria, Volcanello, Vacheluse, Lisca, Dattolo, and Tila Navi. They produce great quantities of alum, sulphur, nitre, cinnabar, and most kinds of fruits, particularly raisins, currants, and figs. Some of their wines are much esteemed, particularly the Malvasia.

LIPARI, the largest and most fertile of the Lipari Islands; about 15 miles in circumference. Pop. 15,000. It has not suffered from subterraneous fires for ages past, though it everywhere bears the marks of its former volcanic state. It abounds with the currant grape: cotton also grows here; and great quantities of pumice are exported. It has a town of the same name, which is a bishop's see, and stands on the S. E. side of the island. It is 26 miles N. N. E. of Patti, in Sicily. Long. 15. 30. E. lat. 38. 35. N.

LIPNO, a town of Poland; in the palatinate of Ploczko; 33 miles N. N. W. of Ploczko.

LIPOUREC, a town of Poland; in the palatinate of Cracow; 22 miles W. of Cracow.

LIPPE, a river of Westphalia, which flows W. by Paderborn, Lippstadt, Ham, and Dorsten, and joins the Rhine above Wesel.

LIPPE-DETMOLD, a principality of Germany, in Westphalia; bounded by the Prussian states and Hanover, and containing an area of 430 square miles, with 73,000 inhabitants. It is mountainous almost throughout, and contains large forests of oak and beech.

LIPPSPRING, a town of Prussian Westphalia; near the source of the Lippe; 6 miles N. of Paderborn.

LIPPSTADT, a strong town of Westphalia; with a good trade in timber. It stands on the river Lippe; 18 miles W. of Paderborn. Long. 8. 28. E. lat. 51. 41. N.

LIQUE, a town of France; department of Pas de Calais; 12 miles W. of St. Omer.

LIRIA, a town of Spain, in the province of Valencia, (the Edera of the Carthaginians, and the Edeta of the Romans.) It has manufactures of linen, soap, and earthenware; also brandy distilleries; 20 miles N. N. W. of Valencia. Pop. 9350.

LIS, a river of Asiatic Russia, which rises in a lake of the same name, and falls into the Yenisei. Long. 90. 14. E. lat. 62. 20. N.

LIS, a river which rises in France, in the department of Pas de Calais, flows by Aire, St. Venant, and Armentieres, into Flanders, where it passes by Menin, Courtray, and Deynse, and joins the Scheldt at Ghent.

LISBON, the capital of Portugal, and the see of a patriarch and an archbishop; with a university. It is seated on the N. side of the Tagus, 10 miles from its mouth, and built in the form of an amphitheatre, on seven hills, not broad, but 6 miles in length. The city is walled round, and it has so increased by degrees, particularly towards the W., that the old walls now divide the two dioceses; the E. part under the archbishop, and the W. under the patriarch. The harbour, which is capable of containing 1000 ships in the greatest safety, is defended by two forts, and before the entrance to the city is the fort of Belem. Near this is a grand aqueduct, between two hills, which conveys water to a great reservoir at one of the extremities of Lisbon. In the middle of the city, on one of the hills, is a citadel, which commands the whole place. The cathedral, on another eminence, is ancient and gloomy; but the riches of the Portuguese have rendered it magnificent. The royal palace, which fronts the river, is large and magnificent, and contains a library, collected at a vast expense by John V. Lisbon was almost destroyed by an earthquake in 1755, but has been handsomely rebuilt. It contains many beautiful edifices; 40 parish churches, 99 chapels, 75 convents of both sexes, and 258,000 inhabitants. There are public walks, two theatres, and a circus for the bull-feasts. The manufactures are in a backward state, but the trade is very considerable, and many foreign merchants, both catholic and protestant, reside here; this city being the grand magazine for all goods brought from Brazil, and the colonies belonging to Portugal. In December, 1807, it was entered by the French, who retained possession till August 1808, when they evacuated it after the battle of Vimiera, in which they were defeated by the British. The inhabitants of Lisbon are described as superstitious, vindictive, and meanly acquiescing under power; 178 miles W. by N. of Seville, and 255 S. by W. of Madrid. Long. 9. 5. W. lat. 38. 42. N. *See* PORTUGAL.

LISBURNE, a borough of Ireland, in the county of Antrim, returning one member to parliament; with manufactures of linen, cloth, muslin, and cambric. It is seated on the Laggan; 8 miles S. W. of Belfast.

LISCA, or LISCA BIANCA, one of the Lipari islands; 3 miles S. W. of Stromboli. It is a small desert spot.

LISIEUX, a town of France, in the department of Calvados. It has a good trade, particularly in linen cloth, and is seated on the Touque; 12 miles from the sea, and 40 S. W. of Rouen. Pop. 11,250. Long. 0. 14. E. lat. 49. 9. N.

LISLE, a strong city of France, in the department of Nord, and one of the most commercial towns in France. The inhabitants are estimated at 69,860. Its citadel is supposed to be the strongest in Europe, next to that of Turin. The streets and squares are adorned with noble buildings, particularly the Great Square and the Little Square; and among the public structures are the exchange, a magazine of vast extent, and a general hospital. The manufactures are numerous, comprising camlets, serges, cotton, linen, silk, velvet, lace, &c. Lisle was taken by the allies in 1708, but was restored by the treaty of Utrecht in 1713, in consideration of the demolition of the fortifications of Dunkirk. In 1792 it sustained a severe bombardment from the Austrians. It is seated in a rich and marshy soil, on the Deule; 18 miles E. of Tournay, and 145 N. N. E. of Paris. Long. 3. 4. E. lat. 50. 38. N.

LISMORE, one of the Hebrides of Scotland; at the entrance of Loch Mull, on the coast of Argyleshire. It is a fertile island, 9 miles long and 2 broad, and was anciently the residence of the bishop of Argyle.

LISMORE, a town of Ireland, in the county of Waterford, and a bishop's see united to Waterford. The cathedral is spacious and handsome, but the town is now a small place. It stands on the Blackwater; 26 miles N. E. of Cork.

LISONZO, a river of Austrian Italy, in Friuli, which enters the Gulf of Trieste.

LISSA, an island in the Gulf of Venice; on the coast of Austrian Dalmatia. Here is a fishery of pilchards and anchovies; and it produces excellent wine, and abundance of oil and almonds. It is 56 miles W. of Ragusa. Pop. 7550. Long. 17. 0. E. lat. 42. 59. N.

LISSA, a town of Prussian Poland; near the borders of Silesia. In 1707 it was laid waste by the Russians; but it has been rebuilt, with great improvement, and carries on a great trade. It is 65 miles W. of Kalisch. Pop. 7550. Long. 16. 35. E. lat. 52. 0. N.

LISSA, a village of Prussian Silesia; on the Weistritz; 6 miles N. W. of Breslau; celebrated for a victory gained by the Prussians over the Austrians, in 1757.

LITCHFIELD, or LICHFIELD, a city of Staffordshire, with markets on Tuesday and Friday. It is a county of itself, and, united with Coventry, forms an episcopal see. It has three parish churches, besides the cathedral, which is a beautiful structure, and walled in like a castle. Litchfield is the birthplace of two celebrated contemporaries, Samuel Johnson and David Garrick. The city is governed by two bailiffs, &c., and sends two members to parliament. It is seated on both sides of a small river, which soon afterwards joins the Trent; 16 miles N. of Birmingham, and 119 N. W. of London. Long. 1. 44. W. lat. 52. 41. N.

LITCHFIELD, a mountainous county of Connecticut, bounded N. by Massachusets, E. by Hartford county, S. E. by New Haven county, S. W. by Fairfield county, and W. by New York; and containing 40,448 inhabitants, chiefly farmers. The soil is fertile, yielding large crops of wheat and Indian corn, and affording fine pasture.

LITCHFIELD, the capital of the above county, situated in an elevated plain. It is a good agricultural town, and contains numerous mills and manufacturing establishments; 8 miles N. N. W. of New Haven. Pop. 4038.

LITHUANIA, the former name of an extensive tract of country lying between Poland and Russia, now forming the three Russian governments of Wilna, Grodno, and Minsk. It was divided into Lithuania Proper, and Samogitia, and in 1569 was united to Poland under one elective king. It is a flat country, fertile in corn, and produces honey, wood, pitch, and vast quantities of wool; also excellent little horses, which are never shod, their hoofs being very hard. There are vast forests, in which are bears, wolves, elks, wild oxen, lynxes, beavers, wild cats, &c.; and eagles and vultures are very common.

LITIZ, a town of Pennsylvania, in Lancaster county, and a settlement of the Moravians; 66 miles W. by N. of Philadelphia.

LITSCHAU, a town and castle of Austria, on the frontiers of Bohemia, 23 miles N. W. of Horn.

LITTAU, a town of Moravia, on the river March, 9 miles N. N. E. of Olmutz. Pop. 2350.

LIVADIA, a province of Greece, bounded on the N. by Epirus and Thessaly, E. by the Archipelago, S. by the Morea, and W. by the Mediterranean. It is 180 miles long, and about 40 in mean breadth, and includes the most celebrated portion of ancient Greece. The soil is very productive in wine, oil, and fruits.

LIVADIA, or LEBADIA, a town of Greece, capital of the above province, with a castle. It has a brisk trade in wool, corn, and rice: it is seated on the Gulf of Lepanto, 50 miles N. W. of Athens. Long. 23. 20. E. lat. 38. 30. N.

LIVENZA, a river of Austrian Italy, which runs on the confines of Trevisano and Friuli, and enters the Gulf of Venice between the mouth of the Piava and the town of Caorlo.

LIVERPOOL, a borough in Lancashire, with markets on Tuesday, Wednesday, and Saturday. Up to the close of the seventeenth century it was a very inconsiderable place, having only one church, which was a chapel of ease to Walton, a village 3 miles off. In 1669 an act was passed to make it a distinct parish, and erect a new church. Since this period it has been gradually advancing in importance; and with respect to population and commerce, it is become the second port in the kingdom. It extends three miles along the E. bank of the river Mersey, and about a mile in average breadth; contains 23 churches and chapels for the Establishment, a much greater number of meeting-houses for dissenters, five Roman Catholic chapels, and a Jews' synagogue. Among the public buildings, which comprise numerous specimens of architectural taste, the most important are the town hall, exchange buildings, lyceum, Wellington rooms, corn exchange, infirmary, St. John's market, blue coat school, dispensary, asylum for the blind, theatre, athenæum, music hall, news room, custom-house, and a borough gaol on the Howardian plan. The streets are generally spacious, some of them elegant, and lighted with gas. At the head of the institutions for literary and scientific pursuits is the Royal Liverpool Institution, opened in 1817, at an expense of 30,000*l.* To enumerate the asylums for the wretched and unfortunate, of every description and denomination, would be altogether incompatible with our limits. The increase and prosperity of Liverpool have been greatly promoted by the enterprise and skill of its inhabitants, by its local advantages, commanding the trade of Ireland and America, and by the wisdom of the corporation, in abolishing all exclusive laws, and encouraging every species of industry and commercial talent. The principal manufactures, besides those connected with the shipping, which employ an immense number of persons, are fine porcelain, watches, glass, iron, salt, copperas, &c. The watch movement and tool business is almost confined to this part of the country, and the breweries, soap works, brass and iron foundries, sugar-houses, &c. are on an extensive scale. Few towns possess accommodations for shipping at all comparable to Liverpool; it has, at present, six docks, the Dry Dock, Salthouse Dock, King's Dock, Queen's Dock, George's Dock, Prince's Dock, North Dock, and Brunswick Dock, which, with their basins, occupy nearly 100 acres of land. The estuary of the Mersey may be properly termed an arm of the sea, opening to this port a ready access to the Western Sea; and ships of any burden may come up fully laden to the town; though the sand-banks which enclose the channels are continually shifting, proper precautions are taken in removing the beacons, buoys, &c.; while the system of canal navigation opens a communication inland with all parts of the kingdom: and the inland trade is still more commanded by the extensive system of railways with which the town is connected. The first of these is that to Manchester, which was the first one of importance opened in the kingdom, Sept. 15th, 1830; by means of this railway and the Grand Junction it is connected with Birmingham, from whence other lines diverge into the N., and to London. This port is now estimated to engross a fourth part of the foreign trade of Britain, a sixth of its general trade, and to furnish one-twelfth of the shipping: its customs amount to nearly 4,000,000*l.* and its exports exceed even those of the metropolis. One of the few eminent individuals to whom Liverpool has given birth, was Legh Richmond, author of the Dairyman's Daughter, and other celebrated tracts. He died at his living of Turvey, in Bedfordshire, in 1827. The town is governed by a mayor, and sends two members to parliament. It is 48 miles S. of Lancaster, and 206 N. W. of London. Long. 3 W. lat. 53. 22. N.

LIVERPOOL, a town of New South Wales, Northumberland county, 20 miles W. by S. of Sydney. It has a straggling appearance, but is very neat and pleasant, and has several public buildings.

LIVERPOOL, a town of Nova Scotia, in Queen's county, with a harbour at the mouth of a river of its name, 58 miles N. W. of Halifax. Long. 64. 15. W. lat. 44. 10. N.

LIVINGSTON, a town of New York, in Columbia county, on the E. side of the Hudson, 11 miles S. of Hudson.

LIVONIA, a province of Russia, which, with that of Esthonia, has been reciprocally claimed and possessed by Russia, Sweden, and Poland, and, for more than two centuries, was a perpetual scene of the most bloody wars. It was finally wrested from the Swedes by Peter the Great: was confirmed to the Russians by the peace of Nystadt, in 1721, and now forms the government of Riga, or Livonia. It is 250 miles long, and 150 broad; bounded on the N. by the government of Esthonia, and S. by Courland. The land is fertile, but is only partially cultivated; the products are rye, barley, flax, and linseed. In the forests are wolves, bears, elks, rein-deer, stags, and hares. The domestic animals are numerous, but the sheep bear very bad wool. The peasantry are in a state of great degradation.

LIVORNO. *See* LEGHORN.

LIZARD, a peninsula on the S. coast of Cornwall, and the most southern point of land in England. On it are two lighthouses. The Lizard Point is in long. 5. 11. W. lat. 49. 58. N.

LIZIER, ST., a town of France, department

of Arriege, seated on the Salat; 50 miles S. E. of Auch. Long. 1. 9. E. lat. 43. 0. N.

LLANBEDER, a corporate town of Wales, in Cardiganshire, with a market on Tuesday, and a considerable traffic in horses, cattle, hogs, salted butter, and tanned and raw hides. It is seated on the Teifi, over which is a bridge into Caermarthenshire; 27 miles E. of Cardigan, and 209 W. by N. of London.

LLANDAFF, an ancient city of Wales, in Glamorganshire, being an episcopal see; but it is a small place, and has no market. The body of its ancient cathedral was rebuilt in 1751, but without cross aisles. Near it are some ruins of the ancient castellated mansion of the bishop. It is seated on the Taafe, and has the benefit of a tolerably good harbour, which opens into the Severn. It is 2 miles N. W. of Cardiff, and 163 W. of London. Long. 3. 13. W. lat. 51. 29. N.

LLANDAFF, a township of the United States, in New Hampshire, Grafton county.

LLANDILO-VAWR, a town of Wales, in Caermarthenshire, with a market on Saturday, and a considerable manufacture of flannel. Near it are the picturesque remains of Dinevwar castle, formerly the residence of the native princes of Wales. It is seated on the side of a hill, on the river Towy, 13 miles E. of Caermarthen, and 202 W. of London.

LLANDOVERY, a town of Wales, in Caermarthenshire, with a market on Friday. It is seated on the Towy, at its conflux with the Braun, 26 miles E. N. E. of Caermarthen, and 191 W. of London.

LLANELLY, a town of Wales, in Caermarthenshire, with a considerable trade in iron and coal; seated on a creek of the Bristol Channel, 16 miles S. S. E. of Caermarthen, and 217 W. of London.

LLANERCH-Y-MEDD, a town of North Wales, in the county of Anglesey, with a manufacture of snuff; 253 miles from London.

LLANFAIR, a town of Wales, with a market on Saturday. It is seated on the banks of the river Verniew, 14 miles W. of Newton, and 180 W. by N. of London.

LLANFYLLIN, a town of Wales, in Montgomeryshire, with a market on Thursday; seated in a flat, among hills, near the river Cain. It is 15 miles N. by W. of Montgomery, and 186 W. of London.

LLANGADDOCK, a town of Wales in Caermarthenshire, with a market on Tuesday; 18 miles E. by N. of Carmarthen, and 195 W. of London.

LLANGOLLEN, a town of Wales, in Denbighshire, in the Vale of Llangollen, with a market on Saturday. Near it, on a steep mountain, are the remains of Castle Dinas, once a strong place; and about 2 miles distant is the beautiful ruin of Valle Crucis abbey. The town stands on the Dee, over which is a beautiful ancient bridge; 2 miles S. S. W. of Wrexham, and 184 N. W. of London.

LLANIDLOES, a town of Wales, in Denbighshire, with a market on Saturday, and a considerable manufacture of fine flannels, &c. It is seated at the confluence of the Severn and Clewedog, 13 miles S. W. of Newton, and 188 N. W. of London.

LLANRWST, a town of Wales, in Denbighshire, with markets on Tuesday and Saturday. Here are two churches, and the town is the centre of the business of the Vale of Conway. It is seated on the Conway, over which is a bridge into Caernarvonshire; 20 miles W. S. W. of Denbigh, and 220 N. W. of London.

LLANTRISSAINT, a town of Wales; in Glamorganshire; with a market on Friday. It is governed by a portreeve, and unites with Cardiff, Swansea, &c., in sending one member to parliament. It had a castle, which is nearly destroyed. It is 12 miles N. W. of Cardiff, and 171 W. of London.

LLAUGHARM, a town of Wales, in Caermarthenshire; with a market on Saturday. It stands at the mouth of the Towy, where, on a low rock, are the ruins of an ancient castle; and on the other side of the river are the remains of that of Llanstephan. Laugharm is 7 miles S. W. of Caermarthen, and 223 W. by N. of London.

LLERENA, a town of Spain; in Estremadura; 63 miles N. of Seville.

LLOUGHOR, or LLYCHWYR, a corporate town of Wales; in Glamorganshire; on the left bank of a river of the same name: it is contributory, with Swansea, in sending one member to parliament. It was the Leucarum of Antoninus. It is 312 miles W. of London.

LO, ST., a town of France, department of La Manche; with manufactures of serges, shalloons, ribbons, and gold and silver lace; seated on the Vire; 125 miles W. by N. of Paris. Pop. 7600.

LOANDO, capital of the Portuguese settlements in Angola. It has a good harbour, formed by the island of Loando, lying a little off the coast. The town is large and handsome, considering the country; containing 3000 houses, built of stone, and covered with tiles, besides a vast number of huts made of straw and earth. It is 260 miles S. S. W. of St. Salvador. Long. 13. 15. E. lat. 8. 50. S.

LOANDO, an island of the Atlantic; near the coast of Angola; about 20 miles long, and only 1 broad, and divided from the continent by a narrow channel. Goats and sheep are numerous. It produces no grain, but yields the best water in all the neighbourhood.

LOANGO, a kingdom of Western Africa; to the N. of the river Zaire or Congo. It includes Loango Proper, and the districts of Mayomba and Malemba, which are subject to the king of Loango: it is said to extend more than 400 miles along the coast, from the Zaire to Cape St. Catherine. The climate is said to be very fine, and never subject to hurricanes, nor even to violent winds. Rain rarely occurs, but the dews are sufficient for vegetation. The land is fertile, yielding, with very little of agricultural skill or labour, three crops of millet in a year. The potato and yam are abundant; and there are a great number of trees whence palm-wine is drawn. The women cultivate the ground, sow, and get in the harvest. The inhabitants are well-made, mild, and tractable.

LOANGO, the capital of the above kingdom; with a harbour, at the mouth of the Quiloa. The streets are wide, and lined with palm-trees, bananas, and bacavas. The houses are oblong, and have only a ground floor; separated from each other, and fenced round with a hedge of palm-twigs, canes, or bulrushes. In the centre of the city is a large square, fronting the royal palace, which forms another square, a mile and a half in compass, surrounded by a palisado of stately palm-trees. The principal trade consists in elephants' teeth, palm-cloth, copper, tin, lead, iron, and slaves. It is 230 miles W. N. W. of St. Salvador. Long. 12. 30. E. lat. 4. 40. S.

LOANO, or LOVANO, a town of the Sardinian states; in the territory of Genoa; near the sea; 6 miles S. S. W. of Finale. Pop. 4000.

LOBAU, a town of West Prussia; with a castle, where the bishop of Culm resides; 45 miles E. by N. of Culm.

LOBAU, a town of Saxony, in Upper Lusatia; which has a trade in grey, striped, and white linens; 13 miles S. E. of Bautzen.

LOBENSTEIN, a town of Saxony; in the circle of Voigtland; seated on the Lemnitz; 22 miles N. N. E. of Culmbach. Long. 11. 52. E. lat. 50. 21. N. Pop. 3000.

LOBOA, a town of Spain; in Estremadura; seated on the Guadiana; 22 miles E. of Badajoz.

LOBSTADT, a town of Saxony; in the circle of Meissen; 10 miles S. S. E. of Leipsic.

LOBURG, a town of Prussian Saxony; in the government of Magdeburg; 22 miles E. of Magdeburg.

LOCANA, a town of the Sardinian states; in Piedmont; seated in a fine valley, on the river Orco; 25 miles S. of Aosta. Pop. 5792.

LOCARNO, a town of Italy, capital of a baliwick belonging to the Swiss. It contains three convents, and a small Franciscan monastery on a rock overhanging the valley, and commanding a view of the lake Maggiore; 56 miles N. by W. of Milan. Long. 8. 31. E. lat. 46. 10. N.

LOCHABER, a district of Scotland; in Inverness-shire; bounded on the E. by Badenoch, W. by Moydart, N. by Glengary, and S. by Lorn. The country is bleak, mountainous, and rugged. The inhabitants pay little attention to any commerce, except the sale of their black cattle; and the only lands cultivated are a few acres around the huts of those who tend their flocks. Here the Pretender erected his standard in 1745.

LOCHENITZ, a town of Prussia; in the province of Bradenburg; on the river Rando; 16 miles N. E. of Prentzlo.

LOCHER MOSS, a morass of Scotland; in Dumfries-shire; 10 miles long and 3 broad, extending down by Dumfries to Solway Frith, and divided into two parts by a river called Locher Water, which abounds with excellent pike. Oak, fir birch, and hazel trees, also anchors, pieces of vessels, &c., have been dug up in different parts of this moss.

LOCHES, a town of France; department of Indre-et-Loire; with a strong castle on a rock. In the collegiate church is the tomb of the celebrated Agnes Sorel, mistress of Charles VII., to whose patriotic exhortations that monarch owed almost all his glory. Loches is seated on the Indre, near a forest; 15 miles S. of Amboise, and 20 S. W. of Tours.

LOCHMABEN, a borough of Scotland; in Dumfries-shire; with a manufacture of coarse linen; seated on the W. side of the Annan; 8 miles N. E. of Dumfries.

LOCHRIDA, or OCRIDA, a town in the province of Albania, and a Greek archbishop's see. It is well fortified, and seated on a hill, near a lake of its name; 62 miles S. E. of Durazzo. Long. 20. 40. E. lat. 41. 40. N.

LOCHTA, a seaport of Sweden; seated on a bay of the Gulf of Bothnia; 30 miles S. of Tornea. Long. 24. 16. E. lat. 64. 20. N.

LOCHWINNOCH, a town of Scotland; in Renfrewshire; with a considerable manufacture of cotton. It is seated on Castle Semple Loch; 6 miles S. W. of Paisley.

LOCHY, LOCH, a lake of Scotland; in Inverness-shire; 14 miles long, and from one to two broad. Out of it flows the river Lochy, which, about a mile below, receives the Spean, and their united stream enters Loch Eil, at Fort William.

LOCKARTSBURG, a town of Pennsylvania, in Luzerne county; situate on the point formed by the confluence of the Tioga with the Susquehanna; 60 miles N. N. W. of Wilkesbarre.

LOCKERBY, a town of Scotland; in Dumfries-shire; with a trade in linen and woollen cloth; and one of the largest lamb fairs in Scotland on the 2nd of August, O.S.; seated near the Annan; 12 miles E. by N. of Dumfries, and 66 from Edinburgh.

LOCLE, a town of Switzerland, in an elevated valley of the same name, in the canton of Neufchatel; famous for watchmakers, laceweavers, goldsmiths, cutlers, and enamellers; 9 miles N. W. of Neufchatel.

LODDON, a town in Norfolk; with a market on Friday; 8 miles S. E. of Norwich, and 112 N. E. of London.

LODEVE, a town of France, department of Herault; with manufactures of silk, hats, &c. During the late war it supplied a great part of the clothing for the army. It is seated on the Lergues; 30 miles W. by N. of Montpelier. Long. 3. 20. E. lat. 43. 43. N. Pop. 9031.

LODI, a town of Austrian Italy, in the government of Milan; capital of a province of the same name, and a bishop's see; with a fortress. It has manufactures of porcelain; and the Parmesan cheese made here is esteemed the best of its kind. The French defeated the Austrians at this place in 1796; at which engagement Napoleon first displayed his heroism; in 1799 they were, however, totally defeated by the Russians, but regained possession in 1800. It is seated on the Adda; 18 miles

S. E. of Milan. Long. 9. 30. E. lat. 45. 18. N. Pop. 12,000.

Lodomeria. *See* Galicia.

Loffingen, a town of Germany, in Baden; with a medicinal bath; 3 miles W. S. W. of Huiffengen.

Loffoden Islands, off the coast of Norway; between lat. 67. 28. and 68. 46. N. They are elevated, and are covered with snow. Five of them are inhabited. Pop. 4520; engaged in the fishery off the coast.

Lofsta, a town of Sweden, in the province of Upland; with extensive iron-works. These works were destroyed by the Russians, in 1719, but have since been again erected. Pop. 2570. It is 39 miles N. of Upsal.

Logierait, a town of Scotland, in Perthshire; noted for its distillation of whisky; seated on the Tummel; 22 miles N. N. W. of Perth.

Logrono, a town of Spain; in the province of Burgos; seated on the Ebro, in a country abounding with excellent fruits and good wines. It is 62 miles E. of Burgos, and 155 N. N. E. of Madrid. Long. 2. 20. E. lat. 42. 22. N. Pop. 7500.

Logrono, a town of Chili; capital of Melipilla. Long. 71. 16. W. lat. 33. 38. N.

Lohagur, a celebrated fortress of Hindostan; province of Dowlatabad; now belonging to the British; 20 miles N. W. of Poonah.

Loheia, a town of Arabia, in Yemen; on the coast of the Red Sea. It has a great trade in coffee, brought from the neighbouring hills; in the vicinity is a mountain which affords a considerable quantity of mineral salt. It has no harbour, and the smallest vessels are obliged to anchor at a distance from the town; 180 miles N. N. W. of Mocha. Long. 42. 50. E. lat. 15. 42. N.

Loja. *See* Loxa.

Loir-et-Cher, a department of France; bounded on the N. E. by the province of Loiret, N. W. by that of Sarthe, S. by that of Indre, S. E. by that of Cher, and S. W. by that of Indre-et-Loire. Area, 2710 square miles. Pop. 227,527. It takes its name from the rivers Loire and Cher; the former of which joins the Sarthe above Angers; and the latter runs into the Loire 10 miles below Tours. Blois is the capital.

Loire, the principal river of France; which rises in the department of Ardeche, and falls into the Atlantic about 40 miles below Nantes, watering a vast plain of more than 600 miles, and dividing France almost into two equal parts. By means of the Languedoc canal it establishes a communication between the Atlantic and Mediterranean, and facilitates the commercial operations of the kingdom.

Loire, a department of France, adjoining those of Rhone and Isere. Area, 2150 square miles. Pop. 343,554. It has its name from the river Loire, which flows N. through its whole length. Montbrison is the capital.

Loire, Upper, a department of France, comprising the Velay and that part of the evennes dependent on the former province of Languedoc. Area, 2000 square miles. Pop. 276,830. It takes its name from the river Loire, which flows through it from the S. to the N. E. Le Puy is the capital.

Loire, Inferieure, a department of France, containing part of the ancient province of Bretagne. Area, 3000 square miles. Pop. 300,000. It has its name from the river Loire, which crosses it from E. to W. and then enters the ocean. Nantes is the capital.

Loiret, a department of France, comprising part of the former province of Orleanois. Area, 2750 square miles. Pop. 291,394. It has its name from a small river that runs into the Loire. Orleans is the capital.

Loitz, a town of Prussia; in Pomerania; with a castle; seated on the Peene; 25 miles S. of Stralsund.

Loldong, a town and fortress of Hindostan; on the N. E. border of the province of Delhi, and on the river Pattereah, 8 miles above its conflux with the Ganges, and 100 N. N. E. of Delhi. Long. 78. 38. E. lat. 29. 47. N.

Lokeren, a large town of Belgium; in East Flanders; with various manufactures, and a considerable trade. It is seated on the Darme; 12 miles N. E. of Ghent. Pop. 15,000.

Lombardo-Venetian Kingdom, or Austrian Italy, a kingdom of Italy, belonging to the House of Austria. It is bounded on the E. by Illyria; S. E. by the Adriatic; S. by the States of the Church, Parma, and Modena; W. by Piedmont; and N. by Switzerland and Austria; and is divided into the governments of Milan and Venice. Pop. 4,065,000. The country is well cultivated, and is watered by the finest lakes and rivers of Italy. It was erected into a kingdom in 1815; and, though declared to be a monarchy inseparable from the Austrian empire, it has a constitution of its own, and a prince of the imperial family at its head, who has the title of viceroy, and resides at Milan.

Lombez, a small town of France; department of Gers. It is seated on the Save; 27 miles S. W. of Toulouse. Pop. 1536.

Lombok, an island of the East Indies; between Bally and Sumbava; 50 miles long and 45 broad. It is very mountainous, but covered with wood and verdure. At the town of Bally on the E. side, in the Strait of Allas, and in the many flourishing villages of the coast, European ships, passing to the E., are well supplied. The inhabitants, originally emigrants from Hindostan, retain most Hindoo customs.

Lombok, a strait formed by the island of Bally W. and that of Lombok E. The S. entrance is in long. 115. 43. E. and lat. 8. 45. S. where is a large island called Banditti Island, to the W. of which there is no passage. Owing to the extreme rapidity of the tides, navigation is here extremely dangerous.

Lomond, Loch, a lake of Scotland, in Dumbartonshire; 30 miles long, and from 1 to 9 wide. It contains several islands, some of which are inhabited, and adorned with antique ruins, concealed among ancient yews; and others rise into high rocky cliffs, the habitation of the osprey. On the E. side is the mountain Benlomond, which rises to the height of 3240 feet; and the river Leven issues from its S. extremity.

LONATO, a town of Austrian Italy; in the government of Milan; 12 miles E. S. E. of Brescia.

LONCARTY, a village of Scotland; in Perthhire; signalized by the great victory obtained by the Scots over the Danes, in 970. It has extensive bleaching grounds; and is seated near the Tay, 5 miles N. of Perth.

LONDON, the metropolis of Great Britain; one of the largest and most opulent cities in the world; mentioned by Tacitus as a considerable commercial place in the reign of the Roman emperor Nero. In its most extensive view, as the metropolis, it may be said to consist of five great portions, viz.: the west end of the town, the city, the east end of the town, Westminster, and the borough. The west end of the town is popularly regarded as extending from Charing Cross to Hyde Park, and from St. James's Park to Paddington. This is the best and most fashionable portion of the metropolis, and is chiefly occupied by the town residences of the nobility and gentry, and fashionable shops. The city includes the central part, and is the great emporium of commerce. The east end of the town is also devoted to commerce, ship-building, manufactures, &c. The southern bank of the Thames, from Deptford to Lambeth, bears a great resemblance to the east end of the town, being occupied by persons engaged in commercial and maritime concerns. London and Westminster are situated in Middlesex, on the N. side of the river Thames. Southwark is situated on the opposite bank in Surrey. The extent of the whole, from Limehouse and Deptford to Milbank and Vauxhall, is about 7 miles; the breadth varies from 3 to 5. The extension of this metropolis, since the middle of the last century, has proceeded with unprecedented rapidity, and covered the fields, gardens, and marshes in the vicinity of London, with new squares and streets. The direction of the principal streets accompanies the course of the river Thames from E. to W.; and the cross streets run mostly in a transverse direction from N. to S. There are two chief lines of streets from W. to E., one of which commences at the N. side of Hyde Park, and, under the successive names of Oxford-street, St. Giles's, Holborn, Skinner-street, Newgate-street, Cheapside, Cornhill, and Leadenhall-street, is continued to Whitechapel and Mile End, on the Essex road; the other begins at the S. side of Hyde Park, and consists of Piccadilly, St. James's-street, Pall Mall, Charing Cross, the Strand, Fleet-street, Ludgate-hill, St. Paul's Church-yard, Watling-street, Cannon-street, and Tower-street; whence, crossing Tower-hill, it may be said to be further extended 2 miles along the river side, in Wapping. The streets near the river, and most of the cross ones in the city, are very narrow; the broadest and handsomest are to the N. of Oxford-street and Holborn. They are all well paved with granite stones, and wood, and on each side with flag-stones, for the convenience of foot passengers. The subterranean works, constructed for the accommodation of the inhabitants, consisting of sewers, drains, water-pipes, and gas-pipes, are most extensive. The houses are mostly built of brick of a pale colour. The principal squares are Grosvenor, Portman, Berkeley, St. James's, Hanover, Manchester, Cavendish, Belgrave, Bedford, Russell, Tavistock, Bloomsbury, Montague, Leicester, Bryanston, and Finsbury-squares, and Lincoln's Inn Fields. Among the public buildings, St. Paul's Cathedral is the most conspicuous. It is 2292 feet in circumference, and 340 in height to the top of the cross, and is inferior to none in Europe, except St. Peter's at Rome. It contains monuments of many illustrious individuals, who have done honour to their country by their talents or their virtues. Westminster Abbey is a grand specimen of Gothic architecture, said to have been founded by Sebert, king of the East Saxons, in 610. Here most of the English sovereigns have been crowned, and many of them interred. It contains also a great number of monuments, erected to the memory of kings, statesmen, heroes, poets, and persons distinguished by genius, learning, and science. The chapel of Henry VII., adjoining, Leland calls The Wonder of the World. St. Stephen's, Walbrook, is a small church of exquisite beauty, the masterpiece of Sir Christopher Wren. Bow Church in Cheapside, St. Bride's in Fleet-street, St. Dunstan's in the East, and several others, are worthy of notice; but the far greater number are of plain and ordinary architecture. The churches and chapels belonging to the Establishment, in the bills of mortality, including those erected under the recent act of parliament, amount to above 300. There are likewise a great number of meeting-houses for Protestant dissenters of all persuasions, 30 foreign Protestant churches, 15 Roman Catholic chapels, and 6 synagogues for the Jews. Besides the royal palaces, there are many fine houses of the princes of the blood, and of the nobility and gentry. The Tower of London is very ancient, but the founder is uncertain. It is surrounded by a wall, and partly by a deep ditch. Here are the jewels and ornaments of the crown, as well as the other regalia. The Grand Armoury was destroyed by fire in 1841. The Mint, on Tower-hill, is a very elegant modern building, of pure Grecian architecture. The bridges are a great ornament to the metropolis. The most ancient, London Bridge, was begun in 1176, and finished in 1209. The length of it was 915 feet. The number of arches was 19, of unequal dimensions, through which, in consequence of their narrowness and clumsy construction, the current rushed with such force as to render the navigation extremely dangerous. This clumsy fabric is, however, now supplanted by the New London Bridge, a noble structure of 5 arches, which was opened by King William IV. on August 1, 1831. Westminster Bridge was commenced in 1739, and opened to the public in 1750. It is 1223 feet in length, and has 13 large, and 2 small semicircular arches. Blackfriars' Bridge, built by Mylne, was completed in 1768. Its length is 995 feet; the breadth of the carriage 28, and of the foot-paths 7 feet each.

It consists of 9 elliptical arches, the centre one of which is 100 feet wide; and both this, and the arch on each side, are wider than the celebrated Rialto at Venice. Waterloo Bridge, commenced in 1811, and opened in 1816, on the anniversary of the battle which it is designed to commemorate, is one of the noblest structures of the kind in the world. It consists of 9 arches, each 120 feet span, and 35 feet elevation. The other bridges are those of Southwark and Vauxhall. Among the other public buildings, which can be merely be enumerated here, are Westminster Hall, containing the supreme courts of justice, and adjoining to which are the Houses of Lords and Commons; the Guildhall of the city; the Sessions House; the Horse Guards, the Treasury, and the Admiralty, at Whitehall; the National Gallery; the noble collection of public offices which form that magnificent structure called Somerset Place; the British Museum; the Royal Exchange; the Bank of England; the Excise Office; the East India House; the Mansion House, for the lord mayor; the Monument, in commemoration of the great fire in 1666; the New Post Office, St. Martins-le-grand, opened in Sep. 1829; the Stock Exchange; the new Customhouse; the new Corn Exchange, erected on the site of the old one, in Mark-lane, in 1829; the Herald's College; and the halls of the various city companies. The inns of court, for the study of the law; the colleges, learned societies, and public seminaries; the noble hospitals and other charitable institutions; the public places of diversion, &c., are too numerous to be here particularly mentioned. Such, on a cursory view of it, is the metropolis of Great Britain, to the extent and opulence of which many causes have contributed. The broad stream of the Thames, flowing between London and Southwark, continually agitated by a brisk current, or a rapid tide, brings constant supplies of fresh air, which no buildings can intercept. The country around, especially on the London side, is nearly open to some distance; whence, by the action of the sun and wind on a gravelly soil, it is kept tolerably dry in all seasons, and affords no lodgment for stagnant air or water. The cleanliness of London, as well as its supply of water, is generally aided by its situation on the banks of the Thames; and the New River, with many good springs within the city itself, further contributes to the abundance of that necessary element. All these are advantages, with respect to health, in which this metropolis is exceeded by few. Its situation, with regard to the circumstance of navigation, is equally well chosen: had it been placed lower on the Thames it would have been annoyed by the marshes; had it been higher, it would not have been accessible, as at present, to ships of large burden. It now possesses every advantage that can be derived from a seaport, and at the same time, by means of its noble river, and its canal navigation, enjoys a most extensive communication with the internal parts of the country, which supply it with necessaries, and in return receive from it such commodities as they require. It contains several large wet docks, particularly those called the West India, the East India, the London, and St. Catherine's docks; also dry docks for repairing, and slips for building of ships; besides the royal yard at Deptford, for building men-of-war. London, therefore, unites in itself all the benefits arising from navigation and commerce, with those of a metropolis at which all the public business of a great nation is transacted; and is thus both the mercantile and political emporium of these kingdoms. It is also the seat of many considerable manufactures; some almost peculiar to itself, as administering to the demands of studied splendour and refined luxury; others in which it participates with the manufacturing towns in general. The most important of its peculiar manufactures is the silk-weaving, established in Spitalfields by refugees from France. A variety of works in gold, silver, and jewellery, the engraving of prints, the making of optical and mathematical instruments, are principally executed here, and some of them in greater perfection than in any other country. The porter-brewery, a business of immense extent, is also chiefly carried on in London. To its port are likewise confined some branches of foreign commerce, as the vast East India trade, and those to Turkey and Hudson's Bay. Thus London has risen to its present rank of the first city in Europe, with respect to wealth and population. The city is divided into 26 wards, each governed by an alderman; and from the aldermen the lord mayor is annually chosen. There are likewise 236 common-councilmen, a recorder, a common-serjeant, two sheriffs (who are also sheriffs of Middlesex), a chamberlain, a town-clerk, a city remembrancer, a water-bailiff, and many inferior officers. Westminster is governed by a high steward, who is generally a nobleman, chosen by the dean and chapter; and he has an under steward who officiates for him. Next to him is the high bailiff, chosen also by the dean and chapter; whose power resembles that of a sheriff. The suburbs are under the jurisdiction of justices of the peace for the county; and there are also several police offices, where magistrates sit every day for the examination of offenders, and the determination of various complaints, in a summary way. Southwark was long independent of London, but Edward III. granted it to the city. It was then called the village of Southwark, and afterward named the bailiwick. In the reign of Edward VI. it was formed into a twenty-sixth ward, by the name of Bridge Ward Without. On the death of the alderman of this ward, he is succeeded by the next in seniority, to whatever ward he may belong, this ward being considered as a sinecure, and consequently the most proper for "the father of the city." The city has likewise a high bailiff and steward here. To attempt an enumeration of the events by which this great capital has been distinguished, within the limits of a work like this, would of course be absurd; but we cannot omit to mention the plague, in 1665, which cut off 68,596 people: and the dreadful conflagration of 1666, by which the cathedral and many other churches, with 13,200 houses, were destroyed. London, in its most extended sense, is divided into 7 districts, called the Metropolitan Boroughs, of which the city of London returns 4 members, and the boroughs of the city of Westminster, Southwark, Mary-le-bone, Finsbury, Tower Hamlets, and Lambeth, 2 members each, or 16 members altogether. London is 225 miles N. N. W. of Paris, 395 S. of Edinburgh, and 338 E. S. E. of Dublin. Long. 0. 5. 7. W. lat. 51. 31. N.

London, New, a seaport of Connecticut; capital of a county of the same name; with the best harbour in the state, defended by two forts. A considerable part of the town was burnt by Benedict Arnold, in 1781, but was subsequently rebuilt. It has a good trade to the West Indies: it is seated on the Thames, near its entrance into Long Island Sound; 54 miles E. by N. of Newhaven. Pop. 5528. Long. 72. 30. W. lat. 41. 25. N.

London, New, a town of Virginia; chief of Bedford county; 110 miles W. by S. of Richmond. Long. 79. 45. W. lat. 37. 20. N. It is also the name of several townships of the United States.

Londonderry, a county of Ireland, in the province of Ulster; 40 English miles long, and 33 broad; bounded on the W. by Donegal, N. by the Ocean, S. and S. W. by Tyrone, and E. by Antrim. It is divided into 31 parishes, and sends two members to parliament. It is a fruitful champaign country; and the greater part of it was given by James I. to an incorporated company of London merchants. The linen manufacture flourishes through every part of the county.

Londonderry, a city and seaport of Ireland, and a county of itself; capital of the foregoing county, and a bishop's see. It is still surrounded by walls, and celebrated for a long siege it sustained against James II. in 1689. It is governed by a mayor, and sends one member to parliament. The principal commerce is with America and the West Indies. It is seated on the river Foyle, over which is a wooden bridge, 1068 feet in length. Londonderry is 4 miles S. of Lough Foyle, and 115 N. W. of Dublin.

Londonderry, a town of New Hampshire, in Rockingham county, with a manufacture of linen, cloth, and thread; seated near the head of Beaver River, which runs into the Merrimac; 38 miles S. S. W. of Portsmouth.

Long, Loch, an arm of the sea, in Scotland; which, from the Frith of Clyde, extends 20 miles N. between the counties of Dumbarton and Argyle. It is from 1 to 2 miles in breadth; and near the middle, on the Argyle side, it sends off a small branch called Loch Goil.

Long Island, an island of the state of New York; separated from Connecticut by Long Island Sound. It extends E. from the city of New York 140 miles, but is not more than 10 broad on a medium; and is divided into three counties, King's, Queen's, and Suffolk. Hence are exported to the West Indies, &c., whale oil, pitch, pine-boards, horses, cattle, flax-seed, beef, &c. The produce of the middle and western parts of the island, particularly corn, is carried to New York.

Long Island Sound, a channel in North America, from 3 to 25 miles broad; extending the whole length of Long Island, and dividing it from Connecticut. It communicates with the Atlantic at both ends of the island.

Long Lake. *See* Rain Lake.

Longford, a county of Ireland, in the province of Leinster; 25 miles long, and 20 broad; bounded on the N. W. by Leitrim, N. E. by Cavan, S. E. by West Meath, and W. by the river Shannon, which parts it from Roscommon. It is divided into 25 parishes, and sends two members to parliament. The country in general is fertile, but interspersed in some parts with bogs, morasses, and forests; the flat parts, along the Shannon, are subject to inundation. It contains several lakes, and besides the Shannon, is watered by the Inny, the Camlin, the Fallen, and numerous inferior streamlets. Oats form the chief article of agricultural export.

Longford, a town of Ireland, capital of the above county. Much linen is manufactured in the town and neighbourhood, and great quantities of flax sent to other parts. It is seated on the Camlin; 70 miles (English) W. N. W. of Dublin. Long. 7. 40. W. lat. 52. 48. N.

Longforgan, a town of Scotland; in the S. E. corner of Perthshire; on the Frith of Tay; 4 miles W. by S. of Dundee.

Long-nan, a city of China, of the first rank; in the province of Se-tchuen. Long. 104. 18. E. lat. 32. 22. N.

Longtown, a town in Cumberland; with a market on Monday; seated on the Esk; 9 miles N. of Carlisle, and 310 N. N. W. of London.

Longue, a town of France; in the department of Maine-et-Loire; 7 miles N. of Saumur.

Longuion, a town of France; in the department of Moselle. Here is a considerable iron forge and cannon foundry; 10 miles S. W. of Longwy, and 36 N. W. of Mentz.

Longwy, a town of France, in the department of Moselle; with a castle. It is divided into the Old and New Town, the latter of which is fortified. It is seated on a rocky eminence, on the river Chiers; 32 miles N.N.W. of Mentz. Long. 5. 44. E. lat. 49. 32. N. Pop. 2500.

Lons le Saulnier, a town of France; capital of the department of Jura. It derives its name from the salt springs in its vicinity: it is seated on the Solvan; 62 miles S. E. of Dijon. Pop. 7350. Long. 5. 30. E. lat. 46. 37. N.

Loo, a town of Belgium; in West Flanders; 10 miles N. N. W. of Ypres. Pop. 1525.

Loodheana, a town and fort of North Hindostan, province of Delhi; on the S. bank of the Sutlej river: it is the most remote military station possessed by the British; 178 miles N. W. of Delhi.

Loo-koo, Lew-chew, or Lieou-kiou, the general name of 36 islands lying between Formosa and Japan. The Great Loo-koo is 50 miles long, and from 12 to 15 broad; the others are inconsiderable. They were very imperfectly known to Europeans, till visited by Captain Hall and Mr. M'Leod, in their return from the late embassy to China. The climate and soil seem to be among the happiest on the globe. The fruits and vegetable productions are of the most exquisite description. The inhabitants are diminutive in their stature, but strong and well made. Their disposition appears to be peculiarly gay, hospitable, and affectionate, but they showed that strong aversion to receive strangers into their country which is characteristic of China, Japan, and all the neighbouring regions. The king is tributary to China, and the government resembles that of the Chinese. The capital is Kintching; about 5 miles from its port of Napakiang. Long. 127. 52. E. lat. 26. 14. N.

Looe, East and West, Cornwall; separated by a creek, over which is a narrow stone bridge. A market is held at East Looe, on Saturday. It is 13 miles W. of Plymouth, and 233 W. by S. of London.

Lookout Cape, a cape of North Carolina, S. of Cape Hatteras, and opposite Core Sound. Long. 76. 48. W. lat. 34. 22. N.

Looz, or Lootz, a town of Belgium; in the province of Liege; 14 miles N. N. W. of Liege.

Lopatka, Cape, the S. extremity of Kamtschatka. Long. 156. 45. E. lat. 51. 0. N. *See* Kuriles.

Lopham, North and South, two adjoining parishes in Norfolk; 4 miles S. E. of East Harling.

Lopo Gonsalve, Cape, a long and narrow peninsula on the coast of Guinea, low, flat, and covered with trees. It affords a good harbour, and near the cape is a village, where provisions are plentiful. Long. 8. 30. E. lat. 0. 45. S.

Lora, a town of Spain in Seville; on the Guadalquiver; 28 miles N. E. of Seville.

Lorbus, (the ancient Laribus Colonia,) a town of the kingdom of Tunis; with a castle, and fine remains of antiquity. It is seated in a plain, fertile in corn; 150 miles S. W. of Tunis. Long. 9. 0. E. lat. 35. 34. N.

Lorca, a town of Spain, in Murcia, divided into the Upper and Lower Town. The former has narrow, crooked, and ill paved streets; the latter is regularly and neatly built. It contains nine churches and several monasteries, and has extensive manufactures of saltpetre. In 1802 the bursting of an immense reservoir, containing water for the purpose of irrigation, occasioned much damage to the town. It is seated on an eminence near the Sengonera; 40 miles W. S. W. of Murcia. Pop. 23,500. Long. 1. 22. W. lat. 37. 25. N.

Lord Howe's Group, an extensive group of islands in the South Pacific, thickly covered with wood, among which the cocoa-nut is very distinguishable. The natives are of a dark copper colour; their hair tied in a knot on the back of the head; and they seem to have some method of taking off the beard, for they appear as clean shaved. Their arms and thighs are tatoeed in the manner described by Captain Cook, of some of the natives of the islands he visited in these seas; and some are painted with red and white streaks. They wear a wrapper round their middle. Long. from 159. 14. to 159. 37. E. lat. 5. 30. S.

Lord Howe Island, an island in the Pacific Ocean; discovered in 1788 by Lieutenant King. Many excellent turtles have been caught here on a sandy beach; and it abounds with a variety of birds, which were so unaccustomed to be disturbed that the seamen went near enough to knock them down with a stick. At its end are two high mountains, nearly perpendicular from the sea, the southernmost named Mount Gower. About 14 miles to the S. is a remarkable rock, named Ball's Pyramid, which at a distance had much the appearance of a steeple. The island is 3½ miles long, and very narrow. Long. 159. 0. E. lat. 31. 36. N.

Lorenzo, San, a town of Mexico, province of New Biscay; with 500 inhabitants, whose employment consist in cultivating the grape. There are numerous settlements and inconsiderable islands of this name in South America.

Loreo, a town of Austrian Italy; in Rovigo; on the Adige; 30 miles E. of Rovigo.

Loretto, a fortified town of Italy; in the papal states. The cathedral contains the Casa Santa, or Holy House, in which it is pretended the Virgin Mary lived at Nazareth. According to the legend, it was carried by angels from Galilee into Dalmatia, and thence to the place where it now stands, in 1295. This house, or chapel, is 31 feet long, 15 broad, and 18 high: the inner part very old, but cased with marble on the outside. The famous Lady of Loretto, who holds the infant Jesus in her arms, stands upon the principal altar, in a niche of silver: this statue is of cedar wood, three feet high; but her face can harply be seen, on account of the numerous gold and silver lamps around her. She is clothed with cloth of gold, set off with jewels; and the child Jesus is covered with a shirt, holds a globe in his hand, and is adorned with rich jewels. Those who go on pilgrimage to Loretto, after having performed their devotion, make the Virgin a present; so that the treasury of this chapel was immensely rich. The inhabitants of this town subsist principally by agriculture and gardening, and many of them are shoemakers, tailors, and sellers of chaplets. Loretto was taken by the French, in 1796, and the church despoiled of its treasures: even the Virgin was carried away, but restored in 1802. It is seated on a mountain; 3 miles from the Gulf of Venice, 12 S. E. of Ancona, and 115 N. E. of Rome. Long. 13. 36. E. lat. 43. 27. N.

Lorgues, a town of France, in Provence; on the Argens; 16 miles W. of Frejus.

L'Orient, a fortified modern seaport of France; department of Morbihan. It is built with considerable regularity; the streets are wide, the public squares spacious and handsome, and the harbour large, secure, and of easy access, Formerly it was a very flourishing town, the French East India Company making it the exclusive entrepôt of their imported goods. It has still some trade, and is a place of importance on account of its magazines for the navy. The chief manufacture is of salt. The British made an unsuccessful attempt upon it in 1746. It is seated on the bay of Port Louis, at the influx of the Scorf; 340 miles W. by S. of Paris. Long. 3. 20. W. lat. 47. 44. N. Pop. 17,250.

LORROCK, a town of Germany; in Baden; 6 miles N. E. of Bale.

LORRAINE, an extensive district of the N. E. of France, between Champagne and Alsace, and now forming the departments of Meurthe, Moselle, and Vosges. It abounds in all sorts of corn, wine, hemp, flax, and rape-seed.

LOSTWITHIEL. *See* LESTWITHIEL.

LOT, a river of France, which rises in the department of Lozere, begins to be navigable at Cahors, and enters the Garonne near Aiguillon.

LOT, a department of France; consisting of the former district of Quercy, in Guienne. It takes its name from the river Lot, which crosses it from E. to W.; it is bounded on the N. by Correze, E. by Cantal and Aveyron, S. by Tarn-et-Garonne, and W. by Lot-et-Garonne and Dordogne. Its pastures feeds numerous flocks, which constitute a great part of the commerce. The climate is mild and healthy; and the soil, consisting of fat rich earth, is cultivated with horses, and yields more than sufficient for its population, estimated at 275,296. Cahors is the capital.

LOT-ET-GARONNE, a department of France, including part of the former province of Guienne; bounded on the N. by Dordogne, by E. Tarn-et-Garonne, S. by Gers, and W. by Landes and the Gironde. It has its name from the rivers Lot and Garonne. Its pastures are but indifferent, and artificial meadows are little known. The land, being much covered with heath, is cultivated with oxen; and a large proportion of the department is incapable of cultivation, consisting of rugged hills or sandy deserts. Pop. 330,000. Agen is the capital.

LOTHIAN. *See* HADDINGTONSHIRE, EDINBURGHSHIRE, and LINLITHGOWSHIRE.

LOUDEAC, a town of France; department of Cotes du Nord; 25 miles S. of St. Brieux.

LOUDON, a county of the United States, in Virginia, on the Potomac; adjoining Fairfax, Berkley, and Faquier counties. It is about 50 miles in length, and 20 in breadth. Leesburgh is the chief town.

LOUDON, a town of France; department of Vienne; 30 miles N. W. of Poitiers. Pop. 5350.

LOUGHBOROUGH, a town in Leicestershire; with a market on Thursday. It has a large church, with a handsome tower, and seven meeting-houses for dissenters; also a free grammar school, and a charity school. The chief manufactures are those of cotton-spinning, lace, and hosiery. By means of the Loughborough canal, the river, and Midland Counties rail-road, it carries on a brisk trade, particularly in coals. Many of the houses have an old and irregular appearance, but great improvements have lately taken place: it is seated near the Soar; 11 miles N. of Leicester, and 109 N. N. W. of London.

LOUGHREA, a town of Ireland, in the county of Galway, near a lake of the same name; 15 miles S. W. of Galway.

LOUHANS, a town of France; department of Upper Saone, situate on a kind of island between the rivers Seilles, Vaillere, and Solman; 18 miles S. E. of Chalons. Pop. 3550.

LOUIS, FORT, a barrier fortress of France; in Alsace, on the Rhine; 12 miles E. of Haguenau.

LOUIS, ST., an island of Africa, at the mouth of the river Senegal; with a fort, built by the French. It was taken in 1758 by the English, and ceded to them in 1763. In the American war it was taken by the French, and kept by them after the peace in 1783. It is a flat, sandy, and barren. Long. 16. 15. W. lat. 16. 0. N.

LOUIS, ST., a seaport and fortress of St. Domingo, on the S. W. coast at the head of a bay of its name. The exports are coffee, cotton, and indigo; 70 miles W. S. W. of Port au Prince. Long. 73. 32. W. lat. 18. 16. N.

LOUIS, ST., a town in the state of Missouri, delightfully situate on the banks of the Mississippi. Most of the houses are of wood; but some are built of stone, and are white-washed. Its situation is more central with regard to the whole territory of the United States than any other considerable town. It is very prosperous, and bids fair to become a great commercial city. It has a Catholic chapel, a theatre, a bank, and two weekly newspapers; 982 miles from Washington. Long. 89. 36. W. lat. 38. 36. N.

LOUIS, ST., a lake of North America; formed by the junction of the Ottawa with the St. Lawrence. It is 12 miles long, and 6 broad.

LOUIS, ST. a river of North America, which has its source near the eastern head waters of the Mississippi, and falls into Lake Superior, on the west shore. It is navigable 150 miles. Long. 91. 52. W. lat. 46. 44. N.

LOUIS DE MARANHAM, ST., a seaport of Brazil; capital of the island of Maranham, and a bishop's see; with a strong castle. It is the residence of a captain-general, and contains a custom-house and treasury. The churches and convents are numerous, and the houses, though only one story high, are many of them neat. The harbour is tolerably large, but the entrance is difficult. It stands on the E. side of the river Mearim, near the Atlantic Ocean. Long. 43. 37. W. lat. 2. 30. S.

LOUISA, a town of European Russia; on a bay of the Gulf of Finland: 30 miles E. N. E. of Helsingfors.

LOUISA, a county of the United States; in Virginia; about 25 miles long, and 20 broad; with 16,151 inhabitants.

LOUISBURG, the capital of the island of Cape Breton, British North America; with a citadel, and an excellent harbour, nearly four leagues in circumference. It was taken by the English in 1745, restored to the French in 1748, taken by the English in 1758, and ceded to them in 1763. The chief source of trade is the cod-fishery. Long. 59. 55. W. lat. 45. 54. N.

LOUISBURG, a town of North Carolina; chief

of Franklin county; situate on the river Tar; 23 miles N. by E. of Raleigh. Long. 78. 40. W. lat. 36. 3. N.

Louisiana, a country of North America; estimated to extend about 2000 miles in length, and 680 in breadth; bounded on the E. by the Mississippi, S. by the Gulf of Mexico, W. by New Mexico, and running indefinitely N. It is agreeably situate between the extremes of heat and cold; the climate varying as it extends toward the N. The timber is as fine as any in the world; and the quantities of oak, ash, mulberry, walnut, cherry, cypress, and cedar, are astonishing. The neighbourhood of the Mississippi furnishes the richest fruits, in great variety. The soil is particularly adapted for hemp, flax, and tobacco; and indigo is a staple commodity. It is intersected by a number of fine rivers, among which are the Missouri, Arkansas, the Red river, the Washita, &c., which all flow into the Mississippi. The chief articles of trade are indigo, cotton, rice, beans, wax, and lumber. This country was discovered by Ferdinand de Soto, in 1541; traversed by M. de la Salle, in 1682; and settled by Louis XIV. in the beginning of the 18th century. In 1763 that part of Louisiana lying on the E. bank of the Mississippi was ceded to England, and the portion to the westward of the river to Spain. Louisiana having been ceded by Spain in 1801 to France, the American government succeeded in purchasing it for 15,000,000 of dollars, and their commissioners took formal possession of it in the year 1804. A small portion of this country is incorporated into the state of Mississippi, the S. E. part forms the states of Louisiana and Missouri. It is rapidly advancing in population and wealth.

Louisiana, one of the United States, formed in 1812. It is situated between 31. and 33. N. lat., and bounded N. and W. by the Missouri territory, S. by the Gulf of Mexico, E. by the Mississippi territory. It is 300 miles in length from E. to W., and 210 broad from N. to S., having an area of 48,000 square miles, or 31,463,000 acres. The south-western part is generally level prairie, and much of its area very productive; the north-western part, a thick forest, and low alluvial soil upon the rivers, which is of great fertility; but at a distance from the streams the land is high, broken, and sterile. That part of West Florida which lies between Pearl River on the E., and the Mississippi on the W. as far as 31. N. lat., has been annexed to this state. Sugar plantations are becoming numerous, and the exports, consisting of sugar, cotton, indigo, rice, molasses, soap, tallow, wax, planks, &c., are rapidly increasing. Population 352,411, including 168,452 slaves. The principal town is New Orleans.

Louisville, a town of Georgia; capital of Jefferson county; seated on the N. side of the Ogeechee; 52 miles S. S. W. of Augusta and 110 N. W. of Savannah. Long. 82. 17. W. lat. 32. 42. N.

Louisville, a flourishing town of Kentucky; capital of Jefferson county; seated on the Ohio, just above its rapids, at the head of which is a fort. Louisville is a port of entry; 50 miles W. of Frankfort. Population 21,210. Long. 85. 32. W. lat. 38. 4. N.

Loule, a town of Portugal; in Algarva; surrounded by antique walls, and seated on a river of the same name; 10 miles N. W. of Faro. Pop. 5350.

Lou-ngan, a city of China, of the first rank; in the province of Chan-sti; situate near the source of the Queyho; 270 miles S. S. W. of Peking. Long. 116. 56. E. lat. 31. 46. N.

Lourde, a town of France; in the department of Upper Pyrenees; with a castle on a rock; 10 miles N. W. of Bagneres.

Louristan, a mountainous but fertile district of Irak; in Persia; bordering upon Khusistan. It is abundantly watered, and the pastures are most luxuriant, but agriculture is quite neglected. The inhabitants are a barbarous and independent race, and reside always in tents. The only town is Khorumabad.

Louth, a corporate town in Lincolnshire; with markets on Wednesday and Saturday. It has manufactures of blankets and carpets, and also a large soap manufactory. Here is a noble Gothic church, with a lofty spire; also five meeting-houses for dissenters, a free school, founded by Edward VI., and another founded in 1677. It has a navigation, by means of the river Lud and a canal, to the German Ocean, at Tetney Creek; 28 miles N. E. of Lincoln, and 141 N. of London.

Louth, a county of Ireland, in the province of Leinster; 27 miles long, and 18 broad; bounded on the N. by Armagh and Carlingford Bay, E. by the Irish Sea, W. by Monaghan and E. Meath, and S. by E. by Meath, from which it is parted by the Boyne. It is a fertile country, contains 61 parishes, and sends two members to parliament.

Louth, a town of Ireland, in the county of the same name; containing the ruins of an ancient abbey, founded by St. Patrick; 18 miles N. N. W. of Drogheda.

Louvain, a city of Belgium; in S. Brabant; with an old castle, and a celebrated university. Its walls are nearly 9 miles in circumference, but within them are many gardens and vineyards. The churches, convents, and public buildings, are magnificent. Large quantities of cloth were formerly made here; but this trade is decayed, and the town is now chiefly noted for good beer. It was taken by the French in 1746, 1792, and 1794. It is seated on the Doyle; 14 miles E. by N. of Brussels, and 20 S. S. E. of Antwerp. Long. 4. 41. E. lat. 50. 53. N.

Louviers, a handsome town of France; in the department of Eure; with a considerable manufacture of fine cloths. It is seated on the Eure: 10 miles N. of Evreux, and 55 N. W. of Paris. Pop. 7100.

Louvres, a town of France, in the department of Seine-et-Oise; 14 miles N. of Paris.

Lowell, a town of the United States; in Middlesex county, Massachusets; 25 miles N. W. from Boston: one of the most flourishing towns in the United States, being the principal seat of the cotton manufacture, and also carpeting, and silk fabrics. Its rise may be inferred from its increase of population, which in 1830 was 6474; in 1840 was 20,796.

LOWENSTEIN, a town of Germany, in Wirtemberg; capital of a county of the same name, 9 miles E. S. E. of Heilbron, and 33. N. N. E. of Stutgard.

LOWENSTEIN, a fort and ancient castle of the Netherlands; in the province of Guelderland; situated at the W. end of the island of Bommelwert. In this castle, in 1618, Hugo Grotius was confined, and after three years' imprisonment was conveyed away by a stratagem of his wife, in a returned box used for the purpose of carrying books. It is 18 miles S. E. of Rotterdam.

LOWESTOFT, a town in Suffolk; with a market on Wednesday. Its church is a fine Gothic building; and it has, beside a chapel of ease, several dissenting meeting-houses, and two grammar-schools. The chief trade is in the mackerel and herring fisheries; and it is much frequented for sea-bathing. Here are forts and batteries for protecting ships in the roads. The coast being dangerous, here are two lighthouses; and a floating-light was stationed off this port in 1815; and in 1830 a harbour and swing-bridge were added to the Lowestoffe and Norwich navigation. It stands on a cliff, the most easterly point of Great Britain; 10 miles S. of Yarmouth, and 114 N. E. of London. Long. 1. 44. E. lat. 52. 29. N.

LOWES-WATER, a lake in Cumberland, one mile long, and a quarter of a mile broad. It is of no great depth, but abounds with pike and perch. In opposition to all the other lakes, it has its course from N. to S., and, under the lofty Mellbreak, runs into the N. end of Cromach-water.

LOWICZ, a town of Poland, with a strong fortress; seated on the Bzura; 42 miles W. of Warsaw. Pop. 2550.

LOWOSITZ, a town of Bohemia; in the circle of Leutmeritz. In 1756 the greatest part of it was burnt in an obstinate engagement between the Saxons and Prussians. It is seated on the Egra; 5 miles W. S. W. of Leutmeritz.

LOXA, or LOJA, a town of Spain; in Granada; with a royal salt-work, and a copper forge; seated in a fertile country, on the river Xenil; 28 miles W. of Granada. Pop. 9000.

LOXA, or LOJA, a town of Quito; republic of Colombia; capital of a province of the same name; famous for producing fine Jesuits' bark and cochineal. Carpets of remarkable fineness are manufactured here, but the town is much decayed. It stands at the head of a N. W. branch of the Amazon; 150 miles E. N. E. of Paita. Pop. 4500. Long 78. 16. W. lat. 4. 5. S.

LOZERE, a department of France, corresponding to the ancient Gevaudan. It is a mountainous, barren country, and receives its name from the principal ridge of mountains. Pop. 145,000. Mende is the capital.

LOZZOLO, a town of North Italy; in Piedmont, kingdom of Sardinia. Pop. 6350.

LU, a town of the Sardinian states; in Piedmont; 8 miles S. S. W. of Alexandria.

LUARCA, a town of Spain, in Asturia; near the sea coast; 23 miles N. W. of Oviedo.

LUBAR, a town of Russia; in the government of Volhynia; with 3000 inhabitants.

LUBAU, a town of Prussian Silesia; 30 miles N. W. of Glatz.

LUBBEN, a town of Lower Lusatia; seated on the Spree, in a swampy country; 50 miles S. S. E. of Berlin. Long. 13. 55. E. lat. 52. 0. N.

LUBEC, or LUBECK, a free city and seaport of Germany; adjoining the duchy of Holstein. It was the head of the famous hanseatic league, formed here in 1164, and the most commercial city of the north; but great part of its trade is transferred to Hamburgh. The city is surrounded with walls, which are planted with rows of trees, but the other defences were demolished by the French, to whom it was surrendered in 1806. The houses are built of stone, in a very ancient style. The town-house is a superb structure, and has several towers. There is also a fine council-house, and an exchange. The inhabitants are Lutherans. There are four large churches, besides the cathedral. The trade consists in the export of corn from the adjoining country, and the import of articles for consumption; and the manufactures, which are on a small scale, comprise woollens, silks, cotton, tobacco, soap, white lead, copper, &c. Lubec is seated on the Trave; 8 miles S.W. of the Baltic, and 53 N. E. of Hamburgh. Pop. 22,500. Long. 40. 49. E. lat. 53. 52. N.

LUBEC, an island in the Indian Ocean; near the island of Madura. Long. 112. 22. E. lat. 5. 50. S.

LUBECK, a seaport of Maine, in Washington county; situated on a beautiful peninsula, on the W. side of Passamaquoddy Bay; 365 miles E. of Boston. It was commenced in 1815, and is now a handsome and flourishing town.

LUBEN, a town of Prussian Silesia; seated on the Katzbach; 14 miles N. of Leignitz.

LUBLENITZ, a town of Silesia; in the principality of Oppeln; 32 miles E. of Oppeln.

LUBLIN, a city of Russian Poland; capital of a palatinate of the same name, and a bishop's see; with a citadel. Three annual fairs are held here, each lasting a month, which are frequented by great numbers of German, Russian, Turkish, and other traders and merchants. It is seated on the Bistricza; 85 miles S. E. of Warsaw. Long. 22. 45. E. lat. 51. 14. N.

LUBLYO, a town of Poland; palatinate of Cracow; 56 miles S. E. of Cracow.

LUC, a town of France; in the department of Var; 25 miles N. E. of Toulon.

LUCAN, a town of Ireland; in the county of Dublin; with a sulphureous spring, the waters of which are much esteemed; 7 miles from Dublin.

LUCANAS, a town of Peru, which gives name to a jurisdiction; containing rich silver mines, and feeding great droves of cattle. It stands near one of the head branches of the Apurimac; 80 miles S. of Guamanga.

LUCAR, CAPE ST., the S. E. end of the

peninsula of California. It lies under the tropic of Capricorn, in long. 111. 30. W.

LUCAR DE BARAMEDA, ST., a seaport of Spain, in Andalusia, and a bishop's see. It has a fine harbour, well defended, at the mouth of the Guadalquiver; 40 miles S. S. W. of Seville. Long. 5. 54. W. lat. 36. 58. N. Pop. 15,500.

LUCAR DE GUADIANA, ST., a strong town of Spain; in Andalusia; on the river Guadiana; 76 miles W. N. W. of Seville. Long. 7. 18. W. lat. 37. 28. N.

LUCAYA ISLANDS. *See* BAHAMA.

LUCCA, a duchy of Italy; lying on the E. coast of the Gulf of Genoa. It is bounded by Tuscany, Modena, and the Mediterranean, and contains about 430 square miles, and a population of 137,500. Much of it is mountainous, but it is well cultivated, and produces plenty of wine, oil, silk, wool, and chestnuts; the oil, in particular, is in high esteem. It was formerly a republic; was constituted a principality by Napoleon, in 1805, and in 1815 erected into a duchy by the Congress of Vienna, and given to the infanta of Spain.

LUCCA, a city of Italy; capital of the above duchy, and an archbishop's see. It is nearly 3 miles in circumference, regularly fortified, and contains 18,000 inhabitants. The state palace, and the cathedral, and other churches, are worthy of notice. Here are considerable manufactures of silk, and gold and silver stuffs. Lucca was entered by the French in 1796, evacuated in 1799, and re-entered in 1800. It is seated in a fruitful plain, near the river Serchio; 10 miles N. E. of Pisa, and 37 W. of Florence. Long. 10. 35. E. lat. 43. 50. N.

LUCE, a spacious bay on the S. coast of Scotland; in Wigtonshire; lying E. of the promontory called the Mull of Galloway. The river Luce enters its N. E. extremity, at the town of Glenluce.

LUCEINSTEIG, ST., a narrow pass from the country of the Grisons into Germany; defended by a fort; 3 miles N. of Mayenfeld; which was taken by General Massena, in March 1799.

LUCENA, a town of Spain; in Cordova; 32 miles S. S. E. of Cordova, and 42 W. N. W. of Granada. Pop. 13,500.

LUCERA, a city of Naples; capital of Capitanata, and a bishop's see. The town is small, but populous, and has a manufacture of cloth. It is 75 miles N. E. of Naples. Long. 15. 34. E. lat. 41. 28. N.

LUCERNA, a town of Piedmont; in a valley of its name; 15 miles S. W. of Turin.

LUCERNE, canton of Switzerland, containing a superficial extent of 740 square miles; and bounded by the cantons of Underwalden, Schweitz, and Zurich. The air is mild, and the soil uncommonly fertile. Freedom and openness of manners characterize the inhabitants, who are Roman Catholics, and computed at 106,500.

LUCERNE, the capital of the above canton, is divided into two parts by a branch of the Reuss, which here enters the Lake of Lucerne. It has no manufactures of consequence, and little commerce, the merchants being principally engaged in the commission business, upon goods passing between Italy and Germany, over Mount St. Gothard and the Lucerne lake. Pop. 6750. It is 30 miles S. W. of Zurich, and 42 E. of Berne. Long. 8. 14. E. lat. 47. 0. N.

LUCERNE, or WALDSTADTER, a lake of Switzerland; between the cantons of Underwalden, Lucerne, Schweitz, and Uri. It consists of a number of detached parts, forming in a manner, separate lakes. It is the largest, as well as the most romantic lake in the interior of Switzerland, being 25 miles long and from 2 to 4 broad.

LUCHOW, a town of Hanover; in the duchy of Luneburg; seated on the Jeetze; 36 miles S. of Luneburg.

LUCIA, ST., one of the Caribbee islands: 27 miles long and 12 broad. It consists of plains well watered with rivulets, and hills furnished with timber; and has several good bays and commodious harbours By the peace of 1763 this island was allotted to France. In 1803 it was taken by the English, and confirmed to them by the treaty of Paris, in 1814. There are two high mountains, by which this island may be known at a considerable distance. Its N. end is 21 miles S. of Martinico. Long. 60. 51. W. lat. 14. 0. N.

LUCIA, ST., one of the Cape de Verde islands, to the W. of that of St. Nicholas. Long. 24. 32. W. lat. 16. 45. N.

LUCIA, ST., a town of Sicily, in Val di Demona; 15 miles W. of Massina.

LUCIA, ST., a town of Buenos Ayres; on a river of the same name; 30 miles N. of Monte Video and 340 N. by W. of Buenos Ayres.—It is also the name of several settlements in S. America, none of which require particular notice.

LUCIANA, a town of Spain; in Andalusia; 8 miles W. N. W. of Ecija.

LUCITO, a town of Naples; in the Molise; 11 miles N. E. of Molise.

LUCKAU, a town of the Prussian states; in Lower Lusatia. It is seated in a swampy country, on the Breste; 55 miles N. of Dresden.

LUCKENWALD, a town of Prussian Saxony; seated on the Nute; 32 miles S. of Berlin.

LUCKFORD, a town of Dorsetshire; W. of Holme; on the river Luckford, which fall into the Frome, and forms the W. boundaries of Purbeck Isle.

LUCKNOW, an ancient city of Hindostan, and capital of Oude. It is a large, but poorly built, and the streets are narrow and crooked. The palace of the nabob is situated on a high bank near the Goomty, and commands an extensive view both of that river and the country on the eastern side. Adjoining the palace is a cantonment of one of the East India Company's regiments of native infantry; and in the vicinity is the dwelling of the British resident.

LUCO, a town of Naples; on the W. bank of the lake Celano; 9 miles S. S. W. of Celano.

LUCON, a town of France; department of

Vendee; seated on a morass, on the canal of Fontenay; 20 miles W. of Fontenay, and 50 S. of Nantes.

LUÇONIA, or MANILLA, the chief of the Philippine islands; 400 miles in length, and 100 in breadth. It is not so hot as might be expected, being well watered by large lakes and rivers, and the periodical rains, which inundate the plains. There are several volcanoes in the mountains, which occasion earthquakes. The produce is wax, cotton, indigo, tobacco, sugar, coffee, wild cinnamon, sulphur, cocoa-nuts, rice, &c. Gold is found in various parts of the island; and horses, buffaloes, and a variety of game abound. The inhabitants are, for the most part, a well disposed people, and, before their subjugation, were distributed into mud villages. Under the tyranny of the Spanish government they have became indolent, and destitute of energy. The interior, however, is occupied by a savage race, whom the Spaniards have not been able to subdue. They carry on a small traffic in gold, wax, and tobacco, in exchange for cattle. Area, 65,000 square miles. Pop. 1,760,000. Long. 122. 0. E. lat. 15. 0. N.

LUCRINO. *See* LICOLA.

LUCY, a town of the Sardinian states, in Savoy; 16 miles N. of Chambery.

LUDAMAR, a county of central Africa; bounded on the S. by Kaarta and Bambarra, and N. by the Sahara or Great Desert. It is inhabited by a race of Moors, who are almost strangers to agriculture, and depend for subsistance on the rearing of cattle. In religion they are Mahomedans of the most bigoted and intolerant character, as was fully proved in the case of Major Houghton, who was murdered here; and of Mr. Park, who was kept in long captivity, and with difficulty made his escape.

LUDENCHEID, a town of Prussian Westphalia; with manufactures of iron and cloth; 28 miles N. E. of Cologne.

LUDGERSHALL, a village in Wiltshire; it is 15 miles N. of Salisbury, and 71 N. by W. of London.

LUDLOW, a borough in Shropshire; with a market on Monday. It has a castle, now fast going to decay, where all business was formerly transacted for the principality of Wales. This castle and town were held for the empress Maud, against king Stephen, and besieged by him. Edward V. resided here at the time of his father's death, and was carried hence to London. Arthur, prince of Wales, son of Henry VII., held a court, and died here. Ludlow has a stately church, an elegant town-house, a commodious market-house, several meeting-houses for dissenters, two alms-houses, a free school, a charity school, and a national school. It returns two members to parliament. It is seated on the Teme; 21 miles from Shrewsbury, and 142 from London. Long. 2. 42. W. lat. 52. 23. N.

LUDWIGSBURG, a town of Germany, in Wirtemberg; with manufactures of cloth, damask linen, and marble paper. It is seated on the Neckar; 6 miles N. of Stutgard. Pop. 4500.

LUDWIGSBURG, a town of the Prussian states, in Pomerania, near the Baltic Sea, 5 miles E. N. E. of Greifswalde.

LUGA, a town of Russia, in the government of Petersburg; on a river of the same name; 96 miles S. of Petersburg.

LUGANO, a town of Italy; capital of the Swiss canton of Ticino; with a considerable trade in silk. It is built round a gentle curve of the lake Lugano, and backed by an amphitheatre of hills. The principal church is seated on an eminence above the town. It is 17 miles N. W. of Como. Pop. 4500. Long. 8. 57. E. lat. 45. 54. N.

LUGANO, a lake in the canton of Ticino; 25 miles in length, and from 3 to 6 in breadth. Its form is irregular, and bending into continual sinuosities. It lies between the lakes Como and Maggiore, but is above 180 feet higher than either of them.

LUDGE, or LUDE, a town of Prussian Westphalia; seated on the Emmer, 24 miles N. N. E. of Paderborn.

LUGO, a city of Spain, in Gallicia, and a bishop's see. It was once the metropolis of Spain, but is now chiefly celebrated for its hot medicinal springs. It is seated on the Minho, 50 miles E. N. E. of Compostella. Pop. 5000. Long. 7. 32. W. lat. 43. 4. N.

LUIS, ST., a town of Buenos Ayres, in the province of Tucuman; 140 miles W. S. W. of Cordova. Long. 67. 52. W. lat. 32. 10. S.

LUIS DE LA PAS, ST., a town of Mexico, in the province of Mechoacan; 120 miles N. by E. of Mechoacan.

LUIS DE POTOSI, ST., a city of Mexico, in the province of Mechoacan; situate in the midst of rich gold mines, and all the comforts of life. The streets are neat and straight, and the churches magnificent. It is 180 miles N. by W. of Mechoacan. Long. 102. 54. W. lat. 22. 25. N.

LUI-TCHEOU, a city of China, of the first rank; in the province of Quang-tong. It is seated in a fertile country, near the sea; 315 miles S. W. of Canton. Long. 109. 25. E. lat. 20. 58. N.

LULEA, a seaport of Sweden, in Bothnia; with a good harbour. Near it is a mountain of iron ore. It stands on a river of the same name, at the N. W. extremity of the Gulf of Bothnia; 115 miles N. N. E. of Uma. Long. 22. 12. E. lat. 65. 32. N.

LUMBERTON, a town of N. Carolina; chief of Robeson county; situate on Drowning Creek; 32 miles S. of Fayetteville, and 65 N. W. of Wilmington.

LUMELLO, a town of the Sardinian states; formerly the residence of the kings of Lombardy, but now a small place. It is seated on the Gogna; 44 miles E. N. E. of Turin. Pop. 3250.

LUND, a town of Sweden, in the province of Scania. It carries on but little trade, and is principally supported by its university, founded by Charles XI., and from him called Academia

Carolina Gothorum. The cathedral is an ancient irregular building. It is 21 miles E. of Copenhagen, and 38 S. W. of Christianstadt. Pop. 3500. Long. 13. 12. E. lat. 55. 42. N.

LUNDEN, a town of Denmark, in N. Ditsmarsch; seated near the Eyder; 22 miles W. of Rendsburg.

LUNDY, an island at the entrance of the Bristol Channel, about 12 miles from the Devonshire coast: it has a lighthouse on its summit. It is about 5 miles long, and 2 broad; and in the N. part is a high pyramidical rock, called the Constable. Long. 4. 8. W. lat. 51. 18. N.

LUNE. *See* LOYNE.

LUNEL, a town of France, in the department of Gard; near the river Ridourle. It has excellent muscadine wine. It is 16 miles E. of Montpelier.

LUNEN, a town of Westphalia; in the county of Marck; situate at the conflux of the Zezisk with the Lippe; 20 miles S. by W. of Munster.

LUNENBURG, or LUNEBURG, a province of Hanover: formerly a duchy of the German empire; lying along the left bank of the Elbe. A small portion, lying on the right bank of the Elbe, now belongs to Denmark; but Hanoverian Lunenburg comprises a superficial extent of 4236 square miles, with 265,000 inhabitants. It is watered by the rivers Aller, Elbe, Ilmenau, Oker, Jeetze, Fuhse, and some smaller streams; and part of it is full of heaths and forests; but near the river it is tolerably fertile.

LUNENBURG, a large fortified town; capital of the foregoing province. The chief public edifices are the places for public worship, the palace, three hospitals, the town-house, the salt magazine, the anatomical theatre, and the academy. The salt springs near this place are very productive. It is situate on the Ilmenau; 36 miles S. E. of Hamburgh, and 60 N. of Brunswick. Pop. 12,000.

LUNEVILLE, a town of France; department of Meurthe. In its castle the dukes of Lorrain formerly kept their court, as did afterwards king Stanislaus. In 1131 a treaty of peace was concluded here between France and Austria. Luneville is seated in a plain between the rivers Vesoul and Meurthe; 14 miles E.S.E. of Nancy, and 62 W. of Strasburg. Long. 6. 30. E. lat. 48. 36. N. Pop. 11,250.

LUNGRO, a town of Naples, in Basilicata; chiefly inhabited by Greeks; 35 miles N. N. W. of Cosenza.

LUPOW, a town of Pomerania, on a river of the same name; 15 miles E. of Stolpe.

LURE, a town of France, department of Upper Saone; celebrated for a late abbey of Benedictines, converted, in 1764, into a chapter of noble canons. It is seated near the Ougnon; 30 miles N. E. of Besançon.

LURGAN, a town of Ireland; in the county of Armagh; with an extensive linen manufacture; 14 miles N. E. of Armagh, and 67 N. of Dublin.

LUSATIA, a margraviate of Germany; 90 miles long, and 60 broad; bounded on the N. by Brandenburg, E. by Silesia, S. by Bohemia, and W. by Saxony. It is divided into Upper and Lower Lusatia, formerly two distinct states, which became subject to Saxony, and formed a province of that power until 1815. The whole of Lower Lusatia, which forms the northern part of the margraviate, now belongs to Prussia, as does also one-half of Upper Lusatia, which is included in the government of Leignitz: the part that remains to Saxony is computed at 1170 square miles, with 195,000 inhabitants. Upper Lusatia abounds more in mountains and hills than the Lower, in which are many boggy and moorish tracts; yet it is the most fruitful. The breeding of cattle is very considerable, and there is plenty of game; but the products of the country do not supply the necessities of the inhabitants. This want is compensated by its numerous manufactures, particularly those of cloths and linens. Chief town, Bautzen.

LUSIGNAN, a town of France; department of Vienne; seated on the Vonne; 15 miles S. S. W. of Poitiers.

LUSO, a river of Italy, which rises in the duchy of Urbino, crosses part of Romagno, and enters the Gulf of Venice; 10 miles N. of Rimini.

LUTON, a town of Bedfordshire; with a market on Monday. The population is principally employed in the straw plait making. It is situate on the river Lea; 18 miles S. of Bedford, and 31 N. by W. of London.

LUTTERBERG, a town of Hanover; in the principality of Grubinhagen; seated on the Oder; 15 miles S. of Gozlar.

LUTTERWORTH, a town in Leicestershire; with a market on Thursday. It has a large and handsome church. Wickliff, the celebrated reformer, was rector, and died here, in 1387. Lutterworth has little trade, being principally supported by the neighbouring opulent graziers. It is seated on the river Swift; 14 miles S. of Leicester, and 88 N. W. of London.

LUTZELSTEIN, a town of France; department of Lower Rhine; with a strong castle; seated on a mountain; 30 miles N. W. of Strasburg.

LUTZEN, a town of Saxony; in the principality of Merseberg; belonging to Prussia; with a castle. Pop. 1350. Near this place, in 1632, Gustavus Adolphus, king of Sweden, was killed in a battle, at the moment of victory. Lutzen is also celebrated for the defeat of the united forces of Russia and Prussia, by Bonaparte, in May, 1813. It is seated on the Elster; 11 miles W. S. W. of Leipsic.

LUXEMBURG, a province of the Netherlands; bounded by the Prussian states on the Rhine, a part of the French frontier, and the Belgic provinces of Namur and Liege, and comprising a superficial area of 2400 square miles, with 293,600 inhabitants. It gives the title of grand duke to the sovereign. The surface is mountainous and woody, being traversed by branches of the Ardennes; and the climate is colder than that of the other provinces. The principal river is the Moselle. Corn, potatoes, flax, and some wine are raised; the rearing of cattle forms an important branch of industry; and there are manufactures of woollen and iron; but the chief wealth of the province consists in its forests, which occupy upwards of 460,000 acres. It is divided into the districts of Luxemburg, Dietkirch, and Neufchateau. In the partition of Europe in 1815, it was ceded to the kingdom of the Netherlands, and on the separation of Belgium from that kingdom, it was claimed by them; and the possession of it is still disputed by those powers.

Luxemburg, the capital of the above province, and one of the strongest towns in Europe. It is divided by the Alsitz into the Upper and Lower Town; the former almost surrounded by rocks, but the latter seated in a plain. In 1795 it surrendered to the French, but was restored in 1814. It is 22 miles W. S. W. of Treves, and 130 S. E. of Brussels. Long. 6. 10. E. lat. 49. 37. N. Pop. 11,500.

Luxeuil, a town of France; department of Upper Saone; near which are some mineral waters and warm baths. It is seated at the foot of the Vosges; 14 miles from Vesoul. Pop. 3250.

Luxor, a village of Upper Egypt; on the site of the ancient Thebes; and in which were two famous obelisks, one of which has been removed to the Place Louis XIV., in Paris. Lat. 25. 41. N. long. 32. 41. E.

Luyo and Chillaos, a province of Peru; bounded E. by mountains, N. and N. W. by the province of Jaen, and S. E. by that of Caxamarca. It is 54 miles in length, and 24 in breadth, and contains 3500 inhabitants. The capital has the same name, and is in long. 77. 41. W. lat. 5. 33. S.

Luz, St. Jean de, a town of France; department of Upper Pyrenees; 27 miles S. W. of Tarbes. Pop. 2250.

Luzara, a strong town of Austrian Italy; in the province of Mantua; where a battle was fought between the Austrians and the French and Spaniards, in 1702, when each side claimed the victory. It is seated near the conflux of the Crostolo with the Po; 16 miles S. of Mantua.

Luzarches, a town of France; department of Seine-et-Oise; 19 miles N. of Paris.

Luzerne, a county of Pennsylvania; bounded N. by Tioga county, New York; E. and S. E. by Northampton, and W. by Lycoming and Northumberland counties. It is about 79 miles in length, and 75 in breadth, and is divided into 12 townships. Pop. 44,006. Wilksbarre is the chief town. Pop. 1718.

Luzon. *See* Luconia.

Lydd, a town of Kent; with a market on Thursday. It is a member of the cinque port of Romney, and seated in Romney Marsh; 25 miles S. W. of Dover, and 72 S. E. of London.

Lyge, a town of Norway; near a lake of the same name; 16 miles N. W. of Christiansand.

Lyme, or Lyme Regis, a borough and seaport in Dorsetshire; market on Friday. It returns one member to parliament. It is seated on the side of a craggy hill, on the river Lyme, at the head of a little inlet; and its harbour is formed by two very thick walls, called the Cobbe. Here the Duke of Monmouth landed, in 1585, for the execution of his ill-judged design against James II. Lyme is the birthplace of Thomas Coram, the benevolent patron and contriver of the Foundling Hospital in London. It is 26 miles E. of Exeter, and 143 S. W. of London.

Lymfiord, a gulf of Denmark, in North Jutland; which has a narrow entrance from the Cattegat, and extends 80 miles across the country, widening gradually, and forming several branches; the W. end is 20 miles long, and separated from the North Sea only by a narrow bank.

Lymington, a borough in Hampshire; governed by a mayor; with a market on Saturday. It is seated on a river of its name, a mile from the sea; and the harbour will admit vessels of 300 tons burden. The chief trade is in salt; and it is much resorted to in summer for sea-bathing. Near it are the remains of a Roman camp; and in 1744 nearly 200lbs. weight of their coins were discovered here in two urns. It returns two members to parliament. It is 18 miles S. S. W. of Southampton, and 88 S. W. of London.

Lynchburg, a town of Virginia, in Campbell county, on the S. side of James River; 166 miles W. of Richmond.

Lyndhurst, a village in Hampshire; on the N. side of the New Forest, 9 miles W. S. W. of Southampton. Here are the king's house and the king's stables, the latter very large; and all the forest courts are held here.

Lynn, a town of Massachusets, in Essex county; with a considerable manufacture of women's silk and cloth shoes. It is 9 miles S. S. W. of Salem, and 10 N. E. of Boston. Pop. 9369.

Lynn, or Lynn Regis, a borough and seaport of Norfolk; governed by a mayor; with markets on Tuesday and Saturday. It sends two members to parliament. By the Ouse, and its associated rivers, it supplies most of the midland counties with coal, timber, and wine; and, in return, exports malt and corn in great quantities: it also partakes in the Baltic trade and Greenland fishery. Lynn has a large market-place, with an elegant cross. It is 42 miles W. N. W. of Norwich, and 96 N. by E. of London. Long. 0. 24. E. lat. 52. 46. N.

Lyonnois, a former province of France; lying on the W. side of the Saone and Rhone; 30 miles in length, and 17 in breadth. This province, with Forez and Beaujolois, now forms the department of the Rhone and the Loire.

Lyons, a city of France; capital of the department of Rhone, and the see of an archbishop. Many antiquities are still observed, which evince its Roman origin. It was long considered as the second city of France, in beauty, size, and population, and superior to Paris in trade, commerce, and manufactures. The quays were adorned with magnificent structures; the cathedral was a majestic Gothic edifice; and the town-house was one of the most beautiful in Europe. The other principal buildings were the exchange, the custom-house, the palace of justice, the arsenal, a theatre, a public library, two colleges, and two hospitals. The bridge which unites the city with the suburb de la Guillotiere is 1560 feet long; and there are three other principal suburbs, six gates, and several fine churches. Such was Lyons in June, 1793, when it revolted against the national convention. Being obliged to surrender in October, the convention decreed that the walls and public buildings should be destroyed, and the name of the city changed to that of Ville Affranchie. The chiefs of the insurgents had fled, but several of them were afterwards taken; and, of 3528 persons who were tried before the revolutionary tribunal, 1682 were either shot or beheaded. In 1794, however, on the destruction of the faction of the jacobins, the convention decreed that the city should resume its ancient name, and that measures should be taken to restore its manufactures and commerce. In 1795 the friends of those who were so wantonly put to death in 1793, avenged their fate by a general massacre of the judges of the revolutionary tribunal, and of all the jacobins who were then confined in the prisons of Lyons. Notwithstanding, Lyons has begun to resume its ancient celebrity, and is now a place of very great trade, which is extended not only through France, but to Italy, Switzerland and Spain; and there are four celebrated fairs every year. The chief article of manufacture now is that of silk; the others are gold and silver brocade, plain, double, and striped velvet, richly embroidered taffeta, and satin; also gold and silver laces, or galloons, gauze, hats, ribbons, leather, carpets, and coloured paper. The printing and bookselling of this place are the next to Paris in importance. It was the scene of several actions between the French and Austrians in 1814; and, on the return of Bonaparte from Elba, in 1815, the princes of the house of Bourbon were obliged to withdraw. The city is seated at the conflux of the Saone with the Rhone; 15 miles N. of Vienne, and 280 S. E. of Paris. Population about 186,000. Long. 4. 49. E. lat. 45. 46. N.

Lyons, a town of North America; state of New York; an improving place; situated on the Western Canal; 16 miles N. of Geneva, and 20 N. E. of Canandaigua.

Lythe, a village of North Yorkshire, on the seacoast; 4 miles W. N. W. of Whitby; noted for its extensive alum-works.

Lytham, a town in Lancashire; 5 miles from Kirkham, and 230 from London.

M.

Maadieh, a lake of Lower Egypt, between Alexandria and Aboukir, on the coast of the Delta; it is divided from Lake Mareotis on the S. W. by a neck of land, on which runs the Alexandrian Canal, or El Kaliss.

Maalmorie, a promontory and small island of Scotland, on the S. E. coast of the Isle of Islay.

Maartensdyke, a town of the Netherlands, in the province of Zealand; on the island of Tholm; 9 miles W. N. W. of Bergen-op-Zoom.

Mabra, a town of Algiers, seated on the Gulf of Bona; 10 miles W. of Bona.

Macao, a town in China, in the province of Quang-tung, in the Bay of Canton, from which it is distant 55 miles. It is the only settlement possessed by Europeans in the extensive empire of China. The town is situated on a sandy peninsula. connected with the island of Macao by a neck of land, on which is a Chinese fort and wall, and beyond which no European is allowed to pass, and which circumscribes the space to about 3 miles long and 1 wide. The Portuguese, to whom the town nominally belongs, and who have a custom-house, and who are masters of the strong fortifications, pay an annual ground-rent for the town. The British and other European nations have factories in the town, which is 30 miles below the island of Lintin, and beyond which no ship of war is allowed to proceed, and 45 miles below Whampoa, where merchant ships stop, 10 miles below Canton. The first Portuguese settlement was in 1537; but they gradually proceeded to gain a firm footing, till it became the centre of the commerce which they carried on with Japan, China, and the eastern islands, and was then a more important place than at present. After 1638 it declined, and is now inhabited by about 5000 Portuguese, and the Chinese are estimated 30,000. Long. 113. 30. E. lat. 22. 13. N.

Macarsca, a seaport of Austrian Dalmatia, and a bishop's see. In its vicinity are many subterraneous grottoes. It is seated on the Gulf of Venice; 36 miles S. E. of Spalatro. Long. 18. 7. E. lat. 43. 49. N.

Macas, a town of Colombia, the capital of a fertile district of Del Escudor. The town was formerly a rich and flourishing place, but it is greatly decayed. It is seated on one of the sources of the Amazon; 138 miles S. by E. of Quito.

Macassar, formerly a considerable kingdom of the island of Celebes. Its princes at one period ruled over almost the whole island, and also over several of the neighbouring ones. Since that time, however, the empire has been completely subverted by the Dutch.

Macassar, the chief settlement of the Dutch in the above territory, called by them Fort Rotterdam; with a respectable fort and a good harbour; but the latter is of difficult access. Chinese junks carry on a direct trade with

China from this place; so that the mixed population, of Dutch and half-castes, Chinese and natives, amounts to about 100,000. The Portuguese settled here about 1525, but were expelled by the Dutch in 1660. The British took possession of it in 1810, but restored it in 1814. It is seated at the mouth of a river, on the S. W. coast, and at the S. end of the Strait of Macassar. Long. 119. 49. E. lat. 5. 9. S.

MACASSAR, a strait which separates the islands of Celebes and Borneo. It is about 350 miles in length, and from 50 to 140 in in breadth, and contains numerous shoals and rocky islands.

MACCLESFIELD, a borough in Cheshire; markets on Tuesday and Saturday. It returns two members to parliament. It has manufactures of mohair, twist, hatbands, buttons, and thread, and mills for the winding of silk. It is a large handsome town, and contains two churches, seven meeting-houses for dissenters, a Roman Catholic chapel, three almshouses for widows; a free grammar-school, founded by Edward VI., and two Sunday-schools. It is seated at the edge of a forest, near the river Bollin; 36 miles E. of Chester, and 167 N. W. of London. Long. 2. 17. W. lat. 53. 15. N.

MACDUFF, a town of Scotland, in Banffshire, with a good harbour, on the Frith of Moray; 2 miles E. of Banff.

MACEDON, or MACEDONIA, a celebrated province of Greece; bounded by Thrace, Bulgaria, Servia, Thessaly, and the Archipelago. The soil is, for the most part, fertile, and the coasts in particular abound in corn, wine, oil, tobacco, &c. Pop. 700,000. Salonica is the capital.

MACEIRA. *See* MAZIERA.

MACERATA, a town of Italy, in the Papal States; it is the see of a bishop, and contains a university, two academies, a public school, and about 10,000 inhabitants. The principal gate is built in the form of a triumphal arch. In 1797 it was taken by the French. It is seated on a hill by the river Chienti; 22 miles S. by W. of Ancona. Long. 13. 27. E. lat. 43. 20. N.

MACHALA, a town of Colombia, in the department of Quito. The environs produce great quantities of excellent cocoa; also large mangrove-trees, the wood of which is very durable, and so heavy as to sink in water. It stands near the Bay of Guayaquil; 86 miles S. of Guayaquil.

MACHERRY, a town of Hindostan, capital of a district of the same name, in the province of Agra. It is 70 miles S. S. W. of Delhi.

MACHIAN, the most fertile of the Molucca Islands, which rises like a conic mountain from the sea. It is 20 miles in circumference, and produces excellent cloves. Long. 126. 55. E. lat. 0. 28. N.

MACHIAS, a seaport of the state of Maine, in Washington county. In 1792 Washington academy was established here. The trade is considerable in fish, lumber, boards, shingles, and hewed timber. It stands on a bay of its name; 65 miles E. N. E. of Castine. Long. 67. 45. W. lat. 44. 40. N.

MACHLIN, a town of Scotland, in Ayrshire; seated on an eminence near the river Ayr; 9 miles E. N. E. of Ayr.

MACHYNLLETH, a town of Wales, in Montgomeryshire, with a market on Wednesday. In the vicinity are extensive slate quarries and several productive lead mines; the staple manufacture is that of flannel. Here Owen Glendwr exercised his first acts of royalty, in 1402. The town is seated near the Dyfi, over which is a bridge into Merionethshire; 37 miles W. of Montgomery, and 207 N. W. of London.

MACKENZIE'S RIVER, a considerable river, of North America, discovered by Mackenzie, in 1780, which issues from the Slave Lake, and flows to the Frozen Ocean, in long. 135. W. and lat. 69. N.

MACON, or MASCON, a city of France, capital of the department of Saone-et-Loire; celebrated for its wine. It is seated on the side of a hill, near the Saone; 40 miles N. of Lyons. Pop. 11,750. Long. 4. 48. E. lat. 46. 20. N.

MACQUARIE HARBOUR, an extensive land-locked basin, on the W. side of Van Diemen's Land. On Sarah Island was a penal settlement for secondary punishments.

MACQUARIE, PORT, a settlement in the E. coast of Australia, at the mouth of the Hastings river, in lat. 31. 22. S. long. 152. 52. E.—Also the name of a large river in New South Wales, rising W. of the Blue Mountains. It was discovered in 1813, and it has since been traced to its junction with the Darling river.

MACRI, or MAKRI, a town of Asiatic Turkey, in Natolia, seated on a gulf of its name, in the Mediterranean. Here are the ruins of an amphitheatre and an old fort, and numerous remains of Greek inscriptions. It is 125 miles S. E. of Smyrna. Long. 29. 24. E. lat. 36. 56. N.

MACRO, or MACRONISI, an island of the Grecian Archipelago, near the coast of Livadia; 20 miles E. of Athens. Long. 24. 16. E. lat. 37. 30. N.

MACROOM, a town of Ireland, in the county of Cork. It has a handsome court-house and chapel. Macroom Castle is a building of great beauty, and of great antiquity; 191 miles from Dublin.

MACTAN. *See* MATAN.

MACULA, a seaport of Arabia, in the province of Hadramaut; 150 miles S. W. of Shibam. Long. 47. 50. E. lat. 13. 25. N.

MADAGASCAR, an island lying on the eastern coast of Africa; about 800 miles in length, 300 in breadth, and 2000 in circumference. It is intersected throughout its whole length by a chain of lofty mountains, the scenery of which is in many places strikingly grand and picturesque. The climate is healthy, and the soil extremely fertile; its products are rice, sugar, and silk; also potatoes. The cocoa-nut, the banana, and other useful trees, flourish here. The island rears no horses, or camels, but large herds of oxen, some of which come to an enormous size. The inhabitants are divided into a number of tribes, and amount to about 4,000,000. The natives, called Madagasses, or Malegasses, are commonly tall and well made, of an olive complexion, which in some is pretty dark. Their hair is usually long and black, curling naturally; their noses are small, though not flat. They seem to have had a great many Arabs among them, with whom they are mixed; and there are some of a yellowish complexion, who have neater features than the rest. Although a populous country, they have no cities or towns, but a great number of villages at a small distance from each other, composed of huts, with doors so low that a boy of 12 years old cannot enter them without stooping. They have neither windows nor chimneys, and the roofs are covered with reeds or leaves. Both men and women are fond of bracelets and necklaces, and anoint their bodies with grease or oil. Those that are dressed in the best manner have a piece of cotton, cloth, or silk, wrapped round their middle; but they generally make little use of clothing. Their beds are only mats spread upon boards, and a piece of wood or stone serves them for a bolster. They are very superstitious, and practise circumcision and polygamy. Madagascar is happily exempt from the ravages of the lion and the tiger, but here are great numbers of locusts, crocodiles, and chameleons. The French have frequently attempted to settle here, but have always been driven hence; and there are only some parts on the coast yet known. The chief settlement was at Port Dauphin, on the S. E. coast, in long. 47. 0. E. lat. 25. 0. S.; and the place most visited by the Europeans is more to the N., called Fouleponte. Long. 49. 50. E. lat. 17. 40. S.

Madalena, a river of Terra Firma, which rises in the mountains to the E. of Popayan, takes a northerly course of above 900 miles, and enters the Caribbean Sea, by several mouths, between Carthagena and St. Martha.

Madeira, an island in the Atlantic Ocean, 54 miles long and 20 broad, and 250 N. by E. of Teneriff. Area, 400 square miles. Population, almost entirely of Portuguese descent, between 90,000 and 110,000. It may be characterized as one mountain, rising in the centre to the height of 5068 feet, and exhibits evidences of volcanic action. The Portuguese discovered this island in 1419; but it was uninhabited, and covered with wood, and on that account they called it Madeira; but it has been asserted that it was visited prior to this, by an Englishman named Macham, who had eloped with a French lady. Prince Henry, the next year, settled a colony here, and not only furnished it with the plants and domestic animals common in Europe, but procured slips of the vine from Cyprus, and plants of the sugar-cane from Sicily; and the sugar and wine of Madeira quickly became articles of some consequence in the commerce of Portugal. The sugar-works have since been removed, but its wine is now in the highest estimation, especially such as has been a voyage to the East or West Indies. It produces from 20,000 to 25,000 pipes annually, two-thirds of which are exported. The scorching heat of summer and the icy chill of winter are here unknown; for spring and autumn reign continually, and produce flowers and fruits throughout the year. The cedar tree is found in great abundance, and the dragon-tree is a native of this island. Flowers nursed in the English greenhouses grow wild here in the fields; the hedges are mostly formed of the geranium, rose, jasmine, and honeysuckle; while the larkspur, fleur-de-lis, lupin, &c., spring up spontaneously in the meadows. There are few reptiles to be seen in the island; the lizard is the most common. Canary birds and goldfinches are found in the mountains. The hog is the food most relished; they are suffered to range among the mountains, and are hunted and caught by dogs. Salted cod is imported from America, and is the chief diet of the poor. Madeira is well watered and populous. The British factory settled in this island consists of upwards of 20 commercial houses, and have considerably more of its trade than the Portuguese. In 1808 it surrendered, conditionally, to the English. Funchal is the capital.

Madely Market, a town in Shropshire, with a market on Friday, held at the foot of Colebrook Dale Bridge. It is celebrated for having afforded refuge to Charles I. after the battle of Worcester. Here are some very extensive iron works. It is 9 miles N. of Bridgenorth, and 147 N. W. of London.

Madhugiri, a town of Hindostan, in Mysore, with a strong hill-fort. In its vicinity much iron is smelted, and a great number of cattle are bred. It is seated amid hills and fertile valleys, 22 miles E. of Sera.

Madian, or Midian, a town of Arabia Petræa, on the E. side of the eastern arm of the Red Sea. The Arabians call it Megar el Schuaid, the Grotto of Schuaid (or Jethro), and suppose it to be the place where Moses tended the flocks of his father-in-law. It is 50 miles N. of Moilah, and 80 S. of Acaba.

Madison, a county of the United States, in New York, erected in 1806.—Also, 2. A county in the state of Virginia. 3. In Georgia, celebrated for its chalybeate springs. Pop. 4510. 4. In Alabama. 5. In Kentucky. 6. In Ohio. 7. In Illinois. This is also the name of numerous townships of Ohio, New York, and Virginia.

Madras, or Fort St. George, a celebrated fort and city of Hindostan. It is the capital of the British possessions on the E. side of the Peninsula, and is a fortress of very great extent. It is close on the margin of the Bay of Bengal, from which it has a rich and beautiful appearance, the houses being covered with stucco, called chunam, which in itself is nearly as compact as the finest marble, and bears as high a polish. The Black town is separated from the fort by an esplanade. In common with all the European settlements on this coast, Madras has no port for shipping, the coast forming nearly a straight line; and it is incommoded also with a high and dangerous surf. It is the seat of an archdeaconry, and of missions from different societies in Britain. In 1746 it was taken by the French, but restored by the peace of Aix-la-Chapelle. Pop. 140,000. It is 100 miles N. by E. of Pondicherry. Long. 80. 25. E. lat. 13. 5. N.

Madras Territory, the countries subject to the presidency of Fort St. George, or Madras; comprehending nearly the whole of India S. of the river Kistnah, and the extensive province denominated the Northern Circars. Within these boundaries, however, three native princes, the rajahs of Mysore, Travancore, and Cochin, still collect their resources, and exercise a certain degree of authority within their territories. The rest of the country is under the immediate jurisdiction of the governor and council of Madras, and is subdivided into 24 districts, over each of which there is a European judge and a collector, with the requisite establishments. There are also four provisional courts of circuit and appeal, to which the above-mentioned judges are subordinate; and a supreme court of appeal, stationary at Madras, consisting of four judges, selected from the Company's civil servants. Pop. about 12 millions.

Madre de Dios, an island in the Pacific Ocean, near the coast of Patagonia; 180 miles in circumference.

Madre de Popa, a town of New Granada, with a celebrated convent. It is much resorted to by the pilgrims of South America, and they pretend that the image of the Virgin has done a great many miracles in favour of the seafaring people. It is seated on the Madelena, 50 miles E. of Carthagena.

Madrid, the capital of Spain, in New Castile. It was formerly an inconsiderable place, belonging to the archbishop of Toledo, but the purity of the air induced the court to remove hither, and it is now a considerable city. It contains 77 churches, 66 convents, 15 gates of granite, and about 201,344 inhabitants. The houses are mostly built of stone, and the principal streets are long, broad, and straight, and adorned at proper distances with handsome fountains. There are above 100 towers or steeples in different places, which contribute greatly to the embellishment of the city. It stands in a plain, surrounded by mountains, and has a high wall, built of mud. There are palaces on a large scale. The Palacio Real, at the W. end, is strongly built, and elegantly ornamented on the outside; the Buen Retiro is situated at the E. of the town, and is chiefly remarkable for its large collection of paintings, and very extensive gardens. The churches and monasteries contain many paintings by the most celebrated masters. The squares are numerous; the finest is the Plaça Mayor, which is 1536 feet in circuit, surrounded by houses five stories high, all of an equal height; every story being adorned with a handsome balcony, and the fronts supported by columns, which form very fine arcades. Here the *autos da fe* were formerly celebrated, with all their terrible apparatus. In the environs are several royal residences, such as the Casa del Campo, where a great many wild animals were formerly kept for the chase. The manufactures of Madrid are very inconsiderable; those for hats, and the royal china and saltpetre works, are the principal. The French took possession of this city in March, 1808, and on the 2d of May the inhabitants rose up in arms to expel them from the city, when a terrible carnage took place for several hours, and it was not till the arrival of more troops that order was enforced among the people. On the 20th of July following Joseph Bonaparte entered it as king of Spain, but was obliged to quit it soon afterwards. On the 2d of December of the same year it was retaken by Napoleon, who reinstated his brother on the throne; and he kept possession till August, 1812, when Madrid was entered by the British army under the Duke of Wellington. The French, however, again took possession of it in November, but finally evacuated it the following year. The inhabitants joined in the revolution of 1820, when the king was obliged to accede to the general desire of restoring the constitution of the Cortes of 1812. *See* Spain. Madrid is on the river Manzanares, over which is a magnificent bridge; 265 miles N. E. of Lisbon, and 650 S. S. W. of Paris. Long. 3. 34. W. lat. 40. 25. N.

Madrigal, a town of Spain, in Old Castile; seated in a plain, fertile in excellent wine, 10 miles N. E. of Medina del Campo.

Madrisio, a town of Italy, in Friuli, 30 miles N. of Venice.

Madrogan, a town of Africa, the capital of Mocaranga, with a spacious royal palace. The upper part of the houses is in the shape of a bell. Long. 29. 40. E. lat. 18. 0. S.

Madura, a town of Hindostan, capital of a district of the same name belonging to the British, and included in the collectorship of Dindigul. It is fortified with square towers and parapets, and has one of the most superb pagodas in Hindostan. It is 130 miles N.N.W. of Cape Comorin, and 270 S. S. W. of Madras. Long. 78. 12. E. lat. 9. 55. N

Madura, an island in the Indian Ocean, on the N. coast of the island of Java. It is 100 miles long, and 15 broad, and the soil is fertile and well cultivated. The chief towns are Samanap, Parmacassan, and Bancallan.

Maeler, a lake of Sweden, 80 miles long and 20 broad, between the provinces of Westmania and Sudermania. It contains several fine islands, is usually frozen during a few weeks in winter, and opens an easy communication, by sledges, between the interior parts of Sweden and the city of Stockholm.

Maelstrom, a dangerous whirlpool on the coast of Norway, in 68 N. lat. and near the island of Moskoe; whence it is also named Moskoestrom. When it is flood, the stream runs up the country with a boisterous rapidity; but the roar of its impetuous ebb to the sea is scarcely equalled by the loudest cataracts. The whirlpool is of such an extent and depth, that, if a ship comes within its attraction, it is inevitably absorbed and beaten in pieces against the rocks below; and when the water relaxes the fragments come up again. The intervals of tranquillity are only at the turn of the ebb and flood, and calm weather; and they last but a quarter of an hour, its violence gradually returning. When the stream is most boisterous, and its fury heightened by a storm, vessels have been reached by it at the distance of 5 miles.

Maerna, a town of Germany, in Tyrol; 23 miles W. S. W. of Trent.

Maese. *See* Meuse.

Maeseyk, a town of Belgium, in the province of Liege, on the river Meuse; 10 miles S. S. W. of Ruremonde.

Maeslandsluys, a town of South Holland, near the mouth of the Meuse; 10 miles W. of Rotterdam.

Maestricht, a city of the Netherlands, capital of the province of Limburg, about 4 miles in circumference, seated on the Meuse, opposite Wyck, with which it communicates by a stone bridge. The number of inhabitants is estimated at 18,000. It has fine long streets, many churches and convents, a college formerly belonging to the Jesuits, a council-house with its library, and considerable manufactures of cloth, leather, hosiery, and hardware. Near it is the lofty mountain of St. Peter, with a fortress; and a stone quarry, with such a number of subterranean passages as to be capable of containing 40,000 persons. The other fortifications, and the situation of Maestricht, are such, that it is deemed one of the strongest places in Europe. The city was besieged by the French in 1748, during the negotiations of Aix-la-Chapelle; was unsuccessfully attacked by them in 1793; and they became masters of it towards the end of the following year. In 1814 it was delivered up to the allied forces. It is 14 miles N. N. E. of Liege, and 58 E. of Brussels. Long. 5. 48. E. lat. 50. 49. N.

Mafra, a town of Portugal, in Estremadura, with a college, founded in 1772. In a sandy and barren spot near this place, John V., in pursuance of a vow, erected a building of extraordinary magnificence, as a Franciscan convent. The town is seated near the sea, 18 miles N. N. W. of Lisbon.

Magadi, or Maghery, a town of Hindostan, in the district of Mysore, seated in a hilly country, abounding in timber-trees, stone, and iron; 24 miles W. of Bangalore.

Magadoxa, the capital of a kingdom of the same name on the coast of Ajan, with a citadel, and a good harbour. It stands at the mouth of a river, which is supposed to have a long course, having regular inundations, that fertilize the country to a great extent. The inhabitants are mostly Mahomedans; but there are also some Abyssinian Christians. They all speak the Arabic tongue, are stout and warlike, and, among other weapons, use poisoned arrows and lances. The city is a place of great commerce, receiving from Adel and other parts cotton, silk, spices, and drugs, in exchange for gold, ivory, wax, and other commodities. Long. 46. 25. E. lat. 2. 10. N.

Magdalen Isles, a group of islets in the Gulf of St. Lawrence, near its entrance. They are inhabited by a few families, whose chief support is derived from fishing.

Magdalena, a large river of New Granada, which rises in the province of Popayan, and, after a course of 900 miles, falls into the sea in lat. 11. 2. N.

Magdalena, a river in New Mexico, which runs into the sea between the rivers Flores and Mexicano.

Magdeburg, a government of the Prussian states in Saxony, composed of part of the duchy of Magdeburg, that portion of the Old Mark on the left of the Elbe, the principality of Halberstadt, the abbey of Quedlinburg, the county of Wernigerode, the barony of Schauen, and the bailiwicks of Kloetze, Barby, and Gommern. It comprises a superficial area of nearly 4400 square miles, is divided into 15 circles, and contains 450,000 inhabitants. The country is in general level, and the parts which are not marshy and overgrown with wood are very fertile. Its commerce is greatly facilitated by the Elbe, which traverses it through its whole extent.

Magdeburg, a fortified city; capital of the foregoing government. It has a handsome palace, a citadel, with a fine arsenal, and a magnificent cathedral, which contains the superb mausoleum of Otho the Great. The inhabitants are computed at 37,500. Here are manufactures of cotton and linen goods, stockings, gloves, porcelain, hats, leather, soap, and tobacco; but the principal are those of woollen and silk. It is well situate for trade, on both sides of the Elbe, by which it has an easy communication with Hamburgh. In the neighbourhood are the monastery of Bergin, and the salt-works of Schœnebeck, producing about 30,000 tons annually. Magdeburg has sustained several sieges. In 1631 it was taken by the Austrians, who burnt the town, except the cathedral and a few houses adjacent, and massacred above 10,000 of the inhabitants; but it was soon handsomely rebuilt. In 1806 it surrendered to the French, and was not restored till 1813. It is 75 miles W. S. W. of Berlin, and 120 S. E. of Hamburgh. Long. 11. 40. E. lat. 52. 10. N.

Magellan, or Magalhaen, a strait of South America; discovered in 1520, by Ferdinando Magellan, a Portuguese, in the service of Spain. It has since been accurately surveyed; but the passage, upwards of 300 miles, being dangerous and troublesome, navigators generally sail round Cape Horn.

Maggeroe, or Mageron, a large island on the coast of Norway, and the most northern land in Europe. It is separated from the continent on the S. by a narrow channel; and its N. extremity in an enormous rock, called North Cape. Long. 25. 57. E. lat. 71. 10. N.

Magherafelt, a town of Ireland; in the county of Londonderry; with a considerable linen manufacture; 13 miles W. of Antrim, and 30 S. E. of Londonderry.

Magia, a river of Switzerland, in the canton

of Tessin; which runs S. with rapidity, through a narrow valley of its name, and enters the lake of Maggiore, near Locarno.

MAGGIORE, a lake of Upper Italy; separating part of the Austro-Italian government of Milan from the states of Sardinia, and extending from Sesto northward, to Locarno; 30 miles in length, and 3 in breadth. The river Tesino runs S. through its whole length; and it contains the celebrated Boromean Isles.

MAGINDANAO. *See* MINDANAO.

MAGLIANO, a town of Italy; province of Sabina; seated on a mountain near the river Tiber; 34 miles N. of Rome. Long. 12. 35. E. lat. 42. 25. N.

MAGNA VACCA, a town and fort of Italy, in the Papal States; seated at the mouth of the Lake of Commachio, in the Gulf of Venice; 3 miles S. E. of Commachio.

MAGNISA, (ancient Magnesia,) a town of European Turkey, in Anadolis; 20 miles N. E. of Smyrna; once the capital of the Greek empire. It is better built than the rest of the towns in the pachalic, and was formerly famous as productive of the loadstone; from whence the name magnet perhaps is derived.

MAGNY, a town of France, department of Seine-et-Oise; 32 miles N. W. of Paris.

MAHALEU, or MAHALLET-EL-KEBEER, a town of Egypt; capital of El-Garbia. It carries on a considerable trade in linen, cotton, and salammoniac; and the inhabitants have ovens to hatch chickens. Long. 33. 30. E. lat. 31. 30. N.

MAHANUDDY, (the large river,) a river of Hindostan, which rises in the N. E. part of Berar, crosses Orissa, and enters the Bay of Bengal, by several mouths, below Cattack. These mouths form an assemblage of low woody islands: and at the mouth of the principal channel, near False Point, is a fortified island, named Cajung, or Codjung.

MAHE, a town of Hindostan, in Malabar; formerly belonging to the French, but taken by the English in 1793. It is situate on high ground, at the mouth of a river; 5 miles S.S.E. of Tellicherry.

MAHLBERG, a town and castle of Germany, in Baden; 17 miles N. of Friburg.

MAHMOODABAD, a town of Hindostan, in Guzerat; 17 miles S. S. E. of Ahmedabad.

MAHMUDPORE, a town of Hindostan, in Bengal; 80 miles N. E. of Calcutta.

MAHOMDY, a town of Hindostan, in the province of Oude; 70 miles N. W. of Lucknow, and 150 E. S. E. of Delhi.

MAHON, a port and town at the eastern end of Minorca. It is a fine harbour, the entrance of which is narrow, and defended by two forts. It was much used by the British, during the late wars.

MAHRATTA TERRITORY, and extensive country of Hindostan; which, till lately, stretched across what is called the Peninsula of India. On the accession of Ram Rajah, in 1740, the peishwa and the paymaster-general confined him to the fortress of Sattarah, and divided the empire between them; the former fixing his residence at Poonah, which became the capital of the Western Mahrattas: the latter founding a new kingdom in the province of Gundwaneh, called the Eastern Mahrattas, and fixing his residence at NAGPORE (which see). The peishwa became dependent on the British, in 1802; but, attempting to shake off his dependence, he was defeated, and deposed. The Mahrattas are Hindoos; and many of the Brahmins are polished and insidious merchants. They are fond of horses, and their army was almost entirely composed of cavalry; they were, however, never very formidable, as a regular force, depending more on the celerity of their motions, and the suddenness of their incursions, than on the boldness with which they met their enemies.

MAHRBURG. *See* MARCHBURG.

MAHUR, a town of Hindostan; capital of a district of its name, in the province of Berar; seated on the Chin Gonga, which flows into the Godavery; 140 miles S. W. of Nagpore. Long. 78. 34. E. lat. 19. 24. N.

MAIDA, a town of Naples, in Calabria Ultra. On the plain near this place, in 1806, a victory was obtained by 5000 British troops over 8000 French. It is 9 miles W. S. W. of Squillace.

MAIDENHEAD, a town in Berkshire; governed by a mayor; with a market on Wednesday, and a good trade in malt, meal, and timber. It is seated on the Thames, over which is a bridge, near which it is also crossed by the Great Western railway; 12 miles E. by N. of Reading, and 26 W. by N. of London.

MAIDENOI, an island of the Pacific Ocean; 36 miles long, and 9 broad. In the N. W. part of it native copper is found. Long. 167. 10. E. lat. 54. 40. N.

MAIDSTONE, a borough, and the county town of Kent; governed by a mayor, with a market on Thursday. It has a brisk trade in exporting the commodities of the county, particularly hops, of which there are numerous plantations around; here are likewise paper mills, and a manufacture of linen. The church is a spacious and handsome edifice. The county gaol and court-house is an extensive range of modern buildings; and there are several meeting-houses for dissenters, a grammar school, eight charity schools, &c. Maidstone is seated on the Medway, over which is a bridge of seven arches; 20 miles W. of Canterbury, and 34 E. S. E. of London. It returns two members to parliament. Long. 0. 38. E. lat. 51. 16. N.

MAIHIDPORE, a town of Hindostan, in Malwal; near which the troops of Holkar were defeated by the British in 1817. It is seated on the Soprah; 20 miles N. of Oojain.

MAILCOTTA, a lofty fortress of Hindostan, in Mysore; and one of the most celebrated places of Hindoo worship. The large temple is a square building of great dimensions, and the jewels belonging to it are very valuable. In 1772 Hyder was completely routed by the Mahratta chiefs near this place; and it was here that the Mahratta chiefs joined Lord Cornwallis, in 1791. It is 17 miles N. of Seringapatam.

MAILLIEZAIS, a town of France; department

of Vendee; seated on an island formed by the Seure and Autize; 22 miles N. E. of Rochelle.

Maina, a seaport of Greece, in the Morea; which gives name to a district that lies between two bays of the Mediterranean Sea. The inhabitants of the district, estimated at 50,000, could never, even nominally, be subjected to the Turks, till the end of the eighteenth century, when they agreed to pay a small tribute to the porte. The town is seated on the Bay of Coron; 46 miles S. by W. of Misitra. Long. 22. 10. E. lat. 36. 34. N.

Maine, one of the United States; formerly a district of Massachusets; 250 miles long, and 192 broad. Area 32,628 square miles. Pop. 501,793. It is bounded on the N. W. and N. by Canada, E. by New Brunswick, S. E. and E. by the Atlantic, and W. by New Hampshire. It comprises the counties of Penobscot, York, Cumberland, Lincoln, Hancock, Washington, Kennebeck, Oxford, and Somerset. The chief rivers are the Penobscot, Kennebeck, Saco, Androscoggin, St. John, and St. Croix; and it has several small lakes. Though an elevated tract, it cannot be called mountainous, and a great proportion of the lands are arable, and exceedingly fertile. Hops are the spontaneous growth of this country. The trees are white pine, spruce, maple, beech, white and grey oak, and yellow birch; these, as ship timber, boards, and every species of split lumber, are the principal exports of the country. The heat in summer is intense, and the cold in winter extreme; all the lakes and rivers are usually passable on ice, from Christmas till the middle of March. Portland is the capital.

Maine, a large river of Germany; formed by two streams called the Red and White Maine, which rises among the mountains of Franconia. It joins the Rhine a little above Mentz.

Maine, Lower, a circle of the Bavarian states; contiguous to Baden, Hesse-Cassel, and Hesse-Darmstadt; comprising a superficial extent of 3000 square miles, with 423,000 inhabitants. The principal products are corn and wine. Wurtzburg is the capital.

Maine, Upper, a circle of the Bavarian states; contiguous to Bohemia and Saxony; comprising an extent of 3460 square miles, with 434,000 inhabitants. The manufactures, though confined to the productions of the province, viz the metals, flax, and timber, are considerable. Bayreuth is the capital.

Maine-et-Loire, a department of France; bounded by the departments of Mayenne, Sarthe, and Indre-et-Loire; comprising an extent of 4000 square miles, with 343,819 inhabitants. The soil is in general fertile, producing corn, flax, hemp, fruit, and wine; and the manufacture of linen is carried on to a considerable extent. Angers is the capital.

Maine and Tauber, a circle of Baden; comprising the N. E. portion of the grand duchy, and a small tract on the Maine, insulated from the rest by part of Bavaria. Wertheim is the chief town.

Mainland, the principal of the Shetland Isles, is 60 miles long, and from 6 to 13 broad, and is divided into eight parochial districts. The face of the country exhibits a prospect of black, craggy mountains, and marshy plains, interspersed with some verdant spots, which appear smooth and fertile. The mountains abound with various kinds of game; the lofty cliffs, impending over the sea, are the haunts of eagles, falcons, and ravens; the deep caverns underneath shelter seals and otters; and to the winding bays resort the swans, geese, scarfs, and other aquatic birds. The seas abound with fish, such as the herring, cod, turbot, and haddock, lobsters, oysters, muscles, &c., are also plentiful; while the rivulets and lakes abound with salmon, trout, &c. The hills are covered with sheep of a small breed, and of a shaggy appearance; but their fleece is very soft, and extremely fine. Their horses are of a diminutive size, but remarkably strong and handsome, and are well known by the name of Shelties. There is an immense store of peat, but no coal. They have some manufactures of linen and woollen cloth, but their chief employment is derived from the fisheries. Lerwick is the capital.

Mainland, the principal of the Orkney Islands. *See* Pomona.

Maintenon, a town of France; department of Eure-et-Loire; seated between two mountains; on the river Eure; 11 miles N. by E. of Chartres.

Maire, Le, a strait of South America; between Terra del Fuego and Staten Land; about 15 miles long, and as many broad.

Maitland, town of considerable importance, about 4 miles from the navigable head of the river Hunter, and 120 miles from Sydney, with which city a constant communication is kept up by steam vessels. It is known as East and West Maitland: the former being the site selected by government, and the latter chosen on the banks of the Hunter by the early settlers. East Maitland contains a Protestant church, Catholic chapel, and courthouse; also a branch of the Bank of Australasia. In West Maitland there is a Protestant church, a Scotch kirk, and a Wesleyan meeting-house, also a branch of the Commercial Bank of Sydney. There are several good inns.

Maixant, St., a town of France; department of Deux Sevres; with a trade in corn, and manufactures of woollen stuffs, &c. It is seated on the Sevre Niortoise; 36 miles S. W. of Poitiers.

Majorca, the principal of the Balearic Isles; 40 miles long, and 35 broad; situate in the Mediterranean Sea, between Ivica and Minorca. The whole coast is lined with strong towers. The N. W. part is mountainous: the rest produces good corn, olive-trees, fine honey, and delicate wine. Pop. 181,900. Palma is the capital.

Makarev, a town of Russia; in the government of Niznei Novogorod; situate on the Volga; 24 miles E. N. E. of Niznei Novogorod.

Makarief, or Makareu, a town of Russia; in the government of Kostroma. It is seated on the river Unza; 140 miles E. of Kostroma. Long. 44. 14. E. lat. 58. 50. N.

Malabar, a maritime province of Hindostan; lying between 10. and 13. N. lat.; now under the dominion of the British. It consists either of flat land washed by the sea, or of different ranges of hills, extending to the foot of the mountains; and it is intersected by a number of mountain streams. Its chief produce is timber, sandal-wood, cocoa-nut, coir, and black pepper. Its principal towns are Calicut, Tellicherry, and Cananore. The inhabitants are principally Hindoos; but there are also Jews, Mahometans, and Christians.

Malacca, or Malaya, an extensive country of India, beyond the Ganges; bounded on the N. by Siam, E. by the ocean, and S. W. by the strait of Malacca, which separates it from Sumatra. It is 775 miles in length, and 125 in breadth; and produces a great many excellent fruits and roots, pepper, and other spices, with some precious gums and woods. There is but little corn, and sheep and oxen are scarce; but hogs and poultry are plentiful. The Malays are rather below the middle stature; their limbs well shaped; their complexion tawny; their eyes large, and their hair long, black, and shining. They are fond of navigation, war, plunder, emigration, adventures, and gallantry; talk incessantly of their honour and bravery, and speak the softest language of Asia; yet they are deemed the most treacherous and ferocious people on the face of the globe. The government is vested in a rajah, or sultan, with a great number of chiefs under him, who generally pay very little regard to his authority. Their religion is a mixture of Mahomedism and Paganism. The inland parts are possessed by a savage and barbarous people.

Malacca, the capital of the above country; situate on the western coast. The Portuguese had a factory here, which was taken from them by the Dutch, in 1640: it was subjected to the English in 1795, restored to the Dutch in 1818, but is now under the authority of Great Britain, and is one of the principal stations of the London Missionary Society. It is seated on the strait of its name; 480 miles S. E. of Acheen. Long. 102. 5. E. lat. 2. 12. N.

Malaga, a seaport and city of Spain; in Granada, with a good harbour, capable of containing 400 merchant vessels, and 20 sail of the line. The cathedral is a stupendous pile, begun by Philip II. while married to Mary of England, and their united arms are over the gate. The inhabitants are about 50,000, who have some trade in raisins and excellent wines, and manufactures of silks, velvets, soap, paper, &c. Malaga was taken by the French, in 1810, and remained in their possession till 1812. It is seated on the Mediterranean: surrounded by hills; 55 miles W. S. W. of Granada. Long. 4. 10. W. lat. 36. 35. N.

Malahide, a town and bay of Ireland, in the county of Dublin, famous for its oysters, 6 miles from the capital. In the vicinity is Malahide Castle, the residence of the Talbot family.

Malambito, a town of S. America, in the province of Carthagena, about 60 miles E. of Carthagena, on the W. side of the river Magdalena.

Malamocco, a small island and town of Austrian Italy, 5 miles S. of Venice.

Malatia, a town of Asia Minor, on the site of the ancient Melitene, once the capital of Armenia Minor; seated 15 miles W. of the Euphrates, and 90 W. N. W. of Diarbekir. Long. 37. 50. E. lat. 37. 30. N.

Malawully, or Malavilly, a town of Hindostan, in Mysore, with a large mud fort, separated into two parts by a transverse wall Here is a fruit-garden of great extent, planted by the late sultans. Tippoo Sultan was defeated here by General Harris, in 1799. It is 35 miles E. of Seringapatam.

Malchin, a town of Germany, in the duchy of Mecklenburg-Schwerin; seated on the river Peene, where it forms the lake Camrow; 22 miles E. of Gustrow.

Malcho, a town of Germany, in the duchy of Mecklenburg-Schwerin, between the lakes Calpin and Plau; 23 miles S. S. E. of Gustrow.

Maldeghem, a town of Belgium, province of East Flanders. Pop. 4850. It is 10 miles E. of Bruges.

Malda, a town of Bengal, capital of a district of the same name, on the N. E. side of the Ganges. It is the residence of the commercial agent of the E. India Company, and carries on an extensive trade in raw silk, and manufactured goods. Long. 88. 4. E. lat. 25. 3. N.

Malden, a town of Middlesex county, Massachusets, 4 miles N. of Boston. It is connected with Charlestown by a bridge over Mystic River, built in 1787.

Maldives, a cluster of small islands in the Indian Ocean; lying S. W. of Cape Comorin, extending from the equinoctial line to 8. N. lat. and situated between 72. and 74. E. long. They are divided in 17 attolons, or provinces, each having its separate governor and its distinct branch of industry, the brewers residing in one, the goldsmiths in another, &c. The inhabitants appear to be a mixture of Arabs and Hindoos from Malabar. They supply ships with sails and cordage, cocoa-nuts, oil, and honey, dry fish, tortoise-shell, and especially cowries.

Maldon, a borough in Essex, governed by a mayor, with a market on Saturday, and a considerable trade, chiefly in corn, salt, coal, iron, deals, and wine. It has two parish churches, a free school, a library, and a town-hall; and returns two members to parliament. Vessels of moderate burden come up to the town, but large ships are obliged to unload at a distance below, in Blackwater Bay. The custom of Borough English, by which the youngest son succeeds to the burgage tenure, is kept up here. It is seated on an eminence, on the river Blackwater, 8 miles E. of Chelmsford, and 37 N. E. of London.

Maldonado, a town of Buenos Ayres, with a harbour sheltered by a small island of its name; seated near the N. entrance of the Plata. Long. 55. 36. W. lat. 34. 50. S.

Maldonado, a small river of Buenos Ayres, which enters the sea in the bay of Maldonado.

Malemba, a seaport on the coast of Loango, Western Africa, 50 miles S. of Loango.

Male, the principal of the Maldive islands, and the residence of the prince. Long. 73. 10. E. lat. 6. 20. N.

Malesherbes, a town of France, department of Loiret; seated on the Essone, 35 miles N. E. of Orleans. Pop. 1150.

Malestroit, a town of France, department of Morbihan; seated on the Ouse, 19 miles E. N. E. of Vannes.

Malham, a village in W. Yorkshire, surrounded on every side by mountains and rising grounds, which abound in natural curiosities; and among them, on a high moor, 'is a circular lake, about a mile in diameter, which is the source of the river Aire, 6 miles E. of Settle, and 233 from London.

Malines. *See* Mechlin.

Malivagonga, a river of Ceylon, which rises among the hills to the S. E. of Candy, nearly encompasses that city, and, after many windings among the mountains, enters the sea at Trincomalee.

Mallicollo, one of the largest of the New Hebrides, in the South Pacific, extending 20 leagues from N. W. to S. E. The inland mountains are very high, and clad with forests; but the soil is rich and fertile, producing cocoa-nuts, bread-fruit, bananas, sugar-canes, yams, eddoes, turmeric, oranges, &c. Hogs and common poultry are the domestic animals. The inhabitants appear to be a different race from those of the Friendly and Society Islands. In many particulars they seem to correspond with the natives of New Guinea, particularly in their black colour and woolly hair. They go almost naked, are of a slender make, have lively but very irregular features, and tie a rope fast round their belly. At the S. end of the island is a port, named Sandwich Harbour. Long. 167. 53. E. lat. 16. 25. S.

Malling, West, a town in Kent, with a market on Saturday; 6 miles W. of Maidstone, and 29 E. by S. of London.

Mallow, a borough of Ireland, in the county of Cork, with considerable linen manufactures, and a fine spring of tepid water. It is seated on the Blackwater, 17 miles N. by W. of Cork. It returns one member to parliament.

Malmedy, a town of the Prussian province of Lower Rhine, government of Aix-la-Chapelle; seated on the Recht; 20 miles S. of Aix-la-Chapelle. Pop. 4575.

Malmoe, a seaport of Sweden, government of Malmohus, with a large harbour and a strong citadel. It has manufactures of woollen, and a considerable trade; seated on the Sound, 18 miles E. by S. of Copenhagen. Long. 13. 7. E. lat. 55. 36. N.

Malmohus, a government of Sweden, including a great part of the ancient Schonen, or Scania. It lies along the Sound and the Baltic, and comprises an area of 1380 square miles, with 137,000 inhabitants.

Malmsbury, a borough in Wiltshire, with a market on Saturday, and a woollen manufacture. Its castle is demolished, bnt there are some remains of its once celebrated abbey. It is seated on a hill, almost surrounded by the Avon, over which it has six bridges; 26 miles E. by N. of Bristol, and 96 W. of London. It returns one member to parliament.

Malo, St., a seaport of France, department of Ille-et-Vilaine, with a strong castle. It has a large harbour, difficult of access, on account of the rocks that surround it, and is a trading place of great importance. It was bombarded by the English, in 1693, but without success. In 1758 they landed in Cancalle Bay, went to the harbour by land, and burnt above 100 ships. St. Malo is seated on an island, united to the mainland by a causeway; 44 miles N. N. W. of Rennes. Pop. 10,500. Long. 2. 2. W. lat. 148. 39. N.

Malpas, a town in Cheshire; with a market on Wednesday. It has a handsome church, an independent chapel, an hospital, a grammar school, and a national school. It is seated on a high hill, near the river Dee; 15 miles S. E. of Chester, and 165 N. W. of London.

Malplaquet, a village of France, in the department of the North; famous for a victory gained over the French by the Duke of Marlborough, in 1709. It is 9 miles S. E. of Mons. Pop. 1225.

Malta, an island in the Mediterranean; between Africa and Sicily; 20 miles long, and 12 broad; formerly reckoned a part of Africa, but now belonging to Europe. It was anciently little else than a barren rock, but is now become a fertile island. The principal objects of cultivation are lemons, indigo, saffron, cotton, and vines, which produce excellent wine. The number of inhabitants is said to be about 80,000, who speak Arabic and Italian. After the taking of Rhodes, the emperor Charles V. gave this island to the grand master of the order of St. John of Jerusalem. It was attacked, in 1566, by the Turks, who were obliged to abandon the enterprise with the loss of 30,000 men. It was taken by Bonaparte in the outset of his expedition to Egypt, on the 12th of June, 1798, when he found in it 1200 cannons, 200,000 lbs. of powder, two ships of the line, a frigate, four galleys, and 40,000 muskets, besides an immense treasure collected by superstition, and 4500 Turkish prisoners, whom he set at liberty. It was soon afterwards taken by the British; was stipulated to be restored to the knights at the peace of Amiens, but retained in consequence of new aggressions from France. In 1803 the war recommenced between the two nations, and the treaty of Paris, in 1814, confirmed the possession of it to Great Britain. Malta is extremely well fortified; the ditches, of a vast size, are all cut out of the solid rock, and extend many miles. Valetta is the capital.

Malton, New, a borough in N. Yorkshire, returning one member to parliament; with a market on Saturday, and a considerable trade in coals, corn, butter, &c. Here are two churches, four dissenting meeting-houses, a free school, and a national school. It is seated on the Derwent, over which is a stone bridge to the village of Old Malton; 48 miles N. E. of York, and 214 N. by W. of London.

Malvern, Great and Little, two villages in Worcestershire. The former is 8 miles W. by S. of Worcester, and had once an abbey, of which nothing remains but the gateway of the abbey, and the nave of the church, now parochial; the latter is seated in a cavity of the Malvern hills, 3 miles from Great Malvern. Between Great and Little Malvern are two celebrated chalybeate springs, one of which is called the Holy Well.

Malvern Hills, a range of hills in the counties of Worcester and Hereford, extending about 9 miles in length, and from 1 to 2 in breadth. They appear to be of limestone and quartz, and the highest point is 1313 feet above the surface of the Severn.

Malwah, a province of Hindostan; bounded N. by the provinces of Agimere and Agra, E. by Allahabad and Gundwaneh, S. by Khandeish and Berar, and W. by Agimere and Guzerat. It is 250 miles in length, by 150 in breadth, and is one of the most extensive, elevated, and diversified tracts in Hindostan. Till lately, the whole territory belonged to the Mahrattas.

Malzieu, a town of France; in the department of Lozere, seated on the Truyere; 12 miles N. N. E. of Mende.

Mamars, a town of France; in the department of Sarthe, seated on the Dive; 14 miles W. of Bellesme.

Man, an island in the Irish Sea, 30 miles long, and 12 broad. It contains 18 parishes, under the jurisdiction of a bishop, called the bishop of Sodor and Man, who is sole baron of the isle, and possesses other important privileges, but has no seat in the British parliament. The air is healthy, and the soil produces more corn than is sufficient to maintain the inhabitants, who are a mixture of English, Scotch, and Irish. The language is a dialect of the Celtic, called Manx. The commodities of the island are wool, hides, butter, tallow, black marble, slate, limestone, lead, and iron. Some manufactures of coarse hats, cotton goods, and linen cloth, are carried on in different parts; but its principal trade arises from the herring fishery. The duke of Athol was formerly lord of this island, the sovereignty of which he sold, in 1765, to the Crown. The chief towns are Castletown, Douglas, Peele, Ruthin, and Ramsay. It is 18 miles S. of Scotland, 40 N. of Wales, 30 W. of England, and 26 E. of Ireland.

Manaar, a small island in the Indian Ocean; on the N. W. side of Ceylon. From this island a bank of sand, called Adam's Bridge, runs over to the continent of Hindostan, which can be passed only by boats. The sea to the S. of this, between the continent and the island of Ceylon, is called the Gulf of Manaar. The Portuguese obtained possession of the island in 1560; but it was taken by the Dutch, in 1658, and in 1795 by the English. Long. 79. 3. E. lat. 9. 6. N.

Manapar, a town of Hindostan, district of Tinevelly; situate on a point of land projecting into the Gulf of Manaar; 40 miles S. E. of Palamcotta. Long. 78. 17. E. lat. 8. 39. N. —Also a town in the province of Tanjore. Long. 78. 30. E. lat. 16. 39. N.

Manbona, a town of Eastern Africa; situate on the sea coast, 60 miles S. of Sofala. Long. 35. 39. E. lat. 21. 15. S.

Mancester, a village in Warwickshire, near Atherstone. It was a Roman station, and here several coins have been dug up: seated on an eminence near the Anker; 106 miles from London.

Mancha, a territory of Spain, lying S. of Old Castile, and N. of Andalusia. It is divided into Upper and Lower, and is nearly surrounded by mountains, producing antimony, vermilion, and mercury. The country is an immense plain, intersected by ridges of low hills and rocks; but it is well cultivated, and produces corn, olives, and wine. Area, 8000 square miles. Pop. 215,000. The inhabitants are affable, and great lovers of music and dancing; and it was here that Cervantes made his hero, Don Quixote, perform his chief exploits.

Manche, a department of France, including the W. part of Normandy, and comprising about 2500 square miles, with 600,000 inhabitants. It is almost surrounded by the English Channel. St. Lo is the capital, but Cherburg is the largest town.

Manchester, a borough in Lancashire, with markets on Tuesday, Wednesday, Thursday, and Saturday; seated between the rivers Irk and Irwell. It returns two members to parliament. It is a place of great antiquity, and has attained greater opulence than almost any of the trading towns in England. It has long been noted for various branches of the linen, silk, and cotton manufactures, and is now principally conspicuous as the centre of the cotton trade. The labours of a very populous neighbourhood are collected at Manchester, whence they are sent to London, Liverpool, Hull, &c. These consist of a great variety of cotton and mixed goods, fitted for all sorts of markets, both at home and abroad, spreading over a great part of Europe, America, and the coast of Guinea. Manufactures of tapes and other small wares, of silk goods, and of hats, are also carried on at Manchester. Its chief ornaments are the college, the exchange, the collegiate church, another large church, and a spacious market-place. The churches and chapels of the Establishment, several of which are recent erections, are nineteen in number. Here are also upwards of forty places of worship for different sects of dissenters, and three for Roman Catholics; one of the latter, opened in 1820, is a beautiful edifice, erected at a cost of 10,000*l.* The charity schools and Sunday schools are numerous. The most important of the other charitable institutions are the Manchester General Infirmary and Dispensary, the Lunatic Asylum, the Fever Hospital, the Lying-in-Hospital, the Strangers' Friend Society, the Samaritan Society, the Lock Hospital, the Female Penitentiary, and the School for the Deaf and Dumb, instituted in 1825. Of the institutions for the promotion of literature and science, the principal are the Literary and Philosophical Society, the Society for the Promotion of Natural History, and the Royal Manchester Institution. The Mechanics' Institute is in a very flourishing state; and there are several valuable libraries, particularly the College Library, and the Portico. Manchester is governed by a corporation, consisting of a Mayor, Court of Aldermen, &c., and has several courts of law. It has risen to its present consequence entirely by its manufactures. By the Irwell it has a communication with the Mersey, and all the late various extensions of inland navigation; and, by means of the various railways, it communicates with all parts of the kingdom. It is 36 miles E. by N. of Liverpool, and 186 N. N. W. of London.

MANCHESTER, a town of Vermont; in Bennington county; situate on Batten River, which flows into the Hudson, above Saratoga. It is 22 miles N. of Bennington, and 35 S. of Rutland. There are several other townships and villages of this name in the United States.

MANDAL, a town of Norway, capital of a province in the government of Bergen; seated near the mouth of a river of the same name; 60 miles W. S. W. of Christiansand. Long. 7. 42. E. lat. 58. 2. N.

MANDAN, a fort and Indian village of North America, on the Missouri; where Captains Lewis and Clarke had their winter encampment, when on their expedition to the Missouri. Long. 100. 50. W. lat. 47. 20. N. The Mandan tribe is now extinct.

MANDAR, a district of the island of Celebes; on the W. and N. coast; bounded W. by the Strait of Macassar, and E. by a tract of desert mountains.

MANDAVEE, a seaport town of Hindostan, in the province of Cutch, at the entrance of the gulf of that name. It is the centre of a considerable commerce with India, and the neighbouring states of Sinde and the Indus; 35 miles S. S. W. of Bhooj. Pop. 35,000.

MANDINGO, a country in the W. part of Negroland, at the sources of the rivers Niger and Senegal. Not only the inhabitants of this state, but the bulk of the people in many other districts in the western part of Africa, are called Mandingoes, probably from having originally emigrated from this country. They are of a mild, sociable, and obliging disposition: the men are above the middle size, well-shaped, strong, and capable of enduring great labour; the women are good-natured, sprightly, and agreeable. The dress of both sexes is composed of cotton cloth, of their own manufacture. Polygamy is common, but the women are not under that restraint which prevails in many other countries. Most of the towns contain a mosque, where public prayers are offered; and a bentang, or coffee-house, where public business is transacted. The private houses are built of mud, with a conical bamboo roof, thatched with grass. The language of the Mandingoes is said to be copious and refined, and is generally understood in all the regions of Western Africa.

MANDSHOOS, or MANTCHOOS, a branch of the Mongul Tartars, whose ancestors conquered China in the thirteenth century, but were expelled by the Chinese, in 1368. They inhabit the three provinces of Eastern Tartary, and retain the customs they brought from China.

MANFREDONIA, a seaport of Naples, in Capitanata; with a castle and good harbour. All sorts of vegetables are in abundance, and most of the corn exported from the province is shipped here. It is seated on a gulf of the same name; 30 miles E. N. E. of Lucera. Pop. 5000. Long. 16. 12. E. lat. 41. 35. N.

MANGALORE, a town of Hindostan; in the province of Canara; seated between the two arms of a fine lake of salt water, each of which receives a river from the Gauts; but the bar at the entrance into this harbour will not admit vessels drawing more than ten feet. It is a place of great trade: the principal exports are rice, betel-nut, black pepper, sandal-wood, (from the country above the Gauts,) cinnamon, and turmeric. Here are the ruins of a fort which Tippo Sultan ordered to be demolished in 1784. In this town a treaty of peace was signed between Tippoo and the English, in 1784; in 1799 it came into the hands of the British, and is now the residence of the judge, collector, &c., of South Canara. Pop. 30,000. It is 130 miles N. N. W. of Calicut, and 190 S. S. E. of Goa. Long. 75. 4. E. lat. 12. 50. N.

MANGEA, an island in the South Pacific; 5 leagues in circumference. In the interior parts it rises into small hills; and Captain Cook, by whom it was discovered in 1777, represents it as a fine island; but he did not find a landing-place. Long. 158. 16. W. lat. 21. 27. S.

MANHEIM, a town of Baden, and capital of the circle of the Neckar. The streets are spacious, straight, and well paved; the houses elegant, and uniform. The palace is a magnificent structure, with a cabinet of natural curiosities and a gallery of pictures. The inhabitants are computed at 21,625. Manheim was frequently taken and re-taken by the French and Austrians, in the late wars: and was finally ceded to Baden in 1802. It is 17 miles N. of Spire, and 42 S. of Frankfort. Long. 8. 31. E. lat. 49. 29. N.

MANICA, an inland kingdom in the S. E. part of Africa; bounded on the N. by Mocaranga, E. by Sofala and Sabia, and S. and W. by unknown regions. It is said to abound with mines of gold, and has a river and capital of the same name; but it is little known to the Europeans.

MANICKDURG, a town and fortress of Hindostan; in the province of Berar; 5 miles S. E. of Chanda.

MANICKPATAM, a town of Hindostan; in the province of Orissa; 12 miles S. W. of Juggernaut.

MANICKPORE, a town of Hindostan; capital of a district of the same name in the province of Allahahad; seated on the Ganges, in lat. 19. 40. N. long. 85. 36. E.

Manilla, the capital of the island of Luzon, as well as of the other Philippine Islands, and the see of an archbishop, who is commonly the Spanish viceroy. It is well fortified, and defended by the castle of St. Philip. Population, about 175,000. The number of Christian inhabitants is estimated at 12,000. Most of the public structures are built of wood, on account of the frequent earthquakes, by one of which, in 1617, a mountain was levelled; and, in 1625, a third part of the city was overthrown by another, when 3000 persons perished. This city is seated near the lake Bahia, on the E. side of a bay, on the S. W. coast. The bay is a circular basin, 10 leagues in diameter, and great part of it land-locked; but the port peculiar to the city, called Cavete, lies 9 miles to the S. W. On account of the pure and mild temperature of the air, it is deemed the most healthy of all the European settlements in the East. In 1762, the English took this city by storm, and humanely suffered the archbishop to ransom it for about 1,000,000*l.* sterling; but great part of the ransom never was paid. In 1821 accounts were received of a dreadful massacre of all foreigners, except Spaniards, when property was destroyed or carried off to the value of 400,000 dollars. Long. 120. 52. E. lat. 14. 36. N.

Manningtree, a town in Essex, with a market on Thursday. The principal imports are deals, corn, coal, and iron. It is seated on a branch of the Stour, called Manningtree-water, 11 miles W. of Harwich, and 60 E. N. E. of London.

Mannhartsberg, a mountain chain of Austria, beginning at the frontier of Moravia, and terminating at the Danube. The products are corn, saffron, and wine. The chief towns are Crems and Kloster-Neuberg.

Manosque, a town of France; in the department of Lower Alps; near the Durance; with a castle; 25 miles N. E. of Aix. Pop. 5400.

Manpurry, a town and fort of Hindostan; in the district of Dooab; seated on Issah; 54 miles E. of Agra.

Manresa, a town of Spain, in Catalonia; with a castle, and manufactures of silk, hats, gunpowder, &c.; seated at the conflux of the Cardonero with the Lobbregat; 20 miles N. W. of Barcelona.

Mans, a town of France; capital of the department of Sarthe, and the see of a bishop. It contains 19,477 inhabitants, and was formerly much more populous. It has excellent poultry, and its wax and stuffs are famous. It is seated on a high hill, near the Sarthe; 20 miles S. of Alençon, and 75 W. by N. of Orleans. Long. 0. 9. E. lat. 48. 0. N.

Mansaroar, a lake of Thibet, from which the southernmost head of the Ganges was long supposed to issue. It was about 115 miles in circumference, and lies about 79 E. long. and 34. N. lat.

Mansfeld, a town of Prussian Saxony: in the government of Merseberg; with a decayed castle on a high rock; seated on the Thalbach; 8 miles N. N. W. of Eisleben.

Mansfield, a town in Nottinghamshire, with a market on Thursday; a trade in corn and malt, and manufactures of lace, hosiery, and cotton-spinning. Here are a commodious church, five meeting-houses, a grammar-school, two charity schools, and twelve almshouses. Coins of several Roman emperors have been dug up near this town, and the relics recently discovered afford indisputable proof that the Romans had a station in the vicinity. It communicates with Pinxton Canal, by a railway 7 miles in length. It is seated on the edge of the forest of Sherwood; 14 miles N. of Nottingham, and 138 N. by W. of London.

Mansfield, a town of Tolland county, Connecticut. Population, 2276.—There are several inconsiderable townships of this name in the United States.

Mansilla, a town of Spain; province of Leon; 10 miles S. S. E. of Leon.

Mansora, a town in the kingdom of Fez; seated near the mouth of the Guir; 60 miles W. of Mequinez.

Mansoura, a town of Lower Egypt; with a considerable trade in rice and sal-ammoniac; built by the Saracens, during the crusades, as a bulwark against the Christians. It is seated on the E. side of the Nile: 24 miles S. S. W. of Damietta and 60 N. of Cairo.

Mantes, a town of France; department of Seine-et-Oise, with a bridge over the Seine, the great arch of which is 120 feet wide. The wines of its vicinity are famous. It is 31 miles N. W. of Paris. Pop. 4300.

Mantua, a province of Italy; contigious to the duchies of Parma and Modena; fertile in corn, flax, fruits, and excellent wine. It comprises a superficial extent of 880 square miles, with 239,436 inhabitants; but the former duchy of Mantua was of greater extent. It was governed by the Gonzago family, with the title of duke, till Charles IV., taking part with the French in the dispute relating to the succession of Spain, was put under the ban of the empire, and died in 1708. Having no heirs, the House of Austria kept possession till 1800, when the French obtained it after the battle of Marengo; but the Austrians obtained possession of it again in 1814.

Mantua, a city of Austrian Italy; capital of the above province. It is seated on an island in the middle of a lake, 20 miles in circumference, and 2 broad, formed by the Mincio, and so very strong by situation, as well as by art, that it is one of the most considerable fortresses in Europe. The only way into this city is by means of two moles or bridges, each of which is defended by a fort and other works. The city is well built, and most of the streets are spacious, regular, and well paved. In the cathedral are paintings by the most celebrated masters; the church of St. Anthony is famous for relics: and the Franciscan church is one of the most elegant of that order in Italy. Here are many other churches, numerous convents, a synagogue for the Jews, who live in a distinct quarter, a university, the ancient ducal palace, with its gallery of paintings, &c. Virgil was born at a village near this city. Mantua surrendered to the French, in 1797 (after a siege of eight months,) was taken by the Austrian and Russian army, in 1799; again ceded to France in 1801, and finally delivered up to the Austrians in 1814. It is 35 miles N. E. of Parma, and 70 E. S. E. of Milan. Long. 10. 50. E. lat. 45. 10. N.

MANZANARES, a town of Spain; in the district of Guadalaxara, province of New Castile; on a river of the same name; 21 miles of Ciudad Real. Pop. 6800.

MAOUNA, one of the Navigator's Islands, in the S. Pacific.—Here, in 1787, Perouse met with his first fatal accident; Captain Langle, Lemanon, the naturalist, and nine sailors, being massacred by the natives. Long. 169. 0. W. lat. 14. 19. S.

MARACAIBO, a province of S. America; now forming part of the Venezuelan province of the Colombian republic, and extending N. to the Caribbean Sea. The soil is in many places exceedingly fertile, and the climate, although excessively hot, is not on the whole unhealthy. The inhabitants are estimated at about 100,000.

MARACAIBO, the capital of the above province; with a harbour which can only admit small vessels, owing to the obstruction of a sand-bar. It has a mean appearance, some of the houses being covered with tiles, others with reeds. The climate is hot, and the storms of thunder and lightning that frequently occur, are accompanied with tremendous rains. Population, 24,000. It is seated on the outlet of the lake of its name; 60 miles W. S. W. of Venezuela, and 420 W. of Caraccas; Long. 71. 46. W. lat. 10. 30. N.

MARACAIBO, a lake of the Caraccas; in the province of Venezuela. It is 150 miles long, and 90 where broadest, with a circumference of 450; and is navigable for vessels of the greatest burden. The banks are sterile, and the air insalubrious; but the water is fresh, except in stormy weather, when the waters of the sea are forced into it. It communicates with the Gulf of Venezuela, by a strait, which is defended by strong forts, and has several Spanish towns seated on its borders.

MARACAY, or MORACAO, a town of Colombia, in the province of Venezuela; in the neighbourhood of which are plantations of cotton, indigo, coffee, corn, &c.; seated on the E. side of the lake Valencia, in the valley of Aragoa. Population, 8400.

MARAGA, a well-built city of Persia; province of Aderbijan; with a spacious bazaar, a glass manufactory and a handsome public bath; situated at the extremity of a well cultivated plain, opening to the lake of Urumea, from which it is distant 10 or 12 miles, and 68 miles N. of Tabreez. Population, 15,000. Long. 46. 25. E. lat. 37. 20. N.

MARANHAM, a northern province of Brazil, which comprehends a fertile and populous island of the same name, 112 miles in circumference. The French settled here in 1812; but they were soon expelled by the Portuguese. St. Luis de Maranham is the chief town.

MARANON. *See* AMAZON.

MARANO, a seaport of Austrian Italy; in the province of Udina; seated on the Gulf of Venice; 27 miles S. by E. of Udina. Long. 13. 5. E. lat. 45. 52. N.

MARANS, a town of France; department of Lower Charente; with a brisk trade in salt, malt, corn, and meal; seated on the Sevre, in the midst of salt marshes; 12 miles N. N. E. of Rochelle.

MARANT, or AMARANT, a town of Persia; in the province of Aderbijan; containing 2500 houses, each with a garden; situate near a river, and watered by canals. Cochineal is found in its neighbourhood. The inhabitants say that Noah was buried here. It is 50 miles N. of Tauris. Long. 47. 46. E. lat. 39. 7. N.

MARASA, a town of W. Africa, in Wangara, on the N. side of the Niger; 160 miles N. E. of Ghanara. Long. 17. 10. E. lat. 15. 50. N.

MARASCH, a town of Asiatic Turkey, in Caramania; the capital of a sangiacate, and the see of a bishop. It is 180 miles E. by S. of Konieh. Long. 37. 25. E. lat. 37. 24. N.

MARATHON, a village of Livadia; formerly a city, famous for the victory obtained by Miltiades, with 10,000 Athenians, over 500,000 Persians, B. C. 490. It is 20 miles N. N. E. of Athens.

MARAVI, a lake of Eastern Africa, behind Mozambique; reported to be about 40 miles in breadth, and of much greater length. At its S. extremity is a district with a town of the same name. Long. 33. 10. E. lat. 13. 10. S.

MARAWAR, a country of Hindostan, situated on the eastern coast, opposite Ceylon, and between 9. and 10. of N. lat. It is 66 miles in length, by 40 in breadth; and is included in the collectorship of Dindigul. The chief towns are Ramnad and Tripatore.

MARAZION, or MARKET JEW, a town in Cornwall; with a market on Saturday. The parish church of St. Hilary is about 2 miles distant, but the town has a chapel of ease, besides several meeting-houses for dissenters. It is seated on Mount Bay, 4 miles E. of Penzance, and 279 W. by S. of London.

MARBELLA, a town of Andalusia; seated at the mouth of the Rio Verde; with a harbour, defended by a castle; 28 miles S. W. of Malaga.

MARBLEHEAD, a town of Massachusets, in Essex county; with a harbour protected by a sea wall, and defended by a battery and citadel. It stands on a neck of land, in Massachusets Bay; 16 miles N. E. of Boston. Pop. 5575. Long. 70. 36. W. lat. 42. 36. N.

MARBŒUF, a town of France, department of Eure; 12 miles N. of Conches.

MARBOZ, a town of France, department of Ain. It is 12 miles N. of Bourg. Population 2500.

MARBROOK, a river in Shropshire, which joins the Severn below Bridgenorth.

MARBURG, a town of Germany; capital of

that part of Upper Hesse which belongs to the elector of Hesse-Cassel. It has a fortified castle on the top of a mountain, a university, an academy, a Lutheran, a Calvinist, and a Catholic church, an hospital, two infirmaries, and an orphan-house. It was taken by the French in 1757; surrendered to the allies in 1759; and again taken by the French in 1760. It is seated on the Lahn; 47 miles S. W. of Cassel. Pop. 6588. Long. 8. 50. E. lat. 50. 48. N.

MARCELLIN, ST., a town of France, department of Isere; seated on the Isere, at the foot of a hill, in an excellent wine country; 30 miles S. S. E. of Vienne.

MARCH, a town in Cambridgeshire; with a market on Friday, and a considerable trade in corn, coals, and timber. Near this place, three urns full of burnt bones, and some small Roman coins, were dug up in 1730. It is seated on the Nen, in the Isle of Ely; 26 miles N. N. W. of Cambridge, and 81 N. of London.

MARCHBURG, or MAHRBURG, a town of the Austrian states, in Styria; capital of a circle of its name, with two castles. In its vicinity are good vineyards. It is seated on the Drave; 36 miles S. S. E. of Gratz. Long. 15. 38. E. lat. 46. 38. N.

MARCHE, a town of France, department of Vosges; situate near the source of the Mouzon; 20 miles S. of Neufchateau.

MARCHECK, a town of Lower Austria; with an old castle; seated on the March, on the frontiers of Hungary; 23 miles E. by N. of Vienna.

MARCHIENNES, a town of Belgium, province of Hainault; seated on the Sambre; 18 miles E. by S. of Mons.

MARCHIENNES, a town of France, department of Nord; seated in a morass, on the river Scarpe; 9 miles W. N. W. of Valenciennes.

MARCIANISI, a town in Naples, in Terra di Lavoro; 13 miles N. N. E. of Naples.

MARCIGNY, a town of France, department of Saone-et-Loire; near the river Loire; 32 miles W. of Macon.

MARCO, ST., a seaport of East Florida, on a river of the same name, at its entrance into Apalache Bay; 180 miles W. N. W. of St. Augustin. Long. 84. 38. W. lat. 30. 18. N.

MARCO, ST., a town of Naples, in Calabria Citra; seated on the Senito. It is 22 miles N. of Cosenza.

MARCOU, ST., two small islands in the English Channel, near the coast of France; 7 miles S. E. of La Hogue.

MARDIKE, a village of France, department of Nord; seated on a canal, to which it gives name; 4 miles W. by S. of Dunkirk.

MAREB, the capital of a district of Arabia, in Yemen. It is 100 miles S. E. of Sana. Long. 47. 30. E. lat. 15. 44. N.

MARENGO, a village of Austrian Italy, in the government of Milan; famous for a decisive victory gained by the French over the Austrians, June 14, 1800. It is 3 miles S. E. of Alessandria.

MARENNES, a town of France, department of Lower Charente; remarkable for the green-finned oysters found near the coast. It is 25 miles S. of La Rochelle, and 270 S. W. of Paris.

MAREOTIS, LAKE, at the S. of Alexandria, Egypt. It was formed by the British, in their siege of that city, by cutting a communication between the canal and the present lake, and which is still open, and affords a considerable supply of water to the ancient lake, which had become almost dry.

MARETIMO, an island in the Mediterranean; on the W. coast of Sicily; 12 miles in circumference. It has a castle, with a few farm-houses; and produces much honey. Long. 12. 15. E. lat. 38. 5. N.

MARGARET'S ISLANDS, in the N. Pacific; were discovered by Captain Magee, in the ship Margaret of Boston, in his voyage from Kamtschatka, in 1780. Long. 141. 12. E. lat. 24. 40. N.

MARGARITA, an island near the coast of Cumana; about 40 miles long and 15 broad; discovered by Columbus in 1498. The continual verdure renders it pleasant; but it has no fresh water. The inhabitants are principally mulattoes and the original natives. The pearl fishery was once prosecuted to a great extent; but in 1620 the Dutch landed and burnt the town and castle, since which it has greatly declined. Its ports are Pampatar, Pueblo de la Mar, and Pueblo del Norte. It was the scene of several sanguinary battles between the independents and the royal troops under General Morillo, who was defeated with great loss near Pampatar, and obliged to retire to the continent. Ascension is the capital. Long. 64. to 65. W. lat. 10. 56. N.

MARGATE, a town in Kent, on the isle of Thanet; with markets on Wednesday and Saturday, and a brisk trade in corn, coals, fish, timber, iron, tar, &c. It is a member of the port of Dover: and, owing to the great resort to it, for sea-bathing, for which its situation is well adapted, it has rapidly increased in population and wealth. The harbour has been greatly improved, and the town is protected from the inroads of the sea by a stone pier. It is situate on the side of a hill; 17 miles E. N. E. of Canterbury, and 71 E. by S. of London. Long. 1. 22. E. lat. 51. 24. N.

MARGUERITE, a small uncultivated island on the S. E. coast of France, opposite Antibes; with a strong castle; in which "the man with the iron mask" was for some time confined. Long. 7. 3. E. lat. 45. 31. N.

MARI, LOCH, a lake of Scotland, in Ross-shire; 16 miles long, and from 1 to 2 broad. There are 24 small islands in it.

MARIA, a river of North America, which rises in the Rocky Mountains, and, after a course of 500 miles, falls into the Missouri; 54 miles below the Great Falls.

MARIA, CAPE, a small island on the N. coast

of New Holland, in the Gulf of Carpentaria. Long. 135. 53. E. lat. 14. 50. S.

Maria, St., an island in the Indian Ocean, near the E. side of Madagascar. It is 45 miles long, and 7 broad; well watered, and surrounded by rocks. The air is extremely moist; for it rains almost every day. It produces rice, sugar-canes, legumes, pine-apples, tobacco, &c., and on the coasts are found white coral and ambergris. Long. 50. 20. E. lat. 17. 0. S.

Maria, St., the most southern island of the Azores; which produces plenty of wheat, and has about 5000 inhabitants. It has a town of the same name. Long. 25. 9. W. lat. 36. 57. N.

Maria, St., a town of Congo; capital of the kingdom of Matamba. It stands on river that flows into the Coanzo; 310 miles E. of Loanda. Long. 18. 0. E. lat. 8. 50. S.

Mariegalante, one of the Caribbee Islands; belonging to the French. It extends 16 miles from N. to S. and 4. from E. to W. On the E. shore are lofty perpendicular rocks; and about half its surface is barren mountains. It is indifferently watered, but produces tobacco, cotton, coffee, and sugar. It was taken by a British frigate in 1808. The S. end is 30 miles N. by E. of Dominica. Long. 61. 12. W. lat. 15. 52. N.

Marian Islands. *See* Ladrone.

Marie aux Mines, a town of France, department of Upper Rhine; divided into two parts by the river Laber. It is 14 miles N. W. of Colmar. Pop. 4000.

Marienburg, a strong town of West Prussia; in the government of Dantzic; with a brisk trade. It is seated on the E. branch of the Vistula; 24 miles S. E. of Dantzic. Long. 19. 1. E. lat. 54. 2. N. Pop. 7200.

Marienburg, a town of Saxony, in the circle of Erzgebirge; near which are mines of silver, iron, vitriol, and sulphur. It is 35 miles S. W. of Dresden. Pop. 2600.

Mariestadt, a town of Sweden, capital of the province of Scarborg; seated on the Lake Wenner; 35 miles S. E. of Carlstadt, and 162 S. W. of Stockholm. Long. 14. 25. E. lat. 58. 28. N.

Marienwerder, one of the two governments into which West Prussia is now divided. It is a long tract of very irregular form, lying N. of Poland, and S. of Pomerania and the government of Dantzic. Area, 6880 square miles. Pop. 302,000.

Marienwerder, a neat town of West Prussia; capital of a government and circle; with a spacious palace, built in the old Gothic taste. The cathedral is the largest church in the kingdom of Prussia, being 320 feet long; and, by its strong breastworks, seems to have formerly served as a fortress. In 1709 Peter the Great and Frederic I. of Prussia had an interview at this place. It is seated near the Vistula; 90 miles S. W. of Konigsberg. Pop. 6000. Long. 18. 52. E. lat. 53. 50. N.

Marietta a town of Ohio, in Washington county, and the oldest town in the state, but liable to inundation; which, from its situation, is irremediable. Here is a church, court-house, public academy, dock-yard, &c.: and in the vicinity were discovered, in 1806, a beautiful tesselated pavement, a large human skeleton, and other curious antiques. It is seated on a peninsula formed by the Muskingum and Ohio rivers; 240 miles W. by N. of Washington, and 159 N. E. of Lexington. Pop. 1814. Long. 81. 19. W. lat. 39. 30. N.

Marignano, a town of Austrian Italy, in the government of Milan; seated on the Lambro; 10 miles S. E. of Milan. Pop. 4000.

Marina, a town of Italy, in the papal states; with a castle; 10 miles E. S. E. of Rome.

Marino, San, a strong town of Italy, duchy of Urbino; capital of a small republic, under the protection of the pope. It is seated on a mountain 2000 feet high, with a small tract around its base of about 40 square miles, forming the smallest state in Europe. Pop. of the town, 6000; of the whole territory, 7000. It is 17 miles N. W. of Urbino. Long. 12. 33. E. lat. 42. 54. N.

Marissa, or **Maritz**, a river of Romania, which flows by Philipopoli, Adrinople, and Eno, into the Archipelago.

Mark, a territory of Prussian Westphalia; bounded N. by the principality of Munster, E. by the duchy of Westphalia, and S. and W. by that of Berg. Ham is the capital.

Mark, St., a seaport and jurisdiction on the W. side of St. Domingo. The town is one of the pleasantest on the island; and the houses are built of freestone, which is abundant in the neighbouring country. It is situate on a bay of the same name; 53 miles S. W. of Cape François. Long. 72. 40. W. lat. 19. 20. N.

Market Jew. *See* Marazion.

Marlborough, a borough in Wiltshire; governed by a mayor, with a market on Saturday. It returns two members to parliament. Here King John had a castle, in which a parliament was held in 1267, when the statute of Marlebridge, for suppressing riots, was enacted. The town contains two churches, several meeting-houses, a free grammar-school, a Lancasterian school, &c. It is seated on the Kennet; 26 miles N. of Salisbury, and 74 W. of London.

Marlborough, a town of Massachusets; in Middlesex county; with a manufacture of Spanish brown, from a kind of loam found in the neighbourhood. It is 25 miles W. by S. of Boston. Pop. 2101.—Also the name of several townships of the United States.

Marlborough-Fort, an English factory, on the W. coast of the island of Sumatra; 3 miles E. of Bencoolen.

Marlborough, Lower, a town of Maryland, in Calvert county, on the Patuxent; 24 miles S. E. of Washington.

Marlborough, Upper, a town of Maryland, chief of Prince George county; situate on the Hatavisit, a principal branch of the Patuxent; 15 miles E. of Washington.

Marlow, Great, a borough in Buckinghamshire, with a market on Saturday, and a manufacture of black silk lace, and paper. It sends two members to parliament. It is seated near the Thames, over which is a bridge into Berkshire; 17 miles N. of Aylesbury, and 31. W. of London.

MARMANDE, a town of France, department of Lot-et-Garonne, with a brisk trade in corn, wine, and brandy. It is seated on the Garonne, 35 miles S. E. of Bordeaux. Long. 0. 15. E. lat. 44. 20. N.

MARMORA, or WHITE SEA, (the ancient Propontis,) an inland sea between Europe and Asia, which communicates with the Archipelago by the Strait of Gallipoli, and with the Black Sea by the Strait of Constantinople. It is 120 miles in length, and 60 in breadth.

MARMORA, an island in the above sea, 30 miles in circumference, with a town of the same name. Long. 27. 34. E. lat. 40. 28. N.

MARMORICE, a seaport on the S. W. coast of Asia Minor, the harbour of which is one of the finest in the world, though the entrance is very narrow. Lat. 36. 52. N. long. 28. 31. E.

MARNE, a department of France, including part of the former province of Champagne, and the district of Brie. It takes its name from a river which rises near Langres, and falls into the Seine a little above Paris. Area, 3200 square miles. Pop. 325,045. Chalons is the capital.

MARNE, UPPER, a department of France, including the S. E. part of the province of Champagne and Brie. It is fertile, and produces considerable quantities of wine. Area, 2560 square miles. Pop. 244,823. Chaumont is the capital.

MARO, a town of the Sardinian states, in the province of Oneglia, seated in a valley, 8 miles N. W. of Oneglia.

MARQUARTSTEIN, a town of Bavaria, with an ancient castle, seated near the river Acha; 22 miles W. of Salzburg.

MARQUESAS, five islands in the Pacific Ocean, named St. Christina, Magdalena, St. Dominica, St. Pedro, and Hood. The first four were discovered by Quiros, in 1595, the last by Cook, in 1774. St. Dominica is much the largest, about 48 miles in circuit. Captain Cook, in his second voyage, lay some time at Christina, in long. 139. 9. W. and lat. 9. 55. S. It is high and steep, but has many valleys, which widen towards the sea, and are covered with fine forests to the summits of the interior mountains. The products of these islands are bread-fruit, bananas, plantains, cocoa-nuts, scarlet beans, paper-mulberries, (of the bark of which their cloth is made,) casuarinas, with other tropical plants and trees. The inhabitants are well made, strong, and active; of a tawny complexion, but look almost black, by being punctured over the whole body. Their language, manner, customs, &c., very much resemble those of the Society Islands.

MARSAL, a town of France, department of Meurthe, with considerable salt-works, seated on the Seille, in a marsh of difficult access, 17 miles E. S. E. of Nancy.

MARSALA, a town of Sicily, in Val-di Mazara, built on the ruins of the ancient Lilybæum, at the most western part of the island, 45 miles W. S. W. of Palermo. Long. 12. 29. E. lat. 38. 4. N. Pop. 10,000.

MARSAQUIVER, a strong seaport of Algier, in the province of Mascara, seated on a rock, near a bay of the Mediterranean, 3 miles from Oran.

MARSCH. *See* MORAW.

MARSEILLES, a flourishing seaport of France, capital of the department of Mouths of the Rhone. The inhabitants are computed at 110,000. It was so celebrated in the time of the Romans, that Cicero styled it the Athens of the Gauls, and Pliny called it the Mistress of Education. It is divided into the Old Town and the New. The former appears like an amphitheatre, to the vessels which enter the port, but the houses are mean, and the streets dirty, narrow, and steep. In this part is the principal church, built by the Goths, on the ruins of the temple of Diana. The New Town is, in every respect, a perfect contrast to the Old, with which it has a communication by one of the finest streets imaginable. The other streets and squares, as well as the public buildings in general are very elegant. With respect to commerce, Marseilles has long been eminent; and it is now sometimes called Europe in Miniature, on account of the variety of dresses and languages. In the environs are nearly 5000 little country boxes of the citizens, called bastides. The port is a basin of an oval form, 3480 feet long, by 960 broad at its widest part, with 18 or 20 feet depth of water. In 1649 the plague raged with great violence in Marseilles, and with still greater in 1720, when it carried off 50,000 of the inhabitants. The late Lord Gardenstone observed, that Marseilles was a little republic within itself; that the citizens elected their own magistrates; and that the expense of a law-suit never exceeded *twopence-half-penny*, which sum was lodged by each party with the clerks of the court, at the commencement of every process; after which no further expense was incurred. Marseilles is seated on the Mediterranean, 15 miles S. of Aix, and 450 S. by E. of Paris. Long. 5. 27. E. lat. 43. 18. N.

MARSHFIELD, a town in Gloucestershire, with a market on Tuesday, seated on the Coteswold Hills, 11 miles E. of Bristol, and 103 W. of London.

MARSICO NUOVO, a town of Naples, in Principato Citra, 21 miles N. N. E. of Policastro. Pop. 6800.

MARSICO VECCHIO, a town of Naples, in Basilicata, near the river Acre, 23 miles N. E. of Policastro. Pop. 2560.

MARSILLY, a town of France, department of Marne, 10 miles S. of Suzanne.

MARSTRAND, a town of Sweden, in the government of Gottenburg. The inhabitants, about 1200 in number, subsist chiefly by the herring fishery, by the number of ships which in bad weather take refuge in the harbour, which, though difficult of entrance, is secure and commodious, and by a contraband trade. It stands at the entrance of the Cattegat, 33 miles N. N. W. of Gottenburg. Long. 11. 36. E. lat. 57. 53. N.

Marta, a town of Italy, in the patrimony of St. Peter, seated on a river of the same name, 10 miles E. of Castro.

Martaban, a province of the Birman empire, part of which has been ceded to the British. The whole population amounts to about 45,000, of which about 25,000 belong to Britain. The religion is Buddhism.

Martaban, a city of the Birman empire, capital of a province of the same name, fertile in rice, fruits, and wines of all kinds. It was at one time a rich trading place, but after it fell into the hands of the Birmans, they caused its harbour to be nearly choked up, and it is now of little importance. It is seated on the bay of Bengal, at the mouth of the Thaluan; 120 miles S. E. of Pegu. Long. 97. 56. E. lat. 16. 30. N.

Martapura. *See* Metapura.

Martel, a town of France, department of Lot, seated near the Dordogne, 18 miles E. of Sarlat. Pop. 2800.

Martha, St., a district of the republic of Columbia, in the territory of New Granada, bounded N. by the Caribbean Sea, E. by Maracaibo, and W. by Carthagena. It abounds with fruit proper to the climate, and there are mines of gold and precious stones, and salt-works. Here commences the famous ridge of mountains called the Andes, which runs S. the whole length of S. America.

Martha, St., a town of Colombia, capital of the above district. The harbour is surrounded by high mountains. It was once flourishing and populous, but has of late years much declined. It has been frequently pillaged by the English, the Dutch, and the Buccaneers: in 1596 it was reduced to ashes by Sir Francis Drake. It is seated on one of the mouths of the Madalena, 100 miles W. by S. of Rio de la Hache. Long. 74. 4. W. lat. 11. 27. N.

Martha's Vineyard, an island near the S. coast of Massachusets, a little to the W. of Nantucket. It is 21 miles long, and from 2 to 10 broad, and belongs to Duke's county. The chief products are Indian corn and rye. Edgarton is the chief town.

Marthalen, a town of Switzerland, canton of Zurich, 6 miles S. of Schaffhausen.

Martigues, a town of France, department of Mouths of the Rhone, seated near a lake 12 miles long, and 5 broad, which produces excellent salt. It is 20 miles N. W. of Marseilles. Pop. 8000.

Martin, Cape, a promontory of Spain, separating the Gulf of Valencia from that of Alicant. Long. 0. 36. E. lat. 38. 54. N.

Martin, St., a town of France, in the Isle of Re, with a harbour and strong citadel, 10 miles W. N. W. of Rochelle. Long. 1. 21. W. lat. 46. 18. N. Pop. 3000.

Martin, St., one of the Leeward Caribbee islands, 44 miles in circumference. It has neither harbour nor river, but several salt-pits, and salt-water lakes. Tobacco is the chief commodity cultivated. It was long jointly possessed by the French and Dutch, was taken by the British in 1801, but subsequently restored. The W. end is 5 miles S. of Anguilla. Long. 63. 16. W. lat. 18. 4. N.

Martinach, a town of Switzerland, in the Valais, on the river Dranse, 12 miles S. W. of Sion.

Martinico, one of the Windward Caribbee islands, 50 miles long, and 18 broad, belonging to the French. There are high mountains covered with trees, several rivers, and many fertile valleys. The chief products are sugar, cotton, ginger, indigo, chocolate, aloes, pimento, plantains, and several other tropical fruits. The island is extremely populous, and it has several safe and commodious harbours, well fortified. It was taken by the English, in 1762, 1794, 1809, but restored in 1815. In 1806 it suffered great damage by a tremendous hurricane. Pop. 96,413. Fortroyal is the capital.

Martinsburg, a town of Virginia, capital of Berkeley county, situate in a fertile country, 10 miles N. N. W. of Shepherdstown, and 22 N.E. of Winchester.

Martinsville, a town of North Carolina, capital of Guildford county. Near this place, in 1781, Lord Cornwallis defeated General Greene. It is seated on Buffalo Creek, 22 miles E. of Salem, and 45 W. by N. of Hillsborough.

Martinsville, a town of Louisiana, situate in a well cultivated district, on the river Zeche.

Martock, a town in Somersetshire, with an elegant church, and markets on Wednesday and Saturday. It is 7 miles S. of Somerton, and 130 W. by S. of London.

Martorano, a town of Naples, in Calabria Citra, and a bishop's see; 18 miles from the sea, and 15 S. of Cosenza.

Martorel, a town of Spain, in Catalonia, at the conflux of the Noya and Lobbregat; 18 miles N. W. of Barcelona.

Martos, a town of Spain, in Andalusia, with a fortress. It is 10 miles W. of Jaen. Pop. 6000.

Maru, a town of Persia, in Khorasan, celebrated for its salt-works; situate on the Morga, 130 miles E. N. E. of Mesched.

Marvao, a town of Portugal, in Alentejo; 8 miles N. E. of Portalegre.

Marvejols, a town of France, department of Lozere; seated on the Colange, 10 miles N. W. of Mende. Pop. 3700.

Marville, a town of France, department of Meuse; seated on the Oshein, 3 miles N. of Jametz.

Mary, St., a seaport of the state of Georgia, in Camden county, at the mouth of St. Mary River; 70 miles S. by W. of Newport. Long. 80. 52. W. lat. 30. 43. N.

Mary River, St., a river of the state of Georgia, navigable for vessels of considerable burden for 90 miles. Its banks afford immense quantities of fine timber, suited to the West India markets. It rises in the Okefonoke swamp, and thence forms the southern boundary of the United States to the ocean, which it enters at the town of St. Mary, between the points of Amelia and Cumberland islands.

Mary Strait, St., a strait in North America, about 70 miles long, which connects Lake Superior and Lake Huron. It contains a number of islands, and at the upper end is a rapid, which, by careful pilots, can be descended without danger.

Maryborough, a town of Ireland, Queen's county, with considerable woollen manufactures. It is the shire and assize town, and has an excellent gaol, and a market-house. It is situate 17 miles S. of Philipstown, and 43 S. W. of Dublin.

Maryland, one of the United States of America, 212 miles long and 120 broad; bounded N. by Pennsylvania, E. by Delaware and the Atlantic, and S. and W. by Virginia. It is divided into 19 counties, 11 of which are on the western, and 8 on the eastern shore of the Chesapeake; those on the W. side are Hartford, Baltimore, Ann Arundel, Frederic, Allegany, Washington, Montgomery, Prince George, Calvert, Charles, and St. Mary; those on the E., Cecil, Kent, Queen Anne, Caroline, Talbot, Somerset, Dorchester, and Worcester. Wheat, Indian corn, and tobacco, are the staple commodities of this state, which, in most respects, resembles Virginia. Inhabitants, 469,232, of whom 89,495 are slaves. Annapolis is the capital, but Baltimore is the mart of trade.

Marylebone, in the county of Middlesex, one of the metropolitan boroughs, returning two members to parliament. *See* London.

Maryport, a town in Cumberland, with markets on Tuesday and Friday, and a good harbour. In 1750 it was only a poor fishing town; the inhabitants employ upwards of 130 vessels, from 50 to 250 tons burden, in the coal or coasting trade. Here are three ship-yards, and some manufactures; and near the town is the Roman station, Virosidum, where several altars and statues have been dug up. Besides the parish church, here are five meeting-houses and a national school. Maryport is situate at the mouth of the Ellen, in the Irish Sea, 28 miles S. W. of Carlisle, and 312 N. N. W. of London. Long. 3. 22. W. lat. 54. 35. N.

Mary's, St., the chief of the Scilly islands. It is about 2½ miles long, and 1½ broad. Newtown, or Hughtown, is the capital of the islands, and has a custom-house, &c., and is guarded by Star Fort. Long. 6. 12. W. lat. 49. 55. N.

Marza, a town in Sicily, in Val di Noto, noted for its salt. It is 10 miles S. by W. of Noto.

Mas d'Agenois, a town of France, department of Lot-et-Garonne, on the river Garonne; 24 miles N. W. of Agen, and 50 S. E. of Bordeaux.

Mas d'Asil, a town of France, department of Arriege, with a Benedictine abbey; seated on the Clisse, 8 miles S. W. of Pamiers.

Masafuera, an island in the Pacific Ocean, 80 miles W. of Juan Fernandez. It is high and mountainous, but lowest to the N., and at a distance appears like one hill or rock. It is uninhabited, except by numerous seals and goats. There is also plenty of wood, but difficult to be got off, as the heavy surf allows of no good landing-place. Long. 81. 40. W. lat. 33. 40. S.

Masbate, one of the Philippines, about 80 miles in circumference. The natives are tributary to the Spaniards. Long. 123. 25. E. lat. 12. 18. N.

Mascara, the western province of Algier, 370 miles long, and 130 broad. It is dry, barren, and mountainous, except on the N., where there are plains abounding in corn, fruit, and pastures. The S. parts are inhabited by independent wandering tribes, particularly the Angad tribe.

Mascara, the capital of the above province, with a strong castle, in which the bey resides. In 1732 it was an inconsiderable place, but is now populous and flourishing. It is not so large as Tremesen, but surpasses it in beauty, having a great number of good houses and mosques. It is seated in a fertile district, 45 miles E. S. E. of Oran, and 190 S. W. of Algier. Long. 0. 40. E. lat. 35. 54. N.

Mascat, or Muskat, a seaport on the E. coast of Arabia, with an excellent harbour. It has a castle on a rock, and is very strong, both by nature and art, though the buildings are mean. It was taken in 1508 by the Portuguese, who retained it for a century and a half. The cathedral, built by the Portuguese, is now the imaum's palace. There is no vegetation to be seen on the sea coast near it, and only a few date trees in a valley at the back of the town, though the inhabitants have all things in plenty. The bazaars are covered with the leaves of date-trees, laid on beams, which reach from the house tops on one side to those on the other. The inhabitants are Mahomedans. Great Britain recognizes the flag of Muscat as neutral, and in time of war it has often been the medium of communication with the enemies' ports. It is seated on a small bay of the Arabian Sea. Long. 59. 26. E. lat. 23. 30. N.

Maseyck, a town of Belgium, province of Limburg, on the Meuse; 9 miles S. S. W. of Roermonde. Pop. 3400.

Masham, a town in North Yorkshire, with a market on Tuesday, and manufactures of coarse woollen cloths; seated on the Ure, 7 miles S. E. of Middleham, and 218 N. N. W. of London.

Mashanagur, a town of Candahar, province of Cabul; situate on the Seward, 48 miles N. of Attock, and 130 E. S. E. of Cabul. Long 71. 7. E. lat. 33. 54. N.

Maskelyne Isle, a small beautiful island in the S. Pacific, lying off the S. E. point of Mallicollo, one of the New Hebrides. Long. 167. 59. E. lat. 16. 32. S.

Masmunster, a town of France, department of Upper Rhine; 25 miles S. S. W. of Colmar.

Masovia, a palatinate of Poland, bounded by Prussian Poland, the palatinates of Sendomir and Kalisch, and the Vistula. Population 318,000. The name formerly included a province of much greater extent. Warsaw is the capital.

Massa, a town of Italy, capital of a duchy of

the same name, which is famous for its quarries of fine marble. The town and its territory belonged to Tuscany, but was given, in 1806, to Lucca. It is seated on the river Frigido, 3 miles from the sea, and 30 N. by W. of Leghorn. Long. 10. 10. E. lat. 44. 2. N.

MASSA, a town of Tuscany, in the Siennese. Borax and lapis lazuli are found in the neighbourhood. It is seated on a mountain near the sea, 35 miles S. W. of Sienna. Long. 11. 3. E. lat. 43. 5. N.

MASSACHUSETS, one of the United States of America, 190 miles long, and from 60 to 100 broad; bounded on the N. by New Hampshire and Vermont, W. by New York, S. by Connecticut, Rhode Island, and the Atlantic, and E. by that ocean and Massachusets Bay. It is divided into 14 counties: Suffolk, Norfolk, Essex, Middlesex, Hampshire, Worcester, Plymouth, Barnstable, Dukes, Nantucket, Bristol, Berkshire, Franklin, and Hampden. There are several railroads in operation in this state, from Boston to Worcester, to the Hudson, and thence to Lake Ontario, parallel with the Grand Canal; to Providence, to Lowell, and from West Stockbridge to the boundary of New York. This state is well watered by a number of small rivers, and produces plenty of maize, wheat, flax, hemp, copper, and iron. Nails have been made here in such quantities, as to prevent, in a great measure, the importation of them from Great Britain. There is a machine for cutting nails at Newbury Port, invented by Mr. Jacob Perkins, which will turn out 200,000 in a day. There are also duck manufactories, manufactures of cotton and woollen, paper mills, several snuff, oil, chocolate, and powder mills, and a number of iron works, and slitting mills besides other mills in common use for sawing timber, grinding grain, and fulling cloth. In fact, there are few articles necessary to the comfort and convenience of life which are not manufactured in this state. Breweries and distilleries have long been established, and shipbuilding is prosecuted with great ardour. The literary, humane, and other societies are numerous. It is estimated that more than one-fourth of the shipping of the United States belong to Massachusets. The inhabitants amount to 737,699. Slavery is, happily, in this state abolished. Boston is the capital.

MASSACHUSETS BAY, a bay of the foregoing state, between Cape Ann and Cape Cod. It is so named, as well as the whole state of Massachusets, from a tribe of Indians of the same name that formerly lived round this bay.

MASSAFRA, a town of Naples, in Terra d'Otranto; 16 miles N. W. of Taranto. Pop. 7000.

MASSAGANO, a town of Congo, in Angola, capital of a province of the same name, seated on the Coanzo, 100 miles E. S. E. of Loango. Long. 14. 30. E. lat. 9. 40. S.

MASSAPA, a town of Africa, in Motapa; near which are rich mines of gold. The Portuguese are settled here. It is seated on a river, 230 miles N. W. of Sofala. Long. 31. 55. E. lat. 18. 5. S.

MASSERANO, a town of the Sardinian states, in Piedmont; 40 miles N. N. E. of Turin. Pop. 3600.

MASSEUBE, a town of France, department of Gers; 14 miles S. of Auch.

MASUAH, a town of Abyssinia, situate on an island on the coast of the Red Sea, with an excellent harbour, distributed into three divisions. The houses in general are built of poles and bent grass, as in the towns in Arabia. Long. 39. 36. E. lat. 15. 35. N.

MASULIPATAM, a city and seaport of Hindostan, in the district of Condapilly; with a good harbour, and a considerable trade in chintzes, painted linens, &c. It formerly belonged to the French, but was taken by the British in 1769. It is seated near one of the mouths of the Kistna, 73 miles S. W. of Rajamundy. Long. 81. 15. E. lat. 16. 10. N.

MASVAUX, a town of France, department of Upper Rhine, at the foot of the Vosges mountains; 10 miles N. of Befort. Pop. 2200.

MATA, a town of Spain, in Valencia. Near it is a lake of the same name, noted for the immense quantity of salt that it produces. The town stands on the sea coast; 28 miles S. S.W. of Alicant.

MATACA, or MATANZA, a commodious bay on the N. coast of the island of Cuba; 35 miles E. of Havanna. Long. 81. 16. W. lat. 23. 12. N.

MATALA, a town and cape on the S. coast of the island of Candia; 30 miles S. of Candia. Long. 24. 51. E. lat. 34. 46. N.

MATAMBA, a country of Africa, in Congo, bounded on the N. by Congo Proper, E. by parts unknown, S. by Bemba and Benguela, and W. by Angola. The chief town is St. Maria.

MATAN, or MACTAN, one of the smaller Philippines, on which Magellan was killed in 1521, after he had conquered the isle of Zebu.

MATAPAN, CAPE, the most southern promontory of the Morea, between the Gulf of Coron and that of Colochina. Long. 22. 20. E. lat. 36. 35. N.

MATARAM, a town of the island of Java. It is strong by situation, and is seated in a fertile and populous country, surrounded by mountains. Long. 111. 55. E. lat. 7. 15. S.

MATARO, a town of Spain, in Catalonia, celebrated for its glass-works, and the best red wine made in the province. Here are also manufactures of calico, silk stuffs, laces, &c. It is seated on the Mediterranean; 20 miles N. E. of Barcelona. Pop. 25,000.

MATERA, a town of Naples, capital of Basilicata, and the see of an archbishop. It is seated on the Canapro; 35 miles W. N. W. of Taranto. Pop. 12,400. Long. 16. 34. E. lat. 40. 50. N.

MATEREA. *See* HELIOPOLIS.

MATHAN, a town of the empire of Bornou; with a royal palace, forming a kind of citadel; situate on a small river; 100 miles S. W. of Bornou.

MATHIEU, a town of France, department of Upper Vienne; 12 miles W. S. W. of St. Junier.

MATHURA, a celebrated town of Hindostan,

province of Agra, much venerated by the Hindoos, as the birthplace of their god Krishna. It is one continued street of temples, the resort of innumerable pilgrims from all parts of India, and is seated on the Jumna. Long. 80. 40. E. lat. 27. 32. N.

MATLOCK, a village in Derbyshire, situate on the Derwent; 4 miles N. of Wirksworth. It is an extensive straggling place, built in a romantic style, on the steep side of a mountain; and near the bridge are two chalybeate springs. A little to the left is Matlock Bath, famous for its warm baths, which are much frequented from April to October. Near the western bank of the river is a petrifying spring.

MATSMAI, a town of eastern Asia, the capital of the island of Jesso, under the domination of the Japanese. Pop. about 50,000.

MATTCHEETZ, or MATSCHEWICE, a town of Poland, memorable for a great victory obtained by the Russians over the Poles, in 1794; 32 miles E. of Warsaw.

MATTHEO, ST., a town of Spain, in Valencia, 10 miles from the Mediterranean, and 50 N. N. E. of Valencia.

MATTHEW, ST., an island in the Atlantic; 420 miles S. by W. of Cape Palmas, on the coast of Guinea. It was planted by the Portuguese, but is now deserted. Long. 8. 10. W. lat. 1. 24. S.

MATTHEW, ST., a small island in the Indian Ocean. Long. 123. 51. E. lat. 52. 3. S.

MATTHEWS, a county of the state of Virginia; 18 miles long, and 16 miles broad; seated on the W. shore of the Chesapeake. Pop. 7442.

MATTO GROSSO, a province of Brazil, bounded N. by the province of Para, S. by that of St. Paul, W. by that of La Plata, and E. by that of Goyar, and lying between 52. and 64. of W. long., and between 10. and 23. of S. lat. It was first visited by the Portuguese, in search of gold, which abounds near the sources of many of its rivers. The country is generally fertile.

MATURA, a seaport of Ceylon, with a small fort. The country round is exceedingly wild, and abounds in elephants. It is seated at the mouth of the Melipu, near the southern extremity of the island; 25 miles E. S. E. of Galle. Long. 80. 28. E. lat. 5. 53. N.

MATURA, a town of Hindostan, in the province of Agra; 22 miles N. E. of Agra, and 70 S. S. E. of Delhi.

MAUBEUGE, a forrified town of France, department of Nord; with manufactures of arms and woollen stuffs. In 1793 the Austrians formed the blockade of this place, but were soon driven from their position. It was one of the fortresses occupied by the allies from 1815 to 1818. Seated on the Sambre; 13 miles S. of Mons. Pop. 4800.

MAULDAH, a town of Hindostan, in Bengal; situate on a river that communicates with the Ganges. It arose out of the ruins of Gour, which are in its neighbourhood; and is a place of trade, particularly in silk; 170 miles N. of Calcutta. Long. 88. 16. E. lat. 25. 3. N.

MAULE, a province of Chili; 132 miles long, and 120 broad. The soil is fertile, and the province is well watered. Pop. 12,000. The capital is Talca. Lat. 34. 47. S.

MAULE, a river of the above province, which rises in the Cordillera, and enters the Pacific in lat. 34. 50. S.

MAULEON, a town in France, department of Vendee; with an ancient castle on a rock. It is seated near the river Oint; 52 miles N. E. of Rochelle.

MAULEON, a town of France, department of Lower Pyrenees; 20 miles W. S. W. of Pau.

MAULEON, a town of France, department of Upper Pyrenees; 23 miles S. E. of Tarbes.

MAURA, ST. (ancient Leucadia), an island in the Ionian Sea, on the W. coast of Greece; 13 miles N. of the island of Cephalonia, and about 50 miles in circuit. Its surface is mountainous and rugged, and it is subject to frequent earthquakes. The chief products are wine, olives, citrons, pomegranates, almonds, and other fruits. It forms part of the Ionian republic, and sends four deputies to the assembly. Pop. 20,000. There are several good ports, but no town of consequence, except the capital, of the same name, situate at the N. extremity of the island. Pop. 6000. Long. 20. 46. E. lat. 38. 40. N.

MAURIAC, a town of France, department of Cantal; famous for excellent horses; seated near the Dordogne; 29 miles E. of Tulle.

MAURICE, ST., a town of Switzerland, in the Valais, situate on the Rhone, between two high mountains; 16 miles N. W. of Martigny.

MAURITIUS. *See* FRANCE, ISLE OF.

MAURUA, one of the smaller Society Islands, in the South Pacific; 14 miles W. of Bolabola. Long. 152. 32. W. lat. 16. 25. S.

MAUTERN, a town of Austria, on the S. side of the Danube, opposite Stein; with which it is connected by a long wooden bridge. It is 11 miles N. by W. of St. Polten.

MAUES, ST., a town in Cornwall; market on Friday. It has no church, but a chapel has been erected at the expense of the late Marquis of Buckingham. It is seated on the E. side of Falmouth Haven; 12 miles S. S. W. of Grampound, and 260 W. by S. of London.

MAXEN, a town of Upper Saxony, celebrated for a victory obtained by the Austrians over the Prussians, in 1759, when 20,000 Prussians surrendered themselves prisoners of war. It is 10 miles S. of Dresden.

MAXIMIN, ST., a town of France, department of Var; seated on the Argens; 21 miles N. of Toulon. Pop. 3300.

MAY, a small island of Scotland, at the mouth of the Frith of Forth, with a lighthouse, 6 miles S. E. of Anstruther.

MAY, CAPE, a cape of N. America, on the N. side of the mouth of the Delaware. Long. 75. 4. W. lat. 39. 0. N.

MAYAMBA, or MAJUMBA, a seaport of Africa, in Loango. The chief trade is in logwood. It stands at the mouth of the Banna; 110 miles N.W. of Loango. Long. 10. 20. E. lat. 3. 40. S.

MAYBOLE, a town of Scotland, in Ayrshire; with a manufacture of cotton goods and coarse blankets; seated on an eminence, surrounded by hills. It is 8 miles S. of Ayr.

Mayen, a town in the Prussian province of Lower Rhine, with a castle and a collegiate church; seated on the Nette; 15 miles W. by N. of Coblentz.

Mayence. *See* Mentz.

Mayenfield, a town of Switzerland, in the Grison county; chief place of the League of the Ten Jurisdictions; with 900 inhabitants; seated on the Rhine, in a romantic valley; 22 miles S. by E. of Appenzel.

Mayenne, a department of France, including part of the former province of Maine It takes its name from a river, which flows S. by the cities of Mayenne and Laval, to that of Angers, where it receives the Sarthe, and soon after joins the Loire. Pop. 34,000. Laval is the capital.

Mayenne, the chief place of an arrondissement in the above department; with a castle on a rock. It has manufactures of linen, woollen, and thread. It is seated on the river Mayenne; 45 miles W. N. W. of Mans. Pop. 9100. Long. 0. 43. W. lat. 48. 18. N.

Maynooth, a town of Ireland, in the county of Kildare. Here is a royal college for students intended for the Romish church; also a college for lay students of the same persuasion, established in 1802. It is 15 miles W. of Dublin.

Mayo, a county of Ireland, in the province of Connaught; 62 miles long, and 52 broad; bounded E. by Roscommon, S. by Galway, W. and N. by the Atlantic, and N. E. by Sligo. It is divided into 76 parishes, and sends two members to parliament. The W. coast is mountainous, and thinly inhabited; but the interior produces excellent pasturage, and is watered by several lakes and rivers. The fisheries are very productive. Mayo gives the title of earl to the family of Bourke. The principal town is Castlebar.

Mayo, a town of Ireland, once the capital of the county of its name, but now a poor place; 9 miles S. E. of Castlebar.

Mayo, one of the Cape Verd islands; 20 miles in circumference. The N. E. end is low, and the land rises gradually till it arrives at a volcanic mountain, to the S. W. of which is irregular ground, soon followed by a high peak, much more lofty than the volcanic cone. The soil in general is barren, and water is scarce; but there are plenty of beeves, goats, and asses; as also some corns, yams, potatoes, plantains, figs, and water-melons. The chief commodity is salt. Long. 23. 5. W. lat. 15. 10. N.

Mayorga, a town of Portugal, in Estremalura; near the Atlantic; 67 miles N. of Lisbon.

Maysville. *See* Limestone.

Maywar. *See* Oudipour.

Mazagan, a seaport of Morocco, near the Atlantic; 8 miles W. of Azamor, and 120 N. of Morocco. It is now almost deserted. Long. 8. 15. W. lat. 33. 12. N.

Mazanderan, a province of Persia, bounded N. by the Caspian Sea, W. by Ghilan, S. by the lofty mountains of Elburz, which separate it from Irak, and E. by Khorassan. It is a fertile country, and the mountains on its S. boundary are covered with timber trees; but the climate is moist and unhealthy. Sari is the capital.

Mazara, a seaport of Sicily, in Val di Mazara, and a bishop's see. It has a capacious harbour, and is built on the ruins of the ancient Sesinuntum: 45 miles S. W. of Palermo. Long. 12. 30. E. lat. 37. 53. N.

Maziera, or **Maceira**, an island in the Arabian Sea, on the coast of Oman; 60 miles long, and from 4 to 8 broad. Long. 59. 30. E. lat. 20. 30. N.

Meaco, a city of Niphon, in Japan, formerly the metropolis of the whole empire. It is still the ecclesiastical capital, the residence of the dairo, or spiritual sovereign, and the centre of literature and science. The palace, and some of the temples, are of extraordinary magnificence. A number of the finer manufactures, particularly japan-work, painting, carving, &c. are carried on here. The town is seated in a fine plain; 160 miles W. S. W. of Jeddo. Pop. 529,000. Long. 153. 30. E. lat. 35. 24. N.

Meadia, a town of Hungary; in the bannat of Temeswar. It was taken by the Turks, in 1738 and 1789. It is 23 miles S. E. of Temeswar. Pop. 1400.

Meco, one of the smaller Moluccas; in the Indian Ocean; with a good harbour. Long. 127. 5. E. lat. 1. 12. N.

Mearns. *See* Kincardineshire.

Meath, or **East Meath**, a county of Ireland, in the province of Leinster; 43 miles (English) long, and 36 broad; bounded on the N. by Cavan and Louth, E. by the Irish Sea, S. by Kildare and Dublin, and W. by Westmeath. It is divided into 18 baronies and 147 parishes, and sends two members to parliament. It formerly contained several small bishoprics, which were gradually united into one see, and received the name of Meath in the twelfth century. There is no cathedral, and the episcopal palace is at Ardbraccan, a village near Navan. The agriculture of this county is now in a very flourishing state. The soil in general is a rich fertile loam, producing abundance of corn, and feeding numerous sheep and cattle. Trim is the capital.

Meath, West, a county of Ireland; in the province of Leinster; 42 miles long, and 35 broad; bounded N. by Cavan, E. by East Meath, S. by King's county, W. by Roscommon (from which it is separated by the Shannon), and N. W. by Longford. It is divided into 11 baronies (besides half the barony of Fore) and 59 parishes, with parts of seven others. It sends two members to parliament. It is very fertile in corn and pasturage, and has several lakes and rivers. This county gives the title of marquis to the family of Nugent. Mullingar is the county town.

Meaux, a large and populous town of France. department of Seine-et-Marne. The marketplace is a peninsula, contiguous to the town, which was formerly well fortified. In the cathedral is the tomb of the celebrated Bossuet, bishop of Meaux. It is seated on both sides of the Marne; 25 miles N. of Paris. Pop. 7000. Long. 2. 53. E. lat. 48. 58. N.

Mecca, a city of Arabia; famous as the birthplace of Mahomet. It is seated in a barren valley, surrounded by many little hills, consisting of a blackish rock. The houses follow the windings of the valley, and are built partly on the declivities upon each side. The streets are regular, level, and convenient. The chief support of the inhabitants is derived from the pilgrims, who flock to this place from every part of the Mahometan world. The principal object of veneration and pilgrimage is the Kaaba, or Beit Allah, (the House of God,) a quadrilateral tower of 34 feet high, enclosing the sacred stone, or Hagera el Assoud, a block of black stone, which is exposed through an opening in an immense black cloth, covering the whole of the Kaaba, except its base. The ceremonies consists in walking seven times round the Kaaba, commencing at the sacred stone at the eastern angle, and kissing and touching it with the right hand, repeating certain prayers. This stone was an object of veneration many ages ago; the same ceremonies were observed 700 years before Mahomet engrafted them into his system. The other objects of Mahometan superstition have been destroyed by the schismatic Wahabees; and the whole ceremonies have much declined in the veneration of the Mussulmans. The city formerly contained 100,000 inhabitants; it now does not amount to above 16,000, whose character is a union of fraud, fanaticism, and poverty. The famous balm of Mecca is not manufactured in this city, but is found and brought hither from the surrounding country. Mecca is governed by a shereef, who is a temporal prince, and his revenue is increased by the donations of Mahometan sovereigns. It is 34 miles E. N. E. of Jidda, the seaport of Mecca, and 220 S. by E. of Medina. Long. 40. 55. E. lat. 21. 40. N.

Mechlin, or Malines, a town of Belgium; capital of a district in the province of Antwerp, and an archbishop's see. The cathedral is a superb structure, with a very high steeple. Here is a great foundry for ordnance of all kinds; and the best Brabant lace, fine linen, damasks, carpets, and leather are made here. Mechlin submitted to the duke of Marlborough, in 1706, and was taken by the French, in 17.6, 1792, and 1794. The system of railroads, which intersects Belgium in all directions, from Ostend to the Rhine, centres in this town, which therefore is a starting point for the traffic of the kingdom. It is seated on the Dyle; 10 miles N.N.E. of Brussels, and 15 S. S. E. of Antwerp. Long. 4. 29. E. lat. 51. 2. N.

Mechoacan. *See* Valladolid.

Meckenheim, a town of the Prussian states; in the province of Berg and Cleves; situate on the Erfft; 8 miles S. W. of Bone.

Mecklenburg, a duchy of Germany, bounded N. by the Baltic, E. by Pomerania, S. by Brandenburg, and W. by Holstein and Lunenburg. It extends 135 miles in length, and 90 where broadest; and abounds in corn, pastures, and game. The country was, for many centuries, under the government of one prince; but on the death of the sovereign, in 1592, it was divided between his two sons; the elder obtaining the duchy of Mecklenburg-Schwerin, and the younger the duchy of Mecklenburg-Strelitz. Both princes received the title of grand duke, at the congress of Vienna, in 1815, and they have each a vote at the diet of the empire. Pop. 475,000. Schwerin and Strelitz are the chief towns.

Mecklenburg, a county of Virginia, bounded N. by Lunenburg, E. by Brunswick, S. by N. Carolina, and W. by Halifax and Charlotte counties. Pop. 20,076. Chief town Boydton.

Meckley. *See* Cassay.

Mecon, a river which rises in the N. E. part of Tibet, flows through the country of Cambodia, and falls into the China Sea by three mouths.

Mecran, or Mukran, a province of Persia; bounded on the N. by Segistan and Candahar, E. by Hindostan, S. by the Indian Ocean, and W. by Kerman. The southern part is dry, and little more than a desert; the northern is less so, but animals are rare, and the soil far from fertile. Kedge is the capital.

Medea, a town of Algier, on the site of the ancient Lamida, in a country abounding in corn, fruit, and sheep; 35 miles S. W. of Algier.

Medea, or Maledia, a seaport of Tunis; formerly a place of importance; seated on a peninsula in the Gulf of Cabes; 8 miles S. by E. of Tunis.

Medebach, a town of Prussia; in the province of Westphalia; 32 miles E. of Cassel.

Medelin, a town of Spain; in Estremadura; the birthplace of the celebrated Fernando Cortes. It is seated in a fertile country, on the river Guadiana; 20 miles E. by S. of Merida.

Medelpadia, a province of Sweden; between the Gulfs of Bothnia and Jamtland. It is 100 miles long, and 45 broad, very mountainous and woody, but interspersed with lakes, rivers, and fertile valleys. Sundswald is the capital.

Medenblick, a seaport of the Netherlands; in North Holland; with a good harbour. The chief commerce is in timber brought from Norway and Sweden; and the vicinity is remarkable for its rich pastures. Medenblick was taken by the English, in 1799. It is seated on the Zuyder Zee; 28 miles N. E. of Amsterdam. Long. 4. 51. E. lat. 52. 46. N.

Medford, a town of Massachusets; in Middlesex county; noted for its distilleries and brick-works. Pop. 2478. It stands on the Mystic, 3 miles from its mouth, and 4 N. of Boston.

Median. *See* Madian.

Medina, a town of Arabia Deserta, celebrated as the burial place of Mahomet. It is a small, poor place, but is walled round, and has a magnificent mosque, in one corner of which is the tomb of Mahomet, enclosed with rich curtains, and lighted by a great number of lamps. Medina is called the city of the Prophet, because here he was protected by the inhabitants, when he fled from Mecca, and here he was first invested with regal power. The time of his death was in 637; but the Mahometan epoch begins in 622, from the time of his flight. Medina is seated on a sandy plain, abounding in palm-trees; 200 miles N. W. of Mecca. Its port is Jambo. Long. 39. 33. E. lat. 24. 20. N.

MEDINA, the capital of the kingdom of Woolly, West Africa. It contains about 1000 houses, and is defended by a high wall, surrounded by a thick hedge. Long. 12. 50. W. lat. 23. 38. N.

MEDINA, a town and fort of the island of Bahrein, near which is a bank containing the finest pearls in the world. The harbour will not admit vessels of more than 200 tons. It is seated near the Arabian shore of the Persian Gulf.

MEDINA, a town of Spain, in Estremadura; seated at the foot of a mountain; 20 miles W. N. W. of Lerena.

MEDINA DEL CAMPO, a town of Spain; province of Leon; in a country abounding with corn and wine; 23 miles S. S. W. of Valladolid. Pop. 6000.

MEDINA DEL RIO SECCO, a decayed town of Leon; near the Sequillo; 25 miles N. W. of Valladolid, and 56 S. S. E. of Leon. Pop. 8000.

MEDINA SIDONIA, a town of Spain, in Andalusia; with a castle; 24 miles S. E. of Cadiz, and 60 S. of Seville. Pop. 5000.

MEDITERRANEAN, a sea between Asia, Africa, and Europe; communicating with the Atlantic Ocean by the Strait of Gibraltar, and with the Black Sea by the Strait of Gallipoli, the Sea of Marmora, and the Strait of Constantinople. It is of very great extent, but its tides are inconsiderable, and a constant current sets in from the Atlantic through the Strait of Gibraltar. It contains many islands, several of them large, as Majorca, Minorca, Corsica, Sardinia, Sicily, Candia, Cyprus, &c. The eastern part of it, bordering on Asia, is sometimes called the Levant Sea.

MEDWAY, a river of England, which rises in Ashdown Forest, in Sussex; entering Kent, it flows by Tunbridge and Maidstone, and thence to Rochester; below which, at Chatham, is a station of the royal navy. Dividing into two branches, the western one enters the Thames, between the isles of Grain and Sheppey, and is defended by the fort at Sheerness. The eastern branch, called the East Swale, passes by Queenborough and Milton, and enters the German Ocean below Faversham. The tide flows up nearly to Maidstone, and the river is navigable to Tunbridge.

MEDWI, a town of Sweden, in Gothland; much frequented on account of its waters, which are vitriolic and sulphureous. The lodging-houses form one street of uniform wooden buildings, painted red. It stands near the lake Wetter; 3 miles from Wadstena.

MEELAH, a town of Algier; province of Constantina; surrounded by gardens producing abundance of herbs and excellent fruit, particularly pomegranates. It is 14 miles N. W. of Constantina.

MEGARA, a town of Greece, in the Isthmus of Corinth; formerly a very large, but now inconsiderable. It has some fine remains of antiquity; 20 miles W. of Athens.

MEGEN, a town of the Netherlands, in North Brabant; seated on the Muse; 15 miles W. S. W. of Nimeguen.

MEGNA. *See* BURRAMPOOTER.

MEHALLET EL KEBEER. *See* MAHALEN.

MEHUN, a town of France; department of Cher. Here are the ruins of a castle built by Charles VII. as a place of retirement; and here he starved himself, in the dread of being poisoned by his son, afterwards Louis XI. It is seated on the Yevre; 10 miles N. W. of Bourges.

MEHWAS, a district of Guzerat, Hindostan; inhabited by a race of marauders, who live by plunder.

MEINAU, a small island in the middle lake of Constance, which produces excellent wine; 5 miles N. W. of Constance.

MEININGEN, a principality of Germany, in Saxony, forming the territory of the Duke of Saxe-Meiningen, comprising an area of 448 square miles, with 56,000 inhabitants.

MEININGEN, the capital of the foregoing principality; with a fine castle, a lyceum, a council-house, &c. The principal manufacture is black crape. It is situate amongst mountains, on the river Werra; 16 miles N. W. of Hildburghausen, and 21 N. of Schweinfurt. Pop. 4500. Long. 10. 43. E. lat. 50. 38. N.

MEISSEN, or MISNIA, a circle of Saxony, formerly a margraviate. Part of it was ceded to Prussia in 1815, but it has still an area of 1600 square miles, with 298,000 inhabitants. It is a fine country, producing corn, wine, metals, and all the conveniences of life. It is situate on both sides of the Elbe, having Bohemia on the S. and Prussian Saxony on the N.

MEISSEN, the capital of the foregoing circle, with a castle, and a famous manufacture of porcelain. The cathedral is the burial-place of the Saxon princes, to the year 1539. The bridge over the Elbe, burnt down by the Prussians in 1757, has been replaced by another of a very handsome construction. Meissen is seated on the rivulet Meisse, at its junction with the Elbe; 12 miles N. N. W. of Dresden. Pop. 400. Long. 13. 31. E. lat. 51. 11. N.

MEISSENHEIM, a town of Bavaria, in a district of the same name, situate on the Glan; 34. miles N. by E. of Deux Ponts, and 30 W. S. W. of Mentz.

MELASSA, a town of Asiatic Turkey, in Natolia, situate on a fertile plain, near a mountain abounding in white marble. It was anciently a city, adorned with many public buildings, especially temples, and is still a large place, but the houses are mean; 80 miles S. of Smyrna. Long. 27. 50. E. lat. 37. 15. N.

MELAZZO. *See* MILAZZO.

MELBOURN, a considerable village in Derbyshire, 8 miles S. by E. of Derby. Here are a church, four meeting-houses, and the vestiges of an ancient castle in which the Duke of Bourbon was confined after the battle of Agincourt.

MELBOURNE, a flourishing town of South Australia, at the head of Port Philip, near the confluence of two rivers, in lat. 37. 48. S. and long. 144. 55. E. It is seated in a country admirably adapted for the pasturing of sheep, and has a considerable population employed in agriculture. The population in 1841 was 4440; of the whole territory, 7681.

MELCK, a town of Austria, with a Benedictine abbey on a high rock, near the Danube; 10 miles W. of St. Polten.

MELCOMBE REGIS, a town in Dorsetshire, united to Weymouth as a port, as a corporation, and as a market-town, and with it returns two members to parliament. It has a good market-place, and a town-hall, in which the corporation of Weymouth and Melcombe transact business. It is seated at the mouth of the river Wey, opposite to Weymouth, with which it communicates by an elegant bridge; 127 miles W. S. W. of London. *See* WEYMOUTH.

MELDERT, a town of Belgium, in South Brabant; 10 miles S. E. of Louvain.

MELDORF, a town of Denmark, in Holstein; seated near the mouth of the Miele; 50 miles N. W. of Hamburgh.

MELDRUM, a town of Scotland, in Aberdeenshire, 17 miles N. N. W. of Aberdeen.

MELFI, a town of Naples, in Basilicata, and a bishop's see, with a castle on a rock, 20 miles N. N. W. of Acerenza.

MELGAZA, a town of Portugal, in Entre Douro e Minho, with a strong castle; seated on the Minho, 27 miles N. by E. of Braga.

MELIDA, an island of Dalmatia, in the Gulf of Venice, with a Benedictine abbey, six villages, and several harbours. It is 30 miles in length, and abounds in oranges, citrons, wine, and fish.

MELILLA, a seaport of Fez, on the coast of the Mediterranean. In 1496 it was taken by the Spaniards, who built a citadel. It is 115 miles N. E. of Fez. Long. 2. 57. W. lat. 34. 58. N.

MELINDA, a kingdom of East Africa; on the coast of Zanguebar. Its products are gold, elephants' teeth, ostriches' feathers, wax and aloes, senna, and other drugs, also plenty of rice, sugar, cocoa-nuts, and other tropical fruits.

MELINDA, the capital of the above kingdom, is a large and handsome place surrounded by fine gardens. It has a good harbour, defended by a fort, but the entrance is dangerous, on account of the great number of shoals and rocks under water. The inhabitants are said to amount to above 200,000, principally negroes; 470 miles S. W. of Magadoxa. Long. 41. 48. E. lat. 2. 15. S.

MELIPILLA, a province of Chili, extending about 25 leagues from E. to W., and abounding in grain and wine. Logrono is the capital.

MELITA. *See* MALTA.

MELITELLO, a town of Sicily, in Val di Noto, 8 miles W. of Leontini.

MELITOPOL, a town of Russia, government of Taurida; situate on a lake, 12 miles from the Sea of Asoph, and 108 S. of Catherineslaf.

MELKSHAM, a town in Wiltshire, with a market every other Thursday, for cattle, and a manufacture of broad cloths. It has a large parish church, and three meeting-houses. It is 99 miles W. of London.

MELLE, a town of Hanover, seated on the Hase; 15 miles E. by S. of Osnaburg.

MELLE, a town of France, in the department of Deux Sevres; 12 miles S. W. of Niort.

MELLINGEN, a town of Switzerland, in the canton of Aargau; seated on the Reuss, 2 miles S. by W. of Baden.

MELNICK, a town of Bohemia, with a castle. Its vicinity yields excellent red and white wine, and near it stands the Augustine convent of Schopka. It is seated on the Elbe, opposite the influx of the Muldau; 18 miles N. of Prague.

MELOUI, a town of Egypt, with a remarkable mosque; seated on the Nile, 3 miles S. of Ashmunein.

MELROSE, a tn. of Scotland, in Roxburghshire. At some distance from the town, on the S. side of the Tweed, are the magnificent remains of Melrose Abbey, founded by David I., in 1136, part of which was used for divine service, till the new church was erected. Alexander II. is said to be buried under the great altar. Abbotsford, the seat of the late Sir Walter Scott, is in the vicinity of the abbey. Melrose is 11 miles N. W. of Jedburgh, and 35 S. of Edinburgh.

MELTON MOWBRAY, a town in Leicestershire, with a market on Tuesday. The fine cheese, called Stilton, is chiefly made in its neighbourhood. The church is a fine Gothic edifice, and here are two meeting-houses, a charity school, a national school, and twelve almshouses, six of which were erected in 1827. It is seated in a rich grazing country, on the river Eye, over which are two handsome stone bridges; 15 miles N. E. of Leicester, and 106 N. by W. of London.

MELUN, a town of France, in the department of Seine-et-Marne. It has a trade with Paris in corn, meal, wine, and cheese. It is seated on the Seine; 25 miles S. E. of Paris. Long. 2. 35. E. lat. 48. 30. N. Pop. 6700.

MEMEL, a strong town of East Prussia, with a castle, a fine harbour, and an extensive commerce. It is seated on a river of the same name, at the N. extremity of the Curische Haff, and on the N. E. side of the entrance into the harbour is a lighthouse. It is 70 miles N. N. E. of Konigsberg, and 130 N. E. of Dantzic. Long. 21. 36. E. lat. 55. 46. N.

MEMMINGEN, a town of Bavaria, defended by art, and surrounded by a morass. It has a considerable trade in fine linen, fustian, cotton, paper, salt, tobacco, and hops. Near this place, in 1795, the French republicans defeated the emigrants under the prince of Conde; and in 1800 the French defeated the Austrians, and took the town. It is seated in a fertile plain, near the river Iller; 28 miles S. by E. of Ulm, Long. 10. 12. E. lat. 48. 0. N.

MEMPHRAMAGOG, a lake of North America, in Canada and Vermont; 35 miles long, and 3 broad.

MENAI, a strait which divides the island of

Anglesey from the other parts of N. Wales. An elegant suspension bridge has been thrown over this strait, which will allow the largest vessels that pass the strait to sail beneath it.

MENAN, a river of the kingdom of Siam, which passes by the city of Siam, and enters the Gulf of Siam below Bancok.

MENANCABOW, a kingdom in the centre of the island of Sumatra. The country is described as a large plain, clear of wood, comparatively well cultivated, and abounding in gold.

MENDE, a town of France, capital of the department of Lozere, and a bishop's see. It has manufactures of serges and other woollen stuffs. It is seated on the Lot, 35 miles S. W. of Puy, and 210 S. by E. of Paris. Long. 3. 30. E. lat. 44. 31. N. Pop. 500.

MENDIP HILLS, a lofty tract in the N. E. of Somersetshire, abounding in coal, calamine, and lead: copper, manganese, bole, and red ochre, are also found. A great portion of these hills, formerly covered with heath and fern, has been brought into cultivation, and produces good corn.

MENDON, a town of Massachusets, in Worcester county; 18 miles S. S. E. of Worcester, and 36 S. W. of Boston.

MENDOZA, a city of Buenos Ayres, in the province of Cugo, on the E. side of the Andes, in a plain adorned with gardens, well watered by canals. It contains four convents, a college, and a church. A river of the same name flows by this town, and finally enters the Atlantic, under the name of Colorado. Long. 70. 12. W. lat. 34. 0. S.

MENDRAH, a province of the kingdom of Fezzan, much of which is a continued level of hard and barren soil; but the quantity of trona, a species of fossil alkali, that floats on the surface, or settles on the banks of its numerous smoking lakes, has given it a higher importance than that of the more fertile districts. It has a town of the same name; 60 miles S. of Mourzouk.

MENDRISIO, a town of Switzerland; canton of Ticino; containing several convents. It is 7 miles W. by N. of Como.

MENEHOULD, ST., a town of France, in the department of Marne. In 1792 the French gave the first check to the progress of the Prussians at this place, which in the end compelled them to a retreat. It is seated in a morass, on the river Aisne, between two rocks; 20 miles E. N. E. of Chalons. Pop. 3400.

MENGEN, a town of Wirtemberg, near the Danube; 50 miles S. of Stutgard.

MENGERINGHAUSEN, a town and castle of Germany, county of Waldeck; 8 miles N. E. of Corbach, and 24 N. W. of Cassel.

MENIN, a town of Belgium, in West Flanders. It has been often taken; the last time by the French, in 1794. It is seated on the Lis; 10 miles N. of Lisle.

MENTONE, a town of Nice, with a castle and a small harbour; 5 miles E. N. E. of Monaco.

MENTZ, or MAYENCE, a city of Germany, in the grand duchy of Hesse, and a bishop's see. It is well fortified and deemed a barrier fortress. The city is built in an irregular manner, and plentifully provided with churches. The principal buildings are the electoral palace, (now much decayed,) the house of the Teutonic knights, and the cathedral. Mentz is one of the towns which claim the invention of printing; and the growth of the best Rhenish wine is limited to a circle of about 5 miles round it. The French took this place by surprise in 1792; and the next year it stood a long blockade and siege before it surrendered to the allies. It was twice re-attacked by the French, in 1795, but they were defeated by the Austrians, who also relieved it from a blockade of two months, in 1796. The siege was soon after resumed, and continued till the signing of the treaty of Udina, in 1797, when the city was taken possession of by the French. By the peace of Luneville, in 1801, it was formally ceded to France, but was delivered up to the allies in 1814. Mentz is seated on the Rhine, just below the influx of the Maine; and on the opposite side is the town of Cassel, connected with it by a bridge of boats. Pop. 27,000. It is 22 miles W. S. W. of Frankfort, and 70 E. by N. of Treves. Long. 8. 10. E. lat. 49. 58. N.

MENUF, a town of Egypt; situate in a well cultivated country, near that branch in the Nile which flows to Rosetta; 40 miles N. N. W. of Cairo. Pop. 5000.

MENZALEH, a town of Egypt; situate near a lake of the same name, 60 miles long, separated from the Mediterranean by a narrow slip of land. It is 20 miles S. S. E. of Damietta, and 73 N. N. E. of Cairo. Long. 32. 2. E. lat. 31. 3. N.

MEPPEN, a town of Westphalia; capital of a district of the same name; 52 miles N. of Munster.

MEQUINENZA, a town of Spain, in Catalonia; with a castle; seated at the conflux of the Segra with the Ebro; 58 miles E. S. E. of Saragossa, and 180 E. N. E. of Madrid.

MEQUINEZ, a city of Morocco; seated in a delightful plain, having a serene and clear air; for which reason the emperor frequently resides in this place, in preference to Fez. The palace stands on the S. side, and is guarded by several hundreds of black eunuchs, whose knives and scimitars are covered with wrought silver. In the middle of the city the Jews have a place to themselves, the gates of which are locked every night, and guarded. Close by Mequinez, on the N. W. side, is a large Negro town, which takes up as much ground as the city, but the houses are not so high, nor so well built. The inhabitants of Mequinez, estimated at 112,000, are considered more polished and hospitable than those of the southern provinces. It is 58 miles W. of Fez. Long. 5. 46. W. lat. 32. 40. N.

MER, a town of France; in the department of Loire-et-Cher; 11 miles N. N. W. of Blois.

MERAN, a town of the Austrian states; in Tyrol, of which it was formerly the capital; seated near the conflux of the Passar with the Adige; 12 miles N. N. W. of Botzen. Long. 11. 5. E. lat. 46. 39. N.

MERDIM, a town of Asiatic Turkey, in Diarbeck, and an archbishop's see; with a castle. The country about it produces a great deal of cotton. It is seated on the summit of a mountain; 45 miles S. E. of Diarbekir. Pop. 20,000. Long. 39. 59. E. lat. 36. 50. N.

MERE, a town in Wiltshire; with a market on Thursday; 28 miles W. of Salisbury, and 100 W. by S. of London.

MERECGA, a town of Algier; in the province of Mascara; celebrated for its warm baths. It is 25 miles S. E. of Shershel, and 50 S. W. of Algier.

MERECZ, a town of Russian Lithuania; government of Wilna; seated at the conflux of the Merecz and Memen; 30 miles N. of Grodno.

MERGENTHEIM, a well built town of Wirtemberg, seated on the Tauber; 20 miles S. S. W. of Wurtzburg. Long. 9. 52. E. lat. 49. 30. N.

MERGHEN, or MERGUEN, a city of East Tartary, province of Tcitcicar; seated on the Nonni; 140 miles N. by E. of Tcitcicar. Long. 124. 55. E. lat. 49. 10. N.

MERGUI, a seaport on the W. coast of Siam; with an excellent harbour. It was wrested from the Siamese by the Birmans, in 1755, but was ceded to Britain in 1824-5. It is 208 miles S. W. of Siam. Pop. 8000. Long. 98. 9. E. lat. 12. 12. N.

MERGUI ARCHIPELAGO consists of islands extending 135 miles along the coast of Tannasserim and the isthmus of the Malay peninsula, with a strait between them and the mainland, from 15 to 30 miles broad, having regular soundings and good anchorage. They are in general covered with trees, but are not inhabited, although the soil appears fertile. The principal of them are King's Island, Clara, St. Matthew's, and Tannasserim.

MERIDA, a strong town of Spain, in Estremadura; built by the Romans, before the birth of Christ. Here are fine remains of antiquity, particularly a triumphal arch. In 1811 it fell into the hands of the French, but was retaken by General (afterwards Lord) Hill in the following year. It is seated in an extensive fertile plain, on the river Guadiana, over which is a noble Roman bridge; 32 miles E. of Badajoz. Long. 5. 58. W. lat. 38. 47. N.

MERIDA, a town of Mexico, capital of a province of the same name, lying between the bays of Honduras and Campeachy. It is situated in an arid plain; 30 miles S. of the Gulf of Mexico, and 70 N. E. of Campeachy. Long. 89. 58. W. lat. 20. 45. N.

MERIONETHSHIRE, a county of Wales; 36 to 46 miles long, and 34 where broadest; bounded N. by the counties of Caernarvon and Denbigh, E. by the latter and Montgomery, S. by Cardiganshire, and W. by the Irish Sea. It contains nearly 500,000 acres, is divided into 5 hundreds and 37 parishes, has four market towns, and sends one member to parliament. The face of the country is varied throughout with a romantic mixture of all the scenery peculiar to a wild and mountainous region. The principal rivers are the Dee and Dyfi. Cader Idris, one of the highest mountains in Wales is in this county.

MERITCH, an important town and fortress of Hindostan in the province of Bejapoor; situate near the N. bank of the Kistna; 62 miles S.W. of Visiapour.

MERO, a strong town of the kingdom of Pegu, 140 miles S. W. of Pegu. Long. 98. 36. E. lat. 16. 0. N.

MEROU, a town of Persia, in Khorassan; seated in a fertile country, which produces salt; 112 miles S. W. of Bokhara. Long. 64. 25. E. lat. 37. 40. N.

MERRIMAC, a river of the United States, formed by the junction of the Pemigewasset and Winnipiscogee; in the centre of New Hampshire. Its course is S. till it enters Massachusets; it then turns E., and passes into the ocean at Newbury. It is navigable for vessels of 200 tons, 20 miles from its mouth, where it is obstructed by the first rapids, called Mitchell's Eddy, a little above Haverhill. It gives name to a township in Hilsborough county.

MERSCH, a town of the Netherlands; in the duchy of Luxemburgh; 8 miles N. of Luxemburg.

MERSEBURG, one of the new divisions of the Prussian states, consisting principally of cessions made by Saxony in 1815. It lies to the S. of Anhalt, and to the E. of the government of Erfurt; and comprises an area of 4000 square miles, with 471,000 inhabitants.

MERSEBURG, the capital of the above government; formerly a bishopric. The most remarkable buildings are the castle, the cathedral, which stands below it, and the academy. The brewing and exportation of strong beer furnish the principal employment of the inhabitants. It is seated on the Saale; 15 miles N. W. of Leipsic.

MERSEY, a river of England; which rises in the N. extremity of the Peak in Derbyshire, receives the Tame at Stockport, and, lower down, the Irwell. It then passes by Warrington, and receives the Weaver at Frodsham, where it forms a broad estuary, that contracts on its approach to Liverpool, below which it enters the Irish Sea. This river not only affords salmon, but it is also visited by annual shoals of smelts, here called sparlings, of a remarkable size and flavour.

MERSEY, an island in Essex, between the mouth of the Coln and the entrance of Blackwater Bay. It has two parishes, called East and West Mersey; 7 miles S. of Colchester.

MERTHYR TYDVIL, a borough of South Wales, in Glamorganshire; with markets on Wednesday and Saturday. It returns one member to parliament. It has a canal to Cardiff, immense mines of iron and coal, and very extensive iron-works; 3 miles distant are the ruins of Morlais Castle, said to have been the residence of the kings of Brecknock. It is seated on the Taafe; 24 miles N. N. W. of Cardiff, and 180 W. of London.

MERTOLA, a strong town of Portugal, in Alentejo; seated near the Guadiana; 60 miles S. of Evora, and 100 S. E. of Lisbon. Long. 7. 37. W. lat. 37. 41. N.

MERTON, a village in Surrey, which formerly had considerable manufactures and bleach-fields.

Here Henry III. held a parliament in 1236, at which were enacted the Provisions of Merton, the most ancient body of laws after Magna Charta. It is seated on the Wandle; 7 miles S. W. of London.

Meru Shah Jehan, a town in Persia, province of Khorassan; founded by Alexander the Great. It was the capital of many of the Persian monarchs; but it has since declined from its greatness. It is 130 miles N. E. of Mesched. Pop. 3000.

Merville, a town of France, department of Nord; seated on the Lys; 15 miles N. of Lisle.

Mesched, or Mushed, a city of Persia; capital of Khorassan. It is fortified with several towers, and is famous for the magnificent sepulchre of Iman Risa, of the family of Ali, to which the Persians pay great devotion. Here is a manufacture of beautiful pottery, and another of skins. Caravans are continually passing through this city from Bokhara, Balkh, Candahar, Hindostan, and all parts of Persia. It is 180 miles E. of Asterabad, and 490 N. E. of Ispahan. Long. 58. 30. E. lat. 35. 56. N.

Mesched Ali, a town of Asiatic Turkey, in Irak-Arabi; near a large lake called Rahema, which communicates with the Euphrates by a canal. It stands on the spot where Ali, one of the successors of Mahomet, was interred; and his tomb is annually visited by Persian pilgrims. It is 110 miles S. of Bagdad. Long. 44. 50. E. lat. 32. 5. N.

Messa, a considerable town of Morocco, on the river Sus; not far from the Atlantic. It is 165 miles S. W. of Morocco. Long. 10. 46. W. lat. 29. 58. N.

Messina, a seaport of Sicily; capital of an intendancy of the same name, in Val di Demona; with a citadel and several forts. It is 5 miles in circumference, has four large suburbs, and contains 36,000 inhabitants. The public buildings and monasteries are numerous and magnificent: there are 50 churches, including the cathedral, which is much admired. The harbour is one of the safest in the Mediterranean, and has a quay above a mile in length. A great trade is carried on here in silk, oil, fruit, corn, and excellent wine. The city suffered much by an earthquake in 1780; and also in 1783, when it was half destroyed. It has since been rebuilt, with elegant houses, only two stories high. For several years prior to the peace of 1814, Messina was the head-quarters of the British troops in Sicily. It is seated on the Faro, or Strait of Messina, which separates Sicily from Calabria; 130 miles E. of Palermo. Long. 15. 50. E. lat. 38. 10. N.

Messing, a town of Franconia, in the principality of Aichstat. It is 14 miles N. N. E. of Aichstat.

Mestre, a town of Austrian Italy, in Treviso; 8 miles N. W. of Venice.

Mesurado, a considerable river of Western Africa, which falls into the Atlantic on the Grain Coast. On its banks is a kingdom of the same name, the boundaries of which are very uncertain.

Mesurata, a seaport of Tripoli, and the residence of a governor. Caravans travel hence to Fezzan, and other interior parts of Africa; by which they carry on a great trade. It is 100 miles E. S. E. of Tripoli. Long. 15. 10. E. lat. 32. 10. E.

Meta, a large river of New Granada, which has its rise opposite to Santa Fe de Bogota, and falls into the Orinoco, about 450 miles from its source, in long. 67. 45. W. lat. 6. 10. N.

Metapura, a town of the island of Borneo; in the kingdom of Banjermassing; 72 miles N. E. of Banjermassing, and 100 S. E. of Negara.

Metelen, a town of Prussia, in the province of Westphalia; seated on the Vechta; 19 miles N. W. of Munster.

Metelin, or Mytilene, an island of the Grecian Archipelago; anciently called Lesbos; to the N. of Scio, and at the entrance of the Gulf of Adramiti. It is about 40 miles long, and 12 broad; somewhat mountainous; and has many hot springs. The soil is very good; and the mountains are in many places covered with wood. It produces good wheat, wine, oil, and the best figs in the Archipelago. Mytilene is the capital.

Methil, a town of Scotland, in Fifeshire; with a safe harbour on the Frith of Forth, whence much coal is exported. It is 6 miles N. E. of Dysart.

Methven, a town of Scotland, in Perthshire; where King Robert Bruce was defeated by the English in 1306; 6 miles W. N. W. of Perth.

Metling, or Moitling, a strong town of the Austrian states, in Carniola; seated on the Kulp; 13 miles N. W. of Carlstadt, and 40 S. E. of Laubach.

Metro, a river of Italy, which rises on the frontiers of Tuscany, crosses the duchy of Urbino, and enters the Gulf of Venice near Fano.

Metropoli, a town of the island of Candia; on the site of the ancient Gortyna, of which many vestiges remain; 22 miles S. S. W. of Candia.

Metz, a town of France, in the department of Moselle, of which it is the capital. The fortifications are excellent, and it has three citadels and noble barracks. The cathedral is one of the finest in Europe. Here are manufactures of cotton, linen, gauze, chintz, fustian, &c.; and a considerable trade in leather, wine, brandy, &c. The sweetmeats made here are in high esteem. Metz is the seat of the departmental administration, and a bishop's see, and contains nearly 42,000 inhabitants. It is seated at the conflux of the Moselle and Seille; 210 miles N. E. of Paris. Long. 6. 10. E. lat. 49. 7. N.

Meudon, a village of France, with a magnificent royal palace and park; seated on the left bank of the Seine, and on one of the Versailles railroads, 6 miles S. of Paris.

Meulan, a town of France, department of Seine-et-Oise; seated on the Seine, over which is a stone bridge of 21 arches; 26 miles N. W. of Paris.

MEULEBEEK, a town of Belgium, province of East Flanders; 14 miles S. of Bruges. Pop. 7000.

MEURS, or MOERS, a town of the Prussian states; capital of a small principality of the same name. It has a castle, and was formerly a place of strength; but its fortifications were destroyed in 1764; 16 miles N. N. E. of Dusseldorf.

MEURTHE, a department of France, including part of the former province of Lorraine. It is bounded by the departments of Moselle, Vosges, and Meuse, and comprises an area of 2500 square miles, with 403,038 inhabitants. The climate is temperate, and the soil in general fertile. Nancy is the capital.

MEURTHE, a river of France, which rises in the department of Vosges, and flows by Luneville and Nancy into the Moselle.

MEUSE, MAESE, or MAAS, a river which rises in France; in the department of Upper Marne. It enters Belgium at Givet, flows to Charlemont, Namur, Huy, Liege, Maestricht, Ruremonde, Venlo, Grave, Battenburg, Ravestein, Gorcum, (where it receives the Waal,) and Worcum. At Dort it divides into four principal branches, the most northern of which is called the Merve. These form the islands of Ysselmonde, Voorn, and Overflackee, and enter the German Ocean below Briel, Helvoetsluys, and Goree.

MEUSE, a department of France, including the former duchy of Bar. It is bounded by the grand duchy of Luxemburg, and the departments of Moselle, Vosges, Marne, and Ardennes, and comprises an area of 2500 square miles, with 306,339 inhabitants. Bar sur Ornain is the capital.

MEWAT, a hilly and woody tract of Hindostan; lying on the S. W. of Delhi; confining the low country, along the W. bank of the Jumna, to a comparatively narrow slip, and extending westward 130 miles. From N. to S. it is 90 miles. Its inhabitants, the Mewatti, have been ever characterized as the most savage and brutal, and are still noted as thieves and robbers. The country contains some strong fortresses on steep or inaccessible hills. It is nominally possessed by the rajah of Macherry.

MEXICANO, or ADAYES, a river of New Mexico, on the confines of Louisiana; which runs into the Gulf of Mexico.

MEXICO, a country of North America, now forming an independent republic; situated between 42. and 113. W. long., and extending from the Pacific Ocean to the Caribbean Sea, the Gulf of Mexico, and the Sabine river. It comprises an area of 1,700,000 square miles, with about 7,500,000 inhabitants. In general, it is a mountainous country, intermixed with many rich valleys; the highest mountains, many of which are volcanoes, are near the coast of the Pacific Ocean. The eastern shore is a flat country, full of impenetrable forests, with bogs and morasses, overflowed in the rainy season, which is from April to September. Although a considerable portion of Mexico is within the torrid zone, the climate in general is temperate and healthy. No country abounds more with grain, fruits, roots, and vegetables, many of them peculiar to the country, or at least to America. It is also celebrated for its mines of gold and silver, and has quarries of jasper, porphyry, and exquisite marble. Cochineal is almost peculiar to this country; its indigo and cocoa are superior to any in America; and its logwood has long been an important article of commerce. Among the quadrupeds are the puma, jaguar, bears, elks, wolves, deer, &c. The puma and jaguar have been inaccurately denominated, by Europeans, lions and tigers; but they possess neither the undaunted courage of the former, nor the ravenous cruelty of the latter. The domestic animals of Europe, particularly horned cattle, have multiplied here, almost with incredible rapidity. Numbers of these, having been suffered to run wild, now range over the vast plains, in herds of from 30,000 to 40,000; they are killed merely for the sake of their hides, which are annually exported, in vast quantities, to Europe. The inhabitants consist of native Spaniards; Creoles, who are descendants of Europeans; Mulattoes, the issue of whites and negroes; Mestizoes, descendants of whites and Indians; Zamboes, descendants of negroes and Indians; and African negroes, with whom are classed a mixed extraction from Europeans, Africans, Indians, and Malays, or others of Asiatic origin. The whole country was long under the dominion of Spain, and governed by a viceroy. The first attempt to assume independence took place in 1810. In 1824 a federal government was established. Numerous disturbances have since arisen, and the country is still far from being in a settled state. A considerable degree of mercantile activity has lately prevailed, and the English houses in Mexico have been unable to supply the demand. The separation of these regions from the domination of Spain is certainly a decided triumph for liberty; and the philanthropist cannot but look forward with pleasing anticipations of prosperity to a state the anniversary of whose independence was signalized by a noble act of national justice—the immediate and entire abolition of slavery, by a decree of the president, September 15, 1829.

MEXICO, the capital of the above country. It was a flourishing city before the Spaniards entered the country. It is seated in a marshy plain. Instead of an "interior sea," as formerly, the lakes Tezcuco and Xochimilco, which originally insulated the city, have been gradually diminishing. It is elevated 7200 feet above the sea. Pop. about 155,000. The circumference of the city, exclusive of the suburbs, was formerly above 10 miles; and it contained at least 80,000 houses, with several large temples, and three palaces. It was taken by Ferdinando Cortes, in 1521, after a siege to nearly three months, and, as the Mexicans defended themselves from street to street, it was almost ruined, but was afterwards rebuilt by the Spaniards. The streets are straight, and so exactly disposed, that, in point of regularity, it is the finest city in the world. The great square, in the centre of the city, and the public buildings, are magnificent. The situation of Mexico is highly favourable for carrying on commerce both with Europe and Asia, being about 69 leagues distant from Vera Cruz on the one hand, and from Acapulco on the other. The working of gold and silver has long been carried to great perfection here, and here are also manufactures of calico, cloth, soap, and tobacco. This city has been frequently inundated by the overflowing of the lakes in its vicinity, particularly in 1629, when 40,000 persons are said to have been drowned. To prevent the recurrence of such calamities, a vast conduit was constructed, to turn the course of the waters, which formerly flowed into the lake Tezcuco, through the mountains. It is 200 miles E. N. E. of St. Juan de Ulhua. Long. 101. 25. 30. W. lat. 9. 25. 45. N.

MEXICO, an immense gulf of North America, lying between the S. coast of East Florida and the N. E. point of Yucatan.

MEYAHOUN, a city of Pegu; with numerous gilded temples and spacious monasteries. Its vicinity is uncommonly fruitful in rice; and here are capacious granaries, always kept filled with grain ready to be transported to any part of the empire in which there happens to be a scarcity. It stretches 2 miles on the S. W. bank of the Irrawaddy; and is 85 miles N. W. of Pegu. Long. 95. 8. E. lat. 18. 18. N.

MEYENFIELD, *See* MAYENFIELD.

MEYRVIES, a town of France, department of Lozere; 23 miles S. of Mende.

MEZEMNA, a seaport of Fez, on the coast of the Mediterranean; 80 miles E. of Tetuan. Long. 4. 1. W. lat. 35. 22. N.

MEZIERES, a town of France, department of Ardennes; with a citadel; seated on an island in the river Meuse; 12 miles W. by N. of Sedan.

MEZIN, a town of France, department of Lot-et-Garonne; 9 miles N. W. of Condom.

MGLIN, a town in European Russia, governed by Czernigov. It has a considerable trade in hemp. Pop. 5000.

MHENDIGAUT, a town of Hindostan, in the province of Agra; on the W. bank of the Ganges. Long. 79. 57. E. lat. 27. 3. N.

MIACO. *See* MEACO.

MIAMI, LITTLE and GREAT, two rivers of the state of Ohio, which run S. into the Ohio, the former just above Columbia, and the latter 21 miles below Cincinnati. The little Miami is 60 miles to its source, but generally so shallow as to afford no navigation. The Great Miami has a navigation, like the Muskingum, that approaches near the navigable waters of Lake Erie. The country between these two rivers is called the Miamis, and is reckoned among the richest belonging to the United States.

MIANA, a town of Persia, in Aderbeitzan. Here the celebrated traveller M. Thevenot died, on his return from Ispahan. It is 57 miles S. E. of Tauris.

MICHA a cape of Dalmatia, which advances into the Gulf of Venice, near the town of Zara.

MICHAEL, ST., the most extensive and populous island of the Azores. It is 54 miles long and from 6 to 15 broad, and contains nearly 80,000 inhabitants. In a valley on the eastern side are a number of boiling fountains; also many sulphureous springs, some of a hot, and others of a cold temperature. The principal towns are Punta del Guda (the capital of the island) and Villa Franca. Long. 25. 42. W. lat. 37. 47. N.

MICHAEL, ST., or MIDSHALL, a town of Cornwall; 8 miles S. W. of St. Columb, and 250 W. by S. of London.

MICHAEL, ST., a town of France, department of Meuse; with a fine hospital, and the rich library of a Benedictine abbey. It is surrounded by mountains. It is seated on the Meuse; 20 miles N. E. of Bar le Duc.

MICHAEL, ST., a town of Mexico, in the province of Nicaragua; on the river St. Michael; 110 miles N. W. of Leon. Long. 87. 45. W. lat. 12. 25. N.

MICHAEL, ST., a town of Mexico, province of Culiacan; near the mouth of the Siguatlan; 30 miles E. S. E. of Culiacan. Long. 107. 40. W. lat. 24. 10. N.

MICHAEL, ST., a city of Tucuman, situate in a fruitful valley, at the foot of a range of rugged mountains; 150 miles N. W. of St. Jago del Estero. Long. 66. 45. W. lat. 27. 0. S.

MICHAEL DE IBARRA, ST., a town of Columbia, in the presidency of Quito; capital of a jurisdiction of its name. It has a large and elegant church, a college, and several convents. It is 70 miles N. E. of Quito. Long. 77. 30. W. lat. 0. 25. N.

MICHAEL DE PIURA, ST., a town of Quito, seated near the mouth of the Piura; 325 miles S. S. W. of Quito. Long. 80. 40. W. lat. 3. 10. S.

MICHAEL, GULF OF ST., to the E. of Panama; that part of the Pacific Ocean which was first discovered by the Spaniards, after their march across the Isthmus of Darien.

MICHIGAN, one of the United States; bounded on the N. by Lake Superior, E. by the lakes Huron, St. Clare, and Erie, S. by Ohio and Indiana, and W. by Lake Michigan. The country possesses immense advantages, resulting from navigation and fisheries; but the soil is marshy and poor, and part of it inundated for six months in the year. The chief exports are furs and peltries, dried hides, bees'-wax, pot and pearl ashes, fish, &c. There are 557 miles of railroad intended in this state, 40 of which, from Ann Arbor to Detroit, the capital, is in operation. The population, which has rapidly increased, is now 212,276.

MICHIGAN, the largest lake which is wholly within the United States, being 280 miles long, and from 50 to 60 broad. It is navigable for vessels of any burden, and communicates with the N. W. end of Lake Huron, by the Strait of Michilimackinac.

MICHILIMACKINAC, a strait of North America which unites the lakes Michigan and

Huron. It is 6 miles wide; and on its S. E. side, in Lake Huron, is an island, with a fort and village of the same name. Long. 84. 30. W. lat. 45. 48. N.

MICHILIMACKINAC, LITTLE, a river of the state of Illinois, which enters the Illinois 200 miles above its junction with the Mississippi.

MIDDLEBOROUGH, a town of Massachusq., in Plymouth county; situate 40 miles S. by E. of Boston

MIDDLEBURG, a large commercial town of the Netherlands, capital of the island of Walcheren, and of all Zealand. The squares and public buildings are magnificent; particularly the townhouse, formerly a celebrated abbey. The harbour is commodious, and has a communication with Flushing by a canal, which will bear the largest vessels. Middleburg was taken by the British in July, 1809, but evacuated in the December following. It is 85 miles S. W. of Amsterdam. Pop. 15,000. Long. 3. 37. E. lat. 51. 29. N.

MIDDLEBURG, a town of the Netherlands, in Flanders; 5 miles S. E. of Sluys.

MIDDLEBURG, one of the Friendly Islands. *See* EAOOWE.

MIDDLEBURY, a town of Vermont, chief of Addison county; seated on the Otter Creek, 37 miles S. of Burlington. Pop. 3168.

MIDDLEHAM, a town in North Yorkshire, with a market on Monday, and a woollen manufacture. Here are the ruins of a once stately castle, in which Richard III. was born, and where Edward IV. was confined after being taken prisoner in his camp. It is seated on the Eure; 11 miles S. by W. of Richmond, and 232 N. N. W. of London.

MIDDLESEX, a county of England; bounded N. by Hertfordshire, E. by Essex, S. by Surrey and Kent, and W. by Buckinghamshire. It contains an area of 179,200 acres, has two cities (London and Westminster,) and seven market towns, and sends two members to parliament. The air is healthy; but the soil in general, being gravelly, is not naturally fertile, though, by means of the vicinity to the metropolis, many parts of it are converted into rich beds of manure, clothed with almost perpetual verdure. Besides the Thames, Lea, and Coln, which are its boundaries to the S., E., and W., Middlesex is watered by several small streams; one of which, called the New River, is artificially brought from near Hertford, for the purpose of supplying London with water.

MIDDLESEX, a county of Massachusets; bounded N. by New Hampshire, E. by Essex county, S. E. by Norfolk county, and W. by Worcester county. Pop. 106,611. The chief towns are Charlestown, Cambridge, and Concord.

MIDDLESEX, a maritime county of Connecticut; bounded N. by Hartford county, E. by New London county, S. by Long Island Sound, and W. by New Haven county. Middletown is the capital. Pop. 27,845.

MIDDLESEX, a county of New Jersey, bounded N. by Essex county, E. by Rariton Bay, and part of Staten Island, S. E. by Monmouth county, and W. by Somerset county. Pop. 21,893. New Brunswick is the chief town.

MIDDLESEX, a county of Virginia; on Chesapeake Bay; about 35 miles in length, and 7 in breadth. Pop. 392. Urbanna is the chief town.

MIDDLESEX, a town of Vermont, in Washington county. — Also, a town in Ontario county, New York.

MIDDLETON, a town in Lancashire, with a market on Friday. The church is an ancient edifice; and there are five meeting-houses, and a free-grammar school. It has the cotton trade in all its branches, a large twist manufacture, considerable bleaching-works, some manufactures of silk, and extensive dye-works. It stands on the Rochdale canal; 6 miles N. by E. of Manchester, and 190 N. N. W. of London.

MIDDLETON IN TEESDALE, a town of Durham, with considerable lead mines in the parish; 255 miles from London.

MIDDLETON, a town of Ireland, in the county of Cork; situated on the N. W. angle of Cork harbour. It is 13 miles E. of Cork.

MIDDLETON, a town of Delaware, in Newcastle county, situate on Apoquinimy Creek; 21 miles S. S. W. of Wilmington.—Also, the name of a number of inconsiderable townships of the United States.

MIDDLETOWN, a town of Connecticut, capital of Middlesex county. It is a pleasant and flourishing town, and has a considerable trade and manufactures. Two miles from the town is a lead mine. Population 7210. It is seated on the W. bank of Connecticut River; 25 miles N. N. E. of New Haven. Long. 72. 54. W. lat. 41. 35. N.

MIDDLETOWN, a town of Pennsylvania, in Dauphin county. It has a trade in corn, and stands on Swatara Creek, 2 miles from its mouth in the Susquehanna, and 62 W. by N. of Philadelphia.

MIDDLETOWN, a town of New Jersey; in Monmouth county, on the S. W. side of the bay within Sandy Hook; 14 miles N. W. of Shrewsbury, and 52 E. N. E. of Trenton.

MIDDLEWICH, a town in Cheshire, with a market on Tuesday. The trade of the place is chiefly derived from the surrounding neighbourhood, which is a great farming district; to which may be added the extensive salt-works, and some silk factories. Here are a spacious church, three meeting-houses, and a free grammar-school. The Trent and Mersey canal runs through the town. It is seated on the Croco, near its confluence with the Dane; 24 miles E. of Chester, and 167 N. W. of London.

MIDHURST, a borough in Sussex, seated on the Arun; 11 miles N. of Chichester, and 50 W. by S. of London. It returns one member to parliament.

MIDNAPOUR, a town of Hindostan, in Orissa, capital of a district of the same name. It is seated near a river that flows into the Hoogly; 70 miles W. by S. of Calcutta. Long. 87. 25. E lat. 22. 30. N.

Mies, a town of Bohemia, in the circle of Pilsen, on the river Misa; 18 miles W. of Pilsen.

Mifflin, a county of Pennsylvania, bounded by the counties of Cumberland, Northumberland, Dauphin, and Huntingdon. Pop. 13,092. Lewistown is the capital.

Mikalida, a town of Asiatic Turkey, in Natolia; with a fort; situate on a river which runs into the Sea of Marmora; 55 miles W. by S. of Bursa.

Milan, or the **Milanese**, a country of Italy, bounded on the N. by the Alps, E. by the Venetian territory, S. by the Apennines, and W. by Piedmont. The soil is every where fertile in corn, wine, fruits, rice, and olives; and there are also plenty of cattle. The rivers are the Seccia, Tesin, Adda, Oglio, and Po. There are likewise several lakes, the three principal of which are those of Maggiore, Como, and Lugano. Milan, with other countries in Italy, was long comprised under the general name of Lombardy. In the fourteenth century it became a duchy. The campaign of Prince Eugene, in 1706, put it in possession of the House of Austria, to whom, with the exception of the Sardinian Milanese, it continued subject during 90 years, until the victories of Napoleon in 1796. In 1797 it was formed into four departments, as the Cisalpine republic; but in 1814, after several other changes, the part belonging to the king of Sardinia was restored, and the remainder incorporated with the Lombardo-Venetian kingdom, or Austrian Italy. The Austrian Milanese forms, along with the duchy of Mantua, and the Valteline, the government of Milan. It is divided into eight delegations, and contains 7700 square miles, with 2,280,063 inhabitants. The Sardinian Milanese, which lies to the W. of the Austrian, is divided into nine districts, comprising an area of 3300 square miles, and containing 560,000 inhabitants.

Milan, a city of Italy, capital of the Lombardo-Venetian kingdom, and the see of an archbishop. The city is 10 miles in circumference; but the garden grounds are so extensive, that it does not contain above 124,647 inhabitants. It stands in a delightful plain, between the rivers Adda and Ticino, which communicate with the city by means of two canals. The cathedral, in the centre of the city, is a splendid specimen of Gothic architecture, and, next to St. Peter's at Rome, is the most considerable in Italy. This vast fabric is built of white marble, supported by 50 columns, and adorned, within and without, by a prodigious number of marble statues. The other public buildings are the university, several colleges, the convents, the hospitals, the theatres, the mansions of the minister of finance, of the minister of the interior, and of the archbishop, and the former ducal palace, now the residence of the Austrian viceroy. In the Piazza di Castello is an arena, in imitation of the amphitheatre of Verona, which is capable of containing 30,000 spectators. The college of St. Ambrose has a library, which, besides a prodigious number of manuscripts, contains 60,000 printed books; and its superb gallery is adorned with rich paintings. The chief trade of Milan is in grain (especially rice), cattle, and cheese; and the manufactures, of silk and velvet stuffs, stockings, handkerchiefs, ribbons, gold and silver lace and embroideries, woollen and linen cloths, glass, porcelain, &c. It has been many times taken in the wars that have desolated Italy. The French took it in 1796. It was retaken by the Austrians and Russians in 1799, but again possessed by the French in 1800, and retained by them till the fall of Napoleon in 1814. It is 280 miles N. W. by N. of Rome. Long. 9. 12. E. lat. 45. 28. N.

Milazzo, or **Melazzo**, a seaport of Sicily; in Val di Demona. It is divided into the Upper and Lower Town; the former stands on a promontory, and is fortified; the latter has a fine square, with a superb fountain. It stands on a rock, on the W. side of a bay of the same name; 20 miles W. of Messina. Long 15. 24. E. lat. 38. 12. N.

Milborn-port, a town in Somersetshire, which has no market. It has manufactures of woollen cloth, linen, and hosiery. It is seated on a branch of the Parret; 2 miles E. by N. of Sherborn, and 114 W. by S. of London.

Mildenhall, a town in Suffolk; with a market on Friday; seated on the Larke, a branch of the Ouse; 12 miles N. W. of Bury, and 70 N. N. E. of London.

Mileto, a town of Naples, in Calabria Ultra; nearly destroyed by an earthquake in 1783. It is 8 miles N. E. of Nicotera.

Milford, a town of Wales, in Pembrokeshire. It is elegantly and uniformly built, and stands on the N. side of Milford Haven, a deep inlet of the Irish Sea. The haven branches off into so many creeks, secured from all winds, that it is esteemed the safest and most capacious harbour in Great Britain. At the entrance on the W. point, called St. Ann's, is an old lighthouse, and a blockhouse. Here the Earl of Richmond, afterwards Henry VII., landed, on his enterprise against Richard III. A quay and several good buildings have been constructed by a company of Quakers from Nantucket, who have formed an establishment here, for the southern whale fishery. It is 6 miles W. N. W. of Pembroke, and 262 W. by N. of London.

Milford, a town of Pennsylvania, in Northampton county; on the W. side of Delaware River; 120 miles above Philadelphia.

Milford, a town of Connecticut; in Newhaven county; situate on a creek of Long Island Sound; 10 miles S. W. of Newhaven. There are a great many townships of this name in the United States.

Milford, New, a town of Connecticut, in Litchfield county; on the side of the Housatonic; 20 miles S. W. of Litchfield.

Milhau, a town of France; department of Aveyron; seated on the Tarn; 20 miles N. W. of Montpelier.

Milhaud, a town of France; department of Gard; seated on the Vistre. It is 9 miles S. W. of Nismes.

Militsch, a town of Prussian Silesia; seated on the river Bartsch; 27 miles N. N. E. of Breslau. Long. 17. 23. E. lat. 51. 32. N.

Milledgeville, a town in North America, county of Baldwin, state of Georgia, of which it is the capital, the legislative assembly being held here; otherwise it is inconsiderable. It is situated on the Oconee; 170 miles S. W. of Savannah. Pop. 1599.

Millport, a neat village and bathing-place on Great Cambray, Buteshire; 24 miles S. of Greenock; the railway to which place affords a great means of communication between it and Glasgow.

Milo, (the ancient Melos,) an island of the Grecian Archipelago; 18 leagues in circumference; with one of the best and largest harbours in the Mediterranean. It produces plentiful crops of corn, excellent fruit, and wine; abounds in very good cattle, especially goats; and has mines of iron and sulphur. In this island are curious subterranean galleries, the roofs of which are covered with genuine capillary or plume alum, and the crevices of the rocks filled with pure sulphur. Here are two bishops; one of the Greek, and the other of the Latin church. At the commencement of the eighteenth century, the inhabitants amounted to above 20,000; but since that period it has groaned under the yoke of Turkish despotism, and a considerable time must elapse before it can recover its former opulence and splendour. The population of the whole island does not at present exceed 1200.—On the E. side of the island is a town of the same name, 60 miles N. of Candia, and 100 S. by E. of Athens. Long. 25. 0. E. lat. 36. 41. N.

Miltenberg, a town of the Bavarian states, principality of Leiningen; with a castle on a hill, seated on the Maine; 20 miles S. S. E. of Aschaffenburg.

Milthorpe, a town in Westmoreland; with a market on Friday; seated on the Betha, near the mouth of the Ken. It is the only port in the county; and hence the fine Westmoreland slates and other commodities are expected. The manufactures consist chiefly of sacking, twine, and paper; there is also a respectable tannery, and in the vicinity are limestone and marble quarries. It is 8 miles S. of Kendal, and 255 N. N. W. of London.

Milton, a town in Kent, with a market on Saturday. It is noted for excellent oysters; and much corn, &c. is shipped here for the London markets. It is a place of great antiquity, and was the residence of the kings of Kent, and of Alfred, who had a palace here. It is 14 miles N. E. of Maidstone, and 40 E. of London.

Milton, a town of Massachusets, in Norfolk county; 7 miles S. of Boston. Pop. 1565.

Milton, a town of Virginia, in Albemarle county, situate on the Rivanna; 76 miles W. N. W. of Richmond.—Also the name of several inconsiderable townships in the United States.

Milton Abbas, or Abbey Milton, a village in Dorsetshire; 7 miles S. W. of Blandford. It formerly had an abbey, founded by king Athelstan; but the whole was swept away, except the church, in 1771, by the Earl of Dorchester, who erected on its site a large Gothic mansion. The village with its church and almshouse were built by the same nobleman.

Milverton, a town in Somersetshire; 152 miles from London: an ancient town. The population are employed in the manufacture of flannel, druggets, &c.

Mina, a town of Persia, province of Kirman; surrounded by a wall with towers, and seated on the Ibrahim, near its entrance into the Gulf of Ormus; 190 miles S. of Kerman. Long. 56. 50. E. lat. 26. 40. N.

Minas, a town of S. America; in Buenos Ayres; seated near the source of the river St. Lucia, 34 miles N. E. of Maldonado. Long. 55. 5. W. lat. 34. 21. S.

Minas Geraes, a province of Brazil; bounded N. by Bahia, W. by Goiaz, and S. by the Paraibuna. It extends 600 or 700 miles from N. to S. and nearly the same from E. to W., and contains 600,000 inhabitants, one-third of whom are slaves. This vast territory produces gold and diamonds in abundance; also iron, antimony, bismuth, platina, chromate of lead, &c. The soil is likewise rich, producing in the valleys sugar, cotton, &c.; and in the higher grounds wheat, and generally all kinds of European grain.

Minch, an arm of the sea, on the W. coast of Scotland, which separates the Isle of Sky from Long Island.

Minching Hampton, a town in Gloucestershire, with a market on Tuesday, and a considerable manufacture of cloth. It is pleasantly situated on a declivity, 10 miles W. of Cirencester, and 98 W. of London.

Mincio, a river of Italy, which flows S. from the lake Garda, forms the lake and marshes that surround the city of Mantua, and afterward runs into the Po.

Minckendorf, a town of Austria, on the Triessing, 6 miles E. N. E. of Baden.

Mindanao, an island in the Eastern seas, and one of the Philippines; about 300 miles long, and 108 broad. The coast is indented by numerous bays, and the interior is intersected by chains of lofty mountains, with intervening plains that afford pasture for immense herds of cattle. The sides of the hills and valleys are stony, and yet there are tall trees, of kinds unknown in Europe. Some of the mountains yield very good gold; and the valleys are well watered with rivulets. Rice is produced in abundance; as are also plantains, cocoa-nuts, sweet potatoes, and all the fruits common to tropical climates. There are neither lions nor tigers; but horses, beeves, buffaloes, goats, hogs, deer, &c., are numerous. The fowls are ducks, hens, pigeons, parrots, parroquets, and turtle-doves, besides many small birds. The inhabitants are generally of a low stature, with little heads, small black eyes, short noses, and large mouths. Their hair is black and straight, and their complexion tawny, but more inclined to yellow than that of other Indians. The chief trades are goldsmiths, blacksmiths, and carpenters, who can build pretty good vessels. Polygamy is practised. The government is partly feudal and partly monarchical. The prevailing religion is Mahomedism, but the Spaniards have been in possession of a large portion of the sea-coast, to the W., N., and N. E., where they have planted colonies of Christians.

MINDANAO, the capital of the above island, and the residence of the sultan and his court, is about 6 miles up the Pelangy. Opposite stands the town of Selangan. Long. 124. 40. E. lat. 7. 9. N.

MINDELHEIM, a town of Bavaria, with a castle on a mountain; situate between the rivers Iller and Lech: 25 miles S. W. of Augsburg.

MINDEN, a government of the Prussian states; comprising the N. E. part of the province of Westphalia, and the former principalities of Minden, Paderborn, Rittberg, and Corvey, the bailiwick of Reckeberg, and the lordship of Rheda. It has area of 2000 square miles, divided into 13 districts, with 330,000 inhabitants. The soil in general is fertile, and the pasturage good.

MINDEN, the capital of the above government, is one of the oldest towns of Germany, and, while the see of a bishop, formed a petty republic. Its convenient situation for trade and navigation, its breweries, sugar-houses, and wax manufactures, are great advantages to the inhabitants. Near this town prince Ferdinand, of Brunswick, defeated the French, in 1759. It was occupied in 1806 by the French, and finally ceded to Prussia in 1814. Pop. 6800. It is seated on the Weser, 43 miles E. of Osnaburg. Long. 8. 56. E. lat. 52. 19. N.

MINDORO, one of the Philippines; separated from Luconia by a narrow channel. It is mountainous, and abounds in palm-trees and all sorts of fruits. The inhabitants are pagans, and pay tribute to the Spaniards.

MINEHEAD, a seaport in Somersetshire; market on Wednesday. It has a good harbour on the Bristol Channel, and carries on a trade in wool, coal, and herrings. It is 35 miles N. of Exeter, and 160 W. by S. of London. Long. 3. 34. W. lat. 51. 12. N.

MINGRELIA, a country of Asia; bounded W. by the Black Sea, E. by Imeritia, S. by the river Phasis, and N. by Georgia. It is governed by a prince who is tributary to Russia. The face of this country, its products, and the customs and manners of the inhabitants, are similar to those of Georgia.

MINHO, a river of Spain; which rises in the N. E. part of Galicia, passes by Lugo, Orense, and Tuy; and, dividing Galicia from Portugal, enters the Atlantic at Caminha.

MINIEH, a town of Egypt, on the left bank of the Nile; 90 miles S. of Fayoum.

MINORVINO, a town of Naples; in Terra di Bari; 24 miles, W. S. W. of Trani.

MINORCA, one of the Balearic islands, lying 50 miles to the N. E. of Majorca. It is 30 miles long, and 12 broad; and is a mountainous country, with some fruitful valleys. Some corn is raised, but the principal products of the island are wine, wool, cheese, and various fruits. It has been frequently in the hands of the British, by whom it was taken without the loss of a man, in 1798, but given up by the peace of 1802. Ciudadella is the capital; but Mahon claims greater consequence, on account of its excellent harbour, Port Mahon, which is defended by two forts. Population, 31,000. 3. 48. E. lat. 39. 51. N.

MINSK, an extensive province of European Russia, comprehending the old palatinate of Minsk and portions of Polotzk, Novogrodek, and Wilna. It extends from the Dwina, N. to the province of Volhynia, comprises an area of 37,000 square miles, is divided into ten circles, and contains 950,000 inhabitants. The surface, productions, &c., are the same as in Lithuania.

MINSK, the capital of the foregoing province, with two citadels, seated on the Swislocz: 80 miles S. E. of Wilna, and 310 E. N. E. of Warsaw. Long. 27. 58. E. lat. 53. 46. N.

MINTAON, an island in the Indian Ocean, 40 miles long, and 14 broad; on the W. coast of the island of Sumatra. Long. 97. 38. E. lat. 0. 25. S.

MIOSS, a lake of Norway, in the province of Hedemarke, 90 miles in circumference. It is almost divided by a peninsula, and contains a fertile island 10 miles in circumference.

MIQUELON, a small desert island, S. W. of Cape Mary, in Newfoundland, ceded to the French, in 1763, for drying and curing their fish. They were dispossessed of it by the English, in 1793, but it was restored to them in 1802. Long. 56. 10. W. lat. 46. 42. N.

MIRA, a town of Portugal, in Beira, 16 miles N. W. of Coimbra.

MIRANDA, a town of Portugal, in Tras los Montes, seated on a rock, on the river Douero, 32 miles E. S. E. of Braganza. Long. 6. 32. W. lat. 41. 46. N.

MIRANDA DE CORVO, a town of Portugal, in Beira, 13 miles S. E. of Coimbra.

MIRANDA DE EBRO, a town of Spain, in the province of Burgos, with a castle, seated in an excellent wine country, on the river Ebro, over which is a handsome bridge. It is 34 miles N. E. of Burgos.

MIRANDE, a town of France, department of Gers. Wool, down, and the feathers of geese, are its principal articles of trade. It is seated on an eminence, near the river Baise. It is 13 miles S. W. of Auch.

MIRANDELA, a town of Portugal, in Tras los Montes, 22 miles S. W. of Braganza.

MIRANDOLA, a city of Italy, in the Modenese, capital of a province of its name, and a bishop's see, with a citadel and fort. Besides the cathedral, it contains many fine churches and convents. It is 18 miles N. N. E. of Modena Pop. 8200. Long 11. 19. E. lat. 44. 52. N.

MIRAVEL, a town of Spain, in New Castile, with a strong castle, seated on the side of a hill, 16 miles S. by W. of Placentia.

MIREBEAU, a town of France, department of Upper Vienne; 14 miles N. by W. of Poitiers.

Mirebeau, a town of France, department of Cote d'Or, 13 miles N. of Dijon.

Mirecourt, a town of France, department of Voges, famous for its violins and fine lace, seated on the Modon, 15 miles W. N. W. of Epinal. Pop. 5100.

Miremont, a town of France, department of Dordogne. Near it is a remarkable cavern, called Cluseau. It is seated near the river Vizere, 15 miles E. of Bergerac.

Mirepoix, a town of France, department of Arriege, seated on the Gers, 15 miles E. N. E. of Foix, and 43 S. S. E. of Toulouse.

Mirow, a town of Saxony, with a castle, 11 miles W. of Strelitz.

Misagno, a town of Naples, in Otranto, 9 miles S. S. E. of Ostuni.

Misitra, a town of Greece, capital of the Morea, and an archbishop's see, with a castle. It was formerly a very considerable place, but, during the possession of the Morea by Turkey, it had much decayed, and not more than one-fourth of the houses are now inhabited. It is seated on the Vasilipotamo; 90 miles S. S. E. of Lepanto. Long. 22. 36. E. lat. 37. 16. N.

Misnia. *See* Meissen.

Mississippi, one of the United States of America, bounded N. by Tennessee, E. by Alabama, S. by Louisiana and the Gulf of Mexico, and W. by Pearl and Mississippi rivers. It is 312 miles long, and 150 broad; comprises an area of about 45,350 square miles, is divided into 56 counties, and contains 375,561 inhabitants. The Mississippi territory was divided, in 1817, into two nearly equal parts, the western part forming the state of Mississippi, and the eastern forming the territory, afterwards the state, of Alabama. The surface is agreeably diversified with hills, plains, and valleys; the climate is mild, and the soil is in general exceedingly fertile in corn, sugar, indigo, garden vegetables, cotton, and various kinds of fruit. Cotton is the staple production. Monticello is the capital, but the largest towns are Natchez and Washington.

Mississippi, a large river of North America, which rises from Turtle Lake, in long. 95. 8. W. lat. 47. 42. N., and falls into the Gulf of Mexico by several mouths, the principal of which is called the Balize: but below New Orleans, the port of the river, 105 miles from the sea, the country is not habitable, consisting of mud-banks, which confine the river above the height of the surrounding districts, as is the case throughout the state of Louisiana. The tributary streams are numerous, the largest is the Missouri, which it receives 1310 miles from its mouth; after which the character of the river is altered, and it becomes a furious, turbid current, bearing a great quantity of trees, &c. torn from the banks, and which it deposits in its course, forming sand and mud-banks, &c. The other affluents are the Illinois, the Arkansas, and the Ohio. The general course of the Mississippi is from N. to S., but below the influx of the Ohio it is exceedingly crooked, and in it are many small islands. The water of this river is clear till it receives the Missouri. It is navigable for boats, upwards of 2000 miles, and its whole course is estimated at 3000. It drains three-fifths of the whole territory of the United States.

Missolonghi, a town of Western Greece; 10 miles W. of Livadia, on a strip of land projecting into the Gulf of Patras. It was taken by the Turks in 1826, when nearly all the inhabitants were slaughtered. Lord Byron died here on April 19th, 1824.

Missouri, one of the United States of North America, formed in 1821, and lying on both sides of the Missouri river. It is the largest state, except Virginia, and contains an area of 60,000 square miles, and 383,702 inhabitants, of whom 58,240 are slaves. The general face of the state consists of immense prairies, which, during the summer, have but little water, and the population is chiefly confined to the neighbourhood of its immense rivers. Its principal feature is the extensive lead mines in the S. E. part of the state, occupying a space of 45 miles by 70 miles, and containing the richest mines in the New Continent, about 170 in number, affording a vast supply of the richest and purest ore. It is divided into 35 counties. The capital is St. Louis, situate on the Mississippi, 13 miles below the junction of the Missouri.

Missouri, a river of North America, which rises in the Rocky Mountains, and falls into the Mississippi, 1200 miles from its mouth. In 1804–5, by direction of the government of the United States, it was ascended its whole length by Captains Lewis and Clarke, who gave the names of Jefferson, Madison, and Gallatin, to the three branches into which it is divided, 2858 miles from its confluence with the Mississippi. The Missouri is deep and rapid, and receives numerous rivers in its course, many of them of considerable extent. The navigation may be deemed good, for 2575 miles, when tremendous cataracts render a portage of about 3 miles necessary. Above these falls, shoals and rapids are frequent; and, as the river issues from the Rocky Mountains, its banks for more than 5 miles are shut in on both sides, by the most tremendous rocks, which rise perpendicularly to the height of nearly 1200 feet. The banks, except a sterile district below the falls, are in general rich and beautiful: in some parts are extensive meadows, with hills beyond them covered with trees; in others, lower down, are long chains of high hills of a dark colour.

Missouri Territory, a country of the United States; which, in its most extended sense, includes all Louisiana not comprised in the state of that name. The chief towns are New Madrid, Girardeau, St. Genevieve, and St. Louis.

Mistaken Cape, the S. point of the easternmost of the Hermit Islands, about 9 miles E. N. E. of Cape Horn.

Mistaken Point, a promontory on the W. of Cape Race, at the S. E. point of the island of Newfoundland.

Mistassin Lake, a lake of New Britain, lying E. of the S. part of James's Bay, and surrounded by mountains called the Great Mis tassins. It is above 250 miles in circuit, of a very irregular shape, being much intersected by long and narrow projections of land, and contains several islands. It is formed of the Mistassin and other rivers from the mountains, and its outlet is the river Rupert.

MISTRETTA, a town of Sicily, in Val di Demona, 50 miles E. S. E. of Palermo. Pop. 6000.

MITCHAM, a village in Surrey, 7 miles S. W. of London. It is seated on the Wandle, on which are some snuff-mills and calico-printing manufactories.

MITCHELDEAN, a town in Gloucestershire, with a market on Monday, seated at the N. extremity of the forest of Dean, 12 miles W. of Gloucester, 116 W. by N. of London.

MITCHELSTOWN, a town of Ireland, in the county of Cork, with a college for 12 decayed gentlemen, and 16 gentlewomen. It is 23 miles N. E. of Cork, and 26 S. S. E. of Limerick.

MITTAU, a town of Russia, capital of the government of Courland, the residence of Louis XVIII. for several years during his exile. The walls and moats of the town are decayed; the houses, for the most part, have no particular elegance, and a great many gardens and open places are contained within its circuit. Here are two Lutheran churches, a beautiful Calvinist church, and a Catholic church. It is seated on the Aa, 45 miles E. of Goldingen, and 270 N. N. E. of Warsaw. Pop. 12,000. Long. 23. 50. E. lat. 56. 40. N.

MITTENWALD, a town of Bavaria, capital of the county of Werdenfels, seated on the Iser, 12 miles N. of Inspruck.

MITTERBURG, a town of Austrian Illyria, with a castle on a rock, 30 miles S. E. of Trieste.

MOBILE, a town of the United States, in Alabama, formerly in West Florida. When it came into the possession of the United States, in 1813, it was a poor mean place, but has since been rapidly increasing in population and commercial importance. It is a great shipping port for cotton. It has a regular fortress, and stands at the mouth of a river, and at the head of a bay, of the same name; 170 miles E. of New Orleans. Pop. 3914. Long. 88. 18. W. lat. 30. 37. N.

MOBILE, a river formed by two main branches, the Alabama and Tombeckby, in the S. part of the state of Georgia. After flowing 4 miles S. it separates into two streams, which soon after enter into West Florida. The river to the W. retains the name of Mobile; that to the E. takes the name of Tensaw; both are equally navigable, and they run nearly parallel into Mobile Bay, which extends 11 leagues S. to the Gulf of Mexico.

MOCARANGA, or MOCARA, a kingdom on the E. coast of Africa, mistakenly called Monomotapa, which is the title of the monarch. It is bounded on the N. by Monomugi, E. by the Mosambique, S. by Sofala and Manica, and W. by unknown regions. It has several rivers, of which the Zambezi is the chief; is fertile in rice, millet, and sugar-canes, which last grow without cultivation; and the pastures feed vast multitudes of cattle, especially of the larger sort, but not any horses. There are a great many ostriches, wild beasts, and elephants; and several mines of gold and silver. The natives possess all the characteristics of the African negro. Their houses are built of wood, and covered with plaster; but they have few towns. Madrogan is the capital.

MOCAUMPOUR, or MOCKWANPORE, a town of Hindostan, capital of a district of the same name, subject to the rajah of Nepaul. It is situate on the E. side of the Nepaul, 48 miles S. S. E. of Catmandu, and 136 N. of Patna. Long. 85. 20. E. lat. 27. 30. N.

MOCHA, or MOKA, a town of Arabia, in Yemen; seated on a small bay of the Red Sea, near the Strait of Babelmandel. On each of the points of land which enclose the road is a fort, but they are wretched structures. The town is of a circular form, surrounded by a wall, in which are six gates, and has a handsome appearance from the sea. It stands in a dreary plain, bounded by mountains, and consisting entirely of arid sand. The English, from Hindostan, at present engross almost exclusively the trade of this place, which is very considerable, especially in coffee; 140 miles S. S. W. of Sana, and 630 S. S. E. of Mecca. Long. 44. 25. E. lat. 13. 10. N.

MODBURY, a town in Devonshire, with a market on Thursday, and a manufacture of plush. It has a spacious church, and two meeting-houses. It is seated between two hills, 36 miles S. S. W. of Exeter, and 208 W. S. W. of London.

MODENA, or MODENESE, a duchy of Italy, bounded on the W. by Parma, N. by the Po, E. by the Papal states, and S. by the Apennines. It now includes the principalities of Massa and Carrara, and contains an area of 2060 square miles, with 370,000 inhabitants. The soil is fertile in corn, wine, oil, and fruits of different kinds. It also feeds a great number of cattle.

MODENA, the capital of the Modenese, and a bishop's see, with a citadel and a magnificent college. The cathedral, several of the churches, and some of the monasteries, are handsome structures. The ducal palace is richly furnished, and contains fine paintings. The inhabitants of Modena, estimated at 27,000, carry on manufactures of hemp, woollens, glass, leather, &c. It is seated between the rivers Secchia and Fanaro, 30 miles E. S. E. of Parma, and 60 N. N. W. of Florence. Long. 11. 12. E. lat. 44. 34. N.

MODICA, a town of Sicily, in Val di Noto, capital of a district of its name; seated near the river Scieli, 10 miles W. of Noto. Pop. 23,500.

MODON, a strong town of the Morea, and a bishop's see, with a safe harbour. It is seated on a promontory projecting into the sea of Sapienza, 15 miles W. of Coron. Long. 21. 31. E. lat. 36. 53. N.

MOERS. *See* MEURS.

MOESKIRCH, a town of Bavaria, 18 miles N. of Constance.

MOFFAT, a town of Scotland in Dumfries-shire, near the river Annan; encompassed on all sides, except the S., by hills of different heights. Its delightful situation and its mineral springs attract much company; 20 miles N. by E. of Dumfries, and 50 S. of Edinburgh.

MOFFAT HILLS, the highest mountains of the S. of Scotland, on the N. border of Dumfriesshire. Hartfel, the most elevated, is 2300 feet above the level of the sea. They feed numerous flocks of sheep, and from them descend, in different directions, the Tweed, Clyde, and Annan; whose sources are but little distant from each other.

MOGADOR, or SUERRAH, a town of the empire of Morocco, with a harbour for vessels of a middling size. It is the emporium of all the foreign, and indeed of the entire trade of Morocco, and contains 10,000 inhabitants. The town is surrounded by walls, with batteries, and at high tides is almost encompassed by the sea. The streets are all in straight lines, and contain a great number of handsome houses. It is supplied with water by means of an aqueduct. The port is formed by a channel between the mainland and an island, above a mile in length. It is 180 miles W. N. W. of Morocco. Long. 9. 35. W. lat. 31. 28. N.

MOHATS, a town of Lower Hungary, in the county of Burany. Here Louis, the last king of Hungary, was defeated in 1526 by the Turks under Soliman II., with the loss of 22,000 men, and, after the battle, suffocated by the fall of his horse in a muddy brook. In 1687 the Turks were defeated by prince Charles of Lorrain, with the loss of 10,000 men, their cannon, and baggage. It is seated at the conflux of the Corasse with the Danube, 23 miles N. by E. of Esseck.

MOHAWK RIVER, a river of the state of New York, which rises 40 miles E. of Lake Ontario, and, after receiving many tributary streams, enters Hudson River, 10 miles above Albany. About 3 miles above its junction with the Hudson it has a cataract, where the stream, 100 yards wide, falls perpendicularly about 70 feet.

MOHAWKS, a once powerful tribe of Indians living on Mohawk River. Most of them emigrated in 1776 into Canada, and none now remain in the United States.

MOHILA, one of the Comoro Islands, between the N. end of Madagascar and the continent of Africa. The inland parts are mountainous and woody. It has a good road for ships. Long. 43. 59. E. lat. 12. 35. S.

MOHILEF, or MOGILEV, a considerable government of the Russian empire, to the E. of the government of Minsk. Its area is 18,500 square miles, and its population about 800,000, of whom the majority are Poles.

MOHILEF, the capital of the above government, is the seat of the government offices, and the residence of a Greek and a Catholic archbishop, and has a castle, surrounded with an earthen mound. The inhabitants carry on a considerable trade with Dantzic, Riga, and Memel. In July, 1812, a severe battle was fought in the neighbourhood of this place between the French and the Russians. It is situate on the Dnieper, 340 miles E. N. E. of Warsaw, and 364 S. of Petersburg. Population 12,500. Long. 30. 14. E. lat. 53. 52. N.

MOHILL, a market town of Ireland, in the county of Leitrim, 94 miles from Dublin.

MOHRIN, a town of Prussia, in Brandenburg, 18 miles N. N. W. of Custrin.

MOHRUNGEN, a town of Prussia, in the government of Konigsberg; situate on a lake of the same name, which almost surrounds it. Here is an old castle, formerly a convent belonging to the knights of the Teutonic order, in consequence of whose wars the town has frequently suffered. It is 56 miles S. S. W. of Konigsberg, and 56 S. E. of Dantzic.

MOILAH, a town and fort of Arabia Petrea, on the coast of the Red Sea, 130 miles S. of Akaba, and 180 N. W. of Medina. Long. 33. 50. E. lat. 27. 30. N.

MOIRA, a market town of Ireland, in the county of Down, with an excellent linen market; 90 miles from Dublin.

MOIRANS, a town of France, in the department of Isere; 25 miles S. E. of Vienne.

MOISSAC, a town of France, in the department of Tarn-et-Garonne, with a trade in corn and flour; situated on the Tarn, near its confluence with the Garonne; 18 miles N. W. of Montauban.

MOLA DI BARI, a town of Naples, in Terra di Bari, seated on the Gulf of Venice; 17 miles E. of Bari. Pop. 7700.

MOLA DI GAETA, a town of Naples, in Terra di Lavoro, seated near the sea; 3 miles N. E. of Gaeta. Pop. 2000.

MOLD, a town of Wales, in Flintshire, with a market on Saturday. It is surrounded by rugged hills, rich in mineral treasures; 5 miles S. of Flint, and 191 N. W. of London.

MOLDAVIA, a province of Turkey in Europe, bounded N. by Austrian Poland, E. by Russia, S. by Turkey, and W. by Transylvania. The principal rivers are the Danube, Pruth, and Sereth. The W. part is mountainous, and there are some uncultivated deserts; but it abounds in good pastures, which feed a great number of horses, oxen, and sheep; it also produces corn, pulse, honey, wax, fruits, with plenty of game and fowls. The sovereign, who is styled hospodar, is tributary to the grand seignior. Jassy is the principal town.

MOLE, a river in Surrey, which rises on the borders of Sussex, flows N. to Dorking, and, passing beneath Box Hill, is said to disappear in its vicinity, and to rise again near Leatherhead, and enters the Thames opposite Hampton Court.

MOLE, a port of St. Domingo. *See* NICHOLAS, ST.

MOLFETTA, a town of Naples, in Terra di Bari, seated on the Gulf of Venice, 10 miles W. by N. of Bari. Pop. 11,500.

MOLIERES, a town of France, department of Tarn-et-Garonne; 11 miles N. of Montauban.

MOLISE, a province of Naples, in the form of a triangle whose sides are 39 miles long, lying between Terra di Lavora, Abruzzo Citra, Capitanata, and Principato Ultra. Pop. 27,000.

It is a mountainous country, but fertile in corn, wine, saffron, and silk. It suffered much damage by an earthquake in 1805, when upwards of 20,000 of the inhabitants perished.

Molise, the capital of the foregoing province, with a castle. It is 50 miles N. N. E. of Naples. Long. 14. 43. E. lat. 41. 36. N.

Mollen, a strong town of Denmark, in the duchy of Lauenburg; seated on the Steckenitz, 8 miles S. of Lubec.

Molsheim, a town of France, in the department of Lower Rhine; seated on the Brusch, 10 miles W. of Strasburg. Pop. 2500.

Molton, South, a town in Devonshire, 178 miles from London, on the river Moule, with a manufacture of serges, &c.

Moluccas, or Spice Islands, a number of islands in the Indian Ocean, lying E. of Celebes. They include those from Mortay in the N. to Banda in the S., and from Mysol in the E. to Bouro in the W. The other principal ones are Gilolo, Ceram, Amboyna, Ouby, Ternate, Tidore, Motir, Machian, and Bachian. Except Gilolo, they produce neither corn, rice, nor cattle; but they have oranges, lemons, and other fruits; and are most remarkable for spices, especially cloves and nutmegs. On the shores there are large rocks of coral, of great variety and beauty. They were discovered in 1511, by the Portuguese, who formed some settlements, but were driven out in 1607 by the Dutch, to whom the islands are at present subject.

Molwitz, a town of Prussian Silesia, in the principality of Brieg; famous for a victory gained by the Prussians over the Austrians in 1741. It is 4 miles W. of Brieg.

Mombaza, a city on the coast of Zanguebar. It was seated on a peninsula, which has been since turned into an island, by cutting a canal through the isthmus. It is defended by a strong citadel, has a commodious harbour for large vessels, and carries on a great commerce with the islands and kingdoms adjacent, in gold, ivory, rice, flesh, &c. The king of Melinda, being a Christian, had a quarrel with the Portuguese governor, took the castle by assault, turned Mahomedan, and murdered all the Christians, in 1631. In 1729 the Portuguese again became masters of this territory; but since that time the natives have regained possession of it, and have treated in the most treacherous and hostile manner all Christians who have attempted to land. Mombaza is 75 miles S. S. W. of Melinda. Long. 39. 30. E. lat. 3. 15. S.

Momflôt, a town of Egypt with manufactures of linen; seated on the left bank of the Nile, 20 miles N. N. W. of Siout.

Mompox, a town of New Granada, republic of Colombia, in the province of Carthagena, on the left bank of the Madalena; 112 miles S. S. E. of Carthagena.

Mona, an island of Denmark, in the Baltic, to the S. W. of the island of Zealand, from which it is separated by a narrow channel. Stege is the chief town.

Monaco, a fortified seaport of Italy, capital of a small principality of the same name, between the county of Nice and the duchy of Genoa. The harbour is good, but not deep enough for large vessels; the principal export is olive oil. It is seated on a craggy rock that projects into the sea, 12 miles E. N. E. of Nice. Long. 7. 30. E. lat. 43. 44. N.

Monaghan, a county of Ireland, in the province of Ulster; bounded N. by Tyrone, E. by Armagh, S. E. by Louth, S. W. by Cavan, and W. by Fermanagh. Its area includes 179,600 Irish acres part of which is occupied by woods and bogs, and a third part taken up by Lough Erne. A great part is, however, in a high state of cultivation. It contains five baronies, is divided into 27 parishes, and sends two members to parliament.

Monaghan, the capital of the foregoing county, was fortified with a castle and a fort, in the reign of Queen Elizabeth. It is 40 miles S. W. of Belfast, and 60 N. N. W. of Dublin. Long. 6. 49. W. lat. 54. 16. N.

Monaster, a town of the kingdom of Tunis, seated near the sea; 70 miles S. E. of Tunis. Long. 11. 6. E. lat. 35. 50. N.

Monasterevan, a town of Ireland, in the county of Kildare, situate on the Barrow, near the Grand Canal; 19 miles N. of Carlow, and 32 S. W. of Dublin.

Monblanc, a town of Spain, in Catalonia, on the river Francoli, 17 miles N. of Tarragona.

Moncaglieri, a town of the Sardinian states, in Piedmont, seated on an eminence near the Po; 5 miles S. E. of Turin. Pop. 7300.

Moncalvo, a town of Piedmont, province of Montferrat, seated on a mountain; 12 miles S. W. of Casal, and 30. E. of Turin. Pop. 3500.

Monçaon, a town of Portugal, in Entre Douro e Minho; with a strong castle; seated near the Minho; 24 miles N. of Braga.

Monchabou, a city of Birmah, and during a short period its capital, is surrounded by a wall and ditch, but is chiefly celebrated as the birthplace of Alompra, who afterwards became the deliverer of his country, and the conqueror of Pegu. It is 40 miles N. of Ummerapoora.

Monçon, a town of Spain, in Arragon, with a castle; 6 miles S. of Balbastro, and 50. N. E. of Saragossa.

Moncontour, a town of France, in the department of Cotes du Nord; 12 miles S. S. E. of St. Brieux.

Moncontour, a town of France, department of Vienne; 27 miles N. W. of Poitiers.

Mondego, a river of Portugal, which has its source near Guardo, crosses Beira by Coimbra, and enters the Atlantic near a cape of the same name.

Mondonedo, a town of Spain, in Galicia, and a bishop's see; 60 miles N. E. of Compostella, and 115 N. W. of Leon. Long. 7. 10. W. lat. 43. 30. N.

Mondovi, a fortified town of Piedmont, capital of a province of its name, and a bishop's see. In 1796 the French gained a victory here over the Austrians, which made them masters of the state of the king of Sardinia; and in 1799 they abandoned this place to a general pillage. It is seated on a mountain, near the river Ellero; 14 miles E. of Coni.

Population 20,000. Long. 8. 3. E. lat. 44. 25. N.

MONDRAGON, a town of Spain, in Guipuscoa; near which are some medicinal springs, and a famous mine of excellent iron. It is seated on the Deva; 24 miles S. S. W. of St. Sebastian.

MONDRAGONE, a town of Naples, in Terra di Lavoro; celebrated for its medicinal waters; 13 miles N. W. of Capua.

MONFIA, an island on the coast of Zanguebar, to the N. E. of Quiloa; tributary to Portugal. Long. 40. 50. E. lat. 7. 50. S.

MONFLANQUIN, a town of France, in the department of Lot-et-Garonne; 20 miles N. N. E. of Agen. Pop. 5000.

MONFORTE, a town of Spain, in Galicia, with a castle; 19 miles N. of Orense.

MONGHYR, a celebrated town and fortress of Hindostan, capital of a district of its name in the province of Bahar; seated on the S. bank of the Ganges, which in the rainy season forms here a prodigious expanse of fresh water. The town, as distinct from the fortress, consists of 16 different bazaars, or market-places, scattered over a space of about a mile and a half long and a mile wide. The population is estimated at 30,000. Since 1816 this has formed one of the stations of the Baptist Missionary Society, whose exertions here have been attended with a pleasing degree of success; 80 miles E. by S. of Patna, and 300 N. W. of Calcutta. Long. 86. 36. E. lat. 25. 24. N.

MONGOLIA, or WESTERN CHINESE TARTARY, is bounded on the N. by Siberia, E. by Eastern Tartary, S. by the Great Wall of China and Leao-tong, and W. by Independent Tartary, and occupying most of the space between China and Asiatic Russia. Almost the whole territory consists of a level plain, which borders on the Altai and other mountain chains that form the Russian frontier. The inhabitants are decidedly distinguished both from the Turks and Tartars. They have neither towns nor houses, but wander in hordes, and live under tents, which they remove from one place to another, according as the temperature of the different seasons, or the wants of their flocks require. They pass the summer on the banks of rivers, and the winter at the foot of some mountain or hill which shelters them from the piercing N. wind. Their ideas of honour, perhaps less ridiculous than those of our contemporaries, induce them rather to be content with the food which their flocks supply them, than cultivate the earth. During the summer they live only on milk, using, without distinction, that of the cow, mare, ewe, goat, and camel. Their ordinary drink is warm water, in which a little coarse tea has been infused; with this they mix cream, milk, or butter, according to their circumstances. They have also a method of making a kind of spirituous liquor of sour milk, especially of that of the mare. The Monguls are free, open, and sincere. They pride themselves chiefly on their dexterity in handling the bow and arrow, mounting on horseback, and hunting wild beasts. Polygamy is permitted among them; but they generally have only one wife. Their religion is confined to the worship of Fo. They have the most superstitious veneration for their lamas, to whom they give the most valuable of their effects in return for prayers, which they go about reciting from tent to tent. The Monguls are now split into a number of petty states, dependent on the empires of Russia and China. Those under the Chinese government may be divided into four principal tribes, which are the Monguls, properly so called, the Kalkas, the Ortous, and the Tartars of Kokonor.

MONHEIM, a town of Bavaria, in Neuburg, 8 miles N. of Donawert.

MONIKENDAM, a seaport of the Netherlands, in North Holland; with manufactures of soap and silk; seated on an arm of the Zuyder Zee; 8 miles N. E. of Amsterdam. Long. 4. 38. E. lat. 52. 28. N.

MONISTROL, a town of France, in the department of Upper Loire. It is 14 miles S. W. of St. Etienne. Pop. 4000.

MONKLAND, OLD and NEW, an extensive district in Lanarkshire, Scotland, which is one of the principal seats of the iron manufacture and collieries in Scotland. The vast abundance of its mineral treasures have advanced it rapidly in population and importance. The soil is also fertile, and is occupied by thriving agriculturists. This district is also connected with no less than four great railways: the Garnkirk and Glasgow, the Monkland and Kirkintilloch, the Ballochine, and the Wishaw and Coltness Railways; besides which it has the Monkland and Glasgow Canal. It is 12 miles distant from Glasgow.

MONMOUTH, a town of Maine; in Lincoln county, seated on the Androscoggin; 15 miles W. by S. of Harrington, and 125 N. by E. of Boston.

MONMOUTH, a borough of England, capital of Monmouthshire, with a market on Saturday. It is governed by a mayor, and joins with Usk and Newport in sending one member to parliament. It was formerly defended by a wall and ditch, and contains the ruins of a castle, in which the warlike Henry V. was born, hence called Henry of Monmouth; his cradle, and the armour which he wore at the battle of Agincourt, are still shown at Troy House, the seat of the Duke of Beaufort, about half a mile from the town. Here are two ancient churches, both curious structures. The inhabitants carry on some trade by means of the Wye, and there are iron and tin-works in the neighbourhood. Monmouth is seated at the conflux of the Wye and Minour; 25 miles W. of Gloucester, and 131 W. by N. of London. Long. 2. 46. W. lat. 51. 49. N.

MONMOUTHSHIRE, a county of England; 24 miles long and 20 broad; bounded on the N. by Herefordshire, E. by Gloucestershire, S. by the Severn, and W. and S. W. by the counties of Brecknock and Glamorgan. It contains 318,720 acres, is divided into six hundreds and 127 parishes, has seven market towns, and sends two members to parliament. Besides the Wye (which parts it from Gloucestershire), the Monnow (which separates it from Herefordshire), and the Rhyney, or Rumney, which divides it from Glamorganshire), this county has, almost peculiar to itself, the river Usk, which divides it into two unequal portions. The eastern and largest part is a tract fertile in corn and pasture, well wooded, and abounding with limestone. The western portion is mountainous, and, in great part, unfavourable for cultivation; whence it is devoted to the feeding of sheep and goats. Monmouthshire was formerly reckoned one of the counties of Wales; and, from the names of its towns and villages, its mountainous rugged surface, and its situation beyond the Wye, which seems to form a natural boundary between England and Wales in this part, it certainly partakes most of the character of the latter country, though now comprehended in the civil division of the former. The higher ranks generally speak English, but the common people use the Welsh language. The chief wealth of the county arises from its agricultural and mineral products. During the last century a great number of iron-works have been established, and some tin-works; and the inland intercourse has been greatly facilitated by the Brecknock and Monmouthshire canals, as also by the several railways.

MONOMOTAPA. *See* MOCARANGA.

MONONGAHELA, a river of the United States, which rises in Virginia, at the foot of Laurel Mountains, flows N. by Morgantown, where it becomes navigable, then enters Pennsylvania, and passes by Redstone to Pittsburg, where it meets the Allegany, and their united streams assume the name of Ohio.

MONOPOLI, a town of Naples, in Terra di Bari, on the coast of the Gulf of Venice; 28 miles E. S. E. of Bari. Pop. 15,600.

MONPAZIER, a town of France, in the department of Dordogne, seated on the Drot; 18 miles S. W. of Sarlat.

MONQUEGNA, or MONQUEQUA, a town of Peru, in the bishopric of Arequipa; capital of a territory of its name, adorned with large vineyards. Its whole commerce is in wine and brandy, which are greatly valued; 100 miles S. E. of Arequipa. Long. 71. 40. E. lat. 17. 34. S.

MONREALE, a town of Sicily, in Val di Mazara. It is an archbishop's see, and the cathedral is an admired specimen of Gothic architecture, 3 miles W. S. W. of Palermo.

MONROVIA, a flourishing town on the coast of Africa, capital of a district named Liberia. It contains a public library, a court-house, meeting-houses, school-houses, an infirmary, &c. The houses are constructed of the same materials and finished in the same style as in the towns of America. In the vicinity good building stone, shells for lime, and excellent clay for bricks, abound. Timber of various kinds, fit for all the purposes of building and fencing, is also plentiful. *See* LIBERIA.

MONS, a strong town of Belgium, capital of Hainault. The most remarkable buildings are the castle, the arsenal, the town-house, and the great church. It is a place of good trade, has considerable manufactures of woollen stuffs, cottons, lace, earthenware, &c., as also iron-foundries and salt-works, and contains 25,000 inhabitants. Mons has been several times taken by the French, Dutch, and Austrians. It stands partly on a hill and partly on a plain, on the river Trouille; 30 miles S. S. W. of Brussels. Long. 3. 57. E. lat. 50. 27. N.

MONSARAZ, a town of Portugal, in Alentejo, seated on the Guadiana, 25 miles S. W. of Elvas.

MONSOL, a town of Guinea, in the country of Anziko, the residence of the micoco, or king; 380 miles N. E. of St. Salvador. Long. 17. 16. E. lat. 0. 40. N.

MONSTIERS. *See* MOUSTIERS.

MONT BLANC, a stupendous mountain of the Pennine Alps, in Savoy; so called from its white appearance. It is supposed to be the highest in Europe, being 15,673 feet above the level of the sea.

MONT DAUPHIN, a town of France; department of Upper Alps; seated on a craggy mountain almost surrounded by the Durance; 16 miles S. of Briançon.

MONT DE MARSAN, a town of France; capital of the department of Landes; seated on the Midouse; 30 miles N. E. of Dax. Long. 0. 30. W. lat. 43. 55. N.

MONT ST. MICHEL, a strong town of France; department of Manche; built on a rock in the sea, which is accessible at low water; 10 miles S. W. of Avranches. Long. 1. 30. W. lat. 48. 37. N.

MONTABAUR, a town of Germany; in the duchy of Nassau; with a fine palace; 7 miles N. of Nassau.

MONTAGU ISLAND, one of the New Hebrides, in the South Pacific; near Sandwich Island. Long. 168. 31. E. lat. 17. 26. N.

MONTAGU ISLAND, an island in the N. Pacific; 50 miles long, and 12 broad; near the W. coast of North America, at the entrance of Prince William Sound. Long. 147. 30. W. lat. 60. 0. N.

MONTAIGU, a town of France, in the department of Vendee; 18 miles S. S. E. of Nantes.

MONTAIGU, a town of France, in the department of Puy de Dome; 33 miles N. N. W. of Clermont.

MONTAIGUE, or SCHERPENHEUEL, a town of the Netherlands; in South Brabant; famous for an image of the Virgin, visited by a great number of pilgrims. It is 14 miles N. E. of Louvain.

MONTALEGRE, a town of Portugal; in Tras los Montes; 25 miles N. E. of Braga, and 42 W. of Braganza.

MONTALVAN, a town of Spain, in Arragon; with a strong citadel; seated on the Rio Martin; 44 miles S. of Saragossa, and 92 N. by W. of Valencia.

MONTALVAO, a town of Portugal, in Alentejo; on the borders of Spain; 18 miles N. N. E. of Portalegre, and 108 from Lisbon.

MONTARGIS, a town of France; department of Loiret; adjacent to the river Loing; from which a navigable canal proceeds to the Seine. It is seated near a fine forest; 15 miles S. of Nemours, and 62 S. by E. of Paris. Pop. 6400.

Montauban, a town of France; department of Tarn-et-Garonne; with a celebrated Protestant university. It is the see of a bishop, restored in 1817. Here are manufactures of silk stockings, stuffs, serges, shalloons, &c. This town was taken from the Huguenots in 1629, and the fortifications were demolished. In the reign of Louis XIV. it was depopulated by the dragonnades, and in 1815 it suffered much from a persecution raised against the Protestants by an infuriated rabble. It is seated on an eminence on the river Tarn; 20 miles N. of Toulouse, and 30 S. of Cahors. Pop. 24,600.

Montbeliard, a town of France; department of Doubs; with a castle on a rock. It has a good trade in linen, leather, and cutlery; and near it is a considerable iron mine. It is seated at the confluence of the Savoureuse with the Luzine; which soon after joins the Doubs; 10 miles S. S. W. of Befort, and 47 N. E. of Besançon. Long. 6. 56. E. lat. 47. 30. N. Pop. 3700.

Montbrison, a town of France; capital of the department of Loire; celebrated for its medicinal waters. It is seated on the Vezize; 40 miles W. S. W. of Lyon. Long. 4. 7. E. lat. 45. 34. N. Pop. 5200.

Montdidier, a town of France; in the department of Somme; seated on a mountain; 22 miles S. S. E. of Amiens, and 58 N. by E. of Paris.

Monte Alcino, a town of Tuscany; famous for producing the best wine in Italy, called Muscatella di Monte Alcino. It is 24 miles S. S. E. of Sienna.

Monte Alto, a town of Italy, in Ancona; 14 miles S. S. W. of Fermo.

Monte Christo, a town, river, bay, and cape on the N. side of St. Domingo. Long. 71. 50. W. lat. 19. 54. N.

Monte Fiascone, a town of Italy; in the papal states; near the Lake Bolsena; 12 miles N. N. W. of Viterbo. Pop. 3000.

Monte Fossoli, a town of Tuscany; in the Pisano; 18 miles E. by N. of Leghorn.

Monte Leone, a town of Naples, in Calabria Ultra; and a bishop's see; 12 miles N.N.E. of Nicotera. Pop. 8000.

Monte Leone, a town of Naples, in Principato Ultra; 9 miles N. of Benevento. Pop. 2100.

Monte Marano, a town of Naples, in Principato Ultra; near the river Cahore; 18 miles S. of Benevento.

Monte Peloso, a town of Naples; in Basilicata; near the river Basiento; 14 miles E. of Acerenza.

Monte Santo. *See* Athos.

Monte Verde, a town of Naples, in Principato Ultra; 16 miles N. E. of Conza.

Monte Video, a seaport of Buenos Ayres; republic of La Plata; with a fort. The town is surrounded by a strong wall, and the principal trade consists in hides. It was taken by the English, in February, 1807; but evacuated in September. It is seated at the foot of a lofty conical mountain, on the N. side of the river Plata, 60 miles from its mouth, and 140 E. of Buenos Ayres. Long. 53. 25. W. lat. 34. 35. S.

Montechio, a town of Austrian Italy; in the province of Brescia; near which the French defeated the Austrians in 1796. It is 10 miles S. E. of Brescia.

Montego Bay, a seaport, on a bay of the same name; on the N. side of the island of Jamaica. Long. 78. 0. W. lat. 18. 30. N.

Montelimart, a town of France; department of Drone; with an ancient citadel, and manufactures of wool, silk, and leather. It is seated in a fertile plain, near the Rhone; 25 miles S. of Valence, and 50 N. of Avignon.

Montemor o Novo, a town of Portugal, in Alentejo; on the Canna; 15 miles W. N.W. of Evora and 55 E. of Lisbon.

Montemor o Velho, a town of Portugal, in Beira, with a castle; seated on the Mondego; 106 miles N. by E. of Lisbon.

Montereau, a town of France; department of Seine-et-Marne; celebrated for a battle fought here, on the 17th February, 1814, between the allies and the French, in which the former were defeated with great loss. It has a trade in corn, &c. It is seated on the Seine; at the influx of the Yonne; 15 miles S. E. of Melun.

Monterey, St. Carlos de, a seaport of New California; republic of Mexico; in a jurisdiction of its name. It comprehends an area of 300 yards long by 250 wide, is walled round, and has a fort. It stands on the S. E. part of a spacious bay of its name. Long. 121. 34. W. lat. 37. 6. N.

Montesa, a town and fortress of Spain, in Valencia; 9 miles W. S. W. of San Felippe.

Montesquieu, a town of France; in the department of Upper Garonne; 15 miles S.S.E. of Toulouse. Pop. 2800.

Montesquieu, a town of France; department of Gers; 11 miles W. S. W. of Auch.

Montferrand, a town of France: now forming a suburb to Clermont (which see).

Montferrat, a duchy of Italy, forming a part of the Sardinian states, and bound by Piedmont, the Milanese, and Genoa, from which last it is separated by the Apennines. It is very fertile and well cultivated, abounding in corn, wine, oil, and silk. Pop. 186,000.

Montfort, a town of France, in the department of Seine-et-Oise; 16 miles W. of Versailles.

Montfort, a town of France; department of Ille-et-Vilaine; 12 miles W. of Rennes.

Montfort, a fortified town of the Netherlands, in Utrecht, seated on the Yssel; 7 miles S. W. of Utrecht.

Montfort, a town of the Austrian states, in Tyrol; 6 miles N. of Feldkirch.

Montgatz, or Munkacs, a town of Hungary, with a fortress, composed of three castles; seated on a craggy rock. It is encompassed by a great morass; and was defended three years by the wife of Count Tekeli, the leader of the Hungarian malcontents, near the close of the seventeenth century. It is 162 miles E. S. E. of Cracow. Long. 21. 55. E. lat. 48. 26. N.

Montgomery, the name of the following counties of the United States:—1. In the central part of New York. 2. In the S. E. part of Pennsylvania. 3. In Maryland. 4. In Ohio. 5. In the S. W. part of Virginia. 6. In the central part of North Carolina. 7. In Kentucky, on the river Licking. 8. On the N. side of W. Tennessee. And, 9. In the central part of Georgia, 750 miles from Washington.—Also, of various inconsiderable townships.

Montgomery, a borough of Wales; capital of Montgomeryshire; with a market on Thursday; it returns one member to parliament. Here are the ruins of a castle, which was destroyed in the civil wars. Of late years the town has received considerable improvements, the market-house has been enlarged, and a new county jail erected; many of the buildings are large and handsome. It stands on the side of a hill, at a short distance from the Severn; 24 miles S.W. of Shrewsbury, and 168 N.W. of London. Long. 3. 5. W. lat. 52. 26. N.

Montgomeryshire, a county of Wales; 36 miles long, and 34 broad: bounded N. by Merionethshire, and Denbighshire, N. E. and E. by Shropshire, S. by Radnorshire, S. W. by Cardiganshire, and W. by Merionethshire. It contains 491,000 acres, is divided into nine hundreds and forty-seven parishes, has seven market towns, and sends one member to parliament. Though barren and mountainous in many parts, it has a greater mixture of fertile vale and plain than several of the Welsh counties. Its riches proceed from its sheep and wool, the hilly tracts being almost entirely sheep walks; and the flocks, like those of Spain, are driven from distant parts to feed on them during the summer. This county also affords mineral treasures, particularly lead; and it abounds with slate and lime; but there is no coal. Its principal rivers are the Plynlimmon, Severn, Vyrnew, and Tannat, all of which are noted for affording a variety of fish, particularly salmon.

Montguyon, a town of France, in the department of Lower Charente; 43 miles S. S. E. of Saintes.

Montiel, a town of Spain, in New Castile; 22 miles W. of Alcaraz, and 70 E. S. E. of Calatrava.

Montignac, a town of France, in the departmont of Dordogne; on the Vezere; 21 miles E. S. E. of Perigeux.

Montilla, a town of Spain, in Cordova: 18 miles S. S. E. of Cordova.

Montivilliars, a town of France, department of Lower Seine, on the small river Lazarde; 6 miles N. of Havre.

Montjoy, a town of the Prussian province of Lower Rhine; with a fortified castle on a hill; situate among rugged rocks; 16 miles S. S. E. of Aix-la-Chapelle.

Montlieu, a town of France, in the department of Lower Charente; 40 miles S. S. E. of Saintes.

Montlouis, a town of France; department of Upper Pyrenees; with a regular fortress on a rock, at the foot of the Pyrenees, for the protection of the frontiers. It is 40 miles W. by S. of Perpignan, and 430 S. of Paris. Long. 2.5. E. lat. 42. 30. N.

Montluçon, a town of France; department of Allier; with manufactures of lace, ribands, serge, &c., seated on the Cher; 35 miles W.S. W. of Moulins. Pop. 5700.

Montluel, a town of France, department of Ain, on the Seraine; 9 miles S. E. of Trevoux.

Montmarault, a town of France; department of Allier; 28 miles S. W. Moulins.

Montmedy, a town of France, department of Meuse; seated on the river Chiers, which divides it into the Upper and Lower Town; 21 miles N. of Verdun. Pop. 2000.

Montmirel, a town of France, department of Marne; rendered memorable for two severe battles fought in its vicinity, between the French and the allies, on the 12th and 14th of February, 1814. It is 33 miles W. by S. of Chalons sur Marne, and 55 E. of Paris.

Montmorency, a town of France, department of Seine-et-Oise; 10 miles N. of Paris.

Montmorillon, a town of France, department of Vienne; seated on the Gartempe; 25 miles S. E. of Poitiers. Pop. 4100.

Montona, a town of Austrian Illyria, in Istria; 16 miles E. S. E. of Umago.

Montpelier, one of the largest, richest, and most beautiful cities of France, in the department of Herault, and a bishop's see, with a university, in which is a celebrated school of medicine, and a botanic garden, the first established in Europe. Here are also one of the great provincial schools, a special school of medicine, erected in 1801, an anatomical theatre, an extensive library, a literary society, &c. The town-house is remarkable for its halls, which are embellished with fine paintings. The number of inhabitants is computed at 33,000. Its trade consists in silks, blankets, carpets, cotton goods, gauzes, hides, &c. The air is extremely healthy, and a great number of invalids flock hither from all parts, though it is unfavourable to consumptive patients. Montpelier is the seat of the departmental administration, and is situated on an eminence between the small rivers Lez and Merdanson; about 5 miles from the Mediterranean, with which it communicates by the Canal de Grave; 30 miles S. W. of Nismes, and 47 N. E. of Narbonne. Long. 3. 58. E. lat. 43. 37. N.

Montpelier, a town of Vermont, in Washington county; the permanent seat of the state government, and a county town. It is a flourishing town, and has considerable trade. Seated on the Onion river; 38 miles E. S. E. of Burlington, and 160 N. N. W. of Boston.—Also, a town of North Carolina, in Richmond county.

Montreal, a district of Lower Canada, comprising the counties of York, Effingham, Leinster, Warwick, Huntingdon, Kent, Surrey Bedford, Richelieu, and Montreal.

Montreal, a fertile island and county of Lower Canada; on the river St. Lawrence; 30 miles long, and 10 broad; surrendered by the French to the English, in 1760.

Montreal, a city on the S. side of the above island. From the river there is a gradual ascent to what is called the Upper Town, in which are the Catholic cathedral, capable of holding 10,000 persons; the English church, and the government-house; and being the grand depôt of the fur trading companies of North America, and the channel through which is carried on the commerce between Canada and the United States, it is rapidly improving in extension. The chief trade is in furs, which are sent to England. Pop. 30,000. It is 110 miles N. of Crown Point, and 170 S. W. of Quebec. Long. 73. 11. W. lat. 45. 50. N.

Montreal, a town of Spain, in Arragon, with a castle; seated on the Xiloca; 25 miles N. of Albaracin.

Montreal, a town of Sicily; in Val di Mazara; and an archbishop's see; seated on a rivulet; 5 miles W. of Palermo, and 50 N. E. of Mazara.

Montreuil, a strong town of France; department of Pas de Calais; on a hill, near the mouth of the Canche; 20 miles S. E. of Boulogne, and 36 S. of Calais. Pop. 3400.

Montreuil Bellay, a town of France; department of Maine-et-Loire, on the Touet; 10 miles S. S. W. of Saumur.

Montrichard, a town of France; department of Loir-et-Cher, with a castle; seated near the Cher; 12 miles S. E. of Amboise.

Montrose, a town and seaport of Scotland; in Angus-shire, at the mouth of the S. Esk, over which a fine suspension bridge was erected in 1829. A little above the town the river expands into a wide lake called the Basin, into which the tide flows; so that at high water the town is almost surrounded by the sea. Fine quays have been erected, and two lighthouses. The harbour is very commodious, and has a dry and wet dock. Here are considerable manufactures of canvas, ropes, sheeting, linen, and thread. The salmon fisheries on the N. and S. Esk form a valuable branch of commerce, and also the exportation of corn; and the town generally has undergone great improvements and extensions within these few years. At this place the Pretender landed on the 22nd of December, 1715, and embarked on the 14th of February following; 28 miles N. E. of Dundee. Long. 2. 22. W. lat. 56. 41. N.

Montsauche, a town of France, department of Nievre; 15 miles N. E. of Chateau-Chinon.

Montserrat, a mountain of Spain, in Catalonia, on which is a monastery, with a chapel dedicated to the Virgin, resorted to by numbers of pilgrims. It is 26 miles N. W. of Barcelona.

Montserrat, one of the Leeward Caribbee Islands, discovered by Columbus, and so named by him from its resemblance to the mountain mentioned in the preceding article. It is about 9 miles in length and breadth; and the hills are covered with cedar and other trees. It belongs to the English, and is 30 miles S. W. of Antigua. Long. 61. 7. W. lat. 16. 48. N.

Monza, a town of Austrian Italy, in the government of Milan; famous for the treasury of St. John the Baptist; where, among other things, is the iron crown of the kingdom of Lombardy. Charlemagne was crowned here with it in 774, and Napoleon in 1805. It is seated on the Lambro; 8 miles N. E. of Milan.

Moon, Mountains of the, (Gebel el Kumri,) mountains of Africa; extending from West Africa, through Abyssinia, to the Indian Sea. They are said to be higher than those of Atlas, but have never yet been visited by Europeans.

Moorfields, a town of Virginia; chief of Hardy county, on the Potomac; 45 miles W. by S. of Winchester, and 18[illegible] N. W. of Richmond. Long. 79. 20. W. lat. 39. 8. N.

Moorshedabad, a city of Hindostan, the capital of Bengal before the establishment of the English power. It is seated near the western arm of the Ganges; 112 miles N. of Calcutta. Long. 89. 15. E. lat. 24. 12. N.

Mootapilly, a town of Hindostan, in the Guntoor circar, at the mouth of the Gondegama. Long. 80. 10. E. lat. 15. 35. N.

Moquehua, a province of Peru, bounded by those of Lampa, Puno, Chucuico, Arica, and Arequipa. The chief products are wine, fruits, and olives. The capital, of the same name, is situate in a fertile valley, at the foot of the Cordilleras; 70 miles S. of Arequipa. Pop. 6000.

Mora, a town of Portugal, in Alentejo, on the Odivor; 29 miles N. W. of Evora.

Mora, a town of Spain, in Catalonia, on the Ebro; 18 miles of Tortosa.

Mora, a town of Spain, in New Castile; 18 miles S. E. of Toledo.

Morant Point, a promontory on the E. coast of Jamaica. Long. 75. 56. W. lat. 17. 56. N.

Morat, or Murten, a town of Switzerland, canton of Friburg, with a castle. This town sustained a siege against the Duke of Burgundy, in 1476, in which his whole army was destroyed. It is 10 miles N. E. of Friburg.

Moratalaz, a town of Spain, in New Castile; 22 miles E. of Ciudad Real.

Moratalla, a town of Spain, in Murcia; 34 miles S. S. W. of Chinchilla.

Morava, a large river of Servia, which rises in Bulgaria, and, running through Servia by Nissa, joins the Danube at Semendria.

Moravia, a province of the Austrian empire; bounded N. and W. by Bohemia, E. by Hungary and S. by Austria Proper. With Austrian Silesia now annexed to it, its area is upwards of 10,000 square miles, and its population 1,680,000. It is intersected by mountain ranges, but the most lofty ridges are diversified with fertile valleys and extensive plains; and it is watered by a great number of rivers and brooks. More corn is grown than the inhabitants consume, and much hemp and flax are raised. The principal manufactures are woollens, linen, cotton, iron, glass, paper, and gunpowder. From this country a sect of Christians takes its name, their doctrines having been first taught here; who have migrated to other countries, in consequence of the intolerance of the government: the inhabitants in general are Roman Catholics. Brunn is the capital.

MORAW, or MARSCH, a river of the Austrian states, which rises in the mountains between Bohemia and Silesia, and, receiving the Teya, on the confines of Austria and Hungary, separates these two countries as far as the Danube, into which it enters; 15 miles above Presburg.

MORAY. *See* MURRAY.

MORBEGNO, a town of Austrian Italy, one of the handsomest and most commercial towns in the Milanese; seated on the Adda; 12 miles S. E. of Chiavenna. Pop. 2000. Long. 9. 36. E. lat. 46. 8. N.

MORBEYS, or OMMIRABIH, a river of Barbary; which rises in Mount Atlas, flows through the empire of Morocco, and enters the Atlantic at Azamor.

MORBIHAN, a department in the N. W. of France, bounded N. by that of Cotes du Nord, and S. by the sea. It takes its name from a bay between Vannes (the capital), and the island of Bellisle. It has extensive fisheries, and contains a population of 403,500.

MORCONE, a town of Naples, province of Molise; 19 miles S. S. E. of Molise.

MOREA, (the ancient Peloponnesus,) a peninsula of the kingdom of Greece, to which it is joined by the Isthmus of Corinth. It is 180 miles long, and 120 broad, and forms the principal port of the new kingdom. The soil is fertile, except in the middle, where there are many mountains; and it is watered by several rivers, of which the Alpheus, Vasili Potamo, and Stromio are the chief. The principal towns are Tripolitza, Argos, Patras, and Nauplia; but the trade is inconsiderable. It was taken by the Venetians from the Turks, in 1687, and retaken in 1715. It remained in their hands till the erection of the kingdom of Greece, and contained above half a million of inhabitants, now reduced by war, &c., to half that number. *See* GREECE.

MORELLA, a town of Spain, in Valencia; seated among high mountains; 80 miles S. of Valencia.

MORET, a town of France, department of Seine-et-Marne, near the Seine; 12 miles S. S. E. of Melun.

MORETON HAMPSTEAD, a town in Devonshire, with a market on Saturday, and a considerable trade; three meeting-houses, and a charity school. Here are the vestiges of two castles, or forts; and in the vicinity, are a Druidical temple, a large rocking-stone, and a cromlech. It is 12 miles W. S. W. of Exeter, and 185 W. by S. of London.

MORETTA, a town of the Sardinian states, in Piedmont; seated on a small river which runs into the Po; 18 miles S. of Turin.

MORGANTOWN, a town of North Carolina, in Burke county, near Catabaw River; 68 miles W. of Salisbury. Long. 81. 53. W. lat. 35. 42. N.

MORGANTOWN, a town of Virginia, chief of Monongahela county, on the E. side of the Monongahela; 75 miles S. of Pittsburg. Long. 80. 10. W. lat. 39. 34. N.

MORGES, a town of Switzerland, in the canton of Vaud; with a castle; 5 miles W. S. W. of Lausanne.

MORHANGE, a town of France, department of Moselle; 21 miles S. S. E. of Mentz.

MORIGEN, a town of Hanover, on the Mohr; 2 miles N. N. W. of Gottingen.

MORITZ, ST., a town of the Swiss canton of Grisons; with a famous mineral spring; 25 miles N. N. E. of Chiavenna.

MORLACHIA, a mountainous country, lying between, and forming part of, the provinces of Croatia and Dalmatia. The inhabitants are called Morlachi, or Moro-blassi, and are said, by some, to be of Wallachian extraction. Segna is the capital.

MORLAIX, a town of France; department of Finisterre; with a castle and a tide harbour. The church of Notre Dame is a singular structure, and the hospital is very handsome. It has a considerable trade in linen, hemp, and tobacco: it is seated on a river of the same name; 30 miles E. N. E. of Brest. Pop. 10,000. Long. 3. 45. W. lat. 48. 33. N.

MOROCCO, or MAROCCO, an empire of Africa, comprehending a considerable part of the ancient Mauritania; bounded W. by the Atlantic, N. by the Mediterranean, E. by Algier, and S. by the Sahara. It greatest length is above 590 miles; but it is nowhere more than 260 broad. Pop. between 4,000,000 and 5,000,000. The soil, though sandy and dry in some places, is fertile in others; and the fruits, as well as the pastures, are excellent; but the country is not properly cultivated. The inhabitants are Mahomedans: of a tawny complexion, robust, and very skilful in managing a horse and wielding a lance; they are jealous, deceitful, superstitious, and cruel. There are a great number of Christian slaves, and some merchants, upon the coast; besides a multitude of Jews, who carry on almost all the trade, especially by land, with the negroes; to whom they send large caravans, which travel over vast deserts, almost destitute of water. Besides woollen goods, their commodities are morocco leather, indigo, cochineal, and ostriches' feathers; in return for which they have silks, muslins, calicoes, coffee, and drugs. In the deserts are lions, tigers, leopards, and serpents of several kinds. The fruits are dates, figs, almonds, lemons, oranges, pomegranates, and many others. There is also much flax and hemp, but very little timber. The emperor is absolute, his will being a law; and he often exercises great cruelties. He can bring 100,000 men into the field, half of whom are foot and half horse; but they are poorly armed, and know little of the art of war. The occupation of Algier by the French will no doubt change the political character of this despotic government.

MOROCCO, a city of the foregoing empire; seated in a beautiful valley, formed by a chain of mountains on the N. and those of Atlas on the S. and E. Though not equal to Fez in magnitude and population, it is generally considered the capital, being the most usual residence of the emperor. It has nothing to recommend it but its great extent, and the royal palace. It is surrounded by strong walls: 8 miles in circumference. The mosques are very numerous, and some of them magnificent. The best houses are enclosed in gardens; but the generality of them serve only to impress the traveller with the idea of a miserable and deserted city. The Jews, who are numerous, have a separate town, walled in, and under the charge of an alcaid, appointed by the emperor. It has two gates, which are regularly shut every evening at nine; after which hour no person can enter or depart. Morocco is 90 miles E. of Mogodor, and 400 S. of Gibraltar. Long. 7. 35. 30. W. lat. 31. 37. 31. N.

Moron, a town of Spain, in Andalusia; with a castle; near it is a mine of precious stones. It is 30 miles S. E. of Seville.

Morotoi, one of the Sandwich Islands; 7 miles W. N. W. of Mowee. Yams are its principal produce; but it has little wood. The coast, on the S. and W. sides, forms several bays. Long. 117. 14. W. lat. 21. 10. N.

Morpeth, a borough in Northumberland; market on Saturday. It stands on the N. bank of the Wansbeck; and on the opposite side are the parish church and the ruins of a castle. Here are also a chapel of ease; a Roman Catholic chapel, two meeting-houses, a free grammar-school founded by Edward VI.; an English free school, erected in 1792; a dispensary, opened in 1817; and a mechanics' institute, commenced in 1825. The other principal buildings are the town-hall, and the new county gaol, house of correction, &c. It returns one member to parliament. It is 15 miles N. of Newcastle, and 289 N. by W. of London.

Morris, a county in the state of New Jersey; bounded by Bergen, Essex, Somerset, Hunterdon, and Sussex counties. Pop. 25,844.

Morristown, the capital of Morris county, has two churches, an academy, &c. It is 28 miles N. W. of New York.

Morsona, a town of Naples; in the Molise; 14 miles N. E. of Molise.

Mortagne, a town of France; department of Orne; famous for its serges and tanneries. It is 19 miles E. N. E. of Alençon, and 70 W. S. W. of Paris. Pop. 5800.

Mortagne, a town in the department of Nord; seated at the conflux of the Scarpe and Scheldt; 8 miles S. E. of Tournay.

Mortagne, a town in the department of Lower Charente; on the Gironde; 24 miles S. S. W. of Saintes.

Mortagne, a town in the department of Vendee, where a battle was fought between the royalists and republicans, in 1793; in which the former are said to have lost 20,000 men. It is 36 miles N. of Fontenay le Compte.

Mortain, a town in the department of Manche; on the rivulet Lances; almost surrounded by craggy rocks; 18 miles E. of Avranches.

Mortara, a town of the Sardinian Milanese; 22 miles S. W. of Milan.

Mortay, or Martero, an island in the Eastern Seas; formerly subject to the sultan of Ternate. It is 80 miles in circumference, and thinly inhabited, but full of sago trees, which are cut by the people of Gilolo. Long. 128. 23. E. lat. 2. 15. N.

Mortlach, a village of Scotland; in Banffshire. The ancient cathedral is now used as the parish church, 6 miles S. W. of Keith.

Morviedro, a town of Spain in Valencia; on the site of the ancient Saguntum; with the ruin of a Roman amphitheatre, &c. It is seated on a river of the same name; 15 miles N. of Valencia.

Mosa, a town of Arabia; in Yemen; 25 miles N. by E. of Mocha.

Mosambique, a strait or channel of the Indian Ocean: between the E. coast of Africa and the island of Madagascar. It is narrowest in the middle, where it is 240 miles over.

Mosambique, a city and seaport; the principal settlement of the Portuguese on the E. coast of Africa. It stands on an island of the same name, not more than 3 miles in length, and half as much in breadth, and about 2 miles from the continent. The city is handsome, and the buildings well constructed, especially the churches and convents; the fort, or castle, is about a musket-shot from the city. The Portuguese have generally a good garrison here, a well-stored magazine, and a large hospital for sick sailors. Their ships always call here in going to the East Indies; and the harbour is so commodious, that whole fleets may anchor and provide themselves with all necessaries. Pop. 2800. Long. 41. 8. E. lat. 15. 5. S.

Mosbach, a town of Germany, in the grand duchy of Baden; with a castle, and manufactures of cloth and salt; seated on the Neckar; 18 miles E. of Heidelberg.

Mosburg, a town of Bavaria; seated at the conflux of the Amber with the Iser; 24 miles N. E. of Munich.

Moscovy. *See* Russia.

Moscow, formerly a duchy, but now a government of Russia; bounded on the N. by the government of Tver, E. by that of Great Volodimir, S. by the government of Kaluga and Resan, and W. by those of Tver and Smolensko. It is a fruitful country; and a considerable portion is laid out in gardens and orchards. Area, 10,000 square miles. Pop. 1,126,000.

Moscow, the capital of the above government, and formerly o the whole empire. Previous to the entry of the French, it was the largest city in Europe, the circumference within the rampart that inclosed the suburbs being 20 miles: but its population did not correspond with its extent. It contained within the ramparts 300,000 souls, and was the most populous city in the empire, notwithstanding the residence of the court was at Petersburg. Moscow is rendered memorable in history, for one of the most extraordinary events that ever took place. In June, 1812, the French entered Russia with such an immense army, that they threatened to sweep every thing before them like a torrent; and it was generally expected that if they once reached this city, which would afford vast resources for their army, as well as comfortable quarters for the winter, the object of the war would have been completed. On the 8th of September, the battle of Borodino took place; victory decided in favour of the French; and the Russians retreated off the field, leaving Moscow to its fate. The road being thus left open, the French entered this city on the 14th of the same month, with little opposition. But a sad reverse of fortune now took place, which preserved the Russian empire from ruin, and paved the way to the downfall of the French military power over Europe. Count Rostopchin, the governor, had formed the desperate resolution of setting the city on fire; which was so completely carried into effect, at the time the French had taken possession, that they were foiled in their last resource, and compelled to attempt their retreat, at the moment they thought themselves securely entrenched for the winter. Nothing now remained but to offer terms of peace to the Russians, which were rejected; they next proposed an armistice, which was refused; and, on the 19th of October following, they commenced their calamitous retreat from Moscow. The conflagration destroyed upwards of three parts of the town; and, shocking to relate, more than 30,000 sick and wounded soldiers, who were in the hospitals, perished in the flames. The old city was distributed into five divisions, all of which, not excepting the suburbs, have been rebuilt, with wider streets and greater uniformity in the private dwellings; and the population has nearly reached its former magnitude. The divisions are—1. The Kremlin, in the central and highest part of the city, surrounded by high walls of stone and brick, two miles in circumference. This division contained the ancient palace of the czars, where Peter the Great was born; also the cathedral with seven towers, besides other churches, the patriarchal palace, and the arsenal. The palace escaped the conflagration of 1812, but was damaged by the French on their leaving Moscow; it has since been rebuilt, with improvements. 2. The Khitagorod, much larger than the Kremlin, contained the university, the printing-house, and many other public buildings, with all the tradesmen's shops. 3. The Bielgorod, or White Town, ran round the two preceding divisions, and took its name from a white wall, by which it was formerly surrounded. 4. The Semlainogorod environed all the other three quarters, and was so denominated from a circular rampart of earth by which it was encompassed. The last two divisions exhibited a grotesque group of churches, convents, palaces, brick and wooden houses, and mean hovels. 5. The Sloboda, or suburbs, formed a vast exterior circle round all the parts already described, and were invested by a low rampart and ditch. These suburbs contained, besides buildings of all kinds, orchards, gardens, corn-fields, much open pasture, and some small lakes, which give rise to the Neglina. The Moskwa, from which the city takes its name, flows through it in a winding channel; but, excepting in spring, is only navigable for rafts. It receives the Yausa in the Semlainogorod, and the Neglina at the western extremity of the Kremlin; but the beds of both these rivulets are nearly dry in summer. Moscow exhibited an astonishing degree of extent and variety, irregularity and contrast; some parts had the appearance of a sequestered desert; others of a populous town; some of a contemptible village; others of a great capital. The streets, in general, were very long and broad: some of them paved; others, particularly in the suburbs, were formed with trunks of trees, or boarded with planks like the floor of a moor. The places of divine worship, including chapels, amounted to above 1500: of these, 484 were public churches, some built of brick, stuccoed or white-washed, but the greater part were of wood, painted red; some had domes of copper, others of tin, gilt or painted green, and many were roofed with wood. They were richly ornamented within; and the pictures of the saints were decorated with gold, silver, and precious stones. Some of their bells were of stupendous size: they hung in belfries detached from the church, were fixed immovably to the beams, and rung by a rope tied to the clapper. In the cathedral of St. Michael the sovereigns of Russia were formerly interred, their bodies being deposited in raised sepulchres, in the shape of coffins, above the pavement. The cathedral of the Assumption of the Virgin Mary was the most magnificent in the city, and had long been appropriated to the coronation of the Russian sovereigns. The foundling hospital, founded by Catherine II., was an immense pile of building, of a quadrangular shape, and capable of containing 8000 foundlings. Since the fire, the churches and chapels are less numerous than before, but those which have been rebuilt occupy the former sites. Moscow is the centre of the inland commerce of Russia, particularly connecting the trade between Europe and Siberia. The principal manufactures are those of silk, linen, cotton, paper, leather, and sugar. The navigation to this city is formed by the Moskwa, which flows into the Occa, near Kolomna, and that river communicates with the Volga and also by a canal to the Don, which river communicates with the sea of Asoph; 425 miles S. E. of Petersburg. Long. 37. 33. E. lat. 55. 46. N. Pop. 349,068.

Moselle, a department of France, including part of the former province of Lorrain. It takes its name from a river which rises in the Vosges, waters Epinal and Toul, receives the Meurthe below Nancy, and, passing by Metz, Thionville, and Treves, enters the Rhine at Coblentz. Pop. 409,000. Metz is the capital.

Mosenia, a town of Persia, in Khusistan; 22 miles S. W. of Suter.

Moskirch, a town of Germany; in the grand duchy of Baden, where the Austrians sustained a defeat in 1800; 22 miles N. of Stutgard.

Moskoe, an island on the coast of Norway,

separated from the mainland by the Vestfiord. On its coast is the whirlpool of MAELSTROM (which see).

MOSQUITO SHORE, a tract of country on the eastern coast of Honduras. It is well watered by navigable rivers and lakes; abounds in fish, game, and provisions of all sorts. It is now included in the Mexican republic. *See* MEXICO.

MOSS, a seaport of Norway, in the government of Aggerhuys; at the mouth of a river of its name, on the E. side of Christiania Bay. Here are many saw-mills, and a large iron foundry; 28 miles S. of Christiania. Long. 10. 48. E. lat. 58. 38. N.

MOSSULA, a town of the kingdom of Congo, at the mouth of the Onzo; 220 miles S. W. of St. Salvador. Long. 12. 10. lat. 7. 50. S.

MOSTAR, a seaport of Dalmatia, and a Greek archbishop's see; seated on the Narenza; 20 miles N. E. of Narenza. Long. 18. 37. E. lat. 43. 48. N.

MOSUL, a town of Asiatic Turkey; in Diarbeck; surrounded by high walls and defended by a castle and citadel. The houses are in several places gone to ruin; but it has a great trade, particularly in cloth, and all sorts of cottons and silks. At some distance from Mosul is a mosque, in which they pretend the prophet Jonah lies; on the opposite bank of the river is the village of Nunia, probably occupying the site of the ancient Nineveh. It is seated on the Tigris; 130 miles S. E. of Diarbekir, and 190 N. E. of Bagdad. Long. 43. 30. E. lat. 36. 20. N.

MOTIR, one of the Molucca Islands; 20 miles in circumference, and valuable for its spices. Long. 127. 0. E. lat. 0. 10. N.

MOTRIL, a seaport of Spain, in Granada; with a good harbour; seated on the Mediterranean; 37 miles S. E. of Granada. Long. 3. 28. W. lat. 36. 32. N.

MOTTA, a town of Austrian Italy, in the Trevisano; at the conflux of the Mottigano and Livenza; 18 miles N. E. of Treviso.

MOTTA, a town of Naples, in Capitanata; 3 miles E. S. E. of Volturara.

MOTTLING. *See* METLING.

MOUAB, a town of Arabia, in Yemen; and the residence of a prince; seated in a fertile country; 90 miles S. E. of Sana. Long. 46. 35. E. lat. 14. 20. N.

MOUDON, a town of Switzerland, in the canton of Vaud; with a castle on the summit of a mountain; 12 miles N. N. E. of Lausanne.

MOULINS, a town of France, capital of the department of Allier. Its manufacture of cutlery is in great esteem; and the houses of the late Chartreux, and of the Visitation, are magnificent. It is seated on the Allier, over which is a fine bridge; 30 miles S. of Nevers, and 225 S. S. E. of Paris. Pop. 14,000. Long. 3. 20. E. lat. 46. 34. N.

MOULINS EN GILBERT, a town in the department of Nievre, at the foot of the mountains of Morvan; 5 miles S. W. of Chateau Chinon.

MOULTAN, a province of Hindostan; bounded by Lahors, Afghanistan, Agimere, Sinde, and Beloochistan. Its products are cotton, sugar, opium, galls, sulphur, &c. In many parts there are fine camels, and a breed of excellent horses. It is governed by an independent prince, protected by the shah of Cabool.

MOULTAN, the capital of the above province, surrounded with a fine wall 40 feet high, and four miles in circumference, is strongly fortified, and has a Hindoo temple of great celebrity. It is famous for its silks and carpets, and is situate in a pleasant and well cultivated district, 4 miles S. E. of the Chenaub, or Acesines River, and 210 N. W. of Lahore. Long. 70. 40. E. lat. 20. 52. N.

MOUNT BAY, a bay in the English Channel, on the S. coast of Cornwall, between the Land's End and the Lizard Point. Within rises a lofty peninsulated rock, called Mount St. Michael, near the town Marazion, to which there is a dry passage at low water.

MOUNT DESERT, a fertile island on the coast of the state of Maine; in Hancock county; 15 miles long, and 12 broad.

MOUNT HOLLY, a town of New Jersey; capital of Burlington county; on the N. side of Anocous Creek; 7 miles S. E. of Burlington.

MOUNT VERNON, the capital of Knox county, Ohio; seated on Owl Creek.—Also the name of several townships and villages.

MOUNTMELLICK, a town of Ireland, in Queen's county, inhabited principally by Quakers. The wool-combing, malting, and tanning businesses, the cotton manufacture, and bleaching, are carried on here. It is seated on a stream which falls into the Barrow; 5 miles N. of Maryborough, and 42 W. S. W. of Dublin.

MOUNTRATH, a town of Ireland, in Queen's county. In its neighbourhood are some iron-works; but the woollen manufacture forms the principal trade; 23 miles N. of Kilkenny, and 47 W. S. W. of Dublin.

MOUNTSORREL, a town in Leicestershire; with a market on Monday; seated on the Soar, at the foot of a high mount or rock, of a sorrel-coloured stone, with which the town is chiefly built and paved. It is 7 miles N. of Leicester, and 102 N. W. of London.

MOURA, a town of Portugal, in Alentejo; with an old castle; 34 miles S. S. E. of Evora. Population, 4000.

MOURAON, a town of Portugal, in Alentejo; with a castle; on the borders of Spain; 28 miles E. by S. of Evora.

MOURZOUK, the capital of Fezzan; with a fortress, in which is the sultan's palace. It is situate on a rivulet, and supplied with water from a multitude of springs and wells. The medley which it presents to the eye, of the vast ruins of ancient buildings, and the humble cottages of earth and sand that form the dwellings of the present Arab inhabitants, is singularly grotesque and strange. It is surrounded by a high wall, with three gates, at which is collected a tax on all goods (provisions excepted) that are brought into the city. Its commerce, which is considerable, consists of foreign merchandise brought by the caravans from Cairo, Bornou, Mesurata, and other smaller troops of traders. Mourzouk is 290 miles S. of Mesurata, and 700 N. W. of Bornou. Long. 15. 35. E. lat. 27. 54. N.

MOUSTIERS, a town of France, in the department of Lower Alps; with a manufacture of porcelain; seated between two craggy mountains; 9 miles E. of Riez.

MOUZON, a town in the department of Ardennes; with a manufacture of serges, seated on the Meuse; 9 miles S. E. of Sedan.

MOWEE, or MAUI, one of the Sandwich islands, 162 miles in circumference. A low isthmus divides it into two circular peninsulas, of which the eastern is double the size of the western. The mountains in both rise to a great height, but the country presents an appearance of verdure and fertility. Near the W. point of the smaller peninsula is a spacious bay, with a sandy beach shaded with cocoa-nut trees. Long. 175. 56. W. lat. 20. 53. N.

MOYALLEN, a town of Ireland, in the county of Down, with a manufacture of linen; 3 miles from Portadown, and 63 from Dublin.

MOYENVIC, a town of France, in the department of Meurthe; noted for its salt spring; 2 miles E. S. E. of Vic, and 16 E. of Nancy.

MOZYR, a town of Russian Lithuania, in the government of Minsk; on the river Pryne; 150 miles S. S. E. of Minsk. Long. 29. 30. E. lat. 52. 10. N.

MOSCISLAW, a town of Russian Lithuania, in the government of Mohilef; formerly the capital of a palatinate. It is seated on the Sofz; 30 miles S. of Smolensko, and 64 E. by N. of Mohilef. Long. 32. 32. E. lat. 54. 28. N.

MUCIDAN, a town of France, in the department of Dordogne; on the river Ille; 18 miles S. W. of Perigueux.

MUCK, one of the Hebrides of Scotland; 4 miles S. W. of that of Egg. It is 3 miles long, and a mile broad; the soil in general is good, and the black cattle thrive well. Kelp is burnt on its shores, and much oil extracted from the livers of the sunfish.

MUDANIA, or MOUDANIEH, a town of Asiatic Turkey, in Natolia; on a gulf of the sea of Marmora. The commerce is very considerable in grain, fruit, wine, saltpetre, silk, and the manufactures of Broussa, which are brought here for exportation. It is 17 miles N. of Broussa. Long. 29. 10. E. lat. 40. 27. N.

MUGELN, NEW, a town of Saxony, in Meissen; with a castle, called Rugethal; 18 miles W. by N. of Meissen.

MUGIA, a town of Spain, in Galicia, on the W. coast; 40 miles W. N. W. of Compostella.

MUGLIA, a town of Austrian Illyria; in Istria, with a castle, and a harbour for barges; 5 miles S. E. of Trieste.

MUGLITZ, a town of Moravia, in the circle of Olmutz; 22 miles N. N. W. of Olmutz.

MUHLBERG, a town of Prussian Saxony, in the government of Merseberg, with a castle; situate on the Elbe; 30 miles N. W. of Dresden.

MUHLDORF, a town of Bavaria, on the Inn; 23 miles S. S. E. of Landschut.

MUIRKIRK, a town of Scotland, in Ayrshire, with manufactures of iron and coal tar; on the river Ayr; 26 miles E. of Ayr.

MUJAXAR, a seaport of Spain, in Granada; with a strong castle on a mountain; seated on a bay of the Mediterranean; 40 miles N. E. of Almeria. Long. 1. 55. W. lat. 37. 7. N.

MULDAU, or MOLDAU, a river of Bohemia, which rises on the confines of Bavaria, and, after receiving a number of rivers, enters the Elbe, opposite Melnick.

MULHAUSEN, a city of Prussian Saxony, in the government of Erfurt. It was formerly an imperial city, but fell to Prussia in 1802, and was confirmed to that power in 1814. Here are various manufactures, and some flourishing schools. It is seated in a fertile country, on the Unstrut; 29 miles N. W. of Erfurt. Pop. 9400. Long. 10. 37. E. lat. 51. 10. N.

MULHAUSEN, a town of France, in the department of Upper Rhine; with manufactures of printed linens and cottons; seated in a fertile plain on the Ille, 24 miles S. of Colmar.

MULIVADDY, a river of Ceylon, which rises at the foot of a high mountain called Adam's Peak, about 60 miles N. E. of Colombo, flows westward, and enters the sea by several branches, 3 miles from Colombo.

MULL, one of the Hebrides of Scotland, 28 miles in length, and in some places of equal breadth, separated from the mainland of Argyleshire by a narrow passage, called the Sound of Mull. There are many good natural harbours, and the ruins of several ancient castles are to be seen. The soil is for the most part rocky and barren, but the hills abound with springs, and are covered with sheep and cattle; these, with the fishery, and a considerable quantity of kelp, are the articles of commerce. The only town is Tobermory.

MULLINGAR, a town of Ireland, capital of West Meath. It is a place of good trade. It stands on the river Foyle, 38 miles W. of Dublin. Long. 7. 50. W. lat. 53. 30. N.

MULLUVIA, a river which rises in Mount Atlas, divides the empire of Morocco from Algier, and runs into the Mediterranean sea.

MULROSE, a town of the Prussian province of Brandenburg, seated on a canal cut between the Spree and Oder; 10 miles S. W. of Frankfort.

MUNCHBERG, a town of Bavarian Franconia, in the principality of Bayreuth, 16 miles E. of Culmbach.

MUNCHENBERG, a town of Prussia, in Brandenburg, with silk and woollen manufactures; 34 miles E. of Berlin.

MUNDA, a town of Spain, in Granada, 30 miles W. N. W. of Malaga.

MUNDEN, a town of Hanover, in the duchy of Brunswick, situate on the Werra, at the influx of the Fulda, where their united streams form the Weser. Good millstones are found in the neighbourhood of the town. In the war of 1756 it was several times in the hands of the French, by whom it was again occupied in 1805. It is 10 miles N. E. of Cassel, and 13 S. W. of Gottingen.

MUNDERKINGEN, a town of Germany, in Wirtemberg, seated on the Danube; 9 miles N. of Buchau.

MUNDU, a town of Hindostan, capital of a district of the same name, extending from 22. to 23. N. lat., in the province of Malwah. It was anciently the capital of the province, and was then 22 miles in circuit, and contained many monuments of ancient magnificence; but it is fallen much to decay. It occupies the top of a large and lofty mountain, 25 miles S. of Ougein, and 110 N. N. W. of Burhanpour. Long. 75. 47. E. lat. 22. 50. N.

MUNGLORE, a town of Afghanistan, in the province of Cabul, 125 miles W. of Cashmere, and 135 E. of Cabul. Long. 71. 15. E. lat. 34. 15. N.

MUNGULHAUT, a town of Bengal, with a manufacture of coarse cotton cloths, situate on the Durlah; 20 miles N. N. E. of Rungpour.

MUNICH, one of the finest towns in Germany, and capital of the kingdom of Bavaria. It contains nearly 70,000 inhabitants. The houses are high, and the streets spacious, with canals in many of them. The palace is a stupendous structure, the interior magnificently adorned; and the cabinet of curiosities, the museum, the library, and the arsenal, merit attention. The cathedral of Notre Dame contains the tomb of one of the emperors, of black marble, adorned with statues of bronze. Institutions for charitable, literary, and scientific purposes are numerous. The large market-place, in which is the town-house, is very beautiful. Manufactures of silk, velvet, woollen cloth, and tapestry are carried on. Near the city are two other palaces, Nymphenburg and Schlesheim. Munich has often suffered in the wars of Germany, and in 1796 and 1800 it was taken by the French. It is seated on the Iser, 33 miles E. S. E. of Augsburg, and 62 S. by W. of Ratisbon. Long. 11. 30. E. lat. 48. 10. N.

MUNKACS. *See* MONTGATZ.

MUNNERSTADT, a town of Germany, in Franconia; situate on the Lauer; 13 miles N. of Schweinfurt.

MUNNYPOUR, a town of Birmah; capital of the province of Cassay; 210 miles N. N. W. of Ummerapoora, and 410 E. by N. of Calcutta. Long. 94. 40. E. lat. 24. 30. N.

MUNSINGEN, a town of Germany, in the kingdom of Wirtemberg; with a castle; 20 miles W. of Ulm.

MUNSTER, a province of Ireland, 135 miles long, and 120 broad; bounded on the N. by Connaught, E. by Leinster, and S. and W. by the Atlantic. It contains the counties of Clare, Tipperary, Waterford, Cork, Limerick, and Kerry, and 820 parishes. The principal place is Cork.

MUNSTER, a government of the Prussian province of Westphalia. It contains 2820 square miles, and is divided into 10 circles or districts; Munster Proper, Tecklenburg, Wahrendorf, Beckum, Ludinghausen, Koesfeld, Recklinghausen, Berken, Ahans, and Steinfurt. Pop. 328,000. The chief rivers are the Ems and Lippe. The country is level, with some agreeable heights, but no mountains; and it has fruitful plains, fine woods, extensive heaths, that feed much cattle, and good quarries of stone. This government consists, for the greater part, of the ancient bishopric of its name, which, on the secularization of church property, in 1802, was divided between Prussia, the duke of Oldenburg, and several other princes, all of whom became subject to Prussia in 1815.

MUNSTER, the capital of the foregoing government. The cathedral, the library of the chapter, and many antiquities, are worthy of notice. In 1535, a tailor, called John of Leyden, king of the anabaptists, made himself master of the city; but it was retaken in 1536, after 14 months' siege, when John and two of his associates were tortured to death with red-hot pincers. The famous treaty, called the Treaty of Westphalia, which ended the 30 years' war, was concluded here in 1648. In the war of 1756 this city sustained several sieges, and was taken in 1759. In 1806 the French laid the inhabitants under a heavy contribution, and stripped the churches of their plate. Munster is seated on the Aa; 50 miles E. N. E. of Wesel, and 52 W. N. W. of Paderborn. Population, 13,000. Long. 7. 36. E. lat. 51. 58. N.

MUNSTER, a town of Switzerland; in the canton of Lucerne; 12 miles N. N. W. of Lucerne.

MUNSTER, a town of Switzerland; in the canton of Grisons; 15 miles N. of Bormio.

MUNSTER, a town of France, in the department of Upper Rhine; 6 miles W. of Colmar.

MUNSTER EYFFEL, a town of the Prussian states, in Westphalia; 16 miles S. S. W. of Cologne.

MUNSTER MEINFELD, a town of the Prussian province of Lower Rhine; 12 miles S. W. of Coblentz.

MUNSTER, NEW. *See* ZEALAND, NEW.

MUNSTERBERG, a town of Prussian Silesia; in the government of Reichenbach; rich in grain, flax, hemp, and hops. It is seated on the Ohlau; 13 miles N. W. of Neisse. Long. 17. 3. E. lat. 50. 31. N.

MUR, or MUHR, a river which rises in the duchy of Salzburg, crosses Styria, and falls into the Drave, near Canischa, in Hungary.

MUR DE BABREZ, a town of France, in the department of Aveiron; 32 miles N. by E. of Rhodez.

MURANO, a town of the Lombardo-Venetian kingdom; on an island of the same name; one of the largest of the Lagunes of Venice. Here the famous Venetian looking-glasses are made. It is 3 miles N. by E. of Venice.

MURAT, a town of France, in the department of Cantal; seated on the Alaignon, near the source; 13 miles N. W. of St. Flour.

MURCIA, a province of Spain; bounded N. by New Castile, E. by Valencia, W. by Andalusia and Granada, and S. by the Mediterranean. It is 90 miles long, and 58 broad; and the principal river is the Segura. The soil is dry, and it produces little corn or wine; but oranges, citrons, lemons, olives, almonds, mulberries, rice, pulse, and sugar are plentiful. It has also a great deal of silk. The vale of Murcia is celebrated for the variety and richness of its culture. Population, 384,000.

Murcia, the capital of the foregoing province; and a bishop's see. The inhabitants are computed at 60,000. A number of hands are employed in the working of bassweed, and there is also an extensive establishment for twisting silk, and a refinery of saltpetre. There are fine gardens about the city, in which are the best fruits in Spain. It is seated on the Segura, over which is a bridge; 27 miles N. of Carthagena, and 212 S. E. of Madrid. Long. 1. 16. W. lat. 37. 58. N.

Murfreesborough, a flourishing town of Tennessee; in Rutherford county; seated on an eminence in a fertile district; 32 miles S. E. of Nashville. Pop. 1000.

Muro, a town of Naples, in Basilicata; seated at the foot of the Apennines; 12 miles S. E. of Conza.

Muros, a town of Spain, in Galicia, at the mouth of the Tambro; 29 miles W. by S. of Compostella.

Murray, or Moray Frith, a considerable inlet of the sea, on the coast of Scotland, between Tarbetness, in Ross-shire, on the N., and Brough-Head, in Murrayshire, on the S. It extends in a S. W. direction as far as Inverness, and thence W. to the town of Beaulie, where it receives the river of that name.

Murrayshire, or Morayshire, or Elginshire, a county of Scotland; 50 miles in length, and 20 along the coast; bounded on the N. by the Frith of Murray, E. by Banffshire, S. by Inverness-shire, and W. by that county and Nairnshire. It is divided into 18 parishes. The S. part is mountainous, and occupied by forests; but the greater part is rich, and produces wheat, barley, oats, and flax. The chief rivers are the Spey, Findhorn, and Lossie. The county town is Elgin. Elgin and Nairnshires return one member to parliament.

Murten. *See* Morat.

Musa, a walled town of Arabia, in Yemen; 18 miles E. of Mocha.

Muska, a town of Prussia, in Upper Lusatia; with a castle; seated on the Neisse; 25 miles N. N. W. of Gorlitz, and 52 N. E. of Dresden.

Muskat. *See* Mascat.

Muskingum, a river of the state of Ohio, which runs S. into the Ohio, at Marietta, where it is 280 yards wide. *See* Cayahoga.

Musselburgh, a seaport of Scotland, in Edinburghshire, near the mouth of the Esk, over which are three bridges to the suburb of Fisherrow. It enjoys many privileges, and has 7 incorporated trades. Besides the parish church, here are an episcopal chapel and four other places of worship. The principal manufactures are of salt, sail-cloth, hair-cloth, and netting. It is 5½ miles E. of Edinburgh, to which it is connected by a railway to its suburb of Musselburgh. It unites with Leith and Portobello in sending 1 member to parliament.

Mustagam, or Mostaganem, a seaport of Algier, in the province of Tremecen, with three castles; 140 miles W. S. W. of the city of Algier. Long. 0. 30. E. lat. 36. 20. N.

Musuela, a town of Spain, in Andalusia; situate on the river Guadalquiver, 7 miles N. E. of Jean, and 50 N. of Granada.

Muteodu, a town of Hindostan, in Mysore; noted for its manufacture of the glass used for making the rings which are worn on the wrists of the native women. It is 3[illegible] miles W. of Sera.

Muyden, a fortified town of the Netherlands, in S. Holland; seated on the Zuyder Zee, at the influx of the Vecht. It is 6 miles E. S. E. of Amsterdam.

Myconi, an island of the Grecian Archipelago; 30 miles in circumference. The soil is dry, and the mountains are of great height. Here are plenty of partridges, quails, woodcocks, turtledoves, rabbits, and wheatears; also excellent grapes and figs. The harbour is open, and deep enough for the largest ships to ride secure from the N. wind. Long. 25. 21. E. lat. 37. 38. N.

Mysol, one of the Moluccas, of a triangular form, with a bold shore. The villages are built in the water upon posts; and there are forests visited by the birds of paradise, which are caught in great numbers. Long. 130. 0. E. lat. 2. 0. S.

Mysore, an extensive province of Hindostan, lying between 11. and 15. N. lat., and now surrounded by the British territories of the Madras Presidency, while the existing rajah is also dependent on British protection. The country is in general dry, rugged, mountainous, and barren; but there are several rivers and mountain torrents, which by artificial means, serve to water rice-grounds, gardens, &c. In the forests are many elephants, and tigers are common. Oxen, buffaloes, and goats are numerous, and in the N. E. part many sheep are bred; but horses and asses are few. The chief products are rice, cotton, pepper, cocoa, and betelnut; sugar-cane, butter, and oil. The whole of this country, with some other territories to the N. and E., and the provinces of Coimbetore, Malabar, and Canara, were subdued by Hyder Ali, a mussulman, who usurped the throne of Mysore, in 1759, and made Seringapatam his capital. He was succeeded by Tippoo Sultan, who continued his father's state of warfare. On the termination of a war, in 1792, Tippoo agreed to pay thirty lacs of rupees, and to cede one half of his dominions to the English and their allies, the Mahrattas and the nizam of the Deccan. In 1799, a new war taking place, his capital was taken by the English on the 4th of May, and himself killed in the assault. A partition of his remaining territories took place, and on the 30th of June following, Kistna Rajah, then only five years old, was placed by the British on the throne of his forefathers. The dominions of the rajah of Mysore are now divided into three great districts; Patana, to the S., Nagara, to the N. W., and Chatrakal to the N. E.; so called from the three places where the chief officers are situate. The Patana district is by far the largest, and of itself comprises a much greater extent of territory than was ever before subject to the Mysore family.

Mysore, the capital of the foregoing province, was ruined by Tippoo Sultan; but since the English restored the ancient family, in 1799, and made it the rajah's seat of government, the town and fortress have been rebuilt, and the population is rapidly increasing. Mysore is 10 miles S. of Seringapatam. Long. 76. 50. E. lat. 12. 15. N.

Mytilene. *See* Metelin.

Myton, a town in N. Yorkshire, 2 miles from Aldborough.

N.

Naas, a town of Ireland, in the county of Kildare; where the assizes are held alternately with Athy. It was anciently the residence of the kings of Leinster. It is 17 miles S. W. of Dublin. Long. 6. 42. W. lat. 53. 13. N.

Nab, a river of Germany, which flows S. through the kingdom of Bavaria, and enters the Danube a little above Ratisbon.

Nabal, a town of the kingdom of Tunis; celebrated for its potteries. Near it are several remains of antiquity. It is seated near the sea, 32 miles S. S. E. of Tunis. Long. 10. 19. E. lat. 53. 13. N.

Nabburg, a town of Bavaria, on the river Nab; 10 miles E. S. E. of Amberg.

Nablous, (anciently Neapolis,) a town of Palestine, capital of a country which was the ancient kingdom of Samaria. It is the residence of a scheik, who farms the tribute to the pacha of Damascus. Here is considerable trade, and the manufactures flourish more than in most cities of the east. The soil of the surrounding country is fertile, and produces a great deal of corn, cotton, olives, and some silk. Nablous is 24 miles N. of Jerusalem, and 90 S. S. W. of Damascus. Long. 35. 24. E. lat. 32. 20. N.

Naco, a town of S. America, in Mexico, 50 miles N. W. of Valladolid.

Nadir, a town of Egypt, on the W. branch of the Nile; 28 miles N. N. W. of Cairo.

Naefels, a tn. of Switzerland, in the canton of Glarus, near which, in 1388, an unparalleled victory was obtained by 350 troops of Glarus, assisted by 50 Schweitzers, over 15,000 Austrians. In memory of his heroic achievement, a chapel was built on the spot, which was re-built in 1779. It is 4 miles N. of Glarus.

Naerden, a strong town of the Netherlands, in S. Holland, at the head of the canals of the province, of which it is considered the key. In 1572 it was taken by Fernande de Toledo, son of the Duke of Alva, and all the inhabitants were massacred. In 1672 it was taken by the French, and retaken by the Prince of Orange, the following year. It is seated on the Zuyder Zee, 14 miles E. S. E. of Amsterdam. Long. 5. 11. E. lat. 52. 19. N.

Nagamangala, a town of Hindostan, in Mysore, with a citadel in the centre, both fortified with mud walls, In the outer town, a wide street extends all round, with short lanes on each side of the outer and inner wall. In the fort are two large temples and a ruinous palace. It is 30 miles N. of Seringapatan.

Nagara, or Hyder-nagara, a city of Hindostan, capital of the district of Bednore. It was formerly called Bidderuru, and by Europeans, Biddenore; but received its present name in 1763, on being taken by Hyder, who made it his principal arsenal, and a place of great magnitude and commerce. It afterwards declined, being neither the seat of a court nor of any public works, except the mint. In 1783 it was taken by the English and re-taken soon after Tippoo; but on his final defeat, in 1799, it was ceded by the English, to the rajah of Mysore. It is 70 miles N. by E. of Mangalore, and 150 N. W. of Seringapatam. Long. 75. 8. E. lat. 13. 48. N.

Nagaz, a town of Candahar, province of Cabul; on the Cowmull, 70 miles W. by N. of Attock, and 120 S. of Cabul.

Nagera, a town of Spain, in Old Castile, with a fort; 3 miles N. W. of Calahorra, and 138 N. of Madrid.

Nagold, a town of Germany, in the kingdom of Wirtemburg, with a ruined castle; situate on a river of the same name, 15 miles W. of Tubingen.

Nagore, a city of Hindostan, capital of a district of the same name, in the province of Agimere; 50 miles N. W. of Agimere. Long. 74. 15. E. lat. 27. 9. N.

Nagpore, a city of Hindostan, capital of the Eastern Mahratta territories. It is extensive and populous, but meanly built; and, excepting a small citadel, is open and defenceless; 500 miles W. by S. of Calcutta. Long. 79. 46. E. lat. 21. 9. N.

Nagpore, Chuta (or Little,) a district of Bahar, Hindostan, constituting the S. W. British frontier, and included in the collectorship of Ramghur. It is one of the wildest and least cultivated districts of British India.

Nagybanja, a town of Hungary, and one of the royal free towns. The gold and silver mines are of great produce, and money is coined here. It is 30 miles N. E. of Zatmar. Long. 22. 54. E. lat. 48. 10. N.

Nahe, a river of Germany, which rises in the territory of Treves, above Birkenfeld, and enters the Rhine at Bingen.

Nahn, a town of Delhi, Hindostan, capital of a district of the same name; and a place of considerable strength. It is the residence of a Hindoo chief, tributary to the rajah of Nepaul. Long. 77. 8. E. lat. 30. 41. N.

Nairn, a town of Scotland, and capital of Nairnshire, with a small harbour. It is seated at the mouth of a river of the same name, on the Murray Frith, 18 miles N. E. of Inverness, and 194 N. N. W. of Edinburgh. Long. 3. 6. W. lat. 57. 38. N.

Nairnshire, a county of Scotland, 15 miles

long, and 10 broad, bounded N. by the Murray Frith, and enclosed on every side by the counties of Inverness and Murray. It is divided into four parishes, and sends one member to parliament in conjunction with Murrayshire. The S. part is mountainous, but towards the N. it is level, and the soil abundantly fertile.

NAKSIVAN, or NAKSCHIVAN, a town of Persian Armenia, formerly a large city, but ruined by Abbas I. who removed the inhabitants into the interior parts of Persia. Here are now some considerable bazaars, caravanseras, baths, and other public buildings. It is 85 miles S. E. of Erivan, and 250 E. of Erzerum. Long. 45. 30. E. lat. 38. 40. N.

NAMAQUAS, a people of South Africa, a branch of the Hottentot race. *See* HOTTENTOTS.

NAMSLAU, a town of Prussian Silesia, with a castle. It is situate among morasses, on the river Weyda, 29 miles E. S. E. of Breslau.

NAMUR, a province of Belgium, 30 miles long, and 20 broad, bounded by the French frontier, and by the provinces of Hainault, South Brabant, and Liege. It is pretty fertile, and has several forests, marble quarries, and mines of iron, lead, and coal. The rivers Meuse and Sambre divide it into three parts, nearly of equal extent. Before the French Revolution of 1789, the greater part of this province belonged to Austria, and the remainder to France. In 1794 the whole was seized by the French, and constituted for 20 years part of the department of Sambre-et-Meuse, and was incorporated with the kingdom of the Netherlands in 1815.

NAMUR, the capital of the above province, and a bishop's see. It has a castle in the middle of The town, on a craggy rock, and several forts. the inhabitants are estimated at 20,000. Fire-arms, swords, knives, and many other kinds of cutlery are made here. This city was the scene of a sanguinary conflict, between the allies and the French, in June, 1815, and is noted in history as the scene of many early battles. It is seated between two mountains, at the confluence of the Maese and Sambre; 24 miles W. S. W. of Liege, and 32 S. E. of Brussels. Long. 4. 45. E. lat. 50. 29. N.

NANCY, a city of France, capital of the department of Meurthe and a bishop's see. It is divided by a canal into the Old and New Town. The former, though irregularly built, is rich and populous, and contains the palace of the ancient dukes of Lorrain; and their tombs are in a rich saloon, which adjoins the church of the late Cordeliers. The New Town, whose streets are perfectly straight, was one of the finest in Europe, even before the magnificent works with which Stanislaus I., titular king of Poland, and duke of Lorrain enriched it. The cathedral is a superb structure, and there are several other elegant churches. It was occupied by the allies in 1814. Nancy is seated in a delightful plain, near the river Meurthe; 30 miles S. of Metz. and 230 E. of Paris. Pop. 30,000. Long. 6. 10. E. lat. 48. 42. N.

NANDIDROOG, a strong fortress of Hindostan, in Mysore. Since the restoration of the rajah, in 1799, it has been garrisoned by English troops. It is 25 miles N. by E. of Bangalore, and 64 E. S. E. of Sera.

NANFIO, an island of the Grecian Archipelagos, a little to the E. of Santorini. It is 16 miles in circumference, but has no harbour, nor springs sufficient to water the fields. The inhabitants are all Greeks, and their chief trade is in onions, wax, and honey. The ruins of the temple of Apollo are yet to be seen, and consist chiefly of marble colums. Long. 26.10. E lat. 36. 15. N.

NANGASAKI, a city of Japan, in the island of Zimo, with a good harbour, and the only one in the empire in which foreign ships are permitted to anchor. The inhabitants carry on a great trade with the Chinese and Dutch. Long. 129. 46. E. lat. 32. 32. N.

NANGIS, a town of France, in the department of Seine-et-Marne; 12 miles W. of Provins.

NAN-KANG, a city of China, of the first rank, in the province of Kiang-si; seated on the lake Po-yang; 637 miles S. of Peking. Long. 113. 58. E. lat. 29. 33. N.

NANKING, a city of China, capital of the province of Kiang-nan. It is 17 miles in circumference, and about 3 miles distant from the great river Yang-tse-Kiang, from which canals are cut, so large that vessels may enter the town. It was formerly the imperial city, whence it is called Nanking, which signifies southern court; but, since the six grand tribunals have been removed to Peking, it is called Kiang-nan in all public acts. The place is greatly fallen from its ancient splendour; for it had a magnificent palace, which is quite destroyed, as well as many ancient monuments, and a third part of the city itself is desolate. The streets are narrow, but handsome and well paved; and on each side are shops neatly furnished. The public buildings are mean, except a few temples, the city gates, and a tower of porcelain 200 feet high. The inhabitants were formerly estimated at 2,000,000, the city being above 30 miles in circumference. The number at present is said to be 1,000,000, without comprehending the garrison of 40,000 men. They have several manufactures in silk and wood. Here the physicians have their principal academy. Nanking is seated on the Yang-tse-Kiang river, 500 miles S. S. E. of Peking. Long. 119. 25. E. lat. 32. 46. N.

NAN-NGAN, a city of China, of the first rank, in Kiang-si. It stands among plantations of sugar-cane, near the source of the Kan-kiang, and the foot of the mountain Me-lin; 200 miles N. E. of Canton. Long. 113. 38. E. lat. 24. 48. N.

NAN-NING, a city of China, of the first rank, in the province of Quang-si; 1145 miles S. S. W. of Peking. Long. 107. 45. E. lat. 22. 44. N.

NAN-TCHANG, a city of China, capital of Kiang-si. It has no trade but that of porcelain, which is made in the vicinity of Jaatcheou. The country is so much cultivated, that the pastures are barely sufficient for the flocks. It is seated on the Kan-kiang, which flows hence into the lake Poyang; 695 miles S. of Peking. Long. 115. 30. E. lat. 28. 36. N.

NANTES, a city of France, capital of the department of Lower Loire, and a bishop's see, with a university. It was formerly the residence of the dukes of Bretagne, who built a strong castle on the side of the river, which still exists. The cathedral contains the tombs of the ancient dukes, besides which there are a collegiate church and 11 parish churches. The bridges over the Loire, in which are some islands, are almost a league in length. The suburbs exceed the city in extent. A great quantity of salt is made in the territory of Nantes, both at the bay of Bourgneuf and in the salt marshes of Guerande and Croisic. Large vessels can come no higher than Port Laubai, which is 12 miles from Nantes. The inhabitants are computed at nearly 80,000. It was here that Henry IV. promulgated the famous edict, in 1598, in favour of the Protestants, which was revoked by Louis XIV. in 1685. Nantes is 58 miles S. by E. of Rennes, and 217 S. W. of Paris. Long. 1. 33. W. lat. 47. 13. N.

Nantua, a town of France, department of Ain; with manufactures of gauzes, taffetas, chintzes, &c.; situate on a lake of the same name; 18 miles E. of Bourg.

Nantucket, an island and county of the state of Massachusets, which lies 8 leagues S. of Cape Cod. It is 15 miles long and 11 broad, including Sandy Point, which makes a fine road for ships. A considerable whale fishery is carried on here; and there are several spermaceti works and a duck manufacture. It has also one town, now called Nantucket, but formerly Sherburne; 93 miles S. E. of Boston. Long. 70. 30. W. lat. 41. 20. N.

Nantwich, a town in Cheshire, with a market on Saturday. It has an elegant church, six meeting-houses, a free school, charity school, &c. The manufacture of salt was formerly considerable, but it is now confined to a single establishment; and the chief trade consists in the manufacture of shoes for the London and Manchester dealers. The principal dairies of Cheshire are about this town; and it has a considerable trade in cheese. It is seated on the Weaver, and by the Chester Canal, which here forms a broad basin; 20 miles S. E. of Chester, and 164 N. W. of London.

Nan-yang, a city of China, of the first rank, in the province of Ho-nan, seated on a small river, and surrounded by mountains; 160 miles S. of Ho-nan.

Nan-yong, a city of China, of the first rank, in the province of Quangtong, seated on the Peikiang, near its source; 170 miles N. N. E. of Canton.

Naples, or the Two Sicilies, a kingdom comprehending the S. part of Italy, bounded on the N. W. by the Ecclesiastical States, N. E. by the Gulf of Venice, and every where else by the Mediterranean. It is 300 miles in length by 100 in breadth, and is divided into 13 provinces; namely, Napoli or Naples, Terra di Lavoro (the ancient Campania Felix), Principato Citra and Ultra, Molise, Basilicáta, Calabria Citra and Ultra, Abruzzo Citra and Ultra, Capitanata, Terra di Bari, and Terra d'Otranto; the last three forming the ancient Apulia, now called Puglia, on the E. side of the kingdom. The climate in general is extremely hot, especially in July, August, and September, and is said to be one of the most inconstant and unfavourable to valetudinarians. In some seasons it rains every day for six or seven weeks together; but the most disagreeable part of the climate is the sirocco, or S. E. wind, which is very common in May, and extremely relaxing. In winter there is seldom any ice or snow, except on the mountains. The country abounds with grain, the finest fruits and vegetables, rice, flax, oil, wine, saffron, and manna, and affords alum, vitriol, sulphur, rock-crystal, marble, minerals, and fine wool and silk. Besides the manufactures noticed in the account of the city of Naples, waistcoats, caps, stockings, and gloves are also made of the hair or filaments of a shellfish, which are warmer than those of wool, and of a beautiful glossy green. The principal mountains are the Apennines (which traverse this country from N. to S. branching out to the two extremities), and the celebrated volcano, Mount Vesuvius. The rivers are numerous, but inconsiderable; the chief are the Garigliano and Volturno. One of the greatest inconveniences to which this kingdom is exposed is earthquakes. The established religion is the Roman Catholic; but Protestants and Jews are allowed to settle here.

Naples, a large and rich trading city of Italy, one of the finest in the world, capital of the above kingdom, with a university. It is situate at the bottom of a bay, and is built in the form of a vast amphitheatre, sloping from the hills to the sea. Although the style of architecture is inferior to what prevails at Rome, and it cannot vie with that city in the number of palaces, or in the magnificence of the public buildings, yet the private houses in general are better built, and the streets are broader and better paved. No street in Rome equals in beauty the Strada di Toledo at Naples; nor can any of them be compared with the beautiful streets which lie open to the bay, where the excessive heat of the sun is often tempered with the sea breezes and gales wafting the perfumes of the Campagni Felice. The houses in general are five or six stories high, and flat at the top; on which are placed numbers of flower vases, or fruit trees in boxes of earth, producing a very gay and agreeable effect. On the mountain St. Elmo, in a most pleasant situation, is a convent of Carthusians, on which much expense has been lavished, to render the building, the apartments, and the gardens, equal to the situation. Naples is admirably situated for commerce, and has all the necessaries and luxuries of life in great profusion. The chief articles manufactured here are silk stockings, soap, snuff-boxes of tortoise-shell, or of the lava of Mount Vesuvius, tables, and ornamental furniture of marble. They are thought to embroider here better than in France; and their macaroni is preferred to that of any part of Italy. They excel also in liquors and confections. The number of inhabitants is computed at 350,000, which is very probable; for, though Naples is not one-third of the size of London, yet many of the streets here are more crowded than the Strand, and a great proportion of the poorest sort are obliged to spend the night in them, as well as the day, for want of habitations. Although the churches and convents of Naples are not to be compared with those of Rome in point of architecture, they surpass them in rich jewels, and the quantity of silver and golden crucifixes, vessels, and other ornaments. The cathedral is a grand Gothic edifice; and of all the palaces that of the king is not only the most magnificent, but in the best style of architecture. The harbour, which is spacious, is protected by a mole. The bay of Naples is one of the finest in the world, being almost of a circular figure, about 30 miles in diameter, shut out from the Mediterranean by the island of Caprea, and three parts of it sheltered by a circuit of woods and mountains. Naples was taken by the French in January, 1799, but retaken by the British fleet under Lord Nelson, in the June following. In 1806 it was again taken possession of by the French, under Massena; soon after which Joseph Bonaparte was here crowned king of Naples; but on his removal to Spain, in 1808, the crown was conferred on Murat. In May, 1815, Naples was surrendered to a British squadron; and in the following month, king Ferdinand entered his capital amidst the acclamations of his subjects. In 1803 the city suffered much damage by an earthquake. It is 110 miles S. E. of Rome, 104 N. E. of Palermo, and 300 S. by E. of Venice. Long. 14. 20. E. lat. 14. 55. N.

Napoli de Romania, or Nauplia, a seaport of the Morea, and an archbishop's see; seated on a peninsula, at the head of a bay of the same name. It has a large harbour, with a narrow entrance, defended by a citadel. This town was taken by the Turks in 1715, and remained under the government of the Porte till the recent dismemberment of Greece. It is 20 miles S. S. W. of Corinth. Long. 22. 44. E. lat. 37. 44. N.

Napoli di Malvasia, a seaport of the Morea, capital of the island of Malvasia. It has a fine harbour, defended by a good citadel, and a long wooden bridge, which joins it to the mainland. It gives name to that excellent wine called Malmsey; and was the ancient Epidaurus, famed for the temple of Æsculapius. It is seated on a rock, at the entrance of the bay of Napoli de Romania; 38 miles S. E. of Misitra. Long. 22. 58. E. lat. 36. 53. N.

Nara, a town of Japan, in the island of Niphon, with a magnificent castle; 25 miles N. W. of Meaco.

Naraingunge, a town of Bengal, in the district of Decca; with manufactures of muslin, and a trade in grain, salt, tobacco, &c. It is seated on the Luckia. Long. 90. 35. E. lat. 23. 36. N.

Narasinghapura, a town of Hindostan, in Mysore, with two considerable temples. It is well built, and stands in a fertile country, on the Cavery, immediately below the influx of the Kapini; 20 miles E. S. E. of Mysore.

Narberth, a town of Wales, in Pembrokeshire, with a market on Wednesday; seated on a hill; 12 miles N. E. of Pembroke, and 242 W. by N. of London.

Narbonne, a city of France, in the department of Aude. In the time of the Romans it was the capital of that part of Gaul called Gallia Narbonensis; and here the emperor Marcus Aurelius was born. Some Roman inscriptions, in different parts of the city, are still visible; and the canal from the river Aude, through the city to the Mediterranean, was cut by the Romans. Narbonne is famous for its honey; and the cathedral is remarkable for its noble choir. It is 5 miles from the Mediterranean, and 80. E. S. E. of Toulouse. Pop. 9000. Long. 3. 0. E. lat. 43. 11. N.

Narborough, an uninhabited island in the South Pacific, on the coast of Chili; where Sir John Narborough refreshed his men when sent to the South Sea, in the reign of Charles II. Long. 74. 35. W. lat. 45. 0. N.

Nardo, a town of Naples, in Terra d'Otranto; 22 miles N. by W. of Otranto.

Narenza, a town of Dalmatia, and a bishop's see; seated on a river of the same name; 42 miles N. N. W. of Ragusa.

Narim, a town of Siberia, in the government of Tobolsk; surrounded by palisades and wooden towers. The environs abound with foxes, ermines, and sables. It is seated at the conflux of the Ket with the Oby; 400 miles E. by N. of Tobolsk. Long. 81. 15. E. lat. 59. 10. N.

Narnalla, a town and fortress of Hindostan; province of Berar; 33 miles W. N. W. of Ellichpour.

Narni, a town of Italy, in the states of the Church. Here are the ruins of a marble bridge, built by Augustus; and also of an aqueduct that brought water from a spring at the distance of 15 miles. It is seated on the Nera; 20 miles S. S. W. of Spoleto, and 40 N. of Rome.

Naro, a town of Sicily, in Val de Mazara; on a river of the same name; 11 miles E. of Girgenti.

Narova, a river of Russia, which issues from the lake Peipus, flows to Narva, and enters the Gulf of Finland, 8 miles below that town. It has two cataracts, pompously described by travellers; but they are far inferior to that of the Rhine at Lauffen.

Narraganset Bay, in North America, makes up from S. to N. between the mainland in the state of Rhode Island. It embosoms many fruitful and beautiful islands, the principal of which are Rhode, Canonicut, Prudence, Patience, Hope, Dyer's, and Hog Islands. This capacious bay affords plenty of lobsters.

Narraguagus, a town of the state of Maine; in Washington county; situate on a bay of the same name; 16 miles N. E. of Goldsborough.

Narsingapatam, a town of Hindostan, in the territory of Cattack, near the coast of the Bay of Bengal; 44 miles S. of Cuttack.

Narva, a strong town of Russia, in the government of Petersburgh. The houses are built of brick, and stuccoed white, and it has more the appearance of a German than of a Russian town. In the suburb called Ivangorod are the stupendous remains of an ancient fortress, built by Ivan Basilowitz the Great, which impend over the steep banks of the Narova. In 1700 Charles XII. of Sweden obtained a victory here over Peter the Great. Five years after, the czar took the town by assault, and by his own personal exertions, saved it from pillage and massacre. The principal exports are hemp, flax, timber, and corn. It is situated on the Narova; 8 miles from its mouth, and 85 W. S. W. of Petersburg. Long. 27. 52. E. lat. 59. 18. N.

Narwar, a town of Hindostan; capital of a fertile district of the same name, in the province of Agra; seated near the Sinde; 115 miles S. of Agra. Long. 78. 17. E. lat. 25. 40. N.

Nasca, a seaport of Peru, in the audience of Lima. It has a good harbour, and stands in a territory, fertile in wine and sugar; 220 miles S. S. E. of Lima. Long. 75. 10. W. lat. 14. 45. S.

Naseby, a village in Northamptonshire, famous for the decisive victory gained by the army of the parliament over that of Charles I. in 1645; 12 miles N. N. W. of Northampton.

Nashville, a flourishing town of Tenessee; capital of Davidson county; seated on Cumberland River; 170 miles W. of Knoxville. Long. 86. 56. W. lat. 36. 2. N.

Naskow, a town of Denmark, in the island of Laaland: with a convenient harbour; seated on a bay of the same name; 15 miles W. by N. of Marieboe.

Nassau, an independent duchy of Germany, formed of the several principalities which formerly bore this name. It is bounded by the Prussian territory on the Lower Rhine, and the states of the princes of Hesse. It contains mines of iron, copper, and lead, and the soil is fertile in some places, but the surface is for the most part woody and mountainous. The rearing of cattle and the culture of the vine are the principal occupations of the inhabitants. Area, 2186 square miles. Pop. 340,000. The Duke of Nassau holds the thirteenth place at the smaller assembly of the German diet, and has two votes in the full assembly.

Nassau, a town of Germany, in the above duchy. Opposite the town, on the other side of the river, and on a high mountain, formerly stood Nassauberg, a place of great antiquity, and the original seat of the Nassau family. Nassau is 32 miles W. N. W. of Frankfort. Long. 7. 52. E. lat. 50. 16. N.

Nassau, an island in the Indian Ocean, on the W. side of the island of Sumatra; about 120 miles in circumference. It abounds with forests, and presents an enchanting verdure. The inhabitants are dissimilar from their neighbours, for they approach the simplicity of manners and personal appearance of the Otaheitans, while their colour is like that of the Malays. Long. 99. 40. E. lat. 2. 50. S.

Nassuck, a town of Hindostan, in the province of Guzerat; 95 miles S. S. W. of Surat. Long. 73. 49. E. lat. 19. 50. N.

Nata, a seaport of Terra Firma, in the province of Panama; seated in a fertile country, on the bay of Panama; 68 miles S. W. of Panama. Long. 81. 5. W. lat. 8. 36. N.

Natal, a country on the S. E. coast of Africa; lying N. E. of the Cape of Good Hope; inhabited by a tribe of Caffres. It is about 500 miles in length, and near the middle is a river and also a bay of the same name. Long. 31. 30. E. lat. 29. 0. S.

Natchez, a town of the state of Mississippi; in Adam's county; with a strong fort. It is seated on the Mississippi, 520 miles W. of Savanna, and 320 miles above New Orleans. It is the chief emporium of the state, and has a great trade in the export of cotton. Pop. 4800. Long. 91. 39. W. lat. 31. 34. N.

Natchitoches, a town of Louisiana; chief of a county of the same name; on the Red River. Long. 93. 10. W. lat. 31. 45. N.

Natolia, or Anadoli, a province of Asiatic Turkey; comprising the W. part of Asia Minor, the whole of which is sometimes called by the name. It is about 400 miles in length, from N. E. to S. W., and 370 miles from E. to W. It is mountainous, but generally fertile, and has considerable commerce. The residence of the bey is at Kutaiah.

Nattam, a town and fortress of Hindostan, in the district of Dindigul; 45 miles S. S. W. of Trichinopoly.

Nattore, a town of Bengal, seated on the river Attri; 47 miles E. N. E. of Moorshedabad.

Nauen, a town of Prussia, in Brandenburg; 18 miles W. N. W. of Berlin.

Naumberg, a town of Germany, in Hesse Cassel, situate on the Eide; 16 miles W. S. W. of Cassel.

Naumburg, a town of Prussian Saxony, in the government of Merseburg, formerly capital of a duchy of the same name. It has a small citadel, and its cathedral is remarkable for its fine altars, paintings, and subterranean chapels. The chief manufactures are leather, soap, starch, gunpowder, turnery wares, &c.; and it carries on a brisk trade. It is seated on the Saale; 18 miles W. S. W. of Merseburg. Pop. 12,000. Long. 12. 0. E. lat. 51. 11. N.

Naumburg, a town of Prussian Silesia, in the government of Leignitz, on the river Queis; 11 miles N. W. of Lowenburg.

Nauplia. *See* Napoli di Romania.

Navan, a town of Ireland, in the county of Meath, seated at the conflux of the Blackwater with the Boyne; 7 miles N. E. of Trim, and 25 N. W. of Dublin.

Navarino, a seaport on the W. coast of the Morea, with a large harbour, defended by two forts. It is memorable for the destruction of the Turkish and Egyptian fleet, by the English, French, and Russians, in 1827. It is seated on a hill; 10 miles N. by E. of Modon, and 88 S. W. of Corinth. Long. 21. 25. E. lat. 37. 5. N.

Navarre, a province of Spain, containing the greater part of the ancient kingdom of Navarre. It is 75 miles long, and 60 broad, containing an area of 2475 square miles. Pop. 230,000. Though a mountainous country, abounding in game and iron mines, some valleys produce good corn and excellent wine. Pampeluna is the capital.

NAVARRE, NEW, a former province of Mexico, now divided into various modern intendancies.

NAVARREINS, a town of France; department of Lower Pyrenees, on the Gave d'Oleron; 26 miles S. E. of Bayonne.

NAVIGATOR'S ISLANDS, a cluster of ten islands in the Pacific Ocean; discovered by Bougainville, and explored by Perouse in 1787. They are called by the natives Opoun, Leone, Fanfoue, Maouna, Oyalava, Calinasse, Pola, Shika, Ossamo, and Ouero. Opoun the most southerly and easterly of these islands, lies in long. 169. 7. W. lat. 14. 7. S. Maouna, Oyalava, and Pola, may be numbered among the largest and most beautiful islands of the South Pacific. They combine the advantages of a soil fertile without culture, and a climate that renders clothing unnecessary. The inhabitants are a strong and lusty race; scarcely a man is to be seen among them less than six feet high, and the women are in proportion. In disposition they are thievish, treacherous, and ferocious. Their villages are situate on creeks, by the seaside, and have no paths between them; so that they pass from one to another in their canoes: and thus they are almost constantly on the water. Their canoes, houses, &c., are well constructed; and they are much more advanced in internal policy than any of the islands in this ocean. *See* MAOUNA.

NAXIA, or NAXOS, an island in the Grecian Archipelago, 15 miles in length and 50 in circumference. It is fertile in grain, wine, oil, cotton, and silk, and its plains abound with orange, olive, lemon, cedar, citron, pomegranate, fig, and mulberry trees. It is inhabited both by Greeks and Latins, and has a great many villages: but the population of the whole island does not exceed 10,000. The highest mountain is Zla, which signifies the mountain of Jupiter; but there are no antiquities, except some small remains of a temple of Bacchus.

NAXIA, the capital of the above island, and one of the most beautiful places in the Archipelago. It has two archiepiscopal sees, the one Greek and the other Latin. Here is no harbour, but the trade is considerable in barley, wine, oil, figs, cotton, silk, flax, cheese, salt, oxen, sheep, and mules. It stands on the S. side of the island, and is defended by a castle. Long. 25. 32. E. lat. 37. 8. N.

NAYAKANAHULLY, a large square town of Hindostan, in Mysore, with a citadel in the centre, both strongly fortified with mud walls. In the town a wide street extends all round, and has short lanes on each side. It has a manufacture of coarse cotton cloth, and in the vicinity are many palm gardens. It is 34 miles S. W. of Sera.

NAZARETH, or NASZERA, a town of Palestine, celebrated as the residence of Christ, in the early part of his life. The Latin convent is spacious, and the church is, after that at Jerusalem, the finest in Syria. Pop. about 3000. 50 miles N. N. E. of Jerusalem.

NAZARETH, a town of Pennsylvania, in Northampton county, and a settlement of the Moravians, 10 miles N. of Bethlehem, and 63 N. by W. of Philadelphia.

NAZE, or LINDENESS, the most southern promontory of Norway. Long. 7. 20. E. lat. 57. 30. N.

NEAGH, LOUGH, a lake of Ireland, 20 miles long, and 15 broad, lying in the counties of Armagh, Down, Antrim, Londonderry, and Tyrone. The river Bann flows through it.

NEATH, a corporate town of Wales, in Glamorganshire, with markets on Wednesday and Saturday. In the neighbourhood are iron forges, smelting works for copper, and coal mines, and on the other side of the river are the extensive remains of an abbey. A great quantity of coal is exported hence in small vessels. It is seated on the river Neath, near the Bristol Channel; 27 miles S. W. of Brecknock, and 198 W. of London.

NEATH, a river of Wales, which rises in Brecknockshire, and runs through Glamorganshire, by the town of Neath, into the Bristol Channel.

NEB, a river in the Isle of Man, which runs into the Irish Sea at Peel Castle.

NEBRA, a town of Prussian Saxony; in Thuringia; on the Unstrut; 12 miles N. N. W. of Naumburg.

NECKAR, a river of Germany; which rises in Wirtemberg, flows by Rothwiel, Tubingen, Esslingen, Heilbron, and Heidelberg, and enters the Rhine at Manheim. This river gives name to three departments of Wirtemberg, Upper, Lower, and Middle, and also to the two following circles.

NECKAR, a circle of the grand duchy of Baden; comprehending that part of the Lower Palatinate lying to the E. of the Rhine. Manheim is the capital.

NECKAR, one of the four circles of Wirtemberg; comprehending the W. part of the kingdom, according to the division made in 1818. Pop. 2180.

NECKARGEMUND, a town of Baden; on the Neckar; 5 miles E. of Heidelberg.

NECKARSULM, a town of Wirtemberg; seated at the conflux of the Neckar and Sulm; 5 miles N. of Heilbron.

NEDROMA, a town of Algiers; in the province of Mascara; surrounded with magnificent ruins. It is 50 miles W. S. W. of Oran. Long. 0. 38. W. lat. 35. 40. N.

NEDSJED, an extensive province of Arabia; bounded N. by the desert of Syria, E. by Lachsa, S. by Hadramaut and Yemen, and W. by Hedsjaz. The soil is various, and in many parts very fertile. The Bedouins inhabit a great part of this province; the remainder is mountainous, and contains a great number of towns, almost every one of which has its own chief.

NEEDHAM, a town in Suffolk, with a market on Wednesday; seated on the Orwell; 9 miles N. W. of Ipswich, and 74 N. E. of London.

NEEDLES, a cluster of rocks in the English Channel, at the W. end of the Isle of Wight; so called from their height and sharp extremities. Here is a lighthouse. Long. 1. 33. W. lat. 50. 44. N.

NEEHEEHOW, one of the Sandwich Islands, in the N. Pacific; 5 leagues W. of Atooi. The E. coast is high, and rises abruptly from the sea; the rest of it consists of low ground, except a round bluff head on the S. E. point. Long. 160. 15. W. lat. 21. 50. N.

NEERWINDEN, a village of Belgium; in N. Brabant; a little N. by W. of Landen. Hence the two celebrated battles of Landen are sometimes called by the name of Neerwinden. *See* LANDEN.

NEFTA, a town of the kingdom of Tunis; 250 miles S. by W. of Tunis. Long. 9. 25. E. lat. 30. 0. N.

NEGAPATAM, a city of Hindostan; in the district of Tanjore, on the coast of Coromandel. The port is not extraordinary; but most of the different nations in India are here settled, and trade under the protection of the fort. It is 50 miles E. of Tanjore, and 166 S. by W. of Madras. Long. 79. 56. E. lat. 10. 46. N.

NEGARA, a town of the isle of Borneo; capital of the kingdom of Banjermassing; situate on the E. side of the river Banjar; 60 miles N. of the town of Banjermassing. Long. 114. 0. E. lat. 1. 40. S.

NEGOMBO, a seaport on the W. coast of the isle of Ceylon; with a fort built by the Portuguese. It was taken in 1640 by the Dutch, who evacuated it to the English in 1796. It is 16 miles N. of Colombo. Long. 79. 55. E. lat. 7. 20. N.

NEGRAIS, an island on the E. side of the Bay of Bengal; at the mouth of the Bassien river, the most western branch of the Irrawaddy; with an excellent harbour. Long. 94. 30. E. lat. 16. 0. N. It gives its name to a district adjoining, containing 9000 square miles, and a population of 80,000.

NEGRIL POINT, the most westerly promontory of the island of Jamaica. Long. 78. 23. W. lat. 18. 17. N.

NEGRO, CAPE, a promontory of Africa; on the coast of Benguela; being the most southerly country to which the Europeans usually resort to purchase slaves. Long. 11. 40. E. lat. 16. 15. N.

NEGROLAND, or NIGRITIA, a large country in the interior of Africa, through which the river Niger flows from W. to E. It is called by the Arabs, Soudan, a word of similar import to the European appellation, signifying the Land of the Blacks. It extends from long. 10. W. to 27. E., and from lat. 10. to 25. N.; being bounded on the N. by the Zahara, and the mountains which separate it from the states of Barbary, on the E. by Nubia and Abyssinia, on the S. by countries unknown and Guinea, and W. by Guinea, Fouli, and Zahara. Of this vast country little is known, more than the names of some of the towns and great kingdoms of which it is composed. Some parts, particularly on the river Niger, are said to be exceedingly fertile; other parts are represented as sandy and desert. The principal territory known is Bornou. The general character of the negroes, who are the inhabitants of this region, is that of levity. They do not appear to want the feelings of humanity, nor are they more destitute of sagacity than other people of an equal degree of education; but, as their country supplies them with food by a very slight degree of industry, and there is little occasion for clothing amid the heat of their climate, they have a general habit of seeking present pleasure, and no care for the future. The only necessary of life that appears to be deficient, is salt, which is the more wanted among them, in consequence of their subsisting chiefly on vegetable food; and it is a proverbial expression of a man's riches, to say that he eats salt with his food. This important article they receive from Zahara, by caravans of trading Arabs. They also receive arms, hardware, glasses, and trinkets from the W., by the Europeans, and in the interior, by the caravans of Cairo, Fezzan, and Morocco. For these they give, in return, gold dust, ivory, and elephants' teeth. The kind of government that exists among the negro nations is by no means uniform. Many districts are governed by a number of independent petty chiefs, who are engaged in frequent wars with each other. In other places, the talents of individual chieftains have been able to reduce considerable tracts of territory under their dominion; and hence some flourishing towns have sprung up. Many of the towns are fortified with ditches and high walls. Domestic slavery prevails in a very great degree among all the negro states. When the tropical rains fall, or are so deficient that the sun burns up the face of the country, it is not uncommon for parents to sell their children, and even themselves, for bread. A free man may also lose his liberty by being taken prisoner in war, or on account of the crimes of murder and sorcery; and also in consequence of insolvency. The knowledge of the negroes, with regard to religion and all speculative subjects, is extremely limited; but they have much superstition, and are implicit believers in witchcraft and magic.

NEGROPONT, or EGRIPOS, an island in the Grecian Archipelago; 100 miles in length, and 18 in breadth; anciently called Eubœa. It is near the N. coast of Livadia, and separated from it by the strait of Euripus, over which is a bridge. It abounds in corn, wine, oil, and fruits. Pop. 60,000.

NEGROPONT, a strong city; capital of the above island, and an archbishop's see; with a good harbour. The walls of the city are 2½ miles in circumference, but the suburbs are much larger. It is seated on a strait of the same name; 30 miles N. E. of Athens, and 260 S. W. of Constantinople. Pop. 16,000. Long. 24. 8. E. lat. 38. 30. N.

NEHAVEND, a town of Irak, in Persia; famous for a battle fought near it, between the caliph Omar and Yex Degerd, king of Persia, in 638, when the latter lost his life and kingdom. It is 200 miles N. W. of Ispahan. Long. 48. 10. E. lat. 34. 20. N.

NEIDENBERG, a town of Prussia, in the government of Konigsburg; with a castle on a mountain; 75 miles E. of Culm. Long. 20. 20. E. lat. 53. 22. S.

NEIDENSTEIN, a town of Germany, in Hesse Cassel; 9 miles S. S. W. of Cassel.

NEIRA, one of the Banda Islands, and the seat of their government. It has a spacious harbour, but difficult to be entered; and ships anchor under the cannon of two forts. Long. 129. 30. E. lat. 4. 50. S.

NEISSE, a city of Prussian Silesia, in the government of Oppeln. It is a place of great strength, and one of the finest towns in Silesia. The inhabitants carry on a considerable trade in linens and wine. This place was taken in 1741 by the Prussians; in 1807 it surrendered to the French; and was finally ceded to Prussia in 1814. It is seated on a river of the same name; 48 miles S. by E. of Breslau. Long. 17. 20. E. lat. 50. 24. N.

NEITRA, a town of Hungary, and a bishop's see; with a castle and a college. It is situate on a river of the same name, 34 miles N. of Gran.

NELISURAM, a town of Hindostan, on the W. coast, 33 miles N. E. of Mangalore, and 40 N. W. of Tellicherry.

NELLENBURG, a former landgraviate of Suabia; now belonging to Baden.

NELLENBURG, a town of Wirtemberg; formerly the capital of a landgraviate of Suabia, with a citadel on a mountain; 22 miles N. of Constance. Long. 9. 5. E. lat. 47. 57. N.

NELLORE, a town and fortress of Hindostan, in the Carnartic, near the Pennar; 85 miles N. by W. of Madras. Long. 79. 57. E. lat. 14. 26. N.

NEMÆA, a village of Greece, in the Morea; 20 miles S. W. of Corinth; anciently celebrated for its games; now a miserable place.

NEMOURS, a town of France, in the department of Seine-et-Marne; with an old castle; seated on the Loing, between two hills; 45 miles S. S. E. of Paris. Pop. 3800.

NEN, a rives which rises in the W. part of Northamptonshire, becomes navigable at Northampton, and runs into the Lincolnshire Wash.

NENAGH, a town of Ireland, in the county of Tipperary; with a castle, seated on the branch of the Shannon; 19 miles N. E. of Limerick, and 23 N. of Cashel.

NEOCASTRO, a town and fort of Romania; on the Strait of Constantinople; 12 miles N. of Constantinople.

NEOT'S, ST. a town in Huntingdonshire, with a market on Thursday, and a considerable trade in coal; seated on the Ouse over which is a strong bridge; 9 miles S. S. W. of Huntingdon, and 56 N. N. W. of London.

NEOUNDOH, a town of Birmah; with manufactures of japanned ware; seated on the Irrawaddy; 4 miles N. N. E. of Pagahm,

NEPAUL, a kingdom of Northern Hindostan; bounded N. by the Himalaya Mountains, S. by the provinces of Bahar, Oude, and Delhi, E. by Bootan and the territory of the rajah of Si Kim. The soil is productive, and in some places yields two crops in the year. The mountains of Nepaul contain mines of copper and iron; and, although commerce is not encouraged, it sends to Bengal ivory, wax, honey, resin, timber, bastard cinnamon, cardamums, walnuts, &c.; and takes, in return, muslins and silks of Bengal, carpets, spices, tobacco, and European goods. In 1814, in consequence of the repeated encroachments of the Nepaulese, the British invaded their territories, and dictated to them a treaty of peace in 1816. By this treaty Nepaul is limited on the W. to the river Gogra; the British have gained possession of the province of Kumaon, and a British envoy constantly resides at Katmandoo, the capital of Nepaul. Pop. 2,000,000.

NEPEAN ISLAND, a small island in the South Pacific, opposite Port Hunter, on the S. coast of Norfolk Island.

NEPI, a town of Italy, in the papal states, remarkable for some Roman ruins, and a fine modern aqueduct, seated on the Triglia; 20 miles N. of Rome.

NERAC, a town of France, department of Lot-et-Garonne, divided by the river Baise into Great and Little Nerac. In the feudal times this was the residence of the lords of Albert, whose stupendous castle is now in ruins. It is 16 miles W. S. W. of Agen, and 67. S. E. of Bordeaux.

NERBUDDA, a river of Hindostan, which issues from a lake on the S. confines of the province of Allahabad, flows W. for 700 miles, and enters the Gulf of Cambay below Baroach.

NERESHEIM, a town of Wirtemburg, with a late Benedictine abbey, on a mountain, whose abbot was a prelate of the empire. It is 15 miles W. N. W. of Donawert.

NERICIA, a province of Sweden, bounded by Sudermania, Westmania, Wermland, and W. and E. Gothland. It is now included in the government of Orebro.

NERONDE, a town of France, department of Loire; 24 miles W. of Lyons.

NERONDES, a town in the department of Cher; 19 miles E. S. E. of Bourges.

NERTSCHINSK, a town of Siberia, capital of a province of the same name, in the government of Irkutsk, with a fort. The adjacent country is mountainous, but yields excellent pasture for cattle, and there are some considerable lead and silver mines. It is seated at the confluence of the Nercha with the Shilka; 440 miles E. of Irkutsk.

NESLE, a town of France, department of Somme, on the Lingon; 25 miles E. S. E. of Amiens, and 66 N. by E. of Paris.

NESS, LOCH, a lake of Scotland, in Inverness-shire, 23 miles long, and from one to two broad. The depth is very considerable, and the high hills on each side present a delightful view of wood, pasture, cultivated lands, and rugged precipices. It was agitated in an extraordinary manner during the great earthquake at Lisbon, in 1755. Its outlet, at the N. extremity, is the river Ness, which runs into Murray Frith, below Inverness.

NESTVED, a town of Denmark, in the island of Zealand, 38 miles S. W. of Copenhagen.

NETHERLANDS, or HOLLAND, a kingdom of Europe, bounded on the W. and N. by the German Ocean, E. by Hanover, and S. by Belgium. It is divided into ten provinces, viz. North and South Holland, Zealand, Utrecht,

Gelderland, Overyssel, Drenthe, Groningen, Friesland, and North Brabant. The capital is Amsterdam, but the seat of government is at the Hague. The area is 11,518 square miles, and the number of inhabitants 2,445,550. The surface of the country is uncommonly level, and is covered with woods, corn fields, and vast meadows of the freshest verdure. The maritime provinces have undergone great physical revolutions, especially from the retreat and encroachments of the sea, along with the changes in the course of the Rhine. So lately as the 15th century, a great salt-water lake was suddenly formed to the S. E. of Dort, which overwhelmed 72 villages, and 100,000 inhabitants are supposed to have perished. To prevent the recurrence of such dreadful calamities, the Dutch began to secure their coasts, as also the banks of the great rivers, by dykes or mounds of earth, the erection of which has been justly considered one of the greatest efforts of human industry. The climate in the maritime provinces is humid and variable ; in the interior it is more constant. The summers are warmer, and the winters colder than in England. The soil is in general fertile, and agriculture has been long prosecuted with care and success. The principal productions are corn, flax, hemp, tobacco, hops, madder, and fruit. Cattle are reared in great numbers, and vast quantities of excellent butter and cheese are made for exportation. The principal rivers are the Rhine, with its different branches, and the Maese. These rivers and the multitude of canals with which the country is intersected, afford an easy and safe navigation, not only to all parts of the kingdom, but to the W. of Germany, the N. of France, and even to Switzerland. The lakes are comparatively inconsiderable ; the principal is that of Haarlem, which it is proposed to drain. During several centuries the Netherlands took the lead of all the neighbouring states, both in trade and manufactures, the linen of Holland, the lace of Brussels, the leather of Liege, the woollens of Leyden and Utrecht, and the silks of Amsterdam and Antwerp, being known several centuries ago throughout Europe. From their situation, at the mouth of so many large rivers, both the Dutch and Flemish had an early and extensive trade. The number of vessels employed by the Dutch in the fisheries, particularly the herring fishery, is said to have exceeded that of all the rest of Europe. At a later date came their acquisitions in the East and West Indies, while they also carried on extensive transactions with America, and the coast of Guinea. The commerce of this country, however, experienced a woeful decline after its connexion with France. The new constitution resembles, in many respects, that of Great Britain ; though it also approximates to the federal government of the United States of America, in consequence of the long existence of provincial customs, particularly among the Dutch. The royal power is vested in the family of Nassau-Orange, with the title of the King of Holland. The parliament is divided into two houses, the upper and lower house, the members of both being paid for their attendance. The supreme courts sit at the Hague. The Dutch have been long distinguished as a laborious and persevering people, not devoid of enterprise, but led much more rarely than the English and Americans into miserable speculations of doubtful success. Calvinism is the established religion ; but there are no political disqualifications on account of religious tenets. The earliest accounts we have of the history of this country are from the Romans, by whom all the southern and central part was conquered, and called by them Belgium. After several political changes, the country came into the possession of the House of Burgundy, and, by marriage, passed to Maximilian of Austria, father of Charles V. The latter united the 17 provinces into one state ; but the bigotry and tyranny of his son Philip II. produced the separation of the seven united provinces. The other ten, however, continued under the Spanish crown till 1702, when Louis XIV. obtained possession ; but after the battle of Ramillies in 1706, the Netherlands were brought under the power of the allies, and assigned to the Austrians by the peace of Utrecht. In 1741 the French, under Marshal Saxe, recovered what the preceding generation had lost ; but at the peace of Aix-la-Chapelle the country was again restored to Austria. In 1792 the French overran the Austrian Netherlands ; they were driven out of the country in 1793, but returned in 1794, and subdued every part of it ; and in 1795 decreed it, with the territories of Liege and Upper Gelderland, an integral part of the French republic. To this country they gave the name of Belgium, and divided it into nine compartments ; but, in 1814, agreeably to the treaty of Paris, they evacuated all that part which formerly belonged to Austria and Holland ; and the 17 provinces were united, and formed into an independent state. In November, 1815, the French also ceded some frontier districts, and two fortresses, to the Netherlands; and in 1830, the southern or Catholic provinces threw off the yoke they had always borne with uneasiness, and formed a new kingdom under the ancient name of BELGIUM (which see).

NETSCHKAU, a town of Saxony, on the Golsch, 12 miles S. W. of Zwickau.

NETTUNO, a town of Italy, in the states of the church, near the ruins of the ancient Antium, at the mouth of the Loracina, 24 miles S. by E. of Rome.

NEUBURG, called also the Younger Palatinate, formerly a duchy of the German empire, but now incorporated in the Bavarian circles of Upper Danube and Regen.

NEUBURG, a town of Germany, in Bavaria. It stands on a hill, on the Danube, and has two gates ; but the fortifications are chiefly gone to decay. The castle is a large building, and contains a hall of extraordinary size, embellished with portraits. It is 11 miles W. of Ingolstadt ; and 60 S. W. of Amberg. Pop. 4000. Long. 11 13. E. lat. 48. 43. N.

Neuburg, a town of Bavaria, seated on the Schwarza; 19 miles E. S. E. of Amberg.

Neuchateau, a town of France, department of Vosges; seated in a soil fertile in corn and good wine, on the river Meuse; 25 miles S. W. of Nancy. Pop. 2700.

Neuchateau, a town of Belgium, in Luxemburg 16 miles S. W. of Bastogne, and 30 W. N. W. of Luxemburg.

Neuchatel, or **Neufchatel**, a canton of Switzerland, between the lake of Neuchatel and the borders of France. It is a hilly country, and is watered by several lakes and rivers. The soil is not equally fertile; but there are large vineyards that produce white and red wine of excellent quality. The pastures on the mountains feed a great number of cattle, and there are plenty of deer in the forests. The inhabitants are Protestants, except in the two districts of Landeron and Cressier, where the Catholics are predominant. This district, along with that of Vallengin, was formerly a separate principality. On the death of the duchess of Nemours, in 1707, the sovereignty was claimed by Frederic I. of Prussia, as heir to the Prince of Orange, and his right was acknowledged by the states of the country, whose privileges and alliances he confirmed. In 1806 Neuchatel was ceded by the king of Prussia to the French marshal Berthier, and the grant was confirmed by Napoleon. In 1814 it was rescued from this subjection, and the Congress of Vienna acknowledged it a Swiss canton, though the nominal sovereignty of Prussia was preserved. Area, 340 square miles. It contains 50,000 inhabitants, who use the French language.

Neuchatel, the capital of the above canton, situate partly on the plain between the lake of Neuchatel and the Jura, and partly on the side of that mountain. The chief article of exportation is wine, produced from the neighbouring vineyards, and much esteemed; and it has manufactures of printed linens and cottons. It is 25 miles N. E. of Lausanne, and 25 W. of Bern. Pop. 5000. Long. 7. 0. E. lat. 47. 5. N.

Neuchatel, a town of France, department of Lower Seine, noted for excellent cheese; 20 miles S. E. of Dieppe. Pop. 3000.

Neuchatel, a lake of Switzerland, about 20 miles long, and 4 broad. At the N. E. extremity it has a communication with the Lake of Biel, by a narrow outlet.

Neuffen, a town of Germany, in Wirtemberg; with a fortress called Hoheneuffen; 17 miles S. E. of Stutgard.

Neuhaus, a town of Bohemia, with a castle; 27 miles E. by S. of Bechin.

Neuhaus, a town of Hanover, in the duchy of Bremen, near the mouth of the Oste. It was once a place of great trade, but a sank-bank arising in the harbour, at the entrance of the Oste into the Elbe, it is now much less frequented. It is 19 miles N. W. of Stade. Pop. 5200.

Neuhausel, a town of Hungary, seated in a marshy plain, on the river Neitra; 43 miles E. S. E. of Presburg.

Neukirchen, a town of Germany, in Hesse Cassel, on the river Fulda; 32 miles S. S. E. of Cassel.

Neumagen, a town of the Prussian province of Lower Rhine; seated on the Moselle; 17 miles N. E. of Treves.

Neumark, a town of Bavaria; on the river Roth; 17 miles S. E. of Landschut.

Neumark, a town of Austrian Illyria; in Carniola; 28 miles N. W. of Laubach.

Neumarkt, a town of Bavaria, where the French, in 1796, met with the first of that series of defeats which led to their retreat across the Rhine. It is seated on the Sulz; 19 miles S. E. of Nuremberg. Pop. 2400.

Neumarkt, a town of Prussian Silesia; near which, at the village of Leuthen, the Prussians gained a decisive victory over the Austrians, in 1757; 20 miles W. by N. of Breslau.

Neurode, a town of Prussian Silesia; in the county of Glatz, on the river Wolitz; 10 miles N. N. W. of Glatz. Pop. 3000.

Neus, a river of North Carolina, which enters Pamtico Sound below Newbern, where it is a mile and a half broad.

Neusatz, a strong town and fortress of Hungary, formerly called Peterwardein Schanz. It is the see of a Greek bishop, and stands on the Danube, opposite Peterwardein in Sclavonia. Pop. 13,400.

Neuseidler, a lake of Hungary; 26 miles long, and 10 broad, and 16 S. S. W. of Presburg. It is almost surrounded by fens. In its vicinity is the castle of Esterhazy, said to rival the palace of Versailles in pomp.

Neusol, a town of Hungary, and a bishop's see, with an old castle, in which is a church covered with copper. In the adjacent mountains are extensive copper mines. It is seated on the Gran; 22 miles N. by E. of Schemnitz. Pop. 10,000.

Neustadt, a town of Austria, with a castle, and an arsenal. It has the staple right over all goods coming from Italy. It stands on the frontiers of Hungary; 28 miles S. by W. of Vienna. Long. 16. 18. E. lat. 47. 50. N.

Neustadt, a town of Bavaria, in the circle of Lower Maine, formerly the capital of the lower part of the principality of Bayreuth; with a castle. The library belonging to the church contains many curiosities. It stands on the river Aisch; 32 miles E. S. E. of Wurtzburg. Long. 10. 43. E. lat. 49. 38. N.

Neustatd, a town of the Bavarian circle of Lower Maine; formerly in the principality of Wurtzburg; seated on the Saale; 16 miles N. by E. of Schweinfurt.

Neustatd, a town of Wirtenburg; seated on the Kocher; 12 miles N. N. E. of Heilbron.

Neustadt, a town of Saxony, in Meissen, capital of a circle of the same name. It has a castle, two churches, and a mine office, and on a mountain near it is another castle, called Arnshaug. It is seated on the Orla; 46 miles S. S. W. of Leipsic. Long. 11. 49. E. lat. 50. 5. N.

Neustadt, a town of Prussia, in the province of Brandenburg. Here are extensive breweries, and manufactures of cloth and cutlery. It stands on the Finow Canal; 31 miles N. E. of Berlin.

NEUSTADT, a town of Brandenburg, in the mark of Pregnitz; celebrated for its manufacture of plate-glass; seated on the Dosse; 8 miles E. N. E. of Havelberg.

NEUSTADT, a town of Denmark, in the duchy of Holstein, with a castle, and a spacious harbour on the Baltic. It suffered greatly from fire in 1817; 20 miles N. by E. of Lubec. Long. 10. 57. E. lat. 54. 10. N.

NEUSTADT, a town of Germany, in the grand duchy of Mecklenburg-Schwerin, with a castle; 17 miles S. of Schwerin.

NEUSTADT, a town of Germany, in the duchy of Brunswick, with a castle, seated on the Leina; 15 miles N. N. W. of Hanover.

NEUSTADT, a town of Germany, in Bavaria, at the conflux of the Abenst with the Danube; 16 miles E. by N. of Ingolstadt.

NEUSTADT, a town of Bavaria, with a castle, seated on the river Nab; 27 miles N. N. E. of Amberg.

NEUSTADT, a town of the Austrian states, in Moravia; 10 miles N. W. of Olmutz.

NEUSTADT, a town of Prussian Silesia, in the principality of Oppeln, with manufactures of linen and woollen, and a trade in wines, seated on the Prudnitz; 14 miles S. E. of Neisse.

NEUSTADT, a town of Bohemia, in the circle of Pilsen; 35 miles W. by S. of Pilsen.

NEUSTADT, a town of Bohemia: 13 miles N. E. of Konigingratz.

NEUSTADT, a town of Westphalia, in the county of Mark; 50 miles E. S. E. of Dusseldorf.

NEUSTADTEL, a town of Bohemia; 66 miles N. E. of Prague.

NEUSTADTEL, a town of Hungary, on the Waag; 52 miles N. N. E. of Presburg.

NEUVILLE, a town of France, department of Loiret; 11 miles N. N. E. of Orleans.

NEUVILLE, a town of Switzerland; 9 miles N. E. of Neuchatel.

NEUWIED, a town of Westphalia, capital of the lower county of Wied; with a fine castle; seated on the Rhine; 7 miles N. W. of Coblentz.

NEVA, a river of Russia, which issues from a Lake Ladoja, flows to Petersburg, where it divides into several branches, and enters the Gulf of Finland; 8 miles W. N. W. of Halle in Suabia.

NEVERS, a town of France, capital of the department of Nievre, and a bishop's see. It is built in the form of an amphitheatre, and contains several fine buildings. The chief manufactures are china, glass, and works of enamel. It is seated on the Loire, at the influx of the Nievre, over which is a handsome bridge of 20 arches; 30 miles N. N. W. of Moulins. Pop. 12,000.

NEVIS, one of the Leeward Caribbee Islands, in the West Indies; divided from the E. end of St. Christopher by a narrow channel. It has but one mountain, which is in the middle, very high and covered with large trees up to the top. Here is a hot bath, much of the same nature as those of Bath, in England. It is a small island, but very fruitful, and subject to the English. Pop. 16,000. Charleston is the capital, on the S. W. side; defended by a fort. Long. 62. 50. W. lat. 16. 10. N.

NEVYN, or NEWIN, a town of Wales, in Caernarvonshire; with a market on Saturday. Here Edward I., in 1284, held his triumph on the conquest of Wales. It is seated on St. George's Channel; 21 miles S. by W. of Caernarvon, and 249 W. N. W. of London.

NEW FOREST, a forest in that part of Hampshire which lies between Southampton water and the river Avon. It is 20 miles in length, and 15 in breadth; and has advantages of situation, with respect to conveyance by water carriage and vicinity to the dock-yards, superior to every other forest, having in its neighbourhood several places for shipping timber. It was afforested by William the Conqueror, and was then 10 miles longer than it is now. His son William Rufus was killed in this forest by an arrow, shot by Walter Tyrrel, that accidentally glanced against a tree, the site of which is now pointed out by a triangular stone. Several considerable towns and villages are now included in the forest. The lord warden is appointed by letters patent, during the king's pleasure, and all the courts of jurisdiction are held at Lyndhurst.

NEW RIVER, an artificial river of England, originally brought from Amwell, in Hertfordshire, to Islington, for the supply of the metropolis with water. It was finished in 1613, by Sir Hugh Middleton, a citizen of London, who expended his whole fortune in the undertaking. It has since been carried up to a spring near Hertford, called Chadwell, where the stream is also increased by a cut from the river Lea. The river, with all its windings, is 42 miles in length, and is under the management of a corporation called the New River Company.

NEW YEAR HARBOUR, a good harbour on the N. coast of Staten Land. Long. 64. 11. W. lat. 54. 49. S.

NEW YEAR ISLANDS, small islands in the South Pacific, near New Year Harbour; the resort of vast numbers of sea lions, seals, and a species of vulture.

NEW YORK. *See* YORK, NEW.

NEWARK, a borough in Nottinghamshire; governed by a mayor, with a market on Wednesday. It returns two members to parliament. Near the river are the splendid ruins of its ancient castle. The church, erected by Henry IV., is reckoned one of the finest in the kingdom. There are also three meeting-houses for dissenters, and a catholic chapel. The schools are a free grammar school, and subscription and national schools. Here, in the midst of his troubles, died King John; and here Charles I., after his defeat at Naseby, put himself into the hands of the Scotch army, who afterwards gave him up to his worst enemies. Newark has a good trade in malt, corn, and coals, manufactures of coarse linens and lace, iron and brass foundries, extensive roperies, &c. Gypsum of a superior quality is found in the neighbourhood. It is seated on the Trent, over which is a bridge; 17 miles N. E. of Nottingham, and 120 N. by W. of London. Long. 0. 45. W. lat. 53. 6. N.

NEWARK, a town of New Jersey; capital of Essex county; with five churches and an academy. It is celebrated for its cider, and has a considerable manufacture of shoes. It stands on the W. side of Passaick River, near its mouth in Newark Bay; 9 miles W. of New York. Long. 74. 18. W. lat. 40. 40. N.

NEWBERN, a town of N. Carolina; in Craven county; capital of a district of its name. It has a considerable trade in tar, pitch, turpentine, timber, corn, &c., and stands on a sandy point of land, formed by the confiux of the Neus and Trent; 96 miles E. S. E. of Raleigh. Pop. 3690. Long. 77. 3. W. lat. 35. 20. N.

NEWBURN, a maritime district of North Carolina; comprehending the counties of Carteret, Jones, Craven, Beaufort, Hyde, Pitt, Wayne, Glasgow, Lenoir, and Johnston.

NEWBOROUGH, or GOREY, a town of Ireland, in the county of Wexford; 25 miles N. by E. of Wexford.

NEWBURGH, a town of Scotland, in Fifeshire; with a good harbour on the Frith of Tay. Here the large vessels belonging to Perth unload their goods into lighters. The principal manufacture is linen, and there is also a considerable export of grain. It is 10 miles S. E. of Perth.

NEWBURGH, a town of Wales, in the isle of Anglesey; governed by a mayor; with a market on Tuesday; 12 miles S. W. of Beaumaris, and 250 N. W. of London.

NEWBURGH, a town of New York, in Orange county, on the W. side of Hudson River. Ships of considerable burden may unload at the wharfs, and many vessels are built here It is 32 miles S. of Kingston, and 54. N. of New York. Population, 8933.

NEWBURY, a town in Berkshire, governed by a mayor; with a market on Thursday. The manufactures of druggets, shalloons, and broad cloths, formerly very extensive, are greatly declined; but a considerable trade is carried on by means of the Kennet and Avon canal. Here is a handsome parish church; also five meeting-houses, a charity school, and 65 almshouses. Two battles were fought near this town, between Charles I. and the parliament, in 1643 and 1644. It is seated on the Kennet; 26 miles S. of Oxford, and 56 W. of London.

NEWBURY, a town of Vermont, in Orange county; situate on the Connecticut; 50 miles N. N. E. of Windsor, and 60. E. S. E. of Burlington. Pop. 2578.

NEWBURY PORT, a seaport of Massachusets, in Essex county, with seven churches and a court-house. Large quantities of rum are distilled here, and the inhabitants have a considerable trade with the W. Indies and the southern states. The harbour is safe and commodious, and the business of ship-building is carried on largely. In 1811 the town suffered severely by fire. It is situate on the river Merrimac; 2 miles from the sea, and 35 N. N. E. of Boston. Long. 70. 50. W. lat. 42. 48. N. Pop. 7161.

NEWCASTLE IN EMLYN, a town of Wales; in Caermarthenshire; with a market on Friday. It had a fine castle, now in ruins. It is seated on the Tivy; 18 miles N. N. W. of Caermarthen, and 229 W. N. W. of London.

NEWCASTLE, a town of Ireland, in the county of Dublin; 10 miles W. S. W. of Dublin.

NEWCASTLE, a town of Delaware; capital of a county of the same name; with two churches. It was settled by the Swedes, in 1627, and called Stockholm; afterwards taken by the Dutch, and called New Amsterdam; and, falling into the hands of the English, it was called Newcastle. It is the oldest town on the river Delaware. It is 35 miles S. W. of Philadelphia. Pop. 2737. Long. 75. 38. W. lat. 39. 37. N.

NEWCASTLE, a town of Virginia, in Hanover county; seated on the Pamunky, a branch of York River; 24 miles N. E. of Richmond.

NEWCASTLE, a town of New South Wales, in Northumberland county; on the entrance of Port Hunter. It is prettily situated, and has several public buildings; but has declined, preference being given to Maitland, at the head of the navigation of the river Hunter; but is now rising rapidly. Near it is a productive coal mine.

NEWCASTLE UNDER LYNE, a borough in Staffordshire; governed by a mayor; with markets on Monday and Saturday, and a considerable manufacture of hats. It returns two members to parliament. The throwing of silk is a very considerable branch of trade, and here are also a cotton mill, tanneries, malt concerns, &c., and in the neighbourhood are some iron-works. The villages around are entirely occupied with the manufactures of porcelain, stone-ware, &c. The principal streets are broad, well paved, and lighted with gas, and the general aspect of the town is much improved of late years. It had four churches, now reduced to one: and the castle, whence it had its name, is quite demolished. Another church has been erected, and here are several meeting-houses, a free-school, and 20 almshouses. It stands on a branch of the Trent; 15 miles N. by W. of Stafford, and 149 N. N. W. of London.

NEWCASTLE UPON TYNE, a borough and seaport in Northumberland; governed by a mayor; with markets on Tuesday and Saturday. It is situate among steep hills, on the Tyne, which is here a fine and deep river, so that ships of 300 or 400 tons burden may safely come up to the town, though the large colliers are stationed at Shields. The haven is so secure, that vessels, when they have passed Tynemouth Bar, are in no danger either from storms or shallows. The town rises on the N. bank of the river, where the streets upon the ascent are exceedingly steep. Many of the houses are built of stone; but some of timber, and the rest of brick. Through this town went part of the wall which extended from sea to sea, and was built by the Romans, to defend the Britons against the incursions of the Picts, after all their trained youth had been drawn from the kingdom to recruit the armies of their conquerors. The castle, which is old and ruinous, overlooks the whole town. There are four parish churches, two chapels of ease, five chapels of the Scotch establishment, one for Roman Catholics, and seventeen meeting-houses belonging to different denominations. The exchange, churches, and other public buildings, are elegant; and the quay for landing goods is long and large. Here are a surgeon's hall; a large hospital, built by the contribution of the keelmen, for the maintenance of the poor of their fraternity; and several charitable foundations. This town has undergone such improvements within these few years, that it may rank with some of the most elegantly built in England. This improvement has been chiefly caused by the enterprise and genius of one individual. It has a railway to Carlisle. Newcastle is situated in the centre of the collieries, which have for centuries supplied London, all the eastern, and most of the midland and southern parts of the kingdom with coal. This trade has been the source of great opulence to Newcastle; which, besides, exports large quantities of lead, salt, salmon, butter, tallow, and grindstones; and imports wine and fruit from the S. of Europe, and timber, iron, hemp, &c., from the Baltic and Norway. Ships are sent hence to the Greenland fishery. It also possesses manufactures of steel, iron, and woollen cloth; and in the town and vicinity are several glasshouses. The first charter which was granted to the townsmen for digging coal, was by Henry III., in 1239; but in 1306 the use of coal for fuel was prohibited in London, by royal proclamation, chiefly because it injured the sale of wood for fuel, great quantities of which were then growing about that city; but this interdiction did not long continue, and we may consider coal as having been dug and exported from this place for more than 400 years. A handsome stone bridge of nine arches connects this town with the ancient borough of Gateshead. It was erected in 1781, in place of the old one, which was carried away by an extraordinary flood in 1771. It sends two members to parliament. Newcastle is 14 miles N. of Durham, 94 N. of York, and 272 N. by W. of London. Long. 1. 14. W. lat. 54. 57. N.

New England, a district of North America; once called by that name; now comprising the six states of New Hampshire, Massachusets, Connecticut, Rhode Island, Vermont, and Maine.

Newenham, Cape, a rocky point of considerable height; on the W. coast of North America. It was discovered by Cook, in 1778. Long. 162. 24. W. lat. 58. 42. N.

Newent, a town in Gloucestershire; with a market on Friday; seated on a branch of the Severn: 8 miles N. W. of Gloucester, and 112 W. N. W. of London.

Newfane, a town of Vermont; chief of Windham county; situate on West River; 28 miles E. N. E. of Bennington, and 80 W. N. W. of Boston. Pop. 1403.

Newfoundland, an island on the E. coast of N. America; between 47. and 52. N. lat. It was discovered by Sebastian Cabot, in 1496; and, after many disputes with the French, it was ceded to the English in 1713. Its form is triangular; the N. point is separated from Labrador by the Strait of Belleisle, and from this apex it is 350 miles in length to the base, which is 300 in breadth. It is a mountainous, woody country, and very cold, being covered with snow five months in the year. The settlements of the British are chiefly confined to the harbours, the country near Placentia, and along the bays E. toward Cape Race and thence to Cape Bonavista. In the fishing season, which begins in May and ends in September, it is resorted to by at least 100,000 people, on account of the great fishing-banks to the S. E. of the island; for here they cure the cod, which is carried not only to England, but to the Mediterranean and the West Indies. Within a few years Newfoundland has rapidly increased in population and industry. In 1789 the number of inhabitants was 25,300; it is now estimated at 100,000. The cutting down of wood still furnishes a large portion of employment during the winter. There is great plenty of game, fish, and fowl, but very little corn, fruit, or cattle. It was, with the Bermudas, made a bishopric in 1842, the city of St. John's being the seat of the bishop.

Newhaven, a town in Sussex; near the mouth of the Ouse; with a small harbour. The entrance of the river is defended by a battery. Ship-building is carried on here to some extent. It is 7 miles S. by E. of Lewes, and 57 S. S. E. of London.

Newhaven, a seaport of Connecticut; capital of a county of its name. The half-yearly assembly of the state is held here in October. Near the centre is the public square, in which are the state-house, two college edifices, and a chapel; three churches for congregationalists, and one for episcopalians. Here are manufactures of card-teeth, linen, butter, cotton, and paper. The harbour has good anchorage, and is defended by a fort. It carries on a considerable trade with New York and the West India islands, and stands at the head of a bay; 4 miles N. of Long Island Sound, and 78 N. E. of New York. Pop. 14,390. Long. 72. 56. W. lat. 41. 17. N.

Newington, an elegant modern suburb of the old town of Edinburgh. It consists of one fine street of villas, and forms the extreme south of the city.

Newmarket, a town of Suffolk; with a market on Thursday. It is the most celebrated place in England for horse-races, which are held several times every year, chiefly in spring and in the months of July and October; and here Charles II. built a house for the sake of this diversion. It is 13 miles W. of Bury, and 61. N. by E. of London.

Newmarket, a town of Virginia, in Amherst

county; on the N. side of James River, at the influx of the Tye; 100 miles above Richmond.

NEWNHAM, a town in Gloucestershire; with a market on Friday, seated on the Severn; 12 miles W.S.W. of Gloucester, and 120 W.N.W. of London.

NEWPORT, a borough of Hampshire; returning two members to parliament; and the chief town in the Isle of Wight; governed by a mayor; with markets on Wednesday and Saturday, and a manufacture of starch. It is seated on the river Cowes, which is navigable for small vessels; 17 miles S. by E. of Southampton, and 91 S. W. of London. Long. 1. 16. W. lat. 50. 42. N.

NEWPORT, a town in Shropshire, with a market on Saturday, and a handsome free-school. The church is of great antiquity, and was formerly collegiate: the other places of worship are one for Roman Catholics, and two for Methodists. Here is a spacious market-hall; and in the neighbourhood are productive mines of coal, iron, and limestone. The surrounding country is very fertile, is enriched by many seats of note, and affords delightful views; 17 miles E. of Shrewsbury, and 139 N. W. of London.

NEWPORT, a village of Cornwall, 3 miles N. of Launceston, and 214 W. by S. of London.

NEWPORT, a town of Monmouthshire, with a market on Saturday. It was formerly walled round, and defended by a castle, considerable remains of which are yet in being. Near it are the vestiges of a camp. It is seated on the river Usk, 19 miles S. S. W. of Monmouth, and 118 W. by N. of London.

NEWPORT, a decayed town of Wales, in Pembrokeshire; governed by a mayor; with a market on Saturday; and the ruins of a castle. It is seated at the foot of a high hill, on a bay of the same name; 18 miles N. E. of St. David, and 320 W. N. W. of London.

NEWPORT, a seaport of Rhode Island; chief town of a county of the same name, and the semi-metropolis of the state. It stands on the S. W. end of Rhode Island, about 5 miles from the sea; and has 11 edifices for public worship, a flourishing academy, an elegant state-house, and a handsome public library. Its harbour is one of the finest in the world; and to the W. of the town is Goat Island, on which is a fort. Newport has a considerable trade. It is 80 miles N. E. of New York. Pop. 8333. Long. 71. 15. W. lat. 41. 30. N.

NEWPORT, a town of the state of Georgia, in Liberty county; situate on a navigable creek, 8 miles above Sunbury, and 34 S. S. W. of Savanna.

NEWPORT, a town of Kentucky, chief of Campbell county; seated on the Ohio, opposite Cincinnati.

NEWPORT, a town of Delaware, Newcastle county; on the N. side of Christiana Creek; 31 miles S.W. of Philadelphia.—There are several inconsiderable townships of this name in the United States.

NEWPORT PAGNEL, a town in Buckinghamshire; with a market on Saturday, and a considerable manufacture of bonelace; seated on the Ouse; 14 miles E. N. E. of Buckingham, and 50 N. N. W. of London.

NEWPORT PRATT, a seaport of Ireland, in the county of Mayo; near the mouth of the Beatta; 8 miles W. of Castlebar. Long. 9. 21. W. lat. 53. 53. N.

NEWRY, a borough of Ireland, in the county of Down; situate on the side of a steep hill, by a river of the same name, which enters Carlingford Bay, 2 miles below the town of Newry. Vessels of 200 tons burden can come up to the town; and, by means of the Newry Canal to the river Bann, it has a communication with Lough Neagh. Newry was burned by the Duke of Berwick, in 1689, but is now become the largest town in the county; and the trade and manufactures are rising rapidly in importance. It sends one member to parliament, and is 49 miles N. of Dublin. Long. 6. 20. W. lat. 54. 15. N.

NEWTON, a village in Lancashire; 5 miles N. of Warrington, and 193 N. W. of London.

NEWTON, a town in the Isle of Wight; governed by a mayor; 5 miles W. of Newport.

NEWTON BUSHEL, a town in Devonshire; with a market on Wednesday, and a manufacture of woollen cloths, seated on the Teign; 15 miles S. by W. of Exeter, and 188 W. S. W. of London.

NEWTON DOUGLAS, or NEWTON STEWART, a town of Scotland, in Wigtonshire; situate on the Cree, which is navigable for small vessels to within two miles of the town. Here are manufactures of cotton and carpets, which have much declined, and several tan-works. It is 8 miles N. of Wigtôn, and 28 E. by N. Port Patrick.

NEWTOWN, a town of Wales, in Montgomeryshire; with markets on Tuesday and Saturday; seated in a beautiful valley, on the Severn. It is the principal seat of the fine flannel manufacture in Wales, and is now in a very flourishing state. A new bridge has been erected, and the town is rapidly extending itself on the opposite shore. An extensive pottery, established in 1823, is carried on with great success. The church is an ancient edifice; beside which there are several meeting-houses, and a free-school; 9 miles S. W. of Montgomery, and 175 W. N. W. of London.

NEWTOWN, a town of New Jersey, the seat of justice in Sussex county; 60 miles N. of Trenton. Long. 75. 2. W. lat. 41. 3. N.

NEWTOWN, a town of New York, in Tioga county; where the judicial courts are held in February. It is situate near Tioga River; 50 miles W. by N. of Union, and 70. S. E. of Williamsburg.

NEWTOWN, a town of Connecticut, in Fairfield county; 9 miles E. by N. of Danbury, and 26 N. W. of Newhaven.

NEWTOWN ARDES, a town of Ireland, in the county of Down; with a considerable linen manufacture. It is situate on the N. point of Strangford Lough; 8 miles E. of Belfast, and 16 N. of Downpatrick.

NEWTOWN-BARRY, a town of Ireland, in the

county of Wexford; seated on the Slaney; 10 miles N. W. of Enniscorthy.

NEWTOWN LIMAVADY, a town of Ireland, in the county of Londonderry; with a linen manufacture. It stands on the river Roe, near the E. side of Lough Foyle; 15 miles E. N. E. of Londonderry.

NEW YORK. *See* YORK, NEW.

NEYLAND, a town in Suffolk; with a market on Friday, and a brisk trade, seated on the Stour; 16 miles S. W. of Ipswich, and 57 N. E. of London.

NEYRAC, a town of France, department of Aveiron; 18 miles N. of Rodez.

NEYVA, a town of New Granada, near the Madalena; 130 miles S. W. of St. Fe de Bogota.

NGAN-CHAN, a city of China, of the first rank; in the province of Koeitcheou; situate in a mountainous district. Long. 105. 32. E. lat. 26. 12. N.

NGAN-KING, a city of China, capital of the W. part of the province of Kiang-nan. It is defended by a fort, and seated on the Kian-ku; 575 miles S. of Peking. Long. 116. 45. E. lat. 30. 37. N.

NGAN-LO, a city of China, of the first rank; in the province of Hou-quang. It has a considerable trade, and stands in a vast plain on the river Han; 175 miles S. S. W. of Peking. Long. 112. 3. E. lat. 31. 14. N.

NIAGARA, a river of North America, which forms the communication between the lakes Erie and Ontario, and flows from S. to N. about 36 miles. At the head of this river, on its western shore, is Fort Erie; and 18 miles below this are those remarkable falls, which are reckoned among the greatest natural curiosities in the world. The river is here 740 yards wide. The half mile immediately above the cataracts is a rapid, in which the water falls 58 feet: it is then thrown, with astonishing grandeur, down a stupendous precipice of 176 feet perpendicular, in three distinct and collateral sheets; and, in a rapid that extends to the distance of 9 miles below, falls nearly as much more. The river then flows in a deep channel till it enters Lake Ontario, at Fort Niagara.

NIAGARA, a town and fort of New York, in a county of the same name; on the E. side of the river Niagara, at its entrance into Lake Ontario, and opposite Newark, in Upper Canada. The fort was erected by the French, in 1751, and was taken from them in 1759, by Sir William Johnson. In 1796 it was surrendered to the United States; it was again taken by the British in 1803, and the town destroyed, but it has since been rebuilt, and is a flourishing place; 18 miles below the cataracts, and 80 N. W. of Williamsburg. Long. 79. 5. W. lat. 43. 4. N.

NIAS, a small island, near the W. coast of the island of Sumatra. Long. 97. 0. E. lat. 0. 40. N.

NIBE, a town of Denmark, in North Jutland, 9 miles W. S. W. of Alburg.

NIBIANO, a town of Italy, in the duchy of Parma; 16 miles S. W. of Piacenza.

NICARAGUA, a province of Central America; republic of Guatimala; bounded on the N. by Honduras, E. by the Atlantic Ocean, S. E. by Costa Rica, and S. W. by the Pacific Ocean. It is 400 miles from E. to W., and 120 from N. to S. It is well watered by lakes and rivers, and produces plenty of sugar, cochineal, and fine chocolate. Leon de Nicaragua is the capital.

NICARAGUA, a lake in the foregoing province; 350 miles in circumference. It is interspersed with islands, and abounds in fishes, but is infested with crocodiles. The S. W. extremity is only a few leagues from the Pacific Ocean, and the S. E. end communicates with the Atlantic Ocean by the river St. Juan.

NICARIA, an island of the Grecian Archipelago, between Samos and Tina; anciently called Icaria. It is 50 miles in circumference, and full of rocks. Long. 26. 30. E. lat. 37. 40. N.

NICASTRO, a town of Naples, in Calabria Ultra, with an ancient castle; 17 miles S. S. E. of Cosenza. Pop. 10,000.

NICE, a county of Sardinia; bounded by the Var, the Maritime Alps, the territories of Genoa, and the Mediterranean. It was anciently an appendage of Provence in France, but afterwards passed to the king of Sardinia. It is 36 miles long, and 18 broad, and contains 173,200 inhabitants.

NICE, an ancient, handsome, and considerable town, on the confines of France and Italy, capital of the foregoing province. It has a strong citadel built on a rock, and on the W. it is fortified with a wall and ditch. On the E. side of the rock is the harbour, called Limpia, from a small river that runs into it. The inhabitants export oil, silk, wine, cordials, rice, oranges, lemons, and all sorts of dried fruits. It was taken by the French in 1792, retaken by the Austrians in 1800, but evacuated in a week afterwards. It is very agreeably situated; 4 miles from the mouth of the Var; 83 miles S. by W. of Turin, and 83. E. of Aix. Pop. 18,500.

NICE, a city of Natolia. *See* ISNIC.

NICHABURG, a town of Persia, famous for a mine of turquois stones in its neighbourhood. It is 37 miles S. of Mesched.

NICHOLAS, ST., one of the largest and most pleasant of the Cape Verd islands, between St. Lucia and St. Jago. It is 75 miles in length, and is the residence of the bishop of the isles. Long. 14. 10. W. lat. 16. 32. N.

NICHOLAS, ST., a town of France, in the department of Meurthe; with a handsome church, to which pilgrims formerly resorted. It is seated on the Meurthe; 7 miles S. E. of Nancy.

NICHOLAS, ST., or MOLE, a town, harbour, and cape, at the N. W. extremity of St. Domingo; commanding the strait called the Windward Passage. The harbour is strongly fortified by nature and art; and ships of any burden may ride at anchor in the basin, even during a hurricane. It was taken by the English, aided by the French royalists, in 1793, but evacuated in 1798. Long. 73. 30. W. lat. 19. 49. N.

Nicholas Island, a small island on the N. coast of the island of Cuba. Long. 79. 40. W. lat. 33. 50. N.

Nicobar Islands, a group of 19 islands, on the E. side of the Bay of Bengal. They are almost entirely uncultivated: but the cocoa-nut, the mellori, or lerum (a kind of bread-fruit), and other tropical fruits, grow spontaneously; there are also yams and sweet potatoes, and the edible birds'-nests, so much esteemed in China. Dogs and hogs are the principal animals. The inhabitants are tall and well proportioned, with black eyes, black lank hair, and dark copper-coloured skins. They live in little huts, having no towns, and go quite naked, except a cloth about the waist with a small string hanging down behind. These islands extend northward, from the N. point of Sumatra. The largest, which gives name to the rest, is 25 miles long, and 10 broad. Its S. extremity is in long. 94. 3. E. lat. 6. 39. N.

Nicolas, St., a town of Belgium, in the province of East Flanders; a handsome town, and has a considerable trade in corn, cattle, and horses. Pop. 11,500. It is 12 miles S. W. of Antwerp.

Nicolayef, a city of Russia, in the government of Catherinenslaf; founded by Catherine II.: on the S. side of the Ingul, in its conflux with the Bog. The public buildings, and a number of private houses, are constructed of a white calcareous stone, but the rest of the houses are of wood. This place, being of easier access by water for vessels than Cherson, is now the capital of the naval establishment of the Black Sea. The admiralty, with a long line of magazines, workshops, wet and dry docks, and every necessary department for shipping, are placed along the bank of the Ingul. It is 30 miles N. N. E. of Oczakow, and 45. N. W. of Cherson. Long. 30. 46. E. lat. 46. 58. N.

Nicolo, St., the most considerable of the isles of Tremeti, in the Gulf of Venice. It has a harbour, defended by a fortress, in which is an abbey with a church. Long. 15. 37. E. lat. 42. 10. N.

Nicolsburg, a town of Moravia, with a castle on a mountain; 12 miles E. N. E. of Laab.

Nicopoli, a town of Bulgaria; famous for the first battle fought between the Turks and the Christians, in 1396, when the Emperor Sigismund was defeated, and had 20,000 men killed. It is seated on the Danube, at the influx of the Osma; 60 miles S. S. W. of Bucharest, and 150 N. N. W. of Adrianople. Long. 25. 43. E. lat. 44. 16. N.

Nicopoli, or Glanish, a town of Turkish Armenia, built by Pompey, in memory of a victory gained over Mithridates. It is 15 miles S. of Erzerum.

Nicosia, the capital of Cyprus, seated near the mountain Olympus. From the time of Constantine the Great, till 1567, it was 9 miles in circumference; but the Venetians, finding it too extensive, reduced it to 3, and fortified it with 11 bastions and three gates; all the rest they razed to the foundation, demolishing temples, palaces, and the most beautiful monuments. In 1570 it was besieged 45 days by the Turks, and then taken by a general assault. The church of St. Sophia is a fine old Gothic structure. The bazaar is extensive, well supplied with provisions, and remarkably clean. Long. 33. 26. E. lat. 35. 14. N. Pop. 15,000.

Nicosia, a town of Sicily, in Val di Demona; 12 miles S. of Cefalu.

Nicotera, a town of Naples, in Calabria Ultra, near the coast of the Mediterranean; 35 miles N. N. E. of Reggio, and 135 S. E. of Naples. Long. 16. 30. E. lat. 38. 34. N.

Nicoya, a town of Guatimala, in Costa Rica, situate on a small river, which runs into the Bay of Salinas, where there is a pearl fishery. It is 98 miles W. N. W. of Cartago. Long. 85. 49. W. lat. 10. 40. N.

Nicsara, a town of Turkey, in Caramania and an archbishop's see; 10 miles N. of Tocat. Long. 36. 9. E. lat. 39. 25. N.

Nidau, a town of Switzerland, in the canton of Bern, with a castle, situate on the Lake of Biel; 15 miles N. W. of Bern.

Nidda, a town of Germany, in Hesse Darmstadt, seated on a river of the same name; 20 miles N. E. of Frankfort.

Niebla, a town of Spain, in Seville; near which is a considerable copper mine; seated on the Tinto; 11 miles N. N. W. of Mogner, and 40 W. of Seville.

Niemeck, a town of Brandenburg, on the river Ada; 16 miles N. of Wittenberg.

Niemecz, a strong town of Moldavia, situate on a mountain, on a river of the same name; 76 miles W. S. W. of Jassy. Long. 26. 10. E. lat. 46. 58. N.

Niemen, a river which rises in Lithuania, and passes by Bielica and Grodno; it then runs through part of Samogitia and East Prussia, and enters the Curisch Haff by several mouths, of which the principal and most northern is called the Russ.

Nienburg, a strong town of Hanover, capital of the county of Hoya, with a considerable trade in corn and wool, seated on the Weser; 37 miles S. S. E. of Bremen. Long. 9. 25. E. lat. 52. 29. N.

Nienburg, a town of Prussia, in the government of Munster, seated on the Dinkel; 33 miles N. W. of Munster.

Nienburg, a town of Germany, in the duchy of Anhalt-Kothen, seated on the Saale; 8 miles N. W. of Kothen.

Nienhaus, a town of Hanover, in the district of Paderborn, with a castle, formerly the residence of the prince; seated on the Lippe; 2 miles N. N. E. of Paderborn.

Nieper. *See* Dnieper.

Niester. *See* Dniester.

Nieuport, a seaport of Belgium, in West Flanders, at the mouth of the Yperlee. Here are sluices, by which the country can be laid under water. The inhabitants principally subsist by the herring fishery, and by making nets and ropes. It is 9 miles S. W. of Ostend. Long. 2. 45. E. lat. 51. 8. N.

Nieuport, a town of the Netherlands, in South Holland, seated on the river Leck; 15 miles E. of Rotterdam.

Nievre, a department of France, including the greatest part of the province of Nivernois. It takes its name from a small river, which rises near Champlemy, and runs into the Loire, at Nevers, the chief town of the department.

Niger, a large river of Africa, which rises in the Korankoo country, in lat. 9. 25. N., and long. 9. 45. W., near to the sources of the Gambia and Senegal, which flow in an opposite or westerly direction. It pursues a north-easterly course as far as Tombuctoo, in about 17. 5. N. lat., and 3. 40. W. long., when it proceeds to the S. E., and falls into the Atlantic by several mouths in the Bight of Benin. This river, for many years, excited the most extraordinary interest in geographers, nothing but the name being known till Mungo Park reached it in 1796, at Sego, in Bambarra; he traced it upwards to Bammakoo, and downwards to Silla, an extent of 300 miles; it was there called the Joliba, the name Niger being unknown in Africa. It was afterwards explored by him to Jenna and Cabra, the port of Tombuctoo, and at Boossa he was killed by the natives. From this point all remained in mystery, till the brothers Lander, in 1830, traced the river from Yaoorie, by Rabba, Egga, Eboe, through which course it is called the Quorra, and finally to the river Nun, or First Brass river, in the Bight of Benin, and which had long been known and frequented by traders, little suspecting that it was the celebrated Niger. Its course has since been accurately surveyed, and several expeditions have been sent to it.

Nigono, a town of Italy, in the duchy of Modena; 22 miles S. W. of Modena.

Nigritia. *See* Negroland.

Nile, a great river of Africa, which has two principal sources, called the Bahr el Abiad, or White River, and the Bahr el Azrek, or Blue River (which see). They unite and form the Nile at Halfaiah, in Sennaar. It receives the Tacazze after having flowed some distance northward, after which it does not receive a single tributary. It then enters into Nubia, through which country it takes a circuitous course, and forms some considerable cataracts. It then flows almost directly S. through Egypt, till it arrives at Cairo; and a little below that city it divides into two great branches, which, with the Mediterranean Sea, form the island called Delta. The ancients reckoned eleven mouths of the Nile, of which seven were considerable; but at present there are only two that are at all times navigable, and those are at Rosetta and Damietta. The fertility of Egypt depends upon the overflowing of the Nile, which takes place regularly every year, from the 15th of June to the 17th of September, when it begins to decrease. It is caused by the periodical rains that fall between the tropics, and more particularly in Abyssinia, which is full of high mountains. In Cairo there is a canal, called Khalis, which is opened when the water is high enough; thence it is conveyed into reservoirs and cisterns, and is afterwards distributed into the fields and gardens, as occasion requires.

Nimeguen, a town of the Netherlands, in Gelderland, with a citadel, an ancient palace, and several forts. The churches are, in general, handsome structures; and the town-house is remarkable for its beauty and magnificence. The inhabitants subsist chiefly by brewing ale, and their trade with Germany. The city is celebrated in history, on account of several treaties of peace concluded here, particularly in 1678. It was taken by the French in 1794. It stands on the Waal; 35 miles E. S. E. of Utrecht. Long. 5. 51. E. lat. 51. 52. N.

Nimptsch, a town of Prussian Silesia, which gives name to a circle in the principality of Brieg. It has a castle on an eminence, and is seated on the Lohe; 26 miles S. W. of Breslau.

Ning-Koue, a city of China, of the first rank, in the province of Kiang-nan; noted for its manufacture of paper, made of a species of reed. Its district is very hilly, but pleasant; and the surrounding mountains, covered with woods, produce excellent medicinal plants. It is seated on a river, which runs into the Kiang-hu; 537 miles S. by E. of Peking. Long. 118 25. E. lat. 31. 2. N.

Ning-po, called by Europeans Liampo, an excellent seaport of China, and a city of the first rank in the province of Tche-kiang. The silks manufactured here are much esteemed in foreign countries, especially in Japan, where they are exchanged by the Chinese for copper, gold, and silver. It is seated on the E. coast, opposite Japan; 660 miles S. S. E. of Peking. Long. 120. 18. E. lat. 29. 58. N.

Ninguta, a city of Eastern Tartary, in the province of Kirin, with considerable trade; particularly in the valuable plant ginseng, which abounds in the neighbourhood. It is seated on the Hurha; 110 miles N. E. of Kirin. Long. 124. 40. E. lat. 44. 30. N.

Ninians, St., a town of Scotland, in Stirlingshire, with manufactures of leather, woollen cloth, and nails. It is 2 miles S. E. of Stirling. In this parish is the village of Bannockburn, the scene of the famous battle.

Ninove, a town of Belgium, in East Flanders, on the Dender; 12 miles W. of Brussels.

Nio, an island of the Grecian Archipelago, to the S. of Naxia, anciently called Nios. It is 35 miles in circumference, and fertile in corn, but has very little wood or oil. The regular manners of the inhabitants, who are all Greeks, revives an idea of the simplicity of the primitive ages; and their kind treatment of strangers appears to be the genuine remains of ancient hospitality. Pop. 1000.

Nion, a town of Switzerland, in the canton of Bern, with a manufacture of beautiful porcelain. It is 12 miles N. by E. of Geneva.

Nions, a town of France, department of Drome, with a mineral spring called Pontais, and some manufactures of soap and woollen cloth. It is seated at the foot of a chain of mountains, on the river Aigues; 21 miles E. S. E. of Montelimart.

Niort, a town of France, capital of the department of Deux Sevres, with manufactures of druggets, serges, and other coarse woollen goods. It is seated on the Sevre Niortoise; 31 miles E. N. E. of Rochelle, and 46. W. S. W. of Poitiers. Pop. 15,000. Long. 0. 33. W. lat. 46. 20. N.

NIPHON, or NIPPON, the largest island of Japan; 750 miles long, and from 150 to 300 broad; containing 55 provinces. It was discovered in 1542, by the Portuguese, who were cast ashore by a tempest. The chief town is Jedo.

NISCHNEI-NOVOGOROD. *See* NOVOGOROD.

NISIBIN, or NISBIN, a town and fortress of Asiatic Turkey, in Diarbeck, now greatly decayed. It is seated in a vast plain, 78 miles S. E. of Diarbekir.

NISIDA, a small island in the Gulf of Naples, very fertile, and laid out in slopes and terraces, like a large garden. It has a harbour, called Porto Pavone, 5 miles W. S. W. of Naples.

NISMES, a city of France, capital of the department of Gard, and a bishop's see. Here are numerous monuments of antiquity, of which the amphitheatre, built by the Romans, is the principal. There are likewise the ruins of a temple of Diana, and a grand tower. The Maison Quarrée, or the Square House, is one of the finest pieces of architecture of the Corinthian order in the world. Here are manufactures of silks, stuffs, stockings, cloth, leather, &c., and a considerable trade in silk, corn, dried fruits, oil, and wine. It is seated in a plain, abounding in wine and oil; 75 miles N. E. of Narbonne. Pop. 40,000, including 25,000 Protestants. Long. 4. 19. E. lat. 43. 50. N.

NISSA, a strong town of Servia. It was taken by the Hungarians, in 1737, but retaken by the Turks the following year. It is seated on a river of the same name; 20 miles E. of Precop, and 120 S. E. of Belgrade. Long. 22. 32. E. lat. 43. 32. N.

NITH, a river of Scotland, which rises in Ayrshire, flows through a part of Dumfriesshire, to which it gives the name of Nithsdale, and enters Solway Frith a little below Dumfries.

NIVELLE, a town of Belgium, chief place of an extensive district in Brabant, with a manufacture of cambrics, seated on the Thienne; 15 miles S. of Brussels.

NIVERNOIS, a late province of France, between Burgundy, Bourbonnois, and Berry. It is pretty fertile, contains mines of iron, and is watered by a great number of rivers, of which the Loire, Allier, and Yonne, are the principal. It now forms the department of Nievre.

NIXABOUR, a town of Persia, in Chorasan; 80 miles S. E. of Mesched. Long. 61. 32. E. lat. 35. 40. N.

NIXAPA, a town of Mexico, in the province of Guaxaca, with a rich Dominican convent. The country near it produces a great deal of indigo, cochineal, and sugar. It is 30 miles S. E. of Antioquiera. Long. 97. 15. W. lat. 16. 42. N.

NIXONTON, a town of North Carolina, chief of Pasquotank county; 28 miles E. N. E. of Edenton.

NIZAMPATAM, a town of Hindostan, in the circar of Guntoor, at the mouth of the Kistnah; 34 miles S. W. of Masulipatam.

NIZZA DELLA PAGLIA, a town of Sardinia, in Piedmont; seated on the Belbo; 14 miles S. E. of Asti. Pop. 5000.

NOACOTE, a town of Hindostan; capital of a district of its name in Nepaul. It has a celebrated temple dedicated to Bhavany. Long. 85. 30. E. lat. 27. 40. N.

NOAILLES, a town of France, department of Vienne, 6 miles S. S. E. of Poitiers.

NOANAGUR, a town of Hindostan, in Guzerat; capital of a district of its name on the coast of the Gulf of Cutch. The chief of the district, by a treaty with the British, engaged to prevent his subjects from plundering British vessels. It is 190 miles W. S. W. of Amedabad. Long. 69. 30. E. lat. 22. 22. N.

NOCERA, a town of Italy, in the duchy of Spoleto; seated at the foot of the Apennines; 18 miles N. E. of Spoleto.

NOCERA DELLI PAGANI, a town of Naples, in Principato Citra; 8 miles N. W. of Salerno, and 20 S. E. of Naples. Pop. 6800.

NOGARA, a town of France; department of Gers; 21 miles S. W. of Condon.

NOGARCOT, a town of Hindostan, in Nepaul; with a celebrated pagoda; 60 miles N. E. of Catmandu.

NOGENT LE ROTROU, a town of France; department of Eure-et-Loire, seated on the Huisne; 35 miles N. E. of Mans.

NOGENT SUR SEINE, a town in the department of Aube, seated on the Seine; 25 miles N. W. of Troyes. Pop. 3200.

NOIR CAPE, a promontory at the S. extremity of Terra del Fuego. Long. 73. 33. W. lat. 54. 32. S.

NOIRMOUTIER, an island of France, in the Bay of Biscay; S. of the mouth of the river Loire. It is 12 miles long and 3 broad; and has good pastures. Pop. 5500. The principal town, of the same name, is defended by a fort. Long. 2. 10. W. lat. 47. 0. N.

NOLA, a town of Naples; in Terra di Lavoro; once a rich Roman colony, and still a handsome place. The silk spun in its neighbourhood is much esteemed. It is 14 miles E. N. E. of Naples. Pop. 8000.

NOLI, a town of Sardinia, with a fort and a good harbour, 30 miles S. W. of Genoa. Long. 8. 41. E. lat. 44. 18. N.

NOMBRE DE DIOS, a town of Guatimala; in the province of Darien, 30 miles E. of Porto Bello, to which its once flourishing trade is now transferred.

NOMBRE DE DIOS, a town of Mexico, the most populous in the province of Zacatecas. It is 170 miles N. of Guadalaxara. Long. 104. 15. W. lat. 24. 0. N. Pop. 6800.

NOMENY, a town of France, in the department of Meurthe, on the Seille, 15 miles N. of Nancy.

NON, or NUN, CAPE, a promontory of the kingdom of Sus, opposite the Canary Islands. The Portuguese, in their first attempts to explore the W. coast of Africa, long considered this promontory as an impassable boundary.

This its name imports; but they doubled it, at last, in 1412. Long. 11. 50. W. lat. 28. 38. N.

NONA, a seaport of Dalmatia, and a bishop's see. It was once a splendid city, but is now a mean place, and its harbour not capable of receiving large vessels. It is almost surrounded by the sea, 7 miles N. by W. of Zara.

NONTRON, a town of France, department of Dordogne, 21 miles N. of Perigueux.

NOOPOUR, a town of Hindostan, in Guzerat, 55 miles E. of Surat. Long. 73. 50. E. lat. 21. 11 N.

NOOTKA SOUND. *See* KING GEORGE SOUND.

NORBERG, a town of Sweden, in Westmanland, near which are the best iron mines in the province. It is 34 miles N. of Stroemsholm. Long. 16. 12. E. lat. 60. 2. N.

NORCIA, a town of Italy, in the duchy of Spoleto, seated among mountains, on the river Fredara, 20 miles S. E. of Spoleto.

NORD, a department of France, so named from its situation. It includes the greater part of the former divisions of Hainault, French Flanders, and Cambresis, and is the principal department, next to Paris, in point of wealth and revenue. Area, 2820 square miles. Pop. 962,648.

NORDBURG, a town of Denmark, at the N. extremity of the Isle of Alsen, with a castle; 9 miles N. N. W. of Sunderburg.

NORDEN, a seaport of Hanover, in East Friesland, with a good harbour. It is 4 miles from the German Ocean, and 14 N. of Embden.

NORDHAUSEN, a town of Prussian Saxony, in the government of Erfurt, with seven Lutheran churches, and a well-built orphan-house. It has a considerable trade in corn, brandy, and rape and linseed oil, and manufactures of marble and alabaster. It was ceded to Prussia in 1802. It is seated on the Zorge, 35 miles N. N. E. of Erfurt. Long. 10. 56. E. lat. 51. 30. N. Pop. 9000.

NORDHEIM, a town of Hanover, situate on the Rhume, at its conflux with the Leina, 10 miles N. of Gottingen.

NORDKIOPING, a seaport of Sweden, in Gothland. It is 10 miles in circumference, but the houses are scattered, and the inhabitants do not exceed 9000. The river Motala flows through the town, forms a series of cataracts, and is divided into four principal streams, which encircle several rocky islands, covered with buildings; but at the extremity of the town it is navigable for large vessels. Here are manufactures of woollen cloth, paper, and fire-arms, some sugar-houses, and a brass-foundry. Corn is exported hence in great quantities, and a salmon fishery gives employment and riches to many of the inhabitants. It is 110 miles S. W. of Stockholm. Long. 15. 50. E. lat. 58. 35. N.

NORDLAND, one of the ancient divisions of Sweden; bounded on the N. by Lapland, E. by the Gulf of Bothnia, S. by Sweden Proper, and W. by the same and Norway. It contains six provinces.

NORDLAND, a province of Norway, having the North Sea on the W. and Swedish Lapland on the E.

NORDLINGEN, a town of Bavaria; fortified in the ancient manner. Here the league of the five western circles of the empire was concluded in 1702. In 1796 it was taken by the French. It is a commercial place, seated on the Eger; 38 miles N. N. W. of Augsburg. Pop. 5800. Long. 10. 34. E. lat. 48. 50. N.

NORDMALING, a town of Sweden, in Angermania; near a bay of the Gulf of Bothnia, 24 miles S. W. of Uma, and 70 N. E. of Hermosand.

NORDSTRAND, an island of Denmark, on the W. coast of South Jutland, 12 miles long, and 5 broad. It has a town called Ham, 28 miles W. of Sleswick. Long. 9. 0. E. lat. 54. 40. N. Pop. 2500.

NORE, a noted part of the river Thames; situated off Sheerness, at the point of a sand-bank, on which is a light vessel. Long. 0. 44. E. lat. 51. 27. N.

NORFOLK, a county of England; 77 miles long and 45 broad; bounded on the N. and E. by the German Ocean, S. E. and S. by Suffolk, and W. by Cambridgeshire and Lincolnshire. It contains 1,292,400 acres, is divided into 33 hundreds and 660 parishes, has one city and 32 market towns, and sends 4 members to parliament for the E. and W. divisions of the county. The products vary according to the soil and situation. The lighter arable lands produce barley in great plenty; wheat is cultivated in the stronger soils; and turnips are grown here in great quantities; buck-wheat is also grown on the light soils, and used for feeding swine and poultry. The fenny parts yield great quantities of butter, which is sent to London under the name of Cambridge butter. The sheep are a hardy small breed, much valued for their mutton. Poultry of all kinds are very plentiful, and the turkeys are reared here to a larger size than elsewhere; rabbits are extremely numerous on the sandy heaths; and there is abundance of game, especially of pheasants. The principal manufactures of the county are silks, bombazines, crapes, camblets, &c. It is watered by the Great Ouse, Nen, Little Ouse, Waveney, Yare, Bure, and some smaller streams. Norwich is the capital.

NORFOLK, a seaport of Virginia; capital of a county of the same name. It was burnt in 1776, by order of the British governor; but is now the most considerable commercial town in the state. The chief exports are tobacco, flour, corn, staves, and lumber. Here are 5 churches, and the harbour is large enough to contain 300 ships. The town stands on the E. side of Elizabeth River, near its entrance into the estuary of James River; 110 miles E. S. E. of Richmond.

NORFOLK ISLAND, an island in the South Pacific; lying to the E. of New South Wales, and settled by a colony of convicts, subordinate to that government. It was discovered in 1774 by Captain Cook, who found it uninhabited, except by birds. It is very hilly, but some of the valleys are tolerably large. Mount Pitt is 12,000 feet high. It is a beautiful spot, the climate being delicious, and the soil wonderfully productive. It would seem to be a perfect garden. The whole island is covered by a thick forest, but has not much underwood; and the principal timber-tree is the pine, which is very useful in building, and seems to be durable. The island is supplied with many streams of good water, which abound with very fine eels. The cliffs round the coast are 240 feet high, quite perpendicular: and anchorage is safe all round the island, on taking the lee-side; but there is no harbour, and, from the heavy seas which constantly beat upon the shore, there is great difficulty in approaching it. It was abandoned for New Norfolk, in Van Diemen's Land, but was again colonized, and is at present a penal settlement. Long. 168. 2. E. lat. 29. 5. S.

Norfolk, New, or Elizabethtown, a town of Van Diemen's Land, in Buckingham county; on the banks of the Derwent, 22 miles from Hobart Town. It was founded by the settlers from Norfolk Island, and the name was afterwards changed to Elizabethtown, but the original name is the one in use.

Norham, a village in the detached part of Durham, called Norhamshire. Its castle, on the edge of a rock above the Tweed, has been many times taken and destroyed by the Scotch, and as often rebuilt by the English; 6 miles S. W. of Berwick.

Normandy, a former province of France, now forming the departments of Calvados, Eure, Manche, Orne, and Lower Seine. The Normans, a people of Denmark and Norway, having entered France, under Rollo, Charles the Simple ceded this country to them in 912, which from that time was called Normandy. Rollo, the first duke, held it as a fief of the crown of France, as did several of his successors after him. In 1066, William, the seventh duke, having conquered England, it became a province of that country, till it was lost in the reign of King John, and reunited to the crown of France. It is one of the most fertile provinces in France, and abounds in all things except wine, which defect is supplied by cider and perry. It contains iron, copper, and a great number of rivers and harbours.

Norridgewock, a town of the state of Maine, capital of Somerset county, situate on the Kennebeck, over which is an elegant bridge, 10 miles W. by N. of Canaan. Pop. 1865.

Norristown, a town of Pennsylvania, capital of Montgomery county. It is seated on the Schuylkill, 15 miles N. W. of Philadelphia. Long. 75. 24. W. lat. 40. 10. N.

Nortelga, or Nor Telge, a seaport of Sweden, in the Baltic. Near it is a forge for making fire-arms; 30 miles N. E. of Stockholm. Long. 10. 32. E. lat. 50. 44. N.

Northallerton, a borough in North Yorkshire, with a market on Wednesday; it returns one member to parliament. Near this place was fought the celebrated battle between the English and Scots, called the Battle of the Standard, in 1138. It is seated in a delightful valley, watered by the river Wisk: 32 miles N. N. W. of York, and 222 N. by W. of London.

North Cape, an enormous rock at the N. end of the island Maggeroe, on the coast of Norway, and the most northern promontory of Europe. Long. 25. 57. E. lat. 71. 10. N.

North Sea. *See* German Ocean.

Northampton, a town of Massachusets; capital of Hampshire county. It has a considerable inland trade, and is situate on the Connecticut, 98 miles W. of Boston.

Northampton, a borough, and the capital of Northamptonshire, governed by a mayor, with a market on Saturday; returning two members to parliament. It was formerly surrounded by a wall, and had a castle, of which there are still some remains. In 1675 it was almost entirely destroyed by fire, but was soon rebuilt. The houses are uniformly built of freestone, and chiefly slated; the streets are regular, and the town is lighted with gas. It has four churches, eight dissenting meeting-houses, a spacious market place, a good free-school, a general infirmary, and a county gaol, on the principles of Mr. Howard. The principal manufactures consists of boots and shoes, chiefly for exportation. In the meadows below the town a battle was fought in 1460 between Henry VI. and the Yorkists, in which the former was defeated and made prisoner. Two miles to the S. is a fine ancient Gothic structure, called Queen's Cross, erected by Edward I., in memory of his queen, Eleanor. Northampton is seated on the Nen; 20 miles S. E. of Coventry, and 66 N. W. of London.

Northamptonshire, a county of England, 65 miles long, and 24 where broadest, bounded S. by Buckinghamshire and Oxfordshire, W. by the latter county and Warwickshire, N. W. by Leicestershire and Rutlandshire, N. by Lincolnshire, and E. by the counties of Cambridge, Huntingdon, and Bedford. It contains 646,810 acres, is divided into 19 hundreds, and 336 parishes, has one city and 11 market-towns, and sends four members to parliament for the N. and S. divisions of the county. In the N. E. part, near Peterborough, commences a fenny tract, extending to the Lincolnshire Wash. With this single exception, Northamptonshire is said to contain less waste ground, and more seats of the nobility and gentry, than any other county. Its greatest defect is a scarcity of fuel, which is but scantily supplied by its woods; and though coal is brought by the river Nen, it is at a very dear rate. This county, however, possesses some considerable remains of its old forests, particularly those of Rockingham, on the N.W., and of Salcey and Whittlebury, on the S. Its products are, in general, the same with those of other farming counties, but it is particularly celebrated for grazing land. Woad for the dyers is cultivated here, but the county is not distinguished for manufactures. The principal rivers are the Nen and Welland; besides which it is partly watered by the Ouse, Leam, Cherwell, and Avon, and the inland trade is greatly facilitated by the construction of canals, and by the Birmingham Railway, which traverses this county.

Northfleet, a village in Kent, seated on the Thames; 2 miles W. of Gravesend. The church contains fragments of monuments as ancient as the 14th century. Vast quantities of lime are made here, and great numbers of extraneous fossils have been dug up.

NORTHOP,* a town of Wales, in Flintshire; 3 miles S. E. of Flint, noted for its manufactures of coarse earthenware, fire-bricks, &c.

NORTHUMBERLAND, the most northern county of England. In the Saxon heptarchy it was a part of the kingdom of the Northumbrians, which contained also the counties of York, Lancaster, Durham, Cumberland, and Westmorland, and received its name from being situate N. of the Humber. It is a triangular form, 64 miles in extreme length, and 50 in extreme breadth; bounded on the E. by the German Ocean, S. by Durham, W. by Cumberland and Scotland, and N. by the detached part of Durham called Norhamshire and Islandshire. It contains 1,157,760 acres, is divided into six wards and 460 parishes, has 12 market-towns, and sends four members to parliament for the N. and S. divisions of the county. The soil is various; the E. part is fruitful in most sorts of corn, with rich meadows on the banks of the rivers; but the W. part is mostly heathy and mountainous. The S. E. part abounds with thick seams of coal, and the S. W. angle has rich lead mines. Limestone and iron ore abound in various parts. The principal rivers are the Tyne, Coquet, Alm, and Blyth. Alnwick is the capital; but the largest town is Newcastle. It gives the title of duke to the ancient family of Percy.

NORTHUMBERLAND, a town of Pennsylvania, in a county of its name; seated in the angle formed by the junction of the W. and E. branches of the Susquehanna; 2 miles above Sunbury, and 138 N. W. of Philadelphia.

NORTHUMBERLAND ISLANDS, a chain of islands in the South Pacific; near the N. E. coast of Australia. Long. 150. E. lat. 22. S.

NORTHUMBERLAND STRAIT, the S. part of the Gulf of St. Lawrence; between the island of St. John and the coast of New Brunswick and Nova Scotia.

NORTHWICH, a town in Cheshire, with a market on Friday, a cotton manufacture, and considerable salt-works; seated on the Dan, at its junction with the Weever; 20 miles N. E. of Chester, and 174 N. W. of London.

NORTON, a town of Massachusets, in Bristol county. A great quantity of nails are made here, and it has a manufacture of ochre, similar to that of Taunton; 28 miles S. of Boston.

NORTON. *See* CHIPPING.

NORTON SOUND, an inlet of the sea, on the W. coast of North America, discovered by Cook in his last voyage. The entrance is between Cape Denbigh, on the E., and Cape Danby, on the W., about 70 miles distant, both lying in lat. 64. 30. N., and the latter in long. 162. 55. W.

NORWALK, a town of Connecticut, in Fairfield county, with two churches, and some ironworks. It has a small trade to the West Indies, and is situate on an inlet of Long Island Sound; 48 miles N. E. of New York. Long. 73. 47. W. lat. 41. 9. N. Pop. 3863.

NORWAY, a country in the N. of Europe, belonging to Sweden, the most westerly part of the ancient Scandinavia. It is bounded on the W. and N. by the Northern Ocean, E. by Swedish Lapland and Sweden, and S. by the Cattegat; extending from the Naze in lat. 57. 30., to the North Cape in lat. 71. 10. Its breadth, which is very unequal, is from 40 to 280 miles. It is naturally formed into two divisions, namely, Northern and Southern, or Proper Norway, separated from each other by the small Swedish province of Herndahl. It is divided into the four governments of Aggerhuys, Christiania or Christiansand, Berghen, and Drontheim. From its rocky soil, and northern position, Norway is not populous in proportion to its extent. The number of inhabitants is calculated at 1,000,000, who, like the Swiss mountaineers, are exceedingly attached to their country. In Norway they have a particular code, called the Norway Law, compiled by Grieffelfeld, at the command of Christian V., the great legislator of this country. By this law—the palladium of Norway—the peasants are free-born. They possess much spirit and fire in their manner; are frank, open, and undaunted, yet not insolent; never fawning, yet paying proper respect. Their principal mode of salute is by offering their hand; and when they are given or paid any trifle, the peasants, instead of returning thanks by words, or by a bow, shake hands with great frankness and cordiality. The same causes which affect the population of Norway operate likewise on the state of tillage; for although in some places vegetation is so quick, that the corn is sown and cut in six or seven weeks, yet the country does not produce sufficient corn for its own consumption. It is however, exceedingly rich in pasture, and consequently produces much cattle. The horses are small, but strong, very active, and hardy. The fisheries, particiularly on the W. coast, find employment and wealth for the natives, and supply the finest sailors for the Danish fleet. The principal fish are salmon, cod, ling, and whiting: their livers also yield train-oil, and the smallest are given as winter fodder to the cattle. The extensive forests of oak and pine produce timber, spars, beams, and planks, besides, charcoal, turpentine, bark, fuel, and even manure; and the birch (the bark of which is used as a covering for the roofs of houses) not only supplies fuel, but also a kind of wine. The general exports are tallow, butter, dried fish, timber, planks, horses, horned cattle, silver, cobalt, alum, Prussian blue, copper, and iron. It abounds in lakes and rivers; the former so large that they appear like inlets of the sea; but the rivers are in general of a short course, except the Glommen. The mountains are numerous, and generally clothed with pines and firs; the grand Scandinavian chain, which runs from S. to N., is known by distinct appellations; the chief are the ridges of Langfial, Dofrafial, Kolen, and Severnoi. The wild animals are the bear, lynx, wolf, fox, and hare; but the most singular creature is the lemming, or Norwegian mouse, of a reddish colour, and about five inches long. These animals proceed in vast numbers from the ridge of Kolen to the sea, devouring every produce of the soil in their course, and at last seem to devour each other. Norway was formerly governed by its own hereditary sovereigns. On the demise of Hasen V., in 1319, without male issue, his grandson, in the female line, Magnus Smek, united in his person the kingdoms of Sweden and Norway. Magnus was succeeded in the kingdom of Norway by his son Hagen VI. husband of the celebrated Margaret, and at his decease, in 1380, Norway was united to Denmark by their son Olof V., who dying without issue, Margaret herself was raised to the throne by the unanimous voice of the nation On her death, it descended, with Denmark and Sweden, to her nephew Eric. Sweden was afterwards separated from Denmark by the valour and address of Gustavus Vasa. By the treaty of Kiel, in Jan. 1814, Norway was ceded by the king of Denmark to Sweden; but the people not approving of this cession, had recourse to arms, in order to resist the entrance of the Swedish troops into their country; and the Diet elected Prince Christian, the king of Denmark's son, who was then governor, to the throne. However, on the conclusion of the war with France, the allied powers, who had previously promised this country to Sweden, if she would take an active part in the coalition against the French empire, now did all in their power to enforce the cession. For this purpose a considerable body of their troops was marched into the Danish territories on the continent, to watch that power, and all the ports of Norway were blockaded by the Swedish and English fleets by sea, while the Swedish army, under the crown prince, entered Norway by land. Amidst such united efforts, it was not to be expected that the brave Norwegians could hold out long. After the capture of Frederickstadt, and the passage of the Glommen by the Swedes, Prince Christian proposed to resign his crown into the hands of the Diet; and on the 20th of October, 1814, that assembly came to the resolution that Norway should be governed by the king of Sweden, but as an integral state, preserving its constitution and laws; to which the Sweden assented. Christiania is the capital.

Norwich, a city and county of itself; the capital of Norfolk, and a bishop's see; with markets on Wednesday and Saturday. It is governed by a mayor, recorder, &c.; and sends two members to parliament. It was formerly surrounded by a strong wall, of which some ruins still remain. Many of the streets are still narrow and ill-disposed, though, during the last ten years, considerable improvements have been effected. Besides the cathedral, which is one of the most spacious and elegant in the kingdom, here are 32 parish churches, two churches for the Flemings, a number of dissenting meeting-houses, and two Roman Catholic chapels. On a hill, commanding an extensive view of the city, is the castle, an ancient and stately edifice, occupied as a shire-house and county gaol. It has recently undergone considerable alteration and enlargement. Among the other public buildings are the Guildhall, St. Andrew's Hall, the assembly-room, the theatre, the Norfolk and Norwich Hospital, the Norwich Dispensary, the Blind Hospital, Lunatic Asylum, and Doughty's Hospital. Here are also a good grammar-school, a public library, a literary institution, a musuem, a society of artists, and other scientific and charitable institutions. The market-place is a spacious area, with a gradual descent. It is occupied on market days by an immense number of moveable shambles, and contrivances for displaying the neatly-trussed poultry, and other provisions, brought from all parts of the county, and has a very striking appearance. On the upper part, but separated by a range of shops and dwelling-houses, is a good fish market, which is well supplied. Near this city, on Mousehold Heath, are the ruins of the castle of Kett, the tanner, by whose rebellion, in the reign of Edward VI., the city was reduced to a ruinous state. Norwich has extensive manufactures of crapes, bombazines, and stuffs of various kinds, and a considerable trade. It is seated on the river Yare; 22 miles W. of Yarmouth, and 110 N. E. of London. Long. 1. 20. E. lat. 52. 40.

Norwich, a city of Connecticut, in New London county; with five churches. It is in three divisions, namely, Chelsea, the Town, and Beau Hill. The executive courts of law are held at this place and New London alternately. Here are made paper of all kinds, stockings, buttons, stone and earthenware, and all kinds of forge work. It is seated at the head of navigation on the Thames; 12 miles N. of New London. Long. 72. 12. W. lat. 41. 34. N.—Also, the name of numerous inconsiderable townships of the United States.

Nossen, a town of Saxony; on the Muldau; 18 miles W. of Dresden.

Noteburg, a town of Russia, in the government of Petersburg; seated on an island in the lake Ladoga, at the place where the Neva issues. It has a good citadel, and was capital of Ingria, before Petersburg was built. It is 25 miles E. of Petersburg. Long. 31. 9. E. lat. 59. 56. N.

Noto, a town of Sicily, capital of Val di Noto. It was ruined by an earthquake in 1693, and near it another town was built, called Noto Nuovo. It is 22 miles S. W. of Syracuse. Long. 15. 19. E. lat. 36. 50. N.

Nottingham, a town of Maryland; in Prince George county; situate on the Patuxent; 26 miles S. E. of Washington.

Nottingham, a town of New Hampshire; in Rockingham county; 14 miles N. N. W. of Exeter.—Also, the name of several townships in the United States.

Nottingham, a borough and the capital of Nottinghamshire; governed by a mayor, with markets on Wednesday and Saturday. It returns two members to parliament. It is situate on the side and summit of a rock, of a soft, sandy nature, out of which many of the cellars and vaults of the town are excavated, and from which the name of the town is derived, *i. e.* "the town of the caves." To the W. of the town, on a rocky eminence, is the castle, a magnificent modern structure, now destroyed by fire, belonging to the Duke of Newcastle, built on the site of an ancient fortress, originally erected in the reign of William the Conqueror, and afterwards the residence of the profligate Isabella, queen of Edward II., and her paramour Roger Mortimer. It was made a garrison by the parliamentarians in the reign of Charles the I., but was taken by the royalists; after the civil war, it was dismantled by order of Oliver Cromwell, and was rebuilt by William Cavendish, Duke of Newcastle. It is a handsome town, distinguished by its spacious market-place, and noted for its excellent ale. It is one of the principal seats of the silk and cotton stocking manufacture; the lace manufacture is also very extensive. It has three parish churches, one extraparochial; a chapel of ease, above 15 meeting-houses for dissenters, two for Roman Catholics, and a synagogue for Jews. The charitable institutions are numerous, and many of them pre-eminent in extent and utility of design. In the neighbourhood are many coal-pits, which afford plenty of fuel at little expense. At this town Charles I. set up his standard, at the commencement of the civil war, which terminated in his destruction. Nottingham is seated on a river which communicates with the Trent 1 mile to the S. It is 16 miles E. of Derby, and 124 N. by W. of London. Long. 1. 8. W. lat. 52. 57. N.

NOTTINGHAMSHIRE, a county of England, 48 miles long, and 25 broad; bounded N. by Yorkshire, E. by Lincolnshire, S. by Leicestershire, and W. by Derbyshire. It contains 533,680 acres, is divided into six hundreds, and 168 parishes, has eight market-towns, and sends four members to parliament for the N. and S. divisions of the county. It enjoys such a temperature of soil and climate as to render it one of the most fertile and healthful counties in England. The principal rivers are the Trent, Idle, and Erwash. Almost the whole of the middle and western parts of the county were formerly occupied by the extensive forest of Sherwood, the only royal forest N. of the Trent; but the greater part is now enclosed and covered with thriving towns, cheerful villages, and extensive parks. The chief products of this county are coal, of which there is a great plenty, gypsum, lead, grain of all sorts, cattle, malt, hops, wool, liquorice, and woad. The manufactures chiefly consist of hosiery, bobbin-net and net lace, glass, and earthenware.

NOVA SCOTIA, a British province of North America; which formerly, till 1784, included the province of New Brunswick. It is bounded on the S. and S. E. by the Atlantic, E. by the Gut of Canso, N. by Northumberland Strait, and N. W. by New Brunswick and the Bay of Fundy. Its length is 235 miles from Cape Sable on the S. W. to Cape Canso on the N. E. Its extreme breadth is 88 miles, but the mean of the peninsular part is not more than 45: it contains an area of 15,617 square miles. It has several lakes, and a vast number of small rivers. It is a peninsula, lying S. E. of New Brunswick, and joined to it by a narrow isthmus, at the N. E. extremity of the Bay of Fundy. The French settled here before they made any establishment in Canada, and called it Acadia. The first grant of lands was made to Sir William Alexander, by James I. of England, from whom it received the name of Nova Scotia. Since its first settlement it has more than once changed rulers and proprietors, nor was it confirmed to England till the peace of Utrecht in 1713. The inhabitants consist of English, Scotch, Irish, and a few Germans: recent accounts state them at 300,000. The soil is in many parts thin and sterile, but there are some tracts not inferior to the best lands in New England. Halifax is the capital.

NOVA ZEMBLA, or NOVAIA ZEMLIA, an island in the Arctic Ocean; separated from the continent of Russia by the Strait of Waigatz. This country was discovered by the English in 1556. In 1595, a Dutch vessel being cast away on the coast, the crew were obliged to winter here, and with great difficulty preserved their lives. The eastern coast was first visited in 1742; from 1762 till 1819 no expedition to these islands is on record; between 1819 and 1824 the W. coasts were explored in five expeditions, by order of the Russian government; the eastern coast was visited in 1832, again in 1834, and in 1837; the result of these discoveries is, that more than the eastern half of the islands, as formerly represented, has no existence; and that, beyond the lat. of Cape Nassau, 76. 17. N., nothing is known. It stretches in a N. N. W. direction about 400 geographical miles, with an average breadth of 50 miles. It is divided into two by the Matoshkin Shar, in lat. 73. 45., long. of W. entrance 54. 10. E. The country is extremely desolate, producing no trees, nor any vegetables but moss, and some few arctic plants. It is inhabited by wild beasts, particularly white bears, white foxes, elks, rein-deer, and rabbits.

NOVALLE, a town of Austrian Italy; in the Trevisano; 10 miles S. W. of Treviso.

NOVARA, a town of Italy; capital of a province of its name, in the Sardinian Milanese. It contains 17 churches, besides the cathedral: and is seated on an eminence; 25 miles W. by S. of Milan. Pop. 13,000.

NOVELLARA, a town of Italy, in the Modenese, with a castle, 17 miles E. by N. of Parma, and 18 N. N. W. of Modena.

NOVI, a town of the Sardinian States, in the territory of Genoa; with a strong castle on a mountain. It is the principal deposit for goods coming from the Levant, which pass into Austrian Italy, and thence into the S. of Germany. Near this place, in 1799, the Austrians and Russians defeated the French, who lost their general (Joubert,) and nearly 10,000 men; 25 miles N. by W. of Genoa. Pop. 5100.

NOVI, a fortified town of Croatia; taken by the Austrians in 1789. It is seated on the right bank of the Unna; 52 miles S. E. of Carlstadt. Long. 16. 53. E. lat. 45. 8. N.

NOVI BAZAR, a town of Servia, seated near the Oresco; 72 miles W. of Nissa, and 95 S. of Belgrade. Pop. 8000. Long. 21. 1. E. lat. 43. 35. N.

NOVIGRAD, a town of Hungary, capital of a

county of the same name; with a castle, seated on a mountain, near the Danube; 25 miles N. of Buda.

NOVIGRAD, a town of Austrian Dalmatia; with a castle, seated on a lake of the same name; near the Gulf of Venice; 17 miles E. of Nona, and 25 N. W. of Zara.

NOVOGOROD, a city of Russia, capital of a government of the same name, and formerly called Great Novogorod, to distinguish it from other towns of the same appellation. It was for a long time governed by its own dukes, and was in fact a republic, under the jurisdiction of a nominal sovereign. It was the great mart of trade between Russia and the Hanseatic cities, and made the most rapid advances in opulence and population. Its power was so great, and its situation so impregnable, as to give rise to a proverb: "Who can resist the gods and Great Novogorod?" But in the 15th century this independent republic was obliged to submit to Ivan Basilowitz I., grand duke of Russia. It continued, nevertheless, the largest and most commercial city in Russia, and contained at least 400,000 inhabitants. It was first desolated by the cruelties of Ivan Basilowitz II.; but its splendour was not totally eclipsed until Peter the Great built Petersburg, to which he transferred all the commerce of the Baltic that had before entered here. It now contains scarcely 8000 souls; and a vast number of churches and convents stand as melancholy monuments of its former magnificence. The town stretches on both sides of the Volkoff, a river of considerable depth and rapidity, which separates it into two divisions, namely, the trading part, and the quarter of St. Sophia; in the latter are the ruins of the cathedral, in which several princes of the ducal family of Russia are interred. Novogorod is situate near the N. end of the lake Ilmen; 120 miles S. S. E. of Petersburg. Long. 31. 45. E. lat. 58. 25. N.

NOVOGOROD, NIZNEI, a city of Russia, capital of a government of the same name, and an archbishop's see. It has a castle, surrounded by stone walls; also two cathedrals, 28 parish churches, and five convents. The trade is considerable, and the shops richly furnished with all kinds of foreign and home goods. It is seated at the conflux of the Occa with the Volga; 250 miles E. by N. of Moscow.

NOVOGOROD, SEVERSKOI, a town of Russia; government of Czernigov, seated on the Desna; 86 miles E. N. E. of Czernigov.

NOVOGRODEK, a town of Russian Lithuania, government of Grodno; seated on a hill in a vast plain; 80 miles S. by E. of Wilna. Long. 26. 8. E. lat. 53. 25. N.

NOVOMIGOROD, a town of Russia, in the government of Catharinenslaf; 160 miles N. N. W. of Cherson. Long. 31. 44. E. lat. 48. 40. N.

NOUTRA, a town of Austrian Poland, near which are mines of gold and silver; 30 miles S. of Cracow.

NOYA, a town of Spain, in Galicia. The chief trade is in ship-building. It stands at the mouth of the Tambro; 15 miles W. of Compostella.

NOYERS, a town of France, department of Yonne; with a castle; seated on the Serin; 19 miles E. S. E. of Auxerre.

NOYON, a town in the department of Oise; the birthplace of the celebrated Calvin. It is an episcopal see, and is seated near the Oise; 25 miles N. W. of Soissons, and 70 N. by E. of Paris.

NOZEROY, a town in the department of Jura; with a castle on a mountain; 20 miles S. E. of Salins.

NUBIA, a country of Africa; bounded on the N. by Egypt, E. by the Red Sea, S. by Abyssinia and Darfoor, and W. by Bornou. It is about 600 miles in length, and 450 in breadth. The Nile runs through it, on the banks of which it is fruitful, but in other places barren, sandy, and destitute of water. The inhabitants make their bread and drink of a small round seed called durra, or dhourra, a kind of millet. Their houses have mud walls, are very low, and covered with reeds. The dress of the better sort is a vest without sleeves, and they have no coverings for head, legs, or feet. The common people wrap a piece of linen cloth about them, and the children go quite naked. They are described as a stupid and debauched people, but profess to be Mahomedans. The productions of the country are gold, elephants' teeth, civet, and sandal-wood; and a great many slaves are sent into Egypt.

NUEZ, a town of Spain, in the province of Leon, on the borders of Portugal; 15 miles E. of Braganza, and 48 W. of Zamora.

NUITZ, a town of France, department of Cote d'Or; famous for its excellent wines. It is seated at the foot of a mountain; 15 miles S. S. W. of Dijon.

NUN, or WADINOON, an extensive country of Africa, of which the emperor of Morocco arrogates to himself the sovereignty, but his real authority is extremely feeble. It is inhabited by different tribes of Arabs, whose camps are scattered over such interior parts of the country as are capable of cultivation. It has a river of the same name, which enters the Atlantic on the N. side of Cape Non.

NUNDYDROOG, a town and fortress of Hindostan, in Mysore. It is built on the summit of a mountain, 1700 feet in height, the greater part inaccessible; but was besieged and taken by the English, under Lord Cornwallis, in 1792. It is 70 miles N. of Seringapatam.

NUNEATON, a town in Warwickshire; with a market on Saturday; and manufactures of woollen cloths and ribbons. It was formerly noted for its nunnery: it is seated on the river Anker, 9 miles N. by E. of Coventry, and 98 N. W. of London.

NUNJINAGODU, a town of Hindostan, in Mysore; with a ruinous fort, and a large square temple. It is situate in the fork formed by the junction of the Kaundini with the Kapini; 12 miles S. by E. Mysore.

Nuremberg, a town of Bavaria, in the circle of Rezat. It is surrounded by an old wall and ditch, more than 3 miles in circumference, formerly flanked with 365 towers; and through the middle of the town flows the river Pegnitz, over which are six stone bridges, and several of wood. The inhabitants are very industrious, and their maps and prints, as well as their musical and mathematical instruments, are in high esteem; nor are they less curious in clock-work, and in the several manufactures of iron, steel, ivory, wood, and alabaster. The toys commonly known in England by the name of Dutch toys are also made here. Among the public institutions are a famous academy for painting, an anatomical theatre, and a public library. The ancient castle, or palace, is still standing at the extremity of the city; and the arsenal is one of the best in Germany. The houses are built of freestone, and are four or five stories high. Nuremberg was given to Bavaria by the treaty of Tilsit, in 1807. It is 95 miles N. by W. of Munich, 250 W. N. W. of Vienna. Pop. 27,000. Long. 11. 4. E. lat. 49. 27. N.

Nurtingen, a town of Wirtemberg; with an hospital, founded in 1481, said to be the richest foundation in the kingdom. It is situate on the Neckar; 14 miles S. E. of Stutgard.

Nusserpour, a town of Hindostan, capital of a district of the same name, in the province of Sindy. It is situate on the Sinde; 58 miles N. E. of Tatta. Long. 69. 10. E. lat. 25. 28. N.

Nyborg, a seaport of Denmark, on the E. coast of the Isle of Funen. The remains of the old palace, in which Christian II. was born, now serve for a magazine and arsenal. It is seated on a bay of the Great Belt; 10 miles E. of Odensee. Pop. 2000. Long. 10. 40. E. lat. 55. 30. N.

Nykioping, a town of Denmark, in North Jutland; with a good harbour; on the Gulf of Lymford. It stands on the E. side of the island of Mors, which is formed by branches of the gulf; 40 miles W. by S. of Alburg. Long. 8. 36. E. lat. 56. 52. N.

Nykoping, a seaport of Denmark, capital of the Isle of Falster; with a royal palace, and one of the best endowed hospitals in the kingdom. It stands on a narrow channel, opposite the Isle of Laland; 60 miles S. S. W. of Copenhagen. Long. 11. 58. E. lat. 54. 50. N.

Nykoping, a government of Sweden; comprehending the W. part of Sudermania. Pop. 99,000.

Nykoping, a neat town of Sweden, capital of Sudermania; with a harbour, and the remains of a strong castle. It is the most ancient town in the kingdom, and was formerly the residence of the kings of Sudermania. It is seated on a river of the same name, near the Baltic; 70 miles S. W. of Stockholm. Pop. 2400. Long. 17. 27. E. lat. 58. 35. N.

Nyland, a province of European Russia, in Finland; lying on the Gulf of Finland, to the W. of Carelia. It is 120 miles long, and from 30 to 60 broad; and is a fertile pleasant country, being better peopled and cultivated than the neighbouring provinces. The inhabitants (about 115,000) carry on some trade in corn, cattle, planks, linen, and dried fish.

Nyslot, a town of Russia, in the government of Wiburg, on the Lake Saima. The castle, which stands on a rock in a river, near the town, is strongly fortified by nature and art. It was taken by the Russians in 1714, restored to the Swedes at the peace of Nystadt, but finally given up to the Russians, by the treaty of Abo, in 1743. It is 50 miles N. W. of Wiburg.

Nyslot, a town of Russia, in the government of Livonia, with a castle; 20 miles S. by W. of Narva.

Nystadt, a town of Russia, in Finland; with a commodious harbour, and a considerable trade in all kinds of wooden vessels. In 1721 a peace was concluded here between Russia and Sweden. It is seated on a bay of the Gulf of Bothnia; 38 miles N. W. of Abo. Pop. 1900. Long. 21. 31. E. lat. 61. 10. N.

Nysted, a town of Denmark, on the S. E. coast of the isle of Laland. It carries on a considerable trade with the provinces of Germany. It is 22 miles E. S. E. of Naxkow.

O.

O, or St. Martin d'O, a town of France, department of Orne; 5 miles S. of Argentan.

Oahaha, a river of Lousiana, which falls into the Mississippi, from the N. W. in lat. 39. 10. N. and 7 miles N. of Riviere au Beauf.

Oahoona, one of the Ingraham Isles, which is said to be the northernmost of all this cluster. It lies about 10 leagues N. E. of Nooheva. To this island Captain Roberts gave the name of Massachusets. Captain Ingraham had before called it Washington.

Oakham, the chief town of Rutlandshire, with a market on Saturday. Near the church are the decaying walls of an old castle; and in 1749 four silver pennies of the later Mercian kings were found here. It is seated in the centre of a fertile valley, called the Vale of Catmore; 28 miles S. by E. of Nottingham, and 98 N. by W. of London. Long. 0. 46. W. lat. 52. 42. N.

Oakhampton, a town in Devonshire, market on Saturday. It has a manufacture of serges, and the remains of a castle, dismantled by Henry VIII. It stand on the river Oak; 24 miles W. of Exeter, and 195 W. by S. of London.

Oakingham. *See* Wokingham.

Oaxaca. *See* Guaxaca.

Oban, a village of modern importance in Scotland, in Argyleshire; seated 3 miles to the S. of the entrance of Loch Etive. Here is an excellent harbour, capable of containing upwards of 500 merchantmen, defended from the westerly winds by the islands of Kerrera and Mull. It is 33 miles N. W. of Inverary, and 136 W. N. W. of Edinburgh.

OBDACH, a town of the Austrian states, in Styria, at the conflux of the Achza and Traun; 9 miles S. E. of Judenburg.

OBERKIRCH, a town of Baden; 15 miles E. of Strasburg.

OBERNBERG, a town of Bavaria, with a castle seated on the Inn; 12 miles S. S. W. of Passau.

OBERNDORF, a town of Wirtemberg, seated on the Neckar; 8 miles N. N. E. of Rothweil.

OBIDOS, a town of Portugal, in Estremadura; with the remains of a castle on a rock. It is 13 miles E. of Peniche, and 40 N. N. E. of Lisbon. Pop. 300.

OBOLLAH, a strong town of Persia, in Irac-Agemi; seated on a branch of the Tigris, near Bassora.

OBSKAIA, a gulf or bay of Siberia, in the Frozen Ocean; about 360 miles from N. to S. and 45 to 60 in breadth. The S. W. extremity, where it is entered by the river Oby, is in long. 69. 15. E. lat. 66. 55. N.

OBVINSK, a town of Russia, in the government of Perm; situated on the Kama; 60 miles N. of Perm. Long. 56. 0. E. lat. 58. 44. N.

OBY, or OB, the largest river of Siberia. It issues from Lake Altyn, in the desert of Ischimska, runs N. W. and W. by Kolivan, Narim, and Surgut, till it receives the Irtysh from Tobolsk, when its flows N. and N. E., and, after a course of 1900 miles, enters the Gulf of Obskaia. It is a large smooth stream, abounds in fish, and is navigable almost to its source. In its course, especially after the influx of the Irtysh, it forms a great number of islands.

OCANA, an ancient town of Spain, in La Mancha; formerly fortified, but now in a state of decay. In 1810 a battle was fought in its vicinity, between the French and Spaniards. Pop. 5000. It is 30 miles S. S. E. of Madrid.

OCANA, a town of the republic of Columbia, in the province of St. Martha; on the Rio de Oro, which flows to the Madalena. It is 240 miles S. by E. of St. Martha. Long. 73. 26. W. lat. 7. 40. N.

OCEANICA, an expressive name given by Malte Brun and other modern geographers to that division of the globe which cannot well be classed with the other quarters. It includes Australasia, or the continent of Australia, and its surrounding islands, and New Zealand, and Polynesia, or the numerous groups of islands which are spread over the Pacific Ocean, and which cannot scarcely be called either American or Asiatic. The term, however, is not universally recognized.

OCHSENFURT, a town of Bavarian Franconia, seated on the Maine; 10 miles S. E. of Wurtzburg.

OCHSENHAUSEN, a town of Wirtemburg, capital of a petty principality (formerly the territory of a rich abbey) which was given to prince Metternich in 1803. It is 14 miles S. of Ulm.

OCKER, a river of Saxony, which rises in the Hartz, flows by Goslar, Wolfenbuttel, and Brunswick, and joins the Aller, E. of Zell.

OCRIDA. *See* LOCHRIDA.

OCZAKOW, or OTCHAHOF, a decayed seaport and fortress of Russia, in the government of Catharinenslaf. It has been frequently an object of contest between the Turks and Russians, many thousands of whom, on both sides, have fallen in its different sieges. The Russians took it by storm in 1788, and it was confirmed to them by the subsequent peace. This important place is the key to both the Bog and the Dnieper, rivers of great consequence to this part of the empire. It is seated near the Black Sea, on the N. side of the estuary of the Dnieper, opposite Kinburn, 50 miles W. of Cherson, and 190 N. by E. of Constantinople. Long. 30. 30. E. lat. 46. 35. N.

ODENBACH, a town of Germany, in the duchy of Deux Ponts, seated on the Glan; 34 miles S. W. of Mentz.

ODENSEE, a town of Denmark, capital of the isle of Funen, and a bishop's see. It supplies the greatest part of the army with all their leather accoutrements, and is particularly famous for gloves. Here are also manufactures of cloth, sugar, and soap. It is situate in a river, 6 miles from the Bay of Stegestrand, and 90 W. by S. of Copenhagen. Pop. 6000. Long. 10. 25. E. lat. 55. 30. N.

ODER, a river of the Austrian empire, which rises in the mountains of Moravia, and flows through the Brandenburg and Pomerania. Below Stettin it forms a large lake or bay, called Gross Haff, and then enters the Baltic Sea by three channels, called Peene, Swin, and Diwenow; between which lie the islands of Usedom and Wollin.

ODERBERG, a town of Moravia, on the confines of Silesia with a castle; seated on the Oser, at the influx of the Elsa; 18 miles N. N. W. of Teschen.

ODERBERG, a town of the Prussian province of Brandenburg, situate on the Oder; 25 miles N. W. of Custrin.

ODERNHEIM, a town of Germany, in Hesse Darmstadt, on the Seltz; 14 miles S. of Mentz.

ODERNHEIM, a town of Germany, in the duchy of Deux Ponts, seated on the Glan, near its conflux with the Nahe; 28 miles S. W. of Mentz.

ODESSA, a fortified seaport of Russia, in the government of Catherinenslaf, founded in 1792 by Catherine II. The town is well-built, and is rapidly increasing in size and importance. The population is estimated at about 60,055, who carry on a good trade and have manufactures of woollens, silks, gunpowder, soap, &c. It is seated on the gulf of the Black Sea; 44 miles W. by S. of Oczakow, and 99 E. of Cherson.

ODEYPORE. *See* OUDIPORE.

ODEYPORE, a town of Hindostan, capital of Jushpour, in the province of Orissa. It is 60 miles N. E. of Ruttunpour, and 220 N. W. of Cuttack. Long. 83. 22. E. lat. 22. 37. N.

ODIHAM, a town in Hampshire, with a market on Saturday. Here are the remains of an ancient castle, and of a royal palace, barns, &c.

It is seated on the Basingstoke Canal; 24 miles N. E. of Winchester, and 42 W. by S. of London.

Oebsfeld, a town of Prussian Saxony, seated on the Aller; 22 miles N. E. of Brunswick.

Olderan, a town of Saxony, in Messen; situate near the Flohe, 9 miles E. N. E. of Chemnitz.

Oeland, an island of Sweden, in the Baltic, separated from the coast of Gothland by a strait 12 miles broad in the narrowest part. It is 80 miles long, but not more than 9 broad. The N. part has fine forests, and quarries of excellent freestone; the S. is more level, and very fertile. Both parts abound in alum mines. Borkholm, the chief town, is seated on the strait; 22 miles E. N. E. of Calmar. Pop. 22,000. Long. 16. 50. E. lat. 56. 48. N.

Oels, a town of Prussian Silesia, capital of a principality of the same name, which now forms part of the government of Breslau, belonging to the duke of Brunswick. The town stands on a river of the same name, is surrounded with walls, and has a palace, formerly occupied by the prince. It is 17 miles E. N. E. of Breslau. Long. 17. 31. E. lat. 51. 12. N.

Oelsnitz, a town of Saxony, on the Elster; 6 miles S. by E. of Plauen.

Oepen, or **Eupen**, a town of the Netherlands, in Limburg; with considerable manufactures of cloth, situate on the Weze; 4 miles E. N. E. of Limburg.

Oesel, an island in the Baltic, on the coast of Livonia, at the entrance of the Gulf of Riga. It is 74 miles long, and 50 broad; defended by two forts, and belongs to Russia. Pop. 30,000. Arensberg is the capital.

Oetting, a town of Bavaria, seated on the Inn; 8 miles N. W. of Burkhausen.

Oettingen, a town of Bavaria, with a well-endowed college. It is seated on the Wirnitz, 28 miles S. of Anspach, and 69 N. N. W. of Munich. Long. 10. 40. E. lat. 48. 56. N. Pop. 3200.

Offa's Dike, an entrenchment of England; cast up by Offa, a Saxon king, to defend England from the incursions of the Welsh. It extends through Herefordshire, Shropshire, Montgomeryshire, Denbighshire, and Flintshire, from the Wye to the Dee.

Ofen. *See* **Buda**.

Offanto, a river of Naples, which rises in the Appennines, and enters the Gulf of Venice, near Barletta. It is the ancient Aufidus.

Offenbach, a town of Germany, in Hesse Darmstadt, and the principal manufacturing town in the duchy, seated on the S. side of the Maine; 5 miles E. of Frankfort. Population, 8000.

Offenburg, a town of Baden, seated on the Kintzig; 10 miles S. E. of Strasburg.

Offida, a town of Italy, in Anconia; 26 miles S. of Loretto.

Ogersheim, a town of the Bavarian circle of the Rhine; 12 miles N. of Spire.

Oglio, a river which rises in the principality of Trent, enters Italy, and joins the Po, above Borgoforte.

Ogmo, a town of the kingdom of Siam, seated at the N. E. point of the Gulf of Siam; 56 miles S. E. of Siam. Long. 101. 28. E. lat. 13. 33. N.

Oheteroa, an island in the S. Pacific; 13 miles in circuit. It has no harbour, and is neither so populous nor fertile as the islands to the N. of it; but its manufactures are of a superior kind, the cloth is of a better dye, and the spears and clubs are better carved and polished. The people are lusty and well made, and rather browner than those of Tahiti. Long. 150. 47. W. lat. 22. 27. S.

Ohio, a river of N. America, formed by the junction of the Allegany and the Monongahela, at Pittsburg. It bounds the states of Ohio and Kentucky in its whole length; and the only disadvantage it has is a rapid, just below Louisville, one mile and a half long. In this place the river runs over a rocky bottom, above 1000 yards broad; and when the stream is low, empty boats only can pass, but when high, boats of any burden may pass in safety. The Ohio carries a great uniformity of breadth, from 400 to 600 yards, except the last 150 miles, where it is from 800 to 900 yards. After a course of 1188 miles, in which it receives many large and small rivers, it enters the Mississippi, in lat. 36. 58. N.

Ohio, one of the United States of America, erected in 1802, lying between 38. 30. and 42. 2. N. lat. and 80. 18. and 83. 53. W. long. It is bounded N. by the territory of Michigan and Lake Erie, E. by Pennsylvania, S. E. and S. by the Ohio, and W. by Indiana. This country, affirmed to be the most healthy and fertile spot in America, is divided into five districts; the North-West, Cincinnati, Chilicothe, Marietta, and New Connecticut. Its principal rivers are the Muskingum, Hockhocking, and Sciota, which runs into the Ohio; and the Cayahoga, which runs into Lake Erie. There are no slaves in this state. The manufactures of cotton, wool, hemp, flax, iron, earthenware, &c., are prosecuted with great success; ship-building is carried on to a considerable extent, and the inhabitants are rapidly increasing in number and wealth. In 1815 the population amounted to 324,070; it is now 1,519,467. Columbus is the seat of the legislature, but Cincinnati is the principal town.

Ohlau, a town of Prussian Silesia; with a fine castle. Great quantities of tobacco are produced in the neighbourhood. It is situate on the Ohla; 16 miles S. E. of Breslau. Pop. 2800.

Ohrdruf, a town of Saxony, in Saxe-Gotha, with a castle, and numerous manufactures. It is 8 miles S. S. E. of Gotha. Pop. 4200.

Ohringen, a town of Wirtemburg, capital of the district of Hohenlohe, with an academy. In the vicinity of the town many Roman antiquities have been found since 1741. It stands on the river Ohrn, which divides it into the Old and New Town; 28 miles S. S. W. of Mergentheim. Long. 9. 42. E. lat. 49. 11. N.

Oich, Loch, a lake of Scotland, Inverness-shire, extending 4 miles from E. to W. and containing some little wooded islands; its outlet at the N. end is the river Oich, which flows by Fort Augustus into the S. extremity of Loch Ness.

OIRE, a town of Naples in Terra d'Otranto; with an old castle, seated at the foot of the Appennines; 20 miles N. E. of Tarento.

OISE, a department of France, including part of the former provinces of the Isle of France and Picardy. Area, 24,000 square miles. Population, 390,000. It takes its name from the river Oise, which has its source in the Ardennes, and joins the Seine below Pontoise. Beauvais is the capital.

OKOTSK, or OKHOTSK, a town of Siberia, capital of a province of the same name, in the government of Irkutsk. It is seated at the mouth of the Okota, in a bay of the Pacific Ocean, called the Sea of Okotsk; 420 miles E. S. E. of Yakutsk. Pop. 1500. Long. 143. 12. E. lat. 59. 20. N.

OLDENBURG, a grand duchy of Germany, consisting of several scattered portions, containing together 2620 square miles, and a population of 240,000. Oldenburg Proper was formerly a county, united with Delmenhorst; and when the line of its counts became extinct, in 1667, it devolved to the royal family of Denmark. In 1773 it was exchanged by Denmark with the grand duke of Russia, for the district of Kiel, in Holstein; and in 1777 the emperor of Germany raised it to the rank of a duchy. The reigning duke was expelled by Napoleon in 1810, but was restored in 1813, and at the congress of Vienna received the title of grand duke. He now possesses, besides Oldenburg Proper (including Delmenhorst and the lordships of Varel, Jever, and Kniphausen), the principality of Eutin (formerly the bishopric of Lubec), in Holstein, and the lordship of Birkenfeld, ceded by Prussia out of the territory on the Rhine. The inhabitants are of the Lutheran religion.

OLDENBURG, a fortified town of Germany, capital of the foregoing duchy, and the residence of the grand duke. The church of St. Lambert contains the tombs of the last counts of Oldenburg, which are very curious. It is seated on the Hunta; 22 miles W. of Bremen, and 76 S. S. W. of Hamburg. Pop. 5000.

OLDENBURG, a town of Denmark, in the duchy of Holstein, seated near the Baltic; 28 miles N. of Lubec.

OLDENSAEL, a town of the Netherlands, in Overyssel; 30 miles E. of Deventer.

OLDESLOHE, a town of Denmark, in Holstein, with extensive salt-works, seated on the Trave; 17 miles W. of Lubec.

OLDHAM, a borough in Lancashire, built on high ground, on a branch of the Medlock, and near the Irk, whose streams give motion to the machinery, &c., of numerous manufactures. In consequence of the great increase of population and wealth, a chapel of ease was erected by voluntary contributions, in 1765, and enlarged in 1804. The ancient parochial chapel has been replaced by a new church, and another is built under the late acts of parliament. Here are also seven places of worship for dissenters, and a free grammar-school. It returns two members to parliament. It is 7 miles N. of Manchester.

OLDTOWN, a town of Maryland, in Allegany county, on the N. side of the Potomac. It is 14 miles S. E. of Cumberland, and 140 W. by N. of Baltimore.

OLERON, a populous and fertile island of France, 5 miles from the W. coast, opposite the mouth of the Charente. It is 20 miles long, and 5 broad, and belongs to the department of Lower Charente. Pop. 19,000. This island was formerly in the possession of the Crown of England; and here Richard I. compiled the code of maritime laws called the laws of Oleron, which are received by all nations in Europe, as the ground and substruction of all their marine constitutions.

OLERON, a town in the department of Lower Pyrenees, on the Gave; 10 miles S. W. of Pau. Pop. 5500.

OLIKA, a town of Poland, in Volhynia; with a citadel; 20 miles E. of Lucko.

OLINDA. *See* PERNAMBUCO.

OLITA, a town of Spain, in Navarre; formerly the residence of the kings of Navarre, but now much reduced. It is seated in a fertile country; 20 miles N. of Tudela.

OLIVA, a seaport of W. Prussia, where a peace was concluded, in 1660, between the emperor of Germany and the kings of Sweden and Poland. It is situate on a bay of the Gulf of Dantzic; 10 miles W. N. W. of Dantzic. Long. 18. 32. E. lat. 54. 24. N.

OLIVENÇA, a town and fortress of Spain, in Estremadura, which, with its territory, formerly belonged to Portugal, but was ceded to Spain in 1801. It is 16 miles S. S. W. of Badajoz. Pop. 4500.

OLMEDO, a decayed town of Spain, in Leon; seated near the Adaja. It is 25 miles S. of Valladolid.

OLMUTZ, a district or circle of the Austrian province of Moravia, containing 2000 square miles, with 347,300 inhabitants. The N. part is mountainous, but the S. level and fertile.

OLMUTZ, the capital of the above district, and formerly of Moravia, is an archbishop's see, and has a famous university. It is fortified, well built, and almost surrounded by the river Morau. In 1741 it was taken by the king of Prussia, who attempted it again in 1758, but was obliged to raise the siege. The emperors of Russia and Austria met here in 1805, previous to the battle of Austerlitz. It is 80 miles N. by E. of Vienna, and 97. S. of Breslau. Pop. 11,000. Long. 17. 15. E. lat. 49. 33. N.

OLNEY, a town in Buckinghamshire, with a market on Monday, and a manufacture of bone-lace; seated on the Ouse; 12 miles S. E. of Northampton, and 55 N. N. W. of London.

OLONETZ, a government of Russia, formerly included in the government of Novogorod. In this district are mines of copper and iron. Area, 87,500 square miles. Pop. 282,000. The capital is Petrozavodsk.

OLONETZ, a town of the foregoing government; near which are a mineral spring and an iron forge. It is situate on the river Olonza, near its entrance into the Lake of Ladoga; 100 miles, across the lake, N. E. of Petersburg. Pop. 2800.

OLONETZ MOUNTAINS, a chain of mountains in the N. W. part of Russia; which runs in a direction almost due N. for the space of 1000 miles, forming part of the boundary between this country and Sweden.

OLONNE, a town of France, department of Vendee; 35 miles W. of Fontenay le Comte.

OLPHEN, a town of Prussian Westphalia; 17 miles S. S. W. of Munster.

OLTEN, a town of Switzerland, in the canton of Soleure; seated on the Aar; 17 miles E. N. E. of Soleure.

OLYMPUS, a celebrated mountain of Natolia. The ancients supposed its top reached the heavens, and from that circumstance placed the residence of the gods there, and made it the court of Jupiter. It is 10 miles S. E. of Broussa, and is 6000 feet high. It is a name also given to other mountains, in Greece, &c.

OMAGH, a town of Ireland, in the county of Tyrone; 14 miles S. of Strabane.

OMAN, a province of Arabia, bounded on the N. W. by the Persian Gulf, N. E. and S. E. by the ocean, and S. W. by extensive deserts. It is possessed by a number of petty sovereigns, the most considerable of whom is the imam of Rostak. The chief town is Mascat.

OMBO, a town of Egypt, on the right bank of the Nile; 26 miles N. of Esne.

OMBRONE, a town of Tuscany, in the Siennese, at the mouth of the river Ombrone; 5 miles S. of Grossetto.

OMEGNA, a town of the Sardinian states, province of Novara, on the N. E. side of Lake Orta; 25 miles N. N. W. of Novara.

OMER, ST., a fortified town of France, in the department of Pas de Calais. It owes its name and importance to a saint, who built a grand monastery here in the seventh century. The cathedral and the church of St. Bertin are magnificent structures. About a league from the town is a great morass, in which are the floating islands, but which have almost disappeared. St. Omer is seated on the Aa, on the side of a hill; 8 miles N. W. of Aire, and 135 N. of Paris. Long. 2. 15. E. lat. 50. 44. N. Pop. 20,000.

OMMEN, a town of the Netherlands, in Overyssel; seated on the Vecht; 17 miles N. E. of Deventer.

OMMIRABIH. *See* MORBEYS.

OMOA, a town of Guatimala, in Honduras, with a strong fortress. In 1779 the British took it by escalade; but the garrison they left could not long retain possession. It is seated on the Bay of Honduras, 80 miles N. N. W. of Valladolid.

OMSK, a town and fortress of Russia, in the government of Tobolsk; situate at the conflux of the Om with the Irtysh; 350 miles S. E. of Tobolsk. Long. 74. 54. E. lat. 54. 14. N.

ONEEHOW, one of the Sandwich Islands, in the North Pacific; 5 leagues W. of Atooi. It produces plenty of yams, and a sweet root called tee. Long. 161. 0. W. lat. 21. 50. N.

ONEGA, a town of Russia, in the government of Archangel; on the river Onega, near the White Sea; 80 miles S. S. W. of Archangel. Long. 37. 54. E. lat. 63. 53. N.

ONEGA, a river and lake of Russia, in the government of Olonetz. The lake is 100 miles long, and 40 broad, and has a communication with the lake Ladoga. The river gives its name to a country full of woods, and flows into the White Sea.

ONEGLIA, a province of the Sardinian states, in Piedmont; surrounded by the territory of Genoa and the sea. It abounds in olive-oil, fruits, and wine. Pop. 29,000.

ONEGLIA, or ONEILLE, a seaport of Piedmont; capital of the above province. In 1792 the French took it by storm, and set it on fire in several places. It is seated at the mouth of the Imperiale; 55 miles S. W. of Genoa. Pop. 5000. Long. 7. 57. E. lat. 43. 58. N.

ONEIDA, a town of New York, chief of a county of the same name; seated on Oneida Creek; 20 miles S. W. of Fort Stanwix. Long. 75. 20. W. lat. 43. 10. N. *See* ONONDAGO.

ONEZKOE, a lake of Russia, in the government of Olonetz; 120 miles long, and 40 broad. It contains several islands.

ONGAR, or CHIPPING ONGAR, a town in Essex, with a market on Saturday; 12 miles W. of Chelmsford, and 21 E. N. E. of London.

ONGOLE, a town of Hindostan, in the Carnatic, capital of a district of its name belonging to Britain. It is 78 miles S. S. W. of Condapilly, and 166 N. by W. of Madras. Long. 79. 56. E. lat. 15. 28. N.

ONION, one of the principal rivers of Vermont; which flows through a fertile country, and, after a course of 70 miles, falls into Lake Champlain.

ONOLZBACH. *See* ANSPACH.

ONONDAGO, or ONEIDA, a lake of New York, lying between the counties of Onondago and Oneida. It is 20 miles W. of Fort Stanwix, and extends westward about 20 miles, where its outlet, the river Onondago, runs into Lake Ontario, at Oswego. At the N. E. corner of the lake is Wood Creek, and at the S. W. corner is Oneida Creek.

ONONDAGO CASTLE, a town of New York, chief of a county of its name; 145 miles W. of Albany.

ONORE. *See* HONAWERA.

ONRUST, a small island near the coast of Java, at the mouth of the harbour of Batavia. Here the Dutch formerly repaired their ships, and had large warehouses, which were destroyed by the British.

ONTARIO, a lake of North America, situate between 75. and 79. W. long., and 43. and 44. N. lat. Its length is 180 miles, and 50 its medium breadth; its depth is from 15 to 300 fathoms. On its S. W. part it receives the waters of Lake Erie (by the river Niagara), and near the S. E. the Onondago river; and on the N. E. is its outlet, the river Iroquois, or

St. Lawrence. It is 500 miles in circumference, and abounds with fish, among which are the Oswego bass, weighing three or four pounds. The islands are principally at the eastern end. The chief harbours are Toronto and Kingston, belonging to the British, and Sackets' harbour, belonging to the Americans.

ONTARIO, a county of New York; bounded N. by Lake Ontario. It is fertile and well watered, and contains 1777 square miles, with 43,501 inhabitants.

OODAMALLY, a town of Hindostan, in Coimbetore; 30 miles S. S. E. of Coimbetore.

OOJEIN. *See* OUGEIN.

OONALASHKA, one of the islands of the Northern Archipelago, visited by Cook in his last voyage. The natives are described as very peaceable. Fish and other sea animals, birds, roots, berries, and even sea-weed, compose their food. They dry quantities of fish during the summer, which they lay up in small huts for their use in winter. Their clothing is chiefly composed of skins. The upper garment, made like a waggoner's frock, reaches down to the knees. Besides this, they wear a waistcoat or two, a pair of breeches, a fur cap, and boots. They manufacture mats and baskets of grass, which are both strong and beautiful; and there is a neatness and perfection in most of their works, which shows that they are not deficient in ingenuity and perseverance. Long. 165. 0. W. lat. 53. 5. N.

OOSTBORCH, a town and fort of the Netherlands, in the Isle of Cadsand; 4 miles N. E. of Sluys.

OOSTENBY, a town of Sweden, in the Isle of Oeland; 27 miles S. of Borkholm.

OOTATORE, a town of Hindostan, in the Carnatic; 22 miles N. N. W. of Tanjore, and 80 S. W. of Pondicherry.

OPHEIM, a town of Norway, in the province of Bergen; 45 miles N. N. E. of Bergen.

OPORTO, or PORTO, a city and seaport of Portugal, in Entre Douro e Minho, and a bishop's see. It is by nature almost impregnable; and is noted for its strong wines, of which large quantities are exported to England; whence all red wines from Spain or Portugal are called Port wines. The other chief exports are oranges, lemons, oil, sumach, and linen cloth. Its commerce greatly increased after the earthquake at Lisbon, in 1755; before that time the population was estimated at 20,000, and it is now said to be 70,000. Oporto was in the hands of the French during part of 1808, and the spring of 1809. The inhabitants readily joined in the late revolution of the kingdom. It is seated on the side of a mountain, near the river Douro, which forms an excellent harbour; 172 miles N. by E. of Lisbon. Long. 8. 22. W. lat. 41. 10. N.

OPPELN, a province of the Prussian states, comprising the greater part of Upper Silesia. It consists chiefly of hills and mountains, abounding with extensive forests, and containing a large store of valuable minerals. Pop. 550,000. The district called the principality of Oppeln, including more than half of this province, was formerly governed by its own duke.

OPPELN, the capital of the above province, with a Catholic collegiate church. It has a great trade in wool, and stands on the Oder, 150 miles S. E. of Breslau. Long. 18. 0. E. lat. 50. 39. N. Pop. 3200.

OPPENHEIM, a town of Germany, in Hesse Darmstadt. The vicinity produces excellent wine. It is seated on the side of a hill, near the Rhine, 12 miles S. S. E. of Mentz. Pop. 1700.

OPPIDO, a town of Naples, in Calabria Ultra, at the foot of the Apennines, 25 miles N. E. of Reggio. Pop. 8000.

OPPIDO, a town of Naples, in Basilicata, 5 miles S. S. E. of Acerenza.

OPPURG, a town of Saxony, in the circle of Meissen, with a castle, 4 miles W. S. W. of Neustadt.

ORACH, a town of European Turkey, in Bosnia, near the river Drino, 60 miles S. W. of Belgrade.

ORAN, a city and seaport of Algier, in the province of Tremecen, with an excellent harbour, almost opposite Carthagena, in Spain. It was taken by the Spaniards in 1509, and retaken in 1708. In 1732 the Spaniards became masters of it again. It is now in the possession of the French. In 1790 it was destroyed by an earthquake, little besides the exterior walls being left standing, when 2000 persons perished; 225 miles W. N. W. of Algier. Long. 0. 5. W. lat. 35. 58. N.

ORANGE, a city of France, in the department of Vaucluse, and a bishop's see. It was an important place in the time of the Romans, but at present is remarkable only for its antiquities. A triumphal arch, 200 paces from the town, was formerly within its limits; and here are also the remains of a fine amphitheatre, some aqueducts, &c. The fortifications were demolished by Louis XIV., in 1682. The chief manufactures are linen, serge, and paper. Orange was the capital of a principality of the same name, 17 miles long, and 12 broad, given by Charlemagne to William au Cornet, as a reward for his military services. It was possessed successively by the Houses of Baux, Chalons, and Nassau; and, on the death of William III. of England, in 1702, Frederic William of Prussia claimed the succession, but in 1713 it was ceded to France. The city is seated in a fine plain, on the river Aigues; 12 miles N. of Avignon, and 57 S. of Valence. Long. 4. 49. E. lat. 44. 9. N. Pop. 7300.

ORANGE, a county of the state of New York; bounded N. by Sullivan and Ulster counties, E. by Hudson, S. E. by Rockland county, and S. W. by New Jersey and Pennsylvania.—2. A county in the central part of Virginia.—3. In North Carolina.—4. In Indiana.—5. In Vermont.—Also, the name of various townships in the United States.

ORANGE, a river of Africa, which falls into the Atlantic. Lat. 28. 30. S.

ORANGE, a river of Jamaica, which runs into the sea 4 miles E. of Montego Bay.

Orangeburg, an inland district of South Carolina, comprehending the counties of Lewisburg, Orange, Lexington, and Winton.

Orangeburg, a town of South Carolina; the capital of Orange county, and of the foregoiug district. It is seated on the N. branch of the river Edisto, 75 miles N. W. of Charleston. Long. 80. 42. W. lat. 33. 23. N.

Orangetown, a town of the state of New York, on the W. side of the Hudson, 28 miles N. of New York. Pop. 2771.

Oranienbaum, a town of Saxony, in the duchy of Anhalt-Dessau; 6 miles S. E. of Dessau.

Oranienbaum, a town of Russia, in Ingria. It is seated in the Gulf of Finland, 20 miles W. of Petersburg.

Oranienburg, a town of Prussia, in the Middle Mark of Brandenburg, situate on the Havel, 18 miles N. of Berlin.

Oratava, a town on the W. side of the island of Teneriffe, and the chief place of trade. It is seated at the bottom of an amphitheatre of mountains, out of which rises the Peak of Teneriffe. Its port is at 3 miles distance. Long. 16. 24. W. lat. 28. 23. N.

Orbassan, a town of Piedmont, with 1700 inhabitants, 6 miles S. W. of Turin.

Orbe, a town of Switzerland, in the Pays de Vaud; 32 miles W. S. W. of Bern.

Orbe, a town of Germany, in the late electorate of Mentz; celebrated for its salt-works; 26 miles E. of Frankfort.

Orbitello, a seaport of Tuscany; in the province of Sienna, with a good harbour protected by several forts. It is seated on the Mediterranean, near the mouth of the Albegna; 63 miles S. by W. of Sienna. Long. 11. 6. E. lat. 42. 28. N.

Orbre, a river of France, which rises in the Cevennes, flows by Beziers, and enters the Gulf of Lyons at Serignan.

Orcades. *See* Orkneys.

Orchies, a town of France, in the department of Nord; 12 miles S. S. E. of Lisle. Pop. 2600.

Orchilla, a cluster of small islands in the Caribbean Sea, N. of the coast of Terra Firma. Long. 65. 20. E. lat. 12. 0. N.

Orchimont, a town of Belgium, in the territory of Luxemburg; situate on the Semoy, 18 miles N. of Sedan.

Ordingen, a town of Germany, in the late electorate of Cologne; seated near the Rhine; 36 miles N. N. E. of Cologne.

Orduna, a town of Spain, in Biscay; seated in a valley, surrounded by high mountains; 20 miles S. W. of Bilboa. Pop. 4000.

Orebro, a government of Sweden; comprising the old province of Nericia, part of Westmannland, and a small part of Warmeland. It contains 1780 square miles, with 100,000 inhabitants.

Orebro, the capital of the above government, has a considerable trade with Stockholm, across the lakes Hielmar and Maeler, by means of the river and canal of Arboga; sending iron, vitriol, and red paint, in particular, to that capital. In the middle of the town, on a small island formed by the Swart, stands the castle, formerly a royal residence. It is seated near the W. extremity of the lake Hielmar: 100 miles W. by S. of Stockholm. Pop. 4000.

Oregon. See Columbia.

Oregrund, a seaport of Sweden, in Upland, on the Gulf of Bothnia, opposite the small island of Ginson. The chief article exported is iron, from the long celebrated mine of Danamora in its vicinity. It is 70 miles N. of Stockholm. Long. 18. 5. E. lat. 60. 21. N.

Orel, a government of Russia, once a province of the government of Beilgorod. Pop. about 1,000,000. Its capital, of the same name, is seated on the Occa and Orel, 207 miles S. S. W. of Moscow. Long. 35. 20. E. lat. 53. 0. N.

Orellana, a town of Spain, in Estremadura; 28 miles E. of Merida.

Orenburg, a government of Asiatic Russia; bounded by European Russia, and the government of Tobolsk. Pop. 629,426.

Orenburg, a town and fortress of the above government. It is a place of considerable commerce, and is seated on the Ural, 260 miles S. S. E. of Ufa. Pop. 10,000. Long. 55. 4. E. lat. 51. 46. N.

Orense, a city of Spain, in Galicia; and a bishop's see. Here are some celebrated tepid and hot springs. It is seated at the foot of a mountain, on the river Minho; 47 miles S. E. of Compostella. Long. 7. 50. W. lat. 42. 22. N.

Orfa, **Ourfa**, or **Rouah**, a city of Turkey, in Diarbeck; said to be the Ur of the Chaldees. The walls are 3 miles in circumference, defended by square towers, and on a rocky hill to the S. is a stately castle. It has a good trade, particularly in carpets and leather, and has a canal to the Euphrates. The country round is fertile in corn and fruit. It is 83 miles N. E. of Aleppo, and 100 S. W. of Diarbekir. Pop. 20,000. Long. 38. 20. E. lat. 36. 50. N.

Orford, a town in Suffolk, with a market on Monday. Here are the remains of a castle, which, with the church, is a seamark. It is 18 miles N. by E. of Ipswich, and 88 N. E. of London.

Orford, a town of New Hampshire, in Grafton county. It is situate on the Connecticut; 11 miles N. N. E. of Hanover. Pop. 1707.

Orford Ness, a cape of England, on the S. E. coast of Suffolk, where a lighthouse is erected for the direction of ships. Long. 1. 34. E. lat. 52. 4. N.

Orgaz, a town of Spain, in New Castile, with a castle, 15 miles S. of Toledo.

Orgelet, a town of France, department of Jura; seated at the source of the Valouse, 30 miles S. S. W. of Salins.

Orgiva, a town of Spain; in the province of Granada; 25 miles S. of Granada.

Orient. *See* L'Orient.

Orihuela, a town of Spain, in Murcia, and a bishop's see; with a university, and a citadel built on a rock. The inhabitants have manufactures of silk, brandy distilleries, and some saltpetre works; and here are made curious snuff-boxes, with the roots of the terebinthus, much esteemed for preserving Spanish snuff. It is seated in a very fertile country, on the Segura; 12 miles N. E. of Murcia. Pop. 20,000.

Orissa, a province of Hindostan; bounded on the N. by Bohar and Bengal, W. by Berar, S. by Golconda, and E. by the Bay of Bengal. The greater part of the province now belongs to the British. It is divided into the districts of Cuttack, Mohurbgunge, and Konjeur.

Oristano, a fortified town of Sardinia, and an archbishop's see, with a good harbour. It is seated on the W. coast, on a bay of the same name; 42 miles N. W. of Cagliari. Long. 8. 51. E. lat. 39. 53. N.

Orizaba, a town of North Amerca, republic of Mexico; seated in a rich valley, 120 miles E. by S. of Mexico, and producing great quantities of tobacco in its neighbourhood. Pop. 8,000.

Orkened, a town of Sweden, in Schonen; 24 miles N. of Christianstadt.

Orkney Islands, the ancient Orcades, a cluster of islands to the N. of Scotland, from which they are separated by Pentland Frith. They lie between 54. 47. and 59. 20. N. lat., and are about 38 in number, of which 29 are inhabited, and besides a very large number of rocky islets or skerries. The largest is sometimes dignified with the appellation of Mainland, but is more frequently called Pomona. Beyond this island, to the N. E., are seen, among others, Rowsa, Eglisha, and Westra; Shapinsha and Eda; Stronsa, Sanda, and North Ronaldsha; and to the S. appear Hoy and South Ronaldsha, with others of inferior note. The currents and tides which flow between these islands are rapid and dangerous, and near the small isle of Swinna are two whirlpools, very dangerous to mariners, especially in calms. The sea-coast swarms with seals and otters, and is visited by whales, cod, ling, haddocks, herrings, and other fish; and on the shores are found large oysters, muscles, cockles, &c. The islands are visited by eagles, falcons, wild geese, and ducks in great variety, herons, hawks, gulls, &c. Springs of pure water are found in all the mountainous parts, and there are numerous lakes and rivulets abounding in fish. The heath on the mountains shelters grouse, plovers, snipes, &c., but there are no partidges, hares, nor foxes. There are great numbers of small sheep and black cattle, swine, rabbits, and red deer. The products of the valleys and plains are chiefly big and oats. Except juniper, wild myrtle, heath, and a shrub called cyorhordon, there is scarcely a tree or plant to be seen; but this nakedness cannot have been their former state, as many trunks of large oaks are to be found in all the mosses. The climate in summer is moist and cold, but in winter there is very little snow, and that lies only a short time. Preceding the autumnal equinox, dreadful storms of wind, rain, and thunder occur. For about three weeks in midsummer these islands enjoy the rays of the sun almost without intermission; but, for the same space in winter, that luminary hardly rises above the horizon, and is commonly obscured by clouds and mists. In this gloomy season the absence of day is supplied partly by moonlight, and partly by the radiance of the aurora borealis, which here gives a light nearly equal to that of a full moon. The coasts afford numerous bays and harbours for the fisheries. The chief exports are linen and woollen yarn, stockings, butter, dried fish, herrings, oil, feathers, and skins of various kinds, and kelp. The English language prevails in all these islands, although there are many words in the Norse or Norwegian still in use. The inhabitants have the general character of being frugal, sagacious, circumspect, and hospitable; but the common people are superstitious. The Orkney and Shetland Isles unite in sending one member to the imperial parliament.

Orlamunda, a town of Germany, in Saxe-Gotha, seated on the Saale, opposite the influx of the Orla; 40 miles W. S. W. of Altenburg. Pop. 2000.

Orlando, a cape on the N. coast of Sicily, 15 miles W. by N. of Patti. Long. 15. 4. E. lat. 38. 14. N.

Orleans, a city of France, capital of the department of Loiret, and a bishop's see. It is seated on the Loire, and has a canal thence to the Loing, near Montargis. Under the sons of Clovis it was the capital of a kingdom. In 1428 it stood a memorable seige against the English, which was raised by the celebrated Joan of Arc, called the Maid of Orleans. It is now considered one of the largest and most pleasant cities in France. The principal public buildings are the cathedral, town-house, court of justice, mint, and theatre. The trade consists in stockings, sheep skins, wine, brandy, corn, grocery, and particularly sugar, which is brought raw from Nantes and Rochelle. The fauxbourg of Paris is of a prodigious length, and that of Olivet, on the left side of the Loire, has a communication with the city by a bridge of nine arches. Near the city is a forest, containing 94,000 acres, planted with oak and other valuable trees. Orleans is 30 miles N. E. of Blois, and 60 S. S. W. of Paris. Pop. 42,000. Long. 1. 54. E. lat. 47. 54. N.

Orleans, a county in the state of Vermont, bounded on the N. by Canada. The chief towns are Irasburg, Craftsbury, and Brownington. Pop. 13,364.

Orleans, an island and town of Lower Canada, on the river St. Lawrence, a little to the E. of Quebec. Long. 69. 50. W. lat. 17 0. N.

Orleans, New, a city and the capital of Louisiana, built in 1720, under the regency of the duke of Orleans. In 1788 seven-eighths of the city were destroyed by fire; but it is now rebuilt on a regular plan, principally in the Spanish and French style, the houses covered with stucco, and is one of the handsomest towns in the union. It is seated in a swampy plain, about 7 feet below the level of the Mississippi, from which it is protected by an artificial embankment called the Levée, 50 miles in length. During the hot months it is very unhealthy, but is one of the most important ports in North America, with an immense export trade in sugar and cotton. It is fortified on the sides exposed to the land, and has a railroad from the city to Lake Pontchartrain, where there is a fort. The inhabitants are about 43,000, and consist of a great variety of manners, language, and complexion; about one-half are black, or coloured; and the French still predominate among the whites. Religion is little attended to; there are not more than eight places of worship; trade engrosses the whole attention, and the morals suffer accordingly. In 1814 it was attacked by the British, who were repulsed with great loss. It is seated on the Mississippi, 105 miles from its mouth. Long. 90. 9. W. lat. 29. 58. N.

ORLENGA, a town of Russia, in the government of Irkutsk; situate on the Lena; 235 miles N. of Irkutsk. Long. 105. 40. E. lat. 56. 0. N.

ORMEA, a town of the Sardinian states, in Piedmont; seated on the river Tanaro; 12 miles S. of Mondovi.

ORMSKIRK, a town in Lancashire, with a market on Thursday. The parish church is remarkable for its two steeples, placed contiguous; one a tower, and the other a short spire; a second church has been erected under the recent acts; and here are also three meeting-houses for dissenters, a grammar-school, and a national school. The chief branch of trade is cotton-spinning; coarse thread is also made for sail-cloth; 3 miles N. by E. of Liverpool, and 209 N. N. W. of London.

ORMUZ, a small island in a strait of the same name, at the entrance of the Gulf of Persia; 9 miles S. of Gombron. In 1505 the Portuguese were permitted to form a settlement here, and it was afterwards frequented by a number of rich merchants. In 1622 the Persians, by the assistance of the English, expelled the Portuguese, and demolished the buildings. Some time after, the Persians rebuilt the fort, and, though they could never bring it to be a place of trade as before, it is still the key of the Gulf of Persia, on account of the commodiousness of the harbour. It is almost deserted; for it produces nothing but salt, which sometimes is two inches deep upon the surface of the earth. Long. 56. 25. E. lat. 27. 20. N.

ORNANS, a town of France, department of Doubs; seated on the Louvre; 10 miles S. E. of Besançon. Pop. 3100.

ORNE, a department of France, including the old province of Perche, and part of that of Normandy. It takes its name from a river which rises in the department, and runs into the English Channel 8 miles below Caen. Pop. 434,300. The capital is Alençon.

ORONOCO, or ORINOCO, a majestic river of South America, which issues from the small lake Ipava, in lat. 5. 5. N., flows E. and S. E. to the lake Parima, from which it runs towards the W.; but, after receiving the Guaviari, it bends N., then N. E. and E., till it enters the Atlantic by an extended delta of mouths opposite the isle of Trinidad; but the principal one is considerably to the S. E. of that island, in lat. 8. 30. N. In this singular winding course, estimated at 1400 miles, it receives many large rivers; and its chief estuary is so deep and impetuous as to stem the most powerful tides. *See* PARIMA.

ORONSA, a small fertile island of Scotland, one of the Hebrides, to the S. of Colonsa, from which it is separated by a narrow channel that is dry at low water. Here are the ruins of an abbey, with many sepulchral statues, and some curious ancient sculpture.

ORONTES. *See* AASZI.

OROPESA, a town of Spain, in Valencia, on a cape of its name, in the Mediterranean, 55 miles E. N. E. of Valencia. Long. 0. 5. E. lat. 40. 8. N.

ORR, a river of Scotland, in Kirkcudbrightshire, which issues from a small lake to the E. of New Galloway, and flows into the Solway Frith, at Dalbeattie.

ORSOVA, a town and fortress of Hungary, on the confines of Servia, seated on the N. side of the Danube; 60 miles S. E. of Tameswar, and 75 E. of Belgrade. Long. 22. 40. E. lat. 45. 10. N.

ORSOY, a town of the Prussian states, seated on the Rhine; 20 miles S. E. of Cleves.

ORSZA, a town of European Russia, in the government of Mohilef, with a castle, seated on the Dnieper; 38 miles N. of Mohilef. Pop. 2500.

ORTA, a town of Italy, in the ecclesiastical states, seated near the Tiber; 10 miles E. of Viterbo.

ORTA, a town of the Sardinian states, in the province of Novara, seated on a lake of its name; 21 miles N. N. W. of Novara.

ORTEGAL, a cape and castle of Spain, on the N. coast of Galicia; 30 miles N. N. E. of Ferrol. Long. 7. 50. W. lat. 43. 46. N.

ORTENBERG, a town of Germany, in Hesse-Darmstadt, with a castle, situate on the Nidder; 17 miles S. E. of Giessen.

ORTENBURG, a town and citadel of Bavaria, in a county of the same name, seated near the river Vills; 10 miles W. of Passau.

ORTENBURG, a town of the Austrian states, in Carinthia, on the S. bank of the Drave, opposite the influx of the Liser; 32 miles W. of Clagenfurt.

ORTHES, a town of France, department of Lower Pyrenees, celebrated for a victory gained here by the allied army over the French in 1814. It is seated on the side of a hill, by the river Pau; 20 miles N. W. of Pau.

ORTON, a town of Westmoreland, with a market on Wednesday; 10 miles S. W. of Appleby, and 276 N. N. W. of London.

ORTONA A MARE, a town of Naples, in Abruzzo Citra, on the Gulf of Venice; 13 miles E. of Civita di Chieti.

ORTRAND, a town of Saxony, in the circle of Meissen, situate on the borders of Lusatia: 16 miles N. E. of Meissen.

ORURO, a town of Peru, capital of a jurisdiction of the same name. The country abounds in cattle, and has many gold and silver mines. It is 150 miles N. W. of Plata. Long. 68. 30. W. lat. 18. 10. S.

ORVIETO, a fortified town of Italy, in the

papal states, capital of a territory of the same name, and a bishop's see, with a magnificent palace, and a fine Gothic cathedral. It is seated on a craggy rock, near the conflux of the Paglia and Chiana; 50 miles N. N. W. of Rome. Long. 12. 20. E. lat. 42. 42. N.

ORWELL, a river in Suffolk, which runs S. E. by Ipswich, and, uniting with the Stour, forms the fine harbour of Harwich.

OSACA, a city of Japan, in the island of Niphon, defended by a magnificent castle. It has a harbour, and is one of the most commercial places of the empire. It stands on the Jedogawa, over which are several bridges of cedar; 30 miles S. by W. of Miaco. Long. 136. 5. E. lat. 35. 5. N.

OSCHATZ, a town of Saxony, in the circle of Meissen, with a college and some manufactures of cloth; seated on the Chemnitz, 16 miles N. W. of Meissen.

OSERO, an island in the Gulf of Venice, having on the N. that of Cherso, to which it is joined by a bridge. The capital is of the same name. Long. 15. 30. E. lat. 44. 56. N.

OSMA, a town of Spain, in Old Castile, and a bishop's see, with a university. The cathedral and episcopal palace are at Borgo d'Osma, a little to the E. It stands on the Douro, 48 miles S. E. of Burgos. Long. 2. 52. W. lat. 41. 50. N. Pop. 2000.

OSNABURG, or OSNABRUCK, a province of Hanover, lying between the grand duchy of Oldenburg and Prussian Westphalia. It is 40 miles long and 20 broad; produces much corn and flax, and plenty of turf, coal, and marble. The most beneficial manufacture is a coarse kind of linen, which is exported to distant parts. Area, 920 square miles. Pop. 126,000, chiefly Lutherans.

OSNABURG, the capital of the above province, with a castle and a university. It is celebrated for the peace of Westphalia, concluded here in 1648. The Catholics and Protestants have each two churches and a gymnasium. It is seated on the Hase; 25 miles N. by E. of Munster. Pop. 9300. Long. 7. 54. E. lat. 52. 18. N.

OSORNO, a town of Chili, seated on Rio Bueno, in a territory where there are mines of gold; 80 miles S. of Valdivia. Long. 73. 20. W. lat. 40. 58. S.

OSRUSHNA, a town of Western Tartary, in Turkestan, capital of a province of the same name. It is 80 miles N. N. E. of Samarcand, and 260 S. of Taras. Long. 66. 20. E. lat. 40. 40. N.

OSSETIA, the country of the Ossi, or Osseti; one of the seven Caucasian nations, between the Black Sea and the Caspian; bounded on the N. by Great Cabarda, E. by the Lesguis Tartars, and S. and W. by Imeritia. It is divided into 19 districts of very unequal size; some containing only five, and others 50 villages, each of which comprises from 20 to 100 families. Their language has some analogy with that of the Persians. Their history is entirely unknown. The Circassians and Tartars call them Kusha.

OSSORY, the western division of Queen's county, in Ireland. It gives name to a bishopric, but the cathedral is now at Irishtown, in the county of Kilkenny.

OSSUNA, a town of Spain, in Andalusia. It was formerly strong, but less by its ramparts than by a fountain in the middle of the town, which furnished the inhabitants with water, while the country for 8 miles round was totally deprived of that necessary article; 50 miles E. N. E. of Seville. Pop. 15,000, Long. 5. 8. W. lat. 37. 22. N.

OSTALRIC, a town of Spain, in Catalonia. It had a strong castle, taken by the French, and demolished in 1695. It is seated on the Tordera; 28 miles N. E. of Barcelona.

OSTEND, a fortified seaport of Belgium, in West Flanders; seated among a number of canals, and almost surrounded by two of the largest of them, into which ships of great burden may enter with the tide; and connected, by means of railroads, with Mechlin, Antwerp, Brussels, &c. It is famous for the long siege it sustained from the Spaniards, from July 1601 to September 1604, when it capitulated on honourable terms. On the death of Charles II., of Spain, the French seized Ostend; but in 1706, after the battle of Ramillies, it was retaken by the allies. It was again taken by the French in 1745, but restored in 1748. In the war of 1756 the French garrisoned this town for the empress queen, Maria Theresa. In 1792 it was once more captured by the French; evacuated in 1793, and repossessed in 1794. In 1798 a body of British troops landed here, and destroyed the works of the Bruges Canal; but, the wind shifting before they could re-embark, they were compelled to surrender to the French; 10 miles W. of Bruges, and 22 N. E. of Dunkirk. Pop. 10,500. Long. 2. 56. E. lat. 51. 14. N.

OSTERHOFEN, a town of Bavaria; seated on the Danube; 20 miles W. N. W. of Passau.

OSTERODE, a town of Hanover, with a manufacture of woollen stuffs; also a magazine for corn, which is delivered out to the miners of Harz Forest at a fixed price. It is seated on the Saale; 18 miles N. N. E. of Gottingen. Population, 4200.

OSTERODE, a town of Prussia; with a castle, situate on the Dribentz; 46 miles S. E. of Marienberg.

OSTERSUND, a town of Sweden, seated on the E. side of the Lake Storsio; 76 miles N. W. of Sundswald. Long. 16. 10. E. lat. 63. 10. N.

OSTERWICK, a town of Prussian Saxony, in the government of Magdeburg; with good woollen manufactures; situate on the Ilse; 17 miles W. by N. of Halberstadt.

OSTIA, a decayed seaport of Italy, in the papal states, and a bishop's see. In the neighbourhood are extensive salt-works. It stands near the eastern mouth of the Tiber, 12 miles S. W. of Rome Near it was the ancient Ostium, the first maritime establishment formed by the Romans.

OSTIAKS, a people of North Asia, forming a considerable portion of the inhabitants of Siberia, and residing principally on the banks of the Obi. They are rude, uncivilized, and idolatrous, and appear to be related to the Fins. They are governed by their own chiefs, who pay their tribute to the Russian government, in the furs they collect.

OSTIGLIA, a town of Austrian Italy, in the province of Mantua, seated on the Po; 15 miles S. E. of Mantua

OSTINGHAUSEN, a town of Westphalia, situate on the Alst; 8 miles W. of Lipstadt.

OSTROG, a town of Russian Poland, in Volhynia; near the river Horin; 30 miles N. N. W. of Constantinow. Pop. 4600.

OSTROGHOSHK, a town of European Russia; government Voronez. Pop. partly Cossacks, 11,000; 50 miles S. of Voronez.

OSTROLENKA, a town of Poland, where the Russians were repulsed by the French in 1806; seated on the Narew; 50 miles N. E. of Warsaw.

OSTROVIZZA, a town of Austrian Dalmatia, with the ruins of a castle, formerly fortified. It is 14 miles N. of Scardona.

OSTROVNO, a village of Russian Lithuania, where the French defeated a body of Russians in 1812. It is 17 miles W. of Vitepsk.

OSTUNI, a town of Naples, in Terra d'Otranto, seated on a mountain, near the Gulf of Venice; 16 miles W. N. W. of Brindisi, and 50 S. E. of Bari.

OSWEGO, a town and fort of the state of New York, seated on the S. E. side of Lake Ontario, at the mouth of a river of the same name, more commonly called Onondago. It was taken from the French, 1756, by the British, who delivered it up to the United States in 1796. It is 156 miles W. N. W. of Albany. Long. 76. 16. W. lat. 43. 20. N.

OSWESTRY, a town in Shropshire, governed by a mayor, with a market on Wednesday. It had a wall and a castle, long since demolished. Of late years the town has been much extended and improved. It has a flourishing cotton manufactory, and a good trade. The church is spacious, and here are four places of worship for dissenters, and an excellent grammar-school. It is 18 miles N. W. of Shrewsbury, and 179 of London.

OSZMIANA, a town of Russian Lithuania, in the government of Wilna; 32 miles S. E. of Wilna.

OTABALO, a town of S. America, republic of Colombia; capital of a province of the same name, pleasantly situate; with a Franciscan convent. Pop. 15,000.

OTAHA, one of the Society Islands, in the South Pacific. It lies N. of Ulitea, and is divided from it by a strait, which, in the narrowest part, is not more than 2 miles broad. This island is smaller and more barren than Ulitea, but has two good harbours.

OTAHEITE, or TAHITI, an island in the South Pacific; discovered in 1767 by Captain Wallis, who called it George the Third Island. Captain Cook, who came hither in 1768 to observe the transit of Venus, sailed round the whole island in a boat, and staid three months; it was visited twice afterwards by that celebrated navigator. It consists of two peninsulas, about 30 leagues in circumference. Great part of it is covered with woods, consisting partly of bread-fruit trees, palms, cocoa-nut-trees, plaintains, bananas, mulberries, sugar-canes, and others peculiar to the climate, particularly a kind of pine-apple, and the dragon-tree. The only quadrupeds found on the island were hogs, dogs, and rats. The inhabitants have mild features, and a pleasing countenance. They are about the ordinary size of Europeans, of a pale mahogany brown, with fine black hair and eyes. Their provisions are chiefly fish, pork, cocoa-nuts, bread-fruit, and bananas; and they employ sea water as a sauce, both to fish and pork. Nothing can exceed their agility in swimming, diving, and climbing trees, and they are praised for their gentleness, good nature, and hospitality. Previously to the introduction of European habits, the men wore a piece of cloth round their middle, and another wrapped about the head, like a turban; the women had a piece of cloth, with a hole in the middle, through which they passed their heads, so that one part of the garment hung down behind and the other before to the knees, a fine white cloth, like muslin, passing over this in various elegant turns round the body. Tattooing was common among both sexes. Their houses had seldom any walls, but consisted only of a roof, thatched with the long prickly leaves of the palm tree, and supported by a few pillars made of the bread-fruit tree. The native cloth is made of the fibrous bark of the mulberry-tree, which is beaten with a kind of mallet; and a glue, made of the hibiscus esculentus, is employed to make the bark cohere. Some of these pieces are two or three yards wide, and 50 yards long. Omai, a native of this island, was brought over to England by Captain Cook, and carried back by him in his last voyage. In 1799 king Pomare ceded the district of Matavai, on the N. side of this island, to some of the missionaries belonging to the London Missionary Society, through whose labours all the inhabitants of Otaheite, and many of the neighbouring islands, have been led to renounce idolatry. The sovereign himself became a decided convert to Christianity. A general reformation of manners has been effected, a number of schools established, the useful arts introduced, and civilization is rapidly advancing. Point Venus is in long. 149. 36. W. lat. 17. 29. S.

OTCHAKOF. *See* OCZAKOW.

OTLEY, a town of West Yorkshire, with a market on Friday, seated on the Wharf, under a high craggy cliff; 25 miles W. of York, and 203 N. N. W. of London.

OTOQUE, an island of South America, in the Bay of Panama. Long. 80. 10. W. lat. 8. 10. N.

OTRANTO, or TERRA D'OTRANTO, a province of Naples; 70 miles long, and 30 broad; bounded on the N. by Terra di Bari, and on all other parts by the sea. It is a mountainous country, abounding in olives, figs, and wine. Pop. 292,000. *See* LECCE.

OTRANTO, a strong city and seaport of Naples, capital of Terra d'Otranto, and an archbishop's see; with a harbour and a citadel. It has a considerable trade, and is seated on the Gulf of Venice; 140 miles S. E. of Bari. Pop. 2400. Long. 18. 35. E. lat. 40. 20. N.

OTRAR, a town of W. Tartary, in Turkestan, near the river Sirr; 70 miles W. S. W. of Taraz.

OTRICOLI, a town of Italy, in the papal states; seated on a hill, near the Tiber; 7 miles N. by E. of Magliano.

OTSEGO, a county in the state of New York, containing 935 square miles, with 49,628 inhabitants. Cooperstown is the capital.

OTSEGO, a lake in the above county, 9 miles long, and little more than a mile broad. Its outlet, at Cooperstown, is the E. branch of the Susquehanna.

OTTAWA RIVER, Canada; flowing from Lake Huron, and falling into the St. Lawrence; 25 miles W. N. W. from Montreal. It has many rapids, but is used for navigation, and was the boundary between the provinces of Upper and Lower Canada.

OTTENDORF, a town of Prussian Saxony; with a castle, situate near the mouth of the Meden; 27 miles N. W. of Stade.

OTTENHEIM, a town of Austria, on the N. side of the Danube; 5 miles W. N. W. of Lintz.

OTTERBERG, a town of Bavaria; in the circle of the Rhine; 5 miles N. of Kayserslautern.

OTTERBURN, a village in Northumberland, on the river Reed, noted for a battle in 1388, between the English and Scotch, when Henry Percy, surnamed Hotspur, was taken prisoner, and Douglas, the Scotch general, killed. On this battle the ballad of Chevy Chase is founded. It is 21 miles N. of Hexham.

OTTERSBERG, a town of Hanover, in the duchy of Bremen, with a fort; 17 miles N. E. of Bremen.

OTTERY ST. MARY, a town in Devonshire, with a market on Tuesday. It has a large church with two square towers, and manufactures of flannels, serges, &c. It is seated on the rivulet Otter; 10 miles E. of Exeter, and 161 W. by S. of London.

OTTMACHAU, a town of Prussian Silesia, in the government of Oppeln, with a castle; seated on the river Niesse; 7 miles W. by S. of Niesse.

OTTWEILLER, a town of Prussia, in the province of Lower Rhine, with an ancient castle, seated among mountains; 16 miles N. N. E. of Sarbruck.

OUBY, one of the Molucca islands, lying to the S. of Gilolo, and subject to the sultan of Bachian. It abounds in clove trees. The Dutch have a small fort on the W. side. Long. 126. 50. E. lat. 1. 30. S.

OUDE, a province of Hindostan, to the N. of Allahabad. It is subject to a nabob, whose dominions lie on both sides of the Ganges, occupying (with the exception of the district of Rampour) all the flat country between that river and the northern mountains, as well as the principal part of that fertile tract lying between the Ganges and Jumna, known by the name of Dooab, to within 40 miles of the city of Delhi. Oude and its dependencies are estimated at 360 miles in length, from E. to W., and in breadth from 150 to 180, and to contain 3,000,000 inhabitants. The nabob is in alliance with the British, and a brigade of the Bengal army is constantly stationed on its western frontier, which answers the purpose of covering Oude as well as Bengal, and of keeping the western states in awe. The capital is Lucknow.

OUDE, a decayed city of Hindostan, in the province of Oude, said to have been the capital of a great kingdom 1200 years before the Christian era. It is frequently mentioned in the Mahaberat, a famous Hindoo work in Sanscrit, under the name of Adjudiah. But no traces of its former magnificence are left. It is seated on the Gogra, nearly adjoining Fyzabad.

OUDENARDE, a town of Belgium, in E. Flanders, in the middle of which is a fort. Here are manufactures of very fine linen and of curious tapestry. This town was besieged by the French in 1708, but the Duke of Marlborough entirely routed their army. In 1745 it was taken by the French, restored by the peace of 1748, again surrendered to the French in 1794, and finally ceded to the Netherlands after the fall of Napoleon. It is seated on both sides of the Scheldt; 12 miles S. of Ghent, and 29 W. of Brussels.

OUDENBURG, a town of Belgium, in West Flanders, 8 miles S. E. of Ostend.

OUDENWATER, a fortified town of the Netherlands; in the province of Utrecht; the birthplace of the celebrated James Arminius, seated on the Little Yssel; 10 miles W. S. W. of Utrecht.

OUDIPOUR, the capital of the territory of Oudipour, Hindostan, is seated on the Banass; 134 miles S. S. W. of Agimere, and 175 N. E. of Amedabad. Long. 74. 4. E. lat. 25. 28. N.

OUEN-TCHEOU, a city of China, of the first rank, in Tche-kian, at the mouth of a river, with a good harbour; 300 miles S. S. E. of Nanking. Long. 121. 10. E. lat. 28. 2. N.

OUGEIN, or OOJEIN, a city of Hindostan, in the province of Malwa; the residence of one of the Western Mahratta chiefs. It is 6 miles in circumference, surrounded by a strong wall, with round towers. Here are four mosques, several Hindoo temples, and a modern palace. It is seated on the Sippara, which flows into the Chumbul; 150 miles N. by W. of Burhampour. Long. 75. E. lat. 23. 26. N.

OULZ, a town of the Sardinian states, in Piedmont; seated in a valley; 12 miles S. W. of Susa.

OUNDLE, a town of Northamptonshire, with a market on Saturday; seated on the Nen, over which are two bridges; 26 miles N. E. of Northampton, and 78 N. by W. of London.

OURAL, or URAL MOUNTAINS. *See* URAL.

OUREM, a town of Portugal; in Estremadura; seated on a mountain; 12 miles W. of Tomar.

OURFA. *See* ORFA.

OURIQUE, a town of Portugal, in Alentejo, celebrated for a victory obtained by Alphonso king of Portugal, over five Moorish kings, in 1139. The heads of these five kings are the arms of Portugal. It is 26 miles S. W. of Beja.

OUSE, a river in Yorkshire, formed by the Ure and Swale, which rise near each other in the romantic tract called Richmondshire, and unite at Aldborough. It flows thence through York, where it is navigable for considerable vessels; and after receiving the Wharf, Derwent, Aire, and Don, it meets the Trent on the borders of Lincolnshire, where their united streams form the Humber.

OUSE, a river in Sussex, formed of two branches, one of which rises in St. Leonard Forest, the other in the forest of Worth, and they unite above Lewes. It flows by that town to Newhaven, below which it forms a considerable haven, and enters the English Channel.

OUSE, GREAT, a river which rises in Northamptonshire, and flows through Buckingham, Stony Stratford, Newport Pagnel, Olney, and Bedford, where it is navigable. Thence it proceeds to St. Neots, Huntingdon, St. Ives, Ely, and Lynn, below which it enters the Lincolnshire Wash.

OUSE, LITTLE, a river which rises in the S. part of Norfolk, and, dividing that county from Suffolk, as it flows westward, becomes navigable at Thetford, and afterwards joins the Great Ouse.

OUSSORE, a town and fort of Hindostan, in Mysore, taken by the English in 1792. It is 19 miles S. E. of Bangalore, and 69 E. N. E. of Seringapatam.

OUTEIRO, a town and fortress of Portugal, in Tras los Montes; seated on a mountain, 9 miles S. E. of Braganza.

OVERFLACKEE, an island of the Netherlands, in South Holland; between the mouths of the Meuse. Sommerdyck is the principal town.

OVERYSCHE, a town of Belgium, in Brabant, seated on the Ysche; 8 miles N. E. of Brussels. Pop. 3500.

OVERYSSEL, a province of the Netherlands; bounded on the N. by Friesland and Groningen, E. by Hanover and Westphalia, S. by Gelderland, and W. by the Zuyder Zee. It is nearly equal in extent to the whole of North and South Holland, and contains many morasses. Its greatest riches consist in turf, which is dug up here, and sent to the neighbouring provinces; the other exports are cattle, butter, cheese, hides, tallow, wool, and linen. Pop. 147,000. Zwolle is the capital.

OVIDOPOL, a town and fort of Russia, in the government of Catherinenslaf. It had its name from a curious antique tomb, supposed to be that of the poet Ovid, discovered in 1795. It is seated at the mouth of the Dniester; 60 miles S. W. of Oczakow. Long. 30. 22. E. lat. 46. 10. N.

OVIEDO, a town of Spain, capital of Asturias, and a bishop's see, with a university. Near it are the hot springs of Rivera de Abajo, which bear some resemblance to those of Bath. It is seated at the conflux of the Ove and Deva, which form the Asta; 55 miles N. N. W. of Leon. Pop. 7500. Long. 5. 53. W. lat. 43. 20. N.

OWEGO, a town of New York, in Broome county; on the E. branch of the Susquehanna; 170 miles W. of Albion.

OWYHEE, or HAWAII, the largest and most eastern of the Sandwich Islands, in the Pacific Ocean. It length from N. to S. is 84 miles, and its breadth 70. It is divided into six districts, two of which, on the N. E. side, are. separated by a mountain, which rises in three peaks, the summits of which are 18,000 feet above the level of the sea; they are perpetually covered with snow, and may be seen at 40 leagues distance. To the N. of this mountain, the coast consists of high and abrupt cliffs, down which fall many beautiful cascades; and the whole country is covered with cocoa-nut and bread-fruit trees. To the S. the ground is covered with cinders, and in many places has black streaks, which seem to mark the course of a lava that has flowed from the mountain to the shore. The southern promontory looks like the mere dregs of a volcano. The projecting headland is composed of broken and craggy rocks piled irregularly on one another, and terminating in sharp points; yet amidst these ruins are many patches of rich soil, carefully laid out in plantations. The fields are enclosed by stone fences, and are interspersed with groves of cocoa-nut trees. Here Captain Cook, in 1779, fell a victim to a sudden resentment of the natives, with whom he unfortunately had a dispute. The inhabitants, formerly devoted to the most degrading superstitions, have within a few years wholly renounced idolatry, and some American missionaries are settled amongst them. They are said to be naturally mild, friendly, and hospitable to strangers. The king and chiefs ceded this island to Great Britain in 1794. Pop. 85,000. Long. 156. 0. W. lat. 19. 28. N.

OXFORD, a town of New York, in Tioga county; 45 miles N. E. of Union.

OXFORD, the capital of Oxfordshire, and a bishop's see; with markets on Wednesday and Saturday. It is seated at the conflux of the Cherwell with the Thames, and has a canal to Braunston, in Northamptonshire. The city, with the suburbs, is of a circular form, three miles in circumference, and was anciently surrounded by walls, of which some remains are yet to be seen; as also of its extensive castle, the tower of which now serves for a county gaol. It has, besides the cathedral, 13 parish churches, a number of dissenting chapels, a famous university, a noble market-place, and a magnificent bridge. The university is generally supposed to have been a seminary for learning before the time of Alfred, although it owed its revival and consequence to his liberal patronage. Here are 20 colleges and four halls, several of which stand in the streets, and give the city an air of magnificence. The colleges are provided with sufficient revenues for the maintenance of a master, fellows, and students. In the halls the students live, either wholly or in part, at their own expense. The colleges are, University, Balliol, Merton, Exeter, Oriel, Queen's, New, Lincoln, All Souls, Magdalen, Brazen Nose, Corpus Christi, Christ Church, Trinity, St. John Baptist, Jesus, Wadham, Pembroke, Worcester, and Hertford. Of these, the most ancient is University College, founded before the year 872; and to Christ Church College, begun by Cardinal Wolsey, and finished by Henry VIII., belongs the cathedral. The halls are Alban, Edmund, New Inn, and St. Mary Magdalen. Among the libraries in the university, the most distinguished is the Bodleian (founded by Sir Thomas Bodley), those of All Souls College, Christ Church, Queen's, New, St. John, Exeter, and Corpus Christi. Among other public buildings are the theatre, the Ashmolean museum, the Clarendon printing-house, the Radcliffe infirmary, and an observatory. Magdalen Bridge, besides the beauty of its architecture, has this singularity, that more than half of it is on dry ground, and the rest covers two small strips of the Cherwell; this bridge is 526 feet long. At Oxford, King John, compelled by his barons, summoned a parliament to meet in 1258, the proceedings of which were so disorderly that it was afterwards known by the name of the Mad Parliament. Charles I. assembled a parliament here in 1625, in consequence of the plague then raging in London; and in 1644 he summoned such of the members of both houses as were devoted to his interests; these were seceders from the parliament then sitting at Westminster. This city was distinguished for its attachment to that unfortunate king, who here held his court during the whole civil war. Without the town are many ruins of the fortifications erected in that war. Oxford is governed by a mayor, dependent on the chancellor and vice-chancellor of the university, and sends four members to parliament, two for the university and two for the city. It is 50 miles S. by E. of Coventry, and 55 W. N. W. of London. Long. 1. 15. W. lat. 51. 46. N.

Oxfordshire, a county of England, bounded E. by Buckinghamshire, W. by Gloucestershire, S. by Berkshire, and N. by Warwickshire and Northamptonshire. The extreme length is 48 miles, and breadth 38, but its form is very irregular. It contains 467,380 acres, is divided into 14 hundreds and 207 parishes, has one city and 12 market towns. The soil, though various, is fertile in corn and grass. The S. part, especially on the borders of Buckinghamshire, is hilly and woody, having a continuation of the Chiltern Hills running through it. The N. W. part is also elevated and stony. The middle is, in general, a rich country, watered by numerous streams running from N. to S., and terminating in the Thames. Of these the most considerable are the Windrush, Evenlode, Cherwell, and Tame; the last, although an inconsiderable rivulet, has obtained some importance from having been supposed to give name to the Thames. The products of Oxfordshire are chiefly those common to the midland farming counties; and a great improvement has taken place of late years in the agricultural system. Its hills yield ochre, pipe-clay, and other earths, useful for various purposes. Corn and malt are conveyed from it by the Thames to the metropolis; and the Oxford Canal affords a direct water communication with Liverpool, Manchester, and the Wednesbury colleries, as well as with London and Bristol. It returns three members to parliament.

Oxus, or Jihon River. *See* Amu.

Oye, a town of France, department of the Straits of Calais, 7 miles N. E. of Calais.

Oyonnas, a town in the department of Ain; 8 miles N. of Nantua.

Ozama, a river of Hispaniola, formed by the confluence of two streams, which unite about a league above the capital. In rainy seasons it is of considerable size, and is very convenient for bringing down the produce from the interior. It runs into the sea below St. Domingo.

Ozwiczin, a town of Poland, covered on one side by a green morass, and on the other defended by a castle, whose walls are of wood. It is situate on the Weichshel; 34 miles W. of Cracow. Long. 19. 10. E. lat. 50. 10. N.

P.

Pacajes, a town of Buenos Ayres, capital of a province of its name, with a great trade in cattle; 10 miles S. W. of La Paz.

Pacem, a town in the N. part of Sumatra, capital of a kingdom of the same name; 120 miles S. E. of Acheen. Long. 97. 15. E. lat. 5. 0. N.

Pachamac, or Pachacama, a town of Peru, in the province of Cercade; situate in a valley of its name; formerly beautified with a magnificent temple, built by the incas, in which the Spaniards, when they conquered Peru, found immense riches. It is 18 miles S. S. E. of Lima.

Pachete, a town and fort of Bengal, formerly the capital of a district of its name, which is now included in the government of Burdwan. It stands near the Dummooda; 10 miles N. E. of Rogonatpour.

Pachuca, a town of Mexico, noted for the rich silver mines in its vicinity; 56 miles N. by E. of Mexico. Long. 100. 41. W. lat. 20. 44. N.

Pacific Ocean, otherwise called the South Sea, lying between Asia and America. It is the largest ocean in the world, extending over more than one-third of its whole surface, and being upwards of 10,100 miles in breadth. When Magellan entered this ocean, through the dangerous strait that bears his name, he sailed three months and 20 days in a uniform direction to the N. W. without discovering land. In the distress he suffered in his voyage, before he discovered the Ladrone Islands he had the consolation of enjoying such calm and gentle weather, with fair winds, that he gave this ocean the name of Pacific. The Spaniards, on passing the Isthmus of Darien from N. to S., at the first discovery of this ocean, named it the South Sea; but, with respect to America, it is more properly the western ocean. On one side of the equator it is called the North, and on the other the South Pacific.

PACY, a town of France, department of Eure, on the Eure; 11 miles E. of Evreux.

PADANG, a seaport on the W. coast of Sumatra, in the possession of the Dutch. It was taken by the British in 1781, and again in 1794; but finally surrendered to the Dutch in 1814. In 1797 it was almost totally destroyed by an earthquake, and upwards of 300 lives were lost. Long. 99. 49. E. lat. 0. 50. S.

PADDINGTON, a village in Middlesex, 1 mile W. by N. of London. From the number of buildings erected of late years, it is now joined to the metropolis. A canal passes hence to the Grand Junction Canal, near Brentford, and the Great Western railway commences here.

PADERBORN, an ancient principality of Westphalia, 40 miles long and 25 broad; remarkable for its bacon and venison. It now belongs to Prussia.

PADERBORN, a fortified town of Prussian Westphalia; formerly capital of a principality of the same name. The rivulet Pader rises under the high altar of the cathedral, and in the collegiate church are the remains of St. Blaise. The most remarkable of the convents is the college formerly belonging to the Jesuits, and here is also a celebrated university. It is 52 miles E. S. E. of Munster. Pop. 5300. Long. 8. 55. E. lat. 51. 41. N.

PADRON, a town of Spain, in Galicia, seated on the Ulla; 12 miles S. of Compostella.

PADSTOW, a town in Cornwall, with a market on Saturday, a convenient harbour, and some coasting trade. It is seated at the mouth of the Camel, on the Bristol Channel; 30 miles W. of Launceston, and 243 W. by S. of London.

PADUA, a province of Austrian Italy, in the government of Venice; 40 miles long, and 35 broad, bounded by Rovigo, Verona, Vicenza, Treviso, and Venice. It is well watered, and one of the most fertile countries in Italy. Area, 860 square miles. Pop. 270,000.

PADUA, a fortified city of Italy, capital of the above province, and a bishop's see. It is 7 miles in circumference, but much less considerable than formerly, for great part of the area within the walls is unbuilt, and the town in general so thinly inhabited that grass grows in many of the streets. The houses are built on piazzas, which, when the town was in a flourishing state, may have had a magnificent appearance; but they now rather give it a gloomy air. The cathedral is one of the richest in Italy: in the sacristy is a statue of the celebrated Petrarch, who was a canon of the church, and left to it a part of his library. The Franciscan church is dedicated to St. Antonio, the patron of the city, whose body is enclosed in a sarcophagus, under an altar in the middle of the chapel. Near this church is the school of St. Antonio, where many of the actions of the saint are painted in fresco, some of them by Titian. The church of St. Justina is remarkable for its rich Mosaic pavement. The hall of the town-house is one of the largest in Europe, and contains the cenotaph of Livy, who was a native of Padua. The university, once so celebrated, is now on the decline, but was remodelled in 1814. Here are manufactures of cloth, silk, ribbons, and leather, all on a small scale. Padua was taken by the French in 1796. It is seated on the Brenta and Bachiglione, in a fine plain; 20 miles W. by S. of Venice. Pop. 47,000. Long. 11. 53. E. lat. 45. 14. N.

PADULA, a town of Naples, in Principato Citra; 14 miles N. of Policastro. Pop. 6000.

PAGAHM, a decayed city of Birmah, anciently capital of a province of the same name. It is said to have been abandoned in the 13th century, in consequence of a divine admonition. The remains of its ancient splendour are numerous mouldering temples, and the vestiges of a fort. It is seated on the Irrawaddy, 110 miles S.W. of Ummerapoora. Long. 94. 34. E. lat. 21. 10. N.

PAGLIANO, a town of Naples, in Abruzzo Ultra; 15 miles E. S. E. of Aquilla.

PAGO, an island in the Gulf of Venice, separated from Dalmatia by a narrow channel. It is 20 miles long and 6 broad, chiefly barren, and the soil stony; but it is well peopled, contains salt-works, and produces wine and honey. The chief town is of the same name. Long. 51. 10. E. lat. 44. 40. N.

PAHANG, a reduced seaport on the E. coast of the peninsula of Malaya, capital of a kingdom of the same name, containing 50,000 inhabitants; famous for a great number of elephants, and for plenty of pepper. It is 140 miles N. E. of Malacca. Long. 103. 30. E. lat. 3. 55. N.

PAIMBŒUF, a seaport of France, department of Loire Inferieure, at the mouth of the Loire. Hence all the ships belonging to Nantes take their departure, and here they anchor on their arrival; 22 miles W. by N. of Nantes. Pop. 4300. Long. 1. 59. W. lat. 47. 17. N.

PAINSWICK, a town in Gloucestershire, with a market on Tuesday. The inhabitants are employed chiefly in the clothing trade. It stands on the side of a hill; 7 miles S. S. E. of Gloucester.

PAISHAWUR. *See* PEISHAWUR.

PAISLEY, a borough in Scotland, the largest town in Renfrewshire. It returns one member to parliament. It has considerable manufactures of shawls of various descriptions, particularly of cashmere wool, and of silk, linen, gauze, lawn, muslin, cambric, thread, &c.; also extensive soap, candle, and cotton works. The river White Cart divides it into the Old and New Town, which communicate by three bridges. The latter stands on the E. side of the river, and consists of many handsome buildings; it also contains the magnificent remains of an abbey church, and the only one which Paisley formerly required; and close by this is a small vaulted chapel, used as the family burial-place of the Marquis of Abercorn, which is famous for a surprising echo. Paisley is divided into three parishes, has six churches belonging to the establishment, and 10 for dissenters, besides several meeting-houses. By means of the river, and a canal, vessels of 40 tons can come up and unload at the quay; and the Glasgow and Ayr railway passes this town. It is 7¾ miles W. of Glasgow, and 52 from Edinburgh. Long. 4. 23. W. lat. 55. 57. N.

PAITA, a seaport of Peru, with an excellent harbour. It has frequently been plundered by buccaneers: and in 1741 it was burnt by Commodore Anson, because the governor refused to ransom it. Long. 80. 49. W. lat. 5. 12. S.

PALACHY, a town of Hindostan, in the district of Coimbetore, with a small fort. In its vicinity a pot was dug up a few years since, containing Roman silver coins of Augustus and Tiberius. It stands in a well cultivated country; 14 miles S. of Coimbetore, and 37 W. of Daraporam.

PALACIOS, a town of Spain, in Andalusia; 12 miles S. of Seville.

PALACIOS, a town of Spain, in Leon; 32 miles W. S. W. of Leon.

PALAIS, a town of France, capital of the island of Belleisle. It has a strong citadel, which stood a long siege against the English in 1761, and then surrendered on honourable terms. It stands on the N. E. side of the island; 30 miles S. S. E. of L'Orient. Pop. 2500. Long. 3. 7. W. lat. 47. 19. N.

PALAIS, ST., a town and district in the department of Lower Pyrenees, which, with the town and district of St. Jean Pied de Port, formed nearly the whole of the former province of Lower Navarre. It is seated on the river Bidouse; 18 miles S. E. of Bayonne. Long. 1. 4. W. lat. 43. 21. N.

PALAMBUAN, or BALAMBUAN, a town on the E. end of the island of Japan, capital of a territory of its name, which abounds with cotton, rice, maize, fruit, horses, antelopes, buffaloes, and oxen. It stands on a bay in the Strait of Bali. Long. 114. 25. E. lat. 8. 10. S.

PALAMCOTTA, a town of Hindostan, in the province of Tinevelly. Long. 77. 46. E. lat. 8. 42. N.

PALAMOS, a strong seaport of Spain, in Catalonia, seated on a bay of the Mediterranean; 18 miles N. E. of Barcelona.

PALAMOW, a town of Bengal, capital of a well-cultivated district of its name, seated on the Coyle, 140 miles S. S. W. of Patna.

PALAOS. *See* PELEW ISLANDS.

PALATINATE OF THE RHINE and BAVARIA. *See* RHINE and BAVARIA.

PALAWAN. *See* PARAGOA.

PALAZUOLA, a town of Austrian Italy; in the province of Brescia; seated on the Oglio; 20 miles W. N. W. of Brescia.

PALEMBANG, a district or kingdom of Sumatra, on the N. E. coast; conquered by the British in 1812. The chief articles of export are gold, tin, pepper, silk, ivory, wax, rice, &c. Pop. about 75,000.

PALEMBANG, the capital of the above district; and the emporium of the inland commerce of Sumatra. The inhabitants consist of Malays, Chinese, and Arabs. The town is seated on a river of its name, about 60 miles from the sea. Long. 104. 54. E. lat. 2. 59. S. Pop. 25,000.

PALENCIA, a town of Spain, in Leon; capital of a district of its name, and a bishop's see; with five churches, 11 convents, and two hospitals. It is seated on the Carrion; 70 miles S. E. of Leon. Pop. 8300. Long. 4. 23. W. lat. 41. 59. N.

PALENO, a town of Naples, in Abruzzo Citra; 9 miles E. S. E. of Solmona.

PALENZUELA, a town of Spain, in Old Castile; seated on the Arlanza, a little above the influx of the Arlanzon; 30 miles S. W. of Burgos.

PALERMO, a fortified city of Sicily, in Val di Mazara; capital of the island, and an archbishop's see. It stands on a bay of the same name, on the N. coast, near the extremity of a kind of natural amphitheatre, formed by high and rocky mountains. The country between the city and the mountains is one of the richest plains in the world; the whole appearing a magnificent garden, filled with fruitful trees, and watered by fountains and rivulets. The two principal streets intersect each other in the centre of the city, where they form a handsome square, called the Ottangolo, from the centre of which is seen the whole of these noble streets, and the four elegant gates which terminate them, each at the distance of half a mile. The Porto Felice opens to the Marino, a delightful walk, which has on one side the wall of the city, and on the other the sea; and in the centre is an elegant kind of temple, frequently made use of as an orchestra. The churches of Palermo are upwards of 300, and many of them very rich and magnificent. The cathedral is a large Gothic structure, supported within by 80 columns of oriental granite, and divided into a great number of chapels, some of which are extremely rich, particularly that of St. Rosolia, the patroness of Palermo. The relics of this saint are preserved in a large box of silver, enriched with precious stones; and they are considered as the greatest treasures of the city. Here are also found the tombs of several of the ancient Norman kings, and of the emperors Henry VI. and Frederick II., of the finest porphyry. This city has suffered greatly at different periods by earthquakes and inundations. The harbour, defended by two castles, is dangerously open to the sea, from the N. E.; and, even at the anchoring place, ships are in danger when a westerly wind rushes through the valley of Colli, between the mountains. About the middle of the 11th century, the Norman king, Roger, established silk manufactures in this city, by means of prisoners taken in his war with the Greeks, and they still flourish, though not so lucrative since the manufacture has extended to Italy. One mile from Palermo is a celebrated convent of Capuchins, in which is a vault, made use of as a receptacle for the dead. It consists of four wide passages, each about 40 feet in length, with arches along the sides, in which the bodies are set upright, clothed in coarse garments, with their heads, arms, and feet bare. On the floor are handsome trunks, containing the bodies of persons of distinction, the keys of which are kept by the relations. In 1799, when the French made themselves masters of Naples, Palermo became the residence of the court; at present it is the seat of the viceroy of the Sicilian parliament, and of the chief boards of the island administration. It is 130 miles W. of Messina, and 200 S. by W. of Naples. Population 168,000. Long. 13. 23. E. lat. 38. 7. N.

PALESTINE, a country of Syria; so called from the Philistines, who inhabited its seacoast. In the scriptures it is styled the Land of Canaan, and the Promised Land: it is also called Judæa, from the patriarch Judah; and the Holy Land, from its having been the scene of the birth, ministry, and death of Jesus Christ. It is divided from the other parts of Syria, on the N. by Mount Libanus, and on the E. by the river Jordan and the Dead Sea, Arabia Petræa on the S., and the Mediterranean on the W. It is in general a fertile country, abounding, where cultivated, with corn, wine, and oil; and it might supply the neighbouring country with all these, as it anciently did, were the present inhabitants equally industrious. The parts about Jerusalem are the most mountainous and rocky; but they feed numerous herds and flocks, and yield plenty of honey, with excellent wine and oil; and the valleys produce large crops of corn. This country has been conquered and occupied by such a variety of foreign races, that it is difficult to say which forms the basis of its present population. It now belongs to the Turkish empire, and is included in the pachalics of Acre and Damascus, the former comprehending the seacoast, and the latter extending over the interior. The name of Palestine is not known in the country itself, but is applied to it only by Europeans. *See* SYRIA.

PALESTRINA, one of the largest of the islands called the Lagunes, near Venice. It has a town of the same name, 6 miles S. of Venice.

PALESTRINA, (ancient Præneste,) an episcopal town of Italy, in the delegation of Rome, with the title of a principality. Here formerly stood a temple dedicated to Fortune, the ruins of which may yet be seen. It is 25 miles E. by S. of Rome. Population, 3000. Long. 13. 5. E. lat. 41. 52. N.

PALHAMPOOR, a town of Hindostan, in the province of Guzerat; capital of the district of Palhampoor. The inhabitants are uncivilized, and amount to about 40,000. It is 80 miles N. by W. of Amedabad.

PALIANO, a town of Italy, in the papal states, situate on a hill; 20 miles E. of Rome.

PALIGUAT, or PALICAUD, a fort of Hindostan, in Malabar; built by Hyder, on his conquest of that province. Around it are scattered many villages, which contain a considerable population, and have some trade. It was taken by the British in 1783, and again in 1790, and was confirmed to them at the peace of 1792. It stands between two rivulets, near their junction, at the foot of the southern extremity of the Gauts; 25 miles W. S. W. of Coimbetore, and 56 E. by N. of Paniany.

PALIGONDA, a town of Hindostan, in the Carnatic; with the remains of a fort, in which is a considerable temple. It is seated on the Paliar, 25 miles W. of Arcot.

PALIMBAN. *See* PALEMBANG.

PALK STRAIT, a strait at the N. end of the island of Ceylon, in the Bay of Bengal, which separates that island from the coast of Coromandel. It is celebrated for the extensive pearl fishery carried on in it, on both shores, formerly by the Dutch, and now by the British.

PALLISER ISLANDS, a group of islands in the S. Pacific; the largest is about 15 miles long and 10 broad. Long. 146. 30. W. lat. 15. 38. S.

PALMA, one of the Canary islands, to the N. of Ferro; 50 miles in circumference, and very fertile. It has a town of the same name, much frequented for its excellent wines and safe harbour. Population 22,600. Long. 17. 50. W. lat. 28. 37. N.

PALMA, a strong city, capital of the island of Majorca, and a bishop's see. The public squares, the cathedral, and the royal palace, are magnificent. It contains 4000 houses, built after the antique manner; a university, more ancient than celebrated; and 22 churches besides the cathedral. Pop. 30,000. The harbour is extremely good. It was taken by the English in 1766, and retaken in 1785. It is seated on the S. W. side of the island. Long. 2. 30. E. lat. 39. 35. N.

PALMA, a town of Spain, in Andalusia; on the Xenil, near its conflux with the Guadalquiver; 30 miles S. W. of Cordova.

PALMA, a town of Portugal, in Estremadura, on the river Cadoan; 20 miles E. of Setuval.

PALMA, a town of New Granada, republic of Colombia. It is 40 miles N. W. of St. Fe de Bogota.

PALMA NUOVA, a strong frontier town of Italy, in the Venetian province of Udina; seated on a canal which communicates with the Lizonzo; 10 miles S. E. of Udina. Pop. 4500. Long. 13. 15. E. lat. 46. 2. N.

PALMA DI SOLO, a seaport of Sardinia, on the S. W. coast; 38 miles S. W. of Cagliari.

PALMAS, a river of Mexico, formed by the junction of the Nassas and Sauceda, in New Biscay, whence it flows E. about 200 miles, between the provinces of Panuco and New Leon, into the Gulf of Mexico.

PALMAS, the capital of the island of Grand Canaria. *See* CANARIES.

PALMAS, one of the Philippine islands; 16 leagues S. E. of Mindanao. Long. 127. 0. E. lat. 5. 33. N.

PALMAS, CAPE, a promontory on the Ivory coast of Guinea. Long. 5. 34. W. lat. 4. 26. N.

PALMELA, a town of Portugal, in Estremadura; with a castle on a rock. It is 8 miles N. N. E. of Setuval.

PALMERSTON ISLE, an island in the S. Pacific, discovered by Cook, in 1774. It consists of about 10 islets, connected by a reef of coral rocks, and lying in a circular direction; the principal one not exceeding a mile in circumference, nor more than three feet above the level of the sea. It abounds with cocoa-nuts, scurvy-grass, and the wharra-tree, but has no inhabitants. Long. 162. 57. W. lat. 18. 0. S.

PALMYRA, or TADMOR, once a magnificent city of Syria; originally built by king Solomon, in the midst of a sandy desert, bounded on three sides by a chain of high mountains. On the decline of the Macedonian empire in the E., it became the capital of a principality, under the name of Palmyra; and it declared for the Romans, on Adrian marching his army through Syria to Egypt. The city flourished and increased to the time of Aurelian, when it resisted the Roman power under queen Zenobia, who was at length taken captive, and led in triumph through the streets of Rome. Soon afterwards the inhabitants massacred the soldiers who had been left in garrison; this occasioned the return of Aurelian, who, having made himself master of the place, caused the inhabitants to be destroyed, and gave up the city to pillage. Its stupendous ruins were visited, in 1751, by Mr. Wood, who published a splendid account of them in 1753. The inhabitants consist of about 40 Arab families, living in mud cottages, erected within the spacious court of a once magnificent temple. It is 100 miles S. E. of Aleppo. Long. 38. 50. E. lat. 33. 20. N.

PALOS, a seaport of Spain, in Andalusia; with a tolerable harbour; celebrated as the place whence Columbus sailed on his first adventurous voyage, in 1492. It is seated at the mouth of the Tinto; 50 miles W. by S. of Seville. Long. 6. 52. W. lat. 37. 10. N.

PALOS, CAPE, a promontory of Spain, in Murcia; 19 miles E. of Carthagena. Long. 0. 40. W. lat. 37. 37. N.

PALOTA, a fortified town of Hungary, 40 miles S. W. of Buda. Long. 18. 0. E. lat. 47. 0. N.

PALOTZA, a town of Hungary, situate on the Poprah; 54 miles N. of Cassovia. Long. 21. 20. E. lat. 47. 42. N.

PALTE, a famous lake of Tibet; lying to the S. W. of Lassa, about 12 miles S. of the river Sanpoo. It is represented as a wide trench, of about 6 miles broad, surrounding an island 30 miles long, and 20 broad. On the W. shore of this island is a monastery, and the seat of the Lamissa Turcepamo, or the Great Regenerate, in whom the Tibetians think that a divine spirit is regenerated, as it is in the Great Lama. The word *lamissa* is the feminine of *lama*, which signifies a priest.

PAMIERS, a town of France, department of Arriege, and a bishop's see. In the vicinity is a mineral spring. It is seated on the Arriege; 36 miles S. by E. of Toulouse. Long. 1. 35. E. lat. 43. 6. N.

PAMPELONNE, a town of France, department of Tarn; 15 miles N. by E. of Alby.

PAMPLIEGA, a town of Spain, in Old Castile; 12 miles S. W. of Burgos.

PAMPLONA, or PAMPELUNA, a city of Spain; capital of Upper Navarre, and a bishop's see; with a strong citadel, and a university. The squares are handsome, and adorned with shops. It was taken by the French on their invasion of Spain: but surrendered to the allied forces in 1813. It is seated on the Arga; 47 miles S. of Bayonne, and 197 N.E. of Madrid. Pop. 14,000. Long. 1. 42. W. lat. 42. 49. N.

PAMPLONA, a town of New Granada, in the republic of Colombia; famous for mines of gold, and numerous flocks of sheep in its vicinity. It is 150 miles N. by E. of St. Fe de Bogota. Long. 71. 30. W. lat. 6. 30. N.

PAMTICO SOUND, a kind of inland sea, on the coast of North Carolina; 100 miles long and from 10 to 20 broad; separated, in its whole length, from the Atlantic by a beach of sand hardly a mile wide. It has several inlets, but that of Ocrecock, in lat. 35. 10. N., is the only one that would admit vessels of burden.

PANAGIA, a town of Romania, in European Turkey; 14 miles N. of Gallipoli.

PANAMA, a city and seaport of Colombia; capital of a district of the same name, in the government of New Granada. It stands on a fine bay of its name, on the S. coast of the Isthmus of Darien, and contains a handsome cathedral, and a number of churches, convents, and monasteries. Before the abolition of the trade by the galleons, it was the emporium for all the merchandise of Chili and Peru intended for Europe *See* PORTO BELLO. The trade and commerce have much declined, and in the harbour is a fine pearl fishery. The city is surrounded by a wall and other fortifications, and is 60 miles S. by W. of Porto Bello. Long. 80. 21. W. lat. 8. 49. N. *See* DARIEN.

PANARAGA, a town of the island of Java, capital of a kingdom of the same name; 60 miles E. by N. of Mataram.

PANARUCAN, a town on the N. coast of Java, formerly the capital of a principality, but now subject to the Dutch. The chief export is long pepper. Long. 113. 25. E. lat. 8. 0. S.

PANA, one of the Philippine islands, between those of Paragoa and Negros. It is of a triangular form, 250 miles in circumference, populous and fertile, and watered by a great number of rivers and brooks. The chief commodity for exportation is rice. Iloila is the capital.

PANCRAS, an extensive parish in Middlesex, 2 miles N. W. of London. The old church and churchyard have long been noted as a burial place for Roman Catholics. An elegant new church has been erected; and here also are several chapels of ease, a Roman Catholic chapel, and several meeting-houses. The Veterinary College, established in 1791, for the improvement of farriery, the Foundling Hospital, and the Smallpox Hospital, are in this parish.

PANCSOVA, a town and fortress of Hungary, seated near the Danube; 10 miles E. N. E. of Belgrade.

PANGASENA, one of the Molucca islands, in

the East Indies; 45 miles long, and 10 broad, lying between Celebes and Bourton.

PANGO, a town of the kingdom of Congo; capital of a province of the same name. It stands on the river Barbela; 95 miles N. N. E. of St. Salvador. Long. 14. 45. E. lat. 4. 20. S.

PANIANY, a town of Hindostan, in the province of Malabar; containing above 40 mosques, 500 houses belonging to traders, and 1000 huts inhabited by the lower orders of people. The port is frequented by small vessels from different places on the coast; and much rice is exported hence to the northern parts of the province. It is seated in a sandy plain, near the mouth of a river; 32 miles S. by E. of Calicut. Long. 75. 58. E. lat. 10. 47. N.

PANIPUT, a town of Hindostan, in the province of Delhi; celebrated for a battle, in 1761, between an army of 200,000 Mahrattas, and Abdallah, sultan of Candahar, at the head of 150,000 Mahomedans, in which the former were totally defeated. Paniput is situate in an extensive plain, 72 miles N. W. of Delhi. Long. 76. 55. E. lat. 29. 13. N.

PANOMI, a town of Macedonia; 16 miles S. of Salonichi.

PANTALARIA, or PANTELLARIA, an island in the Mediterranean; belonging to Sicily, and situated between that island and the coast of Tunis. It 30 miles in circumference, and abounds in cotton, fruits, and wine. Pop. 6000.

PANUCO, or GUASTECA, a province of Mexico; bounded on the E. by the Gulf of Mexico, and W. by Mechoacan and New Biscay. The tropic of Cancer divides it in two parts; the S. part abounds with provisions, and has some veins of gold and mines of salt; but the other is poor and barren.

PANUCO, the capital of the above province, and a bishop's see, is situate near a river of the same name, which falls into the Gulf of Mexico; 210 miles N. N. E. of Mexico. Long. 98. 50. W. lat. 22. 50. N.

PAO-KING, a city of China, of the first rank, in the province of Hou-quang; 830 miles S. S. W. of Peking. Long. 111. 0. E. lat. 27. 5. N.

PAO-NING, a city of China, of the first rank, in the province of Se-tchuen; on the river Kialing; 700 miles S. W. of Peking. Long. 105. 35. E. lat. 31. 3. N.

PAOOM, one of the New Hebrides, in the South Pacific, to the S. of Mallicollo. Long. 168. 29. W. lat. 16. 30. S.

PAO-TING, a city of China, of the first rank, the most considerable in the province of Petcheli, next to Peking. The country around is pleasant, and as fertile as any part of China; 78 miles S. S. W. of Peking. Long. 115. 25. E. lat. 38. 54. N.

PAPA, a town of Hungary, in the county of Vesprin; 45 miles W. of Buda.

PAPOUL, ST., a town of France, in the department of Aude, on the Lande; 13 miles N. W. of Carcassone, and 35 S. E. of Toulouse.

PAPPENBURG, a town of Hanover, in East Friesland, with two churches, and numerous yards for ship-building. It is seated on a canal, which communicates with the river Ems; 23 miles S. of Embden. Pop. 3400.

PAPPENHEIM, a town of Bavaria, formerly the capital of a county of the same name; seated on a hill near the Altmuhl; 43 miles N. E. of Donawert. Pop. 2000.

PAPUA. *See* GUINEA, NEW.

PARA, a handsome city of Brazil, capital of an extensive government of the same name, with a citadel and castle. The chief business is cultivating tobacco and sugar-canes, and gathering cotton, which grows wild here. It is seated on the estuary of the Tocantin; 80 miles from the ocean. Pop. 10,000. Long. 49. 25. W. lat. 1. 50. S.

PARACELS, or PRACELS, a vast multitude of small islands and rocks in the China Sea, lying off the coast of Cochin-China. They extend 300 miles in length by 60 in breadth, and the intercurrents among them render their navigation dangerous.

PARADELLA, a town of Portugal, in Beira; 12 miles S. E. of Lamego.

PARAGOA, or PALAWAN, the most westerly of the Philippine islands, being 180 miles long, and from 20 to 40 broad, divided between the king of Borneo and the Spaniards, with some independent natives in the interior parts, who are black, and have no fixed place of abode. The Spaniards have a garrison at the N. end of the island, at a place called Tatay. Long. 118. 45. E. lat. 11. 0. N.

PARAGUAY, an extensive country of South America, bounded on the N. by Amazonia, E. by Brazil, S. by Patagonia, and W. by Chili and Peru. It contains numerous lakes and rivers; of the latter, the three principal are the Parana, Paraguay, and Uruguay, the united streams of which form the celebrated Rio de la Plata. These rivers annually overflow their banks. The climate is in general moist and temperate, though in some places it is cold. In the temperate parts the soil is extremely fertile, producing grain, beans, peas, cotton, tobacco, and the valuable herb called paraguay, which is peculiar to this country, and the infusion of which is drunk instead of tea. Here are also a variety of fruits and very rich pastures; but the country is destitute of woods. Cattle, sheep, horses, and mules are in great abundance; of the last many thousands are annually sent to Peru. In the mountain towards Tucuman, the condor, the largest bird of the vulture tribe, is not unfrequent, and the ostrich is found in the wide plains. Several independent tribes of indigenes live in the interior, on the Rio Grande; one of them, called Abipons, are a warlike race, and, by a novelty in American manners, chiefly cavalry, securing and taming the wild horses introduced by the Spaniards. In 1515 the Spaniards discovered this country by sailing up the Rio de la Plata, and in 1535 founded the town of Buenos Ayres. In 1580 the Jesuits were admitted into these fertile regions, and in the next century founded the famous missions of Paraguay. In 1757 Spain exchanged the colonies on the E. shore of the

Uruguay for the Portuguese colony of St. Sacrament, which caused that river to become the boundary of the respective possessions of the two crowns. In 1767 the court expelled the Jesuits, and the natives were put upon the same footing with the other Indians of the Spanish part of South America. The country is now included in the republic of the United Provinces of La Plata, and in the province of Buenos Ayres.

Paraiba, a province of Brazil, between those of Rio Grande and Tamarica. It abounds in sugar-canes, bram-wood, tobacco, and cotton. The chief town, which is of the same name, is seated on the river Paraiba. Pop. 4000. The Dutch obtained possession of it in 1635, and fortified it with a slight rampart; but the Portuguese retook it soon after.

Paramaribo, the capital of Surinam, in Guiana, and the chief place of the Dutch colonies in South America. It has a small but strong citadel, and a noble road for shipping, where there are seldom fewer than 80 vessels, loading coffee, sugar, cotton, and indigo. The streets are straight, and lined with orange, shaddock, tamarind, and lemon trees, in continual bloom. It surrendered to the English in 1799 and in 1803. It is situate on the E. side of the river Surinam, 16 miles from its mouth. Pop. 6000. Long. 55. 25. W. lat. 5. 48. N.

Paramythia, a town in the kingdom of Greece, in the province of Albania; capital of a district, but without any regular government. Population together, about 15,000. The town is 19 miles S. W. of Joannina.

Parana, a province of Paraguay; so named from a large river, which receives the Paraguay at Corrientes, and, afterwards joining the Uruguay, forms the river Plata.

Parchwitz, a town and castle of Prussian Silesia, with a considerable manufacture of cloth; seated on the Katzbach; 10 miles N. E. of Leignitz.

Pardubitz, a town of Bohemia, in the circle of Chrudin, with a fortified castle, and a manufacture of knives and sword blades. It is seated on the Elbe; 23 miles E. by S. of Prague. Pop. 3000. Long. 15. 41. E. lat. 49. 51. N.

Parechia. *See* Paros.

Parenza, a seaport of Istria, on a peninsula in the Gulf of Venice; with a harbour for large vessels. It is 28 miles S. by W. of Capo d'Istria. Long. 13. 50. E. lat. 45. 18. N.

Parga, a seaport on the coast of Albania, opposite to the southern point of the island of Corfu; memorable as the only place which bade defiance to the arms of Ali Pacha, tyrant of Albania, to whom it was eventually surrendered on condition of his paying an indemnity to those of the inhabitants who should refuse to remain. The evacuation took place in 1819, most of the inhabitants removing to the Ionian Islands. It is 30 miles S. W. of Joannina.

Paria, a district of South America, province of Buenos Ayres, lying to the S. E. of Cumana, on the banks of the Oronoco, and including the delta of that river. On the N. of this province between Cumana and the island of Trinidad, is a large bay called the Gulf of Paria.

Paria, the capital of the above province. Here are some silver mines; and its cheeses, made from the milk both of sheep and cows, are in high esteem. It is 140 miles W. N. W. of Plata. Long. 68. 32. W. lat. 18. 30. S.

Paridrong, a strong town of Tibet, on the borders of Bootan; 45 miles W. N. W. of Tassasudon.

Parilla, or Santa, a town of Peru, in the province of Lima, at the mouth of a river of the same name; 80 miles S. E. of Truxillo, and 280 N. W. of Lima. Long. 77. 50. W. lat. 8. 56. S.

Parima, a lake of South America, near the borders of Amazonia and Guiana, of a square form, 80 miles long and 40 broad. It seems to be a kind of inundation formed by the Oronoco; for that river enters on the N. and issues on the W. side of the lake, near its N. W. angle. From the S. E. of this lake issues the White River, called also the Parima, which flows S. to the Black River, and thence S. E. to the river Amazon. To the W. of this lake, before the main stream of the Oronoco turns to the N., there are two other branches that flow from it to the Black River. Hence there are three communications between those two great rivers, the Oronoco and the Amazon.

Paris, the capital of France, one of the largest, finest, and most populous cities in Europe. The river Seine, which crosses it, forms two small islands, called Isle du Palais, and Isle Notre Dame; the former of which was the ancient city of Paris. Paris has 16 gates, and is 17 miles in circumference, including the suburbs. That part of it which is called the ville is situate to the N., the university to the S., and the city in the centre. The houses are built of freestone, many of them seven stories high, and often contain a different family on every floor. The number of inhabitants is estimated at 720,000. There are nine principal bridges in Paris, but only three of them occupy the whole breadth of the Seine, which is not half so large as the Thames at London. There are a great number of public fountains, and some triumphal arches. Of the squares, the finest is the Place de Louis Quinze, of an octagon form, in which was an equestrian statue in bronze of that monarch. This square was the fatal scene of the execution of Louis XVI., of his consort Marie Antoinette, and of his sister the princess Elizabeth. Besides the cathedral of Notre Dame, which is one of the largest in Europe, and contains 45 chapels, Paris has many fine churches. The abbey of St. Genevieve was founded by King Clovis, whose monument is still to be seen in the church; it has a library of 24,000 printed books and 2000 MSS.; also a valuable cabinet of antiquities and natural curiosities. The pantheon, or new church of St. Genevieve, has a front adorned with elegant sculpture, and with colossal pillars. It is the place of interment for illustrious public characters. The university, founded by Charles the Fat, consists of five faculties; namely divinity, civil and canon law, physic, classics, and the sciences; its head is the rector, who is always chosen from the faculty of the sciences. The finest college in Paris is that of the Four Nations, called also Mazarin, from the cardinal, its founder. Among the public libraries, that called the Royal holds the first rank in respect both to the extent of the buildings and the number of volumes. The royal observatory is built of freestone, and neither iron nor wood has been employed in the erection. The botanical garden is worthy of its appellation of royal. The four principal palaces are the Louvre, the Tuileries, the Palais Royal, and the Luxemburg. In the Louvre is deposited the finest collection of paintings and statues in the world, the principal of them brought from various parts of Italy. The garden of the Tuileries, in front of the palace, and on the banks of the Seine, is the finest public walk in Paris. The Luxemburg is famous for its gallery, in which are 20 exquisite paintings by Rubens. The hospital general, which also goes by the name of la Salpetrière (saltpetre being formerly made here), is a most noble foundation for the female sex, nearly 7000 of whom are here provided for, and live under the inspection of 60 sisters. To this foundation belongs the castle of Bicestre, defended on all sides by a wall of considerable circuit, which contains within it many large buildings and several open places; and here nearly 4000 persons of the other sex are maintained. The hospital de la Pitie, where poor children are brought up, constitutes also a part of the hospital general. These three foundations, with the Hotel Dieu, have one common fund, amounting to full 2,000,000 of livres a year. The Hotel des Invalides, for the wounded and superannuated soldiery, built by Louis XIV., is a magnificent structure; as is also the military school in the Champ de Mars, founded by Louis XV. The two principal theatres are the Theatre de la Nation, and the Italian Theatre; which, in point of elegance and convenience, are worthy of the capital of a great nation. The monnoie, or mint, is a noble building, situate on that side of the Seine opposite the Louvre. The Samaritan is a beautiful edifice, at the end of the bridge leading to the Louvre, and contains an engine for conveying the water of the Seine to all parts of the ville. The Hotel de Ville, memorable for having been repeatedly taken and re-taken during the late struggles, is an ancient structure. The most interesting of the manufactures of Paris are those of plate glass, and tapestries made after the pictures of the greatest masters. In the environs are excellent freestone and abundance of gypsum. In the revolution of July, 1830, the inhabitants of Paris distinguished themselves by their courage, their firmness, and their moderation; and in three days achieved a victory over priestcraft and tyranny unparalleled in the annals of history. *See* FRANCE. Paris now forms, with a small district round it, one of the departments of France. It is 210 miles S. S. E. of London, 625 W. of Vienne, and 630 N. N. E. of Madrid. Long. 2. 20. 22½. E. lat. 48. 50. N.

PARIS, a town of Kentucky, chief of Bourbon county; situate in a fine plain, watered by a small river, 30 miles E. of Frankfort.

PARKGATE, a village in Cheshire, situate on the estuary of the Dee; 12 miles N. W. of Chester. Packet-boats frequently sail hence to Ireland, and it has become a frequented and commodious bathing-place.

PARMA, a duchy of Italy, under which name are included the duchies of Parma Proper, Placenza, and Guastalla. It is bounded on the W. and N. by the Milanese, E. by the Modenese, and S. by Tuscany and Genoa. The soil is fertile in corn, wine, oil, hemp, and pasturage; and there are some inconsiderable mines of copper and silver. The celebrated Parmesan cheese is no longer made in this country, but at Lodi, in the Milanese, and some other places. By the treaty of Paris, in 1814, this duchy was given to the ex-empress Maria Louisa. Area, 2300 square miles. Pop. 380,000.

PARMA, an ancient, rich, populous, and handsome town of Italy, capital of the foregoing duchy. It has a university, a magnificent cathedral, and the largest opera-house in Europe, which has seats for 8000 people. The dome, and the church of St. John, are painted by the famous Correggio, who was a native of this place. The other most remarkable places are the ducal palace, with its gallery and collection of artificial curiosities; the large Benedictine convent, in which 12,000 soldiers were quartered in 1724; the Palazza Giardino, a ducal palace, connected with the town; and the promenade between the town and citadel. Charles, king of the Two Sicilies, carried away a library from this place to Naples, which contained 18,000 volumes, and a very valuable cabinet of curiosities, with a rich collection of medals. The inhabitants, about 33,000, trade in silk and silk stockings. In 1734 a bloody battle was fought here between the Austrians and the French and Sardinians, in which the former were defeated. Parma is situated on a river of the same name, which divides it into two parts, united by three bridges; 40 miles N. W. of Modena, and 60 S. E. of Milan. Long. 10. 30. E. lat. 44. 50. N.

PARNASSUS, or PARNASSO, a celebrated mountain of Greece, in Livadia. It has two heads, one of which was famous for being consecrated to Apollo and the Muses, and the other to Bacchus. It is the highest in Greece, and has a fine fountain, supposed to be the ancient Castalia. It is 8 miles N. of Livadia. The ancient Delphi, now called Castri, was on its south face.

PARO, or PORROGONG, a town of Hindostan, capital of a district of its name in the province of Bootan; with a castle, the residence of a governor. It is famous for the manufacture of idols, and the forging of swords, daggers, and arrows. It stands on the Patchieu, in a fertile valley; 20 miles S. by E. of Tassasudon.

PAROS, an island in the Grecian Archipelago, one of the Cyclades, to the W. of Naxia. It is 10 miles long and 8 broad, and the soil is well cultivated. The trade consists in wheat, barley, wine, and pulse, and in calicoes. Pop. 2000.

It formerly produced a great deal of oil, but the Venetian army burnt all the olive-trees. This island was anciently dedicated to Bacchus, on account of its excellent wines; and has been so famous for its marble, that the best carvers would make use of no other. The celebrated statuaries Phidias and Praxiteles were natives of this island; and the famous Arundelian marbles, at Oxford, were brought from this place in 1667.

PAROS, or PARECHIA, the capital of the Isle of Paros, and a bishop's see. It was anciently the largest and most powerful town of the Cyclades, but is greatly decayed. The walls of the castle are built of ancient pieces of marble, and most of the columns are placed long-wise; some of them, that stand upright, support cornices of amazing size. The natives build their houses of marble, which they find ready cut to their hands; but they take no care to place the pieces in a regular manner; their fields, likewise, are enclosed with friezes, altars, and basso-relievos. The present inhabitants are so ignorant, that instead of great sculptors, and skilful architects, they have nothing but carvers of mortars and salt-cellars. Paros is situate on the W. coast of the island. Long. 25. 44. E. lat. 37. 8. N.

PARRAMATTA, a town in New South Wales, with a curious church, with a double steeple, an observatory of great repute, a government-house, court-house, hospital, orphan-house, gaol, &c.; the soil in most places is remarkably good. It is seated at the head of the harbour of Port Jackson: 15 miles W. by N. of Sydney.

PARRET, a river which rises in the S. part of Somersetshire, receives the Ordred, Ivel, and Thone, and enters the Bristol Channel, at Bridgewater Bay.

PARTENKIRCH, a town of Bavaria; 48 miles S. S. W. of Munich.

PARTHENAY, a town of France, department of Deux Sevres; with a considerable trade in cattle and corn, and manufactures of serge, hats, leather, and earthenware. It is seated on the Thoue; 21 miles S. of Thours, and 28 N. N. E. of Niort.

PARTONCRAIG, a ferry-town of Scotland, in Fifeshire; near the mouth of the Frith of Tay; 9 miles N. N. W. of St. Andrew.

PARU, a town and fort of Brazil, in the jurisdiction of Para; situate on the N. side of the head of the estuary of the Amazon; 200 miles from the ocean. Long. 54. 20. W. lat. 1. 50. S.

PAS, a town of France, department of Pas de Calais; 12 miles S. W. of Arras.

PAS DE CALAIS, a department of France, containing the provinces of Artois and Boulonnois. It comprises a superficial area of 2500 square miles, with 570,000 inhabitants. The climate is humid and changeable, several districts are marshy, but the soil in general is fertile in corn, hemp, flax, &c. Arras is the capital.

PASEWALK, a town of Prussian Pomerania; near which are some iron-works. It stands on the Ucker; 28 miles W. of Stettin.

PASQUA, a town of Mexico, in Xalisco; 1000 miles S. S. W. of Compostella.

PASQUARO, a town of Mexico, in Mechoacan; 24 miles S. W. of Mechoacan.

PASSAGE, a town of Ireland, in the county of Cork. It is situated about midway between the city of Cork and Cove, and is much frequented during the summer season; 173 miles from Dublin.

PASSAGE, a seaport of Spain, in Biscay; between those of Fontarabia and St. Sebastian; 3 miles E. of the latter.

PASSAMAQUODDY, a town of the state of Maine, in Washington county; on a bay of the same name; 20 miles N. N. E. of Machias. The river Passamaquoddy, falling into the bay, is the division between the United States and the British territory.

PASSAO, CAPE, a cape of South America, in Quito. Long. 80. 50. W. lat. 0. 50. S.

PASSARO, CAPE (anciently called Pachinum), the most southerly point of Sicily. It has a fort to protect the country from the incursions of the Barbary corsairs. Off this cape Sir George Byng defeated a Spanish squadron in 1735. Long. 15. 22. E. lat. 36. 35. N.

PASSAROWITZ, a town of Servia, where a peace was concluded in 1718 between Charles VI. and Achmet III. It is situate near the river Moravia; 33 miles E. S. E. of Belgrade.

PASSARUAN, a town of the island of Java, capital of an extensive principality; with a trade in cotton and rice; 30 miles W. of Panarucan. Pop. together, 109,000.

PASSAU, a fortified city of Bavaria, capital of the circle of Lower Danube, and formerly of a principality of its name, which in 1815 was divided between Bavaria and Austria. It stands on the Danube, where it receives the Inn and Ilz, and by these rivers is divided into four parts; namely, the town of Passau, Instadt, Ilstadt, and the fortified castle of Oberhaus, on the mountain of St. George. This city is celebrated for the treaty, or religious peace, concluded here in 1552. In 1662 the cathedral and greatest part of the town were consumed by fire, but they have been handsomely rebuilt. It is 65 miles E. S. E. of Ratisbon, and 135 W. by N. of Vienna. Long. 13. 32. E. lat. 48. 34. N. Pop. 10,000.

PASSENHEIM, a town of Prussia, in the government of Konigsberg; 73 miles S. of Konigsberg.

PASSIGNANO, a town of Italy, in the papal states; 17 miles N. W. of Perugia.

PASSY, a village of France, department of Paris, near the town of St. Denys. Here is a manufacture of considerable extent for speedily bleaching cotton and linen cloth. Pop. 3000.

PASTO, or ST. JUAN DE PASTO, a town of Colombia, in New Granada, capital of a district of its name; seated in a valley, 120 miles N. by E. of Quito. Pop. 7000. Long. 76. 55. W. lat. 1. 50. N.

PASTRANA, a town of Spain, in New Castile, 32 miles E. of Madrid.

PATAGONIA, a country in the most southern part of South America, bounded on the N. by Buenos Ayres, and extending 1100 miles on the eastern coast, from Rio de la Plata to the

Straits of Magellan. This country has no timber in the S. parts, though the N. contains an immense quantity, and numerous flocks of cattle. The E. coast is generally low. The natives are tall, stout, and well made, some of them six feet five inches in height; but their hands and feet are remarkably small. Their colour is a kind of bronze. They have no other clothing than skins, which they wear with the hair inwards, and a little apron of leather. The principal harbour is that of Port St. Julian.

PATAK, a town of Hungary, with a Protestant college; situate on the Latoreza, 25 miles S. S. E. of Cassovia.

PATANA, a city and district of Mysore. *See* SERINGAPATAM.

PATANI, a town on the N. E. coast of the peninsula of Malaya, capital of a district of the same name, with a well defended harbour. The inhabitants have some trade with the Chinese; 300 miles N. by W. of Malacca. Long. 100. 50. E. lat. 7. 5. N.

PATAY, a town of France, department of Loiret, where the English were defeated in 1429, by Joan of Arc; 15 miles N. W. of Orleans.

PATELI. *See* PUTALA.

PATERNO, a town of Sicily, in Val di Demona, built on the ruins of Hybla, so celebrated for its honey; 15 miles W. of Catania.

PATMOS, or PATINOS, an island in the Grecian Archipelago, lying 26 miles S. of the Isle of Samos, famous for being the place where St. John wrote the Apocalypse. It is 25 miles in circumference, but produces very little, only a few valleys being capable of cultivation: partridges, rabbits, quails, turtles, pigeons, and snipes abound. In the midst of the island rises a mountain, terminated by the convent of St. John, the abbot of which is the prince of the country. The hermitage of the Apocalypse is situate on the side of the mountain between the convent and the port of Scala. It leads to the church of the Apocalypse, which is built against a grotto in a rock, pointed out as the asylum of St. John during his exile. The inhabitants are chiefly sailors or ship-builders, and have some trade in cotton and stockings of their own manufacture. Long. 26. 24. E. lat. 37. 24. N.

PATNA, a city of Hindostan, capital of Bahar, seated on the right bank of the Ganges, opposite the influx of the Gunduck, and fortified with a wall and citadel. In the citadel were confined the British prisoners taken in 1764, by Meer Cossim, nabob of Bengal, by whose order they were brutally massacred. This occasioned the storming of the city; since which period it has acknowledged the British sway, and is the residence of the provincial courts, &c. The buildings are high, but the streets are narrow. It is a place of considerable trade; 320 miles N.W. of Calcutta. Pop. 312,000. Long. 85. 10. E. lat. 25. 35. N.

PATRAS, a seaport of Greece, in the Morea, and an archbishop's see. The Jews, who are one-third of the inhabitants, have four synagogues, and there are several handsome Greek churches. The principal articles of trade are silk, leather, honey, manna, pomegranates, citrons, and oranges. It is seated on the side of a hill, near the entrance of the Gulf of Lepanto; 14 miles S. W. of Lepanto. Pop. 8000. Long. 21. 45. E. lat. 38. 17. N.

PATRIA, a town of Naples, in Terra di Lavoro, situate near a lake of the same name; 13 miles N. W. of Naples.

PATRICA, a town of tne papal states, in Campagna di Roma; 13 miles S. of Rome.

PATRIMONY OF ST. PETER, a province of Italy, in the papal states; 43 miles long and 30 broad; bounded N. by Orvietto, E. by Umbria and Sabina, S. by Campagni di Roma, and S. W. by the sea. It was granted by the emperor Constantine, to support a church he had built in honour of St. Peter, and for the use of the bishop of Rome. The country is fertile in corn and fruit, and produces much alum.

PATRINGTON, a town in East Yorkshire, with a market on Saturday. Here the Roman road from the Picts' wall ended. It is seated near the mouth of the Humber; 18 miles E. S. E. of Hull, and 188 N. of London.

PATSCHKAU, a town of Prussian Silesia, on the river Neisse; 13 miles W. of Neisse.

PATTA, an island on the coast of Zanguebar, 10 miles in circuit, inhabited chiefly by Arabians; seated at the mouth of a river of the same name. Long. 43. 0. E. lat. 1. 56. N.

PATTAN, a town of Hindostan, in Nepaul, containing several temples, and about 24,000 houses; 40 miles E. S. E. of Catmandu.

PATTENSEN, a town of Hanover, 7 miles S. by E. of Hanover.

PATTI, a seaport of Sicily, in Val di Demona, and a bishop's see, seated on the Gulf of Patti; 38 miles W. of Messina. Long. 15. 22. E. lat. 38. 11. N.

PATTIARY, a town of Hindostan, in the province of Oude; 55 miles N. W. of Canogue, and 55 E. N. E. of Agra.

PATTUN, a town of Hindostan, capital of a district of the same name, in Guzerat. It is seated on the Surswatty; 48 miles N. of Amedabad. Long. 72. 30. E. lat. 23. 45. N.

PATUXENT, a navigable river of Maryland, which flows into the W. side of Chesapeake Bay; 30 miles S. of Annapolis.

PATZOW, a town of Bohemia, in Bechin, with a Carmelite convent, and manufactures of cloth; 17 miles E. of Tabor.

PAU, a town of France, capital of the department of Lower Pyrenees, with a castle where Henry VI. was born. It was the ancient residence of the kings of Navarre; and, before the revolution, the capital of Bearn. Here are manufactures of cloth, linen, &c., and the environs are productive in wine and fruit. It is seated on an eminence by the river called the Gave de Pau; 97 miles S. of Bordeaux. Pop. 9000. Long. 0. 23. W. lat. 43. 7. N.

PAUL, ST., an island in the Indian Ocean. *See* AMSTERDAM.

PAUL, ST., a town of Brazil, in a district of its name; founded by a colony of Jesuits and Indians, in 1570. The inhabitants are estimated at 20,000, the greater part of whom are farmers. The town is pleasantly situated on an eminence, surrounded on three sides by low meadow-land, and washed at the base by rivulets which almost insulate it in rainy weather. It is 36 miles from the sea, and 190 W. of Rio Janeiro. Long. 45. 56. W. lat. 23. 26. S.

PAUL, ST., a town of France, department of Pas de Calais; 18 miles W. N. W. of Arras.

PAUL, ST., a town in the department of Upper Vienne; 10 miles S. E. of Limoges.

PAUL, ST., a town in the department of Var; 7 miles W. of Nice.

PAUL DE FENOUILHET, ST., a town in the department of the Eastern Pyrenees; 18 miles W. N. W. of Perpignan.

PAUL DE LEON, ST., a town in the department of Finisterre; seated on a bay of the English Channel; 30 miles N. E. of Brest. Long. 4. 0. W. lat. 48. 41. N.

PAUL DE OMAGUAS, ST., a town of Amazonia, on the S. side of the river Amazon, and on the borders of Peru. Long. 69. 20. W. lat. 4. 10. S.

PAUL TROIX CHATEAUX, ST., a town of France, department of Drome; on the side of a hill; 16 miles S. of Montelimar.

PAULA, a town of Naples, in Calabria Citra; 12 miles W. N. W. of Cosenza.

PAULOGRAD, a town of Russia, in the government of Catharinenslaf; 32 miles E. of Catharinenslaf. Long. 35. 54. E. lat. 47. 10. N.

PAUSA, a town of Saxony, in Voigtland; 7 miles N. N. W. of Plauen.

PAUSILIPPO, or POSILIPPO, a mountain 5 miles W. of Naples; celebrated for a grotto, which is a passage cut through the mountain, nearly a mile in length, 20 feet in breadth, and 30 in height. People of fashion drive through this passage with torches; but the country people find their way by the light which enters at the extremities, and at two holes pierced through the mountain, near the middle of the grotto. On this mountain is the tomb of Virgil; and its N. and E. sides are covered with villas and gardens.

PAUZK, a town of West Prussia, in Pomerelia; near the W. coast of the Gulf of Dantzic; 25 miles N. W. of Dantzic.

PAVIA, a province of Austrian Italy, in the government of Milan; called, for its fertility, the Garden of the Milanese. It is bounded by Parma, Milan, and Lodi, and comprises an area of 320 square miles, with about 117,000 inhabitants.

PAVIA, the capital of the foregoing province, and a bishop's see; with a celebrated university, and a citadel. Besides the cathedral, there are 18 churches, and numerous convents. The chief articles of commerce are corn, hemp, cheese, and wine. It was once the capital of Lombardy, and has undergone various changes. In 1706 it fell into the hands of Austria; in 1796 it was taken by the French, and retained till the peace of 1814. It is seated in a beautiful plain, on the Tesino, near its conflux with Po; 17 miles S. of Milan. Pop. 23,350. Long. 9. 15. E. lat. 45. 13. N.

PAVOASAN, the capital of the isle of St. Thomas, on the coast of Guinea; and the see of a bishop, with a fort and a good harbour. It lies under the equator, in long. 8. 30. W.

PAXO, one of the Ionian islands, a little S. of Corfu; about 15 miles in circumference; inhabited by about 6500 Greeks. It produces wine, oil, and almonds. Long. 20. 20. E. lat. 39. 21. N.

PAYERNE, a town of Switzerland, in the canton of Bern, on the river Broye; 22 miles S. W. of Bern.

PAYMOGO, a town of Spain, in Andalusia; 42 miles N. by E. of Ayamonte, and 73 N. W. of Seville.

PAYS DE VAUD, a canton of Switzerland, extending along the lake of Geneva, and rising gradually from the edge of that lake. It is richly laid out in vineyards, corn-fields, and meadows, and chequered with many villages and towns. The prevailing language is the French; and it contains 150,000 inhabitants. Area, 1500 square miles. Lausanne is the capital.

PAZ, LA, a city of Bolivia, capital of a district of its name, and a bishop's see. Besides the cathedral, it contains four churches, an hospital, a college, and several convents. It is seated at the foot of a mountain, in a valley abounding in wine and fruits; 220 miles N. W. of Plata. Pop. 20,000. Long. 68. 50. W. lat. 17. 0. S.

PAZZY, a town of Romania, and a bishop's see; 8 miles S. W. of Gallipoli.

PEAK, a mountainous tract in the N. W. part of Derbyshire, which abounds in lead, iron, millstones, marble, alabaster, coal, and a coarse sort of crystals. It is much visited on account of its extraordinary caverns and other curiosities. The "Wonders of the Peak," which have been celebrated both in prose and verse, are noticed in this work, under the articles BUXTON, CASTLETON, CHATSWORTH, and TIDESWELL.

PEARL ISLANDS, islands lying in the Bay of Panama. The inhabitants of Panama have plantations on them.

PEARL RIVER, a navigable river of the state of Mississippi, which, after flowing through a fertile territory, falls into Lake Borgne, a little E. of Lake Pontchartrain.

PECHLARN, a town of Austria, on the right bank of the Danube. The river is very wide; and here the Romans, who called it Præclara, had a harbour for their navy. It is 14 miles W. of St. Polten.

PEDEE, a navigable river in the United States, which rises in North Carolina, and is there called Yadkin River. On entering South Carolina it takes the name of Pedee, and flows into Wynyaw Bay, at Georgetown.

PEDENA, a town of Austrian Illyria, in Istria; 25 miles S. E. of Capo d'Istria.

PEDERNEIRA, a town of Portugal, in Estremadura, on the seacoast; 33 miles S. W. of Leiria.

PEDIR, a town of Sumatra, on the W. coast; 40 miles E. S. E. of Acheen. Long. 96. 36. E. lat. 5. 22. N.

PEDRAZA, a town of Spain, in Old Castile; with a castle, in which the two sons of Francis I. were confined. It was the birthplace of the emperor Trajan. It is 25 miles N. E. of Segovia.

PEDRO, POINT, the most northern point of the island of Ceylon; opposite Point Calymere, on the continent of Hindostan. Long. 80. 27. E. lat. 9. 52. N.

PEDRO, ST., one of the islands in the Pacific Ocean called Marquesas. Long. 138. 51. W. lat. 9. 58. S.—Also the name of a large river of Mexico, which runs into the Rio del Norte, on the borders of Cohahuila, a river of Brazil which falls into the Atlantic; and several inconsiderable settlements in South America, consisting only of a few scattered families of Indians.

PEEBLES, a borough of Scotland, capital of Peeblesshire; seated on the Tweed, over which is an ancient stone bridge, and also an iron bridge for foot passengers. It is divided by Eddlestone Water into the Old and New Town, has manufactures of carpets and serges, and is noted for its excellent ale. On a projecting rock, near the Tweed, stands Nidpath Castle, and on an eminence on the E. stands Horseburg Castle. It is 22 miles S. of Edinburgh. In conjunction with Linlithgow it sends one member to parliament. Long. 3. 7. W. lat. 55. 40. N.

PEEBLESSHIRE, a county of Scotland, 30 miles long, and 12 broad; bounded N. by Edinburghshire, E. by Selkirkshire, S. by Dumfriesshire, and W. by Lanarkshire. It is divided into 16 parishes, and sends one member to parliament. Its hills, among which are those of Tweedsmuir, abound with salubrious springs, and feed numbers of sheep and cattle. The principal rivers are the Tweed and Lyne; the former runs through the county, whence it is sometimes called Tweeddale.

PEEKSHILL, a town of New York, in West Chester county; on the N. side of a creek of its name; 5 miles from its entrance into Hudson River, and 50 N. of New-York.

PEEL, a town on the W. coast of the Isle of Man, situate on a spacious bay. At the S. extremity of the bay is Peel Isle, a rock of great magnitude and height, on the summit of which is a castle, and the dilapidated cathedral of the isle, dedicated to St. Germain, the first bishop, who lived in the fifth century. The town is much decayed, and the inhabitants are indolent and poor. It is 10 miles W. of Douglas. Long. 4. 40. W. lat. 54. 13. N.

PEENE, a river of Germany, which rises out of some lakes in Mecklenburg, flows through Hither Pomerania to the western branch of the Oder, which is thence called Peene, and runs by Wolgast into the Baltic Sea, at Peenemunde.

PEENEMUNDE, a town and fort of Prussian Pomerania, in the isle of Usedom, and the residence of the governor of the island. It commands the entrance and mouth of the Peene, near which it stands; 6 miles N. by E. of Wolgast. Long. 13. 55. E. lat. 54. 8. N.

PEER, a town of the Netherlands, in the province of Limburg; 24 miles N. N. W. of Maestricht.

PEGAU, a town of Saxony, on the Elster; 10 miles S. S. W. of Leipsic.

PEGAU, a town of the Austrian states, in Styria, near which are considerable lead mines. It is seated near the Meur; 9 miles N. N. W. of Gratz.

PEGU, a province of Birmah, bounded N. by Arracan and Ava, W. and S. by the bay of Bengal, and E. by Siam. It is very fruitful in corn, roots, pulse, and fruits; its products are teak timber, elephants' teeth, bees-wax, lac, saltpetre, iron, tin, petroleum, very fine rubies, small diamonds, and plenty of lead. The inhabitants are generally of low stature, and have small eyes, and are a distinct race from the Burmese. The women are much fairer than the men, small, but well proportioned. In the low flat part of the country, which is liable to be overflowed, the houses are built upon stakes, and in time of inundation the inhabitants communicate with each other by boats. Pegu was long an independent kingdom, and in 1752 conquered the kingdom of Birmah; but Alompra, whom the king of Pegu had continued as chief at Monchabou, soon afterwards revolted, and in 1757 reduced Pegu to a dependent province.

PEGU, a city of the above province, erected on the site of the former city, which was ruined by Alompra in 1757. The ancient city was a quadrangle, each side measuring nearly a mile and a half, and surrounded by strong walls and other fortifications, now in ruins. The magnificent temple of Shoemadoo still exists as a monument of its ancient greatness. The present city occupies about one-fourth of the former area. On the N. and E. sides it borders on the old wall, and is fenced round by a stockade. It is seated on a river of the same name; 300 miles S. of Ummerapoora. Pop. about 15,000. Long. 96. 11. E. lat. 17. 40. N.

PEI-HO, or WHITE-RIVER, a river of China, in Pe-tche-li, which passes near Peking, and by the cities of Tong-tchou and Tiensing, into the Yellow Sea. The tide flows 110 miles, and frequently submerges the flat country on its banks.

PEINA, a town of Hanover, in the principality of Hildesheim; with a palace and a Capuchin convent; 20 miles E. of Hanover.

PEIPUS, or TCHUDSKOI, a large lake of Russia, between the governments of Petersburg and Livonia. The river Narova issues from this lake, by which it has a communication at Narva with the Gulf of Finland.

PEISHORE, or PESHAWUR, a town of Afghanistan, capital of a fine and populous district of its name. The inhabitants are estimated at 100,000. Here the Hon. M. S. Elphinstone had his audience with the Afghan king, in 1809; 95 miles S. S. E. of Cabul. Long. 70. 37. E. lat. 33. 32. N.

PEISKRETSCHAM, a town of Prussian Silesia, in the government of Oppeln; 39 miles S. E. of Oppeln.

PEITZ, a town of Prussia, in the Ucker Mark

of Brandenburg, with manufactures of cloth and yarn, and in the neighbourhood are iron-works. It stands on the Maukse, which runs into the Spree; 10 miles N. N. E. of Cotbus, and 37 S. S. E. of Frankfort.

Peking, the capital of the empire of China, in the province of Pe-tche-li. Its name signifies the Northern Court, to distinguish it from Nanking, the Southern Court, where the emperor formerly resided. This capital forms an oblong square, and is divided into two cities; one inhabited by Chinese, the other by Tartars. Those two cities, exclusive of the suburbs, are nearly 14 miles in circumference. The walls of the city are 28 feet high, 24 thick at the base, and 12 at the top; and there are spacious towers at 70 feet distance from each other. The gates are high, and well arched, supporting buildings of nine stories high, the lowest of which is for the soldiers when they come off guard: they are nine in number, three in the S. wall, and two in each of the other sides. The middle gate, on the E. side, opens into the Tartar or imperial city, which is a space within the general enclosure, about a mile from N. to S. and three-quarters of a mile from E. to W. with a rivulet winding through it. A wall of large red polished bricks, 20 feet high, covered with a roof of tiles painted yellow and varnished, surrounds this space, in which are contained the imperial palace and gardens, the public offices, and lodgings for the ministers, the eunuchs, artificers, and tradesmen belonging to the court. Between the two other gates in the S. wall and the opposite ones on the N. side of the city, run two straight streets, each 4 miles in length, and 120 feet wide. One street of the same width runs from one of the eastern to the corresponding western gate, but the other is interrupted by the imperial city, round the walls of which it is carried. The other streets branch from these main streets at right angles, and are very narrow. The houses have no windows nor openings to the street, except the great shops; most of them are poorly built, and have only a ground floor. It is astonishing to see the concourse of people in the main streets, yet not one Chinese woman among them, and the confusion occasioned by the number of horses, camels, mules, asses, waggons, carts, and chairs; without reckoning the several mobs which gather about the jugglers, ballad-singers, &c. Persons of distinction have always a horseman to go before them and clear the way. All the great streets are guarded by soldiers, who patrol night and day with swords by their sides, and whips in their hands, to chastise those who make any disturbance, or take them into custody. The minor streets have lattice gates at their entrance into the great streets, which are shut up at night, and guarded by soldiers, who suffer no assemblies in the streets at that time. The emperor's palace and garden, which occupy two-thirds of the Tartar city, is surrounded by a brick wall, 2 miles in length, with a pavilion at each corner, encompassed by galleries supported by columns: the architecture of the stupendous pile of buildings of which the palace consists is entirely different from that of the Europeans. The temples and the towers of Peking are so numerous that it is difficult to count them. The surrounding country is sandy and unproductive, but provisions of all kinds are exceedingly plentiful, being brought, as well as the merchandise, from all parts by canals from the rivers, which are always crowded with vessels of different sizes. An earthquake, which happened here in 1731, buried above 100,000 persons in the ruins of the houses. The inhabitants are estimated at 2,000,000; 60 miles S. of the Great Wall. Long. 116. 27. E. lat. 39. 54. N.

Pelagnisi, an island in the Grecian Archipelago, about 8 miles in circumference. Long. 24. 12. E. lat. 39. 30. N.

Pelegrino, a mountain on the N. coast of Sicily, nearly 2 miles W. of Palermo. On this mount is a cavern, in which is the image of St. Rosolia, the patroness of Palermo, who is said to have died here: and round this cave a church is built, where priests attend to watch the precious relics, and receive the offerings of the pilgrims.

Pelew Islands, or Palaos, a group of islands in the Pacific Ocean lying between 134. and 136. E. long. and 6. and 8. N. lat. They are encircled on the W. side by a reef of coral; and are 18 in number, of which the principal ones are Oroolong, Emungs, Emillegue, Artingal, Coroora, and Pelelew. They are well covered with trees of various kinds and sizes; and every part of that called Coroora bears the marks of industry and good cultivation. Captain Wilson, of the Antelope East India packet, who was wrecked here in 1783, found the natives simple in their manners, delicate in their sentiments, and friendly in their disposition. The astonishment which they manifested on seeing the English plainly showed that they had never before seen a white man. They had no idea of the nature of powder and shot, and were exceedingly amazed on seeing its effects. Their principal arms consist of bamboo darts, from five to eight feet long, pointed with the wood of the betel-nut tree; but there are short ones for different marks, which are thrown by means of a stick two feet long. The chiefs wear a bone round one of their wrists, in the form of a bracelet, which being a mark of great honour conferred by the king, is never to be parted with but with life. They are not all of the same degree, as appeared from the difference in the bone they wore. Captain Wilson was invested with the highest order of the bone. With respect to property, in these islands, a man's house or canoe is considered as his own, as is also the land allotted to him, as long as he occupies and cultivates it; but whenever he removes to another place, the ground reverts to the king. The natives make canoes out of the trunks of trees, some large enough to carry 30 men. Yams and cocoa-nuts, being their chief articles of subsistence, are attended with the utmost care, and the milk of the latter is their common drink. On particular occasions they add to their ordinary fare certain sweetmeats, and a sweet beverage, obtained by the aid of a syrup extracted either from the palm-tree or the sugar-cane. Their houses are raised about three feet from the ground, the foundation beams being laid on large stones, whence spring the upright supports of their sides, which are crossed by other timbers grooved together, and fastened by wooden pins, the intermediate space being closely filled up with bamboos and palm-tree leaves, plaited together: the inside is without any divisions, forming one great room. They have little baskets, nicely woven from slips of the plantain-tree, and wooden baskets with covers, neatly carved, and inlaid with shells. No one goes abroad without a basket, which usually contains some betel-nut, a comb, a knife, and a little twine. The best knives are made of a piece of the large mother-of-pearl oyster, ground narrow, and the outward side a little polished. The combs are made of the orange tree, of which there are a few of the Seville kind; the handle and teeth are fastened to the solid wood. The fishing-hooks are of tortoiseshell; and twine, cord, and fishing-nets are well manufactured from the husks of the cocoa-nut. Of the plantain leaf are formed mats, which serve the people as beds. They also use a plantain leaf at meals, instead of a plate; and the shell of a cocoa-nut supplies the place of a cup. There are vessels of a kind of earthenware, of a reddish brown colour, in which they boil their fish, yams, &c. A bundle of cocoa-nut husks serves them for a broom; and thick bamboos, with bores five or six inches in diameter, are their buckets or cisterns. The shell of the tortoise is here remarkably beautiful, and the natives have discovered the art of moulding it into little trays or dishes, and spoons. Some of the great ladies have also bracelets of the same manufacture, and ear-rings inlaid with shells. The Pelewans, in general, are stout and well made, rather above the middle stature, and of a deep copper colour. Their hair is long, and generally formed into one large loose curl round their heads. The men are entirely naked; but the women wear two little aprons, one before, the other behind. Both sexes are tattooed, have their teeth made black by art, and the cartilage between the nostrils bored, through which they frequently put a sprig or blossom of some plant or shrub. The men have the left ear bored, and the women both; a few of the former wear beads in the perforated ear, the latter either a leaf, or an ear-ring of inlaid tortoise-shell. Both sexes are very expert swimmers; and the men are admirable divers Such an opinion had Abba Thulle, the king of the island, entertained of the English, that, on their departure, he permitted his second son, Lee Boo, to accompany them to England, where he arrived in 1784. In a few months after, this hopeful youth died of the small pox, and the East India Company erected a monument over his grave in Rotherhithe church-yard. The directors of the East India Company, sensible that there remained obligations for them to fulfil, equipped two vessels at Bombay, under the command of Captain M'Cluer, which arrived at these islands in January, 1791. A joyful and affecting interview took place between the English and the Pelewans; and the good Abba Thulle bore the intelligence of the death of Lee Boo with great fortitude. When the presents were landed, consisting of cattle, sheep, goats, pigs, &c., together with arms, grindstones, shovels, saws, and other utensils, the natives were struck with amazement, and the king himself was for some time at a loss how to express his gratitude. The king, in return, made a present of one of the islands to the English, which was taken possession of with the usual formalities. Captain M'Cluer, leaving one ship behind to superintend the gardens, plantations, and live stock, proceeded with the other to Canton, some of the natives voluntarily accompanying him. He returned to Pelew in June; but thinking his benevolent mission not yet completed, he sailed with both ships to New Guinea and Bencoolen, and returned again in January, 1793, with two full cargoes of cattle and stores. During his absence Abba Thulle had died, and his brother had succeeded to the sovereignty. The munificent gratitude of the East India Company has been attended with complete success, the live stock having greatly multiplied, and the rice producing two abundant crops every year. A small trade has been established between Pelew and China.

PELISSANE, a town of France, department of Mouths of the Rhone; 15 miles W. N. W. of Aix.

PELLERIN, a town in the department of Lower Loire, situate on the Loire, with a harbour for small vessels; 10 miles N. of Nantes, and 22 S. E. of Paimbœuf.

PEMBA, an island in the Indian Ocean, near the coast of Zanguebar; about 100 miles in circumference. Long. 41. 10. E. lat. 4. 50. S.

PEMBA, a town of the kingdom of Congo, capital of a province of the same name. It is seated on the Loze; 90 miles S. S. E. of St. Salvador. Long. 14. 40. E. lat. 6. 45. S.

PEMBRIDGE, a town in Herefordshire, with a manufacture of woollen cloth, seated on the Arrow; 7 miles W. of Leominster, and 145 W. N. W. of London.

PEMBROKE, a town of Massachusets, in Plymouth county; situate on North River, remarkable for its depth of water, though in some places not more than 50 feet wide. Vessels of 300 tons are built here, and descend to Massachusets Bay, 18 miles distant. It is 51 miles S. S. E. of Boston.

PEMBROKE, a borough of Wales, capital of Pembrokeshire, governed by a mayor; with a market on Saturday. It returns one member to parliament. It stands on the innermost creek of Milford-haven, over which are two bridges; but the harbour is become injured by the rubbish of the neighbouring lime-stone quarries. It was anciently suronded by walls, and had a magnificent castle; the remains of which still give it an appearance of uncommon grandeur. Here are three churches, several meeting-houses, and a free grammar-school. It is 10 miles S. by E. of Haverfordwest, (where the assizes of the county are held,) and 263 W. by N. of London. Long. 4. 48. W. lat. 51. 43. N.

PEMBROKESHIRE, a county of Wales, 37

miles long, and 28 broad; surrounded on all sides by the sea, except on the E., where it is bounded by Caermarthenshire and Cardiganshire. It contains 335,600 acres, is divided into seven hundreds and 145 parishes, has one city and seven market-towns, and sends one member to parliament. The rivers are inconsiderable. A great part of the county is plain and tolerably fertile, consisting of rich meadow and arable land. The N. E. part alone is mountainous, which, however, yields good pasturage for sheep and cattle. This county abounds with objects of antiquarian interest, such as Druidical circles and cromlechs, single stone monuments, castles, &c.

Pena de Francia, a town of Spain, in Leon; 27 miles S. S. E. of Ciudad Rodrigo.

Penafiel, a town of Spain, in Leon, with a palace, and a strong castle. It is seated at the foot of a mountain, near the Douro; 38 miles E. S. E. of Valladolid. Long. 4. 0. W. lat. 41. 33. N.

Penafirme, a town of Portugal, in Estremadura, at the mouth of the Mongola; 36 miles N. N. W. of Lisbon.

Penaflor, a town of Spain, in Asturias, seated on the Pravia; 8 miles N. W. of Oviedo.

Penaflor, a town of Spain, in Andalusia; 48 miles N. E. of Seville.

Penagarcia, a town of Portugal, in Beira; 36 miles E. of Castel Branco.

Penamacor, a fortified town of Portugal, in Beira, with a castle; 31 miles E. N. E. of Castel Branco. Long. 6. 52. W. lat. 40. 6. N.

Penaranda, a town of Spain, in Old Castile; 39 miles S. by E. of Burgos.—Another, 33 miles N. N. W. of Avila.

Penitz, a town of Bavarian Franconia, on a river of the same name, near its source; 10 miles S. of Bayreuth.

Penon de Velez, a seaport and fortress of Morocco, seated on a rock in the Mediterranean, near the town of Velez. It was built by the Spaniards in 1508, taken by the Moors in 1522, and retaken in 1664. It is 73 miles S. E. of Ceuta. Long. 4. 16. W. lat. 35. 12. N.

Penang. *See* Prince of Wales Island.

Penautier, a town of France, department of Aude; 4 miles N. of Carcassone.

Pendennis, a castle in Cornwall, on a hill of the same name, on Falmouth Bay. It was built by Henry VIII. for the security of the coast; and on the opposite side of the bay is another, called St. Maws. It is a little to the S. E. of Falmouth, the harbour of which it defends.

Pendleton, a large village in Lancashire, 2 miles W. N. W. of Manchester. The inhabitants are principally employed in the trade and manufactures of the various Manchester goods.

Peniche, a strong seaport of Portugal, in Estremadura; with a good harbour and a citadel; seated on a peninsula, 48 miles N. W. of Lisbon. Pop. 2800. Long. 9. 20. W. lat. 39. 22. N.

Penigk, a town of Saxony, and the chief place of one of the lordships forming the county of Schomburg; with a manufacture of woollen stuffs and a pottery; seated on the Mulda, 11 miles N. W. of Chemnitz. Pop. 3000.

Peniscola, a town of Spain, in Valencia, seated on a high point of land, surrounded on three sides by the sea, and of difficult access by land. It is 30 miles S. by W. of Tortosa, and 80 N. N. E. of Valencia. Pop. 2200. Long. 0. 24. E. lat. 40. 24. N.

Penishehr, a town of Afghanistan, capital of a district in the province of Cabul; 46 miles N. of Cabul.

Penistone, a town in West Yorkshire, with a market on Thursday, and a small woollen manufacture. It has a handsome parish church, three meeting-houses, a grammar-school, and three other schools free to the whole parish. The environs, especially to the W., have rather a dreary and barren appearance. The town is seated on the right bank of the river Don, 13 miles S. S. E. of Huddersfield, and 177 N.N.W. of London.

Penkridge, a decayed town in Staffordshire; seated on the river Penk, 6 miles S. of Stafford, and 129 N. W. of London.

Penkum, a town of Prussian Pomerania, seated on the Randow, between two small lakes; 15 miles S. W. of Stettin.

Penmaenmawr, a mountain of Wales, in Caernarvonshire, overhanging the sea, and rising to the height of 1540 feet. It is 4 miles W. by S. of Aberconway, and the road to Holyhead crosses it on the side of a dreadful precipice, from which it is defended by a wall.

Pennar, a river of Hindostan, which rises in Mysore, flows by Gooty, Gandicotta, Cuddapa, and Vellore, and enters the Bay of Bengal at Gangapatnam.

Pennsylvania, one of the United States of America, 288 miles long, and 156 broad, bounded N. by New York, E. by the river Delaware, S. by Delaware, Maryland, and Virginia, W. by the latter and Ohio, and N. W. by Lake Erie, on which it has a considerable front and a good port. It is divided into 50 counties, subdivided into 647 townships, contains three incorporated cities, and sends 23 representatives to congress. The climate of this state is changeable; the heat of summer is seldom oppressive, except in low situations; in all the hilly parts the air is healthy, but near the seacoast the temperature of winter is severe. The country is well watered by the Delaware, Schuylkill, Susquehanna, Monongahela, Allegany, and other navigable rivers. It is intersected from N. E. to S. W. by the different ridges of the Allegany mountains, some of which admit of cultivation almost to their summits; and between the numerous ridges there are delightful valleys, with a very rich soil. The other parts of the state are generally level, or agreeably diversified with hills and valleys. Wheat, Indian corn, buckwheat, rye, barley, oats, flax, hemp, beans, peas, and potatoes, are extensively cultivated. Cherries, peaches, apples, and cider are abundant. Wood is plentiful; in the western parts are found the oak, chestnut, beech, sugar maple, ash, black walnut, bass wood, elm, hickory, white ash, butternut, hemlock, and locust. Cattle and sheep are numerous; the merino breeds of sheep have been introduced, and thrive well. There are mineral waters in different parts of the state, and also salt springs. Iron ore is distributed in large quantities, and in some places copper, lead, and alum are found. Here are also numerous limestone quarries, and various kinds of marble, and coal. The principal manufactures are iron, copper, tin, leather, paper, gunpowder, hats, cotton, sugar, and tobacco. The canals are the Union, Susquehanna, Schuylkill, Chesapeake, Pittsburg, and Pennsylvania; total length, 428 miles; and the railroads are the Philadelphia and Norristown, passing German-town; and the Columbia railroad from Philadelphia to Columbia, a distance of 83 miles. The name was given to it by Charles II. in honour of admiral Sir William Penn, father of the illustrious founder of the colony, William Penn. Area of the state, 46,000 square miles. Pop. 1,734,033. Philadelphia is the capital.

PENNYGANT, one of the highest mountains of England, in Yorkshire, 7 miles N. of Settle. Its summit is 3930 feet above the level of the sea. On its sides are two awful orifices, called Hulpit and Huntpit holes; through each of them runs a brook, both of which run under ground for about a mile, and cross each other in the bowels of the earth, without mixing their waters.

PENOBSCOT, a capacious bay of the state of Maine, at the mouth of a river of the same name. Its E. side is lined with a cluster of small islands.

PENRICE, a town of Wales, in Glamorganshire; with a market on Thursday. Here are the ruins of a Norman castle, and 3 miles to the N., on a mountain, is a Druidical monument, called Arthur's Stone. Penrice is seated on the Bristol Channel, 20 miles S. E. of Caermarthen, and 220 W. of London.

PENRITH, a town in Cumberland, with a market on Tuesday. The parish church is a neat plain structure, partly rebuilt in 1722; in the churchyard is a singular monument of antiquity, called the Giant's Grave. Here are meeting-houses for Independents, Presbyterians, Quakers, Methodists, and Ranters; also a free grammar-school. The ruins of the ancient castle overlook the town from the W., and on the heights to the N. is a square stone building called the "Beacon," well situated for giving alarm in times of danger. The ascent to it is difficult, but the prospects from the summit of the hill are extensive and beautiful. Penrith is seated under a hill, near the river Eamont; 18 miles S. of Carlisle, and 283 N. N. W. of London.

PENRYN, a borough in Cornwall, governed by a mayor; with markets on Wednesday, Friday, and Saturday. It returns two members to parliament. Here are large warehouses for flour and grain imported from the Isle of Wight, and several good breweries, which supply the shipping at Falmouth; and it has a great trade in the pilchard and Newfoundland fisheries. It is seated on a creek of Falmouth Haven, 3 miles N. W. of Falmouth, and 263 W. by S. of London.

PENSACOLA, a city of West Florida, seated on a bay of the Gulf of Mexico, which forms a safe and commodious harbour. The entrance into the bay is defended by a small fort and a battery. It was ceded to the United States, along with the rest of the country, in 1821. Pop. 2000. Long. 87. 14. W. lat. 30. 24. N.

PENSFORD, a town in Somersetshire, with a market on Tuesday, and a manufacture of hats; seated on the Chew: 6 miles S. by E. of Bristol, and 117 W. by S. of London.

PENTLAND FRITH, a strait which divides the Orkney Islands from Caithness-shire, in Scotland. It is 20 miles long, and 10 broad, and dangerous to those who are not acquainted with its tides and currents, especially in passing the Pentland Skerries, a cluster of rocks at the E. end of the frith. On the largest of these rocks are 2 lighthouses. Long. 2. 42. W. lat. 58. 35. N.

PENTLAND HILLS, a ridge of hills in Scotland, 4 miles W. of Edinburgh.

PENZA, a government of Russia; formerly a province of Kasan. Pop. 800,000. Its capital, of the same name, is seated on the Sura, where it receives the rivulet Penza; 220 miles S. W. of Kasan. Pop. 10,000. Long. 45. 38. E. lat. 53. 30. N.

PENZANCE, a seaport in Cornwall; governed by a mayor; with markets on Thursday and Saturday. It was burnt by the Spaniards in 1593, but soon rebuilt, and made one of the tin coinage towns. In the town is a chapel of ease to the mother church of Madron, which is nearly 2 miles to the W.; and here are meeting-houses for Independents, Quakers, Baptists, and Methodists, and a synagogue for the Jews; also a grammar-school. The trade of Penzance is considerable, and consists chiefly in pilchards and other fish, and in shipping lead, tin, and copper, which abound in the vicinity. In consequence of the mildness and salubrity of the air, and the agreeableness of its situation, Penzance is much frequented by invalids, for whose accommodation there are cold and hot seawater baths, &c. It is seated on a creek of Mount Bay, 10 miles N. E. of the Land's End, and 280 W. by S. of London. Long. 5. 35. W. lat. 50. 11. N.

PEQUIGNY, a town of France, in the department of Somme; memorable for an interview and treaty between Louis XI. of France and Edward IV. of England, in 1475, on a bridge built for that purpose It is seated on the river Somme; 15 miles S. E. of Abbeville.

PERAC, a seaport of Malaya; capital of a kingdom on the W. coast. It is seated on a river of the same name, 180 miles N. W. of Malacca. Long. 100. 0. E. lat. 4. 23. N.

PERAY, ST., a town of France; in the department of Ardeche; noted for its wines. It is seated on the Rhone, opposite Valence, 32 miles N. of Viviers.

PERDU, MOUNT, a lofty mountain of the Pyrenees, with a double summit, of which the higher is computed at 11,000 feet above the sea. It is of very difficult access, as the calcareous rock often assumes the form of perpendicular walls, from 100 to 600 feet in height; and glaciers increase the difficulty. About 2000 feet from the summit is a lake, which throws its waters to the E., into the Spanish valley of Beoussa.

PERECOP. *See* PRECOP.

PERGA, a town of Albania, on the Gulf of Venice, 25 miles W. N. W. of Arta.

PERGAMAR, a town of Romania, and a bishop's see; 60 miles S. W. of Adrianople. Long. 25. 55. E. lat. 41. 10. N.

PERGAMO, a town of Asiatic Turkey, in the pachalic of Natolia, and a bishop's see; with a palace and a castle. It is not so considerable as formerly, but has 9 mosques, and occupies an oblong circumference of 3 miles, at the foot of a mountain. Here parchment was invented. It is seated on the Germasti, 15 miles from its mouth, and 37 N. of Smyrna. Long. 27. 27. E. lat. 39. 5. N.

PERIA, a town of Persia, in the province of Irac; 90 miles W. of Ispahan. Long. 51. 25. E. lat. 32. 20. N.

PERIAC, a town of France, in the department of Aude; celebrated for its salt-works. It is seated on a lake of its name, 6 miles S. W. of Narbonne.

PERIAPATAM, a town of Hindostan, in Mysore. The environs are rich and beautiful, and abound in sandal-wood. It is 40 miles W. by S. of Seringapatam.

PERIERS, a town of France, in the department of Manche; 9 miles N. of Coutances.

PERIGORD, a former province of France, now forming the department of Dordogne.

PERIGUEUX, a town of France, capital of the department of Dordogne, and a bishop's see. Here are the ruins of a temple of Venus, an amphitheatre, &c. It is seated on the river Ille, 50 miles S. W. of Limoges. Pop. 6200. Long. 0. 43. E. lat. 45. 11. N.

PERINDA, a town of Hindostan, capital of a district of its name; in the province of Dowlatabad, 188 miles N. W. of Hydrabad. Long. 75. 50. E. lat. 18. 33. N.

PERINDURA, a town of Hindostan, in the province of Coimbetore; 12 miles S. S. W. of Bhawanikudal.

PERLEBERG, a town of Prussia, in Brandenburg, with considerable cloth manufactures. It is seated on the Stepenitz, 42 miles W. N. W. of Ruppin. Long. 12. 3. E. lat. 53. 8. N.

PERM, a government of Russia, in Europe and Asia, formerly a province of Kasan. It is divided into two provinces, Perm and Catharinenberg; the capitals of which are of the same names. It has mines of copper and iron, and contains an area of 116,000 square miles, and 1,100,000 inhabitants.

PERM, a town of Russia; capital of a government and province of the same name. It is seated on the Kama, at the influx of the Zegochekha; 620 miles E. by N. of Moscow, and 810 E. by S. of Petersburg. Pop. 3800. Long. 55. 10. E. lat. 57. 55. N.

PERMACOIL, a town of Hindostan, in the Carnatic; it is situate on a mountain, 20 miles N. N. W. of Pondicherry.

PERNELLA, a town of Hindostan, in Guzerat; 38 miles S. of Surat.

PERNAMBUCO, a province of Brazil; bounded N. and E. by the Atlantic Ocean, S. by Bahia, and E. by the desert territory. It is about 470 miles from N. to S., and 370 from E. to W., and abounds in sugar-cane, cotton, and Brazil wood.

PERNAMBUCO, capital of the above province, consists of three divisions, Recife, St. Antonio, and Boa Vista. The two former are situated on two flat sand-banks, surrounded by the sea, and connected together by a bridge, partly of stone and partly of wood; the other division is connected with Boa Vista, situated on the continent, by a narrow wooden bridge. The greatest part of the extent of sand between Olinda, a town about a league distant, on the same sand-bank as Recife, and the latter, remains uncovered, is open to the sea, and the surf is very violent. The tide enters between the bridges, and encircles the middle compartment. The first division of the town is composed of brick houses, of three, four, and even five stories in height; most of the streets are narrow, and there are no public buildings that require notice. St. Antonio, the principal division of the town, is composed chiefly of large houses and broad streets. It contains the governor's palace (formerly the Jesuits' convent), the treasury, the town-hall and prison, the barracks, and the Franciscan, Carmelite, and Penha convents. It comprises several squares, and has, to a certain degree, a gay and lively appearance. The river Capibaribe discharges its waters into the channel between St. Antonio and Boa Vista. The harbour belonging to Recife, called the Mosqueiro, situated on the outward bank, is formed by a reef of rocks, which runs parallel with the town, at a very small distance. Pernambuco is daily increasing in opulence and importance, and European fashions prevail. Pop. 20,000. Long 35. 20. W. lat. 8. 13. S.

PERNAU, a fortified town of Russia, in Livonia, with a castle; seated near the mouth of a river of the same name; 95 miles N. of Riga. Long. 24. 30. E. lat. 58. 30. N.

PERNES, a town of France, in the department of Vaucluse; noted as the birthplace of the celebrated orator Flechier, bishop of Nismes; 12 miles E. by N. of Avignon. Pop. 3500.

PERNES, a town in the department of Pas de Calais; seated on the Clarence, 17 miles N. W. of Arras.

PERNO, a town of Sweden; in the province of Nyland, on the coast of the Baltic; 36 miles E. of Helsingfors.

PERONNE, a strong town of France, in the department of Somme. It was called Pucelle, because never taken, though often besieged, till the 29th of June, 1815, when it was stormed by the British. Charles the Simple was imprisoned in the castle, where he miserably died ·

and the duke of Burgundy detained Louis XI. here three days, till he consented to sign a disadvantageous treaty. It is seated on the Somme, 27 miles S. W. of Cambray, and 80 E. by N. of Paris. Pop. 3700. Long. 3. 2. E. lat. 49. 55. N.

PEROUSA, a town of the Sardinian states, in Piedmont; seated on the river Cluson; 6 miles N. W. of Pignerol. Pop. 2300.

PERPIGNAN, a fortified town of France; capital of the department of Eastern Pyrenees; with a good citadel and a university. The inhabitants carry on a trade in corn, wool, iron, and wine, and have manufactures of silk, woollen, soap, liqueurs, &c. This town was the scene of two battles between the French and Spaniards, in 1793. It is seated partly on a gentle declivity and partly on a plain, on the Tet, near the Mediterranean; 97 miles S. E. of Toulouse. Pop. 20,000. Long. 2. 54. E. lat. 42. 42. N.

PERSAIM. *See* BASSIEN.

PERRY, a county in the state of Ohio; formed in 1818. Pop. 19,344. Somerset is the capital.

PERSEPOLIS, anciently the capital of the Persian empire. It was taken by Alexander the Great, who set it on fire. Its magnificent ruins are 50 miles N. E. of Shiraz.

PERSHORE, a town in Worcestershire, with a market on Saturday. Here are two churches, and that of Holy Cross contains several ancient monuments. It is seated on the Avon; 9 miles E. S. E. of Worcester, and 102 W. N. W. of London.

PERSIA, a large kingdom of Asia, consisting of several provinces, which, at different times, have had their particular kings. It is bounded on the N. by the Caspian Sea, Russian Tartary, and the mountains of Caucasus; W. by the Euphrates and Tigris; S. by the Gulf of Persia; and E. by Cabool and Beloochistan: in its most extended sense it embraces these last also. It is about 1225 miles in length from E. to W., and 900 in breadth from N. to S. The chief river is the Tigris. In the N. and E. parts it is mountainous and cold; in the middle and S. E. parts, sandy and desert; and in the S. W., level and fertile, though for several months very hot. The soil produces various sorts of pulse and corn, and cotton in great abundance. In several places, naphtha, a sort of bitumen, rises out of the ground, and here are numerous mines of gold, silver, iron, turquois stones, and salt; but the first two of these are not worked, on account of the scarcity of wood. This country produces all the various sorts of fruits, excellent wine, and a great number of mulberry trees; likewise dates, pistachio-nuts, and trees which produce manna. Sheep and goats are abundant; as are also camels, buffaloes, and horses. The principal manufactures are silks, silks mixed with cotton or with camels' or goats' hair, brocades, gold tissues, gold velvet, carpets, calicoes, camlets, &c. The Persians are subjected to a despotism similar to that which presses upon all oriental nations; yet their character is materially different. They are more gay, lively, and active. They are said to be extremely ostentatious, and to surpass all other nations in politeness, if the most profuse and hypocritical flattery may be so called; while falsehood is proverbially their characteristic. Their dress is less graceful than that of the Turks; sombre colours predominate, and the head-dress of all, from the sovereign to the meanest subject, is a cylindrical cap of jet black lamb-skin. The beard is held in high estimation, and every art employed to render it thick and tufted. They are, however, the most learned people of the east; poetry and the sciences may even be considered as their ruling passion. In the former their fame is decidedly superior to that of any other oriental nation. The names of Hafiz, Ferdusi, and Sadi, are classic even in Europe. The religion of the country is Mahomedism, of the sect of Ali, or Sheeahs. In the beginning of the last century Persia was overrun by the Afghans, who carried fire and sword through its remotest extremities, and reduced its proudest capitals to ashes. The atrocities of the Afghans were avenged, and the independence of Persia vindicated, by Nadir Shah; but though the victories of this daring chief threw a lustre on his country, after his death the country was almost torn to pieces by civil war, till the fortune of arms gave a decided superiority to Kurreem Khan. His death gave rise to another disputed succession, with civil wars as furious as before. At length, Aga Mahommed, a eunuch, raised himself to the sovereignty, and not only retained it during his lifetime, but transmitted it to his nephew, who assumed the title of Futteh Ali Shah. He is represented as an accomplished prince; and his son Mahommed is the present shah. The seat of government is Teheran. The other principal towns are Ispahan and Shiraz.

PERSIAN GULF, a sea or inland lake between Persia and Arabia; which receives the united streams of the Euphrates and Tigris, under the name of the Shat el Arab. The entrance near Ormus is not above 30 miles over; but within it is from 120 to 250 in breadth, and the length from Ormus to the mouth of the Euphrates is 500 miles. The southern side is particularly celebrated for its pearl fishery.

PERTH, a borough of Scotland, capital of Perthshire; with two parish churches, one of which formerly belonged to a fine abbey. Here is also a Gaelic chapel belonging to the establishment, and the dissenters have places of worship in almost every part of the town. The grammar-school is accounted one of the best in Scotland; and there is also an excellent academy, with other literary institutions. One of the chief ornaments of the town is the beautiful building for county courts, &c. erected in 1819. It has been the residence of the sovereigns of Scotland, and the seat of the parliament and of the supreme courts of justice. It sends one member to parliament. Near the town are some saline springs, called Pitcaithly Wells, deemed beneficial in scorbutic cases. Perth is beautifully seated on the S. W. side of the Tay, which is navigable for small vessels, but the largest vessels are obliged to partly unload at Newburg. Over the river is a modern bridge of 10 arches, to the town of Kinnoul. Here are several incorporated trades, some of which have halls. The salmon fishery is a great article of trade, shipbuilding is extensively followed, and the manufactures of linen and gingham are considerable. It is 39 miles N. by W. of Edinburgh. Long. 3. 6. 20. W. lat. 56. 24. N

PERTH, a delightful village in Van Diemen's Land, on the South Esk River, 12 miles from Launceston, in Cornwall county. Here are some flour mills, barracks, &c.

PERTH AMBOY, a city and seaport of New Jersey, in Middlesex county; seated on a neck of land between the river Rariton and Arthur Kull Sound. It lies open to Sandy Hook, and has one of the best harbours on the continent. It is 35 miles S. W. of New York, and 74 N. E. of Philadelphia. Long. 75. 0. W. lat. 40. 35. N.

PERTHES, a town of France, department of Seine-et-Marne; 6 miles S. W. of Melun.

PERTHES, a town in the department of Upper Marne; 6 miles N. W. of St. Dizier.

PERTHSHIRE, a county of Scotland, 76 miles long, and 68 broad; bounded W. by Argyleshire, N. by the shires of Inverness and Aberdeen, E. by Angus-shire, S. E. by the Frith of Tay and the counties of Fife and Kinross, and S. by the Frith of Forth and the counties of Clackmannan, Stirling, and Dumbarton. It contains 4,068,640 English acres, is divided into 76 parishes, and returns one member to parliament. The country exhibits scenes of rugged and striking magnificence, contrasted with the most beautiful ones of cultivation. The Grampian mountains cross it from S. W. to N. E., the highest of which is Benlawers. The country N. W. of this ridge is mountainous, and contains several lakes; but the opposite side, though not free from hills, is more low and fertile. There are no canals in the county, and but one short railway, that from Dundee to Cupar-Angus, which passes one of its districts. The principal rivers are the Forth and Tay. Perth is the capital.

PERTIGI, a town of the island of Sardinia; 19 miles S. E. of Castel Aragonese.

PERTUIS, a town of France, department of Vaucluse; near the Durance; 11 miles N. of Aix, and 38 S. E. of Avignon.

PERU, an independent state of South America, the largest of the former Spanish vice-royalties; bounded on the N. by the republic of Columbia, W. by the Pacific Ocean, S. by Chili, and E. by Brazil. It is 750 miles in medium length, from N. to S., and about 500 in breadth. Rain is unknown in the S. parts; but in the N., where the mountains are not so high, it often rains excessively. There are large forests on the side of the mountains, which advance near the sea; but none of the trees are like those in Europe. Peru has been long celebrated for its mines of gold and silver, which are the chief or only source of its riches. Besides the produce of the mines, the commodities exported are sugar, Vienna wood, cotton, Peruvian bark, copper, and cocoa. The fiercest beasts of prey in Peru are the puma and jaguar, inaccurately called lions and tigers by Europeans; for they possess neither the undaunted courage of the former, nor the ravenous cruelty of the latter. The lama, and another species of American camel, inhabit the cold districts, and the elk, bear, deer, armadilloes, monkeys, &c., are numerous. Among the birds, the most remarkable is the condor, which is entitled to pre-eminence over the flying tribe, in bulk, strength, and courage. The river Guayaquil abounds with alligators, and the neighbouring country swarms almost as much with snakes and vipers as that round Porto Bello does with toads. When the Spaniards landed in this country, in 1530, they found it governed by sovereigns called incas, who were revered by their subjects as divinities; and the inhabitants were found to be much more polished than the natives of other parts of America, those of Mexico excepted. These were soon subdued by the Spaniards, under the command of Francis Pizarro. After the assassination of Pizarro, in 1541, the country continued a prey to civil contentions and insurrections, till about the year 1562, when Tupac Amaru, the son of Manco Capac, who had taken refuge in the mountains, was attacked by the viceroy, Toledo. The inca surrendered himself, and was led to the scaffold amid the tears of the people. The royal authority, thus established, continued without interruption till 1781, when a descendant of Amaru began an insurrection. After two years of varied success, he was, however, surprised and taken prisoner, together with his family, who were all executed. Peru now remained in subjection to Spain, and in a comparative state of tranquillity for some time; and in 1809, when juntas were established in La Paz and Quito, Peru sent out troops which suppressed their rising efforts. In 1817 the Peruvian army was compelled to evacuate Chili; and Chili, in return, sent an army into Peru, under General San Martin, who, in 1821, in conjunction with the fleet under Lord Cochrane, succeeded in liberating it from the Spanish yoke. By the latest accounts, it appears that the country is far from being in a settled state. Lima is the capital.

PERUGIA, a province of Italy, in the pope's dominions; comprehending the ancient province of Perugino. It is 25 miles long, and 24 broad, and is bounded W. by Tuscany, S. by Orvieto, E. by Spoleto and Urbino, and N. by Citta di Castello. The soil is fertile in corn and good wine. Pop. 182,000.

PERUGIA, the capital of the above province, and a bishop's see; with a strong citadel and a university. The churches, and many other buildings, public and private, are very handsome. It is seated on a hill, near the Tiber; 85 miles N. of Rome. Pop. 16,000. Long. 12. 20. E. lat. 43. 6. N.

Perugia, a lake of Italy; 8 miles W. of the city of its name. It is almost round, 5 miles in diameter, and in it are three islands.

Pesaro, a seaport of the ecclesiastical states, in the delegation of Urbino, and a bishop's see. The cathedral is magnificent, and it has several handsome churches, with exquisite paintings. The environs are remarkable for producing olives and excellent figs. It is seated on an eminence, at the mouth of the Foglia, on the Gulf of Venice. It is 17 miles E. N. E. of Urbino. Pop. 10,000. Long. 13. 2. E. lat. 45. 52. N.

Pescara, a strong town of Naples, in Abruzzo Citra; at the mouth of a river of the same name, on the Gulf of Venice. It is 9 miles N. N. E. of Chieti.

Peschiera, a strong town of Austrian Italy, in the Veronese. It was taken by the French in 1796; and the garrison surrendered to the Austrians in 1799. It is seated on the river Mincio, where it proceeds from the Lake Garda; 16 miles W. of Verona. Pop. 2500.

Pescia, a town of Tuscany, in the province of Florence; celebrated for its fine oil; 25 miles N. E. of Florence.

Pescina, a town of Naples, in Abruzzo Ultra; near the Lake Celano. It is 20 miles S. by E. of Aquila.

Pesenas, a town of France, department of Herault; on the river Herault; 12 miles N. E. of Beziers. Pop. 7000.

Pesth, a town of Hungary, capital of a palatinate of the same name; with a fortress, a royal palace, and a university; the only one in the kingdom. Pop. 42,000. Here are many Greek merchants, who conduct the Levant trade to Germany and the northern nations. The town was nearly destroyed in 1839, by the eruption of the Danube, which did immense mischief; but it has been rebuilt, and some of the new erections are handsome. It is seated on the E. side of the Danube, opposite Buda; 96 miles E. S. E. of Presburg. Long. 19. 8. E. lat. 47. 30. N.

Pesto, a town of Naples, in Principato Citra; seated near the magnificent ruins of the ancient Pæstum; 20 miles S. E. of Salerno.

Petapa, a town of Mexico, 25 miles S. E. of Guatimala.

Petaguel, a province on the N. coast of Brazil, between the provinces of Seara and Rio Grande. It contains mines of silver.

Pe-tche-li, the principal province of China, bounded on the N. by the Great Wall and part of Tartary, E. by the Yellow Sea, S. by Chang-tong and Ho-nan, and W. by the mountains of Chan-si. It contains nine cities of the first class, which have many others under their jurisdiction. Although Pe-tche-li extends no further than 42. N. lat., yet all its rivers are so much frozen during four months in the year, that waggons with the heaviest loads may safely pass them. The soil is sandy, and produces very little rice; but it abounds with all other kinds of grain, and with the greater part of the fruit-trees common in Europe. But what renders this province the most considerable, is that the riches of the whole empire are brought hither, the southern provinces furnishing it with every thing they produce that is most uncommon and delicious. The inhabitants, in general, are reckoned not so polite, nor so apt to learn the sciences, as those of the southern provinces; but they are stronger and more warlike. Their number is estimated at 38,000,000. Peking is the capital.

Peter Botte, a remarkable mountain in the Mauritius, near the coast of Madagascar, between 2000 and 3000 feet high.

Peter and Paul, St., or **Petropaulonskoi**, a seaport of Russia, in Kamtschatka. The town consists of some log-houses, and a few conical huts. Captain Clerke, who succeeded Captain Cook, and died at sea, was interred here. It is seated on the E. side of Awatska Bay. Long. 158. 48. E. lat. 53. 1. N.

Peter le Port, St., a market-town in the island of Guernsey; with an excellent harbour, defended by two castles.

Peterborough, a city in Northamptonshire, governed by a mayor; with a market on Saturday. It is a bishop's see, but has only one parish church, besides the cathedral, which was formerly a monastery. The market-place is spacious, the streets regular, and many of the buildings extremely neat. The manufacture of stockings is extensive, and considerable trade is carried on in corn, coal, and timber. It sends two members to parliament. It is seated on the Nen, over which is a bridge into Huntingdonshire; 42 miles N. E. of Northampton, and 81 N. of London. Long. 0. 4. W. lat. 52. 30. N.

Peterhead, a seaport of Scotland, in Aberdeenshire; situate on a peninsula, about ¾ of a mile S. of the mouth of the Ugie. It has two harbours, defended by piers, a considerable trade in the whale-fishery, and in the export of grain and butter. Here is a small fort and a battery. A mineral spring, of a powerful diuretic quality, and the sea-bathing, bring a great resort of company, for whose accommodation there is a ball-room, and many elegant houses. It stands a little to the W. of Buchanness, the most eastern promontory of Scotland; 32 miles N. E. of Aberdeen. Long. 1. 35. W. lat. 57. 27. N.

Petersburg, a town of New Hampshire, in Hillsborough county; 18 miles E. of Keene, and 73 W. by S. of Portsmouth.

Petersburg, a town of Pennsylvania, in York county; 25 miles S. W. of York, and 58 N. of Washington.

Petersburg, a town of Virginia, in Dinwiddie county. It has a considerable trade, particularly in tobacco and flour. It is seated on the S. side of the Appomatox; 25 miles S. of Richmond.

Petersburg, a government or province of Russia, at the E. extremity of the Gulf of Finland. The greater part of this province was formerly called Ingermanland, or Ingria. It comprises an area of 18,000 square miles, with

700,000 inhabitants. Timber forms the chief source of wealth.

PETERSBURG, the metropolis of the Russian empire, in the government of the same name, is situated on the river Neva, near the Gulf of Finland, and is built partly upon some islands in the mouth of that river, and partly upon the continent. So late as the beginning of the last century, the ground on which Petersburg now stands was only a vast morass, occupied by a few fishermen's huts. Peter the Great first began this city in 1703. He built a small hut for himself, and some wretched wooden hovels. In 1710 the Count Golovkin built the first house of brick, and the next year the emperor, with his own hand, laid the foundation of a house of the same material. From these small beginnings rose the imperial city of Petersburg; and, in less than nine years after the wooden hovels were erected, the seat of empire was transferred from Moscow to this place. The streets, in general, are broad and spacious; and three of the principal ones, which meet in a point at the admiralty, are at least two miles in length. The mansions of the nobles are vast piles of building, furnished with great cost, in the same elegant style as at Paris or London, and situated chiefly on the S. side of the Neva, either in the admiralty quarter, or in the suburbs of Livonia and Moscow, which are the finest parts of the city. The views upon the banks of the Neva exhibit the grandest and most lively scenes imaginable. That river is in many places as broad as the Thames at London: it is also deep, rapid, and as transparent as crystal; and its banks are lined on each side with a continued range of grand buildings. On the N. the fortress, the academy of sciences, and the academy of arts, are the most striking objects. On the opposite side are the imperial palace, the admiralty, the mansions of many Russian nobles, and the English line, so called because it is mostly occupied by English merchants. In the front of these buildings, on the S. side, is the quay, which extends three miles, except where it is interrupted by the admiralty; and the Neva, during the whole of that space, has been embanked by a wall, parapet, and pavement of hewn granite. There are no fewer than 35 great churches, (almost every sect of Christians being tolerated,) and the number of inhabitants is estimated to be about 470,202. It is said that 3000 one-horse sledges are employed for passengers in the streets, in winter. From its low and marshy situation, it is subject to inundations, which have sometimes risen so high as to threaten the town with a total submersion. The opposite divisions of Petersburg, situated on each side of the Neva, are connected by two bridges on pontoons, which, on account of the large masses of ice driven down the stream from Lake Ladoga, are usually removed when these masses first make their appearance; and, for a few days, till the river is frozen hard enough to bear carriages, there is no communication between the opposite parts of the town. Among the noblest ornaments of Petersburg is an equestrian statue of Peter the Great, in bronze, erected by Catherine II. in 1782. It is of colossal size, and stands on a huge pedestal of rock, brought there at great expense. Within the walls of the fortress is the cathedral of St. Peter and St. Paul, in which are deposited the remains of Peter the Great, and of the successive sovereigns, except Peter II., who was buried at Moscow. The literary and scientific institutions are numerous; but the most important is the university, founded in 1819. A Bible society is established on an extensive scale, having upwards of 200 auxiliaries in different parts of the empire. Of the charitable institutions, the principal are the foundling hospital, the sailor's hospital, the lazaretto, the asylum for the blind, the asylum for the deaf and dumb, the humane society, &c. The manufactures are various, and some of them of considerable extent; and the commercial intercourse is important from its extensive communication with the interior, this being the only great maritime outlet in the Gulf of Finland. The principal exports are hemp, flax, skins, leather, iron, tallow, &c.: the imports, sugar, coffee, cotton, indigo, dyewood, spices, hardware, &c. The number of ships that enter the Neva annually, of which nearly half are British, varies from 1000 to 1700. Petersburg is 355 miles N. W. of Moscow, 430 N. E. of Stockholm, and 1400 E. N. E. of London. Long. 30. 20. E. lat. 59. 56. N.

PETERSDORF, a town of Prussia, in the province of Samland; 24 miles S. of Konigsberg.

PETERSFIELD, a borough in Hampshire; market on Saturday; seated on the Loddon; 18 miles N. E. of Portsmouth, and 54 S. W. of London. It returns one member to parliament.

PETERSHAGEN, a town of Prussian Westphalia; with a castle; seated on the Weser; 7 miles N. N. E. of Minden.

PETERSHAM, a town of Massachusets, in Worcester county, on the E. branch of Swift River; 28 miles N. W. of Worcester. Pop. 1775.

PETERSHAUSEN, a town of Germany, in Baden; with a Benedictine abbey, and a fort; seated on the N. side of the Rhine, opposite Constance.

PETERWARDIEN, a town of Sclavonia; one of the strongest frontier places the House of Austria has against the Turks, over whom, in 1716, Prince Eugene here gained a great victory. It is seated on the Danube, opposite the fortress of Neusatz, in Hungary; 40 miles N. W. of Belgrade. Pop. 3700. Long. 20. 30. E. lat. 45. 23. N.

PETHERTON, SOUTH, a town in Somersetshire; with a market on Thursday, and a manufacture of dowlas; seated near the Parret, over which is a bridge; 24 miles S. S. E. of Wells, and 130 W. by S. of London.

PETIGLIANO, a town of Tuscany, in the Siennese; 8 miles W. of Castro, and 45 S. E. of Sienna.

PETIT GUAVE, a seaport of St. Domingo; seated on a bay at the W. end of the island. It is 200 miles E. of Jamaica. Long. 72. 52. W. lat. 18. 27. N.

PETOUNE, a city of Eastern Tartary, in the province of Kirin; inhabited principally by Tartar soldiers and Chinese condemned to exile. It is seated on the Songari; 150 miles N. by W. of Kirin. Long. 125. 55. E. lat. 45. 10. N.

PETRELLA, a town of Naples, in the Principato Citra; 11 miles E. of Molise.

PETRELLA, a town of Albania; 26 miles S. E. of Durazzo.

PETRIKOW, a town of Poland, and for some time the meeting-place of the Polish diets; 80 miles S. W. of Warsaw. Long. 19. 46. E. lat. 51. 12. N.

PETRINA, a strong town of the Austrian states, in Croatia; seated on the Kulpa; 37 miles E. of Carlstadt.

PETROZAVODSK, a town of Russia, capital of the government of Olonetz; with manufactures of stoneware, leather, lead, &c., and a foundry for cannon. It is seated on Lake Onega; 65 miles N. E. of Olonetz.

PETTAPOLLY, a town of Hindostan, in the district of Guntoor; seated on the Bay of Bengal; 38 miles S. S. E. of Condavir, and 48 N. E. of Ongole.

PETTAW, a town of the Austrian states, in Styria; with considerable manufactures; seated on the Drave; 15 miles S. E. of Marchburg.

PETTYCUR, a harbour of Scotland, in Fifeshire; 1 mile W. of Kinghorn; in the Frith of Forth. It is the usual landing-place of passengers from Leith, on the opposite shore.

PETWORTH, a town in Sussex; with a market on Saturday. In the centre of the town is a very handsome market-house of stone; and in the church are interred the remains of many of the Percies, earls of Northumberland; seated near the Arun; 12 miles N. E. of Chichester, and 48 S. W. of London.

PEVENSEY, a village in Sussex; 14 miles W. S. W. of Hastings; situate on a small river which runs into a bay of the English Channel, called Pevensey Harbour. Here is an ancient castle, which belonged to Robert, earl of Morton, and is said to be the largest and most entire remain of Roman building to be seen in Britain. Pevensey was anciently a famous haven, though now it is nearly 2 miles from the sea. Here Sweyn landed in 1049, when he carried off his cousin Beorn and murdered him; and here William the Conqueror landed, when he invaded England.

PFAFFENHOFEN, a town of Bavaria, with a Benedictine monastery at a small distance. It is seated on the Ilm; 15 miles S. of Ingoldstadt. —Also, a town of Wirtemberg, on the Zaber; 18 miles N. of Stutgard.—A town of the Austrian states, in Tyrol, seated on the Inn; 15 miles W. of Innspruck;—and a village of Bavaria; 8 miles S. E. of Ulm.

PFALZEL, a town of Prussia, in the province of Lower Rhine. It has a convent, which was formerly a palace of the kings of the Franks, and is seated on the Moselle; 3 miles N. E. of Treves.

PFEDDERSHEIM, a town of Germany, in Hesse Darmstadt; seated on the river Prim; 5 miles W. of Worms.

PFEFFIKON, a town of Switzerland, in the canton of Zurich; 12 miles E. of Zurich.

PFETER, a town of Bavaria, on a river of the same name, near its conflux with the Danube; 14 miles E. by S. of Ratisbon.

PFINZ-AND-ENTZ, one of the ten circles of the grand duchy of Baden, lying along the two rivers Pfinz and Entz, from the Rhine to the frontiers of Wirtemberg. Bruchsal is the chief town.

PFORTEN, a town of Lusatia; 10 miles S. of Guben.

PFORZHEIM, a town of Germany, in Baden, with a castle; a considerable trade in wood, and manufactures of cloth, stuffs, stockings, jewellery, and watches. It is seated on the Entz; 15 miles E. by S. of Durlach.

PFREIMBT, a town of Bavaria, with a castle; seated at the conflux of the Pfreimbt with the Nab; 10 miles E. of Amberg.

PFULLENDORF, a town of Baden; seated on the Andalspach; 22 miles N. by E. of Constance.

PFULLINGEN, a town of Wirtemberg; 8 miles S. E. of Tubingen.

PHALSBURG, a fortified town of France, in the department of Meurthe, near the Vosges mountains; 27 miles W. N. W. of Strasburg.

PHANAGORA, a town of Russia, in the island of Taman; with a strong fort. The ruins still show that it has formerly been large and magnificent. It is seated on a gulf of the Black Sea; 70 miles E. by N. of Caffa. Long. 36. 40. E. lat. 45. 12. N.

PHAROS, a small island in the Mediterranean Sea, opposite Alexandria, in Egypt; the space between which and the continent forms an extensive harbour. Long. 31. 11. E. lat. 30. 24. N.

PHARZA, anciently Pharsalia, a town of Greece, in Thessaly; famous for the decisive victory gained by Julius Cæsar over Pompey, in 48 B. C. It is an archiepiscopal see; and seated on the Enipeus; 10 miles S. of Larissa.

PHASIS. *See* RIONI.

PHILADELPHIA. *See* ALLA-SHEHR.

PHILADELPHIA, the capital of Pennsylvania, and formerly the metropolis of the United States of America; situate in the county of its name, on the W. bank of the Delaware, which is here a mile broad. It was originally laid out by William Penn, in 1683, and settled by a colony from England, and was increased by a constant influx of foreigners to so great a degree that in less than a century, and in the lifetime of the first person born in it of European parents, it was computed to contain 6000 houses and 40,000 inhabitants in the city and suburbs. The population has been constantly increasing, and is now estimated at 228,991. The streets intersect each other at right angles; the principal one is Broad-street, 113 feet wide, running N. and S., which is crossed by High-street, 100 feet wide, extending from river to river; the other streets, in general, are 50 feet wide; they are all paved, and have broad bricked footways. The public buildings are numerous, and many of them splendid edifices. It has 62 places of public worship for Christians of various denominations, and a synagogue for the Jews. A university was incorporated here in 1791; its funds partly given by the state, and partly taken from the old college. Among the other literary and scientific institutions, the principal are the Philadelphia library, containing upwards of 22,000 volumes, a museum, philosophical apparatus, &c.; the American Philosophical Society; the Society for Agriculture; the Athenæum, incorporated in 1815; the Academy of Natural Sciences; and the library of the Society of Friends. The benevolent institutions are highly honourable to the inhabitants. The Pennsylvania Hospital, established in 1752, is the most respectable institution of the kind in the union. On the lawn in the front is a handsome statue of William Penn; and in 1817 a building was erected for the celebrated painting of West, representing Christ healing the sick, which is a source of considerable income to the hospital. The manufactures of Pennsylvania surpass in excellence, variety, and extent, those of all other towns in the United States; and printing is here carried on most extensively. The city contains 5 markets, which are well supplied with provisions. It is connected with Columbia by the Columbian railroad, 83 miles in length. It is governed by a mayor, recorder, &c. In August, 1793, it was visited by a malignant fever, which carried off nearly 5000 of the inhabitants in the course of three months. It is 95 miles S. W. of New York, and 130 N. E. of Washington. Long. 75. 8. W. lat. 39. 57. N.

Philip, St., a town of Spain. *See* Xativa.

Philip, St., a town of Brazil. *See* Louis de Maranham, St.

Philip Islands, two islands in the South Pacific, discovered by Captain Hunter in 1791. They are 5 miles asunder, but almost joined by a sandy spit above water. They are covered with shrubs, have few tall trees on them, and the land is low. Long. of the eastern island 140. 3. E. lat. 8. 6. S.

Philippeville, a fortified town of Belgium; 22 miles S. by W. of Namur.

Philippi, a town of Macedonia, and an archbishop's see. Near this place, commonly called the plains of Philippi, Cassius and Brutus were defeated by Augustus and Mark Antony, in 42 B. C. It is greatly decayed, but an amphitheatre and several other monuments of its ancient grandeur remain. It is 60 miles E. of Salonica. Long. 24. 18. E. lat. 40. 40. N.

Philippine, a strong town of Belgium, in Flanders. It was taken by the French in 1747, and again in 1794, but restored in 1814. It is seated on an arm of the Scheldt; 15 miles N. by W. of Ghent.

Philippine Islands, a large cluster of islands, said to be 1100 in number, in the East Indian Ocean. They were discovered by Magellan in 1519. The principal is Luzon, or Luçonia. The air is very hot and moist, and the soil fertile in rice, &c. The trees are always green, and there are ripe fruits all the year. There are many wild beasts and birds, quite unknown in Europe. The inhabitants are affable, hospitable, and honest. They cultivate the land with considerable skill, and rear pigs, fowls, goats, and buffaloes, under the same roof with themselves. The houses are of bamboo, covered with palm leaves, raised on pillars to the height of nine feet. The chief food consists of rice, cocoa-nuts, and salted fish. The total population is about 2,250,000. Further particulars are given under the name of their respective islands.

Philippopoli, a town of Macedonia, founded by Philip, the father of Alexander the Great. It was nearly destroyed by an earthquake in 1818. It is seated on a small island formed by the Marizza; 95 miles W. N. W. of Adrianople.

Philipsburg, a town of New Jersey, in Sussex county; 41 miles N. W. of Trenton.

Philipsburg, a town of New York, in Duchess county, near which is a mine that yields virgin silver. It stands on the E. side of Hudson River; 28 miles N. by E. of New York.

Philipsburg, a town of Germany in the grand duchy of Baden, formerly fortified, and considered as one of the bulwarks of the empire. It was taken by the French in 1734, when the duke of Berwick was killed at the siege; but it was restored the year following, by the treaty of Vienna. In 1799 it was four times blockaded by the French republicans, and was at length completely dismantled. It is seated on the Rhine; 17 miles N. of Durlach. Pop. 1100.

Philipstadt, a town of Sweden, in Wermeland, seated in a mountainous country, abounding in iron mines, between two lakes, and watered by a rivulet; 29 miles N. E. of Carlstadt, and 160 W. by N. of Stockholm.

Philipstown, a town of Ireland, capital of King's county; 40 miles W. of Dublin. Long. 7. 13. W. lat. 53. 18. N.

Piacenza. *See* Placenza.

Pianezza, a town and castle of the Sardinian states, in Piedmont; seated on the Dora; 6 miles W. of Turin.

Pianoza, an island off the coast of Tuscany; 6 miles S. of that of Elba. It is level and low, as the name imports. Long. 10. 34. E. lat. 42. 46. N.

Piave, a river of Austrian Italy, which rises in the delegation of Feltre, flows through the Venetian territory, and falls into the Gulf of Venice; 16 miles N. E. of Venice.

Piazza, a town of Sicily, in Val di Noto; situate almost in the centre of the island; 38 miles W. N. W. of Lentini. Pop. 13,500.

Picardy, a former province of France, on the English Channel, now chiefly included in the department of Somme.

Pickering, a town in North Yorkshire, with a market on Monday. It had a strong castle, in which Richard II. was confined, now in ruins. The parish church is an ancient and spacious building, with a fine lofty spire; and here are meeting-houses for Independents, Wesleyans, Primitive Methodists, and Friends; 26 miles N. E. of York, and 222 N. by W. of London.

Pickersville, a town of South Carolina, in Pendleton county, capital of Washington district; 52 miles W. N. W. of Cambridge.

Pico, one of the Azores, or Western Islands.

It has a volcanic mountain, called Pico, about 8000 feet in perpendicular height, from the surface of the sea to the summit of the peak; on its sides are numerous craters, several of which are now almost concealed by trees. The last eruption of the peak happened in 1718, and destroyed several vineyards. The island is about [illegible] miles in circumference, and produces a great deal of wine. Long. 28. 26. W. lat. 38. 29. N.

Pictou, a small island, between that of St. John, and the continent of Nova Scotia, at the E. end of Northumberland Strait. Long. 62. 15. W. lat. 45. 50. N.

Picts' Wall, in England, a famous barrier against the Picts, of which some remains are left. It began at the entrance of Solway Frith, in Cumberland, and, passing E. by Carlisle, was continued across the island to Tynemouth.

Pidaura, a town of the Morea, the ancient Epidaurus. It is situate on the W. coast of the Gulf of Engia; 25 miles E. of Napoli di Romania. Long. 23. 22. E. lat. 37. 40. N.

Piedmont, a principality of Italy, 150 miles long, and 90 broad, bounded on the N. by the Valais, E. by the Milanese, S. by the county of Nice and the territory of Genoa, and W. by France. Area, 13,000 square miles. Pop. about 2,250,000. It contains many high mountains, among which are rich and fruitful valleys, as populous as any part of Italy. In the mountains are rich mines of several kinds, and the forests afford a great deal of game. The principal rivers are the Po, Tanaro, Sturia, and Doria. This country has a great trade in raw silk, and it produces corn, rice, wine, fruits, hemp, flax, and cattle. It belongs to the king of Sardinia, whose authority was restored in 1814. Turin is the capital.

Pienza, a town of Tuscany; 25 miles S. E. of Sienna.

Pierre, St., a small island, near Newfoundland, ceded to the French in 1763, for drying and curing their fish. They were dispossessed of it by the English in 1793. Long. 56. 0. W. lat. 46. 39. N.

Pierre, St., a town of the island of Martinico, situate on a round bay, on the W. coast; 15 miles N. W. of Fortroyal. Pop. 10,000. Long. 61. 21. W. lat. 14. 44. N.

Pierre le Moutier, St., a town of France, department of Nievre; 15 miles N. W. of Moulins, and 150 S. of Paris.

Pietola, a village of Austrian Italy, near Mantua, the birthplace of Virgil, to whose memory an obelisk was erected in 1797, by Bonaparte.

Pietro, St., an island in the Mediterranean; 13 miles long and 3 broad, near the S. W. coasts of Sardinia, taken by the French in 1793, but retaken soon after.

Pignerol, or Pignerola, a town of Piedmont, and a bishop's see; with manufactures of woollen, silk, paper, and leather, and a trade in corn, wine, spirits, &c. It is seated on the Cluson; 20 miles S. W. of Turin. Pop. 10,000.

Pilgram, a town of Bohemia, in the circle of Bechin, at the source of the Iglau; 28 miles E. of Tabor.

Pillau, a seaport of Prussia, on the Baltic. The harbour is good, and it is well fortified, being considered as the bulwark and key of the kingdom. Here is a magazine for military stores; and below the gate of the castle is a [illegible] equestrian statue of Frederick William the Great. The streets are broad and straight, and the houses built in the Dutch taste. In 1807 it was taken by the French, and retaken by the Russians in 1813. It is 20 miles W. by S. of Konigsberg, of which it is the port. Pop. 3000. Long. 20. 20. E. lat. 54. 38. N.

Pilnitz, a town of Saxony, in Meissen, with a royal palace, celebrated for a treaty entered into by the princes of Europe against France, in 1792. The palace was burned down in 1818, but has since been rebuilt. It is 7 miles S. E. of Dresden.

Pilsen, a town of Bohemia, capital of a circle of the same name, which is particularly rich in sheep, and noted for excellent cheese, and contains 170,000 inhabitants. The town is fortified and well built. It is seated at the conflux of the Radbuza and Walta; 55 miles S. W. of Prague. Pop. 7400. Lon. 13. 39. E. lat. 49. 42. N.

Pilsno, or Pilzow, a town of Austrian Poland, seated on the Wisloka; 60 miles E. of Cracow.

Pilten, a town of Russia, in Courland, capital of a fertile district of its name; seated on the river Windau; 18 miles N. N. W. of Goldingen.

Pinckney, an island district of South Carolina, comprehending the counties of York, Chester, Union, and Spartanburg.

Pinckneyville, a town of South Carolina, in Union county, capital of Pinckney district. It is situate on Broad River, at the influx of the Pacolet; 75 miles N. W. of Columbia. Long. 81. 40. W. lat. 34. 52. N.

Pines, Isle of, an island in the South Pacific, off the S. end of New Caledonia; 14 miles in length. It is a pointed hill, sloping toward the extremities, which are very low, and on the low land are many tall pine-trees. Long. 167. 38. E. lat. 22. 38. S.

Piney, a town of France, department of Aube; 12 miles E. N. E. of Troyes.

Ping-king, or Ping-yuen, a city of China, of the first rank, in the province of Koeitcheou; 930 miles S. S. W. of Peking. Long. 107. 28. E. lat. 26. 38. N.

Ping-liang, a city of China, of the first rank, in the province of Chen-si; seated on the river Kin-ho; 550 miles S. W. of Peking. Long. 106. 25. E. lat. 35. 35. N.

Pinhel, a strong town of Portugal, in Beira, capital of a territory of the same name, and a bishop's see. It is seated on the Coa; 28 miles N. by W. of Guarda. Long 6 40. W. lat. 40. 46. N.

Pinneberg, a town of Hanover, in the duchy of Holstein, capital of a small province of its name, with a castle. It is seated on the Owe; 10 miles N. W. of Hamburg.

PINOS, an island of the West Indies, on the S. side of Cuba; 25 miles long, and 15 broad, mountainous, and covered with pines. Long. 82. 33. W. lat. 22. 2. N.

PINSK, a town of Russian Lithuania, in the government of Minsk. There are many Jews among the inhabitants, and the Greeks have a bishop. The chief manufacture is dressing Russian leather. It is surrounded by morasses, and stands on a river of the same name; 90 miles E. of Brzesc. Pop. 4500. Long. 26. 20. E. lat. 52. 18. N.

PIOMBINO, a small principality of Italy, on the coast of Tuscany, to which was annexed the island of Elba, separated by a channel 7 miles broad. Area, 190 square miles. Pop. 18,000.

PIOMBINO, a seaport of Italy, capital of the above principality. It has a good harbour, defended by a citadel, and is seated on a peninsula; 40 miles S. S. E. of Leghorn. Pop. 4000. Long. 10. 23. E. lat. 42. 57. N.

PIPERNO, a town of the ecclesiastical states, in Campagna di Roma, built out of the ruins of the ancient Privernum, and seated on a mountain; 9 miles N. N. W. of Terracina.

PIPLEY, a town of Bengal, seated on the Subanreeka, not far from its mouth; 53 miles S. of Midnapore.

PIRANO, a small seaport of the Austrian states, in Istria, seated on a peninsula, 6 miles S. W. of Capo d'Istria. Pop. 6200.

PIRITZ, a town of Pomerania, seated near the lake Meldui; 12 miles S. by W. of New Stargard.

PIRMASENS, a town of Bavaria, in the circle of the Rhine. Near this place, in 1793, the French were defeated by the Russians. It is 13 miles E. of Deux Ponts. Pop. 3200.

PIRNA, a town of Saxony, celebrated for a battle fought in its neighbourhood, between the allies and the French, in 1813. It has a castle on a mountain, called Sonnenstein, which was almost destroyed by the Prussians in 1756 and 1758, and is now an asylum for invalids, &c. It is a place of considerable trade, situate on the Elbe; 12 miles S. E. of Dresden. Population 38,000.

PISA, a city of Tuscany, capital of the Pisano, and an archbishop's see, with a famous university, and three forts. The river Arno runs through Pisa, and over it are three bridges, one of which is constructed of marble; and there is a canal hence to Leghorn. This city formerly contained 100,000 inhabitants; but there are not at present above 20,000. The manufactures consist of steel, jewellery, embroidery, damasks, velvet, taffeta, and calico. The cathedral is a magnificent structure, and on the right side of the choir is a leaning tower, built of marble, 188 feet high, and 15 feet out of the perpendicular. There are upwards of 30 other churches: that of St. Stephen, belonging to an order of knights, is particularly deserving of notice. The other remarkable buildings are the palaces of the grand duke and archbishop, the arsenal, the great hospital, and the magnificent exchange, which last is almost superfluous, as the trade of Pisa is removed to Leghorn. It is seated in a fertile plain, at a small distance from the Mediterranean; 11 miles N. N. E. of Leghorn, and 42 W. by S. of Florence. Long. 10. 23. E. lat. 43. 43. N.

PISANO, a territory of Tuscany; lying N. of the Florentino, on the Mediterranean. It is 47 miles long, and 25 broad, abounds in corn, oil and wine, and is well cultivated. Pop. 295,640. Pisa is the capital.

PISCADORES. *See* PONG-HOU.

PISCATAQUA, a river of New Hampshire, the mouth of which forms the only port in that state; and at its entrance is a lighthouse, in long. 70. 41. W. lat. 43. 4. N.

PISCATAWAY, a town of Maryland, in Prince George county, on a creek of its name, which flows W. into the Potomac; 14 miles S. of Washington.

PISCO, a town of Peru, in the province of Sca, with a good road for ships. It is seated in a country fertile in excellent fruits and good wine; 130 miles S. S. E. of Lima. Long. 75. 55. W. lat. 13. 36. S.

PISEK, a town of Bohemia, capital of the circle of Prachin. Bohemian diamonds are found here. It is seated on the Wotawa, near its conflux with the Muldau; 58 miles S. S. W. of Prague. Long. 14. 0. E. lat. 49. 21. N.

PISTOIA, a city of Tuscany, and a bishop's see, with a citadel. There are several fine churches, magnificent palaces, and handsome streets; but it is almost deserted, in comparison to what it was formerly. The Austrians defeated the Neapolitans here in 1815. It is seated near the river Stella; 20 miles N. W. of Florence. Pop. 10,000. Long. 11. 29. E. lat. 43. 55. N.

PITCAIRN'S ISLAND, an island in the South Pacific, where the mutineers of the Bounty resorted after they left Otaheite. One of them was found to be alive in 1808, and there were several of their descendants who inhabited the island. Long. 133. 21. W. lat. 25. 2. S.

PITCAITHLY, a village of Scotland, seated in a sequestered vale; 5 miles S. of Perth. Its mineral waters have been long famed in scorbutic complaints, and it has good accommodation for invalids.

PITHA, a seaport of Sweden, in West Bothnia, seated on a small island, at the mouth of a river of its name, in the Gulf of Bothnia. It is joined to the continent by a wooden bridge. It is 95 miles N. N. E. of Uma. Long. 20. 58. E. lat. 65. 15. N.

PITCHEN, a town of Prussian Silesia, in the government of Breslau, on the frontiers of Poland; 50 miles E. of Breslau.

PITTENWEEM, a town of Scotland, in Fifeshire, with a harbour on the Frith of Forth. In the vicinity are coal mines and salt-works. It is 10 miles S. by E. of St. Andrew, and 24 N. E. of Edinburgh.

PITTSBURG, a town of North Carolina; chief of Chatham county. It is famous for pure air and water, and stands on a rising ground, in a rich and well cultivated country; 16 miles W. of Raleigh.

PITTSBURG, a city of Pennsylvania, capital of

Allegany county, situate on a point of land between the rivers Allegany and Monongahela, and at the termination of the great Pennsylvanian canal, about 500 miles in length. It is the staple of commerce for Philadelphia with the western country, and also for the numerous establishments formed on the two rivers above mentioned, which here unite and take the name of Ohio; and, by this river and the Mississippi, it has a trade with Louisiana and New Orleans. Here was fort Du Quesne, which was abandoned by the French in 1758, on the approach of General Forbes, and its name changed to Fort Pitt; but it is now gone to decay. Fort Fayette, a recent structure, stands on the bank of the Allegany. Steam-engines of great efficiency are made here; ship-building is carried on to a considerable extent; and here are also manufactures of glass, nails, hats, tobacco, &c. It is 300 miles W. by N. of Philadelphia, and contains a population of 21,115, or, including the suburbs of Allegany, &c., 31,204. Long. 80. 8. W. lat. 40. 22. N.

PITTSFIELD, a town of Massachusets, in Berkshire county, situate in a rich vale, on the Housatonic; 33 miles W. of Northampton, and 136 of Boston. Pop. 3747.

PITTSTOWN, a town of New Jersey, in Hunterdon county; 32 miles N. of Trenton.

PITTSTOWN, a town of the state of Maine, in Lincoln county, situate on Kennebec River; 22 miles N. by W. of Wiscasset.

PIURA, a town of Peru; capital of a province of the same name. This was the first Spanish settlement in Peru, being founded by Pizarro in 1531. It is 25 miles S. E. of Paita. Pop. 7000. Long. 80. 29. W. lat. 5. 15. S.

PIZZIGHETONE, a town of Austrian Italy, with a strong castle, in which Francis I., of France, was kept prisoner. It was taken by the French in 1733, again in 1796, and retaken by the Austrians and Russians in 1799. It is situate on the Adda; 10 miles N. W. of Cremona, and 30 S. E. of Milan.

PIZZO, a town of Naples, in Calabria Ultra, on the Gulf of St. Euphemia; 4 miles W. by N. of Monte Leone.

PLACENTIA, a town of Spain, in Estremadura, and a bishop's see, with a castle. It is seated in a plain, almost surrounded by mountains; 50 miles N. E. of Alcantara, and 110 W. S. W. of Madrid. Long. 5. 55. W. lat. 40. 6. N.

PLACENTIA, a town of Spain, in Biscay, seated on the Deva; 25 miles E. by S. of Bilboa.

PLACENTIA, a seaport of Newfoundland, on the E. side of a large bay on the S. part of the island. The harbour is capacious, and defended by a fort, called St. Louis. It is 60 miles W. S. W. of St. John. Long. 53. 43. W. lat. 47. 15. N.

PLACENZA, a fortified town of Italy; capital of a duchy, included in that of Parma, and a bishop's see, with a good citadel, and a celebrated university. The churches, squares, streets, and fountains are beautiful. The inhabitants, about 20,000, have scarcely any other employment than the manufacture of silk stuffs. At this place the Austrians gained a decisive victory over the Spaniards and French in 1746. In 1796 it was taken by the French, who were forced to evacuate it in 1799. In 1800 it again fell into the hands of the French, and was retained till 1814. It is of greater extent than Parma, and is seated in a well cultivated country, near the river Po; 38 miles W. N. W. of Parma. Long. 9. 38. E. lat. 45. 5. N. *See* PARMA.

PLAINFIELD, a town of Connecticut, in Windham county, on the E. side of the Quinabang; 10 miles E. S. E. of Windham.—Also, the name of several inconsiderable townships in the United States.

PLAN, a town of Bohemia, in the circle of Pilsen; with a castle; 20 miles S. E. of Egra.

PLASSEY, a town of Bengal, in the district of Nuddeah, memorable for a great victory obtained by Colonel Clive, 1757, over the nabob Surajah Dowlah. It is 25 miles S. of Moorshedabad.

PLATA, or CHUQUISACA, a rich and populous city of Peru, capital of the province of Los Charcas, and an archbishop's see, with a university. The cathedral is large, and finely adorned with paintings and gildings. It is seated on the Chimao; 600 miles S. E. of Cusco. Long 66. 34. W. lat. 19. 16. S.

PLATA, or RIO DE LA PLATA, (Silver River,) a large river of South America, formed by the union of the great rivers Parana and Uruguay. It was discovered in 1515 by Juan Diaz de Solis, a Spanish navigator, who was slain by the natives in endeavouring to make a descent into the country. It forms the S. boundary of Brazil, and enters the Atlantic between the Capes of St. Anthony and St. Mary, the latter in lat. 35. S. It is 150 miles broad at its mouth, and at Monte Video, 60 miles up the river, the land is not to be discerned on either shore when a vessel is in the middle of the channel. This river has many islets and shoals, which cause adverse currents, and render its navigation intricate; and the only safe port on its shores, for ships of considerable burden, is Monte Video. The Argentine republic derives its name from this river. *See* BUENOS AYRES.

PLATE, a town and castle of Pomerania; on the river Rega; 19 miles E. by S. of Camin.

PLATTEN, a lake of Hungary; 60 miles to the S. E. of that of Neusidler. It is 46 miles in length, from 3 to 8 in breadth, and abounds with fish.

PLATTEN, a town of Bohemia, in the circle of Saatz, on the frontiers of Saxony; 14 miles N. of Elnbogen.

PLATTSBURG, a town of New York, the chief of Clinton county, situate on Lake Champlain; 50 miles N. of Crown Point. Pop. 6416.

PLAU, a town of Saxony, in the grand duchy of Mecklenburg, with a castle, seated on a lake of the same name; 20 miles S. S. E. of Gustrow.

PLAUEN, a town of Saxony, capital of Voigtland, with a castle. It has considerable cotton manufactures. It is seated on the Elster; 80 miles S. W. of Dresden. Pop. 6100. Long. 12 12. E. lat. 50. 28. N.

Plauen, a town of Prussia, in Brandenburg, on a lake formed by the Havel, from which is a canal to the Elbe. It has a manufacture of porcelain. It is 5 miles W. N. W. of Brandenburg.

Plescof. *See* Pskof.

Plesse, a town of Prussian Silesia, in the government of Oppeln; capital of a lordship, with a fine castle. It is surrounded by walls flanked with towers. It is seated on the Vistula; 36 miles E. S. E. of Ratibor. Long. 19. 3. E. lat. 49. 57. N.

Plettenberg, a town of Westphalia, with an ancient castle, situate on the Else and Oester; 13 miles S. S. W. of Arensberg.

Pleyberg, a town and castle of Austria, in Carinthia, seated on the Feistez, at the foot of a mountain; 20 miles E. of Clagenfurt.

Plock, a town of Poland, capital of a palatinate of the same name, and a bishop's see, with a castle. It is seated on a hill, near the Vistula. 75 miles N. W. of Warsaw. Pop. 3000. Long. 19. 29. E. lat. 52. 46. N.

Ploen, a town of Denmark, in the duchy of Holstein. It has a castle on a mountain, and is seated on the N. side of a lake; 24 miles N. N. W. of Lubec. Long. 10. 30. E. lat. 54. 11. N.

Ploermel, a town of France; department of Morbihan, on the river Duc; 27 miles N. E. of Vannes. Pop. 4500.

Plotzkau, a town of Saxony, in the principality of Anhalt, with a castle, seated on the Saale; 10 miles W. of Kothen.

Pludenz, a town of Austria, in Tyrol, capital of a lordship of its name. It is seated on a plain, on the river Ille; 12 miles S. S. E. of Felkirch.

Plumstead, a town of Pennsylvania, in Bucks county; seated on Delaware River; 36 miles N. of Philadelphia.

Pluviers, or **Pithiviers**, a town of France, in the department of Loiret; 20 miles N. N. E. of Orleans.

Plymouth, a borough and seaport in Devonshire, governed by a mayor; with a market on Monday, Thursday, and Saturday. It is seated at the mouth of the Plym, and, next to Portsmouth, is the most considerable harbour in England for men-of-war. There are, properly speaking, three harbours, called Catwater, Sutton Pool, and Hamoaze. The first is the mouth of the Plym, and is a commodious harbour for merchant ships, but is seldom entered by ships of war. The second, frequented by merchant ships only, is almost surrounded by the houses of the town, and further secured by an extensive pier. The third is the mouth of the Tamar, and is the harbour for large ships, having moorings for 92, and a good anchorage for a much greater number. These harbours unite in a capacious bay, called the Sound, which affords fine anchorage for ships, particularly since the construction of the magnificent breakwater across its entrance. The other buildings connected with the port are the Naval Hospital, one of the finest in Britain, and, opposite to the Military Hospital, extensive barracks and a magnificent victualling office, built of marble, at the entrance to the Hamoaze. The theatre, assembly-rooms, and royal hotel, together form the grandest architectural ornaments of Plymouth. There is a railway, 24 miles long, to Dartmoor. The Eddystone lighthouse is off this town, at a distance of 15 miles S. S. W. Plymouth is the fishery for pilchards, which extends no further E. than this port, whence great quantities are exported to Italy, and other catholic countries. Plymouth contains two parish churches, various meeting-houses, and a Jews' synagogue, and carries on a considerable foreign and domestic trade. The charitable institutions are numerous; and, among those for literary purposes, are the Athenæum, and a public library, containing several thousand valuable books. The town is well supplied with fresh water, first brought here from a place 7 miles off, by the famous Sir Francis Drake. It carries on a considerable trade, but has no manufactures of any consequence. It returns two members to parliament. It is 43 miles S. W. of Exeter, and 216 W. by S. of London. Long. 4. 7. W. lat. 50. 23. N.

Plymouth, a seaport of Massachusets, capital of a county of the same name. It is the oldest settlement in New England; and the *rock* on which the first settlers landed was conveyed in 1774, from the shore to a square in the centre of the town. The principal business of the place is the cod fishery, in which 2000 tons of shipping are employed. It is situated at the S. end of Plymouth Bay; 42 miles S. S. E. of Boston. Pop. 5281. Long. 70. 45. W. lat. 41. 58. N.

Plymouth, a town of New Hampshire, in Grafton county, situate on the Pemigewasset; at the mouth of Baker River; 45 miles N. of Concord. Pop. 1281.

Plymouth, a town of North Carolina, capital of Washington county, on the S. side of Roanoke River; 4 miles above Albemarle Sound, and 23 S. S. W. of Edenton.

Plymouth-Dock. *See* Devonport.

Plympton, a town in Devonshire, with a market on Saturday. It is one of the stannary towns for tin. It is seated near the Plym; 4 miles E. of Plymouth, and 218 W. by S. of London.

Plynlimmon, a vast mountain of Wales, partly in Montgomeryshire, and partly in Cardiganshire, 2463 feet high. The Severn, the Wye, and other rivers, have their source in this mountain.

Po, the principal river of Italy, which has its source at Mount Viso, in Piedmont, flows N. E. to Turin, and thence proceeding in an easterly course, it divides Austrian Italy from the states of Parma, Modena, and the pope's dominions, and enters the Gulf of Venice by four principal mouths; in its course it receives several rivers, and often overflows its banks, as most of those rivers descend from the Alps, and are increased by the melting of the snow. It is crossed like the Rhine by flying bridges.

Po, a river of China, in the province of

Kiang-si; which runs into the Po-yang-hou, a small distance from Jao-tcheou.

Pocklington, a town in East Yorkshire, with a market on Saturday; seated on a stream that runs into the Derwent; 14 miles E. of York, and 194 N. by W. of London.

Podenstein, a town of Bavarian Franconia, near the source of the Putlach; 30 miles S. E. of Bamberg.

Podgoriza, a free city of the Austrian empire, in Galicia; seated on the Vistula, opposite to Cracow. Pop. 4000.

Podlachia, one of the eight palatinates of Poland; bounded N. and E. by the river Bog, S. by the palatinate of Lublin, and W. by the Vistula. It has an area of 5520 square miles, with 438,000 inhabitants. The capital is Siedlec.

Podolia, a government of Russia, wrested from Poland in 1793. The Dniester separates it from Moldavia on the S. W., and the Bog crosses it from the N. in a S. E. direction. It has an area of 20,400 square miles, with 1,330,000 inhabitants.

Podolsk, a town of Russia, in the government of Moscow; 28 miles S. of Moscow.

Podor, a fortress of Africa, on the river Senegal; built by the French. It was ceded to the English in 1763, but afterwards taken by the French, and confirmed to them by the peace of 1783. Long. 14. 20. W. lat. 17. 1. N.

Poggio, a town of Tuscany, with a handsome palace; 8 miles S. E. of Florence.

Poggiobonzi, a town of Tuscany, with the ruins of a citadel; seated near the Elsa; 20 miles S. of Florence.

Poggy, an island in the Indian Ocean, on the W. side of the island of Sumatra, and separated from the N. end of that of Nassau by a narrow channel, which contains a number of smaller islands, the whole of which are sometimes called the Nassau or Poggy islands. It is triangular, and about 20 miles in length. Long. 99. 33. E. lat. 2. 20. S.

Poirino, a town of the Sardinian states; in Piedmont, seated on the Bonna; 14 miles S. E. of Turin.

Poissy, a town of France, department of Seine-et-Oise; the birthplace of Louis XI.; seated near the forest of St. Germain; 15 miles N. W. of Paris.

Poitiers, a town of France, capital of the department of Vienne, and a bishop's see. Its population is not in proportion to its extent; for it includes a number of gardens and fields within its circuit. It has several Roman antiquities, particularly an amphitheatre, partly demolished, and a triumphal arch, which serves as a gate to the great street. Here, in 1356, Edward the Black Prince gained a victory over the French, taking prisoners king John and his son Philip, whom he brought to England. The principal manufactures are stockings, woollen caps, gloves, and combs. It is seated on a hill, on the river Clain; 85 miles S. W. of Tours, and 120 N. by E. of Bordeaux. Pop. 21,500. Long. 0. 21. E. lat. 46. 35. N.

Poitou, a province of France, which now forms the three departments of Vendee, Vienne, and Deux Sevres.

Pola, a strong seaport of Istria, and a bishop's see. Here are large remains of a Roman amphitheatre and a triumphal arch. It is seated on a mountain, near a bay of the Gulf of Venice; 38 miles S. of Capo d'Istria. Long. 14. 9. E. lat. 45. 13 N.

Poland, a large country of Europe, bounded on the N. by Prussia, Courland, Livonia, and Russia, W. by the Baltic, Brandenburg, and Silesia, S. by Hungary and Moldavia, and E. by Russia, and the territories wrested by that power from the Turks. It was formerly divided into four principal parts, Great Poland, Little Poland, Red Russia, and Lithuania. In 1772 a partition of this country, projected by the king of Prussia, was effected by that monarch, in conjunction with the empress of Russia and the emperor of Germany. By this partition one-third of the country was wrested from the republic, the diet being compelled, by a foreign force, to make and to ratify this important cession. The three partitioning powers, moreover, forcibly effected a great change in the constitution. In 1791, however, the king and the nation, in concurrence, almost unanimously, and without any foreign intervention, established another constitution, and one so unexceptionable every way, that it was celebrated by Mr. Burke, as a revolution whereby the conditions of all were made better, and the rights of none infringed. By it the broils of an elective monarchy, by which Poland, on almost every vacancy of the throne, had been involved in the calamities of war, were avoided, the throne being declared hereditary in the house of Saxony. A few of the nobility, however, discontented at the generous sacrifice of some of their privileges, repaired to the court of Russia; and, their representations concurring with the ambitious views of the empress, she sent an army into Poland, under pretext of being guarantee of the constitution of 1772. Her interference was too powerful to be resisted; and this new constitution was overthrown. But the principal object for which the Russian army entered Poland was not yet attained. The empress had planned, in conjunction with the king of Prussia, a second partition of this country, which took place in 1793. Such multiplied oppressions at last roused the spirit of the nation. General Kosciusko appeared, in 1794, at the head of a Polish army, to assert the independency of his country, and to recover the provinces wrested from it. He was successful at first, against the king of Prussia, but was at length overpowered by numbers; the country was in different parts desolated, the houses burnt, and the inhabitants massacred in crowds. The brave Kosciusko was taken prisoner, and sent with a number of other patriots into confinement at Petersburg, for having dared to defend his native country against foreign aggression. The king formally resigned his crown at Grodno, in 1795, and was afterwards removed to Petersburg, where he remained a kind of state prisoner, till his death, in 1798. The whole of the country was divided among the three partitioning powers. Austria had Little Poland, and the greatest part of Red Russia and Podolia, which is now called the kingdom of Galicia; Prussia had Great Poland, Polish Prussia, a small part of Lithuania, and Polachia; and Russia had Samogitia, the remainder of Lithuania, Volhynia, and Podolia. In the war with Prussia, in 1806, the French penetrated into Poland, and proclaimed their desire to restore its ancient independence, when, treaties of peace having been adjusted with Russia and Prussia, the project was for the most part abandoned. By the peace of Tilsit, the king of Prussia renounced the possession of the greater part of his Polish provinces, when they were erected into the dukedom of Warsaw, in favour of the king of Saxony. In 1809 Austria was compelled to cede part of Galicia to Russia, and a further portion to the new states. But on the retreat of the French army out of Poland, in 1813, the Russians took possession of the duchy of Warsaw, and the congress of Vienna not only confirmed to that power all the Polish and Lithuanian provinces acquired before 1795, but added the sovereignty of the central provinces. On the downfall of Bonaparte, and the settlement of the continent in 1815, a part of the territory of Poland, comprising the central portion, with an area of 47,000 square miles, and a population of 3,000,000, was formed into a separate kingdom, subject to the emperor of Russia, but governed by its own laws, with such modern improvements in legislature as the liberal policy of the emperor Alexander thought necessary to the welfare of the kingdom, which was governed by his viceroy. On the accession of Nicholas, his despotic conduct towards the conquered nation roused them again to resistance; in 1833 they flew to arms, and made a noble effort to gain their independence, but which only ended in their entire destruction; and the policy of Russia now seems to be the total annihilation of the unfortunate Poles, as a people, in language and character; and Poland, once powerful, and containing a population of 15,000,000, has been annihilated from among the nations of the earth, and even its name almost obliterated from the map of Europe. The religion was Roman Catholic, but the Protestants nearly equalled them in numbers; there were also a great number of Jews, who had many important privileges. The towns of Poland are for the most part built with wood; and the villages consist of mean cottages, or huts. The country is so fertile in corn, in many places, that it supplies Sweden and Holland with large quantities, and it has extensive pastures. Peat, ochre, chalk, agate, chalcedony, carnelians, onyxes, jasper, rock crystals, amethysts, garnets, topazes, sapphires, and even rubies and diamonds, are found in Poland; also talc, spar, lapis calaminaris, coal, iron, lead, and quicksilver. Here is much leather, fur, hemp, flax, saltpetre, alum, manna, honey, and wax; and there are mines of salt, of great depth, out of which is dug rock-salt. Horses are numerous, very strong, swift, and beautiful; and horned cattle are bred in immense numbers. Warsaw is the principal city.

POLERON. *See* POOLOROON.

POLESIA, a name commonly given to the palatinate of Brzesc, in Lithuania.

POL, ST., a town of France; department of Pas de Calais; noted for its mineral waters. It is 16 miles N. W. of Arras.

POLICANDRO, an island in the Grecian Archipelago; one of the Cyclades; 20 miles in circumference. Here are a few villages, a castle, and a harbour; but it consists, in general, of barren rocks and mountains. It lies between Milo and Paros. Long. 25. 31. E. lat. 36. 32. N.

POLICASTRO, a town of Naples, in Principato Citra; seated on a gulf of the same name; in the Mediterranean; 85 miles S. E. of Naples. Long. 15. 40. E. lat. 40. 15. N.

POLIGNANO, a town of Naples, in Terra di Bari; seated on a craggy rock, near the Gulf of Venice; 16 miles E. of Bari. Pop. 7000.

POLIGNY, a town of France, department of Jura; seated on a rivulet, 23 miles S. S. W. of Besançon. Pop. 5400.

POLINA, a town of Albania, 12 miles S. of Durazzo.

POLITZ, a town of Pomerania, in the government of Stettin; celebrated for its hops. It is 8 miles N. of Stettin.

POLITZKA, a walled town of Bohemia, in the circle of Chrudim, on the frontiers of Moravia; 23 miles S. E. of Chrudim.

POLIZZI, a town of Sicily, in Val di Mazara; at the foot of the mountain Madonia, 28 miles S. E. of Palermo.

POLKOWITZ, a town of Silesia, in the principality of Glogau, 13 miles S. of Glogau.

POLLOCKSHAWS, a town of Scotland, in Renfrewshire; on the river White Cart, 3 miles W. S. W. of Glasgow.

POLNO, a town of Prussia, in Pomerania, on the river Grabow; 38 miles E. S. E. of Colberg.

POLORE, a town of Hindostan, in the Carnatic; 36 miles S. S. W. of Arcot, and 55 N. W. of Pondicherry.

POLOTSK, a strong town of Russia, in the government of Vitepsk; celebrated for a number of battles having been fought in its vicinity between the French and Russians, in 1812. It is seated on the Dwina, at the influx of the Polota; 60 miles S. W. of Vitepsk. Long. 27. 50. E. lat. 55. 43. N.

POLTAVA, a government of Russia, between those of Catharinenslaf and Charkov. It has an area of 16,000 square miles, with 1,500,000 inhabitants; is fertile in corn, and affords very rich pasturage.

POLTAVA, the capital of the foregoing government, with a considerable trade in cattle, corn, flax, hemp, wax, &c. It is famous for a battle, in 1709, between Peter the Great and Charles XII. of Sweden, in which the latter was totally defeated; 737 miles S. E. of Petersburg. Population, 9000.

Polten, St., a town of Austria, the residence of a great number of the nobility. The adjacent country yields excellent saffron. It is seated on the Dracam; 33 miles W. of Vienna, Pop. 4300. Long. 15. 41. E. lat. 48. 13. N.

Poltzin, a town of Prussia, in Pomerania, near which are medicinal springs and baths; 50 miles N. E. of Stargard.

Polynesia, (many islands), a term applied by modern geographers to numerous islands in the Pacific Ocean, from the Ladrones to Easter Island. The principal groups are the Ladrones, Carolinas, Pelew, Sandwich, Society, Friendly, Navigators', Hervey, Georgian, and the Marquesas Islands.

Pombal, a town of Portugal, in Estremadura; 16 miles N. E. of Leiria, and 21 S. of Coimbra. Pop. 3800.

Pomegue, a small island in the Mediterranean, near the coast of France, at the entrance into the harbour of Marseilles, defended by a tower.

Pomerania, an extensive province of Prussia; lying along the S. coast of the Baltic, and comprising an area of 12,000 square miles, with 670,000 inhabitants. It is divided into the governments of Stettin, Stralsund, and Coslin, and is watered by several rivers, of which the Oder, Peene, Ucker, Rega, Persante, Ihna, Stolphen, and Lebo, are the most considerable. The air is pretty cold, but compensated by the fertility of the soil, which abounds in pastures and corn, of which a great deal is exported. The country is flat, contains many lakes, woods, and forests, and has several good harbours. It was formerly an independent duchy of the German empire, and was divided into Hither and Further Pomerania. The latter, and part of Hither Pomerania, were seized by the king of Prussia, and confirmed to him in 1720; the remainder N. of the Peene was ceded by the king of Sweden, at the treaty of Kiel, in 1814, to the king of Denmark, in exchange for Norway, but soon after came to Prussia in exchange for Saxe-Lunenburg.

Pomerelia, a district of West Prussia; extending W. from the river Vistula to the duchy of Pomerania, of which it was formerly a part. It is now included in the government of Dantzic.

Pomeroy, a market town of Ireland, in the county of Tyrone; 96 miles from Dublin.

Pomfret, a town of Connecticut, in Windham county; 12 miles N. N. E. of Windham.

Pomona, or **Mainland**, the largest of the Orkney Islands, being 24 miles long, and from 6 to 10 broad; but intersected by numerous arms of the sea. The general appearance of the country is much the same as the Mainland of Shetland; but the soil is more fertile, and in some parts better cultivated. Kirkwall is the capital. *See* **Orkneys**.

Pompeii, the ruins of an ancient town at the base of Mount Vesuvius, which was destroyed with Herculaneum, by an eruption, in 79 A. D. The volcanic matter is much less hard than at Herculaneum, and, since its discovery in 1811, much of the town has been excavated, and many interesting discoveries have been made relating to the domestic manners of the ancient Romans. It once stood on the sea-shore, but is now a considerable distance from it.

Pondicherry, a town of Hindostan, in the Carnatic. It was first settled by the French in 1674, and, previously to the war of 1756, was a fine city. It extended along the sea-coast above a mile, was three-quarters of a mile in breadth, and had a citadel, then the best of its kind in India. The city has been repeatedly taken by the English, particularly in 1761, (when it was immediately razed, in retaliation of M. Lally's conduct towards Fort St. David), and the last time in 1793. It was restored to the French at the general peace; 85 miles S. by W. of Madras. Long. 79. 53. E. lat. 11. 42. N.

Pondico, a small uninhabited island of the Grecian Archipelago, near the coast of Negropont. Long. 23. 29. E. lat. 39. 9. N.

Ponferrada, a town of Spain, in Leon, on the river Sill; 40 miles S. W. of Leon.

Pong-hou, or **Piscadores**, a cluster of islands in the China Sea, which lie about six leagues from the W. coast of the island of Formosa. They are only sand-banks or rocks, and not a shrub is to be seen upon them. The harbour of Pong-hou, the principal island, is good, and was fortified by the Dutch, while they were masters of Formosa. A Chinese garrison is kept here, with one of the mandarins called literati, whose chief employ is to watch the trading vessels between China and Formosa. Long. 121. 25. E. lat. 25. 30. N.

Pons, a town of France, department of Lower Charente; with a mineral spring; seated on a hill, near the river Sevigne; 10 miles S. of Saintes. Pop. 4000.

Pons, St., a town in the department of Herault, and a bishop's see. It is seated in a valley surrounded by mountains, in which are fine marble quarries; 24 miles N. of Narbonne. Pop. 4700. Long. 2. 47. E. lat. 43. 29. N.

Pont Audemer, a town in the department of Eure; with manufactures of woollen, linen, and leather, and a brisk trade in corn, cattle, and cider; seated on the Rille; 23 miles W. S. W. of Rouen. Pop. 5200.

Pont a Mousson, a town in the department of Meurthe. It had once a university, which was removed to Nancy in 1769. It is seated on the Moselle, which divides it into parts; 14 miles N. N. W. of Nancy.

Pont de Camare, a town in the department of Aveiron; celebrated for its mineral waters; 40 miles S. S. E. of Rodez.

Pont de Ce, a town in the department of Maine-et-Loire; seated on the Loire; 3 miles S. of Angers. Pop. 3000.

Pont de l'Arche, a town in the department of Eure, seated on the Seine; 18 miles N. of Evreux.

Pont l'Eveque, a town in the department of Calvados. It is a trading place, seated on the Touque; 4 miles from the sea, and 40 W. S. W. of Rouen. Pop. 2500. Long. 0. 10. E. lat. 49. 17. N.

Pont de Vaux, a town in the department of

Ain, seated on the Resouze, near its conflux with the Saone; 8 miles S. of Macon. Population, 2800.

PONT DE VESLE, a town in the department of Ain, with manufactures of stuffs and tapestry; seated on the Vesle; 12 miles W. of Bourg.

PONT DU GARD. *See* GARD.

PONT GIBAUT, a town in the department of Puy de Dome; 10 miles W. N. W. of Clermont.

PONT ST. ESPRIT, a town in the department of Gard, on the river Rhone; over which is one of the finest bridges in Europe, consisting of 19 great, and 4 small arches. To facilitate the passage of the water, in time of floods, apertures are made through each pier, six feet above the common level of the river; and, to stem the rapidity of the river, the bridge is not built in a right line, but in a curve. Here are manufactures of silk, and a good trade in wine, oil, and fruits; 17 miles S. of Viviers, and 55 N. E. of Montpelier. Long. 4. 40. E. lat. 44 15. N.

PONT ST. MAXENCE, a town in the department of Seine-et-Oise, seated on the Oise; 5 miles N. of Senlis.

PONT-SUR-SEINE, a town in the department of Aube, with a castle, seated on the Seine; 20 miles N. W. of Troyes, and 55 S. E. of Paris.

PONT-SUR-YONNE, a town in the department of Yonne, seated on the Yonne; 8 miles N. W. of Sens.

PONTA DELGADA, a seaport of St. Michael, one of the Azores. It is defended by a citadel, and contains about 8000 inhabitants. Long. 25. 40. W. lat. 37. 45. N.

PONTARLIER, a town of France, department of Doubs, with a strong castle on a mountain. It is seated on the Doubs, and the frontiers of Switzerland; 22 miles W. of Neufchatel, and 35 S. E. of Besançon. Pop. 4500. Long. 6. 26. E. lat. 46. 55. N.

PONTE, a town of the Sardinian states, in Piedmont, seated at the conflux of the Saono and Orco; 19 miles N. N. W. of Turin. Pop. 3600.

PONTE DE LIMA, a town of Portugal, in Entre Douro e Minho, seated on the Lima, over which is a magnificent bridge; 13 miles N. W. of Braga.

PONTE STURA, a town of the Sardinian states, in the duchy of Montferrat; seated at the conflux of the Stura and Po, 5 miles W. S. W. of Casal.

PONTA VETA, a town of Spain, in Galicia, near the mouth of the Leris; 26 miles N. of Tuy.

PONTEBA, or PONTE IMPERIALE, a town of the Austrian states in Carinthia; seated on the Fella, over which it has a bridge to Ponteba Veneta, a small town of the province of Friuli. It is 20 miles N. N. W. of Friuli, and 25 S.W. of Villach.

PONTEFRACT, a borough in West Yorkshire, governed by a mayor, with a market on Saturday, returning two members to parliament. It is situate in a very rich soil, noted for its gardens and nurseries. Its castle, now in ruins, has been the scene of various tragical events in the English history, particularly the murder of Richard II.; 22 miles S. W. of York, and 175 N. N. W. of London.

PONTIAN ISLANDS, a cluster of small islands in the Mediterranean, opposite to the coast of Terra di Lavoro.

PONTIANA, a river of Borneo, which enters the ocean by several mouths, at the W. side of the island, under the equinoctial line, where the Dutch have a factory.

PONTIVY, a town of France, department of Morbihan, with a linen manufacture; seated on the river Blavet, 25 miles N. of Vannes. Pop. 3100.

PONTOISE, a town in the department of Seine-et-Oise, with a castle. The parliament of Paris was transferred to this place in 1652, 1720, and 1753. It is seated on an eminence near the Oise, 20 miles N. W. of Paris. Pop. 5200. Long. 2. 6. E. lat. 49. 3. N.

PONTORSON, a town in the department of Manche, on the Coesnon, with a tide-harbour; 10 miles S. S. W. of Avranches.

PONTREMOLI, a town of Tuscany, with a strong castle, seated at the foot of the Appennines, on the river Magra; 40 miles S. W. of Parma. Pop. 2500. Long. 9. 40. E. lat. 44. 25. N.

PONTRIEUX, a town of France, department of Cotes du Nord, on the river Trieux; 10 miles N. W. of St. Brieux.

PONTYPOOL, a town in Monmouthshire, with a market on Saturday, extensive iron-works, and a manufacture of japanned ware. It is seated between two hills on the river Avon, 15 miles S. W. of Monmouth, and 148 W. by N. of London.

PONZA, one of the Pontian Islands, in the Mediterranean; containing a town, harbour, and considerable salt-works. It was taken by the British in 1813. Long. 13. 10. E. lat. 40. 53. N.

PONZONE, a town of the Sardinian states, in the duchy of Montferrat; 20 miles W. N. W. of Genoa.

POOLE, a borough and seaport in Dorsetshire; with a market on Monday and Thursday. It is a county of itself, and sends two members to parliament. It is governed by a mayor, and situate on a peninsula projecting into a capacious bay, which branches into many creeks, and forms several islands. The parish church, formerly a chapel of ease to Lanford, is a very ancient structure. Here are also various places of worship for dissenters, a grammar-school, and several charity schools. The harbour admits vessels of moderate size only; but for them it is very secure. Poole rose into some consequence when the ancient town of Wareham fell into decay. The principal branch of business here is the Newfoundland fishery. It has also a large importation of deals from Norway, a general commerce with America and various parts of Europe, and a fine coasting trade, particularly in corn and coal. Near the mouth of the harbour is an oyster bank, from which vast quantities are carried to be fattened in the creeks of Essex and the Thames. Poole is 40 miles W. S. W. of Winchester, and 105 W. by S. of London. Long. 1. 59. W. lat. 50. 43. N.

Pooloroon, or Poleron, one of the Banda islands; 100 miles S. E. of Amboyna. Long. 130. 0. E. lat. 4. 20. S.

Poolo Woy, one of the Banda islands, on which the Dutch have a regular pentagon, called Fort Revenge.

Poona, a city of Hindostan, the modern capital of the Mahratta empire. At the bottom of Parvate Hill, in the vicinity, is a large square field, enclosed with high brick walls, where the peishwa used to assemble the Brahmins, to whom he gave alms at the great feast, when the rainy season terminated. The view from this hill commands the town, with all its gardens and plantations, the cantonments, and the British residency at the Sungum. The town is entirely defenceless, the streets long and narrow, and the houses very irregularly built. The more respectable dwellings are raised with large blocks of granite to the height of about 14 feet, after which the superstructure is composed of timber frames, with slight brick walls; those of the common people are only one story high, with tiled roofs. The palace is surrounded by high and thick brick walls, with round towers at the angles, and has only one entrance. The affairs of government are under the direction of the British resident. It is 100 miles S. E. of Bombay. Pop. 110,000. Long. 73. 55. E. lat. 18. 30. N.

Poorunder, a fortress of Hindostan, in Bejapore, where the archives of Poona are kept; seated on a mountain, 18 miles E. S. E. of Poona.

Poote, a town of France, in the department of Mayenne; 6 miles W. S. W. of Alençon.

Popayan, a province in the W. part of New Granada; republic of Colombia. A chain of barren mountains runs through the country from N. to S., and the soil near the sea is flat, marshy, and often flooded by the rains.

Popayan, the capital of the foregoing province, and the most ancient city erected by Europeans in this part of America. It contains a cathedral, several churches and convents, and two nunneries. The trade is considerable, and the inhabitants are estimated at 25,000, chiefly mulattoes. It stands in a large plain, 290 miles W. S. W. of Santa Fe, and 240 N. E. of Quito. Long. 75. 55. W. lat. 2. 35. N.

Popedom, or Ecclesiastical States, a country of Italy; bounded N. by the Po, which separates it from the Austrian states, E. by the Adriatic, S. by Naples, and W. by Tuscany. It is 120 miles long, and from 80 to 100 broad, divided into the delegations of Bologna, Ferrara, Forli, Ravenna, Urbino and Pesaro, Ancona, Fermo, Pontecorvo, Macerata, Perugio, Spoleto, Viterbo, Ascoli, Benevento, Camerino, Civita Vecchia, and Rieti. The papal government is a bar to industry, and ill calculated to promote the happiness of its subjects; the country is consequently badly cultivated and thinly inhabited. Trade and manufactures are but little encouraged; and, were it not for dates, figs, almonds, olives, and other fruits, which grow spontaneously, the indolence of the inhabitants is such that they would be absolutely starved. The pope, according to the ancient canon law, is the supreme, universal, and independent head of the church, and is invested with sovereignty over all Christian sovereigns, communities, and individuals. He has the titles of Holy Father and Holiness, and is elected at every vacancy from among the cardinals, each of whom is styled his Eminence. Their number was fixed by Sixtus V. at 70, in allusion to the number of the disciples sent out by Christ to teach the world—an allusion without any singular propriety, as no two classes of people could be more unlike. The annual revenue of the pope, which formerly amounted to upwards of 2,000,000*l.* sterling, is now reduced to about 600,000*l.*, including the exactions in foreign countries. His military force is inconsiderable; his naval force consists of a few galleys, stationed at Civita Vecchia. In 1798 this state was taken possession of by the French, who overturned its ancient government, and erected it into a republic, styled the Roman republic, under the direction of five consuls. They obliged the pope, Pius VI., to remove from Rome, first into Tuscany, and afterwards into France, where he died at Valence, August 19th, 1799. In December following a conclave was held at Venice, and on March 13th, 1800, cardinal Chiaromonti was elected to the papal chair, under the title of Pius VII., and assumed the sovereignty. A concordat was concluded for France in 1802, and in 1804 Napoleon was crowned by the pope; but in 1807 the emperor became imperious, while the pope maintained a strong feeling of independence. Measures of violence were resorted to; Rome was occupied by French troops; the pope was removed into France, and his states transformed into a kingdom, under Napoleon's son. He continued a kind of prisoner till the allies had invaded France in 1814, when he was restored to most of his former prerogatives. He died in 1823, and was succeeded by cardinal Hannibal della Genga, under the the title of Leo XII., on whose death, in 1829, cardinal Francesco Saverio Castiglioni was elected to the papal chair, and took the title of Pius VIII. Rome is the capital.

Poperinghe, a town of Belgium, in West Flanders, on a river of the same name, 6 miles W. of Ypres.

Popo, a kingdom of Africa, on the slave coast. The inhabitants have scarcely any houses, except the king's village, which is on an island in the midst of a river. Long. 2. 33. E. lat. 6. 18. N.

Pora, an island in the Indian Ocean, on the W. coast of Sumatra; 54 miles long, and from 9 to 12 broad. Long. 98. 30. E. lat. 1. 10. S.

Porcah, a seaport of Hindostan, in Travancore, taken by the English in 1795. It is populous, and carries on a considerable trade. It is 85 miles N. W. of Travancore. Long. 76. 20. E. lat. 9. 15. N.

PORCO, a town of Buenos Ayres, capital of a province which commences on the W. side of Potosi, from which it extends 60 miles. It has its name from a mountain, in which is a rich silver mine, the first worked by the Spaniards after their conquest of the country. It is 25 miles W. S. W. of Potosi. Long. 67. 20. W. lat. 19. 40. S.

PORCUNA, a town of Spain, in Andalusia, on the Salado; 22 miles N. W. of Jaen.

PORENTRUI, a town of Switzerland, canton of Bern; seated on the Hallan, near Mount Jura, 24 miles W. S. W. of Basel. Long. 7. 10. E. lat. 47. 27. N.

PORLOCK, a town in Somersetshire, with a trade in coal and lime. It is seated on a bay of the Bristol Channel, surrounded by hills; 7 miles W. of Minehead, and 170 W. of London.

PORROGONG. *See* PARO.

PORSELOU, a rich and commercial town of the kingdom of Siam. It is surrounded by 14 bastions, and situate on a large river, 300 miles N. of its mouth in the Gulf of Siam. Long. 100. 2. E. lat. 17. 48. N.

PORTARLINGTON, a borough of Ireland, in Queen's county; 44 miles from Dublin. It consists principally of one handsome avenue, and has a market-hall, 2 churches, and 3 chapels. It returns one member to parliament.

PORT AU PRINCE, a seaport of St. Domingo; seated on a bay on the W. side of the island; with considerable trade. It was nearly burnt down in 1791, by the revolting negroes, and was taken by the English and royalists in 1794. Long. 72. 10. W. lat. 18. 40. N.

PORT BALTIC. *See* ROGERWICK.

PORT DALRYMPLE, a harbour on the N. coast of Van Diemen's Land, where a British settlement was established in 1804. Launceston is at the extremity of the river Tamar, which forms the port.

PORT DESIRE, a harbour on the E. coast of Patagonia, where ships sometimes touch in their passage to the Pacific Ocean. Long. 67. 56. W. lat. 47. 50. S.

PORT DISCOVERY, a harbour on the W. coast of North America, in the Gulf of Georgia. Long. 237. 20. E. lat. 48. 7. N.

PORT EGMONT, one of the finest harbours in the world, on the N. W. coast of Falkland Islands, discovered by Commodore Byron, in 1765. The whole navy of England might ride here in perfect security from all winds; and every thing for the refreshment of ships is to be obtained in abundance. Long. 55. 0. W. lat. 51. 27. S.

PORT FRANÇAIS, a harbour on the W. coast of North America, discovered by Perouse in 1786. It is of a circular form, not to be fathomed in the middle, and bordered by peaked mountains, of an excessive height, covered with snow. Long. 137. 30. W. lat. 58. 37. N.

PORT GLASGOW, a town of Scotland; in Renfrewshire; near the mouth of the Clyde; erected in 1710, to serve as the port of the city of Glasgow, whose magistrates appoint a bailiff for its government. The harbour is excellent, and there are extensive warehouses on the quay, belonging to the Glasgow merchants. Contiguous to the town, and near the shore, stands the castle of Newark, a strong fortified edifice. It unites with Dunbarton, Renfrew, &c. in sending one member to parliament. It is 2 miles E. of Greenock, and 20 N. W. of Glasgow.

PORTGLENONE, a town of Ireland, in the county of Antrim. It consists of one street, and has a linen market; 130 miles from Dublin.

PORT JACKSON, a bay and harbour on the coast of New South Wales; 13 miles N. of Botany Bay. The capes that form its entrance are high, rugged, and perpendicular cliffs; and the harbour is one of the noblest in the world, extending 14 miles in length, with numerous creeks or coves. The name of Port Jackson was given to it by Captain Cook, who observed it in sailing along the coast. *See* SYDNEY.

PORT LOUIS, a strong town of France, in the department of Morbihan; with a citadel and a good harbour. It stands on the extremity of a peninsula, at the mouth of the Biavet; 27 miles W. of Vannes. Long. 3. 18. W. lat. 47. 40. N.

PORT LOUIS, the capital of the Island of Mauritius, or Isle of France, situate on the W. side of the island, in a low and flat valley, surrounded by mountains. In 1817 it was almost entirely burnt down, but has since been rebuilt. It was long the chief settlement of the French in this part of the world, but now belongs to the British. Long. 57. 32. E. lat. 20. 10. N.

PORT MAHON, a seaport and chief place of a district of the island of Minorca, with an excellent harbour. It is built chiefly on lofty rocks. The houses are in general good, and are all provided with cisterns, and many with terraces. The Place d'Armes is large and handsome; on one side are barracks capable of containing 1200 men. The only public walk is the Alameyda, which is merely an alley of trees. On one side of the harbour is a dock-yard, and on the other a natural mole. Long. 4. 5. E. lat. 36. 17. N.

PORT PAIX a town on the N. coast of St. Domingo, with a good harbour, opposite the island of Tortue. Long. 73. 2. W. lat. 19. 58. N.

PORT PATRICK, a seaport of Scotland, in Wigtonshire, confined by the sea on one side, and on the other by overhanging rocks and hills. It is nearly opposite Donaghadee, in Ireland, from which it is only 20 miles distant; and packet-boats sail hence for that place every day. The harbour is good, and has one of the finest quays in Great Britain, with a reflecting light-house. It is 28 miles W. of Wigton, and 107 S. W. of Edinburgh. Long. 5. 3. W. lat. 54. 58. N.

PORT PENN, a town of Delaware; in Newcastle county, with a secure harbour, opposite Ready Island, in the Delaware. It is the rendezvous of outward-bound ships, waiting for a favourable wind; 56 miles below Philadelphia.

PORT ROSEWAY. *See* SHELBURNE.

PORT ROYAL, a seaport of Jamaica; once a considerable town, abounding in riches and trade. In 1692 it was destroyed by an earthquake, in 1702 by a fire, in 1722 by an inundation of the sea, and in 1744 by a hurricane. After these extraordinary calamities, the custom-house and public offices were removed, and no market suffered to be held here in future. It now consists of about 200 houses, built on a neck of land which juts out several miles into the sea, and is guarded by a strong fort. Pop. 1000. The harbour is deep, and 1000 ships may ride in it secure from every wind. It is 6 miles across the bay, S. S. W. of Kingston. Long. 76. 45. W. lat. 18. 0. N.

Port Royal, a town of Virginia, in Caroline county, with three churches, situate on the Rappahannoc; 22 miles S. E. of Fredericsburg, and 58 above Urbanna.

Port Royal, an island on the coast of South Carolina, separated from the neighbouring continent by an arm of the sea, called Broad River, which forms the most commodious harbour in the state, at the town of Beaufort.

Port St. Anne. *See* Killough.

Port St. Julian, a harbour on the E. coast of Patagonia, where ships bound for the Pacific usually touch. Long. 68. 44. W. lat. 49. 10. S.

Port St. Mary, a seaport of Spain, in Andalusia, on the Bay of Cadiz. The principal trade is in salt. The English made a descent here in 1702, with a design to besiege Cadiz, but without success; 10 miles N. E. of Cadiz.

Port sur Saone, a town of France, in the department of Upper Saone, on the river Saone; 8 miles N. W. of Vesoul.

Port Tobacco, a town of Maryland, chief of Charles county, situate on a creek of its name, which enters the Potomac, 4 miles below the town. In its vicinity are the celebrated cold waters of Mount Misery; 30 miles S. of Washington.

Port Vendre, a town of France, in the department of Eastern Pyrenees, with a small harbour on the Mediterranean, defended by two forts. It is 25 miles S. S. E. of Perpignan.

Port William, a town of Kentucky, capital of Gallatin county, at the confluence of the Kentucky and the Ohio.

Portadown, a town of Ireland, in the county of Armagh; with a linen manufacture, situate on the river Bann; 16 miles N. of Newry.

Portalegre, a strong town of Portugal, in Alentejo, and a bishop's see. It has a manufacture of woollen cloth, and is seated at the foot of a high mountain; 30 miles N. of Elvas. Pop. 5600.

Portici, a village 4 miles E. S. E. of the city of Naples, on part of the site of the ancient Herculaneum, near Mount Vesuvius. Here is a palace of the king of Naples, enriched with a vast number of fine statues, and other remains of antiquity, taken out of the ruins of Herculaneum. Pop. 5200.

Portland, a peninsula in Dorsetshire, connected with the main land by a ridge of pebbles, called the Chesil Bank, extending above 7 miles up the S. W. coast. Between this bank and the mainland is a narrow arm of the sea, called the Fleet. Portland Isle is 4 miles long, and 2 broad, surrounded by inaccessible rocks, except at the landing-place, at the N. W. end, where there is a strong castle, called Portland Castle, built by Henry VIII. The peninsula is noted for its freestone, which is used for building the finest structures, and about 9000 tons of it are annually exported. It lies on the S. W. side of Weymouth Bay, and on its S. extremity, called Portland Point, two light-houses have been erected. Long. 2. 27. W. lat. 50. 31. N.

Portland, the capital of the state of Maine; in Cumberland county; with a capacious harbour, defended by a fort, a citadel, and a battery. It was almost laid in ashes by the British fleet in 1775, but has been entirely rebuilt, and has three churches. It is situate on a promontory in Casco Bay; with a light-house at the entrance of the harbour; 120 miles N. N. E. of Boston. Pop. 12,601. Long. 70. 20. W. lat. 43. 40. N.

Portland Islands, a cluster of small islands in the South Pacific. They are low and covered with wood; and the centre one is in long. 149. 8. E. lat. 2. 38. S.

Porto, a small seaport of the papal states, in the patrimony of St. Peter. It is the see of a bishop, (who is generally a cardinal,) dependent only on the pope. It is seated on the W. side of the Tiber; 10 miles S. W. of Rome.

Portobello, a modern watering place of Scotland, 3 miles E. of Edinburgh, and 2½ miles from Musselburgh; in 1765, it consisted of a solitary, humble public-house, called the Portobello, which is still in existence in the High-street. The present town is nearly a mile in length, along the beach, and consists of several streets, which are thinly lined with detached houses. It is much frequented for bathing, and contains several handsome houses. There is no accommodation for shipping, and it is seated near the line of the Dalkeith and Edinburgh railway. It unites with Leith and Musselburgh, in sending a member to parliament.

Porto Bello, a seaport of Central America; republic of Colombia; on the N. coast of the Isthmus of Darien, nearly opposite Panama, on the S. coast. It is a very unhealthy place, and the country around it swarms with toads and other reptiles in the rainy season. Before the abolition of the trade by the galleons, in 1748, and the introduction of register ships, this place was the great mart for the rich commerce of Peru and Chili. The town stands close to the sea, on the side of a mountain that surrounds the harbour, which is safe and commodious. It was taken in 1742 by Admiral Vernon, who demolished the fortifications; but it has since been strongly fortified. It is 60 miles N. by E. of Panama, and 300 W. of Carthagena. Long. 79. 50. W. lat. 9. 33. N.

Porto Cabello, a seaport of Venezuela, South America; with a good harbour defended by forts. It is a flourishing place, containing a population of 8000, and is the centre of the navigation and commerce of Venezuela; 70 miles W. by S. of Jago de Leon. Long. 67. 32. E. lat. 10. 31. N.

Porto Farino, a seaport of the kingdom of Tunis. Long. 10. 16. E. lat. 37. 12. N.

Porto Ferrajo, the capital of the island of

Elba, with a good harbour, capable of containing the largest fleets. This town is celebrated as having been the residence of Napoleon, from May 4, 1814, to February 26, 1815, when he sailed on his final expedition to France. Its position is central in the Mediterranean; and it perfectly commands the coast of Italy. It is a very pretty town, built on a shelving rock, that closes in a circular bay, about 2 miles deep and as many in breadth. The land all round is high and woody, and the entrance to the bay is high and easy to hit. The streets and fortifications rise one above another, like rows of seats in an ancient amphitheatre, and present a most beautiful spectacle to those who approach by water. A commodious quay communicates, by means of large flights of steps, with all the streets. Porto Ferrajo was built and fortified by Cosmo I., duke of Florence, in 1548; but the fortifications were not finished till 1628, when Cosmo II. completed them with a magnificence equal to that displayed by the old Romans in their public undertakings; and it is now deemed impregnable. The gates are decorated with sculpture, and the rings for fastening cables to are of carved bronze; 7 miles S. W. of Piombino, on the coast of Italy. Pop. 3000. Long. 12. 17. E. lat. 42. 53. N.

Porto Fino, a small seaport on the coast of Genoa, with a fort, situate between two mountains; 13 miles S. E. of Genoa.

Porto Galete, a town of Spain, in Biscay, seated in a small bay; 10 miles N. W. of Bilboa.

Porto Greco, a town of Naples, in the Capitanata, near the Gulf of Venice; 16 miles N. W. of Manfredonia.

Porto Gruaro, a town of Austrian Italy, in Friuli, seated on the Lema; 20 miles W. by S. of Palma Novo.

Porto Longone, a seaport on the S. E. side of the Isle of Elba; with a good harbour, and a fortress upon a rock, almost inaccessible. It is 4 miles S. E. of Porto Ferrajo, and 35 N. W. of Orbitello, on the coast of Italy. Long. 10. 20. E. lat. 42. 50. N.

Porto Marin, a town of Spain, in Galicia; 48 miles E. of Compostella.

Porto Praya, a town and bay of St. Jago, one of the Cape de Verd Islands. The town stands on an elevated plain, and is the residence of the Portuguese governor of the islands. Long. 23. 29. W. lat. 14. 54. N.

Porto del Principe, a seaport on the N. coast of Cuba, with a good harbour. Near it are several springs of bitumen. Long. 78. 15. W. lat. 21. 52. N.

Porto Real, a seaport of Spain, in Andalusia, on the E. side of the bay of Cadiz; 7 miles E. of Cadiz.

Porto Rico, an island of the West Indies, 60 miles E. of St. Domingo, belonging to the Spaniards. It is 120 miles long, and 40 broad, diversified with woods, valleys, and plains, and watered by springs and rivers, but unhealthy in the rainy season. It produces sugar, rum, ginger, cotton, maize, and rice; and there are so many cattle that they are often killed for the sake of the skins alone. St. Juan de Porto Rico is the capital.

Porto Santo, an island in the Atlantic, the least of the Madeiras; 15 miles in circumference. In 1518 a Portuguese ship, coasting along the African shore, was driven out to sea by a sudden squall, and, when they all expected to perish, they discovered this island, which, on account of their escape, they named Porto Santo; and hence they descried the island of Madeira. It produces little corn, but there are oxen and wild hogs, and a vast number of rabbits. Its most valuable productions are dragons'-blood, honey, and wax. It has no harbour, but good anchorage in the road. Long. 16. 25. W. lat. 32. 58. N.

Porto Seguro, a fertile province of Brazil, S. of that of Ilheos, and N. of Spiritu Santo. The capital, of the same name, is seated on the top of a rock, at the mouth of a river that flows into the Atlantic. Long. 40. 0. W. lat. 16. 20. S.

Porto Vecchio, a seaport of Corsica, seated on a bay on the E. coast of the island; 38 miles S. E. of Ajaccio. Long. 9. 10. E. lat. 41. 40. N.

Porto Venero, a seaport on the coast of Genoa, at the entrance of the Gulf of Spezzia. It has a good harbour, and is seated on the side of a hill, at the top of which is a fort; 5 miles S. of Spezzia. Long. 9. 38. E. lat. 44. 5. N.

Port Patrick, a town in Wigtonshire, opposite the town of Donaghadee, in Ireland, and is the nearest point of Britain to Ireland. A magnificent harbour has recently been formed, and the principal support of the place consists in its being a great international ferry station. It is 34¼m. W. of Wigton, and 131½ S. W. of Edinburgh.

Port Phillip, an extensive bay at the S. E. extremity of Australia; it is 35 miles long and 45 broad: the entrance is in long. 144. 36. E. and lat. 38. 18. S. At the head of the bay is the town of Melbourne and the flourishing S. Australian colony. Western Port is to the east of it.

Portsea, an island between Chichester Bay and the harbour of Portsmouth, in Hampshire. It is a low tract, about 14 miles in circumference, separated from the mainland on the N. by a creek, over which are two bridges, one for the entrance and the other for the departure of passengers. At the S. W. extremity of it is situate the town of Portsmouth.

Portsmouth, a borough and seaport of Hampshire, governed by a mayor, with markets on Thursday and Saturday. It sends two members to parliament. It is the most considerable haven for men of war, and the most strongly fortified place in England. Its capacious harbour is made by a bay running up between the island of Portsea (on which the town is situate), and the opposite peninsula, having a narrow entrance, commanded by the town and forts. Many of the largest ships are always laid up here; and, in the time of war, it is the principal rendezvous of the grand channel fleet. The docks, arsenals, storehouses, barracks, &c., are all of great magnitude, and kept in the most perfect order. To the S. of the town is the noted road of Spithead, where the men-of-war anchor when prepared for actual service. Portsmouth has one spacious church. Portsea, built on what was formerly called Portsmouth Common, is now become much larger than the parent town. Here are two chapels belonging to the establishment, and several places of worship for dissenters. Portsmouth is the birthplace of the celebrated philanthropist Jonas Hanway. It is 20 miles S. S. E. of Winchester, and 72 S.W. of London. Long. 1. 6. W. lat. 50. 47. N.

Portsmouth, a town in N. America, the capital of New Hampshire, in Rockingham county, with seven churches. It is the largest town and the only seaport in the state ; seated on the Piscataqua, two miles from the ocean. Its harbour is one of the finest on the continent, well defended by nature, both against storms and an enemy. It is 56 miles N. by E. of Boston. Pop. 7887. Long. 70. 42. W. lat. 43. 5. N.

Portsmouth, a town of Virginia, in Norfolk county, on the W. side of Elizabeth River, opposite Norfolk, from which it is one mile distant. It is 107 miles E. S. E. of Richmond.

Portsmouth, a town of Ohio, capital of Scioto county, on the E. side of the Scioto, at its confluence with the Ohio. It has a court-house, and is the depôt for the merchandise of the settlements of the upper parts of the Sciota. It is 60 miles S. of Chillicothe. Pop. 1117. Long. 83. 8. W. lat. 38. 22. N.

Portsoy, a seaport of Scotland, in Banffshire. The vicinity is celebrated for its minerals, especially for a fine vein of serpentine, called Portsoy marble ; a species of asbestos, of a greenish colour, which has been wrought into an incombustible cloth ; and a brilliant kind of granite, of a flesh colour. Portsoy stands on a point of land projecting into Murray Frith. It is 9 miles W. of Banff.

Portugal, the most western country on the continent of Europe, bounded on the W. and S. by the Atlantic Ocean, and E. and N. by Spain. It extends from 36. 56. to 42. 20. N. lat. and from 6. 25. to 9. 30. W. long., and is divided into the provinces of Entre Douro e Minho, Tras los Montes, Beira, Estremadura, Alentejo, and Algarve. Though Spain and Portugal are in the same climate, yet the air of the latter is much more temperate than that of the former, on account of the neighbourhood of the sea. Agriculture is in a very backward state ; the implements of industry are of the rudest construction, and very little corn is raised. Indian corn, imported from Africa, is used by the peasants instead of wheat. Olives, vineyards, oranges, lemons, nuts, almonds, figs, and raisins are plentiful, and in the low grounds rice and maize are cultivated. The inhabitants also make considerable quantities of salt with the sea water, especially in the bay of St. Ubes, whence a great deal is exported. Their export trade consists of the produce of their own country, and the merchandise which they receive from their foreign possessions, comprising Madeira, Cape Verd Islands, some settlements in Africa, Goa, and Macao ; the latter consists of wine, sugar, tobacco, cotton, indigo, hides, and many excellent drugs. The horses of Portugal were formerly in great esteem ; but they are now so fond of mules, that horses are scarce. Towards the frontiers of Spain there are mountains, in which gold and silver were formerly found ; and the river Tajo was anciently celebrated by the poets for its golden sands. There are also mines of iron, tin, lead, quarries of marble, and some precious stones. The Portuguese are indolent and luxurious. Plays and church festivals, bull-fights, balls, music, &c., engross the whole attention of those who are not compelled to labour for their subsistence. The peasants are in a state of vassalage, and subsist on the hardest fare. In many respects they bear a striking resemblance to the Highlanders of Scotland. The principal rivers are the Tagus, Douro, Guadiana, Mondego, and Caldao. The government is an absolute monarchy. Formerly it had its cortes or representative body, but, from 1697 to the recent revolution, they were never assembled. The established religion is the Roman Catholic ; and there are two archbishops and 13 bishops. Portugal appears to have been known at an early period to the Phœnicians and Carthaginians. It subsequently followed the fortune of Spain, and, after being the scene of various military operations, was finally reduced and constituted a Roman province, under Augustus. The Romans were succeeded by the Goths and other barbarians. The Saracens, or Moors, invaded the peninsula from Africa, and, after the battle of Xeres, A. D. 712, set up several kingdoms, and were not expelled from Portugal till the 13th century. In 1092, Alphonso VI., king of Castile and Leon, made Henry of Burgundy, grandson of Robert king of France, count of Portugal, as a reward for assisting him against the Moors. Alphonso, son of Henry, was the first king. The last of his descendants by the male line dying in 1580, Philip II. of Spain took possession of the throne in right of his mother. The rapacity of the Spanish viceroys was so great, that in 1640 the Portuguese revolted, and made John IV., duke of Braganza, king. His successors were, 1656, Pedro II.; 1706, John V.; 1750, Joseph ; 1777, Pedro III.; 1786, Mary, daughter of Joseph, and widow of Pedro III.; 1816, John VI.; 1826, Pedro IV.; 1828, Miguel I. The family compact, or the agreement of France, Spain, and the Two Sicilies, Parma, and Placentia, to guarantee each others' dominions, was concluded in August, 1761. The first effect of this confederacy was an attempt by France and Spain upon the independence of Portugal, and the Spaniards had not only passed the frontiers, but had actually taken several towns, when, by the aid of Britain, they were repelled, and Portugal was delivered from apparently inevitable destruction. Upon the death of Pedro III. the mental faculties of his widow began to decline, and in 1799 her son assumed the reins of government, as regent. In 1807 the British fleet preserved the royal family from falling into the hands of Bonaparte, and conveyed them to Brazil. Portugal itself, also, after a long and severe contest, was delivered from the French yoke by English armies under the command of the duke of Wellington and other generals. The queen died at Rio Janeiro, March 20, 1816, in the 82d year of her age, and the prince regent became king. At the conclusion of the general peace, the people became discontented, partly through the degradation of the kingdom to the situation of a dependent colony, and partly through the maladministration of the regency. Plot after plot was formed, in which many officers of distinction were implicated, who, as soon as they were detected, were removed, and replaced by British officers. This only served to increase the discontent both of the people and of the army, and to hasten a revolution. Every thing having been previously arranged between the civil and military authorities, a new constitution was announced at Oporto, August 24, 1820, and in September, a council of regency was formed at Lisbon, and letters issued to assemble the cortes. John VI. by a royal decree issued at Rio Janeiro, February, 1821, approved of the constitution, and, leaving his eldest son, Don Pedro, as regent of Brazil, returned to Portugal, and took an oath to maintain the new constitution, July 4, 1821. On the 12th of October, 1822, the Brazilians proclaimed the prince regent constitutional emperor of Brazil, and the independence of that empire has been since acknowledged by the court of Lisbon. On the 30th of April, 1824, Don Miguel, the king's youngest son, general of the army, surrounded with guards the palace of his father, in order to depose him, and to make his nephew regent. The foreign ambassadors discountenanced the conspiracy; the king took refuge on board an English man-of-war; under the protection of Britain he resumed the government, and Don Miguel left the kingdom. John VI. died in March, 1826. As soon as Pedro IV. heard of his father's death, he declared his determination to remain in Brazil, and to abdicate the throne of Portugal in favour of his daughter Donna Maria da Gloria (who was born in 1819), on condition that his brother Don Miguel should marry her, and that a free constitution should be adopted as contained in a charter which he sent over from Brazil. The acceptance of this charter was resisted by the ultra-royalist faction at Lisbon, and a rebellion took place under the direction of the marquis of Chaves. In consequence of the invasion of the kingdom by the rebels, who had mustered their armies in Spain, the sister of Pedro IV., who had by him been appointed regent, claimed the assistance of George IV.; who, in compliance with ancient treaties between the two kingdoms, sent an army to Lisbon in 1827, which checked the rebellion. Don Miguel, who resided at Vienna, returned to Lisbon in the spring of 1828, having first visited Paris and London, at both which places he professed his determination to adhere to the constitution. The English army then retired on board their fleet, having performed all that was required of them by the treaties between the two kingdoms. The professions of Don Miguel soon appeared to be insincere, and on the 30th of June he assumed the title of king of Portugal and Algarve. A weak resistance was made by the garrison and inhabitants of Oporto, but it was soon overcome. He was obliged to relinquish his sovereignty by the troops of his brother Don Pedro, late emperor of Brazil, who, before his death, succeeded in placing his daughter, the Infanta Donna Maria, on the throne. Lisbon is the capital.

Portumna, a town in Ireland; county Galway. It is a great thoroughfare, and is irregularly built; 99 miles from Dublin.

Posados, a town of Spain, in Andalusia; seated on the Guadalquiver; 19 miles S. W. of Cordova.

Posata, a town on the E. coast of the island of Sardinia; 45 miles E. S. E. of Castel Aragonese. Long. 9. 30. E. lat. 40. 36. N.

Posega, a town of Sclavonia; capital of a palatinate of the same name. It was taken from the Turks by the Austrians, in 1687. It is seated near the Orlava; 18 miles N. N. W. of Brod.

Posen, Grand Duchy of, a province of the Prussian states, comprising that part of Poland which was restored to Prussia in 1815. On the E. it is bounded by the new kingdom of Poland, and S. and W. by Silesia and Brandenburg. It is divided into the two governments of Posen and Bromberg, contains about 12,000 square miles, with 800,000 inhabitants, and is watered by the Netz, the Wartha, the Obra, and the Brahe.

Posen, the capital of Prussian Poland, and of the government of the same name, is a bishop's see, and has a university, and a castle on an island on the river Warta. The cathedral is magnificent. The suburbs are extensive, and contain many fine buildings. The river Warta frequently inundates the town, but is very beneficial to its trade with Germany. By the partition of Poland, in 1773, Posen became subject to the king of Prussia. In 1806 it was entered by the French army, under Marshal Davoust, and added to the duchy of Warsaw till 1815, when it was restored to Prussia. It is seated in a pleasant plain; 27 miles W. by S. of Gnesna. Pop. 20,000. Long. 17. 0. E. lat. 52. 24. N.

Posneck, a town of Saxony, in the principality of Altenburg. It has manufactures of cloth and leather. It is seated on the Gams, near its conflux with the Orla; 8 miles N. E. of Saalfeld.

Possession Island, an island in the South Pacific; near the N. point of New Holland. Here Captain Cook hoisted the British colours, and took possession of all the E. or N. E. coast of New Holland, in the name of King George III., which he called New South Wales. Long. 141. 39. E. lat. 10. 33. S.

Possession Island, an uninhabited island in the South Pacific. Long. 141. 40. E. lat. 46. 30. S.

Possinko, a town of Portugal, in Estremadura; 10 miles N. E. of Santarem.

Potenza, a town of Naples, in Basilicata; seated near the source of the Basiento; 11 miles S. by W. of Acerenza.

Potomac, a river of the United States, which rises in the N. W. part of Virginia, and separates that state from Maryland, almost its whole course, till it enters the W. side of Chesapeake Bay. It is navigable for nearly 300 miles.

Potosi, a town of Bolivia; capital of a department of its name. Here are the best silver mines in all America, in a mountain in the form of a sugar-loaf. Silver was as common in this place as iron is in Europe; but the mines are now much exhausted, or at least little is obtained in comparison of what was formerly. The country around is naked and barren. The town is seated at the bottom of the mountain of Potosi; 260 miles W. N. W. of Arica. Pop. 30,000. Long. 67. 30. W. lat. 19. 50. S.

Potosi, San Luis. *See* Luis.

Potsdam, a province of the Prussian states, in Brandenburg; comprehending the districts formerly termed the Ucker Mark, the Mark of Pregnitz, and the greatest part of the Middle Mark. It is bounded N. by Pomerania and W. Prussia, and S. and W. by Saxony. The city of Berlin, with a small district lying around it, forms a distinct government. Potsdam contains an area of about 8000 square miles, with 488,000 inhabitants.

Potsdam, the capital of the foregoing government; situated on an island formed by the rivers Spree and Havel. The public buildings display great magnificence and taste. The royal palace is an admirable structure; and the houses near it are almost all built in the Italian style. In the market-place is a marble obelisk, 75 feet in height; also marble statues of the first four kings of Prussia. The garrison church is large, and has a marble pulpit, under which is the tomb of the Great Frederick, whose remains are enclosed in a wooden coffin, covered with copper, without any ornament or victorious trophies, to recall the memory of his actions. On a hill, near the city, is the royal palace of Sans Souci, which is only one story high, yet remarkable for its grandeur and magnificence. The inhabitants of Potsdam have manufactures of silk, velvet, cotton, linen, &c. It was entered without opposition on the 24th of October, 1805, by the French, who carried away with exultation the sword and scarf worn by the immortal Frederick during the seven years' war. It is 13 miles W. S. W. of Berlin, to which there is a railway. Population, 17,000. Long. 13. 49. E. lat. 52. 52. N.

Potteries, The, a district in Staffordshire, extending about 10 miles in length, and one and a half in breadth. It comprises the towns and villages of Burslem, Hanley, Lane End, Etruria, Stoke-upon-Trent, Tunstall, Longport, Shelton, Brownhills, &c., situated in a part of the country abounding in coal, and clays of great variety in colour and texture, which, together with the great canal intercourse kept up with all parts of the kingdom, furnish a large portion of industry and wealth.

Potton, a town in Bedfordshire, with a market on Saturday; 12 miles E. of Bedford, and 48 N. by W. of London

Pottsgrove, a town of Pennsylvania, on the Schuylkill; 35 miles N. W. of Philadelphia.

Poughkeepsie, a town of New York; capital of Duchess county; with five churches, an academy, &c. Pop. 10,005. It is situate on the E. side of the Hudson; 74 miles N. of New York.

Pougues, a village of France; department of Nievre; noted for its ferruginous mineral spring. It is five miles N. W. of Nevers.

Poulton, a town in Lancashire, with a market on Monday. It is much frequented in the bathing season, and the population is increasing; the parish church is a plain and commodious edifice, erected in 1751, on the site of the old edifice, which had stood nearly 700 years. Here are four places of worship for dissenters, with various schools. It is 18 miles S. W. of Lancaster, and 234 N. N. W. of London.

Pourçayn, St., a town of France; department of Allier; seated on the Sioule; 19 miles S. by W. of Moulins. Pop. 3000.

Poyang-hou, a lake of China; in the N. part of the province of Kiang-si; formed by the confluence of several rivers, which meet here from every point of the compass. It is 250 miles in circumference, and surrounded by a most desolate region.

Pozzuolo. *See* Puzzuoli.

Prabat, a town of the kingdom of Siam; 100 miles N. of Siam. Long. 101. 10. E. lat. 15. 40. N.

Pracels. *See* Paracels.

Prachatitz, a town of Bohemia, in the circle of Prachin; 23 miles S. by W. of Pisek.

Prachin, a mountain of Bohemia, on which formerly stood a castle of the same name. It gives name to a circle on the W. side of the Muldau, of which Pisek is the capital.

Prades, a town of France; department of Eastern Pyrenees; seated in a fine plain, on the river Tet; 24 miles W. S W. of Perpignan.

Prades, a town of Spain, in Catalonia; near which is a magnificent abbey, where the ancient kings of Arragon were interred. It is 39 miles N. W. of Barcelona.

Praga, a town of Poland, on the Vistula; opposite Warsaw, of which it is considered as a suburb.

Pragilas, a town of the Sardinian states, in Piedmont; 7 miles W. of Turin.

Prague, the capital of Bohemia, and formerly an archiepiscopal see. It comprehends four towns, the Old, New, and Little Town, and the Hradschin. It is 15 miles in circumference, is built upon seven hills, and contains 85,000 inhabitants. The Muldau runs through the city, separating the Old Town from the New; and over it is a bridge of 18 arches, with a strong tower at each end. The Old Town is very populous; the houses are high, and the streets narrow. In this part are the remains of a palace, where the ancient kings resided; but the finest ornament is the university, frequented by a great number of students: here also is a magnificent college, formerly belonging to the Jesuits; and the Jews have nine synagogues, and are about 7000 in number. The New Town contains fine structures, handsome gardens, and large streets; also an arsenal, and a secular foundation, whose abbess was a princess of the empire. The Little Town, which is the most ancient part of Prague, has broad streets, and is very populous. The Hradschin once belonged to the Little Town, but, in 1756, it was made the fourth town of Prague. Its principal buildings are the royal palace, in which is a hall, 100 paces long and 40 broad, without any pillar to support the roof; the cathedral of St. Veit, containing the burial place of the kings, and many relics; the chapel of Our Lady of Loretto; the magnificent archiepiscopal palace; and the large palace of Tschernin. Prague has suffered frequent devastations by war. The White Mountain, without the gate of Strahow, is celebrated for the victory gained in 1620, by the Austrians, over Frederic V., the elector palatine, whom the Bohemians had chosen for their king. In 1631 Prague was taken by the Saxons; and by the Swedes in 1648. It was taken by storm in 1741 by the French, who were obliged to leave it in 1742. In 1757 it was besieged by the king of Prussia, after a great victory, obtained near this city, over the Austrians; but the defeat at Kollin obliged him to raise the siege. It is 75 miles S. E. of Dresden. Long. 14. 30. E. lat. 50. 6. N.

Prasto, a small town of Greece, in the Morea; situate to the W. of the Gulf of Napoli; 16 miles N. by E. of Misitra.

Prato, a town of Tuscany; with a citadel, and a handsome cathedral built of marble. Pop. 10,500. It is 10 miles N. W. of Florence.

Prats de Molo, a fortified town of France, department of Eastern Pyrenees; on the Tet; 29 miles S. W. of Perpignan. Pop. 3000.

Prausnitz, a town and castle of Prussian Silesia. It has a fine church, containing the tombs of the counts of Hatzfeld. It is 18 miles N. of Breslau.

Praya. *See* Porto Praya.

Precop, or Perecop, a town and fortress of Russia, in the government of Catharinenslaf, and province of Taurida; seated on the isthmus that joins the Crimea to the continent. A deep trench, four miles in length, is cut across the isthmus, over which is a bridge, and upon that a vaulted gate, called the Golden Gate of the Tartars. Pop. 1200. Long. 35. 34. E. lat. 46. 8. N.

Precopia, a town of Servia, on the river Morave; 20 miles W. of Nissa. Pop. 6000.

Pregel, a river of East Prussia, which issues from the lake Augerburg, and flowing by Insterburg, Welau, and Konigsberg, enters the eastern extremity of the Frisch Haff.

Premislau, a town of Poland, with a strong castle, and a Greek and Latin bishop's see; seated on the Sana; 60 miles W. by S. of Lemburg. Long. 21. 0. E. lat. 49. 0. N.

Prenzlo, a town of Brandenburg, capital of what was formerly called the Ucker Mark. It contains six churches, and has a brisk trade in corn, tobacco, and cattle. Seated on the lake and river Ucker; 58 miles N. N. E. of Berlin. Pop. 8000. Long. 13. 55. E. lat. 53. 19. N.

Prerau, a town of Moravia, capital of a circle of the same name. It is seated on the Beczwa; 13 miles S. E. of Olmutz. Long. 17. 29. E. lat. 49. 23. N. Pop. 2300.

Presburg, a city of Hungary. It is seated on the Danube, which is here very rapid, and about 250 yards in breadth. The inhabitants are estimated at 30,000. Its castle, a noble Gothic structure, was burnt down in the commencement of the present century. This town was declared by a royal decree of 1536 the capital of Hungary, on account of its vicinity to Vienna, and the sovereigns are still crowned in its cathedral; but the principal officers of government reside at Buda, and the diets and supreme courts of judicature meet at Pesth. In December, 1805, a treaty of peace was concluded here between Austria and France; 38 miles E. by S. of Vienna, and 95 W. N. W. of Buda. Long. 17. 9. E. lat. 48. 9. N.

Prescot, a town in Lancashire, with markets on Tuesday and Saturday. It is a long straggling town, and may be said to be almost built over coal-pits, several being worked close to its extremities. The parish church is a spacious edifice, dedicated to St. Mary. In the chancel is a large upright figure of John Ogle, one of the captains who defended Lathom House. The dissenters have places of worship, with various schools; and here is a free-school, established at an early period by the township. At the east entrance of the town are several almshouses, erected in 1708, by Oliver Lyme. It is estimated that 2000 persons are employed in the collieries of Prescot, whence Liverpool is chiefly supplied with fuel by the railway, which passes about a mile from this town. Here are manufactures of watch-movements, pinion wire, small files, and coarse earthenware; and also some manufactories of cotton, hats, &c.; 8 miles E. of Liverpool, and 197 N. N. W. of London.

Presenzano, a town of Naples, in Terra di Lavoro. It appears, by an inscription, to be the ancient Rufæ, and its territory has the name of Costa Rufraria. It is 28 miles N. of Naples.

Presteign, a town of Wales, in Radnorshire, with a market on Saturday. It may be deemed the modern capital of the county, for here the assizes are held, and in it is the county gaol. The site of its castle is now laid out in public walks. It is seated near the source of the Lug, in a rich valley; 23 miles N. N. W. of Hereford, and 151 N. N. W. of London. Long. 2. 58. W. lat. 52. 15. N.

Prestima, a town of Portugal, in Beira; 11 miles N. of Coimbra.

Presto, a seaport of Denmark, in Zealand, with a good harbour in a bay of the Baltic; 42 miles S. S. W. of Copenhagen. Long. 12. 6. E. lat. 55. 9. N.

Preston, a borough in Lancashire, governed by a mayor; with markets on Wednesday, Friday, and Saturday. It returns two members to parliament. Here is a court of chancery, with other offices of justice, for the county palatine of Lancaster. The chief manufactures are the various branches of cotton and muslin, which are now carried on to a considerable extent. Here are five churches, two catholic chapels, eight meeting-houses for dissenters, and several schools and other charitable institutions. It is noted for the defeat of the Pretender's adherents in 1715, when most of them were made prisoners; also for a kind of public carnival, or jubilee, held every 20 years, the last of which was in 1822. It is seated near the Ribble and the Lancaster Canal; 22 miles S. S. E. of Lancaster, and 217 N. N. W. of London. Long. 2. 53. W. lat. 53. 46. N.

Prestonpans, a town of Scotland, in Haddingtonshire, with a safe harbour, called Morison's Haven, on the Frith of Forth. It has manufactures of salt, and a considerable oyster fishery. At this place the royal army was defeated by the Pretender's adherents, in 1745; 8 miles E. of Edinburgh.

Pretsch, a town of Prussian Saxony, with a fine castle, seated on the Elbe; 10 miles S. of Witte berg.

Prettin, a town of Saxony, on the Elbe; 18 miles S. by E. of Wittenberg.

Prevesa, a town of Greece, in Albania, and a bishop's see. It stands on the ruins of the ancient Nicopolis, built by the emperor Augustus, in memory of his victory over Antony. It was taken by the Venetians in 1684, was ceded to the Turks in 1718, taken by the French in 1798, and retaken the following year by the Turks, in whose hands it remained till the recent liberation of Greece. It is seated on a mountain, on the Gulf of Larta; 70 miles N. W. of Lepanto. Pop. 8000. Long. 21. 5. E. lat. 39. 14. N.

Preuilly, a town of France, department of Indre et Loire. Near it are mines of iron. It stands on the Claise; 18 miles S. of Loches.

Priaman, a town on the west coast of the island of Sumatra, where the Dutch had formerly a factory. The environs produce but little pepper; but the air is healthy. It stands on a small river, in which gold is found. The English East India Company formed a settlement here in 1685. Long. 98. 0. E. lat. 1. 0. S.

Primkenuu, a town of Prussian Silesia, in the government of Leignitz; with an iron forge, and a manufacture of paper; 16 miles S. W. of Glogau.

Prince Edward Island. See John, St.

Prince Frederic, a town of Maryland, chief of Calvert county; 35 miles S. E. of Washington.

Prince of Wales Cape, the north-western extremity of America; discovered by Captain Cook in 1778. It is on the side of Behring Strait.

Prince of Wales Fort, the most northern settlement of the Hudson Bay Company, on the W. side of Hudson Bay, at the mouth of Churchill River. Long. 94. 7. W. lat. 58. 47. N.

Prince of Wales Island, or Pulo-Penang, an island two miles from the W. coast of Malacca, 18 miles long, and 8 broad, divided longitudinally by a ridge of mountains. The channel to the mainland is a safe road for ships. This island was purchased of the king of Queda by the English East India Company, who formed a settlement here in 1786; and, in five years after, Georgetown, its capital, was established as a seaport. The inhabitants were estimated, in 1805, at 14,000, since which time they have considerably increased. Long. 98. 50. E. lat. 5. 36. N.

Prince William Henry's Island, an island in the Eastern Ocean, lying W. N. W. of Tench Island. It is pretty high, well wooded, and about 70 miles in circuit. The population is estimated at 50,000. It was discovered by Lieutenant Ball in 1790, and a high mountain in the centre was called Mount Philip. Long. 149. 30. E. lat. 1. 32 S.—Also, the name of an island in the Pacific Ocean; discovered by Captain Wallis, in 1767. Long. 141. 6. W. lat. 17. 0. S.

Prince William Sound, a gulf on the N. W. coast of America, discovered by Cook in 1778, and visited and explored by Vancouver in 1794. Long. 147. 21. W. lat. 59. 33. N.

Prince's Island, an island near the west coast of Guinea; 90 miles in circumference; discovered by the Portuguese in 1471. It is elevated and fertile, and has a town on the N. part, with a good harbour. Long. 7. 40. E. lat. 1. 40. N.

Prince's Island, a small island in the Indian Ocean, near the W. entrance of the strait of Sunda. It is visited by European ships for wood and water. Long. 104. 30. E. lat 6. 15. S.

Prince's Islands, four small islands in the Sea of Marmora, near the strait of Constantinople, called Prinkipo, Prote, Kalke, and Antigone. The first is the largest, and has a town containing above 2000 inhabitants. Long. 28. 56. E. lat. 40. 51. N.

Princess Ann, a town of Maryland, in Somerset county; situate on Chesapeake Bay, on the E. side of the Monokin river; 25 miles W. S. W. of Salisbury.

Princeton, a town of New Jersey, in Middlesex county. Here was a college called Nassau Hall, which was burnt down in 1802. It is 12 miles N. E. of Trenton, and 18 S. W. of Brunswick.

Princeton, a town of North Carolina, in Gates county; situate on the Meherrin; 3 miles above Murfreesborough, and 28 E. N. E. of Halifax.

Principato, a province of Naples, divided into Principato Citra and Ultra; that is, the Further and Hither Principato. The former is 60 miles long, and 30 broad; the soil is fertile in wine, corn, oil, and saffron; and it has a great deal of silk, and several mineral springs. Area, 2400 square miles. Pop. 503,000. Salerno is the capital. Principato Ultra is 37 miles long, and 30 broad; the soil is not fertile in corn or wine, but it produces chestnuts, and has excellent pastures. Area, 1800 square miles. Avellino is the capital.

Pristina, a town of Romania, and a bishop's see, which was pillaged by the Austrians in

1689. It is seated on the Rusca; 150 miles S. by E. of Belgrade. Long. 21. 36. E. lat. 42. 43. N.

PRITZWALK, a town of Prussia, in Brandenburg, seated on the Domnitz; 13 miles E. N. E. of Perleberg.

PRIVAS, a town of France, capital of the department of Ardeche. It is seated on a hill, near the confluence of three small rivers; 68 miles S. of Lyons. Pop. 3000. Long. 4. 36. E. lat. 44. 45. N.

PROCIDA, an island in the Gulf of Naples, near that of Ischia; 8 miles in circumference, and very fertile and populous. The capital, of the same name, is a small fortified place, on a high craggy rock, by the sea side. Pop. 12,000. Long. 14. 8. E. lat. 40. 43. N.

PRODANO, an island in the Mediterranean, near the W. coast of the Morea, formerly called Sphacteria. It is 36 miles S. S. E. of Zante. Long. 21. 24. E. lat. 37. 15. N.

PROME, a city of Birmah, province of Ava. It was formerly more considerable, having been greatly reduced by frequent wars, but has attained something of its former magnitude. Much teak timber is sent hence to Rangoon. It is seated on the Irrawaddy; 120 miles N. W. of Pegu. Long. 95. 0. E. lat. 18. 50. N.

PROSPECT, a town of the state of Maine, in Hancock county, on the W. side of Penobscot River; 12 miles N. N. E, of Belfast. Pop. 2381.

PROSPEROUS, a village of Ireland, in the county of Kildare; 16 miles S. W. of Dublin. It has a considerable manufacture of cotton.

PROSNITZ, a town of Moravia, in the circle of Olmutz; 8 miles S. S. W. of Olmutz. Pop. 7000.

PROVENCE, a former province of France, which now forms the departments of Var, Lower Alps, and Mouths of the Rhone.

PROVIDENCE, one of the Bahama islands, and the best of those planted by the English. It was taken by the Spaniards in 1782, but retaken the next year. A lighthouse was erected in 1804, on an eminence overlooking Nassau, the chief town. Pop. 5090. Long. 77. 20. W. lat. 25. 3. N.

PROVIDENCE, an island in the Atlantic, which the bucanneers fortified, but afterwards abandoned. It is 150 miles E. of the coast of Nicaragua. Long. 80. 44. W. lat. 13. 25. N.

PROVIDENCE, a river that rises in the state of Massachusets, and waters the town of Providence, whence it is navigable for ships to Narraganset Bay, which it enters on the W. side of Rhode Island.

PROVIDENCE, the oldest town of the state of Rhode Island; chief of a county of its name, and the semi-capital of the state. It has several manufactures, and a large foreign and inland trade. Here are eight edifices for public worship; a handsome court-house, in which is a library for the use of the town and county; and a flourishing seminary, called Rhode Island College. Providence is seated on both sides of the river of the same name; 30 miles N. W. of Newport. Pop. 23,171. Long. 71. 26. W. lat. 41. 51. N.

PROVINCETOWN, a town of Massachusets, in Barnstable county; situate on the hook of Cape Cod. Its harbour is one of the best in the state, and was the first port entered by the English in 1620, when they came to settle in New England. The houses are only one story high, and set upon piles, that the driving sands may pass under them. The inhabitants are wholly dependent on Boston and the towns in the vicinity for every vegetable production; 50 miles E. S. E. of Boston.

PROVINS, a town of France, in the department of Seine et Marne; celebrated for its mineral waters. It has a considerable trade in corn, and some woollen manufactures, and is seated on the Vouzie; 60 miles S. E. of Paris.

PRUCK. *See* BRUCK.

PRUSSIA, a large country of Europe, occupying a great part of the N. of Germany, and extending, with little interruption, from the confines of Lithuania to those of the Netherlands. It is a very fertile country, producing a great deal of flax, hemp, and corn. There are a great number of domestic animals; and the sea, the rivers, and lakes, supply abundance of fish. Game abounds; and elks, wild asses, and uri, are found in the forests: these last are of a huge size, and have some resemblance to beeves; their hides are extremely thick and strong, and they are sold to foreigners at a great price. One of the most remarkable productions of this country is yellow amber, which is found along the seacoast. There are two large lakes, besides the rivers Vistula and Pregel. The inhabitants are generally of a good constitution, laborious, and robust. There are a great number of mechanics; but the principal business is husbandry, with the feeding of cattle. In the 13th century Prussia belonged to the knights of the Teutonic order. In 1454 that part since denominated Polish, or West Prussia, revolted to Casimir IV., king of Poland, and was incorporated into the dominions of the republic. At the same time the knights were constrained to hold the remaining part, called Ducal or East Prussia, as a fief of the crown of Poland. In 1525 Albert, the grand master, betrayed the interests of his fraternity, and concluded a treaty with Sigismund, king of Poland, by which East Prussia was erected into an hereditary duchy, and given him as a Polish fief. Having adopted the tenets of Luther, he married a princess of Denmark, and transmitted this rich inheritance to his descendants; one of whom, Frederic William, was the duke that threw off his dependence on Poland. The foundation of the Prussian monarchy was established by him, between 1640 and 1688. His son and successor, Frederic, in 1701 assumed the title of King of Prussia, which was soon after acknowledged by all the Christian powers, except Poland, which did not acknowledge it till 1764. In 1742 Frederic II. acquired the duchy of Silesia from the house of Austria; and by his wonderful victories, and the still more wonderful resources by which he repaired occasional defeats, he became the admiration of the age. In 1772 he compelled the Poles to cede to him Western Prussia, excepting the cities of Dantzic and Thorn. He cultivated the arts of peace as well as war, distinguishing himself as a poet, philosopher, and legislator, and expending large sums in the improvement of the country. He was succeeded by his nephew, Frederic William II., in 1786, who forcibly annexed to his kingdom Dantzic and Thorn, with several considerable provinces, which he styled Southern Prussia. He had also a share in the general contest against France, in the early part of the revolution; but made peace with that country in April, 1795; and died at Berlin in 1797. His son, Frederic William III., continued on amicable terms with France, till the dissolution of the Germanic body in 1806, and the consequent formation of the Confederation of the Rhine; when, thinking himself aggrieved, he declared war against France. This war was of short duration, but of most disastrous consequences to Prussia. By the peace of Tilsit, the whole of the Polish dominions belonging to Prussia, with a few exceptions noticed under the article Poland, were transferred to another prince; and the king of Prussia had further to renounce his right to all the territories, without exception, situated between the Elbe and the Rhine; to those belonging to Saxony and the house of Anhalt on the right bank of the Elbe; and, lastly, to the circle of Rothus, in Lower Lusatia, which was ceded to Saxony. Thus was Prussia reduced to the lowest rank among the powers of Europe; an event solely owing to her acquiescence in the projects and policy of France against Austria, and her absurd system of neutrality during those great political contests, by which she hoped to raise herself to the rank of the first power in Germany, while she was in fact degraded to a situation among the weakest of the weak. On the memorable retreat of the French armies from Russia, and the arrival of the Russians within the territories of Prussia, she, however, threw off her alliance with France, joined Russia in the war, and made such extraordinary efforts to retrieve her lost character, by the magnitude of her armies and the courage which she maintained in the field, that, on the conclusion of the war, all the countries which had been wrested from her by the treaty of Tilsit were restored. The kingdom is now divided into 10 provinces, namely East Prussia, West Prussia, Brandenburg, Pomerania, Westphalia, Cleves and Berg, Silesia, Posen, Saxony, and Lower Rhine; which are subdivided into 28 governments. For military purposes, the kingdom is divided into five great parts, viz., Prussia, Brandenburg and Pomerania, Silesia and Prussian Poland, Saxony, and, finally, Westphalia with the Lower Rhine. Area, 115,795 square miles. Population, 12,552,278. Berlin is the capital of all Prussia.

Prussia Proper, an extensive division of the Prussian states, between the northern frontier of Poland and the Baltic. It comprises the provinces of East and West Prussia, divided formerly by the Vistula, and now by a line a few miles to the E. of that river. East Prussia lies between 19. 20. and 24. 15. of E. long., and 52. 32. and 56. 3. of N. lat., and has a superficial extent of 16,146 square miles, with 1,000,000 inhabitants. It is divided into the governments of Konigsberg and Gumbinnen. West Prussia is a less extensive country, its area being 10,695 square miles, its population 590,000. It is divided into the governments of Dantzic and Marienwerder.

Pruth, a river that rises in Marmarosch, in Hungary, crosses part of the palatinate of Lemburg, flows through Moldavia, and enters the Danube above Reni, in Bessarabia.

Pruym, a town of the Prussian province of Lower Rhine, with a princely abbey, seated on the river Pruym; 30 miles S. S. E. of Aix-la-Chapelle.

Przesmislia, a town of Austrian Poland, capital of a circle of its name; with a castle seated on the river San; 54 miles W. by S. of Lemberg. Pop. 7400.

Przibram, a town of Bohemia, in the circle of Beraun; with a siver mine, and an iron-foundry; seated near the river Muldau; 28 miles S. S. W. of Prague.

Pskof, a government of Russia, lying between those of Livonia and Smolensko. It comprises an area of 22,000 square miles, with 700,000 inhabitants.

Pskof, the capital of the above government, and an archbishop's see; with a strong castle. It is seated on the river Welika, at its entrance into the lake Tchudskoi; 80 miles S. of Narva, and 170 S. by W. of Petersburg. Pop. 7000. Long. 27. 52. E. lat. 57. 38. N.

Pucculoe, a town of Bengal, 40 miles N. W. of Dacca.

Puckholi, a town of Hindostan, in the province of Lahore; 86 miles S. W. of Cashmere, and 145 N. W. of Lahore. Long. 75. 5. E. lat. 33. 45. N.

Pudda, a river of Hindostan, which rises in the S. W. part of Agimere, divides the provinces of Cutch and Guzerat, and runs into the Gulf of Cutch.

Pudoga, a town of Russia, in the government of Olonetz; situate on the E. coast of the Lake of Onezkoe; 108 miles E. of Olonetz. Long. 36. 30. E. lat. 61. 36. N.

Puebla, a town of Spain, in Galicia; seated near the Atlantic; 29 miles S. S. W. of Compostella.

Puebla de los Angelos, a city of Mexico, capital of a province of its name. The streets are broad and straight, and the buildings, in general of stone, lofty and elegant. In the centre of the city is a large square, adorned on three sides with uniform porticoes, where are shops filled with rich commodities, and, on the other, with the cathedral, which has a beautiful front, and two lofty towers. Besides the cathedral, there are several other churches and convents, well built and finely adorned. A small river runs through the town, and the adjacent valley produces vines and all sorts of European fruits. It is 80 miles E. S. E. of Mexico. Population of the province, 1,303,000; of the town, 100,000. Long. 99. 22. W. lat. 19. 30. N.

PUEBLA NUEVA, a town of Mexico, in the province of Veragua; seated near the Pacific Ocean; 100 miles W. of St. Jago. Long. 83. 0. W. lat. 8. 34. N.

PUEBLA DE SANABRIA, a town of Spain, in the province of Leon; 45 miles S. W. of Astorga.

PUENTE, a town of Spain, in Navarre, on the river Agra; 8 miles S. S W. of Pamplona.

PUERTO BELLA, PUERTO RICO, &c. *See* PORTO.

PUGLIA, the ancient Apulia, containing the three provinces of Capitanata, Bari, and Otranto; on the E. side of the kingdom of Naples.

PULHELY, or PWLLHELI, a town of Wales, in Caernarvonshire; with a market on Wednesday; seated on an inlet of Cardigan Bay, between two rivers; 16 miles S. of Caernarvon, and 243 N. W. of London.

PULO CONDORE, *see* CONDORE; and so with other islands that have sometimes Pulo (island) prefixed.

PULLICATE, a town of Hindostan, in the Carnatic; on the seacoast, and at the S. end of a large lake to which it gives name; 23 miles N. of Madras.

PULTENEYTOWN, a suburb of the royal burgh of Wick, in Caithness-shire; which it outvies in extent and architecture; and is the principal seat of its fisheries and trade.

PULTOUSK, a town in the interior of Poland, where in 1807 a battle was fought between the French and Russians, in which both sides claimed the victory. It is seated on the Narew; 30 miles N. of Warsaw.

PULTOWA. *See* POLTAVA.

PUNA, an island in the Pacific Ocean; 35 miles long, and 12 broad; lying at the entrance of the bay of Guayaquil. It has an Indian town, of the same name, on its S. side. It is 115 miles N. of Paita.

PUNHETE, a town of Portugal, in Estremadura; at the conflux of the Zezere with the Tajo; 6 miles N. W. of Abrantes.

PUNJAUB, or PUNJAB, a territory on the N. W. frontier of India; comprised between the Indus, on the W., and Sutlej River, on the E. Its name signifies "the country of five waters," from the number of the rivers which intersect it, and which all fall into the Indus. It is the country of the Sikhs, an extraordinary sect of India, combining the principles of Hindooism and Mahometanism. It was founded in the 15th century, and first became powerful in the last century, when they favoured the Mahrattas; but, on the downfall of that nation, their sacred city, Umritzir, was entirely destroyed; they, however, quickly recovered, and Runjeet Singh, one of their governors, took possession of the whole kingdom of Lahore, or the Punjaub, which he retained until his death, and was succeeded by his son, who was soon deposed in favour of his grandson, who was unpopular; which renders it not improbable that it may fall into the hands of the British ultimately. Lahore is the capital. As a frontier country, this is of great importance, as it is the only side from which it can be menaced with invasion; and, were the Russians to advance to the Indus, their success would depend chiefly on their having the Sikhs for enemies or allies; and to the British it is doubly important, as it lies between their territory and that of their new ally, in Cabul.

PUNTA DEL GUDA, the capital of St. Michael, one of the Azores, with a strong castle. It is situate on the S. side, and contains 10,000 inhabitants. The streets are regular and of convenient width; and the churches, religious houses, and public edifices, may be deemed elegant. There is no harbour in the vicinity of the town, and vessels usually anchor at a distance from the shore, in an open road. Long. 25. 42. W. lat. 37. 47. N.

PURBECK, ISLE OF, a rough and heathy tract in Dorsetshire, to the S. of Poole Bay. It is insulated by the sea and rivers, and is famous for its stone quarries, the principal part of which lie at its eastern extremity, near Swanage, whence the stone is exported; it is of the calcareous kind, but distinguished into numerous sorts, the finest of which deserves the name of marble, and is used for chimney-pieces, hearths, &c.; while the coarser kinds are made use of in paving. Tobacco-pipe clay is dug up in several parts of the island, the finest near Corfe Castle, of which much is exported, particularly for the Staffordshire potteries.

PURCHENA, a town of Spain, in the province of Granada; 70 miles E. of Granada. Long. 2. 25. W. lat. 37. 19. N.

PURFLEET, a village in Essex, situate on the Thames; 4 miles W. of Grays-Thurrock. It has extensive lime-works, and a large magazine for gunpowder.

PURIFICATION, a town of Mexico, in the province of Xalisco; 90 miles S. by E. of Compostella. Long. 105. 30. W. lat. 19. 58. N.

PURMEREND, a strong town of the Netherlands, in N. Holland. It is 10 miles N. by E. of Amsterdam.

PURNEAH, a town of Bengal, capital of a fertile and populous district of its name; seated on the Seraw; 125 miles N. N. W. of Moorshedabad.

PURYSBURG, a town of S. Carolina, in Beaufort district; built by a colony of Swiss, with a view to the culture of silk. It is seated on the river Savanna; 20 miles N. N. W. of the town of Savanna. Long. 81. 5. W. lat. 32. 12. N.

PUSCHIAVO, a town of Switzerland, in the canton of Grisons; 3 miles N. from a lake to which it gives name. It is 17 miles W. S. W. of Bormio, and 20 E. of Chiavenna.

PUTALA, or PATELI, a mountain of Tibet, near the banks of the Burrampooter; 7 miles E. of Lassa. On its summit is the palace of the grand lama, the high priest of Tibet.

PUTLITZ, a town of Prussia, in the province

of Brandenburg, with an old castle; 11 miles N. N. E. of Perleberg.

PUTNEY, a village in Surrey, seated on the Thames, over which is a wooden bridge; 4 miles W. S. W. of London. It was the birthplace of Thomas Cromwell, earl of Essex, whose father was a blacksmith; and of Nicholas West, bishop of Ely, his contemporary, a great statesman, whose father was a baker; and of Gibbon the Roman historian.

PUTTAN SOMNAUTH, or PUTTAN, a town of Hindostan, near the southern extremity of the Guzerat peninsula. Somnauth is one of the twelve images of Seeb, which are said to have descended from heaven to earth; and the great fame of its temple attracted the cupidity, while it stimulated the bigotry of Sultan Mahmood, of Ghizni. According to Mahomedan authors, the image was destroyed, but the Hindoos assert that the god retired into the ocean. The symbol placed in the temple is deemed peculiarly propitious to those who desire offspring. It is visited by pilgrims from every quarter, who pay a trifling duty to the nabob for permission to perform their devotions at this favourite shrine. The Bombay Presidency is stated to have used its influence with the Junaghar State, in 1816, to secure greater freedom of pilgrimage to Puttan. It stands near the sea; 95 miles S. of Noanagur. Long. 69. 40. E. lat. 21. 2. N.

PUY, a city of France, capital of the department of Upper Loire, and a bishop's see. The cathedral is famous for a prodigious quantity of relics; and Our Lady of Puy is celebrated in the annals of superstition. Puy has manufactures of blankets, linen, lace, silk stuffs, and stoneware. It is seated on the mountain Anis, near the river Loire; 45 miles N. E. of Mende, and 65 S. E. of Clermont. Pop. 12,000. Long. 3. 58. E. lat. 45. 58. N.

PUY DE DOME, a department of France; containing part of the former province of Auvergne. It has its name from a mountain, situate to the W. of Clermont, the capital of the department. Pop. 566,000.

PUY EN ANJOU, a town in the department of Maine-et-Loire. It is 10 miles S. S. W. of Saumur.

PUY L'EVEQUE, a town in the department of Lot; 16 miles W. by N. of Cahors.

PUY LA ROQUE, a town in the department of Tarn-et-Garonne; 18 miles S. S. E. of Cahors.

PUY MOISSON, a town in the department of Lower Alps; 15 miles S. of Digne.

PUYCERDA, a town of Spain, in Catalonia, capital of the county of Cerdagna; seated at the foot of the Pyrenees, near the source of the Segra; 48 miles W. by S. of Perpignan, and 78 N. by W. of Barcelona. It was taken by the French in 1794. Long. 1. 50. E. lat. 42. 36. N.

PUYLAURENS, a town of France, department of Tarn; 28 miles S. by W. of Alby.

PUZZUOLI, or POZZUOLO, a celebrated, but now inconsiderable city of Italy, on the Bay of Naples. Here are the remains of the temple of Jupiter Serapis, an interesting monument of antiquity, being different from the Roman and Greek temples, and built in the manner of the Asiatics; probably by the Egyptian and Asiatic merchants settled at Puzzuoli, which was the great emporium of Italy, till the Romans built Ostia and Antium. It has been converted into a Christian cathedral, and so much modern work added, that at present only the front of the ancient edifice is visible. Many other remains of temples, amphitheatres, and other public buildings in this city, afford convincing proofs of its former magnificence. The ruins of Cicero's villa, near this place, are of such extent as to give a high idea of the wealth of that great orator. It is 9 miles W. of Naples.

PYRAMIDS, a range of ancient and stupendous Egyptian monuments, extending northward from Cairo for about 20 leagues; but on the opposite side of the river.

PYRBAUM, a town of Bavaria, capital of a lordship of its name; situate on the frontiers of Franconia; 13 miles S. E. of Nuremburg.

PYRENEES, a range of mountains which divides France from Spain, and the most celebrated in Europe, except the Alps. They reach from the Mediterranean to the Atlantic, about 212 miles in length, and have different names, according to their different situations. The passages over them are not so difficult as those of the Alps. One of the most frequented is that from Pampeluna to St. Jean de Pied de Fort, by which the French under Soult marched to attack the British before Pampeluna, in July 1813. These mountains contain iron, copper, lead, silver, gold, cobalt, and zinc; they also furnish great quantities of timber, for ship-building, and an abundance of pitch and tar. The highest summits are Nethon, 10,722 feet, Mont Perdu, 10,576 feet, and Pic du Midi, 8958 feet; at the height of 7200 feet, snow is perpetual. *See* PERDU, MOUNT.

PYRENEES, EASTERN, a department of France, containing the provinces of Roussillon, Cerdagne, and part of Languedoc. Its area is estimated at 1650 square miles, and the population at 151,500. Although great part of the country is mountainous, yet it is fertile in corn, excellent wine, olives, oranges, &c. Perpignan is the capital.

PYRENEES, LOWER, a department of France, comprehending the provinces of Bearn and Navarre. The principal products are corn, wine, flax, chestnuts and other fruits; the manufactures woollen, linen, leather, and recently cotton. The province contains an area of about 3000 square miles, with 383,000 inhabitants. Pau is the capital.

PYRENEES UPPER, a department of France, including the province of Bigorre, and comprising an area of 1800 square miles, with 200,000 inhabitants. Here are excellent horses, and good partridges. The valleys are very fertile, furnishing rye, millet, Spanish corn, and flax. The mountains have mines of lead, iron, and copper, and quarries of slate, marble, and jasper. Tarbes is the capital.

PYRMONT, a town of the N. W. part of Germany, capital of a small district of the same name, belonging to the prince of Waldeck. Near it are mineral waters, well known to all Europe, and frequented by persons of the highest rank. It is seated in a delightful valley, between high mountains, 38 miles S. W of Hanover. Pop. 2000. Long. 9. 20. E. lat. 51. 57. N.

PYSTEIN, a town of Bavaria, in the principality of Passau, insulated in Austria. It is 10 miles N. W. of Lintz, and 22. E. of Passau.

Q

QUACKENBRUCK, a town of Hanover, in the principality of Osnaburg, seated on the Hase; 28 miles N. of Osnaburg.

QUADRA AND VANCOUVER'S ISLAND, an island on the N. W. coast of America, on the S. W. side of which is Nootka Sound. It was so named by Captain Vancouver, in compliment to Senor Quadra, the Spanish commandant at Nootka. It is about 300 miles in length, and 80 in its greatest breadth.

QUADRELLO, a town of Naples, in Terra di Lavoro; 20 miles E. N. E. of Naples.

QUANG-PING, a city of China, of the first rank, in the province of Pe-tche-li; 212 miles S. S. E. of Peking. Long. 114. 30. E. lat. 36. 47. N.

QUANG-SI, an inland province in the S. of China. It produces plenty of rice, being watered by several large rivers. The southern part is a flat country, and well cultivated; but the northern is full of mountains, covered with trees. It contains mines of all sorts, and particularly a gold mine. Here is a tree called quang-lang, the pith of which is made into bread; and a small species of insect, which produces white wax. Quei-ling is the capital.

QUANG-TONG, a province of China, bounded on the E. by Kiang-si and Fo-kien, on the S. by the ocean, and on the W. by Tonquin. It is diversified by valleys and mountains, and yields two crops of corn in a year. The northern frontier consists of a range of lofty mountains, which abound in gold, jewels, tin, quicksilver, copper, and iron; ebony and several sorts of odoriferous wood are produced in this province, as well as various sorts of fruit. There is a species of lemon as large as a man's head; and another sort which grows out at the trunk of the tree, whose rind is very hard, and contains a great number of little cells, full of an excellent yellow pulp. A prodigious number of ducks are bred in this province, their eggs being hatched in ovens. The mountains are covered with a kind of osiers, which creep along the ground, and are so tough that they make baskets, hurdles, mats, and even ropes of them. Here is also a tree, the timber of which is remarkably hard and heavy, and is thence called ironwood. Canton is the capital, but the viceroy resides at Chao-king.

QUANGTONG, a town on the N. borders of Birmah; in the province of Ava, with a fort, seated on the Irrawaddy; 150 miles N. N. E. of Ummerapoora.

QUARITZ, a town of Prussian Silesia, in the government of Leignitz; 10 miles W. S. W. of Glogau.

QUARRE, a town of France, department of Yonne; 6 miles S. of Avallon.

QUARTO, two towns of Naples, in Capitanata; the one 6 miles W. and the other 12 S. W. of Salpes.

QUARTEN, a town of Switzerland, near Wallenstadt Lake; 5 miles E. of Glaris.

QUATRE BRAS, a hamlet of the Netherlands; which was the scene of an obstinate conflict between the British and the French, on the 16th of June, 1815.

QUEAUX, a town of France, department of Vienne; 21 miles S. E. of Poitiers.

QUEBEC, the capital of Canada, and of British America, is situated at the confluence of the rivers St. Lawrence and St. Charles, (or the Little River,) about 320 miles from the sea. It is built on a rock, which is partly of marble and partly of slate, and is divided into Upper and Lower. Near it is a fine lead mine. At the time it was founded on the site of the Indian village of Hochelaga, in 1608, the tide, it is said, reached the foot of the rock; but since that period, this river has sunk so far that a large spot of ground is left dry, and on this an extensive suburb is built, styled the Lower Town, which stands at the foot of a rocky precipice, about 48 feet in height, and is chiefly inhabited by merchants. The houses in both towns are of stone, strong and well built. The fortifications are extensive, but irregular. The natural situation of the town renders its defence easy. If attacked by ships from the river, their guns cannot injure the works of the Upper Town, though the ships themselves would be liable to great injury from the cannon and bombs from these elevated ramparts. The Lower Town is defended by a platform, flanked with two bastions, which, at high water and spring tides, are almost level with the surface of the water. A little above the bastion, to the right, is a half bastion, cut out of the rock; a little higher a large battery, and higher still a square fort, the most regular of all the fortifications, and in which the governor resides. The passages which form a communication between these rocks are extremely rugged. The rock which separates the Upper from the Lower Town extends, with a bold and steep front, a considerable distance W. along the river St. Lawrence. The Lower Town is well supplied with water, which is sometimes scarce in the Upper Town. This city was erected by the French, in 1608; the English reduced it, with all Canada, in 1629, but it was restored in 1632. In 1711 it was besieged by the English, without success; in 1759 it was again conquered, after a battle memorable for the death of General Wolfe in the moment of victory, and was confirmed to them by the peace of 1763. In 1775 it was attacked by the Americans, under General Montgomery, who was slain, and his army repulsed. Of late years great improvements have been effected, and the present population amounts to nearly 20,000. The chief exports are grain, flour, timber, lumber, &c. The basin of Quebec is capable of containing 100 sail of the line. It is 330 miles N. of Boston. Long. 70. 48. W. lat. 46. 55. N.

QUEDA, a kingdom of Asia; in the peninsula of Malacca. The king is tributary to Siam. The principal town is of the same name, has a harbour, and is 300 miles N. of the city of Malacca. Long. 100. 5. E. lat. 7. 5. N.

QUEDLINBERG, a town of Prussian Saxony, in the principality of Anhalt; with a castle. The river Bode divides it into the Old and New Town. It has a trade in brandy and linen. It is 10 miles S. by E. of Halberstadt. Long. 11. 10. E. lat. 51. 50. N.

QUEEN ANN, a county of Maryland, on the E. of Chesapeake Bay. Centreville is the chief town.

QUEEN ANN, a town of Maryland, in Prince George county; situate at the foot of a hill, on the Patuxent; 13 miles S. W. of Annapolis and 22 E. of Washington.

QUEEN CHARLOTTE ISLAND, an island in the South Pacific; 6 miles long and 1 broad; discovered by Captain Wallis in 1767. Long. 138. 4. W. lat. 19. 18. S.

QUEEN CHARLOTTE ISLANDS, a group of islands in the North Pacific; explored by Captain Carteret in 1767. The most considerable he named Egmont, but the Spaniards call it Santa Cruz. It is 60 miles long, and from 20 to 30 broad, woody and mountainous, with many valleys intermixed. The inhabitants are very nimble, vigorous, and active; and their weapons are bows and arrows pointed with flint. On the N. side is a harbour named Swallow Bay. Long. 164. 26. E. lat. 10. 42. S.

QUEEN CHARLOTTE SOUND, a sound at the N. extremity of the S. island of New Zealand, near Cook Strait. Long 174. 14. E. lat. 41. 6. S.

QUEENBOROUGH, a town in Kent, in the Isle of Sheppey; market on Monday. It had once a strong castle, remains of which are still to be seen. The town is seated near the mouth of the Medway; 20 miles N. W. of Canterbury, and 45 S. by E. of London. Long. 0. 10. E. lat. 51. 23. N.

QUEENBOROUGH, a town of South Carolina, on the W. side of the Great Pedee River; 32 miles N. N. W. of Georgetown.

QUEEN'S COUNTY, a county of Ireland, in the province of Leinster; about 30 miles long, and 29 broad; bounded on the N. by King's county, E. by Kildare, S. E. by Carlow, S. by Kilkenny, and W. by Tipperary and King's county. It is divided into nine baronies and 55 parishes, and sends two members to parliament. It was formerly full of woods and bogs, but is now much improved in cultivation. Maryborough is the capital.

QUEEN'S COUNTY, a county of New York, in the W. part of Long Island. Pop. 22,276. Jamaica is the chief town.

QUEENSFERRY, a borough of Scotland, in Linlithgowshire; seated on the Frith of Forth, where it is not more than 2 miles wide. It has a trade in soap, and a much frequented ferry. In conjunction with Stirling, &c., it sends one member to parliament. It is 9 miles W. N. W. of Edinburgh.

QUEENSTADT, a town of Prussian Saxony; 5 miles N. E. of Halberstadt.

QUEENSTOWN, a town of Upper Canada, on the river Niagara, just below the last rapid. Here all the merchandise and stores received from Kingston, for the upper part of the province, are sent in waggons to Chippawa, a distance of 10 miles, the falls and broken course of the river rendering the navigation impracticable for that space. It is 7 miles above Fort Niagara, and 20 N. by E. of Fort Erie.

QUEICH, a river of Bavaria, which passes by Anweiller and Landau, and enters the Rhine near Germersheim.

QUEI-LING, a city of China, capital of the province of Quang-si. It has its name from a flower called quei, which grows on a tree resembling a laurel, and emits such a sweet odour, that it perfumes the whole country. It stands on a river that runs into the Ta, but with such rapidity as not to be navigable. It is 180 miles N. by W. of Canton, and 587 S. of Peking. Long. 109. 51. E. lat. 25. 12. N.

QUENTIN, ST., a strong town of France, department of Aisne; with a considerable manufacture of lawns and cambrics; also gauze, linen, and thread. Near this place, in 1557, Philip II. of Spain gained a signal victory over the French, and afterwards took the town by storm, but it was restored to France in 1559. It is seated on an eminence, on the river Somme; 21 miles S. of Cambray, and 83 N. by E. of Paris. Pop. 11,000. Long. 3. 20. E. lat. 49. 50. N.

QUERCY, a province of France; now forming the department of Lot.

QUERETARO, a city of North America, republic of Mexico; elevated 6347 feet above the sea. It has a magnificent church, and several grand squares. Pop. 45,000. It is 95 miles N. W. of Mexico.

QUERFORT, a town of Prussian Saxony, in the government of Merseberg; formerly the capital of a principality of its name; with a castle; 14 miles W. of Merseberg. Long. 11. 50. E. lat. 51. 23. N.

QUERIMBA, a cluster of small islands on the coast of Mosambique; fertile in fruits and pastures. The principal one, of the same name, is in long. 41. 30. E. lat. 11. 40. S.

QUESNOY, a fortified town of France; department of Nord; with an old castle. In 1793 it was taken by the Austrians, but retaken the next year. It is seated in an extensive plain, on the rivulet Ronelle. It is 9 miles S. E. of Valenciennes, and 122 N. E. of Paris. Long. 3. 40. E. lat. 50. 15. N.

QUIBERON, a town in the department of Morbihan, with a fort; situate at the extremity of a peninsula, to the N. of Belleisle. In 1795 it was taken by some French royalists in the pay of Great Britain; but, owing to the desertion and treachery of some of the soldiers, the republicans soon took it by surprise. It was taken by the English in 1800, but evacuated soon afterwards; 17 miles S. S. E. of Port Louis. Pop. 2000.

QUICARO, an island in the Pacific Ocean; near the coast of Veragua; about 20 miles long, and 6 broad. Long. 82. 39. W. lat. 7. 50. N.

QUILIMANCY, a seaport of Zanguebar, in the kingdom of Melinda. It stands at the mouth of a river of the same name; 26 miles S. S. W. of Melinda. Long. 41. 40. E. lat. 3. 10. S.

QUILLAN, a town of France, department of Aude; 25 miles S. S. W. of Carcassone.

QUILLEBŒUF, a town in the department of Eure, seated on the Seine; 37 miles W. of Rouen, and 42 N. W. of Evreaux.

QUILOA, a seaport of Zanguebar, capital of a kingdom of the same name, with a small citadel. This country was for some time in the possession of the Portuguese, from whom it was wrested by the imam of Mascat. It produces abundance of rice, millet, fruits, cattle, and poultry. The inhabitants are Mahomedans, partly black, and partly tawny. The capital is well built, and stands on an island at the mouth of the river Coava. Long. 40. 0. E. lat. 8. 38. S.

QUIMPER, a city of France, capital of the department of Finisterre, and a bishop's see. It is seated at the conflux of the Oder and Benaudet; 34 miles S. S. E. of Brest, and 112 W. by S. of Rennes. Pop. 7000. Long. 4. 6. W. lat. 47. 58. N.

QUIMPERLE, a town in the department of Finisterre, seated on the Isolle; 30 miles E. S. E. of Quimper. Pop. 4200.

QUINCY, a town of Massachusets, in Norfolk county; 10 miles S. by E. of Boston.

QUINGEY, a town of France, in the department of Doubs, seated on the Louve; 12 miles S. W. of Besançon.

QUIN-NONG, or CHIN-CHI, a bay on the coast of Cochin-China, much frequented by the vessels of the country, being an excellent harbour. The entrance is narrow, and ships of burden can get in only at high water. At the head of the harbour is the city of Quin-nong. Long. 109. 15. E. lat. 13. 52. N.

QUINSON, a town of France, department of Lower Alps; 29 miles S. of Digne.

QUINTIN, a town in the department of Cotes du Nord, seated in a valley, on the Goy; 10 miles S. S. W. of St. Brieuc.

QUIRPON, an island in the Atlantic, near the N. coast of Newfoundland. Long. 53. 22. W. lat. 51. 40. N.

QUISTELLO, a town of Austrian Italy, famous for an action between the French and Austrians in 1734, when Marshal Broglio was surprised in his bed. It is seated on the Seccia; 15 miles S. of Mantua.

QUITO, a presidency of the republic of Colombia, forming part of the new state of Ecuador, lying between two chains of the high mountains called the Andes. The eastern governments are chiefly immense tracts, thinly scattered with missionary villages. The vegetable productions vary with the elevation of the ground. The champaign country produces abundant crops of maize; and the deep ravines, where the temperature is hot, produce sugar-cane. The elevated lands possess a colder climate, and produce, wheat, barley, &c. Immense flocks of sheep are reared in the mountain plains, and their wool furnishes materials for the manufactures of this province. The lands are generally well cultivated, and there are a great number of towns and villages inhabited almost entirely by Indians. The streets are generally straight, and in the direction of the four cardinal points; and the roads are laid out in a line, crossing each other; so that the aspect of the country is that of a large garden. Although this country is situate on both sides the equator, yet it lies so high, and so near the snow-clad mountains, that the air is very temperate. There are no noxious animals; for the tigers and serpents are below in the forests. The state of society in this province has undergone considerable improvement since its deliverance from Spanish domination, and the manufactures are in a flourishing state. Hats, cotton stuffs, and coarse woollen cloths, are made here in great quantities, and exported to other parts of South America.

QUITO, the capital of the above country, is seated on the skirts of the volcanic mountain of Pinchincha, in a pleasant valley, but on high ground, 9510 feet above the level of the sea. Having no mines in its neighbourhood it is chiefly famous for its manufactures of cotton, wool, and flax. The town is plentifully supplied with water, and enjoys a delightful climate; but it is subject, together with the whole country, to the awful calamity of earthquakes. Of these a very destructive one was experienced in 1755. In 1797 the face of the whole district was changed by a most dreadful concussion, and 40,000 persons were in one moment hurled into eternity. Violent shocks of earthquakes have since been frequently experienced. It is, notwithstanding, very populous, and inhabited by several families of distinguished rank; 400 miles S. W. of St. Fe de Bogota. Pop. about 70,000. Long. 77. 55. W. lat. 0. 13. S.

QUIZAMA, a province in the south part of Angola, west coast of Africa. It is mountainous and badly cultivated, but produces abundance of honey, wax, and salt. The inhabitants are warlike, and have never submitted to the Portuguese.

QUINZINA, a chain of mountains in the kingdom of Fez; 100 miles in length, extending from the desert of Gret, to the river Nocor.

QUOJA, an inland country of Africa, lying E. of Sierra Leone. It is well cultivated, but has little commercial intercourse.

QUOVEDO, a town of Austrian Illyria, in Istria; 4 miles S. of Capo d'Istria.

R

Raab, a town and fortress of Hungary, capital of a county of its name, and a bishop's see. It is a strong frontier bulwark against the Turks. It is seated at the conflux of the Raab and Rabnitz, not far from the Danube; 38 miles S. S. E. of Presburg. Pop. 11,000. Long. 17. 7. E. lat. 47. 38. N.

Raajegur, a town of Hindostan, in the province of Malwa; 74 miles N. E. of Ougein, and 214 S. S. W. of Agra. Long. 76. 56. E. lat. 24. 2. N.

Raasay, one of the Hebrides of Scotland, between the mainland of Ross-shire, and the Isle of Skye. It is annexed to the parish of Portree, in the county of Inverness, and is about 12 miles long, and 4 broad, rising with a gentle ascent from the W. side to a great height on the E. side, which is nearly perpendicular. It is famous for its millstone quarries; and at the N. E. end stands Castle Brochel, which is a noted sea-mark. Long. 6. 0. W. lat. 57. 32. N.

Rabasteins, a town of France, department of Tarn, with a castle, seated on the river Tarn; 18 miles N. E. of Toulouse. Pop. 6000.

Rabat, a seaport of Algier, in Tremesen, with a castle. It has fine mosques and handsome palaces. It is seated at the mouth of the Buregreg, between Fez and Tangier. Long. 5. 28. W. lat. 30. 40. N.

Rabenstein, a town of Bohemia, on the river Ottava; 21 miles W. S. W. of Rakonitz.

Racca, a town of Turkey, in Diarbekir, at the conflux of the Beles with the Euphrates. Near it are the ruins of Old Racca, once a magnificent city. It is 110 miles S. by W. of Diarbekir.

Rachore, a city of Hindostan, in the province of Bejapore, capital of a district of its name, subject to the nizam of the Deccan. It is seated on the S. bank of the Kistna; 80 miles S. W. of Hydrabad. Long. 78. 3. E. lat. 16. 22. N.

Raconigi, a town of Piedmont, with a magnificent castle belonging to the prince of Carignano, seated in a plain; 18 miles S. of Carignano. Pop. 10,500.

Radeberg, a town of Saxony, near which is a bath, called Augustus Bath, discovered in 1717. It is seated on the Roder; 8 miles E. N. E. of Dresden.

Radeburg, a town of Saxony, with a castle. It is celebrated for earthenware; seated on the Roder, 14 miles N. of Dresden.

Radicofani, a town of Tuscany, in the former province of Sienna; seated on a steep hill, 40 miles S. E. of Sienna.

Radimpour, or **Radunpour**, a town of Hindostan, in the province of Agimere; situate on the Puddar, 175 miles N. of Surat, and 250 S. W. of Agimere. Long. 71. 48. E. lat. 23. 58. N.

Radnor, New, a borough of Wales, in Radnorshire, with a market on Saturday. It is nominally the county town, though a small place, and the assizes are held at Presteign. It returns one member to parliament; 3 miles E. of it is Old Radnor, said to have been the Magoth of Antoninus, but now an insignificant village. New Radnor is seated near the source of the Somergil, at the foot of a hill, on which a castle formerly stood; 24 miles N. W. of Hereford, and 159 W. N. W. of London.

Radnorshire, a county of Wales; 30 miles long and 25 broad, bounded on the E. by Shropshire and Herefordshire, N. by Montgomeryshire, N. W. by Cardiganshire, and S. W. and S. by Brecknockshire. It contains 310,000 acres, is divided into six hundreds and 25 parishes, has four market-towns, and sends one member to parliament. Its principal rivers are the Wye and Tend, the former dividing it from Brecknockshire, and the latter from Shropshire. The E. and S. parts are tolerably level and productive of corn. The other parts are rude and mountainous, devoted chiefly to the rearing of cattle and sheep.

Radom, a town of Poland, in the palatinate of Sandomir; 60 miles N. N. W. of Sandomir.

Radomsk, a town of Poland, in the palatinate of Siradia; 50 miles S. E. of Siradia.

Radstadt, a town of Bavaria, near the source of the Ens; 35 miles E. S. E. of Salzburg. Long. 13. 26. E. lat. 47. 18. N.

Ragivolo, a town of Austrian Italy, in the province of Mantua; 19 miles S. of Mantua.

Ragland, a village in Monmouthshire, famous for its castle, where Charles I. passed much of his time, and lived in a magnificent style. This castle was the last, in Cromwell's time, which surrendered to General Fairfax; 5 miles N. E. of Usk, and 8 E. of Monmouth.

Ragnit, a town of Russian Lithuania, with a very ancient castle, in which is a large royal magazine for provisions, &c. It is situate on the Niemen; 56 miles E. N. E. of Konigsberg. Long. 21. 30. E. lat. 55. 30. N.

Ragoogur, a town of Hindostan, in the province of Malwa; 116 miles N. E. of Oudein, and 256 S. of Delhi. Long. 77. 30. E. lat. 24. 23. N.

Ragusa, a district of Austrian Dalmatia, containing the territory of the ancient republic of Ragusa, and several islands. It has an area of 700 square miles, with 60,000 inhabitants. The soil is so barren that the inhabitants receive the greatest part of their necessaries from the neighbouring islands and Turkish provinces. The chief rivers are the Drino, Gliuta, and Ombla.

Ragusa, the capital of the above district, and an archbishop's see. It is two miles in circumference, and strong by situation, having an inaccessible mountain on the land side, and a strong fort on the Gulf of Venice. It has a considerable trade with the Levant and Italy. It is 66 miles W. of Scutari. Pop. 10,000. Long. 17. 55. E. lat. 42. 32. N.

Ragusa, a populous town of Sicily, in Val di Noto, near the river Maulo; 18 miles W. N. W. of Noto. Pop. 20,000.

RAIATEA, or IORETEA (the Ulitea of Captain Cook), the largest of the Society Isles, in the South Pacific, about 40 miles in circumference. The mountains are lofty and picturesque. The lowland is extensive, and the valleys, which are capable of the highest cultivation, are not only spacious, but conveniently situated for affording to the inhabitants an intercourse with other parts of the island. It is well supplied with rivers and streams of excellent water. On the N. W. is a small but very secure harbour, called Hamanino, which is sheltered from the strong E. and S. winds by the mountains of the interior. Long. 151. 38. W. lat. 16. 45. S.

RAIN, a fortified town of Bavaria, seated on the Acha; 12 miles W. of Neuburg.

RAIN, LAKE, a lake of North America, lying E. of Lake of the Woods, and W. of Lake Superior. It is nearly 100 miles long, but in no part more than 20 wide.

RAISIN, MARKET, a town in Lincolnshire, with a market on Thursday; situate near the source of the Ancholm, 16 miles N. E. of Lincoln, and 147 N. of London.

RAJAMUNDRY, a town of Hindostan, capital of an extensive and fertile district of its name, in the province of the Circars. The principal riches consist in teak timber. It is the residence of the British civil establishment. It is seated on the Godavery, 35 miles from its mouth, and 170 S. W. of Cicacole. Long. 81. 57. E. lat. 17. 0. N.

RAJAPOUR, a town of Hindostan, in the province of Bejapore; seated at the mouth of a river of the same name; 6 miles N. of Geriah.

RAJEMAL, a district of Bengal, separated by a range of hills from Bahar. It is now annexed to the collectorship of Boglipore.

RAJEMAL, a decayed town of Bengal, seated on the W. bank of the Ganges; 68 miles N. N. W. of Moorshedabad.

RAKELSBURG, a town of the Austrian states, in Styria, with a considerable trade in wine and iron. It is a frontier fortress towards Hungary. It is situate on an island in the river Muer; 36 miles S. E. of Gratz. Long. 15. 58. E. lat. 46. 45. N.

RAKONITZ, a town of Bohemia, capital of a circle of the same name. Very good beer is brewed here, and forms the principal article of trade. It is seated on the Miza; 30 miles W. of Prague. Pop. 2000. Long. 14. 0. E. lat. 50. 5. N.

RALEIGH, the capital of North Carolina, in Wake county. It was named after the celebrated Sir Walter Raleigh, under whose direction the first settlement in North America was made at Roanoke Island. Here is a large and handsome state-house, with several other public buildings. The remoteness from navigation is its greatest disadvantage. It is 95 miles W. N. W. of Newbern, the former capital, and 145 W. S. W. of Petersburg in Virginia. Pop. 2244. Long. 78. 52. W. lat. 35. 40. N.

RAMA, or RAMULA, a decayed town of Palestine, with many fine ruins of Christian churches and other buildings, which attest its former magnificence; 20 miles W. by N. of Jerusalem.

RAMADA, a town of Colombia, in New Granada, 100 miles E. of St. Martha. Long. 72. 20. W. lat. 11. 10. N.

RAMAGIRI, a town of Hindostan, in Mysore seated on the W. side of the Arkawatti; with a strong fort on the opposite bank, on a large rocky hill, 50 miles N. E. of Seringapatam.

RAMBERT, ST., a town of France, department of Ain, with a linen manufacture and considerable iron-works; seated near the river Albeline, 24 miles S. S. E. of Bourg en Bresse. Pop. 2300.

RAMBERT, ST., a town in the department of Loire; 12 miles S. E. of Montbrison. Pop. 2400.

RAMBERWILLER, a town in the department of Vosges, 30 miles S. E. of Nancy.

RAMBOUILLET, a town in the department of Seine-et-Oise. Here was a royal palace, which was demolished in 1793; 27 miles S. W. of Paris. Pop. 2600.

RAME HEAD, a promontory on the S. coast of England, the W. point of the entrance into Plymouth Sound. On its summit is a church (a seamark) belonging to the village of Rame. Long. 4. 12. W. lat. 50. 19. N.

RAMERY, a town of France, department of Aube, seated on the river Aube, 18 miles N. E. of Troyes.

RAMILLIES, a town of Belgium, in South Brabant, memorable for a signal victory obtained by the Duke of Marlborough over the French in 1706. It is seated at the source of the Geete, 10 miles N. of Namur, and 24 S. E. of Brussels.

RAMISERAM, an island in the Gulf of Manara, at the W. end of Adam's Bridge, and separated from Marawar, on the continent of Hindostan, by a narrow channel. It is 30 miles in circuit, and contains some beautiful trees, a few villages, and a celebrated temple, to which a vast concourse of pilgrims resort. Long. 79. 22. E. lat. 9. 18. N.

RAMLA, a town of Palestine (the ancient Arimathea), now in a ruinous state. Here is a manufacture of soap, which is sent into all parts of Europe; 18 miles N. W. of Jerusalem.

RAMMEKENS, a seaport of Zealand, in the isle of Walcheren. It was one of the towns put into the hands of the English as a security for a loan in the reign of Queen Elizabeth; 4 miles S. of Middleburg. Long. 3. 40. E. lat. 51. 28. N.

RAMMELBURG, a lofty and extensive mountain of Germany, in that part of the Hartz Forest which lies within the principality of Grubenhagen. On this mountain are several silver mines, and at the foot of it is the city of Goslar.

RAMNAD, a town of Hindostan, capital of a district of its name in the province of Marwar. Long. 78. 49. E. lat. 9. 24. N.

RAMOO, a town of Bengal, in the district of Chittagong. Long. 92. 15. E. lat. 21, 28. N.

RAMPOUR, a town of Hindostan, in Delhi; 32 miles S. of Cossipour, and 105. E. of Delhi.

RAMSAY, a town of the Isle of Man, situate on a large bay on the N. E. coast. The bay affords good anchorage, but the harbour will only admit small vessels. Near it is a lighthouse, and the entrance is defended by a fort. It is 15 miles N. by E. of Douglas. Long. 4. 26. W. lat. 54. 18. N.

RAMSAY, a town in Huntingdonshire, with a market on Saturday. It had formerly an extensive abbey, of which only the ruins of a gateway remain. It is seated in the fens, near the mere of Ramsey and Whittlesey; 12 miles N. E. of Huntingdon, and 69 N. of London.

RAMSEY, an island on the coast of Wales, separated from Pembrokeshire by a narrow channel, called Ramsey Sound. Near it is a group of dangerous rocks, known by the name of the Bishop and his Clerks, frequented in the breeding season by vast multitudes of sea-fowls. The island is two miles long, and one and a quarter broad; 4 miles W. by S. of St. David. Long. 5. 20. W. lat. 51. 55. N.

RAMSGATE, a seaport in Kent, in the Isle of Thanet, near the Downs, with a market on Wednesday and Saturday. It was formerly an obscure fishing-town, and in the reign of Queen Elizabeth contained only 25 inhabited houses. His late majesty (George IV.) conferred upon it the rank of a royal harbour. It has of late years greatly increased in size and population, and contains a good market-place, an assembly-room, two libraries, a neat chapel of ease, and places of worship for Methodists, Independents, and Baptists. The harbour is nearly circular, and has two fine stone piers, a dry dock, and a lighthouse. Ramsgate is a member of the port of Sandwich, and is much frequented as a bathing-place; 17 miles W. by N. of Canterbury, and 72 E. S. E. of London. Long. 1. 24. E. lat. 51. 20. N.

RAMTEAK, a town of Hindostan, in Berar, held sacred to Ram by the Hindoos, who have a temple here; 18 miles N. N. E. of Nagpore.

RANAI, one of the Sandwich Islands in the Pacific Ocean, about three leagues W. of Mowee. The S. part is high and craggy, but the other parts have a better aspect, and are well inhabited. It produces very few plantains and bread-fruit trees, but abounds in yams, sweet potatoes, and taro.

RANDERADT, a town of Prussia, province of Lower Rhine, seated on the river Worm; 10 miles N. W. of Juliers.

RANDERS, a town of Denmark, in N. Jutland, near the mouth of the Gude, 25 miles E. of Wiburg.

RANGAMATTY, a town of Bengal, capital of a district of its name, in the collectorship of Rungpore. It has a celebrated pagoda. It stands near the Burrampooter, on the confines of Assam and Bootan; 170 miles N. E. of Moorshedabad. Long. 90. 8. E. lat. 26. 10. N.

RANGOON, a seaport of Pegu, and the principal mart for teak timber in the Birman empire. It was founded by Alompro, king of Birmah, in 1755, and is the residence of a governor, who lives within the fort. Here is a custom-house, built of brick, but the wharfs and dwelling-houses are all constructed of wood. In its neighbourhood are numerous convents, and, 2 miles N. of the town, on a rocky eminence, is a very grand temple, which is a splendid object at the distance of many miles. Rangoon surrendered to the British, February 1, 1825. It is seated on the most eastern branch of the Irrawaddy, which, hence to the sea, is called the Rangoon, or Syrian River; 18 miles N. of its mouth, and 60 S. of Pegu. Long. 96. 10. E. lat. 26. 48. N.

RANNOCH, LOCH, a lake of Scotland, in the N. part of Perthshire; 11 miles in length. It receives the waters of Loch Ericht from the N. and communicates with Loch Tumel on the E. and Loch Lidoch on the W. On its S. side is a forest of birch and pine.

RANTAMPOUR, a town and fortress of Hindostan, capital of a district of its name, in the province of Agimere; 96 miles E. of Agimere. Long. 76. 57. E. lat. 26. 35. N.

RANTZOW, a town of Denmark, in the duchy of Holstein, 24 miles N. by W. of Lubec.

RAOLCONDA, a town of Hindostan, in Visiapour, near which is a rich diamond mine; 20 miles N. N. W. of Sollapour.

RAON L'ETAPE, a town of France, in the department of Meurthe, seated at the conflux of the Etape and Meurthe; 30 miles S. E. of Nancy.

RAPALLO, a town of the Sardinian states, in the province of Genoa, seated on a bay of its name; 16 miles E. S. E. of Genoa.

RAPHOE, a town of Ireland, in the county of Donegal, and a bishop's see. The cathedral serves as a parish church; 11 miles S. W. of Londonderry, and 21 N. E. of Donegal.

RAPOLLA, a town of Naples, in Basilicata, 5 miles W. of Venosa.

RAPPAHANNOC, a river of Virginia, which rises in the mountains called the Blue Ridge, and flows by Falmouth, Fredericsburg, Portroyal, Leeds, Tappahannoc, and Ubanna, into Chesapeake Bay.

RAPPERSCHWEIL, a town of Switzerland, in the canton of Zurich; seated on a neck of land that advances into the lake of Zurich, over which is a wooden bridge, 1850 feet long. It is 18 miles S. E. of Zurich, and 20 N. W. of Glaris.

RAPPS, a town of Austria, on the river Teya, 8 miles N. by W. of Horn.

RARITAN, a river of New Jersey, which runs by Brunswick and Amboy into Arthur Kull Sound, and helps to form the fine harbour of Amboy.

RASCIA, the eastern division of Sclavonia, watered by the river Rasca, which runs into the Morave. The inhabitants are called Rascians.

RASEBORG, a seaport of Sweden, capital of a canton in Nyland. It is seated on the Gulf of Finland; 37 miles S. E. of Abo. Long. 23. 18. E. lat. 60. 16. N.

RASTADT, a town of Germany, in Baden, with a noble castle. In 1714 a treaty was negotiated here between the French and Austrians, and in 1796 the former defeated the latter near this place. It is seated on the Merg, near the Rhine, 5 miles N. E. of Baden, and 24 S. W of Philipsburg. Pop. 4200.

RASTENBURG, a fortified town of East Prussia, with a castle; seated on the small river Guber, 50 miles S. E. of Konigsberg.

RATENAU, a town of Prussia, in Brandenburg, seated on the Havel, 15 miles N. by W. of Brandenburg.

RATHANGAN, a town of Ireland, in the county of Kildare, 38 miles from Dublin.

RATHCOOLE, a town of Ireland, in the county of Dublin, 10 miles from Dublin.

RATHCORMAC, a town of Ireland, in the county of Waterford.

RATHDOWNEY, a town of Ireland, in Queen's county, 75 miles from Dublin.

RATHDRUM, a town of Ireland, in the county of Wicklow, with a manufacture of flannel; 38 miles from Dublin.

RATHFARNHAM, a town of Ireland, in the county of Dublin, 3 miles from Dublin.

RATHKEALE, a town of Ireland, in the county of Limerick, 137 miles from Dublin.

RATIBOR, a town of Prussian Silesia, formerly the capital of a principality of the same name, with a castle. The cathedral and town-house are worthy of notice. It is seated on the Oder, 15 miles N. E. of Troppau, and 85 S. S. E. of Breslau. Pop. 3500.

RATISBON, a strong city of Bavaria, and the see of an archbishop, transferred from Mentz to this place in 1798. The abbey of St. Emmeran contains the relics of St. Denys, a valuable library, and a fine collection of mathematical instruments. The town-house is magnificent, and in its hall the general diets of the empire used to meet. Ratisbon has a great trade in salt, for which it is a depôt, and sends large quantities of corn and wood to Vienna. In 1809 a battle was fought in the vicinity between the Austrians and French, in which the latter were victorious. It has an ancient bridge of 15 arches over the Danube, and stands on the S. side of that river, at the influx of the Regen; 62 miles N. by E. of Munich, and 195 W. by N. of Vienna. Pop. 22,000. Long. 12. 6. E. lat. 48. 58. N.

RATOATH, a town of Ireland, in the county of Meath; 12 miles E. of Trim, and 12 N. W. of Dublin.

RATMANSDORF, a town of the Austrian states, in Carniola, with a castle; 20 miles S. by W. of Clagenfurt.

RATSHA, or RATSKA, a town and fortress of Sclavonia, on the N. side of the Save, opposite the influx of the Drin; 30 miles S. W. of Peterwardein.

RATTAN. *See* RUATAN.

RATTENBERG, a fortified town of the Austrian states, in Tyrol, with a citadel. In its vicinity are copper mines, which also yield some silver. It is situate on the Inn; 26 miles E. N. E. of Inspruck, and 44 S. W. of Salzburg.

RATZEBURG, a fortified town of Germany; capital of a principality, subject to the duke of Mecklenburgh-Strelitz. It is seated on an island, in the midst of a lake 30 miles in circumference. The buildings are of brick, and almost every house is shaded with a tree. From the lake of Ratzeburg issues the river Waknitz, which joins the Trave near Lubec. Ratzeburg is noted for its excellent beer. It is 14 miles S. by E. of Lubec, and 22 S. of Lauenburgh. Long. 10. 52. E. lat. 53. 43. N.

RAUDNITZ, a town and castle of Bohemia, seated on the Elbe; 20 miles N. of Prague.

RAUMO, a town of Russia, in Finland; 20 miles S. of Biorneburg, and 55 N. by W. of Abo.

RAUSCHENBERG, a town of Germany, in Hesse-Cassel; 7 miles N. N. E. of Marburg, and 32 S. S. W. of Cassel.

RAUVEE, or RAVEE, a river of Hindostan; one of the five E. branches of the Indus. It rises in Lahore, on the borders of Tibet, flows by the city of Lahore to Toulomba, in the country of Moultan, and, 28 miles below, joins the Chunaub. The Rauvee is the Hydraotes of Alexander.

RAVELLO, a town of Naples, in Principato Citra, and a bishop's see; 10 miles W. of Salerno, and 25 S. E. of Naples.

RAVENGLASS, a seaport in Cumberland, with a market on Saturday. It stands on an inlet of the Irish Sea, between the Mite and Esk, which, with the Irt, run into this inlet, and form a good harbour; but, the adjacent country furnishing little for exportation, its chief trade is in oysters; 2 miles from the town, on the S. side of the Esk, are ruins of 3 miles in circumference, called the city of Burnscar, of which no historical documents appear to exist. Ravenglass is 16 miles S. S. E. of Whitehaven, and 279 N. N. W. of London. Long. 3. 30. W. lat. 54. 22. N.

RAVENNA, a city of Italy, in the states of the church, and an archbishop's see, with several colleges, a great number of religious houses, and a ruinous citadel. It has a celebrated harbour, but the sea has gradually withdrawn 4 miles from the town. Theodoric, king of the Goths, resided here, and afterwards the exarchs of the Greek emperors. The mausoleum of Theodoric is still to be seen, and is covered by a single stone, 21 feet in diameter and 15 thick. Ravenna is seated on the river Mantone; 37 miles S. E. of Ferrara, and 162 N. of Rome. Pop. 12,000. Long. 12. 5. E. lat. 44. 25. N.

RAVENSBERG, a town of Prussian Westphalia, capital of a county of its name, now included in the government of Minden; 36 miles S. W. of Minden.

RAVENSBURG, a town of Germany, in Wirtemberg, with a considerable trade, particularly in paper, seated on the Cheus; 18 miles N. of Lindau.

RAVENSTEIN, a town of the Netherlands, in North Brabant, with a castle, seated on the Maese; 8 miles W. S. W. of Nimeguen.

RAVITZ, a town of Prussian Poland, near the confines of Silesia, with a considerable manufacture of cloth; 55 miles S. of Posen. Pop. 8000.

RAWA, a town of Poland, with a strong castle, seated in a morass, and almost surrounded by the river Rawa; 55 miles S. W. of Warsaw. Long. 19. 55. E. lat. 51. 51. N.

RAYNHAM, a town of Massachusets, in Bristol

county, with manufactures of iron, seated near Taunton River; 4 miles N. N. E. of Taunton, and 32 S. of Boston.

Raypour, a town of Hindostan, in Orissa; 60 miles S. of Ruttunpour, and 80 W. of Sumbulpour.

Re, an island in France; 16 miles long, and 4 broad; separated from the coast of Lower Charente by the Strait of Breton, above 7 miles wide. The products are bitter wine, salt, brandy, and the liquor called aniseed. St. Martin is the capital.

Reading, a borough, and the capital of Berkshire; governed by a mayor; with a market on Saturday. It has three churches, and several meeting-houses. The principal manufactures are canvas, blankets, gauze, ribbons, and pins; and a great trade in malt, flour, and timber. It sends two members to parliament. Here are the ruins of a rich abbey, in which Henry I. was interred. It is seated on the Kennet, near its confluence with the Thames; 26 miles S. S. E. of Oxford, and 37 W. of London.

Reading, a town of Pennsylvania, capital of Berks county, with four edifices for public worship, and a large one for the public offices. In 1795 the county voted 12,000*l.* for building a bridge over the Schuylkill, on which the town is seated; 54 miles N. W. of Philadelphia. Pop. 8410. Long. 76. 10. W. lat. 40. 22. N.

Realego, a seaport of Guatemala in the province of Nicaragua, with three churches. The chief trade is in pitch, tar, and cordage. It is situate among swamps, near the mouth of a river of its name, 20 miles W. N. W. of Leon, to which it serves as a harbour. Long. 87. 46. W. lat. 12. 43. N.

Realville, a town of France, in the department of Tarn-et-Garonne; 8 miles N. E. of Montauban, and 20 S. of Cahors.

Reccan. *See* Aracan.

Reccanati, a town of Italy, in the papal states, and delegation of Ancona. It has a great fair in September, which continues 15 days. It is seated on a mountain, near the river Munsone; 14 miles S. of Ancona. Pop. 4000.

Reckem, a town of the Netherlands, near the Meuse; 5 miles N. of Maestricht.

Recklinghausen, a town of Prussian Westphalia, capital of a county belonging to the duke of Aremberg. It has a strong citadel, seated on the Lippe; 20 miles S. S. W. of Munster. Pop. 1200. Long. 7. 36. E. lat. 51. 38. N.

Reculver, a village in Kent, at the mouth of a small branch of the Stour; 8 miles N. E. of Canterbury. It is the Regulbium of the Romans, and its ancient church has two spires, which are called by mariners the Two Sisters.

Red Head, a cape of Scotland, in Angusshire, the S. point of Lunan Bay. Here are the ruins of a castle, almost surrounded by the sea.

Red Lake, a lake of North America, lying S. of Lake of the Woods. It is 60 miles long, and 15 broad, and on the N. side is fed by several small rivers. Its outlet, at the S. E. extremity, in lat. 47. 20., is called Red River, and flows into the Mississippi, a little above St. Anthony Falls.

Red Sea, a sea celebrated in holy writ. It extends 1300 miles from N. to S., dividing Africa from Arabia, and is 200 broad in the widest part. It is separated from the Mediterranean Sea on the N. by the Isthmus of Suez, and communicates on the S., by the Strait of Babelmandeb, with the Indian Ocean.

Redbridge, a village in Hampshire, at the mouth of the Test; 3 miles W. of Southampton. It has a considerable trade in coal, timber, corn, &c.

Redcar, a township of North Yorkshire; 7 miles from Guisborough, and 240 from London. It has lately become a fashionable bathing-place, and is much frequented.

Redditch, hamlet in Tardebigg parish, in the county of Worcester, near Bromsgrove; famous for its manufactures of fish-hooks and needles.

Redon, a town of France, in the department of Ille-et-Velaine. It serves as a mart for the commerce of Rennes. It is seated on the Vilaine; 20 miles E. of Vannes, and 62 S. S. W. of Rennes. Pop. 4000. Long. 2. 10. W. lat. 47. 48. N.

Redondela, a town of Spain, in Galicia, with a strong castle. It stands on Vigo Bay; 8 miles N. E. of Vigo.

Redonda, a town of Portugal, in Beira, with a castle, seated on the Mondego; 17 miles W. of Coimbra.

Redondo, a town of Portugal, in Alentejo; 23 miles S. W. of Elvas.

Redruth, a town in Cornwall, with a market on Friday. It is seated in the very heart of the mining country; 12 miles N. by E. of Helstone, and 263 W. by S. of London.

Redstone, a town of Pennsylvania, in Allegany county, with a manufacture of paper, and a rope-walk, situate on the Monongahela; 30 miles S. by E. of Pittsburg.

Reepham, a town in Norfolk, with a market on Saturday, and a trade in malt; situate on the Eyre, over which it has a ford; 11 miles N. E. of Dereham, and 112 N. by E. of London.

Rees, a town of Westphalia, in the duchy of Cleves, seated on the Rhine; 10 miles N. W. of Wesel.

Rees, or Rens, a town of the Prussian states, in the province of Lower Rhine. Hard by it, on the Rhine, is the Konigstuhl, or Thronus Regalis, a remarkable piece of antiquity, consisting of a round vault, built of freestone, and resting on 9 stone pillars, one of which stands in the middle. The vault is 80 feet in circumference, and has two stout doors, the ascent to which is by 28 stone steps. It is furnished with seven seats, agreeably to the number of electors at that time; and on this regal chair the electors of Germany formerly held consultations relative to the election of a king and emperor, and other weighty matters of the empire. Rees is seated near the Rhine; 5 miles S. by E. of Coblentz.

Reetz, a town of Brandenburg; 18 miles E. S. E. of New Stargard.

Regen, a circle of Bavaria, adjacent to Bohemia, with the circle of Upper Maine on the N. W., and that of Lower Danube on the S. W. Pop. 358,000. Ratisbon and Alenburg are the chief towns.

Regen, a town of Bavaria, on a river of the same name; 12 miles N. N. E. of Deckendorf, and 49 E. of Ratisbon.

Regensberg, a town of Switzerland, in the canton of Zurich, capital of a bailiwick of the same name, with a strong castle. It is seated on a rock called the Lagerberg; 9 miles N. W. of Zurich.

Regensburg. *See* Ratisbon.

Regenstauf, a town of Bavaria, in the principality of Neuburg, on the river Regen; 8 miles N. by E. of Ratisbon.

Regenstein, a town of Germany, in Saxony; 6 miles S. of Halbertstadt.

Regenswalde, a town of Prussian Pomerania, with a castle, seated on the Rega; 24 miles E. S. E. of Camin.

Reggio, a seaport of Naples, in Calabria Ultra, and an archbishop's see. The churches, convents, and many houses, are built of stones from ancient edifices, and numerous inscriptions are to be met with on the walls. The environs produce the best silk in Calabria; and on the coast is found a species of a muscle (pinna), that yields a kind of wool, of which gloves and stockings are made. Reggio was nearly destroyed by an earthquake in 1783. It is seated on the strait of Messina; 12 miles E. S. E. of Messina, and 95 S. by W. of Cosenza. Pop. 16,500. Long. 16. 50. E. lat. 38. 4. N.

Reggio, a city of Italy, capital of a duchy of the same name, included in that of Modena, and a bishop's see, with a strong citadel. In the cathedral are paintings by the greatest masters; and in the square is the statue of Brennus, chief of the Gauls. The principal trade is in silk. It was taken by Prince Eugene in 1706, and by the king of Sardinia in 1742. In 1796 the inhabitants were the first Italians that renounced allegiance to their sovereign, and solicited the protection of the French. Reggio is the birth-place of the poet Ariosto. It is seated in a fertile country, on the river Tessone; 13 miles N. W. of Modena, and 80 S. E. of Milan. Pop. 13,000. Long. 11. 5. E. lat. 44. 43. N.

Reghebil, a town of Negroland, in Wangara; situate on a lake at the influx of a branch of the Niger; 240 miles E. by S. of Ghanara. Long. 19. 10. E. lat. 13. 20. N.

Regina, a town of Naples, in Calabria Citra; 14 miles N. of Cosenza.

Regis, St., a town of Lower Canada, situate on the boundary line that separates Canada from the United States, and on a river of its name, at its junction with the St. Lawrence; 50 miles S. W. of Montreal. Long. 74. 10. W. lat. 45. 0. N.

Regnano, a town of the papal states, seated near the Tiber; 17 miles N. of Rome.

Reichenau, an island in the Zeller Zee, or lower lake of Constance; 3 miles long and 1 broad; abounding with vines and other fruit-trees. It is 4 miles W. of Constance.

Reichenau, a town of Bohemia, with a castle; 18 miles E. N. E. of Konigingratz.

Reichenbach, one of the four governments into which Prussian Silesia was divided in 1815. It comprises the county of Glatz, the principalities of Munsterberg, Brieg, and Schweidnitz, and a considerable part of that of Jauer; and has an area of 2500 square miles, with 470,000 inhabitants.

Reichenbach, the capital of the foregoing government, has considerable manufactures of linen, canvas, and fustian. It is seated on the rivulet Peil; 10 miles S. E. of Schweidnitz. Pop. 3300.

Reichenbach, a town of Saxony, in Voigtland. The inhabitants are principally clothiers; and their method of dyeing, particularly scarlet, is brought to great perfection. It is 10 miles S. S. W. of Zurickau.

Reichenburg, a town of Bohemia, in the circle of Buntzlau; with a considerable manufacture of cloth. It is 28 miles N. of Jung Buntzlau. Pop. 12,000.

Reichenfels, a town of the Austrian states, in Carinthia; 24 miles N. E. of Clagenfurt.

Reichenhall, a town of Bavaria, with a rich salt spring. Some salt is made here; but, for want of fuel, most of the brine is carried over the hills to Traunstein, a distance of 14 miles, by engines and pipes. It is seated on the Sala; 9 miles S. W. of Salzburg.

Reichshofen, a town of France, department of Lower Rhine; with a castle; 9 miles N. of Haguenau.

Reifferscheid, a town of the Prussian states; formerly the capital of a county in the duchy of Juliers. It is seated on the Effel; 30 miles S. S. W. of Cologne, and 52 N. by W. of Treves.

Reigate. *See* Ryegate.

Rein, a town in the Austrian states, in Styria; on the river Save; 25 miles S. S. E. of Cilly.

Reiner, a town of Prussian Silesia, in the government of Reichenbach, with a mineral spring, and manufactures of cloth and paper; 11 miles W. of Glatz.

Reisenburg, a town of East Prussia, 78 miles S. W. of Konigsberg.

Remberviller, a town of France, department of Vosges; 17 miles N. N. E. of Epinal.

Remich, a town of Belgium, on the Moselle; 20 miles S. E. of Luxemburg.

Remiremont, a town of France, department of Vosges; 11 miles S. E. of Epinal. Pop. 4000.

Remo, St., a town of the Sardinian states, in the territory of Genoa; situate in a fruitful valley, with a good harbour, in the Mediterranean; 7 miles E. by N. of Vintimiglia, and 66 S. E. of Genoa. Pop. 7500.

Rems and Fils, one of the 12 departments of the kingdom of Wirtemburg; situate E. of that of Rothenburg. Goppingen is the capital.

REMY, ST., a town of France, department of Mouths of the Rhone. A triumphal arch, and a mausoleum, in the neighbourhood, display the taste of the Augustan age; the former is not entire, but the latter is in the best state of preservation. It is 10 miles N. E. of Arles. Pop. 5100.

RENDSBURG, a fortified town of Denmark, in the duchy of Holstein, on the frontiers of Sleswick, and on the river Eyder. It is composed of three parts, the Old Town, the Schlosskule, and the New Town; the former of which stands on an island formed by the river. The principal manufactures are porcelain, earthenware, and gold and silver lace; and the trade in timber, by means of the Eyder canal, is considerable. It is 15 miles W. of Kiel, and 16 S. S. E. of Sleswick. Pop. 4500. Long. 9. 53. E. lat. 54. 20. N.

RENFREW, a borough of Scotland, and the county town of Renfrewshire. It sends, with its contributories, one member to parliament. The principal branch manufacture is that of thread, but many looms are employed in the silk and muslin. Robert II. had a palace here. It is seated near the Clyde, to which there is a canal; 6 miles W. by N. of Glasgow, and 13 E. by S. of Greenock. Long. 4. 26. W. lat. 55. 54. N.

RENFREWSHIRE, a county of Scotland, 30 miles long, and from 10 to 14 broad; bounded on the W. and N. by the Frith of Clyde, E. by Lanarkshire, and S. by Ayrshire. It is divided into 20 parishes, and returns one member to parliament. In the N. part, towards the borders of the Clyde, the soil is fertile, but the S. part is mountainous and rather barren. Besides the Clyde, it is watered by the Gryfe, and the White and Black Cart. The largest town is Paisley.

RENI, a town of European Turkey, in Bessarabia; seated on the Danube; 135 miles S. W. of Bender.

RENNES, a city of France, capital of the department of Ille-et-Vilaine; and a bishop's see. It contains eight parish churches, besides the cathedral, several convents, and a small university. The streets are broad and straight, but they were narrow before the fire in 1720, which lasted seven days, and consumed 850 houses. In the great square are the Palace of Justice, and the Hotel de Ville. It is seated on the Vilaine, which divides it into two parts. It is 190 miles W. S. W. of Paris. Pop. 30,000. Long. 1. 42. W. lat. 48. 7. N.

RENS, or RENSE. *See* REES.

RENSSELAER, a county of New York, bounded E. by Vermont and Massachusets, N. by Washington, S. by Columbia, and W. by the Hudson. Pop. 60,295. Troy and Lansingburg are the chief towns.

RENTON, a village of Scotland, near which is one of the most considerable printfields in Scotland; also the old mansion of Dalquhurn, where Dr. Smollet was born, and the lofty column erected to his memory, on the bank of the Leven; 4 miles N. W. of Dumbarton.

RENTY, a town of France, department of Pas de Calais; seated on the Aa; 12 miles S. W. of Aire, and 50 N. W. of Arras.

REOLLE, a town in the department of Gironde; seated on the Garonne; 30 miles S. E. of Bordeaux. Pop. 3800.

REPAILLE, a town of the Sardinian states, in Savoy; famous for the retreat of Amadeus, duke of Savoy, in 1440, when he went to enjoy the pleasures of a country life; seated on a river which runs into the lake of Geneva; 20 miles N. E. of Geneva.

REPPEN, a town of Brandenburg; 16 miles S. S. E. of Custrin.

REPTON, a village in Derbyshire, 8 miles S. S. W. of Derby; celebrated as the burial-place of several of the Saxon kings of Mercia, and for several antiquities. Here is a noted free-school, which appears to have been the refectory of a priory.

REQUENA, a town of Spain, in New Castile; with a castle, and a considerable manufacture of silks. It was taken by the English in 1706, and retaken by the French the next year. It is seated on a hill, on the borders of Valencia; 64 miles E. S. E. of Cuenza. Long. 1. 9. W. lat. 39. 44. N.

RESHD, a city of Persia, capital of Ghilan. It has a considerable trade, particularly in silk; and much rice grows in the environs. It is seated on a river; 6 miles from the Caspian Sea, and 100 N. of Casbin. Pop. about 10,000. Long. 49. 50. E. lat. 37. 28. N.

RESOLUTION ISLAND, an island in the North Atlantic; 50 miles long and 20 broad; on the N. side of the entrance into Hudson Strait. Long. 65. 0. W. lat. 61. 40. N.

RESOLUTION ISLE, a small island in the South Pacific; 160 leagues E. of Otaheite; so called from the ship in which Cook made his second voyage. Long. 141. 15. W. lat. 17. 23. S.

RETEL, a town of France, department of Ardennes; seated on a hill, near the Aisne; 26 miles N. E. of Rheims. Pop. 4900. Long. 4. 24. E. lat. 49. 32. N.

RETFORD, EAST, a borough in Nottinghamshire; with a market on Saturday; returning two members to parliament. It is in general well built, and consists of three principal streets, disposed nearly in the form of a Roman Y. The market is held under the town-hall, where the election of members for the borough takes place. The Chesterfield Canal, which was opened in 1777, is conveyed by an aqueduct over the river Idle, to the south-west of the town. It has a handsome and commodious church, three meeting-houses, an hospital, and almshouses for eighteen poor women. The chief trade is in malt, and it has manufactures of hats and bobbinnet. It is seated on the Idle; 29 miles N. by E. of Nottingham, and 144 N. by W. of London. West Retford is situated on the opposite side of the river, and has a small church, a free-school, and an hospital for 16 poor men.

RETHEM, a town of Hanover, seated on the Aller; 35 miles N. N. W. of Hanover.

RETIMO, a seaport of Candia, and a bishop's see; with a citadel. It was taken by the Turks in 1645. Its silk, wool, honey, wax, laudanum, and oil, are preferred to all others. It is seated on the N. coast of the island; 42 miles W. of Candia. Pop. 6000. Long. 24. 38. E. lat. 35. 20. N.

RETZ, a town of Bavaria, on the Schwara; 28 miles E. S. E. of Amberg.

REUS, a town of Spain, in Catalonia, with manufactures of silk, cotton, leather, and hats; and a considerable trade in wine, brandy, &c.; seated in the middle of a most fruitful plain; 17 miles S. W. of Tarragona. Pop. 20,000.

REUSS, a principality of Saxony, lying between the Prussian and Bavarian territories; comprising an area of 600 square miles, with 85,000 inhabitants, of whom the greater part are Lutherans. Gera is the chief town.

REUSS, a river of Switzerland, which rises in the Lake of Locendro, on the N. W. of St. Gothard; flows through the Lake of Lucern, and the town of that name, and joins the Aar below Bruck.

REUTLINGEN, a town of Germany, in Wirtemburg. In the town-house is preserved an ancient battering-ram; and in the vicinity are many paper and powder-mills. It is seated on the Echetz, near the Neckar; 17 miles S. of Stutgard. Pop. 8300.

REVEL, a town of France, department of Upper Garonne, near the canal of Languedoc; 27 miles S. E. of Toulouse.

REVEL, a government of Russia. *See* ESTHONIA.

REVEL, a seaport of European Russia, capital of the government of Esthonia; and a bishop's see. It is surrounded by high walls and deep ditches, and defended by a castle and good bastions. The houses are well built, and have fine gardens. It is become a place of great trade, since the Russians obtained possession of it in 1710; and there are two great fairs, in May and September, frequented by English and Dutch merchants. It is seated on the Gulf of Finland, partly in a pleasant plain, and partly on a mountain; 160 miles N. by E. of Riga, and 220 W. by S. of Petersburg. Population, 13,000. Long. 24. 17. E. lat. 59. 18. N.

REVELLO, a town of the Sardinian states, in Piedmont, seated near the Po, on the top of a mountain, fortified by nature and art; 8 miles N. W. of Saluzzo. Pop. 5000.

REVERO, a town of Austrian Italy, in the Mantuan, seated on the Po, opposite Ostiglia; 20 miles S. E. of Mantua.

REVIN, a town of France, department of Ardennes, seated on the river Meuse; 6 miles E. of Rocroy.

REVOLUTION ISLES, a group of islands in the Pacific Ocean, to the N. W. of the Marquesas, of which they may be deemed a continuation. They were discovered in 1791. The most considerable are Baux and Marchand. The latter is about 15 miles in circuit, and was taken possession of in the name of the French nation, by Captain Marchand. Long. 140. 5. W. lat. 9. 21. S.

vince of Allahabad, the residence of a Hindoo chief, tributary to the British; 57 miles S. S. W. of Allahabad.

REWARI, a town of Hindostan, capital of a district in the province of Delhi. It is the residence of a chief, tributary to the British, and is seated on the Sadi; 55 miles S. W. of Delhi Long. 76. 52. E. lat. 28. 13. N.

RHAMANIE, a town and fort of Egypt, on the W. branch of the Nile, where the canal of Alexandria enters that river. It is 25 miles above Rosetta, and 58. E. S. E. of Alexandria.

RHAYADERGWY, a town of Wales, in Radnorshire, with a market on Wednesday. It is situate on the Wye, where there was formerly a cataract, which is now destroyed, and a neat bridge erected, and on an eminence near it is the site of an ancient castle, of which no ruins remain. In the neighbourhood are lead and copper mines; 19 miles W. N. W. of New Radnor, and 178 of London.

RHEDA, a town of Prussian Westphalia; 10 miles N. of Lipstadt.

RHEIMS, a city of France, department of Marne; and an archbishop's see. The inhabitants are estimated at 38,000. The principal church, built before the year 406, is a very beautiful structure; and that of St. Nicaise is remarkable for its fine architecture. Behind the high altar of the church of St. Remy, the corpse of that archbishop is preserved in a magnificent shrine. The kings of France have been successively crowned at Rheims; probably because Clovis, the founder of the French monarchy, when converted from paganism, was baptized in the cathedral here, in the year 496. The remains of an amphitheatre, a castle, and a triumphal arch, are among the ancient monuments of the Romans. The streets are wide and straight, but the houses are low. Here are manufactures of flannel, coverlets, and other woollen stuffs. This city was taken and retaken several times by the French and allied armies, in 1814. It is seated in a plain, surrounded by hills that produce excellent wine, on the river Vesse; 62 miles N. of Troyes, and 75 N. E. of Paris. Long. 4. 2. E. lat. 49. 15. N.

RHEIN, a town of Prussia, with a large fortified castle, seated on a lake; 75 miles S. E. of Konigsberg. Long. 21. 38. E. lat. 53. 48. N.

RHEINAU, a town of Switzerland, in the canton of Thurgau, with an abbey; on an island formed by the Rhine; 5 miles S. S. W. of Schaffhausen.

RHEINBACH, or RHYNBACH, a town of the Prussian states, in the province of Cleves and Berg; 20 miles S. of Cologne.

RHEINBERG, a town of the Prussian states, in the government of Cleves, seated near the Rhine; 13 miles E. of Gelders, and 48 N. by W. of Cologne.

RHEINE, a town of Prussian Westphalia, seated on the Ems; 18 miles W. N. W. of Osnaburg.

RHEINECK, a town of Germany, seated on the Rhine; 16 miles N. W. of Coblentz.

RHEINECK, a town of Franconia, capital of [illegible] with a castle, on the river Șinn; 25 miles N. by W. of Wurtzburg.

Rheineck, a town of Switzerland, capital of the Rheinthal, in the canton of St. Gall, with a castle, seated on the Rhine; 25 miles S. E. of Constance.

Rheinfelden, a town of Germany, in Baden, the best of the four forest-towns, seated on the Rhine, over which is a bridge; 8 miles E. of Basel.

Rheinfels, a strong fortress of Germany, in the Prussian states. It is one of the most important places on the Rhine, and stands on a stupendous craggy rock, at the foot of which is the fortified town of St. Goar. It was taken by the French in 1794; 16 miles S. of Coblentz.

Rheinmagen, a town of the Prussian states, in the government of Coblentz, situate on the Rhine; 19 miles N. W. of Coblentz.

Rheinthal, a district of Switzerland; in the canton of St. Gall, lying along the Rhine. It is a fertile valley, 30 miles long, and from 3 to 8 broad, and produces excellent wine. Rheineck is the capital.

Rheinzaburn, a town of France, department of Lower Rhine, seated on the Erlbach; 10 miles S. E. of Landau.

Rhena, a town of Germany, in the duchy of Mecklenburg, on the river Radegast; 14 miles E. S. E. of Lubec.

Rhenen, a town of Belgium, in the province of Utrecht, seated on the Rhine; 20 miles S. E. of Utrecht.

Rhine, a great and remarkable river of Europe, which rises in Switzerland, in the canton of Grisons. It is formed of three streams—the Further Rhine, from the head of the valley of Disentis; the Middle Rhine, from the valley of Medelo, an appendage of St. Gothard; and the Hither, or Upper Rhine, from the mount Avicula. The first two torrents united take the name of Lower Rhine, which receives the Upper Rhine at Richenau, and the height is here about 6180 feet above the sea. Flowing by Coire, at the distance of a mile, the Rhine here becames navigable for rafts. It is, soon after, the boundary between the Rheinthal and a territory of Austria, and passes through the Lake of Constance from E. to W. Leaving this lake, it flows W. by Schaffhausen, below which it forms a celebrated cataract. It continues in a westerly course to Basle, when it turns to the N., and enters the Netherlands in which course it waters many considerable cities and towns, and receives some large rivers. Below Emmerick, in the duchy of Cleves, it divides into two streams. That which bends to the W., and flows by Nimeguen, is called the Waal, but loses that name on its junction with the Meuse at Worcum. Below Gorcum, it divides into four principal branches, forming the isles of Ysselmonde, Voorn, and Overflackee: the most northern branch is called the Merwe, and, passing by Rotterdam and Schiedam, is joined by the branch from the S. side of Ysselmonde and enters the German Ocean below Briel: the other two branches make their exit at Helvoetsluys and Goree. The other stream, which had branched off to the N. W. below Emmerick, retains its name; but below Huessen, another branches off to the N., takes the name of Yssel, and enters the Zuyder Zee below Campen. The old river proceeds W. by Arnheim to Duerstede, when it again divides into two streams: that to the left is called the Leck, and enters the Merwe above Rotterdam. The branch to the right, which retains its name, passes on to Utrecht, when it divides once more into two streams: the smaller one is called the Vecht, which runs N. into the Zuyder Zee at Muyden; and the other, the remains of the noble Rhine, flows W. by Woerden to Leyden, where it divides into several channels, and afterwards is lost among hills of sand near the village of Catwyck.

Rhine, a province of the grand duchy of Hesse, to the N. of the Bavarian circle of the Rhine; comprising an area of 1000 square miles, with 155,000 inhabitants.

Rhine, Circle of, a province of Bavaria; situate to the W. of the Rhine, between Weissemburg and Worms. It was ceded to Bavaria in 1814. It contains an area of 1800 square miles, with 308,000 inhabitants.

Rhine Lower, a grand duchy of the Prussian states, composed of territories taken from France and the grand duchy of Berg, in 1814, and assigned to Prussia by the congress of Vienna. It is bounded N. by the province of Cleves and Berg, E. by Nassau and Hesse-Darmstadt, S. by the French and W. by the Dutch frontier. It has an area of 5700 square miles, with 950,000 inhabitants. Aix-la-Chapelle is the capital.

Rhine, Lower and Upper, two divisions of Germany, abolished in 1806.

Rhine, Lower, a department of France, containing the late province of Lower Alsace. It has an area of 1900 square miles, with 440,000 inhabitants. Strasburg is the capital.

Rhine, Upper, a department of France, consisting of the late province of Upper Alsace, and containing an area of about 1700 square miles, with 320,000 inhabitants. Colmar is the capital.

Rhode Island, one of the United States of America, bounded on the N. and E. by Massachusets, S. by the Atlantic, and W. by Connecticut. These limits comprehend what has been called Rhode Island and Providence Plantations. It is divided into the counties of Newport, Providence, Washington, Bristol, and Kent. Area, 1350 square miles. Pop. 108,830. The state is intersected in all directions by rivers, the chief of which are Pawtucket, Providence, and Taunton rivers, which flow into Narraganset Bay. Iron-ore and limestone are found in great plenty in this state, which is principally a country for pasture. Providence and Newport are the chief towns.

Rhode Island, an island in the above state; 15 miles long, and 4 broad. It is exceedingly fertile, and between 30,000 and 40,000 sheep are fed here, besides beeves and horses. This island is a noted resort of invalids from the southern climates, being exceedingly pleasant and healthful. At its S. W. extremity is the town of Newport.

Rhodes, an island of the Grecian Archipelago, at the entrance of the Gulf of Macri; 40 miles long, and 15 broad. The soil is pretty fertile, but badly cultivated. This island is much celebrated in ancient history, having been frequently under the dominion of different masters. The Saracens became possessors of it in 665; and in 1309, it was taken from them by the Knights of St. John of Jerusalem, who afterwards took the name of Knights of Rhodes. They retained it till 1623, when it was taken by the Turks, after an obstinate resistance; and the small number of knights that remained were afterwards removed to Malta. Like the neighbouring islands, it has been reduced by the oppression of the Porte to a state of great poverty and wretchedness. Pop. about 20,000.

RHODES, the capital of the above island, and an archbishop's see, was anciently 9 miles in circumference, and was regarded by Alexander, who deposited his last will here, as the first city in the world; but the present town occupies only a quarter of the extent of the ancient city. It has a good harbour, with a narrow entrance between two rocks, on which are two towers to defend the passage. Pop. 6000. Here, in all probability, stood the famous Colossus, a statue of bronze, 70 cubits high, reckoned one of the seven wonders of the world: it was thrown down by an earthquake; and, when the Saracens became masters of the island, they knocked it to pieces, and sold the fragments to a Jew of Edessa, nearly 900 years after its fall. Rhodes was deemed an impregnable fortress, being surrounded by triple walls and double ditches, which have long been in a state of dilapidation. Long. 28. 20. E. lat. 36. 27. N.

RHODEZ, *See* RODEZ.

RHONE, a large river that rises in Switzerland, in Mount Furca, and soon joins a more considerable stream from an extensive glacier called that of the Rhone. After passing through the vale of Valais, it runs through the Lake of Geneva, and, separating Savoy from Bresse, it flows W. to Lyons, then S. to Vienne, Tournon, Valence, Viviers, Pont St. Esprit, Avignon, Beaucaire, Tarascon, and Arles, and enters the Mediterranean by several mouths.

RHONE, a department of France, so named from the river Rhone, which flows on its E. border. It includes the late provinces of Beaujolois and Lyonnois, and contains an area of 1050 square miles; with 416,000 inhabitants. Lyons is the capital.

RHONE, MOUTHS OF THE, a department of France, on the coast of the Mediterranean, at the influx of the Rhone; containing the W. part of the late province of Provence. It comprises an area of 2000 square miles, with 326,000 inhabitants. Marseilles is the capital.

RHONHOUSE, a village of Scotland, in Kirkcudbrightshire. It is 8 miles N. N. W. of Newton Douglas.

RHUDDLAN, a town of Wales, in Flintshire, on the river Clwyd; an ancient town, now inconsiderable; with a noble castle.

RHUDEN, a town of Prussian Westphalia, on the Monne; 12 miles S. S. E. of Lipstadt.

RHYNBECK, a town of New York, in Duchess county, on the E. side of Hudson River, opposite Kingston, and 18 miles N. of Poughkeepsie.

RHYNBERG, or RHINSBERG, a town of Brandenburg, with a handsome palace, built by Frederic II., when hereditary prince. It is seated on the Rhyn; 10 miles N. of Ruppin.

RHYNEY. *See* RUMNEY.

RHYNOW, a town of Brandenburg, at the conflux of the Rhyn with the Havel; 9 miles S. E. of Havelberg.

RIAZAN, a government of Russia, formerly a province of the government of Moscow. It comprises an area of 13,000 square miles, with 1,000,000 of inhabitants, and had anciently its own princes. The soil is fertile in corn, hemp, and flax.

RIAZAN, the capital of the above government, and an archbishop's see, was formerly considerable for its extent and riches, but was almost ruined by the Tartars, in 1568. It is seated at the conflux of the Trubesh with the Occa; 100 miles S. E. of Moscow. Pop. 5000. Long. 40. 37. E. lat. 54. 55. N.

RIBA DE SELLA, a small seaport of Spain, in Asturias, on the Bay of Biscay; 29 miles E. by S. of Gijon.

RIBADAVIA, a town of Spain, in Galicia, seated at the conflux of the Avia with the Minho, in a territory that produces the best wine in Spain; 15 miles W. S. W. of Orense.

RIBADEO, a seaport of Spain, in Galicia, with a good harbour, defended by two castles. It is seated on a rock, at the mouth of the Rio de Mirando; 45 miles N. by E. of Lugo. Long. 6. 47. W. lat. 43. 38. N.

RIBAS, a town of Spain, in New Castile, on the river Xarama; 8 miles E. of Madrid.

RIBBLE, a river which rises in W. Yorkshire, runs across Lancashire, and enters the Irish Sea below Preston.

RIBEMONT, a town of France, department of Aisne, seated on an eminence near the Oise; 10 miles S. of St. Quentin. Pop. 2400.

RIBERAC, a town in the department of Dordogne; 17 miles E. of Perigueux.

RIBNIK, a town of Prussian Silesia, in the principality of Ratibor. It is 20 miles E. by N. of Ratibor.

RIBNIK, or RIMNIK, a town of European Turkey, in Walachia, and a bishop's see. Here, in 1789, the Austrians and Russians gained a great victory over the Turks. It is seated on a river of the same name; 68 miles E. N. E. of Tergovist.—Another, on the Alth; 50 miles W. by S. of Tergovist.

RIBNITZ, a town of Germany, in the grand duchy of Mecklenburg-Schwerin; seated on a bay of the Baltic, near the influx of the Reckenitz; 13 miles N. E. of Rostock.

RICHELIEU, a town of France, department of Indre-et-Loire, founded by Cardinal Richelieu, in 1637, seated on the Amable and Vide; 33 miles S. S. W. of Tours. Pop. 3200.

RICHMOND, a borough in North Yorkshire, governed by a mayor, with a market on Saturday. It was formerly surrounded by a wall, with three gates, and had a strong castle, (now in a ruinous condition,) on an inaccessible mount. It is the capital of a district called Richmondshire, (now included in the duchy of Lancaster,) which abounds in lead mines, and was formerly a county of itself. Richmond has a manufacture of woollen stockings, caps, &c. It returns two members to parliament. It is seated on the Swale, over which is a bridge. It is 40 miles N. W. of York, and 230 N. N. W. of London. Long. 1. 35. W. lat. 54. 28. N.

Richmond, a village in Surrey, with an elegant stone bridge over the Thames. It was anciently called Sheen; but Henry VII. called it Richmond, on account of his having been earl of Richmond in Yorkshire. Here was a palace, in which Edward III., Henry VII., and Queen Elizabeth expired. Here is an extensive royal park, called Richmond, or the New Park; surrounded by a brick wall, built by Charles I. It is 9 miles W. S. W. of London.

Richmond, a town of New South Wales, in the county of Cumberland; 36 miles from Sydney. It is rapidly increasing. It is seated on the Nepean river, in an exceedingly fertile district.

Richmond, a county of New York, comprehending Staten Island. Chief town, Southfield.

Richmond, a county in the N. of Georgia. Chief town, Augusta. Pop. 11,932.—Also, a county in N. Carolina. Pop. 8900.—And another county in Virginia. Pop. 5965.

Richmond, the capital of Virginia, in Henrico county, on the N. side of James River, at the foot of the Falls. It contains a state-house, and court-house, jail, almshouse, penitentiary, two market-houses, a public library, a museum, and places of worship for Episcopalians, Presbyterians, Baptists, Methodists, Quakers, and Jews. Here is a floating toll-bridge over the river; and the Falls above the bridge are 7 miles in length. Vessels of burden lie at City Point, 20 miles below, to which goods from Richmond are sent down in boats. It is 90 miles S. S. W. of Alexandria. Pop. 20,153. Long. 77. 55. W. lat. 37. 35. N.

Rickmansworth, a town in Hertfordshire, with a market on Saturday, seated on the Coln; 8 miles S. W. of St. Albans, and 18 W. N. W. of London.

Ricla, a town of Spain, in Arragon, on the Xalon; 28 miles W. S. W. of Saragossa.

Ridgfield, a town of Connecticut, in Fairfield county; 14 miles N. W. of Fairfield, and 48 N. N. E. of New York. Pop. 2474.

Ried, a town of Upper Austria, circle of the Inn. Here the French had a victory over the Austrians, in 1805. It is 18 miles S. of Passau.

Riedlingen, a town of Germany, in Wirtemberg, seated on the Danube; 25 miles S. W. of Ulm.

Riesengebirge, a chain of mountains in Central Germany, separating Bohemia and Moravia, and joining the Carpathians; they are the highest in Central Germany, the loftiest Schneeberg, being 5270 feet.

Rietberg, a town of the Prussian states, in the government of Minden, capital of a county of the same name, with a castle; situate on the Ems; 17 miles W. by N. of Paderborn.

Rieti, a town of Italy, in the papal states, capital of a delegation of its name, and a bishop's see. Besides the cathedral, it contains three collegiate and six parish churches, and 12 convents. It is seated on the river Velino, near the Lake Rieti; 37 miles N. E. of Rome. Long. 13. 5. E. lat. 42. 23. N.

Rieux, a town of France, department of Upper Garonne, seated on the Reze; 25 miles S. S. W. of Toulouse.

Riez, a town in the department of Lower Alps, seated in a plain abounding with wine and fruits; 20 miles S. S. W. of Digne. Population, 2900.

Riga, a government of Russia. *See* Livonia.

Riga, a strong town of Russia, capital of the government of Livonia, and, next to Petersburg, the most commercial place in the empire. It stands on the river Dwina, 5 miles from its mouth, in a gulf of the Baltic, called the Gulf of Riga or Livonia. The trade is chiefly carried on by the foreign merchants resident here; those belonging to an English factory enjoy the greatest share of the commerce. The principal exports are corn, hemp, flax, iron, timber, masts, leather, and tallow. The population of Riga is estimated at 36,000. Here is a floating wooden bridge, over the Dwina, 2600 feet long, and 40 broad; in winter, when the ice sets in, it is removed; and in spring it is replaced. In 1812, on the approach of the French army, under Marshal Macdonald, to besiege this place, the governor of the town set fire to the suburbs, which consumed upwards of 2000 houses. Riga is 220 miles N. E. of Konigsberg, and 310 S. W. of Petersburg. Long. 24. 15. E. lat. 56. 50. N.

Rimini, a town of Italy in the papal states, with an old castle, a strong tower, and many remains of antiquity. The sea having receded from this city for some centuries, its harbour will now admit only small vessels. It is seated in a fertile plain, at the mouth of the Marrechia, on the Gulf of Venice; 28 miles S. E. of Ravenna, and 145 N. by E. of Rome. Pop. 8000. Long. 12. 34. E. lat. 44. 4. N.

Ringkioping, a seaport of Denmark, in N. Jutland. It has a considerable trade with Holland and Norway. It is seated on a gulf of the German Ocean; 43 miles S. W. of Wiburg, and 55 N. N. W. of Ripen. Long. 8. 15. E. lat. 56. 8. N.

Ringleben, a town of Germany, belonging to Saxe-Weimar; 6 miles N. of Erfurt, and 26 E. N. E. of Eisenach.

Ringsted, a town of Denmark, in the isle of Zealand. It was formerly a city; and in the great church are interred several kings, and other persons of distinction. It is 30 miles S. W. of Copenhagen.

Ringwood, a town in Hampshire with a

market on Wednesday. It has a manufacture of woollen cloths and stockings, and is famous for its strong beer and ale. It is seated on the Avon; 30 miles S. W. of Winchester, and 91 W. by S. of London.

Rinteln, a strong town of Germany, capital of the district of Schauenburg, with a university. It is seated on the Weser; 12 miles S. E. of Minden, and 35 W. S. W. of Hanover. Long. 9. 10. E. lat. 52. 12. N.

Rio de la Hacha, a seaport of Colombia, in Venezuela, at the north of a river of the same name; 100 miles E. of St. Martha. Long. 72. 34. W. lat. 11. 30. N.

Rio de la Plata. *See* Plata.

Rio de Mirando, a river of Spain; which rises in the mountains of Asturias, separates that province from Galicia, and enters the Bay of Biscay at Ribadeo.

Rio del Norte, a considerable river of North America, the source of which is unknown, but it flows from N. to S. through the whole country of New Mexico; and enters the Gulf of Mexico on the N. border of New Leon.

Rio Grande, a province in the N. part of Brazil, between those of Petaguel and Paraiba. It is watered by a river of the same name, which runs W. into the Parana, of which it is the principal branch. Pop. 250,000.

Rio Grande, a river which rises in the Sierra Leone mountains, and flows through the kingdom of Biguba into the Atlantic. It is navigable for boats 400 miles.

Rio Janeiro, one of the richest provinces of Brazil; lying near the tropic of Capricorn, on a river of the same name. It produces cotton, sugar, coffee, cocoa, pepper, indigo, and tobacco, with abundance of fruit and garden-stuff, but no bread-corn; so that the people here have no wheat-flour, but what is brought from Portugal. As a succedaneum for bread, there are yams and cassada in plenty. The riches of the country consist in its mines of gold, and in precious stones. The latter are found in such plenty that a certain quantity only is allowed to be collected in a year, which is sometimes obtained in less than a month. St. Sebastian is the capital.

Rio, or Rio de Janeiro. *See* St. Sebastian.

Riobamba, a province of Quito; 9 miles long, and 4 broad, adjoining that of Latacunga on the N. It produces abundance of sugar-cane, wheat, maize, barley, and various fruits. Cattle are numerous; and, from the wool of the lama, the inhabitants manufacture stockings, cloth, &c.

Riobamba, the capital of the foregoing province, is situate at the extremity of an extensive valley. The productions and manufactures of its district are superior to any other in Quito; and in some parts of it are very rich mines of gold and silver. It is 98 miles S. by W. of Quito. Long. 77. 20. W. lat. 1. 38. S.

Riom, a town of France; department of Puy de Dome; seated on a hill; 8 miles N. E. of Clermont, and 115 S. of Paris. Pop. 13,500.

Rioni, or Phasis, a considerable river of Asia, which rises in Georgia, forms the S. boundary of Mingrelia, and enters the Black Sea.

Rions, a town of France; department of Gironde; seated on the Garonne; 18 miles S. E. of Bordeaux.

Riopar, a town of Spain; province of La Mancha; situate among mountains, in which are some rich mines of calamine. It is 17 miles S. W. of Alcacaz. Pop. 4600.

Ripa Transone, a town of Italy; in the papal states; 8 miles S. of Fermo.

Ripen, a seaport of Denmark, in North Jutland; capital of a diocese of the same name; with a castle, two colleges, and a public library. The tombs of several kings of Denmark are in the cathedral, which is a very handsome structure. The harbour is at a small distance, at the mouth of the Gram, in a country which supplies the best beeves in Denmark. It is 65 miles N. W. of Sleswick, and 78 S. by W. of Wiburg. Long. 8. 40. E. lat. 55. 23. N.

Ripley, a town of West Yorkshire; with a market on Wednesday; principally noted for its castle, the ancient seat of the Ingilby family; seated on the river Nyd; 23 miles W. N. W. of York, and 211 N. by W. of London.

Ripon, a borough in W. Yorkshire; governed by a mayor; with a market on Thursday. It sends two members to parliament. In its neighbourhood is the celebrated park of Studley, including the venerable remains of Fountain Abbey. Ripon was once famous for its religious houses; it has a collegiate church, a church erected in 1827, four meeting-houses, a free-school, and some other excellent charitable institutions. Its noted manufacture of spurs has long since declined, and at present the principal manufactures are linens and saddle-trees, and a considerable varnish manufacture. The market-place is one of the finest squares of the kind in England. It is seated near the Ure, over which is a handsome bridge of 17 arches; 28 miles N. N. W. of York, and 209 N. N. W. of London. Long. 1. 29. W. lat. 54. 11. N.

Riquier, St., a town of France; department of Somme; seated on the Cordon; 24 miles N. W. of Amiens.

Risborough, Prince's, a town in Buckinghamshire; with a market on Saturday; 20 miles S. of Aylesbury, and 37 W. N. W. of London. It is called Prince's Risborough, because Edward the Black Prince is said to have had here a palace and large possessions.

Ritzebuttel, the chief place of a bailiwick of the same name, belonging to the city of Hamburg; with a castle; seated half a mile S. of Cuxhaven, and 54 miles W. N. W. of Hamburgh.

Riva, a town of Germany, in the principality of Trent; on the river Riva, at its entrance into the Lake Garda; 17 miles S. W. of Trent. Pop. 3100.

Riva, a town of Austrian Italy; in the Valteline; seated on the N. end of the Lake Como; 8 miles S. of Chiavenna.

Rivadeo. *See* Ribadeo.

Rivalta, a town of Piedmont; situate on the Sangeon; 8 miles N. N. E. of Turin.

Rivalta, a town of Austrian Italy; situate on the Lake of Mantua; 5 miles W. of Mantua.

Rivarolo, a town of Piedmont; situate on the Orco; 15 miles N. of Turin.

Rivesaltes, a town of France; department of Eastern Pyrenees; seated on the Egly; 8 miles N. of Perpignan.

Rivoli, a town of Piedmont, with a magnificent castle; 9 miles W. of Turin. Population, 5000.

Rivoli, a small town of Austrian Italy, near which Bonaparte obtained one of the most remarkable of his victories, in January 1797. It is seated on the Adige; 12 miles N. W. of Verona.

Rivolo, or Rolo, a town of Italy, in Modena; between Novellara and Mirandola.

Roa, a town of Spain, in the province of Burgos; with a castle, and a splendid mansion belonging to the counts of Sizuela. It is situate on the Douro; 25 miles N. by E. of Segovia. Pop. 2500.

Roanne, a town of France; department of Loire; seated on the Loire, where it begins to be navigable for barks. Hence the merchandise of Lyons is conveyed to Paris, Orleans, Nantes, &c. It is 45 miles W. N. W. of Lyons, and 210 S. S. E. of Paris. Pop. 7000. Long. 3. 58. E. lat. 46. 4. N.

Roanoke, an island of North Carolina; on the S. side of Albermarle Sound; famous as the place where Sir Walter Raleigh made the first British settlement in North America.

Roanoke, a river of the United States; formed by the junction of the Staunton and Dan, in the S. part of Virginia. It is subject to inundations, and, on account of the falls, is navigable for shallops only, about 60 or 70 miles. It enters, by several mouths, into the S. W. part of Albemarle Sound.

Robben Island, sometimes called Penguin Island; a barren sandy island, near the Cape of Good Hope, at the entrance into False Bay. Long. 18. 22. E. lat. 33. 50. S.

Robel, a town of Germany, in the duchy of Mecklinburg-Strelitz; seated on the lake Muritz; 24 miles W. of Strelitz.

Robert Bay, a capacious bay of the island of Martinico; formed by two points called that of the E. part of La Rosa, and that of the W. part of Los Galeones.

Robin Hood Bay, a bay on the coast of Yorkshire; between Scarborough and Whitby, about one mile broad. Here is a village of fishermen, who supply the city of York, and the adjacent country, with all sorts of fish in their season. It is 6 miles S. E. of Whitby. Long. 0. 10. W. lat. 54. 25. N.

Roca, Cape, a cape of Portugal; the most western extremity of Europe. On its summit is a remarkable monastery, said to be 3000 feet above the sea; and on the E. of the mountain is a summer palace, of Moorish architecture. Here is also a small vineyard, that of Carcavella, yielding a peculiar grape; and the environs supply most of the fruits and greens used at Lisbon. This cape is called generally, by the English sailors, the Rock of Lisbon. Long. 9. 36. W. lat. 38. 42. N.

Rocamadour, a town of France; department of Lot; 23 miles N. of Cahors.

Rocella, a town of Naples, in Calabria Ultra; near which is a coral fishery; 10 miles N. E. of Gierace.

Rochdale, a borough in Lancashire; with markets on Monday and Saturday, and considerable manufactures of baize, flannels, serges, and other woollen goods; also calicoes, strong cotton goods, and hats. It has four churches, eight meeting-houses, a free grammar-school, a free-school, and national and Sunday schools. A canal from Manchester passes hence to the Calder navigation, near Halifax. The manor of Rochdale was held for the last three centuries by the Byrons, but in 1823 was sold by Lord Byron, the celebrated poet, to James Dearden, Esq. The town is seated on the river Roch, at the foot of the Yorkshire hills; 11 miles N. by E. of Manchester, and 197 N. N. W. of London. It returns one member to parliament, and is near the Manchester and Leeds railway.

Roche, a town of the Sardinian states, in Savoy; seated near a large rock, on the river Borne; 12 miles N. E. of Annecy.

Roche, or Rochefort en Ardennes, a town of Belgium, in the province of Luxemburg; with a strong castle; seated on a rock near the river Ourte; 22 miles S. of Liege, and 32 N. W. of Luxemburg.

Roche Beaucour, a town of France, department of Dordogne; 22 miles N. W. of Perigueux.

Roche Bernard, a town in the department of Morbihan, on the Vilaine; 22 miles S. E. of Vannes.

Roche Guyon, a town in the department of Seine-et-Oise; on the river Seine; 21 miles W. of Pontoise.

Roche Posay, a town in the department of Vienne, with a mineral spring; seated on the Creuse; 32 miles E. N. E. of Poitiers.

Roche sur Yon, a town in the department of Vendee; 20 miles N. W. of Luçon.

Rochechouart, a town in the department of Upper Vienne, with a castle on a mountain; 18 miles W. of Limoges.

Rochefort en Ardennes. *See* Roche.

Rochefort, a seaport of France; department of Lower Charente; with a commodious harbour, one of the most famous in France. The streets are broad and straight, and the houses low, but regular. It has a magnificent hospital, the finest hall of arms in France, a noble arsenal, a foundry for cannon, and all the other magazines necessary for the construction and equipment of ships of war. It stands on the Charente, 15 miles from its mouth, which is defended by several forts. It is 18 miles S. S. E. of Rochelle, and 127 S. W. of Paris. Pop. 15,000. Long. 0. 58. W. lat. 45. 56. N.

Rochefort, a town in the department of

Jura; on the river Doubs; 6 miles N. E. of Dole, and 22 W. S. W. of Besançon.

ROCHEFORT, a town in the department of Maine-et-Loire; on the river Loiret; 10 miles S. S. W. of Angers.

ROCHEFORT, a town in the department of Puy de Dome; 17 miles S. W. of Clermont.

ROCHEFOUCAULT, a town in the department of Charente; seated on the Tardoire; 12 miles N. E. of Angouleme. Pop. 2400.

ROCHELLE, a fortified seaport of France; capital of the department of Lower Charente, and a bishop's see. The houses are supported by piazzas, and the haven is surrounded by a prodigious mole, 4482 feet in extent. The inhabitants carry on a considerable trade, especially in wine, brandy, sugar, salt, paper, linen, and serges. Rochelle was the birthplace of Reaumur, the celebrated naturalist. It is seated in a plain at the bottom of a small gulf of the Atlantic; 78 miles S. by E. of Nantes, and 330 S. W. of Paris. Pop. 17,500. Long. 1. 10. W. lat. 46. 9. N.

ROCHEMAUR, a town in the department of Ardeche; seated on the Rhone; 8 miles N. N. E. of Viviers.

ROCHESTER, a city in Kent; with a market on Friday. It returns two members to parliament. Its castle, now in ruins, once rendered it of great importance; and here also are some remains of a priory. Rochester is a bishop's see, and has, besides the cathedral, two parish churches. The inhabitants are chiefly tradesmen and innkeepers, no sort of manufacture being now carried on here. It has two free-schools, one called the King's, and the other the City School; an hospital, liberally endowed for 12 poor people; and an almshouse for six poor travellers, who are supplied for one night with lodging, entertainment, and fourpence: an inscription over the door intimates that rogues and proctors are excepted. Rochester is united to the town of Stroud by a stone bridge of eleven arches over the river Medway, and is contiguous to Chatham on the E. It is 26 miles W. N. W. of Canterbury, and 29 E. S. E. of London.

ROCHESTER, a town in North America; United States, New Hampshire. Pop. 431.—Also a town in Monroe county, New York; 7 miles from Lake Ontario, at the falls of Genessee. Pop. 20,191. Here are some very extensive flour-mills, and an aqueduct over the Genessee.—Also a town in Plymouth county, Massachusets; 48 miles S. of Boston. Pop. 864.

ROCHFORD, a town in Essex, with a market on Thursday; 16 miles S. E. of Chelmsford, and 40 E. by N. of London.

ROCHLITZ, a town of Saxony, with a castle on a rock, and a handsome bridge over the Mulda; 24 miles S. E. of Leipsic.

ROCKAWAY, a town of New Jersey, in Morris county, on a river of its name; 15 miles N. by W. of Morristown.

ROCKBRIDGE. *See* CEDAR CREEK.

ROCKFORD, a town of North Carolina, in Wilkes county, on the Yadkin; 33 miles E. by N. of Wilkes.

ROCKINGHAM, a town in Northamptonshire, with a market on Thursday. It is seated on the Welland, 12 miles S. of Oakham, and 83 N. by W. of London.

ROCKINGHAM, a town of North Carolina, chief of Richmond county; 46 miles W. N. W. of Fayetteville.

ROCKINGHAM, a town of Virginia, chief of a county of its name, situate on a branch of Shenandoah River; 40 miles S. W. of Woodstock, and 55 E. N. E. of Bath.

ROCKY MOUNT, a town of Virginia, chief of Franklin county; seated near the source of the Staunton, 35 miles S. W. of New London.

ROCKY MOUNTAINS, a ridge of mountains which traverse the whole length of the continent of North America, from its southern to its northern extremity, where they terminate in the Icy Sea, in lat. 70.

ROCKY RIVER, a river of Louisiana, which falls into the Mississippi on the E.—Several other rivers of this name also water the United States.

ROCROY, a town of France, department of Ardennes; celebrated for the victory gained by the French over the Spaniards in 1643. It is seated in a plain, surrounded by forests, 26 miles N. of Rethel. Pop. 2900.

RODACH, a town of Germany, in the principality of Saxe-Coburg, on a river of its name, 9 miles N. W. of Coburg.

RODBY, a seaport of Denmark, in the island of Laland. The passage hence to Heiligenhaven, in Holstein, and to the island of Femern, is much frequented. It is 10 miles N. E. of Naxkow. Long. 11. 45. E. lat. 54. 45. N.

RODENBURG, a town and castle of Germany, in the district of Schauenberg, near which is a mineral spring. It is 11 miles W. by S. of Hanover.

RODEZ, or RHODEZ, a town of France, capital of the department of Aveiron, and a bishop's see. Here are four great annual fairs, and some manufactures of grey cloths and serges. The lofty steeple of its cathedral is admired for its architecture. It is seated in the midst of mountains, on a hill, at the foot of which flows the Aveiron; 30 miles W. by S. of Mende. Pop. 6500.

RODING, a river in Essex, which rises near Dunmow, runs S. to Ongar, and gives the name of Rodings to this part of the county. It then flows between Epping and Hainault forests to Barking, below which it joins the Thames.

RODINGS, a district of Essex, comprising eight parishes, each of which is called Roding; but they are distinguished by the additional appellation of Beauchamp, Eythorp, High, Leaden, White, Abbot's, Berner's, and Margaret's.

RODOK, a town of Hindostan, in the province of Delhi; 50 miles E. of Hissar, and 60 W. N. W. of Delhi

RODOSTO, a seaport of European Turkey, in Romania, and a bishop's see, seated on the side of a hill on the Sea of Marmora; 62 miles W. of Constantinople. Pop. 1600. Long. 27. 37. E. lat. 41. 1. N.

Rodriguez, an island in the Indian Ocean, 30 miles long and 12 broad, lying 100 leagues E. of Mauritius. The country is mountainous, and in many parts rocky, though in some places the soil is excellent; but the best production of the island is the land turtle, which are in great abundance. On the N. side is a bay, that affords secure shelter for ships, and ample supplies of wood and water. Long. 63. 0. E. lat. 19. 30. S.

Roer, a river of the Prussian states, which rises in Westphalia, flows by Arensberg, Schwerte, Werden, and Duysburg, and enters the Rhine at Roerort.

Roerort, a town of the Prussian states, in the duchy of Cleves, at the conflux of the Roer with the Rhine; 17 miles S. by E. of Vesel.

Roeulx, a town of Belgium, in Hainault; 8 miles N. E. of Mons.

Rogersville, a town of Tennessee, chief of Hawkins county, on the N. side of the Holston; 60 miles N. N. E. of Knoxville.

Rogerwick, or **Port Baltic**, a seaport of Russia, in the province of Revel, seated on a fine bay at the entrance of the Gulf of Finland; 40 miles W. N. W. of Revel. Long. 23. 20. E. lat. 59. 10. N.

Rogonatpour, a town of Bengal, capital of the district of Pachete. It is 126 miles N. W. of Calcutta. Long. 86. 47. E. lat. 23. 32. N.

Roha, or **Rouah**. *See* **Orfa**.

Rohan, a town of France, department of Morbihan, on the Aoust; 20 miles N. of Vannes.

Rohilcund, or **Rohilla**, a territory of Hindostan, inhabited by the Rohillas, and formerly belonging to the province of Delhi, but now included in the district of Bareilly. It was conquered by the nabob of Oude, with the assistance of the British, in 1774. But in 1801 it was ceded to the British, and is now governed by a civil establishment.

Rokitzan, a town of Bohemia, with good cloth manufactures and a trade in iron; 7 miles E. by N. of Pilsen.

Rolduc, a town of the Netherlands, in the late duchy of Limburg; 10 miles S. W. of Juliers.

Rom, an island of Denmark, on the E. coast of South Jutland. It is 7 miles long, and nearly 3 broad, and contains a few villages.

Romagna, the former name of a province of Italy, in the papal states; bounded on the N. by the Ferrarese, E. by the Gulf of Venice, S. by Tuscany and Urbino, and W. by Bologna and Tuscany. It is fertile in corn, wine, oil, and fruits; and has also mines, mineral waters, and salt-works, which make its principal revenue. Ravenna is the capital.

Romainmotier, a town of Switzerland, in the Pays de Vaud, capital of a bailiwick, with a castle; seated in a narrow valley, through which flows the river Diaz; 11 miles S. W. of Yverdun.

Romani, a town of European Turkey, in Moldavia, and a bishop's see; seated on the Siret, 50 miles W. S. W. of Jassy.

Romania, a province or division of European Turkey, about 200 miles long, and 130 broad; bounded on the N. by Bulgaria, E. by the Black Sea, S. by the Sea of Marmora and the Archipelago, and W. by Macedonia. The whole of this fine country, comprising Thrace and Macedon, is at present in a very backward state, owing to the oppression and arbitrary exactions of the Turks. Area, 120,000 square miles. Pop. 6,000,000.

Romano, a town of Austrian Italy, on a river that runs between the Oglio and Serio; 26 miles E. of Milan.

Romans, a town of France, in the department of Drome, on the Isere; 22 miles S. W. of Grenoble, and 30 S. of Vienna. Pop. 6500.

Rome, a celebrated city of Italy, the capital of the pope's dominions. It is situate on the Tiber, over which it has four bridges. The walls are of brick, in which are 15 gates; and its whole circumference, including that part beyond the Tiber and all belonging to the Vatican, is upwards of 16 miles; but not more than a third of this space is occupied by the present city, which was almost entirely rebuilt on the ruins of the ancient city at the close of the 15th century, and is about 14 or 15 feet above the former level, in consequence of the accumulated rubbish occasioned by its destruction. It is computed to contain 150,000 inhabitants, which, though greatly inferior to what it could boast in the days of its ancient power, is considerably more than it could number at some former periods since the fall of the empire. Some of the principal streets are of considerable length, and perfectly straight. That called the Corso is the most frequented. The shops on each side are three or four feet higher than the street, and there is a path for foot passengers on a level with the shops. The palaces, of which there are several in this street, range in a line with the houses, having no courts before them. The Strada Felice, and the Strada di Porta Pia, are also very long and noble streets. Rome exhibits a strange mixture of magnificent and interesting, and of common and beggarly objects; the former consist of palaces, churches, fountains, and the remains of antiquity; the latter comprehend all the rest of the city. The principal object of attraction is the church of St. Peter, which surpasses in size and magnificence the finest monuments of ancient architecture. It was begun to be built in 1506, finished in 1621, and is entirely covered, both within and without, with marble. Its length is 730 feet, the breadth 520, and the height, from the pavement to the top of the cross which crowns the cupola, 450. The high altar under the cupola is 90 feet in height, and of extraordinary magnificence. It is approached by a splendid double colonnade, enclosing an oval space, in which stands the noble Egyptian obelisk, and two fountains, upwards of 50 feet high. A complete description of this church, and of its statues, basso-relievos, columns, and various other ornaments, would fill volumes. The cathedral of St. John Lateran, the Romans say, is the most ancient of all the churches of Rome, and the mother of all the churches in Christendom. It contains the Scala Santa, of 28 white marble steps, brought from Jerusalem, by which Christ is said to have ascended to the palace of Caiaphas. To this church every new pope constantly goes first in a magnificent procession, to take possession of the holy see. The Pantheon, which, from its circular form, has obtained the name of the Rotunda, is the most perfect of the Roman temples which now remain, and, notwithstanding the depredations it has sustained from Goths, Vandals, and popes, is still a beautiful monument of Roman taste. The pavilion of the great altar of St. Peter, and the four wreathed pillars of Corinthian brass which support it, were formed out of the spoils of the Pantheon, which, after nearly 2000 years, has still a probability of outliving its proud and capacious rival. Its height is 150 feet, and its width nearly the same. There are no pillars to support the roof, which is constructed in the manner of a cupola; neither has it any windows, a sufficiency of light being admitted through a central opening in the dome. As the Pantheon is the most entire, the amphitheatre of Vespasian is the most stupendous monument of antiquity in Rome. About one-half of the external circuit still remains, from which a pretty exact idea may be formed of the original structure; and, by computation, it could contain 85,000 spectators. But the antiquities of Rome are too numerous to be minutely described; so that the ancient Forum, now a cow-market, the beautiful column of Trajan, &c., must be passed over. The Campidoglio, built by Michael Angelo, is a beautiful structure, standing on the site of the ancient capitol, so long the centre of the empire of the world. The body of this palace is the residence of the senators of Rome, and the wings are inhabited by the conservators of the city. The pope has three superb palaces, of which the principal is the Vatican, near St. Peter's church. The library of this palace is the largest and most complete in the world; rich especially in MSS. in all languages, and of all ages. In Rome the connoisseur will meet with innumerable paintings by the greatest masters, and with the finest works of sculpture, &c. Besides the university, which consists of several noble colleges, there are numerous academies and literary societies. The castle of St. Angelo serves more to keep the city in awe than to repel any foreign attack. Rome was formerly the metropolis of one of the greatest empires that have ever existed, and may be regarded as the parent of all the cities, the arts, and states of modern Europe. The ancient Romans were governed by seven kings, for about 220 years. During the next 488 years they were governed by consuls, tribunes, decemvirs, and dictators, in their turns. They were afterwards governed by 60 emperors, for the space of 518 years. Their wars with the Carthaginians, Spaniards, Gauls, Mithridates of Pontus, Parthians, and Jews, were the most noted. The Roman empire was afterwards much distracted by various commotions, and in 410 Rome was taken and burnt. In May, 1527, Rome was invested by the army of the emperor Charles V.; and the general, to prevent a mutiny, promised to enrich them with the spoils of this opulent city. The general, however, was himself killed, as he was planting a scaling-ladder against the walls; but his soldiers, not discouraged by his death, mounted to the assault with the utmost valour, and, entering the city, exercised all those brutalities that may be expected from ferocity aggravated by resistance. In the wars which attended the French revolution Rome was again a considerable sufferer. Large contributions and severe military exactions were drawn from the inhabitants, and a great number of the most valuable statues and paintings were sent off to Paris. The pope was finally restored in 1814. *See* Popedom. Rome is 110 miles N. W. of Naples, 410 S. S. W. of Vienna, and 600 S. E. of Paris. Long. 12. 29. E. lat. 41. 54. N.

Rome, a town of New York, in Herkimer county, near which, to the E., is Fort Stanwix. It is seated at the head of Mohawk River, 8 miles W. N. W. of Whitestown. Pop. 4360.

Romenay, a town of France, in the department of Soane-et-Loire; 15 miles N. N. E. of Maçon.

Romerstadt, a town of Moravia, in the neighbourhood of which are some iron-mines; 20 miles N. N. E. of Olmutz.

Romford, a town in Essex, with a market on Tuesday for hogs, calves, and sheep, and on Wednesday for cattle, corn, &c.. It is 12 miles E. N. E. of London.

Römhild, a town of Germany, in the duchy of Saxe-Meiningen, with a castle; 13 miles S. of Meiningen.

Romkala, a town of Syria, with the remains of an ancient and strong castle, and two churches. It is seated on the Euphrates, at the influx of the Simeren, and is used by the Turks as a place of banishment for great men in disgrace; 85 miles N. N. E. of Aleppo.

Romna, a town of Russia, in the government of Tchernigof; 88 miles E. S. E. of Tchernigof.

Romney, a town of Virginia, chief of Hampshire county, seated on the S. W. branch of the Potomac; 50 miles W. N. W. of Winchester. Long. 59. 5. W. lat. 39. 20. N.

Romney, New, a town in Kent, with a market on Thursday. It is one of the cinque-ports; but, since the sea has retired, it is much reduced. It is seated on a hill in Romney Marsh. About a mile to the W. is Old Romney, the original port, which is now a small place; 22 miles S. W. of Dover, and 71 S. E. of London. Long. 0. 56. E. lat. 50. 59. N.

Romney Marsh, a tract in the most southern part of Kent, between Dungeness and Rye Haven, defended from the sea by a strong embankment, called Dymchurch Wall. It is 20 miles long and 8 broad, containing about 50,000 acres of firm land, and some of the richest pastures in England. Vast flocks of sheep and herds of cattle are fattened here for the London market. It has two towns and 19 parishes, which were incorporated in the reign of Edward

IV., by the name of a bailiff, 24 jurats, and the commonalty of Romney Marsh.

Romont, a town of Switzerland, in the canton of Friburg; seated on a mountain, 10 miles N. W. of Friburg.

Romorentin, a town of France, in the department of Loire-et-Cher, with a castle, and manufactures of serges and cloths; seated on the Saudre, 26 miles S. E. of Blois, and 40 S. by W. of Orleans. Pop. 6100.

Romsdal, a town of Norway, capital of a province in the government of Drontheim; 100 miles S. W. of Drontheim. Long. 7. 54. E. lat. 62. 28. N.

Romsey, a town in Hampshire, governed by a mayor, with a market on Saturday. It has a manufacture of shalloons, and several paper-mills. It is seated on the Andover canal and the river Test; 8 miles N. W. of Southampton, and 72 W. by S. of London.

Ronaldshay, North and South, two small islands of the Orkneys.

Ronay, one of the Hebrides, situate between the Isle of Skye and the mainland.

Roncevallos, a town of Spain in Navarre, situate in a valley to which it gives name; 14 miles N. N. E. of Pampelona.

Ronciglione, a town of Italy, in the States of the Church, with a fortified castle. It is seated on the Tereia, near a lake of the same name; 28 miles N. N. W. of Rome. Long. 12. 32. E. lat. 42. 18. N.

Ronda, a strong town of Spain, in Granada, with a castle, situate on a craggy rock, near the river Guadiaro; 43 miles N. by E. of Gibraltar. It contains but few works of art, but its natural curiosities render it one of the most interesting towns on the peninsula. Pop. 20,000.

Ronne, a seaport of Denmark, in the island of Bornholm, and the residence of the governor. The harbour is fortified, but not deep. Long. 14. 55. E. lat. 55. 10. N.

Ronneburg, a town and castle of Germany, in the principality of Altenburg, belonging to Saxe-Gotha; 14 miles S. W. of Altenburg.

Roopat, an island in the Straits of Malacca, separated from Sumatra by a narrow channel. Long. 101. 9. E. lat. 3. 0. N.

Roosebecke, a town of Belgium, province of West Flanders; 20 miles S. W. of Ghent. Pop. 4000.

Roque, St., a town of Spain, in Andalusia, at the entrance of the isthmus which separates Gibraltar from the continent. It stands on the top of a hill, overlooking the bay; 17 miles N. E. of Tariffa, and 58 S. E. of Cadiz.

Roquefort, a town of France, department of Landes; seated on the Douese, 15 miles E. N. E. of Mont de Marsan.

Roquemaure, a town in the department of Gard; 22 miles N. E. of Nismes. Pop. 3200.

Roquetas, a town of Spain, in Granada, on the coast of the Mediterranean; 10 miles S. W. of Almeria, and 52 S. E. of Granada.

Roras, a town of Norway, in Drontheim, noted for important mines of copper; 68 miles S. of Drontheim. Pop. 3000.

Rosa, a singular mountain of the Pennine Alps, at the N. E. boundary of Piedmont, little inferior in height to Mont Blanc. It forms, as it were, a circus of gigantic peaks, round the village of Macugnaga; and its appearance is supposed to impart the name, from some resemblance to an expanded rose.

Rosamarino, a town of Sicily, in Val di Demona, at the mouth of a river of its name; 22 miles W. by S. of Patti.

Rosana, a town of Russian Lithuania, in the government of Grodno; seated near the Zolva, 56 miles S. W. of Novogrodec.

Rosaria, El, a town of Mexico, 400 miles N. W. of Mexico, near the mines of Copala, now filled with water. Pop. 5600.

Rosbach, a village of Prussian Saxony, famous for a victory obtained by Prussia over the French and Austrians in 1757; 10 miles S. E. of Merseburg.

Roschad, a town of Switzerland, with a castle on a mountain, seated on the Lake of Constance; 7 miles E. N. E. of St. Gall.

Roschild, a town of Denmark, in the Isle of Zealand, and a bishop's see. It is now a poor place, but was the residence of the kings of Denmark for several centuries before Copenhagen was founded; and the cathedral has long been the place of their sepulture. A treaty of peace was concluded here in 1658. It is seated at the end of a deep gulf; 16 miles W. of Copenhagen.

Roscommon, a county of Ireland, in the province of Connaught; 60 miles long and 37 broad; bounded on the N. by Sligo and Leitrim, E. by Longford and West Meath, S. by Galway, and W. by Galway and Mayo. It is divided into 56 parishes, and sends two members to parliament. It is a tolerably level country, producing excellent corn and pasturage, yet there are some extensive bogs.

Roscommon, a town of Ireland, capital of the above county; 80 miles W. by N. of Dublin. Long. 8. 42. W. lat. 55. 34. N.

Roscrea, a town of Ireland, in Tipperary. Two miles to the S. E. are the singular ruins of an abbey, on an island of about three acres, in the centre of a bog. It is 20 miles W. S. W. of Maryborough, and 32 N. of Cashel.

Roseau. *See* Charlotte Town.

Rosemarkie. *See* Fortrose.

Rosenburg, a town of the Prussian states, in the principality of Oppeln, with a small castle; 25 miles N. E. of Oppeln.

Rosenheim, a town of Bavaria, seated at the conflux of the Manguald with the Inn; 34 miles S. E. of Munich.

Roses, or Rosas, a seaport of Spain, in Catalonia, with a citadel. It was taken by the French in 1693, and again in 1793. It is seated on a bay of the same name, in the Mediterranean; 27 miles N. E. of Gerona. Pop. 2600. Long. 3. 7. E. lat. 42. 17. N.

Rosetta (Raschid), a town of Egypt, one of the pleasantest in the country. It has a great manufacture of striped and other coarse linens; but its chief business is the carriage of goods to Cairo; for all European merchandise is brought hither from Alexandria by sea. The rice grown, in its vicinity, called sultani, is chiefly sent to Constantinople, and its exportation to any other place is prohibited. Rosetta was taken by the French in 1798, and here the English were defeated by the Turks in 1807. It stands on an island formed by the W. branch of the Nile; 25 miles E. N. E. of Alexandria, and 100 N. N. W. of Cairo. Pop. about 9000. Long. 30. 23. E. lat. 31. 23. N.

Rosienne, a town of Russia, in the government of Wilna, formerly the capital of Samogitia. It is seated on the Dubisse, 70 miles S. of Mittau. Long. 23. 35. E. lat. 55. 30. N.

Rosiers aux Salines, a town of France, department of Meurthe, formerly celebrated for its salt-works; seated on the Meurthe, 10 miles S. of Nancy. Pop. 2200.

Rosoy, a town in the department of Seine-et-Marne, with a magnificent castle; 16 miles E. N. E. of Melun, and 30. S. E. of Paris.

Ross, a town in Herefordshire, with a market on Thursday. It owes most of its improvements and charitable institutions to John Kyrle, commonly called the Man of Ross, whose benevolent character is so interestingly delineated by Pope. Four miles to the S. W. are the massive remains of Goodrich Castle; and near it are the ruins of Flanesford Priory, the chapel of which is converted into a barn. Ross is seated on an elevated rock, on the Wye; 12 miles S. E. of Hereford, and 120 W. by N. of London.

Ross, or Ross Carbery, a seaport of Ireland, in the county of Cork, and united to Cork as an episcopal see. The harbour was formerly famous, but has been gradually filled up with sand, so that the town is sunk from its former splendour. It is seated on a bay of the Atlantic, 20 miles S. W. of Kinsale. Long. 8. 53. W. lat. 51. 32. N.

Ross, New Town, a borough of Ireland, in the county of Wexford; situate on the Barrow; which is navigable for large vessels up to the quay. The town has a considerable trade, and exports a great quantity of wool, butter, and beef. It returns one member to parliament. It is 12 miles N. E. of Waterford, and 19 W. of Wexford.

Rossano, a strong town of Naples, in Calabria Citra; and an archbishop's see. The adjacent valleys yield oil, capers, saffron, and excellent pepper. It is seated on an eminence, surrounded by rocks; 3 miles from the Gulf of Tarento, and 136 S. E. of Naples. Pop. 7000. Long. 16. 38. E. lat. 39. 48. N.

Rosslau, a town of Germany, in the principality of Anhalt; with a castle; seated at the conflux of the Rosslau with the Elbe; 10 miles S. S. E. of Zerbst.

Ross-shire, a county of Scotland; 80 miles long, and 50 broad; bounded on the N. by Sutherlandshire and the Frith of Dornoch, W. by the Minch, S. by Inverness-shire, and E. by the Frith of Murray and the county of Cromarty, which last it almost encloses. It is divided into 30 parishes. It sends, in conjunction with Cromarty, one member to parliament. The middle and N W. parts are mountainous and dreary; the E. part is variegated with woods, lakes, and rivers. The hills feed horses, beeves, sheep, and goats, and abound with game; the rivers and lakes teem with fish and water-fowl; and the E. coast is visited regularly by a shoal of herrings. Agriculture has undergone great improvements within these few years, and large quantities of corn are grown. The island of Lewis is attached to this county. Tain is the capital.

Rosswein, a town of Saxony; with a good trade in wool, flannel, and cloth; seated on the Muldau; 23 miles W. of Dresden. Pop. 2700.

Rostak, a town of Arabia, in the province of Oman, and the seat of a sovereign prince. It is 120 miles W. of Mascat. Long. 57. 30. E. lat. 23. 30. N.

Rostock, a fortified town of Germany, in the duchy of Mecklenburg-Schwerin; with a university, a good harbour, a strong citadel, an arsenal, and three churches. It is divided into three parts, the Old, the New, and the Middle Town, and carries on a large trade. It is seated on the river Warnow, 10 miles from its entrance into the Baltic, and 32 E. N. E. of Wismar. Pop. 13,000. Long. 12. 20. E. lat. 154. 10. N.

Rostof, a town of Russia, in the government of Jaroslaf; and an episcopal see. It is seated on the Lake Nero, or Rostof, which communicates with the Volga by the river Kotorost; 95 miles N. E. of Moscow. Pop. 5000.

Rostrenan, a town of France, department of Cotes du Nord; near the Blavet; 35 miles S. W. of St. Brieux.

Rostrevor, a seaport of Ireland, in the county of Down; with a considerable salt-work and a pottery. It is much frequented for sea-bathing, and the peculiar beauty of its situation renders it one of the most delightful summer retreats in the province. Adjoining the town is Rostrevor Hill, a romantic mountain of extraordinary elevation and beauty. The town is seated on Carlingford Bay; 9 miles S. E. of Newry.

Rota, a town and castle of Spain, in Andalusia; and at the entrance of the Bay of Cadiz; 9 miles N. N. W. of Cadiz. Pop. 6000.

Rotas, a town of Hindostan, in the province of Lahore; 85 miles N. W. of Lahore. Long. 71. 52. E. lat. 32. 4. N.

Rotas, a town of Hindostan, in the province of Bahar; 108 miles S. W. of Patna.

Rotenberg, a town and fortress of Bavaria; capital of a lordship of the same name; situate on a mountain; 18 miles N. E. of Nurenburg, and 27 S. S. W. of Bayreuth. Pop. 5700.

Rotenburg, a town of Switzerland, in the canton of Lucern; 4 miles N. of Lucern.

Rotenburg, a town of Wirtemburg, in the county of Hohenburg; with a castle. Near it is a famous mineral spring. It stands on the Neckar; 6 miles W. S. W. of Tubingen.

Rotenburg, a town of Hanover, in the duchy of Verden; on the river Wumme; 15 miles N. by E. of Verden.

Rotenburg, a town of Germany, in the electorate of Hesse with a palace; seated on the Fulda; 24 miles S. S. E. of Cassel. Pop. 3000.

ROTENFELS, a town of Bavaria, in the circle of Lower Maine; seated on the Maine; 13 miles N. W. of Wurtzburg.

ROTH, a town and castle of Bavaria, in the district of Anspach; noted as the birthplace of the celebrated Gessner. It stands at the conflux of the Roth with the Rednitz; 18 miles S. of Nurenburg.

ROTHBURY, a town in Northumberland; with a market on Friday; situate on the Coquet, in a sequestered and romantic glen, sheltered from the northern blasts by towering hills; on the S. an abrupt bank rises in a pyramidal form, the summit of which is crowned by a stately tower. The Duke of Northumberland is lord of the manor, though he possesses very little freehold property in the town; 12 miles S. W. of Alnwick, and 303 N. by W. of London.

ROTHENBURG, a town of Prussian Silesia, on the river Neissa; 15 miles N. of Gorlitz.

ROTHENBURG, a town of Bavarian Franconia; surrounded by moats and ramparts. It stands on a mountain, by the river Tauber, from which it is supplied with water by means of a machine; 15 miles W. N. W. of Anspach. Pop. 5700. Long. 10. 18. E. lat. 49. 22. N.

ROTHER, a river which rises in Sussex, forms the boundary between that county and Kent for a short space, and enters the English Channel at Rye.

ROTHERHAM, a town in West Yorkshire; with a market on Monday, celebrated for the sale of cattle. It has a spacious church, four meeting-houses, a charity school, a free school, a subscription library, an extensive brewery, a central station for the N. Midland Railway, &c. It is famous for the extensive iron works in its vicinity at Masbrough, and has an ancient castle on an eminence near the town. It is seated at the conflux of the Rother with the Don, 32 miles S. of Leeds, and 165 N. by W. of London.

ROTHERHITHE, a suburb of London, in Surrey; situate on the S. bank of the Thames, and communicates with the northern side by means of a tunnel, a magnificent work, commenced by Mr. Brunel in 1823, and completed in 1843.

ROTHSAY, a borough of Scotland, the capital of the Isle of Bute. Here is an ancient castle, once a royal palace. The inhabitants are actively engaged in the herring fishery, and several cotton-works are also established. Rothsay joins with Ayr, Irvine, Campbeltown, and Inverary, in sending one member to parliament. It is situate on the E. side of the island, and has an excellent harbour and pier; 80 miles W. by S. of Edinburgh. Long. 4. 53. W. lat. 55. 48. N.

ROTHWEIL, a town of Germany, in Wirtemburg; seated on the Neckar, near its source; 27 miles S. S. W. of Tubingen. Long. 8. 37. E. lat. 48. 8. N.

ROTTENMANN, a town of the Austrian states, in Styria; with a college of regular canons; 20 miles N. N. W. of Judenburg.

ROTTERDAM, a city of South Holland; with one of the finest harbours in the Netherlands. Next to Amsterdam, it is the most considerable place in Holland, for the beauty of its buildings, and for its trade; and the inhabitants are computed at 60,000. There are so many deep canals, that ships may unload at the very doors of the warehouses. On the E. side of the city is a large basin and dock, for the purpose of building and launching vessels employed in the service of the admiralty of the East India Company. This port is more frequented than Amsterdam, because the ice breaks up sooner, and the tide, in two or three hours, will carry a ship into the open sea. The town-house, the bank, and the arsenal, are magnificent. Some of the houses are built in the old Spanish style, with the gable ends embattled in front; but there is a great number of modern brick houses, which are lofty and spacious, particularly on that magnificent quay called the Bomb Tees. On this quay is a handsome Jewish synagogue. In an open place at the head of one of the canals is a bronze statue of Erasmus, who was born here in 1467. This city was in a very flourishing state previously to the admission of the French troops in January, 1795, and the war with England, when the commerce of Holland was suspended. It had begun to recover in 1809, when it was again rapidly depressed by the renewal of war. After the fall of Napoleon, its prosperity greatly increased, and it is thought that the separation of Belgium from Holland will operate favourably on the commerce of this town. It is seated at the influx of the Rotte with the Merwe, (the most northern branch of the Meuse,) 36 miles S. S. W. of Amsterdam. Long. 4. 29. E. lat. 51. 56. N.

ROTTERDAM, one of the Friendly Islands, in the Pacific Ocean; discovered by Tasman, in 1643. Long. 174. 30. W. lat. 20. 16. S.

ROTTINGEN, a town of Bavaria, in the circle of Lower Maine; situate on the Tauber; 17 miles S. of Wurtzburg.

ROUAH, or ROIHA. *See* ORFA.

ROUBAIX, a town of France, department of the North; 6 miles N. of Lisle. Manufactures, woollens, camlets, and spinning thread. Pop. 8000.

ROUEN, a city of France, capital of the department of Lower Seine; and an archbishop's see. It is 7 miles in circuit, and stands on the N. side of the Seine, over which is an elegant stone bridge. The streets are narrow and crooked, and many of the houses are built of wood; notwithstanding which, it is one of the most opulent and commercial places in France. Among the public buildings, the most distinguished are the great hall of the palace, in which the parliament of Rouen met: the old castle; and the principal church, ornamented with three towers. Near this church, which is not the only remarkable one, is the public library. In the market-place is a statue of the celebrated Maid of Orleans, who was burnt here by the English as a witch. The inhabitants have manufactures of woollen, linen, cotton, ironware, paper, and pottery; also sugar-refineries and salt works. Rouen is the birthplace of the two Corneilles, and of Fontenelle. It is 50 miles S. W. of Amiens, and 70 N. W. of Paris. Pop. 87,000. Long. 1. 5. E. lat. 49. 26. N.

ROUERGUE, a former province of France, which now forms the department of AVEIRON, (which see).

ROUSAY, one of the Orkneys, lying N. W. of the mainland. It is about 9 miles long, and 4 broad.

ROUSSELART, a town of the Netherlands, in West Flanders; seated on the Mandel; 10 miles N. E. of Ypres.

ROUSSILLON, a former province of France, now included in the department of Eastern Pyrenees. *See* PYRENEES, EASTERN.

ROVEREDO, a town of the Austrian states, in Tyrol; seated near the Adige, at the foot of a mountain, on the river Lens, over which is a bridge, defended by a strong citadel. It has a very considerable trade in silk, and a great quantity of tobacco is raised here. In 1796 the Austrians were defeated near this place by the French, who took possession of the town; but they were obliged to abandon it soon afterwards; 13 miles S. of Trent. Pop. 12,000. Long. 10. 55. E. lat. 45. 50. N.

ROVIGNO, a seaport of Austrian Illyria, on the coast of Istria; with two good harbours. The inhabitants are estimated at 10,000, who are chiefly employed in the pilchard fishery, ship-building, and the sale of wood. Near it are quarries of fine stone. It is seated on a peninsula in the Gulf of Venice; 36 miles S. of Capo d'Istria. Long. 13. 58. E. lat. 45. 11. N.

ROVIGO, a town of Austrian Italy; capital of a province or delegation of its name, and the residence of the bishop of Adria, to the decline of which town it owes its present prosperity. It is seated on the Adige; 37 miles S. W. of Venice. Pop. 9000. Long. 12. 4. E. lat. 45. 8. N.

ROWAN, a county in the W. part of North Carolina; with 12,109 inhabitants. Chief town, Salisbury.

ROWLEY, a town of Massachusets, in Essex county; 28 miles N. E. of Boston. Pop. 1203.

ROXBOROUGH, a town of North Carolina; capital of Person county.

ROXBURGHSHIRE, a county of Scotland, sometimes called Teviotdale; bounded N. by Berwickshire, E. and S. by Northumberland and Cumberland, and W. by the shires of Dumfries and Selkirk. It is of an irregular figure, and the greatest extent in every direction is about 30 miles. It is divided into 31 parishes, and returns one member to parliament. The principal rivers are the Tweed, Teviot, and Liddel. The face of the country exhibits a rough appearance of mosses, hills, and mountains, interspersed with narrow valleys, well watered and fertile in corn. The hills feed great numbers of sheep and cattle. Some remains are still visible of the Catrail, or Picts-work ditch, a stupendous British work, probably constructed in the fifth century, as a line of defence against the Saxons. It appears to have been a vast fosse, 26 feet broad, with a rampart 8 or 10 feet high on either side. In many parts of the county there are sepulchral tumuli, in which coffins and urns have been found. There are also Druidical circles, and other antiquities. The county had its name from the once magnificent city and castle of Roxburgh, situate between the Teviot and the Tweed, nearly opposite Kelso: of the city few traces are now evident, and the castle, near the mouth of the Teviot, is entirely a ruin. At this castle, in 1460, James II. of Scotland lost his life by the bursting of a cannon. About 2 miles from the castle, on the banks of the Teviot, is a village called Roxburgh. The present capital of the county is Jedburgh.

ROXBURGH, a town of Massachusets, in Norfolk county; 2 miles S. S. W. of Boston. Pop. 8089.—Also, a number of inconsiderable townships in the United States.

ROYALSTON, a town of Massachusets, Worcester county; 70 miles W. N. W. of Boston. Pop. 1667.

ROYALTON, a town of Vermont, in Windsor county. Pop. 1997.

ROYAN, a town of France, department of Lower Charente. It was fortified by the Huguenots, and vigorously defended against Louis XIII. in 1622. It is seated at the mouth of the Garonne; 18 miles S. W. of Saintes. Pop. 2700.

ROYE, a town in the department of Somme; 26 miles S. E. of Amiens. Pop. 3100.

ROYSTON, a town in Hertfordshire, with a market on Wednesday. Part of the town extends into Cambridgeshire. Under the market-place is a kind of subterranean crypt, dug out of the solid chalk, supposed to be a Saxon construction; 14 miles S. of Cambridge, and 37 N. of London.

RUATAN, an island in the bay of Honduras; 30 miles long, and 9 broad, with a fine harbour. Long. 86. 45. W. lat. 16. 23. N.

RUBICON, the ancient name of a small river of Italy, which runs into the Gulf of Venice, to the northward of Rimini; celebrated in history as the limit prescribed to Cæsar by the Roman senate, when the ambitious views of that commander became suspected.

RUCKINGEN, a town of Germany, in Hesse-Cassel; which was the scene of an obstinate engagement between the French and Bavarians in 1813. It is seated on the Kinzig; 5 miles E. of Hanau.

RUDAW, a town of East Prussia, formerly fortified with a castle, now in ruins. It is remarkable for the victory obtained by the Teutonic knights over Kinstud, great duke of Lithuania, in 1370; in memory of which a stone pillar was erected, which is still remaining; 12 miles N. N. W. of Konigsberg.

RUDELSTADT, or RUDOLSTADT, a town of Germany; capital of the county of Schwartzburg Rudolstadt; with a fine castle on a mountain. It has manufactures of flannel and stuffs. It is seated on the Saale, over which is a stone bridge; 22 miles S. E. of Erfurt. Pop. 4000. Long. 11. 50. E. lat. 50. 44. N.

Rudelstadt, a town of Prussian Silesia, in the principality of Schweidnitz; with a mine-office and copper-works; seated on the Bober; 18 miles W. of Schweidnitz.

Rudesheim, a town of Germany, in the duchy of Nassau; celebrated for its wine; 3 miles N. of Bingen.

Rudisto. *See* Rodosto.

Rudkioping, a seaport of Denmark, in the island of Langeland. It has a considerable trade in corn and provisions. Long. 11. 0. E. lat. 55. 1. N.

Rudolfswerd, a town of Austrian Illyria, in Carniola; with a large collegiate church; seated on the Gurck, in a country fertile in wine; 45 miles S. E. of Laubach.

Rue, a town of France; department of Somme; 15 miles N. W. of Abbeville.

Ruffach, a town in the department of Upper Rhine; 7 miles S. of Colmar. Pop. 3300.

Ruffec, a town in the department of Charente; 24 miles N. of Angouleme.

Rufia, (ancient Alpheus,) a river of Greece, in the Morea; which falls into the Gulf of Arcadia opposite the island of Zante.

Rugby, a town in Warwickshire, with a market on Saturday, celebrated for its well endowed grammar-school. It has a commodious church and two meeting-houses, and is seated on the Avon, near the junction of the Midland Counties and Birmingham railways. It is 13 miles S. E. of Coventry, and 85 N. N. W. of London.

Rugely, or Rudgley, a town in Staffordshire; with a market on Thursday, and manufactures of felts and hats, sheet iron, and of verdigris. The parish church is a modern erection, standing close to the ancient edifice, which has long been dismantled, and is fast wasting by the hand of time. The town is rapidly advancing into notice, and two new streets (Albion Street and Church Street) have been built. It is seated on the Trent; 9 miles E. S. E. of Stafford, and 126 N. W. of London.

Rugen, an island in the Baltic, on the coast of Pomerania, opposite Stralsund, the channel between which town and the island is not above a mile in breadth. Including the indentions of the sea, which are considerable, the island is 23 miles long, and 18 broad. It abounds in corn and cattle, and contains numerous gardens and plantations. This island became subject to Prussia, with the rest of Pomerania, in 1814. Pop. 28,000. The chief town is Bergen.

Rugenwald, a town of Prussian Pomerania, in the government of Coslin; with a castle. Here is a good salmon-fishery, and a trade in linen. It is seated on the Wipper; 3 miles from the Baltic, and 35 N. E. of Colberg. Long. 16. 17. E. lat. 54. 25. N.

Ruhland, a town of Prussia, in Upper Lusatia, with a trade in fish and beer; seated on the Elster; 25 miles N. by E. of Dresden.

Rum, one of the Hebrides; 7 miles W. of the S. extremity of Skye. It is 8 miles long, and 6 broad, the surface hilly and rocky; but it feeds a considerable number of small sheep, whose flesh and wool are valuable. The only harbour is Loch Scresort, on the E. coast. Long. 6. 20. W. lat. 57. 10. N.

Rumigny, a town of France, department of Ardennes; 12 miles S. W. of Rocroy.

Rumilly, a town of the Sardinian states, in Savoy; situate on an elevated plain, at the conflux of the Seram and Nepha; 7 miles W. S. W of Annecy. Pop. 3100.

Rummelsburg, a town of Prussia, in Pomerania; with manufactures of cloth, seated on the Wipper, 14 miles N, of New Stettin.

Rumney, or Rhyney, a river of Wales; which rises in Brecknockshire, and, separating the counties of Glamorgan and Monmouth, enters the Bristol Channel to the S. E. of Cardiff.

Runcorn, a township in Cheshire. It is a place of some importance, from being the termination of the Duke of Bridgewater's canal, which here joins the Mersey, and is also frequented for sea-bathing.

Rungpour, a town of Bengal, capital of a fertile district, governed by a judge, collector, &c., and subservient to the court of circuit and appeal of Dacca. The chief produce of the district is rice, but there is also much tobacco and some indigo. The inhabitants carry on considerable trade with Assam, Bootan, and Calcutta. It is 124 miles N. N. E. of Moorshedabad. Pop. of the district, 2,735,000; of the town, 15,000. Long. 80. 4. E. lat. 25. 44. N.

Runkel, a town of Germany, in the duchy of Nassau, with a citadel on a high hill; formerly the residence of the counts of Wied-Runkel. It is seated on the Lahn; 14 miles E. N. E. of Nassau.

Rupelmonde, a town of the Netherlands, in E. Flanders; 8 miles S. W. of Antwerp.

Rupert, a river of the Hudson's Bay territory, which issues from the lake Mistassin, and flows W. into the S. E. part of James Bay. In its course it forms several small lakes; and at its mouth are the remains of Fort Rupert, formerly a settlement of the Hudson Bay Company. Long. 76. 58. W. lat. 51. 3. N.

Ruppin, a town of Prussia, in Brandenburg. It stands on the W. side of a lake, formed by the river Rhin; and on the opposite side of the lake is Old Ruppin, with an ancient castle, the residence of its former counts, whose burial place is at New Ruppin. This town was entirely consumed by fire in 1787, but is rebuilt in a handsome manner, and greatly augmented. It has a considerable trade, a manufacture of cloth, and noted breweries. It is 33 miles N. N. W. of Berlin. Pop. 4600. Long. 13. 0. E. lat. 52. 56. N.

Ruremonde, or Roermonde, a strong town of the Netherlands, in the province of Limburg; seated at the conflux of the Roer with the Meuse; 28 miles N. N. E. of Maestricht. Pop. 4600. Long. 6. 4. E. lat. 51. 11. N.

Ruscek, or Rustschuk, a town of Bulgaria, defended by a castle, with manufactures of silk, cotton, linen, woollen, tobacco, &c It was taken by the Russians in 1810, and a Turkish army was defeated near it in 1811. It is seated on the Danube; 135 miles N. by E. of Adrianople. Pop. 24,000. Long. 26. 50. E. lat. 44. 12. N.

Rush, a town of Ireland, in the county of Dublin; consisting of one street, parallel with the shore. The inhabitants are engaged in fishing.

Russ, a town of E. Prussia, on the Niemen; 28 miles S. by E. of Memel.

Russel, a county in the S. W. part of Virginia; bounded on the N. by Kentucky.

Russelville, a town of Kentucky; capital of Logan county; 85 miles S. of Louisville.

Russelsheim, a town of Germany, in Hesse-Darmstadt, situate on the Maine; 6 miles E. of Mentz, and 13 N. W. of Darmstadt.

Russey, a town of France, department of Doubs; 34 miles E. by S. of Besançon.

Russia, a vast empire, partly in Asia and partly in Europe; bounded on the N. by the Frozen Ocean, E. by the Pacific, S. by Great Tartary, the Caspian Sea, Persia, Turkey in Asia, and the Black Sea, and W. by Turkey in Europe, Poland, the Baltic Sea, and Sweden. There were three countries that had the name of Russia: namely, Red Russia, which formed the S. part of Poland; White Russia, which comprehended the E. part of Lithuania; and Black Russia, which included the governments of Kaluga, Moscow, Tula, Rezan, Volodimir, and Yaroslaf; and hence his imperial majesty takes the title of emperor and autocrat of all the Russias. It is 11,000 miles in length, with an average breadth of 1500 miles; containing an area of 7,000,000 square miles, with a population of 63,000,000. This vast territory, forty-two times the extent of France, has not double its population, and the revenue of Great Britain is quadruple that of Russia. A great portion of the country may be considered as the waste land of Europe, and the Asiatic provinces are scarcely habitable. It is divided into 51 provinces; 41 and part of 4 are in Europe, and 6, and the remaining portions of the 4, are in Asia. A country of such vast extent must lie in different climates, and the soil and products must be as different. The most fertile part is near the frontiers of Poland, the inhabitants of which are able to supply their neighbours with corn. The N. part is not only colder, but very marshy, and overrun with forests, inhabited chiefly by wild beasts. The country affords a variety of commodities, which, being of great use to foreigners, produce a considerable annual balance of trade in favour of Russia. The home commodities are chiefly sables, black furs, the skins of black and white foxes, ermines, hyænas, lynxes, bears, panthers, wolves, martins, white hares, &c., red and black juchte or Russian leather, (which for colour, smell, and softness, is not equalled in the world), copper, iron, talc, tallow, wax, honey, potash, tar, linseed and train oil, castor, isinglass, hemp, flax, thread, sail-cloth, calimanco, Siberian musk, soap, feathers, timber, &c. To these commodities may also be added almost all the merchandise of China, India, Persia Turkey, and some European countries. The principal towns are St. Petersburgh, Moscow, Riga, Odessa, Tula, Wilna, &c. The religion is that of the Greek or Eastern Church, which is governed by a patriarch, under whom are the archbishops and bishops. Every priest is called a *papa* or pope, and of these there were formerly 4000 in Moscow alone; at present their number is about 68,000. A considerable number of the Russians profess the Mahomedan religion, and many are still pagans. The inhabitants of the Swedish provinces are Lutherans; and Protestants as well as Papists enjoy full liberty of conscience. There are many convents for both sexes, but it has been wisely ordained that no male can enter into a monastic life before he is 30 years of age, and that no female can take the veil till she is 50, and even then, not without the license of the holy synod. The inhabitants in general are robust, well-shaped, and of pretty good complexions. They are great eaters, and very fond of brandy. They use bathing, but smoke no tobacco, lest the smoke should dishonour the images of the saints, which they keep in great veneration; however, they take a great deal of snuff, made of the tobacco brought from the Ukraine. The Russians were formerly wholly employed in agriculture, feeding of cattle, hunting, and fishing; and he was thought a learned man who could read and write. But Peter the Great undertook to introduce arts and sciences; and in 1724 the first university was founded that ever was in Russia; there is also an academy of sciences at Petersburg, supplied with eminent professors. With respect to dress, a long beard is in high estimation with the people of Russia, notwithstanding the efforts of their monarchs to root it out; and it is only those depending upon government, in the army and navy, who have yet complied with the custom and wish of the court. Those who retain their beards retain likewise the ancient dress; the long swaddling coat, either of skins, or of coarse cloth lined with skins, in winter, and in summer, with cloth only. About their middle they have a sash of any colour; but what they most effect is green or yellow. Their shirts are fashioned as women's; and their necks, being exposed to the cold, become very hard and impenetrable from this practice. Government continue to exert every nerve to compel the subjects to adopt the German dress. The clergy alone excepted, none can procure any place, or favour from court, upon other conditions than banishing the Asiatic sheep-skin robes. The worn-out veteran retires with a pension, upon the express terms of never again assuming the habit of his fathers. But so jealously attached are the multitude to former manners, and so honourable do they esteem them, that a Russian, dressed in his beard and gown, acquires the greatest respect. The dress of the women is the reverse of that of the men, both in fashion and colour, every part of being as short and tight as decency will allow, and very gaudy. It resembles that of the Highland women in Scotland. The Russian women are, however, far more rich in their attire; nor is gold lace wanting, any more than the art of painting, to complete the Russian belle. The rising generation are modernizing their antique vestments, the stiff embroidered napkin is supplanted by one of flowing silk; the jacket and petticoat are of muslin, or other fine stuffs; and the plaid is exchanged for a silk or satin cloak, in the cold season lined with fur. The richer class of females wear velvet boots. The dress of the higher ranks is after the French and English fashion; and all must have a covering of fur, six months of the year. Thus equipped, the prince and the peasant are drawn in their chaises and sledges through the dreary Scythian winter. The principal rivers are the Dnieper, Volga, Don, Duna or Dwina, and Oby. The sovereigns of Russia are absolute. They were formerly called Grand Dukes, which is still the title of the heir apparent. They afterwards assumed the title of *czar*, and, in the sequel, that of emperor. The first who bore the title of *czar* was Basil, son of John Basilides, who freed his country from its subjection to the Tartars, about the year 1470. The title of *emperor* was first assumed by Peter I., who, by his illustrious actions, justly acquired the surname of Great. He died in 1725; and perhaps no country ever exhibited, in so short a time, the wonders that may be effected by the genius and exertions of one man. Peter the Great at his accession to the throne, found his subjects of all ranks involved in the grossest ignorance and barbarism; his numerous armies ferocious and undisciplined; and he had neither merchant ships nor men-of-war; which, added to the remoteness of her situation, rendered the influence of Russia in the politics of Europe of little consideration. Peter civilized his barbarous subjects, disciplined his armies, built cities and fortresses, and created a navy. These national improvements have been still further prosecuted since his time, and Russia now holds a rank among the nations of the world, of which human foresight, at the commencement of the 18th century, could have formed no conception. An account of the invasion of this country, in 1812, will be found under the head of FRANCE. The campaign of 1315 afforded the Russians but little opportunity to display their military qualities: but these have had full scope in the more recent conflict with the Turks, whose power is completely, and probably for ever crippled. Petersburg is the capital of the whole empire.

RUSTGADEN, a town of Sweden, in the government of Fahlun; 23 miles S. S. W. of Fahlun.

RUSTSCHUK. *See* RUSCEK.

RUTCHESTER, a village in Northumberland, (the Vindobala of the Romans), containing some remarkable ruins of its once considerable fort. Severus's wall runs on the middle of the E. rampart, and Adrian's vallum passes about the distance of a chain to the S. of it.

RUTHERFORD, a town of North Carolina, chief of a county of the same name; situate on a branch of Broad River; 30 miles S. by E. of Morgantown, and 60 W. of Charlotte.

RUTHERGLEN, a borough of Scotland, in Lanarkshire; once a place of considerable note, but now reduced to one principal street, and a few lanes. It sends, with Glasgow, Renfrew, &c., one member to parliament. It is seated near the Clyde; 3 miles S. E. of Glasgow.

RUTHIN, or RHUTHYN, a borough of Wales, in Denbighshire, with markets on Monday and Saturday. It had a stong castle, now in ruins. It is seated on an eminence, by the river Clwyd; 15 miles S. W. of Holywell, and 205 N. W. of London. In conjunction with Holt and Denbigh, it sends one member to parliament.

RUTIGLIANO, a town of Naples, in Terra di Bari; 12 miles S. E. of Bari. Pop. 4300.

RUTLAM, a town of Hindostan, in the province of Malwa; 48 miles W. of Ougein, and 136 E. of Amedabad. Pop. 10,000.

RUTLAND, a town of Vermont, chief of a county of the same name. This town and Windsor are alternately the seat of the state legislature. It is seated on Otter Creek; 40 miles W. by N. of Windsor, and 57 N. of Bennington. Long. 73. 20. W. lat. 43. 30. N.

RUTLAND, a town of Massachusets, in Worcester county; 14 miles N. of Worcester, and 56 W. of Boston, Pop. 1260.

RUTLANDSHIRE, the smallest county in England; 18 miles long, and 14 broad; bounded on the W. and N. by Leicestershire, N. and N. E. by Lincolnshire, and S. and S. E. by Northamptonshire. It contains 95,360 acres, is divided into four hundreds and 50 parishes, has two market towns, and sends two members to parliament. The soil varies much, but in general is fertile, particularly the rich vale of Catmose; which runs from the W. side to the centre of the county. The principal rivers are the Welland and the Guash or Wash. Oakham is the county town.

RUTTUNPOUR, a city of Hindostan, in Orissa, and the capital of a small district of its name. It is 210 miles S. by W. of Benares, and 360 W. of Calcutta. Pop. 8000. Long. 82. 36. E. lat. 22. 16. N.

RUTZEN, a town of Prussian Silesia, principality of Wolau; 20 miles N. of Wolau.

RUVO, a town of Naples, in Terra di Bari; 16 miles W. of Bari. Pop. 3300.

RUZA, a town of Russia, in the government of Moscow; 48 miles W. N. W. of Moscow.

RYACOTTA, a town and fortress of Hindostan, in Mysore. It was taken in 1791 by the British, to whom it was afterwards ceded by Tippoo Sultan. It is 85 miles E. of Seringapatam, and 98 W. S. W. of Arcot. Long. 78. 6. E. lat. 12. 26. N,

RYAN, LOCH, a bay of Scotland, in the N. W. angle of Wigtonshire. The sea flows into it through a narrow pass, and it affords excellent anchorage.

RYDAL, a fertile valley in North Yorkshire, so called from the river Rye, which passes through it and falls into the Swale, near Richmond.

RYDAL-WATER, a lake in Westmoreland, a little to the W. of Ambleside. It is one mile in length, spotted with little islands, and communicates by a narrow channel with Grasmere-water to the W., and by the river Rothay, with Windermere-water, to the S.

Ryde, a town on the N. E. coast of the Isle of Wight, in the county of Southampton. It has become one of the principal watering-places in the S. of England. It stands on a declivity, and is delightfully situated. It has several handsome buildings, and a pier.

Rydroog, a town and fortress of Hindostan, in Mysore, on the river Hindenny; 60 miles N. N. E. of Chittledroog. Long. 76. 52. E. lat. 14. 40. N.

Rye, a borough and seaport in Sussex, with markets on Wednesday and Saturday. It is an appendage to the cinque ports; governed by a mayor and jurats. It returns one member to parliament. The church is a very large structure; and there are, besides, meeting-houses for Methodists, Baptists, Quakers, &c., and a chapel for the French refugees settled here during the last war. On the edge of the cliff is a small battery, and behind it Ipres tower, a square building, now a gaol. The old port is so choked up with sand, that it can admit only small vessels. In 1726 a new harbour was opened, in which vessels of 360 tons burden may safely ride. The exports are corn, malt, hops, and other products of the county; and hence are sent considerable supplies of fish to the London markets. It is 10 miles N. E. of Hastings, and 63 S. E. of London. Long. 0. 44. E. lat. 50. 57. N.

Ryegate, or Reigate, a borough in Surrey, market on Tuesday. It returns one member to parliament. Here was formerly a castle built in the time of the Saxons, and called Holmes Castle; some ruins of it are to be seen, particularly a long vault, with a room at the end, where, it is said, the barons who took up arms against king John held their private meetings. The market-house was formerly a chapel, dedicated to Thomas à Becket. It is seated in a valley, called Holmsdale; 16 miles E. of Guildford, and 21 S. W. of London.

Rymenaut, a town of Belgium, in Brabant, on the Dyle; 5 miles E. of Mechlin.

Ryssen, a town of the Netherlands, in Overyssel; on the river Regge; 16 miles E. N E. of Deventer.

Ryswick, a town of South Holland, remarkable for a treaty concluded in 1697 between England, Germany, Holland, France, and Spain, It is seated between Hague and Delft; 30 miles S. W. of Amsterdam. Pop. 1700.

Rzeczica, a town of Bohemia; 52 miles S. E. of Prague.

Rzemien, a town of Poland, in the palatinate of Sandomir; 36 miles S. S. W. of Sandomir.

Rzeva, a town of the Russian empire, and capital of a province of the same name, situate on the Volga, near its source.

Rzeszow, a well built town of Austrian Poland, capital of a circle of its name; with a brisk trade in corn and peltry, situate on the Wisloka; 80 miles E. of Cracow, and 70 W. of Lemberg. Population of the town, 4600, of the circle, 225,000.

S.

Saaba, a kingdom of Negroland; with a capital of the same name; W. of Timbuctoo, on the river Senegal.

Saada, or Saade, a strong town of Arabia, in Yemen, aud the residence of a sheik. It has a custom-house, which brings in a considerable revenue; and manufactures of Turkey leather. It is 140 miles W. N. W. of Sanaa. Long. 44. 55. E. lat. 17. 50. N.

Saalfeld, a town of Germany, in the duchy of Saxe-Coburg, with a mint, a mine-office, and manufactures of cloth, and of gold and silk stuffs. On an eminence near the town stands the once celebrated and princely abbey of St. Peter. In 1806 prince Louis Ferdinand, of Prussia, was killed here in a skirmish with the French. It stands on the Saale; 34 miles N. N. E. of Coburg, and 46. S. W. of Altenburg. Pop. 3700. Long. 11. 32. E. lat. 50. 41. N.

Saalfeld, a town of East Prussia; on the Lake Mebing; 23 miles S. E. of Marienberg.

Saar, a town of Moravia, in the circle of Brunn, on the confines of Bohemia; 42 miles N. W. of Brunn.

Saar-Louis, a town of Prussia, province of Lower Rhine, ceded by France in 1815. It is situate on a peninsula formed by the Sarre; 34 miles E. of Thionville. Pop. 4100.

Saarmund, a town of Prussia, in Brandenburg; 6 [illegible]

Saatz, a town of Bohemia, capital of a circle of the same name, which contains some of the best corn land in Bohemia, and yields hops of the best quality. The town is seated on the Eger; 48 miles W. N. W. of Prague. Population, 3800.

Saba, a fertile island of the West Indies, 12 miles in curcumference, inhabited by a few Dutch families, almost all shoemakers. The island was taken by the English in 1781, in 1801, and in 1810. It has no port, and lies a little to the W. of St. Christopher. Long. 63. 17. W. lat. 17. 39. N.

Sabanja, a town of Natolia. Here all the roads from Asia to Constantinople meet. It is situate on a lake which abounds in fish; 60 miles E. N. E. of Brusa, and 62 E. S. E. of Constantinople. Long. 29. 40. E. lat. 40. 30. N.

Sabatz, or Saboaz, a town and fortress of Servia, taken by the Austrians in 1719. It is situate on the Drave; 22 miles S. of Peterwardein, and 28 W. of Belgrade.

Sabi. *See* Xavier.

Sabia, a kingdom on the E. coast of Africa; bounded on the N. by Sofala, E. by the Mosambique Channel, S. by unknown regions, and W. by Manica. The country is fertile and populous, is crossed by a river of the same name, has mines of gold, and many elephants. Manbona is the capital.

SABIE, a seaport of Denmark, on the E. coast of North Jutland, at the mouth of a river of the same name; 23 miles N. N. E. of Alburg. Long. 10. 18. E. lat. 57. 20. N.

SABINA, a province of Italy, in the pope's dominions; 28 miles long, and 20 broad; bounded by the Tiber, the Teverone, the duchy of Spoleto, and the Neapolitan frontier. It is watered by several small rivers, and abounds in oil and wine. Magliano is the capital.

SABINE RIVER, North America, forming the boundary between the United States and the Texas territory; falling into the Gulf of Mexico.

SABIONCELLA, a town of Austrian Dalmatia, situate on the extremity of a peninsula to which it gives name. This peninsula runs a considerable way into the Adriatic, having the island of Lesina on the N., and those of Curzola and Melida on the S., all separated by a narrow channel. The town is 45 miles N. W. of Ragusa. Long. 17. 40. E. lat. 43. 20. N.

SABIONETTA, a town of Austrian Italy, formerly capital of a principality of its name, with a strong citadel; 20 miles E. of Cremona. Population, 6000.

SABLE, a town of France, in the department of Sarte, near which are some quarries of black marble. It is seated on the Sarte; 25 miles N. E. of Angers. Pop. 3100.

SABLE, CAPE, the most southerly point of Nova Scotia, near which is a fine cod-fishery. Long. 65. 39. W. lat. 43. 23. N.

SABLES, D'OLONNE, a town of France, in the department of Vendee, with a port capable of containing vessels of 150 tons. It is seated on the Bay of Biscay; 40 miles W. of Fontenay le Compte. Pop. 5200. Long. 1. 50. W. lat. 46. 28. S.

SACAI, a city and seaport of Japan, in the island of Niphon; with several castles, temples, and palaces, and a mountain on one side, which serves as a rampart; 43 miles S. by W. of Meaco. Long. 136. 5. E. lat. 34. 58. N.

SACCANIA, a province of Greece, in the Morea, comprising the ancient districts of Corinth, Sicyon, and Argos.

SACHSENBERG, a town of Germany, county of Waldeck; 10 miles S. W. of Waldeck.

SACHSENHAGEN, a town of Germany, in the principality of Schauenburg; 13 miles W. of Hanover.

SACHSENHAUSEN, a town of Germany, making part of Frankfort on the Maine. It is situate on the S. side of the river, and communicates with the rest of the city by a stone bridge.

SACHSENHAUSEN, a town of Germany, county of Waldeck; 6 miles N. W. of Waldeck.

SACHSENHEIM, a town in the kingdom of Wirtemberg; 12 miles N. N. W. of Stutgard.

SACKET'S HARBOUR, a town of New-York, in Jefferson county, with one of the best harbours in the state. It has a dock-yard, with large store-houses, and is strongly defended by forts and batteries. The Americans have attached much importance to it, and have spared no exertion to render it formidable, and it is rapidly increasing in population and importance. It is seated at the mouth of Black River, on Hungry Bay, at the E. end of Lake Ontario, 176 miles N. W. of Albany.

SACO, a considerable town of the state of Maine, in York county, seated on the Saco, opposite Biddeford, with which it is connected by three bridges. It is favourably situate for trade and manufactures; 100 miles N. N. E. of Boston. Pop. 4408.

SACO, a river of the United States, which rises in New Hampshire, and runs into the sea below the town of Saco.

SACRAMENT, ST., a town of South America, in Buenos Ayres, settled by the Portuguese, but taken in 1777 by the Spaniards. It stands on the river Plata, nearly opposite Buenos Ayres; 100 miles W. by N. of Monte Video.

SACRAPATAM, a town of Hindostan, in Mysore, on the Cavery; 73 miles N. W. of Seringapatam. Long. 75. 52. E. lat. 13. 16. N.

SADDLEBACK, a mountain in Cumberland, so called from its form. It is upwards of 3000 feet above the level of the sea; and on one side is an immense cavity, once the crater of a volcano, at the bottom of which is a lake about 20 acres in dimension; 5 miles E. N. E. of Keswick.

SADRAS, a decayed town of Hindostan, in the Carnatic, on the coast, near the mouth of the Paliar. A little to the N. are seven pagodas, hollowed out of a solid rock; 38 miles S. of Madras.

SAFFI, a strong seaport of Morocco; with a castle. It was long the centre of the commerce carried on with Europe, but now has little trade; 16 miles S. of Cape Cantin. Long. 8. 58. W. lat. 32. 28. N.

SAGAN, a town of Prussian Silesia, capital of a principality of the same name. It has double walls, a fine palace, a priory of the Augustine order, a Lutheran school, and good cloth manufactures. It is seated on the Bober; 80 miles N. W. of Breslau. Long. 15. 22. E. lat. 51. 42. N. Pop. 4700.

SAGAR, a town of Hindostan, in Mysore, with a considerable trade in pepper, betel-nut, and sandal-wood. It stands on the Varada, near its source; 25 miles N. of Nagara.

SAGARA, a celebrated mountain of Greece (the ancient Helicon,) a few miles N. of the Gulf of Corinth. It has a village of its name, formerly called Ascras, noted as the birthplace of Hesiod. From its summit may be seen great part of Greece.

SAGG HARBOUR, a seaport of New York, in Suffolk county, at the E. end of Long Island. The whale fishery from this place produces 1000 barrels of oil annually; 12 miles N. W. of Southampton, and 87 E. of New York.

SAGHALIAN, or AMOUR, a river of Chinese Tartary, which rises near the Yablonoi mountains, where it is first known by the names of Kerlon and Argun, and forms part of the boundary between Siberia and Eastern Tartary where it receives the Schilka, and takes its present name. It then takes a circuitous eastern course of 1850 miles, during which it receives many other rivers, and enters the Sea of Okotsk, opposite the N. part of the island of Saghalian.

SAGHALIAN, or TCHOKA, a large island, or peninsula, in the Sea of Okotsk, separated from the continent by the channel of Tartary on the W., and from the island Jesso by Perouse Strait on the S. and is joined to the continent by a sandy neck, in lat. 52. N. It extends from lat. 46. to 54. or not less than 550 miles in length, by about 90 of medial breadth. The centre is mountainous, and well wooded with pine, willow, oak, and birch; but the shores are level, and well adapted for agriculture. The natives resemble the Tartars in form, and the upper lip is commonly tattooed blue. The dress is a loose robe of skins, or quilted nankeen, with a girdle. Their huts are of timber, thatched with grass, with a fire-place in the middle. In the S. are found some Japanese articles; and there is a little trade with the Mantchous and Russians.

SAGHALIAN OULA, a city of Eastern Tartary, in Mantchouria. It is rich and populous, and very important on account of its situation, as it secures to the Mantchou Tartars the possession of extensive deserts covered with woods, in which a great number of sables are found. It is seated on the river Saghalian, opposite to the ruins of Ai-holm; 200 miles N. N. E. of Tcitcicar. Long. 127. 25. E. lat. 50. 6. N.

SAGRES, a strong town of Portugal, in Algarva, with a harbour and a fort; seated on a tongue of land at the S. W. extremity of the province; 20 miles W. S. W. of Lagos. Long. 9. 0. W. lat. 37. 2. N.

SAGUR, a town of Hindostan, capital of a district in the province of Malwa, situate near the Bunnas; 87 miles N. W. of Gurrah, and 112 S. of Agra. Long. 78. 53. E. lat. 23. 45. N.

SAHAGUN, a town of Spain, in Leon, with a rich abbey; seated in a fertile plain, on the river Cea; 32 miles S. E. of Leon.

SAHAR. *See* SHAHAR.

SAHARA. *See* ZAHARA.

SAHEBGUNG, or JESSORE, a town of Bengal; capital of the district of Jessore; seated on the Boirah; nearly 80 miles E. N. E. of Calcutta.

SAID, or SAHID, a province of Upper Egypt, bordering on Nubia and the Red Sea, (anciently called Thebaid) celebrated for having been the retreat of a great number of Christians, who lived here in a solitary manner. It is the least fertile and populous part of Egypt, being full of deserts.

SAIDA, a town of Syria, on the coast of the Mediterranean (the remains of the ancient Sidon); with a fort and castle. To the W. of the castle is a shoal 200 paces long, and the space between them is a road for vessels, but not safe in bad weather. The shoal, which extends along the town, has a basin, enclosed by a decayed pier: this was the ancient port, but it is now so choked up by sands that boats only can enter its mouth, near the castle. Saida is a trading town, and the chief emporium of Damascus and the interior country. The manufacture of cotton is the principal employment of its inhabitants, who are about 7000 or 8000 in number; 45 miles W. S. W. of Damascus. Long. 35. 20. E. lat. 33. 30. N.

SAIGONG, a town of Cochin China, on the river Donnai. It consists of two cities, extending about 6 miles along the western bank. Bingeh, the modern town, is about a mile from the old town, and contains a citadel built on European principles, a royal palace, and immense magazines of military and naval stores; the houses are of wood, and the town possesses some commerce. Pop. 180,000. Long. 107. 5. E. lat. 10. 47. N.

SAINT GEORGE. *See* GEORGE, ST.

SAINTES, three of the Leeward Caribbee Islands, in the West Indies, between Guadaloupe and Dominica. The middle one seems nothing more than a large barren rock, but contributes to form a good harbour. Long. 61. 45. W. lat. 15. 52. N.

SAINTES, a town of France, capital of the department of Lower Charente. Here are several monuments of antiquity, of which the most famous are the amphitheatre, the aqueducts, and the triumphal arch on the bridge over the Charente. The castle, built on a rock, is deemed impregnable; and the ancient cathedral has one of the largest steeples in France. It is seated on the Charente; 40 miles S. S. E. of Rochelle, and 76 S. W. of Poitiers. Pop. 10,300. Long. 0. 38. W. lat. 45. 45. N.

SAINTONGE, a former province of France, which now forms the greater part of the department of Lower Charente, and part of that of Charente.

SAL, one of the Cape Verd Islands, 42 miles in circumference, lying to the E. of St. Nicholas. It has its name from the number of salt ponds that from time to time are filled by the sea, where the water crystallizes into a beautiful salt, the chief production of the island. Long. 22. 56. W. lat. 16. 38. N.

SALA, or SALBERG, a town of Sweden, in the government of Westernas, near which is a silver mine; seated on a river; 30 miles W. of Upsal, and 50 N. W. of Stockholm.

SALADO, a river of South America, which rises in Tucuman, about 60 miles W. of Salta, and flows S. S. E. to the Parana at Santa Fe.

SALAMANCA, a city of Spain, in Leon, and a bishop's see; with a famous university, consisting of 24 colleges. The structure called the Schools, where the sciences are taught, is very large and curious. There were formerly 7000 students, when the Spanish monarchy was in a flourishing condition; but at present the number does not exceed 400, who are all clothed like priests. Here are 25 magnificent churches, a large public square, fine fountains, and every thing that can contribute to the beauty and commodiousness of the city. The cathedral is one of the handsomest in Spain; and there are several fine convents, with churches belonging to them, adorned with images, and some with curious pictures. The town is seated partly on a plain and partly on hills, and is surrounded by a wall. The river Tormes, which washes its walls, has a bridge over it 300 paces long, built by the Romans. Salamanca is celebrated for a memorable victory obtained over the French by the allied army under Lord Wellington, on the 22nd of June, 1812; 85 miles S. by W. of Leon, and 120 N. W. of Madrid. Pop. 13,600. Long. 5. 48. W. lat. 41. 24. N.

SALAMANCA DE BALCALAR, a town of Mexico, in Jucatan; 140 miles S. E. of Campeachy. Long. 89. 58. W. lat. 17. 55. N.

SALANCHE, a town of Sardinia, in Savoy, with a considerable trade in horses, cattle, cheese, woollen stuffs, iron tools, &c. It is situate in a mountainous district, on the river Arve; 30 miles S. E. of Geneva.

SALANKEMEN, a town of Sclavonia, where a victory was obtained by the prince of Baden over the Turks, in 1691. It is seated on the Danube, opposite the influx of the Teisse; 20 miles N. W. of Belgrade, and 25 S. E. of Peterwardein.

SALBERG. *See* SALA.

SALBOE, a town of Norway, in Drontheim, with a copper-mine; 45 miles S. E. of Drontheim.

SALDANA, a town of Spain, in the province of Leon; 37 miles N. W. of Palencia.

SALECTO, a town of the kingdom of Tunis, near which are the remains of a large castle. It is seated near the Mediterranean, 22 miles S. S. E. of Monaster. Long. 11. 3. E. lat. 35. 13. N.

SALEM, a town of Hindostan, in the Carnatic; capital of a district of its name, included in that of Barramaul. It is the residence of the judge, collector, &c. It is seated on a river that flows into the Cavery; 120 miles S. E. of Seringapatam. Long. 78. 15. E. lat. 11. 37. N.

SALEM, a seaport of Massachusets, capital of Essex county. It carries on a large trade to the East Indies, has some ship-building, and the harbour is defended by a fort and citadel. Here are 11 edifices for public worship, and a bridge, 1500 feet long, which connects the town with Beverley. It is situate on a peninsula, formed by two small inlets of the sea, called North and South Rivers; 20 miles N. E. of Boston. Pop. 15,082. Long. 70. 50. W. lat. 42. 30. N.

SALEM, a town of New Jersey, capital of a county of the same name. It has four edifices for public worship. It is seated on a branch of Salem Creek, 3 miles from its mouth in Delaware Bay, and 37 S. S. W. of Philadelphia. Long. 75. 37. W. lat. 39. 37. N.

SALEM, a town of North Carolina, in Surry county, on the W. side of Wack Creek, a branch of the Cargalis, which flows into the Yadkin. It is the principal settlement of the Moravians in this state; 70 miles W. of Hillsborough. Long 80. 21. W. lat. 36. 2. N.

SALEM, a town of New York, in Washington county; 46 miles N. E. of Albany. Pop. 2855.—There are also several inconsiderable townships of this name in the United States.

SALERNO, a fortified seaport of Naples, capital of Principato Citra, and an archbishop's see, with a castle and a university, principally for medicine. It is seated on a bay of the same name; 27 miles S. E. of Naples. Pop. 10,000. Long. 14. 53. E. lat. 40. 35. N.

SALERS, a town of France, department of Cantal, seated among mountains; 9 miles N. of Aurillac.

SALFORD, a borough in Lancashire, adjoining to Manchester. It returns one member to parliament. Market on Saturday. The population is employed in the manufactures peculiar to Manchester. The principal attraction of Salford is the Crescent, commanding a rich view through which the Irwell meanders.

SALIES, a town in the department of Lower Pyrenees, where are springs from which fine salt is made; 7 miles W. of Orthes.

SALIGNAC, a town of the department of Upper Vienne; 10 miles S. of Limoges.

SALINA, a town of North America, state of New York; 130 miles W. of Albany. It is a collection of four villages, employed in the manufacture of salt, from the brine springs and Onondago Lake. Pop. 11,013.

SALINAS, a town of Spain, in Biscay, seated on the Deva, at the foot of a mountain; 16 miles N. N. E. of Vittoria, and 28 S. S. E. of Bilboa.

SALINS, a town of France, department of Jura, with a strong fort and famous salt-works. In the neighbourhood are quarries of jasper, alabaster, and black marble. It is seated in a fertile valley; 29 miles S. of Besançon. Pop. 8200.

SALISBURY, or NEW SARUM, a city, and the capital of Wiltshire, and a bishop's see, with markets on Tuesday and Saturday. It is situate in a chalky soil, almost surrounded by the Avon, Willy, Nadder, and Bourn; and is rendered particularly clean by a small stream flowing through every street. It has a fine cathedral, the spire of which is the loftiest in the kingdom. The town-hall is a handsome building, and stands in a spacious marketplace. Salisbury is governed by a mayor, returns two members to parliament, and has manufactures of flannel, linseys, hardware, and cutlery; 38 miles S. E. of Bath, and 81 W. by S. of London. Long. 1. 47. W. lat. 51. 4. N.

SALISBURY, a fertile district of North Carolina, comprehending the counties of Rockingham, Guilford, Montgomery, Stokes, Surry, Iredell, Rowan, Cabarras, and Mecklenburg.

SALISBURY, a town of North Carolina, in Rowan county, capital of the district of its name, 110 miles W. of Raleigh. Long. 80. 35. W. lat. 35. 38. N.

SALISBURY, a town of Massachusets, in Essex county, where some ship-building is carried on. It is seated at the junction of the Powow with the Merrimac; 3 miles N. N. W. of Newbury Port. Pop. 2739.

SALISBURY, a town of Maryland, in Somerset county, with a considerable lumber trade; 15 miles S. E. of Vienna.

SALISBURY CRAIG, a hill in Scotland on the

E. side of Edinburgh, remarkable for a great precipice of solid rock, about one mile long, and in some parts 100 feet high, which passes with some regularity along its brow.

SALISBURY PLAIN, an open tract in England, which extends from the city of Salisbury, 25 miles E. to Winchester, and 25 W. to Shaftsbury, and is, in some places, from 35 to 40 miles in breadth. There were so many cross roads on it, and so few houses to take directions from, that Thomas, earl of Pembroke, planted a tree at each mile-stone from Salisbury to Shaftsbury, as a guide for travellers. That part of it about the city is a chalky down; the other parts are noted for feeding numerous and large flocks of sheep. In this plain, besides the famous Stonehenge, are traces of many Roman and British antiquities.

SALLEE, or SLA, a seaport of the kingdom of Fez, with several forts. The harbour is one of the best in the country; but on account of a bar, ships of 200 tons are forced to lighten their burden before they can enter. There are docks to build ships, but they are seldom used, for want of skill and materials. It is divided into the Old and New Town, or Rabat, by the river Guero, and was formerly noted for its pirates; 100 miles W. of Fez, and 150 S. of Gibraltar. Long. 6. 31. W. lat. 34. 0. N.

SALLIEZ, a town S. of France, department of Lower Pyrenees; 9 miles W. by S. of Orthes. Pop. 6400.

SALM, a town of Belgium, in the province of Luxemburg, on the borders of Liege; with an ancient castle on a mountain; 30 miles S. S. E. of Liege, and 45 N. of Luxemburg.

SALM, a town of France, department of Meurte, with a castle; seated at the source of the Sarre; 26 miles E. of Luneville.

SALMUNSTER, a town of Germany, in the district of Fulda; on the river Kinz; 19 miles S. S. W. of Fulda.

SALO, a town of Austrian Italy, in the Brescian; near the Lake Garda; 17 miles N. E. of Brescia.

SALOBRENO, a town of Spain, in Granada; with a castle. It carries on a great trade in sugar and fish. It is seated on a rock, near the mouth of a river of the same name; 12 miles E. of Almunecar, and 36 S. of Granada.

SALON, a town of France, department of Mouths of the Rhone; seated on the canal of Craponne; 20 miles W. N. W. of Aix.

SALONA, a town of Austrian Dalmatia, seated on a bay of the Gulf of Venice. It was formerly an important place, and its ruins show that it was 10 miles in circumference; 7 miles N. of Spalatro.

SALONA, a town of Greece, in Livadia; and a bishop's see; seated at the foot of Mount Parnassus, on the top of which is a citadel; 50 miles N. E. of Lepanto. Pop. 8000.

SALONICA, (the ancient Thessalonica,) a city of European Turkey, capital of Macedonia; and an archbishop's see. It is 10 miles in circumference, and is a place of great trade. The Greeks have 30 churches, and the Jews nearly as many synagogues. The inhabitants are computed at 70,000. It is surrounded by walls, and defended on the land side by a citadel, and near the harbour by three forts. It is seated at the head of a noble gulf of the Archipelago; 310 miles W. of Constantinople. Long. 23. 5. E. lat. 40. 53. N.

SALPE, a town of Naples, in Capitanata; near which are some salt-works. It is situate on a lake, near the sea; 23 miles S. of Manfredonia, and 92 E. N. E. of Naples.

SALSE, a town and fortress of France, department of Eastern Pyrenees; seated on the Lake of Leucate; 10 miles N. of Perpignan.

SALSETTE, an island of Hindostan, lying off the coast of Concan, to the N. of Bombay, from which it is separated by a narrow channel, across which a causeway was carried in 1805, which has much benefited the island. This island is about 15 miles square, and is fertile in rice, fruits, and sugar-canes. It has subterraneous temples cut out of the rock, in the manner of those of Elephanta. In 1773 the English conquered it from the Mahrattas; and it has proved a valuable acquisition to Bombay, which formerly depended on foreign supplies for its subsistence. Pop. 50,000. Chief town, Tanna.

SALTA, a town of Tucuman, republic of Buenos Ayres; of great resort on account of the large quantities of corn, meal, wine, salt, cattle, and other commodities, which are sent hence to most parts of Peru; 280 miles N. N. W. of St. Jago del Estero. Long. 66. 30. W. lat. 24. 40. S.

SALTASH, a town in Cornwall; market on Saturday, and a trade in malt. It is seated near the mouth of the Tamar; 5 miles N. W. of Plymouth, and 220 W. by S. of London.

SALTCOATS, a seaport of Scotland, in Ayrshire; with a considerable trade in salt and coal, and also in ship-building. It is situate on the Frith of Clyde; 7 miles W. of Irvine, and 32 S. W. of Glasgow. Long. 4. 45. W. lat. 55. 40. N.

SALTFLEET, a town in Lincolnshire, formerly a place of considerable importance. About 30 years ago it had a good market, and shipped large quantities of corn, but it is now an insignificant place; situate on a creek of the German Ocean; 33 miles E. N. E. of Lincoln, and 158 N. by E. of London.

SALTILLO, a town of North America, republic of Mexico; state of Cohahuila; seated in an arid plain. Long. 100. 5. W. lat. 25. 20. N. Pop. 6500.

SALUZZO, a town of Piedmont, capital of a district of its name; with a castle. The cathedral is magnificent and rich. It is seated on an eminence near the Po; 24 miles S. by W. of Turin. Pop. of the district, 126,000; of the town, 10,000.

SALVADOR, ST., one of the Bahama islands. *See* GUANAHANI.

SALVADOR, ST., the capital of Congo, stands on a large mountain, the summit of which forms a plain 10 miles in circuit, which is well cultivated. The city has 12 churches, besides the cathedral; also a large palace, in which the king and a Portuguese bishop reside. It is 230 miles E. S. E. of Loango. Long. 14. 20. E. lat. 5. 40. S.

SALVADOR, ST., now called BAHIA, a city of Brazil; capital of the province of Bahia, and an archbishop's see; with several forts. The cathedral is large, but the most superb structure in the city is the grand church of the ex-jesuits, built of European marble, and the internal part exceedingly rich. The houses are two or three stories high, and built of stone. The principal streets are good, but the generality are narrow and dirty. In the royal square are the governor's house, the mint, and the public offices; and along the beach are the custom-house, dockyard, storehouses, &c. There are many gardens, full of a great variety of fruit-trees, herbs, and flowers. The chief commodities are cotton, sugar, tobacco, coffee, gums, wood, hides, tallow, and train-oil. The inhabitants are estimated at upwards of 100,000. It is seated on an eminence, in the bay of All-Saints; 120 miles S. W. of Sergipe. Long. 39. 30. W. lat. 13. 30. S.

SALVADOR DE JUJUI, ST., a city of Tucuman, republic of La Plata; situate at the foot of a high mountain, on a river of its name, which flows E. to the Vermejo. It is 280 miles N. N. E. of St. Jago del Estero. Long. 66. 20. W. lat. 24. 5. S.

SALVAGES, small uninhabited islands, lying between the Canaries and Madeira; 27 leagues N. of Point Nago, in Teneriffe. Long. 15. 54. W. lat. 30. 0. N.

SALVATERRA, a town of Portugal, in Estremadura; with a royal palace; seated on the Tajo; 35 miles N. E. of Lisbon.

SALVATERRA, a strong town of Portugal, in Beira. It was taken by the French in 1704, and by the allies in 1705. It stands on the frontiers of Spain; 12 miles N. N. W. of Alcantara, and 37 E. by S. of Castle Branco.

SALVATIERRA, a town of Spain, in Galicia; seated on the Minho; 7 miles N. E. of Tuy.

SALVATIERRA, a town of Spain, in Leon; seated on the Tormes; 23 miles S. of Salamanca.

SALVATIERRA, a town of Spain, in Biscay; seated at the foot of Mount St. Adrian; 18 miles E. N. E. of Vittoria.

SALZA, a town of Prussian Saxony, in the government of Magdeburg; famous for its salt-works. It is seated near the Elbe; 12 miles S. S. E. of Magdeburg.

SALZBURG, a province of the Austrian empire; bounded on the N. by Bavaria; E. by Styria, S. and W. by Tyrol and Bavaria. It is a mountainous country, but pretty fertile, and contains mines of copper, silver, and iron. It was formerly subject to an archbishop, who was a prince of the empire, and primate of Germany. In 1802 it was made an electorate, and given to the Grand Duke of Tuscany; incorporated with the Austrian states in 1806, and transferred in 1809 to Bavaria. On the fall of Napoleon it was restored, with the exception of a part of its territory, to Austria. It now comprises an area of 2800 square miles, with 142,000 inhabitants.

SALZBURG, the capital of the above province, has a strong castle on a mountain, and two noble palaces. The inhabitants are estimated at 13,000. The cathedral of St. Rupert is very fine, and contains five organs. The university, founded in 1623, was converted, in 1810, into a lyceum, with a theological and surgical school. Near Salzburg are some very productive salt-works. The French became masters of this city in 1800, and again in 1805. In 1818 upwards of 100 houses were destroyed by fire. It is situate between three mountains, on both sides the river Salza; 45 miles S. by W. of Passau; 155 W. by S. of Vienna. Long. 13. 4. E. lat. 47. 46. N.

SALZKOTEN, a town of Prussian Westphalia, with a good salt-mine; 7 miles S. W. of Paderborn.

SALZUSTEN, a town of Germany, in the county of Lippe-Detmold, with a salt-mine; 12 miles N. W. of Detmold.

SALZUNGEN, a town of Germany, in the duchy of Meiningen; with a castle called Schnepfenburg, on an eminence, and several salt-works. It is seated on the Werra; 10 miles S. of Eisenach.

SALZWEDEL, a town of Prussian Saxony, in the government of Magdeburg; with manufactures of woollen, linen, and cotton, and a considerable trade in corn, cattle, and hops. It is seated on the Jeetze; 72 miles E. of Hamburg. Pop. 6000.

SAMANA, an island of the West Indies, on the N. E. side of that of St. Domingo, from which it is separated on the W. by a narrow channel. It is 33 miles long and 8 broad, and has a town and bay of the same name on the coast. It was taken by the British in 1808. Long. 69. 20. W. lat. 19. 10. N.

SAMANDRAKI, or SAMONDRACHI, an island of the Grecian Archipelago, between Stalimeni and the coast of Romania, and to the N. of the isle of Imbro. It is 17 miles in circumference, and has a town of the same name, with a spacious harbour. Long. 25. 17. E. lat. 40. 34. N.

SAMAR, or TENDAY, one of the Philippine islands; S. E. of that of Luçonia, from which it is separated by a strait. It is 320 miles in circumference, and is full of craggy mountains, among which are fertile valleys.

SAMARA, a town of Russia, in the government of Simbirsk; seated on the Volga; 95 miles S. S. E. of Simbirsk. Pop. 2600.

SAMARANG, a fortified town in the N. E. part of the island of Java, and, next to Batavia, the most considerable settlement in the island. It stands at the mouth of a river of the same name; 290 miles E. by S. of Batavia. Pop. 20,000. Long. 110. 38. E. lat. 6. 54. S.

SAMARCAND, an ancient city of Asia, formerly the capital of Usbec Tartary, in Bokharia; with a castle and a university. It was the birthplace and seat of Tamerlane the Great, and afterwards the residence of a Tartar prince. The city falls short of its ancient splendour; yet it is still very large, and fortified with strong bulwarks of earth. The houses are mostly of hardened clay, but some are of stone, from quarries in the neighbourhood. The silk paper made here is in great request; and it has a considerable trade in excellent fruits. It is seated on the Sogd; 138 miles E. by N. of Bokhara. Long. 65. 15. E. lat. 39. 40. N.

SAMAROF, a town of Siberia, in the government of Tobolsk; seated on the Irtysh; 135 miles N. of Tobolsk.

SAMATAN, a town of France, department of Gers; with a castle on a mountain; seated on the Save; 6 miles N. by E. of Lombez.

SAMBA, a seaport of Terra Firma, in the province of Carthagena; 33 miles N. E. of Carthagena. Long. 75. 16. W. lat. 10. 45. N.

SAMBALLAS, a multitude of small uninhabited islands, on the N. shore of the Isthmus of Darien. Most of them are low, flat, and sandy, covered with a variety of trees, and abound with several kinds of shell-fish; some few afford springs of fresh water. Long. 78. 25. W. lat. 9. 26. N.

SAMBAS, a town of Borneo, near the W. coast; inhabited by pirates, against whom a British force was sent out in 1812 and 1813, which proved completely successful. In its vicinity diamond mines are found. Long. 109. 0. E. lat. 2. 20. N.

SAMBOR, a town of Austrian Poland, capital of a circle of its name; seated on a large plain, on the Dniester; 46 miles S. W. of Lemberg. Pop. 6400.

SAMBRE, a river which rises in Picardy; flows by Landrecy, Maubege, Thun, and Charleroy, and joins the Meuse at Namur.

SAMIRI, a town of Asiatic Turkey, in Irac Arabi, on the Tigris; 70 miles N. N. W. of Bagdad.

SAMISAT, a town of Asiatic Turkey, in the sangiacat of Marasch, on the Euphrates; 30 miles E. of Marasch.

SAMOGITIA, a country in the N. W. of Prussian Lithuania; bounded on the N. by Courland, S. by Russia Proper, and W. by the Baltic. It is full of forests and high mountains, which feed a great number of cattle, and produce abundance of honey. Here are also very active horses, in high esteem. The inhabitants are clownish, but honest; and they will not allow a young woman to go out in the night without a candle in her hand, and two bells at her girdle.

SAMOS, an island of the Grecian Archipelago, on the coast of Natolia; about 32 miles long and 22 broad, and extremely fertile. Pop. 60,000. It contains two ranges of lofty mountains, between which are rich and well cultivated plains, producing abundance of grain, melons, lentils, kidney-beans, and excellent muscadine grapes; also white figs, four times as big as the common sort, but not so well tasted. The silk is very fine, and the honey and wax admirable. The island abounds with partridges, woodcocks, snipes, thrushes, wood-pigeons, turtle-doves, wheatears, and excellent poultry. It has emery, stone, and iron-mines, and most of the soil is of a rusty colour. All the mountains are of white marble. Their bishop resides at Cora. The principal harbour is that of Vati.

SAMOYEDES, once a numerous and powerful nation of Tartary. They are now dispersed; some of them are found in small detached bodies among the mountains to the W. of Lake Baikal; others are supposed to be within the Chinese frontiers; others are scattered among the deserts which extend along the Frozen Ocean; and some nearly as far to the W. as Archangel. The Samoyedes have a large head, a flat face, high cheek-bones, small eyes, a wide mouth, a yellow complexion, straight black hair, and little or no beard: they still preserve the manners of a pastoral people, and retain the use of moveable habitations, with which they wander from place to place. They neither have, nor appear ever to have had, any kind of regular government. Their traditional songs mention only certain heroes, who, in better times, led their ancestors to battle. These songs form their principal amusements; but the exploits they celebrate are never likely to be renewed.

SAMSOE, an island of Denmark; on the E. coast of N. Jutland; 12 miles long and 3 broad, and very fertile. It has a town of the same name, and the inhabitants carry on some commerce in small vessels. Long. 10. 33. E. lat. 56 2. N.

SAMSON, ST., a town of France; department of Eure; on the Rille; 5 miles N. of Pont Audemer.

SAMSON, ST., a town in the department of Maine-et-Loire; 4 miles N. E. of Angers.

SAN, a river of Austrian Poland, which rises in the Carpathian Mountains, in Hungary, and falls into the Vistula near Sandomir. It forms part of the boundary between Austrian Galicia and Russian Poland.

SANA, a city of Arabia, capital of Yemen; with a castle on a hill, in which are two palaces. The city, properly so called, is not very populous; for gardens occupy a part of the space within the walls, which are 4 miles in circuit, and contain 7 gates. Here are a number of mosques, some of them built by Turkish pachas; also several palaces, 12 public baths, and some large caravanserais. Fruits are very plenteous, particularly grapes; and the exportation of raisins is considerable, one kind of which is without stones. The city stands near the source of a river, which flows S. into the Arabian Sea, and at the foot of Mount Nikkum, on which are to be seen the ruins of a castle, said to have been built by Shem. It is 250 miles N. N. E. of Mocha, and 490 S. E. of Mecca. Long. 45. 10. E. lat. 15. 24. N.

SANA, or ZANA, a town of Peru; capital of a province of its name. It is situate in a valley fertile in fruit and corn, and adorned with the most beautiful flowers; whence it has been sometimes called Miraflores. It is 90 miles N. of Truxillo. Long. 78. 30. W. lat. 40. 35. N.

SANASHYGOTTA, a flourishing town of Bengal, seated on the Mahanuddy; 165 miles N. of Moorshedabad.

Sancerra, a town of France, department of Cher; seated on a mountain, near the Loire; 22 miles N. W. of Nevers, and 110 N. of Paris.

Sancian, an island of China, on the coast of Quang-tong; 40 miles in circumference; famous for being the burying-place of Francis Xavier, whose tomb is to be seen on a small hill.

Sancoins, a town of France, department of Cher; seated on the Argent; 15 miles S. W. of Nevers.

Sanda, or **Sanday**, one of the Orkney islands, about 12 miles in length, but of an irregular form, and seldom above a mile in breadth. It lies N. of that of Stronsay, from which it is separated by a narrow channel. Much kelp is made here in summer, and it feeds many sheep and beeves. On the Start Point is a light-house. Long. 2. 15. W. lat. 59. 21. N.

Sanda, a small island on the W. coast of Scotland, near the Mull of Cantyre; famed for having been the rendezvous of the Danish fleets during their expeditions to the western coasts. On it are the remains of a chapel, dedicated to St. Columba.

Sandbach, a town in Cheshire, with a market on Thursday; formerly famous for the manufacture of worsted yarn, the weaving of stuffs, and shoe-making, which have now given place to the manufacture of silk. It contains an ancient church, several meeting-houses, national and Sunday schools, &c. In the market-place are two stone square crosses, which were replaced in 1816, and their deficient ancient beauties supplied by modern art. It is seated on the Wheelock; 25 miles E. of Chester, and 162 N. N. W. of London.

Sandec, New, a town of Austrian Galicia, capital of a circle of its name, which is covered with extensive forests; 44 miles S. W. of Cracow. Pop. 3700. Six miles farther N. is Old Sandee, which is now a small place.

Sandhamn, a seaport of Sweden, in the province of Upland, where all vessels to and from Stockholm are examined; 10 miles E. of Stockholm.

Sando, an island of Japan, 87 miles in circumference, on the N. coast of Niphon, with a town of the same name. Long. 139. 30. E. lat. 38. 35. N.

Sandomir, a strong town of Poland, capital of a palatinate of the same name, with a castle on a steep rock, and several colleges. It is seated on a hill, on the Vistula; 75 miles E. by N. of Cracow, and 112 S. by E. of Warsaw. Pop. 2100. Long. 22. 0. E. lat. 50. 21. N.

Sandomir, a palatinate of Poland, bounded on one part by the Vistula, on another by the Pilica, and the palatinate of Cracow. It contains, according to the territorial division of 1815, 4700 square miles, with 448,000 inhabitants.

Sandagal, a town of Portugal, in Beira; seated on the Coa; 12 miles S. S. E. of Guarda.

Sandvliet, a town of Belgium, in the province of Antwerp; seated on the Scheldt; 12 miles N. W. of Antwerp.

Sandwich, a borough in Kent, with markets on Wednesday and Saturday. It is one of the cinque-ports, governed by a mayor. It returns two members to parliament. It is walled round, but the walls are greatly decayed, and only one of the gates is standing. Its trade is much diminished, the river Stour, on which it is seated, being so choked up with sand as to admit only small vessels; 13 miles E. of Canterbury, and 68 E. by S. of London. Long. 1. 20. E. lat. 51. 16. N.

Sandwich, a town of Massachusets, in Barnstable county; 18 miles S. E. of Plymouth.

Sandwich Island, an island in the Pacific Ocean, near the W. coast of New Ireland. Long. 149. 17. E. lat. 2. 53. S.

Sandwich Island, one of the New Hebrides, in the Pacific Ocean. Long. 168. 33. E. lat. 17. 41. S.

Sandwich Islands, a group of islands in the North Pacific; discovered by Cook in 1778. They are 11 in number, extending from 18. 54. to 22. 15. N. lat., and from 150. 54. to 160. 24. W. long. They are called by the natives, Hawaii, or Owhyee, Mowee, Ranai, Morotoi, Tahoorowa, Woahoo, Atooi, Neeheehou, Oneehoua, Morotinnee, and Takoora, all inhabited except the last two. The climate differs little from that of the West Indies in the same latitude; but there are no traces of those violent winds which render the stormy months in the West Indies so dreadful. There is also more rain at the Sandwich isles. The vegetable productions are nearly the same as those of the other islands in this ocean, but the taro root is here of a superior quality. The bread-fruit trees are not in such abundance as in the plains of Otaheite, but produce double the quantity of fruit. The sugar-canes are of a very unusual size, some of them measuring eleven inches in circumference, and having fourteen feet eatable. There is also a root of a brown colour, shaped like a yam, and from 6 to 10 pounds in weight, the juice of which is an excellent substitute for sugar. The quadrupeds are hogs, dogs, and rats. The fowls are of the common sort; the birds beautiful and numerous, though not various. Goats, pigs, and European seeds were left by Captain Cook; but the possession of the goats soon gave rise to a contest between two districts, in which the breed was destroyed. The inhabitants are of the same race with those of the islands S. of the equator, and in their persons, language, and manners, approach nearer to the New Zealanders than to their less distant neighbours, either of the Society or Friendly Islands. They are in general above the middle size, and well made; they walk gracefully, run nimbly, and are capable of bearing great fatigue. Many of both sexes have fine open countenances; and the women, in particular, have good eyes and teeth, with an engaging sweetness and sensibility of look. There is one peculiarity characteristic of every part of the nation, that even in the handsomest faces there is a fulness of the nostril, without any flatness or spreading of the nose. The dress of both men and women nearly resembles those of New Zealand, and both sexes wear necklaces of small variegated shells. Tattooing the body was formerly practised by every colony of this

nation. The hands and arms of the women were very neatly marked, and they had the singular custom of tattooing the tip of the tongue. They lived in villages, containing from 100 to 200 houses, built closely together, without any order, and having a winding path between them. Towards the sea they were generally flanked with detached walls, intended both for shelter and defence. Some of the houses were from 40 to 50 feet long, and from 20 to 30 broad; others were mere hovels. The food of the lower class still consists principally of fish and vegetables, to which the people of higher rank add the flesh of hogs and dogs. The making of canoes, mats, &c., formed the occupations of the men; the women were employed in manufacturing cloth, and the servants principally engaged in the plantations and fishing. They had various amusements, such as dancing, boxing, wrestling, &c.; all of which have now entirely ceased. The bottoms of their canoes are of a single piece of wood, hollowed out to the thickness of an inch, and brought to a point at each end; the sides consist of three boards, each about an inch thick, neatly fitted and lashed to the bottom part. Some of their double canoes measure 70 feet in length, three and a half in depth, and 12 in breadth. The government is monarchical and hereditary. The same system of subordination prevails here as at the other islands; absolute authority on the part of the chiefs, and unresisting submission on the part of the people. So long as idolatry prevailed here, human sacrifices were frequent; not only the commencement of a war, or a signal enterprise, but the death of any considerable chief, called for a repetition of these horrid rites. From their intercourse with Christians, they had renounced idolatry before any missionaries were settled among them; and of late years they have made great advances in civilization. They live in the utmost harmony with each other; and, in hospitality to strangers, they are not exceeded even by the inhabitants of the Friendly Islands. Their natural capacity seems in no respect below the common standard of mankind. It was estimated by the discoverers, that these islands contained a population of 400,000; but from the destructive wars between themselves, the effects of disease introduced by foreign shipping, and, till recently, the consequences of infanticide, the present number is not more than 150,000, of which 85,000 occupy Hawaii. They are now increasing in importance, in a mercantile view, and are visited by many vessels trading to China and India, as well as by the sperm whale-fishers.

Sandwich Land, a desolate country in the southern ocean, to the S. E. of the island of Georgia. The mountains are of a vast height, their summits wrapped in clouds, and their bases covered with snow to the water's edge. Thule, the southern extremity of Sandwich Land, seen by Cook in 1775, lies in 27. 45. W. long. and 59. 54. S. lat.

Sandy Hook, a small island on the coast of New Jersey, formerly a peninsula; but in 1778 the sea broke through the isthmus, and formed it into an island. On the N. point is a lighthouse, 100 feet high; 7 miles S. of the W. end of Long Island. Long. 74. 2. W. lat. 40. 30. N.

Sandy Lake, a lake of North America, about 25 miles in circuit; not far from the source of the Mississippi. Lat. 46. 9. N.

Sandy Point, a seaport of St. Christopher, West Indies; on the N. W. side of the island, in Figtree Bay; defended by two forts. Long. 63. 28. W. lat. 17. 20. N.

Sandy River, a river in the state of Maine, which runs into the Kennebeck; 6 miles above Norridgewock.

Sandy River, Big, a river which rises in the Laurel Mountains, and forms part of the boundary between Virginia and Kentucky. It falls into the Ohio; 40 miles above the Scioto.

Sanen, or Gessenay, a town of Switzerland, in the canton of Bern, with a castle; situate on a river of the same name; 20 miles S. W. of Thun.

Sanford, a town of the state of Maine, in York county; 15 miles N. of Berwick, and 20 N. N. W. of York.

Sangerhausen, a town of Prussian Saxony, in Thuringia, with a castle; seated near the Hartz Mountains; 14 miles E. S. E. of Stolberg.

Sanguesa, a town of Spain, in Navarre; 32 miles S. E. of Pamplona.

Sanore, a district of Hindostan; lying to the S. of Visiapour, and N. of Mysore. It was ceded to the Mahrattas in 1792.

Sanore, a town and fortress of Hindostan, capital of the above district; seated on the left bank of the Toom, 15 miles before its junction with the Nigouden to form the Tungebadra.—On the opposite bank is another town called Sanore Bancapour. It is 103 miles N. by W. of Chitteldroog, and 130 S. by E. of Visiapour.

Sanpoo. *See* Burrampooter.

Sanquhar, a borough of Scotland, in Dumfries-shire, with a ruined castle, once the residence of the Crichton family. It has a trade in coal, and manufactures of carpets and cottons. It is seated on the Nith; 27 miles N. W. of Dumfries, and 56 S. W. of Edinburgh. In conjunction with Dumfries, &c., it returns one member to parliament.

Sansanding, a considerable town in Central Africa, kingdom of Bambarra, on the Niger. It has a great trade, especially in salt. It is 25 miles N. E. of Sego.

Santa. *See* Parilla.

Santaella, a town of Spain, in Andalusia; 24 miles S. of Cordova.

Santander, a strong seaport of Spain, in Asturias; capital of a small district of its name, and a bishop's see. The harbour is good, and large enough to contain a numerous fleet; defended by two castles, and a mole that advances into the sea. It is 11 miles N. E. of Santillana. Long. 3. 47. W. lat. 43. 27. N.

Santarem, a town of Portugal, in Estremadura, with a citadel on a mountain; seated on the river Tajo, in a country fertile in wheat, wine, and oil; 55 miles N. E. of Lisbon. Pop. 8000. Long. 8. 20. W. lat. 39. 18. N.

Santee, a river of S. Carolina, the largest

and longest in that state. It enters the ocean by two mouths, a little S. of Georgetown. About 120 miles from its mouth, it branches into the Congaree and Wateree; the latter, which is the N. branch, passes the Catabaw Indians, and bears the name of Catabaw River, from this settlement to its source.

SANTEN, a town of Germany, in the duchy of Cleves; seated on the Rhine. It is 15 miles S. E. of Cleves.

SANTIANES, a town of Spain, in Asturias; 17 miles S. S. W. of Oviedo.

SANTILLANA, a town of Spain, seated in a fruitful valley, near the Bay of Biscay; 96 miles E. of Oviedo, and 200 N. of Madrid. Long. 3. 58. W. lat. 43. 23. N.

SANTORIN, (the ancient Thera,) an island of the Grecian Archipelago, to the S. of Nio. It is in the form of a crescent, 10 miles from N. to S. and from one to four in breadth. Between its two points, to complete the circle, are the small islands of Therasia and Aspronisi; and within these are three other islands, between which and Santorin is a road for ships; but it affords no anchorage, on account of its depth in some places, and rocky bottom in others. All these islands are of volcanic origin, but the three interior ones are evidently of much later date. Santorin, in proportion to its extent, is the richest and most populous island of the Archipelago. There are two bishops; the one Latin, whose see is Scauro, and the other Greek, whose residence is at Pirgos, near the middle of the island. The soil is very dry, and far from fertile; but it produces plenty of barley, cotton, and wine, in which, and the cotton manufactures, its trade consists. Fruit is scarce, except figs, and it has only cistern water. The inhabitants, about 12,000 in number, are almost all Greeks. Scauro is the capital.

SANTOS, a seaport of Brazil, on an island called Amiaz, on the W. side of the entrance into Santos Bay. It is defended by a rampart and two castles. The town of St. Vincent stands on the same island, which is 18 miles in circuit. It is 10 miles from the sea, and 190 S. W. of St. Sebastian. Pop. 7000. Long. 46. 30. W. lat. 24. 15. S.

SAONE, a large navigable river of France, which rises in the Vosges Mountains, and, after a course of about 200 miles, falls into the Rhone, at Lyons.

SAONE, UPPER, a department of France, including part of the former province of Franche Comte; bounded N. by the department of Vosges, and E. by that of Upper Rhine. It comprises an area of 2500 square miles, with 326,000 inhabitants. The capital is Vesoul.

SAONE-ET-LOIRE, a department of France, including part of the former province of Burgundy; bounded by the departments of Jura, Rhone, and Allier, and comprising an area of 3500 square miles, with 516,000 inhabitants. It is named from two rivers, which flow through it in different directions. Maçon is the capital.

SAORGIO, a town of the Sardinian states, in the county of Nice; situate on the top of a rock, which is nearly enclosed by the Roia and the Bendola. On the opposite side of the Roia is a sharp rock, completely insulated, with an ancient fortress on the summit; and near the town is a strong fort. Saorgio was taken by the French in 1794. Population 3100. It is 19 miles N. E. of Nice.

SAPIENZA, three small islands, and a cape, in the Mediterranean, near the S. coast of the Morea. The largest island was formerly called Sphacteria, and is famous in ancient history for a victory obtained by the Athenians over the Lacedemonians. Long. 21. 35. E. lat. 36. 50. N.

SARACENS, a people celebrated some centuries ago, who came from the deserts of Arabia; *sarra*, in their language, signifying a desert. They were the first disciples of Mahomet, and within 40 years after his death conquered a great part of Asia, Africa, and Europe. They kept possession of Spain till 1511, when they were expelled. For a long time they maintained a war in the Holy Land against the Western Christians, and at length drove them out of it. There are now no people known by this name, for the descendants of those who conquered Spain are called Moors.

SARAGOSSA, or ZARAGOZA, a city of Spain, capital of Arragon, and an archbishop's see; with a university. It is said to have been built by the Phœnicians, and the Romans sent a colony hither in the reign of Augustus; whence it had the name of Cæsarea Augusta, which by corruption has been changed into Saragossa. Before this city was taken by the French, in 1809, there were many magnificent buildings; 17 large churches, and 14 handsome convents, besides others less considerable. The Ebro runs through the city, dividing it into two parts; and on its banks is a handsome quay, which serves for a public walk. The Holy Street is the largest, and so broad that it may be taken for a square. The cathedral is a spacious Gothic building; but the finest church is that of Nuestra Senora del Pilar, and a place of the greatest devotion in Spain. They tell us that the Virgin, while yet living, appeared to St. James, who was preaching the gospel, and left him her image, with a handsome pillar of jasper. This image stands on a marble pillar, with a little Jesus in her arms, ornamented with a profusion of gold and jewels, and illuminated by a multitude of lamps and wax lights. The town-house is a sumptuous structure; and in the hall are the pictures of all the kings of Arragon. Saragossa has no manufactures, and but little trade. It is seated in a large plain, (where the Ebro receives two other rivers,) which produces all kinds of fruit in great abundance. A victory was obtained here over the French and Spaniards in 1710, but it was abandoned by the allies soon after. Saragossa is also celebrated for the brave defence it made under General Palafox, when besieged by the French, in 1808-9. It is 150 miles W by N. of Barcelona, and 180 N. E. of Madrid Pop. 50,000.

SARATOF, a government of Russia, lying along both sides of the Wolga, and having, on one side, the country of Astracan, and on the other, that of the Don Cossacks. The extent is estimated at 91,000 square miles, with a population not exceeding 1,000,000. It is divided into 12 districts, of which that of the same name is the principal.

SARATOF, the capital of the above government, is surrounded by a wall, and is neatly built, chiefly of wood. The inhabitants (about 5000) have a brisk trade in fish, caviar, salt, &c. It is seated on the side of a mountain near the Wolga; 374 miles N. by W. of Astracan. Long. 46. 1. E. lat. 51. 32. N.

SARATOGA, a town and fort of New York, in a county of the same name, memorable for the surrender of an army of British and Hessians, under General Burgoyne, to the Americans, in 1777. It is now the principal summer resort of the fashionable, for its mineral springs, the principal of which are the Saratoga and Ballston Spas. It may be called the American Cheltenham. The permanent population is about 2500. It stands on the E. side of Hudson River; 31 miles N. of Albany.

SARBRUCK, a town of Germany, capital of a county of its name, with a handsome palace, and a magnificent Lutheran church. It is seated on the W. side of the Sarre; 14 miles W. of Deux Ponts. Long. 7. 5. E. lat. 49. 16. N.

SARBURG, a town of France, department of Meurthe; 40 miles E. by N. of Nancy.

SARDAM, or SAARDAM, a town of the Netherlands, in North Holland, where there are vast magazines of timber for ships and naval stores, and a great number of shipwrights. In this town Peter the Great resided for some time, and work(d as a shipwright. It is seated on the Y, 7 miles N. W. of Amsterdam.

SARDINIA, an insular and continental kingdom of Southern Europe; containing, besides the island of Sardinia, Piedmont, Savoy, the county of Nice, the duchy of Montferrat, part of that of Milan, and the territory of Genoa. The government is monarchical, with few definite limits, except the privileges guaranteed to particular states. Popery is the religion of the royal family and the state. The reigning family is descended from the ancient counts of Savoy, whose dominions became progressively extended by purchase, conquest, and donation. In the war of the French Revolution, in 1792, the Sardinians were aided by Austrian troops and a British subsidy; but, on Bonaparte assuming the command, the allied forces were speedily overthrown, all the continental dominions of the king of Sardinia were seized and incorporated with the French territory, and afterwards parcelled out anew into departments of the French empire. The changes of 1814 reinstated the king of Sardinia in all his continental dominions, except the duchy of Savoy; and in 1815 this also was restored, and the Genoese territory added to the kingdom. The total area comprises 27,000 square miles, and a population of 4,092,000. For an account of soil, agriculture, commerce, &c., see the several divisions of the country.

SARDINIA, an island in the Mediterranean, 160 miles from N. to S., and 70 from E. to W.; separated from Corsica on the N. by the strait of Bonifacio. This island has been neglected by the government; for, exclusive of the mountains, the chief part of the country may be regarded as waste, but where cultivated it is fertile in corn, wine, oranges, citrons, and olives. Here are mines of silver, lead, sulphur, and alum; and quantities of cheese and salt are made. The frequent wastes abound with wild ducks, but the cattle and sheep are not numerous, and the morasses yield pernicious exhalations. On the coast is a fishery for anchovies and coral. This island has undergone various revolutions: in 1708 it was taken from the Spaniards by the English, and allotted to the emperor of Germany, at the peace of Utrecht. The Spaniards recovered it in 1717, but were obliged to abandon it two years after; and in 1720 it was ceded to the duke of Savoy, as an equivalent for Sicily. In 1794 the inhabitants rose against their Piedmontese rulers, and caused the viceroy and others to be sent out of the island; but he was afterwards received, on the king pledging himself to assemble the cortes every ten years, and confirming all the ancient laws and privileges of the inhabitants. The island continues to be governed as a province of the kingdom to which it gives name. Area, 9250 square miles. Pop. 490,000. Cagliari is the capital.

SARECTO, a town of North Carolina, chief of Duplin county; 80 miles N. of Wilmington.

SARGANS, a town of Switzerland, in the canton of St. Gall, with a castle on a rock. Near the town are mineral springs and a productive iron mine. It stands on the summit of a hill, near the Rhine; 14 miles N. of Coire, and 47 S. E. of Zurich.

SARGEL, a seaport of Algier, in the province of Mascara, with a castle. Near this town Andrew Doria was defeated by Barbarossa. It is 25 miles S. S. W. of Algier. Long. 2. 15. E. lat. 36. 30. N.

SARI, a town of Persia, in Mazanderan, the residence of one of the Persian princes, situate in a country abounding in rice, oranges, cotton, sugar, and silk; 25 miles S. W. of Ferabad.

SARK, a small island in the English Channel, near the coast of France, and about two leagues E. from the island of Guernsey, on which it is dependent.

SARK, a river of Scotland, which rises in the central part of Dumfries-shire, and flows S. into Solway Frith. Its mouth forms a good harbour, at the village of Sarkfoot; 8 miles E. by S. of Annan.

SARLAT, a town of France, department of Dordogne; 27 miles S. E. of Perigueux.

SARLOUIS, a strong town in the department of Moselle, seated on the isthmus of a peninsula formed by the river Sarre; 32 miles N. E. of Metz.

SARNEN, a town of Switzerland, capital of the canton of Underwalden, near a lake to which it gives name. It is 9 miles S. of Lucerne. Pop. 2000. Long. 8. 14. E. lat. 46. 52. N.

SARNO, a town of Naples, in Principato Citra; seated near the source of a river of its name;

12 miles N. N. W. of Salerno, and 20 E. S. E. of Naples. Pop. 20,000.

SAROS, a strong castle of Hungary, in a county of the same name; seated on the Tariza, at the foot of Mount Krapach; 5 miles N. N.W. of Eperies.

SARP, or SARPEN, a town of Norway, in the province of Christiansand. Near it is a great cataract, the noise of which may be heard at the distance of 20 miles. It is 10 miles W. S. W. of Frederickstadt.

SARREAL, a town of Spain, in Catalonia, near which are quarries of alabaster, so transparent that it is used for windows. It is seated on the Francoli; 11 miles N. of Tarragona.

SARSANA, a town of the Sardinian states, in Genoa, with a fortress, and near it is a fort in the mountains, called Sarsanello. It stands on the river Magra, 5 miles from its mouth, and 45 E. S. E. of Genoa. Pop. 3500. Long. 9. 58. E. lat. 44. 9. N.

SARSINA, a town of Italy, in Romagna; on the river Savio. It is 21 miles W. S. W. of Rimini.

SART, a town of Asia Minor. It was the ancient Sardis, capital of Lydia, and, under the Romans, was a large city, but was almost destroyed by an earthquake in the reign of Tiberius. Here are many remains of massive buildings, a mosque (which was formerly a Christian church), and a large caravansera. The inhabitants are chiefly shepherds, who feed their flocks in the adjacent plains. It is 35 miles E. N. E. of Smyrna.

SARTE, or SARTHE, a department of France, including part of the ancient province of Maine, and containing an area of 2400 square miles, with 446,000 inhabitants. The climate is mild and salubrious, and the soil in general fertile. The manufactures are hardware, woollens, paper, leather, &c. It takes its name from a river which flows by Mans to Angers, where it joins the Mayenne. The capital is Mans.

SARVAR, a town and fortress of Hungary, at the conflux of the Guntz with the Raab; 40 miles S. S. E. of Presburg.

SARUM, OLD, Wiltshire, now reduced to a single house, and scarcely any thing remains to indicate its former importance, though it formerly sent two members to parliament. It is 2 miles N. of New Sarum, or Salisbury.

SARUN, an extensive district of Hindostan, in the province of Bahar, one of the most prosperous in the British territories. It is situate on the N. side of the Ganges, in lat. 26. N. Pop. 1,200,000.

SARWERDEN, a town of France, department of Moselle; seated on the Sarre, 33 miles W. N. W. of Haguenau, and 45 E. N. E. of Nancy.

SAS VAN GHENT, a town and fortress of the Netherlands, in Flanders, situate on the canal from Ghent to the river Scheldt, and fortified with sluices, by means of which the country can be laid under water. It was built by the inhabitants of Ghent as a bulwark to that city, but was taken in 1664 by the Dutch, from whom the French took it in 1747, and again in 1794. It is 10 miles N. of Ghent, on the borders of Belgium.

SASKATCHAWINE, a large river of N. America, rising in the Rocky Mountains. The two principal streams unite about 60 miles E. of Hudson's House, after which it flows into Lake Winnepeg, in lat. 51. 45. N.

SASCRAM, a town of Hindostan, in Bahar; seated at the foot of a mountain, near a lake, 64 miles S. E. of Benares, and 83 S. W. of Patna.

SASSARI, a city of the island of Sardinia, and an archbishop's see, with a castle and a university. Here is a fountain called Rossel, said to be more magnificent than the best at Rome; and in the neighbourhood are mines of gold and silver. It is seated on the river Torres, 7 miles from the sea, and 64 N. of Oristagni. Pop. 30,000. Long. 8. 45. E. lat. 40. 48. N.

SASSUOLO, a town of Italy, in the duchy of Modena, with a castle; seated on the Secchia, 10 miles S. W. of Modena. Pop. 3100.

SATALIA, or ADALIA, a strong seaport of Asia Minor, in Karamania. It is divided into three towns, and is so situate, that from the harbour the streets appear to rise behind each other like an amphitheatre. The country around is very fertile, and the citrons and oranges are extremely fine. The chief trade is in wool, cotton, goats' hair, agaric, tragacanth, opium, and bees'-wax. It is seated on a gulf of the Mediterranean, to which it gives name; 150 miles S. W. of Konieh. Pop. 8000. Long. 31. 21. E. lat. 37. 1. N.

SATGONG, or SATAGONG, a village of Bengal, formerly an important city, in which the European traders in Bengal had their factories. It is seated on a creek of Hoogly River, 4 miles N. W. of Hoogly.

SATHMAR, a town of Hungary, on the Szamos river, consisting of two towns on the opposite sides of the river Sathmar on the N., and Nemethi on the S. The principal trade is in wine; and in the neighbourhood are salt mines; 225 miles E. of Presburg. Pop. 10,000

SATIMANGALAM, a town of Hindostan, in the province of Coimbetore, with a large stone fort, and a considerable temple. It has manufactures of cotton cloths, and a great trade to Seringapatam. In its vicinity the troops of Tippoo Sultan maintained a severe conflict with the British. It is 30 miles W. of Bhawanikudal, and 75 S. S. E. of Seringapatam.

SATRIANO, a town of Naples, in Calabria Ultra; 8 miles S. of Squillace.

SATTARAH, a town and fort of Hindostan, in the province of Visiapour, the residence of the Mahratta prince who was restored by the British in 1818. It is situate near the source of the Kistnah; 50 miles S. of Poonah, and 77 W. of Visiapour.

SATTEAGALA, a town of Hindostan, in the province of Coimbetore, with a fort of considerable size. It stands near the Cavery, which, 3 miles below, forms an island 9 miles in length, with noble cataracts on each side. It is 36 miles S. E. of Seringapatam.

SAUCEDA, a town of Mexico, in New Biscay,

on a river of the same name, which joins the Nassas, to form the Palmas. It is 100 miles N. N. W. of Durango. Long. 105. 36. W. lat. 25. 18. N.

Saugur Island, an island of Hindostan, well known as a place of pilgrimage. The temple of Kapila Muni, on the S. coast of Gunga Saugur, is under the alternate charge of a Byragee and Sunyasee, who levy a tax of 4 annas on each person visiting the temple, the amount of which is divided among five different establishments of Ramanandi Byragees in the vicinity of Calcutta. In 1802, during the administration of the Marquis Wellesley, the horrid practice of infanticide was abolished on this island. It is seated at the mouth of the Hoogly river, 100 miles from Calcutta.

Saulgen, or **Saulgau**, a town of Germany, in Wirtemberg; 5 miles S. W. of Buchau.

Saulieu, a town of France, department of Cote d'Or, noted as the birthplace of the celebrated Vauban. Here was anciently a college of the Druids, and in a wood where they performed their sacrifices the ruins of a druidical temple are still visible. It is seated on an eminence, 38 miles W. of Dijon, and 46 S. E. of Auxerre. Pop. 3000.

Saumur, a town in the department of Maine-et-Loire, with an ancient castle, and manufactures of woollen, linen, and leather, and some trade in wine and brandy. Here is a famous bridge over the Loire, consisting of 12 elliptical arches, each 60 feet in diameter. Pop. 10,000. It is 27 miles S. E. of Angers, and 38 W. S. W. of Tours.

Saunder's Island, one of the Society Islands, in the South Pacific, called by the natives Tapooamanoo. It is about 6 miles long, and has in the centre a mountain of considerable height. Long. 150. 40. W. lat. 17. 30. S.

Saurungpour, a town of Hindostan, in the province of Malwa; 42 miles N. N. E. of Indore, and 43 N. E. of Ougein.

Sauve, a town of France, department of Gard, on the Vidoure; 12 miles S. W. of Alais.

Sauveterre, a town in the department of Lower Pyrenees, with an old ruined castle; seated on the Gave d'Oleron, 20 miles W. N. W. of Pau.

Sauveterre, a town in the department of Aveiron; 15 miles S. W. of Rodez.

Sauveterre, a town in the department of Gironde; 26 miles S. E. of Bordeaux.

Sava, a town of Persia, in Irak, surrounded by walls of earth. The environs produce exquisite fruits, particularly pomegranates and almonds, and a considerable quantity of rice and cotton. It is 60 miles S. of Casbin, and 110 E. of Amadan. Long. 52. 15. E. lat. 34. 30. N.

Savage Isle, an island in the South Pacific, about 35 miles in circumference, discovered by Cook in 1774. It received this name from the rude and inhospitable behaviour of the inhabitants, who were stout well-made men, naked except round the waists; some of them had their face, breast, and thighs painted. It is of a round form, and covered with trees, shrubs, &c. Long. 169. 30. W. lat. 19. 2. S.

Savanna, a river of the United States, which separates Georgia from South Carolina. It is navigable for boats of 100 feet keel, from Augusta to Savanna, and thence for large vessels to its entrance into the Atlantic Ocean, at Tybe Island.

Savanna, a state of the town of Georgia, chief of Chatham county, and formerly the capital of the state. More than two-thirds of the town was destroyed by fire in 1796. It is regularly built, in the form of a parallelogram. It is seated on a high sandy bluff, on the S. side of Savanna River, 17 miles from its mouth, and 100 S. E. of Louisville. Long. 80. 57. W. lat. 31. 57. N.

Savanna la Mar, a town of Jamaica, in Cornwallis county, with a good anchorage for large vessels. In 1780 great part of the town was destroyed by a dreadful hurricane and inundation of the sea, but it has since been rebuilt. It is seated on the S. side of the island. Long. 78. 6. W. lat. 18. 12. N.

Savatopoli. *See* **Sebastopolis**.

Save, a river of the Austrian empire, which has its source on the N. W. confines of Carniola, runs E. through that country, separates Sclavonia from Croatia, Bosnia, and Servia, and joins the Danube near Belgrade.

Savenay, a town of France, department of Lower Loire; 18 miles N. W. of Nantes.

Savendroog, or **Severndroog**, a strong fortress of Hindostan, in Mysore, situate on the top of a vast rock, rising half a mile in perpendicular height, from a base of above 8 miles in circumference, and divided at the summit by a chasm that forms it into two hills; these, having each its particular defences, serve as two citadels, capable of being maintained, independently of the lower works, which are also wonderfully strong. Notwithstanding this, it was taken by the English, in 1791, after a siege of seven days; 85 miles N. E. of Seringapatam.

Saverdun, a town of France, department of Arriege, with a castle; seated on the Arriege, 25 miles S. S. E. of Toulouse. Pop. 3000.

Saverne, a town in the department of Lower Rhine, seated at the foot of Mount Vosges, in a country which produces plenty of wine; 20 miles W. N. W. of Strasburg. Pop. 4000.

Savigliano, a town of the Sardinian states in Piedmont, with a rich Benedictine abbey. Here the French were repulsed in 1799 by the Austrians. It is seated in a fertile plain, on the river Maira, 30 miles S. of Turin.

Savolax, a district of the Russian empire, in the province of Finland, 200 miles long, and 100 broad; consisting mostly of woods, lakes, rivers, and morasses, and abounding in elks and reindeer. The inhabitants are thinly dispersed, and subsist by cultivating buck-wheat, breeding cattle, hunting, fishing, and making wooden ware. Kuopia is the capital.

Savona, a strong town of the Sardinian states, in the territory of Genoa, with a citadel on a rock, and several fine churches. The Genoese, fearing that it would hurt their trade, ruined the harbour, and rendered it unfit for large vessels. It was taken by the king of Sardinia in 1746, restored to the republic of Genoa in 1748, and taken in 1795 by the French, who surrendered it to the Austrians in 1800, through famine. In 1810 and 1811 it was the residence of the Pope, during his dispute with Bonaparte. By the congress of Vienna it was ceded, with the whole Genoese territory, to the king of Sardinia. It is seated on the Mediterranean, 24 miles W. S. W. of Genoa. Pop. 10,000. Long. 8. 20. E. lat. 44. 18. N.

Savoniers, a town of France, department of Indre-et-Loire, near which are caverns, famous for their petrifactions; 8 miles S. W. of Tours.

Savoy, a duchy of Europe, belonging to the kingdom of Sardinia, 85 miles long, and 67 broad, bounded on the N. by the Lake of Geneva, which separates it from Switzerland; E. by the Alps, which divide it from Vallais and Piedmont; S. by the latter and France; and W. by France. The air is cold, on account of high mountains, which are almost always covered with snow; but the valleys are fertile in corn and wine, and many of the mountains abound with pastures that feed a great number of cattle. The principal rivers are the Isere, Arc, and Arve. The Savoyards, from the nature of their country, are generally very poor, and great numbers of them seek a livelihood in France, England, and other countries, in quality of showmen, &c. Area, 3800 square miles. Pop. 467,080. The French subdued this country in 1792, and made it a department of France, by the name of Mont Blanc, which was confirmed to them by the treaty of Paris in 1814; but in 1815 it was restored to Sardinia, with the exception of a small district (the commune of St. Julian) ceded to the Swiss canton of Geneva. Chambery is the capital.

Savu, an island in the Indian Ocean, to which the Dutch have a kind of exclusive trade, having entered into an agreement with the rajahs that their subjects shall trade with no other ships. It is 26 miles in length, and very fertile. Pop. 5000. Long. 122. 30. E. lat. 10. 35. S.

Sax, a town of Spain, in Murcia, near which is an ancient citadel on the summit of a rock. It is seated on the Elda, on the borders of Valencia; 25 miles W. N. W. of Alicant, and 42 N. N. E. of Murcia.

Sax, a town and district of Switzerland, in the canton of St. Gall, with a castle; 16 miles S. of Rheineck. Pop. 3000.

Saxenburg, a town of the Austrian states, in Carinthia, near which are three forts and a strong pass. It is situate on the Drave, 38 miles W. of Clagenfurt. Long. 13. 12. E. lat 46. 44. N.

Saxmundham, a town in Suffolk, with a market on Thursday, seated on a hill, 20 miles N. E. of Ipswich, and 89 of London.

Saxony, in its most comprehensive sense, denotes a vast tract of country in the N. of Germany, extending from the Weser on the W. to the frontier of Poland on the E., but, in consequence of the territorial changes to which it has been subject, the name has been used with great latitude of signification. The division of Germany into circles took place towards the close of the 15th century, and the large tract of country known vaguely by the name of Saxony was formed into three circles, Westphalia, Upper Saxony, and Lower Saxony. Upper Saxony comprised the electorates of Saxony and Brandenburg, the duchy of Pomerania, and a number of small principalities, forming an extent of about 43,000 square miles, with nearly 4,000,000 of inhabitants. It was bounded E. by Poland, Silesia, and Lusatia, and S. by Bohemia and Franconia. Lower Saxony was bounded N. by the duchy of Sleswick and the Baltic, and W. by Westphalia and the Rhine. It comprised the electorate of Hanover, the duchies of Brunswick, Mecklenburg, and Holstein, the free towns of Hamburgh, Bremen, and Lubeck, with a number of small states, forming an extent of 26,000 square miles. In 1806 the distinction of circles was finally abolished, and the names of Upper and Lower Saxony are now of use only for the elucidation of history.

Saxony, a modern kingdom of Europe, situate towards the N. E. of Germany, and bounded S. by Bohemia, and N. by the Prussian states. It comprises an area of 7188 square miles, with 1,400,000 inhabitants; but previously to 1814 it was of much greater extent, having been greatly reduced by the congress of Vienna. No part of Europe, in the same latitude, enjoys a milder climate. The mountainous districts in the S. contain extensive forests, which are kept up with care, as the chief supply of fuel for the mines. In the southern and mountainous parts of Saxony the valleys only are well cultivated, but in the level districts in the N., particularly the circles of Meissen and Leipsic, tillage is general: the products are wheat, barley, oats, and other grain; also some tobacco and hops. Hogs and sheep are very numerous, and the greatest care has been bestowed on the Merino rams, first imported about 1768. Few countries equal Saxony in mineral riches, and in none has this department of natural history been more fully described. The principal are silver, iron, copper, lead, limestone, coal, arsenic, cobalt, antimony, zinc, alum, &c. The principal rivers are the Elbe, the two Elsters, the two Muldas, and the Queiss. The manufactures are of considerable extent, and consist principally of linen, cotton, silk, and leather. The machinery used, though inferior to the English, has of late years been much improved. The position of Saxony is not favourable for commercial intercourse. The exports consist of wool (which has long been considered the best in Germany), minerals, linen, yarn, woollens, and lace. The imports are silk, flax, cotton, coffee, sugar, wine, and, in certain seasons, corn. A great majority of the inhabitants are Lutherans, but the reigning family have been Catholics since 1697. The institutions for education are numerous and well conducted, and the lower classes are generally taught to read and write. In no country of equal extent is the number of printing and book establishments so great. Of the universities, Halle now belongs to Prussia, but Leipsic remains to Saxony, and retains all its former reputation. Saxony was for many centuries an electorate, but in consequence of the occupancy of Prussia by Bonaparte, in 1806, it was formed into a kingdom. This change of title was not, however, accompanied by any extension of prerogative, the sovereign continuing to share the legislative functions with the states, and imposing no tax without their concurrence. The states are divided into two houses, viz., the prelates and nobles in one, and the country gentry and deputies of the towns in the other. The higher offices of administration are entrusted to a cabinet council, a board of finance, a military board, a high court of appeal for judicial questions, and an upper consistory for ecclesiastical. The country is divided into the circles of Meissen, Leipsic, Erzgebirg, and Vogtland, with part of Merseburg, and Upper Lusatia. Each circle has a court of justice, and offices for the transaction of provincial business; and the peasantry are here in the enjoyment of complete personal freedom. The king, as a member of the Germanic confederation, has the fourth rank in the smaller and four votes at the larger assembly. The army amounts to 12,000 men; the revenue exceeds 1,000,000*l.* sterling; and the national debt is 3,700,000*l.* The Saxons are first mentioned in history by Ptolemy, who describes them about the year 160 as a rude tribe, inhabiting Holstein and part of Jutland. Soon after, they appear to have advanced to the S. and W., acquiring an extension of territory. In the 5th century, on the migration of a part of the Franks into Gaul, the Saxons acquired a further extension of territory, viz. the country now forming the grand duchy of Oldenburg, with part of Hanover and Prussian Westphalia. When the Britons were forsaken by their Roman defenders, they applied and obtained assistance from the Saxons, against the Scots and Picts. After maintaining, during many years, a firm resistance to the arms of Charlemagne, the Saxons were at last obliged to submit to his conditions, which involved the payment of an annual tribute and their conversion to Christianity. The title of duke of Saxony was conferred on Wittikind, their chief, whose family, after ruling some time, was succeeded by that of Billung, and afterwards by a branch of that of Guelf, which ruled in Bavaria. The electoral dignity was subsequently conferred on the Wittemberg line of the House of Ascania, and, on its extinction, on the Margraves of Meissen, with the title of elector. The first elector, surnamed Frederick the Warlike, began his reign in 1422; he was the founder of the university of Leipsic. The next memorable event in the history of Saxony was the reformation, in the beginning of the 16th century. The prince did not openly espouse the cause of Luther, but, by protecting him from persecution, he contributed much to the establishment of his doctrines. His successor, John Frederick, styled "the magnanimous," being defeated by Charles V., was stripped of his states and dignity, which the emperor conferred on Maurice, margrave of Meissen, the cousin of the elector, and the ancestor of the present House of Saxony. Maurice, putting himself at the head of the Protestant interest, proved a full match for the artful Charles, who, in 1552, had almost fallen into his hands, and was compelled to sign the convention of Passau, since considered the bulwark of the religious freedom of Germany. The Saxons took an active part in the thirty years' war, which terminated in the peace of Westphalia, in 1648. In 1697 the temptation of the crown of Poland, vacant by the death of Sobieski, induced the reigning elector, Augustus I., to profess himself a Catholic, a change which, however, did not prosper. The Swedes, under Charles XII., not only conquered Poland, but invaded Saxony, bringing great distress upon the country until 1708, when relief was obtained by the march of Charles into Russia, and its disastrous issue; after which, the crown of Poland was resumed by Augustus. In the war of 1740, between Prussia and Austria, Saxony remained neutral. In that of 1756, the elector was tempted to take a part by the flattering promises of Austria; but, instead of an accession of territory, his dominions were ravaged, and many of his subjects ruined in this dreadful contest. In the war against France no decided part was taken by Saxony, until 1806, when the elector sent all his troops to the field, in support of the king of Prussia, whose subsequent overthrow enabled Bonaparte to attach the Saxons to his cause. The title of elector was changed to that of king. Prussian Poland was afterwards added to the Saxon dominions, and in 1809 was nearly doubled by cessions obtained from Austria. But these acquisitions, disproportioned to the inherent strength of Saxony, led, as formerly, to disastrous results. The Russians re-occupied Poland in the beginning of 1813, and, joined by the Prussians, made Saxony the scene of the great continental struggle against Bonaparte. The battles of Lutzen and Bautzen, the attacks on Dresden, and the decisive engagements at Leipsic, were followed by the retreat of Bonaparte to the Rhine, and his too faithful ally, the king of Saxony, was deprived of the government of his territories. By the decision of the congress of Vienna, the northern and eastern part, containing no fewer than 850,000 inhabitants, was separated from the kingdom, and transferred to Prussia. The king of Saxony protested against this dismemberment, but, dreading insurrection and bloodshed, he at length acquiesced. Dresden is the capital.

Saxony, a province of the Prussian states; comprising almost the whole of the cessions made by the king of Saxony at the congress of Vienna, and the principalities lying to the N. of the duchy of Anhalt, and to the W. of the rivers Elbe and Havel. It contains an area of

9830 square miles, with more than 1,000,000 of inhabitants, and is divided into the governments of Magdeburg, Merseburg, and Erfurt. The surface is in general level; but the soil varies greatly, being in some places dry and sandy, and in others a heavy loam. The principal productions are corn, hemp, flax, and chicory. The inhabitants, except in the small district called Eichsfeld, are almost all Protestants, and are in general active and industrious. Magdeburg is the chief town.

SAXTON'S RIVER, a river in the state of Vermont, which joins the Connecticut at Westminster.

SAYBROOK, a town of Connecticut, in Middlesex county, with a fort. It is the most ancient in the state, and situate near the mouth of Connecticut River; 18 miles W. by S. of New London. Long. 72. 25. W. lat. 41. 20. N.

SAYCOCK, one of the islands of Japan; divided from Niphon by a narrow channel. The Dutch factors are permitted to reside in the little island of Disnia, which is on the W. side of this. Long. 132. 28. E. lat. 34. 0. N.

SAYN, a town and castle of the Prussian state; in the duchy of Nassau, which gives name to a small county. It is 6 miles N. of Coblentz, and 50 N. W. of Frankfort.

SAYPAN, the pleasantest and most fertile of the Ladrone islands; 40 miles in circuit, with a safe port called Cantanhitda, on the W. side. Long. 146. 10. E. lat. 15. 22. N.

SCAGEN, a town of Denmark, in N. Jutland; on a promontory of the same name, at the entrance of the passage from the ocean into the Cattegat. Long. 10. 0. E. lat. 57. 31. N.

SCALANOVA, a seaport of Asia Minor, near the site of the ancient Ephesus, with a castle. The trade, which is considerable, consists chiefly in wine, raisins, corn, and leather. It is 40 miles S. S. E. of Smyrna. Pop. about 8000. Long. 27. 31. E. lat. 37. 54. N.

SCALEA, a town of Naples, in Calabria Citra, formerly a large city, but now greatly decayed. It is seated on the W. coast; 25 miles S. E. of Policastro. Long. 15. 54. E. lat. 40. 0. N.

SCANDEROON. *See* ALEXANDRETTA.

SCANIA. *See* SCHONEN.

SCARBOROUGH, a seaport and borough in N. Yorkshire. It has a market on Thursday, and sends two members to parliament. It is seated on the declivity of a high rock, which has such craggy sides that it is almost inaccessible. On the top of this rock is a large green plain, with a little well of fresh water, and the remains of a castle, built by Henry II. This town is greatly frequented on account of its mineral waters, and also for sea-bathing; on which account it is much improved in the number and beauty of its buildings. The new buildings on the cliff stand almost unrivalled in extent of prospect, having in front a beautiful terrace, elevated nearly 100 feet above the level of the sands. Amongst other improvements are the formation of a reservoir, covered with a dome, capable of containing 4000 hogsheads of water, for the supply of the town; and the erection of an elegant iron bridge over the wide chasm through which the stream called the Mill-beck flows, and connecting two lofty dissevered cliffs. Scarborough had formerly four churches, all of which are now demolished, except St. Mary's, and even this has sustained considerable injury. A new church has been erected; and here are meeting-houses for Independents, Baptists, Catholics, Quakers, and Methodists, a free grammar-school, a Lancasterian school, several hospitals, almshouses, and other charitable institutions. The harbour is one of the best in the kingdom, with a commodious quay, several ship-yards, and a strong battery. It is 40 miles N. E. of York, and 216 N. of London. Long. 0. 10. W. lat. 54. 18. N.

SCARBOROUGH, a town and fort on the S. E. side of the island of Tobago. It was taken by the English in 1793. Long. 60. 30. W. lat. 11. 6. N.

SCARDONA, a town of Austrian Dalmatia, and a bishop's see, seated on the Cherca; 8 miles N. of Sebenico. Long. 17. 1. E. lat. 44. 29. N.

SCARLINO, a town of Tuscany, with a castle, seated on the sea coast; 7 miles S. of Massa.

SCARPANTO, an island in the Mediterranean; 18 miles long, and 6 broad; lying S. W. of Rhodes. It is mountainous and rocky, abounds in cattle and game, and has quarries of marble. The principal town on the W. coast has a good harbour. Long. 27. 40. E. lat. 35. 45. N.

SCARPE, a river of France, which rises near Aubigny, in the department of Pas de Calais, passes by Arras, Douay, and St. Amand, and enters the Scheldt at Mortagne.

SCARPERIA, a town of Tuscany, celebrated for its steel manufactures; seated at the foot of the Appennines; 13 miles N. of Florence.

SCAURO, the capital of the island of Santorin, and the see of a Latin bishop. It stands on a lofty volcanic rock, which projects into the roadstead, on the W. coast of the island. Long. 25. 26. E. lat. 16. 28. N.

SCHAFFHAUSEN, a canton of Switzerland; 15 miles long, and 10 broad, with 32,000 inhabitants. The reformation was introduced here in 1529, and the religion is Calvinism. The principal article of trade is wine, and the manufactures are inconsiderable.

SCHAFFHAUSEN, a town of Switzerland, capital of the above canton, is seated on the Rhine, and owes its origin to the interruption of the navigation of that river by the cataract at Lauffen; huts being at first constructed for the conveniency of unloading the merchandise from the boats, which by degrees increased to a large town. Though a frontier town, it has no garrison, and the fortifications are weak. The Rhine, which is here nearly 400 feet wide, is crossed by a kind of hanging bridge; the road not passing over the arch, but being suspended from it, and almost level. It was burnt by the French, when they evacuated the town, after being defeated by the Austrians in 1799, but has since been rebuilt, nearly in the same state as before. It is 22 miles N. by E. of Zurich, and 39 E. of Basel. Pop. 6000. Long. 3. 41. E. lat. 47. 39. N.

SCHALHOLT, or SKALHOLT, a town of Ireland, and a bishop's see, with a college. Long. 22. 20. W. lat. 64. 40. N.

SCHAMACHI, a town of Caucasia, capital of Schirvan. It was formerly very large, but is now decayed, above 6000 houses having been thrown down by an earthquake. It stands in a valley, between two mountains; 24 miles W. of the Caspian Sea, and 250 N. E. of Tauris. Long. 51. 5. E. lat. 40. 50. N.

SCHARDING, a town of Bavaria, with a fortified castle, seated on the Inn; 7 miles S. of Passau.

SCHARNITZ, a fortified town of Germany, in Tyrol, which defends a pass over the mountains, of considerable importance. It surrendered to the French and Bavarians in 1805. It stands on the confines of Bavaria; 12 miles N of Inspruck.

SCHAUENBERG, a principality of Germany, in Westphalia. It is mountainous and woody, but contains much fertile land, quarries of limestone and freestone, and mines of alum, coal, copper, and iron. Area, 172 square miles. Pop. 25,000. The line of its ancient counts was extinct in 1640, and in 1647 it became the property of the landgrave of Hesse-Cassel, of whom the count of Lippe holds a part as fief. Rintel is the capital.

SCHAUENSTEIN, a town of Bavaria, in the principality of Bayreuth; 18 miles N. E. of Culmbach.

SCHAUMBURG, a town and castle of Germany; which gives name to a lordship in the duchy of Nassau. Pop. 7000. It is 25 miles W. S. W. of Wetzlar.

SCHEER, a town and castle of Wirtemberg, capital of a lordship of its name, seated on the Danube; 36 miles S. W. of Ulm. Long. 9. 24. E. lat. 48. 5. N.

SCHEIBENBERG, a town of Saxony; near which are mines of silver and iron; 22 miles S. of Chemnitz.

SCHELDT (L'ESCAUT), a river which rises in France, in the department of Aisne; passes by Cambray, Bouchain, Valenciennes, Conde, Tournay, Oudenard, Ghent, Dendermond, Antwerp, and Fort Lillo, below which it divides into two branches. One of these, called the Eastern Scheldt, flows by Bergen-op-Zoom; the other, the Western Scheldt, proceeds to Flushing, and, both forming several islands, enter the German Ocean, after a course of 200 miles.

SCHELESTAT, or SCHLETSTAT, a fortified town of France, department of Lower Rhine, on the river Ille; 20 miles S. W. of Strasburg. Population, 7500.

SCHELLA, a town of Hungary, seated on the Waag; 25 miles N. E. of Presburg.

SCHELLENBERG, a town of Saxony, frequently called Augustusburg, from a castle of that name standing on the mountain of Schellenberg, close by the town. It is seated on the Zschopa; 8 miles E. of Chemnitz.

SCHOLLENBURG, a town of Bavaria, where a victory was obtained by the allies, over the French and Bavarians, in 1704; 12 miles W. of Neuburg.

SCHELLING, an island of the Netherlands; 12 miles long, and 3 broad, lying at the entrance of the Zuyder Zee. It was taken by the British in 1799. Long. 5. 0. E. lat. 53. 20. N.

SCHEMNITZ, a town of Hungary, one of the seven mountain towns, with three castles. It is famous for mines of silver and other metals; as also for its hot-baths. Near it is a high rock of shining blue stone, mixed with green, and some spots of yellow; 80 miles E. N. E. of Presburg. Pop. 23,000. Long. 18. 56. E. lat. 48. 30. N.

SCHENCK, a fortress of the Netherlands, in Guelderland, seated in the angle where the Rhine divides into two branches, the Rhine and the Wahal. It is now in ruins; 13 miles E. of Nimeguen.

SCHENECTADY. *See* SKENECTADY.

SCHENING, a town of Sweden, in East Gothland, seated in a fertile country; 10 miles S. E. of Wastena.

SCHENINGEN, a town of Germany, in the duchy of Brunswick, near which is a Lutheran convent, and a salt mine; 18 miles E. of Wolfenbuttel.

SCHEPPENSTADT, a town in the duchy of Brunswick; 12 miles E. of Wolfenbuttel.

SCHERPENHEUL. *See* MONTAIGUE.

SCHESBURG, a fortified town of Transylvania, with a castle; 60 miles N. E. of Weissenburg.

SCHIEDAM, a town and harbour of the Netherlands, in South Holland, noted for its numerous distilleries of gin (Hollands). It is seated on a canal, called the Schie, which communicates with the Meuse; 6 miles W. by S. of Rotterdam. Pop. 9000.

SCHIERLING, a village of Bavaria, noted as the scene of an obstinate conflict, generally called the battle of Abensberg, in 1809, between Buonaparte and the archduke Charles. It is 11 miles S. of Ratisbon.

SCHIEVELBEIN, a town of Prussian Pomerania; with a castle, seated on the Rega; 17 miles N. of Dramburg.

SCHILTACH, a town of Germany, in the kingdom of Wirtemberg, on the river Schiltach; 14 miles N. N. W. of Rothwell.

SCHINTA, a town of Hungary, on the river Waag; 28 miles E. of Presburg.

SCHINTZACH, a town of Switzerland, in the canton of Aargau. Here are some tepid mineral waters; and near it, on a lofty eminence, are the ruins of the famous castle of Hapsburg. It is seated on the Aar; 10 miles W. of Baden, and 20 S. E. of Basel.

SCHIRAS. *See* SHIRAZ.

SCHIRVAN, a province of Caucasia; 150 miles long, and 90 broad, bounded on the N. by Daghestan, E. and S. E. by the Caspian Sea, S. W. by Erivan, and W. by Georgia. The soil is very fertile, producing abundance of rice, wheat, and barley; and the pastures feed numerous cattle. Vines are planted along the hedges, and fastened to the trees. Here are vast quantities of wild fowls, particularly pheasants; also hares in abundance. It formed part of the Persian dominions from 1500 till the decline of the Sefti dynasty, when it asserted its independence; it has, however, become nominally subject to Russia. Schamachi is the capital.

SCHLACKENWELD, a town of Bohemia; with a good tin-mine; 5 miles S. of Carlsbad.

SCHLACKENWERTH, a town of Bohemia, with a fine castle, seated on the Weisseritz; 7 miles N. N. E. of Carlsbad.

SCHLADEN, a town of Hanover, in the province of Hildesheim; 28 miles E. S. E. of Hildesheim.

SCHLAN, a town of Bohemia, in the circle of Rakonitz, with a castle. It is surrounded by walls and vineyards. It is 16 miles N. E. of Rakonitz. Pop. 3000.

SCHLAWA, a town of the Prussian states, in the principality of Glogau; 18 miles N. of Glogau.

SCHLAWE, a town of Prussian Pomerania; on the river Wipper; 10 miles W. S. W. of Stolpe.

SCHLEUSINGEN, a town and castle of Saxony, in the county of Henneberg; seated on the Schleuss; 18 miles S. E. of Smalkald, and 19 N. N. E. of Schweinfurt.

SCHLITZ, a town of Germany, in the principality of Fulda, on a small river that runs into the Fulda; 7 miles N. N. W. of Fulda.

SCHLITZ, a town of Germany, in Voigtland; with a castle; 13 miles N. W. of Plauen.

SCHLUSSELBURG, a town and fortress of Russia, situate on the Neva, near Lake Ladoga. The fortress stands on an island in the river, and has frequently been used as a state prison; 34 miles E. of St. Petersburg. Long. 39. 55. E. lat. 59. 55. N.

SCHMALKALDEN. *See* SMALKALDEN.

SCHMALENBERG, a town of Westphalia, on the river Lenne; 14 miles E. of Altendorn.

SCHMIEDEBERG, a town of Prussian Silesia, in the principality of Jauer. The vicinity abounds in iron-ore, and almost all the inhabitants are smiths. It is seated at the foot of a mountain, near the source of the Bauber; 25 miles W. S. W. of Schweidnitz. Pop. 3800.

SCHMIEDEBURG, a town of Prussian Saxony; 14 miles S. of Dresden.

SCHMOLLEN, a town of Germany, in the principality of Altenburg, on the river Sprotta; 7 miles S. W. of Altenburg.

SCHNEEBURG, a town of Saxony, with manufactures of thread, silk, gold and silver lace, &c.; and in the neighbourhood are silver mines. It is situate on an eminence near the Mulda; 9 miles S. S. E. of Zwickau. Pop. 4400.

SCHOHARIE, a town of the state of New York, capital of a county of the same name. It stands on the Schoharie River, which runs N. into Mohawk River; 40 miles W. of Albany. Long. 74. 42. W. lat. 42. 40. N.

SCHONBECK, a town and castle of Prussian Saxony, in the duchy of Magdeburg, with some salt-works, seated on the Elbe; 9 miles S. S. E. of Magdeburg. Pop. 5100.

SCHONBRUNN, a village of Austria; 3 miles S. W. of Vienna. Here is an imperial palace, the usual residence of the court. It was much improved by the empress Maria Theresa; and has also a botanic garden and fine conservatories.

SCHONECK, a town of Saxony, in Voigtland; 15 miles S. E. of Plauen.

SCHONECKEN, a town of Germany, in the territory of Treves, seated on the Nyms; 28 miles N. by W. of Treves.

SCHONEN, or SCANIA, a province of Sweden; in Gothland; almost surrounded by the Sound and the Baltic. It is 70 miles long, and 50 broad, and the most level, pleasant, and fertile spot in the kingdom, producing all the necessaries of life in abundance. Lund is the capital

SCHONGAU, a town of Bavaria, surrounded by a plain wall and some towers. The great square is adorned with three fountains of a kind of marble, the product of the country. It stands on the side of an eminence, by the river Lech. It is 14 miles S. of Lansburg, and 40 S. W. of Munich.

SCHONHOVEN, a town of the Netherlands, in South Holland, with a commodious haven. It is celebrated for its gardens, and its salmon fishery, seated on the Leck; 14 miles E. by N. of Rotterdam.

SCHORNDORF, a town of the kingdom of Wirtemberg, with a strong castle, and productive salt-springs. It is seated on the Rems; 17 miles S. S. E. of Stutgard.

SCHOUTEN ISLAND, an island in the Pacific Ocean, near the N. E. coast of New Guinea; 60 miles long, and 20 broad, discovered by William Schouten, a Dutchman, in 1616. Long. 135. 50. E. lat. 0. 40. S.

SCHOUWEN, an island of the Netherlands, forming the N. part of Zealand, at the mouth of the Scheldt. It is 15 miles long, and 16 broad. Ziriczee is the capital.

SCHRATTENTHAL, a town and castle of Austria; 9 miles S. S. W. of Znaim.

SCHROBENHAUSEN, a town of Bavaria, on the river Par; 16 miles S. S. W. of Ingolstadt.

SCHUT, an island of Hungary, formed by the Danube; immediately below Presburg. It is 40 miles long, and 12 broad; abounds in fruit and herbage, and has plenty of game, wood, and fish. The chief town is Comorn.

SCHUYLER FORT, Old and New, both in the state of New York, on Mohawk River; the Old 4 miles below, and the New, 7 above Whitestown. The latter is more usually called Fort Stanwix.

SCHUYLKILL, a river of Pennsylvania; which rises N. W. of the Kittatinny Mountains. It is navigable from above Reading to its entrance into the Delaware; 5 miles below Philadelphia.

SCHWABACH, a town of Bavaria, in the principality of Anspach, with numerous manufactures. It stands on a river of the same name, which flows into the Rednitz; 12 miles E. by N. of Anspach.

SCHWALBACH, a town of Germany, in the duchy of Nassau, frequented for its mineral waters, seated on the river Aa; 32 miles W. of Frankfort.

SCHWALENBURG, a town of Westphalia, in the county of Lippe; 18 miles N. E. of Paderborn.

SCHWAN, a town of Germany, in the duchy of Mecklenburg, on the river Warnow; 10 miles N. of Gustrow.

SCHWANDORF, a town of Bavaria, in the principality of Neuburg, on the river Nab; 21 miles N. of Ratisbon.

SCHWANENSTADT, a a town of Austria, near which the French gained a decisive victory over the Austrians in 1800. It is seated on the Ager; 25 miles S. W. of Lintz.

SCHWARTZBURG, an ancient castle of Germany, which gives name to a district belonging to the House of Saxony. The district is divided into two parts, the Upper and Lower, each bearing the name of county. Area, 1166 square miles. Population, about 108,000. Rudolstadt and Sondershausen are the chief towns. The castle is seated on the Schwartz; 7 miles S. W. of Rudolstadt.

SCHWARTZENBERG, a town of Bavarian Franconia, in a principality of the same name; with a castle; seated on the Leck; 24 miles E. S. E. of Wurtzburg.

SCHWARTZENBERG, a town of Saxony, with wire and lace manufactures. In the vicinity are iron-forges, and mines of tin and lead. It is 10 miles W. S. W. of Annaberg.

SCHWARTZENBURG, a town of Switzerland, capital of a bailiwick, in the canton of Bern; 10 miles S. E. of Friburg, and 17 S. S. W. of Bern.

SCHWATZ, a town of Austria, in Tyrol; with a silver and copper mine; seated on the river Inn; 14 miles N. E. of Inspruck. Pop. 4000.

SCHWEDT, a town of Prussia, in Brandenburg; with a magnificent castle; seated on the Oder, 24 miles S. E. of Prenzio. Pop. 4700.

SCHWEIDNITZ, a strong city of Prussia, in the government of Reichenbach; capital of a principality of the same name; with a castle. Half of the magistrates are Catholics, but most of the inhabitants are Protestants, who have a church without the town, as also a public school. All kinds of leather, particularly cordovan, are manufactured here. In 1716 the greatest part of this city was burnt down, but it was rebuilt in an elegant manner. The Austrians took it in 1757, from the Prussians, who retook it the next year. In 1807 it surrendered to the French. It is seated on an eminence on the river Weistritz; 22 miles S. W. of Breslau. Pop. 8000. Long. 16. 32. E. lat. 50. 44. N.

SCHWEINFURT, a town of Bavarian Franconia; with a palace. The inhabitants carry on a large trade in wine, woollen and linen cloth, goose quills and feathers. This town was taken by the French in 1796, and was given to Bavaria in 1802. It is seated on the Maine; 21 miles N. E. of Wurtzburg. Pop. 5200. Long. 10. 35. E. lat. 50. 6. N.

SCHWEINITZ, a town of Saxony, on the river Elster; 14 miles S. E. of Wittenberg.

SCHWEINSBERG, a town of Germany, in Hesse-Cassel; on the river Ohm; 7 miles S. E. of Marburg.

SCHWEITS, a canton of Switzerland, containing an area of 466 square miles, and a population of 30,000; bounded on the W. by the Waldstadter See, S. by the canton of Uri, E. by that of Glarus, and N. by those of Zurich and Zug. This canton, with that of Uri and Underwalden, threw off the yoke of Austria in 1308, and formed a perpetual alliance in 1315, which was the grand foundation of the Helvetic confederacy. The name of Schweitzerland, Swisserland, or Switzerland, originally comprehended only these three cantons, but was afterwards extended to all Helvetia. The whole country, being rugged and mountainous, consists chiefly of pasture, raises little corn, and has no wine; but this soil, naturally barren, has been improved by the natives to a great degree of fertility. The inhabitants made a spirited but unavailing resistance to the French in 1798, and they suffered severely in 1799, when Switzerland became the scene of military operations. The Roman Catholic is the established religion.

SCHWEITZ, the capital of the above canton, is seated near the Waldstadter See; on the slope of a hill, at the bottom of two high and rugged rocks, called the Schweitzer Haken. The church is a large magnificent building; 18 miles E. by S. of Lucern. Pop. 5000. Long. 8. 31. E. lat. 46. 56. N.

SCHWEITZ, LAKE OF. *See* WALDSTADTER SEE.

SCHWELM, a town of Prussian Westphalia, in the county of Mark, near which are some medicinal springs; 26 miles E. of Dusseldorf.

SCHWERIN, a town of Germany, capital of the grand duchy of Mecklenburg-Schwerin. It is divided into four parts; namely, Schwerin, the New Town, the island of Schelf, and the Moor, which are all nearly encircled by a beautiful lake. The principal church is a fine Gothic pile, with a lofty spire. The ducal palace and gardens are on an island in the lake, and have a communication with the town by a drawbridge. This town was taken by the Prussians in 1759, and in 1806 it was occupied by the French. It is 35 miles W. S. W. of Gustrow. Pop. 8500. Long. 11. 33. E. lat. 53. 56. N.

SCHWERTE, a town of Prussian Westphalia, in the county of Mark; on the river Roer; 7 miles S. of Dortmund.

SCHWETZ, a town and castle of Prussia, on the Vistula; 7 miles N. of Culm.

SCHWIEBUSSEN, a town of Prussia, in the principality of Glogau. It has a castle, a Catholic parish church, a Protestant church, good cloth manufactures, and fertile gardens and vineyards; 13 miles N. of Zullichau. Long. 15. 47. E. lat. 52. 21. N.

SCHWINBURG, a town of Denmark, on the S. coast of the island of Funen; with the best harbour in the island, and manufactures of woollen and linen; 23 miles S. S. E. of Odensee. Long. 10. 30. E. lat. 55. 10. N.

SCIACCA. *See* XACCA.

SCIATI, an island of the Grecian Archipelago, 14 miles N. N. E. of Negropont, and almost at the entrance of the Gulf of Salonichi. It is 10 miles long, and 4 broad. Long. 23. 40. E. lat. 39. 24. N.

SCIGLIO, a town of Naples; in Calabria

Ultra; on the side of a rocky promontory, called Scylla, or Cape Sciglio. In the terrible earthquake in 1783, the sea was thrown furiously 3 miles inland, and on its return swept off about 2500 of its inhabitants, with the prince of Sciglio, who, hoping to find security, were then on the Scylla strand, or in boats near the shore. It is 10 miles N. by E. of Reggio.

SCILLY, a cluster of isles and rocks, at the entrance of the English and Bristol Channels; lying almost 10 leagues W. of the Land's-end, in Cornwall. They are 17 in number. Of these only five or six are inhabited. They are a resort for seafowl, and feed many sheep and rabbits. The inhabitants principally subsist by fishing, burning kelp, and acting as pilots. The chief isle is that of St. Mary, nearly 3 miles long, and 2 broad, which has a good port, is well fortified, and contains more inhabitants than all the rest put together. In this isle, and in two or three others, are various antiquities, particularly the remains of a temple of the Druids, and ancient sepulchres. On that of St. Agnes is a lighthouse, which, with the gallery, is 51 feet high, and is a very fine column. At the outermost extremity of the isle of St. Martin is a seamark, built with rockstone, and as conspicuous by day as the lighthouse on St. Agnes, but not so high and large. The Scilly rocks have been fatal to numbers of ships entering the English Channel. One of the most disastrous events of this kind happened in 1707, when three men-of-war perished, with Admiral Sir Cloudesley Shovel and all their crews. St. Agnes lighthouse is in long. 6. 19. W. lat. 49. 54. N.

SCILLY, a group of isles or shoals, in the South Pacific; discovered by Captain Wallis in 1767, and described as extremely dangerous. Long. 155. 30. W. lat. 16. 30. S.

SCIO, (anciently called Chios,) an island of the Grecian Archipelago, near the coast of Natolia; 36 miles long, and 13 broad. It is a mountainous country; but fruits of various kinds grow in the fields, such as oranges, citrons, olives, mulberries, and pomegranates, interspersed with myrtles and jasmines. The wine of Scio, so celebrated by the ancients, is still in great esteem; but the island is now principally distinguished by the profitable culture of mastich; it has also some trade in silk, cotton, and figs. Besides the town, of the same name, it contains 68 villages, all inhabited by Greeks; and those which furnish mastich are the most rich and populous. In 1822 this island became the scene of unparalleled barbarity, in consequence of the Greek population having joined their countrymen in their struggle for liberty. The Turks landed several thousand men, and massacred all the men, and the male children above 12 years of age; the women and young children were sent into captivity, and the male children were circumcised in token of conversion to Mahomedism. From the 11th of April to the 10th of May, the number of slain amounted to 25,000, and that of captives to 30,000. But the sanguinary proceedings of the Ottoman power were at length arrested, the oppressed Greeks liberated, and Turkish despotism effectually chastised.

SCIO, the capital of the above island, and a bishop's see. It is the best built town in the Archipelago; the houses being commodious, some of them terraced, and others covered with tiles. The castle, an old citadel built by the Genoese, is now in ruins. The harbour is a rendezvous for ships that go to or come from Constantinople: it will contain 80 vessels, is protected by a low mole, and has two lighthouses. It stands on the E. side of the island; 67 miles W. of Smyrna. Long. 26. 2. E. lat. 38. 28. N.

SCIOTO, a county of the United States; lying on both sides of a river of its name, which rises in the state of Ohio, near the sources of the Sandusky, and falls into the Ohio at Portsmouth, in lat. 38. 34. N. Pop. 11,192. Portsmouth is the chief town.

SCIPIO, a town of New York; in Cayuga county; seated on the E. side of Cayuga Lake; 95 miles W. of Cooperstown.

SCIRO, or SCIROS, an island of the Grecian Archipelago, to the W. of Metelin; 15 miles long, and 8 broad. The country is mountainous, but has no mines. The vines make the beauty of the island, and the wine is excellent; nor do the natives want corn or wood. It contains only the village and convent of St. George, both built on a conical rock; 10 miles from the harbour of St. George. Long. 24. 38. E. lat. 38. 54. N.

SCITUATE, a town of Massachusets, in Plymouth county; situate on an inlet of the sea, which forms a harbour; 16 miles N. of Plymouth, and 28 S. E. of Boston. Pop. 3886.

SCITUATE, a town of Rhode Island; in Providence county; near which is a foundry for cannon and bells; 11 miles S. S. W. of Providence, and 27 N. W. of Newport. Population 4090.

SCLAVONIA, a province of Austria, situate between the rivers Drave and Danube on the N., and the Save on the S.; bounded on the W. by Croatia, from which, to the conflux of the Save with the Danube, it is 150 miles in length, and from 45 to 25 in breadth; containing an area of 6600 square miles, with a population of 550,000. A chain of lofty mountains, covered with forests, extends from E. to W. nearly through its whole length; but the remainder is a fertile level country, producing wheat, barley, maize, flax, hemp, madder, and a variety of fruits. The eastern part is called Ratza, and the inhabitants Rascians. These form a particular nation, and are of the Greek church. The ancient Sclavonia contained many large countries: some have extended it from the Adriatic to the Euxine Sea, and say that it had its name from the Sclavi, a Scythian nation, who conquered Greece and this country in the reign of the emperor Justinian. The language of Sclavonia is the mother of four others; namely, those of Hungary, Bohemia, Poland, and Russia.

SCONE, or SCOON, a village of Scotland, in Perthshire; noted for an ancient palace, where the kings of Scotland used to be crowned. It is situate on the E. side of the river Tay; a mile N. of Perth.

SCOPELO, an island of the Grecian Archipelago, 10 miles long and 5 broad. It is very fertile, produces plenty of good wine, and contains 12,000 inhabitants; 5 miles S. of Sciati. Long. 23. 50. E. lat. 39. 24. N.

SCOPIA, or USKUP, a town of Macedonia, in European Turkey, and an archbishop's see. It is seated on the Vardar, over which is a bridge of 12 arches; 150 miles N. N. W. of Salonica. Pop. 8000. Long. 21. 45. E. lat. 42. 40. N.

SCOTLAND, the northern of the two kingdoms into which the island of Great Britain was formerly divided. It is bounded on the W. by the Atlantic Ocean, N. by the North Sea, E. by the German Ocean, S. E. by England, and S. by the Irish Sea. To Scotland also appertain the islands on its western coast, called the Hebrides, or Western Islands, and those to the N. E. called the Orkney and Shetland Islands. From N. to S. it extends 270 miles, and its greatest breadth is 150, but in some places not above 30, and no part is distant above 40 miles from the coast. It contains about 20,000,000 acres, of which only 2,500,000 are arable, and about the same quantity is meadow-land, and the remainder is barren, or uncultivated. Scotland is divided into two districts, the Highlands and the Lowlands; the former comprising the mountainous part to the N. and N. W., and the latter the more level district on the E. and S. E. But nature seems to have pointed out three grand divisions in Scotland. The first, or N. division, is formed by a chain of lakes, which crosses the country from the Frith of Murray to the island of Mull, in a S. W. direction; the second, or middle division, is bounded on the S. by the Friths of Forth and Clyde, and the great Canal by which they are united; and on the S. side of this boundary is the third, or S. division. The N. division is chiefly an assemblage of vast dreary mountains; not, however, without some fertile valleys on the northern and eastern shores. The middle division is traversed, in different directions, by several ranges of mountains; and though cultivation here is also found chiefly on the eastern shore, yet of this division, as well as of the former, the arable land bears a small proportion to the mountainous and barren tracts. The S. division has a great resemblance to England, and, with respect both to the general aspect of the country, and to the progress of cultivation, exhibits every kind of rural variety. The civil division of the country is into 33 counties; namely, Shetland and Orkney, Caithness, Sutherland, Ross, Cromarty, Inverness, in the N. division; Argyle, Bute, Nairn, Murray, Banff, Aberdeen, Kincardine, Angus, Perth, Fife, Kinross, Clackmannan, Stirling, Dumbarton, in the middle division; and Linlithgow, Edinburgh, Haddington, Berwick, Renfrew, Ayr, Wigton, Lanark, Peebles, Selkirk, Roxburgh, Dumfries, Kirkcudbright, in the S. division. The principal rivers are the Spey, Don, Tay, Tweed, Clyde, Forth, Northern Dee, Esk, Annan, Nith, and Southern Dee. The lochs, or lakes, are numerous, and some of them extensive. The climate is very various. The northern extremity, which is in the same latitude with some parts of Norway, is extremely cold; but, from its insular situation, the frosts are far from being so intense as in parts of the continent equally as far to the N. Its W. coast is subject to frequent rains in the summer, and to sudden changes of weather. In many places on the eastern shore, and in the whole S. division, the climate is not inferior to the N. part of England. The products of the country are grain, flax, woods of oak and fir, coal, lead, iron, freestone, limestone, slate, the most beautiful marble, fine rock-crystals, pearls, variegated pebbles, &c. It feeds vast herds of cattle, and flocks of sheep, which are much valued for the delicacy of their flesh; and the fleece of the latter emulates the finest Spanish wool. On the high grounds the cattle are very diminutive; but in many parts of the country, the horses and cows are not excelled in size and beauty by those of the English breed. Among the wild animals are the roe, stag, fox, badger, otter, hedge-hog, rabbit, weasel, mole, and other small quadrupeds. Among the feathered race are the capercailzie, or the cock of the wood, the eagle, falcon, partridge, quail, snipe, plover, black game, &c. Scotland was governed by a king before the Romans visited England, and continued an independent kingdom till the death of the English queen Elizabeth, when James VI. of Scotland, the most immediate heir, was called to the throne of England, and constantly resided in the latter; he and his successors calling themselves kings of England and Scotland, and each country having a separate parliament, till the year 1707, in the reign of queen Anne, when both kingdoms were united under the general name of Great Britain. The counties send one member each to parliament, except Bute and Caithness, Cromarty and Nairn, Kinross and Clackmannan, which send members in conjunction; so that the counties send 30 members, which, with 23 sent by the cities and boroughs, make the 53 commoners sent by Scotland; and 16 peers are elected to represent the nobility. The established religion is the Presbyterian, which is modelled principally after the Calvinistical plan settled at Geneva, and on a general principle of an equality of ecclesiastical authority among its presbyters. There are few Roman Catholics, but the Protestant Dissenters are numerous. With respect to the trade and manufactures, they are noticed under the respective cities and towns. Edinburgh is the capital.

SCOTT, a county of tne United States, at the N. part of Kentucky. Pop. 13,668. Georgetown is the capital.—Also, a county in the S. W. part of Virginia, formed part of the counties of Russel, Lee, and Washington, in 1814. Pop. 5702.

SCUTARI, or ISKENDERJE, a strong town of Albania, and a bishop's see; seated on the lake Zeta, near its outlet, the river Boiana·

70 miles N. by W. of Durazzo. Pop. 12,000. Long. 19. 16. E. lat. 42. 33. N.

SCUTARI, a town of Asiatic Turkey, in Natolia, which may be considered as a suburb of Constantinople. It stands on the strait opposite that city; and presents itself in the form of an amphitheatre, affording a very picturesque view, from the mixture of trees, houses, mosques, and minarets. This town serves as an emporium and a rendezvous to the caravans of Asia, and has some manufactures of silk and cotton stuffs. Here are extensive burying grounds, shaded with lofty cypresses. The rich Turks of Constantinople prefer being interred here; for they consider Asia as a land belonging to the true believers, and believe that the land of Europe will one day fall into the hands of Christians, and be trodden on by infidels. Scutari is 1 mile E. of Constantinople. Pop. 30,000.

SCYLLA, a rock near the entrance of the strait of Messina, on the coast of Calabria, opposite the celebrated Charybdis. It forms a small promontory in the narrowest part of the strait, and is the famous Scylla of the ancient poets. It does not come up to the formidable description given by Homer, nor is the passage so narrow and difficult as he represents it; but it is probable that its breadth is greatly increased since his time. The rock is nearly 200 feet high; and on the side of it stands the town of Sciglio, whence the promontory is sometimes called Cape Sciglio.

SEAFORD, a town in Sussex, and one of the cinque ports. Its trade and harbour are now of little consequence. It is 10 miles S. E. of Lewes, and 61 S. by E. of London.

SEARA, a province of South America, republic of Brazil, at the N. E. part. It contains a population of 10,000. Seara, the capital, is in long. 38. 28. W. lat. 3. 31. S., and contains 1200 inhabitants.

SEATON, a town of Scotland, in Haddingtonshire. Here is a ruinous palace, in which Mary Queen of Scots occasionally kept her court, after her return from France. It has a considerable trade in salt and coal. It is situate on the Frith of Forth; 9 miles E. of Edinburgh.

SEBASTE, a town of Palestine, the remains of the ancient city of Samaria; 34 miles N. N. E. of Jerusalem.

SEBASTIAN, ST., a seaport of Spain, in Biscay, seated at the foot of a mountain, on the top of which is a strong citadel. The harbour is secured by two moles, and a narrow entrance for the ships. The town is surrounded by a double wall, and fortified towards the sea. It carries on a great trade, particularly in iron, steel, and wool. St. Sebastian was taken by the French in 1719, in 1794, and again in 1808. On the 31st of August, 1813, it was taken by storm, by the allied forces, under General Graham, after a short siege, during which it sustained a most heavy bombardment, which laid nearly the whole town in ruins. It has since been rebuilt. It is 50 miles E. of Bilboa, and 50 N. W. of Pamplona. Pop. 12,000. Long. 1. 56. W. lat. 43. 24. N.

SEBASTIAN, ST., RIO, or RIO JANEIRO, the capital of the province of Rio Janeiro, and of all Brazil; with a citadel on a hill, and numerous forts. The city stands 4 miles W. of the harbour, and behind it are high hills crowned with woods, convents, houses, and churches. It is 3 miles in circumference; the streets are straight, and most of them narrow, intersecting each other at right angles: and the houses in general are of stone, and two stories high. The churches are very fine, and there is more religious parade in this city, than in almost any town of Europe. The harbour is very commodious, with a narrow entrance defended by two forts. Here are manufactures of sugar, rum, and cochineal. The different mechanics carry on their business in distinct parts of the town, particular streets being set apart for particular trades. On the S. side of a spacious square is a palace: and there are several other squares, in which are fountains, supplied with water by an aqueduct of considerable length, brought over a valley by a double tier of arches. The mint is one of the finest buildings existing, and furnished with all the conveniences necessary for coining with the greatest expedition. A Benedictine convent, and a fort, are on the extreme point, jutting into the harbour, opposite which is Serpent Island, where there are a dockyard, magazines, and naval store-houses. In another part of the harbour, at a place called Val Longo, are warehouses, formerly appropriated for the reception and preparation for sale of slaves imported from Africa. It is the principal emporium of South Brazil, and of the mining districts, but is considered unhealthy, from its low situation, and the adjacent marshes, and also from the filthiness of the streets and inhabitants, who are devoted to pleasure and indolence, and have the character of being more immoral than any European capital. The population consists of about two-thirds mulattoes and negroes, the remainder of a great mixture of nations, and amount to 150,000. It was founded by the Portuguese in 1565, and was made the capital of Brazil in 1763. It was the residence of the Portuguese court till 1821, and in 1831 was the scene of a revolution, in consequence of which the emperor Pedro abdicated in favour of his son Pedro II. St. Sebastian is a bishop's see: seated near the mouth of the Rio Janeiro, in the Atlantic. Long. 42. 39. W. lat. 22. 54. S.

SEBASTIAN CAPE, ST., a cape at the N. W. extremity of Madagascar. Long. 46. 25. E. lat. 12. 30. S.

SEBASTOPOL, or SEVASTOPOL, a seaport of Russia, and the first maritime town of the Crimea. It has one of the finest and most secure harbours in the world, capable of containing all the Russian fleets; and it is the chief station of the Black Sea fleet. The city is built on the side of a hill, which divides two of its fine basins. The old Tartar houses are small and ill-built; but along the quay are some new buildings in a good taste. It stands on part of the site of the ancient Greek city of Cherson, where was the famous temple of Diana Taurica; and considerable ruins of them are yet discoverable. It is 40 miles S. S. W. of Simferopol, and 350 N. E. of Constantinople. Pop. 31,155. Long. 33. 22. E. lat. 44. 25. N.

SEBENICO, a strong seaport of Austrian Dalmatia; and a bishop's see; with four citadels. The cathedral is a magnificent fabric, and its roof is composed of large flat pieces of marble. The Turks have often attempted in vain to take this town. It is seated near the mouth of the Cherca, in the Gulf of Venice; 30 miles S. E. of Zara. Pop. 6300. Long. 16. 46. E. lat. 44. 17. N.

SEBOURG, a town of France, department of Nord; 5 miles E. of Valenciennes.

SEBU. *See* ZEBA.

SECHURA, a town of Peru, inhabited by Indians, who are chiefly employed in fishing or driving of mules. Here commences a sandy desert, which extends southward about 80 miles. The town stands on a river of the same name; 3 miles from the ocean, and 18 N. N. W. of Truxillo. Long. 81. 10. E. lat. 5. 55. S.

SECKAU, a town of the Austrian states, in Styria; seated on the Gayle. It is 9 miles N. of Judenburg.

SECKINGEN, a town of Baden; the smallest of the four Forest Towns. Here is a convent of noble nuns, whose abbess was a princess of the empire. It is seated on an isle, formed by the Rhine, over which is a bridge. It is 11 miles W. of Basel.

SEDAN, a strong town of France, capital of the department of Ardennes, and formerly the seat of a Protestant university. It is deemed one of the keys of the country, and has a strong castle, an arsenal, a cannon foundry, and a manufacture of fine cloth. The famous Marshal Turenne was born in the castle. Sedan is seated on the Meuse; 30 miles S. E. of Charlemont. Pop. 11,000. Long. 4. 58. E. lat. 49. 42. N.

SEDASIVAGUR, a town of Hindostan, the most northern on the coast of Canara. It is seated on the N. side of the estuary of a river, which enters into a deep bay, sheltered by three islands, one of them fortified, and the entrance defended by a fort on a lofty hill. Three miles up the river, on the opposite bank, are the remains of Carwar, formerly a noted place of European commerce, but totally ruined during the reign of Tippoo Sultan. It is 50 miles E. of Goa, and 95 N. N. W. of Kundapura. Long. 74. 15. E. lat. 14. 51. N.

SEDBERGH, a town in West Yorkshire, with a market on Wednesday, and a manufacture of cotton. It has a parish church, two meeting-houses for Methodists, and one for Quakers, and an amply endowed free grammar-school. It is seated near the Rother, which abounds with trout; 10 miles E. of Kendal, and 269 N. W. of London.

SEDGEFIELD, a town in the county of Durham; 251 miles from London.

SEEHAUSEN, a town of Prussia, in the Old Mark of Brandenburg; nearly surrounded by the river Aaland; 12 miles W. of Havelberg.

SEELBURG, a town of Russia, in the government of Courland, on the river Dwina; 58 miles S. E. of Riga.

SEELOW, a town of Brandenburg, 10 miles S. W. of Custrin.

SEER, a seaport of Arabia, capital of a principality in the province of Oman. It has a good harbour, and the navy of the prince is one of the most considerable in the Gulf of Persia. It is 108 miles W. S. W. of Julfar. Long. 54. 58. E. lat. 25. 10. N.

SEESEN, a town of Germany, in the duchy of Brunswick; 14 miles S. W. of Goslar.

SEEZ, a town of France, department of Orne, and a bishop's see. It is seated in a fine country, near the source of the Orne; 14 miles N. of Alençon, and 120 W. by S. of Paris. Pop. 5500. Long. 0. 11. E. lat. 48. 36. N.

SEGEBERG, a town of Denmark, in the duchy of Holstein; with a castle on a high mountain, consisting of limestone, large quantities of which are carried to Hamburg and Lubec. It is seated on the Trave; 15 miles W. N. W. of Lubec.

SEGEDIN, a strong town of Hungary, with a castle; taken from the Turks in 1686. It is seated near the Teisse, opposite the influx of the Maros; 105 miles S. S. E. of Pest. Long. 20. 35. E. lat. 46. 18. N.

SEGESWAR, a town of Transylvania, capital of a county of the same name. It is built in the form of an amphitheatre on the side of a hill, near the river Kokel; 47 miles N. of Hermanstadt. Long. 24. 55. E. lat. 47. 4. N.

SEGNA, a seaport of Morlachia; capital of Hungarian Dalmatia, with a fort. It was declared a free port, and erected into a bishopric, in 1785. It is seated on the Gulf of Venice; 100 miles N. W. of Spoleto. Long. 15. 21. E. lat. 45. 22. N.

SEGNI, a town of the papal states, in Campagna di Roma, and a bishop's see. Organs are said to have been invented here. It is seated on a mountain, 30 miles S. E. of Rome.

SEGO, a city of Negroland, the capital of Bambarra. It consists of four walled towns, two on each side of the river Niger, which contain about 30,000 inhabitants; and, as the Moors form a considerable proportion, their mosques appear in every quarter. The houses are built of clay, of a square form, with flat roofs; some of them have two stories, and many of them are whitewashed. The current money consists of cowries. It is 296 miles W. S. W. of Timbuctoo. Long. 2. 46. W. lat. 14. 15. N.

SEGORBE, a town of Spain, in Valencia, and a bishop's see. It is seated on the side of a hill, by the river Marvedro, 35 miles N. by W. of Valencia. Pop. 15,000.

SEGOVIA, a city of Spain, in Old Castile; capital of province of its name, and a bishop's see; with a castle. It stands on two hills, and the valley by which they are separated, on the S. W. side of the Erasma. It is surrounded by a strong wall, flanked with towers and ramparts. It is supplied with water by a Roman aqueduct, 3000 paces in length, supported by 177 arches of a prodigious height, in two rows, one above the other. Here the best cloth in Spain is made. The other branches of industry are dyeing, and the manufacture of paper, pottery, and lead. The cathedral stands on one side of the great square, and is one of the handsomest Gothic structures in Spain; besides which there are 27 other churches. The castle is seated in the highest part of the town, and has 16 rooms richly adorned with tapestry, and ornaments of marble and porphyry. The royal chapel is magnificently gilded, and embellished with very fine paintings. The mint, for some years the only one in Spain, is surrounded by the river, on which are mills, employed in coining. Segovia was occupied by the French in 1808, but was evacuated in 1813. It is 43 miles N. N. W. of Madrid. The area of the province is 3650 square miles, with a population of 171,000. Population of the city, 10,000. Long. 4. 12. W. lat. 41. 3. N.

SEGOVIA, NEW, a town of Mexico, in Nicaragua; seated near the source of a river of its name, which flows into the Caribbean sea; 90 miles N. by E. of Leon. Long. 87. 5. W. lat. 13. 45. N.

SEGOVIA, NEW, a town in the isle of Luçonia, and a bishop's see, with a fort. It is seated at the N. end of the island, near the mouth of the Cagayan; 245 miles N. of Manilla. Long. 120. 59. E. lat. 18. 39. N.

SEGRA, a river of Spain, which rises in the Pyrenees, and runs S. W. through Catalonia, passing by Puicerda, Urgel, Belaguer, and Lerida, to Mequinenza, where it joins the Ebro.

SEGRE, a town of France, in the department of Maine-et-Loire; 20 miles N. W. of Angers.

SEGURA, a river of Spain, which rises in the mountains of Segura, in Murcia, crosses that province and the S. part of Valencia, and enters the Mediterranean at Guardaman.

SEGURA, a town of Spain, in Murcia, seated among mountains; 34 miles N. E. of Ubeda, and 96 W. N. W. of Murcia.

SEGURA, a town of Spain, in Arragon; 35 miles S. E. of Calatajud, and 38 N. of Teruel.

SEGURA, a town of Portugal, in Beira, with a fort on a mountain. It stands on the frontiers of Spain; 15 miles W. N. W. of Alcantara, and 35 E. S. E. of Castel Branco.

SEHAURANPOUR, a town of Hindostan, in Delhi; capital of a district of the same name, between the Jumna and the Ganges. It is 86 miles N. by W. of Delhi. Long. 77. 15. E. lat. 30. 4. N.

SEIDENBERG, a town of the Prussian states, in Upper Lusatia; with manufactures of cloth and stockings. It is 8 miles S. S. E. of Gorlitz.

SEIKS, or SIKHS, a powerful nation in the N. W. part of Hindostan, consisting of several small independent states, that have formed a kind of federal union, inhabiting the Punjaub. The founder of their sect was Nanock, who lived in the beginning of the 15th century; and they are the descendants of his disciples, the word seiks, in the Sanscrit language, signifying disciples. They are in general strong and well made, accustomed from their infancy to the most laborious life and hardest fare. A pair of long blue drawers, and a kind of chequered plaid, a part of which is fastened round the waist, and the other thrown over the shoulder, form their clothing and equipage. The chiefs are distinguished by wearing some heavy gold bracelets on their wrists, and sometimes a chain of the same metal round their turbans, and by being mounted on better horses; otherwise no distinction appears among them. The government of the Seiks is a military aristocracy. Their army consists almost entirely of horse, of which a Seik will boast they can bring 300,000 into the field; and it is supposed they might bring 200,000. They have commonly two, some of them three horses each. They indeed consider this animal as necessary to their existence; and, while it is customary with them to make merry on the demise of one of their brethren, they mourn for the death of a horse. The Seiks are tolerant in matters of faith, and require only a conformity in certain signs and ceremonies; but, unlike the Hindoos, they admit proselytes, although those from among the Mahomedans are not much esteemed. The capital is Lahore. *See* PUNJAUB.

SEIL, an island of Scotland, one of the Hebrides, 3 miles long and 2 broad; separated from the mainland by a narrow strait, over which is a bridge.

SEINE, a river of France, which rises in the department of Cotes d'Or, flows by Troyes, Melun, Paris, and Rouen, and enters the English Channel at Havre de Grace.

SEINE, a department of France, the smallest but by no means the least important in the kingdom. It has an area of about 260 square miles, with 780,000 inhabitants. The surface is level, and the soil fertile in corn and wine; also fruits and vegetables for the supply of Paris, which is the capital.

SEINE, LOWER, a department of France, including the N. E. part of Normandy. It has an area of 2500 square miles, with 660,000 inhabitants. Rouen is the capital.

SEINE-ET-MARNE, a department of France, including the western part of Champagne. It has an area of 2300 square miles, with 313,000 inhabitants. Melun is the capital.

SEINE-ET-OISE, a department of France, comprising the district of Paris, under the name of Department of the Seine. Exclusive of that district it contains 2200 square miles, with 425,000 inhabitants. Versailles is the capital.

SEINSHEIM, a town of Bavarian Franconia, in a lordship of the same name; with a castle; 18 miles S. E. of Wurtzburg.

SEISSEN, a town of France, department of Gers; 9 miles S. of Auch.

SEISTAN, or SEGESTAN, a province of Persia, bounded on the N. by Korasan and Balkh, E. by Candahar, S. by Mukran, S. W. by Kerman, and W. by Cohestan and Farsistan. The country is in general mountainous. The valleys are the only habitable parts, for the plains are barren, and covered with fine sand, which is sometimes raised by whirlwinds to such a degree as to overwhelm whole caravans. Dooshak is the capital.

SELAM, a town of Mexico, in Jucatan, near the seacoast; 45 miles N. W. of Merida.

SELBOSOE, a town of Norway, in the province of Drontheim; 18 miles S. E. of Drontheim.

SELBY, a town in West Yorkshire; with a market on Monday. It is the birthplace of Henry I., whose father, William the Conqueror, built an abbey here; and the conventual church is now the parish church. The other places of worship are a Catholic chapel, and meeting-houses for Wesleyan and Primitive Methodists, Calvinists, Quakers, and Unitarians. Besides the free grammar-school, founded by Edward VI., here are several charity-schools, almshouses, &c. A canal passes from this place to Leeds, and large ships are built here. It is seated on the Ouse, over which is one of the most complete timber bridges in the kingdom. It is connected with Hull, Leeds, &c., by the Hull and Selby and Leeds railways. It is 14 miles S. of York, and 177 N. by W. of London.

SELENGINSK, a fortified town of Russia, in the government of Irkutsk; with a fort, and 3000 inhabitants. The adjacent country is mountainous, but yields a great quantity of rhubarb. It stands on the Selenga, at the influx of the Chilok; 160 miles S. E. of Irkutsk. Long. 107. 28. E. lat. 51. 16. N.

SELENTI, a town of Asia Minor, in Caramania, at he mouth of a river of the same name; 50 miles W. S. W. of Selesk.

SELEFKEH, (ancient Seleucia,) a town of Asiatic Turkey, in the province of Karamania, at the mouth of the Ghiuk Sooyoo. It is an assemblage of wooden and mud huts.

SELIGENSTADT, a town of Germany, in Hesse-Darmstadt, with a Benedictine abbey; seated at the conflux of the Gernspentz with the Maine; 14 miles E. of Frankfort.

SELIBRIA, or SILIVRI, (ancient Selymbria,) a town of Romania, and an archbishop's see; formerly a large place, but now much decayed. It is seated on the Sea of Marmora; 35 miles W. of Constantinople. Pop. 6000.

SELKIRK, a town of Scotland, the capital of Selkirkshire. Its branches of industry are the spinning of woollen yarn, and extensive manufactures of woollen goods called "Tweeds," which originated in this town; stockings, and a manufacture of boots and shoes. It is seated on the Ettrick, 36 miles S. S. E. of Edinburgh.

SELKIRKSHIRE, a county of Scotland. It is bounded on the N. E. by Edinburghshire, E. by Roxburghshire, S. by Dumfries-shire, and W. and N. by Peebles-shire. It is a hilly country, 20 miles long, and 10 broad. It returns one member to parliament. The chief rivers are the Tweed, Ettrick, Yarrow, and Gala.

SELLES, a town of France, in the department of Loire-et-Cher, on the river Cher; 10 miles S. W. of Romorentin. Pop. 3600.

SELTZ, a town in the department of Lower Rhine, seated on the Rhine; 25 miles N. N. E. of Strasburg.

SELTZER, or LOWER SELTZER, a town of Germany, in the duchy of Nassau; celebrated for a spring of mineral water, which is exported in great quantities. It is situate on the Emsbach; 30 miles E. of Coblentz.

SEMAUAT, a town of Asiatic Turkey, in Irac Arabi; seated on the Euphrates, where a toll is collected. It is 120 miles N. W. of Bassoar. Long. 46. 15. E. lat. 32. 2. N.

SEMBEW-GHEWN, a town of Birmah, from which is the principal road through the western hills into Arracan. It was entirely destroyed by the Burmese, in 1826. It stands 3 miles W. of the Irrawaddy, and 30 S. by W. of Pagahm.

SEMEGONDA, a town of Negroland, in the country of Wangara; seated on a lake formed by a branch of the Nile; 330 miles S. S. W. of Bornou. Long. 21. 30. E. lat. 14. 58. N.

SEMENDRIA, a town of European Turkey, in Servia, with a citadel; seated on the Danube; 20 miles S. E. of Belgrade. Pop. 9000.

SEMENNUD, a town of Egypt, on the E. branch of the Nile; 8 miles S. S. W. of Mansoura, and 53 N. of Cairo.

SEMIGALLIA, a duchy of European Russia, about 100 miles long and 20 broad, forming the E. part of the government of Courland. Mittau is the capital.

SEMINARI, a town of Naples, in Calabria Ultra, with an abbey belonging to the united Greek church. It suffered severely from an earthquake in 1783, but now contains 2000 inhabitants. It is 22 miles N. E. of Reggio.

SEMLEN, a town of Sclavonia, in the Austrian empire, on the south side of the Danube; the principal place for carrying on the transit trade between Turkey and Sclavonia. Pop. 8000. It is 4 miles W. of Belgrade.

SEMPACH, a town of Switzerland, in the canton of Lucerne; celebrated for the battle in 1386, which established the liberty of the Swiss, and in which Leopold, duke of Austria, was defeated and slain. It is seated on a small lake of the same name; 7 miles N. W. of Lucerne.

SEMUR EN AUXOIS, a town of France, in the department of Cotes d'Or, with a castle on a rock. It has a manufacture of cloth. It is seated on the Armançon; 34 miles W. by N. of Dijon, and 135 S. E. of Paris. Pop. 6000.

SEMUR EN BRIENNOIS, a town in the department of Saone-et-Loire; 33 miles W. by S. of Maçon, and 45 S. of Autun.

SENA, or MARZALI, a town of Mocaranga, in East Africa; on the river Zambeze, where the Portuguese have a factory. Pop. 2000. Long. 35. 3. E. lat. 7. 40. S.

SENECA, a lake and river of New York, in Onondago county. The lake is 30 miles long and 2 broad, and lies N. and S. between those of Canandagua and Cayuga. At the N. end is the town of Geneva, and on the E. side, between it and Cayuga Lake, are the military townships of Romulus, Ovid, Hector, and Ulysses. The river rises to the W. of Geneva, passes by that town, and receives the waters of the lake. It afterwards receives the waters of Cayuga Lake, Canandagua Creek, and Salt Lake, and then flows into Onandago River.

SENECA, a county in the state of New York, with 24,874 inhabitants. Waterloo and Ovid are the chief towns.

SENECA, a town of New York, in Onondago county; situate on the N. side of the falls in Seneca River, 14 miles from its mouth, and 28 S. of Oswego. Pop. 4281.

SENEFFE, a town of Belgium, in the province of Hainault; noted for a battle gained by the French over the prince of Orange in 1674. It is 4 miles S. of Nivelle.

SENEGAL, a large river which rises in the mountains of Kong, in Negroland, and flows W. on the southern confines of Zahara, into the Atlantic Ocean; 120 miles N. E. of Cape Verd. Its course is flexuous, till it arrives within 6 miles of the sea, when it takes a sudden turn to the S., and for 75 miles is separated from the sea only by a ridge of sand. Its mouth, not more than half a league over, is incommoded by a shifting bar, which renders the passage difficult and dangerous.

SENEGAL, a country on the W. coast of Africa, lying on a river of the same name. *See* FOULI. The French have a fort and factory in an island at the mouth of the river, and are masters of the gum trade. It is called Fort Louis, was taken by the English in 1758, confirmed to them by the peace of 1763, but restored in 1783. Pop. 10,000. Long. 16. 31. W. lat. 15. 53. N.

SENEGAMBIA, a name applied to the countries on the W. coast of Africa, between the parallels of 8. and 18. N. latitude, and through which the rivers Senegal, Gambia, and Rio Grande flow. It comprises many districts, inhabited by negroes of different languages, and part of it abounds with metals, especially gold. The actual limits are undefined.

SENEZ, a town of France, in the department of Lower Alps, seated in a rough barren country; 15 miles S. S. E. of Digne.

SENFTENBERG, a town of Prussia, in Lower Lusatia, with a castle; 35 miles N. N. E. of Meissen.

SENLIS, a town of France, in the department of Oise; seated on the river Nonette, and almost surrounded by a forest; 20 miles N. W. of Meaux, and 27 N. E. of Paris. Pop. 4300.

SENNAAR, a kingdom of Eastern Africa; bounded E. and S. by Abyssinia, W. by Darfur, and N. by Dongola and the independent districts of Nubia. The Nile flows through this immense plain above a mile broad, full to the very brim, but never overflowing. For several miles from the banks of this river, the soil is of very remarkable fertility; and at the time of the rains, about the end of August and beginning of September, the country assumes a most delightful appearance, resembling the pleasantest parts of Holland. Soon after the rains cease, the dhourra ripens, the leaves turn yellow and rot, the lakes putrify, smell, and are full of vermin, all the beauty disappears, and bare scorched Nubia returns, with all its terrors of poisonous winds and moving sands, glowing and ventilated with sultry blasts. The trade consists chiefly in exchanging the various productions of interior Africa with those of Egypt and Arabia. The kingdom of Sennaar was founded by a body of Shilluk negroes in 1505. The government is despotic, but the king may lawfully be put to death whenever the chief officers decide that his reign is no longer a public benefit.

SENNAAR, a city of Nubia, and capital of the above kingdom, is 5 miles in circumference, and very populous. It is said to contain 100,000 inhabitants. The houses are chiefly of one story, with flat roofs; but the suburbs contain only cottages covered with reeds. The palace is surrounded by high walls, and is a confused heap of buildings. The heats are almost insupportable in the day-time, except in the rainy season, at which time the air is unwholesome. The commodities are elephants' teeth, tamarinds, civet, tobacco, and gold dust. There is a market near the palace, where slaves are sold; the females sit on one side, and the males on another; the Egyptians buy great numbers of them every year. The merchandise required here consists of spices, paper, brass, hardware, glass beads, and a black drug which is used to colour the eyebrows. The women of quality have slight garments of silk, and wear rings of various metals on their hair, arms, legs, ears, and fingers. Women of a low rank, and girls, have clothes wrapped round them from the waist to the knees. The men go almost naked. Sennaar is seated on an eminence, near the river Nile. Long. 33. 0. E. lat. 13. 4. N.

SENS, a town of France, in the department of Yonne, and an archbishop's see, with a handsome Gothic cathedral. Several ecclesiastical councils have been held here; in that of 1140 the well-known Abelard was condemned. Sens was taken by the allies in 1814, but soon after evacuated. It is seated in a fertile country, at the conflux of the Vanne with the Yonne; 25 miles N. of Auxerre, and 80 S. E. of Paris. Long. 3. 17. E. lat. 48. 12. N.

SEPULVEDA, a town of Spain, in Old Castile; 30 miles N. E. of Segovia.

SERA, or SIRA, a town of Hindostan, in Mysore, with a stone fort of a good size. It is the principal place in the central division of the rajah's dominions N. of the Cavery, and carries on a considerable inland commerce. The whole of the cloth made here is used in the neighbourhood. Since the restoration of the rajah, in 1799, the fort has been garrisoned by British troops. It is 48 miles S. E. of Chitteldroog, and 84 N. of Seringapatam. Long. 76. 53. E. lat. 13. 36. N.

SERAI, a town of European Turkey, capital of Bosnia; and the see of a Catholic bishop, appointed by the king of Hungary. It is a large commercial place, and is seated on the river Bosna; 130 miles W. S. W. of Belgrade. Long. 19. 15. E. lat. 44. 14. N.

SERAMPORE, a town of Bengal, belonging to the Danes. The houses are of brick, plastered with mortar, and have flat roofs, with balconies and Venetian windows. The inhabitants carry on some trade with Europe, China, &c. But the town is principally distinguished as the early seat of the Baptist mission in India, and as the residence of British subjects who take refuge here from their creditors. It is seated on the W. bank of the Hoogly; 12 miles N. of Calcutta.

Serdobol, a town of Russia; in the government of Wiburg, on the lake Ladoga; 60 miles N. N. E of Wiburg.

Sered, or Szered, a town of Hungary, on the river Waag; 30 miles E. N. E. of Presburg.

Seres, a town of European Turkey, province of Macedon; 45 miles N. E. of Salonica. It has a number of mosques, and other public edifices, and a manufacture of cotton and linen stuffs. Pop. 30,000.

Seafo, or Serfante, an island of the Grecian Archipelago; 8 miles long, and 5 broad, and full of mountains and rocks, in which are mines of iron and loadstone. The inhabitants are all Greeks, and have but one town, called St. Nicholo; which is a poor place. It is 50 miles N. W. of Naxia. Long. 25. 10. E. lat. 37. 19. N.

Sergag, a town of Russia, in the government of Niznei Novogorod; 48 miles S. E. of Niznei Novogorod.

Sergippe, a province on the coast of Brazil, to the S. of Pernambuco. It produces sugar and tobacco in considerable quantities, and has some silver mines.

Sergippe, a seaport of Brazil, capital of the above province, seated at the mouth of the Sergippe; 120 miles N. E. of St. Salvador. Long. 37. 44. W. lat. 12. 10. S.

Serignan, a town of France, department of Herault, at the mouth of the Ombre, in the Gulf of Lyon; 8 miles S. E. of Beziers.

Serinagur, or Guwal, a province of Hindostan, situated chiefly between 30. and 32. of N. lat. and between 77. and 79. of E. long. It is estimated at 140 miles in length, by 60 in breadth. It is governed by a rajah, under the protection of the British.

Serinagur, the capital of the above province, is about three-quarters of a mile long, the houses built of rough stone and mud, and covered with slate, but seldom more than two stories high. The streets are narrow and dirty, but there are some good shops. It is situate in a valley on the river Alcananda, which is crossed by a bridge of ropes. On the opposite side of the river, at the village of Ranihut, is a temple sacred to Raja Ishwara, principally inhabited by dancing women, whose lives are devoted to prostitution, as a religious service. Serinagur is 38 miles from Hardwar. Long. 79. 18. E. lat. 30. 10. N.

Seringapatam, a city of Hindostan, the modern capital of Mysore, is situate in an island 3 miles long and 1 broad, formed by the Cavery, which is here a large and rapid river, with a wide and rocky channel. The streets are narrow and confused, and the generality of the houses mean. The city is strongly fortified; notwithstanding which Lord Cornwallis, in 1792, here compelled Tippoo to sign a treaty, by which he ceded half of his dominions, and agreed to pay a vast sum of money to the English and their allies; and, a new war taking place in 1799, the British troops carried the fort by an assault, in which Tippoo was killed. The city and the island have since been retained by the English, towards the support of the late sultan's family. The palace is very large, and surrounded by a massy wall of stone and mud: it is now the residence of a surgeon. The seraglio of Hyder has been converted into an European hospital, that of Tippoo into a barrack for artillery; the private apartments of the latter are occupied by the resident, and the public ones by European troops. Without the walls of the city are two gardens and palaces; and near to one of them is the mausoleum of Hyder, where rests all that was mortal of this Mahomedan dynasty, consisting of Hyder and his wife, and Tippoo, who lie under tombs covered with rich cloths at the expense of the British government; and the establishment of priests to offer up prayers, and of musicians to perform the nobut, is retained as formerly. In the space between the city and the two gardens is the suburb called Shahar Ganjam, which is rapidly increasing on a regular plan. Seringapatam is 10 miles N. of Mysore, and 290 W. by S. of Madras. Pop. 10,000. Long. 76. 50. E. lat. 12. 24. N.

Seringham, an island in the S. of India; in the district of Trichinopoly; celebrated for its Hindoo temple, to which pilgrims from all parts of Hindostan resort for absolution; and here, as in all great pagodas, the Brahmins live in a subordination that knows no resistance, and slumber in voluptuousness that feels no want. At present the allowance made by the British government, for the support of the temple and its establishment, amounts to about 6240*l.* sterling.

Seronge, a town of Hindostan, in Malwa; celebrated for its manufacture of painted cottons and chintzes. It is situate on the river Cavery; half a mile N. of the fortress of Trichinopoly, and 140 miles E. N. E. of Ougein. Long. 78. 4. E. lat. 24. 5. N.

Serpa, a town of Portugal, in Alentejo, with a castle, seated on a rugged eminence, near the Guadiana; 38 miles S. by E. of Evora. Population 4000.

Serravalle, a town of Austrian Italy, in the government of Venice, with a castle. It has cloth, woollen, and silk manufactures, and a trade in corn, wine, and honey. The cathedral contains some fine paintings, and the church of St. Augusta is a noble edifice. It is situate between two mountains, and at the source of the Maschio; 22 miles N. of Treviso.

Serres, a town of France, department of Upper Alps; 23 miles S. W. of Gap.

Servan, St., a town of France, department of Ille-et-Vilaine; with considerable manufactures of linen, sail-cloth, soap, and tobacco, and 9000 inhabitants. It is seated at the mouth of the river Rance, about a mile S. of St. Malo, from which it is separated by a narrow arm of the sea, dry at low water.

Servia, a province of European Turkey, 190 miles long, and 95 broad; bounded N. by the Danube and Save, which separate it from Hungary; E. by Bulgaria; S. by Macedonia and Albania; and W. by Bosnia. The climate is less mild than might be expected in 43. and 44. o

N. lat., the winter being of considerable length, and spring not beginning till April. This is owing partly to the height of the great ridge of the Argentaro or Glubotin Mountains, extending along its southern boundary; partly to the number of forests, and the general neglect of cultivation in its interior. The soil is in general fertile, but a small proportion of the country is as yet under tillage. The products are wheat, barley, oats, rice, hemp, flax, and tobacco; also vines, and fruit of various kinds; and in the valleys, and other warm spots, cotton is raised. Mines of iron have been discovered in several parts; but they are almost entirely neglected. The only manufactures are of woollen, cotton, and hardware, for home consumption. Servia was formerly an independent kingdom, but yielded to the Turks in 1365. In 1801 an insurrection took place against their authority, under the standard of Czerni Georges, previously known as the head of a band of robbers, but now honoured with the name of avenger of his country. In 1814 he judged proper to withdraw into Russia; and by a convention concluded between his country and the Porte, in 1815, the Servians acknowledged the sovereignty of the sultan, but preserved the free exercise of their religion, as well as their civil rights. Population 1,000,000. Belgrade is the capital.

SESSLACH, a town and castle of Bavarian Franconia; 16 miles N. of Bamberg.

SESTO, a town of Austrian Italy; in the Milanese; seated on the Ticino, where it issues from the lake Maggiore; 25 miles W. N. W. of Milan.

SESTRE, GRAND, or GREAT PARIS, a town of Guinea, on the Grain Coast; near which is Petit Sestre. It is one of the largest and most commercial towns in the country. Long. 7. 0. W. lat. 4. 50. N.

SESTRI DI LEVANTE, a town of the Sardinian states, in the territory of Genoa; 30 miles E. S. E. of Genoa.

SE-TCHEOU, a city of China, of the first rank, in the province of Koei-tcheou. It is situate among mountains, which yield cinnabar and quicksilver; 980 miles S. S. W. of Peking. Long. 108. 25. E. lat. 27. 10. N.

SE-TCHUEN, a province of China, bounded on the N. by Chen-si, E. by Houquang, S. by Koei-tcheou, and W. by Tibet. It is watered by the Kian-ku, and is rich, not only on account of the great quantity of silk it produces, but also in iron, tin, lead, amber, sugar-canes, lapis lazuli, musk, rhubarb, &c. Tching-tou is the capital.

SETEEF, a town of Algier, in the province of Constantina. It was the ancient Sitipha, capital of a part of Mauritania; but scarcely a fragment is left of its former greatness, except the fountains. It is 50 miles S. W. of Constantina. Long. 5. 36. E. lat. 35. 58. N.

SETIMO, a town of the Sardinian states, in Piedmont; seated on the Po; 8 miles N. of Turin.

SETLEGE. *See* SUTLUJ.

SETTE, a town of Western Africa, in a district of its name, lying between Loango and Benin. It has a great trade in logwood, sent in vessels to Mayamba; and stands on a river of the same name, 60 miles from its mouth, and 110 N. N. E. of Mayamba. Long. 10. 20. E. lat. 20. S.

SETTINIL, a town of Spain, in Granada. It is situate 8 miles N. of Ronda, and 38 N. W. of Malaga.

SETTIA, a town of the island of Candia, and a Greek bishop's see; 48 miles E. S. E. of Candia. Long. 26. 2. E. lat. 35. 3. N.

SETTLE, a town of W. Yorkshire, with a market on Tuesday. About 2 miles to the E. is Attermire Cave, containing numberless chinks and recesses, fluted pillars, and hanging petrifactions. At the like distance to the N. is Giggleswick Well, a reciprocating spring, which will sometimes rise and fall nearly a foot, in a stone trough about a yard square, every ten or fifteen minutes. Settle is seated on the Ribble, 38 miles N. N. W. of Halifax, and 235 of London.

SETUVAL. *See* UBES, ST.

SEVEN ISLANDS, a cluster of islands in the Frozen Ocean, lying in long. 18. 48. E. lat. 80. 31. N. Here Captain Phipps, with two ships, was surrounded by the ice, from the 1st to the 10th of August, 1773, when a brisk wind at N. N. E. effected their deliverance.

SEVEN ISLANDS, islands near the coast of Canada, on the N. side of the mouth of the St. Lawrence, at the entrance of a small bay. Long. 66. 5. W. lat. 50. 10. N.

SEVEN ISLANDS. *See* IONIAN ISLANDS.

SEVENBERGEN, a town of the Netherlands, in N. Brabant; 8 miles W. N. W. of Breda.

SEVENOAKS, a town in Kent, with a market on Saturday. It contains a church, a meeting-house for Baptists, an hospital, and a free-school, first erected by Sir William Sevenoaks, lord mayor of London in 1418, who is said to have been a foundling, charitably educated by a person of this town. Queen Elizabeth having augmented its revenues, it was called Queen Elizabeth's School; and the whole was rebuilt in 1727. Near this town is Knole, an ancient palace of the see of Canterbury, which archbishop Cranmer exchanged with the Crown for other lands, and which was given by Queen Elizabeth to Thomas lord Buckhurst, afterwards earl of Dorset. In 1450 John Cade defeated the royal army near this town; 16 miles N. W. of Maidstone, and 23 S. S. E. of London.

SEVER, ST., a town of France, in the department of Landes, seated on the Adour; 20 miles E. of Dax, and 69 S. by E. of Bordeaux. Pop. 9000.

SEVERAC, a small town in the department of Aveiron, on the river Aveiron; 23 miles E. of Rodez.

SEVERIN, a town of European Turkey, in Walachia, on the Danube; 6 miles W. of Czernetz.

SEVERINA, ST., a fortified town of Naples, in Calabria Ultra, and an archbishop's see. It is seated on a craggy rock, on the river Neto; 8 miles from the sea, and 45 S. E. of Rossano. Pop. 6000. Long. 17. 14. E. lat. 39. 15. N.

SEVERINA, ST., a town of Italy, in the papal states; 13 miles W. S. W. of Macerata.

SEVERINA, ST., a town of Naples, in Principato Citra; on the river Sarno; 10 miles W. S. W. of Policastro.

SEVERN, a river which has its rise in the mountain of Plynlimmon, in Wales. Flowing first across Montgomeryshire, it enters Shropshire above the Brythen Hills, and is navigable in its whole course through this country. It then enters Worcestershire, and runs through its whole length into Gloucestershire. In its course it waters Llanydlos, Newton, Welshpool, Shrewsbury, Bridgenorth, Bewdley, Worcester, Upton, Tewkesbury, Gloucester, and Newnham, where it begins to widen considerably; and, entering the sea, its mouth is called the Bristol Channel. This river has a communication with the Thames, the Trent, the Dee, and the Mersey, by different canals.

SEVERN, a river of Maryland, which waters Annapolis, and enters by a broad estuary into Chesapeake Bay.

SEVERO, ST., a town of Naples, in Capitanata; seated in a plain, 26 miles W. by N. of Manfredonia, and 75 N. E. of Naples.

SEVERUS'S WALL, commonly called Graham's Dike, in the W. of Scotland. It is a work of the Romans, supposed to be done by the emperor whose name it bears, to prevent the incursions of the Picts and Scots. It began at Abercorn, on the Frith of Forth, 4 miles N. E. of Linlithgow, and ran W. to the Frith of Clyde, ending at Kirkpatrick, near Dumbarton.

SÉVIGNY, a town of France, in the department of Ardennes; 12 miles N. W. of Rethel.

SEVILLE, a province of Spain, forming the western half of Andalusia, and still retaining the title of kingdom. It has an area of 9500 square miles, with 800,000 inhabitants. The surface is diversified with beautiful plains and hills, covered with vines and fruit trees. Agriculture is in a very backward state, and the manufactures are all on a small scale. The chief towns are Seville (the capital), Cadiz, Ecija, Xeres, Ossuna, and St. Mary's, near Cadiz.

SEVILLE, a city of Spain, capital of the above province, and an archbishop's see; seated on the Guadalquiver. It is fortified by strong walls flanked with high towers, and takes up more ground than Madrid, although it now has not above 100,000 inhabitants. The Phœnicians called it Hispatis, and it is the Julia of the Romans, who embellished it with many magnificent buildings. The Moors built an aqueduct, still to be seen, 6 miles in length. The cathedral is by some supposed to be the largest church in the world next to St. Peter's at Rome; the steeple is of curious workmanship, and extremely high, consisting of three towers, one above another, with galleries and balconies. The churches and convents are opulent and beautiful; of the latter, that of St. Francis is adorned with a handsome public square, in the midst of which is a fine fountain. The university consists of many colleges; and the professors enjoy rich pensions. The royal palace, called Alcazar, was partly built after the antique, by the Moors, and partly in the modern taste, by King Pedro; it is a mile in extent, and flanked by large square towers, built with stones taken from the ancient temple of Hercules. Here is a foundry, and one of the largest depôts for artillery in the kingdom. The principal manufactures are silk; and behind the Alcazar is a royal snuff manufacture, which is strictly examined and guarded. The exchange is a square building of the Tuscan order, each front 100 feet in length, and three stories high. The town-house is adorned with a great number of statues, and there is a large square before it, with a fine fountain in the middle. There are 120 hospitals richly endowed. The suburb of Triano stands on the other side of the river, over which is a long bridge of boats. In this suburb stood the house of the Inquisition; and there are public walks, where most of the inhabitants go to take the air. The situation of Seville renders it one of the most commercial towns of Spain. All the trade of that kingdom with the New World centred originally in its port; but that of Cadiz being found more commodious, the galleons sailed from that place after the year 1720. Such vast employment did the American trade give, at one period, that in Seville alone there were no fewer than 16,000 looms in silk or woollen work; but, before the end of the reign of Philip III., they were reduced to 400. The country around is extremely fertile in corn, wine, &c., and there is abundance of oil; for, to the W. of the river is a grove of olive-trees, 30 miles in length. Seville was taken by the French in 1810, but they evacuated it after the battle of Salamanca, in 1812. It is 45 miles from the Atlantic, and 212 S. S. W. of Madrid. Pop. 100,000. Long. 5. 59. W. lat. 37. 14. N.

SEVRES, DEUX, a department of France, including part of the ancient province of Poitou. It is so named from two rivers that rise here; one, called Sevre Niortois, flowing W. by St. Maixent, Niort, and Marans, into the Bay of Biscay, opposite the Isle of Re; and the other named Sevre Nantois, which takes a N. W. direction, passes by Clisson, and enters the river Loire, opposite Nantes. The department comprises an area of 2500 square miles, with 288,000 inhabitants, about one-eighth of whom are Protestants. Niort is the capital.

SEVRES, a town of France, 4 miles W. by S. of Paris; celebrated for its glass works and potteries, which are said to produce the finest porcelain in the world.

SEWALICK, a chain of mountains in Hindostan, bordering on the country of Serinagur and the province of Delhi.

SEYSSEL, a town of France, in the department of Ain, divided into two parts by the Rhone, which here begins to be navigable; 14 miles N. by E. of Bellay.

SEZANNE, a town in the department of Marne; 27 miles N. W. of Troyes, and 65 S. E. of Paris. Pop. 4200.

SEZZA, or SESSE, a town of Naples, in Terra di Lavoro; 14 miles N. W. of Capua. Pop. 3800.

SHABUR, a town of Egypt, on the W. branch

of the Nile; 48 miles S. E. of Alexandria, and 50 N. N. W. of Cairo.

SHAFTESBURY, a borough in Dorsetshire, with a market on Saturday. It returns one member to parliament. It stands on a hill, where water is so scarce that the poor get a living by fetching it from a great distance. It had formerly 10 parish churches, now reduced to four. The other places of worship are meeting-houses for Methodists, Quakers, and Presbyterians; 25 miles N. N. E. of Dorchester, and 100 W. by S. of London.

SHAFTSBURY, a town of Vermont, in Bennington county; 10 miles N. of Bennington. Pop. 1885.

SHAHAR, or SAHAR, a seaport of Arabia, in Hadramaut; 110 miles S. S. W. of Shibam. Long. 48. 40. E. lat. 13. 50. N.

SHAHJEHANPORE, a town of Hindostan, capital of a district of its name, in the province of Malwa; 20 miles N. E. of Ougein, and 196 S. of Agimere.

SHAHJEHANPORE, a town in the province of Delhi, district of Bareily, seated on the Gurrah. Long. 79. 50. E. lat. 27. 52. N.

SHANNON, the largest river of Ireland, which issues from Lough Allen, in the county of Leitrim, and, running S., divides the provinces of Leinster and Connaught; it then turns S. W., passes by the city of Limerick, and enters the Atlantic Ocean between the counties of Clare and Limerick.

SHAP, a village in Westmoreland, at the source of the Loder, between Orton and Penrith. It has become a place of some business, from the visitors to Shap Well, a mineral spring in the vicinity. It had once a famous abbey, which stood about a mile W. from the church, of which little remains, except the tower of its church, and the ruins of a bridge. In the vicinity are some great stones, like pyramids, from 10 to 12 yards apart, placed almost in a direct line for a mile together, of such immense weight that carriages now in use could not support them.

SHAPINSHA, one of the Orkney Islands, lying 3 miles from the N. E. part of Pomona. It is 7 miles long and 5 broad. The coasts are level and produce grass and corn, but the middle part is high, and fit only for sheep pasture.

SHARPSBURG, a town of Maryland, in Washington county; 2 miles from the Potomac, and 60 N. W. of Washington.

SHEERNESS, a maritime town in Kent, on the point of the Isle of Sheppy, at the mouth of the Medway, 3 miles N. of Queensborough. A fort was built here by Charles II., after the insult of the Dutch, who burnt the men-of-war at Chatham in 1667; and it has since been considerably augmented and strengthened. There are also an ordnance-office, a dock-yard, and a chapel.

SHEFFIELD, a borough in West Yorkshire, with markets on Tuesday and Saturday, and returns two members to parliament; situate on an eminence surrounded by a beautiful valley, with a range of romantic hills in the perspective. It has 6 churches, 15 meeting-houses, a Romish chapel, a large infirmary, and numerous charitable foundations. Here are also a large theatre and an assembly room. The houses are well built, and many of them elegant; and few places can boast of more handsome or regular streets, which are well lighted with gas, introduced here in 1819. This town has been long celebrated for its various hardware manufactures, which consist particularly of cutlery ware, plated goods, buttons, &c., immense quantities of which are now exported to all parts of the habitable globe. In the town and neighbourhood are foundries for iron, brass, and white metal; and numerous works are established on the banks of the rivers, for the purpose of preparing the iron and steel for the manufactures, and the neighbourhood abounds in coal. It has received a royal charter for a mayor and corporation. The master cutlers are about 600, incorporated by the style of the Cutlers of Hallamshire. Sheffield is seated at the conflux of the Sheaf with the Don, which is now rendered navigable up to the town; the North Midland railway also communicates with it; 53 miles S. S. W. of York, and 163 N. N. W. of London. Long. 1. 29. W. lat. 53. 20. N.

SHEFFIELD, a town of Massachusets, in Berkshire county; 145 miles W. by S. of Boston. Pop. 2322.

SHELBEVILLE, a town of Kentucky, capital of Shelby county, seated on Brashan's Creek, 12 miles above its junction with Salt River.

SHELBURNE, a town of Nova Scotia, at the head of a bay called Port Roseway. It extends two miles on the water side, and one mile backward, with wide streets crossing each other at right angles. The harbour is deep, capacious, and secure. About a mile from Shelburne, and separated from it by a small river, is the Black Town, peopled by about 1200 free blacks, who served on the royal side during the American war. Shelburne is 100 miles S. W. of Halifax. Long. 65. 0. W. lat. 43. 46. N.

SHELLA, a decayed town of Morocco, which none but Mahomedans are allowed to enter; 4 miles E. of Salle.

SHELLIF, the largest river of Algier, which takes its rise in the desert, flows N. through the Lake Titeri, then turns to the W. and enters the Mediterranean to the N. of Mustagam.

SHEPHERD'S ISLES, a cluster of islands, part of the New Hebrides, in the South Pacific, to the S. of Malicolli. Long. 168. 42. E, lat. 16. 58. S.

SHEPHERDSTOWN, a town of Virginia, in Jefferson county, seated on the Potomac, at the influx of the Shenandoah; 60 miles N. W. of Alexandria.

SHEPPY, an island in Kent, at the mouth of the Thames, separated from the main land by a branch of the Medway, called the East Swale. It yields plenty of corn, and feeds numerous flocks of sheep. It contains the borough of Queensborough and the fort of Sheerness.

SHEPTON MALLET, a town in Somersetshire; with a market on Friday, and a considerable manufacture of woollen cloth. It has a large handsome church, and meeting-houses for

Methodists, Quakers, and Presbyterians. The town is seated under the Mendip Hills; 17 miles S. W. of Bath, and 116 W. of London.

SHERBORNE, a town in Dorsetshire; with markets on Thursday and Saturday, and manufactures of linen and silk. It was formerly a bishop's see, and the parish church, which was the cathedral, and in which are interred the Saxon kings Ethelbald and Ethelbert, is a magnificent pile of building. Formerly here were two other churches, a castle, and an abbey, of which scarcely a vestige remains. Here are meeting-houses for dissenters, a free-school, founded by Edward VI., and other charitable institutions. It is seated on the Parret; 16 miles N. by W. of Dorchester, and 116 W. by S. of London. Long. 2. 41. W. lat. 50. 54. N.

SHERBRO, a fort of Guinea, seated at the mouth of Sherbro River, which separates the country of Sierra Leone from the Grain Coast. It belongs to the English. It is 100 miles S. E. of the mouth of the river Sierra Leone. Long. 11. 0. W. lat. 7. 0. N.

SHERBURN, a town in West Yorkshire, with a market on Friday, seated in a well cultivated and fertile district, famous for its fine orchards; on the Werk, which soon joins the Ouse; 15 miles S. W. of York, and 184 N. by W. of London.

SHEREZUR, a town of European Turkey, in Kurdistan; the residence of a pacha; 160 miles N. by E. of Bagdad.

SHERIFF-MUIR, a heath of Scotland, in Perthshire, near Dumblane, famous for a bloody but indecisive battle in 1715, between the royal army under the duke of Argyle, and the rebel forces under the earl of Mar.

SHERSEL, a town of Algier, in the province of Mascara, formerly of great importance. It is said to have been anciently destroyed by an earthquake, when the arsenal and many other buildings were precipitated into the harbour, the ruins being still visible at low water. It is built after the Moorish manner, and is famous for its pottery, and steel and iron manufactures; 60 miles W. by S. of Algier. Long. 2. 48. E. lat. 32. 42. N.

SHETLAND, or ZETLAND, the general name of about forty islands, besides a number of small holms or rocky islets used only for pasturage, lying 100 miles N. N. E. of Caithness-shire, in Scotland, between 59. 48. and 60. 52. N. lat. The names of the principal are Mainland, Yell, Unst, Bressay, and Fula. The description given of the largest, or MAINLAND, will give an idea of the others; and the particulars of the climate, inhabitants, &c., are much the same as in the ORKNEYS. Shetland unites with Orkney in forming one of the counties of Scotland.

SHEVAGUNGA, a town of Hindostan, in Mysore; 25 miles N. W. of Bangolore.

SHIBAM, a city of Arabia, capital of the province of Hadramaut, and the residence of a powerful sheik; 300 miles E. of Sana. Long. 49. 40. E. lat. 15. 25. N.

SHIELDS, NORTH, a seaport in Northumberland, with a market on Saturday, and a considerable trade in coal and salt. The town extends to Tynemouth on the E., and many elegant detached mansions are erected in the neighbourhood. It has wide and airy streets in every direction, well paved, and lighted with gas. Besides the church, which is the parochial church of Tynemouth, here are 12 meeting-houses for dissenters and Catholics, and a Jews' synagogue; also several valuable charities, libraries, a mechanics' institute, and a theatre. This town, together with South Shields, may be deemed the port of Newcastle; for the largest vessels are stationed here to take in their lading, which is brought down in barges and lighters. It is seated on the N. bank of the Tyne, near its mouth, and is connected with Carlisle by a railway; 6 miles E. by N. of Newcastle, and 279 N. by W. of London. Long. 1. 4. W. lat. 54. 58. N.

SHIELDS, SOUTH, a borough in the county of Durham, with a market on Wednesday, seated on the river Tyne, opposite North Shields, with which place it enjoys all the advantages of trade and commerce, in common with Newcastle. It consists principally of one narrow street, two miles in length, with an open square in the middle. Many trading vessels are built here, and it has several salt-works and glass-works. The church, situated on the S. side of the market-place, was rebuilt, except the steeple, in 1810-11, at an expense of more than 4000*l*. The other places of worship are a chapel of ease, (situate on the Sunderland road,) a Scotch chapel, united session chapel, and meeting-houses for Independents, Baptists, Wesleyan, New Connexion, and Primitive Methodists. The societies and institutions, several of which are of recent establishment, reflect great honour upon the inhabitants. It is to a society of gentlemen belonging to this town that the life-boat owed its origin. It returns one member to parliament, and is connected with Gateshead by the Brandling Junction Railway; 22 miles N. N. W. of Durham, and 281 N. by W. of London.

SHIFNALL, a town in Shropshire; with a market on Tuesday. It has a handsome church, two meeting-houses, a grammar-school, a national-school, and a subscription library; 11 miles N. E. of Bridgenorth, and 136 N. W. of London.

SHIN, LOCH, a lake of Scotland; in the S. part of Sutherlandshire; 15 miles long, and 2 broad. At its S. E. extremity issues the rapid river Shin, which flows into the head of the Frith of Dornoch.

SHIPPENSBURG, a town of Pennsylvania; in Cumberland county, on a branch of Conedogwinnet Creek, which flows into the Susquehanna; 21 miles W. S. W. of Carlisle.

SHIPSTON-ON-STOUR, a town in a detached part of Worcestershire; surrounded by Warwickshire, with a market on Friday, seated on the Stom; 14 miles W. of Banbury, and 83 N. W. of London.

SHIRAS, or SHIRAUZ, a city of Persia; capital of Farsistan, seated at the end of a spacious plain, bounded on all sides by lofty mountains. It is surrounded by a wall 5 miles in circuit, with round towers at the distance of 80 paces. The city is built of brick, and adorned with many fine mosques and noble edifices. Here are many good bazars and caravanserais; also a manufacture of swords. This city was the seat of government under Kerim Khan, who erected many of the fine buildings in and near this place. In its vicinity are numerous summer-houses, with gardens; and the rich wines of Shiras are deemed the best in all Persia. The tomb of the celebrated poet Hafiz is in a large garden on the N. E. side of the city, about 2 miles from the wall; and at the foot of the mountains, in the same direction, is the tomb of Sadi; 175 miles S. by E. of Ispahan. Pop. 40,000. Long. 52. 40. W. E. lat. 29. 37. N.

SHIEVAN. *See* SCHIRVAN.

SHOALS, or ISLES OF, seven small islands on the coast of New Hampshire They lie conveniently for the cod-fishery, which was formerly carried on here to great advantage.

SHOGR, DJISSR, a town of Syria, with an excellent caravanserai; seated on the Asi; 18 miles S. by E. of Antioch, and 45 S. W. of Aleppo.

SHOOMSKA, one of the Kurile Islands, three leagues S. of Cape Lopatka, in Kamtschatka. Its inhabitants consist of a mixture of natives and Kamtschadales.

SHOOTER'S HILL, a village in Kent, situate on a hill so called, which affords a very extensive and delightful prospect. On the W. part of the hill is a tower, erected to commemorate the reduction, in 1756, of Severndroog, a strong fort in Hindostan: it is called Severndroog Castle, and contains some of the arms, ornaments, &c., taken from the enemy; 8 miles E. S. E. of London.

SHOREHAM, a borough in Sussex; with a market on Saturday. It sends two members to parliament. It is commonly called New Shoreham, to distinguish it from the Old, which lies near it, and is now of little account. It stands on an arm of the sea, into which vessels can enter with the tide; and many small vessels are built here. It has a railroad to Brighton; 19 miles W. N. W. of Newhaven, and 56 S. by W. of London.

SHREWSBURY, a borough and the capital of Shropshire, governed by a mayor; with markets on Wednesday and Saturday. It sends two members to parliament. It is seated on a peninsula formed by the Severn, over which are two bridges, and is surrounded by a wall, in which are three gates. Here were formerly a castle and abbey, both now in ruins. It contains 6 churches, a Roman Catholic chapel, and meeting-houses for the various sects of dissenters. Here are 16 incorporated trading companies, of which the dressers and mercers are the principal. Shrewsbury is the chief mart for a coarse kind of woollen cloth, made in Montgomeryshire, called Welsh webs; and for all sorts of Welsh commodities, which are generally bought in a rough state at Welshpool, and finished here. It is also famous for its excellent brawn and delicate cakes; and in the environs is a large manufacture of coarse linens. Here is a free school founded by Edward VI., and afterwards rebuilt and more largely endowed by queen Elizabeth; also several charity-schools, and other benevolent institutions. In 1283, Edward I. held a parliament here, when the lords sat in the castle, and the commons in a barn. Another parliament was held here in 1397, by Richard II. In 1403 a battle was fought in the vicinity between Henry V. (then prince of Wales) and Henry Percy, nicknamed Hotspur, in which the latter was defeated and slain. James II. held his court here in 1687; 40 miles S. S. E. of Chester, and 154 N. W. of London. Long. 2. 41. W. lat. 52. 43. N.

SHREWSBURY, a town of New Jersey, in Monmouth county, with three edifices for public worship. It is a place of genteel resort in the summer months, seated near the sea-coast; 45 miles E. by N. of Trenton.

SHROPSHIRE, or SALOP, a county of England; 48 miles long, and 40 broad, bounded N. by Cheshire, and a detached part of Flintshire, E. by Staffordshire, S. E. by Worcestershire, S. by Herefordshire, S. W. by Radnorshire, and W. by the counties of Montgomery and Denbigh. It contains 858,240 acres, is divided into 15 hundreds and 230 parishes, has 12 market-towns, and sends four members to parliament for the northern and southern divisions of the county. The soil is generally fruitful, especially in the N. and E. parts, which produce plenty of wheat and barley; the S. and W. being mountainous, are less fertile, but yield sufficient pasture for sheep and cattle. This county abounds with lead, copper, iron, limestone, free-stone, pipe-clay, bitumen, and coal; it has also some salt-springs, numerous iron-works, and manufactures of porcelain and flannel. The principal rivers are the Severn and the Teme. The capital is Shrewsbury.

SHUMLA, or SCHOUMLA, a strong town of European Turkey; in Bulgaria. It commands the pass over the mountains, and is 120 miles N. N. W. of Constantinople. Pop. 300,000.

SHUSA, a town of European Russia, capital of the province of Karabegh, with 2000 inhabitants, 500 of whom are Armenians, and the remainder Tartars; 225 miles S. E. of Tiflis.

SHUSTER, a city of Persia; capital of Kusistan, with a considerable manufacture of woollen stuffs, which are exported to Bassorah, in return for Indian commodities. The streets are narrow and dirty, but the houses are good, and it contains ruins which testify it to have been formerly of great extent and magnificence. Its present population is estimated at 15,000, Persians and Arabs. It is situate at the foot of a range o mountains, on an eminence which overlooks the rapid course of the Karoon. Long. 49. 2. E. lat. 32. 5. N.

SHUTESBURY, a town of Massachusets, in Franklin county. After an earthquake, in 1815, a medicinal spring appeared, which is now much resorted to; 80 miles W. of Boston.

SIAM, a kingdom of Asia, bounded on the N. E. by that of Laos, E. by Cochin-China and Cambodia, S. by a gulf of its name, and W. by the Bay of Bengal. It is 550 miles in length, and 250 in breadth, though in some places not above 50; and is divided into the Higher and Lower. The country is level, and in the rainy season is overflowed; for which reason most of the houses are built on pillars, and they have no communication for some months but by boats. The soil produces plenty of rice, cotton, and a variety of fruits different from those of Europe. Many authors have extolled it as the finest and richest country in the world. There are mines of gold, silver, tin, and copper; and plenty of pepper, aloes, benzoin, and musk. Wild animals roam in the woods, as elephants, rhinoceroses, leopards, and tigers. Their tame cattle are beeves, buffaloes, and hogs, of which they have plenty about their farms. There are large and dangerous crocodiles, and serpents 20 feet long. The inhabitants have large foreheads, little noses, plump lips, and black sparkling eyes. The men are of an olive complexion, with little beards; but the women are of a straw complexion, and some have their cheeks a little red. Both sexes go bare-headed, and almost naked, except the wealthy, who wear rich garments for ostentation. The king shows himself but once a year to the people. He is the proprietor of all the lands in the country, and no one can buy any merchandise till he has first had the choice of them. He generally keeps a numerous army, besides 3000 elephants, and can take 25,000 men into the field. The mandarins, that is, the principal men who daily attend the palace, are 3000 in number, and are whipt very severely with split rattans for the least fault. The temples and priests are very numerous; the latter are distinguished from the laity by an orange-coloured garment, and by keeping their heads, beards, and eye-brows close shaved. They have schools for the education of their children, and scarcely any are found among them who cannot read and write. This country has been much oppressed by the Birmans, to whom the king of Siam, after a long and destructive war, ceded the W. maritime towns on the Bay of Bengal, in 1793. Bang-kok is the capital.

Siam, or Juthia, a city, the former capital of the foregoing kingdom. It contains a great number of Buddhist temples, convents, columns, and other decorations. The king's palace, and some others, differ from the common habitations, by occupying a more extensive space, being better constructed, and of a greater height, but they never exceed one floor. The Dutch have a factory here, and merchants from different countries come here to trade. In 1766 this city was taken by the Birmans. It is situate on an island in the river Menan, 50 miles N. of its mouth, in the Gulf of Siam, and 360 S. E. of Pegu. Long. 100. 50. E. lat. 14. 18. N.

Siang-yang, a city of China, of the first class, in the province of Hou-quang, on the river Han; 530 miles S. S. W. of Peking. Long, 111. 40. E. lat 32. 5. N.

Siaskoi, a town of Russia, in the government of Petersburg, near the Lake Ladoga; 24 miles N. E. of New Ladoga. Long. 30. 47. E. lat. 60. 16. N.

Siberia, a large country, comprehending the northern part of the Russian empire in Asia. It is bounded on the E. by the Pacific Ocean, S. by Great Tartary, W. by European Russia, and N. by the Frozen Ocean. It extends 3500 miles in length from E. to W., and 1200 in breadth, from N. to S. Area, 5,000,000 square miles, with a population of 2,000,000. The S. part produces all the necessaries of life, but the N. is extremely cold, almost uncultivated, and thin of people. The principal riches of this country consist of fine skins and furs; but there are also rich mines of iron and copper, and several kinds of precious stones, particularly topazes of a beautiful lustre, magnets of an extraordinary size, and even whole mountains of loadstone. The inhabitants are of three sorts, Pagans, or the natives of the country, Mahomedans, and Russians. The former dwell in forests in the winter, and in the summer on the banks of rivers. Their garments are the skins of wild beasts. All their riches are comprised in their bows, arrows, a knife, and a kettle. They make use of reindeer and dogs, instead of horses, to draw their sledges, and live in huts, which they remove from place to place. Those in the southern parts are somewhat more civilized. They have horses with which they go hunting, and their houses, though poor, are not shifted from place to place. The Russians settled here are much the same as in their native country. It is through this vast tract of land that the Russian caravans travel every year, when they carry their merchandize to China. The principal rivers are the Oby, Lena, Irtish, Yenisei, and Okota. The western part of Siberia is comprised in the Russian government of Tobolsk, and is divided into the circles of Tobolsk Proper, Tomsk, Yeniceisk, and Kolyvan; all the eastern part is contained in the government of Irkutsk, and divided into the circles of Irkutsk Proper, Nertschink, Yakoutsk, and Okhotsk, which last includes Kamtschatka and the islands. Siberia is the place to which criminals, as well as persons under the displeasure of the court, are commonly banished from Russia. Christianity has at present made little progress in this country, though considerable efforts have of late years been made by the Russian government as well as by the British Missionary Societies. Tobolsk is the capital, and the residence of the viceroy.

Sical, a town of Mexico, on the N. coast of Yucatan; 70 miles N. W of Merida. Long. 90. 30. W. lat. 39. 30. N.

Sichem, a town of Belgium, in South Brabant; to the S. of which is a celebrated monastery. It is seated on the Demer; 18 miles E. of Mechlin.

Sicily, an island of the Mediterranean Sea, about 165 miles long, and 112 broad. Its form is that of a triangle, terminating in three capes; that which is nearest Italy is called Capo del Faro; that next the Morea, Capo Passaro; and the third, which points to Africa, Capo di Boco. Sicily is separated from the kingdom of Naples by a narrow strait, called the Faro; but, as Messina is situated on it, it is called the Faro of Messina. The two kingdoms of Naples and Sicily have nearly the same climate, and the productions are much the same; but Sicily abounds much more in corn, particularly in the valleys of Noto and Mazara. The valley of Demona has more forests and fruit-trees than the two others. The three great divisions of Sicily are named from those valleys; but since 1815 it has been divided into seven intendancies: viz. Palermo, Messina, Catania, Girgenti, Syracuse, Trapani, and Calatanissetta. The chief towns in the Val di Mazara are Palermo, Marsala, Trapani, Termini, and Mazara; in the Val di Noto, Modica, Ragusa, Noto, Syracuse, and Castro Giovanna; in the Val di Demona, Messina, Catania, and Nicosia. This country produces corn, wine, oil, silk, excellent fruits, and almost every necessary of life in wonderful abundance. The only manufacturing establishments of extent are Palermo, Messina, and Catania; they consist of silk, cotton, and linen, and some woollens, though the wool of the island is of a different quality; to which we may add a few articles, such as hats, cutlery, harness, carriages, and household furniture, made at the principal towns. The commerce of Sicily is comparatively trifling, though, from the variety of its products, the excellence of several of its harbours, and the general safety of its coast for navigation, it might, under an enlightened government, become very extensive. In the darkness of their complexion, and the indolence of their habits, the Sicilians resemble the Italians and Spaniards; and education is in a very backward state, but the new plan of teaching (of Bell and Lancaster) is beginning to be employed with some success. The religion is the Catholic; and the number of ecclesiastics is said to amount to 70,000, exclusive of the monks and nuns. The assembly long dignified with the name of parliament was, until 1810, merely a feudal institution, possessing hardly any marks of the elective franchise. Sicily was successively occupied by the Phenicians, the Carthaginians, and Romans. In the 8th and 9th centuries it was conquered by the Saracens, who retained possession of the island about 200 years. They gave way to the Normans, who, attracted to Sicily on their progress to the crusades, made the conquest of the island in the 11th century. It passed successively into the possession of France, Germany, and Spain. By the peace of Utrecht, in 1713, it was given to the duke of Savoy, with the title of king; but in 1720 the Austrians prevailed on the new possessor of Sicily to exchange it for Sardinia, and added the former to the kingdom of Naples. The war carried on by France and Spain against Austria, in 1734, transferred the crown of Naples to a branch of the royal family of Spain, in whose hands it remained until the progress of the French revolutionists, in 1799, led to the expulsion of the royal family from Naples. They took refuge in Sicily, where they remained till 1815, when the overthrow of Murat, by the Austrians, led to the restoration of the former family to the throne of Naples, which they continue to possess. In 1820 the Sicilians made an attempt to establish a free government, but the country was invaded by the Austrians, and the king re-established in all his former absolute authority. Area, 12,500 square miles. Pop. 1,800,000. Palermo is the capital.

SICLOS, a town of Hungary, with a castle on a mountain, in which the emperor Sigismund was imprisoned; 12 miles S. of Funfkirchen.

SICNLIANA, a town in the S. of Sicily. It has a harbour, and a trade in sulphur and wheat. Pop. 6000. It is 8 miles N. by W. of Girgenti.

SIDAYE, a strong town on the N. coast of the island of Java, with a harbour. Long. 113. 15. E. lat. 6. 40. S.

SIDEROCAPSO, a town of Macedonia, famous for a gold mine in its neighbourhood. It is 5 miles from the Gulf of Contessa, and 40 E. S. E. of Salonichi.

SIDMOUTH, a town in Devonshire, with a market on Saturday. It is much frequented in the bathing season, and was formerly a seaport, but its harbour is now choked up. It is seated on the English Channel, at the mouth of the Sid; 12 miles S. E. of Exeter, and 158 W. by S. of London.

SIDRA, or SYDRA, a spacious gulf of the Mediterranean, on the coast of Tripoli, anciently called Syrtis.

SIEDENBERG, a town of Hanover, in the county of Hoya; 9 miles S. W. of Hoya.

SIEGBERG, a town of Prussian Westphalia, in the duchy of Berg, on the river Sieg; 15 miles S. E. of Cologne.

SIEGEN, a town and castle of Prussian Westphalia, formerly the capital of a principality belonging to the House of Nassau. In the neighbourhood are iron-mines, forges, and foundries. It is seated on the Sieg; 24 miles N. W. of Wetzlar. Long. 8. 12. E. lat. 50. 47. N.

SIENNA, or SIENNESE, a province of the grand duchy of Tuscany, bounded by the Florentine and the territory of Pisa. The soil is pretty fertile, especially in mulberry-trees, which feed a great number of silk-worms; and there are several mineral springs. It is 62 miles long, and nearly the same broad, and has an area of 3000 square miles, with 190,000 inhabitants.

SIENNA, a city of Tuscany, capital of the foregoing province, and an archbishop's see, with a university and a citadel. It is surrounded by a wall above 4 miles in circumference. The Gothic metropolitan church is built with black and white marble, and the pavement is of Mosaic work. Sienna is not very populous; it once contained 85,000 inhabitants, but it has declined to 15,000. It is adorned with a great number of palaces, fountains, and superb churches. The great area is round, and the houses about it are of the same height, supported by piazzas, under which people may walk in all weathers. The Italian language is spoken in Sienna in its greatest purity. It is seated on three eminences, 26 miles S. of Florence, and 120 N. N. W. of Rome. Long. 11. 11. E. lat. 43. 24. N.

Sierk, a town of France, in the department of Moselle, near the river Moselle; 10 miles N. N. E. of Thionville.

Sierra Leone, a country of Africa, in the W. part of Guinea; so named from being mountainous, and the mountains abounding in lions. It is situated on the Atlantic, and is distinguished for the colony formed there by the British nation, from motives of generosity and philanthropy. This country is traversed by a considerable river, derived from the interior, called the Mitomba, or Sierra Leone. Its limits are from the Grain Coast on the S. E. to Cape Verga on the N. W.; that is, between 7. and 10. N. lat. In the open and plain parts, on the banks of the river, the heat of the sun, before any breeze arises, is almost intolerable; but a refreshing gale constantly springs up about noon, which renders the country supportable. The wet season, from May to October, is ushered in and terminated by stormy weather. It is considered very unhealthy, but probably not more so than New Orleans; and far better than the French settlements on the Senegal. The whole tract, on each side of the river, is rich in rice and millet, which is the chief sustenance of the inhabitants; and, upon the whole, it is one of the best countries on the coast. The natives are in general of mild external manners, and noted for their hospitality; but they possess a great share of pride, and are easily affected by an insult. Of all the tribes, those who have embraced Mahomedism are the most civilized and respectable; and those on the coast, from their intercourse with the European slave-factors, are much inferior in every thing, except the art of making a bargain, to those who reside higher up the country. In 1791 an act of parliament was obtained, incorporating a company, called the Sierra Leone Company, for the purpose of cultivating West India and other tropical productions on the banks of the river. The first settlers amounted to 200 white persons, besides a number of free blacks from Nova Scotia. In 1793 the colonists were all put into possession of small lots of land, and a new town, on a regular and extended scale, was begun to be built. The next year a French squadron destroyed the settlement, and captured several of the company's ships: from this disaster they recovered, and a factory was established in the Rio Pongos in 1795. The colony, however, still continued to languish, and in 1808 it was transferred from the company to his majesty. It was soon after placed under the management of the African Institution; and, notwithstanding all its disadvantages, the colony has been rapidly advancing in prosperity, and the population is continually augmenting by the capture of negroes, on their way to the West Indies, by vessels employed to put a stop to the slave trade. The number landed in 1824 was 1530; in 1825, 2337; in 1826, 2727; and in 1827, 2857. The whole population of the liberated Africans in the villages (exclusive of 2562 persons resident in Freetown, or employed at the timber factories) is now upwards of 20,000. Independently of Freetown, but including the isles de Los and Freetown, the number of settlements now amount to 14, of which Regent and Wellington are the richest and most populous. The inhabitants are by no means wanting in industry. The markets of Freetown are supplied with fruit and vegetables almost exclusively by the mountain villages; and from 80 to 100 persons are to be seen daily on the hill leading to Gloucester Town, with the produce of their own farms and gardens. The Church and Wesleyan Missionary Societies are aiding by their efforts in promoting the happiness and prosperity of the colony; education is rapidly extending, and numbers of degraded negroes are rising into respectability, and even wealth. Freetown is the capital.

Sierra Morena, mountains of Spain, dividing Andalusia from Estremadura and New Castile, rendered famous by the wars of the Christians and Mahomedans, and for being the scene where Cervantes has placed the most entertaining adventures of his hero.

Sigeth. *See* Ziget.

Sigilmessa. *See* Sugulmessa.

Sigmaringen, a town of Germany, with a castle, which gives name to a branch of the House of Hohenzollern. It is seated on the Danube, 18 miles E. S. E. of Hollenzollern.

Signau, a town of Switzerland, in the canton of Bern; 12 miles S. E. of Bern.

Sigluna, a town of Sweden, in Upland, 10 miles N. of Stockholm.

Siguenza, a town of Spain, in Guadalaxara, and a bishop's see, with a castle, in which is an arsenal. It had formerly a university, consisting of several colleges. The most considerable structure is the cathedral. It is seated on a hill, at the foot of Mount Atienca, 65 miles N. E. of Madrid. Pop. 5000. Long. 2. 51. W. lat. 40. 58. N.

Sihon, a river. *See* Sirr.

Silagutta, a town of Hindostan, in Mysore, celebrated for its kitchen-gardens. Coarse cotton cloths are made here, and some tobacco grows in the neighbourhood. It is 20 miles N. W. of Colar, and 32 N. E. of Bangalore.

Silberberg, a strong town of Prussian Silesia. It has its name from a mine of lead and silver, the working of which has been discontinued; 11 miles N. N. E. of Glatz.

Silchester, a village in Hampshire, once a celebrated city, and said to have been the place where Arthur was crowned. There are considerable remains of its walls and ditches, enclosing an area of 80 acres; and two military roads from the S. gate, one to Winchester, and the other to Old Sarum. It is 6 miles N. of Basingstoke.

Silesia, a province of the Prussian states, formerly belonging to the kingdom of Bohemia. It is 200 miles long, and 170 broad; bounded on the N. by Brandenburg, E. by Poland, S. by Moravia, and W. by Bohemia, from which it is separated by a long chain of mountains: the highest, called Zotenburg, is in the principality of Schweidnitz. There are mines of coal, lead, copper, and iron, and quarries of various stones, besides antimony, saltpetre, sulphur, alum, vitriol, quicksilver, agate, jasper, and even some gems. The principal rivers are the Oder, Bober, Neisse, Queis, and Oppa. The chief manufacture is linen cloth; there are also some woollen manufactures, potteries, iron-foundries, and glass-houses. In this country are a great number of cattle, large studs of horses, and plenty of game in the woods; also a few lynxes, bears, foxes, otters, and beavers. There are many lakes, full of pike, carp, and other good fish; also plenty of bees, which produce much honey and wax. Wheat, maize, barley, oats, millet, and in some places saffron, are cultivated; but its wine is bad, and chiefly used for vinegar. Silesia was formerly divided into Upper and Lower: the former comprising the S. part, where the inhabitants are generally Roman Catholics, and speak the Polish language: in the latter they are almost all Protestants, and speak their mother tongue. The country of Glatz, and a portion of Lusatia, are now annexed to this province, which forms a military division along with Posen, and is divided into the governments of Breslau, Liegnitz, Oppeln, and Reichenbach; containing together an area of 15,000 square miles, and a population of 2,000,000. This country was ceded to the king of Prussia, in 1742, by the treaty of Breslau. In 1807 it was overrun by the French, but was restored to Prussia at the peace of Tilsit. Breslau is the capital.

Silhet, a town of Bengal, capital of a district of the same name, seated on the Soorma, 120 miles from Dacca. The district is separated from Assam by a range of mountains, and is bounded on the other sides by Muneepoor, Burmah, and Tipperah. Coal has been found in the lower hills, and it exports rice, oranges, and lemons. It belongs to the British, and contains an area of 2861 square miles, and a population of 492,945. The town is agreeably situated, and, from its cool situation, has been used as a sanative station by the inhabitants of Calcutta; 325 travelling miles distant.

Silistria, or Dristra, a town of European Turkey, in Bulgaria, and an archbishop's see, with a citadel. It is seated on the Danube, at the influx of the Missovo, 155 miles N. N. E. of Adrianople. Long. 27. 6. E. lat. 44. 15. N.

Silkeburg, a town of Denmark, in N. Jutland, with a castle, 18 miles W. of Arhusen.

Silla, a town of Negroland, in Bambarra, on the right bank of the Niger; remarkable as the place where Park was obliged to terminate his first journey, after having penetrated 1090 miles in a direct line E. from Cape Verd. It is 75 miles N. E. of Sego.

Sillabar, a seaport on the W. coast of Sumatra, with a good and safe harbour, 30 miles S. S. E. of Bencoolen. Long. 102. 10. E. lat. 4. 0. S.

Sille le Guillaume, a town of France, department of Sarthe; 19 miles N. W. of Mans.

Sillee, a town of Bengal, seated on the Subanrecka, 173 miles W. N. W. of Calcutta.

Silvis, a town of Portugal, in Algarve, on a river of the same name, 35 miles W. N. W. of Tavira.

Simancas, a town of Spain, in Valladolid, with a strong castle, in which Philip II. ordered the archives of the kingdom to be kept. It is situate on the Douro, 10 miles S. W. of Valladolid, and 60 N. E. of Salamanca.

Simbirsk, a government of Russia, formerly a province of the kingdom of Kasan. It has an area of 30,000 square miles, with 850,000 inhabitants, the greater part of whom profess the religion of the Greek church. The capital, of the same name, is seated on the Volga; 100 miles S. by W. of Kasan. Long. 48. 34. E. lat. 54. 22. N.

Simi, or Symi (the ancient Syme), an island in the Mediterranean, between the island of Rhodes and the continent, in a bay of its name. It has a town containing about 2000 houses, built near the summit of a high rocky mountain; 2 miles N. W. of Rhodes. Long. 27. 23. E. lat. 36. 35. N.

Simmern, a town of Prussia, in the province of Lower Rhine, seated on a river of the same name; 25 miles S. of Coblentz.

Simogay, a town of Hindostan, in Mysore, district of Bednore, with a manufacture of coarse cotton cloth. Tippoo Sultan was defeated near this place by the Mahrattas, aided by a detachment of British, in 1790. It is seated on the Tunga, 34 miles E. by N. of Nagara.

Simons, St., an island of the United States, on the coast of Georgia, at the mouth of the Alatamaha. It is 15 miles long, and 3 broad, and has a town called Frederica.

Simonthurn, or Simontornya, a town of Hungary, with a strong castle, taken from the Turks in 1686. It is seated on the Sarvita, 32 miles S. S. W. of Buda. Long. 18. 52. E. lat. 46. 45. N.

Simplon, a celebrated pass leading from Valais into Piedmont, over the Alps. It was formed by Bonaparte, and has been considered his greatest work. It commences at Brieg, and terminates at Duomo D'Ossola.

Sinai, a mountain of Arabia Petrea, in a peninsula formed by the two arms of the Red Sea. The Mahomedans hold it in great veneration; and here the Greek Christians have a monastery, surrounded by a high wall; and those who go in and out are drawn up and let down in baskets. Long. 34. 15. E. lat. 29. 2. N.

Sincapour, or Singapoor, an island at the southern extremity of the peninsula of Malaya, from which it is separated by a narrow channel; and, to the S., it gives name to the narrow sea called the Strait of Sincapour. It has a town of the same name. It was ceded to the British in 1824, and was made a depôt for ships passing to China, &c., and in 5 years became a seat of commerce and population almost unexampled for increase. It is inhabited by Chinese emigrants, and has a safe harbour. Long. 103. 15. E. lat. 1. 10. N.

Sinde, a river of Asia. *See* Indus.

Sinde, a province of Hindostan, bounded on the W. by Persia, N. by the territories of the king of Kandahar, N. E. by those of the Seiks, E. by a sandy desert, and S. by Cutch. It extends along the course of the Indus, from its mouth to the frontiers of Moultan, 300 miles; and its breadth in the widest part is 160. In soil and climate, and the general appearance of the surface, it resembles Egypt—the country being an extended valley, confined on one side by a ridge of mountains, and on the other by a desert, and the Indus, equal at least to the Nile, winding through the midst of this level valley, and enriching it by its annual inundations. During great part of the S. W. monsoon, or at least in July, August, and part of September, (the rainy season in most other parts of India,) the atmosphere is here generally clouded; but no rain falls, except near the sea. Owing to this, and the neighbourhood of the sandy deserts on the E. and on the N. W., the heats are so violent, and the winds from those quarters so pernicious, that the houses are contrived so as to be occasionally ventilated by apertures on the top, resembling the funnels of small chimneys. When the hot winds prevail, the windows are closely shut, excluding the hottest current of air, and a cooler part descends into the house through the funnels. By this means are also excluded vast clouds of dust, the entrance of which would alone be sufficient to render the houses uninhabitable. The roofs are composed of thick layers of earth instead of terraces. Few countries are more unwholesome to European constitutions, particularly the lower part called the Delta. The Hindoos, who were the original inhabitants of Sinde, have been treated with great rigour by the Mahomedan governors, and vast numbers have in consequence retired into other countries. The inland parts of Sinde produce saltpetre, sal-ammoniac, borax, bezoar, lapis lazuli, and raw silk. Here are manufactures of cotton and silk of various kinds; and also of fine cabinets, inlaid with ivory, and finely lacquered. Great quantities of butter are exported, which is clarified and wrapt up in duppas, made of the hides of cattle. Here are large beeves, fine sheep, and small hardy horses. The wild game are deer, hares, antelopes, and foxes, which are hunted with dogs; also leopards, and a small fierce creature called a shiahgush. This province is now governed by three chiefs, called ameers, tributary to the sultan of Kandahar. The Bombay government sent an embassy to the chief in 1808; and the East India Company have now a native agent, or chargé d'affaires, residing at the fort of Hydrabad, the capital. The area is about 24,000 square miles, with a population of not above 1,000,000.

SINDELFINGEN, a town of Germany, in the kingdom of Wirtemberg; 10 miles S. S. W. of Stutgard.

SINES, a town of Portugal, in Alentejo; on a cape to which it gives name; 74 miles S. W. of Evora. Long. 8. 46. W. lat. 37. 58. N.

SING, a strong town of Austrian Dalmatia; built by the Turks in opposition to Clissa, and taken by the Venetians in 1686. It is 8 miles N. of Clissa, and 14 of Spalatro.

SIN-GAN, a city of China, in the province of Chen-si, and one of the largest and most beautiful in the empire. The walls are 12 miles in circuit, nearly a square, and surrounded by a deep ditch; they are well fortified with towers, and some of the gates are very lofty and magnificent. It has a great trade, especially in mules, which are bred up in great numbers and sent to Peking. Here is a strong garrison of Tartars in a separate part of the city, from which it is parted by a strong wall. It is 540 miles S. W. of Peking. Long. 108. 44. E. lat. 35. 16. N.

SINGILIEF, a town of Russia, in the government of Simbirsk, situate on the Volga; 24 miles S. of Simbirsk.

SINGOR, a town in the peninsula of Malacca; seated at the mouth of a small river, in the bay of Patani. Long. 101. 25. E. lat. 6. 40. N.

SINIGAGLIA, a strong seaport of Italy; in the duchy of Urbino, with a castle and two harbours. It is the see of a bishop, and contains several fine churches and convents, and a mint. An annual fair is held here from the middle to the end of July, frequented by merchants from distant parts. It stands at the mouth of the Nigola, in the Gulf of Venice; 17 miles S. E. of Pesaro. Pop. 6200. Long. 13. 15. E. lat. 43. 43. N.

SI-NING, a city of China, of the second rank, in the western extremity of the province of Chen-si, It has a considerable trade with the Tibetians, particularly in tea. It is 450 miles W. N. W. of Singan. Long. 101. 35. E. lat. 36. 45. N.

SINOB, or SINOPE, a seaport of Asiatic Turkey, in Natolia; surrounded by walls and double ramparts, but the castle is much neglected. Diogenes, the cynic philosopher, was born here. It is seated on the isthmus of a peninsula, in the Black Sea; 280 miles E. of Constantinople. Pop. 5000. Long. 33. 55. E. lat. 41. 5. N.

SINTZHEIM, a town of Baden, seated in a morass; 12 miles S. S. E. of Heidelberg.

SION, a mountain of Palestine, on the S. side of Jerusalem; of great celebrity in sacred history. *See* JERUSALEM.

SION, or SITTEN, a town of Switzerland; capital of Valais, and an episcopal see. It is situate on the river Sitten, near the Rhone, at the foot of three insulated rocks, which rise immediately from the plain. On the highest, called Tourbillon, is the old deserted episcopal palace; on the second, denominated Valeria, are the remains of the old cathedral, and a few houses belonging to the canons; on Majoria, the third rock, stands the present episcopal palace. Sion was formerly the capital of the Seduni, and some Roman inscriptions still remain. It is 56 miles E. of Geneva. Pop. 5000. Long. 7. 22. E. lat. 46. 9. N.

SIOUT, or ES SIOUT, a town of Egypt, which has several mosques, and is the see of a Coptic bishop. It is surrounded by fine gardens, and palm-trees that bear the best dates in Egypt. Here are the ruins of an amphitheatre, and some sepulchres, of the Romans. The place is the rendezvous of those who go in the caravan to Sennaar, in Nubia. It stands on an artificial mount; 2 miles from the Nile, and 185 S. of Cairo. Long. 31. 24. E. lat. 27. 25. N.

SIPHANTO, the ancient Siphnos; one of the best cultivated islands of the Grecian Archipelago; situate W. of Paros. It is 36 miles in circumference, and, though covered with marble and granite, produces corn sufficient for its inhabitants; also olives, vines, figs, cotton, and excellent silk, but not in any considerable quantity. The chief articles of commerce are calicoes, straw hats, figs, onions, honey, wax, oil, and capers. Long. 25. 15. E. lat. 37. 9. N.

SIR CHARLES HARDY ISLAND, an island in the Pacific Ocean, discovered by Captain Carteret in 1767. It is low, level, and covered with wood. Long. 154. 20. E. lat. 4. 41. S.

SIRA. *See* SERA.

SIRADIA, a town of Prussian Poland, with a strong castle. It is surrounded by a wall, and seated in a plain, on the river Warta; 62 miles N. E. of Breslau, and 105 N. W. of Cracow. Long. 18. 55. E. lat. 51. 32. N.

SIRAF, a town of Persia, in the province of Laristan; situate on the Persian Gulf; 30 miles S. W. of Lar. Long. 43. 23. E. lat. 35. 20. N.

SIRAVAN, a town of Persia, in Kusistan; 48 miles N. N. E. of Suster.

SIRE, a town of Abyssinia, in Tigre; famous for a manufacture of coarse cotton cloths. It is 40 miles W. of Axum, and 100 W. N. W. of Auzen.

SIRGAN. *See* KERMAN.

SIRHIND, a city of Hindostan, capital of a country of the same name, in the province of Delhi. Procopius takes notice that in the time of Justinian (the sixth century) silk was brought from Serinda, a country in India. It is 175 miles N. W. of Delhi. Long. 75. 35. E. lat. 30. 15. N.

SIRIAM, a seaport of Pegu; frequented by the French, English, and Dutch. It is seated on Pegu River, 30 miles from its mouth, and 80 S. of Pegu. Long. 96. 12. E. lat. 16. 32. N.

SERINAGHUR. *See* CASHMERE.

SIRIUS, an island in the South Pacific, about 18 miles in circuit; discovered by Lieutenant Ball in 1790. Long. 162. 30. E. lat. 10. 52. S.

SIRMICH, or SIRMIUM, a town of Sclavonia; and a bishop's see; seated on the Bosworth, near the Save; 42 miles S. E. of Essek. Long. 20. 19. E. lat. 45. 13. N.

SIROWY, a town of Hindostan, in a district of the same name, in Agimere; seated near the Puddar; 70 miles S. W. of Agimere. Long. 74. 27. E. lat. 26. 1. N.

SIRPY, a town and fort of Hindostan, in Mysore; 14 miles N. of Sera, and 37. S. E. of Chittledroog.

SIRR, or SIHON, a river of Independent Tartary, (the ancient Jaxartes,) which issues from the mountains of Imaus, or Belur, on the confines of Cashgur, and, taking a N. W. course of about 550 miles, enters the N. E. part of the lake Aral. It formerly flowed to the Caspian Sea, but the Tartars, to free themselves from pirates, turned its course.

SISIZAN, a seaport on the E. coast of Luçonia, one of the Philippine Islands. It is situate almost opposite Manilla, and in the vicinity of very high mountains, which render the air extremely moist. Long. 123. 45. E. lat. 14. 20. N.

SISSAC, a town of Switzerland, in the canton of Basel; 17 miles S. E. of Basel.

SISSEK, or SISZEG, a strong town of the Austrian states, in Croatia, situate on the Save, at the influx of the Kulpa; 40 miles E. of Carlstadt. Long. 16. 56. E. lat. 45. 33. N.

SISSOPOLI, a town of Romania, and an archbishop's see; seated on a peninsula of the Black Sea; 25 miles S. of Mesembria. Long. 28. 9. E. lat. 42. 30. N.

SISTERON, a town of France, department of Lower Alps, with a citadel on the top of a rock, which was the prison of Casimir V. king of Poland. It is seated on the Durance, 45 miles N. E. of Aix, and 407 S. E. of Paris. Pop. 4000. Long. 5. 56. E. lat. 44. 12. N.

SISTOVA, a town of Bulgaria, where a peace was concluded between the Austrians and Turks in 1791. It is seated on the Danube, 25 miles E. of Nicopoli. Pop. 20,000.

SITIA, a town on the N. coast of the isle of Candia, on a bay of the same name, 58 miles E. S. E. of Candia. Long. 26. 29. E. lat. 35. 0. N.

SITTARD, a town of the Netherlands, in the province of Limburg, seated near the Meuse; 12 miles N. of Maestricht.

SITTINGBORN, a corporate town in Kent; 15 miles W. N. W. of Canterbury, and 40 E. S. E. of London.

SITTIVACCA, a village of Ceylon, the chief place of intercourse between the Candians and their European neighbours; 28 miles E. of Colombo.

SIVAS, a city of Asia Minor, and the see of a bishop, with a castle. It is noted as the theatre of the great contest between Timur and Bajazet, in which the latter was finally defeated and taken prisoner. It is 180 miles W. S. W. of Erzerum, and 210 E. N. E. of Cogni. Long. 38. 40. E. lat. 38. 55. N.

SIVRAY, or CIVRAY, a town of France, department of Vienne; seated on the Charente; 27 miles S. of Poitiers.

SIVRY, a town of Belgium, in Hainault; with 2500 inhabitants; 18 miles S. W. of Charleroi.

SIWAH, a territory of Africa, on the confines of Egypt and Barca; mentioned by the ancients under the name of the Oasis of Ammon. The fertile part is about 20 miles in circumference, containing several villages, besides the capital. It affords abundance of vegetable productions, with corn and oil, and is well supplied with water from small streams, but none of them flow beyond its territory, being either evaporated before they reach the surrounding desert, or lost in the sterile sand. Pop. 8000. The capital, of the same name, contains the ruins of the celebrated temple of Jupiter Ammon; and in the neighbourhood are many catacombs, which were the burying places of the ancient inhabitants. It is the theatre of considerable trade, being situate on the great caravan route; 220 miles E. of Augila, and 280 W. by S. of Cairo. Pop. about 2500. Long. 27. 10. E. lat. 29. 12. N.

Six Nations, or Iroquois, a confederacy of American Indians; comprising the Mohawks, Gayugas, Oneidas, Onondagas, Linecas, and Tuscarawas.

Skara, a town of Sweden, in W. Gothland, a bishop's see, and formerly the capital of the kingdom of Gothland. It was totally destroyed by fire in 1719. The ruins of several churches and convents are still to be seen, and it has a college, a botanical garden, a medical school, and a large cathedral. It is seated on the Lida, in a morass, 77 miles N. E. of Gotheburg. Long. 14. 0. E. lat. 58. 16. N.

Skeen, a town of Norway, in the government of Aggerhuys; noted for its mines of iron and copper; seated near a lake; 26 miles S. W. of Kongsburg.

Skenectady, or Schenectady, a town of New York; capital of a county of its name. Here are four churches, and a seminary incorporated in 1794, called Union College, from its being established by various denominations of Christians. It has a considerable trade with the back country, and stands on the W. side of the Mohawk river, above the falls; 16 miles N. W. of Albany.

Skibbereen, a town of Ireland, in the county of Cork; 219 miles from Dublin. It is ill-built, but is flourishing, and has a considerable trade in yarn and coarse linens.

Skiddaw, a mountain in Cumberland, near Keswick; 3270 feet in perpendicular height from the surface of the lake Derwentwater, to the N. of which it is situate. It is not difficult of access, and is almost covered with grass, which gradually grows coarser in the ascent. The whole top is covered with a loose brown slaty stone.

Skilskuer, a town of Denmark, in the island of Zealand; situate on a bay of the Great Belt; 52 miles S. W. of Copenhagen. Long. 11. 27. E. lat. 55. 16. N.

Skipton, a town in W. Yorkshire, with a market on Saturday. It has a spacious church, three meeting-houses, a free grammar-school, and two national schools. The river Aire and the Leeds and Liverpool canal pass through the town, and near it are some cotton works. It is seated in the midst of a rough mountainous district, called Craven, well adapted to the grazing and feeding of cattle. It is 22 miles N. by W. of Halifax, and 211 N. N. W. of London.

Skye, an island of Scotland, one of the largest of the Hebrides, being 54 miles long, and from 3 to 30 broad, containing 350,000 acres. The S. E. end is separated from Inverness-shire (to which it belongs) by a channel called the Inner Sound, in the narrowest part of which, named the Kyle, cattle are made to swim across. This side of the island swells gradually from the shore, in a verdant slope, over which are seen the naked hills of Strath; and above these rises the rugged top of Cullin or Cuchullin. Towards the S. W. are rude mountains, black and red, as if discoloured by fire; and on the E. a long extent of lofty hills. There is, notwithstanding, a great portion of level ground, with excellent pasturage; and it has numbers of deer and different kinds of game. It abounds with limestone, marble, &c., but the basaltic columns, resembling the Giant's Causeway in Ireland, are its greatest curiosity. A cave in this island afforded an asylum, in 1746, to the disappointed Pretender and his faithful guide, for two nights. Many thousands of beeves and sheep are annually exported hence. Some small horses are bred, and a great quantity of kelp is manufactured here. Portree is the principal town. The S. extremity is a peninsula, terminating in a rugged promontory, called the Point of Slate. Long. 6. 12. W. lat. 57. 12. N.

Slagelse, a town of Denmark, in the island of Zealand; 45 miles W. S. W. of Copenhagen.

Slaguen, a town of Prussian Pomerania, seated on the Wipper; 10 miles E. by S. of Rugenwald.

Slaithwaite, a village in W. Yorkshire, on the Huddersfield canal; which has manufactures of the various Manchester goods. It is 5 miles S. W. of Huddersfield.

Slane, a town in Ireland, in the county of Meath; 38 miles from Dublin. It is a handsome and well-built town, with a magnificent castle, the seat of the Marquis of Conyngham.

Slatina, a town of European Turkey, in Walachia, on the river Alaut; 59 miles W. of Bucharest.

Slave Coast, a name given to a maritime tract of Guinea, between the Gold Coast and Benin, comprehending the kingdoms of Ardra, Popo, and Whidah.

Slave Lake, a lake of North America, 250 miles in length from E. to W., and 60 to 100 in width. It is full of wooded islands, and its outlet at the W. extremity, in long. 119. 30. W. lat. 61. 30. N., flows N. W. into the Arctic Ocean.

Sleaford, New, a town in Lincolnshire, with a market on Monday. It is a well-built and flourishing town, and contains a handsome Gothic church, three meeting-houses, and an hospital. It had formerly a castle, now in ruins. It is seated on the Slea, which is navigable hence to the Witham. It is 18 miles S. of Lincoln, and 113 N. of London. The hamlet of Old Sleaford is about a mile distant.

Sleswick, a duchy of the Danish dominions, bounded N. by Jutland, S. by Holstein, and E. and W. by the sea. It is about 72 miles long, and from 30 to 56 broad. Area, 3600 square miles. Pop. 340,000. Having no mountains, and few elevations entitled to the name of hills, most parts of it are fit for tillage. The products are wheat, barley, oats, rye, hemp, flax, &c. It has good pasture, on which are bred horses and horned cattle. Woollen and linen are the chief manufactures, which are carried on, not in collective establishments, but in the cottages of the manufacturer. Fishing forms a considerable occupation on the coast, as well as in the arms of the sea.

Sleswick, the capital of the foregoing duchy, is a long irregular town. The houses are chiefly of wood, and few are more than one story high, but very neat. The inhabitants dress like the Dutch, and many of them speak their tongue, though the usual languages are the German and Danish. The buildings most worthy of notice are the cathedral, with its altar and the monuments of the princes, the five churches, the town-house, the orphan-house, and the nunnery of St. John. Near the city is the old ducal palace of Gottorp. Sleswick has manufactures of refined sugar, earthenware, leather, and sail-cloth. It is situate on the N. side of an arm of the Baltic, called the Sley; 60 miles N. W. of Lubec, and 125 S. W. of Copenhagen. Pop. 7000. Long. 9. 40. E. lat. 54. 35. N.

Sligo, a county of Ireland, in the province of Connaught; 39 miles long, and nearly as many broad; bounded on the E. by Leitrim, S. E. by Roscommon, S. W. and W. by Mayo, and N. by the Atlantic. It is divided into 39 parishes, contains about 260 square miles, and sends two members to parliament. The soil is in general fertile, but rather boggy towards the coast.

Sligo, a borough of Ireland, sending one member to parliament; capital of the preceding county, and a place of considerable trade; seated near the mouth of a river which flows from Lough Gill into the bay of Sligo; 42 miles N. by W. of Roscommon, and 100 N. W. of Dublin. Long. 9. 18. W. lat. 54. 15. N.

Slonim, a town of Russian Lithuania, in the government of Grodno, with a castle; seated on the Sezraa; 40 miles S. W. of Novogrodeck, and 60 S. E. of Grodno. Long. 24. 57. E. lat. 53. 0. N.

Sloten, a fortified town of the Netherlands, in Friesland; seated on the rivulet Ee, which flows into the Zuyder Zee; 8 miles E. of Staveren, and 20 S. S. W. of Lewarden.

Sluck, a town of Russian Lithuania, in the government of Minsk; with three Greek churches; seated on the river Sluck; 52 miles S. of Minsk. Long. 27. 54. E. lat. 52. 30. N.

Sluys, a town of Belgium, in Flanders; opposite the island of Cadsand; with a good harbour. It has its name from its fine sluices, by which the whole country may be laid under water. It was taken by the Spaniards in 1587, retaken by the Dutch in 1604, and taken by the French in 1794. It is 10 miles N. of Bruges. Long. 3. 25. E. lat. 51. 19. N.

Smaland, a province of Sweden, in Gothland; lying between the Baltic and the province of Halland. Its area is 7750 square miles; its population is 315,000. It is well watered, both by rivers and lakes, but great part of it consists of marshes, heaths, and barren rocks. In some parts are immense forests of pine and fir; and the approach to the villages is announced by groves of oak, beech, and birch, and numerous plots of arable. Calmar is the capital.

Smalkalden, a town of Germany, in a district of its name, belonging to Hesse-Cassel. It is famous for the league entered into by the Lutherans, against the emperor, in 1531, to defend their religion and liberties. It has a fine castle on a mountain, and in the vicinity are salt-pits and mines of iron. It stands on a river of the same name, which flows into the Werra; 25 miles S. W. of Erfurt, and 56 of Hesse-Cassel. Long. 10. 47. E. lat. 50. 45. N.

Smithfield, a town of Virginia, in Isle of Wight county; seated on Pagal Creek, which flows into James River, 83 miles S. E. of Richmond.

Smithfield, a town of North Carolina; capital of Johnson county; seated on the river Neus, in a beautiful plain; 25 miles S. E. of Raleigh, and 70 W. N. W. of Newbern. It is also the name of several townships of the United States.

Smithtown, a town of the state of New York, in Suffolk county; on the N. side of Long Island; 52 miles E. by N. of New York.

Smithville, a town of North Carolina, in Brunswick county; seated near the mouth of Cape Fear River; 25 miles S. S. W. of Wilmington. Long. 78. 30. W. lat. 33. 50. N.

Smolensko, a government of Russia, on the frontiers of Lithuania. After having been an object of contention, and reciprocally possessed by Poland and Russia, it was conquered by Alexay Michaelovitch, in 1654, and ceded to Russia by the peace of Moscow, in 1666. It contains an area of 21,400 square miles, with 1,050,000 inhabitants; and is fertile in corn, hemp, and flax. Horses, black cattle, and sheep are numerous. The principal rivers are the Duna, Dnieper, Desna, Sosha, Kasplia, and Viasma.

Smolensk, a city of Russia, capital of the foregoing government, is situate on the Dnieper, and extends over two mountains and the valley between them. It is surrounded by walls 30 feet high, and 15 thick, the lower part of stone, the upper of brick, and their circumference 4 miles and three quarters. The houses are mostly of wood, and only one story high, except a few, scattered here and there, which are dignified with the title of palaces. The city is divided, through its whole length, by one straight paved street; the others are circular, and floored with planks. The cathedral stands on an eminence, where there is a view of the whole city. Notwithstanding its extent, it contains only about 13,000 inhabitants, and has no considerable manufactures, but carries on, with Dantzic, Riga, and the Ukraine, a traffic in linen, hemp, honey, wax, leather, furs, &c. In 1812 several severe engagements were fought in the neighbourhood of this city, between the French and Russian armies, in one of which it sustained a bombardment, which destroyed most of the buildings. It is 197 miles S. E. of Novogrodeck, and 235 W. S. W of Moscow. Long. 32. 14. E. lat. 54. 50. N.

SMYNHUSEN, a town of Denmark, in the duchy of Holstein; 16 miles W. of Rendsburg.

SMYRNA, a seaport of Asia Minor, and one of the largest and richest cities of the Levant. The goodness of the harbour has caused it to be rebuilt several times, after having been destroyed by earthquakes. It is the rendezvous of merchants from almost all parts of the world, and the magazine of their merchandise. The population is computed at 100,000 persons. The streets are more open, better paved, and the houses better built, than in any other towns on the continent. The street of the Franks is the finest in Smyrna, and lies all along the harbour. The imports from England consist of woollen cloths, camlets, lead, tin, and hardware; these are exchanged for cotton, coffee, mohair, drugs, galls, raisins, figs, &c. The English and Dutch factors have Protestant chapels, and taverns are as open here as in Europe. The fortifications consist of a fort, a castle, a mountain, and an old citadel. Smyrna is eight days' journey from Constantinople by land; 25 days from Aleppo by the caravans; six from Konieh, seven from Cataya, and six from Satalia. It is seated at the head of a large bay; 190 miles S. S. W. of Constantinople. Long. 27. 7. E. lat. 38. 28. N.

SNAITH, a town in West Yorkshire, with a market on Thursday; seated on a gentle declivity on the S. bank of the Ayre, 5 miles from its confluence with the Ouse; 20 miles S. of York, and 175 N. by W. of London.

SNECK, or SNITZ, a fortified town of the Netherlands, in Friesland, seated on a lake of the same name, in marshy land; 12 miles S. S. W. of Lewarden.

SNEIRNE, a town of Prussia, in the province of Irac; 57 miles W. N. W. of Amadan.

SNIATIN, a town of Austrian Galicia, on the river Pruth; 28 miles W. of Czernowitz. Long. 22. 50. E. lat. 48. 33. N.

SNOWDEN, a mountain of Wales, in the centre of Caernarvonshire, and the most noted in the whole region of the Welsh hills. It has several craggy summits, deep dells, moors, and chasms; also two lakes that abound with fish, particularly the char and the guiniard. The height of this mountain, from the quay of Caernarvon to its highest peak, is 3658 feet. It was held sacred by the ancient Britons, as Parnassus was by the Greeks. Pieces of lava, and groups of columnar stones of vast size, have been found lying in all directions on the summit of this mountain, which commands a delightful and extensive view. In a clear day, and when the mountain is free from clouds, a part of Ireland and of Scotland, the Isle of Man, the mountains of Westmoreland and Cumberland, parts of Lancashire and Cheshire, and all North Wales, the Irish and British seas, and a vast number of lakes, may be seen from its summit.

SNOWHILL, a town of Maryland, capital of Worcester county, which has considerable trade, situate on the Pokomoke, which enters 12 miles below into the Chesapeake; 30 miles S. E. of Vienna. Long. 75. 40. W. lat. 38. 8. N.

SOANE, a river of Hindostan, which issues from a lake on the S. confines of Allahabad, the same that is the source of the Nerbudda, and, flowing in an opposite direction to that river, enters the Ganges above Patna.

SOAR, a river in Leicestershire, which rises from two sources in the S. W. part of the county, flows by Leicester and Mountsorrel, passes a little to the E. and N. of Loughborough, and then separates this county from Nottinghamshire to its entrance into the Trent.

SOBERNHEIM, a town of Prussia, in the province of Lower Rhine, seated on the Nahe; 11 miles W. by S. of Creutznach.

SOBIESLAU, a town of Bohemia, in the circle of Bechin, with good cloth manufactures; 12 miles E. S. E. of Bechin.

SOBOTKA, a town of Bohemia, in the circle of Buntzlau; situate 8 miles E. by N. of Jung Buntzlau.

SOCIETY ISLES, islands in the South Pacific Ocean, discovered by Cook in 1769; situate between 150. 57. and 152. 0. W. long., and 16. 10. and 16. 55. S. lat.. They are seven in number; namely, Huaheine, Raiatea, Tahaa, Borabora, Maurua, Tubuai, and Sir C. Saunders' Island. The soil, productions, &c., are nearly the same as at Otaheite. Nature has been equally bountiful in uncultivated plenty, and the inhabitants are as luxurious and as indolent. They are generally above the middle stature; but their limbs are less muscular and firm than those of the Sandwich islanders, whom in many respects they resemble. Though more robust than the Marquesans, they are inferior in size and physical power to the New Zealanders. In person they resemble the Friendly islanders as much as any others in the Pacific. Their limbs are well formed, and they are generally active in their movements, graceful and stately in their gait, and perfectly unembarrassed in their address. They are remarkably curious and inquisitive, and, compared with other Polynesian nations, may be said to possess considerable ingenuity and mechanical skill. Totally unacquainted, till recently, with the use of letters, their minds could not be improved by any regular or continued culture; yet the distinguishing features of their civil polity, the imposing nature, numerous observances, and diversified ramifications of their mythology, the legends of their gods, the historical songs of their bards, the beautiful, figurative, and impassioned eloquence sometimes displayed in their national assemblies, and, above all, the copiousness, variety, precision; and purity of their language, together with their extensive use of numbers, warranted the conclusion that they possessed no contemptible mental capacities. This conclusion has been abundantly confirmed since the establishment of schools and the introduction of letters. Multitudes, who were upwards of 30 or 40 years of age when they commenced with the alphabet, have in 12 months learned to read distinctly in the New Testament, large portions of which some of them have in a short period committed to memory. The missionaries, who for a long time laboured in these islands amidst discouragements and disappointments, have at length witnessed the complete abandonment of idolatry. Christianity is now universally professed, and the moral character of the people has been raised by it to a high degree of excellence. It is stated that in 1829 not fewer than 10,000 persons had learned to read the scriptures.

SOCONUSCO, a province of Guatimala, 88 miles long, and nearly as many broad; bounded on the N. by Chiapi, E. by Guatimala, S. by the Pacific Ocean, and W. by Guaxaca. The soil is not very fertile, and, being sheltered from the N. winds by high mountains, the air is exceedingly hot and unhealthy.

SOCONUSCO, or GUEVETLAN, the capital of the foregoing province, is seated on a small river, near the Pacific Ocean; 460 miles S. E. of Mexico.

SOCOTORA, or SOCOTRA, an island in the Indian Ocean, lying about 45 leagues from Cape Gardefan, on the coast of Africa. It is 80 miles long, and 22 broad, abounds in fruit and cattle, and is particularly noted for its fine aloes, known by the name of Socotrine aloes. The natives are chiefly Mahomedans, and are governed by a king who depends on Arabia. Tamara is the capital.

SODBURY, or CHIPPING SODBURY, a town in Gloucestershire, with a market on Thursday; seated in a bottom near the Downs, 15 miles E. N. E. of Bristol, and 110 W. of London.

SODERHAMN. *See* SUDERHAMN.

SODOR, a village in the celebrated island of Icolmkill, one of the Hebrides of Scotland. It was formerly a bishop's see, which comprehended all the islands, together with the Isle of Man; the bishop of Man is still called the bishop of Sodor and Man.

SODUS, a town of the state of New York, in Ontario county; situate on the S. side of Lake Ontario, on a bay 7 miles long and 3 broad, which forms an excellent harbour when the rest of the lake is agitated by a storm. It is 80 miles E. of Niagara. Long. 77. 5. W. lat. 43. 10. N.

SOEBORG, a town of Denmark, in the island of Zealand, situate on an island in a fresh-water lake; 15 miles W. N. W. of Elsinore.

SOEST, a large town of Prussian Westphalia, in the government of Arensberg, with a good trade in corn; 12 miles W. S. W. of Lipstadt, and 30. S. E. of Munster. Pop. 5400.

SOFALA, a kingdom on the E. coast of Africa, bounded on the W. and N. by the states of Mocaranga, E. by the Mozambique Channel, and S. by Sabia. It is about 150 miles along the coast, and 250 up the country. The country is wild, and thinly inhabited, but contains rich mines of fine gold.

SOFALA, the capital of the above kingdom, with a fort built by the Portuguese, which is of great importance for their trade to the East Indies. It is seated on a small island, near the mouth of the Cuama. Long. 35. 40. E. lat. 20. 22. S.

SOFIA, or SOPHIA, a city of European Turkey, capital of Bulgaria, and an archbishop's see. The trade is considerable, and the inhabitants are computed at 50,000, but the houses are meanly built. It is seated at the foot of the mountains of Argentaro, on the river Bogana; 160 miles W. N. W. of Adrianople. Long. 23. 52. E. lat. 43. 0. N.

SOFROY, a town of the kingdom of Fez, noted for a very handsome mosque. It is seated on a hill, at the foot of a mountain of the same name, part of Mount Atlas, and between two rivers; 12 miles E. of Fez.

SOGNO, a town of Africa, capital of a province of the same name, in the kingdom of Congo. The inhabitants are said to be Christians, converted by the Portuguese, and the Capuchins have a church here. It is seated on the Zaire, near its mouth; 160 miles W. S. W. of St. Salvador. Long. 11. 55. E. lat. 6. 0. S.

SOHAGEPOUR, a town of Hindostan, capital of a district in the province of Allahabad; 130 miles S. of Allahabad. Long. 81. 52. E. lat. 23. 30. N.

SOHAM, a town in Cambridgeshire, with a market on Saturday, seated on a fen of the same name, near Soham-mere, which takes up 1000 acres of land; 5 miles S. E. of Ely, and 70 N. by E. of London.

SOHO, a village in Staffordshire, 2 miles N. W. of Birmingham. It was founded by Mr. Boulton, for the manufacture of every article common to the Birmingham trade, the plated ware usually made at Sheffield, and of elegant pieces of silver, both light and massive. Here are also made the improved steam-engines now adopted in numerous concerns throughout the kingdom. In 1797 an apparatus for the coinage of copper was employed here by government, and the Bank of England dollars were also stamped at this mint.

SOIGNIES, a town of Belgium, in Hainault, near a forest of its name, on the river Senne; 8 miles N. N. E. of Mons. Pop. 4700.

SOISSONNOIS, a territory of France, in the Isle of France, which, with that of Vermandois, now forms the department of Aisne. It abounds in corn, wood, and pastures.

SOISSONS, a city of France, in the department of Aisne, anciently the capital of a kingdom of its name. It is a bishop's see; and the cathedral has one of the most considerable chapters in the kingdom. Here St. Louis, Philip the Bold, and Louis XIV. were crowned. The castle, though ancient, is not that in which the kings of the first race resided. The inhabitants carry on manufactures of coarse linen, stockings, thread, leather, ropes, &c., and some trade in corn. Soissons was repeatedly taken and retaken by the allied and French armies in 1814, when the town sustained considerable injury. It is seated in a fertile valley, on the river Aisne; 30 miles W. by N. of Rheims, and 60 N. E. of Paris. Pop. 7500. Long. 3. 19. E. lat. 49. 23. N.

SOLANTO, a town of Sicily, in Val di Mazara, which gives name to a cape and bay on the N. coast; 10 miles E. of Palermo.

SOLDIN, a town of Prussia, in the New Mark of Brandenburg, of which it was formerly the capital. It has cloth and woollen manufactures, and a trade in hops. It stands on a lake of the same name; 26 miles N. by E. of Custrin. Long. 15. 7. E. lat. 53. 2. N.

SOLENOF, a salt-water lake of Independent Tartary; 80 miles long, and 20 broad, lying midway between the Caspian Sea and Lake Aral.

SOLEURE, or SOLOTHURN, a canton of Switzerland, which stretches partly through the plain and partly along the chains of the Jura; 36 miles in length, and 25 in breadth. Pop. 50,000. The soil, for the most part, is fertile in corn; and the districts within the Jura abound in excellent pastures. In the mountainous parts are iron, lead, alabaster, marble, and coal. The inhabitants are nearly all Roman Catholics.

SOLEURE, the capital of the above canton, is surrounded by regular fortifications. The church of St. Urs is a noble edifice of a whitish-grey stone, which is a species of rude marble drawn from the neighbouring quarries. The arsenal and the town-house which has two towers, make a good appearance. Soleure stands in a delightful plain on the river Aar; 18 miles N. of Bern, and 30 S. S. W. of Basel. Pop. 4200. Long. 7. 30. E. lat. 47. 9. N.

SOLFATARA, or LAGO DI BAGNI, a lake of Italy, in Campagna di Roma, near Tivoli, formerly called Lacus Albulus. In this lake are several floating islands, formed of matted serge and herbage, with a soil of dust and sand blown from the adjacent ground, and glued together by the bitumen and sulphur with which its waters are impregnated. Some of these islands are 15 yards long, and will bear five or six people, who, by means of a pole, may move to different parts of the lake. From this lake issues a whitish stream, which emits vapour of a sulphureous smell, till it reaches the Teverone. The water of this rivulet has a petrifying quality, which increases in strength the further it has flowed from the lake. Fish are found in the Teverone, both above and below Tivoli, till it receives this lake; after which, during the rest of its course to the Tiber, there are none.

SOLFATARA, a mountain of Naples, in Terra di Lavoro, surrounded by other mountains, in the form of an amphitheatre. It has a kind of cavity, above a mile in diameter, which was no doubt the crater of a volcano now extinct. The earth here is warm and white, and, if opened to some depth, is insupportable from the heat and exhalations. The ground is almost every where hollow, and is supposed to have a subterraneous communication with Mount Vesuvius. Here are manufactures of sulphur, vitriol, and alum.

SOLIMAN, a seaport of Africa, in Tunis; 20 miles E. S. E. of Tunis.

SOLINGEN, a town of Prussian Westphalia, in the county of Berg, with manufactures of cutlery and all kinds of iron-work, seated near the Wipper; 15 miles E. S. E. of Dusseldorf.

SOLKAMSK, a town of Russia, in the government of Perm; famous for its salt-pits and good horses, seated on the Ussolka, which flows into the Kama; 430 miles N. E. of Kasan Long. 57. 26. E. lat. 59. 16. N.

SOLLAPOUR, a town of Hindostan, in Visiapour, capital of a district celebrated for mines of diamonds. It is seated near the Kistna; 130 miles S.E. of Visiapour. Long. 77. 10. E. lat. 16. 23. N.

SOLMS, or SALMS, a county of Germany, in Wetteravia, formerly a principality, but deprived of that rank in 1815. It is subject in part to Hesse-Darmstadt, and in part to Prussia. The decayed castle of Solms, the seat of the ancient counts, is seated on a hill, one mile E. of Braunfels, the present capital.

SOLOMON ISLANDS. *See* DANGER, ISLES OF.

SOLOR, an island of the East Indies; 70 miles in circuit, to the S. of Celebes, and W. of Flores. Long. 123. 53. E. lat. 9. 0. S.

SOLRE LE CHATEAU, a town of France, department of Nord; 7 miles S. E. of Maubeuge.

SOLSERINA, a town of Italy, in the province of Mantua; 17 miles N. W. of Mantua.

SOLSONA, a town of Spain, in Catalonia, and a bishop's see; seated at the foot of a mountain; 51 miles N. N. W. of Barcelona. Pop. 3000.

SOLTAU, a town of Hanover, on the river Bohme; 28 miles N. N. W. of Zell.

SOLTCAMP, a town of the Netherlands, in Groningen, with a large fort, at the mouth of the river Hunse, which is called Groningen Deep; 17 miles N. W. of Groningen.

SOLWAY FRITH, an arm of the sea, between Cumberland in England, and Dumfries-shire and Kirkcudbrightshire in Scotland. It is navigable for vessels of 100 tons, within 6 miles of its extremity; and the fisheries, especially of salmon, are very considerable. At its head on the Cumberland side, near the river Esk, is Solway Moss. This was a level tract, about 2 miles long, and 1 broad; but in 1771, being swollen by rains, it burst out at the eastern extremity, and spread over a neighbouring valley; by this means the surface of the moss was reduced 24 feet, and sunk into its present hollow form.

SOMBRERE, one of the Nicobar Islands, in the Indian Ocean; 30 miles N. of Nicobar. It gives name to a channel nearly in the middle of those islands.

SOMBRERO, a cluster of uninhabited islands in the West Indies, belonging to the English. The most remarkable of them is a league long, and consists of an eminence, to which the Spanish discoverers, finding some resemblance to a hat, gave the name of *Sombrero*. It is 80 miles N. W. of St. Christopher. Long. 63. 37. W. lat. 18. 38. N.

SOMERSET, a county of Maryland; to the E. of Chesapeake. Pop. 19,508. Chief town, Princess Anne.

SOMERSET, a town of Pennsylvania, chief of a county of its name, situate on the S. road from Pittsburg to Bedford, upon the Conemaugh river; 35 miles W. of Bedford. Pop. 649.

SOMERSET, a town of Massachusets, in Bristol county, seated on Taunton River; 50 miles S. by W. of Boston.

SOMERSET, a town of New Jersey, chief of a county of its name, seated on Millstone River; 23 miles N. of Trenton.

SOMERSETSHIRE, a county of England 65 miles long, and 45 broad; bounded on the N. W. by the Bristol Channel, N. by Gloucestershire, E. by Wiltshire, S. E. by Dorsetshire, and S. W. by Devonshire. It contains 1,050,880 acres; is divided into 40 hundreds and 480 parishes; has two cities, five boroughs, and 27 other market towns, and sends 4 members to parliament, for the eastern and western divisions of the county. The soil in the N. E. quarter is in general stony, and possesses a lofty mineral tract, called Mendip Hills. Towards the centre, where its principal rivers unite, were formerly fens and marshy moors of vast extent, a large portion of which has been divided, drained, and brought under cultivation. On the W. side are the Quantock Hills, with many downs and open heaths; and in the N. W. corner is the sterile region of Exmoor. The S. part, towards Dorsetshire, is high, but well cultivated; and throughout the county, especially in its S. W. quarter, are vales of the greatest fertility. The principal rivers are the Parret, Ivel, Thone, Brue, and Avon. Cattle, nearly equal in size to the Lincolnshire, are fed in fine meadows, about the head of the Parret. The cider of this county is a purer and stronger liquor than that of Herefordshire. It is the universal beverage of the working classes, and the consumption of it within the county is very considerable; some is also sent to distant parts. The chief manufactures are those of woollen, coarse linen, stockings, &c. Ilchester is usually considered the county town, from its having a goal and county court, and the elections being held there; but the assizes are held in the spring at Taunton, and in the summer alternately at Wells and Bridgewater.

SOMERTON, a town in Somersetshire, with a market on Tuesday. It was formerly a considerable place, and gave name to the county; some of the ruins of its ancient castle now form a part of the Bear Inn. Between this town and Bridgewater is a tract of land, called Sedgmoor, memorable for the defeat of the duke of Monmouth in 1685; 13 miles S. of Wells. and 123 W. by S. of London.

SOMMA, a town of Naples, in Terra di Lavoro, with a castle. The vicinity annually produces above 7000 pounds of silk of the best quality. It is seated at the foot of Mount Vesuvius; 10 miles E. of Naples.

SOMME, a department of France, including part of the ancient province of Picardy. Its extent is 2380 square miles; its population 495,000, nearly all Catholics. It takes its name from a river which rises in the department of Aisne, flows by St. Quentin, Peronne, Amiens, Abbeville, and St. Valery, and enters the English Channel. Amiens is the capital.

SOMMELSDYCK, a town of the Netherlands, in South Holland; chief place of the island of Overflakkee. It is situate 5 miles E. S. E. of Helvoetsluys.

SOMMERFELD, a town of Prussia, in Lusatia, with manufactures of fine cloths, seated on the Lupa; 15 miles S. S. W. of Crossen.

SOMMERGHEM, a town of Belgium, in the province of East Flanders, with a manufacture of lace; 8 miles N. W. of Ghent. Pop. 6400.

SOMMIERES, a town of France, in the department of Gard, with a manufacture of thick serges, seated on the Vidourle; 14 miles W. by S. of Nismes. Pop. 3400.

SOMORROSTRO, a town of Spain, on the coast of Biscay, with a famous iron-mine; 14 miles N. W. of Bilboa.

SONCINO, a town of Austrian Italy, in the Cremonese; 20 miles N. by W. of Cremona. Pop. 4000.

SONDERBORG, a seaport of Denmark, in the island of Alsen, with one of the best harbours in Denmark, and a royal palace, in which Christian II. was confined as a prisoner for 13 years. It is 16 miles E. N. E. of Flendsburg. Pop. 2700. Long. 9. 49. E. lat. 54. 57. N.

SONDERSHAUSEN, a town of Germany, capital of the lower county of Schwartzburg, with a fine castle on a mountain. It is situate on the Wipper; 24 miles N. of Erfurt.

SONDRIO, a town of Switzerland, capital of a district in the Valteline. It stands in a romantic situation, at the extremity of a narrow valley, and occupies both sides of the Malenco, a furious torrent, which runs into the Adda; 10 miles N. E. of Morbegno, and 14 S. W. of Tirano.

SONEPOUR, a town of Hindostan in Orissa, seated on the Mahanudda; 45 miles S. of Sumbulpour.

SONG-KIANG, a city of China, of the first rank, in the province of Kiang-nan. It has a large trade in cotton cloth, which is sent to different parts of the empire. It is situate amid several canals near the sea; 500 miles S. of Peking. Long. 120. 45. E. lat. 31. 0. N.

SONNEBERG, a town of Germany, in Saxe-Meiningen, with a great trade in looking-glasses, nails, whet-stones, &c.; 11 miles N. N. E. of Coburg.

SONNEBERG, or SONNENBURG, a town of Prussia, in the New Mark of Brandenburg, with a castle. It stands on the Lenze, 9 miles E. of Custrin.

SONNEWALD, a town of Prussia, in Lusatia, on the river Dober. It is situate 12 miles S. W. of Luckau.

SONORA, a province of Mexico, on the E. side of the Gulf of California. It comprises an area of 19,143 square leagues, with about 123,000 inhabitants, and is divided into the districts of Sonora, Sinoloa, and Ostimury. Rich mines of gold were discovered by the Spaniards in 1771, in an expedition against some tribes of Indians. Arispe is the capital.

SOOLOO, a chain of islands in the Eastern Indian Ocean, lying S. W. of Mindanao, almost midway between that island and Borneo. They are said to be 60 in number, and are named from the principal island, which is 36 miles long, and 12 broad, and contains about 60,000 inhabitants, who are Mahomedans. It is governed by a sultan, but the legislative power resides in an assembly composed of the sultan and 15 nobles, the former having two votes. The situation of Sooloo renders it a great mart, particularly for pearls, sago, and edible birds'-nests. The chief town is Bewar, on the N. W. part of the island, where the English East India Company have a resident. Long. 121. 15. E. lat. 5. 57. N.

SOONDA, or SUDHA, a town of Hindostan, in Canara, capital of a district of its name. It was formerly an extensive and populous place. The space within the inner wall was 3 miles square, and fully occupied by houses. When Hyder took possession there still remained 10,000 houses, but the subsequent wars have reduced them under 100. It is seated above the Gauts, on the Gangawali; 60 miles N. by W. of Nagara, and 75 N. by S. of Kundapura.

SOPHIA. *See* SOFIA.

SOPHIANIA, a town of Persia, in Aderbeitzan; seated in a valley, 25 miles N. W. of Tauris.

SOPHIENBERG, a town of Denmark, in Zealand, with a royal palace, near the coast of the Sound, 13 miles N. of Copenhagen.

SORA, a town of Naples, in Terra di Lavoro. with a castle, seated on the Garigliano, 46 miles E. by S. of Rome. Pop. 7200. Long. 14. 4. E. lat. 41. 54. N.

SORAU, a town of Prussian Silesia, 21 miles E. of Ratibor.

SORAU, a town of Prussia, in Lusatia, with manufactures of cloth, and a trade in yarn and linen; 8 miles W. of Sagau.

SORBON, or SORBONNE, a village of France, in the department of Ardennes, 6 miles N. of Rethel; famous for being the birthplace of Robert Sorbon, confessor to St. Louis, who founded the celebrated college at Paris called after his name.

SOREL, a river of Lower Canada, which issues from Lake Champlain, and flows N. to the St. Lawrence, which it enters at the town of William Henry.

SORENTO, a seaport of Naples, in Principato Citra, and an archbishop's see. It is the birthplace of Torquato Tasso, and stands on a peninsula in the Bay of Naples, at the foot of a mountain of its name; 17 miles S. by E. of Naples. Long. 14. 24. E. lat. 40. 36. N.

SORIA, a province of Spain, in Old Castile, bounded on the E. by Navarre and Arragon. Its extent is about 4300 square miles, its population 200,000. The breeding of sheep forms a principal object of attention, and there are a few manufactures of linen, woollen, paper, and leather.

SORIA, the capital of the foregoing province, stands on the site of the ancient Numantia; near the source of the Douro; 74 miles E. S. E. of Burgos. Long. 2. 18. W. lat. 41. 50. N.

SORIANO, a town of Naples, in Calabria Ultra; 17 miles E. N. E. of Nicotera. Pop. 3600.

SOROE, a town of Denmark, in the island of Zealand, with a royal college, endowed with the revenues of a once rich convent; 37 miles W. S. W. of Copenhagen.

SOSILA, a town of Hindostan, in Mysore, with a large fort; 25 miles S. E. of Seringapatam.

SOSPETTO, a town of the Sardinian states, in the county of Nice, with a trade in dried fruits, particularly figs, seated at the foot of three high mountains on the river Bevera; 13 miles N. E. of Nice. Pop. 3200.

SOUBICE, a town of France, in the department of Lower Charente; 23 miles W. N. W. of Saintes.

SOUDAK, a town of the Crimea, with the remains of an old fort on a mountain close by the shore. It was formerly a considerable seaport, and stands at the end of a valley, which produces the best grapes and wine in the whole peninsula; 26 miles S. W. of Caffa.

SOUDAN. *See* NEGROLAND.

SOUILLAC, a town of France, in the department of Lot; seated on the Borese, 32 miles N. of Cahors.

SOUND, a strait between Sweden and Denmark, through which ships usually sail from the Categat into the Baltic. It is about 4 miles broad, and the Danes take a toll of all merchant ships that pass through the channel. *See* ELSINORE.

SOUR, in Syria. *See* SUR.

SOUR, a river of the Netherlands, which flows from N. to S. through Luxemburg, and enters the Moselle, a little above Treves.

SOURABAYA, a town of Java, capital of a district of the same name, on the N. E. coast. It is situate within the narrow strait formed by the islands of Java and Madura, and is defended by batteries. The houses are good, and some are elegant, particularly the country seats of private individuals. There is a fine arsenal, with other extensive works, calculated for equipments on a very large scale. Vessels also, with their various appointments, are built and equipped at Sourabaya. The French, when in possession of the island of Java, intended to have erected Sourabaya into a port of consequence; large sums were expended in the construction of works for the defence of the harbour, and General Daendols was proceeding in his plans, when the island was taken by the British. It is seated on a river which separates the European part of the town from the Chinese and the native quarter. Pop. 24,574. Long. 112. 55. E. lat. 7. 14. S.

SOURI, a town of Persia, in Laristan, situate on the Persian gulf; 115 miles S. W. of Ormus. Long. 55. 30. E. lat. 26. 18. N.

SOUSA. *See* SUSA.

SOU-TCHEOU, a city of China of the first rank, in the province of Kiang-nan. It is so intersected by canals of fresh water, that Europeans compare it to Venice. The country round it is almost unequalled in point of fertility; in consequence of which the Chinese call this city the paradise of the world. The brocades and embroideries made here are esteemed throughout the whole empire. The population is prodigious, and the commercial intercourse with strangers so great, that the trade of all the provinces might be supposed to centre here. It is seated on the Grand Canal, and on a river which communicates with the lake Tai; 560 miles S. by E. of Peking. Long. 120. 0. E. lat. 31. 22. N.

SOUTERRAINE, a town of France, in the department of Creuse; 24 miles N. of Limoges.

SOUTH SEA. *See* PACIFIC OCEAN.

SOUTHAM, a town in Warwickshire, with a market on Monday. Most of the houses are old and meanly built, but the church is a handsome edifice, with a lofty spire. The only other place of worship is a Baptist chapel. Charles I. slept in this town the night before the battle of Edge Hill. It is situate on a branch of the river Watergall, 10 miles S. of Coventry, and 82 N. W. of London.

SOUTHAMPTON, a borough and county of itself, and the county town of Hampshire; governed by a mayor, with markets on Tuesday, Thursday, and Saturday. It sends two members to parliament. It stands between the Itchen and Test, which here flow into an inlet of the sea, called Trissanton Bay, or Southampton Water. The inlet is navigable almost to the head, for vessels of considerable burden, and the two rivers admit small craft some way up the country. Extensive docks are constructing in connexion with the South Western railway from London, and which will probably render Southampton a point of great commerce. It contains five churches, several meeting-houses for dissenters, free grammar, national, and Lancasterian schools, Sunday schools, almshouses for 18 poor widows, an asylum for the orphans of soldiers, &c. Southampton is a fashionable place of resort for sea-bathing, and has manufactures of silks and carpets. Three miles S. E. are the picturesque remains of Netley Abbey. Southampton is the birthplace of the celebrated Dr. Isaac Watts. A mail-packet sails from this place every morning at seven, for Cowes in the Isle of Wight. It is 12 miles S. by W. of Winchester, and 74 W. S. W. of London. Long. 1. 24. W. lat. 50. 54. N.

SOUTHAMPTON, a town of New York, in Suffolk county, on the S. side of Long Island; 75 miles E. of New York. Pop. 6205.

SOUTHBURY, a town of Connecticut, in New Haven county; 21 miles N. W. of New Haven.

SOUTHEND, a village in Essex, at the mouth of the Thames, nearly opposite Sheerness; much resorted to for sea-bathing, and containing handsome accommodation for the company. It is 44 miles E. of London.

SOUTHFLEET, a village in Kent, 3 miles S. W. of Gravesend. Some stone coffins, urns, &c. have been dug up here since the commencement of the present century, which evince it to have been a Roman station; probably the Vagniaca of Antoninus.

SOUTHOLD, a town of New York, in Suffolk county, on the N. side of an inland bay at the E. end of Long Island; 100 miles E N. E. of New York.

SOUTHWARK, a borough in Surrey, sending two members to parliament; which may be considered as part of the metropolis, being seated on the opposite side of the Thames, and under the jurisdiction of the corporation of London. It is called the Borough, by way of distinction, and contains six parish churches, several chapels of ease, a Roman Catholic chapel, and many places of worship for dissenters, amongst which is that called Surrey Chapel, capable of containing 5000 persons. Here are several charitable foundations, particularly the hospitals of St. Thomas and Guy; also the Queen's Bench and Marshalsea prisons, a county gaol, &c. *See* LONDON.

SOUTHWELL, a town in Nottinghamshire, with a market on Saturday. It is an ancient place, enjoying several privileges different from the county, and has a collegiate church. Here are the ruins of a grand palace, demolished in the civil wars of the 17th century. The principal trade is in malt and hops. The town is seated on a gentle eminence, on the small river Greet, and in the midst of an amphitheatre of hills, which are fertile, well-wooded, and picturesque. It is 13 miles N. E. of Nottingham, and 132 N. N. W. of London.

SOUTHWOLD, a seaport in Suffolk, with a market on Thursday. It is seated on a cliff, near a fine bay, with a harbour to the S., and the river Blythe and a drawbridge on the W., so that it is almost surrounded by water, especially at every high tide. Here a much esteemed salt is made, and it has also a trade in corn, beer, and herrings. It is sometimes called Sowle, or Sole, and its bay is named Solebay. In this bay was the great sea-fight in 1672, between the Dutch admiral, De Ruyter, and James, duke of York, in which the victory was undecided. It is 26 miles S. of Yarmouth, and 105 S. E. of London. Long. 1. 54. W. lat. 52. 24. N.

SOUTO MAJOR, town of Portugal in Beira; 14 miles N. W. of Pinhel.

SOUVIGNY, a town of France, in the department of Allier; seated on the river Quesne; 10 miles W. by S. of Moulins.

SOVANO, a town of Italy, in the grand duchy of Tuscany; 45 miles N. N. W. of Rome.

SOW, a river in Staffordshire, which rises in the W. part of the county, flows by Eccleshall to Stafford, below which it receives the Peak, and soon afterwards joins the Trent.—Also, a river in Warwickshire, which runs into the Avon near Stoneleigh Abbey.

SOW AND PIGS, large rocks on the coast of Massachusets, lying off the S. W. end of Catahunk Island.

SPA, a town of Belgium, in the province of Liege; famous for its mineral waters. That called the Old Spa consists of miserable cottages, and is properly nothing but the suburb to the other. The houses of the New Spa are mostly of wood and plaster; but the more modern ones are of brick and stone. The church of the Capuchins, and the parish church, are both seated upon eminences. The names of the five principal wells are Pouhon, Geronferd, Saviniere, Watpotz, and Tunnelet. The inhabitants are employed in making toys for strangers. Spa was taken by the French in

1794, and afterwards annexed to France; but in 1814 they delivered it up to the allies. It is seated in a valley surrounded by mountains; 17 miles S. E. of Liege.

Spain, a kingdom of Europe, 700 miles long, and 500 broad; bounded on the N. by the Bay of Biscay, N. E. by the Pyrenees, which separate it from France, E. and S. by the Mediterranean, S. W. by the Atlantic, and W. by Portugal and the Atlantic; with an area of 176,372 square miles, and a population of 13,000,000. It contains the provinces of Old and New Castile, Andalusia, Arragon, Estremadura, Galicia, Leon, Catalonia, Granada, Valencia, Biscay, Asturias, Murcia, and Navarre, some of which have been separate kingdoms, and still retain the title. The air is dry and serene, except during the equinoctial rains; but excessively hot in the southern provinces in June, July, and August. The vast mountains, however, that run through Spain, are beneficial to the inhabitants by the refreshing breezes that come from them in the S. parts; though those in the N. and the N. E. are in the winter very cold. The soil is very fertile, but there are large tracts of uncultivated ground; and the superior attention paid to the large flocks of sheep greatly impedes the progress of agriculture. The produce of the country consists in wheat, barley, saffron, honey, silk, salt, saltpetre, hemp, barilla, and even sugar-canes, with the richest and most delicious fruits that are to be found in France and Italy; and its wines are in high esteem. Wolves are the chief beasts of prey that infest Spain. The wild bulls have so much ferocity, that bull-fights were the most magnificent spectacle the court of Spain could exhibit. The domestic animals are horses, (which are remarkably swift,) mules, asses, beeves, and sheep. Spain abounds in minerals and metals. Carnelian, agate, jacinth, loadstone, torquois stones, quicksilver, iron, copper, lead, sulphur, gypsum, calamine, crystal, marbles of several kinds, porphyry, the finest jasper, and even diamonds, emeralds, and amethysts are found here. Anciently it was celebrated for gold and silver mines; but since the discovery of America no attention has been paid to them. The principal rivers are the Douro, Tagus, Guadiana, Guadalquiver, and Ebro. Spain, formerly the most populous kingdom in Europe, is now very thinly inhabited; to which various causes have contributed, as the expulsion of the Moors, the emigration to the colonies, the vast numbers and celibacy of the clergy, the indolence of the natives, and the late desolating war. Here are some considerable manufactures, especially of silk and woollen, but these are far short of that flourishing condition which they might attain, being checked by the royal monopolies, which extend to broad cloth, china, glass, pottery, paper, saltpetre, salt, sulphur, tobacco, and some others. The Spaniards in general are tall, their complexion swarthy, their countenances expressive. The beauty of the ladies reigns chiefly in their novels and romances: in their persons they are small and slender. Jealousy is no longer the characteristic of a Spanish husband: the married ladies have here their cortejo, or male attendant, in the same manner as the Italians have their cicisbeo. The established religion is popery; and that execrable tribunal the Inquisition has reigned here in all its horrors, but has been abolished. There are 8 archbishoprics, 46 episcopal sees, and 24 universities, or rather academies. The Spanish language springs from the Roman, but many of the words are derived from the Arabic used by the Moors, who for seven centuries held dominion in the country: their speech is grave, sonorous, and very melodious. In 1808 Spain excited the interest of all Europe by the rapid and extraordinary revolution which it underwent, in consequence of the domineering influence and intrigues of the court of France. The king of Spain, as the ally of the French emperor, in the war with Great Britain, was required, in the beginning of 1807, to furnish a body of troops to assist in the campaign then going on against Russia and Prussia. For that purpose the flower of the Spanish army was placed at the disposal of France, and marched to the N. of Germany, to take possession of the newly acquired territories of that power. However, the war being soon after terminated by the peace of Tilsit, these troops were still detained in garrison at a great distance from their country; and the views of the French emperor towards Spain and Portugal began now to develope themselves. Towards the close of this year, he prevailed on the court of Spain to acquiesce in his projects against the House of Braganza, and to allow a free passage for his troops through Spain, to take possession of Portugal. A large force, therefore, entered Spain on the 18th of October, to proceed to that country. In the meantime, the agents of France were not idle at Madrid; and, in the beginning of 1808, that city was thrown into the greatest confusion, in consequence of the prince of Asturias assuming the sovereignty, by the title of Ferdinand VII., and Charles IV. his father treating it as an act of rebellion. But as the prince was very popular, and had a numerous party to support his pretensions, the French ambassador urged both parties to refer their disputes to the mediation of Napoleon. While this was going forward, the French armies kept pouring into Spain; and on the 23rd of March they entered Madrid, under Prince Murat. The French having thus obtained possession of Portugal, and a great part of Spain, succeeded in persuading the royal family to repair to Bayonne, to lay their case personally before the emperor: but they had not been there many days before they were compelled to sign a renunciation of the crown of Spain in favour of Bonaparte. On the 13th of May they were sent into the interior of France, to the places assigned them by the French government, as their future residence; and the throne of Spain was transferred to Joseph Bonaparte, the brother of Napoleon. The French emperor having now the royal family in his power, and a formidable army in the heart of the country, thought he had acquired quiet possession of this vast peninsula: but in this he soon found himself deceived; for the storm, which had been long gathering, was about to burst forth in all its fury. The Spaniards could not but view with a jealous eye the entry of so many foreign troops into their country, without any reasonable cause having been assigned; and no sooner did they hear of the captivity of their monarch, and the appointment of a new one, than their indignation was roused to the highest pitch. All Spain rose, as if by one consent, on their invaders, Madrid setting the example, notwithstanding the presence of the enemy. A Supreme Junta of Government was established by the people at Seville, who formally declared war against France, in the name of Ferdinand VII. The military force, being small, was augmented by new levies; and their arms were successful, at the commencement, in several instances, particularly on the 20th of July, when General Dupont surrendered with nearly 20,000 men to the Spanish general Castanos. The new government lost no time in seeking the aid of Great Britain, who generously sent them both arms and money. The British likewise sent an army into Portugal, which, by the decisive battle of Vimiera, cleared that country entirely of the French forces under Junot. After these successes, the French army in Spain were under the necessity of retreating towards the Ebro, where they acted on the defensive for some time; and the Spaniards entered Madrid in triumph. About this time also 10,000 Spanish troops, who were in the N. of Germany, effected their escape on board a British fleet, which conveyed them to Corunna, whence they proceeded to join their countrymen in arms. Bonaparte, perceiving that his affairs were in a bad state in the peninsula, drew a large portion of his forces from Germany and Italy, at the head of which he put himself on the 3rd of November; and such was his progress, that, after defeating and dispersing the Spanish armies of Generals Blake and Castanos, he pushed on to Madrid, without further opposition, and entered it on the 4th of December following. The British general Moore also, who had been sent from Portugal with an army to assist the Spaniards, was forced to make a precipitate retreat to Corunna, and the army compelled to embark, after sustaining a severe action with the enemy, in which their brave commander was killed. In all probability Spain must now have fallen beneath the power of Napoleon, had not his attention been drawn off by the war with Austria. The French emperor, in consequence, quitted Spain in order to conduct the war in person against that power; and in the meantime exertions were made by the Spanish and British governments to make head against the enemy. The British sent another army into the peninsula, who distinguished themselves in the hard-fought battle of Talavera, on the 27th of July, 1809; but from the exhausted state of the country, and a want of energy in the Spanish government, affairs continued in a languishing state till 1810, when, the war being closed with Austria, the French began to collect a formidable army on the frontiers of Portugal, under the command of Marshal Massena, for the avowed purpose of driving the British army out of that kingdom. But finding it hopeless to attack them in the formidable position which Lord Wellington had chosen, and being unable to furnish subsistence for his army any longer, from the wretched state of the country, Massena at length commenced a retreat, on the 5th of March, 1811, followed by the British and Portuguese army. From this time it may be said that the British nation, from auxiliaries, became principals in the war, as the Spanish forces, notwithstanding their numbers, were by no means able to stand against the superior discipline of their adversaries. The government now underwent several changes, in the last of which the cortes were assembled, and proceeded to form a new constitution, by which the executive government was placed in the hands of a regency; the Inquisition was abolished; the liberty of the press established, and several excellent laws, tending to meliorate the condition of the people, were recognized. In 1812 the British army once more ventured to pursue active operations in Spain; and the glorious victory of Salamanca, on the 22nd of July, was followed by the most important advantages. Cadiz, which had been besieged by the French for more than two years, was abandoned, and Joseph Bonaparte expelled from Madrid. But, towards the close of this campaign, the allied army was again compelled to retire into Portugal, through the negligence of the Spanish general Ballasteros, and the failure of the attack on the castle of Burgos. In the following year the British general opened the campaign with a most formidable army, consisting of British, Portuguese, and Spaniards, and amounting to nearly 120,000 men. The progress of the allied army was unusually rapid, and on the 21st of June they defeated the enemy's army, of about 70,000 men, in the vicinity of Vittoria, which was followed by the loss of all their artillery, baggage, &c. This battle decided the fate of Spain; and Bonaparte, finding his armies driven from the country, and the war carried into France, thought proper to release Ferdinand, and send him back to his dominions. The war, nevertheless, continued; and the allied army, under their illustrious commander, gained immortal fame in the battles of the Pyrenees, and those of Orphies and Toulouse. After the capture of Toulouse, on the 12th of April, 1814, their victorious arms were arrested by news being brought them of the capture of Paris, and the consequent conclusion of the war. Ferdinand arrived at Madrid on the 14th of May; but the first acts of his government were to revive the Inquisition, with all the other abuses against which the new constitution had provided, and banish and imprison those men who, to the best of their power, had contributed to his re-establishment.

The dissatisfaction and indignation which this conduct excited, produced in 1820–21 a revolution, by which the constitution of the cortes, as established in 1812, was restored. Madrid is the capital.

SPAIN, NEW. *See* MEXICO.

SPAITLA, a town of Barbary, in the kingdom of Tunis; near which are extensive and magnificent ruins. It is situate on a rising ground, shaded all over with juniper-trees; 90 miles S. W. of Tunis, and 100 S. S. E. of Bona. Long. 9. 15. E. lat. 35. 40. N.

SPALATRO, or SPALATTO, a strong seaport of Austrian Dalmatia; and an archbishop's see. The harbour is large and deep, and well frequented. Without the walls is a sulphureous spring, of great benefit in chronical diseases. Here are the ruins of the palace of Diocletian, and of a magnificent aqueduct. In 1784 Spalatro was nearly depopulated by the plague. It is seated on a peninsula, in the Gulf of Venice; 70 miles S. of Zara, and 102 N. W. of Ragusa. Pop. about 7500. Long. 17. 31. E. lat. 44. 4. N.

SPALDING, a town in Lincolnshire, with a market on Tuesday. It is seated on the Welland, and from its neatness, and the canals in its streets, resembles a Dutch town. The church is a large and neat structure of the 13th century, and here are six meeting-houses, two grammar-schools, a charity-school, and two alms-houses. A new house of correction was erected here in 1824. The inhabitants are not employed in manufactures, but derive their chief support from agriculture, and the extensive grazing carried on in the neighbourhood. Much hemp and flax is grown in the vicinity, and there is a good carrying trade in corn and coal. It is 14 miles S. by W. of Boston, and 96 N. of London.

SPALT, a town and castle of Bavarian Franconia, in the district of Anspach. The vicinity produces excellent hops. It is seated on the Retzat; 16 miles E. S. E. of Anspach.

SPANDAU, a town of Prussia, in the Middle Mark of Brandenburg; with a fine fortress. The arsenal is in subterranean vaults, and there is a prison for state criminals. Bayonets, ramrods, sword-blades, and sabres, are made here; also musket-barrels, which are sent hence to Potsdam to be finished. It is seated on the Havel, opposite the influx of the Spree; 8 miles W. N. W. of Berlin, and 12 N. E. of Potsdam. Pop. 5000.

SPANGENBERG, a town and castle of Germany, in Hesse-Cassel; seated on a mountain; 28 miles S. E. of Cassel.

SPANISHTOWN, or JAGO DE LA VEGA, a town of Jamaica, where the legislative assembly and the grand courts of justice are held. It is seated in a pleasant valley, on the river Cobre; 16 miles W. N. W. of Kingston. Pop. 5000.

SPARTEL, CAPE, a promontory on the coast of Barbary; at the entrance of the Strait of Gibraltar. Long. 5. 56. W. lat. 35. 50. N.

SPARTIVENTO, CAPE, a promontory of Naples, at the S. E. extremity of Calabria Ultra. Long. 16. 40. E. lat. 37. 50. N.

SPEIGHTS TOWN, a seaport of Barbadoes, formerly much frequented by the Bristol traders, and thence called Little Bristol. It is situate on the N. W. coast of the island, and defended by two forts. Long. 58. 31. W. lat. 13. 15. N.

SPELLO, a town of Italy, in the duchy of Spoleto. Here are the ruins of a theatre, and other remains of antiquity. It is seated on a hill; 13 miles N. of Spoleto.

SPEY, a rapid river of Scotland, which issues from a small lake in the centre of Inverness-shire, flows N. E. into Murrayshire, then divides that county from Banffshire for more than 20 miles, and enters the German Ocean at Garmouth.

SPEZZIA, or SPECIA, a town of the Sardinian states, in the territory of Genoa; with a good harbour. It is seated at the foot of a hill, on a gulf of the same name; 47 miles S. E. of Genoa. Pop. 4000. Long. 9. 37. E. lat. 44. 10. N.

SPEZZIA, an island of Greece, 6 miles long, and 2 broad. It has a town of the same name, containing 3000 inhabitants. It is situate about 20 miles from Napoli di Romania.

SPICE ISLANDS. *See* MOLUCCAS.

SPIELBERG, a town of Germany, in the principality of Oettingen; 8 miles N. E. of Oettingen, and 13 S. S. E. of Anspach.

SPIETZ, a town of Switzerland, in the canton of Bern; seated on the W. side of the lake Thun; 40 miles S. S. E. of Bern.

SPIGELBURG, a town and castle of Hanover, capital of a county of the same name, lying within the principality of Calenberg; belonging as a fief to the king of the Netherlands. It is 12 miles E. by S. of Halem.

SPIGNO, a town of Sardinia, in the duchy of Montserrat; with a castle; seated on the Belbo; 11 miles S. S. W. of Acqui, and 40 S. E. of Turin.

SPILEMBERGO, a town of Austrian Italy, in Friuli; seated on the Tagliamento; 14 miles W. of Udina.

SPILSBY, a town in Lincolnshire, with a market on Monday. It has an ancient church, two meeting-houses, a small free-school, and a subscription library. Here is also a town-hall, in which the general quarter-sessions for the S. division of the ports of Lindsey have been held for upwards of 100 years. It is seated on the side of a hill, 31 miles E. of Lincoln, and 133 N. by E. of London.

SPINALONGA, a seaport of the island of Candia, with a good harbour and a citadel. It is situate near a cape of the same name; 30 miles E. of Candia. Long. 25. 48. E. lat. 35. 20. N.

SPIRE, a city of Bavaria, capital of the province of Rhine, and formerly of a bishopric of its name. In ancient times, the emperors held many diets at Spire, and it was the seat of the imperial chamber till 1689, when the city was burnt by the French; and it was not rebuilt till after the peace of Ryswick, in 1697. Most of the citizens are Lutherans; but there are 15 Catholic churches and convents, among which the college formerly belonging to the jesuits claims the first place. Spire was taken by the French in 1734; and in 1792 it surrendered to the republican troops of France, who evacuated it the next year, but re-entered it in 1794. In 1814 it was ceded to Bavaria. It is seated on the W. side of the Rhine, at the influx of the Spirebach; 54 miles S. by E. of Ments. Pop. 4000. Long. 8. 29. E. lat. 49. 19. N.

Spiritu Santo, a province of Brazil, between that of Porto Seguro and Rio Janeiro. The soil is fertile, and watered by a river of the same name, which flows into a large bay of the Atlantic. The capital, of the same name, has a castle, and its port is a small bay about 10 miles from the Ocean. Long. 41. 10. W. lat. 20. 10. S.

Spiritu Santo, a town of Cuba, near the middle of the island; 155 miles E. S. E. of Havanna. Long. 79. 37. E. lat. 22. 15. N.

Spital, a town of Austrian Illyria, in Carinthia; seated on the Liser, near the Drave; 15 miles W. N. W. of Villach.

Spithead, a famous road in the English Channel, between Portsmouth and the Isle of Wight, where the royal navy frequently rendezvous.

Spitzbergen, a group of dreary islands, lying between 9. and 20. E. long., and 76. 46. and 80. 30. N. lat.; having Greenland to the W. and Nova Zembla to the E. The Mainland, or principal island, is 300 miles in length. It was discovered in 1533, by Sir Hugh Willoughby, who called it Greenland, supposing it to be a part of the western continent. In 1595 it was visited by Barentz and Cornelius, two Dutchmen, who pretended to be the original discoverers, and called it Spitzbergen, or sharp mountains, from the many sharp-pointed and rocky mountains with which it abounds. The glaciers on the N. E. present a singular appearance, being high cliffs of an emerald colour, impendent over the sea, with cataracts of melted snow, and a background of black conic hills, streaked with white. In the winter it is continual night for four months. The animals are deer, bears, and foxes. To the N. E. of this group are small isles called the Seven Sisters, the most arctic land yet discovered.

Splugen, a town of Switzerland, in the Grisons; seated near the source of the Rhine; 16 miles N. W. of Chiavenna.

Spoleto, a duchy of Italy, in the Ecclesiastical States; 55 miles long, and 40 broad; bounded on the N. by Ancona and Urbino, E. by Naples, S. by Sabina, and W. by Orvieto and Perugino. It comprises the greatest part of the ancient Umbria, and contains 105,000 inhabitants.

Spoleto, the capital of the foregoing duchy, and a bishop's see. The houses are in general well built, but the only edifices that have any claim to distinction are the castle, which stands on a hill, and is connected with the town by a bridge, and the cathedral, which is certainly a fine structure. Spoleto suffered greatly from earthquakes in 1703 and 1767. Here are the ruins of an amphitheatre, a triumphal arch, and an aqueduct. It is seated in a country noted for good wine, near the river Tessino; 40 miles E. of Orvieto, and 60 N. by E. of Rome. Pop. 7000. Long. 13. 6. E. lat. 42. 45. N.

Sponheim, a town of Germany, and the capital of a county of its name. It is seated among hills, covered with vineyards; 27 miles W. by S. of Mentz. Long. 7. 38. E. lat. 49. 54. N.

Sporades, the ancient name of those islands of the Grecian Archipelago which are scattered irregularly along the shores of Europe and Asia, in contradistinction to the Cyclades, which are grouped circularly around Delos.

Spotsylvania, a county of Virginia, bounded N. by the Rappahannock, N. W. by Orange county, S. E. by Caroline county, and S. W. by the counties of Hanover and Louisiana. It contains 15,161 inhabitants, about one-half of whom are slaves.

Spree, a river which rises in the mountains of Bohemia, passes through Lusatia into Brandenburg, flows by Berlin, and joins the Havel, opposite Spandau.

Spremberg, a town of the Prussian states, in Lusatia; situate on an island formed by the river Spree; 14 miles S. by E. of Cotbus.

Springfield, a village in the parish of Gretna, Dumfries-shire, and is notorious as the scene of the inglorious marriage-trade of Gretna; 9 miles from Carlisle.

Springfield, a town of Massachusets, capital of Hampden county. It has a considerable inland trade, a woollen manufactory, a rope-walk, two paper-mills, two public libraries, a very extensive establishment for the manufacture of arms, &c. It stands on the Connecticut; 90 miles W. S. W. of Boston. Pop. 10,985.

Springfield, a town of Kentucky, in Bourbon county; situate on the Licking; 60 miles W. by N. of Frankfort.—There are several inconsiderable townships of this name in the United States.

Sprottau, a town of Prussian Silesia, in the principally of Glogau; on a river of the same name, at its confluence with the Bober; 20 miles W. S. W. of Glogau.

Spurn Head, a promontory on the S. E. coast of Yorkshire, at the mouth of the Humber, on which is a lighthouse. Long. 0. 15. E. lat. 53. 38. N.

Squillace, a town of Naples, in Calabria Ultra; which was much injured by the earthquake of 1783. It is seated on the Favolono, near a gulf of its name; 35 miles S. W. of St. Severino. Long. 16. 40. E. lat. 39. 3. N.

Stablo, a town of Belgium, in the province of Liege; with a celebrated Benedictine abbey. Here is a manufacture of leather, and a trade in cloths and stuffs. It is seated on the Rect; 12 miles S. of Limbourg.

Stabroek, a town in S. America, Dutch Guayana; on the river Demerara. It consists of 2 rows of houses, built wide apart; with canals. The public buildings are the government-house, town-house, custom-house, and colonial hospital. Pop. 8500.

Stade, a town of Hanover, in the duchy of Bremen, with a fortress, a college, and three churches. It is the seat of the regency and chief courts of justice of the duchies of Bremen and Verden, and has manufactures of lace, flannels, stockings, hats, and spirituous liquors. The foreign trade is chiefly confined to the transit business. It stands on the Swingel, near its confluence with the Elbe; 43 miles N. E. of Bremen. Pop. 4800. Long. 9. 28. E. lat. 55. 36. N.

Stadt-am-Hof, a town of Bavaria; on the N. side of the Danube, connected by a bridge with the city of Ratisbon.

Stadtberg, a town of Prussia, in the province of Westphalia; on the frontiers of the county of Waldeck. Part of it, called Marsberg, stands on the site of the famous Saxon fort of Elmesburg, which was taken by Charlemagne, who built a church here in honour of St. Peter and St. Paul. Stadtberg is situate on the Dumel; 16 miles S. of Paderborn.

Stadthagen, a strong town of Prussian Westphalia, in the principality of Schauenberg; with a palace, belonging to the prince of Schauenberg-Lippe, in the garden of which is a mineral spring. It is 8 miles E. of Minden.

Stafarda, a town of Sardinia, in Piedmont, with a rich abbey. In 1690 a victory was gained near this place by the French, over the duke of Savoy. It is seated on the Po; 3 miles N. of Saluzzo.

Staffa, a small island of Scotland, one of the Hebrides, on the W. side of that of Mull. It is the greatest natural curiosity in Europe, if not in the world. The whole S. W. end is supported by ranges of basaltic pillars, mostly above 50 feet high, and four feet in thickness. Here is also a magnificent cavern called Fin-macoul, or Fingal's Cave, which extends 250 feet in length. Its entrance is a natural arch, 53 feet wide and 117 high, from which the cavern is lighted, so that its furthest extremity may be seen. It is supported on each side by ranges of columns, and roofed by the fragments of others that have been broken off in forming it. The bottom of the cave is filled by the sea reaching to the extremity, and in very calm weather a boat may sail into it. This singular island is every where supported by basaltic rocks and pillars, and so much hollowed by various caves, that its whole surface is shaken in stormy weather.

Staffelstein, a town of Bavaria; situate on the Lauter; 16 miles N. N. E. of Bamberg.

Stafford, a borough, and the county town of Staffordshire, governed by a mayor; with a market on Saturday. It sends two members to parliament. A castle was built here by William the Conqueror, which was garrisoned by the troops of Charles I., and, being taken, was demolished by order of the parliament. It has two parish churches, one of which was formerly collegiate. The other places of worship are a Roman Catholic chapel, and meeting-houses for Independents, Quakers, Methodists, and Presbyterians. Here are also two national schools, a free grammar-school, several almshouses, a handsome infirmary, and a fine square market-place, in which is the shire-hall, and under it is the market-house. The principal trade consists in the manufacture of boots and shoes, which at one time was very considerable, but has greatly declined. Hats and cutlery are also manufactured here, and a considerable tanning business is carried on. It is seated on the river Sow; 144 miles N. W. of London. Long. 2. 4. W. lat. 52. 48. N.

Staffordshire, a county of England, 55 miles long, and 35 broad, bounded on the W. by Shropshire, N. W. by Cheshire, N. E. and E. by Derbyshire, S. E. by Warwickshire, and S. by Worcestershire. It contains 765,800 acres, is divided into five hundreds and 181 parishes, has one city and 19 market towns, and sends four members to parliament for the N. and S. divisions of the county. The principal rivers are the Trent, Dove, Sow, Churnet, Stour, Peak, and Manyfold. The soil in the S. part is good and rich, though not without heaths, which take up a large tract of ground: it abounds in coal and iron. The middle is level and plain, the N. hilly and barren, being full of heaths and moors. There are good stone quarries, plenty of alabaster, and limestone. Tin and brass are among the productions in Staffordshire, and there are several smelting and brass-works near the copper mines. Within the last half century material improvements have been introduced into the agriculture of this county; whilst on the rich lands bordering the Trent the dairy has become a source of considerable profit. The trade and manufactures have been greatly extended by the inland navigation, which connects this county, not only with the metropolis, but with the Severn, the Mersey, and the Humber, and the three corresponding ports of Bristol, Liverpool, and Hull. The iron-foundries, blast-furnaces, slitting-mills, and other branches of the iron trade, employ great numbers of people. The cotton manufactures are very considerable, and the silk trade is carried on to some extent. The S. parts of the county are distinguished for the manufactures of locks, buckles, steel toys, (particularly watch chains,) and a variety of plated, lacquered, japanned and enamelled goods. In the vicinity of Stourbridge the manufacture of glass is considerable. There are also manufactures of tobacco and snuff-boxes, shoes, hats, &c. But the chief manufacture of the county is that of earthenware, for which it has been long and deservedly celebrated, and which may now be ranked among the most important manufactures of the kingdom.

Stagira, a town of European Turkey, in Macedonia, celebrated for being the birthplace of Aristotle; whence he is called the Stagirite. It is now called Stavros. It is seated on the Gulf of Contessa; 16 miles W. N. W. of Contessa.

Stagno, a seaport of Austrian Dalmatia, and a bishop's see, seated on a peninsula, in the Gulf of Venice; 30 miles N. W. of Ragusa Long. 17. 50. E. lat. 43. 12. N.

Staines, a town in Middlesex, with a marke on Friday, seated on the Thames, over which i a new stone bridge. At some distance above the bridge, at Coln Ditch, is the London Mark Stone, which is the ancient boundary to the jurisdiction of the city of London on the Thames, and bears the date of 1280. The town has of late years been greatly improved. It has a spacious church, meeting-houses for Methodists, Baptists, and Quakers, and a Lancasterian school. It is 16 miles W. by S. of London.

STALBRIDGE, a town in Dorsetshire, with a market on Monday, and a considerable manufacture of stockings. Here is an ancient cross of one stone, 21 feet high, on a base of eight feet. It is seated near the Stour; 20 miles N. by E. of Dorchester, and 112 W. by S. of London.

STALIMENE. *See* LEMNOS.

STAMFORD, a borough in Lincolnshire, sending two members to parliament, governed by a mayor, with markets on Monday and Friday, and a good trade, particularly in malt and freestone. One of its parishes, St. Martin's, is situate in Northamptonshire, but the greater part is built on the side of a hill in Lincolnshire, and, when approached from the S., presents an interesting and picturesque appearance. The notable custom of Borough English prevails here, by which the younger sons inherit the lands and tenements of the father dying intestate. Here are six parish churches, places of worship for Roman Catholics and several denominations of Protestant dissenters, three free-schools, and several charitable institutions. Stamford had formerly a college, whose students removed to Brasenose College, in Oxford. It is seated on the Welland, which is navigable hence. It is 44 miles S. of Lincoln, and 89 N. by W. of London. Long. 0. 31. W. lat. 52. 42. N.

STAMFORD, a town of Connecticut, in Fairfield county; 44 miles N. E. of New York. Pop. 3516.

STAMPALIA, an island of the Grecian Archipelago; 12 miles long and 5 broad. It is destitute of fresh water, and almost without inhabitants. It is 30 miles W. of Stanchio.

STANCO, a fertile island of the Grecian Archipelago, near the coast of Natolia. It is the ancient Cos, the birthplace of Hippocrates and Apelles, and is 25 miles long, and 10 broad. It abounds with cypress and turpentine trees, and a great variety of medicinal plants. The capital, of the same name, is a bishop's see, seated at the foot of a mountain, at the bottom of a bay, and has a good harbour, defended by a castle. It is 40 miles N. W. of Rhodes. Long. 26. 54. E. lat. 36. 45. N.

STANDON, a town in Hertfordshire, with a market on Friday, seated on the river Rib; 8 miles N. E. of Hertford, and 27 N. by E. of London.

STANFORD, a town of Kentucky, chief of Lincoln county; 10 miles S. S. E. of Danville, and 40 E. by W. of Lexington.

STANHOPE, a parish in the county of Durham, chiefly inhabited by miners. It is seated on the Wear; 20 miles W. of Durham, and 263 N. by W. of London.

STANLEY, a town in Gloucestershire, with a market on Saturday; 12 miles S. of Gloucester, and 105 W. of London.

STANWIX, FORT, a fort in the state of New York; sometimes called New Fort Schuyler. It is seated on Mohawk River, near its source; 68 miles N. W. of Albany. Long. 74. 56. W. lat. 43. 18. N.

STANZ, a town of Switzerland, in the canton of Underwalden. Near this place, in 1798, the troops of the canton were totally defeated by the French, who afterwards burnt the town and put the inhabitants to the sword. It is seated in a plain, at the foot of the Stanzberg; 8 miles S. E. of Lucern, and 38 E. of Bern.

STARA RUSA, a town of Russia; in the government of Novogorod, on the river Polista, near the lake Ilmen; 40 miles S. of Novogorod. Long. 33. 2. E. lat. 57. 40. N.

STARENBERG, a town and castle of Bavaria, near the N. end of the lake Wurmsee; 14 miles S. W. of Munich.

STARGARD, NEW, a town of Prussian Pomerania, with a college, fine manufactures of wool, and a considerable trade. In 1758 it was taken by the Russians. It stands on the river Ihna; 20 miles E. of Stettin. Pop. 8600. Long. 15. 13. E. lat. 53. 26. N.

STARKENBURG, one of the three great divisions of Hesse-Darmstadt, situate between the Rhine and the Maine, and forming the southern part of the grand duchy. Its extent is 1060 square miles, its population 200,000. Darmstadt is the capital.

START POINT, a promontory on the coast of Devonshire; 14 miles S. by W. of Dartmouth. Long. 3. 48. W. lat. 50. 13. N.

STASFURT, a town of Prussian Saxony, in the duchy of Magdeburg, with some good salt-works; 21 miles S. S. W. of Magdeburg.

STATEN ISLAND, an island of New York, 18 miles long, and 6 broad, which forms the county of Richmond. On the S. side is a tract of level land, but the island in general is rough, and the hills are high. Pop. 10,965. Richmond is the chief town.

STATES OF THE CHURCH. *See* POPEDOM.

STATESBURG, a town of South Carolina, chief of Clermont county; situate on Beech Creek, which joins the Wateree a few miles W. of the town. It is 20 miles E. of Camden, and 95 N. by W. of Charleston.

STAUFFEN, a town of Germany, in Baden; situate on the Mehlbach, 8 miles S. of Friburg.

STAUFFENBURG, a town and castle of Germany, in Hesse-Darmstadt; situate on the Lohn, 5 miles N. N. E. of Giessen.

STAUNTON, a town in Virginia, chief of Augusta county; situate on Middle River, a water of the Potomac, 100 miles S. S. W. of Winchester. Pop. 2000. Long. 79. 35. W. lat. 38. 15. N.

STAVANGER, a seaport of Norway, in the government of Bergen. Near it is a fortress, called Deswick. It is seated on a peninsula, 95 miles S. of Bergen. Long. 5. 55. E. lat. 58. 58. N.

STAVEREN, a town of the Netherlands, in Friesland; formerly a rich city and seaport, but now much decayed, and the harbour choked up.

The ancient kings of Friesland made it their ordinary residence; and there remains enough of its former splendour to make it a considerable town. It has still some trade, especially in fishing, and in passage-boats over the pools and lakes of the neighbourhood. It is seated on the Zuyder Zee, 8 miles W. of Sloten, and 17 N. E. of Enchuysen. Long. 5. 13. E. lat. 52. 54. N.

STAVROS. *See* STAGIRA.

STEENBERGEN, a town of the Netherlands, in North Brabant; formerly a strong place, with a convenient harbour, but the sea has retired from it about 3 miles, which, with the calamities it has suffered by war, has reduced it to a poor town. It has a communication with the Meuse. It is 7 miles N. of Bergen-op-Zoom. Population, 4200.

STEENKEER, a town of Norway, in the province of Drontheim; 36 miles N. E. of Drontheim.

STEENKIRK, a village of the Netherlands, in Hainault; famous for the victory obtained by the French over William III. of England, in 1692. It is 15 miles N. of Mons.

STEENWYCK, a town of the Netherlands, in Overyssel; seated on the river Aa, 18 miles N. of Zwoll.

STEGE, a seaport of Denmark, on the N. coast of the Isle of Mona, almost surrounded by a lake; 42 miles S. by W. of Copenhagen. Long. 12. 15. E. lat. 55. 4. N.

STEGEBURG, a seaport of Sweden, in East Gothland, seated on the Baltic; 9 miles N. of Calmar, and 82 S. W. of Stockholm. Long. 16. 40. E. lat. 58. 16. N.

STEIN, a small independent town of Switzerland, in the canton of Zurich; seated on the N. side of the Rhine, where it issues from the lake of Constance. Near it is the ancient castle of Hohenlingen, now converted into a watchtower. The church is on the opposite side of the Rhine, in a place called Berg, which is connected to the town by a bridge; 15 miles W. by N. of Constance, and 25 N. E. of Zurich.

STEIN, a town of Austria, on the N. side of the Danube, over which is a long wooden bridge to Mautern. Between Stein and Krems is a military manufacture, in which metal articles, sabres, cloth, and clothes are made and kept; 2 miles W. of Krems, and 12 N. by W. of St. Polten.

STEIN, a town and castle of Austrian Illyria, in Carniola, on the Feistritz; 11 miles N. of Laubach.

STEIN, a town and castle of the Austrian states, in Carinthia, on the Drave; 12 miles S. of Clagenfurt.

STEINAU, a town of Prussian Silesia; formerly the capital of a circle, in the principality of Wolau. It has manufactures of cloth. It is seated near the Oder; 16 miles N. N. E. of Lignitz.

STEINFURT, a town of Prussia, in the province of Westphalia; capital of a county of its name, with a Calvinist academy; seated on the Aa; 10 miles S. S. E. of Bentheim, and 33 N. W. of Munster.

STEINHEIM, a town of Germany, in Hesse-Darmstadt; with a castle, near the river Maine; 4 miles S. E. of Hanau.

STEINHUDE, a town of Germany, in the county of Schauenburg-Lippe; on the S. side of Steinhuder-mere, in which is the strong fortress of Wilhemstein; 15 miles N. W. of Hanover.

STEINHURST, a town of Denmark, in Holstein, with a castle; 14 miles S. S. W. of Lubec.

STELLENBOSCH, a district of the Cape of Good Hope; bounded on the W. by the Cape district, S. by False Bay and Zwellendam, E. by Tulbagh, and N. by Clanwilliam; and Stellenbosch, 20 miles N. of False Bay, is the capital. It is mountainous, but contains some of the finest land in the colony.

STENAY, a town of France, department of Meuse, on the river Meuse; 22 miles N. N. W. of Verdun.

STENDAL, a town of Prussia, in Brandenburg, formerly capital of the Old Mark. Here is a colony of French Calvinists, who carry on manufactures of wool, leather, &c. It stands on the rivulet Ucht; 5 miles W. of the Elbe, and 36 N. by E. of Magdeburg. Pop. 5000. Long. 11. 58. E. lat. 52. 35. N.

STERNBERG, a town of the Prussian states, in the New Mark of Brandenburg, with a great trade in cattle; 20 miles E. N. E. of Frankfort.

STERNBERG, a town of Germany, in the grand duchy of Mecklenburg-Schwerin; situate on a lake; 16 miles S. E. of Wismar.

STERNBERG, a town and castle of the Austrian states, in Moravia; 10 miles N. E. of Olmutz. Pop. 8000.

STERZINGEN, a town of the Austrian states, in Tyrol; celebrated for its manufacture of sword-blades, and for the silver-mines in its vicinity. It is seated at the foot of a mountain, on the Eysoch; 12 miles N. W. of Brixen.

STETTIN, a government of Prussia, comprising the middle of Pomerania, and containing an area of 6625 square miles, with 300,000 inhabitants.

STETTIN, a fortified seaport of Prussia, capital of Pomerania. It is a handsome town; contains about 21,000 inhabitants, exclusive of the garrison; has numerous manufactures, particularly of cloths, stuffs, hats, stockings, yarn, cotton, ribbons, paper, and canvas, and carries on a considerable trade to all parts of Europe. Timber and corn are the principal articles of exportation, and ship-building is a very profitable branch of employment. In 1795 a fire consumed a great number of houses. In 1806 this place, furnished with 160 pieces of cannon and a garrison of 6000 men, surrendered to the French. It was garrisoned by them after the disastrous retreat from Russia, in 1812, but in 1813 was obliged to capitulate, when the Dutch troops, belonging to the garrison, hoisted the orange cockade. It is seated on the Oder, 80 miles N. N. E. of Berlin. Long. 14. 44. E. lat. 53. 30. N.

STETTIN, NEW, a town of Pomerania, in the government of Coslin, with a castle; situate on the Willem; 41 miles E. of Coslin, and 62 E. N. E of New Stargard.

STEUBENVILLE, a flourishing town of Ohio; capital of Jefferson county. It contains four churches, an academy, two banks, and manufactures of woollen, cotton, &c. The population is 5203. It stands on the Ohio, 40 miles below Pittsburg.

STEVENAGE, a town in Hertfordshire; 31 miles from London.

STEVENSBURG, a town of Virginia, in Culpepper county, on the road from Philadelphia to Staunton; 13 miles S. W. of Winchester.

STEVENSTON, a town of Scotland, in Ayrshire, famous for the coal strata in its vicinity. The Ardrossau and Kilwinning railway traverses the parish. It is situate on a hill, 5 miles N. W. of Irvine.

STEVENSWERT, a fortress of the Netherlands, in the province of Limburg, seated on the Meuse; 6 miles S. S. W. of Ruremonde.

STEWART ISLANDS, five islands in the South Pacific; discovered by Captain Hunter in 1791, and named by him in honour of Admiral Keith Stewart. Long. 163. 18. E. lat. 8. 26. S.

STEWARTON, a town of Scotland, in Ayrshire, with a noted manufacture of bonnets; 6 miles N. of Irvine.

STEWARTON, a town of Ireland, in the county of Tyrone; 5 miles N. N. E. of Dungannon.

STEYNING, a town in Sussex; market on Wednesday. It is 10 miles W. by N. of Brighton, and 50 S. W. of London.

STEYR, a town of Austria, which has a great trade in articles of iron and steel. The French entered it in 1800, and concluded an armistice for a peace with the Austrians. It is seated at the conflux of the Steyr with the Ens; 20 miles S. E. of Lintz. Pop. 10,000.

STEYREG, a town and castle of Austria, situate on a mountain, on the N. side of the Danube; 8 miles E. of Lintz.

STICKHAUSEN, a town and castle of Hanover, in the principality of East Friesland; 22 miles E. S. E. of Emden.

STIGLIANO, a town of Naples, in Basilicata, famous for its baths; seated near the Salandrella, 26 miles S. S. E. of Acerenza.

STILLWATER, a town of New York, in Saratoga county, on the W. side of the Hudson; 25 miles N. of Albany.

STILTON, a town in Huntingdonshire, celebrated for a rich kind of cheese. It is 14 miles S. by E. of Stamford, and 75 N. by E. of London.

STINCHAR, a river of Scotland, in the S. part of Ayrshire, which has a rapid course of 26 miles, and enters the ocean below Ballantrae.

STIRIA. *See* STYRIA.

STIRLING, a borough of Scotland, capital of Stirlingshire; seated on the river Forth, on a hill which terminates abruptly in a steep basaltic rock. On this rock is an ancient castle, once a place of great strength, and often the scene of bloody contention. The palace, erected by James V., is a stately building, the outside curiously ornamented with grotesque figures. Here are two churches, and a famous grammar-school. In the town and its neighbourhood are manufactures of carpets, shalloons, and other woollen stuffs, and the cotton trade is flourishing. A salmon-fishery, belonging to the town, is let to a company, who send the fish chiefly to the London and Edinburgh markets. Stirling has undergone considerable improvement within the last few years; several new streets have been built on a modern and improved plan on the N. side of the town, and, in the old part of the town, numbers of houses have been rebuilt. From its commodious situation, Stirling commands the pass between the N. and S. part of Scotland. It returns one member to parliament. It is 35 miles W. N. W. of Edinburgh. Long. 3. 50. W. lat. 56. 12. N.

STIRLINGSHIRE, a county of Scotland; 35 miles long, and 10 broad; bounded on the N. by Perthshire, N. E. by Clackmananshire and the Frith of Forth, S. E. by Linlithgowshire, S. by Lanarkshire and Dumbartonshire, and W. by Dumbartonshire. It is divided into 24 parishes, and sends one member to parliament. The principal rivers are the Forth, Carron, and Avon; and the great canal crosses it from the mouth of the Carron. The S. part of the county is mountainous, but the part near the Forth is fertile. It abounds in coal, ironstone, and limestone.

STIRUM, a town of Prussia, in the grand duchy of Lower Rhine; seated on the Roer; 12 miles N. of Dusseldorf.

STOCKACH, a town of Germany, in Baden, near which the Austrians gained a victory over the French in 1799, and in 1800 the latter defeated the former, and took possession of the town. It is seated on a river of the same name; 17 miles N. E. of Constance.

STOCKBRIDGE, a town in Hampshire; market on Thursday; 9 miles N. W. of Winchester, and 66 W. by S. of London.

STOCKBRIDGE, a town of Massachusets, in Berkshire county; 44 miles W. by N. of Springfield, and 130 W. of Boston.

STOCKEM, a town of the Netherlands, in the territory of Leige; seated on the Meuse, 11 miles N. of Maestricht.

STOCKERAU, a town of Austria, situate near the Danube; 14 miles N. N. W. of Vienna.

STOCKHOLM, a province of Sweden, comprising the eastern parts of Upland and Sudermania, or the districts of Roslagen and Sodertorn. It has an area of 2736 square miles, with 100,000 inhabitants.

STOCKHOLM, the capital of Sweden, lies in a situation remarkable for its romantic scenery. It is very long, irregular, and occupies, besides two peninsulas, three rocky islands, situate in the Maeler, in the streams which issue from that lake, and in a bay of the Baltic. There are four smaller islands, or rather islets, on which are situate forts or buildings for naval purposes. A variety of contrasted and beautiful views are formed by numerous rocks of granite, rising boldly from the surface of the water, partly bare and craggy, and partly dotted with houses, or feathered with wood. The harbour is an inlet of the Baltic; the water is of such depth that ships of the largest burden can approach the quay. At the extremity of the harbour, several streets rise one above another in the form of an amphitheatre, and the palace, a magnificent building, crowns the summit. Except in the suburbs, where several houses are of wood, painted red, the generality of the buildings are of stone, or of brick whitened with stucco. There is a royal academy of science, instituted by the celebrated Linnæus, and a few other learned men, in 1741; and also a royal academy of arts. The arsenal contains an immense number of trophies and standards taken from different nations. Stockholm, with a small territory surrounding it, forms a separate government, has its own magistrates, and contains nearly 80,000 inhabitants, who manufacture glass, china, silk, woollen, &c. It is 320 miles N. E. of Copenhagen, 1000 N. E, of Paris, and 900 N. E. of London. Long. 18. 9. E. lat. 59. 20. N.

STOCKPORT, a borough in Cheshire, market on Friday, and considerable manufactures of cotton, printed goods, and hats. It returns two members to parliament. The present parish church was erected on the site of the ancient church, in 1813. The other places of worship are a church erected in 1822, under the million act, a chapel erected and endowed by W. Wright, Esq., a Catholic chapel, and nine meeting-houses. Here is a free grammar-school founded in 1487, and also a national school erected in 1826. From its contiguity to Manchester, and the facilities of its canal navigation, Stockport partakes of the prosperity of that town. It is seated on the Mersey, 7 miles S. S. E. of Manchester, on the Manchester and Birmingham railway, and 179 N. N. W. of London.

STOCKPORT, a town of Pennsylvania, in Northampton county, on the W. side of the Popaxtunk branch of Delaware River. It stands on Susquehanna River; 18 miles E. S. E. of Harmony.

STOCKTON-UPON-TEES, a borough in the county of Durham, markets on Wednesday and Saturday. It returns two members to parliament. Here are two docks for ship-building; manufactures of canvas and ropes to a considerable extent; also of diapers, huckabacks, checks, &c.; and a trade in lead, corn, pork, butter, sail-cloth, leather, &c. Besides the church, which is a handsome brick building, the town contains meeting-houses for Presbyterians, Quakers, and Methodists, a Roman Catholic chapel, and several schools and almshouses. It is seated on the river Tees, not far from its mouth; 18 miles S. S. E. of Durham, and 243 N. by W. of London.

STOKE, or STOKE POGES, a village in Buckinghamshire, 4 miles N. N. E. of Windsor. Its churchyard is the scene of Gray's celebrated Elegy.

STOKE-UPON-TRENT, or ETRURIA, a borough in Staffordshire, near Newcastle. It returns two members to parliament. It is the principal seat of the potteries in this county, and here the most elegant vases and other articles are made. Josiah Wedgewood was the founder, and died here in 1795. It is 1½ mile W. of Newcastle-under-Line, and 150 N. N. W. of London.

STOKES, a town of North Carolina, chief of Montgomery county; seated near the Yadkin, 46 miles W. of Averysborough.

STOKESLEY, a small but neat town in North Yorkshire, with a market on Saturday. It has a church, two meeting-houses, two national schools, and a dispensary. It is seated on the river Wisk; 20 miles N. by E. of Thirsk, and 238 N. by W. of London.

STOLBERG, a town of Prussian Saxony, capital of a county of the same name, with a castle. It is seated in a valley between two mountains, in which are mines of copper and iron; 12 miles N. E. of Nordhausen, and 55 W. N. W. of Leipsic. Population, 2000. Long. 11. 5. E. lat. 51. 36. N.

STOLBERG, a town of Saxony, where great quantities of cloth are made; 2 miles S. W. of Chemnitz.

STOLBOFEN, a town of Germany, in the grand duchy of Baden; 8 miles S. W. of Baden.

STOLPE, a town of Prussian Pomerania, with a castle, three churches, and a Lutheran nunnery. The inhabitants, estimated at 4500, carry on a considerable trade in linen and wood; and here is also a fine salmon fishery. It is seated on the Stolpa, 10 miles from its mouth, in the Baltic, and 56 E. N. E. of Colberg. Long. 16. 48. E. lat. 54. 27. N.

STOLPEMUNDE, a town of Pomerania, on the Baltic Sea, with a harbour at the mouth of the Stolpa; 10 miles N. W. of Stolpe.

STOLPEN, a town of Saxony, with a castle on a mountain; 15 miles E. of Dresden.

STOLZENAU, a town of Hanover, in the county of Hoya; seated on the Weser, 14 miles S. S. W. of Nienburg.

STOLZENBURG, a town of West Prussia, formerly a suburb of the city of Dantzic, but, with the adjacent suburbs of Old Scotland, St. Albert, and Schidlitz, was formed into a separate town, having its own magistrates and municipal rights, in 1772. Pop. 8000.

STONE, a town in Staffordshire, with a market on Tuesday, and a considerable manufacture of shoes; seated on the Trent, 7 miles N. by W. of Stafford, and 140 N. W. of London.

STONEHAVEN, or STONEHIVE, a seaport of Scotland, and the county town of Kincardineshire. It consists of the old and new towns, the latter of which is the principal, and is regular, spacious, and well built. The harbour is secured by a high rock and stone pier. Near it are the ruins of the castle of Dunnottar, on a lofty perpendicular rock, almost surrounded by the sea. The town has a manufacture of brown linen, and some trade in dried fish and oil. It is situated 23 miles N. N. E. of Montrose. Long. 2. 6. W. lat. 56. 55. N.

STONEHENGE, a remarkable monument of antiquity, in Wiltshire, on Salisbury Plain; consisting of several very large stones, some placed upright, and others horizontally across them. Most antiquarians suppose this work to have been a temple of the Druids, because it is in a circular form, and seems to have been much more regular than it appears to be at present. It has puzzled many diligent inquirers to account for the bringing and placing of those enormous stones; for it is thought no method now known is sufficient to have raised those that lie across to that height. It is 6 miles N. of Salisbury.

Stonehouse, a town in Devonshire, with markets on Tuesday and Saturday. It contains two episcopal chapels, two meeting-houses, a national school, very extensive barracks, a royal naval hospital, &c. It is situate about half way between Plymouth and Devonport.

Stoneleigh, a town in Warwickshire, with a market on Thursday; seated on the river Low, 5 miles S. W. of Coventry.

Stonington, a seaport of Connecticut, in New London county. The harbour sets up from Long Island Sound, opposite Fisher Island. In 1814 this town was bombarded, but without effect, by the British; 14 miles E. of New London. Pop. 3898. Long. 71. 58. W. lat. 41. 26. N.

Stony Point, a town of New York, taken by the British in 1779, but recovered soon after by the Americans, and the British garrison made prisoners of war. It is seated on the Hudson, opposite Verplantis Point.

Storkau, a town of Prussia, in the Ucker Mark of Brandenburg; 27 miles S. E. of Berlin.

Stornoway, a seaport of Scotland, on the E. side of the Isle of Lewis, at the head of Loch Stornoway, which is a good harbour for ships of any burden. It is a port of the custom-house, and has a post-office and a regular packet weekly. Long. 6. 38. W. lat. 58. 18. N.

Stortford, or Bishop's Stortford, a town in Hertfordshire, with a market on Thursday. On the E. side are the ruins of a castle, on an artificial mount. It is seated on the side of a hill, on the river Stort, which is navigable hence to the Lea; 10 miles E. N. E. of Hertford, and 30 N. N. E. of London.

Stossen, a town of Saxony, 6 miles S. of Weissenfels.

Stoughton, a town of Massachusets, in Norfolk county, whence great quantities of charcoal, baskets, and brooms are sent to Boston; 9 miles S. E. of Dedham, and 15 S. of Boston.

Stour, a river which rises on the most northerly point of Dorsetshire, passes by Stourminster, Blandford, and Winborn, then enters Hampshire, and flows into the Avon, opposite Christchurch.

Stour, a river in Kent, which rises in the Weald, flows by Wye and Canterbury, and, 7 miles below, divides into two streams; the smaller one passes into the sea at Reculver, and the main branch flows by Sandwich into Hope Bay.

Stour, a river which forms the entire boundary between Essex and Suffolk, passes by Clare, Sudbury, Neyland, and Manningtree, and, being joined by the Orwell, from Ipswich, forms the harbour of Harwich.

Stour, a river which rises in the S. part of Staffordshire, enters Worcestershire at Stourbridge, and flows by Kidderminster into the Severn, opposite Stourport.

Stourbridge, a corporate town in Worcestershire, with a market on Friday, and manufactures of glass, iron, and earthenware, particularly crucibles for glass-melters. Here are a neat church, meeting-houses for Methodists, Independents, Presbyterians, and Quakers, and a free-school founded by Edward VI.; in the neighbourhood is a noble hospital for the maintenance and education of 60 boys. It is seated on the Stour, 22 miles N. of Worcester, and 126 N. W. of London.

Stourbridge, a town of Massachusets, in Worcester county, famous for its excellent butter and cheese; 22 miles S. W. of Worcester.

Stourminster, a town in Dorsetshire, with a market on Thursday, and a manufacture of white baize. Near it are the ruins of a castle, which was the seat of the W. Saxon kings. It is seated on both sides the Stour, over which is a bridge; 20 miles N. E. of Dorchester, and 108 W. by S. of London.

Stourport, a handsome town in Worcestershire. It is a busy centre of inland navigation, being seated opposite the place where the river Stour and the Staffordshire and Worcestershire canal enters the Severn, over which river it has an elegant iron bridge. It is 4 miles S. of Kidderminster.

Stow Market, a thriving town in Suffolk, with a market on Thursday, a manufacture of sacking, ropes, &c., and a considerable malting business. It has a navigable canal to Ipswich. It is seated on the Orwell, 12 miles N. W. of Ipswich, and 70 N. N. E. of London.

Stow on the Wold, a town in Gloucestershire, with a market on Thursday, and a manufacture of shoes; seated on a bleak hill, 22 miles E. of Gloucester, and 80 W. by N. of London.

Stowey, a small town in Somersetshire, with a market on Tuesday. It had once a castle, of which no vestiges remain, except the ditch. It is 8 miles W. by N. of Bridgewater, and 147 W. by S. of London.

Strabane, a town of Ireland, in the county of Tyrone, situate on the Mourne, near the Foyle; 11 miles S. S. W. of Londonderry.

Strabane, a town of Pennsylvania, in Washington county.

Stradbally, a town of Ireland, Queen's county. It is 49 miles from Dublin.

Stradella, a strong town of the Sardinian states, in the Milanese, with a castle. The French became masters of it in 1800. It is seated on the Versa, near the Po; 10 miles S. E. of Pavia. Pop. 3900.

Strakonitz, a town of Bohemia, in the circle of Prachin, with a castle, seated on the Wotawa; 11 miles S. W. of Piseck.

Stralsund, a government of the Prussian states, comprising the part of Pomerania formerly belonging to Sweden, along with Rugen and other islands on the N. coast. It has an area of 1400 square miles, with 115,000 inhabitants.

Stralsund, a seaport of Prussia, formerly the capital of Swedish Pomerania. It contains about 11,000 inhabitants, and its trade and commerce are considerable. The churches and other public buildings are handsome, and the library belonging to the college has a capital collection of coins. Charles XII., in 1714, came hither after his return from Turkey, and ennobled the magistracy. Stralsund was forced to submit to the allies in 1715, was restored in 1720, surrendered to the French in 1807, and was finally ceded to Prussia in 1813. It is almost surrounded by the Baltic and the lake Francen, and has a harbour separated from the Isle of Rugen by a narrow channel. The manufactures are various, but most of them on a small scale, and the trade is considerable, particularly in corn. It is 40 miles E. N. E. of Rostock, and 85 N. W. of Stettin. Long. 13. 16. E. lat. 54. 20. N.

STRAMMEL, a town of the Prussian states, in Pomerania, on the river Rega; 21 miles N. E. of New Stargard.

STRANGFORD LOUGH, a large bay, or inlet of the sea, in the county of Down, on the E. coast of Ireland, about 17 miles long and 5 broad, abounding with excellent fish, particularly smelts; and off the bar, about August, is a periodical herring-fishery. It contains a great many small islands; and the burning of kelp profitably employs a great number of hands in them. The bar or entrance into it, from the Irish Sea, is 3 miles below Strangford, and not a mile in breadth.

STRANRAWER, or STRANRAER, a seaport of Scotland, in Wigtonshire, with considerable manufactures of cotton and linen. Vessels employed in the coasting trade and herring-fishery frequent this place, and some ships sail hence to the Baltic and Ireland with corn. It is situate at the head of Loch Ryan; 26 miles W. by N. of Wigton, to which, with Whithorn and N. Galloway, it unites in sending a member to parliament. Long. 4. 57. W. lat. 55. 0. N.

STRASBURG, a city of France, capital of the department of Lower Rhine, and a bishop's see. It is situate near the Rhine, and the river Ill runs through it, and forms many canals, over which there are several bridges to connect the different quarters of the city. It is a place of considerable commerce, and has manufactures of tobacco, porcelain, steel, lace, carpets, cloth, leather, &c. The inhabitants are computed at 50,000. The principal structures are built of a red stone, dug from the quarries which are along the Rhine. This town, formerly imperial, was taken by Louis XIV. in 1681. The citadel and fortifications which he constructed have been so much augmented, that Strasburg may be considered one of the strongest places in Europe. It was confirmed to France by the peace of Ryswick in 1697. The university, which had been curtailed of its classes during the French revolution, was replaced on its former footing in 1803. The town is entered by six gates. In the cathedral is a clock, which showed the motions of the constellations, the revolutions of the sun and moon, the days of the week, the hours, &c. Another remarkable circumstance in this cathedral is its pyramidical tower, which is 549 feet high, next to the great pyramid the highest building in the world. In the church of St. Thomas is the magnificent tomb of the famous Marshal Saxe. It is 65 miles N. of Basil, and 75 E. of Nancy. Long. 7. 45. E. lat. 48. 35. N.

STRASBURG, a town of West Prussia, in the circle of Culm, with a castle, seated on the Drigentz; 30 miles E. N. E. of Thorn.

STRASBURG, a town of Prussia, in Brandenburg; 15 miles N. by W. of Prenzlo.

STRASBURG, a town of Austrian Illyria, in Carinthia, seated on the river Gurk; 13 miles N. of Clagenfurt.

STRASBURG, a town of Virginia, in Shenandoah county, on a branch of the Shenandoah river; 18 miles S. S. W. of Winchester.

STRASBURG, a town of Pennsylvania, in Lancaster county; 58 miles W. of Philadelphia.

STRASNITZ, a town of the Austrian states, in Moravia, with a castle and a college, on the river Marsch; 12 miles S. S. W. of Hradisch. Pop. 4100.

STRATFORD, a town of Connecticut, in Fairfield county, situate on a river of the same name; 5 miles from its mouth, and 14 W. S. W. of Newhaven. Pop. 1807.

STRATFORD, a village in Essex, separated from Bow in Middlesex by the river Lea, over which was a bridge, said to be the most ancient stone arch in England. It is 3 miles E. N. E. of London.

STRATFORD, FENNY, a town in Buckinghamshire, with a manufacture of thread lace, seated on the Lyssel, and the Roman highway called Watling-street; 12 miles E. of Buckingham, and 45 N. W. of London.

STRATFORD, STONY, a town in Buckinghamshire, with a market on Friday. Here are two churches, several meeting-houses, and a neat market-place. The cross, built by Edward I. in memory of his queen Eleanor, was demolished during the civil wars, and in 1743 a fire happened, which destroyed 150 houses. The inhabitants are principally lace-makers. It is seated on the Ouse and the Roman Watling-street; 8 miles N. E. of Buckingham, and 52 N. W. of London.

STRATFORD-ON-AVON, a town in Warwickshire, governed by a mayor; with a market on Friday. It is memorable as the birthplace of Shakspeare, who was buried here in 1616. Here is a manufacture of silk buttons, and some trade in corn and malt. The town is situate on the Avon, over which is a long bridge: 8 miles S. W. of Warwick, and 95 N. W. of London.

STRATHAVEN, a town of Scotland, in Lanarkshire, with a manufacture of cotton, seated on the Avon; 8 miles S. of Hamilton, and 12 W. of Lanark.

STRATHMORE, a river of Scotland, in Sutherlandshire, which flows into a bay of the North Sea, called Loch Hope.

STRATHY, a river of Scotland, in Sutherlandshire, which issues from a small lake, and flows into a bay of the North Sea, sheltered to the W. by a large promontory, to which it gives name.

STRATTON, a town in Cornwall, with a market on Tuesday. It is noted for a victory obtained by the royalists over the parliamentary army in 1643. It is 18 miles N. N. W. of Launceston, and 222 W. by S. of London.

STRAUBING, a town of Bavaria, capital of a territory of the same name, with a castle. It has broad streets, handsome churches, a flourishing academy, and a convent of Ursuline nuns. In 1743 it was taken by the Austrians, who demolished the fortifications; but it was restored in 1745. It is seated on the Danube; 22 miles S. E. of Ratisbon, and 68 N. E. of Munich. Pop. 6200. Long. 12. 28. E. lat. 48. 50. N.

STRAUSBERG, a town of Prussia, in the Middle Mark of Brandenburg, with an old castle on a mountain. It has manufactures of baize and cloth, and stands on the lake Strauss; 21 miles E. N. E. of Berlin.

STREHLA, a town of Saxony, in Meissen, near which the Prussians were defeated by the Austrians in 1760. It is seated on the Elbe; 14 miles N. W. of Meissen.

STREHLEN, a town of Prussian Silesia, with manufactures of woollens, stockings, and leather. It is seated on the Ohla; 22 miles S. of Breslau.

STRELITZ, NEW, a town of Lower Saxony, capital of the duchy of Mecklenburg-Strelitz. It owes its origin to the destruction of the ducal palace in Old Strelitz; in consequence of which, in 1713, the duke began to erect a magnificent palace, 2 miles from the site of the old one, at a place called Glienke, which was before his hunting-seat; and in 1733 he founded a town adjoining to the palace, and ordered it to be called New Strelitz. The centre is a spacious market-place, and thence a number of streets branch out in straight lines; the chief street leads to the palace, and the next to a pleasant lake. It is seated among lakes; 55 miles S. E. of Gustrow, and 56 N. by W. of Berlin. Pop. together, 7000. Long. 13. 18. E. lat. 53. 21. N.

STRENGNES a town of Sweden, in Sudermania, and a bishop's see, seated on the Lake Maerler; 30 miles W. by S. of Stockholm. Long. 17. 4. E. lat. 59. 20. N.

STRIEGAU, a town of Prussian Silesia, in the principality of Schweidnitz. It seated on a river, at the foot of a mountain; 11 miles N. of Schweidnitz. Pop. 2700.

STROEMSHOLM, a town of Sweden, in Westmania, situate on the Lake Maerler; 45 miles S. W. of Upsal. Long. 16. 24. E. lat. 59. 30. N.

STROMA, a small island of Scotland, on the coast of Caithness-shire, in Pentland Frith. Its caverns were once used by the inhabitants of the neighbouring islands as places of interment. Near its N. end is a dangerous whirlpool.

STROMBERG, a town of Prussian Westphalia, in the government of Munster; 20 miles E. N. E. of Munster, and 20 N. W. of Paderborn.

STROMBOLI, the most northern of the Lipari Islands. It is a volcano, which rises in a conical form to the height of 3000 feet; and on the E. side are three or four little craters ranged near each other, nearly at two-thirds of its height. Notwithstanding its fires it is inhabited, and produces a great deal of cotton. Of all the volcanoes regarded in history, Stromboli seems to be the only one that burns without ceasing; and it has long been looked upon as the great lighthouse of the Mediterranean, the flames being seen by night at a great distance. Long. 15. 40. E. lat. 38. 40. N.

STROMNESS, a town of Scotland, on the S. W. side of the island of Pomona, with a good harbour; 14 miles W. by S. of Kirkwall.

STROMOE, the principal of the Feroe Islands, in the Northern Ocean; 30 miles in length, and 10 in breadth. It has a town called Thorshaven, which is the capital of all the islands, and the common market. Long. 7. 0. W. lat. 62. 10. N.

STROMSOE, a town of Norway, in the province of Aggerhuys; 18 miles S. W. of Christiania. *See* DRAMMEN.

STROMSTADT, a town of Sweden, in West Gothland, celebrated for its shell-fish. It stands on the coast of the North Sea; 43 miles N. N. W. of Uddevalla. Long. 11. 4. E. lat. 59. 4. N.

STRONGOLI, a town of Naples, in Calabria Ultra, seated on a high rock; 3 miles from the sea, and 7 N. of St. Severino.

STRONSA, one of the Orkney islands, situate N. E. of that called Pomona. It is 7 miles from N. to S., and nearly the same in breadth, but so indented by bays, that no part of it is above a mile and a half from the sea. It produces much kelp, and feeds many sheep and cattle.

STRONTIAN, a village of Scotland, in Argyleshire, and in the district of Ardnamurchan, noted for its lead-mines, in which a kind of mineral was discovered in 1790, and named *strontites*.

STROUD, a borough in Gloucestershire, market on Friday. It returns two members to parliament. It is seated on a brook, the waters of which are peculiarly adapted to the dyeing of scarlet, and its banks are consequently crowded with the houses of clothiers; a navigable canal accompanies its progress to the Severn, and is now extended to join the Thames at Lechlade. Stroud is 9 miles S. by E. of Gloucester, and 100 W. by N. of London.

STROUD, a considerable village in Kent; which joins the N. end of Rochester bridge, being parted from that city by the river Medway.

STUHLINGEN, a town of Baden, in a lordship of the same name, with a castle on a mountain; 9 miles S. of Furstenburg.

STUHLWEISSENBURG, a town of Hungary, capital of a county of its name, and the see of a bishop; situate in marshy ground, occasioned by the river Sarwitz. It was formerly the place for the coronation of the kings, and generally also of their interment, but it is much decayed since its works were dismantled in 1702. The number of inhabitants is estimated at 13,000; 36 miles S. W. of Buda, and 80 S. E. of Presburg. Long. 18. 28. E. lat. 47. 18. N.

Stutgard, a city of Germany, capital of the kingdom of Wirtemberg. It is surrounded by walls and ditches, and has an ancient castle, with a rich cabinet of curiosities, a magnificent palace, an orphan-house, a college, a ducal academy and observatory, a military academy, and one of the largest libraries in Germany. It has manufactures of silks, stockings, ribbons, &c., and around it are innumerable vineyards and gardens. The streets are narrow in the city, and the houses generally of wood; but there are fine houses and straight streets in one of the suburbs. Stutgard was repeatedly entered by the armies on both sides, between 1796 and 1815. It is seated in a plain among mountains near the river Neckar; 36 miles E. of Baden, and 52 N. E. of Strasburg. Pop. 160,000. Long. 9. 21. E. lat. 48. 44. N.

Styria, a province of Austria, 125 miles long, and 17 broad; bounded on the E. by Hungary, S. by Carniola, and W. by Carinthia and Salzburg. It is divided into Upper and Lower Styria; the former containing the circles of Judenburg and Bruck, and the latter those of Gratz, Marchburg, and Cilley. Though a mountainous country, there is much land fit for tillage, and the soil is fertile. The mountains are clothed with oak, beech, and pine; every kind of grain is well cultivated, and the white wine is very pleasant. It contains mines of excellent iron, whence the arms made here are in great esteem; also mines of lead and coal. The principal rivers are the Enns, Muhr, Drave, and Save. The inhabitants are for the most part Catholics, but Protestants are tolerated, and Jews in a limited degree. Pop. 840,000. Gratz and Judenburg are the chief towns.

Suabia, the former name of one of the ten circles of Germany; bounded on the N. by Franconia and the circle of Lower Rhine; W. by that circle and Alsace, S. by Switzerland, and E. by Bavaria. It comprised the greater part of the kingdom of Wirtemberg, the grand duchy of Baden, and some other territories.

Suakem, or **Suakin**, a seaport, seated on a small island of the same name, in the Red Sea. It is the residence of a Turkish governor under the bashaw of Cairo, and was once a very flourishing place, but is now gone to decay. Long. 37. 55. E. lat. 19. 56. N.

Subiacco, a town of the Papal States, in Campagna di Roma; seated on the Teverone; 33 miles E. by N. of Rome.

Succadana, a town on the S. W. coast of Borneo, capital of a kingdom of the same name. The chief products of the country are camphor and diamonds. It is seated at the mouth of a river. Long. 110. 15. E. lat. 1. 10. S.

Success Bay, a bay on the S. E. coast of Terra del Fuego. The S. promontory, at its entrance, is called Cape Success. Long. 65. 27. W. lat. 55. 1. S.

Suczava, a town of Austria, in Galicia; formerly a flourishing city, but now much declined. It is seated on a river of the same name; 70 miles N. W. of Jassy. Long. 25. 52. E. lat. 47. 57. N.

Suda, a strong fort of the isle of Candia: situate on an islet, in a gulf of its name, which is one of the finest and safest harbours in the Levant. This fort was constructed by the Venetians, who preserved it a great while after Candia was no longer in their possession. It is 8 miles E. of Canea.

Sudbury, a borough in Suffolk, governed by a mayor, with a market on Saturday. It sends two members to parliament. It has three churches, and was one of the first seats of the Flemings, who were brought over by Edward III. to teach the English art of manufacturing their own wool. Its trade is now diverted, in a great part, into other channels; but many kinds of thin stuffs are still made here. It is seated on the Stour, which is navigable hence to Manningtree; 14 miles S. of Bury St. Edmund, and 54 N. E. of London. Long. 0. 50. E. lat. 52. 11. N.

Suderhamn, a town of Sweden, in the government of Gefleborg; with a considerable trade in linen, butter, timber, and flax; situate at the mouth of a river, near the Gulf of Bothnia; 20 miles N. of Gefle. Long. 17. 5. E. lat. 63. 20. N.

Suderkoping, a town of Sweden, in East Gothland; seated on a navigable river; 10 miles S. S. E. of Nordkoping.

Sudermania, a province of Sweden Proper; 62 miles long, and 42 broad; containing an area of 3470 square miles, and 156,000 inhabitants; bounded by Upland, Westmania, Nericia, and the Baltic. It is the most populous part of Sweden, and abounds in corn, and mines of divers metals. Nykoping is the capital.

Sudertelge, a town of Sweden, in Sudermania; with a manufacture of worsted and silk stockings; 16 miles W. S. W. of Stockholm.

Suderoe, one of the Feroe Islands, in the Northern Ocean; remarkable for a dangerous whirlpool near it, which is occasioned by a crater, 61 fathoms deep in the centre. The danger, especially in storms, is very great; but at the reflux, and in very still weather, the inhabitants venture in boats, for the sake of fishing.

Suen-hoa, a city of China, of the first rank, in the province of Pe-tche-li; seated amid mountains, near the Great Wall; 77 miles N. N. W. of Peking. Long. 114. 39. E. lat. 40. 38. N.

Suez, a seaport of Egypt, with a castle; seated at the N. end of the W. arm of the Red Sea, called the Gulf of Suez. This gulf is separated from the Mediterranean by an isthmus, 125 miles over, which joins Asia to Africa. The town is surrounded by a sandy country, and is without water. It is now a wretched and unhealthy place; but in the 16th century was of considerable importance. Several vessels are employed in the navigation between this port and Jidda, where the commodities are bartered for Indian goods and the coffee of Arabia. The commerce of Cairo with Suez is carried on by caravans, which wait the arrival, and set out on the departure of the vessels, that is, about the end of April, and in the course of July and August. The merchandise consists in corn, wood, iron, lead, wool, cloth, cordage, &c.; 65 miles E. of Cairo. Long. 32. 51. E. lat. 30. 2. N.

SUFFIELD, a town of Connecticut, in Hartford county; 17 miles N. of Hartford. Pop. 2669.

SUFFOLK, a county of England, 58 miles long, and 28 broad; bounded on the S. by Essex, W. by Cambridgeshire, N. by Norfolk, and E. by the German Ocean. It contains 1,002,240 acres, is divided into 21 hundreds, and 510 parishes, has 29 market towns, and sends four members to parliament for the Eastern and Western divisions. The soil is of various qualities, but the country, in general, is level. Near the shore it is sandy and full of heaths, but abounds in rye, peas, turnips, carrots, and hemp, with numerous flocks of sheep. Copious beds of petrified shells, called crag, which are found in various parts between Woodbridge and Orford, have for many years been made use of for improving light land. High Suffolk, or the woodlands, which is in the inland parts, yields good pasture, which feeds abundance of cattle. That part on the confines of Essex and Cambridgeshire affords also excellent pasture; and to the N. and N. W. it is fruitful in corn. Its chief produce is butter and cheese; but the latter has gained, almost proverbially, the character of the worst in England. The principal rivers are the Stour, Waveney, Little Ouse, Larke, Deben, Gipping, and Orwell. Ipswich is the principal town; but the assizes are held at Bury St. Edmund.

SUFFOLK, a county of New York, comprising about two-thirds of Long Island. Pop. 32,469. Chief towns, Riverhead, Sagharbour, Satauket, and Huntingdon.

SUFFOLK, a county of Massachusets. Chief town, Boston. Pop. 95,773.

SUFFOLK, a town of Virginia, chief of Nansemond county; situate on the river Nansemond; 28 miles W. by S. of Portsmouth.

SUGULMESSA, or SIGILMESSA, a town of the kingdom of Tafilet, S. W. of Morocco; the capital of a district which abounds in corn, dates, and other fruits; and has mines of iron, lead, and antimony. It is seated on the Zig; 140 miles N. N. E. of Tafilet. Long. 5. 5. W. lat. 29. 40. N.

SUHLA, a town of Prussian Saxony, capital of Henneberg; with manufactures of fustian, linen, leather, and steel. It is seated on the Hasel; 7 miles N. of Schleusingen. Pop. 6000.

SUHLINGEN, a town of Hanover, in the county of Hoya, on a river of its name; 22 miles W. by N. of Nieuburg.

SUIRE, a river of Ireland, which rises in Tipperary, flows by Clonmel and Carrick to Waterford, and meets the Barrow at the head of Waterford Haven.

SULAU. *See* ZULAUF.

SULI, a district of Albania, in European Turkey, containing 18 villages; 20 miles from St. Maura. It was subdued by Ali Pacha in 1803.

SULIMANIEH, a town of Asiatic Turkey, capital of the pachalic of Bagdad. It was built 50 years ago, on the site of the ancient town, which had gone to decay. It has considerable trade, and contains a population of 15,000.

SULLIVAN, a town in the state of Maine, in Hancock county, situate on a bay, opposite Mount Desert Island; 12 miles N. W. of Goldsborough.

SULLY, a town of France, in the department of Loiret; seated on the Loire. It is 20 miles S. E. of Orleans.

SULMONA, a town of Naples, in Abruzzo Citra; and a bishop's see. It contains 11 churches and 12 convents, and was the birthplace of the poet Ovid. It is seated on the Sora; 26 miles S. W. of Civita di Chieti. Pop. 4000. Long. 14. 55. E. lat 42. 0. N.

SULTANIA, a decayed town of Persia, in Irak; with a magnificent mosque, which contains the tomb of sultan Chodabend, or Hodabunda. It is 50 miles N. W. of Casbin. Long. 51. 53. E. lat. 36. 16. N.

SULTANPORE, a town of Hindostan, in the province of Lahore; 62 miles S. E. of Lahore.

SULTANPORE, a town of Hindostan in the province of Oude; the station of a British detachment; 32 miles S. of Fyzabad, and 50 N. of Allahabad.

SULTZ, a town of Germany, in Mecklenburg, with a salt mine; seated on the Rekenitz; 18 miles E. S. E. of Rostock.

SULTZ, a town of France, in the department of Upper Rhine, with a medicinal spring; 13 miles S. S. W. of Colmar. Pop. 4000.

SULZ, a town of Germany, in the kingdom of Wirtemberg, with some salt-works; seated near the Neckar; 12 miles N. of Rothwell.

SULZA, a town in the grand duchy of Saxe-Weimar, with a salt-mine; seated on the Ilme; 13 miles E. N. E. of Weimar.

SULZBACH, a town and castle of Bavaria, in a duchy of its name, the regency of which is united to Amberg. It stands in a mountainous country, fertile in hops; 6 miles N. W. of Amberg.

SULZBURG, a town of Germany, in Baden; with a fine palace; seated in a territory fertile in good wine; 8 miles S. W. of Friburg.

SUMATRA, the most western of the Sunda Islands, in the Indian Ocean. Its general direction is nearly N. W. and S. E. The equator divides it into almost equal parts; the one extremity being in 5. 53. N., the other in 5. 56. S. lat., and Acheen Head, its N. extremity, is in long. 95. 34. N. It is 950 miles in length, and from 150 to 200 in breadth; and is separated from Malacca by the strait of that name, and from Java by the Strait of Sunda. A chain of mountains runs through its whole extent, the ranges, in many parts, being double and treble; yet their altitude is not sufficient to occasion their being covered with snow during any part of the year. Between these ridges are extensive plains, considerably elevated above the surface of the maritime lands. In these the air is cool; and, from this advantage, they are esteemed the most eligible portion of the country, are the best inhabited, and the most cleared from woods, which elsewhere, in general, cover both hills and valleys with an eternal shade. Here too are found many lakes and rivers, which facilitate the communication between the different parts. The inhabitants consist of Malays, Achenese, Battas, Lampoons, and Rejangs; the latter are taken as a standard of description, with respect to the person, manners, and customs of the Sumatrans. They are rather below the middle stature, their bulk in proportion; their limbs, for the most part, slight, but well-shaped, and particularly small at the wrists and ancles. Their hair is strong, and of a shining black. The men are beardless, great pains being taken to render them so, when boys, by rubbing their chins with a kind of quick-lime. Their complexion is properly yellow, wanting the red tinge that constitutes a copper or tawny colour. Those of the superior class, who are not exposed to the rays of the sun, and particularly the women of rank, approach to a considerable degree of fairness; but the major part of the females are ugly. The rites of marriage among the Sumatrans consist simply in joining the hands of the parties, and pronouncing them man and wife, without much ceremony, excepting the entertainment which is given upon the occasion. But little apparent courtship precedes their marriages: their manners do not admit of it, the young people of each sex being carefully kept asunder, and the girls being seldom trusted from their mothers. The opportunities which the young people have of seeing and conversing with each other are at the public festivals, where the persons who are unmarried meet together, and dance and sing in company. A man, when determined in his choice, generally employs an old woman as his agent, by whom he sends a present. The parents then interfere, and, the preliminaries being settled, a feast takes place. At these festivals, a goat, a buffalo, or several, according to the rank of the parties, are killed, to entertain not only the relations and invited guests, but all the inhabitants of the neighbouring country who choose to repair to them. The greater the concourse, the more is the credit of the host, who is generally, on these occasions, the father of the girl. Polygamy is allowed; but it is extremely rare that an instance occurs of a man having more than one wife, and that only among a few of the chiefs. This continence they owe, in some measure, to their poverty. Mothers carry their children straddling on the hip, and usually supported by a cloth tied in a knot on the opposite shoulder. The children are nursed but little, and are not confined by any swathing or bandages. The original natives of Sumatra are pagans; but it is to be observed, that when the Sumatrans, or any of the natives of the eastern islands, learn to read the Arabic character, and submit to circumcision, they are said to become Malays, the term Malay being understood to mean Mussulman. The wild beasts of Sumatra are tigers, elephants, rhinoceroses, bears, and monkeys. The tigers prove to the inhabitants, both in their journeys, and even their domestic occupations, most destructive enemies; yet, from a superstitious prejudice, it is with difficulty they are prevailed upon to use methods for destroying them, till they have sustained some particular injury in their own family or kindred. Alligators likewise occasion the loss of many inhabitants; and yet a superstitious idea of their sanctity also preserves them from molestation. The other animals of Sumatra are buffaloes, a small kind of horses, goats, hogs, deer, bullocks, and hog-deer. This last is an animal somewhat larger than a rabbit, the head resembling that of a hog, and its shanks and feet those of the deer; the bezoar stone found on this animal has been valued at ten times its weight in gold. Of birds there is a greater variety than of beasts. The coo-ow, or Sumatran pheasant, is a bird of uncommon beauty. Here are storks of a prodigious size, parrots, dunghill fowls, ducks, the largest cocks in the world, wood-pigeons, doves, and a great variety of small birds, remarkable for the beauty of their colours. The reptiles are lizards, flying lizards, and chameleons. The island swarms with insects, and their varieties are no less extraordinary than their numbers. Rice is the only grain that grows in the country. Here are sugar-canes, beans, peas, radishes, yams, potatoes, pumpkins, and several kinds of pot-herbs unknown to Europe; and also most of the fruits to be met with in other parts of the East Indies, in the greatest perfection. Indigo, saltpetre, sulphur, arsenic, brazil-wood, two species of the bread-fruit tree, pepper, cassia, camphire, benzoin, coffee, and cotton, are likewise the produce of this island. Here also are the cabbage-tree and silk cotton tree; and the forests contain a great variety of valuable species of wood, as ebony, pine, sandal, eagle or aloes, teak, manchineel, and iron-wood, and also the banyan tree. Bees'-wax is a commodity of great importance here; and there are likewise edible birds' nests. Gold, tin, iron, copper, and lead are found in the country; and the first is as plentiful here as in any part of Asia. Sumatra is divided into many petty kingdoms, the chief of which are Acheen, Indrapore, Palimban, and Jambi. The English and Dutch have factories on this island; the principal one of the former being Fort Marlborough, at Bencoolen, where, as also at the Dutch settlement at Pedang, Christian missionaries have been for some time established. The total population is estimated at about 3,000,000.

Sumbawa, an island in the Eastern seas, about 200 miles long and 40 broad. It is divided into the districts of Beema, Dempoo, Tambora, Sangur, Pekat, and Sumbawa, all governed by their respective chiefs. The island furnishes sappan-wood, rice, horses, saltpetre, sulphur, wax, birds'-nests, tobacco, &c., though but little trade is at present carried on. In the W. part of the island is a town of the same name, with a good harbour.

Sumbhoonaut, a town of Hindostan, in the province of Nepaul; with a celebrated temple, which is annually visited by an immense number of pilgrims from Bootan and Thibet. Long. 85. 38. E. lat. 27. 33. N.

SUMBUL, a town of Hindostan, in a territory of its name; lying E. of Delhi; subject to the nabob of Oude. It is 52 miles W. N. W. of Bereilly, and 75 E. of Delhi.

SUMBULPOUR, or SUMELPOUR, a town of Hindostan, in a district of its name; in the province of Orissa; 144 miles W. N. W. of Cuttack, and 280 W. of Calcutta. Long. 83. 40. E. lat. 21. 25. N.

SUMEH, a town of Asiatic Turkey, in Natolia, 14 miles E. of Pergamo.

SUMEREIN, a town of Hungary, in the island of Schut; 16 miles S. S. E. of Presburg.

SUMMEI-KIOUM, a town of Birmah, the inhabitants of which are chiefly employed in the manufacture of saltpetre and gunpowder. It is seated on the Irrawaddy; 68 miles S. by W. of Ummerapoora.

SUMY, a town of European Russia, in the government of Kharkov. It is fortified, and has four annual fairs, which are considerable. Pop. 11,000.

SUNART, LOCH, an inlet of the sea, on the W. coast of Scotland; which extends 20 miles E. into the county of Argyle, from the N. end of the island of Mull.

SUNBURY, a seaport in the state of Georgia, in Liberty county; with a safe and convenient harbour. The town, being very healthy, is the resort of the planters from the adjacent country, during the sickly months. It is 34 miles S. by W. of Savanna. Long. 81. 0. W. lat. 31. 33. N.

SUNBURY, a town of Pennsylvania, chief of Northumberland county; with two churches. It stands on the E. side of the Susquehanna; 120 miles N. W. of Philadelphia. Pop. 1057.

SUNDA ISLANDS, islands in the S. E. part of the Indian Ocean. The chief of them are Borneo, Sumatra, and Java; the two latter separated by a channel, called the Strait of Sunda.

SUNDERBUNDS, a tract of country in Bengal, consisting of that part of the delta of the Ganges which borders on the sea. In extent it is equal to the principality of Wales. It is completely enveloped in wood, infested with tigers, and composed of a labyrinth of rivers and creeks, all of which are salt, except those that immediately communicate with the principal arm of the Ganges. Here salt, in quantities equal to the whole consumption of Bengal and its dependencies, is made and transported with equal facility; and here also is found an inexhaustible store of timber for boat-building.

SUNDERBURG, a town of Denmark, in the island of Alsen, with a castle. It is seated on a strait called Sunderburg Sound; 12 miles E. of Flensburg. Pop. 2700. Long. 10. 0. E. lat. 54. 51. N.

SUNDERDOO, a fortified island and seaport of Hindostan, in Concan; reduced by Commodore James in 1756. It is 36 miles N. N. W. of Goa. Long. 73. 20. E. lat. 16. 3. N.

SUNDERLAND, a borough and seaport in the county of Durham, governed by a mayor; with a market on Saturday. It sends two members to parliament. For the exportation of coal, it is next in consequence to Newcastle. Its port, at the mouth of the Wear, will admit vessels of 400 tons; the entrance is defended by a battery, and a pier, on which is a lighthouse. Here are several small dockyards, manufactures of salt, glass, copperas, and earthenware, and a trade in lime, grindstones, and other articles. The commerce and population of this port have been gradually increasing during the last century, and the general appearance of the town has been greatly improved. The parish church is a handsome brick building; besides which are St. John's Chapel, and the church in John Street, the foundation stone of which was laid June 10, 1827. There are also in the town and suburbs 19 chapels not belonging to the establishment, besides several licensed meeting-rooms, and a Jews' synagogue. Sunderland is much frequented during the bathing season, and the neighbourhood, for several miles round, is enriched by many elegant seats and mansions. It is situate on the river Wear, over which is a magnificent iron bridge, of one immense arch, which will admit ships of 200 tons burden to sail under it. It is 13 miles N. E. of Durham, and 269 N. by W. of London. Long. 1. 2. W. lat. 54. 52. N.

SUNDERLAND, a town of Massachusets, in Hampshire county; on the E. side of the Connecticut; 10 miles N. of Hadley, and 100 W. by N. of Boston.

SUNDI, a province of Congo, which lies along the river Zaire. Its rivers render it extremely fertile, and in the mountains are mines of several metals. The capital is of the same name. Long. 17. 55. E. lat. 4. 50. N.

SUNDSWALD, a seaport of Sweden, and the capital of Medelpadia. The chief trade is in tar, birch-bark, deals, hops, flax, and linen. It is seated near the Gulf of Bothnia, 210 miles N. by W. of Stockholm. Pop. 1500. Long. 17. 50. E. lat. 62. 25. N.

SUNERGONG, or SUNNERGAUM, a town of Hindostan, in Bengal, once a large city, and famous for a manufacture of fine cotton cloth. It is seated between the Burrampooter and a branch of the Ganges, 15 miles S. E. of Dacca.

SUNK ISLAND, an island within the mouth of the Humber, 9 miles in circuit; separated from Yorkshire by a channel nearly two miles broad. It produces grain, wood, and black rabbits.

SUPERIOR, LAKE, a lake of North America, above 1500 miles in circumference, and supposed to be the largest body of fresh water on the globe. It contains many islands, two of them very large, especially Isle Royale, which is 100 miles long, and in many places 40 broad. The Indians suppose these islands to be the residence of the Great Spirit. Upwards of 30 rivers enter this lake, some of which are of considerable size, and its water is unrivalled in purity and transparency. It abounds with fish, particularly trout and sturgeon. Storms are even more dreadful on this lake than on the ocean. It discharges its water from the S. E. corner, through the Strait of St. Mary, into Lake Huron; but the quantity does not appear to be one-tenth part of what is conveyed into it by the rivers.

SUPINO, a town of Naples, in the Molise, with a castle; seated at the source of the Tamara, 17 miles N. by W. of Benevento.

SUR, or SOUR, a town of Syria, in Palestine, on the coast of the Mediterranean, where stood the famous city of Tyre, destroyed by Alexander the Great. It is now no more than a village, situate on a peninsula which projects from the shore into the sea, in the form of a mallet with an oval head. The village consists of about 60 families, who live obscurely on the produce of their little grounds, and a trifling fishery. It is 18 miles S. S. W. of Saida, and 60 S. W. of Damascus.

SURA, a town of Sweden, in Westmanland, 15 miles N. of Stroemsholm.

SURABAYAH. *See* SOURABAYA.

SURAT, a city of Hindostan, in Guzerat, with a strong citadel. The squares are large, and the streets spacious, but not paved, so that the dust is troublesome. Each street has gates of its own, with which it is shut up in times of turbulence. The larger houses are flat-roofed, with courts before them; and those of the common people are high-roofed. It is said to have 600,000 inhabitants; and its trade is considerable, notwithstanding the sand-banks that obstruct the entrance of the Tapty, which cause large vessels to load and unload at Swally, 15 miles to the W. of Surat. In this city are Mahomedans of several sects, many sorts of Gentoos, and Jews and Christians of various denominations. It is one of the stations of the London Missionary Society. The Mahomedans at Surat are not by far so strict as they are in Arabia or in other Turkish countries, nor are the distinctions of tribes among the Hindoos who reside here strictly observed. The latter are almost all of the caste of the Banyans; and their skill and dexterity in matters of calculation and economy often raise them to places of considerable trust. Some of them are very rich, but all live in a style of moderate simplicity, and wear only a plain robe of white cotton. All people of distinction in Surat, and through the rest of India, speak and write the Persian language; but in trade, corrupt Portuguese is the language used. This city was long the emporium of the most precious productions of Hindostan, for hither were brought from the interior parts an immense quantity of goods, which the merchants carried in their ships to the Red Sea, the Persian Gulf, the coasts of Malabar and Coromandel, and even to China. Since the rise of Bombay, however, the traffic of this place has greatly declined, and now consists chiefly of raw cotton and a few of its own manufactures. One thing singular in Surat is, that though there is no hospital for human beings, there is an extensive establishment of this nature for sick or maimed animals. When the Europeans turn out an old horse, or any other domestic animal, to perish, as useless, the Banyans voluntarily assume the care of it, and place it in this house, which is full of infirm and decrepit cows, sheep, rabbits, hens, pigeons, &c. The country round Surat is fertile, except towards the sea, where it is sandy and barren. Before the English East India Company obtained possession of Bombay, Surat was the seat of their presidency, and the centre of their eastern trade. It is situate 20 miles up the river Tapty, and 147 N. of Bombay. Long. 72. 48. E. lat. 21. 11. N.

SURGOOJA, a town of Hindostan, capital of a circar of the same name, in the province of Orissa. It is 75 miles N. E. of Ruttenpour, and 210 S. S. W. of Patna. Long. 83. 32. E. lat. 23. 6. N.

SURGUT, a town of Asiatic Russia, in the government of Tobolsk, surrounded by palisadoes. It is seated on the Oby, 285 miles N. N. E. of Tobolsk. Long. 73. 30. E. lat. 61. 30. N.

SURINAM, a country of Guiana, extending 75 miles along a river of the same name. It abounds with game, and singular animals of different kinds; the toad, in particular, being remarkable for its enormous size and ugly form. The products are coffee, fruits, indigo, sugar, cotton, tobacco, gums, and wood for dyeing. The woods are full of monkeys, and it is said there are serpents 30 feet long. This country was ceded by the English to the Dutch for the province of New York, in 1774. It was taken by the British in 1799, and again in 1804, but restored in 1814. The capital is Paramaribo.

SURINGIA, a seaport of Japan, in the island of Niphon, capital of a province of the same name, with a castle, where the emperors formerly resided. It is 170 miles E. of Meaco. Long. 139. 5. E. lat. 39. 30. N.

SURREY, a county of England, 37 miles long and 27 broad; bounded on the N. by Middlesex, E. by Kent, S. by Sussex, and W. by Hampshire and Berkshire. It contains 485,120 acres, is divided into 13 hundreds and 140 parishes, has six boroughs, and eight other market-towns, and sends four members to parliament for the E. and W. divisions of the county. The soil is very different in the extreme parts from that in the middle, whence it has been compared to a coarse cloth with a fine border; for the edge of the county on all sides has a rich soil, extremely fruitful in corn and grass, particularly on the N. and W. towards the Thames; but it is far otherwise in the heart of the county, where are wide tracts of sandy ground and barren heath, and in some places long ridges of hills. It produces corn, boxwood, walnuts, hops, and fullers'-earth. Medicinal herbs are raised to a considerable extent, and about 3500 acres of land consist of gardens for the supply of the London market. The principal rivers, besides the Thames (which is the boundary of this county on the N.), are the Mole, Wey, and Wandle. The spring assizes are held at Kingston, and the summer at Guildford and Croydon alternately.

Sursee, a town of Switzerland, in the canton of Lucerne, seated on the river Sur, near the Lake of Sempach; 12 miles N. W. of Lucerne.

Sus, a river of Morocco, which rises in Mount Atlas, flows through the kingdom of Sus, and enters the Atlantic at Messa. Its annual inundations enrich the country.

Sus, or Suse, a kingdom or province of the empire of Morocco, bounded on the W. by the Atlantic, N. by Morocco Proper, E. by Tafilet, and S. by Darah. It is a flat country, abounding in corn, sugar-canes, and dates. The inhabitants, who are chiefly Berebers, or ancient natives, are distinguished by their industry, and many of them who live in towns become opulent, and are much more polite than the natives of Fez and Morocco. In the mountainous part they are entirely free, and are governed by their own chiefs. The principal town is Tarudant.

Susa, or Sousa, a seaport of Tunis, the chief mart of the kingdom for oil and linen, and formerly a place of some repute; near it are considerable remains of ancient buildings. It stands on the E. coast, 75 miles S. E. of Tunis. Long. 11. 15. E. lat. 35. 40. N.

Susa, a province of the Sardinian states, in Piedmont, consisting of a broad valley interspersed with steep rocks. It has an area of 700 square miles, with 65,000 inhabitants.

Susa, a town of Piedmont, with a strong fort, called Brunette. Here are four churches and several religious houses, and near it is a triumphal arch to the honour of Augustus Cæsar. It is seated on the Doria, among pleasant mountains, and is the principal passage out of France into Italy. It was taken by the French in 1799, but was restored in 1814; 23 miles W. N. W. of Turin. Pop. 1700. Long. 7. 16. E. lat. 45. 10. N.

Susdal, a town of Russia, in the government of Volodimir, and a bishop's see. It is built of wood. It is seated on the Nerl, 90 miles N. E. of Moscow. Long. 40. 25. E. lat. 56. 26. N.

Susquehanna, a river of the United States, which issues from the Lake Otsego. It crosses three times the line that divides the state of New York from Pennsylvania, after which it flows S. E. to Wilkesbarre, and then S. W. to Sunbury, where it meets the W. branch of the Susquehanna. It then flows by Harrisburg to Havre de Grace, where it enters the head of Chesapeake Bay.

Sussac, a town of France, department of Upper Vienne, 15 miles S. E. of Limoges.

Sussex, a county of England, 70 miles long, and 28 where broadest; bounded on the N. by Surrey, N. E. and E. by Kent, S. by the English Channel, and W. by Hampshire. It contains 935,040 acres, is divided into six rapes, subdivided into 65 small hundreds, and 342 parishes. It sends four members to parliament for the eastern and western divisions of the county. The soil is various; that of the downs, and thence to the sea, is fertile in corn and grass, the latter feeding sheep, whose wool is remarkably fine; the middle abounds with meadows and rich arable ground, and the N. side is shaded with extensive woods, that used to supply fuel for the iron-works when they were in a flourishing state. The chief commodities are corn, malt, cattle, wool, wood, iron, chalk, and glass. Sussex is not distinguished for any manufacture but that of gunpowder, at Battle, and of needles, at Chichester. The principal rivers are the Arun, Adar, Ouse, and Rother. Chichester is the capital, but the spring assizes are held at Horsham, and the summer at Lewes.

Suster. *See* Tostar.

Susteren, a town of the Netherlands, in the province of Limburg; 2 miles from the river Meuse, and 10 S. of Ruremonde.

Sutherlandshire, a county of Scotland, 52 miles long, and 50 broad; bounded on the N. by the North Sea, E. by Caithness-shire and the German Ocean, S. by the Frith of Dornoch and Ross-shire, and W. by the Minch. It is divided into 14 parishes. It returns one member to parliament. Some parts of this county, called forests, are trackless deserts, destitute of trees; or bleak mountains, abounding with wild roes. In these parts there are few inhabitants, and no villages; but along the Frith of Dornoch the country is populous and well cultivated. It has abundance of ironstone, limestone, and slate, and many veins of lead-ore. Within the last 30 years the most important improvements have been effected in this county. New roads have been formed and bridges erected to facilitate the communication with other parts of the country; the feudal system, which had been tenaciously preserved here, long after it had been banished from other parts of the country, has at length been superseded, and almost all the lands, having been disencumbered of the superfluous tenants by whom they were held under the tenure of military service, are now occupied by active improvers. Dornoch is the county town.

Sutluj, or Setlege, (ancient Hyphasis,) a large river of N. W. India, tributary to the Indus, and scarcely inferior to it in magnitude. It rises in Chinese Tartary; but the true source is unknown It has been traced as far as Shipkee, on the Chinese frontier, at an elevation of 9267 feet. Flowing to the south-west, it forms the eastern boundary of Lahore, and is the eastern stream of the Punjaub. It receives the Chunaub (Acesines,) the Behoot (Hydaspes,) and the Ravee (Hydraotes,) and falls into the Indus. The rapidity of its course prevents it from being used for navigation.

Sutri, a town of the Papal States, in the patrimony of St. Peter, seated on the Puzzola; 22 miles N. W. of Rome.

Sutton, a town of Massachusetts, in Worcester county; 10 miles S. by E. of Worcester, and 46 W. S. W. of Boston.

Sutton Colefield, a corporate town in Warwickshire, with a market on Monday. It is situate in the N. W. part of the county, on a bleak eminence, surrounded by a rather barren soil; but the air is excellent, and the prospects from the high lands extensive and picturesque. Here is a stately Gothic church, and a neat Baptist meeting-house. In 1826 corporation schools were established, and almshouses have since been erected for five poor widows and as many widowers. The inhabitants have the privilege of free pasturage in a large well-wooded tract of land, called Sutton Park. Hardware forms the principal article of trade; 24 miles N. N. W. of Warwick, and 110 N. W. of London.

SUTTON-UPON-TRENT, a small town in Nottinghamshire, with a market on Monday, seated on the Trent; 6 miles S. E. of Tuxford.

SUZANNE, ST., a town of France, in the department of Mayenne; with a considerable pepper manufacture; 24 miles W. of Mans.

SVEABORG, a strong fortress of Sweden, built on several rocky islets in the Gulf of Finland. In 1808 it surrendered to the Russians. It is 3 miles S. of Helsingfors.

SVENBORG, a seaport of Denmark, in the island of Funen, with the best harbour in the island. Here are manufactures of woollen and linen; 22 miles S. of Odensee. Long. 10. 37. E. lat 55. 9. N.

SWAFFHAM, a town of Norfolk, with a market on Saturday, noted for butter. The church is handsome, and in the form of a cathedral. The other places of worship are meeting-houses for Baptists and Quakers. It is seated on a hill; 28 miles W. of Norwich, and 93 N. E. of London.

SWALE, a river in Yorkshire; which rises on the confines of Westmoreland, flows E. by Richmond, and then S. E. to its junction with the Ure, a little below Aldborough, where their united stream forms the Ouse. This river was held sacred by the Saxons, from the circumstance of upwards of 10,000 persons having been baptized in it by Paulinus, archbishop of York, upon their conversion to Christianity.

SWALLY, a town of Hindostan, in Guzerat; with a harbour, where ships receive and deliver their cargoes for the merchants of Surat. It is seated near the Gulf of Cambay; 15 miles W. of Surat. Long. 72. 33. E. lat. 21. 10. N.

SWAN RIVER. *See* AUSTRALIA, SOUTH.

SWANAGE, a town of Dorsetshire, seated on a bay of the same name, in the English Channel; 4 miles E. S. E. of Corfe Castle. It has a trade in herrings; also quarries of fine stone, of which many thousand tons are shipped here annually.

SWANSBOROUGH, a town of North Carolina; chief of Onslow county, to the N. E. of Wilmington; 40 miles S. S. W. of Newbern.

SWANSEA, a seaport and borough of Wales, in Glamorganshire; governed by a portreeve, with markets on Wednesday and Saturday; it has an old castle, and two churches. It returns one member to parliament, with its contributories. Coal, iron, and limestone abound in its neighbourhood, and great quantities are exported. It has a considerable trade to Bristol, and extensive works for the smelting of copper and lead-ore. Many ships have been built here, and it is resorted to for sea-bathing. It is seated near the mouth of the Tawy; 32 miles S. W. of Brecknock, and 206 W. of London. Long. 3. 56. W. lat. 51. 37. N.

SWANSEA, a town of Massachusets, in Bristol county, on the river Taunton; 10 miles S. W. of Taunton.—Also, a town of New Hampshire, in Cheshire county; 6 miles S. of Keene.

SWANSHALS, a town of Sweden, in West Gothland; 25 miles W. S. W. of Lindkoping.

SWANTON, a town of Vermont, in Franklin county, situate on Lake Champlain, at the mouth of Mischiscoui River; 30 miles N. by E. of Burlington.

SWARTEBERG, a town of Sweden; in West Gothland; 18 miles N. W. of Uddevalla.

SWARTSLUYS, a town and fortress of the Netherlands, in Overyssel, seated on the Vecht, 4 miles from its mouth, and 8 N. of Zwoll.

SWEDEN, a kingdom of Europe; extending 1000 miles from N. to S.; and 300 from E. to W., bounded on the N. by Norwegian Lapland, E. by Russia, S. by the Gulf of Finland and the Baltic, and W. by the Sound, the Categat, and Norway. It was formerly divided into five general parts; Sweden Proper, Gothland, Nordland, Lapland, and Finland, and each of these subdivided into provinces. Sweden Proper contained Upland, Sudermania, Nericia, Westmania, and Dalecarlia. Gothland included East Gothland, Smoland, West Gothland, Wermeland, Bahus, Dalia, Schonen, Halland, Blekingen, and the isles of Gothland and Oeland. Nordland contained Gestricia, Helsingia, Medelpadia, Jemptia, Angermania, and W. Bothnia. Swedish Lapland comprised Umea, Pitea, Lulea, Tornea, and Kemi; these have no towns, and take their names from rivers that rise near the borders of Norway and flow into the Gulf of Bothnia. Finland contained Finland Proper, E. Bothnia, Tavasteland, Nyland, Savolax, and part of Kymene, and Carelia. The greater part of Finland, however, was ceded to Russia in 1808, but in 1814, on ceding the small province of Swedish Pomerania, it acquired Norway, including which, and Norwegian Lapland, the total extent of surface may be computed at 343,000 square miles, with a population scarcely exceeding 4,500,000. The whole country is now divided into 23 governments; Umea, Hernosand, Gefleborg, Upsal, Stockholm, Westeras, Nykoping, Orebro, Stora Kopparberg or Fahlun, Carlstadt, Lindkoping, Jonkoping, Kronoborg or Wexico, Calmar, Carlscrona, Scaraborg, Elfsborg, Gottenburg, Halmstadt, Christianstadt, Malmohus, and Wisby. Though enclosed by mountains on the W. and N., it is in general a very flat country; and it is remarkable, that along the whole road from Gottenburg in the W. to Stockholm in the E., there is not a single acclivity of consequence, till within a few miles of the latter. It is well watered by rivers, (though not a single navigable one worth mentioning,) numerous lakes, and inland pieces of water, on the banks of which the palaces and villas are usually built. At Stockholm, spring and autumn are scarcely to be perceived; for winter continues nine months, and summer during the remaining three. In winter the cold is excessive, and the heat in summer is considerable, the air being serene all that time. During this season, all the rocks are quite covered with flowers, and the gardens have plenty of fruits. The trees are early in blossoming, the soil being fat and sulphureous; but the fruits have not so good a taste as in more southern countries. The animals are horses, cows, hogs, goats, sheep, elks, reindeer, bears, wolves, foxes, wild cats, and squirrels. The horses are so little and feeble that seven are put to a travelling carriage, four a-breast in the first line, and three in the second; but a lame or foundered horse is seldom to be seen, which is attributed, in a great degree, to the manner of stabling them on perforated boards, without litter. Here are several sorts of fowls; and partridges, woodcocks, and falcons in great plenty. In some parts are rich silver, copper, and iron-mines, and vast forests of timber trees. The articles of export are boards, gunpowder, leather, iron, copper, tallow, skins, pitch, resin, and masts; and the imports salt, brandy, wine, linen cloth, stuffs, tobacco, sugar, spice, and paper. The inhabitants are of a robust constitution, and able to sustain the hardest labour. They are, however, more polished than formerly, and have several public schools and colleges, where the arts and sciences are taught. Their houses are generally of wood, with very little art in their construction. The roofs in many places are covered with turf, on which their goats often feed. The form of the Swedish government has frequently varied. Before the accession of Gustavus I. it was an elective monarchy. By the union of Calmar, in 1397, it was stipulated that the same monarch should rule over Denmark, Sweden, and Norway; and hence Sweden became a merely tributary kingdom to Denmark. From this state of subjection to a tyrannical foreign yoke it was rescued by Gustavus Vasa, on whom the Swedes, in 1523, conferred the sovereignty, and made the crown hereditary in his male issue. He was entrusted with great prerogatives; and these were augmented by Gustavus Adolphus, the right of succession being extended, at the same time, to the female line. In the minority of his daughter Christina, the regal powers were greatly circumscribed, and the nobles acquired such an exorbitant authority as gave great umbrage to the clergy, citizens, and peasants. This proved a favourable opportunity for Charles XI. to obtain from the states a formal cession of absolute sovereignty, which quietly devolved upon his son, Charles XII. Upon the death of the latter, the Swedes conferred the crown upon Ulrica Eleonora, his youngest sister, stipulating, at the same time, great limits to the prerogative. Ulrica resigned the crown to her consort Frederic I. From this period, the Swedish monarchy was the most limited one in Europe, till 1772, when Gustavus III. effected a revolution, by which he regained the most essential royal prerogatives, without, however, being an absolute monarch. He was assassinated in 1792, leaving his son Gustavus Adolphus a minor, who attained his majority in 1796. This prince was deposed on the 1st of May, 1809, and his uncle, the duke of Sudermania, was called to the throne. But soon after his accession, in consequence of the sudden death of his son, the crown prince, he assembled the diet of the kingdom, in order to choose a successor to the throne. This Swedish diet met for this purpose at Orebro, on the 8th of August 1810, and, after a short speech from the king, they elected the French marshal, Bernadotte, prince of Ponte Corvo, to the dignity of crown prince of Sweden. This person, though a Frenchman, and raised to rank and eminence under Bonaparte, greatly distinguished himself in the service of the allies, in 1813, at the head of the Swedish army, and in 1814 secured Norway to Sweden by the treaty of Kiel. The established religion is the Lutheran, and they have one archbishop and 13 bishops. Stockholm is the capital.

Sweden Proper, formerly one of the five grand divisions of Sweden; bounded on the S. by Gothland, W. by Norway, N. by Nordland, and E. by the Baltic Sea. It comprehended five provinces, and Stockholm, the capital of all Sweden.

Swedesborough, a town of New Jersey, in Gloucester county, on Rariton Creek; 20 miles S. by W. of Philadelphia.

Sweiny, a town of the kingdom of Darfoor, and a place of general resort for merchants trading to Egypt. It is 45 miles N. of Cobbo.

Swift, a river of England, in the counties of Leicester and Warwick. It runs into the Avon, above Rugby.

Swindon, a town in Wiltshire, with a market on Monday, situate on an eminence; 28 miles N. of Salisbury, and 83 W. of London.

Swinemunde, a town of the Prussian states, in Pomerania, in the isle of Usedom, situate at the mouth of the river Swine; 13 miles E. by N. of Usedom. Long. 14. 12. E. lat. 53. 56. N.

Swineshead, a town in Lincolnshire, with a market on Thursday. The sea formerly came up to the town, and there was a haven near the present market-place; and, about 30 years since, a bridge was taken down which crossed a navigable river, now choked up. It is six miles E. of Boston, and 110 N. of London.

Swinna, a small island of Scotland, one of the Orkneys; situate near the middle of the Pentland Frith. Here are two whirlpools that are dangerous to mariners, particularly in a calm.

Switzerland, a country of Europe, bounded on the N. and E. by Germany, S. by Italy, and W. by France. It is 220 miles long, and 140 broad, and is separated from the adjacent countries by high mountains, called the Alps. Area, 18,681 square miles. Pop. 2,250,000. Switzerland has been divided, since 1815, into 22 cantons, namely, Lucerne, Uri, Schweitz, Underwalden, Zug, Friburg, Soleure, Ticino, Valais, Bern, Basel, Schaffhausen, Zurich, Vaud, Neufchatel, Geneva, Appenzel, Glarus, Grisons, St. Gall, Thurgau, and Aargau. The first nine are Catholics, the next seven are Calvinists, and the others contain both religions. Each canton has its distinct internal goverment. The general government of the country is by a diet, composed of a member from each canton, which assembles annually in June, at Friburg, Bern, Soleure, Basil, Zurich, or Lucerne, in rotation; and the president is styled Landamman of Switzerland. The diet declares war, concludes peace, makes alliances with foreign states, and also decides on all treaties on commerce. The armed force is fixed at 30,000 men. There are four passages over the Alps into Italy from Switzerland; the first is beyond the lake of Geneva, over Mount Cenis, which leads to Savoy; the second begins in the country of the Grisons, crosses Mount St. Bernard, and leads to the valley of Aosta, in Piedmont; the third, the celebrated Simplon pass, begins in the country of the Grisons, crosses Mount Simplon, and leads to the duchy of Milan; the fourth crosses Mount St. Gothard, and the bailiwicks of Italy, and terminates in the Milanese. The principal lakes are those of Constance, Geneva, Lucerne, Zurich, and Neufchatel. The most considerable rivers are the Rhine, Rhone, Aar, Arve, Reuss, and Limmat. Switzerland exceeds every country in the world in diversity of appearance: the vast chain of Alps, with enormous precipices, extensive regions of perpetual snow, and glaciers that resemble seas of ice, are contrasted by the vineyard and cultivated field, the richly-wooded brow, and the verdant valley with its crystal stream. Agriculture cannot of course be carried to great extent, but the grain produced is sufficient for domestic consumption. The chief riches consist of excellent pastures, in which many cattle are bred and fattened, and the goats and chamois feed on the mountains and in the woods. The men are strong and robust. The women are tolerably handsome, and are in general very industrious. The peasants retain their old manner of dress, and are content to live upon milk, butter, and cheese; and there are some of the mountaineers who never have any bread. In 1797, the partizans of France having excited disturbances in Switzerland, the French entered the country; and, after defeating the troops and the peasants, who opposed them in several battles, they abolished the constitutions of the principal cantons, erected what was termed the Helvetic Republic, and vested the government in two councils and a directory. This constitution was abolished in 1802, by the first consul of France, and another was presented for their acceptance, but rejected; he offered them a new one in 1803, which they consented to accept. In December, 1813, the allied armies traversed the country, for the purpose of invading France, when some partial changes again took place in the administration of Switzerland, which was the cause of violent commotions amongst several of the cantons; but in 1814, on the meeting of the diet, these disturbances were appeased, and on the 8th of September a federal compact was signed at Zurich.

Switzerland, New, a settlement of Indiana; commenced in 1805 by emigrants from the Pays de Vaud, for the purpose of cultivating the vine. Pop. 7111.

Swords, a town of Ireland, in the county of Dublin, 9 miles from Dublin. It has a spacious church, a Catholic chapel, and infantry barracks. Here are the ruins of a monastery, an archiepiscopal palace and a pillar tower.

Sya, a town of Sweden, in West Gothland; 13 miles S. W. of Lindkoping.

Sydney Bay, a bay on the S. side of Norfolk Island, in the South Pacific. Long. 168. 12. E. lat. 29. 4. S.

Sydney, the capital of New South Wales, founded by Governor Philip, in 1788, as a British settlement for the colony of convicts originally intended for Botany Bay. It is now a corporate city and the principal seat of government, has three Episcopal churches, with a cathedral (in course of erection), two Catholic chapels, an extensive gaol, military barracks, hospitals (for military and convicts), a naval yard, an excellent market, &c. The governor's residence, which fronts the harbour, is of recent erection, and presents a very striking appearance. Sydney has also chapels for dissenters: 7 banking companies, insurance offices, benevolent and literary institutions. It is situate on the S. side of the harbour of Port Jackson, on the E. of an inlet called Darling Harbour. Long. 151. 23. E. lat. 33. 48. S.

Syene, or Essouan, a town of Egypt, with a small fort, on the right bank of the Nile. It was anciently a city, and celebrated for the first attempt to ascertain the circumference of the earth, by Eratosthenes, a native of Cyrene, about the year 275 B.C. The remains of the ancient town are on an eminence to the S., where columns and pillars of granite, scattered here and there, denote its situation. Near it, on a small island in the Nile, anciently called Elephantina, are the ruins of a temple of Cnuphis. It is 400 miles S. of Cairo. Long. 33. 20. E. lat. 24. 0. N.

Sylt, an island of Denmark, on the W. coast of Jutland, of an irregular form, about 40 miles in circumference, but in no part above 2 miles from the sea. Great quantities of oysters are found here. The chief town is Morsum. Long. 8. 26. E. lat. 54. 57. N.

Sylves, a town of Portugal, in Algarva, situate on a river of the same name; 15 miles E. N. E. of Lagos, and 42 W. of Tavira.

Symi. *See* Simi.

Sympheropol, or Simferopol, the capital of the Crimea, or Russian province of Taurida. The houses are built of stone, and roofed, in the ancient Greek style, with tiles. There are likewise numerous modern handsome buildings, for the residence of the governor, judges, and other civil officers. The old Tartar part of the town, called Achmetshet, is dirty and ill-built. The environs are beautiful; and, 2 miles to the E. of the city, is the mountain Tchatirdagh, the highest in the Crimea, and the Mons Berosus of the ancients. Sympheropol is situate on the Salgir, the principal river of the province; 65 miles W. by S. of Caffa, and 90 S. by E. of Precop. Long. 34. 0. E. lat. 44. 52. N.

Syracuse, a seaport of Sicily, in Val di Noto, and a bishop's see, with a fine harbour, defended by a castle. It was once the metropolis of all Sicily; but war, tyranny, and earthquakes have reduced it to less than one-fourth of its former size, when it was deemed one of the most famous cities in the world, and 22 miles in compass. Near this place, in 1718, there was a sea-fight between the Spaniards and English, in which the latter were victorious. It is seated near the sea; 72 miles S. by W. of Messina, and 110 S. E. of Palermo. Pop. 15,000. Long. 15. 10. E. lat. 37. 5. N.

Syria, (El Sham,) a province of Turkey in Asia, bounded on the N. by Natolia and Diarbeck, E. by the latter and the deserts of Arabia, S. by Arabia Petræa, and W. by the Mediterranean. Under the general name of Syria was included the ancient Phœnicia, lying S. of Syria Proper. This province abounds in oil, corn, and several sorts of fruits, as well as peas, beans, and all kinds of pulse and garden-stuff but it would produce much more than it does, if it were well cultivated; for there are the finest valleys in the world between the mountains, whose sides are proper for the cultivation of tobacco, olives, and vines. The inhabitants have a trade in silk, camlets, and salt. Syria was possessed by a succession of foreign nations, before the time of Ptolemy, when it became a province of the Roman empire. Five centuries after, when the sons of Theodosius divided their immense patrimony, this country was annexed to the empire of Constantinople. In this situation it continued till the year 622, when the Arabian tribes, under the banners of Mahomet, seized, or rather laid it waste. Since that period it has been torn to pieces by the civil wars of the Fatimites and Ommiades; wrested from the khalifs by their rebellious governors; taken from them by the Turkoman soldiers; invaded by the European crusaders; retaken by the Mamelukes of Egypt; and ravaged by Tamerlane and his Tartars; it fell, at length, into the hands of the Ottoman Turks, who have been its masters nearly three centuries. It is divided into pachalics, or governments; Aleppo, Tripoli, Damascus, Acre, and Gaza. The whole area amounts to 51,778 square miles, and the population probably is about 2,000,000. Aleppo is the capital.

Syriam, a seaport of Birmah, in Pegu, seated at the head of a river of the same name, opposite the mouth of Pegu River; 2 miles to the S. is the great pagoda of Syriam. It is 8 miles E. by N. of Rangoon, and 60 S. of Pegu. Long. 96. 17. E. lat. 16. 50. N.

Syrk, a town of France, in the department of Moselle; 14 miles S. E. of Luxemburg.

Szekely, a town of Hungary, 18 miles E. S. E. of Debreczen.

Szluin, a district of Austria, in Croatia, comprising an area of 320 square miles, with 43,000 inhabitants. It has a small town of the same name, on the Crona; 24 miles S. by E. of Carlstadt.

Szucca, a town of West Prussia, seated on the Vistula; 12 miles S. by W. of Culm.

T.

Taafe, or Tave, a river of Wales, which rises in Brecknockshire, and flows through Glamorganshire, by Merthyr Tidvil, Pont y Prydd, and Cardiff, into the Bristol Channel.

Taaif, a town of Arabia, in the province of Hedjas, with a considerable trade in raisins and almonds, and other fruits. It is situate on a lofty mountain; 60 miles S. E. of Mecca. Long. 41. 35. E. lat. 21. 5. N.

Taas, a strong city of Arabia, in the province of Yemen, with a fortress. Here is the tomb of a saint, who, according to tradition, was king of the country. The city is seated at the foot of a fertile hill; 48 miles E. N. E. of Mocha. Long. 44. 10. E. lat. 13. 45. S.

Taasinge, an island of Denmark, between those of Langeland and Funen; 8 miles long, and 4 broad. Long. 10. 37. E. lat. 54. 48. N.

Taata, a town of Upper Egypt, one mile from the Nile. It is the residence of a governor, has many curious remains of antiquity, and is 200 miles S. of Cairo. Long. 31. 25. E. lat. 26. 56. N.

Tabaga, an island in the Bay of Panama, 4 miles long, and 3 broad. It is mountainous, but abounds with fruit-trees. Long. 80. 16. W. lat. 7. 50. S.

Tabarca, an island on the coast of Barbary, at the mouth of the Zaine. It was fortified, and had a populous city of the same name, when under the dominion of the Genoese, who had a coral-fishery here. But in 1757, on the Genoese attempting to transfer the island to France, the Tabarcans surrendered their city to Tunis; and they were cruelly deceived by the bey, for he razed the fortifications, and took away most of the inhabitants as slaves. It is 50 miles W. N. W. of Tunis. Long. 9. 16. E. lat. 36. 50. N.

Tabaria (the ancient Tiberias), a town of Palestine, situate on the W. side of a lake, formerly called the Sea of Tiberias; 50 miles N. N. E. of Jerusalem, and 70 S. S. W. of Damascus. Long. 35. 45. E. lat. 32. 40. N.

Tabasco, a province of Mexico, bounded on the N. by the Bay of Campeachy, E. by Jucatan, S. by Chiapa, and W. by Guaxaca. It is 100 miles long, and 50 broad; and its chief riches consist in cocoa-nuts. There are showers every day for nine months in the year.

Tabasco, the capital of the above province, called by the Spaniards Nuestra Senora de la Vittoria, from a great victory obtained here by Cortes on his first arrival. It is situate on an island of the same name, 30 miles long and 10 broad, formed by the river Tabasco and that of St. Peter and Paul; and on the Bay of Campeachy; 270 miles N. E. of Chiapa. Long. 93. 20. W. lat. 18. 20. N.

Taberg, a town of Sweden, noted for its rich mines of iron; 10 miles S. of Jonkoping.

Table Island, one of the New Hebrides, in the South Pacific. Long. 167. 7. E. lat. 15. 38. S.

Taboo, a town of Cassina, the capital of a country lying to the E. of Zahara. It is 280 miles N. by W. of Agades. Long. 12. 10. E. lat. 24. 0. N.

Tabor, a town of Bohemia, in the circle of its name. The Hussites, under their celebrated general Zisca, fortified it, and made it their principal retreat. It is seated on a mountain of the same name, by the river Luschnitz; 11 miles N. N. E. of Bechin. Pop. 3800.

Tabor, a mountain of Palestine, which commands a view of the Jordan, the lake Gennesareth, and the Mediterranean. It is 6 miles S. of Nazareth.

Tabriz. *See* Tauris.

Tacames. *See* Atacama.

Tacazze, a river which rises in Abyssinia, flows N. W. into Nubia, and joins the Nile at Ilak.

Tachau, a town of Bohemia, in the circle of Pilsen, on the river Mies; 28 miles W. of Pilsen.

Tacuba, a town of the republic of Mexico, in a district of its name. It is 6 miles W. N. W. of Mexico.

Tacurga, a town of Columbia, capital of a district of the same name; seated at the foot of the Andes, 18 miles from the volcano of Cotopaxi. It was destroyed by an earthquake in 1698, and suffered again in 1743 and 1757. It has several convents, and a manufacture of cloth; 44 miles S. of Quito. Pop. 12,000.

Tadcaster, a town in West Yorkshire, with a market on Wednesday. Besides the parish church, here are places of worship for Independents, Inghamites, and Methodists; the Methodists, who form a numerous and respectable congregation, have erected a chapel capable of seating 900 persons. Limestone is procured in great abundance in the neighbourhood of this town. It is seated on the river Wharf, over which is one of the finest bridges in the county, built with the materials which once formed the castle that stood on the S. bank of the river. It is 10 miles S. W. of York, and 186 N. by W. of London.

Tadivan, or **Taduan**, a town of Persia, in Farsistan; situate in a fruitful valley; 60 miles S. of Shiras.

Tadmor. *See* Palmyra.

Tadousac, a town of Lower Canada, which is of great resort for trading with the Indians, who bring hither furs to exchange for cloth and other European goods. It is situate at the mouth of the Saguenay, on the river St. Lawrence; 98 miles N. E. of Quebec. Long. 68. 35. W. lat. 48. 5. N.

Tafalla, a town of Spain, in Navarre, with a university. Charles II., king of Navarre, built a palace here, which he made his ordinary residence; and Philip IV. honoured the town with the title of city. It is seated on the Cidazzo, in a country producing good wine; 18 miles S. of Pamplona. Pop. 3000. Long. 1. 36. W. lat. 42. 29. N.

Tafilet, a kingdom of Barbary, on the E. side of Mount Atlas, tributary to Morocco. It is bounded on the N. by Algier, E. by the Berberes, S. by Zahara, and W. by Darah and Morocco. The country is sandy and mountainous, but produces wheat and barley by the sides of the rivers. The inhabitants live upon camels' flesh and dates, and they breed horses to sell to foreigners. The Arabs live in tents, and the Berberes, the ancient inhabitants, dwell in villages. Pop. 600,000.

Tafilet, the capital of the above kingdom, with a castle. It is a trading-place, and seated on a river of its name; 275 miles S. E. of Morocco. Long. 4. 20. W. lat. 30. 40. N.

Taganrog, a seaport and fort of Russia, situate on the N. W. extremity of the Sea of Asoph. It is the largest and best port on this sea, and carries on a considerable trade with Constantinople and the Archipelago, particularly in corn and butter. It is employed in ship-building; 33 miles W. N. W. of Asoph. Pop. 6000. Long. 18. 40. E. lat. 47. 14. N.

Tagliacozza, a town of Naples, in Abruzzo Ultra; 18 miles S. W. of Aquila, and 33 E. N. E. of Rome.

Tagliamento, a river of Austrian Italy, which rises in the Alps, on the frontiers of Germany, and runs S. through Friuli and Trevisano, into the Gulf of Venice.

Tagoast, or **Tagavast**, a town of Western Africa, in the province of Sus, by some said to have been the birthplace of St. Augustine. A great many Jews live here, who carry on considerable trade. It is seated in a fertile plain, 37 miles S. of Tarudant.

Tagumadert, a town of the kingdom of Darah, North Africa, with a strong castle on a mountain; seated on the river Darah, 20 miles S. of Tattah.

Tagus, or **Tajo**, a river which has its source on the confines of Arragon, in Spain, runs through New Castile, by Aranjuez, Toledo, and Talavera, whence it proceeds by Alcantara, in Estremadura, when, entering Portugal, it flows by Abrantes and Santarem, below which it forms the harbour of Lisbon, and then enters the Atlantic Ocean.

Tahiti. *See* Otaheite.

Tai, a lake of China, in the provinces of Kiang-nan and Tche-kiang; nearly 50 leagues in circumference, and 75 miles S. E. of Nanking.

Taief, a town of Arabia Deserta, in Hedjas, with a castle on a mountain; 60 miles S. E. of Mecca.

Tailleborg, a town of France, department of Lower Charente; 30 miles S. E. of Rochelle.

Tain, a borough of Scotland, in Ross-shire, with a large square tower adorned with five spires, and an elegant church, formerly collegiate. It is seated near the Frith of Dornoch, 10 miles N. of Cromarty. In conjunction with Dingwall, &c. it sends one member to parliament. Long. 3. 51. W. lat. 57. 46. N.

Tai-ouan, a city and seaport, capital of the island of Formosa. The streets are nearly straight, from 30 to 40 feet in breadth, and some of them above two miles in length. They are covered seven months in the year with awnings, to defend them from the heat of the sun. The harbour is sheltered from every wind. It is seated on the W. side of the island. Long. 120. 30. E. lat. 23. 25. N.

TAI-PING, a city of China, of the first rank, in the province of Kiang-nan; seated on the Kian-ku, 25 miles S. S. W. of Nanking. Long. 118. 15. E. lat. 32. 26. N.

TAI-PING, a strong city of China, of the first rank, in the province of Quang-si; seated on a point of land almost surrounded by a river, 360 miles W. by S. of Canton. Long. 107. 0. E. lat. 22. 36. N.

TAI-TCHEOU, a city of China, of the first rank, in the province of Tche-kiang; seated on the bank of a river, in a mountainous country, 720 miles S. S. E. of Peking. Long. 121. 2. E. lat. 28. 55. N.

TAI-TONG, a strong city of China, of the first rank, in the province of Chan-si; seated near the Great Wall, in a mountainous country, 155 miles W. of Peking. Long. 113. 2. E. lat. 40. 5. N.

TAI-YUEN, a city of China, capital of the province of Chan-si. It is 8 miles in circumference, but much decayed since it was the residence of the princes of the last imperial family of Tai-ming-tchao; 220 miles S. W. of Peking. Long. 111. 56. E. lat. 37. 54. N.

TALACUDA, a town of Hindostan, in Mysore, with a celebrated temple. It is 24 miles E. S. E. of Mysore.

TALAVERA DE LA REYNA, a town of Spain, in New Castile, with a fort. It has manufactures of silk, and a pottery. A very obstinate battle was fought in its vicinity between the British and French armies in 1809. It is seated on the Tagus, in a valley abounding in corn, fruits, and excellent wine; 58 miles S. W. of Madrid. Pop. 8000. Long. 4. 1. W. lat. 39. 41. N.

TALCAGUANA, a seaport of Chili, on the S. E. shore of the Bay of Conception, and near the ruins of the Old City of Conception. It is now the only Spanish settlement in the bay; 9 miles from the New City of Conception. Long. 73. 0. W. lat. 36. 42. S.

TA-LI, a city of China, of the first rank, in the province of Yun-nan. Here are made curious tables and ornaments of fine marble, which is naturally beautiful with different colours, representing mountains, flowers, trees, and rivers; 160 miles W. N. W. of Yun-nan. Long. 100. 6. E. lat. 24. 54. N.

TALLAHASSEE, a town of North America, Florida, of which it is the capital. It was founded in 1824, and has become of some importance. It is seated on the river Tuzabona. Lat. 30. 27. N. long. 84. 25. W.

TALLANO, a seaport of Corsica, situate on the Gulf of Tallano, 24 miles N. N. W. of Bonifacio, and 30 S. S. W. of Corte. Long. 9. 18. E. lat. 51. 20. N.

TALLERD, a town of France, department of Upper Alps; seated on the Durance, 9 miles S. of Gap.

TALMONT, a town in the department of Lower Charente, with a harbour, near the mouth of the Gironde; 20 miles S. W. of Saintes.

TALNERE, a celebrated town and fortress of Hindostan, in the province of Khandeish; taken by the British in 1818. Long. 75. 2. E. lat. 21. 13. N.

TAMALAMECA, a town of Terra Firma, in the province of St. Martha, seated on the Madalena, 140 miles S. of St. Martha. Long. 74. 15. W. lat. 9. 6. N.

TAMAN. See PHANAGORIA.

TAMANAH, a town of Hindostan, in the province of Concan; 24 miles S. by E. of Gheriah.

TAMAR, a river which rises in the N. part of Cornwall, on the borders of Devonshire, takes a southerly course, separating the two counties, and forms the harbour of Hamoaze, at Plymouth.

TAMARA, the capital of the island of Socotra, with a good harbour. The trade consists chiefly in aloes, frankincense, ambergris, and dragons'-blood. It is seated on a bay, on the N. coast of the island. Long. 53. 45. E. lat. 11. 56. N.

TAMARICA, or ITAMARICA, a province of Brazil, between Paraibo on the N. and Pernambuco on the S. On the coast is an island of the same name, 24 miles in length, which has a harbour, and good fresh water. Long. 35. 5. W. lat. 7. 56. N.

TAMBOV, a government of European Russia, to the W. of those of Penna and Saratov. It is divided into 12 circles, and contains an area of 21,000 square miles, with 1,140,000 inhabitants. The soil in the S. part is very fertile; in the N. it is sandy, and in many parts woody and fertile. It is watered by a number of lakes and rivers.

TAMBOV, a town of Russia, capital of the above government, and a bishop's see; with manufactures of woollen, linen, canvas, and alum. It is seated on the Tzna, which flows into the Mokscha; 228 miles S. E. of Moscow. Pop. 10,700. Long. 41. 45. E. lat. 52. 44. N.

TAME, a river which rises in Staffordshire, and, entering Warwickshire, flows first E. and then N. till it re-enters its native county at Tamworth, below which it joins the Trent, 7 miles above Burton.

TAME, a river which rises in Hertfordshire. See THAME.

TAMIEH, a town of Egypt, on a canal which communicates with the Nile; 12 miles N. E. of Fayoum.

TAMISE, a town of Belgium, province of East Flanders, with manufactures of linen and lace; 8 miles N. of Dendermonde. Pop. 5700.

TAMWORTH, a borough in Staffordshire, returning two members to parliament; with a market on Saturday, and manufactures of carpets and narrow cloths. In the neighbourhood are many streams of water, upon which are corn and cotton-mills; and near it are several coal-mines. The church, formerly collegiate, is a very handsome structure, and is said to be the largest parish church in England. The different denominations of dissenters have five meeting-houses; and here are several almshouses, a free grammar-school, a national school, several other charitable institutions, and an excellent library. The E.

part of the town is in Warwickshire. Tamworth Castle is the seat of Sir Robert Peel. It is seated at the confluence of the Aker and the Tame, the latter, which is much the larger river, giving name to the town; 7 miles S. E. of Litchfield, and 111 N. W. of London.

TANA, a river of North Europe, dividing Swedish Lapland from Russia, for 150 miles, and falling into a gulf of the same name, in the Arctic Ocean.

TANARO, a river of the Sardinian States, which rises in Piedmont, flows by Cherasco, Alba, Asti, and Alexandria, and joins the Po below Valenza.

TANCOS, a town of Portugal, in Estremadura; 12 miles S. S. E. of Tomar.

TANCROWAL, a town of Africa; seated on the Gambia, where the English have a fort. Long. 14. 27. W. lat. 13. 10. N.

TANDA, or TANRAH, a town in Bengal, of which it was the capital in the 17th century. It is seated on the Ganges, 120 miles N. W. of Dacca. Long. 87. 56. E. lat. 23. 25. N.

TANDERAGEE, a town of Ireland, in the county of Armagh; with an extensive linen manufacture, and a considerable trade. It stands near the Newry Canal; 11 miles E. N. E. of Armagh, and 13 N. N. W. of Newry.

TANEYTON, a handsome town of Maryland, in Frederick county, with two churches; 27 miles N. by E. of Fredericktown.

TANGERMUNDE, a town of Prussia, province of Saxony, with a castle; 24 miles W. N. W. of Brandenburg. Pop. 3200.

TANGIER, a seaport of the kingdom of Fez, with a castle, and surrounded by a wall. The trade consists in supplying the opposite coasts with provisions. It was taken by the Portuguese in 1471, and ceded to Charles II. of England, on his marriage with the princess Catherine, but he did not think it worth the expense of keeping, and in 1683 caused the works to be blown up. It is seated on the Strait of Gibraltar, 140 miles N. W. of Fez. Long. 5. 48. W. lat. 35. 46. N.

TANJORE, a province of Hindostan, on the coast of Coromandel; 95 miles long, and 50 broad. It is an appendage of the Carnatic, but subject to its own rajah, who pays an annual subsidy to the English East India Company. The Mahomedans never having actually occupied this territory, or effected any permanent establishment in it, the Hindoo religion has been preserved in considerable splendour, and the ancient temples, with their vast endowments, remain untouched. In almost every village there is a temple, with a lofty gateway of massive but not inelegant architecture, where a great many Brahmins are maintained, either by the revenues formerly attached to them, or by an allowance from government. The Brahmins are here the chief holders of land, and perform almost every office of husbandry, except holding the plough. They are all extremely loyal, on account of the protection they receive, and also the allowance granted by the British government, of 45,000 pagodas (about 18,000*l.* sterling) annually, which is distributed for the support of the poorer temples. Population, 903,000.

TANJORE, a city of Hindostan, capital of the foregoing province. Here is one of the handsomest temples in the S. of India; also the rajah's palace, which is a grand square, surrounded by a wall and a wet ditch. It is seated on a branch of the Cavery; 205 miles S. by W. of Madras. Long. 79. 12. E. lat. 10. 46. N.

TANKIA, a town and fortress of Tibet, at the foot of a mountain; 275 miles W. S. W. of Lassa. Long. 87. 22. E. lat. 29. 5. N.

TANNA, a fertile island in the South Pacific, one of the New Hebrides, on which are a volcano and some hot springs. It is 22 miles long, and 10 broad, and was discovered in 1774 by Cook, who named the harbour where he lay Port Resolution, from the name of his ship. The inhabitants are brave and hospitable; their arms are bows and arrows, slings, spears, and clubs. Long. 169. 41. E. lat. 19. 32. S.

TANNA, a town of Hindostan, in the island of Salsette, on the E. coast; 15 miles N. E. of Bombay.

TANORE, a seaport of Hindostan, in the province of Malabar, belonging to the British; 28 miles S. S. E. of Calicut. Long. 75. 50. E. lat. 10. 55. N.

TAORMINA (the ancient Tannomenium,) a seaport of Sicily, in Val di Demona; seated on a rocky eminence, on the E. coast; 34 miles S. S. W. of Messina. Pop. 4000.

TAOUKA, a small island in the South Pacific; 65 leagues N. E. of Otaheite. Long. 145. 9. W. lat. 14. 30. S.

TAPAJOS, a large river of Brazil, which rises in Matto Grosso, near the sources of the Paraguay, which flows in an opposite direction. It flows to the N. N. E., and falls into the Amazons at Santarem.

TAPOOR, a town of Hindostan, in Mysore; 83 miles E. S. E. of Seringapatam.

TAPPAHANNOC, a town of Virginia; chief of Essex county. It has some export trade, and stands on the S. W. branch of the Rappahannoc; 54 miles N. E. of Richmond. Pop. 7000.

TAPPAN, a town of New York, in Orange county; 3 miles from the W. bank of the Hudson, and at the S. end of the broad part of it called the Tappan Sea. Here, in 1780, Major André was tried, and suffered as a spy, being taken on his way to New York, after concerting a plan with General Arnold for delivering up West Point to the British. It is 25 miles N. of New York.

TAPPANOOLY, a seaport on the W. side of the island of Sumatra, situate on a small island called Punchongkecheel. The bay is very deep, and capable of containing the united navies of Europe. The English East India Company have a factory here. It was taken by the French, but restored at the peace in 1763. Long. 98. 50. E. lat. 1. 40. N.

TAPTY, a river of Hindostan, which rises at Maltoy, in the country of Berat, and runs into the Gulf of Cambay, 20 miles below Surat.

TAR, or PAMTICO, a river of North Carolina,

which flows by Louisburg, Tarborough, Greenville, and enters Pamtico Sound, 40 miles S. E. of Washington.

TARANSA, one of the Western Islands of Scotland, 4 miles in length, and 2 where broadest. Long. 8. 55. W. lat. 58. 2. N.

TARANTAISE, a province of Sardinia, in Savoy; between Savoy Proper, Aosta, Faucigny, and Maurienne. It has an area of 780 square miles, with 39,000 inhabitants. The surface is rugged and mountainous.

TARARE, a town of France, in the department of Rhone; situate at the foot of a mountain; 20 miles W. N. W. of Lyons.

TARASCON, a town in the department of Mouths of the Rhone, with a castle; seated on the Rhone, opposite Beaucaire, with which it communicates by a bridge of boats. It has a trade in oil, brandy, starch, and silk stuffs; 10 miles N. of Arles, and 14 E. by S. of Nismes. Pop. 12,000.

TARASCON, a town in the department of Arriege; 7 miles S. S. E. of Foix.

TARAZ, a city of Western Tartary, and the capital of Turkestan. It is seated on a river which flows into the Sirr, 350 miles N. by E. of Samarcand. Long. 66. 30. E. lat. 44. 20. N.

TARAZONA, a strong town of Spain, in Arragon, and a bishop's see. It is seated partly on a rock and partly in a fertile plain; 60 miles W. N. W. of Saragossa, and 120 N. E. of Madrid. Pop. 4000.

TARBERT, a town of Scotland, in the county of Cromarty; 6 miles E. of Tain.

TARBES, a town of France, capital of the department of Upper Pyrenees, and a bishop's see; with an ancient castle, and a college, and manufactures of linen, paper, and leather. It is seated on the Adour; 42 miles S. W. of Auch, and 112 S. by E. of Bordeaux. Pop. 8000. Long. 0. 4. E. lat. 43. 14. N.

TARBOROUGH, a town of North Carolina, capital of Edgecombe county. Large quantities of tobacco, maize, pork, and beef are collected here for exportation. The town stands on the Tar; 56 miles E. by N. of Raleigh. Long. 77. 45. W. lat. 33. 58. N.

TARENTO, a seaport of Naples, in Terra d'Otranto, and an archbishop's see. It is seated on a peninsula, and defended by a strong castle; but the harbour is become shallow, and its trade is consequently diminished; 75 miles N. W. of Otrano, and 150 E. by S. of Naples. Pop. 18,500. Long. 17. 29. E. lat. 40. 35. N.

TARGA, a town of the kingdom of Fez, on the Mediterranean, with a castle on a rock; 90 miles S. E. of Tangier.

TARIFFA, (the Julia Traducta of the Romans,) a fortified seaport of Spain, in Andalusia; with a castle. In 1811 a British party, lodged here, baffled all the efforts of the French to take the town, after a long siege. It is seated on an eminence, and on the Strait of Gibraltar; 52 miles S. E. of Cadiz. Pop. 1800. Long. 5. 36. W. lat. 36. 5. N.

TARIJA, or ST. BERNARDO DE TARIJA, a town of the republic of Bolivia, in the province of Charcas, which abounds in pastures that feed a vast number of cattle and sheep. It stands near the source of the Tarija, which flows into the Vermejo; 196 miles N. N. E. of St. Salvador de Jujui. Long. 64. 50. W. lat. 21. 40. S.

TARKU, the capital of the province of Daghestan, seated on the W. coast of the Caspian Sea; 52 miles S. S. E. of Terki, and 300 N. N. E. of Tauris. Long. 47. 5. E. lat. 45. 50. N.

TARMA, a town of Peru, capital of a province of its name, which has many mines of silver, and feeds abundance of cattle; 120 miles N. E. of Lima.

TARMUTOLA, a town of Italy, in the kingdom of Sicily; 28 miles N. E. of Policastro. Pop. 4000.

TARD, a department of France, including part of Languedoc. It takes its name from a river which rises in the department of Lozere, and flows by Mithoud, Alby, Guillac, Montauban, and Moissac, into the Garonne. The superficial extent is estimated at 2100 square miles, with 296,000 inhabitants, of whom upwards of 40,000 are Protestants. Castres is the capital.

TARN-ET-GARONNE, a department of France, formed of portions of the departments of Lot and Upper Garonne, in 1808. It has an area of 1500 square miles, with 240,000 inhabitants, of whom about 30,000 are Protestants. Montauban is the capital.

TARNOPOL, a town of Austrian Galicia; capital of a circle of its name, with a brisk trade; seated on the Sereth; 84 miles E. of Lemberg. Pop. 7100.

TARNOW, a town of Austrian Galicia; capital of a circle of the same name, and a bishop's see; seated on the Danajee; 47 miles E. of Cracow. Pop. 4300.

TARNOWITZ, a town of Prussian Silesia, with a valuable iron-mine. It stands near the frontiers of Poland; 38 miles E. S. E. of Oppeln.

TARO, a town of Italy, in the grand duchy of Parma, on the river Taro; 28 miles S. W. of Parma.

TARPORLEY, a town in Cheshire, with a market on Thursday; 11 miles E. S. E. of Chester, and 173 N. W. of London.

TARRAGONA, a seaport of Spain, in Catalonia, and a bishop's see. It was very powerful in the time of the Romans, and has many noble monuments of antiquity. The cathedral is worthy of notice for its vast dimensions, the elegance of its Gothic architecture, and a magnificent chapel built with rich marble and jasper. The ordinary exports are wine and brandy; but its harbour is dangerous, and not much frequented. This town was taken by storm, by the French, in 1810, when it was nearly reduced to ashes. It is seated on a hill, at the mouth of the Francoli, in the Mediterranean; 54 miles W. S. W. of Barcelona, and 260 E. by N. of Madrid. Pop. 9000. Long. 1. 16. E. lat. 41. 10. N.

TARREGA, a town of Spain, in Catalonia; situate on a hill, on the river Cervera; 33 miles N. by W. of Tarragona. Pop. 3600.

TARSUS. *See* TERASSO.

TARTARY, or TATARY, a country of Asia, which, taken in its utmost limits, reaches from the Eastern Ocean to the Caspian Sea, and from Corea, China, Tibet, Hindostan, and Persia, to Russia and Siberia. It lies between 55. and 135. E. long., and between 35. and 55. N. lat., being 3600 miles in length, and 960 in extreme breadth, but not above 330 in the narrowest part. It may be considered under two grand divisions, namely, Eastern and Western Tartary. The greatest part of the former belongs to the emperor of China, is tributary to him, or is under his protection. It is divided into three provinces, Tcitcicar, Kirin, and Leao-tong. A considerable part of Western Tartary has been conquered by the Russians; and that part of it E. from the mountains of Imaus, or Belur, to the Caspian Sea, has for many ages been attached to Persia, and is called Independent Tartary. These vast countries include all the central parts of Asia, and are inhabited by Tartars of different denominations and different manners. For various particulars concerning them, see the articles CIRCASSIA, CRIMEA, COSSACS, GEORGIA, IMERITIA, KALMUCS, MANDSHARS, MINGRELIA, MONGOLIA, SAMOYEDES, and USBECS.

TARTAS, a town of France, in the department of Landes. The Midouse runs through it; and, on one side of this river, it rises in the form of an amphitheatre. It is 12 miles N. E. of Dax. Pop. 3200.

TARUDANT, a town of West Africa, capital of the province of Suse, and the residence of a governor, or some sheriff related to the emperor of Morocco. It is 120 miles S. W. of Morocco. Pop. 25,000. Long. 8. 35. W. lat. 29. 58. N.

TARWIS, a town of Austrian Illyria, in Carinthia; seated on the rivulet called Gailitz. It is 28 miles W. S. W. of Clagenfurt.

TASHKUND, a city of Independent Tartary, formerly capital of the province of Turkestan. It is seated on the Sihon, 210 miles N. of Samarcand. Long. 64. 48. E. lat. 42. 40. N.

TASMANIA, a name given to Van Diemen's Land from its discoverer, and the title of the bishop's diocese. See VAN DIEMEN'S LAND.

TASSACORTA, a town of the isle of Palma, one of the Canaries. It lies S. W. of St. Cruz, and, being exposed to westerly winds, is little frequented but by boats. Long. 17. 58. W. lat. 28. 38. N.

TASSASUDON, the capital of Bootan, a feudatory country of Tibet. The castle, or palace, is an extensive quadrangular building of stone, with accommodation for the raja, or lama, all the officers of state, a very numerous establishment of Gylongs, and a temple of the great idol Mahamoonie. It is seated on the Tchintchieu, in a well cultivated valley, surrounded by mountains; 280 miles S. S. W. of Lassa. Long. 89. 40. E. lat. 27. 49. N.

TASSING, an island of Denmark, between Funen and Langeland; separated from the former by a strait. It is 18 miles in circuit, and has a town of the same name. Long. 10. 47. E. lat. 55. 7. N.

TATA, a town in the W. of Hungary. The inhabitants are employed in the woollen manufacture; 64 miles E. S. E. of Presburg. Pop. 8600.

TATTA, a city of Hindostan, capital of an extensive district of its name, in the province of Sinde. It is seated on a branch of the river Sinde or Indus. In the 17th century it was very extensive and populous, possessing manufactures of silk, wool, and cotton; and it was celebrated for its cabinet ware. Little of these now remain, and the limits of the city are very circumscribed. The Indus and its branches admit of an uninterrupted navigation from Tatta to Moultan, Lahore, and Cashmere, for vessels of nearly 200 tons; and a very extensive trade was carried on between those places in the time of Aurungzebe; but this trade is now much diminished, owing to a bad government in Sinde, and to a hostile disposition of the Seiks. It is 280 miles W. N. W. of Amedabad, and 390 S. S. W. of Moultan. Pop. 15,000. Long. 67. 37. E. lat. 24. 50. N.

TATTAH, a town on the common frontiers of Morocco, Darah, and Tafilet, and in the route from Morocco to Timbuctoo. It is 170 miles S. by E. of Morocco. Long. 6. 15. W. lat. 28. 25. N.

TATTERSHALL, a small town in Lincolnshire, with a market on Thursday. It contains the remains of an ancient castle, and stands on the Bane; 21 miles S. E. of Lincoln, and 128 N. E. of London.

TAUCKEL, a town of Prussia, in Pomerelia; seated on the Verd; 30 miles N. W. of Culm.

TAUMACO, a town of European Turkey, in the province of Janna; 18 miles N. W. of Zeiton.

TAUMAGO, a fertile island in the Pacific Ocean, 24 miles in circuit; discovered by Quiros in 1606. Long. 170. 45. W. lat. 13. 0. S.

TAUNTON, a town of Massachusets, chief of Bristol county; seated on Taunton River, which is navigable hence for small vessels to Narraganset Bay. Here are various manufactures of iron, and also a manufacture of ochre into pigments of a dark yellow colour. It is 36 miles S. of Boston. Pop. 6045.

TAUNTON, a borough in Somersetshire, governed by a mayor; with markets on Wednesday and Saturday. It sends two members to parliament. It is situate in an extensive and fertile valley, called Taunton Dean, on the river Tone, which is navigable hence to the Parret. The silk trade furnishes the principal employment of the inhabitants, the manufacture of coarse woollen goods, which was formerly carried on here to a considerable extent, having been transferred to Wellington and other neighbouring towns. Here was once a strong castle, part of which still remains, and is converted to various uses. The town is well built, and has undergone great improvement of late years. It contains two parish churches, several meeting-houses, a free grammar-school, an hospital or infirmary, and other charitable institutions. The spring assizes are held here. Taunton was the scene of many bloody executions in the reign of James II., after the defeat of the Duke of Monmouth, at Sedgemoor, near this town. It is 31 miles N. E. of Exeter, and 141 W. by S. of London. Long. 3. 17. W. lat. 50. 59. N.

Taureau, an isle of France, department of Finisterre; at the mouth of the river Morlaix; with a fort to defend the port of Morlaix.

Taurida. *See* Crimea.

Tauris, or Tabriz, a city of Persia, capital of Azerbjan, and formerly the capital of Persia. It is of an irregular figure, and has neither walls nor fortifications. The river Spingtcha flows through it, and the Agi passes on the N. side of the city. The bazaars, from their largeness, the beautiful domes with which they are covered, and the merchandise with which they are filled, make as fine an appearance as any in Asia. Here were formerly 300 caravanserais so spacious that 300 persons might lodge in each; and the mosques and baths were grand and magnificent structures. In 1724 it was terribly shaken by an earthquake, and nearly 100,000 persons perished. Soon after this calamity the Turks laid siege to it, and they were driven away with great loss; but they took it the next year, after a bloody contest, in which the Persians lost 30,000 men, and the Turks 20,000. Of 250 mosques, mentioned by Chardin, the ruins of three only are visible. The inhabitants carry on a good trade in cotton, cloth, silks, gold and silver brocades, fine turbans, and shagreen leather. It is seated in a fertile plain, at the foot of a mountain, 95 miles S. E. of Naksivan, and 320 N. W. of Ispahan. Pop. 30,000. Long. 48. 0. E. lat. 38. 28. N.

Taurus, or Kuron, a chain of mountains in Asia, which begins near the shores of the Archipelago, and extends 600 miles to the river Euphrates. The Taurian chain was formerly considered as extending to the sources of the Ganges, and the extremities of Asia, as far as discovered by the ancients; but various parts of it were known by different names.

Taus, a town of Bohemia, in the circle of Pilsen; 31 miles S. S. W. of Pilsen. Pop. 4400.

Tavastland, a district of European Russia, in the middle of Finland; 150 miles long, and 100 broad. The N. part is mountainous and woody, but the greater part consists of fertile plains, watered by numerous rivers and lakes. Notwithstanding the goodness of the soil, which is scarcely surpassed by any province in Sweden, it is far from being well cultivated; and the peasants are generally poor. The chief traffic is in corn, flax, hemp, dried fish, cattle, leather, tallow, and lime.

Tavastus, or Tavastborg, a town of Finland, formerly capital of the district of Tavastland. It has a strong castle, and is seated on a river which flows into the lake Wana; 110 miles E. N. E. of Abo.

Taverna, a town of Naples, in Calabria Ultra; 20 miles E. N. E. of Nicastro.

Tavira, or Tavila, a seaport of Portugal, in Algarve; with a castle, and one of the best harbours in the kingdom, defended by two forts. It is seated at the mouth of the Gilaon, in the Gulf of Cadiz; 96 miles N. W. of Cadiz, and 136 S. E. of Lisbon. Pop. 5000. Long. 7. 36. W. lat. 37. 8. N.

Tavistock, a borough in Devonshire, returning two members to parliament; with a market on Saturday, and a manufacture of serges. In its vicinity was born the famous Sir Francis Drake. It is seated on the river Tavy; 32 miles W. by S. of Exeter, and 207 of London.

Tavoy, a seaport on the W. coast of Siam, in a district of its name, which was wrested from the Siamese by the Birmans, and subsequently ceded to the British in 1824–5. Area, 15,000 square miles. Pop. 26,000. The town is 150 miles W. N. W. of Siam. Long. 98. 20. E. lat. 14. 45. N.

Tavy, a river in Devonshire, which rises in Dartmoor, flows by Tavistock, and enters the harbour of Hamoaze, above Plymouth.

Taw, a river in Devonshire, which rises in Dartmoor, flows by Chimleigh and Barnstaple, and joins the Trowbridge at its mouth in the Bristol Channel.

Tawy, a river of Wales, in Glamorganshire; which flows parallel to the Neath, and enters the Bristol Channel at Swansea Bay.

Tay, a river of Scotland, which rises on the W. borders of Perthshire, flows through Loch Tay to Dunkeld, Perth, and Newberg, below which to the sea, (above 20 miles,) it may be deemed a continued harbour, and is called the Frith of Tay, having Fifeshire on one side, and the counties of Perth and Angus on the other.

Tay, Loch, a lake of Scotland, in Perthshire, 15 miles long, and in most parts above one broad, formed by several streams and the river Tay, which flows through its whole length.

Tazowskaia, a bay of Siberia, in the Obskaia Gulf, about 140 miles long, and 3 broad.

Tchad, an extensive fresh water lake in the interior of Africa, into which the river Shary flows on the S., and the Jeir on the W. It is probable it communicates with the river Tchadda, which flows into the Niger at King William's Mount. The lake is 185 miles long, and 110 miles broad. Long. of the W. end 12. 5. E. lat. 14. 0. N.

Tchang-tcha, a city of China, capital of the S. part of Hou-quang. It is seated on the river Heng, which has a communication with an extensive lake, called Tong-ting-hou; 740 miles S. by W. of Peking. Long. 112. 25. E. lat. 28. 11. N.

Tchang-tcheou, a city of China, of the first rank, in Fo-kien. It has a considerable trade with Emony, Pong-hou, and Formosa. It is 950 miles S. of Peking. Long. 117. 35. E. lat. 24. 32. N.

Tchang-te, a city of China, of the first rank, in Ho-nan. It is remarkable for a fish like a crocodile, the fat of which is of such a singular nature, that when once ignited it cannot be extinguished Near it is a mountain, so steep and inaccessible, that in the time of war it affords a safe asylum to the inhabitants. It is

255 miles S. S. W. of Peking. Long. 111. 5. E. lat. 29. 2. N.

TCHAO-KING, a city of China, of the first rank, in Quang-tong, seated on the river Si; 70 miles W. of Canton,

TCHAO-TCHEOU, a city of China, of the first rank, in Quang-tong, seated on the Peikiang; 86 miles E. of Canton.

TCHE-KIANG, a province of China, one of the most considerable in extent, riches, and population. It is bounded on the N. and W. by King-han, S. W. by Kiang-si, S. by Fo-kien, and E. by the ocean. In this province whole plains are covered with dwarf mulberry trees, purposely checked in their growth; and prodigious quantities of silk-worms are bred. The principal branch of trade consists in silk stuffs; and those in which gold and silver are intermixed are the most beautiful in China. The tallow tree grows here, and a species of mushrooms, which are transported to all the provinces of the empire; and here also are found the small gold-fish with which ponds are commonly stocked. In Tche-kiang are reckoned 11 cities of the first rank, 72 of the third, and 18 fortresses, which in Europe would be deemed large cities. Hang-tcheou is the capital.

TCHEOU-CHAN, an island near the W. coast of China, belonging to the province of Tche-kiang. It is about 24 miles long, and from 5 to 10 broad.

TCHERKASK, OLD and NEW, towns of European Russia, capital of the Don Cossacs. Old Tcherkask is seated on the Don, near the S. of Azof, and has a splendid cathedral, but has much decayed since the foundation of the New Town, in 1810. It is on high ground, free from inundations, and has much increased. It is 40 miles N. E. of Azof. Pop. together, 15,000.

TCHERNIGOF, a government of Russia, formerly a part of the Ukraine. Its capital, of the same name, is seated on the Desne; 345 miles S. S. W. of Moscow. Long. 66. 45. E. lat. 51. 24. N.

TCHESNE, a town on the W. coast of Natolia, with a citadel. It stands almost opposite Scio, at the head of a spacious road, which is famous for the destruction of the Turkish fleet by the Russians, in 1770. It is 48 miles W. of Smyrna. Long. 26. 26. E. lat. 38. 26. N.

TCHING-KIANG, a city of China, of the first rank, in Se-tchuen; 910 miles S. W. of Peking. Long. 104. 26. E. lat. 27. 18. N.

TCHING-KIANG, a strong city of China, of the first rank, in Kiang-nan, and the key of the empire towards the sea. Its situation and trade, and the beauty of its walls, give it a preeminence over the other cities of the province. It is seated on the S. of the Kian-ku; 470 miles S. S. E. of Peking. Long. 118. 55. E. lat. 32. 14. N.

TCHING-KIANG, a city of China, of the first rank, in the province of Yun-nan; 36 miles S. by E. of Yun-nan. Long. 102. 40. E. lat. 24. 44. N.

TCHING-TCHEOU, a city of China, of the first rank, in Hou-quang, seated on an angle formed by two rivers. Under it are five cities of the third class, in which a kind of plain earthenware is prepared, which the Chinese prefer to the most elegant porcelain. It is 765 miles S. S. W. of Peking. Long. 109. 40. E. lat. 28. 23. N.

TCHING-TING, a city of China, of the first rank, in the province of Pe-tche-li; 136 miles S. S. W. of Peking. Long. 114. 21. E. lat. 38. 9. N.

TCHING-TOU, a city of China, of the first rank, in the province of Se-tchuen. It was formerly the residence of the emperors, and one of the largest and most beautiful cities in the empire; but in 1646, during the civil wars that preceded the last invasion of the Tartars, it was almost entirely destroyed. Its temples, and the ruins of ancient palaces, are objects of admiration to strangers. It is 810 miles S. W. of Peking. Long. 103. 44. E. lat. 30. 40. N.

TCHIN-NGAN, a city of China, of the first rank, in Quang-si; 1250 miles S. S. W. of Peking. Long. 106. 0. E. lat. 23. 21. N.

TCHI-TCHEOU, a city of China, of the first rank, in Kiang-nan, seated on the river Kiang; 570 miles S. of Peking. Long. 117. 0. E. lat. 30. 45. N.

TCHI-YUEN, a city of China, of the first rank, in Koei-tcheou; 980 miles S. S. W. of Peking. Long. 107. 51. E. lat. 27. 1. N.

TCHOKA. *See* SAGHALIEN.

TCHONG-KING, a city of China, of the first rank, in Se-tchuen. It is seated on a mountain, rising in the form of an amphitheatre, at the conflux of the Kincha with the Kian-ku; 750 miles S. W. of Peking. Long. 106. 20. E. lat. 29. 42. N.

TCHOU-KIONG, a city of China, of the first rank, in the province of Yun-nan; 75 miles W. of Yun-nan. Long. 101. 20. E. lat. 25. 6. N.

TCHUDSKOI. *See* PEIPUS.

TCHUKOTSKI, the most eastern part of Siberia, in the province of Okotsk. The attention of the natives is confined chiefly to their deer, with which the country abounds. They are a well-made, courageous, warlike race, and are formidable neighbours to the Koriacs, who often experience their depredations.

TCHUKOTSKOI, a cape of Siberia, on the eastern extremity of Asia, and the S. W. limit of Behring Strait. Long. 172. 30. W. lat. 64. 15. N.

TCHU-TCHEOU, a city of China, of the first rank, in Tche-kiang; 730 miles S. S. E. of Peking. Long. 120. 33. E. lat. 28. 36. N.

TCITCICAR, the largest of the three provinces of Chinese Tartary; bounded on the N. by Siberia, N. E. by the Sea of Okotsk, S. E. by the province of Kirin, and W. by Western Tartary and Siberia. It is a mountainous country, watered by the river Saghalien, which receives many others in its course.

TCITCICAR, a city of Chinese Tartary, capital of the foregoing province, and the residence of a Mandshur general. This city was built by the emperor of China, to secure its frontiers against the incursions of the Russians. It is seated on the Nonni; 355 miles N. N. E. of Peking. Long. 123. 30. E. lat. 47. 25. N.

TEBESTA, or TINSA, a town of Tunis, in Africa, on the borders of Algier, with a castle, and several remains of antiquity. It is seated at the foot of a mountain; 130 miles S. E. of Tunis.

TECUIT, a town of Morocco, in the province of Sus, seated in a country abounding in grain, dates, and sugar-canes. It is 4 miles E. of Messa.

TECKLENBURG, a town of Prussian Westphalia, capital of a fertile county of the same name. It has manufactures of linen cloth. It is seated 22 miles N. by E. of Munster. Long. 7. 47. E. lat. 52. 14. N.

TECUANTEPEC, or TEHUANTEPEC, a seaport of Mexico, in Oaxaca, with a fortified abbey and several handsome churches. It is seated on a large bay of the same name, in the Pacific Ocean. Long. 95. 55. W. lat. 16. 28. N.

TECRIT, a town of Asiatic Turkey, in the government of Mosul. It is seated on a rock, near the W. side of the Tigre; 130 miles S. of Mosul.

TECULET, a town of Morocco, with an old castle. It is seated at the mouth of a river of the same name; 99 miles W. of Morocco. Long. 9. 45. W. lat. 31. 5. N.

TEDELEZ, a town of Algier, on the coast of the Mediterranean, with a castle; 45 miles E. of Algier.

TEDNEST, a town of Morocco, in the province of Hea, almost surrounded by a river. It was taken by the Portuguese in 1517; but they were driven away soon after. It is 40 miles N. E. of Mogador.

TEDSI, a town of Morocco, in the province of Sus, seated in a plain abounding in corn; 20 miles S. E. of Tarndant.

TEEMBO, a city of Central Africa, capital of the kingdom of Foota Jalloo. The inhabitants, estimated at 8000, carry on manufactures of cloth, iron, silver, wood, leather, &c. It is 160 miles E. of Sierra Leone.

TEES, a river which rises on the confines of Cumberland, separates the counties of Durham and York, and enters the German Ocean below Stockton.

TEFESSAD, a town of Algier, with mines of iron in its neighbourhood. It is 32 miles S. W. of Algier.

TEFFLIS, a city of Asia, the capital of Georgia, called by the inhabitants Thilis-Caba (Warm Town), from the warm baths in its neighbourhood. It contains 30,000 inhabitants, of whom more than one-half are Armenians. The streets seldom exceed seven feet in breadth, and the houses are of stone, with flat roofs, which serve as walks for the women. Here is a foundry for cannon, mortars, and balls; also a public school founded by the emperor Alexander. The most flourishing manufactures are those of silks and printed linens; but the chief trade is in furs, sent to Turkey and the S. of Persia. In 1723 it was taken by the Turks, and in 1734 retaken by Kouli Khan. It is seated on the Kur, a dirty river, at the foot of a hill; 300 miles S. S. W. of Astracan. Long. 45. 3. E. lat. 42. 20. N.

TEFZA, a strong town of Morocco, capital of a district of the same name, seated on the side of a mountain; 70 miles N. N. E. of Morocco. Long. 5. 55. W. lat. 32. 0. N.

TEFZRA, a town of Algier, in the province of Mascara; 55 miles S. S. W. of Oran.

TEGAZA, a town of Zahara, capital of a territory of that name; remarkable for mountains of salt. Long. 6. 30. W. lat. 21. 40. N.

TEGERHY, a town of the kingdom of Fezzan; 80 miles S. W. of Mourzook.

TEGERN, a town of Bavaria, with a celebrated abbey, seated on a lake, called the Tegern See; 30 miles S. S. E. of Munich.

TEGLIO, a town of Austrian Italy, in the Valteline; 9 miles S. W. of Tirano.

TEHRAN, or TEHERAUN, a city of Persia, the present capital of the empire. It was an inconsiderable place, till Aga Mahomed, uncle to the present shah, made this his royal residence. It is about four miles in circumference, and surrounded by a strong wall, and strengthened with towers, &c. It is strikingly seated, at the foot of Mount Elburz, and N. of the ruins of the city of Rey. Though it has been much enlarged and adorned, it contains no public building, except the Ark, which combines the character of a fortress and a palace. Pop. 60,000.

TEIGN, a river in Devonshire, composed of two branches, which rise in the E. part of Dartmoor, and, uniting, enter the English Channel at Teignmouth.

TEIGNMOUTH, a seaport in Devonshire, with a market on Saturday. At this place the Danes first landed, and committed several outrages. It was almost entirely destroyed by the French, who set fire to it in 1690. Since that period the town has become of more consequence, and it is now a fashionable watering-place. It sends a number of vessels to the Newfoundland fishery, and has a considerable trade in carrying fine clay to the potteries in Staffordshire, Liverpool, &c., whence are brought coal, salt, earthenware, &c. It is seated at the mouth of the Teign, 15 miles S. of Exeter, and 187 W. by S. of London. Long. 3. 29. W. lat. 50. 32. N.

TEINITZ, a town of Bohemia, in the circle of Pilsen, with a castle and a convent, seated on the Radbuza; 30 miles W. S. W. of Pilsen.

TEISENDORF, a town of Austria, in the province of Salzburg; 12 miles N. W. of Salzburg.

TEISSE. *See* THEISSE.

TEJUCO, a district of Brazil, about 50 miles long, and 24 broad, particularly noted for its production of diamonds.

TEJUCO, the capital of the above district, is situate on the side of a hill, and is very irregularly built. The circulation of property created by the diamond-works renders it a flourishing town. British cottons, baizes, cloths, and other manufactured goods, are abundant; also cheese, butter, hams, porter, and other articles of consumption. But the inhabitants carry on no manufactures. Pop. 6000. Long. 42. 30. W. lat. 18. 11. S.

TEKEN. *See* BENDER.

TELESE, a town of Naples, in Terra di Lavoro; 18 miles E. N. E. of Capua.

TELGEN, or TELGA, a town of Sweden, in Sudermania, on the lake Maeler; 12 miles S. W. of Stockholm.

TELGET, a town of Prussian Westphalia; 5 miles E. N. E. of Munster.

TELLES, a town of the kingdom of Fez; with a small harbour, on the Mediterranean; 100 miles E. S. E. of Tetuan.

TELLICHERRY, a town of Hindostan, in Malabar. It has a considerable trade. It is seated at the mouth of a river, 42 miles N. N. W. of Calicut. Long. 75. 38. E. lat. 11. 48. N.

TELTOW, a town of Prussia, in Brandenburg, on a lake of the same name; 7 miles S. S. W. of Berlin.

TELTSCH, a town of Austria, in Moravia; 16 miles S. of Iglau.

TEME, a river which rises in Radnorshire, flows through Shropshire and Worcestershire, and falls into the Severn, one mile below Worcester.

TEMENDEFUST, a town of the kingdom of Algier; 10 miles E. of Algier.

TEMESWAR, a strong town of Hungary, capital of a territory called the Bannat of Temeswar; containing an area of 9450 square miles, and a population of 700,000. It stands on the river Bega, which forms a morass round it, and the fortress requires a garrison of 14,000 men. This place formerly passed for impregnable, but it was taken by Prince Eugene, in a dry season, in 1716. It is 80 miles N. N. E. of Belgrade, and 160 S. E. of Buda. Population, 11,000.

TEMISSA, a town of Fezzan, where the caravans from Timbuctoo, Bornou, &c., which travel by way of Cairo to Mecca, usually provide the stores of corn, dates, dried meat, and other requisites for their dreary journey; 120 miles E. N. E. of Mourzook.

TEMPELBORG, a town of the Prussian states, in Pomerania; on the S. side of a lake, and on the frontiers of Poland; 43 miles E. by N. of New Stargard.

TEMPIO, a town of Sardinia. Pop. 5000. It is 32 miles E. of Sassari.

TEMPLEMORE, a town of Ireland, county of Tipperary; 86 miles from Dublin; with a free-school on Erasmus Smith's foundation.

TEMPLIN, a town of Prussia, in Brandenburg, with a great trade in timber. It was totally consumed by fire in 1735, but has been rebuilt in a beautiful manner. It stands between the Bodensee and Dolgensee; 18 miles S. W. of Prenzlo, and 42 N. by E. of Berlin.

TENASSERIM, a town of Birmah, capital of a district of its name; situate on a large river 47 miles S. E. of Mergui. Long. 98. 50. W. lat. 11. 35. N.

TENBURY, a town in Worcestershire, with a market on Tuesday. It has a spacious parish church, a Baptist meeting-house, and a good national school. A mile S. of this town is a course where horse-races take place annually in July. Here is a considerable malting business, and a large tannery, and the town enjoys a good local trade. It is seated on the Teme, over which is a bridge of six arches, forming a communication with the county of Hereford; 11 miles W. by N. of Worcester, and 133 W. N. W. of London.

TENBY, a seaport of Wales, in Pembrokeshire; with markets on Wednesday and Saturday. Its castle was demolished in the civil wars. The principal trade is in coal, and it is a place of fashionable resort for bathing; 4 miles W. S. W., on the sea coast, are the massive remains of Manorbeer Castle. Tenby is seated on a narrow rock projecting into the sea; 10 miles E. of Pembroke, and 253 W. of London. Long. 4. 40. W. lat. 51. 44. N.

TENCH ISLAND, an island in the South Pacific, 2 miles in circumference; discovered by Lieutenant Ball in 1790. It is low, but entirely covered with cocoa-nut and other trees. Long. 151. 31. E. lat. 1. 39. S.

TENDA, a town of the Sardinian states, in Piedmont; with a fortified castle on a rock. It stands on the Roia, 65 miles S. of Turin.

TENDAY. *See* SAMAR.

TENEDOS, an island of the Grecian Archipelago, on the coast of Asia Minor; 14 miles S. of the Strait of Gallipoli. It is 11 miles long, and 7 broad; is inhabited almost wholly by Greeks, and its muscadine wine is the best in all the Levant. On the E. side is the town, at the foot of a mountain; with a harbour, defended by a castle. Pop. 4000. Long. 26. 0. E. lat. 39. 50. N.

TENERIFFE, one of the Canary Islands, and the most considerable of them for riches, trade, and population. It lies W. of the Grand Canary, is 70 miles long, and 22 broad, and abounds in wine, different sorts of fruits, cattle, and game. One part of this island is surrounded by inaccessible mountains, of which one in particular, called the Peak of Teneriffe, is 12,072 feet above the level of the sea, and the distance to the Peak from the port of Orotava, at the base of the mountain, is above 11 miles. This island is subject to volcanic eruptions, and in 1704 one destroyed several towns and many thousand people. The laborious works in this island are chiefly performed by oxen and mules, horses being scarce, and reserved for the use of the officers. Hawks and parrots are natives of the island, as are swallows, seagulls, partridges, canary-birds, and blackbirds. There are also lizards, locusts, and dragon-flies. St. Cristophe de Laguna is the capital, but the governor resides at St. Cruz.

TENERIFFE, a town of the republic of Colombia, in the former viceroyalty of New Granada; seated on the Madalena; 100 miles S. S. W. of St. Martha.

TENEZ, or TENIS, a town of Algier, in the province of Mascara; capital of a district of its name, with a fort. It has a considerable trade in corn. It is seated on a river, 4 miles from the sea, and 85 W. S. W. of Algier.

TE-NGAN, a city of China, of the first rank; in Hou-quang; 550 miles S. by W. of Peking Long. 113. 21. E. lat. 31. 20. N.

Tennessee, one of the United States of America, situate between the parallels of 35. and 36½. of N. lat.; bounded on the S. by Georgia, W. by the Mississippi, N. by Kentucky and Virginia, and E. by the Iron and Bald Mountains, which separate it from North Carolina. It is 400 miles in length, and 104 in breadth; is divided into 38 counties, and has an area of 43,000 square miles, with a population of 829,210, including 153,059 slaves. The principal rivers are the Mississippi, Tennessee, Cumberland, and Holston; and it is watered by other rivers and creeks. The Cumberland mountains, a lofty ridge nearly 30 miles broad, cut this state into the eastern and western divisions, which were originally known by the names of the establishments of Holston and Cumberland; but the latter is much the larger part. The climate, soil, and produce of Tennessee are nearly the same as in the adjoining state of Kentucky; but West Tennessee, or Cumberland, is less salubrious, having a warmer and more humid temperature. Nashville is the capital.

Tennessee, a river of the United States, formerly called the Cherokee River, and the largest of all those which flow into the Ohio. Its commencement is formed in the state to which it gives name, by the junction of the Clinch with the Holston, 35 miles below Knoxville. It flows S. W. on the E. side of Cumberland Mountains, into Georgia, where it makes a circuit to the W., called the Great Bend; it then re-enters the state of Tennessee, which it passes quite through into that of Kentucky, where it enters the Ohio, 50 miles above the conflux of that river with the Mississippi. The Tennessee is 600 yards broad at its mouth, and is thence navigable by vessels of great burden for 260 miles, to the Muscle Shoals, in the Great Bend: here the river widens to between 2 and 3 miles, for nearly 30 miles; and these shoals can only be passed in small boats: hence it may be navigated, by boats of 40 tons burden, 400 miles further to its commencement.

Tennis, a town of Egypt, situate on an island in a lake of the same name, sometimes called Lake Menzaleh; 28 miles S. E. of Damietta.

Tenos Island, Grecian Archipelago, between Andros and Myconi; 35 miles in circumference; producing silk, wine, and fruits, and but little corn. Pop. 25,000.

Tenstadt, a town of Prussian Saxony, 10 miles N. E. of Langensalza.

Ten-tcheou, a city of China, of the first rank; in Chang-tong; with a good port and a strong garrison. It is seated on the N. side of a peninsula of the Yellow Sea; 250 miles S. E. of Peking. Long. 120. 50. E. lat. 37. 20. N.

Tenterden, a town in Kent, governed by a mayor; with a market on Friday. It has a handsome church, the steeple of which is very lofty, and, at the time of the Spanish invasion, in 1588, was made use of as a beacon. Here are also three meeting-houses and a free-school; 24 miles S. W. of Canterbury, and 56 E. by S of London.

Tentugal, a town of Portugal, in Beira 8 miles W. S. W. of Coimbra.

Teramo, a town of Naples, in Abruzzo Ultra, 25 miles N. E. of Aquila.

Terceira, one of the Azores, of a circular form, about 55 miles in circumference, and very fertile. It contains several towns and villages, with a number of forts. Pop. 50,000. Angra is the capital.

Terchiz, or **Tersiz**, a town of Persia, in the province of Khorasan; situate on the borders of the Great Salt Desert; 160 miles W. N. W. of Herat. Long. 57. 25. E. lat. 35. 5. N.

Terek, a river in Asiatic Russia, forming the boundary between that power and the Caucasus, over which the Russians hold an unacknowledged authority.

Terga, a town of Morocco, seated on the Omirabi; 90 miles N. of Morocco.

Tergovist, or **Tervis**, a town of European Turkey, in Walachia. Here is a fine palace, belonging to the hospodar, or reigning prince; but he chiefly resides at Bucharest. It stands on the Jalonitz; 35 miles N. N. W. of Bucharest. Long. 25. 48. E. lat. 45. 28. N.

Tergouw. *See* **Gouda**.

Termed, a town of Usbec Tartary, capital of a district in Bokharia, seated in an angle formed by the union of two rivers; 150 miles S. of Samarcand. Long. 65. 35. E. lat. 37. 15. N.

Termini, a town on the N. coast of Sicily, in Val di Mazara, with a strong castle. Its mineral waters are much celebrated, and it has a considerable trade. It is situate on a rocky eminence, near the mouth of a river of the same name; 20 miles S. E. of Palermo. Pop. 8700.

Termoli, a town of Naples, in Capitanata, seated near the sea; 32 miles S. E. of Lanciano.

Ternate, one of the Molucca islands, lying to the W. of Gilolo, formerly the seat of sovereignty. It abounds in cocoa-nuts, bananas, citrons, oranges, almonds, and other fruits proper to the climate. There are also a great number of birds of paradise. It is a mountainous country, and contains a great number of woods, which furnish abundance of game. It is in the possession of the Dutch, from whom it was taken by the British in 1810, but restored, with their other Indian possessions, in 1814. The inhabitants are Mahomedans, and very indolent; 100 miles E. of Celebes. Long. 127. 4. E. lat. 0. 50. N.

Terneuse, a town and fort of the Netherlands, in Flanders, on the W. branch of the Scheldt, called the Hondt. It is 8 miles N. of Sas van Ghent, and 25 W. N. W. of Antwerp.

Terni, a town in the ecclesiastical states, in the duchy of Spoleto, seated on the Nera, near the influx of the Velino, which has a famous cataract a mile from the town. Terni was the birthplace of Tacitus the historian. It is 15 miles S. S. W. of Spoleto, and 46 N. of Rome.

Ternova, a town of Bulgaria, and an archbishop's see. It was formerly the seat of the princes of Bulgaria, and a strong place, but the fortifications are ruined. It is seated on a mountain, near the Jenera; 88 miles N. W. of Adrianople, and 97 N. E. of Sofia. Long. 26. 2. E. lat. 43. 1. N.

TEROUENC, a town of France, department of Pas de Calais, seated on the Lis; 6 miles S. of St. Omer.

TERRA DI BARI, LAVORO, and OTRANTO. *See* BARI, &c.

TERRA DEL ESPIRITU SANTO, the largest and most western island of the New Hebrides, in the South Pacific, being 40 leagues in circuit. The land is exceedingly high and mountainous, and in many places the hills rise directly from the sea. Except the cliffs and beaches, every part is covered with wood, or laid out in plantations. Besides the bay of St. Philip and St. Jago, on the N. side of it, the isles which lie along the S. and E. coast form several good bays and harbours. Long. 167. E. lat. 15. S.

TERRA FIRMA, a name applied sometimes to the provinces of Central America, or Darien, Panama, and Veragua.

TERRA DEL FUEGO, a large island, separated from the southern extremity of America by the Strait of Magellan, and so called from the volcanoes observed on it. The sea intersects it into several islands, all of them barren and mountainous; but on the lower grounds are found several sorts of trees and plants, and a variety of birds. The natives are short in stature, not exceeding five feet six inches; their heads large, their faces broad, their cheek-bones prominent, and their noses flat. They have little brown eyes, without life; their hair is black and lank, hanging about their heads in disorder, and besmeared with train-oil. They wear no other clothing than a small piece of seal-skin, hanging from their shoulders to the middle of the back, being fastened round the neck with a string. They live chiefly on seals' flesh, of which they prefer the oily part. There is no appearance of any subordination among them, and their whole character is a strange compound of stupidity, indifference, and inactivity.

TERRACINA, a decayed town of the ecclesiastical states, in Campagna di Roma, with a castle on a rock. Formerly it was called Auxur, and was the capital of the Volsci, and its cathedral was originally a temple of Jupiter. It is seated near the sea, on the frontiers of Naples; 54 miles S. S. E. of Rome. Pop. 9000. Long. 13. 15. E. lat. 41. 24. N.

TERRANOVA, a seaport of Sicily, in Val di Noto, seated near the mouth of a river of the same name; 20 miles E. S. E. of Alicata. Long. 14. 10. E. lat. 37. 9. N. Pop. 9000.

TERRANOVA, a seaport of Sardinia, seated at the bottom of a bay on the N. E. coast; 62 miles E. N. E. of Sassari. Long. 9. 35. E. lat. 41. 3. N.

TERRASSON, a town of France, in the department of Dordogne, seated on the Vesere; 28 miles E. of Perigueux.

TERRIDON, LOCH, an inlet of the sea, on the W. coast of Scotland, in Ross-shire; between Gairloch and Applecross. It has many creeks and bays.

TERRIORE, a strong town and fortress of Hindostan, in the Carnatic; 25 miles N. of Trichinopoly.

TERSOOS, a seaport of Asia Minor, on the coast of Karamania, and an archbishop's see. It was formerly called Tarsus, and was the capital of Cilicia, the literary rival of Athens and Alexandria, and the birthplace of the apostle Paul. It is seated on the Mediterranean; 100 miles W. by N. of Alexandretta. Long. 35. 15. E. lat. 37. 4. N.

• TERUEL, a town of Spain, in Arragon, and a bishop's see, with a citadel. It is 80 miles S. W. of Saragossa, and 112 E. of Madrid. Pop. 5500. Long. 1. 0. W. lat. 40. 25. N.

TERVERE, or VEERE, a fortified seaport of the Netherlands, in Zealand, on the N. E. coast of the isle of Walcheren. It has a good harbour, and a fine arsenal; 4 miles N. by E. of Middleburg, with which it communicates by a canal. Long. 3. 42. E. lat. 51. 36. N.

TESCHEN, a town of Austrian Silesia, capital of a circle of the same name. It is surrounded by a wall, and at a little distance, on an eminence, is the old castle where the ancient dukes resided. The inhabitants carry on a trade in leather, woollen stuffs, and wine, and make excellent fire-arms. This town was taken by the Prussians in 1757, but restored in 1763. In 1779 a treaty of peace was concluded here, between the emperor of Germany and the king of Prussia. It is seated in a morass, near the river Elsa; 36 miles E. S. E. of Troppau, and 60 E. by N. of Olmutz. Pop. of circle 152,000; of town, 5400. Long. 18. 32. E. lat. 49. 43. N.

TESEGDELT, a town of Morocco, seated on a craggy rock, said to be impregnable, at the mouth of the Techubit; 140 miles W. N. W. of Morocco.

TESHOO LOOMBOO, the capital of Tibet, or of that part which is immediately subject to the Teshoo lama, who is sovereign of the country, during the minority of the grand lama. Its temples and mausoleums, with their numerous gilded canopies and turrets, and the palace of the lama, render it a magnificent place. It stands at the N. end of a plain, upon a rocky eminence; 220 miles S. W. of Lassa, and 470 N. by E. of Calcutta. Long. 89. 7. E. lat 29. 4. N.

TESINO, a town of the Austrian States, in Tyrol; 25 miles E. N. E. of Trent.

TESSET, a town of Zahara, capital of a district of the same name. It is 350 miles S. S. W. of Tafilet. Long. 5. 45. W. lat. 25. 54. N.

TESSIN. *See* TICINO.

TEST, or TESE, a river in Hampshire, which rises near Whitchurch, flows by Stockbridge and Romsey, and enters the head of the Bay of Southampton at Redbridge.

TETBURY, a town of Gloucestershire, with a market on Wednesday, and a trade in yarn and wool. It is 25 miles E. N. E. of Bristol, and 99 W. of London.

Tetschen, or **Tetzen**, a town of Bohemia, in the circle of Leutmeritz, with a castle on a rock, on the river Elbe. It is 29 miles S. E. of Dresden.

Tettnang, a town of Germany, in the kingdom of Wirtemberg; 8 miles N. of Lindau.

Tetuan, a city of the kingdom of Fez, with a castle. The houses have only small holes towards the streets, which are very narrow; and the windows are on the other side, facing a court-yard, which is surrounded by galleries, and in the middle is generally a fountain. The houses are two stories high, flat at the top; and the women visit each other from the tops of them. The shops are very small, and without any door; the master sits cross-legged on a counter, with the goods disposed in drawers round him, and all the customers stand in the street. Several European consuls formerly resided in this city: the English are still allowed to touch here, and considerable communication is kept up with Gibraltar. It is seated on the river Cus, near the Mediterranean; 110 miles N. N. W. of Fez. Long. [illegible] W. lat. 35. 37. N.

Teverone, a river of Italy, the ancient Anio, which rises in the Appennines, 50 miles above Tivoli, glides through a plain till it comes near that town, when it is confined for a short space between two hills, covered with groves. These were supposed to be the residence of the sibyl Albunea, to whom an elegant temple was here dedicated. The river moving with augmented rapidity, as its channel is confined, at last rushes over a lofty precipice, and the noise of its falls resounds through the hills and groves of Tivoli. Having gained the plain, it soon afterwards receives the waters of the lake Solfatara, and then joins the Tiber, near Rome.

Teupitz, a town of Prussia, in Brandenburg, with a castle on a lake; 25 miles S. by E. of Berlin.

Teuschnitz, a town and castle of Bavarian Franconia; 17 miles N. of Culmbach.

Teviot, a river of Scotland, which rises in the mountains in the S. W. of Roxburghshire, and, passing N. W. through the county, unites with the Tweed a little above Kelso.

Tewsing, a town of Bohemia, in the circle of Pilsen; 30 miles N. W. of Pilsen.

Tewkesbury, a borough in Gloucestershire, returning two members to parliament. Markets on Wednesday and Saturday. Here is one of the noblest parish churches in the kingdom, which is almost the only remains of the celebrated monastery to which it formerly belonged. The other places of worship are meeting-houses for Methodists, Independents, Baptists, and Quakers. The principal manufacture is that of stockings, and the inhabitants carry on a considerable trade in malt. Here, in 1441, Edward IV. gained a decisive victory over the Lancastrians. Tewkesbury is seated on the Avon, near its union with the Severn, and on the Birmingham railway; 10 miles N. of Gloucester, and 103 W. N. W. of London. Pop. 5000.

Texas, a district of North America, on the N. of the Gulf of Mexico, between 27. and 33. of N. lat., with a length of 1200 miles by 350 of average breadth, being one-half larger than Great Britain. It consists of undulating plains, or prairies, of exuberant fertility and great beauty. In some parts are rolling prairies, with insulated groups of trees, the whole scenery being of surpassing beauty. It is very thinly populated by settlers from the United States. There are some deer, and herds of wild ponies called mustangs. The climate is tropical, and the vegetation is consequently of rapid growth, producing abundance of wild fruits, including grapes, nuts, peaches, walnuts, &c., and large quantities of honey. On the separation of Mexico from Spain, in 1822, Iturbide, under the title of Augustin I., invited settlers from the United States into this tract, which was then a part of the Mexican territory; but after his deposition and execution, and the consequent disturbances, General Santa Anna seized the government, and abolished the existing legislature of the States, and enforced the observance of the Roman Catholic religion. The Texians consequently revolted in 1835; a civil war ensued, which caused much bloodshed; in the conclusion of which Santa Anna was taken prisoner, which led to a settlement of their affairs.

Texel, an island of the Netherlands, separated from North Holland by a narrow channel of the same name, defended by a strong fort on the mainland, called the Helder. This channel is the best and most southern entrance into the Zuyder Zee, and through it most of the ships pass that are bound to Amsterdam. In 1799 the fort was taken by the English, and the whole of the Dutch fleet lying within the channel surrendered to them; but the English abandoned the fort soon afterwards. Pop. 5000. Long. 4. 59. E. lat. 53. 10. N.

Teya, or **Theya**, a river of the Austrian states, which rises near Teltsch, in Moravia, flows E. by Znaim, on the borders of Austria, and enters the Moraw on the confines of Hungary.

Teyn, a town of Bohemia, in the circle of Bechin, seated on the Muldau; 10 miles S. E. of Piseck.

Tezar, a town of Fez, capital of the province of Cuzi; containing a mosque half a mile in circumference. It is seated on a small river, 45 miles E. of Fez. Long. 4. 15. W. lat. 33. 40. N.

Tezcuco, a town of Mexico, once the capital of a rich kingdom. Here Cortez caused a canal to be dug, and built 18 brigantines, to carry on the siege of Mexico. It is seated near the Lake of Mexico; 20 miles E. of Mexico. Pop. about 5000.

Tezela, a town of Algier, in the province of Mascara; with a castle; 15 miles S. W. of Oran.

Tezout, a town of the kingdom of Fez, seated on the point of a rock; 15 miles S. of Melilla.

Tezzoute, an ancient town of Algier, in the province of Constantina. Its ruins extend 10 miles in circumference, among which are magnificent remains of city gates, an amphitheatre, a temple dedicated to Æsculapius, and other elegant structures. It is 90 miles S S. W. of Constantina.

THAINEE, a town of the kingdom of Tunis, near the mouth of a river of the same name; 120 miles S. of Tunis. Long. 10. 15. E. lat. 34. 50. N.

THAME, or TAME, a river which rises near Tring, in Hertfordshire; crosses Buckinghamshire to the N. of Aylesbury, enters Oxfordshire at the town of Thame, whence it is navigable for barges to Dorchester, where it joins the Thames. This river has been erroneously supposed to give name to the Thames.

THAME, a town in Oxfordshire, with a market on Tuesday. It is seated on the river Thame; 12 miles E. of Oxford, and 44 W. by N. of London.

THAMES, the finest river in Great Britain, which takes its rise from a copious spring, called Thames Head, 2 miles S. W. of Cirencester, in Gloucestershire. It has been erroneously stated that its name is Isis till it arrives at Dorchester, 15 miles below Oxford, when, being joined by the Thame, or Tame, it assumes the name of Thames. But Camden says that the river was always called Thames, or Tems, before it came near the Thame; and in several ancient charters granted to the abbey of Malmesbury, as well as that of Ensham, and in the old deeds relating to Cricklade, it is never considered under any other name than that of Thames. All the historians who mention the incursions of Ethelwold, and of Canute, into Wiltshire, concur likewise in the same opinion, by declaring that they passed over the Thames at Cricklade in Wiltshire. About a mile below the source of the river, it is not more than nine feet wide in the summer, yet, in the winter, becomes such a torrent as to overflow the meadows for many miles. The stream proceeds to Cricklade, where it receives many other rivulets, which cause it to widen considerably in its way to Lechlade; and, being there joined by the Coln and Lech, at the distance of 138 miles from London, it becomes navigable for vessels of 90 tons. At Oxford (in whose academic groves its poetical name of Isis has been so often invoked) it is joined by the Cherwell, and, proceeding by Abingdon to Dorchester, it receives the Thame. Passing by Wallingford to Reading, and forming a boundary to Berkshire, Buckinghamshire, Surrey, and Middlesex, it waters Henley, Marlow, Maidenhead, Windsor, Staines, Chertsey, Kingston, and Brentford, in its course to London; during which it receives the Kennet, Loddon, Coln, Wey, Mole, Brent, and Wandle. From London the river proceeds to Greenwich, Woolwich, Grays-Thurrock, Gravesend, and Leigh, into the German Ocean, in which course it parts Essex from Kent, and receives the Lea, Roding, Darent, and Medway. The tide flows up the Thames as high as Kingston, which, following the winding of the river, is 70 miles from the ocean—a greater distance than the tide is carried by any other river in Europe. Though the Thames is said to be navigable 138 miles above London Bridge, there are so many flats that in summer the navigation westward would be stopped, were it not for a number of locks; but the first lock is 52 miles above that bridge. The plan of new cuts has been adopted, in some places, to shorten the navigation; there is one near Lechlade, and another a mile from Abingdon. A still more important undertaking was effected in 1789—the junction of this river with the Severn. A canal had been made from the Severn to Stroud, which canal was afterwards continued to Lechlade, where it joins the Thames, a distance of above 30 miles. A communication between this river and the Trent and Mersey has likewise been effected, by a canal from Oxford to Coventry; and another canal extends from this, at Braunston, to the Thames at Brentford, called the Grand Junction Canal.

THAMES, a river of Connecticut, formed of two principal branches, the Shetucket and the Norwich, or Little River, which have their junction at Norwich. From this place the Thames is navigable 15 miles to Long Island Sound, which it enters below New London.

THANET, an island comprising the E. angle of Kent, being separated from the mainland by the two branches of the Stour. It produces much corn, and the S. part is a rich tract of marsh land. It contains the towns of Margate, Ramsgate, and Broadstairs, and several villages.

THANHAUSEN, a town of Bavaria, on the river Mindel; 14 miles N. of Mindelheim.

THASOS, an island of the Grecian Archipelago, on the coast of Macedonia; at the entrance of the Gulf of Contessa. It is 12 miles long, and 8 broad, and abounds in all the necessaries of life. The fruits and wine are very delicate; and there are some quarries of fine marble. The chief town, of the same name, has a harbour, frequented by merchants. Long. 24. 33. E. lat. 40. 59. N.

THAXTED, a town in Essex, with a market on Friday. It has a beautiful and spacious church, two meeting-houses, almshouses, a school, and other charities. It is seated near the source of the Chelmer; 20 miles N. by W. of Chelmsford, and 44 N. N. E. of London.

THEAKI, an island in the Mediterranean Sea, 24 miles long, and 7 broad; separated from the N. E. part of that of Cefalonia by a narrow channel. It is the ancient Ithaca, celebrated as the birthplace and kingdom of Ulysses. The chief town is Vathi, which has a spacious harbour. Long. 20. 40. E. lat. 38. 25. N.

THEBAID, a country of Upper Egypt, now called SAID, which see.

THEBES, the ancient name of a city of Upper Egypt. It was celebrated for having 100 gates; and there are many tombs and magnificent remains of antiquity. Three villages, named Carnak, Luxor, and Gournou, are seated among its ruins, which extend 7 or 8 miles along the river, and are hence called the antiquities of Carnak and Luxor.

THEBES, in Greece. *See* THIVA.

Theisse, a river of Hungary, which rises in the Carpathian Mountains, flows above 1000 miles in a western direction to Tokay, when it turns to the S., passes by Tsongrand and Segeden, and, after receiving a great number of rivers, falls into the Danube, below Titul.

Themar, a town of Germany, in the duchy of Saxe-Coburg, near the river Werra; 10 miles S. E. of Meiningen.

Theodosia. *See* Caffa.

Theresienstadt, a town in the S. of Hungary, 100 miles N. by W. of Belgrade. It is an assemblage of villages, and received its name, and the privileges of a royal free city, in 1779, from the empress Maria Theresa. Pop. 22,000.

Thermia, an island of the Grecian Archipelago, S. of the island of Zia, and near the Gulf of Engia, 12 miles long, and 5 broad. The soil is good and well cultivated, and it has a great deal of silk. The principal town, of the same name, is the residence of a Greek bishop. Pop. 6000. Long. 24. 59. E. lat. 37. 31. N.

Thermopylæ, a narrow passage in the N. E. of Greece, near Mount Œta; with high cliffs on one side, and an impassable marsh on the other. It is noted in history for the brave stand made by Leonidas with 300 Spartans against the army of Xerxes.

Thessaly. *See* Janna.

Thetford, a borough in Norfolk, governed by a mayor; with a market on Saturday. It returns two members to parliament. It is seated on the Little Ouse, which here divides Suffolk from Norfolk, and is navigable from Lynn. It has three parish churches, (one of which is on the Suffolk side of the river,) and a considerable manufacture of woollen cloth and paper. The spring assizes for the county are held here. It is 30 miles S. S. E. of Lynn, and 80 N. E. of London. Long. 0. 50. E. lat. 52. 28. N.

Thiel, or **Tiel**, a strong town of the Netherlands, in Gelderland; seated on the Waal; 18 miles W. of Nimeguen.

Thielt, a town of Belgium, in West Flanders; 10 miles N. of Courtray.

Thiengen, a town of Baden, on the river Wuttach; 13 miles W. of Schaffhausen.

Thiers, a town of France, in the department of Puy de Dome; with manufactures of paper; thread, leather, and cutlery. It is seated on the side of a hill; 21 miles E. by N. of Clermont. Pop. 10,600.

Thionville, a strong town in the department of Moselle. The Austrians bombarded it in 1792, but were obliged to raise the siege. It is seated on the Moselle, over which is a bridge defended by a horn-work; 14 miles N. of Mentz, and 33 S. W. of Treves. Pop. 4384.

Thirlmere. *See* Leathes-water.

Thirsk, a borough in North Yorkshire; market on Monday, and manufactures of coarse linens, sacking, &c. It has a handsome church, which was erected out of the ruins of its strong castle, destroyed by Henry II. The other places of worship are meeting-houses for Wesleyan and Independent Methodists, and a Quakers' chapel. It returns one member to parliament; 23 miles N. W. of York, and 214 N. by W. of London.

Thiva, or **Thebes**, a celebrated city of Greece, and a bishop's see. The ancient city was 4 miles in circumference, but only that part of it is now inhabited which was originally the castle, called Cadmæa, from Cadmus the founder. In the vicinity is a fine sort of white clay, of which bowls for pipes are made, that dry naturally and become as hard as stone. It is seated between two rivers; 28 miles N. W. of Athens. Pop. 5000.

Thiviers, a town of France, in the department of Dordogne; 18 miles N. N. E. of Perigueux.

Tholen, a town of the Netherlands, in an island of its name belonging to the province of Zealand; 4 miles N. W. of Bergen-op-Zoom.

Thomas, St., an island of the Atlantic, lying under the equator, near the W. coast of Guinea; discovered in 1640 by the Portuguese. It is almost round, is about 30 miles in diameter, and consists chiefly of hills, intermixed with valleys, which are often filled with a thick fog. The soil is fertile, and produces plenty of sugar-canes, rice, and millet. On the same vines are blossoms and green and ripe grapes, all the year round. The climate is unwholesome to the Portuguese, but agrees well with the original inhabitants, and also with the cattle, which are larger and finer here than on the coast of Guinea. In 1641 this island was taken by the Dutch; but they soon relinquished it in consequence of the insalubrity of the climate. Pavoacan is the capital.

Thomas, St., one of the Virgin Islands, in the West Indies, with a harbour, a town, and a fort. It is 15 miles in circumference, and the trade is considerable, particularly in times of peace. It surrendered to the English in 1807, but was restored to the Danes in 1814. Population, 5000. Long. 65. 26. W. lat. 11. 22. N.

Thomas, St., a town of Hindostan, in the Carnatic, formerly a powerful city. It is inhabited by weavers and dyers, and noted for making the best coloured stuffs in India; 3 miles S. of Madras.

Thomaston, a town of the state of Maine, in Lincoln county, which has a great trade in lime. It stands on the W. side of Penobscot Bay, 30 miles E. by N. of Wiscasset. Pop. 6227.

Thomastown, a town of Ireland, in the county of Kilkenny, on the river Noire; 10 miles S. S. E. of Kilkenny.

Thonon, a town of the Sardinian states, in Savoy, with a palace and several convents, seated on the Lake of Geneva, at the influx of the river Drama; 16 miles N. E. of Geneva.

Thorda, a town of Austria, in the province of Transylvania, capital of a county of the same name. Pop. 100,000. The town is seated near the river Aranjos, with some salt mines, which have been wrought by the Romans. Pop. 8000.

Thorn, a city of West Prussia, formerly a Hanseatic town. In the church of St. John is the epitaph of the celebrated Nicholas Copernicus, who was born here. It is divided into the Old and New Town, and has a celebrated Protestant academy. In 1703 it was taken by the Swedes, who demolished the fortifications; and in 1793 it was seized by the king of Prussia, and annexed to his dominions. It was taken by the French in 1806, and remained in their hands till 1812. It is seated on the Vistula, over which is a long wooden bridge; 67 miles S. of Dantzic, and 105 N. W. of Warsaw. Pop. 8500. Long. 18. 42. E. lat. 53. 6. N.

THORN, a small but thriving town in West Yorkshire, with a market on Wednesday. It contains a neat parish church, six meeting-houses, and two charity schools. It is situate in a marshy soil, near the river Don; 11 miles N. E. of Doncaster, and 165 N. by W. of London.

THORNBURY, a borough in Gloucestershire, governed by a mayor, with a market on Saturday. It is 24 miles S. W. of Gloucester, and 122 W. of London.

THORNEY, a small island in a bay of the English Channel, near the coast of Sussex; with a village of the same name, at the mouth of the Levant; 7 miles S. W. of Chichester.

THORNHILL, a town of Scotland, in Dumfries-shire, with manufactures of coarse linen and woollen cloth; seated near the river Nith, 15 miles N. N. W. of Dumfries.

THOUARS, a town of France, department of Deux Sevres. The castle of its ancient dukes is on a rock, surrounded by walls 120 feet high, built of white stone. It is seated on a hill, by the river Thone, 32 miles S. E. of Angers, and 162 S. W. of Paris.

THOUROUT, a town of Belgium, province of West Flanders. It is an ancient town, with a manufacture of hats; 12 miles S. E. from Ostend. Pop. 5000.

THRAPSTON, a town of Northamptonshire, with a market on Tuesday; seated on the Nen, 20 miles S. W. of Peterborough, and 73 N. N. W. of London.

THREE HILLS ISLAND, one of the New Hebrides, in the South Pacific; 12 miles in circumference, lying to the S. of Malicollo.

THREE RIVERS, or TROIS RIVIERES, a town of Lower Canada, situate on a river of the same name, which, before its conjunction with the St. Lawrence, was divided by two islands into three branches. It has two churches, a convent, and an hospital; 9 miles up the river is a considerable iron-foundry; 70 miles W. S. W. of Quebec.

THUIN, a town of Belgium, in the territory of Liege; seated on the Sambre, 8 miles S. W. of Charleroy, and 15 S. E. of Mons.

THUN, a town of Switzerland, capital of a bailiwick, in the canton of Bern, with a castle. It is seated on a lake of the same name, 14 miles long, and 3 broad, where the river Aar issues from it; 15 miles S. by E. of Bern.

THUR, a river of Switzerland, which rises in the S. part of the county of Toggenburg, and flows into the Rhine; 7 miles S. S. W. of Schaffhausen.

THURGAU, a canton of Switzerland, which lies along the river Thur; bounded on the S. by the canton of St. Gall, W. by that of Zurich, and N. and E. by the lake and territory of Constance. It is extremely populous, and the most pleasant and fertile part of Switzerland, though somewhat mountainous towards the S. Its area is computed at 350 square miles, with 77,000 inhabitants, one-third of whom are Catholics, and the other two-thirds Calvinists. Frauenfeld is the capital.

THURINGIA, the former name of a province of Germany, in Saxony; bounded on the E. by Meissen, S. by Franconia, W. by Hesse and Eichfeld, and N. by the duchy of Brunswick and the principality of Anhalt. It is 73 miles in length, and nearly as many in breadth, abounding in corn, fruits, and wood.

THURLES, a town of Ireland, county of Tipperary, with a handsome church, Catholic chapel, market-house, and two convents; also some infantry barracks, 95 miles from Dublin.

THURSO, a town of Scotland, in Caithness-shire, at the mouth of the river Thurso, on the S. W. side of a spacious bay. It has a considerable trade in corn and fish, and manufactures of woollen and linen cloth; 21 miles N. W. of Wick, and 56 N. N. E. of Dornoch. Long. 3. 18. W. lat. 58. 30. N.

TIAGAR, a town of Hindostan, in the Carnatic, 50 miles W. S. W. of Pondicherry, and 75 S. of Arcot.

TIANO, a town of Naples, in Terra di Lavoro, with a famous nunnery and a mineral spring; 15 miles N. W. of Capua. Pop. 3100.

TIBER, a river of Italy, which rises in the Appennines; flows through the Pope's dominions by Borgo, St. Sepulchro, Citta di Castella, Orto, and Rome; 10 miles below which it enters the Mediterranean Sea, between Ostia and Porto.

TIBET, or THIBET, a country of Asia, bounded on the N. W. and N. by the Desert of Kobi, in Tartary, E. by China, S. by Assam and Birmah, and S. W. and W. from Hindostan and Bootan, by the Himalaya mountains. This country is one of the highest in Asia, being a part of that elevated tract which gives rise not only to the rivers of India and China, but also to those of Siberia and Tartary. Its length from E. to W. cannot be less than 2500 miles; its breadth about 500, but very unequal. It may be described as a vast plateau, or table-land, 15,000 feet above the sea, and from which rise the lofty summits of the Himalaya range to the height of 27,000 feet. The country is described as pleasant, and the climate and temperature delightful, though at a height that in other countries is uninhabitable; but vegetation is found on the northern slopes at the elevation of 17,500 feet. It is divided into four great provinces, and Lassa, Teshoo Lomboo, which are separated by a vast tract of unexplored country from Undes and Lahdak. The Indus and Sutluj have their sources in this region; but the principal river of Tibet is the Sampoo, or Burrampooter, of which little is known. The Irrawaddy also rises here, and flows through Burmah and Pegu. The principal exports are gold-dust, diamonds, pearls, lambskins, shawls, woollen cloths, rock-salt, musk, and tincal, or crude borax. The nature of the soil prohibits the progress of agriculture; but wheat, peas, and barley are cultivated. Here are many beasts of prey, and great abundance and variety of wild fowl and game, with numerous flocks of sheep and goats, and herds of cattle of a diminutive size, as well as small horses. The religion is a modification of Buddhism, called Lamaism, and they are governed by the grand lama, who is not only submitted to and adored by them, but is also the great object of adoration for the various tribes of pagan Tartars who walk through the vast tract of continent which stretches from the river Volga to Corea. He is not only the sovereign pontiff, the vicegerent of the Deity on earth, but by the more remote Tartars is absolutely regarded as the Deity himself. Even the emperor of China, who is of a Tartar race, does not fail to acknowledge the lama, in his religious capacity, although, as a temporal sovereign, the lama himself is tributary to that emperor. The opinion of the most orthodox Tibetians is, that when the grand lama seems to die, either of old age or infirmity, his soul, in reality, only quits a crazy habitation, to animate another younger and better; and it is discovered again in the body of some child, by certain tokens known only to the lamas, or priests, in which order he always appears. The lamas, who form the greatest and most powerful body in the state, have the priesthood entirely in their hands. At the head of their hierarchy are three lamas: the Dalai lama, who resides at Lassa; the Teshoo lama, who lives at Teshoo Loomboo; and the Taranat lama, whose seat is Kharca, in the N. The priests constitute many monastic orders, which are held in great veneration among them. The most numerous sect are called Gylongs, or Buddhist monks, who are exempt from labour, enjoined temperance, and interdicted all intercourse with the female sex: they abound over all Tibet and Bootan, notwithstanding the severity of discipline; since every family consisting of more than four boys is obliged to contribute one of them to this order; and it is also encouraged by ambition, as the officers of state are usually selected from this sect. Besides the religious influence and authority of the grand lama, he is possessed of unlimited power throughout his dominions. His residence is at a vast palace on the mountain Putala, 7 miles from Lassa. The religion of Tibet, though in many respects it differs from that of the Indian brahmins, yet, in others, has a great affinity to it. The practice of polyandry is universally prevalent in Tibet; and one female associates with all the brothers of a family, without any restriction of age or number: the choice of a wife is the privilege of the elder brother. This extraordinary custom, and the celibacy of the priests, may have been intended to guard against too numerous a population in an unfertile country. The Tibetians preserve entire the mortal remains of their sovereign lamas only; every other corpse is either consumed by fire or exposed to be the promiscuous food of beasts and birds of prey. They have a great veneration for the cow, and highly respect the waters of the Ganges, the source of which they believe to be in heaven. The sunniasses, or Indian pilgrims, often visit Tibet as a holy place; and the grand lama always maintains a body of nearly 300 of them in his pay. The country became subject to China in 1720, and has been tranquil under its government, except in 1790, when it was invaded by the Ghoorkas of Nepaul; but they were repulsed with great loss. The population is estimated at 5,000,000. *See* PALTE.

TIBURON, a cape at the most western extremity of the island of St. Domingo; with a town and fort, on an open road, opposite Port Antonio in Jamaica. Long. 74. 32. W. lat. 18. 25. N.

TICINO, or TESSIN, a canton of Switzerland, to the W. of the canton of Grisons, on the S. side of the Alps, and almost encircled by Italy. It is rich in pastures and cattle, and has an area of 1130 square miles, with 90,000 inhabitants. Bellinzona is the capital.

TICINO, or TESSIN, a river which has its source in Switzerland, on the S. side of St. Gothard, flows through the canton of Ticino and the Lake Maggiore, then passes to Pavia, in the Milanese, and a little after joins the Po.

TICKHILL, a town in West Yorkshire, with a market on Friday. It was formerly much noted for its malting business, which is still the principal trade of the place. Here was formerly a castle, the ruins of which still bear ample testimony to its former strength and magnitude. The church is a handsome and spacious edifice, and here are two meeting-houses for dissenters, a free-school, and alms-houses for 14 poor women; 7 miles S. of Doncaster, and 156 N. by W. of London.

TICONDEROGA, a fort of the state of New York, built by the French in 1756, on the narrow passage between the lakes George and Champlain. It was taken in 1759 by General Amherst, and in 1777 by General Burgoyne, but evacuated soon after the convention of Saratoga. It had all the advantages that art or nature could give it, but is now a heap of ruins, and forms an appendage to a farm. The town of Ticonderoga is on the W. shore of Lake Champlain, and has a valuable iron-mine; 95 miles N. of Albany, and 14 S. of Crown Point. Pop. 2169.

TIDESWELL, a town in Derbyshire, on the S. confines of the Peak, with a market on Wednesday. Here is a well, deemed one of the wonders of the Peak, which after great rains ebbs and flows two and three times in an hour, the waters gushing from several cavities at once, for the space of five minutes: the well is three feet deep and broad, and the water rises and falls two feet; 22 miles N. W. of Derby, and 160 N. N. W. of London.

TIDORE, an island in the eastern seas, one of the Moluccas. It is 20 miles in circumference, and produces cloves and flax. The woods and the rocks that surround it render it a place of defence. It is governed by a sultan, who possesses also the S. part of Gilolo, and claims tribute from Mysol; 16 miles S. of Ternate. The Dutch have a factory here, first built in 1527. Long. 126. 40. E. lat. 1. 0. N.

TIEL. *See* THIE.

TIEN-SING, a city of China, in Pe-tche-li; which has a great trade in salt. It is seated on the Pei-ho, at the influx of the Eu-ho, 90 miles from its mouth, and 90 S. E. of Peking.

TIGRE, a province in the N. E. part of Abyssinia, 200 miles long, and 120 broad, through which passes all the merchandise of the kingdom destined to cross the Red Sea for Arabia. Adowa is the capital; and the port of the Mosuab on the Red Sea is in this province.

TIGRIS, (the Hiddekel of the sacred writings,) a river of Asia, which has its source in Diarbek. It flows by Diarbekir, Gezira, Mosul, and Tecrit, in which course it separates Diarbeck from Curdistan, then passes by Bagdad and Corna, and soon after joins the Euphrates, 35 miles above Bassora. It has been navigated by steam-boats as high as Mosul; but the current is swift, and above Bagdad it cannot be navigated, except by vessels of light draught. The ancient cities of Nineveh, Seleucia, and Ctesiphon were on this river, and which bounded, on the E., Mesopotamia (the modern Irak Arabi), having the Euphrates on the W. It may be considered as the boundary between the Ottomans and Persia.

TILBURY FORT, a fortress in Essex, situate on the Thames, opposite Gravesend. It has a double moat, the innermost of which is 180 feet broad, and its chief strength on the land side consists in its being able to lay the whole level under water. On the side next the river is a strong curtain, with a platform before it; on both which, and the bastions, are planted a great number of guns. It was made a regular fortification in 1667, after the attack of the Dutch fleet, when they burnt the shipping at Sheerness. It was originally a blocktown built in the reign of Henry VIII It is 28 miles E. by S. of London.

TILLIERS, a town of France, department of Eure; 6 miles N. E. of Verneuil.

TILSIT, a town of Prussian Lithuania, with a castle, and a considerable trade in corn, linseed, butter, cheese, and other provisions. In 1807 it was taken by the French; soon after which two treaties of peace were made between France and Prussia, and France and Russia, the three sovereigns being here in person. It is situate on the Memel; 50 miles N. E. of Konigsberg, and 95 S. S. W. of Mittau. Pop. 9000. Long. 22. 8. E. lat. 55. 8. N.

TIMANA, a town of Colombia, in Popayan, capital of a territory of the same name, which abounds in fruits and pastures. It is seated on a river, 130 miles E. S. E. of Popayan. Long. 74. 55. W. lat. 1. 35. N.

TIMBUCTOO, a city of Central Africa, and the great emporium of the interior trade of that continent. It was for many years enveloped in mystery, and the most extravagant ideas respecting its magnificence were formed, but have been dissipated by the reality. It was first visited by the unfortunate Major Laing, in 1826, but he was assassinated on his homeward route. M. Caille was more fortunate, and from his descriptions most of our knowledge is derived. It is situated in an immense plain of white sand, having no vegetation but stunted trees and shrubs, such as the mimosa ferruginea, which grows no higher than three or four feet. The city is not closed by any barrier, and may be entered on any side. It forms a sort of triangle about three miles in circuit. The houses are large, but not high, consisting entirely of a ground floor; they are built of bricks of a round form, rolled in the hands and baked in the sun. The streets are clean, and sufficiently wide for three horsemen to pass abreast. Both within and without the town there are many straw huts, which serve as dwellings for the poor, and for the slaves, who sell merchandise for their masters. The city contains seven mosques, two of which are large. The number of inhabitants is stated not to exceed 12,000, who are all engaged in trade; but the population is sometimes augmented by the Arabs, who arrive with the caravans and remain awhile in the city. In the plain several species of grass and thistle afford food for the camels. Fire-wood is very scarce, being all brought from the neighbourhood of Cabra, and camel-dung forms the only fuel of the poorer classes. The soil being totally unfit for cultivation, the inhabitants are obliged to procure from Jenné everything requisite for the supply of their wants, such as millet, rice, vegetable butter, honey, cotton, Soudan cloth, preserved provisions, candles, soap, allspice, onions, dried fish, pistachios, &c.; and, to prevent immediate famine, in case the vessels from Cabra should chance to be stopped by the Tooariks, the inhabitants take care to have their warehouses amply stored with every kind of provision. Water is also scarce, and is sold in the market-place, where a measure containing about half a pint is procured for a cowrie. To the W. S. W. of the town there are large excavations, from 30 to 40 feet deep, for preserving the rain-water. These reservoirs have no covering; and the water, being consequently exposed to the sun and the hot wind, though tolerably clear, has a disagreeable taste, and is very hot. Near the reservoirs are some small plantations of tobacco, the only plant which is here cultivated, and which grows no higher than five or six inches, and that only by dint of watering. All the native inhabitants of Timbuctoo are zealous Mahomedans. Their dress is similar to that of the Moors. They are represented as gentle and complaisant to strangers, industrious in their habits, and not wanting in intelligence. The men are of the ordinary size, generally well made, upright, and walk with a graceful step. Their colour is fine deep black. Their noses are a little more aquiline than those of the Mandingoes, and like them they have thin lips and large eyes. The women attend to domestic occupations. They are not veiled, like those of Morocco, and are allowed to walk out when they please. Those of the richer class have always a great number of glass beads about their necks and in their ears. Like the women of Jenné they wear nose-rings; and the female who is not rich enough to procure a ring substitutes a piece of red silk for it: they wear silver bracelets, and ancle-rings of plated steel, the latter of which are made in the country. The female slaves of rich masters have gold ornaments about their necks, and instead of wearing ear-rings, as in the environs of the Senegal, they have little plates in the form of a necklace. The interior of the dwellings in Timbuctoo, as well as the dress of the inhabitants, is exceedingly neat. Their domestic articles consist of calabashes and wooden platters: knives and forks are unknown here, and the natives imagine that, like them, all people in the world eat with their fingers. Their furniture consists merely of mats for sitting on; and their beds are made by fixing four stakes in the ground at one end of the room, and stretching over them some mats or a cow hide. The rich have cotton mattresses and coverlets, which the neighbouring Moors manufacture from camels' hair and sheep's wool. The people are well fed. Their meals, of which they take two in a day, consist of rice, and couscous made of a small millet, dressed with meat or dried fish. Those negroes who are in easy circumstances breakfast on wheaten bread, tea, and butter made from cow's milk; those of inferior circumstances use vegetable butter. Generally speaking, the negroes are not so well lodged as the Moors: the latter have great influence over them, and indeed consider themselves far their superiors. Cloth and other European merchandise, and salt, are brought to Timbuctoo by caravans from Barbary; these are exchanged for ivory, slaves, senna, gold-dust, dates, ostriches' feathers, &c., brought from the interior and more maritime parts of Africa. This city is subject to a well-regulated police, and many of the inhabitants are very rich. Cabra, its port, 3 miles N., is a narrow town of mud huts, containing about 1000 inhabitants, who are all employed either in landing the merchandise brought from Jenné, or in conveying it to Timbuctoo: it has a small mosque with a minaret, but is a dirty and miserable-looking place. Long. 3. 40. W. lat. 17. 50. N.

Timerycotta, a town and fortress of Hindostan, in the Carnatic, chief place in the district of Palnaud. It is 72 miles S. E. of Hydrabad, and 82 W. by S. of Condapilly. Long. 79. 26. E. lat. 16. 20. N.

Timon, or Timoan, an island on the E. coast of the peninsula of Malaya, 30 miles in circumference. It is mountainous and woody, and produces plenty of cocoa-nuts and rice. Long. 104. 25. E. lat. 3. 0. N.

Timor, an island in the Indian Ocean, to the W. of the N. W. point of New Holland. It is 200 miles long, and 60 broad, and abounds in sandal-wood, wax and honey. The Dutch have a fort here, from which they expelled the Portuguese in 1613. It is situate at Coepang, the principal town, on the S. W. point of the island. Long. 124. 0. E. lat. 10. 23. S.

Timorlaut, or Timor-Laoet, an island in the Indian Ocean, between Timor and New Guinea. It is 60 miles in circumference, and the S. point is in long. 131. 54. E. lat. 8. 15. S.

Tinevelly, or Tinnevelly, a town of Hindostan, capital of a district of its name, at the S. extremity of the Carnatic. It is seated on a river which flows into the Gulf of Manaar; 85 miles S. S. W. of Madura. Long. 71. 46. E. lat. 8. 42. N.

Ting-tcheou, a city of China, of the first rank, in Fo-kien; 980 miles S. of Peking. Long. 116. 30. E. lat. 25. 48. N.

Tinian, an island in the North Pacific, one of the Ladrones, 12 miles long, and 6 broad. The soil is dry, and somewhat sandy, but produces abundance of cocoa-nuts, paupaus, guavas, limes, sour oranges, and bread-fruit; also much cotton and indigo. The road is dangerous, for the bottom consists of hard sand and large coral rocks. Long. 146. 0. E. lat. 15. 0. N.

Tino, the ancient Tenos, an island of the Grecian Archipelago, to the S. of Andros, from which it is separated by a channel of a mile in width. It is 15 miles long, and 8 broad, and produces 16,000 pounds of silk every year. The fortress stands on a rock; and here is a bishop's see of the Latin church, though the Greeks have 200 papas or priests. Pop. 25,000. The capital is St. Nicholo. Long. 25. 10. E. lat. 37. 40. N.

Tintagel, a village in Cornwall, noted for the splendid remains of a castle, on a bold promontory in the Bristol Channel, said to have been the birthplace of king Arthur, and the seat of the ancient dukes of Cornwall. It is 1 mile W. of Bossiney.

Tintern, a village in Monmouthshire, noted for the venerable remains of an abbey, which is a beautiful specimen of Gothic architecture. It is seated on the river Wye, 5 miles N. by E. of Chepstow.

Tinto, a river of Spain, which rises in the province of Seville, and has its name from the water being tinged of a yellow colour. Near its springs it has a petrifying quality; no fish will live in it, nor any plants grow on its banks; these properties continue till other rivulets enter and alter its nature; for when it passes by Niebla it is not different from other rivers; and 18 miles below it enters the Bay of Cadiz, at Huelva.

Tinzeda, a town of Barbary, in the county of Darah; on the river Dras. Long. 6. 13. W. lat. 27. 30. N.

Tiorn, an island on the W. coast of Sweden, 25 miles in circumference, and abounding in excellent pastures. Long. 11. 29. E. lat. 58. 0. N.

Tipera, a district of Bengal, on the borders of Birmah. Pop. 750,000. The chief town is Comillah, which is the residence of the rajah, and the seat of the British civil establishment.

Tipperary, a county of Ireland, in the province of Munster; 70 miles long, and 40 broad; bounded on the N. by King's county, E. by Queen's county and Kilkenny, S. by Waterford, and W. by Galway, Clare, Limerick, and Cork. It is divided into 147 parishes, and sends two members to parliament. The S. part is fertile; but the N. is rather barren, and terminates in a range of twelve mountains, the highest in Ireland, called Phelem-dhe-Madina. The river Suire runs through it from N. to S. Clonmel is the capital.

Tipperary, a town of Ireland, in the county of the same name; 9 miles W. S. W. of Cashel, and 20 N. W. of Clonmel.

Tipsa. *See* Tebesta.

Tirano, a town of Austrian Italy, capital of a district in the Valteline. It contains several handsome buildings, but from the narrowness of the streets, and many ruinous houses, its general appearance is desolate. Its staple commerce consists in the exportation of wine and silk. Near the town is the magnificent church of the Madonna, much visited by Catholic pilgrims. The massacre of the Protestants of the Valteline, in 1620, began in this town. It is seated on the Adda, 15 miles E. of Londris. Pop. 3700. Long. 9. 58. E. lat. 46. 20. N.

Tireh, a town of Asia Minor, in Natolia; situate on the Meinder; 32 miles S.S.E. of Smyrna.

Tiree, an island of Scotland, one of the Hebrides; lying to the W. of Mull. It is 16 miles long, and 3 broad. The surface in general is even, and it is noted for its marble quarry, and a handsome breed of little horses.

Tirlemont, a town of Belgium, in South Brabant; formerly one of the most considerable cities in that duchy, but ruined by the wars, and by a great fire in 1701. Near this place the Austrians were defeated in 1792 by the French, who the year following were routed by the former. It is seated on the river Greete, 10 miles E. S. E. of Louvain.

Tirnau, a town of Hungary, in the country of Neitra; seated on the Tirna; 26 miles N. E. of Presburg.

Tirschenreid, a town of Bavaria, seated on a lake; 10 miles S. of Egra.

Titan, or **Cabaros**, an island of France, the largest and most eastern of the Hieres, in the Mediterranean.

Titchfield, a town in Hampshire, noted for the remains of a mansion where Charles I. was concealed, in his flight from Hampton Court, in 1647. It is seated on the river Aire, 3 miles W. of Fareham.

Titeri, the middle or southern province of the kingdom of Algier, in which is a lake of the same name, formed by the river Shellif, near its source. Towards the N. the country is mountainous and narrow, and to the S. it extends far into the desert. It contains some of the highest mountains in the kingdom, part of which are inhabited by the Cabyls, an independent tribe, who have never been subdued by the Algerines. The principal town of this province is Belida.

Titicaca, or **Chucuito**, a lake of South America, in the state of Peru. It is of an oval figure, with an inclination from N. W. to S. E., and 240 miles in circumference. Many streams enter into it, but its waters are so muddy and nauseous as to be unfit for drinking. One of the most splendid temples in the empire was erected on an island in this lake, by the incas.

Titlisberg, one of the highest mountains in Switzerland, in the canton of Uri; 11 miles S. S. W. of Altorff.

Titschein, New, a well-built town of the Austrian states, in Moravia; defended by walls; 28 miles E. by N. of Prerau.

Tittmaning, a town of Bavaria, in the duchy of Salzburg; seated on the Salza; 20 miles N. N. W. of Salzburg.

Titul, a town of Hungary, seated on the Theisse; 23 miles E. S. E. of Peterwardein, and 24 N. N. W. of Belgrade.

Tiumen, a town of Siberia, in the province of Tobolsk, on the river Tura, at the influx of the Pischma; 170 miles S. W. of Tobolsk.

Tiverton, a borough in Devonshire, governed by a mayor; with markets on Tuesday and Saturday. It returns two members to parliament. It has long been noted for its woollen manufactures, particularly kerseys. Here are two churches, several meeting-houses, and a free-school, (founded by a clothier of the town,) which has an endowment for the maintenance of four scholars at Balliol College, Oxford, and four at Sidney Sussex, Cambridge. Near the old church are the remains of a castle, part of which is converted into the offices of a farm. Tiverton has suffered very severely by fire, particularly in 1731. It is seated on the river Ex; 14 miles N. N. E. of Exeter, and 161 W. by S. of London. Long. 3. 38. W. lat. 50. 54. N.

Tivoli, a town of the papal states, in Campagna di Roma; and a bishop's see. Though now poor, it boasts of greater antiquity than Rome, being the ancient Tibur, which was founded by a Grecian colony. It was the favourite country residence of the ancient Romans, as Frascati is of the moderns. The cathedral is built on the ruins of a temple of Hercules. In the market-place are two images of oriental granite, representing the Egyptian deity Isis. The adjacent country yields excellent oil. Near Tivoli are the ruins of the magnificent villa built by the emperor Adrian, a celebrated cascade, a temple of Vesta, and another of the sibyl Albunea, a famous villa called the Villa Esteme, and the remarkable lake of Solfatara. Tivoli is seated on an eminence, on the river Teverone; 16 miles E. N. E. of Rome. Pop. 14,000.

Tizzano, a town of Italy, in the duchy of Parma; 13 miles S. of Parma.

Tlascala, a province of Mexico, bounded on the N. by Panuco, E. by the Gulf of Mexico, S. by Guaxaca and the Pacific Ocean, and W. by Mexico Proper. On the W. side there is a chain of mountains for the space of 55 miles, well cultivated; and on the N. is a great ridge of mountains, the neighbourhood of which exposes it to violent tempests and frequent inundation. It produces so much maize, that hence it had the name of Tlascala, the Land of Bread. Pop. 59,177. Puebla de los Angelos is the capital.

TLASCALA, a town of Mexico, formerly the capital of the province of the same name; seated on a river; 15 miles N. by E. of Puebla de los Angelos. Pop. 3400.

TLEMSAN. *See* TREMESAN.

TOBAGO, the most southern of the islands of the West Indies, and the most eastern except Barbadoes. It is 30 miles long, and 10 broad; and near its N. E. extremity is Little Tobago, an island 2 miles long, and 1 broad. The climate is not so hot as might be expected from its situation so near the equator; nor is it visited by such dreadful hurricanes as frequently desolate the other islands. It is diversified with hills and vales, and is equal in richness of produce to any island in these seas. In 1748 it was declared a neutral island, but in 1763 it was ceded to the English. It was taken by the French in 1781, and confirmed to them in 1783; but it was taken by the English in 1793, and restored in 1802. It was again taken by the English in 1803, and confirmed to them by the treaty of Paris in 1814. Pop. 14,500. The principal place is Scarborough.

TOBERMORY, a town of Scotland, in the island of Mull; with a good harbour, and a custom-house; seated on a fine bay, near the N. W. end of the sound of Mull. Long. 5. 58. W. lat. 56. 46. N.

TOBOLSK, a government of the Russian empire, which comprehends the greatest part of Western Siberia. It is divided into the two provinces of Tobolsk and Tomsk. Population 622,422.

TOBOLSK, a considerable and populous city of Russia, formerly capital of Siberia, and at present of the government of Tobolsk. It is divided into the Upper and Lower Town: the former is properly the city, and stands very high, with a fort built of stone, in which are the governor's court, the governor's house, the archbishop's palace, the exchange, and two of the principal churches, all built of stone, but the houses in general are of wood, and are very low. The Tartars, who live round this town, for several miles, are all Mahomedans, and their mufti is an Arabian: in general they behave very quietly, and carry on some commerce, but practise no mechanic trades. There are also a great number of Calmuc Tartars, who serve as slaves. All the Chinese caravans pass through this town, and all the furs furnished by Siberia are brought here, and hence forwarded to Moscow. The Russians commonly send their state prisoners to this city. It is seated at the confluence of the rivers Tobol and Irtysch; 1100 miles E. by N. of Moscow, and 1200 E. by S. of Petersburg. Pop. 16,200. Long. 68. 35. E. lat. 58. 12. N.

TOCANTIN, a large river of Brazil, which rises in lat. 18. S., and flows N. E. at the foot of a ridge of mountains for above 700 miles; then enters a more open country, and pursues its course 400 miles further to the Atlantic Ocean, which it enters by a large estuary, below the city of Para. The estuary of this river has a communication with that of the Amazons to the W.; and the space included by them and the ocean is an island, 150 miles in diameter, called Maraso or Joanes.

TOCAT, a city of Asia Minor, in Sivas. The houses are handsomely built, and the streets paved, which is an uncommon thing in these parts; but the town makes a very odd appearance, being built on uneven ground. There are two rugged perpendicular rocks of marble, with an old castle upon each; and so many streams, that each house has a fountain. The inhabitants are computed at 60,000. The chief trade is in copper vessels, but much yellow leather and silk is manufactured. It is seated in a district which abounds in fruit and excellent wine; 45 miles W. N. W. of Sivas, and 150 N. of Marash. Long. 36. 35. E. lat. 39. 10. N.

TOCAYMA, a town of Colombia, in a country abounding in fruit and sugar-canes. Here are hot baths between two cold springs: and near the town is a volcano. It is seated on the Pati, near its entrance into the Madalena; 34 miles W. of St. Fe de Bogota. Long. 74. 58. W. lat. 4. 5. N.

TOCRUR, a kingdom of Negroland, lying to the E. of Timbuctoo, on both sides the Niger. The capital is of the same name, seated on the S. side of the Niger; 320 miles E. of Timbuctoo. Long. 6. 18. W. lat. 16. 38. N.

TOCUYO, a town of the republic of Colombia, in the province of Venezuela, near the source of the Tocuyo, famous for its excellent wheat; it has also a trade in salt; 60 miles N. of Truxillo. Pop. 10,200.

TODI, a town of the papal states, in the duchy of Spoleto, seated on a hill, near the Tiber; 22 miles E. of Spoleto.

TODMORDEN, a town in Lancashire, and partly in Yorkshire, 207 miles from London. The inhabitants are occupied in the manufacture of cotton, fustian, velveteen, &c. The Manchester and Leeds railway passes through the town.

TOISSEY, a town of France, in the department of Ain, with a college, seated near the conflux of the Saone and Chalarone; 15 miles N. of Trevoux.

TOKAY, a town of Hungary, with a castle. It is celebrated for its wine, which is preferred to all others in Hungary; and near it are large salt-works. It stands at the conflux of the Bodrog with the Theisse; 105 miles E. N. E. of Buda. Pop. 4200. Long. 21. 15. E. lat. 48. 8. N.

TOLEDO, a city of Spain, in New Castile, of which it was formerly the capital. It is seated on a conical hill on the river Tagus, which nearly surrounds it, and on the land side is an ancient wall, flanked with 100 towers. There are a great number of superb structures, besides 17 public squares, where the markets are kept. It is an archbishop's see, and the cathedral is the richest in Spain: the Segrario, or principal chapel, contains 15 large cabinets let into the wall, full of gold and silver vessels, and other works. Here are numerous religious houses and churches, with some hospitals; and formerly it had a university, which was suppressed in 1807. The inhabitants, once estimated at 200,000, are now reduced to 25,000. Without the town are the remains of an amphitheatre and other antiquities. It has a royal castle, and several manufactures of arms, silk, and wool. Toledo was occupied by the French in 1808; 37 miles S. of Madrid. Long. 3. 20. W. lat. 39. 50. N.

TOLEN, a fortified town of the Netherlands, in Zealand, in an island of the same name, separated by a narrow channel from Brabant. On the Brabant side it has a fort, called Schlyckenburg; 5 miles N. W. of Bergen-op-Zoom. Long. 4. 20. E. lat. 51. 30. N.

TOLENTINO, a town of the Ecclesiastical States, in Ancona, where the relics of St. Nicholas are kept. A treaty of peace was concluded here between Bonaparte and the papal court in 1797. It is seated on the Chiento; 8 miles S. E. of St. Severino. Pop. 4000.

TOLESBURG, a seaport of Russia, in the government of Riga, seated on the Gulf of Finland; 60 miles W. of Narva. Long. 26. 4. E. lat. 59. 38. N.

TOLFA, a town of Italy, in the States of the Church. In the environs are warm baths, mines of alum and iron, and quarries of alabaster and lapis lazuli. It is 6 miles N. E. of Civita Vecchia.

TOLHUYS, a town of the Netherlands, in Guelderland, seated on the Rhine; 8 miles E. of Nimeguen.

TOLLAND, a town of Connecticut, chief of a county of its name; 18 miles N. E. of Hartford. Pop. 1562.

TOLMEZO, a town of Austrian Italy, in Friuli with a castle. Near it is an extensive linen manufacture. It stands on the Tagliamento; 16 miles N. W. of Udina.

TOLMINO, a town of the Austrian states, in Carniola; 12 miles N. of Goritz.

TOLNA, a town of Hungary, formerly the capital of a county of the same name; producing excellent wine. It is seated on the Danube; 65 miles S. of Buda. Long. 19. 15. E. lat. 46. 30. N.

TOLNANI, a town of Hindostan, in the country of Baglana; 70 miles W. of Burhampour, and 124 E. of Surat. Long. 75. 3. E. lat. 21. 15. N.

TOLOMETA, a seaport of Barbary, in Barca, anciently called Ptolemais. It is seated on the Mediterranean; 100 miles W. of Derna. Long. 20. 30. E. lat. 32. 44. N.

TOLOSA, a town of Spain, in Biscay, capital of the district of Guipuscoa, celebrated for its steel manufactures, particularly of sword-blades. It was taken by the French in 1794, and again in 1808. It is seated in a valley, between the Araxis and Oria; 36 miles E. of Bilboa. Pop. 4200. Long. 2. 5. W. lat. 43. 12. N.

TOLU, a seaport of Colombia, in Carthagena, famous for its balsam, produced from a tree like a pine. It is seated on a bay; 70 miles S. of Carthagena. Long. 75. 16. W. lat. 9. 30. N.

TOMAR, a town of Portugal, in Estremadura, on the river Naboan, at the foot of the mountains, where there is a castle belonging to the knights of Christ. It is 40 miles S. by E. of Coimbra, and 65 N. E. of Lisbon.

TOMBUCTOO. *See* TIMBUCTOO.

TOMINA, a province of Buenos Ayres, 72 miles long, and 210 in circuit. The surface is mountainous, but the valleys are fertile.

TOMINI, a town on the E. coast of the island of Celebes, on a bay to which it gives name. Long. 111. 0. E. lat. 0. 45. S.

TOMSK, a town of Asiatic Russia, capital of a province of its name, in the government of Tobolsk. On the highest part stands a wooden castle, defended by 14 pieces of cannon; and in it are a cathedral built of wood, the chancery, and an arsenal. The inhabitants carry on a great trade, this town lying on the great road through all the E. and N. parts of Siberia. Here are all kinds of artificers and tradesmen, but they are extremely indolent and slothful. It contains above 2000 houses, with 12,000 inhabitants. It is seated on the river Tom; 590 miles E. by S. of Tobolsk. Long. 84. 19. E. lat. 57. 4. N.

TONDERN, a well-built town of Denmark, capital of a district of its name, in the duchy of Sleswick, with a considerable trade in corn, cattle, silk, and fine lace. It is seated on the river Widaw, and on a bay of the German Ocean; 28 miles S. by E. of Ripen, and 40 N. W. of Sleswick. Long. 9. 40. E. lat. 54. 58. N.

TONGATABOO, one of the Friendly Islands, 20 leagues in circuit. It was discovered by Tasman, who called it New Amsterdam, and was visited in 1773 and 1777 by Cook, who lay at anchor on the W. part. It has the best harbour, or anchoring-place, to be found among these islands. The land is low, with many gentle risings, and very fertile, being wholly laid out in plantations, with roads or lanes for travelling. It is the seat of government for all the other islands, and the ordinary residence of all the principal chiefs. Long. 174. 46. W. lat. 21. 9. S.

TONGERON, or TONGRES, a town of Belgium, in the territory of Liege; formerly one of the most flourishing cities in the Roman province of Gallia Belgica. It is seated on the Jeckar; 13 miles N. W. of Liege.

TONG-GIN, a city of China, of the first rank, in Koei-tcheou; 850 miles S. S. W. of Peking. Long. 108. 37. E. lat. 27. 40. N.

TONGHO, a city of Birmah, capital of a province of the same name, noted for producing the best betel-nut. It has a fort deemed the strongest in the Birman empire. It is seated near the Setang; 90 miles N. of Pegu. Long. 96. 45. E. lat. 18. 45. N.

TONG-TCHANG, a city of China, of the first rank, in Chang-tong, seated near the N. end of the Grand Canal; 210 miles S. of Peking. Long. 116. 12. E. lat. 36. 30. N.

TONG-TCHOU, a small city of China, in Petche-li, seated on the Pei-ho, 170 miles from its mouth, and 12 E. by S. of Peking.

TONG-TCHUEN, a fortified city of China, of the first rank, in the province of Se-tchuen. The inhabitants are all soldiers, who have followed the profession of arms from father to son. It is 1000 miles S. W. of Peking. Long. 102. 30. E. lat. 25. 56. N.

TONGUSIANS, or TONGUSES, a people who inhabit the E. part of Siberia, and are subject to the Russians. They are all pagans, and subsist chiefly by grazing and hunting of sables. They live in huts, which they take down and remove with them from place to place. These huts are composed of wooden poles, covered all over with hair and rubbish, except a hole left at the top to let out the smoke. Their fire is made in the middle, and they all sit round it upon turfs. Both sexes are very strong, and broad-faced, and they all ride on horseback, not excepting the girls. Both men and women dress alike, in a sort of frock, with boots of skins on their legs, and their common drink is water. Their number is supposed not to exceed 45,000.

TONNA, a town of Germany, in Saxe-Gotha, 6 miles N. of Gotha.

TONNAY BOUTONNE, a town of France, department of Lower Charente, on the river Boutonne; 17 miles N. of Saintes.

TONNAY CHARENTE, a town in the department of Lower Charente, with a castle. It is seated on the Charente; 3 miles E. of Rochfort, and 15 N. W. of Saintes.

TONNEINS, a town in the department of Lot-et-Garonne, seated on the Garonne; 7 miles E. of Marmande. Pop. 600.

TONNERRE, a town in the department of Yonne, famous for its good wines. It is seated on the Armançon; 27 miles S. of Troyes, and 102 E. of Paris.

TONNINGEN, a seaport of Denmark, in the duchy of Sleswick. The harbour is commodious, and defended by three batteries. It is seated on a peninsula, formed by the river Eyder; 25 miles W. S. W. of Sleswick, and 70 N. N. W. of Hamburgh. Long. 9. 10. E. lat. 54. 30. N.

TONQUIN, or TONGKING, a country of Asia; bounded on the N. by China, E. by China and the Gulf of Tonquin, S. by Cochin-China, and W. by Laos. It is 1200 miles in length and 500 in breadth, and one of the finest countries of the East, for population, riches, and trade. It contains about 18,000,000 of inhabitants. The commodities are gold, musk, silks, calicoes, drugs of many sorts, woods for dyeing, lacquered and earthen wares, salt, aniseed, and wormseed. The lacquered ware is not inferior to that of Japan, which is accounted the best in the world. The natives in general are of a middling stature, and clean limbed, with a tawny complexion; their faces oval and flattish, and their hair black, long, and coarse, hanging down their shoulders. They dye their teeth black. They are dexterous, active, and ingenious in mechanic arts. Their garments are made either of silk or cotton; but the poor people and soldiers wear only cotton of a dark tawny colour. Their houses are small and low, and the walls either of mud, or hurdles daubed over with clay. They have only a ground floor, with two or three partitions, and each room has a square hole to let in the light. They have stools, benches, and chairs; and on the side of a table in every house is a little altar, on which are two incense-pots. The country abounds with villages, which consist of 30 or 40 houses, surrounded by trees; and in some places are banks to keep the water from overflowing their gardens, where they have oranges, betels, pumpkins, melons, and salad herbs. In the rainy season they cannot pass from one house to another without wading through the water, but sometimes they have boats. The Tonquinese in general, are courteous to strangers; but the great men are haughty and ambitious, the soldiers insolent, and the poor thievish. They buy all their wives, of which the great men have several. The men are so addicted to gaming that, when every thing else is lost, they will stake their wives and children; and in hard times they will sell them to buy rice for themselves. When a man dies he is buried in his own ground, and, if he was a master of a family, they make a great feast. The first new moon that happens after the middle of January is a great festival, when they rejoice for ten days together; and they have another great feast in May or June, when their first harvest is got in. Their religion is paganism, but they own a Supreme Being. Their principal idols have human shapes; but they have likewise some resembling elephants and horses, placed in small low temples built of timber. The language is very guttural, and some of the words are pronounced through the teeth: it has a great resemblance to the Chinese. Tonquin became an independent kingdom in 1368, but it has been entirely subdued by Cochin-China, so that, with Cambodia, and all the countries between Siam and China, it is now united under the Chinese empire. Cachao, or Kestro, is the capital.

TONSBERG, a seaport of Norway, in the province of Aggerhuys. It has some commerce in timber; and near it is Walloe, the most considerable salt-work in the kingdom. It is 46 miles S. of Christiania. Long. 10. 14. E. lat. 58. 50. N.

TONURU, a town of Hindostan, in Mysore, formerly a city of great extent, as appears by some ruins of the walls. Here are three temples, in good preservation, and near it is an immense tank, or reservoir of water, between two rocky hills. It is 10 miles N. of Seringapatam.

TOOBOUAI, an island in the South Pacific Ocean, one of the Society Islands, discovered by Cook. It is not in any direction above 6 miles over, but there are hills in it of a considerable elevation, covered with herbage, except a few rocky cliffs, with patches of trees interspersed to their summits. It is plentifully stocked with hogs and fowls, and produces ceveral kinds of fruits and roots. *See* SOCIETY ISLANDS. Long. 210. 23. W. lat. 23. 25. S.

TOPEL, or TOPL, a town of Bohemia, in the circle of Pilsen, at the source of a rivulet of the same name; 25 miles N. W. of Pilsen.

TOPETINO, a town of Mexico, in the province of Mechoacan, at the mouth of a river, near the Pacific Ocean; 55 miles N. W. of Zacatula.

TOPLITZ, a town of Bohemia, in the circle of Leutmeritz, celebrated for its warm baths. Near this place the Austrians defeated the Prussians in 1762, and here the allied sovereigns had their head-quarters a considerable time in 1813. It is 16 miles N. W. of Leutmeritz.

TOPOLTZAN, a town of Hungary. 60 miles N. E. of Presburg.

TOPSHAM, a seaport of Devonshire, with a market on Saturday. Here is a spacious and convenient quay, belonging to the city of Exeter, of which this town is the port. Most of the inhabitants are employed in the shipping business. It is seated at the head of the estuary of the Ex, 5 miles S. E. of Exeter, and 170 S. W. of London.

TOR, a seaport of Arabia, with a good harbour, defended by a castle. Here is a Greek convent, in the garden of which are fountains of bitter water, pretended to be those which Moses rendered sweet by throwing in a piece of wood. It stands on the W. side of the peninsula formed by the two arms of the Red Sea, 150 miles S. S. E. of Suez. Long. 33. 40. E. lat. 28. 10. N.

TORBAY, a bay of the English Channel, on the coast of Devonshire, to the E. of Dartmouth; formed by two canals, called Berry Head and Bob's Nose. Here the prince of Orange landed in 1688, when he came over from Holland by the invitation of many principal persons, to preserve the country from popery and arbitrary power. The S. point, Berry Head, is in long. 3. 28. W. lat. 50. 24. N.

TORBIA, a town of the Sardinian states, in Piedmont, 7 miles E. of Nice.

TORBOLE, a town of Austrian Italy, in the circle of Trent; 14 miles S. E. of Trent.

TORCELLO, a town of Austrian Italy, in a small island of the same name in the Gulf of Venice. It is a bishop's see, and has several churches and an elegant nunnery. It is 7 miles N. of Venice. Pop. 9000.

TORDESILLAS, a fortified town of Spain, in Leon, with a palace, where queen Joan, mother of Charles V., ended her melancholy days. It is seated on the Douro, 15 miles S. W. of Valladolid, and 75 S. S. E. of Leon.

TOREE, a town of Bengal, 235 miles W. N. W. of Calcutta. Long. 84. 55. E. lat. 23. 38. N.

TORELLO, a town of Spain, in Catalonia, famous for a battle gained by the French over the Spaniards in 1694. It is seated near the mouth of the Ter, 19 miles E. by S. of Gironna, and 60 N. E. of Barcelona.

TORGAU, a strong town of Prussian Saxony, in the government of Merseburg, with a castle. The inhabitants brew excellent beer, and have manufactures of woollens, leather, and soap. Here the king of Prussia obtained a great victory over the Austrians in 1760. The town was taken by the allies in 1814. It is seated among groves and lakes on the river Elbe, 26 miles N. N. W. of Meissen, and 46 N. W. of Dresden. Pop. 4500. Long. 13. 3. E. lat. 51. 32. N.

TORIGNY, a town of France, department of Manche, with a castle, 7 miles S. E. of St. Lo.

TORMES, a river of Spain, which rises in the mountains of Avila, in Castile, passes by Alva, Tormes, and Salamanca, and joins the Douro below Mirande de Douro. The battle of Salamanca, July, 1812, was fought on its banks.

TORNA, a town of Hungary, capital of a district of the same name, with a castle seated on an eminence on the river Sayo; 22 miles W. of Cassovia. Long. 20. 43. E. lat. 48. 50. N.

TORNEA, a river of Sweden, which rises on the borders of Norway, forms a lake of the same name, and flows S. E. into the Gulf of Bothnia, below Tornea.

TORNEA, a seaport of European Russia, in the government of Finland, with a good harbour. It is a place of some trade, for the Laplanders in those parts come and exchange their skins and other articles for what they want. The houses are low, and the cold so severe, that sometimes people lose their fingers and toes. In its vicinity is an entire mountain of iron ore. It is seated on the river Tornea, at the N. extremity of the Gulf of Bothnia, 165 miles N. E. of Uma. Long. 24. 12. E. lat. 65. 51. N.

TORO, a town of Spain, in Leon, capital of a district of its name, and a bishop's see. It is seated on a hill, on the river Douro, over which is a bridge; 20 miles E. N. E. of Zamoro, and 30 N. N. E. of Salamanca.

TORON, a town of Macedonia, situate on a neck of land between the Gulfs of Monte Santo and Cassandra; 90 miles S. E. of Salonica. Long. 24. 10. E. lat. 39. 58. N.

TORONTO, late YORK, which see.

TORQUAY, a town in Devonshire, near the N. side of Torbay, 7 miles S. E. of Newton Bushel. It has two piers, and a neat range of buildings for summer visitors, who may here enjoy convenient bathing and a romantic situation. Near it is a singular cavern, called Kent's Hole, which is full 200 yards long, and in no part more than 20 feet high.

TORRE DE LAS SALINAS, a town of Spain, in Valencia, with a great trade in salt, procured from a small lake formed by saline springs. This is the most considerable salt-work in all Spain. The town is situate near the coast of the Mediterranean, 20 miles S. E. of Origuela, and 37 N. N. E. of Carthagena.

TORRE DEL GRECO, a town of Naples, in Terra di Lavoro; destroyed by an eruption of Vesuvius in 1631, and by another in 1794. The present town is built on the lava that covers the former habitations. It stands on the Bay of Naples, 5 miles S. E. of that city. Pop. 16,000.

TORRE DE MONCORVO, a town of Portugal, in Tras los Montes, surrounded by a wall, and defended by a bastion and a castle. It is 27 miles S. E. of Mirandela, and 42 S. S. W. of Braganza.

TORREJO, a town of Spain, in New Castile, 15 miles S. of Madrid.

TORRES, a town of Spain, in Granada, seated on the Mediterranean. It is 45 miles S. W. of Granada.

TORRES NOVAS, a town of Portugal, in Estremadura, with a castle; seated in a fertile plain, 38 miles N. by E. of Santaren.

TORRES VEDRAS, a town of Portugal in Estremadura, noted for the lines erected in its vicinity by Lord Wellington, in 1810. It has a castle, four churches, &c. It is seated near the Atlantic, 27 miles N. of Lisbon. Population, 2300.

TORRIDGE, a river in Devonshire, which rises on the summit of a high moor, within a few yards of the source of the Tamar, not far from the Bristol Channel. It flows S. E. to Hatherly, and then, receiving the Oak, from Oakhampton, turns short to the N., and, passing by Torrington and Biddeford, enters the Bristol Channel at Barnstable Bay.

TORRIGLIA, a town of the territory of Genoa, 14 miles N. E. of Genoa.

TORRINGTON, a town in Devonshire, governed by a mayor, with a market on Saturday. It has two churches, several meeting-houses, some almshouses, a charity school, a manufacture of stuffs, and some remains of a castle. It is seated on the Torridge, 11 miles S. by W. of Barnstable, and 194 W. by S. of London.

TORSHOK, a town of European Russia, in the government of Iver. It has several churches, a castle, and a manufacture of woollen and coarse linen. It is seated on the river Treiza, 45 miles W. of Iver. Pop. 10,000.

TORSILLA, a town of Sweden, in Sudermania, 43 miles W. of Stockholm.

TORTOLA, the principal of the Virgin Islands, in the W. Indies; 18 miles long, and 7 broad. It formerly belonged to the Dutch, who built a strong fort, from which they were expelled by the English in 1666. The town and harbour are at the E. end of the island. In 1802 it was made a free port, since which period the island has undergone great improvements. It produces excellent cotton, sugar, and rum. Long. 63. 0. W. lat. 18. 33. N.

TORTONA, a town of the Sardinian states, in a province of its name, with a good citadel on an eminence. It was formerly deemed a considerable frontier place; was taken by the allies in 1744, by the Spaniards in 1745, by the French in 1796, by the Russians and Austrians in 1799, regained by the French the same year, and by them delivered up to the Austrians in 1814. It is seated on the Scrivia, 27 miles S. W. of Milan. Population of the province, 40,000; of the town, 8000. Long. 8. 58. E. lat. 44. 54. N.

TORTORELLA, a town of Naples, in Principato Citra; 5 miles N. E. of Policastro.

TORTOSA, a town of Spain, in Catalonia, and a bishop's see, with a citadel. It is divided into the Old and New Town, both surrounded by fortifications. The entrance is over a large bridge of boats, on the river Ebro. The cathedral, the royal college of Dominicans, and the convent of the Carmelites, are the most remarkable edifices. Here is a great deal of silk and oil, and very fine potter's-ware, which resembles porcelain. Tortosa was taken by the French in 1810, after a short siege, but restored in 1814. It is seated partly on a plain and partly on a hill, in a country fertile in corn and fruits, and abounding with quarries and mines of silver, iron, alabaster, jasper of divers colours, and stones with veins of gold. It is 48 miles S. W. of Tarragona, and 96 S. E. of Saragossa. Pop. 11,000. Long. 0. 35. E. lat. 40. 48. N.

TORTOSA (the ancient Orthosia), a town of Syria, with a castle. It is surrounded by lofty walls, and stands near the Mediterranean; 35 miles N. N. E. of Tripoli.

TORTUE, an island of the West Indies, near the N. coast of St. Domingo, so named from the great number of tortoises found on and near it. Here the French buccaneers used to fortify themselves. It is about 20 miles long, and 4 broad, and has a safe harbour, but difficult of access. Long. 73. 10. W. lat. 20. 10. N.

TORTUGA, or SAL TORTUGA, an uninhabited island near the coast of Colombia, 60 miles W. of the island of Margaretta, and about 36 in circumference. There are a few goats on it; and the tortoises come upon the sandy banks to lay their eggs. At the E. end is a large salt-pond, where the salt begins to kern in April; and for some months after, ships come here to lade salt. At the W. end is a small harbour, with fresh water. Long. 64. 46. W. lat. 11. 16. N.

TOSA, a seaport of Spain, in Catalonia, on a bay which forms a good harbour. It is built partly on a plain, and partly on a steep hill, which projects into the sea. On the top of the hill is a strong citadel, with other fortifications. It is 57 miles N. E. of Barcelona. Long. 2. 54. E. lat. 41. 42. N.

TOSCANELLA, a town of Austrian Italy, 5 miles E. N. E. of Salo.

TOSENA, a town of Sweden, in West Gothland; 20 miles W. N. W. of Uddevalla.

TOSSO, a town of Sweden, in West Gothland; 42 miles N. N. E. of Uddevalla.

TOST, a town of Prussian Silesia, in the principality of Oppeln, with a castle; 25 miles E. S. E. of Oppeln.

TOTNESS, a borough in Devonshire; governed by a mayor, returning two members to parliament, with a weekly market on Saturday, and a monthly one on Tuesday; also a manufacture of serges, &c. It had formerly a castle and walls, and two gateways are yet standing. It is seated on the river Dart, on the side of a hill; 26 miles S. W. of Exeter, and 196 W. by S. of London.

TOTTENHAM, a village in Middlesex, 5 miles N. of London. Here are three almshouses; one of them founded in 1596, by Balthazar Zanches, who was confectioner to Philip II. of Spain, and the first that exercised that art in this country.

Toul, a fortified town of France, department of Meurthe. The cathedral and episcopal palace are handsome structures. It is seated on the Moselle, in a plain almost surrounded by mountains; 13 miles W. by S. of Nancy, and 34 W. S. W. of Metz. Pop. 7000.

Toulon, a fortified city and seaport of France, capital of the department of Var. It is divided into the Old and New quarter; the former, which is ill-built, has nothing remarkable in it but the town-house, and a long street, shaded with trees, called the Rue aux Arbres; the other contains the magnificent works constructed by Louis XIV., many fine houses, and a grand oblong square, lined with trees, and serving as a parade. The Old and New harbour communicate with each other by means of a canal. The old haven has a noble quay, and is protected by two moles, begun by Henry IV. The new haven was constructed by Louis XIV., as were the fortifications; it contains an arsenal, a ropewalk, a park of artillery, dockyards, basins, and every thing to be expected in the second port for men-of-war in this country. The galleys, transferred from Marseilles some years ago, occupy a basin in the new port. Many of the galley-slaves are artisans, and some merchants: they no longer sleep on board the galleys, but are provided with accommodations on shore, in a vast building erected for that purpose. Both the old and new port have an outlet into the outer road, or harbour, which is 10 miles in circuit, surrounded by hills, and the entrance defended on both sides by a fort and batteries. Toulon is the only mart in the Mediterranean for the re-exportation of the products of the East Indies. In 1706 it was bombarded by the allies, both by land and sea, by which almost the whole town was reduced to a heap of ruins, and several ships burned; but they were at last obliged to raise the siege. In 1721 it experienced the dreadful ravages of a pestilence. In 1793 it capitulated, in the name of Louis XVII., to the British, who, not finding the place tenable, evacuated it the same year, after having destroyed the arsenal, &c. Toulon is seated on a bay of the Mediterranean; 37 miles S. E. of Marseilles, and 517 S. S. E. of Paris. Pop. 30,000. Long. 5. 55. E. lat. 43. 7. N.

Toulouse, a city of France, capital of the department of Upper Garonne; and an archbishop's see. It contains 60,000 inhabitants, and is the most considerable city in France, next to Paris and Lyons, although its population bears no proportion to its extent. It was the capital of the Tectosages, who made so many conquests in Asia and Greece. It was next a Roman colony, and was successively the capital of the Visigoths, (who destroyed the superb amphitheatre, of which there are still some remains, the capitol, and other Roman monuments,) and that of Aquitaine. The walls of the city, as well as the houses, are built with bricks. St. Stephen's, the metropolitan church, would be incomparable if the nave were equal to the choir, and the archbishop's palace is magnificent. The town-house forms a perfect square, 324 feet long, and 66 high: the principal front occupies an entire side of the grand square called the Place Royale. In the great hall called the Hall of Illustrious Men is the statue of the Chevalier Isaure, with the busts of all the great men to whom Toulouse has given birth. Communicating with the Atlantic on one side by the river Garonne, and with the Mediterranean on the other by the canal of Languedoc, Toulouse might have been a very commercial city; but the taste of the inhabitants has been principally for the sciences and belles-lettres. The little commerce they have, consists in leather, wool, drapery, blankets, mignonettes, oil, iron, mercury, hardware, and books. The bridge over the Garonne, equal to that of Tours, forms a communication with the suburb of St. Cyprian. The allied army entered this city on the 12th of April, 1814, after a severe action with the French army the preceding day. Toulouse is 145 miles S. E. of Bordeaux, and 400 S. by W. of Paris. Pop. 52,000. Long. 1. 26. E. lat. 48. 30. N.

Tour, a town of France, department of Puy de Dome; 22 miles S. of Clermont.

Tour de Roussillon, a town in the department of Eastern Pyrenees; 3 miles E. of Perpignan.

Tour du Pin, a town in the department of Isere, seated on the Bourbre; 24 miles S. of Vienne.

Tour la Blanche, a town in the department of Dordogne; 15 miles N. W. of Perigueux.

Tour la Ville, a town in the department of La Manche, celebrated for its manufacture of glass. It is separated from Cherburg by a river.

Touraine, a late province of France, which now forms the department of Indre-et-Loire.

Tourancourchy, a town of Hindostan, in the Carnatic. It is 35 miles S. S. W. of Tritchinopoli.

Tournan, a town of France, department of Seine-et-Marne; 20 miles E. S. E. of Paris.

Tournay, a city of Belgium, in Flanders, and a bishop's see. It has several fine manufactures, and is particularly famous for good stockings. The cathedral, and the abbey of St. Martin, are very magnificent. It was taken by the allies in 1709, and ceded to the House of Austria by the treaty of Utrecht; but the Dutch were allowed to place a garrison in it, as one of the barrier towns. In 1792 it was taken by the French, who were obliged to abandon it in 1793, but re-entered it again on the conquest of Flanders in 1794; and retained it till 1814. It is seated on both sides the Scheldt, over which is a bridge; 14 miles E. S. E. of Lisle, and 30 S. S. W. of Ghent. Population 23,000. Long. 3. 24. E. lat. 50. 33. N.

Tournehem, a town of France, department of Pas de Calais; 9 miles N. W. of St. Omer.

Tournon, a town in the department of Ardeche, with a fine college, and a castle, seated on the side of a mountain, on the river

Rhone; 38 miles N. of Viviers, and 48 S. of Lyons. Pop. 4600.

TOURNUS, a town in the department of Saone-et-Loire; 15 miles S. of Chalons. Pop. 5200.

TOURS, a city of France, capital of the department of Indre-et-Loire, and an archiepiscopal see. It is seated on the Loire, and near the Cher. Over the former is one of the finest bridges in Europe, consisting of 15 elliptic arches, each 75 feet in diameter. The principal church is remarkable for the delicacy of its structure, curious clock, mosaic pavement, and rich library of manuscripts. Under the ministry of Cardinal Richelieu, 27,000 persons were here employed in the silk manufacture; and now the whole number of inhabitants is about 23,000. The red wines of Tours are much esteemed. In one of the suburbs is the abbey of Marmoutier, reputed the most ancient in the west. Near this city is Plessis-les-Tours, a palace built by the profligate and superstitious Louis XI., who died here in 1483. Tours is 52 miles N. N. E. of Poitiers, and 127 S. W. of Paris. Long. 0. 42. E. lat. 47. 24. N.

TOWCESTER, a town in Northamptonshire, with a market on Tuesday and manufactures of lace and silk. It was once strongly fortified, and the Roman Watling-street passes through the town. It is seated on the Weeden; 9 miles S. S. W. of Northampton, and 60 N. W. of London.

TOWER HAMLETS, one of the metropolitan boroughs, returning two members to parliament. *See* LONDON.

TOWTON, a village in West Yorkshire, famous for that bloody battle between the forces of the Houses of York and Lancaster, so fatal to the latter, on Palm Sunday, 1461; 3 miles S. E. of Tadcaster.

TOWY, a river of Wales, which rises in Cardiganshire, enters Carmarthenshire at its N. E. extremity, and flows by Llanymddoory, Llandilovawr, and Carmarthen, into the Bristol Channel.

TRACHENBERG, a town of Prussian Silesia, capital of a principality of the same name, abounding in corn, cattle, and timber. It has a fine castle. It is seated on the Bartch; 26 miles N. N. W. of Breslau. Long. 16. 56. E. lat. 51. 27. N.

TRAFALGAR, a promontory of Spain in Andalusia, at the entrance of the Strait of Gibraltar. Off this cape, in 1805, Admiral Lord Nelson, with 27 sail of the line, engaged the combined fleets of France and Spain, consisting of 33 sail of the line, 19 of which were taken, sunk, or destroyed, and the French commander in chief, (Admiral Villeneuve,) and two Spanish admirals made prisoners; this unparalleled victory was obtained without the loss of one British ship: but the noble commander fell by a musket-ball, near the close of the engagement. This cape is 20 miles S. S. E. of Cadiz. Long. 6. 2. W. lat. 36. 11. N.

TRAGONARA, a town of Naples, in Capitanata, 20 miles N. W. of Lucera.

TRAIN, a town of Bavaria, on the river Ambs, 5 miles S. of Abensperg, and 20 E. of Ingolstadt.

TRAINA, a town of Sicily, in Val di Demona, 25 miles N. W. of Catania.

TRAJANOPOLI, a town of European Turkey, in Romania, and a Greek archbishop's see. It is seated on the Marissa; 40 miles S. of Adrianople, and 135 W. by N. of Constantinople. Population 15,000

TRAJETTO, a town of Naples, in Terra di Lavoro, built on the site of the ancient Minturna; 25 miles N. W. of Capua. Long. 14. 4. E. lat. 41. 20. N.

TRALEE, a borough of Ireland, returning two members to parliament, capital of the county of Kerry; near which is a chalybeate spring. It stands on a small river, which flows into a shallow bay of its name; 50 miles S. W. of Limerick. Long. 10. 0. W. lat. 52. 4. N.

TRAMORE, a town of Ireland, in the county of Waterford. It is frequented for sea-bathing, and is well built, with a handsome church, market-house, and assembly-room; 102 miles from Dublin.

TRANCOSO, a town of Portugal, in Tras los Montes, with a castle; 9 miles W. by S. of Pinhel.

TRANENT, a town of Scotland, in Haddingtonshire; 9½ miles E. of Edinburgh, and 17½ W. of Haddington.

TRANI, a city of Naples, in Terra di Bari; the see of an archbishop, and the usual residence of the governor of the province, which is sometimes called Terra di Trani. Since the harbour has been choked up, the town has fallen greatly to decay. It stands on the Gulf of Venice, 26 miles W. by N. of Bari, and 125 N. by E. of Naples. Pop. 14,000. Long. 16. 36. E. lat. 41. 18. N.

TRANQUEBAR, a seaport of Hindostan, in the district of Tanjore, with a fort and factory, belonging to the Danes, who pay an annual rent to the rajah. The town is surrounded by a wall and bastions, and contains three Christian churches, a large mosque for the Mahomedans, and several pagodas for the Gentoos. In 1807 it was taken by the English. It is seated at the mouth of the Cavery, 165 miles S. of Madras. Long. 79. 53. E. lat. 11. 1. N.

TRANSYLVANIA, a country of Europe, formerly annexed to Hungary; bounded on the N. by Hungary, E. by Moldavia, S. by Wallachia, and W. by Hungary. It is 160 miles long, and 150 broad, containing 23,700 square miles, and 1,712,000 inhabitants. It is surrounded by high mountains, which, however, are not barren. It produces as much corn and wine as is wanted, and there are rich mines of gold, silver, lead, copper, quicksilver, and alum. The manufactures, which are in an extremely backward state, consist of woollen, cotton, glass, &c. It has undergone various revolutions, and now belongs to the House of Austria. The inhabitants are of various religions, as Roman Catholics, Lutherans, Calvinists, Socinians, Arminians, Greeks, and Mahomedans. The government is aristocratical; and, since the year 1722, rendered hereditary to the princes and princesses of the House of Austria.

TRAPANI, a seaport on the N. W. coast of

Sicily, in Val di Mazara; with a fort, and an excellent harbour in the form of a sickle, whence its ancient name, Drepanum. It is a trading place, famous for its salt-works, and fisheries of tunnies and coral. It stands on a small peninsula, 30 miles N. of Mazara, and 45 W. of Palermo. Pop. 20,000. Long. 12. 20. E. lat. 38. 10. N.

Tras los Montes, a province of Portugal, beyond the mountains with regard to the other provinces of this kingdom, whence it has its name. It is bounded on the N. by Galicia, W. by Entre Douro e Minho, S. W. and S. by Beira, and E. by Leon; and contains an area of 5500 square miles, with 350,000 inhabitants. The valleys are fertile in corn, wine, and oil, and are numerous. The Douro divides it into two parts. Miranda is the capital.

Trasmaur, a town and castle of Austria, seated on the Trasen, 12 miles W. of Tuln.

Trau, a strong seaport of Austrian Dalmatia, and a bishop's see. It is seated on the Gulf of Venice, in a small island joined to the mainland by a long bridge of wood, and to the Isle of Bua by another of stone; 22 miles S. E. of Sebenico. Long. 17. 52. E. lat. 44. 0. N.

Traunstein, a town and castle of Bavaria. Great quantities of salt are made here, from water brought above 14 miles over mountains, by means of engines and pipes, from Reichenhall. It is seated on the river Traun; 16 miles W. N. W. of Salzburg.

Trauntenau, a town of Bohemia, in the circle of Konigingratz; 21 miles N. of Konigingratz.

Travancore, a province of the peninsula of Hindostan, extending along the coast of Malabar, from Cape Comorin to the province of Cochin, 140 miles in length, by 70 in breadth at the N. extremity, and contracting gradually to the S. point. It is subject to a rajah, who is under British protection. Pop. 1,500,000.

Travancore, the ancient capital of the above province, is surrounded by strong and extensive lines, but is much decayed; 110 miles S. S. W. of Madura, and 230 S. S. E. of Calicut. Long. 77. 15. E. lat. 8. 25. N.

Trave, a river of Denmark, in the duchy of Holstein, which flows by Segeberg, Oldeslo, and Lubeck, and enters the Baltic at Travemunde.

Travemunde, a strong town of Germany, seated on the Baltic, at the mouth of the Trave. It is the port of Lubeck, to which it belongs. It is 12 miles N. E. of that city.

Traverse, a town of Switzerland, in a district of its name, in the canton of Neufchatel; 11 miles W. of Neufchatel.

Trayguera, a town of Spain, in Valencia; 30 miles S. W. of Tortosa.

Trebbin, a town of Prussia, in Brandenburg; 22 miles S. S. W. of Berlin.

Trebia, a river of Italy, which rises in the territory of Genoa, flows by Bobio in the Milanese, and joins the Po above Placentia.

Trebigna, a town of Turkish Dalmatia, and a bishop's see, seated on the Gulf of Venice, at the mouth of the Trebenska; 14 miles N. of Ragusa.

Trebisaccia, a town of Naples, in Calabria Citra, on the Gulf of Tarento; 10 miles E. N. E. of Cassano.

Trebisond, a seaport of Asia Minor, in Natolia, and a Greek archbishop's see. The walls are square and high, with battlements; and are built with the ruins of ancient structures, on which are inscriptions not legible. The town is not populous, for there are many gardens in it, and the houses are but one story high. The castle is seated on a flat rock, with ditches cut in it. The harbour is at the E. end of the town, and the mole built by the Genoese is almost destroyed. It stands at the foot of a very steep hill on the Black Sea; 104 miles N. N. W. of Erzerum, and 440 E. of Constantinople. Pop. 15,000. Long. 40. 25. E. lat. 39. 45. N.

Trebitz, a town of the Austrian states in Moravia, with manufactures of cloth, iron, and glass; seated on the Igla, 21 miles S. E. of Iglau.

Trebnitz, a town of Prussian Silesia, in the principality of Oels, with a Cistercian nunnery; 12 miles N. of Breslau.

Trebsen, a town of Saxony, on the Mulda; 14 miles E. by S. of Leipsic.

Treffurt, a town of Prussian Saxony, with a castle, seated on an eminence, 30 miles S. E. of Gottingen.

Tregarron, a town of Wales, in Cardiganshire, governed by a mayor, with a market on Thursday. It is seated on a branch of the Tyvy; 15 miles S. by E. of Aberystwith, and 204 W. by N. of London.

Tregony, a town in Cornwall, market on Saturday; seated on the Fale, 6 miles E. of Truro, and 253 W. by S. of London.

Treguier, a seaport of France, department of Cotes du Nord, seated on a peninsula near the English Channel; 22 miles N. W. of St. Brieux. Long. 3. 13. W. lat. 48. 47. N.

Trelleborg, a town of Sweden, in Schonen, seated on the Baltic; 26 miles S. of Lund.

Tremesen, or **Tlemsan**, a city of Algier, capital of a district of its name, in the province of Mascara. It is surrounded by strong walls, and inhabited by poor Arabs, Moors, and Jews. In the time of the Arabs it was the residence of powerful princes, but is now dwindled to scarcely a fifth part of the ancient city. Its once flourishing manufacture of carpets and woollen coverlets is in a state of decay, and the former masterpieces of architecture have disappeared; for there is not a single building of excellence now to be seen. It is 50 miles S. S. W. of Oran. Long. 1. 12. W. lat. 34. 56. N.

Tremiti, three islands of Naples, in the Gulf of Venice, 15 miles from the N. coast of Capitanata. They are called Tremiti, or St. Nicolo, St. Domino, and Capraria. The first, which is the principal of them, has a Benedictine convent and a castle. Long. 15. 30. E. lat. 42. 10. N.

Tremouille, a town of France, department of Vendee, seated on the Bennaile; 35 miles E. by S. of Poitiers.

Tremp, a town of Spain, in Catalonia; 20 miles N. of Balaguer.

Trenschin, a town of Hungary, capital of a county of its name, with an ancient castle on a rock. It has celebrated hot baths. It is seated near the Waag; 70 miles N. N E. of Presburg. Pop. 3100. Long. 18. 0. E. lat. 48. 58. N.

Trent, a circle of the Austrian empire, in the S. part of Tyrol, among the Alps; bounded by Tyrol Proper and the territories of Venice. It produces excellent wine.

Trent, a fortified city, capital of the above circle, and formerly of a principality; famous in church history for a celebrated council which was held from 1545 to 1563. It has a handsome castle, a cathedral, three parish churches, a college, and some convents. In 1796 it was taken by the French, under Massena, with 6000 prisoners and 20 cannon. It is situate between two mountains, on the river Adige; 67 miles N. W. of Venice. Pop. 10,000. Long. 10. 55. E. lat. 46. 2. N.

Trent, a river which rises in Staffordshire, from three springs to the W. of Leek, and flows S. E. through the county to the S. W. borders of Derbyshire, where it receives the Tame. It then takes a N. E. direction, between the two counties, till it receives the Dove, when it enters Derbyshire, crosses its S. angle, and forming, for a short space, its separation from the counties of Leicester and Nottingham, it enters the latter county at its S. W. extremity; thence crossing obliquely to the E., it flows along its whole eastern side, forming, towards the N. part, the boundary between that county and Lincolnshire, a corner of which it crosses, and, below Gainsborough, meets the Ouse on the borders of Yorkshire, where their united stream forms the Humber. This river is of itself navigable from Burton, in Staffordshire; and, by canals, it has a communication with the Mersey, the Severn, and the Thames.

Trent, a river of North Carolina, which runs into the Nens at Newbern.

Trenton, a town of New Jersey, in Hunterdon county, and the capital of the state. Here are four edifices for public worship, and a flourishing academy. It is seated on the Delaware, 30 miles N. N. E. of Philadelphia. Pop. 3925. Long. 75. 0. W. lat. 40. 15. N.

Trenton, a town of North Carolina, chief of Jones county, on the river Trent, 18 miles S. W. of Newbern.

Trenton, a town of the state of Maine, in Hancock county, opposite the N. end of Mount Desert Island, 30 miles E. N. E. of Castine.

Treport, a town of France, department of Lower Seine, seated on the English Channel, at the mouth of the Bresle. It is the port for the town of Eu, nearly 2 miles distant, and is 17 miles N. E. of Dieppe.

Trepto, a town and castle of Prussia, in Pomerania, seated on the river Tollensee, and frontiers of Mecklenburg; 25 miles N. of New Strelitz.

Trepto, New, a town of Pomerania, with manufactures of stockings and woollen stuffs; seated on the Riga, near its mouth in the Baltic; 16 miles E. N. E. of Camin. Population, 3400

Treshanish Isles, four fertile islands on the W. coast of Scotland; between the island of Coll and that of Mull.

Treves, a government of Prussia, comprising the old electorate of Treves, a small portion of the duchy of Luxemburg, with some other petty districts, and containing an area of about 2500 square miles, with 300,000 inhabitants. There are many mountains and forests; but near the Rhine and Moselle the soil is fruitful, abounding in corn and wine.

Treves, a city of Germany, formerly the capital of an electorate and archbishopric of the same name, and now of the preceding government. It has a castle, a university (now termed a gymnasium), numerous remains of antiquities, and many fine churches and palaces; but has greatly suffered by war, and is now neither large nor populous. It was taken by the French, under Jourdan, in 1794, and retained till 1814. It is seated on the Moselle, over which is a handsome bridge, between two mountains covered with vineyards; 20 miles N. E. of Luxemburg, and 55 S. by E. of Cologne. Pop. 10,000. Long. 6. 43. E. lat. 49. 47. N.

Trevi, a town of Italy, in the duchy of Spoleto; 12 miles N. by W. of Spoleto.

Trevico, a town of Naples, in Principato Ultra; 25 miles E. of Benevento.

Trevier de Courtes, St., a town of France, in the department of Ain; 26 miles N. N. W. of Bourg en Bresse.

Trevier en Dombes, St., a town in the department of Ain; 18 miles S. W. of Bourg en Bresse.

Trevino, a town of Spain, in Biscay, with a citadel; 10 miles S. of Vittoria.

Trevisano, a province of Austrian Italy, in the government of Venice, bounded on the W. by Vicentino, N. by Feltrino and the Bellunese, E. by Friuli, and S. by the Gulf of Venice, Dogado, and Padua. The soil is fertile, and produces corn, wine, and wood; and the exports are cattle, silk, and woollen cloth. Area, 1310 square miles. Population, 233,000. Treviso is the capital.

Treviso, or **Trevigio**, a fortified city of Italy, capital of Trevisano, and a bishop's see. It is the residence of many noble families, and is seated on the Sile, at the influx of the Piavesella; 18 miles N. N. W. of Venice. Pop. 15,000. Long. 12. 18. E. lat. 45. 44. N.

Trevoux, a town of France, in the department of Ain, and formerly the capital of the principality of Dombes. The most remarkable buildings are the ancient mint, the parliament-house, the governor's house, and the printing-office. The last is celebrated for the literary journals, composed by the Jesuits of the college of Louis le Grand. Trevoux is seated on the side of a hill, on the river Saone; 12 miles N. of Lyons, and 188 S. by E. of Paris. Pop. 2600. Long. 4. 51. E. lat. 45. 54. N.

Treysa, a town of Germany, in Hesse-Cassel; 16 miles E. N. E. of Marburg.

TRIBAU, a town of the Austrian states, in Moravia; 30 miles N. W. of Olmutz.

TRIBSEES, a town of Prussia, in Pomerania, with a castle, seated on the Trebel; 22 miles S. S. W. of Stralsund, and 28 E. S. E. of Rostock.

TRICALA, or TRIKALA, a town of Macedonia. It is the see of a Greek bishop, and contains ten churches, seven mosques, and two synagogues. The town is of considerable extent, seated on a low ridge of hills, near the river Selembria. Pop. 12,000. It is 50 miles E. N. E. of Salonica.

TRICARICO, a town of Naples, in Basilicata; 13 miles S. E. of Acerenza, and 21 S. W. of Matera.

TRICETO, a town of Naples, in Calabria Citra; 14 miles S. E. of Scalea.

TRICOLORE, a town of Hindostan, in the Carnatic, where Tippoo Sultan was defeated by the British in 1790. It is 44 miles W. of Pondicherry.

TRIERS. *See* TREVES.

TRIESTE, a government of the Austrian empire, bounded by the government of Lambach, the Adriatic, and Croatia. It comprises the southern part of Illyria, is divided into three circles, and contains an area of about 5000 square miles, with 1,124,000 inhabitants.

TRIESTE, a seaport of Austrian Illyria, capital of a circle of its name, in the foregoing government, and a bishop's see. The harbour is spacious, screened by a wall fortified with a bastion. In the old town the houses stand on the side of a mountain, extending themselves quite to the sea; and on the top of the mountain is a castle. On the side N. W. of the old town, where formerly were salt-pits, a beautiful suburb, or new town, has been built. The fixed inhabitants, estimated at 40,000, have a good trade in salt, oil, almonds, iron, copper, &c., brought from Laubach; and they make good white wines. Trieste was taken by the French in 1797, but evacuated in the same year. In 1809 it again fell into the hands of the French, who retained it till 1814. It stands on a gulf of its name, which is the N.E. part of the Gulf of Venice; 12 miles N. of Capo d'Istria, and 70 N. E. of Venice. Long. 14. 3. E. lat. 45. 51. N.

TRIM, a town of Ireland, capital of the county of Meath, seated on the Boyne, 23 miles N. W. of Dublin. Long. 6. 48. W. lat. 53. 32. N.

TRINCOMALEE, a seaport on the E. coast of Ceylon, with a harbour, reckoned the finest in the East Indies, but situate in the most barren part of the island. The nearest farm villages, from which the inhabitants are supplied with provisions, are upwards of 12 miles distant. The harbour is defended by two forts, Trincomalee and Ostenburg, the latter built upon a cliff, projecting 1500 paces into the sea. Its circumference within the walls is about 3 miles, but in this space is included a rising point, immediately over the sea, covered with thick jungle. Trincomalee was taken from the Dutch, by the English, in 1782, retaken by the French in the same year, restored to the Dutch by the peace of 1783, and again taken by the English in 1795. It stands on a spacious bay of the same name; 100 miles N. N. E. of Candy. Long. 81. 25. E. lat. 8. 32. N.

TRINCOMALE, a town of Hindostan, in the Carnatic, near which the troops of Hyder Ali were defeated by the British in 1768. It is 45 miles S. S. W. of Arcot, and 52 W. N. W. of Pondicherry.

TRING, a town in Hertfordshire, with a market on Friday, seated near the Birmingham railway and the Grand Junction canal; 22 miles W. of Hertford, and 31 N. W. of London.

TRINIDAD, an island on the N. E. coast of Terra Firma, separated from Paria on the S. by a channel about 10 miles over, and from Cumana on the W. by the Gulf of Paria, the N. entrance into which is called Boca del Drago (Dragon's Mouth,) on account of the adverse currents and tempestuous waves encountered here, when this island, with the neighbouring continent, was discovered by Columbus, in 1498. It is 80 miles long, and 56 broad; produces sugar, cotton, maize, fine tobacco, indigo, and fruit; but the air is unhealthy. It was taken in 1595 by Sir Walter Raleigh, and in 1676 by the French, who plundered and left it. In 1797 it was captured by the English, and afterwards ceded to them by the treaty of Amiens. The capital is Port d'Espagne, on the Gulf of Paria, near the Boca. Pop. 45,000. Long. 61. 30. W. lat. 10. 0. N.

TRINIDAD, a seaport of Guatimala, on a bay of the Pacific Ocean. It is a place of great trade, the harbour being the nearest landing to Guatimala for all merchandise that comes from Mexico and Peru. The town is 9 miles from the harbour, and 110 E. S. E. of Guatimala. Long. 90. 40. W. lat. 14. 0. N.

TRINIDAD, a seaport of Cuba, in a bay on the S. part of the island; 40 miles S. W. of Spiritu Santo. Long. 80. 3. W. lat. 21. 58. N.

TRINIDAD, a town of Colombia, seated on the Madalena; 58 miles N. W. of St. Fe de Bogota.

TRINIDADA, three rocky islets in the Atlantic Ocean, 200 leagues E. of Spiritu Santo, in Brazil. Long. 29. 35. W. lat. 20. 30. S.

TRINITY, a seaport on the N. side of Martinico, with a spacious and safe harbour, and a considerable trade. Long. 61. 8. W. lat. 14. 53. N.

TRINO, a town in the Sardinian states, in Piedmont, 8 miles N. W. of Casal, and 35 N. E. of Turin. Pop. 5500.

TRIPATORE, a town of Hindostan, in Marawar; 36 miles E. N. E. of Madura, and 58 S. W. of Tanjore.

TRIPOLI, a country of Barbary, bounded on the N. by the Mediterranean, E. by Barca, S. by Fezzan, and W. by Biledulgerid and Tunis. The fertile districts of Ghadian and Mesurata are in a mountainous tract to the S. E. of the town of Tripoli, and are inhabited by Arabs. In the immediate neighbourhood of the capital the tract called the Messeah is of exuberant fertility; but the supply of water is precarious, there being no rivers: it was anciently the granary of the Romans. To the E. is the Great Syrtis, a bay much dreaded by the ancient mariners for its supposed quicksands, &c., but which do not exist. It was colonized by the Greeks, and called by them Cyrene. The total population has been variously stated from 660,000 and 2,000,000. It is probably about 1,500,000. It is 925 miles along the coast, but the breadth is various. It is governed by a dey, under the protection of the Turks.

Tripoli, a city and seaport of Barbary, capital of the foregoing country, with a castle and a fort. It contains some ruins, which mark its origin, particularly of a beautiful triumphal arch of marble, erected in honour of the emperor Antoninus. It was taken by the emperor Charles V., who settled the knights of Rhodes here; but they were expelled by the Turks in 1551. The Americans made an attempt upon the town in 1804, but without success. It was formerly very flourishing, and has now some trade in ashes, ostriches' feathers, and skins. The population is of a motley character, consisting of all nations; and some Europeans have had high situations in the government. It was famous for its piracies, and derived considerable revenues from the ransom and sale of the prisoners. The inhabitants amount to about 25,000, including 2000 Jews, who are better treated than in other Mahomedan states. The general character of the people is vicious and depraved, though they are not so bigoted as other Moslems. The common language is a bad Italian; but Arabic is that used by the court. Tripoli is seated on the Mediterranean, and surrounded by a wall; 275 miles S. E. of Tunis, and 570 E. S. E. of Algier. Long. 13. 5. E. lat. 32. 54. N.

Tripoli, a town of Syria, capital of the pachalic of Tripoli, on the Mediterranean, defended by a citadel. There is one handsome mosque, and all the houses have fountains belonging to them. Before it is a sand-bank, which increases so much that it is expected to choke up the harbour, which is 2 miles W. of the town, and formed by a round piece of land, united to the mainland by an isthmus. On each side is a bulwark to defend the entrance. It is the residence of a bashaw, who also governs the territory about it, where there are great numbers of mulberry-trees, and other fruits. The commerce of Tripoli consists almost wholly in coarse silk, which is made use of for laces. It is 90 miles N. W. of Damascus, and 120 S. of Scanderoon. Pop. 15,000. Long. 36. 20. E. lat. 34. 50. N.

Tripolitza, or Tripolizza, a town of Greece, in the Morea, of which it is the capital. It is a gloomy, dirty town, and badly situated. It was taken in 1821 by the exasperated Greeks, in their struggle for independence, when 6000 Turkish soldiers and inhabitants were barbarously massacred. Pop. 12,000.

Tripstadt, a town of Bavaria, in the province of the Rhine; 16 miles E. N. E. of Deux Ponts.

Tripura, a town of Hindostan, in the province of Coimbetore, with a fort at a little distance, called Palar. It is seated on the Noyelar; 27 miles N. N. W. of Daraporam.

Trist, an island of Mexico, on the coast of Tabasco, in the Bay of Campeachy, separated by a narrow channel, on the E., from the Isle of Port Royal. It is 18 miles in circuit. Long. 92. 45. W. lat. 18. 15. N.

Tristan d'Acunha, an island in the Atlantic Ocean, 15 miles in circuit. The land is extremely high, and rises gradually towards the centre of the island (where there is a lofty conical mountain) in ridges, covered with trees of a moderate size and height. The coast is frequented by sea-lions, seals, penguins, and albatrosses. Long. 11. 44. W. lat. 37. 6. S.

Tritchinopoly, a town of Hindostan, in the Carnatic, surrounded by a double wall, flanked with towers, and encompassed with a ditch. It was taken by the British in 1751; 30 miles W. of Tanjore, and 208 S. S. W. of Madras. Population 80,000. Long. 78. 46. E. lat. 10. 49. N.

Trivadi, a town of Hindostan, in the Carnatic, with a large pagoda, which forms a citadel. It is 26 miles S. W. of Pondicherry.

Trivandipatam, or Trivanderam, an extensive and populous town of Hindostan, capital of Travancore, and the summer residence of the rajah, who has a palace built in the European style; 50 miles from Cape Comorin. Long. 76. 50. E. lat. 8. 30. N.

Trivento, a town of Naples, in the Molise, seated on a hill, 11 miles N. of Molise.

Trochtelfingen, a town of Germany, in the principality of Hohenzollern; situate on the Schoneicha, 14 miles E. of Hechingen, and 29 S. of Stutgard.

Trogen, a town of Switzerland, and the chief place of the Protestant part of the canton of Appenzel. It has manufactures of cloth, and near it is a mineral spring. It is 7 miles N. N. E. of Appenzel.

Trois Rivieres. *See* Three Rivers.

Troja, a town of Naples, in Capitanata, on the river Chilaro; 32 miles E. N. E. of Benevento, and 60 N. W. of Naples.

Troki, a town of Lithuania, capital of a palatinate of the same name. It is seated among lakes, 18 miles W. of Wilna, and 85 N. N. E. of Grodno. Long. 25. 13. E. lat. 54. 38. N.

Trolhatta, a town of Sweden, in W. Gothland; seated on the Gotha-Elf, which here forms several cascades, that afterwards unite into a cataract, upwards of 60 feet in height. Here is also a canal for vessels to pass by these falls, wrought through the midst of rocks, and deemed one of the boldest works of the kind in the world. It is 45 miles N. N. E. of Gotheburg.

Tron, St., a town of the Netherlands, in the territory of Liege, with a Benedictine abbey; 20 miles N. W. of Liege.

Troon, a thriving seaport of Ayrshire, 6 miles N. of Ayr, and 31 S. W. of Glasgow. It has a good harbour, &c. and great quantities of coal are shipped from this port, which are brought down by a railway from Kilmarnock.

Tropea, a town of Naples, in Calabria Ultra, seated on a high rock on the Gulf of St. Eufemia, 10 miles N. W. of Nicotera.

Tropez, St., a seaport of France, in the department of Var, with a citadel; seated on a bay of the Mediterranean, 38 miles E. N. E. of Toulon. Napoleon Bonaparte embarked at this place for the isle of Elba, in 1814. Long. 6. 40. E. lat. 43. 16. N.

Troppau, a strong town of Silesia, capital of a principality of the same name, which belongs partly to Austria, and partly to Prussia. Here are an ancient palace of the princes, three churches, a college, four convents, and a commandery of the order of St. John. It was taken by the Prussians in 1741 and 1756, but restored to the House of Austria by a treaty subsequent to each capture; and it is the seat of regency for all the Bohemian part of Silesia. In 1758 the greatest part of the town was destroyed by fire. It stands in a fruitful country, on the river Oppa, 40 miles N. E. of Olmutz, and 90 S. S. E. of Breslau. Pop. 10,000. Long. 17. 54. E. lat. 49. 52. N.

Trosa, a seaport of Sweden, in Sudermania, seated on the Baltic, 35 miles S. W. of Stockholm. Long. 17. 29. E. lat. 59. 0. N.

Trosachs, certain rugged and stupendous mountains of Scotland, in Perthshire, which have been greatly visited since they have been made the scene of the adventures of the Lady of the Lake.

Trowbridge, a town in Wiltshire, with a market on Saturday, and considerable manufactures of broad cloth and kerseymeres. It is seated on a hill by the river Were, over which is a stone bridge; 23 miles S. W. of Marlborough, and 99 W. of London.

Troy, a flourishing town of New York, capital of Rensselaer county, with a court-house, market-house, five churches, &c. The manufactures are various, and the trade considerable. It is 3 miles S. of Lansinburg. Pop. 11,405.

Troyes, a city of France, capital of the department of Aube, and a bishop's see; with a castle, in which the ancient counts of Champagne resided. It is surrounded by good walls, but almost all the houses are of wood, and good water is wanting. Its commerce, once very flourishing, now consists only in some linens, dimities, fustians, wax-chandlery, candles, and wine. Troyes was captured and recaptured several times by the allied and French armies, in 1814. It is seated on the Seine, 28 miles E. by N. of Sens, and 105 S. E. of Paris. Pop. 27,000. Long. 4. 5. E. lat. 48. 18. N.

Truns, a town of Switzerland, in the canton of Grisons; seated on the Rhine, 7 miles W. of Ilantz.

Truro, a borough in Cornwall, governed by a mayor, with markets on Wednesday and Saturday. It returns two members to parliament. It is a stannary town, and the chief business is in shipping tin and copper ore, found in abundance in its neighbourhood. Here, after the battle of Naseby, the forces of Charles I., under Lord Hopeton, surrendered to General Fairfax. Truro is seated between the rivers Kenwyn and St. Allen, at the head of Falmouth Haven, 10 miles N. of Falmouth, and 257 W. by S. of London.

Truro, a town of Nova Scotia, in Halifax county, at the head of a narrow gulf in the Bay of Fundy, 40 miles N. by W. of Halifax.

Truro, a fishing town of Massachusetts, in Barnstable county, on the N. part of the peninsula of Cape Cod; 9 miles S. of Provincetown.

Truxillo, a town of Spain, in Estremadura, with a citadel on the top of a hill. It was the birthplace of the noted Francis Pizarro. It is situate on the side of a hill, near the river Magasca, 70 miles N. E. of Badajoz, and 90 S. W. of Toledo. Pop. 4000. Long. 5. 43. W. lat. 39. 26. N.

Truxillo, a city and seaport of Peru, capital of a province of its name, and the see of a bishop. It was built by Francis Pizarro in 1553. In its territory are above 50,000 native Americans. It is surrounded by a wall, and seated in a fertile country, on a small river near the Pacific Ocean, 300 miles N. W. of Lima. Pop. 5800. Long. 70. 5. W. lat. 8. 1. S.

Truxillo, a seaport of South America, government of Venezuela, republic of Colombia, on the Gulf of Honduras. It stands 3 miles from the sea, between two rivers, the mouths of which, and some islands before them, form the harbour. It is 140 miles N. E. of Valladolid. Pop. 7600. Long. 86. 30. W. lat. 15. 46. N.

Truxillo, or Nuestra Senora de la Paz, a town of Venezuela, 150 miles S. E. of Maracaybo. Long. 70. 15. W. lat. 8. 15. N.

Tsanad, a town of Hungary, on the river Meros, 23 miles E. by S. of Segedin.

Tschernahora, a town of the Austrian states, in Moravia, with a castle on a mountain, 13 miles N. N. W. of Brin.

Tschernemt, a town of Austria, in Carniola, with a castle, and a commandery of the Teutonic order. It is 33 miles S. E. of Laubach.

Tschirne, a town of Prussian Silesia, in the principality of Glogau; with a castle and good cloth manufactures. It is 22 miles E. N. E. of Glogau.

Tschopau, a town of Saxony, celebrated for its blue manufacture. It stands on a river of the same name, 7 miles S. E. of Chemnitz.

Tsiampa. *See* Ciampa.

Tsi-nan, a city of China, capital of Chang-tong. It is much respected by the Chinese, on account of its having been formerly the residence of a long series of kings, whose tombs, rising on the neighbouring mountains, afford a beautiful prospect. It is seated on the river Tsi, or Tsing-ho, 230 miles S. by E. of Peking. Long. 117. 25. E. lat. 36. 46. N.

Tsi-ning, a city of China, of the second rank, in Chang-tong; situate on the Grand Canal; 275 miles S. of Peking. Long. 116. 24. E. lat. 35. 24. N.

TSIN-TCHEOU, a city of China, of the first rank, in Chang-tong; 250 miles E. S. E. of Peking. Long. 119. 2. E. lat. 36. 40. N.

TSONG-MING, an island of China, 50 miles long, and 10 broad; lying at the mouth of the Kiang-ku, and separated from the province of Kiang-nan by two channels, 13 miles broad. Its principal revenue arises from salt, which is made in such abundance on the N. side of the island, that it can supply most of the neighbouring countries. It contains only one city, but villages are very numerous. The country is delightful, and intersected by many canals. The city, of the same name, is of the third class. It is situate at its S. E. end. Long. 121. 55. E. lat. 30. 15. N.

TSONGRAD, a town of Hungary, capital of a county of the same name, seated on the Theisse, opposite the influx of the Koros; 26 miles N. of Segedin.

TUAM, a city of Ireland, in the county of Galway, and an archbishop's see, though now a small place. The cathedral serves as a parish church. It is 20 miles N. N. E. of Galway, and 25 W. S. W. of Roscommon.

TUARICK, a people of Central Africa, S. of Soudan. They are a remarkably fine race, and subsist in some measure on plunder. They are of various tribes and complexions. Some are Mahomedans and some Pagans. They are all, however, of the Berber race, and the language is still exclusively spoken by some tribes in Sockna, Augila, and Irwah.

TUBAN, one of the strongest towns of Java, with a harbour, and a king of its own. It is seated on the N. coast of the island. Long. 111. 51. E. lat. 6. 0. S.

TUBINGEN, a town of Germany, in the kingdom of Wirtemberg, with a celebrated university, and a fortified castle on a mountain. Here are good snuff manufactures, and in the town-house is a very curious clock. It is seated on the Neckar, in a country abounding in corn and wine, 20 miles S. of Stutgard, and 59 E. by S. of Strasburg. Pop. 6000. Long. 9. 10. E. lat. 48. 32. N.

TUCUMAN, a province of South America, in the republic of La Plata, between Chili and Paraguay, to the E. of the Andes, and W. of Rio de la Plata. This province, with the country S. of the river Plata, forms an extensive plain, almost without a tree. The soil is a deep fertile mould, watered by many streams from the Andes, and clothed in perpetual verdure. In this rich pasturage the horses and cattle imported from Europe have multiplied to an almost incredible degree. This has enabled the inhabitants not only to open a lucrative trade with Peru, by supplying it with cattle, horses, and mules, but to carry on a commerce equally beneficial, by the exportation of hides to Europe; notwithstanding which, the towns in this country are no better than paltry villages. The Spaniards endeavoured to add some dignity to these towns when in their possession, by erecting them into bishoprics.

TUCUMAN, or SAN MIGUEL DE TUCUMAN, the capital of the foregoing province, and a bishop's see, is situate in a pleasant plain, and has considerable trade in oxen and mules. It is 200 miles E. of Copiapo. Long. 64. 35. W. lat 27. 2. S.

TUDELA, a town of Spain, in Navarre, with a castle. A battle was fought here, in 1808, between the Spaniards and French, in which the latter were victorious. It is seated in a country that produces good wine, on the river Ebro; 44 miles S. of Pamplona, and 100 E. of Burgos. Pop. 7300. Long. 1. 38. W. lat. 41. 12. N.

TUGGURT, a town of Barbary, capital of a country lying S. of Algier. It is 310 miles S. S. E. of Algier. Long. 5. 50. E. lat. 32. 40. N.

TUGGURT, a town of Zahara, capital of a district called Wadreag. It is 420 miles N. E. of Timbuctoo. Long. 6. 15. E. lat. 20. 35. N.

TULA, a government of Russia, formerly a province of the government of Moscow. It has an area of about 12,000 square miles, with 960,000 inhabitants. The climate is healthy, and the soil better cultivated than in some other governments. Its capital, of the same name, has manufactures of fire-arms, all sorts of cutlery and iron-work, and leather, &c.; hence it has been styled the Sheffield of Russia. It is seated on the Upha, 115 miles S. by W. of Moscow. Pop. 51,735. Long. 37. 24. E. lat. 54. 10. N.

TULEBROS, a town of Spain, in Navarre; situate on the Queis, 7 miles W. of Tuleda.

TULLAMORE, or KILLBRIDE, a town of Ireland, in King's county; on a river of the same name, and near the great canal; 10 miles W. by S. of Philipstown.

TULLE, a town of France, capital of the department of Correze. The cathedral is famous for its steeple, which is very high and curious. It is seated at the conflux of the Correze and Solane, in a country surrounded by mountains and precipices; 37 miles S. S. E. of Limoges, and 62 S. W. of Clermont. Pop. 9000. Long. 1. 42. E. lat. 45. 16. N.

TULLOW, a town of Ireland, in the county of Carlow; 8 miles E. S. E. of Carlow, and 38 of Dublin.

TULN, a town of Austria, and a bishop's see, seated near the Danube; 15 miles W. N. W. of Vienna.

TULSK, a hamlet of Ireland, in the county of Roscommon, containing the ruins of towers, castles, &c., which sufficiently attest its former importance; 9 miles N. of Roscommon.

TUMBEZ, a town of Peru, noted as the place where the Spaniards first landed in these parts, under Pizarro. It is seated on a river of the same name, which flows into the Bay of Guayaquil; 270 miles S. by W. of Quito. Long. 79. 51. W. lat. 3. 40. S.

TUMCURU, a town of Hindostan, in Mysore, with a well-built fort; 32 miles S. E. of Sera.

TUMEN, a town of Russia, in the province of Tobolsk; 150 miles W. S. W. of Tobolsk. Long. 150. 15. E. lat. 57. 3. N.

TUNBRIDGE, a town in Kent, with a market on Friday. Here are the ruins of a large castle, erected by Richard, Earl of Clare, natural son of Richard I., Duke of Normandy; and here is a famous free-school, founded by Sir Andrew Judd, Lord Mayor of London, in 1551. It is seated on the Tun, one of the five branches into which the Medway here divides itself, and over each of which is a stone bridge, and on the London and Dover railway. It is 12 miles W. S. W. of Maidstone, and 30 E. S. E. of London.

TUNBRIDGE WELLS, a town in Kent, much resorted to on account of its chalybeate waters, discovered in 1606 by Dudley, Lord North, who recovered from a deep consumption by drinking them. The old town is seated at the bottom of three hills, called Mount Sion, Mount Ephraim, and Mount Pleasant. The town has increased much of late years, towards the S. and E., and contains some handsome churches, a Roman Catholic chapel, and many fine ranges of building for the accommodation of its numerous visitors. It is built irregularly, and resembles an extended and romantic village, rather than a town. The surrounding country is picturesque, and abounds in a sandstone, of which many of the buildings are erected. On Rustall Common, about a mile and a half from the town, are some picturesque rocks of a singular form, and great height. The only manufacture is of inlaid turnery and toys, for which it is famous. It is 5 miles S. of Tunbridge, and 35 S. S. E. of London.

TUNGINSKOI, a town of Russia, situate on the Irkut; 80 miles S. W. of Irkutsk. Long. 103. 15. E. lat. 51. 18. N.

TUNEGOOSES. *See* TONGOUSI.

TUNIS, a country of Barbary, bounded on the N. and E. by the Mediterranean, S. by Tripoli and Biledulgerid, and W. by Algier. It extends 200 miles from N. to S., and 120 from E. to W. This country was formerly a monarchy, but in 1574 it became a republic, under the protection of the Turks, and pays a certain tribute to the bashaw that resides at Tunis. The soil in the E. part is but indifferent, for want of water. Towards the middle the mountains and valleys abound in fruits; but the west part is the most fertile, being watered by rivers. The environs of Tunis are very dry, and corn is generally dear; but there are plenty of citrons, lemons, oranges, dates, grapes, and other fruits; also olive trees, roses, and odoriferous plants. In the woods and mountains are lions, bisons, ostriches, monkeys, roebucks, hares, pheasants, partridges, and other sorts of birds and beasts. The principal rivers are the Wad-el-Kebir, Magrida, Magerada, and Caps. The form of government is by a divan, or council, whose president is the bey. The members of the divan are chosen by the bey. The inhabitants are a mixture of Moors, Turks, Arabs, Jews, and Christians, merchants and slaves; and they carry on a great trade in linen and woollen cloth, morocco leather, gold-dust, lead, horses, oil, soap, and ostriches' eggs and feathers. The established religion is Mahomedanism. All public instruments are written in the Arabic tongue, but commerce is usually carried on by that of the Lingua Franca. Population, between 4,000,000 and 5,000,000.

TUNIS, the capital of the above country, stands on a point of the Gulf of Goletta, surrounded by lakes and marshes. It is in the form of an oblong square, 5 miles in circumference, with a lofty wall, five gates, and 35 mosques. The houses are all built of stone, though but one story high; and it has a citadel on an eminence, on the W. side of the city. Without the walls are two suburbs, which contain upwards of 100 houses. The divan, or council of state, assembles in an old palace, where the bey resides. The harbour has a very narrow entrance, which is well fortified. The Mahomedans here have 9 colleges for students, and a great number of smaller schools. Tunis is a place of great trade, and has manufactures of velvets, silks, linen, and red caps worn by the common people. It is 10 miles from the sea, 275 N. W. of Tripoli, and 380 E. of Algier. Pop. 130,000. Long. 10. 16. E. lat. 36. 45. N.

TUNJA, a town of New Granada, capital of a district of the same name. Near it are mines of gold and emeralds. It is seated in a fertile valley; 90 miles N. by E. of St. Fe de Bogota. Long. 73. 8. W. lat. 5. 20. N.

TUNKAT, a town of Western Tartary, in Turkestan, seated in a large plain, on the river Ilak; 100 miles S. E. of Taraz.

TUNKERSTOWN. *See* EPHRATA.

TURCOIN, a town of France, department of Nord, where the allies, under the Duke of York, were defeated by the French in 1794. Pop. 11,000. It is 6 miles N. N. W. of Lille.

TURCOMANIA, a province of Turkey in Asia, now called ARMENIA, (which see.)

TURENNE, a town of France, department of Correze, with a castle; 16 miles S. S. W. of Tulle.

TURIN, a fortified city of Piedmont, capital of the dominions of the king of Sardinia, and an archbishop's see, with a university founded in 1405 by Amadeo, duke of Savoy. There are many large squares, among which that of St. Charles is the most spacious; the buildings are handsome, and it has extensive arcades on each side. Most of the streets are well built, uniform, and straight, and terminate on some agreeable object; the Strada di Po, the finest and largest, leads to the royal palace, and is adorned with piazzas filled with shops, as are various others of the best streets; all of which are kept clean by means of a canal from the Doria, with sluices that flow through them into the Po. The palace consists of two magnificent structures, joined together by a gallery, in which are several pictures, statues, and antiquities of great value. The citadel, which was demolished by the French after the battle of Marengo, was a regular pentagon, comprehending an extensive and well-furnished arsenal, a cannon-foundry, a chemical laboratory, &c. There are fine walks on the ramparts and walls of the city, fine gardens on the side of the river Po, and a charming public place called the Corso, where many people assemble in an

evening to exhibit themselves and their equipage. Near this city, on the banks of the Po, is the beautiful castle of Valentin, the garden of which is applied to botanical studies. It contains 110 churches, all richly endowed and decorated. In 1798 the French republican army took possession of this city, seized all the strong places and arsenals of Piedmont, and obliged the king and his family to remove to the island of Sardinia. In 1799 the French were driven out by the Austrians and Russians; but shortly afterwards the city and all Piedmont surrendered to the French. In 1814 it was delivered up to the allies, when they restored it to the king of Sardinia. It is seated in a fertile plain, at the confluence of the Doria with the Po; 68 miles N. W. of Genoa, and 80 S. W. of Milan. Pop. 114,000. Long. 7. 40. E. lat. 45. 4. N.

Turinge, a town of Sweden, in the province of Sudermanland; 24 miles W. S. W. of Stockholm.

Turinsk, a town of Russia, in the government of Tobolsk, with a fort; 190 miles W. by S. of Tobolsk.

Turivacary, a town of Hindostan, in Mysore, consisting of an outer and inner fort, strongly defended by a ditch and mud wall, and an open suburb at a little distance. Here are two small temples of curious workmanship; 34 miles S. of Sera, and 50 N. of Seringapatam.

Turkestan, a country of Western Tartary, bounded on the N. and E. by the country of the Kalmucs, S. by Bokharia, and W. by the Lake Aral. The chief of this country is generally called the khan of the Karakalpaks. The capital is Taraz.

Turkey, a large empire, extending over part of Europe, Asia, and Africa. European Turkey formerly comprehended Moldavia, Bessarabia, Walachia, Bulgaria, Servia, Bosnia, part of Croatia and Dalmatia, Romania, Macedonia, Albania, Janna, Livadia, and the Morea. Bessarabia and part of Moldavia were, however ceded to Russia in 1812, and in 1830, the independence of Greece being established by the allied powers, the territory of the sultan in Europe became greatly contracted. *See* Greece. Asiatic Turkey is bounded on the N. by the Black Sea and Circassia, E. by Persia, S. by Arabia, and W. by the Mediterranean and the Sea of Marmora. It lies between 27. and 46. E. long., and 28. and 45. N. lat., and contains the countries of Irac-Arabi, Diarbek, Curdistan, Armenia, Caramania, Natolia, and Syria, with Palestine. In Africa, the Turkish power may be considered as nominal, the Barbary states merely acknowledging the porte as the head of the Moslems, while Egypt is independent, though governed by a Turkish pacha. Of these countries (which see respectively) the climate, productions, manners, &c., must be various. The Turks are generally robust, and well-shaped. They shave their heads, but wear long beards, except those in the seraglio, or palace, and military men, who wear only whiskers. The turban worn by the men is white, and consists of long pieces of thin linen made up together in several folds. No one but a Turk must presume to wear a white turban. Their clothes are long and full. They sit, eat, and sleep on the floor, on cushions, mattresses, and carpets. In general they are very moderate in eating, and their meals are despatched with great haste. Their principal food is rice; and the frugal repast is followed by fruit and cold water, which are succeeded by hot coffee, and pipes with tobacco. With opium they procure what they call a kief, or placid intoxication. Chess and draughts are favourite games; and the coffee-houses and baths furnish other sources of amusement. Polygamy is allowed among them; but their wives, properly so called, are no more than four in number. The fair sex here are kept under a rigorous confinement: the Arabic word Haram, which signifies a sacred or prohibited thing, is in its fullest sense used both of the habitation of the women and of the women themselves. The Turks believe in one God, and that his great prophet is Mahomet; they appropriate to themselves the name of Moslemim, which has been corrupted into Mussulman, signifying persons professing the doctrine of Mahomet, which he calls Islam. Drinking wine is prohibited by this prophet, in the Koran, yet the Turks make use of it occasionally, without any scruple; though instead of it they generally use sherbet, a liquor made of honey, spices, and the juice of fruits; in this, as in other points, their character is one of extremes. They seldom drink wine, but when they do they get intoxicated. They are usually mild and placid; but when provoked, they are infuriated. They are not habitually cruel, but in their cruelty they are remorseless; and though they have many virtues, yet their vices are great, and spring from a pharisaical and sensual creed, and the debasing effects of a despotic government. They expend great sums on fountains, not only in the towns, but in the country, and other solitary places, for the refreshment of travellers and labourers. The grand seignior is absolute master of the goods and lives of his subjects, insomuch that they are little better than slaves. The grand vizier is the chief officer under the grand seignior: besides discharging the functions of prime minister, he is commander of all the forces of the empire. The divan, or cabinet council, consists of the vizier, the mufti, and the kiaya bey. The other ministers are the reis effendi (whose office corresponds in part to that of chancellor, and in part to that of secretary for foreign affairs in Britain); the tefterdar, or minister of finance; the tschelebi, or master of the ordnance; and the capitan pacha, or commander of the forces. The pachas, or governors of provinces, act also as farmers-general of the revenue, for their respective provinces. The sangiac beys are the governors of districts under the pachas, and invested, like them, with both civil and military functions. The ulemas are a numerous body, whose functions consist in explaining the Koran, and in applying its injunctions to the circumstances of the times. They thus combine the character of clergy and lawyers, having at their head the grand mufti. The imans, or priests, are a body altogether distinct from the ulemas, their duty being merely to perform public worship in the mosques. Turkey in Europe is divided into the beylerbeyliks of Romania or Roumelia, and Bosnia, the island of Cyprus, and the province of Walachia; and contains an area of 183,458 square miles, and a population of 9,650,000, of whom one-third are Turks, the remainder Greeks, Albanians, Jews, Franks, &c. Asiatic Turkey probably contains 21,250,000 inhabitants, and are not less mixed. The area is about 655,134 square miles.

TURKHEIM. *See* DURKHEIM.

TURKIN, a town of Russia, in the government of Caucasia, situate on the Caspian Sea. It is 140 miles S. of Astracan. Long. 47. 15. E. lat. 44. 15. N.

TURN-AGAIN CAPE, a cape on the E. side of the northern island of New Zealand. Long. 176. 56. E. lat. 40. 28. S.

TURNAU, a town of Bohemia, in the circle of Buntzlau, on the river Iser; 12 miles N. N. E of Jung Buntzlau.

TURNHOUT, a town of Belgium, in Brabant, near which, in 1596, prince Maurice, of Nassau, with only 800 horse, totally defeated the Spaniards, consisting of 6000. It is 24 miles N. E. of Antwerp. Pop. 11,000.

TURON, a seaport of Cochin-China, situate on a bay of the same name, which affords a safe retreat for the largest ships in the most tempestuous season. In the vicinity are plantations of sugar-canes and tobacco. Turon is 40 miles S. E. of Hue. Long. 107. 40. E. lat. 16. 9. N.

TURSHEEZ, or TOORSHEEZ, a town of Persia, in the province of Khorasan, on the borders of the Great Salt Desert; with an export trade in iron. It imports rice, wool, and cloth from Herat, from which it is distant about 160 miles W. N. W. Pop. 20,000.

TURSI, a town of Naples, in Basilicata, on the river Sino; 8 miles W. of the Gulf of Tarento, and 30 S. of Matera.

TUSCANY, a sovereign state of Italy, with the title of a grand duchy, belonging to the House of Austria. It is bounded on the N. by Modena, on the E. and S. by the pope's territories, and on the W. by the Mediterranean. It is about 130 miles in length, and 100 in breadth, and is watered by several rivers, of which the Arno is the chief. There are several mountains, in which are found mines of iron, alum, and vitriol. There are also quarries of marble, alabaster, and porphyry, besides hot baths and mineral waters. Many parts of it are fruitful in corn and wine, and produce abundance of citrons, oranges, pomegranates, and other fruits. The inhabitants apply themselves to trade; they chiefly manufacture silks, stuffs, fine earthenware, and gilt leather. They are much visited by foreigners, on account of their politeness, and because the Tuscan language is accounted the purest in all Italy. This duchy is divided into three provinces, Florence, Pisano, and Sienna, to which some add the islands. Upon the flight of the grand duke, in 1799, it was erected by the French into the kingdom of Etruria, but was soon afterwards transformed into an appendage to the crown of Italy. In 1814, however, the duchy was restored to the Austrians, when Ferdinand, the grand duke, returned to his dominions. Area, 9270 square miles. Pop. 1,500,000. Florence is the capital.

TUSIS, a town of Switzerland, in the canton of Grisons, seated near the torrent Nolla; 16 miles S. by W. of Coire.

TUTBURY, a village, and formerly a market-town, in Staffordshire (with a considerable cotton manufacture); noted for its ancient castle, of which several towers and a small part of the wall still remain. It is seated on the river Dove, 4 miles N. W. of Burton, and 134 of London.

TUTICORIN, a town of Hindostan, in the Carnatic, seated on the Gulf of Manaar; 29 miles E. by N. of Palamcotta, and 67 S. of Madura.

TUTLINGEN, a town of Germany, with a castle on a mountain, belonging to the kingdom of Wirtemberg. Near it is the celebrated foundry of Ludwigsthal. It is seated on the Danube, over which is a bridge; 58 miles S. S. W. of Stutgard. Long. 8. 48. E. lat. 48. 2. N.

TUTURA, a town of Russia, in the government of Irkutsk, situate on the Lena; 160 miles N. of Irkutsk. Long. 105. 40. E. lat. 54. 40. N.

TUXFORD, a town in Nottinghamshire, with a market on Monday, and a good free-school. It is 12 miles N. N. W. of Newark, and 137 N. by W. of London.

TUY, a town of Spain, in Galicia, and a bishop's see. It is surrounded by walls and ramparts, and well furnished with artillery, being a frontier town towards Portugal. It stands on a mountain near the river Minho; 60 miles S. of Compostella, and 260 W. N. W. of Madrid. Pop. 4000. Long. 8. 32. W. lat. 42. 4. N.

TUZLA, a town of Asiatic Turkey, in Caramania, situate at the western extremity of a lake to which it gives name. It is 28 miles N. of Konieh.

TVER, a government of Russia, formerly a province in the government of Novogorod. It was the first province modelled according to the code of laws of Catherine II. It comprises an area of 24,000 square miles, with 1,000,000 inhabitants. The country produces abundantly all kinds of corn and vegetables. Its forests yield the most valuable timber. The quadrupeds and the feathered race are the same as in all the N. of Europe. Besides the fishes common to most lakes and rivers, there is one peculiar to the waters of these northern regions, called the sterlet: it is the *acipenser ruthenus* of Linné, and is a species of sturgeon, highly esteemed for the flavour of its flesh, and for its roe, of which the finest caviare is made.

TVER, the capital of the foregoing government, and an archbishop's see, with a fortress. It is a place of considerable commerce, being seated at the conflux of the Tverza and Volga, along which is conveyed all the merchandise sent by water from Siberia and the S. provinces towards Petersburg. It is divided into the Old and New Town; the former, situate on the opposite side of the Volga, consists almost entirely of wooden cottages; the latter has risen with lustre from the ashes of the conflagration of 1763. Catherine II., at her own expense, raised the governor's house, the episcopal palace, the courts of justice, the exchange, the prison, and some other public edifices; and, to every person who engaged to build a house of brick, she offered a loan of 300*l.* for 12 years, without interest. The streets are broad and long, extending in straight lines from an octagon in the centre; the houses of this octagon, and of the principal streets, are of brick, stuccoed white, and make a magnificent appearance. Here is an ecclesiastical seminary, which admits 600 students. In 1776 the empress founded a school for the instruction of 200 burghers' children; and in 1779, an academy for the education of 120 of the young nobility of the province. Tver is 99 miles N. N. W. of Moscow. Pop. 20,000. Long. 36. 5. E. lat. 56. 7. N.

TWEED, a river of Scotland, which rises from numerous springs in the S. part of Peebleshire, called Tweedsmuir. It divides that county almost into two equal parts, crosses the N. part of Selkirkshire and Roxburghshire, then forms the boundary between Berwickshire and England, and enters the German Ocean at Berwick.

TWEEDMOUTH, a town in the detached part of Durham, called Islandshire; situate on the Tweed, and communicating by a bridge with Berwick, of which it may be deemed a suburb.

TWICKENHAM, a village in Middlesex, adorned with many handsome villas, of which two are particularly celebrated: that which was the favourite residence of Pope, and Strawberry Hill, the elegant Gothic retreat of the celebrated Horace Walpole, earl of Orford. It is seated on the Thames, 3 miles S. S. W. of Brentford.

TYCOKZIN, a town of Poland, on the Narew; 22 miles N. E. of Bielsk.

TYDORE, one of the Molucca Islands, three leagues S. of Ternate.

TYLER, a county in the N. W. of Virginia, formed from a part of Ohio county, in 1814.

TYNE, a river in Northumberland, formed by a branch from the E. part of Cumberland, and another from the hills on the borders of Scotland. These, uniting a little above Hexham, form a large river, which flows by Newcastle, and enters the German Ocean at Tynemouth.

TYNE, a river of Scotland, in Haddingtonshire, which rises on the borders of Edinburghshire, flows by Haddington, and enters the German Ocean to the W. of Dunbar.

TYNEMOUTH, a borough in Northumberland, near the mouth of the Tyne, noted for its ancient castle, seated on a high rock, inaccessible on the sea-side. Tynemouth has some considerable salt-works; and here, and at Shields, large vessels take in their loading of coal and goods brought from Newcastle. During the bathing season it is a place of fashionable resort, and in the neighbourhood are some mineral springs. It returns one member to parliament. It is 9 miles E. N. E. of Newcastle.

TYRE. *See* SUR.

TYROL, a princely county of the Austrian empire; bounded on the N. by Bavaria, E. by Salzburg and Carinthia, S. by Austrian Italy, and W. by Switzerland. Though a mountainous country, its valleys are fertile in corn and wine, and it has an excellent breed of cattle. It likewise yields salt, all kinds of ores, and various sorts of precious stones. Its copper contains not only silver, but also some gold. The principal rivers are the Inn, Adige, and Eysach. The country is divided into seven districts or circles. It was overrun by the French and Bavarians in 1805, and, by the treaty of Presburg, was ceded to Bavaria. In 1809 it was ceded to Italy, but was restored to Austria in 1814. Area, 11,000 square miles. Pop. 720,000. Innspruck is the capital.

TYRONE, a county of Ireland, in the province of Ulster, 46 miles long, and 37 broad; bounded on the N. by Londonderry, E. by Armagh and Loch Neagh, S. W. by Fermanagh, and W. by Donegal. It is divided into 35 parishes, and sends two members to parliament. It is a rough country, but tolerably fertile. The capital is Dungannon.

TYSTED, a town of Denmark in North Jutland, with a citadel; seated on the Gulf of Lymford, 46 miles W. of Alburg. Long. 8. 25. E. lat. 56. 54. N.

TYVY, or TEIFE, a river of Wales in Cardiganshire, which issues from a lake on the E. side of the county, and flows by Tregannon, Llanbeder, Newcastle, and Cardigan, into Cardigan Bay.

TZARITZYN, a town of Russia, in the government of Saratof; seated on the Volga; 120 miles N. W. of Astracan. Long. 45. 25. E. lat. 48. 0. N.

TZERNITZ, a town of European Turkey, in Romania, near the river Tzerna; 32 miles N. N. E. of Adrianople.

TZIVILSK, a town of Russia, in the government of Kasan; 56 miles W. of Kasan. Long. 47. 25. E. lat. 55. 40. N.

TZURUCHATU, STAROI, a town of Russia, in the government of Irkutsk; seated on the Argunia, on the borders of China; 160 miles S. E. of Nertchinsk Long. 119. 32. E. lat. 49. 18. N.

U.

Ubeda, a town of Spain, in Andalusia, with a strong castle, seated in a fertile country, near the river Guadalquiver; 22 miles N. E. of Jaen. Pop. 16,000.

Uberlingen, a town of Baden, in the district of Furstenburg. The principal trade is in corn to Switzerland; and near it are famous baths. It is seated on a high rock, 7 miles N. of Constance.

Ubersko, a town of Bohemia, in the circle of Chrudin; 10 miles E. N. E. of Chrudin.

Ubes, St., or **Setuval**, a fortified seaport of Portugal, in Estremadura; with a strong citadel and a good harbour, defended by three forts. It is built on the ruins of the ancient Setobriga, at the head of a bay, near the influx of the Cadaon, and has a good trade, particularly in salt, of which a great quantity is sent to the colonies in America. It stands at the end of a plain, 5 miles in length, extremely fertile in corn, wine, and fruits; the N. end bounded by mountains, covered with pines and other trees, and containing quarries of jasper of several colours; 20 miles S. E. of Lisbon. Long. 8. 54. W. lat. 38. 22. N.

Ubigau, a town of Saxony, seated on the Elster; 28 miles S. E. of Wittenburg.

Uby, an island on the E. side of the entrance of the Gulf of Siam, 20 miles in circumference. It yields good water and plenty of wood. Long. 104. 46. E. lat. 8. 55. N.

Ucayal. *See* Apurimac.

Ucedo, or **Uzeda**, a town of Spain, in New Castile, with a castle; seated on the Xarama; 32 miles N. N. E. of Madrid.

Ucker, a river which issues from a lake of the same name, near Prenzlo, in Brandenburg, flows N. into Pomerania, and, being joined by the Rando, enters the Frisch Haff at Uckermunde.

Ucker Mark, the former name of that part of Brandenburg which bordered on Pomerania, between Mecklenburg and the Oder. It now forms part of the Prussian government of Potsdam.

Uckermunde, a town of Prussia, in Pomerania; seated on the Frisch Haff, at the influx of the Ucker; 32 miles N. W. of Stettin.

Uddevalla, a seaport of Sweden, in the province of Bahus. The streets are spacious, but the houses are built of wood; and the town was therefore almost entirely destroyed in the fire of 1806. The chief trade is in iron, planks, and herrings. It is situate on a bay of the Cattegat; 50 miles N. by W. of Gotheburg. Long. 11. 50. E. lat. 58. 24. N.

Udina, or **Udine**, a city of Austrian Italy, capital of a delegation of its name, which comprises almost the whole of the former Venetian Friuli; with a citadel. It is the see of an archbishop, and contains 17,000 inhabitants. A treaty between the Austrians and French was signed here in 1797. It is seated in a large plain, on the river and canal called La Roia; 20 miles N. W. of Aquileia, and 65 N. E. of Venice.

Udinskoi, a town of Siberia, in the government of Irkutsk; seated on the Selinga; 150 miles E. of Irkutsk. Long. 108. 20. E. lat. 52. 0. N.

Udipu, a town of Hindostan, in Canara; near which is a small fort. Here are three temples, placed in a common square, and surrounded by 14 large convents. It stands amid rice fields, beautifully intermixed with palm gardens; 2 miles from the sea, and 36 N. N. W. of Mangalore.

Udskoi, a town of Siberia, in the province of Okhotsk; situate on the Ud; 300 miles S. W. of Okhotsk. Long. 135. 30. E. lat. 55. 6. N.

Udvarhely, a town of Transylvania, capital of a district of its name; with a considerable trade in honey, wax, &c.; 22 miles E. N. E. of Schœsburg, and 78 S. E. of Clausenburg. Pop. 6000.

Uelzen, a town of Hanover, in Luneburg; noted as the birthplace of Zimmerman. It is situate on an island in the river Ilmeran; 22 miles S. of Luneburg.

Ufa, a government of Asiatic Russia, formerly included in the government of Tobolsk. It is divided into the two provinces of Ufa and Orenburg.

Ufa, the capital of the above government, seated on the river Ufa, near its confluence with the Bielaia; 760 miles E. by S. of Moscow. Long. 56. 0. E. lat. 54. 50. N.

Uffenheim, a town of Bavarian Franconia, in the district of Anspach, with a castle; situate on the Gollace; 15 miles N. by E. of Rotenburg, and 22 S. E. of Wurtzburg.

Ugento, a town of Naples, in Terra d'Otranto, and a bishop's see; 8 miles W. of Alessana, and 20 S. W. of Otranto.

Ugliani, a town of the Sardinian states, in Piedmont; 9 miles N. of Ivrea, and 16 E. S. E. of Aosta.

Uglich, a town of Russia, in the government of Jaroslavl; with a trade in leather and soap; seated on the Volga, 45 miles W. of Jaroslavl. Pop. 5500.

Ugogna, a town of Austrian Italy; 45 miles N. W. of Milan.

Uist, North and **South**, two islands of the Hebrides, on the W. side of Scotland. North Uist is 22 miles long and 17 broad, and the face of the country corresponds with that of Lewes. South Uist is 23 miles long, and 7 broad, and trees are here equally unknown. Many cows are annually exported; but the staple commodity is kelp. The island of Benbecula lies between them, and they are each about 16 miles to the W. of the most western point of the Isle of Skye.

Ukenskoi, a town of Russia, in the government of Tobolsk, at the conflux of the Irtisch and Oby; 196 miles N. of Tobolsk. Long. 69. 15. E. lat. 61. 10. N.

UKRAINE, a country of Europe, lying on the borders of Poland, Russia, and Little Tartary. Its name signifies *a frontier*. By a treaty between Russia and Poland, in 1693, the latter remained in possession of the Ukraine, on the W. side of the Dnieper, which constituted a palatinate called Kiov; while the E. side was allotted to Russia, and called the government of Kiov; but Russia, having obtained the Polish part, by the treaty of partition in 1793, the whole belongs now to that power. That part of the Ukraine on the W. side of the Dnieper is but indifferently cultivated; but that on the E. side, inhabited by the Cossacs, is in much better condition. The principal town is Kiov. *See* COSSACS.

ULALA, a town of Hindostan, in Canara; 3 miles S. W. of Mangalore.

ULAPOOL, a town of Scotland, in Ross-shire; on the E. side of the entrance of Loch Broom; at the mouth of a river of its name; with a good harbour and commodious road. It is a great fishing station, and situate in the midst of a wool country; 48 miles W. by N. of Tain. Long. 5. 5. W. lat. 57. 50. N.

ULEA, or ULABORG, an extensive province to the N. of Finland, and extending along the S. coast of the Gulf of Bothnia. It was long subject to Sweden, but, since 1809, it forms a circle of the Russian government of Abo. The population is thinly scattered, the chief part of the surface being covered with forests, marshes, and rocks.

ULEABORG, the capital of the preceding province, and the largest town in East Bothnia; with a castle on an island, and a commodious harbour. In 1714 this town was demolished by the Russians, to whom the Swedes surrendered it in 1808. It is situate at the mouth of a river of the same name; 340 miles N. by E. of Abo. Pop. 3500. Long. 24. 40. E. lat. 65. 30. N.

ULIETEA, one of the Society Isles, in the South Pacific. *See* RAIATEA.

ULLSWATER, a lake on the borders of Westmoreland and Cumberland; 10 miles N. of Ambleside. It is 8 miles long, and abounds with char and other fish. The report of guns, discharged in certain stations on the lake, is reverberated from rock to rock, promontory, cavern, and hill, with every variety of sound. The river Eamont flows through this lake, and by Penrith to the Eden, forming that part of the boundary line between the two counties.

ULM, a city of Germany, in Wirtemberg. It is a fortified, large, and handsome place, in which the archives of the late imperial towns of Suabia were preserved, and where the diet of the circle was generally held. The cathedral is a large magnificent structure. Here is an excellent college, with a theological seminary annexed; and a convent for the daughters of the nobility and citizens, who are here educated and afterwards at liberty to marry. Its other most remarkable buildings are the abbey of St. Michael, commonly called Wengen, the town-house, the arsenal, the magazines, and the valuable town library. The inhabitants are Protestants, and estimated at 16,000; they have a good trade in linens, fustians, paper, wine, and wool. The Duke of Bavaria took it in 1702, by stratagem; but surrendered it after the battle of Blenheim in 1704. In 1796 it was taken by the French, and it surrendered to them in 1805, with the flower of the Austrian army, under General Mack, consisting of 60,000 men. In 1810 it was transferred to Wirtemberg. It is seated at the confluence of the Blau with the Danube, opposite the influx of the Iler; 38 miles W. by N. of Augsburg, and 40 S. E. of Stutgard. Long. 9. 56. E. lat. 48. 24. N.

ULOTHO, or VLOTHOW, a town of Prussian Westphalia, in the county of Ravensburg; near which is a medicinal spring. It is 6 miles S. of Minden.

ULRICHSTEIN, a town of Germany, in Hesse-Darmstadt; with a fortified castle. It is 25 miles S. E. of Marburg.

ULRICHSHAMN, a town of Sweden, in W. Gothland; formerly called Bogesund; the present name being given it in 1741, in compliment to queen Ulrica Eleanora. It has a considerable trade in cattle, provisions, tobacco, &c. It is 50 miles E. of Gotheburg.

ULSTER, a province of Ireland, 116 miles long, and 100 broad; bounded on the E. by the Irish Sea, N. by the Northern Ocean, W. by the Atlantic Ocean, S. W. by the province of Connaught, and S. by that of Leinster. It contains the counties of Donegal, Londonderry, Antrim, Tyrone, Fermanagh, Monaghan, Armagh, Down, and Cavan. The principal place is Londonderry.

ULSTER, NEW. *See* ZEALAND, NEW.

ULTZEN, or VELTZEN, a town of the Netherlands, in N. Holland; with a trade in flour and wool. It is 50 miles N. of Haarlem.

ULVERSTONE, a town in Lancashire, with a market on Thursday. It is seated at the foot of some hills, near a shallow arm of the Irish Sea, and has a canal to the estuary of the Leven. The parish church, situate a small distance from the town, at the foot of a steep hill, is a handsome structure, rebuilt in 1804, after its ancient pattern of the age of Henry VIII. Here are also an additional church, erected under the recent acts, three places of worship for dissenters, the ancient Quakers' meeting-house at Swartz Moor, and a Roman Catholic chapel. At the intersection of two of the principal streets was an ancient cross, which was replaced by one of cast iron in 1821. Since the decline of Dalton, this town has considerably increased; and has manufactures of cotton, check, canvas, and hats. It is the port of the district of Furness, and exports much corn, limestone, iron-ore, and blue slate. It is 22 miles N. W. of Lancaster, and 261 N. N. W. of London. Long. 3. 12. W. lat. 54. 14. N.

UMA, or UMEA, a province of Sweden, comprising W. Bothnia, Umea, Lapmark, and nearly all Swedish Lapland. It has an area of

65,000 square miles, with about 80,000 inhabitants.

UMA, or UMEA, a seaport of Sweden, in W. Bothnia, capital of the above province, at the mouth of the river Uma, in the Gulf of Bothnia. The houses are built of wood, and it was twice burnt by the Russians. It is 310 miles N. by E. of Stockholm. Long. 19. 18. E. lat. 63. 58. N.

UMAGO, a small seaport of Austrian Illyria, in Istria, seated near the Gulf Largona; 12 miles S. W. of Capo d'Istria.

UMBRIA, a province of Italy, now called the duchy of Spoleto.

UMBRIATICO, a town of Naples, in Calabria, seated on the Lipuda; 15 miles N. by W. of St. Severina. Pop. 10,000.

UMMERAPOORA, or AMARAPURA, one of the most flourishing and well-built cities of Asia; the metropolis of Birmah; with a spacious and regular fort, completely fortified after the eastern manner. It was founded in 1783 by the emperor Minderagree; 4 miles N. E. of Ava, the ancient capital. The houses are raised on posts from the ground; the smaller supported by bamboos, the larger by strong timber. The streets are all straight, many of them wide, paved with brick, and frequently crossed by others at right angles. The royal palace is a splendid edifice, within the fort, and not any nobleman of the court is permitted to enter it with his feet covered. The temples and monasteries are numerous, and, though in general composed of wood, are very magnificent. The unbounded expenditure of gilding, which is bestowed on the outside of the roofs, particularly on the lofty spires, renders them objects of extraordinary splendour. Ummerapoora is situate on a peninsula, formed by the Irrawaddy on the W. and a narrow channel branching E. from the river, which soon takes a N. direction, and expands to a lake on the E. side of the city, 7 miles long, and one and a half broad. It is 250 miles E. of Calcutta, and 620 N. N. W. of Siam. Pop. 150,000. Long. 76. 7. E. lat. 21. 57. N.

UMRITSIR, a city of Hindostan, in the kingdom of Lahore, or Punjaub, once the principal city of the Sikhs, who now occupy the whole of the territory, and is by them esteemed sacred. It was razed to the ground in 1761.

UNDERWALDEN, a canton of Switzerland, bounded on the N. by the canton of Lucerne and the Lake of the Four Cantons, E. by high mountains which separate it from the canton of Uri, S. by Mount Brunich, which parts it from the canton of Bern, and W. by that of Lucern. It is 24 miles long, and 20 broad, contains an area of 300 square miles, with 23,000 inhabitants, and is divided into the Upper and Lower Valley by a forest called Kesterwald, which crosses the canton from N. to S. The country abounds in fruit and cattle, but produces little corn, and no wine. The inhabitants are Roman Catholics. Stanz is the capital of the Lower Valley, and Sarnen of the Upper, and of the whole canton.

UNGVAR, a town and fort of Hungary, capital of a palatinate of the same name. It stands in an island formed by the Ung; 57 miles E. of Cassovia. Pop. 5000. Long. 22. 23. E. lat. 48. 42. N.

UNIEGO, a town of Poland, in the palatinate of Lenczicz, with a fine castle belonging to the archbishop of Gnesen, seated on the Warta; 20 miles S. S. W. of Lenczicz.

UNION, a town of Pennsylvania, chief of Fayette county, situate on Redstone Creek. It is 14 miles S. by E. of Brownsville, and 28 N. E. of Morgantown.

UNION, a town of New York, in Tioga county, where the judicial courts are held in October. It is situate on the Susquehanna, W. of the influx of the Chenango. It is 50 miles E. by S. of Newtown, and 150 N. W. of New York.

UNITED PROVINCES OF THE NETHERLANDS, a name given to the seven Protestant states of the Netherlands, which threw off the yoke of Spain, and became an independent republic. *See* HOLLAND and NETHERLANDS.

UNITED STATES OF AMERICA, a republic of North America, consisting originally, in 1783, of thirteen states, namely, Massachusetts, New Hampshire, Rhode Island, Connecticut, New York, New Jersey, Pennsylvania, Delaware, Maryland, Virginia, North Carolina, South Carolina, and Georgia: Kentucky, Vermont, Tennessee, Maine, Mississippi, Indiana, Illinois, Missouri, Alabama, Louisiana, and Ohio, having since been formed, and added to them, the present number of the states that constitute this great American republic is 30; including the territories of Michigan, Arkansaw, Wisconsin, and Iowa, and the district of Colombia. These districts are all described in this work in their proper places. The population of this republic has wonderfully increased since they acquired their independence, in 1783. The number of inhabitants in 1770 was estimated at 1,500,000; in 1791, 3,929,326; in 1800, 5,319,762; in 1810, 7,239,903; in 1820, 9,654,415; in 1831, 13,358,171; and in 1841, 17,068,666. No part of the globe is so well supplied with rivers, great and small, springs, and lakes, as the United States; so that a communication by water from one extremity to the other is more easy than in England; and a great multitude of bays and excellent harbours are on the coast of every maritime state. In the large towns, the houses are of brick; in the others, and their environs, the half, and often the whole of them are of planks: but 80 miles from the sea, in the central and southern states, and particularly in those W. of the Allegany mountains, a large portion of the inhabitants still live in what are called log-houses, made of the trunks of trees, from 20 to 30 feet long, and four or five inches in diameter, laid one upon another, and supported by letting their ends into each other: the spaces between the trunks are filled with clay; they have two doors, which are hung upon wooden hinges, and these frequently supply the place of windows: neither nails nor iron of any sort are used. The thirteen original states long flourished as provinces of Great

Britain; but parliament attempting to tax them by its sole authority, without the intervention of their assemblies, a civil war ensued. The Americans formed a congress, which in 1776 disclaimed all dependence on the mother country; the French king entered into an alliance with them in 1778; the colonies, powerfully assisted by France, were successful; and Great Britain acknowledged their independence by the peace of 1783. From this period they continued to flourish until they became involved in the wars that raged between Great Britain and France, and at length, in June 1812, took up arms against the British for the vindication of their rights as a neutral power. The American commerce now fell off to a very low ebb, and the states suffered considerably from the more direct consequence of the war. In 1814, peace having been concluded in Europe, the question in dispute between Britain and America ceased entirely, in a practical view, to possess any interest. Accordingly, the commissioners of the two powers, who had met at Ghent, agreed to adjourn the controversy, and in December a treaty of peace was signed between them. The manufactures and commerce have since been rapidly increasing, and the country is progressively advancing in population and importance. The federal constitution of the United States is governed by a congress, consisting of a president, a vice-president, senate, and house of representatives. The representatives are elected every second year; the senators are chosen for six years, and the president and vice-president for four. General Washington was elected the first president in 1788. In the United States there is no national establishment of religion, but every man is left to support that which is agreeable to him by his own voluntary contributions. The great mass of the people profess Christianity, and are divided into various sects, but as no one sect is taken under state patronage, or distinguished by peculiar privileges, the difference of religious sentiment excites no feeling of rancour, and all classes live together in the utmost harmony. Education receives every possible encouragement from the government, and colleges, medical and law schools, and academies, are numerous throughout the union. In some of the states slavery is abolished, and the disgrace which its prevalence in other states reflects on a free nation is beginning to be felt by the government, who, it cannot be doubted, will, at no remote period, eradicate for ever this abominable stigma on their country. The city of Washington is the metropolis.

Unna, a town of Prussian Westphalia, in the county of Mark, environed by walls and ditches, and formerly a considerable Hanseatic town. It is seated on the Kottolbeck; 10 miles S. S. W. of Ham.

Unna, a river of European Turkey, which rises in Bosnia, on the frontiers of Croatia, passes by Wihitsch, and joins the Save, 16 miles above Gradisca.

Unnary, a town of Sweden, in the province of Smoland; 43 miles W. of Wexio.

Unst, the most northern of the Shetland Islands, 10 miles long, and 4 broad, and more level than the other isles. It feeds many sheep, horned cattle, and hogs, and about 80 tons of cured fish are annually exported. Long. 1. 10. W. lat. 61. 10. N.

Unterseen, a town of Switzerland, in the canton of Bern, near which is the famous cavern of St. Pat. It is seated on the river Aar, between the lakes Brientz and Thun; 25 miles S. S. E. of Bern.

Unza, a town of Russia, in a province of the same name, in the government of Kostroma. It is situate on the river Unza; 92 miles E. N. E. of Kostroma.

Upland, a province of Sweden, between Sudermania, Westmania, Gestricia, and the Baltic. It is 70 miles long, and 45 broad, contains an area of 500 square miles, with 250,000 inhabitants, and is extensively covered with shapeless stones and impenetrable woods, but enriched with inexhaustible mines of copper, iron, and silver. Stockholm is the capital.

Uppingham, a town in Rutlandshire, with a market on Wednesday, seated on an eminence; 6 miles S. of Oakham, and 89 N. by W. of London.

Upsal, a city of Sweden, in Upland, and an archbishop's see, with a university. It is divided into two almost equal parts by the river Sala, and the streets are drawn at right angles from a central kind of square. A few of the houses are built of brick, but the generality are constructed of wood, painted red, and the roofs are covered in with turf. Upsal was formerly the metropolis of Sweden, and near it is the morasten, or stone on which the kings used to be crowned. The cathedral, a large structure of brick, contains the remains of the celebrated Gustavus Vasa, and of Charles Linné. The university is the most ancient in Sweden, and the first seminary in the N. for academical education. The Royal Society here is likewise the oldest literary academy in the N. Here is an observatory, planned by the celebrated Celsius, from which the Swedish geographers compute the longitude; also a botanical garden, of which Linné was superintendent. Upsal is seated in a vast open plain, fertile in corn; 35 miles N. N. W. of Stockholm. Pop. 5000. Long. 17. 39. E. lat. 59. 52. N.

Upton-upon-Severn, a town in Worcestershire, with a market on Thursday, and a great trade in cider. It is seated on the Severn, 10 miles S. of Worcester, and 111 W. N. W. of London.

Urach, a town of Germany, in the kingdom of Wirtemberg. It has a great trade in paper, damasks, and linen, and is 21 miles S. S. E. of Stutgard.

Ural, or Oural, a river of Russia, which rises in Mount Caucasus, flows by Orenburg, Uralsk, and Gurief, and enters the Caspian Sea by three mouths.

Ural Mountains, a chain of mountains extending from the 50th to nearly the 67th degree of N. lat., or about 1150 miles, and sometimes called by the Russians "the back of the world." The central part of this chain abounds in metals, and they contain fine white marble. Pauda, one of the highest mountains, is said to be 4512 feet above the level of the sea. This chain forms a considerable part of the boundary between Europe and Asia.

URALIAN COSSACS, a Tartar tribe that inhabit the Russian province of Orenburg, on the S. side of the river Ural. These Cossacs are descended from those of the Don, and are a valiant race. They profess the Greek religion, but they are dissenters from the established religion, whom the Russians called Roskolniki, or Separatists, and who styled themselves Staroverski, or Old Believers. They consider the service of the established church as profane, and have their own priests and ceremonies. The Uralian Cossacs are all enthusiasts for the ancient ritual, and prize their beards almost equal to their lives. A Russian officer having ordered a number of Cossac recruits to be publicly shaved in the town of Yaitsk, in 1771, this wanton insult excited an insurrection, which was suppressed for a time; but in 1773 an impostor, Pugatchef, who assumed the name of Peter III., appeared among them, and, taking advantage of this circumstance, roused them once more into open rebellion. This was suppressed by the defeat and execution of the impostor; and, in order to extinguish all remembrance of this rebellion, the river Yaik was called the Ural, the Yaik Cossacs were denominated Uralian Cossacs, and the town of Yaitsk was named Uralsk. The Cossacs are very rich, in consequence of their fisheries in the Caspian Sea. Their principal fishery is for sturgeons and beluga, whose roes supply large quantities of caviare; and the fish, chiefly salted and dried, afford a considerable article of consumption in the Russian empire.

URALSK, a town of Russia, capital of the country of the Uralian Cossacs, was formerly called Yaitsk; and is seated on the river Ural, 375 miles N. N. E. of Astracan. Pop. 3600. Long. 50. 10. E. lat. 52. 0. N.

URANIBURG, a once magnificent castle of Denmark, in the island of Huen, now in ruins. It was built by Tycho Brahe, a celebrated astronomer, who called it Uraniburg, or Castle of the Heavens, and here made his observations.

URBANIA, a town of Italy, in the delegation of Urbino, built by Urban VIII., seated on the Metro; 7 miles S. S. W. of Urbino.

URBANNA, a town of Virginia, in Middlesex county, on the Rapahannoc; 73 miles N. E. of Richmond.

URBINO, a delegation of Italy, in the pope's dominions, comprising the greater part of the former duchy of Urbino, with some adjoining districts. The air is not deemed wholesome, nor is the soil fertile. The chief production is silk, and game is plentiful. Pop. 200,000.

URBINO, a city of Italy, capital of the foregoing delegation, and an archbishop's see. The university contains a noble college and 16 convents. Great quantities of fine earthenware are made here; and it is famous for being the birthplace of the illustrious painter Raphael. It stands on a hill, 58 miles E. of Florence, and 120 N. of Rome. Pop. 10,800. Long. 12. 40. E. lat. 43. 46. N.

URE, a river in Yorkshire, which rises on the confines of Westmoreland, flows by Middleham, Ripon, Boroughbridge, and Aldborough, and a little below joins the Swale, where the united stream forms the Ouse.

UREDEN, a town of Prussian Westphalia, in the government of Munster, with manufactures of excellent linen; seated on the Berckel, 26 miles W. N. W. of Munster.

URGEL, a town of Spain, in Catalonia, and a bishop's see. It is seated on the Segra, in a fertile plain, surrounded by mountains planted with vineyards; 78 miles N. N. W. of Barcelona. Long. 1. 28. E. lat. 42. 24. N.

URGHENZ, a town of Tartary, in Kharasm, of which it was formerly the capital; seated on a small river which runs into the lake Aral, 90 miles N. N. W. of Khiva. Long. 58. 30. E. lat. 42. 24. N.

URI, a canton of Switzerland, 30 miles long, and 12 broad; bounded on the N. by the canton of Schweitz and the Waldstadter See, E. by the cantons of Grisons and Glarus, S. by the bailiwicks of Italy, and W. by the cantons of Underwalden and Bern. It has an area of 640 square miles, with 15,000 inhabitants. Altorf is the capital. *See* SCHWEITZ.

URI, LAKE OF. *See* WALDSTADTER SEE.

URSEREN, a town of Switzerland, in the canton of Uri; situate on the Reuss, 17 miles S. S. E. of Altorf.

URSITZ, ST., a town in Switzerland, in the canton of Bern; indebted for its origin to a hermitage, built in the 7th century by St. Ursinius. It is seated on the Doubs, 6 miles S. of Porentrui.

URUGUAY, a province of South America, in the Argentine republic; bounded on the N. by Guayra, S. by the river La Plata, E. by the province del Rey, and W. by the river Parana; 600 miles long, by 400 broad. It is divided by the river Uruguay, which flows from N. to S. through it, and falls into the Plata, 25 miles N. W. of Colonia. It is inhabited by Indians, and is well wooded, and has good pastures.

URUMEA, or ORMIA, a great lake of Persia, in the province of Azerbijan, about 47 miles long, and 25 broad. Its depth does not exceed six feet, and is in some parts not more than one foot. The waters are extremely salt, and emit sulphureous vapours. It receives 14 rivers, and has no outlet. There are several islands, which are increased in the dry season.

URUMEA, a town from which the preceding lake is named, on its S. W. shore, on a noble plain watered by the Shur; 90 miles S. S. W. of Tabriz. It is walled, and contains 12,000 inhabitants.

USBEC TARTARY, a vast country of Western Tartary; bounded on the N. by the country of the Kalmucs and Turkestan, E. by Tibet, S. by Hindostan and Persia, and W. by the Caspian Sea. These Tartars are divided into several tribes, governed by their respective khans, or princes. When under one sovereign, they were the most powerful of all the Tartarian nations. The principal khans pride themselves in being descended from Tamerlane, whose birthplace was the ancient city of Samarcand. The Usbecs, in their persons, are said to have better complexions and more engaging features than the Kalmucs. Their religion is Mahomedism, and they differ, in general, very little from the people of the northern provinces of Hindostan.

USEDOM, an island of the Prussian states, in Pomerania, in the Baltic Sea, between the mouths of the Peene and Swin; with two forts named after these two rivers. Pop. 12,000. It has a town of the same name, on the S. W. coast; 40 miles N. W. of Stettin. Pop. 1000. Long. 14. 2. E. lat. 53. 58. N.

USHANT, an island of France, on the coast of the department of Finisterre, opposite Conquet. It is 8 miles in circumference, and contains several hamlets and a castle. Pop. 1700. Long. 5. 5. W. lat. 48. 28. N.

USINGEN, a town of Germany, in the duchy of Nassau. It has a handsome castle. It is seated on the Usbach; 12 miles S. S. E. of Wielburg.

USK, a river which rises in Wales, on the W. side of Brecknockshire, flows by Brecknock, and, entering Monmouthshire, passes by Abergavenny, Usk, Caerleon, and Newport, into the Bristol Channel.

USK, a town in Monmouthshire, with a market on Friday, and a manufacture of japanned-ware. It returns one member to parliament, in conjunction with Monmouth, &c. Here are the ruins of a castle and priory; part of the latter is converted into a farm-house, and its church is now the parish church. It is seated on the river Usk; 12 miles S. W. of Monmouth, and 142 W. by N. of London.

USKUP. *See* SCOPIA.

USSEL, a town of France, department of Correze; 32 miles N. E. of Tulle, and 53 E. S. E. of Limoges.

USTARITZ, a town in the department of Lower Pyrenees; 6 miles S. S. E. of Bayonne.

USTICA, a small island in the Mediterranean, 25 miles N. of the coast of Sicily. It was for centuries uninhabited, except by wild goats, till, in the year 1765, a citadel was built and a colony settled. The island is without springs, and its only supply of fresh water consists of rain kept in cisterns. Long. 13. 26. E. lat. 38. 42. N.

USTING, a town of Russia, in the government of Vologda; capital of a large district of its name, and an archbishop's see. Great quantities of grain are sent hence to different parts. It is seated on the Dwina, 464 miles N. E. of Moscow.

UTICA, a city of North America, New York, on the S. bank of the Mohawk. It is the commercial capital in the W. part of the state; 93 miles W. by N. of Albany. Pop. 12,782.

UTRECHT, one of the Dutch provinces, 30 miles long, and 20 broad; bounded on the N. and W. by Holland and the Zuyder Zee, and E. and S. by Guelderland. The soil is fertile, and there are no inundations to fear, as in the other provinces. Area, 490 square miles. Pop. 110,000.

UTRECHT, a fortified city of the Netherlands, capital of the foregoing province, with a famous university. It is of a square form, about 3 miles in circumference, exclusive of the suburbs, which are considerable. The inhabitants are estimated at 35,000. The most distinguished of the public buildings is the cathedral, the tower of which is very lofty, and said to be one of the handsomest in the kingdom. The town-house is also a noble building, and there are a great many churches and hospitals, schools for the fine arts, a hall of paintings, several valuable libraries, &c. The principal manufactures are silk and fire-arms; and in a palace called the Mall is an extensive foundry for cannon-balls. Two canals, called the New Graft and the Vaert, run through the city, and over them are 36 stone bridges. The environs are full of gardens, walks, and groves, which, added to the purity of the air, render Utrecht one of the most agreeable places for residence in these parts. Here the union of the Seven United Provinces was begun in 1579; and here was concluded, in 1713, the peace which terminated the wars of Queen Anne. Utrecht surrendered to the Prussians in 1787, and to the French in 1795, each time without resistance. It is seated on the Rhine; 18 miles S. E. of Amsterdam, and 35 N. N. W. of Nimeguen. Long. 5. 8. E. lat. 52. 6. N.

UTRERA, a town of Spain, in Andalusia, near which is a salt-spring; 21 miles S. of Seville. Pop. 9000.

UTTOXETER, a town of Staffordshire, with a market on Wednesday, and manufactures of cabinet-ware, and a considerable trade in corn and cheese. The parish church, the body of which has been recently rebuilt, is a spacious Gothic edifice. The other places of worship are two meeting-houses for Methodists, and one for Quakers. It is seated on a rising ground, near the river Dove; 14 miles N. E. of Stafford, and 135 N. N. W. of London.

UTZNACH, a town of Switzerland, capital of a bailiwick belonging to the cantons of Schweitz and Glarus. It is 8 miles N. from the Lake of Zürich, and 15 N. by W. of Glarus.

UXBRIDGE, a town in Middlesex, with a market on Thursday, and a great trade in corn and flour. The Coln flows through it in two streams, and the Grand Junction Canal passes close by. A treaty was carried on here between Charles I. and the parliament in 1644; and the house in which the plenipotentiaries met is still called the Treaty-house. Near this town are the remains of an ancient camp. Uxbridge is 15 miles W. by N. of London.

UXBRIDGE, a town of Massachusetts, in Worcester county; 16 miles S. by E. of Worcester, and 40 S. by W. of Boston.

UZEL, a town of France, department of Cotes du Nord; 17 miles S. W. of St. Brieux.

UZERCHE, a town in the department of Correze; 10 miles N. N. W. of Tulle, and 36 S. S. E. of Limoges.

UZES, a town in the department of Gard, with a spring that supplies the aqueduct of Nismes. It is seated in a country abounding in corn, oil, silk, and good wine; 12 miles N. of Nismes. Pop. 6400.

V.

Vaast, St., a town of France, department of Manche; with a small harbour and some salt-works; 14 miles E. S. E. of Cherburg.

Vabres, a town in the department of Aveiron. It has manufactures of serges, dimities, and cottons. It stands at the confluence of two small rivers that flow into the Tarn; 30 miles S. S. E. of Rodez, and 32 E. of Alby.

Vacha, a town of Germany, in Saxe-Weimar; on the river Werra; 16 miles W. S. W. of Eisenach.

Vache, an island of the West Indies, of a triangular form; 24 miles in circuit. It is 12 miles from the S. coast of St. Domingo, opposite St. Louis.

Vacheluse, one of the Lipari Islands; 3 miles S. of Stromboli.

Vada, a town of Tuscany, at the mouth of the Cecina; 26 miles S. S. E. of Leghorn.

Vadacurray, or Vadaghery, a town of Hindostan, in Malabar; with a neat fort on the top of a hill. It is a place of considerable trade, and stands on the seacoast, at the N. end of a long inland navigation; 12 miles S. S. E. of Tellichery.

Vadin, a town of Bessarabia, situate on the Danube; 92 miles W. of Nicopoli.

Vado, a town of the Sardinian states, in the territory of Genoa, on a bay of the Mediterranean; 3 miles S. of Savona, and 24 S. W. of Genoa.

Vadestein, a town of Sweden, in East Gothland; where the kings of Sweden had a palace, now in ruins. It is seated on the Lake Wetter, near the river Motala; 32 miles W. of Nordkioping.

Vadutz, a town and castle of Germany, in the principality of Lichtenstein; 26 miles S. of Lindau.

Vaena, a town of Spain, in Andalusia; seated on the Castro; 23 miles S. E. of Cordova.

Vaigatch. *See* Waigatz.

Vaihend, a town of Persia, in Segestan, on a river of the same name; 40 miles E. S. E. of Arokhage.

Vaihingen, a town of Germany, in Wirtemburg, seated on the Enz; 18 miles N. N. W. of Stutgard.

Vaison, a town of France, department of Vaucluse; noted as the birthplace of Trogus Pompeius, the Roman historian. It is seated on a mountain, near the river Oreze, and the ruins of ancient Vaison, which was one of the largest cities of the Gauls; 22 miles N. E. of Avignon, and 23 S. S. E. of Montelimar.

Val, a village of the Netherlands, 3 miles W. of Maestricht; where, in 1744, Marshal Saxe obtained a victory over the Duke of Cumberland.

Val di Demona, a province in the N. E. angle of Sicily. It means the valley of demons, and is so called because Mount Ætna is situate in this province, which occasioned ignorant and superstitious people, at the time of its fiery eruptions, to believe it was a chimney of hell. The capital is Messina.

Val di Mazara, a province in the W. angle of Sicily, so called from the town of Mazara. It contains Palermo, the capital of the whole island.

Val di Noto, a province in the S. E. angle of Sicily; so called from the town of Noto, its capital.

Valais, a canton of Switzerland, which consists of a valley 100 miles long, and 20 broad, between ridges of very high mountains, among which are the Great St. Bernard, Simplon, Grimsel, Furca, and others, whose summits are never free from snow. The S. chain separates it from the Milanese, Piedmont, and Savoy; the N. divides it from the canton of Bern. The country is divided into Upper and Lower Valais. The former reaches from Mount Furca, its E. boundary, to the river Morge, below Sion, and the latter from that river to St. Gingou, on the Lake of Geneva. A country consisting of plains, elevated valleys, and lofty mountains, must necessarily exhibit a great variety of climates and prospects. The productions must vary also according to its singular diversity of climates; for strawberries, cherries, plums, pears, and grapes in their natural growth, may be tasted in the same day. It has more than sufficient wine and corn for interior consumption; the soil in the midland and lower districts being exceedingly rich and fertile; but in the more elevated parts barley is the only grain that can be cultivated with success. The inhabitants profess the Roman Catholic religion, and the lower class are extremely indolent and dirty; they have no manufactures of any consequence. In 1802 the Valais was constituted an independent republic, under the guarantee of France, Switzerland, and Italy; but in 1814 it was annexed to Switzerland. Area, 1850 square miles. Pop. 60,000. Sion is the capital.

Valckowar, a town of Sclavonia, seated on the Walpo, near its confluence with the Danube; 70 miles W. N. W. of Belgrade.

Valdai, a town of Russia, in the government of Novogorod; on the side of a lake of the same name. The lake is 20 miles in circumference, and has an island in the middle, on which is a convent surrounded by trees. The town contains several brick buildings; and the wooden houses are more decorated than the generality of Russian cottages. It is 72 miles S. E. of Novogorod. Pop. 3100. Long. 33. 44. E. lat. 57. 50. N.

Valdasnes, a town of Portugal, in Tras los Montes, 9 miles E. S. E. of Mirandela.

Valdeburon, a town of Spain, in Leon; near the source of the Esla; 38 miles N. E. of Leon.

Valdecabras, a town of Spain, in New Castile; 10 miles N. N. E. of Cuenza.

Valdecona, a town of Spain, in Catalonia; 15 miles S. by W. of Tortosa.

Valdemoro, a town of Spain, in New Castile; 13 miles S. of Madrid.

Valdepennas, a town of Spain, province of La Mancha; with a manufacture of soap and excellent red wine; 113 miles S. of Madrid. Pop. 8000.

Valdivia, or **Baldivia**, a seaport of Chili; built in 1552, by the Spanish General Valdivia, after he had conquered the country. It is surrounded by walls built of earth, and defended by several forts and batteries; the entrance of the harbour has also numerous pieces of cannon on each side. In the vicinity are many gold mines. It stands on a bay of the Pacific Ocean; 200 miles S. of Conception. Long. 73. 10. W. lat. 39. 40. S.

Valence, a city of France, capital of the department of Drome, and a bishop's see; with a citadel, and a school of artillery. It is surrounded by walls; and the greatest part of the public places, and many private houses, are adorned with fountains. Besides the handsome cathedral, there are many other churches, as well as convents. It is seated on the Rhone; 30 miles N. by E. of Viviers, and 335 S. by E. of Paris. Long. 4. 52. E. lat. 44. 55. N.

Valence, a town of France, department of Lot-et-Garonne, on the river Garonne; 12 miles S. E. of Agen.

Valencia, a province of Spain, formerly a kingdom; bounded on the N. by Arragon, N. E. by Catalonia, E. by the Mediterranean, S. and S. W. by Murcia, and W. by New Castile. It is 220 miles long, and from 20 to 60 broad, with a population of 800,000, and the most pleasant and populous country in Spain; for here they enjoy a perpetual spring. It is watered by a great number of streams, and fertile in all the necessaries of life, especially fruits, oil, and wine. In the mountains are mines of iron and alum, and quarries of marble, jasper, and lapis calaminaris. Here is also much silk, cotton, and hemp; the manufactures of which are the cause of a considerable population.

Valencia, a city of Spain, capital of the above province, and an archbishop's see; with a university. The Moors were expelled from it in the 12th century. It was taken by the Earl of Peterborough in 1705, and lost again in two years after. In 1811 it was taken by the French under Suchet, with a garrison of 16,000 men, and immense stores. It contains 12,000 houses within the walls, besides those in the suburbs and pleasure gardens around it, which amount to the same number. The cathedral has a steeple 130 feet high; and one side of the choir is incrusted with alabaster, and adorned with fine paintings of scripture history. The palace of the viceroy, that of Ciuta, the monastery of St. Jerome, the exchange, and the arsenal, are all worthy of notice. Here are manufactures of cloth and silk, and several remains of antiquity. It is seated on the Guadalavia, near the Mediterranean, 130 miles E. S. E. of Madrid. Pop. 80,000. Long. 0. 24. W. lat. 39. 27. N.

Valencia, a town of South America, in Venezuela, republic of Colombia; seated on the lake Tocarigua; 57 miles S. W. of Porto Cavallo. Pop. 8000. Long. 65. 30. W. lat. 9. 50. N.

Valencia d'Alcantara, a town of Spain, in Estremadura, with an old castle. It is surrounded by walls, and stands on a rock, near the frontiers of Portugal; 28 miles S. W. of Alcantara, and 45 N. N. W. of Badajoz.

Valenciennes, a city of France, in the department of Nord; seated on the Scheldt, which flows through it in several branches, and here begins to be navigable. It is large and populous, but the streets are narrow and crooked, and many of the houses are of wood. The citadel and fortifications were constructed by order of Louis XIV., who took this town from the Spaniards; and it was confirmed to him by the treaty of Nimeguen in 1678. In 1793 it was taken by the allies, under the Duke of York, after a severe siege. But in 1794 it again surrendered to the French by capitulation, and was confirmed to them by the treaties of 1814 and 1815. Besides lace, this city is noted for manufactures of woollen stuffs and cambric. It is 28 miles S. E. of Lisle, and 120 N. N. E. of Paris. Pop. 17,000. Long. 3. 32. E. lat. 50. 21. N.

Valentine, a town of France, in the department of Upper Garonne; 9 miles N. E. of St Bertrand.

Valenza, a town of Austrian Italy, in the government of Milan; seated on a mountain, near the river Po; 12 miles E. S. E. of Casal and 35 S. S. W. of Milan.

Valenza, a fortified town of Portugal, in Entre Douro e Minho; seated on an eminence near the river Minho, opposite Tuy, in Spain, and 30 miles N. N. W. of Braga.

Valery, St., a town of France, in the department of Somme, on the river Somme. Here William the Conqueror embarked, in 1066, for England; 50 miles N. W. of Amiens. Pop. 3200.

Valery en Caux, St., a town of France, in the department of Lower Seine, with considerable fisheries and trade; 33 miles N. by W. of Rouen. Pop. 5000.

Valetta, a city of Malta, the capital of that island, and wonderfully strong both by nature and art. It is seated on a peninsula, between two of the finest ports in the world, which are defended by almost impregnable fortifications. Valetta has three gates, and the streets are all paved with flat square stones. The houses are neat, and built of stone, the rooms forming a flat terrace, plastered with pozzolana, and most of them have a balcony to the street, where the inhabitants pass a great part of their time. The principal buildings are the palace of the grand master, the infirmary, the conservatory, and the magnificent church of St. John. The pavement of this church is composed entirely of sepulchral monuments of the finest marbles, porphyry, lapis lazuli, and a variety of other valuable stones, admirably joined together, representing the arms, insignia, &c., of the persons whose names they commemorate. The great source of water that supplies Valetta rises near Citta Vecchia, and is thence conveyed by an aqueduct, erected at the expense of one of the grand masters. Valetta is situate opposite Cape Passero, in Sicily. Pop. 36,000. Long. 15. 34. E. lat. 35. 54. N.

VALETTE, a town of France, in the department of Charente; 12 miles S. by E. of Angouleme.

VALKENBURG, or FAUQUEMONT, a town of the Netherlands, in Limburg. In 1672 it was taken by the French, who demolished the fortifications. It is seated on the Geule; 8 miles E. by N. of Maestricht. Long. 5. 58. E. lat. 51. 0. N.

VALLADOLID, a city of Spain, in Leon, capital of a province of the same name, and a bishop's see, with a university. It has long and broad streets, and is adorned with handsome buildings, squares, and fountains. The market-place, called El Campo, is 700 paces in circumference, surrounded by a great number of convents. There are numerous monasteries and nunneries, the finest of which is that of the Dominicans, remarkable for its church, which is one of the most magnificent in the city. The kings formerly resided at this place; and the royal palace, which still remains, is of very large extent, though but two stories high. The town-house takes up the entire side of a square. Here are some woollen manufactures, and many goldsmiths and jewellers. The environs of the city are covered with gardens, orchards, vineyards, meadows, and fields. Valladolid was taken and retaken several times by the French and Spaniards, during the late peninsular war. It is seated on the Escurva, near the Pisuerga; 74 miles S. S. E. of Leon, and 100 N. N. W. of Madrid. Pop. 20,000. Long. 4. 47. W. lat. 41. 42. N.

VALLADOLID, a province of the republic of Mexico, bounded N. by the Rio de Lerma, S. by the Pacific, W. by New Galicia, and E. by Mexico Proper. It is very rich, abounding in all the necessaries of life; and the climate in general is mild and salubrious. At the period of the Spanish conquest, this province formed part of the kingdom of Mechoacan, which was independent of the ancient Mexican empire. Area, 10,338 square miles. Population, 376,400.

VALLADOLID, or MECHOACAN, a city of Mexico, capital of the foregoing province, with a fine cathedral, and some handsome houses; situate on a river, near its source; 120 miles W. of Mexico. Pop. 18,000.

VALLADOLID, or COMAYAGUA, a city of South America, capital of Honduras, seated in a plain; 280 miles E. of Guatimala. Long. 88. 20. W. lat. 14. 35. N.

VALLELONGA, a town of Naples, in Calabria Ultra; 18 miles E. N. E. of Nicotera.

VALLENCAY, a town of France, in the department of Indre, on the Nabon; 28 miles N. by W. of Chateauroux.

VALLENGIN, a town of Switzerland, in a county of its name, united to the principality of Neufchatel. It is seated on the Seyon; 3 miles N. N. W. of Neufchatel.

VALLERS, a town of France, in the department of Indre-et-Loire, noted for its mineral waters; 4 miles N. W. of Tours.

VALLIER, ST., a town in the department of Drome; near the river Rhone; 18 miles N. of Valence.

VALOGNE, a town in the department of La Manche, noted for cloth and leather; 10 miles S. S. E. of Cherburg, and 50 W. N. W. of Caen. Pop. 7000.

VALONA, or AVLONA, a seaport of Albania, and an archbishop's see; seated at the entrance of the Gulf of Venice, near the mountains of Chimera; 50 miles S. of Durazzo. Long. 19. 40. E. lat. 40. 54. N.

VALPARAISO, a seaport of Chili, with a well-frequented harbour, defended by a strong fort. Its proximity to St. Jago has drawn hither all the commerce formerly carried on between that city and Callao, which consists principally of wheat, tallow, leather, cordage, and dried fruits. It is seated on a bay of the Pacific Ocean, at the foot of a high mountain; 75 miles N. W. of St. Jago. Long. 72. 19. W. lat. 33. 3. S.

VALPERGA, a town of the Sardinian States, in Piedmont; 16 miles N. of Turin.

VALREAS, a town of France, in the department of Vaucluse; 18 miles N. E. of Orange.

VALS, a town in the department of Ardeche, celebrated for mineral springs, seated on the Ardeche; 18 miles N. W. of Viviers.

VALTELINE, or VALLE-TELINO, a fertile valley of Austrian Italy, 50 miles long, and from 12 to 15 broad, enclosed between two chains of high mountains; the N. chain separates it from the Grisons, the S. from the Venetian territories; on the E. it is bounded by the county of Bormio, and on the W. by that of Chiavana. The river Adda flows through its whole length into the lake Como; and it is divided into three districts, Upper, Middle, and Lower. The inhabitants are all Roman Catholics, and have no manufactures; but they export wine, silk, plants, cheese, butter, and cattle. On the 20th of July, 1620, there was a general massacre of the protestants in this valley. Chief town, Sondio. Pop. 81,000.

VALVA, a town of Naples, in Abruzzo Citra; 18 miles S. S. W. of Civita di Chieti.

VAN, a strong town of Curdistan, with a castle on a mountain, in which the Turks keep a numerous garrison. It is governed by a beglerbeg, and seated on a lake of its name, 120 miles in circumference; 80 miles E. by S. of Betlis. Pop. 50,000. Long. 44. 30. E. lat. 37. 10. N.

VANDALIA, a town of North America, in the state of Illinois, of which it has been selected as the capital, and a court-house and other government offices have been recently erected. It is seated on the river Kaskasia; 55 miles from St. Louis.

VAN DIEMEN'S LAND, or TASMANIA, is between 40. and 44. S. lat., and 144. and 149. E. long. It is about 210 miles long from N. to S., and 150 from E. to W., and contains an area of 23,437 square miles, or 14,999,680 acres, a very large proportion of which is unfit for cultivation. It was discovered by A. J. Tasman, on Dec. 1st, 1642, and named by him after the Dutch governor-general of the East Indies. It was not again visited till 1773, when Captain Furneaux passed the E. coast; and in 1777 Captain Cook landed on Bruné Island. It is also probable that the ill-fated La Perouse touched here in 1788. It was partially explored by the French expeditions under D'Entrecasteaux, in 1792 and 1793. Up to this time it was supposed to form part of the continent of Australia, till, in 1797, Bass Strait, which separates it, was discovered by Captain Flinders, upon whose representations, and the fear of the French forming an establishment on it, a party under Lieutenant Bowen settled at Risdon, in August, 1803, 5 miles from the present Hobart Town; and here the first encounter with the natives took place, in which some of them were killed. This place was abandoned for that of Hobart Town, in 1804, under Lieutenant-governor Collins. For several years the colonists endured the greatest privations, being sometimes compelled to subsist on the flesh of the kangaroo, and a species of seaweed. In 1810 a great number of cattle and sheep were introduced. From 1813 the whole colony was in a state of alarm from the atrocities of the bush-rangers, or escaped convicts, which led to the establishment of martial law for a time, and confidence was again restored on the capture and death of the ringleaders. On June 14, 1825, Van Diemen's Land was declared to be independent of the government of New South Wales, under which the administration was hitherto carried on by a lieutenant-governor. The existence of the colony was now threatened by the aborigines, who had ever shown a hostile spirit toward the settlers, and which had increased to such an extent that life and property were equally unsafe; this led to active measures on the part of the colonists, in 1830, but which were ineffectual; but at the latter end of that year, a number of them were induced, by the humane endeavours of Mr. Robinson, to accompany him to Swan Island, and afterwards to King's Island, in Bass Strait, where they are now domesticated; and thus the greatest drawback on the colony has been removed. It was made the diocese of a bishop in 1842. The colonized part of Van Diemen's Land is divided into eleven counties, viz., Kent, Buckingham, Pembroke, Monmouth, Cumberland, Somerset, Glamorgan, Westmoreland, Cornwall, Dorset, and Devon. The western side, except on the margins of the rivers, and the N. W. corner, which is occupied by the Van Diemen's Land Agricultural Company, is barren and unfit for agricultural purposes, and is generally covered with forest. The principal rivers are the Derwent, Huon, and Gordon in the S.; and the North and South Esk, Hellyer, and Arthur on the N. On the W. coast is a remarkable land-locked basin, Macquarrie Harbour, 20 miles long, and 5 broad, in which, on Sarah's Island, was a penal settlement, which was left for the penal settlement at Port Arthur, founded in 1830, in a remarkably fine harbour, between Cape Raoul and Cape Pillar, formed of basaltic columns, similar to the Giant's Causeway, in Ireland. The chief mountains are St. Valentine's Peak; Ben Lomond, 4200 feet; Peak of Teneriffe, 4500 feet; Mount Wellington, 3750 feet, &c.; and many in the S. W. which are covered with snow for a great part of the year. The chief towns are Hobart Town, or Hobarton, the capital; Launceston, George Town, New Norfolk, Campbell Town, and Perth. The staple production is wool, which is of superior quality, and principally exported to England; besides which, wheat, oats, and the usual European crops are cultivated with success. The wild animals are five species of kangaroos, now becoming scarce; the opossum, and other marsupial animals, similar to those of Australia. The black whale resorts to its shores, and forms a lucrative branch of commerce. Iron ore abounds in most parts, and coal has been found. The climate is capricious, but healthy; the thermometer frequently ranging from 90 deg. and upwards down to 50 deg. in a single day; but it may be generally characterized as warm. The population is about 32,000, including 11,000 convicts, who are spread over an area of 11,760 square miles, or nearly one-half larger than Wales, of which about 60,000 acres are brought into cultivation.

VANIAM BADY, a town of Hindostan, in Mysore; 55 miles W. S. W. of Arcot, and 130 E. of Seringapatam.

VANNES, a seaport of France, capital of the department of Morbihan, and a bishop's see. The principal trade is in corn, bar-iron, and fish. It is seated on the Gulf of Morbihan; 56 miles S. W. of Rennes, and 255 W. by S. of Paris. Pop. 10,500. Long. 2. 46. W. lat. 47. 39. N.

VAR, a department of France, which takes its name from a river that rises in the county of Nice, and enters the Mediterranean 4 miles W. of Nice. The surface is rugged, and the soil very various. It contains an area of 2900 square miles, with 290,000 inhabitants. Toulon is the capital.

VARALLO, a strong town of the Sardinian States, on the frontiers of Piedmont, 33 miles E. of Aosta, and 57 N. N. E. of Turin. Pop. 3300.

VARAMBON, a town of France, in the department of Ain; on the river Ain, 14 miles S. S. E. of Bourg en Bresse.

VATHI, or BATHI, the capital of Ithaca; one of the Ionian islands. It has a port. Pop. 3000.

VERASDIN, a town of Croatia, with a castle and a citadel, situated near the Drave; 65 miles N. N. E. of Carlstadt. Long. 16. 32. E. lat. 46. 25. N.

VARDAR, a river of Greece, which rises in

Mount Scardus, and flows S. through Macedonia, into the Gulf of Salonica.

VARELLA, a cape on the E. coast of the kingdom of Ciampa. Behind it is a mountain, remarkable for having a high rock like a tower on its summit. Long. 109. 17. E. lat. 12. 50. N.

VARENNES, a town of France, department of Allier, seated on an eminence near the river Allier; 20 miles S. of Moulins.

VARENNES, a town in the department of Meuse, where Louis XVI., his queen, sister, and two children, were arrested in their flight from the Tuileries, in 1791, and conducted back to Paris. It is 13 miles W. by N. of Verdun.

VARESE, a town of Austrian Italy, in the government of Milan. It is 30 miles N. W. of Milan.

VARHELY, a town of Transylvania; 40 miles S. of Weissenburg.

VARNA, a seaport of Bulgaria, and an archbishop's see; seated near the mouth of the Varna, in the Black Sea. It is 22 miles N. of Mesembria, and 145 N. W. of Constantinople. Long. 27. 48. E. lat. 45. 48. N.

VARZEY, a town of France, department of Nievre; 24 miles N. of Nevers.

VASIL, a town of Russia, in the government of Novogorod, situate on the Volga. It is 60 miles E. of Novogorod. Long. 45. 44. E. lat. 56. 16. N.

VASSALBOROUGH, a town of the state of Maine, in Lincoln county. It is seated on the Kennebeck, 9 miles N. of Hallowell. Population, 2761.

VASSY, a town of France, department of Upper Marne, where, in 1562, a bloody persecution of the protestants began, by order of the duke of Guise. It is seated on the Blaise; 10 miles N. W. of Joinville.

VATAN, a town in the department of Indre, 8 miles N. W. of Issoudun.

VATICA, a seaport of the Morea, situate on a large bay, to which it gives name. It is 44 miles S. E. of Misitra. Long. 23. 2. E. lat. 36. 38. N.

VAUCLUSE, a department of France, including the county of Venaissin and territory of Avignon. The superficial extent is estimated at 1400 square miles, with 210,000 inhabitants. It takes its name from the fountain of Vaucluse, 12 miles E. of Avignon, celebrated by Petrarch. The chief town is Avignon.

VAUCOULEURS, a town of France, department of Meuse; seated on the side of a hill on the river Meuse. It is 23 miles S. E. of Bar le Duc.

VAUD, PAYS DE. *See* PAYS.

VAUDEMONT, a town of France, department of Meurthe; 18 miles S. by W. of Nancy.

VAUVILLE, a town in the department of Manche, on a bay to which it gives name; 9 miles W. of Cherburg.

VAYPURA, a town of Hindostan, in Malabar, seated at the mouth of a fine river, down which much teak timber is floated. It is 7 miles S. of Calicut.

VECHT, a river that rises in Westphalia, near Munster, crosses the counties of Stenfort and Bentheim, and, entering Overyssel, passes by Ommen, Hasselt, and Swartsluys, below which it enters the Zuyder Zee.

VECHT, a river of Holland, which branches off from the old channel of the Rhine at Utrecht, and enters the Zuyder Zee at Muyden.

VECHTA, a town and fortress of Germany, in the principality of Oldenburg; seated on a river of the same name; 27 miles S. of Oldenburg, and 35 N. N. E. of Osnaburg.

VEDENSKOI, a town of Russia, in the government of Archangel; situate on the Vokscha, 200 miles S. S. E. of Archangel. Long. 46. 44. E. lat. 58. 45. N.

VEERE. *See* TERVERE.

VEGA, a town of Spain, in Asturias, near the coast; 34 miles N. W. of Oviedo.

VEGA, a town of Spain, in the province of Leon; 22 miles N. N. E. of Leon.

VEGAYMAN, a town of Spain, in the province of Leon; 28 miles N. N. E. of Leon.

VEGLIA, an island in the Gulf of Venice, on the coast of Dalmatia. It is 90 miles in circuit, rocky, and badly cultivated, but it produces wine and silk, and has small horses, in high esteem. Pop. 10,000. The town, of the same name, has a good harbour, a strong citadel, and is the see of a bishop. Pop. 1200. Long. 14. 56. E. lat. 45. 22. N.

VEGLIANA, a town of the Sardinian states, in Piedmont; seated on an eminence near the river Doria; 12 miles N. W. of Turin.

VEH, a town of Hindostan, in Moultan, seated at the junction of the Setledge with the Indus; 63 miles S. S. W. of Moultan. Long. 70. 5. E. lat. 29. 8. N.

VEIROS, a town of Portugal, in Alentejo; seated on the Anhaloura; 10 miles S. S. W. of Portalegre.

VEISENBURG, a town of Russia, in the government of Revel, near the Gulf of Finland; 56 miles E. of Revel.

VEIT, ST., a town of Austrian Illyria, in Carinthia, with an old castle; seated at the conflux of the Glan and Wunich, 8 miles N. of Clagenfurt.

VELA, a cape on the N. coast of Terra Firma; 160 miles E. N. E. of St. Martha. Long. 71. 25. W. lat. 12. 30. N.

VELAY, a district of France, which is full of high mountains, covered with snow the greater part of the year, but abounds in cattle. It forms a part of the department of Upper Loire.

VELBURG, a town of Bavaria, in the principality of Neuburg, with a decayed castle; 22 miles N. W. of Ratisbon.

VELDENTZ, a town of Prussia, in the province of Lower Rhine, with a castle. The environs produce excellent Moselle wine. It is seated on the Moselle, 16 miles N. E. of Treves.

VELETRI, a town of Italy, in Campagna di Roma, the residence of the bishop of Ostia, whose palace is magnificent, and there are large squares adorned with fine fountains. It is seated on an eminence, 18 miles S. E. of Rome. Pop. 12,000.

VELEZ DE GOMARA, a seaport of the kingdom of Fez, with a castle, seated between two high mountains on the Mediterranean; 120 miles N. N. E. of Fez. Long. 4. 0. W. lat. 55. 10. N.

VELEZ MALAGA, a town of Spain, in Granada, seated in a large plain, between two rivers, near the Mediterranean; 13 miles E. by N. of Malaga, and 62 N. W. of Granada. Pop. 15,000.

VELIKA, a town of Sclavonia, on the river Bakawa; 10 miles E. of Cruetz, and 60 N. W. of Fosega.

VELORE, a town of Hindostan, in the Carnatic, with a large and beautiful fort, strongly garrisoned by English forces. The town is pretty large, and well built. Above it are three small forts on as many hills. It is seated in a fine valley, on the Paliar; 14 miles W. of Arcot.

VELTZEN. *See* ULTZEN.

VENAFRO, a town of Naples, in Terra di Lavoro; 25 miles N. by W. of Capua.

VENAISSIN, a small but fertile district of France, now included in the department of Vaucluse.

VENANT, ST., a town of France, department of Pas de Calais, on the river Lis. It is 6 miles N. by W. of Bethune, and 27 S. E. of Dunkirk.

VENASQUE, a town of Spain, in Arragon, in a valley of the same name, and on the river Essarn; 47 miles N. N. E. of Balbastro.

VENASQUE, a town of France, department of Vaucluse, on the river Nasque; 10 miles E. S. E. of Carpentras, and 18 E. N. E. of Avignon.

VENCATICHERY, a town of Hindostan, in the E. part of Mysore, ceded to the English by the treaty of Seringapatam. Here are the remains of the rajah's palace, and the ruins of a fort. Near this place iron is smelted from black sand. It is 57 miles W. of Arcot, and 58 E. of Bangalore.

VENCE, a town of France, department of Var; 9 miles N. of Antibes, and 9 W. of Nice.

VENDEE, a department of France, including part of the former province of Poitou. It is so called from a small river of the same name. The surface is level and the soil fertile. It contains an area of 2600 square miles, with 280,000 inhabitants. Bourbon Vendee is the capital.

VENDEN, a town of Russia, in the government of Riga, on the river Aa; 36 miles E. N. E. of Riga.

VENDOME, a town of France, department of Loir-et-Cher, on the river Loire; 30 miles N. E. of Tours, and 95 S. W. of Paris. Pop. 8000.

VENDRELL, a town of Spain, in Catalonia; 25 miles W. S. W. of Barcelona.

VENERIA, a town of Piedmont, which took its name from a magnificent hunting-seat built by a duke of Savoy. It has manufactures of wool and silk. It stands on the Stura, 8 miles N. N. W. of Turin.

VENEZUELA, a province of the republic of Colombia; bounded E. by the province of Cumana, W. by Maracaybo, N. by the Caribbean Sea, and S. by the plains of Varinas and the Orinoco. It spreads round a gulf of the same name (which reaches 90 miles within land, and is 80 in breadth), and the lake of Maracaybo. When the Spaniards landed here in 1499, they observed some huts built upon piles in an Indian village named Coro, in order to raise them above the stagnated water that covered the plain: and this induced them to give it the name of Venezuela, or Little Venice. Near the seacoast are high mountains, the tops of which are barren, but the lower parts in the valley are fertile, and gold is found in the sands of the rivers. The province is said to contain 100,000 inhabitants, who raise great numbers of sheep, manufacture some cotton stuffs, and cultivate excellent tobacco, cocoa, and sugar. Leon de Caraccas is the capital.

VENICE, formerly a celebrated republic of Italy, the government of which was aristocratic, for none could have any share in it but the nobles. The doge was elected by a plurality of votes, obtained in a peculiar manner by means of gold and silver balls; and after his election the ducal cap was placed on his head with great ceremony, on his public entrance into St. Mark's church. He held his dignity for life, and his office was to marry the Adriatic Sea, in the name of the republic; to preside in all assemblies of the state; to have an eye over all the members of the magistracy; and to nominate to all the benefices annexed to the church of St. Mark. On the other hand, his power was so limited, that he has been justly defined to be, in habit and state, a king; in authority a counsellor; in the city a prisoner; and out of it a private person. There were five councils: the first was called La Signoria, composed of the doge and six counsellors. The second was Il Consiglio Grande, in which all the nobles, amounting to 2500, had a voice. The third was Il Consiglio dei Pregadi, consisting of about 250 of the nobility. The fourth was Il Consiglio Proprio, which was united to the Signoria: its members consisted of 28 assessors; this council gave audience to the ambassadors. The fifth and last was Il Consiglio dei Dieci, composed of ten counsellors, took notice of all criminal matters; and the doge himself, when accused, was obliged to appear before them: there was no appeal from this council, which was a severe state inquisition. This constitution, however, no longer exists. In 1797, a tumult having happened at Venice, in which some French soldiers were killed, the French seized the city, and instituted a provisionary democratic government; but soon after, by the treaty of Campo Formio, the city and territory of Venice, lying to the N. and W. of the river Adige, was ceded to Austria as a duchy, in equivalence for the dominions that house had lost in the Netherlands; and the remainder of the territory was annexed to what the French then styled the Cisalpine republic. In 1805 commenced a short war between Austria and France, and, by the treaty of peace at Presburg, the duchy of Venice was given up, and the whole territory of Venice was annexed to the kingdom of Italy The Austrians, however, took possession of this country in 1814. The Venetian territories on the continent, enumerated above, (and which, by way of distinction, are sometimes called the Terra Firma,) are described in their respective places. Venice was once one of the most powerful commercial and maritime states in Europe. For this it was indebted, at first, to the monopoly of the commerce of India; the products of that country being conveyed, in the middle ages, up the Gulf of Persia, the Euphrates, and the Tigris, as far as Bagdad; thence by land, across the desert, to Palmyra; and thence to the Mediterranean ports; and afterwards the supplying of the crusaders with provisions and military stores was an additional source of opulence and power. All this declined, however, after the discovery of the Cape of Good Hope by the Portuguese, in 1486; which, in its consequences, has reduced Venice from a state of the highest splendour to comparative insignificance. The Venetians are lively and ingenious, extravagantly fond of amusements, with an uncommon relish for humour. They are in general tall, well made, and of a ruddy brown colour, with dark eyes. The women are of a fine style of countenance, with expressive features, and a skin of a rich carnation; they are of easy address, and have no aversion to cultivate an acquaintance with strangers who are properly recommended. Whatever degree of licentiousness may prevail among them, jealousy, poison, and the stiletto have been long banished from their gallantry. The common people display some qualities very rarely to be found in that sphere of life, being remarkably sober, obliging to strangers, an gentle in their intercourse with each other.

Venice, a city of Italy, and a long time the capital of a territory of the same name. In the 4th century, when Attila, king of the Huns, ravaged the N. part of Italy, many of the inhabitants abandoned their country, and retired into the islands of the Adriatic Sea, now called the Gulf of Venice. These islands being near each other, they found means to join them by driving piles on the sides, and forming the channels into canals, on which they built houses; and thus the superb city of Venice had its beginning. It is the see of a patriarch, and stands on 72 little islands, about 5 miles from the mainland, in a kind of laguna or lake, separated from the Gulf of Venice by some islands at a few miles' distance. These islands in a great measure break the force of the Adriatic storms before they reach the laguna. The number of the inhabitants is computed at 130,000; and they have a flourishing trade in silk manufactures, bone-lace, and all sorts of glasses and mirrors, which make their principal employments. Most of the houses have a door opening upon a canal, and another into a street, by means of which, and of the bridges, a person may go to almost any part of the city, by land as well as by water. The streets in general are narrow, and so are the canals, except the Grand Canal, which is very broad, and has a serpentine course through the middle of the city. There are nearly 500 bridges in Venice; but most of them are only paltry single arches thrown over the canals. The Rialto consists also of a single arch, but a very noble one, and of marble, built across the Grand Canal, near the middle, where it is the narrowest; this celebrated arch is 90 feet wide on the level of the canal, and 24 feet high. The beauty of it is impaired by two rows of booths or shops, which divide its upper surface into three narrow streets. The view from the Rialto is equally lively and magnificent, the canal being covered with boats and gondolas, and flanked on each side by magnificent palaces, churches, and spires. The patriarchal church of St. Mark, one of the richest and most expensive in the world, is crowned by five domes; and the treasury is very rich in jewels and relics. In the numerous churches and convents are the most admirable paintings; and indeed Venice, highly renowned for valuable paintings, far surpasses, in this respect, even Rome itself. The ducal palace, before the subversion of the republic, contained the apartments of the doge, halls and chambers for the senate and the different councils and tribunals, and an armoury, in which a great number of muskets were kept, ready charged, that the nobles might arm themselves on any sudden insurrection. The arsenal is a fortification of three miles in compass; before it was possessed by the French, it contained arms for 60,000 foot and 20,000 horse, arranged in an ornamental manner; and 2800 men were daily employed in building ships, casting cannons, making cables, sails, anchors, &c. The handsome structure, called Il Fontica di Tedeschi, containing 22 shops, and 100 rooms, is that where the German merchants lay their commodities. The bank of Venice is supposed to be the first of the kind in Europe, after the model of which those of Amsterdam and Hamburgh were established. In this city a famous carnival is held from Christmas till Ash Wednesday, in all which time libertinism reigns through the city, and thousands of foreigners frequent it from all parts of Europe. The chief diversions are ridottos and masquerades; and St. Mark's Place is the general rendezvous. Venice is included in the province called the Dogado. It is 125 miles N. N. E. of Florence, and 140 E. of Milan. Long. 12. 23. E. lat. 45. 27. N.

Venice, Gulf of, a sea or gulf of the Mediterranean, between Italy and Turkey in Europe. It is the ancient Adriaticum Mare, and is still sometimes called the Adriatic Sea. There are many islands in it, and many bays or small gulfs on each coast. The grand ceremony of the doge of Venice marrying the Adriatic annually on Ascension Day, by dropping into it a ring from his bucentaur, or state barge, attended by all the nobility and ambassadors in gondolas, was intermitted in 1797, for the first time for several centuries.

Venlo, a strong town of Belgium, in Limburg, and a place of trade for merchandise coming from the adjacent countries. In 1702 it surrendered to the allies, and was confirmed to the Dutch by the barrier treaty in 1715. It was taken by the French in 1794, but ceded to the allies in 1814. It is seated on the E. side of the Meuse, opposite Fort St. Michael; 12 miles N. of Ruremonde. Pop. 5000. Long. 6. 6. E. lat. 51. 22. N.

VENOSA, a town of Naples, in Basilicata, noted as the birthplace of Horace, seated on the river Ofanto; 13 miles N. W. of Acerenza. Pop. 3500.

VENTA DE CRUZ, a town of Colombia, in the Isthmus of Darien; seated on the river Chagre. Here the Spaniards used to bring the merchandise of Peru and Chili on mules from Panama, and embark it on the river for Porto Bello, 20 miles N. of Panama.

VENZONE, a town of Austrian Italy, in Friuli, situate on the Tagliamento; 18 miles N. N. W. of Friuli.

VERA, a town of Spain, in Granada, 34 miles N. N. E. of Almeria, and 80 E. of Granada.

VERA CRUZ, a province of Mexico, comprising a considerable part of the eastern coast. It has an area of about 32,000 square miles, with 160,000 inhabitants. The soil of the lower grounds is abundantly productive, but the climate is so various that in the space of one day the traveller may pass from the regions of perpetual snow through all the intermediate temperatures, to the suffocating heat of the plains near the sea; and within the compass of a few miles the naturalist may range through the scale of vegetation.

VERA CRUZ, a city and seaport of Mexico, capital of the above province. The harbour is defended by a fort, situate on a rock of the island of St. Juan de Ulhua, nearly adjoining. This port is the natural centre of the treasure and merchandise of Mexico. The city is regularly built, its streets broad and straight, and its edifices constructed of materials drawn from the bottom of the ocean; for no rock is to be procured in the neighbourhood. It is situate in an arid plain, without running water, and on which the N. winds blow with dreadful impetuosity from October to April, forming vast hills of moving sand. People in easy circumstances drink rain water collected in cisterns, and it is in contemplation to erect public cisterns within the precincts of the city; but at present the common people are obliged to use water which proceeds from the filtration of the marshes, and which, having been in contact with the roots of vegetables, is of very bad quality. The old town, 16 miles to the N. W., is famous on account of the landing of Cortez, with 500 Spaniards, when he undertook the conquest of Mexico. Vera Cruz is 200 miles E. S. E. of Mexico. Pop. 17,000. Long. 96. 50. W. lat. 19. 5. N.

VERA PAZ, a province of South America, in Guatimala, bounded on the N. by Jucatan, E. by the bay and province of Honduras, S. by Guatimala Proper, and W. by Chiapa. It is full of mountains and forests; but there are many fertile valleys, which feed a great number of horses and mules. There are also many towns and villages of the native Americans. The capital, of the same name, is a bishop's see, but is inconsiderable. It is 120 miles N. E. of Guatimala. Long. 90. 55. W. lat. 15. 30. N.

VERAGUA, a province of Colombia, bounded on the N. by the Caribbean Sea, E. by the province and bay of Panama, S. by the Pacific Ocean, and W. by Costa Rica. It is 125 miles long, and 40 broad, and is a mountainous and barren country, but abounds in gold and silver. St. Jago is the capital.

VERBERIE, a town of France, in the department of Oise, on the river Oise; 10 miles N. E. of Senlis.

VERCELLI, a city of the Sardinian States, in Piedmont, capital of a lordship of the same name, and a bishop's see. The townhouse, the governor's palace, and the hospital, are handsome structures. The inhabitants, estimated at 16,000, are chiefly employed in the manufacture of silk. It is seated at the conflux of the Cerva with the Cesia; 40 miles N. E. of Turin. Long. 80. 24. E. lat. 45. 31. N.

VERCHOLENSK, a town of Russia, in the government of Irkutsk, seated on the Lena; 120 miles N. of Irkutsk. Long. 105. 35. E. lat. 54. 0. N.

VERCHOTURA, a town of Russia, in the government of Perm, and a bishop's see. This was the first town the Russians built in Siberia. It is situate near the river Tura; 120 miles N. of Catharinenburg. Long. 60. 15. E. lat. 58. 45. N.

VERD, CAPE, a promontory on the W. coast of Africa, 145 miles N. W. of the mouth of the Gambia. Long. 17. 37. W. lat. 14. 44. N.

VERD ISLANDS, CAPE, islands in the Atlantic, about 300 miles W. of the coast of Africa, between 13. and 19. N. lat. They were discovered in 1446, by Anthony Noel, a Genoese, in the service of Portugal, and received their general name from their situation opposite Cape Verd; but they are said to have been known to the ancients under the name of Gorgades. They are ten in number, lying in a semicircle. The names are St. Antonio, St. Vincent, St. Lucia, St. Nicolas, Sal Bonavista, Mayo, St. Jago, Fuego, and Brava. St. Jago is the principal.

VERDEN, a duchy of Hanover, 28 miles long, and nearly as many broad; bounded on the W. and N. by the duchy of Bremen, and E. and S. by the duchy of Lunenburg. Pop. 23,000. It consists chiefly of heaths and high dry lands; but there are good marshes on the rivers Weser and Aller. It was formerly a bishopric, which, at the peace of Westphalia, was secularized, and ceded to Sweden; in 1712 it was taken by the Danes, who, in 1715, ceded it to the electoral house of Brunswick, which cession was confirmed, in 1718, by the Swedes. The inhabitants are Lutherans.

VERDEN, the capital of the foregoing duchy, contains four churches. It is seated on a branch of the Aller; 18 miles E. S. E. of Bremen. Pop. 3600. Long. 9. 20. E. lat. 52. 52. N.

VERDUN, a strong town of France, in the department of Meuse, and a bishop's see The citadel, which is a regular fortification, was constructed by Vauban, who was a native of this place. Besides the cathedral there are a collegiate church and nine parish churches, and it is divided into the Upper, Lower, and New Town. Verdun surrendered to the Prussians in 1792, but was retaken soon after. Here Bonaparte confined those Englishmen whom he detained after the rupture of 1803. It is seated on the Meuse; 28 miles N. by E. of Bar le Duc, and 140 E. by N. of Paris. Pop. 9000. Long. 5. 23. E. lat. 49. 9. N.

VERDUN, a town in the department of Saone-et-Loire, seated on the Saone, at the influx of the Doubs; 30 miles E. by S. of Autun.

VERDUN, a town in the department of Upper Garonne, seated on the Garonne; 20 miles N. N. W. of Toulouse.

VEREA, a town of Macedonia, 48 miles W. of Salonica. It has large manufactures of cotton and thread. Pop. 8000.

VERERIA, a town of Russia, in the government of Moscow; 56 miles W. S. W. of Moscow. Pop. 6000.

VERGENNES, a flourishing town of Vermont, in Addison county; seated on Otter Creek; 6 miles from its mouth in Lake Champlain, and 10 N. of Middlebury. Pop. 1017.

VERINU, a town of Colombia, in Cumana; celebrated for its tobacco. It is situate on a gulf of the Atlantic; 45 miles E. of Cumana. Long. 63. 44. W. lat. 10. 8. N.

VERMANDOIS, a territory of France, in Picardy; which is now included, with the territory of Soissonnois, in the department of Aisne. It abounds in corn and excellent flax.

VERMANTON, a town of France, in the department of Yonne; 14 miles S. S. E. of Auxerre.

VERMEJO, a river which rises in Tucuman, on the borders of Peru, flows S. E. to the Paraqua, and enters that river a little above its junction with the Parana.

VERMONT, one of the United States of America, bounded N. by Canada, E. by the Connecticut, which divides it from New Hampshire, S. by Massachusets, and W. by New York. It is 157 miles long, and 65 broad, and is divided into 13 counties; Addison, Bennington, Caledonia, Chittenden, Essex, Franklin, Grand Isle, Orange, Orleans, Rutland, Washington, Windham, and Windsor. A chain of high mountains, running N. and S., divides the state nearly in the centre, between the river Connecticut and Lake Champlain. The natural growth upon this chain consists of hemlock, pine, spruce, and other evergreens: hence they are called the Green Mountains, and give name to the state. The country is generally hilly, but not rocky, and the soil is fertile. It has numerous streams and rivers, which all rise in the Green Mountains; the largest are on the W. side, and the chief are Otter Creek, Onion River, La Moille, and Mischiscoui; the most numerous are on the E. side, and the largest are West River, White River, and Poousoomsuc. Iron ore abounds in this state, and renders it the seat of flourishing manufactures of every thing that can be made of iron and steel; the other chief manufactures are pot and pearl-ash, maple-sugar, and spirits. The principal denominations of Christians are Baptists and Congregationalists; there are also some Episcopalians, Quakers, &c. Area 10,212 square miles. Pop. 291,948. Montpelier is the chief town.

VERNET, a town of France, in the department of Eastern Pyrenees; 4 miles S. of Prades.

VERNEUIL, a town in the department of Eure, seated on the Aure; 22 miles S. W. of Evreux, and 65 W. by S. of Paris. Population, 5300.

VERNEUIL, a town in the department of Allier, 3 miles from the river Allier, and 15 S. of Moulins.

VERNON, a town in the department of Eure, with a fortress at the end of the bridge over the Seine; 27 miles S. E. of Rouen, and 42 N. W. of Paris. Pop. 4000.

VEROLI, a town of Italy, in Campagna di Roma; seated on the Cosa; 3 miles S. of Alatri.

VERONA, a province of Austrian Italy, in the government of Venice; 35 miles long, and 27 broad. Pop. 285,000. It is a very fertile country, abounding in corn, wine, fruit, and cattle.

VERONA, a city of Italy, capital of the foregoing province, and a bishop's see. It has three forts, and is surrounded by thick walls, deep ditches, and good ramparts. The river Adige divides it into two parts, which communicate by four bridges. Most of the buildings are of marble, above thirty kinds of which are found in the neighbourhood; but the streets are neither clean nor straight: the best is that called the Corso, which is pretty long; and there is a handsome square called the Piazza d'Armi. This city is famous for antiquities, the most remarkable of which is the Roman amphitheatre, of which seven rows of benches of white marble are still entire; but various repairs have been made from time to time. In the town-house are the statues of five illustrious natives of Verona; namely, Catullus, Æmilius Marcus, Cornelius Nepos, the elder Pliny, and Vitruvius. Besides the cathedral there are a great number of churches and convents, and several hospitals. The palaces of Bevilacqua and Scipio Maffei contain many valuable paintings, antiques, and other curiosities. The principal trade arises from the manufactures of silk and woollen, and next to them are those of gloves and leather. Near the city is a delightful place, called Campo Marzo, where two annual fairs are held in May and November. Verona has been often taken, and, when Italy was invaded by the French, it was added to the kingdom of Italy. In 1814 it was ceded to Austria, and in 1822 the members of the Holy Alliance met here to deliberate on the affairs of Europe. It is 20 miles N. N. E. of Mantua, and 54 W. of Venice. Pop. 60,000. Long. 11. 18. E. lat. 45. 26. N.

VEROVITZA, a strong town of Sclavonia,

seated near the Drave; 65 miles N. W. of Essek.

VERREZ, a town of the Sardinian states, in Piedmont; with a fortress so strong by nature as to be deemed impregnable. It is 15 miles S. S. E. of Aosta, and 35 N. of Turin.

VERRIERES, a town of Switzerland, in the canton of Neufchatel. The environs are celebrated for excellent cheese. It is 6 miles E. N. E. of Pontarlier, and 20 W. S. W. of Neufchatel.

VERSAILLES, a town of France, capital of the department of Seine-et-Oise, and a bishop's see. In the reign of Louis XIII. it was only a small village, in a forest 30 miles in circuit; and here this prince built a hunting-seat in 1630, which Louis XIV. enlarged into a magnificent palace, and it was the usual residence of the kings of France till 1789, when Louis XVI. and his family were removed from it to Paris. The buildings and gardens were adorned with a vast number of statues, by the greatest masters, and the water-works are magnificent. The gardens, with the park, are 5 miles in circumference, and surrounded by walls. Versailles is 10 miles W. S. W. of Paris, and has two railroads to the capital. Pop. 30,000. Long. 2. 7. E. lat. 48. 48. N.

VERSAILLES, a town of Kentucky, chief of Woodford county; 23 miles W. by S. of Lexington.

VERSETZ, a town of Hungary, in Temeswar, and a bishop's see. It contains some extensive barracks, and near it are the ruins of a castle; 18 miles N. of Vipalanca, and 40 S. of Temeswar. Pop. 5000.

VERSOIX, a town of France, in the department of Aisne. Here, in 1768, an attempt was made to form a harbour, in opposition to Geneva, and great sums were expended for that purpose; but it was soon after relinquished. It is seated on the lake of Geneva, at the influx of the river Versoix; 6 miles S. E. of Gex, and 7 N. of Geneva.

VERT BAY. *See* FUNDY.

VERTUS, a town of France, in the department of Marne; seated at the foot of a mountain on which are good vineyards; 17 miles S. W. of Chalons, and 78 N. E. of Paris.

VERVIERS, a town of Belgium, in the province of Liege; which has a considerable traffic in cloth. It is seated on the Weze; 4 miles S. W. of Limburg, and 17 E. S. E. of Liege. Pop. 10,000.

VERVINS, a town of France, in the department of Aisne; famous for a treaty, in 1598, between Henry IV. of France and Philip II. of Spain. It is seated on the Serre; 40 miles N. E. of Soissons.

VERZUOLO, a town of the Sardinian states, in Piedmont, with a castle. It is surrounded by an ancient wall, flanked with towers, and seated in a very fruitful soil. near the Vratia; 3 miles S. of Saluzzo.

VESLEY, a town of France, in the department of Aisne, on the river Aisne; 10 miles E. N. E. of Soissons.

VESOUL, a town of France, capital of the department of Upper Saone. In its vicinity is a medicinal spring. It is seated at the foot of a mountain, near the river Durgeon; 24 miles N. of Besançon, and 106 E. S. E. of Troyes. Pop. 5700. Long. 6. 8. E. lat. 47. 36. N.

VESPRIN, or VESZPRIM, an episcopal town of Hungary, capital of a county of the same name; with a castle. It is seated on the Sed; 19 miles W. by S. of Stuhlweissenburg, and 70 S. S. E. of Presburg. Pop. 4500. Long. 17. 57. E. lat. 47. 16. N.

VESUVIUS, a volcanic mountain of Italy, 7 miles E. of Naples. It is nearly 30 miles in circuit at the base, and 3730 feet high. Towards the sea it is covered with fruit-trees and vineyards, but on the S. and W. sides, and on the top, nothing is to be seen but black ashes, cinders, and stones. The top of Vesuvius is divided into two points, the southernmost of which is called Mont de Somma. The eruption in the year 79, under Titus, was accompanied by an earthquake, which overturned several cities, particularly Pompeii and Herculaneum; and this eruption proved fatal to Pliny the naturalist. Great quantities of ashes and sulphureous smoke were carried not only to Rome, but also beyond the Mediterranean, into Africa; birds were suffocated in the air, and fell down upon the ground; and fishes perished in the neighbouring waters, which were made hot, and infected by it. Another very violent eruption, in 1631, totally destroyed the town of Torre del Greco. The eruption in 1767 was the 27th from the time of Titus; since which there have been 12 others, the last of which was in 1819 and 1831, which was the 47th on record. Next to those in 79 and 1631, that of 1794 was the most violent and destructive. In this eruption the lava flowed over 5000 acres of rich vineyards and cultivated lands, and the town of Torre del Greco was again destroyed; the top of the mountain likewise fell in, and the crater is now little short of 2 miles in circumference.

VEUDRE, a town of France, department of Allier, on the river Allier; 17 miles N. W. of Moulins.

VEVAY, a town of Switzerland, capital of a bailiwick in the Pays de Vaud. The principal manufacture is watches and jewellery, it has a large trade in cheese, and its wine is in great estimation. It stands near the lake of Geneva, 10 miles E. by S. of Lausanne. Pop. 3800. Long. 7. 0. E. lat. 46. 25. N.

VEVAY, a town of Indiana, capital of Switzerland county; in the neighbourhood of which the vine is successfully cultivated by Swiss emigrants. It is seated on the Ohio, 8 miles above the mouth of the Kentucky.

VEYNE, a town of France, in the department of Upper Alps; 12 miles W. by S. of Gap.

VEZELAY, a town in the department of Yonne, noted for the noble stand made by the Calvinists, in 1560, against Charles IX., who besieged the town, but was obliged to retire after the loss of 1500 men. Theodore Beza was a native of Vezelay. It is seated on the top of a mountain, near the river Cure; 26 miles E. by S. of Auxerre.

VEZELIZE, a town in the department of Meurthe, seated on the Brenon; 12 miles S. of Nancy, and 14 S. E. of Toul.

VIANA, a town of Portugal, in Entre Douro e Minho, at the mouth of the Lima, with a good harbour for small vessels, defended by a fort; 20 miles W. by N. of Braga. Pop. 8000.

VIANDEN, a town of Belgium, in Luxemburg, divided into the Old and New Town by the river Uren. It has a castle on an inaccessible rock, and considerable manufactures of cloth and leather. It is 22 miles N. of Luxemburg, and 22 N. W. of Treves.

VIANEN, a town of the Netherlands, in S. Holland, with a castle. It is seated on the Leck; 7 miles S. of Utrecht.

VIATKA, a government of Russia, which was formerly a province of Kasan; containing an extent of 47,000 square miles, with not more than 1,100,000 inhabitants. It takes its name from the river Viatka, which flows through the country, and joins the Kama.

VIATKA, formerly called Khlynof, a town of Russia, capital of the foregoing government, and a bishop's see, with a castle. It is seated on the river Viatka; 100 miles N. of Kasan. Pop. 8500. Long. 54. 15. E. lat. 57. 25. N.

VIAZMA, a town of Russia, in the government of Smolensk, seated on an eminence; 80 miles N. E. of Smolensk.

VIBORG. *See* WIBURG.

VIC, a town of France, department of Meurthe, seated on the Seille; 15 miles E. N. E. of Nancy. Pop. 3100.

VIC, or VIQUE, a town of Spain, in Catalonia, and a bishop's see. It is seated in a fertile plain; 35 miles N. of Barcelona. Pop. 8400.

VIC BIGORRE, a town of France, department of Upper Pyrenees, situate on the Adour; 12 miles N. of Tarbes.

VIC FEZENSAC, a town in the department of Gers, seated on the Douze; 15 miles W. of Auch. Pop. 3000.

VIC LE COMPTE, a town in the department of Puy de Dome, with a palace, where formerly the counts of Auvergne resided. About a mile from it are mineral springs. It is seated near the Allier; 15 miles S. E. of Clermont.

VICEGRAD, a town of Hungary, with a castle on the top of a rock, in which the crown of Hungary was formerly kept. It is seated on the S. side of the Danube; 8 miles S. E. of Gran, and 16 N. W. of Buda.

VICENZA, or VICENTINO, a delegation of Austrian Italy, in the government of Venice; 35 miles long, and 27 broad, and so pleasant and fertile, that it is called the garden and flesh-market of Venice. Here are also mines of silver and iron, and quarries of stone, almost as fine as marble. Pop. 310,000.

VICENZA, a city of Italy, the capital of the foregoing province, and a bishop's see. It is without walls, but is a large place, adorned with about 20 palaces, from the designs of Palladio, who was a native of this place. The cathedral is embellished with marble, and has some good paintings; besides which there are above 60 other churches, and in that of St. Corona, the high altar, and the painting by Paul Veronese, of the Magi paying adoration to Christ, attract particular notice. In the fine square before the town-house are two lofty columns, with St. Mark's winged lion on one of them, and on the other a statue of our Saviour. The other remarkable places are the Monte della Pieta, with its fine library; the Palazzo Vecchio, with its admirable paintings; the Theatrum Olympicum, after the model of the amphitheatre of Palladio, and the triumphal arches in the public promenade of Campo Marzo. The principal manufactures are silk, damask, and taffeta. About four miles from the city, on a mountain, is the church Della Madonna di Monte Berrico, which is much frequented by pilgrims, and has a fine frontispiece, with a convent close by. Vicenza is seated in a fertile plain, between two hills, at the union of the rivulets Bachiglione and Rerone; 22 miles E. of Verona, and 32 W. of Venice. Pop. 30,000. Long. 11. 40. E. lat. 45. 28. N.

VICHY, a town of France, department of Allier; near which are some mineral springs. It is seated on the Allier; 40 miles S. of Moulins.

VICO, a town of Naples, in Principato Citra, near the Bay of Naples. It is 5 miles N. E. of Sorento.

VICO, a town of Corsica, in which is the cathedral of the bishop of Sagona, a town now in ruins. It is 15 miles S. W. of Corte, and 30 S. of Calvi.

VICOVARO, a town in the Ecclesiastical States, in the district of Sabina; seated near the Teverone; 10 miles N. E. of Tivoli.

VICTORIA, a settlement in North Australia, in Port Essington. *See* AUSTRALIA, NORTH.

VICTORIA LAND, discovered in January, 1841, by Captains Ross and Crozier; the most southern known land, extending from lat. 71. 56. S. long. 171. 16. E. to 79. S. In lat. 77. 31. S. is an active volcano, 12,400 feet high, called Mount Erebus; and a ridge of lofty mountains extends southward of it. To the westward is a barrier of ice cliffs, 150 feet high, and 300 miles long.

VICTORIANA, a tract on the north coast of North America, discovered by Messrs. Dease and Simpson in 1839; lying to the S. of the Boothian Gulf.

VIELSK, a town of Russia, in the goverment of Vologda, situate on the Vaga; 156 miles N. N. E. of Vologda. Long. 41. 45. E. lat. 61. 40. N.

VIENNA, a city of Lower Austria, the capital of the empire, and an archbishop's see. It stands in a fertile plain, on the right bank of the Danube, at the influx of the little river Vien. The city itself is not of great extent, nor can it be enlarged, being limited by fortifications; but it is very populous. The streets in general are narrow, and the houses high; but there are several fine squares; and in that called Joseph Square is a colossal equestrian statue in bronze, of Joseph II. Some of the public buildings are magnificent; the chief of them are the imperial palace, the palaces of the princes Lichtenstein, Eugene, &c., the imperial chancery, the extensive imperial arsenal, the city arsenal, the mint, the general hospital, the town-house, the custom-house, the bank, the library, and the museum. No houses without the walls are allowed to be built nearer to the glacis than 600 yards, so that there is a circular field of that breadth all round the city, which has a beautiful and salutary effect. The eight suburbs are said to contain 220,000 inhabitants, but they are not populous in proportion to their size, for many houses have extensive gardens. The circumference of the city and suburbs is upwards of 18 miles. Many families who live during the winter within the fortifications, spend the summer in the suburbs. The cathedral is built of freestone, and the steeple contains a bell of uncommon magnitude, cast out of the cannon taken from the Turks. Adjoining to this church is the archbishop's palace, the front of which is very fine. Vienna was ineffectually besieged by the Turks in 1589 and 1683. At the latter period the siege was raised by John Sobieski, king of Poland, who totally defeated the Turkish army. The university had several thousand students, who, during the siege, mounted guard, as they did also in 1741. The archducal library is much frequented by foreigners, as it contains above 300,000 printed books, and 12,000 MSS. The archducal treasury, and a cabinet of curiosities of the house of Austria, are great rarities. The Danube here is very wide, and contains several woody isles, one of which is the prater, or imperial park; it also forms a sort of harbour, where are magazines of naval stores; and ships have been fitted out to serve on that river against the Turks. The trade of Vienna is in a flourishing state, and it has manufactures of silk stuffs, gold and silver lace, tapestry, looking-glasses, &c. In 1805 this city surrendered to the French, but was given up by the peace of Presburg. In 1809 it again surrendered to the French, but they again restored it on the conclusion of peace. In 1830 it experienced a severe calamity; after a frost of 118 days, a thaw set in on the 26th of February, and about midnight on the 28th the ice broke, and inundated the dwellings of 50,000 inhabitants, many of whom were drowned, together with a great number of horses, cows, pigs, &c. It is 50 miles W. of Presburg, 350 N. N. E. of Rome, and 570 E. of Paris. The total population is about 300,000. Long. 16. 16. E. lat. 48. 13. N.

VIENNA, a town of Maryland, in Dorchester county. It carries on a brisk trade with the neighbouring seaports. It is situate on the Nanticoke; 10 miles S. E. of Cambridge.

VIENNE, a town of France, department of Isere, and an archbishop's see. In the 5th century the Burgundians made it the capital of their kingdom. The cathedral is a handsome Gothic structure. In 1311 a general council was held here, at which Pope Clement V. presided, and, among other matters, the suppression of the Knights Templars was determined. The commerce of Vienne consists in wines, silk, and sword-blades. It is seated on the Rhone; 15 miles S. S. E. of Lyons, and 33 N. W. of Grenoble. Pop. 12,200. Long. 4. 56. E. lat. 45. 32. N.

VIENNE, a department of France, formed of part of the province of Poitou, and bounded N. by the department of Indre-et-Loire, and S. by that of Charente. It takes its name from a river which rises in the department of Correze, and flows into the Loire 5 miles above Saumur. Poitiers is the capital. Area, 2800 square miles. Pop. 252,000.

VIENNE, UPPER, a department of France, comprising the greater part of the province of Limosin. Limoges is the capital.

VIERRADEN, a town of Prussia, in Brandenburg, seated on the Vesle, near its conflux with the Oder; 22 miles E. S. E. of Prenzlo.

VIERZON, a town of France, department of Cher; famous for its forges. It is seated on the Cher, near the influx of the Yevre; 17 miles N. W. of Bourges. Pop. 5800.

VIESTI, a town of Naples, in Capitinata, seated on the Gulf of Venice, at the foot of Mount Gargano; 25 miles N. E. of Manfredonia. Pop. 4700. Long. 16. 40. E. lat. 41. 51. N.

VIET, ST., or ST. VITH, a town of Belgium, in Luxemburg, near the source of the Uren; 24 miles S. S. E. of Limburg, and 48 N. of Luxemburg.

VIGAN, a town of France, department of Gard; 22 miles W. S. W. of Alais, and 38 W. N. W. of Nismes. Pop. 4000.

VIGEVANO, a town of Austrian Italy, in the province of Milan, with a strong castle on a rock; seated near the Tesino, 16 miles S. W. of Milan. Pop. 12,000.

VIGNOT, a town of France, department of Meuse, on the river Meuse; 16 miles E. of Bar le Duc, and 24 S. S. E. of Verdun.

VIGO, a seaport of Spain, in Galicia, situate on a bay of the Atlantic, defended by a fort on an eminence, and an old castle. It has a good harbour, into which, in 1702, the English and Dutch fleets forced their passage, and made themselves masters of the Spanish Plate-fleet, when just arrived from America. In 1719 the English obtained possession of Vigo, but relinquished it after raising contributions. It stands in a fruitful country; 14 miles W. N. W. of Tuy, and 47 S. of Compostella. Long. 8. 40. W. lat. 42. 14. N. Pop. 2500.

VIGONA, a town of Italy, in Piedmont; 12 miles E. by S. of Pignerolo. Pop. 5300.

VIHIERS, a town of France, department of Maine-et-Loire; 20 miles S. of Angers, and 20 W. by S. of Saumur.

VILAINE, a river of France, which rises in the department of Mayenne, passes by Vitre and Rennes, divides the department of Morbihan from that of Lower Loire, and enters the Bay of Biscay below Roche Bernard.

VILLA DO CONDE, a town of Portugal, in Entre Douro e Minho, at the mouth of the Ave; 20 miles N. of Oporto. Pop. 4500

VILLA DE HORTA, the capital of the island of

Fayal, one of the Azores. It is seated on the W. coast, and has a harbour, land-locked on every side except the E. and N. E., and defended by several forts. Long. 28. 41. W. lat. 38. 32. N.

VILLA D'IGLESIAS, a town of the island of Sardinia, and a bishop's see; 35 miles W.S.W. of Cagliari.

VILLA FLOR, a town of Portugal, in Tras los Montes; 28 miles S. by W. of Braganza.

VILLA FRANCA, a seaport of Sardinia, in the county of Nice, with a castle and fort. The harbour is capacious, and the mountains which enclose it extend into the sea like promontories. It was taken by the French in 1705, by the French and Spaniards in 1744, and by the French in 1792. Of late years it has become the resort of consumptive invalids, in preference to Nice. It is 3 miles E. of Nice. Pop. 2200.

VILLA FRANCA, a town of Portugal, in Estremadura, on the estuary of the Tagus; 20 miles N. E. of Lisbon.

VILLA FRANCA, a town on the S. coast of St. Michael, one of the Azores, defended by a fort and other works. Opposite this place, half a mile from the shore, is a small island, which has a basin with a narrow entrance, where 50 vessels may anchor in security. It is 16 miles E. by N. of Punta del Gada. Pop. 2000. Long 25. 30. W. lat. 37. 50. N.

VILLA FRANCA DE PANADES, a town of Spain, in Catalonia; 18 miles W. by S. of Barcelona.

VILLA HERMOSA, a town of Spain, in Valencia, near the river Millas; 58 miles N. of Valencia.

VILLA HERMOSA, a town of Mexico, in the province of Tabasco, on the river Tabasco; 60 miles S. W. of Tabasco, and 70 N. E. of Chiapa. Long. 94. 5. W. lat. 17. 45. N.

VILLA JOIOSA, or JOYOSA, a town of Spain, in Valencia, on the coast of the Mediterranean; 18 miles E. N. E. of Alicant, and 24 S. of Gandia.

VILLA NOVA D'ASTI, a fortified town of the Sardinian States, in Piedmont; 14 miles W. of Asti.

VILLA NOVA DE CERVERA, a town of Portugal, in Entre Douro e Minho, situate on the Minho, near its mouth; 27 miles N. W. of Braga, and 45 N. of Oporto.

VILLA NOVA DE PORTIMAO, a fortified seaport of Portugal, in Algarva, on a river which forms a spacious and secure harbour, defended by two forts. It is 9 miles E. N. E. of Lagos, and 42 W. by S. of Tavari. Pop. 3500. Long. 8. 27. W. lat. 37. 12. N.

VILLA NOVA DO PORTO, a town of Portugal, in Entre Douro e Minho, seated on the Douro, opposite Oporto (on which it depends), and defended by several forts. Pop. 10,000.

VILLA NOVA DE PRINCIPE, a town of Brazil, in Rio Janeiro, situate near the diamond mines; 130 miles W. of Porto Seguro.

VILLA REAL, a town of Portugal, in Tras los Montes, seated at the conflux of the Corgo and Ribera; 12 miles N. by E. of Lamego, and 38 S. E. of Braganza. Pop. 4000.

VILLA REAL, a town of Spain, in the province of Valencia, near the Minjares; 40 miles N. N. E. of Valencia. Pop. 7000.

VILLA REAL, a town of Brazil, in the province of Spiritu Santo; 150 miles W. by S. of Spiritu Santo.

VILLA RICA, a town of Chili, on the Lake Malabangen; 60 miles N. E. of Valdivia.

VILLA RICA, a town of South America, republic of Brazil. It is seated near some exhausted gold-mines, in the province of Minas Geraes, of which it is the capital. When the mines were in their greatest abundance, between 1730 and 1750, they yielded upwards of 6,000,000*l.* sterling annually; but on their decline the town was comparatively deserted, and has now lost its original splendour and importance. Population, 20,000.

VILLA VICIOSA, a town of Spain, in Asturias, seated on the Bay of Biscay; 32 miles N. E. of Oviedo.

VILLA VIÇOSA, a fortified town of Portugal, in Alentejo, with an old castle, and a palace where the dukes of Braganza formerly resided. In the suburb is an ancient temple, originally built to the honour of Proserpine, and in the neighbourhood are quarries of fine green marble. It is 12 miles S. W. of Elvas, and 33 N. E. of Evora. Pop. 3000.

VILLACH, a town of Austrian Illyria, in Carinthia, with a castle. Near it are medicinal baths. It is seated at the conflux of the Geil with the Drave; 16 miles W. by S. of Clagenfurt. Population, 3000.

VILLAINE, a town of France, department of Mayenne; 16 miles E. by N. of Mayenne.

VILLALPONDO, a town in the W. of Spain, province of Leon, on the S. bank of the river Valderaguay; 40 miles S. of Leon. Population, 6700.

VILLAMIEL, a town of Spain, in Leon; 48 miles S. of Ciudad Rodrigo.

VILLARINO, a town of Spain, in Leon, on the river Douro, and confines of Portugal; 45 miles W. N. W. of Salamanca.

VILLEDIEU, a town of France, department of Loire-et-Cher. It is 20 miles W. S. W. of Vendome.

VILLEDIEU, a town in the department of Manche; 8 miles N. N. E. of Avranches.

VILLEFORT, a town in the department of Lozere; 18 miles E. of Mende, and 19 N. of Alais.

VILLEFRANCHE, a town in the department of Rhone, surrounded by walls, and seated on the Saone; 18 miles N. by W. of Lyons. Pop. 6700.

VILLEFRANCHE, a town in the department of Eastern Pyrenees, with a fort, seated on the river Tet; 25 miles W. S. W. of Perpignan.

VILLEFRANCHE, a town in the department of Aveiron, with a great trade in linen and cloth, seated on the Aveiron; 20 miles W. of Rodez. Pop. 10,000.

VILLEFRANCHE, a town in the department of Upper Garonne, on the Canal Royale; 22 miles S. E. of Toulouse.

VILLEJUIVE, a town in the department of Paris; 4 miles S. of Paris.

VILLEMUR, a town in the department of Upper Garonne, seated on the Tarn; 12 miles N. N. E. of Toulouse. Pop. 4000.

VILLENA, a town of Spain, in Murcia, with a castle, formerly of great strength. In the neighbourhood is a morass, from which salt is made. It is 18 miles S. S. E. of Almanza, and 50 N. by E. of Murcia. Pop. 12,500.

VILLENEUVE, a town of France, department of Lot-et-Garonne, on the river Lot; 17 miles N. of Agen. Pop. 5500.

VILLENEUVE, a town in the department of Gard, on the Rhone, opposite Avignon, with which it communicates by a bridge; 21 miles E. N. E. of Nismes. Pop. 3300.

VILLENEUVE, a town of Switzerland, in the canton of Pays de Vaud; situate at the E. extremity of the Lake of Geneva, 3 miles from the influx of the Rhone, and 14 E. S. E. of Lausanne.

VILLENEUVE DE BERG, a town of France, department of Ardeche; 18 miles S. of Privas.

VILLERS COTERETS, a town in the department of Aisne; 12 miles S. W. of Soissons, and 44 N. E. of Paris.

VILLINGEN, a town of Germany, in Baden, strong by nature, on account of the surrounding mountains and narrow passes. Here is a Benedictine abbey; and in the vicinity is a good bath. It is 20 miles E. by N. of Friburg.

VILSECK, a town of Bavarian Franconia, near which are several foundries. It is seated on the Vils; 20 miles N. of Amberg.

VILSHOFEN, a town of Lower Bavaria. In 1745 the Austrians took it by storm. It is situate on the Danube, at the influx of the Vils; 11 miles W. by N. of Passau.

VILVORDEN, a town of Belgium, in South Brabant, with an ancient castle, seated at the confluence of the Woluwe and the Senne; 7 miles N. N. E. of Brussels.

VIMIEIRO, a town of Portugal, in Alentejo; 12 miles W. by N. of Estremos.

VIMIERA, a village of Portugal, in Estremadura; 30 miles N. of Lisbon. Here, in 1808, a battle was fought between the British and French, in which the latter were defeated.

VIMIOSA, a town of Portugal, in Tras los Montes; 15 miles W. N. W. of Miranda, and 17 S. E. of Braganza.

VINCENNES, a town of France, in the department of Paris, remarkable for its castle, which for three centuries was the country residence of the royal family, but which is now used as a state prison. Here the unfortunate duke d'Enghien was shot in 1804; 3 miles E. of Paris. Pop. 4600.

VINCENNES, or VINCENT, a town of the United States, and capital of Knox county, Indiana, with a fort. It is seated on the Wabash, opposite the influx of the Ombra; 160 miles W. N. W. of Frankfort, in Kentucky. Pop. 1500. Long. 85. 30. W. lat. 39. 0. N.

VINCENT, CAPE ST., the S. W. promontory of Portugal, 25 miles W. by S. of Lagos, off which the naval victory was gained in 1797, by Sir John Jervis, created Earl St. Vincent. Long. 9. 0. W. lat. 37. 3. N.

VINCENT, ST., one of the Windward Caribbee Islands, in the West Indies, 24 miles long, and 18 broad, and about 70 miles W. of Barbadoes. It is extremely fertile, and well adapted for the raising of sugar and indigo; and here the bread-fruit trees brought from Tahiti thrive remarkably well. The original inhabitants were Caribs, a warlike race, manifestly distinguished from the aborigines of the larger islands. They are conjectured tó have been originally a colony from North America, their fierce manners approaching nearer to those of the original natives of that continent than they do to that of South America, and their language also having some affinity to that spoken in Florida. In their wars they preserved their ancient practice of destroying all the males, and preserving the women either for servitude or for breeding. St. Vincent was long a neutral island; but at the peace of 1763 the French agreed that the right to it should be vested in the English. The latter, soon after, engaged in a war against the Caribs, on the windward side of the island, who were obliged to consent to a peace, by which they ceded a large tract of land to the crown. The consequence of this was, that in 1779 they greatly contributed to the reduction of this island by the French, who, however, restored it in 1783. In 1795 the French landed some troops, and again instigated the Caribs to an insurrection, which was not subdued for several months. It was almost desolated in 1812 by an eruption of the Souffrier mountain, which had continued quiet for nearly a century before. It contains 84,000 acres. Pop. 24,000. Kingston is the capital.

VINCENT, ST., one of the Cape Verd Islands, 12 miles long, and three broad, and uninhabited. On the N. W. side of it is a good bay, where ships may wood and water, and wild goats may be shot. Long. 25. 30. W. lat. 17. 30. N.

VINCENT, ST., a town of Spain, in Asturias, seated on the Bay of Biscay; 9 miles W. by S. of Santillana.

VINGORLA, a town of Hindostan, in Visiapour, belonging to the British. About 10 miles to the W. N. W. are some rocks in the sea, called Vingorla Rocks. The town is situate near the mouth of a river; 25 miles N. N. W. of Goa. Long. 73. 27. E. lat. 15. 51. N.

VINTIMIGLIA, a town of the Sardinian states, in the territory of Genoa, with a small harbour, and a strong castle on a high rock. It is seated on the Mediterranean, at the mouth of the Rotta; 20 miles N. E. of Nice, and 24 S. W. of Oneglia. Pop. 5000. Long. 7. 37. E. lat. 43. 53. N.

VIPALANCA, or UJ PALANKA, a town of Hungary, in Temeswar, with a fortress. It stands on the Karass, near its entrance into the Danube. It is situate 42 miles E. of Belgrade, and 58 S. of Temeswar.

VIQUE. *See* VIC.

Vire, a town of France, department of Calvados, with several manufactures of coarse woollen cloths. It is seated on the Vire; 30 miles S. E. of Coutances, and 150 W. of Paris. Pop. 7500.

Virgin Gorda, or Spanish Town, one of the Virgin Islands in the West Indies. It has two good harbours, and is defended by a fort. Long. 64. 0. W. lat. 18. 18. N.

Virgin Islands, about 40 islands and keys in the West Indies, between St. Juan de Puerto Rico and the Leeward Caribbee Islands. They are possessed by the English and Danes. In the first division, belonging to the English, is Tortola, to which belong Jost Van Dike, Little Van Dike, Guana, Beef, and Thatch Islands. In the second division is Virgin Gorda, to which belong Anegada, Nicker, Prickly Pear, the Muskitos, the Commanoes, &c. Of the Danish islands the principal are St. Thomas and St. John.

Virginia, one of the United States of America, bounded on the S. by North Carolina and Tennessee, W. by Kentucky, N. by Pennsylvania and the river Ohio, and E. by the Atlantic Ocean. It is 446 miles long, and 224 broad, and is divided into 104 counties. Several ridges of mountains cross the country from N. to S., the most easterly above 100 miles from the Atlantic. Here are mines of gold, lead, copper, iron, and coal; marble and limestone are found in great quantities; and many medicinal springs have been discovered in different parts. The principal rivers are James, York, Rappahannoc, and Potomac, which are full of convenient harbours; and there are many other rivers, some of which are capable of receiving the largest merchant ships. The land towards the mouths of the rivers is generally low, and fit for rice, hemp, and maize; that higher up is generally level, and watered with springs. Near the sea it is generally sandy, and without stones, for which reason the horses are seldom shod. The richest lands lie near the branches of the rivers, and abound with various sorts of timber, surprisingly large. The superficial extent is about 64,000 square miles, with 1,239,797 inhabitants. The principal produce is tobacco, wheat, and maize; but the culture of tobacco has considerably declined in favour of that of wheat. The capital is Richmond.

Vernenberg, a town of Prussia, in the government of Treves, seated near the Nesse; 26 miles W. N. W. of Coblentz.

Virton, a town of the Netherlands, in Luxemburg; 22 miles W. of Luxemburg.

Visagapatam, a town of Hindostan, capital of an extensive district in the province of the Northern Circars, and the residence of the judge, collector, &c. of the district. It has a harbour, and carries on a considerable trade; 100 miles N. E. of Rajamundry, and 480 N. E. of Madras.

Vischma, a town of Russia, in the government of Tobolsk; 268 miles S. W. of Tobolsk.

Vise, a fortified town of the Netherlands, in the province of Liege; seated on the Meuse, 6 miles S. of Maestricht.

Viseu, a town of Portugal, in Beira, and a bishop's see; 32 miles S. of Lamego, and 49 N. E. of Coimbra. Pop. 5000.

Vishnei-Volotschok, a town of Russia, in the government of Tver. It has a canal, which, by uniting the Tverza and the Masta, connects the inland navigation between the Caspian and the Baltic. It is seated on the river Zua; 50 miles N. W. of Tver.

Visiapour, or Bejapour, a province of Hindostan, 350 miles long, and about 200 broad; bounded N. and E. by the provinces of Aurungabad and Beder, S. by Canara and the river Toombuddra, and W. by the sea. The soil is in general fertile, and provisions are plentiful and cheap.

Visiapour, or Bejapour, the capital of the foregoing province, was formerly a great city, and is said to have contained immense wealth, some of which has been found among the ruins. It was besieged by Aurungzebe, and obliged to capitulate in 1689. It is situate in a fertile plain, 150 miles S. E. of Poonah, and 340 N. by W. of Seringapatam. Long. 75. 40. E. lat. 17. 16. N.

Viso, a mountain of the Maritime Alps, in Piedmont; noted as the source of the river Po.

Vistula, a river which rises in the Carpathian mountains, on the confines of Moravia and Hungary, flows through Poland and Prussia, by Cracow, Sandomir, Warsaw, Culm, Marienburg, and Dantzic, and enters the Baltic by three mouths.

Vitepsk, a government of Russia, lying between Courland and Livonia; it has an area of about 20,000 square miles, and contains 750,000 inhabitants. The surface is flat, and covered with extensive forests.

Vitepsk, a city of Russia, capital of the foregoing government. It is divided into two parts by the river Dwina, and is surrounded by a wall. In the campaign of 1812 it was entered by the French. It is 297 miles W. of Moscow, and 320 S. of St. Petersburg. Population, 13,000.

Viterbo, a town of Italy, capital of a delegation of its name, in the pope's dominions, and a bishop's see. Its streets are broad and well paved, and it contains 16 parish churches, and numerous convents, palaces, and fountains. Near the city is a hot mineral spring, much frequented. It is seated at the foot of a mountain, in a beautiful valley, 40 miles N. N. W. of Rome. Long. 12. 26. E. lat. 42. 25. N. Pop. 10,000.

Vith, St. *See* Viet, St.

Vitre, a town of France, department of Ille-et-Vilaine, with a trade in linen cloth, knit stockings, and gloves; seated on the Vilaine, 20 miles N. E. of Rennes, and 52 S. E. of St. Malo. Pop. 10,000.

Vitry le Brule, a village of France; 2 miles N. E. of Vitry le François. It was formerly a considerable town, but was burnt by Louis VII., and on this account called Brule. The English and Burgundians, in the war with

Charles VII., set fire to Vitry, with 60 villages. It was a third time burned and ruined by the troops of the emperor Charles V.

VITRY LE FRANÇOIS, a town of France, department of Marne, built by Francis I. after the destruction of Vitry le Brule by the emperor Charles V. It has a great trade in corn: it is seated on the Marne; 15 miles S. E. of Chalons, and 100 E. of Paris. Pop. 600.

VITTEAUX, a town in the department of Cote d'Or, seated on the river Braine, among the mountains, where there are quarries of marble; 12 miles S. E. of Semur, and 27 W. of Dijon.

VITTORIA, a town of Spain, capital of the province of Alaba, in Biscay. It is surrounded by double walls, and the large streets are bordered with trees. In the principal square are the town-house, two convents, and a fine fountain. It has a great trade in hardware, particularly in sword-blades, which are made here in large quantities. Vittoria is famous for a victory obtained in its vicinity by the allies, under Lord Wellington, on the 21st of June, 1813. It is seated on an eminence at the end of a plain, fertile in corn and grapes; 32 miles S. E. of Bilboa, and 155 N. of Madrid. Pop. 6500. Long. 2. 38. W. lat. 42. 45. N.

VITTORIA, a town of Sicily, in the Val di Noto; 40 miles W. by S. of Syracuse. Population, 11,000.

VIVAREZ, a territory of France, in the N. E. part of Languedoc, on the banks of the Rhone, now forming the department of Ardeche.

VIVERO, a town of Spain, in Galicia, seated at the foot of a steep mountain, near the river Vivero, or Landrova, which flows into the Bay of Biscay; 22 miles N. W. of Mondonnedo.

VIVIERS, a town of France, department of Ardeche, seated among rocks, (on one of which the cathedral is built,) on the river Rhone; 16 miles S. by E. of Privas.

VIZZINI, a town of Sicily, in the Val di Noto; 28 miles S. W. of Catania. Pop. 8000.

VLAARDINGEN, a town of Holland, province of South Holland, on the Maas; 6 miles S. by W. of Rotterdam. Pop. 6000.

VLADIMIR. *See* VOLODIMIR.

VLIELAND, an island of the Netherlands, about 8 miles long, and 3 broad, situate at the entrance of the Zuyder Zee; 5 miles N. of Texel.

VOGHERA, a province of the Sardinian states, adjacent to Austrian Italy; comprising an area of 100 square miles, with 110,000 inhabitants. The soil is fertile in corn and wine, and much silk is produced.

VOGHERA, a town of Italy, capital of the above province, and a bishop's see. The chief manufacture is that of silk. It is seated on the Staffora; 9 miles N. E. of Tortone. Pop. 10,000.

VOGLABRUCK, a town of Austria, on the river Vogel; 28 miles N. E. of Salzburg, and 38 S. W. of Lintz.

VOID, a town of France, department of Meuse; 18 miles E. S. E. of Bar le Duc.

VOIGTLAND, a circle of the kingdom of Saxony, adjoining that of Erzgebirge; comprising an area of 700 square miles, with 90,000 inhabitants. It is very hilly, and abounds in wood; but the valleys afford plenty of corn, and pastures that feed great numbers of excellent cattle. Plauen is the capital.

VOIGTSBERG, a town and citadel of Saxony, in Voigtland; 5 miles S. by E. of Plauen.

VOIGTSBERG, a town of the Austrian states, in Styria, seated on the Kainach; 18 miles W. by S. of Gratz.

VOKELMARK, or VOLKENMARK, a town of Austrian Illyria, in Carinthia, seated on the Drave; 17 miles E. by S. of Clagenfurt.

VOLCANO, one of the most considerable of the Lipari Islands, in the Mediterranean, lying S. of the island of Lipari, from which it is separated by a deep channel, a mile and a half broad. It is 12 miles in circumference, and is a volcano in the form of a broken cone, but now emits smoke only. It is uninhabited.

VOLCANELLO, a small volcanic island in the Mediterranean, between that of Lipari and Volcano.

VOLGA, a river of Russia, which forms part of the boundary between Europe and Asia. It has its source in two small lakes in the government of Pleskof, about 80 miles W. of Tver, begins to be navigable a few miles above that town, and is there augmented by the influx of the Tverza. It waters some of the finest provinces in the Russian empire, passes by Yaroslaf, Kostroma, Nishnei Novogorod, Kasan, Simbirsk, Saratof, Tzaritzin, and Astracan, and enters the Caspian Sea by several mouths. This is supposed to be the largest river in Europe, its length being about 2700 miles; and by means of it, the river Tverza, and a canal thence to the Neva, there is a navigable communication between the Caspian Sea and the Baltic.

VOLHYNIA, a government of Russia, 220 miles long, and 130 broad. Area, 29,300 square miles. Pop. 1,200,000. It is bounded on the N. by Polesia, E. by Kiof, S. by Podolia, and W. by the kingdom of Poland. It consists chiefly of fertile plains, watered by a great number of rivers.

VOLLENHOVEN, a town of the Netherlands, in Overyssel, with a castle, seated on the Zuyder Zee; 8 miles S. W. of Steenwich, and 12 N. W. of Zwoll.

VOLMAR, a town of Russia, in the government of Riga, on the river Aa; 60 miles N. E. of Riga.

VOLO, an ancient town of Greece, in Thessaly, with a citadel and a fort. It was taken, and almost ruined, in 1655, by the Venetians. It it seated on a gulf of the same name, from which the N. boundary of the kingdom of Greece commences, where there is a good harbour; 30 miles S. E. of Larissa. Long. 22. 55 E. lat. 39. 21. N.

VOLODIMIR, or VLADIMIR, a government of Russia, formerly a province of the government of Moscow. It contains an area of 19,500 square miles, with about 1,000,000 of inhabitants. The soil is extremely fertile, and in the forests are innumerable swarms of bees.

VOLODIMIR, the capital of the foregoing government, is seated on the Kliasma; 110 miles E. by N. of Moscow. Pop. 3000.

Vologda, a government of Russia, divided into the two provinces of Vologda and Ustiug, and comprising an area of 149,000 square miles, with about 660,000 inhabitants. It is a marshy country, full of forests, lakes, and rivers, and noted for its fine wool.

Vologda, the capital of the above province, and an archbishop's see, has a magnificent cathedral, several churches, a castle, and a fortress. The principal trade is in hemp, matting, leather, and tallow. It is seated in a marsh, on the river Vologda, which flows into the Sukhona; 257 miles N. by E. of Moscow. Pop. 11,000. Long. 39. 46. E. lat. 59. 20. N.

Volsk, a town of Russia, in the government of Saratof; situate on the Volga; 76 miles N. E. of Saratof. Pop. 4600.

Volta, a river of Guinea, which separates the Gold Coast from the Slave Coast, and enters the Atlantic Ocean.

Voltagio, a town of the Sardinian States, in the territory of Genoa; 15 miles N. by W. of Genoa.

Volterra, a walled town of Italy, in the grand duchy of Tuscany, containing several antiquities. It is the see of a bishop, and is seated on a mountain; 30 miles S. S. W. of Florence, and 32 S. E. of Pisa. Pop. 5000.

Voltri, a town of the Sardinian States, in the territory of Genoa, near which the Austrians were defeated by the French in 1796. It is 6 miles W. of Genoa.

Volturara, a town of Naples, in Capitanata, 20 miles W. of Lucera, and 52 N. E. of Naples.

Volturno, a river of Naples, which rises in the Appennines, passes by Isernia and Capua, and enters the Gulf of Gaieta.

Volvic, a town of France, in the department of Puy de Dome, near which are immense quarries, which furnish materials for the building of the adjacent towns, and for the statues of the churches. It is 6 miles N. of Clermont.

Vonizza, a town of European Turkey, in the province of Epirus, with a considerable trade in timber for ship-building. It is 50 miles S. of Joannina.

Voorn, an island of the Netherlands, in South Holland, between two mouths of the Meuse, 20 miles long, and 5 broad. This island, with Goree and Overflackee, form the territory called Voornland, which anciently belonged to Zealand. Briel is the capital.

Vorden, a town of Hanover, in the principality of Osnaburg; 20 miles N. N. E. of Osnaburg.

Vordon, a town of Poland, on the Vistula, where a toll is collected from ships going up and down that river. It is 15 miles S. S. W. of Culm.

Voringen, a town of Germany, in the principality of Hohenzollern. It is 10 miles S. E. of Hohenzollern.

Voronez, a government of Russia, bordering on the Ukraine, which it resembles in climate, soil, and productions. It comprises an area of 31,000 square miles, with about 800,000 inhabitants.

Voronez, the capital of the above government, and an archbishop's see, is seated on the river Voronez, near its junction with the Don; 230 miles S. S. E. of Moscow. Long. 39. 14. E. lat. 51. 36. N. Pop. 15,000.

Vosges, a department of France, including the S. E. part of the former province of Lorrain; so called from a chain of mountains, formerly covered with wood, that separates this department from those of Upper Saone and Upper Rhine. It has an extent of 2400 square miles, with 357,727 inhabitants. Epinal is the capital.

Vouille, a village of France, in the department of Vienne, where Clovis gained a battle, in 507, against Alaric, king of the Visigoths, which extended the French empire from the Loire to the Pyrenees; 10 miles W. of Poiters.

Vourla, a town of Asia Minor, in Natolia; 30 miles W. by S. of Smyrna.

Vou-tchang, a city of China, capital of the province of Hou-quang, and the rendezvous, as it were, of all the commercial people in the empire. As every branch of trade is carried on here, its port, on the Kian-ku, is always crowded with vessels, the river being sometimes covered with them to the distance of two leagues. The beautiful crystal found in its mountains, the plentiful crops of fine tea, and the prodigious sale of the bamboo paper made here, contribute no less to make it famous than the continual influx of strangers. It is 655 miles S. of Peking. Long. 112. 25. E. lat. 30 30. N.

Vouziers, a town of France, in the department of Ardennes, seated on the river Aisne; 32 miles E. N. E. of Rheims.

Vriezen-Veen, a town of the Netherlands, in Overyssel; 20 miles E. by S. of Zwolle.

Vukovar, a town of the Austrian states, in Sclavonia, with a manufacture of silk, seated on the Danube, at the influx of the small river Vuko, which divides it into two parts. It is 21 miles S. E. of Eszek. Pop. 5700.

Vulturara, a town of Naples, in Principato Ultra; 65 miles N. E. of Naples.

W.

Waag, a river of Hungary, which rises in the Carpathian mountains, flows by Leopoldstadt, and joins the Danube below Comorn.

Waal, a river of the Netherlands, being the S. branch from the Rhine below Emmerick. It flows W. through Gelderland, passes by Nimeguen, Tiel, Bommel, and Gorcum, and joins the Meuse at Briel.

Wabash, a river of the United States, in Indiana, which rises near some lakes to the W. of Lake Erie, and, taking a S. S. W. course of 400 miles, enters the Ohio 100 miles above the confluence of that river with the Mississippi. It is navigable for 340 miles, and approaches within 9 miles of the navigable waters of Lake Erie.

Wachenheim, a town of Bavaria, in the circle of the Rhine; 17 miles S. S. W. of Worms.

Wachovia, a tract of land in North Carolina, between the rivers Dan and Yadkin, in the county of Surrey, consisting of 100,000 acres, purchased by the Moravians in 1751, and named by them from an estate of Count Zinzendorf's, in Austria. In 1755, by an act of assembly, it was made a separate parish, called Dobb's Parish. It contains several settlements, of which Salem is the principal.

Wachtersbach, a town of Germany, in Wetteravia, with a castle, in which the count of Isenburg-Wachtersbach resides. It is 20 miles E. N. E. of Hanau.

Wadebridge, a town in Cornwall, with a trade in corn; 239 miles from London.

Wadesborough, a town of North Carolina, chief of Anson county, seated on a lofty hill; 50 miles S. S. E. of Salisbury.

Wadstena, a town of Sweden, in East Gothland, with a castle built by Gustavus Vasa, in 1544, and inhabited by his son Magnus, who was insane. It is seated on the Lake Wetter; 46 miles W. of Nordkoping. Long. 14. 53. E. lat. 58. 28. N.

Wageningen, a town of the Netherlands, in Gelderland, with a good trade in cattle and tobacco. It is seated on the Rhine; 12 miles W. of Arnheim.

Wahren, a town of Germany, in the duchy of Mecklenburg, seated near the Lake Calpin; 12 miles S. of Malchin, and 27 W. N. W. of New Strelitz.

Waiblingen, a town of Germany, in the kingdom of Wirtemberg, on the river Rems; 7 miles E. N. E. of Stutgard.

Waidhoven, Bairisch, a town of Austria, on the river Ips; 23 miles S. W. of St. Polten.

Waidhoven, Bohmisch, a town and castle of Austria, on the river Teya; 10 miles N.N.W. of Horn.

Waigatz, or **Vaigatch**, an island and strait between Nova Zembla and Russia. Long. 93. 30. E. lat. 69. 30. N.

Wainfleet, a town in Lincolnshire, with a market on Saturday, seated on the river Limb, near a creek of the sea; 14 miles N. E. of Boston, and 131 N. by E. of London.

Waitzen, a town of Hungary, and a bishop's see. A large annual fair is kept here. It has frequently been taken by the Turks, and was burnt by them in 1685. It is situate on the Danube; 98 miles E. S. E. of Presburg. Long. 19. 15. E. lat. 47. 45. N.

Wakefield, a borough in West Yorkshire, with a market on Friday. It returns one member to parliament. Here are two churches, several meeting-houses, and an ancient stone bridge over the Calder, on which Edward IV. erected a chapel to the memory of his father, who lost his life in the battle near this place, in 1460; but it has long been used as a warehouse. Here are considerable manufactures of woollen cloth and stuffs, and a hall for the sale of the goods; also a free grammar school, which has several exhibitions to both the universities. It is situate in the heart of a rich and fertile district; 29 miles S. W. of York, and 178 N. N. W. of London.

Walachia, or **Wallachia**, a province of European Turkey, 250 miles long, and 160 broad, bounded on the N. by Transylvania, E. by Moldavia, S. by the river Danube, which separates it from Bulgaria, and W. by Hungary. It is watered by numerous rivers, abounds in good horses and cattle, has mines of several kinds, and produces wine, oil, and all manner of European fruits. Its area is estimated at 23,000 square miles; its population at 800,000. It was ceded to the Turks by the treaty of Belgrade, in 1739. Bucharest is the capital.

Walcheren, an island of the Netherlands, the principal one of Zealand, and the most westerly, at the mouth of the Scheldt. It is 9 miles long, and 8 broad, and, being low, is subject to inundations, but has good arable and pasture lands. This island was taken by the British in July 1809, with a view to the destruction of the ships and arsenal at Antwerp; but a number of untoward circumstances first rendered the principal object of the expedition abortive, and then the pestilential nature of the island, at that particular season of the year, obliged the British to relinquish every advantage they had gained. The capital of this island, and of the whole province, is Middleburg.

Walcour, a town of the Netherlands, in the province of Namur, which was entirely destroyed by fire in 1615; seated on the Heura; 27 miles S. W. of Namur.

Waldburg, a castle of Germany, which gives name to a county between the Danube and the Iller. It stands on a mountain; 7 miles N. of Wangen, and 38 S. by W. of Ulm.

Waldeck, a principality of Germany, 30 miles long, and 24 broad, bounded on the E.

and S. by Hesse-Cassel, W. by the Prussian province of Westphalia, and N. by the principality of Paderborn. It consists of two counties, Pyrmont and Waldeck, the latter containing 424 square miles, with 40,000 inhabitants; the former, 31 square miles, with 10,000 inhabitants. The country is mountainous and covered with woods, and has mines of iron, copper, quicksilver, and alum.

WALDECK, a town of Germany, in the county of the same name, with a castle; seated on the Steinbach; 6 miles S. E. of Corbach.

WALDEN, or SAFFRON WALDEN, a town in Essex, governed by a mayor; with a market on Saturday, and a trade in malt. It has a fine large church. It is seated on a hill, among fields that were formerly cultivated with saffron. The other places of worship are meeting-houses for Quakers, Baptists, and Independents. The keep of its ancient castle is still to be seen. It is 27 miles N. N. W. of Chelmsford, and 42 N. by E. of London.

WALDENBURG, a town and castle of Saxony, situate on the Muldau. The old town, on the opposite side of the river, is famous for its brown and white earthenware. It is 12 miles N. N. E. of Zwickau. Pop. 3000.

WALDENBURG, a town of Wirtemburg, in the principality of Hohenlohe, with an ancient castle on a mountain; 6 miles E. by N. of Ohringen.

WALDENSES, VALLEYS OF THE, a district of Piedmont, bordering on France; 24 miles long and 10 broad. It was formerly called the four valleys of Perusa, Lucerna, St. Martino, and Angrogna, but the last does not now belong to them. Pop. 20,000, who are remarkable as being the first community of Western Europe who separated from the church of Rome.

WALDHEIM, a town of Saxony, with an ancient monastery, now converted into an orphan-house, and house of correction, in which various manufactures are carried on. It is situate on the Zschopa; 30 miles S. E. of Leipsic.

WALDMUNCHEN, a town of Bavaria, on the river Schwarza; 32 miles E. S. E of Amberg.

WALDOBOROUGH, a town of Maine, in Lincoln county; 16 miles E. of Wiscasset, and 180 N. E. of Boston.

WALDOSSEN, a town of Bavaria, near which is a rich Cistercian abbey, the abbot of which was formerly a prince of the empire. It is 44 miles N. N. E. of Amberg.

WALDSHUT, a strong town of Baden, in the circle of Wiesen; one of the four Forest Towns; seated on the Rhine, at the entrance of the Black Forest; 19 miles W. S. W. of Schaffhausen.

WALDSTADT, a name given to the Swiss cantons of Lucern, Uri, Schweitz, and Underwalden. It signifies Forest Towns, these cantons containing a great number of forests. For the Waldstadt of Baden, see FOREST TOWNS.

WALDSTADTER SEE, or LAKE OF THE FOUR CANTONS, one of the finest lakes in Switzerland. It consists of three principal branches, called the lakes of Lucern, Schweitz, and Uri. The upper branch, or lake of Lucern, is in the form of a cross, the sides of which stretch from Kussnatcht to Dullenwal, a village near Stantz. It is bounded towards the town by cultivated hills, sloping gradually to the water, contrasted on the opposite side by an enormous mass of barren and craggy rocks, Mount Pilati, one of the highest mountains in Switzerland, rising boldly from the lake. Towards the E. of this branch, the lake contracts into a narrow creek, scarcely a mile across. Soon after, it again widens, and forms the second branch, or lake of Schweitz; on the W. side is the canton of Underwalden, on the E. that of Schweitz. Here the mountains are more lofty, and infinitely varied; some covered to the very summits with verdure, others perpendicular and craggy. Near Brumen commences the third branch, or lake of Uri, which takes a S. E. direction. It is deep and narrow, about 9 miles long, and bordered on both sides by rocks uncommonly wild and romantic, with forests of beech and pine growing down their sides to the very edge of the water. The river Reuss flows through this lake.

WALES, a principality in the W. of England, 150 miles long, and 80 broad; bounded on the N. by the Irish Sea, W. by that sea and St. George's Channel, S. by the Bristol Channel, and E. by the counties of Chester, Salop, Hereford, and Monmouth. It has an area of 5,206,900 acres, of which 900,000 are arable, 2,600,000 pasture, and 1,700,000 waste, of which much is capable of improvement. It sends 24 members to parliament. It is divided into North and South Wales, each containing six counties, namely, Anglesea, Carnarvon, Denbigh, Flint, Merioneth, and Montgomery, in North Wales; Brecknock, Cardigan, Carmarthen, Glamorgan, Pembroke, and Radnor, in South Wales. It is the country to which the ancient Britons fled when Great Britain was invaded by the Saxons. They are now called Welsh, and continue to preserve their own language. They were long governed by independent kings, till in the reign of Edward I., their last prince, Llewellyn, being vanquished and slain in the year 1283, the country was united to England. The natives submitted to the English dominion with extreme reluctance; and Edward, as a conciliatory means, promised to give them for their prince a Welshman by birth, and one who could speak no other language. This notice being received with joy, he invested in the principality his second son, Edward, then an infant, who had been born at Carnarvon. The death of his eldest son, Alphonso, happening soon after, young Edward became heir also of the English monarchy, and united both nations under one government; but some ages elapsed before the animosity which had long subsisted between them was totally extinguished. From the time of Edward II. the eldest son of the king of England has always been created prince of Wales. The general aspect of the country is bold, romantic, and mountainous, consisting of almost continued ranges of lofty mountains and impending crags, intersected by numerous deep ravines, with extensive valleys, and affording endless views of wild mountain scenery. Agriculture is in a backward state, but the soil is by no means barren, producing all the necessaries of life; the cattle and sheep are numerous, but small. It is watered by many rivers, the principal of which, and other particulars, are noted in the different counties.

WALES, NEW SOUTH, a name given to the E. portion of Australia. It was first explored by Captain Cook in 1770; and a design was formed, in consequence of his recommendation, to settle a colony of convicts at Botany Bay. Captain Philip, being appointed governor of the intended settlement, sailed from Portsmouth, in May, 1787, with a detachment of marines, and 778 convicts, of whom 220 were women. He arrived at Botany Bay in January, 1788, but, subsequently, finding this bay very ineligible for a colony, he fixed upon Port Jackson, about 13 miles further to the N.; and here a settlement was begun, to which he gave the name of Sydney. It has regularly increased since that time, by the influx of emigrants from the mother country, to whom the colony offers peculiar agricultural, or rather pastoral, advantages, and also by the transportation of convicts, which has largely increased their population. The inhabitants are now spread over a vast extent of country, in proportion to their numbers. The flocks now range over an extent of 900 miles long, by 300 miles wide, from Moreton Bay on the N. to the boundaries of South Australia and Port Philip on the S. and W. The peculiar character of Australia, differing from every other European colony, has been the cause of this remarkable dispersion. The absence of dense forests, or swamps, combined with the remarkable dryness of the soil, render travelling over the whole country a work of facility. As a proof of its accessible nature, a road has been opened from Melbourne, at Port Philip, to Yass, on the confines of the colony, a distance of 380 miles, at a very trifling expense to a few individuals, and which is easy throughout for carriages of any description. The land, in its natural state, is far from rich, but consists of pasturage, which is available to the settler without the outlay of a large amount of capital; and the flocks are reared for the wool, and migrate in the interior as the pasturage varies, and as far as the limits of land carriage for the produce render it profitable, which, in the opinion of many, has been already attained. The alluvial lands on the banks of the Nepean and Hawkesbury, within the colony, are of the greatest fertility, being a rich vegetable mould many feet in depth, formed by depositions from these rivers during their inundations. Wheat and maize are extensively cultivated by the colony, and barley, oats, rye, &c., are also raised. Every species of culinary vegetable known in Britain is produced in New South Wales, and many of them attain a superior degree of perfection, though a few also degenerate. The fruits are excellent, and of great variety; oranges, peaches, apricots, nectarines, grapes, pears, plums, pomegranates, raspberries, strawberries, melons, &c., attain the highest degree of maturity in the open air. The colony is divided into 19 counties, but which are only used to distinguish certain tracts of country, as they are not used for any civil or ecclesiastical divisions: for purposes of jurisdiction it is divided into 30 police districts, of very unequal size, each having a magistrate and a bench of petty sessions. The extreme boundary of the counties, however, are the limits of location; that is, no lands are sold beyond their limits; beyond this, the country is on a different regulation: it is divided roughly into districts, in each of which is a commissioner of crown lands, who is also the magistrate, and has a small force of mounted, or border police. Beyond the limits of location, land is neither sold nor let on lease, as within the colony, but licenses are granted for allotments of land for pasturage, in stations of from 5000 to 30,000 acres. The quantity of stock thus pastured was stated, in January, 1840, as 7088 horses, 371,699 cattle, 1,334,593 sheep, which is probably under the real amount. The number of stations was 604. The persons who form these stations are the real explorers of the country; they push themselves into the interior with extraordinary rapidity, and perhaps do not become known, even to the crown commissioner, till some accidental circumstance, as a collision with the aborigines, brings them under his notice. This hostility of the natives, and its dreadful consequences, are the greatest drawback on the colony. Wherever a river presents itself, its banks are lined with stations, which the general aridity of the intervening tracts prevents from being tenanted so early. The district of Port Philip, in the southern part of New South Wales, was opened, and the town of Melbourne, at the head of the Port, was founded in 1837, by Governor Sir Richard Bourke; since which it has increased in population and prosperity in an eminent degree: the quantity of land sold at the end of 1840 exceeded 160,000 acres. The net amount of the revenues, without the sales of land, was, in 1837, 2539*l.*; in 1838, 2820*l.*; in 1839, 14,703*l.*; and in the first six months of 1840, 11,747*l.*; affording a satisfactory proof of the flourishing state of the settlement, and which the proximity of Australia Felix, a rich and beautiful district to the W. and N., discovered in 1836, by Sir Thomas Mitchell, and also of Gipps Land, discovered in 1840, by Count Strelcski, and named after the present governor, must tend to increase. In October, 1841, a township was formed at Portland Bay, 185 miles S. by W. from Melbourne, and which will be a central point for the colonization of the rich tracts of Australia Felix to the N. W., in its immediate neighbourhood; on the coast between which and Australia Felix, is an intervening tract of nearly 40 miles in extent. Of the interior of the continent, to the westward of the colony, no attempt has been made to explore it, but from the general character of the limits of the country now colonized. it may be inferred that it is a desert, perhaps sometimes inundated from the tropical rains, but not of any permanent inland sea, which has been a favourite theory concerning this remarkable country. The native quadrupeds are principally of the marsupial kind, or bear their young in an abdominal pouch, of which the most remarkable is the kangaroo. The native dogs are extremely fierce, and cannot be brought to the same degree of familiarity as those with which we are acquainted. There are also weasels and anteaters, with that singular animal the ornithorhyncus paradoxus, or duck-billed platypus, in which the jaws of a quadruped are elongated into the complete bill of a bird. There are many beautiful birds of various kinds; among which the principal is a black swan, its wings edged with white, its bill tinged with red; and the emu, or Australian ostrich, which frequently reaches the height of seven feet or more. Several kinds of serpents, large spiders, and scolopendras, have also been met with; and three or four species of ants, particularly green ants, which build their nests upon trees, in a very singular manner. There are likewise many curious fishes; though the finny tribe seem not to be so plentiful here as they generally are in higher latitudes. The aborigines of New South Wales are represented as perhaps the most miserable and debased race of men existing. Their colour is rather a deep chocolate than a full black; but the filth with which their skin is covered prevents its true colour from appearing. Their hair is generally clotted with a red gum, and they paint themselves with various colours: they will also sometimes ornament themselves with beads and shells, but make no use of the beautiful feathers of their birds. Most of the men want one of the fore teeth in the upper jaw, which appears to be a badge of honour among them; and it is common for the women to cut off two joints of the little finger. Of the cultivation of the ground they have no notion; hence they depend entirely for subsistence on the fruits and roots they can gather, and the animals and fish they catch. Their canoes are nothing more than large pieces of bark tied up at both ends with vines; and, considering the slight texture of these vessels, the dexterity with which they are managed, and the boldness with which they venture out to sea in them, are wonderful. Their huts consist of pieces of bark laid together in the form of an oven, open at one end, very low, but long enough for a man to lie at full length: but they seem to depend more for shelter on the caverns with which the rocks abound. They possess a great power of imitation; they can imitate the songs and language of the Europeans almost instantaneously. In person they are active and vigorous, though generally lean. They are very expert at throwing their waddies or lances, and will hit a mark at a considerable distance. Their number seems to be small, in comparison to the extent of the country. The colony of New South Wales lies between 31. 40. and 36. 0. S. lat., and 148. 40. and 152. 35. W. long., and extends from the Manning river, and Liverpool range on the N., to the Munnoo river on the S., and is bounded on the W. by the Goulburn, Cudgeegong, Lachlan, and Morumbidgee rivers, and the Warragong mountains, or Australian Alps; which limits contain an area of 34,505 square miles, or 22,083,200 acres, and is divided into 19 counties, viz. Bligh, Brisbane, Durham, Gloucester, Philip, Hunter, Northumberland, Wellington, Roxburgh, Cook, Cumberland, Bathurst, Georgiana, Westmorland, King, Argyle, Camden, Murray, and St. Vincent. This extensive district contains a great variety of soil, which on the coast is generally of inferior quality, and which extends for 12 or 14 miles inland, after which there are many rich tracts, particularly on the margins of the rivers. From the first establishment of the colony in 1788, till 1813, a very small portion of this vast continent was known; the Blue Mountains, a range extending for upwards of 1000 miles in length, under different names, and lying 50 or 60 miles from the coast, was for 25 years a barrier between the coast and interior. In 1813, a season of distressing drought, a pass was discovered through these mountains, and a vast extent of valuable country was thrown open to the settlers; fresh expeditions were set on foot in 1817, when the Lachlan river was explored, and in 1818 the Macquarie was traced: these rivers flow into the interior in a N. W. direction, and join the Darling river in lat. 30. 0., which was discovered in 1828: the waters are salt; it flows in a S. W. course to the Murray, which enters the Pacific at Encounter Bay in South Australia: these are by far the largest rivers that have been discovered in Australia, but they flow through a level, arid country, totally useless for colonization. The principal rivers of the colony are the Hunter, in the N. part, flowing through a rich and beautiful country, and falling into the sea at Newcastle, in Port Hunter; S. of this is the Hawkesbury, rising in the Blue Mountains, and flowing eastward to Broken Bay; the banks are fertile and populous: the Nepean, also fertile, and falling into the Hawkesbury; and in the S. the Shoalhaven, debouching N. of Jervis Bay, and rising to the E. of the sources of the Morumbidgee, a large river tributary to the Murray, and one of the principal rivers of the province. The principal towns are Sydney, the capital, Paramatta, Richmond, Maitland, Liverpool, and Carrington.

Walet, the capital of Beeroo, in Negroland. It is 100 miles N. by W. of Sego, and 270 W. by S. of Timbuctoo. Long. 3. 0. W. lat. 15. 45. N.

Walhof, a town of Russia, in the government of Courland, near which the Poles were defeated by Gustavus, king of Sweden, in 1626. It is 34 miles E. of Mittau.

Wallajapetta, a populous and well-built town of Hindostan, in the Carnatic, which is the emporium of the trade between the country above the Gauts and the seacoast. It is seated on the N. bank of the Paliar, nearly opposite Arcot; 63 miles W. by S. of Madras.

Wallenburg, a town of Switzerland, in the

canton of Basel, with a castle on a high rock, seated on the Ergetz; 12 miles S. by E. of Basel.

WALLENSTADT, a town of Switzerland, in the canton of St. Gall. It is a great thoroughfare for merchandise passing from Germany, through the country of the Grisons, to Italy, and stands at the E. end of a lake of the same name; 9 miles W. of Sargans, and 15 N. W. of Coire.

WALLENSTADT, a lake of Switzerland, 10 miles long, and 2 broad, bounded by high mountains, except to the E. and W. Through this lake flows the Mat, which soon after joins the Linth, and forms the river Limmat.

WALLERSTEIN, a town of Bavaria, with a castle; 6 miles S. W. of Oettingen.

WALLINGFORD, a borough in Berkshire, markets on Tuesday and Friday, and a great trade in corn and malt. It was once surrounded by a wall, and had a magnificent castle, some ruins of which still remain. There were formerly four churches, only one of which is now in use. The town has, however, of late years much increased in population and extent, and now contains three meeting-houses for dissenters, a handsome market-house, a town-hall, a free-school, almshouses, &c. It is seated on the Thames, over which it has a handsome stone bridge of 19 arches. It returns one member to parliament. It is 14 miles N. W. of Reading, and 46 W. of London.

WALLINGFORD, a town of Connecticut, in Newhaven county; 13 miles S. W. of Middleton, and 13 N. E. of Newhaven.

WALLKILL, a town of New York, in Orange county, on a creek of its name; 19 miles W. of Newburg.

WALNEY, an island of England, on the coast of Lancashire. It is 9 miles long, and 1 broad, and serves as a bulwark to the hundred of Furness, against the waves of the Irish Sea.

WALPO, a town of Sclavonia, capital of a county of the same name, with a castle. It is seated on the river Walpo; 20 miles W. of Essek, and 110 S. of Buda.

WALPOLE, a town of New Hampshire, in Cheshire county, seated on the Connecticut; 14 miles N. by W. of Keene.

WALSALL, a borough in Staffordshire, market on Tuesday, and several manufactures of hardware. It returns one member to parliament. In the neighbourhood are valuable lime-works. The parish church is a beautiful Gothic edifice, erected on the site of the old church, which was taken down in 1819. The other places of worship are a new episcopal chapel, opened in September, 1826, a Roman Catholic chapel, and three meeting-houses for dissenters. Here are two free-schools, a national school (with which is incorporated the blue-coat charity school), and several charitable institutions. The town is pleasantly situated on the side of a hill, on the Grand Junction railway; 18 miles S. of Stafford, and 115 N. W. of London.

WALSHAM, NORTH, a town in Norfolk, with a market on Thursday; 10 miles E. of Norwich, and 123 N. N E. of London.

WALSINGHAM, a town in Norfolk, with a market on Friday. It is famous for the ruins of a monastery, containing a chapel of the Virgin, which was greatly frequented by pilgrims. Much saffron is grown in the neighbourhood. It is 25 miles N. W. of Norwich, and 113 N. N. E. of London.

WALSRODE, a town of Hanover, in the duchy of Lunenburg, with a convent of nuns of noble extraction, seated on the Bohme; 15 miles E. by S. of Verden.

WALTENBUCH, a town of Germany, in the kingdom of Wirtemberg, on the river Aich; 10 miles S. by W. of Stutgard.

WALTERSHAUSEN, a town of Germany, in the duchy of Saxe-Gotha, with manufactures of cloth, seated on the Horsel; 6 miles S. W. of Gotha.

WALTHAM ABBEY, a town in Essex, with a market on Tuesday. It derives its name from a magnificent abbey, founded by king Harold, some fragments of which remain. Harold and his two brothers, after the battle of Hastings, were interred here, and a stone coffin, supposed to have been his, was discovered in the reign of Elizabeth. Here are some gunpowder-mills, and manufactures of printed linens, and pins. The town is seated on the E. side of the river Lea, which here forms several islands; 12 miles N. by E. of London.

WALTHAM, BISHOP, a town in Hampshire, with a market on Friday; 9 miles S. S. E. of Winchester, and 65 W. by S. of London.

WALTHAMSTOW, a village in Essex, near the river Lea, with a large and handsome church, two meeting-houses, a free-school, and many elegant villas; 5 miles N. E. of London.

WALTON, a village in Surrey, seated on the Thames, over which is a handsome bridge; 6 miles W. by S. of Kingston.

WALTON-LE-DALE, a populous village in Lancashire, with considerable manufactures common to the county; seated near the Lancaster canal and the river Ribble; 2 miles S. S. E. of Preston.

WALUR, a town of Hindostan, in Mysore, with a castle, and manufactures of cotton cloth and coarse blankets. It stands in a fertile country; 20 miles E. by N. of Bangalore.

WANDIWASH, a town of Hindostan, in the Carnatic, noted for a victory obtained by the British over the French in 1760; 27 miles S. S. E. of Arcot, and 38 N. N. W. of Pondicherry.

WANDSWORTH, a village in Surrey, with manufactures for bolting cloth, the printing of calicoes and kerseymeres, and the whitening and pressing of stuffs; also oil, iron, and white lead-mills, vinegar-works, and distilleries. It is seated on the Wandle, near its confluence with the Thames; 5 miles W. S. W. of London.

WANDFRIED, a town of Germany, in Hesse-Cassel, situate on the Werra; 15 miles W. of Mulhausen, and 36 E. S. E. of Cassel.

WANGARA, a fertile country of Negroland, lying to the S. of Bornou. It is watered by the Niger, which here divides into several branches. Ghanara is the capital.

Wangen, a town of Germany, in Wirtemberg, with a great trade in wine, fine paper, linen, and hardware. It is seated on the Overarg; 18 miles N. E. of Lindau, and 21 W. of Kempton.

Wangen, a town of Switzerland, in the canton of Bern, capital of a bailiwick. It is seated on the Aar; 10 miles E. of Soleure, and 23 N. N. E. of Bern.

Wangen, a town of France, department of Lower Rhine, seated on the side of a hill, and surrounded by a wall; 12 miles W. of Strasburg.

Wanlockhead, a village of Scotland, in Dumfries-shire, to the northward of Sanquahar, and near the lead-mines. It has a considerable number of smelting-houses.

Wantage, a town in Berkshire, with a market on Saturday, and a manufacture of sacking. It is celebrated for being the birthplace of king Alfred; and many battles with the Danes have been fought in the vicinity. It stands on a branch of the Ock; 12 miles S. by W. of Oxford, and 60 W. of London.

Wantzeneau, a town of France, department of Lower Rhine; 6 miles N. of Strasburg.

Wantzleben, a town of Saxony, in the government of Magdeburg; 12 miles W. S. W. of Magdeburg.

Wara, a town of Negroland, capital of the country of Bergoo; 320 miles S. S. E. of Bornou. Long. 25. 25. E. lat. 15. 30. N.

Warangole, a ruinous town of Hindostan, (the Arinkill of Ferishta,) once the capital of Golconda. The site of it is still evident from the old ramparts, which are amazingly extensive. A modern fortress is constructed within it, and is in possession of the nizam of the Deccan; 62 miles N. N. E. of Hydrabad. Long. 79. 30. E. lat. 13. 6. N.

Warberg, a seaport of Sweden, in Holland, with a castle at the mouth of the harbour, on a rock surrounded by water. It is seated near the Cattegat; 34 miles S. S. E. of Gotheburg. Long. 11. 56. E. lat. 57. 12. N.

Warburg, a town of Prussian Westphalia, in the principality of Paderborn, seated on the Dymel; 17 miles S. S. E. of Paderborn.

Warde, a town of Denmark, in North Jutland, near the mouth of a river of the same name; 15 miles N. of Ripen.

Wardein, Great, a strong town of Hungary, capital of a county of the same name, and a bishop's see, with a citadel. The town itself is not large, but has three suburbs of very considerable extent. It was taken by the Turks in 1660, but the Austrians retook it in 1692. It is seated on the Keres; 117 miles N. E. of Peterwardein, and 150 E. S. E. of Buda. Pop. 7000. Long. 21. 50. E. lat. 47. 5. N.

Wardein, Little, a strong town of Croatia, capital of a county of the same name, seated on the Drave; 34 miles N. by E. of Agram, and 50. S. E. of Gratz. Long. 15. 55. E. lat. 46. 40. N.

Wardhuys, a seaport of Norway, capital of a district of its name. It stands on a small island of the same name, near the continent, and has an old fort, where the governor resides; 120 miles E. S. E. of the North Cape. Long. 31. 7. E. lat. 70. 23. N.

Wardsbridge, a town of New York, in Ulster county; 16 miles W. by S. of Newburg.

Ware, a town in Hertfordshire, with a market on Tuesday. It is seated on the river Lea, by which large quantities of malt and corn are sent to London, and the barges return with coal, &c.; 2 miles E. by N. of Hertford, and 21 N. by E. of London.

Waree, a town of Guinea, capital of a country of its name, in the kingdom of Benin; 70 miles S. S. W. of Benin. Pop. 5000. Long. 6. 0. E. lat. 5. 38. N.

Wareham, a borough in Dorsetshire, market on Saturday. It returns one member to parliament. It had formerly eight churches, now reduced to three; also a wall of earth, and a castle; but it has suffered much by the various turns of fortune, and the harbour is almost choked up. In 1762 two-thirds of the town were destroyed by fire, but it has since been rebuilt. Above the bridge, over the Frome, is a good salmon-fishery; and in the neighbourhood fine tobacco-pipe clay is dug, of which nearly 10,000 tons are annually sent coastwise. Wareham is the birthplace of the celebrated Horace Walpole. It is seated between the Frome and the Piddle, at their entrance into Lochford Lake, the W. part of Poole harbour; 20 miles E. of Dorchester, and 112 W. by S. of London.

Warendorf, a fortified town of Prussian Westphalia, in the government of Munster, with good linen manufactures, seated on the Ems; 12 miles E. by S. of Munster. Pop. 3300.

Warka, a town of Poland, in the palatinate of Masovia, on the river Pisa; 45 miles S. by E. of Warsaw.

Warkworth, a town in Northumberland, with a market on Thursday. It has a castle, the seat of the Duke of Northumberland; and near it, on the bank of the river, is a hermitage, divided into three apartments, cut out of a rock, at the mouth of the Coquet; 5 miles S. E. of Alnwick.

Warminster, a town in Wiltshire, with a market on Saturday, a woollen manufacture, and a great trade in malt. It has two churches, four meeting-houses, a free grammar-school, a market-house, an assembly-room, &c. It is seated at the source of the Willy; 22 miles N. W. of Salisbury, and 96 W. by S. of London.

Warminster, a town of Virginia, in Amherst county; 70 miles W. by N. of Richmond.

Warnemunde, a town of Germany, in the grand duchy of Mecklenburg-Schwerin, 9 miles N. N. W. of Rostock.

Warneton, a town of Belgium, in West Flanders; 8 miles N. W. of Lisle. Pop. 5300.

Warren, the name of several counties in the United States: viz., 1. In Kentucky, S. of Green River, with 15,446 inhabitants. Chief town, Bowling Green. 2. In North Carolina, with 12,929 inhabitants. 3. In the S. W. of Ohio, with 23,141 inhabitants. Chief town, Lebanon. 4. In the central part of Georgia, with 9789 inhabitants. Chief town, Warrenton. 5. In West Tennessee, with 10,803 inhabitants. Chief town, M'Minnville. 6. In the state of Mississippi, with 15,820 inhabitants. 7. In the N. W. part of Pennsylvania, with 41,279 inhabitants.

WARREN, a town of Pennsylvania, capital of Warren county, seated on the Allegany river, where it receives the Connewango.

WARREN, a town of Rhode Island, in Bristol county, which has a good trade, particularly in ship-building. It stands on Warren River, and the N. E. part of Narraganset Bay; 10 miles S. S. E. of Providence. Pop. 2437.

WARREN, a town of Virginia, on the N. side of James River; 10 miles E. N. E. of Warminster, and 21 S. S. W. of Charlottesville.

WARRENTON, a town of North Carolina, chief of Warren county; 35 miles W. by N. of Halifax, and 54 N. N. E. of Raleigh.

WARRENTON, a town of Georgia, capital of Warren county.

WARRENTON, a town of Virginia, capital of Fanquier county; 40 miles N. N. W. of Fredericksburg.

WARRINGTON, a borough in Lancashire, markets on Wednesday and Saturday; manufactures of muslins, velveteens, canvas, cottons, checks, hardware, pins, and glass, and a considerable traffic in malt. Here are two churches, six meeting-houses for dissenters, a Roman Catholic chapel, an excellent free school, two charity schools, and an infant school, opened in 1826. It is seated on the Mersey, over which is a bridge; 18 miles E. of Liverpool, and 182 N. N. W. of London. It returns one member to parliament.

WARRIORE, a town of Hindostan, in the Carnatic; 32 miles N. N. E. of Tanjore, and 55 S. S. W. of Pondicherry.

WARSAW, the metropolis of the present kingdom of Poland, and formerly of the whole country of that name. It is built partly in a plain, and partly on a gentle rise from the Vistula; extending, with the suburbs of Kraka and Praga, over a vast extent of ground, and containing above 140,571. inhabitants. The streets are spacious, but ill paved; the churches and public buildings large and magnificent; the palaces of the nobility numerous and splendid; but the greatest part of the houses, particularly in the suburbs, are mean and ill-constructed wooden hovels. The manufactures comprise woollen stuffs, carpeting, gold and silver wire, soap, tobacco, &c. Here are several wholesale mercantile houses, employed in the import of articles for the supply of the interior, and the export of Polish produce. Two great annual fairs have, since 1817, been established here, on the plan of those of Frankfort, Leipsic, &c. They are held in May and November, each continuing three weeks. In the beginning of 1794 the empress of Russia put a garrison into this city, in order to compel the Poles to acquiesce in the usurpation she had in view; but this garrison was soon expelled by the citizens. The king of Prussia besieged Warsaw in July, but was compelled to raise the siege in September. It was undertaken by the Russians, who, in November, took by storm the suburb of Praga, massacred the inhabitants, and nearly reduced it to ashes. The immediate consequence was the surrender of the city to the Russians, who, in 1796, delivered it up to the king of Prussia. Towards the end of 1800, the French occupied this place; and by the treaty of Tilsit, the city, with this part of Poland, was given to Saxony, to be held under the title of the duchy of Warsaw. The Russians, however, overran this duchy in 1813, and took possession of the city of Warsaw. It was the residence of the viceroy, and the place of meeting of the Polish parliament, till the insurrection of the Poles in 1833, which failed in restoring their ancient privileges, and was the means of annihilating the political existence of the Poles; since which it must be considered as forming a part of the Russian empire. It is 170 miles S. of Konigsberg, and 180 E. N. E. of Breslau. Long. 21. 0. E. lat. 52. 14. N.

WARTA, a river of Poland, which rises in the palatinate of Cracow, flows by Siradia and Posnan, passes by Driessen and Landsberg in Brandenburg, and enters the Oder at Custrin.

WARTENBERG, a town of Prussian Silesia, capital of a lordship of the same name, with a castle. In 1742 it was entirely reduced to ashes, except the old castle, which is now used as a brewhouse. It is 28 miles N. E. of Breslau.

WARTENBERG, a town of Prussian Silesia, in the principality of Glogau; 20 miles N. W. of Glogau.

WARWICK, a borough, and the capital of Warwickshire, governed by a mayor, returning two members to parliament. Markets on Tuesday and Saturday. It was fortified with a wall, now in ruins, but has still a noble castle of the ancient earls of Warwick, inhabited by the present possessor of that title. The town was nearly destroyed by fire in 1694, but was subsequently rebuilt with greater regularity. The streets are spacious, and meet nearly in the centre of the town. It had formerly six parish churches, of which two only remain. There are likewise meeting-houses for Baptists, Independents, Methodists, Presbyterians, and Quakers; and a mile distant is a Roman Catholic chapel. The charitable institutions are numerous, and conducted upon a scale of liberality and extent which reflect great honour upon the inhabitants. The chief manufactures are in worsted and hats; there are also silk-throwing concerns, and a good malting business. The town is situate on a rocky eminence, on the river Avon, over which is a stone bridge, erected by the late earl of Warwick, at his own expense. It is 10 miles S. S. W. of Coventry, and 92 N. W. of London. Long. 1. 35. W. lat. 52. 17. N.

WARWICK, a town of North America, in the state of New York, in Orange county, containing five places of worship, and large iron-works; 54 miles N. W. of New York. Population, 5113.

Warwick, a town of Virginia, capital of a county, seated on the right bank of James River; 15 miles S. E. of Richmond.

Warwick, a town of Rhode Island, chief of Kent county. It has a cotton manufacture, and is situate at the head of Narraganset Bay; 8 miles S. of Providence. Pop. 6726.

Warwickshire, a county of England; 47 miles long, and 30 broad; bounded on the N. by Derbyshire, N. E. by Leicestershire, E. by Northamptonshire, S. E. by Oxfordshire, S. W. by Gloucestershire, W. by Worcestershire, and N. W. by Staffordshire. It contains 577,280 acres; is divided into four hundreds and one liberty, and 209 parishes. It sends four members to parliament for the N. and S. divisions of the county. The climate of this county is healthy, and the air mild and pleasant: its salubrity is increased by the great consumption of wood for the iron-works, many parts being entirely cleared and converted to tillage and pasture. The N. part, called the Woodlands, is divided from the S., called the Feldon, by the river Avon; and the soil of both is in general rich and fertile. It produces corn, flax, wood, wool, cheese, coal, iron, and limestone, and its breeds of cattle and sheep are of a superior kind. The principal rivers are the Avon, Tame, and Arrow. It is also intersected by several canals, which, communicating with others that proceed to the rivers Thames, Severn, Mersey, and Trent, are of considerable advantage to its trade and commerce. The manufactures are various and important, comprising ribbons, gauzes, and other silk fabrics, lastings and thread, and all descriptions of hardware. The capital is Warwick, but Birmingham is the largest town.

Wasa, a seaport of Sweden, in East Bothnia, on the Gulf of Bothnia; 40 miles N. by E. of Christianstadt.

Washington, a city, and the metropolis of the United States of America. It is seated on the river Potomac, at the junction of the Eastern Branch, extending about 4 miles up each; including a tract of territory called Columbia, scarcely to be exceeded in point of convenience, salubrity, and beauty, by any in the world. The plan of this city combines every thing grand and beautiful that can be introduced into a city. It is divided into squares or grand divisions, by streets running due N. and S., and E. and W.; which form the ground-work of the plan. But from the capitol, the president's house, and some of the important areas in the city, run diagonal streets, from one material object to another, which not only produce a variety of prospects, but remove the insipid sameness which renders some great cities unpleasing. The great leading streets are 160 feet wide, including a pavement of 10 feet, and a gravel walk of 30 feet, planted with trees on each side, which will leave 80 feet of paved street for carriages. The rest of the streets are, in general, 110 feet wide, with a few only 90 feet, except North, South, and Capitol streets, which are 160 feet. The diagonal streets are named after the respective states composing the Union, while those running N. and S. are, from the capitol eastward, named East First street, East Second street, &c., and those W. of it are, in the same manner, called West First street, West Second street, &c. Those running E. and W. are, from the capitol northward, named North A street, North B street, &c.; and those S. of it are called South A street, South B street, &c. The squares, or divisions of the city, amount to 1150; the rectangular ones contain from three to six acres, and are divided into lots of from 40 to 60 feet in front, and their depth from 110 to 300, according to the size of the square. In 1800, after the adjournment of congress, at their last session in Philadelphia, the public offices, records, and property were removed to this city; and here, on the 22nd of November, the congress assembled for the first time. In 1804, a society of agriculture was incorporated here. On the 19th of August, 1814, a British army, of about 5000 men, under General Ross, landed at Benedict, on the right bank of the Patuxent, and, after defeating the Americans at Bladensburg, entered this city on the 24th, and destroyed all the public edifices; but they have subsequently been rebuilt, and some of them on an improved plan. The houses are all brick or stone. The capitol (or house for the legislative bodies) is on an eminence, about a mile from the Eastern Branch, and not much more from the Potomac, commanding a full view of the city, as well as a considerable extent of the country round. It is built of white free-stone, and is an edifice of great elegance and grandeur. The president's house is also an elegant building, of the same material, situate on a rising ground, not far from the Potomac, and possessing a delightful water prospect, with a view of the capitol, and some other material parts of the city. Due S. from the president's house, and due W. from the capitol, run two great pleasure parks, or malls, which intersect and terminate upon the banks of the Potomac, and are ornamented at the sides by a variety of elegant buildings, houses for foreign ministers, &c. Interspersed through the city, where the most material streets cross each other, are a variety of open areas, formed in various regular figures, which, in great cities, are extremely useful and ornamental. The more spacious of these areas are appropriated to the different states composing the Union; not only to bear their respective names, but as proper places to erect statues, obelisks, or columns, to the memory of their celebrated men. Upon a small eminence, where a line due W. from the capitol, and due S. from the president's house, would intersect, is erected an equestrian statue of General Washington, the first president of the United States. The general post-office is a large brick building, containing, besides the different offices of that establishment, the general land office, the patent office, &c. Other public buildings have been commenced, as a marine hospital, with its gardens; a general exchange, and its public walks; a fort, magazines, and arsenal; a city hall, churches, colleges, market-houses, theatre, &c. The city being situate on the great post road, equidistant from the N. and S. extremities of the Union, and nearly so from the Atlantic Ocean to the river Ohio, upon the best navigation, and in the midst of the richest commercial territory in America, is by far the most eligible situation for the residence of the congress. The Eastern Branch is one of the safest and most commodious harbours in America, being sufficiently deep for the largest ships, for 4 miles above its junction with the Potomac; while the channel lies close along the edge of the city, and is abundantly capacious. The Potomac produces a communication by water between the city and the interior parts of Virginia and Maryland, by means of the Shannandoah, the South Branch, Opecan, Cape Capon, Patterson Creek, Conoochegue, and Monocasy, for upwards of 200 miles, through one of the most healthy regions in America, producing tobacco of superior quality, hemp, maize, wheat, and other small grain, with fruits and vegetables in abundance. The lands upon the Potomac, above the city of Washington, all around it, and for 60 miles below, are high and dry, abounding with innumerable springs of excellent water, and well covered with timber trees, of various kinds. A few miles below the city, upon the banks of the Potomac, are inexhaustible mountains of excellent freestone, of which the public edifices in the city are built. Above the city also, upon the banks of the river, are immense quantities of excellent coal, limestone, and marble, with blue slate of the best quality. The Tyber, which is the principal stream that passes through the city, is to be collected in a grand reservoir, near the capitol, whence it will be carried into pipes to different parts of the city; while its surplus water will fall down in cascades, through the public gardens W. of the capitol, into a canal. The plan of this city was formed by Major L'Enfant; but the scale is so gigantic, that it may be considered rather as consisting of four distinct towns lying on the principal streets, and about a mile distant from each other; and it is improbable that it ever will become the centre of attraction that the ideas of the originators seemed to anticipate. Except during the sitting of congress, it presents a dull and deserted aspect, and possesses but little trade; and whatever may be the plan, it is much inferior to many other towns of the Union. It is 144 miles S. W. of Philadelphia, the late capital of the United States. Long. 77. 2. W. lat. 38. 58. N.

Washington, a district of Tennessee, comprehending the counties of Washington, Sullivan, Greene, and Carter. The capital is Jonesborough.

Washington, a hilly district in the N. W. part of S. Carolina, comprehending the counties of Pendleton and Greenville. Pickensville is the capital.

Washington, the name of several counties in the United States, viz.: 1. A county in the state of Maine, lying W. of New Brunswick. Chief town, Machias. 2. In Alabama. Chief town, St. Stephens. 3. In the central part of Georgia. Chief town, Saundersville. 4. In Kentucky. Chief town, Springfield. 5. In Maryland, bounded S. by the Potomac. Chief town, Elizabeth Town. 6. In New York, bounded by Essex, Vermont, Saratoga, and Warren counties. Chief town, Salem. 7. In the S. E. part of Ohio. Chief town, Marietta. 8. In Pennsylvania, to the E. of Virginia. Chief town, Washington. 9. In Rhode Island. Chief town, South Kingston. 10. In East Tennessee. Chief town, Jonesborough. 11. In Indiana, lying W. of Clark county. Chief town, Salem. 12. In North Carolina. Chief town, Plymouth. 13. In the central part of Vermont. Chief town, Montpelier. 14. In the S. W. part of Virginia. Chief town, Abingdon.

Washington, a town of North Carolina, in Beaufort county. It was formerly called Bath, and has a good harbour near the mouth of the river Tar; 38 miles N. E. of Newbern.

Washington, a town of the state of Georgia, chief of Wilkes county. A mile and a half E. of the town is a medicinal spring, which has been found beneficial in scorbutic cases: it rises from a hollow tree, the inside of which is covered with a coat of matter an inch thick, and the leaves around the spring are incrusted with a substance as white as snow. It is 50 miles W. N. W. of Augusta. Long. 82. 30. W. lat. 33. 12. N.

Washington, a town of Pennsylvania, chief of a county of the same name, and noted for a variety of manufactures. It stands on a branch of Chartier Creek; 10 miles above Morganza, and 22 S. S. W. of Pittsburg. Pop. 2062. Long. 80. 10. W. lat. 40. 11. N.

Washington, a town of Kentucky, chief of Mason county. It is a commercial place, situate in a fine country, near the Ohio; 70 miles E. N. E. of Frankfort. Long. 84. 15. W. lat. 38. 32. N.

Wassenberg, a town of Prussia, in the duchy of Juliers, seated on the Roer; 17 miles N. W. of Juliers.

Wasserburg, a town of Bavaria, with a castle and four churches. The principal trade is in salt. In 1800 the French took it by storm. It is seated on the Inn; 28 miles E. of Munich, and 38 N. W. of Salzburg.

Wasser-trudingen, a town of Bavarian Franconia, in the principality of Anspach. It is 6 miles N. of Oettingen.

Westwater, a lake in Cumberland, 7 miles N. N. E. of Ravenglass. It is 3 miles long, and above half a mile broad, lying in Wastdale, among the western mountains. The Screes, a very high ridge of mountains, run along the S. E. side of the lake. Its outlet, at the S. end, joins the river Irt, which enters the sea at Ravenglass.

Wasungen, a town of Germany, in the duchy of Saxe-Meiningen, seated on the Werra; 5 miles N. of Meiningen.

Watchet, a town in Somersetshire, with a market on Saturday. It is seated on the Bristol Channel, at the mouth of a harbour, frequented by coal ships, which are freighted hence with limestone, alabaster, and kelp. It is 14 miles N. W. of Taunton, and 156 W. by S. of London.

Watehoo, an island in the S. Pacific, discovered by Captain Cook. It is six leagues in circuit, diversified by hills and plains, and covered with verdure. Long. 158. 15. W. lat. 21. 1. S.

Waterbury, a town of the state of Maine, in York county, seated on Mousom River; 15 miles N. W. of Wells.

Waterford, a county of Ireland, 50 miles long, and 29 broad; bounded on the S. by St. George's Channel, W. by Cork, N. and N. E. by the river Suir, which separates it from Tipperary and Kilkenny, and E. by Waterford Haven, which parts it from Wexford. It is divided into 73 parishes, and sends one member to parliament. It presents a diversity of soil and prospect, but in general is pleasant and fertile, yet in many parts mountainous and rocky. The chief rivers are the Suir and Blackwater.

Waterford, a city and seaport of Ireland, capital of a county of the same name, and a bishop's see, united with Lismore. It has an excellent harbour, where ships of the greatest burden may ride at the quay. The bishop's palace and the Roman Catholic chapel are the most elegant elevations in the city. Among the other public buildings are a gaol, new court-house, exchange, custom-house, assembly-rooms, &c. &c. The streets are generally narrow, but improvements in this respect are daily in progress. The chief boast of Waterford, however, is the noble river that rolls before her walls, and her beautiful quay, nearly a mile in length. The commerce with England and other countries is very considerable; and packet-boats sail regularly hence for Milford Haven. The principal exports are beef, pork, corn, live stock, butter, and linen. It sends two members to parliament. It stands on the river Suir; 8 miles N. of St. George's Channel, and 94 S. by W. of Dublin. Long. 7. 24. W. lat. 52. 10. N.

Waterloo, a village of Belgium, celebrated as the scene of the signal victory of the 18th of June, 1815, which completed the downfall of Napoleon. It is 10 miles S. of Brussels. Pop. 1600.

Watertown, a town of Massachusets, in Middlesex county, seated on Charles River, 7 miles from its mouth in Boston harbour, and 9 S. S. E. of Concord.

Watford, a town in Hertfordshire, with a market on Tuesday. It has a spacious church, a large Baptist meeting-house, a free-school, market-house, eight almshouses, &c. It is seated on the Colne, near the Birmingham railway; 7 miles S. by W. of St. Albans, and 15 N. W. of London.

Watlington, a town in Oxfordshire, with a market on Saturday, seated near the Chiltern Hills, on a brook, which, with the continued ridge, divides the county from Buckinghamshire. It is 14 miles S. E. of Oxford, and 46 W. of London.

Watton, a town in Norfolk, with a market on Wednesday; 18 miles W. by S. of Norwich, and 91 N. N. E. of London.

Waveren, or **Wavre**, a town of Belgium, in S. Brabant, situate on the Dyle; 12 miles S. of Louvain. Pop. 4100.

Waxholm, a fortress on the coast of Sweden, in the Baltic, situate on a small island at the entrance of the lake Maeler. Here all homeward-bound ships are searched. It is 16 miles E. of Stockholm.

Way, or **Pulo Way**, an island near the N. point of that of Sumatra. It is the largest of the islands that form the entrance of the channel of Acheen, and is peopled by men banished from Acheen. Long. 94. 50. E. lat. 5. 35. N.

Wayne, a county in the central part of N. Carolina.—Also a county in the central part of Ohio, formed in 1808, and containing 870 square miles.—A county on the S. side of Kentucky; chief town, Monticello.—A county in the state of Georgia;—and another in Alabama.

Waynesborough, a town of the state of Georgia, chief town of Greene county; 22 miles S. of Washington.

Waynesborough, a town of N. Carolina, the capital of Wayne county, seated on the Neuse; 50 miles S. E. of Raleigh.

Waynesborough, a town of Georgia, capital of Burke county, seated on Brier Creek; 24 miles E. N. E. of Louisville.

Wear, a river which rises in the W. part of the county of Durham, flows S. E. by Stanhope to Bishop Auckland, and thence N. E. by Durham to Sunderland, where it enters the German Ocean.

Wearmouth, Bishop, a town in the county of Durham, on the S. side of the Wear, adjoining Sunderland. It has an iron bridge over the river, of one arch, 236 feet span, erected in 1796, and the first ever constructed of parts so formed as to unite in the manner of keystones. It has manufactures of canvas, and partakes in the commerce of Sunderland.

Wearmouth, Monk, a town in the county of Durham, on the N. side of the mouth of the Wear, opposite Sunderland. Here was an extensive monastery, which was destroyed by the Scots. It shares in the growing prosperity of Sunderland. It is on the Brandling Junction railway from Gateshead to South Shields.

Wedenschweil, a town of Switzerland, in the canton of Zurich; 10 miles S.E. of Zurich.

Wednesbury, a town in Staffordshire, with a market on Friday, and manufactures of hardware, several iron forges, and mines of excellent coal. Here is an elegant church, built on the site of an ancient castle; also three meeting-houses for dissenters. It is 13 miles S. S. W. of Litchfield, and 118 N. W. of London.

Weert, a town of Belgium, in the province

of Liege, seated on the river Brey; 10 miles W. N. W. of Ruremonde. Pop. 5300.

WEEVER, a river which rises in the N. part of Shropshire, crosses Cheshire, and, receiving the Dane from the E., enters the estuary of the Mersey. It is navigable to Winsford, some miles above Northwich, in Cheshire.

WEIBSTADT, a town of Prussia, in the province of the Rhine. It is 15 miles E. S. E. of Heidelberg.

WEICHSELBURG, a town of Austrian Illyria, in Carniola, with a castle on a mountain, and a manufacture of fine stockings; 10 miles S. E. of Laubach. Pop. 4000.

WEICHTERBACH, a town of Germany, in the county of Isenberg, with a castle, seated on the Zinzig; 20 miles S. E. of Giessen, and 23 N. E. of Frankfort.

WEICKERSHEIM, a town of Wirtemberg, in the district of Hohenlohe, with a fine castle, on the river Tauber; 3 miles E. of Mergentheim.

WEIDA, a town of Germany, in Saxe-Weimar; 32 miles E. of Weimar.

WEIDEN, a town of Bavaria, with manufactures of linen, woollen stuffs, and saltpetre, seated on the Nab; 18 miles N. E. of Amberg.

WEIL, or WEILERSTADT, a town of Germany, in Wirtemberg, seated on the Worm; 12 miles W. of Stutgard.

WEIL, or WYL, a town of Switzerland, in the canton of St. Gall, seated on the river Thur; 19 miles S. S. W. of Constance.

WEILBURG, a town of Germany, in the duchy of Nassau, seated on the Lahn, over which is a bridge. It is 12 miles S. W. of Wetzlar, and 25 N. N. W. of Frankfort.

WEILE, a seaport of Denmark, in N. Jutland, situate on a bay in the Little Belt; 35 miles S. S. W. of Arhusen, and 38 N. E. of Ripen. Long. 9. 30. E. lat. 55. 45. N.

WEILHEIM, a town of Bavaria, with a castle, on the river Amper. It is 28 miles S. S. W. of Munich.

WEILHEIM, a town of Wirtemberg, on the river Lauter; 20 miles S. E. of Stutgard.

WEIMAR, SAXE, a grand duchy of Germany, comprising the duchies of Weimar, Jena, and Eisenach, part of the principality of Altenburg, the chief part of the district of Neustadt, the petty districts of Alstadt, Ilmenau, and Oldisleben, and some districts to the E. of the Hesse-Cassel territory. It is divided into two great provinces, and contains an area of 1450 square miles, with upwards of 200,000 inhabitants.

WEIMAR, the capital of the foregoing duchy. In the duke's palace is one of the most considerable libraries in Germany, with a cabinet of coins and medals; and it had a gallery of paintings, which, with some other parts of the castle, was destroyed by fire in 1774. It is seated on the Ilm; 12 miles W. of Erfurt, and 26 W. S. W. of Naumburg. Pop. 8000. Long. 11. 27. E. lat. 51. 2. N.

WEINHEIM, a town of Germany, in Baden, seated on the river Welchnitz; 10 miles N. of Heidelberg. Pop. 4000.

WEINSBERG, a town of Wirtemberg, with a ruined castle on a hill. In 1707 the greatest part of the town was destroyed by fire. It stands partly on the hill, and partly in a valley, famous for wine; 5 miles N. E. of Heilbron.

WEISSELMUNDE, a fortress of West Prussia, seated at the W. mouth of the Vistula, to defend the harbour of Dantzic.

WEISSENBURG, a town of France, in the department of Lower Rhine. Between this place and Lauterburg are the famous lines from which the French drove the Austrians in 1744; and in 1793 the Prussians drove the French from the same situation. It is seated on the Lauter; 10 miles S. W. of Landau, and 22 N. E. of Strasburg. Pop. 4000. Long. 8. 11. E. lat. 48. 53. N.

WEISSENBURG, a town of Bavarian Franconia, seated on the Rednitz; 5 miles N. of Pappenheim, and 30 S. W. of Nuremburg. Pop. 3300.

WEISSENBURG, or CARLSBURG, a city of Transylvania, capital of a county of the same name, and a bishop's see, with a university. It is seated on the side of a hill, near the river Maros; 42 miles W. N. W. of Hermanstadt.

WEISSENBURG, a town of Switzerland, in the canton of Bern, celebrated for its mineral waters; 20 miles S. of Bern.

WEISSENFELS, a town of Prussian Saxony, on the Saal; 17 miles S. W. of Leipsic. Upon a white rock above the town is a fine citadel, called Augustusburg.

WEISSENHORN, a town and castle of Germany, in a county of its name, seated on the Roth; 10 miles S. E. of Ulm, and 28 W. of Augsburg.

WEISSENSEE, a town of Prussian Saxony, with a superintendency and commandery of the knights of Malta. The lake formerly in its neighbourhood was drained, and converted into arable land, in 1705. It was 21 miles N. E. of Langensalza.

WEISSKIRCHEN, a town of Hungary, bannat of Temeswar; 53 miles S. by E. of Temeswar. Pop. 4300.

WELAU, a town of East Prussia, celebrated for the treaty concluded here with Poland in 1657, when the elector, Frederic William, was invested with the sovereignty of Ducal Prussia. It is seated on the Pregel, at the influx of the Alla; 30 miles E. of Konigsberg.

WELLAND, a river which rises in Northamptonshire, and separates that county from Leicestershire, Rutlandshire, and Lincolnshire: it passes by Market Deeping to Stamford, and is thence navigable to the Fossdike Wash, which it enters below Spalding.

WELLINGBOROUGH, a town in Northamptonshire, with a market on Wednesday. Here are manufactures of shoes and lace, and near it is a fine chalybeate spring called Redwell. A fire happened here in 1738, which consumed above 800 houses. It is seated on the side of a hill, on the river Nen; 12 miles N. E. of Northampton, and 67 N. by W. of London.

WELLINGTON, a town in Shropshire, with a market on Thursday. In the neighbourhood are foundries, iron-mines, and coal-works. It is situate near Wrekin Hill; 12 miles E. of Shrewsbury, and 150 N. W. of London.

WELLINGTON, a town in Somersetshire, with a market on Thursday, and manufactures of serges, druggets, and earthenware. The duke of Wellington takes his title from this place. It is seated on the Tone; 15 miles N. E. of Exeter, and 148 W. by S. of London.

WELLINGTON, or DURHAM, a town founded in 1838, in Port Nicholson, on the N. island of New Zealand. It is seated on the W. side of the port in Lambton Harbour, and near Cook's Strait, which separates the two islands.

WELLS, a city of Somersetshire, governed by a mayor; with markets on Wednesday and Saturday. It returns two members to parliament. It has its name from the wells and springs about it; and is a bishop's see, jointly with Bath. The cathedral is a stately pile; and the bishop's palace is like a castle, being surrounded by walls and a moat. The city is well built and neatly paved. The summer assizes are held here alternately with Bridgewater It is seated at the foot of the Mendip Hills; 16 miles S. of Bristol, and 120 W. of London. Long. 2. 37. W. lat. 51. 12. N.

WELLS, a town in Norfolk, which has a large church, and a considerable corn trade. It stands near the sea; 34 miles N. N. E. of Norwich, and 118 N. N. E. of London.

WELLS, a town of Maine, in York county, situate on a bay of its name; 88 miles N. by E. of Boston. Long. 70. 52. W. lat. 43. 20. N.

WELLS, a town of West Florida, on the W. side of St. Andrew Bay; 60 miles W. of St. Marco.

WELS, a town of Upper Austria, with a castle, and a great trade in timber, seated on the Traun, near a large forest; 15 miles S. S. W. of Lintz.

WELSHPOOL, a corporate town of Wales, in Montgomeryshire, with a market on Monday. It is the great mart for Welsh cottons, flannels, &c., which are sent hence to Shrewsbury. Near the town are the remains of Powis Castle, a large structure, built on an eminence. It is seated in a rich vale, on the river Severn; 9 miles N. of Montgomery, 19 W. of Shrewsbury, and 176 N. W. of London.

WELWARN, a town of Bohemia, in the circle of Rakonitz; 13 miles N. of Prague.

WELWYN, a village in Hertfordshire, 5 miles N. of Hatfield. Dr. Young was rector of this place, and here he wrote his celebrated Night Thoughts.

WELZHEIM, a town of Wirtemberg, seated on the Lein; 19 miles E. of Stutgard.

WEM, a town in Shropshire, with a market on Thursday; 9 miles N. of Shrewsbury.

WENDLINGEN, a town of Wirtemberg, situate on the Neckar; 12 miles S. S. E. of Stutgard.

WENDOVER, a town in Buckinghamshire, with markets on Tuesday and Thursday; 5 miles S. E. of Aylesbury, and 35 N. W. of London.

WENLOCK, or MUCH WENLOCK, a borough in Shropshire, sending two members to parliament, with a market on Monday; 12 miles S. E. of Shrewsbury, and 148 N. W. of London.

WENNER, the largest lake of Sweden, lying in West Gothland, to the N. W. of the Lake Wetter. It is 100 miles in length, and in some places 40 in breadth, and contains several islands. It receives 24 rivers, and its only outlet is the river Gotha.

WENNERSBORG, a town of Sweden, in West Gothland, with a castle. It is the staple for all the iron sent from the province of Wermeland to Gotheburg. It is seated on the Gotha, near the S. W. extremity of the Lake Wenner; 50 miles N. by E. of Gotheburg.

WENTERSWYK, a town of Holland, in the province of Gelderland, seated on the river Sling; 25 miles W. S. W. of Zutphen. Pop. 5700.

WEOBLEY, a town in Herefordshire, noted for its excellent ale; with a market on Tuesday. It is 10 miles N. W. of Hereford, and 147 W. N. W. of London.

WERCHTEREN, a town of Belgium, in Brabant; 9 miles E. S. E. of Mechlin.

WERDAU, a town of Germany, in the kingdom of Saxony; 6 miles W. of Zwickau; on the river Pleisse. Pop. 3000.

WERDEN, a town of Prussian Westphalia, seated on the Roer; 13 miles N. E. of Dusseldorf.

WERDENBERG, a town of Switzerland, in the canton of St. Gall, on the Rhine; 8 miles N. of Sargans. Pop. 4000.

WERDENFELS, a town and castle of Bavaria, giving name to a county on the frontiers of Tyrol; 16 miles S. of Weilheim, and 22 N. W. of Inspruc.

WERDERBERG, a fortified town of Switzerland, capital of a bailiwick in the canton of Glarus; with a castle on an eminence. It is seated near the Rhine; 10 miles S. S. E. of Appenzel, and 26 E. N. E. of Glarus.

WERFEN, a town and fortress of Austria, in the province of Salzburg, situate on the Salza; 22 miles S. by E. of Salzburg.

WERL, a town of Prussian Westphalia, with a castle, seated on the Sisek; 8 miles S. of Ham. Pop. 2300.

WERMELAND, a former province of Sweden, the N. part of Gothland, between Dalecarlia and the lake Wenner; 100 miles long, and 50 broad. The country is fertile, diversified by mountains, rocks, hills, and dales, clothed with forests of birch, poplar, mountain ash, pine, and fir. It also abounds with lakes, which succeed each other almost without intermission; and numerous rivulets flow from these lakes. The chief river is the Clara, or Stor Elbe, in which is a good salmon-fishery. It has mines of silver, lead, copper, and iron, with forges, foundries, &c., belonging to them.

WERN, a town of Prussian Westphalia, seated near the Lippe; 6 miles W. of Ham.

WERNIGERODE, a town of the Prussian states, capital of a county of the same name, abounding in mountains, the principal of which is the Great Brocken, or Blocksberg. The principal business of the town consists in brewing, distilling, and manufactures of cloth and stuffs. It is 12 miles W. by S. of Halberstadt, and 23 S. S. E. of Wolfenbuttel. Pop. 5100. Long. 10. 58. E. lat. 51. 53. N.

Werra, a river of Germany, which rises in the principality of Coburg; 3 miles above Eissfeld; flows by Hildburghausen, Meiningen, Salzungen, Vacha, Trefurt, Wanfried, Allendorf, and Witzenhausen; it then enters the duchy of Brunswick, passes by Munden, and a little below that town joins the Fulda, where the united stream forms the Weser.

Wertheim, a town of Germany, in Baden; capital of a county of the same name, which yields excellent wine. It is seated at the conflux of the Tauber with the Maine; 16 miles W. of Wurtzburg. Population of the county, 12,000; of the town, 3200.

Werwick, a town of the Netherlands, in Flanders, seated on the Lis; 8 miles S. E. of Ypres.

Wesel, a town of the Prussian states, in the duchy of Cleve, with a strong citadel. Here are two Calvinist churches, one for the Lutherans, and another for the Papists. It is seated on the Rhine, at the influx of the Lippe; 25 miles S. E. of Cleve, and 50 W. S. W. of Munster. Pop. 8000. Long. 6. 37. E. lat. 51. 38. N.

Wesenburg, a fortified town of Russia, in the government of Esthonia, seated on the Wiss; 45 miles E. of Revel.

Weser, a river of Germany, formed by the union of the Werra and Fulda, in the duchy of Brunswick, at Munden. It flows along the confines of Westphalia and Saxony, by Corvey, Hamelin, Minden, and Hoye, receives the Aller from Verden, and, passing by Bremen, enters the German Ocean at Carlsburg.

West Chester, a county in the S. E. part of New York, with 48,686 inhabitants. Chief towns, Bedford and White Plains.

West Chester, a town in the foregoing county, seated on East River; 12 miles N. E. of New York. Pop. 4154.

West Chester, a town of Pennsylvania, capital of Chester county. It contains several public institutions, and is connected by a branch to the Columbia railroad; 24 miles W. of Philadelphia. Pop. 2152.

West Point, a village and military post of New York, in Orange county, on the W. bank of the Hudson. It is situate amid the high lands, and so strongly fortified by nature and art, that it is called the Gibraltar of America. It is 20 miles S. of Poughkeepsie, and 54 N. of New York.

Westbury, a borough in Wiltshire, with a market on Friday, and a manufacture of broad cloth. On a hill to the E. of the town is Bratton Castle, the remains of a fortification, where the Danes held out 24 days against the English. It returns one member to parliament. It is 21 miles N. W. of Salisbury, and 98 W. of London.

Westeras, a town of Sweden, capital of a government of its name, and a bishop's see, with a citadel, and a famous college. It carries on a considerable commerce with Stockholm, particularly in copper and iron from the neighbouring mines. Here are the ruins of an ancient palace, formerly inhabited by the kings of Sweden. The cathedral, built of brick, is celebrated for its tower, esteemed the highest in the kingdom. In this cathedral is the tomb of the unfortunate Eric XIV. Westeras is seated on the Lake Maeler; 46 miles N. W. of Stockholm. Pop. 3000. Long. 17. 0. E. lat. 59. 38. N.

Westerburg, a town of Germany, in the duchy of Nassau, with a castle; 22 miles S. W. of Dillenburg, and 40 N. of Mentz.

Westerham, a town in Kent, with a market on Wednesday, on the Darent, which rises near this town. It is pleasantly seated in a vale, at the foot of the chalk range. The church is a handsome structure, and contains a monument of General Wolfe, the conqueror of Quebec, who was born here, January 2nd, 1727; 21 miles S. S. E. of London.

Westerly, a town of Rhode Island, in Washington county, with a good coasting trade, and extensive fisheries. It stands at the mouth of Paukatuk; 5 miles E. of Stonington, in Connecticut. Pop. 1912.

Western Islands. *See* Azores and Hebrides.

Westerwald. *See* Wetteravia.

Westerwick, a seaport of Sweden, in Smaland, with a good harbour, a commodious quay, a cloth manufacture, and a trade in ship-timber and all sorts of naval stores. It is seated on the Baltic; 56 miles N. of Calmar, and 126 S. W. of Stockholm. Long. 16. 0. E. lat. 57. 40. N. Pop. 3000.

Westfield, a town of Massachusets, in Hampden county, on a river of its name; 10 miles W. of Springfield. Pop. 3526.

Westhofen, a town of Germany, in the palatinate of the Rhine. It has three churches. It is 7 miles N. W. of Worms.

Westhofen, a town of France, in the department of Lower Rhine; 12 miles W. of Strasburg.

Westmania, a former province of Sweden, between Upland, Sudermania, Nericia, Wermeland, and Dalecarlia. It is 75 miles long, and 45 broad. Pop. 110,000. It abounds in copper and iron-mines. The face of the country is diversified like Wermeland.

Westmeath. *See* Meath.

Westminster, a city of Middlesex, the residence of the monarch, the seat of the parliament, and of the high courts of justice, and constituting, with London and Southwark, the metropolis of the British empire. On the dissolution of its abbey, in 1541, Henry VIII. erected it into a bishopric, appointing the whole of Middlesex, (Fulham excepted,) for the diocese. It had, however, only one prelate; for Edward VI. soon after dissolved it, and the abbey is now only a collegiate church. Westminster, through courtesy, still bears the title of a city, and sends two members to parliament, who are chosen by its householders, there being no freemen nor incorporated companies.

Besides the churches of the establishment, Westminster contains places of worship for dissenters of almost every denomination, and a Jews' synagogue. In the city are two parish churches, St. Margaret and St. John; and seven in the liberties, namely, St. Clement, St. Mary, St. Paul, St. Martin, St. Ann, St. James, and St. George. The precinct of St. Martin-le-Grand, though within the city of London, is under the jurisdiction of Westminster. *See* LONDON.

WESTMINSTER, a town of Vermont, in Windham county, on Connecticut River, opposite Walpole, in New Hampshire, with which it communicates by a bridge; 40 miles N. E. of Bennington.

WESTMORELAND, an inland county of England, 42 miles long, and from 16 to 40 broad; bounded on the N. and N. W. by Cumberland, E. and S. E. by Yorkshire, and S. W. by Lancashire. It contains 462,080 acres, is divided into four wards, and 32 parishes, has eight market-towns, and sends two members to parliament. It is a region of lofty mountains, naked hills, dreary forests, and barren moors; but is watered by numerous rivers, and several lakes. The soil, of course, is various; that on the mountains being very barren, while that in the valleys is fertile, producing good corn and grass, especially in the meadows near the rivers. In the hilly parts on the W. borders are some mines of copper, but the ore lies very deep. This county yields abundance of limestone, and the finest blue slate; and many excellent hams are cured here. Its manufactures are a coarse woollen cloth, worsted stockings, flannels, tanned leather, and gunpowder. The principal rivers are the Eden, Lune, and Ken; and the chief lake is Winandermere, the largest in England. Appleby is the county town.

WESTOE, a borough in the county of Durham, a suburb of South Shields, the market-place, and many of the principal streets of which are in this township; and, in conjunction with it, it sends one member to parliament.

WESTPHALIA, one of the former circles of Germany, bounded on the E. by Lower Saxony, S. by Hesse, Wetteravia, and Treves, W. by the Netherlands, and N. by the German Ocean. The climate is cold, and there are a great many marshes, but the soil produces pastures, and some corn. The horses are large, and the hogs in high esteem, especially the hams, known by the name of Westphalia hams. The principal rivers are the Weser, Ems, Lippe, and Roer. This circle contained the bishoprics of Munster, Liege, Paderborn, and Osnaburg; the principalities of Emden, or East Friesland, Meurs, Minden, and Verden; the duchies of Westphalia, Berg, Juliers, Cleve, Oldenburg, and part of the territories of the princes of Nassau; the counties of Mark, Ravensberg, Steinfurt, Tecklenburg, Lingen, Bentheim, Diepholt, Hoya, Schauenburg, Spigelburg, Lippe, Ritberg, and other smaller ones; and several lordships and abbeys. In 1800 all the parts of the circle lying on the left bank of the Rhine, being full one-third of the whole territory, became united to France; and in 1808 the French emperor erected the remainder into a kingdom, in favour of his brother Jerome, and added to it the electorates of Hesse-Cassel and Hanover. Cassel was the capital. After the celebrated battle of Leipsic, in 1813, this new kingdom was overrun by the allies, and the government overthrown. The whole territory now belongs to Prussia, Hanover, and Oldenburg.

WESTPHALIA, a province of the Prussian states, bounded W. by the Netherlands, and E. by Hanover and Hesse-Cassel. It is divided into the districts of Arensberg, Minden, and Munster. It contains an area of 8300 square miles, with 1,000,000 of inhabitants. The soil in general is not fertile, but large quantities of flax are raised, and the rearing of cattle is carried to a great extent. There are mines of lead, iron, and coal in the mountainous districts, and extensive salt-works in different parts of the province.

WESTPHALIA, a duchy of Germany, in the Prussian province of Westphalia, and government of Arensberg; 40 miles long, and 25 broad; bounded on the N. by the principalities of Munster and Osnaburg, and the county of Lippe; W. by that of Mark; S. by the territories of Nassau; and E. by the counties of Witgenstein, Hartzfeld, Waldeck, and Hesse. It is a mountainous country, full of wood, but moderately fertile. Area, 1700 square miles. Pop. 150,000. It formerly belonged to the elector of Cologne, but was ceded to the prince of Hesse-Darmstadt in 1802, and made over to Prussia in 1814.

WESTPORT, a town of Ireland, in the county of Mayo; 8 miles W. of Castlebar.

WESTPORT, a town of Massachusets, in Bristol county, seated on Buzzard's Bay; 24 miles S. of Taunton. Pop. 2820.

WESTRA, one of the Orkney Islands, 9 miles long, and from 1 to 3 broad. It has a trade in kelp, and a good harbour for small vessels on the N. W. side; 9 miles N. N. E. of Pomona. Long. 2. 52. W. lat. 69. 8. N.

WETHERBY, a town in West Yorkshire, with a market on Thursday, seated on the Wharf, over which is a handsome stone bridge; 15 miles W. by S. of York, and 191 N. by W. of London.

WETHERSFIELD, a town in the United States, in the state of Connecticut, famous for its onions. It is situated on the W. bank of the river Connecticut; 4 miles S. of Hartford. Population, 3824.

WETTER, a lake of Sweden, in Gothland, S. E. of the lake Wenner. It is 100 miles in length, and in some places 20 in breadth. Above 40 small streams enter this lake, and its only outlet is the river Motala, which flows E. by Nordkoping into the Baltic.

WETTEREN, a town of Belgium, in the province of East Flanders, on the river Scheldt, with a considerable manufacture of lace, linen, and woollens. It is 7 miles E. of Ghent. Population, 7200.

Wetteravia, or Weteraw, a name originally applied to a district of Germany, lying on the banks of the river Wetter, but now so extended as to denote all the country between the Lahn, the Rhine, and the Maine.

Wettin, a town of Prussian Saxony, in the duchy of Magdeburg, with a castle on a mountain, seated on the Saal, over which is a ferry; 9 miles N. N. W. of Halle. Pop. 2700.

Wettingen, a town of Switzerland, in the county of Baden, celebrated for its wooden bridge, 240 feet long, of a single arch, over the river Limmat. It is 1 mile S. of Baden.

Wetzlar, a town of Germany, in Wetteravia, capital of a county of the same name. It is surrounded by ditches, and walls flanked with towers. It is seated at the confluence of the Lahn, Disle, and Dillen; 30 miles N. of Frankfort. Long. 8. 37. E. lat. 50. 33. N.

Wevelghem, a town of Belgium, in the province of West Flanders, on the river Nederbeeke, with a manufacture of dimities. Population, 3100.

Wevelsburg, a town and citadel of Westphalia, in the principality of Paderborn; 9 miles S. of Paderborn.

Wexford, a county of Ireland, in the province of Munster, 47 miles long, and 30 broad, bounded on the N. by Wicklow, E. by St. George's Channel, S. by the Atlantic Ocean, W. by Waterford and Kilkenny, and N. W. by Catherlough. It contains 142 parishes, has two boroughs, and sends two members to parliament. The surface is mountainous, but the soil in general is fertile in corn and grass. The principal rivers are the Barrow and Slaney.

Wexford, a borough of Ireland, sending one member to parliament, and capital of the foregoing county. It has a spacious harbour at the mouth of the Slaney, on a bay of St. George's Channel, but the water is not deep enough for large vessels. Much woollen cloth is manufactured here, and in the neighbourhood. It is 33 miles E. N. E. of Waterford, and 60 S. of Dublin. Long. 6. 30. W. lat. 52. 22. N.

Wexio, a town of Sweden, in Smaland, seated on the Lake Helga, which contains a group of woody islands. It is a bishop's see, though small. It is 50 miles W. of Calmar.

Wey, a river which rises in Hampshire, flows through Surrey by Godalming and Guildford, and enters the Thames at Weybridge.

Weybridge, a village in Surrey, seated on the Wey, near its entrance into the Thames, and near the South Western railway; 2 miles E. of Chertsey.

Weyhill, a village in Hampshire, famous for an annual fair for all kinds of cattle and sheep, leather, hops, cheese, and pedlary. It is one of the largest fairs in England, lasting 10 days; 3 miles W. of Andover.

Weymouth, a seaport and borough in Dorsetshire, with markets on Tuesday and Friday. It stands on a bay of its name, in the English Channel, and on the S. side of the mouth of the Wey, which separates it from the borough of Melcomb Regis. The two boroughs are united as one corporation, returning two members to parliament, governed by a mayor; and the communication between them is by means of a bridge. *See* Melcomb Regis. The harbour is injured by the sand, so that its trade, which was once considerable, is much reduced. This decline is in some degree compensated by the great resort of persons of all ranks, for the purpose of sea-bathing, for which it is excellently fitted by its remarkably fine beach; and the royal family have often honoured it with their residence for many weeks. Here is a handsome battery, a royal assembly-room, and an elegant theatre. In the church is a fine altar-piece, executed and presented by Sir James Thornhill, who was born at Melcomb Regis. A few plain and striped cottons are made here. Near it, at the village of Nottington, is a famous sulphureous spring. Weymouth is 9 miles S. of Dorchester, and 128 W. S. W. of London. Long. 2. 34. W. lat. 50. 40. N.

Whampoa, a town of China, province of Quangtung, on an island in the Canton river. Merchant vessels stop at this town and communicate with Canton by means of boats. It is 45 miles N. of Macao, and 10 S. of Canton.

Wharnside, the highest mountain in England, situate in the N. W. part of Yorkshire, amid other mountains, and about 6 miles to the N. of that called Ingleborough. Its summit is 4050 feet above the level of the sea. Near the top are four or five tarns or small lakes. Its base contains several spacious caverns, of which the principal are Yordas, Gatekirk, and Greenside caves.

Wheeling, a town of Virginia, in Ohio county, which participates with Pittsburg in the trade to the western country. It is situate at the mouth of a creek on Ohio River; 45 miles S. W. of Pittsburg.

Whidah, a country of Guinea, on the Slave Coast, extending about 10 miles along the Atlantic, and 12 miles inland. Europeans who have been in this country extol it as the most beautiful in the world, and assert that spring and autumn reign perpetually in alternate succession. The country is so populous that one single village contains as many inhabitants as some entire kingdoms on the coast of Guinea. The people, in their manners, have been compared to the Chinese; the same persevering industry, ceremonious civility, jealous affection for their women, and thievish inclinations in trade, prevail in both countries. Bows, arrows, assagays, and clubs, are the principal weapons of the Whidanese. They have no distinction of hours, days, weeks, or stated periods; and yet, without pen, ink, or the assistance of artificial arithmetic, they calculate any thing with great accuracy. They are said to have a faint idea of a Supreme Being, to whom they attribute omnipotence, and consider him as the Creator of the universe. He is, they say, too highly exalted to have any concern about his creatures; and the government of the world he leaves to the fetiches, to whom, therefore, they apply as the mediators between God and them.

These fetiches are divided into three classes, snakes, tall trees, and the sea; and sometimes they add a fourth, namely, the chief river of the kingdom, the Euphrates. The deified snakes are about a yard long, amazingly tame and familiar; and no insult or injury can be offered to them by a native under pain of death. Here are oxen, cows, goats, sheep, hogs, turkeys, ducks, and hens; also elephants, buffaloes, tigers, several kinds of deer, and a sort of hares. The fruits are citrons, lemons, oranges, bananas, tamarinds, &c., and there are vast numbers of palm-trees, from which much wine is made. The trade consists chiefly of elephants' teeth, wax, and honey; and the principal manufactures are cloths, umbrellas, baskets, pitchers for pito or beer, plates and dishes of wood, gourds finely ornamented, white and blue paper, &c. In 1727 the king of Dahomy reduced this country to the state of a dependent province. Xavier, or Sabi, is the capital.

Whitby, a borough and seaport in North Yorkshire, with a market on Saturday. It returns one member to parliament. It has a considerable manufacture of canvas, and a great traffic in the building of ships, and in the carrying business. In the neighbourhood are some large alum works. The principal public buildings are the church, a chapel of ease, several places of worship for dissenters, a town-hall, a dispensary, a library, and a commodious news-room. Its harbour is the best on this coast, and has a fine pier; but it has no river communication with the inland country. Several ships are sent hence to the Greenland fishery. In 1787 a strong new-built quay, running parallel to a high cliff, fell into the sea, followed by large masses of the cliff. The remains of an abbey church stood on this cliff, and since the above accident several parts have fallen to the ground. Whitby is the birthplace of James Cook, the great circumnavigator. It is seated at the mouth of the Esk; 48 miles N. N. E. of York, and 243 N. of London. Long. 0. 30. W. lat. 54. 30. N.

Whitchurch, a town in Hampshire, market on Friday; seated on the Test, near its source; 12 miles N. of Winchester, and 56 W. by S. of London.

Whitchurch, a town in Shropshire, with a market on Friday. It is noted for its annual races, and contains a handsome church, several places of worship for dissenters, an excellent free-school, a charity-school, almshouses, &c.; 20 miles N. of Shrewsbury, and 160 N. W. of London.

White Mountains, the highest part of a ridge of mountains in the state of New Hampshire. They extend N. E. and S. W.; their height above an adjacent meadow is 5500 feet, and the meadow is 3500 feet above the level of the sea. The snow and ice cover them nine or ten months in the year; and during that time they exhibit the bright appearance from which they are denominated the White Mountains. Although they are 70 miles inland, they are seen many leagues off at sea, and appear like an exceedingly bright cloud in the horizon. Their highest summit is in lat. 44. N.

White Sea, a large bay of the Frozen Ocean, on the N. part of Russia, on the E. side of which stands the city of Archangel.

Whitehall, (formerly Skenesborough,) a town of New York, in Washington county. It has a considerable trade, and is the great thoroughfare between New York and Montreal; 70 miles N. of Albany. Pop. 3 13.

Whitehaven, a borough and seaport in Cumberland, with markets on Tuesday, Thursday, and Saturday. It returns one member to parliament. It is seated on a creek of the Irish Sea, on the N. end of a great hill, washed by the tide on the W. side, where there is a large whitish rock, and a strong stone wall that secures the harbour. Near it are excellent coal mines, some of which run a considerable way under the sea, and are the chief source of its wealth; but its trade is now extended to foreign parts. Here are yards for ship-building, an extensive canvas manufacture, large roperies, and several copperas works. The town is defended by batteries, and has four neat churches, and several meeting-houses. It is 41 miles S. W. of Carlisle, and 320 N. N. W. of London. Long. 3. 35. W. lat. 54. 25. N.

Whithorn, a borough of Scotland, in Wigtonshire, near the bay of Wigton. It contributes, with Wigton, &c., in sending one member to parliament. It is a place of great antiquity, having been a Roman station, and the first bishopric in Scotland; 11 miles S. of Wigton.

Whitestown, a town of New York, in Herkimer county; 50 miles W. N. W. of Canajohary. Pop. 5156.

Whitstable, a town on the coast of Kent, 7 miles N. N. W. of Canterbury. It is a small port, whence Canterbury is supplied with coal by means of a railroad, and has several trading vessels to London.

Whitsuntide Island, one of the New Hebrides in the South Pacific; 30 miles long, and 8 broad; discovered by Captain Wallis on Whit-sunday, 1767. Long. 168. 20. E. lat. 15. 44. S.

Whittlebury Forest, a forest in the S. part of Northamptonshire; 9 miles long, and 3 broad. In 1685 the first Duke of Grafton was appointed hereditary ranger of this forest, in which is a fine seat, called Wakefield Lodge.

Wiburg, or Viborg, an extensive district of Russia, in the government of Finland It was ceded by the Swedes to the Russians, partly by the peace of Nystadt in 1721, and partly by the treaty of Abo in 1743. Besides pastures, the country produces rye, oats, and barley, but not sufficient for the inhabitants.

Wiburg, a fortified seaport of Russia, capital of the foregoing district, and a bishop's see, with a strong citadel. The houses are almost entirely built of stone. The chief exports are planks, tallow, pitch, and tar. The surrounding country is pleasant; and near it, at Imatra, is the famous cataract of the Woxa, which makes a noise more stunning than that of the Rhine at Lauffen. Wiburg stands on the N. E. point of the Gulf of Finland; 100 miles N. N. W. of Petersburg. Long. 29. 10. E. lat. 60. 56. N.

WIBURG, a city of Denmark, in North Jutland, capital of a diocese of the same name, and the seat of the chief court of justice in the province. In 1726 the cathedral, a church, the town-house, and the bishop's palace, were destroyed by fire; but they have all been magnificently rebuilt. It is seated on a lake, in a peninsula; 120 miles N. of Sleswick. Long. 9. 50. E. lat. 56. 20. N.

WICK, a borough of Scotland, and the capital of Caithness-shire; united with Cromarty, Dingwall, &c., in sending one member to parliament; with a harbour on an inlet of the German Ocean, at the mouth of a river of the same name. Much kelp is made here, but the herring-fisheries are the chief object of importance. It is 55 miles N. E. of Dornock. Long. 2. 51. W. lat. 58. 01. N.

WICK, a fortified town of the Netherlands, in the duchy of Limburg, seated on the Meuse, opposite Maestricht, with which it communicates by a bridge.

WICK DUERSTEDE, a town of Prussian Westphalia, with two castles; 12 miles N. of Juliers.

WICKLOW, a county of Ireland, in the province of Leinster; 36 miles long, and 25 broad; bounded on the N. by Dublin, E. by the Irish Sea, S. by Wexford, W. by Catherlough and Kildare, and N. W. by Kildare. It is divided into 58 parishes, and sends two members to parliament. It is very mountainous and woody, interspersed with rocks and bogs, but the valleys are fertile and well cultivated, and watered by numerous small rivers.

WICKLOW, the capital of the foregoing county, is seated on the Irish Sea, with a narrow harbour, at the mouth of the river Leitrim; 26 miles S. S. E. of Dublin. Long. 6. 12. W. lat. 52. 58. N.

WIDDIN, a fortified town of Bulgaria, and an archbishop's see. It has often been taken and retaken by the Austrians and Turks. It is seated on the Danube; 100 miles N. by W. of Sossa, and 140 E. S. E. of Belgrade. Pop. 20,000. Long. 24. 27. E. lat. 44. 12. N.

WIED, a county of Germany, at the conflux of the rivers Wied and Rhine. It is composed of two parts, the Upper County, or Wied-Runkel, and the Lower County, or Wied-Nieuwied. Area, 170 square miles. Pop. 24,000.

WIED, a town of Germany, in the Lower County of Wied; 9 miles N. N. W. of Coblentz.

WIELUN, a town of Prussian Poland, with a good castle; 16 miles S. of Siradia.

WIELITSKA, a village of Austrian Poland, in Galicia, celebrated for its salt mines, which extend under the whole town, and to a considerable distance on each side. In these mines are several small chapels, excavated in the salt; and many of the inhabitants reside chiefly in the mines. It is 8 miles S. E. of Cracow. Pop. 2200.

WIESENSTEIG, a town of Wirtemberg, with a castle, seated on the Fils; 16 miles W. N. W. of Ulm, and 25 E. S. E. of Stutgard.

WIESENTHAL, a town of Saxony, in Meissen, with manufactures of iron, steel, and fire-arms, and a considerable trade in leather. It stands on a rivulet of the same name, on the frontiers of Bohemia; 15 miles N. by E. of Carlsbad.

WIGAN, a borough in Lancashire, governed by a mayor, with markets on Monday and Friday. It returns two members to parliament. It has manufactures of strong checks and other articles of linen and cotton. Braziery has long been a staple article; and there is a large pottery of fine ware. Here are two churches, two Roman Catholic chapels, five meeting-houses for dissenters, a free-school, a blue-coat school, a school of industry, a dispensary, a mechanics' institute, &c. The town is lighted by gas, under a company chartered in 1823, and is well supplied with water. In the neighbourhood are very extensive iron-works; a mineral spring of a somewhat similar nature with that of Harrowgate, and plenty of that species of coal called cannel, which is so soft before it is brought into the open air, that snuff-boxes and a variety of toys are made of it. In 1650 a battle was fought here between the forces of Charles I. and those of the parliament, in which the latter were victorious; the Earl of Derby, who commanded the former, being then taken prisoner and afterwards beheaded. Wigan is seated on the rivulet Douglas, which is made navigable to the Ribble, and joins a canal from Liverpool, and on the N. the Union railway. It is 39 miles S. of Lancaster, and 196 N. N. W. of London. Long. 2. 50. W. lat. 53. 34. N.

WIGHT, an island in the English Channel, on the S. coast of Hampshire, from which it is separated by a narrow strait. It is about 21 miles in length, and 13 in breadth, and is nearly divided into two equal parts by the river Medina, or Cowes, which, rising in the southern angle, enters at the northern into the channel, opposite the mouth of Southampton Bay. The S. coast is bordered with very steep cliffs of chalk and free-stone, hollowed into caverns in various parts. The W. side is fenced with ridges of rocks, of which the most remarkable are those called the Needles. Between the island and the main are various sand-banks, especially off the E. part, where is the safe road of St. Helens. Across the island from E. to W. runs a ridge of hills, forming a tract of fine downs, with a chalky or marly soil, which feeds a great number of rabbits and fine fleeced sheep. To the N. of this ridge the land is chiefly pasture; to the S. of it is a rich arable country, producing great crops of corn. The variety of prospects which this island affords, its mild air, and the neat manner in which the the fields are laid out, render it a very delightful spot. It is devoted almost entirely to husbandry, and has no manufactures of any consequence. Among its products are to be reckoned a pure white pipe-clay, and a fine white crystalline sand, of the latter of which great quantities are exported for the use of the glass-works of various parts. The other articles of export are wheat, flour, barley, malt, and salt. Its principal town is Newport. It returns one member to parliament.

WIGTON, a town in Cumberland, with a market on Tuesday, and manufactures of linen and cotton; also an extensive calico-printing establishment, and a hat manufactory. Besides the parish church, which is a neat structure, here are meeting-houses for Independents, Quakers, and Methodists; also a free grammar-school, Brookfield-school, established by the Quakers, in 1826, and an hospital for six clergymen's widows. It is seated among the moors; 12 miles S. W. of Carlisle, and 304 N. N. W. of London.

WIGTON, a borough and seaport of Scotland, capital of Wigtonshire. It sends one member to parliament, with Whithorn, &c. Here are manufactures of woollen and cotton, the former chiefly of plaids and flannel. It is situate on a hill which overlooks the bay of Wigton; 105 miles S. S. W. of Edinburgh. Long. 4. 23. W. lat. 54. 57. N.

WIGTONSHIRE, or WEST GALLOWAY, a county of Scotland, bounded on the N. by Ayrshire, N. E. by Kirkcudbrightshire, and on all other sides by the Irish Sea. Its greatest extent, in any direction, does not exceed 30 miles, and its figure is very irregular. It is divided into 17 parishes. It returns one member to parliament. The Bays of Luce and Ryan extend inland, forming by their approximation a peninsula, called the Rhyns of Galloway. The principal rivers are the Luce, Cree, and Bladenoch. The coast is tolerably fertile, but the interior and northern parts are mountainous, fit only for the pasturage of sheep and black cattle, and a small breed of horses called galloways.

WIHACS, a frontier town of European Turkey, in Bosnia, seated on a lake formed by the river Unna; 40 miles S. E. of Carlstadt, and 220 W. of Belgrade. Long. 16. 10. E. lat. 45. 34. N.

WILDBAD, a town of Germany, in Wirtemberg, with a celebrated warm-bath, seated on the Enz; 24 miles W. of Stutgard.

WILDBERG, a town of Wirtemberg, situate on the Nagold; 19 miles S. W. of Stutgard.

WILDBERG, a town of Prussia, in Brandenburg; 28 miles N. of Brandenburg.

WILDESHAUSEN, a town of Germany, in the duchy of Oldenburg, seated on the Hunte; 20 miles S. W. of Bremen. Long. 8. 27. E. lat. 52. 53. N.

WILDUNGEN, a town of Germany, in the county of Waldek, with a castle. Near it are mineral springs, and mines of copper, iron, and lead. It is 14 miles S. S. E. of Corbach.

WILHELMSTEIN, a fortress of Germany, in the county of Schauenburg, on an island formed of stones sunk for the purpose, in Steinhudermere. It was erected in 1768, by William, count of Schauenburg-Lippe, for the improvement of his new inventions in the art of war. It stands near the town of Steinhude, 18 miles W N. W. of Hanover.

WILKES, a town of North Carolina, capital of a county of its name, seated on the Yadkin, near its source; 50 miles W. of Morgantown.

WILKESBARRE (formerly Wyoming), a town of Pennsylvania, chief of Luzerne county, on the E. branch of the Susquehanna; 118 miles N. W. of Philadelphia. Pop. 1718.

WILKOMIERS, a town of Russia, in the government of Wilna, seated on the Sweita; 45 miles N. N. W. of Wilna.

WILLIAM, FORT, a fort of Scotland, in the county of Inverness, at the extremity of Loch Linne, where that arm of the sea bends to the W. and forms Loch Eil. It is of a triangular figure. It is 64 miles S. W. of Inverness.

WILLIAM HENRY, a town of Lower Canada, situate at the conflux of the Sorel with the St. Lawrence. It has a Protestant and a Roman Catholic church. The principal channel of intercourse with this country and the United States is through this town. It is 40 miles N. E. of Montreal, and 120 S. W. of Quebec. Long. 73. 22. W. lat. 45. 55. N.

WILLIAMSBOROUGH, a town of North Carolina, chief of Granville county, with a flourishing academy. It has a brisk trade with the back country, and stands on a creek that flows into the Roanoke; 50 miles W. N. W. of Halifax.

WILLIAMSBURG, a town of Virginia, formerly the capital of that state. The college of William and Mary is fixed here, but since the removal of the seat of government, this and other public buildings are much decayed. It is situate between two creeks; 60 miles E. S. E. of Richmond. Long. 77. 3. W. lat. 37. 10. N.

WILLIAMSPORT, a town of Maryland, in Washington county, seated on the Potomac, at the mouth of Conegocheaque Creek; 6 miles S. W. of Elizabethtown, and 75 N. N. W. of Washington.

WILLIAMSTADT, a strong seaport of the Netherlands, in North Brabant, built by William I., prince of Orange, in 1585. It is well built, has a good harbour, and stands on that part of the Meuse called Butterfliet; 15 miles W. N. W. of Breda. Long. 4. 30. E. lat. 51. 30. N.

WILLIAMSTON, a town of Massachusets, in Berkshire county, with a flourishing seminary called William's College, in honour of its liberal founder. It is 28 miles N. of Lenox, and 140 W. N. W. of Boston. Pop. 2153.

WILLIAMSTON, a town of North Carolina, chief of Martin county, situate on the Roanoke; 24 miles W. of Plymouth, and 55 S. E. of Halifax.

WILLIS ISLE, a rocky island at the N. end of the island of Southern Georgia. It was discovered in 1775, and contained the nests of many thousands of shags. Long. 38. 30. W. lat. 54. 0. S.

WILLISAU, a town and bailiwick of Switzerland, in the canton of Lucern, seated among mountains on the river Wiger; 16 miles W. N. W. of Lucern.

WILMANSTRAND, a town of Russia, in the government of Finland, near which an obstinate battle was fought in 1741, between 3000 Swedes and 16,000 Russians, when the former were obliged at length to yield to superiority of number. It is seated on the S. side of the lake Saima; 40 miles N. N. W. of Wiburg, and 100 N. N. W. of Petersburg.

WILMINGTON, a maritime district of North Carolina, comprehending the counties of Brunswick, New Hanover, Onslow, Duplin, and Bladen.

WILMINGTON, a town of North Carolina, chief of New Hanover county, and of the district of its name. It has a considerable trade to the West Indies. It stands on the N. E. branch of Cape Fear River; 34 miles from the sea, and 90 S. S. W. of Newbern. Pop. 4744.

WILMINGTON, a city and seaport of Delaware, in Newcastle county. Here are ten edifices for public worship, and the town, with its neighbourhood, is deemed the greatest seat of manufactures in the United States. Almost the whole of the foreign exports of Delaware are from this place. It is situate on the N. side of Christiana Creek; 2 miles W. of the river Delaware, and 28 S. W. of Philadelphia. Pop. 8367. Long. 75. 40. W. lat. 39. 43. N.

WILNA, a government of Russia, comprising the N. part of Lithuania, and containing an area of 2300 square miles, with about 1,000,000 of inhabitants.

WILNA, a town of Russia, capital of the foregoing government, and a bishop's see, with a university, an ancient castle, and a royal palace. It stands on several little eminences, and has two considerable suburbs, called Antokollo and Rudaiska. Here are upwards of 40 churches, and the magnificent one belonging to the castle has a very rich treasury. In 1748 a dreadful conflagration destroyed 13 churches, and in 1749 another fire happened by lightning, which consumed 6 churches: besides these, the Jewish synagogue, the council-house, 33 palaces, numerous stone edifices, and other buildings were destroyed. The churches have been rebuilt, and some of them in a more elegant manner than before; but the city has not recovered its former grandeur. Wilna was taken by the Russians in 1794, and, with its territory, annexed to that empire. The French took possession of it in 1812, but evacuated it the same year. It is seated on the Vilia; 180 miles E. of Konigsberg, and 240 N. E. of Warsaw. Pop. 54,499. Long. 25. 20. E. lat. 54. 41. N.

WILSDORF, a town of Saxony, in Meissen, near which the Saxons were defeated by the Prussians in 1745. It is 9 miles W. of Dresden.

WILSNACH, a town of Prussia, in Brandenburg; 14 miles N. W. of Havelberg.

WILSOWITZ, a town of the Austrian states, in Moravia; 15 miles E. N. E. of Hradisch.

WILTON, a borough in Wiltshire, market on Wednesday, and a manufacture of carpets and thin woollen stuffs. It returns one member to parliament. It was formerly the capital of the county, but is now much reduced. Here is Wilton House, the magnificent seat of the earl of Pembroke, in which is a celebrated collection of antiques. Wilton is seated between the rivers Willy and Nadder; 3 miles W. by N. of Salisbury, and 85 W. by S. of London.

WILTSHIRE, a county of England, 53 miles long, and 38 broad; bounded on the E. by Berkshire and Hampshire, S. by Hampshire and Dorsetshire, W. by Somersetshire, and N. W. and N. by Gloucestershire. It contains 869,620 acres, is divided into 29 hundreds and 304 parishes, and sends 4 members to parliament for the N. and S. divisions of the county. The air is sharp on the hills in winter, but is mild during that season in the vales. The land in the N. parts is generally hilly and woody, but affords excellent pasture for cattle; and here is made the N. Wiltshire cheese, so much esteemed. In the S. the soil is rich and fertile; in the middle it chiefly consists of downs, that afford the best pasture for sheep; and in the valleys, which divide the downs, are corn fields and rich meadows. Its principal commodities are sheep, wool, wood, and stone; of this last there are excellent quarries on the banks of the Nadder, where some of the stones are 23 yards in length, and four in thickness, without a flaw. The chief manufactures are the different branches of the clothing trade. The principal rivers are the Upper and Lower Avon, the Nadder, Willy, Bourn, and Kennet. Salisbury is the capital.

WIMBLEDON, a village in Surrey, on an elevated heath, 7 miles S. W. of London. On the S. W. angle of the common is a circular encampment, including seven acres; the trench very deep and perfect.

WIMBORNE, or WIMBORNE MINSTER, a town in Dorsetshire, with a market on Friday. It had a monastery, in which were interred the W. Saxon kings Ethelred and Sigeforth, and queen Ethelburga. Its noble church, called the Minster, was formerly collegiate. The town is seated between the Stour and Allen; 6 miles N. of Poole, and 100 S. W. of London.

WIMMIS, a town of Switzerland, in the canton of Bern, seated on the Sibnen. It is 18 miles S. of Bern.

WIMPFEN, a town of Germany, in Hesse-Darmstadt, consisting properly of two towns, called Wimpfen on the Hill, and Wimpfen in the Vale. A salt-work was established here in 1761. It is seated on the Neckar; 8 miles N. of Heilbron, and 22 E. of Heidelberg.

WINCAUNTON, or WINCANTON, a town in Somersetshire, with a market on Wednesday, and manufactures of ticking, dowlas, serges, &c., and a considerable trade in cheese. It is 24 miles S. of Bath, and 108 W. by S. of London.

WINCHCOMB, a town in Gloucestershire, with a market on Saturday. It was formerly noted for its abbey, whose mitred abbot sat in parliament. Near the town is the ruin of Sudeley Castle, where Catherine Parr, queen of Henry VIII., and afterwards wife to Sir Thomas Seymour, died in childbed, not without suspicion of poison. It is 15 miles N. E. of Gloucester and 99 N. N. W. of London.

Winchelsea, a town in Sussex, an appendage to the cinque ports, market on Saturday. It is seated on a rocky cliff, on an inlet of the sea; 4 miles S. W. of Rye, and 64 S. E. of London.

Winchester, a city in Hampshire, governed by a mayor, with markets on Wednesday and Saturday. It sends two members to parliament. It is one mile and a half in circumference, and has eight churches, besides the cathedral, in which were interred several Saxon kings and queens, whose bones were collected by bishop Fox, put into six small gilded coffins, and placed on a wall in the S. side of the choir. In this cathedral is the marble coffin of William Rufus. There are also several meeting-houses for dissenters, and a Roman Catholic chapel. On a fine eminence, overlooking the city, stood the castle, which was taken from Charles I., and afterwards demolished, except the magnificent hall, in which the assizes are now held. Near the site of this castle is the shell of a palace built by Charles II., but never finished: some years since, a part of it was fitted up for the reception of prisoners of war. In the vicinity is St. Mary's College, founded by William of Wykeham, for a warden, 70 scholars, 10 fellows, &c., with exhibitions for New College, Oxford; and contiguous to it is a spacious quadrangular edifice for commoners or gentlemen not on the foundation. At the S. end of the city is the hospital of St. Cross, founded by a bishop of this see, for a master, nine poor brethren, and four out-pensioners. All travellers who call at this hospital have a right to demand some bread and beer, which is always brought to them. Near the E. gate of the city is St. John's hospital, in the hall of which the corporation give their entertainments. Winchester was of great note in the time of the Saxons, and here Egbert was crowned the first sole monarch of England. Here Henry II. held a parliament, king John resided, Henry III. was born, Richard II. held a parliament, and Henry IV. was married, as was also Mary I. Winchester is seated on the river Itchen, which is navigable hence to Southampton; 21 miles N. W. of Chichester, and 62 W. by N. of London. Long. 1. 12. W. lat. 51. 4. N.

Winchester, a town of Virginia, capital of Frederick county. It has edifices for public worship. It is 70 miles W. N. W. of Washington. Pop. 3454. Long. 78. 34. E. lat. 39. 15. N.

Windau, a seaport of Russia, in the government of Courland, with a castle. The exports are pitch, tar, wax, &c., and some ships are built here. It stands at the mouth of a river of the same name, in the Baltic; 76 miles N. W. of Mittau, and 100 N. by E. of Memel. Pop. 1000. Long. 21. 50. E. lat. 57. 15. N.

Windermere, or **Winandermere**, the most extensive lake in England, lying between Westmoreland and Lancashire. It extends 15 miles from N. to S., but is not more than a mile broad. It is famous for its fine char, and abundance of trout, perch, pike, and eel. Its principal feeders are the rivers Rothay and Brathay, and its outlet the river Leven. This lake is intersected by several promontories, and spotted with islands. Among these, the Holme, or Great island, an oblong tract of 30 acres, crosses the lake in a diagonal line, surrounded by a number of inferior isles, finely wooded.

Windham, a town of Connecticut, in a county of its name, seated on the Shetucket, 31 miles E. of Hartford. Pop. of the county, 28,080; of the town, 3832.

Windlengen, a town of the kingdom of Wirtemburg, seated on the Lauter; 12 miles S. E. of Stutgard.

Windsbach, a town and castle of Germany, in the district of Anspach, on the Rednitz; 10 miles S. E. of Anspach.

Windsheim, a town of Germany, in Bavaria, surrounded with ramparts which serve for a promenade. It is seated on the Aisch; 30 miles S. E. of Wurtzburg, and 32 S. S. W. of Bamberg. Pop. 4500.

Windsor, a borough in Berkshire, seated on an eminence, on the Thames, with a market on Saturday. It has been a royal demesne ever since the time of William the Conqueror, who received it from the hands of the abbot of Westminster, in exchange for lands in Essex. The picturesque beauty of its scenery, its noble forest, and the interesting historical associations connected with the vicinity, all combine to confer upon it peculiar attractions; but it owes its chief celebrity to its magnificent castle, the favourite residence of a long line of kings. This castle stands upon a high hill, which rises from the town by a gentle ascent; and its fine terrace, faced with a rampart of free-stone, 1870 feet in length, is one of the noblest walks in Europe, with respect to strength, grandeur, and prospects. It was built originally by William the Conqueror, and enlarged by Henry I. Edward III. (who was born in it) caused the greater part of the edifice to be taken down and rebuilt in its present form. Great additions were made to it by Edward IV., Henry VII., Henry VIII., and Elizabeth. Charles II. enlarged the windows and made them regular, furnished the royal apartments with paintings, enlarged the terrace walk on the N. side, and carried it round the E. and S. sides. After the accession of the illustrious House of Brunswick, and in particular during the reign of George III., splendid improvements were made; and under his late majesty George IV. it assumed its present grand and magnificent appearance. It has undergone many improvements by William IV., and her present majesty. The castle is divided into two large courts, separated from each other by the round tower, allotted for the residence of the governor. On the N. side of the upper court are the state apartments, on the E. the private apartments of his late majesty, and on the S. the suite of rooms set apart for the officers of state. In the centre of the court is an equestrian statue of Charles II. The royal apartments are adorned with a splendid collection of paintings, chiefly formed by his late majesty, and the royal chapel is embellished with a variety of superb carvings, by the celebrated Gibbons. In the lower ward of the castle is St.

George's chapel, an elegant and highly finished structure, of pointed architecture, begun by Edward III. in 1437, in honour of the order of the garter. Edward IV. enlarged the design, and it was completed and embellished as it is now seen, during the reign of Henry VIII. The interior architecture is greatly admired, particularly its stone roof, the whole of which was repaired and beautified in 1790. In this chapel are interred Henry VI., Edward IV., Henry VIII., and his queen Jane Seymour, and Charles I.; and here also is the new royal cemetery commenced by George III., under the direction of the late James Wyatt, the entire dimensions of which are 70 feet long, 28 wide, and 14 deep. The cemetery has already received the remains of the princess Amelia, the duchess of Brunswick, the princess Charlotte, queen Charlotte, George III., the duke of York, the duke of Kent, George IV., and William IV. Connected with the chapel is the charitable institution of the poor knights of Windsor, who receive a yearly allowance of about 40*l.*, and blue cloaks embroidered with the cross of St. George. Opposite the S. E. side of the castle is a mansion called the Queen's Lodge; and below this is the Lower Lodge, for the accommodation of the younger branches of the royal family. Adjoining the Queen's Lodge is the little park, which extends round the E. and N. sides of the castle, and forms a beautiful lawn, 4 miles in circumference. On the S. side of the town is the great park, which is 14 miles in circumference. From that part of the castle called the round tower, the eye embraces one of the most noble and extensive prospects in England; for not fewer than 12 counties may be discerned with the naked eye; while the landscape presents every combination of picturesque beauty. The Thames, winding its serene and majestic course amidst green and luxuriant foliage, which forms the most agreeable and refreshing shade—the vivid green, or deeper brown shades of the forest—hamlets, villas, and hills—all combine to present to the beholder a rural panorama of unrivalled brilliancy and effect. In the interior of the tower is a guard-chamber filled with various kinds of warlike weapons and ancient armour, among which are the coats of mail said to have been worn by John, king of France, and David of Scotland, both of whom are known to have been prisoners in the castle. Windsor is governed by a corporation of 30 brethren, 10 of whom are called aldermen, and the rest benchers and burgesses. From the former of these are annually elected a mayor and justice, and two bailiffs from the latter. It received its first charter from Edward I., and its last from William III. It returns two members to parliament. The parish church is an ancient Gothic edifice, and contains monuments of great interest to the antiquary. The guildhall is a stately edifice, containing several noble apartments, and is decorated chiefly with portraits of the English sovereigns. Here are also many handsome buildings, a free-school, almshouses, and other charities, &c. It is 17 miles E. by N. of Reading, and 22 W. of London. Long. 0. 36. W. lat. 51. 30. N.

WINDSOR, a town of Vermont, chief of a county of its name. The assembly of the state holds its session here and at Rutland alternately. It is seated on the river Connecticut; 40 miles E. by S. of Rutland, and 70 N. E. of Bennington. Pop. 2744 ; of the county, 40,356. Long. 72. 40. W. lat. 43. 27. N.

WINDSOR, a town of Connecticut, in Hartford county, on the river Connecticut; 7 miles N. of Hartford. Pop. 2383.

WINDSOR, a town of North Carolina, chief of Bertie county, situate on the Cushai; 23 miles W. by S. of Edenton.

WINDSOR, a town of New South Wales, near the Hawkesbury river, it has a handsome church. 34 miles from Sydney

WINDSOR, a town of Nova Scotia, with a college, founded by royal charter in 1802. It is seated on a river of the same name; 25 miles N. W. of Halifax.

WINDSOR, NEW, a town of New York, in Ulster county, on the W. side of the Hudson, just above the high lands ; 6 miles N. of West Point.

WINDSOR FOREST, a forest in the E. part of Berkshire, 50 miles in circumference. Though the soil is generally barren and uncultivated, it is finely diversified by hills and dales, woods and lawns, and delightful villas. It contains several towns and villages, of which Oakingham is the principal.

WINDWARD ISLANDS, such of the Caribbee islands in the West Indies as commence at Martinico, and extend to Tobago.

WINDWARD PASSAGE, the strait between Point Maizi, the E. end of the island of Cuba, and Cape St. Nicholas, the N. W. extremity of St. Domingo.

WINNENDEN, a town and castle of Wirtemberg; 12 miles E. N. E. of Stutgard.

WINNICZA, a town of Austrian Poland, with a castle, seated on the river Bog; 35 miles N. of Bracklau.

WINNIPEG, a lake of Upper Canada, N. W. of Lake Superior. It is 240 miles long, and from 50 to 100 broad, and exhibits a body of water next in size to Lake Superior. It contains a number of small islands, receives the waters of several small lakes in every direction, and discharges them by the Nelson and Severn into Hudson's Bay. A very narrow ridge divides its sources from those of the Mississippi. The lands on its banks produce vast quantities of wild rice, and the sugar-maple in great plenty.

WINNSBOROUGH, a town of South Carolina, chief of Fairfield county, with a seminary called Mount Zion College. It stands on Wateree Creek, which flows into the river of that name; 30 miles N. by W. of Columbia.

WINSCHOTEN, a fortified town of the Netherlands, in Groningen. Here, in 1568, was fought the first battle between the revolted Dutch and the Spaniards, who were defeated by Lewis, brother to the prince of Orange. It is 6 miles

S. of Dolbart Bay, and 19 E. S. E. of Groningen.

WINSEN, a town of Hanover, with a castle, seated on the Luhe, near its confluence with the Ilmenau; 15 miles N. W. of Lunenburg. —Another, seated on the Aller; 6 miles below Zell, and 47 S. S. W. of Lunenburg.

WINSLOW, a town in Buckinghamshire, with a market on Tuesday; 7 miles N. W. of Aylesbury, and 49 W. N. W. of London.

WINSLOW, a town of the state of Maine, in Lincoln county, seated on the Kennebec; 18 miles N. of Harrington.

WINSTER, a town in Derbyshire, with a market on Saturday. It is situate among rich lead mines; 26 miles N. N. W. of Derby.

WINTERBERG, a town of Bohemia, with a celebrated glass manufactory; 77 miles S. by W. of Pryne.

WINTERTHUR, a town of Switzerland, in the canton of Zurich, where there are mineral baths. The articles made here by the smiths and turners are in great estimation; and it has manufactures of earthenware, striped camlets, and cotton. It is seated in a fertile plain, on the river Alach; 12 miles E. N. E. of Zurich.

WINTERTON, a village on the E. coast of Norfolk, near a promontory called Wintertonness, on which is a lighthouse; 8 miles N. by W. of Yarmouth.

WINTHROP, a town of Maine, in Kennebec county; 10 miles W. by S. of Harrington.

WINTON, a town of North Carolina, chief of Hartford county, situate on the Chowan; 12 miles S. S. E. of Murfreesborough, and 30 N. W. of Edenton.

WINWEILER, a town of Germany, capital of the county of Falkenstein; 24 miles W. S. W. of Worms, and 27 N. E. of Deux Ponts.

WIPPERFURT, a town of Prussia, in the province of Cleves and Berg, seated on the Wipper; 30 miles E. S. E. of Dusseldorf. Pop. 4800.

WIPPRA, a town of Prussian Saxony; 10 miles W. N. W. of Eisleben.

WIRKSWORTH, a town in Derbyshire, with a market on Tuesday. Lead ore is found in great abundance in the vicinity, and it is the greatest mart for lead in England. Millstones and grindstones are also found in the neighbourhood, as well as veins of antimony. It is seated in a valley, surrounded by hills, near the source of the Ecclesborn; 13 miles N. by W. of Derby, and 140 N. N. W. of London.

WIRTEMBERG, or WURTEMBURG, a kingdom of Germany, bounded E. by Bavaria and W. by Baden, and comprising an area of 8000 square miles, with 1,580,000 inhabitants. It is one of the most populous and fertile countries in Germany, though there are many mountains and woods. It produces plenty of pasture, corn, fruit, and a great deal of Neckar wine—so called from the river Neckar, which runs through the kingdom. There are also mines and salt springs, and much game. This country was erected into a kingdom by Napoleon, in 1305; and he made considerable additions to it by the territories taken from Austria. In 1813 the allies, having engaged to preserve the king in his various acquisitions, received his support in the invasion of France. Stutgard is the capital.

WISBADEN, a town of Germany, in the duchy of Nassau. It has some warm baths of great repute; 6 miles N. of Mentz, and 22 W. of Frankfort. Pop. 3500.

WISBEACH, a town in Cambridgeshire, with a market on Saturday. The parish church is a spacious edifice, and here are, besides, four meeting-houses for dissenters, a free-school, two charity schools, &c. The town is seated in the Isle of Ely, between two rivers, and has a considerable trade in corn, and oil pressed from seeds at mills in its neighbourhood. It is 34 miles N. N. W. of Cambridge, and 89 N. of London.

WISBY, a seaport of Sweden, capital of the isle of Gothland, with a castle. It is seated on the side of a rock, on the Baltic; 120 miles S. by E. of Stockholm. Long. 18. 41. E. lat. 57. 36. N. Pop. 400.

WISCASSET, a seaport of Maine, capital of Lincoln county, which has a considerable trade. The judicial courts for the county are held here and at Harrington alternately. It is seated on the Sheepscut, near the sea; 56 miles N. E. of Portland. Pop. 2314. Long. 69. 45. W. lat. 43. 57. N.

WISMAR, a strong seaport of Germany, in the duchy of Mecklenburg Schwerin, with a citadel. It has suffered frequently by war, and in 1716 it was taken by the northern confederates, who blew up and razed its former fortifications. The three principal churches, the town-house, and the palace of Mecklenburg, are its most remarkable buildings. It is seated on a bay of the Baltic; 30 miles E. by N. of Lubec, and 33 W. S. W. of Rostock. Pop. 6700. Long. 11. 34. E. lat. 53. 56. N.

WISTON, or WHISTON, a town of Wales, in Pembrokeshire, governed by a mayor, with a market on Wednesday. It had formerly a castle, which is now a gentleman's seat; 6 miles E. N. E. of Haverford-West, and 248 W. N. W. of London.

WITGENAU, a town of Bohemia, in the circle of Bechin, on the river Lausnitz; 14 miles E. of Budweis.

WITGENSTEIN, a castle of Germany, which gives name to a small county belonging to Hesse-Darmstadt. It stands on a high rock; 13 miles N. W. of Marburg.

WITHAM, a river in Lincolnshire, which flows N. by Grantham to Lincoln, and thence S. E. to Tattershall and Boston into the German Ocean. From Lincoln it has a communication with the Trent, by a navigable canal, called the Fossdike, cut by king Henry I.

WITHAM, a town in Essex, with a market on Thursday, seated on a rivulet, near its confluence with the Blackwater; 8 miles N. E. of Chelmsford, and 38 E. N. E. of London.

WITLICH, a town of Prussia, in the province of Lower Rhine. It has a castle, called Ottenstein, and in its neighbourhood are many copper-mines. It is seated on the Leser; 19 miles N. N. E. of Treves.

WITNEY, a town in Oxfordshire, with a market on Thursday. Here are manufactures of the finest blankets, and other thick woollens, called bear-skins and kerseys. It has a handsome church and three meeting-houses, and is seated on the Windrush; 11 miles W. N. W. of Oxford, and 65 of London.

WITSTOCK, a town of Prussia, in Brandenburg, with celebrated cloth manufactures, seated on the river Dosse; 17 miles N. N. W. of Ruppin. Pop. 3800.

WITTENBURG, a strong town of Prussian Saxony, with a famous university and a castle. The celebrated Martin Luther began the Reformation here, in 1517, and is buried in a chapel belonging to the castle. In 1821 a colossal statue was erected here to his memory. Wittenberg has suffered greatly by wars, particularly in the siege by the Austrians in 1760; and in 1813 it was taken by the allies after a short siege. It is seated on the Elbe, over which is a bridge; 65 miles N. W. of Dresden. Pop. 5000. Long. 12. 45. E. lat. 51. 54. N.

WITTENBURG, a town of Prussia, in Brandenburg, seated on the Elbe; 7 miles S. S. W. of Perleberg.

WITTENBURG, a town of Germany, in Mecklenburg; 15 miles W. S. W. of Schwerin.

WITTENSTEIN, a town of Russia, in the government of Livonia; 40 miles S. E. of Revel.

WITTLESEY-MERE, a lake in the N. E. part of Huntingdonshire; 6 miles long, and 3 broad. It is 4 miles S. of Peterborough.

WITZENHAUSEN, a town of Germany, in Hesse-Cassel, seated on the Werra; 18 miles E. by N. of Cassel.

WIVELISCOMB, a town in Somersetshire, with a market on Saturday, and a considerable manufacture of blanketing, kerseys, and other coarse cloths. It stands on the Thone; 20 miles N. of Exeter, and 153 W. by S. of London.

WIVENHOE, a village in Essex, seated on the Coln; 3 miles S. E. of Colchester, of which it is the port. The Colchester oysters are chiefly barrelled at this place.

WLADISLAW, a town of Poland, capital of a palatinate of its name, and of the province of Cujavia, with a fort. It stands on the Vistula; 98 miles W. N. W. of Warsaw. Long. 18. 50. E. lat. 52. 54. N.

WOAHOO, one of the Sandwich islands; 7 leagues N. W. of Morotoi. From the appearance of the N. E. and N. W. parts, it is the finest island of the group. A bay is formed by the N. and W. extremities, into which a fine river flows, through a deep valley; but the water is brackish for 200 yards from the entrance. It is supposed to contain 60,000 inhabitants. Lieut. Hergist, who had been sent from England in 1791, with a supply of provisions for Captain Vancouver, then on a voyage of discovery, was here surprised and murdered by the natives, together with Mr. Gooch, the astronomer. Long. 157. 51. W. lat. 21. 43. N.

WOBURN, a town in Bedfordshire, with a market on Friday. It had an ancient abbey, on the site of which stands the magnificent building called Woburn Abbey, the seat of the Duke of Bedford. The town was burnt down in 1724, but was subsequently rebuilt with considerable improvement. Near it is found great plenty of fuller's earth. It is 12 miles S. of Bedford, and 42 N. N. W. of London.

WODNIAN, a town of Bohemia, seated on the Bianitz; 12 miles S. of Piseck.

WOERDEN, a town of the Netherlands, in South Holland, seated on the Rhine; 10 miles W. of Utrecht.

WOKEY, or OKEY, a village in Somersetshire, on the S. side of the Mendip Hills, 2 miles W. of Wells. Here is a famous cavern, called Wokey Hole, the mouth of which is only six feet high, but it soon expands into a spacious vault, 80 feet in height, the roof composed of pendent rocks, whence a clear water, of a petrifying quality, continually drops. From this grotto a narrow passage descends to another of less height; and beyond a second narrow passage is a third grotto. The extremity is above 200 yards from the entrance.

WOKING, a village in Surrey, on the river Wey; 5 miles N. N. E. of Guildford, near the South Western railroad. In the manor-house here died Margaret Countess of Richmond, mother of Henry VII.

WOKINGHAM, or OAKINGHAM, a corporate town in Berkshire, with a market on Tuesday, noted for its great supply of poultry. Here all the courts for Windsor Forest are held, and, 4 miles to the S. E. are vestiges of some Roman entrenchments called Cæsar's Camp. It is 7 miles E. S. E. of Reading, and 31 W. by S. of London.

WOLAU, a strong town of Prussian Silesia, capital of a principality of the same name, with a fine castle, many handsome buildings, and a great woollen manufacture. It is seated near the Oder, surrounded by a morass; 20 miles N. W. of Breslau. Population of the principality, 50,000, and of the town, 1300. Long. 16. 45. E. lat. 51. 18. N.

WOLBECK, a town of the Prussian states, in the government of Munster; 7 miles S. S. W. of Munster.

WOLDECK, a town of Germany, in the duchy of Mecklenburg; 21 miles E. N. E. of Strelitz.

WOLFACH, a town of Baden, on a river of the same name, at its confluence with the Kinzig; 19 miles N. E. of Friburg.

WOLFENBUTTEL, a principality of Germany, which constitutes part of the duchy of Brunswick. It is divided into two parts by the principalities of Hildesheim and Halberstadt: the northern borders on the duchies of Lunenburg and Magdeburg; the southern lies between the principality of Hildesheim, the abbey of Corvey, and the county of Wernigerode. The N. part produces abundance of grass, grain, flax, hemp, silk, and various kinds of pulse and fruit. The S. part is hilly, and has little arable land, but yields plenty of timber and iron, and has manufactures of glass and fine porcelain, with a very rich mine and salt works in the Hartz Forest. The principal rivers are the Weser, Leine, and Ocker. The established religion is the Lutheran.

WOLFENBUTTEL, a strong city of Germany, capital of the foregoing principality. It has a castle, formerly the residence of the dukes, in which is an excellent library, with a cabinet of curiosities relating to natural history. In the principal church is the burial-place of the princes, which is an admirable piece of architecture. Wolfenbuttel is seated in a marshy soil, on the Ocker; 7 miles S. by W. of Brunswick, and 30 W. of Halberstadt. Pop. 6700. Long. 10. 45. E. lat. 52. 10. N.

WOLFERSDIKE, a small island of the Netherlands, in Zealand, between N. and S. Beveland.

WOLFSBERG, a town of Austrian Illyria, in Carinthia, with a castle, seated on the Levant, at the foot of a mountain; 26 miles E. N. E. of Clagenfurt.

WOLGA. *See* VOLGA.

WOLGAST, a seaport of Prussia, in Pomerania, with one of the best harbours on the Baltic. Only the tower of its ancient castle is now standing. It is seated on the Peene, or W. channel of the Oder; 54 miles N. W. of Stettin. Pop. 4000. Long. 13. 52. E. lat. 54. 4. N.

WOLKENSTEIN, a town of Saxony, in the circle of Erzgeberg, with a castle on a rock, seated near the Zschopa; 15 miles S. S. E. of Chemnitz.

WOLKOMYSK, a town of Prussia, in the government of Grodno, seated on the Ros; 23 miles S. E. of Grodno.

WOLLIN, a fortified town of Pomerania, capital of a fertile island of the same name, between the two eastern branches of the Oder. It is seated on the Diwenow; 12 miles S. W. of Camin, and 30 N. of Stettin. Long. 14. 40. E. lat. 53. 50. N.

WOLMIRSTADT, a town of Prussian Saxony, in Magdeburg, on the river Ohra; 10 miles N. of Magdeburg.

WOLOCZOK, a town of Russia, in the government of Novogorod; 100 miles S. E. of Novogorod. Long. 34. 20. E. lat. 57. 30. N.

WOLSINGHAM, a town in the county of Durham, with a market on Tuesday, situate on the Wear, amid mines of lead and coal; 16 miles W. of Durham, and 257 N. N. W. of London.

WOLVERHAMPTON, a borough in Staffordshire, with a market on Wednesday. It returns two members to parliament. It has a collegiate church, annexed to the deanery of Windsor, two other churches of modern erection, and several meeting-houses for dissenters, and one for Catholics. It is a town of considerable antiquity, and is seated in a district abounding in coal, iron, and limestone, and has long been celebrated for the manufacture of locks, which is carried on to a great extent, and also manufactures of various kinds of iron, brass, steel, and tin goods, japanned and paper wares, &c. The town is well lighted with gas, and has within the last few years undergone considerable improvements in other respects. It is seated on a hill, nearly encompassed by canals; 16 miles S. of Stafford, and 122 N. W. of London.

WOMELDORF, a town of Pennsylvania, in Berks county; 68 miles N. W. of Philadelphia.

WOODBRIDGE, a town in Suffolk, with a market on Wednesday, seated on the E. side of a sandy hill on the river Deben; 8 miles from the sea. It has docks for building ships, convenient wharfs, and a great corn trade; 7 miles E. N. E. of Ipswich, and 77 N. E. of London.

WOODBRIDGE, a town of New Jersey, in Middlesex county; 3 miles N. by W. of Amboy. Pop. 3969.

WOODBURY, a town of New Jersey, chief of Gloucester county, situate near the Delaware; 9 miles S. of Philadelphia.

WOODCHESTER, a village in Gloucestershire, 2 miles S. of Stroud. It has a broad-cloth and a silk manufacture. A great tessellated pavement and other splendid Roman antiquities have been discovered here.

WOODS, LAKE OF THE, a lake of North America, 90 miles long, and 30 where broadest, but very irregular in its shape. It lies between the Winnipeg and Lake Superior, chiefly in Upper Canada, but the S. part is in the territory of the United States. The lands on its banks are covered with oaks, pines, firs, &c.

WOODSTOCK, a borough in Oxfordshire, market on Tuesday and Friday. It is chiefly noted for Blenheim-house, built at the expense of the nation for the duke of Marlborough, in memory of his signal victory over the French and Bavarians in 1704. In Blenheim park originally stood a royal palace, the favourite retreat of several kings of England till the reign of Charles I., when it was almost wholly in ruins. In this palace king Ethelred held a parliament, and here Alfred the Great translated Boetius de Consolatione Philosophiæ. It was beautified by Henry I., became the residence of Rosamond, mistress of Henry II.; Edmund, second son of Edward I., and Edward, eldest son of Edward III., were born here; and here the princess Elizabeth was confined by her sister Mary. After the building of Blenheim every trace of the ancient edifice was removed, and two elms were planted on its site. Woodstock has a manufacture of gloves, and of steel watch-chains. The poet Chaucer was born, lived, and died here. It is 8 miles N. W. of Oxford, and 62 W. N. W. of London.

WOODSTOCK, a town of Virginia, chief of Shenandoah county, on a branch of Shenandoah River; 24 miles S. S. W. of Winchester, and 80 W. N. W. of Alexandria.

WOODSTOCK, a town of Vermont, capital of Windsor county; seated on the Waterqueechy; 14 miles N. W. of Windsor. Pop. 3315.

WOODSTOWN, a town of New Jersey, in Salem county; 12 miles N. by E. of Salem, and 26 S. S. W. of Philadelphia.

WOOLER, a town in Northumberland, with a

market on Thursday. In a plain near this town the Scots were defeated on Holyrood day, 1402, and the battle was so bloody, that it gave the name of Redriggs to the place where it was fought. Wooler is seated on the river Till, near the Cheviot Hills; 14 miles S. of Berwick, and 317 N. by W. of London.

WOOLWICH, a town of Kent, with a market on Friday. It is the most ancient military and naval arsenal in England, and has a royal dockyard, where men-of-war were built as early as the reign of Henry VIII. At the eastern part of the town is the royal arsenal, in which are vast magazines of great guns, mortars, bombs, balls, powder, and other warlike stores; a foundry, with three furnaces, for casting ordnance; and a laboratory, where fireworks and cartridges are made, and bombs, carcases, grenadoes, &c., charged for the public service. A little to the S. of the arsenal are extensive artillery barracks, for the accommodation of the officers and privates; and a little further S. a royal military academy, where the mathematics are taught, and cadets instructed in the military art. The parish church is a spacious brick edifice, the interior of which is elegantly fitted up in the Grecian style. Here are also not fewer than 12 meeting-houses for the several denominations of dissenters. Woolwich is seated on the Thames, which is here so deep that large ships may at all times ride with safety. It is 8 miles E. of London.

WORCESTER, a town of Massachusets, capital of a county of its name, and the largest inland town of New England. It has manufactures of pot and pearl-ash, cotton and linen goods, and some other articles. It is situate in a healthy vale; 45 miles W. by S. of Boston. Pop. 4797. Long. 71. 55. W. lat. 42. 20. N.

WORCESTER, one of the most ancient and respectable cities of England; the capital of Worcestershire, and a bishop's see, with markets on Wednesday and Saturday. It contains eleven churches, besides the cathedral, also a number of meeting-houses for various sectaries, as well as Roman Catholics. Edgar's Tower, a strong portal, is part of its ancient castle; here are also three grammar-schools, seven hospitals, a public infirmary, and a well-contrived quay. Worcester is governed by a mayor, carries on a considerable trade in hops, carpets, and gloves, has a large manufacture of elegant china-ware, manufactures of fine lace, an extensive iron-foundry, distillery, &c. It returns two members to parliament. Here Cromwell, in 1651, obtained a victory over the Scotch army which had marched into England to reinstate Charles II., who, after this defeat, escaped with great difficulty into France. Worcester is seated on the Severn; 36 miles N. N. E. of Bristol, and 111 W. N. W. of London. Long. 2. 0. W. lat. 52. 9. N.

WORCESTERSHIRE, a county of England, 44 miles long, and 24 broad; bounded on the N. by Shropshire and Staffordshire, E. by Warwickshire, S. E. and S. by Gloucestershire, and W. by Herefordshire. It contains 431,360 acres, is divided into five hundreds and 152 parishes, and sends four members to parliament for the eastern and western divisions of the county. The soil in the vales and meadows is very rich, particularly the vale of Evesham, which is styled the granary of these parts. The hills have generally an easy ascent, except the Malvern Hills in the S. W. part of the county, which feed large flocks of sheep. The other hills are the Licky, near Bromsgrove, towards the N., and the Bredon Hills, towards the S. E. Here are plenty of fruits of most sorts, especially pears, which are in many places found growing in the hedges. The commerce and manufactures are considerable. The chief exports are coal, corn, hops, cloth, cheese, cider, perry, and salt. The principal rivers are the Severn, Teme, and Avon.

WORCUM, a town of the Netherlands, in South Holland, seated on the S. side of the Meuse, just below the influx of the Waal; 8 miles N. N. W. of Heusdon.

WORCUM, a town of the Netherlands, in Friesland; 18 miles S. W. of Lewarden.

WORDINGBORG, a seaport of Denmark, on the S. coast of the island of Zealand, from which there is a much-frequented passage to the islands Falster and Laland. It is 46 miles S. S. W. of Copenhagen. Long. 11. 58. E. lat. 55. 3. N.

WORKINGTON, a seaport in Cumberland, with markets on Wednesday and Saturday, seated at the mouth of the Derwent, on the coast of the Irish Sea. The river admits vessels of 400 tons burden, and the harbour is commodious. Here are two churches belonging to the Establishment, and several meeting-houses for dissenters. This was the landing-place of Mary queen of Scots, when she was driven to take refuge in England. In the neighbourhood are a large iron-foundry, some salt-works, and numerous collieries. The principal manufactures are canvas and cordage, but the coal trade is its chief support. It is 7 miles W. by S. of Cockermouth, and 312 N. N. W. of London. Long. 3. 27. W. lat. 54. 31. N.

WORKSOP, a town in Nottinghamshire, with a market on Wednesday. Here was once an abbey, of which the church still remains. On the W. side of the town is a circular hill, which was the site of a castle. Quantities of liquorice are grown in its vicinity. Two miles to the S. E. is Clumber Park, the seat of the duke of Newcastle. The canal from Chesterfield to the Trent passes near this town. It is 22 miles N. W. of Newark, and 146 N. by W. of London.

WORMS, a city of Germany, in Hesse-Darmstadt, formerly the capital of a princely bishopric of the same name. It is famous for a diet held in 1521, at which Luther assisted in person. The cathedral is magnificent, and the principal Lutheran church has a beautiful altar and fine paintings. In the war of 1689 it was taken by the French, who almost reduced it to ashes. In 1743 a treaty was concluded here between Great Britain, Hungary, and Sardinia. In 1792 Worms surrendered to the French, who were obliged to evacuate it the next year, after the loss of Mentz; but it was again taken by them in 1794. It is seated on the Rhine; 27 miles S. S. W. of Mentz. Pop. 5700. Long. 8. 28. E. lat. 49. 36. N.

WORSLEY, a town in Lancashire, celebrated for the immense quantity of coal in its vicinity, and for being the place where the duke of Bridgewater first commenced his canal navigation. It is 6 miles N. N. W. of Manchester.

WORSTEAD, a town in Norfolk, with a market on Saturday. This place is noted for the introduction of that sort of twisted yarn called worsted; and was formerly a place of considerable trade, though now reduced to a mere village. It is 12 miles N. of Norwich, and 121 N. E. of London.

WORTHING, a town in Sussex, on the coast, 11 miles W. of Brighton; like which, it has, from an obscure fishing village, become a fashionable watering-place. It is pleasantly seated, and has fine sands, and is much frequented for sea-bathing. It possesses a theatre, good libraries, and some spacious hotels, though it cannot boast of the gaieties and grandeur of its proud neighbour. There is also a considerable fishery off the town; 56 miles from London.

WORTHINGTON, a town of Massachusets, in Hampshire county; 19 miles W. by N. of Northampton.

WOTTON BASSET, a town in Wiltshire, market on Tuesday. It is a mean town; 12 miles N. W. of Marlborough, and 88 W. of London.

WOTTON-UNDER-EDGE, a town in Gloucestershire, governed by a mayor, with a market on Friday, and extensive manufactures of cloth. It is seated under a fertile eminence; 20 miles N. E. of Bristol, and 109 W. N. W. of London.

WRAGBY, a town in Lincolnshire, with a market on Thursday; 11 miles E. N. E. of Lincoln, and 143 N. of London.

WRATH, CAPE, a promontory of Scotland, in Sutherlandshire, which is the N. W. point of Great Britain. Against its rugged and lofty cliffs the rapid tide bursts with incredible fury. Long. 4. 47. W. lat. 58. 34. N.

WREKIN, a noted hill or mountain in Shropshire, 8 miles E. S. E. of Shrewsbury. It was a famous station of the Romans, and its height is reckoned 1200 feet.

WRENTHAM a town of Massachusets, in Norfolk county , 30 miles S. S. W. of Boston.

WREXHAM, a town of Wales, in Denbighshire, with markets on Monday and Thursday. It is a great mart for flannel, and a place of considerable traffic. Here is a large church, a beautiful specimen of the florid Gothic, with a lofty steeple; also two large meeting-houses, and a well endowed free-school. Near Wrexham is a foundry for cannon and other articles; and the adjacent country affords plenty of lead. It is seated on a river which flows into the Dee; 13 miles W. by S. of Chester, and 180 N. W. of London. Long. 3. 10. W. lat. 53. 2. N.

WRIEZEN, or BRIETZEN, a town of Prussia, in Brandenburg, situate on a lake formed by the inundations of the Oder; 37 miles E. N. E. of Berlin. Pop. 3200.

WRINGTON, a town in Somersetshire, with a market on Tuesday. Much teasel is grown in the vicinity, and sold to the cloth manufacturers. It was the birthplace of the celebrated Locke. It is seated near the source of the Yeo; 10 miles S. W. of Bristol, and 125 W. of London.

WROTHAM, a town in Kent, with a market four times a year. The church is a large edifice, dedicated to St. George, attached to which was an archiepiscopal palace, the materials of which were removed to Aylesford. It is 11 miles W. N. W. of Maidstone, and 24 S. E. of London.

WROXETER, a village in Shropshire, said to have been formerly a city built by the Britons. It appears to have been surrounded by a thick wall and a deep trench, 3 miles in circuit, which may be traced in several places; 5 miles S. E. of Shrewsbury.

WUNNENBERG, a town of Prussian Westphalia, which received its name from a victory gained by Charlemagne over the Saxons in 794. It is 14 miles S. of Paderborn.

WUNSIEDEL, a town of Bavarian Franconia, near which are mines of copper and iron, and quarries of marble. It is seated on the Rosslau; 12 miles W. of Egra, and 34 E. of Bayreuth. Pop. 2600.

WURTEMBURG. *See* WIRTEMBERG.

WURTZBURG, a district of Bavaria, in the circle of Lower Maine, comprehending a great part of Franconia. It is 65 miles long, and 50 broad, and is bounded on the N. by Henneberg, E. by Bamberg, S. by Anspach, Hohenlohe, and Mergentheim, and W. by Wertheim, Mentz, and Fulda. The soil is very fertile, and produces more corn and wine than the inhabitants consume. This territory was formerly a bishopric, and its sovereign was one of the greatest ecclesiastical princes of the empire; but it was given as a principality to the elector of Bavaria in 1803; and by the treaty of Presburg, in 1805, it was ceded to the archduke Ferdinand, whose electoral title was transferred from Salzburg to this place. In 1814, however, it was again transferred to Bavaria, in exchange for the Tyrol, when the archduke Ferdinand was reinstated in his Tuscan dominions.

WURTZBURG, a fortified city of Bavaria, capital of the circle of Lower Maine, with a magnificent palace, a university, an arsenal, and a handsome hospital. The fortress stands on an eminence, and communicates with the city by a stone bridge. Besides the cathedral, there are several collegiate and parish churches, colleges, abbeys, and convents. Here is a cannon and bell foundry; also cloth and stuff manufactures, established in the house of correction. Wurtzburg was taken by the French in 1796, and again in 1800. It is seated on the Maine; 40 miles W. S. W. of Bamberg, and 65 E.S.E. of Frankfort. Pop. 20,000. Long. 10. 14. E. lat. 49. 46. N.

WURZACH, a town of the kingdom of Wirtemberg, in the county of Waldburg, with a castle, situate on the Aitrach; 17 miles N. of Wangen, and 28 S. by W. of Ulm

WURZEN, or WURTZEN, a town of Saxony, with a castle, a cathedral, and two churches. Here are fine bleaching-grounds for linen; but the principal trade is in beer, of which great quantities are exported. It is situate on the Muldau; 15 miles E. of Leipsic. Pop. 2400.

WUSTERHAUSEN, a town of Prussia, in Brandenburg, seated on the Spree; 15 miles S.S.E. of Berlin.—Another, seated on the Dosse; 17 miles E. N. E. of Havelburg, and 44 N. W. of Berlin.

WUSTRAU, a town of Hanover, in the duchy of Lunenberg, seated on the Dumme, at its confluence with the Jetzo; 14 miles S. of Danneberg.

WYBORG. *See* WIBURG.

WYCOMB, or HIGH WYCOMB, a borough in Buckinghamshire, returning, with its contributories, two members to parliament, governed by a mayor. Market on Friday. In the vicinity are many corn and paper mills; and a Roman tesselated pavement was discovered in an adjacent meadow in 1744. It is seated on the Wyck; 12 miles S. S. E. of Aylesbury, and 31 W. N. W. of London.

WYE, a town in Kent, whose market is now disused, seated on the Stour; 10 miles S.S.W. of Canterbury, and 55 S. E. of London.

WYE, a river of Wales, celebrated for its romantic scenery. It issues from Plynlimmon Hill, in the S. part of Montgomeryshire, very near the source of the Severn, and crosses the N. E. corner of Radnorshire, giving name to the town of Rhayadergowy, (fall of the Wye,) where it is precipitated in a cataract; then, flowing between this county and Brecknockshire, it enters Herefordshire, passing by Hay to Hereford, a few miles below which it receives the Lug; it then flows by Ross and Monmouth, and, separating the counties of Monmouth and Gloucester, it enters the Severn below Chepstow. This river is navigable almost to Hay, and a canal forms a communication between it and the Severn, from Hereford to Gloucester.

WYMONDHAM, a town in Norfolk, with a market on Friday, and manufactures of bombasins, Norwich crapes, &c. The church is the eastern part of an ancient abbey, and has a lofty steeple, on which Ket, the leader of the rebellion in the reign of Edward VI., was hanged. Here is a free school, founded by Queen Elizabeth. It is 9 miles W. S. W. of Norwich, and 100 N. N. E. of London.

WYRE, a river in Lancashire, which rises 6 miles S. E. of Lancaster, passes by Garstang, and enters the Irish Sea below Poulton, at Fleetwood, which is connected with Preston and Liverpool by railways.

X.

XABEA, a seaport of Spain, in Valencia, near the coast of the Mediterranean; 44 miles N. E. of Alicant. Long. 0. 3. E. lat. 38. 48. N.

XACCA, or SCIACCA, a seaport of Sicily, in Val di Mazara, with an old castle. Here are large granaries for the reception of corn intended to be exported, and manufactures of beautiful vases. It is seated on the S. coast, at the foot of a mountain; 20 miles S. E. of Mazara, and 41 S. S. W. of Palermo. Pop. 12,000. Long. 13. 2. E. lat. 37. 41. N.

XAGUA, a seaport on the S. coast of the island of Cuba, seated on a bay, which is five leagues in circumference, and surrounded by mountains. It is one of the finest ports in the West Indies. It is 84 miles S. E. of Havannah. Long. 80. 45. W. lat. 22. 10. N.

XALAPA, a town of Mexico, in Vera Cruz, and a bishop's see. This town is said to give name to the purgative root called jalap, or xalap. It is 60 miles E. of Angelos, and 80 E. of Mexico. Pop. 13,000. Long. 98. 20. W. lat. 19. 32. N.

XALISCO, a town of Mexico, in a province of its name; 14 miles N. W. of Compostella.

XATIVA, or ST. PHILIP, a town of Spain, in Valencia. Having taken the part of Charles III. in 1707, Philip V. ordered it to be demolished, and a new town to be built called St. Philip. It is seated on the side of a hill, at the foot of which runs the Zucar; 32 miles S. W. of Valencia, and 50 N. W. of Alicant. Long. 0. 14. W. lat. 39. 4. N.

XAUXA, or JAUXA, a province of Peru; 36 miles long, and 45 broad; bounded by the mountains of the Indians, and the provinces of Tarma, Huanta, Angaraes, Xauyos, and Guarochiri. The climate is highly salubrious, and the soil fertile in corn and fruits. Population, 52,286.

XAUXA, a town of Peru, capital of the foregoing province, noted for its silver mines. It is seated on a river of the same name; 100 miles E. of Lima.

XAVIER, or SABI, the capital of the kingdom of Whidah, in Guinea. It is populous, and a great market is held every Wednesday and Saturday, at the distance of a mile from the town. The market-place is surrounded by suttlers' booths, which are only permitted to sell certain sorts of meat, as beef, pork, and the flesh of goats and dogs. Here slaves of both sexes are sold, as well as oxen, sheep, dogs, hogs, fish, and birds; also the various commodities of Whidah manufacture, and every thing of European, Asiatic, or African production. Xavier is seated near the river Euphrates, about 7 miles from the sea. Long. 2. 30. E. lat. 6. 40. N.

XAVIER, a town of Spain, in Navarre, noted as the birthplace of the celebrated Romish saint and missionary of that name. It is 35 miles S. E. of Pamplona.

XAVIER, ST., a town of Paraguay, in the province of La Plata. It is 200 miles W. of Rio Janeiro.

XENIA, a flourishing town of Ohio, capital of Green county, seated on the Shawnoe Creek; 30 miles S. W. of Urbana.

XENIL, a river of Spain, which rises in the E. part of Granada, and flows by Granada, Loxa, and Ecija, into the Guadalquiver.

XERES, a town of Mexico, in Nicaragua, seated on a river that flows into Fonseca Bay; 70 miles N. W. of Leon.

XERES DE LA FRONTERA, a large and well-built town of Spain, in Andalusia, famous for that excellent wine corruptly called sherry. It is seated on the small river Guadalette, 15 miles N. E. of Cadiz, and 38 S. S. W. of Seville. Pop. 25,000.

XERES DE LA FRONTERA, a town of Mexico, in the S. part of the province of Zacatecas; 80 miles N. by E. of Guadalaxara. Long. 103. 35. W. lat. 22. 22. N.

XERES DE GUADIANA, a town of Spain, in Andalusia, seated on the Guadiana, 28 miles N. by E. of Ayamonte.

XICOCO, an island of Japan, between Niphon and Ximo; 250 miles in circumference.

XILOTOPEC, a town of Mexico, capital of a district of its name; 60 miles N. of Mexico.

XIMO, an island of Japan, the second in size and eminence, situate to the S. W. of Niphon, from which it is divided by a narrow channel. It is 450 miles in circumference.

XIXONA, a town of Spain, in Valencia, with a castle, seated among mountains, in a country that produces excellent wine, and the valuable drug called kermes. It is 15 miles N. of Alicant.

XUCAR, a river of Spain, which rises in the N. E. part of New Castile, passes by Cuenza, and, entering the province of Valencia, runs into the Gulf of Valencia at the town of Cullera.

XUDNOGROD, a town of Croatia; 17 miles N. of Sebenico, and 37 E. of Kzara.

Y.

YACHTA, a fort of Russia, in the government of Irkutsk, on the borders of Chinese Tartary; 48 miles S. S. W. of Selenginsk.

YADKIN. *See* PEDEE.

YAITSK. *See* URALSK.

YAKUTSK, or JAKUTSKOI, a town of Russia, capital of a province of the same name, which contains a scattered population of 185,000, in the government of Irkutsk, with a wooden fort. It is seated on the Lena; 960 miles N. E. of Irkutsk. Pop. 3000. Long. 129. 48. E. lat. 62. 2. N.

YALE, the capital of a province of the same name, in the island of Ceylon; 56 miles S. E. of Candy.

YAMBURG, a town of Russia, in the government of Petersburg, situate on the Luga; 20 miles E. of Narva.

YAMINA, a town of Negroland, in Bambara, near the river Niger; 66 miles S. W. of Sego.

YANG-TCHEOU, a city of China, of the first rank, in the province of Kiang-nan. Its district is intersected by a number of canals, and it carries on a great trade, particularly in salt, which is made on the seacoast of this jurisdiction. It stands on the left bank of the Kian-ku, where the Imperial canal crosses that river; 485 miles S. by E. of Peking. Long. 118. 54. E. lat. 32. 26. N.

YAO-GAN, a city of China, of the first rank, in the province of Yun-nan. Its territory is intermixed with mountains, fine forests, and fruitful valleys, and produces abundance of musk. Near the city is a salt-spring, which produces very white salt. It is 100 miles W. by N. of Yun-nan. Long. 100. 45. E. lat. 25. 12. N.

YAO-TCHEU, a city of China, of the first rank, in Kiang-si; on the W. side of the lake Po-yang; 700 miles S. of Peking. Long. 116. 40. E. lat. 29. 8. N.

YARE, a river in Norfolk, formed by the confluence of several streams that rise in the heart of the county. It passes through Norwich, whence it is navigable to Yarmouth, where it enters the German Ocean.

YARKUND, a town of Tartary, in the country of Cashgur; with a large palace, where the khan of the Eluth Tartars generally resides. It has a considerable trade, and stands in a fertile country, on a river of the same name; 100 miles S. E. of Cashgur. Long. 79. 4. E. lat. 38. 40. N.

YARM, a town in North Yorkshire, with a market on Thursday, seated on the Tees; 17 miles N. by E. of Northallerton, and 239 N. by W. of London.

YARMOUTH, a seaport and borough in Norfolk, returning two members to parliament, governed by a mayor, with markets on Wednesday and Saturday. It is seated at the mouth of the Yare. The harbour is convenient for business, the vessels lying in the river along a very extensive quay. Its foreign trade is considerable. A great number of herrings are cured here, and also a large quantity of mackarel are caught and sent to London. The town is much frequented for sea-bathing, and has three churches, seven meeting-houses, a charity school, an hospital, a theatre, a large gauze silk factory, extensive ship yards, &c. The market-place is very spacious, but the streets in general are narrow. Off the mouth of the harbour is a bar, which prevents the entry of ships of large burden; and the many sand-banks off the coast form the Yarmouth Roads, so noted for frequent shipwrecks. It is 23 miles from Norwich, and 124 N. E. of London. Yarmouth gives the inferior title of earl to the Marquess of Hertford. Long. 1. 45. E. lat. 52. 38. N.

YARMOUTH, a town in Hampshire, on the north-western coast of the Isle of Wight, with a market on Friday, a fortified castle, and a convenient quay. It is 9 miles W. of Newport.

YARMOUTH, a seaport of Massachusets, in Barnstable county, on the N. side of the peninsula of Cape Cod; 5 miles N. N. W. of Barnstable. Long. 70. 12. W. lat. 41. 52. N.

YARMOUTH, NORTH, a town of Maine, in Cumberland county, on a small river that falls into Casco Bay; 14 miles N. of Portland.

YARUQUI, a village of Peru, near a plain of the same name; 12 miles N. E. of Quito. This plain was chosen for the base of the operations for measuring an arc of the meridian, by Ulloa and the French mathematicians.

YAYNAN-GHEOUM, a town of Birmah, celebrated for the oil wells in its neighbourhood, which supply the whole empire, and many parts of India, with petroleum. The inhabitants are employed in making jars to contain the oil. It stands on a creek of the Irrawaddy; 28 miles S. by E. Shillahmew

YEA, a town of Peru, in Lima, with a trade in glass, wine, brandy, &c. It is seated in a valley, watered by a river. It is 50 miles E. S. E. of Pisco, and 170 S. S. E. of Lima.

YELL, one of the Shetland Islands, to the N. of that called Mainland. It is 20 miles long, and 8 broad, and has several good harbours.

YELLOW RIVER. *See* HOAN-HO.

YELLOW SEA, or LEAO-TONG, a gulf of China; between the provinces of Pe-tche-li and Chang-tong on the W., and the peninsula of the Corea on the E.

YEMEN, a province of Arabia Felix, comprehending the finest and most fertile part of Arabia, and lying on the coast of the Red Sea and Indian Ocean. Millet is the grain chiefly cultivated, but the principal object of cultivation is coffee, which is all carried to Beit el Fakir. Nearly the whole commerce of the country is carried on by Mocha, but Sana is the capital.

YENIKALE, an important fortress of the Crimea; 8 miles E. of Kertch. *See* JENIKALE.

YENISEI, or JENISA, a large river of Siberia, which runs from S. to N., and enters the Frozen Ocean to the E. of the Bay of Oby.

YENISEISK, or JENISKOI, a town of Russia in the government of Tomsk, on the river Yenisei; 310 miles E. N. E. of Tomsk. Pop. 6000. Long. 92. 5. E. lat. 57. 20. N.

YENNE, a town of the Sardinian states, in Savoy, near the Rhone. It is 13 miles N. W. of Chambery.

YEN-NGAN, a city of China, of the first rank, in Chen-si, on the river Yen; 390 miles S. W. of Peking. Long. 108. 50. E. lat. 36. 44. N.

YEN-PING, a city of China, of the first rank, in Fokien, seated on the brow of a mountain, by the river Minho; 820 miles S. of Peking. Long. 116. 54. E. lat. 26. 40. N.

YEN-TCHEOU, a city of China, of the first rank, in Chang-tong, situate in a well-cultivated district, which is enclosed between two considerable rivers. It is 270 miles S. of Peking.

YEN-TCHEOU, a city of China, of the first rank, in Tche-kiang. In the neighbourhood are mines of copper, and trees that yield an excellent varnish, which, when once dry, never melts again, and will bear boiling water. The paper made here is in high esteem. It is 650 miles S. S. E. of Peking. Long. 119. 14. E. lat. 29. 38. N.

YENTCHING, a town of China, in Chang-tong, where a kind of glass is made, so delicate that it will not endure the inclemencies of the air. It is 45 miles S. E. of Tsi-nan.

YEOVIL, a corporate town of Somersetshire, with a market on Friday. It contains a handsome parish church, five meeting-houses, a free-school, and several other charitable institutions. Here was formerly a considerable manufacture of woollen cloths, but the principal manufacture at present is of leather gloves, and the trade in hemp and flax is considerable. It is seated on the Yeo or Ivil; 20 miles S. of Wells, and 122 W. by S. of London.

YESD, a town of Persia, in the province of Irac, on the road from Kerman to Ispahan. It has a silk manufacture, and here are made the finest porcelain and carpets. It is 200 miles E. S. E. of Ispahan. Population supposed to be 80,000. Long. 56. 50. E. lat. 33. 0. N.

YLO, a seaport of Peru, in Los Charcos; 70 miles N. N. W. of Arica. Long. 71. 13. W. lat. 17. 36. S.

YONNE, a department of France, containing part of the former provinces of Burgundy and Champagne, and comprising an area of 2900 square miles, with 350,000 inhabitants. The climate is temperate, and the soil fertile in corn, hemp, flax, wine, and fruits. It receives its name from a river which rises in the department of Nievre, flows by Chateau-Chinon, Clameci, Auxerre, Joigny, and Sens, and joins the Seine at Montereau. Auxerre is the capital.

YORK, a city, the capital of Yorkshire, and an archbishop's see, with markets on Tuesday, Thursday, and Saturday. It returns two members to parliament. It is the Eboracum of the Romans, and many of their coffins, urns, coins, &c., have been found here. It has always been considered as the capital of the North, and, in point of rank, as the second city of the kingdom; but is now surpassed in wealth and populousness by many of the more modern trading towns. The cathedral of St. Peter, generally called the Minster, is reckoned the largest and most magnificent Gothic structure in the universe. The E. window, which is said hardly to have its equal for tracery, painting, and preservation, was the work of John Thornton, a glazier, of Coventry, in 1405. This beautiful edifice sustained considerable injury from fire, occasioned by a frantic incendiary, in 1829. It was restored to its original splendour by public subscription, and was again destroyed in 1840, by one of the towers accidentally taking fire and falling on the nave, which has again rendered this beautiful pile a mass of ruins. Besides the cathedral, York contains but 20 churches in use, though in the reign of Henry V. it had 44 parish churches, 17 chapels, and 9 religious houses. Here are also a number of meeting-houses for dissenters and catholics. The city is divided by the Ouse into two parts, united by a stone bridge of five arches, the centre one 81 feet wide. The river is navigable to this city for vessels of 70 tons burden, although it is 60 miles from the sea. The castle is a noble structure, and was formerly a place of great strength, but is now used as a county prison. Near it, on an artificial mount, is Clifford's Tower, a round shell, said by some to have been raised by William the Conqueror, but others deem it a Roman work. It was used as a garrison in the civil wars, and till the year 1683, when the magazine, blowing up, reduced it to its present form. York is a county of itself, governed by a lord mayor, the prefix of lord being given by Richard II.; and its county includes Ainsty Liberty, in which are 35 villages and hamlets. The guildhall, built in 1466, is a grand structure, supported by two rows of oak pillars, each pillar a single tree. The corporation built a mansion-house in 1728, for the lord mayor; and, among the other public buildings, are a noble assembly-house, designed by the Earl of Burlington, an elegant court-house on the right of the castle, a theatre royal, a county hospital, and an asylum for lunatics. It is connected with the metropolis by means of the N. Midland and Birmingham railways. York is 70 miles S. by E. of Durham, 190 S. S. E. of Edinburgh, and 195 N. by W. of London. Long. 1. 7. W. lat. 53. 59. N.

YORK, now called TORONTO, a city of Upper Canada. It is situate on the N. W. side of Lake Ontario, and has an excellent harbour, formed by a long peninsula, which embraces a basin of water sufficiently large to contain a considerable fleet. On the extremity of the peninsula called Gibraltar Point, are stores and blockhouses, which command the entrance of the harbour; and on the mainland, opposite this point, is the garrison. The front of the city is a mile and a half in length, and it contains several handsome squares, particularly one open to the harbour. It is 45 miles N. N. W. of Fort Niagara, and 140 W. by S. of Kingston. Pop. 3500. Long. 79. 36. W. lat. 43. 35. N.

YORK, a town of Pennsylvania, capital of a county of the same name. It has eight edifices for public worship, and stands on the Codorus Creek, which flows into the Susquehanna, 88 miles W. of Philadelphia. Population of the county, 47,016, of the town, 4779.

YORK, a seaport of Maine, capital of a county of the same name. The river of its name enters York harbour below the town. It is 75 miles N. N. E. of Boston. Population of the county, 54,034, of the town, 3111. Long. 70. 55. W. lat. 43. 7. N.

YORK, a county in the E. part of Virginia, with 4720 inhabitants. York Town is the capital.

YORK, a town of South Carolina, capital of a district of its name; 30 miles N. of Columbia.

YORK, NEW, one of the United States of America, 350 miles in length, and 240 in breadth; bounded on the N. by Lower Canada, E. by Vermont, Massachusets, and Connecticut, S. by the Atlantic and New Jersey, and W. by Pennsylvania, Lake Erie, and Upper Canada. It contains 58 counties, the chief of which are New York, Richmond, Suffolk, West Chester, Queen's, King's, Orange, Ulster, Duchess, Columbia, Rensselaer, Washington, Clinton, Saratoga, Albany, Montgomery, Herkimer, Onondaga, Otsego, Ontario, Tioga, &c. New York, in general, is intersected by ridges of mountains running in a N. E. and S. W. direction. Beyond the Allegany mountains, however, the country is quite level, of a fine rich soil, covered in its natural state with various kinds of trees. East of these mountains it is broken into hills and valleys; the hills are thickly clothed with timber, and, when cleared, afford fine pastures; while the valleys produce wheat, hemp, flax, peas, grass, oats, and maize. Of the commodities produced from culture, wheat is the staple, of which immense quantities are raised and exported. The manufactures of the state are important and flourishing. The noble river Hudson traverses this state from N. to S., and it is connected to Lake Erie by the great Erie canal, 360 miles in length. It is also joined to Lake Champlain, by a shorter canal; and another connects it with the Delaware. Owing to these singular advantages of situation, and the unequalled extent of inland navigation, this state has become the principal of the N. states, and now contains a population of 2,428,921, being nearly equal to all the states of New England.

YORK, NEW, the capital of the foregoing state, is situate on the S. W. point of Manhattan Island, at the confluence of Hudson and E. rivers, and is 5 miles in circumference. Surrounded on all sides by water, it is refreshed by cool breezes in summer, and the air in winter is more temperate than in other places under the same parallel. The island is 15 miles in length, but hardly one in breadth; and is joined to the mainland by a bridge called King's Bridge. There is no basin or bay for the reception of ships, but the road where they lie, in East River, is defended from the violence of the sea by some islands which interlock with each other. Here are upwards of 100 edifices for public worship, a well endowed university, a noble theological seminary, an institution for the education of the deaf and dumb, and numerous other charitable institutions. The most magnificent edifice is Federal Hall, in front of which is a gallery 12 feet deep, where the illustrious Washington took his oath of office, at the commencement of the federal institution, in 1789. An academy of the fine arts, and a botanical garden, were established here in 1804. This city has more commercial business than any town in the United States, owing to its situation at the mouth of a noble river, and its fertile and populous back country. It is 97 miles N. E. of Philadelphia. Long. 74. 11. W. lat. 40. 40. N.

YORK FORT, a settlement of the Hudson Bay Company, on the W. side of Hudson Bay, at the mouth of Nelson, or York River. Long. 88. 44. W. lat. 57. 15. N.

YORK TOWN, a seaport of Virginia, capital of York county, with the best harbour in the state. Here, in 1781, Lord Cornwallis and his army were captured by the combined forces of the United States and France. It is seated on

York River, near its entrance into Chesapeake Bay; 13 miles E. of Williamsburg. Pop. 1000. Long. 76. 52. W. lat. 37. 18. N.

Yorkshire, the largest county of England, bounded on the N. by Westmoreland and Durham, E. by the German Ocean, S. by Lincolnshire, Nottinghamshire, and Derbyshire, S. W. by Cheshire, W. by Lancashire, and N. W. by Westmoreland. It extends 80 miles from N. to S., and 115 from E. to W., and contains 3,847,420 acres. From its great extent it has been divided into three parts, called the North, East, and West Ridings, each of which returns two members to parliament, and subdivided into 26 wapentakes: it has two cities, 60 market-towns, and 604 parishes. The air and soil of this county vary extremely. The East Riding is less healthy than the others, but this inconvenience decreases in proportion as the county recedes from the sea. On the hilly parts of this riding, especially in what is called the York Wolds, the soil is generally barren, dry, and sandy; but great numbers of lean sheep are sold here, and sent into other parts to be fattened. The West Riding, which is much the largest, enjoys a sharp but healthy air, and the land on the western side is hilly, stony, and not very fruitful; but the intermediate valleys consist of much good arable ground, and pasture for the largest cattle. It also produces iron, coal, lime, jet, alum, horses, and goats. Here the clothing manufactures principally flourish. The North Riding, in general, exceeds the other two in the salubrity of the air. The worst parts breed lean cattle; but, on the sides of the hills, in the valleys, and in the plains, it produces good corn and rich pastures. Richmondshire, on the N. W. of this riding, was formerly a county of itself; here many lead-mines are worked to great advantage. In Yorkshire, likewise, are the districts of Holderness, on the borders of the Humber; Cleveland, on the confines of Durham; and Craven, on the borders of Westmoreland and Lancashire. In this last district are three of the highest hills in England, named Warnside, Ingleborough, and Pennygant, which form a sort of triangle from their tops, at the distance of 5, 6, and 8 miles, while their monstrous bases nearly unite. The principal rivers are the Ouse, Don, Derwent, Calder, Aire, Warf, Nid, Ure, and Hull, and they all terminate in the Humber, which enters the German Ocean between Yorkshire and Lincolnshire.

Yo-tcheou, a city of China, of the first rank, in Hou-quang, and one of the richest cities in the empire. It is seated on the river Kian-ku, and on the Lake Tong-ting, which is more than 70 leagues in circuit; 700 miles S. by W. of Peking. Long. 112. 35. E. lat. 29. 23. N.

Youghall, a borough and seaport of Ireland, in the county of Cork, sending one member to parliament, with a commodious harbour, and a well defended quay. It has a manufacture of earthenware. It is seated on the side of a hill, on a bay of its name; 28 miles E. by N. of Cork. Long. 8. 10. W. lat. 51. 49. N.

Ypres, a fortified city of Belgium, in Flanders, and a bishop's see. It has considerable manufactures of silk, linen, lace, cotton, thread, &c., and the canal of Boisingen, and the New Cut, greatly expedite the conveyance of goods to Nieuport, Ostend, and Bruges. Ypres was taken by the French in 1794, and retained till the downfall of Napoleon. It is seated on the Yperlee; 15 miles W. of Courtray. Pop. 15,000. Long. 2. 48. E. lat. 50. 51. N.

Yriex, St., a town of France, department of Upper Vienne; 20 miles S. by W. of Limoges. Pop. 6400.

Ysendyk, a strong town of the Netherlands, in the Isle of Cadsand; 8 miles E. of Sluys, and 18 N. W. of Ghent.

Yssel, or Issel, a river of the Netherlands, which branches off from the Rhine below Huessen, and, flowing by Doesburg, Zutphen, Deventer, and Campen, enters the Zuyder Zee by two channels.

Yssel, or Little Issel, a river of the Netherlands, which flows by Ysselstein, Montford, Oudewater, and Gouda, and enters the Merwe above Rotterdam.

Yssel, or Old Issel, a river which rises in Westphalia, in the duchy of Cleve, flows by Ysselburg into the county of Zutphen, and enters the Yssel at Doesburg.

Ysselmond, an island of the Netherlands, in South Holland, situate between the Merwe on the N., and another branch of the Meuse on the S. It has a town of the same name, nearly 3 miles W. of Rotterdam.

Ysselstein, a town of the Netherlands, in South Holland, with a castle on the river Yssel; 5 miles S. S. W. of Utrecht.

Ystadt, or Ydsted, a town of Sweden, in the province of Schonen, on a bay of the Baltic, opposite Stralsund; 26 miles S. E. of Lund. Long. 13. 44. E. lat. 55. 22. N.

Ythan, a river of Scotland, in Aberdeenshire, which crosses the county in a S. E. direction, and enters the German Ocean at the village of Newburg; 15 miles N. N. E. of Aberdeen.

Yucatan, a peninsula of Mexico, in the province of Merida, bounded N. W. by the waters of the Mexican Gulf, S. E. by the Bay of Honduras, S. W. by Vera Cruz, and S. by Vera Paz. Area, 80,000 square miles. Pop. 750,000.

Yuen-kiang, a city of China, of the first rank, in the province of Yun-nan, on the river Ho-ti; 145 miles S. S. W. of Yun-nan. Long. 101. 44. E. lat. 23. 37. N.

Yuen-tcheou, a city of China, of the first rank, in Kiang-si; 750 miles S. of Peking. Long. 113. 58. E. lat. 27. 50. N.

Yuen-yang, a city of China, of the first rank, in Hou-quang, on the river Han; 515 miles S. S. W. of Peking. Long. 100. 30. E. lat. 32. 50. N.

Yuma, Exuma, or Long Island, one of the Bahama islands, in the West Indies, lying to the N. of the E. end of Cuba, and its N. part under the tropic of Cancer. It is 70 miles in length, and 10 in breadth.

Yumetos, a cluster of small islands, among the Bahamas, lying to the S. W. of Yuma.

YUNG-NING, a city of China, of the first rank, at the N. extremity of the province of Yun-nan, on the borders of Tibet; 230 miles N. N. W. of Yun-nan. Long. 100. 24. E. lat. 27. 50. N.

YUNG-PE, a city of China, of the first rank, in the province of Yun-nan; 170 miles N. W. of Yun-nan. Long. 100. 34. E. lat. 26. 44. N.

YUNG-PING, a city of China, of the first rank, in Pe-tche-li, on a river that enters the Gulf of Leao-tong. Near it stands the fort Chun-hai, which is the key of the province of Leao-tong; 115 miles E. of Peking. Long. 108. 34. E. lat. 39. 55. N.

YUNG-TCHANG, a city of China, of the first rank, in the province of Yun-nan. The neighbouring country produces gold, honey, wax, amber, and a vast quantity of fine silk; 210 miles W. of Yun-nan. Long. 99. 2. E. lat. 25. 5. N.

YUNG-TCHEOU, a city of China, of the first rank, in Hou-quang; 885 miles S. S. W. of Peking. Long. 111. 15. E. lat. 26. 10. N.

YUN-HING, a city of China, of the first rank, in the province of Ho-nan; 430 miles S. of Peking. Long. 113. 52. E. lat. 33. 0. N.

YUN-NAN, a province of China, at the S. W. extremity; 300 miles long, and 250 broad; bounded on the N. by Tibet and Se-tcheuen, E. by Koei-tcheou and Quang-si, S. by Tonquin and Laos, and W. by Pegu and Birmah. It is mountainous, but the soil in general is fertile, and it is reckoned the richest province in China, from its productive mines of gold, copper, and tin, its amber, rubies, sapphires, agates, pearls, and marble, its musk, silk, elephants, horses, gums, medicinal plants, and linen; 21 cities of the first rank, and 55 of the second and third, are included in this province. The number of inhabitants is estimated at upwards of 8,000,000.

YUN-NAN, a city of China, capital of the foregoing province, formerly celebrated for its extent, magnificent buildings, vast gardens, tombs, triumphal arches, and elegant squares; but it has suffered greatly from the Tartars, in their different invasions, and the city at present contains nothing remarkable. It stands at the N. extremity of a lake; 1260 miles S. S. W. of Peking. Long. 102. 30. E. lat. 25. 6. N.

YURCUP, a town of Asiatic Turkey, in Caramania, on the Kizil-Irmak; 125 miles N. E. of Konieh. Long. 34. 30. E. lat. 39. 40. N.

YUTHIA. *See* SIAM.

YVERDUN, a strong town of Switzerland, in the Pays de Vaud, capital of a bailiwick of its name, with a castle, a college, and an hospital. Near the town is a sulphurous spring, with a commodious bathing-house. The principal trade is in wine, and merchandise passing between Germany, Italy, and France. It has some remains of Roman antiquities. It stands on the Lake of Neufchatel, at the influx of the Orbe and Thiele; 38 miles W. S. W. of Bern. Pop. 25,000. Long. 6. 59. E. lat. 46. 44. N.

YVETOT, a town of France, department of Lower Seine; 7 miles N. N. W. of Caudebec. Pop. 10,000.

YVRY, a town of France, department of Eure, on the river Eure; 16 miles S. of Evreux.

Z.

ZAAB, a district of Algier, in the desert behind Mount Atlas, belonging to the province of Constantine. The people of Zaab are free, and pay no tribute; but they are poor and indigent, as may be expected of the inhabitants of so barren a soil. Dates are the principal article of food; and they have extensive plantations of palm-trees. They carry on some commerce in ostriches' feathers. The chief place of the district is Biscara.

ZABOLA, a town of Transylvania, on the confines of Moldavia; 5 miles S. W. of Denmark.

ZACATECAS, a province of Mexico, bounded on the N. by New Biscay, E. by Panu, S. by Mechoacan and Guadalaxara, and W. by Chiametlan. It abounds with large villages, and its mines are deemed the richest in America. Pop. 150,000.

ZACATECAS, a city of Mexico, capital of the above province, surrounded by rich silver mines; 260 miles N. E. of Mexico. Pop. 33,000.

ZACATULA, a town of Mexico, in the province of Mechoacan, on a river of the same name, near the Pacific Ocean; 180 miles S. W. [illegible]

ZACHAN, a town of Prussia, in Pomerania; 13 miles E. of New Stargard.

ZAFRA, a town of Spain, in Estremadura, with a castle; 20 miles S. W. of Medina. Pop. 6000.

ZAGARA, a mountain of Greece, in Livadia, one of the tops of Mount Parnassus. It was the ancient Helicon, from which issued the fountain Hippocrene, and was sacred to the Muses, who had here a temple.

ZAGHARA, a town of Negroland, in Bornou, on the river Fittree; 170 miles S. E. of Bornou.

ZAGORA. *See* DEVELTO.

ZAHARA, or the GREAT DESERT, a vast country of Africa, 1900 miles in length, by 840 in breadth; bounded on the N. by Barbary, E. by Fezzan and Cassina, S. by Negroland and Fouli, and W. by the Atlantic Ocean. The air is very hot, but not unwholesome to the natives. The soil is generally sandy and barren, but there are verdant valleys, in which water either springs or stagnates, and it is here and there interspersed with spots of astonishing fertility, which are crowded with inhabitants. These fertile spots in the desert are called oases, or islands, bearing some resemblance to islands in the sea; and they abound most in the northern and eastern parts; but the smaller ones are not always permanent, for a furious wind from the desert, bringing along with it an immense quantity of sand, sometimes overwhelms an oasis, and reduces it to barrenness. These oases are formed into a number of states, governed by petty princes; and those of which some intelligence has been obtained are noticed in this work in their proper places. The inhabitants, consisting of various tribes, are wild and ignorant; and the Mahomedan religion is professed throughout the country, unless where they approach the country of the Negroes. They maintain towards each other the maxims of apparent hostility, but a Christian is every where odious. Their language is chiefly a dialect of the Arabic; and their only intercourse with other nations is carried on with the caravans, which periodically traverse these immense deserts. The Zahara abounds in antelopes, wild boars, leopards, apes, ostriches, and serpents. There are few horses and beeves, but many sheep, goats, and camels.

Zahara, a town of Spain, in Andalusia, with a citadel, seated on a craggy rock; 42 miles S. E. of Seville.

Zahna, a town of Prussian Saxony; 6 miles N. E. of Wittenberg.

Zaina, a town of Algier, in the province of Constantina, supposed, from some considerable ruins, to have been the ancient city of Zama. It is 28 miles S. E. of Seteef, and 46 S. W. of Constantina.

Zaine, a river of Barbary, which separates the kingdoms of Algier and Tunis, and enters the Mediterranean at the island of Tabarca.

Zaire, a river of Congo, which rises in the kingdom of Matamba, flows N. to the extreme borders of Congo, where it turns to the W., then separates the kingdoms of Loango and Congo Proper, and enters the Atlantic Ocean below Sogno.

Zalamea, a town of Spain, in Andalusia, 12 miles N. of Niebla, and 38 W. N. W. of Seville.

Zalamea, a town of Spain, in Estremadura, anciently called Ilapa. It contains many vestiges of its former splendour. It is 38 miles S. E. of Merida.

Zambezi, a large river of East Africa, in Mocaranga. It falls into the Indian Ocean, at Quilimane, of which it is the port. The sources are unknown. It has many Portuguese settlements on its banks, among which is Sena: gold is found on its banks, and much ivory is brought from the interior of it.

Zamora, a strong town of Spain, in Leon, and a bishop's see. In its environs fine turquoise stones are found. It is seated on a hill, on the river Douro, over which is a bridge; 32 miles N. by W. of Salamanca, and 146 N. W. of Madrid. Population, 9000. Long. 5. 56. W. lat. 41. 50. N.

Zamora, a town of Quito, in the neighbourhood of which are rich mines of gold. It is seated near the Andes; 230 miles S. of Quito. Long. 78. 20. W. lat. 4. 6. S.

Zamora, a town of Mexico, in Guadalaxara, 40 miles S. E. of Guadalaxara. Long. 103. 30. W. lat. 20. 52. N.

Zamora, a town of Algier, in the province of Constantina; 250 miles W. of Hamamet. Long. 6. 25. E. lat. 36. 20. N.

Zamoski, a town of Poland, with a citadel, a cathedral, and several other churches. It is 37 miles S. S. W. of Chelm, and 44 W. N. W. of Betz. Pop. 6600.

Zampago, a town of Mexico, seated on a small lake; 30 miles N. of Mexico.

Zanfara, a kingdom of Negroland, to the S. of Zegzeg, between Cassina and Bornou. The inhabitants are tall in stature, of very black complexion, with broad faces, and savage dispositions. The capital, of the same name, stands on a river that forms a lake N. of Ghana, and then flows through that city into the Niger. It is 230 miles N. E. of Ghana, and 450 W. S. W. of Bornou. Long. 16. 0. E. lat. 18. 30. N.

Zanguebar, or Zanzibar, a country on the E. coast of Africa, between 3. N. and 9. S. lat. It includes several petty kingdoms, in which the Portuguese have settlements. The inhabitants are all blacks, with curled woolly hair, and, except those converted by the Portuguese, are either Mahomedans or Pagans, the latter much the more numerous. The principal territories are Jubo, Melinda, Mombaza, and Quiloa. The Portuguese trade for slaves, ivory, gold, ostriches' feathers, wax, and drugs. The productions are much the same as in the other parts of Africa, between the tropics.

Zante, an island in the Mediterranean, forming part of the Ionian republic. It is situate near the coast of the Morea, 17 miles S. of the island of Cephalonia, and is 14 miles long, and 8 broad. Its principal riches consist in currants, which are cultivated in a large plain, under the shelter of mountains, and it has some tar-springs, or petroleum. Here are also the finest peaches in the world, with other choice fruits, and excellent wine and oil. The natives speak both Greek and Italian, though there are very few Roman Catholics among them; but they have a bishop as well as the Greeks. Area, 160 square miles. Pop. 40,000.

Zante, the capital of the foregoing island, is pleasantly situate on an eminence on the E. side of the island, at the bottom of a small bay. The houses are built partly of brick, and partly of wood, and seldom more than one or two stories in height, on account of the frequency of earthquakes: the last visitation of this kind was in 1820, when several hundreds of houses were overthrown. The harbour is capacious, and is protected by a mole. It is 12 miles W. of Cape Tornese, in the Morea. Pop. 18,000.

Zanzibar, an island in the Indian Sea, on the coast of Zanguebar, between the islands of Pemba and Monsia. It abounds in sugar-canes and citrons. The inhabitants are Mahomedan Arabs, and are governed by a sheik appointed by the iman of Muscat. Long. 41. 0. E. lat. 6. 0. S.

Zara, a city of the Austrian states, capital of a circle of the same name, and of the whole of Austrian Dalmatia, with a harbour. It is situated in a plain, upon a small peninsula, joined to the continent by an isthmus of about 25 paces broad. On the side of the citadel it is very well fortified. Near the church, which the Greeks called St. Helia, are two handsome fluted columns of the Corinthian order, said to have been part of the Temple of Juno. This place was formerly more considerable than at present, the number of the inhabitants being now not above 8000. The circle contains an area of 2150 square miles, with 100,000 inhabitants. There are very fine paintings in the churches, done by the best masters; and they pretend to have the body of Simeon, brought from Judea, and kept in a shrine with a crystal before it. Zara is seated on the Gulf of Venice; 80 miles S. W. of Jaicza, and 150 S. E. of Venice. Long. 16. 6. E. lat. 44. 30. N.

Zareng, a town of Persia, in the province of Segestan. It is celebrated for its beautiful porcelain. It is seated on the Hirmund; 350 miles E. of Ispahan. Long. 61. 10. E. lat. 32. 28. N.

Zaril, a town of Greece, in the Morea; 22 miles E. of Misitra.

Zarnate, a town in the Morea, seated on an eminence; 20 miles S. W. of Misitra.

Zarnowitz, a town of Prussia, in Pomerelia, on a bay of the Baltic; 38 miles N.N.W. of Dantzic.

Zaslaw, a town of Poland, in Volhynia, seated on the Horin; 30 miles N. N. W. of Constantinow.

Zatmar, a strong town of Hungary, capital of a county of the same name. It is seated on a small lake, formed by the river Samos; 50 miles E. by S. of Tokay, and 130 E. of Buna. Long. 22. 34. E. lat. 47. 50. N.

Zator, a town of Poland, in the palatinate of Cracow, with a castle, seated on an eminence, near the river Vistula; 20 miles S. W. of Cracow, and 50 S. E. of Ratibor.

Zaweh, a town of Persia, in the province of Khorasan, situate on the Tedjen; 20 miles from the Caspian Sea, and 80 N. of Mesched.

Zbaras, a town of Austrian Poland, 28 miles E. of Zborow, and 68 N. by W. of Kaminieck.

Zborow, a town of Austrian Poland, in the circle of Lemburg. Here, in 1649, John Casimir, king of Poland, with 20,000 men, was attacked by 110,000 Cossacks and Tartars, for three days successively, but defended himself so bravely, that the latter consented to terms of accommodation. Zborow is 52 miles E. by S. of Lemburg. Long. 25. 46. E. lat. 49. 46. N.

Zealand, or Zeeland, an island of Denmark, of a triangular form; 230 miles in circumference, and the largest of the isles belonging to the king of Denmark. Area, 2600 square miles. Pop. 125,000. It lies at the entrance of the Baltic, having the Cattegat on the N., the Sound on the E., and the Great Belt on the W. The coast is much intersected by large bays; and within the country are several lakes, which, as well as the rivers, abound in fish. It is exceedingly fertile, producing grain of all sorts, with excellent pasture, and in most parts plenty of wood. It is particularly famous for its breed of horses. Copenhagen is the capital of this island, and of the whole kingdom.

Zealand, a province of the Netherlands, comprising the ancient county of Zealand, and Dutch Flanders; bounded on the N. by the isles of Holland, E. by Brabant, S. by Flanders, and W. by the German Ocean. It is composed of several islands, the principal of which are Walcheren, Schowen, North and South Beveland, Tolen, Duyveland, and Wolversdike. Area, 570 square miles. Pop. 120,000. The surface is generally level, and lies so low that the inhabitants are obliged to defend themselves from encroachments of the sea, by vast dykes, which are kept up at a great expense. The river Scheldt forms the most of these islands, and the soil of them is fruitful. The province carries on considerable trade in corn, madder, flax, salt meat, linen yarn, rape-seed, oil, &c. The greater part of the inhabitants are Calvinists, but there are also many Catholics and Lutherans, and some Mennonite Baptists. The principal towns are Middleburg and Flushing.

Zealand, New, a group of islands in the Pacific Ocean, lying between lat. 34. 25. and 47. 17. S. and long. 166. 5. and 178. 35. E., was discovered by Tasman in 1642. He traversed the eastern coast from lat. 34. to 45. S., and entered a strait; but, being attacked by the natives soon after he came to an anchor, he did not go ashore. From the time of Tasman, the whole country, except that part of the coast which was seen by him, remained altogether unknown, and was by many supposed to make part of a southern continent, till 1770, when it was circumnavigated by Captain Cook, who found it to consist of two large islands, separated by the strait above mentioned, and to which he gave his own name. In the year 1814 several missionary stations were established, which have continued their exertions in the civilization and instruction of the natives in their vicinity, up to the present time. These islands have been the resort of the South Sea whalers, particularly the middle islands; and a great quantity of land has been purchased, or procured from the native chiefs, from time to time, by various adventurers who had established themselves among the numerous harbours and fine rivers with which the northern island abounds. Up to the year 1840 New Zealand was not regularly colonized, though the number of Europeans was gradually increasing. In the commencement of that year, a company was formed in London for the purchase and cultivation of land in that country; and a number of emigrants sailed from England for Port Nicholson, in the S. part of the north island, the territory on each side of Cook Strait having been purchased from the natives; this colony, which was unauthorized by the British government, led to many speculations in the purchase of large districts by private individuals, and others. To prevent the dissensions consequent upon this, it was judged expedient by the government to commission a lieutenant-governor under New South Wales, to proclaim the sovereignty of the Queen over the whole territory. Lieutenant-governor Hobson accordingly issued a proclamation to that effect on the 23rd of May, 1840, and immediately proceeded to procure the submission of the chiefs, who unanimously acceded to the British domination. This deliberate act, and cession of the chiefs, and of their having been formerly recognized by Great Britain as an independent state, form strong claims for protection on the part of the government. Among the many barbarous tribes that our extended colonial empire brings us in contact with, there are none whose claims are greater. They are not mere wanderers over an extended surface, in search of a precarious subsistence, nor tribes of hunters, or of herdsmen, but a people among whom the arts of government have made some progress; they have a regular division and appropriation of the soil, have some agricultural skill, and have a certain subordination of ranks, and large bodies of them have been converted to the Christian faith. These islands were established into a separate colony by a royal charter, dated November 16, 1840, and Lieutenant-governor Hobson was appointed the first governor, assisted by a legislative council. By the same charter it is directed that the northern island be called New Ulster; the middle island, New Munster; and the south, or Stewart Island, New Leinster. New Ulster, or Eaheinomauwe, or North Island, is the most populous, as it is probably the most fertile, of the New Zealand group; at least, it is the best adapted for colonization, from its numerous fine harbours, and the rich valleys which intersect it. It is about 520 miles long, and 140 in its greatest breadth, but is very irregular in figure. The occupation of its inhabitants will be almost exclusively agricultural, as the remarkable deficiency of pasturage will prevent the increase of cattle in any great degree. In this circumstance a marked difference will exist between this and the neighbouring colonies of Australia. The numerous missionary stations, which have been long established, are all on the north island, the principal of which are in the Bay of Islands in the N. E. The first colony was founded at Wellington, in Port Nicholson, a splendid harbour in Cook Strait. The future capital, Auckland, has been fixed at Waitemata harbour, in the Shouraki gulf, or Frith of the Thames, in lat. 36. 51. S. long. 174. 45. E. The temporary seat of government is at Russell, a settlement near Paheha, in the Bay of Islands. In the interior are the extensive lakes of Roturoa and Taupo, and numerous fine streams intersect the country; the mountains are not so extensive as in New Munster, though some attain a great elevation, as Ruafauhu, always covered with snow, and near it the Tongouro volcano, 10,000 feet high. The forests, with which the interior abounds, contain the finest timber for ship-building, and have been extensively used for that purpose. Another native production is the phormium tenax, or New Zealand flax, a species of flag growing on the margins of streams, and which has been prepared for cordage in great quantities by the natives. New Munster, Tavai Poenammoo, or the middle island, is of a much more regular figure; it is 580 miles long, and from 100 to 160 broad, and contains about 23,000,000 acres, and the mountains which traverse it have a remarkably bleak and savage appearance, which contrasts strongly with the real amenity of the climate, and the fertility of the land near the coast. In the N. part are some fine harbours and rivers, which have been colonized, particularly the Oyerri or Pelorus river, which has some fine land on its banks. A settlement has been formed by the French on Banks Peninsula, on the eastern coast; the English have also a settlement here, and it is frequented by the whalers on the S. side. This peninsula consists of a succession of hills, which are clothed with verdure to their summits, and well adapted for agricultural and pastoral purposes. The climate of the middle island is represented as being delicious. The productions of Europe flourish here, and potatoes and cattle are raised in many parts of it. Stewart's Island, or New Leinster, is the southernmost of the group, and is much smaller than the other two, being only 38 miles broad by 40 long. It has some fine harbours, particularly Port Pegasus, on the S. E. From its being more to the S. the climate is somewhat colder than in the others; but it is a beautiful and fertile island; the number of paroquets giving rather the appearance of a tropical climate. There is plenty of timber, among which are several varieties of pine: all the trees appear to be evergreens. The Europeans resident on it raise pigs, poultry, potatoes, and wheat, for the whalers who visit its shores. The number of Europeans estimated to be in the colony, at the commencement of 1841, was about 4000. The only native quadrupeds are dogs and rats; the former are domesticated. The birds, like the vegetables, are almost entirely peculiar to the country. The creeks swarm with fish, which are equally delicious with those of Europe. The rocks are furnished with great quantities of excellent muscles, one sort of which measures above a foot in length, and with great variety of other shell-fish. The natives are stout and fleshy, but not corpulent, and are exceedingly vigorous and active. The women, in general, are smaller than the men, and are chiefly distinguished by the softness of their voices. The bodies of both sexes are marked with black stains, which is the same as tattooing at Tahiti. Their dress is also the same with that of the natives of that island. Their houses are miserable lodgings, and their only furniture consists in a few small baskets, in which they put their fishing-hooks and other trifles. Their food consists chiefly of fish, with which, instead of bread, they eat the root of a kind of fern, which they scorch over the fire, and then beat with a stick till the bark or dry outside falls off. Besides their dogs they also contrive to kill birds; and in most parts of the northern island they have sweet potatoes, cocoas, and yams; but in the southern nothing is raised by cultivation. Their cookery consists wholly in roasting and baking, which last is performed in the same manner as at Tahiti. The eastern coast of the north island is by far the most populous, tillage, weaving, and the other arts of peace, being here best known and most practised. The canoes are more decorated, the plantations more numerous, and the clothes and carving finer than any where else. In other parts the inhabitants are scattered along the coast in families or tribes. A bishop of New Zealand was appointed in 1842.

ZEBID, a city of Arabia, in the province of Yemen. It was once very considerable, but its walls are demolished, and its present buildings scarcely occupy the half of its ancient extent. It is seated on a river; 10 miles from the Red Sea, and 140 N. of Mocha. Long. 44. 28. E. lat. 15. 10. N.

ZEBU, or SEBU, one of the Philippine islands, between those of Leyta and Negros. It is 140 miles long, and 30 broad, and has a town of the same name, on the E. coast. Long. 122. 30 E. lat. 10. 36. N.

ZEDIC, a town of Barbary, in Tripoli, seated on a bay of the Mediterranean; 120 miles S. E. of Tripoli.

ZEGEDIN, or SZEGED, a strong town of Hungary, with a trade in salt, tobacco, wool, and corn, situate on the Theisse, opposite the influx of the Maros; 65 miles N. W. of Temeswar, and 98 S. E. of Pest. Long. 20. 25. E. lat. 46. 20. N.

ZEGZEG, a kingdom of Negroland, to the N. of Zanfara, between Cassina and Bornou. The capital is of the same name; 380 miles N. E. of Cassina. Long. 16. 0. E. lat. 20. 45. N.

ZEHDENICK, a town of Prussia, in Brandenburg, noted for a large foundry; 30 miles N. of Berlin.

ZEIL, a town of Bavarian Franconia, seated on the Maine; 10 miles N. W. of Bamberg.

ZEILA, a seaport of the kingdom of Adel, and a place of considerable trade, seated on a bay of the Arabian Sea. Long. 44. 22. E. lat. 11. 9. N.

ZEITON, a town of Greece, in Janna, and an archbishop's see, with a castle. It is seated on a gulf of its name; 50 miles S. S. E. of Larissa, and 62 N. of Corinth.

ZEITZ, a town of Prussian Saxony, with a magnificent castle, and a collegiate church. It has good cloth and stuff manufactures. It is seated on the Elster; 23 miles S. S. W. of Leipsic. Pop. 5400.

ZELL, a town of Hanover, formerly the capital of a duchy of the same name, in the principality of Lunenburg. It is surrounded by ditches and ramparts, on which are planted chesnut and lime-trees. The high courts of appeal for all the territories of the electoral house of Brunswick-Lunenburg were held here; and also the diets for the principality. The castle was repaired by George III. of England, for the residence of his unfortunate sister, the queen of Denmark, who died here in 1775. Zell is seated on the Aller; 28 miles E. N. E. of Hanover. Pop. 8200. Long. 10. 14. E. lat. 52. 42. N.

ZELL, a town of Baden, seated on the river Kintzig; 18 miles S. E. of Strasburg.

ZELL IN THE PINZGAU, a town of Austria in the province of Salzburg, seated on a lake; 30 miles W. of Radstadt, and 34 S. S. W. of Salzburg.

ZELL IN ZILLERTHAL, a town of Austria, in the Tyrol, seated on the Ziller; 24 miles E. of Inspruck.

ZELLERFELD, a town of Hanover, in the Upper Hartz, with a mine-office and a mine; 9 miles S. S. W. of Goslar.

ZELUIA, a town of Russia, in the government of Grodno; 50 miles W. S. W. of Novogrodek.

ZEMPLIN, a town of Hungary, in a palatinate of the same name, seated on the Bodrog; 25 miles S. E. of Cassovia, and 27 N. E. of Tokay.

ZENGAN, a town of Persia, in the province of Irac; 80 miles N. N. E. of Amadan.

ZENGUIA, a town of Asiatic Turkey, in the pachalic of Aleppo, situate on the Euphrates; 55 miles N. N. E. of Aleppo.

ZENTA, a town of Hungary, memorable for a signal victory gained by prince Eugene over the Turks in 1697. It is seated on the Theisse; 52 miles N. of Belgrade.

ZERBST, a town of Germany, in the duchy of Anhalt-Dessau, with a fine castle. It is famous for good beer, and has manufactures of gold and silver; 10 miles N. N. W. of Dessau. Pop. 8000.

ZEREA, a town and fortress of Persia, in Farsistan; 18 miles N. N. E. of Shiras.

ZETLAND. *See* SHETLAND.

ZEULEN, a town of Bavarian Franconia, on the river Rosach; 21 miles N. E. of Bamberg.

ZEULENRODO, a town of Germany, in the principality of Reuss, with manufactures of stuffs and stockings; 14 miles N. W. of Plauen.

ZIA, an island of the Grecian archipelago, to the S. of Negropont, 15 miles long, and 8 broad. Pop. 6000. It abounds in barley, wine, and silk; also a fine sort of oak, whose fruit, called valonia, used by dyers and tanners, is the best trading commodity in the island. The principal town, of the same name, seated on an eminence, is a bishop's see, and has a good harbour, with about 2500 houses, all flat at the top. Long. 34. 24. E. lat. 37. 48. N.

ZIEGENHALS, a town of Prussian Silesia, with several foundries, and a manufacture of excellent glass. It is seated on the Biela; 10 miles S. of Niesse.

ZIEGENHAYN, a fortified town of Germany, capital of a province of its name in the electorate of Hesse, with a fine castle and an arsenal. The suburb called Weinhausen is a handsome place, and more extensive than the town. In 1757 it was taken by the French, and in 1761 it was ineffectually besieged by the allies, who reduced two-thirds of the town to ashes by their cannonade. It stands in a morass, surrounded by the river Schwalm; 28 miles S. S. E. of Cassel. Pop. 1100.

ZIEGENRUCK, a town of Saxony, on the river Saal; 10 miles S. of Neustadt.

Ziegeser, or **Ziesar**, a town and castle of Prussia, in Brandenburg; 18 miles W. S. W. of Brandenburg.

Zielenzig, a town of Prussia, in Brandenburg, with manufactures of cloth; 20 miles E. S. E. of Custrin.

Zierenberg, a town of Germany, in Hesse-Cassel; 8 miles W. N. W. of Cassel.

Ziget, a town of Hungary, on the river Theisse, near its source; 42 miles E. by N. of Nagybanja.

Zigeth, a strong town of Hungary, which has been several times besieged and taken by the Turks and Austrians. It stands on the Alma, by which it is surrounded; 48 miles S. E. of Canischa. Long. 18. 16. E. lat. 46. 8. N.

Ziriczee, or **Zierikzee**, a strong town of the Netherlands, in Zealand, and capital of the isle of Schouwen. It was the ancient residence of the counts of Zealand. It is 12 miles N. E. of Middleburg, and 18 S. W. of Briel. Pop. 6300.

Zittau, a fortified town of Saxony, in Upper Lusatia, surrounded by a wall, with four large and six small gates. It has a very extensive trade in linen, white damasks, woollen cloth, and blue paper. The cathedral has three organs; and near it is a college, where the languages, drawing, and other arts, are taught gratis. Adjoining to the cloisters is an excellent library, and at a small distance from it is an orphan-house. It is seated on the Neisse; 17 miles S. W. of Gorlitz, and 47 S. E. of Dresden. Long. 15. 1. E. lat. 50. 54. N. Pop. 7200.

Znaim, a strong town of the Austrian states, in Moravia, capital of a circle of the same name, with a castle, in which are a great many pagan antiquities. The vicinity yields excellent wine. It is seated on the Teya; 35 miles S. W. of Brinn, and 42 N. N. W. of Vienna. Pop. 5200. Long. 16. 0. E. lat. 48. 40. N.

Zoara, a fortified town of Tripoli, with a good harbour. It is seated on the Mediterranean; 60 miles W. of Tripoli. Long. 11. 53. E. lat. 32. 45. N.

Zoblitz, a town of Saxony, in Meissen. The inhabitants subsist principally by working the serpent-stone, which is found in the neighbourhood, into pitchers, bowls, tea and coffee-cups, &c. The red species of this stone, which is considered as the finest, belongs solely to the sovereign. It is 17 miles S. of Freyberg.

Zobten, a town of Prussian Silesia, in the government of Reichenbach; 9 miles E. N. E. of Schweidnitz.

Zoffingen, a town of Switzerland, in the canton of Bern, with an elegant church, and a public library, containing several curious manuscripts. It is seated on the Wigger; 19 miles N. N. W. of Lucern.

Zolnock, a town of Hungary, capital of a county of the same name. In 1554 it was taken by the Turks, but retaken in 1685. It is seated on the Theisse, at the influx of the Sagelia; 62 miles N. E. of Colocza, and 62 E. of Buda. Long. 20. 50. E. lat. 47. 10. N.

Zombor, a town of Hungary, near the river Moszlonga; 50 miles N. W. of Neusatz.

Zorbig, a town of Prussian Saxony, with a citadel; 24 miles N. N. W. of Leipsic.

Zorndorf, a village of Prussia, in Brandenburg, where the king of Prussia, after a dreadful conflict, totally defeated the Russians in 1758; 5 miles N. of Custrin.

Zossen, a town and castle of Brandenburg, situate on the Notte; 19 miles S. of Berlin.

Zout-Pan, a curious salt lake, in the country of the Hottentots, lying a few miles N. of Point Padron, in a plain much above the level of the sea, and between 3 and 4 miles in circumference. At some seasons of the year it is formed into an entire mass of fine white salt, with a hard crust resembling ice.

Zowan, a town of the kingdom of Tunis, famous for the dyeing of scarlet caps and the bleaching of linen; 36 miles S. W. of Tunis.

Zuckmantel, a town of Austrian Silesia, and a bishop's see. It has mines of gold, silver, copper, and iron. It is 15 miles S. of Neisse.

Zueela, a town of the kingdom of Fezzan, situate in a district of remarkable fertility. The remnants of ancient buildings, the number and size of the cisterns, and the construction of the vaulted caves, intended perhaps as repositories for corn, exhibit wonderful vestiges of its ancient splendour. It is 60 miles E. N. E. of Mourzook. Long. 16. 34. E. lat. 27. 59. N.

Zug, the smallest canton of Switzerland, containing an area of 125 square miles; bounded on the E. and N. by Zurich, W. by Lucern, and S. by Schweitz. It is rich in pasturage, has plenty of various kinds of stone fruit, as well as walnuts and chesnuts, and wine of a very acid flavour. The inhabitants, estimated at 15,500, are Roman Catholics.

Zug, a capital of the foregoing canton, containing several handsome churches, a good town-house, &c. It is seated on a lake of its name; 12 miles N. W. of Schweitz. Pop. 2000. Long. 8. 24. E. lat. 47. 4. N.

Zulauf, or **Sulay**, a town of Prussian Silesia; 5 miles S. W. of Militsch.

Zullichau, a town of Prussia, in the province of Brandenburg, with a castle, which stands without the walls of the town, and has a rampart and ditches. The suburbs contain more houses than the town itself, and among them is a large orphan-house, to which is annexed a school, an academy, &c. Here are good cloth manufactures, and the vicinity produces much corn and wine. In 1759 a battle was fought near this town, between the Prussians and the Russians, in which the former were defeated. It is situate in a plain, near the Oder; 24 miles E. by N. of Crossen. Pop. 5500. Long. 15. 52. E. lat. 52. 9. N.

Zulpha, or **Julfa**, a town of Persia, almost close to Ispahan, to which it is a sort of suburb, and separated from it by the river Sanderon. It was peopled by a colony of Armenians, brought hither by Shah Abbas. It contains several churches and monasteries.

Zulz, a town of Austrian Silesia, in the principality of Oppeln; 14 miles E. by S. of Neisse, and 26 S. S. W. of Oppeln.

Zulz, a town of Switzerland, in the canton of Grisons, on the river Inn; 26 m. S. E. of Coire.

Zumampa, a town of Tucuman, on the river Dolce; 110 miles S. S. E. of St. Jago del Estero.

Zumaya, a town of Biscay, near the coast; 5 miles W. by S. of St. Sebastian.

Zumpango, a town of Mexico; 100 miles N. by E. of Acapulco, and 105 S. of Mexico.

Zurich, a canton of Switzerland, bounded on the N. by Schaffhausen, E. by Thurgau and the county of Tockenburg, S. by Glarus, Schweitz, and Zug, and W. by Lucern and the county of Baden. Zurich was admitted a member of the Helvetic confederacy in 1351, and obtained the privilege of being the first canton in rank; it is also the most considerable in extent, both of territory and power, next to that of Bern, having an area of 950 square miles, with upwards of 185,000 inhabitants. It abounds in wine and excellent pasture, but the supply of corn is not sufficient for interior consumption. The inhabitants are all Calvinists; and two thirds of them derive their livelihood by spinning thread and silk, and making linen for the manufacture of the town.

Zurich, a city of Switzerland, capital of the foregoing canton, stands at the northern extremity of the Lake of Zurich, and occupies both sides of the rapid and transparent Limmat, which issues from that lake and divides the town into two unequal parts, communicating by three bridges. It was formerly an imperial city, and is one of the best built in this country, but the streets are narrow and the houses high. Zurich was the first town in Switzerland that separated from the church of Rome. Among its charitable foundations are an orphan house, an hospital for incurables, that for the sick of all nations, which usually contains between 600 and 700 patients, and the Almosen-Amt, or foundation for the poor, which puts out children as apprentices, and distributes money, clothes, and books, to poor persons, not of the town only, but of the canton, to the amount of upwards of 5000*l.* a year. The inhabitants carry on manufactures of muslins, cottons, linens, and silk handkerchiefs. It is 35 miles S. W. of Constance, 40 S. E. of Basil, and 55 N. E. of Bern. Pop. 11,000. Long. 8. 32. E. lat. 47. 20. N.

Zurich, a lake of Switzerland, 24 miles long and 4 broad. The adjacent country is finely cultivated and well peopled, and the S. part of the lake appears bounded by the stupendous mountains of Schweitz and Glarus. The scenery is picturesque, lively, and diversified. The river Limmat runs through the whole length of this lake to Zurich.

Zurita, a town of Spain, in New Castile, with a castle, seated on the Tagus; 38 miles E. of Madrid.

Zurz, a town of Switzerland, in the canton of Grisons, seated on the Inn; 20 miles N. N. W. of Bormio.

Zurzach, a town of Switzerland, in the county of Baden, seated on the Rhine, just above the influx of the Aar. It is 9 miles N. of Baden.

Zurzonza, a town of Mexico, in the province of Mechoacan, situate on an island in a lake; 25 miles W. S. W. of Mechoacan.

Zutphen, a strong town of the Netherlands, in Gelderland, capital of a county of its name. It is seated at the conflux of the Berkel with the Yssel; 9 miles S. by E. of Deventer, and 55 E. by S. of Amsterdam. Long. 6. 13. E. lat. 52. 10. N.

Zuyder Zee, a great bay of the German Ocean, which extends from N. to S., in Holland, between the provinces of Friesland, Overyssel, Gelderland, and North Holland.

Zuyst, a village of the Netherlands, which abounds in plantations and shady walks, and is inhabited by Moravian manufacturers. It is much frequented, in the summer months, by merchants who have no country seats of their own. It is 5 miles from Utrecht.

Zvenigorod, a town of Russia, in the government of Moscow, situate on the Moskva; 28 miles W. of Moscow.

Zwellendam, a district of the Cape of Good Hope, on the S. coast, bounded on the N. by Tulbagh and Stellenbosch, and on the E. by George. Area, 9000 square miles. Pop. 6663. It produces some corn, wine, and cattle. Port Beaufort, in St. Sebastian's Bay, enjoys a considerable coasting trade. To the W. are some salt pans, and to the N., over the Zwartberg mountains, some remarkable caverns were discovered in 1780. Zwellendam is the chief town.

Zwenkau, a town and castle of Saxony, seated on the Elster; 6 miles S. of Leipsic.

Zwetl, a town of Austria, at the conflux of the Zwetl with the Kemp; 26 miles W. N. W. of Krems.

Zwick, a town of Saxony, with a citadel, three churches, and a Latin school, in which is a good library. The inhabitants have manufactures of cloth and leather, and a trade in corn and beer. It is seated on the Mulda; 26 miles N. N. E. of Plauen, and 21 S. of Altenburg.

Zwingenberg, a town of Germany, in Hesse-Darmstadt; 8 miles S. of Darmstadt.

Zwittau, a town of Moravia, in the circle of Olmutz; 40 miles W. N. W. of Olmutz.

Zwoll, a fortified town of the Netherlands, in Overyssel, with three handsome suburbs. A canal begins near this place, and extends to the river Yssel, which is defended by several forts. Zwoll is the most opulent town in the province, and stands on an eminence, on the river Aa; 14 miles N. of Deventer, and 31 S. W. of Coevorden. Pop. 12,800. Long. 6. 3. E. lat. 52. 31. N.

Zwonitz, a town of Saxony; 14 miles S. S. W. of Chemnitz.

Zwornick, a town of Bosnia; 60 miles E. of Seraio, and 68 S. W. of Belgrade.

Zytomierz, a town and fortress of Russia, capital of the government of Volhynia, and a bishop's see, seated on the Ciecirief; 120 miles E. of Lucko. Long. 29. 22. E. lat. 50. 35. N

J. Haddon, Castle Street, Finsbury.